THE TENTH MENTAL MEASUREMENTS YEARBOOK

EARLIER PUBLICATIONS IN THIS SERIES

EDUCATIONAL, PSYCHOLOGICAL, AND PERSONALITY TESTS OF 1933 AND 1934

EDUCATIONAL, PSYCHOLOGICAL, AND PERSONALITY TESTS OF 1933, 1934, AND 1935

EDUCATIONAL, PSYCHOLOGICAL, AND PERSONALITY TESTS OF 1936

THE NINETEEN THIRTY-EIGHT MENTAL MEASUREMENTS YEARBOOK

THE NINETEEN FORTY MENTAL MEASUREMENTS YEARBOOK

THE THIRD MENTAL MEASUREMENTS YEARBOOK

THE FOURTH MENTAL MEASUREMENTS YEARBOOK

THE FIFTH MENTAL MEASUREMENTS YEARBOOK

TESTS IN PRINT

THE SIXTH MENTAL MEASUREMENTS YEARBOOK

READING TESTS AND REVIEWS

PERSONALITY TESTS AND REVIEWS

THE SEVENTH MENTAL MEASUREMENTS YEARBOOK

TESTS IN PRINT II

ENGLISH TESTS AND REVIEWS

FOREIGN LANGUAGE TESTS AND REVIEWS

INTELLIGENCE TESTS AND REVIEWS

MATHEMATICS TESTS AND REVIEWS

PERSONALITY TESTS AND REVIEWS II

READING TESTS AND REVIEWS II

SCIENCE TESTS AND REVIEWS

SOCIAL STUDIES TESTS AND REVIEWS

VOCATIONAL TESTS AND REVIEWS

THE EIGHTH MENTAL MEASUREMENTS YEARBOOK

TESTS IN PRINT III

THE NINTH MENTAL MEASUREMENTS YEARBOOK

THE SUPPLEMENT TO THE NINTH MENTAL MEASUREMENTS YEARBOOK

INSTITUTE DIRECTOR
BARBARA S. PLAKE

PRODUCTION AND SECRETARIAL
DEBRA S. RUTHSATZ
ROSEMARY G. SIECK

RESEARCH ASSISTANTS

JANET ALLISON
STEPHEN AXFORD
CAROL BERIGAN
JERENE BISHOP
MICHAEL BONNER
CRYSTAL GROW
HAEOK KIM
JULIE KREJCI
CHRISTOPHER MILNE
BUNNY POZEHL
DEBRA SABERS
MARK SHRIVER
RICHARD SONNENBERG

THE TENTH MENTAL MEASUREMENTS YEARBOOK

JANE CLOSE CONOLEY and JACK J. KRAMER

Editors

LINDA L. MURPHY

Managing Editor

The Buros Institute of Mental Measurements
The University of Nebraska-Lincoln
Lincoln, Nebraska

1989
Distributed by The University of Nebraska Press

LC 39-3422
ISBN 0-910674-31-0

Manufactured in the United States of America

The paper used in this publication meets the minimum requirements of American National Standard for Information Sciences—Permanence of Paper for Printed Library Materials, ANSI Z39.48–1984.

Note to Users

The staff of the Buros Institute of Mental Measurements has made every effort to ensure the accuracy of the test information included in this work. However, the Buros Institute of Mental Measurements and the Editors of *The Tenth Mental Measurements Yearbook* do not assume, and hereby expressly and absolutely disclaim, any liability to any party for any loss or damage caused by errors or omissions or statements of any kind in *The Tenth Mental Measurements Yearbook.* This disclaimer also includes judgments or statements of any kind made by test reviewers, who were extended the professional freedom appropriate to their task; their judgments and opinions are their own, uninfluenced in any way by the Buros Institute or the Editors.

All material included in *The Tenth Mental Measurements Yearbook* is intended solely for the use of our readers. None of this material, including reviewer statements, may be used in advertising or for any other commercial purpose.

TABLE OF CONTENTS

INTRODUCTION

The publication of the *Tenth Mental Measurements Yearbook* (*10th MMY*) completes the first cycle of the new production schedule for the *Yearbook* series. Our goal of making critical, scholarly evaluations of test materials available to consumers on a regular basis has been achieved through publication of *The Supplement to the Ninth Mental Measurements Yearbook* in 1988 and now the *10th MMY* in 1989. As with previous *Yearbooks*, the *10th MMY* consists of descriptive information, references, and critical reviews of commercially published English-language tests. Criteria for inclusion of a test in the *10th MMY* are that the test be new or revised since last reviewed in the *MMY* series. Descriptive information about the contents and use of the newest Buros Institute of Mental Measurements publication is provided below.

THE TENTH MENTAL MEASUREMENTS YEARBOOK

The *10th MMY* contains reviews of tests that are new or significantly revised since the publication of the *Ninth MMY* in 1985. We have included reviews of tests that were available before our production deadline of April 1, 1989. Reviews, descriptions, and references associated with older tests can be located in other Buros publications such as previous *MMY*s and *Tests in Print III*.

The contents of the *10th MMY* include: (*a*) a bibliography of 396 commercially available tests, new or revised, published as separates for use with English-speaking subjects; (*b*) 569 critical test reviews by well-qualified professional people who were selected by the editors on the basis of their expertise in measurement and, often, the content of the test being reviewed; (*c*) bibliographies of references for specific tests related to the construction, validity, or use of the tests in various settings; (*d*) a test title index with appropriate cross-references; (*e*) a classified subject index; (*f*) a publishers directory and index, including addresses and test listings by publisher; (*g*) a name index including the names of all authors of tests, reviews, or references; (*h*) an index of acronyms for easy reference when a test acronym, not the full title, is known; and (*i*) a score index to refer readers to tests featuring particular kinds of scores that are of interest to them.

The volume is organized like an encyclopedia, with tests being ordered alphabetically by title. If the title of a test is known, the reader can locate the test immediately without having to consult the Index of Titles.

The page headings reflect the encyclopedic organization. The page heading of the left-hand page cites the number and title of the first test listed on that page, and the page heading of the right-hand page cites the number and title of

TABLE 1
TESTS BY MAJOR CLASSIFICATIONS

Classification	Number	Percentage
Vocations	100	25.3
Personality	72	18.2
Miscellaneous	43	10.9
Developmental	31	7.8
Intelligence and Scholastic Aptitude	28	7.1
English	24	6.1
Reading	24	6.1
Speech and Hearing	22	5.6
Education	20	5.1
Achievement	12	3.0
Mathematics	9	2.2
Social Studies	3	.8
Fine Arts	2	.5
Foreign Languages	2	.5
Sensory-Motor	2	.5
Neuropsychological	2	.5
Total	396	100.0

the last test listed on that page. All numbers presented in the various indexes are test numbers, not page numbers. Page numbers are important only for the Table of Contents and are indicated at the bottom of each page.

TESTS AND REVIEWS

The 10*th MMY* contains descriptive information on 396 tests as well as 569 test reviews by 303 different authors. The reviewed tests have generated 1,153 references in the professional literature and reviewers have supplied 727 additional references in their reviews. Table 1 presents statistics on the number and percentage of tests in each of the 16 major classifications. Two new categories have been added since the publication of the 9*th MMY*, Education and Foreign Language. Two areas, Multi-Aptitude and Science, had no tests included in the 10*th MMY*.

Table 2 provides the percentages of new and revised or supplemented tests according to major classifications. Overall, slightly more than half of the tests included in the 10*th MMY* are new and have not been listed in a previous *MMY*. The Index of Titles can be consulted to determine if a test is new or revised.

Our goal is to include all English language, commercially published tests that are new or revised. No minimal standards exist and inclusion of a test in the *MMY* does not mean that a test has met any standard of "goodness." We attempt to gather all tests, good and bad alike. We select our reviewers carefully and let well-informed readers decide for themselves about the quality of the tests.

Table 3 presents statistics on the review coverage for the various classifications. The 10*th MMY* contains 569 original reviews spread across 351 tests. Almost 90% of the tests included in the 10*th MMY* are reviewed, with more than 60% of the tests having two reviews.

Because there are too many new and revised tests to permit all to be reviewed, some tests have had to be given priority over others. The highest priority has been given to tests sold commercially in the United States. Some tests have not been reviewed because (*a*) they were published too late to meet our production schedule; (*b*) competent reviewers could not be located; (*c*) persons who agreed to review did not meet their commitment; or (*d*) reviews were rejected as not meeting minimum *MMY* standards.

The selection of reviewers was done with great care. The objective was to secure measurement and subject specialists who represent a variety of different viewpoints. It was also important to find individuals who would write critical reviews competently, judiciously, and fairly. Reviewers were identified by means of extensive searches of the professional literature, attendance at professional meetings, recommendations from leaders in various professional fields, previous performance on earlier reviews, and through what might best be described as

TABLE 2
NEW AND REVISED OR SUPPLEMENTED TESTS BY MAJOR CLASSIFICATIONS

Classification	Number of Tests	Percentage New	Percentage Revised
Achievement	12	41.7	58.3
Developmental	31	58.1	41.9
Education	20	65.0	35.0
English	24	58.3	41.7
Fine Arts	2	50.0	50.0
Foreign Languages	2	50.0	50.0
Intelligence and Scholastic Aptitude	28	60.1	39.9
Mathematics	9	88.9	11.1
Miscellaneous	43	60.5	39.5
Neuropsychological	2	0.0	100.0
Personality	72	52.8	47.2
Reading	24	62.5	37.5
Sensory-Motor	2	100.0	0.0
Social Studies	3	100.0	0.0
Speech and Hearing	22	59.1	40.9
Vocations	100	47.0	53.0
Total	396	55.8	44.2

TABLE 3
TEST REVIEWS IN THE 10TH MMY

Classification	Number of Reviews	Number of Tests Reviewed	Percentage of Tests 1 or More Reviews	Percentage of Tests 2 or More Reviews
Achievement	20	12	100.0	66.7
Developmental	56	31	100.0	80.6
Education	31	19	95.0	60.0
English	36	22	91.7	58.3
Fine Arts	3	2	100.0	50.0
Foreign Language	2	1	50.0	50.0
Intelligence and Scholastic Aptitude	51	28	100.0	78.6
Mathematics	10	6	66.7	44.4
Miscellaneous	64	41	95.3	55.8
Neuropsychological	3	2	100.0	50.0
Personality	111	70	97.2	58.3
Reading	41	23	95.8	75.0
Sensory-Motor	3	2	100.0	50.0
Social Studies	1	1	33.3	0.0
Speech and Hearing	36	21	95.5	68.2
Vocations	101	70	70.0	30.0
Total	569	351	88.6	55.1

general professional knowledge. Perusal of reviews in this volume will also reveal that reviewers work in and represent a cross-section of the places in society in which tests are taught and used: universities, public schools, business, community agencies, private practice, and beyond. These reviewers represent an outstanding array of professional talent, and their contributions are obviously of primary importance in making this *Yearbook* a valuable resource.

Readers of test reviews in the 10*th MMY* are encouraged to exercise an active, analytical, and evaluative perspective in reading the reviews. Just as one would evaluate a test, the reader should evaluate critically the reviewer's comments about the test. The reviewers selected are outstanding professionals in their respective fields, but it is inevitable that their reviews also reflect their individual learning histories. The *Mental Measurements Yearbooks* are intended to stimulate critical thinking about the selection of the best available test for a given purpose, not the passive acceptance of reviewer judgment. Active, evaluative reading is the key to the most effective use of the professional expertise offered in each of the reviews.

REFERENCES

This yearbook lists a total of 1,880 references related to the development, psychometric quality, and use of specific tests. This figure may be slightly inflated because a reference involving more than one test may be listed under each of the tests in question, or because of overlap between the "Test References" section and the "Reviewer's References" section for a given test. The "Reviewer's References" section groups the reviewer's references in one convenient listing for easy identification and use by the reader. Of the total of 1,880 references, 1,153 are included under "Test References" and 727 are included under "Reviewer's References."

All references listed under "Test References" have been selected by Buros Institute staff searching through hundreds of professional journals. Because of the great proliferation of tests in recent years, it was decided to increase test and review coverage but to limit the increase in references by not including theses and dissertations. There is ample justification for this in that the findings from theses and dissertations, if worthwhile, usually find their way into the journal literature.

As has been traditional with Buros Institute publications, all references are listed chronologically and then alphabetically by author within year. The format for references in journals is author, year, title, journal, volume, and page numbers; for books it is author, year, title, place of publication, and publisher. A large number of additional references are listed in *Tests in Print III*, which was published in 1983.

Table 4 presents all tests in this yearbook that generated more than 10 references. Within the table the tests are also rank-ordered according to number of references. This table refers only to those references listed under "Test References." The references are valuable as additions to our cumulative knowledge about specific tests, particularly as supplements to in-house studies, and are also a useful resource for further research.

INDEXES

As mentioned earlier, *The* 10*th MMY* includes six indexes invaluable as aids to effective use: (*a*) Index of Titles, (*b*) Index of Acronyms, (*c*) Classified Subject Index, (*d*) Publishers Directory and Index, (*e*) Index of Names, and (*f*) Score Index. Additional comment on these indexes will be presented below.

Index of Titles. Because the organization of the 10*th MMY* is encyclopedic in nature, with

TABLE 4
NUMBER OF REFERENCES FOR MOST FREQUENTLY CITED TESTS

NAME OF TEST	NUMBER OF REFERENCES
Wide Range Achievement Test—Revised	161
Stanford-Binet Intelligence Scale, Fourth Edition	89
Multiple Affect Adjective Check List, Revised	84
Bayley Scales of Infant Development	80
California Achievement Tests, Forms E and F	68
Personality Research Form, 3rd Edition	68
Iowa Tests of Basic Skills, Forms G and H	45
Metropolitan Achievement Tests, Sixth Edition	45
Myers-Briggs Type Indicator	42
Woodcock Reading Mastery Tests—Revised	38
Maslach Burnout Inventory, Second Edition	34
Personality Inventory for Children, Revised Format	20
The Self-Directed Search: A Guide to Educational and Vocational Planning	19
Learning-Style Inventory	17
Vocational Preference Inventory, 1985 Revision	17
Boehm Test of Basic Concepts—Revised	16
Classroom Environment Scale, Second Edition	16
Eating Disorder Inventory	16
Detroit Tests of Learning Aptitude (Second Edition)	15
Gray Oral Reading Tests, Revised	15
Cognitive Abilities Test, Form 4	13
Diagnostic Interview for Borderline Patients	12

the tests ordered alphabetically by title, the test title index does not have to be consulted to find a test for which the title is known. However, the title index has some features that make it useful beyond its function as a complete title listing. First it includes cross-reference information useful for tests with superseded or alternative titles or tests commonly (and sometime inaccurately) known by multiple titles. Second, it identifies tests that are new or revised. It is important to keep in mind that the numbers in this index, like those for all *MMY* indexes, are test numbers and not page numbers.

Index of Acronyms. Some tests seem to be better known by their acronyms than by their full titles. The Index of Acronyms can help in these instances; it refers the reader to the full title of the test and to the relevant descriptive information and reviews.

Classified Subject Index. The Classified Subject Index classifies all tests listed in the 10*th MMY* into 16 major categories: Achievement, Developmental, Education, English, Fine Arts, Foreign Language, Intelligence and Scholastic Aptitude, Mathematics, Miscellaneous, Neuropsychological, Personality, Reading, Sensory-Motor, Social Studies, Speech and Hearing, and Vocations. Each test entry includes test title, population for which the test is intended, and test number. The Classified Subject Index is of great help to readers who seek a listing of tests in given subject areas. The Classified Subject Index represents a starting point for readers who know their area of interest but do not know how to further focus that interest in order to identify the best test(s) for their particular purposes.

Publishers Directory and Index. The Publishers Directory and Index includes the names and addresses of the publishers of all tests included in the 10*th MMY* plus a listing of test numbers for each individual publisher. This index can be particularly useful in obtaining addresses for specimen sets or catalogs after the test reviews have been read and evaluated. It can also be useful when a reader knows the publisher of a certain test but is uncertain about the test title, or when a reader is interested in the range of tests published by a given publisher.

Index of Names. The Index of Names provides a comprehensive list of names, indicating authorship of a test, test review, or reference.

Score Index. The Score Index is an index to all scores generated by the tests in the 10*th MMY*. Test titles are sometimes misleading or ambiguous, and test content may be difficult to define with precision. But test scores represent operational definitions of the variables the test author is trying to measure, and as such they often define test purpose and content more adequately than other descriptive information. A search for a particular test is most often a search for a test that measures some specific variables. Test scores and their associated labels can often be the best definitions of the variables of interest. It is in fact a detailed subject index based on the most critical operational features of any test—the scores and their associated labels.

HOW TO USE THE YEARBOOK

A reference work like *The Tenth Mental Measurements Yearbook* can be of far greater benefit to a reader if a little time is taken to become familiar with what it has to offer and how one might most effectively use it to obtain the information wanted. The first step in this process is to read the Introduction to the 10*th MMY* in its entirety. The second step is to become familiar with the six indexes and particularly with the instructions preceding each index listing. The third step is to make actual use of the book by looking up needed information. This third step is simple if one keeps in mind the following possibilities:

1. If you know the title of the test, use the alphabetical page headings to go directly to the test entry.
2. If you do not know, cannot find, or are unsure of the title of a test, consult the Index of Test Titles for possible variants of the title or consult the appropriate subject area of the Classified Subject Index for other possible leads or for similar or related tests in the same area. (Other uses for both of these indexes were described earlier.)
3. If you know the author of a test but not the title or publisher, consult the Index of Names and look up the author's titles until you find the test you want.
4. If you know the test publisher but not the title or author, consult the Publishers Directory and Index and look up the publisher's titles until you find the test you want.
5. If you are looking for a test that yields a particular kind of score, but have no knowledge of which test that might be, look up the score in the Index of Scores and locate the test or tests that include the score variable of interest.
6. Once you have found the test or tests you are looking for, read the descriptive entries for these tests carefully so that you can take advantage of the information provided. A description of the information provided in these test entries will be presented later in this section.
7. Read the test reviews carefully and analytically, as described earlier in this Introduction. There is much to be gained from reading these reviews, and you are well advised to take the time and make the effort to read them thoroughly and with understanding.
8. Once you have read the descriptive information and test reviews, you may want to order a specimen set for a particular test so that you can examine it firsthand. The Publishers Directory and Index has the address information needed to obtain specimen sets or catalogs.

Making Effective Use of the Test Entries. The test entries include extensive information. For each test, descriptive information is presented in the following order:

a) TITLES. Test titles are printed in boldface type. Secondary or series titles are set off from main titles by a colon.

b) PURPOSE. For each test we have included a brief, clear statement describing the purpose of the test. Often these statements are quotations from the test manual.

c) DESCRIPTIONS OF THE GROUPS FOR WHICH THE TEST IS INTENDED. The grade, chronological age, or semester range, or the employment category is usually given. "Grades 1.5–2.5, 2–3, 4–13, 13– 17" means that there are four test booklets: a booklet for the middle of first grade through the middle of the second grade, a booklet for the beginning of the second grade through the end of third grade, a booklet for grades 4 through 12 inclusive, and a booklet for undergraduate and graduate students in colleges and universities.

d) DATE OF PUBLICATION. The inclusive range of publication dates for the various forms, accessories, and additions of a test is reported.

e) ACRONYM. When a test is often referred to by an acronym, the acronym is given in the test entry immediately following the publication date.

f) SPECIAL COMMENTS. Some entries contain special notations, such as: "for research use only"; "revision of the ABC Test"; "tests administered monthly at centers throughout the United States"; "subtests available as separates"; and "verbal creativity." A statement such as "verbal creativity" is intended to further describe what the test claims to measure. Some of the test entries include factual statements that imply criticism of the test, such as "1980 test identical with test copyrighted 1970" and "no manual."

g) PART SCORES. The number of part scores is presented along with their titles or descriptions of what they are intended to represent.

h) INDIVIDUAL OR GROUP TEST. All tests are group tests unless otherwise indicated.

i) FORMS, PARTS, AND LEVELS. All available forms, parts, and levels are listed.

j) COST. Price information is reported for test packages (usually 20 to 35 tests), answer sheets, all other accessories, and specimen sets. The statement "$17.50 per 35 tests" means that all accessories are included unless otherwise indicated by the reporting of separate prices for accessories. The statement also means 35 tests of one level, one edition, or one part unless stated otherwise. Because test prices can change very quickly, the year that the listed test prices were obtained is also given. Foreign currency is assigned the appropriate symbol. When prices are given in foreign dollars, a qualifying symbol is added (e.g., A$16.50 refers to 16 dollars and 50 cents in Australian currency). Along with cost, the publication date and number of pages on which print occurs is reported for test booklets, manuals, technical reports, profiles, and other nonapparatus accessories (e.g., '85, 102 pages). All types of machine-scorable answer sheets available for use with a specific test are also reported in the descriptive entry.

k) SCORING AND REPORTING SERVICES. Scoring and reporting services provided by publishers are reported along with information on costs. In a few cases, special computerized scoring and interpretation services are given in separate entries immediately following the test.

l) TIME. The number of minutes of actual working time allowed examinees and the approximate length of time needed for administering a test are reported whenever obtainable. The latter figure is always enclosed in parentheses. Thus, "50(60) minutes" indicates that the examinees are allowed 50 minutes of working time and that a total of 60 minutes is needed to administer the test. A time of "40–50 minutes" indicates an untimed test which takes approximately 45 minutes to administer, or—in a few instances—a test so timed that working time and administration time are very difficult to disentangle. When the time necessary to administer a test is not reported or suggested in the test materials but has been obtained through correspondence with the test publisher or author, the time is enclosed in brackets.

m) AUTHOR. For most tests, all authors are reported. In the case of tests that appear in a new form each year, only authors of the most recent forms are listed. Names are reported exactly as printed on test booklets. Names of editors are generally not reported.

n) PUBLISHER. The name of the publisher or distributor is reported for each test. Foreign publishers are identified by listing the country in brackets immediately following the name of the publisher. The Publishers Directory and Index must be consulted for a publisher's address.

o) CLOSING ASTERISK. An asterisk following the publisher's name indicates that an entry was prepared from a firsthand examination of the test materials.

p) FOREIGN ADAPTATIONS. Revisions and adaptations of tests for foreign use are listed in a separate paragraph following the original edition.

q) SUBLISTINGS. Levels, editions, subtests, or parts of a test available in separate booklets are sometimes presented as sublistings with titles set in small capitals. Sub-sublistings are indented and titles are set in italic type.

r) CROSS REFERENCES. For tests that have been listed previously in a Buros Institute publication, a test entry includes—if relevant—a final paragraph containing a cross reference to the reviews, excerpts, and references for that test in those volumes. In the cross references, "T3:467" refers to test 467 in *Tests in Print III*, "8:1023" refers to test 1023 in *The Eighth Mental Measurements Yearbook*, "T2:144" refers to test 144 in *Tests in Print II*, "7:637" refers to test 637 in *The Seventh Mental Measurements Yearbook*, "P:262" refers to test 262 in *Personality Tests and Reviews I*, "2:1427" refers to test 1427 in *The* 1940 *Yearbook*, and "1:1110" refers to test 1110 in *The* 1938 *Yearbook*. In the case of batteries and programs, the paragraph also includes cross references—from the battery to the separately listed subtests and vice versa—to entries in this volume and to entries and reviews in earlier yearbooks. Test numbers not preceded by a colon refer to tests in this *Yearbook*; for example "see 45" refers to test 45 in this *Yearbook*.

If a reader finds something in a test description that is not understood, the descriptive material presented above can be referred to again and can often help to clarify the matter.

ACKNOWLEDGEMENTS

The publication of the 10*th Mental Measurements Yearbook* could not have been accomplished without the contributions of many individuals. The editors acknowledge gratefully the talent, expertise, and dedication of all those who have assisted in the publication process. Foremost among this group is Linda Murphy,

Managing Editor. Her constant effort, knowledge, editorial skill, and cheerful attitude made our job as editors easier than we could have imagined. Nor would the publication of this volume be possible without the efforts of Debbie Ruthsatz, Secretarial Specialist, and Rosemary Sieck, Word Processing Specialist. As always, their efforts go far beyond that required as part of normal job responsibilities. We are also pleased to acknowledge the continuous assistance available from the Director of the Buros Institute, Dr. Barbara Plake. Her enthusiasm for our work, visionary leadership, and skill in building a cohesive team effort are important to us all. The sense of accomplishment and pride we feel with the publication of the 10*th MMY* is shared by our entire staff and our heartfelt thank you is extended to the four individuals mentioned above. During the early stages of the preparation of the 10*th MMY*, James V. Mitchell, Jr. served as the Director of the Buros Institute of Mental Measurements. His dedication to the mission of the Institute and his efforts in providing leadership during the period in which the Institute was established at the University of Nebraska-Lincoln are acknowledged.

Our gratitude is also extended to the many reviewers who have prepared test reviews for the Buros Institute. Their willingness to take time from busy professional schedules to share their expertise in the form of thoughtful test reviews is appreciated. The *Mental Measurements Yearbook* would not exist were it not for their efforts.

Many graduate students have contributed to the publication of this volume. Their efforts have included reviewing test catalogs, fact checking reviews, looking for test references, and innumerable other tasks. We thank Janet Allison, Stephen Axford, Carol Berigan, Jerene Bishop, Michael Bonner, Crystal Grow, Haeok Kim, Julie Krejci, Christopher Milne, Bunny Pozehl, Debra Sabers, Mark Shriver, and Richard Sonnenberg for their assistance.

Appreciation is also extended to our National and Departmental Advisory Committees for their willingness to assist in the operation of the Buros Institute. During the period in which this volume was prepared the National Advisory Committee has included Luella Buros, T. Anne Cleary, Roger Lennon, Robert Ebel, Stephen Elliott, William Mehrens, Ellis Page, Daniel Reschly, Lawrence Rudner, Lyle Schoenfeldt, Richard Snow, Julian Stanley, Douglas Whitney, and Frank Womer. The Buros Institute is part of the Department of Educational Psychology of the University of Nebraska-Lincoln and we have benefitted from the many departmental colleagues who have contributed to our Departmental Advisory Committee including Robert Brown, Roger Bruning, Collie Conoley, David Dixon (now at Ball State University), Terry Gutkin, Ronn Johnson, Kenneth Orton, Wayne Piersel, Barbara Plake, Royce Ronning, Toni Santmire, and Steven Wise. We are also grateful for the contribution of the University of Nebraska Press, which provides expert consultation and serves as distributor of the *MMY* series.

This volume would have taken much longer to produce were it not for the efforts of Dave Spanel and his colleagues at the UNL Computing Resource Center.

Elsewhere in this volume, Luella Buros' presentation at the Sixth Buros-Nebraska Symposium on Measurement and Testing has been reproduced. Her continued interest in and involvement with the Buros Institute are vital to the Institute's continuing mission. We are inspired by her unflagging commitment to the work begun by Oscar Buros over a half century ago.

Finally, none of what we accomplish as editors would be as meaningful without the support of our families. Thanks Collie, Brian, Colleen, Collin, and Jeannie, Jamie, and Jessica.

SUMMARY

The preparation and production of the 10*th MMY* has taken a good deal of time and involved many different individuals. Our hope is that this volume continues to fill an important need for critical reviews of testing products. The 10*th MMY* will fulfill its purpose if its use creates substantive gains in the selection, use, and interpretation of commercially published tests.

PRESENTATION
by
MRS. LUELLA BUROS
at the 50th Anniversary Celebration
of the *Mental Measurements Yearbooks*
Buros-Nebraska Symposium on Measurement and Testing
October 6–7, 1988

I should like all of you to know how delighted I am to be here to celebrate the 50th Anniversary of the *Mental Measurements Yearbooks*, dedicated to Oscar's memory. I know he would have loved being here to thank all of you for this beautiful tribute, but most of all, to thank Barbara Plake, Jim Mitchell, Jane Conoley, Jack Kramer, the Institute staff, and all you wonderful people here at the University of Nebraska, Lincoln, for making our long-cherished dreams come true.

I know that Oscar would also want me to express our deepest thanks and appreciation to all of you present, across our nation, and in the English-speaking world, who have contributed so generously in helping to make this landmark celebration possible.

Over the years, numerous individuals, professional organizations and others, have cooperated, by providing information and materials essential to the publication of the *Yearbook*, for which we are very grateful. But, as many of you know, Oscar's most heartwarming reward in preparing the *MMY*s was his relationship with contributing reviewers, whose critical evaluations of tests constitute the very heart of the *Yearbooks*, so to all of you, our eternal thanks and gratitude, for your conscientious loyal commitment to the crusading objectives and values for which the *Yearbooks* were founded.

When the first *MMY* was published in 1938, it was Oscar's hopes and dreams to publish a *Yearbook* annually. Unhappily, however, we were never able to muster the time or financial resources to do this. The time lag between *Yearbooks* was very disturbing to him, and in later years, he believed it was imperative for the Institute to adopt computer technology for greater flexibility and ease in preparing future publications. I know that Oscar would be thrilled beyond words, to know that not only have these dreams been realized, but in addition, the Institute has established an *MMY* online database with monthly updates which, combined with annual *MMY*s, must surely make it the most updated, comprehensive, and reliable information service for test users, in existence.

I feel deeply grateful and indebted to the Administrators of the University of Nebraska Foundation (especially Woody Varner), and the University of Nebraska, Lincoln, for their confidence, trust, and support in continuing the vital work and services of the Buros Institute, and also to the Department of Educational Psychology, Teachers College, of which the Institute is a part, and to their Departmental Advisory Committee for their valuable help and support.

I wish to give special thanks to Dr. Cecil R. Reynolds for his sincere initial efforts in helping to bring the Institute to UNL.

I also wish to warmly thank members of the National Advisory Committee, and participants of the Buros-Nebraska Symposium on Measurement and Testing, for your invaluable contributions and support to the Institute, in behalf of the measurement and testing community, education, and society.

Most of all, however, I wish to express our deepest thanks and gratitude to Dr. James V. Mitchell, Jr., the Institute's first director and editor at UNL, for his untiring dedicated commitment, vision, and inspired leadership, during the Institute's crucial first seven years at UNL, and also to his highly competent professional associates, Dr. Barbara S. Plake, now director of the Institute, to Dr. Jane Close Conoley and Dr. Jack J. Kramer, Editors, and the loyal supporting Institute staff, for their solid record of achievement, in advancing the Institute's progress and growth, in both production and services over the past nine years.

I know that Oscar would be very pleased, as I am, that the Institute, and professional staff, are continuing to receive distinguished awards and honors at home and abroad, for outstanding contributions to the profession.

As many of you know, the *Supplement to the Ninth MMY*, published July 1988, marks an important milestone in the history of the Institute, since it not only commemorates the 50th Anniversary of the *MMY*s, but ushers in a new era of annual productions of the *Yearbooks*, making the designation *Yearbook* in the title, a reality—and our long cherished dreams come true.

What a magnificent 50th Anniversary gift to Oscar's memory (and to me) from the Buros Institute staff—and to repeat, from all of you wonderful people, who over the years, have contributed so much in helping to make this historic and memorable 50th *MMY* Anniversary celebration possible.

We thank you all from the bottom of our hearts.

A message given in appreciation by Mrs. Luella Buros, commemorating the 50th Anniversary of the Mental Measurements Yearbooks, *dedicated to the memory of Oscar Krisen Buros, Founder of the* MMY*s, at the Annual Buros-Nebraska Symposium on Measurement and Testing, University of Nebraska, Lincoln, on October 7, 1988.*

Tests and Reviews

[1]

The ABC Inventory to Determine Kindergarten and School Readiness. Purpose: Measures kindergarten and school readiness and identifies children too immature for kindergarten or first grade before enrollment. Ages 3.5–6.5; 1965–85; individual; an individualized computer-generated narrative report, The Learning Temperament Profile (based on child's ABC Inventory scores), available from publisher; 1985 price data: $8 per 50 copies of Inventory and administration and scoring procedures ('85, 4 pages); $.48 per child per Learning Temperament Profile; (10) minutes; Normand Adair and George Blesch; Educational Studies & Development.*

See T3:7 (2 references); see also T2:1691 (2 references); for a review by David P. Weikart, see 7:739 (2 references).

Review of The ABC Inventory to Determine Kindergarten and School Readiness by CARL J. DUNST, Director, Family, Infant and Preschool Program, Western Carolina Center, Morganton, NC:

The ABC Inventory is a screening instrument designed for use with preschoolers to determine readiness for kindergarten or first grade placement. The authors indicate the scale can be completed in about 10 minutes, and that administration does not require any special training on the part of the test examiner.

The scale is organized according to four groups of items: Section I asks a child to draw a man, Section II includes items that require identification and discrimination (e.g., "What has wings?"), Section III requires answers to a series of questions (e.g., "How do we hear?"), and Section IV involves completion of simple tasks (e.g., repeating a four-digit sequence). The scores obtained from each section are summed to obtain a total scale score that is used for both categorization (classification) purposes and determination of a "Readiness Age." A child is assigned to one of four readiness categories based on his or her score. Readiness ages vary from 3-6 to 6-7 years in 1-month intervals. The authors report a correlation of $r = .78$ between the readiness ages and mental ages (Stanford-Binet) for a small pilot sample ($N = 14$).

No measures of reliability for the raw scores, categorization scheme, or readiness ages are reported in the test manual nor could any studies be located that specifically assessed the reliability of the ABC. The lack of adequate reliability studies is a serious problem given the fact the behavior of preschoolers is so much more variable than that of older children.

The authors argue they have established the reliability of the ABC by finding no significant differences in the mean scale scores for matched samples of children enrolled in the same school district 2 years apart. The mean ABC scores were 65.51 and 66.71 for the two separate samples. For comparable samples from other school districts, mean ABC scores have varied from as low as 54.60 (Schooler & Anderson, 1979) to as high as 80.91 (Van Horn & Holland, 1974). What the authors have established is that the average group scores are stable for children in the same community across time, not that there is stability in the individual scores of children in the same community cohort. The method the authors used for determining stability does not constitute adequate evidence for the reliability of the ABC.

The principal method used by the authors for establishing the validity of the ABC has been to ascertain whether or not scale scores accurately predicted school failure. In a study of 166 preschoolers, a total scale score less than 70 correlated $r = .71$ with kindergarten failure. In another analysis of the same data, the sample was divided into equal subgroups of 83 subjects each based on a median split, and the percentage of children failing first grade ascertained. Of the 43 children failing first grade, 37 or 86% were identified accurately based on the group assignment. While this seems impressive, it should also be noted that this categorization method failed to identify 46 or 37% of the children who passed first grade.

The extent to which the ABC is related to other readiness tests as well as school achievement has been reported by a number of investigators. Van Horn and Holland (1974) administered, respectively, the ABC and Metropolitan Readiness Test to a large sample of kindergartners 12 months apart, and found that the two verbal subtests of the ABC had a multiple $R = .57$, and the two perceptual-motor subtests had a multiple $R = .56$ with the Metropolitan Readiness Test. However, when an ABC cutoff score of 69 was used to determine readiness for first grade based on Metropolitan Readiness Test performance, only 15% of the children not deemed ready according to the ABC were classified correctly, whereas 97% of children deemed ready were classified correctly. (A score of 69 approximately divided the standardization sample into high and low ABC score groups.) At least in terms of predicting Metropolitan Readiness performance, the ABC does a remarkably poor job of identifying children who are likely to have subsequent learning difficulties. In a study predicting first and third grade academic achievement from both ABC and Metropolitan Readiness Test scores, Randel, Fry, and Ralls (1977) found an $r = .19$ for the ABC and $r = .34$ for the Metropolitan for first grade performance, and an $r = .23$ for the ABC and $r = .51$ for the Metropolitan for third grade performance. Taken together, these various sets of data indicate the ABC is not very accurate in terms of predicting school failure. The Metropolitan is a better predictor of school-age academic standing.

SUMMARY. The ABC is a screening instrument designed to identify children who are and are not ready for kindergarten and first grade placements. Although the scale has promise as a simple cost-efficient screening instrument, its potential usefulness awaits adequate reliability and validity studies. Until such studies are conducted, it is better to consider an alternative instrument for screening purposes.

REVIEWER'S REFERENCES

Van Horn, K. R., & Holland, J. M. (1974). Relationship between the ABC Inventory and the Metropolitan Readiness Test. *Psychology in the Schools*, 11, 396-399.

Randel, M. A., Fry, M. A., & Ralls, E. M. (1977). Two readiness measures as predictors of first- and third-grade reading achievement. *Psychology in the Schools*, 14, 37-40.

Schooler, D. L., & Anderson, R. L. (1979). Race differences of the Developmental Test of Visual Motor Integration, the Slosson Intelligence Test, and the ABC Inventory. *Psychology in the Schools*, 16, 453-456.

Review of The ABC Inventory to Determine Kindergarten and School Readiness by J. JEFFREY GRILL, Professor of Special Education, The College of Saint Rose, Albany, NY:

The stated purpose of The ABC Inventory to Determine Kindergarten and School Readiness is to "identify children who are immature for a standard school program." This purpose is appropriate, but the standard school program for kindergarten and first grade is not now what it was when the ABC Inventory was constructed between 1960 and 1962.

The ABC Inventory consists of a one-page (two-sided) protocol containing all Inventory items, space for the demographic data, and a table to convert raw scores to "Ready Ages." Items are arranged in four sections: Section I requires the child to draw a man (in the 6 inch x 6 inch space provided on the face page of the protocol); Section II requires one-word responses to questions on general information; Section III requires one-word answers to questions that seem to assess reasoning ability; Section IV requires performance on four tasks (i.e., counting four squares, folding a paper triangle, repeating digits, and copying a square).

Although the instrument is appealing in its simplicity and its use of several time-honored indices of school readiness (Sections I and IV), the ABC Inventory shows its age in both items and their presentation on the protocol. For example, Section I needs editing to remove sexist language. More appropriate wording would replace "man" with "person." Further, this section should be completed on a separate, clean sheet of paper in order to avoid the clutter of the demographic and tabular portions of the face page.

Scoring of the inventory is direct, but seems arbitrary and simplistic. In Section I, 4 points are awarded for each of 16 body parts and each article of clothing included. In Sections II and III, 2 points are given for each correct response, but in Section IV, 8 points are awarded for successful performance on each task. No rationale is provided for this weighting of raw scores.

For about half the items in Section II, correct responses are indicated in parentheses for the convenience of the examiner. These items could elicit a variety of appropriate responses, but only one is considered correct. Such scoring may penalize many children. For example, in item 2 the examiner asks the child to "Tell me the color" of: (*a*) grass (green), (*b*) an apple (red), (*c*) a banana (yellow). For each of these at least two or three colors could be accurately named by the child, yet, only the one response indicated as correct is given credit.

Section III, consisting of six questions (e.g., "What is ice when it melts?"; "What make a cloudy day bright?"; "How do we hear?"), seems to assess a child's comprehension and reasoning abilities. For most of these items correct responses are indicated for the examiner.

The four tasks in Section IV seem most directly related to school activities. The authors state that this section was found to be "most discriminating [of the four sections] in the group studied." That is, the authors state "Two thirds of the lower group [which is not clearly identified] failed in items 2, 3 and 4." A careful reading of the "Notes on Construction" leads one to conclude the lower group consisted of 83 of the 166 children in the standardization group who obtained raw scores below 68.

More important than the shortcomings of some of the Inventory's items are the major problems with its technical aspects and its meager, confusing manual. First, the normative sample apparently consisted of 166 children between the ages of 4 years 9 months and 4 years 11 months. However, at various points in the manual, and in promotional literature, other groups are mentioned so that the reader has no accurate understanding of the sample from which the Ready Age scores were derived. No indication of the ratio of girls to boys is given, nor are separate norms provided for girls and boys, despite the appropriateness of such norms for preschool children. The severely restricted age range of the normative sample is not appropriate for an instrument intended to determine readiness for both kindergarten and first grade. No demographic data are provided for the normative sample, thus rendering the norms useless.

Reliability is reported as a comparison of two groups of children, the 1962 group of 166, and a 1964 sample of 314. A *t*-test comparison of group means yielded no significant difference between groups. Such a comparison is not evidence of reliability. The authors offer no test-retest, split-halves, Kuder-Richardson, or alternate forms reliability data.

Information on validity, appropriately for a readiness measure, focuses on the prediction of later school performance. Unfortunately, the data presented are confusing and incomplete. Apparently the standardization group was equally divided using a median raw score of 68. The authors state that of 43 children who failed their first year of school, 37 were identified accurately and that "Seventy-seven or 63% passing, scored above 68." The reader is left to decide if such proportions are adequate evidence of predictive validity. However, because no criteria for failing are specified, and because the first year of school is not identified as kindergarten or first grade, no conclusion can be reached. The authors offer no information on content or on criterion-related validity, although they state that with a sample of 14 children a product-moment correlation of .78 was obtained between ready age and Stanford-Binet mental age.

Throughout the manual, contradictory and misleading information is presented. Section I (draw-a-man) is suggested as useful for establishing initial rapport. In the next sentence the authors state, "Frequently, children find this threatening." The normative sample is presented as consisting of 166 children, yet the authors report that, "A ready age scale was constructed by combining all test scores over a 3 year period ($N = 619$)," but no data are presented to describe the additional children.

Available at a small additional cost per child is a Learning Temperament Profile that provides individualized statistical and narrative information including test age (which may be the ready age) and percentile scores for each section and total test, a ratio IQ, descriptions of characteristics of children who scored similarly to the child being profiled, and brief, broad suggestions for instruction. Such information may be appealing, but it is practically useless and can be dangerously misleading. For example, the authors state, in the manual, that the ABC Inventory is not an intelligence test, yet the Profile provides a ratio IQ, with no indication as to how this outdated form of IQ is derived. Because no rationale is given for the division of the Inventory into four sections, age and percentile scores for the sections are meaningless.

In summary, the ABC Inventory is a quick, easily administered and scored instrument of little value. It is outdated, poorly normed, and lacking usable evidence of validity and reliability. Ironically, its title suggests that knowledge of the alphabet (for many kindergarten teachers, a favored predictor of first grade success) is assessed; oddly, no Inventory item refers to the ABCs.

[2]

Ability-Achievement Discrepancy. Purpose: "To help educators assess the degree of academic underachievement a child is experiencing based upon ability and achievement tests administered by school personnel." Students in potential need of special education programs; 1985; AAD; educator enters child's scores from ability and standardized achievement tests into computer program; 3 scores: Correlation, Discrepancy Score, Lower Bound; requires IBM PC or Apple II, +, e, or c computer, and printer; 1986 price data: $149 per complete program including 2 program disks and one data disk and user manual (36 pages); $49 per additional disk after purchase of a program; Psychoeducational Software Systems, Michael J. Furlong, and Davis C. Hayden; Southern MicroSystems.*

Review of Ability-Achievement Discrepancy by MARIBETH GETTINGER, Associate Professor, Department of Educational Psychology, University of Wisconsin-Madison, Madison, WI:

The Ability-Achievement Discrepancy (AAD) program includes a manual (36 pages) and diskette designed to facilitate a determination of "the degree of academic underachievement a child is experiencing based upon ability and achievement tests." As part of their introduction to the program, the authors clarify that although a significant ability-achievement discrepancy may be calculated with AAD, this information *alone* should not be used in making special education placement decisions. In fact, the first page of the AAD report reiterates this caution and outlines additional information or issues that should be considered by a multidisciplinary team in determining eligibility for special education services (e.g., classroom observations, work samples, etc.). Thus, the authors have carefully and appropriately delimited the purpose and use of the AAD program.

The manual and various program commands and options are easy to understand and fairly straightforward in terms of implementation. The derivation and interpretation of "discrepancy scores" and "lower bounds" are more complex; however, the authors have done an excellent job of simplifying their explanations of the psychometric justifications and statistical formulae involved. To implement the AAD program, the user enters three types of information in the following order: ability test standard scores, achievement test standard scores, and background information (e.g., age and gender of examinee). The program automatically requests four ability tests (composite and subtest scores)—Wechsler Intelligence Scale for Children—Revised (WISC-R), Kaufman Assessment Battery for Children (K-ABC), Woodcock-Johnson Psychoeducational Battery (Broad Cognitive Ability), and Stanford-Binet (1972 edition). The user may enter information (name, score, mean, standard deviation, and internal consistency reliability coefficient) for up to three additional ability tests. Three additional test slots are insufficient to accommodate the Stanford-Binet, Fourth Edition (i.e., composite and four area scores). Although the program allows the user to update particular components of the program (e.g., correlations between tests), the manual does not indicate that standard ability test information per se can be updated. Thus, for Stanford-Binet, Fourth Edition users, this is one limitation. Similarly, the program automatically requests scores from four achievement tests (subtest scores)—Wide Range Achievement Test (WRAT; 1978 or 1984 editions), K-ABC, Peabody Individual Achievement Test (PIAT), and Woodcock-Johnson (cluster scores). Information from up to four additional tests may be entered; this is probably sufficient to cover most achievement tests and batteries published since 1985 (e.g., Kaufman Test of Educational Achievement).

The program itself has several notable strengths explained with remarkable clarity in the manual. First, the determination of a child's "estimated" achievement level uses a procedure that corrects for "regression to the mean" by considering the correlation between the ability and achievement tests being compared. Thus, when an alternate ability or achievement test is used, it is the *user's* responsibility to locate (perhaps, in the test's manual) and enter the necessary correlation coefficient(s). This may be a potential drawback to using alternate tests; however, the program invokes a "default" ability-achievement correlation of .60 when none is available.

A second strength is the discrepancy information is reported as a *z*-score allowing for normal-curve comparisons and interpretations) and as a "lower bound" (i.e., the lower limit of the confidence interval for the obtained discrepancy *z*-score). This emphasis on the lower bound seems to be "pro-discrepancy." In other words, if a severe discrepancy criterion of -2.0 is used (as recommended), the lower bound values may allow a greater number of children to meet the criterion. For example, even if a child's obtained discrepancy of -1.8 does not meet the criterion, his/her lower bound score of -2.4 indicates there is a 95% probability that the true score *does* exceed the criterion. Conversely, if a child's obtained discrepancy is -2.4, his/her upper bound score of -1.8 indicates there is a 95% probability that the true score does *not* exceed the criterion. Upper bound scores can be easily calculated, however, their inclusion in the AAD program would have been appropriate and more objective.

In addition to these two particular strengths (i.e., accounting for regression to the mean and using *z*-scores with confidence intervals), there are several other positive features about the program's treatment of test information and scores that are highlighted in the manual. For example, the severe discrepancy criterion (-2.0) is automatically adjusted and reported on the printout when multiple comparisons are being made. Another interpretive aid is the transformation and reporting of all test scores as common standard scores with a mean of 100 and standard deviation of 15. Interestingly, however, Stanford-Binet scores are *not* transformed; they retain the distribution with a mean of 100 and standard deviation of 16. Users will need to remember this when entering Stanford-Binet (1972 edition) scores. The program also allows for several user options (e.g., changing the severe discrepancy criterion, instituting a comprehensive and systematic recordkeeping procedure on a data storage disk).

In summary, the AAD program is clearly presented, appropriately and carefully developed, easy to implement, and potentially useful when a determination of a severe ability-achievement discrepancy is required. It is important to remember that AAD is only an interpretive framework for test data. The upper limit, so to speak, on the reliability and validity of conclusions derived from this program is the psychometric properties of the ability and achievement tests themselves. When requisite information concerning a test is not available, the AAD does have respectable default options (e.g., .90 internal consistency), which a test may or may not exceed. Thus, AAD should be viewed as a supplement to, *not* a replacement for, the selection and utilization of ability and achievement tests with documented reliability and validity for the areas they assess.

Review of Ability-Achievement Discrepancy by JONATHAN SANDOVAL, Professor of Education, University of California, Davis, Davis, CA:

The Ability-Achievement Discrepancy (AAD) software program permits a psychological examiner to determine the rareness of a difference in a child's performance on a standardized ability test and on a standardized achievement test. An unusually large difference in favor of the ability measure is often taken as a sign of a learning disability. Output from the program includes a discrepancy score, a lower bound discrepancy score, and the correlation between the two measures. The discrepancy score is expressed as a *Z* score, which means that zero equals no discrepancy, negative numbers indicate an achievement score lower than an ability score and positive numbers indicate the reverse. The advantage of the *Z* score is that it can be compared to the normal distribution in determining the estimated frequency of the discrepancy. In addition to the discrepancy, the program also computes the standard error of measurement of the discrepancy score and uses this statistic to produce a lower bound estimate of the discrepancy. This lower bound estimate indicates the greatest discrepancy that is likely to be obtained from an individual. Thus, the lower bound estimate gives the "worst case scenario" to the interpreter. The correlation listed in the output is the correlation between the two measures that was used in the calculation of the significance of the discrepancy score. Having this value available helps the user understand why a particular value is or is not significant.

For the most part, the manual is clearly written and leads the reader carefully through the rationale behind the program's calculations. It contains appropriate cautions about the confidentiality of information generated by the program and the use of the program with minority individuals. Nice features of the program are the capacity to store data on the data disk for later institutional studies, and a number of simple error trapping routines to catch mistakes in entering numbers. The manual also contains a complete listing of the data used in the program and the formulas used in the program's operation.

Built into the program are analyses based on the Wechsler Intelligence Scale for Children—Revised (WISC-R), the 1972 Stanford-Binet, the Kaufman Assessment Battery for Children, and the Woodcock-Johnson Broad Cognitive Ability Full Scale. Each time the program is used, three optional ability tests may be entered if the user provides the mean, the standard deviation, and internal consistency reliability estimates. Many users might like to use the WISC-R factor scores or the Stanford Binet Fourth Edition full scale score, for example. The achievement tests already built into the program are the Wide Range Achievement Test, 1978 and 1984 edition, the Peabody Individual Achievement Test, the achievement measures from the Woodcock-Johnson Psycho-educational Battery and the achievement tests of the Kaufman Assessment Battery for Children. Again, other achievement tests may be added if the user has the relevant data. Because the provided tests are probably the most commonly used by school psychologists, the program will have utility for most school practitioners. It is surprising the Wechsler Preschool and Primary Scale of Intelligence (WPPSI) and the Wechsler Adult Intelligence Scale—Revised (WAIS-R) are missing. Within the program, it is possible to change the correlation between ability and achievement variables. This feature allows the program to be kept current as new data become available.

At first, the user will find the discrepancy score and the lower bound score will take some getting use to, because they are on a scale that is fairly unfamiliar to them. It might be a useful addition to have the program compute the actual difference in points on the scale of 100 with a standard deviation of 15. Users might be more comfortable with the scale used on the Wechsler and Kaufman tests, rather than the one used by the program. Another desirable feature the program lacks is the translation of the discrepancy score into an estimate of the frequency of occurrence. Although a user might look this up easily enough, it is curious that it was not included in the program.

A nice feature of the program is an adjustment for the number of comparisons made to bring the obtained discrepancy in line with probability theory. In addition, when a correlation between the ability and achievement test is not known, the program provides an estimate based on $r = .60$ and an estimated test reliability $= .90$. These are, however, fairly liberal estimates.

The manual contains a useful example of a test report and record forms to keep aggregate data. The printout includes an appropriately worded narrative.

The manual is fairly clear on how to get the program running on a computer and the program assists the user to use it to good advantage. Unfortunately the examination disk provided this reviewer did not work properly in printing discrepancies entered for optional tests (i.e., those tests not on the program's list of tests). It also did not automatically calculate an estimate based on the default values.

In summary, this program may be useful to some practitioners in spite of a limited number of features. It may not save a great deal of time in instances where tables indicating critical discrepancies using local criteria have been prepared for the practitioner.

[3]

Academic Advising Inventory. Purpose: "Designed to measure three aspects of academic advising: (1) the nature of advising relationships, seen along a developmental-prescriptive continuum, (2) the frequency of activities taking place during advising sessions, and (3) satisfaction with advising." Undergraduate students; 1984–86; AAI; manual entitled *Evaluating Academic Advising*; 5 parts: Developmental-Prescriptive Advising, Advisor-Advisee Activity Scales, Student Satisfaction With Advising, Demographic Information, Locally Generated Items (optional); 1985 price data: $17.50 per 50 inventories; $5 per 50 answer sheets; $5 per 100 advising conference records; $5.50 per manual (37 pages); $6 per specimen set; scoring service available from publisher; (20) minutes; Roger B. Winston, Jr. and Janet A. Sandor; Student Development Associates, Inc.*

Review of the Academic Advising Inventory by ROBERT D. BROWN, Professor of Educational Psychology, University of Nebraska-Lincoln, Lincoln, NE:

The Academic Advising Inventory (AAI) is designed to serve several purposes, primarily for conducting formative and summative evaluation of academic advising programs. It can be used to help monitor and improve an academic advising program and for making comparisons of advising programs across departments, colleges, or universities.

The AAI has four parts: Part I assesses the nature of advising relationships along a developmental-prescriptive continuum, Part II looks at the frequency of advising activities, Part III assesses student satisfaction with advising, and Part IV gathers demographic information.

Part I, Developmental-Prescriptive Advising, consists of 28 statements; half of these represent a developmental approach to advising, and the other half are matched items representing a prescriptive approach to advising. Overall scores indicate whether or not prescriptive advising or developmental advising is prevalent. Prescriptive advising is when the advisor primarily diagnoses student problems, prescribes remedies, and provides instructions. These activities usually center around academic matters such as course selection. Developmental advising is characterized as a caring and friendly relationship in which responsibilities are shared and the focus is on the student's total education. Respondents decide first whether the advising was prescriptive or developmental (statements are paired and randomly placed on the left or right) and then indicate the extent to which the statement is true. Mark sense scanner answer sheets are available.

This scale is divided into three subscales: Personalizing Education (8 items) reflects the extent to which advising focuses on academic *and* personal interests and concerns, the latter including career planning, extracurricular activities, personal concerns, goal setting, and use of resources on campus; Academic Decision Making (4 items) looks at the process of monitoring academic progress and collecting related information about student interests and abilities; and Selecting Courses (2 items) focuses specifically on course selection.

Part II, Advisor-Advisee Activities (30 items), asks students to report the frequency of activities during the academic year. The activities are "typical of 'good academic advising.'" The scale has five activity subscales: Exploring Institutional Policies (EIP) (5 items), which looks at policies regarding transfer of credit, probation, dismissal, and related issues; Providing Information (PI) (6 items), which includes activities related to providing information about course requirements, job placement, financial aid, and campus resources; Personal Development and Interpersonal Relationships (PDIR) (12 items), which relates to personal concerns about careers, values, goals, and activities; Registration and Class Scheduling (4 items), which looks specifically at the registration process; and Teaching Personal Skills (3 items), which looks at teaching students how to study, manage time, and set goals.

Part III, Satisfaction with Advising, has 5 items that assess overall student satisfaction, accuracy in information, notice of deadlines, availability of advising, and amount of time available.

Part IV, Demographic Information, solicits information about student age and gender and about the type and amount of advising they have had.

The authors suggest that the AAI takes about 20 minutes to complete and is best administered in group settings with the sample instructions provided. Also available is an Advising Conference Record form that can be used by students and advisors to record results of their planning and goal-setting during advising sessions.

Reliability and validity estimates are provided for the Developmental-Prescriptive Advising Scale. This scale went through several pilot testings and refinement, including factor analysis, before it appeared in its current form. Cronbach's alpha for the total score, based on 476 students, was .78. Subscale coefficients were .42 for Selecting Courses, .66 for Academic Decision-Making, and .81 for Personalizing Education. Interscale correlations ranged from .02 to .64. Validity support comes from two sources reported in the manual. One source was comparison of responses of 53 students in a relatively intensive program to 74 regularly admitted students. This study found statistically significant differences on the Developmental-Prescriptive Advising Scale and the Personalizing Education Scale but not on the other scales. Another validity source the authors present is examination of correlational relationships between the advising subscales and the activities scales. Except for the subscale dealing with selecting courses, the advising scales correlated moderately (range .16 to .60, median .35) with the activities scales.

Part II, Advisor-Advisee Scales, is not intended to be viewed as psychometrically unitary scales and, in fact, the authors strongly suggest that for evaluative purposes users examine the results from each item of this scale. Confirmation of the scale structures was reported in a 1986 Addendum to the Manual. Factor loadings for items ranged from .43 to .79 for their assigned scales and all items loaded highest on their assigned scale. Intercorrelations among items are provided for Part III, Satisfaction with Advising, and these are moderately high. The authors note as well that the more developmental the advising relationship is portrayed by the student, the greater the satisfaction with the advising.

Evaluating an academic advising program is complex and multifaceted. Students' perceptions are an important element of an evaluation. This inventory represents an excellent first step in providing institutions with a short and relatively reliable assessment tool. Its availability could save faculty committees much labor in devising their own form and, as the inventory authors attest, this inventory can be valuable in making comparisons across groups as well as providing useful information for improving advising efforts. The presence of the tool itself may stimulate departments and colleges to conduct a systematic evaluation of advising efforts.

The developmental-prescriptive continuum as presented implies that developmental advising is best. If use of the tool is coupled with faculty discussions about the purpose of advising and advising roles, faculty might consider alternative roles and activities rather than simply signing registration sheets. Not all faculty, however, may agree. Some may question the developmental role, believing that the appropriateness of this role may depend upon the context of the advising situation and the developmental level of the student. This tool can be used as an important resource in testing these questions empirically. Some institutions may be misguided enough to focus exclusively on outcomes, primarily retention, as the index of advising effectiveness. This instrument may help them consider also the process of advising and study its relationship to student satisfaction and retention.

Institutions will want to supplement the AAI with questions specific to their setting and their concerns. They may also want to gather faculty opinion and monitor faculty loads and responsibilities. As a minimum, studying this instrument and its rationale can provoke faculty and their institution to re-examine advising activities. Concerned stakeholders in either planning or evaluating advising approaches would be well served, however, by studying developmental literature cited by the authors that pertains to advising.

The authors note in the preliminary manual that these are exploratory efforts and more research is needed, but it is clear they have made an excellent start. Revisions and competing inventories may approach an evaluation differently, but this instrument can serve as the core for evaluating advising programs in many institutions.

[4]

ACER Primary Reading Survey Tests. Purpose: To provide teachers with assessments of the status of their students in the areas of reading vocabulary and reading comprehension. Grades 3, 4, 5, 6; 1971–84; 2 scores: Word Knowledge, Comprehension; revised teacher's handbook ('84, 32 pages); price information available from publisher; Word Knowledge [20] minutes, Comprehension [30] minutes, (with parallel format); Graham Ward (revised handbook); Australian Council for Educational Research [Australia].*

See T3:42 (4 references).

Review of the ACER Primary Reading Survey Tests by MARILYN FRIEND, Assistant Professor of Learning, Development, and Special Education, Northern Illinois University, DeKalb, IL:

The revised editions of the Australian Council for Educational Research Primary Reading Survey Tests are group administered, timed screening instruments designed to "test the language skills of primary school students" in grades 3, 4, 5, and 6 (Levels A, B, C, and D, respectively). This purpose is accomplished through two subtests: Word Knowledge and Comprehension. For Word Knowledge students select from four alternatives a synonym for a stimulus word presented in boldface type. For Comprehension (for which two forms are available) students read short passages and then respond to several related multiple-choice items. The testing materials include student test booklets, machine-readable answer sheets, answer keys in the form of clear acetate overlays, and a teacher's handbook.

The information contained in the handbook demonstrates that this set of tests is the product of considerable research and development effort. The handbook includes detailed instructions on the proper administration of the test, explanations of the scores obtained (reported in percentile ranks and stanine scores), suggestions on using the test results, cautions about their use, and technical information. It is conveniently organized and well written; its contents should be readily understood by even novice test users, yet the information is precise and detailed.

On the basis of technical quality, the ACER Primary Reading Survey Tests are quite sound. Content validity was established by experts (i.e., teachers, test developers, subject specialists), who rated the correspondence between item content and curricular emphases. Users are urged to carefully assess item suitability for themselves. Further, the developers established the differences in relative difficulty of the tests for the four grade levels for which the test is standardized. For the Reading Comprehension test, variations in the complexity of the topics, vocabulary, overall reading level, and types of questions (factual recall vs. inference) were also evaluated. A final strategy for establishing validity was trial testing followed by revisions and detailed item analyses.

The reliability section of the teacher's handbook begins with a discussion of what reliability is and how it can be established. The KR-20 values reported are acceptable: For the Word Knowledge subtest they range from .79 to .92 for the four test levels, and for the Comprehension subtest the values range from .84 to .93. The handbook mentions test-retest reliability as appropriate for this type of instrument; surprisingly, no data of this sort are presented.

The problems with this set of tests for potential users in the U.S. are primarily the result of its development for Australian students. For example, the norms are based on a rigorous 1983 standardization study in which careful attention was paid to the sampling design in order to accurately represent the school populations in the Australian states. However, it remains unknown how the norms relate to U.S. populations.

The occasional variations in spelling are another drawback for U.S. students. While many students would probably understand "colour" for "color," translating "tonnes" for "tons" might prove more difficult. In a speed test of language skill the potential negative impact of such variations on students' performance is a risk to be considered.

Other cautions concerning these tests should also be noted. First, the Word Knowledge subtest is actually a type of comprehension exercise since students must independently read the stimulus word and then likewise read and select the correct response alternative. Second, in the Comprehension subtest, the short passages limit the types of questions posed, thus tapping only a limited number of comprehension skills. Finally, and hopefully not trivially, the bright pink paper on which the student test booklets are printed seemed to be an unnecessary distractor.

In summary, the ACER Primary Reading Survey Tests are exactly what the developers intended: technically sound assessment instruments for assisting teachers to evaluate students' reading skills. Despite the overall quality, their use cannot be recommended for U.S. students. So many adequate similar assessment instruments have been developed in this country that no reason exists to contend with the vocabulary and norming difficulties presented by these Australian tests. Such qualifications would not apply to use in Australia.

Review of the ACER Primary Reading Survey Tests by JULIA A. HICKMAN, Assistant Professor of School Psychology, The University of Texas at Austin, Austin, TX:

The ACER Primary Reading Survey Tests are part of a series of Primary Reading Survey tests developed by the Australian Council for Educational Research. The ACER Primary Reading Survey Tests are designed to assess word knowledge and reading comprehension skills of children in grades 3 through 6. The authors group word knowledge and passage comprehension under the rubric of language learning skills.

The Word Knowledge tests consist of one form, Form R, with four levels, one at each grade 3 through 6. Each level of the test is comprised of 40 to 45 multiple-choice items in which the student is required to select among three or four alternatives the one word that has the meaning most similar to the stimulus word. To administer the test, the examiner reads three sample questions to a group of students to insure that they understand the nature of the task. The students then have 20 minutes to complete the remaining items.

A raw score for word knowledge is obtained by summing the number of items the student answers correctly. It may be that the derived score obtained from the raw score is not a valid measure of word knowledge due to the fact that children may choose the correct answer even if they do not recognize the stimulus word. It is impossible to ascertain word knowledge precisely on a paper-and-pencil, multiple-choice test administered in a group format.

There are two forms of the comprehension tests, Forms R and S, each with four levels, one for each grade 3 through 6. The student reads a passage silently and then answers multiple-choice questions (each with four options) concerning the factual meaning or inferred knowledge of the paragraph.

The comprehension tests are also administered in a group format. Prior to administering the actual test, the examiner presents three sample items again to insure the students understand the nature of the tasks. The students are given 30 minutes to complete the remaining items independently. Here again, it is questionable to consider this a complete assessment of reading comprehension as the results may simply reflect a student's word-recognition skills. That is, a student may understand what a paragraph means but may be unable to demonstrate this in the testing situation because of poorly developed word-recognition skills. When only a measure of silent reading is used as an indicator of reading comprehension, the results have little if any diagnostic value. In the test manual, the authors do provide appropriate cautions to test users regarding the limitations of the scores obtained.

Raw scores obtained on the ACER Primary Reading Survey Tests are converted to standard scores. Norm-referenced scores are also presented in the form of percentile ranks and stanine scores. The authors explain the weaknesses of percentile scores and advantages of stanine scores. Although it is preferable to use age-based standard scores when making norm-referenced comparisons, both percentile ranks and stanine scores are superior to age- or grade-equivalent scores often presented in test manuals.

The standardization and technical data reported in the test manual are adequate in some areas but lacking in most. For example, the procedures for construction and standardization of the ACER Primary Reading Survey Tests are described inadequately. The authors state that initial and revised test items were presented to "committees of critics" for review and selection, but no specification of who these critics were or how they chose the final items is forthcoming in the manual. It is implied that item-discrimination and item-difficulty indices were calculated and used to select appropriate test items, but the actual procedures are not described in the test manual.

In addition, although an entire page in the manual is devoted to description of norming procedures, little substantive information is provided. For example, a detailed, albeit confusing, description is presented regarding standardization sampling procedures. Although it is clear that many schools were used as sites from which the standardization sample was drawn, it is not explicit how many subjects were included or how the sample was representative of a normal population according to such relevant variables as sex, socioeconomic status, race, and so forth.

Data regarding the tests' reliability and validity are also incomplete. Kuder-Richardson reliability coefficients are appropriately presented as evidence of the internal consistency of the Primary Reading Survey Tests. The coefficients seem adequate except for the .79 value reported for Level D of the Word Recognition Test. Otherwise, the values range from .84 on Level D of Form S of the Comprehension Test to .92 on several levels of the Word Recognition and Comprehension Test.

It is unfortunate that the authors present no data assessing reliability of the alternate forms of the Comprehension Tests. This is a glaring omission for the Primary Reading Survey Tests.

Standard errors of measurement (*SEM*s) were calculated for the Word Recognition and Comprehension tests using internal-consistency reliability coefficients. The authors give a brief but adequate explanation of *SEM*s and their appropriate use in test interpretation. Cautions concerning interpretation of individual test scores without consideration of this and other sources of errors are adequately described in the manual.

Confirmation of the tests' validity consists of the author's written assurance that the method of item development and selection resulted in satisfactory test content validity. Although content validity is an important and necessary part of the evidence needed to establish the validity of a test, content validity is not sufficient to determine that a test in fact measures what it says it measures. Many more empirical studies supporting the tests' concurrent and construct validity are needed.

In conclusion, although it is not possible to make comparative judgments regarding the Primary Reading Survey Tests and other tests normed in Australia, it is possible to consider its adequacy and usability in relation to other reading tests normed specifically for use in the United States. This reviewer regretfully concludes that the Primary Reading Survey Tests as presented in the test manual do not meet the technical standards described in the *Standards for Educational and Psychological Testing* (AERA, APA, NCME, 1985). The tests also do not realize the purposes stated in the test manual. It is hoped that future manuals will include the data and information necessary to use the Primary Reading Survey Tests in conjunction with other instruments in the never-ending search for good reading diagnostic information.

REVIEWER'S REFERENCE

American Educational Research Association, American Psychological Association, & National Council on Measurement in Education. (1985). *Standards for educational and psychological testing*. Washington, DC: American Psychological Association, Inc.

[5]

Achievement Identification Measure. Purpose: "Determine the degree to which children exhibit the characteristics of underachievers so that preventive or curative efforts may be administered." School-age children; 1985; AIM; parent report inventory; 6 scores: Competition, Responsibility, Control, Achievement Communication, Respect, Total; 1987 price data: $80 per 30 tests, manual for administration (8 pages), manual for interpretation of scores (7 pages), and computer scoring of 30 tests; $10 per specimen set; (20) minutes; Sylvia B. Rimm; Educational Assessment Service, Inc.*

Review of the Achievement Identification Measure by HOWARD M. KNOFF, Associate Professor of School Psychology, Department of Psychological Foundations, University of South Florida, Tampa, FL:

The Achievement Identification Measure (AIM) is a 77-item rating scale completed by parents of school-aged children which, according to its manual, "was developed to provide a measure of the characteristics which distinguish achieving students from underachievers" and to identify underachievers "so that preventive or curative efforts may be administered." The AIM was developed by Dr. Sylvia B. Rimm, who is described as having specialized in the identification and treatment of underachievers, the latter through her work with identified children and their parents and schools. The conceptualization of the AIM and its rating-scale items are based on Dr. Rimm's clinical work. The AIM has six scores (Competition, Responsibility, Control, Achievement Communication, Respect, and a Total Score), which are reported using percentile, normal curve equivalent (Mean = 50, Standard Deviation = 21.06), and stanine scores. Two manuals are provided with the AIM materials, one describing its administration and the other describing the interpretation of its scores.

The six-page Manual for Administration has sections addressing the AIM's purpose and background, administration and scoring, and research base. While the discussion of the AIM's purpose is admirably succinct, it does not define underachievers ("children whose performance in school is below their ability level") in sufficient detail. For example, not specified is whether all exceptional children (e.g., learning disabled, emotionally disturbed, mentally retarded) can be underachievers, nor what effects their exceptionality might have on underachievement in general or their AIM profile in particular. Gifted underachieving children are noted briefly in the manual (this appears to be an area of specialization with Dr. Rimm), but again there is no elaboration that would suggest anything other than one AIM profile or criterion level to identify all underachieving students. The background section of the manual, meanwhile, simply refers to Dr. Rimm's experience and clinical findings with underachieving students; no other studies or information are referenced to provide a broader foundation towards understanding the AIM.

The background material in the manual would be significantly strengthened by a comprehensive review of the literature on underachieving students, noting interrelationships with various exceptionalities, and a demonstration that the AIM is related to empirical results that are meaningful and replicable. Unfortunately, the AIM does not appear to be founded on empirical research. The test appears to be based on one individual's perception of underachievement which, at the very least, may be specific to a limited geographic area and/or a select group of students who have been referred for outside counseling or academic support. This is a serious limitation of the AIM affecting the very roots of its validity. Because of the limited information presented in this manual, these are the only comments possible at this time. Perhaps, with a more extensive background section, different conclusions would be warranted.

The administration and scoring section of the manual is fairly easy to follow. The manual recommends that both parents complete the AIM together unless there are serious disagreements. In such cases separate forms can be completed. The possible effects of single versus joint versus separate parent completion of the AIM are not explored, statistically or conceptually. This section also notes that the AIM evaluates underachievement for all school-aged children, yet the possible use of the AIM with exceptional children, who may be educated in the public schools until age 21, is unspecified. Further, the AIM's standardization sample is not fully described. Thus, it is not clear whether the AIM was standardized with parents who had children who fully represent "all school aged children." The breadth and applicability of the AIM with all school-aged children, therefore, is unclear, is not demonstrated, and cannot be determined. Finally, the acceptability of comparing a completed AIM protocol to the entire standardization sample or the need to compare it to an age-specific subset of the sample, comparable to the target child's specific age, is not addressed.

Unfortunately, the only way the AIM can be scored is to send the completed protocol to the scale's publishers. This is a serious flaw, which is compounded by the lack of reported norms in the manual. Without these norms, this test cannot be fully evaluated, and the accuracy of the publisher's scores and interpretations cannot be determined. This scoring approach may also reduce test users' understandings of the AIM's important details and nuances, while introducing an unnecessary delay between administering the scale and implementing an intervention program based on its results (the manual states that the AIM scoring will be returned within one month, or within one week for special "rush" jobs). The lack of AIM norms also discourages the comparative research that is desperately needed to further validate this test.

The research background section of the manual *appears* to describe the AIM's test construction and psychometric properties; however, the discussion is only cursory at best. The test construction section again alludes to the clinical work of Dr. Rimm, while other parts of the research background section are vague or limited in their scope. There is no description of how the scale items were chosen, whether a group of pilot items were tested and statistically discarded or retained to create the present scale, or whether a factor-analytic procedure was used to identify and/or validate the five AIM scales. A comprehensive discussion of the AIM's reliability is missing, no construct-validity statistics are reported, and criterion-related validity support is based on an author-generated study with an undefined subject pool and methodology. Finally, there is only a vague description of the AIM's standardization and normative sample (500 school-aged children from rural, suburban, and urban geographic areas in this country), with no statistical or stratification data presented. Overall, the development, integrity, utility, reliability, and validity (construct, concurrent, convergent, and discriminant) of this scale cannot be evaluated or are not present. The manual provides insufficient information in almost all technical areas—even the accomplishment of the AIM's stated goals and purposes cannot be determined. It would surely be unwise to use the AIM for any clinical purpose, or for that matter, any research-oriented purposes.

In five pages, the Manual for Interpretation describes how to evaluate and interpret the percentile scores that are returned with a scored protocol along with the scores for the five AIM dimensions. Again, the validity of these dimensions and interpretations must be seriously questioned—the manuals provide no empirical support for them either through a factor analysis of the present scale or a review of previous research.

The manual reports that total AIM scores above the 80th percentile indicate students who are high achievers. This use of the AIM as a tool which evaluates high *and* low achievers (rather than the latter only) is commendable. However, the manual's statement that those scoring between the 40th and 60th percentiles "probably are having some problems related to school achievement already" is inconsistent with common interpretations of these percentiles as being within average ranges. Finally, the designation of students scoring below the 40th percentile as being at high risk for underachievement is troublesome. First, this cutoff score is not empirically supported, and more importantly, it appears to be unusually high—higher than one might expect from a randomly sampled standardization group. If this is true, the potential for identifying numerous "false-positive" underachievers within a typical population is significant, both in terms of the costs involved in serving them and the possible stigmatization from an inappropriate label.

The remainder of this manual is devoted to describing the five AIM dimensions. Once again, there are no citations to validate the interpretation; they appear to be drawn from the clinical experience of the author. Thus, more questions related to the validity of the AIM's interpretations arise.

To summarize, the AIM manuals do not present sufficient description, standardization data, and/or psychometric support to permit any recommendation for its use—clinically or in research. Indeed, the apparent dependence on the author's clinical experience, devoid of any empirical support for the conceptualization, development, or interpretation of the AIM, is a significant weakness. The validity and utility of the AIM has not been demonstrated, or at least reported, in its manuals. In fact, the notion that parents, who have their own biases and perceptions of schools' academic processes, can reliably identify their children as underachievers, has not been discussed or demonstrated. It is strongly recommended that any revision of the AIM provide the comprehensive information noted above in a *single* manual. While the author has alluded to a forthcoming book and other studies with the AIM, these should be reported in this manual so that users are able to independently evaluate and use the tool for their own purposes.

Review of the Achievement Identification Measure by SHARON B. REYNOLDS, Assistant Professor of Education, Texas Christian University, Fort Worth, TX:

The stated purpose of the Achievement Identification Measure (AIM) is to measure characteristics that distinguish between achieving and underachieving school-age children. The author describes a theoretical framework in which underachievement is viewed as a pattern, learned in early childhood, related to attention "addiction," expressed in either dependent or domineering modes.

ITEMS. The inventory is a Likert-type scale in which the parent checks, for each of the items, one of the following responses: *no, to a small extent, average, more than average, definitely*. The 70 items to which all parents are asked to respond can be categorized as follows: 19

items related to the child's behavior with respect to school, 17 items related to the child's behavior or characteristics in general, 12 items about the child's relationship with either the child's father or mother, 8 items related to the parent's behavior or characteristics, 6 items about the child's behavior toward other children, 3 items about the child's siblings, 2 items about the behavior or attitudes of the child's father or mother toward school, 1 item about the child's health, 1 item about the child's relationship with grandparents, 1 item about the parents' relationship with each other.

Of these 70 items, some are repeated and some are opposites. An additional seven questions are to be answered only by two-parent families. These questions all refer to differences between the father and mother.

Some of the items do not use the full range of the scale. These require a yes or no response. Some of the items require factual information or information based on direct observation. Other items require the parent to compare the child to "normal" or "reasonable" behavior. There is no information within the inventory that provides the parent with appropriate norm reference with respect to these items.

No information is given regarding the source of the original set of items, or on the criteria for selecting the final set. The authors stated that item analysis revealed gender differences for some items. These differences resulted in a change in scoring procedures such that some items are now scored for only one gender.

RELIABILITY AND VALIDITY. Reliability coefficients are reported, but the size and characteristics of the reliability sample were not described. In the absence of such information, the reliability coefficients are not useful in assisting the user to determine the suitability of the instrument for the user's purposes.

The information provided on construct validity is just a restatement of the theoretical basis for the inventory, with no empirical data provided. Criterion-related validity is reported as a correlation between AIM scores and parent ratings of their child's achievement on a 5-point scale. The size and characteristics of the validity sample were not described. Thus, in the absence of information about the sample on which the test was validated, the validity coefficients are not useful in assisting the user in determining the suitability of the test for the user's purposes.

MANUALS. The inventory includes two manuals: Manual for Administration and Manual for Interpretation of Scores. The Manual for Administration is divided into three sections: Background Information, Administration and Scoring, and Research Background. The administration and scoring section includes instructions, time suggestions, materials, and age restriction ("school age"). It states that "small problems should be considered more serious when identified in younger children since they are likely to increase with age unless there is intervention." No empirical evidence is cited in support of this assertion.

The Manual for Interpretation of Scores is divided into four sections: Introduction, Scores, Dimension Descriptions, and Further Information.

ADMINISTRATION AND SCORING. The directions for administration of the instrument are clear and simple. Directions for scoring are not included because scoring is provided by Educational Assessment Service, Inc.

The inventory provides scores for overall achiever characteristics as well as "dimension" scores for Competition, Responsibility, Control, Achievement, Communication, and Respect. The Manual for Interpretation of Scores states that scores are reported as percentiles, Normal Curve Equivalent scores, and stanine scores for the five separate dimensions. The instructions for interpreting scores states that the total score is reported as a percentile and Dimension scores are reported as stanines. It does not give any information about the Normal Curve Equivalent Scores. Directions for interpreting both types of scores are given in terms of ranges. A general description of the way in which the theory relates the Dimension score to the overall score is provided. The relationship is not supported by quantitative data. Incomplete information is provided about the reference group on which these norms were established.

SUMMARY. The major flaw in this instrument is its lack of empirical data. It is not possible to determine the appropriateness of the instrument, the relevance of the norms, or even the relationship between the Dimension scores and the overall score. The major advantage of the instrument is its ease of administration. In the absence of empirical data, however, one is left with the opportunity to easily measure something that cannot be interpreted with any level of confidence.

[6]

ACT Proficiency Examination in Abnormal Psychology. Purpose: "To give adult learners the opportunity to earn college credit for knowledge gained outside the classroom and to provide institutions with an objective basis for awarding such credit" in abnormal psychology. College and adults; 1984–86; test administered 6 times annually (February, March, May, June, October, November) at centers established by the publisher; 1986 examination fee: $40 (includes reporting of score to the candidate and one college); 180(190) minutes; developed by the faculty of The University of the State of New York; American College Testing Program.*

For information on the entire ACT Proficiency Examination Program, see 9:45 (1 reference).

Review of the ACT Proficiency Examination in Abnormal Psychology by PAUL F. ZELHART, Associate Academic Vice President and Professor of Psychology, East Texas State University, Commerce, TX:

The American College Testing Program Proficiency Examination Program (ACT PEP) is one mechanism through which universities may offer credit for knowledge gained outside the classroom. Examinations are offered in selected subject areas in the arts and sciences, business, education, and nursing at specified times and locations. The results can be forwarded to schools at the request of the examinee.

The PEP examination in Abnormal Psychology is one of the New York Regent's College examinations. It assesses the material normally taught in a 1-semester, undergraduate course. It is also assumed that students taking the examination have mastered the concepts presented in a 1-semester introductory psychology course. The examination tests for knowledge of the history of abnormal psychology and its major concepts. Included are elements of the description, definition, classification, etiology, and treatment of psychological disorders. Thirty percent of the questions assess knowledge of background and basic concepts, 55 percent assess knowledge of disorders, and 15 percent are devoted to approaches to treatment.

The test was designed by a committee of two applied psychologists and three academic psychologists. The primary references for the content were seven well-known abnormal psychology texts, including the standard work by Coleman (7th Ed., 1984). Supplementary references include Skinner's *Walden Two* (1976) and several popular novels and texts. In developing the content the committee made reference to seven test objectives that assess: (*a*) the recognition or recall of facts, terms, persons, categories, or principles; (*b*) the understanding of such material; (*c*) the implications and consequences of presented data; (*d*) the use of abstractions in concrete situations; (*e*) the ability to see relationships between parts of a conceptual framework; (*f*) the ability to assemble conceptual elements into a coherent structure; and (*g*) the ability to make value judgements about purposes, ideas, works, methods, or materials.

The test consists of 156 objective items. The examinee selects the best of four alternatives. There is no correction for guessing. The items are clearly stated. The average item difficulty was .64; that is, on the average 64 percent of examinees responded correctly to the items of the test. It should be noted, however, the norm group is heterogeneous with regard to disciplinary identification. Only 37 percent of the norm group were psychology majors. The test would not be challenging for most upper division majors in psychology. Because a cutoff score of one half a standard deviation below the mean is suggested, many individuals "passing" the examination may have a modest understanding of abnormal psychology.

The test development process attended to content validity concerns through the use of test objectives, a committee of experts, pretesting, and test revision. Data supporting criterion-related validity, however, are not presented for this specific test. The general statement is made that there is a positive relation between course grades and scores on PEP tests in general.

The test appears to be reliable. The estimated alpha (Kuder Richardson Formula 20) is reported to be .94. The standard error of measurement (scaled score units) is 2.55.

Test scores are presented in terms of standard scores with a mean of 50 and a standard deviation of 10 (range 20 to 80). Norms are reestablished every 3 to 4 years.

The demographic characteristics of examinees for the period 1985–1986 show 91 percent were female, 71 percent were over 30 years of age, 89 percent were Caucasian, and most were employed, part-time students who were seeking a college degree.

Overall the ACT PEP examination in Abnormal Psychology appears to be a reliable and valid measure of the content of a semester course in abnormal psychology. Users should, however, assess their specific use of the examination, and the subsequent success of students given credit for the course. Such experience may dictate adjustment in the cutoff score.

REVIEWER'S REFERENCES

Skinner, B. F. (1976). *Walden two*. New York: Macmillan.
Coleman, J. C., Butcher, J. N., & Carson, R. C. (1984). *Abnormal psychology and modern life* (7th ed.). Glenview, IL: Scott, Foresman and Co.

[7]

ACT Proficiency Examination in Statistics. Purpose: "To give adult learners the opportunity to earn college credit for knowledge gained outside the classroom and to provide institutions with an objective basis for awarding such credit" in statistics. College and adults; 1984–86; test administered 6 times annually (February, March, May, June, October, November) at centers established by the publisher; 1986 examination fee: $40 (includes reporting of score to the candidate and one college); 180(190) minutes; developed by the faculty of The University of the State of New York; American College Testing Program.*

For information on the entire ACT Proficiency Examination Program, see 9:45 (1 reference).

Review of the ACT Proficiency Examination in Statistics by ROBERT P. MARKLEY, Professor of Psychology, Fort Hays State University, Hays, KS:

The ACT Proficiency Examination in Statistics (PEP) test is designed to provide a measure of knowledge or achievement in the topics contained in a traditional elementary statistics course. The purpose of the test (and the PEP program) is to provide a measure of college-equivalent life experiences. Presumably, one could take the test, submit the score to a local educational institution, and (if the score is satisfactory) be given credit for three units of statistics without having formally attended or enrolled in the traditional class. For institutions, there are available a Technical Handbook and User's Guide which provide general information about the total PEP program and some technical information about the Statistics test. A very thorough Study Guide is provided to the enrollee upon registration.

The first version of the test itself has 97 items in multiple-choice format. Items are placed on alternate pages with an interleaved blank page for notes and figuring. According to the Technical Handbook, an attempt was made to have 20% of the items tap rote-memory knowledge, 25% of the items deal with comprehension of the subject, 25% applications and higher order operations, and 25% applications and higher order operations with computations. (Either there is a misprint in the Handbook or 5% of the items are unaccounted for.) Almost all of the topics that are found in the traditional elementary text book appear in test items, including descriptive statistics, graphs, probability, probability distributions, sampling and sampling distributions, estimation and hypothesis testing—including large and small sample tests on single means and pairs of means, Chi Square, regression and correlation, and one-way ANOVA. There are no items dealing with nonparametric statistics. Topics are, for the most part, sequenced in a manner similar to their order of appearance in a standard text. The test taker is provided with a booklet containing a list of standard formulas and excerpts from statistical tables that can be used during the test. Calculators cannot be used during the test.

A group of 1,327 introductory statistics students at 37 U.S. colleges and universities was used to norm the test. The raw score mean for this group was 53.5 items correct (out of 97) with a standard deviation of 12.4. A coefficient alpha of .86 is reported by the ACT. Scores are reported in a standard score form ($M = 50$, $SD = 10$, range = 80 to 20). The SE_m is estimated as being 3.7 scaled-score units. The ACT recommends that a scaled score of 45 be considered a passing score. Thirty-one percent of the norm group failed this standard.

As yet there is no information available on performance of actual candidates who are taking this test for course equivalency purposes.

Score reports include a scaled score, percent of items correct, and (apparently) a projected final grade (based upon the norm sample). Apparently there is no provision for a breakdown of topics or areas missed, which the candidate could use for diagnostic or remedial purposes. It would be very helpful for a failed candidate to be informed that further study in a subarea (e.g., probability or correlation) would be beneficial. Such diagnostics would also be helpful to an instructor who might be interested in using this standardized exam to assess students' achievement against a national norm (even though this is not the purpose of the test).

An instructor could quarrel with the relative weighting of topics on the test. There is more coverage of probability on this test than I would want on my final exam and not enough coverage of ANOVA and experimental design. I suppose that a decision-theory-oriented business statistics instructor would like the emphasis upon probability topics. As an instructor, I personally am somewhat put off and frustrated by the traditional textbook reliance upon one and two sample designs to illustrate and introduce inferential hypothesis testing. We just begin to get students to understand what is going on and then tell them that real researchers almost never use the statistical tests they have just learned—that the main action is in ANOVA and various multivariate procedures which we don't have time to teach in a one-semester course.

Some really minor quibbles: There is at least one item that is pure algebra and not statistics. Throughout the test the lower case x or x_1 is used to refer to individual scores; most social science and psychology texts are now using the upper case X or X_1 to refer to an individual raw score and reserving the lower case x or x_1 to refer to the deviation quantity, $X_1 - M$. Finally, the technical manual consistently commits the error of saying "data is."

Finally, despite some quibbles and reservations, I would, provisionally and until local experience proves otherwise, judge an applicant for a social science graduate program who presents a high score on this test to have satisfied an undergraduate statistics prerequisite and thus allow the student entry to discipline-oriented graduate level methods and statistics courses.

Review of the ACT Proficiency Examination in Statistics by STEVEN L. WISE, Assistant Professor of Educational Psychology, University of Nebraska-Lincoln, Lincoln, NE:

The ACT Proficiency Examination in Statistics (PEP) is intended to be used by postsecondary institutions in decisions regarding the awarding of college credit to individuals who have studied elementary statistical methods. The PEP Statistics examination, currently consisting of 97 multiple-choice items, was developed to test knowledge of material that is normally taught in a one-semester introductory course in statistics.

The test materials include three types of supporting information: a User's Guide, a Study Guide, and a Technical Handbook. The PEP User's Guide provides generic information about thc PEP program and examinations. A description of the test development procedures and psychometric properties of the PEP examinations are presented in a general fashion. Because the PEP Statistics examination is administered by ACT, detailed administration instructions are not contained in the User's Guide. Candidates for the PEP Statistics examination are provided a Study Guide containing a general description of the examination, a list of objectives, a description of the content domain covered by the items, the proportion of the items measuring each content area, a list of reference materials for candidate preparation, a list of the tables and formulas used in the examination, and several sample test items. The Technical Handbook contains psychometric and normative information for each of the PEP examinations.

The PEP User's Guide gives a comprehensive description of the PEP program. The test development procedures used in all of the PEP examinations are clearly presented. General descriptions of the methods used to insure reliability and validity of the examinations are also given in the User's Guide. In addition, several methods are presented for choosing an appropriate cutoff score for a PEP examination.

Several aspects of the Study Guide merit discussion. First, the content domain presented in the Study Guide is very broad. I feel that there are few instructors of introductory statistics who cover more than about 90% of these topics within the time constraints of a one-semester course. Several of the topics, such as hypergeometric distributions and Bayes' theorem, are only rarely addressed in an introductory course. Moreover, 25% of the test items deal with probability theory and probability distributions. This is substantially more coverage of probability than is given in many introductory statistics courses. Users should take into account the scope and emphasis of the content domain when choosing cutting scores for the examination.

A second problem with the Study Guide concerns the list of four primary reference textbooks. This list is preceded by the statement "any one of the following general purpose textbooks may be used to study the material listed in the content outline." Inspection of the four textbooks reveals that only one, Freund's *Modern Elementary Statistics*, provides an exhaustive coverage of the content domain. Hence the statement in the Study Guide that any of the textbooks in the list may be used is misleading, because a candidate who studied Freund's textbook would be at a clear advantage over a candidate who studied only one of the other "primary" textbooks. It would be clearer (and more accurate) to state that the content of the PEP Statistics examination is based on Freund's textbook.

The Technical Handbook provides little evidence of the reliability and validity of the PEP Statistics examination. Only one estimate of reliability is given—a coefficient alpha value of .86. No validity evidence is presented. This is somewhat surprising, given the high overall quality of the testing materials. In the beginning of the Technical Handbook, general procedures for obtaining evidence of both content and concurrent validity of the PEP examinations are described. Apparently the user is expected to accept on faith that the validity evidence for a particular examination is adequate. I find this practice to be unacceptable, and hope that ACT will soon provide detailed validity evidence for each of the PEP examinations.

Overall, I feel that the PEP Statistics examination should provide postsecondary institutions with useful information regarding statistics proficiency. In view of the scanty psychometric evidence available for this examination, however, it is difficult to provide a more detailed assessment of the psychometric quality of the PEP Statistics examination.

[8]

The Activity Completion Technique. Purpose: Assessment of personality through sentence completion technique. High school and over; 1984; ACT; developed from the Sacks Sentence Completion Test; 4 areas: Family, Interpersonal, Affect, Self-Concept; 1987 price data: $24.95 per 25 tests, 25 rating sheets, and manual (33 pages); $12 per 50 tests; $8 per 25 rating sheets; $8.50 per manual; (30–40) minutes; Joseph M. Sacks; Psychological Assessment Resources, Inc.*

Review of The Activity Completion Technique by FRED M. GROSSMAN, Assistant Professor of Special Education and Communication Disorders, University of Nebraska-Lincoln, Lincoln, NE:

The Activity Completion Technique (ACT) is a revision of the Sacks Sentence Completion Test (SSCT) (Sacks & Levy, 1959) and, as such, attempts to assess personality characteristics by requesting individuals to complete sentence stems within a standard sentence completion format. According to the author, the test can be administered individually or in groups with an average completion time of 30–40 minutes. Administration procedures are clearly delineated within the ACT manual as are suggestions for the examiner on how to respond to frequently asked questions by examinees. ACT respondents are asked to silently read and subsequently to complete each sentence stem in writing, although the author recommends that for particularly anxious test-takers it may be advantageous for the examiner to read the stimulus items orally and then record the client's oral responses. In addition, examiners are encouraged to conduct an inquiry by asking follow-up questions relating to selected responses that appear to be of clinical significance.

The entire instrument is comprised of 15 categories that are grouped under four major areas. Each category includes 4 stimulus items, resulting in a total of 60 sentence completion items. The four major areas are: (*a*) Family, which has three categories (e.g., relationship with mother, early family relationships, etc.); (*b*) Interpersonal, which is comprised of four categories (e.g., peers, authority figures, etc.); (*c*) Affect, of which anxiety and hostility are the two components; and (*d*) Self-Concept, which has six categories (e.g., competence, needs, fantasy, etc.). The four stimulus items within each category are scored together as a constellation of responses, which is a departure from previous sentence completion methods. In effect, based upon the clinical judgment of the examiner, each category is globally scored on a rating sheet as either (1) no significant disturbance; (2) mildly disturbed; (3) severely disturbed; or (X) unknown, insufficient evidence. Space is provided under each category on the rating sheet for clinicians to write a brief interpretive summary (i.e., usually a phrase or sentence) regarding their impressions of the test-taker's set of responses. After completion of the scoring for all categories, the examiner is expected to complete a clinical summary with respect to outlined areas provided on the rating sheet.

In addition to the previously mentioned scoring procedures, selected ACT items can be scored in accordance with criteria for Self-Actualization personality characteristics. Further scoring criteria are also available for Activity-Passivity personality tendencies and can be assessed for any of the ACT items that the examiner chooses to evaluate in this manner. To the author's credit, several scoring samples are provided in the test manual as are two illustrative cases to aid the clinician in the ratings and narrative interpretations of response constellations.

Although some reliability and validity indices are reported in the manual for the original SSCT, no such data are presented for the ACT. In fact, psychometric data on the ACT are totally lacking, with the exception of minimal summaries of a few correlational studies regarding Self-Actualization and Activity-Passivity constructs. In effect, standardization information, normative data, and reliability and validity indices are conspicuously absent.

In summary, although the ACT differs from some of the previous sentence completion methods in a positive manner (e.g., first-person stimuli, scoring a constellation of responses rather than a single response, etc.), the lack of psychometric data suggests that diagnostic and classification decisions not be made solely on the basis of the results of this instrument. The major problem with the ACT is best represented by the comment of the test author that the validity of ratings is greatly determined by the clinical impressions, experience, and insight of the examiner. This type of interpretive approach poses the potential danger of idiosyncratic and subjective scoring by individual examiners and points to the need for substantially more research on the ACT, particularly with regard to reliability and validity data. In effect, while clinically-oriented psychologists may feel comfortable using the ACT, psychometrically-inclined clinicians are advised to direct their attention toward the use of personality instruments that have more objective scoring systems and psychometrically-derived interpretive systems.

REVIEWER'S REFERENCE

Sacks, J. M., & Levy, S. (1950). The Sentence Completion Test. In L. E. Abt & L. Bellak (Eds.), *Projective psychology* (pp. 357-402). New York: Knopf.

Review of The Activity Completion Technique by MARCIA B. SHAFFER, School Psychologist, Steuben/Allegany BOCES, Bath, NY:

Joseph M. Sacks is known for his development of the Sacks Sentence Completion Test (SSCT), which has been widely used in research and in clinical practice. He is the originator, also, of the Activity Completion Technique, or ACT. The ACT consists of 60 items, each of which is intended to probe a specific characteristic or experience of the subject. In scoring, each item is grouped with three others, e.g., "authority role" is described by items 14, 29, 32, and 47. Finally, these areas are grouped under the four categories listed in the test, e.g., "affect" includes anxiety and hostility. Administration of the ACT is like that of other sentence completion tests, with the addition of an inquiry.

The ACT is described as "a revised form of the Sacks Sentence Completion Test in which the items have been reworded to elicit responses in terms of behavioral, emotional, or cognitive activity." This symbiotic affinity to the SSCT is so strong that there are few statistics in the manual which are based on the actual ACT. There is no reference to factor analysis. The comments on validity and reliability tend to be ambiguous, evasive, or patently derived from SSCT research done several years ago.

The dubious data comprise the major flaw in the construction and interpretation of the ACT. There is one other criticism which might be made, although some potential users may not find it of primary importance. The criticism is of the method of scoring. "The validity of the ACT is dependent . . . upon . . . the clinical acumen of the examiner. . . . [and] highly dependent on the psychologist's experience, insight, and knowledge of the dynamics of behavior." Accuracy in understanding is supposedly enhanced by 20 pages of examples of responses, with interpretation by experts. Whether examples are a safe substitute for the expertise of the examiner is an important question, but is not addressed here. Warning about ethical use of the ACT is contained in a single statement: "For those who have little experience with this method, examples of interpretation and ratings are presented." No additional cautionary advice is given.

Among its assets, the ACT offers the advantage of being in the first person, which has been found to "elicit more valid clinical content than stimuli referring to others." The use of several responses in combination produces information of a richer nature than use of a single response. It is adaptable, it may be given to groups as well as individuals, and it may be read to a subject if necessary. In addition, the ACT places emphasis on strengths, assets, and coping ability rather than simply on pathology.

The ACT is definitely in need of research, and a more carefully written, more explicatory manual. Still, it has a strong visual appeal for possible purchasers; the rating sheet is neatly arranged with the categories defined and a place for the scorer's interpretive summary. The questions appear relevant and the test can be said to possess a face validity. It would be easy to forget about psychometric data and test interpretation when looking at so tidy a test. In fact, the ACT might be a satisfactory part of an extensive battery in a hospital, an industrial setting, or a college admissions office. Unfortunately, the test's integrity rests chiefly on faith rather than proven performance.

[9]

Adaptive Behavior Inventory. Purpose: Helps to "evaluate a student's day-to-day ability to take care of her/himself, communicate with others, interact socially, perform academic tasks, and perform work-related or prevocational tasks." Mentally retarded students ages 6-0 through 18-11 and normal students ages 5-0 through 18-11 years; 1986; ABI; inventory is completed by classroom teacher or other professional having regular contact with the student; 6 scores: Self-Care Skills, Communication Skills, Social Skills, Academic Skills, Occupational Skills, Composite Quotient; ABI-Short Form available for research and screening purposes; individual; 1987 price data: $39 per complete kit including 25 profile and response sheets, 25 short form response sheets, and examiner's manual (69 pages); $14 per 25 profile and response sheets; $7 per 25 short form response sheets; $21 per examiner's manual; $49 per optional PRO-SCORE in-house computerized scoring system (specify Apple or IBM); (20–25) minutes; Linda Brown and James E. Leigh; PRO-ED, Inc.

Review of the Adaptive Behavior Inventory by STEWART EHLY, Associate Professor of School Psychology, The University of Iowa, Iowa City, IA:

The Adaptive Behavior Inventory (ABI) was developed to "evaluate a student's day-to-day ability to take care of her/himself, communicate with others, interact socially, perform academic tasks, and perform work-related or prevocational tasks." The ABI is intended for use with mentally retarded students ages 6-0 to 18-11 and nonretarded students ages 5-0 to 18-11. The manual accompanying the instrument could serve as a model for publishers introducing new assessment instruments to consumers. The overall excellence of presentation in the manual convinces the reader to consider the ABI as the instrument of choice in assessing adaptive behavior of school-aged children.

The authors begin their presentation with a short review of the adaptive behavior concept and selected instruments that have been developed for use with children. A welcomed focus in an early section involves a discussion of the rationale for the ABI. Brown and Leigh assume that any instrument addressing the adaptive behavior construct must provide information on general and specific factors of behavior, complement the information from intelligence tests, provide data from routine aspects of life as well as activities in academic settings, and reflect the child's response to societal and situational demands.

The authors argue that assessment of adaptive behavior will add valuable information to the process of instructional decision-making for students other than those labelled mentally retarded. Indeed, current research would support the consideration of adaptive behaviors with students of average intelligence, but who are experiencing difficulty coping with the demands of the classroom and the broader community.

By providing a norm-referenced instrument for school-aged children, Brown and Leigh offer an alternative source of data gathering from that provided by the Adaptive Behavior Inventory (Mercer & Lewis, 1977) and the Vineland Adaptive Behavior Scales (Sparrow, Balla, & Cicchetti, 1984). The success of the ABI in the marketplace will center on its ability to provide information to educators that can be integrated into programming in the classroom. The rating (on a 4-point scale) of the student's Self-Care Skills (30 items), Communication Skills (32 items), Social Skills (30 items), Academic Skills (30 items), and Occupational Skills (28 skills) is conducted by the teacher or staff person most familiar with the student's behavior. Ratings range from "student does not perform skill" to "student has mastered skill."

Items are presented in order of difficulty on each scale. The authors' rationale for the structure is to allow basal and ceiling scores to be obtained. Norms were developed for each scale independently. Users can complete the entire instrument or any combination of scales. The Short-Form is an alternative to selecting entire scales, providing the educator with a 50-item sample of the complete instrument. Brown and Leigh present the Short-Form as a research and screening tool that can also be used in reevaluation of students.

A final point in the description of the instrument that may be attractive to educators is the authors' attempt to provide multiple routes to applying the information on adaptive behaviors. Options include comparison of the student to two sets of norms (one sample representative of all school-age children nation-wide, the second that is representative of children already diagnosed as mentally retarded and enrolled in special education programs), identification of the child's strengths and weaknesses, determination of the need for additional assessment, and the measurement of child change or program effectiveness. Again, whether the ABI will succeed in providing each form of information awaits the results of classroom applications.

The authors do document early research on the ABI. Internal-consistency reliability and test-retest statistics are indicative of a sound instrument. Evidence on content validity, criterion-related validity, and construct validity is reviewed. Of special interest is the presentation of results from correlations with intelligence tests. The authors note that 85% of correlation coefficients were statistically significant. Data on discrimination among students with varying intelligence quotients, discrimination among children enrolled in different educational placements, and correlations with tests of academic achievement are available in the manual. Whether the information provided by the ABI will be seen by psychologists as justifying administration (in addition to intelligence and achievement measures) rests more on the perceived value of the instrument for influencing programming decisions than on the uniqueness of the information provided.

The Adaptive Behavior Inventory does provide psychologists with a tool for use in schools and other educational settings. The age range covered, the ease and length (under 30 minutes) of administration, and the options in administration and interpretation will attract interest from educators and psychologists. The ABI, with the authors' attention to development and initial application, awaits extended investigation of its merits.

REVIEWER'S REFERENCES

Mercer, J. R., & Lewis, J. (1977). SOMPA: System of Multicultural Pluralistic Assessment. New York: The Psychological Corporation.

Sparrow, S. S., Balla, D. A., & Cicchetti, D. V. (1984). Vineland Adaptive Behavior Scales. Circle Pines, MN: American Guidance Service.

Review of the Adaptive Behavior Inventory by CORINNE ROTH SMITH, Associate Professor of Special Education and Rehabilitation, Syracuse University, Syracuse, NY:

The Adaptive Behavior Inventory (ABI) was designed to reflect the ability of school-age youngsters to meet age-appropriate sociocultural expectations for personal responsibility. Teachers or other professionals who have had daily contact with the student complete 150 ratings of the student's behavior. Parents and the student can be asked for input if the respondent is unclear regarding how to rate a particular skill and cannot set up a situation to observe that skill in the school. Approximately 30 items comprise each of the five scales: Self-Care, Communication, Social, Academic, and Occupational Skills. The rating process takes approximately 5 minutes per scale. Scaled scores are derived for each scale, and an Adaptive Behavior Quotient can be calculated from four or five scales. For the very young or severely impaired, the authors recommend the Occupational Skills scale be omitted. Ratings are done on a Likert-type scale of 0 to 3: 0 means the child does not perform the skill, 1 means the skill is emerging, 2 indicates the skill is performed most of the time, 3 represents skill mastery. Items are arranged by difficulty level, with suggested starting points for different ages. A basal is established at five items in a row receiving a perfect rating of 3 points. A ceiling occurs with five consecutive ratings of 0.

The ABI has two normative samples, a "normal intelligence" group of 5-0 to 18-11 year olds and a mentally retarded group of 6-0 to 18-11 year olds. The norms on mentally retarded (MR) students are particularly useful because at the low end of the normal intelligence norms, a few raw score points can dramatically alter a student's adaptive behavior quotient. The MR norms distribute these scores over a broader range, allowing greater discrimination when considering classification issues, intervention efficacy, and child change over time. Although the authors refer to the full range norms as the "Normal Intelligence sample," this is a misnomer. These norms actually derive from a representative sample of school-aged children. Therefore, test users might be misled into believing that low performers' ratings are underestimated due to a higher than typical functioning normative group.

The ABI also contains a Short Form intended for research and screening purposes. Every third item from each scale was selected to comprise the 50-item Short Form. Rating time is 5 to 10 minutes. Only an Adaptive Behavior Quotient is derived as the scales are too brief (9 to 11 items) to offer findings reliable for strength/weakness determinations.

ABI item selection began with 406 items chosen from perusal of other adaptive behavior measures. These items were edited by special educators, psychometrists, professors, and students in special education and school psychology for imprecise or ambiguous wording, elimination of unimportant and redundant items, addition of items, and assignment to one of the five scales. The resulting 357 items were analyzed for item difficulty and discrimination with ratings of 157 students aged 5-0 to 18-11 in three midwestern states. A similar analysis was conducted with 143 MR students (ages 5-0 to 19-11) drawn from schools in Missouri and Texas. In selecting the final items, care was taken that two or three items on each scale had mean ratings below 1. This avoided a ceiling effect for the normal population. Conversely, two or three items per scale had mean scores of above 2 to assure basals for the MR population. The remaining items had means ranging between 1 and 2. The retained items generally correlated with their scale's score between .30 to .80, indicating adequate item discrimination power. Because the same scale is used for all ages, this necessarily results in some items at each age interval not making a significant contribution to their assigned scale, and some items that duplicate information already provided by other items within the scale. Median item discriminating power seems well distributed for all scales, except for the Occupational Scale for the normal intelligence sample. Here, the median correlation ranges from .71 at ages 7 and 8, to .80–.93 at ages 9 through 18. This suggests that approximately half of the scale items are so highly intercorrelated that many contribute information that is redundant with other items on the scale.

Good attention was given to standardization. The "Normal Intelligence" sample (CA 5-0 to 18-11) included 1,296 students while 1,076 students comprised the MR sample (CA 6-0 to 18-11). Data were gathered in 24 states. In most respects, the samples were comparable to the percentages of the U.S. school-age population indicated in the 1980 census. In the MR sample, females and institutional educational settings were slightly overrepresented, as were numbers of teachers teaching 6–10 years and numbers of teachers with Master's degrees. Special day school students, numbers of teachers teaching 11–15 years, and numbers of teachers with Bachelor's degrees were somewhat underrepresented. The authors do not list the percentage of the normal intelligence sample that is handicapped, or break the group down by handicapping condition. They merely state the sample "is representative of all school age children nationally." Approximately 80–100 students were tested at each age level for the normal intelligence sample, with the exception of 68 in the 5 to 6-5 year interval. In the MR sample, 6-year-olds ($N = 71$; CA range 6-0 to 7-5) and 18-year-olds ($N = 70$) appear underrepresented.

As the mean differences from year to year were largely insignificant, age groups were collapsed into different intervals for each scale. At times the same scaled scores are derived for children varying as much as 3 and 4 years in age from one another. In addition, the standard deviations on each scale are so large (often 1/3–1/2 the mean score, and in one instance surpassing the mean) that this variability necessitates careful scrutiny of the norms to determine whether the scaled score findings are clinically meaningful. For example, with a mean score of 63.68 and *SD* of 24.66 (age 9-6 to 10-11) on the Communication Skills scale (Normal IQ sample), it is common for students to equal the mean score of 18-11-year-olds (mean = 82.11) and for others to equal the mean ratings of 5-year-olds (mean = 40.48). Similarly, a student earning a rating of 78 on the Social Skills scale places at the 50th percentile for any age distribution from age 10 to 18-11.

Internal consistency for each scale is high when calculated for 50 students from each standardization sample spanning primarily 2-year intervals. Test-retest reliability was determined for 39 normal intelligence students (ages 5 to 18; mean = 13.3) and 56 MR students (ages 6 to 18, mean = 13.6) after a 10-to-14-day interval. Coefficients ranged from .91–.98, indicating scores to be stable over short time periods.

A validity study correlated ABI ratings for the majority of the two samples with a 9-point teacher rating of the student's ability relative to same age peers in each scale's area. Coefficients ranged from .67 to .84, indicating a positive relationship between professional judgements on two types of measures. Criterion-related validity coefficients also were derived from correlations with three other adaptive behavior measures (*N* ranged from 15 to 62 per comparison). The ABI quotients correlated approximately .75, and individual scale correlations with the predicted criteria all exceeded .35. These results are not unexpected given that the ABI items were derived from perusal of the three criterion measures, among others. Construct validity studies reported a significant correlation of ABI scores with several intelligence measures, a moderate relationship with academic achievement, significant discrimination of four groups of children with differing IQ levels (IQ 90+, 55–70, 40–54, below 39), and three instructional settings (regular class, regular/resource combination, self-contained). The Short Form correlated .94 (normal IQ sample) and .96 (MR sample) with the full scale, reflecting the equivalence of the two forms ($^1/_3$ overlap of the scales was corrected statistically).

The ABI record sheets are well-designed, with room to graph standard scores on six additional measures. Place is provided to record the Standard Error of Measurement, administration conditions, interpretations, and recommendations. The manual gives Standard Error of Differences between each scale, and describes how to calculate the Standard Error of Differences, so that the examiner can determine the significance of differences between measures.

The authors, Brown and Leigh, are to be commended for their excellent presentation throughout the examiner's manual. They offer an interesting overview of various definitions of adaptive behavior, the early history of adaptive behavior scales, and the more recent spurring on of adaptive behavior measurement by civil rights and normalization movements. They rightfully caution that because adaptive behavior measures are designed to tap acquired skills rather than innate abilities, these scales are in fact more culturally loaded and biased than well-designed individualized intelligence tests. Nevertheless, multiple sources of information are preferable and fairer in making diagnostic and placement decisions. Brown and Leigh offer a useful schema for hypothesizing about the meaning of various discrepancies between adaptive behavior and intelligence quotients.

For the test user not well-versed in statistics, the authors offer an easy-to-follow explanation of many critical variables: the value of percentile ranks and standard scores, types of reliability and validity, sources of test error, the importance of calculating the Standard Error of Difference between two measures before making judgments about whether discrepancies represent true differences, the fact that significant differences in test scores may be clinically insignificant, and the knowledge that comparing a child's test performance to the norms is not equivalent to comparing the performance to what is normal. Brown and Leigh offer very explicit scoring procedures and examples.

The ABI authors note that the assessment of adaptive behavior is important for several reasons, among them the need to identify adaptive skills training goals so as to facilitate normalization, and the need to address test bias concerns in MR identification of cultural and ethnic minorities. Unfortunately, however, their measure accomplishes neither of these.

Brown and Leigh warn that the ABI has insufficient item numbers and breadth per scale to warrant using the findings for planning specific instructional objectives. Furthermore, despite the fact that performance means at adjacent age intervals on the normative tables are significantly different, many do not appear to be sufficiently discrepant to warrant clinical decisions. The large standard deviations highlight the commonality of large individual variations in adaptive behavior at any one age interval. The authors also state that the ABI is intended to aid in program evaluation and the measurement of child change over time. Given the large number of years one would have to wait to expect a statistically significant gain from maturation and programming, using the ABI for these purposes in most cases is not the pragmatic choice.

The best purpose fulfilled by the ABI appears to be determination of general strengths and weaknesses in several adaptive areas, identification of areas for further assessment in order to plan instructional programs, and the addition of one more piece of data in determining whether a student might be mentally retarded and whether special education related to the adaptive weaknesses might be beneficial. The scales also serve a useful research purpose. Given the high correlation of scale scores to the full scale score, and Short Form to full scale scores, it is suggested the primary focus of measurement be the full scale or Short Form quotients, with subscale interpretations being made only after careful scrutiny of the norm distributions.

[10]

Adolescent Language Screening Test. Purpose: "Developed to screen for deficits in the dimensions of language use, content, and form" in adolescents. Ages 11–17; 1984; ALST; 7 subtests: Pragmatics, Receptive Vocabulary, Concepts, Expressive Vocabulary, Sentence Formation, Morphology, Phonology; individual; 1988 price data: $69 per complete kit including 50 record booklets, stimulus easel, and administration manual (26 pages); (10–15) minutes; Denise L. Morgan and Arthur M. Guilford; PRO-ED, Inc.*

Review of the Adolescent Language Screening Test by LINDA CROCKER, Professor of Foundations of Education, University of Florida, Gainesville, FL:

The Adolescent Language Screening Test (ALST) is an individually administered test of developmental speech and language, designed for use with examinees from middle school through high school grades. Its seven subtests include Pragmatics (responses to simple instructions and conversational skills), Concepts (answering questions based on information obtained from a sentence spoken by the examiner), Receptive Vocabulary (understanding/identifying words spoken by the examiner), Expressive Vocabulary (picture identification, definitions, and word usage), Sentence Formation (scored for complexity of sentence structure when sentences are generated using specified words), Morphology (sentence completion), and Phonology (pronunciations requiring various consonant blends). Based upon these subtests three separate subscores and a total score are determined. Subtest 1 yields a Language Use score; subtests 2, 3, and 4 yield a Language Content score; and subtests 5, 6, and 7 are combined to obtain a Language Form score.

The ALST is easily administered and easily scored. The notebook format for task presentation is conveniently arranged to facilitate administration. While no special qualifications are needed to administer the test, some practice with the materials is essential for smooth administration. For several subtests the examiner must present stimulus words or sentences and the instructions are explicit that these can be presented only once (without repetition). Consequently there is no margin for examiner error in oral presentation of the stimuli and no alternative items are provided. The manual offers no instructions about the pacing or speed of presentation of verbal stimuli or the length of time that should be allowed between oral presentation of a sentence and questions that follow about the content of that sentence. In giving this test I noted that variations in examiner presentation could result in variations in examinee performance on these items. These matters should be addressed in any future revisions of this scale and manual.

Because of the heavy dependence on oral stimuli and the strictures against repetition of the verbal items, the ALST would not appear to be suitable for administration to hearing-impaired students.

The standardization sample consisted of 775 examinees (approximately 100 at each age level from 11 to 17). The process by which these examinees were selected is not described. The sample included 68 black and 35 Hispanic examinees ranging in numbers from 3–19 across age levels for blacks and 1–13 across age levels for Hispanics. Approximately 26% of the standardization sample were classified as learning disabled or needing speech therapy. Means and standard deviations are reported by age group for examinees receiving special services, those receiving no services, and the two groups combined. The means increase progressively over age-level groups but the standard deviations are noticeably smaller for the 16–17-year-olds, suggesting a possible ceiling effect on the test, at least for normal examinees. The standard deviations, however, remain large for the special services older students.

No data are presented on validity or reliability. Evidence of concurrent criterion-related validity might be inferred from the fact that at every age level the means for examinees qualifying for special services were substantially lower than means for examinees not receiving special services, but the test authors do not mention this. A more serious omission is the lack of any consideration of construct validity. An important issue in developing or reviewing any language test is whether it measures a construct that is distinct from general verbal aptitude as measured by standardized intelligence measures. Another aspect of construct validity is the internal structure of the scale and its subtests. Collapsing seven separate subtest scores for reporting purposes is a practice that should have some empirical justification. Correlational data or results of a factor-analytic study are sorely needed to support the subscale structure and reporting format of the test. Further evidence of internal consistency of subtest and total scores, test-retest reliability, and reliability of classifications of examinees at the recommended cut-scores (the 25th percentile rank) are also essential before this instrument is used for screening or placement of students.

In summary, the desirable features of the ALST are that it is easy to administer and covers the age range from 11–17, making longitudinal follow-up possible over a wide age span using the same instrument. Norm-group sample sizes at each age level are adequate. These positive features, however, are outweighed by the serious lack of data relating to validity and reliability of the test scores. Until such studies are published or conducted by test users in local settings, use of this test for clinical or educational decision making will remain open to question.

Review of the Adolescent Language Screening Test by ROBERT T. WILLIAMS, Associate Professor of Occupational and Educational Studies, Colorado State University, Fort Collins, CO, and AMY FINCH-WILLIAMS, Assistant Professor of Speech/Language Pathology, University of Wyoming, Laramie, WY:

The authors of the Adolescent Language Screening Test (ALST) maintain there is a need for a screening test of language abilities for adolescents. This test was designed to screen for deficits associated with spoken language in the areas of use, content, and form, as identified by Bloom and Lahey (1978). The authors build a strong rationale for their theoretical position relative to the language tasks included in the screening. The manual includes a review of the language characteristics of language-learning disabled adolescents. The development of this theoretical position and the review of the research establishes the content validity for this instrument.

Although content validity is established, the specific items selected and the scoring procedure for some subtests reduces the value of the screening instrument. This is apparent in both the Language Use and Language Form sections. For example, in the first section of Language Use a good rationale is made for the use of higher-level indirect speech acts with adolescents. However, the stimulus item chosen reflects an earlier developing indirect speech act.

Further, in the second section of Language Use the authors evaluate conversational skills, but the scoring system does not allow differentiation between impaired and normal populations. This problem is reflected in the fact that each subcategory has both early and later developing skills that are weighed equally. A point may be earned for the subcategory by demonstrating only the early developing skill. For example, in the second subcategory the authors are evaluating the functions of language (e.g., imperative, question, and declarative). The students may receive a point for using any function. In screening the language abilities of adolescents, it would be more appropriate to give differentiated credit for use of the question function or higher-level cognitive uses of language (Bereiter & Engelmann, 1966; Simon, 1985).

This same type of problem is found in the Language Form section. The authors state that the Sentence Formulation subtest was modified to evaluate a variety of sentence constructions. Although the scoring criteria for this section differentiate among various constructions, neither the directions nor the stimulus words suggest the expectation of a response more complex than simple, active, declarative sentences. The lack of this expectation could well affect the individual's score on this subtest.

Overall, the Language Content section is appropriate for adolescents. However, at least one of the pictures in the Receptive Vocabulary subtest is confusing. For the stimulus word "destruction" the possible responses include pictures of (1) a building under construction, (2) a car with a dented front bumper and fender behind a car with a dented rear bumper and fender, (3) a building being destroyed, and (4) a building burning. The keyed responses are 3 and 4, but response 2 seems justifiable. In addition the instructions to the examiner and to the student are contradictory. The examiner reads to the examinee, "I will only say each statement one time, so be sure to listen carefully." Then the manual tells the examiner, "At the student's request, one repetition may be given for each item without penalty."

The authors state in their rationale that language-learning disabled adolescents have been noted to have word retrieval difficulties. They maintain that the ALST screens vocabulary knowledge and word-finding skills. The "Naming to Confrontation" section of the Expressive Vocabulary subtest does not adequately screen word-finding skills. It is an expressive vocabulary test (i.e., vocabulary knowledge) because the student is not timed during his/her naming responses.

The manual provides no further evidence of validity or reliability. Caution, therefore, should be used in generalizing the results of this screening instrument.

The authors of the ALST attempt to provide normative data. Additionally, they attempt to account for ethnic diversity by including Black, Hispanic, and other minorities within the 775 students used in the standardization sample. Within the standardization sample they also include information on 208 students who were identified as needing special services. In the tables in which the means and standard deviations are presented, the total sample is divided into two groups: those students identified as needing special services and those identified as not needing special services. However, there is no information indicating in which of these groups the various ethnic groups are to be found. Further, because the group needing special services included a variety of handicapping conditions as well as levels of impairment, the usefulness of these norms is limited. The pass/fail criteria are based on the total sample population ($N = 775$), including students needing special services, 27% of the total population. The reviewers question the inclusion of students needing special services to establish standardizations of screening for normal language functions.

Visual inspection suggests small differences among means and standard deviations across age groups and between various subgroups. The authors do not discuss any significant differences between their populations for any of the subtests or for the total test. Nor do they provide this information for the age groups. The inclusion of this information would enhance the usefulness of the data provided.

In summary, this instrument provides a strong rationale and theoretical position for the need for a screening test of language abilities for adolescents and for the items selected for screening. The review of the research for each subtest is relevant for individuals working with adolescents with language-learning disabilities. However, the overall implementation of this information is affected by the selection of certain items and scoring procedures that reduce the value of the instrument as a screening tool. The normative data provided are affected by the fact that 27% of the standardization sample presents various handicapping conditions with varying levels of impairment. Therefore, the pass/fail criteria are lowered and do not reflect criteria that are based on normal adolescents. Because the authors do not provide any information on validity, reliability, or significant differences among the age groups, the usefulness of this screening instrument is limited.

REVIEWER'S REFERENCES

Bereiter, C., & Engelmann, S. (1966). *Teaching disadvantaged children in the preschool.* Englewood Cliffs, NJ: Prentice-Hall.

Bloom, L., & Lahey, M. (1978). *Language development and language disorders.* New York: John Wiley and Sons, Inc.

Simon, C. (1985). Functional flexibility: Developing communicative competence in speaker and listener roles. In C. Simon (Ed.), *Communication skills and classroom success: Therapy methodologies for language-learning disabled students* (pp. 135-178). San Diego: College-Hill Press.

[11]

AH6 Group Tests of High Level Intelligence. Purpose: Tests for general reasoning ability, effecting discrimination among selected high ability groups. "Highly intelligent" individuals age 16 through college and university; 1970–83; 3 scores: Verbal, Numerical Plus Diagrammatic, Total; 2 tests; 1987 price data: £11.50 per 10 AG or SEM test booklets; £4.25 per set of 3 keys; £4.95 per 25 AG or SEM answer sheets; £7.95 per manual ('83 26 pages); £14.95 per specimen set including 1 each test booklets AG and SEM, answer sheets AG and SEM, key AG/SEM, manual; A. W. Heim, K. P. Watts, and V. Simmonds; NFER-Nelson Publishing Co., Ltd. [England].*

a) SEM. Intended for potential or qualified scientists, engineers, and mathematicians; 40(70) minutes.

b) AG. Intended for historians, linguists, economists, philosophers, and all others not included for SEM; 35(70) minutes.

Review of the AH6 Group Tests of High Level Intelligence by THOMAS J. KEHLE, Professor of Educational Psychology, University of Connecticut, Storrs, CT:

The AH6 is a British group test of general reasoning ability designed for highly intelligent individuals age 16 through college and university. There are two versions intended for different populations. The SEM version was designed to test the potential and qualifications of scientists, engineers, and mathematicians. The AG version (Arts and General) is intended for everyone else including historians, linguists, economists, and educators. The authors state that the AH6 was designed to discriminate among highly intelligent groups of individuals. According to the authors, the AH6 is unlike other existing instruments also designed to discriminate among the highly intelligent (i.e., Concept Mastery, Intelligence Tests Grade III, and the Miller Analogies Test), in that it does not rely solely on the subject's verbal reasoning ability.

The procedures for administration and scoring are clearly and concisely presented in the manual. However, since the test was developed in England, American users may find some of the test administration instructions awkward. The question books and answer sheets are easy to use and score. The AG version has 60 items of which 30 are verbal, 15 are numerical, and 15 are diagrammatic. Although a Verbal score is obtainable, along with a Numerical Plus Diagrammatic score, the most important score is supposedly the Total score. The SEM version is comprised of 72 items of which 24 are verbal, 24 are numerical, and 24 are diagrammatic. Scores for each of these areas are obtainable; however, as in the case of the AG version, the Total score appears to be the most significant. The authors state that both versions of the AH6 contain numerous questions in common and that the two versions are of equal difficulty. However, no statistical data are presented to support the statement of comparability. The authors also state that in both versions the items are arranged cyclically along a gradient of increasing difficulty; however, no statistical support for rank-order difficulty of items is presented. Subjects can answer items in any order they choose. The AH6 incorporates an 18-item preliminary practice test that is completed immediately prior to the test administration. The preliminary test is not timed and functions, according to the authors, to: (*a*) dispel tension; (*b*) familiarize the subjects with some unique aspects of the items; (*c*) help compensate the slow starters; (*d*) decrease the possibility of less intelligent subjects feeling injured; and (*e*) lessen the effects of subjects' different levels of test-taking ability. The test procedure employs a time limit of 35 minutes for the AG version and 40 minutes for the SEM version, exclusive of the preliminary untimed practice test.

The consistency or reliability for the AG version is based on a nonrandom sample of 112 subjects (representing a 44% mortality from the first testing session) and involved a test-retest after an interval of 5 months. The reliability coefficients were .79 for the Verbal score, .72 for the Numerical Plus Diagrammatic score, and .83 for the Total score. The split-half correlations for the AG were low, ranging from

.59 for the Verbal items to .71 for the Total test. The relatively low split-half reliabilities are probably due to the low number of test items and the fact that the subjects were instructed to take the test in whatever order they choose. No test-retest data are presented in the manual for the SEM version of the AH6. A split-half correlation based on a nonrandom sample of 100 university students yielded a coefficient of .70. No pre- and post-test means or standard deviations are reported for either the AG or SEM versions. The data presented in support of the reliability of the AH6 are insufficient.

The concurrent validity data for the AG version consists of comparisons between the AG Total score and three other tests (Thurstone's Primary Mental Abilities, Experimental Test of Academic Aptitude of Committee of Vice-Chancellors and Principals of Universities, and Progressive Matrices) and an earlier edition of the AH6 (i.e., AH5). Data are also presented on the two components (Verbal and Numerical Plus Diagrammatic) of the AG version. Inspection of the validity data, comparing the AG Total score with the Thurstone IQ and the Progressive Matrices total, indicates relatively low coefficients of .44 and .42 respectively. A serious omission is the lack of tables depicting the means and standard deviations. The validity data for the SEM version consist of comparisons between the SEM scores and four other tests. Of particular significance is the relationship between the SEM Total score and scores on the Progressive Matrices and the Differential Aptitude Test. These coefficients were .19 and .29 respectively, and support the argument that there is little practical relationship between the AH6 SEM and these other established tests of intellectual ability. As in the case of the AG validity data, no means or standard deviations were presented. The authors also present data indicating the relationship between AH6 AG and the English examination compulsorily ($r = .31$). Finally, mean data are presented to illustrate the relationship between students' SEM and AG scores and university place gained for Oxford science scholarship candidates, and final examination class results of Oxford and Cambridge students. According to the authors, these data indicate that the AH6 is more sensitive for selection purposes at the lower, rather than the top, end of the scale.

The authors also present validity data based on nontest criteria. However, the nontest criteria involve the number of 'O'-levels passed, grade of 'O'-level obtained, summed grades on subjects' best performance on four 'O'-levels, and summed grades on the subjects' best performances on two 'A'-levels. These criteria are interrelated and are designed to measure assimilated knowledge and not necessarily high intellectual capacity. Correlations between the AG Total score and 15 various academic criteria reflected in the 'O'-level examinations ranged from -.16 to .57, with a mean of .27.

With regard to the AH6 standardization sample, the authors fail to include information on gender, race, ethnicity, social class, or other demographic characteristics. The norms presented involve five grade levels, from A (top 10 percent) to E (lowest 10 percent), for fifth and sixth form grammar school children and three groups of university students (i.e., students in education, arts, and students reading science). The groups that comprised the standardization sample were not randomly selected, but were based on a restricted range of students from a few select grammar schools and universities.

In summary, based on insufficient support for the instrument's reliability and validity, the value of the AH6 is seriously questioned. Given the unacceptably low validity data presented, it is difficult, if not impossible, to determine the degree in which accurate information can be gained about highly intelligent subjects' general reasoning ability. The authors' statement that the instrument discriminates among highly intelligent groups of individuals is not justified. The standardization sample is meager, severely restricted, and not representative of highly intelligent individuals. The AH6 is psychometrically a very poor measure of general reasoning. To employ the AH6 for any purpose other than further attempts at refinement would be an error and inconsistent with ethical professional practice.

Review of the AH6 Group Tests of High Level Intelligence by PAUL ZELHART, Associate Academic Vice President and Professor of Psychology, East Texas State University, Commerce, TX:

The AH6 Group Tests of High Level Intelligence are the most recent additions to the AH series of intelligence tests. AH6 was created to improve upon AH5 which also measures high level intelligence. The still earlier AH4 measures general intelligence. The two forms of AH6 measure either the abilities of scientists, engineers, and mathematicians (Form SEM), or the abilities of those in arts and other non-science-based (general) endeavors (Form AG). Both forms were designed to discriminate among selected highly intelligent individuals. Both forms assess intelligence by means of posing verbal (V), numerical (N), and diagrammatic (D) problems in the forms of analogies, relations, and series. SEM has equal numbers of each item type (72 items in all). AG uses proportionately more verbal items (V = 30 items, D = 15 items, N = 15 items) on the premise that verbal items are better predictors for nonscientists.

The manual provides scant coverage of the conceptual framework in which the tests are embedded. The types of items included and the validation procedures used, correlations with school achievement, clearly require that to score well on the tests a subject must be sophisticated in terms of formal education. Moreover, some items require a knowledge of British culture. The use of terms like "spanner," and numerical problems requiring knowledge of British currency are examples.

The manual is clear and complete on matters of test administration. A set of pretest items, which are common to both forms, require the administrator(s) be well informed in order to aid examinees in orienting themselves to the types of items used. The manual is very helpful in this regard. Scoring procedures are also clear. Obviously missing, however, is a discussion of item selection and test development methods. Such a discussion would be of interest to those studying the cognitive capacities and characteristics of subgroups of intelligent individuals.

The validity of AH6 was established through correlations with other measures, and through measures of school achievement by selected groups of superior university-bound or university students. In general, the pattern of results shows AH6 to be predictive of scores on other measures of higher intelligence and school performance. Although the bulk of the correlations presented are statistically significant, the values are only modest. Correlations with other tests range from .193 to .648. The latter value is the relationship between AH6 and AH5. Moreover, the numbers of subjects involved in the various validation studies tend to be relatively small (20 to 174 students per study).

The specialization of Forms AG and SEM is also generally supported by the pattern of results of the validation studies. The necessity for Form AG might be questioned, however. Only seven items from Form AG do not appear on Form SEM, and as noted earlier, the 18 pretest practice items are identical for both forms. The time alloted for SEM (40 minutes) is only 5 minutes longer than the limit for AG. So, the utility of two forms over only one form should be established empirically. Also, the relative contribution of item types to the scores of individuals from different disciplines needs to be determined.

Test-retest reliabilities for AH6 are good (total score = .827). Test-retest reliabilities for the various item types (V, N, and D) range from .588 to .706. Correlations between types of items (V to N + D) ranged from .504 to .706 for Form AG. For Form SEM intercorrelations of the item types ranged from .538 to .607.

Norms are presented for various school levels. Presenting norms by age groups would be helpful for those not familiar with the British school system. Norms are given for the top 10 percent (A), the next 20 percent (B), the middle 40 percent (C), the next 20 percent (D), and the lowest 10 percent (E).

AH6 is an interesting and promising instrument. The items are engaging and demanding. The assessment of the contribution of diagrammatic items to the intelligence scores of individuals from specific academic disciplines is a research question of some interest.

[12]

Alcohol Dependence Scale. Purpose: "Provides a brief [quantitative] measure of the extent to which the use of alcohol has progressed from psychological involvement to impaired control." Problem drinkers; 1984; ADS; title on test is Alcohol Use Questionnaire; 4 scale scores: Loss of Behavioral Control, Psychophysical Withdrawal Symptoms, Psychoperceptual Withdrawal Symptoms, Obsessive-Compulsive Drinking Style; 1984 price data: $6.25 per 25 questionnaires; $14.25 per user's guide (41 pages); $15 per specimen set; (5–10) minutes; Harvey A. Skinner and John L. Horn; Addiction Research Foundation [Canada].*

TEST REFERENCES

1. Davidson, R. (1987). Assessment of the alcohol dependence syndrome: A review of self-report screening questionnaires. *British Journal of Clinical Psychology*, 26, 243-255.

Review of the Alcohol Dependence Scale by ROBERT E. DEYSACH, *Associate Professor of Psychology, Department of Psychology, University of South Carolina, Columbia, SC:*

The theoretical context in which the Alcohol Dependence Scale (ADS) is set reflects the practice (i.e., exercised by the World Health Organization and others) of separating primary alcohol dependence from alcohol-related physical, psychological, and social disabilities stemming from alcohol dependence. According to this formulation, levels of alcohol dependence (including characteristics of drinking pattern disturbance) can be independently identified and placed on a continuum of severity. Recently, *DSM III-R* (APA, 1987) has acknowledged the centrality of an alcohol-dependence syndrome by broadening the definition introduced in *DSM III*, by limiting the importance of the dependence/abuse distinctions and by reducing "abuse" to a "residual" status.

The ADS is a 25-item self-report derivative of the Alcohol Use Inventory (AUI), a scale that has enjoyed long service as a research tool and comprehensive clinical device. The ADS is limited to measuring those behaviors specifically linked to reports of compulsive drink seeking, to loss of behavioral control with alcohol use, and to physical and perceptual disturbances associated with withdrawal. A major advantage of the ADS is its brevity and ease of administration. Adaptable for use in either an interview or questionnaire format, the authors recommend the economy of a self-administered questionnaire. Although a clinical interview may afford opportunity to challenge deceptive responses, direct examiner contact may further lower a client's threshold for defensiveness. The ADS questionnaire requires approximately 10 minutes to complete.

Scoring is based on a 2- or 3-point scale with resulting raw scores ranging from 0 to 47. The higher scores describe greater reported levels of dependence. Available in the manual are percentile and standard scores generated on normative data from four clinical samples of clients seeking treatment. The samples (with *N*s ranging from 70 to 225) were taken from admissions to the Clinical Institute of Addiction Research Foundation in Toronto. The ADS manual provides tentative interpretative guidelines in the form of brief characterizations of patients in each quartile together with a promise for inclusion of additional material as more research is conducted with the questionnaire. The authors promise to update interpretative material as a result of future research investigations.

Reported reliabilities of the ADS are in the low .90s and appear acceptable. These reliabilities, however, seem to be drawn primarily from a single large sample of moderate problem drinkers admitted to a short term treatment facility and are based on data gathered with the parent instrument and utilizing a slightly altered set of ADS items. (The authors report that after research conducted in 1982 three more discriminating items were introduced to replace seven less discriminating ones from the AUI, reducing the items from 29 to the present number of 25.) Initial comparisons between the two data sets indicate the original and revised ADS share common properties and are considered by the authors to be "operationally equivalent."

At all levels of analysis of the ADS, concern must be directed toward the accuracy of the self-reported symptoms. Analysis of the internal structure of the ADS suggests that it serves best as a measure of the signs of perceived physical disability resulting from alcohol use and withdrawal and concomitant psychological distress. However, high correlations between self-reported drinking behavior and behavioral control and independent measures of Social Desirability suggest that patients are routinely less candid on these items. Although the authors acknowledge that use of the ADS "demands caution" because of the correlations with Social Desirability, they conclude that such effects are inevitable if items are going to retain content validity.

Additional validational efforts undertaken in Toronto have raised similar concern regarding the adequacy of patient report as a measure of private perceptions. Although the authors do cite evidence for a solid relationship between alcohol dependence as measured by the ADS and alcohol-related disabilities (i.e., with correlations approximating .70), the scale appears less adequate as an index of perceived psychological and social disabilities than of physical ones. Such a finding might be better accounted for in terms of patients' greater facility in externalizing responsibility for ill health than in admitting limited self-control or emotional difficulties.

The most encouraging signals for the utility of the ADS appear to be found in the authors' claims of its ability to successfully predict patterns of help-seeking behavior among a "socially stable" sample of problem drinkers. The authors found that those problem drinkers who report high levels of alcohol dependence are more willing to admit a need for a firm, restrictive treatment program than are a similarly constituted group of drinkers who report lower levels of alcohol dependence. Unfortunately, the tenuous relationship between insight and behavior may account for the increased tendency for self-reported highly alcohol-dependent patients to fail to keep their initial treatment appointments.

On the other hand, problem drinkers reporting low to moderate levels of alcohol dependence are more likely to deny the need for programs of abstinence in favor of a controlled drinking approach to treatment. Among this sample, however, it is those who acknowledge moderate dependence who appear more likely to demonstrate sustained motivation to comply with controlled drinking programs (i.e., compared to those acknowledging only low levels of dependence). The authors report these effects to be present in follow-up assessments of up to 2 years.

Overall, the ADS offers an opportunity to sample an array of physical, social, and psychological consequences reported by problem drinkers. However, it is clear from the research that this self-report measure is limited in its ability to depict actual behavior or private perceptions of such behavior. In point of fact, the ADS seems to accurately depict only perceived physical symptoms and disability. The authors' contentions aside that examiner skill can limit patient deceptiveness, the private beliefs of problem drinkers regarding social, behavioral, and psychological consequences of drinking are heavily masked by social demand characteristics when they are asked to make their beliefs public on the ADS.

While validity of the scale as a measure of the alcohol dependence construct remains largely undemonstrated, the ADS' ability to predict motivation for treatment and treatment response is encouraging. It is a frequently offered speculation that degree of motivation is associated with alcohol treatment outcome. Equally common, however, are disagreements regarding identifying the best measure of motivational level. To the extent the ADS depends on the willingness of the problem drinker to acknowledge a number of the consequences of alcohol abuse, it may serve as a vehicle by which a patient may "project" his/her level of openness to treatment. In combination with other data about an individual's drinking history, environmental determinants, and therapist and treatment attributes, the ADS may well serve as a useful component of a multifaceted assessment of alcoholism.

REVIEWER'S REFERENCE

American Psychiatric Association. (1987). *Diagnostic and statistical manual of mental disorders* (3rd ed. rev.). Washington, DC: Author.

Review of the Alcohol Dependence Scale by NICK J. PIAZZA, Department of Counselor Education, The University of Toledo, Toledo, OH:

The Alcohol Dependence Scale (ADS) was derived from the larger Alcohol Use Inventory. The Alcohol Use Inventory is based on a "multidimensional" conceptualization of alcoholism that includes many different types or styles of alcoholic drinking behavior. One such type of alcoholic use identified in the Alcohol Use Inventory was the alcohol dependence syndrome, which is characterized by impaired control over alcohol consumption, increased tolerance for the effects of alcohol, presence of withdrawal symptoms when alcohol consumption is discontinued, compulsion to drink excessively, and alcohol-seeking behavior. The ADS was developed to provide a brief, yet "psychometrically sound measure of this syndrome."

Skinner and Horn (1984) complain that too often alcohol dependence is thought of as a dichotomous condition, that is, either someone is alcohol dependent or they are not. The ADS is designed to reflect the authors' contention that the alcohol dependence syndrome exists in "degrees rather than as an all-or-none state." The authors cite numerous research articles to support their belief that alcohol dependence is developmental and that it progresses from the merely "psychologically involved" to impaired control over alcohol use. Consequently, the authors intend for the ADS to be used not only to identify the presence of the alcohol-dependence syndrome, but also to provide a "brief measure of the extent to which the use of alcohol has progressed from psychological involvement to impaired control."

Skinner and Horn attribute much of the theoretical foundation for the alcohol-dependence syndrome to work done initially by Edwards and Gross, and the authors appear to have made every effort to develop items that reflect this theoretical orientation. Concurrent validity seems adequate, with the authors reporting a correlation of .69 with scores on the Michigan Alcoholism Screening Test (MAST). This finding strongly suggests that the items on the ADS are, in fact, a measure of problematic drinking.

The authors report very favorable reliabilities for their instrument. They report an internal-consistency (alpha) reliability of .92 and test-retest reliability of .92 as well. Based on these reliability coefficients, the authors claim that "one may have considerable confidence that the ADS will exhibit substantial reliability with individuals who are seeking treatment for their alcohol-related problems."

While the authors identify several uses for the ADS, it is obvious they foresee its greatest use in predicting "compliance with abstinence versus controlled drinking goals." Skinner and Horn cite ample research data to indicate that persons scoring in the low to moderate ranges on the ADS would be more likely to accept and comply with controlled-drinking goals and reject treatments based on total abstinence than persons who score in the higher ranges. The results reported by the authors would appear to support using the ADS in differential diagnosis and treatment planning.

Since Skinner and Horn intend for the ADS to be used in a variety of treatment settings with persons presenting a range of alcohol dependence, they recognize that no single norm group would be sufficient. Consequently, they provide normative data on both outpatient and inpatient groups as well as samples of individuals assigned to both controlled drinking and abstinence-oriented treatment conditions. Consistent with their intent that the instrument be used to determine appropriate treatment goals based on degree of measured dependence, the authors provide an ADS interpretation guide to assist the professional in using the results obtained.

The ADS consists of a 25-item Alcohol Use Questionnaire and a User's Guide. The items, which are multiple forced-choice, are easy to read, have from two to four alternatives, and come in a booklet with clear instructions. Administration is estimated to take about 10 minutes. The questionnaire could be given to groups or individuals and could just as easily be given as an oral interview. The questionnaires appear to be relatively inexpensive and would fit easily into a client or patient record.

The documentation provided in the User's Guide consists of background information on the ADS and on the concept of alcohol dependence as well as all the necessary information to score and interpret the instrument. The materials are clear, and pertinent information is easy to find. Procedures for scoring the questionnaire and for scaling the raw scores are fairly straightforward and adequately documented. Scaled scores are presented as percentiles, z scores, and T scores.

Skinner and Horn claim several advantages to using the ADS: (*a*) The ADS is well-grounded theoretically, (*b*) the ADS gives an index of the degree of alcohol dependence, (*c*) the ADS is brief and easy to administer and interpret, (*d*) the ADS appears to possess high reliability and validity, and (*e*) the ADS is useful as both a diagnostic and a research tool.

There are, however, several limitations inherent in the questionnaire. Limitations would include: (*a*) The items on the questionnaire seem to be vulnerable to deception or poor recall, (*b*) too much emphasis may be given to the instrument in treatment planning or in setting treatment goals, and (*c*) research does not yet seem to be adequate to support any rules for making treatment-planning decisions.

Overall, the ADS appears to be a sound instrument to use clinically as part of a more complete survey of drug and alcohol use. It would also appear to be very useful in evaluating the appropriateness of treatment referrals and program effectiveness with different types of clients. Having instruments such as the ADS available will become increasingly important in determining which groups of individuals respond best to which treatments and in justifying admissions to very expensive and restrictive programs.

[13]

Armed Services-Civilian Vocational Interest Survey. Purpose: Allows "a student to 'self report' and organize interests; and, to use this input, with ASVAB reinforcement, to make informed career decisions about military and/or civilian jobs." High school through adult; 1983; ASCVIS; self-administering, self-assessing, and self-scoring; 8 occupational groups: Administrative/Clerical Personnel, Communications, Computer and Data-Processing, Construction/Engineering/Craft, Mechanical/Repairer/Machining, Service and Transportation, Health and Health Care, Scientific/Technical/Electronic; 1986 price data: $16 per 35 individual folders (6 pages) and user's guide (6 pages); $.50 per individual folder; (30) minutes; Robert Kauk; CFKR Career Materials, Inc.*

Review of the Armed Services-Civilian Vocational Interest Survey by BRUCE W. HARTMAN, Professor of Education, Seton Hall University, South Orange, NJ:

The Armed Services-Civilian Vocational Interest Survey (ASCVIS) is neatly packaged and is offered as a comprehensive, well-structured career assessment instrument (i.e., interest survey) that is self-administering, self-assessing, and self-scoring. I encountered several problems in completing the instrument that created, for me, the image of raising my hand and asking for assistance. Two of the most annoying difficulties I had with managing the format of the ASCVIS were: (*a*) The numbered steps to follow are different from the page numbers on which they fall. For instance, the student is directed to go to step 2 on page 3. That created no problem when step and page were consistently mentioned together, but this was not the case in the directions on page 3. Also a step 3 is printed on page 4 directions. This adds to the confusion between page numbers and step numbers. (*b*) The author switches from using the term "occupational group" to "job group" in step 4 on page 5. This is confusing to the student who is asked a question about job groups when that term has never been used before. This also happens when the term "FIRST-CHOICE JOB GROUP" is used later in the same section. These two terms have not been used before but the student is expected to be familiar with their meaning.

The solution for managing these and other ambiguities is to assume that the ASCVIS is not self-directed. If you plan to distribute this to teachers for administration during their homeroom, you should complete the ASCVIS first, then administer it to the teachers. In this way students encountering difficulties can be guided through them. These are relatively innocuous problems, yet combined with other minor annoyances such as typographical errors and inappropriate use of statistical terminology, I was left wondering about the construction of the instrument itself.

The goals and objectives of the ASCVIS are based on the predictive validity of interests in precise job duties for future job satisfaction. Yet, the author seems to believe that validity and reliability issues do not pertain to the ASCVIS because only concrete job activities that directly relate to armed services-civilian jobs are included. Thus, it is not surprising that evidence for the validity and reliability of the ASCVIS is either missing or insufficiently reported. For instance:

(*a*) The concurrent validity that is presented is insufficient because the description of the "number of occupations" administered the ASCVIS was missing. Predictive validity is not mentioned.

(*b*) The construction of the eight occupational groups is a content validity question of major importance. The author makes reference to the groupings being a "consensus of the major technical occupational groupings found in handbooks published by the various branches of the Armed Services and the latest edition of the OCCUPATIONAL OUTLOOK HANDBOOK" and that his groupings were very similar to Clark's (1961). These are not sufficient explanations of the systematic and objective process the author should have employed for arriving at these particular eight groups.

(*c*) Where student reactions to taking the ASCVIS are presented, the reader should not be uncritical. That students report the "ASCVIS provided new information that helped me make career decisions" does not demonstrate, as the author implies, that these decisions were better than decisions made if students had not taken the ASCVIS.

SUMMARY. The idea for the ASCVIS is good, but because the author dismisses the importance of validity and reliability issues, serious deficiencies of the instrument may not be addressed. During administration of the ASCVIS I would plan for the possibility that some students may not find the ASCVIS "self-administering, self assessing, and self scoring." It may be that the ASCVIS is a valid and reliable interest survey, but the information provided by the author is not sufficient to make that determination at this time.

REVIEWER'S REFERENCE

Clark, K. E. (1961). *The vocational interests of nonprofessional men.* Minneapolis, MN: University of Minnesota Press.

Review of the Armed Services-Civilian Vocational Interest Survey by FREDRICK A. SCHRANK, Associate Academic Dean, Griffin College, Tacoma, WA:

The Armed Services-Civilian Vocational Interest Survey (ASCVIS) costs 50 cents. You get what you pay for.

The ASCVIS is a six-page, self-scoring career assessment leaflet intended to (*a*) assist high school students or young adults in exploring training and job opportunities in high-tech fields not requiring a college degree; (*b*) orient users to technical and specialized jobs in the military and private sector; (*c*) relate armed services training opportunities to civilian jobs; (*d*) show how the military can be a source of advanced technical training and immediate employment; (*e*) bridge a gap in public perception that military training is unrelated to public sector employment; (*f*) augment aptitude information obtained through use of the Armed Services Vocational Aptitude Battery (ASVAB); (*g*) allow students to self-report, organize, and clarify their interests; and (*h*) help individuals develop educational plans and reach preferred career goals. Such grandiose and ambitious goals are promised to be realized within a simple, highly-motivating, concise, and easily-understood package.

Rationale and theoretical foundation for this test is touted as the extension of "authoritative writers in the field of career development." Only four references are listed, and these are 8, 17, 27, and 33 years old. Some of these are related to this test only by the wildest stretch of the imagination: Goldman's (1971) book is listed as presenting "a format for good counseling." The reference to Cronbach (1955) is suggested as an encapsulation of the value of short tests. The work by Clark (1961) is said to be the theoretical model for the development of the ASCVIS. The only recent reference is to Berk (1980), who wrote a book about criterion-referenced measurement. Was nothing else published in the last 27 years that supports this theoretical model?

The actual survey begins with an introduction to the goals of the ASCVIS, a description of who should take this instrument, and a disclaimer about what the ASCVIS "can't do." One curious anomaly is that the survey is described as a "decision-maker." This statement flies in the face of the accepted counseling standard that no single test should be used to make important decisions. The author of this test apparently does not understand that tests do not make decisions, people do.

The instrument proceeds with a self-rating of interests in eight groups of job activities. The directions contain spelling and grammatical errors. Some of the directions are contained in a footnote. Following that, test-takers are asked to transfer ratings to a list of corresponding occupational groups. Based on this unsophisticated and limited framework, respondents are asked to list the civilian and military jobs that best match their interests and aptitudes, and then develop an educational plan for the career goal selected.

No research on validity is reported. The issue is skirted by references to the above-mentioned authorities. Written requests for validity information produced no response from the publisher.

Test-retest reliability is reported as .96, using a sample of 100 11th and 12th grade students over a 2-week period. No information is provided as to where, when, how, and according to what standards this research was conducted.

As it stands, this inventory is not recommended. The author was too ambitious in this undertaking. One six-page folder simply cannot meet the all-encompassing goals described earlier. No research has shown that this inventory meets these goals. In fact, one could suggest that this instrument will do more harm than good. More and better research is needed, especially on the validity of this instrument. In future revisions of this instrument, it is recommended that the author correct the spelling and grammatical errors and update his knowledge of career development by doing some reading of current sources in the field.

REVIEWER'S REFERENCES

Cronbach, L. J. (1955). New light on test strategy from decision theory. Princeton, NJ: Educational Testing Service Conference, The Educational Testing Service.

Clark, K. E. (1961). *The vocational interests of nonprofessional men.* Minneapolis: University of Minnesota Press.

Goldman, L. (1971). *Using tests in counseling* (2nd ed.). New York: Appleton-Century-Crofts.

Berk, R. (Ed.). (1980). *Criterion-referenced measurement: The state of the art.* Baltimore: Johns Hopkins University Press.

[14]

Articulation Screening Assessment. Purpose: To evaluate articulation and identify sounds that a student has not yet mastered. Preschool and elementary; 1983; ASA; 3 scores: Articulation While Naming Isolated Pictures, Articulation in Elicited Speech, and Articulation During Reading; individual; 1986 price data: $32 per complete kit including 50 each of forms I and II and manual ('83, 11 pages); $15 per 50 each of forms I and II; administration time not reported; Jean Gilliam de Gaetano; PRO-ED, Inc.*

[The publisher advised us in January 1988 that this test is no longer available.]

Review of the Articulation Screening Assessment by HAROLD A. PETERSON, Director, Clinical Services and Professor of Audiology and Speech Pathology, University of Tennessee-Knoxville, Knoxville, TN:

The Articulation Screening Assessment (ASA) is neither a diagnostic nor a screening test. It may only loosely be termed an assessment procedure. The ASA is in fact a set of cutely drawn pictures, designed to elicit articulation productions.

There are three sections or choices of stimuli: Section I has pictures for words in isolation in order to elicit spontaneous or imitative naming (e.g., pictures of a fish, a leaf, and an elephant); Section II has the pictures arranged to generate a story description (the fish holding the leaf and tickling the elephant); and Section III has a sentence for readers ("A fish tickles an elephant with a leaf"). The stated purpose of the ASA is "to simply identify the sounds that student has not yet mastered and to determine on what level the errors occur (isolated words or elicited speech). The information is to then be used in determining whether or not the student is in need of additional testing and to be considered for therapy."

Twenty-one single phonemes plus /l/, /r/, and /s/ blends are included—more or less in an "initial, medial and final" word position with few available exceptions. The voiced /th/, /ng/, and /hw/ phonemes are omitted. No rationale is given for the inclusion nor omission of any phonemes or phoneme positions. Occasionally a number of examples of the target sounds may be elicited by the picture and sentence stimuli. (Picture: two angels squeezing orange juice in a jar. Sentence: "Two angels squeeze oranges to make orange *j*uice. They put the orange *j*uice in a *j*ar.") No rationale is given for choosing pictures or words (e.g., frequency of occurrence of words or ease of identifying the pictures), and no advice is provided on the treatment of consistent or inconsistent production of tested phonemes.

There are no data on validity, reliability, or anything else. Instructions on one score sheet (Form I, which lists the target words) suggest marking the target sounds for errors of substitution, or omission, and three degrees of severity of distortion. Again, this suggestion is provided with neither rationale nor description. The second response form (Form II) includes the target word pictures and blank spaces. Instructions are to use Form II with the Section II sequential pictures if the clinician wishes to record the exact response of the individual being tested.

In other words, the purchaser is paying $32 for a set of stimulus pictures and a choice of two forms (one is blank) on which to record the responses. With truth in advertising, this Articulation Screening Assessment would better be termed Selected Articulation Sampling Stimuli. It is neither a test nor a particularly complete inventory of phonemes.

If the clinician is searching for a set of cartoon-cute pictures to aid in eliciting a "free-flowing speech" sample, Part II of this procedure has some usefulness. If, however, the clinician is interested in a comparative measure of articulation skill, he/she will need a different instrument. By virtue of its design, the interpretation of the ASA could only be from an age-of-acquisition base. And there are at least five sets of age-of-acquisition "norms" for when individual phonemes are expected to be mastered. These range from the 2-to-4+-year span reported by Prather et al. (1975), to the 3½-to-7½-year age span reported by Wellman et al. (1931). The problem with age-normed interpretations is that they do not allow an estimate of the normal range in variations of performance.

For the stated purpose of "identifying sounds not yet mastered" one of the more useful and meaningful tests would be the McDonald Screening Deep Test. If the interest is the relative mastery of particular sounds, the McDonald has the advantage of a specified variety of contexts in which frequently erred sounds are tested, and the additional advantage of percentile rank interpretations for those levels of mastery in a kindergarten to third grade population.

REVIEWER'S REFERENCES

Wellman, B. L., Case, I. M., Mengert, I. M., & Bradbury, D. E. (1931). Speech sounds of young children. *University of Iowa Studies in Child Welfare*, Vol. 5, No. 2.

Prather, E. M., Hedrick, E. L., & Kern, C. A. (1975). Articulation development in children aged two to four years. *Journal of Speech and Hearing Disorders*, 40, 179-191.

McDonald, E. T. (1976). A Screening Deep Test of Articulation. Tucson, AZ: Communication Skill Builders, Inc.

[15]

The Assessment of Aphasia and Related Disorders, Second Edition. Purpose: Provides "insight into the patient's functioning and [serves] as a bridge to relating test scores to the common aphasic syndromes recognized by neurologists." Aphasic patients; 1972–83; individual; 2 tests; 1986 price data: $32.50 per complete kit containing both tests, scoring booklets, and manual ('83, 102 pages); Harold Goodglass, with the collaboration of Edith Kaplan; Lea & Febiger.*

a) BOSTON DIAGNOSTIC APHASIA EXAMINATION. 45 scores: Severity Rating, Fluency (Articulation Rating, Phrase Length, Melodic Line, Verbal Agility), Auditory Comprehension (Word Discrimination, Body-Part Identification, Commands, Complex Ideational Material), Naming (Responsive Naming, Confrontation Naming, Animal Naming), Oral Reading (Word Reading, Oral Sentence Reading), Repetition (Repetition of Words, High-Probability, Low-Probability), Paraphasia (Neologistic, Literal, Verbal, Extended), Automatic Speech (Automated Sequences, Reciting), Reading Comprehension (Symbol Discrimination, Word Recognition, Comprehension of Oral Spelling, Word-Picture Matching, Reading Sentences and Paragraphs), Writing (Mechanics, Serial Writing, Primer-Level Dictation, Spelling to Dictation, Written Confrontation Naming, Sentences to Dictation, Narrative Writing), Music (Singing, Rhythm), Spatial and Computational (Drawing to Command, Stick Memory, 3-D Blocks, Total Fingers, Right-Left, Map Orientation, Arithmetic, Clock Setting), plus 8 ratings: Melodic Line, Phrase Length, Articulatory Agility, Grammatical Form, Paraphasia in Running Speech, Repetition, Word Finding, Auditory Comprehension; $15 per 25 examination booklets ('83, 32 pages); $4 per set of 16 test stimulus cards; (75–150) minutes.

b) BOSTON NAMING TEST. Ages 5.5–59; $7.50 per test ('83, 64 pages); $6 per 25 scoring booklets ('83, 8 pages); administration time not reported.

See 9:86 (2 references); see also T3:308 (28 references) of *a* only; for reviews by Daniel R. Boone and Manfred J. Meier of *a* only, see 8:955 (1 reference).

TEST REFERENCES

1. Liederman, J., Kohn, S., & Wolf, M. (1986). Words created by children versus aphasic adults: An analysis of their form and communicative effectiveness. *The Journal of Genetic Psychology*, 147, 379-393.

2. Albert, M., Duffy, F. H., & Naeser, M. (1987). Nonlinear changes in cognition with age and their neuropsychologic correlates. *Canadian Journal of Psychology*, 41 (2), 141-157.

3. Lovett, M. W. (1987). A developmental approach to reading disability: Accuracy and speed criteria of normal and deficient reading skill. *Child Development*, 58, 234-260.

Review of The Assessment of Aphasia and Related Disorders, Second Edition by RITA SLOAN BERNDT, Associate Professor of Neurology, University of Maryland School of Medicine, Baltimore, MD:

SUMMARY. The Boston Diagnostic Aphasia Examination (BDAE) is a comprehensive test of language and other cognitive functions in adults who have suffered damage to the brain. The first edition of this test, published in 1972, is widely used for both clinical and research purposes. The goal of the test is to classify each patient into one of the "classical" aphasia types: Wernicke, Broca, Conduction, Anomic, Transcortical Motor, Transcortical Sensory, or Global Aphasia. This is accomplished by a subjective rating scale applied to patients' spontaneous speech (which provides separate assessments of characteristics such as phrase length, grammatical form, etc.) and by objectively-scored subtests assessing auditory comprehension, sentence repetition, and confrontation naming. These subtests, as well as others investigating automatic speech, reading, writing, and rhythmic abilities, provide information on a wide range of linguistic capabilities. Supplemental tests are included for the assessment of other cognitive capacities, such as arithmetic and spatial abilities, that might also be compromised.

CRITIQUE. The second edition of the BDAE introduces minimal changes in test procedures; the first edition stimulus materials can be used with the new test booklets. Several well-considered changes have been made in the order of test items within subtests, with only minor changes to the items themselves. Modification has been made to the scoring procedures, all of which are explained in some detail in the test manual. Subtest scores are now expressed in terms of percentiles, rather than *z*-scores, and several modifications have been made to the rating scale profile of speech characteristics, which is central to the classification decision. In general, these changes are clearly explained and well justified. In addition, significant (and welcome) changes have been made in the procedures for scoring patients' attempts to write.

One major contribution of the second edition is the publication of new normative data on 242 aphasic patients and 142 neurologically-intact adults. The data were subjected to a number of different statistical analyses, including discriminant and factor analyses. These analyses provide useful information about the clustering of subtests, as well as about the subtests that contribute most information to the ultimate classification of the patient. The data from control subjects are particularly useful in interpreting patients' performance on the supplementary non-language tests. These tests indicate considerable variability in normal performance.

A clear strength of the Boston approach to aphasia testing is its solid grounding in a theoretical model of language, and of language/brain relationships. That model is clearly articulated in the new test manual, and the relationship of the aphasic syndromes to the model is demonstrated with well-selected examples. One particularly positive aspect of this approach is its explicit statement that many individual aphasic patients will not be classifiable into one of the types, but will demonstrate some combination of symptoms that does not constitute a "syndrome." Unlike other similar tests, the BDAE allows a considerable proportion of patients to be called "unclassifiable." Thus, the classes that are formed tend to be relatively homogeneous groupings. The classification criteria are not blurred to admit unclear cases. This issue of homogeneity within the aphasia types is of great importance to researchers who group patients into the classical types for subsequent testing.

The BDAE is a comprehensive assessment instrument, and therefore it cannot be administered quickly or by untrained examiners. Several hours are typically required to administer the entire test, and the scores obtained must be interpreted by a trained Speech/Language Pathologist or other specialist. There is considerable flexibility, however, in actual administration procedures, and subtests can be ordered to minimize patient fatigue, or to focus on specific aspects of performance that may be of interest.

SUMMARY. The Boston Diagnostic Aphasia Examination is a theoretically-driven assessment instrument for use with brain-damaged adults. Its subtests probe a wide range of language and other cognitive capacities, yielding data in the form of subtest percentiles for individual patients. In addition, the test provides a means for interpreting subtest scores, along with a profile of spontaneous speech characteristics, in terms of the classical aphasia typology. The manual contains a clear theoretical rationale for the inclusion of test items, as well as comprehensive information about the psychometric properties of the test. This is an excellent test that should be useful in a variety of clinical settings.

Review of The Assessment of Aphasia and Related Disorders, Second Edition by MALCOLM R. MCNEIL, Professor, Department of Communicative Disorders, University of Wisconsin-Madison, Madison, WI:

Alterations in The Assessment of Aphasia and Related Disorders, Second Edition from the first (1972) edition entitled the Boston Diagnostic Aphasia Examination (BDAE) involved: (*a*) reordering some items within subtests, (*b*) the addition of three body-part names to the Confrontation Naming subtest, and (*c*) elimination of the Body-Part Naming subtest. Substantive changes were made in the organization of the test record booklet including a new subtest summary page, percentiles replacing *z*-scores and new norms on 242 aphasic subjects as well as original norms on 147 neurologically normal adult men. Seven subtests (Oral Word Reading, Visual Confrontation Naming, Symbol and Word Discrimination, Word-picture Matching, Mechanics of Writing, Serial Writing, and Primer-level Dictation) were eliminated from this norming procedure based on the assumption that no failures would occur on them. Test stimuli have remained essentially unchanged from the first edition except for the addition of the Boston Naming Test.

PURPOSE. The authors suggest the BDAE was designed to meet several aims: (*a*) detection of the presence of aphasia, (*b*) classification of aphasic syndromes that lead to inferences about (*c*) cerebral lesion localization, (*d*) classification by overall severity of aphasia, (*e*) measurement of patient change, and (*f*) a tool with which the speech/language pathologist can focus treatment. The intended users of this information are neurologists, psychologists, and speech/language pathologists.

TEST STRUCTURE. The test is organized into five major sections: (*a*) *Conversational and Expository Speech*; from the tasks in this section, eight characteristics of the patient's speech and language (listed in the description above) are rated on a 7-point equal-appearing interval scale. The purposes of these ratings are to derive a profile that corresponds to a particular aphasia syndrome or "type." The format for eliciting speech and communication include conducting an "informal exchange" with suggested questions and responses to social, hospital-related, and open-ended conversational topics. An action picture is also used for eliciting a more predictable verbal sample. Other than the rating of speech characteristics, no further linguistic or psycholinguistic analyses are made of this speech sample. Additional analyses of these speech/language data have, however, been suggested by other researchers (e.g., Yorkston & Beukelman, 1980).

(*b*) *Auditory Comprehension*, the second major section, is assessed with four subtests (listed above). The format and stimuli, along with the scoring conventions and criteria are heterogeneous for each of these auditory comprehension subtests. The tasks used in these four subtests are not unlike the auditory comprehension and processing tasks of several other aphasia tests (e.g., the Minnesota Test for Differential Diagnosis of Aphasia [MTDDA], Schuell, 1965; T3:1513). In this sense these tasks may have concurrent validity. However, no formal correlations among these tests have been undertaken and these relationships remain unreferenced in the test manual. The "objectively" derived score for Auditory Comprehension is converted to a percentile and graphed along with the rating of the seven speech/language characteristics for the eventual derivation of the profile.

The order of presentation of the test stimuli are left to the discretion (whims) of the tester for the Word Discrimination subtest, with an instruction to "rotate at random from one category to another." This nonstandard presentation could have a great influence on performance, both among persons and within the same person on repeated testing due to selective and idiosyncratic semantic priming or interference effects. The scoring conventions, which encompass points of 2, 1, 1/2, and 0 for the Word Discrimination subtest, can probably be reliably assigned with the instructions given for scoring. However, the justification for the differential point assignment (e.g., 2 points if identified correctly within a 5-second time limit) and the ordinality and intervality of this scoring procedure are not addressed. The scores are, however, treated as ordinal (probably interval) level data for statistical purposes.

(*c*) The *Oral Expression* section is composed of 11 subtests (listed above under Naming, Oral Reading, Repetition, Automatic Speech Subtests, along with the Boston Naming Test). Scoring is primarily plus-minus although the Nonverbal and Verbal Agility Subtests use a 2-point equal-appearing interval scoring system. The scores for these tasks are dependent on the number of alternating movements produced in 5 seconds. As with the other rated scores that are assigned in the test battery, nowhere is there a rationale or supporting data for the ordinal or interval nature of these scoring conventions. The Oral Agility Subtest assesses selected nonspeech lip, jaw, and tongue movements in response to oral commands. These are standard tasks for the assessment of the speech mechanism (Darley, Aronson, & Brown, 1975) and do not reveal aphasia per se, unless deficient performance is the result of an auditory processing/comprehension deficit. The results of this subtest are not formally graphed on the subtest summary profile. Performance on these tasks may, however, subjectively influence the rating of articulatory agility in the Rating Scale Profile of Speech Characteristics used to judge the presence and nature of aphasia.

The Verbal Agility Subtest is described qualitatively, with paraphasias and "articulatory difficulty (dysarthria)" assuming mutually exclusive classifications. The assumptions underlying the differentiation of these categories and the description given for their scoring are contradictory and unsupported by contemporary views of neurogenic disorders of speech production. The authors define articulatory difficulty as the "loss of accuracy in forming individual phonemes, so that the sounds that emerge—particularly difficult consonants and blends—are not standard English phonemes." In this case, only non-English speech sound productions could be considered as articulatory (motor) in origin. Only those speech errors that cross categorical perceptual boundaries are considered as errors of phonological (linguistic) origin and then those that do cross categorical boundaries are always assumed to arise from linguistic origins. These definitions and the conceptual framework from which they are derived are indefensible. That is, some sound alterations that do not cross categorical boundaries could result from a failure of the "linguistic" system. Likewise, some sound substitutions could be attributable to motoric mechanisms. Perceived ease of production is a critical feature that is supposed to separate literal paraphasias from articulatory disorders. Related to the ease of articulation is a judgment of "stiffness" of articulation that is defined as "no transcribable phonemic error, but perceptibly awkward." However, narrow phonetic transcription allows for and describes sound alterations that do not cross categorical boundaries. In addition, stiffness of articulation receives no further definition, a condition shared by other constructs inherent in the perceptual differentiations required for making the ratings of speech characteristics. The personal experience of this reviewer, teaching these ratings to graduate students sophisticated in making a variety of auditory perceptual ratings and transcriptions of normal and pathological voice, speech, and language, attests to the difficulty and unreliability in making them. No interjudge, intrajudge, or test-reliability data are provided for these ratings. Although the manual does attempt to provide more objective descriptions and rating criteria for the enhancement of this subtest's scoring reliability, it is insufficient. Training tapes, or other supplementary training procedures are not available with or separate from the test.

The inclusion of the Automatized Sequences Subtest is well justified in the aphasia testing literature, and the Reciting, Signing, and Rhythm Subtests are well justified in the aphasia research literature. However, each of the subtests' scoring procedures suffer from the same lack of justification or evidence (ordinality or intervality) for the assignment of points as the Oral Agility Subtest.

The Repetition of Words Subtest has adequate concurrent validity in the aphasia testing literature. The words in this subtest are described in terms of the articulation and the linguistic manner in which they are produced. Only the linguistic aspect is judged on a plus-minus basis and the total correct words forms the final score. Reliance on the skills and biases of the test administrator for providing a stimulus repetition creates a potential source of unreliability and bias in the performance on this test.

The Repeating Phrases Subtest, with its high and low probability phrases is unique in aphasia testing and is well supported as a valuable task, both in the factor analyses reported in the test manual and in the aphasia literature. Explicit instructions for the verbal presentation of the stimuli (e.g., speech rate, intonational level, intensity level, etc.) are not specified in the manual and are a potential source of bias and unreliability.

The Word Reading, Responsive Naming, and Visual Confrontation Naming Subtests are appropriate tasks from a content validity point of view. However, they suffer from the same absence of evidence for the ordinality of the 4-point scoring system based on response delay (3 points are awarded for a correct response given within 3 seconds, 2 points for 3–10 seconds, 1 point for 10–30 seconds, and 0 points for a failed item). The test administrator is not given explicit directions for deciding when an item has been failed. Although the articulation is rated as normal, stiff, distorted, or failed, and paraphasias are rated as neologistic distortions, literal, verbal, or other, directions are not provided for the determination of which of these paraphasias is correct (it is inferred that all but the failed articulation is correct). Using a literal interpretation of the instructions, *any* response that meets the time requirements should be awarded a score, even if it is a verbal or neologistic paraphasia.

The rationale and concurrent validity for the Animal Naming and Oral Sentence Reading Subtests justify their inclusion in the test battery. Unlike several other subtests in this section, administration and scoring procedures for these two subtests are probably sufficiently explicit to allow for reliable interjudge and intrajudge agreement.

(*d*) The *Understanding Written Language* section of the test assesses a number of elementary associative skills that underlie or are a byproduct of reading. In general, the rationale given by the authors and the concurrent validity provided by other aphasia batteries justifies the inclusion of the various subtests in this section of the test. The administration and scoring procedures are clear for these subtests. One potential weakness in many of these subtests (and in several other subtests throughout the test) is that there are few (usually only one) stimulus items at any level of difficulty. Given the extreme variability in aphasic performance on all tasks, it is highly unlikely that performance on a single item will be the truest (i.e., reliable) reflection of the patient's capabilities at that difficulty level. A relatively high Kuder-Richardson reliability coefficient for these and most of the other subtests suggests the items within subtests tend to vary together. However, this does not measure internal consistency and does not establish item homogeneity on a severity basis, a highly prized attribute of any aphasia test.

(*e*) *Writing*. The writing tasks sample a moderate range of graphic abilities that are typically sampled in some form by other aphasia test batteries (e.g., automatic and serial language; writing sentences, words, letters and numbers to dictation; written naming; and elicited narrative writing). Some of the administration procedures are vague and unspecified in the test manual. For example, it is unclear whether the numbers to be dictated in the primer-level dictation task are read as a sequence of numbers (i.e., one-five) or as a single number (i.e., fifteen). The ordinality of the scoring categories for the Mechanics of Writing, Narrative Writing, and Sentences Written to Dictation Subtests have not been established and cannot be employed without considerable skepticism.

The Supplementary Language Tests are not standardized in terms of administration or scoring and are not norm referenced (with the exception of the Boston Naming Test) and will therefore not be discussed. The Boston Naming Test is normed on a small sample of normal ($N = 30$ children and $N = 84$ adult) and aphasic ($N = 82$) subjects. These norms are reported by grade and age level for the children, by age level for normal adults, and by BDAE severity rating level for the aphasics. These norms are not particularly useful clinically for differential diagnosis, as the ranges overlap considerably across age and severity levels. In addition, the severity breakdown for the aphasic group is not consistent with the theoretical construct of syndromes on which the test is based. This naming test is, however, widely used and does sample a wide difficulty range of picture names based on justifiable psycholinguistic variables such as semantic category and frequency of usage.

The Supplementary Nonlanguage Tests (16 in number) are better standardized than the supplementary language tasks, both in terms of reference data and administration procedures. Their exact use as differential diagnostic tasks are not well delineated in the test manual, and their differentiation from other language tasks is not always made clear (e.g., the Acalculia tasks).

VALIDITY. From a construct validity perspective, the BDAE is based on the premise that components of language can be impaired selectively due to aphasia. Although the authors do not refer to a formal model for the structure of the test, it is clear the classic Wernicke-Lichtheim Model, with its necessary tie to structure (lesion location) and syndromes, dominates the underpinnings of the test. This theoretical position represents what is probably the most subscribed to paradigm governing research and clinical practice in aphasiology. In the rationale for the areas of deficit that are assessed (articulation, loss of verbal fluency, word-finding difficulty, repetition, seriatim speech, loss of grammar and syntax, paraphasia, auditory comprehension, reading, and writing) and the tasks used to elicit behaviors, it is evident (although not always explicitly stated) that differential lesion location is required for conceptual admissibility of particular patterns of linguistic, modality, or communicative functions to be included in the behaviors sampled in the test.

The theoretical justification for patient classification according to this paradigm, using the eight ratings of speech characteristics is based upon an abundance of research that is in great measure reported elsewhere. The theoretical justification for classifying subjects according to the paradigm that motivates this test is, however, not addressed adequately in the test manual and has, in recent times, come under considerable criticism on theoretical (Caramazza, 1984; Schwartz, 1984) and clinical (Darley, 1982) grounds.

It should be noted there is an equally popular and viable alternate and opposing view (i.e., a competing paradigm) of the fundamental nature of aphasia. This view portrays aphasia as a unidimensional, central language processing disorder, and has been discussed by Schuell, Jenkins, and Jimenez-Pabon (1964), Darley (1982), and others. In this theoretical framework, classically defined syndromes do not guide the selection of tasks. Rather, variables that may be more directly related to describing interpersonal communicative ability (e.g., the Communicative Abilities in Daily Living [CADI], Holland, 1980 [69]) or those psycholinguistic or information processing variables or operations that are the target of treatment (e.g., the Porch Index of Communicative Ability [PICA], Porch, 1981 [9:963]; or the MTDDA, Schuell, 1965) are more likely to be sampled, and provide the aphasiologist with this particular theoretical persuasion, a more parsimonious description of behavior. Only after a potential user of the BDAE has made a philosophical commitment to the "centers and pathways" model of aphasia, with its resultant emphasis on deriving a classification in which to place the individual, would the BDAE be chosen as a tool for assessing aphasia. One other standardized aphasia test is based on very similar theoretical constructs (the Western Aphasia Battery; Kertesz, 1980) and competes with the BDAE for its potential as a patient classification instrument.

The test was not designed to have *predictive validity* in the classic sense and the authors make no claims for its ability to predict future performance from current test results. In the sense that lesion location is predictable from profile analysis, the test claims predictive (correlational) validity. However, no data are provided in the test manual to document the degree with which it achieves this test aim. There are, however, several reports that provide some indirect support for the profile's high correlation with lesion location (e.g., Goodglass, Quadfasel, & Timberlake, 1964).

Concurrent validity is not reported in the test manual. However, a correlation with the Communicative Abilities in Daily Living (Holland, 1980) [r = 84] reported by Holland (1980) provides some concurrent validity information suggesting the test is in fact assessing attributes of the aphasic person that are shared by the constructs of another contemporary aphasia test instrument.

Content validity, in terms of the tasks chosen for the assessment, is probably the strongest attribute of the BDAE's construction. The stimuli used to elicit the behaviors to be judged and the tasks themselves are well supported in the aphasia literature. This literature is primarily derived from studies that have researched the notions of modality and linguistic level dissociations and from literature attempting to demonstrate the correlation between specific linguistic functions (or deficits) and focal cerebral hemispheric lesions. As alluded to in other sections of this review, however, there are substantive problems with some of the scoring conventions as well as with potential unreliability of administration instructions. This unreliability is caused by administrator freedom in administering the stimuli within a subtest and in the ambiguity of instructions provided to the test administrator.

MAJOR STRENGTHS. The BDAE is to be praised for attempting to objectify, through operationalized definitions and standardized assessment procedures, the diagnosis of the previously ill-defined and poorly assessed syndromes of aphasia (Darley, 1977; Duffy, 1978). The BDAE assesses a large sample of behaviors to accomplish the differentiation among aphasia syndromes. From a content validity perspective, the tasks and the test items are research-based and are appropriately included in the test battery. The test's content reflects current psycholinguistic research and knowledge better than other standardized aphasia test batteries.

Extensive statistical treatment of the test using simple correlations, cluster analysis, discriminant function analysis, and factor analysis provides useful information about the test's internal structure and about its success in accurately classifying aphasic individuals according to the theoretical schema of the test. While cross validation studies using unselected groups of aphasic subjects or other neurologically involved subjects have not been accomplished, a discriminant function analysis on the scores of 41 subjects from four preselected aphasic syndromes (Broca, Wernicke, Conduction, and Anomic), accurately classified 37 subjects.

MAJOR WEAKNESSES. Because no test-retest or intrajudge reliability and minimal interjudge reliability data are reported, many of the aims of the test are not achieved. The rationale offered by the authors for omitting test-retest reliability was that aphasic patients vary so greatly from day to day and within the day that reliability is not obtainable until neurological (recovery) stability has been reached. Without these data, however, the ability to document patient change as a function of treatment, physiological recovery, or additional neuropathology is impossible. In addition, the ability to focus treatment would be impossible if the patient's performance on the test would be expected to change from hour to hour or from day to day. This is particularly true of aphasia treatment that involves an intense, long-term treatment plan. A test incapable of providing a stable description of abilities and disabilities (for those tasks sampled) cannot be considered an instrument useful in inferring lesion location. Likewise, it is unlikely that classification by syndrome or by severity could be offered with any confidence if the test were unstable from administration to administration. Nowhere in the manual was there a caveat indicating the test as appropriate for only those patients with a stabilized course of recovery.

The test is generally (although not for all subtests) equipped with poor test administration instructions. This weakness could lead to poor interjudge, intrajudge, and test-retest reliability as well as patient performance bias.

The items within subtests do not appear to be, and have not been established as, homogeneous. Given the extreme moment-to-moment variability in aphasic performance, and the small number of subtest items of equal difficulty, there is a high likelihood the test will provide an unreliable and possibly inaccurate assessment of the patient's abilities on a particular task.

None of the rating scales used for the various subtests have established ordinality or intervality. This represents a potential fatal error in the test's construction that, unless successfully addressed and statistically established, can lead to serious theoretical misrepresentation and clinical misinterpretation of the test data.

The major theoretical construct of the test is the existence of classic aphasia syndromes. Further, the purpose of the test is to categorize aphasic subjects into these classic syndromes. No data are presented, however, as to how many patients from an unselected clinical population can be classified according to this schema.

In terms of the clinical use of the test, the elimination of seven subtests from the norming sample creates a serious test interpretation problem. Although one of the aims of the test is to provide the speech/language pathologist with a treatment focus, no discussion is offered as to how to most validly and efficiently employ test results for this use. The test does, however, offer a large sample of behaviors relevant to clinical hypothesis generation by the clinician.

SUMMARY. The BDAE is unique and comprehensive in many respects. It is based upon the most prevalent and classic notion of the validity of aphasic syndromes. Content validity in terms of the tasks used to assess aphasia is its major strength. An absence of established test-retest, intrajudge, and interjudge reliabilities, along with an absence of established ordinality for its scoring system, explicit administration procedures, within subtest item homogeneity, and complete normative data make the test poorly suited to achieving many of its stated aims. There is some evidence the profile derived from the Rating of Speech Characteristics correlates with anterior versus posterior lesions; however, this profile is derived from rating only the expository speech and the scores from speech repetition and auditory comprehension. The great majority of the test battery is not used for the two purposes achieved by the test (classifying and predicting site of lesion). The test has promise, but presents too many concerns to recommend it for clinical use.

REVIEWER'S REFERENCES

Schuell, H., Jenkins, J. J., & Jimenez-Pabon, E. (1964). *Aphasia in adults: Diagnosis, prognosis and treatment.* New York, Hoeber Medical Division: Harper and Row, Publishers.

Goodglass, H., Quadfasel, A., & Timberlake, W. H. (1964). Phrase length and the type and severity of aphasia. *Cortex,* 1, 133-153.

Schuell, H. (1965). *The Minnesota Test for Differential Diagnosis of Aphasia.* Minneapolis: University of Minnesota Press.

Sarno, M. T. (1969). *The functional communication profile.* New York: Institute of Rehabilitation Medicine.

Darley, F. L., Aronson, A. E., & Brown, J. R. (1975). *Motor Speech Disorders*. Philadelphia: W. B. Saunders Co.

Darley, F. L. (1977). A retrospective view: Aphasia. *Journal of Speech and Hearing Disorders*, 42, 161-169.

Duffy, J. R. (1979). Boston Diagnostic Aphasia Examination (BDAE). In F. L. Darley (Ed.), *Evaluation of appraisal techniques in speech and language pathology* (pp. 198-202). Reading, MA: Addison-Wesley Publishing Company, Inc.

Holland, A. L. (1980). Communication Abilities in Daily Living: A Test of Functional Communication for Aphasic Adults. Baltimore: University Park Press.

Kertesz, A. (1980). *Western aphasia battery*. New York: Grune & Stratton, Inc.

Yorkston, K. M., & Beukelman, D. R. (1980). An analysis of connected speech samples of aphasic and normal speakers. *Journal of Speech and Hearing Disorders*, 45, 27-36.

Porch, B. E. (1981). Porch Index of Communicative Ability. Palo Alto: Consulting Psychologists Press.

Darley, F. L. (1982). *Aphasia*. Philadelphia: W. B. Saunders Co.

Caramazza, A. (1984). The logic of neuropsychological research and the problem of patient classification in aphasia. *Brain and Language*, 21, 9-20.

Schwartz, M. F. (1984). What the classical aphasia categories can't do for us, and why. *Brain and Language*, 21, 3-8.

[16]

Assessment of Career Decision Making.

Purpose: "Assesses a student's career decision-making style and progress on three career decision-making tasks." Adolescents and adults; 1985; ACDM; 9 scales: Rational, Intuitive, Dependent, School Adjustment, Satisfaction With School, Involvement With Peers, Interaction With Instructors, Occupation, Major; 1986 price data: $32 per 2 answer sheets including scoring service and manual (84 pages); $17.50 per manual; WPS scoring service, $4.80 or more per answer sheet; (40) minutes; Jacqueline N. Buck and M. Harry Daniels; Western Psychological Services.*

TEST REFERENCES

1. Phillips, S. D., & Strohmer, D. C. (1983). Vocationally mature coping strategies and progress in the decision-making process: A canonical analysis. *Journal of Counseling Psychology*, 30, 395-402.

2. Phillips, S. D., Pazienza, N. J., & Ferrin, H. H. (1984). Decision-making styles and problem-solving appraisal. *Journal of Counseling Psychology*, 31, 497-502.

3. Phillips, S. D., Pazienza, N. J., & Walsh, D. J. (1984). Decision making styles and progress in occupational decision making. *Journal of Vocational Behavior*, 25, 96-105.

4. Pinder, F. A., & Fitzgerald, P. W. (1984). The effectiveness of a computerized guidance system in promoting career decision making. *Journal of Vocational Behavior*, 24, 123-131.

5. Remer, P., O'Neill, C. D., & Gohs, D. E. (1984). Multiple outcome evaluation of a life-career development course. *Journal of Counseling Psychology*, 31, 532-540.

6. Thomas, R. G., & Bruning, C. R. (1984). Cognitive dissonance as a mechanism in vocational decision processes. *Journal of Vocational Behavior*, 24, 264-278.

7. Phillips, S. D., Friedlander, M. L., Pazienza, N. J., & Kost, P. P. (1985). A factor analytic investigation of career decision-making styles. *Journal of Vocational Behavior*, 26, 106-115.

8. Gordon, V. N., Coscarelli, W. C., & Sears, S. J. (1986). Comparative assessments of individual differences in learning and career decision making. *Journal of College Student Personnel*, 27, 233-242.

Review of the Assessment of Career Decision Making by BRUCE J. EBERHARDT, Associate Professor of Management, University of North Dakota, Grand Forks, ND:

The Assessment of Career Decision Making (ACDM) is a 94-item, self-report instrument, the major focus of which is the process of career decision making. The theoretical basis of the ACDM is the Harren Model of Career Decision Making (Harren, 1979), which is "a comprehensive model that takes into account many of the important factors involved in the career decision-making process of students." The instrument assesses aspects of three of the four major components of the model: decision-making process, decision-making styles, and developmental tasks.

Three 10-item scales measure the degree to which students utilize three strategies—Rational, Intuitive, and Dependent—in making career decisions. A 24-item scale, labeled School Adjustment, consists of three 8-item subscales and measures students' satisfaction with school, involvement with peers, and interaction with instructors. These subscales represent the developmental tasks of autonomy, interpersonal maturity, and sense of purpose. Finally, the Occupation and Major scales are both 20-item scales that "measure the degree of commitment and certainty the student feels towards his or her choice of future occupation" or major or field of study, respectively. Both scales represent single, bipolar continua and assess the planning and commitment phases of the career decision-making process.

The ACDM can be administered to students either individually or in groups. The publisher recommends that the purpose of the instrument be explained to students before distribution. The ACDM was intended for use with adolescents and adults. However, particular sections of the test should be deleted when used with certain populations. The entire test can be used for college and university students. For high school students the Major scale should be deleted except for those individuals who have plans for some form of further education. Because of their general wording the Decision-Making Styles scales and the Occupation scale can be used with nonstudents. However, the publisher recommends not using the test with this group because relevant normative data are not available. Although the reading difficulty of the instrument has been estimated at the sixth-grade level, users are cautioned that students with low verbal skills or learning disabilities may have problems completing the test.

The scoring of the ACDM is both a strength and a potential weakness of the instrument. All completed forms must be scored through the publisher's scoring service. The computerized report which is generated from the scored ACDM actually consists of three separate reports: a Group Summary, a Counselor's report, and a Student's report. All of these reports provide extensive, detailed information. Especially impressive in the Counselor's report is a section labeled "Validity Considerations." This section considers two types of validity checks: "(*a*) invalid responses due to random or systematic response biases, and (*b*) threats to validity associated with relevant moderator variables such as age or ethnic group membership." The first type of validity concern is assessed using a Random Response Index. This scale was designed to detect random response patterns in the ACDM and was based on the supposition that certain pairs of items are inconsistent, contradictory, or at least statistically unlikely.

The only potentially negative aspect of ACDM scoring is that no hand-scoring option is available. Although the publisher states that for the average user the scoring turn around time is from 2 to 6 working days, it is easy to predict that in some circumstances, depending on the postal service, delays could be longer. For the user wishing to provide immediate feedback to test takers this delay may be prohibitive.

The publishers have done a first-rate job in providing test users with a manual that supplies extensive information concerning the test's theoretical development and standardization and its psychometric properties. The ACDM was standardized on samples of 550 high school and 2,495 college students. For scales where sex and grade-level differences were discovered, separate norms were established for males and females and individuals in the various grades. A shortcoming in the normative data, as noted by the publisher, is that the representation of ethnic minorities in the normative sample is limited. Therefore, caution should be taken when using the norms to interpret the scores of minority group members.

The manual presents the results of several studies investigating both the internal consistency and the test-retest reliabilities of the ACDM. In studies using the present form, alpha coefficients ranged from .49 to .84 for the Decision-Making Styles scales and from .78 to .92 for the Decision-Making Tasks scales. These figures indicate that the ACDM possesses adequate internal consistency for research purposes. However, the .49 for the one Decision-Making Style scale is relatively low and caution should be exercised when using the scale for individual interpretation. The studies examining the temporal stability of ACDM scores all involved only college students; data on test-retest reliability were lacking for high school students. The research investigating the test-retest reliability of the ACDM in its present form yielded correlation coefficients ranging from .66 to .84 with a 2-week time interval.

Numerous studies are cited in the manual that report on the ACDM's validity. Evidence is presented for the content, criterion-related, and construct validity of the test. When considered together, these studies present an impressive argument for the validity of the ACDM. However, more information on the predictive validity of the test would be desirable.

In summary, the ACDM appears to be a useful tool for individuals interested in the career decision-making process. Potential users include teachers, career counselors, and school staff responsible for career orientation programs. Used in combination with instruments assessing vocational interests, it provides students with information to assist in their career decision making. Potential users, however, should be careful when expanding its application to groups for which normative data are not presently available. These groups include non-students and members of certain ethnic minorities.

REVIEWER'S REFERENCE

Harren, V. A. (1979). A model of career decision making for college students. *Journal of Vocational Behavior*, 14, 119-133.

Review of the Assessment of Career Decision Making by NICHOLAS A. VACC, Professor and Coordinator of Counselor Education, University of North Carolina, Greensboro, NC:

The Assessment of Career Decision Making (ACDM) is a 94-item measure that assesses, through self-report, an individual's style of career decision making and progress on career decision-making tasks. Originally designed and developed by Vincent A. Harren, the ACDM is based on the Tiedeman and O'Hara theory of career decision. The present form of this instrument is the result of further development and refinement by Jacqueline N. Buck and M. Harry Daniels.

The ACDM is a self-report instrument with a true or false checkoff answer sheet and requires approximately 40 minutes to administer. The price of the answer sheet (i.e., $7.95 per sheet for quantities less than 10 with a slightly reduced cost for quantities greater than 10) includes computer processing, an individualized Counselor's Report, Student's Report, Group Summary if applicable, and postage and handling for returning the reports.

The manual indicates the ACDM, which was designed for high school and college students, can be used individually or with a group. As reported by the authors, the purpose of the instrument is to assist students in making career decisions and "selecting college majors and occupations that are compatible with their interests, skills, and environmental constraints." It is further stated that the test helps determine the "need for career counseling and best type of counseling to use." The latter purpose is particularly ambitious considering that the counseling literature indicates disagreement concerning who needs counseling and the type to use for different groups of clients.

Norms for the instrument are reported based on the performance of 550 high-school-age students and 2,495 college-age students over a 7-year period. As the authors indicate, use with individuals outside schools is limited. Grade-level norms are reported from ninth grade through the senior year in college. The normative sample for the ninth-grade level consists of only 60 subjects. A related concern is the demographic section of the answer sheet, which includes responses for students below the ninth grade; norms are not available for this group. In addition, reporting grade norms for college students is of questionable value because of the wide range of ages among those attending college. For example, differences between 40-year-old college students and stereotypic students who recently graduated from high school would be great. In general, standardization appeared to be nonsystematic, evolving from a series of studies completed over a number of years, with some studies using different forms of the test. The authors, however, have not clearly indicated how many subjects were administered earlier versions of the ACDM.

Several reliability studies were reported. The authors reported alpha coefficients for the ACDM ranging from .49 ($N = 143$) to .84 ($N = 264$) for the Decision-Making Styles scales, and from .78 ($N = 264$) to .92 ($N = 143$) for the Decision-Making Tasks scales. The reliability evidence presented is supportive, but further reliability estimates are needed. A number of validity studies by a variety of authors reported on content validity and estimates of criterion-related and construct validity. Again, earlier versions of the ACDM were used in some of the reported validity studies. Hence, this reviewer believes that the validity data cannot be interpreted with confidence.

Of concern is the interpretation of test results. The authors have reported that the Student Report is "designed to be used as part of a broader effort of giving feedback, including, at a minimum, a face-to-face meeting." However, the 1985–86 Western Psychological Services sales catalog indicates a report that is "jargon-free" and easily understood by the student. In making counselor, student, and group reports readily available, it appears that despite the manual warning, the Student Report is designed to be distributed without an interview with a counselor. This would not be a serious concern except the interpretive language of the Student Report is inappropriately dogmatic. Phrases such as "you are" and "your decision-making style also includes . . . " are prescriptively emphatic and not as tentative as they should be.

In summary, the ACDM has evolved over a period of 20 years. Some of the studies cited in the manual reflect earlier versions of the present instrument, i.e., Vocational Decision Making Q-Sort (1964–65) and Vocational Decision-Making Checklist (1968). Normative information is somewhat fragmented and has been generated from a variety of investigations whose purposes were other than addressing the psychometric properties of the ACDM.

Although recommended for high-school and college students, it seems the ACDM is most appropriately used at the college level. The majority of standardization studies focus on college populations, and the terms used in the instrument (e.g., instructor, course, and major) seem more appropriate to college students than to high school students. Terms more familiar to the latter group would include teacher, class, and program. The authors' recommendation that the ACDM be used with students only is well advised.

The concept of assessing career decision-making components is intriguing. At this time, however, there is a lack of sufficient confidence that the ACDM can provide this information. Until more empirical data using the present instrument are available, the manual and catalog announcement for the ACDM should temper their claims of the instrument's uses and effectiveness.

[17]

Assessment of Children's Language Comprehension, 1983 Revision. Purpose: "To determine how many word classes in different combinations of length and complexity a child would be able to understand." Ages 3-0 to 6-5; 1969–83; ACLC; 4 scores: Vocabulary, Two Critical Elements, Three Critical Elements, Four Critical Elements; individual; may be administered in abbreviated form for screening purposes; 1987 price data: $22.50 per complete kit including 50 recording sheets, card set, and manual ('83, 32 pages); $6 per 50 recording sheets; $13.75 per set of 41 spiral-bound cards; $3.75 per manual; Spanish-language version on reverse side of recording form; (10–15) minutes; Rochana Foster, Jane J. Giddan, and Joel Stark; Consulting Psychologists Press, Inc.*

See T3:212 (8 references); for additional information and a review by James A. Till of an earlier version, see 8:452 (3 references).

TEST REFERENCES

1. Aram, D. M., Ekelman, B. L., & Nation, J. E. (1984). Preschoolers with language disorders: 10 years later. *Journal of Speech and Hearing Research*, 27, 232-244.

2. Perozzi, J. A. (1985). A pilot study of language facilitation for bilingual, language-handicapped children: Theoretical and intervention implications. *Journal of Speech and Hearing Disorders*, 50, 403-406.

3. Brinton, B., Fujiki, M., Winkler, E., & Loeb, D. F. (1986). Responses to requests for clarification in linguistically normal and language-impaired children. *Journal of Speech and Hearing Disorders*, 51, 370-378.

Review of the Assessment of Children's Language Comprehension, 1983 *Revision by MARY ELLEN PEARSON, Professor of Special Education, Mankato State University, Mankato, MN:*

PURPOSE. The Assessment of Children's Language Comprehension (ACLC) determines how many of 50 words a child comprehends (Part A) and how many of those words combined into 2-, 3-, and 4-word sentences the child understands (Parts B, C, and D). The instrument was developed to provide information for the language teacher to develop a training program in vocabulary and in comprehension of increasing numbers of syntactic units.

The authors refer to the test as a criterion-referenced measure, and the ACLC is appropriately used for program planning. It is not appropriately used as a norm-referenced, valid, and reliable instrument for identifying a child as delayed even though the authors include a confusing implication about its norm-referenced qualities. Professionals must use the ACLC only for program planning because percentiles, standard scores, and adequate reliability and validity data are not provided.

Three other specifications concerning purpose include the measurement of comprehension, not expression; the measurement of comprehension through picture verification; and the measurement of comprehension with emphasis on auditory memory.

CONTENT OF THE ACLC. The test contains a manual, recording sheet, and a set of 41 cards with drawings in a spiral book. The 32-page manual includes a brief description of language development, impairment, and training as well as the following information about the ACLC: administration and scoring, statistical properties, and clinical applications. The manual's general discussions are somewhat dated with the 18 references ranging from 1954 to 1972.

The 8 1/2 inch x 11 inch record sheet is clear and easy to use, and the picture book is also easy to use. One picture book page at a time is presented to the child, who is asked to point to a drawing that matches the common vocabulary word or combination of words. The 41 cards contain the correct drawing and 3 or 4 distractors. In general the drawings or silhouette drawings are clear, but examples of minor criticisms would include unclear pictures (ball, can, box, behind), unusual pictures (woman jumping, happy cup), and cluttered pictures (pages 32 and 36).

DIRECTIONS FOR ADMINISTRATION AND SCORING. The authors provide acceptable general instructions for administration of a criterion-referenced instrument; they do not provide word-for-word directions, so the ACLC will not be administered in a completely standard manner. They do provide information concerning seating, praise, feedback, reinforcement, and repetitions; however, the teacher must decide if Parts B, C, and D should be given as no cutoff score for Part A is provided.

MEAN SCORES. The mean-score data were gathered in 1974 and 1976 on 818 nursery, Head Start, and elementary school children. The children came from Ohio (48%), Florida (39%), and Vermont, California, and Illinois (13%). The authors did not test a random nor stratified sample, but they did indicate that socioeconomic status and educational levels of parents were mixed with 30% from low and 70% from low-middle to high-middle classes. In addition, 25% of the children represented minority groups.

The data are presented as mean scores at 6-month intervals; intervals of 3 or 4 months are preferable for the younger children. The mean-score information is adequate for a criterion-referenced instrument.

RELIABILITY. The only reliability information provided concerns internal consistency. The authors report odd-even reliability coefficients of .86 for Test A and .80 for Tests B, C, and D on an unspecified number of children. The coefficients provide only moderate support for internal consistency. At a minimum information should be made available in the manual concerning interrater reliability and test-retest reliability.

VALIDITY. The steady and gradual increase in mean scores from age 3 to 6 1/2 years provides some evidence of construct validity. In addition, an unreported number of handicapped children scored lower than the norm group, and 148 mentally retarded persons scored lower as the severity of their retardation increased.

McCauley and Swisher (1984) found the ACLC met only one of 10 criteria appropriate for norm-referenced tests. The teacher must conclude that overall the technical information is not adequate for a norm-referenced test, and care must be taken to use the test appropriately.

SCREENING. The authors provide a screening version but do not provide cutoff scores to separate risk from no-risk children. Nor are reliability or validity data presented. The ACLC screening version does not meet acceptable standards for a screening instrument and should not be used for that purpose.

SPANISH TRANSLATION. The ACLC can be administered in Spanish with the items listed on the back of the record sheet. No reliability, validity, or norm data are provided for the Spanish version.

LITERATURE. Rizzo and Stephens (1981) reported the inability of the ACLC to separate delayed and nondelayed children due to low sample means. In addition, they reported the ACLC did not consistently correlate with other measures of vocabulary and comprehension. The format of verifying comprehension through picture identification may unnecessarily complicate the task for children with learning disabilities and language delays (Silliman, 1979). Millen and Prutting (1979) have noted similar concerns for mentally retarded children. Semel and Wiig (1975), however, recommended the ACLC for identifying older children with learning disabilities.

Finally, questions have been raised about the common use of the ACLC with adults (Pickett & Flynn, 1983), and its limited content has been criticized (Owens, Haney, Giesow, Dooley, & Kelly, 1983).

SUMMARY. The ACLC may be a useful criterion-referenced tool for determining how many words in sequence a child comprehends. The test may also be useful for planning appropriate programs. The research literature, however, has not supported its usefulness. The instrument is widely used and may be misused as a norm-referenced test because mean scores are included; therefore, the authors need to clarify the appropriate use of the instrument. In addition, the screening version should not be used because reliability, validity, standard scores, and cutoffs are not provided.

REVIEWER'S REFERENCES

Semel, E. M., & Wiig, E. H. (1975). Comprehension of syntactic structures and critical verbal elements by children with learning disabilities. *Journal of Learning Disabilities*, 8, 53-58.

Millen, C., & Prutting, C. A. (1979). Inconsistencies across three language comprehension tests for specific grammatical features. *Language, Speech, and Hearing Services in Schools*, 10, 162-170.

Silliman, E. R. (1979). Relationship between pictorial interpretation and comprehension of three spatial relations in school-age children. *Journal of Speech and Hearing Research*, 22, 366-388.

Rizzo, J. M., & Stephens, M. I. (1981). Performance of children with normal and impaired oral language production on a set of auditory comprehension tests. *Journal of Speech and Hearing Disorders*, 46, 150-159.

Owens, R. E., Haney, M. J., Giesow, V. E., Dooley, L. F., & Kelly, R. J. (1983). Language test content: A comparative study. *Language, Speech, and Hearing Services in Schools*, 14, 7-12.

Pickett, J. M., & Flynn, P. T. (1983). Language assessment tools for mentally retarded adults: Survey and recommendations. *Mental Retardation*, 21, 244-247.

McCauley, R. J., & Swisher, L. (1984). Psychometric review of language and articulation tests for preschool children. *Journal of Speech and Hearing Disorders*, 49, 34-42.

[18]

Assessment of Fluency in School-Age Children. Purpose: "To determine speech, language, and physiological functioning." Ages 5–18; 1983; AFSC; "criterion-referenced"; assessment includes classroom observation, parent interview, teacher evaluation of child's speech, multi-factored evaluation of child, and post therapy; multi-factored evaluation assesses 5 areas: Automatic Speech, Cued Speech, Spontaneous Speech, Physiological Components, Interview With Student/Assessing Attitudes; individual; 1983 price data: $32.50 per complete set including 32 of each form; $8 per 32 assessment of fluency forms; $2.25 per 32 parent interview, teacher evaluation, or dismissal from therapy program forms; $14.75 per resource guide (220 pages); (45) minutes for student evaluation; (30) minutes for parent interview; (15) minutes for classroom observation; (15) minutes for teacher evaluation; Julia Thompson; The INTERSTATE Printers & Publishers, Inc.*

Review of the Assessment of Fluency in School-Age Children by LYNN S. FUCHS, Assistant Professor of Special Education, George Peabody College, Vanderbilt University, Nashville, TN:

Assessment of Fluency in School-Age Children is designed to assess fluency for the purposes of screening and making program placement and planning decisions. It incorporates assessment information from different sources, within multiple settings, employing a variety of measurement strategies, on a range of variables including fluency, articulation, voice, semantics, syntax, pragmatics, breath control, and auditory memory. The potential of such an ambitious instrument is great. Unfortunately, the author fails to fulfill this potential because of (*a*) inaccurate and inconsistent representation of the nature of the test, (*b*) confusing and insufficiently standardized directions and procedures as well as a poorly designed protocol, and (*c*) inadequate empirical development and documentation.

With respect to representation of the nature of the assessment, the author makes some questionable and confusing assertions. Examples include inconsistent and vague application of the term *differential evaluation* and the author's definition of stuttering. Perhaps most troublesome is the use of the descriptor *criterion-referenced*, in which the notion of a "threshold" for identifying ineffective communicators is proposed. This concept is promising and suggests a basis for related empirical work. Nevertheless, no relevant empirical development is presented; moreover, no criterion for fluency program placement or for speech and language screening is provided. Rather, the resource guide presents normative guidelines for certain determinations, such as acceptable phonation times and inhalation/exhalation rates, and one set of undocumented guidelines for classifying numbers of performative errors, with no age breakdowns. Most often, however, evaluation decisions are purely subjective. The author states, "There is no formula for making decisions as to whether therapy is indicated. . . . In the final analysis, the decision . . . is . . . individual . . . based on the uniqueness of the assessment." Such unsystematic, subjective decision making not only is unacceptable from a measurement viewpoint, but also is contradicted by some of the author's own recommendations. For example, the author notes that practitioners must determine whether "the child meets . . . eligibility criteria of the . . . district," and should set a fluency training goal representing "normal, human speech, operationally defined as a stuttering rate of 0.5 SW/M."

Directions for administration and protocol design also contribute to the inadequacy of the assessment. The first problem is one of confusion. The protocol has four numeral 2s, each subsumed under a different letter, but the resource guide refers to 2s without clarifying whether A2, B2, C2, or D2 is the relevant item. The top portion of the last page of the protocol has no heading to indicate the summative nature of this section, and this summative section precedes the scoring of the speech sample on the protocol. The level of headings in the outline under "Preliminary Activities" fails to reflect the organization. The "Overview of Activities" misleadingly implies corresponding activities for child and tester. One-to-one correspondence is not maintained between the scoring code and definitions (see pages 32–35). The three-item code for scoring performatives is operationalized dichotomously, with no functional meaning assigned to the "None" code.

Second, directions are incomplete, with (*a*) no clear instructions on what to score/write for many sections of the test/protocol (in fact, the author contends the only "test" scored is No. 2), and (*b*) inadequate guidelines and protocol format for integrating data from multiple sources, for summarizing information, and for determining whether performance is adequate (examiners are told to make these decisions using "general impressions"). Because no information is provided concerning appropriate examiner training, the confusing and incomplete nature of directions and protocol and the lack of interpretive guidelines represent serious problems.

Of even more serious consequence, however, is the lack of standardized instructions for administration. Few directions to students are provided; the examiner is required to identify relevant storybooks, four-sequence stories, and reading materials, with no guidelines for determining difficulty; the tester is directed to create another test of spontaneous speech for older students if the material provided seems juvenile; the examiner is required to select syntax and articulation tests to include in the assessment; the tester is instructed to choose between a stopwatch and second hand of watch when several items seem to require a stopwatch for reliable scoring. This lack of standardization requires validation studies across a variety of testing materials and formats.

Unfortunately, test development and validation are incomplete. Two pilot studies, with a total N of 48 spanning grades K–7, report only minimal descriptive results. Obvious problems are the omission of reliability and validity information, procedures used to develop test items, and norms or empirical guidelines for criterion-referenced decisions. Additionally, it appears that in the studies reported, grades 8–12 were omitted. This is inappropriate because the author claims the assessment is designed for ages 5–18 (although the materials are juvenile and the author repeatedly refers to "young children" in the resource guide). A clinic population of fluency disorders also was excluded, and the percentages of students with high rates of disfluencies are, in fact, low for a sample specifically identified for fluency difficulties. These low percentages are especially problematic because disfluencies included whole word repetitions, which are not usually considered stuttered blocks. Therefore, the samples in these studies are unrepresentative not only of overall demographic variables, but also of the age range and fluency-disordered population the measure was designed to cover.

This test suffers from serious problems including lack of accurate and consistent representation, unclear directions, protocol deficiencies, unstandardized procedures, and insufficient development and validation. Given these problems along with the instrument's time-consuming nature (105 minutes for data collection and 30 minutes for summary and transcription), I can think of no decision-making purpose for which I can recommend its use.

Review of the Assessment of Fluency in School-Age Children by E. CHARLES HEALEY, Associate Professor of Speech-Language Pathology, University of Nebraska-Lincoln, Lincoln, NE:

TEST OVERVIEW. The Assessment of Fluency in School-Age Children (AFSC) by Julia Thompson is one of the few assessment instruments that provides a speech-language pathologist with a comprehensive examination of stuttering in young children. The author has provided a data-based rationale for the assessment approach along with a rather complete set of questions and test items for the professional to use. This assessment instrument includes color-coded forms along with a Resource Guide that provides directions for administration and descriptions of case studies, therapy methods, future research needs, and published materials on fluency disorders.

The major strength of this assessment tool is the multi-factor approach to the evaluation of school-age, nonfluent children. The author recognizes the complex and idiosyncratic nature of this disorder and provides a speech-language pathologist with a number of areas to test that might relate to the detection of problematic stuttering in children. The approach and assessment areas included in this test are sound and organized in a logical fashion.

The Resource Guide that accompanies the AFSC provides the necessary data and information about the test. The procedures used are justified by past research findings and/or commonly accepted opinions by highly regarded professionals in this field. The color-coded forms accompanying the test are easy to understand and provide adequate space for recording information.

The "Directions for Administration" chapter in the Resource Guide gives complete explanations of procedures to be followed in administering this test. The author offers suggestions about the types of questions to be asked to elicit responses from a child as well as specific items to present in order to collect the necessary data for the evaluation. It is also a plus to find definition of terms, normative data on certain test items, and a generous number of examples of responses one could anticipate in each section of the AFSC.

Another strength of the assessment instrument is the inclusion of rather detailed information regarding treatment. Specific treatment techniques and methods are given for those children diagnosed as stutterers. Thus, not only does the author provide an assessment tool, but a fairly complete description of therapeutic methods as well. Justification and rationale for each method is given along with some specific examples of instructions and procedures clinicians might follow. Many professionals will find this information helpful as reference or review information even if they do not use the assessment materials.

The test has some weaknesses, however. Most of the information provided in the AFSC is taught in graduate level coursework in most training programs. Thus, most professionals do not need to purchase this particular instrument to perform an adequate differential diagnosis of school-age stutterers. None of the forms provided with the kit are unique in their content and most professionals could probably develop better ones than those provided. The assessment tool relies heavily on the evaluation procedures specified in an article by Gregory and Hill (1980), and professionals could easily refer to that article for suggestions regarding the diagnostic procedures supplied in the AFSC.

Another major weakness is the lack of clearly specified reliability and validity data. There is no evidence in the Resource Guide of any test-retest, interjudge, or intrajudge reliability data or standard errors of measurement. Statistical comparisons between data derived from the AFSC and another popular assessment device such as *The Stoker Probe Technique* (Stoker, 1980) are lacking. This lack of validity data is a serious oversight. Moreover, the total sample of young stutterers making up the normative group is also extremely small. All of the assessment data were acquired from children in the east-central Ohio area, a rural, small industrial region of the United States. The author even admits to this weakness in the Preface by stating, "there is a need for data from urban and rural areas in different geographic locations." When the test is used to track the improvement of students (criterion-referenced), this may not be a weakness. However, as a tool used to place children in special programs the small norming group does raise some concern.

SUMMARY. The AFSC is a practical and useful guide to professionals interested in a thorough differential evaluation and assessment of school-age children with a fluency disorder. The Resource Guide that accompanies the test forms provides complete and easy-to-understand materials. In addition to the information provided in the guide about assessment, there are chapters dealing with treatment, criteria for dismissal from therapy, and directions for future research. The major strength of this instrument is the material in the Resource Guide. It is complete, thorough, and represents sound, objective evaluation of literature in the area of fluency disorders.

Perhaps the biggest concern this reviewer has about the instrument is its relative simplicity and the lack of any really novel assessment procedures for this type of problem. Most, if not all, of the tasks performed in AFSC are those that any professionals could develop on their own. Thus, the basic evaluation tasks included are ones that professionals have been using for several years. Additionally, there is no evidence that the author has conducted any reliability and validity studies. Despite these serious shortcomings, many professionals might find the AFSC helpful in planning assessment and treatment procedures for young stutterers.

REVIEWER'S REFERENCES

Gregory, H., & Hill, D. (1980). Stuttering therapy for children. In W. Perkins (Ed.), *Strategies in stuttering therapy. Seminars in Speech, Language and Hearing*. New York: Thieme-Stratton.

Stoker, B. (1980). *The Stoker Probe Technique* (2nd ed.). Tulsa: Modern Education Corporation.

[19]

Assessment of Intelligibility of Dysarthric Speech. Purpose: "To provide clinicians and researchers with a means of measuring intelligibility and speaking rate of dysarthric individuals." Adult and adolescent dysarthric speakers; 1981; AIDS; 6

scores: Single Word Intelligibility (Transcription, Multiple Choice), Sentence Intelligibility (Transcription, Speaking Rate, Rate of Intelligible Speech, Communication Efficiency Ratio); individual; Apple 48K computer with single disk drive and monochrome monitor necessary for administration of computerized version; 1988 price data: $69 per complete kit containing portfolio of stimulus words and manual ('81, 60 pages); $139 per computerized version containing 2 software disks and clinician manual; administration time not reported; Kathryn M. Yorkston, David R. Beukelman, and Charles Traynor (computer program); PRO-ED, Inc.*

Review of the Assessment of Intelligibility of Dysarthric Speech by KATHARINE G. BUTLER, Professor of Communication Sciences and Disorders, and Director, Center for Research, Syracuse University, Syracuse, NY:

The Assessment of Intelligibility of Dysarthric Speech (AIDS) is particularly well designed by the authors to provide quantitative data regarding a dysarthric individual's level of intelligible speech under single-word and sentence conditions (i.e., a measure of severity), and speaking rate, as measured by either imitated or read sentences. Both transcription and multiple-choice formats are available.

Administration, judging of responses, scoring, and interpretation require that the examiner perform only specific portions of those tasks. The examiner first audio-records the subject's oral production of single words selected by the examiner and presented as a reading or an oral imitation task. Prior to the recording session, the examiner creates a key for a word list ($N =$ 50) by randomly selecting (by means of a Random Numbers Table) from a total of 50 groups of words, each 12 items in length. Only the subject's responses are recorded to both the "single word intelligibility" task and the sentence intelligibility task. The sentences are also randomly selected from sentence lists that range from sentences 5 words in length to those 15 words in length, with the examiner randomly selecting two sentences from each sentence length set (total $N =$ 100 sentences).

Raters other than the examiner assess the intelligibility of the subject's responses. The number of raters is left to the examiner's judgement and can vary according to the purpose of assessment (e.g., researchers may prefer multiple judges, while ongoing clinical monitoring of a patient's performance may require only one). Either professionals or nonprofessionals may be used as judges. Judges are asked to be familiar with the pool of items, but not with specific words, so that knowledge is general and recognition of items is not fostered when the subject's speech is unintelligible. The judges record in writing their understanding of the subject's audio-taped single word or sentence utterances for scoring and interpretation. The examiner calculates an intelligibility percentage score based upon judges' responses, the speaking rate (words per minute), the rate of Intelligible Speech (IWPM), the rate of Unintelligible Speech (UWPM), and the Communication Efficiency Ratio (a comparison of the dysarthric speaker's rate of intelligible speech with that of a group [$N =$ 20] of normal speakers [190 IWPM]).

The authors provide considerable background research data in the "Interpretation of Results" chapter of the manual, reporting on research from 1969 to the present, including perceptual, component, and overall assessment. They note their test may be used as an index of severity, including a rank-ordering of dysarthric speakers, comparison with normal performance, and the monitoring of changing performances over time. Speech-language pathologists may find the ability to monitor changing performance over time to be quite valuable. This is one of the few more quantitative methods of assessing efficacy of treatment, which is important in verifying change of status in third party reimbursement.

The authors also carefully delineate not only those areas in which their instrument is helpful but provide cautions regarding possible misinterpretation. They are scrupulous in this regard and readers of the manual will be well rewarded for a thoughtful perusal of the 60-page document.

The theoretical and research basis for the development of the instrument are also described. Reliability measures of the multiple-choice and transcription formats range between .90 and .87 (Pearson Product-Moment correlations, interjudge reliability ranged from .88 to .99, depending on the task). Reliability for judging sentences varies between .93 and .99 while intersample reliability is reported to range from .92 to .99 (Pearson Product-Moment correlations).

STRENGTHS AND WEAKNESSES. AIDS attempts to assess a very important area of clinical treatment. It is probably the best instrument available at this time for assessment and monitoring of dysarthric speech production. While validity has not been addressed, reliability measures, albeit on small samples, lend credence to the authors' statements regarding the usefulness of the instrument. The manual is substantial and carefully written. All forms are provided and may be duplicated at will. Examiners must have high quality audiotaping equipment available, as well as the ability to identify appropriate and repeatable placement of a microphone for recording examinees' responses, and access to several judges in order to meet the requirements of the described procedures.

Examiners, who do not function in a group setting with other professionals, may find their use of the instrument is limited by a lack of reliable judges. Although the availability of independent raters is basic to the construct of the AIDS, and may be considered one of the test's strengths, this requirement may also preclude its use in settings where the examiner engages in solo practice. Because a judge need not be a professional, any literate adult with normal hearing may also function as a judge, and thus it is possible that secretarial staff might also be used.

This untimed test may prove to be time-consuming when the requirements of audiotaping, judge listening and recording of subject responses, examiner construction of a key, and data scoring and interpretation are considered. Users indicate that examiner time is approximately 30 minutes and that judges' scoring time is not significant.

The AIDS' greatest usefulness may be as a research tool due to the need for both examiners and judges. Nevertheless, it should prove particularly appropriate for use by clinical personnel who must document progress of their patients for third-party payment purposes or patient care adults.

The utility of the computerized revision cannot be assessed, because only the 1981 version of the instrument was available for review. The 1981 version provides the five necessary answer sheets, graphs, and cumulative data forms for user replication, as necessary. This version consists of a spiral-bound manual and a spiral-bound set of stimulus materials. Both are well prepared, clear, and well designed. The manual provides all the necessary information and is well written if occasionally redundant. Statistical data are well presented. The instrument is viewed as a complement and supplement to other approaches in assessment of dysarthric speech, which are also well described and documented.

SUMMARY. The AIDS is a reliable tool for quantifying single word intelligibility, sentence intelligibility, and speaking rate, including rates of both intelligible and nonintelligible speech. Test procedures require that each administration be individualized and a specific key be constructed by the examiner to identify the randomly chosen words and sentences selected for use. Further data on validity is yet to be garnered. Given the state of the art, while face validity appears favorable, other validity factors, such as predictive validity and content validity must be considered. The choice of words and sentences, generated randomly, has been carefully controlled. Such factors as the reading ability of the subject may play some as yet undetermined role. However, the test may be administered to nonreaders orally. Overall, this instrument advances the measurement of dysarthria and provides an interesting approach to measuring a hitherto ill-defined intelligibility issue, that is, the "ear" of the examiner is now supported by a more clearly articulated view of perceptual events. The authors have contributed a valuable addition to both the research and clinical armamentarium in assessing and monitoring change in dysarthric speech.

Review of the Assessment of Intelligibility of Dysarthric Speech by C. DALE CARPENTER, Associate Professor of Special Education, Western Carolina University, Cullowhee, NC:

INTRODUCTION. The authors of Assessment of Intelligibility of Dysarthric Speech (AIDS) state that clinicians and researchers can use their instrument to "(1) rank order different dysarthric speakers; (2) compare performance of a single dysarthric speaker to normal performance; and (3) monitor changing performance over time." They also suggest the measure can help to plan treatment. These are important potential uses. The instrument is standardized in that specific directions are provided for administering the test to individuals. The only reference to a norm sample pertains to the rate of intelligible speech that is represented as intelligible words per minute spoken by normal, nondysarthric speakers.

The materials required to administer the test include a portfolio of stimulus words and sentences and a manual. The manual contains the expected components of administration and interpretation instructions, technical information, and references. To help with interpretation and use, three case histories are presented. The manual also includes forms that must be duplicated to record assessment information. Permission to duplicate is printed on each form. Therefore, one advantageous feature of this instrument is that it eliminates the need for the continual purchase of record forms required with many tests. A high-quality tape recorder is needed to administer the test and the manual stresses the importance of obtaining consistently high-quality recordings. Specific microphone equipment and procedures are suggested. This should pose no problems for speech professionals who are the most likely users of the test and who are familiar with the need for accurate recordings of speech samples. The test might have required videotaping of clients producing speech samples. Because the purpose is to assess intelligibility of speech, audio tapes are an acceptable and parsimonious choice. A computerized version of this test is available but was not provided and is not included in this review.

TASKS. The AIDS can be administered as either a reading or imitation task. The choice is determined by the examiner. The client may read single words and sentences or repeat words and sentences spoken by the examiner. Imitation is technically more difficult because the examiner's voice must not be recorded and (according to the manual) imitation scores are likely to be higher than reading scores. One or more judges are employed in scoring. Their task is to listen to recordings once for single word tasks and no more than twice for sentences. Judges transcribe or select from a multiple-choice list what is heard. Examiners score the record forms and figure rate and efficiency measures.

One of the features of the test is the choice of selecting how clients will take the test—by imitation or reading. Another feature is the choice of selecting the judging format—transcription or multiple choice. Both choices are made dependent on the characteristics of the client and the purpose of the assessment. To make appropriate choices, examiners need to be thoroughly familiar with the manual and need to understand accurately why the assessment is necessary. The desirable flexibility of the test design could also be an obstacle for some examiners who are not adequately prepared.

The format of the tasks and scoring procedures appear to be consistent with best practices (Darley, Aronson, & Brown, 1975; Rosenbek & LaPointe, 1978). Although one or more judges are required depending on the assessment purpose, random sample selection and scoring by the examiner rather than judges eliminate the expected need for several unbiased judges. They have also introduced the unique multiple-choice format for severely dysarthric speakers, who often do not score at all using the transcription format because of the unintelligibility of their speech. The multiple-choice format allows clinicians to measure small progress. Such subtle measurement would not always be possible using the transcription format. The tables of random numbers used to select words and sentences are easy to use for those familiar with them. More directions might be needed for those who previously have not used random number tables.

SCORING AND INTERPRETATION. Scoring is not difficult and directions are clear. The instrument avoids subjective ratings of intelligibility by providing a means to objectively score speech intelligibility. However, examiners are required to calculate percentages given number correct and number possible. The manual should have percentages calculated based on number correct because number possible is constant for words and sentences. This minor improvement would eliminate opportunities for scoring errors.

Interpretation is based on the mode of stimulus for examinee (i.e., imitation or reading), and the judging format (i.e., multiple choice or transcription). Interpretation is also specific to the particular information used. No simple interpretations are provided. The examiner can look at no chart or table to classify the client's performance based on scores achieved. Interpretations are also influenced by the purpose of the assessment. Rank ordering different dysarthric speakers requires different procedures and interpretation than evaluating changing performance over time. As in choosing testing and judging formats, the examiner needs to be well-versed in theory, practice, and the use of this instrument to do appropriate interpretations. The manual could be better organized to assist the examiner in each purpose and design.

TECHNICAL PROPERTIES. Because most scores are used for intraindividual comparisons over time, dysarthric speaker norms are not a major issue. Norms are the basis for determining normal rates of intelligible speech. The manual states that 20 normal speakers were used to determine that normal speakers produced 190 intelligible words per minute on the sentence production task. Besides stating that half were male, no other information is known about the sample.

Reliability is addressed comprehensively in the manual. Test-retest coefficients were near .90 or better and interjudge coefficients were usually above .90 for all tasks. The authors have previously researched and published the formats used in the test. No doubt, test users would like to see the authors' results replicated by other researchers using these procedures.

Content validity in the test is apparent to this reviewer by examining the items and the format used. The authors have used their knowledge and experience well to select and design the tasks to measure intelligibility of the speech of dysarthric individuals. They do not report using any other expert panel to establish content validity. Construct validity is addressed in the manual by a review of research on different performances of dysarthric speakers using different test formats. The research is not conclusive and does not demonstrate the construct validity of the AIDS. The research cited using similar tasks supports this instrument's tasks, but fails to provide needed information about this test. Criterion-related validity is critical given the purposes stated, but is not demonstrated by information provided in the manual. The authors have shown why the tasks were designed as they were using previous research and have demonstrated the reliability of the test. They have not provided criterion-related validity, which would support the usefulness of the instrument.

SUMMARY. This test is well designed to provide the user with a standardized, objective measure of dysarthric speech intelligibility. It is flexible enough to allow clinicians and researchers to choose the testing and judging mode most appropriate for their purposes and the characteristics of the client. It is a sophisticated, but practical, approach to the assessment of dysarthric speech. Diagnosticians must be careful and purposeful in selecting testing and judging formats. They must be diligent in following manual directions in administering, scoring, and interpreting results. The opportunity to make inappropriate decisions and other errors is greater than desired. Reliability appears adequate. Validity has not been appropriately addressed. Because this area is, to this reviewer's knowledge, without much competition in standardized assessment devices, Assessment of Intelligibility of Dysarthric Speech is welcome. A revision with more precise guidelines regarding testing and judging formats, scoring and interpretation, and with evidence in support of test validity would be more welcome.

REVIEWER'S REFERENCES

Darley, F. L., Aronson, A. E., & Brown, J. R. (1975). *Motor speech disorders*. Philadelphia: W. B. Saunders.

Rosenbeck, J. C., & LaPointe, L. L. (1978). The dysarthrias: Description, diagnosis, and treatment. In D. F. Johns (Ed.), *Clinical management of neurogenic communicative disorders* (pp. 251-289). Boston: Little, Brown and Company.

[20]

A.S.S.E.T.S.—A Survey of Students' Educational Talents and Skills. Purpose: "Helps in the identification of children's gifts and talents and in planning enrichment experiences for these students." Kindergarten–grade 3, grades 4–6; 1978–79; A.S.S.E.T.S.; separate inventories completed by student, teacher, and parent; 5 scores: Interests, Talent Areas (Academic Aptitude, Motivational Characteristics, Creative Thinking Ability, Visual/Performing Arts Aptitude/Talent); 2 levels: Early Elementary, Later Elementary; 1986 price data: $5.95 per examination kit (specify Early Elementary or Later Elementary); $39.60 per complete set (specify Early Elementary or Later Elementary) including 30 Parent, 30 Teacher, and 30 Student inventories, sample student profile report form, instructions checklist, user's guide ('79, 18 pages), and complete scoring and data report services for 30 students; administration time not reported; Learning Publications, Inc.*

Review of A.S.S.E.T.S.—A Survey of Students' Educational Talents and Skills by DIANNA L. NEWMAN, Assistant Professor of Education, University at Albany/SUNY, Albany, NY:

A.S.S.E.T.S.—A Survey of Students' Educational Talents and Skills consists of a series of instruments designed to aid in the identification of elementary-aged children's skills and talents and in the planning of instructional curriculum for these children. It is designed to consider both the cognitive and the affective perceptions of children with special gifts and talents from multiple perspectives. Three sources of information about each child are obtained by A.S.S.E.T.S.: parents, teachers, and the student. This information is collected separately and combined to form a profile of Talent Areas and Interests.

THE INSTRUMENTS. Each of the three surveys (parent, teacher, and student) covers two major topics: talent area skills and special interests and activities. The talent areas or skills covered include Academic Aptitude, Motivational Characteristics, Creative Thinking Ability, and Visual/Performing Arts. The teacher survey contains 30 Likert-type statements describing characteristics or activities that exemplify each of these constructs. After reading each descriptive statement, teachers respond to a 4-point scale indicating how much or how frequently (almost always, often, sometimes, almost never) the individual child displays the characteristic. Some of the items are related to direct observation ("can grasp underlying principles in instruction" or "likes to tell funny stories") while other items are more subjective in nature ("seems to enjoy reading on his/her own" or "would enjoy acting in a play").

The parent inventory is similar to the one for teachers; it consists of 29 Likert-type items covering the same four constructs of Aptitude, Motivation, Creativity, and Talent in Visual/Performing Arts. Parents are asked to read each description and indicate how well that statement describes their child. Many of the items are identical to that of the teacher survey; however, the intent is to determine parents' perceptions of how the child is succeeding in school ("Shows better understanding of school work than children his/her age") or how the child functions in nonschool settings ("Reads at home every day"). On some of the items, however, although the concepts are similar, stimuli for parents are phrased at a lower reading/vocabulary level than are stimuli for teachers. (Teacher: "Enjoys having conversations with peers." Parent: "Enjoys talking with friends and classmates.") No justification for this variation is available in the documentation, giving rise to the question of why it was necessary. Although it is laudable the authors realized the possible need for a lower vocabulary level for parents, one wonders why it was felt necessary to couch teacher items at the higher level, instead of creating identical forms.

Both parent and teacher forms have an open-ended section measuring student interests. Respondents are asked to provide information about students' favorite books, activities, hobbies, ideal trips, and interest in learning a foreign language. Parents are to solicit the information from the child, in addition to providing their own perceptions. No documentation is provided for the selection of these items, nor is any documentation provided on how these open-ended items are to be scored.

An additional difficulty with the parent survey is the lack of explicit directions on administering the interest section of the instrument to the child. Parents are instructed to conduct an interview by asking the child about special interests and activities and then to add anything that the parent may know about the child's interests. No directions on coaching, asking leading questions, or interpretation of the child's responses are given. Also, no directions on how to record the child's verbal information are provided.

The student survey consists of 26 questions which teachers either read or administer to students (depending on student age) in a group setting. The questions once again reflect the four constructs of Academic Aptitude, Motivational Characteristics, Creative Thinking, and Visual/Performing Art Aptitudes. Using a question format, students are asked if they can do, like to do, or know how to do, a variety of activities ("Do you like talking with adults?" "Can you figure out the answers to hard questions?" "Do you know how to find out the meaning of new words?") Students respond to each question by circling a yes or a no or by responding to a Likert scale (again, depending on student age).

There appear to be two major difficulties with the student instrument. First, the instrument is to be used for multiple grade levels: K–3 elementary. There are no variations for each of the four grades. In addition, the manual suggests that the form be administered in a class setting. The diversity of student vocabulary and test-taking ability, both within and among these four grade levels, may make the form difficult to administer and decreases the content validity of the results.

Second, poor formatting of the student answer sheet also decreases the ease of administration and the validity of results. In general, the directions to the students appear to be confusing and distracting. To avoid the use of item numbers, the test authors have used a series of symbols. Because the symbols are not related to the question, their presentation distracts from the concept presented in the survey question. In addition, the item symbols are larger than either of the appropriate responses (the words "yes" or "no") making the symbol more appealing than the responses. Problems related to the use and size of symbols are further augmented by the overall size of the answer sheet. Each question is to be answered in a small box (approximately 3/4 inch by 1 1/4 inch) containing a symbol and two words ("yes," "no"). This small size makes it difficult for primary grade children to complete the task of identifying and circling the appropriate response. Again, because this task is designed to be conducted as a group task or in a classroom setting, the instrument is difficult to administer and prone to incorrect responses.

SUMMARY. In summary, the general concept of A.S.S.E.T.S. is appealing. The inventory attempts to use multiple measures and multiple sources of information concerning children's abilities when judging talents and skills. It is the process of collecting the information that appears to be faulty. Several difficulties in the procedure have been discussed above. Some of them (development of identical forms for parents and teachers, clearer answer sheets for students) would require only minor modifications on the part of the authors. Other difficulties, such as the use of one inventory for students with a wide variety of skills, would require more development. Finally, the attempt to include parents in the assessment process in a direct manner is to be commended; however, the present format necessitates an assumption that all children have a parent who is willing and able to conduct that portion of the instrument. This may result in social stereotyping of placement due to parental interest and ability. Users of this inventory must be aware of this assumption and its possible consequences when using the instrument for decision making or diagnostic purposes.

Review of A.S.S.E.T.S.—A Survey of Students' Educational Talents and Skills by JAMES O. RUST, Professor of Psychology, Middle Tennessee State Unversity, Murfreesboro, TN:

A.S.S.E.T.S.—A Survey of Students' Educational Talents and Skills purports to identify talented students. It also aims to improve instruction by pinpointing students' strengths and weaknesses. The survey is comprised of a parent inventory, teacher inventory, and two student inventories. The inventories contain approximately 30 questions to be answered on NCS computer response sheets. The parents are asked questions such as whether their children read at home. The teachers are given items such as whether the students are alert observers, and the students themselves are asked questions such as whether they enjoy telling jokes.

The chief strength of the survey is that the parent's, child's, and teacher's opinions are all used. It makes good sense to include a broad range of opinions in developing instructional decisions about talented youngsters. A second relative strength of the survey is its focus on student interests. These are useful contributions to the education of talented children.

The A.S.S.E.T.S. User's Guide and promotional literature provide the rationale, purpose, steps to follow in administration, and two testimonials regarding the merits of the survey. However, the User's Guide provides no information about the construction, reliability, or the validity of A.S.S.E.T.S. The author's name is omitted from the manual. The survey relies on face validity. Items were presumably selected because the author felt they would identify talented children or because the items would assist in setting instructional goals. No normative information is provided, but a scoring service is available. The service reports are said to contain talent area scores that highlight special student abilities.

It is important to include a wide range of information in decisions about gifted and talented students. A.S.S.E.T.S. provides an opportunity to gather such information. However, it does so in a purely subjective manner. Renzulli, Smith, White, Callahan, and Hartman (1976) have authored an instrument for identifying gifted children. The advantage of the Renzulli et al. approach is that they provide psychometric data concerning their Scales for Rating the Behavioral Characteristics of Superior Students, while no such data are provided with the A.S.S.E.T.S. survey.

A.S.S.E.T.S. is conceptually interesting because it includes three views of the talented children, and because the children's interests are investigated. The survey is weakened by its lack of information about reliability, validity, and normative data.

REVIEWER'S REFERENCE

Renzulli, J. S., Smith, L. H., White, A. J., Callahan, C. M., & Hartman, R. K. (1976). *Scales for rating the behavioral characteristics of superior students.* Mansfield Center, CT: Creative Learning Press, Inc.

[21]

Autistic Behavior Composite Checklist and Profile. Purpose: "May be used to establish and support a diagnosis of autism. . . . to follow a student's behavioral changes over a period of time to denote progress or regression. . . . [and] provide aid in prioritizing problem areas as a basis for establishing a Behavior Intervention Plan." Autistic or emotionally handicapped students; 1984; ratings by teacher, clinician, or informant; 8 categories: Prerequisite Learning Behaviors, Sensory Perceptual Skills, Motor Development, Pre-Language Skills, Speech/Language/Communication Skills, Developmental Rates and Sequences, Learning Behaviors, Relating Skills; individual; 1987 price data: $19.95 per 20 test booklets ('84, 22 pages); administration time not reported; Anita Marcott Riley; Communication Skill Builders, Inc.*

Review of the Autistic Behavior Composite Checklist and Profile by JOHN M. TAYLOR, Executive Director, Developmental Disabilities Center, Boulder, CO:

The Autistic Behavior Composite Checklist and Profile (ABCCP) was designed to "establish and support a diagnosis of autism"; "to follow a student's behavioral changes over a period of time"; and to "aid in prioritizing problem areas as a basis for establishing a Behavior Intervention Plan."

The checklist is composed of 148 items, considered to be "interfering behaviors", grouped into eight categories: Prerequisite Learning Behaviors, Sensory Perceptual Skills, Motor Development, Pre-Language Skills, Speech Language and Communication Skills, Developmental Rates and Sequences, Learning Behaviors, and Relating Skills. Scoring for each item is based upon the informant's estimate of the frequency of occurrence of the interfering behavior: Frequent—behavior occurring 70% to 100% of the time; Intermittent—behavior occurring 30% to 70% of the time; Seldom—behavior occurring less than 30% of the time; and Not Applicable. The scores are then transferred from the checklist to a Profile Sheet that presents the results in a visual/graphic form.

Unfortunately, absolutely no statistical information is available regarding item selection, standardization, validity, or reliability and, as such, the test should be used with great caution, and probably not at all for diagnostic/placement purposes. The test does contain appropriate items, useful when developing an individual program for a child with autistic-like behaviors, but there is no information provided in the test booklet to substantiate the author's suggestion the test could be used to diagnose autism. As a diagnostic tool, the ABCCP adds little to the armamentarium of the School Psychologist or Special Education Diagnostician.

Review of the Autistic Behavior Composite Checklist and Profile by RICHARD L. WIKOFF, Professor of Psychology, University of Nebraska at Omaha, Omaha, NE:

The Autistic Behavior Composite Checklist and Profile (ABCCP) is a pencil and paper checklist designed for use with autistic individuals. It consists of 148 items to be marked using a code indicating the frequency of occurrence of different interfering behaviors. A profile sheet is included for the purpose of graphically presenting an overview of these behaviors.

As the name implies, the ABCCP is simply a checklist. It may have some subjective, clinical value, but should not be thought of, in any way, as a psychometric instrument. There is no manual. The booklet containing the Checklist and Profile presents one page of information stating the purposes of the ABCCP and the method suggested by the author for marking the items. A second page makes some suggestions about working with autistic students.

The Checklist is divided into eight categories that are further divided into subcategories. The subcategories contain from one to eight items each. No rationale is presented for the use of these particular categories.

The Profile is three pages long and simply repeats the frequency coding of the checklist. Those subcategories that have more than one item in the checklist are represented in the

Profile by only one item. No directions are given for combining the information from the individual items.

There are no norms presented and reliability and validity are never mentioned. No research concerning the ABCCP is reviewed.

The ABCCP is wholly inadequate. There is no manual, and essential information regarding norms, reliability, and validity are not discussed. While there might be some value to a checklist in the hands of a trained clinician, there is a danger the instrument might be used by the untrained to diagnose autism. For this reason, the author feels that the ABCCP should be considered useful for research purposes only. A much better instrument for identifying autistic children is the Autism Screening Instrument for Educational Planning, reviewed in the *Ninth Mental Measurements Yearbook* (9:105).

[22]

Bader Reading and Language Inventory. Purpose: "Designed to determine appropriate placement of students in instructional materials." Children and adolescents and adults; 1983; a compilation of graded reading passages, word recognition lists, phonics and word analysis subtests, spelling tests, cloze tests, visual discrimination tests, auditory discrimination tests, unfinished sentences, and evaluations of language abilities; individual; manual including all tests (233 pages); price data available from publisher; administration time not reported; Lois A. Bader; Macmillan Publishing Co., Inc.*

Review of the Bader Reading and Language Inventory by KRISTA J. STEWART, Associate Professor of Psychology and Director of the School Psychology Training Program, Tulane University, New Orleans, LA:

The Bader Reading and Language Inventory is a battery of informal tests developed for use by reading specialists, resource teachers, and classroom teachers. Primary emphasis is on the set of graded reading passages, but the other tests allow examination of specific areas (some more related to reading than others) in which the student might also be having difficulty.

The manual gives little information on the development of the Bader's many tests; less than four pages are dedicated to this discussion. The bulk of this description focuses on the development of the graded passages, but even that information is sketchy at best. Three sets of 12 passages were developed for the graded passages: one set for children; one for children, adolescents, and adults; and one for adults. The passages were either written by the author or, as the author indicates, were selected from materials that appeared to be typical for the grade level designations. After the initial passages were written, they were administered to a total of 70 students. According to the author, passages that were not considered appealing were dropped although no indication is given of how this determination was made.

The author reports that the sets of passages were tested for equivalence, resulting in correlations in the upper .70s and low .80s but does not indicate specifically what scores were correlated (i.e., word recognition, comprehension, or both). To give evidence of the validity of these passages, the author reports a study of 30 students whose performance on the test was compared to teacher report of the child's level of placement in basal reading materials; 60% of these comparisons were identical. The author, however, does not describe the sample used.

Literal comprehension of the passages is assessed by having the child summarize the passage, followed by a series of questions to prompt recall of information not given in the summary. From these responses, total number of "memories" is determined. Interpretative questions are asked but are not counted in the total number of memories. The author gives criteria for instructional reading level, criteria that are less stringent than those used in current practice. The author justifies this difference by stating that traditional cutoffs result in students usually being placed in materials that are too easy for them. No further rationale is given, however, for the precise cutoffs that are used. The author does indicate that if the student's reading is extremely slow, the instructional level may be one level lower than the passage on which comprehension was adequate.

Cutoffs are also given for frustration and independent levels. Comprehension can be determined for oral and silent reading as well as for listening, although the author encourages omitting testing for comprehension after oral reading, which is usually lower than comprehension after silent reading. The author advises that oral reading be tape recorded so that scorer accuracy of the evaluation of reading errors can be checked.

The major purpose for another part of the test, the Graded Word List, is to determine entry level for the graded passages. According to the author, the lists can also serve as a check on the student's word attack skills and provide a comparison with contextual reading. As was the case for the written passages, little specific information is given on how the words were selected for the lists. According to the author, words were chosen from graded sight-word lists and basals that appeared to be appropriate for each level. Validity was evaluated by comparing reading specialists' placement of 64 students and the child's performance on the lists. Besides the Graded Word List, four supplementary functional word lists are included: a list of words frequently used in instructional materials, two lists of words encountered in daily life, and a list of words encountered in completing forms and managing personal affairs.

The remaining parts of the inventory are to be given as desired and are to be interpreted based on the need of the student to perform the skill being evaluated. Virtually no information is given on the development of any of these tests. In some cases the author gives recommended cutoff points and indicates that they are those suggested by research; no specific research is cited, however.

The Phonics and Word Analysis Test contains 14 subtests that, according to the author, may be pertinent to some areas of knowledge and abilities that may underlie word recognition. These subtests are to be given selectively.

Seven Spelling Tests are provided and categorized according to the type of skill being evaluated and the reading level of the child for which the test would be appropriate. Skills being evaluated include words with silent letters, words spelled phonetically, words illustrating common spelling conventions, and commonly misspelled high frequency words.

The four Cloze Tests each contain unrelated sentences rather than a paragraph format. The first test is for beginning readers; the others are a semantic cloze test, a syntactic cloze test, and a grammatical cloze test.

The two Visual Discrimination Tests require matching letters, syllables, words, and phrases. The first test is for children through grade one, and the second is for readers at second grade level or above. A general guide for evaluating performance is provided although no indication is given of how those guidelines were established.

The first of the Auditory Discrimination Tests requires discrimination of word pairs. Cutoff scores (with no rationale cited) for six-, seven-, and eight-year-olds are given. The second test involves having the student name the initial letter in words that are presented.

The author refers to the Unfinished Sentences task as a "projective technique." The purpose of this test is to evaluate the child's concerns and interests that should be considered during assessment and remediation. The author notes that often students will share problems about which the examiner can do little, a comment that reflects the inappropriateness of untrained personnel administering this test.

The Arithmetic (calculation) Test is included to provide an estimate of the student's ability to perform a skill that is not dependent on reading. Grade equivalents for raw scores are provided, but the method of score derivation is not indicated.

Several methods are described for evaluating expressive language and include describing, retelling, dictating, completing sentences, repeating sentences, and syntax matching. A Sentence Repetition Test and a Syntax Matching Test are included in this section. Also provided are suggestions for evaluating receptive language.

Finally, evaluation of writing is discussed. A checklist for evaluating written language expression is provided.

Also included in the manual are several other forms: a teacher's reading referral form, a form for summarizing the assessment and recommendations, and two checklists for evaluating the student's own learning priorities. In addition, a graphic representation of a model for the test battery is presented. This model, however, is never discussed in the text.

In summary, the Bader is a battery that may be most useful to the expert diagnostician who is particularly interested in evaluating skill development. The test does provide an interesting assortment of materials to be used in assessment; but the user should keep in mind that the tests, because of the lack of psychometric data, must be considered strictly informal. The cutoffs or grade equivalent scores can be considered only rough estimates at best.

Review of the Bader Reading and Language Inventory by DAN WRIGHT, School Psychologist, Ralston Public Schools, Ralston, NE:

The Bader Reading and Language Inventory was designed as a flexible and largely qualitative inventory of reading and reading-related skills. Constructed for use primarily by reading specialists, resource teachers, and classroom teachers, the actual administration of the inventory could be mastered by anyone with training in individual assessment. The time required for administration will depend not only on student abilities, but on the depth and breadth of inquiry desired by the examiner. Test materials, scoring sheets, and other forms can be detached from the manual, duplicated as needed, and organized and stored to accommodate the examiner's uses.

The central feature of the inventory is a series of graded reading passages, ranging from preprimer through twelfth grade, and providing alternate passages on three levels of interest at each grade level. The purpose of the graded passages, as succinctly stated in the manual, is "to find the highest instructional level at which the student can comprehend and to analyze oral reading to discover student strengths and problems in reading so that the student can be appropriately placed in materials for instruction." The word recognition lists function primarily to indicate an appropriate entry level to the graded passages, and the other tests generally provide information supplementary to test interpretation.

The manual is somewhat ambiguous regarding test development. The graded word lists and graded word passages rightly appear to have received the most intensive attention, but item selection or construction in these areas seems to have been rather subjective and there is no indication that items were added, deleted, or modified as a result of field testing. Some testing with small, poorly-defined samples was conducted to demonstrate that items were indeed presented in order of increasing difficulty, that alternate passages were roughly equivalent, and that results were in agreement with current reading placements. However, a much stronger case for the adequacy of all the items needs to be built. Reliability is not addressed, and validity is dismissed with reference to a single, unpublished study.

Shaky as the support may be for the word lists and reading passages, the remaining parts of the inventory fare worse. No information is presented on the development or adequacy of the remaining tests, and there is no coherent articulation on the utility of any results. A student's performance on tests of visual and auditory discrimination, for example, may be of some relevance in interpreting performance on the reading passages, but the examiner is left alone to infer the nature or extent of such relevance.

In summary, it would be better not to consider this inventory as a "test" at all in the sense of providing useful quantitative results. Examiners must make independent and subjective judgements on the appropriateness of the inventory for their populations of students, its relevance to curriculum in use locally, and any inferences to draw regarding instructional programming. What the inventory does offer is a structured series of tasks that provide an opportunity to observe and record much qualitative information regarding students' reading and reading-related abilities. However, there is little reason to recommend this inventory over teacher-constructed, informal reading inventories, and nothing that causes it to stand out positively among other commercially available inventories.

[23]

Basic Language Concepts Test. Purpose: To screen children and identify those having serious language-concepts problems and provide diagnostic information to aid in developing effective remedies. Ages 4–6.5 and "older language-deficient children in elementary schools or clinic settings"; 1966–82; BLCT; revision of Basic Concept Inventory; "criterion-referenced"; 5 scores: Receptive Language Skills, Expressive Language Skills (Sentence Repetition, Answering Questions), Analogy Skills, Total; individual; 1986 price data: $35 per 40 test forms and manual ('82, 105 pages); $10 per 40 test forms; (10–20) minutes; Siegfried Engelmann, Dorothy Ross, and Virginia Bingham; Science Research Associates, Inc.*

TEST REFERENCES

1. Cole, K. N., & Dale, P. S. (1986). Direct language instruction and interactive language instruction with language delayed preschool children: A comparison study. *Journal of Speech and Hearing Research*, 29, 206-217.

Review of the Basic Language Concepts Test by AMY FINCH-WILLIAMS, Associate Professor of Speech/Language Pathology, University of

Wyoming, Laramie, WY, and ROBERT T. WILLIAMS, Associate Professor of Occupational and Educational Studies, Colorado State University, Fort Collins, CO:

The Basic Language Concepts Test (BLCT) is a direct result of field testing of the Basic Concept Inventory (BCI) (Engelmann, 1966). "The major goal was to retain what was valuable from the original test and add norms." One reviewer of the BCI indicated that "the author's goals are worthwhile, the inventory plan is potentially valuable, the test content is promising" (McCandless, 1972, p. 1152). The weaknesses of the BCI were "typical of those inherent in any research edition . . . . since the criteria for selection [of test items] are not given, we must infer that they are subjective. . . . None of the criteria of formal test construction is satisfied" (McCandless, 1972, p. 1152).

Some of the same strengths and weaknesses continue in the Basic Language Concepts Test. All items in the BLCT were in the BCI. The only change in test content was the reduction of scorable items from 110 to 81. It appears that the authors' views of language and concept development have remained consistent between 1966 and 1982. There has been no effort to incorporate recent research in language and concept development (Bates, 1976; Bloom & Lahey, 1978; Miller, 1978; Rees, 1978).

The authors state that the purposes of the BLCT are (*a*) to screen children with respect to language skills important for initial school learning, (*b*) to diagnose specific skill deficiencies in a way that implies instructional remedies, (*c*) to serve as a basis for IEPs, (*d*) to obtain baseline measures against which to evaluate progress, and (*e*) to provide norms against which to compare individual children in language-concept development. The major aspects assessed are the (*a*) receptive function in which the child must demonstrate understanding of concepts such as negation, plurality, and tense by pointing to pictures; (*b*) imitative function in which the child must repeat spoken sentences which range from four to nine words (the reviewers count three to nine words); (*c*) representational function in which the child must answer questions related to the sentences they have imitated; and (*d*) pattern function in which the child must generalize on the basis of auditory and visual patterned information.

The authors provide minimal information on validity. They provide no information about content or construct validity. Although the authors state that the BLCT assesses skills related to academic success, there is no discussion on the theoretical basis or rationale for the items selected or the functions assessed. Neither the academic skills needed for school, the development of language and concepts, nor the relationships between and among these areas are discussed.

The authors use teacher judgment in establishing predictive and concurrent validity since "there was no other applicable measure of performance available for children in the age range of 4–6 1/2 years." Although there may not be other "screening" instruments available, assessment instruments are available to evaluate language and concept development to which the BLCT could have been compared (Baker & Leland, 1959; Boehm, 1971; Carrow, 1973; Newcomer & Hammill, 1977).

The procedures used to establish examiner reliability are discussed completely and are appropriate. A "stability over time" study of three different groups of children assessed in the fall of their kindergarten year is the only other reliability information offered. This seems inadequate.

The norms were drawn primarily from Lane County, Oregon. The "general population" ($N = 2{,}541$) seems to be drawn primarily from middle class homes. The poverty population ($N = 327$) was drawn from special programs in Oregon and seven other states and consisted primarily of Blacks, Hispanics, and Native Americans. No information is given about the number of children in each of these minority groups nor how the poverty group was distributed across the age groups assessed. The clinic population ($N = 39$) was a group of children diagnosed as being language delayed by speech-language pathologists at the Eugene (Oregon) Hearing and Speech Center. There was no information on the number of clinic children in each age group. There is some confusion on the part of the present reviewers regarding the general population and the poverty group. The authors state that norms are provided for "a general population, an economically disadvantaged population, and a clinic population. About 13% of the general population is a poverty group consisting of Head Start children in Oregon and children in other geographical locations who met federal guidelines for disadvantaged." The reviewers do not know if the "poverty group" is part of the general population or a separate group. Table XIV would suggest that the poverty group is separate from the general population. In addition, the reviewers do not know if the disadvantaged group is separate from the poverty group.

These norms seem appropriate for a screening test, but are limited by geography. Most of the tables are clear and easy to read. However, there needs to be clarification of the make-up of the general population, poverty, and disadvantaged groups.

The authors provide extensive interpretation of test performance. This interpretation begins with the analysis of the raw score, which is considered in relation to a pass-fail criterion. For example, if a kindergarten or first-grade child makes up to 29 errors, the authors declare that "no serious language problem" is indicated. However, users need to be aware that 29 errors could include all items in some parts or the majority of items in other parts of the test and that a serious language problem could be present. Although the authors of the BLCT provide no further analysis at this point, users will want to be aware of where and how frequently errors occur.

If a "serious language problem" is evident, further analysis of errors is recommended and outlined. The first aspect of this analysis examines performance on Part IIa (Imitative Function), which requires the imitation of eight declarative statements. These items seems inadequate for diagnosing a serious language problem in that they evaluate only declarative statements, have a limited number of morphological markers, and may be within the short term memory capabilities of the children tested, especially the upper age group. Further, the value of these items is called into question by the fact that although children in the clinical population performed below the other populations on these items, they performed approximately the same as the other populations in answering questions about these items (Part IIb/c).

The next level of analysis involves using a circle chart in which the user may determine deficient language strategies children are using. Even though the skills assessed are limited, this analysis seems to be valuable, especially to guide the user in further, more comprehensive language evaluation.

The authors of the BLCT also provide some instructional suggestions. Users are cautioned that these suggestions are limited by the authors' viewpoint of language and concepts.

The present reviewers believe that this test is a reasonable screening device and the norms provided may be used as screening norms. However, the language concepts and language systems assessed are limited. Therefore, users must be cautious with this test. Because of the limited concepts and language systems assessed (i.e., primarily semantics, syntax, and morphology), the present reviewers believe that this test cannot be used to diagnose specific skill deficiencies that imply instructional remedies or to serve as a basis for IEPs. The test, however, may help the specialist determine areas for further evaluation. The BLCT should not be used to obtain baseline measures since it is primarily a screening device and only one form is available.

Users of the BLCT are urged to be aware that language and concept development are broader, more complex processes than that suggested by the BLCT. The lack of assessment of some areas, such as the use of language in various contexts and the development of narrative and metalinguistic skills, is considered a serious omission.

Beyond a gross screening instrument, the value of the BLCT is seriously questioned. Instruments such as the Boehm Test of Basic Concepts (Boehm, 1971), Bracken Basic Concept Scale (Bracken, 1984), Detroit Tests of Learning Aptitude—Primary (Hammill & Bryant, 1986), Test of Auditory Comprehension of Language—Revised (Carroll, 1985), Test of Early Language Development (Hresko, Reid, & Hammill, 1981), and Test of Language Development—Primary (Newcomer & Hammill, 1982) are more comprehensive and diagnostic. An investment in time yields depth and specificity in the assessment of language and concept development. These complex processes do not lend themselves to quick screening procedures.

REVIEWER'S REFERENCES

Baker, H., & Leland, B. (1959). Detroit Tests of Learning Aptitude. Indianapolis, IN: Bobbs-Merrill Co., Inc.

Engelmann, S. (1966). The Basic Concept Inventory, Field Research Edition. Chicago: Follett Educational Corporation.

Boehm, A. E. (1971). Boehm Test of Basic Concepts. New York: The Psychological Corporation.
McCandless, B. (1972). [Review of the Basic Concept Inventory, Field Research Edition.] In O. K. Buros (Ed.), *The seventh mental measurements yearbook*, pp. 1151-1152. Highland Park, NJ: The Gryphon Press.
Carrow, E. (1973). Test of Auditory Comprehension of Language. Boston: Teaching Resources.
Bates, E. (1976). Pragmatics and sociolinguistics in child language. In D. Morehead & A. Morehead (Eds.), *Normal and deficient child language*. Baltimore: University Park Press.
Newcomer, P. L., & Hammill, D. D. (1977). Test of Language Development. Austin, TX: PRO-ED, Inc.
Bloom, L., & Lahey, M. (1978). *Language development and language disorders*. New York: John Wiley & Sons.
Miller, J. (1978). Assessing children's language behavior: A developmental process approach. In R. Schiefelbusch (Ed.), *Bases of language intervention*. Baltimore: University Park Press.
Rees, N. (1978). Pragmatics of language: Applications to normal and disordered language development. In R. Schiefelbusch (Ed.), *Bases of language intervention*. Baltimore: University Park Press.
Hresko, W., Reid, D. K., & Hammill, D. D. (1981). Test of Early Language Development. Austin, TX: PRO-ED, Inc.
Newcomer, P. L., & Hammill, D. D. (1982). Test of Language Development—Primary. Austin, TX: PRO-ED, Inc.
Bracken, B. (1984). Bracken Basic Concept Scale. Columbus: Charles E. Merrill.
Carrow-Woolfolk, E. (1985). Test of Auditory Comprehension of Language—Revised. Allen, TX: DLM Teaching Resources.
Hammill, D. D., & Bryant, B. (1986). Detroit Tests of Learning Aptitude—Primary. Austin, TX: PRO-ED, Inc.

[24]

Basic Living Skills Scale. Purpose: Determining the skills levels of pupils in seven necessary behavior areas. Grades 3–8; 1980; 8 scores: Self-Concept, Interpersonal Relations, Responsibility, Decision Making, Study Skills, Citizenship, Career Planning, Total; 1987 price data: $30.80 per 35 response booklets and manual (17 pages); (15–20) minutes; Bob Percival; Dallas Educational Services.*

Review of the Basic Living Skills Scale by BONNIE W. CAMP, Professor of Pediatrics and Psychiatry, University of Colorado School of Medicine, Denver, CO:

DESCRIPTION. This scale was developed to meet the need for a method to evaluate achievement in "affective skills" important in everyday living. The test consists of 50 positive statements written at a third-grade reading level that cover feelings and thoughts about such things as the self in relation to peers, school, authority, and growing up. The response to each item involves reading the statement, comparing oneself with the statement, then responding on a 6-point Likert scale ranging from *Least Like Me* (score 1–2) to *Most Like Me* (score 5–6). The test is expected to require 15–20 minutes for administration and may be given in a group. It is targeted for grades 3 through 8.

A pool of 70 items was developed to cover each of seven categories: Self-Concept, Interpersonal Relations, Responsibility, Decision Making, Study Skills, Citizenship, and Career Planning. The items were then submitted to a jury of 10 professional counselors, 11 classroom teachers, and 2 elementary counselors. The jury rated each item on a scale of 0–3 for how well it evaluated each of the seven selected areas.

The resulting test of 50 items consists of the 10 statements with the highest average score in each category (reduced from a total of 70 items because of overlapping). Items in each category are clustered together. Standardization consisted of one administration to 1,020 pupils in grades 3 through 8 drawn from schools in five different geographic locations in Texas. Ethnic representation was 70% Anglo, 16% Black, and 14% Mexican American.

The only statistical treatment of the data presented in the manual consists of means for each grade level on each item and means for each grade on each category. The standard deviation for each item "was approximately .5." Some future analyses are planned including a study of the relationship between categories and statements and correlations with other measures of achievement and intelligence to be calculated on selected populations.

This scale is clearly in the initial stages of development. The face validity of the items is high and the preliminary item selection process insured consensus on content validity of the items. The test itself is presented in a clear and understandable fashion, which should make it usable with the majority of pupils even at the lowest grade level targeted. There may, however, be some problems with test interpretation. The test is basically a test of self perception; yet it is presented as a "criterion-referenced test" and suggested interpretations sometimes slip into assuming that the self perceptions are accurate (e.g., "A high score in this category [Study Skills] indicates organization ability and thus good grades," or "A high score in this category [Interpersonal Relations] indicates ability to get along well with others").

There is certainly need for information on internal consistency, test-retest reliability, and validity, particularly with respect to proposed interpretations. From information currently available, however, test users should be cautious about assuming stability of response patterns or interpretations of low average or high scores. Nevertheless, this scale is likely to be a welcome addition to the evaluation methodology available to school counselors and, hopefully, additional technical information will be forthcoming to substantiate its use.

Review of the Basic Living Skills Scale by LOUIS J. HEIFETZ, Professor, Division of Special Education and Rehabilitation, School of Education, Syracuse University, Syracuse, NY:

My first impressions of this instrument were colored by two remarkable errors. On the cover of the Basic Living Skills Pupil Record Form (i.e., the score sheet), one of the subtest names is misspelled in large letters as "CAREER AWARNESS" (sic). On page 2 of the accompanying manual, the author refers to "Burros (sic) Tests in Print." The worst, however, is yet to come. On virtually every important dimension of test construction and validation, this instrument is fundamentally flawed. The remainder of this review will highlight several of the problems but, because of the extent of test deficiencies, this review cannot cover all of them.

The Basic Living Skills Scale (BLSS) consists of seven subscales, as described above. Each subscale consists of 10 self-report items, rated on a 6-point Likert-type scale (1 = *never like me*; 2 = *almost never like me*; 3 = *often like me*; 4 = *more often than not like me*; 5 = *almost exactly like me*; 6 = *exactly like me*). Subscale scores are the sum of their 10 item scores. There is also a "Grand Total" score, which is the sum of the seven subscale scores.

On the 6-point self-rating scale, the relative positions of the two middle points are not well defined (3 = *often like me*, 4 = *more often than not like me*). I have asked a dozen colleagues to decide which of the two phrases sounds stronger. About half of them felt the unqualified "often" was stronger (i.e., more characteristic description), while the other half felt that "more often than not" was stronger. For individuals who regard "often like me" as the stronger statement, their 4s will be misrepresented as 3s and vice versa. Another problem concerns the two highest points on the scale (5 = *almost exactly like me*; 6 = *exactly like me*). In order for these labels to be consistent with the labels of points 1 through 4, they should be phrased "almost *always* like me" and "*always* like me." These two problems with the labels for the numbers on the scale raise serious questions about the interpretability of the subscale scores.

The skimpy (16 pages) manual that accompanies the BLSS is not at all clear or consistent about the purpose of the instrument (quality and clarity of writing in the manual are generally low). "The purpose was to develop a scale for determining the skills level of seven necessary behavior areas." "The seven categories measured by the Basic Living Skills Scales . . . were chosen because they cover most (sic) any skill essential for everyday life." "The entire scale could measure self-concept if one uses a broad definition of the term. For our purposes we limit the meaning and broaden the skills base to the seven categories included." "Basic Living Skills—Behavior needed for happy, successful everyday living." "Accountability in education is a thrust everyone must recognize. Achievement in cognitive skills has been realized and has resulted in adequate program evaluation. Achievement in affective skills has been very difficult to determine."

It is also not clear how the domains of the seven subscales were conceptualized. For example, Interpersonal Relations is defined as "measuring ability to 'get along,'" while Citizenship is defined as "measuring respect and consideration for others." This is both a peculiar definition of "citizenship" and a close synonym to the previous definition of "interpersonal relations." There is substantial overlap in the items assigned to each of the seven subscales (each subscale contains 10 items). Two subscales (Self-Concept and Interpersonal Relations) have 5 of their 10 items in common. Two other subscales (Responsibility and Citizenship) have 4 of their 10 items in common. None of the subscales is completely distinct from all others; each subscale shares items with at least two of the other six subscales. Out of the total set of 50 items, 12 items appear on two different subscales, while 4 items appear on three different subscales. Consequently, in calculating the Total Score (which is merely the sum of the seven subscale scores), certain items receive double or triple weight. This scoring system needs to be more clearly explained.

There are also problems with the language level of several items in the BLSS. The author claims that items are written at the third-grade level. Because many third-grade students read below the third-grade level—and some students in higher grades also do not yet read at a third-grade level—certain items will not be fully understood by all pupils in grades 3 through 8, for whom the BLSS is intended. Particularly prone to misunderstanding are items containing words like "dependable," "consider," "goals," "schedule," "observe," "enforce," "responsibility," "destroy," "physical," "several," and "leisure." Responses to misunderstood items will undermine the validity of subscale scores containing those items. Depending on the nature of the students' misinterpretations, scores on these items might systematically inflate (or deflate) their subscale scores. This could create an apparent (but artificial) relationship between subscale scores and students' reading levels.

A major weakness of the BLSS is the total lack of information on its reliability. For example, how consistent are students' scores from one administration of the test to a second administration (test-retest reliability)? Are some of the subscales more stable than others? Is reliability higher in areas that are, by their nature, more stable (e.g., Study Skills), and is it lower in areas that are likely to be more variable (e.g., Self Concept)? Without any information on the reliability of the BLSS, it is impossible to interpret apparent improvements—whether spontaneous or pre/post some systematic intervention—because the changes in BLSS scores will reflect both the unreliability of the instrument and the actual change in the characteristics being measured.

There are also no data on the BLSS's validity—the degree to which it is measuring what it purports to measure. For example, do students' scores on Study Skills correlate with teachers' ratings? To what extent do the various subscale scores correlate with measures of academic achievement? Is the pattern of these correlations plausible (e.g., are the correlations higher for Study Skills than for Interpersonal Relations)? What about demonstrating validity through "known group differences"? For example, do children with a history of disciplinary problems also tend to score lower on Responsibility and Citizenship?

A classic threat to the validity of self-report inventories is the distortion introduced by "social desirability" (i.e., wanting to appear in a favorable light to figures of authority such as parents, teachers, testers, etc.). Although the author states repeatedly that "this is not a test of right or wrong answers," most of the items on the BLSS have an obviously "appropriate" quality that students would likely want to attribute to themselves (e.g., "I have good ideas," "I am a good person," "I like to make good grades," etc.). The author himself states that, "All statements are of a positive nature," but does not appear to recognize how vulnerable such items are to distortions of social desirability. In test construction, under conditions that raise the possibility of distortion by social desirability, it is common to administer a test of social desirability (e.g., the Marlowe-Crowne) in conjunction with the test in question. It is then possible to determine if individuals' susceptibility to the demands of social desirability is related to their responses on the other test. No such analysis is reported by the author.

Another contradiction concerns the amount of time suggested for administering the BLSS. Each of the 50 statements must be read, related to the student's sense of self, and then rated on a 1-to-6 scale calling for fairly fine discriminations. On page 4 of the manual the author states: "Allow 15 to 20 minutes for completing the 50 statements," which translates into 18–24 seconds per item. For students with limited reading skills (see previous comments), this might be insufficient time for merely reading/comprehending the item, leaving no time at all for careful introspection and response. Later in the manual, the author contradicts his earlier time limit: "There are no time limits but a long drawn out time can prove wasteful and unnecessary."

A final problem is the author's contention that the BLSS "was designed to be used as a Criterion Reference (sic) Scale; low scores indicating need for programs for improvement, high scores indicating necessary skills are present." The author seems not to understand the basic distinction between criterion-referenced tests and norm-referenced tests. He proceeds to provide quasi-normative data for subscales and individual items, even though this is supposed to be a criterion-referenced measure. Criterion-referenced tests typically deal with directly observed performance (not self-ratings of ability or attitude) of hierarchically organized task-items. The BLSS does not bear much resemblance to a criterion-referenced instrument.

In conclusion, the Basic Living Skills Scale violates most of the important principles of sound test construction. There is no basis whatsoever for recommending its use in actual practice.

[25]

Battelle Developmental Inventory. Purpose: To identify the developmental strengths and weaknesses of handicapped and nonhandicapped children in infant, preschool, and primary programs. Birth to 8 years; 1984; BDI; individual; 30 profile scores: Adult Interaction, Expression of Feelings/Affect, Self-Concept, Peer Interaction, Coping, Social Role, Personal-Social Total, Attention, Eating, Dressing, Personal Responsibility, Toileting, Adaptive Total, Muscle Control, Body Coordination, Locomotion, Gross Motor, Fine Muscle, Perceptual Motor, Fine Motor, Motor Total, Receptive, Expressive, Communication Total, Perceptual Discrimination, Memory, Reasoning and Academic Skills, Conceptual Development, Cognitive Total, Total; screening test available as a separate; 1988 price data: $165 per complete set including 15 scoring booklets, 30 screening test booklets, test items, examiner's manual (168 pages), screening manual (118 pages), and domain manuals: personal-social (92 pages), adaptive (64 pages), motor (103 pages), communication (94 pages), and cognitive (81 pages); $15 per 15 scoring booklets; $15 per 15 screening test booklets; (60) minutes; Jean Newborg, John R. Stock, Linda Wnek, John Guidubaldi, and John Svinicki; DLM Teaching Resources.*

TEST REFERENCES

1. Guidubaldi, J., & Perry, J. D. (1984). Concurrent and predictive validity of the Battelle Development Inventory at the first grade level. *Educational and Psychological Measurement*, 44, 977-985.

Review of the Battelle Developmental Inventory by JUDY OEHLER-STINNETT, Assistant Professor, University of Wisconsin-Whitewater, Whitewater, WI:

The Battelle Developmental Inventory (BDI), a relatively new developmental battery covering the age range from birth to 8 years, is a welcome addition to available testing instruments for infants and young children. The battery is divided into five domains, assessing all areas of typical concern: Personal-Social (social/emotional adjustment), Adaptive, Motor, Communication, and Cognitive. Each domain is further divided into subdomains. In this regard, the BDI is more comprehensive and easier to interpret than comparable batteries. The ambitious purposes of the BDI include assessment and identification of handicapped children, assessment of nonhandicapped children, determination of individual strengths and weaknesses, development of Individual Education Plans (IEPs), tracking of individual progress, and planning and evaluation of instructional programs. The test's organization and comprehensiveness, inclusion of a Screening Test, standardized test scores, empirically-based age placement of items, wide age range, and behaviorally-based item descriptions all facilitate its usefulness for each of these purposes. The BDI was designed to be used by teachers, diagnosticians, and multidisciplinary teams. The manual is carefully written, explaining statistical terms for those less experienced in testing and providing detailed examples of interpretation and IEP development based on a BDI assessment.

Items were drawn initially from a pool of 4,000 items in use in developmental testing and programming. The original version was administered to 152 children in order to standardize procedures and include adaptations for the handicapped. In 1980 a pilot study involving 500 children was conducted to further refine the BDI and develop the Screening Test. Items were assigned to an age level based on the empirical criteria of 75% passage of an item at that particular age level. Thus, efforts comparable to IQ test development were implemented with the BDI. Final standardization was conducted from December 1982 to March 1983, using a stratified quota sampling technique similar to that used with the Wechsler Intelligence Scale for Children—Revised (WISC-R). In all, 800 children were tested, approximately 50 of each gender at each age level. These normative data could have included a larger sample size; however, they represent a significant improvement over norms available for more widely used developmental inventories. Geographically, the sample was 75% urban, 25% rural. Racially, the sample was 84% white and 16% minority (mainly Black and Hispanic children). Socio-economic status was not specifically controlled but was considered widely distributed. The breakdown by gender shows 49% male and 51% female. This sample is purported to represent the U.S. population as it is currently distributed. Examination of the standardization data shows no significant performance differences by race or gender; however, further investigation is needed to determine that the BDI does not discriminate based on gender, race, SES, or geographic location. Users are cautioned to consider this when interpreting results for rural, low SES, or minority children. In addition, while administration procedures for handicapped children were developed during standardization, no normative data for handicapped children were reported, and only normal children were included in the standardization data.

Excellent reliability data are reported. The standard error of measurement (*SEM*) for all domain scores is very small, and the *SEM* for the BDI total score ranges from 1.30 (84–95 months) to 5.47 (36–47 months). Subdomain *SEM*s are also adequate. Test-retest reliability ($n = 183$), reported across domains and age levels for a 4-week retest time, ranges from .71 to .99 (BDI Total = .99), with most coefficients above .80. Stability of test scores over a longer period of time is not reported. Interrater reliability ($n = 148$) ranges from .70 to 1.0 (BDI Total = .99), again with most coefficients above .80. Split-half reliability is not reported.

Initial validity information supports the BDI as a measure of development and to a lesser extent the Domain organization of the battery. Content validity was ensured by the item selection and test development procedures described above. Except for the absence of a vocabulary measure, the BDI displays an excellent sampling of developmental skills. The BDI is not intended to be an achievement test and would have to be supplemented in this area, most notably in the upper age ranges. Item-Total score and Domain-Total score correlations are also very good, suggesting the BDI is a homogeneous measure of development. The validity of the developmental nature of the BDI is supported by significant *t*-test comparisons between adjacent age groups on components of the BDI. High age-score correlations also support the developmental organization of the battery.

Several studies support the construct and criterion-related validity of the BDI and its domains. According to the authors, factor analyses of the pilot data lend moderate to good support for the BDI Domain organization. Actual data were not available for review and have not been published. For children under age 2, three general factors emerge; therefore, Domain interpretation should be limited for these children. For children above age 2, factor analyses support the Domain structure of the BDI, although there is some overlap between the Communication and Cognitive domains. Additional factor analyses of the battery in its present form need to be conducted, as well as analyses for specific handicapped groups of children.

The manual reports moderately high correlations with the Vineland Social Maturity Scale and the Developmental Activities Screening Inventory. Telzrow (1982) found that for preschool and kindergarten children, the BDI adequately predicts performance on the Peabody Picture Vocabulary Test—Revised (PPVT-R), the Developmental Test of Visual Motor Integration (VMI), and reaction time (RT). Pezzino, Mott, and Waidler (1986) found the BDI was significantly correlated with the Bayley Scales of Infant Development, the Minnesota Child Development Inventory, and the Stanford-Binet (S-B) for a 3-to-5-year-old group of moderately to severely handicapped children. Moderate correlations (BDI manual) with the Stanford-Binet, the WISC-R, and the PPVT indicate the BDI is measuring some similar skills but is distinct from intelligence tests. Lower than expected correlations between the BDI Cognitive Domain and the S-B and WISC-R would suggest this domain is not, for the most part, measuring the same cognitive skills assessed by these IQ tests. However, Christie (1982) found the BDI to be correlated with traditional measures of IQ for small groups of 3–4-year-old hearing-impaired, visually-impaired, and orthopedically-impaired children and found the Cognitive Domain score to be the best predictor of IQ. Guidubaldi and Perry (1984) compared BDI domain scores to scores on tests purported to measure similar constructs and found that all domains except Adaptive were correlated with most measures given, lending little support for the predictive validity of the Domain scores to only tests measuring the same construct. However, results lend support to the internal consistency of the scale as a developmental measure. Mott (1987) correlated the BDI with the PPVT-R, the Preschool Language Scale—Revised (PLS-R), and the Arizona Articulation Proficiency Scale—Revised (AAPS-R) for a group of preschool language-disordered children. Results supported use of the Communication Domain for "assessing general language functioning," gave limited support to the Expressive Domain, and suggested caution in use of the Receptive Domain alone. The Cognitive Domain was correlated with the PLS-R and the Total BDI score was correlated with the PPVT-R and the PLS-R, indicating further that the BDI cannot be considered a nonverbal measure of development. While Mott favors use of the BDI with language-impaired children, interpretation should be cautious, and a nonverbal measure of cognition should be used to make eligibility decisions for these children. An additional study involving handicapped children (BDI manual) shows the BDI discriminates between a heterogenous group of handicapped children and a group of normal children. Discriminative studies involving specific groups are needed.

Guidubaldi and Perry (1984) also compared the BDI's ability to predict achievement (first grade Wide Range Achievement Test [WRAT] scores) and found that it outperformed such instruments as the Metropolitan Readiness Test. The BDI correlated .70 with WRAT Reading and .71 with WRAT Math. Guidubaldi (1987), in a follow-up study, and Gerassimakis (1981) found the Personal-Social, Communication, and Cognitive domains to be the best predictors of academic achievement and the Total BDI score and Cognitive score to correlate with measures of IQ and achievement. No studies have been conducted so far comparing the usefulness of the BDI to that of such popular tests as the Learning Accomplishment Profile or the Brigance Inventory of Early Development for diagnostic and predictive purposes, program planning, IEP development, or validity of domains. Also, there are limited validity data for the upper age ranges. As in all areas reviewed above, further validity studies are needed.

Each domain has its own manual, allowing specific diagnosticians (e.g., speech pathologists, adapted P.E. specialists, psychologists) to administer the appropriate section of the test. Until further validation of each domain is conducted, users should view the BDI as an overall measure of development and use it as such for eligibility and placement decisions. However, each specialist could administer and/or interpret the appropriate domain and include the results with other data in making diagnostic decisions. For program planning, progress checks, or IEP development, separate domains could be administered independently.

Administration of the Screening Test takes from 10 to 30 minutes. Based on these results, the BDI or appropriate domains would be administered. Administration of the entire battery takes from 1 to 2 hours. Children in the 3-to-5-year range typically take the maximum administration time due to an increased number of items in this age range. This administration time is somewhat longer than that of other developmental batteries, mostly due to the comprehensiveness of the test (as opposed to, for example, the Bayley Scales of Infant Development) and the fact that many tests now used for eligibility were designed as screening instruments (e.g., the Denver Developmental Screening Test; Developmental Activities Screening Inventory). Examiners are encouraged to weigh the BDI's advantages over the disadvantage of its relatively lengthy administration time. The BDI now appears to be the test of choice over the Bayley, based on test construction, normative information, and comprehensiveness. While additional validity studies are needed and the test has limitations, it is preferable to other tests in their current form. Although the Screening Test must be investigated further, it does have the advantage of norms based on part of the full BDI standardization group. The validity section of the manual suggests the Screening test could be cautiously used as the assessment instrument for eligibility decisions. Based on its high correlation with the total battery ($r > .90$; $n = 164$), this use is permissible when a global picture of development is needed and additional instruments will be used. However, the total battery should be administered whenever possible.

There are several concerns regarding administration of the BDI: (*a*) The examiners must initially gather testing materials; these should be well organized and easily reached when in the process of test administration. Considerable familiarity with the BDI is needed. (*b*) Ample space is needed for the Motor Domain assessment. (*c*) While many items are administered in a structured format, some items can be scored based on interview or observation methods, or structured items can be corroborated with the other two methods. Considerable expertise is needed in interpreting discrepant data so that accurate scores are obtained. The manual suggests that when two interviewees disagree (such as the parent and teacher), credit should be given if the child performs a task in at least one setting (e.g., home vs. school). This helps to clarify Adaptive and Personal-Social items, which are often difficult to score on other tests such as the Vineland. However, there are no guidelines for scoring when there is disagreement between observation and interview data. Users are cautioned to gather all relevant data and give credit only when it is clear the child performs the behavior on an habitual basis. Therefore, the use of the observation method of assessment would be most appropriate for a teacher who has daily contact with the child. Assessment specialists who do not know the child should validate teacher observation with other assessment methods. When items are scored based on interview only, it would be desirable to interview both the teacher and the parent. (*d*) While the manual is well organized, on items that require exposing a visual stimulus to the child, the picture is on the page following the instructions, making it difficult to read instructions and display the stimulus at the same time. (*e*) The basal is a score of 2 on all subdomain items at an age level, while the ceiling is 0 on two consecutive items. While the examiner's manual states that to obtain a basal the tester should move to a lower level if the child scores a 0 on an item at an age level (not a 1 or 0), this would disagree with the basal rule of a score of 2 on all items. Clarification is needed. (*f*) While administration instructions for handicapped children are detailed and an admirable departure from tests that instruct examiners to "modify as needed," users should be cautioned there are no normative data established for these procedures indicating how the modifications may affect scoring. Also, the modifications for some items are said to be for instructional purposes only, and no explanation is given for scoring when these items are omitted from testing. If they are to be administered in the standard fashion, some discrimination may occur. (*g*) Finally, there are no modifications for language-impaired children, and the test instructions are verbally loaded. While modifications listed for the hearing impaired may be appropriate for language-impaired students, further investigation is needed to make this determination.

Scoring is relatively straightforward, on a 3-point scale. For the most part, the scoring is: 0 = *rarely or never*, 1 = *sometimes* (50%), or 2 = *typical* (90%); however, some items have specific criteria. The manual should be closely followed for scoring criteria. As noted, corroboration of data is recommended when necessary. Changing raw scores to percentiles and standard scores is easily managed, and appropriate cautions regarding age- and grade-equivalent scores are included in the manual. To the relatively new examiner, the inclusion of several standard score types on one table may be confusing; however, the relationship between each type of score is clearly demonstrated. For comparison to other tests and eligibility determination, the Developmental Quotient (DQ) is the score of choice. There is a provision for interpolating DQ scores below 65 on the last page of the manual. As many handicapped children will score below the floor of the norms table, this additional table is useful. Users are advised to calculate scores in the suggested manner when a child falls in the first percentile on a subdomain, domain, or the full battery score. Considering the purpose of the test, however, it would be most desirable to obtain norms at the lower functioning levels. There also appears to be a ceiling effect for some subdomains with increasing age. When a child achieves a perfect score on several subdomains, interpretation should indicate the child's skills may be underestimated by the obtained score.

Overall, the BDI was developed within respected guidelines, and initial data suggest it to be a commendable assessment instrument in early childhood development. Further validity studies should be conducted to continue development of the Battelle Developmental Inventory.

REVIEWER'S REFERENCES

Gerassimakis, N. (1981). A two year longitudinal study of early childhood multifactored predictors for later academic and social competencies. *Dissertation Abstracts International*, 43 (3-A), 660-661.

Christie, A. E. (1982). A comparison of the McCarthy Scales of Children's Abilities and the Battelle Developmental Inventory for use with handicapped preschool children. *Dissertation Abstracts International*, 43 (4-A), 1033.

Telzrow, K. (1982). Longitudinal prediction of PPVT, VMI, and reaction time performance by the Battelle Development Inventory and the Minnesota Child Development Inventory for three ages of preschool children. *Dissertation Abstracts International*, 43 (4-A), 1095.

Guidubaldi, J., & Perry, J. D. (1984). Concurrent and predictive validity of the Battelle Development Inventory at the first grade level. *Educational and Psychological Measurement*, 44, 977-985.

Pezzino, J., Mott, S. E., & Waidler, J. (1986). *The concurrent validity of the Battelle Developmental Inventory*. Unpublished manuscript, Utah State University, Early Intervention Research Institute, Logan, UT.

Guidubaldi, J. (1987). Predictive validity of the Battelle Developmental Inventory: A 4-year comparative study [Summary]. *Proceedings of the National Association of School Psychologists*, 19, 141-142.

Mott, S. E. (1987). Concurrent validity of the Battelle Developmental Inventory for speech and language disordered children. *Psychology in the Schools*, 24, 215-220.

Harrington, R. [Review of Battelle Developmental Inventory]. Unpublished manuscript, University of Kansas, Lawrence, KS.

Review of the Battelle Developmental Inventory by KATHLEEN D. PAGET, Associate Professor, Department of Psychology, University of South Carolina, Columbia, SC:

Unlike many tests that are shrouded from the beginning of their development in an entrepreneurial cloak, the Battelle Developmental Inventory (BDI) had a more noble genesis. It took root in 1973 when the U.S. Bureau of Education for the Handicapped (BEH), now the Department of Education's Special Education Program, initiated a project with the Columbus Laboratories of Battelle Memorial Institute to evaluate the effectiveness of the Handicapped Children's Early Education Programs (HCEEP). Having been involved in an HCEEP project at that time, this author writes with an appreciation for the void filled by these early program evaluation efforts. More specific purposes of the BDI are stated in the manual as (*a*) assessment and identification of the handicapped child; (*b*) assessment of the nonhandicapped child; and (*c*) planning and providing instruction.

The development of the BDI, administration and scoring guidelines, standardization procedures, psychometric properties, and normative data (by age, not race or gender) are all provided in the manual. Special features of the manual are five case studies useful to interpretation of the Screening Test, the full BDI, and the development of individualized education plans. In addition, guidelines for conducting interviews and assessing handicapped children are given. Reading these guidelines and practicing the interview skills are imperative activities for the attainment of reliable and valid results, and should be done with an eye toward avoiding simplistic interpretations and "teaching to the test" (Molitor & Kramer, 1987). These points need to be emphasized more strongly in the manual, especially because of the varied backgrounds of professionals who will be administering the BDI. A noteworthy feature of the battery's development is the method used to select and sequence its items. An empirical approach involving a decision rule common to psychophysics (75% of children passing) was used to determine item difficulty and assign an item to an age. Although this procedure resulted in item assignments that occasionally are contrary to test users' conceptual expectations, it allows for normative comparisons of the performance of same-age children, as well as ipsative analyses leading to program planning for individual children.

STANDARDIZATION PROCEDURES. Commendable procedures were followed in standardizing the BDI. The sample of 800 children, though smaller than samples for some other standardized developmental assessment instruments (e.g., McCarthy Scales, Binet 4th Edition), was stratified at each age level by geographic region, race, and sex; and it represented 24 states in four major geographical regions of the United States. The distribution by race and sex reflected the distribution of these characteristics in the U.S. population according to 1981 census data. In addition, all high and low incidence handicaps were represented in proportions equivalent to BEH percentages, with modification made in instructions, scoring criteria, and test materials (Telzrow, 1985). However, the manual does not report that handicapped children were included in the standardization sample, and the normative data do not reflect inclusion of these clinical subsamples. A table of normative data for clinical samples would be a helpful addition to a future revision of the manual.

ADMINISTRATION AND SCORING. A unique feature of the BDI is that items may be administered using either a structured testing format, observation, or parent/teacher interviews. On one hand, this feature affords the examiner freedom to use the method believed to optimize valid results. On the other hand, reliability and validity of BDI administration must be evaluated carefully within the context of this multisource, multimethod administration format. In addition, the manual states that the prescribed order of items must be followed when administering the BDI. This requirement may add to administration time and interfere with the examiner's spontaneity in capturing and maintaining the momentary interest of a young child.

Administration is reported to require from 1 to 2 hours, which is a long period of time for preschool-age children. Nevertheless, administration may take place conveniently over different sessions because procedures for each domain are contained in separate booklets. This format is intended to foster multidisciplinary administration of the BDI. In this respect, a school psychologist, speech clinician, occupational therapist, and social worker could administer separate domains for which they are best trained and then provide a collective report of their results. Although this procedure meets legislative mandates for interdisciplinary communication, all examiners involved must be aware that it introduces a potential threat to the reliability of results.

It is important for test users to realize that all necessary materials are not included in the kit. Although most materials can be found in preschool and primary settings, frustration is likely to occur if the examiner is unable to locate all of them. A complete list of materials, including adapted materials for handicapped children, appears in an appendix, but some are poorly described with respect to color, size, and type. Thus, a major source of error is introduced. Although a supplemental materials kit has recently become available, many of the materials necessary for administration to the handicapped (e.g., the beeper ball, raised drawings, brailled letters, etc.) are missing. Furthermore, for some items, particularly in the communication and cognitive domains, actual assembly of items is required. Thus, the test user must cut out puzzles, pictures, etc., that may not have much longevity.

A 3-point scoring system (0, 1, 2) reflects a necessary emphasis on emerging versus fully-acquired developmental skills. These scores are assigned on a percentage basis, as determined by a parent, a teacher, or the examiner's observations in the evaluation setting or classroom. A score of 0 is assigned if the behavior or skill occurs rarely or never; a score of 1 if it occurs 50% of the time; and a score of 2 if it is a typical behavior occurring 90% or more of the time. Given the need for low-inference assessment procedures for young children (Neisworth & Bagnato, 1986), a caveat must be stated regarding the inferential nature of these data. The percentages are not based on exact frequency of behavior, and only with specific interview probes and observations over time would situationally-specific data be obtained. Helpful guidelines to be included in a revision of the manual would emphasize the need for the test user to observe across settings and over time, and to provide other informants the proper structure and encouragement to do the same. Data that are situationally specific and based on actual frequency of occurrence would assist in the development of more specific curricular objectives and, thus, would tighten the assessment-intervention connection.

An appropriate caution is stated in the manual with respect to the use of age-equivalent scores. Thus, the normative tables report a variety of derived scores for each domain (i.e., percentiles, *z*-scores, *t*-scores, deviation quotients, and normal curve equivalents), and a profile to plot Standard Scores is included in the protocol score summary section of the BDI. Despite this provision of varied scores, the floor of the test is inadequate for many children with special needs because the tables report scores only to the first percentile, or to a Deviation Quotient of 65. Although the manual describes a procedure for computing *t*-scores from raw scores and converting these to other standard score units, it would be helpful if tables of low scores were included in the manual, to save time and reduce the potential for scoring errors.

PSYCHOMETRIC PROPERTIES. In general, the available psychometric information *suggests* good consistency and validity of the results obtained with the BDI, although the manual lacks sufficient detail to derive firm conclusions. The standard error of measurement for the BDI is reported as small, thus suggesting assurance that the obtained score is close to the child's "true score." Test-retest and interrater reliability coefficients are reported in the .90 range and above, thus suggesting the BDI is a stable instrument that produces accurate scores. Studies of long-term stability are needed, particularly because (*a*) the BDI is described as being appropriate for program evaluation, and (*b*) the wide range of ages reflected in the standardization sample provides for longterm follow-up of individual children. Future reliability studies should also focus on derivation of internal consistency coefficients for the subtests and total test and replication of previously-conducted studies with larger sample sizes.

Concurrent validity studies comparing domain scores and the total Developmental Quotient with other measures have been promising, as has a study predicting first grade achievement from the BDI (Guidubaldi & Perry, 1984). Nevertheless, validity studies are needed that use actual classroom and home behavior as the criterion to which BDI results are compared. Evidence for construct validity is reported in the manual based primarily on intercorrelations among subdomains, which are generally high and positive. The only factor analysis reported in the manual (Newman & Guidubaldi, 1981) was based on pilot data, and limited detail about the study is provided. Clearly, factor analyses with large sample sizes are needed to lend credibility to the marketing of the BDI as a multifactored instrument. Some of these studies should be designed to evaluate the factorial invariance of the BDI across race and gender. Although the manual reports no statistically significant gender or social differences across ages, caution must be exercised in interpreting these results, again because details about the study (e.g., sample size, whether the data were taken from pilot or standardization samples) are missing. Finally, from information in the manual, conclusions regarding the validity of the BDI with minority children must be limited to black and Spanish-origin groups.

The validity of the Screening Test was evaluated by administering it to a total of 164 children in the norming and clinical samples prior to their receiving the full BDI. Because the correlations were all above .90, a child's performance on the Screening Test should be an excellent predictor of performance on the full BDI. Thus, although it is inappropriate for diagnostic or instructional purposes, the Screening Test appears to predict well those children who should receive a comprehensive evaluation that includes the BDI.

SUMMARY. In general, this review suggests the Battelle joins the ranks of other evaluation instruments that necessarily possess both strengths and limitations. Despite its limitations, the Battelle appears to have a promising future. It already has been adopted as the instrument of choice for several current, large-scale program evaluation efforts; and test users give it high marks for assessing current developmental status and documenting the progress made by individual children. Future research investigations are welcome to further validate its use with specific populations of children and its unique contribution to early assessment and intervention efforts.

REVIEWER'S REFERENCES

Newman, I., & Guidubaldi, J. (1981). Factor validity estimate of the Battelle Developmental Inventory for three age groupings. Paper presented at the annual meeting of the National Association of School Psychologists.

Guidubaldi, J., & Perry, J. D. (1984). Concurrent and predictive validity of the Battelle Developmental Inventory at the first grade level. *Educational and Psychological Measurement*, 44, 977-985.

Telzrow, C. (1985). Test review: Battelle Developmental Inventory. *Preschool Interests*, 1, 6-7.

Neisworth, J. T., & Bagnato, S. J. (1986). Curriculum-based developmental assessment: Congruence of testing and teaching. *School Psychology Review*, 15, 180-199.

Molitor, D. L., & Kramer, J. J. (1987). Review of the Battelle Developmental Inventory. *Journal of Psychoeducational Assessment*, 3, 287-291.

[26]

Bayley Scales of Infant Development. Purpose: Provide a "basis for the evaluation of a child's developmental status in the first two and one-half years of life." Ages 2–30 months; 1969–84; BSID; revision consists of a manual supplement, which provides classifications of the directions for administration and scoring; 2 scores: Mental and Motor, and 30 behavior ratings; individual; the Mental and Motor Scales "draw heavily upon" the California First-Year Mental Scale, the California Preschool Mental Scale, and the California Infant Scale of Motor Development; 1988 price data: $449 per complete set including accessories, 25 each of 3 record forms, carrying case and manual ('69, 185 pages); $22 per 25 Mental Scales record forms; $16 per 25 Motor Scale or Infant Behavior record forms; $39 per 25 combined record forms (each of 3); $75 per carrying case; $750 or less per 2 training film videotapes (available in 16 mm, 1/2 inch reel-to-reel, 1/2 inch cassettes, 3/4 inch cassettes, 1 inch reel-to-reel); $35 per manual; $10 per manual supplement ('84, 32 pages); (45) minutes; Nancy Bayley, Leanne Rhodes (manual supplement), Ben C. Yow (manual supplement), Jane Hunt (training films), and Paul Rush (training films); The Psychological Corporation.*

See 9:126 (42 references); see also T3:270 (101 references); for a review by Fred Damarin, see 8:206 (28 references); see also T2:484 (11 references); for reviews by Roberta R. Collard and Raymond H. Holden, see 7:402 (20 references).

TEST REFERENCES

1. Larson, K. A. (1982). The sensory history of developmentally delayed children with and without tactile defensiveness. *The American Journal of Occupational Therapy*, 36, 590-596.

2. Bagnato, S. J., & Neisworth, J. T. (1983). Monitoring developmental progress of young exceptional children: The Curricular Efficiency Index (CEI). *The Journal of Special Education*, 17, 189-193.

3. Egeland, B., Sroufe, L. A., & Erickson, M. (1983). The developmental consequence of different patterns of maltreatment. *Child Abuse & Neglect*, 7, 459-469.

4. Haynes, C. F., Cutler, C., Gray, J., O'Keefe, K., & Kempe, R. S. (1983). Non-organic failure to thrive: Decision for placement and video taped evaluations. *Child Abuse & Neglect*, 7, 309-319.

5. Haynes, C. F., Cutler, C., Gray, J., O'Keefe, K., & Kempe, R. S. (1983). Non-organic failure to thrive: Implications of placement through analysis of videotaped interactions. *Child Abuse & Neglect*, 7, 321-328.

6. Mundy, P. C., Seibert, J. M., Hogan, A. E., & Fagan, J. F., III. (1983). Novelty responding and behavioral development in young, developmentally delayed children. *Intelligence*, 7, 163-174.

7. Tsai, L. Y., & Beisler, J. M. (1983). The development of sex differences in infantile autism. *British Journal of Psychiatry*, 142, 373-378.

8. Adams, J. L., Campbell, F. A., & Ramey, C. T. (1984). Infants' home environments: A study of screening efficiency. *American Journal of Mental Deficiency*, 89, 133-139.

9. Bradley, R. H., & Caldwell, B. M. (1984). The relation of infants' home environments to achievement test performance in first grade: A follow-up study. *Child Development*, 55, 803-809.

10. Brooks-Gunn, J., & Lewis, M. (1984). Maternal responsivity in interactions with handicapped infants. *Child Development*, 55, 782-793.

11. Call, J. D. (1984). Child abuse and neglect in infancy: Sources of hostility within the parent-infant dyad and disorders of attachment in infancy. *Child Abuse & Neglect*, 8, 185-202.

12. Coates, D. L., & Lewis, M. (1984). Early mother-infant interaction and infant cognitive status as predictors of school performance and cognitive behavior in six-year-olds. *Child Development*, 55, 1219-1230.

13. Coll, C. G., Kagan, J., & Reznick, J. S. (1984). Behavioral inhibition in young children. *Child Development*, 55, 1005-1019.

14. Collaborative Group on Antenatal Steroid Therapy. (1984). Effects on antenatal dexamethasone administration in the infant: Long-term follow-up. *The Journal of Pediatrics*, 104, 259-267.

15. Daniels, D., Plomin, R., & Greenhalgh, J. (1984). Correlates of difficult temperament in infancy. *Child Development*, 55, 1184-1194.

16. Egeland, B., & Farber, E. A. (1984). Infant-mother attachment: Factors related to its development and changes over time. *Child Development*, 55, 753-771.

17. Esenther, S. E. (1984). Developmental coaching of the Down syndrome infant. *The American Journal of Occupational Therapy*, 38, 440-445.

18. Gaensbauer, T. J., Harmon, R. J., Cytryn, L., & McKnew, D. H. (1984). Social and affective development in infants with a manic-depressive parent. *American Journal of Psychiatry*, 141, 223-229.

19. Giblin, P. T., Starr, R. H., Jr., & Agronow, S. J. (1984). Affective behavior of abused and control children: Comparisons of parent-child interactions and the influence of home environment variables. *The Journal of Genetic Psychology*, 144, 69-82.

20. Gottfried, A. W. (1984). Measures of socioeconomic status in child development research: Data and recommendations. *Merrill-Palmer Quarterly*, 31, 85-92.

21. Hakimi-Manesh, Y., Mojdehl, H., & Tashakkori, A. (1984). Short communication: Effects of environmental enrichment on the mental and psychomotor development of orphanage children. *Journal of Child Psychology and Psychiatry*, 25, 643-650.

22. Haynes, C. F., Cutler, C., Gray, J., & Kempe, R. S. (1984). Hospitalized cases of nonorganic failure to thrive: The scope of the problem and short-term lay health visitor intervention. *Child Abuse & Neglect*, 8, 229-242.

23. Honig, A. S. (1984). Risk factors in infants and young children. *Young Children*, 39 (4), 60-73.

24. Jeremy, R. J., & Bernstein, V. J. (1984). Dyads at risk: Methadone-maintained women and their four-month-old infants. *Child Development*, 55, 1141-1154.

25.Mundy, P., Seibert, J. M., & Hogan, A. E. (1984). Relationship between sensorimotor and early communication abilities in developmentally delayed children. *Merrill-Palmer Quarterly*, 30, 33-48.

26. Olson, S. L., Bates, J. E., & Bayles, K. (1984). Mother-infant interaction and the development of individual differences in children's cognitive competence. *Developmental Psychology*, 20, 166-179.

27. Parette, H. P., Jr., Holder, L. F., & Sears, J. D. (1984). Correlates of therapeutic progress by infants with cerebral palsy and motor delay. *Perceptual and Motor Skills*, 58, 159-163.

28. Ramey, C. T., & Campbell, F. A. (1984). Preventive education for high-risk children: Cognitive consequences of the Carolina Abecedarian Project. *American Journal of Mental Deficiency*, 88, 515-523.

29. Ramey, C. T., Yeates, K. O., & Short, E. J. (1984). The plasticity of intellectual development: Insights from preventive intervention. *Child Development*, 55, 1913-1925.

30. Ruff, H. A., McCarton, C., Kurtzberg, D., & Vaughan, H. G., Jr. (1984). Preterm infant's manipulative exploration of objects. *Child Development*, 55, 1166-1173.

31. Stancin, T., Reuter, J., Dunn, V., & Bickett, L. (1984). Validity of caregiver information on the developmental status of severely brain-damaged young children. *American Journal of Mental Deficiency*, 88, 388-395.

32. Stith, S. M., & Davis, A. J. (1984). Employed mothers and family day-care substitute care-givers: A comparative analysis of infant care. *Child Development*, 55, 1340-1348.

33. Yarrow, L. J., MacTurk, R. H., Vietze, P. M., McCarthy, M. E., Klein, R. P., & McQuiston, S. (1984). Developmental course of parental stimulation and its relationship to mastery motivation during infancy. *Developmental Psychology*, 20, 492-503.

34. Allen, R., & Wasserman, G. A. (1985). Origins of language delay in abused infants. *Child Abuse & Neglect*, 9, 335-340.

35. Aram, D. M., Ekelman, B. L., Rose, D. F., & Whitaker, H. A. (1985). Verbal and cognitive sequelae following unilateral lesions acquired in early childhood. *Journal of Clinical and Experimental Neuropsychology*, 7, 55-78.

36. Barclay, A., & McWay, J. (1985). A factor analytic study of responses to the Bayley Scales of Infant Development by a disadvantaged population. *Perceptual and Motor Skills*, 60, 713-714.

37. Cardoso-Martins, C., & Mervis, C. B. (1985). Maternal speech to prelinguistic children with Down syndrome. *American Journal of Mental Deficiency*, 89, 451-458.

38. Cardoso-Martins, C., Mervis, C. B., & Mervis, C. A. (1985). Early vocabulary acquisition by children with Down syndrome. *American Journal of Mental Deficiency*, 90, 177-184.

39. Coleman, M., Sobel, S., Bhagavan, H. N., Coursin, D., Marquardt, A., Guay, M., & Hunt, C. (1985). A double blind study of vitamin B6 in Down's syndrome infants. Part 1-Clinical and biochemical results. *Journal of Mental Deficiency Research*, 29, 233-240.

40. Crittenden, P. M. (1985). Maltreated infants: Vulnerability and resilience. *Journal of Child Psychology and Psychiatry*, 26, 85-96.

41. Cunningham, C. C., Glenn, S. M., Wilkinson, P., & Sloper, P. (1985). Mental ability, symbolic play and receptive and expressive language of young children with Down's syn-

drome. *The Journal of Child Psychology and Psychiatry and Allied Disciplines*, 26, 255-265.

42. Drotar, D., Nowak, M., Malone, C. A., Eckerle, D., & Negray, J. (1985). Early psychological outcomes in failure to thrive: Predictions from an interaction model. *Journal of Clinical Child Psychology*, 14, 105-111.

43. Eckerman, C. O., Sturm, L. A., & Gross, S. J. (1985). Different developmental courses for very-low-birthweight infants differing in early head growth. *Developmental Psychology*, 21, 813-827.

44. Feldman, M. A., Case, L., Towns, F., & Betel, J. (1985). Parent education project I: Development and nurturance of children of mentally retarded parents. *American Journal of Mental Deficiency*, 90, 253-258.

45. Fox, N. A., & Porges, S. W. (1985). The relation between neonatal heart period patterns and developmental outcome. *Child Development*, 56, 28-37.

46. Gunn, P., & Berry, P. (1985). The temperament of Down's syndrome toddlers and their siblings. *The Journal of Child Psychology and Psychiatry and Allied Disciplines*, 26, 973-979.

47. Haskins, R. (1985). Public school aggression among children with varying day-care experience. *Child Development*, 56, 689-703.

48. Kashani, J. H., Carlson, G. A., Horwitz, E., & Reid, J. C. (1985). Dysphoric mood in young children referred to a child development unit. *Child Psychiatry and Human Development*, 15, 234-242.

49. MacTurk, R. H., Vietze, P. M., McCarthy, M. E., McQuiston, S., & Yarrow, L. J. (1985). The organization of exploratory behavior in Down syndrome and nondelayed infants. *Child Development*, 56, 573-581.

50. Molfese, V. J., & Thomson, B. (1985). Optimality versus complications: Assessing predictive values of perinatal scales. *Child Development*, 56, 810-823.

51. Rose, S. A., & Wallace, I. F. (1985). Cross-modal and intramodal transfer as predictors of mental development in full-term and preterm infants. *Developmental Psychology*, 21, 949-962.

52. Rose, S. A., & Wallace, I. F. (1985). Visual recognition memory: A predictor of later cognitive functioning in preterms. *Child Development*, 56, 843-852.

53. Ross, G. (1985). Use of the Bayley Scales to characterize abilities of premature infants. *Child Development*, 56, 835-842.

54. Sankey, C. G., Elmer, E., Halechko, A. D., & Schulberg, P. (1985). The development of abused and high-risk infants in different treatment modalities: Residential versus in-home care. *Child Abuse & Neglect*, 9, 237-243.

55. Shaner, J. M., Peterson, K. L., & Roscoe, B. (1985). Older adolescent females' knowledge of child development norms. *Adolescence*, 20, 53-59.

56. Stahlecker, J. E., & Cohen, M. C. (1985). Application of the strange situation attachment paradigm to a neurologically impaired population. *Child Development*, 56, 502-507.

57. Thompson, L. A., Plomin, R., & DeFries, J. C. (1985). Parent-infant resemblance for general and specific cognitive abilities in the Colorado Adoption Project. *Intelligence*, 9, 1-13.

58. Wasserman, G. A., Allen, R., & Solomon, C. R. (1985). At-risk toddlers and their mothers: The special case of the physical handicap. *Child Development*, 56, 73-83.

59. Wilson, R. S. (1985). Risk and resilience in early mental development. *Developmental Psychology*, 21, 795-805.

60. Adamakos, H., Ryan, K., Ullman, D. G., Pascoe, J., Diaz, R., & Chessare, J. (1986). Maternal social support as a predictor of mother-child stress and stimulation. *Child Abuse and Neglect*, 10, 463-470.

61. Bendell, R. D., Culbertson, J. L., Shelton, T. L., & Carter, B. D. (1986). Interrupted infantile apnea: Impact on early development, temperament, and maternal stress. *Journal of Clinical Child Psychology*, 15, 304-310.

62. Breitmayer, B. J., & Ramey, C. T. (1986). Biological nonoptimality and quality of postnatal environment as codeterminants of intellectual development. *Child Development*, 57, 1151-1165.

63. Heinicke, C. M., Diskin, S. D., Ramsey-Klee, D. M., & Oates, D. S. (1986). Pre- and postbirth antecedents of 2-year-old attention, capacity for relationships, and verbal expressiveness. *Developmental Psychology*, 22, 777-787.

64. Hourcade, J. J., & Parette, H. P., Jr. (1986). Early intervention programming: Correlates of progress. *Perceptual and Motor Skills*, 62, 58.

65. Lewis, M., Jaskir, J., & Enright, M. K. (1986). The development of mental abilities in infancy. *Intelligence*, 10, 331-354.

66. Maisto, A. A., & German, M. L. (1986). Reliability, predictive validity, and interrelationships of early assessment indices used with developmentally delayed infants and children. *Journal of Clinical Child Psychology*, 15, 327-332.

67. Messer, D. J., McCarthy, M. E., McQuiston, S., MacTurk, R. H., Yarrow, L. J., & Vietze, P. M. (1986). Relation between mastery behavior in infancy and competence in early childhood. *Developmental Psychology*, 22, 366-372.

68. Olson, S. L., Bayles, K., & Bates, J. E. (1986). Mother-child interaction and children's speech progress: A longitudinal study of the first two years. *Merrill-Palmer Quarterly*, 32, 1-20.

69. Pianta, R. C., Egeland, B., & Hyatt, A. (1986). Maternal relationship history as an indicator of developmental risk. *American Journal of Orthopsychiatry*, 56, 385-398.

70. Plimpton, C. E. (1986). Effects of water and land in early experience programs on the motor development and movement comfortableness of infants aged 6 to 18 mo. *Perceptual and Motor Skills*, 62, 719-728.

71. Power, T. G., & Chapieski, M. L. (1986). Childrearing and impulse control in toddlers: A naturalistic investigation. *Developmental Psychology*, 22, 271-275.

72. Schwethelm, B., & Mahoney, G. (1986). Task persistence among organically impaired mentally retarded children. *American Journal of Mental Deficiency*, 90, 432-439.

73. Seibert, J. M., Hogan, A. E., & Mundy, P. C. (1986). On the specifically cognitive nature of early object and social skill domain associations. *Merrill-Palmer Quarterly*, 32, 21-36.

74. Sloper, P., Glenn, S. M., & Cunningham, C. C. (1986). The effect of intensity of training on sensori-motor development in infants with Down's syndrome. *Journal of Mental Deficiency Research*, 30, 149-162.

75. Whiteley, J. H., & Krenn, M. J. (1986). Uses of the Bayley mental scale with nonambulatory profoundly mentally retarded children. *American Journal of Mental Deficiency*, 90, 425-431.

76. Crano, W. D., & Mendoza, J. L. (1987). Maternal factors that influence children's positive behavior: Demonstration of a structural equation analysis of selected data from the Berkeley Growth Study. *Child Development*, 58, 38-48.

77. Ernhart, C. B., Marler, M. R., & Morrow-Tlucak, M. (1987). Size and cognitive development in the early preschool years. *Psychological Reports*, 61, 103-106.

78. Loveland, K. A. (1987). Behavior of young children with down syndrome before the mirror: Exploration. *Child Development*, 58, 768-778.

79. Slade, A. (1987). A longitudinal study of maternal involvement and symbolic play during the toddler period. *Child Development*, 58, 367-375.

80. Sostek, A. M., Smith, Y. F., Katz, K. S., & Grant, E. G. (1987). Developmental outcome of preterm infants with intraventricular hemorrhage at one and two years of age. *Child Development*, 58, 779-786.

Review of the Bayley Scales of Infant Development by MICHAEL J. ROSZKOWSKI, Research Psychologist, The American College, Bryn Mawr, PA:

The Bayley Scales of Infant Development (BSID) represent the realization of almost half a century of study of this subject by Nancy

Bayley, an eminent developmental psychologist. Although this instrument was first released for general distribution in 1969, various portions of it were used experimentally as research tools much earlier, and revisions were made along the way in accordance with the results of empirical data. This instrument's precursors, also devised by Bayley, date back to the 1930s (i.e., The California First-Year Mental Scale, The California Preschool Mental Scale, and The California Infant Scale of Motor Development). The latest refinement of the BSID consists of a Manual Supplement, published in 1984, that clarifies issues regarding its proper administration.

The BSID does not contain the term "intelligence" in its title, but along with instruments such as the Cattell Infant Intelligence Scale (CIIS; T3:381), the Griffiths Mental Development Scales (GMDS; 9:450), and the Užgiris-Hunt Scales of Infant Psychological Development (UHSIPD; 9:83), it is usually considered to be a major contemporary device for measuring what can be termed loosely as infant "intelligence." (The GMDS is relatively unknown in the United States, but it is quite popular in Great Britain. The UHSIPD, which approaches the measurement of cognitive development from a Piagetian framework, must still be viewed as an experimental device even though a manual describing the administration and interpretation of this scale, along with record forms, are being published commercially). Of the four scales mentioned, only the BSID and the CIIS are standardized instruments; the other two can be more appropriately described as criterion-referenced. In most cases, the BSID's chief competitor remains the CIIS. Hence, in order to evaluate the BSID, it is helpful to compare and contrast it with the CIIS.

The BSID consists of three parts, namely, the Mental Scale (163 items), the Motor Scale (81 items), and the Infant Behavior Record (30 items). Thus, with the BSID, a comprehensive assessment is possible. The Mental Scale deals with skills such as perception (i.e., responses to visual and auditory stimuli, discrimination of shapes), memory, learning (e.g., imitation), early verbal skills (e.g., naming objects), and rudimentary problem solving. The items forming the Motor Scale involve various fine motor (i.e., grasping objects) and gross motor abilities (i.e., sitting, standing, walking, climbing). In contrast to the Mental and Motor Scales, which are actual "tests" of performance, the Infant Behavior Record (IBR) is a "rating scale" that calls for a subjective evaluation of the infant by the examiner on personality/temperament variables such as attention span, persistence, endurance, activity level, etc. It is completed after the infant has left the test situation, the ratings being based on behaviors exhibited during the test situation.

Inclusion of the IBR in the BSID battery marks a noteworthy innovation in "intelligence" testing. According to some experts, at any age, the addition of personality to ability variables can significantly increase the percentages of explained variance in achievement. Furthermore, in the case of infants, the attributes tapped by the IBR may be complexly intertwined with how well the individual "performs" in a test situation. It is the opinion of a number of researchers that given our methods of assessment, infant intelligence is as much a function of motivational and affective factors as it is a function of purely cognitive factors. At the very least, consideration of the IBR may allow the psychologist to better judge whether the performance shown by the child on a particular day is an accurate reflection of his/her abilities.

The premise underlying the BSID is that there exists a progression in the maturation of the infant's abilities and that this pattern can be described normatively. The developmental period covered by the BSID is between 2 and 30 months of age. The items on the Mental and Motor Scales, arranged in order of difficulty from easiest to hardest, are identified by their normative age. The age placement of items is very precise, in tenths of a month. Procedures used to determine item selection and placement are well-defined and rigorous. The criterion was the point at which 50% of the infants of a particular chronological age could pass it. This procedure for item placement represents a more objective rationale than the one used in the construction of the CIIS.

The test materials come in a sturdy briefcase, large enough to resemble a suitcase. A majority of the materials necessary to administer and interpret the test are contained therein. Notable exceptions are the stairs and walking board, which must be built by someone experienced in carpentry according to the specifications contained in the Manual. The test materials are not only durable and washable, but they are objects that are contemporary and should be familiar to today's infants. Four of the test pieces (doll with detached head, sugar pellets, rabbit, yellow cubes) are small enough to pose a potential choking or ingestion hazard (Ridenour & Reid, 1983). Thus, the test administrator should not view them as "toys" (Bayley & Hunt, 1983) and he/she needs to be sure the child does not accidently get hold of these items outside of the specific test situation in which their use is necessitated. During the administration of the test item requiring these four pieces, the examiner needs to focus his/her attention to the ongoing activity. There is no special spot in the case for each specific test object, so unless one creates some sort of system for storage, locating the proper materials quickly may prove to be difficult. A helpful organizational feature that does exist is the color code on the test record form that refers the tester to the appropriate section of the manual. Because some stimuli are used for a number of different items, a similarly beneficial feature is the situation code, which allows one to group items based on the stimuli they require.

The directions in the Manual regarding the proper administration of the test are extensive and well-written, but the test is difficult to learn to give due to the large number of items, each one with specific instructions. The 1984 supplement to the Manual, while serving to make more explicit the administrative and scoring procedures for items that have been found to confuse both the novice and experienced psychometrician, at the same time also imposes an additional burden on one's memory because a person is forced to remember even more detailed directions.

Infant intelligence tests are inherently more difficult to score than similar tests geared for adults because a more subjective judgment is typically involved in deciding whether an item was passed or failed. The more precise guidelines and clarifications introduced in the supplement to the Manual should serve to further standardize the administration and scoring of the BSID. Considerable experience is still required, however, to become proficient with this instrument. To remain facile, one needs to administer it on more than just an occasional basis.

The order of presentation is flexible, although the Mental Scale is usually given first. According to the Manual, the typical amount of time needed to administer the BSID is about 45 minutes, although on a rare occasion testing can last as long as an hour and a half. Basal and ceiling items are established to keep the test session within reasonable limits. Clues as to where to begin testing are the situation codes and the age placements of the items. In inexperienced hands, however, the test session could easily become fatiguing to the infant. The comprehensive nature of the BSID also limits its suitability for screening purposes even with an experienced test administrator.

By providing ample space for making notes, the test protocol allows for a qualitative description of the infant's reactions to the test items. For each item, there are three standardized response options on the test protocol: Pass (P), Fail (F), and Other (O). Under the (O) column, the tester can use codes such as O-omit, R-refused, and RPT-reported by mother as being able to do. Only P items can be used to compute the actual scores, but the Other items, especially the RPT, can serve as some indication of the validity of a particular test session.

An infant's performance on the Mental and Motor Scales of the BSID is determined by summating the number of items that are passed on each scale into their respective raw scores. These raw scores are then converted into normalized standard scores reflecting the infant's standing relative to other infants of the same chronological age. The standard score derived from the Mental scale is named the Mental Developmental Index (MDI). Its counterpart on the Motor scale is called the Psychomotor Developmental Index (PDI). Both the MDI and the PDI, standardized to have a mean of 100 with a standard deviation of 16, have a possible range of scores from 50 to 150. In addition, a "mental age" equivalent is available for each raw score.

If the MDI or PDI falls below 50, it is necessary to consult the tables on age equivalents to get some estimate of the infant's level of development. The age equivalents have a particularly useful application in the evaluation of profoundly retarded individuals who, while they may fall outside the chronological age range covered by the test, nonetheless have such a limited repertoire of behaviors that it is best to assess them with an infant intelligence scale. It is worth mentioning that Naglieri (1981) presents extrapolated indices for developmental scores below 50, but as with the age equivalents, one needs to exercise care not to overinterpret their significance. This same caution applies even more to the practice of converting the age equivalents into ratio IQ-like scores by dividing the mental or motor age by the chronological age. At best, such scores can only be considered approximations. No standardized scores are provided for the Infant Behavior Record portion of the BSID, although the distribution of the ratings from the standardization sample is reported in the Manual.

The BSID was not designed to provide for a finer breakdown of functions beyond the general categories of mental and motor abilities, because Bayley maintains that in the first two years of life human abilities do not cluster into any neat, discrete factors. She believes that any grouping at this age range is strictly artificial or if real, limited to a very short age span. Nonetheless, a number of systems have been created by others to allow for a more detailed analysis of the infant's strengths and weaknesses. For example, with the Kohen-Raz (1966) scoring system, it is possible to further divide the Mental Scale into five subscales: (*a*) eye-hand coordination, (*b*) manipulation, (*c*) object relations/conceptual ability, (*d*) imitation-comprehension, and (*e*) vocalization-social. According to another system, presented in an article by Haskett and Bell (1978), the Mental Scale items can be subdivided into 13 categories. Perhaps because clinicians like to identify "strengths" and "weaknesses," they seem to prefer having items assessing similar abilities grouped together, as is done on the Wechsler Scales. Notably, even the new edition of the Stanford-Binet (S-B; 4th Edition) has abandoned its traditional format of grouping items by successive age levels, and now organizes the items into separate tests. Such subscores on the BSID may have some clinical significance, but one needs to be cautious in making decisions based on subscale profiles given their larger standard errors of measurement. More research on these systems is needed before the profiles they yield can be used with confidence.

While there have been attempts to break down the Mental and Motor Scales into a larger number of components, the converse has been occurring with respect to the IBR section of the BSID. Several systems have been proposed for research purposes. Matheny, Dolan, and Wilson (1974) subjectively group the items into two composites, "primary cognition" and "extraversion." Using the more objective methodology of factor analysis, Matheny (1980, 1983) reveals that it is possible to group the items into three stable factors: "task orientation," "task affect-extraversion," and "activity." On the basis of a principal-components analysis by McGowan, Johnson, and Maxwell (1981) the IBR can be divided into five sets of items.

The value of a standardized test ultimately rests on its ability to provide an accurate appraisal of the performance of a given individual on some variable relative to an appropriate comparison group. For this reason, it is extremely important for the test developer to identify a representative normative group when developing a standardized test. For infant tests, this is no easy task as there is no single source, like a public school, from which a representative sample may be drawn. Frequently, the samples used to norm infant tests are small and have a strong potential for bias. For example, the CIIS was standardized in the 1930s on only 274 children, mostly from a lower middle class neighborhood in Boston.

In this respect, the BSID stands in marked contrast. The standardization sample used to build the norms for it was large and seems to have been selected with the utmost of care to be representative of the population of the United States. The stratified (quota) sample of 1,262 children that was drawn by Bayley and her colleagues tried to control for sex, race, urban-rural residence, and parental educational and occupational level.

Upon close scrutiny, however, one finds that even this scale's norms are not above reproach. Participation in the norming of the BSID was voluntary, so as one would expect, there are certain discrepancies between the standardization group and the U.S. population circa 1960 (which Bayley tried to approximate). As Bayley acknowledges, her sample overrepresents infants from urban areas (87.6% in the sample compared to 69.2% in the general population).

Moreover, in terms of geographical region of residence, the sample overrepresents the West at all age levels, but especially after 18 months of age. Conversely, it underrepresented the South at all age levels. The Northeast is overrepresented between ages 2 and 15 months and underrepresented between 18 and 30 months. The educational level of the head of the household in the infant's family appears to be higher than in the general population. According to Bayley, though, these variables were not related to any significant differences on either the Mental or Motor Scales, other than for minor race differences on the Motor Scale at ages 3 through 14 months.

The reliability data presented in the BSID Manual are in the form of internal consistency, temporal stability, and interobserver agreement. Thus, it would appear that all possible means of gauging reliability have been considered. Unfortunately, these data deal only with the Mental and Motor Scales and do not provide any indication of the IBR's reliability.

The internal consistency aspect of the BSID's reliability was studied in the standardization sample through the split-half method, using raw scores as input and correcting for length differences with the Spearman-Brown formula. The split-half reliability coefficients for each of the 14 age groups were calculated, and as reported in the manual, they range from .81 to .93 (median of .88) on the Mental Scale and from .68 to .92 (median of .84) on the Motor Scale. Along with these reliability coefficients, the Manual presents the associated standard errors of measurement for each age as well as the differences between MDI and PDI scores that may be considered statistically significant at the 15% and 5% levels of confidence. This latter type of presentation of information about reliability should prove to be meaningful to the clinician on a practical level, and probably needs to be done more often in manuals.

According to the BSID Manual, the instrument's reliability from the perspective of interobserver agreement and temporal stability can be inferred using data collected on the immediate precursor to the current edition of the BSID (the 1958–60 version of the Mental and Motor Scales), which is said to be very similar to the present test. These statistics, based on an 8-month-old sample, are presented in the Manual in "percent agreement" form. The agreement between the tester and an observer in scoring each of a selected set of items (59 mental, 20 motor) for a sample of 90 infants was found to be, on average, about 89% (*SD* = 7%) on the Mental Scale and about 93% (*SD* = 3%) on the Motor Scale.

The test-retest information, also at the item level, was collected from a subsample of 28 of these same 90 infants, relying on the same 59 Mental Scale items and 20 Motor Scale items. The agreement between the two sets of scores administered 1 week apart was about 76% (*SD* = 14%) and 75% (*SD* = 15%) for the Mental and Motor Scales, respectively. These statistics are again quite respectable although it must be kept in mind that they are based on the BSID's predecessor rather than the new scale, that only one age group was studied, and that the index used to gauge reliability, namely "percent agreement," has been criticized by some authorities for failing to control for chance agreements.

Additional data about the BSID's reliability, not available in the Manual, have accumulated since the release of this instrument for commercial use. Various populations, age groups, items, intervals between testings, and statistical procedures for measuring degree of association have been considered in this literature.

A number of studies have involved disadvantaged minority groups. Spit-half reliability in a sample of firstborn black male infants from Harlem was studied by King and Seegmiller (1973), who reported coefficients (Mental/Motor) of .77/.75 at 14 months of age (*N* = 49); .89/.77 at 18 months of age (*N* = 34); and .84/.86 at 22 months of age (*N* = 32). Bayley did not study internal consistency reliability at 14 months of age, so a direct comparison is not possible, but at 18 and 22 months of age, their estimates are similar. Also presented in this study are the test-retest correlation coefficients at these three ages. For the 27 subjects who were available for all three test sessions, the MDI correlations were .62 between the 14-month and 18-month sessions, .70 between the 18-month and 22-month sessions, and .57 between 14-month and 22-month sessions. The corresponding correlations between the PMI scores were lower, namely .17, .38, and .42. The 1-year stability of the MDI between ages 6 months and 18 months in another sample of disadvantaged black infants was lower, .27 (Yeates, MacPhee, Campbell, & Ramey, 1983). Data from an article by McGowan, Johnson, and Maxwell (1981) show that the MDI scores of Mexican-American infants from low SES backgrounds correlated .47 for males ($N = 64$) and .54 for females ($N = 61$) between administrations conducted 1 year apart (at ages 12 and 24 months).

Horner (1980) examined the test-retest reliability of the BSID in a sample of 48 normal, primarily white, full term babies divided evenly between 9-month-olds and 15-month-olds. They were tested twice, about 7 days apart on the two occasions, with the one session being held at the infant's house and the other in a clinic. The item reliabilities from Horner's study, which used the actual BSID rather than its immediate precursor, are somewhat better than those cited in the Manual. The average 1-week test-retest item reliability of the Mental Scale for both the 9-month-olds and the 15-month-olds was 85%. Test-retest reliability of the total scores from the Mental Scale, computed in terms of Pearson correlations and broken down by the infant's age-sex, ranged between .42 (9-month-old females) and .96 (15-month-old females). Ruddy and Bornstein (1982) report that for a sample of infants ($N = 20$) born to middle-class college-educated parents, the correlation between a BSID at age 4 months and age 12 months is .47.

Other researchers (DuBose, 1977; Haskett & Bell, 1978; Maisto & German, 1986; Mastropieri, 1987; Siegel, 1981; Whiteley & Krann, 1986; Wilson & Harping, 1972) have provided information on reliability with various populations. The available data on the reliability of the BSID can best be summarized in the following terms. Considered in the context of other individual tests for infants and preschoolers, the reliability of the BSID equals or is better than that of the other tests of its genre. The internal consistency and interobserver agreement estimates of reliability are acceptable for an instrument designed for use in making decisions about individual cases, however, few studies find the BSID's reliability to be comparable with cognitive tests designed for children or adults in terms of test-retest reliability. The problem may not be with the test itself, however. Infants are quite volatile, and their performance is easily affected by daily fluctuations in mood, attention, etc. Furthermore, research seems to indicate that the rate of development is quite erratic in infancy, not really stabilizing until age 3 years. The test-retest reliability on the BSID, like all cognitive measures in infancy, improves progressively with increasing age. When used with mentally retarded persons, it has greater stability among the more impaired individuals.

The Manual accompanying the BSID presents surprisingly sparse information about the instrument's validity, especially in view of the immense effort that went into the development of the test materials and the norms. It would seem, based on the information in the Manual, that only a single form of validity, namely concurrent, was examined and that only one study was conducted. In that study, MDI scores were compared to IQ scores from the Stanford-Binet (S-B), Form L-M in a sample of 24-month-old ($N = 22$), 27-month-old ($N = 41$), and 30-month-old ($N = 57$) children residing in California who were able to reach the basal level on the S-B. These 120 children were part of an original sample of 350 and represent the upper half of the distribution of talent (which could potentially limit the generalizability of the results). The correlation between the two instruments was .53 for the 24-month-olds, .64 for the 27-month-olds, .47 for the 30-month-olds, and .57 when the subjects are considered in toto. These correlations are modest, but as Bayley observes, they would probably have been higher were it not for the restriction in the range of scores that were included in the study. There is no mention in the Manual of any validation studies of the Motor Scale. Neither does the Manual discuss the validity of the IBR per se. Generally, IBR behaviors show correlations with the Mental Scale in the .20s to .40s. Items dealing with coordination, activity level, and attention appear to differentiate between neurologically-impaired and normal subjects. However, Bayley suggests that further research is needed before we can tell if the IBR can serve as a predictor of later mental ability.

Bayley believes that the BSID, like all infant scales, should be used principally to assess current levels of behavior, and she does not see attempts to demonstrate the BSID's predictive validity (of later intelligence) to be of much relevance (see also, Pease, Wolins, & Stockdale, 1973). In fact, she purposely avoided using the term "intelligence" in the title of the BSID, claiming that the instrument is a measure of "developmental status," but this may be skirting the issue because she fails to define the term developmental status explicitly in the Manual and she attempts to demonstrate the validity of the BSID by correlating it with the S-B, an acknowledged measure of intelligence.

While Bayley reports on the relationship between her test and the S-B only at the age in which the two tests overlap, the professional literature has served as a conduit for a more extensive body of information about the validity of the BSID. Studies published in the academic literature deal not only with validity per se, but also with factors and test situations which may compromise the BSID's validity. Interestingly, despite Bayley's lack of interest in questions regarding the BSID's usefulness for the prediction of future intelligence, considerable effort seems to have been devoted by others to an examination of this issue, perhaps because a primary reason for assessing the infant's current level of general ability in the first place involves some sort of concern regarding the infant's potential (see Berk, 1979; Broman, Nichols, & Kennedy, 1975; Goffeney, Henderson, & Butler, 1971; Maisto & German, 1986; Ramey & Smith, 1977; Rubin & Balow, 1979; Siegel, 1981; VanderVeer & Schweid, 1974; Yeates, et al., 1983).

In general the BSID is not a good predictor of future intelligence with normal infants. Its predictive power is better at the upper age range encompassed by the scale and is good for impaired infants.

Some work has also been done that allows one to gauge the construct validity of the BSID. Because the BSID is constructed on a developmental model, an age differentiation criterion can be used to infer the test's validity. In this vein, it can be noted that for premature infants, there exists a high degree of association (r = .72–.82) between gestational age and MDI scores determined on chronological age (Hunt & Rhodes, 1977). In nonambulatory profoundly mentally retarded persons who are above the chronological age range of the instrument, the frequency with which the 45 "mat" items on the Mental Scale are passed corresponds to the age placements of these items (Whiteley & Krenn, 1986), which is some evidence for the correctness of item placement.

Although the relative difficulty of the items may be similar in normal infants and nonambulatory, profoundly retarded children and adults, there seems to be some difference in the factor structure of the BSID in normal full-term infants compared to pre-term infants who are delayed in development (Lasky, Tyson, Rosenfield, Priest, Krasinski, Heartwell, & Gant, 1983). A principal component analysis of the BSID, given 92 weeks postconception, reveals considerable agreement between the item composition in the pre-term and full-term babies (congruence coefficient of .75), but while the first principal component accounted for 27% of the total variance in the former, it only accounted for 16% in the latter. Moreover, more of the items loaded on the first principal component in the pre-term group. In essence, these results indicate that for the pre-term infants (considered high-risk), the responses are intercorrelated to a greater extent than in the normal, full-term babies (which perhaps explains the greater temporal stability of the BSID in impaired groups).

The Manual presents a table listing the correlation between the Mental and Motor Scales in terms of both raw scores and standard scores at each age level. The range of correlations is .24–.78 for the raw scores and .18–.75 for the standard scores. In both instances, the median correlation is .46, and there is some tendency for the degree of association to decrease with increasing age, although the pattern is erratic, due perhaps to sample-specific variance. Reports on the correlation between the Mental and Motor Scales have been made by other investigators (e.g., Gottfried & Brody, 1975; King & Seegmiller, 1973; Wilson & Harping, 1972), and such studies appear to support the clearer differentiation between mental and motor skills with increasing age. There is evidence to suggest that at the earlier ages even the Mental Scale is heavily dependent on motor skills (Gottfried & Brody, 1975). Some instances of low degrees of association between the Mental and Motor Scales can be found even at the earliest ages covered by the BSID, but they can perhaps be best attributed to the instability of the correlation coefficient based on small samples (e.g., Sostek & Anders [1977] computed a correlation of .27 at 10 weeks in a sample of 18 infants being placed for adoption).

Investigations of the relative merits of the Mental and the Motor Scales suggest that the Mental Scale may be more prognostic of later status among normal infants, and that it becomes an increasingly better predictor with progressing age (King & Seegmiller, 1973; Ramey, Campbell, & Nicholson, 1973).

Increasingly, the BSID is emerging as the standard by which the validity of other measures is judged. Examples of this include efforts to validate such scales as Brazelton's Neonatal Behavioral Assessment Scale (Vaughn, Taraldson, Crichton, & Egeland, 1980); The Minnesota Child Development Inventory (Saylor & Brandt, 1986); The Mental Development Scales: Birth to Three Years (Wagner, 1983); The Home Observation for Measurement of Environment (Bradley & Caldwell, 1981); the Kent Infant Development Scale (Stancin, Reuter, Dunn, & Bickett, 1984); and the revision of the Denver Developmental Screening Test (German, Williams, Herzfeld, & Marshall, 1982).

Situational factors impacting on the validity of the BSID that should be noted by examiners include maternal presence during testing (Haskins, Ramey, Stedman, Blacker-Dixon, & Pierce, 1978), and perhaps familiarity with the setting in which testing takes place (Durham & Black, 1978), both of which appear to result in higher scores. Repeated testing every 3 months between ages 4 and 28 months does not appear to create any sort of biasing effect on subsequent BSID scores or on the S-B given at 31 months of age (Haskins, et al., 1978).

The BSID has generated a very impressive body of research since its publication. This data base is much more extensive than the one for the CIIS even though the CIIS has been in existence for a longer time. Given the current emphasis on intervention at earlier ages and the present popularity of the BSID, the volume of research in which the BSID is somehow involved should continue to grow. Even if these new studies do not have as their primary focus an investigation of the BSID's psychometric properties, evidence regarding the BSID's measurement qualities will be a likely by-product.

Because of the space limitations, only the more critical findings from the existing research literature could be mentioned in this review. After consideration of all the data available at this point, it is only appropriate to conclude that the BSID is the premier instrument in its category. An examination of this test and its accompanying materials gives one an appreciation of the painstaking work that went into its development. The statistical data in the Manual have been supplemented extensively by other research, and it can now be said that the BSID has psychometric integrity. The lack of temporal stability is troubling because one tends to think of intelligence as a relatively constant and enduring characteristic, but this problem is common to all scales purporting to measure infant intelligence and appears to be due to factors within the organism rather than the scale. The BSID can be used with confidence to assess the infant's current level of development and appears to have considerable value in the early identification of infants at risk for mental impairments, but it is much less useful in the prediction of subsequent cognitive ability in infants scoring within the normal range of ability. Nonetheless, there is some evidence to suggest that considered in conjunction with measures of socio-environmental circumstances, it may even be appropriate for the latter application.

REVIEWER'S REFERENCES

Kohen-Raz, R. (1966). The ring-cube test: A brief time sampling method for assessing primary development of coordinated bilateral grasp responses in infancy. *Perceptual and Motor Skills*, 23, 675-688.

Goffeney, B., Henderson, N. B., & Butler, B. V. (1971). Negro-white, male-female eight-month developmental scores compared with seven-year WISC and Bender test scores. *Child Development*, 42, 595-604.

Wilson, R. S., & Harping, E. B. (1972). Mental and motor development in infant twins. *Developmental Psychology*, 7, 277-287.

King, W. L., & Seegmiller, B. (1973). Performance of 14 to 22 month old black, firstborn male infants on two tests of cognitive development: The Bayley Scales and the Infant Psychological Development Scale. *Developmental Psychology*, 8, 317-326.

Pease, D., Wolins, L., & Stockdale, D. F. (1973). Relationship and prediction of infant tests. *Journal of Genetic Psychology*, 122, 31-35.

Ramey, C. T., Campbell, F. A., & Nicholson, J. E. (1973). The predictive power of the Bayley Scales of Infant Development and the Stanford-Binet Intelligence Test in a relatively constant environment. *Child Development*, 44, 790-795.

VanderVeer, B., & Schweid, E. (1974). Infant asessment: Stability of mental functioning in young retarded children. *American Journal of Mental Deficiency*, 79, 1-14.

Broman, S. H., Nichols, P. L., & Kennedy, W. A. (1975). *Preschool IQ: Prenatal and early developmental correlates*. Hillsdale, NJ: Lawrence Erlbaum Associates.

Gottfried, A. W., & Brody, D. (1975). Interrelationships between and correlates of psychometric and Piagetian scales of sensorimotor intelligence. *Developmental Psychology*, 11, 379-387.

Matheny, A. P., Jr., Dolan, A. B., & Wilson, R. S. (1976). Within-pair similarity on Bayley's Infant Behavior Record. *Journal of Genetic Psychology*, 128, 263-270.

DuBose, R. F. (1977). Predictive value of infant intelligence scales with multiply handicapped children. *American Journal of Mental Deficiency*, 8, 388-390.

Hunt, J. V., & Rhodes, L. (1977). Mental development of preterm infants during the first year. *Child Development*, 48, 204-210.

Ramey, C. T., & Smith, B. J. (1977). Assessing the intellectual consequences of early intervention with high risk infants. *American Journal of Mental Deficiency*, 81, 318-324.

Sostek, A. M., & Anders, T. F. (1977). Relationships among the Brazelton Neonatal Scale, Bayley Infant Scales, and early temperament. *Child Development*, 48, 320-323.

Durham, M., & Black, K. N. (1978). The test performances of 16–21-month-olds in home and laboratory. *Infant Behavior and Development*, 1, 216-223.

Haskett, J., & Bell, J. (1978). Profound developmental retardation: Descriptive and theoretical utility of the Bayley Mental Scale. In C. E. Meyers (Ed.), *Quality of life in severely and profoundly mentally retarded people* (pp. 327-352). Washington, DC: American Association on Mental Deficiency.

Haskins, R., Ramey, C. T., Stedman, D. J., Blacker-Dixon, J., & Pierce, J. E. (1978). Effects of repeated assessment on standardized performance by infants. *American Journal of Mental Deficiency*, 83, 233-239.

Berk, R. A. (1979). The discriminative efficiency of the Bayley Scales of Infant Development. *Journal of Abnormal Child Psychology*, 7, 113-119.

Rubin, R. A., & Balow, B. (1979). Measures of infant development and socioeconomic status as predictors of later intelligence and school achievement. *Developmental Psychology*, 15, 225-227.

Horner, T. M. (1980). Test-retest and home-clinic characteristics of the Bayley Scales of Infant Development in nine- and fifteen-month-old infants. *Child Development*, 51, 751-758.

Matheny, A. P., Jr. (1980). Bayley's Infant Behavior Record: Behavioral components and twin analyses. *Child Development*, 51, 1157-1167.

Vaughn, B. E., Taraldson, B., Crichton, L., & Egeland, B. (1980). Relationships between neonatal behavioral organization and infant behavior during the first year of life. *Infant Behavior & Development*, 3, 47-66.

Bradley, R. H., & Caldwell, B. M. (1981). Home environment and infant social behavior. *Infant Mental Health Journal*, 2, 18-22.

McGowan, R. J., Johnson, D. L., & Maxwell, S. E. (1981). Relations between infant behavior ratings and concurrent and subsequent mental test scores. *Developmental Psychology*, 17, 542-553.

Naglieri, J. A. (1981). Extrapolated developmental indices for the Bayley Scales of Infant Development. *American Journal of Mental Deficiency*, 85, 548-550.

Siegel, L. S. (1981). Infant tests as predictors of cognitive and language development at two years. *Child Development*, 52, 545-557.

German, M. L., Williams, E., Herzfeld, J., & Marshall, R. M. (1982). Utility of the revised Denver Developmental Screening Test and the Developmental Profile II in identifying preschool children with cognitive, language, and motor problems. *Education & Training of the Mentally Retarded*, 17, 319-324.

Ruddy, M. G., & Bornstein, M. H. (1982). Cognitive correlates of infant attention and maternal stimulation over the first year of life. *Child Development*, 53, 183-188.

Bayley, N., & Hunt, J. V. (1983). Are test materials toys? A reply to Ridenour and Reid. *Perceptual and Motor Skills*, 57, 1270.

Lasky, R. E., Tyson, J. E., Rosenfeld, C. R., Priest, M., Krasinski, D., Heartwell, S., & Gant, N. F. (1983). Principal component analyses of the Bayley Scales of Infant Development for a sample of high-risk infants and their controls. *Merrill-Palmer Quarterly*, 29, 25-31.

Matheny, A. P., Jr. (1983). A longitudinal twin study of stability of components from Bayley's Infant Behavior Record. *Child Development*, 54, 356-360.

Ridenour, M. V., & Reid, M. (1983). Inspection of the Bayley Mental Scale test materials for potential hazards of choking, aspiration, and ingestion when used outside of test situation. *Perceptual and Motor Skills*, 57, 1077-1078.

Wagner, B. S. (1983). Reliability, scalability, and validity of an instrument to assess developmental levels of children from birth to three years of age. *Psychological Reports*, 52, 217-218.

Yeates, K. O., MacPhee, D., Campbell, F. A., & Ramey, C. T. (1983). Maternal IQ and home environment as determinants of early childhood intellectual competence: A developmental analysis *Developmental Psychology*, 19, 731-739. .

Stancin, T., Reuter, J., Dunn, V., & Bickett, L. (1984). Validity of caregiver information on the developmental status of severely brain-damaged young children. *American Journal of Mental Deficiency*, 88, 388-395.

Maisto, A. A., & German, M. L. (1986). Reliability, predictive validity, and interrelationships of early assessment indices used with developmentally delayed infants and children. *Journal of Clinical Child Psychology*, 15, 327-332.

Saylor, C. F., & Brandt, B. J. (1986). The Minnesota Child Development Inventory: A valid maternal-report form for assessing development in infancy. *Journal of Developmental & Behavioral Pediatrics*, 7, 308-311.

Whiteley, J. H., & Krenn, M. J. (1986). Uses of the Bayley Mental Scale with nonambulatory profoundly mentally retarded children. *American Journal of Mental Deficiency*, 90, 425-431.

Mastropieri, M. A. (1987). Age at start as a correlate of intervention effectiveness. *Psychology in the Schools*, 24, 59-62.

Review of the Bayley Scales of Infant Development by JANE A. RYSBERG, Associate Professor of Psychology, California State University, Chico, CA:

To open a Bayley Scales of Infant Development (BSID) suitcase is to view a piece of psychological history. Some of the items from the Mental Scale, for example, "prolonged regard of the red ring," appeared in the 1933 California First Year Mental Scale, and were actually conceptualized when Dr. Bayley was a graduate student at the University of Washington, 1922 to 1924 (Coe, 1987).

This is not to suggest that the Bayley should be honored as a mere relic. There is a great need today for instruments to assess the development of infants and very young children. This need reflects both an awareness of the importance of the earliest segment of life, and the existence of early educational and therapeutic facilities, particularly for high-risk infants.

THE TEST SETTING. There are few other developmental instruments for children under 2 1/2 years of age. Some of the available tests, for example the Kent Infant Development Scale (2 to 13 months), depend upon parental report, whereas the Bayley is a behavioral performance measure. Few infant scales exist, partly because of the nature of early childhood. Children under 2 years of age do not reliably respond to instructions to solve a problem; they respond where reflex or interest takes them. The Bayley is a progressive series of tasks novel enough to be motivating, yet similar enough to daily experience (e.g., the manipulation of balls, cups, and books) to be comfortable.

Typically parents remain in the testing area to make the experience a calm and natural one for the infant. Parents are usually very interested in the results of interactions between their child and a diagnostic professional. The format of the Bayley makes providing feedback to caregivers very easy. Three aspects of infant development are assessed by the Bayley. These are motor skills (Psychomotor Development Index, PDI), mental ability (Mental Development Index, MDI), and social and attitudinal orientations (Infant Behavior Record, IBR). The PDI and the MDI permit easy comparisons with the performance of age-mates. It is also possible to make estimates of the effective level of functioning. It is not necessary to discuss "intelligence," which may be misunderstood by parents and professionals alike. Examples from specific test items can illustrate for caregivers the performance difficulties of the child, for example, lack of wrist rotation or selective listening.

THE MANUAL. The Bayley kit contains 39 items and item sets. The manual includes four pages on how to build additional apparatus. The manual is appropriately hefty, containing all the necessary information for the manipulation of this large array of materials. The administration and scoring information is very well written and comprehensive, even providing suggestions on furniture placement and rapport building. The Bayley is a complex test to administer. Experienced testers will need to return frequently to the manual and its supplement lest their techniques become too casual.

PSYCHOMETRIC CHARACTERISTICS. A correlation of .57 was found between the MDI and the Stanford-Binet IQ for 120 children between 24 and 30 months of age. This is the only validity study cited. The lack of validity statistics is not an oversight, but a direct result of the premise of the Bayley. The BSID was designed to "provide the basis for establishing a child's current status, and thus the extent of any deviation from normal expectancy."

Split-half reliability estimates are presented. Coefficients are available for 14 age groups. For the Mental scale, the figures range from .81 to .93 (median = .88) and for the Motor scale, from .68 to .92 (median = .84). In addition, standard errors of measurement were computed for this data set, and range from 4.2 to 6.9 and 4.6 to 9.0, respectively.

Tester-observer and test-retest reliabilities were calculated for the 1958–1960 version for the Mental and Motor scales. The authors stated the current Bayley is so similar to the original in content and procedures the reliabilities are still relevant.

The standardization sample was composed of between 83 and 95 children at each month level from 2 to 30, approximately equally divided between males and females. The 1,262 children of the sample came from households that conformed to the distribution of head-of-household variables described by the 1960 United States census. No significant differences emerged on either the MDI or the PDI in relation to the census variables, except for a persistent superiority of black children between 3 and 14 months on the PDI.

The almost 30-year-old norms are problematic. The present Bayley manual and kit date from 1969. A manual supplement was added in 1984, with a primary purpose of amplifying the administration and scoring information found in the original. The meticulously collected standardization sample conformed to the 1960 census figures. In 1960, 29.2% of Americans graduated from high school. In December 1986, the California Postsecondary Education Commission reported that 85% of Americans had completed 12 years of education, with 48% having some college. In 1960 only 10.2% of the population had completed some college. Standardization, on the order originally done for the Bayley, is a Herculean undertaking and may result in no changes to the test. However, dramatic changes in the basic descriptions of the American people may warrant such an undertaking.

CONCLUSION. The Bayley Scales of Infant Development is a superbly crafted behavioral assessment instrument for children between birth and 30 months. Test specialists, such as Sattler (1982) and Anastasi (1982) rate the BSID as the best test in its category. The Bayley was once almost the only test of infant development. Recent entries, such as the Kaufman Infant and Preschool Scale, have not seriously challenged the leadership of the Bayley.

REVIEWER'S REFERENCES

Bayley, N. (1933). *The California first year mental scale.* University of California Syllabus Series, No. 243.

Anastasi, A. (1982). *Psychological testing,* (5th ed.). New York: Macmillan Publishing Co., Inc.

Sattler, J. M. (1982). *Assessment of children's intelligence and special abilities,* (2nd ed.). Boston: Allyn and Bacon.

Coe, A. (1987). Nancy Bayley: A brief biography. *SRCD Newsletter,* Spring 1987, 1-2.

[27]

Behavior Rating Profile. Purpose: "An ecological approach to behavioral assessment." Ages 6-6 through 18-6 and/or grades 1–12; 1978–83; BRP; ratings by student, teacher, parents, and peers; 5 checklists: Student Rating Scales (Home, School, Peer), Teacher Rating Scale, Parent Rating Scale, and 1 Sociogram score; scales may be administered in any order, separately or in combination with any of the other scales; 1987 price data: $72 per complete kit including 50 each of Teacher, Parent, and Student rating forms, 50 profile sheets, and examiner's manual ('83, 48 pages); $19 per 50 student rating forms (4 pages); $13 per 50 teacher rating forms (2 pages); $13 per 50 parent rating forms (2 pages); $13 per 50 profile forms (2 pages); $19 per examiner's manual; Spanish version (Perfil de Evaluacion del Comportamiento, '82) available; (15–30) minutes; Linda L. Brown and Donald D. Hammill; PRO-ED, Inc.*

For reviews by Thomas R. Kratochwill and Joseph C. Witt, see 9:130 (1 reference); see also T3:273 (1 reference).

TEST REFERENCES

1. Slate, N. M. (1983). Nonbiased assessment of adaptive behavior: Comparison of three instruments. *Exceptional Children,* 50, 67-70.

2. Nunn, G. D. (1987). Concurrent validity between children's locus of control and attitudes toward home, school, and peers. *Educational and Psychological Measurement,* 47 (4), 1087-1089.

Review of the Behavior Rating Profile by ELLEN H. BACON, Assistant Professor of Special Education, Western Carolina University, Cullowhee, NC:

The Behavior Rating Profile (BRP) provides the user with information about a target student's behavior from four sources: the teacher, the parents, the target student, and the student's peers. The teacher and the parent rating scales contain 30 descriptions of problem behaviors rated by respondents in four categories from *Very much like my child or student* to *Not at all like my child or student.* The Student Rating Scale asks students to complete 60 true-false items describing their behaviors at home, in school, and with peers. The fourth component is a Sociogram. The student's classroom peers are asked to answer questions indicating their preferences among classmates.

ADMINISTRATION AND SCORING. The BRP is easy to administer and score, yielding standard scores that can be charted on a profile indicating average, above average, and below average ratings on problem behaviors. The Sociogram is an exception. Scoring the sociogram is complicated and interpretation may be difficult. Another positive feature is that users are encouraged to obtain ratings from several teachers and from both parents and to chart all scores on the student's profile. However, many of the items may be difficult for respondents to rate because behavioral language is not used and terms are not defined. Guidelines for assessing frequency of occurrence, recency, duration, and intensity of behaviors are not provided. Scores are changed easily to standard scores and percentiles, but standard error of measurement and confidence intervals are not readily available.

ITEM SELECTION AND STANDARDIZATION. The Behavior Rating Profile was standardized on a sample of 1,966 students, 955 teachers, and 1,232 parents. The description of the demographic characteristics in the manual provides information to demonstrate the standardization sample is representative of the U.S. population and provides sufficient information for users to determine if the population is representative of their community. Unfortunately, no information is presented on the development of scaled scores and percentiles for the Sociogram. It is unclear why Sociogram data are not provided.

The items for the BRP were selected by examination of other behavior checklists and by analyzing written descriptions that parents and teachers made of children with behavior problems. A large pool of items was reduced by use of item analysis. Although the manual describes careful development of the scales, one area of student behavior not assessed in the BRP is depression and unhappiness (McCarney, 1984).

Reliability of the BRP is argued on the basis of test-retest reliability and internal consistency using coefficient alpha. Coefficient alphas, calculated at five different grade levels, indicate the test is sufficiently internally consistent to be used as a screening instrument. Parent rating scales range from .82 to .91, Teacher Rating

Scales range from .87 to .98, and Student Rating Scales range from .74 to .87. Test-retest reliability was evaluated on 36 normal high school students with coefficients ranging from .78 to .91. This measure of stability was evaluated also with 17 emotionally disturbed adolescents with coefficients ranging from .76 to .81. No information on test-retest reliability at the elementary school level is provided.

The standard error of measurement (*SEM*) is given at five grade levels. The manual describes how an examiner might use *SEM* to determine the confidence interval for a student's score. However, the authors must report *SEM*s for all grades at several score levels. This is especially important for those scores indicating behavior outside of the normal range (AERA, APA, NCME, 1985).

The Behavior Rating Profile does not provide any evidence of interrater reliability. Filling out the checklists requires a number of judgments to be made by teachers and parents. No explanation or clarification of items is provided in the manual. Teachers make judgments based on their own personal standards on such items as "is lazy" and "has unacceptable personal habits." Parents also must make subjective judgments on whether they consider their child lazy, shy, or self-centered. Given the lack of clearly defined behaviors, the authors need to make a strong case for interrater reliability (AERA, APA, NCME, 1985).

The authors present evidence for three types of validity. For content validity, they refer to the extensive item selection and item analysis procedures. For criterion-related validity, the manual lists the correlations of each subtest score with the Walker Problem Behavior Identification Checklist, the Quay Peterson Behavior Problem Checklist, and the Vineland Social Maturity Scale. Four groups were compared: a normal group, an institutionalized emotionally disturbed group, a public school emotionally disturbed group, and a public school learning disabled group. The manual lists significant correlations between the Behavior Rating Profile and the three other measures for 64 of 72 comparisons. Of these groups the relationship between the Behavior Rating Profile and other behavior checklists was weakest for the public school emotionally disturbed group.

Construct validity is demonstrated by high intercorrelations (median .81, range .49–.96) between subtests for the four groups. The manual also reports a study to determine whether the BRP discriminates among groups of students. The results demonstrated that normal children had fewer behavior problems than handicapped children and that institutionalized emotionally disturbed students had the most problem behaviors. However, the BRP ratings by parents and teachers did not discriminate between learning disabled and emotionally handicapped students.

Another finding of the construct-validity study was that children rated themselves highest, parents rated their children lowest, and teachers produced intermediate ratings. This result was reported also by Reisburg, Fudell, and Hudson (1982) with the additional finding that regular class teachers rated students more positively than special class teachers. These results should be considered in interpreting discrepancies and patterns in rating scales so that what may be a systematic bias in the ratings is not overly interpreted as meaningful for an individual student.

On the student rankings for home, school, and peers, the students in the public school handicapped groups of emotionally disturbed and learning disabled ranked themselves as not having problem behaviors out of the average range. Institutionalized emotionally disturbed groups fell slightly below average. A question must be raised about the validity of the student scales if public school learning disabled and emotionally disturbed students rate themselves as having only an average number of behavior problems when parents and teachers rate them as having a greater than average number of problems.

These data indicate the BRP can discriminate between students who are handicapped and nonhandicapped, but does not provide evidence the instrument can be used to discriminate between students who have behavioral or emotional problems and those who have learning problems. The BRP should be used only as a screening instrument to obtain information on a student's problems from a variety of settings and perspectives. It is not the best instrument to diagnose or describe a student's behavior problems.

SUMMARY. The BRP has the unique advantage of offering rating scales for parents and teachers, a sociogram for assessing problems with peers, and a checklist for measuring the student's perception of his or her home, school, and peer group. The BRP is easy to use and score. Development of the items and norms are adequately described. Internal reliability and test-retest coefficients are good but no interrater reliability is reported. This is a critical shortcoming as many items are not descriptions of behavior, but require the rater to make subjective judgments on ambiguous terms without guidelines as to frequency, intensity, or duration. The inclusion of nonbehavioral items limits the use of the instrument in helping teachers focus on behaviors to change, and makes interpreting the scores needlessly difficult.

If users are seeking a behavior rating scale to aid in identification and diagnosis of behaviorally and emotionally handicapped students, they should consider the Behavior Evaluation Scale by McCarney, Leigh, and Cornbleet (1983). This scale lists specific behaviors that can be used as objectives in school and behavioral programs. This scale also offers guidelines for raters as to frequency, duration, and intensity. However, if an evaluator needs to compare perceptions concerning a child across different settings, the Behavior Rating Profile would be a good choice. Additional evaluation will be necessary if users must distinguish between students who have learning problems and those who have emotional problems.

REVIEWER'S REFERENCES

Reisberg, L. E., Fudell, I., & Hudson, F. (1982). Comparison of responses to the Behavior Rating Profile for mild to moderate behaviorally disordered subjects. *Psychological Reports*, 50, 136-138.

McCarney, S. B., Leigh, J. E., & Cornbleet, J. A. (1983). *The Behavior Evaluation Scale*. Columbia, MO: Educational Services.

McCarney, S. B. (1984). *The Behavior Evaluation Scale*. Columbia, MO: University of Missouri. (ERIC Document Reproduction Service No. ED244 460).

American Educational Research Association, American Psychological Association, & National Council on Measurement in Education. (1984). *Standards for educational and psychological testing*. Washington, DC: American Psychological Association, Inc.

Review of the Behavior Rating Profile by C. DALE POSEY, Licensed Psychologist, C. M. E. Psychology Consultants, Boca Raton, FL:

The Behavior Rating Profile (BRP) was designed to provide a measure of a child's behavior in different environments based upon reports from multiple respondents. The environments include home and school, and the respondents include parents, teachers, peers, and the student in question. There are several existing scales measuring each of these respondent perceptions and environments, but this is the first published scale to incorporate them all into one measure. This is a worthy task, and one which, if properly executed, could provide a useful and economical tool for professionals interested in the treatment of children with behavior problems.

The BRP was standardized on a sample of almost 2,000 students. The national sample was relatively representative of the general population in terms of demographic variables. An attempt was made to select a wide range of items from existing inventories and checklists and from anecdotal reports of parents and teachers. The 120 items retained for the scales demonstrated a high degree of internal consistency.

Reliability studies are reported based upon 2-week retesting intervals, standard errors of measurement, and internal consistency. In general, the scales were shown to be fairly consistent over short intervals. The scales were also found to have high internal consistency and a relatively small amount of variance attributable to error. Thus, the BRP appears to measure one dimension in a relatively consistent manner.

The test authors examine criterion-related validity by correlating the BRP with other well-known behavior rating scales. In general, significant correlations were obtained for both normal groups and children with emotional and learning problems.

Construct validity was investigated by obtaining the intercorrelations of the scales of the BRP. The scale scores obtained from different respondents and from the child regarding different environments demonstrated a relatively high degree of intercorrelation, ranging from .49 to .96; the highest correlation was with the child's rating of his or her school behavior and the teacher's rating of the child.

A study was performed to investigate the ability of the BRP to differentiate known groups of children. Normal children had fewer problem behaviors on every measure, while institutionalized children with emotional problems had the most problem behaviors on each of the scales. Children with learning problems and children with behavior problems in school were roughly equivalent on the BRP.

The authors assert that face validity and content validity are the same. This erroneous conclusion points out one of the limitations of the instrument. There is no reported attempt to choose items based upon a complete sampling of the domain of possible problem behaviors. As a result, well over half of the items on all of the scales pertain to antisocial behavior. The remaining items sample depressive characteristics, withdrawal, poor academic performance, and anxiety symptoms. In order for a child to score high on the scales, however, the predominant behavior pattern would almost have to be antisocial acting out. Thus, while the items appear to be quite face valid, content saturation does not appear to have been achieved.

Another shortcoming of the BRP is the direction in which the items are keyed. On every item, pathological behavior is indicated by *true* (for the student scales) and *very much like* the child (for parent and teacher ratings). Thus the scales are all vulnerable to response sets such as denial or exaggeration of pathology.

The BRP yields six scores: a teacher rating, a parent rating, the child's rating of her or his behavior at school, home, and with peers, and a score derived from classroom sociometric ratings. Thus there are six different perspectives regarding one aspect of the child: behavior. As broadly based as this dimension is, all one can really say about a child from the BRP is that he or she behaves appropriately or inappropriately according to several significant people. This information could be accessed by asking the respondents a question about the child. No particular insight is gained as to the types of behaviors the child is exhibiting. There is little diagnostic utility in this one bit of information. Thus, more multidimensional scales such as the Devereux, Burkes, and Walker behavior scales are more useful.

In summary, the BRP is a well-constructed inventory of behavior as assessed in different situations from the point of view of different respondents. Reliability appears to have been demonstrated, and with the exception of content validity, the scales appear to be valid indices of inappropriate behavior. The scale is of limited utility, however, due to its unidimensionality and vulnerability to the effects of response bias. Perhaps the authors will revise the scales at some point with the inclusion of factor analytic studies and multiple dimensions of behavior. These revisions would likely improve the BRP.

[28]

Behaviordyne Retirement Service. Purpose: "Designed to help you plan for a satisfying retirement." Pre-retirees and people in retirement; 1982–85; BRS; 5 areas: Leisure, Health, Housing, Finances, Legal Issues; 1983 price data: $25 per test including report ('85, 161 pages) and scoring service; (30) minutes; John H. Lewis; Behaviordyne, Inc.*

[This service has been temporarily withdrawn; the Editor has been informed that it will be reintroduced after revision, at a later date.]

Review of the Behaviordyne Retirement Service by CAMERON J. CAMP, Associate Professor of Psychology, University of New Orleans, New Orleans, LA:

The Behaviordyne Retirement Service (BRS) consists of a computer-scored questionnaire, which has 100 statements such as "Most retirement villages are occupied by people with small incomes." Each of these statements is judged to be "true," "false," or "don't know." The items are distributed across five categories of information, ranging from Leisure to Legal. The number of items in each category ranges from 14 to 28. In addition, topics are listed under each category, and respondents can obtain further information on any of these topics by indicating their interests on the questionnaire form. For example, under the category Health the respondent can get additional information about Death and Dying, Heart Disease, Diabetes, Stress, etc. In addition, the questionnaire concludes with a potpourri of "Retirement Specials," which are additional topics of information ranging from Women and Retirement to how to get the President of the United States to send you a birthday card or anniversary greeting.

Upon sending in the questionnaire/booklet, respondents receive a listing of the "actual" answers to the true/false questions, brief (generally 2–3 pages) narratives about the general topics, and information related to the "additional information" choices requested. The additional information usually includes addresses where publications can be obtained from other agencies.

The BRS is not a test, nor is it an interest inventory in the tradition of standardized inventories. The true/false statements "stimulate your thinking about retirement and help us determine if there is retirement information that might be of value to you." The same key of "correct" answers is sent to all respondents, while "additional information packets" are identical and sent to all persons indicating interest in such information. No attempt is made to match patterns of responses with national norms or other profiles. Therefore, issues such as reliability, validity, etc., are superfluous to discussion of this questionnaire.

Basically, the BRS is a marketing tool. It is used as a "hook" to arouse the interest of prospective respondents who then purchase a "product," in this case information. The value or worth of the BRS therefore is best determined by free market forces rather than by criteria of good test design. It is certainly worthwhile for older adults to plan for retirement, and the information that the BRS provides is easily understood and apparently updated on a regular basis. Whether the BRS is "good" can only be judged on the basis of "getting your money's worth." If $25 seems to be a good buy for obtaining this information, then the BRS is a good questionnaire. If the same or better information can be obtained more easily and/or cheaply (as through the local chapter of the AARP or Administration on Aging), then the BRS is "not good," (i.e., overpriced).

SUMMARY. The Behaviordyne Retirement Service (BRS) contains a questionnaire that has 100 true/false items dealing with respondents' attitudes and knowledge about five aspects of retirement, and also allows respondents to indicate topics dealing with retirement about which they would like to receive more information. After sending in the questionnaire, respondents are sent an answer key for the 100 items, along with narrative information about aspects of retirement and more specific information concerning additional topics of interest. Not a test, the BRS is instead an information dissemination service for individuals interested in planning for retirement.

Review of the Behaviordyne Retirement Service by KEVIN W. MOSSHOLDER, Associate Professor of Management, Auburn University, Auburn, AL:

The Behaviordyne Retirement Service (BRS) is designed to aid in retirement planning. The goal of the BRS is to provide timely retirement information in a nonthreatening manner in order to increase the potential for a satisfactory retirement. Though ideally used prior to retirement, the service could be helpful to many persons who have been retired for some years.

The initial step in using the BRS requires the respondent to answer a series of true-false questionnaire items that tap five areas: Leisure, Health, Housing, Finances, and Legal Issues. The format of the questionnaire booklet allows for individuals to request additional information pertinent to each of the above areas. After responses have been processed, the BRS returns a computer-generated report containing the "correct" responses to the true-false items, extensive narrative concerning topics broached by the items and/or requested by the respondent, and bibliographies indicating sources of further topical, relevant information.

The BRS offers a product that could prove beneficial to an increasing portion of the population. Its ultimate purpose is educational rather than evaluative. Accordingly, the BRS might be more properly judged with respect to this goal rather than more traditional criteria used to assess standardized tests. A positive feature is that its objective format may, in a nonthreatening way, allow the BRS to attract attention to topics that are important but overlooked or taken for granted by the prospective retiree. The BRS questionnaire items are laid out for optical scanning and instructions for completing the questionnaire are adequate. Few if any respondents should have trouble understanding how to use the questionnaire. The instructions emphasize the nonevaluative purpose of the process, which may ease reservations some respondents might have about assessing their beliefs and views on less positive aspects of retirement.

According to the BRS, the computer-generated report should have impact because it contains only information relevant to the respondent. Since the report is not assembled from preprinted material, it can be kept more up-to-date. Apprehensions about others knowing the respondents' feelings on sensitive items are reduced because the resulting report belongs solely to the respondent and can be read in private. Judging from the sample report accompanying the BRS package, the average person should be able to comprehend its contents.

Information is presented in a well-organized, straightforward manner. Bibliographies accompanying the narrative portions of the report appear to be current and potentially helpful.

There are some questions that need to be answered about the BRS and some features that could be improved. The BRS emphasizes that reports are individualized, but does not explain further. Individualized could mean the amount of information contained in any of the five areas depends on the correctness of an individual's responses (i.e., how much was known). Individualized could also mean simply that a respondent receives unique information in the reports only because of having specifically requested it. Certainly, the former definition indicates greater sophistication and a higher quality report. The BRS package does not make clear which definition of individualized applies and this information should be made available.

The correctness of a response to the questions in the response booklet may depend on one's perspective. In some cases, presenting answers as being true (or false) when matters of perspective are involved could cause a respondent to discount other information that is actually based on facts. (A BRS advertising flyer indicates that there are no right or wrong answers, but this is not stated in the questionnaire booklet or report.) It is not clear if the respondent's answers are fed back along with the report. It would be desirable if this were done so the respondent could assess areas where more education is needed.

Needless to say, the BRS would not be recommended for research or psychological assessment purposes. However, as a nonthreatening, relatively inexpensive educational tool for retirement, it is acceptable. The BRS could benefit from improved explanations about report generation and information updating. The computer-generated report might also include an expanded introduction section (in addition to its suggestions for use section) to provide better overall integration of the areas of the report. This type of information could strengthen the report overall by promoting the perspective that, while some of the five content areas of the questionnaire may be of greater interest, all are of sufficient importance to satisfactory retirement planning and should receive the respondent's attention.

[29]

Behaviour Assessment Battery, Second Edition. Purpose: "To assess cognitive and self help skills with a view to implementing appropriate teaching programmes." Severely mentally handicapped children and adults; 1977–82; BAB; 13 assessments: Reinforcement and Experience, Inspection, Tracking, Visuo-Motor, Auditory, Postural Control, Exploratory Play, Constructive Play, Search Strategies, Perceptual Problem Solving, Social, Communication, Self-Help Skills; individual; 1987 price data: £12.60 per book ('82, 190 pages) including tests, information, and score sheets; untimed, administration time not reported; Chris Kiernan and Malcolm C. Jones; NFER-Nelson Publishing Co., Ltd. [England].*

Review of the Behaviour Assessment Battery, Second Edition by DIANE BROWDER, Associate Professor of Special Education, Lehigh University, Bethlehem, PA:

PURPOSE. The Behaviour Assessment Battery (BAB) was developed as a formal test of skills for individuals with profound mental retardation. The purpose of the BAB is to identify areas for teaching. The authors question strict adherence to developmental sequences for this population and so, provide a criterion-referenced rather than norm-referenced test.

EDUCATIONAL AND SOCIAL VALIDITY. The BAB does not reflect a functional focus, that is, skills related to daily living (Snell, 1986). The authors' use of existing instruments and literature on infant development has, however, yielded a developmental checklist with skills of dubious value to individuals beyond the chronological age of early childhood. Even though the authors question adherence to developmental sequences, they have retained a developmental focus in their test. Current alternatives such as The Functional Skills Screening Inventory (123) will have more utility for educational planning of skills that will best enhance independence or partial autonomy for individuals with severe and profound handicaps.

Although the assessment of communication was given special attention in this second edition and includes a detailed appraisal of motor and sign imitation, it does not reflect current research and practice in communication training (Warren & Rogers-Warren, 1985). Assessment of functional use of language is not considered. No content is included on skills related to vocational preparation, leisure skills, domestic skills, or interaction with community resources.

ADMINISTRATION. One of the interesting aspects of the BAB is the use of preidentified reinforcers to encourage test performance. Providing motivation to assess the learner's best performance is often a concern with individuals who cannot be motivated through a verbal discussion of a test's purpose. However, educational assessment for functional skills can rarely be conducted in a traditional test setting because of the varying materials and environments of concern. By contrast, functional settings may provide more motivation than artificial test settings to perform responses to be assessed and thus preclude the need to find artificial reinforcers.

The administration of the BAB requires six or seven 20-minute sessions and additional interviews. This investment of time does not seem warranted given the results yielded.

TECHNICAL MERIT. The technical quality of the BAB is not well documented. The BAB was field tested with 174 children in five programs. The children ranged in age from 2 to 17. The number of children included in the test statistics is unclear in the report with variations from 54 to 111 children included in various subscales. Interrater reliability was at or above the .90 level for four of the nine subscales included in these test statistics with a reliability range of .67 to .96. Test-retest reliability ranged from .76 to .95 with four out of nine subscales assessed receiving correlations above .90. No further statistics were reported.

SUMMARY. The BAB is a time-consuming test that is based heavily on infant development and does not reflect a functional-skills focus. Even for use with young children with severe handicaps, the results should be interpreted cautiously given the weak support for technical quality provided and the omission of consideration of skills for community living.

REVIEWER'S REFERENCES

Warren, S. F., & Rogers-Warren, A. K. (Eds.). (1985). *Teaching functional language*. Baltimore: University Park Press.

Becker, H., Schur, S., Paoletti-Schlep, M., & Hammer, E. (1986). Functional Skills Screening Inventory. Austin, TX: Functional Resources Enterprises.

Snell, M. E. (1986). *Systematic instruction of people with severe handicaps* (3rd ed.). Columbus, OH: Charles E. Merrill.

Review of the Behaviour Assessment Battery, Second Edition by LELAND C. ZLOMKE, Clinical Director of the Intensive Training Service, and BRENDA R. BUSH, Psychologist, Beatrice State Developmental Center, Beatrice, NE:

DESCRIPTION. The Behaviour Assessment Battery (BAB), Second Edition, is a modification of the 1977 Battery and an expansion on the 1981 Revision. This criterion-referenced developmental assessment instrument has been developed to measure cognitive and self-help skill levels of severely and profoundly handicapped children and adults. Unlike some other instruments (e.g., Brigance Inventory of Early Development), this assessment provides no normative comparisons or age/ability levels. The BAB is packaged as a single 190-page manual supplying none of the needed assessment equipment or materials. All scoring sheets and lattices must be copied from the manual. In addition to the manual more than 50 pieces of testing equipment are described for examiners to obtain. The items range from a small torch (flashlight) to some undescribed search and perceptual problem-solving apparatus. Examiners expecting to use this assessment may find the acquisition of this equipment costly and time consuming. The manual, in addition to providing directions for use of the instrument and technical information, also discusses some of the difficulties inherent in assessing severely and profoundly handicapped clients. Recognizing those difficulties several useful strategies are provided to "fine tune" assessment procedures through the use of pretraining, prompts, and incentives to improve client performance.

The BAB is comprehensive with sufficient detail to detect discrete changes in behavior. Due to the detailed behavioral samples, the reported testing time for a complete assessment is six to seven sessions each 20 minutes in length. Additional time must be allowed for interviews with parents and teachers. The authors encourage the use of relevant portions of the instrument to meet specific diagnostic needs as a means to shorten the assessment time commitment. The full BAB measures demonstrated and emerging skills under optimal client performance conditions over 13 separate domains. Six domains: Reinforcement/Experience, Auditory, Postural Control, Social, Communication, and Self-Help are assessed by interview with limited direct testing. The remaining seven domains: Inspection, Tracking, Visuo-Motor, Exploratory Play, Constructive Play, Search Strategies, and Perceptual

Problem-Solving involve direct testing with the client.

SCORING. Each domain consists of items ordered by difficulty as established according to the frequency of demonstration by the sample population. These items are then summarized on a scoring lattice with each lattice having several vertical stems. Stems individually represent a particular type of task, function, or situation. Items that the client demonstrates at criterion are checked off on a scoring sheet or on the lattices. The authors explain that missing skills represent "hypotheses about logical sequencing of development." They caution that critical steps in learning may have been omitted. Due to the lack of adequate task analyses of the skills measured, the BAB is not considered to be a prescriptive measure in regard to selection and development of training experiences. Therefore, the BAB's primary use is reportedly to assist in understanding clients and stimulating ideas.

Technical Adequacy.

ITEM GENERATION. Unlike other developmental instruments the BAB does specify the processes used in item selection. The "item bank" was established through three procedures: (*a*) existing test and interview batteries ($n = 71$), (*b*) experimental and theoretical literature, and (*c*) as need or suggestion indicated during testing. Items were then divided into observation and interview categories, assumedly by the author's subjective choice.

ITEM CONTENT. During development of the battery, 174 children in five different settings were tested. General items, items requiring reliance on verbal instructions, "distressful" items, and items on which none or all of the examinees scored were eliminated from the battery. Other items were eliminated based on low ($<90\%$) interobserver agreement. Based on the information in the manual, items were eliminated on subjective decisions rather than based on empirical measures available such as low test-retest reliability.

SAMPLE. A total of 174 children participated in the development of the BAB with 103 assessed on the final Battery. The age range was 2 years, 2 months to 17 years, 1 month. All subjects were enrolled in hospitals or schools for the handicapped in Great Britain. All individuals tested were "classified as severely or profoundly retarded by relevant authorities." The manual does not detail the examinees' characteristics sufficiently to judge whether the classifications are based on accepted schemes or are idiosyncratic to the various settings. This lack of specificity further limits the extent that the results can be generalized to other populations especially to populations outside of Great Britain.

STATISTICAL ANALYSIS. Content validity appears adequate for the BAB based on the item bank. Using coefficients of reproducibility, provided by a Guttman Analysis, the authors hoped that "items would scale in such a way as to suggest a progression from simpler to more complex tasks." This procedure is a weak attempt to establish construct validity. Guttman scales are easily contaminated by a small number of responses being analyzed. Thus the ordering found for the small sample may not hold up when other groups are tested (Allen & Yen, 1979). This is a good beginning at developing empirical support for the ordering of items but further evidence is desired.

Reliability studies provided interrater agreement (where relevant) and test-retest statistics. Test-retest reliabilities were computed with 3 months between sessions ($n = 51$). Reliabilities ranged from .67 to .95 on the 9 of the 13 domains analyzed. Earlier analyses required 90% interobserver agreement for items to be maintained. Agreement per domain ranged from 72% to 92.8% with 7 of the 9 domains analyzed having percentages less than 90%. The Auditory and Social domains were the lowest on both test-retest and interobserver percentages. The manual gives no evidence of criterion-related validity and concurrent-validity studies are missing to validate the instrument's applicability and usefulness.

CRITIQUE. The lack of prescriptive information, normed comparisons, specific task analyses, or a systematic means to establish priority training needs for individualized educational plans are considerable weaknesses of the BAB. Several developmental assessments such as the Brigance Inventory of Early Development and The Developmental Assessment for the Severely Handicapped are appropriate for use with clients demonstrating significant handicaps and provide normed comparisons and prescriptive program information for use in selection of curriculum goals.

To the authors' credit they have carefully examined the difficulties that severely handicapped clients experience in expressing their skills, knowledge, and abilities. This most recent revision of the BAB provides items within the communication interview to make the interview more appropriate for clients without speech and those who have sign and/or symbol abilities. In conjunction with these revisions are the special procedures included with many of the items of the assessment that encourage the use of pretraining, prompting, and incentives to improve client performance. Together, these procedures make the BAB a leader in "client friendly" assessment instruments for use with individuals displaying severe-profound developmental delays.

SUMMARY. The BAB is a criterion-referenced assessment that was developed to examine the strengths and weaknesses of severely-profoundly handicapped clients. The apparent content validity, sufficiently specific behavioral examples to detect discrete changes in skills, and "client friendly" use of pretraining, prompting, and incentives are the Battery's most significant strengths. The authors are commended in their attention to the problem-solving skills of severely-profoundly handicapped examinees. An instrument that assesses the relative strengths and weaknesses of a client's ability to "think better, as well as, know more skills" is a new addition to the developmental scale field. The overall technical adequacy of the BAB is the battery's most significant weakness. This is not unusual among criterion-referenced instruments. There are, however, psychometric procedures available to adequately address the instrument's technical weaknesses. It is hoped that future revisions will provide more data regarding validity and reliability. The usefulness of the BAB by applied clinicians in education and treatment environments is limited by the battery's failure to provide prescriptive information or individualized curriculum construction references. The domains of Search Strategies and Perceptual Problem-Solving are unique and could provide interesting information to the practitioner and aid in choosing appropriate instructional strategies. However, in applied habilitation settings the considerable time commitment required for administration of the full BAB could be more productively spent. This time and effort would yield more meaningful information if either informal behavioral assessments on the level of development of critical skills or with one of several developmental scales that contain prescriptive curriculum development links (e.g., Developmental Assessment for the Severely Handicapped, Brigance Inventory of Early Development, or The Uniform Performance Assessment System).

REVIEWER'S REFERENCES

Hambleton, R. K., & Eignor, D. R. (1978). Guidelines for evaluating criterion-referenced tests and test manuals. *Journal of Educational Measurement*, 15 (4), 321-327.

Allen, M. J., & Yen, W. M. (1979). *Introduction to measurement theory*. Monterey, CA: Brooks/Cole Publishing Co.

[30]

The Ber-Sil Spanish Test. Purpose: Screening and evaluation of Spanish-speaking children. Ages 5–12, 13–17; 1972–84; individual; 2 levels; 1987 price data: $85 per combination elementary and secondary complete kits including 50 of each test booklet; $50 per elementary or secondary complete kit including 50 test booklets; $28 per book of picture plates; $10 per cassette tape; Marjorie L. Beringer; The Ber-Sil Co.*

a) ELEMENTARY LEVEL, 1987 REVISED EDITION. Ages 5–12; 7 scores: Vocabulary, Response to Directions, Writing, Geometric Figures, Draw a Boy or Girl, Math Skills, English Vocabulary; $8 per 50 test booklets; $15 per manual ('87, 83 pages); $15 per translation for available languages; Cantonese, Mandarin, Ilokano, Tagalog, Korean, and Persian translations available; (45–55) minutes.

b) SECONDARY LEVEL, 1984 EDITION. Ages 13–17; 4 scores: Vocabulary, Dictation in Spanish, Draw a Person, Mathematics; $8 per 50 test booklets; $15 per manual ('84, 69 pages); (45) minutes.

For reviews of an earlier edition by Giuseppe Costantino and Jaclyn B. Spitzer, see 9:141.

Review of the Ber-Sil Spanish Test, Elementary and Secondary Levels, by J. MANUEL CASAS, Associate Professor, University of California, Santa Barbara, CA, and DAVID STRAND, Counseling Psychologist, University of Colorado, Boulder, CO:

The Elementary and Secondary levels of the Ber-Sil Spanish Test have been developed as individual screening devices to assess the abilities and achievement level of students in their native language, and to aid in initial placement decisions. The instruments were developed in response to the influx of Hispanic students into the California school system. The number of Hispanic children in California schools has risen dramatically since the early 1970s. For example, in the Los Angeles Unified School District over half of the students are now of Hispanic origin. Because many new students arrive with no record of their prior education, there is a need for accurate assessment of school-related abilities. To this end, the California Education Code mandates that children must be evaluated to determine their dominant language, and that subsequent intelligence tests must be administered in that language. Recent court decisions have barred the use of intelligence tests for educational placement purposes. These decisions have created an urgent need for alternative means of assessment to insure that Spanish-speaking children are placed in appropriate educational programs.

In 1972 an experimental edition of the Elementary Ber-Sil Test for use with children between the ages of 5 and 12 was developed. Four years later, after cross validation of the experimental edition was conducted using a very diverse sample of Spanish speaking children, the 1976 version of the test was published. It was comprised of three sections: Section I assessed vocabulary; Section II assessed understanding and following directions; and Section III measured visual motor ability, including a sample of the child's writing, the copying of geometric figures, and the drawing of a boy or girl. The 1987 version is similar in format and content to the 1976 version with the exception that two additional sections have been added: Section IV, which enables examiners to quickly screen basic mathematic skills, and Section V, which assesses basic knowledge of English.

In 1977, 5 years after developing the elementary test, an experimental edition of the Ber-Sil Secondary Test for use with children ages 13 to 17 was developed. The rationale for developing this test was that "The information needed from screening a secondary student is somewhat different than the basic information obtained at earlier ages." Content validity and reliability testing was conducted during the 1976–77 and 1980–81 school years with a similar sample to that used in the cross validation of the elementary test. The 1984 version retains the same format as the experimental edition and purports to measure vocabulary, knowledge of spelling and grammar as evidenced from written responses to dictation, the student's level of development as determined from drawing a person, and mathematical skills.

There are several noteworthy features inherent in both levels of the Ber-Sil. An audiotape recording gives directions in Spanish. The numbers and letters of the items on the test are spoken in English so the examiner who does not understand Spanish will be able to follow the tape easily. Furthermore, in the directions for the test, the English translation is written below the Spanish. The picture book used in Section I is the same for both levels and contains attractive professionally prepared drawings.

However, many aspects of both tests raise serious concerns about their efficacy as screening devices. These concerns include proper standardization procedures, adequate content and concurrent validity, omission of raw and normative data, and test material design.

Directions for administering both levels of the Ber-Sil are clear, but the procedures suffer from lack of standardization. In the Spanish vocabulary section, 100 words are presented. Two trial words are administered first. The manual suggests that students can be helped during these trials but explicit directions are not provided for how this help is to be given. This is especially important in light of the fact that in many instances the examiner and student speak different languages.

During the administration of the vocabulary section, students listen to audiotaped words and are asked to point to one of three pictures that best represents each word. The Examiner turns the picture book pages after each student response. Unfortunately, instead of creating a new picture book for the Secondary Level, the author retained the picture book from the Elementary Level. More difficult and abstract words have been generated for students to match to these same pictures. As a result, many word/picture associations are ambiguous or ill-matched, and consequently detract from the power of the test to assess vocabulary per se. Developing a new picture book for the Secondary Level around words that effectively discriminate vocabulary ability is strongly recommended.

Relative to Section I of both tests, the author provides general information on how the face and content validity was determined yet fails to provide specific data and details to corroborate this information. For instance, the face validity of Elementary Level is essentially based on the questionnaire responses of 45 psychologists who had varying degrees of experience in administering this test. In a similar vein, some of the more gross omissions inherent in the Secondary Level test include a lack of demographic information of the 82 high school-aged students who comprised the 1980 sample. In comparing results from the 1976–1977 and 1980 studies, only percentages are provided. Inclusion of raw data and statistical analysis for both tests are necessary to gauge content validity. Comparing both levels of the Ber-Sil to comparable instruments used in the schools would be helpful in assessing the concurrent validity of this instrument. Though minimal, the information on reliability provided in both tests shows them to be fairly reliable.

ELEMENTARY LEVEL. Section two of the Elementary Level is comprised of 13 verbal instructions that help to gauge the student's ability to comprehend verbal directions and perform motor tasks. Since the examiner is asked to assess the student's level of functioning relative to his/her age group, familiarity with child developmental stages is crucial. In Section III the child is asked to write his/her name as well as draw a circle, a square, a triangle, a diamond, and a boy or girl. The rationale for including this section in the test is to provide the Examiner with the opportunity to observe the following functions: visual-motor coordination, distractibility, perseveration, disinhibition, and recall of nonverbal visual stimuli. If a marked age discrepancy is apparent, the Examiner is instructed to take steps for further examination of the child's visual, perceptual, and fine motor abilities. Section IV consists of 70 math problems and was added in order to provide a quick screening of students' mathematical skills. Charts are included in the scoring section to enable the Examiner to quickly determine specific problem areas. Finally, Section V attempts to roughly assess the child's familiarity with the English language. To this end the child is presented with an English word and then asked to point to the picture of that word. The words included in this section were selected to match the pictures already contained in the picture book. According to the author "an entire new list of concepts are in the new list so there will be no perseveration from the Spanish to the English." It should be noted that the English word list is in an experimental stage and relevant validity and reliability statistics are yet to be reported.

SECONDARY LEVEL. With respect to the content of the Secondary Level, Sections II, III, and IV provide examiners with rough estimates of writing, drawing, and mathematical skills respectively. In Section II, four sentences of increasing length and complexity are read via the audiotape while students attempt to write them down. The number of errors in spelling, grammar, and punctuation are added up and compared to norms from the 1976 sample. Results from the 1980 sample are not reported, so it is unclear how useful these normative data are.

Students are asked to draw a girl or a boy in Section III, in an effort to get a quick estimate of their current drawing age. No attempt at interpretation is made. Test users are referred to outside sources such as the Goodenough-Harris Drawing Test Manual for this purpose. The usefulness of this section for academic screening seems quite tenuous.

Section IV has students completing mathematical problems in an effort to assess basic math skills. While potentially valuable as a placement tool, no norms are presented from either the 1976 or 1980 sample for comparative purposes. A minor concern for both levels of the Ber-Sil is that some of the 70 math questions require some reading ability, and may confound the results.

If Sections II, III, and IV are to be useful to examiners, specific criteria for interpretation and placement considerations need to be included, beyond reference to outside sources.

Both Levels of the Ber-Sil Spanish Tests will be attractive to counselors and psychologists primarily because of their ease of administration. They have a significant advantage in that non-Spanish speaking examiners are able to quickly screen students in their primary language, obviating placement errors that result from problems with the English language. However, poor reporting of norms and raw data, concerns about the test materials themselves, and lack of standardization raise serious questions about the efficacy of the tests in their present form as screening instruments. Further test development and refinement is recommended.

Review of The Ber-Sil Spanish Test, Elementary and Secondary Levels, by GIUSEPPE COSTANTINO, Executive Director, Sunset Park Mental Health Center of Lutheran Medical Center, Brooklyn, NY, and Research Associate, Hispanic Research Center, Fordham University, Bronx, NY:

A prominent issue in psychological and educational assessment is the validity, for ethnic minority examinees, of tests that have been conceived, standardized, and validated with middle-class, nonminority populations (Olmedo, 1981; Padilla, 1979). Other tests such as the TEMAS (Costantino, Malgady, & Rogler, 1988; Costantino & Malgady, 1983; Malgady, Costantino, & Rogler, 1984; Malgady, Rogler, & Costantino, 1987) have attempted to avoid this problem by conceiving, standardizing, and validating tests with Hispanic children. The Ber-Sil Spanish Test has used the latter strategy.

Recent litigation has prompted several states to mandate that all school children who are "Limited-English-Proficient" (LEP) be tested for language dominance before they are administered a traditional intelligence test. Hence there is a strong need to develop reliable and valid tests for the assessment of language dominance in Hispanic children. Both versions of the Ber-Sil Spanish Test (Elementary Level, 1976; Secondary Level, 1977) were reviewed in the *Ninth Mental Measurements Yearbook* (9:141). The 1987 edition of the Elementary Level of the Ber-Sil Spanish Test is a further attempt to standardize and validate the earlier edition of the test. The 1984 edition of the Secondary Level of this test represents the standardized version of the 1977 experimental edition.

ELEMENTARY LEVEL. The Elementary Level is divided into five sections. Section I—Vocabulary/Receptive Language presents a table comparing means and standard deviations of 1976 and 1987 studies. This represents the only section having percentile data for both the 1977 and 1987 editions. An improvement over the previous edition is the addition of an English vocabulary test to the Spanish test. Unfortunately, this is an experimental subtest and it is not known whether the Spanish and English vocabulary subtests provide a valid assessment of language dominance. Furthermore, it needs to be clarified that the English Vocabulary subtest is presented in Section V of the Manual.

Sections II and III remain basically the same as in the 1976 Edition.

Section IV presents a comprehensive Mathematics subtest for grades 1 through 12. No rationale is given for including secondary level scoring guidelines. The addition of this subtest gives a more complete assessment of the academic abilities of the Hispanic children, however, percentile scores should be developed for a more accurate assessment of mathematical abilities.

In summary, the 1987 edition of the elementary level represents some improvement over the 1976 edition, however, the endeavor is not sufficient to obviate the biases of traditional intelligence and educational tests. More comprehensive standardization and validation is necessary if this test is to become an unbiased instrument for assessing cognitive functioning in LEP children.

SECONDARY LEVEL. The 1984 revision of the Secondary Level of the Ber-Sil Spanish Test represents another endeavor to standardize and validate the 1977 experimental edition of this test. Developed as a quick assessment instrument of students in secondary schools, the test is comprised of four subtests: Spanish Vocabulary, Dictation of Spanish Sentences, Mathematics, and Drawing of a Person. The theoretical rationale for the development of the subtests in compelling.

Content validity data for the Vocabulary subtests are provided in the form of percentages of correct responses for each of the 100 words for ages 13–17 (1977 Edition) and for ages 15–17 (1984 Edition). A useful table showing the items in ascending difficulty (*p*) indicates that 52 items have *p*s ranging from .80 to 1.00, whereas only 7 items have *p*s below .40. There are too many easy items. The items may have poor discriminating power. There are no content validity data for the items in the other three subtests.

The internal consistency reliability coefficient estimated in a 1980 study is .82, calculated by the rational equivalence method, while the index of reliability is .91, with 4 points as the standard error of measurement. There is no test-retest reliability reported. The median score of the 1980 sample was 5.5 points, higher than the median of the 1977 study for 17-year-old students. The sample size for the 1977 study is not reported; however, the 1980 study was based on 82 Spanish-dominant students.

The instructions for administration of the four subtests, and the scoring for the Dictation, Mathematics, and Draw a Person subtests remain the same as the previous edition. The scoring for the Vocabulary reports quartile equivalents for raw scores and mean scores for ages 13–17 (1977 Edition) and percentile scores for ages 15–17 for the 1980 sample.

The 1984 edition of the test indicates some beginning efforts to validate and standardize the instrument. However, significant work remains to be accomplished in order to enhance the utility of this screening instrument. A larger standardization sample is needed. Eighty-two subjects are inadequate. The normative group should be stratified by socioeconomic status and national origin. Various forms of validity studies must be conducted. Content validity and reliability should be determined for all subtests, including the Draw a Person, and complete age norms should also be developed.

The publication of the latest editions of the Ber-Sil Spanish Test, Elementary and Secondary Levels, is an initial effort to validate and standardize a screening instrument to assess language dominance and cognitive abilities in Elementary and Secondary students with Spanish-language dominance. However, much more work needs to be conducted in order to make this instrument a reliable, valid, and unbiased test for Hispanic LEP children. In its present form, the test should be used with caution.

REVIEWER'S REFERENCES

Padilla, A. M. (1979). Critical factors in the testing of Hispanic Americans: A review and some suggestions for the future. In R. Taller & S. White (Eds.), *Testing, teaching and learning: Report of a conference on testing*. Washington, DC: National Institute of Education.

Olmedo, E. L. (1981). Testing linguistic minorities. *American Psychologist*, 36, 1078-1085.

Costantino, G., & Malgady, G. R. (1983). Verbal fluency of Hispanic, Black and White Children on TAT and TEMAS, a new Thematic Apperception Test. *Hispanic Journal of Behavioral Sciences*, 5, 199-206.

Rogler, L. H., Santana-Cooney, R., Costantino, G., Earley, B., Grossman, B., Gurak, D., Malgady, R., & Rodriquez, O. (1983). *A conceptual framework for mental health research on Hispanic populations*. Bronx, NY: Hispanic Research Center.

Malgady, G. R., Costantino, G., & Rogler, H. L. (1984). Development of a Thematic Apperception Test (TEMAS) for urban Hispanic children. *Journal of Consulting and Clinical Psychology*, 52, 986-996.

Malgady, R. G., Rogler, L. H., & Costantino, G. (1987). Ethnocultural and linguistic bias in mental health evaluation of Hispanics. *American Psychologist*, 42, 228-234.

Costantino, G., Malgady, G. R., & Rogler, H. L. (1988). TEMAS, (Tell-Me-A-Story) A Multicultural Thematic Apperception Test for Minority and Nonminority Children. Los Angeles: Western Psychological Services.

[31]

Bipolar Psychological Inventory. Purpose: "To provide a fairly comprehensive personality assessment instrument that has utility in institutions, clinics, educational settings, industry, private work, or in any situation where personality functioning is of interest." College and adults; 1971–82; BPI; 16 scores: Invalid/Valid, Lie/Honest, Defensive/Open, Psychic Pain/Psychic Comfort, Depression/Optimism, Self Degradation/Self Esteem, Dependence/Self Sufficiency, Unmotivated/Achieving, Social Withdrawal/Gregariousness, Family Discord/Family Harmony, Sexual Immaturity/Sexual Maturity (Form A only), Problem Index High/Problem Index Low (Form B only), Social Deviancy/Social Conformity, Impulsiveness/Self Control, Hostility/Kindness, Insensitivity/Empathy; 2 forms: A, B; may be hand scored, machine scored, or administered and scored by computer; computer version can be administered on IBM-PC or Apple II computer; 1985 price data: $.50 per test booklet (indicate Form A or B); $10 per set of 16 scoring keys; $.15 per answer sheet; $.15 per profile sheet (indicate Peace Officer, Normal, or Offender); $2 per administration manual ('75, 8 pages); $2 per scale items booklet ('71, 17 pages); $2 per studies booklet ('72, 12 pages); $15 per sample kit containing test booklet, 16 answer sheets, keys, 16 profiles, administration manual, scale items booklet, and studies booklet); $250 per BPI computer program including disk, backup disk, and instructions ('82, 5 pages); (30–60) minutes; Allan V. Roe, Robert J. Howell, and I. Reed Payne; Diagnostic Specialists, Inc.*

See T3:294 (4 references) and 8:507 (11 references).

TEST REFERENCES

1. Gibb, G. D. (1984). A comparative study of recidivists and contraceptors along the dimensions of locus of control and impulsivity. *International Journal of Psychology*, 19, 581-591.

Review of the Bipolar Psychological Inventory by BRUCE W. HARTMAN, Professor of Education, Seton Hall University, South Orange, NJ:

The term bipolar in the title of the Bipolar Psychological Inventory (BPI) refers to labelling, in the title of a dimension, what a low score on the dimension being measured represents. For example, in the authors' judgment, a low score on the depression dimension represents optimism so the subscale is labelled Depression-Optimism. Because other measures of personality provide descriptions of low scores on the dimension being measured, the bipolar nature of this scale is not a unique (just a more obvious) feature.

While completing this inventory I felt that I had been asked some of the items twice, and I was certain the Lie-Honest subscale was constructed from repeated presentations of the same items. I was surprised to find that it was not. In the manual of individual scale items provided by the authors, I found what appeared to me to be a number of fairly similar items. This apparent item redundancy would tend to reduce the variance generated by the inventory and may make it difficult to find within-group differences. That is, the inventory may differentiate prisoners from college students, but do poorly at discriminating among college students themselves.

The authors provide a manual of research studies done using the BPI. The majority of the studies are unpublished papers written by the authors. The most problematic material presented in these studies was information on differences between populations without an analysis of the differences. For example, the authors examined individual scale differences broken down into affect and behavior dimensions (these two dimensions are measured but not scored separately) between university students and prison inmates. The authors concluded, "that of the thirteen affect scores only the Sexual Immaturity Scale failed to significantly differentiate prisoners from university students" (Roe, 1972). Yet the authors failed to mention that university students were significantly more dependent, sexually immature, and insensitive than the prison inmates. The same is true for the behavior dimension of the scale with the exception of the Hostility scale. The authors use the differences reported between populations as a rationale for constructing separate norms. The studies on which the norms are based are not included in the manual of studies.

The Bipolar Psychological Inventory can be administered and scored by IBM or Apple II compatible personal computers. The scores derived from the paper-and-pencil and computer versions are intended to be used interchangeably, yet no data are provided concerning the parallelism of the forms. The computer version presents the items and scores, plots the dimension scores according to the desired norms, and reports items marked in the problem direction for scale scores that are at the 70th percentile or above for the norm group selected. The computer-scored inventory does not provide an enhanced interpretative report. Hand scoring is easy with the templates provided and transferring scores to the desired norm sheet is a trivial task. The BPI is not keyed to the DSM-III-R.

SUMMARY. The Bipolar Psychological Inventory is not new, yet, to date, too few studies have been conducted by too few researchers to conclude the scale has sufficient validity and reliability. The manual of studies that accompanies the BPI should be updated. It appears from a brochure that the BPI is marketed as a personnel selection tool for police officers. Although requested, I did not receive the manuals reporting the validity studies of the BPI used for this purpose. After careful study of this instrument, I am left with a sense of frustration regarding recommending the BPI for use.

REVIEWER'S REFERENCE

Roe, A. (1972). *Bipolar psychological inventory studies.* Orem, UT: Diagnostic Specialists.

Review of the Bipolar Psychological Inventory by KEVIN E. O'GRADY, Assistant Professor of Psychology, University of Maryland, College Park, MD:

The Bipolar Psychological Inventory (BPI) consists of two separate forms, A and B, each of which contains 300 true-false items. Each form contains items common to 14 subscales: Invalid-Valid, Lie-Honest, Defensive-Open, Psychic Pain-Psychic Comfort, Depression-Optimism, Self Degradation-Self Esteem, Dependence-Self Sufficiency, Unmotivated-Achieving, Social Withdrawal-Gregariousness, Family Discord-Family Harmony, Social Deviancy-Social Conformity, Impulsiveness-Self Control, Hostility-Kindness, and Insensitivity-Empathy. Form A contains items that yield a Sexual Immaturity-Sexual Maturity subscale score, and Form B contains items that yield a Problem Index (High)-Problem Index (Low) subscale score. The number of items on any given subscale varies from a minimum of 10 to a maximum of 25, with all but two subscales containing 20 or more items. Each item is scored for only a single subscale. Instructions to respondents ask that they "Read each statement and decide how you feel about it. If you agree with the statement, or it is TRUE of you, fill in the 'T' space on the answer sheet. If you disagree with a statement, or if you feel it is FALSE of you [sic], fill in the 'F' space on the answer sheet."

The Administration Manual states the BPI was "designed for use with both normal and clinical populations." The intentions in developing the BPI were stated as "broader coverage, better discrimination, relevant dimensions, and the combining of the best known psychometric techniques in construction are possibilities in the development of a new and hopefully improved objective personality test."

The manual itself is quite brief, and generally does not contain sufficient information regarding either the development of the BPI or its current psychometric properties to allow a potential user the possibility of an evaluation of the instrument. There are several major problems with the BPI: (*a*) The rationale for the development of the BPI is contained in three brief paragraphs, which do not allow for a reasonable evaluation of the underlying theoretical orientation of the test itself, or the subscales. For example, the manual simply states that "The word 'bipolar' has reference to the bipolar nature of the personality dimensions." Questions any reasonable reader might raise under such circumstances include: Are all personality dimensions bipolar? Are the bipolar dimensions included in the BPI important, either because they are somehow central to personality, or because they allow for meaningful prediction of human behavior? (*b*) The descriptions of the subscales rely largely on the use of adjectival synonyms to describe high and low scores in a given subscale. Hence, no definitions of the bipolar dimensions are offered. (*c*) How the original pool of 700 items was reduced to the final set of 300 items is not discussed in sufficient detail to allow for a reasonable evaluation of the adequacy of scale development procedures. For example, the number of subjects utilized in the first scale construction study is not provided. (*d*) The test-retest reliabilities reported in the manual do not indicate the time period elapsed between the two administrations of the BPI. (*e*) No estimate of internal consistency reliability for each subscale is provided. (*f*) No subscale intercorrelations are provided, so even the most basic information regarding convergent and discriminant validity is missing. I should state that there are further criticisms that might be offered, most notably regarding the Manual's sections on Interpretation and Use of the BPI, which I will forego.

In summary, I cannot recommend the use of the BPI for either clinicians or researchers without considerable further substantive research. Certainly, the fact the manual does not provide what might be regarded as basic, fundamental information regarding the psychometric characteristics of the BPI would argue strongly against its use in clinical circumstances. Moreover, the fact the subscales themselves are defined solely by analogy suggests a continuing difficulty in hypothesizing what behaviors and attitudes each subscale should and should not predict. Thus, its utility to researchers in testing hypotheses of interest is quite limited. The manual needs to provide considerably more information of both a conceptual and psychometric nature before the BPI could be used with confidence by psychologists.

[32]

Boehm Test of Basic Concepts—Revised. Purpose: "Designed to assess children's mastery of the basic concepts that are both fundamental to understanding verbal instruction and essential for early school achievement." Grades K–2; 1967–86; Boehm-R; 3 forms: Form C and Form D (alternate forms) and Applications (concepts used in combination); 1988 price data: $39 per 35 sets of test booklets 1 and 2 (specify Form C or Form D) including key, class record, and directions ('86, 8 pages); $25 per 35 sets of Applications test booklets 1 and 2 including key, class record, and directions ('86, 7 pages); $2.50 per class record and keys for hand scoring test booklets (specify Form C, D, or Applications); $3 per directions (specify Form C, D, or Applications); $18 per 35 parent-teacher conference reports; $15 per manual ('86, 69 pages); $19 per examination kit containing one copy of each booklet of Form C, D, and Applications, directions for each form, key for hand scoring each form, class record, parent-teacher conference report, and manual; test booklets, directions, and parent-teacher conference reports available in Spanish; (30–40) minutes for Form C or D, (15–20) minutes for Applications Form; Ann E. Boehm; The Psychological Corporation.*

a) THE TACTILE TEST OF BASIC CONCEPTS. Blind children grades K–2; 1976–86; TTBC; a tactile analog to the Boehm Test of Basic Concepts, Form A; individual; 1986 price data: $25.97 per complete test including 50 test cards, 5 practice cards, TTBC manual ('86, 22 pages), and Boehm manual ('71, 30 pages); administration time not reported; Hilda R. Caton; American Printing House for the Blind Incorporated.

See T3:302 (18 references); for additional information and an excerpted review by Theodore A. Dahl, see 8:178 (22 references); see also T2:344 (1 reference); for reviews by Boyd R. McCandless and Charles D. Smock, and excerpted reviews by Frank S. Freeman, George Lawlor, Victor H. Noll, and Barton B. Proger, see 7:335 (1 reference).

TEST REFERENCES

1. Ernhart, C. B., Spaner, S. D., & Jordan, T. E. (1977). Validity of selected preschool screening tests. *Contemporary Educational Psychology*, 2, 78-89.

2. Obrzut, J. E., Hansen, R. L., & Heath, C. P. (1982). The effectiveness of visual information processing training with Hispanic children. *Journal of General Psychology*, 107, 165-174.

3. Piersel, W. C., & McAndrews, T. (1982). Concept acquisition and school progress: An examination of the Boehm Test of Basic Concepts. *Psychological Reports*, 50, 783-786.

4. Piersel, W. C., Plake, B. S., Reynolds, C. R., & Harding, R. (1982). Bias in content validity on the Boehm Test of Basic Concepts for White and Mexican-American children. *Contemporary Educational Psychology*, 7, 181-189.

5. Silverstein, A. B., Begler, K. A., & Morita, D. N. (1982). Social class differences on the Boehm Test of Basic Concepts: Are they due to bias? *Psychology in the Schools*, 19, 431-432.

6. Manning, B. H. (1984). Problem-solving instruction as an oral comprehension aid for reading disabled third graders. *Journal of Learning Disabilities*, 17, 457-461.

7. Nelson, R. B., & Cummings, J. A. (1984). Educable mentally retarded children's understanding of Boehm basic concepts. *Psychological Reports*, 54, 81-82.

8. Piersel, W. C., & Kinsey, J. H. (1984). Predictive validity of the First Grade Screening Test. *Educational and Psychological Measurement*, 44, 921-924.

9. Price, G. G. (1984). Mnemonic support and curriculum selection in teaching by mothers: A conjoint effect. *Child Development*, 55, 659-668.

10. Connelly, J. B. (1985). Published tests—which ones do special education teachers perceive as useful? *Journal of Special Education*, 19, 149-155.

11. Evans, E. D. (1985). Longitudinal follow-up assessment of differential preschool experience for low income minority group children. *Journal of Educational Research*, 78, 197-202.

12. Gallivan, J. (1985). Absence of sex differences on the Boehm Test of Basic Concepts. *Perceptual and Motor Skills*, 61, 1322.

13. Jordan, T. E. (1985). Prospective longitudinal study of superior cognitive readiness for school, from 1 year to 7 years. *Contemporary Educational Psychology*, 10, 203-219.

14. Smith, E. F. (1986). The Boehm Test of Basic Concepts: An English standardisation. *British Journal of Educational Psychology*, 56, 197-200.

15. Smith, E. F. (1986). The validity of the Boehm Test of Basic Concepts. *British Journal of Educational Psychology*, 56, 332-344.

16. Gallivan, J. (1988). Concept knowledge as a predictor of first- and fourth-grade reading achievement. *Perceptual and Motor Skills*, 66 (2), 407-410.

Review of the Boehm Test of Basic Concepts—Revised by ROBERT L. LINN, Professor of Education, University of Colorado at Boulder, Boulder, CO:

The Boehm Test of Basic Concepts—Revised (Boehm-R) is intended to provide classroom teachers with a means of identifying (*a*) "individual children whose overall level of concept mastery is low and who therefore may need special attention," and (*b*) "individual concepts with which large numbers of children in a class may be unfamiliar." Teachers are advised to provide small-group remedial instruction directed at concepts with low percentage passing rates when the class average is low. When the class average is high, however, it is suggested that group instruction is best limited to "the occasional concepts that are missed by a large proportion of the class," while special individual attention is provided to help those children who score well below the class average.

As was true of the original Boehm Test of Basic Concepts (BTBC), the Boehm-R consists of a set of 50 relational concepts (e.g., front, below, fewest). The revisions were relatively modest. A few concepts, mostly antonyms of concepts already included in the BTBC, were added and a few concepts were deleted or moved to the Preschool Version or the Applications booklet. Some improvements in the artwork were also made. However, Forms C and D of the Boehm-R are otherwise much the same as Forms A and B of the BTBC.

Forms C and D are each divided into two booklets. Each booklet has 3 practice and 25 operational pictorial items arranged roughly in order of increasing difficulty. The two forms are parallel in the sense that like-numbered items measure the same concepts. A typical item consists of line drawings of three objects or sets of objects (e.g., a lamp, a shirt, and a shoe). Items are read by the teacher. The format of the instructions is parallel throughout. First a sentence is read instructing the children to look at a particular picture. This is followed by a sentence of instructions (e.g., "Mark the thing that a child should *never* wear"). The instructional sentence is repeated and teachers are instructed to emphasize the key word.

EVALUATION. The administration instructions are detailed and clearly written. Although one might prefer more colorful or interesting illustrations, the black-and-white line drawings are generally clear and appear unambiguous.

The manual does not provide sufficient information to evaluate the norming samples. The sample was apparently stratified by region of the country and size of school district, but the details of participation rates and the match between the sample and the population in terms of racial-ethnic group representation or socioeconomic status is not provided.

The use of common conversion tables to obtain percentile equivalents of raw scores for both forms is questionable. Although the forms are conceptually parallel, the Manual does not provide extensive information regarding their statistical relationship. On the contrary, the tables that report the percent passing each item at the beginning of kindergarten (Tables 7 and 8 of the Manual), suggest that Form C with an average *p*-value of .733 is more difficult than Form D with an average *p*-value of .774). The corresponding mean number-right scores are 36.6 and 38.7, which is equivalent to a difference in percentiles of approximately 10 points.

Generally, the difficulties of the matched pairs of items from the two forms are quite similar with, as the above comment indicates, Form D items being slightly easier than Form C items at the beginning of kindergarten. Indeed, the simple correlation between the beginning kindergarten *p*-values across the 50 item pairs is .82. However, there are a few deviant item pairs. For example, the Form C item for the concept "half" is answered correctly by 74% of the beginning kindergarteners whereas the corresponding percentage correct for the Form D item is 38%. The Form C item for "half" shows three pies cut into six pieces that have 1, 2, or 3 pieces missing. On Form D the item shows three egg cartons containing 4, 6, or 12 eggs. Recognizing when half the eggs are "gone" is apparently a good deal harder than recognizing when half the pie is "gone."

As in the case of the two items for the concept "half," the other large discrepancies in percent correct for matching item pairs appear to make sense. While such differences are not necessarily a problem, they might have been avoided with more pretesting of items, thereby reducing the likelihood that the choice of test form will determine whether or not a teacher is encouraged to spend time teaching a concept to a whole class.

The reliability of the Boehm-R, whether estimated by split-half or the alternate-forms coefficients, depends on the grade level. The test has reasonable reliability at the end of kindergarten and at the end of grade 1 (low to mid .80s) but poor reliability at the end of grade 2 (alternate form correlation of .65 and split-half coefficients of .64 and .73 for Forms C and D, respectively). The reduction in reliability is due to the increasing severity of the ceiling effect that causes a high negative skew and small variance by grade 2. In a norm-referenced sense, the test is simply much too easy by the end of grade 2 to provide useful distinctions among any but the lowest scoring students. This is evident from the fact that a child who answered 45 of the 50 items correctly would rank only at the 10th percentile at the end of grade 2. Even at the end of grade 1, a raw score of 45 would have a percentile equivalent of only 30.

The discussion of validity in the Manual touches the traditional bases (i.e., content, criterion-related, and construct). However, as is too often the case, the construct-validity discussion lacks any clear conception or direction. Similarly, the criterion-related validity evidence consists of a summary of available correlations with other tests which, while in keeping with what might be expected, are not integrated into a conceptual framework or accompanied by much explanation. For example, 17 correlations (ranging from .28 to .64, median = .44) with the composite or reading scores from four achievement tests that were obtained at kindergarten, grade 1, or grade 2 at one of three school districts are reported. From these correlations it is concluded that "the findings support the use of the Boehm-R as a screening measure." If "screening" means simply the identification of children who need special attention from the teacher (one of the two primary purposes of the test) then the correlation results are not particularly relevant. Worse, if "screening" means holding children back a year or assigning them to special classes, then the list of correlations is a completely inadequate basis for the conclusion.

The strongest argument for the validity of the test for its stated purposes comes under the heading content validity. There is reasonable support for the claim that the test concepts are used frequently by teachers and in instructional materials and achievements tests. Evidence that targeted instruction based on the test results is beneficial is limited. The suggestions that such instruction might be useful are reasonable, however, and the risk of negative consequences from instructional applications are minimal.

SUMMARY. The Boehm-R assesses the understanding of relational concepts that are used frequently in school. Except for occasional statements about the use for purposes of screening, the claims for the measure are modest and the recommended uses are in keeping with common sense—if a concept is not understood, then it is desirable to teach it. Due to the test ceiling, it is most likely to be useful in kindergarten or the beginning of first grade. The main basis for concluding that the test is valid for the intended uses comes from the frequent use of the concepts in classrooms.

Review of the Boehm Test of Basic Concepts—Revised by COLLEEN FITZMAURICE, *Graduate Associate, and* JOSEPH C. WITT, *Associate Professor of Psychology, Louisiana State University, Baton Rouge, LA:*

The Boehm Test of Basic Concepts—Revised (Boehm-R, 1986) is a revision of the 1971 Boehm Test of Basic Concepts. The stated purpose of the test is to assess children's acquisition of basic concepts that are in the author's opinion "both fundamental to understanding verbal instruction and essential for early school achievement." Basic concepts include primarily relational concepts (e.g., more-less) but also include concepts that help children make decisions in relation to a standard (e.g., left-right). It is used for children in kindergarten through second grade, but is most useful as a screening device for children entering school in either kindergarten or first grade. As a screening test, it can detect children with deficiencies in the basic concepts assessed. In addition, specific concepts that are not understood by the child become the focus for instruction. The revision places greater emphasis on relational concepts such as more-less and first-last than did the original Boehm. The original test consisted of two alternate Forms A and B. The revision consists of Forms C and D and an Applications test. Forms C and D are comprised of 50 items each measuring basic concepts similar to those in the original Boehm. The Applications test, which is something new in the revision, consists of 26 items to assess mastery of basic concepts that are used frequently in combinations with other basic concepts. Thus, Forms C and D tap a child's knowledge of the concept and the Applications tests ask a child to apply that knowledge often within the context of multiple-step directions.

The test can be administered in groups by a teacher reading each question; however, with young children it may be necessary to limit the number per group. The complete test (i.e., Form C or Form D and the Applications test) can be administered in approximately 1 hour. For children with short attention spans, the test can be divided into sections and administered separately. The test manual gives specific instructions, including a script, making it easy for teachers to administer. Scoring of the test is straightforward and simple. A single test protocol can be used for all children tested in one class, which makes an analysis of errors easy.

The norms are reported to be representative of the national school population with respect to size of school district, geographic region, and socioeconomic level of students, according to the 1980 U.S. Census. However, only 15 states are represented. The percentage of students passing each item by grade level (K–2), socioeconomic level (low, medium, high) and time of testing (beginning, end of year) are provided in easy-to-read tables. In addition, percentile equivalents of raw scores are given.

Forms C and D are represented as equivalent forms; however, the correlations between total scores for C and D ranges from a high of .82 for kindergarten and a low of .65 for second grade. These correlations are low for alternate forms and caution must be taken when comparing performance of students who have been administered different forms. Split-half reliabilities are also reported and range from a high of .87 (Form D, kindergarten) to a low of .55 (Form C, second grade).

Content validity is the primary form of validity that the Boehm-R can claim. Test items were chosen because of the frequency of use in school curricular materials, and teachers' verbal instructions. The manual states the Boehm-R correlates well with other tests of achievement; however, the correlations with other achievement tests (e.g., Comprehensive Tests of Basic Skills, California Achievement Tests, Iowa Tests of Basic Skills) ranged from .24 to .64. These correlations do very little to support the validity of the Boehm-R. Despite these data, some question remains as to whether students who do poorly on the test actually do more poorly in school or preschool.

Overall, the Boehm-R seems to be an improved version of the Boehm with a more representative standardization sample and stronger content validity. Given that the author states the test is primarily a screening device, use of the test for this purpose seems warranted. As a screening instrument, the Boehm-R would appear to be most appropriate as a rough measure of language development. If a test user were interested in screening readiness for academic tasks, then other measures (e.g., the readiness section of the BRIGANCE Preschool Screen, 36) would seem to be more appropriate for that purpose. If some indications of a child's cognitive functioning were needed, then there are numerous instruments, specifically designed for that purpose, which may be more appropriate.

[33]

Bracken Basic Concept Scale. Purpose: "To measure a subset of children's receptive vocabulary—basic concepts." Ages 2-6 to 7-11, ages 5-0 to 7-0; 1984–86; BBCS; can be supplemented with the Bracken Concept Development Program; 2 tests; 1988 price data: $98 per complete program including Screening Test Forms A and B; $60 per Diagnostic Scale stimulus manual ('84, 243 pages); $13 per 25 Diagnostic record forms; $15 per examiner's manual ('84, 124 pages); untimed; Bruce A. Bracken; The Psychological Corporation.*

a) DIAGNOSTIC SCALE. Ages 2-6 to 7-11; 8 scores: School Readiness Composite Score, Direction/Position, Social/Emotional, Size, Texture/Material, Quantity, Time/Sequence, Total; individual; $60 per stimulus manual; $13 per 25 record forms and 2 sample screening tests; $15 per examiner's manual.

b) SCREENING TESTS. Ages 5-0 to 7-0; 30 concepts in 8 areas: Comparisons, Shapes, Direction/Position, Social/Emotional, Size, Texture/Material, Quantity, Time/Sequence; 2 forms: A and B; $13 per 12 Screening Test booklets (specify Form A or Form B); $15 per examiner's manual.

Review of the Bracken Basic Concept Scale by TIMOTHY L. TURCO, Assistant Professor of School Psychology, Lehigh University, Bethlehem, PA:

Due to the limitations of our present technology, every psychoeducational instrument and curriculum contains specific conceptual prerequisites. For example, in order to write his/her name at the top of a worksheet, the child must at least understand the following concepts: (*a*) top, for the proper location on the page, (*b*) alphabet recognition for the formation of the letters, and (*c*) left/right, for the proper ordering of the letters. If we are able to identify what concepts each task demands and we are able to assess what concepts each child has mastered, then we can better understand and possibly predict the child's task performance. The Bracken Basic Concept Scale (BBCS) was developed to identify what concepts a child has mastered.

The BBCS contains three norm-referenced instruments. First, there is a 258-item Diagnostic Scale designed "for an in-depth assessment of an individual child's conceptual knowledge." The Diagnostic Scale (DS) assesses 258 concepts clustered into 11 subtests. The first five subtests of the DS (Color, Letter Identification, Numbers/Counting, Comparisons, Shapes) are combined to form a School Readiness Composite Score (SRC), which is used to determine the starting point for the administration of the remaining six subtests (Direction/Position, Social/Emotional, Size, Texture/Material, Quantity, Time/Sequence).

The remaining instruments in the BBCS are two parallel forms of a group-administered 30-item Screening Test. The Screening Test (ST) was designed to identify kindergarten and first-grade children who may benefit from a more intensive diagnostic assessment of conceptual knowledge.

The test administration formats for all the BBCS instruments are identical. Children are shown four monochrome pictures and asked to identify the picture that depicts a particular concept. Minor exceptions to stimulus format occur in two subtests of DS. The Color subtest contains one color plate with 12 geometric shapes. The Letter Identification subtest has two plates with five monochrome stimuli.

One of the major strengths of the BBCS is the detailed and well-organized Examiner's Manual. The Manual can serve easily as a model for other test manuals in its thorough explanation of the instruments and its self-critical evaluations. After reading the Manual, the evaluator will have an appropriately detailed understanding of the test's: (*a*) theoretical and conceptual basis, (*b*) development and standardization, (*c*) administration and scoring, (*d*) interpretation and uses in remediation, and (*e*) technical characteristics.

The Examiner's Manual will meet the needs of paraprofessionals primarily interested in how to administer, score, and interpret the tests. For example, Chapter 4 describes how the DS can be interpreted using norm-referenced, ipsative, and criterion-referenced methods. In addition, the chapter gives 10 practical general guidelines for writing I.E.P. concept objectives and providing remedial instruction in basic concepts.

The Manual also contains an ample amount of technical information of interest to more critical test users who want to understand the details of the test's construction, standardization, and even the author's personal views about the test's constructs. For example, in Chapter 2, Bracken describes: (*a*) other published tests that touch upon the content of the BBCS, (*b*) the 12 criteria that influenced item design and the test's format, (*c*) the specific skills assessed by each subtest, (*d*) what concepts were deleted from the final version of the BBCS as a result of the first item field testing, and (*e*) the race, gender, location, and city size of the 1,109 children included in the DS standardization sample.

The test administration procedures for the DS were fairly well planned and coordinated. The test administration protocol for the DS was very easy to use and was self explanatory. It supplied the examiner with enough administration and scoring prompts that reference to the Examiner's Manual was not necessary during test administration. The stimulus manual uses a spiral-bound easel format. The easel was somewhat temperamental to use because occasionally the spiral wiring twisted, which prevented the pages from flipping easily and lying flat.

The administration procedures of the screening tests do require concept prerequisites. Unlike the DS, in order for a child to make a correct response on the ST, the child must have mastered the concepts of top/bottom, on/off, and be able to write the letter "X." Thus, the ST appears to have some of the conceptual prerequisities confounding the task.

One of the technical problems with the BBCS concerns the scoring system. The raw scores of each of the seven major subtests of the DS are summed and converted into standard scores with means of 100 and standard deviations of 15. These standard scores range from 50 to 150. Apparently, the range of raw scores from the standardization sample did not allow direct computation of the full range of standard scores. For example, the standardization sample did not contain a sufficient number of extremely low functioning 7-year-olds to extend the distribution down to a standard score of 50. Thus, in several places in the standard score tables, the author used extrapolation to derive some of the standard scores. Bracken correctly alerts the test user to be cautious of any test interpretation based on extrapolated scores. However, no provision is made to let the test user know what scores are extrapolated in any of the raw score to standard score conversion tables. This leaves the test user uncertain as to whether each test score is empirically based on the performance of the standardization sample or a linear extrapolation. The author needs to provide the user with more information.

Another point of concern is the treatment of color-blind children. As previously mentioned, the Color subtest contains one plate with 12 colored geometric shapes. A color-blind child would not perform as well on the Color subtests as other children and some adaptation of the BBCS should probably be made. However, Bracken makes the adjustment to the BBCS scoring based upon a post hoc prorating procedure instead of a standardization of the test with color-blind children. The 1,109 children included in the standardization sample were not selected based upon not being color blind, so conceivably many of the children in the sample may have been color blind. Therefore, any post hoc prorating of color-blind children's scores is not appropriate.

The test-retest reliability of the BBCS was evaluated on 27 children over a 14-day intertest interval. The lowest reliability coefficient was on the Size subtest ($r = .67$). The remaining subtests ranged from .85 to .98. However, it is important to note that the number of children used to evaluate the reliability of the BBCS was very small in comparison to the number of students utilized in other portions of the standardization of the Scale.

The content validity of the BBCS was established during the development of the Scale. The concepts initially included in the BBCS were extracted from the content of 13 commonly used preschool and primary school tests. From the original concept pool, 33 items were removed because they failed to adequately discriminate.

The BBCS manual summarizes the results from seven empirical studies that established the concurrent validity of the Scale. In these studies the BBCS standard scores of children were correlated with other norm-referenced assessment instruments (e.g., Boehm Test of Basic Concepts and the Peabody Picture Vocabulary Test—Revised). The correlations ranged from .68 to .88.

Unfortunately, none of the studies evaluated the predictive validity of the BBCS. Based upon the data presented in the manual, we do not know whether a low BBCS score is predictive of any academic deficits.

The alternate forms reliability of the ST was computed using the data from the 850 children in the standardization sample. These coefficients ranged from .71 to .80.

Because the ST items were extracted from the BBCS, the content validity of the ST is contingent upon the acceptance of the content validity of the BBCS. The concurrent and predictive validity of the ST was not evaluated.

The BBCS would probably be of most use to curriculum developers and assessment personnel interested in identifying the concept mastery of preschool and primary school children. It can serve to provide a link between traditional psychometric assessment and the formulation of remedial interventions. The BBCS is relatively easy to administer and flexible in allowable response modes. In addition, the alternate forms ST facilitates periodic norm-referenced evaluations.

Review of the Bracken Basic Concept Scale by JAMES E. YSSELDYKE, Professor of Educational Psychology, University of Minnesota, Minneapolis, MN:

Knowledge of basic concepts, like concepts of size, number, shape, and direction, is necessary to succeed in preschool and kindergarten settings. The Bracken Basic Concept Scale (BBCS) is among several tests designed to enable professionals who work with young children to assess children's knowledge of basic concepts. In developing a measure of knowledge of basic concepts, an author is confronted with the relatively difficult task of deciding those concepts to be included in the scale. In this case, Bracken surveyed commonly used preschool and primary psychometric measures and made lists of the concepts required for performance on those measures. Then he categorized the concepts into 11 conceptual categories or subtests. He added "very few" items based on review of preschool curricula and solicitation of concepts from preschool teachers. Items were given to a limited sample of 50 children; some items were eliminated and other placed in order of difficulty based on the performance of this group. Later, following standardization, additional items were eliminated and others were rearranged in order of difficulty.

The BBCS is a screening test, one designed to be used in spotting children who may be "at risk" for failure in situations requiring knowledge of basic concepts, and one designed to be used in developing instructional programs to teach unknown basic concepts. The BBCS is made up of two separate instruments: a diagnostic full scale instrument that measures 258 concepts, and two alternative form (A and B) screening tests, each measuring knowledge of 30 basic concepts. Items for the screening tests are taken entirely from the Diagnostic Scale.

Materials for the BBCS include a set of stimulus drawings that are in easel format. The drawings are of sufficient size and clarity for use with young children.

Several different scores are obtained for children who take the BBCS. One may obtain a total score with a mean of 100 and a standard deviation of 15, or one may obtain scaled scores (mean = 10, standard deviation = 3) for the subtests. Five subtests (numbers 1–5) are grouped to provide a composite score called the School Readiness Composite. Users may also obtain Concept Ages, NCEs (normal curve equivalents), and percentile ranks for each of the subtests. Those who use this measure will probably find most useful for instructional purposes a simple listing of the concepts about which students do and do not demonstrate knowledge.

The BBCS was standardized on a sample of 1,109 students selected on the basis of age, sex, ethnic heritage, geographic region, socioeconomic status, and community size. Cross tab information is provided on sex and ethnic heritage only. Thus, we do not know how many minority students, for example, came from each of the specific geographic regions, or from specific SES levels. A weakness is the socioeconomic status was determined on a site basis rather than on an individual student basis. Effort was made to represent all socioeconomic levels in the standardization.

The author of this scale has done a commendable job of providing users with the necessary information to make judgments about the technical adequacy of the Diagnostic Scale of the BBCS. And, for the most part, this is a technically adequate test. When tests are used with very young children, it is often difficult to know whether there are enough easy items to discriminate very young low-functioning children. That is, it is difficult to know whether the test has sufficient floor. For example, for some preschool measures the average number of items correct for children who are 2 to 3 years of age is less than one. Bracken goes to considerable length to provide information on ceiling and floor items for each of the 11 subtests. He shows the test has good floor down to age 2-6 and excellent floor at ages 4-2 to 7-6. The test has excellent ceiling to age 6-6. It has a poor ceiling after 7-6 years of age.

Two kinds of reliability data are provided for the Diagnostic Scale of the BBCS. Internal consistency reliabilities were calculated by correlating performance of the standardization sample on odd and even items of the scale. Reliabilities ranged from .47 to .96 for the subtests. The reliability of the Size subtest ranges from .47 to .73 depending on the ages of the students assessed. These coefficients are indicative of reliability that is too low for screening purposes. Reliabilities for the Social Emotional, Texture/Material, and Time/Sequence subtests are too low for screening purposes at age 6.

Internal consistency reliability is also reported for the two 30-item screening tests. Reliabilities ranged from .76 to .80. These are borderline reliabilities for use of this instrument for screening purposes.

Test-retest reliability data on the Diagnostic Scale are reported for a limited sample of 27 children who took the test 14 days apart. The ages of these children are not specified, though the author reports that age was "restricted." Reliabilities of the subtests are sufficiently high for screening purposes, with the exception once again of the Size subtest.

Test-retest reliability information is reported for the two forms of the screening test. Data were taken from the performance of the standardization sample. Test-retest reliability for the screening test ranged from .71 to .80.

Bracken claims the BBCS has good content validity because the items on the scale are used very often in preschool and primary tests typically given to young children. He also reports eight validity studies for the Diagnostic Scale. Performance on the BBCS is shown to correlate sufficiently and about as would be expected with measures of basic concepts (the Boehm Test of Basic Concepts and the Token Test) and receptive vocabulary (the Peabody Picture Vocabulary Test—Revised).

Those who want to assess knowledge of basic concepts at the preschool, kindergarten, and first grade level will find the BBCS very useful. It will be most helpful in identifying concepts that students do and do not know and in the planning of interventions designed to teach basic concepts. The Diagnostic Scale should be helpful in identification of "at risk" students, provided a district is willing to establish local norms. The Screening Scale is limited in the numbers and kinds of behaviors sampled, and has lower reliability than the Diagnostic Scale. Those who wish to make screening decisions might better use the BBCS Diagnostic Scale, though they will have to put limited confidence in the Size subtest.

[34]

Brief Index of Adaptive Behavior. Purpose: Provides a quick acceptable measure of adaptive behavior in non-borderline cases. Ages 5–17; 1984; BIAB; 4 domains: Independent Functioning, Socialization, Communication, Total; responded to by a third party informant, preferably a teacher or parent; 1986 price data: $8 per starter set including 20 response sheets and manual ('84, 10 pages); $5 per 20 response sheets; $3.50 per manual; $6 per specimen set; administration time not reported; R. Steve McCallum, Maurice S. Herrin, Jimmy P. Wheeler, and Jeanette R. Edwards; Scholastic Testing Service, Inc.*

TEST REFERENCES

1. McCallum, R. S., Helm, H. W., Jr., & Sanderson, C. E. (1986). Local norming and validation of an adaptive behavior screening unit. *Educational and Psychological Measurement*, 46, 709-718.

Review of the Brief Index of Adaptive Behavior by MICHAEL J. ROSZKOWSKI, Research Psychologist, The American College, Bryn Mawr, PA:

As suggested by its title, the Brief Index of Adaptive Behavior (BIAB) was designed to provide a quick appraisal of adaptive behavior status. Intended for use in screening for developmental disabilities, this instrument is a short (one-page) rating scale on which informants familiar with the child/adolescent being assessed record their impressions of whether, relative to others of the same age, the individual is "below average," "average," or "above average" on such skills (items) as eating, toileting, dressing, working with others, speaking, etc.

The 39 items comprising the BIAB are distributed equally among the three domains believed to best define the construct of adaptive behavior (i.e., Independent Functioning, Socialization, Communication). Raw scores for each domain are calculated by applying the respective weights of 1, 2, and 3 to the response options of below average, average, and above average. In turn, the three domain scores can be summated into a Total Score. The nature of the response options and their weights (1 = below average, 2 = average, 3 = above average) are supposed to convey meaning to the raw scores on the scale. That is, "average" skill level on each domain is set by definition at 26 (13 items multiplied by a weight of 2), and, similarly, a raw score of 78 constitutes an "average" overall level of adaptive behavior. After summating the items into raw domain scores and a raw total scale score, the rater is instructed to also provide an "estimated functioning age" (EFA) for the child on each of the three domains as well as on his/her total adaptation. The EFA is described as having clinical value, but the specific uses for this score (conceptually similar to mental age) are not discussed. The EFA score appears to be tangential rather than central to the purpose of the BIAB.

Only limited normative data, based on 206 persons, are presented in the BIAB Manual. The norms are in terms of raw score means and standard deviations for each of 11 age cohorts. In the Appendix of the Manual there is a condensed table of derived scores, presenting raw score to standard score equivalents. The standard scores, set to have a mean of 100 with a standard deviation of 15, seem to be based on the linear transformation of raw scores that were collapsed across age. The creators of the BIAB suggest that "local" norms can be developed by the test's users. A request is made in the Manual that those attempting any local standardization share the results with the creators of the BIAB so that this information can be incorporated into the next edition of the BIAB manual. According to the instructions in the Manual, more extensive and precise testing is to be conducted if the person being screened scores one or more standard deviations below the mean of the appropriate comparison group. However, if need be, a different cutoff score can be selected.

The short technical manual accompanying the BIAB concisely summarizes the results of an item analysis, internal consistency reliability analysis, and a factor analysis. All of this information is derived from the protocols of the same randomly selected sample of 206 children from three states who were used to develop the norms. These children were rated by either their teachers or guardians, although in a majority of the cases, the rater was a teacher. The correlation of the items with their respective domain scores ranged from .65 to .85, while the correlation between the items and the total score computed from the sum of the three domains ranged from .56 to .79. The Cronbach's alphas were uniformly high, ranging from .93 to .95 for the domain scores, with the total scale score showing an alpha of .97.

A factor analysis with a three-factor solution, accounting for 56% of the variance, is cited. The three factors, rotated orthogonally, correspond to the three domains of the BIAB and all but three of the items (from the Independent Functioning domain) have their highest loading on the factor/domain they were meant to measure. Item loadings on the appropriate factors range from .39 to .75 on Independent Functioning, .44 to .72 on Socialization, and .45 to .76 on Communication. Over half the items are factorially pure (loading at .35 or higher on only one of the three factors).

Additional psychometric information is available in a journal article authored in part by the senior developer of the BIAB (see McCallum, Helm, & Sanderson, 1986). Here, another item-analysis and internal consistency reliability analysis are reported and a second factor analysis is documented to further support the scale's construct validity. Correlations between the BIAB and two comprehensive adaptive behavior scales (The AAMD Adaptive Behavior Scale-SE and The Vineland Adaptive Behavior Scale-SE) are also presented as evidence of concurrent validity. In addition, local norms for the state of Mississippi are introduced in this article. The item analysis, internal consistency reliability estimates, and the local norms are based on a stratified random sample of children drawn from 20 elementary and junior high schools in Mississippi. Ratings were provided by the children's teachers, with each teacher rating about three children. The correlations between the BIAB and the AAMD Adaptive Behavior Scale are based on a subsample of 39 children (rated by 10 teachers with each teacher rating approximately four children). The concurrent validity study with the Vineland Adaptive Behavior Scale, on the other hand, involved a different sample of 100 children and 21 teachers (from Mississippi and Alabama).

The new set of item-domain correlations ranged between .66 and .87 while the item-total test score correlations were slightly lower, falling in the .64 to .79 range. The Cronbach's alphas computed on these data ranged from .94 to .98. The three factors derived from these new data, based on a principal factor analysis with an orthogonal rotation, showed a significant overlap in factor structure with the analysis performed on the original standardization sample. (One could argue that given the purpose of this analysis, namely the construct validation of a three-factor model, a confirmatory factor analysis method would have been preferable. However, this is a minor point and it is open to debate.) The correlations between the BIAB and the AAMD Adaptive Behavior Scale were moderate in content areas thought to measure similar constructs (.38 to .55). Relatively higher correlations (.43–.75) were derived between comparable domains on the BIAB and the Vineland Adaptive Behavior Scale. The area of least overlap between the BIAB and the Vineland occurred on Independent Functioning, where the correlations were between .43 and .56 (computed separately at each grade). The Socialization scores on these two scales correlated between .63 and .75, and the Communication scales correlated between .64 and .71. Thus, there appears to be some convergent validity between the BIAB and the Vineland Adaptive Behavior Scale.

When developing a scale that is meant to measure a construct through ratings, one needs to decide on the size of the unit of behavior that is to be considered as the object of the rating. Generally, it is believed that the smaller (i.e., more specific, detailed) the unit of behavior to be rated, the greater will be the accuracy of this rating because respectively lower levels of inference are required of the rater. Despite their apparent simplicity, ratings requested for global characteristics frequently constitute a very hard task for the rater because (*a*) the rater may have difficulty in deciding what behaviors are to be excluded and what behaviors are to be included under the large unit of analysis, and (*b*) because no explicit guidelines are provided on how to weigh the ratee's potentially discrepant standing on the different small units of behavior when combining them mentally into a single large unit rating. A long-standing advice has been that if global ratings are desired, they should be developed from the summation of the individual ratings on the specific behaviors. Accordingly, when eating behavior is appraised on the comprehensive adaptive behavior scales, (like the AAMD Adaptive Behavior Scale) the rater is required to provide information about whether the ratee can use a spoon, fork, knife, glass, napkin, etc., rather than simply being asked to indicate the overall quality of the person's eating behavior in terms of just one rating. Unfortunately, this level of detail demands quite a bit of the rater's time.

Likewise, it is generally felt that response options should be as free as possible from subjective interpretation. Traditionally, rating scale values such as "average" have been discouraged because it has been argued that the term lacks uniformity in meaning across raters. Therefore, most of the comprehensive adaptive behavior scales ask the rater to indicate whether a certain behavior is absent or present (or the degree to which it is present). The evaluation of the behavior's quality relative to an appropriate comparison group is typically a second-stage process, involving the norming of the scale.

The economy in administration time achieved by the BIAB is brought about through a focus on relatively large units of adaptive behavior and correspondingly more subjective response options. The format of the BIAB is thus controversial. However, global ratings do not necessarily have to be of low reliability and validity. If the characteristic being rated has salience to the individual, then there is little reason to suppose that the rating will be unreliable. Indeed, even extremely global ratings have been shown to be quite adequate in some situations and, under certain circumstances, global ratings may even be better measures of a construct than a summation of the many individual responses that define it (see Scarpello & Campbell, 1983).

Nonetheless, the format of the BIAB makes it impossible to interpret the scores without due consideration of the rater because the accuracy of the scores on this instrument depends very heavily on the qualifications of the person who is the source of the information. In order to judge whether the individual being rated is below average, average, or above average on a certain skill relative to others of his/her age, the rater not only needs to be familiar with the ratee, but must also know what behavior is typical of a child of that age.

The psychometric properties of the scores from the BIAB (based on the reported studies) are quite acceptable, despite the potential drawbacks of the format. In fact, I would note that the correlation between the BIAB and two very popular comprehensive measures of adaptive behavior (i.e., AAMD Adaptive Behavior Scale—School Edition, Vineland Adaptive Behavior Scale—School Edition) as reported in the McCallum, et al. (1986) article, compare favorably in magnitude to correlations that other studies have found between these two comprehensive scales themselves (see Harrison, 1987). It must be recognized, however, that the ratings in the BIAB validation studies were produced, for the most part, by teachers. Because of their training as well as experience with different children, teachers presumably have a more accurate frame of reference than laypersons. Studies using parents as raters could lead to different results.

No investigations of interrater agreement on the BIAB have been reported. The results of such studies could tell us whether different raters are defining the boundaries of each item and the scale values within the same parameters. Comparison between different groups of raters (e.g., fathers vs. mothers vs. teachers) would be especially helpful in establishing the degree of accuracy that the BIAB ratings typically have among different classes of raters. There is considerable evidence based on various rating-type measures to suggest that mothers tend to overestimate their children's skills (e.g., Bagnato, 1984).

The issue of norms for the BIAB is rather perplexing, perhaps because they are still evolving. By the BIAB authors' own account, the aged-based norms presented in the Manual have limited utility due to the small size of the standardization group. (The 11 age norms are derived from cohorts ranging in size from only 11 to 26 children.) The authors of the BIAB recommend construction of local norms by the BIAB's users, but the term local is not explicitly defined in the Manual. If too parochial, the norms can lose meaning for diagnostic purposes. The article by McCallum et al. (1986) implies that state-based norms are one appropriate approach. At this point, children from only a few states seem to have been studied.

Based on the premise that it is less acceptable to miss identifying a pathological case than to recommend further assessment for a normal case, it is generally believed that a good screening instrument should have a bias toward false positives rather than toward false negatives. Although there are no empirical data to indicate the number of hits, false negatives, and false positives that result from relying on 1 *SD* below the mean on the BIAB as the cutoff score for deciding on whether to conduct a more comprehensive assessment of adaptive behavior, on the face of it, this criterion should result in a larger proportion of false positives than false negatives. The mean raw total score for the standardization group (reported in the Manual) is about 81 with a standard deviation of about 16. Hence, an individual who was rated "average" on 26 (67%) of the items and "below average" on the remaining 13 (33%) items would already qualify for more elaborate testing based on the guidelines presented in the BIAB Manual. For a better understanding of the BIAB scores, though, empirical data on the detection efficiency of different cutoff scores should be sought.

The local norms for Mississippi presented in the McCallum et al. (1986) article are in terms of raw score standard deviations only; the means associated with these *SD*s are not indicated. Total score *SD*s for the eight reported age levels range from 13 (at age 9) to 19 (at age 7). According to the authors of that paper, only the variability (*SD*) in the cohort needs to be considered because the means of the BIAB scales are set by definition. Interestingly, the grand raw score mean for the standardization group reported in the Manual is 81, quite close to the theoretical mean of 78 one would expect in a representative sample that was rated accurately on the 39 items comprising the scale using the 3-point scale on which average has a numerical value of 2. The concept presented in the article, however, represents a change from the procedures specified in the BIAB manual, where one *SD* below the standardization group's actual mean was to serve as the benchmark for deciding whether a more extensive assessment of adaptive behavior was necessary. The logic underlying this new procedure could stand further elaboration and needs to be reconciled with the instructions in the BIAB Manual.

Given the nature of the verbal anchors on this rating scale (above average, average, and below average), one has to wonder if there is any systematic reason for the differences between the age-based cohorts in the size of their respective *SD*s. More than likely they simply represent random error variance in sampling and/or in the accuracy of the assigned rating. With these response options, the child being rated is being compared to an intrinsic set of norms already formulated in the rater's mind. Consequently, it seems to me that it should be possible to interpret the scores even without reference to any external norms. However, knowledge of the variance and the shape of the distribution curve would serve to show how raters typically allocate ratings using the categories of below average, average, and above average.

For screening purposes, a global approach to measurement such as found on the BIAB may be necessary in order to achieve the needed reduction in administration time. The only other alternative to screening involves the administration of a limited but very specific number of items from one of the comprehensive scales of adaptive behavior and then inferring more global information from this small sample of behavior. Articles have appeared in the professional literature on how certain popular comprehensive measures of adaptive behavior can be abbreviated, and screening-level assessment has been incorporated formally into instruments such as the Scales of Independent Behavior (321; Bruininks, Weatherman, Woodcock, & Hill, 1984), on which 32 items rather than the total set of 226 items can be used for screening purposes. Generally, the reduced set of items is selected purposely based on the strength of the items' relationship with the other items measuring the same domain of behavior. A potential problem with the reduced item set approach to screening exists in situations where a child has received training on the skills measured by the smaller subset of items. If the training does not generalize to the other items constituting that domain, then the subset's natural relationship to the other items is distorted, thereby compromising the validity of the short-form measure.

My overall impression is that the BIAB can meet the need for a screening-level measure of adaptive behavior. With the BIAB, it should be possible to assess a large number of children in a short time period. This scale probably has no equal in terms of economy of time. The apparent simplicity of the scale should also make it appealing to the user. However, it must be realized that this scale provides an evaluation of adaptive behavior at a molar rather than a molecular level, and unfortunately, this type of format may be more susceptible to certain rating errors. Particular care must be exercised in interpreting the scores obtained from raters with limited knowledge about normal developmental patterns, especially if young children are being evaluated. The authors of the BIAB seem aware of the limitations of their instrument and appropriately caution the user not to overinterpret the scores.

This is a new scale and although only a limited set of psychometric data about it are reported in the Manual, further empirical work seems to be ongoing and the results are being reported in the professional literature. I look forward to the publication of the promised expanded and revised edition of the Manual that, I hope, will contain further data on the characteristics of the BIAB in diverse samples of raters and ratees, thus allowing us to better gauge the most appropriate conditions for the use of this instrument.

REVIEWER'S REFERENCES

Scarpello, V., & Campbell, J. P. (1983). Job satisfaction: Are all the parts there? *Personnel Psychology*, 36, 577-600.

Bagnato, S. J. (1984). Team congruence in developmental diagnosis and intervention: Comparing clinical judgment and child performance measures. *School Psychology Review*, 13, 7-16.

Bruininks, R. H., Woodcock, R. W., Weatherman, R. F., & Hill, B. K. (1984). Scales of Independent Behavior. Allen, TX: DLM Teaching Resources.

McCallum, R. S., Helm, H. W., Jr., & Sanderson, C. E. (1986). Local norming and validation of an adaptive behavior screening instrument. *Educational and Psychological Measurement*, 46, 709-718.

Harrison, P. L. (1987). Research with adaptive behavior scales. *The Journal of Special Education*, 21, 37-68.

Review of the Brief Index of Adaptive Behavior by JANE A. RYSBERG, Associate Professor of Psychology, California State University, Chico, CA:

The Brief Index of Adaptive Behavior (BIAB) is a 39-item instrument designed to measure adaptive behavior in nonborderline cases. The eight-page manual presents a fine historical account of the need for behavioral measurement in the assessment of mental retardation. The authors admit the BIAB is actually an instrument in the making, and indicate a need for more normative data, including concurrent validity.

The manual identifies teachers and parents as potential users of the BIAB. The preamble to the scoring sheet, however, is addressed to "school personnel well acquainted with the child" and advises that contacting a parent may be necessary.

The purpose of the BIAB is the identification of a "deficit." Test users are referred to their state guidelines for an appropriate definition of a "deficit." The scoring instructions amplify this association with law-making bodies: "State and federal regulations stipulate that children considered for special education (MR) receive an adaptive behavior assessment." The manual clearly identifies the BIAB as a screening device for adaptive behavior assessment. This is not done on the scoring sheet unless one counts the implications of "return this sheet to the appropriate professional."

The Brief Index of Adaptive Behavior includes three subscales: the Independent Functioning domain (IF), the Socialization domain (SOC), and the Communication domain (COMM). Each domain has 13 items, but are not equal slices of a child's behavioral repertoire. The IF items are very diverse, ranging from appropriate eating behaviors to prevocational/vocational skills. The SOC and COMM tap smaller, more homogeneous categories of behavior. Sample items include: "works well with others" to "is flexible," and "uses appropriate speech" to "communicates appropriate feelings," respectively. Exhaustive item analyses are presented. The conclusion from these is simply that each item "contributes meaningfully to the total." The question arises—what is the total? No diagnostic function is assigned to the total of the combined IF, SOC, and COMM scores. An appendix to the manual provides a table for converting IF, SOC, COMM, and total scores to standard scores. Although the manual suggests the standard scores will be useful in providing feedback, the precise utility of the scores is left undefined.

A study of the standardization sample does not cast light on the question of utility. The 206 respondents in the sample were teachers attending workshops on adaptive behavior, and guardians who completed the BIAB individually. Estimates of the socioeconomic status of target children were available for 59% of the sample; race and gender were known for 96%. The relationship between these variables and the BIAB scores was not reported. It was also not reported whether the standardization sample was representative of the school-age population in the three states where standardization testing was conducted.

The age range covered by the BIAB is 5 to 17 years. In general, teachers may find the accurate rating of older students, especially on the IF scale, quite difficult. Examples of item meanings are given, but they are not generally helpful; for example, "Observes safety rules (e.g., obeys traffic signals, fire warnings; cautious of pools, traffic)." In the instruction section, respondents are advised that a lack of opportunity to observe a behavior does not preclude giving that behavior a rating. Furthermore, teachers are advised that a purpose of gathering adaptive behavior information is to determine potential for performance. No attempt is made to operationalize "potential." The instruction to rate unknown behaviors and the conceptualization of the scale as measuring "potential" rather than current levels of performance both invite unreliable results.

BIAB respondents are requested to give a total estimate of functioning age (EFA), as well as an EFA for each domain. The instructions on how to make such estimates are vague. This vagueness may be related to the overall utility of an EFA. The only sentence referring to the EFA in the manual describes it as for "clinical use." No hows or whys are provided.

In defining the need for the Brief Index of Adaptive Behavior, the authors state that existing measures such as the Vineland Adaptive Behavior Scales and the Adaptive Behavior Inventory for Children are generally too time-consuming and ill-standardized, and demonstrate limited reliability and validity. The newest edition to the arsenal, the BIAB, is likewise ill-standardized, and presents no evidence of reliability or validity. It does, however, take virtually no time to complete.

[35]

The Brief Symptom Inventory. Purpose: "Designed to reflect the psychological symptom patterns of psychiatric and medical patients as well as nonpatient individuals." Psychiatric patients and nonpatients; 1975-82; BSI; essentially the brief form of the SCL-90-R; self-report; 9 primary dimension scores (Somatization, Obsessive-Compulsive, Interpersonal Sensitivity, Depression, Anxiety, Hostility, Phobic Anxiety, Paranoid Ideation, Psychoticism), plus 3 global indices (Global Severity Index, Positive Symptom Distress Index, Positive Symptom Total); 1987 price data: $30 per 100 test forms; $17.50 per manual ('82, 48 pages); (7–10) minutes; Leonard R. Derogatis and Phillip M. Spencer; Clinical Psychometric Research.*

See 9:160 (1 reference).

TEST REFERENCES

1. Cochran, C. D., & Hale, W. D. (1985). College student norms on the Brief Symptom Inventory. *Journal of Clinical Psychology*, 41, 777-779.

2. Cella, D. F., & Tross, S. (1986). Psychological adjustment to survival from Hodgkin's disease. *Journal of Consulting and Clinical Psychology*, 54, 616-622.

3. Friedman, A. S., Utada, A., & Glickman, N. W. (1986). Outcome for court-referred drug-abusing male adolescents of an alternative activity treatment program in a vocational high school setting. *The Journal of Nervous and Mental Disease*, 174, 680-688.

4. Verinis, J. S., Wetzel, L., Vanderporten, A., & Lewis, D. (1986). Improvement in men inpatients in an alcoholism rehabilitation unit: A week-by-week comparison. *Journal of Studies on Alcohol*, 47, 85-88.

5. Kiecolt-Glaser, J. K., & Williams, D. A. (1987). Self-blame, compliance, and distress among burn patients. *Journal of Personality and Social Psychology*, 53, 187-193.

6. Noyes, R., Jr., Clarkson, C., Crowe, R. R., Yates, W. R., & McChesney, C. M. (1987). A family study of generalized anxiety disorder. *The American Journal of Psychiatry*, 144, 1019-1024.

7. Sarason, B. R., Shearin, E. N., Pierce, G. R., & Sarason, I. G. (1987). Interrelations of social support measures: Theoretical and practical implications. *Journal of Personality and Social Psychology*, 52, 813-832.

Review of The Brief Symptom Inventory by BERT P. CUNDICK, Professor of Psychology, Brigham Young University, Provo, UT:

The Brief Symptom Inventory (BSI) is a 53-item self-report symptom inventory designed to reflect the psychological systems of psychiatric, medical, and normal individuals. It is a brief form of the SCL-90, which was also devised by Derogatis. It is designed to provide a multidimensional symptom measurement in about 10 minutes.

Although only four to seven items are used on each of the symptom scales, the internal consistency reliabilities (Cronbach's alpha) are very acceptable, ranging from a low of .71 on Psychoticism to a high of .83 on Obsessive-Compulsive. The test-retest reliabilities are also good, ranging from a low of .68 on Somatization to a high of .91 on Phobic Anxiety. The three global scores all have test-retest reliabilities above .80. The 53-item total may be somewhat misleading because the response format utilizes a 5-point continuum, which greatly increases score points over what would be obtained from a T-F format. A variation of alternate form reliability is also presented where the specific items on the BSI were taken from the answer sheets obtained from a group who had taken the SCL-90 and correlated with the symptom scales they matched. These correlations ranged from .92 on Psychoticism to .99 on Hostility. The effort to represent reliability is thorough and establishes the fact that the scores on the BSI are very acceptable for this kind of measure and that the instrument is an adequate substitute for the SCL-90.

Concurrent validity is reported by showing the correlations on the symptom dimensions of the BSI with the Wiggins content scales and the Tryon cluster scores obtained on the MMPI. The reported correlations range from .30 to .72 with the most relevant average score correlations averaging above .5. A factor analysis on a 1,002-psychiatric-outpatient sample was performed. The results confirmed to a remarkable degree the a priori construction of the symptom dimensions; only the four-item Interpersonal Sensitivity scale was not essentially found as hypothesized.

Predictive and construct validity will take some time to establish. However, the method of deriving the BSI from the SCL-90 suggests that previous studies involving the SCL-90 might reflect on the validity of the BSI.

The norms on the BSI are well described; however, they do not appear to be representative of many areas in the United States and it might be desirable for users to develop local norms. The psychiatric norm groups appear heavily weighted toward lower social classes and also overrepresent blacks. It would have been interesting and more informative to show comparisons with U.S. Bureau of the Census data.

Derogatis has been very careful to look at reading level in developing his items. However, neither the SCL-90 nor the BSI include an attempt at validity scores. Confusion, faking, and illiteracy could all produce individual profiles which might be highly misleading.

In summary, the BSI appears to be technically sound in its test construction procedures. The manual is well written and complete and is convincing on matters of score reliability and initial efforts to establish validity. The BSI would be a good initial screening measure. However, future efforts might be directed at improving the test norms and addressing the issue of validity scores.

Review of The Brief Symptom Inventory by CHARLES A. PETERSON, Staff Clinical Psychologist, VA Minneapolis Medical Center, and Clinical Assistant Professor, Department of Psychology, University of Minnesota, Minneapolis, MN:

The Brief Symptom Inventory (BSI) is a brief form of the SCL-90-R (9:1082). It is a self-report inventory "designed to reflect the psychological symptom patterns of psychiatric and medical patients as well as non-patient individuals." The authors state the BSI may be used for a "single, point-in-time assessment of an individual's clinical status, or it may be utilized repeatedly either to document trends through time, or in pre-post evaluations." No comparative data are provided, but the authors insist that the BSI can be reliably administered in a narrative mode to patients who cannot read. Brief, clear instructions to the test will enable all but the very deranged to rate each of the 53 items on a 5-point scale of distress (0–4), ranging from *not at all* (0) to *extremely* (4). Subjects are asked to consider "the past seven days including today" when rendering their self-observing assessment on an easy-to-comprehend answer sheet.

Item content appears to have face validity and is simply stated. A typical example asks, "HOW MUCH WERE YOU DISTRESSED BY:" "Poor appetite?" "Feeling uneasy in crowds?" "Your mind going blank?" Nine symptom dimensions and three global indices can be assessed by the clinician after receiving the answer sheet, quickly scoring the test, and plotting the profile on conveniently normed profile sheets. Interpretation takes place on three different, but interrelated, levels: the global level, the dimensional level, and the level of discrete symptoms. Profile interpretation may be unwarranted, given that no information was provided in the manual on intercorrelations among scales. Scale intercorrelations are "moderate to high, ranging from the mid .40s to the mid .70s" (L. R. Derogatis, personal commmunication, January 27, 1987). Interpretations should be based on the relevant norms provided in the manual: male and female outpatients, male and female nonpatients, male and female psychiatric inpatients, and male and female adolescents. Additional norms are available for college students (Cochran & Hale, 1985) and for the elderly (Hale, Cochran, & Hedgepeth, 1984).

There is every reason to believe that this test will work as promised. The psychometric underpinnings are impressive and are the result of a careful, sequential research program. Internal consistency ranges from a low of .71 on Psychoticism to a high of .85 on Depression. Test-retest reliability over a 2-week period is excellent, ranging from a low of .68 on Somatization to a high of .91 in Phobic Anxiety. The Global Severity index, touted as "the most sensitive" of the macroscopic measures of psychopathology, has a test-retest reliability of .90. These test-retest reliabilities sound good, but theory-derived predictions of those scales most likely to change over time (states?) and those likely to remain stable over time (traits?) should have been provided. The authors use the parent SCL-90-R as an alternate form and find reliability coefficients ranging from .92 to .99. In line with Loevinger (1957) and Messick (1981), the BSI has been evaluated primarily in terms of construct validity. When correlated with the MMPI, convergent validity is good but attenuated by less impressive discriminant validity. Factor analytic results demonstrate impressive agreement between the factor precipitates and the a priori dimensional structure. Predictive validity has been underresearched, a sad state of affairs common to most tests in the *Mental Measurements Yearbooks*. Multimodal assessments of BSI constructs could be made by using compatible instruments from the Psychopathology Rating Scale Series; for example, the Hopkins Psychiatric Rating Scale (9:483) allows a clinician to rate the same constructs from interview data.

Surely it is no secret that clinician time has become increasingly expensive and scarce. Less available time and higher costs have prompted many changes in traditional psychological assessment, including less testing, abbreviated testing, and more automated testing. We have witnessed the MMPI shrink from maxi to midi to mini. Tests may become so brief that we must fearfully wonder if psychologists—following Allport (1953)—will simply dispense with tests and just ask the patient, "Are you depressed?" Psychologists must consider carefully the indications for and the implications of this hurried understanding. Compared to the significant interpersonal relationship in traditional psychological testing (cf., Schafer, 1954; especially Chapter 2), a measure such as the BSI may signal a treatment relationship that may seem ephemeral and superficial. Expressed somewhat differently, what patient would be comforted by the sight of a physician reading a book titled *Rapid Interpretation of Grave Conditions*?

The SCL-90-R takes 15–20 minutes to administer, apparently an unacceptable amount of time to today's fevered clinician, causing the BSI's authors to reduce administration time to 7–10 minutes. Is this difference significant? Is the reduction in time sufficient to justify the BSI's existence? In the spirit of brevity, the answer is "Yes," particularly in light of the solid psychometric foundation, the multiple norms which help the clinician remain sensitive to fluctuations in base rates of psychopathology, and the test's ability to survey a fairly broad range of psychopathology. No doubt potential users would be happier if a "Mania" symptom dimension were included, and if the authors more honestly called the test by its true name, The SCL-53.

REVIEWER'S REFERENCES

Allport, G. W. (1953). The trend in motivational theory. *American Journal of Orthopsychiatry*, 23, 107-119.

Schafer, R. (1954). *Psychoanalytic interpretation of Rorschach testing*. New York: Grune & Stratton.

Loevinger, J. (1957). Objective tests as instruments of psychological theory. *Psychological Reports*, 3, 635-694.

Messick, S. (1981). Constructs and their vicissitudes in educational and psychological measurement. *Psychological Bulletin*, 89, 575-588.

Hale, W. D., Cochran, C. D., & Hedgepeth, B. E. (1984). Norms for the elderly on the Brief Symptom Inventory. *Journal of Consulting and Clinical Psychology*, 52, 321-322.

Cochran, C. D., & Hale, W. D. (1985). College student norms on the Brief Symptom Inventory. *Journal of Clinical Psychology*, 41, 777-779.

[36]

BRIGANCE® Preschool Screen. Purpose: Screens a child's basic "skills and behavior in order to identify the child who should be referred for more comprehensive evaluation." Ages 3–4; 1985; BPS; "criterion-referenced"; individual; 1987 price data: $35.90 per screen (assessment book, 88 pages, and building blocks); (10–20) minutes; Albert H. Brigance; Curriculum Associates, Inc.*

a) AGE 3. 11 skills: Personal Data Response, Identifies Body Parts, Gross Motor Skills, Identifies Objects, Repeats Sentences, Visual Motor Skills, Number Concepts, Builds Tower with Blocks, Matches Colors, Picture Vocabulary, Plurals; $11.95 per 30 three-year-old child 3-part no-carbon data forms; $39.95 per 120 three-year-old child 3-part no-carbon data forms.

b) AGE 4. 11 skills: Personal Data Response, Identifies Body Parts, Gross Motor Skills, Tells Use of Objects, Repeats Sentences, Visual Motor Skills, Number Concepts, Builds Tower with Blocks, Identifies Colors, Picture Vocabulary, Prepositions and Irregular Plural Nouns; $12 per 30 four-year-old child 3-part no-carbon data forms; $40 per 120 four-year-old child 3-part no-carbon data forms.

Review of the BRIGANCE® Preschool Screen by EDITH S. HEIL, Administrative Assistant for Special Programs, Crowley Independent School District, Crowley, TX:

The BRIGANCE® Preschool Screen (BPS) was developed by the author following the publication in 1982 of the Brigance K & 1. The Brigance Diagnostic Inventory of Early Development (birth to age 7) is the more in-depth predecessor of the Preschool Screen. The author's stated purpose is to assess a child's basic "skills and behavior in order to identify the child who should be referred for more comprehensive evaluation."

The 11 subtests for each of the two levels include: Personal Data Response, Identifies Body Parts, Gross Motor Skills, Identifies Objects, Repeats Sentences, Visual Motor Skills, Number Concepts, Builds Tower with Blocks, Matches Colors, Picture Vocabulary, and Plurals.

The test is easily administered by professional or paraprofessional staff with limited background and training in test administration. This makes it an attractive choice for the mass screenings held by school districts to identify children to be considered for in-depth assessment of potential learning problems. The directions and scoring sheet are easy to follow. The average time of administration per child, in trials by this reviewer, was 15 minutes as contrasted to the more lengthy Brigance Diagnostic Inventory.

In describing the test development, the author indicates that a subtest, Visual Discrimination, was eliminated after field testing and critiquing. However, the item development discussion gave no background on the item content of this eliminated scale. In this reviewer's opinion, visual discrimination can be a critical area for academic readiness skills and failure to demonstrate appropriate maturation in this area would be a strong reason to consider a more in-depth assessment.

While 36 different program sites were listed as taking part in the field testing and critiquing, no information is given on how many of the personnel listed in the Appendices actually administered the instrument and how many reviewed the test only for critical purposes. No ethnic, sex, or geographical information is included concerning the test development population. In fact, statements such as "three percent of the children failed those items" are meaningless because the actual number of students participating in the refining process for selection of items is not reported. This serious oversight should be corrected.

Although the BPS is a criterion-referenced test, the delineation of items by age level is troublesome. Since the author indicated the careful selection of items based on the number of children consistently passing or failing, the test giver might feel a level of concern should the child not master any particular item. What consitutes a total score that justifies referral? What is failure or at risk for a 4-year-old student? The author suggests that a child who scores 60 or below should be considered for additional assessment. The manual indicates each program needs to develop its own cutoff score for referral.

There is a supplemental assessments section with more advanced items available for further child assessment. If the basic purpose of the screening is to indicate students who are in need of more in-depth assessment, the directions and items in this section would be rarely used in this reviewer's opinion. In addition the teacher rating form would be rarely used in a public school setting because most of the children being screened for public schools would not have had prior educational experiences. Information gained from the screening can be utilized for additional classroom assessment and instructional purposes by transferring the screening data to the Brigance Diagnostic Inventory of Early Development.

Despite the shortcomings listed above, the BRIGANCE® Preschool Screen appears to be a very cost-effective instrument, both in terms of time of administration and personnel utilization. Its special use would be in conducting preschool screening of large numbers of children for possible consideration for referral for in-depth testing. Some more adequate description of the population upon which the items were developed is necessary, however, before the test can be used with confidence.

Review of the BRIGANCE® Preschool Screen by TIMOTHY L. TURCO, Assistant Professor of School Psychology, Lehigh University, Bethlehem, PA:

Many school districts concerned with the identification of handicapped preschool children are adopting prereferral screening procedures. The general goal of these procedures is to quickly screen large numbers of children to identify those in need of more thorough individual evaluations. Properly conducted screenings are a fairly efficient means for school districts to reduce the number of work hours pupil appraisal personnel must spend assessing nonexceptional preschool children.

Probably the most important decision that must be made as school districts plan their screening procedures is what the screenings should include. Ideally, the results of the screening tests would be highly correlated with: (*a*) the assessment measures used by pupil appraisal personnel during complete psychoeducational evaluations (concurrent validity), and (*b*) the actual identification of handicapping conditions (construct validity). Thus, in part, the validity of preschool screening procedures depends upon the school district's ability to identify the content of the psychoeducational instruments used by pupil appraisal personnel. This is probably the best reason for a school district to consider adopting the use of the BRIGANCE® Preschool Screen for Three-

and Four-Year-Old Children (BPS). The BPS was written specifically to include items similar to those found in 16 psychoeducational assessment tests. In addition, the items included in the BPS were designed to be quick, objectively scored, and procedurally simple.

The BPS makes use of three types of information about each preschool child: (*a*) ratings from the child's parents and preschool teacher(s), (*b*) the child's actual performances on screening tasks, and (*c*) observational data from the child's evaluator. The BPS manual contains self-administered 38-item rating forms for teachers and parents to evaluate a child's skill levels. The content of these rating forms varies slightly between the 3- and 4-year-olds, but is identical for parents and teachers. Despite the fact that the content of the rating forms is identical, a separate form was created for parents and for teachers. This seems to unnecessarily complicate the evaluator's form management problems. Not only must the evaluator insure that the correct form is distributed to the appropriate person, but the evaluator must have an ample supply of forms dedicated to teachers and a separate supply of forms for parents. These forms should be combined and incorporate a box for the evaluator to indicate whether the respondent is a parent or a teacher.

The evaluator has one mandatory and two supplemental one-page forms to use during the screening process. Children's responses to the BPS's 11 basic skill areas are recorded on the mandatory Child Data Sheet. This Sheet prompts the evaluator: (*a*) to collect demographic data, (*b*) on how to assess the child's skills, (*c*) on how to score the child's responses, (*d*) to make some basic behavioral observations, (*e*) on how to rate the child in reference to a group of children screened, and (*f*) to write recommendations. This is a considerable amount of material on a single page, so the print is small and there is not much room for the evaluator to make many legible comments or notes.

In addition to the 11 basic skill areas, the BPS has 8 supplemental skills that can be assessed. Each 3- and 4-year-old child's responses to each of the supplemental skills is recorded on the Supplemental Assessment Data Sheet. The format of the Supplemental Sheet is similar to the Child Data Sheet, except there is no provision to formally score these skills.

The final evaluator form is the Screening Observations Form. This checksheet is designed to cue the evaluator to observe conditions in the child that may warrant referral for additional screenings or treatments (e.g., speech evaluation).

The administration procedures for the BPS are clear, concise, and behaviorally objective. The BPS manual provides complete descriptions of each test administration procedure and the Child Data Sheets also provide prompts for each item.

It is important to remember the BPS is a criterion-referenced test. Therefore, a BPS score does not represent how well the child performed compared to other children the same age. A BPS score indicates only how many points out of 100 the child made. The BPS score is not a simple percentage, but is a summation of weighted raw scores. How these summation scores are used is left to the discretion of the school district. However, the BPS materials suggest a couple of recommendations. First, the scores of cohorts can be rank ordered, and the lowest scoring children can be considered for further evaluation. Second, school districts can set cutting scores, so that any child scoring below the cutting score is referred for a full evaluation. Brigance recommends that any student scoring below 60 is given a full evaluation.

Although the BPS is a criterion-referenced instrument, several validity and reliability issues are vital to consider in determining the technical adequacy of the BPS. Most of the important empirical validity and reliability questions are not answered in the BPS manual. There is a brief description of how educators from 12 different states were asked to evaluate the content validity of the BPS. However, there is no mention of any attempts to assess the construct validity, criterion-related validity, test-retest reliability, or internal constancy of the measure. Thus, assessment personnel who decide to use the BPS must be willing to assume responsibility for appraising its validity and reliability. One way school districts can accomplish this goal, although this is not discussed in the BPS manual, is to use the BPS raw scores to create local standard scores. These standard scores would allow comparisons of student performances on the BPS to: other norm-referenced evaluations in the district (concurrent validity), actual school performances or handicapping conditions (predictive validity), and later BPS scores (test-retest reliability).

Thus, school districts interested in identifying a screening instrument with similar types of test items to instruments used by pupil appraisal personnel should consider the BPS. However, the decision to use the BPS should also be accompanied by a district-wide commitment to standardize and evaluate the screening results.

[37]

Burns/Roe Informal Reading Inventory: Preprimer to Twelfth Grade, Second Edition. Purpose: Allows teacher "to determine students' strengths and weaknesses in reading as well as the levels of reading skills they've attained." Beginning readers–grade 12; 1985; IRI; 2 scores: Word Recognition, Comprehension; 14 levels: Preprimer, Primer, First Reader, Second Grade, Third Grade, Fourth Grade, Fifth Grade, Sixth Grade, Seventh Grade, Eighth Grade, Ninth Grade, Tenth Grade, Eleventh Grade, Twelfth Grade; 1987 price data: $17.50 per manual ('85, 174 pages) containing instructions and graded word lists and graded passages; (30) minutes; Paul C. Burns and Betty D. Roe; Houghton Mifflin.*

Review of the Burns/Roe Informal Reading Inventory: Preprimer to Twelfth Grade, Second Edition by CAROLYN COLVIN MURPHY, Assistant Professor of Teacher Education, San Diego State University, San Diego, CA and ROGER H. BRUNING, Professor of Educational Psychology, University of Nebraska-Lincoln, Lincoln, NE:

The Burns/Roe Informal Reading Inventory is an informal test used to discover the kinds of materials students can and cannot read without assistance. Most often, informal reading inventories (IRIs) are administered by classroom teachers. In the case of the Burns/Roe Informal Reading Inventory, student oral and silent reading of graded word lists and passages is assessed, yielding grade-equivalent scores for independent reading (student can read with understanding alone and with ease), instructional reading (student can read and comprehend with teacher assistance), frustration level (student is unable to function adequately), and capacity (student level of listening comprehension). These scores are seen as suitable for placing students at the correct level in reading programs, for supplying appropriate content-area reading material, and for recommending recreational reading.

Among the many classroom teachers who use it, the Burns/Roe appears to enjoy a generally favorable status. The materials have high interest; there are equivalent forms, which makes the Burns/Roe flexible for use in a variety of situations; it uses the familiar concepts (to reading teachers) of independent, instructional, and frustration levels in reading; and the Burns/Roe is one of the few IRIs that go up to the twelfth grade level. For knowledgeable users, it provides a relatively quick source of information about problems students may be experiencing with reading.

At the same time, the implication of diagnostic capability (e.g., separate scores for different types of comprehension questions) and the fact that the Burns/Roe yields scores used in making individual decisions about students require certain basic psychometric qualities. These are completely lacking. There is no technical manual. There are no data on reliability, standard errors of measurement, comparability of the four forms, or relationship to other measures. No basis for the criteria used to determine levels is given (e.g., in grades 1 and 2, instructional level equals 85 percent or higher in word recognition and 75 percent or higher on comprehension questions). A two-page appendix to the manual contains all the information presented on scale development and validation. Neither the numbers nor characteristics of the students who took part are described.

As a consequence, use of the Burns/Roe Informal Reading Inventory must be an act of faith. While clinical judgments may lead users to the conclusion that the Burns/Roe's assessments may be valid, there are no data to substantiate that claim. The lack of that data severely detracts from what, otherwise, might be considered one of the better informal inventories. Certainly, reading teachers would react with much greater confidence to a measure in which they could make a judgment of probable error in any score, correspondence to other, more formal measures of reading, and expected relationship to classroom performance. In its present form, the Burns/Roe Informal Reading Inventory, Second Edition falls far short of accepted standards for test development and revision.

Review of the Burns/Roe Informal Reading Inventory: Preprimer to Twelfth Grade, Second Edition by EDWARD S. SHAPIRO, Associate Professor and Director, School Psychology Program, Lehigh University, Bethlehem, PA:

The Burns/Roe Informal Reading Inventory (IRI) is a set of informal reading inventories from preprimer through twelfth grade reading levels. The instrument contains both graded word lists and reading passages. The current version is a revision of an earlier edition.

Two sets of word lists, 20 words each, are provided at each level. Words were selected from the Rand McNally and Scott Foresman reading series, although the authors do not provide information regarding which particular series of those publishers were used. Words were assigned to grade levels during field testing; the criteria for classifying a word at a given grade level were that 80% or more of the students at that grade level could successfully pronounce the word, less than 80% of the students could successfully pronounce the word at the grade level below, and more than 80% could pronounce it at the grade level above.

Passages were constructed from the same basal reading series as the word lists and from the reading and literature series of the Houghton-Mifflin company. Again, the authors do not indicate the specific series employed. Passages were evaluated for readability levels using the Spache and Fry formulae. Comprehension questions were constructed to evaluate six areas: Main Idea, Detail, Sequence, Cause and Effect, Inference, and Vocabulary. For each passage, 8 to 10 questions are provided. The questions were evaluated by graduate students in reading education and then revised. Subsequent field testing was conducted, although the authors do not indicate with whom or how many students were tested. Based on the feedback from these students, however, revisions on comprehension questions were made.

Included in the instrument are a number of excellent tables, charts, and clear examples on the administration, scoring, and interpretation of the IRI. The authors discuss their definitions for independent reading level, instructional reading level, frustration reading level, and capacity reading levels. In addition, they offer a suggested system for marking errors and conducting a miscue analysis. Appropriate cautions about the use of error analysis from the limited sample of the IRI are included.

The authors make clear that the intent of their measure is primarily to determine appropriate reading levels. Implied in this use is that a teacher would then be able to accurately place a child within the basal series. Unfortunately, there may be a significant problem with the degree to which IRI results may be generalized beyond the particular basal reading series from which the IRI was developed. Jenkins and Pany (1978), Armbruster and Rosenshine (1977), and Leinhardt, Zigmond, and Cooley (1981) have all provided data that suggest the overlap between the content of assessment instruments and basal reading series is questionable. As such, results on a particular measure may be very different if a different reading series was employed. The IRI measures were all derived from the Rand McNally, Scott Foresman, and Houghton Mifflin series. Although the results may be generalizable to students placed into these series, the authors did not adequately report the exact series employed in developing the inventories.

In addition to the problem of test/curriculum overlap, there are only limited details provided in the manual regarding the field testing. It is difficult to evaluate the degree to which the measures were effectively piloted before publication.

Another concern of this reviewer is the lack of psychometric data reported. Although I would agree the measures are designed as informal inventories, the authors do suggest the use of the measures in a retest format to evaluate student progress. There are no data on test-retest reliability reported. Further, if the measures are to be used to determine placement, validity data should be reported; yet there are no validity data presented. Indeed, the authors have provided very little discussion of potential uses of the measures.

An additional weakness of these measures is their limited usefulness in monitoring student performance across a short period of time. Given that only two equivalent forms of each grade level are provided, any attempt to readminister the IRI frequently would result in biased data due to retesting on the identical information. The authors do not explicitly caution against using the measures to monitor performance. Such cautions should be included in the manual.

Despite these weaknesses, the IRI measure does have a number of significant strengths. The authors have provided all forms, charts, tables, and instructions necessary for conducting IRIs. These items are very clear and easily reproducible. As such, the measure would be particularly valuable as an adjunct assessment measure for reading specialists or classroom teachers.

The measure does offer one of the few available, commercially produced IRIs. Although users should be careful about the potential lack of overlap with the basal reading series employed by their school, the measure may provide an important component to an overall reading assessment.

REVIEWER'S REFERENCES

Armbruster, B. B., Stevens, R. J., & Rosenshine, B. (1977). *Analyzing content coverage and emphasis: A study of three curricula and two tests*. Technical Report No. 26, Center for the Study of Reading, University of Illinois at Urbana-Champaign.

Jenkins, J. R., & Pany, D. (1978). Standardized achievement tests: How useful for special education? *Exceptional Children*, 44, 448-453.

Leinhardt, G., Zigmond, N., & Cooley, W. W. (1981). Reading instruction and its effects. *American Educational Research Journal*, 18, 343-361.

[38]

Bury Infant Check. Purpose: Aids in identifying children with special needs. Children in second term of infant school; 1986; BIC; individual; 2 versions; 1986 price data: £6.95 per teacher's set including Full Check record booklet, Quick Check record form and manual ('86, 36 pages); Lea Pearson and John Quinn; NFER-Nelson Publishing Co., Ltd. [England].*

a) QUICK CHECK. Teacher-rated; 3 scores: Language Expression, Learning Style, Total; £2.95 per 25 Quick Check record forms; (3–4) minutes.

b) FULL CHECK. 12 scores: Language Skills (Comprehension, Expression, Total), Learning Style, Memory Skills (Visual, Auditory, Total), Number Skills, Perceptual Motor Skills (Copying Shapes, Visual Discrimination, Total), Total; £3.45 per 10 Full Check record booklets; (20) minutes.

Review of the Bury Infant Check by STEPHAN A. HENRY, Director of Research and Evaluation, Topeka Public Schools, Topeka, KS:

PURPOSE AND DESCRIPTION. The Bury Infant Check is an individually administered screening instrument for use in identifying kindergarten children with special needs. It is not intended to identify children who may be exceptionally talented or gifted. The instrument consists of 60 items, 13 of which are ratings completed independently by the teacher. This brief instrument should take about 15 minutes to administer. There are eight subtests including Language Comprehension, Language Expression, Learning Style, Visual Memory Skills, Auditory Memory Skills, Number Skills, Copying Shapes, and Visual Discrimination. This test emphasizes language and developmental processes rather than academic skills. Correct responses are assigned a score of one while incorrect responses are scored zero. The total score is obtained by summing the correct response across all subtests. The authors have generally succeeded in attempts to keep the administration and scoring simple. The Copying Figures subtest, however, lacks explicit scoring rules, which may contribute to unreliable scoring. In general, teachers who study the manual and practice the administration of the test a few times should be able to successfully administer the test. The examiner records responses in an individual record book that also has space for children to copy geometric patterns, letters, and words. Visual stimuli for several of the items are contained in the teacher's manual.

Intervention is recommended for children obtaining 47 or less on the total score, 7 or less on the combined number-skills, and 17 or less on the combined language-skills subtests. Since a decision to intervene or not is made based on scores on the Bury Infant Check, it appears that the authors view this instrument as a diagnostic device. Most practitioners would consider the Bury Infant Check to be a screening device and would want to do a more comprehensive assessment before assigning interventions. A short form of this instrument called The Quick Check uses 13 items from the Language Expression and Learning Style subtests. Intervention is recommended for children scoring less than 9 on The Quick Check.

NORMS. The norms are quite limited, consisting of 1,751 children in their second term of "infant school" at Bury, England. Data on socioeconomic and racial groupings are lacking. There is only a reference that the normative group provides "a reasonably representative cross-section of the UK population." Any use of the Bury Infant Check in the USA should incorporate the development of local norms, cutoff scores, and validation.

The ages of the children included in the norm group are loosely described as including children mostly between 5 years and 5 years 6 months with some being under five years. Infant school in England is apparently equivalent to kindergarten in the USA, at least in terms of the ages of students served.

There are separate norms for the eight subtests plus a total score. The norms consist of a table of raw scores with associated percentile equivalents. In general, this test has a good floor. There are several easy items per subtest, which will help with sorting out the lowest functioning students.

TECHNICAL DATA. The teacher's manual provides only vague references to the process of development of the scale and item analyses. Teachers and district psychologists reportedly provided input regarding the content of the test. Easy items passed by students scoring low overall were eliminated. Test-retest reliability coefficients were computed for a group of 42 children with a gap between test administrations of about 3 weeks. The reliabilities were as follows: total score, .67; language items, .89; number items, .74; and teacher-rated items, .99. Reliability coefficients for the Perceptual Motor and Memory Skills subtests were notably absent. The reliability of the total score is too low to support its use for assigning children to interventions. It is most unusual that the total score reliability is considerably lower than the reliabilities reported for various subtest groupings based on far fewer items. Perhaps the unreported reliabilities for the Perceptual Motor and Memory subscales are extremely low, impairing the reliability of the total score. Reliability information is also missing for the short-form version of this test.

The item content of the Bury Infant Check is consistent with its stated purposes. A table in the teacher's manual reveals surprisingly low intercorrelations between most of the subtests. Most are below .25 and several are below .05. These subtests are so independent of one another that summing performance to obtain a total score has questionable meaning. Predictive validity was assessed by administering reading and math tests to random samples of children 2 years after they had been tested with the Bury Infant Check. The reading test subsample included 255 children, while the math test was given to 177 children. The authors tabulated data to determine the extent of pass versus fail agreement between the Bury Infant Check and each criterion test. A standard score of 90 was set as the passing criterion on the math and reading tests. Contingency tables based on using the Bury Infant Check total score, language score, and teacher-rated items to predict the reading test score are presented in the teacher's manual in Tables 4a to 4c.

SUMMARY. The Bury Infant Check is a potentially useful screening instrument for identifying children of kindergarten age who may have special needs. The standardization sample was limited to Bury, England, however, and the use of this instrument in other localities, particularly outside of England, would require the development of local norms and validation studies. Readers are encouraged to consider the use of the Developmental Indicators for the Assessment of Learning—Revised (DIAL-R)(Mardell-Czudnowski & Goldenberg, 1983; 89) when looking for a screening instrument for use with children under 6 years of age. The DIAL-R has many more items, is based on a stratified sample representative of the USA population, and has considerable technical data to support its use.

REVIEWER'S REFERENCE

Mardell-Czudnowski, C. D., & Goldenberg, D. S. (1983). Developmental Indicators for the Assessment of Learning—Revised. Edison, NJ: Childcraft Education Corp.

[39]

Business Analyst Skills Evaluation. Purpose: "Measures practical and analytical skills required for the position of Business Systems Analyst." Candidates for non-computer Business Analyst positions; 1984; 20 subtests: Logic/Flowcharting/Problem Solving, Systems Analysis, Communication Skills, Memory, Emotional Stability, People Contact Desired, Extroversion, Maturity, Dominance, Enthusiasm, Consistency, Adventurousness, Toughmindedness, Practicality, Sophistication, Self-Confidence, Self-Sufficiency, Participating, Leadership Potential, Initiative and Drive; manual ('84, 6 pages); 1987 price data: $175–400 per administration and scoring (depending on version); (210) minutes; Wolfe Personnel Testing & Training Systems, Inc.*

Review of the Business Analyst Skills Evaluation by LENORE W. HARMON, Professor of

Educational Psychology, University of Illinois, Champaign, IL:

The Business Analyst Skills Evaluation (BASE) consists of two sections. The six problems that form Section 1 of the evaluation are apparently the original contributions of the test publishers. Section 2 contains personality subtests, and tests for memory and fluency. It appears that the personality subtests are based on the 16PF. No examples of Section 2 items are given in the manual. Neither did the publisher provide copies of these tests to the Buros Institute of Mental Measurements. This reviewer infers that Section 2 is composed of tests not developed by the authors of the BASE.

Scores can be obtained by phoning the responses to the publisher, mailing the inventory to the publisher, or the user can score the inventory. Scales are divided into Technical Skills and Personality Factors. The six problems in Section 1 are apparently used to assess technical skills. The manual is unclear about how many technical skills are measured but the report form lists three scales under the topic of technical skills that are apparently derived, at least partially, from these problems. They are: (*a*) Logic, Flowcharting, & Problem Solving, (*b*) Systems Analysis, and (*c*) Communications Skills. The other scale in this cluster is Memory, which is not derived from Section 1. There is also an Overall Technical Rating, which seems to be based on all four scales. The only items available for review were the six problems in Section 1.

The six problems are interesting and appear to be appropriate for testing business analysis skills. Unfortunately, no evidence is given that they are. All but one of the problems can be scored objectively but several scores might be obtained from one problem, and the manual does not tell how they are derived, how they contribute to the scales, or how the scales are related to the traits required in a business analyst that are listed in the manual. One wonders how the user who elects to score the inventory is told to handle the one problem that does not appear to lend itself to any type of objective scoring.

The manual offers various formats of score reports containing one, three, or six pages, and then gives an example of a two-page report. This is typical of the generally confusing style of this manual. The report form lists what are apparently stanine scores for the individual and for the "ideal" on each scale. No evidence is given regarding the groups tested to provide norms or regarding how the ideal scores were determined. They are clearly not averages.

In addition to the fact that the manual presents no evidence as to how the test was scaled or normed, or how it is scored, or whether it is reliable, there is no evidence that it is useful as a "hiring, promotion, or training tool," as claimed. The manual itself is so inadequate and confusing that one wonders how clear the instructions for user scoring are. There seems to be no plausible reason to use this evaluation as currently presented. The publishers might, however, explore the reliability and validity of the scores derived from the six problems in Section 1, write a clear informative manual, and hope for a better evaluation in the future. It is too bad these steps were not taken prior to publication.

[40]

Buying My Food. Purpose: Evaluates upper elementary school students' application of their food purchasing knowledge. Grades 5–6; 1985; price data for complete set including manual (8 pages), test, and answer key available from local Dairy Council; (20–50) minutes; National Dairy Council and Iowa State University; National Dairy Council.*

[The publisher advised in April 1989 that this test will be discontinued.]

Review of Buying My Food by HAZEL M. FOX, Professor of Human Nutrition, Emeritus, University of Nebraska-Lincoln, Lincoln, NE:

Buying My Food is described as a practical inventory for evaluating upper elementary school (fifth and sixth grades) students' application of their food purchasing knowledge. The food purchasing behaviors the test attempts to measure are: Food Quality, Labeling, and Shopping Techniques. The test consists of 29 pictorial items in a multiple-choice format with three options provided for each item. In addition to selecting the best response, students must provide a rationale for their choice. Only correct answers accompanied by a correct reason are given credit. Eleven test items deal with Food Quality, seven with Labeling, and 11 with Shopping Techniques.

The authors do not state specifically how they determined that these three content areas represent the areas of knowledge most pertinent to food buying in this age group. Apparently, elementary food and nutrition curriculum guides were consulted to translate the three concepts into test items. In developing the test, 38 fifth and sixth grade students took part in a series of simulated food purchase situations that portrayed consumer choices students in this age group might experience. Actual food items were used. Students were asked to choose the foods to buy from a group of similar foods. Responses were analyzed and the behaviors identified were used to develop a paper-and-pencil test appropriate for administering to a large group.

The test was field-tested under three situations. First it was administered to four classrooms of fifth and sixth grade students who were able to complete the test in a reasonable length of time (approximately 25 minutes). Second, criterion-related validity was obtained through a field test with 160 students in four midwestern schools. Students selected appropriate food items from pictures or from actual food samples. Third, a national field test was conducted with 496 fifth and sixth grade students in 21 different schools. Schools were from nine states and represented low, middle, and high socioeconomic levels, different social and ethnic backgrounds, and three major geographical areas.

Content and criterion validity were assessed. Content validity, the degree to which the inventory measures specified content, was established by four nutrition and education specialists, who confirmed that the items were appropriate and accurate. Criterion-related validity, the extent to which responses to the paper-pencil instrument agreed with responses given using actual food products, revealed similar ability to discriminate. Students provided similar rationales for their answers whether responding to the paper-and-pencil format or the actual food product models.

The 29 test items are straightforward, unambiguous, and easy to understand. In general, the items appear to measure the concepts which the authors have attributed to them. Thirteen of the 29 items depend on previous knowledge, while answers to the remaining 16 items can be determined from the information presented in the test material. Mathematical ability is stressed rather heavily with 11 answers directed to calculating cost per serving or nutrient content per serving. The calculations are used to determine least cost or highest or lowest nutrient content of the food items presented.

Seven items refer to food costs. While some of the calculations required are simple, others are sufficiently complex to require paper and pencil or a calculator. It is quite possible that students may answer incorrectly not because they do not understand the principle involved, but rather because they were unable to perform the mathematical calculation. This, then, tests mathematical skill instead of the nutrition knowledge. It seems somewhat unreasonable to expect fifth and sixth grade students to perform rather complex mathematical operations as a routine part of grocery shopping.

Other test items stress ingredient labelling, dating of food products, and ingredient listing. These items concern very useful information that fifth and sixth graders may be expected to master.

Internal measures of consistency were calculated. The resulting coefficients were .82 for the fifth grade and .83 for the sixth grade. These are acceptable. The authors present mean scores and standard deviations for each grade level and suggest using these as norms for other users.

Overall, the test is well conceived, measures the subject matter it proposes to measure, and has adequate psychometric qualities.

Review of Buying My Food by GWENDOLYN NEWKIRK, Professor and Chairman, Department of Consumer Science and Education, University of Nebraska-Lincoln, Lincoln, NE:

Buying My Food is described by the authors as an inventory that can be used to assess the application of food purchasing knowledge and behaviors of fifth- and sixth-grade students. Three major food purchasing concepts are identified for purposes of instrumentation: Food Quality, Labeling, and Shopping Techniques. The test manual includes an answer key and the 16-page test that contains 29 items. The easily removed perforated test pages can be used indefinitely as masters making it possible to reproduce the test in quantities for classroom use.

TEST DEVELOPMENT. The inventory is designed so that respondents are asked what to do in a specific situation. Three pictorial drawings of possible responses follow each question. The respondent selects one of the three responses and writes a statement of the reason for the choice. This format enhances the ability to clarify the food purchasing behaviors, offering a better opportunity to plan curriculum in keeping with the appropriate level of student knowledge. Instrument development included devising a test plan for purposes of organizing the food purchasing situations, preliminary testing of behaviors using actual food items, and adapting the items to a paper-pencil format. A three-stage national field test of 496 fifth and sixth graders in 21 different schools was accomplished to determine understanding of inventory items, establish validity, and obtain evidence of statistical qualities. The national field test students lived in three major geographical areas, represented varying socioeconomic levels, and different racial and ethnic backgrounds.

While the authors interchangeably use the terms test plan and table of specifications, the latter is not clarified nor presented to compare level of behaviors/knowledge being tested by the three major concepts. Therefore, referring to the summary as a test plan is more appropriate for user interpretation.

STATISTICAL CHARACTERISTICS. Using data from the national field test respondents, the test manual was written to present descriptive evidence of content and criterion-related validity, difficulty, and discrimination indices. Internal consistency was calculated, using Kuder-Richardson formula 20 with coefficients of .82 for fifth grade, and .83 for sixth grade. The highest possible total score is 29. Mean score for fifth grade was 16.8 with a range of 3–27, and 16.9 for sixth grade with a range of 3–28. While completion time ranged between 20–50 minutes for each group of students, average completion time was 35 minutes. At least four situations require mathematical calculations to answer. It is not clear whether the time needed to complete the inventory reflected use of a calculator or not. Incorrect responses to these items may be the result of improper calculations rather than deficits in food knowledge.

The test is designed to be administered at the same time to all members of a class. A practice question is included to insure that students understand how to respond. An ingenious teacher could convert the drawings into simulations of the actual food items, if there were the desire to present the situations in other than a paper-pencil format.

SUMMARY AND LIMITATIONS. Ascertaining pupil food buying behaviors can be useful to teachers in judging levels of understanding of nutrition knowledge, and can provide teachers with substantive information for curriculum planning to enhance this knowledge base.

The questions on the instrument are presented to be eye-appealing and easily read. Given some assistance, students with minor learning disabilities could respond to the items with little difficulty.

An advantage of the test is that it can be used with other instruments described in the test manual to judge the general effectiveness of nutrition education programs. The technical aspects of this test are quite strong.

Although nutrition education specialists verified that items conformed to the test plan and were accurate, this reviewer perceived some limitations in content validity.

One limitation observed in the test was the inconsistency in categorization of the items into the three identified concepts. With the exception of the identifying nutrient and the pictorial representation, five items used the same basic wording in the stem (8, 12, 22, 26, 29). Yet, three of these items (12, 22, 26) were classified under the concept of labeling and the remaining two (8 and 29) were identified with the concept of food quality. No logical rationale could be discerned for this differentiation among these items. To retain a reasonably even distribution of items among the three concepts, other item choices would have strengthened the instrument.

The authors refer to two items frequently missed in the pilot of the instrument although these items were not identified. Should one of the items have been that selected by this reviewer (Item 24), the "miss-rate" could be attributed to drawings unrelated to the question. Example "C" in this item moves away from food buying and becomes an unrelated choice. Rewording of the stem for this item also would be appropriate. This restatement might be "select the shopping list which gives the most information for making food purchases." However, being unaware of the intent in presenting the item in this manner, the additional word might not resolve this reviewer's concern. The item in its present form may be considered a weak indicator of food buying behavior.

In accepting the classification of items into the three food purchasing behaviors, one must adhere to the definitions of the authors, although in general usage, items are apt to be classified differently by the educator. This can lead to a problem in designing curriculum that is enabling in helping learners to reason about ends.

IN CONCLUSION. Buying My Food can measure buying behaviors of fifth and sixth grade students. Instrument development is clearly described in the test manual and adheres to criteria for sound test construction. Although there is concern about the classification of the items into the three concepts, and the apparent weakness in the construction of at least one item in a limited number of items, the instrument represents a creative effort to assess food buying behaviors. Teachers will undoubtedly wish to use additional measures to complement the results obtained by this test.

[41]

California Achievement Tests, Forms E and F. Purpose: "To measure achievement in the basic skills commonly found in state and district curricula." Grades K.0–K.9, K.6–2.2, 1.6–3.2, 2.6–4.2, 3.6–5.2, 4.6–6.2, 5.6–7.2, 6.6–8.2, 7.6–9.2, 8.6–11.2, 10.6–12.9; 1957–85; CAT/E & F; 2 forms; 11 overlapping levels; Form F available in Levels 13–20 only; 1986 price data: $13.30 per 35 locator tests with answer sheets and directions (specify No. 1 for grades 1–6 or No. 2 for grades 6–12); $18.60 per set of 3 hand-scoring stencils for use with CompuScan answer sheets (specify Level 14, 15, 16, 17, 18, 19, or 20 and Level E or F); $13 per 50 CompuScan Complete Battery answer sheets, Levels 14–20; $7.65 per 50 CompuScan answer sheets, Levels 14–20 (specify Reading, Mathematics, or Listening Test/Writing Assessment/Optional Testing); $10.10 per 25 SCOREZE answer sheets (specify Reading and Study Skills, Mathematics, Language and Spelling, or Science and Social Studies and indicate Level 14–20); $10.90 per 50 answer sheets for Locator Tests 1 and 2; $.65 per class record sheet for hand recording; $17.45 per 100 student diagnostic profile sheets for hand recording (specify Level 10–20); $3.80 per Directions, Locator Tests 1–2; $7 per Test Coordinator's Handbook; $7 per Preliminary Technical Report; $11.60 per Class Management Guide; $4.95 per Multi-Level Norms book (specify Fall, Winter, or Spring); $29.25 per Form E Multi-Level examination kit (K–12); $17.35 per Form E review kit (indicate Primary/Grades K–3, Intermediate/Grades 4–6, or Secondary/Grades 7–12); scoring service available from publisher; CTB/McGraw-Hill.*

a) LEVEL 10. Grades K.0–K.9; 6 scores: Reading (Visual Recognition, Sound Recognition, Vocabulary, Comprehension), Language Expression, Mathematics Concepts and Applications; 2 editions; $4.60 per 35 practice tests; $4.95 per Form E examiner's manual ('85, 45 pages); (154–169) minutes in 3 sessions.

1) *Hand-Scorable Booklet*. $29.75 per 35 Form E Complete Battery Booklets including examiner's manual and scoring key.

2) *Machine-Scorable Booklet*. $45.50 per 35 Form E Complete Battery booklets including examiner's manual.

b) LEVEL 11. Grades K.6–2.2; 6 scores: Reading (Word Analysis, Vocabulary, Comprehension), Language Expression, Mathematics (Mathematics Computation, Mathematics Concepts and Applications); 2 editions; $5 per 35 practice tests for Levels 11–12; $4.95 per Form E examiner's manual ('85, 44 pages); (175–190) minutes in 3 sessions.

1) *Hand-Scorable Booklet*. $29.75 per 35 Form E Complete Battery booklets (examiner's manual and scoring key included with each set of 35 booklets); $21.35 per 35 Form E Reading or Form E Mathematics booklets.

2) *Machine-Scorable Booklet*. $45.50 per 35 Form E Complete Battery booklets including examiner's manual; $31.85 per 35 Reading or Mathematics booklets (each including examiner's manual).

c) LEVEL 12. Grades 1.6–3.2; 10 scores: Reading (Word Analysis, Vocabulary, Comprehension), Spelling, Language (Language Mechanics, Language Expression), Mathematics (Mathematics Computation, Mathematics Concepts and Applications), Science (optional), Social Studies (optional); 2 editions; $4.95 per Form E examiner's manual ('85, 49 pages); (315–330) minutes in 3 or 4 sessions (including optional tests).

1) *Hand-Scorable Booklet*. $33.25 per 35 Form E Complete Battery booklets (examiner's manual and scoring key included with each set of 35 booklets); $29.75 per 35 Form E Basic Skills Battery booklets; $21.35 per 35 Form E Reading or Form E Mathematics booklets.

2) *Machine-Scorable Booklet*. $49.70 per 35 Form E Complete Battery booklets; $45.50 per 35 Form E Basic Skills Battery booklets; $31.85 per 35 Form E Reading or Form E Mathematics booklets (each set of 35 including examiner's manual).

d) LEVEL 13. Grades 2.6–4.2; 10 scores: same as for *c*; 2 editions; 2 forms; $5 per 35 practice tests;

$4.95 per Form E or Form F examiner's manual ('85, 49 pages); (354–369) minutes in 3 or 4 sessions.

1) *Hand-Scorable Booklet.* Prices same as for Level 12; Complete Battery booklet available in both Form E and Form F.

2) *Machine-Scorable Booklet.* Prices same as for Level 12; Complete Battery booklet available in both Form E and Form F.

e) LEVEL 14. Grades 3.6–5.2; 11 scores: Reading (Word Analysis, Vocabulary, Comprehension), Spelling, Language (Language Mechanics, Language Expression), Mathematics (Mathematics Computation, Mathematics Concepts and Applications), Study Skills, Science (optional), Social Studies (optional); $5 per 35 practice tests; $45.85 per 35 Complete Battery Form E or Form F reusable test booklets; $44.10 per 35 Form E Basic Skills Battery reusable test booklets; $21.70 per 35 Form E Reading or Form E Mathematics reusable test booklets; $4.95 per Form E and Form F examiner's manual for Levels 14–20 ('85, 51 pages); (408–423) minutes in 3 or 4 sessions.

f) LEVEL 15. Grades 4.6–6.2; 11 scores: same as for Level 14; examiner's manual, prices for reusable test booklets and time same as for Level 14.

g) LEVEL 16. Grades 5.6–7.2; 11 scores: same as for Level 14; examiner's manual, prices for reusable test booklets, and time same as for Level 14.

h) LEVEL 17. Grades 6.6–8.2; 10 scores: same as for Level 14 but without Word Analysis; examiner's manual and prices for reusable test booklets same as for Level 14; (393–408) minutes.

i) LEVEL 18. Grades 7.6–9.2; 10 scores: same as for Level 17; examiner's manual and prices for reusable test booklets same as for Level 14; time same as for Level 17.

j) LEVEL 19. Grades 8.6–11.2; 10 scores: same as for Level 17; examiner's manual and prices for reusable test booklets same as for Level 14; time same as for Level 17.

k) LEVEL 20. Grades 10.6–12.9; 10 scores: same as for Level 17; examiner's manual and prices for reusable test booklets same as for Level 14; time same as for Level 17.

For reviews by Bruce G. Rogers and Victor L. Willson of the 1978 edition, see 9:180 (19 references); see also T3:344 (68 references); for reviews by Miriam M. Bryan and Frank Womer of the 1970 edition, see 8:10 (33 references); for reviews by Jack C. Merwin and Robert D. North of the 1957 edition, see 6:3 (19 references); for a review by Charles O. Neidt, see 5:2 (10 references); for reviews by Warren G. Findley, Alvin W. Schindler, and J. Harlan Shores of the 1950 edition, see 4:2 (8 references); for a review by Paul A. Witty of the 1943 edition, see 3:15 (3 references); for reviews by C. W. Odell and Hugh B. Wood of an earlier edition, see 2:1193 (1 reference); for a review by D. Welty Lefever and an excerpted review by E. L. Abell, see 1:876. For reviews of subtests, see 8:45 (2 reviews), 8:257 (1 review), 8:719 (2 reviews), 6:251 (1 review), 5:177 (2 reviews), 5:468 (1 review), 4:151 (2 reviews), 4:411 (1 review), 4:530 (2 reviews, 1 excerpt), 2:1292 (2 reviews), 2:1459 (2 reviews), 2:1563 (1 review), 1:893 (1 review), and 1:1110 (2 reviews).

TEST REFERENCES

1. Howe, A. C., Hall, V., Stanback, B., & Seidman, S. (1983). Pupil behaviors and interactions in desegregated urban junior high activity-centered science classrooms. *Journal of Educational Psychology*, 75, 97-103.

2. McDermott, P. A., & Watkins, M. W. (1983). Computerized vs. conventional remedial instruction for learning-disabled pupils. *The Journal of Special Education*, 17, 81-88.

3. Powers, S., Slaughter, H., & Helmick, C. (1983). A test of the equipercentile hypothesis of the TIERS norm-referenced model. *Journal of Educational Measurement*, 20, 299-302.

4. Baldwin, L., Medley, D. M., & MacDougall, M. A. (1984). A comparison of analysis of covariance to within-class regression in the analysis of non-equivalent groups. *The Journal of Experimental Education*, 52, 68-76.

5. Bos, C. S., & Filip, D. (1984). Comprehensive monitoring in learning disabled and average students. *Journal of Learning Disabilities*, 17, 229-233.

6. Butler-Omololu, C., Doster, J. A., & Lahey, B. (1984). Some implications for intelligence test construction and administration with children of different racial groups. *The Journal of Black Psychology*, 10, 63-75.

7. Chandler, H. N. (1984). The American public school: Yes, we have no standards. *Journal of Learning Disabilities*, 17, 186-187.

8. Coie, J. D., & Krehbiel, G. (1984). Effects of academic tutoring on the social status of low-achieving, socially rejected children. *Child Development*, 55, 1465-1478.

9. Dunkelberger, G. E., & Heikkinen, H. (1984). The influence of repeatable testing on retention in mastery learning. *School Science and Mathematics*, 84, 590-597.

10. Karnes, F. A., Whorton, J. E., & Currie, B. B. (1984). Correlations between the Wide Range Achievement Test and the California Achievement Test with intellectually gifted students. *Psychological Reports*, 54, 189-190.

11. Labaree, D. F. (1984). Setting the standard: Alternative policies for student promotion. *Harvard Educational Review*, 54, 67-87.

12. Levi, G., Musatti, L., Piredda, M. L., & Sechi, E. (1984). Cognitive and linguistic strategies in children with reading disabilities in an oral storytelling test. *Journal of Learning Disabilities*, 17, 406-410.

13. Peterson, P. L., Swing, S. R., Stark, K. D., & Waas, G. A. (1984). Students' cognitions and time on task during mathematics instruction. *American Educational Research Journal*, 21, 487-515.

14. Powers, S., & Jones, P. B. (1984). Factorial invariance of the California Achievement Tests across race and sex. *Educational and Psychological Measurement*, 44, 967-970.

15. Price, P. A. (1984). A comparative study of the California Achievement Test (Forms C and D) and the Key Math Diagnostic Arithmetic Test with secondary LH students. *Journal of Learning Disabilities*, 17, 392-396.

16. Russell, T., Brunson, L. D., & Bryant, C. A. (1984). Effects of verbal-mediated modeling on concrete-operational reasoning for a sample of ESN children. *Psychology in the Schools*, 21, 504-511.

17. Sandoval, J. (1984). Repeating the first grade: How the decision is made. *Psychology in the Schools*, 21, 457-462.

18. Slavin, R. E., Madden, N. A., & Leavey, M. (1984). Effects of team assisted individualization on the mathematics achievement of academically handicapped and nonhandicapped students. *Journal of Educational Psychology*, 76, 813-819.

19. Swanson, H. L. (1984). Effect of cognitive effort on learning disabled and nondisabled readers' recall. *Journal of Learning Disabilities*, 17, 67-74.

20. Swartz, J. P., & Walker, D. K. (1984). The relationship between teacher ratings of kindergarten classroom skills and second-grade achievement scores: An analysis of gender differences. *Journal of School Psychology*, 22, 209-217.

21. Weiner, M., & Kippel, G. (1984). The relationship of the California Achievement Test to the Degrees of Reading Power Test. *Educational and Psychological Measurement*, 44, 497-500.

22. Abadzi, H. (1985). Ability grouping effects on academic achievement and self-esteem: Who performs in the long run as expected. *The Journal of Educational Research*, 79, 36-40.

23. Amlund, J. T., Gaffney, J., & Kulhavy, R. W. (1985). Map feature content and text recall of good and poor readers. *Journal of Reading Behavior*, 17, 317-330.

24. Beck, S., Collins, L., Overholser, J., & Terry, K. (1985). A cross-sectional assessment of the relationship of social competence measures to peer friendship and likeability in elementary-age children. *Genetic, Social, and General Psychology Monographs*, 111, 43-63.

25. Burke, J. P., Ellison, G. C., & Hunt, J. P. (1985). Measuring academic self-concept in children: A comparison of two scales. *Psychology in the Schools*, 22, 260-264.

26. Carnine, D., Gersten, R., Darch, C., & Eaves, R. (1985). Attention and cognitive deficits in learning-disabled students. *Journal of Special Education*, 19, 319-331.

27. Childers, J. S., Durham, T. W., Bolen, L. M., & Taylor, L. H. (1985). A predictive validity study of the Kaufman Assessment Battery for Children with the California Achievement Test. *Psychology in the Schools*, 22, 29-33.

28. Colledge, N. J., & Wurster, S. R. (1985). Intergenerational tutoring and student achievement. *The Reading Teacher*, 39, 343-346.

29. Conklin, R. C. (1985). Teacher competency testing: The present situation and some concerns on how teachers are tested. *Education Canada*, 25, 12-15.

30. D'Angelo Bromley, K. (1985). Précis writing and outlining enhance content learning. *The Reading Teacher*, 38, 406-411.

31. Evans, E. D. (1985). Longitudinal follow-up assessment of differential preschool experience for low income minority group children. *Journal of Educational Research*, 78, 197-202.

32. Fitzgerald, J., Spiegel, D. L., & Webb, T. B. (1985). Development of children's knowledge of story structure and content. *The Journal of Educational Research*, 79, 101-108.

33. Gallegos, R., & Franco, J. N. (1985). Effects of a bilingual education program on language and academic achievement. *Perceptual and Motor Skills*, 60, 438.

34. Holliday, B. G. (1985). Differential effects of children's self-perceptions and teachers' perceptions on black children's academic achievement. *Journal of Negro Education*, 54, 71-81.

35. Hoy, W. K., & Ferguson, J. (1985). A theoretical framework and exploration of organizational effectiveness of schools. *Educational Administration Quarterly*, 21 (2), 117-134.

36. Kickbusch, K. (1985). Minority students in mathematics: The reading skills connection. *Sociological Inquiry*, 55, 402-416.

37. Kippel, G. M. (1985). Use of forms C and D of the California Achievement Test as equivalent forms. *Psychological Reports*, 57, 1049-1050.

38. Medina, M., Jr., Saldate, M., IV, & Mishra, S. P. (1985). The sustaining effects of bilingual instruction: A follow-up study. *Journal of Instructional Psychology*, 12, 132-139.

39. Runco, M. A., & Albert, R. S. (1985). The reliability and validity of ideational originality in the divergent thinking of academically gifted and nongifted children. *Educational and Psychological Measurement*, 45, 483-501.

40. Sizemore, B. A. (1985). Pitfalls and promises of effective schools research. *Journal of Negro Education*, 54, 269-288.

41. Slavin, R. E., & Karweit, N. L. (1985). Effects of whole class, ability grouped, and individualized instruction on mathematics achievement. *American Educational Research Journal*, 22, 351-367.

42. Smith, E. R. (1985). Community college reading tests: A statewide survey. *Journal of Reading*, 28, 52-55.

43. Tolfa, D., Scruggs, T. E., & Bennion, K. (1985). Format changes in reading achievement tests: Implications for learning disabled students. *Psychology in the Schools*, 22, 387-391.

44. Valenzuela de la Garza, J., & Medina, M., Jr. (1985). Academic achievement as influenced by bilingual instruction for Spanish-dominant Mexican American children. *Hispanic Journal of Behavioral Sciences*, 7, 247-259.

45. Vertiz, V. C., Fortune, J. C., & Hutson, B. A. (1985). Teacher leadership styles as they relate to academic gain for unsuccessful students. *Journal of Research and Development in Education*, 18 (3), 63-67.

46. Wakefield, J. F. (1985). Towards creativity: Problem finding in a divergent-thinking exercise. *Child Study Journal*, 15, 265-270.

47. Willson, V. L., & Reynolds, C. R. (1985). Another look at evaluating aptitude-achievement discrepancies in the diagnosis of learning disabilities. *The Journal of Special Education*, 18, 477-487.

48. Baglin, R. F. (1986). A problem in calculating group scores on norm-referenced tests. *Journal of Educational Measurement*, 23, 57-68.

49. Boone, H. C. (1986). Relationship of left-right reversals to academic achievement. *Perceptual and Motor Skills*, 62, 27-33.

50. Curry, J. F., Logue, P. E., & Butler, B. (1986). Child and adolescent norms for Russell's revision of the Wechsler Memory Scale. *Journal of Clinical Child Psychology*, 15, 214-220.

51. Dirgi, D. R. (1986). Does the Rasch model really work for multiple choice items? Not if you look closely. *Journal of Educational Measurement*, 23, 283-298.

52. Entwisle, D. K., Alexander, K. L., Cadigan, D., & Pallas, A. (1986). The schooling process in first grade: Two samples a decade apart. *American Educational Research Journal*, 23, 587-613.

53. Fitzgerald, J., & Spiegel, D. L. (1986). Textual cohesion and coherence in children's writing. *Research in the Teaching of English*, 20, 263-280.

54. Friedman, A. S., Utada, A., & Glickman, N. W. (1986). Outcome for court-referred drug-abusing male adolescents of an alternative activity treatment program in a vocational high school setting. *The Journal of Nervous and Mental Disease*, 174, 680-688.

55. Kinard, E. M., & Reinherz, H. (1986). Birthdate effects on school performance and adjustment: A longitudinal study. *Journal of Educational Research*, 79, 366-372.

56. Kinard, E. M., & Reinherz, H. (1986). Effects of marital disruption on children's school aptitude and achievement. *Journal of Marriage and the Family*, 48, 285-293.

57. Mboya, M. M. (1986). Black adolescents: A descriptive study of their self-concepts and academic achievement. *Adolescence*, 21, 689-696.

58. Midkiff, R. M., Burke, J. P., Hunt, J. P., & Ellison, G. C. (1986). Role of self-concept of academic attainment in achievement-related behaviors. *Psychological Reports*, 58, 151-159.

59. Papay, J. P., & Spielberger, C. D. (1986). Assessment of anxiety and achievement in kindergarten and first- and second-grade children. *Journal of Abnormal Child Psychology*, 14, 279-286.

60. Powers, S., Escamilla, K., & Haussler, M. M. (1986). The California Achievement Test as a predictor of reading ability across race and sex. *Educational and Psychological Measurement*, 46, 1067-1070.

61. Powers, S., Jones, P. B., & Barkan, J. H. (1986). Validity of the Standard Progressive Matrices as a predictor of achievement of sixth and seventh grade students. *Educational and Psychological Measurement*, 46, 719-722.

62. Spiegel, D. L., & Fitzgerald, J. (1986). Improving reading comprehension through instruction about story parts. *The Reading Teacher*, 39, 676-682.

63. Wood, K. D. (1986). The effect of interspersing questions in text: Evidence for "slicing the task." *Reading Research and Instruction*, 25, 295-307.

64. Wright, J. P., & Wright, C. D. (1986). Personalized verbal problems: An application of the language experience approach. *The Journal of Educational Research*, 79, 358-362.

65. Young, T. W., & Shorr, D. N. (1986). Factors affecting locus of control in school children. *Genetic, Social, and General Psychology Monographs*, 112, 407-417.

66. Crane, P., Wright, C. R., & Michael, W. B. (1987). School-related variables as predictors of achievement on the National Council Licensure Examination (NCLEX-RN) for a sample of 418 students enrolled in a diploma nursing program. *Educational and Psychological Measurement*, 47 (4), 1055-1069.

67. Dudek, S. Z., Strobel, M., & Thomas, A. D. (1987). Chronic learning problems and maturation. *Perceptual and Motor Skills*, 64, 407-429.

68. Whorton, J. E., & Karnes, F. A. (1987). Correlation of Stanford-Binet Intelligence Scale with various other measures used to screen and identify intellectually gifted students. *Perceptual and Motor Skills*, 64, 461-462.

Review of the California Achievement Tests, Forms E and F by PETER W. AIRASIAN, Professor of Education, Boston College, Chestnut Hill, MA:

The California Achievement Tests (CAT) have been a well-respected test battery for over 50 years. The latest version of the CAT, Forms E and F, is a revision of the 1978 Form C and D edition, and is designed to provide "valid measurement of academic basic skills." New features of Forms E and F include: the addition of an advanced level for high school testing; optional science and social studies tests for grades 2 through 12; lengthening of the tests to minimize ceiling effects; use of item response theory scoring; and a restructuring of many test objectives to bring them more in line with current practice and emphasis (e.g., adding words in context to the Reading Vocabulary Test; inclusion of a proofreading objective in the Language Mechanics Test; emphasizing reasoning skills in the Mathematical Concepts Test, etc.). As has been the case with past revisions, the publication of Forms E and F of the CAT represents an improvement on an already creditable test battery.

ITEMS. The CAT utilizes multiple-choice items at all levels. The genealogy of the items, from identification of the objectives to be measured to the writing, editing, reviewing, and final selection is excellent. The items were subjected to various bias reviews and statistical analyses during the test construction process to identify and eliminate items that manifested ethnic or sexual bias. The procedures followed were appropriate and state of the art.

The items appear to measure the objectives they are intended to measure. The presentation of the items in the test booklets is clear and uncluttered, conducive to maintaining pupil attention. Art work in the Study Skills and Mathematics Concepts Tests is excellent. Overall, the development, try out, selection, relation to state objectives, and reproduction of the items in the test are appropriate and well done.

TEST CONSTRUCTION AND NORMS. The tests were normed on 300,000 pupils in grades K through 12 in Fall, 1984 and Spring, 1985. The sampling design stratified public schools on the basis of geographic region (4 levels), community type (rural, suburban, urban), district size (large-small), and a measure of district social class. Catholic and private schools also were included in the norming sample. The sampling plan was acceptable, but it would have been informative to know how well it was implemented by having information about the number of primary sampling units that refused to participate and had to be replaced by back-up units. Two commendable features provided in Technical Bulletin 2 are a detailed comparison of the Fall and Spring norming samples over a variety of characteristics and comparisons of Fall and Spring norming samples with 1983 U.S. Census Data. These comparisons indicate the Fall and Spring norming groups were similar and are representative of the school population of interest. Mid-year norms also are available, derived presumably from interpolation of the Fall and Spring norms. It is important to note the CAT Form E is more difficult than the previous edition CAT Form C. The authors attribute this difference to the fact that "students in 1984–85 were achieving at a higher level than in 1977, when CAT/C was normed."

A three-parameter item response theory model was used to link all levels of the CAT to an equal interval scale ranging from 0 to 999. A similar procedure was used to equate scores on Form F to scores on Form E. In both situations, the procedures used were appropriate. The scale scores provided the basis for deriving other norm-referenced scores the CAT uses to describe a pupil's test performance: percentile ranks, normal curve equivalents, stanines, and grade equivalents. Grade mean equivalent scores also are provided as a group performance indicator.

In addition to norm-referenced comparisons, the CAT seeks to provide criterion-referenced information about how students have performed on the Category Objectives the test is designed to measure. Information about whether each pupil has attained mastery, partial mastery, or nonmastery on each objective is provided. Although such information, particularly for the class as a whole, may be helpful to teachers when used in conjunction with their own observations and perceptions of pupil performance, heavy reliance upon such objective level performance data should be avoided for two reasons. First, many of the objectives are assessed by only a few items, so scores are likely to be of low reliability. Second, no justification or validation is provided for the definition of the cut points for the mastery, partial mastery, and nonmastery categories.

INTERPRETIVE MATERIALS. This reviewer has examined the following interpretive materials that support the CAT: Technical Bulletins 1 and 2, detailing test construction and norming, bias review, validity evidence, and reliability studies; Examiner's Manuals; Norms Booklets; and the Class Management Guide, which presents a description of test content, examples of test items, guidelines to interpret scores, score report formats, and general information about conducting a successful testing program. The Examiner's Manuals and the Class Management Guide are the interpretive materials most likely to be used by teachers and guidance personnel. The Examiner's Manuals are direct, easy to follow, and pertinent to the testing exercises.

The authors of the CAT are to be particularly commended for the Class Management Guide. In a clear and direct manner they have provided the test user a resource that clarifies the nature of the tests and guides the proper interpretation of scores from the test. In a time when many test publishers overwhelm users with manual after manual overexplaining and overinterpreting information about and from the test, it is refreshing to read the Class Management Guide. The chapter describing the test content is the clearest and most informative chapter of this type that this reviewer has ever read. In a concise manner, the rationale, item format, general trait measured, relationship of tested content to various popularly used textbooks, and information about how distractors were chosen to represent common pupil errors is presented for each subtest of the CAT. After reading this chapter, the user is in an optimum position to determine the content validity of the test vis a vis instruction. To clarify test content further, a chapter that contains sample items from various test levels in various subject areas is presented. This combination of content description and test items maps out the content domain of the test with exceptional clarity.

The chapter on interpreting test scores is readable and informative. It is refreshing not to see extravagant claims for a variety of potential test uses made by the authors. Essentially the authors claim the test assesses a pupil's norm-referenced performance in basic skills areas and provides objective-referenced information about a pupil and class attainment of specific objectives. Examples of types of score reports are presented and clear explanations provided about how to interpret information therein. The authors highlight the existence of measurement error and its relationship to score interpretations. They also are properly cautious regarding interpretations of grade equivalent scores and provide examples of improper interpretations. Overall, the Class Management Guide will enhance test use and interpretation by virtue of its concise, lucid, and pertinent discussions. The Guide could be improved if cautions regarding interpretation of objective level mastery scores were made more explicit (as they are in Technical Bulletin 2, which few users will ever read) and if at least one specific example of how the standard error of measurement influences score interpretation was provided in the section that presents score report forms.

VALIDITY AND RELIABILITY. The content validity of an achievement test or test battery rests ultimately upon the user's judgment of the match between test content and the local curriculum. It is unlikely that every item or subtest is content valid for every school or classroom, but within the confines imposed by the goal of producing a nationally normed and used achievement test battery, the authors of the CAT have done about all that can be expected to identify common, representative, and relevant test content. Moreover, the authors have provided a detailed description of the objectives and curriculum emphases the test is designed to measure so that potential CAT users will be able to make sound judgments about content validity.

Additional validity evidence is also presented by the authors. Evidence that the construct measured in the various subtests is related to instruction is provided by data showing that mastery of an objective increases with grade level and, within a grade level, on Spring compared to Fall test administrations. Intercorrelations among the subtests of the CAT are relatively high, in the .5 to .8 range. This indicates there is substantial overlap, from 25 to 65 percent depending upon the subtests, within the battery and suggests that a general construct undergirds the battery. Further, the correlation between total scale score on the CAT Form E and total scale score on the Test of Cognitive Skills ranges from .6 at Level 13 to .8 at Level 16, indicating substantial overlap between the achievement battery and an ability test. Many of the achievement-ability correlations are higher than the correlations among the achievement subtests, although this is partially a function of the number of items on the tests being correlated. The achievement/ability issue is an important one, and becomes more important as a test seeks to move from measuring factual recall to measuring more general understandings, skills, and processes as the CAT does. The authors should provide the user with some interpretation of this somewhat contradictory construct validity evidence. The failure to address the ability/achievement construct validity issue is a common lack among most published standardized achievement test batteries, not just the CAT. Other criterion-related validity studies might shed light on this issue.

The within-level Kuder Richardson 20 internal consistency reliabilities for the subtests and total test score generally are high. Above the kindergarten and early first grade level tests, where smaller numbers of test items produce reliabilities in the high .6s and .7s, the internal consistency reliabilities are typically in the high .8s and .9s. Standard errors of measurement are provided in the norms booklets for various points in the score range. Except at extreme score levels, the standard errors indicate reliable measurement. Stability reliabilities for tests in levels 10, 11, and 12 of the CAT are in the .8 to .95 range. Equivalent forms reliabilities for levels 13 to 20 have median across subtest values around .85 for the Reading, Language, and Mathematics Tests and median values of around .75 for the Science, Social Studies, and Study Skills Tests. Overall, the stability, equivalence, and internal consistency of the test scores are high.

SUMMARY. The CAT, Forms E and F, is technically state of the art, well constructed, and well documented. Users will appreciate the interpretive materials, especially the Class Management Guide, which is succinct and informative as regards test content and score interpretations. The CAT is strong in all areas associated with the construction of a standardized achievement test battery and compares very favorably to other achievement batteries of its genre such as the Stanford Achievement Tests, the Iowa Tests of Basic Skills (155), and the Metropolitan Achievement Tests (200).

Review of the California Achievement Tests, Forms E and F by JAMES L. WARDROP, Associate Professor of Educational Psychology, University of Illinois at Urbana-Champaign, Champaign, IL:

Standardized achievement batteries continue to be an essential component of school testing programs in an overwhelming majority of school districts. The California Achievement Tests (CAT) rank as one of the most popular of such batteries. This latest version (Forms E and F) is a revision and extension of the 1978 edition (Forms C and D). Form E consists of 11 levels (10 through 20) covering grades K–12, while Form F contains 8 levels (13–20) and is intended to cover the latter half of grade 2 through grade 12. Adjacent levels of each form are intended to have approximately a half-year overlap, permitting fall-and-spring testing within a grade using two different levels of the same form.

Additionally, levels 14 to 20 are designed so that several different levels can be administered within a class at the same time, to facilitate what the publishers call "functional level testing," in which some pupils may be tested at levels above or below their grade placement. Optional "locator tests" can be given to "match students in the same grade with different levels" of the test. Authors of the Class Management Guide emphasize that when making decisions about what test to use, these locator tests should be used to supplement, not supplant, teacher judgments about a student's general level of achievement.

AIDS TO USE AND INTERPRETATION. Two major documents are available that prospective and actual users of the CAT-E and F series will find helpful both for deciding whether to use these tests and, if they are used, how to use the results effectively. The Class Management Guide "has been designed to help educators interpret and use results" of the tests. In addition to describing the test's content and rationale, it includes extensive consideration of how to interpret test results and communicate those results to parents and others. The Technical Report (404 pages plus appendices) is extraordinarily thorough and detailed, including a description of item response theory (IRT)—spread over several parts of the manual—and chapters dealing with validity, norming, reliability, bias, and supplementary data. In addition, there are two appendices, one listing school districts that participated in the fall standardization and the other presenting a technical description of the Objective Performance Index (OPI), discussed below. Of the 404 pages in this document, over 350 are tables and figures, dealing with such diverse aspects of test development as proportion passing every item in every form, within- and between-form correlations, data on subtest performance by members of various ethnic groups (Hispanic, Black, Other) and by gender, and the percentage of students "mastering" each category objective at every level for both forms. Also available, but not seen by this reviewer, are the Test Coordinator's Handbook and a Norms Book.

CONTENT. Subtests in CAT-E and F cover the traditional verbal and quantitative topics (reading, spelling, language; computation, concepts and applications). In addition, at levels 14 and above there is a study skills subtest, and optional subtests for science and social studies are available for levels 12 and above. The lack of tests in these latter two areas was seen as a possible limitation of the previous edition. Another difference between the current edition and the previous one is the inclusion of an additional level for use in high school. CAT C and D used one level to cover grades 9.6 to 12.9, while CAT E and F has one for grades 8.6 to 11.2 and another for 10.6 to 12.9. Other major changes from the previous edition that seem likely to strengthen the CAT are the use of a new format for the Spelling subtests, in which examinees must choose the correct spelling for a word from four alternatives; and increased emphasis on problem-solving skills at the upper grade levels in the mathematics tests. To test problem-solving skills in a way that minimizes the effect of computation is a challenging task. Authors of CAT E and F have done a fair job of this by including some questions about problem-solving processes that do not require computation of a numerical answer. This is an area of testing where considerable additional attention and effort would be justified.

Test developers have done what I consider a commendable job of defining the content domains, using an excellent set of representative curriculum guides and materials for determining what should be included in the subtests. Test content is structured in terms of 95 "objectives" and three thinking skills: recall and recognition, inference, and evaluation. Exactly what constitutes an objective is not really clear: Labels within a single level range from "short vowels," "addition of whole numbers," and "consonant sounds," to "character analysis," "geometry," and "botany." Nevertheless, the presentation of an objectives-by-thinking-skills classification table in the Class Management Guide is very helpful. (The lack of such information for the previous edition of the CAT was noted with displeasure by a reviewer in *The Ninth Mental Measurements Yearbook*.)

During my examination of this item-classification table, I discovered an anomaly that may be of some importance to potential test users. For the science subtests at all levels except 19, items classified as "evaluation" appear to be concentrated in Form F, with an average of almost eight items per level as contrasted with two items per level for Form E. For level 19, there are fewer evaluation items in Form F than in Form E (three vs. four). In fact, at this level 25 of the 40 items in Form F are "recall and recognition" items, while only 14 of the 40 Form E items are in this category. Schools or districts that wish to emphasize the higher-level thinking skills would generally choose Form F, but would then have a mismatch at this one level. The choice is complicated even more by the fact that, on the average, there are over six more science "inference" items at each level in Form E than Form F. Thus, for measurement of scientific inference skills, one would choose Form E; but for measuring evaluation skills, Form F would be preferred.

I did not carry out an exhaustive analysis of item classification information to see whether other such anomalies exist, but it seems to me that the test assembly process should incorporate a procedure that would better match the representation of thinking-skill levels for alternate forms and across levels of the same form.

In spite of the above concerns, an overall judgment must be that the development, implementation, and presentation of item content in the CAT E and F batteries is as good as can be found for any broad-spectrum achievement test series.

STANDARDIZATION AND NORMS. The standardization procedures are carefully and thoroughly described in the Technical Report, including an appendix that lists the public, private, and Catholic schools that participated in the fall, 1984 standardization. Concerns expressed by Rogers in his *Ninth Mental Measurements Yearbook* review of CAT C and D (Rogers, 1985) are equally relevant here: Data about how many first-choice schools refused to participate are not given, and discrepancies between family income data from the standardization sample and from the U.S. Census (lower for the standardization sample) are "explained" by suggesting that "these estimates are more nearly guesses than the responses to other questions," and "parents of school-age children are likely to be less affluent than the adult population as a whole." The alternative suggested by Rogers and others, that poorer districts are more likely to participate, is not acknowledged at all. In other respects, however, the standardization samples appear to be solidly representative of the population in general.

Fall and spring testing were done using some 300,000 students on each occasion, chosen using a multistage sampling procedure: district, school, and classroom. Fall testing used Form E and "a special set of test books used to link adjacent levels" of that form, while spring testing was done using Form E, Form F, or "special . . . books used to link the forms." This use of "linking" test books permitted scaling across levels within each test form, so that scores could be reported on a common scale ranging from 0 to 999. Item response theory (using a 3-parameter logistic model) was used to carry out this scaling. The equating of Forms E and F was also accomplished using the "linking" tests from spring testing. This strategy permitted scaling the Form F results in terms of Form E, so that the scaled scores from the two forms are tau-equivalent. Although one might raise questions about the extent to which the 3-parameter logistic IRT model is applicable to these tests, the vertical articulation and horizontal equating procedures are as good as current theory and technology permit.

In the test development process, careful attention was given to the possibility of ethnic or gender bias, and results of bias studies are provided in considerable detail. Again, these studies were conducted using the best available techniques and stand as exemplars that all test publishers would do well to emulate.

RELIABILITY. Unfortunately, the description of "reliability" on page 74 of the Class Management Guide thoroughly confounds stability estimates (obtained using a test-retest procedure) and homogeneity estimates (obtained using internal consistency procedures like KR-20). As is the case with virtually every standardized achievement battery, internal consistency reliability is emphasized. KR-20 coefficients are reported for every subtest at every level. As we have come to expect, these reliabilities are almost uniformly high. Somewhat lower reliabilities are reported at the lower grades/levels, as is typical; and the study skills subtests are almost uniformly less reliable than those in the areas where instructional content is more standardized: reading, language, and mathematics. With the exception of grade 2 science, both the science and social studies subtests have reliabilities comparable to the other content-area tests. For grades 2 and above, median subtest reliabilities are all at least .88.

It is not unusual for publishers to report little or no data on test-retest reliability estimates. This edition of the CAT E is no exception. Such estimates are reported only for Form E, grades K–2 (levels 10–12) for two administrations within a 2½-week period in the spring of 1985. These estimates are higher than or comparable to the internal consistency estimates for the same time period. Also reported are alternate form reliabilities for Form E subtests for grades 3–12 (levels 13–20), obtained during the same time period. These estimates average about .10 lower than the corresponding internal consistency values, with especially large discrepancies for the social studies subtest (median alternate form reliability, .75; median internal consistency reliability, .91). It is gratifying to find these values reported, but it would be desirable to have more complete information about test-retest reliabilities.

In addition to reliability estimates, the Technical Manual contains a very complete description of the standard errors of measurement for all subtests, including figures portraying the IRT standard error curves (important because IRT standard errors vary by performance level, in contrast to the traditional standard errors). There is much to praise and only a little to criticize about the availability and presentation of reliability data for these tests.

VALIDITY. For years, *Mental Measurements Yearbook* reviewers, among others, have complained that publishers of standardized achievement tests overemphasize content validity and neglect construct validity. The CAT E and F is no exception. In the Class Management Guide, the reader is told, "There are several types of validity. The one of greatest concern to the classroom teacher is content validity," whether the items "accurately represent the subject matter that the test was designed to cover." The part of the Technical Manual titled "validity" has as subsections the following: Rationale (two paragraphs summarizing how content representativeness was achieved), Comparison of CAT E and F with CAT C and D (approximately two pages describing E and F subtests and how they compare to subtests from C and D), Test Development (summarizing "methods were applied to ensure the accuracy, currency, and curricular relevance" of the test materials), Tryout and Item Selection (nearly six pages explaining what was done to end up with items that minimize the standard error of measurement, maximize fit to the IRT model, minimize ethnic and gender bias, and whose answer choices performed in a reasonable manner), Typical Administration Times (including a number of tables demonstrating the lack of speededness of the tests), Passage Dependency of Reading Comprehension Items (describing, with nine pages of tables, the study of passage dependency), and Statistical Data Related to Validity (presenting percentages of students "mastering" each of the 95 objectives, the IRT location and guessing parameter estimates, correlations with the Test of Cognitive Skills, and intercorrelations of subtests from CAT-E with those of CAT-C).

Some of this content has to do with validity of score interpretation (eliminating speededness and bias from the scores, supporting the claim that reading comprehension items relate to passages with which they are associated), but none of it deals with construct validity. Yet, if one looks at the kinds of verbal descriptions contained in some of the score reports available with CAT E and F, one finds reference to a student's strengths or weaknesses in such "skills" as "analyzing characters in passages" or "understanding number theory." These "skills" are constructs that exist in the minds of test developers. Evidence that they are valid representations of the workings of the minds of test takers is called for. Construct validity studies are not easy to do, often cannot be done in a timely manner to be included in manuals when a test publication deadline looms, and are unlikely to increase the market for the tests. However, if we are going to use test scores to identify someone as lacking in the skill of "understanding [mathematics] problem solving" or "understanding the physical environment," evidence needs to be provided that these are indeed meaningful "skills."

SCORES AND REPORTS. Seven different types of scores are available for the CAT E and F: scale scores, percentile ranks, normal curve equivalents, stanines, grade equivalents, "anticipated achievement scores," and "objective performance indices." Scale scores are based on computerized pattern scoring derived from the three-parameter IRT model. If computerized scoring is not used, less accurate approximations to scale scores are obtained by converting number of correct responses to the scale using tables in the Norms Book. The scale is continuous across all levels of CAT E or F and ranges from 0 to 999. Scale scores for a subtest can be directly compared from year to year, but scales from different subtests are not directly comparable. Most other scores are derived from the scale scores. Scale scores are a standard component of achievement batteries these days, and those for CAT E and F are technically the best that can be provided.

The next four scales: percentile ranks, normal curve equivalents, stanines, and grade equivalent scores, are all standard measurement scales used for many tests. Appropriate guidelines for and cautions about the uses of each are presented in the Class Management Guide. Anticipated achievement scores are essentially regression estimates of CAT performance, using scores from the Test of Cognitive Skills as regressors. Why these scores are available or what to do with them is not discussed in either the Class Management Guide or the Technical Manual. They are treated so briefly that one might well wonder if their inclusion is simply a legacy from previous editions.

The most controversial scores reported for the CAT E and F are the Objective Performance Indices (OPI). For those objectives having at least four items on a subtest, an OPI is available. The OPI is ideally a Bayesian estimate of the proportion of items a student would answer correctly from a (hypothetical) pool of all items measuring an objective. It is obtained by using performance on the remaining items in the test to created a Bayesian prior distribution, along with observed performance on the items actually in the test that relate to the objective, to create a posterior estimate of performance level. More simply, the OPI can be thought of as the proportion of items measuring an objective that the student has answered correctly. For some subtests at some levels, there may be as few as 4 or as many as 20 items referenced to a single objective. Needless to say, the standard errors for OPIs based on small numbers of items can be quite large. In order to highlight these standard errors, OPIs are reported with (68%) confidence bands. Given the inherent instability of these estimates, it might be better to report only the intervals and not include the point estimates.

More troubling is the categorization of each OPI as representing a "level of mastery." Levels are arbitrarily defined: nonmastery, an OPI less than .50; partial knowledge, an OPI between .50 and .74; and mastery, an OPI of .75 or greater. This kind of labelling of student performance, based frequently on quite fragile evidence, is difficult to justify. Carrying the analysis one step further, one of the available reports is the Class Grouping Report, in which all pupils in a class are categorized by "mastery," "partial knowledge," or "non-mastery" for each objective. Would it not be sufficient to provide a rank-ordered listing of students according to the number of items answered correctly for each objective, then let teachers make judgments about what constitutes mastery or nonmastery?

A rich variety of report forms is available for the CAT E and F. The Class Record Sheet, Individual Test Record, and Right Response Record are all carefully and usefully designed to provide test performance information to teachers and administrators. The Student Interpretive Report should be helpful to teachers who want to use the test results as one means of better understanding their students' academic strengths and weaknesses. The Parent Report is well thought out and presents performance data in a nontechnical way for parents. The Objectives Performance Report and Class Grouping Report are created by aggregating students' OPIs. If not taken too seriously, they can provide a helpful summary of curricular strengths and weaknesses and help teachers tailor instruction to the apparent needs of their classes.

I find it surprising that there is not more information about uses of test scores provided in the materials accompanying the CAT. If I could make just one recommendation to CTB/McGraw-Hill it would be to develop a booklet focussing on just this topic. Fine examples are available in connection with several other achievement batteries, including the SRA Achievement Series and Iowa Tests of Basic Skills. Such a document, whether issued separately or incorporated in the Class Management Guide, would be a welcome addition to the CAT materials.

SUMMARY. For all its strengths, the CAT E and F battery is not without flaws: the Technical Manual could be organized in a more useful way. (For example, to compare test-retest or alternate form reliability estimates with internal consistency estimates required repeatedly flipping back and forth between Parts 4 and 6 of the Manual, and material in the final part seems to be an accumulation of miscellaneous data that could be integrated into the remainder of the Manual. Only limited test-retest reliability data are presented; there is an overreliance on content validity, very little data relating test scores to an external criterion (one study predicting Algebra I grades from Level 18 mathematics scores), and a complete neglect of construct validity; the Objective Performance Indices have a weak theoretical and empirical foundation; and, in spite of the overall excellence of supporting and descriptive materials in both the Classroom Management Guide and the Technical Manual, relatively little guidance is given about how to interpret and use the various scores and score reports.

Even taking into account the concerns summarized above, this latest revision of the CAT is one of the best standardized achievement batteries available. The available data about test quality are comprehensively and (usually) clearly reported; the standardization process appears to have been carried out as well as is possible; reported reliabilities are at least as good as the best of the competing batteries, with a laudable emphasis on standard errors; content validity is clearly and thoroughly described, and procedures used to minimize ethnic and gender bias and to evaluate the passage dependency of reading comprehension items were exemplary; scales and reporting formats for results are carefully designed and effectively presented. Whether it is the battery of choice for any setting should be determined by the extent to which the content coverage, item formats, and administrative requirements fit the needs in that setting.

REVIEWER'S REFERENCE

Rogers, B. G. (1985). [Review of California Achievement Test, Forms C and D]. In J. V. Mitchell, Jr. (Ed.), *The ninth mental measurements yearbook* (pp. 243–246). Lincoln, NE: The Buros Institute of Mental Measurements.

[42]

Canadian Cognitive Abilities Test, Form 3. Purpose: "Designed to assess the development of cognitive abilities related to verbal, quantitative, and nonverbal reasoning and problem solving." Grades K.5–3, 3–12; 1954–84; CCAT; Canadian revision of Cognitive Abilities Test, Form 3; Form 1 is still available; 1985 price data: $3.90 per 10 class record sheets; $8.50 per technical notes ('84, 31 pages); original edition by Robert L. Thorndike and Elizabeth P. Hagen; Canadian revision by Edgar N. Wright; Nelson Canada [Canada].*

a) PRIMARY BATTERIES. Grades K.5–1.9, 2–3; 2 levels: Primary 1, 2; $21.70 per 35 test booklets; $2.20 per scoring key; $5.35 per examiner's manual ('82, 43 pages); $5.75 per examination kit; (60) minutes in two sessions.

b) MULTILEVEL EDITION. Grades 3–12; 3 scores: Verbal, Nonverbal, Quantitative; $5.55 per test booklet; $9.95 per 35 hand-scorable answer sheets; $26.75 per 100 machine-scorable answer sheets; $118 per 250 NCS answer sheets; $7.30 per scoring masks; $9.95 per examiner's manual ('82, 95 pages); $15.75 per examination kit; (150) minutes in three sessions.

See T3:361 (5 references) and 8:180 (2 references).

TEST REFERENCES

1. Shapson, S. M., & Day, E. M. (1982). A comparison study of three late immersion programs. *The Alberta Journal of Educational Research*, 28, 135-148.

2. Brailsford, A., Snart, F., & Das, J. P. (1984). Strategy training and reading comprehension. *Journal of Learning Disabilities*, 17, 287-290.

3. Fagan, W. T. (1987). A comparison of the reading processes of adult illiterates and four groups of school age readers. *The Alberta Journal of Educational Research*, 33, 123-136.

Review of the Canadian Cognitive Abilities Test, Form 3 by GIUSEPPE COSTANTINO, Clinical Director, Sunset Park Mental Health Center of Lutheran Medical Center, Brooklyn, NY, and Research Associate, Hispanic Research Center, Fordham University, Bronx, NY:

All psychoeducational tests should be constructed to achieve the following three basic goals: (*a*) Tests should assess the learning abilities of the students without penalizing those students with poor academic achievement associated with psychosocial and linguistic barriers; (*b*) tests should predict the academic achievement of the examinees; and (*c*) tests should enable the integration of both assessment of deficits and remediation program. The Canadian Cognitive Abilities Test (CCAT), Form 3, achieves the first goal quite fully, but the second and third goals only partially.

DESCRIPTION. The CCAT, Form 3, has evolved from its predecessors, the Cognitive Abilities Test (standardized in the United States), the Canadian Lorge-Thorndike Intelligence Test, and the Canadian Cognitive Abilities Test, Form 1. The CCAT comprises a Primary Battery for grades K–3 and a Multilevel Edition with three batteries for grades 3–12. Level 1 of the Primary Battery is for testing children from the second half of kindergarten through grade 1, and Level 2 is for testing children in grades 2 and 3. Levels A–H of the Multilevel Edition are for testing children in grades 3–12.

Levels 1 and 2 of the Primary Battery, which is a nonreading test, are composed of four subtests: Relational Concepts, Object Classification (Multimental), Quantitative Concepts, and Oral Vocabulary. The Primary Battery yields a single score. The test items are administered one at a time, without time limits. However, each subtest has an average time limit estimate that should be used as a guideline. The four subtests should be administered in two sessions, on separate days if possible.

Levels A–H of the Multilevel Edition are divided into three distinct batteries: Verbal, Quantitative, and Nonverbal. The Verbal Battery consists of four subtests: Vocabulary, Sentence Completion, Verbal Classification, and Verbal Analogies. Time limits range from 34 to 49 minutes, in addition to 5–10 minutes for preparation and pretest exercises. The Quantitative Battery is made up of three subtests: Quantitative Relations, Number Series, and Equation Building. Time limits range from 32 to 45 minutes, plus 5 minutes for preparation. The Nonverbal Battery is made up of three subtests: Figure Classification, Figure Analogies, and Figure Synthesis. Time limits range from 32 to 45 minutes, plus 5 minutes for preparation. All three batteries should be administered in three separate periods. For elementary school children, the batteries should be administered on three separate days; for older children, on two separate days. The tests can be administered to small groups, with a maximum of 15 students. Each group should be homogeneous with respect to academic achievement. A chart is provided for the examiner to determine the basal level for the testing of "slow," "normal," and "rapid" students in cognitive development. The degree of cognitive development for each student should be determined on the basis of reading scores.

ITEM SELECTION. Item selection for the Primary Battery was conducted in grades K–3 by administering items to a pilot group of 250–300 students at each grade level. For the Multilevel Edition, most items were tested in two grade groups. All items showing satisfactory discrimination, based on biserial correlations, were included in the subtests. No single-item data are shown; however, means and standard deviations for each subtest based on 261–2,723 students (Primary Battery) and 1,623–3,009 students (Multilevel Battery) are reported. Difficulty level of the Primary Battery subtests averages 70% correct for grades 1 and 2, and 80% correct for grade 3. These relatively high percentages make the battery less effective in discriminating among students of average ability, but more effective in discriminating among students of below average ability. Conversely, the items of the Multilevel Edition are more discriminating. In fact, the average difficulty level for the overall Verbal Battery is 57% correct; for the Quantitative Battery, 68% correct; and for the Nonverbal Battery, 71% correct. Although some of the subtests within each battery have more discriminating value than others, in general the values are within the optimal range.

The CCAT Primary Battery assesses the same basic cognitive skills as its predecessors; however, new items were constructed and new pictures were developed. The new pictures are attractive and contemporary. However, the following pictorial items may need revision. The "thermometer" item, which is depicted without numbers, should be numbered. Other similar items (e.g., scale, ruler, clock), are numbered. This pictorial inconsistency may create difficulty in the selection of the correct item on page 14 of the test form. The "fireman hat," which is the item constructed as "not belonging to the four female wear categories," would seem to be biased because there are female firefighters. Perhaps the items should be reversed by presenting typical male wear as the same-category items and typical female wear (e.g., a skirt), as the item that does not belong. The Verbal, Numerical, and Geometric design items of the Multilevel Edition appear to be free of any bias.

NATIONAL STANDARDIZATION PROGRAM. The standardization of the CCAT was conducted in the fall of 1980, concomitantly with the standardization of the Canadian Tests of Basic Skills, using a large stratified random sample ($N = 32{,}137$) of English-language dominant students in 102 Canadian schools. Upon completion of the standardization, the percentages of students within each stratification category were weighted to approximate the total school population in most categories. Furthermore, additional testing was conducted at the third-grade level where students were administered both Level 2 and Level A in order to establish longitudinal equivalence of both the Primary and Multimodal Batteries.

Notwithstanding the magnitude of the standardization program and the efforts made to test the representative sample of the Canadian schools, the authors recognize they encountered some limitations. For example, it would have been desirable to stratify the probability sample according to community size and socioeconomic status, especially because the latter factor seems to be related to school achievement.

NORMS. The raw scores on each battery are transformed into Universal Scale Scores (USS), which are also converted into Standard Age Scores (SAS). The SAS are normalized standard scores with a mean of 100 and a standard deviation of 10. Furthermore, USS are converted into percentile ranks for grades and stanines for ages. This complete normative system allows for continuity of measurement and comparison of scores at different grade and age levels. There are not separate norms for racial, ethnic, or linguistic minority groups. However, the authors indicated that a number of items were tested with minority students to determine the item difficulty value. In order to reflect accurately the academic progress of students, Fall, Winter, and Spring norms are provided.

RELIABILITY. Kuder-Richardson 20 reliability estimates by levels and grades for the multimodal batteries average .92 for the Verbal, .89 for the Quantitative, and .90 for the Nonverbal; for the Primary Battery they are approximately .87. There is no indication that test-retest studies were conducted.

CORRELATIONS AMONG BATTERIES. Intercorrelations among battery scores are moderately high, ranging from the high .50s to .70s. Intercorrelations of subtests are lower, but still within the moderate range of values. Reliabilities between pairs of scores can be estimated from the intercorrelations of multimodal batteries. Because the reliabilities of the separate batteries are moderately high, differences between scores tend to be accurate. However, the authors caution that differences on the Standard Age Score scale should be considered significant only if they range between 10 and 15.

VALIDITY. The authors discuss content validity, criterion-related validity, and construct validity. However, they report only correlations between the Standard Age Scores on the CCAT and the Grade-Equivalent Scores on the CTBS, Elementary Multilevel Battery. Typical validity coefficients for composite scores are .85 for the Verbal Battery, .75 for the Quantitative Battery, and .63 for the Nonverbal Battery. These values, however, refer to concurrent validity. The authors note that predictive validity has not been established.

The utility of a psychoeducational test or subtest rests upon its effectiveness in "predicting" academic achievement. Both the Verbal and Quantitative batteries seem to be effective indicators of academic achievement. However, the Nonverbal Battery seems to be a poor indicator. In the technical manual, the various types of validity are not fully discussed. In the United States edition of the Cognitive Abilities Test (CAT), construct validity is supported by moderately high correlations of the CAT with the Stanford-Binet. Content validity is also briefly described, but it is not clear why the item-selection data were not included under the caption of content validity. The item-selection data, together with single-item data, and the relationship of the items to those cognitive abilities measured would give a fuller understanding of the content validity of the CCAT.

SEX DIFFERENCES. Examination of sex differences was not considered in the standardization of the CCAT; however, information taken from the CAT (U.S. edition) indicates that in one subsample girls in grades 3–8 were superior to boys on the Verbal, Quantitative, and Nonverbal batteries. But in a second subsample, girls scored higher on the Verbal Battery at all grade levels, whereas boys scored higher on the Quantitative Battery, and both sexes scored identically on the Nonverbal Battery.

ADMINISTRATION AND SCORING. Details of administration are provided in the general description of the test. The instructions for administration are easy to follow and they are sufficiently detailed without being redundant. The instructions for scoring are clear and concise. The authors point out pitfalls associated with facile or biased interpretation of the results. Furthermore, they offer some general guidelines for possible remediation of deficits identified by the batteries. However, a more detailed remediation program for students would be extremely helpful to teachers. A complete theoretical framework justifying the cognitive abilities measured is necessary in order to develop a more detailed remediation program.

SUMMARY. The CCAT, Form 3, is a further development of the CAT (U.S. edition), basically patterned on the same type of items and measuring the same cognitive abilities as its

American counterpart. However, a number of items have been rewritten, and the pictorial items of the Primary Battery have been redrawn to reflect more contemporary features. The Primary Battery, Levels 1 and 2, is for testing in grades K–3 and the Multimodal edition, Levels A–H, is for testing in grades 3–12. Instructions for administration and scoring are concise and clear. The CCAT has high reliability, but test-retest reliability research was not conducted. Its criterion-related validity is moderately high; predictive validity studies should be conducted. The standardization program in Canadian schools was carefully planned and executed. The standardization sample presents some minor problems that were beyond the authors' control. Norms are adequate and afford a good interpretation of the test results. The CCAT would be enhanced by the formulation of a theoretical framework explaining the cognitive abilities measured by the test, and by a more detailed formulation of a remediation program.

Review of the Canadian Cognitive Abilities Test, Form 3 by JACK A. CUMMINGS, Associate Professor of Counseling and Educational Psychology, Indiana University, Bloomington, IN:

Similar to the Cognitive Abilities Test (66; Thorndike & Hagen, 1983), the Canadian Cognitive Abilities Test (CCAT) is based on the premise that "individuals differ in their abilities to work with three basic types of symbols—verbal, quantitative, and geometric or spatial" (Thorndike & Hagen, 1982). It is proposed that individual differences in the pattern (intraindividual differences) and level (interindividual differences) of these measured abilities have implications for matching instructional techniques/materials to individuals. Thus, given the information generated by the CCAT the teacher should better be able to design instruction to meet the "varied needs, skills and cognitive styles of individual students" (Thorndike & Hagen, 1982).

STANDARDIZATION. The standardization of the CCAT was conducted in the Fall of 1980. The CCAT was normed concurrently with the Canadian Test of Basic Skills. Schools where the primary language of instruction was English provided the starting point in selecting the sample. The target sample was drawn from schools in each of the 10 Canadian provinces. Within each province the schools were divided into four categories based on third grade enrollment: 30 pupils or fewer, 31 to 60 pupils, 61 to 90 pupils, and greater than 90. There were 137 schools identified in the target sample; 117 agreed to participate, and 102 followed through. There were 32,137 children sampled as part of the standardization. In grades 1–8, there were in excess of 2,500 students sampled per grade level. In grades 9–10, the sample fell slightly below 2,500, while grades 11–12 had roughly 1,700 students sampled at each grade level. To accommodate the attrition a weighting procedure was used to statistically adjust the sample. Inspection of the distribution of the sample across provinces relative to the actual province populations reveals that the obtained sample closely approximates the actual population within the province. Likewise the distribution of the pupils by school size within the sample is comparable to the actual population percents.

It is stated in the technical notes (Thorndike & Hagen, 1984) that as part of the standardization a portion of the third grade students were administered both Level A and Level 2. This was for the purpose of examining the equivalence of forms. Unfortunately data are not given to document the relationship between these two levels. It is merely stated that this was done.

A student's performance may be referenced to either age or grade. Standard scores, percentiles, and stanines provide age-based comparisons, while percentiles and stanines are available for grade-based comparisons. These scores may be used to indicate a child's performance on the three facets (verbal, quantitative, geometric/spatial) of the CCAT. A total score is not calculated, because the test authors believe the pattern of scores would be officiated. Individuals with the same total score could have very different ability scores (e.g., high verbal, low quantitative, low spatial vs. low verbal, low quantitative, high spatial).

On the whole, the technical manual reveals careful attention to the standardization.

ADMINISTRATION AND SCORING. The teacher's directions for administration are concise and lucid. Practical suggestions are provided regarding the necessary materials and the general arrangements for testing. These include comments about the advance preparation of students, seating arrangement, avoidance of interruptions, and the importance of the students understanding the practice questions before starting the test. For young children or those who would be expected to have problems, a practice test may be used to familiarize students with the test format.

As would be expected of a group-administered cognitive ability measure, both machine-scoring and hand-scoring procedures are available to the test user. Nelson Canada scoring services provide computerized results for the machine-scored version. As part of the basic service the Nelson Canada processes lists of pupils, their demographic data and performance according to various derived scores, a report of building averages, and system averages. Optional computerized services include pressure-sensitive labels for each student, frequency distributions for each building and the total system, local norms based only on the system, and score suppression for derived scores that a system may choose to delete.

RELIABILITY. Reliability was determined by KR 20 (coefficient alpha). For versions of the CCAT appropriate for grades 3–12, the Verbal KR 20s equalled or exceeded .91, the Quantitative and Nonverbal KR 20s exceeded .88. For grades 1 and 2 the KR 20s were .88 and .86 respectively. Thus, the internal consistency of the CCAT scales is quite satisfactory.

Stability data are not given for the CCAT although means across time are provided for the Canadian or Lorge-Thorndike (the predecessor of the CCAT). A more helpful table would have reported correlations over time in addition to the means.

VALIDITY. Two types of validity are discussed in the technical manual: content and criterion-referenced validity. It is difficult to judge the adequacy of the content validation approach taken by the CCAT authors. The introduction of the examiner's manual states that steps were taken to eliminate irrelevant sources of difficulty. Among the potential irrelevant sources of difficulty would be vocabulary that children may not understand included in the teacher's oral directions, and directions with complex sentence structures. Unfortunately, the technical manual (Thorndike & Hagen, 1984) does not indicate what steps the authors took to ensure the teacher's directions to students were lucid or the vocabulary level was controlled. Likewise, the manual does not detail how test items were modified or adapted based on potential differences between Canadian English and U.S. English.

Evidence of criterion-related validity is presented in terms of correlations with achievement tests. As part of the standardization process the Canadian Test of Basic Skills (CTBS) was given concurrently with the CCAT. As would be expected the composite CTBS score correlated highest with the Verbal scale of the CCAT (median $r = .85$). The Quantitative scale also correlated well with the median falling at $r = .73$, while the Nonverbal scale predicted the CTBS at a level below either of the other scales (median $r = .64$). These correlations were interpreted to mean that the Verbal scale is the best indicator of general academic competence (Thorndike & Hagen, 1984). Construct validity is mentioned in the technical manual as a means of examining the degree to which the measure assesses an individual with respect to a defined trait. However, the manual provides no further discussion of this important aspect of validity.

INTERPRETATION. Five pages of the Examiner's Manual are devoted to the interpretation of the CCAT. A table is provided that shows how the various derived scores compare (percentile rank of 96 = standard age score of 128 = stanine of 9). Four of the five pages are devoted to nine illustrative case studies. The case studies exemplify typical nuances in interpretation. Random guessing, giftedness, differences between age and grade norms, average performance, and uneven patterns of scores are among the concepts illustrated in the case studies. The section on interpretation is concluded with well-conceived rules of thumb (e.g., asterisk scores indicate the test performance is unreliable, differences of 15 standard score points are required for two scores to indicate a reliable difference between the abilities assessed by the two scales, look at pattern and level, and remember that test scores represent estimates to be interpreted within the context of other achievement test data, grades, and teacher judgment).

Only one and a half pages of the Examiner's Manual are devoted to the use of the test scores. If the CCAT is "to be used constructively to enhance the students' chances of success in learning" (Thorndike & Hagen, 1982), one would expect detailed and explicit instructions for the teacher. Very general suggestions are covered in the one and a half pages of the manual. The teacher is told that students who score higher on the nonverbal sections (quantitative and spatial) than on verbal process information "quite differently" than high verbal students. The test authors continue stating that these children "tend to organize and handle data in complex wholes and patterns. They frequently have rich visual imagery which they can use effectively for learning. Certainly instructional methods can be devised to take advantage of these types of abilities!" (Thorndike & Hagen, 1982). The present reviewer believes it is incumbent upon the test authors to be more explicit. Specific examples of instructional techniques should be outlined for the teacher. The examples should be numerous and illustrate adaptations appropriate at various levels. Research should also be cited to support the aptitude by treatment approach embodied in the concept of differential instruction based on the student's aptitudes.

CONCLUSION. The CCAT is a carefully standardized measure of cognitive ability. The authors are to be praised for avoiding a composite score, something that would probably have been misinterpreted as a unidimensional IQ. In lieu of a single score an individual's performance is broken into three scales: Verbal, Quantitative, and Nonverbal. The teacher's administration is straightforward and reflects the fact that this is a revision and not a new measure. The major shortcomings of the CCAT are failures of the authors to provide explicit and detailed instructional implications of patterns and/or levels for the three scales, and the obvious omission of a discussion of construct validity in the manual.

REVIEWER'S REFERENCES

Thorndike, R. L., & Hagen, E. (1982). Canadian Cognitive Abilities Test: Examiner's manual, (revised). Scarborough, Ontario: Nelson Canada.

Thorndike, R. L., & Hagen, E. (1983). Cognitive Abilities Test. Chicago: Riverside Publishing Co.

Thorndike, R. L., & Hagen, E. (1984). Canadian Cognitive Abilities Test: Technical notes. Scarborough, Ontario: Nelson Canada.

[43]

Career Assessment Inventory—The Enhanced Version. Purpose: A vocational interest assessment tool focusing on careers requiring up to 4 years of college. Junior high school and above; 1975–86; CAI; provides scores on a broader range of occupational scales than the original version; earlier Vocational Version still available; 142 scores: 6 themes (Realistic, Investigative, Artistic, Social, Enterprising, Conventional), 25 basic interest (Mechanical/Fixing, Electronics, Carpentry, Manual/Skilled Trades, Protective Service, Athletics/Sports, Nature/Outdoors, Animal Service, Mathematics, Scientific Research/Development, Medical Science, Writing, Creative Arts, Performing/Entertaining, Educating, Community Service, Medical Service, Religious Activities, Public Speaking, Law/Politics, Management/Supervision, Sales, Office Practices, Clerical/Clerking, Food Service), 111 occupational (Accountant, Advertising Artist/Writer, Advertising Executive, Aircraft Mechanic, Architect, Athletic Trainer, Author/Writer, Auto Mechanic, Bank Manager, Bank Teller, Barber/Hairstylist, Biologist, Bookkeeper, Bus Driver, Buyer/Merchandiser, Cafeteria Worker, Camera Repair Technician, Card/Gift Shop Manager, Carpenter, Caterer, Chef, Chemist, Child Care Assistant, Chiropractor, Computer Programmer, Computer Scientist, Conservation Officer, Cosmetologist, Counselor-Chemical Dependency, Court Reporter, Data Input Operator, Dental Assistant, Dental Hygienist, Dental Lab Technician, Dentist, Dietitian, Drafter, Economist, Elected Public Official, Electrician, Electronic Technician, Elementary School Teacher, Emergency Medical Technician, Engineer, Executive Housekeeper, Farmer/Rancher, Firefighter, Florist, Food Service Manager, Forest Ranger, Guidance Counselor, Hardware Store Manager, Hospital Administrator, Hotel/Motel Manager, Insurance Agent, Interior Designer, Janitor/Janitress, Lawyer, Legal Assistant, Librarian, Machinist, Mail Carrier, Manufacturing Representative, Mathematician, Math-Science Teacher, Medical Assistant, Medical Lab Technician, Military Enlisted, Military Officer, Musical Instrument Repair, Musician, Newspaper Reporter, Nurse Aide, Nurse/LPN, Nurse/RN, Occupational Therapist, Operating Room Technician, Orthotist/Prosthetist, Painter, Park Ranger, Personnel Manager, Pharmacist, Pharmacy Technician, Photographer, Physical Therapist, Physician, Piano Technician, Pipefitter/Plumber, Police Officer, Printer, Private Investigator, Psychologist, Purchasing Agent, Radio/TV Repair, Radiologic Technician, Real Estate Agent, Religious Leader, Reservation Agent, Respiratory Therapy Technician, Restaurant Manager, Secretary, Security Guard, Sheet Metal Worker, Surveyor, Teacher Aide, Telephone Repair Technician, Tool and Die Maker, Travel Agent, Truck Driver, Veterinarian, Waiter/Waitress; Mail-In scoring, Arion II teleprocessing, or MICROTEST assessment software available from publisher and provide a Narrative Report or a Profile Report or optional group reports for large volume users; 1987 price data: $8.75 or less (Narrative Report) and $4.40 or less (Profile Report) per prepaid Mail-In answer sheets including test items and the cost of scoring and reports; $9.25 per 25 answer sheets including test items to be used with Arion II or MICROTEST; 25 interpretive guides entitled "Understanding Your Results" free with each 25 answer sheets; $15 per manual ('86, 218 pages); $19.50 per specimen set including manual and one prepaid answer sheet for both the Profile and Narrative Reports; $8.75 (Narrative Report) or $4.40 (Profile Report) per report scored via Arion II teleprocessing (billed monthly; for use with any microcomputer); $68 (Narrative Report) or $35 (Profile Report) per disk containing 10 tests for use with MICROTEST assessment software (50 tests: $255/$140; 100 tests: $435/$245); (35–40) minutes; Charles B. Johansson; National Computer Systems, Inc.*

See T3:367 (1 reference); for reviews by Jack L. Bodden and Paul R. Lohnes of an earlier edition, see 8:993.

TEST REFERENCES

1. Galassi, M. D., Jones, L. K., & Britt, M. N. (1985). Nontraditional career options for women: An evaluation of career guidance instruments. *Vocational Guidance Quarterly*, 34, 124-130.

2. Thompson, R. A. (1985). Vocational interests of vocational/technical and non-college bound students using the Career Assessment Inventory. *Journal of Research and Development in Education*, 18 (4), 61-67.

Review of the Career Assessment Inventory—The Enhanced Version by JAMES B. ROUNDS, Associate Professor of Educational Psychology, University of Illinois at Urbana-Champaign, Champaign, IL:

The Career Assessment Inventory (CAI), when introduced in 1975, was intended for use with individuals seeking careers not requiring a baccalaureate degree. With successive updates in 1978, 1982, and the current 1986 edition, "The Enhanced Version," the intended audience for the CAI has been expanded to include individuals seeking professional careers.

The 1986 enhanced edition represents a major revision of the 1975 vocational edition. The enhanced version contains 370 items in contrast to its 305-item predecessor, increasing the administration time to about 40 minutes. The original 22 Basic Interest Area scales now number 25. The 1975 version had 42 Occupational scales with 14 scales for males, and 8 scales for females. Only 10 occupations had joint male and female scales. Beginning with the 1982 edition, combined-sex occupational scales were introduced, a new and bold development for commercial interest inventories, because separate-sex occupational scales have been the mainstay of the Strong and Kuder inventories. By the 1986 edition, 111 combined-sex Occupational scales had been constructed.

GENERAL THEME SCALES. While the Theme scales were ostensibly developed to measure Holland's six occupational types, the manual discusses neither standard methods for coding Theme profiles, nor the relationship of the Themes to Holland's comprehensive occupational classification (both of which are common approaches to the use of Holland-type scales). The manual does, however, provide clients and counselors with interpretations of the six Themes based on Holland's (1985) elaboration and description of these types.

Data presented in the manual provide an equally confusing picture for how adequately the Theme scales measure Holland's typology. For example, there is no demonstration that the spatial representation of the Themes meets the requirements of the hexagonal model; without such evidence the Theme scales cannot be interpreted as Holland-type scales (Rounds & Zevon, 1983). Instead, the internal relationships among the Themes were "eyeballed," a poor substitute for model testing procedures, and the author reports, "The linear model is used to present scores on the six General Theme scales in the results reports, since this model corresponds best to the correlational data."

On the other hand, the Theme scales, with the exception of the Enterprising and Conventional scales, show expected relationships with similar scales from the Strong-Campbell Interest Inventory (SCII), Kuder, and Jackson Vocational Interest Survey. In addition, item analyses of descriptors from two personality measures elaborate the meaning and interpretation of the theme categories in predicted directions. Overall, the manual needs to be more carefully written because the typical user is likely to form an impression that Theme scales can be used as Holland-type scales when this is not the case.

BASIC INTEREST AREA SCALES. The Basic Interest Area (BIA) scales are intended to suggest occupations for career exploration and decision making and to suggest avocational activities for people planning for retirement. Evidence to support these intended interpretations is limited to displaying the mean scores on the BIA scales for 111 occupational samples used in the development of the Occupational scales. The reader is left to peruse 25 tables. It would be much more helpful if these data were summarized to indicate which occupations score high and low. Validity data are not provided about the inferences concerning avocational and extracurricular activities although the inferences are described as useful. The manual also claims, without supporting evidence, the BIA scales can be used with the Occupational scales to increase predictive validity.

The manual asserts the CAI provides more basic interest scales than does the SCII, but the high correlations among several scales raise questions regarding how well the CAI scales distinguish among their corresponding basic interest areas. Given the scale intercorrelations and reliability estimates, scales such as Mechanical/Fixing, Electronics, Carpentry, and Manual/Skilled Trades cannot be used to reliably differentiate these interest areas.

OCCUPATIONAL SCALES. The procedures used to develop 64 of the 111 combined-sex scales may tend to limit the career options of men or women, contrary to the intentions expressed in the manual. At best, these procedures could provide scores that are misleading. In the case of 30 scales, the item selection and weighting is based on either a male or female occupational criterion sample. For 33 of the scales, when the occupational criterion group for one sex numbered less than 50 (for example, the size of the female janitor/janitress criterion group was 3), the larger criterion group was used for item selection and weighting with the smaller opposite-sex group used only to exclude items. Essentially, these procedures produce separate-sex scales—not a problem in itself, but these scales are not so labelled on the profile.

How well did the combined-sex strategy work when it was used to construct Occupational scales? Only an incomplete answer can be given because the manual provides data based on the same criterion samples used for development of the empirical keys. For those 52 scales developed on female and male criterion samples having a size of 40 or more (the only data given), the mean scores for these same criterion samples are within 2 to 3 points for the majority of Occupational scales. For 10 scales the mean score differences are approximately half a standard deviation or greater (e.g., females score 47.7 and males 52.2 on the Mathematician scale), indicating that caution should be exercised in interpreting these scales.

A second problem with the Occupational scales, possibly more critical than the first, is the small size of the CAI occupational criterion groups. Only six female criterion groups are greater than 200 and only five male criterion groups are greater than 200. E. K. Strong (1943) thought criterion samples of 400 were desirable; Campbell (1971) suggested "samples of 400 are preferable, samples of 300 are sufficient, and samples of 200 are adequate." Even if the male and female criterion groups are combined (an approach not taken for developing the Occupational scales here), only 40 of the 111 scales had combined-sex groups greater than 200 subjects. With such small criterion samples, the empirical scale construction strategy capitalizes on chance differences raising questions about the generalizability of the items and weights composing these Occupational scales.

The manual provides validity data about relationships of the Occupational scales with the CAI General Themes and appropriate SCII and Kuder occupational scales. Yet these validity data are derivative, not addressing the primary concern of users: how well the Occupational scales distinguish between people who are currently employed or who will eventually enter different occupations. This information is necessary because the Occupational scales, like the General Theme and Basic Area scales, are used to make vocational decisions. The Occupational scales were constructed using an empirical strategy; validity data are, therefore, required that are *not* based on the same samples used for scale construction purposes.

SUMMARY. Like most vocational interest inventories, the primary goal of the CAI is to help clients find highly satisfying occupations. The evidence for this intended purpose is not given; instead, the manual concentrates on providing information concerning scale construction. Although necessary for initial evaluation of the CAI, these data cannot then be advanced, as they are here, as primary evidence for the validity of the same scales. Until resources are invested in obtaining the combination of evidence to support the intended purpose of the CAI, I suggest users rely on the Strong-Campbell Interest Inventory or the Self-Directed Search. These inventories have provided solid evidence that their scales are related to current and future occupational membership and job satisfaction.

REVIEWER'S REFERENCES

Strong, E. K. (1943). *Vocational interests of men and women.* Stanford: Stanford University Press.

Campbell, D. P. (1971). *Handbook for the Strong Vocational Interest Blank.* Stanford: Stanford University Press.

Rounds, J. B., Jr., & Zevon, M. A. (1983). Multidimensional scaling research in vocational psychology. *Applied Psychological Measurement,* 7, 491-510.

Holland, J. L. (1985). *Making vocational choices* (2nd ed.). Englewood Cliffs, NJ: Prentice-Hall.

[44]

Career Directions Inventory. Purpose: "Designed to identify areas of greater or lesser interest from among a wide variety of occupations" to assist in educational and career planning. High school and college and adults; 1982–86; CDI; 15 Basic Interest Scales: Administration, Art, Clerical, Food Service, Industrial Arts, Health Service, Outdoors, Personal Service, Sales, Science & Tech., Teaching/Social Service, Writing, Assertive, Persuasive, Systematic; 1987 price data: $6 per question and answer document (includes price of machine scoring); $8 per manual ('86, 61 pages); $12 per examination kit including manual, question and answer document, computerized scoring for 1 document; French edition available; (30–50) minutes; Douglas N. Jackson; Research Psychologists Press, Inc.*

Review of the Career Directions Inventory by DARRELL L. SABERS, Professor of Educational Psychology, University of Arizona, Tucson, AZ:

The Career Directions Inventory (CDI) is intended to be differentiated from (Jackson's) Vocational Interest Survey "by its broad applicability to the general population, highlighting 'blue collar' as well as professional careers, and its relatively easy vocabulary level. It is differentiated from many other vocational interest measures by its advanced methods of item selection and scale construction, by the relatively limited linguistic demands it makes on respondents, by its up-to-date and continuing compilation of a wide range of specialty groups, by its use of modern multivariate techniques to identify stable clusters of educational and occupational groupings, by the broad applicability and generalizability of the groupings, and by the application of sophisticated computer-based means for detecting unreliable records." This review reports the extent to which these intentions are met.

The CDI consists of 100 forced-choice triads presenting 300 statements decribing job-related activities or a certain kind of work environment or work role. The respondent is to "decide which one of the activities you would most like to do and which one of the activities you would least like to do." Many of the statements do not describe activities, but the respondent would have little difficulty following the directions.

The CDI answer sheet must be machine scored by the publisher, but the advantage of central scoring is the completeness of the profile produced by the scoring program. The "CDI Profile" is a 10-page computer-generated report that should be understandable by most of its intended readers. One aspect of the report is questionable—each standard score is expressed twice as an exact number with no provision for the standard error of measurement. The graphic representation of each standard score could easily be shown as a confidence interval rather than as a bar starting at 30 and extending to the score obtained.

The items are written in unisex terms and appear to be easy to read and understand. If it were not for the extensive piloting procedures and numerous reviews, one might question the acceptability of some items; for example, "never arriving late for an appointment" and "never wasting time unnecessarily." The forced-choice triads eliminate the possibility of the respondent "faking good," but, of course, cannot stop the respondent from faking a particular interest.

The manual is easy to read and presents useful case summaries to assist in interpretation of results. However, the description of the development of the CDI is inconsistent. The steps followed are clearly presented, but the reader does not learn what the instructions to participants were during the item development. This last point seems important because the items were tried out prior to forming the triads. The manual reports, "We requested of the entire group that they identify any words that were found to be difficult." It is clear how this procedure would assist in identifying statements needing revision, but the manner of the respondents' endorsement is unclear.

The three items combined into any triad had approximately equal endorsement proportions in early tryouts. However, it is not obvious from reading the manual whether these endorsement proportions were established with much precision. The degree to which the error in endorsement is controlled is the degree to which acquiescence is eliminated from the resulting scores. When principal components analyses were conducted on 450 and 316 respondents, one believes that adequate sample size was not an important criterion for item development. Another possible problem is the triads were formed prior to the last screening for readability. Because some words were substituted for words identified as causing comprehension problems in this final readability check, some of the statements included in the published instrument apparently have never been subjected to item tryout in their present forms. It is unfortunate the extensive care taken to ensure readability included a step that now detracts from the final instrument's credibility.

Although extensive item writing and editing are reported to ensure the items measure the appropriate scales, empirical item analyses were used to document that each item measures the appropriate scale and not other scales. The procedures used should result in lower correlations among scales and increase the meaningfulness of profile interpretation. The documentation of the steps in validating the scales and the explanation for these steps is adequate. The names for the scales seem appropriate and informative, although the reader learning about the infrequency scale may experience difficulty because Figure 4-2 in the manual is labelled incorrectly.

The "norming group" is an unidentified group of 1,000 respondents who are not intended to be representative of any specific population. The 1,000 (500 males, 500 females) are a subsample of the 12,846 respondents drawn from 138 specialty groups identified for validation purposes. The institutions contributing data to the standardization are listed in the manual, but this list should not be used in an attempt to define a population for the norms. The scores of this group do not provide usable norms based on any representative group, and this group should probably always be referred to with the phrase "people enrolled in many different career training programs" as presented on the scoring report rather than with "people in general" as used in the validity section of the manual. The problem with the norm group may be less serious, however, than using the results of achievement tests developed with interpolation, extrapolation, and imperfect scaling techniques.

The strange and unknown composition of the normative group should not introduce a major problem for the validation of the scales. The validity information is based on comparing the distribution of scores on different specialty groups with scores obtained by the 1,000 people forming the normative group. Because the scores of people unlikely to take the inventory are not of interest in this comparison, it is possible the normative group as used here is actually preferred to a census-representative norming sample. The contrasted-groups validation technique was used repeatedly, and the manual provides abundant data for judging the validity of the many scores. Because the data presentation emphasizes visual rather than numerical bases for validity, some users may look unsuccessfully for validity "coefficients" or indices of group separation.

The reliability information consists of test-retest and alpha coefficients. The test-retest coefficients are based on 70 respondents over a period of about 4 weeks, and there is no indication of the lack of precision in an estimate based on such a small sample. Of more interest to the user would be stability estimates based on longer periods of time, yet it is not unusual for that type of information to be absent even for instruments that have been available for several years. The reader would do well to ignore the differences in reliabilities among the scales because few such differences would be statistically significant. The coefficient alpha reliabilities are based on the norming sample of 1,000 respondents, a sample size that is adequate for this purpose. These internal consistency coefficients for the separate scores range from below .70 to above .90, and are likely to be judged as acceptable or high.

The manual contains adequate warning against overinterpretation of the scores, and misuses should be minimized by repeated cautions in the score report. Among points emphasized are what CDI is not, that there is a need for local validation, and that the CDI should be used as only one source of information on which to base a decision. One shortcoming in this respect is the statement in the manual that "low scores represent rejected activities"; a more accurate statement because of the forced choice nature of the task is that these are relatively less attractive activities for the individual. The CDI report's suggestions for obtaining additional information to validate the information reported in the profile are commendable.

Although the manual presents detailed information on the differences between the CDI and the Jackson Vocational Interest Survey (158) by the same author, the reader may be more interested in a comparison with Super's Career Development Inventory, especially because the abbreviation for that instrument is also CDI. It is this reviewer's opinion that such a similarity is more than unfortunate; rather, it should be the responsibility of an author to avoid using the identical initials of an existing instrument when confusion is to be expected. Actually, the instruments are different enough that they should not be considered to be competitors. A likely competitor to the CDI is the Strong-Campbell Interest Inventory (SCII; 9:1195), an instrument that has received much praise from reviewers of previous *Mental Measurements Yearbooks*. The SCII will be preferred by those who accept the response format of *Like, Indifferent, Dislike* to each statement. For those among us who prefer the ipsative nature of the forced-choice triads, the CDI appears to be more like the Kuder Occupational Interest Survey (167). Which of these instruments is actually better for a given purpose is an empirical question.

In summary, the CDI appears to be a quality instrument based on well-documented research. There are a number of shortcomings noted in this review, but these are to be expected for a new instrument and can easily be addressed. It is not uncommon to end a review with the statement "the instrument can be recommended for research purposes only." This reviewer has no doubt there are more positive than negative aspects to the CDI, and that there is no question it can be recommended for more than research. The CDI is already a good instrument, and will likely improve greatly as the author receives information from its users.

Review of the Career Directions Inventory by FREDRICK A. SCHRANK, Associate Academic Dean, Griffin College, Tacoma, WA:

This review will reflect mixed opinions about the Career Directions Inventory (CDI).

The CDI is intended to measure vocational interests in trade and skilled occupations. In purpose it is differentiated from other interest inventories by broad applicability to the general population, assessing patterns of interest in skilled and technical occupations as well as professional careers. The test places limited linguistic demands on examinees. Vocabulary is at about the sixth grade level, items are simply worded, and activities which are described are either familiar or easy to understand.

Administration, scoring, and report generation of this test are impressive with the software available for an IBM or IBM-compatible microcomputer. Two double-sided double-density disk drives are required. This program assumes only basic familiarity with personal computers. Program functions are easily accessed through menus. A toll-free number for professional assistance with any computer software problems is provided. This service was found to be immediately responsive and helpful in problem resolution.

Theoretical interpretation of this test and occupational search procedures that follow may be problematic. The test's general occupational themes are based, in part, on Holland's theory of careers, but the basic structure of the theory has been supplemented with an additional theme (which was determined through factor analysis). Counselors who use the Holland coding system to expand the career search process will find the additional theme unexplainable with the Holland typology. Additionally, the basic interest scales contain an odd mix of measured interest in certain types of roles (such as teaching, food service, and writing) and temperaments (such as assertive, persuasive, and systematic). Measurement of the latter appears to be done as an afterthought and would probably best be left to more sophisticated measures of temperament, such as the Temperament and Values Inventory (9:1233). Inclusion of the temperament scales within the basic interest profiles complicates interpretation and raises an additional question about the purity of the theoretical model used to design the inventory.

Standardization of this test is peculiar. The manual presents a convoluted rationale for inadequate research with occupational specialty groups. In the place of research on workers data were obtained from student groups. Traditionally, interest correlations are obtained by comparing a respondent's pattern of preferences to those of individuals already employed in an occupation and who report they are satisfied with their work. The author reports this type of research was too difficult to obtain and instead substituted research with students enrolled in educational programs and thought likely to represent an occupation. Although the interpretive report identifies these groups as "educational specialty groups," the existence of occupational titles implies measurement against occupational groups, not students who intend to enter the occupation. Further, there is no evidence to suggest those students would actually be successful or satisfied with the occupation they have been selected to represent if, in fact, they pursued it. Because of this serious flaw, it is important to caution examinees that this test should not be used to infer similarities between their scores and those of successful members of an occupation.

Psychometric characteristics are inconclusive. Information on the validity of the CDI is unconvincing. The author presents a dizzying list of specialty group score distributions compared to a 1,000-person normative group defined as "people in general" to establish a concurrent validity thesis. The reported test-retest reliability scores are satisfactory and range from .67 to .96 using a 4-week interval with a sample of 34 males and 36 females.

Despite these serious anomalies, examinee response to this test has been highly positive. Measurement of vocational interests in trade and skilled occupations has been seriously neglected, and this instrument provides a tool for career exploration for a large population of individuals who are considering technical or skilled careers. This reviewer's case studies with adults already employed in career fields supports the thesis of concurrent validity, but this research was merely of the catch-as-catch-can variety. Student response to this test has been unusual, and has, in most cases, stimulated action in the career search process.

In summary, the CDI is enjoyable to use and is well-received by examinees. The software program represents the state-of-the-art in test administration, scoring, and reporting. Theoretical interpretation and ensuing career search procedures may be problematic, but can be overcome. The CDI is not well researched. To make this test a better one, information on validity, especially predictive validity, is needed.

[45]

Career Profile System. Purpose: Selection tool predicting a candidate's "odds of succeeding as an insurance sales representative." Insurance sales representatives and candidates for insurance sales representative positions; 1983–87; earlier edition called Aptitude Index Battery (AIB); 2 levels: Initial, Advanced; distribution restricted to home offices of member insurance companies; 1989 price data: $12 per administrator's kit including kit folder, Initial Career Profile questionnaire, Advanced Career Profile questionnaire, and manual ('87, 37 pages); $5 per questionnaire booklet; $1,475 or less per 100 Initial Career Profile or Advanced Career Profile answer sheets and card-envelope sets including mandatory LIMRA scoring and other services; $4 per manual; English-speaking Canada, French-speaking Canada, and United Kingdom/Republic of Ireland editions also available; 55(65) minutes; Life Insurance Marketing and Research Association, Inc.*

Review of the Career Profile System by EDWIN L. HERR, Professor and Head, Division of Counseling and Educational Psychology and Career Studies, The Pennsylvania State University, University Park, PA:

The Career Profile System (CPS) has been developed by and is a service of the Life Insurance Marketing and Research Association (LIMRA), a cooperative research organization supported by over 600 member insurance companies around the world. The CPS in its first edition in 1983 is, in fact, the twelfth edition of a paper-and-pencil questionnaire earlier known as the Aptitude Index and, subsequently, the Aptitude Index Battery.

The CPS is described as central to a selection process for insurance representatives who either have no or some sales experience in insurance. The CPS Questionnaire completed by candidates for insurance sales positions is computer scored by LIMRA and then returned to the potential employer with a multipage score report and additional information to be used in the rest of the selection process. The CPS includes two questionnaire forms and a variety of documents designed for different purposes.

The CPS includes initial and advanced career profile reports, initial and advanced career profile interview guides, and initial and advanced career combination guides. Each of these items is accompanied by interview manuals and other material to guide the interpretation of and the extension of the information included in the report of the candidate's Career Profile results. These manuals and supporting information are well-written, systematic in their content, and attractive.

The predictive validity research that led to the CPS began in 1919 and was directed principally to the two earlier instruments—the Aptitude Index (AI) and the Aptitude Index Battery (AIB). In both of these instruments and the current Career Profile System, the intent is to provide a rating of a candidate for an insurance position relative to the probability of on-the-job success based on a comparison of his or her scores to those of similar candidates who have become sales representatives. The resulting rating of the candidate indicates that chances of success are above average, average, or below average.

The more than 60 years of research underlying the CPS has been directed largely to identifying questions that differentiate successful and unsuccessful insurance agents. These questions are included in two sets of forms. The Initial Career Profile is designed to be used with candidates who do not have any insurance sales experience. The 183 items comprising the questionnaire are divided into six sections dealing with the candidate's past, present, and future (Sections I, II, and III) and with the details of the career opportunity (Sections IV, V, and VI). The questions included in these sections assess the candidates' career expectations, motivating goals, concerns about the career, self-assessment of skills and abilities appropriate to the career, and satisfaction with present job and potential client markets. The Advanced Career Profile is used with candidates who have insurance sales experience. It is comprised of 158 items divided across seven sections that assess the candidate's clients; market potential; sales results, types, and methods; self-assessment of sales activities appropriate to the career; insurance income, income needs, and income expectations; satisfaction with present insurance sales position; and, managerial background.

The candidate rating system is a 19-point scale derived from the candidate's completed initial or advanced Career Profile. The rating indicates the degree of success that managers have had when they selected sales representatives. The higher the rating, the better the candidate survival and production is likely to be. Companies or managers are encouraged to set specific cutoff scores pertinent to their needs. Managers are encouraged to not use the rating score alone in deciding whether or not to employ the candidate. Rather, if a candidate's score exceeds the cutoff score for that company, LIMRA encourages a manager to continue the candidate through a careful screening process involving in-depth interviews. LIMRA provides managers with an excellent multipage report on the candidate and interview guides and manuals that detail how to conduct effective interviews and use the Career Profile Report on the candidate with insight and sensitivity to EEO and other criteria.

LIMRA provides several pieces of information about the research conducted on the CPS and its antecedents. One document, *Agent Selection Questionnaire Research: Selected Literature*, summarizes the research procedures used to construct and validate the Aptitude Index and the Aptitude Index Battery. According to this literature review, from the beginnings of the research to the present, the procedures used include control on age for personal history items, the use of multiple regression techniques for the addition of items to the scoring system, cross-validation of the scoring system, testing the validity across a variety of companies in both the United States and Canada, weighing the personality and personal history items based on age because of differential validities, use of a predictive validity model, and insistence on a continuing program to be sure the questionnaire continues to provide valid data. This review of the selected literature identifies 47 studies and books relating to the development of the AI or AIB and 30 references related to the search for alternative and additional selection tests. There then follow 13 classic articles beginning in the 1930s and ending in the 1970s relating to the construction and validation of the AI or AIB. In order to understand the psychometric properties of the AI, AIB, or Career Profile, a potential user must read each of these studies. Unfortunately, this reviewer found no clear summary or chart in the manual or elsewhere that condensed the large literature on these instruments. However, when one reads these studies there is impressive evidence of the predictive validity of the rating system and of the personal history (questionnaire) form over extended periods of time (e.g., up to 38 years). In addition, these studies show that specific scale values for individual items do change over time and need to be rescaled and that some items gain or lose validity over time. However, the studies also show that with adequate key development, scoring key confidentiality, and large sample sizes, well-developed personal history items tend to retain validity even when economic conditions have changed.

A variety of tables in the manual and separate tables for the Career Profile System present data related primarily to predictive validity. The criterion for assessing predictive validity with regard to the Career Profile ratings is on-the-job performance: A sales representative is defined as a success if earned commissions or income from all lines of business during the first 12 months are in the top 20 percent as compared with other first-year company sales representatives. The scoring systems have been developed using multiple-regression techniques with modification for the use of moderator variables. These scoring procedures were then cross-validated or cross-checked on a sample of candidates who were not used in the development of the systems. In terms of predictive validity, the data show the probability of success for an individual who receives a score of 19 is twice that of an individual rated 11, nearly three times that of an individual rated 9, and nearly 10 times that of an individual rated 2. Data are also available about the cost savings that accrue to companies using the Career Profile Questionnaire versus those who do not in terms of how many persons would have to be hired to get one successful representative at different rating score levels. For those insurance companies using the Career Profile System, the percent reductions in total costs are estimated at 29% to 43% at different cutoff scores from 9 to 19. Separate predictive validity tables are provided for Canadian operations, U.S. multiple-line operations, U.S. combination, and U.S. ordinary operations.

The generalizability of the validity of the Career Profile System to minority groups, women, different age groups, candidates with different educational backgrounds, and others is asserted in several manuals and in other information. The data supporting such assertions are not reported in the manual. Nor are specific data reported about the concurrent validity of the Career Profile with other somewhat comparable instruments (e.g., Strong-Campbell Interest Inventory). There is a list in the manual of annotated references of past studies of alternative or additional selection procedures (e.g., the Adult Placement Test, the Allport-Vernon Study of Values, the Activity Vector Analysis) with the implication that none of these was found to be useful in predicting on-the-job performance of insurance representatives. Presumably, these studies do assess concurrent validity.

In summary, the Career Profile System manifests a long history of apparently sophisticated studies of key development, interviewing procedures, personal history items, and other components. The reporting system, interview guides, and other supporting material are useful and well developed. Additional data on concurrent validity and on the utility of the personal history items in the Career Profile System with occupational groups other than insurance sales representatives are warranted. The system, with some modification, could provide important contributions to career guidance beyond that of selecting insurance representatives.

Review of the Career Profile System by MARY L. TENOPYR, Selection and Testing Director, AT&T, Morristown, NJ:

The Career Profile System consists of two biodata inventories, a 183-item instrument for selection for initial entry into the life insurance sales field and a 158-item blank for advanced entry. The instrument upon which these inventories are based was originally named the Aptitude Index Battery. Distribution is restricted to member companies of the Life Insurance Marketing and Research Association, Inc. (LIMRA). The biodata blanks are administered in local offices of insurance companies and mailed to LIMRA for scoring.

It is extremely difficult to review proprietary instruments such as the Career Profile Records on the basis of typical standards by which more available instruments are evaluated. For example, much of the material is developed appropriately for the user naive in psychometrics. The key and scoring methods are, as is absolutely necessary, kept confidential. Nevertheless, there is some information available by which one may judge the most important features of the Career Profile Records.

Initial research and development work was begun on the predecessor Aptitude Index Battery in 1919 and continues to this day. A booklet, which may serve some of the purposes as a manual, lists available publications relative to the inventories. Both publications for scientific audiences and lay persons are listed therein. Validity data are summarized in terms of an expectancy table, and expected cost-reduction data associated with the use of the inventories in selection are given. Verbal descriptions of generalization data and the feasibility of alternate selection procedures are provided. A list of references to previous studies on alternatives to the inventories is in this booklet. The document ends with a discussion of the confidentiality of scoring and records.

Another document, which is designated as a manual for the inventories, gives lucid instructions for administration and use of the instruments, but not the traditional data found in a test manual. Each user company selects its own critical score, and guides for interviewing based upon Career Profile Record results are furnished with actual score reports.

A book of reprints of selected journal articles and internal reports is available. Although the book contains much material supporting the validity of the inventories the data are scattered through the various articles, and reporting is thin in areas such as current reliability and appropriateness of the inventories for women and minorities.

What is needed to review this instrument adequately is a recent summary of scientific data. How much information should be given wide distribution considering the confidential nature of the inventory keys and related data is open to question; however, in view of the widespread use of biodata in various employment situations, publishing of such data would be a service to many personnel psychologists and scientists, alike.

[46]

Career Survey. Purpose: "To provide students, clients, and their counselors with information which may stimulate the counseling process . . . . to encourage students and clients to explore career areas which they may not have previously considered . . . . to provide a means for self-reflection and clarification of long-range plans in order to make short-range educational decisions which are consistent with those plans." Grade 7 through adults; 1984; 12 interest scales: Accommodating/Entertaining, Humanitarian/Caretaking, Plant/Animal Caretaking, Mechanical, Business Detail, Sales, Numerical, Communications/Promotion, Science/Technology, Artistic Expression, Educational/Social, Medical; 2 ability scales: Verbal, Nonverbal; 1987 price data: $26.25 per 35 career survey booklets, 35 orientation booklets, and directions for administration (16 pages); $23.85 per 35 interest survey booklets (includes interests only), 35 orientation booklets, and directions for administration; scoring service and additional packages available from publisher; (60) minutes; American Testronics.*

Review of the Career Survey by CHRISTOPHER BORMAN, Professor of Educational Psychology, Texas A&M University, College Station, TX:

The Career Survey is a guidance instrument consisting of two parts: an interest survey called the Ohio Career Interest Survey and an ability test called the Career Ability Survey. The interest test has 12 scales with 11 items per scale. The 132 items in the interest test (Part 1) are scored on a 5-point scale going from *dislike very much* to *like very much*. As a part of the Ohio Career Interest Survey, there are seven additional items (Part 2) relating to expressed interests, and these questions ask about best-liked job tasks, best-liked school subjects, and future educational goals. The Career Ability Survey contains two parts: (*a*) Verbal reasoning is measured by 22 verbal analogy items; and (*b*) Nonverbal reasoning is measured by 18 items divided equally between two item types—number series and figural relationships.

A two-dimensional model was used to develop the Ohio Career Interest Survey. Test materials indicate that this survey was developed by staff members from the Ohio Department of Education who worked with Ohio schools in using the Ohio Vocational Interest Survey (OVIS) and used this experience to develop the Ohio Career Interest Survey. Dimensions of the test model are people-things and data-ideas. Twelve interest scales were developed to fit this bipolar model, and these scales can be displayed graphically along the diagonals of a square. Opposite sides of the square are labeled people-things and data-ideas.

Originally 600 items were written to relate directly to 1 of the 12 scale definitions, and then the number of items was reduced until there were 11 items per scale. The Counselor's Guide (provided with the test and similar to a test manual) explains how the items were assigned to scales and how the final items were selected, but no data are given to back up this selection process. The items of the interest inventory are stated as job tasks. The Ohio Career Interest Survey results are linked to the Worker Trait Group arrangement of jobs developed by the Department of Labor and to the Military Occupation Specialties used by the Department of Defense.

In developing the Career Ability Survey, approximately 500 ability test items were written and field tested with approximately 8,000 students per grade (7–12). The authors state that from this pool three types of items were selected for inclusion in the test—verbal analogy, number series, and figural relationships. Item selection criteria are described in the Counselor's Guide, but no data are given to support the selection of the 40 items that comprise the ability test.

The Career Survey was designed for students in grades 7 through 12 and for use with adults. The instrument was nationally normed in the fall of 1983 and the spring of 1984. A list of participating schools is included in Part 4 of the Counselor's Guide. The norm sample seems to be similar to a representative sample of students from across the country, but this observation is based only on a visual examination of a table that lists school districts and the number of participants per grade level included in the norm sample. National percentile ranks are provided for both the interest and ability scales. For the 12 interest scales, separate norm tables are provided for males, females, and combined groups (both sexes) for the following grade combinations: 7/8, 9/10, and 11/12. Norm tables for 11–12 are also used for college/young adult. For the two ability subtests (Verbal and Nonverbal), norm tables are provided separately for each grade. It is stated that there are not separate tables for males and females because sex differences on the ability tests were negligible.

Using Cronbach's coefficient alpha, internal consistency of the Ohio Career Interest Survey was tested with Ohio studies of 6,000 to 7,000 students per grade level. The coefficients for the 12 scales range from .86 to .93 indicating very respectable internal consistency for the instrument. Test-retest reliability coefficients, with 10-day intervals, were calculated for samples of students in grades 8, 9, and 10. Test-retest reliability coefficients for the interest survey range from .79 to .92 with the median reliability being .86. Test-retest reliability data indicate that results from the 12 interest scales are stable over time. Reliability of the Career Ability Survey was assessed by the Kuder-Richardson Formula 20 and odd-even approaches with a sample of approximately 1,500 students in grades 7–12. Reliability coefficients for the verbal and nonverbal sections of the test range from .62 to .84 when the coefficients are examined separately for each grade level. Coefficients for all grades combined are .80 (KR-20) and .81 (odd-even) for the verbal test, and .73 (KR-20) and .78 (odd-even) for the nonverbal test. These data indicate satisfactory internal consistency of the ability test, but no data are reported on the test-retest reliability of the ability test.

Construct validity for the interest survey was established by a two-step process: (*a*) Theoretical relationships were predicted from the two-dimensional model used to develop the instrument, and (*b*) the "fit" between observed and theoretical relationships was examined. Data presented in the Counselor's Guide tend to support predictions from the test model. Criterion validity of the 12 interest scales was investigated by relating measured interests to satisfaction with the job training experiences in selected vocational training programs. The sample consisted of 996 graduates from nine vocational training programs at 16 vocational schools. Students involved in the validation study completed the interest survey and a questionnaire measuring overall satisfaction with the job tasks that they were trained to perform. The hypotheses that were tested in this study were that a satisfied group of students in a particular training program would show significantly higher interest on certain specified items and scales than a dissatisfied group and that the satisfied group means would be significantly higher than the standardization means for the same scales. The data presented generally support these hypotheses and provide evidence for criterion validity for the 12 scales of the Ohio Career Interest Survey. Additional validation studies with students in other training programs or with actual workers in different occupations would add considerable support to the validity of the instrument.

The Career Ability Survey was written by the four authors who wrote the Developing Cognitive Abilities Test (DCAT), and one of the validity studies described in the Counselor's Guide compares Career Ability measures with DCAT results. Data indicate that the Verbal subtest is moderately to highly correlated with the DCAT Verbal subtest. The Nonverbal subtest of the Career Ability Survey is moderately correlated with the DCAT Quantitative and Spatial subtests. The Career Ability Survey has also been correlated with the General Aptitude Test Battery (GATB), the American College Test (ACT), and the Scholastic Aptitude Test (SAT). Data indicate a substantial relationship between the Verbal scale of the Career Ability Survey and the Verbal scale of the GATB. There is a moderate relationship between the Nonverbal scale of the Career Ability Survey and the Numerical and Spatial scales of the GATB. Finally, the Career Ability Survey subtests have substantial correlations with subtests of the ACT and SAT.

The interest test (Ohio Career Interest Survey) and ability test (Career Ability Survey) are included in one test book and can be taken together. Also, the interest survey is included by itself in a separate booklet if the desire is only to administer the interest test. Directions for administration of the Career Survey are clear and easy to follow. The instrument can be hand scored and scoring directions are given in the Counselor's Guide. Machine scoring is recommended and provided by the test publishers. A career profile is provided where the scores are presented in a visual fashion. Also, the profile reports results in words as a part of a personalized narrative for each student.

The Career Survey is a new instrument among career guidance instruments, but it offers the potential for being a very useful instrument, especially since the Career Survey includes both an interest inventory and an ability test. Reliability data for the interest inventory indicate respectable internal consistency and stability over time. Reliability data for the ability survey indicate satisfactory internal consistency, but no information is reported on test-retest reliability of the test. Evidence is presented supporting the construct validity and criterion validity of the interest survey, but further studies with more diverse populations are needed to add support to the criterion validity of the instrument. Considerable evidence is given in the Counselor's Guide supporting the criterion validity of the ability survey. The Career Survey is well developed in terms of providing support materials for clients or students taking the survey and also providing good reference materials for those administering and interpreting the instrument.

Review of the Career Survey by GEORGE DOMINO, *Professor of Psychology, University of Arizona, Tucson, AZ:*

The Career Survey is designed to provide measures of a person's interests and abilities through the administration of three separate subtests: (*a*) the Ohio Career Interest Survey (Part 1), made up of 132 items (e.g., pick fruits or vegetables, analyze data from computer printouts) for which the respondent indicates degree of liking on a 5-point scale ranging from "*like this activity very much*" to "*dislike this activity very much*"; (*b*) the Career Planning Survey (designated as Part 2 of the Ohio Career Interest Survey), a set of seven multiple-choice questions that explore the kinds of job tasks respondents like and assesses plans for further education or training (e.g., What school subjects do you like best? In what high school program are you enrolled?); (*c*) the Career Ability Survey, a 40-item timed (24 minutes) test of reasoning ability that consists of 22 verbal analogies, 9 number series, and 9 spatial or concept relationship items.

The use of the words "career" and "survey" for both the overall questionnaire and each of the parts is quite confusing. Adding further to the confusion is the fact that Part 1 was originally called the Ohio Interest Survey, and this in turn was based on the Ohio Vocational Interest Survey.

The Career Survey is designed for students in grades 7 through 12 and for adults, and has three primary purposes: (*a*) to provide students, clients, and counselors with information that will stimulate the counseling process; (*b*) to encourage exploration of career areas not previously considered; and (*c*) to provide a link between long-range career plans and short-range educational decisions. The Career Survey was developed to meet three criteria: (*a*) "efficiency and flexibility in administration and interpretation," (*b*) "high technical quality in materials development and standardization," and (*c*) "links with one or more existing career information systems."

Part 1 of the Ohio Career Interest Survey yields scores on 12 interest scales, each based on 11 items, ranging from Accommodating/Entertaining to Medical. These interest scales are said to cover all 66 job clusters defined by the U.S. Department of Labor. The items that form these scales require a sixth-grade reading level and are free of any racial, gender, or cultural bias. The 12 interest scales appear to intercorrelate substantially, ranging from .88 between Business Detail and Sales (for females), to a low of .14 between Accommodating/Entertaining and Science/Technology (for males). At least 1/2 of the intercorrelations between the scales are at or above .35.

The normative sample included almost 3,000 junior high school students, over 7,000 high school students, and 681 freshman and sophomore college students, from diverse geographical areas. Little information is given about these subjects, however, and the impression is that these were samples of convenience rather than selected to be representative.

The reliability of Part 1 was assessed by both internal homogeneity and 10-day test-retest analyses. Results seem quite satisfactory, with median coefficient alphas in the .89/.90 range, and a median test-retest coefficient of .86. Validity information is fairly extensive and centers on (*a*) the construct validity of the 12 scales as related to a two-dimensional model with "poles" designated as data-ideas and people-things, as well as (*b*) criterion validity based on comparison of measured interests with satisfaction in training experiences in selected vocational training programs. Much more information is required, but these validity data represent a good beginning.

Part 2, the Career Planning Survey, seems to be disregarded by the test authors, and perhaps that is the way it ought to be. It seems pretentious to call something a "survey" that only asks the respondent which of the 12 career fields is most liked and in which school program the respondent is enrolled. Nonetheless, it would have been nice to know to what degree a person's first and second career choices on this part actually match the results of Part 1.

Part 3 of this battery is the Career Ability Survey and yields two scores, a Verbal Reasoning Ability score based on 22 items, and a Nonverbal Reasoning Ability score based on 18 items. Since each score is based on so few items, the resulting percentile distribution is highly misleading. For example, for seventh graders a raw score of 3 equals the 34th percentile, but a raw score of 5 equals the 50th percentile. Thus on the basis of 2 items, the typical counselor would arrive at quite different conclusions regarding a student's ability.

Reliability seems satisfactory and was estimated by both Kuder-Richardson Formula 20 and odd-even approaches. The reported coefficients for all grades combined are in the .73 to .81 range, but it is not indicated whether the odd-even coefficients were corrected by the Spearman-Brown formula.

The test authors indicate that Part 3, the Career Ability Survey, allows one to predict a student's ACT, SAT, and/or GATB-G scores. This prediction is based on linear regression analyses of two samples of 11th- and 12th-grade students who took the ACT and the SAT ($N = 142$) or the GATB-G ($N = 62$) in addition to the Career Ability Survey. Given the rather large normative samples, one wonders why these analyses are based on smaller samples, the nature of which is not described. In addition, no information is given on how accurate the prediction is, and the typical counselor might well assume a degree of correspondence between tests that is not warranted.

The validity of the Career Ability Survey is explored by relating the Verbal and Nonverbal scores to scores on the Developing Cognitive Abilities Test, the General Aptitude Test Battery, the American College Test, and the Scholastic Aptitude Test. It should be pointed out that the two Career Ability Survey scores (Verbal/Nonverbal) correlate with one another substantially, from .44 to .68 in various samples, and hence one would question whether these two are in fact measuring different aspects of reasoning ability. The two do correlate significantly with the various measures indicated above, and many of the resulting coefficients are in the .50s and .60s.

The Career Survey can be hand scored, although for Part 1 this represents a rather herculean task. Computer scoring services are available from the test publisher, who provides both individual reports for the client and group reports for the counselor. The package of test materials is quite comprehensive and includes very detailed administration guidelines. Most of the materials are clearly written, and a careful reading revealed only one typographical error.

In summary, Part 1 seems quite promising and represents a reliable and well validated questionnaire. Part 2 adds little and one would hope the typical counselor would already have this information. Part 3 is suspect, and much more evidence needs to be presented that in fact the Career Ability Survey measures two types of reasoning abilities, and that these are indeed differentially related to career choice. Finally, there is no evidence presented that would support what the authors state are the three primary purposes of the Career Survey. There is no empirical evidence that the information generated by the Career Survey (*a*) stimulates the counseling process, (*b*) encourages the exploration of new career areas, and (*c*) provides a link between long range career plans and short range educational decisions. Unless such evidence is forthcoming, career counselors are advised to use other, better validated instruments.

[47]

Certificate of Proficiency in English. Purpose: Indicates an advanced level of competence in English at University study level. Candidates whose mother-tongue is not English; 1913–86; CPE; oldest in the range of Cambridge Examinations in English as a Foreign Language; 5 scores: Reading Comprehension, Composition, Use of English, Listening Comprehension, Interview; tests administered in June and December at over 450 local centers throughout the world; price data available from publisher; (350) minutes; University of Cambridge Local Examinations Syndicate in collaboration with the British Council; the Syndicate [England].

[48]

Certified Picture Framer Examination. Purpose: "To provide professional recognition to competent individuals who are engaged in the business of picture framing." Individuals actively involved in the business of picture framing for one year; 1986: CPF; test administered on specific dates at centers established by the publisher; 1987 price data: registration fee $125 for members of PPFA or $170 for nonmembers; 210(225) minutes; Certification Advisory Committee of the Professional Picture Framers Association; Professional Picture Framers Association.

[49]

Chelsea Diagnostic Mathematics Tests. Purpose: "Designed as diagnostic instruments to be used both for ascertaining a child's level of understanding and to identify the incidence of errors." Ages 10–15; 1984–85; 10 tests: Algebra, Fractions 1, Fractions 2, Graphs, Measurement, Number Operations, Place-Value and Decimals, Ratio and Proportion, Reflection and Rotation, Vectors; 1985 price data: £65 per 10 of each test booklet, teacher's guide ('85, 154 pages), and marking overlays for Reflection and Rotation test; £4.45–6.45 per 10 of any one test; £11.95 per teacher's guide; £4.45 per marking overlays; £16.95 per specimen set; (30–70) minutes per test; Kathleen Hart, Margaret Brown, Daphne Kerslake, Dietmar Kuchemann, and Graham Ruddock; NFER-Nelson Publishing Co., Ltd. [England].*

[50]

The Child Abuse Potential Inventory, Form VI. Purpose: "To assist in the screening of suspected physical child abuse cases." Male and female parents or primary caregivers who are suspected of physical child abuse; 1980–86; CAP Inventory; 10 scale scores: Abuse scale (Distress, Rigidity, Unhappiness, Problems With Child and Self, Problems With Family, Problems With Others, Total Physical Child Abuse), Validity scales (Lie Scale, Random Response Scale, Inconsistency Scale), and 3 Response Distortion Indexes (Faking-Good, Faking-Bad, Random Response); individual administration recommended; 1988 price data: $12 or less per 10 inventory booklets; $18 per basic scoring template set; $38 per complete scoring template set; $1 per Inconsistency scale scoring sheet set; $1 per 10 raw score summary sheets; $24 per manual ('86, 112 pages); $40 per CAPSCORE Program 1.02 or $50 per CAPSCORE Program 2.02 (Apple IIe, IIc, and IBM PC, PCjr) for computer scoring and research; (12–20) minutes; Joel S. Milner; Psytec Inc.*

TEST REFERENCES

1. Milner, J. S., Gold, R. G., Ayoub, C., & Jacewitz, M. M. (1984). Predictive validity of the Child Abuse Potential Inventory. *Journal of Consulting and Clinical Psychology*, 52, 879-884.

2. Ayoub, C. C. (1985). Failure to thrive: Parental indicators, types, and outcomes. *Child Abuse & Neglect*, 9, 491-499.

3. Stringer, S. A., & LaGreca, A. M. (1985). Correlates of child abuse potential. *Journal of Abnormal Child Psychology*, 13, 217-226.

4. Milner, J. S., & Gold, R. G. (1986). Screening spouse abusers for child abuse potential. *Journal of Clinical Psychology*, 42, 169-172.

5. Milner, J. S., Gold, R. G., & Wimberley, R. C. (1986). Prediction and explanation of child abuse: Cross-validation of the Child Abuse Potential Inventory. *Journal of Consulting and Clinical Psychology*, 54, 865-866.

Review of The Child Abuse Potential Inventory, Form IV, by STUART N. HART, Associate Professor of Educational Psychology, Indiana University-Purdue University at Indianapolis, Indianapolis, IN:

The primary and general goal set for the Child Abuse Potential Inventory (CAP), was to produce "an instrument that could be employed by protective services workers to screen for physical abuse." The author combined psychiatric and interpersonal orientations to the etiology of physical abuse, in the absence of a widely accepted unified theoretical base, to guide the construction of the scale. It is a self-administered screening instrument offering "Agree" and "Disagree" as response options to 160 items.

The manual (second edition) for this instrument is very well organized, presenting information on development and applications in a detailed, logical, and clear fashion, which displays a high level of respect for the criteria set forth in *Standards for Educational and Psychological Testing* (AERA, APA, & NCME, 1985). The CAP is sufficiently simple to allow supervised nonprofessionals to administer it, while requiring interpretation by a qualified professional. Administration, which requires only a four-page booklet and pencil, may be by individual or group procedure. The estimated third grade reading level should allow most subjects to work unassisted, or the inventory may be read to subjects. Scoring to produce the 10 scales (one primary, six factor, and three validity) involves computations with weighted scores. It is possible to hand score by using templates, but computer scoring, as advised by the author to decrease time and increase accuracy, appears to be justified.

Reliability information is available for both internal consistency and temporal stability estimates. Corrected split-halves and KR-20 internal consistency estimates presented for the 77-item Physical Abuse scale, are high, ranging from .92–.96 for controls and .95–.98 for abusers. The overall *SEM* for the Abuse scale is the equivalent of 3.9 on a 100-point scale and fairly uniform across groups. Lower internal consistency estimates were produced for factor and validity scales, adequate for their purposes, with abuser estimates generally higher than those for controls. Data were produced by 2,610 subjects representing control, at-risk, neglect, and abuse groups, and as a function of location, gender, age, educational level, and ethnic background. Temporal stability estimates (Pearson Product-Moment correlation coefficients) for the Abuse scale range from .91 (125 controls) to .75 (150 controls) for 1-day and 3-month intervals, respectively. Temporal stability estimates were adequate to strong for validity and factor scales. Temporal stability information for abusers was not available. While this information should be sought, it is recognized that it may by necessity be of limited interpretive value because of the impact of treatments during intervening periods.

Validity information in content, construct, concurrent predictive, and future predictive forms is available. Content validity has been established through (*a*) creation of items expressing child abuse associates identified in an extensive literature review, representing both psychiatric and interactional models; (*b*) judgments of knowledgeable professionals; and (*c*) through evidence of strong internal consistency. Construct validity has been established through (*a*) numerous correlational studies indicating expected relationships between performance on the CAP and characteristics having known or assumed relationships with child abuse (e.g., history of childhood abuse, locus of control, self-esteem, life stress); (*b*) studies finding decreased CAP scores following periods of treatment; (*c*) factor analysis producing six subscales consistent with child abuse literature; and (*d*) the discriminant validity characteristics described next.

Concurrent predictive and future predictive validity are essential for a screening device applied to an area of such great consequence. Three major concurrent validity studies have been conducted by the author and associates, while several studies by others have been analyzed. Available data support expectations that, using a cutoff of 215 points, correct identification of active, nontreated, moderate to severe physical abusers in a high risk population will cluster near the 80% level and that correct identification of controls will be near or above the 90% level. These percentages may rise to a level identifying 88% of physical abusers and 100% controls, with application of Milner's recommended complete interpretation procedure (i.e., rounded, weighted scores and valid protocols only—responses for more than 90% of items, totals prorated for missing responses, and acceptable response distortion indexes). Information on factor scales indicates that, while five of six and the combined set discriminate between abusers and nonabusers, they do not equal the strength of the Abuse scale to do so and they produce increased misclassifications when used in a factor scoring approach. The author has properly relegated them to inclusion in client factor profiles for assessment and treatment purposes. One major future predictive study has been reported (Milner, Gold, Ayoub, & Jacewitz, 1984). Subjects (200) participating in an at-risk parent-child program were followed until they left the program or were reported for child maltreatment (average of 6.5 months after initial testing). All subjects reported for abuse (11) had CAP scores elevated beyond the Abuse scale 215-point cutoff; however, the majority of subjects with elevated scores were not reported for abuse. The misclassifications may be due to treatment effects, reporting failures, or prediction failures. These results and the strong relationships found between the CAP Abuse scale scores and subsequently reported abuse or neglect, provide preliminary support for the use of the CAP for future prediction.

The CAP Abuse scale's potential to identify categories of maltreating adults other than active, nontreated, moderate to severe physically abusive parents has received some investigation. Results have been promising for identifying institutional abusers, while mixed for neglectful parents, and poor for mildly physically abusive parents and for failure-to-thrive consequences. Additionally, a recent study raises questions about the effectiveness of the scale to identify abusers who may have previously experienced social system intervention (Holden, Willis, & Foltz, 1987). With justification, Milner states a relative strength of the scale "is the low misclassification rate of nonabusive and nurturing parents."

This is clearly the best standardized instrument available for the intended purposes. Other promising self-report instruments intended to screen for maltreatment potential (e.g., Michigan Screening Profile for Parenting and Parental Awareness Scale paper and pencil self-report procedures, Life Stress Scale interview procedure) do not approach the psychometric strengths of the CAP. However, this instrument should not be used in isolation as the basis for intrusive, coercively applied intervention. The possibility of false positives argues against this on ethical and moral grounds. Its best uses in work with abuse-suspected populations could be to focus comprehensive evaluation resources efficiently on most likely subjects after establishing the instrument's power for this use under local conditions. For other populations at various degrees of risk, it could be used to identify groups to be offered prevention and improvement programs, if further research supports this. Further research is also recommended to determine the potential of the CAP, in modified forms, to identify maltreaters outside the active, severe, untreated physical abuser category, and to determine the usefulness of factor scores in treatment and prevention.

REVIEWER'S REFERENCES

Milner, J. S., Gold, R. G., Ayoub, C., & Jacewitz, M. M. (1984). Predictive validity of the Child Abuse Potential Inventory. *Journal of Consulting and Clinical Psychology*, 52, 879-884.

American Educational Research Association, American Psychological Association, & National Council on Measurement in Education. (1985). *Standards for educational and psychological testing*. Washington, DC: American Psychological Association, Inc.

Holden, E. W., Willis, D. J., & Foltz, L. (1987, August). *Child abuse potential and parenting stress: Relationships in maltreating parents*. Paper presented at 95th annual meeting of the American Psychological Association, New York City.

Review of The Child Abuse Potential Inventory, Form VI by GARY B. MELTON, Carl A. Happold Professor of Psychology and Law, University of Nebraska-Lincoln, Lincoln, NE:

The Child Abuse Potential Inventory (CAP) is a model of rapid, meticulous test development. Although the instrument was first published just a few years ago (1980) with research having begun in 1976, about 50 published articles and theses are already available on the CAP. The manual for the CAP, revised in 1986, is 100 pages long and unusually detailed and well organized. Moreover, not only has test author Joel Milner shown commendable care in development of the CAP, but, as we shall see, the CAP's hit rate in identifying known abusers *in highly selected samples* is simply uncanny. It is hard to imagine another instrument of similar age with better established psychometric properties.

At the same time, however, the potential for misuse of the CAP is so great that I question its clinical utility. The CAP is designed to provide protective services workers with a convenient means of screening suspected cases of physical child abuse. In keeping with that purpose, the initial validation samples consisted of equal numbers of known child abusers and matched nonabusers. The manual makes clear the CAP is intended to be used only in high-baserate populations and then only in conjunction with other sources of information. Unfortunately, some of the articles about the CAP have reported hit rates without qualification about the nature of the sample involved (see, e.g., Milner, Gold, Ayoub, & Jacewitz, 1984; Milner, Gold, & Wimberly, 1986).

Several problems arise in the application of the CAP. First, although the qualifications in the manual are well specified, my experience in conducting continuing legal education workshops leaves me virtually certain that such qualifications about the application of baserates will seldom be provided in practice and, if provided, rarely understood or heeded. Second, whatever the empirical baserates in the population referred to child protective services, a strong argument can be made that the law requires that the referred parent is assumed to be drawn from the general population, not a high-baserate population. Without such an assumption, the presumption of innocence is, in effect, obliterated. Third, although the construct the CAP purports to measure is mere *potential* for child abuse, the question the protective service worker must answer is postdictive: Did an abusive act occur? Fourth, if as some later work suggests, the CAP might be used for preventive purposes (see, e.g., Milner et al., 1984), the likelihood is the baserate, even in a high-risk population, will be substantially lower than the initial validation samples, and the risk of false positives will rise concomitantly. Although such a risk is less grievous than in child protective interventions, it still is significant because of the heightened vulnerability to compelled intrusions on family privacy that may result from a high CAP score. Milner also has suggested the CAP might be used preventively to screen a variety of child-care workers and groups outside the aegis of child protective jurisdiction (e.g., spouse abusers). As the consequences of a high score become more aversive (e.g., denied employment), the cost of a false positive becomes more serious.

The CAP consists of 160 agree/don't-agree items written at a third grade reading level. Although a number of content and validity scale scores are obtainable, the key scale (the only one to be used for screening) is the 77-item Child Abuse scale. The items were derived from review of over 700 articles and books about child abuse.

In the initial validation studies, the goal was to discriminate substantiated physical abusers (according to North Carolina law) from matched nonabusive comparison parents. Participants resided in North Carolina or Tulsa, Oklahoma. When validity scales have been applied to delete uninterpretable protocols, more than 90% of participants have been correctly classified, with the false negative rate being higher than the false positive rate. The false-positive rate rises substantially, however, when the CAP is used predictively (Milner et al., 1984).

CAP scores have been found to be correlated with a personal history of abuse, even though items specifically asking about such a history did not discriminate abusers from nonabusers and therefore were dropped during the test development. CAP scores also tend to be elevated among parents of handicapped children, especially when other stressors or possible support deficits (e.g., single parenthood) are present (Kirkham, Schinke, Schilling, Meltzer, & Norelius, 1986). At a personal level, CAP scores have been found to be related to a wide variety of measures of general mental health and ego strength, and an ego strength scale has been developed from the CAP itself (Milner, in press).

The CAP Abuse scale has excellent internal-consistency reliability (.92–.96 for comparison participants and .95–.98 for abusers). Test-retest reliability is also quite adequate (.91 for 1-day and .75 for 3-month intervals).

In short, the CAP is an impressive, relatively new instrument that has strong validity and reliability. It has been the subject of research involving a sufficiently broad range of populations that norms are potentially available for a variety of groups. However, the problems in application of CAP scores to individuals are sufficiently serious that I do not recommend the instrument for its intended purpose of screening in child protective services. The CAP does have considerable promise, though, as a research instrument (e.g., as a measure of outcome in interventions intended to promote parental skills or diminish parental mental health problems).

REVIEWER'S REFERENCES

Milner, J. S., Gold, R. G., Ayoub, C., & Jacewitz, M. M. (1984). Predictive validity of the Child Abuse Potential Inventory. *Journal of Consulting and Clinical Psychology*, 52, 879-884.

Kirkham, M. A., Schinke, S. P., Schilling, R. F., II, Meltzer, N. J., & Norelius, K. L. (1986). Cognitive-behavioral skills, social supports, and child abuse potential among mothers of handicapped children. *Journal of Family Violence*, 1, 235-245.

Milner, J. S., Gold, R. G., & Wimberley, R. C. (1986). Prediction and explanation of child abuse: Cross-validation of the Child Abuse Potential Inventory. *Journal of Consulting and Clinical Psychology*, 54, 865-866.

Milner, J. S. (in press). An ego-strength scale for the Child Abuse Potential Inventory. *Journal of Family Violence*.

[51]

Child Language Ability Measures. Purpose: Measures vocabulary and grammatical language development. Ages 2–7; 1979; CLAM; 6 tests: Vocabulary Comprehension, Grammar Comprehension, Inflection Production, Grammar Imitation, Grammar Formedness Judgment, Grammar Equivalence Judgment; individual; tests may be administered separately or in any of 11 combinations; 1986 price data: $20 per test administration book one ('79, 238 pages) or book two ('79, 162 pages); $12 per manual ('79, 103 pages); (15-25) minutes per test; Christy Moynihan and Albert Mehrabian; Albert Mehrabian.*

Review of the Child Language Ability Measures by ALLEN JACK EDWARDS, Professor of Psychology, Southwest Missouri State University, Springfield, MO:

The purpose of the Child Language Ability Measures (CLAM), according to the Manual, is "to measure language development of children in the two- to seven-year age range." The assessment includes phonological, semantic, and syntactic rules of a child's language development, with emphasis on the last. Six subtests are included: Vocabulary Comprehension, Grammar Comprehension, Inflection Production, Grammar Imitation, Grammar Formedness Judgment, and Grammar Equivalence Judgment. Content of each of the first three subtests uses black-and-white line drawings, requiring only that the child point to a choice of drawing for an answer. The last three subtests require oral responding to indicate the child's choice. Subtests may be used independently or in combinations. Testing time requires 1 to 2 hours to complete.

The authors state that test administrators require no training other than practice with the instructions and an ability to work successfully with children on a one-to-one basis. Unfortunately, score interpretation is left at the level of percentile rankings, standard scores, or age equivalent scores. Further, all tests are not appropriate for the total age range; in fact, only the Grammar Comprehension subtest is suitable for all ages supposedly covered by the test, and the Grammar Equivalence Judgment subtest is recommended only for ages 6 and 7. Such constraints limit the potential utility and meaning of the purpose as stated above.

There is a disclaimer, due to sample selection in norming, that the CLAM reflects Standard English and is inappropriate for Nonstandard users. Direct reference is made to Black dialect, but the test may be restricted for other groups as well (see statements under Norming, below).

The Manual is in two parts. Part I deals with test rationale, description of subtests, norming, and statistical evidence of reliability and validity. Part II describes subtest qualities, administration, and score calculation. There follow tables of norms for each subtest and 11 combinations of subtests. These combinations are described briefly on pages 39 and 40. The authors point out that if one is concerned only about test administration, Part I may be skipped "without loss of continuity." Psychometrically, such advice is questionable at best.

TEST AND SUBTEST RATIONALE. Perhaps the strongest element in this Manual is the description of rationales used in deciding appropriate content for the subtests, and the reasons for the subtests included. Although the decisions are based on theoretical, and not empirical, arguments, the authors are persuasive. Essentially, they have tried to assemble content that includes phonology, semantics, and syntax. This combination, they state, is an unconventional approach in such tests but does yield a more comprehensive measure of the total language development of a child between the ages of 2 and 7-11. At the same time, the initial subtest offers a measure of vocabulary development while the other five reflect grammar development. Interestingly, the authors point out that, with subtests 1 through 3 where pictures are used, both sexes are represented equally and various racial groups in proportion to their occurrence in the population at large—this despite the earlier disclaimer that Standard English only is tested.

NORMING. The appealing arguments for kinds of measures selected assumes little importance when one reads Chapter 2: Test Construction. The initial sample consisted of 1,196 native English-speakers between the ages of 2 and 7-11. Of these, 25 children did not take any tests (noted as "unable or unwilling") leaving a final sample of 1,171. The age levels had different numbers of participants: For years 2 through 5, half-year intervals were used, yielding a total sample of 263 at age 2, for example. Ages 6 and 7 are full-year samples, with an *N* of 81 for age 7. There are clear discrepancies in *N*s throughout the year levels.

Even more condemning is the sample selection procedure. Advertisements were placed in newspapers, apparently largely in the Westwood area of Los Angeles. In any event, the children came "primarily"(sic) from middle- and upper-middle-class homes within a 10-mile radius of UCLA. Such a sample contains biases that may render scores of little utility or meaning except for the area represented. The norms derived may have unfortunate outcomes for Blue Eye, MO, Dothan, AL, or Brohman, MI, should the test be used there. Further evidence of sample bias is presented in demographic data on such factors as education level of parents, income, and the like. The authors must be commended for reporting the data (despite noting the test administrator might skip such information earlier).

The Procedures section describes item selection and follows conventional procedures. Numbers of items for subtests ranged from 55 for Inflection Production to 152 for Grammar Formedness Judgment after pilot testing. Because the final subtest forms include 40 and 50 items, there was obviously more room for selection in some cases than others. Standardization numbers also varied by subtest, with 549 used for Vocabulary Comprehension and 123 with Grammar Equivalence Judgment. None of these differences are explained. Cross-validation was conducted for all subtests except Grammar Equivalence Judgment, again with unequal *N*s. The authors point out that they administered tests in increasing level of test difficulty. As a result, *N*s decrease with test difficulty. Further, two sessions were required and the Manual notes that not all children returned for the second session. How many did not return and what the effects of such attrition might be simply are not stated.

STATISTICAL DATA. Given the limitations imposed by selection of the norming sample, and the several unexplained losses of subjects, interpretation of statistical results is questionable. The authors report test-retest and interscorer reliabilities with product-moment coefficients. The Kuder-Richardson 20 Formula was used to calculate internal consistency. Partial correlations are given by age level. All are adequate, ranging from moderate to high.

Validity was principally convergent. Coefficients were low to moderate for most intercorrelations, with a few not achieving even statistical significance. Subtest performance was correlated also with age, sex, socioeconomic status, Peabody Picture Vocabulary Test score, and an interview schedule (Bentler Interview Developmental Scale published in an Office of Economic Opportunity Report in 1970). Although many of the resulting coefficients achieve statistical significance, their robustness is unimpressive.

Although the Manual was published in 1979, no evidence of predictive validity (in terms of further language development and/or usage) is quoted. Given the fact the Manual states the congruences reported are "preliminary assessments of validity," it seems a deficiency that 9 years later there is no improvement in the status of validity data.

SUMMARY. This test has severe limitations. Theoretical models support the rationale used for test selection and testing procedure, but standardization is so biased as to render use of scores meaningless for most children in this country. Statistical evidence of reliability and validity is narrow and restricted, and no evidence of predictive validity is given even nearly 10 years after test and manual publication.

Despite the cosmetic appeal of the test, this reviewer cannot recommend its use as a standard measure of language development.

[52]

The Children of Alcoholics Screening Test. Purpose: "Measures children's attitudes, feelings, perceptions, and experiences related to their parents' drinking behavior." School-age children of possible alcoholics; 1981–87; CAST; may be administered as paper-and-pencil test or by computer; 1987 price data: $10 or less per 25 test forms; $25 per

Clinician/Researcher set including manual ('87, 36 pages) and 30 test forms; $195 for CAST Assessment Software (for IBM-PC and 100% Compatibles); (5–10) minutes; John W. Jones; Camelot Unlimited.*

For reviews by Susanna Maxwell and Barrie G. Stacey, see 9:217.

Review of The Children of Alcoholics Screening Test by STUART N. HART, Associate Professor of Educational Psychology, Indiana University-Purdue University at Indianapolis, Indianapolis, IN:

The Children of Alcoholics Screening Test (CAST) is intended for use (*a*) in identifying children in schools and clinics who are "at risk" due to having adult caretakers (e.g., parents) who are alcoholics, (*b*) to assist in the diagnosis of a parent's alcoholism, (*c*) as a clinical counseling tool for children of alcoholics, and (*d*) for research on children of alcoholics. The CAST consists of 30 one-sentence items designed to measure "children's attitudes, feelings, perceptions, and experiences related to their parents' drinking behavior." Children are instructed to answer yes or no to items about "(*a*) psychological distress (of child) associated with a parent's drinking," "(*b*) perceptions (of child) of drinking-related marital discord between their parents," "(*c*) attempts (by child) to control a parent's drinking," "(*d*) efforts (by child) to escape from the alcoholism," "(*e*) exposure (of child) to drinking-related family violence," "(*f*) tendencies (of child) to perceive their parents as being alcoholic," and "(*g*) desire (of child) for professional counseling."

The Ninth Mental Measurements Yearbook contained two reviews of the CAST (Maxwell, 1985; Stacey, 1985). At that time a preliminary manual was available. A test manual, presented as in nonpreliminary form, was available for my review. No substantive changes appeared to have been made that would justify modification of the major findings of the previous reviews. The major findings reaffirmed by this review and additional comments follow.

The rationale for the test remains strong, although it has not been updated with support more recent than 1983 references. The administration, indicated to require 5–10 minutes, seems simple enough, but information/instructions have not been modified to adequately address the appropriateness of the test and procedures for children under 9 years of age. The manual (copyright 1983, fifth printing 1987), presents an order of instructions for the tester which must be in error (i.e., first administer, secondly read the instructions, page 6).

Reliability support is limited to the split-half internal consistency findings previously available (Spearman Brown coefficient of .98), leaving questions about stability of findings over time unanswered. Validity support is limited to face validity of items as judged by an undisclosed number of alcoholism counselors and grown-up children of alcoholics, and the findings of two validity studies previously available, one study of latency-age and adolescent children and one of adult children of alcoholics. The findings for latency-age and adolescent children are interpreted by the author to support the following cutoffs for decision making: With possible scores ranging from 0–30, 6 or higher identifies children of alcoholics, 2–5 identifies the children of problem drinkers, and 0–1 identifies children of nonalcoholics. The 6 or higher cutoff identified 100% of those who were known to be children of alcoholics accurately, and 23% of those in the control group, presumed but unsubstantiated to have nonalcoholic parents, as false positives. The grown-up children of alcoholics (5 of the 81 subjects) scored significantly higher than the grown-up children of nonalcoholics and scores on the CAST were positively correlated with children's judgment of the quantity of alcohol consumed by their parents. The relevance of false positives and the possibilities for "faking good" were recognized but not clarified in these studies, while no consideration was given to sex, ethnic background, and age/developmental stage differences. Additionally, the new manual contained three sections describing procedures for intervention/treatment programs which did not further clarify the psychometric qualities of the instrument.

Information, not included in the manual, was available for this review from 11 studies incorporating the CAST (published 1984–86). They provided no evidence to further clarify CAST reliability and validity, or the relevance of specific examinee factors. Most of these studies applied the CAST to sort groups into those who were and were not children of alcoholics, assuming adequate reliability and validity, for the purposes of investigating presumed associated characteristics (e.g., personality, adjustment, role in family). The majority (7 of 11) of the studies were dissertation projects.

At this time the CAST should be considered to be an experimental instrument appropriate for carefully designed use in research and in therapeutic relationships where problem drinking is likely to be a factor for individuals or families. Its use to identify children at risk within schools appears to represent an inappropriate invasion of privacy, especially in consideration of the high levels of false positives it produces. Its use to diagnose or validate the drinking problem of a parent may create substantial child-adult relationship problems unless handled very carefully. Though the author presents interesting case study information in the manual, he does not address special administration strategies that would reduce the dangers for these last mentioned two uses. The potential application strengths of this instrument are significant; for example, the CAST might be useful in the study of "stress-resistant" or "invulnerable" children. However, the instrument's reliability and validity, with consideration of special factors (e.g., age, sex, race, ethnicity), require much more research and are presently overstated in the CAST manual. Most of these concerns were raised in previous reviews and appear not to have been addressed during the intervening period.

REVIEWER'S REFERENCES

Maxwell, S. (1985). [Review of the Children of Alcoholics Screening Test]. In J. V. Mitchell, Jr. (Ed.), *The ninth mental measurements yearbook*, (pp. 307-308). Lincoln, NE: Buros Institute of Mental Measurements.

Stacey, B. G. (1985). [Review of the Children of Alcoholics Screening Test]. In J. V. Mitchell, Jr. (Ed.), *The ninth mental measurements yearbook*, (pp. 308-309). Lincoln, NE: Buros Institute of Mental Measurements.

Review of The Children of Alcoholics Screening Test by STEVEN P. SCHINKE, Professor, School of Social Work, Columbia University, New York, NY:

STRENGTHS. The Children of Alcoholics Screening Test (CAST) offers a clinically helpful means for determining how children will respond to questions and items concerning their parents' drinking. As such, the CAST seems most profitably used to stimulate discussions and interventions with children and families where drinking is an issue. The CAST represents a pioneer effort to assess and quantify what children think about their parents and alcohol and to confront parents about the effects of their drinking behavior on their children.

WEAKNESSES. Despite its potential value, the CAST has several flaws. Together, these flaws indicate that the CAST is more fittingly used as a therapeutic process than as a diagnostic, evaluation, or research tool. For example, the CAST manual is accompanied by two treatment programs. One program is for children of alcoholics and the other is for marital group therapy for alcoholics and their spouses. Because these manuals are included with the CAST manual, the test is placed in the context of a therapeutic tool. Further expressing the therapeutic use of the CAST are the many anecdotes in the manual describing how the administration of the measure led to clinically significant insights among the target family members and alcohol abusers.

The potential for confusing clinical assessment, research data collection, and program evaluation baseline development tasks with treatment and therapy weakens the CAST as a stand-alone psychometric device. Added to this weakness are rather vague and undocumented statements about the construction and application of the CAST. For instance, on page four of the CAST manual, the author states: "All items [on the CAST] were judged to be face valid by a number of alcoholism counselors and grown-up children of alcoholics."

The author of the CAST grounds the measure in publications that are largely outside of the peer-reviewed, scientific literature. Of the three cited papers he has written on the measure, one is an earlier version of the screening manual, one is a conference paper, and one is a technical report from the company that produces the CAST.

Finally, the author of the CAST overstates the instrument's value, and deemphasizes its possible problems. Illustrative is the statement on page 14 of the CAST manual, "The CAST can then be used to gain an objective measure of alcoholism from the viewpoint of the children." Yet, on an earlier page (12), the author says, "When using the diagnostic criteria, remember that some children might have been motivated to 'fake good' on the CAST. Interpret with caution." Though not entirely contradictory, these statements express opinions that seem inappropriate for the process of instrument development, testing, and dissemination.

RELIABILITY, VALIDITY, NORMATIVE DATA. Internal consistency scores reported for the CAST show Spearman-Brown coefficients of .98 based on samples of children and adults. Validity data on the CAST also support the measure's psychometric properties. From information provided in the manual, sufficient numbers of children have taken the CAST to yield adequate normative data.

SUMMARY. Due to its psychometric properties, the potential contribution of the CAST to clinical activities with children of alcoholic parents cannot be discounted. Still, the confusing presentation of treatment and therapeutic guidelines along with instrumentation data call into question the authors' understanding of the purposes and applications of a diagnostic, evaluation, and research tool. Furthermore, the CAST manual's lack of published, peer-reviewed scientific support for the instrument, combined with the anecdotal and therapeutic tone of the accompanying materials, put doubt on the instrument's research grounding. In sum, the CAST seems more fitting to therapy and treatment settings than to research, diagnosis, or evaluation tasks.

[53]

Children's Abilities Scales. Purpose: Furnishes a broad assessment of a pupil's abilities as the pupil enters a secondary school. Ages 11-0 to 12-6; 1982–84; CAS; maximum 3 scores per child; 10 Scores: Verbal (Word Pairs, Word Overlap, Total), Spatial (Flags [part 1], Flags [part 1 and 2], Dice, Total), Non-Verbal (Symbols, Shapes, Total); 1986 price data: £76 per introductory pack including 30 pupil's books, 30 answer sheets, 30 pupil's performance records, set of scoring overlays, 3 class header sheets, and manual ('84, 39 pages); £1.95 per reusable pupil's book; £2.95 per answer sheet pack including 10 answer sheets, 10 pupil's performance records, 1 class header sheet; £4.75 per set of 2 hand-scoring overlays; £5.95 per manual; (140) minutes for the battery, (15–35) minutes for any one test; Chris Whetton and Roy Childs, The National Foundation for Educational Research in England and Wales; NFER-Nelson Publishing Co., Ltd. [England].*

Review of the Children's Abilities Scales by STEPHEN N. ELLIOTT, Associate Professor of Educational Psychology, and JAMES J. MAZZA, University of Wisconsin-Madison, Madison, WI:

The Children's Abilities Scales (CAS) is a rather brief (175 items) pencil-and-paper, group-administered test designed primarily to measure reasoning skills of children transferring into a British secondary school. The CAS consists of six subtests, two each contributing to what the authors call a Verbal Scale, a Spatial Scale, and a Non-Verbal Scale. Information about the use and psychometric characteristics of the CAS is well laid out in a Teacher's Guide, with the items themselves presented in a rather durable and neatly prepared Pupil's Book. All children's responses are coded on a computer scoreable sheet and each individual's performance can be recorded and charted on a visually appealing Pupil Performance Record.

The test was designed to facilitate general placement and instructional decisions for British students ranging in age from 11 to 12½ years. The authors apparently believe that use of ability tests is a fairer and more accurate means than use of achievement tests for placing students into secondary school curriculums. Unfortunately, the authors present no data to support their contention. In fact, logic and research in the area of curriculum-based assessment suggests that more accurate and meaningful instructional information is gained by testing students directly on what they will be taught. Thus, we seriously question the use of ability tests, even one like the CAS which psychometrically has many redeeming qualities, for use in placing children into mathematics, science, and language arts courses. With this major reservation noted, we briefly will review the psychometric characteristics of the CAS.

STANDARDIZATION. The CAS was standardized in the Fall of 1982 in 69 schools, stratified by size and setting, located in England and Wales. The final standardization sample included 1,947 students between 11 years 1 month and 12 years 1 month of age. No data are provided to establish the representativeness of the final sample.

RELIABILITY AND VALIDITY. The authors of the CAS clearly appreciate high psychometric standards and have done an excellent job educating potential users of the CAS about measurement error, reliability, and validity. For the most part, tabular correctional data and concise summaries are offered to substantiate the test-retest reliability (range r = .83–.92), internal consistency (range KR 20 r = .89–.95), concurrent validity (range r = .52–.64), and predictive validity (r = .40 with a math achievement test only).

No data concerning or discussion of the content validity of the test are offered. However, an analysis of the interscale correlations (range $r = .51–.73$) and an inspection of the items caused us to question the validity of the Verbal and Non-Verbal characterization of the items. Certainly formal reading is required only for the Word Pairs and Word Overlap subtests; however, a student also must "decode" the symbols and pictoral schemes in each of the Flags, Dice, Symbols, and Shapes subtests. In conclusion, we believe it is misleading to emphasize the verbal and nonverbal dichotomy to characterize the CAS (the factor analysis data also supports this position). Rather, all the items seem to stress *reasoning* that involves determining similarities and differences in concepts or designs.

With regard to the factor structure of the CAS, the authors reported a "principal factor analysis" where the factors were rotated using a varimax criterion. The results were interpreted to support a two-factor solution with a "large Reasoning Factor and a smaller Verbal Ability Factor." Given the substantial correlations among the tests (range $r = .66–.73$), it seems that an oblique rotation would have been more appropriate and may have more strongly substantiated the authors' theoretical bias for verbal and nonverbal factors.

One final point concerns scoring and the use of difference scores for pairs of CAS scales. Specifically, the authors seem to encourage the calculation and use of difference scores for Verbal versus Spatial, Verbal versus Non-Verbal, and Non-Verbal versus Spatial. Although they present a sound, conservative method of calculating and interpreting such scores, there is absolutely no evidence the scores are valid for placing students in different instructional curriculums.

SUMMARY. The CAS is a psychometrically sound test of reasoning skills standardized on an age-restricted sample of children in Great Britain. The instrument was designed to facilitate placement of students who transfer into secondary schools. Although the need for instructional placement information is valid, the use of an ability test such as the CAS is questioned. It certainly minimizes curriculum differences experienced by transferring students, but at the expense of low-inference, curriculum-valid cognitive tasks. Researchers may find the test of use to gain a rather quick measure of children's reasoning ability. Educators, however, would be advised to look for a more curricular-relevant instrument if their goal is accurate instructional placement for students.

Review of the Children's Abilities Scales by STEPHAN A. HENRY, Director of Research and Evaluation, Topeka Public Schools, Topeka, KS:

PURPOSE AND DESCRIPTION. The Children's Abilities Scales (CAS) was developed by the National Foundation for Educational Research of England. The authors envision the test being used to provide a picture of student's mental abilities as they make the transition to secondary schools at 11 to 12 years of age. The test results are purported to provide an assessment of the differential nature of student's abilities with regard to various subject areas and curricular decisions. The primary uses for the test are screening, placement, and curricular adaptation. There are three separate scales, each of which consists of two subtests that are summed to obtain a total scale score. There is no overall summary score. The Verbal scale consists of two verbal reasoning tests called Word Pairs and Word Overlap and consists primarily of verbal analogies. The Spatial scale consists of subtests called Flags and Dice, which assess the capacity for spatial visualization and manipulation of objects. The Nonverbal subscale tests are called Symbols and Shapes and consist of items similar to Raven's Progressive Matrices. Any number of subtests may be given and the authors assume that few would wish to give the entire battery, which would take 140 minutes. This test is administered to groups of students with administration instructions that are clear and helpful. Machine-scoring and hand-scoring templates are available. Test materials are attractive and well produced. The manual provides a thoughtful presentation of basic measurement concepts and issues to be considered by users of this test and does so at a level comprehensible to the layman.

NORMS AND SCORING. The normative sample consists of 1,947 students ranging in age from 11-1 to 12-1 who were making the transition to secondary school at various locations in England and Wales. The sample design incorporated random selection and stratification to insure good representativeness. Relatively few tests are normed with this degree of care. Applicability of the norms to settings outside of England is highly questionable at best. There is, however, nothing unique in the item content to prevent the test from being used with other English-speaking populations. With translation and renorming, the spatial and nonverbal subscales could even be used with non-English speaking populations. The scoring of the CAS is straightforward. All items are multiple choice. Subtest and subscale raw scores are obtained by summing the correct responses. The manual contains conversion tables for obtaining standard scores with a mean of 100 and a standard deviation of 15. A table is also provided for obtaining percentile ranks. The authors have done a commendable job in providing information and clear procedures for computing confidence intervals and determining whether observed differences between subscale scores are significant.

RELIABILITY AND VALIDITY. The authors provided good evidence of internal consistency for the subscales. Test-retest reliability was assessed with a sample of 258 students from nine schools over an interval of 1 to 5 weeks. The reliability coefficients for the Verbal, Spatial, and Nonverbal subtests were .88, .92, and .83 respectively. The authors appropriately assert that these reliability figures suggest that the test is adequate for use with other sources of information as part of a student guidance process. The six tests comprising the CAS were selected from 16 that were originally piloted in a study examining factor structure and predictive validity. A factor analysis of the finalized CAS indicated that it is primarily a global measure of reasoning and that it secondarily measures verbal ability. The factor analysis provided strong support for the organization of the three subscales and the placement of the subtests. An examination of the test items reveals good face and content validity. Data are also provided concerning concurrent and predictive validity. Moderate correlations, generally in the range of .50s to .60s, are reported between various CAS subtests and the NFER Verbal Test D and Basic Mathematics DE. Similar data are provided relating the CAS to locally developed mathematics tests. Moderate correlations between the CAS and an unnamed standardized test of verbal and nonverbal reasoning were also reported. Meager evidence of predictive validity was provided through a study with 110 students, which yielded correlations in the .30s between the CAS and a mathematics test given a year later. Although the CAS was normed in 1982 and published in 1984, there do not appear to be any published studies featuring its use.

SUMMARY. The CAS is a well constructed test of reasoning ability that may be useful for student guidance and evaluation in educational settings. The normative data were collected carefully but should be used cautiously when testing outside England. This instrument has adequate reliability and validity for its stated purposes. The authors are to be commended for producing an examiner's manual that provides a thoughtful yet highly readable treatment of the basic measurement issues and concepts confronting the potential user of the CAS.

[54]

Children's Academic Intrinsic Motivation Inventory. Purpose: "To measure academic intrinsic motivation . . . . defined as enjoyment of school learning characterized by an orientation toward mastery, curiosity, persistence, and the learning of challenging, difficult, and novel tasks." Grades 4–8; 1986; CAIMI; self-report inventory; 5 scales: Reading, Math, Social Studies, Science, General; 1987 price data: $39.95 per kit including 25 test booklets (10 pages), 25 profile forms, and manual (24 pages); $27.50 per 25 test booklets; $6.50 per 25 profile forms; $7 per manual; (20) minutes individual; (60) minutes group; Adele Eskeles Gottfried; Psychological Assessment Resources, Inc.*

Review of the Children's Academic Intrinsic Motivation Inventory by C. DALE POSEY, Licensed Psychologist, C. M. E. Psychology Consultants, Boca Raton, FL:

The Children's Academic Intrinsic Motivation Inventory (CAIMI) is based upon a theoretical model of academic motivation conceived by Adele Gottfried, the author of the test. Intrinsic motivation is conceptualized as being specific for each primary subject area. There is also a general motivational variable related to the child's overall orientation toward learning. Thus, the CAIMI is comprised of four content scales related to reading, math, science, and social studies attitudes. There is also a separate scale related to "general orientation toward school learning." Each specific scale is comprised of 24 Likert-scale items and two forced-choice items. The general scale is made up of 18 Likert-scale items. The items are presented in a rather unusual format. There are 44 questions; the 26 relevant to the specific scales each require four responses, one for each content category. Thus, each question requires four responses on different Likert scales. In spite of this seeming complexity, the items appear to be understandable for students at least in the fourth grade, and scoring is surprisingly simple, requiring no templates or scoring keys. The author has, thus, developed an economical and simple method of obtaining a substantial amount of information.

The CAIMI was developed in three stages. An initial pool of theoretically derived items was administered to 141 white children attending one public school. Items demonstrating internal consistency and positive correlations with the total scale were retained. A biracial group from another public school was then used to assess racial and intellectual moderation, select additional items, and to investigate reliability. A third group of private school students was given the complete battery and further reliability studies were done.

An attempt was made to control for response bias. A social desirability scale was found to be uncorrelated with CAIMI scores, and items were balance-keyed to counteract yea-saying or nay-saying. Reverse-keyed repeated items were also included.

Reliability of the CAIMI appears to be adequate. Two-month retest coefficients ranged from .66 to .76. Internal consistency coefficients range from .83 to .93. Thus, reliability has been demonstrated, with no differences found as a function of race, sex, or IQ. An average shared variance of .15 indicates relative independence of the CAIMI scales.

CAIMI scores were significantly correlated with achievement test results on matched subject areas. Correlations ranged from .24 to .44. Thus, measured intrinsic motivation was related to achievement, but the two variables were largely independent. Achievement accounted for no more than 18 percent of the variance in matched subject CAIMI scores. Math CAIMI scores were especially strongly related to math achievement.

CAIMI scores were found to be negatively correlated with measures of subject-related academic anxiety (r = -.38 to -.52). Thus, intrinsic motivation is inversely related to anxiety within each subject area. In addition, the General CAIMI score was significantly correlated (r = .49 to .62) with the children's ratings of their academic competence. Teachers' ratings of a child's intrinsic motivation were significantly related to CAIMI Reading (r = .27), Math (r = .22), and General Motivation (r = .25). CAIMI Reading and Math scores were also correlated with these areas of achievement after controlling for IQ. Finally, the CAIMI was found to be significantly correlated with another measure of intrinsic motivation (r = .17 to .64).

In summary, the CAIMI appears to be a reliable and unique measure of an attribute labeled "academic intrinsic motivation." The operational definition of this construct is provided, and is based upon internal cognitive constructs. Studies of convergent and discriminant validity indicate these scales provide a fairly good measure of a child's academic ability, thoughts regarding self efficacy as it relates to school work, and teacher perception of a child's motivation. Academic intrinsic motivation also appears to be independent of intelligence and largely independent of achievement. The scales appear to be free of sex and racial bias, and should be fairly resistant to response sets. The only problem noted in the scale's development is the size and representativeness of the normative sample. The samples were adequate for the development of a research scale, but a commercially marketed scale should have national stratified norms. The scale is promising, but the author must conduct a more extensive normative study. Further validity studies would also be helpful in behaviorally defining academic intrinsic motivation. It is recommended that the scale be used, but caution should be exercised in drawing unreplicated conclusions. As part of a larger battery it may provide useful information regarding academically unsuccessful children.

[55]

Childrens Adaptive Behavior Scale, Revised. Purpose: Provides a means to gather information on the relevant knowledge and concepts requisite to adaptive functioning. Ages 5–11; 1980–83; CABS; 6 scores: Language Development, Independent Functioning, Family Role Performance, Economic-Vocational Activity, Socialization, Total; individual; other test materials (e.g., coins, blocks, scissors, paper) must be supplied by examiner; 1987 price data: $1 per student booklet; $14.95 per manual ('83, 42 pages); $19.95 per specimen set including 5 student booklets, picture book, and manual; (45) minutes; Richard H. Kicklighter and Bert O. Richmond; Humanics Limited.*

For reviews by Thomas R. Kratochwill and Corinne R. Smith of the original edition, see 9:218; see also T3:395 (1 reference).

TEST REFERENCES

1. Telzrow, C. F. (1984). Practical applications of the K-ABC in the identification of handicapped preschoolers. *The Journal of Special Education*, 18, 311-324.

Review of the Childrens Adaptive Behavior Scale, Revised by KENNETH A. KAVALE, Professor and Chair, Division of Special Education, The University of Iowa, Iowa City, IA:

The Childrens Adaptive Behavior Scale (CABS) is designed to assess adaptive functioning in children ages 5 through 10 years. Adaptive functioning is measured with from 16 to 30 items on five dimensions of adaptability: Language Development (LD), Independent Functioning (IF), Family Role Performance (FRP), Economic-Vocational Activity (EVA), and Socialization (S). Every item is administered to every child and the testing takes up to approximately 45 minutes. In terms of efficiency, this is considerably less time than most of the popular adaptive behavior measures.

Although dispute exists over the concept of adaptive behavior, a measure of adaptive behavior is suggested to be included in any comprehensive psychoeducational evaluation. The CABS views adaptive behavior as operative in all social settings where "Children act, interact, react, mesh with, or conflict with the flow of social currents that affect them every minute of their school day." Adaptive behavior is what individuals do, not what they know. While acknowledging the importance of a total view of adaptive functioning, the CABS is designed specifically for use in school settings. This is an advantage because other adaptive behavior measures were not designed for use in educational settings. The CABS determines what children do by asking them directly in contrast to other available adaptive behavior measures that ask others (e.g., parents, teachers) to provide information about a child. This "return to the source" is a significant advantage because the child's perspective is now included in the overall assessment of adaptive functioning. Of course, the CABS should be combined with other adaptive behavior measures to provide a total picture.

The CABS was developed initially from a review of known indices of adaptive functioning where the obtained indicators were extracted, analyzed, and grouped into five domains. Factor analyses showed the CABS to be independent of other adaptive behavior measures and to load on two factors accounting for about 69% of the variance. Although individual items were selected carefully, it is unclear whether or not the items in any domain represent a hierarchical sequence even though CABS scores reveal a significant increase with increasing chronological age. Intercorrelations among domains suggests substantial overlap but it is argued these relationships indicate little contamination and the presence of a unidimensional trait (i.e., adaptive behavior).

Validity evidence is presented in several ways. Content validity was judged by experts who rated about 50 items per domain on a 5-point scale. The data indicating a relationship between increasing age and higher test scores were assumed to indicate a congruence between chronological age and adaptive behavior. Data are also presented indicating a consistently significant relationship between adaptive behavior and intelligence wherein older children do better than younger children and slow learners do better than mentally retarded children. Concurrent validity was established through positive and significant correlations with the AAMD-Adaptive Behavior Scale (Public School Version) (ABS) for both teachers and parents and the Adaptive Behavior Inventory for Children (ABIC). This evidence of validity is satisfactory only to a point. The correlations with the ABS and ABIC, although significant, were only modest and left substantial variance unexplained. It appears this variance can be explained only by examining the relationship between CABS scores and behavior in natural settings in order to determine what the CABS does not measure.

Reliability was reported in two ways. Reliability coefficients (KR-21) ranged from .63 to .83 for subtests with the Total Score being .93. Test-retest reliabilities for 2-week intervals were high (.98 or .99). The CABS appears to possess adequate reliability.

Normative data were based originally on 250 mildly mentally retarded public school children in South Carolina and Georgia. This sample was too small and not representative enough to be used with confidence. The Revised CABS includes additional normative data on regular classroom pupils and are more geographically representative. These data are positive additions allowing for more confident comparisons. The normative data reveal quite large standard deviations at individual age ranges across domains. It is correctly suggested the greatest weight be placed on Total Score and a range of age scores be reported instead of a single age equivalent score. To assist this process, CABS scores by chronological age showing the range of $-1/2$ to $+1/2$ standard deviation are provided.

The CABS is administered individually by a trained examiner. Individual items are described adequately and scoring guidelines are outlined so as to make the process simple and objective. Interpretation of scores is described in relation to the normative data and includes sufficient warning about overinterpreting the CABS. The user is warned against using the CABS in deciding whether or not a child may be retarded and against relying upon subtest scores in making decisions about areas of strength and weakness in adaptive functioning. The necessity for corroborating evidence like direct observation of adaptive functioning in real settings for such decisions is rightly stressed.

In summary, the Revised CABS is a useful instrument that is getting better. The CABS remains efficient, school-focused, and child-centered. The additional information provided about administration, interpretation, validity, and norms has strengthened and refined the CABS. The process is not complete, however, and more psychometric information is needed to clarify exactly what skills and abilities the CABS is tapping as well as the exact nature of the relationship between the CABS and intelligence. Adaptive behavior is an important focus for special education and the CABS offers the unique advantage of providing a direct assessment of a child's adaptive behavior without reliance upon retrospective data supplied by parents, teachers, or other caretakers.

Review of the Childrens Adaptive Behavior Scale, Revised by ESTHER SINCLAIR, *Associate Professor of Psychiatry and Biobehavioral Sciences, UCLA School of Medicine, Los Angeles, CA:*

The Childrens Adaptive Behavior Scale, Revised (CABS-R) measures adaptive behavior in five domains of competency: Language Development, Independent Functioning, Family Role Performance, Economic-Vocational Activity, and Socialization. Raw scores, which correspond to age scores, are yielded in each domain as well as for the total test. There are 16–30 items in each domain that are administered directly to the 5–10-year-old child. The CABS-R is designed for use in an educational setting and reflects the view that adaptive behavior, however defined, is operative in all social settings including school.

Measures of adaptive behavior have long been part of the psychoeducational diagnostic workup of children being evaluated for possible placement in school programs for the mentally retarded. Currently, adaptive behavior scales are becoming increasingly popular in assessing learning disabled and behavior disordered children as well. Thus, the concept of adaptive behavior and specific instruments to assess adaptive behavior remain important in the assessment of children for special education programs for the learning disabled, behavior disordered, and mentally retarded.

CABS-R is easy to score and can be administered in 45 minutes. Because the child is the respondent, it is essential the test administrator be sensitive to issues of establishing rapport and trained in the techniques relating to educational testing of children. Although items in each domain seem to be arranged hierarchically in terms of difficulty of mastery in a general sense, no information regarding item analysis or justification for inclusion of a particular item in a particular scale is presented in the manual.

The most obvious way in which the CABS-R differs from other widely used adaptive behavior scales such as the Vineland Social Maturity Scale and the AAMD-Adaptive Behavior Scale (Public School Version) is that the child himself or herself is the respondent. Furthermore, as these other scales are based on naturalistic observations they are more time-consuming to administer.

Because the child must repond to each item in the scale, CABS-R seems to be inappropriate for children with specific disabilities or impairments such as Cerebral Palsy, Aphasia, serious seizure disorders, severe Attention Deficit Disorder, and other specific medical problems.

Children who have difficulty verbally communicating effectively and efficiently would have difficulty completing the items on the scale. Because the child is the test respondent, the manual urges test administrators to corroborate scores with a third person when making diagnostic and placement decisions. While the added corroboration would provide the test administrator with "insurance" that children are accurately identifying abilities and skills, this recommendation seems to detract from the overall uniqueness and strength of the scale which is, namely, that children themselves are the respondents. Inclusion of the corroboration recommendation seems to alter the focus of the scale in the direction of measurement of the degree of interrater reliability between the child/respondent and his or her teacher, parent, or caretaker.

The original CABS was criticized for limited normative data. The manual states the revised version contains new normative data on regular class students, more nationally representative normative samples, and additional technical information on validity and psychometric quality. Yet the Tables presented in the manual are all based on CABS scores with no differentiation between CABS and CABS-R, thus making comparisons difficult. Table 2 of the manual states that CABS was normed on 60 children identified as slow learners and 60 children identified as educable mentally retarded. This yields a total sample size of 120. Tables 6, 7, and 8 further mention the total sample size of 120 broken down into 60 slow learners and 60 mildly mentally handicapped children. Yet, the reliability section of the manual mentions a sample size of 250 children. It is unclear if this is indeed a renorming of the original CABS or an error in print.

In relation to the slow learner and mildly mentally handicapped groups, the slow learners scored higher on all domains than the other group. However, the mean scores for both groups appear to be so close that individual inferences about specific children and the different educational needs of these specific children would be difficult to make. Furthermore, the manual indicates that it would be useful for the classroom teacher to tie curriculum plans and instructional objectives to domain scores. However, there is no justification for this based on overall group mean differences. Perhaps it would be more useful to design curriculum and instructional objectives based on deficits and strengths as measured by responses to specific items in each domain. This strategy may prove unreliable as well, however, because responses to a single item or a few items may or may not represent mastery of a certain educational objective.

The CABS-R reliability data appear adequate for the total test scale. Reliability indices were obtained by a test-retest paradigm using a 2-week interval. The reliability coefficient for the total test was .93 but considerably lower in 4 of the 5 individual domains ($r = .63$, $r = .76$, $r = .79$, $r = .72$).

It is interesting to note that Black EMR children scored higher on all domains than did White EMR children. Although more demographic information is needed to interpret this finding, the authors suggest the scale may measure social adaptive competence in a way that does not penalize the Black child. As in the earlier version, the authors encourage users of the CABS-R to develop local norms. This is a good suggestion but one wonders why the authors did not address the limited normative population more comprehensively in the CABS-R.

In summary, the CABS-R seems to be an adequate adaptive behavior scale. It is unique in that the child is the respondent. This self-reporting would appear to limit the range of testable populations in that children with specific disabilities such as those previously mentioned would be unable to participate in the self-report. The limited normative data provided in the original CABS do not seem to have been sufficiently improved upon. Because of these limitations, the CABS-R needs to be supplemented with naturalistic environmental observation especially when diagnostic and programming decisions are being made about children.

[56]

Children's Problems Checklist. Purpose: "To identify relevant problems, establish rapport, and provide written documentation of presenting problems consistent with community standards of care." Ages 5–12; 1985; CPC; ratings by parent or guardian; 11 areas: Emotions, Self-Concept, Peers and Play, School, Language and Thinking, Concentration and Organization, Activity Level and Motor Control, Behavior, Values, Habits, Health; no manual; 1987 price data: $12.95 per 50 checklists; (10–20) minutes; John A. Schinka; Psychological Assessment Resources, Inc.*

Review of the Children's Problems Checklist by WAYNE C. PIERSEL, Associate Professor of Educational Psychology, University of Nebraska-Lincoln, Lincoln, NE:

The author's stated purpose of the Children's Problems Checklist (CPC) is to aid in the evaluation and assessment of children's behavior and emotional difficulties. There is no manual accompanying the CPC. No normative data, no rationale for the development of the checklist, and no directions for administration or use of the CPC are provided. Users do not know how the questions were selected nor how the author intended the CPC to be employed.

The CPC is a set of 202 structured stimuli (descriptive phrases) that a parent or teacher or some other significant adult can respond to by checking the problems that apply to the target child and circling the problems that are most important. The CPC is a pencil and paper interview that, if completed and made available to the clinician prior to the initial interview, could provide a general idea of the concerns of the adult completing the checklist.

The CPC is subdivided into 11 categories. The labels for each of the categories are abbreviations. With no manual or other information available, the user must depend on his or her own creative skill to determine what the author intended for each of these 11 categories to be called. For example, one section is labeled "SCH." Examination of the 14 items listed under this heading leads this author to conclude that "SCH" is the abbreviation for School. The abbreviation "SEL" remains a mystery to this author. However, the term "self" does appear in 2 out of 18 of the descriptive phrases in this section.

The 202 CPC items sample a broad range of behaviors and situations that typically can become problem areas for children and youth. However, without any information regarding this scale, it is virtually useless. One cannot even comment on the adequacy of the author's rationale or the checklist's basic psychometric properties except to note that they are an unknown. For example, users do not know if the descriptive phrases elicit reliable responses from adult raters; or if the descriptive phrases suggest the same meaning to different raters. These are just two basic psychometric essentials requiring specification.

There are many other behavior rating scales and checklists available to record the concerns of teachers, parents, and other significant adults (e.g., Achenbach & Edelbrock, 1981; Peterson & Quay, 1982; Swift, 1982). These scales not only have test manuals that provide such basics as rationale, appropriate populations, and instructions for administration, these checklists also provide a description of their standardization samples and an array of psychometric data to permit the consumer to make an informed decision regarding use of the instrument.

In summary, I cannot conceive of any reason to employ this scale. If a teacher's or parent's or other individual's observations and recollections are needed and that significant adult is willing to spend his or her valuable time reading and responding to a series of statements and questions, then they and the target child or youth deserve the professional courtesy of responding to a pencil and paper interview that meets minimal standards of educational and psychological practice. The three instruments mentioned above and other instruments reviewed in the *Mental Measurements Yearbook* do meet minimal standards and do a much better job of providing the clinician with potentially useful and minimally harmful information. Unless the CPC author provides an examiner's manual that contains essential information as specified in the *Standards for Educational and Psychological Testing* (AERA, APA, NCME, 1985), the consumer is well advised to choose another instrument.

REVIEWER'S REFERENCES

Peterson, D. R., & Quay, H. C. (1979). Behavior Problem Checklist. Coral Gables, FL: H. C. Quay.

Achenbach, T. M., & Edelbrock, C. (1981). Child Behavior Checklist. Burlington, VT: University of Vermont, Psychiatry Associates.

Swift, M. (1982). Devereux Elementary School Behavior Rating Scale II. Devon, PA: The Devereux Foundation Press.

American Educational Research Association, American Psychological Association, & National Council on Measurement in Education. (1985). *Standards for educational and psychological testing*. Washington, DC: American Psychological Association, Inc.

[57]

Children's Version of the Family Environment Scale. Purpose: "Provides a measure of young children's subjective appraisal of their family environment." Ages 5–12; 1984; CVFES; downward extension of the Family Environment Scale (9:408); 10 scores: Cohesion, Expressiveness, Conflict, Independence, Achievement Orientation, Intellectual-Cultural Orientation, Active-Recreational Orientation, Moral-Religious Emphasis, Organization, Control; 1987 price data: $17 per 10 test booklets; $6 per 50 answer sheets; $7 per 50 profiles; $6 per 50 examiner's worksheets; $6 per manual (17 pages); administration time not reported; Christopher J. Pino, Nancy Simons, and Mary Jane Slawinowski; Slosson Educational Publications, Inc.*

Review of the Children's Version of the Family Environment Scale by NANCY A. BUSCH-ROSSNAGEL, Associate Professor of Psychology and Research Associate, Hispanic Research Center, Fordham University, Bronx, NY:

The Children's Version of the Family Environment Scale (CVFES) is a downward extension of the Family Environment Scale (FES) of Moos and Moos (1981). As such, its purpose is to enable children, ages 5 to 12, to provide self-reports of family relationships. Children's perceptions of 10 dimensions in three general areas of family functioning are assessed: Relationship Dimensions (Cohesion, Expressiveness, and Conflict); Personal Growth Dimensions (Independence, Achievement Orientation, Intellectual-Cultural Orientation, Active-Recreational Orientation, and Moral-Religious Emphasis); and System Maintenance Dimensions (Organization and Control).

The CVFES is a 30-item test, with 3 items for each of the 10 scales. These items were taken from the Family Environment Scale (FES) of Moos and Moos (1981). Each item has 3 pictures; each picture is a cartoon-like drawing of a mother, father, son, and/or daughter. The pictures vary along some dimension, for example, proximity of the family members. The child is asked to pick the picture that "looks like your family." Although the test is described as pictorial, many items require a third-grade reading level. The family's verbalizations are presented in a balloon, comic-strip style. In half of the items, the three pictures are identical except for the written information. The parents' comments differ among the pictures, but the visual cues, such as facial expression and posture, are the same in each of the three pictures in these items. Because of the reliance on reading for many distinctions, the test should be given to younger children (up to fourth grade) only in an individual format. The authors suggest this practice, but do not follow it themselves in their content-validity study.

The validity of the CVFES rests on the validity of the FES and the pictures developed to tap its content. While the FES has adequate reliability, the evidence for its validity is weak (Busch-Rossnagel, 1985). In developing the CVFES, the authors grouped the items of the FES so that a smaller number of items would tap the same content as the adult version. They then chose those items which "best" cut across the nine FES scales, but they do not indicate what their criteria were.

The content validity of the pictures is unclear. The authors state that an effort was made to make each item unidimensional, (i.e., to vary only one feature in each of the three pictures comprising the item). However, the variability in facial expression is difficult to see on some items, making the item a test of visual perception rather than family environment. In addition, some items vary two features among the pictures, making the content unclear, (e.g., item 3 varies both proximity and facial expression). The authors attempted to address the issue of content validity of the items in two studies. The first study had a small sample ($N = 16$), but no information was given about the results. The second study raises more questions than it answers (e.g., why include seventh-grade subjects when the standardization sample included only first- through sixth-graders? How many children were unable to understand the items?).

There are problems with scoring as well. Scoring is done by assigning each response a 1, 2, or 3, with 3 representing the highest level in each dimension; the responses for each subscale are then summed. No information is provided as to how the rankings of the pictures were established. The rankings for items 11 and 12 go against common sense: the parents saying "we'll do it for you" is scored as a 2, showing more independence than "if you need help, we'll help you" which is scored as a 1.

The authors report that the 4-week test-retest reliability was .80. No range of reliabilities is given, so one presumes that this is the reliability for the total score, even though no indication is given that a total score should be computed. Because the scoring is done by scales, the reliabilities for each scale should be reported.

Information about differences in reliabilities for different ages should also be given.

As noted by the authors, the standardization sample for the CVFES is very restricted: 158 children from grades 1 to 6 of the Buffalo parochial schools. No specific breakdown of the sample is provided, and this seriously limits the usefulness of the norms. For example, family size may affect FES scores, and the authors of the CVFES suggest that children from single-parent families may have difficulty identifying with the four-person family of the picture. Likewise, the authors present the subscale means by grade level and state there are important differences in them, but they do not indicate which differences are significantly different or why they are important. If the grade level differences are important, and if family size may affect responses, the norm sample should be broken down by at least these two factors. Because of the restricted sample and paucity of information, the norms as presented are inadequate. This norm group problem limits the potential for comparison between children's perceptions of the family with the CVFES and parents' and adolescents' perceptions with the FES.

One potential application of the CVFES is for feedback in family therapy, and the authors primarily tie the test to the program for family enrichment they have developed. The authors present a case study using the CVFES and the parents' responses to the FES. Such an application requires comparisons between the CVFES and the FES which, as noted above, should not be done with the current norms. In addition, specifics about this application are not given, (e.g., how is the "line of best fit" determined? What magnitude of differences between parent and child scores should be considered important?).

In summary, the CVFES should be considered as an experimental, downward extension of the FES. The utility of the test rests primarily with the validity of the pictorial format. The content validity studies presented make that validity very questionable. The standardization sample is so restricted the present norms should not be used, thus limiting the potential comparison of the CVFES results with the FES and such applications in therapy. The authors should be encouraged in their efforts to overcome these limitations because a valid evaluation of family environment from children's perspectives would be useful for therapists and researchers alike.

REVIEWER'S REFERENCES

Moos, R. H., & Moos, B. S. (1981). *Family Environment Scale.* Palo Alto, CA: Consulting Psychologists Press, Inc.

Busch-Rossnagel, N. A. (1985). [Review of the Family Environment Scale.] In J. V. Mitchell, Jr. (Ed.), *The ninth mental measurements yearbook* (pp. 573-574). Lincoln, NE: The Buros Institute of Mental Measurements.

[58]

Clark-Madison Test of Oral Language. Purpose: "To evaluate children's expressive capacity with various grammatical and syntactical components of language." Ages 4-0 to 8-11; 1981–84; individual; 1988 price data: $69 per manual ('84, 35 pages) and stimulus materials, and 50 test forms; $19 per 50 test forms; (10–20) minutes; John B. Clark and Charles L. Madison; PRO-ED, Inc.*

Review of the Clark-Madison Test of Oral Language by BARRY W. JONES, Associate Professor of Communicative Disorders, San Diego State University, San Diego, CA:

The theoretical construct for the Clark-Madison Test of Oral Language "is based on the premise that verbal responses to an event are shaped by the individual's ability to discriminate the antecedent stimuli and utilize appropriate rules to construct specific language units." This construct is grounded in the work of Bloom and Lahey (1978) who described the components of language in terms of form (structure), content (semantics), and use (pragmatics or context). The purpose of the test is to provide an evaluation of children's abilities to express "various grammatical and syntactical components of language." The test is, therefore, designed to assess, primarily, syntactic components of English when given verbal, visual, and structural information that should constrain children's responses to test stimuli.

The test consists of 97 probes assessing five areas. These include (*a*) 16 items assessing syntax, (*b*) 21 items on modifiers, determiners, and prepositions (MDP), (*c*) 21 items on verbs, (*d*) 18 items assessing inflections, and (*e*) 21 items on pronouns. All of the probes are accompanied by pictures (visual stimuli) and verbal information provided by the examiner. The test is administered individually and all materials necessary for administration of the test are included in the test manual.

The scoring procedures permit one to easily compute the percentage scores for both the total test and each of the five areas. Initial normative data are provided for 234 children with no histories of language disorders or delays distributed unevenly among five age levels. The summary statistics include what appear to be mean raw scores, standard deviations, and standard errors of measurement for 1-year intervals between the ages of 4-0 and 8-11 years for the total test score only. The authors did not, however, explicitly state whether the mean scores were based on raw scores or percentage scores and the analysis form accompanying the test directs the test user to calculate percentage scores. Therefore, a strong possibility of misinterpretation of test scores exists. Also, the authors provided no additional information on their standardization sample and failed to discuss their sampling procedures. The test user does not have, as a result, information on the representativeness of their standardization sample. The authors did indicate, however, their sample was minimal and that more extensive research was in progress.

Clark and Madison suggest using the total test score as an indication of the examinee's "functional capacity with language structure." According to their criteria, children who score more than one standard deviation below the mean scores of the standardization sample should be considered as candidates for language remediation. Again, the small standardization sample, the lack of information on the sample and the manner in which it was selected, and the absence of information on whether one should use raw or percentage scores for the analysis should lead the test user to interpret the results on their own examinees with caution.

The authors presented evidence of content, construct, and concurrent validity for their test. To establish the content validity, they demonstrated the content in the five areas of the test had been identified as developmentally sensitive in a number of previous research studies. Additionally, they performed analyses to show that each item would yield the target responses 85% of the time in "linguistically mature respondents." They did, however, retain an unspecified number of items not meeting this criterion if the items were thought to be "developmentally sensitive or discriminating."

The construct validity of the test was established primarily by submitting the five subtests to correlational analyses to ascertain "whether or not they represented sufficiently distinct structural categories to be so designated." Of the 10 possible comparisons, four were found to have significant correlations. Three of these four significant correlations involved the MDP subtest suggesting the authors should investigate further whether this subtest represents a "distinct structural" category. It should also be noted that these correlations were based on a sample of only 25 first grade children with normal language. Clark and Madison also cited a study by Becker (1981) to demonstrate the test and its subtests discriminate between normal children and those with language problems. The information they provided on the study was, however, insufficient to permit any definitive judgments.

The concurrent validity of the test was established by correlating the Clark-Madison Test of Oral Language with the Test of Language Development ($r = .73$), the Kindergarten Language Screening Test ($r = .89$), and spontaneous language samples ($r = .65$). These results, although significant, are based on small and disparate samples.

The reliability of the test was established using test-retest procedures. Based on a sample of 16 children retested after 7 to 9 days, a correlation coefficient of .99 was found on the total test and coefficients ranging from .88 to .98 on each of the subtests. Additional studies cited by the authors confirmed the test-retest reliability of the test.

The Clark-Madison Test of Oral Language presents a potentially viable alternative to procedures for assessing the structural components of language for individuals. The test user, however, must be aware the normative data and the data related to the validity and reliability of the test are based on small samples of children. Additionally, analysis procedures described on the analysis form are, potentially, not consistent with information in the test manual. All interpretations must, therefore, be made with caution. It is hoped that as the test developers continue their research they will provide the test consumer with a more adequate statistical base for a test that, from procedural and content considerations, could substantially benefit the profession.

REVIEWER'S REFERENCES

Bloom, L., & Lahey, M. (1978). *Language development and language disorders.* New York: Wiley.

Becker, M. J. (1981). *Grammatical distinctions produced on the Clark-Madison Test of Oral Language compared to a spontaneous language sample.* Master's degree project, Washington State University, Pullman, WA.

[59]

CLASS—The Cognitive, Linguistic and Social-Communicative Scales. Purpose: "Created to provide the speech-language pathologist, early childhood educator, physician, or other professional concerned with language development in preschool children with an efficient means of assessing cognitive, linguistic and social-communicative systems development in children from birth through five years of age." Ages birth through 72 months; 1984; CLASS; indirect assessment from informant reports; 3 scales: Cognitive, Linguistic, Social-Communicative; individual; 1985 price data: $60 per complete set including manual (91 pages); (45) minutes; Dennis C. Tanner and Wendy M. Lamb; PRO-ED, Inc.*

[The publisher informed us in January 1988 that this test has been discontinued.]

Review of CLASS—The Cognitive, Linguistic and Social-Communicative Scales by DORIS V. ALLEN, Professor of Audiology, Wayne State University, Detroit, MI:

CLASS—The Cognitive, Linguistic and Social-Communicative Scales is intended as an indirect assessment of language behaviors of preschool children. Information concerning language and speech is derived, not from the child, but from the parent. The three systems (Cognitive, Linguistic, and Social-Communicative) are assessed separately. The 157 items comprising this scale have been derived from the research literature. The items span the developmental period from birth through 5 years of age. Within each system, the items are arranged in 11 successive developmental levels. The authors estimate that testing time is about 15 minutes per section, giving a total time of 45 minutes. The directions specify that the child being assessed should not be present during the interview. Each item has two examples that are presented to the parent. The parent indicates whether the child currently exhibits the target behavior or has done so at some time in the past (a positive response), or that the child has never exhibited such behavior (negative response). If the parent expresses uncertainty about whether the child has ever exhibited the target behavior, this is scored as an inadequate response. Directions are given in the manual for identifying the basal and ceiling levels. Performance is summarized ultimately on graphs representing each system and a composite graph, each showing the child's level of performance relative to chronological age.

The manual includes two audiocassette tapes intended for parent training. One tape is an introduction to behavior modification of speech and language and the other covers principles of language development. The manual itself contains no suggestions or directions regarding the use of the tapes. It is not clear how, when, or by whom these tapes should be distributed to parents. The tapes themselves state that they "have been designed to offer constructive advice and general instruction to provide a home program of speech and language therapy to your child" and should be used "under the supervision of a speech-language pathologist." Presumably the tapes should be distributed at the discretion of a speech-language pathologist but this information is not explicitly stated. In addition, the level of the concepts involved and the language used on the tapes suggest that the tapes are best suited for the educated, well-motivated parent.

Using parent report as a source of information regarding speech and language development has both advantages and disadvantages. Studies have found that parents are an accurate source of information about behaviors of their children; however, it is also recognized that parent report is subject to error (e.g., denial, exaggeration). Obviously, the accuracy of a specific parent report is unknown. Thus, the outcomes from administration of this instrument are best viewed as tentative until additional data are obtained from other sources to serve as a referent or basis for comparison. Consistencies across different sources would support the accuracy of the parent report but provide little additional information about the child. Inconsistencies, on the other hand, may be due either to assessment or parent "error"; these would need to be resolved before an accurate evaluation of the child can be made. This weakness precludes the use of this instrument by other than speech-language pathologists. Even these clinicians might elect to use this instrument following language assessment (rather than preceding or replacing such assessment), to gain further information about the child's language behavior in other than the clinical setting.

Another aspect of this instrument that has both advantages and disadvantages is the derivation of the items from the research literature. Research findings and their interpretations form the knowledge base for any discipline, but the status of such information is, at best, tentative until those facts have been confirmed by independent replication. Use of small sample sizes and available samples often produces results that are not replicable. Items in this instrument that are based upon findings reported in several research studies by independent authors may be viewed as valid. However, many of the linguistic and social-communicative scale items are based on single sources. The validity of the placement of the items in terms of developmental level should not be considered as confirmed at this time.

The authors provide no other information concerning either the validity or the reliability of this instrument; normative data are not reported but are promised. A reference entitled "Unpublished Pilot Study Data" by the authors is included in the reference list and serves as a source of some items, but details of the pilot study are not given (e.g., sample size, characteristics, etc.). Analysis suggests that this pilot study was used primarily to obtain linguistic data from infants ranging in age from birth through one year.

In conclusion, while CLASS attempts to provide an alternative approach to assessment of a child's speech and language development, it has serious weaknesses that a potential user should consider. It should not be used by individuals lacking professional training in speech-language pathology. Decisions should not be based solely on CLASS but the test may be used to supplement other assessment procedures. CLASS could provide further insight into the child's behavior as reported by the parent, but, in many instances, the information will be redundant. Without further research, the developmental levels derived from CLASS must be viewed as being of unknown or uncertain validity and reliability.

Review of CLASS—The Cognitive, Linguistic and Social-Communicative Scales by JANICE SANTOGROSSI, Instructor of Special Education and Communication Disorders, University of Nebraska-Lincoln, Lincoln, NE:

CLASS—The Cognitive, Linguistic and Social-Communicative Scales is a standardized instrument for indirect assessment of the language skills of preschool children. The authors' purpose in developing CLASS was to create an assessment tool to supplement direct assessment procedures. The three sections of CLASS assess the child's conceptual development, use and comprehension of English grammar, and communicative effectiveness.

The behaviors assessed by CLASS were selected from "several descriptive studies of child language development, as well as from parental reports and the authors' clinical experience." Items in each section are arranged in 11 levels in developmental sequence. The age ranges assigned to each level are approximate ages at which children typically acquire the behaviors. The sequence was determined from studies of development in young children and from the authors' experience in administering CLASS. The authors present adequate references to support selection and placement of the behaviors at various developmental levels, but no information about their pilot studies with CLASS. The authors do report that they are conducting normative studies, the results of which will be reported when the studies are completed. The authors suggest that "locally developed" norms may be more useful to users of CLASS. While this may be true, it is this reviewer's opinion that conducting such studies is beyond the resources and time constraints of most test users.

The authors report no reliability data for CLASS. In the introduction to the CLASS manual they mention, almost in passing, that "the content validity of the test items is determined by the research on which they are based." There is no mention of attempts to establish other kinds of validity.

CLASS includes a readable manual that contains clear and complete instructions for administering the instrument. For each section of CLASS the manual provides a synopsis of development in preschool children, instructions to be given to the informant, and the test items. The manual also contains information about interpretation and application of the results and one set of response forms. (These forms are apparently to be photocopied for use, though this reviewer could find no mention of this anywhere in the CLASS materials.) A separate

Presentation Booklet, which has instructions to the informant and the test items to be used when administering CLASS, is also included. In addition, the CLASS materials include two parent training tapes "Introduction to Behavior Modification of Speech and Language" and "Principles of Language Development." The parent training tapes are an interesting addition, but this reviewer feels such materials are outside the scope of an assessment tool. The authors would have been better advised to have spent their time conducting reliability, validity, and normative studies on CLASS.

CLASS is based on the premise that a knowledgeable informant such as a parent (the authors recommend the child's mother) can provide reliable, accurate, and complete information about the language skills of young children that is equivalent to or, in fact, superior to information that can be obtained from direct testing. The authors offer results of studies reporting high correlations between data from parental report and direct testing to support this premise. The authors provide further justification for using an informant format from their experience that direct testing of young children may "yield inaccurate or incomplete data and result in inappropriate and ineffective intervention programs" due to the difficulty of getting a child's best performance in a formal evaluation situation. The informant format is an advantage and, at the same time, a problem. It is this reviewer's experience that it is indeed difficult at times to obtain from a young child results that are truly representative of the child's skills with direct testing procedures. At the same time, I have found that some parents are reliable informants while others are not. It would require a skilled, experienced interviewer who is familiar with the parent, the child, and the family situation to facilitate and recognize complete and accurate reporting from the informant.

The authors state that CLASS requires 45 minutes to administer (i.e., 15 minutes for each section). The interviewer would need to be thoroughly acquainted with the behaviors and administration/scoring procedures in order to complete CLASS in that time. A procedure for determining basal and ceiling levels for each section precludes the necessity of administering all the items. The scoring procedures for CLASS stress the importance of the interviewer's judgement of the appropriateness of the example of each behavior given by the informant in crediting a child with the behavior. The authors, however, provide no guidelines for making such judgements and, again, report no studies of inter-judge reliability.

The results of CLASS are plotted on bar graphs (one for each section and a cumulative graph). These graphs provide a clear, convenient visual representation of the child's results. The child's ceiling level is his/her "age equivalent" for each section (i.e., the level at which the child is assumed to be functioning). The authors caution that the age range for each level is an approximate age of acquisition of the behaviors and should be used as a general guideline to compare the child's chronological age to his/her developmental age achieved for each of the CLASS sections. The items the child did not achieve below his/her chronological age should be targeted for training in developmental sequence. In this way the results of CLASS may be used to determine objectives for remediation.

SUMMARY. CLASS could serve as a useful adjunct to a direct language assessment battery especially for difficult-to-test children, provided it is administered by an experienced, skilled interviewer to a knowledgeable, reliable informant. The format and content of CLASS promise to fulfill the need for a standardized measure of a child's communicative functioning in real-life situations. However, in the absence of data to show that CLASS is a reliable, valid instrument with appropriate norms, this reviewer cannot recommend it for use.

[60]

Classroom Environment Scale, Second Edition. Purpose: To "assess the social climate of junior high and high school classrooms. It focuses on teacher-student and student-student relationships and on the organizational structure of a classroom." Junior high and senior high teachers and students; 1974–87; CES; one of ten Social Climate Scales; 9 scores: Relationship dimensions (Involvement, Affiliation, Teacher Support), Personal Growth/Goal Orientation dimensions (Task Orientation, Competition), System Maintenance and Change dimensions (Order and Organization, Rule Clarity, Teacher Control, Innovation); 3 forms: Real Form (Form R), Ideal Form (Form I), Expectations Form (Form E), and a Short Form (Form S) by administering and scoring the first 36 items of Form R; 1987 price data: $6 per 25 reusable tests; $1.50

per scoring key; $6 per 50 answer sheets; $3.50 per 50 profiles; $9.50 per manual ('87, 61 pages); $15 per specimen set; administration time not reported; Rudolf H. Moos and Edison J. Trickett; Consulting Psychologists Press, Inc.*

See T3:409 (9 references); for reviews by Maurice J. Eash and C. Robert Pace of an earlier edition, see 8:521 (3 references). For a review of The Social Climate Scales, see 8:681.

TEST REFERENCES

1. Harpin, P. M., & Sandler, I. N. (1979). Interaction of sex, locus of control, and teacher control: Toward a student-classroom match. *American Journal of Community Psychology*, 7, 621-632.

2. Trickett, E. J., & Quinlan, D. M. (1979). Three domains of classroom environment: Factor analysis of the Classroom Environment Scale. *American Journal of Community Psychology*, 7, 279-291.

3. Trickett, E. J., & Wilkinson, L. (1979). Using individual or group scores on perceived environment scale: Classroom Environment Scale as example. *American Journal of Community Psychology*, 7, 497-502.

4. Fraser, B. J. (1982). Development of short forms of several classroom environment scales. *Journal of Educational Measurement*, 19, 221-227.

5. Fraser, B. J., & Fisher, D. L. (1982). Predicting students' outcomes from their perceptions of classroom psychosocial environment. *American Educational Research Journal*, 19, 498-518.

6. Haladyna, T., Olsen, R., & Shaughnessy, J. (1982). Relations of student, teacher, and learning environment variables to attitudes toward science. *Science Education*, 66, 671-687.

7. Trickett, E. J., Trickett, P. K., Castro, J. J., & Schaffner, P. (1982). The independent school experience: Aspects of the normative environments of single-sex and coed secondary schools. *Journal of Educational Psychology*, 74, 374-381.

8. Fisher, D. L., & Fraser, B. J. (1983). A comparison of actual and preferred classroom environments as perceived by science teachers and students. *Journal of Research in Science Teaching*, 20, 55-61.

9. Fraser, B. J., & Fisher, D. L. (1983). Development and validation of short forms of some instruments measuring student perceptions of actual and preferred classroom learning environment. *Science Education*, 67, 115-131.

10. Fraser, B. J., & Fisher, D. L. (1983). Use of actual and preferred classroom environment scales in person-environment fit research. *Journal of Educational Psychology*, 75, 303-313.

11. Schultz, R. A. (1983). Sociopsychological climates and teacher-bias expectancy: A possible mediating mechanism. *Journal of Educational Psychology*, 75, 167-173.

12. Humphrey, L. L. (1984). Children's self-control in relation to perceived social environment. *Journal of Personality and Social Psychology*, 46, 178-188.

13. Wright, S., & Cowen, E. L. (1985). The effects of peer-teaching on student perceptions of class environment, adjustment, and academic performance. *American Journal of Community Psychology*, 13, 417-431.

14. Zatz, S., & Chassin, L. (1985). Cognitions of test-anxious children under naturalistic test-taking conditions. *Journal of Consulting and Clinical Psychology*, 53, 393-401.

15. Fraser, B. J., & Fisher, D. L. (1986). Using short forms of classroom climate instruments to assess and improve classroom psychosocial environment. *Journal of Research in Science Teaching*, 23, 387-413.

16. Smilansky, J., & Halberstadt, N. (1986). Inventors versus problem solvers: An empirical investigation. *The Journal of Creative Behavior*, 20, 183-201.

Review of the Classroom Environment Scale, Second Edition by RICHARD A. SAUDARGAS, Associate Professor of Psychology, University of Tennessee, Knoxville, TN:

This Classroom Environment Scale (CES) is designed to assess the psychosocial environment of the classroom and is derived from Murray's concept of environmental press. According to this perspective, groups within an environment will perceive the environment in consistent ways. These perceptions will "press" the individuals and groups to behave in a manner consistent with that environment. The CES consists of 90 statements asking respondents to consider whether each statement is mostly true or mostly false about the classroom. The only difference between the Real and Ideal Forms is in the instructional set.

The Second Edition of the manual has been updated to include recent CES research. Norms are provided based on students in 382 classrooms and teachers in 295 classrooms. Although the manual suggests the CES is appropriate for both junior high and high school classrooms, only 27 junior high classrooms were used in the normative sample. Separate norms are also given for English and Social Studies Classes, Science Classes, Mathematics Classes, and Business and Technical Classes. Sample sizes for these latter norms range from 46 to 92 classrooms. Normative data for the Short Form and preliminary normative data for the Ideal Form are also presented. Using the Kuder-Richardson Formula-20, the subscale internal consistency for 22 classrooms is good ranging from .67 to .86. Six-week subscale test-retest reliabilities for 52 students ranged from .72 to .90. Subscale intercorrelations for 465 students in 22 classrooms indicated that several of the subscales are interrelated. The subscales of Involvement, Affiliation, Teacher Support, Order and Organization, and Innovation intercorrelated from .45 to .49. Teacher support was negatively correlated with Task Orientation (-.25) and Teacher Control (-.48) but had a high positive correlation with Innovation (+.51). There are other subscale intercorrelations of equal magnitude.

The high subscale intercorrelations beg the question of a CES factor structure. The manual briefly reports on a number of factor analytic studies. The numbers of factors reported ranged from three to six. The manual concludes this section by stating the "variations in the factor solutions point to the value of using a standard set of conceptually relevant dimensions to describe classroom settings." However, the manual does not report whether individual's scores or classroom scores were used as the unit of analysis for the factor analytic studies. One study (Haladyna, 1982) tested whether the unit of analysis and sample led to different factor solutions. Different units of analysis (individual vs. classroom) disclosed alternate factor structures. Likewise, different academic domains (social studies vs. mathematics) indicated varying factor structures. A brief, trenchant analysis of the importance of units of analysis was presented in the *Eighth Mental Measurements Yearbook* (8:681, 1978) by Richards in a general review of the Social Climate Scales. A potential user of the CES is encouraged to become familiar with this issue.

Although validity issues are of great importance in determining the usefulness of the CES, only limited information is provided. Construct validity is supported by some data concerning how the CES subscales related to different observable behaviors in classrooms. However, the report is so scanty (i.e., no tables, *N* sizes, etc.) that it is impossible to evaluate the adequacy of the conclusions stated.

The last two sections of the manual present brief, noncritical summaries of recent research findings on clinical, program evaluation, and research applications. The aim of these sections is to inform the potential user how the CES has been used, as well as how the CES could be used for research and applied purposes. Headings under these sections include profile interpretation, changing social climates, evaluating programs, describing and comparing classrooms, and determinants of classroom climate. Most of the research summarized is correlational. For example, research is reported correlating the CES with absenteeism, self-concept, academic motivation, and sociometric status. As with all correlational research, one does not know what the functional variables are. Research on the relationship of the CES with academic achievement is sparse and equivocal. Much of the research summarized in these two sections comes from research on elementary school students. As noted, the CES is designed for and norms are provided for only junior and senior high school students. It would be clearly inappropriate to use the norms tables provided in the manual for converting raw scores to standard scores when doing research with elementary school students. The authors do not make clear how one should deal with elementary school data or, indeed, if the CES is appropriate at all for elementary school use.

In summary, the CES is a fairly good instrument for measuring what it purports to measure. The questions are straightforward and the true/false response format is simple (others have suggested, however, that a scale format for the items might be more valid). The CES has been used in research projects very frequently since its first publication, and the manual provides many up-to-date references. A potential user is advised to know exactly how the CES would be useful for his/her clinical or research purposes and to become familiar with the research literature pertinent to those purposes. Given the existing literature, the CES should not be used as a sole dependent measure for attempting to assess the impact of an academic or social intervention in the schools.

REVIEWER'S REFERENCE

Richards, J. M., Jr. (1978). [Review of The Social Climate Scales]. In O. K. Buros (Ed.), *The eighth mental measurements yearbook* (Vol. 1, pp. 1085-1087). Highland Park, NJ: The Gryphon Press.

Review of the Classroom Environment Scale, Second Edition by CORINNE ROTH SMITH, Associate Professor of Special Education and Rehabilitation, Syracuse University, Syracuse, NY:

The Classroom Environment Scale (CES), originally published by Moos and Trickett in 1974, evaluates the extent to which a classroom is perceived to provide conditions in which students can learn with effective supports and opportunities for positive peer relationships. Moos and Trickett's 1987 CES manual retains the original standardization data and scoring criteria, but provides additional information regarding clinical, research, and program evaluation applications.

One of a set of 10 Social Climate Scales, the CES specifically addresses the social climate of junior high and high school classrooms. The Real Form (Form R) of the CES assesses perceptions of the current classroom by means of 90 statements that tap three social climate dimensions: Relationship, Personal Growth and Goal Orientation, and System Maintenance and Change. Each dimension further divides into several subscales of 10 items each, as summarized in the descriptive entry above. Students and teachers read from a reusable booklet, and, for each statement, mark a box on an answer sheet labelled T (true or most true for your class) or F (false or mostly false). The Ideal Form (Form I) of the CES rewords each statement so that teachers and students can express the goals, values, and operational characteristics they would ideally like in their classes. Likewise, the Expectations Form (Form E) of the CES rewords each item to reflect student and teacher expectations about a classroom they are about to enter. A Short Form (Form S) provides a rapid assessment of a classroom's social climate by utilizing only the first 36 items of Form R, four items from each of the nine subscales.

CES items are arranged so that an item belonging to the first subscale is first, an item from subscale two is second, and so forth through the ninth item. The sequence then repeats itself. Scoring is accomplished with a template, each column of responses constituting one scale. Standard score equivalents on each subscale are provided for classroom mean scores, individual scores, teacher scores calculated on the basis of student norms, and teacher scores calculated on the basis of teacher norms.

The CES item development process was excellent. Initially, 242 items had been formulated from classroom observation and interviews with students, teachers, and administrators. After tryouts of several forms in 71 high school classrooms, items were dropped that did not correlate sufficiently with others on their assigned subscales, correlated too highly with other subscales, or that did not differentiate classrooms. Eighty of the 90 final items correlated .40 or above with their subscale, 87 items differentiated among classrooms at the .05 level, and 74 items were characteristic of nonextreme classrooms (item splits between 30% and 70%).

The CES standardization process sampled a broad range of classrooms on the east and west coasts, including large, suburban middle-class white schools, medium-sized rural white schools, small private schools, an integrated inner-city alternative high school, a large primarily black inner-city school, and a large integrated inner-city school. Although the authors state that "these classrooms are reasonably representative of the entire range of high school classes," no comparison with census data is presented with respect to geographic location, race, community size, or urban-rural setting.

The CES, Form R, was standardized on students from 382 classrooms and teachers from 295 classrooms. Two-hundred-eighteen classes were from general high schools, 97 from vocational high schools, 40 from alternative and private high schools, and 27 from junior high schools. Class size ranged from 4 to 34 students, with the majority ranging between 20–30 students. Classroom means and standard deviations are presented for the total sample, as well as 58 Science classes (53 teachers' rooms), 48 Math classes (46 teachers' rooms), and 67 Business and Technical classes (typing, bookkeeping, auto mechanics, machine and wood shops; 64 teachers' rooms). The means and standard deviations for 92 English, history, government, economics, and social studies classes (85 teachers' rooms) were combined due to the similarity of their average CES profiles. It is presumed the 465 randomly selected students for whom *SD*s are reported (computer power didn't permit total group computations; personal communication, Consulting Psychologists Press) are representative of the sampling distribution and classroom means, although neither are reported.

Reliability of the scales is strong. Internal consistencies calculated for 22 classrooms (N = 465) range from .67 to .86, with six of the subscales being above .80. Average item to subscale correlations range around .50. Subscale intercorrelations range from .00 to .49 (mean = .27; approximately 1/3 over .40), suggesting that some of the scales are measuring distinct aspects of classroom environments while others are somewhat related. A 6-week test-retest in four classrooms (n = 52) indicated subscale reliabilities of .72 to .90 (mean = .82). Stability of profiles for the most part above .90 was indicated by 2-, 4-, and 6-week intraclass test-retest correlations.

Construct validity has been demonstrated in a number of studies that find strong CES (Form R) subscale associations with classroom observational and teacher interview data. When examining how the subscales relate to the three dimensions the authors purport to measure, factor analysis studies have found the items to cluster on three to six factors. Therefore, evaluation of CES results is best conducted using subscale comparisons or factor analysis, rather than grouping subscales by the three original dimensions.

The CES has been used to explore a wide variety of questions. The authors devote a substantial portion of the manual to illustrating how the various CES forms can be used to determine the congruence of student and teacher values, goals, and expectations, what each perceives as the preferred environment, how the real and ideal ratings can be subtracted from one another to yield goals for change, how the effect of innovations and interventions on learning environment can be monitored, and how prior expectations impact on achievement and class relations. Moos and Trickett report the utility of the CES in providing students' perceptions to parents, thus assisting in program selection. CES profiles have been helpful to teachers in determining how to enhance the class learning environment and measure subsequent changes. The impact of grouping practices and cooperative learning projects on perceived classroom environment also has been an interesting application. The CES has been used to identify environmental factors predictive of outcome in intervention programs and to choose heterogenous environments for research purposes. Other studies have reported provocative results when using the CES to evaluate the relationship of teacher/student characteristics (sex, personality, behavior, race), teacher style, subject matter, work climate, and student morale and adjustment, to perceived classroom environment, which together influence achievement, social relationships, and self-concept.

The large number of studies that have utilized the CES attest to its well-founded respect for clinical and research applications. Possibilities for adaptations of the CES are numerous. The authors report that investigators have used a 5-point rating scale instead of the T/F recording format, the scale has been extended to primary grade children, the school rather than classroom has been the focus of ratings, and several foreign translations have produced results similar to those in American classrooms, with acceptable internal consistencies and intercorrelations.

With respect to the Short Form, Moos and Trickett warn that it has too few items to validly make interindividual comparisons. However, it is useful for comparing classroom units. Form S norms were based on 315 classrooms (256 teachers' rooms). In support of the reliability and validity of the Short Form for studying class patterns, Moos and Trickett report Fraser's (1982) and Fraser and Fisher's (1983) studies of six CES Short Form subscales (24 items) in a sample of 116 junior high school science classes. Analyzing class means, internal reliabilities were acceptable (alpha coefficients .59 to .78). Correlations with the Real Form ranged from .78–.95 and the subscales significantly discriminated between classes. Criterion validity was demonstrated in the finding that students who rated their classes as more task-oriented and well-organized also were more interested in science and learned more about it.

Preliminary Form I norms are presented for 50 classrooms (1,013 students; 42 teachers' rooms). No reliability or validity studies are reported.

The CES Real Form is a well-constructed instrument that merits clinical and research use in the schools. There is preliminary evidence the Short Form may prove of equal technical adequacy. In the last decade, educators have become more alert to the great impact that classroom environment has on student satisfaction, achievement, and peer relations. Consequently, it has become more important that we have a technically adequate instrument with which to assess a youngster's and teacher's perceptions and expectations. An understanding of incongruities and weaknesses on the CES profiles is of direct instructional relevance, as is an understanding of the optimal teacher-pupil environment match that will maximize personal and academic success.

Nevertheless, the CES norms are over 14 years old. With all the clinical activity involving the CES, it is surprising the authors have not compared data from recent studies to the original norms, assuring the user the scaled score values remain representative of today's perceptions regarding classroom environments. High schools in America have changed, and it is appropriate to wonder if norms for teacher and student attitudes gathered 14 years ago are equally valid today. In the absence of such information, and because the authors do not break down the standardization data by geographic location, class and school size, suburban/rural/urban setting, public/private, integrated/nonintegrated schools, and number of classes sampled per school, the user is advised to develop local norms. These would more adequately aid interpretation of local performance. In fact, the content validity of the items lend themselves to subscale interpretation even without reference to scaled scores and norms.

REVIEWER'S REFERENCES

Fraser, B. (1982). Development of short forms of several classroom environment scales. *Journal of Educational Measurement*, 19, 221-227.

Fraser, B., & Fisher, D. (1983). Development and validation of short forms of some instruments measuring student perceptions of actual and preferred classroom learning environment. *Science Education*, 67, 115-131.

[61]

Classroom Reading Inventory, Fourth Edition. Purpose: "Attempts to identify the student's specific word-recognition and comprehension skills." Grades 2–8, high school and adults; 1965–82; CRI; 6 scores: Independent Reading Level, Instructional Reading Level, Frustration Reading Level, Hearing Capacity Level, Word Recognition, Comprehension; individual in part; Forms A, B, C, (for use with grades 2–8), D (for use with high school and adults); manual ('82, 170 pages, includes all forms); price data available from publisher; (24) minutes; Nicholas J. Silvaroli; Wm. C. Brown Co., Publishers.*

For a review of an earlier edition by Marjorie S. Johnson, see 8:749; see also T2:1618 (1 reference); for an excerpted review by Donald L. Cleland, see 7:715.

TEST REFERENCES

1. Paris, S. G., & Jacobs, J. E. (1984). The benefits of informed instruction for children's reading awareness and comprehension skills. *Child Development*, 55, 2083-2093.

2. Connelly, J. B. (1985). Published tests—which ones do special education teachers perceive as useful? *Journal of Special Education*, 19, 149-155.

3. Olson, M. W. (1985). Text type and reader ability: The effects on paraphrase and text-based inference questions. *Journal of Reading Behavior*, 17, 199-214.

4. Gildemeister, J., & Friedman, P. (1986). Sequence memory and organization in recall of black third and fifth graders. *Journal of Negro Education*, 55, 142-154.

Review of the Classroom Reading Inventory, Fourth Edition by IRA E. AARON, Professor Emeritus of Reading Education, and SYLVIA M. HUTCHINSON, Associate Professor of Reading Education, University of Georgia, Athens, GA:

The Classroom Reading Inventory, Fourth Edition, consisting of three forms (A, B, and C) for grades 2–8 and a form (D) for high school and adult students, is a useful inventory for assisting teachers to pinpoint strengths and weaknesses in student reading and in estimating student reading level (Independent, Instructional, and Frustration). It also furnishes an estimate of hearing capacity level, and Forms A, B, and C include Spelling Surveys.

The instructions and discussion in the test booklet are sufficient for teachers and prospective teachers to learn how to administer the inventory. However, 16 teachers, asked to review the instructions, concluded that certain sections should be improved. The marking system for recording oral reading errors is practical and easy to master. The two samples of inventory results and accompanying explanations are of considerable help in illustrating inventory administration and interpretation.

Forms A, B, and C contain Graded Word Lists of 20 words each for eight levels, preprimer through sixth grade; Form D contains eight lists, from grade 1 through 8. Though how and why these particular words were selected is not discussed, the difficulty from level to level appears appropriate. Mispronunciations are analyzed for word-recognition errors.

The Graded Oral Paragraphs are interesting and appropriate in difficulty at the various levels from preprimer through grade 8. Approximately three-fourths of the 38 oral reading selections in the four forms of the inventory are informational in content, mainly about science and sports. Several readability formulas were used in checking selections for difficulty levels. No comment was made about equal comprehensibility across levels and forms, but selections appear to be written satisfactorily. Form D selections, designed for use with older readers and not meant to be interchanged with selections in the other three forms, begin at grade 1 rather than at preprimer level as in the other forms.

Each Graded Oral Paragraph in all four inventory forms is followed by five comprehension questions. For the most part the questions are good. However, six Yes/No and True/False questions are included in the total of 190 questions across all four forms. Because of the 50/50 chance of a correct answer just from guessing, such questions are poor. One answer also is given in the title and not in the text, though titles are not included in the word count.

The author states that editing was done to assure that questions were passage dependent. However, a panel of 16 teachers, asked to review the passages and comprehension questions, concluded that many (at least 14 in Form

A alone) could be answered by some children from their experiences, independent of the selections. A few examples are these: "At what time of year do we see more spiders?" "Why do you think they called the horse Midnight?" "What does in excess of 90 m.p.h. mean?" The panel of teachers also questioned the effectiveness of the illustrations accompanying each paragraph; these are in black and white and are of poor quality. The information relative to speed of reading the oral paragraphs is not likely to be of much use since speed of comprehension in silent reading is what teachers are concerned about. Further, rate of oral reading is limited at higher levels by rate of speaking.

Comprehension questions are classified as Fact, Inference, or Vocabulary. According to the labels given the 190 questions on the four forms, 61 percent are classified as Fact, 23 percent as Inference, and 16 percent as Vocabulary. Five questions labeled as Fact appear to be Inference questions, and two Vocabulary questions actually check interpretations of figurative language (i.e., "sensitive nostrils feeling the air") and could have been classified as Inference.

Spelling Surveys, consisting of six 10-word lists, ranging in difficulty from grade 1 to grade 6, are included in each of Forms A, B, and C. This test may be given in a group setting, with responses checked following the administration of each list. As in the case of the Graded Word Lists, the basis for the selection of these particular words is not given, though the spelling words do appear to be suited to the difficulty level assigned them (grades 1–6). On the summary sheet, there is no place to record Spelling Survey results. This test, which is optional, is likely to be far less useful to most teachers than the first two sections of the inventory.

The criteria for determining the hearing capacity and the various reading levels are explained clearly. A good case is made in the instructions for teacher judgment—along with the criteria—for making decisions about levels. As would be expected because of the differing lengths of selections, the error percentages for Independent, Instructional, and Frustration levels are not the same at the different grade levels; (i.e., the error range for the lower limits of the Instructional level varies from 3 to 8 percent [92 to 97 percent correct pronunciation]).

Overall, the Classroom Reading Inventory is a useful tool in the hands of a knowledgeable teacher. This particular inventory compares favorably with the best of other published inventories. To control testing time, this inventory uses brief selections—especially at early levels, and checks comprehension following oral reading, with no assessment of silent reading. Longer selections likely would have increased reliability, and checking comprehension following silent reading would have been more in keeping with school practice. The author does suggest that teachers may use the Graded Oral Paragraphs in Forms B and C to check on comprehension following silent reading for those children who do not react well to the oral reading. Some teachers may prefer to build their own tests to use in place of or in addition to a published inventory such as this—if they have the knowledge and time. Teacher-made tests have the added advantage of instructional and testing passages being comparable because test passages may be taken from student textbooks.

Review of the Classroom Reading Inventory, Fourth Edition by JANET A. NORRIS, Assistant Professor of Communication Disorders, Louisiana State University, Baton Rouge, LA:

The stated purpose of the Classroom Reading Inventory, Fourth Edition (CRI) is to provide a diagnostic tool for teachers that can be used both to identify specific word-recognition and comprehension skills, and to determine the grade levels at which a child reads independently, instructionally, at frustration, and potentially. The test is designed to be administered quickly, within the classroom setting, and individually in order to provide the teacher with some specific insights into a child's reading strengths and weaknesses. The manual provides case examples to illustrate some of the information that can be obtained from the inventory.

The fourth edition of the CRI includes the addition of a fourth form of the test designed to assess the reading ability of more mature students exhibiting low reading achievement levels. Other revisions include the modification of a few of the reading passages, changes or rewording of some of the comprehension questions, the provision of a motivational statement prior to the reading of each graded passage, and revised drawings to accompany the reading passages.

The CRI is designed for use by classroom teachers, and does not purport to be an instrument used to ascertain achievement levels, diagnose reading disorders, or identify handicapping conditions. However, although the test may not have to meet the rigorous test construction or normative procedures of a diagnostic test, the provision of some information in the manual concerning test construction would be useful. For example, the manual states that the passages were evaluated for their readability level and cites several procedures used. No further information is provided about selection criteria, number of measures an individual passage was subjected to, level of agreement of readability between measures for the same passage, or level of agreement of readability between passages among alternate forms graded at the same level by the inventory. The agreement among alternate forms is particularly important because the author states the forms can be used for posttesting, a comparison of oral reading to silent reading, and/or a comparison of oral reading to hearing capacity, therefore implying the forms are equivalent. No studies or evaluations are reported indicating the reliability coefficients across the alternate forms of the test. Variations between passages, such as differences in the complexity of the sentence structures seen between the fourth-grade passages of Forms A and B, may create differences in performance. Similarly, no information is provided on the manner in which the sight words were selected for the word recognition portion of the test.

In this fourth edition of the CRI, modifications were made in the comprehension questions in an attempt to eliminate correct responses derived from general knowledge rather than reading comprehension. The author states that all questions are passage dependent, meaning they can be answered correctly only by reading the corresponding passages. However, several passage-independent questions still remain, such as, "Is there more than one kind of spider?" or "Where do ants live?" Several of the vocabulary questions ask for a generic definition that can be answered if the child knows the word without regard to the reading passage, such as, "What does the word 'grind' mean?" or "What does the word 'submerge' mean?" There are inferential questions such as, "Why do you think they called the horse Midnight?" that not only can be answered independently of the text, but which have very little to do with the theme of the story towards which inferences should be directed. For some questions, such as, "At what time of year do we see more spiders?" the answers are not contained within or implied by the text. The examiner is instructed to accept the answer typical for the area of the country in which the child lives. In general, there are too many factual questions that the child can answer without really understanding the theme, story, or significance of the passage, so that many comprehension problems could go undetected by this inventory. The inferential questions that are asked tend to be relatively low-level inferences, and many of them are only tangentially related to the theme or purpose of the passage. Therefore, the comprehension questions remain the most problematic aspect of the inventory.

The material presented to the child to read is not ideal, and could have an effect on reading performance. The print is small, and is the same size and typeface at all levels. There is only single spacing between lines of the text, even at the preprimer and primer reading levels. Many children reading at that level are accustomed to reading print of larger type and could easily be confused or intimidated by the type size and spacing. Because of the minimal spacing between words and lines, some children may experience a greater number of errors related to skipping across lines of text. The story in Form C, Level 2 is written in paragraph form, while the equivalent passages in Forms A and B are written in the somewhat easier format of one sentence per line. Similarly, on the word recognition lists, there is barely a character of space between the number of the word and the word to be read, making the visual discrimination harder for some children. The numbers themselves on the child's form seem superfluous and may serve as irrelevant distractions.

The pictures accompanying the text in this edition consist of abstract sketches with poorly defined lines, unclear details, and poor use of shading. It is difficult to determine what some of the sketches are supposed to represent. Such ambiguity may mislead a child in predicting what the text is about. Unlike the pictures in previous editions of the CRI, these sketches tend to depict isolated objects hanging within an empty space of dark background rather than a scene representative of the story. Many of the drawings are hard to recognize because much of the object is not visible, such as a sketch of the back end of a bus, or an airplane with the wing tips and tail end cut off. The penciled lines are so faintly drawn it is hard to distinguish shapes or figures within the pictures. Any child with visual discrimination problems would find it extremely difficult to get any information from these pictures. Rather than supporting the text, the pictures add confusion.

The manual has clear and complete instructions for administration and scoring. Adequate guidelines and explanations are provided to enable an inexperienced examiner to understand the significance of the various obtained reading levels, and to generate some useful interpretations of this information. The examples also help to clarify procedures.

In summary, the CRI is designed to provide the classroom teacher with a quick method of evaluating an individual child's word recognition and comprehension abilities for relative strengths and weaknesses. While there are many problems in the construction of the inventory, the author does not make diagnostic claims that go beyond its use as an informal analysis, and, therefore, the test can be useful in accomplishing its stated purposes. As a quick inventory, it can provide the teacher with information about an individual child that is not available from achievement test scores or group reading activities.

[62]

Clerical Staff Selector. Purpose: "Evaluates the suitability of candidates of all levels of experience for the position of clerk." Candidates for clerks; 1954–84; 4 tests: Problem Solving Ability, Numerical Skills, Attention to Detail, N.P.F. (emotional stability); 1987 price data: $75 per set of tests including manual (no date, 5 pages) and scoring guide; information on scoring service available from distributor; French edition available; (5–15) minutes per test; tests from various publishers compiled, distributed, and scored (optional) by Wolfe Personnel Testing & Training Systems, Inc.*

Review of the Clerical Staff Selector by RUTH G. THOMAS, Associate Professor of Education, University of Minnesota, St. Paul, MN:

The purpose of the Wolfe Clerical Staff Selector is described as aiding in the selection of applicants of all levels of experience for clerical positions including inventory control, order desk, filing, accounting, and miscellaneous positions requiring similar skills. The test is described as measuring problem-solving and logical ability, numerical skills, attention to detail, and emotional stability.

The Wolfe Clerical Selector is published in English and in French. It was introduced in 1977 according to the test manual; the four tests bear 1984, 1983, and 1955 copyright dates. Administration is described as requiring only clerical supervision.

The Wolfe Clerical Staff Selector consists of three speeded tests and one nonspeeded test. The manual suggests the total test administration time is approximately 30 minutes. The three timed tests (which must be timed to the second according to the instructions) take 5 minutes each. The first, identified as a test of Problem Solving Ability, is comprised of 30 items, each consisting of a series of four groups of letters or numbers or letter/number combinations. These items are meant to test the examinee's skills in determining the principle underlying the series of letters and numbers. The second timed test, identified as Numerical Skills, is composed of 60 items requiring various mathematical calculations. The third timed test, Attention to Detail, involves 45 items, each containing four sets of symbols that must be compared for similarity and difference. The fourth test, although untimed, is estimated to take approximately 15 minutes. This is the emotional stability measure. It is NPF, Edition A, Employee Attitude Series (9:552) published by Industrial Psychology, Inc. with a 1983 copyright and 1955 prior copyright.

Scoring may be done by the client or by Wolfe. Phone scoring is available from Wolfe, with results available in a few minutes after an applicant completes the tests. Scoring guides are available to clients who wish to do the scoring.

An extremely brief manual provides one to four sentences concerning each of the following: test purpose, suggested uses, positions for which use of the Wolfe Clerical Staff Selector is appropriate, job criteria measured, test administration, and scoring options available. The manual also includes sample questions and a sample score profile.

Neither reliability nor validity data are provided with this test. Validation studies are mentioned as in progress. Wolfe offers to undertake a validation study on the Clerical Staff Selector at no cost but for the tests. It is stipulated that such a study requires the involvement of 30 persons. Such offers to do validation studies are no substitute for the validation data that should have been gathered prior to the marketing of the test and provided with the test. Further, such an approach to identifying validation samples is unsystematic and must be questioned.

Because this is a selection test, criterion validity is of utmost importance. No discussion of a criterion is provided. It is not clear to what criterion (e.g., work performance ratings, productivity, low error rates) the test items or subtests are linked. Some data indicating that people who score high on this test perform better in clerical positions than those who score low need to be provided for this test to be considered positively against more established tests such as the Minnesota Clerical Test for use in clerical hiring decisions.

Further, there is no definition or discussion of the four constructs (i.e., problem solving, numerical skills, attention to detail, and emotional stability) measured by this test. No substantiation that the test actually measures these constructs is provided. Furthermore, a sample profile included in the manual includes a statement about the candidate's level of general intelligence even though this test does not purport to measure general intelligence.

Because normative data are not presented, it is impossible to identify the population to which the test's job criteria should apply, for what samples of workers and kinds of organizations this test is appropriate, if the test has been piloted with any samples of workers, or upon what reference group the score profile is based.

No stability, equivalence, or internal consistency reliability nor any estimate of standard error is reported. Neither is the absence of such information noted nor are any cautions provided regarding interpretation of results without such information. On the contrary, instead of saying this is tentative information requiring external sources of verification, the manual provides a profile of a sample case in which very specific predictions about the likely performance of the person are stated and guidance is provided to hire or not hire the candidate on the basis of the scores on the four tests.

In summary, the materials accompanying this test do not contain sufficient information for the test to be considered a valid and reliable instrument for providing information on which to base selection decisions for clerical personnel. It can, at best, be considered an experimental test.

[63]

Clinical Articulation Profile. Purpose: "Designed to assess young children who have severe articulation difficulties." Young children; 1983; CAP; 3 scores: Omissions, Substitutions, Total; individual; 1985 price data: $20 per 100 profiles and information sheet (2 pages); administration time not reported; PRO-ED, Inc.*

[The publisher informed us in January 1988 that this test has been discontinued.]

Review of the Clinical Articulation Profile by JOHN A. COURTRIGHT, Professor and Chair of Communication, University of Delaware, Newark, DE:

The most notable aspect of the Clinical Articulation Profile (CAP) is the complete absence of any information about its reliability, and only the most minimal discussion of its content validity. The CAP has no manual containing this essential information, but rather is accompanied by a single-page instruction sheet. This sheet provides three pieces of information: (*a*) a brief description of "four features of the CAP"; (*b*) an equally brief set of instructions for the administration and scoring of the CAP; and (*c*) an incomplete reference to an article by the authors of the test.

Given the brevity of this instruction sheet, my natural reaction was to locate and read the cited article: Hurvitz, Rilla, and Pickert (1983). Unfortunately, the article is little more than a slightly amplified version of the instruction sheet. At least part of this amplification addresses the issue of content validity, but reliability again receives not the slightest mention.

Hurvitz et al. (1983) present the same four features of the CAP that are outlined in the instruction sheet. In their article, however, they indicate why these features are important and explain how several existing tests are lacking because they do not possess these attributes. There is no doubt as to what the "performance domain" of an articulation test must be: all of the possible sounds in the initial, medial, and final positions of words. How a test assesses the child's ability to produce these combinations of sounds and positions is the issue.

Children with severe articulation disorders—the specified target population for this test—pose a particularly difficult problem for assessment. Hurvitz et al. (1983) make a relatively persuasive case that their approach will provide a more representative assessment of a child's ability to produce combinations of sounds in various positions than do several existing instruments. Without question, these arguments should have appeared in the test materials.

Neither the Hurvitz et al. (1983) article nor the instruction sheet contains information about concurrent validity. What other established tests or diagnostic instruments are related to the CAP? Even though the rationale for the CAP is that it overcomes "difficulties" inherent in several other articulation tests, it surely is not completely unrelated to these tests. The authors have a responsibility to evaluate and discuss where both commonalities and uniquenesses exist between the CAP and other instruments. Their failure to provide this essential information on concurrent validity is a serious shortcoming of the test materials.

Similarly, the authors of the CAP have provided absolutely no information about the reliability of the instrument. For the CAP, test-retest reliability (without intervening therapy, of course) would have been most useful for estimating the stability of the instrument. The authors maintain that the CAP is a "quantifiable method for documenting change and progress" due to therapy (Hurvitz et al., 1983). Accordingly, it should have been demonstrated empirically that differences between administrations are the result of actual changes in client performance, and not the result of random fluctuations due to measurement error.

In addition, coefficients of interrater reliability should have been obtained by having more than one qualified clinician score the same administration of the test. Given the relatively straightforward method of administering and scoring the CAP, it is likely that interrater reliability would be high. Information on interrater reliabilities is necessary to rule out a potentially significant source of measurement error. Interrater reliability coefficients would also have an important bearing on the interpretation of the test-retest reliability of the instrument. Clearly, the authors are responsible for providing this information and its omission constitutes another serious shortcoming of the test materials.

In summary, the Clinical Articulation Profile has failed to comply with several essential standards for published tests. The CAP offers absolutely no assessment of its reliability or its relationship to other measures of articulation. Moreover, content validity is addressed only indirectly in a separately published article. Because tests of articulation have such a well-defined performance domain, there is no confusion about what should be measured. In contrast, the accuracy and consistency of those measurements, as well as the relationship of the obtained scores to other recognized tests of articulation, are very important to establish in a new test.

Consequently, the authors of the CAP should be strongly encouraged to provide information essential to the evaluation of this test. If the appropriate data were gathered, I suspect the CAP would prove to be highly reliable and acceptably valid. I also believe that clinicians would find this test quite appealing. It presents an efficient way to assess the articulation of a highly problematic population, and it has the potential (assuming reliability and validity) to measure therapeutic progress, even when a child's overall intelligibility is lacking. These are very strong points favoring the utility of the CAP. Nevertheless, until the essential empirical information is provided, it is impossible to recommend its use without several serious reservations.

REVIEWER'S REFERENCE

Hurvitz, J. A., Rilla, D. C., & Pickert, S. M. (1983). Measuring change in children with severe articulation disorders. *Language, Speech, and Hearing Services in Schools*, 14, 195-198.

Review of the Clinical Articulation Profile by LYNN S. FUCHS, Assistant Professor of Special Education, George Peabody College, Vanderbilt University, Nashville, TN:

The Clinical Articulation Profile requires examinees to imitate sounds in isolation as well as at beginning, medial, and ending positions within words and syllables. The authors contend this instrument improves upon other articulation measures for assessing young children with severely impaired speech, because it (*a*) incorporates sounds in isolation and in syllables to permit assessment of skills prerequisite to successful word production, (*b*) measures only one sound within each word or syllable to facilitate reliable scoring, (*c*) uses imitation instead of picture naming to reduce administration time, and to separate effects of word knowledge and retrieval from articulation proficiency, and (*d*) provides a method for monitoring student growth over time. A measure combining these features is potentially useful. Unfortunately, the two-page supporting document, along with the four-page referenced article and accompanying instructions on the protocol, fail to satisfy primary standards on test and technical manuals as stated in *Standards for Educational and Psychological Testing* (APA, AERA, NCME, 1985). These materials omit most supporting information necessary for meaningful and accurate interpretation of the test results.

Specifically, technical data are inadequate. First, information on test development is limited to the statement in the referenced article that developers were speech-language pathologists at a city hospital, working with preschool speech and language impaired children. Discussions of the development of test stimuli, item order, and other aspects of content and format are omitted. Second, the reliability of the instrument is never addressed. Third, authors' statement on validity are limited to assertions that the instrument provides "a quantifiable method for documenting change and progress," "documentaion of whether therapy objectives were attained," claims of sensitivity to growth, and curricular validity (Yalow & Popham, 1983), respectively. However, only one case study is presented to support these assertions, rather than the necessary empirical documentation for sensitivity to growth, curricular validity, and criterion-related validity. Given (*a*) that the 50 syllabic and 50 word items, across three positions, contain certain redundancies, (*b*) the authors' statement that the overall intelligibility of the case-study child's connected speech did not coincide with improvement on the test, and (*c*) the nature of sample objectives provided, one might question the outcome of such studies. Additionally, the failure to document content validity, along with no clear definition of the universe represented by the test, violates Standard 1.6 of the *Standards for Educational and Psychological Testing* (APA, AERA, NCME, 1985).

Furthermore, directions for administration and scoring are incomplete and at times questionable. No guidelines concerning tester experience and training are provided. This is an omission with potentially serious implications given the lack of information on interrater reliability and the well-known potential for inaccuracy in scoring articulation errors. Specific directions to examinees are not provided, and it is unclear whether the examiner's production of the stimuli should be visible to the child. Without instructions for standardized administration, decisions based on comparisons between students and intra-individual comparisons over time could be affected. A questionable direction is for examiners to code unintelligible responses as substitutions, when the possibility that targeted sounds are omitted seems equally plausible.

Finally, insufficient information is provided on interpretation of scores. There is no clear statement on what decisions can be based on the measure, or the pupils for whom the measure was designed. In terms of decisions, the authors imply a dual purpose in their summary: "provides a . . . tool for assessment of children who have severe articulation disorders . . . also . . . a . . . method for documenting . . . progress." However, the first "assessment" purpose is never specified, and no guidelines for formulating any norm- or criterion-referenced decisions are delineated. With respect to relevant populations, the appropriate age range for the test is omitted, and the supporting document and referenced article provide different information concerning the severity of articulation disorders for which the test was designed. Additional details necessary for adequate test interpretation also are lacking. For example, explanation for the I, M, and F codes on the protocol is omitted, and the articulation categories (e.g., bilabial, tip-alveolar) are neither defined nor addressed for interpretation. Although one might assume that the "profile" aspect of this measure, referenced in the instrument's title, refers to these articulation categories, appropriate profile analysis is never discussed.

The Clinical Articulation Profile has little to recommend it over other measures. It suffers from serious problems of inadequate technical development, unclear purpose, insufficient administration and scoring directions, and inadequate guidelines on test interpretation.

REVIEWER'S REFERENCES

Yalow, E. S., & Popham, W. J. (1983). Content validity at the crossroads. *Educational Researcher*, 12 (8), 10-14, 21.

American Psychological Association, American Educational Research Association, & National Council on Measurement in Education. (1985). *Standards for educational and psychological testing*. Washington, DC: American Psychological Association.

[64]

Coarticulation Assessment in Meaningful Language. Purpose: Designed to assess coarticulatory variability in children using meaningful multisyllabic words and word strings. Ages 2.5–5.5; 1984; CAML; 14 scores: 8 specific phoneme scores, 3 Manner scores (Liquid, Fricative, Stop), 2 Position scores (Arrest, Release), Total; individual; 1987 price data: $20 per 25 scoring forms, test booklet, and manual (36 pages); $7 per 25 scoring forms; (10–20) minutes; Kathryn W. Kenney and Elizabeth M. Prather; Communication Skill Builders.*

TEST REFERENCES

1. Kenney, K. W., & Prather, E. M. (1986). Articulation development in preschool children: Consistency of productions. *Journal of Speech and Hearing Research*, 29, 29-36.

Review of the Coarticulation Assessment in Meaningful Language by JANET A. NORRIS, Assistant Professor of Communication Disorders, Louisiana State University, Baton Rouge, LA:

No purpose is stated in the test manual for the Coarticulation Assessment in Meaningful Language (CAML). This lack of definition leads to methodological problems in the test's design and standardization. The rationale provided for the CAML includes a description of the coarticulation model, as contrasted to phoneme-based models of articulation, and a discussion of the problems inherent in the existing test instruments. However, the CAML never establishes its own purposes, and so it is unknown whether the test is designed as a screening device, a diagnostic instrument, a measure of normal and/or disordered articulation, or as a method for obtaining an in-depth analysis of selected phonemes in various coarticulation contexts. This lack of clear purpose results in many methodological errors in test construction. The errors negate the positive intentions of the test as a standardized instrument.

The CAML reflects 2 decades of research demonstrating that phoneme productions are strongly influenced by the sounds that precede and follow them. The CAML, therefore, systematically tests each of eight targeted phonemes in contexts that both precede and follow bilabial, alveolar, velar-stop, and fricative sounds, to determine effects related to place and manner of production, and to identify contexts of best production. Considerable planning went into the construction of appropriate stimulus items. Efforts were made to control for factors related to stimulus complexity, including the selection of meaningful words and phrases such as "watchdog" or "her shoe," rather than nonsense words or syllables, thereby more closely approximating natural speech productions. Also, stimulus words were selected to be within a preschool child's vocabulary, to maintain simple syllable structure (91% are bisyllabic), and to be composed of the simple canonical forms characteristically used by children in continuous speech samples (89% represent simple CVC, CV, and VC syllabic shapes). Overall, item construction is a strength. Although some of the word combinations are unfamiliar to many preschool children and unlikely to be elicited spontaneously (i.e., pushpin, catbird, steel table, keep right), the protocol specifies that a delayed imitation procedure be used. This reviewer administered the test to a small sample of children ($N = 6$). The delayed imitation procedure was successful in obtaining a response for approximately 80% of the items. For the remaining items, a direct imitation was required to elicit the stimulus words.

The most problematic aspect of the CAML is related to the standardization procedures used and the resulting standard scores. Some major assumptions of a normal curve distribution were violated in both subject selection and in deriving the norms for this test. The 60 children included in the standardization population at each of the six age intervals fall short of the minimum 100 recommended for any normative sample. The problems created by the insufficient numbers are greatly compounded by the lack of representativeness in the normative sample. The 360 subjects in the standardizing population formed a homogeneous and nonrepresentative group across nearly every dimension, including geographic area, socioeconomic status, and most importantly, range of abilities. The children all attended preschool, were all from a single metropolitan area, were all from middle- and upper middle-class homes, were all rated as "normal" across seven developmental areas including intelligence, language, and motor ability, were not members of minority groups, and were all selected voluntarily on the basis of parent permission. Each of these characteristics factors out variability and representativeness as it relates to standardization in general. Several of these variables, such as socioeconomic status, intelligence, motor ability, and language ability, have been shown to strongly influence articulation performance. The resulting population is biased and nonrepresentative of any population other than developmentally normal, white, middle-class children with preschool exposure. Rather than representing a normal distribution of preschool coarticulation abilities, the normative data available for the CAML represent only a narrow range of normal articulation variability. Therefore, the scores ranked as representing extremely poor performances on the CAML (i.e., greater than 2 standard deviations from the mean) in actuality are within the average range of articulation abilities for preschool-aged children. This bias renders the standard scores useless in assessing and making comparisons among children likely to display articulation problems. In their manual, the authors recommend administration of the test to children with delayed and/or disordered articulation development, and provide case histories to illustrate this use. This generalization of use to children not represented in the norm group results in several statistically and diagnostically unsound interpretations. For example, because only normally developing children were used to establish the norms, when children with relatively mild articulation disorders are assessed, they appear to be in the severely disordered range of performance.

Standard scores are based on the distribution of the normal curve, with less than 1% of all scores falling more than three standard deviations from the mean. The misuse of the norms of the CAML, when applied to children with delayed articulation development, is evident in the manual's reporting of scores up to 12 standard deviations from the mean for children with moderate articulation problems.

Two studies of CAML test-retest reliability yielded adequate results. The authors also established adequate reliability for their scoring procedure. Several studies were conducted to establish validity, including a comparison of performance on the CAML to the McDonald's Screening Deep Test, and a comparison of performance on the CAML to intelligibility of spontaneous speech. A comparison of performance on the CAML with articulation performance within a story-retelling task is erroneously reported as content validity; it is essentially a further confirmation of concurrent validity, and not content validity. Thus, the last three studies cited supported the concurrent validity of the instrument.

Problems were evident in the data the authors used as support for construct validity. The manual reports that the data collected from the normative population support construct validity in that the younger children with normally developing articulation made significantly more errors than older children. However, analysis of their standard score tables reveals that for several of their standard scores across age groups, this relationship did not hold. For example, children between 3.6 and 3.11 years of age received a lower standard score in the category of "stop" productions than children between 3.0 and 3.5 years, indicating that with increasing age the same number of errors would reflect an improved within-age performance according to these norms. These differences were as large as two standard deviations for some scores. This problem was prevalent across all age levels and several production categories, including stops, /r/, /k/, and /t/ at the 3.6–3.11 year age level; fricative, /s/, and /f/ at 4.0–4.5 years; /f/, /l/, and /r/ at 4.6–4.11 years; and arrests, stops, /sh/, and /k/ at the 5.0–5.5 year age levels.

Aside from the problem in supporting construct validity on the basis of the normative data, these discrepancies in the scores across ages also create problems for use of these norms for diagnostic purposes, despite the authors' claims. Without changing any articulation productions, a child's performance can be judged to show improvement as he or she transitions into an older age level, when in fact the results should be the opposite. With increasing age, a continuing error should reflect a greater developmental problem. Furthermore, the interpretation of the scores is confusing by virtue of the manner in which they are reported. When reporting standard scores, the normal distribution is conventionally used in such a way that those respondents displaying the least proficiency in a skill or behavior are distributed below the mean. However, the CAML uses a distribution of errors rather than relative performance. Therefore, the worse a child's articulation performance is, the higher he or she places above the mean. This can add confusion in interpretation, particularly when guidelines for diagnosis of handicapping conditions among preschool-aged children often stipulate a performance below the mean on a standardized measure.

Another problem created by the lack of clarity or purpose in its design concerns the phonemes selected for inclusion on the CAML. The test assesses only eight phonemes, and therefore is not comprehensive enough to constitute a diagnostic test of articulation performance. As a screening device, it does assess high-frequency error phonemes. However, the test is designed to be administered to preschoolers between the ages of 2.5 to 5.5. Of the eight phonemes tested, seven have been normed as relatively late developing sounds, not considered mastered by the majority of children until 4 to 7 years of age (Shames & Wiig, 1986). Therefore, it is questionable whether preschoolers below the age of 4 should be screened on these phonemes. Because the CAML used only average or above preschoolers in its normative population, it is questionable whether these norms can be used as a basis of comparison for many children. Additionally, the manual suggests that an error analysis, reflecting various phonological processes, can be conducted from the phonetic transcription, but neither the stimuli nor the score sheet are systematically set up for this analysis.

The test is easy to administer and score, and does provide some information about production in various phonetic contexts that may be useful in the analysis of a child's articulation. The line drawings used to elicit the target words are sufficiently clear for most children to interpret accurately if they know the concepts depicted. The durability of the stimulus booklet is questionable, consisting of lightweight paper through which pictures and print from other pages can easily be seen, creating a distraction to children during test administration.

In summary, the CAML is a test instrument with well developed test stimuli designed to elicit phonemes in a variety of coarticulatory frames, but with serious problems in its test construction and norms. These problems render the test inappropriate for the assessment of the population to which it is most likely to be administered (i.e., children with articulation delays and/or disorders), at least as a standardized instrument. If used as a criterion-referenced assessment of selected phonemes, it may provide useful information about productions in a variety of phonetic contexts.

REVIEWER'S REFERENCE

Shames, G. H., and Wiig, E. H. (1986). *Human communication disorders* (2nd ed.). Columbus: Charles E. Merrill.

Review of the Coarticulation Assessment in Meaningful Language by RICHARD J. SCHISSEL, Associate Professor and Chair, Department of Speech Pathology and Audiology, Ithaca College, Ithaca, NY:

The Coarticulation Assessment in Meaningful Language (CAML) is designed to assess the effects of coarticulation on the articulatory accuracy of preschool children. It was constructed to overcome some of the purported weaknesses of the Screening Deep Test of Articulation (SDTA).

The CAML elicits production of eight of nine sounds examined by the SDTA (/s, f, ch, t, k, sh, l, r/) in meaningful words and word strings.

Each of the eight target phonemes is examined in eight contexts. Each sound is tested as part of an abutting pair: four times each in syllable arresting (bu*s* ride), and syllable releasing (big *s*un) position. The authors attempted to control canonical form (syllable shape), phonetic context, syllable structure, and linguistic structure. For example, 91% of the 57 stimulus items presented are bisyllabic. Eighty-nine percent of the 115 syllables are simple shapes of the type most frequently used by children in continuous speech: CVC, CV, VC. Phonetic context is controlled for place and manner of production. Linguistically the test contains 10 multisyllabic nouns and 47 word strings composed of verbs, adjectives, and possessive pronouns with nouns. Stimulus items are words normally included in a preschool child's vocabulary.

The test was standardized on 360 children between the ages of 2½ and 5½ years of age. All were native English speakers from middle- and upper middle-class homes. Based on the performance of this group, norms are provided for children at 6-month intervals between 2½ and 5½ years of age. Norm tables allow conversion from raw scores (total number of errors) to standard scores for easier interpretation and to allow comparison across children. Norms are provided for the total number of errors on the entire test, errors in releasing position only, arresting position only, liquids, fricatives, stops, and for each of the eight individual phonemes.

The test utilizes a delayed imitation format. Stimulus items consist of black and white line drawings. Each item is identified for the child by the examiner. For example, the examiner would say "This is a pet cat. This is a catbird. What is this?" (points to pet cat). "It's a ______." "What's this?" (points to catbird). "It's a ______."

The manual clearly presents instructions for administering, scoring, and interpreting the results. The rationale for the test is clear. Test materials are unambiguous and the scoring sheet is easy to follow. Most clinicians would find this a useful addition to their test battery. I do not recommend this test, however, and my reservations follow.

First, the content validity of the test is questionable. Content validity was not established on the published version of the test but on "an earlier, but similar version." From material presented in the manual, it appears that the canonical form and phonetic context of 28 of the 64 items were altered. Thus, there is no assurance the data provided in support of content validity are applicable to the version the clinician will be using.

The procedure used to establish this form of validity was flawed. The authors used an analysis of variance to compare total number of errors made by 30 "normally developing children" on the CAML and a story-retell task. The children were between the ages of 4 years 4 months and 4 years 8 months. The authors claim content validity on the basis of finding no significant difference in the total number or type of errors on the two tasks. There are problems with this. First, absence of evidence is not evidence of absence. The fact that the authors found no difference between performance on the two tasks does not mean that no differences existed. The authors did not include a statement regarding the power or ability of their analysis to detect a difference if one existed. Second, their subject group was too limited and homogeneous. They used only 30 "normally developing children," within a 4-month age range. The literature clearly shows that children will make more sound-production errors on spontaneous speech tasks than picture-naming tasks. The use of such a restricted sample decreased the likelihood that these differences would emerge.

The use of the total number of errors in the analysis is misleading. It is possible that subjects made errors on different sounds on the two test conditions, but that the total number of errors did not differ to a statistically significant degree. Such a finding would have suggested that the CAML does not tap the same skills as the story-retell task.

In addition, the authors' treatment of validity issues is incomplete. The approach described in the manual (comparing errors made by normally developing children on a CAML task and a spontaneous story-retell task) is informative but should be supplemented with expert opinions about the content of the test.

An effort to establish predictive validity also should have been made. The relationship between performance on the CAML and a criterion measure must be published, thereby confirming (or disconfirming) the usefulness of the CAML in meaningful treatment decisions.

Of most concern is that an effort was made to establish content validity using children only within a 4-month age range. The test is to be used with, and norms are provided for, children across a 3-year age range. It is incumbent upon test developers to establish validity of the test for all subjects for whom it is intended. Even had the authors successfully established content validity on their sample there is no assurance that the test would have been equally valid for all other children for whom it was designed.

The concurrent validity of the test also is of concern. Concurrent validity is demonstrated when there is evidence that the test correlates highly with external, independent criteria of the variable measured. The authors first compared performance on the CAML with performance on the SDTA and found very close agreement. The SDTA was a poor choice of criterion measure. The SDTA itself has never been validated. To demonstrate that the CAML measures the same behavior as the SDTA is of little usefulness because no evidence exists to show what the SDTA measures.

A further effort to establish concurrent validity was made by comparing performance on the CAML with errors in a spontaneous speech sample of 35 children of unspecified age. This procedure was well done and the results encouraging. The data suggest the test will distinguish between children with and without articulation disorders. However, there remains the problem of a restricted sample. In their comparison with the SDTA the authors used only kindergarten children. In the spontaneous speech comparison the age range of the children was not provided. It is impossible to know whether such concurrent validity as might exist for the test exists across all ages for which the test was developed.

The problems with validity are unfortunate. This test has the potential to be a popular and useful tool. However, I cannot recommend its adoption until such time as its validity has been established.

[65]

Cognitive Abilities Scale. Purpose: Allows a comprehensive assessment of cognitive development relevant to later school success. Ages 2-0 through 3-11; 1987; CAS; 6 scores: Language, Reading, Mathematics, Handwriting, Enabling Behaviors, Total; individual; 1987 price data: $93 per complete kit including 25 examiner record books, child's book, picture cards, toys, examiner's manual ('87, 87 pages); $26 per 25 examiner record books; $5 per child's book; $9 per picture cards; $39 per toys; $19 per manual; (30–45) minutes; Sharon Bradley-Johnson; PRO-ED, Inc.*

Review of the Cognitive Abilities Scale by A. DIRK HIGHTOWER, Associate Director, Center for Community Study, Psychology Department, University of Rochester, Rochester, NY:

The Cognitive Abilities Scale (CAS) fills the gap between infant assessment scales such as the Bayley Scales of Infant Development and the more traditional intelligence tests (i.e., the Stanford-Binet and the WPPSI). The CAS also provides information in pertinent areas related to school success. Recognizing tests tap only a sample of behavior within a given domain, the author of this test has chosen a truly representative sample of important school-related domains.

ADMINISTRATION AND SCORING. Descriptions of examiner competence, general testing procedures, assessing of nonvocal children, testing time, and specific subtest instructions are reasonable, clearly written, and obviously piloted with the examiner and child in mind. In conjunction with the examiner record book, those individuals familiar with standardized testing procedures will find the manual easy to use for both administration and scoring. Scoring criteria are clear and unambiguous. Suggested prompts are easy to use and flow with the test. One criticism is the test materials come in a bag and are generally of poor quality. This, however, does not affect 2- or 3-year-olds' interest in the materials, which have obviously been piloted and designed for them. An examiner who uses this kit often would want to purchase or make some type of box, briefcase, etc. to keep the materials organized during and after administrations.

INTERPRETING CAS RESULTS. The manual provides procedures to establish percentiles and standard scores for the subtests and it reports two cognitive quotients. Appropriate cautions are provided throughout the manual in regard to uses and abuses of these quotients. The author has followed the emerging standard of a mean of 100 with a standard deviation of 15 for the cognitive quotient and a mean of 10 and a standard deviation of 3 for the subtest. In addition, a 'nonvocal cognitive quotient' can be computed for nonvocal items allowing for adaptation of this test with shy, nontalkative children. Many 2- and 3-year-old children may seem shy and nonvocal during testing. Tables of standard errors of measurement are provided for both raw scores and standard scores. These allow easy interpretation and description to various interested parties such as parents and teachers. After computation of scores, the scores can then be shifted to a profile of test scores where a child's relative strengths and weaknesses can be plotted and used in planning. In fact, the author has taken note of recent criticism regarding the need for tests to provide for realistic educational planning and suggests means of doing this at both the subtest and the item profile interpretation levels. A somewhat primitive cognitive ability summary sheet is provided that allows for the examiner to list the skills learned and the skills needed to be learned under the five subtest areas.

DEVELOPMENT OF THE CAS. Item selection was obviously well researched and piloted.

Children respond well to the items and the rationale for the items is described adequately. Standardization procedures used to select the 536 students for the normative sample represent well the diverse characteristics of the major demographic characteristics of typical interest such as sex, residence, occupation of parents, race, geographic area, ethnicity, and age. One shortfall in the description of the sample is that no interaction such as race by occupation of parents or race by geographic area are provided. What was good to see, however, was that the sample did include a proportional amount of mentally retarded students in the norming sample. Alpha reliability coefficients are adequate for the subscales and range from .80 to .94 with a median of .87 for 2-year-olds with a similar range for 3-year-olds. Both the nonvocal total and the total test score are .93 or higher and more than adequate. Test-retest or stability reliability for two samples ($N = 40$ and $N = 30$) showed moderately high coefficients and are adequate for a test such as this. These scale validity coefficients appear to be adequate, although, like all measures additional information in this domain is needed.

In sum, this reviewer would not hesitate to recommend this test to other professionals who need to assess the cognitive abilities of 2- and 3-year-old children. The author appears to have fulfilled her duties regarding test development and now it is up to the test user to appropriately use the materials provided.

Review of the Cognitive Abilities Scale by GARY J. ROBERTSON, Director, Test Division, American Guidance Service, Inc., Circle Pines, MN:

The Cognitive Abilities Scale (CAS) is an "educationally relevant" individually administered assessment device for children 2 and 3 years of age. Designed for administration within 30–45 minutes, CAS contains 88 items arranged in five subtests: Language, Reading, Mathematics, Handwriting, and Enabling Behaviors. The author recommends that examiners have had graduate training in individual assessment.

RATIONALE. CAS has a dual purpose: to provide a norm-referenced assessment useful in identifying children with developmental delays and to provide information about the acquisition of specific skills useful in planning educational intervention programs. Development of CAS was motivated by the dearth of appropriate assessment instruments for 2- and 3-year-olds, the ages at which most available tests either begin or end. The dual purposes of the CAS pose an identity problem, for it is neither an intelligence test nor an achievement test, yet its results are apparently interchangeable for either type of measure. Confusion over the construct(s) measured is raised further by grouping the test content into the traditional elementary school curricular rubrics of Reading, Mathematics, and Handwriting. Items in these subtests are, at most, very elementary precursors of skills developed at later ages in these curricular areas. The author provides no justification for the imposition of this standard elementary school curriculum pattern on test content for 2- and 3-year-olds, nor does she address the lack of agreement among early childhood educators with respect to what should be taught and the age at which such teaching is most appropriate developmentally. Users who agree that the behaviors measured by CAS are appropriately taught to 2- and 3-year-olds will find the most comfort with the author's philosophy of assessment.

PRACTICAL FEATURES. Materials required to administer the CAS are the manual, record book, picture cards, story book, and small toys. Directions for administering and scoring seem clear and easy to follow. Use of a wire-o binding for the manual would have permitted examiners to keep the directions open flat during test administration; the saddlestitched binding precludes this and makes referring to the directions during testing cumbersome and awkward. The small storybook is a novel way to test for orientation to print and book-handling skills. Use of the small toys should aid in maintaining rapport as well as providing the most appropriate assessment for certain of the items.

STANDARDIZATION. The CAS was standardized on a national sample of 536 children (203 2-year-olds and 333 3-year-olds). Comparative data for the total sample and the entire U.S. are provided on selected demographic variables. The CAS sample matches the U.S. figures reasonably well except for race. According to the 1980 U.S. Census, about 27% of the sample should be minorities. Data are reported for the CAS sample in such a way that race/ethnicity are separated. It is apparent, however, that minorities are significantly underrepresented. Finer demographic breakdowns within age group and geographic region would have provided more complete information. There is no explanation of how the sample was selected, how the standardization sites were chosen, who administered the tests, nor the date of the standardization testing. The number of cases tested is sufficient to provide stable normative data.

INTERPRETATION. Standard scores (M = 10, SD = 3) are provided for the five subtests and the total test (M = 100, SD = 15). Percentile ranks are available for subtests, but not for the total battery. Unfortunately, the author labeled the battery composite standard score a quotient, when it is actually a standard score. The attempt to portray the Cognitive Quotient (CQ) as an intelligence quotient is puzzling, especially in a test developed in the mid-1980s. The provision for an interpretive index called the Nonvocal Cognitive Quotient (NCQ) for children who either do not verbalize their responses or whose speech is unintelligible is excellent; however, caution is needed in interpreting NCQ because the subtests contribute unequally to it (whereas they do contribute equally to the Cognitive Quotient). Furthermore, no data are presented correlating NCQ and CQ so it is impossible to determine the extent of overlap. The author is to be commended for encouraging confidence bands in the interpretation of standard scores and for not providing age equivalents. More explicit rules are needed, however, for standard score comparisons among subtests. This reviewer strongly objects to the author's advocacy of the use of item response data to formulate individualized education plans. In fact, the use of item responses for curricular planning is especially troublesome for two reasons: (*a*) the wide variability among the item difficulty indexes, and (*b*) the marked difficulty of the Reading subtest for both 2- and 3-year-olds and the Mathematics subtest for 2-year-olds.

RELIABILITY AND VALIDITY. Both internal consistency and test-retest reliability coefficients are presented for the CAS. Subtest internal consistency estimates range from .75–.94, with a majority of the coefficients in the .80s. The Nonvocal and Cognitive Quotients are above .90 for both ages 2 and 3. Two small samples of 2- and 3-year-old subjects provided the data for the test-retest reliability study. For subtests, the test-retest coefficients range from .69–.98, with a median of .85. For the Nonvocal and Cognitive Quotients, the test-retest coefficients range from .88–.99, with all but two values above .90. Reliability of the CAS seems generally good and quite comparable to other tests for this age range. More complete information about the two test-retest samples is needed.

The validity section is divided into three parts: content, criterion-related and construct, and predictive. Correlations between CAS Cognitive Quotients and the Stanford-Binet, the K-ABC Mental Processing Composite and Achievement Composite, and the CAS Nonvocal and K-ABC Nonverbal score are presented. These coefficients range from .69–.84 and indicate substantial overlap. Correlations of the CAS Reading subtest, Language subtest, and total test with the Test of Early Reading Ability (TERA) and the Test of Early Language Development (TELD) are reported also. Although the correlations cluster around .70, the CAS subtests and total test correlate to about the same degree with the TERA and TELD measures. No criterion-related validity data are reported for the Handwriting and Mathematics subtests.

The validity section is the weakest part of the manual. Treatment of validity in three discrete sections leads to a fragmented discussion that does not provide the overall broad unification of data and information advocated by recognized authorities (e.g., Anastasi and Cronbach). Data presented to document predictive validity would be better presented as long-term stability (relationship between CAS retests 1 year apart) and construct validity (CAS vs. Stanford-Binet). The very organization of the validity section into the three divisions cited above demonstrates the author's confusion about the topic and how best to present it. Additional data for performance on CAS versus other tests listed as having been examined during item development would help to establish the construct(s) measured by CAS.

SUMMARY. The major test development operations are, for the most part, reasonably well executed for the CAS. There are a few more subtle omissions or errors (e.g., failure to correct subtest-total test intercorrelations for spurious overlap), but these are not serious enough to interfere with the use of the test.

This reviewer's reservations about CAS stem from the author's philosophical position that CAS measures important learned behaviors that, when missed by a particular child during the test, have direct immediate implications for instruction. Developmental and maturational factors seem overlooked. The confusion about what the CAS measures is heightened by direct contradictions in the manual such as that on page 42 where the general statement is made that only skills directly related to school success were considered for inclusion, followed two paragraphs later by the statement that, for the Language subtest, the relationship of the structures measured to school success is unknown. What does CAS really measure? What skills should early childhood educators attempt to teach to 2- and 3-year-olds? Early childhood specialists who find that their views about what constitutes appropriate early childhood education assessment and intervention match those of the CAS author may find the test useful.

[66]

Cognitive Abilities Test, Form 4. Purpose: "To assess the development of cognitive abilities related to verbal, quantitative and nonverbal reasoning and problem solving." Grades K–1, 2–3, 3–12; 1954–86; CogAT; third component of the Riverside Basic Skills Assessment Program; Form 3 is still available; 1986 price data: $6.84 per 35 class record folders for Levels 1 and 2 and A–H; $9.90 per Technical Manual; Robert L. Thorndike and Elizabeth Hagen; The Riverside Publishing Co.*

a) PRIMARY BATTERY. Grades K–1, 2–3, 1979–86; 2 levels: Primary Battery, Level 1 and Primary Battery, Level 2; 3 scores: Verbal, Quantitative, Nonverbal; $6.60 per 35 practice tests for Levels 1 & 2 including directions for administration; $1.50 per directions for Levels 1 & 2 practice tests ('86, 8 pages); $42 per 35 MRC machine-scorable test booklets including Examiner's Manual and materials needed for machine-scoring (specify Level 1 or Level 2); $33.75 per 35 hand-scorable test booklets including Examiner's Manual with answer key and class record folder (specify level); $47.10 per 35 NCS test booklets including NCS directions for administration (specify level); $1.26 per scoring key (indicate level); $2.70 per NCS directions for administration ('86, 21 pages each level); $6.15 per Examiner's Manual for Levels 1 & 2 ('86, 42 pages); scoring service available from publisher; 90(110) minutes in at least 3 sessions.

b) MULTILEVEL EDITION. Grades 3–12; 1978–86; 8 overlapping levels: Level A through Level H; 3 scores: Verbal, Quantitative, Nonverbal; $16.86 per 100 practice tests for Levels A–H including 3 directions for administration; $3.66 per Multilevel Battery test booklet, Levels A–H ('86, 76 pages); $39.45 per 35 separate-level test booklets including directions for administration (specify Level A, B, C, D, E, F, G, or H); $15 per 35 MRC answer sheets including Examiner's Manual and materials needed for machine-scoring (specify level); $24 per 100 MRC answer sheets and materials needed for machine-scoring (specify level); $114.99 per 500 MRC answer sheets and materials needed for machine-scoring (specify level); $96 per 250 NCS 7010 answer folders (specify level); $9 per MRC scoring masks (specify level); $1.95 per scoring key booklet, Levels A–H, $1.50 per directions for Levels A–H practice tests ('86, 14 pages); $2.70 per directions for administration for separate-level booklets ('86, 29 pages); $6.15 per Examiner's Manual for Levels A–H ('86, 36 pages); scoring service available from publisher; 90(140) minutes in 3 sessions.

For review by Charles J. Ansorge of an earlier edition, see 9:240 (5 references); see also T3:483 (32 references); for reviews by Kenneth D. Hopkins and Robert C. Nichols, see 8:181 (12 references); for reviews by Marcel L. Goldschmid and Carol K. Tittle and an excerpted review by Richard C. Cox of the primary batteries, see 7:343.

TEST REFERENCES

1. Holzman, T. G., Pellegrino, J. W., & Glaser, R. (1983). Cognitive variables in series completion. *Journal of Educational Psychology*, 75, 603-618.

2. Sternberg, R. J., & Gardner, M. K. (1983). Unities in inductive reasoning. *Journal of Experimental Psychology: General*, 112, 80-116.

3. Burton, E., & Sinatra, R. (1984). Relationship of cognitive style and word type for beginning readers. *Reading World*, 24 (1), 65-75.

4. Harty, H., & Beall, D. (1984). Attitudes toward science of gifted and nongifted fifth graders. *Journal of Research Teaching*, 21, 483-488.

5. Wilson, L. R., & Cone, T. (1984). The regression equation method of determining academic discrepancy. *Journal of School Psychology*, 22, 95-110.

6. Alderton, D. L., Goldman, S. R., & Pellegrino, J. W. (1985). Individual differences in process outcomes for verbal analogy and classification solution. *Intelligence*, 9, 69-85.

7. Fennema, E., & Tartre, L. A. (1985). The use of spatial visualization in mathematics by girls and boys. *Journal for Research in Mathematics Education*, 16, 184-206.

8. Harty, H., Hamrick, L., & Samuel, K. V. (1985). Relationships between middle school students' science concept structure interrelatedness competence and selected cognitive and affective tendencies. *Journal of Research in Science Teaching*, 22, 179-191.

9. Holmes, B. C., & Allison, R. W. (1985). The effect of four modes of reading on children's comprehension. *Reading Research and Instruction*, 25, 9-20.

10. Martin, D. J., & Dunbar, S. B. (1985). Hierarchical factoring in a standardized achievement battery. *Educational and Psychological Measurement*, 45, 343-351.

11. Bender, W. N. (1986). Instructional grouping and individualization for mainstreamed learning disabled children and adolescents. *Child Study Journal*, 16, 207-215.
12. Berk, L. E. (1986). Relationship of elementary school children's private speech to behavioral accompaniment to task, attention, and task performance. *Developmental Psychology*, 22, 671-680.
13. Lochman, J. E., & Lampron, L. B. (1986). Situational social problem-solving skills and self-esteem of aggressive and nonaggressive boys. *Journal of Abnormal Child Psychology*, 14, 605-617.

Review of the Cognitive Abilities Test, Form 4 by ANNE ANASTASI, Professor Emeritus of Psychology, Fordham University, Bronx, NY:

NATURE OF THE REVISION. While retaining the major features of the earlier forms, this revision of the Cognitive Abilities Test (CogAT) incorporates the periodic updating and refinements expected in a well-constructed instrument. In both the Primary Battery and Multilevel Edition, Form 4 provides more nearly equal coverage of the Verbal, Quantitative, and Nonverbal areas than did Form 3. The two levels of the Primary Battery (K–1, 2–3), which formerly yielded only a single total score derived from four tests, now yield separate Verbal, Quantitative, and Nonverbal scores, each derived from two tests.

In the Multilevel Edition (3–12), each battery now contains three tests and requires 30 minutes of actual working time, slightly less than in Form 3. Each battery utilizes one type of symbols or concepts, namely verbal, numerical/quantitative, or geometric/spatial; all the batteries, however, use some pictorial content, especially at the lower levels. The tests include: (Verbal Battery) Verbal Classification, Sentence Completion, Verbal Analogies; (Quantitative Battery) Quantitative Relations, Number Series, Equation Building; (Nonverbal Battery) Figure Classification, Figure Analogies, Figure Analysis—the last-named is a new test, replacing the Figure Synthesis test of Form 3. This new test is essentially a printed adaptation of the familiar paper folding and cutting test, using diagrams to show folding and position of punched holes, as well as appearance of paper when unfolded. All tests now use multiple-choice items and all provide 5 choices except for Quantitative Relations, which provides 3 (requiring essentially a judgment of greater, less, or equal).

As in the earlier forms, CogAT Form 4 uses overlapping multilevel testing to adapt the difficulty level of items to broad ability differences. In the Multilevel Edition, "Start" and "Stop" points for each of the 9 levels are printed on the test booklet and also given orally by the examiner. These levels correspond to the student's grade placement, but the selection may be modified from supplementary information, such as the student's reading competence.

STANDARDIZATION AND NORMS. In its present form, CogAT has again been jointly normed with two achievement batteries, the Iowa Tests of Basic Skills (ITBS) for grades K–9 and the Tests of Achievement and Proficiency (TAP) for grades 9–12, thereby providing comparability of scores across the two types of tests. The standardization sample of over 160,000 students comprised three subsamples representative of the national student population in public schools, Catholic schools, and private non-Catholic schools. Within the total sample, approximately 16,500 were retested from fall to spring. The stratification variables were size of enrollment within school districts, geographic region, and socioeconomic status. The actual sample percentages were weighted so as to bring them closer to the national percentages for the computation of norms. Additional standardization samples for grades K–12 were tested with CogAT Forms 3 and 4 in order to equate the two forms; and a sample of third-grade pupils took Primary Level 2 and the lowest level of the Multilevel Edition to provide common anchoring data for item scaling across the entire K–12 span.

Normative tables are provided to convert raw scores on Verbal, Quantitative, and Nonverbal cognitive areas into Standard Age Scores (SAS). These are normalized standard scores (M = 100, SD = 16) within age groups. Also available are percentile ranks and stanines within age and within grade. The normative tables provide four 3-month age levels within each year of age, and three levels within each grade (for fall, winter, and spring testing). As a further interpretive aid, the final version of the Examiner's Manual (Multilevel Edition, 1986) provides interpretive cautions and 11 abbreviated case studies. This is a welcome addition in view of the growing recognition of the key role of the test user in the interpretation of test results and in their appropriate utilization in action recommendations. Similar interpretive aids are included in the final version of the *Examiner's Manual for the Primary Battery* (1986).

ITEM ANALYSES. In 1983, a national item tryout was conducted for the three tests that were being jointly revised (CogAT, ITBS, TAP). The sample included approximately 47,000 students in 38 states and was designed to oversample minority students in order to provide sufficient data to analyze group differences in performance. Both traditional and Item Response Theory techniques were used to select items and to identify those that were potentially unfair. Successive qualitative reviews for both ethnic and gender bias were also conducted, including a final review by a panel of independent experts selected on the basis of geographic region and ethnic composition.

RELIABILITY AND VALIDITY. The Preliminary Technical Summary available when CogAT-4 was first released for operational use in 1986 covers all three jointly developed tests, with relatively meager information on CogAT interspersed between coverage of the two achievement batteries. The data analyses are only tentative because of the use of small subsamples, raw scores rather than scaled scores, unweighted percentages of cases in standardization sample, and other limitations specific to particular analyses. It is apparent that for a direct evaluation of the psychometric properties of CogAT-4, the test user must examine the forthcoming Technical Manual (1987) devoted exclusively to CogAT-4. Were this a new test, it should not have been released for operational use until the information provided in the complete Technical Manual was available.

For the present instrument, however, the situation differs in two major respects. First, CogAT is a well-established and widely known test, for which detailed information is available in the technical manuals of earlier editions. Second, the changes introduced in the present edition are relatively minor and of such a nature as to represent technical improvements. Hence, it is reasonable to expect that the psychometric quality of the current instrument is either essentially unchanged or slightly better.

The available data on preliminary analyses support this expectation. K-R 20 reliability coefficients for Verbal, Quantitative, and Nonverbal batteries cluster around the low .90s. *SEM*s are available for use in setting "accuracy bands" around obtained battery scores. Long-term stability has been investigated with earlier forms. With the present form over intervals of 2 and 4 years, the coefficients are in the .80s for Verbal and Quantitative batteries and in the .70s for the Nonverbal battery. Intercorrelations and factor analyses of Verbal, Quantitative, and Nonverbal scores indicate a large general factor through the three batteries, although some additional common variance is accounted for by the separate battery scores. The Verbal and Quantitative scores are better predictors of achievement test performance and school grades than are the Nonverbal scores, but the latter are recommended for possible usefulness for students with reading disabilities and for foreign-language speakers with inadequate facility in English. These Nonverbal scores may also have some predictive value for success in specialized academic or occupational areas.

OVERVIEW. This well-established, group-administered measure of educationally relevant aptitude areas has undergone some moderate content revisions and a complete restandardization, conducted jointly with ITBS and TAP. The changes are such as to improve the technical quality and practical usefulness of the instrument. Detailed evaluation of the present edition requires an examination of the forthcoming complete Technical Manual.

Review of the Cognitive Abilities Test, Form 4 by DOUGLAS FUCHS, Associate Professor of Special Education, George Peabody College, Vanderbilt University, Nashville, TN:

The Riverside Basic Skills Assessment Program includes (*a*) two achievement tests, the Iowa Test of Basic Skills (ITBS) and Tests of Achievement and Proficiency (TAP), and (*b*) an aptitude test, the Cognitive Abilities Test (CogAT), Form 4. The CogAT, Form 4 consists of a Primary Battery for grades K–3 and a Multilevel Edition for grades 3–12. This overlapping of grades "provides for . . . flexibility in adapting the type and difficulty level of the tests to individual differences among students" (p. 1, Preliminary Examiner's Manual, Primary Battery hereafter described as "Examiner's Manual—Primary").

PRIMARY BATTERY. *General description*. The Primary Battery was first introduced in 1968 as a measure of grade K–3 students' development of cognitive skills. In keeping with earlier editions, Form 4 comprises two levels: Level 1 for grades K–1 and Level 2 for grades 2–3. This version also continues to measure three "cognitive skill areas." Unlike prior editions, however, Levels 1 and 2 have been expanded from four to six subtests, with 24 to 30 items per subtest, and the user now may calculate separate scores for each cognitive skill area. Skill areas and corresponding subtests follow: Verbal (Vocabulary and Verbal Classification); Quantitative (Relational Concepts and Quantitative Concepts); and Nonverbal (Figure Classification and Matrices).

The Examiner's Manual—Primary states these skill areas should be important to teachers because they are necessary precursors to progress in school tasks like reading: "If an individual does not develop an adequate set of these basic learning skills, he or she is likely to be handicapped in dealing successfully with school tasks throughout his or her school years" (p. 2). There is an implicit suggestion that if a pupil demonstrates an inadequate grasp of the CogAT's developmental or precursor "basic learning skills" then the teacher's responsibility is to teach those skills (see p. 2). In other words, CogAT subtests should be regarded as assessment tasks as well as potential foci of instruction. This suggested assessment-to-instruction linkage will be welcomed by many test users. However, the links in this chain appear hypothetical. No empirical evidence is offered to substantiate the notion that mastery of the CogAT skill areas is necessary for eventual mastery of basic school tasks like reading.

Administration and scoring. The Primary Battery has no time limit. Items are presented one at a time with rate of presentation determined by the test administrator. The Examiner's Manual—Primary (p. 7) indicates that each subtest can be presented in 12 to 18 minutes. It is recommended that, for Levels 1 and 2, the six subtests be administered in three sessions, two subtests per session. The suggested duration of each testing session ranges from 35 to 40 minutes (p. 7). Specific and helpful suggestions are provided with respect to preparing pupils for testing, pacing the presentation of items, and scheduling sessions (see pp. 6–8). The test booklets have been designed to be machine scored, however, a hand-scorable edition of the booklets is available. All six subtests must be completed for machine scoring (pp. 4–5, Examiner's Manual—Primary).

MULTILEVEL EDITION. *General description.* The Multilevel Edition is a revision and extension of the Lorge-Thorndike Intelligence Tests and earlier editions of the CogAT. The Multilevel Edition's tripartite organization is similar to that of the Primary Battery: Verbal, Quantitative, and Nonverbal. Each of these so-called "batteries" subsumes three subtests: For Verbal, there is Sentence Completion, Verbal Analogies, and Verbal Classification; for Quantitative, there is Equation Building, Number Series, and Quantitative Relations; and for Nonverbal, there is Figure Analogies, Figure Analysis, and Figure Classification. The Figure Analogies subtest is new, which, according to the authors, contributes to a more balanced representation of subtests among the three batteries. Additionally, testing time has been shortened and test directions clarified.

For each subtest, items are arranged in ascending order of difficulty and are assigned to eight levels ranging from A–H. Separate scores are reported for each battery; there is no total score that "can give a misleading picture of the cognitive development of an individual whose cognitive skills in one area are much more highly developed than in the other areas" (p.5, Preliminary Examiner's Manual, Multilevel Edition hereafter described as Examiner's Manual—Multilevel). It is claimed that the Verbal and Quantitative batteries are good predictors of school success, and that scores on the Nonverbal battery "are significantly correlated with success in secondary and higher level mathematics, in the physical sciences, and . . . architecture and engineering" (p. 6, Examiner's Manual—Multilevel). There are no data presented in the Examiner's Manual—Multilevel nor in the Preliminary Technical Summary (referred to below as Technical Manual) to substantiate these claims.

Administration and scoring. A 76-page spiral-bound reusable test booklet contains Verbal, Quantitative, and Nonverbal batteries for grades 3–12. Single-level test booklets (A through H) are also available. Whereas the Primary Battery is a power test, the Multilevel Edition is a speed test. Number of items and time limits for each battery follow: for Verbal,

75 items, 30 minutes; for Quantitative, 60 items, 30 minutes; and for Nonverbal, 65 items, 30 minutes. Permissible work time and estimated overall administration time for each subtest is provided in a useful table (p. 10, Examiner's Manual—Multilevel). This table also suggests use of three test sessions and administration of one battery (three subtests) per session. A "Preparations for Testing" section in the Examiner's Manual—Multilevel (pp. 9–11) provides useful information to prepare test administrators and students by discussing test directions and format, scheduling, necessary materials, and general procedures. Scores for each battery include: number of items attempted, number of items correct, Standard Age Score, percentile rank and stanine for age group, and percentile rank and stanine for grade group. The Multilevel tests may be machine or hand scored.

ITEM SELECTION. Primary Battery and Multilevel Edition items were explored qualitatively and quantitatively for possible ethnic and gender bias. The qualitative analysis comprised three steps (see p. 8, Technical Manual). First, items were reviewed by author-assembled "editorial teams," which are never defined. Second, the publisher's editorial staff conducted an independent review. Third, the items were studied by "a panel of independent experts selected on the basis of geographic region and ethnic composition" (p. 8). Following this qualitative review, test items from the CogAT, ITBS, and TAP were evaluated for fairness as part of a National Item Tryout Study in Fall 1983. Whereas it is reported on page 8 of the Technical manual that 47,000 students in 38 states participated, one reads on the next page that 48,000 pupils in 35 states were included.

On page 5 of the Examiner's Manual—Multilevel it is reported that, "Separate analyses of item difficulty and discrimination were made for white and for minority students and for males and females. Items that showed atypical patterns of difficulty between white and minority students or between males and females were eliminated from the final test." Neither the Technical Manual nor either of the two examiner's manuals describe findings from these analyses. And, whereas the Technical Manual presents evidence on (*a*) floor and ceiling characteristics, (*b*) completion rates, and (*c*) summary difficulty and discrimination statistics for the ITBS and TAP (see Tables 4.9–4.12, pp. 44–62), no such information is provided for CogAT, Form 4 items.

NORMS AND STANDARDIZATION. Standardization of Form 4 was accomplished in October/November 1984 and April/May 1985. Because it was normed jointly with the ITBS and TAP, users can compare a student's performance on either achievement test with performance on the CogAT, thereby "helping to identify those students whose achievement deviates significantly from their level of cognitive development" (p. 8, Examiner's Manual—Multilevel). The educational importance of this information, however, is unclear. A "preliminary" count indicated that 550 schools and 153,000 pupils participated in the Fall 1984 standardization (see Table 3.8, p. 18, Technical Manual), with more than 14,000 per grade (p. 11, Technical Manual). The Spring 1985 sample reportedly comprised the students who paticipated in Fall testing (see p. 11). However, there is no discussion of probable attrition among the Fall standardization population.

Selecting public schools. All public school districts in the nation were stratified into nine size-of-enrollment categories(see Table 3.1, p. 13, Technical Manual), grouped by four geographic regions (see Table 3.2, p. 14, Technical Manual), and divided into five levels of SES on the basis of the 1980 census (see Table 3.3, p. 14). Accompanying such sorting was "a random selection procedure" (p. 12, Technical Manual) to choose representative districts. This procedure, however, is not described. Moreover, there is no discussion of probable situations in which one or more chosen districts refused to participate in the standardization. Was there a replacement pool from which districts were selected randomly? How many districts decided *not* to participate and why? Were these noncooperative districts different from cooperative ones?

After a school district agreed to participate, "one of three sampling plans" (p. 12) was used to select school buildings representative of the district's academic achievement. Although the three sampling plans are not described, they appear to have depended on a rank ordering of the school buildings by administrators who "were requested to use objective data (preferably previous achievement test results)" (p. 12).

There is no documentation for the accuracy of these ratings.

Selecting private schools. All Catholic schools were stratified (*a*) by five enrollment categories based on the size of the diocese of which the schools were members and (*b*) by the four geographic regions used for the public school sample (see Tables 3.4 and 3.5, p. 16, Technical Manual). Private non-Catholic schools were stratified by five types of school (e.g., Baptist, Lutheran, Seventh-Day Adventist) and the same four geographic regions (see Tables 3.6 and 3.7, p. 17, Technical Manual).

Sample weighting. Following Fall testing, the proportions of pupils within each stratification category (e.g., geographic region) were adjusted by weighting so they would approximate national percentages. Size of school district, geographic region, SES, and public-private balance were considered simultaneously in assigning these weights (see p. 20, Technical Manual).

RELIABILITY. Table 4.3 (pp. 27–28, Technical Manual) shows means, standard deviations, standard errors of measurement, and internal reliability (K-R 20) by grade level and Verbal, Quantitative, and Nonverbal skill areas. These summary data are based on unweighted distributions of scores from the Fall 1984 testing. Internal reliability coefficients range from .82 to .94. No other form of reliability is reported. The test authors caution that these data are preliminary and promise that, "More complete technical descriptions . . . will be included in subsequent guides and manuals" (p. 21, Technical Manual). Such caution and promises, however, do not prevent the authors from claiming that, "reliabilities of the tests of the Riverside Basic Skills Assessment Program are quite high" (p. 22, Technical Manual) and that, "users can have confidence in the scores from these tests, and in interpretations for individual students as well as for classes, buildings, or districts" (p. 22).

Given the preliminary and limited nature of the CogAT's reliability data, these claims appear unjustified. Internal consistency reliability is often viewed as less important than test-retest reliability, and, as stated in the *Standards for Educational and Psychological Testing* (American Educational Research Association, American Psychological Association, & National Council on Measurement in Education, 1985), "Coefficients based on internal analysis should not be interpreted as substitutes for alternate-form reliability or estimates of stability over time" (Standard 2.6, p. 22). Stability over time data for Verbal, Quantitative, and Nonverbal skill areas *are* presented in Table 4.8 (p. 42, Technical Manual), but they come from "earlier Cognitive Ability Test manuals" (p. 41, Technical Manual), and may not be viewed as indicative of the long-term stability of the CogAT, Form 4.

VALIDITY. Currently, the CogAT, Form 4 has scant validity data. Table 4.7 (p. 41, Technical Manual) displays raw score intercorrelations among Verbal, Quantitative, and Nonverbal skill areas. These correlation coefficients, which range from .53 to .84, are presented as evidence of the test's construct validity (p. 41). However, there is no interpretation of the correlation coefficients, and the reader is left to guess at their possible theoretical or practical importance. Moreover, they were "based on a small sample identified for a special study" (footnote to Table 4.7, p. 41), raising the issue of whether they are representative of the entire standardization population.

The authors do not discuss the test's content validity nor do they present data on its concurrent or predictive validity. Instead, they describe findings from studies on earlier versions of the test, which related performance on the CogAT to contemporaneous reading and math grades and scores on the Stanford-Binet and Differential Aptitude Tests (see p. 42, Technical Manual). The authors appear to acknowledge implicitly the absence of clear and meaningful validity data in their current examiner and technical manuals when they promise, "Statistical evidence on the construct . . . criterion . . . and factorial validity will be found in the [non-preliminary] Technical Manual for Form 4, to be available shortly" (p. 4, Examiner's Manual—Multilevel). Thus, it is difficult to understand the assertion that, "Such [reliability and validity] studies for these three test batteries [CogAT, ITBS, and TAP] . . . have been reported earlier in Part 4 [of the Technical Manual]. With the use of such reliability and validity information, test users . . . can help to insure fairness to all students by recognizing possible errors in all scores and by using the scores in conjunction with other information about the student so that correct educational decisions can be made" (p. 63, Technical Manual).

SUMMARY. The CogAT, Form 4 is a revision of Form 3. Modifications include the expansion of Levels 1 and 2 of the Primary Battery from four to six subtests, and the opportunity now to derive separate scores for Verbal, Quantitative, and Nonverbal skill areas. Regarding the Multilevel Edition, there is a new Figure Analogies subtest and testing time has been reduced. Additionally, Form 4 was renormed in 1984–85. Test materials and guidelines for administration reflect careful design. Unfortunately, much important information on the technical characteristics of this new version is missing from the two preliminary examiner manuals and technical manual. Unsubstantiated claims for the test's reliability and validity are a poor proxy for pertinent data.

REVIEWER'S REFERENCE

American Educational Research Association, American Psychological Association, & National Council on Measurement in Education. (1985). *Standards for educational and psychological testing*. Washington, DC: American Psychological Association, Inc.

[67]

College Student Experiences Questionnaire. Purpose: Measures "the quality of effort students put into using the facilities and opportunities provided for their learning and development in college." College students; 1979–87; CSEQ; 6 areas: College Activities, Conversations, Reading/Writing, Opinions About College, The College Environment, Estimate of Gains; 1986 price data: $175 basic participation fee and $1 per questionnaire processed (includes all student responses and scores on tape, plus summary computer report of results); $.40 per questionnaire and information booklet; $12 per test manual and norms ('87, 154 pages); National Computer Systems scoring service, $1 per test; (35–45) minutes; C. Robert Pace; Center for the Study of Evaluation.*

For reviews by Robert D. Brown and John K. Miller, see 9:246 (1 reference).

Review of the College Student Experiences Questionnaire by DAVID A. DECOSTER, Vice President for Student Affairs, Indiana University of Pennsylvania, Indiana, PA:

Students learn not only because of what takes place in the college classroom but because of all the experiences, opportunities, and interactions that occur during the college years. The author of the College Student Experiences Questionnaire (CSEQ) understands that the educational process is not synonymous with intellectual growth and has incorporated a developmental perspective in this survey instrument designed to evaluate the college experience. Thus, in addition to cognitive growth, the questionnaire includes items relating to personality development and the extent to which students utilize major campus facilities.

Another underlying concept of the CSEQ that will be attractive to developmental educators is that the "process" of education has an importance distinct from the "product." Consequently, the CSEQ assesses student behavior that has the potential to enhance learning through a positive utilization of the social-psychological environment as well as the physical environment offered by the institution. The CSEQ asks students to respond to statements intended to measure the "quality of effort" that they contribute to the educational process or, stated another way, the amount of time and initiative that they invest toward enhancing their own growth and development. Once we analyze how well students take advantage of the institution's resources, inferences can be made regarding facilities that might be improved, opportunities that could be created, or programs that should be revised to provide a more fulfilling college experience.

Approximately 50 percent of the questionnaire's content is devoted to measuring "quality of effort" through students' self-reported responses regarding the frequency in which they engage in activities that comprise 14 separate scales: Course Learning; Library; Art, Music, Theater; Science/Technology; Student Union; Athletic and Recreation Facilities; Dormitory or Fraternity/Sorority; Experiences with Faculty; Clubs and Organizations; Experiences in Writing; Personal Experiences; Student Acquaintances; Topics of Conversation; and Information in Conversations. Each scale is composed of 6 to 12 activities or items with most of the scales having 10 items each. Students are asked to indicate how frequently they engage in each of the 142 separate activities: "never," "occasionally," "often," or "very often." For example, "In your experience at this college during the current school year, about how often have you done each of the following? . . . Discussed your career plans and ambitions with a faculty member" (Experiences with Faculty Scale) or "Attended a concert or other music event at the college" (Art, Music, Theater

Scale). Each of the Quality of Effort scales arrange the activities in a hierarchy or Guttman-type scale with the beginning activities requiring less effort to achieve than the latter activities.

The questionnaire also contains a "Background Information" section consisting of 17 demographic items commonly used to profile student characteristics as well as: two items requiring reading and writing activities, two items relating to student satisfaction with their college experience, and an item asking the degree to which students agree that "they have to take the initiative" in order to benefit from college.

Another major section of the CSEQ concentrates on characteristics of the college environment by asking students to judge the emphasis their college places on developing five qualities: scholarly and intellectual; aesthetic, expressive, and creative; critical, evaluative, and analytical; vocational and occupational competence; and the personal relevance and practical value of courses. Students rate each dimension from "strong emphasis" to "weak emphasis" on a 7-point scale. On three additional items students rate their relationships with other students, with faculty members, and with administrative officials.

The last major section entitled "Estimate of Gains" consists of 21 items that each describe a learning outcome. Students are asked to reflect on the progress they have made in achieving a variety of commonly recognized objectives of a college education by responding "very little," "some," "quite a bit," or "very much." Examples include: "Gaining a broad general education about different fields of knowledge"; "Becoming aware of different philosophies, cultures, and ways of life"; and "Ability to learn on your own, pursue ideas, and find information you need." As the test author notes, this section asks students to make self-defined, "value added" judgments regarding the progress they have made toward fulfilling specific learning objectives since entering college.

Test administrators have the benefit of two publications, *CSEQ: Test Manual and Norms* and a research monograph entitled *Measuring the Quality of College Student Experiences* that summarize the rationale for the questionnaire and report data regarding norms, item and scale intercorrelations, and factor analysis for each of the scales. Both publications are authored by the CSEQ author and both present information in a logical, readable, and understandable format. The monograph is particularly helpful in relating the results of studies conducted since 1979 that have relevance to the development of the CSEQ and how the questionnaire has been utilized effectively for purposes of institutional research and evaluation.

The CSEQ was first published in 1979 and a slightly revised second edition was available in 1983. Norms for the second edition are reported for student samples from 74 institutions ($N = 25,606$) during the time period from 1983 to 1986. The responses to every item are reported in percentages and it is especially helpful that the normative data are categorized by four institutional types: doctoral granting universities, comprehensive colleges and universities, general liberal arts colleges, and selective liberal arts colleges. All groups contain an adequate sample size although the selected liberal arts category has considerably fewer institutions and a smaller number of students represented than the other three populations.

Utilizing a 10% random sample of the same diverse student populations, statistical properties for the CSEQ are described. Alpha reliability coefficients are reported in a range from .82 to .92 for the Quality of Effort scales—slightly higher than those reported for the first edition. Exploratory factor analysis data are presented and discussed for each of the 14 scales. In general, items within each scale are correlated positively suggesting that the activities have been clustered and collectively contribute to a well-defined scale. Factor analysis of these scales produced four factors: academic, scholarly activities; informal interpersonal activities; group facilities and organized activities; and science activities. The science factor has a relatively low correlation with the other three factors. Of special interest is that both the interpersonal factor and group facilities factor correlate positively with the academic factor providing an indication of the mutually supportive relationship between cognitive and affective aspects of the college experience.

The distribution of student responses to the eight items regarding the college environment are all skewed toward positive perceptions. Item intercorrelations reveal that the items are all positively related and, further, factor analysis resulted in three factors that are also positively correlated: supportive personal relationships; scholarly, intellectual emphasis; and vocational, practical emphasis.

Item intercorrelations for the Estimate of Gains section vary from -.03 to .80 with a median intercorrelation of .24. Factor analysis of the 21 items resulted in five factors with the item regarding computer skills remaining independent of these factors: Personal/Social; Science and Technology; General Education, Literature and the Arts; Intellectual Skills; and Vocational Preparation.

The CSEQ is a well-conceived standardized survey that has considerable utility for college educators and administrators. It is relatively easy to administer, provides for a centralized scoring service, and offers national norms for four types of institutions. The author demonstrates how the questionnaire can be used effectively in self-studies, program evaluations, accreditation reviews, and in comparing special student populations. The CSEQ has excellent potential for institutions involved in student outcomes assessment programs because of the broad applicability of the data for all constituency groups of an institution. Although somewhat cumbersome for working with individual students, the questionnaire could provide meaningful information for educator-student discussions within the context of a mentoring relationship or a developmental advising program—a use that is not presently recommended or intended by the test author.

Review of the College Student Experiences Questionnaire by SUSAN MCCAMMON, Assistant Professor of Psychology, East Carolina University, Greenville, NC:

The College Student Experiences Questionnaire (CSEQ) is a battery of tests that measures three aspects of college experience. The 14 Activity scales measure the Quality of Effort (QE) students put into using facilities available at most colleges, capitalizing on opportunities for personal experiences, and becoming involved in campus groups. Eight features of the College Environment are assessed through questions reflecting students' perceptions of the purposes of the organization and the supportiveness of personal relationships within the environment. In the Estimate of Gains section the students rate the progress they have made in 21 general goals of undergraduate education. In addition, data are collected on students' satisfaction with college, how much reading and writing they have done, and students' backgrounds and status. There is also space on the answer sheet for 10 locally constructed questions.

The CSEQ was originally published in 1979, slightly revised in content in 1983, and modified in format in 1986. Description and discussion of the CSEQ are presented in a monograph (Pace, 1984) and in the recent Manual. The most recent normative data are based upon responses of 25,606 undergraduates from 74 colleges and universities from 1983–86. The data are presented according to institutional type (doctoral granting universities, selective liberal arts colleges, etc.). The test developers believe the current norms are fairly stable but have promised a supplemental update if new studies reveal significant changes. Data on psychometric properties of the CSEQ are provided by a 10% random sampling of respondents from the norm population. Students report on their activities and perceptions during the current school year. Therefore, testing time is recommended for the spring of the year.

Pace offers the CSEQ as providing a descriptive profile of student life; a new dimension for understanding college outcomes (quality of effort); and measures of the quality of undergraduate experience, education, and development. He suggests it would be useful in college self-study, institutional research (e.g., evaluation and assessment of student recruitment and retention), and accreditation review.

The approach employed in the CSEQ is based on a theory of student involvement, with practical implications for college administrators, staff, and faculty. As Astin (1984) observed, the involvement approach encourages educators to concentrate on what students *do*, and suggests that getting students involved is a more useful construct than motivating them. It is a twist from our usual concern with focusing on content (preparing our lectures) and resources (creating physical facilities) to view *student time* as the most important institutional resource. Empirical support for this stance is provided in Astin's (1975) study, which linked student persistence versus dropping out with student involvement. Pace's "effort" variable is a similar but narrower term, and forms the conceptual basis for his Activity Scales.

ACTIVITY SCALES. On 11 of 14 scales the mean is near the midpoint of the scale, with useful variability of obtained scores. The test Manual reports high reliabilities for the scales; Cronbach's coefficient-Alpha values range from .82 to .92. However, in Smart and McLaughlin's (1986) study employing three groupings of the scales, the internal consistency (also using Cronbach's alpha) ranged from modest (.54 for group effort) to strong (.74 for academic effort). The scales are assumed to consist of one dominant factor but multifactor solutions were also identified. In the earlier CSEQ manuscript the scales were described as Guttman scales, but in the current Manual this claim has been dropped. Instead the scales are described as "Guttman-like," revealing a range of difficulty in the responses, reflecting that some activities require more effort than others with potentially greater impact on educational and developmental outcomes.

COLLEGE ENVIRONMENT SCALES. Eight features of the college environment are rated on a 7-point scale. These ratings cluster toward the more favorable end of the scale with few negative ratings.

ESTIMATE OF GAINS. Five factors, and an independent issue of computer use, were identified from analyzing responses estimating gains or progress made in college. The authors concluded the internal structure of these measures of gains "is stable and dependable." This conclusion seems to be based on intercorrelations among the gain scores and the fact that the most current factor analysis results match those obtained in 1983. Looking at developmental changes to see if upperclass students report more progress than freshmen would reflect one aspect of construct validity, but the manual does not present the data by college class.

RELATIONSHIP BETWEEN EFFORT AND GAINS. The QE scales were related to estimates of gains to study the relationship between QE measures and outcomes. For example, the correlations between QE in science activities was .66 with gains in Science and Technology and .35 with gains in Intellectual Skills. The new Manual presents no new regression data using QE to predict gains. However, Smart and McLaughlin (1986) used multiple regression to identify the unique ability of the QE scales (separated from influences of precollege variables) to explain outcomes. When QE scales were added to precollege information, increases in proportions of explained variance ranged from .17 to .28 across the outcome measures.

LIMITATIONS OF RELIABILITY AND VALIDITY INFORMATION. Reliability is explored only through study of interitem consistency. No test-retest reliabilities are reported and alternate form reliability is not examined. That type of investigation could address the critique by Miller (1984) that homogeneity of the scales may be an artifact of the grouping and physical presentation of items. Face validity is good as evidenced by the high response rate of students. Most subjects completed all items, with most scales missing about 2% of cases and none missing more than 4%. Validity information remains dependent on data relating sets of CSEQ variables to each other and to factorial analysis. These relationships do make sense. I found myself predicting the findings of the activity frequency ratings based on my teaching experience. Yes, students are more likely to have discussed personal problems with a faculty member than to have worked on a research project with her. Yes, scale means for library use were lower than means for most other activities. However, users might feel greater confidence in the CSEQ if measures external to it confirmed its findings or revealed moderately high correlations. The Manual provides no reports comparing the CSEQ scales to other measures.

Those interested in using the CSEQ are advised to heed McLaughlin and Smart's (1986) suggestion that investigators examine the reliabilities of the QE scales, and that they use multivariate procedures to identify independent relationships among the QE scales and outcome measures. With these caveats, those interested in assessing student behaviors and educational/personal outcomes have a valuable tool in the CSEQ. Grounded in a credible theoretical base, the QE measures offer a way to quantify and gauge the quality of student involvement. Extensive normative data allow institutions of varied types and sizes to compare with other schools. Those involved in institutional research and programming will find this a very useful measure in meeting accountability demands and giving insight into student development and design of more effective learning environments.

REVIEWER'S REFERENCES

Astin, A. W. (1975). *Preventing students from dropping out.* San Francisco: Jossey-Bass.

Astin, A. W. (1984). Student involvement: A developmental theory for higher education. *Journal of College Student Personnel,* 25, 297-308.

Pace, C. R. (1984). *Measuring the quality of college student experiences.* Los Angeles: Higher Education Research Institute, UCLA.

Miller, J. K. (1985). [Review of College Student Experiences.] In J. V. Mitchell, Jr. (Ed.), *The ninth mental measurements yearbook* (pp. 366-368). Lincoln, NE: Buros Institute of Mental Measurements.

Smart, J. C., & McLaughlin, G. W. (1986). Outcomes assessment and the quality of student involvement. Paper presented at the Forum of the Association for Institutional Research, Orlando, FL.

[68]

Communications Profile Questionnaire. Purpose: To teach the "Johari Window" communication model, identify one's communication style, learn techniques to give feedback and get information effectively, and to develop a plan for modifying one's communication style as appropriate. Managers and employees; 1974–83; 4 versions: Generic Management, Sales Management, Health Care Management, Non-Manager; 1987 price data: $6 per set including 1 participant form, 2 companion forms, and scoring and interpretation booklet ('83, 15 pages); $15 per leader's guide (no date, 16 pages); Spanish version of Generic Management available; 195(225) minutes; Don Michalak; Michalak Training Associates, Inc.*

Review of the Communications Profile Questionnaire by DANIEL J. MUELLER, Professor of Educational Psychology, Indiana University, Bloomington, IN:

The Communications Profile Questionnaire is actually two questionnaires for rating the interpersonal communication effectiveness of "managers." One instrument is for self rating; the other for employees to rate the managers. The items on the two instruments are parallel in focus and wording. Each instrument is designed to give two scores: one for *telling* (giving information), the other for *asking* (receiving information). Combinations of high and low scores on these two scales are proffered as diagnostic of communication style.

The printing and format of the instruments are of professional quality. Both the items and the manual are well written. But the manual is only for scoring and interpretation of scale scores. There is no information about the construction of the scales. Nor is there any evidence of psychometric quality. No data concerning reliability or validity are presented. It is simply assumed by the author that the questionnaire is measuring what it is hoped it is measuring. Apparently, the author expects users to assume the same thing.

Because a profile of the two scores is necessary in interpretation of the questionnaire results, it is important for the two scales to be measuring distinct and substantially independent components of communication skill. But the manual does not report the correlation between the two scales. A close look at the questions shows that most of the "telling" questions have the word *tell* in them. (E.g., "If one of my best employees was coming in late and it was affecting his/her job performance, I would tell him/her how I felt about it.") And most of the "asking" questions have the word *ask* in them. (E.g., "If one of my employees took several days off [personal time allowed by company policy], I would ask him/her what the problem was.") Many of the items, on both scales, are about confronting others (mostly employees, but also one's boss, colleagues, and friends) when there is a problem. Some items are about asking for others' opinions or feelings. All items describe socially desirable behaviors, and it is likely that both scales are substantially affected by social desirability response set. My estimate is that the telling and asking scales correlate highly.

On the questionnaire form for employees to rate their managers, the items asking the employee how the manager would behave in a confrontation with *his/her* boss are necessarily very speculative. (E.g., "If the manager's boss gave him/her a direct order to do something that he/she felt was unnecessary, he/she would ask the boss why it had to be done.")

Just for fun, I administered the self-rating questionnaire to one of my graduate classes in measurement, and to myself ($N = 16$). My students and I are not managers, but we imagined ourselves to be managers. (We have some level of telling and asking communication skills, just as do managers.) Based on these data, the *telling* scale had an alpha reliability of .39. But item 20, the only item on the inventory that asked respondents about sharing their personal problems with others, correlated highly negatively with total scale score. When this item was deleted, the reliability jumped to

.64. The *asking* scale had an alpha of .60. These reliabilities are not high enough to warrant decision making based on individual scores, but at least some of the items in each scale are focusing on a single underlying psychological construct.

The scales intercorrelated .52. This is as high as their respective reliabilities will allow, and indicates the two scales are measuring essentially the same construct. When the two scales were combined into one (not a procedure suggested by the test author), the alpha was .68. With item 20 removed, the combined scale reliability increased to .74—a respectable level. These are very meager psychometric data for judging any psychological instrument, but perhaps better than none at all.

Another curious finding in our small data set was the configuration of item response distributions. On an 11-point rating scale, ranging from "0, Not Like Me At All" to "10, Exactly Like Me," 7 was the first or second most frequently occurring response on 13 of the 20 items. This is an artifact. Response category 7 is anchored with the words "Quite Like Me." Except for 0 and 10, 3 is the only other response category so anchored.

This instrument is designed to be used in a kind of personal growth workshop. In addition to a measurement function, it is intended to stimulate introspection about one's communication behaviors. In this capacity, not only are the telling and asking scores utilized (both manager's self-rating and their rating by employees), but individual item responses are also studied and discussed. Remediation exercises for improving communication skills in each area are included in the manual. This may be a useful personal growth exercise; there are no psychometric criteria that can be applied.

The idea of measuring communication skills is a good one, and the Communications Profile Questionnaire has some promise for measuring at least one dimension of interpersonal communication skill (probably not two). But it is still in a developmental stage, and should not be used other than for research purposes until sound evidence of reliability and validity can be demonstrated.

Review of the Communications Profile Questionnaire by LYLE F. SCHOENFELDT, Professor of Management, Texas A&M University, College Station, TX:

The conceptualization underlying the Communications Profile Questionnaire is that one's communications effectiveness depends on his/her skill and sensitivity with respect to giving (telling) and receiving (asking) information. The relationship between telling and asking is illustrated through a model developed by Joseph Luft and Harry Ingham in the late 1960s and called the Johari Window, not an esoteric term, but merely the combination of the first two names of the developers. The Communications Profile Questionnaire is designed to measure one's skill at telling and asking, information that would be used in conjunction with a training session on the Johari Window.

The Leader's Guide which accompanies the materials outlines a 3¹/₄-hour training session. Potential participants would be asked to arrange for two employees, if they are managers, or two coworkers to complete the Companion Form of the Communications Profile Questionnaire. The "companions" are asked to return the completed forms to the workshop leader in an envelope provided. The participant would fill out a separate Participant Form of the Communications Profile Questionnaire and bring it to the workshop.

The Participant and Companion forms each have 20 questions, and differ only in the reference to the target person (i.e., self, manager, or coworker). The respondent is asked to rate each item on an 11-point scale ranging from "Not Like Me At All" (rated 0) to "Exactly Like Me" (rated 10). ("Her/him" is substituted for "Me" on the companion forms.) Half the items are combined to determine the Telling Score and the other half the Asking Score.

As an example, one of the items contributing to the Telling Score inquires, "If I were at a meeting and totally ignorant on the subject being discussed (and everyone else seemed to understand the subject), I would confess my ignorance at the first opportunity." An item which contributes to the Asking Score reads, "If I had a heated argument with one of my employees and I suspected he/she still felt bad about it, I would ask the employee how he/she was feeling." With each question, the "Exactly Like Me" rating is the response which indicates openness in communication (i.e., telling and asking).

At the workshop the participant is given a Scoring and Interpretation Booklet and proceeds to score his/her Communications Profile Questionnaire along with those of his/her employees or coworkers. The scores are marked on the respective Telling/Asking axes, and lines drawn across (Telling) or down (Asking) to form four rectangles, typically of unequal size, the four "panes" of the participant's Johari Window. In fact, three separate windows are constructed, one based on the participant responses and two from ratings by companions. The 11-page Booklet includes background information on the concepts of the Johari Window, information on analyzing the ratings, and guidelines the participant can use to change his/her communications style.

The 15-page Leader's Guide includes lists of materials and activities that precede the workshop. In terms of the workshop itself, the Guide contains a 6-point summary outline followed by five pages of detailed notes. Also included is a test to assess understanding of the concepts and a sample letter to use as a cover to those completing the companion form.

The effectiveness of the Communications Profile Questionnaire could be evaluated in a variety of ways. First, while it is possible that individuals would see themselves differently than would coworkers or employees, do the two companions solicited to complete the Questionnaire tend to agree in how they evaluate the communication skills of the workshop participant? Such information would speak to the reliability of the Questionnaire. Second, does the Questionnaire really measure telling and asking? This would provide an indication of the construct validity. Third, can people change their communication style, as intended by the workshop, and will this be detected when companions are resurveyed at a later date? Such data would provide evidence of the empirical validity of the Questionnaire. Finally, what can a participant learn about his/her own communication style by knowing the scores of others in similar situations, for example, managers at a comparable level? Normative data should allow participants to put their own scores in perspective and to understand communication styles typical of their situation.

All are open questions because no psychometric information is provided on the Communications Profile Questionnaire, either in the Scoring and Interpretation Booklet or as a part of the Leader's Guide. There is no evidence that the Communications Profile Questionnaire is effective in identifying a meaningful individual communication style. It is interesting that an instrument designed to assess the asking and telling sophistication of communications does not apply these principles in communicating with users (i.e., does not tell users what they need to know to evaluate the usefulness of the Communications Profile Questionnaire).

In summary, the Communications Profile Questionnaire is designed to provide feedback on communications style to be used in conjunction with a workshop on the Johari Window communications model, an approach that was popular at the height of the human relations movement in the late 1960s and 1970s but used less at the present time. No psychometric evidence is provided attesting to the value of the Questionnaire for the intended purpose. The information on procedures for administering and scoring the Questionnaire is good. The interpretative guidance is minimal, especially given the challenge of attempting to understand and modify a communication style developed over a long period of time.

There is always some potential for harm when one becomes privy to feedback from companions with respect to communication effectiveness, or lack thereof. Given the absence of evidence that the instrument is sound, the potential costs would seem to outweigh benefits of using the Communications Profile Questionnaire.

[69]

Communicative Abilities in Daily Living. Purpose: "To assess the functional communication skills of aphasic adults." Aphasic adults; 1980; CADL; intended as a supplemental test; individual; other test materials (e.g., shoe lace, watches, white jacket) must be supplied by examiner; 1986 price data: $79 per complete kit including scoring kit, picture book, administration manual ('80, 125 pages), and audiotape cassette (for training/administration); $9 per scoring kit; $39 per picture book; $18 per audiotape cassette; $17 per administration manual; (40–50) minutes; Audrey L. Holland; PRO-ED, Inc.*

TEST REFERENCES

1. Behrmann, M., & Penn, C. (1984). Non-verbal communication of aphasic patients. *British Journal of Disorders of Communication*, 19, 155-168.

2. Skenes, L. L., & McCauley, R. J. (1985). Psychometric review of nine aphasia tests. *Journal of Communication Disorders*, 18, 461-474.

Review of Communicative Abilities in Daily Living by RITA SLOAN BERNDT, Associate Professor of Neurology, University of Maryland School of Medicine, Baltimore, MD:

SUMMARY. The Communicative Abilities in Daily Living (CADL) is a test of functional communication for aphasic adults. The goal of the test is to assess the ability of the aphasic patient to communicate, by whatever means, despite an essential disorder of language. The test employs an interactive role-playing technique, in which examiner and patient pretend to go shopping, to use the telephone, to travel in a car, and to make a visit to the doctor. A wide range of communicative functions is tested, including the ability to give biographical information, to notice mistakes on the examiner's part, to recognize a variety of nonverbal sounds, and to respond appropriately in everyday situations. Because the administration of the test requires somewhat unusual behavior from the examiner, an extensive self-training procedure, including a test tape containing possible responses, is provided. Data are given for 130 aphasic patients and an equal number of normal subjects, that allow evaluation of individual test items and of the performance of different types of aphasic patients on the test.

CRITIQUE. The CADL represents a creative approach to the difficult question of evaluating aphasic patients' *actual* ability to communicate and to function in society, despite what are often enormous language impairments. An optimal assessment of this capacity would be done in the patient's normal surroundings, as he or she goes about typical activities. This kind of observational assessment is usually not possible in the clinical setting, and family members' observations are not always accurate. This instrument seeks to recreate these "natural" settings to the extent possible, while maintaining some control over the content and order of the interactions. The role-playing approach adopted here is at once the strongest point and the weakest aspect of this test. If a patient has the cognitive capacity to understand the concept of pretending, much useful information can be gained. However, if the patient cannot grasp this central concept, very little will be learned about his or her communicative capacities.

The actual form the interaction takes in the CADL, though it appears very informal and relaxed, is quite structured. The questions, and the order in which they are asked, clearly have been carefully chosen and arranged. The administration of the CADL requires an astute examiner who can adapt flexibly to a variety of possible patient responses. Considerable effort has been expended in the development of this test to provide suitable training exercises for new examiners. The tape recording that accompanies the manual is well done, although the voices of the examiner and patient are sometimes difficult to distinguish.

The normative data provided with the CADL contain useful information about the performance to be expected from different types of aphasic patients in different kinds of settings. Extensive item analysis is also provided, allowing a direct comparison of an individual patient's responses with those of other patients on specific items. All of these data are presented clearly, in a format that is relatively easy to use.

SUMMARY. The CADL is a test of functional communication for aphasic adults that utilizes a role-playing format to assess patients' ability to communicate in everyday situations. It is intended to supplement other formal tests of specific language functions. The CADL manual is clearly written, well documented with normative data, and contains extensive training materials. The test is well designed to assume an important place in the clinical test inventories of Speech/Language Pathologists and other specialists in adult communication disorders.

[70]

Comprehensive Drinker Profile. Purpose: "Provides an intensive and comprehensive history and status of the individual client with regard to his or her use and abuse of alcohol." Problem drinkers and alcoholics; 1984–87; CDP; 3 adjunct instruments available as separates; individual; 1987 price data: $49.95 per complete kit including 25 interview forms, manual (81 pages), and 8 reusable card sets used in the administration of the interview; $35 per 25 interview forms; $6 per card sets; $12 per manual; price data for manual supplement ('87, 54 pages) and interview booklets for adjunct forms available from publisher; (60–120) minutes; G.

Alan Marlatt and William R. Miller; Psychological Assessment Resources, Inc.*

a) BRIEF DRINKER PROFILE. 1987; BDP; abbreviated version of the Comprehensive Drinker Profile; 50 minutes.

b) FOLLOW-UP DRINKER PROFILE. 1987; FDP; to be used in conjunction with the CDP or BDP; (30–50) minutes.

c) COLLATERAL INTERVIEW FORM. Friends and family of client; 1987; CIF; to provide information not available from client; administration time not reported.

TEST REFERENCES

1. Laberg, J. C. (1986). Alcohol and expectancy: Subjective, psychophysiological and behavioral responses to alcohol stimuli in severely, moderately and non-dependent drinkers. *British Journal of Addiction*, 81, 797-808.

Review of the Comprehensive Drinker Profile by ROBERT R. MOWRER, Assistant Professor of Psychology and Sociology, Angelo State University, San Angelo, TX:

The term "comprehensive" is certainly applicable to this extensive instrument intended to address the diagnosis and treatment of alcoholism and problem drinking. In addition, there are also related materials available to assess the efficacy of treatment (Follow-up Drinker Profile, FDP) and the Collateral Interview Form (CIF), which allows for information from friends and relatives. Finally, there is a shorter version available that is an abbreviation of the Comprehensive Drinker Profile (CDP). An examination of these materials indicates the combination of these measures is unique in its purpose.

The full-length CDP is divided into three main sections: demographics, drinking history, and motivational information. It is intended for use in a structured interview setting and requires 1 to 2 hours to complete (the shorter version, the Brief Drinker Profile [BDP], requires approximately 1 hour).

An especially interesting aspect of the drinking history section is the use of a set of six cards describing "drinker types" ranging from nonalcoholic to alcoholic. The client is then asked to choose which card best describes the drinking habits of various significant others (mother, father, spouse, partner). This type of forced-choice procedure is used also with regard to drinking location, social situation (who you drink with), other drugs used, and beverage preference. In the motivational section, this procedure is used to determine effects of drinking, other life problems, and drinker type.

I think this approach may be especially useful and effective in reducing the ambiguity of an interview. A second plus is the incorporation of aspects of the Michigan Alcoholism Screening Test (MAST) into this instrument. Third, several sections of the CDP are converted into quantitative indices increasing the reliability of the instrument (similar quantitative indices are derived in the abbreviated version). All four instruments (CDP, BDP, FDP, and CIF) are logically structured into major sections, another advantage in terms of consistency. In sum, I like the forced-choice cards, the incorporation of the MAST, the quantitative indices, and the consistency of the instrument.

On the negative side, although this instrument clearly has face validity, it is difficult to see how it could be incorporated with something such as the MMPI (as the MacAndrew [1965] can be). A second potential weakness is its psychometric characteristics. The normative sample was small and no attempt was made to obtain a cross-validation sample. The normative sample consisted of 103 problem drinkers at a University-related clinic. I think it is important that additional normative data be obtained especially from a sample of "social," nonproblem drinkers to show this set of instruments can differentiate problem drinkers from those not identified as problems. Further supportive data could be obtained from a "normal" sample, randomly selected without regard to drinking behavior. The research potential of this instrument is extremely rich and strongly merits pursuit.

Some other minor problems with the CDP involve its administration. Although the CDP manual is fairly extensive, it is clear that competent administration will require quite a bit of practice. The entire manual is 79 pages long with the "instruction" portion garnering 41 of these pages. The manual points out that style and consistency are extremely important.

All in all, I feel this is an extremely important and promising diagnostic tool. With further validation studies this may become the instrument of choice for family systems therapists and practitioners due to its emphasis on functional impairments within the examinee's various systems. The idea of a comprehensive set of inventories is a very good one with significant advantages over other assessment approaches.

REVIEWER'S REFERENCE

MacAndrew, C. (1965). The differentiation of male alcoholic outpatients from nonalcoholic psychiatric outpatients by means of the MMPI. *Quarterly Journal of Studies on Alcohol*, 26, 238-246.

Review of the Comprehensive Drinker Profile by NICK J. PIAZZA, Assistant Professor, Department of Counselor Education, The University of Toledo, Toledo, OH:

The Comprehensive Drinker Profile (CDP) is not so much an assessment device as it is a structured interview. As such, the CDP is able to provide the clinician or researcher with a structured data base. However, the consumer should be aware that the CDP offers little that is not already available or that could not be easily duplicated with materials produced locally.

The CDP interview consists of a sequence of questions encompassing three different areas: demographics, drinking history, and motivation. Materials necessary for the interview include the manual, an interview booklet, and numerous color-coded cards that are to be sorted by the client. The authors suggest that the CDP be administered in one session approximately 1 to 2 hours in length. The authors also recommend that the CDP not be administered to persons who are withdrawing from alcohol or who have blood alcohol concentrations exceeding .05%.

The CDP, because of its comprehensive nature and complexity of administration, should only be administered by a trained interviewer. Training to use the CDP could be done quickly with someone with good basic interviewing skills and should not need to consist of more than a few practice administrations.

Much of the interview consists of eliciting information from the interviewee and then recording it into the CDP booklet. With several items, however, there is the need to present the client with a series of cards that are arrayed on the table before the interviewee. The interviewee is then asked, depending on the nature of the information needed, to either select the appropriate card or to sort the cards into an order that represents the interviewee's drinking experiences or feelings.

Several problems were immediately apparent with the card-sort technique as suggested by the authors of the CDP. First, using this technique adds greatly to the time needed to conduct the interview. Second, the card-sort technique makes it impossible to administer the interview in more efficient group settings. This could be an important limitation when the CDP is employed in research or assessment situations. Third, there is an obvious alphanumeric identification number on the face of the cards that could influence the interviewee as he or she sorts the cards. An interviewee might use these identification numbers in an effort to "second guess" the purpose of the interview. Fourth, the identification numbers do not correspond to the item and section numbers within the interviewer's booklet. Consequently, the identification numbers do not contribute to the ease of training or administration of the CDP. Fifth, having the interviewee sort cards requires the interviewer to transcribe the results into the booklet later. It would seem much more efficient to merely give the interviewee a set of forms to fill out that could then be inserted into the booklet. Such forms could be given to the interviewee either before or after the interview for completion outside of the interview setting.

The authors provide a mechanism for quantifying much of the data within the CDP. The methods employed can be fairly complicated at first, but are well documented in the manual. Scoring should become quite easy for anyone familiar with the administration of the interview. The only serious deficiencies in the documentation occur when scoring the subsections on Family History and Alcohol-Related Life Problems. In both cases, weights are assigned to various items, but no indication was given of how the weights were determined. It would seem desirable for the manual to include documentation for how scoring weights were determined or to at least reference articles in the literature where that information may be obtained.

In interpreting the results, the authors offer no information on the validity or reliability of the information obtained using the CDP. A subsection of the CDP includes the Michigan Alcoholism Screening Test (MAST). It would seem reasonable to assume that information obtained on that subsection would be comparable to a separate administration of the MAST and that research relevant to the validity and reliability of the MAST would apply as well.

Normative data for the CDP is based on a single sample of 103 outpatient "problem drinkers" at the University of New Mexico. The relatively narrow scope of the authors' sample calls into question the utility of the interview in other than outpatient settings. While the authors claim that information obtained using the CDP is "relevant to the selection, planning, and implementation of treatment," it would appear that the interviewer must rely on his or her clinical judgment or knowledge of other research in utilizing this data with groups different than the sample. The authors do provide suggestions from the research and an appendix with suggested rules for interpreting the data; however, the final analysis of the information seems too dependent on the clinical intuition or experience of the interviewer or interpreter.

Overall, the CDP is a comprehensive, structured interview such as the authors claim. It should prove useful to anyone seeking to establish a large, uniform data base of information relevant to alcoholic clients. In fact, the ease with which the CDP could be coded for entry into a computer is perhaps this instrument's greatest strength. The limitations evident within the administration, scoring, and interpretation of the CDP suggest that clinicians and researchers may be better served by an assessment tool that is easier and more efficient to administer, offers better documentation of validity and reliability, and/or is developed and tailored to meet local needs.

[71]

Comprehensive Screening Tool for Determining Optimal Communication Mode. Purpose: "To evaluate the clients' performative skills in the areas of vocal production (Oral Skills Battery), gestural and motor production (Manual Skills Battery), and response to symbols and pictorial content (Pictographic Skills Battery)." Low functioning non-speaking clients; 1984; CST; 9 subtests: Manual Training Prerequisites, Movement Patterning, Cognitive Correlates for Manual Communication, Prerequisites Visual Training, Attending Behaviors and Accuracy Movement, Cognitive Correlates, Pre-Speech and Oral Awareness, Pre-Articulatory and Articulatory Skills, Auditory Awareness; individual; 1986 price data: $53 per 25 scoring summary/profile sheets, 25 record sheets per subtest, and manual (50 pages); (45) minutes; Linda Infante House and Brenda S. Rogerson; United Educational Services, Inc.*

Review of the Comprehensive Screening Tool for Determining Optimal Communication Mode by MARILYN E. DEMOREST, Associate Professor of Psychology, University of Maryland-Baltimore County, Catonsville, MD:

The purpose of the Comprehensive Screening Tool for Determining Optimal Communication Mode (CST) is to promote formal and objective assessment of nonspeaking individuals. Its development was motivated by the authors' awareness of the subjective and unsystematic nature of many clinical assessments. Accordingly, the CST has been designed to be a theoretically and empirically based tool for systematically eliciting, observing, and evaluating communicative behaviors. The primary goal of this behavioral assessment is selection of an appropriate communication mode such as vocal production, an augmentative communication system, or a combination of both. Secondary goals include (*a*) providing an empirical basis for recommendations to parents, teachers, and administrators; (*b*) justification of a previously selected communication mode; and (*c*) planning and evaluation of intervention procedures.

The instrument was designed for clients who are mentally retarded and/or physically limited and suggestions are offered for adapting the testing procedures to the special needs of multiply-handicapped individuals. The target population is not confined to any particular age group, but tasks contained in the CST reflect skills appropriate for a developmental age of at least 6 months.

Steps or stages in the development of the CST, if any, are not described in the manual. The starting point for item construction was the authors' clinical experience and expert judgment, which was corroborated by a review of the literature. Brief reference is made to discussions with other professionals and to field testing of the instrument, but no details are given other than the fact that a variety of ages and handicapping conditions was represented. Whether the amount and type of feedback from other professionals was sufficient to insure that the CST reflects collective clinical judgment and practice is unknown and remains to be determined.

The CST manual is most comprehensive in its presentation of the rationale for inclusion of each behavioral objective. The behavioral domain is divided into three areas (Manual,

Pictographic, and Oral Skills, respectively), and within each there are three subtests, each comprising two or more sections. Theoretical arguments and empirical studies are offered in support of each of the 151 CST items. Although the rationale for individual items is excellent, other aspects of test design are not so well documented. For example, a 5-point rating scale is used for evaluating each task, but there is no discussion of how or why this scheme was adopted. Scoring is accomplished by adding the ratings for items within each battery. Nowhere is it pointed out that these battery scores are each based on 46 items and that the appropriateness of directly comparing battery totals hinges on this fact. Indeed, items in Subtest III of the Oral Skills Battery (Auditory Awareness) are excluded from the battery total because "the authors feel these items are important to oral communication but not necessary for successful use of the oral mode of communication." Had they been included, the battery total would have been based on 59 items; it is tempting to speculate that this fact may also have played some role in the decision to exclude them.

CST materials consist of a recording sheet for each subtest and a scoring summary/profile sheet. The recording sheet states each behavioral objective and gives a brief description of the task to be performed. The manual offers further comments and guidelines on procedures and scoring. Although the manual gives a general guideline for using the 5-point rating scale, its adaptation to individual items is not straightforward. Full credit (4 points) is to be awarded when the client meets the objective without delay and without assistance from the observer. Ratings of 3, 2, 1, and 0 are given for delayed, assisted, partial, and inaccurate responses respectively. It is not clear how this strategy is to be employed when the objective involves *absence* of a response (e.g., absence of startle, self-stimulatory behavior, or rooting reflex). Suggestions are made for awarding partial credit for many items, but they are not sufficiently specific. For example, one objective is to assess the chewing reflex. Up-and-down movement is the target, but 1 point is to be awarded for rotary movement. It is not clear whether or how ratings of 2 or 3 are to be used with this item. Given the raison d'être of the CST is to improve objectivity in assessment, scale values should be more clearly defined for each objective. Clinical judgment should play a role in deciding whether performance satisfies the description for a particular rating; it should not be used to define the scale values themselves.

The authors repeatedly state that the CST is not a standardized test. Although the scope of the assessment and the behavioral objective of each task are given in detail, flexibility in the selection of test materials and in the test procedures are both permitted and encouraged in the interest of eliciting maximum performance from each client. It is also recommended that the test format and the test setting be adapted to the individual. Although these features of test content and administration are justifiable, they do not preclude evaluations of reliability and validity. In fact, given that items are scored and that total scores are calculated, plotted, and interpreted, it is imperative that the psychometric properties of these scores be documented.

Given the ambiguity of the scoring system, it is important that its reliability be established. Both intra- and interscorer agreement should be evaluated using videotaped samples of client performance. In addition, the reliability of the behavioral sample should be evaluated through multiple assessments of the same clients. At present, the only evidence of interobserver reliability for the CST comes from a sample of 10 clients who were independently evaluated by the authors with "consistent scoring on all items." However, there is no indication that other users of the CST will be able to administer and score the items in the same manner. Thus there is little evidence the goal of an objective assessment procedure has been attained.

The most serious omission in the CST manual is the failure to provide evidence supporting the recommended interpretation of battery scores. The authors propose the skill battery or batteries with the highest score "should be considered for training potential." Although this interpretation has strong face validity, it has not been demonstrated that scores on the different batteries are equivalent. That is, there is no evidence that equal scores on different batteries represent equal potential for training or that they would predict equal levels of proficiency after training. Such issues can be addressed only through carefully designed and controlled outcome research. Test users should also beware of claims the CST can be used to support a selected mode of training or to evaluate intervention procedures. The absence of standardization and the potential for observer bias are likely to seriously compromise its validity in such applications.

In summary, the CST represents an important step toward systematic and objective assessment of nonspeaking individuals. The rationale for its scope and for inclusion of individual items is clearly documented, but as a tool for behavioral assessment it suffers from a lack of precision in the definition and application of the rating scale. The manual provides no empirical data on the psychometric characteristics of battery scores and, therefore, it is essential that studies be undertaken to demonstrate (*a*) the interobserver and retest reliability of the assessment, and (*b*) the validity of recommended battery-score interpretations.

Review of the Comprehensive Screening Tool for Determining Optimal Communication Mode by KENNETH L. SHELDON, School Psychologist, Edgecombe County Schools, Tarboro, NC:

The Comprehensive Screening Tool for Determining Optimal Communication Mode (CST) is a nonstandardized assessment instrument used to determine the existence of prerequisite skills necessary for alternative modes of communication in nonspeaking individuals. It was developed by two speech/language professionals for use by speech/language pathologists. The authors reasoned that a tool to assess skills for alternative communication modes was needed, that alternative communication modes are desirable for those unable to use the traditional communication channels, and that many nonspeaking people are not too physically handicapped to be able to use an alternative communication system. Three assumptions derived from an interpretation of current research, discussion with other professionals, and field testing with low-functioning nonspeaking individuals were used to develop the test. The assumptions are that manual communication, communication with a communication board, or oral communication are viable alternatives for communication if the person possesses the appropriate skills.

The goal of the instrument is to determine what alternative communication mode is appropriate and what prerequisite skills may be needed before teaching the new communication mode. Appropriate skills, based on the Piagetian view of the interaction of cognition and language development, are identified for each of the three communication modes. Each of the nine subtests cited above in the test description are further divided into skill areas that follow a developmental sequence of prerequisite skills. ationale for the inclusion of the subtests is well documented in the easily read manual. The concise manual lists the objectives, tasks, and guidelines for scoring. Stimuli used to assess each skill are selected by the clinician based on his/her knowledge of the client's likes. This indicates the clinician needs to know the client well before administering the tasks. The authors include a list of materials needed. These are readily available household items.

Administration of the instrument requires a thorough understanding of the task and materials that are organized and ready to use. The entire battery is recommended so that the clinician has information about the client for all three modes of communication. Additional testing is also highly recommended to more fully understand the client. While there is no limit on chronological age, the client must have at least a mental age of 6 months.

Scoring is based on a numerical scale of 0 to 4, with 4 being an accurate, complete, and prompt response without clinician assistance, while 0 is an incorrect or incomplete response. The scores from the items are summed and plotted for each battery. The highest battery score suggests training in that mode. While the guidelines are clear, interpretation is enhanced by the clinician's professional knowledge and observational skills.

Stressed throughout the manual is that the CST is not a standardized instrument. It is behavioral in nature and used only as a tool to give the clinician help in determining the mode of communication for a nonspeaking client. Validity and reliability are mentioned but no rigorous statistical procedures are described. For content validity, the authors note the instrument is representative of the goals and objectives for which it was developed. Interrater reliability was established by the authors of the instrument and was based on the assessment of 10 clients. Field testing was completed on 50 clients. A description of these clients is not given and would obviously have been extremely helpful. Modifications for use with the mentally retarded, cerebral palsy or neurologically impaired, visually impaired, and/or hearing impaired are included.

Helpful additions to the manual would include: behavior examples with numerical ratings, a case history, interpretation guidelines and examples, and suggestions for training deficient skills. Interrater reliability needs to be established for clinicians other than the authors.

In summary, the CST appears theoretically sound. The authors have developed a useful instrument for assessing a client's potential for different communciation modes. The tasks for assessing skills appear complete and well organized along a firm developmental sequence necessary for oral communication, manual communication, and pictographic communication modes. With more field testing, the CST seems promising.

[72]

Computer Aptitude, Literacy, and Interest Profile. Purpose: "Developed to meet the needs of vocational counselors and personnel managers in assisting junior and senior high school students and adults in making career decisions." High school and adults; 1984; CALIP, 7 scores: Aptitude (Estimation, Graphic Patterns, Logical Structures, Series, Total), Interest, Literacy; 1984 price data: $45 per complete test including manual (56 pages), 50 answer booklets, and 10 test booklets; $18 per 50 answer booklets; $12 per 10 test booklets; $18 per manual; (60) minutes; Mary S. Poplin, David E. Drew, and Robert S. Gable; PRO-ED, Inc.*

TEST REFERENCES

1. Gable, R. S., Drew, D. E., & Poplin, M. S. (1985). Is there an aptitude for learning about computers? *Claremont Reading Conference Yearbook*, 49, 101-106.
2. Levinson, E. M. (1986). A review of the Computer Aptitude, Literacy, and Interest Profile (CALIP). *Journal of Counseling and Development*, 64, 658-659.

Review of the Computer Aptitude, Literacy, and Interest Profile by SAMUEL JUNI, Associate Professor of Counselor Education, New York University, New York, NY:

The Computer Aptitude, Literacy, and Interest Profile (CALIP) manual is well written and organized with lucid lecture-like material explaining psychometric methodology and basic statistics to the novice as background to reliability and validity data. The purposes of the test are presented as: (*a*) identifying talented persons who might otherwise lack the opportunity to demonstrate aptitudes being measured, (*b*) broadening the range of options for those choosing careers, (*c*) providing an empirical base for allocation of resources, and (*d*) documenting progress in training.

The manual is comprehensive in presenting test development data. A discussion comparing the relative merits of the CALIP, as compared with alternate tests, correctly points out the advantage of the test in predicting competence in high school and college students, in contrast to such established tests as IBM's revised Programmer Aptitude Test and Science Research Associates' Computer Programmer Aptitude Battery, which are designed and normed for adults. A defect in the CALIP, conversely, is its reliance on skills that are presumed to predict competence rather than corresponding to actual tasks of working adult programmers.

The test is ostensibly oriented to both computer-experienced and inexperienced students. Such an orientation is consonant with a review of the content of the items and test instructions. Experience in programming would make the test materials more familiar and less mysterious, and may increase scores regardless of actual ability. The test authors also attempt to make the CALIP more robust by attempting to measure aptitude in such fields as computer sales, where actual computer skills are not essential. In the opinion of the reviewer, such identification of potential is outside the reasonable range of a test designed to measure computer literacy, as the qualitative requirements for computer sales seem more sales oriented than computer oriented.

The statistics presented in the manual support the psychometric merit of the test. Split-half reliability coefficients exceeded .80 for all subtests except Series and Literacy at the earliest age grouping. Test-retest reliabilities were statistically significant, but several were lower than .80. Reliability data, as presented in the manual, speak against use of the Interest subtest for the younger age groupings. The subtests' intercorrelations ranged from .12 to .89 (median $r = .34$). A comparison of scores of expert versus non-expert programmers indicated that experts did score higher than non-experts. The Literacy subtest was shown to correlate with age while the Interest subtest did not. Males score somewhat higher on the CALIP total aptitude score than females, but the difference is not statistically significant except for Interest and Literacy.

There are several problems in the design of the test booklet and item presentation: (*a*) The initial example requires the subject to look at the answer sheet in conjunction with the test booklet—this may confuse the subject. Examples should be self-contained. (*b*) The use of arrows directing the student to the next item is confusing, and can be taken as related to the other symbols within items by anxious subjects. (*c*) Section III contains a mixture of analogies and logical structure problems. The interspersing of these items is disorienting and needlessly distracting. This is compounded by the presentation of introductory examples for analogies but not for logical structures. (*d*) In Section III, the analogy items utilize the colon (:) as symbol for "is to" in the analogies problems. The correct interpretation of this symbol should not be prerequisite for performing well on the test; substituting the term "is to" is more appropriate. (*e*) The test is confounded with skills in reading comprehension. Although authors suggest the possibility of reading the items for some subjects, normative data are not presented for that administration method.

A problem with the normative samle is that the distribution is biased. Twenty-one percent of the sample placed themselves at or above the top 25% in achievement in computer classes, and 24% had home computers. This bias may limit the test's validity when seeking to identify aptitude in the computer novice.

There is also a problem in the way the scoring is computed. The manual calls for the computation of the "Computer Aptitude Quotient" by summing the four aptitude subtests. No psychometric rationale is given for the use of a straight sum in the formula. Although the validity data on the quotient seem impressive, authors should have utilized appropriate regression weights in summing the subtests.

The problems noted are minimal in light of the excellent work represented in the test development. The CALIP is an apparently valid and acceptable measure of computer aptitude, interest, and literacy in adolescents and adults. The CALIP has the distinction of being the most acceptable test available for use with children and adolescents.

Review of the Computer Aptitude, Literacy, and Interest Profile by DAVID MARSHALL, Associate Professor of Computer Science, The Texas Woman's University, Denton, TX:

The Computer Aptitude, Literacy, and Interest Profile (CALIP) is intended to identify people having high potential for computer programming. It consists of six subtests. The Estimation subtest is the only timed subtest (2 minutes) and is presented first. It contains 24 blocks of small white and black squares in varying patterns. The examinee is explicitly instructed to write an estimate of the number of black squares in a block and move on as quickly as possible. In view of the instruction set, this subtest is scored inappropriately because a point is earned only if the estimate written is exactly equal to the number of black squares in the block. The number of black squares varies from dozens to nearly 100. Close approximations are not given credit. The subtest score seems an inadequate measure of quantitative and visual-spatial abilities, the stated computer skills for which Estimation was included.

The Graphic Patterns subtest contains items of a sort found in tests of fluid or nonverbal intelligence: selecting a figure from four or six alternatives which best completes a pattern, testing logical and visual-spatial abilities. The Logical Structures subtest presents analogies and problems in finding similarities between apparently unrelated stimuli, and is designed to measure logical, sequential, translation, and quantitative abilities. The Series subtest, a measure of the same abilities as Logical Structures, is a set of number and/or letter series completion items. The Interest subtest is a self-rating checklist of examinee attributes and preferences which reportedly correlates with self-reported interest in and participation with computer activities. The only such correlational evidence provided in the manual is based on analyses of the standardization sample and no other evidence is presented to support the inclusion of Interest in the CALIP. Interest is also intended to measure reading comprehension.

Literacy, a computer vocabulary and knowledge subtest, appears last because it is not appropriate for all examinees. According to the manual, this subtest also assesses reading comprehension and personal interests.

All raw subtest scores are converted to standard scores (mean = 10, standard deviation = 3). Experienced examinees also respond to a Computer Experience Survey in which they report their competency in computer activities, and programming and computer use experiences. A total Computer Aptitude Quotient (CAQ) is determined as the sum of the four standardized aptitude subtest scores converted to a standard score (mean = 100, standard deviation = 15). Together the CAQ, Interest, and Literacy scores are used to determine relative potential for, and achievement, experience, and interest in computer programming. The test can be completed in 1 hour.

The test was standardized on a sample of 1,236 children, adolescents, and adults, stratified according to the 1980 census figures across the four census regions. The manual does not indicate to what degree random sampling was done. Separate norm tables are given for males and females combined within each of four age groups (12 to 14, 15 to 19, 20 to 29, and 30 to 60) on all but the Interest subtest, which may be sex biased favoring males. Separate male and female norms are provided for Interest within each of the four age groups. Age grouping was based on statistical comparisons of subtest means.

The manual reports that the subtests were chosen to provide measures of the major computer skills identified in the computer aptitude literature. The final items chosen and subtest item order were based on analyses of item discriminating power and difficulty. Items are presented in increasing order of difficulty within each subtest. The manual presents scanty information regarding preliminary item testing, suggesting that only one sample was tested on a large number of potential items, after which item analyses were performed and final items were selected, without subsequent rounds of testing on fresh samples. No information is given about preliminary subtest reliabilities, difficulties, or discrimination coefficients. Power medians and ranges are presented for each aptitude subtest within each of the four age groups in the standardization sample, and are acceptable (medians of .30 and higher) except for Series in the lowest age group (median of .28).

Reliability analyses within each age level of the standardization sample include test-retest, split-half, coefficient alpha, and standard errors of measurement for all but the Estimation and Interest subtests. For these subtests only test-retest and standard errors are properly presented because Estimation is timed and Interest is composed of heterogeneous items. Reliabilities are quite good (.80 and above) except within the youngest age level where all coefficient alphas range from .72 to .78 and split-halves are .75 and .76 for Series and Literacy, respectively. The reliability of Estimation is lower than is desirable (.71), and that for Interest is unacceptably low (.50) when computed on data for persons under 20 years of age.

The manual urges caution when interpreting the subtests for younger people, and suggest that the CAQ, rather than the aptitude subtests, be interpreted because it is more reliable than any subtest. Nothing is currently known about the predictive validity of a given aptitude subtest profile. The authors recommend aptitude profile interpretation for adults, but this seems unwarranted because no evidence exists to date regarding the predictive validities of either the CAQ or the subtests.

The manual presents preliminary information about concurrent validity. Analyses of covariance controlling for age were performed on each subtest and the CAQ between the following groups identified in the standardization sample: males versus females; expert programmers versus random others; those knowing two or more programming languages versus thôse knowing one or none; those having written intermediate to advanced programs versus those not having done so; and those having had two or more computer courses versus those having had one or none. The manual does not give the criteria used in defining expertise, but does say that cases were selected based on the self-report experience survey. Every analysis between more experienced people versus any others resulted in significantly higher averages in the experienced groups. No information is given about how often the same experienced people were contrasted with another group, but it seems likely that a core of people having more courses, greater expertise, and advanced programming skills was repeatedly contrasted with another cluster of those having little or no experience, coursework, or ability, thus rendering those four analyses highly redundant because the selection criteria are most certainly correlated (e.g., having no coursework probably relates more often to not having written programs than to having written advanced programs). However, these findings do lend support to the construct validity of the CALIP. As predicted, males were significantly higher than females on Interest and Literacy, a known sex difference, and aptitude and Literacy increase from childhood to adulthood while Interest remains fairly stable.

While the foregoing results support the construct validity of the test, they do not constitute evidence of predictive validity. The CALIP must be researched on new samples of untrained, inexperienced people in studies of predictive validity before the test can be used with confidence in guidance or personnel selection.

Subtest and CAQ intercorrelations are also presented. The correlations of Estimation with the other three aptitude subtests are disturbingly low (.16 to .22), while the other three measures intercorrelate satisfactorily (.71 to .89). The reviewer performed a principal components analysis on the subtest intercorrelation matrix, obtaining one significant component upon which Estimation loaded only .32 while the other aptitude subtests loaded .87 to .94. Estimation is only minimally related to the aptitude measured by the other subtests, a point noted in the manual. It seems inappropriate to sum the Estimation score together with the others because it is clearly measuring something else. Studies are needed regarding the separate validities of Estimation and the CAQ computed without including Estimation, and of subtest interrelationships when Estimation is scored more appropriately, that is, when close approximations are given credit.

The manual gives excellent information on group-, individual-, and self-administration, scoring, and test interpretation and uses. No information is provided about any ethnic or racial biases possible in the test. The authors stress the importance of local research and norming, and sharing of results. The manual alternates between portraying the CALIP as a research instrument and one ready for use in career counseling and personnel selection.

In summary, the CALIP contains measures of aptitude, interest, and computer literacy, and was developed in a basically sound manner. It is easy to administer, score, and interpret. The validity evidence is insufficient and all based on self reports in the standardization sample, but the known reliabilities and concurrent validities do support the CALIP as being worthy of further study. If used in guidance or selection activities, extreme caution must be observed, and it must be used as one of several information sources. Examinees should be informed that the test is experimental in nature, until the predictive validities are known. Either the instruction set for Estimation or its scoring scheme may have to be changed, as well as the way Estimation is used in partially determining the CAQ, because this subtest is a poor measure of general aptitude. The test manual gives sufficient information on administration, scoring, interpretation, uses, and limitations of the CALIP to allow a trained examiner to use the test efficiently.

[73]

Computer Competence Tests. Purpose: "Assesses student knowledge in the areas of historical development, the current impact of computers, computer operations and application of computer technology." Junior and senior high and adults; 1986; CCT; 5 test modules may be administered separately or in any combination; 1988 price data: \$140 per 35 test booklets for each module and directions for administering; \$85 per Level 1 package including 35 test booklets each for Modules 1, 2A, and 3A and directions for administering; \$55 per Level 2 package including 35 test booklets each for Module 2B and 3B and directions for administering; \$30 per 35 test booklets (specify module) and directions for administering (17 pages); \$17.50 per 35 Ready Score® Answer Documents (specify module) and class record folder; \$2.50 per class record folder; \$4 per directions for administering; \$7.50 per manual (18 pages); \$10 per examination kit including test booklet and Ready Score® Answer Document for each module, directions for administering, class record folder, and manual; 20(30) minutes per test; The Psychological Corporation.*

a) MODULE 1: DEVELOPMENT AND IMPACT.
b) MODULE 2A: COMPUTER OPERATIONS LEVEL 1.
c) MODULE 2B: COMPUTER OPERATIONS LEVEL 2.
d) MODULE 3A: APPLICATIONS LEVEL 1.
e) MODULE 3B: APPLICATIONS LEVEL 2.

Review of the Computer Competence Tests by MICHAEL J. STAHL, Professor and Head,

Department of Management, School of Business, Clemson University, Clemson, SC:

The authors of the Computer Competence Tests should be complimented for their thorough test development and reporting. Students from grades 7–12 and adults totalling 6,880 subjects were used to develop the tests and provide norms. The five different tests, entitled Development and Impact, Computer Operations—Level 1, Computer Operations—Level 2, Applications—Level 1, and Applications—Level 2, are each contained in separate manuals making administration of the separate tests easy. The tests all have satisfactory reliabilities ranging from .73 to .85.

The authors should be encouraged to undertake and report validity studies. What criteria does performance on the tests predict? Do the scores predict subsequent choice of major in college? Do the scores predict subsequent performance in collegiate computer courses? Do those who score high on the Computer Operations Test tend to pick Computer Science as a collegiate major? Do those who score high on the Applications tend to pick Business as a major? Do current computer professionals score higher on the tests than others?

The missing validity data are the only apparent shortcoming of the tests.

[74]

Coping Inventory. Purpose: "Assess the behavior patterns and skills that are the resources a person uses to meet personal needs and to adapt to the demands of the environment." Ages 3–16, adults; 1985; 2 levels; 9 scores: 3 scores (Productive, Active, Flexible) for Coping With Self, Coping With Environment, plus Adaptive Behavior Index; individual; administration time not reported; Shirley Zeitlin; Scholastic Testing Service, Inc.*

a) SELF-RATED FORM. Adults; self-report ratings of adaptive behavior; 1985 price data: $10 per 10 inventories; $5 per manual (27 pages); $9 per specimen set.

b) OBSERVATION FORM. Ages 3–16; ratings of adaptive behavior by adult informant; $15 per 20 inventories; $10 per manual (75 pages); $14 per specimen set.

TEST REFERENCES

1. Abelson, A. G., & Henritz, S. (1984). Generalization of coping skills in a group of retarded students. *Psychological Reports*, 54, 498.

2. Abelson, A. G., & Mutsch, M. A. (1985). A measure of adaptive behavior of learning disabled students. *Perceptual and Motor Skills*, 61, 862.

Review of the Coping Inventory by ALFRED B. HEILBRUN, JR., Professor of Psychology, Emory University, Atlanta, GA:

The Coping Inventory appeared in its earliest form as an observational measure of child or adolescent coping behaviors and required an adult rater as the source of evaluation. A self-report form was developed subsequently for use with older individuals. Despite the fact that the self-report version was deemed worthy of an independent manual, this manual includes essentially nothing not found already in the manual for the observation form. It also lacks any hint of the technical information that should be included. The self-report manual is clearly premature, and this review must depend upon the observation form for whatever technical information is available for the Coping Inventory. Before leaving the self-report form, however, I am compelled to wonder why the test developer chose to convert the declarative structure of her items into interrogative statements in seeking self-descriptions while maintaining a (1) *not effective* to (5) *effective most of the time* self-rating format. If my own experience is at all typical, self-raters must inhibit answering a question (e.g., "Do you stay with a task until it is completed?") by shadings of "yes" or "no," convert the statement back to declarative form (i.e., "To stay with a task until it is completed"), and then rate the behavior according to whether they perceive themselves as more or less effective in it. If interrogative item form is desired, a probabilistic rating format should be provided (e.g., 1 = *almost never* to 5 = *almost always*).

A more profound problem regarding the Coping Inventory is that its nature remains discomfortingly mysterious. It could turn out that this test measures something, perhaps something important, but the jury is certainly out as to whether "coping" properly describes what is measured. Zeitlin attempts to distinguish between adaptive behaviors that allow the person to survive and prosper and one type of adaptive behavior, coping, that allows the person to meet personal needs and environmental demands. Unfortunately, the distinction is not achieved, with the result that "adaptation" and "coping" become synonymous. This does not mean that the Coping Inventory is without worth, but it does suggest that its merits cannot be established until the conceptual cloud is lifted. Right now the Coping Inventory looks like a measure of general adjustment. Coping is more consensually reserved to describe behaviors directed toward the short-term or long-term resolution of stress, and the construct as used by Zeitlin lends nothing but confusion.

The fact that the test confounds adaptive outcomes and coping strategies is not the only conceptual problem I encountered. One assumption underlying the test is that the form of coping behaviors is the same for everybody, although the specific actions may vary. By this it is meant that all coping behaviors can be described in terms of their productive-nonproductive, flexible-rigid, and active-passive qualities. The test proceeds to assess these qualities in behaviors directed toward need fulfillment or meeting environmental demands. I have no argument with developing a measure of these three qualities of adaptive behavior. However, why ignore current views of coping (Billings & Moos, 1984; Lazarus, 1975) that stipulate discrete categories of coping behavior varying in adaptive value and differentially represented across individuals? The specific actions by which coping is implemented, the form of coping behavior, is exactly what requires measurement.

The second major issue with this instrument is how well it measures whatever it measures—general adaptation (my version) or coping behavior (Zeitlin's version). Reliability figures for the observer form, reported both in terms of interjudge agreement and alpha coefficients, were quite satisfactory. Amazingly, the self-report manual was published without a reliability figure. Some type of internal consistency index could have been provided at the very least. The question of validity was treated only within the observer-form manual, and to the test developer's credit she did make a concerted effort to marshall as much evidence as she could on the matter. Unfortunately, she has a far more relaxed view of what constitutes evidence of validity than I do. Validity is not confirmed, as Zeitlin contends, by reference to the source of test content or by the processes of inventory development. This view simply confounds the process of development with its outcome.

The observer-form manual includes evidence of relationships with other instruments that bear upon validity, although the selection is somewhat uneven in quality. For examples, Coping Inventory scores are reported to be uncorrelated with another measure of adaptive behavior (which seems rather strange), and its scales are found to include content beyond that found on measures of specific variables such as intelligence, temperament, and social competence. This is less than compelling as a statement of validation. The most relevant validity evidence presented in the manual is the normative figures for normal children and comparable figures for a number of impaired groups such as children with communication handicaps, emotional problems, neurological impairments, and perceptual deficits. Normal children do a lot better as evidenced by higher scores on all scales. These figures point to the inferior adaptive skills of children with handicaps, at least a start for determining the value of the Coping Inventory. However, there is not a shred of evidence that would link this instrument with coping behaviors as they are generally understood.

REVIEWER'S REFERENCES

Lazarus, R. S. (1975). A cognitively oriented psychologist looks at biofeedback. *American Psychologist*, 30, 553-561.

Billings, A. G., & Moos, R. H. (1984). Coping, stress, and social resources among adults with unipolar depression. *Journal of Personality and Social Psychology*, 46, 877-891.

[75]

Correctional Officers' Interest Blank. Purpose: To predict performance of correctional officers. Applicants for jobs in penal institutions and correctional agencies; 1953–82; COIB; 1987 price data: $8 per 25 test booklets; $16 per handscoring stencils; $7.50 per manual ('82, 24 pages); $8 per specimen set; (10) minutes; Harrison G. Gough and F. L. Aumack (test); Consulting Psychologists Press, Inc.*

Review of the Correctional Officers' Interest Blank by ROBERT J. HOWELL, Professor of Psychology and Director of Clinical Psychology, Brigham Young University, and R. LYNN RICHARDS, Doctoral Student, Brigham Young University, Provo, UT:

The Correctional Officers' Interest Blank (COIB) is designed to evaluate correctional officers and applicants by assessing their personal preferences and attitudes. Individual scores are compared with the scores of other correction officers. The manual recommends that "scores on the COIB should never be used as the sole or even principal basis for selection or evaluation." The COIB score functions only as collaborative data in the employment evaluation process. It is also recommended that the COIB be evaluated for its usefulness within the specific institutional setting and for particular duty assignments.

Administration time for the COIB is approximately 10 minutes. It is a two-part test consisting of 40 total items. The first part measures personal preferences and consists of 18 triads. The respondent must choose one activity that he/she would like the most and one activity that he/she would like the least from each of the triads. The second part of the test assesses personal attitudes and consists of 22 personal statements to which the respondent must choose true or false.

Scoring is completed with a stencil. The results are then compared to a smoothed frequency distribution of scores from 1,272 correctional officers. The normative group has not been clearly identified as to demographics, the type of institution, duty assignments and experience, the year in which the data were collected, the sampling design, or the participation rates.

Evidence concerning the fakability of the COIB indicates that it is resistant to the creation of false impressions on an individual basis. However, there is considerable overlap in the distributions and as such faking would be difficult to detect.

The COIB purports to measure responsibility, dependability, and good judgement. Evidence supporting the validity of these constructs was obtained by correlating the COIB with The California Psychological Inventory (CPI). This represents a major flaw in determining the construct validity of the COIB because many of the items for the second part of the test were drawn from the item pool of the CPI. Therefore, a significant number of the correlations between the CPI and COIB scales may be due to replicated items. Other evidence of construct validity is provided from more modest positive correlations, ranging from .20 to .25, that are available for the 10 highest positive descriptors on the Adjective Check List (ACL). A possible problem with this evidence is that the sample was drawn from college students and not correctional officers. Therefore, the effectiveness of the COIB in describing psychological qualities of correctional officers remains unknown.

The manual reports a median validity coefficient of .31 for the cross-validating samples, which when corrected for a reliability rating of .75 raises the coefficient to .36. It is not clear which studies are used to support this reported validity coefficient. Cross-validational data are presented both for the older version of the COIB (50 items) and the newer version (40 items), which creates some confusion as to which studies were utilized in determining the correlation coefficient. A cross-validation study is reported in which the 50-item version was given to the respondents, and the results were item analyzed. This analysis resulted in the elimination of the lower 10 items and the present 40-item version of the test. The manual avoids using coefficients derived from item analysis of the earlier 150- and 100-item versions of the test; however, the same caution is not followed with the 50-item version. Subsequent cross-validation evidence utilizing the 40-item format reported only two studies—one using 37 eastern state correction officers yielded a validity coefficient of .31, and a second study of 252 officers from the state of Ohio whose overall job rating was correlated .22 with the COIB. This coefficient was corrected for criterion unreliability which raised it to .25. The median validity coefficient of .31 seems to have been derived from item analysis of the 50-item version as well as the current 40-item version, which creates confusion as to what the true cross-validation correlation coefficient is.

Predictive validity coefficients ranging from .17 to .30 are reported for job stability. The coefficient of .30 appears to have been derived from the 50-item version of the test rather than the current 40-item version thus confusing the picture as to the true predictive validity of the current instrument.

Six-month test-retest reliability for the 50-item version of the COIB is .69. Odd-even reliability from the 50-item version appears to be approximately .71.

The manual correctly identifies the need for research with minorities, women, and correctional facilities other than state or federal correctional institutions.

The COIB appears to be moderately valid as an adjunct to the employment evaluation process. There needs to be more research into the constructs that the test purports to measure, other than from correlation with the instrument from which many of the original items were drawn. More research needs to be done using the current version of the test instead of relying on item analysis of the older 50-item version. The manual provides an excellent background section that demonstrates the evolution of the test. However, there needs to be a clearer distinction between which studies are being used to support the psychometric properties of the test.

Review of the Correctional Officers' Interest Blank by SAMUEL ROLL, Professor of Psychology and Psychiatry, University of New Mexico, Albuquerque, NM:

The Correctional Officers' Interest Blank was developed to identify and measure the personality and attitudinal factors related to successful performance as a correctional officer. Empirical and intuitive explorations lead to an emphasis on personal qualities like "sense of responsibility," "integrity," "resourcefulness," "dependability," "leadership," and "self-criticism." Other factors deemed important but already reliably measured by other instruments (e.g., intelligence and occupational background) were not included.

The original format involved having the officers respond to a set of three items indicating which one they "liked best" and which one they "liked least." An example of one set of three choices is: "(*a*) reprimand an inmate in front of others, (*b*) reprimand an inmate in private, and (*c*) turn in a report on an inmate for disciplinary action." On the current form of the test 18 of 40 items are of that variety. The rest of the items (22 out of 40) were added to the inventory later and are personality inventory items answered as "true" or "false." Most of these items are taken from the California Psychological Inventory (Gough, 1957). Sample items include "I always follow the rule: business before pleasure," "I am a better talker than listener" and "I never make judgments about people until I am sure of the facts."

A series of careful validation studies was used to decide which of the original items were useful in differentiating correctional officers according to how well the officers were ranked by their supervisors. The Correctional Officers' Interest Blank turns out to be only moderately affected by age, education, years of experience, and (according to preliminary studies) race and gender. Throughout the 35-year history, and across various forms, the test has consistently shown moderate predictive correlations with job ratings of correctional officers by supervisors, (roughly a correlation of .36) and less extensive and more modest correlations related with job stability (correlation between .17 and .30).

In addition to its careful validation, repeated cross-validation, construct validity, face validity, and moderate predictive validity the Correctional Officers' Interest Blank has a number of other positive features. It can be administered easily and quickly, individually or in groups. The reading requirement is minimal and the items are generally inviting and nonthreatening. Scoring is simple and made even simpler by a scoring stencil accompanying the test. The test manual is clearly written with the empirical support for the test objectively described. The test is also relatively impervious to "faking good." Also, at least judging from preliminary findings, the test is probably nondiscriminatory between white and black officers and between men and women. A correlation between the Correctional Officers' Interest Blank and the California Psychological Inventory indicates the psychological qualities being measured by the Correctional Officers' Interest Blank can best be summarized as "responsibility and socialization," which share a common emphasis on internalization of values, acceptance of society norms, and ability to perform well in settings where rules must be respected.

In sum, the Correctional Officers' Interest Blank is an example of a solidly-based instrument with a specific, limited aim, a careful empirical base, careful validation and cross validation, and a history of programmatic research that has yielded the most that can probably be expected in such a complex area of personnel selection, namely a practical, fair, carefully built instrument with modest potential for prediction.

REVIEWER'S REFERENCE

Gough, H. G. (1957). *Manual for the California Psychological Inventory*. Palo Alto, CA: Consulting Psychologists Press, Inc.

[76]

Data Entry Operator Aptitude Test. Purpose: "Evaluates a candidate's aptitude for success as a Data Entry Operator." Candidates for data entry operators; 1982; DEOAT; 5 scores: Coding, Numerical Skills, Manual Dexterity, Clerical Accuracy/Detail/Editing, Overall; 1987 price data: $20

($35 if scored by publisher) per test including manual (no date, 7 pages); French edition available; 20(30) minutes; Wolfe Personnel Testing & Training Systems, Inc.*

Review of the Data Entry Operator Aptitude Test by DAVID O. HERMAN, Measurement Research Services, Inc., New York, NY:

The DEOAT is intended primarily for selecting "data entry operators," presumably the computerized successors to keypunch operators. Each of the four sections of the test has a 5-minute time limit and is described as a test of both speed and accuracy. Thus if the test lived up to its claims it would be an attractive and brief instrument to help select workers in an increasingly important occupation. This review will present evidence about how well the DEOAT and its supporting documents meet current test standards.

The first section of the test, Coding, involves substituting one set of letter or number codes for another. The task is similar to that of the familiar Digit Symbol test of the Wechsler scales, but probably calls for more mental processing than does the Wechsler task. Section II, Numerical Skills, requires the examinee to perform one or two arithmetic operations sequentially. The items include no words, but only numbers and the four conventional operations signs. The first 40 items involve only integers, but the remaining 20 items require manipulation of fractions and decimals.

For each item of Section III, Manual Dexterity, the examinee must draw a line along a maze-like pathway without touching the path walls. An unusual feature of the test is that the examinee traces one or more figures with one hand, then draws identical figures with the other hand, and finally traces the figure with both hands simultaneously using pathways printed side by side. The pathways become narrower and the figures smaller as the test progresses, making the task increasingly difficult.

Each item of Section IV, Clerical Accuracy, Detail & Editing, presents four sets of letters, numbers, symbols, or letter-number-symbol combinations. Any number of these sets, from none to all four, may be identical, and the examinee must identify the ones that are the same.

The administration instructions indicate that the DEOAT is essentially self-administering in that examinees read for themselves the directions for each section and work the sample problems. The instructions offer no guidance to the tester should the examinee have trouble understanding the tasks. Although the manual emphasizes that the test must be administered under supervision, it fails to caution users to be alert for applicants who disobey the instructions for Section III and thereby make the task easier. For example, an inattentive examiner may not see an applicant use his preferred hand to mark pathways intended for the nonpreferred hand.

Scoring is usually done by a scoring center in New Jersey, which sends a report of the results to the client company. Under certain restrictions, however, clients may obtain a special Scoring Guide from the publisher and do their own scoring locally. According to instructions in this guide, the raw score on each section of the test is the number of correct answers (weighted in the case of Section III), less some function of the number of errors. Critical portions of the scoring directions are ambiguous, but it appears that the section scores are then weighted and summed to yield an overall total score. In turn the total score is transformed to a "percent score," a needless step and a misleading name for the score that is to be interpreted. (The percent score is not the percentage of items answered correctly, as its name implies.)

The percent score appears to be the only score interpreted. Although the manual notes that the section subscores are converted to stanines, which implies interpretation of performance on the separate parts, the manual and the Scoring Guide are otherwise silent on the issue.

Percentile norms for the percent score are available for a sample of 93 experienced candidates for positions as data entry operators. The sample is in other respects undescribed. The manual presents no reliability data.

An empirical validity study is reported for 40 female data entry operators employed by 12 different companies. The correlation of the DEOAT percent score with supervisory ratings was .41. The relationships between the subscores and the criterion are not reported.

COMMENT. The DEOAT materials include no meaningful discussion of the relevance of its tasks to the job of data entry operator. Measures of an applicant's speed and accuracy in coding and clerical checking tasks have a surface relevance to the work in question. Other abilities tapped by the DEOAT do not share this face validity, however, and should be supported by evidence. An important example relates to the Manual Dexterity section. How does precise line-drawing with a pencil relate to operating a computer or terminal keyboard? This question is most relevant for the portions of Section III that involve drawing with the nonpreferred hand and drawing simultaneously with both hands.

Similarly, the relevance of numerical computation to data entry tasks may be in question, especially because one-third of the items of Section II require facility with fractions and decimals. It must be added that one of the numbers in this section is printed as "10.001 1/2," reflecting unconventional notation, to say the least; that two of the answers provided in the Scoring Guide are wrong; and that three other answers in the guide have been truncated back to one or two decimal places, so that inexperienced scorers may deny credit to the correct, longer answers.

Three of the four sections of the DEOAT resemble the kinds of tests often used in clerical selection. It is to the author's credit that item formats have novel aspects that should minimize practice effects from exposure to previous employment testing. However, the novelty of the dexterity task appears to offer no advantage, for neither data nor appropriate discussion of construct validity addresses the critical issue of why the dexterity section is included at all. The one empirical validity study summarized in the test materials presents no criterion correlations for the subscores, as noted earlier; these might have provided some of the missing evidence.

Further, it is the reviewer's opinion that the manual indefensibly recommends using the DEOAT for certain secondary purposes. These include determining whether examinees need more training, measuring the effectiveness of training, and reviewing employees' career goals. Such purposes would be met better with measures of job performance than with aptitude measures such as the DEOAT. Unsupported and illogical claims of this kind should have been avoided.

Incompleteness and ambiguity in the directions for obtaining and transforming scores, errors in the scoring key, and lack of reliability information all reflect carelessness in preparing the DEOAT materials. Many of these flaws could be repaired by editing and revision. At present, however, there is little to recommend the DEOAT for its stated purpose on anything but a cautious, experimental basis.

Review of the Data Entry Operator Aptitude Test by RICHARD W. JOHNSON, Associate Director and Adjunct Professor, University Counseling Service, University of Wisconsin-Madison, Madison, WI:

The Data Entry Operator Aptitude Test (DEOAT) was designed to aid in the selection of data entry or terminal operators. It consists of four subtests (Coding Skill, Numerical Facility, Manual Dexterity, and Clerical Accuracy), each of which has a time limit of 5 minutes. Relatively little information is available for evaluating this test.

The brief manual for the DEOAT offers no rationale for the selection of the four subtests. It gives no information concerning the intercorrelations of the subtests or their relative effectiveness in predicting job performance. It provides no data to help determine the influence of speed and guessing on the test results.

Normative data reported in the manual are based on "93 experienced candidates" who are not further described. The degree to which this group is representative of the entire population of data entry operators is unknown.

There is limited information on scoring. According to the Scoring Guide, raw scores for three of the subtests (all but Coding) must first be multiplied by a weighting factor (ranging from 1.5 to 2.0) before they are converted to percentages. No explanation is provided as to why the weighting factors are used. The score for the Manual Dexterity subtest is calculated by subtracting points from a set amount each time a candidate "touches or crosses a boundary line." No data are given regarding the interjudge reliability of this scoring procedure. It is also unclear why so many points are assigned to the Manual Dexterity subtest (210 of 465 total possible points). After the raw scores are converted to percentages, the percentages are interpreted in terms of four categories ranging from "HIRE—candidate is likely to be a superior performer" (84% to 100%) to "DO NOT HIRE" (0% to 44%). No empirical data (e.g., expectancy tables) are provided to justify using these particular cutoff scores.

The test authors provide no information regarding the reliability of candidates' scores. Because of the heavy emphasis on speed, candidates' scores may change considerably upon retesting once they have become familiar with the nature of the test. A test-retest study would be helpful in determining to what extent scores may be expected to change upon retesting.

Only one validity study has been conducted. This study showed a moderate degree of relationship $r = .41$) between the DEOAT total score and supervisor ratings for a sample of 40 workers. It is not clear if the supervisors who evaluated the performance of the data entry operators had knowledge of their test scores or not. If they did, the correlation coefficient could be spuriously high. At any rate, additional validity studies with larger sample sizes are needed before one can place much confidence in the results.

The DEOAT cannot be recommended for commercial use because of the limited amount of information available for evaluating it and because so little research evidence is provided to support its use. According to recent research, the performance of data entry operators and related workers may be predicted with a fair degree of accuracy by special tests of reasoning ability, quantitative ability, or perceptual speed or by general tests of mental ability or clerical aptitude (Pearlman, Schmidt, & Hunter, 1980). Meta-analyses of a large number of studies (Hunter & Hunter, 1984) indicate that ability tests are more successful in predicting performance in clerical jobs or other types of jobs than are nearly all alternative predictors (e.g., biographical inventories, reference checks, interviews, or training and experience ratings). Previous research which indicated that the predictive validity of ability tests varied substantially from job situation to job situation appears to have been unduly influenced by sampling errors and other statistical artifacts (errors of measurement and restriction of range in the criterion variable). When the statistical artifacts are taken into account, the predictive validities of the different types of ability tests are similar for different jobs within broad occupational categories (e.g., computing and account-recording occupations). With this body of research in mind, the test user may wish to select a combination of ability tests from the PSI Basic Skills Tests for Business, Industry, and Government, a general mental ability test such as the Wonderlic Personnel Test, or an established clerical aptitude test such as the Short Employment Tests to help predict the job performance of data entry operators and related workers. Any of these possibilities would be preferable to the DEOAT.

REVIEWER'S REFERENCES

Pearlman, K., Schmidt, F. L., & Hunter, J. E. (1980). Validity generalization results for tests used to predict job proficiency and training success in clerical occupations. *Journal of Applied Psychology*, 65, 373-406.

Hunter, J. E., & Hunter, R. F. (1984). Validity and utility of alternative predictors of job performance. *Psychological Bulletin*, 96, 72-98.

[77]

Decision Making Inventory. Purpose: "To assess an individual's preferred style of decision making." High school and college students; 1983; DMI; 4 scores: 2 Information-Gathering Styles (Systematic, Spontaneous), 2 Information-Analysis Styles (Internal, External); 1984 price data: $6 per 30 inventories; $1 per 2 scoring grids; $10 per manual (72 pages); specimen set included with manual; (10–15) minutes; William Coscarelli, Richard Johnson (test), and JaDean Johnson (test); Marathon Consulting & Press.*

TEST REFERENCES

1. Coscarelli, W. C. (1983). Development of a decision-making inventory to assess Johnson's decision making styles. *Measurement and Evaluation in Guidance*, 16, 149-160.

2. Ferrell, B. G. (1983). A factor analytic comparison of four learning-styles instruments. *Journal of Educational Psychology*, 75, 33-39.

3. Gordon, V. N., Coscarelli, W. C., & Sears, S. J. (1986). Comparative assessments of individual differences in learning and career decision making. *Journal of College Student Personnel*, 27, 233-242.

Review of the Decision Making Inventory by GEORGE DOMINO, Professor of Psychology, University of Arizona, Tucson, AZ:

The DMI is intended to operationalize a theoretical model (Johnson, 1978) that was formulated to assist counselors' understanding of clients' decision-making styles as well as to assist researchers in their investigation of the process of decision making. The theory, based on Johnson's work in a college counseling center, proposes that there are two basic processes of gathering information, the Spontaneous and the Systematic, and two basic processes of analyzing information, Internal and External. The spontaneous and systematic approaches are differentiated along five dimensions: goal orientation, choosing among alternatives, thinking patterns, speed of commitment to new ideas, and reaction to events. The result is a fourfold typology of systematic-internal, systematic-external, spontaneous-internal, and spontaneous-external.

The current DMI is apparently the sixth version, although prior versions seemed to be significantly different from one another; for example, the first version consisted of 29 forced-choice items, while the second version consisted of 66 items of unspecified form. The current version consists of 20 items, but only 12 are scored so that each of the four scales is based on only three items. The items are standard personality-type items, each to be responded to on a 6-point scale where only the end points are labeled. A representative (but made up) item is: I prefer to think carefully before making a decision (never o o o o o o always). Each item is scored on a 1 to 7 scale, with 4 omitted, so that scores on each scale (e.g., Spontaneous-External) can range from 3 to 21.

The manual presents the results of five administrations of the DMI to: (*a*) Sample 1—73 undergraduate students enrolled in an introductory interpersonal communication course, in which the DMI was followed by either a 10-, 20-, or 30-minute presentation on the constructs assessed by the DMI, and students were then asked to guess their decision-making style; (*b*) Sample 2—316 students in freshman orientation courses; (*c*) Sample 3—113 students also in freshman orientation courses, 58 of whom were retested a week later; (*d*) Sample 4—313 students enrolled in a second year chemistry course, where information on high school rank, college GPA, chemistry course grade, and ACT scores was obtained (the manual does not indicate whether these were students' reports, registrar's records, etc.); (*e*) Sample 5—67 students enrolled in a freshman orientation course, who were administered the Kolb Learning Style Inventory, Harren's Decision Making Style subscale of the Assessment of Career Decision Making questionnaire, and the DMI. These five samples are clearly captive samples, with the results of the first three cited in the body of the manual, while the last two are relegated to an appendix.

The first and most striking result from those studies is the low reliability of the DMI. For sample 1, alpha coefficients range from .40 to .68, for sample 2 from .36 to .60, and for sample 3 from .29 to .69; test-retest coefficients for sample 3 range from .41 to .71. Considering the brevity of the scales, these low coefficients are not surprising, and certainly not acceptable. Considering that each scale is actually made up of three different versions of the same item, greater internal consistency might be expected. The results from the various samples are consistent in indicating that the External scale is the most reliable and Spontaneous the least.

The results of each DMI administration were also factor analyzed, and these analyses support the presence of four factors, accounting for approximately 54 to 60 percent of the total score variance. Scale intercorrelations, however, indicate substantial correlations between the External and Internal scales (-.33 to -.48), the Systematic and the Internal scales (.48 to .66), the External and Spontaneous (.31 to .52), and the Systematic and Spontaneous (-.19 to -.41), calling into question the relative independence of the four scales.

Validity data is scant and the reader has to wade through a variety of tables for which no statistical tests of significance are given. For example, for sample 4, the fourfold typology is analyzed in terms of high-school rank, college GPA, chemistry grade, and ACT scores. The only presumably significant difference is that spontaneous-internal students had a substantially lower high school rank than did the other groups. There is no indication in this table of the relative frequency or sex composition of each type, or whether a statistical analysis such as ANOVA was performed.

Two tables address the question of sex differences, one based on 216 students (part of sample 2), the other on 282 students (part of sample 4). Both tables present the raw frequencies and the percent of the total samples, with no chi-square or other statistical test of significance. It is left up to the reader to do the appropriate analysis, which is made more challenging by the typographical error found in Table A-4, where 112 + 43 is made to equal 185.

Given that Johnson's theoretical observations evolved in a counseling center setting, it would seem natural to test the validity of the DMI in such a setting, but the manual reports no such efforts. Similarly, it would seem basic to assess the validity of the DMI not only against other questionnaires, but against real world criteria. For example, the manual states that spontaneous thinkers excel in divergent thinking, but no evidence to support this claim is presented.

The manual is to a large extent a repetition of the information found in several journal articles, and lacks organized coherence. It contains a discussion of decision making using simple-minded analogies from physics, and a theoretical analysis of task groups, both of which seem out of place in a test manual. Incidentally, the manual gives 16 references, but 7 of these are to convention papers, personal communications, and unpublished manuscripts—all sources unavailable to the typical reader. The manual contains a number of typographical errors and reads like a series of studies rather than a coherent piece of work. Johnson's observations are given the status of a theory, which seems too grandiose a term, and the response options are called a "Likert" scale, simply because they involve something more than a true-false response.

In summary, the DMI has low reliability and there is little evidence of validity. Use of this instrument for any purpose is not recommended.

Review of the Decision Making Inventory by BARBARA A. KERR, *Assistant Professor of Counselor Education, The University of Iowa, Iowa City, IA:*

The Decision Making Inventory is based on a theory developed by one counselor based on his clinical observations. As such, it is probably most useful to adherents who wish to engage in research related to that theory. As an instrument to measure decision-making style for diagnostic or classification purposes, it is severely flawed by its isolation from any empirical work in the areas of information processing and cognition. The test author's (Johnson, 1978) theory states that individuals may be classified as gathering information in either a systematic or spontaneous manner and as analyzing information either internally (that is, silently) or externally (that is, out loud). The Decision Making Inventory is a set of 12 items embedded in a 20-item scale, designed to place individuals on both continua so as to determine a "decision-making style."

The author admits to using a combination of inductive and deductive methodologies in the development of this inventory, and perhaps that is what makes this scale difficult to evaluate. Much work has been put into validation and establishment of reliability by Johnson's colleagues, but the methodologies used in these studies were often inadequate, and the overall results provide weak support for the theory and the instrument. In the three studies reported in the manual, reliability as measured by internal consistency of the scales ranged from moderate (.69 for External) to very low (.29 for Spontaneous). Validity research consisted of weak techniques such as teaching students the theory, asking which style they thought they might be, and comparing their responses to the scores on the instrument. An instrument which required teaching the construct in order to obtain construct validity is not a strong one. Factor analyses of the inventory did not lead to impressive amounts of variance being accounted for by the posited factors, and overlap with other measures of decision-making style was small or nonexistent.

In short, the development of the Decision Making Inventory seems to have been hampered by the original inadequacy of the theory upon which it is based. This instrument would probably not be useful unless completely overhauled, with a comprehensive review of the literature of decision-making as the first step for the developers.

REVIEWER'S REFERENCE

Johnson, R. H. (1978). Individual styles of decision-making: A theoretical model for counseling. *The Personnel and Guidance Journal*, 56, 530-536.

[78]

Decoding Skills Test. Purpose: Measures the reading levels and decoding skills of elementary school readers and identifies reading disabled children and provides a diagnostic profile of their decoding skill development. Grades 1.0–5.8+; 1985; DST; "criterion-referenced"; 3 subtests yielding 22 scores: Basal Vocabulary (Instructional Level, Frustration Level), Phonic Patterns (Monosyllabic, Polysyllabic [Long Vowel, Short Vowel, Vowel Digraph, Single Consonant, Consonant Blend, on real and nonsense words]), Contextual Decoding (Instructional Level [Reading Rate, Error Rate, Phonic Words, Comprehension], Frustration Level [Reading Rate, Error Rate, Phonic Words, Comprehension]); individual; 1985 price data: $56.50 per complete kit including 24 scoring booklets (15 pages), presentation book (22 pages), and manual ('85, 57 pages); $8 per 24 scoring booklets; (30–45) minutes; Ellis Richardson and Barbara DiBenedetto; York Press, Inc.*

Review of the Decoding Skills Test by STEPHEN N. ELLIOTT, Associate Professor of Educational Psychology, University of Wisconsin-Madison, Madison, WI:

The Decoding Skills Test (DST) is a diagnostic, criterion-referenced test for elementary school children (grades 1–5) that lives up to its name and purpose. Specifically, the test provides instructionally relevant indices of basal vocabulary recognition, decoding in context, and phonic skill development for fundamental vowel and consonant patterns. The experienced reading teacher or clinician will find it a well-structured test that yields a rich array of diagnostic information; the novice user, however, may find it challenging to administer and score.

The DST was developed originally as part of a grant from the National Institute of Child Health and Human Development to study the discrete decoding skills of disabled readers. Consequently, several major investigations have been reported in which the DST has been used to characterize the reading behaviors of children. The various research projects provide a strong field-test component for the DST and have facilitated the refinement of interpretative information and the documentation of psychometric qualities. The resulting DST package is comprised of three subtests: Basal Vocabulary, Phonic Patterns, and Contextual Decoding. An 11-level word difficulty index derived from a content analysis of basal reading series (preprimer through fifth grades) is used to organize materials within both the Basal Vocabulary and Contextual Decoding subtests. The materials in the DST test package include an easel-style test book (black print on white pages); a test manual with test administration, interpretation, and psychometric information; a 14-page scoring booklet; a Phonic Profile Worksheet; and a basal/ceiling and error scoring key. This latter component is redundant with content in the test manual, but it serves to highlight critical administration procedures. Now to some comments about technical aspects of this test.

STANDARDIZATION. The sample of children (N approximately 1,500) used to develop the DST involved both good and poor readers in grades 1 through 5 from New York City and Atlanta schools. Gender and race characteristics of the children are not provided in the manual; however, over 1,400 of the children were described as being from low SES neighborhoods.

In the development of a criterion-referenced test, the sampling of test content is as (or more) important than the sample of individuals used to validate the test. With regard to the DST, its authors appear to have done a thorough job of selecting relevant words from 10 widely used reading programs. These programs are listed in the manual and represent a balance between "meaning emphasis" and "code emphasis" approaches to reading. In sum, the authors seem to have done a very good job of content selection and an adequate job of sampling children representative of good and poor readers.

SCORING AND INTERPRETATION. The three DST subtests provide the content and a complex array of objective scores giving the experienced user information about (*a*) words in a child's basal vocabulary, (*b*) the effects of context on word recognition, (*c*) a child's knowledge of basic phonic patterns (VC, VCe, and VV) in real and nonsense words, and (*d*) oral fluency and error types at both instructional and frustration levels of text. In addition to these basic decoding skills, recall comprehension is evaluated on the Contextual Decoding subtest. To derive all this information requires approximately 60 minutes of administration time and 15 minutes of scoring. This is a rather substantial time investment that cannot easily be reduced with practice. It is a simple fact that users of the DST must be prepared to invest about 1½ hours of their time for each child they evaluate; but as with many other endeavors, you get what you pay for! Let me elaborate on some of what you get.

From the Basal Vocabulary subtest you get a functional list of words a child can and cannot recognize in isolation. The summation of a child's performance on this array of words of ever increasing difficulty is a raw score that can be transferred easily to Instructional Level and Frustration Level indices. Although the concepts of instructional and frustration level are widely used in reading assessment, the criteria for operationalizing them vary across experts. The authors of the DST do not provide any specific information about the criteria they employed to derive these two reading levels, however, the combination of ecologically valid content and a conservative basal/ceiling rule seems to have resulted in a pragmatic characterization of Instructional and Frustration levels of reading.

From the Contextual Reading subtest, one is able to characterize a child's reading rate, error rate, phonic words, and comprehension for both Instructional and Frustration levels of reading. One unique and valuable design feature of this subtest is that 10 words from each level of the Basal Vocabulary subtest are used in each of the passages the child is required to read aloud. Thus, one is able to get a sense of the influence of context on the recognition of this subset of basal target words at each difficulty level. The authors note that one could use the Basal Vocabulary and Phonic Patterns subtests alone as a short form version of the DST. This would probably save about 35 minutes of administration and scoring time.

The Phonic Patterns subtest is comprised of monosyllabic and polysyllabic real and nonsense words that are divided into four subsets accordingly. From responses to this array of words, one can derive four phonic pattern profiles: a phonic transfer index, which provides a sense of reader's ability to generalize phonic knowledge from monosyllabic words to polysyllabic words; a vowel pattern profile across vowel-consonant, vowel-consonant with an ending e, and vowel-vowel constructions; a consonant pattern profile across single consonants and blends; and finally, a syllabic patterns profile based on responses to the monosyllabic and polysyllabic words. Scoring of this rather lengthy set of profiles is facilitated by the Phonic Profile Worksheet. The four phonic pattern profiles are intuitively appealing and have been found to differentiate good and poor readers; however, the use of different scale metrics (e.g., 0 to 1.0 for the Phonic Transfer Index and 0 to 40 on Vowel Patterns) across the various profiles is never adequately explained.

RELIABILITY AND VALIDITY. The authors stress the major validity issue for a criterion-referenced test should concern content. This reviewer agrees that content validity is important and consequently, must be somewhat critical of the authors for not doing a better job at clearly documenting the degree of overlap between the words on the DST and the popular basal reading series from which the words were derived.

With regard to standard indices of psychometric qualities, the authors reported adequate interrater reliabilities, high test-retest (over a 5-month period) reliabilities, and very high indices of internal consistency. Correlational evidence from several different samples provide support for construct and predictive validity. Of note are data indicating the DST is highly correlated with teacher-generated program placements for children across elementary grades. Thus it seems the DST does provide information on the mastery of discrete decoding skills and that this information is predictive of performance in classroom reading programs.

SUMMARY. The DST is a new criterion-referenced, diagnostic test of elementary students' decoding skills. The selection of content from major basal reading series enhances the overlap between testing and teaching, and coupled with a rich array of interpretative scores, seems to offer teachers an instructionally relevant tool for programming for disabled readers. The test compares favorably with the decoding subtests of established diagnostic reading tests such as the Woodcock Reading Mastery Tests and yet allows for more informal performance analyses that many educators have come to value in the Brigance Diagnostic Inventories. The major limitation of the DST is that it requires nearly 1 1/2 hours to administer and score. Many experts will also certainly note the standardizaton sample was small and nonrepresentative of the U.S. population. All in all, however, this reviewer found the DST to be a welcome addition to the evaluation and programming arsenal of educators working with young readers.

Review of the Decoding Skills Test by TIMOTHY S. HARTSHORNE, Assistant Professor of Counseling and School Psychology, Wichita State University, Wichita, KS:

Models of reading typically refer to two primary processes: decoding and comprehension. The Decoding Skills Test (DST), identified by the authors as a "diagnostic, criterion-referenced instrument," addresses the first.

The DST is a well-packaged instrument. The manual is clear, with numerous examples of both scoring and interpretation. Test presentation is by the increasingly popular spiral booklet that stands up with testing instructions on one side, and child materials on the other. The pages, with the exception of page 1, are numbered, so instructions to place the book so that page 1 faces you create momentary confusion. Also, because six word lists typically reside on the same page, children can get lost, requiring the tester to lean over the book to help locate the correct spot. But these are minor problems. The scoring protocol is nicely designed to facilitate scoring, with plenty of space for markings and diagnostic notations in addition to those typically scored.

Criterion-referenced tests are becoming popular in education due to their link to instructional intervention. Although there are different definitions of criterion referenced, most refer to a comparison of the testee's score with mastery. Unfortunately, mastery of decoding skills is not something that has been clearly defined. The authors do an admirable job of breaking down decoding skills into pronouncing basic vocabulary words, pronouncing words with particular consonant and vowel patterns, and pronouncing words in context. However, the choice of words came from an analysis of 10 "widely used reading programs." Thus mastery is defined in terms of commonalities in vocabulary between the 10 programs. Scores for the DST can then be reported in terms of grade equivalents for instructional and frustration reading levels. But grade equivalents are essentially norm-referenced scores (e.g., "The child's score places him at the beginning third grade level with regard to decoding"). In fairness to the authors, there is probably no other viable alternative for constructing the test, but it might more accurately be described as a "curriculum-referenced" instrument.

Norms for the test might, in fact, be useful. Raw scores are derived that have no meaning other than as a measure of progress between administrations. Norms could aid in the definition of "good" versus "poor" readers, as well as provide an interesting comparison with grade equivalent scores. The authors do provide some normative interpretation for scores on the contextual decoding subtest as an aid in interpretation, but with no supporting evidence.

Reliability and validity methods for criterion-referenced instruments are still in the development stage. Data from a small number of studies of the DST are reported, two of good and poor readers and another of two schoolwide samples in two states. Reliability is reported in terms of interrater agreement (.84–1.00, "with most above 90%"), split-half coefficients (.95–.99, with no mention of whether corrected by Spearman-Brown or not), coefficient Alphas (.97–.99), Guttman Lambdas (.97–.99), and test-retest. The test-retest was over a 5-month period, and both full and partial correlations were calculated, the latter with grade placement partialed out. The correlations were quite high, the zero order ranging from .85 to .96, and the partial from .84 to .93. The authors note in the test manual that "the relationship between scores remains relatively constant across five months in spite of the influence of other variables (e.g., instruction and individual ability), (indicating) that the DST is a highly reliable instrument." This seems to be a strange virtue in a criterion-referenced test. Would it not be desirable to have a test that is highly sensitive to the effects of instruction?

As the authors note, content validity is of great significance in a criterion-referenced test. They present a very clear description of how content was selected, but their justification relies heavily on the work of curriculum developers, and no concrete evidence is presented to support the validity of those reading programs. However, it is clear the authors took painstaking care to select items that are highly representative of the domain.

Other validity data for the DST are basically concurrent and predictive. Correlations with Iowa Test of Basic Skills (ITBS), New York City-Wide Reading Test, Gilmore Oral Reading Test, and Gates-MacGinitie Reading Tests are typically in the .70 to .90 range. Convergent construct validity is provided by the slightly higher correlations with vocabulary over comprehension subtests of the above instruments. Evidence of predictive validity comes from correlations between DST subtests and ITBS scores 7 months later. These show the same convergent trend noted above, but with ITBS vocabulary, correlations are .93 for Basal Vocabulary, .83 for Phonic Patterns, and .93 for Contextual Decoding. Correlations with grade partialed out are only slightly lower.

Although these validity studies are encouraging, one other concurrent and predictive correlation is more perplexing, and that is with program placement. For program placement at the present time, (calculated separately for basal reader and phonics), the coefficients range from .83 to .94. For future program placement, the coefficients range from .83 to .93. What this really suggests is that teachers do an excellent job of matching the children to their appropriate reading level, as one might determine from the DST, without the use of the DST.

This is probably the major concern in choosing this instrument. Although the authors estimate one-half hour for administration, this reviewer spent an hour and a half administering it to one first grader. Thus test users must make the decision as to whether the diagnostic quality of the instrument is worth the time invested, particularly because the test authors have found such a close correspondence between test results and program placement. Other tests are available that measure not only decoding skills but comprehension as well. With only a limited amount of time to invest, other tests may provide more appropriate information.

However, for those children whose primary difficulty seems to be in the area of decoding, the authors of the DST are quite correct that the instrument yields a wealth of data, and can provide evidence for different kinds of decoding difficulties. Reliability and validity data are promising, and test users should have confidence in the test results. The extent to which these results lead to differential instruction and successful intervention will be critical in the ultimate evaluation of the DST's utility.

[79]

Defense Mechanisms Inventory. Purpose: Measures "the defense mechanisms of individuals in clinical and other applied settings." Adolescents, adults, and elderly; 1968–86; DMI; adolescent and elderly versions are for research purposes only; 5 scores: Turning Against Object, Projection, Principalization, Turning Against Self, Reversal; 2 forms (male, female) for each of 3 versions (Adolescent, Adult, Elderly); 1989 price data: $45 per comprehensive kit including male and female test booklets for Adolescents, Adults, and the Elderly, 25 answer sheets, male and female profile sheets for college students and general adults, scoring key, instructions for hand scoring, set of 5 scoring templates (for all age groups), manual ('86, 179 pages), DMI Bibliography ('88, 12 pages); $10 per 10 reusable test booklets (specify male or female and Adolescent, Adult, or Elderly); $5 per 25 answer sheets; $10 per set of scoring templates; $5 per 25 profile sheets (specify adult or student and male or female); $22 per manual; $5 per bibliography; $8 per specimen set (specify Adolescent, Adult, or Elderly) including male and female test booklet, 2 answer sheets, scoring key, instructions for hand scoring, and DMI bibliography; (45) minutes; David Ihilevich and Goldine C. Gleser; DMI Associates.*

See T3:665 (14 references); see also 8:534 (30 references), and T2:1152 (5 references); for a review by James A. Walsh, see 7:63 (4 references).

TEST REFERENCES

1. Frank, S. J., McLaughlin, A. M., & Crusco, A. (1984). Sex role attributes, symptom distress, and defensive style among college men and women. *Journal of Personality and Social Psychology*, 47, 182-192.

2. Greenberg, R. P., & Fisher, S. (1984). Menstrual discomfort, psychological defenses, and feminine identification. *Journal of Personality Assessment*, 48, 643-648.

3. Minskoff, S., & Curtis, J. M. (1984). Comparison of defense mechanisms utilized in perception by congenitally blind and sighted respondents. *Psychological Reports*, 55, 228-230.

4. Peglar, M., & Borgen, F. H. (1984). The defense mechanisms of coronary patients. *Journal of Clinical Psychology*, 40, 669-679.

5. Pekarik, G., Blodgett, C., Evans, R. G., & Wierzbicki, M. (1984). Variables related to continuance in a behavioral weight loss program. *Addictive Behaviors*, 9, 413-416.

6. Juni, S., & Cohen, P. (1985). Partial impulse erogeneity as a function of fixation and object relations. *The Journal of Sex Research*, 21, 275-291.

7. Moses, I., & Reyher, J. (1985). Spontaneous and directed visual imagery: Image failure and image substitution. *Journal of Personality and Social Psychology*, 48, 233-242.

8. Assor, A., Aronoff, J., & Messé, L. A. (1986). An experimental test of defensive processes in impression formation. *Journal of Personality and Social Psychology*, 50, 644-650.

Review of the Defense Mechanisms Inventory by JAMES J. HENNESSY, Associate Professor of Psychological and Educational Services, Fordham University, New York, NY:

The Defense Mechanisms Inventory (DMI), which measures most and least likely responses to hypothetical conflicts, is essentially unchanged in content, format, and rationale since the review by Walsh (7:63). It is a 200-item, forced-choice inventory that yields scores on five defense mechanism scales: Turning Against Object (TAO), Projection (PRO), Principalization (PRN), Turning Against Self (TAS), and Reversal (REV). These five encompass the many specific defense mechanisms uncovered in clinical and research settings. Each mechanism is assessed in four domains (feelings about a conflict, fantasized behavior in response to it, thoughts about it, and anticipated actual response to it) in response to 10 stories that represent five commonly-experienced types of conflict (authority, independence, competition, sexual identity, and situations).

The major change in the DMI is the development of an extensive manual in which theoretical, psychometric, and clinical issues are presented in great detail. The manual is really a monograph on defense mechanisms rather than a user's manual for an inventory. It is only after 121 pages of text that a reader finds an appendix describing the administration, scoring, and interpretation of the inventory.

The extensive discussion of theoretical issues and research findings not specifically related to the DMI clouded the presentation about the inventory itself. For example, much of the material in the validity sections pertained to studies in which the DMI was not used, but from which statements about the validity of it were extrapolated. Also, the discussion in several places about the critical differences between conscious, intentional coping styles and unconscious, automatic defensive reactions was not sufficiently focused to support assertions that the inventory measures stable response dispositions or psychological reflexes that are activated by unconscious processes. The psychological entities purportedly measured by the DMI were not clearly or concisely explained or differentiated.

The evidence for the reliability of the DMI is impressive, especially in light of its ipsative format and the vagueness of its underlying construct. Averaged internal consistency coefficients for a combined sample of over 1,000 late-adolescent and adult respondents ranged from .61 to .80 for the five defense scales. Stability coefficients for those scales ranged from .62 to .82 for samples of over 400 college students tested at intervals of 17 to 28 days. The internal consistency estimates of the four level scores (feelings, thoughts, etc.) varied considerably leading the authors to state there was not sufficient justification to warrant treating them as separate entities.

While the DMI appears to be as reliable as most well-developed personality measures, the evidence for its validity in most instances is scant. Trained clinicians and graduate students in psychology in two separate studies could not accurately match DMI items with their respective defense mechanisms, and a principal component analysis indicated the DMI was composed of two (not five) stable factors. Thus the internal and factor validity of the inventory is equivocal. A host of unrelated studies were presented to support the DMI's validity as a predictor of clinically important issues including differential diagnosis, response to therapeutic treatment, and hemispheric specialization. Most of the research reviewed did not include the DMI, but rather used instruments that in other studies were found to correlate at varying magnitudes with the DMI. These one-step-removed analyses do not provide direct evidence of the validity of the DMI; that point should be clearly stated in the manual to avoid unintentionally misleading a user.

The findings from studies in which the DMI was used are inconclusive at best. Virtually all of them were correlational in which the correlates were either easily-obtained, but clinically questionable, characteristics of respondents (age, sex, SES, etc.) or ill-defined criteria such as psychosocial adaptation, anxiety, or self-esteem. The substantive meaning of many of the significant correlations could not be readily explained and in some instances seemed to be opposite those expected. In the few studies in which a highly explicit outcome or criterion was specified (weight-loss, length of survival after surgery) the DMI did not operate as expected. The authors' claim, following their reporting these negative findings, that the studies "give some indication of the potential clinical value of the DMI" is misleading almost to the point of being disingenuous.

Normative data are available derived from either a college or general adult male and female sample. Means and standard deviations by sex also are reported for several groups tested between 1969 and 1978 and it was from aggregating these that the two larger, primary norms tables were generated. Raw scores are transformed to *T*-scores on the profile report form using the sex-appropriate general adult or college norms.

The rationale for converting ipsatively-computed raw scores to what are called "standardized," though not normalized, *T*-scores is not given. The shifting between an intraindividual/ipsative focus and an interindividual/normative one exemplifies the basic problem with the DMI. If its intent is to identify the consistent way in which a person deals with a perceived threat, the within-person differentiation of response patterns is of paramount concern. Determining that person's response profile does not require considering the ranking of the person's preferences in relations to other people. Given that virtually all of the research reviewed in the manual treated DMI scores normatively, its value as an intraindividual measure has not yet been determined. The adequacy of its norms is of secondary importance to its usefulness in identifying cross-situational response consistencies within an individual.

In summary, the DMI continues to have a number of problems. It has not demonstrated how to differentiate measures of automatic defense styles from intentional coping styles. It reliably measures responses to hypothetical conflict situations, but the relationships between those response tendencies and important clinical or theoretical functions are tenuous at best. The authors state that the recently developed versions for adolescents and the elderly are intended for research purposes only; that same caveat must also apply to the standard version. While the authors are to be commended for bringing together all of the DMI literature, the findings reported are not promising for the inventory itself.

[80]

DeGangi-Berk Test of Sensory Integration. Purpose: "Designed to overcome problems in detecting sensory integrative dysfunction in the early years." Ages 3–5; 1983; TSI; 4 scores: Postural Control, Bilateral Motor Integration, Reflex Integration, Total; individual; other test materials (e.g., stopwatch, carpeted scooter board, hula hoop) must be supplied by examiner; 1986 price data: $42.75 per complete kit including set of test materials in carrying kit, 25 star designs, 25 record booklets, and manual (48 pages); $12.50 per set of test materials; $12.10 per 100 star designs; $7.90 per 25 record booklets; $12.50 per manual; $11.80 per carrying case; (30) minutes; Ronald A. Berk and Georgia A. DeGangi; Western Psychological Services.*

Review of the DeGangi-Berk Test of Sensory Integration by R. A. BORNSTEIN, Assistant Professor of Psychiatry and Psychology, Ohio State University, Columbus, OH:

This test appears to represent an extension of previous tests (most notably the Southern California Sensory Integration Tests) for use with preschool children. The basic underlying rationale is that early identification of children with various problems may permit initiation of treatment and thus ameliorate or avoid later academic consequences. The test itself is predicated on the rather tenuous assumption that vestibular-based sensory integration deficits may lead to problems in the development of laterality, learning, language, and visual-spatial skills.

In this regard, there appear to be some rather simplistic assumptions about the neural mechanisms underlying the role of the vestibular system. For example, the authors state that "Since the vestibular system is located at the junction of the brain halves, it is hypothesized that the vestibular system contributes to communication between hemispheres. Consequently, coordination of the two body sides should be affected by dysfunctions of the vestibular system." Curiously, in support of the argument the authors cite a study of monkeys who failed to transfer objects between hands following section of the corpus callosum, which clearly is the primary pathway for interhemispheric communication but is not part of the vestibular system. In spite of the weaknesses of the theoretical assumptions underlying this (and related) measures, the "sensory integration" approach is employed by a considerable group of professionals; therefore, tests related to this theory are of some value.

The present authors have made an admirable effort in the development and documentation of this instrument. Although a true normative study has not been performed, there is a relatively large normal sample, and data are presented with respect to several aspects of validity and reliability. The present form of the test incorporates 36 items selected from a larger pool of items. The rationale for item selection is presented and the criteria for rating the response for each item are clearly specified. In the test instructions, refusal of an item is interpreted as an inability to perform the task and thus a score of 0 is assigned. The validity of this approach is not clear, and an alternate approach might have been to assign no score and prorate on the basis of attempted items.

A more serious problem is apparent in the statistical procedures employed for item selection. The criteria used for evaluation of individual items yield ordinal data, although interval data on many items form the basis for the derived scores. In fact, eight of the selected items are dichotomous (scored 0 or 1), and all of the items on the Reflex Integration subscale are scored 0, 1, or 2. Nevertheless, the authors have employed *t* tests in the evaluation of differences between the normative and delayed samples. This is clearly inappropriate, and nonparametric procedures (e.g., Mann-Whitney U) should have been employed. This is a rather significant flaw and raises questions about the clinical validity of the scale. Similarly the discussion of discrimination indices based on differences between means is of limited value for the same reason. In addition, the different degrees of freedom for the variables in Table 4 suggest that not all items were given to all subjects, or that variances were unequal. This would represent another reason for using nonparametric analyses. The entire pool of 73 items should be reexamined with appropriate statistical technique.

There also appear to be problems with the samples upon which these data are based, some of which are acknowledged by the authors. Thus, although the test is intended for use with children 3–5 years old, only seven normal and four delayed children were 5 years of age. This is without question insufficient to permit generalization. The sample of delayed children is rather small. Although apparently all had fine or gross motor delay, 7 (almost 20%) were mentally retarded, and 14 (nearly 40%) of the motor-delayed children also had language delay. In the section on classification accuracy it is not stated which of the delayed children are identified. If the multiple-problem children are more consistently distinguished from normals, the contribution of the sensory integration by itself is thus open to question.

In terms of the subscales of the test, the Reflex Integration subscale is consistently weak, most conspicuously in terms of interrater reliability. The authors attribute this partially to the small number of items in the scale and stress that "Reflex Integration scores should not be employed for any type of decision making." This reviewer wonders why the authors did not improve the psychometric qualities of the scale by lengthening it and whether interrater problems can be explored by length of scale. The other two subscales appear to possess adequate reliability and may be appropriate for use.

In summary, this test has been developed to apply the theoretical assumptions related to sensory Integration to 3–5-year-old children. The endorsement of this theory by a considerable group of professionals makes such an endeavor worthwhile. The DeGangi-Berk Test of Sensory Integration is a preliminary step toward this goal. Setting aside questions of the validity of the theoretical assumptions, there are a number of significant problems including inappropriate statistical derivation of items included in the test, unrepresentative samples, and lack of acceptable reliability of some scales. The authors should be encouraged to continue the development of this test. However, the above noted weaknesses should caution against clinical use of this test in its present form.

[81]

Dental Assistant Test. Purpose: Developed to help screen for dental assistant positions. Dental assistant applicants; 1975; self-administered; 8 tests: Attention to Details, Organization Skills, Perception of Objects in Space, Perception of Spatial Perspective, Following Directions, Detail Judgments, Dexterity, Logic and Reasoning; no manual; 1985 price data: $2 per test; $12 per scoring key; (40–45) minutes; Mary Meeker and Robert Meeker; SOI Systems.*

[82]

Dental Receptionist Test. Purpose: Developed to help screen for dental receptionist positions. Dental receptionist applicants; 1975; self-administered; 8 tests: Attention to Details, Vocabulary, Verbal Reasoning, Following Directions, Management of Details, Management of Numerical Information, Dexterity, Logic and Reasoning; no manual; 1985 price data: $2 per test; $12 per scoring key; (45–50) minutes; Mary Meeker and Robert Meeker; SOI Systems.*

[83]

Denver Handwriting Analysis. Purpose: "Task analysis approach to the identification of specific handwriting difficulties for the purpose of remedial intervention." Grades 3–8; 1983; DHA; 5 subtests, 7 scores: Near-Point Copying, Writing the Alphabet (Capitals, Lower Case), Far-Point Copying, Total, Manuscript-Cursive Transition, Dictation; 1988 price data: $32 per kit including 25 record forms, 25 scoring profiles and 50 remedial checklists; $8.50 per 25 record forms and scoring profiles; $7 per 50 remedial checklists; $13.50 per set of manual (69 pages) and wall chart; $13.50 per specimen set; (25–65) minutes; Peggy L. Anderson; Academic Therapy Publications.*

Review of the Denver Handwriting Analysis by EDWARD A. POLLOWAY, Professor of Education, Lynchburg College, Lynchburg, VA:

The Denver Handwriting Analysis (DHA) test manual describes the tool as a "method of handwriting evaluation that offers a detailed analysis of the student's performance and provides results that are relevant to instructional programming." The test author describes the DHA as an informal, criterion-referenced test applicable to students in grades 3 through 8 with possible extension to usage with both older and younger students. Although not specifically labeled as being designed primarily for handicapped learners, the test clearly developed out of remedial efforts undertaken with learning disabled students.

The DHA is presented as a task analysis approach to handwriting assessment that can provide an alternative to instruments having only a more general concern for level of legibility. The test is not designed for the identification of writing disorders; instead, the author indicates that once a problem or disorder is identified the DHA provides an approach to scrutinizing it. The objectives of the DHA are summarized as assessing handwriting across a classroom-relevant multi-task format, identifying specific types of errors that interfere with legibility and efficiency, and translating assessment data into remedial planning. Clearly the DHA is quite different in purpose from the more global focus of assessment tools such as the Handwriting subtest of the Test of Written Language (Hammill & Larsen, 1983).

No technical characteristics are presented with the DHA and, thus, no data are available on reliability and validity. These topics are not discussed in the manual. Information is lacking on how individual subtests were selected, how the test was validated, whether administration procedures yield a high interscorer agreement and, therefore, whether the tool represents a reliable measure of performance. The author notes that the DHA is a remedial tool rather than a diagnostic test. Regardless of how the term diagnostic might be defined, a discussion on the development and usage of the test, accompanied by relevant data, would have been beneficial to potential users.

The test can be administered individually and to large and small groups. If the objective is, however, to scrutinize writing problems, only individual administration would seem advisable. The time requirements of administration to students at various age levels range from 23 to 63 minutes for third and eighth graders, respectively. Clear directions are provided for prospective examiners.

The DHA contains five parts: Near-point Copying, Writing the Alphabet, Far-point Copying, Manuscript/Cursive Transition, and Dictation. Near-point Copying requires the student to copy a four-line poem onto the bottom of the page of his or her booklet. Writing the Alphabet includes two sections for writing the upper and lower cases respectively from memory. Far-point Copying is based on a stimulus of a three-sentence story posted on a wall chart. The Manuscript/Cursive Transition subtest requires the student to produce cursive letters when presented with their manuscript counterparts. Finally, the Dictation part includes directions to students to write sequences of two to nine letters per line on either the right or left side of a center line.

The first three parts of the DHA yield two forms of data: subskill analysis and performance analysis. Subskill analysis represents a specific task analysis approach with a focus on 10 possible errors in individual letters (e.g., closure, looping, rounding, connection, transition, reversal, poor formation, substitution, omission, and insertion). These were selected, in part, from Newland's (1932) often cited research on errors in legibility. Samples are provided for comparative purposes; ultimately, however, determination must rely on application of the evaluator's own standards.

Performance analysis, the second type of data available, is a more global approach to assessment. Foci include spatial organization, speed, slant, and appearance. In addition, total mastery scores can be determined as a ratio of the number of errors and the sample size of letters written.

The last two parts of the test (Manuscript/Cursive Transition and Dictation) can be used to generate a raw score. This score represents the number of correct versus incorrect responses on the subtest and is to be expressed as a percentage figure. This percent score is used to determine a mastery level for each of these respective subtests. Ostensibly, this level is to provide a basis for evaluating intra-individual differences.

The author provides a section on interpretive analysis that provides some guidance through the evaluative process. Specific questions are presented to orient the teacher to the task of interpretation. In addition, brief case studies illustrate written summaries of students who have been administered the tool, and sample individual reports integrate profiled DHA results with other test data as a basis for deriving general conclusions leading to recommendations for needed educational services and instructional programs. This additional information is an advantage of the DHA over other criterion-referenced tools such as the Diagnosis and Remediation of Handwriting Problems (Stott, Moyes, & Henderson, 1985).

The DHA manual contains a useful chapter on remedial suggestions that can assist the teacher in using the assessment data in instructional programming. General teaching strategies are discussed and specific methods are provided for common problem areas in handwriting.

No research on the use of the DHA is presented in the manual. A review of the literature yielded only one peripheral reference to the instrument.

In summary, the Denver Handwriting Analysis presents a potentially useful approach to the informal assessment of handwriting as a basis for remedial programming. Primary concerns, in addition to the absence of data related to the use of the test, revolve around basic questions concerning the test's rationale. For example, why were particular test items or procedures selected? Why does this approach present the most valid set of procedures for evaluation? The test's lack of attention to these areas necessarily results in poor comparisons with formal tools in the area of handwriting, although it must be noted that these other tools have different purposes than does the Denver Handwriting Analysis.

REVIEWER'S REFERENCES

Newland, T. (1932). An analytic study of the development of illegibilities in handwriting from the lower grades to adulthood. *Journal of Educational Research*, 26, 249-258.

Hammill, D. D., & Larsen, S. C. (1983). *Test of Written Language*. Austin, TX: PRO-ED.

Stott, D. H., Moyes, F. A., & Henderson, S. E. (1985). *Diagnosis and Remediation of Handwriting Problems*. Guelph, Canada: Brook Educational.

[84]

Detroit Tests of Learning Aptitude—Primary. Purpose: "Designed to measure intellectual abilities in children ages 3 through 9." Ages 3–9; 1986; DTLA-P; 8 subtests: Verbal, Nonverbal, Conceptual, Structural, Attention-Enhanced, Attention-Reduced, Motor-Enhanced, Motor-Reduced, plus a General Intelligence score; individual; 1986 price data: $64 per complete kit including examiner's manual (89 pages), 25 student response forms, 25 profile/examiner record forms, and picture book; $9 per 25 student response forms; $9 per 25 profile/examiner record forms; $29 per picture book; $21 per examiner's manual; $49 per software scoring system; (15–45) minutes; Donald D. Hammill and Brian R. Bryant; PRO-ED, Inc.*

TEST REFERENCES

1. Lovett, M. W. (1987). A developmental approach to reading disability: Accuracy and speed criteria of normal and deficient reading skill. *Child Development*, 58, 234-260.

Review of the Detroit Tests of Learning Aptitude—Primary by CATHY F. TELZROW, Psychologist and Director, Educational Assessment Project, Cuyahoga Special Education Service Center, Maple Heights, OH:

The Detroit Tests of Learning Aptitude—Primary (DTLA-P) is an adaptation of the Detroit Tests of Learning Aptitude—2 (DTLA-2) designed for children ages 3 through 9 years. The DTLA-P is composed of 130 items ordered by difficulty level. Two dichotomous subtests are used to assess each of four theoretical domains incorporated in the DTLA-2: Linguistic, Cognition, Attention, and Motor. Scores (raw scores, percentiles, and standard scores or quotients [$M = 100$, $SD = 15$]) are reported for each of eight subtests and a total score, but not for the four domains.

Three major purposes of the DTLA-P are described in the manual: (*a*) to assess intraindividual variability, (*b*) to assist in measuring mental ability for special education placement decisions, and (*c*) as a research tool. The test is clearly portrayed by the test authors as a test of intelligence. As such it may be considered a restricted test in some states, where intelligence testing is limited to persons with appropriate credentials. The test manual addresses this issue rather explicitly.

A number of characteristics about this instrument make it fairly appealing to test users. The test's age span is attractive to professionals who desire a scale that spans the period from preschool to primary levels. Test materials are confined to three easy-to-manage items: an Administration and Picture Book; a response form, wherein the child records certain responses; and the Examiner Record Form, upon which items are marked correct or incorrect, raw scores are tallied, and derived scores are reported. Items are ordered by difficulty level, and basal and ceiling rules are applied, thus restricting items administered to critical levels and reducing testing time. The manual includes a fairly comprehensive discussion of the theoretical underpinnings of aptitude testing. Scoring guidelines are addressed adequately in most cases, and there is a very thorough discussion of the application of basal and ceiling rules, as well as several illustrations of computing raw scores from various basal and ceiling configurations. The Examiner Record Form includes brief abstracts of certain technical aspects of the test (e.g., item selection, normative data, reliability, and validity). The authors indicate this feature, uncommon for a test record form, is included to facilitate reporting results to others.

Other features of the DTLA-P are less attractive to test users. The stimulus items are black-and-white line drawings, which may lack appeal for many young children. No manipulatives are included, and two-dimensional stimuli may have limitations for the youngest populations. Directions to examiners are boxed and included on the same page as stimulus pictures, rather than on an opposing page in the commonly used easel-kit format. The test authors specify that examiners should sit beside children during evaluation rather than across from them, stating that this enhances test conditions. Nevertheless, having examiner directions on the same page as item stimuli could well be distracting to children, especially those who read. Another characteristic of this test that appears to interfere with ease of administration is the order of item administration. As noted earlier, items are arranged by difficulty level rather than by item type. This results in dramatic changes in task types from one item to the next, and frequent circling back and repetition of a single task as it is scored at various levels. In addition to contributing to an awkward administration, the sometimes dramatic shift in types of tasks may be confusing to young children. This problem might be addressed by an administrative format similar to the Stanford-Binet, Form L-M, or the Bayley, wherein certain types of tasks are introduced only once and tested to ceiling levels. Only one task (drawing of a person) is treated in this fashion on the DTLA-P. Inadequate directions for administration and scoring criteria are provided for certain items. For example, the directions do not state whether or not to drop the voice at the end of digit sequences. Scoring criteria for Design Reproduction items appear insufficient; only a single model is provided for each item, and no descriptive criteria are included.

The technical adequacy of the DTLA-P appears mixed. The standardization sample appears adequate with regard to both the size (N = 1,676) and demographic representativeness (36 states, with close match to 1985 *Statistical Abstract of the United States*). However, it is not clear from the manual how children in the standardization sample were selected. Some concern about the selection of this sample derives from the authors' discussion of criterion-related validity. In this section of the manual, it is noted that "professionals who tested children in the normative sample were asked to note the names of other tests given to children. . . . with the exception of the subjects given the DTLA-2, SRA, CAT, and MRT who were normal in cognitive ability, most of these children were either enrolled in special education classes (mostly classes for the mentally retarded and the learning disabled) or were being screened for exceptional education placement." Further description of the process by which subjects were selected appears essential, as does the inclusion of descriptive statistics on the scale for the standardization sample.

The manual reports reliability coefficients for content sampling, test-retest, and standard error of measurement. All data meet minimum standards for reliability. While content validity appears adequately addressed, data with respect to criterion-related and construct validity are sparse. The manual reports data from eight studies, all with extremely small samples, wherein the DTLA-P was correlated with other measures of intelligence (e.g., WISC-R), specific abilities (e.g., PPVT-R), or achievement (e.g., WRAT). The sample sizes ranged from 28 to 81 subjects, with six of the eight studies having fewer than 50 subjects. While the data reported are favorable, reflecting high correlations (typically in the .80s) with other aptitude tests and moderate correlations (typically in the .40s and .50s) with achievement tests, further investigation of criterion-related validity seems necessary.

Greatest concerns are raised with regard to construct validity of the DTLA-P, particularly in light of the eight subtests and four domains. As indicated above, one of the test's stated purposes is the "intraindividual assessment of psychological assets and deficits." Such a statement implies some demonstrated validity for the separate scales on the DTLA-P. Furthermore, the interpretation section of the manual includes a description of detailed inferences to be drawn from scores on the four domains and each domain's dichotomous subtests: (e.g., "Low scores on this subtest [Conceptual Aptitude] are made by individuals who think concretely, express shallow ideas in speaking, and see neither abstract nor meaningful relationships in material that is seen or heard"). Despite these claims that the DTLA-P can contribute to the elucidation of intraindividual variability, no construct validity data are reported to support this contention. In fact, the construct validity section is limited fairly exclusively to the construct of *g* and the DTLA-P's sensitivity to the general ability factor. At the very least, factor-analytic data to demonstrate the validity of independent subtests/domains appears essential.

In summary, the DTLA-P appears to promise considerably more than it delivers. Despite its claim to provide a measure of "strengths and weaknesses among intellectual abilities," the DTLA-P appears at best to provide a brief estimate of mental ability. Furthermore, insufficient data are provided to determine whether or not it is a valid measure for that purpose. While its brevity may be appealing, other measures of mental ability appropriate for some or all of this age range (e.g., Stanford-Binet, Form L-M; WPPSI; WISC-R) are preferable because of their extensive validity data.

REVIEWER'S REFERENCE

Statistical abstract of the United States. (1985). Washington, DC: U.S. Bureau of the Census.

Review of the Detroit Tests of Learning Aptitude—Primary by STANLEY F. VASA, Professor of Special Education and Communication Disorders, University of Nebraska-Lincoln, Lincoln, NE:

The Detroit Tests of Learning Aptitude—Primary (DTLA-P) is a primary age-level aptitude scale assessing four separate domains: Linguistic, Cognitive, Attentional, and Motoric. The DTLA-P is a revision and adaptation of the original Detroit Tests of Learning Aptitude (Baker & Leland, 1935) and a companion measure to the DTLA-2.

The rationale for the DTLA-P is well documented in the test manual and a clear description of the uses of the DTLA-P is provided by the authors. They cite three primary purposes for the scale: to inventory a child's relative strengths and weaknesses; to identify those children who are markedly deficient in intellectual ability; and to provide an instrument to be used in research.

The test manual provides background information on the assumptions of the scale and clear instructions for administration. The authors recommend that individuals who administer and interpret the scale have some formal training in assessment. They also recommend that users of the test have supervised practice in using mental ability tests. Overall, the test is relatively straightforward and easy to administer. Qualified examiners should have little difficulty administering the scale. The test itself contains 130 items and takes approximately 15 to 45 minutes to administer depending upon the child's age and ability level. The scoring and administration guides are well written and provide sufficient explanation.

The four domains of the scale, Linguistic, Cognitive, Attentional, and Motoric, each yield two scores or quotients. The Linguistic domain consists of a Verbal Aptitude Quotient (48 items) and Nonverbal Aptitude Quotient (73 items) and purports to assess the understanding and use of language. This domain and the two subscores are designed to provide for a comparison between the verbal and nonverbal abilities of the child. The Attentional domain contains Attention-Enhanced Aptitude Quotient (62 items) and Attention-Reduced Aptitude Quotient (67 items) and assesses primarily short-term memory and attention span. The Cognitive domain is composed of Conceptual Aptitude Quotient (59 items) measuring reasoning, problem solving, and language, and Structural Aptitude Quotient (69 items) measuring skills in dealing with physical properties such as form, texture, size, and sequence. The Motoric domain includes Motor-Enhanced Aptitude Quotient (57 items) and Motor-Reduced Aptitude Quotient (55 items), which measure the effects of motor-dependent and relatively motor-free sets respectively. Motor-dependent activities include drawing, coloring, and performing imitative actions of the examiner. Motor-reduced activities include verbal responses and matching by pointing.

Cautions and guidelines are provided for interpretation of the scale and the authors are conservative in their suggestions for its use. The authors do not recommend an aptitude-treatment interaction interpretation of subscales of the DTLA-P. They judiciously point out the need for assessment data beyond the DTLA-P in making decisions about identification of students as handicapped and in planning instructional interventions.

The DTLA-P has limited usefulness in the identification of students with specific learning disabilities or any other handicappping condition. The observational data and information gained from the test administration may be helpful, however, in better understanding the child's learning strengths and weaknesses. The profile of subscale scores is not intended to be used in planning specific intervention strategies.

The standardization procedures used in the development of the scale include a norm population of 1,676 children from 36 states. The authors report the normative sample was representative of the national population as indicated by Census Bureau statistics and represented diverse geographic, ethnic, and social class backgrounds. The standardization sample was small for ages 3 and 9 with only 105 and 89 subjects in each cell respectively. This may limit the ability to adequately compare children at the extremes of the scale's age range. In other age ranges the sample sizes varied from 214 to 354.

Reliability for the scale was presented in the form of both internal consistency and stability. Two studies containing a total of 109 students, ages 3 through 9, were cited for the test-retest reliability. Reliability coefficients ranged from .63 to .89 for the domains and .85 to .89 for the total scale. The standard error of measurement for the general intelligence score ranges from 3 to 5 scaled score points. The standard error of measurement for subscales ranges from 4 to 8 scaled score points.

Content validity for the scale was supported by statements that the subscales were readily identifiable with respect to "currently popular models of intellect." In this regard, the items on the scale are similar to those utilized in other general intelligence measures for young children. Behavioral domains addressed by the authors in item construction include: discrimination, generalization, vocabulary, motor, general information, induction, comprehension, sequencing, detail recognition, analogies, abstract reasoning, memory, and pattern recognition. Items were also based on the existing item pool from the DTLA-2. A review of the subscales would indicate the DTLA-P does have face validity. Items on the subscales generally appear to reflect the domain they purport to measure and are evenly distributed across all domains.

Evidence of concurrent validity is provided by comparing the DTLA-P with the SRA Achievement Series, the California Achievement Test, and the Metropolitan Readiness Test as measures of achievement ability; and the Wechsler Intelligence Scale for Children, the Slosson Intelligence Test, and the Peabody Picture Vocabulary Test—Revised for the relationship to tests of cognitive ability. A median correlation coefficient of .74 is reported between the DTLA-P scores and these aptitude and achievement scales, indicating that similar characteristics are being assessed.

SUMMARY. DTLA-P, a downward-age extension of the DTLA-2, provides one overall score for general aptitude, but unlike many others, it also contains subtests that produce eight separate subscores in four domains. The DTLA-P's standardization procedure is good and the authors have followed the *Standards for Educational and Psychological Testing* (AERA, APA, NCME, 1985) in the development of the scale. The manual is easy to read. Caution is recommended in using the scale to make specific instructional planning recommendations. The scales do provide another means of systematically gathering considerable and diverse information about a young child in a relatively short testing session.

REVIEWER'S REFERENCES

Baker, H. J., & Leland, B. (1935). Detroit Tests of Learning Aptitude. Austin, TX: PRO-ED.

American Educational Research Association, American Psychological Association, & National Council on Measurement in Education. (1985). *Standards for educational and psychological testing*. Washington, DC: American Psychological Association, Inc.

[85]

Detroit Tests of Learning Aptitude (Second Edition). Purpose: "To determine strengths and weaknesses among intellectual abilities, to identify children and youths who are significantly below their peers in aptitude, and to serve as a measurement device in research studies investigating aptitude, intelligence, and cognitive behavior." Ages 6–18; 1935–85; DTLA-2; 20 scores: 11 subtest scores (Word Opposites, Sentence Imitation, Oral Directions, Word Sequences, Story Construction, Design Reproduction, Object Sequences, Symbolic Relations, Conceptual Matching, Word Fragments, Letter Sequences) and 9 composite scores (Verbal Aptitude, Nonverbal Aptitude, Conceptual Aptitude, Structural Aptitude, Attention-Enhanced Aptitude, Attention-Reduced Aptitude, Motor-Enhanced Aptitude, Motor-Reduced Aptitude, Overall Aptitude); individual; 1987 price data: $88 per complete kit including 25 student response forms, 25 examiner record forms, 25 summary and profile sheets, picture book, and manual ('85, 135 pages); $11 per 25 student response forms; $11 per examiner record forms; $8 per 25 summary and profile sheets; $39 per picture book; $24 per manual; $59 per software scoring system; (50–120) minutes; Donald D. Hammill; PRO-ED, Inc.*

See 9:320 (11 references) and T3:691 (20 references); for a review by Arthur B. Silverstein of an earlier edition, see 8:213 (14 references); see also T2:493 (3 references) and 7:406 (10 references); for a review by F. L. Wells, see 3:275 (1 reference); for reviews by Anne Anastasi and Henry Feinburg and an excerpted review by D. A. Worcester (with S. M. Corey), see 1:1058.

TEST REFERENCES

1. DeSoto, J. L., & DeSoto, C. B. (1983). Relationship of reading achievement to verbal processing abilities. *Journal of Educational Psychology*, 75, 116-127.

2. Olson, J., & Midgett, J. (1984). Alternative placements: Does a difference exist in the LD populations? *Journal of Learning Disabilities*, 17, 101-103.

3. Perlmutter, B. F., & Bryan, J. H. (1984). First impressions, ingratiation, and the learning disabled child. *Journal of Learning Disabilities*, 17, 157-161.

4. Simner, M. L. (1984). Predicting school readiness from stroke directions in children's printing. *Journal of Learning Disabilities*, 17, 397-399.

5. Tobey, E. A., & Cullen, J. K., Jr. (1984). Temporal integration of tone glides by children with auditory-memory and reading problems. *Journal of Speech and Hearing Research*, 27, 527-533.

6. Weithorn, C. J., & Kagen, E. (1984). Verbal mediation in high-active and cognitively impulsive second graders. *Journal of Learning Disabilities*, 17, 483-490.

7. Weithorn, C. J., Kagen, E., & Marcus, M. (1984). The relationship of activity level ratings and cognitive inpulsivity to task performance and academic achievement. *The Journal of Child Psychology and Psychiatry and Allied Disciplines*, 25, 587-606.

8. Brown, R. T., & Alford, N. (1984). Ameliorating attentional deficits and concommitant academic deficiencies in learning disabled children through cognitive training. *Journal of Learning Disabilities*, 17, 20-26.

9. Brown, R. T., Wynne, M. E., & Medenis, R. (1985). Methylphenidate and cognitive therapy: A comparison of treatment approaches with hyperactive boys. *Journal of Abnormal Child Psychology*, 13, 69-87.

10. Webster, R. E. (1985). The criterion-related validity of psychoeducational tests for actual reading ability of learning disabled students. *Psychology in the Schools*, 22, 152-159.

11. Bowers, P. G., Steffy, R. A., & Swanson, L. B. (1986). Naming speed, memory, and visual processing in reading disability. *Canadian Journal of Behavioural Science*, 18, 209-223.

12. Brown, R. T., Borden, K. A., Wynne, M. E., Schleser, R., & Clingerman, S. R. (1986). Methylphenidate and cognitive therapy with ADD children: A methodological reconsideration. *Journal of Abnormal Child Psychology*, 14, 481-497.

13. Kashani, J. H., Horwitz, E., Ray, J. S., & Reid, J. C. (1986). DSM-III diagnostic classification of 100 preschoolers in a child development unit. *Child Psychiatry and Human Development*, 16, 137-147.

14. Shinn-Strieker, T. (1986). Patterns of cognitive style in normal and handicapped children. *Journal of Learning Disabilities*, 19, 572-576.

15. Silverstein, A. B. (1986). Organization and structure of the Detroit Tests of Learning Aptitude (DTLA-2). *Educational and Psychological Measurement*, 46, 1061-1066.

Review of the Detroit Tests of Learning Aptitude (Second Edition) by ARTHUR B. SILVERSTEIN, Professor of Psychiatry, University of California, Los Angeles, CA:

The original Detroit Tests of Learning Aptitude (DTLA) appeared 50 years ago. When the DTLA was introduced, the second revision of the Stanford-Binet was still 2 years in the future and the Wechsler Intelligence Scale for Children (WISC) was not to appear for another 14 years. The fourth edition of the Stanford-Binet has been recently released and 11 years have passed since the WISC was revised. Thus, to say that the second edition of the DTLA (DTLA-2) is long overdue is quite an understatement. How does the new DTLA compare with its predecessor and competing tests, and has it been worth waiting for?

Instead of the 19 subtests that made up the old DTLA, from which the examiner was to select from 9 to 13 to meet the needs of the individual subject, the DTLA-2 has just 11, all of which are to be administered except in special circumstances. Seven subtests—those preferred by a sample of users of the first edition—have been retained more or less intact, although most of them have been retitled; four subtests are new. The order in which the subtests are to be given is the same as that used in the standardization, and the time required is said to vary from approximately 50 minutes to 2 hours. For comparison, the time required for the Wechsler Intelligence Scale for Children—Revised (WISC-R) is said to be approximately 50 to 75 minutes.

Raw scores on the 11 subtests are first transformed into standard scores with a mean of 10 and a standard deviation of 3, just as with the WISC-R. The standard scores are then summed in various ways. The resulting sums are converted into a series of composite scores, which, in keeping with tradition, are termed quotients. These quotients are actually standard scores with a mean of 100 and a standard deviation of 15, again just as with the WISC-R. Mental ages have been abandoned, which is a change for the better. Provision is made on the examiner record form for presenting both the subtest scores and the composite quotients in profile form.

The standardization was based on a sample of over 1,500 subjects—roughly 100 or more at each age level from 6 through 17 years—living in 30 states, and closely comparable to the population of the United States with respect to sex, place of residence (urban vs. rural), race (white, black, or other), and geographical area. However, much of the psychometric information is based on a stratified random subsample of 300 subjects, 25 at each age level, pooled into six groups of 50 subjects each (ages 6/7, 8/9, . . . 16/17). This information includes a summary of the results of item analyses conducted on each subtest (median discriminating powers and percentages of difficulty), internal consistency data (Cronbach's alpha coefficients and associated standard errors of measurement), and the intercorrelations among the subtests and the composities. The values of alpha, averaged across age groups, are impressively high, ranging from .81 to .95 for the subtests and from .95 to .97 for the composites. For comparison, split-half reliability coefficients for the WISC-R, again averaged across age groups, range from .70 to .86 for the subtests and from .90 to .96 for the Verbal, Performance, and Full Scale.

Additional psychometric information is based on smaller samples. Stability coefficients over a 2-week interval range from .63 to .91 for the subtests and from .80 to .93 for the composites. Corresponding values for the WISC-R, over a 1-month interval, range from .65 to .88 for the subtests, and from .90 to .95 for the three scales. Validity data of various sorts are also presented. These include correlations between the DTLA-2 and the WISC-R (.83), the Peabody Picture Vocabulary Test (.75), and the SRA Achievement Series (from .58 to .93 for students at different grade levels). However, these coefficients should not be taken at face value—they are too high by some unknown amount—because they were "attenuated [sic] to account for imperfect reliability" (of course, *dis*attenuated is what is meant).

A novel feature of the DTLA-2 is the variety of composite scores that it yields. Besides a General Intelligence Quotient, there are quotients for four pairs of composites: Verbal versus Nonverbal, Conceptual versus Structural, Attention-Enhanced versus Attention-Reduced, and Motor-Enhanced versus Motor-Reduced. All 11 subtests contribute to the General Intelligence Quotient, and every subtest enters into one or the other composite in each pair. The correlations between composites in the same pair range from .61 to .68. For comparison, the correlation between the Verbal and Performance IQs on the WISC-R, averaged across age groups, is .67. Because of overlap in their makeup, the correlations between composites in different pairs are generally higher (range: .63 to .95), as are the correlations with the General Intelligence Quotient (range: .78 to .87). Clinicians are likely to find discrepancies between the composite quotients a fruitful source of hypotheses to account for intraindividual variability in performance. The manual is appropriately cautious in suggesting interpretations of these discrepancies, but if all four are evaluated routinely, the discrepancies required for significance at the .05 level, based on the Bonferroni procedure, are about 12 points rather than the 9 points that the manual suggests.

From a psychometric perspective, the DTLA-2 appears vastly superior to the old DTLA, although users of the first edition will have to make a number of adjustments in administration and scoring if they choose to switch. The toughest competition will almost certainly come from the WISC-R (the new Stanford-Binet is an unknown quantity at this time). Practitioners and researchers are encouraged to try the DTLA-2 . . . they may well like it.

Review of the Detroit Tests of Learning Aptitude (Second Edition) by JOAN SILVERSTEIN, Assistant Professor of Psychology and Director, School Psychology Program, Montclair State College, Upper Montclair, NJ:

The Detroit Tests of Learning Aptitude (Second Edition) (DTLA-2), a revision of the DTLA, is an individual intelligence scale which can be administered to children and adolescents ranging in age from 6 through 17 years. The DTLA-2 consists of 11 subtests, all of which are administered to each subject.

Serious efforts were made to retain and improve the reported strengths of the DTLA, while modifying the weaknesses. Recognized standards for test construction were consulted for decisions related to reliability, validity, normative data, and methods for reporting scores. The representativeness and size of the normative sample have been greatly improved. The scoring criteria for some subtests have been revised in order to make them "objective and easy to apply." Some of the subtests have been shortened through extensive item analysis; others have been lengthened to increase reliability. Standard scores have replaced the mental age equivalents for each subtest and the former ratio IQ has been replaced by a series of composite quotients and the General Intelligence or Aptitude Quotient.

Suggestions have been heeded to improve the level of sophistication and the usability of the test manual; technical data on reliability and validity have been added. Useful sections on testing the limits, sharing the results, and cautions on interpreting test results have been included. The pictures have been improved and updated so that they are generally more readily recognizable by current test takers. (See further discussion of this issue below under discussion of test design.) The straightforward physical layout of the material has been retained, making the test fairly simple to administer.

Based on a survey of test users, seven of the original subtests were retained, generally in modified form and with titles revised in an attempt to reflect more closely the skills tapped (Word Opposites, Sentence Imitation, Oral Directions, Word Sequences, Design Reproduction, Object Sequences, Letter Sequences). Four new subtests have been added (Story Construction, Symbolic Relations, Conceptual Matching, Word Fragments). Subtests have been grouped into eight composite domains, including two for each of four specific aptitude domains (linguistic, cognitive, attentional, and motoric) plus the General Intelligence or Aptitude Quotient. The statistical basis for the selection of the new subtests and for the development of the domains is not reported.

Three principal uses for the DTLA-2 are specified: (*a*) to determine strengths and weaknesses among intellectual abilities, (*b*) to identify children and youth who are significantly below their peers in aptitude, and (*c*) to serve as a measurement device in research studies. Many professionals have used the DTLA and will, presumably, now adopt the DTLA-2 to diagnose individuals "to qualify them for placement in programs for special groups such as the mentally retarded, learning disabled, and other categories of handicap." Therefore, the results of the test can have serious implications for a child's future. Unfortunately, significant areas of concern affect the usefulness of the DTLA-2:

1. *Qualifications for test administrators.* Given the significance of the DTLA-2's uses, it is extremely important that test administrators be adequately trained, particularly for the complex task of interpretation. As discussed below, fairly sophisticated levels of knowledge and skill in areas such as test construction, test administration, diagnosis, and interpretation are necessary if the DTLA-2 is to be used effectively. Otherwise, findings may be misinterpreted. However, the only discussion in the manual about the need for properly trained, qualified examiners is a warning that tests do not diagnose, but that "in the end, practical diagnoses rest on the clinical skills and experience of examiners." No attention is devoted to describing the qualifications, skills, and knowledge required to effectively administer and interpret the DTLA-2.

2. *Issues related to statistical properties of the scale.* While there has been a substantial improvement in the reporting of statistical data concerning reliability and validity, there remain concerns with time sampling and criterion-related validity, as well as the need for more precise statistical data to document some aspects of the author's decision making.

In order to determine stability over time, 33 students from the Hilltop Baptist Academy were tested twice with a 2-week period between tests. A larger, more representative sample and a longer time period is clearly necessary. Criterion-related validity was determined by testing 76 students who were either enrolled in special education classes (mostly for the mentally retarded or learning disabled) or were being screened for possible special education placement. DTLA-2 values were correlated with WISC-R scores. However, this selection of a subset of possible scores has resulted in a truncation of the sample and of the potential correlation.

In addition, as mentioned above, it is important that test users have access to precise factor analytic data, describing the relationship of the specific subtests to *g*, and providing factor loadings to illustrate how the composition of the domains was determined.

3. *Issues related to language bias, design of materials, test procedures, and interpretation.* Because many of the subtests—including those that measure nonverbal abilities—require proficiency in English for understanding of directions and, at times, for responses, the DTLA-2 "has a decided bias regarding the English language." The manual warns that "test results should be viewed with unusual caution when testing persons known to speak English poorly. Of course, the DTLA-2 should not be given at all to non-English speakers." Unfortunately, this very important warning is not prominently displayed in the manual.

As mentioned in the manual, several of the subtests are complex in demands. At one point, for example, the author states in his discussion of the Oral Directions subtest, "At present, we do not know which of these abilities is the most important for doing well on this subtest. All that is known is that the subtest's results are reliable and valid indicators of general learning aptitude (i.e., it seems imbued with lots of Spearman's *g* factor)." In some cases, this complexity may affect a child's ability to succeed on specific subtests. For example, the response sheet for Oral Directions is complex, containing a large number of stimuli on each page. Two other subtests, Object Sequences and Letter Sequences, require a written response on an answer sheet with very tiny spaces. It is possible that such factors as visual perceptual and motor difficulties, developmental delays, or immature motor development common in 6-year-old children may affect a child's ability to perform effectively on these tasks.

Test procedures may also affect performance. For example, the Conceptual Matching subtest measures the ability to see theoretical or practical relationships between objects. Although most of the line drawings are clear, some of the drawings may be confusing to some children either because of the content or the abstractness of the design (e.g., a dome of a capitol building, a tower for power lines, and a schematic of an atom). At no point is the examiner instructed to check to determine whether the child has correctly identified the symbols. Therefore, failure on this subtest may be due to the child's misinterpretation of the symbols, rather than to lack of ability to identify relationships. However, with the current procedures, the examiner may not realize the cause of the error.

Although the manual lists generic suggestions for limit testing, the causes of failure on specific subtests may be subject to misinterpretation. Unfortunately, due to the complex demands of some tasks and the lack of ample guidance in teasing out the factors affecting test performance, the success of interpretation of these complex tasks relies heavily on the sophistication of the test administrator.

It is important that the publishers provide the additional technical information and clarify issues of interpretation. Clarification of the qualifications of test administrators and test takers, including the need for caution when testing persons with limited English skills, should be stated clearly at the beginning of the manual. Specific factors affecting test performance (such as construction of test materials and test procedures) should be discussed in detail, with specific recommendations for testing limits in order to aid accurate interpretation. Without these modifications, there is a significant concern that poor test performance due to linguistic, visual, perceptual, and motor factors may be misinterpreted as due to cognitive difficulties. Unless these issues are resolved, there are major concerns about the use of the DTLA-2 as a test of cognitive ability for purposes of diagnosis, classification, and placement.

[86]

[Re Detroit Tests of Learning Aptitude, Second Edition.] DTLA-2 Report. Purpose: Produces the following report interpretations from input of client information and subtest standard scores: demographic data, standard scores table, profile of standard scores, composite quotient table, report of findings. Ages 6–18; 1986; 2 sections: General Intellect, Composite Aptitudes; printer is required; 1987 price data: $199 per report program (available for Apple II Plus, IIe, IIc, or IBM PC, XT, AT, and compatibles); $35 per manual (8 pages) and sample printout; administration time not reported; John J. Trifiletti; Precision People, Inc.*

For information regarding the actual test see 9:320 (11 references); see also T3:691 (20 references); for a review by Arthur B. Silverstein of an earlier edition of the test, see 8:213 (14 references); see also T2:493 (3 references) and 7:406 (10 references): for a review by F. L. Wells of an earlier edition of the test, see 3:275 (1 reference); for reviews by Anne Anastasi and Henry Feinburg and an excerpted review by D. A. Worcester (with S. M. Corey) of an earlier edition of the test, see 1:1058.

Review of the [Detroit Tests of Learning Aptitude, Second Edition] DTLA-2 Report by STEPHEN R. HOOPER, Assistant Professor of Psychiatry, Psychology Section Head, The Clinical Center for the Study of Development and Learning, University of North Carolina School of Medicine, Chapel Hill, NC:

The [Detroit Tests of Learning Aptitude, Second Edition] DTLA-2 Report is a computerized psychoeducational report program designed to be used with the second edition of the Detroit Tests of Learning Aptitude (Hammill, 1985). As such, it purports to provide an integrative report based on the standard scores obtained from the Detroit. Given that the DTLA-2 Report is a computerized aid to be used with the Detroit, users should be aware of the psychometric properties and clinical utility of the test prior to using this diskette (for reviews of the Detroit Tests of Learning Aptitude-2, see 87 and Radencich, 1986).

The DTLA-2 Report is a software package that can be used with IBM PC, Apple, or compatible computer systems. A disk drive and a printer are required in order to operate the program. It is command driven and, consequently, user friendly. Only several minutes are required to input the data and obtain a report. The Report yields basic demographic data, a listing of the standard scores and their respective percentile ranks, a profile of the standard scores, and a two-page narrative report. Although the DTLA-2 Report was not designed to be a scoring diskette, it does combine the standard scores into their respective composites, thus offering some time-savings to the user with respect to scoring. These composite scores are listed in the printout as well.

The narrative report itself is better than most computer-derived reports in that it provides the user with more than a test-bound reiteration of levels of functioning based upon subtest scores. The report yields integrative statements, largely due to its dependence on the composite scores, and it offers conjectures regarding an individual's academic and vocational functioning. The report does not provide a summary paragraph. Such an addition would have been useful. Perhaps to the developers' credit, however, the DTLA-2 Report does not engage in diagnostic hypotheses generation, leaving this and other clinical activities (e.g., the inclusion of qualitative observations) to the examiner. Generally, the overall report is well organized, logical, and has potential clinical utility. The DTLA-2 Report also has a standard 90-day limited warranty that consumers should read carefully prior to using the diskette. Despite these relative advantages of the report, there are a number of potential difficulties associated with the DTLA-2 Report package.

First, the program for the DTLA-2 Report was written in a somewhat dated and unspecified version of the BASIC language. Although this is not inappropriate, it is not contemporary with the computer language of most current computer systems. For this diskette to be used immediately with most contemporary computer systems, particularly the IBM PCs, additional changes in the DTLA-2 Report program are required in order to accommodate the changes in newer versions of BASIC. Another problem is the diskette was designed to be used exclusively with a color monitor. If a user does not have access to a color monitor, then the program will not run. Again, this is not listed in the manual and changes in the program are required in order for the program to become operational on these systems.

Second, the program was designed to output the report to a printer instead of to a data storage file. Although this is not a major problem, it does not contribute to the creation of data files for users interested in data collection or, more practically, for those wishing to edit the computer-generated report. With respect to this latter concern, given that the narrative report does not provide a summary paragraph, this option would have strengthened the printout by building in flexibility for the user.

Third, the user is required to input the standard scores derived from the subtests of the Detroit. This requirement offers little time savings to the examiner with respect to scoring, aside from the time saved by the program combining the subtest standard scores into their respective composite scores. The program would have provided a greater time savings to the examiner and contributed to error reduction if raw scores were entered for each subtest instead of the examiner-calculated standard scores.

A fourth concern also pertains to the entry of the data. Although only several minutes are required to enter the data and obtain a printout, there is no data verification step written into the program. The program does provide opportunities for the user to change entries, however, it does not require data verification. Given the relatively short amount of time required to enter these data, this would have been a useful procedure to include in the program in order to increase the reliability of data entry and results. On the positive side, the program does not allow out-of-range standard score entries and it will prorate for any single missing subtest score when calculating the composite scores.

Finally, the manual for the DTLA-2 Report is only seven scant pages in length. Potential consumers should recognize that in addition to the cost of the diskette, they must purchase the manual which, given its contents, is grossly overpriced. It would have been more reasonable to include the manual with the cost of the DTLA-2 Report package. The manual briefly describes the DTLA-2 Report and basic start-up procedures for using the diskette with the Apple and IBM PC computer systems (e.g., copying the program onto an IBM PC hard drive). Although these are necessary inclusions, they are brief and list none of the concerns or pitfalls described above. The manual did provide a copy of the report generated from the DTLA-2 Report, but the narrative portion was not included for appraisal. The manual does include an address and telephone number for users to contact should they encounter difficulties with their diskette.

The DTLA-2 Report is one of an ever-widening array of computer software packages designed to assist the clinician and researcher with issues such as time management and clinical biases. This computerized package was designed to generate a psychoeducational report based on standard scores obtained from the Detroit Tests of Learning Aptitude-2 and, based on this single criterion, it performs in a better than average fashion. Aside from the lack of a summary paragraph in the narrative report, the actual product holds potential clinical utility and contributes to a moderate time savings for the user. The major problems with the DTLA-2 Report are embedded in the program structure of the diskette and, perhaps, the language in which it is written. With several modifications in the program structure (e.g., flexibility for the user to add/delete information in the narrative report, data verification, entry of subtest raw scores for scoring purposes, data storage options), the DTLA-2 Report would become a better complement to the Detroit. In tandem with these concerns, the manual should be enhanced to address potential pitfalls the user may encounter and be more descriptive of the actual inner workings of the program. As currently designed, the DTLA-2 Report package does not describe all of the pitfalls that exist in the programming, and users may not be able to use this report-writing program without having the exact computer system or a substantial background in computer programming. It is hoped that these concerns will be addressed in subsequent versions of the DTLA-2 Report.

REVIEWER'S REFERENCES

Hammill, D. (1985). Detroit Tests of Learning Aptitude (Second Edition). Austin, TX: PRO-ED, Inc.

Radencich, M. D. (1986). Test review: Detroit Tests of Learning Aptitude (DTLA-2). *Journal of Psychoeducational Assessment*, 4, 173-181.

[87]

Developmental Activities Screening Inventory—II. Purpose: "Designed to provide early detection of developmental difficulties." Birth to 60 months; 1977–84; DASI-II; behavior checklist; individual; some test materials (formboard, bell) must be supplied by examiner; 1984 price data: $39 per set of testing materials including manual ('84, 103 pages), picture cards, and 50 response forms; $11 per 50 response forms; $12 per set of picture cards; $19 per manual; (25–30) minutes; Rebecca R. Fewell and Mary Beth Langley; PRO-ED, Inc.*

See 9:323 (1 reference).

Review of the Developmental Activities Screening Inventory—II by DENNIS C. HARPER, Professor of Pediatrics, The University of Iowa, Iowa City, IA:

The intended use of the revised edition of the Developmental Activities Screening Inventory—II (DASI-II) is as an individually administered "informal screening measure" for children. The authors maintain the DASI-II fills a gap in the screening literature by focusing on outcome data that can be translated into practical applications. Furthermore, the instrument is also presented as a "nonverbal test" to avoid penalizing those with potential auditory or language handicaps. Modifications are also noted to enable equitable assessment of the visually impaired. Classroom teachers or those with a basic knowledge of child development are described as appropriate test administrators.

General suggestions are given to teach the basic concepts assessed by the DASI-II in the form of a "Sample Instructional Program" for a hypothetical child. The manual concludes with a rational analysis of the 11 major perceptual and conceptual components measured by the test.

Test materials consist of 67 test items from a variety of standard early assessment surveys and batteries, a series of pictures (objects, words, symbols, numbers), a one-page record form, a manual with directions/interpretations, and an extensive list (Materials Needed) of approximately 60 items (i.e., rattle, cups, toys, common objects, etc.) that must be obtained by the potential user.

Test administration directions are straightforward (begin one level below your estimate of developmental age) and testing continues until a basal (all passes) and ceiling (all fails) are ascertained. The test is not timed, the sequence of testing is flexible, and a variety of suggestions are offered to obtain maximum performance. Scoring consists of an age by item sequence and a calculated Developmental Quotient (DQ, DQ = DA/CA x 100), and a series of categories for interpretation (e.g., 140 = Superior; Below 60 = Poor). No other scoring or interpretive aids are provided.

The test manual reports the only available data on reliability and validity. This reviewer's specific request (Dykes, 1980) for an earlier study from the test publisher was not honored. Pearson product-moment correlations of .91 are reported between the DASI (earlier version) and the Infant Intelligence Scale and the Merrill-Palmer Scale of Mental Tests. The sample was not described. Dykes (1980) completed a comparison of the DASI and the Developmental Assessment of the Severely Handicapped on 15 "severely and multiply handicapped children" resulting in a Pearson of .98. A series of additional comparison studies are noted, all reporting concurrent correlations ranging from .87 to .97. The authors report the DASI was administered to "over 200 multiply handicapped children" and note that the "DASI can be used with a reasonable degree of confidence for the purpose of screening children for possible developmental delays." This information is encouraging but is not interpretable given the insufficient sample descriptors reported in the manual. There is no basis upon which to judge if the DASI-II is a useful screening device or is a practical addition to the literature on the basis of the data reported in the manual.

The test manual is clearly written, scoring is simple, and items are well described. However, the testing skills needed for administration are substantial and interpretation on screening outcome (when to refer) is left to the evaluator. A nonverbal test is very much needed in early childhood screening, but whether the DASI-II satisfies this purpose is unknown. The instrument is more suited to obtaining a picture of a child's strengths and weaknesses rather than a specified DQ.

In summary, the DASI-II presents itself as a screening instrument with a nonverbal orientation aimed at offering practical suggestions for remediation. The test requires more than beginner's level of skills to administer, and is too unstructured to be called a screening test as it is currently presented. The manual's data on reliability and validity are not interpretable. The Developmental Profile II (9:327) or the Denver Developmental Screening Test (9:311) are still more useful as screening instruments with young children.

REVIEWER'S REFERENCE

Dykes, M. K. (1980). *Developmental assessment for the severely handicapped.* Austin, TX: PRO-ED, Inc.

Review of the Developmental Activities Screening Inventory—II by WILLIAM B. MICHAEL, Professor of Education and Psychology, University of Southern California, Los Angeles, CA:

The Developmental Activities Screening Inventory—II (DASI-II) constitutes a revised edition of an earlier form of the scale. The scale has been extended in scope by adding two lower age levels (1 to 3 months and 3 to 5 months). The DASI-II was constructed to furnish an informal scorable screening device for children between the ages of 1 month and 60 months. Intended to provide an early screening for and assessment of developmental disabilities and to minimize the customary dependence of many infant and preschool tests upon substantial receptive and expressive language abilities, DASI-II is a nonverbal scale consisting of 67 items. In the opinion of the test authors the DASI-II can be administered relatively easily by teachers who have had only limited testing experience, but who do possess some knowledge of child development. This test samples a broad range of skills including tasks emphasizing perceptual, motor, and cognitive functions. DASI-II contains 11 developmental scales, the first two of which span intervals from 1 to 2 months of age and 3 to 5 months of age, respectively, the next eight of which cover modules of 6 months of age, and the last one of which corresponds to the growth period from 54 to 60 months.

Materials included in the test package include five types of cards, a pad of 50 response forms, and a manual. Approximately 30 other kinds of additional materials are required—all the way from a pacifier or bottle with a nipple to four objects against which to match picture cards (hammer, watch, apple, and shoe). The manual also furnishes comprehensive instructions for the administration of each item including (*a*) materials needed; (*b*) the precise procedure to be followed; (*c*) the adaptation required, if any, in presenting the item to the visually-impaired child; (*d*) exact instructions concerning how the responses are to be scored; and (*e*) an occasional instruction for inserting a higher-level task out of its customary order if a given item has been passed previously. In addition to the inclusion of both a table of developmental ages corresponding to reported raw scores and a procedure for the calculation and interpretation of a developmental quotient, the manual also furnishes a testing record form for a 28-month-old visually impaired child named Ben Smith and outlines a sample instructional program. An appendix entitled "Item Analysis" sets forth for each of the 11 developmental scales a two-dimensional grid with the vertical dimension listing the item activities (usually six for each developmental level) and with the horizontal dimension delineating 15 psychologically related behaviors (sensory intactness, sensorimotor organization, visual pursuit/object permanence, means-ends relationships, causality, imitation, behaviors relating to objects, construction objects in space, memory, discrimination, association, quantitative reasoning, seriation, spatial relationships, and reasoning). Check marks are inserted within the cells of the grid to reveal what the authors have interpreted to be the psychological behaviors associated with performance on each item (activity).

Although the manual for the DASI-II has provided a sound and convincing rationale for the construction of the instrument and although the procedures for administration and scoring are clear and precise, data pertaining to norms, validity, and reliability are quite fragmented and incomplete. Admittedly, a reasonable amount of time must be given to generate comprehensive validity and reliability data. Concurrent validity evidence is given in the form of correlation coefficients of scores on the original DASI with other published developmental scales. One promising finding was that the DASI exhibited statistically significant coefficients (in excess of .90) with other behavior (nonverbal) scales. Within the same sample of children ($N = 45$) having known language delays, a correlation of only .19 was found with a test yielding receptive language scores—a statistical outcome which the test authors interpreted to support their position that the DASI does not penalize children with identified language deficits. Encouraging as the validity evidence may seem, the samples studied were small, and the number of investigations cited—all with respect to the original form—was only five.

Although a section of slightly more than one page entitled "Validity and Reliability" was included in the manual, no data pertaining to reliability appear in this section. Somewhat disturbing also is the fact that the table in which total raw scores were converted to developmental ages in months is not accompanied by any rationale or empirical evidence to demonstrate the appropriateness of the conversions made. Apparently no normative data have been obtained in a school setting to afford a basis for the assessment of the behaviors of preschool children against those of what could be considered a representative population.

In summary, the manual for the DASI-II presents detailed descriptive information concerning each test item that seems to indicate substantial face and content/process validity in the developmental functions sampled, but fails to furnish any reliability and normative data. Validity evidence is relatively scant. Although teachers will probably find this instrument quite useful and informative in understanding individual child behaviors, great caution must be exercised in interpreting the scores and in forming any diagnoses regarding the possible presence of developmental disabilities. It is strongly recommended that professionally trained and highly qualified school psychologists work closely with teachers in any kind of detailed psychological assessment and that the same school psychologists supplement any information obtained from the DASI-II with data from well standardized instruments of demonstrated reliability and validity.

[88]

Developmental Articulation Profile. Purpose: "Provides a method for rapid examination of the articulation errors relative to frequency of occurrence and the approximate developmental ages for each phoneme." Ages 3.0–7.3; 1977–79; DAP; individual; no manual, 2-page explanation; 1986 price data: $15 per 100 profile forms; Dennis C. Tanner, Kathryn E. Mahoney, and Gale Derrick; PRO-ED, Inc.*

[The publisher advised us in January 1988 that this test is no longer available.]

Review of the Developmental Articulation Profile by KATHARINE G. BUTLER, Professor of Communication Sciences and Disorders, and Director of Center for Research, Syracuse University, Syracuse, NY:

Information accompanying the protocol of the Developmental Articulation Profile (DAP) indicates the DAP was designed for use by public school speech-language pathologists and has proven useful in the authors' clinical experience. This instrument, as noted above, has no manual, a two-page explanation, and a one-page protocol or profile form. Additional information was requested from the senior author of the instrument, who indicated the DAP "cannot be plotted without information provided by a standard articulation test such as the Goldman-Fristoe, Fisher-Logemann, Henja, or other similarly constructed instrument" (personal correspondence, August 1, 1987). It would be helpful if the need to administer a standardized articulation test prior to plotting the information on the profile was highlighted in the DAP packet, because some purchasers might be under the impression the DAP can be used as the single assessment measure for articulation disorders.

This brief instrument may be used by a speech-language pathologist to create a visual display of a child's performance on 24 consonants (no vowels are included) arranged in order of phoneme acquisition, and with frequency of occurrence of those consonants also provided. The authors used three sources for the construction of the profile: the Frequency of Occurrence Table in *Phonetic Science: A Program of Instruction* (Faircloth & Faircloth, 1973), M. Templin's (1957) seminal study *Certain Language Skills in Children, Their Developmental and Interrelationships*, and Wellman, Case, Mengert, and Bradbury's (1931) earlier study, *Speech Sounds in Young Children*. More recent work, for example that of Prather in 1975 and Sander in 1972 (as reported in Steckol, 1977), indicates that a significant number of phoneme acquisition data reported by Templin and Wellman have been modified over the decades. Acquisition of the 24 consonants studied by all sources noted above is consistently reported in the more recent studies as occurring months to years earlier, with the earliest phonemes occurring at age 2 or before, and the latest between ages 5 and 7. Thus, for those who wish to use the DAP, reference to the more current norms may be useful. The authors of the DAP note the profile provides approximate developmental ages and that the criteria for diagnostic placement remains with the clinician and should be used as only one of many considerations when determining intervention. This reviewer concurs with that statement.

In summary, the profile is not, in and of itself, a diagnostic instrument. It is intended to provide the display of a child's performance on 24 phonemes as obtained from other instruments. Its use with parents or other professionals may be appropriate.

REVIEWER'S REFERENCE

Steckol, K. F. (1977, November). *An overview of children's development of language: Linguistic production.* Paper presented at the meeting of the American Speech-Language-Hearing Association, Chicago, IL.

Review of the Developmental Articulation Profile by RICHARD J. SCHISSEL, Associate Professor of Speech Pathology and Audiology, and

Chair, Speech Pathology and Audiology Department, Ithaca College, Ithaca, NY:

The Developmental Articulation Profile (DAP) consists of a single sheet on which may be plotted the results from "any standard articulation test." The DAP itself is not a test but a form for charting results of other tests.

The DAP allows the charting of errors on 24 consonant sounds. It provides norms on the ages at which each of the consonants should be mastered as well as the frequency of occurrence of each consonant tested. Instructions for plotting the client's profile are provided on the back of the form. The form allows the clinician a quick visual comparison of her/his client's error sounds with the age at which the sound had been mastered by 75% of the children in the studies from which the norms were derived. Information on the frequency of occurrence of each sound provides additional data that the clinician could use in making decisions regarding the need for therapy.

The form itself is clear and very simple to use. It is accompanied by a two-page description of the rationale and design of the form. Most of the information included here focuses on the selection of age norms. There is no discussion on how the information on frequency of occurrence was developed, from where it came, or how it might best be used. A citation in the list of references gives some clue, but no direct mention of these data is made in the discussion of the rationale of the profile.

The intent here, clearly, was to provide a quick visual aid that clinicians could use with parents, administrators, and others. The authors also suggest that the form will provide the clinician with a profile of each child's articulation errors and provides an "objective method of test-retest comparison." However, this and all such forms suffer from a major flaw.

In the case of the DAP, data on the age of acquisition of each consonant charted on this form were derived from two of the classic studies on speech sound acquisition in children. These data were obtained using procedures and stimulus items different from those utilized by many tests today. Research consistently has shown that children's sound production is affected by many variables, not the least of which are phonetic context and canonical form. Age of acquisition data would be expected to be a function of stimulus items used and test format (cf. Smit, 1986).

Children would not be expected to perform similarly on, for example, the McDonald Screening Deep Test of Articulation, the Arizona Articulation Proficiency Scale, and the Goldman-Fristoe Test of Articulation, and research has borne out this expectation (Schissel & James, 1979; Ritterman, Zook-Herman, Carlson, & Kinde, 1982). Further, the norms provided for the Arizona Articulation Proficiency Scale itself are quite different from the age of acquisition data provided by the DAP.

It is a fundamental tenet of psychometry that any test be accompanied by normative data describing normal performance on that specific test. There can be no universal set of norms against which performance on any "standard" articulation test can be compared. All norms are test specific. Any attempt to compare performance on different tests against the same set of normative data will result in meaningless comparisons at best and misleading ones at worst.

The DAP is a tempting shortcut that replaces scrupulous rigor in individual test interpretation with speed and ease of visual presentation of results. With consideration given to the dangers involved, as discussed above, I do not recommend its use. Virtually all articulation tests on the market today provide an easily interpretable scoring or summary sheet which may be used for the same purposes as the DAP without the inherent problems.

REVIEWER'S REFERENCES

Schissel, R., & James, L. B. (1979). A comparison of children's performance on two tests of articulation. *Journal of Speech and Hearing Disorders*, 44, 363-372.

Ritterman, S. I., Zook-Herman, S., Carlson, R. L., & Kinde, S. W. (1982). The pass/fail disparity among three commonly employed articulatory screening tests. *Journal of Speech and Hearing Disorders*, 47, 429-433.

Smit, A. B. (1986). Ages of speech sound acquisition: Comparisons and critiques of several normative studies. *Language, Speech, and Hearing Services in Schools*, 17 (3), 175-186.

[89]

Developmental Indicators for the Assessment of Learning—Revised. Purpose: "To meet the obvious and continued need for an adequately standardized, valid, and reliable measure of early motoric, conceptual, and language development." Ages 2–6; 1983; DIAL-R; 4 scores: Motor, Concepts, Language, Total; individual; some testing materials (e.g., play dough) must be supplied by examiner; 1986 price data: $159.95 per complete kit; $4.95 per set of 3 administration booklets;

$4.95 per 50 scoresheets; $4.95 per 100 cutting cards; $4.95 per 50 parent questionnaires; $8.95 per manual (108 pages); $6.95 per coordinator handbook (47 pages) not included in complete kit; $100 per DIAL-LOG computerized scoring/reporting/suggested activities/recording system; (20–30) minutes; Carol D. Mardell-Czudnowski and Dorothea S. Goldenberg; Childcraft Education Corp.*

TEST REFERENCES

1. Docherty, E. M., Jr. (1983). The DIAL: Preschool screening for learning problems. *The Journal of Special Education*, 17, 195-202.

2. Broadhead, G. D., & Church, G. E. (1985). Movement characteristics of preschool children. *Research Quarterly for Exercise and Sport*, 56, 208-214.

3. Spillman, C. V., & Lutz, J. P. (1985). Focus on research: Criteria for successful experiences in kindergarten. *Contemporary Education*, 56, 109-113.

4. Mardell-Czudnowski, C., Chien-Hou, H., & Tien-Miau, W. (1986). Cross-cultural adaptation of a developmental test (DIAL-R) for young children in Taiwan. *Journal of Cross-Cultural Psychology*, 17, 475-492.

5. Miller, L. J., & Sprong, T. A. (1986). Psychometric and qualitative comparison of four preschool screening instruments. *Journal of Learning Disabilities*, 19, 480-484.

6. Chew, A. L., & Morris, J. D. (1987). Investigation of the Lollipop Test as a pre-kindergarten screening instrument. *Educational and Psychological Measurement*, 47 (2), 467-475.

Review of the Developmental Indicators for the Assessment of Learning—Revised by DAVID W. BARNETT, *Associate Professor, School Psychology, University of Cincinnati, Cincinnati, OH:*

Developmental Indicators for the Assessment of Learning—Revised (DIAL-R) is an individual screening instrument for use with young children in potential need of further diagnostic evaluation or curricular modification. DIAL-R consists of three *areas* or stations, each containing eight tests.

The Motor Area tasks are comprised of catching a bean bag, jumping, hopping, skipping, building with blocks, touching fingers (e.g., finger to thumb), cutting with scissors, matching, copying shapes and letters, and writing one's name. Concepts Area tasks include color naming, identifying body parts, counting, identifying basic concepts (e.g., spatial, size), naming letters, and sorting (i.e., by shape). Language tasks include articulating, giving personal data (a photo taken during screening or mirror is used), remembering (patterns of hand claps, digit span, sentences), picture vocabulary (nouns, verbs), problem solving (e.g., similar to the Comprehension subtest of the Wechsler Preschool and Primary Scale of Intelligence), and length of utterance.

Behavioral Observations, described as subjective impressions related to social and affective skills, are also recorded based on occurrences of behavior at each screening station. Behaviors evaluated include difficulties with separation, crying/whining, refusals, perseveration, distractibility, hyperactivity, and disruptiveness. A Parent Information Form is also included in the materials and potentially contains useful information about perceptions of development and behavior. However, since the authors state that other adults who know the child well, such as neighbors or babysitters, can provide the information, its usefulness as a standardized technique is reduced due to possible rater differences.

ADMINISTRATION AND SCORING. The DIAL-R requires a professional coordinator, three professional or paraprofessional "operators," and optional volunteers. The coordinator should have a background in one of the following areas: special education, early childhood education, or speech/language. The administration time is estimated to be 20–30 minutes.

Detail is given concerning desirable conditions and facilities for testing. Parents are allowed to observe the process and assist in interpreting performance. The order of activities is flexible (e.g., a reticent child attends the Language area last).

RESTANDARDIZATION. DIAL-R represents a substantial improvement over its predecessor. The latent trait method was used to evaluate item characteristics of the scale based on a sample of 2,447 children (ages 2-0 to 5-11), including an impressive number of nonwhite children (1,089). A subsample of 1,861, adjusted to match the 1980 census, was used to establish cutoff points for screening decisions. Stratification variables included age, sex, ethnicity, geographic region, and size of community. Supplementary norms are available for the all-white and nonwhite samples.

Information on the education level of parents and second language in the home was also obtained from many parents, but was insufficient for stratification purposes. The correlations between DIAL-R performance and education level were low but significant. Although only a small percentage had a second language, the number for the nonwhite families was three times that found for the white sample. Handicapped children were *not* excluded from the norming study, but they were not identified as such.

VALIDITY. Content validity was established in the earlier DIAL through interviews with teachers and reviews by early childhood consultants. Item characteristics strongly reflect developmental trends. However, factor analysis revealed that the Motor and Concepts areas were highly related and formed one factor (unnamed). Language was the second factor. Therefore, the total DIAL-R score is given emphasis. The correlations between all three subtests are high (ranging from .77 to .85).

Evidence for criterion-related validity was examined through a comparison of DIAL-R scores with the Stanford-Binet ($r = .40$, $N = 125$, with the DIAL-R total). A decision matrix revealed 82% agreement between the two scales based on the DIAL-R screening categories. A study of predictive validity is presented based on the earlier DIAL.

RELIABILITY. Internal consistency reliabilities reported by age levels vary widely across areas, and range from .41 to .88 (the median for the three areas combined was approximately .74). The median reliability for the total score was approximately .86. Test-retest reliabilities, with an N of 65 and variable intervals between administrations, were .76 (Motor), .90 (Concepts), .77 (Language), and .87 (Total).

INTERPRETATION. Means, standard deviations, standard errors, and internal consistency reliabilities are available for all scores by 3-month intervals. The total score is used to classify a child as belonging to one of three groups: *potential problem*, *ok*, or *potential gifted*. Cutoff points are based on performances of 1.5 or more standard deviations below the mean, within 1.5 standard deviations above and below the mean, and 1.5 standard deviations above the mean (73% white/27% nonwhite sample). The authors recommend that children scoring in the "potential problem" and "potential gifted" categories receive further diagnostic evaluation. Tables with other cutoff points are available in the manual. Furthermore, decisions may be based on white or nonwhite samples. Minimal interpretative information is given to the behavioral observations except that the scores are inversely related to total score and age. However, cutoff points are likewise included for referral decisions in the "social/affective" area.

CONCLUSIONS. The DIAL-R has marginal to acceptable technical qualities and contains engaging materials for children. As with any instrument, a number of issues and concerns can also be raised.

It is likely that many screening errors will result from the use of DIAL-R. The arbitrary flexibility in proportions of screened children identified hints at longstanding philosophical and technical issues involved in early identification and classification. Labeling issues are *not* resolved through the use of the DIAL-R descriptors. If a child does poorly on a screening measure, it may be more logical to implement prereferral intervention procedures rather than formal diagnostic measures. In subsequent revisions, categories such as "rescreen along with in-depth structured interview" and various categories tied to curricular decisions based on emerging skills and needed experiences should be explored. Standard errors should be incorporated into suggested cutoff points. The "potential gifted" category will lead to unnecessary misunderstandings when based on a cutoff that includes 6.68% of the population. As the authors point out, a need exists for validity studies. A question remains about the usefulness of DIAL-R for educational planning.

Preschool screening is best employed through an organizational approach, implied by the authors. Further, the authors recommend that vision and hearing screening be incorporated into the procedures. However, screening instruments such as the DIAL-R give more emphasis to information acquired from the child than the information acquired by parents (or teachers) and perpetuate emphasis on certain narrow stategies related to child study. In subsequent revisions, it would be helpful if parental questions and concerns received formal attention, not only with respect to clarifying the child's performance during screening, but more importantly, with respect to the role of parents in creating learning experiences and for altering maladaptive patterns of behaviors. Similarly, the section on communicating results to parents could be meaningfully improved.

Review of The Developmental Indicators for the Assessment of Learning—Revised by G. MI-

CHAEL POTEAT, Assistant Professor of Psychology, East Carolina University, Greenville, NC:

The Developmental Indicators for the Assessment of Learning—Revised (DIAL-R) was developed for use in the developmental screening of young children. The test is a revision of the DIAL first published in 1972. The test materials are accompanied by a 102-page manual containing details on administering, scoring, and interpreting the test. Information is provided on the technical characteristics of the DIAL-R including standardization procedures, establishment of norms, and reliability. Test instructions are well written and can be followed easily; but the manual is poorly organized. All materials necessary for administration are included in the test kit and the test materials appear durable.

The authors characterize the DIAL-R as an untimed, team-administered measure of motoric, conceptual, and language skills for children from 2 to 6 years of age. The testing team consists of three operators (who each administer a subscale) and a coordinator who supervises the group testing process. The test is administered individually to children who rotate between different test stations within one room. Criteria for the selection of operators consists only of a demonstrated competency in working with young children. The requirements for a coordinator are expanded to include expertise (e.g., a degree) in special education, early childhood education, or a related field. Both operators and coordinators are to demonstrate competency in the administration of the DIAL-R, but no criteria for judging competency are provided. Brief instructions for training operators are included in a Coordinator Handbook, but a training packet must be purchased separately.

The authors present the DIAL-R as a norm-referenced, developmental screening instrument, and repeatedly emphasize that it is neither a measure of intelligence nor a diagnostic test. The test follows a developmental model conceptualized as consisting of three domains. The Motor, Concept, and Language domains are measured by subscales (subareas). Each subarea consists of eight test items worth 31 points. However, a factor analysis indicates the DIAL-R measures only two factors. The motor and concept items contribute to one factor, while the second is comprised of the language items. No details of the factor analysis are presented. No new evidence is presented for the content validity of the DIAL-R. The content validity of the DIAL is reviewed and the authors appeal to the similarities between the two instruments. A subjective behavioral checklist is also included at the end of each subscale. These behavioral impressions are not used in determining test scores, and no evidence of reliability or validity is provided.

Given the expressed intent of the test to be a "definitive first step" in identifying young children at the extremes of the continuum of readiness skills and potentially in need of further services, criterion-related validity should be the primary basis for evaluating the DIAL-R. Moderate evidence for concurrent criterion-related validity is presented through correlations between Stanford-Binet IQs and DIAL-R total and subscale scores for a sample of 125 children. Correlations with the Stanford-Binet were .40 for the Total score, .33 for Language, .50 for Concepts, and .28 for the Motor subscale. Cross tabulation tables comparing DIAL-R total scores and Stanford-Binet IQs with classifications as a potential problem, a potential advanced, or an okay child are also presented for the same sample. Thirteen children identified as either potentially advanced or as having potential problems on the DIAL-R had IQs within the Stanford-Binet cutoffs. Nine students who had Stanford-Binet IQs outside of the cutoff scores were not identified using the DIAL-R. No evidence of predictive validity for the DIAL-R is provided, and no research on predictive validity was found in a search of the literature.

Test-retest correlation coefficients are presented for a sample of 65 children. The modal length of time between assessments was 2 weeks. The Motor (r = .76) and Language (r = .77) subscales were moderately reliable. The Concept subscale (r = .90) and the Total scores (r = .87) were more stable. Cronbach's alpha based on the 24 items composing the Total scale was .96, with alphas for the subscales ranging from .86 to .92. Alphas are also presented for subscales and the Total score across 2-month age increments. The DIAL-R appears to have adequate internal consistency but the Language subscale has a pattern of declining internal consistency associated with increasing age. No data are presented on interrater (interoperator) reliability. Interrater reliability is not usually a major concern with objective measures of ability, but it should be addressed when individuals not trained in assessment are used as test administrators.

The DIAL-R uses cutoffs for the identification of potentially advanced and potentially problem children of 1.5 standard deviations from the mean. No rationale for the selection of these cutoffs is provided. However, alternative cutoff scores based on the 10th and 90th percentiles and the 5th and 95th percentiles are included in an appendix. Cutoffs based on only white or only nonwhite children in the normative sample are also provided. The normative sample for the DIAL-R ($N = 2{,}447$) was made up of approximately equal percentages of males and females. In the initial sample, nonwhites were overly represented (44.5% of the total sample). The total sample was then truncated to resemble the 1980 U.S. census figures of 73% white and 27% nonwhite. Because the sample was also stratified by geographical region, age (in 6-month intervals), and size of the community (above or below 50,000) before the truncation, more information is needed to interpret the resulting norms. In addition, the number and location of the testing sites was not sufficient to insure a representative sample of the U.S. population. Of the eight primary sites, both southern sites were located in Florida, and both north central sites were in Illinois. One primary, and four of the five supplemental sites, were in Hawaii. No attempt was made to stratify the sample on the basis of socioeconomic status nor is there any indication of a strategy to identify representative samples at any of the sites. No information on how the samples were recruited is provided. Research suggests that a potentially large difference in performance exists across samples of children from diverse settings (Derevensky & Mardell-Czudnowski, 1986). It is recommended the norms be used with caution because of the lack of information on the recruitment of subjects, the possible effects of the truncation procedure, the small number of standardization sites, and the failure to stratify by socioeconomic status.

Despite problems, the DIAL-R can still be recommended for use in developmental screening programs and it compares favorably with other instruments designed for the same purpose (cf. Miller & Sprong, 1986). Used only as a screening instrument, it should provide an initial basis for the identification of children requiring early intervention services. Educational systems using the DIAL-R should consider developing local norms, collecting data on the utility of different cutoff scores, and establishing objective measures of administrative competency. However, the use of the extrapolated norms for children between ages 6-0 and 6-11 cannot be recommended; the behavioral impressions have no demonstrated reliability or validity; and the psychometric properties of the subscales are not sufficient to warrant their separate interpretation. The DIAL-R can be characterized as an adequate screening test of developmental readiness, but further test refinement is encouraged.

REVIEWER'S REFERENCES

Derevensky, J. L., & Mardell-Czudnowski, C. (1986). *The use of the Developmental Indicators for the Assessment of Learning—Revised (DIAL-R) preschool screening test for the early identification of learning disabled children in a Canadian population*. Quebec, Canada: Ministry of Education. (ERIC Document Reproduction Service No. ED 269 449).

Miller, L. J., & Sprong, T. A. (1986). Psychometric and qualitative comparison of four preschool screening instruments. *Journal of Learning Disabilities*, 19, 480-484.

[90]

Developmental Profile II. Purpose: "Designed to assess a child's functional, developmental age level." Birth to age 9.5; 1972–86; DP-II; ratings in 5 areas: Physical Age, Self-Help Age, Social Age, Academic Age, Communication Age; may be administered and scored by hand or using computer program; IBM PC, XT, AT, or compatibles needed for administration or in-house scoring by computer; 1986 price data: $50 or less per complete kit including 2 prepaid WPS Test Report answer sheets, 25 scoring/profile forms, and manual ('86, 95 pages); $5.95 or less per prepaid WPS Test Report answer sheet; $22.50 or less per 25 scoring/profile forms; $21 per manual; $149.50 or less per microcomputer diskette for administration, scoring, and interpretation (25 uses per diskette); (20–40) minutes; Gerald Alpern, Thomas Boll, and Marsha Shearer; Western Psychological Services.*

For reviews by Dennis C. Harper and Sue White, see 9:327; see also T3:698 (5 references); for a review by Jane V. Hunt of the original edition, see 8:215 (1 reference).

TEST REFERENCES

1. Tsai, L. Y. (1983). The relationship of handedness to the cognitive, language, and visuo-spatial skills of autistic patients. *British Journal of Psychiatry*, 142, 156-162.

2. Tsai, L. Y., & Beisler, J. M. (1983). The development of sex differences in infantile autism. *British Journal of Psychiatry*, 142, 373-378.

3. Ritvo, E. R., Freeman, B. J., Yuwiler, A., Geller, E., Yokota, A., Schroth, P., & Novak, P. (1984). Study of fenfluramine in outpatients with the syndrome of autism. *The Journal of Pediatrics*, 105, 823-828.

Review of the Developmental Profile II by A. DIRK HIGHTOWER, Associate Director, Center for Community Study, Psychology Department, University of Rochester, Rochester, NY:

The Developmental Profile II (DP-II) manual has six chapters with each describing a major component typically associated with the standards for psychological testing. As such, this review will appraise each chapter in sequence and conclude with an overall summary.

GENERAL DESCRIPTION. Although the DP-II sequentially assesses developmental behaviors from birth to 9 1/2 years, the functional utility of this scale, as noted in the manual, goes only to about age 7. The manual suggests the scale is appropriate for handicapped children of any age, but does not provide psychometric information for this population. One strength of this chapter, and the test manual in general, is that it gives very good descriptions of specific scale limitations.

ADMINISTRATION AND SCORING. Although the DP-II manual states it may be administered as: (*a*) an interview to parents, (*b*) a combination of an interview and direct testing of the child, or as (*c*) a self-interview completed by a teacher, only norms based upon parental reports are provided. If parental reports are used, however, the authors suggest an over estimation of skills will likely result. Additional norms specific to other sources would be informative. If a test user, however, decides to do direct testing, the authors have provided a table of material needed for a criterion-referenced assessment. Directions to administer the scale are adequate. Examples provide additional clarity. Computerized scoring and interpretation are available, but the service is expensive for what you get. There is little advantage in using the computer scannable answer sheets, as it is difficult to score items directly onto the sheet. Instead, the manual suggests a transfer of the information after the interview has been conducted, which is time consuming. In fact, it takes almost more time to transfer item responses onto the scan form than it does to manually score the scale. Although the personal computer administration procedure saves professional time, the program provided, if used on a PC or XT model, is *extremely* slow. For example, between each item it takes approximately 17 seconds for the computer screen to clear itself and write the next item; it definitely does not respect parent's time. Another drawback of the personal computer scoring disk is that it cannot be loaded onto a hard disk without considerable effort. Once loaded onto a hard drive, however, the speed of the program becomes more reasonable. Last, the computer-generated reports provide an excessive number of pages (14) with little unique information.

INTERPRETATION AND USE. This scale appears to be "clinically" versus empirically derived. For example, items in the physical scale are classified into gross motor or fine motor subscales and items in the communication scale are divided into receptive, expressive, and speech articulation items, but no empirical support nor psychometric properties are provided. Also, these classifications are not typically representative of the entire age range. For example, there are five speech and articulation items, and all of them assess development during the infancy period. In general, the manual is strong on providing "clinical" interpretations and guidelines, but weak on supporting the suggestions with empirical data.

DEVELOPMENT AND STANDARDIZATION. Although many items are easy to read, significant differences occur if interviewers and/or parents are not specifically trained in making distinctions between such words as "can," "does," and "usually." Pilot testing by this reviewer suggested significant discrepancies can occur without adequate operational definitions of words such as these. Also, some items seem to assess parental development versus child development. For example, in the social scale, "Is a child allowed to play in his/her own neighborhood without being watched by an adult?" may be more reflective of parenting style, or location of the child's habitat, versus the child's actual social development. Another disturbing type of item such as, "Has the child been promoted from regular first grade?" may discriminate those in second grade from those in first grade and below, but does not speak to the child's development.

Infant assessment is particulary weak in that there are too few items per developmental period. This period of development is not assessed adequately as not enough of the skills are broken down into small enough increments.

For assessment of infants of less than 30 months, the Bayley Scales of Infant Development are recommended.

The large (3,008) normative sample was a pleasing surprise, but finding out that 91% of those came from the state of Indiana and 9% from the state of Washington reduces quickly the enthusiasm regarding the potential generalizability. What is nice, as mentioned before, the authors describe these limitations clearly. Also, the standardization sample collected in 1970 requires caution in the late 1980s.

PSYCHOMETRIC PROPERTIES. The reliability of this scale has not been adequately assessed. For example, for test-retest stability, only 11 mothers were interviewed on two occasions and these interviews were separated by 2-to-3-day intervals. A longer time period between testing intervals and larger sample sizes are needed before test-retest stability can be determined. Although internal consistency coefficients are computed on a large sample of over 1,000 children, and are reasonable ranging from .78 to .87, the manual does not specify if this is a split half coefficient or a Kuder Richardson-20. Also, these internal consistency coefficients were determined on a modified version of the developmental profile and not the DP-II.

Although various validity indices are provided, most of the studies reported have small sample sizes and frequently use earlier editions of this scale. As the authors point out, there is "limited support for convergent validity" and "the high correlations within scales may reflect a strong method bias."

SUMMARY. The Developmental Profile II is strong on clinical judgements and interpretations and weak in empirical foundations. In fact, this scale may have its strengths in more of the criterion-referenced areas versus the norm-referenced arena to which the manual seemed to be written. If paraprofessionals can be trained to reliably and accurately administer this instrument, the scale might best serve as a screening device, especially for those professionals without a strong foundation in normal development. The computer scoring and reports are not worth the money. In general, this test is not particularly strong nor is it extremely weak. If a professional is going to assess the child on his own time, however, some combination of the McCarthy Scales of Children's Abilities in combination with either the Vineland or the AAMD Adaptive Behavior Scale would probably provide a more accurate description of the child's developmental functioning.

Review of the Developmental Profile II by E. SCOTT HUEBNER, Associate Professor, Department of Psychology, Western Illinois University, Macomb, IL:

The Developmental Profile II (DP-II) is a 186-item inventory designed to assess a child's development in five areas of functioning: Physical, Self-Help, Social, Academic, and Communication. The inventory is intended for use with children from birth through 9 1/2 years (birth through 7 years for normal children). According to the manual, the scale can be administered as a direct test or by interviewing parents, teachers, or others who are well-acquainted with the child. However, the scale was normed exclusively by interviewing parents, who typically report higher levels of functioning than teachers (Gradel, Thompson, & Sheehan, 1981).

The manual states the DP-II can be used to accomplish a variety of objectives. These include, but are not limited to the following: "(*a*) to determine eligibility for receiving special education and/or related services; (*b*) as a planning tool to develop an individualized education plan (IEP) consistent with the child's strengths and weaknesses; (*c*) to measure a child's progress by comparing profile scores at the beginning of the school year (pretest) with scores achieved at the end of the school year (posttest)."

It should be noted the current revision represents a revision of items based upon feedback from users, not a restandardization. The modifications were limited to deleting items above the age of 9 years, 6 months; clarifying some directions, and removing sexist items and language.

With the exception of the Academic scale, raw scores can be converted only into age scores. Neither percentile ranks nor standard scores are available. The Academic scale score can also be converted into an IQ equivalency score "only if such a score is required for administrative purposes or to determine program eligibility." It should be underscored that this score is essentially a ratio IQ score. Ratio IQs are obsolete and misleading, and they should be abandoned, particularly for purposes of determining program eligibility.

Item analysis data are reported in the manual. However, these data were derived from the original standardization study and do not reflect the items in the current revision. In fact, much of the reliability and validity data reported below apply to the original version of the scale. Thus, the psychometric properties of the scale must be interpreted cautiously.

An examination of the standardization data reveals numerous problems. The sample consisted of 3,008 children between birth and age 12 years, 6 months from Indiana (91%) and Washington (9%) assessed during the early 1970s. Only normally developing children were included in the standardization sample, despite the fact that one of the stated purposes of the test is to determine eligibility for special education or related services. The major problems involving the norms include: (*a*) The sample is disproportionately urban, middle class, and Midwestern; (*b*) although blacks are adequately represented, other minority groups (e.g., Asians and Hispanics) are not; (*c*) although sample sizes are generally satisfactory, ages 1-7 to 2-0 and 2-1 to 2-6 are smaller ($n =$ 91 and 95, respectively). To summarize, the DP-II standardization group is biased and thus does not represent a nationally standardized instrument.

As noted previously, the DP-II was standardized using only parent (mother) ratings. Separate norms for teachers would add greatly to its usefulness. Using maternal reports limits the ability of the instrument to achieve one of its stated objectives, that is, to measure a child's progress in school.

Reliability data are inadequate. Reliability was assessed in three ways: test-retest, internal consistency, and interscorer reliability. Test-retest reliability was investigated by interviewing 11 mothers, separated by 2–3 day intervals, using the original version of the scale. Such a small sample precludes generalizing from the results of the study. Internal consistency reliability coefficients were computed for each of the five subtests for a sample of 1,050 children ages 3–5 years. The coefficients range from .78 to .87 with a median of .82, all falling below desirable standards for making individual decisions. Interscorer reliability data, however, indicate satisfactory consistency among scorers. Overall, however, the data do not reflect adequate reliability for this instrument.

In a related vein, the manual fails to provide information related to the *SEM* for the test and subtests nor does it provide information related to subtest specificity. Without such information, users are left with no defensible methods to interpret subtest fluctuations. Unfortunately, the authors compound this problem by presenting a table to interpret subtest strengths and weaknesses (i.e., to determine which scores reflect significant delays) based totally on clinical judgment. Such nonempirical methods serve only to provide confidence in interpretation when there should be none.

Validity studies are described in detail in the manual. With regard to concurrent validity, the majority of the correlations reported between criterion measures (e.g., Binet, Slosson Intelligence Test, Learning Accomplishment Profile) were satisfactory. However, predictive validity studies are noticeably absent. Also, factor analytic studies investigating the structure of the DP-II have not been conducted. Finally, the usefulness of the inventory with minority children (e.g., differential construct and predictive validity studies) remains to be demonstrated. Overall, although the available validity data are promising, much additional work needs to be done to substantiate the claims of the authors.

In conclusion, the use of the DP-II is fraught with difficulty. The identification of children needing special education services (i.e., the primary objective of the DP-II) requires a technically sound norm-referenced instrument. Unfortunately, the DP-II is simply technically inadequate for the task. Given the many problems related to its standardization, reliability, and validity, I recommend alternative devices (e.g., Vineland Adaptive Behavior Scales) for diagnostic, instructional, or research purposes.

REVIEWER'S REFERENCE

Gradel, K., Thompson, M. S., & Sheehan, R. (1981). Parental and professional agreement in early childhood assessment. *Topics in early childhood and special education*, 1 (2), 31-39.

[91]

Diagnosis and Remediation of Handwriting Problems. Purpose: "To provide the teacher with a systematic means of identifying faults of handwriting . . . as remedial materials . . . for clinical assessment and empirical research . . . teacher education." Children with at least 2 years of instruction in writing; 1985; DRHP; 2 scores: Faults of Concept and Style, Faults Suggestive of Motor or Perceptual Problems; 1985 price data: $39.50 per complete kit including 20 student writing sheets, 20 diagnostic record forms, 6 student's specimens of writing sheets, 1 group score sheet, 1 diagnostic template, and manual (64 pages); $1.92 per 20 student writing sheets; $4.02 per 20 diagnostic record forms; $2.43 per 10 student's specimens of writing sheets; $3 per 10 group score sheets; $19.50 per 10 diagnostic templates; $15 per manual; (20) minutes; Denis H. Stott, Fred A. Moyes, and Shelia E. Henderson; Hayes Publishing, Ltd. [Canada].*

Review of Diagnosis and Remediation of Handwriting Problems by EDWARD A. POLLOWAY, Professor of Education, Lynchburg College, Lynchburg, VA:

The Diagnosis and Remediation of Handwriting Problems (DRHP) is described as having multiple purposes, that is, the assessment of handwriting deficits, a basis for remedial programming, teacher education, facilitation of clinical evaluation, and a tool for empirical research. Its authors indicate it is a measure of legibility appropriate for children (not clearly identified by age or grade) who have a minimum of 2 years of handwriting instruction.

The DRHP program focuses on the detection of patterns of particular faults resulting in poor legibility or poor performance. Therefore, it is intended to be a basis for systematic analysis of handwriting that can then serve as the basis for remedial efforts. Seventy specimens of children's writing are included to illustrate specific faults.

There are three major parts to the diagnostic procedures included within the DRHP. The first, faults of concept and style, includes the following four sections: conceptual errors, such as incorrect letter forms and improper joining of letters; inappropriate spacing between or within words; stylistic distractors such as extreme slants or unusual letter size; and slurring, defined as the degeneration of letters (i.e., partial or total elimination). Each of these sections is scored through an analysis of a writing sample. A total score is derived for this whole part covering concepts and style.

The second part focuses on faults that suggest perceptual or motor problems. The problems identified by the authors include: inconsistency of slant, inconsistency of letter size, irregular word alignment, random letter distortion, and tremor. Samples are provided for each of these five faults with a total score again available for this part of the test.

The third part of the DRHP, faults of writing position, focuses on diagnostic indicators gathered by the teacher or clinician through observations of the child. The three subsections relate to posture, physical disadvantages (e.g., vision defects, compulsive movements), and faults in the way the task is addressed (e.g., impulsivity, haste, overcaution). This part is to be used for general interpretative purposes; no total score is generated.

The instrument is presented as an experimental edition published before a full evaluation of its merits could be accomplished. The authors expressed their belief that this was necessary to fill a void because "teachers themselves do not in general know how to diagnose the illegibilities of their students' handwriting." This degree of relative professional neglect of this curricular domain was thus cited as a contributing factor in the publication of the test in its current form. The experimental flavor of the test is evidenced in the manual's discussion of reliability and validity.

The question of reliability is addressed through the evaluation of interscorer agreement. Data are presented indicating a correlation of .56 for Part 1 and .66 for Part 2. Subsequent modifications in scoring procedures were reported to have had a modest positive effect on these coefficients. Again the point is made by the authors that these data provide direction for further research and refinement of the tool. Unfortunately a review of the literature reveals no such efforts reported to date.

Limited attention is given to the questions of how the parts of the test were selected and why these particular areas are central to the diagnosis of handwriting errors. Although many of the fault patterns addressed in Part 1 are generally consistent with common informal error analysis procedures, the subcategories in Part 2, though apparently clinically derived, warrant further discussion. This concern is particularly important given the somewhat controversial nature of the assessment and treatment of perceptual and perceptual-motor abilities of children. Additional attention to the implications of these analyses would seem particularly apt for this program.

Because of the technical limitations of the DRHP, the primary strength of the tool lies in the identification and analysis of specific handwriting difficulties. The sections of the manual devoted to scoring procedures provide very clear illustrations of the specific faults deserving attention.

The DRHP program concludes with considerations for instruction. A variety of helpful suggestions related to instruction are provided. However, unlike other tools with similar purposes, such as the Denver Handwriting Analysis (Anderson, 1983), there is no provision for direct linkage from specific assessment results from this tool to the development of specific educational programs. Such an addition would clearly be of benefit to practitioners. It should be noted that three remedial programs are discussed which have as their respective purpose to restyle the writing of poor performers, to train students in critical self-awareness, and to enhance posture and pen-grip. However, the value of these programs would be enhanced if the specific implications of the assessment data for teaching were further emphasized. To some extent, this concern could be alleviated by a reorganization of the manual itself.

In summary, the DRHP is an interesting project warranting further attention and future development by the authors. Its model and corresponding focus is variant enough to demand greater attention to validation. It certainly can provide some direction to teachers interested in informal handwriting evaluation but it lacks the systematic administration and scoring procedures necessary for precise evaluation by persons relatively unskilled in this curricular area.

REVIEWER'S REFERENCE

Anderson, P. L. (1983). Denver Handwriting Analysis. Novato, CA: Academic Therapy Publications.

[92]

Diagnostic Achievement Test for Adolescents. Purpose: Measures the achievement level of secondary students. Grades 7–12; 1986; DATA; 14 scores: 9 subtest scores (Word Identification, Reading Comprehension, Math Calculation, Math Problem Solving, Spelling, Writing Composition, Science, Social Studies, Reference Skills), and 5 composite scores (Reading, Mathematics, Writing, Achievement Screener, Total Achievement); individual in part; PRO-SCORE System in-house computerized scoring system available for use with Apple or IBM computer; 1987 price data: $53 per complete kit including student booklet, 25 student response forms, 25 profile/examiner record forms, and examiner's manual (76 pages); $14 per student booklet; $9 per 25 student response forms; $13 per 25 profile/examiner record forms; $21 per examiner's manual; $49 per optional PRO-SCORE System (specify Apple or IBM); (60–120) minutes; Phyllis L. Newcomer and Brian R. Bryant; PRO-ED, Inc.*

Review of the Diagnostic Achievement Test for Adolescents by RANDY W. KAMPHAUS, Assistant Professor of Educational Psychology, University of Georgia, Athens, GA:

The Diagnostic Achievement Test for Adolescents (DATA) was published in 1986 by PRO-ED, Inc. According to the test's authors the DATA "provides examiners with an estimate of a student's knowledge of information commonly taught in the schools." The DATA seems to be an eminently practical instrument for use by teachers, and a variety of school clinicians. It is conveniently packaged and easily administered and scored.

Administration of the scale is facilitated by the use of item formats that are familiar to school personnel. The Spelling subtest, for example, uses a dictation format that is much more familiar to school clinicians than the multiple-choice format used by some individually administered tests of school achievement such as the Peabody Individual Achievement Test. The use of familiar item formats also contributes to a sense of content validity. The item pool was selected as a result of reviews of popular textbooks. Other tests of achievement were also reviewed in order to develop test items. The practice of relying on other tests' items is not impressive for the establishement of content validity as it may perpetuate the use of poor items that have been included in tests with little content validity.

A strength of the DATA, related to its content validity, is the breadth of achievement areas assessed by the test. This is an improvement over many of its predecessors such as the Wide Range Achievement Test that measure only a few areas of academic achievement and yet are used widely by clinicians for diagnosis. The broad coverage offered by the DATA makes it time efficient to use because clinicians can get a large sample of achievement behavior without having to switch instruments.

The DATA is also practical for other reasons. It is inexpensive in comparison to some of its competitors. It is also convenient in that there are very few component parts; only a manual and a record form are needed.

Despite the DATA's convenience and ease of use, concerns must be raised regarding psychometric rigor. The standardization, reliability, and validity data for the test are minimal, occasionally unsupportive of the test, and sometimes not described adequately enough to allow critical evaluation of the instrument.

The standardization of the DATA is substandard. The most crucial stratification variable for any standardization sample is some measure of socioeconomic status because this variable produces the largest differences in ability or achievement test scores. There is no statistical evidence in the manual indicating a close match between the DATA sample and the national population on SES. The data presented for race and ethnicity are also confusing. Specifically, the manual reports the sample was made up of 86% Whites, 10% Blacks, and 4% Others. Later in the manual the ethnic composition of the sample is described as 3% American Indian, 4% Hispanic, and 2% Asian. These figures do not add up to the 4% figure reported earlier for the "Other" racial category. Where are these ethnic groups subsumed under race?

With regard to norms development the authors are to be applauded for their rejection of age and grade equivalent norms. The DATA could have offered the popular alternative developmental norm, latent trait scaled scores, as does the Basic Achievement Skills Individual Screener (BASIS). However, the failure to offer this interval scale developmental norm is not a major weakness.

More disconcerting aspects of the norms include the use of the antiquated term "quotients" to describe composite scores. In addition, an incomplete percentile rank table is provided in the manual for the interpretation of these quotients. Most importantly, no information is given in the manual on the procedures used to develop the standard score norms. They look like normalized standard scores because a percentile rank of 50 always corresponds to the mean standard score, but there is no way of knowing this or other aspects of the norms, such as the extent and type of smoothing procedures used.

Internal consistency and stability coefficients are adequate. The test-retest coefficients were low for some of the subtests. The test-retest coefficient for Writing Composition, for example, was only .71. Some of the concurrent validity coefficients are also disturbingly low. The correlation between total math on the Stanford Diagnostic Mathematics Test and the DATA math total was .62. The correlation of this same DATA math total score with the math composite on the Iowa Tests of Basic Skills (ITBS) was reported as not significant. It is appropriate to report exact correlations even when they are not significant. The consumer should not have to guess. The correlation between the DATA math computation score and the computations test of the ITBS was only .41. The consumer should not have to guess. These coefficients, and others reported in the manual, do not engender confidence that all DATA scores are likely to agree with the scores from other popular and well-developed achievement tests.

In summary, the DATA is a practical achievement testing tool that is convenient for use in schools. It has several appealing features. It does, however, have significant psychometric weaknesses making it difficult to have confidence in the obtained scores. The most glaring weakness is the inadequate standardization program. In terms of psychometric qualities, other individually administered tests of academic achievement are clearly superior. Tests such as the Kaufman Test of Educational Achievement (K-TEA)—Comprehensive Form are much stronger in terms of psychometric quality. Because of these psychometric weaknesses the DATA should be carefully evaluated on a local level before it is used. One way of doing this would be to administer the DATA to children on a trial basis with other achievement tests that have earned the confidence of school personnel. Another procedure would be to develop local norms. The DATA may have potential not apparent from early research findings. This potential, however, is not evident without more convincing research findings.

Review of the Diagnostic Achievement Test for Adolescents by JAMES E. YSSELDYKE, Professor of Educational Psychology, University of Minnesota, Minneapolis, MN:

The Diagnostic Achievement Test for Adolescents (DATA) is designed to measure "retention of content material that is usually, but not always, presented in schools." The Battery was developed in response to a perceived need for a comprehensive achievement test that was specific to the content taught in secondary schools. The authors identify four purposes of the DATA: identification of students who are significantly below their peers in the content areas assessed, identifications of individual students' specific strengths and weaknesses, documentation of progress as a result of intervention, and use in research. Four kinds of scores are obtained using the DATA: raw scores, percentile scores, subtest standard scores, and composite standard scores. The authors are commended for not including age or grade scores, scores that are often misinterpreted on achievement batteries.

Content areas selected for inclusion in the DATA are reading, writing, mathematics, science, social studies, and reference skills. In selecting items for the test the authors relied on searches of textbooks used in grades 7–12. Reading and spelling words were generated using the EDL Core Vocabularies in Mathematics, Science, and Social Studies. And, items for the Science, Social Studies, Mathematics, and Reading subtests were based on *Barron's How to Prepare for the New High School Equivalency Examination (GED)*. Items were reviewed by content specialists for wording and relevancy. The authors do not specify the extent to which items were rewritten or excluded on the basis of this review process. Selection and placement in the test of final items was based on the performance of an unspecified number of junior and senior high school students attending only one school system: Huntington, West Virginia. I view this as a limited sample for purposes of calibrating the difficulty of items and of the extent to which the items discriminate between students who know specific academic content and those who do not.

The DATA was standardized on 1,135 children in 15 states. A specific stratified sampling plan was not used. Rather, the authors contacted users of the Diagnostic Achievement Battery (Newcomer & Curtis, 1983) and asked them to administer 20 to 30 DATAs. The sample is voluntary, and rate of participation is not specified. As indicated in the APA *Standards for Educational and Psychological Testing* (APA, AERA, & NCME, 1985), norms of a volunteer group of schools cannot be assumed to apply to schools in general. The authors of the DATA provide information showing sample distribution in comparison to census data for sex, residence, race, geographic area, ethnicity, and age. The data may be misleading. For example, while 17% of the norm sample came from the western geographic region, data were collected in only two western states (Arizona and California).

In describing the normative sample for the DATA, the authors do not provide crosstabulated information. Thus, while we know that 10% of the normative sample was Black, that 76% came from urban residences, and that 24% were from the Northeast, we do not know how many Black students were from urban environments in the Northeast. It may be that all Black students in the norm sample were from urban environments in the Northeast, or it may be that none were from urban residences in the Northeast. The normative sample and the sampling plan are insufficiently described to enable a user to make judgments about the nature of the group to which tested students are being compared.

Two kinds of data on reliability are presented. Internal consistency of all subtests was computed and in all instances exceeded .88. This is commendable. Data on test-retest reliability, though, are limited to performance of 58 students ages 12–18 attending school in Cedar Park, Texas. Coefficients ranged from .71 to .94. Coefficients for three of the nine subtests (Writing Composition, Reading Comprehension, and Reference Skills) are below the desirable standard of .80 (Salvia & Ysseldyke, 1988).

Although the authors state four purposes for using the DATA, they do not provide data on the validity of the test for each of these purposes. Data on criterion-related validity are limited to comparison of scores earned on DATA to those earned on other measures of achievement by members of the norm group. Those examiners who agreed to participate in standardization of DATA were asked to submit scores earned on other achievement tests by the children they tested. Scores were available for 234 students. Differing numbers of students took the various tests, and we are not told the dates of testing or the ages of those who took the tests. Data on content validity are based on expert opinion. The authors provide sufficient data on the construct validity of the test.

The Diagnostic Achievement Test for Adolescents is the only individually administered achievement test that provides users with scores in Reading, Mathematics, Spelling, Social Studies, Science, and Use of References. As such, it should provide very useful information to secondary school personnel. Those who use the test to compare the performance of students to a normative group should exercise caution, as the procedures for standardization of this test are neither adequate nor carefully described.

REVIEWER'S REFERENCES

Newcomer, P. C., & Curtis, D. (1984). *Diagnostic Achievement Battery*. Austin, TX: PRO-ED, Inc.

American Educational Research Association, American Psychological Association, & National Council on Measurement in Education. (1985). *Standards for educational and psychological testing*. Washington, DC: American Psychological Association, Inc.

Salvia, J., & Ysseldyke, J. E. (1988). *Assessment in special and remedial education*. Boston: Houghton-Mifflin Co.

[93]

A Diagnostic Achievement Test in Spelling. Purpose: Measures spelling ability and diagnoses specific spelling deficiencies. Grades 2–10; 1980; administered to determine pupil's proper placement in the Prescriptive Spelling Program; 4 forms; manual ('80, 24 pages); price data available from publisher; [20–25] minutes; William Wittenberg; Barnell Loft, Ltd.*

Review of A Diagnostic Achievement Test in Spelling by C. DALE CARPENTER, Associate Professor of Special Education, Western Carolina University, Cullowhee, NC:

A Diagnostic Achievement Test in Spelling, part of the Diagnostic and Prescriptive Spelling Program, is a standardized spelling test in dictation format, consisting of four equivalent forms of 100 words each. Grade scores are available for grades 2.0 through 10.0. The test is intended to diagnose specific types of spelling errors and to aid in placing students in the accompanying instructional program called A Prescriptive Spelling Program, which is designed to teach spelling principles usually taught in grades 2 through 8. This review is not intended to reflect on the worth of the intact program.

Apparently the test may be administered to individuals or to groups because the manual provides suggestions concerning the number of sessions recommended for groups at various age levels. The directions for administering the test are scant. For example, "[t]he teacher at any level may terminate the test when certain that the remaining words are too difficult for all the pupils." No specific instruction is given for establishing a ceiling or ending point; therefore, no standard procedure is followed. The test may not be a standardized test if it lacks standard procedures.

No information is provided to indicate how the test words were selected. One must infer they were chosen because they contain elements comprising the principles systematically assessed by each of the four forms. This includes 19 sets of principles, some of which are subgroups of a larger group (e.g., word endings, comprising three subgroups). The manual does not state these principles are usually taught or mastered in grades 2 through 8. That information is stated in a separate four-page publication titled PROOF-APPROACH COMPLIANCE provided by the publisher at this reviewer's request. It is assumed that most consumers would not have the same information.

Although grade scores are available, no information is provided in the manual stating how these scores were determined or describing the norming sample. The publisher's fact sheet states that 14,400 pupils were tested but does not state that the grade scores were derived from such sampling. Consequently, the potential consumer has no basis to judge the adequacy or relevancy of the norming sample or to positively determine that one exists.

Data concerning reliability and validity are also missing from the manual. No reliability or validity information is available from the publisher on request. The publisher's fact sheet states that computer analysis helped to determine equality of the four forms, difficulty of test items, and placement utility of the test into the accompanying instructional program. No other supporting information is provided.

The test purports to diagnose specific spelling deficiencies. Yet, 8 of the 19 error categories use only three items or words to measure the student's proficiency. On the basis of three items the teacher is supposed to determine if the student's skills in that category are on the Independent Level or Needs Instruction. In categories with four or more items three levels of proficiency are possible: Independent Level, Needs Reinforcement, and Needs Instruction. It is unlikely that three items are sufficient to determine the student's mastery of a particular skill. The reliability of this instrument for diagnostic purposes is suspect. In diagnosing particular errors, Spellmaster might be preferred because more items are used.

The consumer has no means to determine how well the test aids in instructional programming using the companion Prescriptive Spelling Program or any other program. It appears the diagnostic test would be well suited to placing students into the instructional program because it was designed to do so. However, no data are provided to support such a claim.

SUMMARY. A Diagnostic Achievement Test in Spelling is part of the Diagnostic and Prescriptive Spelling Program and should be considered in this context only. No data support use of A Diagnostic Achievement Test in Spelling as a stand-alone standardized diagnostic spelling measure. Psychometric qualities are undetermined. Although the 400 test words measuring different spelling categories may be useful to educational diagnosticians, the test as constituted lacks evidence that it is a valid or reliable measurement instrument.

Review of A Diagnostic Achievement Test in Spelling by JEFFREY K. SMITH, Associate Professor of Educational Psychology, Rutgers, The State University, New Brunswick, NJ:

A Diagnostic Achievement Test in Spelling was designed to serve two purposes: first, to provide an overall spelling ability score in grade equivalents, and second, to diagnose spelling problems into 19 clusters. The format of the 100-item test is free-response; that is, the word to be spelled is dictated by the teacher, placed in a sentence by the teacher, and then the student writes his/her answer on paper. The teacher is responsible for grading and translation of scores into the clusters and grade equivalents using forms and tables provided by the publisher.

The grade equivalent table ranges from 2.0 to 10.0. The 19 clusters of spelling skills provide for determination of the following levels: "independent level," "needs reinforcement," and "needs instruction." The 100-item test is ordered from easy (words such as can, pet, ride) to hard (words such as criticize, thorough, plateau). There are four forms of the test. Performance on the test is correlated with the Prescriptive Spelling Program by the same publisher. There are no time limits specified in the manual (which is appropriate for a test given in the manner described).

There is no technical information available on the test. A discussion with the individual listed as the supervisor for the statistical analysis revealed the grade equivalents were empirically-based, but no report of the details of the study were available from the publisher. The same table of grade equivalents is used for all four forms of the test. That is, a raw score of 51 provides a grade equivalent of 4.9 no matter which of the four forms is administered. It seems highly unlikely that all four forms of the test were perfectly parallel, which would be necessary in order for the grade equivalent table to be correct. There is no reliability or validity information reported for the test. There is no information provided on the development of the test or the source material for the words chosen to be on the test.

An examination of these tests would suggest they are fairly appropriate for their intended purposes: to diagnose spelling strengths and weaknesses and to measure achievement. There are problems underlying this conclusion, however, and in the absence of technical information, the tests cannot be recommended for classroom use as proposed in the published materials. In order to move one grade-equivalent year (up to the eighth grade level), a student has to improve his or her score by 8–15 items on a 100-item test. If the equating is off by 3–4 items at any given level on a given form, this can result in a fairly substantial error in the estimated growth of a student during a school year. This, of course, would be in addition to measurement error. Because the test is to be used over eight grade levels, the measurement error within a 1-to-2 year range could be substantial.

There are also validity concerns with the measure. Construct validity is a particular concern. Do students who perform poorly on this measure also have trouble with spelling in their everyday writing? If a student misspells one word in the "contractions" cluster, but does not make his or her mistake in the contraction aspect of the word, does he or she really "need instruction" in contractions as indicated by the diagnostic evaluation form? Should students receive instruction on the words on the test or should the test words be saved from direct instruction in order to produce a purer measure of spelling ability? For such a seemingly straightforward domain, spelling raises a number of intriguing validity concerns. Unfortunately, the author does not address any of them.

Overall, A Diagnostic Achievement Test in Spelling appears to be a well-constructed set of spelling measures that would be easy for classroom teachers to administer. In the absence of any technical data, however, it is not possible to recommend its use at this time.

[94]

Diagnostic and Achievement Reading Tests. Purpose: "Used to diagnose skills deficiencies or proficiencies and to measure whether a learner's mastery of skills is categorized as weak, marginal, or proficient." Children who have received instruction in whichever skills objectives selected to be tested; 1977; DART; "criterion-referenced"; 10 tests divided into three program levels measuring sixty-six different objectives-based sections that focus on a standard array of word-attack skills; no manual, directions for administration for each test; 1988 price data: $64.08 per complete program; $29.55 per Level A; $17.97 per Level B or Level C; administration time not reported; Modern Curriculum Press.*

Review of the Diagnostic and Achievement Reading Tests by ROBERT G. HARRINGTON, Associate Professor, Department of Educational Psychology and Research, University of Kansas, Lawrence, KS:

Reading difficulties are among the most common referral problems encountered by school personnel (Witt & Bartlett, 1982). Reading problems of school-age children are usually manifested in three ways: (*a*) ineffective word attack strategies; (*b*) inconsistent comprehension of materials; and (*c*) a negative attitude toward reading (Poostay & Aaron, 1982). There is increasing agreement that from among these three areas the acquisition of phonics skills is of fundamental importance in learning to read (Weaver & Resnick, 1979; Williams, 1979). Perhaps this agreement is possible because a great deal of research has been done on decoding, the process involved, and how to teach this aspect of reading (Weaver & Resnick, 1979). In keeping with this emphasis on phonics the Diagnostic and Achievement Reading Tests (DART) was designed to assess skills in attacking, recognizing, and pronouncing words.

Many reading specialists tend to view the reading process within a hierarchical framework, wherein the global skills such as word attack skills are reduced to a sequence of subskills, with each subskill consisting of one or more prerequisite skills that are usually interrelated and often difficult to assess in isolation (Fry & Lagomarsino, 1981). Therefore, when a reading specialist analyzes a child's reading problem, an attempt is usually made to pinpoint the child's strengths and weaknesses in relation to the hierarchy of reading skills within that reading curriculum. The DART is a criterion-referenced test intended to identify strengths and weaknesses within such a reading skills hierarchy. As such, the DART can be used to evaluate individual learners' reading skills against objectives rather than against national norms or the reading achievement scores of peers. In fact, nowhere in the test manual are suitable age or grade ranges for DART examinees mentioned. A table outlining at what age or grade levels these word attack skills are typically taught and mastered would have been helpful especially for novice examiners. Without this information new examiners using the DART should be cautious to compare the performance objectives assessed by the DART with the scope and sequence charts outlining the reading skills being taught within the particular reading series the teacher is employing.

The DART consists of 10 booklets of criterion-referenced tests covering three test series (A, B, and C). Test series A contains four booklets, while test series B and C consist of three booklets each. Within the 10 test booklets there are test units composed of varying numbers of sections each designed to assess specifically stated performance objectives. For example, the performance objective for Test Unit A-1, Section B is the following: Given a picture stimulus, the pupil will correctly identify from among an array of pictures that picture which is the same as the picture stimulus. In total, the 10 booklets of the DART include 66 sections focusing on different sets of word-attack skills. The number of word-attack skills covered on the Phonics DART, as evidenced by the 66 Test Sections, appears to be quite extensive. Mimeograph master copies of each test section are provided at the back of each of the 10 Test Unit manuals so copies of sections can be reproduced to administer to groups of child examinees rather easily without the need to purchase individual test record booklets. Some examples of the variety of reading skills assessed within each of the 10 test units on the DART are the following: identifying both similarities and differences by visual discrimination (Test Unit A-1); recognizing specific letters in words (Test Unit A-2); recognizing vowel sounds (Test Unit A-3); recognizing consonant blends visually and aurally (Test Unit A-4); recognizing alphabet letters (Test Unit B-1); recognizing words in which the letter 'y' stands for a vowel sound (Test Unit B-2); recognizing words in which prefixes have been added to certain base words (Test Unit B-3); distinguishing long and short vowel sounds in words (Test Unit C-1); identifying words that make up various contracted forms (Test Unit C-2); and syllabification skills (Test Unit C-3).

According to the test developers it is unnecessary to administer the entire DART to a group of children, but rather the examiner is free to select skills sections from among those test units in which children have received reading instruction previously. Unfortunately, no rationale is offered in the test manual to justify how the 10 Test Units were grouped into their three respective Test Series and no research evidence is presented to verify the sequential hierarchy of phonics skills purportedly assessed by the DART do, in fact, represent an accurate sequential ordering of milestone reading/decoding skills.

The Phonics DART is untimed. It may be administered individually or in groups small enough so the examiner is able to observe each child's performance on the test and to ensure that each child is both comprehending and following the test directions. Directions for administering, scoring, and interpreting the test sections are contained in each of the 10 manuals. The directions for test administration appear to be complete and rather simple. General suggestions and directions for the examiner as well as test information to be given to the children are provided in the examiner's manual. Each Test Section in the three Test Series of the Phonics DART is preceded by an additional introductory section that reviews with the pupils the procedures they will need to follow in responding to the various sections of the test. No scoring is necessary for this introductory section of the test but is included to help the examiner determine whether or not a child is capable of following the test directions, moving the cardboard item marker correctly, and drawing a ring around pictures or words they choose as their answers. All items on the DART are presented in a multiple-choice format. Before proceeding with the actual Test Sections, the examiner is supposed to observe and attempt to correct any difficulties a child may have in recognizing rows, using the marker, recognizing pictures, drawing rings, or following directions. Only those children who can follow the test procedures should continue with the other sections. Once it is clear that each child can follow the test procedures correctly a sample item is administered prior to each section to make sure the children understand the specific word attack skill being tested in that section. These preliminary test procedures are laudable because they ensure that all children understand what is expected of them before they take the test. These procedures are especially important in group test administrations in which some children may receive low scores because they did not comprehend the directions or the concept being assessed.

To facilitate scoring the Test Sections, miniature facsimile pages of each Test Section with answers keyed appear in the examiner's manual for that Test Unit. The score for each Test Section is the total number of a child's correct responses for that section. Incomplete responses and multiple responses to the same item are scored as errors. There is no total test score for the DART and no attempt should be made to compute one. All scores are reported as Test Section raw scores and no transformations to standard scores or grade or age equivalents are made. Of course, raw scores are extremely difficult to interpret and most such interpretations should probably be made with regard to specific reading skills development assessed by the DART relative to the performance of peers within a specific classroom.

The results of the DART are intended for use in profiling children's phonics skills and deficiencies and in classifying a reader's skills in phonics as weak, marginal, or proficient compared to the stated performance objectives. Raw scores on Test Sections falling within the range of 0–6 correct responses are considered weak; 7–8 correct responses is marginal; and children with raw scores of 9–10 correct responses on a particular Test Section are considered to have proficient skills in that area. No data are presented in the manual regarding how these diagnostic classifications were made or whether (as one might expect) the criteria changes depending upon the age, grade, or sex of the child. The score for each Test Section is recorded on the cover page of the test booklet for that Test Unit by darkening the number representing the child's raw score on a scale from 0 to 10. When a child receives scores on a Test Section in the proficient range then the child is considered to have mastered those word attack skills and should be ready to be instructed in new skills. For marginal performance, it is recommended the child receive remedial instruction in that skill area before progressing to new skills. When weak skills are detected the authors recommend the child be given additional instruction in the skill involved but with new instructional material, not the same material on which the child experienced failure.

In summary, the strengths and weaknesses of the DART are similar to those shared by other criterion-referenced reading tests. The advantages are the following: (*a*) the child's performance is assessed in relation to a specific reading criterion (Wallace & Larsen, 1978); (*b*) the emphasis on the direct assessment of specific reading skills helps the examiner understand exactly what skills the reader does or does not possess (Hively & Reynolds, 1975); (*c*) the test can be adapted to target specific skills deficits for assessment; (*d*) student progress can be assessed continuously; and (*e*) the DART can be adapted to closely match the reading skills being taught in the current reading curriculum.

On the other hand, the major disadvantages of the DART are the following: (*a*) The authors of the DART fail to report any reliability or validity data. It has been suggested by Salvia and Ysseldyke (1981) that in such situations the examiner should consider employing repeated observations using the same criterion-referenced test to confirm or disconfirm initial impressions and increase the reliability of diagnostic decisions. This strategy, however, does not compensate sufficiently for the lack of technical data according to the latest version of the *Standards for Educational and Psychological Testing* (AERA, APA, & NCME, 1985). (*b*) Another problem with a test like the DART arises when it is administered to a group. The multiple-choice format may tend to encourage impulsive guessing (Compton, 1980). Consequently, the group version of the DART is recommended for screening purposes only when a general range of a client's reading skills is desired and not for diagnostic or classification uses.

In conclusion, there is no simple answer to the question whether the Phonics DART is a useful measure of reading skills. In deciding whether to use the Phonics DART, reading specialists would do well to consider several questions posed by Ysseldyke and Marston (1981): What reading skills do I wish to assess? What kinds of reading scores do I wish to report, if any? Do I need a group or individually administered test? Will I be satisfied with the results of an informal reading test or do I require a norm-referenced reading measure? What kinds of decisions about reading am I trying to make? Answers to these questions should preface every reading assessment and, in the case of the Phonics DART, will help individual examiners confirm or disconfirm the utility of this informal reading measure in addressing the unique kinds of referral problems presented by a particular child with a suspected reading disability.

REVIEWER'S REFERENCES

Hively, W., & Reynolds, M. C. (Eds.). (1975). *Domain-referenced testing in special education*. Reston, VA: The Council for Exceptional Children.

Wallace, G., & Larsen, S. C. (1978). *Educational assessment of learning problems: Testing for teaching*. Boston: Allyn & Bacon, Inc.

Weaver, P. A., & Resnick, L. B. (1979). The theory and practice of early reading: An introduction. In L. B. Resnick & P. A. Weaver (Eds.), *Theory and practice of early reading: Volume 1* (pp. 1-27). Hillsdale, NJ: Lawrence Earlbaum Associates, Publishers.

Williams, J. (1979). Reading instruction today. *American Psychologist*, 34, 917-922.

Compton, C. (1980). *A guide to 65 tests for special education*. Belmont, CA: Fearon Education.

Fry, M. A., & Lagomarsino, L. (1982). Factors that influence reading: A developmental perspective. *School Psychology Review*, 11, 239-250.

Poostay, E. J., & Aaron, I. E. (1982). Reading problems of children: The perspectives of reading specialists. *School Psychology Review*, 11, 251-256.

Witt, J. C., & Bartlett, B. J. (1982). School psychologists as knowledge-linkers in the solution of children's reading problems. *School Psychology Review*, 11, 221-228.

Ysseldyke, J. E., & Marston, D. (1982). A critical analysis of standardized reading tests. *School Psychology Review*, 11, 257-266.

American Educational Research Association, American Psychological Association, & National Council on Measurement in Education. (1985). *Standards for educational and psychological testing*. Washington, DC: American Psychological Association, Inc.

Review of the Diagnostic and Achievement Reading Tests by DEBORAH KING KUNDERT, Assistant Professor, Educational Psychology and Statistics, SUNY-Albany, Albany, NY:

The Diagnostic and Achievement Reading Tests (DART) are a set of 10 criterion-referenced tests, designed to assess mastery of specific phonics skills in grades 1 through 3. Each of the 10 tests consists of several sections, with each section measuring a specific performance objective. Student performance is evaluated against these clearly stated objectives to determine strengths and weaknesses in word-attack skills. While the DART series was originally developed as a companion to the Modern Curriculum Press Phonics Programs, DART can be used with any phonics or reading program.

The DART program is divided into three levels, A, B, and C, with each level assessing specific skills. The tests ascend gradually in order of difficulty (e.g., readiness skills to syllabication), though the sequence does not have to be followed rigidly. Examiners may select those objectives that they want to assess. The DART can be administered to individual students or to small groups with no time limits.

Each DART test unit provides clear, specific administration, scoring, and interpretation instructions. Each test contains 10 items, with the number correct as the child's score. These scores are interpreted as weak (0–6), marginal (7–8), or proficient (9–10). As such, weak performance indicates the need for additional instruction with new material, marginal performance indicates the need for reinforcement work prior to going on to new skills, and proficient performance indicates that the child is ready for further instruction in new skills.

DART is a criterion-referenced test, thus traditional norm-referenced test evaluation criteria are inappropriate. Requirements for evaluating criterion-referenced tests are suggested by Popham (1978) and these criteria were used to examine the DART. In all cases, items on the DART coincide with the described behaviors stated in the performance objectives. Thus, the test seems to possess a suitable descriptive framework. Furthermore, an adequate number of items are used to assess mastery of each objective. The focus of this test is best evaluated through an examination of each level of the series (A, B, or C). Level A assesses 28 separate objectives, Level B assesses 17 separate objectives, and Level C assesses 22 separate objectives. Within each level, there is some overlap among the individual test units (e.g., two tests of initial and final consonants). As such, it appears that effort was made in test construction to limit the focus of the DART within each level. Information on reliability is not included with the test materials. Validity issues are indirectly addressed in various sections of the test instructions. Items were selected to correlate with Modern Curriculum Press Phonics series, which have been in existence for over 25 years; therefore, the domain-selection validity criterion is met. Descriptive or content validity may be implied from a statement in the test booklets that many experts in the field of reading and testing were consulted during test construction. Criterion-related validity is alluded to in the test results interpretation section. That is, weak performance indicates the need for additional instruction with alternate materials, marginal performance indicates the need for reinforcement work, and proficient performance indicates skill mastery and the need to move ahead. Information on how these performance levels (weak-proficient) were developed is not provided. The last factor to address in evaluating criterion-referenced tests is the availability of comparative test data. Comparative test data are not reported for the DART.

As outlined by Popham (1978), the concept of comparative data entails the gathering of data upon which to base comparisons of criterion test results. Essentially, this process involves collecting field trial data indicating how other students perform on the test. By collecting the comparative data, examiners have some measure of how well an examinee should perform with respect to the behavior in question. When criterion-referenced tests are accompanied by comparative data, then the examiner can determine what the examinee can and cannot do, as well as have information that will help judge the adequacy of the examinee's test performance.

In summary, the DART is a series of criterion-referenced test units developed to assess the mastery of phonics skills in early elementary grades. A technical analysis of its characteristics indicates that it is a moderately well-developed instrument. School personnel would find it useful as a measure of pupil progress and as a source of information for individual educational program planning in the area of phonics and early reading development. Information provided by the publisher indicated that the DART is not widely distributed, and that there are no plans to revise this test.

REVIEWER'S REFERENCE

Popham, W. J. (1978). *Criterion-referenced measurement*. Englewood Cliffs, NJ: Prentice-Hall, Inc.

[95]

Diagnostic Interview for Borderline Patients. Purpose: Designed to discriminate borderline patients from patients with schizophrenia, neurotic depression, and mixed diagnoses. Patients; [1982–83]; 6 scores: Social Adaptation, Impulse Action Patterns, Affects, Psychosis, Interpersonal Relations, Total; individual; manual ('83, 21 pages); price data available from distributor; (50–90) minutes; John G. Gunderson (interview), Pamela S. Ludolph (manual), Kenneth R. Silk (manual), Naomi E. Lohr (manual), and Dewey G. Cornell (manual); interview distributed by Pfizer; manual distributed by Pamela S. Ludolph.*

TEST REFERENCES

1. Andrulonis, P. A., & Vogel, N. G. (1984). Comparison of borderline personality subcategories to schizophrenic and affective disorders. *British Journal of Psychiatry*, 144, 358-363.
2. Frances, A., Clarkin, J. F., Gilmore, M., Hurt, S. W., & Brown, R. (1984). Reliability of criteria for borderline personality disorder: A comparison of DSM-III and the Diagnostic Interview for Borderline Patients. *American Journal of Psychiatry*, 141, 1080-1084.
3. McManus, M., Brickman, A., Alessi, N. E., & Graphentine, W. L. (1984). Borderline personality in serious delinquents. *Comprehensive Psychiatry*, 25, 446-454.
4. Hurt, S. W., Clarkin, J. F., Frances, A., Abrams, R., & Hunt, H. (1985). Discriminant validity of the MMPI for borderline personality disorder. *Journal of Personality Assessment*, 49, 56-61.
5. Reich, J. (1985). Measurement of DSM-III, Axis II. *Comprehensive Psychiatry*, 26, 352-363. Patients):
6. Chopra, H. D., & Beatson, J. A. (1986). Psychotic symptoms in borderline personality disorder. *American Journal of Psychiatry*, 143, 1605-1607.
7. Greenman, D. A., Gunderson, J. G., Cane, M., & Saltzman, P. R. (1986). An examination of the borderline diagnosis in children. *American Journal of Psychiatry*, 143, 998-1003.
8. Hurt, S. W., Clarkin, J. F., Koenigsberg, H. W., Frances, A., & Nurnberg, H. G. (1986). Diagnostic Interview for Borderlines: Psychometric properties and validity. *Journal of Consulting and Clinical Psychology*, 54, 256-260.
9. Nace, E. P., Saxon, J. J., & Shore, N. (1986). Borderline personality disorder and alcoholism treatment: A one-year follow-up study. *Journal of Studies on Alcohol*, 47, 196-200.
10. Gardner, D., Lucas, P. B., & Cowdry, R. W. (1987). Soft sign neurological abnormalities in borderline personality disorder and normal control subjects. *The Journal of Nervous and Mental Disease*, 175, 177-180.
11. Pope, H. G., Jr., Frankenburg, F. R., Hudson, J. I., Jonas, J. M., & Yurgelun-Todd, D. (1987). Is bulimia associated with borderline personality disorder?: A controlled study. *The Journal of Clinical Psychiatry*, 48, 181-184.
12. Zubenko, G. S., George, A. W., Soloff, P. H., & Schulz, P. (1987). Sexual practices among patients with borderline personality disorder. *The American Journal of Psychiatry*, 144, 748-752.

Review of the Diagnostic Interview for Borderline Patients by ROBERT E. DEYSACH, Associate Professor of Psychology, University of South Carolina, Columbia, SC:

It is perhaps apt that a nosological entry as controversial as the Borderline designation be assessed via an interview schedule as complex as the Diagnostic Interview for Borderline Patients (DIB). The revised DIB outlines a semistructured interview designed to standardize collection of information regarding the presence or absence of Borderline symptom patterns. Additional Guidelines for Administration are available but unpublished.

The DIB is a rating scale based primarily on patient report of history and symptoms. In the face of potentially unreliable or unavailable patient reports, information can be obtained from other sources (e.g., family, case records). Five section scores are generated on the DIB that provide estimates of: Social Adaptation (stability in work history, underuse of talents, marketing social style); Impulse Action Patterns (flagrant acts against self, serious substance abuse, unstable sexual behavior, brushes with the law); Affects (depression, anger, or other signs of poorly regulated mood states); Psychosis (psychotic experiences that are subclinical, brief, or linked to intense mood states, to drug use, or to the process of therapy); and Interpersonal Relations (needy, ambivalent, intense, manipulative, self-defeating styles in intimate social or therapy relationships). Twenty-nine individual Statements (four of which identify symptoms exclusive of borderline diagnoses) are rated on a 3-point scale reflecting presence or absence of symptoms, with the middle value reflecting ambiguous judgments. To accommodate uneven Statement frequencies across the five areas, individual Section Scores are each converted to a single score (also on a 3-point scale), and the five resulting scores are totalled. A cutoff score is provided (i.e., a score of 7 or higher out of a possible 10 points) that reportedly identifies the presence of Borderline Personality Disorder as distinct from other clinical syndromes.

The DIB is designed to be administered in 50 to 90 minutes within an interview format. While some individual cue words are included to prompt examiners to the main content of items, general instructions regarding the manner of item presentation are not provided. To accommodate varying levels of examiner experience, the interview consists of 132 additional items designed to elicit additional information in each of the five areas. Although the schedule itself stops short of generating a prototypic context to anchor the examiner's clinical judgments, the additional items appear to provide useful descriptors to help stabilize ratings regarding the critical Statements and more adequately operationalize the five diagnostic clusters.

The DIB protocol, in combination with scoring Guidelines developed in collaboration with the author, offers fairly explicit criteria for inferring traits and behavior patterns. In spite of this, the complexity of the scale (e.g., use of different time frames in judging individual symptoms and statement composites that admit incompatible symptom patterns) renders it difficult for use by the inexperienced examiner.

The author reports satisfactory interrater reliabilities on DIB total scores (i.e., with percent agreements ranging from the mid-80s to low 90%). Similar levels of interrater reliability have been found by others but only following extensive examiner training in the use of the scale. Reliability of judgments of the five component scores has yielded satisfactory interrater reliabilities for only three of the five scales. Test-retest reliabilities have ranged from .47 to .64 on individual scales even when doctoral level clinicians were specifically trained in DIB interviewing and scoring. Overall, while reliabilities are generally of the order to warrant continued use of the DIB, cautiousness regarding the reliability would seem in order if the instrument is used to make individual treatment decisions.

On inspection, the DIB appears to capture the essential characteristics described in the literature on borderline behavior patterns. Formal validational efforts of the DIB, however, are lacking at the present time. It has been reported in the literature that the DIB is useful in generating diagnostic judgments of Borderline Personality Disorder comparable to those based upon the criteria presented in *DSM-III*. Parallel studies using *DSM-III-R* criteria have not been attempted to date.

In general, the DIB is an unpretentious attempt to add stability to diagnostic judgments regarding borderline symptoms and traits. It appears the utility of the DIB may be judged from three separate perspectives. Although the first of these is not listed by the authors as a potential use, the DIB appears to have considerable potential as a diagnostic training tool for those attempting to differentiate borderline behavior patterns. The delineation of five major diagnostic criteria, the provision of 19 subgroupings under which to organize patient report and case record material and, finally, an exhaustive listing of symptoms encompassing behaviors both inclusive and exclusive of borderline symptoms combine to provide a systematic review of a rich set of clinical information.

The author of the DIB highlights its value as a research tool. However, although the general content of the rating scale parallels *DSM-III*'s major criteria, the range of symptoms tapped by the DIB tends to be more inclusive than those described in *DSM-III*. Integration of findings based on the DIB and *DSM-III* has yet to be attempted. The DIB has eliminated references to family relationships and focuses primarily on patient social and emotional adjustment in the recent past. In so doing, the measure appears to provide an independent source of information for studying the role of parent-child relationships in the development of borderline functioning. The investigation of variables linked to response to treatment appears slightly more problematic in light of inclusion on the DIB of diagnostic statements directly rating the quality of therapeutic relationships.

Finally, although the DIB offers some promise as a clinical tool, it contains problems, some of which have been noted above. The first of these mirrors the controversies existing in the definition of the category itself. While some clinicians accent the links between borderline patterns and the spectrum of affective symptoms, others have highlighted the role of manipulative and irresponsible social behaviors in describing the syndrome. The existence of such controversy regarding theory governing borderline traits, combined with confusion specifically tied to DIB diagnostic Statements, is likely to severely limit the value of the DIB in drawing valid clinical inferences. The solutions to such diagnostic dilemmas are not easy ones. Although those most familiar with the DIB have recommended staff conferences to resolve controversies, this solution appears to side-step the issues of generalizability of this diagnostic consensus beyond the immediate clinical setting.

Overall, the DIB is an instrument of some psychiatric utility, but unfortunately it is also one that embodies the problems all too evident in psychiatric diagnosis. In point of fact, recent attempts to cast psychiatric diagnosis in a form emphasizing operationalized criteria and atheoretical perspectives have served only to mask the set of assumptions and premises upon which the field turns. As concluded by its supporters, reliable and valid use of the DIB depends upon variables such as examiner experience, preliminary team meetings, training tapes, and ongoing diagnostic consultation. Although such practices may in fact "untangle" nagging "diagnostic differences," they also may serve to foster a great deal of rater bias, limiting researchers to obtaining no more than what they expect. Similarly, it is for the clinician-in-training that the DIB (like most of the other attempts to structure psychiatric judgment) may be of greatest value. For the experienced clinician its use is likely to simply be "gilding the lily."

Review of the Diagnostic Interview for Borderline Patients by CHARLES A. PETERSON, Staff Clinical Psychologist, VA Minneapolis Medical Center and Clinical Assistant Professor, Department of Psychology, University of Minnesota, Minneapolis, MN:

Now that "borderline" has become a "star word . . . seeming to illuminate a great deal" (Pruyser, 1975), clinicians everywhere have sought ways to psychometrically apprehend this elusive patient: The clinical interview (e.g., Kernberg, 1981)?—too subject to bias and countertransference; the traditional psychological test battery with an intact WAIS and a deviant Rorschach (e.g., Kwawer, Lerner, & Sugarman, 1980)?—too time consuming, too tied to psychoanalytic object relations theory. Should we slash our psychometric wrists? Should we despair at the unavailability of a sustaining instrument? Maybe "Yes" and maybe "No." Along comes the Diagnostic Interview for Borderline Patients (DIB), a semistructured interview designed to diagnose borderline personality disorder. The alert potential user should ask "But which borderline?" "Whose conceptualization of the borderline is now psychometrically incarnate?" Test construction is basically rational-intuitive (Hase & Goldberg, 1967) but guided by a prior review of the clinical literature on borderline patients (Gunderson & Singer, 1975; note the pre-DSM-III origins of this test!)

The 161 items—a mix of query and observation—have been grouped into five major sections: Social Adaptation (sample question, "Is patient aware of social conventions—even if in defiance of them?"), Impulse Action Patterns ("Have you ever behaved self-destructively, even threatening to kill yourself?"), Affects ("Have you been argumentative?"), Psychoses ("Do you ever feel like your actions or speech are controlled by something other than yourself?"), Interpersonal Relations ("Do you tend to feel sorry for animals or people with problems?"), culminating in a Total Score to rule in borderline personality disorder. The items vary in the depth of inference and degree of clinical judgment required, but, in the main, call for a high degree of clinical skill and favor a psychodynamic orientation. Items are scored "2, 1, or 0" and reflect the "interviewer's best clinical judgment" as "Yes, Probably, or No." The interviewers are given considerable leeway on how to conduct the interview and are encouraged to probe as needed. No suggestion is made as to who should use this test, and whether it is suited for research or clinical practice. The consumer will have difficulty evaluating the DIB for potential use, not to mention making sense of its product because the test itself is not accompanied by any descriptive literature on test development, reliability, or validity. Available under separate cover and authored by an independent research group, the alleged manual bears no resemblance to the *Standards for Educational and Psychological Testing* (AERA, APA, & NCME, 1985). The manual is, in fact, a photocopied collection of loosely organized tips designed to "facilitate" the achievement of reliability *within* research groups and to insure that the DIB can be administered and uniformly scored *across* research settings (Ludolph, Silk, Lohr, & Cornell, undated [1982–83]; emphasis in the original). The manual advocates DSM-III definitions of vague terms used in DIB ratings and offers recommendations ranging from group discussion (presumably to articulate the nomothetic network surrounding the borderline construct) to individual and group consensus ratings of videotaped interviews. A growing literature (Cornell, Silk, Ludolph, & Lohr, 1983; Frances, Clarkin, Gilmore, Hurt, & Brown, 1984; Gunderson & Singer, 1975; Gunderson, Kolb, & Austin, 1981; Hurt, Clarkin, Koenigsberg, Frances, & Nurnberg, 1986; Kolb & Gunderson, 1980) suggests that interrater, test-retest reliability, and internal consistency are generally acceptable but show great variation across items and sections. Factor analytic studies are premature and presumptuous. The several validity studies suggest the DIB does distinguish borderline personality disorder from schizophrenia and other psychoses as well as from other personality disorders, but *may* show some compromised efficiency across in- and out-patient settings and with disorders in varying stages of compensation. The DIB does correlate significantly with DSM-III but the two are not measuring identical constructs, given there are areas on the DIB (e.g., psychotic functioning) not assessed by DSM-III.

This is not the first test (don't forget the Rorschach, TAT, and Bender-Gestalt) devised by a psychiatrist that shows some clinical promise despite some very suspect psychometric underpinnings. Insecure clinicians may use the DIB as a "transitional object" to help them sustain the illusion that Gunderson himself will accompany them on ward rounds, diagnosing borderlines no matter the Axis I veneer. Researchers may choose to use the DIB in a multimethod assessment in order to avoid a "criterion problem" (Wiggins, 1973) when studying borderline personality disorder. The more psychometrically responsible will question the test's absence of a scaling algorithm that equally weights items or scales with obviously different predictive power, the too simple advocacy of one cutting score despite local fluctuations in base rate prevalence of borderlines (Meehl & Rosen, 1955), the absence of an adequate test manual, and the unanswered but basic question of whether the DIB outperforms or otherwise adds incremental validity to DSM-III diagnoses of borderline personality disorder. The sociopolitically sensitive will take offense at some of the value-laden items and judgments required of the rater. "Homosexuality," "promiscuity," and "repetitive sexually deviant practices" are implicitly linked. Another question asks "Have you had any strange or dramatic sexual or religious experiences or adventures?" Are we talking sodomy in Georgia or hot tubs in Marin County? Are we ruling in the noetic moment or ruling out adult baptism? Will borderline become the DIB diagnosis for those who do not honor the commandment "Thou Shalt Adjust!"? (Linder, 1952). Like the patients it is designed to assess, the DIB will enthrall some users and disgust others.

REVIEWER'S REFERENCES

Lindner, R. M. (1952). *Prescription for rebellion.* New York: Rinehart.

Meehl, P. E., & Rosen, A. (1955). Antecedent probability and the efficiency of psychometric signs, patterns, or cutting scores. *Psychological Bulletin*, 52, 194-216.

Hase, H. D., & Goldberg, L. R. (1967). Comparative validity of different strategies of constructing personality inventory scales. *Psychological Bulletin*, 67, 231-248.

Wiggins, J. S. (1973). *Personality and prediction: Principles of personality assessment.* Reading, MA: Addison-Wesley.

Gunderson, J. G., & Singer, M. T. (1975). Defining borderline patients: An overview. *American Journal of Psychiatry*, 132, 1-10.

Pruyser, P. W. (1975). What splits in "splitting"? *Bulletin of the Menninger Clinic*, 39, 1-46.

Kolb, J. E., & Gunderson, J. G. (1980). Diagnosing borderline patients with a semistructured interview. *Archives of General Psychiatry*, 37, 37-41.

Kwawer, J. S., Lerner, H. D., & Sugarman, A. (Eds.). (1980). *Borderline phenomena and the Rorschach test.* New York: International Universities Press, Inc.

Gunderson, J. G., Kolb, J. E., & Austin, V. (1981). The Diagnostic Interview for Borderline Patients. *American Journal of Psychiatry*, 138, 896-903.

Kernberg, O. (1981). Structural interviewing. *Psychiatric Clinics of North America*, 4, 169-195.

Ludolph, P. S., Silk, K. R., Lohr, N. E., & Cornell, D. G. [1982-83]. *Guidelines for the administration of the Diagnostic Interview for Borderlines.* Ann Arbor, MI: Pamela Ludolph.

Cornell, D. G., Silk, K. R., Ludolph, P. S., & Lohr, N. E. (1983). Test-retest reliability of the Diagnostic Interview for Borderlines. *Archives of General Psychiatry*, 40, 1307-1310.

Frances, A., Clarkin, J. F., Gilmore, M., Hurt, S. W., & Brown, R. (1984). Reliability of criteria for borderline personality disorder: A comparison of DSM-III and the Diagnostic Interview for Borderline Patients. *American Journal of Psychiatry*, 141, 1080-1084.

American Educational Research Association, American Psychological Association, & National Council on Measurement in Education. (1985). *Standards for educational and psychological testing.* Washington, DC: American Psychological Association, Inc.

Hurt, S. W., Clarkin, J. F., Koenigsberg, H. W., Frances, A., & Nurnberg, H. G. (1986). Diagnostic Interview for Borderlines: Psychometric properties and validity. *Journal of Consulting and Clinical Psychology*, 54, 256-260.

[96]

Drumcondra Criterion Referenced Mathematics Test, Level 6. Purpose: "To assess pupil's mastery of the objectives of the primary school mathematics curriculum." Pupils in 6th class or in first-year post primary; 1977–84; DCRMT; formerly Level C; "criterion-referenced"; item scores only for 58 objectives in 10 sections: Operations With Whole Numbers, Whole Number Structure, Fractional Number Structure, Operations With Fractions, Decimals, Sets, Algebra, Geometry, Charts, Problems; 1985 price data: 50p per test booklet ('84, 14 pages); 20p per answer sheet; 35p per scoring stencil; 35p per Pupil Mastery Record; 35p per Class Mastery Record; 50p per manual (no date, 36 pages); £3 per specimen set; price data for machine scoring service available from publisher;

(180) minutes total to be administered on 3 or 5 separate days; John S. Close and Peter Airasian; Educational Research Centre [Ireland].*

Review of the Drumcondra Criterion Referenced Mathematics Test, Level 6 by IRVIN J. LEHMANN, Professor of Measurement, Michigan State University, East Lansing, MI:

The Drumcondra Criterion Referenced Mathematics Test (DCRMT), Level 6 is designed to be used with students in Irish schools "to evaluate pupils' mastery of the objectives of the mathematics curriculum for sixth standard in primary school . . . . [or] pupils in first year in post-primary school." This reviewer would interpret this as meaning the DCRMT could be used for American students in middle or junior high school. Because of the possible differences in the mathematics curriculum between American and Irish schools, potential users must exercise extreme care and caution in evaluating the DCRMT.

Fifty-eight instructional objectives are measured by 156 multiple-choice questions. With the exception of one objective that is tested with five items, all others are tested with two to three items. The major emphasis of the test is, according to the test authors, on "mathematical knowledge and comprehension to reflect emphasis of the new curriculum on the development of mathematical understandings." A careful examination of the test blueprint indicates that the authors were somewhat successful in this endeavor as there are items measuring sets, algebra, geometry, and word problems, as well as measurement, charts, and graphs.

As would be expected in any achievement test, and particularly for a criterion-referenced test, content validity was stressed in the test's construction. After a "detailed analysis" of the sixth class mathematics curriculum and textbooks and a consensus of opinion of experienced primary teachers regarding curricular objectives, a list of test objectives was developed. Unfortunately, users are provided with no information concerning some important facts. For example, what textbooks and curricula were surveyed and by whom? How many primary teachers were surveyed? Are these teachers representative of the primary teachers in Ireland? Were any mathematics teachers used in the development of objectives? Was a master list of instructional objectives drawn up by the test developers and given to a panel to obtain a consensus of opinion? Without answers to such questions it is very difficult to draw any valid interpretation regarding the strength of content-validity claims.

Evaluation of the validity of criterion-referenced tests (CRT), like reliability to be discussed later, has been a source of disagreement among psychometricians. However, if and when CRTs are used for instructional decision-making, as most criterion-referenced or mastery tests normally are, should we not have some evidence of empirical validity? This reviewer believes that we should have such evidence; unfortunately, the authors of the DCRMT do not provide these data.

Regretfully, no information is presented regarding the reliability of the test. Granted there is disagreement among measurement experts as to how to best assess reliability of a criterion-referenced test. Regardless of the point of view of the DCRMT's authors, this reviewer believes they should have presented their position. Instead, they appear to have ignored the significance of this very important psychometric property of tests, be the test criterion- or norm-referenced.

Criterion or cutoff or mastery scores were determined in a somewhat simplistic fashion. For the one instructional objective that had five items, the criterion score was set at 4, that is, the pupil had to answer four items correctly to be classified as having mastered the objective. For the remaining 57 objectives, each of which was measured with two or three items, the criterion score was 2. What justification was there in setting the mastery scores in the DCRMT? If there were some empirical studies conducted in order to set these mastery scores, this information should have been provided. If the test authors simply picked some numbers out of the air (and they are entitled to do so) this should also have been stated. This reviewer feels very strongly that when there are empirical ways to do something, such as setting criterion scores or estimating validity and reliability, they should be used; and data should *not* be reported without an explanation of how it was derived.

Although users may not expect to see a CRT test manual with a description of standardization procedures or normative data, this reviewer strongly believes that data must be presented somewhere in the examiner's/administrator's or technical manual describing in detail the procedure used to select the final items. The test authors allude to the fact that more items than needed were prepared "by an experienced mathematics teacher and 2 or 3 items were selected to represent the objective in the test." Who were these "experienced" teachers and how was it determined that they were "experienced"? How were the two to three items selected, that is, what criteria were used? What *p*-values are associated with the final selection of items? Are most of them "easy," and if not, should they not be since this is construed to be a mastery test? Again, this type of information would be most desirable and not too difficult to obtain.

The test authors are to be commended for the manner in which the test items are presented. The 11 sections as well as the items within each section are presented in order of increasing difficulty. This reviewer cannot think of anything more frustrating and traumatic than an examinee sitting down to take a test and not being able to answer, for instance, the first four to five items.

The quality of printing and the diagrams used are good. The overall layout of the items is fine. Even though there are many items presented per page, the use of boxes/cells makes for a good separation. The use of bold type helps for those items dealing with fractions.

Although the test is untimed, the authors suggest that it will take about 3 hours to complete and therefore should be administered in three to five testing sessions. The authors also suggest that the test could be administered "section by section as required throughout the school year"; however, this reviewer is somewhat ambivalent regarding this recommendation. Trying to maintain test security in such an endeavor might prove to be an exercise in futility. There is, however, value in such an approach as testing and feedback could immediately follow instruction and provide evidence of whether remedial instruction is needed. Because of the instructional benefit of this approach, we strongly urge the test authors and publisher to give serious consideration to reformatting the sections so that each section appears on a separate page. In this way, section by section testing could take place without compromising test security.

The Temporary Examiner's Manual has sections dealing with the typical phases of test administration—preparing the pupils, planning for effective test administration, test administrator's responsibilities, handscoring, and the like. In addition, instructions are provided on how to prepare the answer sheets for machine scoring, completing the pupil mastery record (PMR), and completing the class mastery record (CMR).

The PMR and CMR provide teachers with information concerning the performance of each individual pupil and the class as a whole on each of the DCRMT's objectives. With this information, the classroom teacher can readily obtain a picture of the strengths and weaknesses of the individual pupils as well as the whole class. Based on this information, appropriate remedial activities may be undertaken. These two charts may also help the teacher evaluate his/her instruction. It would be valuable if the test authors were to provide users with either a list of suggested activities or teaching strategies that could be used for remediation in the areas tested by various sections as is done in some achievement test batteries such as the Stanford or Metropolitan Achievement Tests.

In summary, the DCRMT is a good test if one defines "good" in terms of acceptable principles of item-writing practices. The DCRMT is also a "good" test in the sense that the instructional objectives are specific and behavioral, rather than general. That is, the objectives are written in terms of what the student is expected *to do*. Regarding the validity of the DCRMT for American schools and pupils, only the user's careful study of the instructional objectives, clearly presented in the test manual, will answer this question. It appears to this writer, at least, that there is an overemphasis on fractions, algebra, and geometry. However, for those teachers who emphasize these content areas, the test might be valid.

The major deficiency, in this reviewer's opinion, deals with the determination of mastery of an objective on the basis of a pupil answering two out of two to three items correctly. Surely, a mastery test should have a *limited* number of instructional objectives with *many* items per objective. But this is not so in the DCRMT, or for that matter, in many mastery tests. In addition, if I were a classroom teacher, I would be very hesitant in ascribing strengths or weaknesses based upon the scores on the DCRMT. To obtain a very limited view of middle or junior high school pupils' knowledge in mathematics, the DCRMT may be valid. However, teachers wishing to evaluate the strengths and weaknesses of their pupils might well consider other mathematics tests. This would be especially true for American middle and junior high school mathematics teachers inasmuch as the curriculum between the Irish and American schools may be too dissimilar.

Review of the Drumcondra Criterion Referenced Mathematics Test, Level 6 by LINDA JENSEN SHEFFIELD, Professor of Education and Mathematics, Northern Kentucky University, Highland Heights, KY:

Even though the Drumcondra test was written in 1977 and reprinted in 1984, the Examiner's Manual is labeled as a Temporary Version. It contains no data whatsoever on validity or reliability.

The objectives for the test were decided upon after an analysis of sixth class mathematics curricula and textbooks currently in use, and a survey of experienced primary teachers about their perceptions of the objectives of the curricula. Although the authors state that the Drumcondra Criterion Referenced Mathematics Test (DCRMT) "is weighted in favour of objectives relating to mathematical knowledge and comprehension to reflect the emphasis of the new curriculum on the development of mathematical understandings," there is no evidence that objectives are based upon recommendations from any professional organizations or that there was any input from mathematics educators concerned with primary mathematics. The objectives do include the use of the commutative and distributive properties, interpreting and analyzing charts and graphs and solving one- or two-step word problems, but there is no mention of such topics as actual problem solving, estimation, mental calculations, predicting, or using computers and calculators. The majority of the objectives deal with the structure of whole and rational numbers and operations with whole numbers, fractions, decimals, and percents. Relatively fewer objectives are concerned with sets, algebra, geometry, charts, graphs, and word problems.

The actual test items were written by an experienced mathematics teacher. No mention is made of any testing of the instrument for validity or reliability, or even any analysis by a "panel of experts" for face validity. Most objectives do seem fairly clear, however, and do appear to match the test items. There are two to three test items for each of 57 objectives and the criterion score for mastery is set at 2. For the objective on reading and interpreting charts and graphs there are five questions (all about a histogram) and the criterion for mastery is set at 4.

Some of the questions would cause difficulty if used by students in the U.S. Problems involving money utilize pounds and pence, metric exercises use British spellings such as grammes and metres, and word problems talk about such things as a chip of tomatoes. The presentation of the directed numbers on the number line may also be unfamiliar. Terms are often varied on the exercises that test the same objective. For example, one question asks for the highest common factor and the next for the highest number which will divide evenly into. This may help students who are familiar with one term but not the other, but it may confuse other students who may think two different processes are being asked for.

Both the individual pupil mastery record and the class mastery record would be useful to a classroom teacher for keeping track of students' progress. It is recommended that the tests be used as a pretest to help with lesson planning and again as a posttest to check progress. Tests may be machine scored, but only if all 10 sections of the test are completed at the same time. If teachers wish to pre- or posttest each section separately (the most useful method for diagnostic-prescriptive testing), they must score the tests themselves. A scoring key is included, which can be placed over students' answer sheets for easy scoring, but it is a bit difficult to align.

To summarize, this test might be useful to Irish teachers of pupils in the sixth standard of primary school or the first year of post-primary school, but other teachers should carefully study the objectives to determine if the test is appropriate for their classes. A final version of the Examiner's Manual with reliability and validity data is needed. Objectives should be examined relative to goals for the 1980s and beyond, such as the NCTM Agenda for Action (1980).

REVIEWER'S REFERENCE

National Council of Teachers of Mathematics. (1980). *Agenda for action*. Reston, VA: NCTM.

[97]

Drumcondra Verbal Reasoning Test 1. Purpose: "Measures the . . . combination of mental abilities which correlate highly with achievement in scholastic tasks." Ages 10-0 to 12-11; no date; DVRT; distribution restricted to qualified psychologists, research workers, and career guidance personnel; 1985 price data: 30p per test booklet; £2 per scoring stencil; 35p per manual (no date, 10 pages); £3 per specimen set; 40(55) minutes; Educational Research Centre; the Centre [Ireland].*

Review of the Drumcondra Verbal Reasoning Test 1 by ALLEN K. HESS, Professor of Psychology and Department Head, Auburn University at Montgomery, Montgomery, AL:

The Drumcondra Verbal Reasoning Test 1 (DVRT-1) is intended to measure the "combination of mental abilities which correlate highly with achievement in scholastic tasks." This reviewer received a blue plastic folder containing Instructions for Administration, a single-sheet practice test, directions for scoring, seven translucent scoring stencils or templates, and an eight-page test booklet containing instructions, a scoring grid, and the 110 test items. The absence of a test manual, technical report, or any other type of informing material that may reveal the standardization sample characteristics, reliability and validity studies, factor analytic studies, theoretical network from which the test was developed, other tests in the same family, or any other of the information that would make a test useful, raises more than the 110 questions contained in the DVRT-1. This is regrettable because the materials present hint at a promising test.

The instructions are clear and seem to be structured to allow for cost-efficient group testing by counselors or teachers. The student is allowed 40 minutes to complete the test, so it can be administered within an hour. The scoring is straightforward, and a single standard score is calculated from a two-page norm table stapled to the instructions. Based on the tables, students ranging in age from 10 years to 12 years 11 months can be assessed on the measure. The standard scores range from 70 to 140 but no information about the means, standard deviations, or normality of the distributions for the age groups is given. In fact, there is no hint about whether or in what proportion both genders were represented in the samples, or what numbers of pupils contributed to the norms. Thus, if I find a pupil earned a 120 on the DVRT-1, I have no idea whether the score is good, bad, or indifferent.

The test per se consists of six areas. All are repeated at least once at harder difficulty levels. The first 5 questions are what we can term symbol processing (e.g., How many letters come after V in the alphabet?), and are followed by 12 questions concerning concept grouping (e.g., Of the following, which does not belong: pencil, radio, crayon, typewriter, fountain pen?). The next 7 items call for identification of an opposite (e.g., loud: white, tall, quiet, heavy, sweet), and the following 10 call for completing a verbal analogy from a choice of four alternatives (e.g., Boy is to girl as brother is to [son, woman, sister, daughter]). Seven items requiring the pupil to supply the missing number in a sequence (e.g., 11, 2, 12, 3, 13, 4, 14, ______) are followed by 6 logic questions that presume three children have certain numbers of different colored boxes of wood or cardboard, and ask how many cardboard boxes would various children have, or how many boxes are red and wooden. The remaining eight sections of the test repeat the above sections, and repeat the missing number and the logic sections a third time. The items are clear, well-developed, unambiguous, and graduated in difficulty over the narrow, less than 3-year, age range. However, the lack of a manual is akin to running into a brick wall in terms of using the test. There is no way to know what a score means from the extant materials. Perhaps the Educational Research Centre, St. Patrick's College, Dublin, Ireland has plans for a manual (it should accompany the test or the test should not be produced). Perhaps they have a DRVT-2 or 3 in their plans. Perhaps they normed the test for girls and boys. These are but a few of the many questions the DVRT-1 presents that are not in the 110-test-item booklet.

Review of the Drumcondra Verbal Reasoning Test 1 by NEIL H. SCHWARTZ, Associate Professor of Psychology, California State University at Chico, Chico, CA, and WILLIAM K. WILKINSON, Research Associate, Northern Arizona University, Flagstaff, AZ:

The Drumcondra Verbal Reasoning Test (DVRT) is a norm-referenced instrument designed to measure the overall verbal reasoning ability of children from 10 to 13 years of age. It consists of six types of verbal-reasoning cognitive tasks, comprising a total of 110 items. The six item-sets are (*a*) verbal oddities, in which an examinee must choose the word in a set of words which does not belong; (*b*) verbal opposites, in which the correct choice is made by correctly identifying the target-word's antonym; (*c*) verbal analogies; (*d*) verbal logical reasoning; (*e*) number series; and (*f*) letter series, in which an examinee may be asked to identify the seventh letter of the alphabet, for example. A global verbal-reasoning score is derived by totalling the number correct for all 110 items, and then locating this raw score in a table of standard scores having a mean of 100 and a standard deviation of 15.

The instrument is professionally packaged, with its materials clearly identified and organized. Its manual comprises a practice test, instructions describing administration and scoring procedures, a set of scoring stencils, and a raw-score conversion table. Indeed, the administration procedure is clear and easy to follow, and the inclusion of a practice test increases the likelihood that examinees understand the task demands before they respond to the target items. Finally, the provision of scoring stencils minimizes the risk of errors associated with hand scoring.

While the DVRT represents a commendable effort to construct a single source from which to estimate the ability to reason verbally, the instrument falls significantly short of real utilitarian value. There are a number of reasons for this shortcoming.

First, the manual offers no technical data relative to the instrument's psychometric properties. Of course, without reliability data the accuracy of an examinee's score is undeterminable. Additionally, there are no construct validity data from which to determine whether an examinee's DVRT performance is reflective of real verbal reasoning aptitude. Verbal reasoning accounts for a major proportion of individual differences in general intellectual ability, and standard tests of intelligence present data of high utility in estimating school performance and predicting future scholastic performance. Thus, the omission of the criterion-related validities seriously restricts the instrument's utility in place of standard tests of intelligence. This is especially pertinent because the DVRT takes approximately 55 minutes to administer and so is not particularly useful for quick screenings.

It was, obviously, the intention of the DVRT authors to provide an instrument that assesses verbal reasoning exclusively, independent of other cognitive processes or activities. However, the authors failed to provide either an operational definition for, or a theoretical discussion of, the verbal reasoning construct. This is a serious shortcoming because a test user cannot be sure if, indeed, his/her concept of the construct is the same as that of the authors. Without validity data, the omission is underscored.

Because no operational definition of verbal reasoning is provided, the only way to make this appraisal is to examine whether the items reflect the construct—the instrument's face validity. Overall, the types of verbal items do seem to reflect an examinee's verbal-reasoning aptitude. Yet, it is unclear whether the items best represent verbal reasoning globally, or six separate components of the construct. The distinction is especially murky, given that six distinct sets of verbal-reasoning items comprise the test.

A final limitation of the DVRT is the absence of pertinent data specifying characteristics of the norming group. That is, information is not provided concerning, for example, the ethnic background, socioeconomic status, gender, or the number of examinees on which the test was normed. Thus, potential test users cannot be sure the DVRT will yield appropriate and meaningful results for different types of examinees.

Given the information presently available on the DVRT, the implications are that the instrument is neither a usable educational tool nor a usable research tool. However, this does not imply that constructive steps cannot be taken to improve the adequacy of the test. What needs to occur, at least as a first step, is (*a*) a clear theoretical definition of the concept, and (*b*) several reliability studies to determine the instrument's stability and internal consistency. Until such steps are taken, DVRT users will find the results of an examinee's performance of little interpretive value.

[98]

The Dyslexia Screening Survey. Purpose: "Screening primary phonetic-auditory, visual, and multisensory processing skills in children who may be dyslexic." Children in primary grades; 1980; checklist of basic developmental skills or criterion tasks divided into 7 steps: Functional Reading Level, Reading Potential, Significant Reading Discrepancy, Specific Processing Skill Deficiencies, Neuropsychological Dysfunctions, Associated Factors, Developmental-Remedial Strategies; individual; no manual; 1988 price data: $7.95 per 10 survey forms; administration time not reported; Robert E. Valett; Fearon Education.*

Review of The Dyslexia Screening Survey by FRED M. GROSSMAN, Associate Professor of Special Education and Communication Disorders, University of Nebraska-Lincoln, Lincoln, NE:

The Dyslexia Screening Survey is described as a "checklist of basic neuropsychological skills involved in the reading process." In effect, the tasks included in the survey are purported by its author to tap representative neuropsychological and processing functions that are important precursors for reading success. The checklist is intended for use by teachers and others interested in screening children for possible reading disabilities.

The author provides a definition of dyslexia in the scoring booklet and introduces the notion that for preschool children of average cognitive ability, dyslexic disorders may be manifested in immature reading readiness skills and psycholinguistic abilities. Additionally, dyslexia is operationally defined for school-age children of average intelligence as a discrepancy of two or more years between learning potential and functional reading. Checklist users are informed that the Survey is not a standardized instrument that provides normative data and are cautioned against making decisions based solely upon the results derived from the checklist. Users of the survey are urged by the author to supplement checklist findings with other data (e.g., standardized tests of intelligence and language skills, behavioral observations, medical examinations, etc.).

The administration of the Survey is described briefly in the scoring booklet. Survey consumers are encouraged to examine the work of Valett (1980) for a more detailed explanation of administration procedures. The Survey booklet describes the problem solving involved in the diagnosis of dyslexia as taking place in seven steps requiring the determination of: (*a*) functional reading level, as measured by oral and silent reading using the child's classroom basal reader and scores on standardized reading tests; (*b*) reading potential, as measured by aptitude or IQ tests (e.g., WISC-R); (*c*) significant reading discrepancy, which is defined as a difference between a child's functional reading level and reading potential; (*d*) specific processing skill deficiencies, which are primarily assessed by administering tasks encompassing phonetic-auditory, visual, and multisensory skills; (*e*) neurological dysfunctions, as measured by a variety of specific tasks used to evaluate sensory integration (e.g., tandem walk, finger to nose coordination, laterality, etc.); and (*f*) associated factors, such as motivation, physical health, anxiety level, self-esteem, etc. A seventh and final section of the Survey instructs the test user to formulate and prioritize instructional objectives based upon an examination of an individual child's strengths and weaknesses relating to the processing skills assessed by the tasks on the checklist. Users are also urged to recommend at least one remedial-prescriptive strategy for each derived objective.

Scoring procedures for the tasks are generally straightforward. In some instances, however, specific criteria for successful performance or skill mastery (i.e., scoring "yes" or "no") are lacking. In addition, the method of administration of several tasks is not specific (e.g., "copies words and sentences," "follows a sequence of oral directions," etc.), which would most likely result in varied forms of presentation. This lack of specificity may also result in inappropriate content in relation to the chronological age of the child being assessed. Furthermore, scoring for some skill areas requires the subjective judgment of the checklist user, particularly when the performance on a specific task is to be evaluated as "good," "fair," or "questionable."

Significant difficulties arise in the author's discussion of methods by which to calculate a reading discrepancy for children. Several methods of determining a significant reading problem are presented in the scoring booklet as well as by Valett (1980), all of which have psychometric weaknesses. For example, the use of mental age and grade equivalent scores presents major problems when conducting discrepancy analyses, particularly for children at the upper grade levels. Eighth-grade students of average intelligence who are reading 2 years below grade expectancy are defined by the author as potentially reading disabled when, in fact, an examination of the more precise standard scores reported by most reading achievement tests would reveal this level of reading skills to be within the low average-average range when compared to other individuals of the same chronological age and level of cognitive functioning. Similarly, the use of the criterion of functional reading approximately 2 years below mental age is inadequate in terms of the identification of reading problems for children in the lower primary grades.

Although the Survey is described as a screening device and is not a norm-referenced instrument, it is inexcusable that reliability and construct-validity data are not reported either in the scoring booklet or adjunct material (Valett, 1980). The absence of psychometric data, the occasional use of qualitative scoring features, the lack of standardized tasks and administration procedures, and the problems associated with the use of mental age and grade level scores present difficulties in the use of the Survey as a diagnostic instrument for the screening of dyslexia or reading disabilities. Educational personnel interested in screening for possible reading problems of individual children would be better advised to consider group standardized achievement tests that have a reading component (e.g., Metropolitan Achievement Test, California Achievement Test, etc.) and are routinely administered to children in school settings. In essence, administration time of The Dyslexia Screening Survey appears lengthy and, perhaps, not worth the effort. This is particularly true when less time-consuming and more psychometrically sound screening approaches are readily available.

REVIEWER'S REFERENCE

Valett, R. E. (1980). *Dyslexia: A neuropsychological approach to educating children with severe reading disorders.* Belmont, CA: Fearon Pitman Publishers.

Review of The Dyslexia Screening Survey by DEBORAH KING KUNDERT, Educational Psychology and Statistics, University at Albany, State University of New York, Albany, NY:

The Dyslexia Screening Survey (DSS) is an informal survey of criterion tasks presented in the author's book *Dyslexia: A Neuropsychological Approach to Educating Children with Severe Reading Disorders* (Valett, 1980). Specifically, the DSS provides a checklist of basic developmental skills which, according to the author, are important for success in reading. Results of the survey, when combined with other information (e.g., observation, standardized tests, and medical examinations), may be used to plan educational interventions.

Dyslexia is defined as "a significant disorder in the meaningful integration of perceptual-linguistic symbols due to neuropsychological immaturity or dysfunction." Following this orientation, tasks on the DSS are organized into 7 categories: Functional Reading Level, Reading Potential, Significant Reading Discrepancy, Specific Processing Skill Deficiencies, Neuropsychological Dysfunctions, Associated Factors, and Developmental-Remedial strategies. The author's book, *Dyslexia*, provides some of the details necessary to complete the survey.

To determine a child's functional reading level, standardized reading tests and direct assessment of reading in the classroom are used. At this step, the examiner determines whether the child has mastered critical perceptual-linguistic skills considered necessary in learning to read. Examiners record test scores and also indicate whether the child can perform 20 developmental reading skills (using Yes, No, or ? ratings). Some of these skills are not described in enough detail, which makes accurate rating difficult.

Determination of reading capacity is based on scores on individual intelligence tests and/or "other evaluations of reading potential." Examiners evaluate the child's level of comprehension of grade level materials.

At the discrepancy step, the examiner determines whether the disability is significant or not (a lag of 2 or more years is defined as significant). To calculate this, the child's functional reading grade level is subtracted from the reading grade level expectancy (based on mental age).

At the processing skills deficiencies step, the child is presented with tasks to assess auditory, visual, and multisensory processing skills. Visual stimuli presented in the survey booklet are small, thus impeding the performance of some children. The examiner records the number correct and incorrect on each task for the various skills. In addition, the author indicates that supplemental tasks may be helpful. Examiners are referred to other texts for information on how these processing skills can be used directly in the classroom.

To assess neurological dysfunction, a variety of tasks in walking, coordination, balance, laterality, stereognosis, and school history are used. Examiners rate these skills as Good/Fair/Questionable, Right/Left, or Yes/No depending on the task. In addition, the author indicates that examiners should obtain medical history and information, as well as use supplemental tasks as needed.

The associated factors step involves rating the child's interest and motivation, physical health, self confidence and esteem, and the adequacy of reading instruction as Good, Fair, or Questionable. The associated text offers no concrete guidelines on which examiners may base ratings.

The final step on the DSS is developmental-remedial strategies. At this point the examiner determines the child's strengths and weaknesses and then establishes priority instructional objectives. In addition, the examiner checks one or more of 12 recommended forms of special education for follow-up consideration. Not all of these strategies seem to follow directly from the survey results, and as such this section would be difficult to complete. The author presents some of the available research on the different interventions in his associated text; however, details are often lacking on how to implement these interventions in the classroom.

The DSS is not a standardized or normative measure. Although informal inventories may serve a purpose, certain, specific information is necessary for examiners to use these instruments appropriately. No manual is included with the survey. The associated text, *Dyslexia*, cannot be considered as a substitute for a manual. Specific information not provided with the DSS includes: indication of the appropriate age range, details on the selection and ordering of items, specific directions for administering and scoring, guidelines for score interpretation, and data on reliability and validity. Other areas of weakness include the vague definition of neuropsychological skills, the limited number of items, and the broad definition of dyslexia.

In summary, the DSS purports to be a screening measure of prerequisite processing skills that are necessary for reading at the upper elementary and secondary school levels. The absence of survey development information, scoring guidelines, and interpretation details, as well as the lack of reliability and validity data, preclude the use of this survey at this time. Additional information from the author and research are needed to determine whether the DSS can contribute useful information in working with children with reading disorders.

REVIEWER'S REFERENCE

Valett, R. E. (1980). *Dyslexia: A neuropsychological approach to educating children with severe reading disorders*. Belmont, CA: Fearon Pitman Publishers.

[99]

The Early Language Milestone Scale. Purpose: Screening instrument for "evaluation of speech and language development during infancy and early childhood." Birth–36 months; 1983–87; ELM Scale; 3 scores: Auditory Expressive, Auditory Receptive, Visual; individual; 1988 price data: $59 per program including 100 score sheets, object kit (bell, ball, cup, spoon, block, crayon), manual ('85, 39 pages); $21 per 100 score sheets; $24 per object kit; $17 per manual; $79 or less per color video training tape (VHS); (1–3) minutes; James Coplan; PRO-ED, Inc.*

Review of The Early Language Milestone Scale by RUTH M. NOYCE, Professor of Curriculum and Instruction, The University of Kansas, Lawrence, KS:

The Early Language Milestone Scale (ELM Scale) measures the general language function of children from birth to age 3. Developed by a pediatrician, the Scale answers the need for an easily-administered, sensitive test of early language development to aid physicians in referral of children with such handicapping conditions as mental retardation, hearing loss, and communicative disorder. The ELM Scale is not intended to be a definitive diagnostic instrument; therefore, children who do poorly on it are candidates for further developmental testing. The ELM Scale is the only norm-referenced, validated screening tool available for measuring the language function of the birth-to-3-year-old age group, according to its author, James Coplan. The instrument most widely used by physicians for this purpose has been The Denver Developmental Screening Test (DDST), which yields scores on gross motor, fine-motor adaptive, language, and personal-social development for ages 2 weeks to 6 years. Because its sensitivity with very young children has been shown to be only about 50% (Frankenburg, 1971), the DDST has not answered the physician's need for a reliable, easy-to-administer instrument for assessing the language function of children younger than age 2.

The ELM Scale, consisting of 41 items categorized in three sections, can be administered in 1 to 3 minutes. A single score sheet contains all the items, each represented by a horizontal bar, which is shaded according to the percentage of children who have passed the item. Three types of linguistic behaviors are measured: Auditory Expressive, Auditory Receptive, and Visual. Auditory Expressive function is defined to include single words, phrases, and sentences, and such prelinguistic behaviors as cooing, reciprocal vocalization, and babbling.

Auditory Receptive behavior encompasses execution of commands, recognition of sounds, and localization of auditory stimuli in space. Visual function is described as visual fixation, visual tracking, visual recognition of familiar objects or people, and response to or initiation of gestures.

In order to determine a child's performance level on the ELM Scale, the administrator draws a vertical line down a score sheet at the level of the child's chronological age. Items falling to the left of the line have been performed successfully by 90 percent of the subjects who have been tested. Starting with the item closest to the line, the administrator works backwards to the left until three consecutive items are passed. This indicates that the subject has succeeded at the basic level of 90 percent of children of the same age, passing that division of the test. Items may be passed by any of three means of elicitation: parental history, direct testing, or incidental observation. The ELM Scale specifies which means are allowable for each item on the score sheet. In order to pass the test, the child must pass each of the three divisions: Auditory Expressive, Auditory Receptive, and Visual.

Test items fall into six hierarchical clusters: Babbling, Orienting to bell, One-step commands, Gesture games, Single words, and Name and use of objects. Because questions on multiple items telescope into one another, the child is given credit for all earlier behaviors in a cluster when a particular language behavior is exhibited, a process that shortens the testing time considerably.

The test manual is well written in an economical style that aids the examiner in the preparation stages; however, another proofreading for typographical errors should have been conducted. The instructions for administering, scoring, and interpreting the test are so clearly articulated in the manual that the audio training cassette is unnecessary for all but the most inexperienced testers. Examples of test score sheets from the author's practice illustrating patterns of item failure that indicate the need for formal testing are included in the test manual. The handicaps represented in the samples are mental retardation, deafness, communication disorder (oromotor apraxia and autism), and dysarthria. An illustration of the usefulness of the ELM Scale for gauging the intellectual level of physically handicapped children is also presented.

Normative data were obtained from a sample of 191 pediatric patients from birth to 3 years of age and the scale was validated with several groups of developmentally delayed children who were referred to the author of the test for evaluation. Results showed that the instrument discriminated between normal and language-delayed children in more than 95 percent of the cases (Coplan, Gleason, Ryan, Burke, & Williams; 1982). One factor that facilitates the rapid administration of the test is the acceptance of parental history data as evidence of the age of emergence of some items. The ease of obtaining information on certain language behaviors from parents rather than from direct testing or observation led the developer to adopt norms derived from parental history and to permit children to pass certain items on this basis, in spite of evidence showing that parents tend to estimate earlier emergence ages than direct testing indicates for some behaviors. The emergence ages of items requiring response to specific commands were established through direct testing in the norming process and must be passed or failed through direct testing.

Since most existing tests of language function are not applicable to children under 18 months of age, the ELM Scale is a unique tool. The instrument facilitates routine developmental screening of very young children, permitting early detection of a variety of handicapping conditions. In view of the fact that the detection of language delay assists physicians in referring very young children for early testing and treatment of handicapping conditions, the ELM Scale should prove to be a valuable contribution. It appears to fill the need for a dependable test that can be administered routinely without demanding undue time or effort for administration.

REVIEWER'S REFERENCES

Frankenburg, W. K., Camp, B. W., & VanNatta, P. A. (1971). Validity of the Denver Developmental Screening Test. *Child Development*, 42, 475-485.

Coplan, J., Gleason, J. R., Ryan, R., Burke, M. G., & Williams, M. L. (1982). Validation of an early language milestone scale in a high-risk population. *Pediatrics*, 70, 677-683.

[100]

Eating Disorder Inventory. Purpose: "A measure of eight attitudinal and behavioral dimensions relevant to anorexia nervosa and bulimia." Ages 12 and over; 1983–86; EDI; 8 subscale scores: Drive for Thinness, Bulimia, Body Dissatisfaction, Ineffectiveness, Perfectionism, Interpersonal Distrust, Interoceptive Awareness, Maturity Fears; 1987 price data: $30 per complete kit including 25 test booklets, 25 profile forms, scoring keys, manual ('84, 34 pages), and manual supplement ('86, 8 pages); $8 per 25 test booklets; $3 per 25 profile forms; $6 per scoring keys; $9 per manual and supplement; (15–25) minutes; David M. Garner and Marion P. Olmsted; Psychological Assessment Resources, Inc.*

TEST REFERENCES

1. Connors, M. E., Johnson, C. L., & Stuckey, M. K. (1984). Treatment of bulimia with brief psychoeducational group therapy. *American Journal of Psychiatry*, 141, 1512-1516.

2. Bourke, M. P., Taylor, G., & Crisp, A. H. (1985). Symbolic functioning in anorexia nervosa. *Journal of Psychiatric Research*, 19, 273-278.

3. Cooper, Z., Cooper, P. J. , & Fairburn, C. G. (1985). The specificity of the Eating Disorder Inventory. *British Journal of Clinical Psychology*, 24, 129-130.

4. Freeman, C., Sinclair, F., Turnbull, J., & Annandale, A. (1985). Psychotherapy for bulimia: A controlled study. *Journal of Psychiatric Research*, 19, 473-478.

5. Garner, D. M., Garfinkel, P. E., & O'Shaughnessy, M. (1985). The validity of the distinction between bulimia with and without anorexia nervosa. *American Journal of Psychiatry*, 142, 581-587.

6. Garner, D. M., Olmsted, M. P., & Garfinkel, P. E. (1985). Similarities among bulimic groups selected by different weights and weight histories. *Journal of Psychiatric Research*, 19, 129-134.

7. Hart, K. J., & Ollendick, T. H. (1985). Prevalence of bulimia in working and university women. *American Journal of Psychiatry*, 142, 851-854.

8. Johnson, C., & Flach, A. (1985). Family characteristics of 105 patients with bulimia. *American Journal of Psychiatry*, 142, 1321-1324.

9. Kirkley, B. G., Schneider, J. A., Agras, W. S., & Bachman, J. A. (1985). Comparison of two group treatments for bulimia. *Journal of Consulting and Clinical Psychology*, 53, 43-48.

10. MicKalide, A. D., & Andersen, A. E. (1985). Subgroups of anorexia nervosa and bulimia: Validity and utility. *Journal of Psychiatric Research*, 19, 121-128.

11. Rodin, G. M., Daneman, D., Johnson, L. E., Kenshole, A., & Garfinkel, P. (1985). Anorexia nervosa and bulimia in female adolescents with insulin dependent diabetes mellitus: A systematic study. *Journal of Psychiatric Research*, 19, 381-384.

12. VanThorre, M. D., & Vogel, F. X. (1985). The presence of bulimia in high school females. *Adolescence*, 20, 45-51.

13. Grant, C. L., & Fodor, I. G. (1986). Adolescent attitudes toward body image and anorexic behavior. *Adolescence*, 21, 269-281.

14. Gross, J., Rosen, J. C., Leitenberg, H., & Willmuth, M. E. (1986). Validity of the Eating Attitudes Test and the Eating Disorders Inventory in bulimia nervosa. *Journal of Consulting and Clinical Psychology*, 54, 875-876.

15. Henderson, M., & Freeman, C. P. L. (1987). A self-rating scale for bulimia: The "BITE". *The British Journal of Psychiatry*, 150, 18-24.

16. Turnbull, J. D., Freeman, C. P. L., Barry, F., & Annandale, A. (1987). Physical and psychological characteristics of five male bulimics. *The British Journal of Psychiatry*, 150, 25-29.

Review of the Eating Disorder Inventory by CABRINI S. SWASSING, Psychologist, Central Ohio Psychiatric Hospital, Columbus, OH:

The Eating Disorder Inventory (EDI) consists of 64 self-report items measuring eight behavioral and psychological traits that are common among anorectics and bulimics. It was designed not to be used as a diagnostic tool but as an adjunct to clinical judgments about eating disorder patients. It is also recommended for use as a screening device, outcome measure, or as an aid in typological research. It was developed on patients diagnosed as having anorexia nervosa. Among these patients was a subgroup who also met the criteria for bulimia. This inventory is unique in that it measures both the cognitive and behavioral characteristics associated with anorexia nervosa and bulimia and also measures the psychological traits that differentiate persons with anorexia from those who are bulimic. It can also be used for outpatient administration.

The test was constructed from a pool of 146 items generated by clinicians who were experienced in treating patients with the disorder and who were also familiar with the research literature in the area. From these items eight constructs were isolated as meeting the necessary reliability and validity requirements. In validating the EDI, two groups of subjects were used. Included in the criterion groups were three subsamples of female patients ($N = 129$) with primary anorexia nervosa (AN) at various stages of treatment. Of the total group, 56 patients were identified as the "restricter" subtype and 73 were also considered "bulimic." There were significant differences ($p < .0001$) between the two groups in mean percentage of average weight. Three independent subsamples of 770 female college students enrolled in first- and second-year psychology courses were used for the female comparison group (FC). Based on results of testing the independent AN and FC samples, items were retained if they met two statistical criteria. They were required to demonstrate significant differentiation between the AN and FC groups and to correlate highly with their own subscales.

Psychometric information reported is based on the final validation sample of 271 college women and 155 anorectics (53 "restricters" and 102 "bulimics"). Internal consistency of each subscale as determined by Cronbach's alpha is above .80 with an average item-total correlation of .63 ($SD = .13$). In order to establish criterion-related validity, self-report EDI patient profiles were compared with judgments made by clinicians who knew the patient's psychological presentation. All correlations were significant ($p < .001$). The EDI has also been shown to differentiate between restricters and bulimics. In an updated sample of 53 restricters and 102 bulimics, the two groups displayed significantly different scores on drive for thinness, ineffectiveness, and interoceptive awareness.

Although the EDI should be interpreted by someone trained in psychometric assessment, it is easily administered in about 20 minutes and does not require professional administration. Handscoring keys are provided for easy scoring. Areas on the profile forms are shaded, showing the 99% confidence intervals for both norm groups. Standard errors of measurement for both groups are also given. Charts are provided for converting raw scores to percentile rankings.

Overall, the EDI is an excellent contribution to the assessment of eating disorders. It is subject to the same precautions regarding distortions in answering as is any self-report instrument. External validity is limited by the fact that the comparison group consisted only of college females enrolled in first- and second-year psychology courses. However, it does add to the clinical knowledge available regarding the psychological and behavioral dimensions of anorexia nervosa and bulimia and can serve as a useful tool in screening for and differentiating between these two disorders as well as differentiating those college women who are simply weight preoccupied from those who are anorectics.

[101]

Eby Elementary Identification Instrument. Purpose: "Developed in order to provide gifted program administrators with an easily administered, objective and comprehensive selection process for an elementary school district that wishes to select students for gifted programming on the basis of performance and behavior." Grades K–8; 1984; additional protocols must be supplied by examiner; individual; 1987 price data: $20 per 50 general selection matrices, 50 teacher recommendation forms, 50 unit selection matrices, and administrator manual (11 pages); $6 per 50 general selection matrices, teacher recommendation forms, or unit selection matrices; $6 per administrator manual; administration time not reported; Judy W. Eby; Slosson Educational Publications, Inc.*

Review of the Eby Elementary Identification Instrument by STEWART EHLY, Associate Professor of Psychology, The University of Iowa, Iowa City, IA:

The Eby Elementary Identification Instrument (Eby) was developed by the author to "provide gifted program administrators with an easily administered, objective, and comprehensive selection process for an elementary school district that wishes to select students for gifted programming on the basis of performance and behavior." The Eby is short and requires minutes to complete by the teacher or administrator responsible for gifted programming. The author's claim to have based the instrument on the work of Renzulli will attract some professionals to this instrument. Unfortunately, limitations in the application of the Eby stem from a dearth of information on the test's development and potential for use in a program for gifted students.

Three test components are provided by the author, a General Selection Matrix, a Teacher Recommendation Form, and a Unit Selection Form. The Matrix is to be completed by the teacher interested in recommending a child for gifted programming. Elements of the Matrix include information on the child's achievement or intelligence test scores, grade point average, Group Inventory for Finding Creative Talent (GIFT) or Group Inventory For Finding Interests (GIFFI) test percentiles, and teacher recommendations. Each component is weighted using a scoring system that is described as based on "four years of use and study to determine reliability."

If the above seems confusing, so is the author's language in describing when and how to use the Matrix. Simply put, the reader is not provided with any justification of the Matrix itself nor any of the means by which it can be interpreted or used. Given these limitations, the author's claim the Matrix can be used with any child nominated for gifted programming by teachers, parents, or self-nomination holds little promise. The Matrix as now described adds nothing to a selection process to determine program eligibility. (The author does suggest using the Slosson Intelligence test if IQ scores are included in a program's requirements.)

The Teacher Recommendation Form can be used to collect information on a student's ability, task commitment, and creativity. As was the case with the Matrix, no support is introduced to justify the selection of items nor is there any explanation of the scoring system (a 4-point scale) provided. The Unit Selection Matrix, with components on task commitment and creativity, is the final section of the Eby.

Recommended for use in conjunction with judging a student's performance on a task prior to selection for gifted programming, the Unit Matrix is presented with no explanation about how the instrument and scoring procedures were created.

The Summary section of the manual provides the author's rationale for developing the instrument. The author views the Eby as a performance-based alternative to judging eligibility for gifted programming. While Eby's preference to consider performance and behavior instead of IQ scores can be supported by the literature, such support is not available for the construction and packaging of this instrument.

The Eby is as likely to confuse the reader as to enlighten him or her. It is not an instrument in the traditional sense but a collection of rating forms and a decision-making matrix. Although educators responsible for programming with gifted students might desire a process by which to evaluate and determine eligibility, neither the Eby nor any other available tool offers the reliability or validity necessary to justify nationwide use. Local school district policies and priorities continue to influence which students will be considered for and placed in gifted programming.

Review of the Eby Elementary Identification Instrument by BRIAN K. MARTENS, Assistant Professor of Psychology and Education, Syracuse University, Syracuse, NY:

The Eby Elementary Identification Instrument (EEII) is a decision-making tool for use with kindergarten through eighth grade students and is described by the author as being based upon Renzulli's three-part definition of giftedness: above average general ability, task commitment, and creativity (Renzulli, 1978). The primary components of the EEII include a 15-item teacher rating scale and a selection matrix for organizing information obtained from multiple sources (e.g., standardized intelligence or achievement tests, student grade-point average, teacher ratings). In addition to the teacher rating scale and selection matrix, the EEII includes a 10-point rating scale for the evaluation of student projects or tasks assigned prior to programming proper. This scale is intended to aid in the identification of students for participation in specific activities by programs delivering services on a "revolving door" basis (Renzulli, Reis, & Smith, 1981).

SELECTION MATRIX. The selection matrix is completed by indicating level of performance in one of five score intervals for each of four assessment areas: performance on a standardized achievement or intelligence test, grade-point average, performance on the GIFT (Group Inventory For Finding Creative Talent) or GIFFI (Group Inventory For Finding Interests) tests, and the composite score on the teacher rating scale. Once the scores have been plotted, the number of entries in each column of score intervals is tallied and multiplied by a whole number weight ranging from one to five. The resulting weight times column scores are summed to yield a total score to be used as a cutoff for determining eligibility. The author suggests a midpoint cutoff score be used to obtain a program composed of "highly qualified students," and recommends use of the Slosson Intelligence Test as the intellectual measure of choice.

In its favor, the manual presents helpful information on potential uses of the EEII that provides the user with great flexibility in selecting students, establishing local norms, and meeting program goals. For example, the manual suggests screening criteria to be considered before completion of the matrix and indicates that eligibility criteria may be chosen to serve several programmatic goals including selection of "highly qualified students," selection of a specific percentage of the school population, or identification of a pool of eligible students for use with the Revolving Door Model. In addition, the selection matrix is clearly organized and can be completed easily by the user.

Unfortunately, report of potential uses of the selection matrix is accomplished in the absence of information concerning its psychometric properties. When choosing a tool for identification of children for gifted programming, the tool's ability to identify individuals likely to succeed in the program (predictive validity), as well as its ability to differentiate among gifted and nongifted populations identified by more extensive procedures, are important selection criteria (Rosenfield, 1983). In the EEII manual, no data concerning the relationship of the suggested (or any other) eligibility criteria to subsequent successful program participation are presented. Similarly, no empirical basis for the selection of weights by which score intervals are multiplied (e.g., multiple regression analyses) is presented in the manual beyond the statement that weights "were selected on the basis of four years of use and study to determine reliability." If this information is available it should be included in the manual; and its absence severely limits the user's ability to evaluate the instrument. Beyond this, the use of a single composite score upon which to decide eligibility may result in the overidentification of children with above average ability in several areas and the underidentification of children who are outstanding in a single area (Rosenfield, 1983).

Other criticisms of information presented in the manual include recommended use of the Slosson Intelligence Test, which is highly questionable given other more psychometrically sound instruments from which to choose, and failure to identify psychometrically sound standardized achievement tests for use in the matrix. In addition, the length of time over which grade-point average should be calculated (an issue likely to affect the predictive validity of this measure) is not specified and it is unclear how the age range of the instrument was determined.

TEACHER RATING SCALES. Both the Teacher Recommendation Form (TRF) and the Unit Selection Matrix (USM) require respondents to rate students on 4-point Likert-type scales ranging from *Highly Superior* to *Below Average*. The TRF is composed of five positively phrased items in each of three categories (ability, task commitment, creativity) and yields only a total score. The USM is composed of five positively phrased items in each of two areas (task commitment, creativity) also yielding a single total score.

Although the manual reports accurately that the TRF can be completed quickly, the statement that the items are "behavior based, allowing teachers to use their skills as observers" is ambitious given that the items do not operationally define observable behavior (Sample item: Is a self-starter; shows initiative). Beyond report that the TRF was "developed with a great deal of input from classroom teachers," criteria for item selection, reliability of total scale and subscale scores (e.g., internal consistency, test-retest), and relationships of ratings on the TRF to other teacher rating scales or information obtained from direct assessment (concurrent validity) are not identified. Further, it is unclear how long the rater should observe the child before completing the scale.

The manual does present a detailed description of the use of the USM in conjunction with a Revolving Door Model of service delivery and suggests further potential uses of the USM in evaluating any student's project. Unfortunately, data concerning USM reliability (interrater, test-retest) and validity are not presented nor is the development of the scale described. In addition, all but one item upon which students are rated are highly subjective (Sample item: Shows care and pride of workmanship), and it is unclear who should serve as judges or how many judges are needed to reliably evaluate a student.

SUMMARY. The EEII is a combination of two brief rating scales and a decision matrix for use in the selection of students for gifted programming between kindergarten and eighth grade. The manual presents helpful information and examples concerning potential uses of the EEII, its flexibility in meeting program goals, and its use in communicating information obtained during assessment to parents. In contrast, information concerning the development of the two rating scales as well as their psychometric properties is not presented, and many items are interpretively ambiguous to the rater. The manual also fails to present data concerning the predictive validity of the selection matrix, and its ability to discriminate between gifted and nongifted populations identified by more extensive procedures is unclear.

REVIEWER'S REFERENCES

Renzulli, J. (1978). What makes giftedness? Reexamining a definition. *Phi Delta Kappan*, 60 (3), 180-184.

Renzulli, J., Reis, S., & Smith, L. (1981). *The revolving door identification model*. Mansfield Center, CT: Creative Learning Press.

Rosenfield, S. (1983). Assessment of the gifted child. In T. R. Kratochwill (Ed.), *Advances in school psychology: Vol. III* (pp. 141-174). Hillsdale, NJ: Lawrence Erlbaum Associates.

[102]

The Edinburgh Questionnaires (1982 Edition). Purpose: "For use in organisational development and in individual placement, guidance and development." Adults; 1982; this preliminary edition is intended mainly for research use; 3 questionnaires; 1987 price data: £14.95 per 25 questionnaires (specify Section 1, Section 2, or Section 3); £19.95 per specimen set including 10 of each of the 3 forms and manual ('82, 8 pages); administration time not reported; John Raven; NFER-Nelson Publishing Co., Ltd. [England].*

a) SECTION 1: QUALITY OF WORKING LIFE. 4 scores: Working Conditions, Type of Work Wanted, Relationships, and General.
b) SECTION 2: IMPORTANT ACTIVITIES.
c) SECTION 3: CONSEQUENCES. 6 scores: Compatibility, Perceptions of Task and Personal Reactions, Reactions of Superiors, Reactions of Colleagues and Workmates, Benefits and Disbenefits to others, Competencies Engaged.

Review of The Edinburgh Questionnaires (1982 Edition) by BRUCE SHERTZER, Professor of Education, Purdue University, West Lafayette, IN:

Raven (1982) uses the word "cluster" as a descriptor of his questionnaires, presumably to suggest that they are both related and successive. However, he states that each one—Quality of Working Life, Important Activities, and Consequences—can stand on its own even though the three are designed to be used together for both organizational development and placement of individuals. Most suggestions about appropriate uses given in the Technical Manual (1982) speak to individual counseling or placement, with comparatively little attention given to how they could be used in facilitating an organization's development.

Raven places the inventories within a context of value-expectancy-instrumentality theory of motivation. First, values and work behaviors important to people are identified; then possible consequences of tackling a problem or behaving in certain ways are examined, followed by perceptions of the benefits or dangers of the consequences. Quality of Working Life, Section 1, contains 98 items ordered into four parts: working conditions, type of work wanted, relationships, and general. For all parts except general, respondents rate how important on a 1 (high) to 5 scale the item is to them as well as their satisfaction on a 1 (very) to 5 scale with that item. The last part, general, contains 22 items for which respondents rate the importance on a 5 (high) to 1 scale of avoiding negative conditions. Important Activities, Section 2, contains 88 items for which respondents indicate the importance (1 = important to do—4 = important not to do) of the activity to them in their work. Consequences, Section 3, is designed to assess the expectations or fears of a worker endeavoring to do something about a work problem (several work problems are presented in the manual). This section contains 105 items organized into six parts: compatibility, perceptions of task and personal reactions, supervisor's reactions, colleague's reactions, benefits and disbenefits of others, and competencies engaged. This reviewer was impressed by the comprehensive array of items in each questionnaire. The items are free of sexist terminology, but the manual is not.

The Technical Manual states that it is best that all three questionnaires be administered for individual guidance and placement, but that some inventory parts (items about relationships and activities important to the respondent) could be omitted if time is a problem. But time always is a problem and the Manual is silent about the consequences of deleting selected parts of the test. The suggestion that it is possible to delete items tapping relationships with colleagues, superiors, and subordinates appears to be contrary to the many research findings that worker relationships are prominent in measures of worker satisfaction or dissatisfaction.

This reviewer agreed with the author that Consequences, Section 3, was "the most important, and most distinctive" of the three questionnaires because of its input to an index of motivation based upon behavior "more likely to be determined by multiple, situationally relevant, value laden, considerations than by a small number of underlying 'traits'" (Technical Manual). Therefore, it was puzzling to learn that for "certain purposes" (not specified in the manual) Section 3 need not be administered in some assessments for organizational development.

Directions for scoring the questionnaires are not provided in the manual. Are the satisfaction and importance ratings of Section 1 summed together or separately? Even the directions for computing an index of motivation, the key outcome measure of these questionnaires, are very fuzzy. This index is calculated by using weighted responses obtained by summing certain items of the Consequences questionnaire and parallel items in Quality of Working Life. These parallel items are identified in a table in the manual. But it is unclear whether the scorer sums the 37 sets of parallel items or simply only the Consequences items for which there is a parallel (four items do not have parallels). Further the table reporting parallel items contains asterisks for which there is no notation. Even if the operation to obtain an index of motivation were completed there is no statement classifying scores. This lack of clarity and specificity characterizes not only the directions given in the manual for scoring, but also those for interpretation and use.

The Technical Manual does not provide any validity or reliability data, results of factor analysis, item selection procedures, normative data, scoring directions (except those for the index of motivation), or interpretation guides. For each of these critical features the user is referred to Raven's (1984) *Competence in Modern Society*. But that simply is not good enough. Further, it is this disappointed reviewer's opinion that the Manual does not meet even the author's stated purpose of providing "a basic understanding of their (the 3 questionnaires) uses and value, including advice on how to use the information they provide" let alone comply with testing standards (AERA, APA, NCME, 1985). Finally, the three questionnaires are described as preliminary versions, published in the hope that normative data and case materials would be shared with or secured by the author. This reviewer concludes that the author must attend to the deficiencies noted here before the potential of this instrument can be realized.

REVIEWER'S REFERENCES

Raven, J. (1984). *Competence in modern society*. London: H. K. Lewis and Company, Ltd.

American Educational Research Association, American Psychological Association, & National Council on Measurement in Education. (1985). *Standards for educational and psychological testing*. Washington, DC: American Psychological Association, Inc.

[103]

Educational Administrator Effectiveness Profile. Purpose: Assesses school administrators' on-the-job skills and behavior. Public school administrators; 1984; EAEP; ratings by self and five coworkers; 11 ratings: Setting Goals and Objectives, Planning, Making Decisions and Solving Problems, Managing Business and Fiscal Affairs, Assessing Progress, Delegating Responsibilities, Communicating, Building and Maintaining Relationships, Demonstrating Professional Commitment, Improving Instruction, Developing Staff; 1987 price data: $25 per complete kit including 1 self inventory, 5 other inventories, item-by-item feedback booklet, administrative skills profile sheet, item-by-item tabulation worksheet, self development guide ('84, 71 pages); $25 per follow-up support materials; $2 per leader's manual ('84, 26 pages); Human Synergistics, Inc. and Tom Webber (leader's manual); Human Synergistics, Inc.*

Review of the Educational Administrator Effectiveness Profile by JAN N. HUGHES, Associate Professor of Educational Psychology, Texas A&M University, College Station, TX:

The stated purpose of the Educational Administrator Effectiveness Profile (EAEP) is to provide educational administrators "accurate, detailed information about healthy human behavior." Purportedly, the EAEP provides "an indepth psychological measure of the basic factors that cause behavior." The manual provides no empirical evidence to substantiate these ambitious claims.

The EAEP is part of a self-improvement program for educational administrators claiming to measure 11 dimensions of leadership critical to administrator success. The EAEP materials are smartly packaged and marketed. The EAEP promises to help administrators keep their skills sharp and become "the more effective leader you want to be."

Use of the EAEP involves several steps. In the first step, the administrator completes a 120-item questionnaire that assesses self-perceptions of leadership behaviors. The administrator selects five raters who can "accurately assess [the administrator's] on-the-job behaviors" and whose opinions the administrator values and trusts. These persons rate the administrator on the same 120 behaviors. Second, a clerical worker scores the self- and other-questionnaires and prepares a feedback sheet that includes both the average self-ratings and average other-ratings for 11 categories of administrator behavior. Optional feedback includes average other-ratings for each item. Third, administrators are provided feedback in a debriefing session. Administrators are encouraged to prioritize categories to work on by examining discrepancies between self- and other-ratings, low other-ratings, low self-ratings, and categories where improvement would be likely to lead to the greatest payoff on the job. Fourth, a self-improvement guide offers suggested strategies for improving performance in each category and suggested readings. A self-improvement option is to enroll in an EAEP follow-up program and receive biweekly mailings on improving leadership behaviors in administrator-selected categories.

The most serious limitation of the EAEP is its failure to include in the test manual evidence of the test's reliability or validity. The EAEP test manual does not provide sufficient information to enable a qualified user to evaluate the claims made for its use or to make sound judgments regarding the interpretation of test scores. The test manual disregards the user's need for the most basic information regarding the development of the test, standardization and norms, reliability, and validity. A statistical report describing the test development process and psychometric properties of the EAEP exists. Similarly a final project report, submitted to the foundation that supported the development of the EAEP, provides necessary technical information. Because no reference to these reports is made in the test manual or in any other materials sent to test users, they are not easily accessible to test users.

The following discussion of the EAEP's technical properties is based on the two supplementary reports mentioned above. The final report describes the development of the test, including the purpose of the test, procedures followed in writing and selecting items, results of pilot testing, and the empirical rationale for revising earlier versions of the EAEP.

Data analyzed for the statistical report came from a sample of 195 administrators and 462 other raters (i.e., persons rating these 195 administrators). The sample is defined in terms of major demographic variables and appears to be representative of those groups for which use of the EAEP is recommended.

Descriptive statistics (mean, standard deviation, range) for the standardization sample are reported for each of the 110 items and 11 subscales. Separate statistics are reported for different rater groups (self-ratings, ratings by others, and combined self- and other-ratings). The distributions of scores are negatively skewed and standard deviations are low, indicating a tendency for raters to evaluate administrators quite positively. The restricted range of ratings limits the test's ability to discriminate among administrators who vary in their effectiveness. The statistical report provides tables for determining an administrator's percentile score for each scale. Separate norm tables for different subgroups (i.e., groups based on gender, years of experience, and work setting) are not provided. The final report states these variables were found to be unimportant.

The internal consistency reliabilities of the EAEP scales were estimated using Cronbach's alpha. Reliability coefficients for the 11 scales range from .71 to .86, based on the combined self- and other-ratings. Thus, the scales possess adequate reliability in terms of internal consistency. Interrater reliability for the ratings by others is moderate (eta-squared statistics average .505 for the 11 scales).

Evidence of the test's content validity includes a list of those experts in the field of educational administration who participated in identifying relevant domains of administrator effectiveness and in writing and selecting items. Item-total matrices provide evidence of the test's construct validity. These matrices demonstrate that 93% of items correlate more highly with their own scale totals than with any of the other scale totals. Thus, items on a given scale tend to measure the same domain.

Additional evidence of the construct validity is provided by correlations between self-ratings and ratings by others for each of the 11 scales. Generally, these correlations are low, with higher correlations for task-oriented skill domains and lower correlations for person-centered skill domains. Thus, one cannot predict how others rate a given administrator from knowledge of the administrator's self-ratings, and vice versa. Given the discrepancy format for reporting and interpreting test results, the low correlations between self-ratings and ratings by others is not necessarily a limitation of the test. However, the question of which type of rating better predicts actual performance has not been empirically addressed. Furthermore, the significance of large versus small discrepancies between self-ratings and ratings by others has not been investigated. Thus, information necessary to accurately and fully interpret test results is not provided.

Critical to evaluating the test's validity is evidence of the test's criterion-related validity. The manual states that the EAEP measures dimensions of leadership critical to administrator success. The final report claims "Evaluations to date prove that the EAEP does identify effective educational administrators and can diagnose levels of proficiency in the domain areas which are assesssed." Virtually no evidence to support this claim is provided. One criterion-related validity study is reported in the final report. In this study, central office supervisors from three high-performing school districts rated 43 principals on a 7-point scale in each of the 11 domains. Correlations between these ratings and the EAEP domain scores based on self-ratings and ratings by others were uniformly low.

The EAEP does have some positive attributes. The self-other discrepancy format for reporting results is interesting, if not innovative. The instructions for administration and scoring and the definitions of each category are clearly detailed. Because most of the items are stated in terms of specific administrator behaviors, the questionnaire provides the user with others' perceptions of his or her behavior. The feedback profiles enhance comprehensibility of the results. The greatest strength of the EAEP is the close connection between questionnaire results and interpretations. The user can easily locate a discussion of each category that includes reasons persons may perform poorly in that area, strategies for changing one's behavior, and suggested readings.

In summary, the EAEP's best use may be as part of an organizational development or human relations exercise led by a trained and skilled organizational consultant. Until evidence of a relationship between EAEP scores and an external criterion of effectiveness is provided, it is a poor choice as a test of educational administrators' effectiveness. For the stated purpose of the EAEP, the Leadership Behavior Description Questionnaire (LBDQ) (8:1175) is a better choice. The LBDQ measures 12 dimensions of leadership, based on supervisee ratings. Extensively researched, the LBDQ possesses adequate psychometric properties.

Review of the Educational Administrator Effectiveness Profile by LESLIE T. RASKIND, School Psychologist, Gwinnett County Schools, Lawrenceville, GA:

The Educational Administrator Effectiveness Profile (EAEP) is a tool for encouraging professional growth in educational administrators. The EAEP package consists of: a self-rating scale to be completed by the administrator, the same scale restated so that up to five other people can rate the administrator, several scoring protocols, and a self-study guide. The EAEP program could be used by a single principal as a self-help guide. However, a Leader's Manual is also available so that several administrators could be accommodated in a workshop format.

An effective administrator is defined as a person who excels in 11 areas: setting goals and objectives, planning, making decisions and solving problems, managing business and fiscal affairs, assessing progress, delegating responsibilities, communicating, building and maintaining relationships, demonstrating professional commitment, improving instruction, and developing staff. These areas are measured by ratings of 120 statements made by five observers using a 7-point scale ranging from *Almost Never* to *Always*. Ratings are then averaged for each domain and across the raters. A visual comparison can be plotted so the administrator can compare the self rating to the average rating given by the participating others. Using the Self-Development Guide, the administrator might choose to study his/her weakest area in depth or the area in which the greatest discrepancy is found between self and others' ratings. The Guide contains 11 chapters summarizing salient research and containing structured activities to plan improvement in the targeted area. An item-by-item tabulation is available so that strengths and weaknesses on individual items can be studied.

The EAEP format is well organized with clear directions, an easily scored protocol, and a visually appealing profile sheet. The strongest feature of this package may be its very readable prose style, both in the Self-Development Guide and in the Leader's Manual. The author's writing is clear, humorous, and quickly understood. The suggested readings are up-to-date, and all examples are relevant to school settings. The goal-setting activities are interesting and would be especially well suited to a workshop format. The content of the Guide takes its direction from the writings of Maslow, Rogers, Carkhuff, and others, and is well adapted to school issues.

The Leader's Manual is equally well done. A trainer could easily manage the logistics of a workshop following the author's suggestions on time-lines, number of participants, activities, scoring, and interpretation. Several different ways of holding the workshop are suggested, which are practical and realistic and consider the time and resource constraints usually found in school systems. In the hands of an adequate trainer, the EAEP materials would be the basis of a very interesting and relevant workshop for school administrators.

The EAEP does not purport to be more than a set of ratings. However, some items are abstractly worded so the rater might need to devote considerable thought before assigning an accurate rating. Ambiguous items seem to occur in the domains that are traditionally difficult to operationalize, such as goal setting and planning. The items relating to fiscal affairs, delegating, and building relationships are more concretely stated. Nevertheless, raters would need to be motivated and conversant with educational terminology to complete the evaluations.

The EAEP scoring is straightforward and requires little skill beyond careful tabulation and averaging. However, the item-by-item feedback method, which is strongly recommended by the authors, is a time-consuming process. Several practical recommendations are made to deal with this disadvantage of the scoring method.

A few guidelines are given to administrators for interpreting results of the evaluation. The guidelines given are stated to be of practical, not statistical, significance. Nevertheless, it would seem the facilitator of a group using the EAEP would need to be skilled in the interpretation of differences between strengths and weaknesses, or between self and others' ratings. Considering the vague wording on some items and the limitations inherent in all rating scales, interpretation of the profile would be critically important in providing an administrator with reasonable feedback on his/her performance.

Information on reliability, validity, or scale construction is not provided in the Leader's Manual. These data are available in an unpublished report entitled: "Final Report: Development of an Educational Administrator Self-Assessment Instrument" available from the publisher. Scale items were developed after an exhaustive literature search and submission to a panel of five experts in educational administration and staff evaluation. The instrument was field tested three times and items revised so as to discriminate the 11 domains more clearly. eliability was measured by analyzing 195 self reports of school administrators and 462 reports made by other persons rating the administrator. The sample was drawn predominantly from public schools in urban, suburban, and rural districts. Seventy-three percent of the participants were male, and 89% were white. Reliability coefficients in a study of interitem consistency ranged from .71 to .86. An interrater reliability study is also reported with these same data, indicating an acceptable level of similarity when the ratings made by others are compared.

Two studies of content and criterion-related validity were conducted. To measure content validity, a factor analysis was conducted to determine whether the 11 domains measured different skills. Three general factors were identified: Planning Skills, Interpersonal Skills, and Professional Skills.

The single study of criterion-related validity compared the self and other EAEP scores of 43 administrators from three districts in Illinois and California with ratings made by these principals' central office supervisors. Correlations were low. The authors suggest the criterion measure may have been inappropriate or that the sample may have been too small and unduly restricted.

The EAEP is a promising instrument for self-study by school administrators. The construction of the questionnaires was based on expert opinion as well as three field studies. Internal consistency and interrater reliability appear to be adequate.

No data are given for the stability of scores over time, but this is not necessarily a major flaw. Optimally, ratings would improve over time for an administrator engaged in a self-improvement program.

The validity data provided are problematic. When self and others' ratings were correlated, only low convergent validity was found, particularly in the area of person-centered skills. When the self ratings were compared with a single rating by a supervisor, correlations were low. If the ratings do not correlate with these two criteria, either more suitable validity studies need to be performed or the EAEP will simply remain a well-written self-help exercise. The author describes future plans to validate the instrument with a larger sample and more variation in the performance of the participating administrators. Until that time, users should be cautioned that differences between self and others' ratings, especially in the person-centered skills, cannot be meaningfully interpreted.

The EAEP provides an avenue for school administrators to focus on the complex set of behaviors that characterize an effective educational leader. Considering its practicality and nominal cost, the EAEP would be an attractive option for districts interested in providing a self-improvement study for administrators with a minimal expediture of time and resources. At this time, validity data are not sufficient for ratings to be used in any normative fashion.

Finally, the information on test instruction, reliability, and validity should be condensed and included in materials that are ordered by prospective users. Failure to include these data violates the most basic standards by which any published test is measured.

[104]

The Effective School Battery. Purpose: "To identify a school's strengths and weaknesses, to develop improvement plans, and to evaluate improvement projects." Grades 7–12, teachers; 1984; ESB; 2 surveys; separate answer sheets must be used; 1987 price data: $3.50 per 10 survey administrator's instructions (3 pages); $2.50 per coordinator's manual (14 pages); $15 per user's manual (105 pages); $20 per introductory kit including user's manual, coordinator's manual, survey administrator's instructions, 1 each of student and teacher answer sheets and reusable survey booklets; scoring service, $50 report fee per school; $.50 per survey; Gary G. Gottfredson; Psychological Assessment Resources, Inc.*

a) STUDENT SURVEY. Grades 7–12; 19 scales: Parental Education, Positive Peer Associations, Educational Expectation, Social Integration, Attachment to School, Belief in Rules, Interpersonal Competency, Involvement, Positive Self-Concept, School Effort, Avoidance of Punishment, School Rewards, Invalidity, Safety, Respect for Students, Planning and Action, Fairness of Rules, Clarity of Rules, Student Influence; $37.50 per 50 survey booklets; $12.50 per 50 answer sheets; (25–50) minutes.

b) TEACHER SURVEY. Teachers; 16 scales: Pro-Integration Attitude, Job Satisfaction, Interaction With Students, Personal Security, Classroom Orderliness, Professional Development, Nonauthoritarian Attitude, Safety, Morale, Planning and Action, Smooth Administration, Resources, Race Relations, Parent/Community Involvement, Student Influence, Avoidance of Use of Grades as a Sanction; $18.75 per 25 survey booklets; $6.25 per 25 answer sheets; administration time not reported.

Review of The Effective School Battery by JAMES R. BARCLAY, Professor of Educational and Counseling Psychology, University of Kentucky, Lexington, KY:

This battery is designed to identify a school's strengths and weaknesses by a survey administered to students and to teachers. It is viewed as a vehicle for developing improvement plans and evaluating improvement projects. The battery was developed both by use of a priori conceptualized scales and extensive field testing in 1982. Approximately 15,000 school-aged individuals from about 10 years of age to 18 years of age were included in the standardization effort. Thirteen student scales were developed which included Parental Education, Positive Peer Associations, Educational Expectation, Social Integration, Attachment to School, Belief in Conventional Rules, Interpersonal Competency, Involvement, Positive Self-Concept, School Effort, Avoidance of Punishment, School Rewards, and Invalidity.

The teacher scales include items that measure the teachers' views towards Pro-Integration, Job Satisfaction, Interaction with Students, Personal Security, Classroom Orderliness, Professional Development, and Nonauthoritarian Attitude. Approximately 1,000 teachers were surveyed.

The battery is administered to both students and teacher in a classroom. The battery is not hand-scorable, but must be returned to the publisher for scoring and reporting.

The manual is well written. The description of the importance of the variables is based on current and past research in both teacher morale and student characteristics. Reliability indices for the scales vary, but appear to be in the acceptable range. A number of independent criterion variables were used in correlational studies with the Effective School Battery Scales. Virtually all of these correlations are significant because of the large samples used. But the absolute magnitude of the relationships is often very low.

In order to utilize the surveys it is necessary to order both student and teacher surveys, administrator instructions, a coordinator's manual, a user's manual, and pay a $50.00 per school scoring service for processing and reporting. In addition there is a scoring fee of $.75 for each student survey. Although the exact per-pupil cost is difficult to predict, it would seem that the cost would be about $4.25 per pupil for a class of 30 students. This cost would, of course, be reduced by larger usage.

The student survey consists of some demographic information and items which, for the most part, call for a true-false, agree-disagree judgment. Included in this section are some estimates of positive peer associations that reflect the known importance of peer relations in schooling. However, positive peer relationships are judged by self-reported true-false alternatives (e.g., "most of my friends think school is a pain"), and by two items that refer to gangs or trouble with the police. To estimate positive peer relationships from eight items, many of which identify clearly antisocial and police-related activities and call for true-false decisions, would invite socially desirable responses. In addition, this scale is simply a self-reported scale and does not truly reflect peer input.

Other items in the student scales are equally difficult to respond to in terms of true-false options. For example, in the social integration scale, item 96 states "life in this town is pretty confusing." I suspect that for many individuals at different times this would be true. At other times it might be false.

Although scaling of items on a Likert scale calls for more decisions, even a three-option choice is better than a true-false one (though some researchers would not agree). In point of fact some scales do include three options (e.g., the Positive Self-Concept and Attachment to School Scales). It is very likely that the low correlations obtained for many of the scales are due to a lot of random responses generated by students as a result of making dichotomous decisions that do not reflect the complexity of reality.

The teacher scales include a number of important dimensions relating to teacher security, job satisfaction, classroom interaction, and professional development. However, some teachers who fill out this inventory might have a concern about who would have access to the results. Since anonymity is not specified, it would seem reasonable that teachers would be quite cautious in their responses and tend to place themselves in a good position, particularly as they respond to race-relations, evaluation of administrators, and parent-community relationships.

Although the reviewer would prefer more options in the scoring of scales to provide a clearer and more graduated set of responses to items, the author's decision to use dichotomous responses is a legitimate one. Moreover, it is extremely difficult to design surveys that provide both a depth of perception and a breadth of content and that are not in some way threatening to either students or teachers. Thus, from an overall point of view, the surveys are clearly described and the manual is succinct.

The major concerns I see with this instrument relate to usability. It would seem costly to administer to an entire school. In junior and senior high schools, students move from teacher to teacher. How would climate be estimated in settings where there is such movement? Moreover, how would the system be used in the "open" school situation where clusters of students interact with clusters of teachers?

But suppose one did use the surveys with a number of schools in a given district. How would the printouts derived from the scoring be used to effect change? The author points out some descriptive differences between schools, but how could these differences be used to effect changes? Both teachers and students may be quite resistant to changes imposed from outside the school. Moreover, because student data reflect means, what can be done about individual differences? In each class there will be some children who do not like teachers, and others who do like them. Mean scores on variables can then be either quite misleading or carry very little information.

If one postulates that knowing group means about these variables is important to effecting change, then this inventory makes a good deal of sense. In point of fact it does provide a profile of a given school's strengths and weaknesses better than other known climate inventories. However, until some direct relationship can be established between using the system and developing improvement plans and evaluating projects, the battery is basically a descriptive survey. To warrant using this system, expensive as it is, requires both some cost-effectiveness studies and some validity studies.

If such studies are completed supporting the usefulness of the instrument in designing and evaluating improvement projects, the battery will be a powerful tool for effecting change. However, much more work remains to be accomplished before such claims can be made.

[105]

The Egan Bus Puzzle Test. Purpose: "Designed to assess language development and some performance skills of young children." Ages 20 months to 4 years; no date on test materials; 6 scores: Expressive Verbal Labels, Comprehension (Verbal Labels, Recognition of Shape, Orientation of Piece to Recess), Comprehension of Sentences, Expressive Language; individual; 1987 price data: £38.50 per complete set including manual (36 pages), board, and 25 forms; £32 per board and manual; £6.25 per 25 forms; (7–8) minutes; Dorothy F. Egan and Rosemary Brown; The Test Agency [England].*

Review of The Egan Bus Puzzle Test by SHELDON L. STICK, Professor, Department of Special Education and Communication Disorders, The University of Nebraska-Lincoln, Lincoln, NE:

PURPOSE. The Egan Bus Puzzle Test is a developmental assessment instrument designed to sample selected aspects of language development and some performance skills of children between 20 and 48 months of age. The authors suggest that professionals could compare a child's pattern of responses against those obtained from the standardization population and determine whether a given child is discrepant in the selected areas of language and performance skills sampled. Raw scores are converted into age equivalencies and judged against the average scores for children in the 50th, 80th, and 90th percentiles of correct responding for 3-month chronological age groups ranging from 21 to 48 months, with a plus or minus variation of 1 month. Standardization information is presented in table and graph forms. The intent is for the instrument to be used by health care professionals, particularly physicians most likely to encounter young children, who are involved in obtaining developmental information on such children. Normative data were not obtained on differing populations of handicapped children. The primary author reportedly has used the test effectively during a period of 10 years while assessing children with a wide range of developmental disabilities. Using the Egan Bus Puzzle Test apparently will allow health care professionals to make reasonably informed decisions for referring children for more definitive assessments when marked variations from normal development are observed.

TEST FORMAT. The Bus Puzzle Test is constructed of plywood on a board approximately 11 1/2 x 17 1/2 inches. It presents a brightly colored street scene with nine life-like pieces each affixed to a small knob that can be held by young children except for those with severe orthopedic difficulties. The objective is for a child to manipulate the puzzle pieces according to directions given by an observer who notes selected aspects of language and performance behaviors.

The language skills assessed are subdivided into three expressive and two receptive sections. Expressively children are required to name selected pieces of the puzzle, respond to six questions pertaining to the illustrated situation contained in the puzzle, and identify objects or items most likely to be contained in a mother's pocketbook. The two receptive subscales involve indicating awareness of selected names of puzzle pieces, and responding to six questions that refer to the puzzle picture. The second major subsection of the test addresses performance skills. The three subareas focus on having a child recognize the outline image of a puzzle piece (shape recognition), moving an appropriate puzzle piece into the space it fits (spatial orientation), and provides an opportunity for the test examiner to observe a child's manual dexterity while manipulating the various puzzle pieces. The authors state that a child can be expected to complete the entire test within 7 to 8 minutes and that it will be attended to fairly well because of the picture's attractiveness and the activity involved, both within the picture itself and the child's involvement with the task.

The 425 children comprising the standardization population came from an inner city area described as a rural market town. English was not necessarily the primary or sole language spoken by the respective families, however, English was spoken by all of the families. Specific information was not provided regarding minority population subjects, but it was stated that the sample consisted of children from several racial backgrounds.

ADMINISTRATION AND SCORING. The authors state the examiner should encourage children to provide their best possible performance and that it is permissible to have a parent close by. However, it is preferable that the child be seated at a small table, or perhaps working on the floor with an examiner instead of seated on a parent's lap. It is recommended that some easy and innocuous task, such as manipulating 1-inch wooden cubes, be given to the child prior to starting the Bus Puzzle Test. Examiners are allowed to repeat and/or encourage a child to respond and provide constant encouragement or praise. Children experiencing difficulty on an initial presentation of a particular task can be given a second opportunity by repeating the original request.

The nine puzzle pieces selected for use in the test are ones reportedly most likely to be familiar to young children in terms of being able to respond with their respective verbal labels. The first part of the language skills section seeks to determine whether a child is able to identify each of the nine items. Children not responding to the tester's question "What is it?" are provided with the name of a particular item and are instructed to take that piece out of the puzzle and place it on the table/floor on the left side of the puzzle tray (tester points to the left side of the tray). The authors indicate that shy or reluctant-to-participate children seem to relax and become more likely to participate after becoming involved with removing the first puzzle piece. However, if a child does not respond with a verbal label, it is recommended the examiner remove each of the remaining eight puzzle pieces while labeling each one. Scoring of the verbal labels subsection is done in terms of 1 point for generic term, 2 points for functional term, and 3 points for applying the proper name to the item. Twenty-four out of a maximum of 27 points is considered acceptable in this subsection, because it takes into account children not responding to the initial item because of shyness or some other cause of reticence.

The second subtest in the language skills area assesses comprehension of verbal labels by asking a child to put each item named into the tray. The authors encourage testers to be cautious to not provide cues and to use the item's proper name as opposed to some idiosyncratic term a child might have provided. Again, children are offered a second opportunity to respond to the selected items if there is an incorrect selection or a child seems confused as to which item should be selected. A point worth noting is that examiners are urged to begin this subtest and the expressive verbal labeling subtest using the stimuli car, dog, bus, and baby because they are likely to be among the earliest terms acquired by young children. There is no prescribed sequence for the remaining five items on the test. Scoring comprehension of verbal labels is done three ways. The first is correct selection of a particular stimulus labeled by the examiner. A child can earn up to a maximum of 9 points for correctly retrieving the appropriate items. The second part of this section also allows earning up to 9 points for correct recognition of the respective shapes in the puzzle in which the items should be placed. The third way in which this subtest is scored is in terms of correct orientation of the particular puzzle piece to the puzzle recess. A maximum of 9 points can be earned by correctly orienting the piece to its recess, even if there is some position experimentation.

The third subsection under language skills provides information on a child's understanding of questions that relate to selected aspects of the puzzle picture. Six questions are presented in a prescribed order. Responses that seem correct using gestures, verbal responses, or a combination of both are given credit. The maximum raw score in this subsection is 6.

The fourth subsection is evaluated concurrently with the responses provided to the questions presented in subsection 3. Subsection 4 analyzes the syntactic/semantic constructions used to answer the six questions presented in subsection 3. Each of the six respective questions are scored as no reply (0 points), gesture or word/gesture (1 point), 2/3 words without a verb or verb only, usually present participle (2 points), and three or more words, including a verb, such as verb/object sentence or better (3 points). The maximum raw score for this subtest is 18 points. Each question given during the presentation of subsection 3 may be repeated once to a child.

The final language skill subsection requires children to tell what they think the mother pictured in the puzzle has in her pocketbook. The question is optional and generally not viewed as appropriate for children under the chronological age of 3 years. In the puzzle picture a mother (who is pushing a baby in a stroller) has a bag hanging over her shoulder. The tester inquires of the child "What do you think Mummy has in her handbag?" Children see only the shoulder bag and must generate possible contents based on experience. The authors indicate that appropriate answers should be viewed as favorable developmental indices. Thirty-four percent of all the children 48 months of age responded correctly with one item; 28% of children 48 months of age named two objects correctly; and 19% of children 48 months of age were able to name three objects correctly.

INTERPRETATION. The raw scores earned on the various parts of the first four subsections are compared to normative data with regard to variation from the average and/or age level equivalencies. The average score is represented as a 50th percentile on the graphs or tables. Moderately below average performances are determined on the basis of scores that fall between the 50th and 80th percentiles. A score at the 80th percentile means that a particular child is performing comparably to children in the lowest 20 percent. The 90th percentile information is interpreted comparably in that it means 90 percent of the children have performed better than that score for a given age level. The authors recommend determining which of the following six profile patterns emerge:

1. Average or above in both language and performance skills—indicative of normal development.

2. Overall low scores—all scores falling in the lowest 10th percentile can be viewed as indicative of mental or neurodevelopmental disorders.

3. Language levels lower than performance—an indication for referral to specialists because of possible problems with (*a*) specific developmental language disorder, (*b*) deafness, and (*c*) difficulty affecting proper social relationships (autism).

4. Mild comprehension—requires determining audiological integrity and/or nonconducive environmental and/or social opportunities for developing language.

5. Mild delay in expressive language—generally of a functional nature which requires intervention by speech-language pathologists.

6. Performance skills markedly delayed in contrast to language skills—possible visual perceptual dysfunction requiring referral to occupational therapists.

CRITIQUE. The Egan Bus Puzzle Test may prove to be useful particularly if it is adopted by large numbers of health care professionals dealing with young children. Using a fairly unstructured play situation in which to gather specific types of language and language-related information could help identify a number of children who would benefit markedly from early intervention procedures and become better candidates for obtaining success in an academic environment. The length of testing time is minimal (7–8 minutes) and the scoring protocol is fairly easy to follow. Because the intent of the test is to obtain estimates of variation from obstensibly normal development, there is no need for a tester to be particularly sophisticated in terms of speech and language development and intervention. Once a decision is made that a child exhibits a variance from normal development, referrals to appropriate specialists would allow for more definitive assessment and subsequent treatment, if appropriate.

If the test is to be employed in the United States, consideration needs to be given to modifying some of the terminology because of the difference in colloquial or everyday speech. Also, a revised version of the picture puzzle should be developed to reflect a scene more commonly found in American communities. In particular, the use of the double-deckered bus, the cylindrical shaped postbox, the traffic man, the woman pushing a buggy, and the disproportionately large child riding a bicycle would need to be changed to better reflect stimuli more common to American children.

[106]

Electronic and Instrumentation Technician Test. Purpose: "To evaluate the knowledge of electronics and instrumentation workers in specific subject areas." Applicants or incumbents for jobs where electronics and instrumentation knowledge is a necessary part of training or job activities; 1985; E&ITT; 8 scores: Motor Control, Digital Electronics/Computers, Analog/Radio, Schematics/Test Instruments, Power Supplies/Power Distribution, AC & DC Theory, Mechanical Maintenance, Total; 1986 price data: $10 per reusable test booklet; $40 per 500 answer sheets; manual ('85, 16 pages) and hand scoring keys also available from publisher; 180(190) minutes; Roland T. Ramsay; Ramsay Corporation.*

Review of the Electronic and Instrumentation Technician Test by ALAN R. SUESS, Professor of Industrial Technology and Education, Purdue University, West Lafayette, IN:

The test manual makes it apparent that at the time of publication, the Electronic and Instrumentation Technician Test was new and relatively untried. Normative estimates were based on responses from fewer than 100 individuals. These small numbers are, however, understandable when the dynamic nature of the content is considered. Individuals or organizations requiring current content will be forced to use tests such as this that cannot accumulate the data bases possible for more stable content areas.

The target audience identified by the developer are applicants for or incumbents in jobs in which electronics and instrumentation knowledge is necessary. It is not altogether clear to this reviewer what the practical purpose of the examination is, given the information in the accompanying manual. The recommended cutoff score for the examination is reported as 114 of 184 possible points. Subjects with scores between 101 and 113 are considered marginally qualified. The one reported normative study was done on a group of 96 individuals who had a mean performance of 82.47 with a standard deviation of 23.20. These results would indicate that even those with scores approximately one standard deviation above the mean would attain only marginal qualification status.

The test was designed to select electronic and instrumentation technicians. A review of the questions for sophistication and balance lead this reviewer to suggest this examination is much more an electronic technician test than it is an instrumentation technician test. There are very few questions in the area of applications of transducers to specific processes, data recording technology, and other instrumentation concerns. Moreover, the section on mechanical and fluid devices does not reveal the same level or sophistication of items that is apparent in the electronic and electrical portions of the test.

This test represents a very comprehensive sampling of electrical distribution, motor, and control elements, as well as the standard analog and digital areas. The questions are very well written and definitely reward individuals who know electronics at a relatively high level. The sophistication of the questions certainly contributed to the low scores of the norm groups. This same item sophistication should make this test very useful for screening applications for positions where intimate knowledge of electrical and electronics systems is imperative for job performance or potential in advanced technical positions.

[107]

The Ennis-Weir Critical Thinking Essay Test. Purpose: "To help evaluate a person's ability to appraise an argument and to formulate in writing an argument in response, thus recognizing a creative dimension in critical thinking ability." High school and college; 1983–85; 1987 price data: $9.95 per complete test including reproducible test, scoring directions, scoring sheet, and manual ('85, 16 pages); (40) minutes; Robert H. Ennis and Eric Weir; Midwest Publications, Inc.*

Review of The Ennis-Weir Critical Thinking Essay Test by JAMES A. POTEET, Professor of Special Education, Ball State University, Muncie, IN:

The Ennis-Weir Critical Thinking Essay Test was designed to be used both as a test and as a teaching instrument. As a test, it is an informal assessment device that requires scoring judgements by examiners who should have had at least a college-level course in informal logic, critical thinking, or the equivalent. The test is most appropriate for high school and college students, although the manual states that it has been used successfully with junior high and sixth-grade students. It takes approximately 40 minutes, which include reading the stimulus and planning and writing the response. The authors grant permission for the purchaser of the manual to reproduce for classroom use the directions to the student, the stimulus letter, and the scoring sheet.

The test stimulus is a letter written to the editor of a fictitious newspaper about the parking problems in a fictitious city. The student must write a response letter to the editor. For each of the eight arguments presented in the stimulus letter, the student is to write a response paragraph judging the quality of those arguments. In addition, a closing paragraph about the stimulus letter's overall quality of argument is to be written by the student. The student is to defend his/her judgments with reasons.

The task described above requires the student to think critically in the context of argumentation in which the student is defending a point. The manual states that "the test is intended to help evaluate a person's ability to appraise an argument and to formulate in writing an argument in response, thus recognizing a creative dimension in critical thinking ability."

For scoring purposes, the examiner is provided with suggested criteria for awarding points for each paragraph written by the student. Thinking ability, not writing ability, is to be judged. The scoring criteria are to be used "flexibly and with judgment." The scoring approach might be described as "loose."

Construct, predictive, and concurrent validity have not been studied, as noted in the manual. Content validity is viewed as acceptable because the stimulus task requires critical thinking. References to earlier works by Ennis are offered to the readers to explore aspects of critical-thinking competence felt to be important by the authors. Interrater reliability for two groups, 27 college students and 28 gifted eighth-grade students, was reported as .86 and .82. The size of these groups, means, and standard deviations are given in the manual. Most of the manual is devoted to offering scoring guidelines and suggestions for each of the paragraphs.

As a teaching instrument, the manual suggests that the instrument can be used by a Socratic teacher by having the students grade either each other's or their own tests followed by a discussion of how to apply the proposed criteria given on the scoring sheet. Also, the students could react to the stimulus letter either orally or in writing and then react to each other's reactions through class discussions. For the didactic teacher, a diagnostic approach might be taken where a teacher evaluates students' responses followed by further instruction based on these responses.

The Ennis-Weir is a cleverly constructed task that is designed to assess a student's skill in critical thinking. Guidelines are given to assist an informed examiner in evaluating student responses. It is not meant to be considered as a norm-referenced test, but more as an informal assessment technique that lends itself well both to informal assessment and to instruction in the area of critical thinking.

Review of The Ennis-Weir Critical Thinking Essay Test by GAIL E. TOMPKINS, Associate Professor of Language Arts Education, University of Oklahoma, Norman, OK:

The Ennis-Weir Critical Thinking Essay Test is "a general test of critical thinking ability in the context of argumentation." According to the authors, the following areas of critical-thinking competence are examined in the test: getting the point, seeing reasons and assumptions, stating one's point, offering good reasons, seeing other possibilities, responding appropriately to and/or avoiding equivocation, irrelevance, circularity, reversal of an if-then relationship, straw-person fallacy, overgeneralization, excessive skepticism, credibility problems, and the use of emotive language to persuade. The Ennis-Weir is not a test of formal or deductive argumentation, and examinees are not required to exhibit technical knowledge or use specialized vocabulary in their essays.

In the Ennis-Weir, examinees read a complex argument presented as a letter to the editor of a newspaper about a local parking problem and are asked to formulate another complex argument in response to the letter. In the letter, a proposal is presented and eight arguments in support of the proposal are offered. Each argument appears in a separate numbered paragraph and exemplifies at least one error in reasoning (e.g., irrelevance, circularity, overgeneralization). Examinees read the letter and then write an essay evaluating the argument of each paragraph and the letter as a whole.

Instructions to examinees are straightforward. During the 40-minute testing period, examinees are directed to spend the first 10 minutes reading and thinking about the letter and the remaining 30 minutes writing the nine-paragraph essay evaluating the argument of the letter.

Graders are provided with detailed evaluation criteria and scoring instructions. A scoring sheet is provided in the manual, and graders are instructed to award from -1 to +3 points for each of the first eight paragraphs and from -1 to +5 points for the ninth paragraph, with a total of 29 points possible. Graders are encouraged to use their own judgment in applying the criteria and to add or subtract points for other insights or errors. The manual contains a detailed discussion, paragraph by paragraph, of the arguments in the letter and comments students might make in response to the arguments. This information should help graders make reasonably sophisticated judgements, but no information is provided about how to interpret the scores or about what might be considered "average" performance on the test.

The authors claim content validity for The Ennis-Weir by arguing that examinees demonstrate critical-thinking skills in appraising the arguments presented in the letter and in formulating arguments in their responses. Furthermore, they have called graders' attention to specific relevant aspects of examinee responses in the scoring guide. However, claims for content validity would be much stronger if the authors had compared the results of this test with other tests of critical thinking.

Scanty information on reliability is provided in the manual. Reliability is based on 27 undergraduate students who took the test as part of an introductory course on informal logic and 28 gifted eighth-graders in an English class who had received some critical thinking instruction. The only reliability information reported was interrater reliabilities (.86 and .82) for the graders who scored the undergraduate and eighth-grade essays, respectively. No other reliability information was reported.

The authors of The Ennis-Weir also suggest that the test can be used as an instructional tool in high school classes. Because of the limited information on validity and the lack of reliability data, this second use may be the more valuable one for this material. The detailed scoring criteria provide useful information for teachers planning a unit on critical thinking, and the test itself can be used as one activity in the unit.

In summary, The Ennis-Weir has the potential to be a valuable test of critical-thinking ability for high school and college students. The authors are to be commended for developing an open-ended and content-specific test that allows students to respond to the arguments presented in the test in a variety of ways. The content of the test minimizes the artificiality of the testing situation, and an interesting and fairly realistic situation is presented in the test. The test manual is another plus. It is easy to read and use, and the detailed scoring criteria simplify grading. Unfortunately, the limited information on validity and the lack of reliability data suggest that The Ennis-Weir may be more appropriately used as a teaching tool than as a testing tool. The essay format of the test prompts another concern. The authors caution that The Ennis-Weir is primarily a test of critical-thinking ability, not of writing ability, and that graders should focus on the quality of thinking in the responses rather than on the quality of writing. But writing ability as well as writing anxiety may influence examinees' performance on the test.

[108]

ENRIGHT® Diagnostic Inventory of Basic Arithmetic Skills. Purpose: To "assess computation skills through error analysis and determine arithmetic performance levels" and to "discover specific error patterns." Grades 1–9; 1983; "criterion-referenced"; a component of the Enright Prescriptive/Diagnostic System; 3-step hierarchical testing system (Wide-Range Placement Test, Skill Placement Tests, Skill Tests, plus Basic Facts Tests) for error analysis of 144 arithmetic skills in 13 sections: Addition of Whole Numbers, Subtraction of Whole Numbers, Multiplication of Whole Numbers, Division of Whole Numbers, Conversion of Fractions, Addition of Fractions, Subtraction of Fractions, Multiplication of Fractions, Division of Fractions, Addition of Decimals, Subtraction of Decimals, Multiplication of Decimals, Division of Decimals; 2 forms (A and B) for each test; 1987 price data: $99 per 10 student tests and arithmetic record books and Tester manual ('83, 326 pages); $4.65 per student tests and arithmetic record book; $399 per 100 student tests and arithmetic record books; administration time not reported; Brian E. Enright; Curriculum Associates, Inc.*

Review of the ENRIGHT® Diagnostic Inventory of Basic Arithmetic Skills by DOUGLAS K. SMITH, Professor of Psychology and Director School Psychology Program, University of Wisconsin-River Falls, River Falls, WI:

This criterion-referenced measure of basic arithmetic skills consists of: the Wide-Range Placement Test, which establishes the starting point for assessment of specific arithmetic skills; the Skill Placement Tests, which "identify, within any skill sequence, the step that needs to be tested further"; the Skill Tests, which indicate whether or not a student can perform a particular skill step correctly; and the Basic Facts Tests, which are used to determine the degree to which a student knows the basic addition, subtraction, multiplication, and division facts. Each component can be given to individuals or to groups.

The Wide-Range Placement Test (Forms A and B) consists of 26 items testing skills from each of the 13 sections of the Inventory. It "identifies the operations that need to be assessed further and the section in which to begin." It is designed for use with middle-grade students to pinpoint skill areas that require more indepth testing. Two items per skill area are presented. The Skill Placement Tests are used to determine the student's knowledge of the 13 arithmetic operations in the Inventory and to identify the need for more specific skill testing. Starting point for testing is based on the results of the Wide-Range Placement Test or the operation to be evaluated. The operations include Addition of Whole Numbers, Subtraction of Whole Numbers, Multiplication of Whole Numbers, Division of Whole Numbers, Conversion of Fractions, Addition of Fractions, Subtraction of Fractions, Multiplication of Fractions, Division of Fractions, Addition of Decimals, Subtraction of Decimals, Multiplication of Decimals, and Division of Decimals. Each test contains one item for each skill measured in the section or operation. The first item missed is the starting point for skill testing. Each Skill Placement Test has two forms (A and B) that can be used as pre- and posttests.

The Skill Tests provide more indepth testing of the skills needed for successful performance in each of the 13 arithmetic operations sampled by the Skill Placement Tests. The skills are arranged in order of difficulty from simple to complex. Each skill is tested by five items. In addition, five review items are presented and these can be used as a posttest. Each skill is defined in the Tester Manual and a chart indicates the average grade level at which the skill is taught along with the grade level at which it is taught in the mathematics textbook series by Holt, Rinehart and Winston; Houghton-Mifflin; D. C. Heath; Scott, Foresman; and Macmillan.

The Inventory can be used flexibly. If the teacher has limited information on a student, the entire hierarchical process can be used beginning with the Wide Range Placement Test followed by the Skill Placement Test, The Basic Facts Tests, and finally the Skill Tests. For students who seem to have a particular skill deficit, testing can begin with the Skill Placement Test.

During development of the Inventory, 233 discrete error types were identified and grouped by common elements into seven error clusters (regrouping, process substitution, omission, directional, placement, attention to sign, and guessing). Student errors on the Skill Tests are analyzed within this framework to pinpoint the specific skill in which remediation is needed. This feature should be useful for the classroom teacher.

Tests are contained in the Student Tests and Arithmetic Record Book. This could be difficult for some students to manipulate. Information is recorded at the back of the book and this procedure could be cumbersome in transferring data from the test to the child's record in the back.

Information needed to use the Inventory is presented clearly in the Tester Manual. Instructions are presented for use of the Inventory, terms are defined, and error analysis is illustrated.

The Inventory was developed using a three-stage field-test procedure. The first stage involved 100 teachers in New Orleans, Louisiana, who used the first draft of the Inventory in their classrooms for several months. Based on teacher feedback and students' errors, the second draft of the Inventory was developed. This draft, including error patterns, was used in the second stage of development by 40 educational assessment specialists throughout Louisiana. After use of the second draft of the Inventory, the specialists critiqued the Inventory and 90% agreement was required for the retention of test items. In the final stage of testing, 11 "selected leaders in the field of educational assessment" reviewed the Inventory and 90% agreement was required for the retention of test items and objectives.

Reliability coefficients were determined using the split-half technique in each of the 13 sections (operations) of the Inventory. Samples ranged between 80 and 100 with a total sample size of 1,170. Additional characteristics of the sample are not provided in the Tester Manual. Reliability coefficients ranged from .90 (Subtraction of Decimals) to .98 (Subtraction of Whole Numbers). Test-retest data are not provided.

Content validity of the Inventory is addressed by the three-stage field-test procedure. Further support for content validity is found through the referencing of each of the 144 skills to the grade level at which each skill is taught in five widely used mathematics texts. The author states that the "face validity of the *Inventory* should stand without question." The author may have more correctly cited content validity in this case.

Although the Inventory appears to be a good, criterion-referenced measure of basic arithmetic skills, the user should be cognizant of the limited reliability data. The lack of test-retest data is particularly troublesome. In developing the Inventory, both the student and teacher samples were exclusively Louisiana-based. Only during the final stage of development was input sought from a more heterogeneous sample of educational assessment leaders from across the country. This may be a serious weakness in the measure.

Review of the ENRIGHT® Diagnostic Inventory of Basic Arithmetic Skills by JEFFREY K. SMITH, Associate Professor of Educational Psychology, Rutgers, The State University, New Brunswick, NJ:

The ENRIGHT® Diagnostic Inventory of Basic Arithmetic Skills represents an effort to provide classroom teachers with a method of assessing students' abilities to perform the four basic arithmetical functions on whole numbers, fractions, and decimals. The intent is to identify specific skill and fact weaknesses and to provide interpretation and categorization of errors that students make when working on problems of this nature. Finally, the skills tested are related to the major published basal mathematics programs.

There are four component tests in the inventory. The first is a Wide Range Placement Test that samples broadly across skills and is used to provide a starting point for the Skills Placement Tests. The second component consists of the Skills Placement Tests, which contain one item for each skill measured under thirteen skill headings ranging from addition of whole numbers to division of decimals. The third component, the Skills Tests, provide a five-item measure of each of the 144 skills in the inventory. The Tester Manual provides information on how to interpret the errors make on the Skills Test and where to find instructional materials for those skills in the major published instructional programs. Over 200 error patterns are identified and grouped into seven clusters. The fourth component is a set of Basic Facts Tests. These are four 50-item tests of the number facts. All components except for the Skills Tests have two forms. All items are free-response format.

The ENRIGHT Inventory is designed to be administered by teachers. It is somewhat daunting at first sight, but the instructions are clear and mastering the administration of the Inventory is more a matter of dedication than intellect.

A research and development report, which describes the development of the Inventory and provides some technical information, is available from the publishers. The skills and error patterns included in the test were generated through a 3-year study of 150 teachers and evaluated later by a second set of teachers and specialists. A content validity study was conducted to match items to objectives with three separate sets of judges. Reliability data are provided for the Skills Tests. Based on sample sizes between 80 and 100, these reliabilities range between .90 and .98. Reliabilities are not reported for the other tests. Given that the test is designed to be useful from grades 2 to 9, it would be very helpful to have reliabilities reported by grade level. Also, reliabilities for various subgroups of children (e.g., learning disabled) would be useful.

The Inventory requires some effort on the part of the examiner, both in administration and interpretation. The Tester Manual provides good descriptions and examples of the various errors that students might make. Successful interpretation of the Inventory requires the examiner, however, to review the student's work in order to reach a solid understanding of the student's strengths and weaknesses. Given that the Inventory requires review and interpretation as well as decision making related to when to stop testing, this measure seems an excellent candidate for computerization.

Overall, the Inventory appears to be a well-conceived and professionally-executed diagnostic tool that should be useful to classroom teachers who need a thorough assessment of students' strengths and weaknesses in basic arithmetic skills. The ENRIGHT® Diagnostic Inventory of Basic Arithmetic Skills would seem particularly appropriate to use in individual or small group settings such as remedial or compensatory programs. For the average student in the typical classroom, the level of detail and analysis contained in the Inventory may not be necessary. As long as a student is progressing well through a sound instructional program, precise diagnosis of difficulties may not be worth the effort. For those students for whom a more complete diagnosis is desired, the ENRIGHT® Inventory seems to be capable of delivering.

[109]

Evaluating Acquired Skills in Communication. Purpose: "Provides the examiner with a systematic tool for assessing a student's communication skills, a simple format for recording the student's performance, and a correlating means for translating that assessment data into an Individual Educational Plan." Language age 3 months to 8 years: mentally impaired, developmentally delayed, preschool language delayed, emotionally handicapped, autistic impaired; 1984, EASIC; 5 levels: Pre-Language (assesses skills prerequisite to meaningful speech), Receptive Level I (assesses skills at a beginning comprehension level), Expressive Level I (assesses skills at a beginning expressive level), Receptive Level II (assesses skills of those students who comprehend more complex semantic, syntactic, morphologic, and pragmatic functions), Expressive Level II (assesses skills of those students who are able to express at more complex levels of semantic, syntactic, morphologic, and pragmatic functioning); individual; other materials must be supplied by examiner; 1987 price data: $69.95 per instructor's manual (28 pages), stimulus picture test book, 54 supplementary picture cards, 142 goals and objectives file cards with dividers, 5 copies of each level test booklet, and 5 copies of each level skill profile; $24.95 per 20 test booklets and 20 skills profiles; administration time not reported; Anita Marcott Riley; Communication Skill Builders.*

Review of Evaluating Acquired Skills in Communication by BARRY W. JONES, Associate Professor of Communicative Disorders, San Diego State University, San Diego, CA:

Evaluating Acquired Skills in Communication (EASIC) is a competency-based informal communication skills inventory. The EASIC is divided into five levels designed for preschool children who are language impaired, mentally impaired, or autistic. Accompanying the inventory are instructionally-related objectives for each level. The levels are designated as 1) Pre-Language; 2) Receptive I; 3) Expressive I; 4) Receptive II; and, 5) Expressive II. With the exception of the Pre-Language level, the inventory and objectives address, at increasing difficulty levels, the areas of semantics, syntax, morphology, and pragmatics. The Pre-Language level "assesses skills prerequisite to meaningful speech."

The technical information related to this inventory was presented in three pages of the instructor's manual. Although a stimulus picture book and supplementary picture cards are provided to assist in the evaluation process, a number of additional common objects are required to administer the inventory. Materials provided to the consumer also include individual record sheets and skills profiles for each of the five levels and a collection of 4 x 6 cards with behavioral objectives for instructional purposes associated with each level.

Administration of the EASIC involves, first, the examiner deciding which of the five levels is most appropriate for the examinee. In order to make this determination the examiner would need to be very familiar with the content of the inventory and the child being assessed. The author provided very little information in the instructor's manual to assist with this decision. The number of items for each level ranges from 24 to 33; however, most of the items require multiple responses. Each item contains information on the targeted behaviors, materials necessary for administration of the item, and the stimuli to be provided by the examiner. The examiner presents the stimuli to the examinee and notes whether the child's responses were spontaneous, cued, imitated, manipulated, wrong, or if the child provided no response. Based on this information the examiner is to determine whether the identified skills are accomplished, emerging, or not yet developed and select appropriate educational goals and objectives.

As an assessment or evaluation tool this inventory leaves much to be desired. At the most basic level, the author presented no information relating to either the validity or reliability of the inventory. Even though the inventory is competency-based one should be able to expect, at a minimum level, information on the content validity of the materials. The instructor's manual, however, contains no bibliographic references for either the five-level taxonomy, the scoring procedure, or the items. In fact, the EASIC is entirely devoid of external references. Also, without reliability information one cannot have confidence in the consistency with which one could assess the identified skills.

In summary, the author has presented insufficient information to inspire confidence in the EASIC. More research is needed before teachers can trust either the results of the inventory or the instructional programs resulting from the evaluation.

Review of Evaluating Acquired Skills in Communication by ROBERT E. OWENS, JR., Associate Professor of Speech Pathology, State University of New York, Geneseo, NY:

Evaluating Acquired Skills in Communication (EASIC) is a nonstandardized informal communication inventory designed for preschool children. EASIC is designed specifically for use with language-impaired, mentally-retarded, and autistic preschoolers, although it was developed through work with autistic individuals only. The author states that the EASIC was developed through work with more than 200 autistic individuals who had an age span of 2–26 years.

The EASIC inventory is divided into five levels labelled Pre-Language, Receptive I, Expressive I, Receptive II, and Expressive II. At each level, syntactic, morphologic, semantic, and pragmatic aspects of language are assessed in a structured manner, although there is considerable overlap between these aspects. Individual test items are arranged from easy to difficult. The Pre-Language level assesses cognitive and social-communicative skills found in nonhandicapped children functioning below Piagetian sensorimotor stage five. This level incorporates many of the skills that the developmental literature considers to be important correlates to the development of symbol use (Owens, 1984). The Receptive I level includes understanding simple noun labels, basic verbs, locations, prepositional commands, primary adjectives and attributives, and basic questions. In the Expressive I level are noun labels, basic verbs, simple location indicators, and the use of primary sentence structures. Receptive II and Expressive II levels include more complex language, such as pronouns, negatives, adjectives of quantity and quality, interrogatives, money concepts, locational pronouns, plurals, and conversational skills. The tester selects the appropriate level for testing, although it is assumed that a child may have both receptive and expressive skills at a given level. Thus, this division is more arbitrary than functional.

There appears to be no organizing principle or rationale for the choice of items in levels I and II beyond the author's belief that the skills selected are important. No literature support is given to demonstrate that these receptive and expressive skills are important for either handicapped or nonhandicapped children. Some skills, such as two-word semantic-syntactic rules, are slighted, while others, such as coin denominations, have been included. The research literature clearly indicates the importance of early semantic-syntactic rules (Bloom & Lahey, 1978). In its defense, however, EASIC does sample a wide variety of communication skills.

In order to be more useful as a descriptive tool, EASIC has been designed to accommodate a variety of child responses and tester cues. For example, the child's response may be scored as spontaneous (S), cued (C), imitated (I), manipulated physically (M), nonresponsive (NR), or wrong/inappropriate (W). This system enables the tester to determine whether the skill is accomplished, emerging, or not developed. Goals and objectives for individualized educational plans are provided in EASIC for these conditions. Unfortunately, there is no similar coding system for the mode of the child's response, such as verbal, vocal-gestural, signed, and the like, although such a system could be easily devised by the tester. Given the variety of communication modes employed clinically with these children, such a notation system seems essential. The often idiosyncratic communication systems of these children, especially the autistic, are also overlooked, and a system of analysis of communication function, such as that suggested by Donnellan, Mirenda, Mesaros, and Fassbender (1984) would seem essential.

This idiosyncratic communication characteristic and the nonnormative design of the EASIC would seem to suggest an even more individualized tool than the one presented. Many diagnostic tools designed for early communication have recognized the individual nature of the content of this communication (MacDonald, 1978). This characteristic of highly individualized content is especially representative of autistic children, who may demonstrate interest in only limited topics initially. Similarly, the use of black and white pictures in EASIC may be too abstract for some children.

In general, EASIC offers a broad-based tool for use in describing the language of preschool children. EASIC is designed as an alternative to the more time-consuming task of collecting a communication sample but could best serve as a supplemental tool. Expansion of the response coding system and the use of individualized content would further expand EASIC's usefulness and applicability. The inclusion of IEP goal statements within EASIC is an added and needed aid for the tester and a good feature of the inventory.

REVIEWER'S REFERENCES

Bloom, L., & Lahey, M. (1978). *Language development and language disorders*. New York: John Wiley & Sons.

MacDonald, J. D. (1978). *Environmental Language Inventory*. Columbus, OH: Charles E. Merrill Publishing Co.

Donnellan, A., Mirenda, P., Mesaros, R., & Fassbender, L. (1984). Analyzing the communicative functions of aberrant behavior. *Journal of the Association for Persons with Severe Handicaps*, 9, 201-212.

Owens, R. (1984). *Language development: An introduction*. Columbus, OH: Charles E. Merrill Publishing Co.

[110]

Evaluating Communicative Competence, Revised Edition. Purpose: "Observe auditory processing, cognitive-linguistic, pragmatic, and stylistic behaviors that seem to enhance or detract from a student's 'communicative image.'" Language age 9–17; 1984–86; 21 tasks: the Interview, Identification of Absurdities in Sentences, Identification of Absurdities in Long Sentences and Paragraphs, Integration of Facts to Solve a Riddle, Comprehension and Memory for Facts, Comprehension of a Paragraph, Comprehension of Directions, Sequential Picture Storytelling, Maintenance of Past Tense in Storytelling, Maintenance of Present Tense in Storytelling, Tense Shifts Based on Introductory Adverbial Phrase, Semantically-Appropriate Use of Clausal Connectors, Stating Similarities and Differences Between Two Stimuli, Sequential Directions for Using a Pay Telephone, Description of Clothing and a Person, Explanation of the Relationship Between Two Items, Barrier Games, Twenty Questions, Creative Storytelling, Situational Analysis and Description, Expression and Justification of an Opinion; individual; some additional materials must be supplied by examiner; 1987 price data: $24.95 per 20 scoring forms; $59 per manual (175 pages), stimulus materials, blocks, 10 scoring forms and 12 picture cards; (60) minutes; Charlann S. Simon; Communication Skill Builders.*

Review of Evaluating Communicative Competence, Revised Edition by ROBERT E. OWENS, JR., Associate Professor of Speech Pathology, State University of New York, Geneseo, NY:

Evaluating Communicative Competence, Revised Edition is a criterion-referenced series of informal multimodality communication probes designed to assess the linguistic abilities needed by 9–17-year-olds for classroom and social discourse. These include auditory processing, metalinguistic skills, and pragmatic and stylistic behaviors. The procedures are designed for those children functioning in Piaget's Concrete Operational Stage and having a mean utterance length of 4.5 morphemes. The selection of tasks and the content rationale suggest that Evaluating Communicative Competence was constructed primarily for the child with a language learning disability. Thus, 7 of the 21 probes included in the procedure involve auditory processing.

The procedure is designed to fill the need for client data that is more conversationally-oriented than standardized tests and more focused but less time-consuming to collect than a conversational free sample. The author states clearly that "This is not a test." Rather, it is a format for obtaining specific descriptive data. According to the author, administration takes approximately 60 minutes. A shortened format is also presented that deletes some tasks from the longer procedure, although all auditory tasks are retained. No rationale is provided for the shorter form, which presumably is as valid as the full version. Several practice administrations are required in order to decrease administration time to the stated target of 60 minutes. This time does not include the extensive period needed for transcription and analysis of many of the responses. The volume of information contained in the manual and needed to administer the protocol is overwhelming. The author offers guidelines in order to ease the burden of familiarization and study. In addition, the Administration and Recording Form contains abbreviated instructions for each probe.

The procedure has received a rough validation of sorts. The author administered the procedure to 25 students from grades K–8 classified by their teachers as good communicators. These children were from Tempe, Arizona and may not be representative of the general United States population. No ethnocultural data on this sample are presented. The only evaluative data on these children were provided by classroom teachers' responses on the Loban Oral Language Scale, a 5-point, seven-category scale of oral language skills needed for success in the middle grades of elementary school (Loban, 1961). The author reports that by age 9, the children in the sample had sufficient control of language to perform within acceptable limits on the ECC probes. While the criterion-referenced nature of this procedure may negate the need for a large norming population, the conclusion that all tasks are within the capabilities of 9-year-olds based on a very limited sample of "good communicators" may be fallacious. In fact, one task, the appropriate use of clausal connectors, is, according to the author, designed for children above age 11. Although no other data are given on validity or reliability, the author suggests that concerns have been minimized by following the design criteria specified by Bennett (1982), such as representative tasks, relevant procedures, and specific criteria. In addition, the author specifies that at least two norm-referenced tests must be used in conjunction with the ECC in order to comply with P.L. 94-142.

The communication tasks chosen for assessment in Evaluating Communicative Competence are those which the professional literature states are valued within the educational system. These include comprehension, direction following, narrative construction, sequencing, description, questioning, and linguistic analysis. As with many evaluative procedures that attempt to isolate various processing modalities, the auditory-receptive probes usually require more than just isolated auditory skills.

While these probes could be designed individually by most knowledgeable clinicians, Evaluating Communicative Competence does provide a prepackaged integrated assessment tool with a formal method of administration. In general, the communication probe techniques used in the Evaluating Communicative Competence procedure provide a structured, time-efficient manner of collecting a comprehensive description of a child's language use within a conversational format.

REVIEWER'S REFERENCES

Loban, W. (1961). *Language ability in the middle-grades of elementary school.* Washington, DC: U.S. Office of Education.

Bennett, R. (1982). Cautions for the use of informal measures in the educational assessment of exceptional children. *Journal of Learning Disabilities,* 15, 337-339.

[111]

Evaluating Educational Programs for Intellectually Gifted Students. Purpose: "Designed to guide the evaluation of educational programming relative to the special educational needs of intellectually gifted students, grades K–12, that have been demonstrated to influence socioemotional and cognitive development." Learning environments for grades K–12; 1984; EEPIGS; ratings by educators; Form A: Socioemotional Needs, Form B: Cognitive Development and Intellectual Needs, Form C: Identified Program Strengths, Form D: Identified Program Weaknesses; 1985 price data: $20 per 50 copies of Forms A and B, 25 copies of Forms C and D, and administrative manual (14 pages); $6 per 50 Form A or Form B; $6 per 25 Form C and Form D; Joanne Rand Whitmore; D.O.K. Publishers, Inc.*

Review of Evaluating Educational Programs for Intellectually Gifted Students by LINDA E. BRODY, Assistant Director, Study of Mathematically Precocious Youth (SMPY), The Johns Hopkins University, Baltimore, MD:

The Evaluating Educational Programs for Intellectually Gifted Students (EEPIGS) scales were designed to assist school systems in evaluating how well their programs meet the needs of intellectually gifted students. The author suggests that the scales can be used for making decisions about the needs of an entire school system, one school, or an individual child. It is designed to assess needs prior to the implementation of special programs for the gifted, as well as for evaluative purposes during and after the development of special services.

The scales include four forms. Form A consists of a list of classroom characteristics related to the socioemotional needs of gifted students, and Form B includes classroom characteristics related to the cognitive development of gifted students. The evaluator is asked to assign a rating from 0 (*not at all*) to 3 (*regularly*) for each item listed based on the frequency with which the characteristic occurs in the program. A total score is computed for each of these scales based on 30 items.

Forms C and D are used to analyze the program strengths and weaknesses identified when Forms A and B are completed. A discussion should follow, and a plan of action for improving the program should be formulated. Then the plan should be reviewed by those affected, and revised if necessary. School systems are encouraged to use these outlined procedures only as a guide and to adapt the instrument to meet their own special needs.

The scales are an outgrowth of the author's extensive experience in designing and evaluating programs for underachieving gifted students. The program characteristics listed reflect the author's philosophical assumptions and beliefs about appropriate programming for gifted students, and these beliefs are listed in the manual. The rationale for the inclusion of each individual item on the scales is not included, however. Users of the instrument need to carefully consider whether the underlying assumptions and the program characteristics are consonant with their own beliefs about educational programming for the gifted and for the particular program being examined before electing to use this instrument.

These scales could be extremely valuable in encouraging schools to do a needs assessment prior to implementing a program for gifted students and also in encouraging schools to include an evaluative component in any program they develop. The inclusion of socioemotional considerations is particularly commendable because they are frequently overlooked in favor of only cognitive results.

I do have some concerns about the scales, however. Although the author encourages schools to adapt the scales for their own purposes, including adding to the list of characteristics, it may be that many schools will use the scales as a checklist and not make any changes. In fact, the computation of total scale scores encourages this. Thus, school systems may be likely to use the scales "as is" without considering whether they agree with the underlying philosophy that the scales reflect or whether the characteristics listed are appropriate for their purposes. Although the manual is well written, my feeling is that the person leading the evaluation may need training in the use of the instrument to ensure its appropriate use in a school's unique situation rather than as a simple checklist.

While traditional measures of validity, reliability, and normative data would not be appropriate for this type of process instrument, some research reporting on the effectiveness of these scales in promoting improvement in a variety of programs would be extremely helpful. The scales may be trying to do too much. It may not be possible to develop one instrument with universally agreed-upon objectives appropriate to evaluate programming for gifted students at all grade levels and in all subject areas. If, on the other hand, the success of the instrument depends upon extensive revision of the scales by school system personnel, a major advantage of the instrument (i.e., ease of administration), is lost.

In conclusion, although instruments are needed to assist schools in evaluating programs, I am not convinced that these scales can be used appropriately for all types of programs without considerable efforts by school personnel to adapt the scales to meet their own needs. If schools fail to make the necessary adaptations, there is danger that inappropriate decisions will be made concerning the programs under consideration. If schools do attempt to modify the instrument, there is reason to be concerned that school personnel may require training in order to do this effectively, and the scales lose their attractiveness as an easily administered instrument. Research is needed to identify the particular kinds of programs for which the scales would be appropriate. Meanwhile, schools are urged to use caution in adopting this instrument without a careful examination of the items.

Review of Evaluating Educational Programs for Intellectually Gifted Students by NICHOLAS COLANGELO, Professor and Chair of Counselor Education, University of Iowa, Iowa City, IA:

Evaluating Educational Programs for Intellectually Gifted Students (EEPIGS) is an instrument designed "to guide the evaluation of educational programming relative to the special educational needs of intellectually gifted students, grades K–12." The EEPIGS has four forms; however, only the first two of these contain items. Form A assesses the socioemotional needs of gifted youngsters, and Form B assesses cognitive development and intellectual needs. Forms C and D will be described later.

The instrument is an outcome of Whitmore's work with gifted underachievers. From this work she found that gifted students become highly motivated to achieve or become underachievers, to various degrees, in response to two sets of characteristics of learning opportunities: (*a*) socioemotional attributes of the learning environment; (*b*) characteristics of the instructional process and curriculum that affect the cognitive development of gifted students. The instrument comprises two scales (Form A and Form B) assessing the attributes of these forces that shape the classroom behavior of gifted students. The author states that both scales are equally important and should not be used separately.

Form A contains 30 items that can be responded to with 0 (*not at all*), 1 (*sometimes, on occasion*), 2 (*often*), 3 (*regularly*). An example of one item from Form A is: "The classroom is well structured for flexibility in learning activities."

Form B contains 30 items with the same 0–3 scale found in Form A. An example of an item from Form B is: "Students are challenged to think critically about what they hear and read and to develop their questioning skills."

It is suggested in the manual that items rated "2" or "3" could be considered a relative strength of the programs whereas ratings of "0" or "1" would signify weaknesses. Scoring for Forms A and B is to be done by adding the "numerical sum of the responses and divide by 30 to obtain the overall rating." It is stated on the forms that a minimally satisfactory score is 60 (or an overall rating of 2.0).

Two other forms are included: Form C is titled, Identified Program Strengths, and Form D is titled, Identified Program Weaknesses. Forms C and D are essentially blank pages divided in half where users of the instrument can list strengths and weaknesses of their program and list what should be done to correct the weakness or sustain the strengths.

The author states that the items for Forms A and B are research-based characteristics of classrooms that foster the full development of the academic potential of intellectually gifted students. However, there is nothing in the manual that gives evidence of the research basis for these items. There is a general reference to three books (Clark, 1983; Purkey, 1978; Whitmore, 1980) but no data on the items themselves. There is no information on how or why some items were selected and others excluded. Also, there is no indication of the relative importance of any single item or cluster of items; I find this a major problem. One can only assume that each item has equal influence. However, an overall score would not provide a sense of what *essential* elements are missing or present in a program.

The EEPIGS is essentially a needs assessment instrument. Instructions are well written and easy to follow. The items do tap a variety of issues in the affective and cognitive development of gifted youngsters.

In summary, EEPIGS is a process tool to help educators make decisions about the educational needs of gifted youngsters. The need for such an instrument is unquestionable. However, EEPIGS does not provide evidence for sound development of items and the scoring system and meaning of scores is ambiguous. The usefulness of the instrument is limited.

[112]

Family Relationship Inventory. Purpose: "Method of examining family relationships, designed to clarify individual feelings and interpersonal behavior." Young children, adolescents, and adults; 1974–82; FRI; based upon Family Relationship Scale; 2 scores: Positive, Negative, for each family member; may be administered individually or to family groups; 1988 price data: $50 per kit including item cards, 25 scoring forms, 50 tabulating forms, 50 individual relationship wheel forms, 25 familygram forms, and test manual ('82, 36 pages); $20 per set of item cards; $10.50 per 100 scoring forms; $5.50 per 50 tabulating forms; $50 per 500 individual relationship wheels, $5.50 per 50 familygrams; administration time not reported; Ruth B. Michaelson, Harry L. Bascom, Louise Nash, W. Lee Morrison, and Robert M. Taylor; Psychological Publications, Inc.*

Review of the Family Relationship Inventory by MARY HENNING-STOUT, Assistant Professor of Counseling Psychology, Lewis and Clark College, Portland, OR:

The Family Relationship Inventory (FRI) was developed to provide a measurement of interpersonal relationships and feelings within a family. This instrument represents positive movement away from isolating psychological distress within an individual and toward considering the functioning of human systems as they affect individual behavior. According to the manual, the FRI assesses each member's perceptions of, effects on, and behaviors toward each other family member.

The FRI is a revision of an instrument developed by Ruth Michaelson, whose position regarding the FRI is quoted in the manual: "A simple test of descriptive feelings and interactions can be constructed to differentiate positive and negative levels of distancing between self and members of a family." The current version of the FRI seems to add several ambitious features to the earlier version, claiming to measure the effects of one family member on another and to assess the behaviors related to interpersonal feelings family members have toward each other. While Michaelson's "levels of distancing" can be determined with this instrument, this reviewer had difficulty discerning how the additional measurements of interpersonal effect and behavior could be gained using the 1982 revision of the FRI.

ADMINISTRATION. The FRI is a 50-item scale composed of simple phrases describing personality characteristics and interpersonal behaviors (e.g., makes me happy, loves me, tells lies). There are 25 positive phrases and 25 negative phrases, each of which is printed on an individual card. The authors state that the FRI may be administered to individuals or family groups and that children as young as 5 years of age may be accurately assessed with the instrument.

Administration is somewhat complicated. Each individual is given a tabulation sheet onto which she or he records family members' names and then places pluses or minuses depending on the phrase card presented. Each card is presented by the examiner and the family members make independent marks on their tabulation sheets under the name of the person the phrase best describes. Pluses are recorded for positive phrases, minuses for negative phrases. The examiner must clarify whether a plus or minus should be recorded for a particular card.

When all items are administered, the examiner summarizes the results for each family member and records them on the graphic sheets provided with the inventory. These sums (positive and negative values) indicate each family member's interpersonal relationship with each other family member and his or her self-esteem level.

Two graphic sheets for recording the scores are provided with the FRI. The Individual Relationship Wheel allows for the responses made by one individual to be recorded. A second graphic, The Familygram, allows for recording all of the participants' responses on one page. Completing the Familygram amounts to transferring the main information from the Individual Relationship Wheels to one page filled with small Individual Relationship Wheels. The Familygram's consolidation of information seems to add confusion to information that can be kept separate and more meaningful by referring to the Individual Relationship Wheels. The one use of the Familygram would be as a tool for explaining the results to the family (i.e., completing the Familygram in the family's presence).

PSYCHOMETRIC PROPERTIES. Reliability of the FRI is discussed with reference to one test-retest effort. This reliability check involved 18 high school students (1 male and 17 females) who rated their families twice with a 2 1/2-week interval between ratings. The highest reliability rating was for siblings ($r = .90$); the lowest was for self ($r = .77$).

Because these results were based on a small, nonrepresentative sample, a convincing indication of the inventory's reliability has not been presented. Additional effort to measure internal consistency and develop some indication of agreement within the positive and negative item pools would greatly improve the psychometric strength of this instrument.

Validity of the FRI was demonstrated in four ways. First, the authors claimed broad professional acceptance of the FRI by "psychiatrists, psychologists, social workers, and marriage and family counselors throughout the United States." Although they gave no demographic descriptions of these mental health professionals, the authors suggested that this acceptance was a strong indicator of validity. While it is possible that the FRI has been useful to these practitioners, utility alone does not indicate that an instrument is measuring what it claims to measure. A more careful assessment of the actual usage of the FRI might strengthen this claim to validity.

The authors also reported their assessment of the content validity of the FRI. They described the item-selection process as beginning with 100 adjectives and phrases that were narrowed to the current pool of 25 positive and 25 negative phrases. Six licensed mental health professionals were asked to help with this process and, thereby, validate the inventory's content. The authors stated that they used "appropriate statistical techniques" to choose the final list. These techniques were not specified.

As a third indication of the scale's validity, the FRI self-esteem measure was compared to outcomes on Rosenberg's Self-Esteem Scale. The agreement between the two measures was sufficient to indicate criterion-related validity ($r = .55$, $p < .02$); however, the self-esteem measure on the FRI is just one of many measures obtained and seems to be less central to the interpretation of FRI results. Thus, this indication of criterion-related validity for a minor section of the FRI does little to strengthen claims for the scale's validity.

Finally, the authors attempted to illustrate validity by providing a long account of the differences in ratings relative to family position (mother, father, sister, brother, daughter, son, etc.). Based on a 1974 study of 40 client families in a California clinic, the authors made generalizations about the response tendencies of individuals in the various family roles. The small, nonrepresentative sample and the statements of response tendencies seem to provide inadequate indication of validity while potentially contributing to unsupported stereotyping.

PRACTICAL AND RESEARCH UTILITY. Until additional research can be done on the FRI to more clearly establish its psychometric properties, this inventory will be of limited research utility. The FRI's potential as a counseling tool seems far more promising. As the authors suggest, the FRI seems capable of serving as a tool for revealing and helping to clarify interpersonal problems in the family that had not formerly been articulated. In this way, the FRI could serve as a vehicle for initiating discussion of these problems.

The FRI would seem to be most useful at the beginning of a therapeutic relationship with a family. Because it can be administered in a game-like fashion, the FRI can facilitate therapeutic rapport building. While the FRI does provide information on the perceptions each family member has for the other members, additional interviewing and observation would be necessary for gathering more subtle information regarding power distribution, actual behaviors, and the functions those behaviors serve.

The authors of the FRI suggest its utility as a diagnostic aid. As with any instrument, the results of the FRI alone would not be sufficient for substantiating a diagnosis. The FRI might be helpful for developing a framework for early therapeutic intervention with a family. It would not seem to be useful for developing a clinical diagnosis.

In summary, the FRI seems to have utility as a counseling tool, particularly early in a therapeutic relationship with a family. Due to the lack of clear validity and reliability data, and small numbers of subjects in the norm group, the FRI is limited in its utility for clinical diagnoses and research. While the inventory does not seem to provide information on actual interpersonal behaviors and the effects one person has on other family members, it does retain the capacity to reflect levels of positive and negative perceptions held by family members with regard to each other. This information can be useful when building a program of therapeutic intervention with a family. If the limits of the FRI are acknowledged, it is likely that mental health professionals can find this instrument a useful tool for counseling with families.

[113]

Fast Health Knowledge Test, 1986 Revision. Purpose: "To measure discrimination and judgment in matters of health." High school and college; 1970–86; 11 scores: Personal Health, Exercise-Relaxation-Sleep, Nutrition, Consumer Health, Contemporary Health Problems, Substance of Abuse, Safety and First Aid, Disease Control, Mental Health, Family Life and Sex Education, Total; 1986 price data: $60 per 50 copies (administrative materials included with each order); 40(50) minutes; Charles G. Fast; the Author.*

For a review by James E. Bryan of the Fast-Tyson Health Knowledge Test, 1975 Edition, see 8:412.

Review of the Fast Health Knowledge Test, 1986 Revision, by LINDA K. BUNKER, Professor of Education, and Associate Dean for Academic and Student Affairs, Curry School of Education, University of Virginia, Charlottesville, VA:

The Fast Health Knowledge Test (FAST; previously called the Fast-Tyson Health Knowledge Test) is a norm-referenced knowledge test designed to evaluate 10 curricular areas: Personal Health; Exercise, Relaxation and Sleep; Nutrition; Consumer Health; Contemporary Health Problems; Substances of Abuse; Safety and First Aid; Disease Control; Mental Health; and Family Life and Sex. It uses a multiple-choice format that can be administered either individually or in a group setting. The authors suggest the test can be used with high school and college students.

The FAST test is purported to "measure discrimination and judgment in matters of health." However, it actually measures knowledge of diseases and health risks, with no evidence the items measure "judgment," or even attitudes or beliefs about health.

The 100 items have been typed and reproduced (not formally type-set or published). Tests may be purchased only in multiples of 50, ranging in price from $60 for 50 copies to $90 per 100 if over 500.

The total kit contains the 1986 Form C version of the test, scoring sheets, a two-page set of instructions, and a list of references in which the FAST has been cited. There are also two unpublished papers by the authors that provide limited additional data.

TEST ITEMS. The test items are comprehensive in breadth and related to major topics of health and illness. Most items are worded clearly and unambiguously.

Two areas of important health information are not represented, or are covered in a very limited fashion: accidents/suicide and smoking habits. Given the prevalence of teenage suicides, and the importance of promoting coping behaviors in teenagers, it would seem appropriate to address some questions to this area. Similarly, the fact that smoking habits, the major preventable cause of heart disease, may become established during these teenage years, would seem to suggest that it would be an important topic. There are also many other forms of substance abuse (e.g., anabolic steroids) that are not addressed in this test. In addition, several other important topics have been omitted including AIDS and compulsive eating behaviors (e.g., anorexia and bulimia; though item 35 uses these terms).

From the information provided by the authors, it appears that all items were developed prior to 1974. This may account for some of the questionable items. For example, item 57 asks about the type of dependence formed as a result of cocaine utilization (physical vs. psychological). This concept has evolved as understanding of addictive behavior and pharmacology has improved, with experts now suggesting that the distinction is somewhat arbitrary. In fact, many now believe that cocaine produces physical dependence, while the correct answer is keyed to psychological dependence.

Other examples of questionable items include item 24, which uses the phrase "oxygen debt." This term has generally been avoided in physiological research since the early 1970s, and therefore leaves the correct response ambiguous. Item 66 illustrates a problem in "foil" design as can be seen in 66C. Most students will see through any item with opposite elements (e.g., alcoholism and excellent nutrition). In addition, statistics now show that alcoholism is the number one cause of fatal automobile accidents. Therefore none of the answers appear to be correct for item 66.

PSYCHOMETRIC PROPERTIES. The author reports that norms for this test were derived from a sample of 25,000 college freshmen and 3,000 high school seniors representing a population of 140,000 and 14,000 students respectively. Given the wide band of developmental and cognitive levels of high school through college-aged students (ages 14–22), the sample provides a very limited basis (grades 12 and 13 only) from which to suggest norms are appropriate for all grade levels in high school and college (grades 8–16).

The normative data were collected from 12 states, most east of the Mississippi River. This seems to limit the generalizability of the norms.

Another questionable characteristic of the norms is their age. They were collected between 1964 and 1974. It would seem obvious to ask if the average knowledge level of students, and the relevant issues in personal health have changed over the past 15 years. It was also unclear as to whether subjects had any health background or previous coursework before completing the questionnaire. Unfortunately, the authors do not address this problem.

There is no information provided about item analyses for this multiple-choice test. It would be very helpful for the authors to provide such data in order to enhance the usefulness of the test, or provide for its modification.

The authors provide an unpublished paper entitled "A Value Added Program that Strives for Excellence: Competency Data on the Health Knowledge of Students Enrolled in PE 100, Health and Physical Fitness Concepts at Northeast Missouri State University, Kirksville, Missouri, Spring, 1986." This paper provides a model for the use of the test as a pretest to facilitate the design of a health-related course for college freshmen. In addition it provides some global data of the knowledge level of college students at one university.

TEST ADMINISTRATION RESTRICTIONS. Individuals wishing to administer this test must "indicate in writing that the test will be used only for diagnostic purposes that result in guided learning in the major health areas, and *shall never* be used to evaluate students or programs against raw score norms or to judge their competency for grades, diplomas, degrees, programs, licenses or entrance requirements." The rationale is that the authors cannot guarantee the validity and reliability if the "confidentiality of the test is not retained." It is unclear why such a promise should be required, rather than merely warning users of the test's limitation, which is true of any norm-referenced test if it is not properly used.

SUMMARY. In summary, the concept for this test is a good one, and may have been a reasonable inventory in the mid-70s. However, some of the items appear to be incorrect, issues out of date, and several important areas are not covered at all. I would therefore not recommend that it be used to assess student knowledge of important health issues in the 80s or 90s.

As is the case with many "health" inventories, this test focuses on diseases and health problems rather than health enhancement. It would seem that most educational programs for high school and college students should focus on the concepts of health promotion and personal responsibility.

[This reviewer wishes to acknowledge the assistance of Ruth Saunders, Assistant Professor of Health Promotion at the University of South Carolina.]

[114]

The First Grade Readiness Checklist. Purpose: To help parents determine a child's readiness for first grade. First grade entrants; 1972; upward extension of the School Readiness Checklist (T3:2090); handbook for both instruments entitled *Ready or Not?*; checklist to be used by parents; 1987 price data: $12 per 50 checklists (8 pages); $12 per *Ready or Not?* handbook ('72, 98 pages); administration time not reported; John J. Austin and J. Clayton Lafferty; Jastak Associates, Inc.*

Review of The First Grade Readiness Checklist by KATHRYN CLARK GERKEN, Associate Professor of Education, The University of Iowa, Iowa City, IA:

Salvia and Ysseldyke (1985) state that the purposes of readiness tests are to predict readiness for regular academic instruction or special programming for developing readiness skills. During the 1960s and 1970s, many different readiness tests appeared. Generally, these tests were administered before entry into kindergarten or first grade. The First Grade Readiness Checklist is one of these tests containing 54 questions grouped under seven headings: Growth and Age, General Activity Related to Growth, Practical Skills, Remembering, Understanding, General Knowledge, and Attitudes and Interests. The number of questions varies from 5 to 13 across areas.

There are no directions for completing the checklist in the four-page booklet entitled "Ready or Not." The booklet contains the checklist and statements regarding the purpose of the checklist, the concept of readiness for learning, and how to use the checklist.

The School Readiness Checklist Handbook serves as the manual for both the "School" and "First Grade" checklists. The Handbook contains information on the concept of readiness, the importance of parents and educators working together to determine school readiness, and educational programs that either should or do consider the readiness of the child when developing the program. Research findings on the School Readiness Checklist are presented in Parts Four and Five of the manual and copies of each checklist complete the manual.

The First Grade Readiness Checklist is compact and easy to complete. However, there are very few other reasons to choose this instrument to determine a child's readiness for first grade. The "Handbook" contains minor spelling and/or typographical errors (e.g., Table 1, p. 58, is missing a number) and is out-of-date in sexist language, inappropriate terminology (culturally deprived), resources cited, and programs described. There is no mention of the leverage, litigation, or legislation (e.g., P.L. 94-142) related to readiness testing. The Handbook lists new readiness instruments, yet all of the instruments listed are at least 20 years old. At a minimum, Parts One, Two, and Three would need to be revised to reflect recent findings regarding the concept of readiness, the programs that meet the needs of children who are at different levels, and the instruments available to assess readiness. Kindergarten is no longer a luxury in school districts but a mandated one-half or whole day program. Many school districts offer various options for kindergarten and first grade placements, ranging from segregated special education programs to alternative regular education programs.

This reviewer believes the authors were attempting to explain the theoretical basis for the instrument in Parts One and Two in the Handbook. However, nowhere is it clearly stated just how the checklist was developed other than the items are based upon data from child growth and development studies. Neither construct nor content validity is clearly addressed by the authors. There are no data presented indicating how the cutoff points for readiness were determined. There is also no information regarding the reliability of the instrument.

The only research information provided are the results of two studies conducted with the School Readiness Checklist rather than the First Grade Readiness Checklist. These two studies attempt to assess the predictive validity of the School Readiness Checklist. In the first study, the results of the checklist completed by parents in August of 1964 were compared to the kindergarten teachers' judgment of readiness in April of 1965 ($N = 278$). If the cutoff suggested by the authors (score of 30 or below = readiness doubtful) was used, then the checklist accurately predicted the teachers' judgment that a child was not ready for kindergarten for 4 out of 22 children (18%) and accurately predicted the teachers' judgment that a child would be ready for kindergarten for 255 out of 256 children (96%).

The researchers also chose to use a score of 36 as a cutoff (score of 35–39 = readiness very probable) and the checklist accurately predicted the teachers' judgment that a child would be ready for kindergarten for 77% of the children and accurately predicted the teachers' judgment that a child would not be ready for kindergarten for 59% of the children.

A follow-up study of 245 children was conducted in May of 1966 in which teachers were asked to rank each child in class (upper or lower half), indicate problems in reading and/or arithmetic, and indicate whether a child was to be retained. Of the 94 children who received checklist scores of 40 or above (score of 40–43 = readiness measurably assured), 23 children were ranked as being in the lowest half of their class and 4 were being recommended for retention. Of the 25 children who scored 34 or below on the checklist, 6 were ranked as being in the upper half of their class.

At best, these studies support the use of the School Readiness Checklist as a gross screening instrument, but provide no evidence regarding the usefulness of the First Grade Readiness Checklist.

Mercer (1979) stated that the prediction of which young children will experience school failure must be approached cautiously and thoroughly. The First Grade Readiness Checklist does neither. It is an instrument that is quick and easy to administer, but lacks needed evidence of reliability and predictive validity. The information provided supports use of the checklist as an informal instrument at best. However, if one is going to use an informal checklist, a specific checklist related to a particular school district or classroom activity would be more appropriate. If a school district or classroom teacher wants to know how well a child will do in first grade compared to other children his/her age, then a norm-referenced instrument with adequate psychometric properties should be selected. The 1986 edition of the Metropolitan Readiness Tests (MRT; Nurss & McGauvran, 1986), is but one example of a good measure of academic readiness for kindergarten or first grade.

REVIEWER'S REFERENCES

Mercer, C. D. (1979). *Children and adolescents with learning disabilities*. Columbus, OH: Merrill Publishing Co.

Salvia, J., & Ysseldyke, J. E. (1985). *Assessment in special and remedial education* (3rd ed.). Boston: Houghton Mifflin.

Nurss, J. R., & McGauvran, M. E. (1986). *Metropolitan Readiness Tests, Levels 1 and 2, Norms Booklet*. San Antonio: The Psychological Corporation.

Review of The First Grade Readiness Checklist by MARIBETH GETTINGER, Associate Professor of Educational Psychology, University of Wisconsin-Madison, Madison, WI:

The First Grade Readiness Checklist was developed for parents as a systematic method for evaluating the readiness of a child for entry into first grade. This 54-item checklist is an extension of The School Readiness Checklist (43 items), which is a kindergarten entry-level checklist. Both checklists are described in one spiral-bound handbook entitled *Ready or Not?*. The checklist can be completed and scored by parents in an estimated 20 minutes. The items are worded as questions (e.g., "Can your child put together a simple puzzle of 6 to 12 pieces?") to which parents simply respond "yes" or "no." Items are grouped under seven general headings: growth and age; general activity related to growth; practical skills; remembering; understanding; general knowledge; and, attitudes and interests. The checklist is scored by tallying the number of items receiving a "yes" response. The authors provide an interpretive table for translating the obtained score (number of "yes" items) into two types of information relative to first-grade placement: (*a*) an "approximate state of readiness for first grade" ranging from "readiness unlikely" (40 or below) to "readiness reasonably assured" (50 to 54), and (*b*) a "possible action," including first-grade placement or consultation with the school concerning other placement options and/or further testing.

The accompanying handbook (77 pages excluding the checklists) has four sections that (*a*) explain the authors' concept of readiness, (*b*) provide a justification for basing kindergarten-entry decisions on both parents' and teachers' perceptions of a child's readiness (*not* age), (*c*) describe educational programs that "respect readiness" (i.e., early childhood approaches, such as the nongraded primary school, that individualize education to match children's readiness levels), and (*d*) present the results of two studies that compare The School Readiness Checklist (kindergarten checklist) with teacher ratings and standardized tests. As such, the handbook cannot be viewed as a manual per se for The First Grade Readiness Checklist. Nonetheless, in that this handbook provides the only available information concerning the development, validation, and utilization of the checklist, it is important to evaluate the information it presents.

Prior to critiquing the specific content of the handbook, however, there are some general concerns to point out—the most obvious being that the information is clearly out of date. The reference citations are primarily from the 1950s and 1960s (and earlier). What are presented as "new programs" (e.g., Head Start, nongraded primary school, early special education) and "new readiness instruments" (e.g., ABC Inventory, Adair & Blesch, 1964; Preschool Inventory, Caldwell & Soule, 1965; School Readiness Survey, Jordan & Massey, 1967) are at least 20 years old. This renders most of the handbook—especially the first three parts—quite limited in terms of its usefulness and accuracy. Another overall concern is that the handbook, in general, is weak in terms of organization and writing. There are several grammatical errors (e.g., "the data is"; "conditions that have effected children"); transitions between paragraphs and sections are weak; and, occasionally, the writing style is too colloquial (e.g., "for those readers . . . who tend towards compulsivity when it comes to scientific methods, a Chi-square check revealed significance at the .01 level").

Aside from these general concerns, the handbook offers very little information (and, in some instances, no information) about the item development, standardization, reliability, or predictive validity of the checklist, and, therefore, it falls considerably short of APA-AERA-NCME standards. According to the authors' instructions to parents, each of the items on the scale is based on "data from child growth and development studies"; however, the handbook provides no evidence of this. In fact, the content validity of some items appears highly questionable (at least for the 1980s). For example, crossing "a major street or highway intersection with or without the aid of a traffic light" or traveling "alone in neighborhood (4–8 blocks) to store, school, playground, or to friend's home" are items to which many parents of developmentally mature 5- and 6-year-old children would probably respond "no." Furthermore, the placement of items in a particular category does not appear to be based on any empirical or research evidence. For example, it is not clear why drawing a square is characterized as "understanding" whereas drawing and coloring a design is a "general activity related to growth." The School Readiness Checklist (kindergarten version) was initially developed "for use in a voluntary program designed to help parents answer the question of school entrance for themselves." There is virtually no information provided in the handbook concerning the number of parents, their socioeconomic status, geographic location, or racial-ethnic status, and age or gender children for whom the checklists were completed.

There are no predictive validity data available in the handbook for The First Grade Readiness Checklist. Evidence for the predictive validity of The School Readiness Checklist was obtained by comparing results of the checklist completed by parents of children entering kindergarten in September ($n = 278$) with teachers' perceptions 7 months later of children's readiness for kindergarten and likelihood of succeeding in first grade. A total of 23 children did not evidence readiness according to teachers; of these, 4 (only about 17%) were tagged as "readiness doubtful" or "readiness unlikely" on the basis of the checklist. This low percentage is not surprising given the apparent ambiguity surrounding the interpretive labels ascribed to obtained scores on the checklist. For example, a child's readiness is "questionable" if his/her score ranges from 31 to 34, whereas readiness is "doubtful" if the score ranges from 26 to 30.

In summary, in view of the inadequacy of supportive research concerning the development and validation of this checklist as well as the out-of-date information upon which the scale was based, I do not recommend The First Grade Readiness Checklist be used by parents to obtain an objective appraisal of their child's readiness for first grade. Information from this checklist does not appear to be an accurate predictor of a child's stage of readiness and can be misleading for parents considering first-grade placement issues.

REVIEWER'S REFERENCES

Adair, N., & Blesch, G. (1965). The ABC Inventory to Determine Kindergarten and School Readiness. Muskegon, MI: Research Concepts.

Caldwell, B. M., & Soule, D. (1965). Preschool Inventory. Princeton, NJ: Educational Testing Service.

Jordan, F. L., & Massey, J. (1967). School Readiness Survey. Palo Alto, CA: Consulting Psychologists Press, Inc.

[115]

Fisher Language Survey (and Process). Purpose: Assesses "the learning abilities of a pupil from use of the auditory and visual learning channels." Grades 1–8; 1978–84; FLS; "criterion-referenced"; 15 tests: Grade 1, second semester–Grade 8, second semester; 1985 price data: $7.75 per complete survey including record forms, profile forms, and manual ('84, 40 pages); $5.25 per 30 record forms; $2 per 10 profile forms; $2.75 per manual; (5–30) minutes; Alyce F. Fisher; Stoelting Company.*

Review of the Fisher Language Survey (and Process) by THOMAS W. GUYETTE, Assistant Professor of Communication Disorders and Sciences, Rush-Presbyterian-St. Luke's Medical Center, Chicago, IL:

The Fisher Language Survey (and Process) (FLS) tests the ability of a person to write sentences dictated by an examiner. The author describes it as "a test of auditory reception with written expression on the part of the pupil." This test was developed to assess students' learning abilities using the auditory and visual channels. The FLS is to be used as a pre-post test with one administration given in the early fall and one in the late spring of the school year. The test can be administered in either group or individual sessions. The target population is school-age children between the first and eighth grades.

Instructions for administering the FLS are clearly written and complete. Instructions for scoring are sometimes confusing. For example, in the scoring section of the test manual it is stated that "EACH AND EVERY error marked on the Fisher Language Survey counts one point." However, on each of the pages that presents the sentence stimuli it is stated that "One error is counted for each word misspelled, omitted, substituted, or added" suggesting that the total number of errors is not greater than the total number of words. These two methods of scoring result in different outcomes, and when interpretation criteria are mentioned later in the test manual it is not always clear upon which method of scoring they are based.

Validity and reliability data are presented in the FLS manual. In the section on Predictive Validity the author reports that "FLS scores correlated with the classroom teacher's estimate of a pupil's instructional reading level at about .70." Interpretation of this information is difficult for the following reasons. First, statements about predictive validity usually involve determining how well scores on a particular test allow prediction of future performance on a criterion variable (Carmines & Zeller, 1979). In other words, predictive validity usually involves a time interval and no time intervals were mentioned in this section. Second, information on the population sample and study design was not reported.

In the section on Concurrent Validity—Construct Validity the author reports "The FLS and the PEP [Pupil Evaluation Program] tests correlate with each other at .60, which suggests that they are related to each other but are not identical." Again, the FLS manual does not state the sample size, composition of the sample, nor give any relevant features of the study design.

Test-retest reliability data are reported. As with the validity research, the number of pupils involved, their ethnic backgrounds, which statistics were used, and how the study was designed are not reported. Without knowing some of this critical information it is impossible to judge the significance of the test-retest reliability data.

Guidelines for interpretation of the test results are ambiguous. For example, the author states that "It has been found that when the percentage of errors is high and when errors are in several categories, the student should be considered for remediation services." However, the author does not define a "high" level of error. Also, although the author talks about failing the FLS, the cutoff score for failure is unclear. At one point the manual reports that "25% significant errors, or above, USUALLY correspond with poor to severe reading disability." In "Chart 2" the cutoff for failure appears to be 10%; however, the reviewer was unable to confirm this with a statement in the text. The test manual does not present data in support of either cutoff point (10% or 25%). Test norms are not presented.

In summary, the FLS is a test of a student's ability to write down sentences from dictation. The directions for administration are clear. Although some validity and reliability data are presented, the FLS manual does not contain sufficient descriptive information regarding test support data. Guidelines for interpretation of test scores are ambiguous and empirical justification for using these guidelines is not present.

REVIEWER'S REFERENCE

Carmines, E. G., & Zeller, R. A. (1979). *Reliability and validity assessment*. Beverly Hills: Sage Publications.

Review of the Fisher Language Survey (and Process) by KATHRYN W. KENNEY, Clinical Supervisor in Speech-Language Pathology, Department of Speech and Hearing Science, Arizona State University, Tempe, AZ:

The Fisher Language Survey (and Process) (FLS) is a criterion-referenced test designed to answer the question: "How does a pupil cope with language when it is heard and has to be written?" The FLS consists of sentence dictation tests, teacher evaluation of reading and math based upon classroom performance, and teacher report of handedness and penmanship. There are two sentence dictation tests per year for grades 2 through 8. The first grade test, administered only once, consists of two forms that vary in difficulty. The first and second grade tests contain three and five sentences and five and eight sentences, respectively. For grades 3 through 8 each test contains 10 sentences.

Children's written sentences are scored for the following competencies: short vowels, blends, digraphs, spelling rules, capitals, periods vs. question marks, handwriting, reversals of letters within words, omissions or additions of letters in words, and other miscellaneous errors.

VALIDITY. The authors report the FLS has high predictive validity. The FLS correlated with classroom reading performance, as evaluated by the teacher, "at about .70." Concurrent validity was addressed by correlating the FLS with the Pupil Evaluation Program (PEP), a test of reading comprehension administered in New York State requiring students to answer questions after reading brief paragraphs. The correlation between the PEP and the FLS was .60. The author suggests that the FLS and PEP are complimentary methods of assessing a child's reading skills. Specific data concerning the number of students, the number of teachers, and the test form used for analyses of validity are not reported in the manual.

Content validity is presumed because the words and sentences used in the FLS are reported to be similar to those found in primary texts. No details regarding the texts from which words or sentences were selected are provided.

RELIABILITY. Test-retest reliability for grades 1 through 8 combined was .94. Test-retest reliabilities of .40 and .83 were reported for the two first-grade tests. Although no correlations were reported for grades 2 through 8, the reliability for third grade was characterized as "somewhat" lower than for these other grades. A standard error of measurement of 1.5 was reported for students in grades 2 through 8. Information concerning the subjects or procedures for these studies are not reported in the manual.

NORMATIVE DATA. The FLS was designed as a criterion-referenced test. The author reported that the FLS has been used with over 6,000 students in five schools within four school districts. She provides descriptive data for only 539 children from grades 1 through 4, 130 to 140 children at each grade level with boys and girls represented equally. For each of the four grade levels the author reports the number and percentage of students who: are left-handed, have poor handwriting, failed the FLS plus had poor reading ability as judged by their teacher, passed the FLS but had poor reading ability by teacher judgement, failed the FLS but had average or above reading ability according to their teacher, combined across categories were below average, and combined across categories were average or above. These data are not available for grades 5 through 8.

Longitudinal data are provided for students who were followed from the end of first grade to the end of fourth grade during a 3-year period from May 1975 to May 1978. The number of students at each test date ranged from 135 to 119. Data included: the number and percentage of students who failed the FLS, the number and percentage of students who had below average reading ability based upon teacher judgement, the combined percentage who failed the FLS or were judged below average in reading, and the percentage of students average or above in reading.

USE OF TEST. The FLS can be group or individually administered at the end of first grade and as a pretest in the fall and a posttest in the spring for grades 2 through 8. Each error on the sentence dictation is marked and counts as one point. The sum of these errors is the raw score. A Significance Table is provided for each test to transform the raw score into a percentage score. Percentage scores of 10% or more are considered significantly below average. A score of 25% or greater represents severely deviant reading or writing. Empirical rationales for these cutoff scores are not provided.

Children's scores on the FLS are ranked from best to worst to construct a class profile. The profile is used to modify the curricula and/or identify students who can benefit from special assistance. The author recommends a priority list for children needing assistance: First priority, a severe deficit in reading and writing (25% or more errors on FLS); Second priority, poor teacher rating in reading but a passing score on the FLS; Third Priority, failure on the FLS, but a satisfactory teacher rating in reading; and Fourth priority, passing score on the FLS, satisfactory teacher rating in reading, but an unsatisfactory teacher rating in math.

SUMMARY. The FLS is a criterion-referenced test of sentence dictation for first through eighth grades that can be group or individually administered. A percent error score of nine or less is considered passing. A classroom profile is constructed by ranking the children's FLS scores. This profile can be used to tailor the curriculum or provide referrals for children who need special assistance. Information concerning the validity and reliability of the FLS is incomplete. Teachers interested in a criterion-referenced test of sentence dictation may want to consider the FLS but should be aware that continued research into its psychometric characteristics is needed.

[116]

The Five P's (Parent/Professional Preschool Performance Profile). Purpose: Helps to "systematically collect information regarding the child's current level of functioning" and "establish a data base for the IEP." Handicapped children functioning between the ages of 6 and 60 months; 1982–87; ratings by parents and teachers; 13 scales in 6 areas of development: Classroom Adjustment, Self-Help Scales (Toileting and Hygiene, Mealtime Behaviors, Dressing), Language Development (Communicative Competence, Receptive Language, Expressive Language), Social Development (Emerging Self, Relationships to Adults, Relationships to Children), Motor Development (Gross Motor/Balance/Coordination Skills, Perceptual/Fine Motor Skills), Cognitive Development/Skills; individual; 1987 price data: $125 per materials for class of 10 children including 20 sets of behavior scales, 10 graphic profiles, 10 IEP forms, 12 Five P's manuals ('87, 46 pages); $48 per specimen set including behavior scales, graphic profile, Individualized Education Program forms, Five P's Manual; Judith Simon Bloch and John S. Hicks (technical manual only); Spanish edition available; Hebrew translation of older edition available; (120) minutes; Variety Pre-Schooler's Workshop.*

Review of The Five P's (Parent/Professional Preschool Performance Profile) by BARBARA PERRY-SHELDON, Associate Professor of Education, North Carolina Wesleyan College, Rocky Mount, NC:

DESCRIPTION. The Five P's (Parent/Professional Preschool Performance Profile) is an assessment tool to be used by parents and teachers twice a year in gathering data about children with language, learning, or behavior problems whose performance level is below 5 years. The ratings are used to develop an Individual Education Program (IEP) for each child. Several materials comprise the Five P's: a manual that includes a glossary and describes the purpose, format, and rating system; five assessment booklets; a profile page; IEP forms; and a technical manual. Included in the review packet were articles written by persons involved in the development of the Five P's. Consolidation of the articles, the technical manual, and the instructional manual into one handbook would create a better organized set of materials.

According to the manual, the Five P's consists of 13 scales representing 6 areas of development organized into five booklets. Positive behaviors, grouped by age norms in months, are listed first in each booklet followed by interfering behaviors. There is also space for comments. The age norms are useful to parents who may need some guidance in understanding normal development. Behaviors are coded by the school and home caregiver in the fall and spring.

ADMINISTRATION/SCORING. The primary caregivers (usually, parents and teachers) must study the scales carefully, observe the child in the home or school environment, interact with the child using suggested items (e.g., scissors, blocks, pictures), and then complete the ratings in a 2-week period early in the school year and again 6 months later. It is implied or assumed that all scales are to be completed for the child. The behaviors are coded Y (yes-always/usually true), S (sometimes true), or N (never/rarely true). The person completing the scales is cautioned against assuming a child's capability and giving too high a rating.

Although not difficult to accomplish, the ratings are time consuming. The manual provides examples to help complete the Five P's. The 1982 handbook outlined a 3-hour training program for both parents and teachers to consist of studying the materials and the completion of a practice rating of a 4-year-old autistic child presented by film. The use of training seems very appropriate but it is not described in the 1987 materials. No information is available on parental willingness to participate in such training.

After the ratings are completed, parents and teachers share their ratings so that each has a complete record. The teacher then completes the Graphic Profile, a bar graph, that visually shows the positive and interfering behaviors and compares home and school ratings. The data are then used to develop an IEP each fall and spring. The IEP lists the current level of functioning and long and short term goals that may be the exact items from the Five P's.

TECHNICAL DEVELOPMENT. The technical manual describes preliminary analyses of the scales for validity and reliability. The developer contends that content validity is supported by two things. One is that items from literature on child development were used to develop the Five P's, and that it was used and continuously revised by the staff of the Variety Pre-Schooler's Workshop. A stronger support would have been the judgment of experts not involved in the Workshop.

A concurrent validity study involving 41 children is included in the review packet. Each of the 5 subscale areas was compared to matching parts of other assessment instruments such as the Preschool Attainment Record, California Preschool Competency Scale, Beery's VMI, Burks Behavior Rating Scale, and the McCarthy. Significant correlations were found, and the strengths of the correlations tend to support concurrent validity of the Five P's.

Using a sample of ratings from 132 boys and 40 girls enrolled at the Workshop, a correlation of age to the items yielded correlations below +.40. This tends to support the developer's contention that the scales do assess non-normal behavior. A factor analysis, reported in detail in the 1982 materials, supports the construct validity of the scale areas. The sample ratio of boys to girls seems high, but more boys are identified as having special needs than are girls. Both the mean and median ages of the children were about 60 months; the sample needed to include more younger children. Other than gender and age no descriptive data are provided about the children.

Several reliability studies using small samples yielded coefficients primarily above .80 with several above .90. Limited test-retest studies yielded coefficients in the .80s and .90s. Further study of all scales is needed with larger samples.

Limited, but positive data regarding interrater reliability were reported. Additional independent testing in many other settings and with younger children is needed.

SUMMARY. The Five P's does seem to be a very promising assessment instrument especially with the new mandates for serving preschool handicapped children in the public schools. Its focus is on assessment of functioning and not labeling. The ratings are intended to supplement clinical or comprehensive evaluations. Whether the Five P's would distinguish the handicapped from the nonhandicapped would be a question for study.

The content and organization of the rating scales are appropriate for assessing handicapped preschoolers or developmentally delayed children. As a data base for writing goals for an IEP, it covers the critical developmental areas. Teachers and parents would still need to carefully plan or select activities for helping the children reach the goals.

The length of the Five P's, 458 items, and the possible need for parent training are two limitations. Cost is another factor. Because most validity and reliability studies involved the Pre-Schooler's Workshop, it would be helpful to prospective users to have more information about the nature of the program, type of families served, workers, etc. Initial validation and reliability studies support its use, but further empirical work is needed.

[117]

Fixing My Food. Purpose: Evaluates elementary school students' application of the nutrition behaviors of selecting, preparing, and serving food. Grades 1–6; 1985; price data for complete set including manual (8 pages), test, and answer key available from local Dairy Council; (15–40) minutes; National Dairy Council and Iowa State University; National Dairy Council.*

[Note: The publisher advised in April 1989 that this test will be discontinued.]

Review of Fixing My Food by HAZEL M. FOX, Professor of Human Nutrition, Emeritus, University of Nebraska-Lincoln, Lincoln, NE:

Fixing My Food is described as a practical and reliable instrument for evaluating elementary school students' application of the nutrition behaviors of selecting, preparing, and serving food. The behaviors relate to the topic of food handling. The concepts identified as basic to the above nutrition behavior are food quality, cleanliness, and personal safety. Behaviors that would demonstrate understanding and use of the concepts are defined as selecting and inspecting food quality prior to using food, storing and preparing food under clean and safe conditions, and maintaining sanitary serving conditions.

In developing the test, elementary food and nutrition guides and textbooks were consulted to identify the test behaviors. Elementary school students (grades 1–6) were interviewed with regard to their behaviors using different instrument formats (e.g., verbal stories with a puppet demonstrating a behavior, written stories with pictures and cartoons depicting the behavior and concept). Because the cartoon format appeared to be most appealing to the students and an effective method of helping students identify with the situations, cartoons were chosen as the vehicle to be used in the evaluation instrument.

The cartoon format was subsequently used in two pilot tests in which multiple-choice options were generated from student responses. A third pilot test was conducted with 419 students in grades 1, 3, 4, and 5 in five schools in 20 classrooms. Responses from this evaluation were analyzed and discrimination indices for each cartoon were calculated by grade level to determine appropriateness of individual items for the various grades.

Finally, Fixing My Food was field-tested with 1,673 students in grades 1 through 6. Schools were in 10 different states and represented low, middle, and high socioeconomic levels, as well as various racial and ethnic backgrounds. Various numbers of cartoons were assigned to different age groups reflecting different levels of maturity and attention span. Grade 1 was assigned 18 cartoons, grade 2, 20 cartoons, grades 3–4, 24 cartoons, and grades 5 and 6, all 26 cartoons. Nine items were classified as measurements of food quality, eleven items, measures of cleanliness, and six items, personal safety.

Content validity was confirmed by three nutrition and education specialists who verified that items conformed to the test plan and reflected accurate nutrition information.

Difficulty was assessed by determining percentage of students at each grade level answering the questions correctly. The average difficulty ranged from 68% to 73% in the six grades compared to a more desirable average difficulty score of 66%. The discrimination index, that is the ability of a test item to differentiate between students with a high total score and those with a low total score, was above .20 at all grade levels. An index of .20 is acceptable for this type of test.

Reliability of the test ranged from .75 in grades 1 and 2 to .87 in grade 6, indicating the test was consistent and would yield the same results if given again.

A Kuder Richardson formula 20 coefficient of internal consistency of .75 was obtained. Mean test scores together with standard deviations are presented for each grade level. Means vary from 12.2 ± 3.6 in grade 1 to 18.9 ± 5.5 in grade 6. These scores serve as a valuable basis of comparison when the test is used with similar groups.

The test appears to have been developed in a conscientious, thorough manner with suitable safeguards used to insure content validity and reliability. Face validity of the test items, however, is questionable. The title, Fixing My Food, appears somewhat misleading in that it does not accurately depict the nature of the content of the test material. The authors state they are measuring the nutrition behaviors of selecting, preparing, and serving food. Somehow this statement conveys the idea of assembling, washing, cutting, peeling, cooking food or presenting the prepared food to an intended eater. It is surprising, then, to discover the test does not deal at all with these concerns. The emphasis of the test material is definitely on sanitation and cleanliness, not on skills needed to prepare the food for eating. Health concerns are much more prominent than nutrition concerns, and while nutrition is part of health, it is only one aspect; food and nutrition as they relate to bodily functions are not dealt with in this test.

Moreover, while food quality and cleanliness are differentiated as separate concerns with different test items designated as measuring these concepts, it is extremely difficult to discriminate between these concepts. Most of the food quality test items refer to cleanliness of the food (e.g., washing the top of the can, washing apples before eating, not eating food that has been dropped on the floor, and not storing food items with cleaning supplies). Cleanliness, on the other hand, refers to personal hygiene (e.g., not using another person's spoon, washing hands before eating, not drinking from another person's glass). Certainly sanitation is an important aspect of food handling, but is is only one concern and does not deal with the total process of food preparation. It seems to be an extremely narrow focus and even somewhat trite. It seems the developers were overly concerned with process and although meticulous in evaluating the test, they lost sight of the real goal and gave too little attention to the subject matter of the test items.

In summary, although the test has some strengths, the over attention to cleanliness and sanitation concerns with food preparation and virtual neglect of nutritional concerns is a great weakness.

Review of Fixing My Food by C. ALAN TITCHENAL, Nutrition Education Consultant, Office of School Food and Nutrition Services, Long Island City, NY:

The focus of this test is the evaluation of behaviors relating to food handling concepts such as food quality, cleanliness, and personal safety. Each test question is presented in a cartoon format depicting a situation that involves either selecting, storing, preparing, serving, or consuming food. Three potential responses to the situation are given with each cartoon. Students are asked to select the answer that is most similar to what they would say in the given circumstance. For example, one typical cartoon is an illustration of a boy offering another boy a glass of milk. The first boy says to the other, "You may have a drink of my milk." Three responses listed for the other boy are, "A. Thank-you, I'm thirsty. B. I don't want to drink from your glass. C. That's nice of you."

As in the above question, correct responses are often negative or curt statements. The incorrect responses listed in each question were determined by using those given most often by students during field testing. One apparent result of this approach is that the incorrect or inappropriate responses are frequently unrelated to food handling and are often expressions of courtesy such as, "May I help?" or "That's nice of you." An incorrect response, therefore, may not always be an incorrect statement. Rather, it is just not the *best* response from the perspective of food handling. Consequently, an incorrect response may not always indicate that the student does not *know* the correct thing to do. Rather, it may only reflect the extent of concern a student has for matters unrelated to food handling.

Perhaps it would be more appropriate for all three response options in a question to have an equal level of courtesy. For example, if the correct response to the question above said, "Thank-you, but I shouldn't drink from your glass," it would have the same level of courtesy as the inappropriate responses. This would allow assessment of food handling behavior without it being confounded by any considerations of manner or courtesy.

The test length varies with the grade of students being tested, allowing the test to be appropriate for a broad range of ages. For example, first grade students answer the first 18 cartoons, whereas sixth grade students answer all 26 cartoons. The test materials state that thorough field testing was conducted with students of diverse socioeconomic, racial, and ethnic backgrounds. However, situations and conditions depicted in the cartoons are those typical of the United States middle class. Normative data, derived from field testing of over 250 students in each grade level, are presented in test materials to assist the instructor in test score interpretation. Reliability coefficients based on this data are at or above .75 for all grade levels, indicating acceptable test performance repeatability.

Content validity of this test was established by a panel of nutrition and education specialists. They certified the questions conformed to the test plan and reflected accurate nutrition information. The lack of criterion-related validity raises questions as to the true value of the test results and the extent to which they represent actual behavior. One means of validation could involve comparison of student's test responses to their responses in the actual situations depicted in the cartoons.

Test content is based on basic information that should provide a reasonable assessment of food handling behavior. Combined changes in knowledge, awareness, and behavior can be evaluated using a pretest/posttest approach to assess teaching effectiveness. The highly visual presentation of information in a cartoon format should facilitate administration to a broad range of ages and language fluencies. An instrument of this type with appropriate objective validation could be a very powerful and reliable tool to assess behavior and behavioral change.

[118]

Food Choice Inventory. Purpose: Assesses food choice behaviors of junior and senior high school students and adults. Junior and senior high school students and adults; 1985; 9 scales: Will Eat (HIGH Nutrient-Value Foods, LOW Nutrient-Value Foods, TOTAL Foods), Like But Try Not to

Eat (HIGH Nutrient-Value Foods, LOW Nutrient-Value Foods, TOTAL Foods), Will Not Eat (HIGH Nutrient-Value Foods, LOW Nutrient-Value Foods, TOTAL Foods); price data for complete set including inventory manual (11 pages), scoring overlay, and group record sheet available from local Dairy Council; (4–10) minutes; National Dairy Council and University of Illinois at Chicago; National Dairy Council.*

Review of the Food Choice Inventory by C. ALAN TITCHENAL, Nutrition Education Consultant, Office of School Food and Nutrition Services, Long Island City, NY:

The Food Choice Inventory (FCI) was developed to assess nutrition education needs or program effectiveness. It provides a quick and abbreviated view of individual and group food choice as an estimate of nutritional quality of the diet. Most dietary assessment tools require a high level of respondent cooperation in recording foods (diet records), remembering foods (dietary recall), or estimating usual consumption of many foods (food frequency questionnaire). These types of demands have been minimized in the FCI at the necessary expense of detailed nutrient information. This, however, provides a simple means of estimating nutritional quality of individual or group food intake by the analysis of food choice. Nutrition education program effectiveness can be assessed by comparing the results of a posttest to those of a pretest.

The FCI uses a list of 40 foods, including familiar foods (eggs, milk, bread), foods about which people often feel either strongly negative or positive (cauliflower, quiche, grits), and foods reflecting different ethnic cultures (gyros, ham hocks, cannoli). Twenty-five of these foods are classified as HIGH Nutrient-Value items and 15 are classified as LOW Nutrient-Value items. This classification is based on the concept of nutrient density (nutrient to calories ratio). Respondents indicate whether they (*a*) *will eat* a food item, (*b*) *like but try not to eat* the food, or (*c*) *will not eat* the food. The total number of the 40 foods an individual will eat provides an estimate of the diversity of their diet. The percentage of foods eaten from the high and low nutrient categories provides an estimate of the nutritional quality of an individual's diet.

The use of only three categories for classifying each food may seem to be a highly restrictive limit to one's position relative to a given food. However, the authors state that this format was developed from a previously tested five-choice scale. Their statistical analyses demonstrated that three choices provided the information needed to produce an index of diet nutritional quality and assess changes in food choice.

However, there seems to be a semantics problem with the third classification, "will not eat." This could more appropriately read, "do not eat." I do not eat cannoli or gyros (two foods in the FCI) because I have never encountered them and do not know what they are. However, I cannot say I will not eat cannoli. If I knew what it was, I might be quite eager to eat it.

Since one objective of this test is the assessment of current food-choice patterns of individuals and groups, it would have been helpful for educators to have a set of standard scores from a normal population. Although no standard scores are given, interpretation of test scores (as described in the test materials) has been designed to provide quantitative information for nutrition education needs assessment. The test user must decide what constitutes need. Scores are totaled for the three response options (eat, avoid, and reject) in each of three food categories (Total Foods, High Nutrient Foods, and Low Nutrient Foods). This provides nine indices of food-choice behavior which serve as indicators of dietary diversity and quality. Preferred directions of change for each index are given in the test materials for interpretation of change between pretest and posttest. The interpretation of these recommended changes is somewhat complex, however, and must be done with some discretion. For example, the authors indicate that a posttest should show an increase in the total number of foods a person will eat, indicating increased variety in the diet. However, since total foods include both high and low nutrient foods, a decrease in low nutrient foods, as recommended, can cause a reduction in total foods if there is little or no change in high nutrient foods. Thus, a positive change in dietary behavior could result in a change in the total foods index that is not preferred. The meaning of posttest changes much be carefully evaluated. This problem is not addressed in the test materials.

Substantial and laudable effort was made in the use of four objective criteria for validation of the FCI. Validation criteria included categorizing food pictures, selection of foods from a printed menu, and both food selection and food consumption during school lunch. Presentation and description of statistical results, however, was somewhat cursory and unclear. Statistical values indicated that three of these validation criteria were strong predictors of FCI results. Correlation between FCI and food selection, however, was low to moderate ($r = 0.5$). Reasons for this were not discussed. Reliability coefficients based on data from 385 respondents indicated an acceptable level of test reliability.

The FCI is an encouraging attempt to develop a simple tool for the assessment of dietary quality in individuals and groups. It places little demand on subjects and is easily administered and scored. It can be used to provide a general assessment of nutritional quality when nutritional detail is unnecessary. A pretest provides results that can assist in nutrition education needs assessment. A posttest can serve as an indicator of change in food-choice behavior. Despite the problems mentioned above, this instrument can be a valuable tool when used for the purposes intended. With the few simple improvements recommended, the FCI would be more effective.

[119]

Food Protection Certification Test. Purpose: "To test persons who have ongoing on-site responsibility for protecting the consumer from foodborne illness in food preparation, serving, or dispensing establishments." Food industry personnel; 1985; tests administered monthly except December at centers established by the publisher; 3 scores: Purchasing/Receiving/Storing Food, Processing/Serving/Dispensing Food, Employees/Facilities/Equipment; 1987 price data: $25 registration fee providing for administration and scoring of the test and mailing of results to examinee; $3 per practice test; 120(135) minutes; Center for Occupational and Professional Assessment; Educational Testing Service.

[120]

Formal Reading Inventory. Purpose: To identify students experiencing difficulties, to identify particular strengths and weaknesses, to evaluate a student's progress, and as a measurement device in research studies. Grades 1–12; 1985–86; FRI; individual; 1986 price data: $52 per complete kit including examiner's manual ('86, 80 pages), student book, and 50 student record forms; $13 per 50 student record forms; $21 per student book; $21 per examiner's manual; administration time not reported; J. Lee Wiederholt; PRO-ED, Inc.*

Review of the Formal Reading Inventory by RICHARD L. ALLINGTON, Professor of Education and Chair, Department of Reading, State University of New York at Albany, Albany, NY:

Recently, there has been a proliferation of published oral reading inventories. Most provide a set of passages of graduated difficulty for use in assessing children's reading development. These inventories are historically linked to either (*a*) teacher-constructed informal reading inventories or (*b*) published diagnostic oral reading tests. Most of the inventories available lack documentation of essential psychometric properties and are, in fact, offered as "informal" assessment instruments and, thus, not approved for serious educational decision making such as placement in remedial or special education programs. There exists a wealth of criticism of these inventories in various published reviews and textbooks.

The Formal Reading Inventory (FRI) overcomes many of the limitations of its predecessors. It compares well with the older, more established diagnostic reading tests, and, often, provides better evidence for the reliability and validity of results obtained. The four alternate forms and the range of textual difficulty presented (grades 1–13) produce an instrument useful for assessing reading development with a broader group of students than any of the established diagnostic reading tests. The information on the construction of the norms and the confidence one can place in results is far better than the information available for any other inventory or individual diagnostic reading test. In short, while the FRI is far from a perfect instrument it does shine in comparison to similar instruments.

The feature of primary concern is the brevity of the passages at all levels. Each is a paragraph, though generally each successive level offers a longer passage. But all passages are less than 200 words, a brief sample at best. While these passages are similar in length to those in some other inventories and tests, their brevity is still a weakness.

The FRI breaks from the tradition of its predecessors and uses comprehension performance alone as the criteria for establishing reading achievement levels. While miscues are recorded during oral reading activities there are no normative comparisons on quantity of errors. Rather, the FRI includes directions for classifying all miscues on several criteria (e.g., meaning similarity between original word and miscue, syntactic function similarity, graphic/phonemic similarity). The arguments against simple quantification of oral reading miscues are well stated and directly derived from recent research (cf. Allington, 1984).

Normative comparisons on student silent-reading comprehension performance are available either in a standard score (silent-reading quotient) or chronological-age percentile rank. Given the unlikelihood that any available inventory or diagnostic test can slice reading ability reliably into tenths of years (grade-equivalent months), this feature seems more straightforward and honest than the methods used in related instruments. The use of both types of normative information will need cautious interpretation in the cases of many remedial and special education students. These students have rarely progressed as steadily through the reading curriculum as their agemates and thus greater reading retardation may be suggested than is appropriate. That is, simply, an 11-year-old who is in grade 3 (due to repeating one or more grades) and is receiving instruction in second-grade material, will be compared with the average 11-year-old in grade 5, who is placed in grade-5 materials. Given that the educational system has not yet presented this student with instruction in a grade-5 curriculum, it can hardly be expected that the student will evidence any mastery of grade-5 (or age-11) tasks presented in the FRI. Examiners will have to look more carefully at the curricular coverage of students assessed.

Finally, unlike most related instruments the FRI uses a multiple-choice format for assessing comprehension. Rather than presenting open-ended questions about the passage, as has been the usual case, after reading the subject is given a sheet with the multiple-choice questions. As with the passage length, the five items for each passage are a concern but a concern allayed, in good part, by the description of the item selection process. Fewer, but better, questions seems preferable in most, if not all, cases.

In sum, the FRI has much to recommend it as an individual diagnostic screening instrument. While departing from historical tradition on a number of features, these evolutionary changes can be viewed as progress based upon our expanded understandings of the reading process and reading failure.

REVIEWER'S REFERENCE

Allington, R. L. (1984). Oral reading. In D. P. Pearson (Ed.), *Handbook of reading research*. New York: Longmans.

[121]

French Reading Diagnostic Tests for Early French Immersion Primary Classes. Purpose: "To provide information of strengths and weaknesses in silent reading performance in French for Early French Immersion (EFI) pupils in Canada and to integrate this information into the reteaching process." Grade 1–3 English-speaking pupils whose main language of instruction is French; 1982; 4 parts: Phonic and Visual Skills, Vocabulary, Sentence Comprehension, Story Comprehension; 1987 price data: $23.25 per 30 tests; $12 per guide (57 pages); administration time not reported; Margaret Tourond; The Ontario Institute for Studies in Education [Canada].*

[122]

The Fullerton Language Test for Adolescents, Second Edition. Purpose: "To determine the differences between normal and language-impaired populations." Ages 11–18; 1980–86; 8 scores: Auditory Synthesis, Morphology Competency, Oral Commands, Convergent Production, Divergent Production, Syllabication, Grammatic Competency, Idioms; individual; 1987 price data: $29 per examiner's kit including 25 scoring forms and profiles (8 pages), set of stimulus items, and manual (55 pages); $13.25 per 25 scoring forms and profiles; $2.50 per set of stimulus items; $15 per manual; $19 per specimen set including profile and scoring form, stimulus items, and manual; (35) minutes; Arden R. Thorum; Consulting Psychologists Press, Inc.*

For a review by Margaret C. Byrne of the Experimental Edition, see 9:428.

Review of The Fullerton Language Test for Adolescents, Second Edition by DIANE J. SAWYER, Associate Professor of Education, Syracuse University, Syracuse, NY:

DESCRIPTION. The revised edition of the Fullerton Language Test for Adolescents "incorporates the suggestions of many of its users" over a 5-year period making it "more comprehensive and useful in both design and content." Changes include revision of the Performance Profile; addition of an optional scoring method; additional directions, examples, and explanations; an expanded section on remediation; and reports of research studies.

The Fullerton consists of eight subtests designed to assess receptive language processing skills (Oral Commands and Syllabication subtests) and expressive language skills (the remaining six subtests). Selection of the specific subtests was based on an extensive review of the research literature on the language performance of adolescents as well as review of commercially available instruments for the assessment of adolescent language (1975–1977).

ADMINISTRATION AND SCORING. The Fullerton was designed to be administered by any professional educator who has become thoroughly familiar with the test prior to its use. Subtests may be given in any order and the test may be completed in one sitting or spread out over two or more sittings. Two scoring options are available within the Second Edition. Traditional pass/fail notations may be made for each item but an examiner may also choose a descriptive approach to scoring. The author has provided a set of five descriptors that may be used to characterize each response (i.e., 1 = correct, immediate response; 2 = correct, delayed response; 3 = correct, self-correction response; 4 = correct, after repeat of stimulus; 5 = error, in second attempt). The numeral representing a descriptor may be noted on the scoring form along with, or in place of, the pass/fail notation.

The two scoring options yield two separate summary profiles of performance. Using the traditional pass/fail scoring procedure, performance on each subtest may be compared with the performance profile (means and standard deviations) of the norming population (N = 762). Standard scores are also provided for mean raw scores and raw scores associated with several standard deviations from the mean. If an examiner chooses to characterize the nature of the responses given using the five descriptors noted above, the percent of items on each subtest that were characterized as 1s or 2s, etc., can serve to establish an estimate of fluency as well as accuracy in language performance as assessed by the Fullerton.

INTERPRETATION AND USE. Suggestions for diagnostic and remedial interpretations of test performance are primarily directed to the speech/language pathologist. However, a brief discussion of the educational implications of deficits in each of the skill areas assessed is also included to aid interpretation of results by psychologists, reading teachers, and special education personnel other than speech/language specialists.

VALIDITY AND RELIABILITY. The Fullerton appears to be a content-valid test of adolescent language performance. The subtests were selected on the basis of a review of research and previously published tests showing these eight skills to be strong indicators of adolescent language competence. In addition, the items on the various subtests appear to elicit the skill described, further supporting the Fullerton's content validity.

Test-retest coefficients range from .84 to .96 for a sample of 75 children. These coefficients are strong and suggest the Fullerton is a stable measure of language performance. Split-half reliability coefficients range from .70 to .85 and suggest the various items within each subtest are measuring the same kind of skill or process.

The Fullerton was developed with a view to distinguish between normal and language-impaired adolescents. Three independent studies are reported showing that performance on the Fullerton does distinguish between the two groups and that differences in performance as a consequence of age (11 to 18+) are not generally apparent.

SUMMARY. The Fullerton appears to be a carefully developed test of adolescent language performance that is easy to administer and capable of identifying students with language impairments that may be related to academic difficulties. Suggestions for interpreting test performance into plans for language therapy make the Fullerton a particularly useful tool.

[123]

Functional Skills Screening Inventory. Purpose: "To be used in natural settings to assess critical living and working skills in persons with moderate to severe handicapping conditions." Age 6 through adult; 1984–86; FSSI; a domain-referenced behavioral checklist; 9 scores categorized into 3 priority levels: Basic Skills and Concepts, Communication, Personal Care, Homemaking, Work Skills and Concepts, Community Living, Social Awareness, Functional Skills Subtotal, Problem Behaviors; individual; 1987 price data: $98 per master copy including assessment booklet for unlimited assessments, scoresheets, and user's guide ('86, 117 pages); $14.50 per sample set including one completed assessment plus user's guide; $380 per FSSI interactive computer program for use with IBM PC (or $340 for use with Apple IIe) plus user's guide;

$22.50 per Demo disk with complete documentation; [60–120] minutes per assessment; Heather Becker, Sally Schur, Michele Paoletti-Schelp, and Ed Hammer; Functional Resources Enterprises.*

Review of the Functional Skills Screening Inventory by DIANE BROWDER, Associate Professor of Special Education, Lehigh University, Bethlehem, PA:

PURPOSE. The Functional Skills Screening Inventory (FSSI) was developed to assess critical living and working skills in individuals with severe handicaps ages 6 to adult. The FSSI is a criterion-referenced behavior checklist with suggested comparison levels for priorities in independent living/competitive employment, supervised living/supportive employment, and partial autonomy in any setting. The domains represented in its content are compatible with those proposed by Halpern, Lehmann, Irvin, and Heiry (1982).

EDUCATIONAL AND SOCIAL VALIDITY. The FSSI adheres to a behavioral assessment approach. The profile obtained is to be interpreted as a description of current skills, and not necessarily as a projection of potential abilities. The checklist is completed across time through informal observations of the person in his or her everyday environments. Because this test provides a detailed behavioral checklist to be used in informal observations, it is well suited for use by classroom teachers for educational screening.

Test content was selected by inviting practitioner input and by reviewing other scales. This dual process is reflected in the detailed and functional items included. The authors also show familiarity with Wehman, Kriegel, and Barcus' (1985) vocational transition model. The ranking of items by priorities reflects a scale that Taylor (1988) has termed "the new community-based LRE continuum model." This ranking helps the practitioner compare performance on the test to performance typical of individuals in semi-independent or independent settings. Some validation of this priority ranking system was provided by the authors by comparing FSSI scores for clients from two Texas programs who were preparing for independent versus semi-independent placements. Significant differences between groups were found for some, but not all subscales. A potential misuse of the scale, mentioned by the authors, would be relying on the FSSI scale alone to make decisions about placement in a service continuum (e.g., supportive versus competitive employment).

ADMINISTRATION. The FSSI is administered by observing the client across time in his or her natural settings. Each item in the behavioral checklist is ranked on a 4-point scale based on the level of supervision or prompting required to complete the item. For problem behaviors, the scale is based on the frequency with which the behavior is exhibited. Caution is required in interpreting the final scores. These are expressed as a percentage because the percentage is computed by total points received per item; not percentage of items mastered. The recommended interpretation is to use the peaks and valleys (within each priority level) in the profile summary to identify areas for further training. A potential weakness of the test may be the informality of the administration procedures that could affect reliability depending on the responder's familiarity with the client and skill in behavioral assessment. The authors suggest a "committee approach" to the assessment. The authors report excellent interrater agreement for a small sample of teachers and aids who had received a training session on the use of the FSSI, but encourage caution in interpreting the scale and the use of supplemental ratings with anecdotal notes.

TECHNICAL MERIT. Besides the interrater reliability statistics, the authors also report test/retest reliability for a sample of nine clients in one program who are deaf/blind and severely retarded. Correlations above .90 are reported for all scales except problem behaviors which was .687. Internal consistency of the scale was computed on a sample of 95 individuals from across Texas with varying handicaps and ages with Cronbach Alpha coefficients of .95 or above reported for all items. Intercorrelations among FSSI scales was also computed for 51 clients in Texas programs for adults with severe handicaps with modest to good correlations found among items (.62 to .94) except for the problem behavior scale. This scale did not correlate well with other categories (.26 to .48). Modest to good correlations were also found with the Vineland and Callier-Azusa. Poorest correlations were found for the Priority III items (independent living/competitive employment). This may be due to the greater number of items in this priority area contained in the FSSI as compared to the other scales. The overall statistics reflect emerging technical quality in reliability and validity of the FSSI as an adaptive behavior scale. The authors report they are conducting continuing evaluation of the test's technical merit. Such evaluation is needed to strengthen users' confidence in the scale's psychometric qualities.

SUMMARY. The most appropriate use of the FSSI is as a screening device to identify educational/habilitative goals for severely disabled clients. More specific teacher-made assessment should also be used to operationalize these goals for ongoing assessment. A computer software edition of the FSSI is available that is easy for the computer novice to learn and offers computer prepared profiles. The FSSI is an informal assessment making it especially crucial that it not be the sole or primary information used for program placement decisions. The FSSI is also not intended for predicting future performance or future placement options.

REVIEWER'S REFERENCES

Halpern, A., Lehmann, J., Irvin, L., & Heiry, T. (1982). *Contemporary assessment for mentally retarded adolescents and adults.* Baltimore, MD: University Park Press.

Wehman, P., Kregel, J., & Barcus, J. (1985). From school to work: A vocational transition model for handicapped students. *Exceptional Children*, 52, 25-38.

Taylor, S. (1988). Caught in the continuum: A critical analysis of the principle of the least restrictive environment. *The Journal of the Association for Persons with Severe Handicaps*, 13, 41-53.

Review of the Functional Skills Screening Inventory by G. MICHAEL POTEAT, Assistant Professor of Psychology, East Carolina University, Greenville, NC:

The Functional Skills Screening Inventory (FSSI) was developed by the authors as an extension of the Basic Life Skills Screening Inventory. The FSSI consists of a manual and a series of forms for recording and summarizing behavioral observations. The authors describe the instrument as a domain-referenced behavioral checklist for assessing critical living and working skills required for functioning at various levels of independence. The eight scales are divided into 27 subscales and consist of 343 behavioral descriptions (items). The instrument is presented as being appropriate for children and adults with moderate to severe and multiple handicapping conditions. The instrument may be completed by any professional or paraprofessional working with handicapped clients. Directions for administering and scoring the scales are provided and emphasize the observation of behavior in unstructured situations over a period of several days to several weeks. The use of informants to describe behaviors not directly observed and the assessment by more than one rater are recommended.

The scales are divided into Parts One and Two. Part Two consists of the Problem Behaviors Scale and is so labeled. Part One is made up of the remaining seven scales and is referred to as Functional Skills. All FSSI items are grouped into three hierarchical priority levels. Priority I items are those necessary for independent functioning in any setting. Priority II items are those skills frequently required for supervised living and noncompetitive employment. Priority III items are identified as skills necessary for independent living and competitive employment. All Functional Skills items are rated using a Likert-type format. An individual who never, under any set of circumstances, performs any part of an item is assigned zero points. Four points are assigned for an item that is consistently performed when appropriate without cueing or assistance. The scoring is reversed for Problem Behaviors so that a low score reflects a frequently observed problem behavior. Scoring standards and cautions are presented in enough detail that even paraprofessionals not trained in assessment should be able to rate the items and tally scores.

The FSSI covers a wide range of behaviors and was constructed to assess a variety of behavioral domains. The content coverage is impressive and should provide a basis for both the assessment of adaptive behavior and the development of intervention programs. However, no item analysis was performed. An analysis comparing individual item scores with both total scores and external criteria would assist the interpretation of content coverage. Test stability was assessed across a short time period for a small sample of multihandicapped students. Test-retest reliability coefficients ranging from .94 to .99 were obtained for all scales used to measure functional skills, but the Problem Behaviors scale was less stable ($r =$ .69). A similar pattern was found on measures of interrater reliability. Interrater correlations for the seven functional scales were all above .84, but was only .16 for Problem Behaviors. All scales have adequate evidence of interitem consistency with alphas above .95. The Functional Scales appear to be reliable measures, but the paucity of information about the training and experience of the raters is a source of concern about generalization to the typical user. Systematic field trials specifying the amount of training received by raters and assessing the reliability of scores obtained by individuals with less extensive contact with clients would greatly assist the potential purchaser in evaluating these scales.

Limited evidence for the criterion-related validity of the FSSI is provided in the form of correlations between the Functional Skills total score and social age obtained on the Vineland Social Maturity Scale. Four subscales on the FSSI (Social Awareness, Communication, Personal Care, and Basic Skills and Concepts) were also significantly correlated with "corresponding" scales on the Callier-Azusa Scale. Evidence for the construct validity of the FSSI is provided by a comparison of subscale scores for groups of residents enrolled in a variety of habilitative programs. Residents in programs designed to serve the less severely handicapped typically had higher scores than residents in more restrictive environments. Norms are not provided, but comparison data (in the form of percentage of possible points scored) are provided for several diverse groups including university students and unimpaired children. However, the small sample sizes used and the lack of representative sampling limits the interpretation of these data. In addition, the comparative data are presented in a poorly organized manner using "raw score sheets" making it difficult to compare groups. A summary of these data would be more helpful in evaluating differences in group performance.

One notable feature of the FSSI is its availability as a computer-based assessment instrument. This system allows the user to record, compare, and print assessment information using a personal computer. The advantages of computer-based assessment have been addressed (see Becker & Schur, 1986) and this modality may have a number of advantages in situations where repeated assessments are conducted. Unfortunately, the demonstration diskette provided by the authors does not allow the potential user to fully evaluate the system because item scores cannot be saved to the diskette. However, the computer scoring system appears to be relatively easy to learn.

Overall, the FSSI can be tentatively recommended for use as a criterion-based measure of adaptive behavior. It is not a norm-referenced measure, and those users needing to compare individual performance to norms should consider using either the Vineland Adaptive Behavior Scales (9:1327) or the appropriate version of the AAMD Adaptive Behavioral Scales (9:3). The FSSI does have some potential as a basis for developing an intervention program for the disabled client. Although more research is indicated, the Functional Scales appear to be stable across time and interrater agreement is acceptable. Use of the Problem Behavior Scale cannot be recommended based on the available data. The content coverage of the Functional Scales is impressive, but additional data on criterion-related validity are needed. Teachers and other instructional staff in institutions and group homes serving clients with severe disabilities or multiple handicaps are the most likely to find the FSSI useful. Potential users are encouraged to purchase the demonstration diskette and user's guide to determine the appropriateness of the instrument for their setting.

REVIEWER'S REFERENCE

Becker, H., & Schur, S. (1986). The advantages of using microcomputer-based assessment with moderately and severely handicapped individuals. *Journal of Special Education Technology*, 8, 53-57.

[124]

GAP Reading Comprehension Test, Third Edition. Purpose: Assesses reading comprehension and can indicate reading progress. Reading ages 7–12; 1965–85; GAP; cloze technique; 2 equivalent forms; 1985 price data: A$24.95 per 48 copies each of Form B and Form R, and teacher manual ('85, 8 pages); 15(20) minutes; John McLeod; Heineman Publishers Australia Pty Ltd. [Australia].*

See T3:928 (4 references), and T2:1550 (3 references); for reviews by Donald B. Black and Earl F. Rankin of an earlier edition, see 7:688.

TEST REFERENCES

1. Beggs, W. D. A., & Howarth, P. N. (1985). Inner speech as a learned skill. *Journal of Experimental Child Psychology*, 39, 396-411.

2. Bowey, J. A. (1986). Syntactic awareness in relation to reading skill and ongoing reading comprehension monitoring. *Journal of Experimental Child Psychology*, 41, 282-299.

3. Marsh, H. W. (1986). Self-serving effect (bias?) in academic attributions: Its relation to academic achievement and self-concept. *Journal of Educational Psychology*, 78, 190-200.

4. Sharpley, C. F., & Rowland, S. E. (1986). Palliative vs. direct action stress-reduction procedures as treatments for reading disability. *British Journal of Educational Psychology*, 56, 40-50.

Review of the GAP Reading Comprehension Test, Third Edition by ALAN S. KAUFMAN, Research Professor of School Psychology, The University of Alabama, Tuscaloosa, AL:

The GAP Reading Comprehension Test is allegedly a "practical by-product from a research study concerned with book readability and the application of information theory to the study of reading"; the test uses a modified cloze procedure to measure reading comprehension. Reliability data are presented for ages 8 to 10 years, but there is nothing else in the eight-page manual of the Third Edition that gives a clue about the suggested age range of the test. Indeed, there is virtually nothing in the test manual: no reference to the study that produced the instrument as a by-product; no explication of the role of information theory in test development; no evidence of a normative sample; and no validity data.

TEST DESCRIPTION AND CONSTRUCTION. The GAP Reading Comprehension Test comprises two supposedly equivalent forms, each with a 15-minute time limit. Although presumably only one form is intended to be given to a child (the manual suggests that there are two forms so that they can be distributed "alternately" to deter cheating), age-equivalent tables are provided for each form separately and for the sum of raw scores on the two forms. Form B3 (which presumably refers to the Third Edition of the blue test) contains seven brief passages (four to six lines), each with four to nine words missing. Form R3 (the red form) contains eight brief passages, each missing four to seven words.

Test-development procedures for the first two editions of the GAP test are discussed sketchily in the current manual, and only a limited description is provided of the construction in 1976 of the Third Edition. Preliminary items for all editions were administered to fluent readers (teachers in training); only items that were answered unequivocally (i.e., by 95 percent or more of the fluent readers) were retained.

Approximately 75 percent of the items selected in this manner for the third revision were from the previous edition of the test; the remaining items were new, written to replace a few of the items that experience had shown to be inappropriate. The revised tests were then administered to 250 children, presumably ages 8 to 10 years, since reliability data are provided for the Third Edition only at ages 8, 9, and 10.

The items on each form are mostly unambiguous, but the passages are not particularly child oriented or interesting, especially on Form B3. The missing words tend to be simple prepositions, auxiliary verbs, articles, and pronouns; very few nonhelping verbs, adjectives (other than articles), adverbs, or nouns are deleted from the passages. The vocabulary in each passage tends to be considerably more difficult than the simple words omitted via the cloze procedure; perhaps reading comprehension would have been assessed with more breadth and depth if a wider variety of words (in terms of part of speech and difficulty level) had been eliminated from the passages.

The format of the test also presents a problem. The print becomes smaller as the items get harder, for no apparent reason. The last two or three items per form are in unnecessarily tiny print.

PSYCHOMETRIC PROPERTIES. The GAP manual is one of the most incomplete I have ever seen. Split-half reliability coefficients are provided for ages 8, 9, and 10, probably for the 250 children tested during the test development phase, but sample sizes for the age groups are not given. The coefficients are good, ranging from .90 to .94 for Form B3 and from .90 to .92 for Form R3. However, the only way that split-half coefficients would be appropriate for the GAP is if all items in a given passage are included on the same "half-test"; otherwise the coefficients would be spuriously high because of experimental interdependence among sets of items. Unfortunately, no mention is made of this important consideration. Of greater concern is the lack of standard errors of measurement to facilitate interpretation of raw scores, and the failure to provide alternate-forms coefficients for the two forms. Test users are asked to accept Forms B3 and R3 as equivalent, but the author of the GAP has provided not one shred of evidence to support the equivalence!

Shockingly, not one validity study is offered in the manual for any edition of the GAP, even though the test was first copyrighted in 1965. There is simply no evidence of any sort that the GAP is a valid measure of reading comprehension.

Normative data are equally lacking. The author states that the sample of 250 children tested during construction of the Third Edition provided data that were used to modify the original norms. How this was done is unclear since 25 percent of the items in the Third

Edition are new. No information about the original sample is offered, and the sample of 250 is described in one word: children. Since the test author is from Canada and the test is published in Australia, the likelihood of the "norms" being appropriate for the United States is nil; indeed, the odds of the norms being appropriate for Canada or Australia are only slightly higher.

Norms tables are provided, namely reading-age equivalents of raw scores. Obviously, age equivalents are not adequate as the only type of norm. Conversion of raw scores to standard scores or percentile ranks for separate age groups would have been decidedly superior to age-equivalent conversion tables for Form B3, Form R3, and for both norms combined. Similarly, the presentation of tables to determine retarded readers based on a criterion of Reading Quotients less than 80 (reading age divided by chronological age multiplied by 100) is psychometrically indefensible.

SUMMARY. The GAP Reading Comprehension Test has little to recommend it. The test construction seems flawed, psychometric data are largely missing, and the only converted scores provided by the test author (reading-age equivalents) are of limited usefulness and questionable meaningfulness because of the unknown nature of the normative sample.

Review of the GAP Reading Comprehension Test, Third Edition by GLORIA E. MILLER, Associate Professor of Psychology, University of South Carolina, Columbia, SC:

The GAP Reading Comprehension Test, authored by J. McLeod, is one of the only published instruments to test reading comprehension using a modified cloze procedure. The third edition of this test, published in 1977, is based on the earlier 1965 version. The author reports that about 75 percent of the original test content is retained in the third revision.

As in the past, there are two versions of the test (Form B3 and Form R3). Each test form consists of seven or eight short reading passages. The test is group administered. The exact instructions to be read orally to the children are provided in the manual. Children are given 15 minutes to fill in an average of five words that have been randomly omitted from each passage. The passages are written and presented at a progressively more difficult readability level.

A child's score on each test form is based on the number of correct word replacements produced. Only exact word replacements are accepted; however, incorrectly spelled versions of the keyed responses are scored as correct. Tables are provided so that a child's total raw score on either of the separate test forms or on the combined test forms can be converted into a reading age equivalency level. In a second set of tables, a cutoff score is provided to allow for a diagnosis of reading deficiency based on a child's chronological age.

The author claims that the GAP Test represents a more valid test of comprehension than other tests, in part because it overcomes the problem of content knowledge. However, it is apparent from reading the passages that this claim certainly is overstated. For example, a child who has experience with or knowledge of gardens and the need for constant weeding would be at a distinct advantage in filling in this blank item: "the gardens are overgrown with _______." Clearly, background knowledge is a factor that affects one's speed and efficiency on a timed test. Poorer performance also might be expected from a child who is a slow or meticulous writer because a written response is required.

The GAP Test is recommended as a screening measure to "facilitate the identification of children who are significantly retarded in reading comprehension." However, caution is recommended in employing this measure to identify children for further assessment because of several problems related to the standardization of the third version of the test.

First, the revised GAP Test was standardized on a small sample of children from Australia ($N = 250$). Moreover, the demographic characteristics of this sample are never presented. Although it is assumed that multiple age groups were employed, there is no breakdown of the age, sex, or socioeconomic status of the standardization sample. Thus, the generalizability of the norms from this population to children in the United States remains unknown.

Second, although the reported split-half reliabilities for the revised GAP Test were quite acceptable (i.e., ranges from .90 to .94), it was unclear just how these were calculated. In a one paragraph description of this procedure, the author states that the reliabilities "were calculated . . . on samples of children at three different age groups." Unfortunately, there is no mention either of the characteristics or number of children in these samples. Also, the exact reliability coefficient employed to obtain these estimates is not reported.

Finally, in contrast to past efforts to establish the validity of cloze procedures, no validity studies were conducted on the third revision of the GAP Test. The cutoff scores used to identify children who are "significantly retarded in reading comprehension" are reportedly set at the expected score of an average child whose age is 80 percent of the tested child's actual chronological age. It is unknown whether children identified as "retarded" comprehenders on the GAP Test actually were similarly identified on other measures. Moreover, there is no mention of how scores on the GAP Test correlate with children's scores on other measures of reading comprehension.

In conclusion, the limited documentation and the above mentioned problems associated with the standardization of the third revision of the GAP Reading Comprehension Test limit its usefulness for accurate reading diagnosis. Though there is considerable reason to believe that a standardized cloze test has the potential to be clinically useful for identifying problem readers, the value of the GAP Reading Comprehension Test in meeting this objective has not yet been clearly demonstrated.

[125]

Gifted and Talented Scale. Purpose: "Designed to identify those children who should be admitted into school programs for the Gifted and Talented." Grades 4–6; no date on test materials; 6 scores: Numerical Reasoning, Vocabulary, Synonyms/Antonyms, Similarities, Analogies, Total; 1985 price data: $50 per 25 pupil record forms and manual (17 pages); $45 per 25 pupil record forms; $7.50 per manual; administration time not reported; Dallas Educational Services.*

Review of the Gifted and Talented Scale by LINDA E. BRODY, Assistant Director, Study of Mathematically Precocious Youth (SMPY), The Johns Hopkins University, Baltimore, MD:

The Gifted and Talented Scale is designed to identify students in grades 4, 5, and 6 for placement in programs for gifted and talented students. Untimed and intended to be used for group administration, the scale attempts to measure abstract concepts through five subtests: Numerical Reasoning, Vocabulary, Synonyms and Antonyms, Similarities, and Analogies.

Programs for gifted and talented students have grown in popularity, creating assessment/identification problems for program administrators. The global intelligence test, once very popular for finding gifted students, is now recognized as somewhat limited in terms of assessing specific strengths and weaknesses for placement purposes. Achievement tests provide useful information but often reflect the adequacy of educational programs more than an individual student's potential. The Scholastic Aptitude Test (SAT) has been used successfully to measure verbal and mathematical reasoning ability in students as young as seventh grade, but the SAT would not be appropriate for younger students except in unusual circumstances. Schools, therefore, usually use a variety of measures of achievement and potential to assess a student's unique pattern of abilities in an effort to predict future performance.

This scale attempts to make the identification task easier by combining in one scale a measure of several types of reasoning abilities in an easily administered format. Unfortunately, the scale has been published prematurely. The research that has been done on the scale is inadequate to justify its use to determine the placement of students.

Norming was done in two school systems and involved the comparison of students in the gifted and talented program with students in the regular program. No other descriptive information about the norm group is provided, such as how they were selected for the gifted program, their socioeconomic level, or the racial and gender composition of the group. In school system A, fourth, fifth, and sixth grade gifted students were tested but only fourth grade regular students. No explanation is given as to why older regular students were not included. In addition, the total number of subjects in this sample is omitted, and the only descriptive information provided about the test results are means and standard deviations. More information is provided about the test results in school system B, including histograms, frequency distributions, analysis of variance and *t*-test results, and some descriptive statistics. However, the population is not described; for example, it is not clear which age groups were tested or how the samples were selected.

Moreover, only 94 students (47 in each group) were tested, certainly an inadequate number for a normative sample. Furthermore, although the gifted students did score higher on the scale than the regular students, the range of scores for both groups in school system B is quite large, suggesting that this measure would not select all of the same students currently placed in the gifted program. There is inadequate information to determine whether the scale or the current identification system used in the school system is more effective in selecting the appropriate students.

The subtests are quite short; therefore assessment of their reliability as well as of the reliability of the total scale is critical. None is reported.

The validity of this instrument is questionable. It would be desirable to compare students' results on this scale with results on other measures such as intelligence and achievement tests to determine just what this scale is measuring. Predictive validity studies are needed to determine the effectiveness of this scale for predicting later achievement. Moreover, the test should be considered in terms of fourth, fifth, and sixth grade curricula. If students currently enrolled in gifted and talented programs, such as those in the norm group, have been exposed to more of the test content because of an enriched program, the test may actually be measuring achievement rather than reasoning ability. This issue needs research attention. The manual provides no information concerning how the test was constructed nor any rationale for the selection of particular items.

In conclusion, I would strongly caution against the use of this scale for placement purposes at this time. Extensive research is needed to validate the scale, to provide representative normative samples, and to ensure adequate reliability of the instrument. It would be inappropriate for any school system to use it to make decisions about the placement of students in programs until this is done. The scale should be used only, and quite cautiously, for research purposes by qualified investigators.

Review of the Gifted and Talented Scale by NICHOLAS COLANGELO, Professor and Chair of Counselor Education, University of Iowa, Iowa City, IA:

The authors claim that the Gifted and Talented Scale (GTS) is designed to identify gifted and talented children in grades 4, 5, and 6. This claim is incredible given the absence of virtually any conceptual or psychometric supporting data in the manual.

The GTS is a power test designed for group administration. There are five categories in the test; all items in every category are designed to measure abstract concepts. No information is provided on how items were developed or selected. In addition, after reviewing each item, I cannot imagine how it was determined that each item measures an abstract concept.

The five categories are Numerical Reasoning, Vocabulary, Synonyms and Antonyms, Similarities, and Analogies. Each category contains 10 items. The Numerical Reasoning category contains a series of numbers. The student is to determine the next logical number in the series. The Vocabulary category consists of items designed to test a student's ability to define words. Students choose among four options for their answers. Synonyms and Antonyms consists of 10 items (five synonyms and five antonyms) designed to test a student's reasoning ability. Similarities is designed to test a student's knowledge of verbal relationships. Ten pairs are presented and a student is to determine how they are alike, choosing one of the four options provided for each pair. The final category is Analogies. This category is designed to test a student's verbal and abstract reasoning abilities.

There are serious conceptual and psychometric problems with the GTS. A major weakness is that no useful definition of gifted or talented is offered. Gifted is defined as "to be endowed with some power, quality or attribute." What human being would not fit this definition? Talented is defined as "possessing talent, special attribute, mentally gifted, skilled in performing art." Both definitions are taken from Webster's *Third New International Dictionary* and offer no guidance to clarify either concept. A confusing, incoherent array of short statements are made about gifted youngsters. Anyone not familiar with the field would not be able to understand what is being communicated. In essence, this is a scale that does not clearly state exactly what is being measured.

The scale is also weak from a psychometric standpoint. Almost no information is provided on item construction or on reliability or validity. Students in the gifted and talented program in two school districts were given the GTS. In addition, students not identified as gifted and talented were given the test. Not surprisingly, the students identified as gifted or talented scored higher than nonidentified students. It is reported that the mean scores of gifted students were significantly higher than the mean scores of regular students. This kind of comparison suggests that if a student scores "high" (i.e., similar to the scores obtained by gifted students in the sample, an acceptable criterion), then this student would be a candidate for a gifted program. No other validity-related information is presented.

Gifted education is receiving considerable attention in schools today. There is a rush to find straightforward, quantifiable data that will clearly determine who is and who is not gifted. I do not recommend the GTS be used to determine giftedness. There is no evidence for the claims made.

[126]

Goldman Fristoe Test of Articulation. Purpose: Provides "a systematic means of assessing an individual's articulation of the consonant sounds." Ages 2 and over; 1969–86; 3 subtests: Sounds-in-Words, Sounds-in-Sentences, Stimulability; individual; filmstrip presentation of stimulus plates also available; 1988 price data: $62 per complete kit containing 25 response forms, test plates in easel, and manual ('86, 33 pages); $6.50 per 25 response forms; $51 per set of test plates in easel; $15 per filmstrip; $7.50 per manual; [10–15] minutes for Sounds-in-Words subtest, administration time not reported for other subtests; Ronald Goldman and Macalyne Fristoe; American Guidance Service.*

See T3:960 (21 references); for additional information, reviews by Margaret C. Byrne and Ralph L. Shelton, and an excerpted review by Dorothy Sherman, see 7:952 (4 references).

TEST REFERENCES

1. Rabe, M. B., & Matlin, M. W. (1978). Sex-role stereotypes in speech and language tests. *Language, Speech, and Hearing Services in Schools*, 9, 70-75.

2. Conners, C. K., & Taylor, E. (1980). Pemoline, methylphenidate, and placebo in children with minimal brain dysfunction. *Archives of General Psychiatry*, 37, 922-930.

3. Johnson, J. P., Winney, B. L., & Pederson, O. T. (1980). Single word versus connected speech articulation testing. *Speech, Language, and Hearing Services in the Schools*, 11, 175-179.

4. Mattison, R. E., Cantwell, D. P., & Baker, L. (1980). Dimensions of behavior in children with speech and language disorders. *Journal of Abnormal Child Psychology*, 8, 323-338.

5. Madison, C.L., Kolbeck, C. P., & Walker, J. L. (1982). An evaluation of stimuli identification on three articulation tests. *Language, Speech, and Hearing Services in Schools*, 13, 110-115.

6. Dworkin, J. P., & Culatta, R. A. (1985). Oral structural and neuromuscular characteristics in children with normal and disordered articulation. *Journal of Speech and Hearing Disorders*, 50, 150-156.

7. Kashani, J. H., Horwitz, E., Ray, J. S., & Reid, J. C. (1986). DSM-III diagnostic classification of 100 preschoolers in a child development unit. *Child Psychiatry and Human Development*, 16, 137-147.

Review of the Goldman Fristoe Test of Articulation by DONALD E. MOWRER, Professor of Speech and Hearing Science, Arizona State University, Tempe, AZ:

The Goldman Fristoe Test of Articulation (GFTA) first published in 1969, revised in 1972, and again in 1986 has been reviewed several times (Mecham, 1979; Byrne, 1972; Shelton, 1972). The reader can refer to these reviews for a general description of the test because few changes have been made in the physical construction, test items, or scoring procedures since the 1972 edition. The comments offered by these reviewers are also appropriate for the 1986 revision with one exception, that being the addition of normative data for age groups 2 to 6 years. Other than this feature there have been no significant changes in this test. The focus of this review will be upon an analysis of the additional normative data, the validity, and the reliability information provided in the test manual.

Normative data for females and males age 2 to 6 years are provided for the Sounds-in-Words Subtest in 2-month increments. These norms were derived from data gathered by Khan and Lewis (1986) who used the GFTA Sounds-in-Words Subtest as a means of evoking responses from young children in their analysis of phonological processes. Khan and Lewis tested 852 children (about 200 in each of four age groups) representing several ethnic groups throughout widely scattered parts of the U.S. (see the current reviews of Khan and Lewis's test in this *Yearbook*, 164). It appears they took necessary precautions to secure a representative sample. In this respect, it can be concluded that an adequate sample was obtained to develop norms for the 2-to-6-year age group.

With respect to the norms established for the 6-to-16+-year age group, the authors of the GFTA relied upon data collected by Hull, Mielke, Timmons, and Willeford (1971) who used the Sounds-in-Words Subtest of the GFTA as part of their test battery for examining 38,802 subjects in their 1969 National Speech and Hearing Survey. The authors of the

GFTA are indeed fortunate to have had access to data from such a large subject pool in which part of their test was used as one of the measuring instruments. It is also stated in the GFTA Test Manual that the Hull et al. study gathered data regarding the Stimulability Subtest from which norms were derived. There is no reference to administration of this Subtest in the Hull et al. published article in *ASHA*. Hull et al. mention only two types of speech responses tested: (*a*) "single word responses to a standard picture articulation test" (the Sounds-in-Words Subtest of the GFTA) and (*b*) "an aggregate of connected speech samples." Each subject's articulation ability was categorized as acceptable, moderate deviation, or extreme deviation for males and females. It is not clear from either the Hull et al. study or from Goldman and Fristoe's report exactly how norms were derived for the GFTA. Evidently, they had access to much more information than was reported in the *ASHA* report.

But aside from this, using the total number of sounds in error as the chief means of establishing percentile rank leaves much to be desired. Of equal or greater importance when making prognostic evaluations or when planning therapy is knowledge about which sounds are in error. Tests like the Arizona Articulation Proficiency Scale (Fudala, 1974) take these factors into account when judging severity of the articulation problem. Consistency of errors and type of errors, factors not used in the GFTA to establish percentile ranks, are also important considerations. One can obtain only a general idea of how many children made more or less errors at a given age level. This information is useful but of limited value for making decisions about the severity of individual cases.

To establish reliability of the GFTA, the authors present data regarding test-retest, interrater, and intrarater studies. Test-retest reliability was determined from evaluations of eight "experienced speech pathologists" who tested and retested 37 children between 4 and 8 years of age. No descriptive data are provided regarding the specific ages of the subjects, sex, or level of education, training, and experience of the judges. Data are reported in terms of the median agreement for the Sounds-in-Words and Sounds-in-Context Subtests. This means that 50% of the agreements were above the specified level and 50% were below. The problem is that the median, as a measure of central tendency, is insensitive to extreme scores. Thus, while the median agreement of 95% for test-retest for the Sounds-in-Words Subtest was very high, we do not know the spread or clusters of the remaining 50%. In some cases, median agreements for type of error in initial and final positions in the Sounds-in-Sentences Subtest were only 70% but the majority were above 80%. Mean and standard deviation data would be much more informative.

Interrater reliability was based solely on the evaluations of only six judges who evaluated four subjects tested on the Sounds-in-Words Subtest. This appears to be a very limited sample although the median agreement was 92%. Again, there is no description of the lower 50% levels.

With respect to intrarater reliability, six judges and four subjects were used. Raters listened to tape recordings of the subjects to determine amount of agreement with their original evaluations. A median agreement of 91% for both presence-absence and type of production was reported. Again, we need to know more about central tendency measures and variability of agreement than was reported in the GFTA Manual.

There was no attempt to compare results of the GFTA with other standardized articulation tests in order to establish criterion validity. Thus, we do not know if the GFTA norms are valid indicators of a child's articulation ability. We know only how one child's articulation compares with the articulation ability of other children who have taken this test. While this is useful information, we can only guess how a child might have performed on another test of articulation.

The authors present no convincing data to indicate the content validity of the GFTA. They state that an in-depth analysis of articulation is too time consuming and that a sample of a sound in three positions of a word plus in a few clusters is sufficient to establish validity. Many would disagree that such a superficial examination could be used to describe one's articulation ability accurately. Of course, repeated assessments involving the other two Subtests would certainly aid in making a more complete assessment of a misarticulated sound. The authors suggest if one is interested in a more thorough study of sounds, The Khan-Lewis Phonological Analysis test should be administered, but this advice is simply begging the question when it comes to establishing validity of the GFTA.

The authors mention the scores from the 37 subjects who were given the Sounds-in-Words Subtest and Sounds-in-Context Subtest were compared. The somewhat low percent of agreement indicated these tests measure different aspects of articulation but this finding offers little support of content validity.

There was also no attempt to establish the predictive validity of the GFTA and little evidence of any attempt to verify construct validity. Efforts to verify the validity of the GFTA remains its weakest point.

In summary, it appears little has been done to improve the GFTA since its inception save the addition of percentile norms for the male and female groups between the ages of 2 and 6 years. This addition is a welcomed one. The same criticisms leveled by other reviewers of the 1972 edition still seem appropriate because no substantial improvements have been made in the areas of establishing further reliability or validity of the test. This reviewer is in agreement with Mecham (1969) and Shelton (1972) who felt the GFTA offers little in the advancement of our knowledge of articulation. On the positive side, the GFTA is a relatively easy test to administer and score once the examiner uses it a few times and it provides a fairly complete picture of a child's articulation skills. This is true not only for sounds in three positions but also for sounds produced in context. The Stimulability Subtest is not an outstanding feature because many examiners routinely test this feature. The GFTA compares very favorably to other similar picture articulation tests that check sounds in three positions and to some degree in spontaneous speech. It will continue to be a favorite of many practicing speech pathologists who want to make a rapid assessment of a child's articulation ability and compare the performance with other children of similar ages who have taken this test.

REVIEWER'S REFERENCES

Hull, F. M., Mielke, P. W., Jr., Timmons, R. J., & Willeford, J. A. (1971). *ASHA*. The National Speech and Hearing Survey: Preliminary results, 13, 501-509.

Byrne, M. C. (1972). [Review of the Goldman-Fristoe Test of Articulation]. In O. K. Buros (Ed.), *The seventh mental measurements yearbook* (p. 1339). Highland Park, NJ: The Gryphon Press.

Shelton, R. L. (1972). [Review of the Goldman-Fristoe Test of Articulation]. In O. K. Buros (Ed.), *The seventh mental measurements yearbook* (pp. 1339-1341). Highland Park, NJ: The Gryphon Press.

Fudala, J. B. (1974). Arizona Articulation Proficiency Scale. Los Angeles: Western Psychological Services.

Mecham, M. J. (1979). [Review of the Goldman-Fristoe Test of Articulation (GFTA)]. In F. L. Darley (Ed.), *Evaluation of appraisal techniques in speech and language pathology* (pp. 103-105). Reading, MA: Addison-Wesley.

Khan, L. M. L., & Lewis, N. P. (1986). Khan-Lewis Phonological Analysis. Circle Pines, MN: American Guidance Service.

[127]

The Golombok Rust Inventory of Sexual Satisfaction. Purpose: Provides "an objective assessment of the quality of a sexual relationship and of a person's function within it." Sex therapy clients; 1986; GRISS; 13 scores: Impotence, Premature Ejaculation, Male Non-sensuality, Male Avoidance, Male Dissatisfaction, Infrequency, Non-communication, Female Dissatisfaction, Female Avoidance, Female Non-sensuality, Vaginismus, Anorgasmia, Total; 2 forms: Male, Female; 1986 price data: £18.95 per complete set including 10 male questionnaires, 10 female questionnaires, and manual ('86, 30 pages); £4.95 per 10 male or female questionnaires; £8.95 per manual; [10] minutes; John Rust and Susan Golombok; NFER-Nelson Publishing Co., Ltd. [England].*

TEST REFERENCES

1. Rust, J., & Golombok, S. (1985). The Golombok-Rust Inventory of Sexual Satisfaction (GRISS). *British Journal of Clinical Psychology*, 24, 63-64.

2. Rust, J., & Golombok, K. S. (1986). The GRISS: A psychometric instrument for the assessment of sexual dysfunction. *Archives of Sexual Behavior*, 15, 157-165.

Review of The Golombok Rust Inventory of Sexual Satisfaction by KEVIN E. O'GRADY, Assistant Professor of Psychology, University of Maryland, College Park, MD:

The Golombok Rust Inventory of Sexual Satisfaction (GRISS) consists of two separate forms, one for males and one for females. Each form contains 28 questions to which respondents indicate frequency of occurrence on a 5-point scale. The points on the scale are: N (Never), H (Hardly Ever), O (Occasionally), U (Usually), and A (Always). Each item is scored, with scores ranging from 0 to 4. On both the male and female forms, responses to 24 of the 28 questions can be summed and then transformed to a 9-point scale to yield a global measure of sexual satisfaction. Moreover, it is possible to obtain seven subscale scores, which likewise can be transformed to 9-point scales. For males, the subscales are: Impotence (4 items); Premature Ejaculation (4); Male Non-sensuality (4); Male Avoidance (4); Male Dissatisfaction (4); Infrequency (2); and Non-communication (2). For females, the subscales are: Infrequency (2); Non-communication (2); Female Dissatisfaction (4); Female Avoidance (4); Female Non-sensuality (4); Vaginismus (4); and Anorgasmia (4). It should be noted that for both the male and female forms, the four items not summed in the global score are included in the Dissatisfaction subscale, and conversely, four items contained in the global score are not used in any subscale. Finally, it is possible to plot the transformed subscale scores for a couple, and obtain a GRISS profile that outlines the sexual functioning of the couple.

The manual describes the GRISS as intending to "provide an objective assessment of the quality of a sexual relationship and of a person's function within it." The manual does provide some detail related to definition of terms and theoretical rationale of the test. Moreover, the authors are quite clear about both the potential strengths of a test such as the GRISS, as well as potential limitations. Finally, a brief, straightforward description of sexual dysfunction and sex therapy is provided, assumedly for those potential test administrators unfamiliar with this material.

The remainder of the manual describes the design and development of the GRISS, and several studies regarding reliability and validity. A critical reading of this material indicates both a number of strengths of the GRISS as well as several significant limitations that need to be addressed by the developers of the test.

The major strengths are apparent in the developers' attention to detail. The manual describes a very careful, thoughtful multistep procedure followed for developing the test. Items were developed for a pilot version of the GRISS, based on considerable input from a number of experts, and this pilot version was revised based on various methods of content and statistical analysis. Moreover, the developers were clearly concerned with examining the utility of the GRISS with various populations, and several studies are reported with different samples and outcome measures.

A major weakness found in the manual is, in a number of cases, the inadequacy of the information provided. In some instances, the amount of information provided is simply too brief for any critical reader to make use of the material. For example, the results of several studies utilizing the GRISS are not described in sufficient detail to allow meaningful evaluation of the research. Some of the material is simply confusing. Results of various factor analyses are difficult to follow, as when a figure simply states that the "correlation between the two main scales is .04" without any additional information provided in the text that would elucidate such a statement. Finally, a standardization sample of only 88 sex therapy clients was used to develop the 9-point "pseudostanine scale." This is a fairly small sample to consider as a standardization sample; furthermore, the sample is not described in sufficient detail (e.g., age, race).

In summary, the GRISS represents a thoughtful first attempt at developing a test potentially useful both in research and clinical screening. The items on the test appear to sample both representatively and comprehensively from the sexual problems that occur in the general population. The items are generally well-written, unambiguous, and balanced between positive and negative statements. Nonetheless, some caution needs to be exercised by anyone who might consider adoption of the GRISS. The two foremost problems are (*a*) the lack of clarity and detail in critical areas in the manual; and (*b*) the use of a relatively small standardization sample. This latter problem is especially troubling in that the risk of diagnosing someone incorrectly, either because the standardization sample is unrepresentative of the population at large and/or the individual (or couple) is from a population not represented in the standardization sample seems significant. Any user of the GRISS should keep the last point keenly in mind.

[128]

Gordon Personal Profile—Inventory. Purpose: Provides a simply obtained measure of eight important factors in the personality domain. Grades 9–16 and adults; 1951–78; GPP-I; a combination of the Gordon Personal Profile and the Gordon Personal Inventory; separate booklet editions are still available; 1988 price data: $79 per 35 profile-inventory booklets; $25 per manual ('78, 105 pages); $35 per examination kit; (20–25) minutes; Leonard V. Gordon; The Psychological Corporation.*

a) GORDON PERSONAL PROFILE. 1953–63; 5 scores: Ascendancy, Responsibility, Emotional Stability, Sociability, Self-Esteem (Total); $43 per

35 booklets, manual, and keys; $36 per 35 answer documents; $35 per key for scoring answer documents; $17 per key for scoring booklets; (15–20) minutes.

b) GORDON PERSONAL INVENTORY. 1956–63; 4 scores: Cautiousness, Original Thinking, Personal Relations, Vigor; prices and time same as *a* above.

See 9:444 (1 reference), T3:966 (6 references), 8:568 (34 references), 8:569 (52 references), T2:1194 (56 references), and P:93 (23 references); for reviews by Charles F. Dicken and Alfred B. Heilbrun, Jr., see 6:102 (13 references) and 6:103 (25 references); for reviews by Benno G. Fricke and John A. Radcliffe and excerpted reviews by Laurance F. Shaffer and Laurence Siegel, see 5:58 and 5:59 (16 references).

TEST REFERENCES

1. Churchill, G. A., Jr., Ford, N. M., Hartley, S. W., & Walker, O. C., Jr. (1985). The determinants of salesperson performance: A meta-analysis. *Journal of Marketing Research*, 22, 103-118.

2. Schippmann, J. S., & Prien, E. P. (1985). The Ghiselli Self-description Inventory: A psychometric appraisal. *Psychological Reports*, 57, 1171-1177.

3. Henkin, B., & Fish, J. M. (1986). Gender and personality differences in the appreciation of cartoon humor. *The Journal of Psychology*, 120, 157-175.

4. Schippmann, J. S., & Prien, E. P. (1986). Individual difference correlates of two leadership styles. *Psychological Reports*, 59, 817-818.

Review of the Gordon Personal Profile—Inventory by DOUGLAS FUCHS, Associate Professor of Special Education, George Peabody College, Vanderbilt University, Nashville, TN:

The Gordon Personal Profile—Inventory (GPP-I) represents the unification of two previously developed self-report measures of personality: the Gordon Personal Profile (GPP) and Gordon Personal Inventory (GPI). The GPP explores four aspects of personality: Ascendancy (A), Responsibility (R), Emotional Stability (E), and Sociability (S). The sum of these four traits yields an additional index of Self-Esteem (SE). The GPI measures four traits: Cautiousness (C), Original Thinking (O), Personal Relations (P), and Vigor (V).

GPP and GPI consist of sets of four descriptive phrases, with each set referred to as a "tetrad." The personality traits (for GPP: A, R, E, S; for GPI: C, O, P, V) are each represented by a descriptive phrase in the tetrad. It is presumed that two phrases are of similar high preference value and two are of equal low preference value. As an example, for trait A, a purportedly high preference value phrase is, "Takes the lead in group discussion." The related low preference value phrase is, "Prefers to let others take the lead in group discussion." A forced-choice format requires that respondents mark one phrase in each tetrad as most like themselves and one as least like themselves.

The GPP-I is self-administered, requires approximately 25 minutes for completion, and is hand scored. Separate scoring keys are provided for GPP and GPI. Both measures, it is claimed, are "appropriate for use with high school, college, industrial, and general adult groups," and "have applications in selection, appraisal, vocational guidance, personal counseling, classroom demonstration, and basic research."

The manual demonstrates several strengths. It is well-organized, written clearly, and contains detailed information on certain procedures such as scoring. Additionally, for the most part, it provides clear information on important aspects of test development and technical adequacy. It also reports findings from studies addressing related practical issues like the potential for "faking" performance and differences in responses for racial-ethnic subgroups. Nevertheless, the GPP-I user should be aware of a number of limitations and concerns associated with item development, the establishment of norms, and indices of reliability and validity.

ITEM DEVELOPMENT. Initial items for GPP and GPI were taken from previous factor analytic investigations of personality and generated by calculating intercorrelations of college students' responses to various trait lists. Early versions of the measures were administered to small homogeneous college samples. Peer ratings were obtained concurrently and used as a criterion index. Because the responses of these samples formed the basis for determining high and low preference value phrases, an obvious question is whether their judgments about the desirability and undesirability of various attitudes and behaviors are representative of the larger population.

On page 32 of the manual the author answers affirmatively: "The GPP-I has been found to be appropriate for use with academic, industrial, and other adult samples, including American minority groups." However, data in the manual appear to contradict this assertion. Results from three studies of Black and Caucasian responses to GPP and GPI indicate that, among 24 possible racial contrasts (three studies x eight traits), eight contrasts (33%) were statistically significant (see Tables 45–47, pp. 61–62). Moreover, the significant contrasts involved six of eight personality traits making up the GPP and GPI. Acknowledging the possibility that population subgroups may demonstrate different preferences for GPP and GPI items, the author suggests that, "These differences may be compensated for by the use of appropriate group norms." However, as indicated below, the GPP-I manual provides limited normative information.

NORMS. Tables 1, 2, and 3 (pp. 8–10) are provided to assist the user in converting obtained trait scores to percentile rank equivalents. They represent female and male college students, adult females, and female and male high school students, respectively. Thus, no norms are provided for adult males, reducing the usefulness of the GPP and GPI.

Furthermore, users have reason to question the representativeness of the normative data that *are* provided. Norms for college students were based principally on freshman and sophomore liberal arts majors from moderately to highly selective institutions. Information on page 7 of the manual is vague concerning geographic representation, and there is an absence of data on the samples' race and SES. Moreover, only 26% responded to both the GPP and GPI. The remainder were administered one *or* the other. Because "The corresponding percentiles, based on smoothed distributions, were found to be almost identical," it is an assumption, not a fact, that the largely different normative groups for GPP and GPI were representative of the same college population.

The GPP normative sample of high school students was from the Northeast and Midwest; the GPI sample was drawn from the South and Southwest. It is claimed without substantiation that "the upper four grade levels (9th through 12th) are about equally represented in both sets of norms." Again, race and SES of the samples are not provided. The adult female sample was drawn exclusively from the Midwest and was "almost exclusively housewives . . . not otherwise employed. Most were in their thirties and 'middle class.'" For the college, high school, and adult normative samples, it is also unclear when the norms were obtained. The *Standards for Educational and Psychological Testing* (American Educational Research Association, American Psychological Association, & National Council on Measurement in Education, 1985) encourages test developers to report such information (see Standard 4.4, p. 33). Because the GPP and GPI were first published in the early and mid-1950s, it is possible these norms may be nearly 35 years old.

Additional norms are presented for various industrial groups (see Tables 4–7). Again representativeness is an issue. Each table represents the responses of a relatively small number of employees from only one company.

RELIABILITY. The author claims the GPP and GPI "provide reliable measures of eight well-established personality traits." However, again, this assertion is not fully supported by evidence in the manual, and requires qualification. Tables 10 and 11 on page 20 provide split-half reliabilities for the personality traits in the GPP (.82 to .89) and GPI (.79 to .84). Test-retest reliability (involving a 29-week hiatus) for all eight traits ranged from .50 to .70 (see Tables 12 and 13, p. 21). No *SEM* or confidence intervals are reported for these data. Moreover, these reliability indices are based on small and highly restrictive samples of college students, managers in a single company, and navy enlisted men. Thus, it remains unclear whether the reliabilities of GPP and GPI generalize to other population groups.

Another concern addresses the suggested use of cutoff scores. The author writes, "In some settings, the Self-Esteem score has been used to identify students to be seen by the counseling service." On page 26 of the manual, a Self-Esteem score of 72 or below (on the GPP) is suggested as the demarcation point of low self-esteem. Contrary to guidelines in the *Standards* (see Standard 2.10, p. 22), no *SEM* is reported for this cutoff score, despite its suggested use in classifying students and selecting them for special treatment.

VALIDITY. A total of 17 studies, many conducted by other investigators, explored the concurrent validity of the GPP and/or GPI with measures of intelligence, ratings by peers, and other self-report personality measures. A majority of these studies were conducted on college students and military personnel between 1951 and 1975, with a median study year of 1966. Correlations are low to moderate in magnitude. Predictive validity, reported as product-moment correlations, is based largely on students in college in the 1950s and 1960s. The magnitude of these correlations tends to be low (see Tables 37–39).

The author describes findings from several studies, which, contrary to his interpretation, demonstrate a consistent pattern among examiners to "fake good" (i.e., choose answers that create a favorable impression). Anastasi (1982) provides much additional evidence that examinees dissemble on personality inventories. It should probably be considered an important limitation of the GPP-I that it does not have a validity score like the MMPI, Edwards Personal Preference Scale, or Personality Research Form.

MANUAL FORMAT AND SCORING. The manual is unclear about the relationship between GPP, GPI, and GPP-I. GPP-I is infrequently mentioned, appearing initially as a footnote on page 5. The first time it is mentioned in the text is on page 32. The manual is also vague about the importance and uses of GPP-I. The pertinent section, "Uses of the Profile and Inventory" is located at the very end of the manual, and is too brief. Finally, it is unclear whether there is a separate GPP-I scoring key in addition to the GPP and GPI scoring keys (see footnote on bottom of page 5).

SUMMARY. The GPP-I is a self-report measure that represents a relatively simple, economical means of obtaining information on eight personality traits. The author contends the GPP-I is appropriate for use with a wide range of groups, and may be put to multiple purposes, such as vocational guidance, personal counseling, and classroom demonstration. Nevertheless, data in the manual on the technical adequacy of this measure do not appear to support the claim; item development and the establishment of norms and indices of reliability and validity were typically based on small homogeneous samples. Moreover, many of these samples were tested as many as 35 years ago.

REVIEWER'S REFERENCES

Anastasi, A. (1982). *Psychological testing* (5th ed.). New York: Macmillan.

American Educational Research Association, American Psychological Association, & National Council on Measurement in Education. (1985). *Standards for educational and psychological testing*. Washington, DC: American Psychological Association, Inc.

Review of the Gordon Personal Profile—Inventory by ALFRED B. HEILBRUN, JR., Professor of Psychology, Emory University, Atlanta, GA:

The Gordon Personal Profile—Inventory, like the Minnesota Multiphasic Personality Inventory and the California Psychological Inventory, is a survivor among personality measures. Construction of the Gordon Personal Profile and Gordon Personal Inventory began in the early 1950s. The two tests, now routinely combined into a single measure, have received sufficient scrutiny over the intervening years by the developer and other interested researchers to allow a confident verdict regarding their worth. By and large, the Personal Profile—Inventory has proven itself to be a valuable tool for measuring personality traits. In addition, the latest manual, published in 1978, is both readable and complete. Not the least of the manual's virtues is a reference section including well over 260 relevant publications bearing upon the Personal Profile—Inventory.

The emergence of this test as one of the dependable personality measurement tools is not accidental. The test development procedures were thorough and based upon sound psychometric principles. The eight personality variables represented in the Profile and the Inventory (see test entry) evolved from the factor-analytic work of Raymond Cattell and found item representation in a forced-choice format that seems to restrict dissimulation and to avoid disadvantages associated with ipsative measurement. Even in its current combined form, the Personal Profile—Inventory requires only about 20 to 25 minutes to complete, and the instructions seem clear enough to allow self-administration without significant problems.

The manual includes a substantial amount of information bearing upon interscale correlation, test reliability, construct validity, dissimulation, and norms. Relationships among the eight scales of the Personal Profile—Inventory are quite low for the most part. The highest correlation reported is .68 between Ascendancy and Sociability, still far short of the scale intercorrelation often found with the Minnesota Multiphasic Personality Inventory. The average absolute interscale correlation is reported to be less than .25. The test scores do not change much even when subjects are tested under conditions, such as employment situations, conducive to creating favorable impressions.

Reliability is quite adequate when considered in terms of internal consistency (.80s) and holds up as well as would be expected over protracted test-retest intervals (.50s).

Two types of percentile normative tables are available. There are large-scale norms, presented separately by sex, that provide expectations for college and high school students. In addition, a number of special-interest norms are provided for those concerned with occupational differences. Actually, one of the few problems I could find with the manual is the failure to include useful general adult norms for testing situations in which the occupational norms are not relevant. There are norms for adult women presented, but these are based upon limited numbers. No general adult standards for men are included. Perhaps the next manual will rectify this problem.

A respectable accumulation of research by Gordon and by many others relevant to the issue of validity is reviewed in the manual. Much of the validity evidence is not very impressive, taken each piece in isolation. Yet, the aggregate of small but statistically significant relationships does add up to a satisfactory construct validation of the instrument. These reservations about test validity are not unique to the Personal Profile—Inventory itself. Similar problems are apparent for personality assessment instruments in general. None of our current tests is powerful enough for individual prediction without considerable risk of error. Gordon's instrument is certainly valid but introduces the same risk if used to predict for the individual.

[129]

Graduate and Managerial Assessment. Purpose: "Intended for use in the recruitment, selection and assessment of graduates; the identification of management and promotion potential; and the recruitment of those such as 'A' level school leavers who may be capable of entering higher education." Undergraduate and graduate students; 1985; GMA; 3 tests: Numerical, Verbal, Abstract; 2 forms: A, B; 1987 price data: £43.25 per reference set; £30 per 10 Numerical test booklets (specify Form A or Form B); £36 per 10 Verbal test booklets (specify Form A or Form B); £47 per 10 Abstract test booklets (specify Form A or Form B); £20 per 25 self-scoring answer sheets (specify test and form); £5.50 per administrator's test records; £9.50 per instruction cards; £19.50 per manual (59 pages); (30) minutes per test; Psychometric Research Unit, The Hatfield Polytechnic; NFER-Nelson Publishing Co., Ltd. [England].*

Review of the Graduate and Managerial Assessment by PHILIP G. BENSON, Assistant Professor of Management, New Mexico State University, Las Cruces, NM:

The Graduate and Managerial Assessment (GMA) is a three-part test of abilities assumed to be relevant in the selection of high level personnel in organizations, most notably in managerial and executive positions. The three subtests consist of Numerical (GMA-N), Verbal (GMA-V), and "Abstract" (GMA-A) components, and would seem to have much in common with many tests of general intellectual ability.

At the outset, it is worthy of note that the test was developed and published in Great Britain at the Psychometric Research Unit of The Hatfield Polytechnic. Because of the British development history, the tests are likely to be awkward with many users outside of the British Commonwealth. In some instances the British influence is trivial, for example, the use of British idioms and examples. However, at times interpretation becomes problematic for non-British audiences. For example, the test of numerical ability is designed to require no more mathematical sophistication than is assumed for "o" level standard, while the verbal test is appropriate for all levels "from sixth-form school-leaver to senior executive." Within the tests themselves, the assumed monetary units are pounds, cars run on petrol, and spellings are British. In short, the test may have much to recommend it to British users, but U.S. users may want to be cautious that these issues are not irrelevant sources of difficulty.

The numerical test (GMA-N) is designed to be a relatively speeded, rather than a power test. The test developers intended this as a way to force test takers to use general estimations and judgments, instead of focusing on long and relatively laborious calculations. The underlying assumption is that useful quantitative thinking in managerial positions is based in seeing general mathematical relationships, and that these capabilities will be better estimated through quick but approximate interpretations. In addition, the item distractors are in many cases developed on the basis of errors typically made by test takers, so that their plausibility is increased. The actual mathematical skills required include ratios and proportions, percentages, simple statistics, simple equations, exchange rates, probability, and the ability to assimilate information presented in tables and graphs. In general, the items tend to have fair face validity for business applications.

The verbal test (GMA-V) is based in the assumption that high-level managerial work requires individuals to reach logical conclusions from verbally presented material, and that often such material is only somewhat familiar. To meet this objective, material is included that is semitechnical, but drawn from general literature so as not to require truly specific technical skills or training. The items vary in the extent to which they deal with overtly business-oriented material, although many of the items have high face validity in this regard.

The test manual suggests the test is in the tradition of the Watson-Glaser Critical Thinking Appraisal, although much of the test content is a closer reflection of the work done at the Psychometric Research Unit. The test's intent is to raise issues of personal relevance to the test takers, and require them to sort out the information needed to draw logical conclusions. It is suggested that such situations are more realistic than simple analogies or basic problems in logic, given the use of the test in business settings.

The abstract test (GMA-A) is highly reminiscent of Raven's Advanced Progressive Matrices, and is designed to measure the ability to see abstract relationships. In particular, the ability to change set and think divergently is suggested as at the core of this subtest. Specific educational attainment is deliberately minimized within the test. In addition, the time allotted is designed to emphasize the power aspects of the test, rather than the element of speed.

The manual suggests two uses for the GMA-A. First, it can be used as a test in its own right, measuring the ability to think flexibly, to see order where none is apparent, and to focus on relevant issues and ignore unimportant details. The second suggested use is to aid in interpretation of the other two tests. In particular, it is suggested that difference scores can be used to identify those individuals whose high scores on the other two tests result from excessive rote learning rather than true creative insight. However, given the problems in the interpretation of difference scores, this reviewer is somewhat skeptical of the practicality of this second suggestion, although theoretically, the notion is interesting. In addition, although the data on difference scores reported in the manual are very limited, the authors do offer to give greater details if contacted.

All three subtests have been developed in two forms, and the manual gives substantial detail on the steps used to ensure comparability. Although much of the documented work is very commendable, at times the developers seem to have gone a bit far. In particular, the GMA-V was developed with the objective of having the same scoring key applicable to both forms, which is not a traditional requirement of parallel tests. In addition, it is worth noting that examinees' scores may vary if the subtests are given in combination versus given in separate sessions. Score correlations are higher when the tests (GMA-N, V, A) are given in a single session. Apparently the similarity of the mental operations across the forms can be remembered, at least over brief periods of time.

Perhaps the greatest reservation raised by the material presented in the manual deals with the data on reliability and validity of the GMA. Essentially, not enough information is available to document the test's value. The manual does a fairly good job of reporting the available data but more information is required before any firm conclusions about the value or usefulness of the test can be reached.

First, the norms presented are based on a very small sample. The initial norming sample consisted of 596 students in British universities; however, the sample was broken down so that each respondent dealt only with a subsample of all of the tests. Thus, the reported sample sizes are relatively small, especially when considering data for specific gender or other groups. The manual explicitly recognizes this problem, and the suggestion is made that local norms should be developed. This is inadequate test development.

Reliability data are somewhat disappointing. Given this is an abilities test, higher interscale correlations should be expected. For Forms A and B of each subtest, reported internal consistency reliabilities are .82 and .82 (GMA-N), .73 and .71 (GMA-V), and .68 and .67 (GMA-A). (Note that the GMA-A test does report higher reliabilities using another scoring method, but the figures reported here are for the recommended method of scoring.) In addition, the GMA-N is relatively speeded, such that the estimate of reliability could be spuriously high. This interpretation is tempered somewhat by the fact that scores reflect both power and speed. Still, although the reliabilities are not unacceptable, they are certainly less than desirable.

In addition, it is worth noting that the GMA-A shows somewhat higher correlations across parallel forms when the two forms are given in the same session. Apparently, the mental operations required by the sets of items can be remembered over relatively short periods of time, making the reasoning tasks sensitive to recall of prior problem solutions. Thus, an adequate value for parallel-forms reliability likely can only be obtained when a brief time is allowed between testings, such that prior items will have largely been forgotten.

Validity data are sparse. The manual points out the authors were more concerned with construct validity than predictive validity for the initial release of the tests and manual. The validity data are inadequate. The manual does suggest that caution be used in using the tests unless the abilities represented can be clearly related to the job. This is especially prudent given the high degree to which the tests resemble tests of general intellectual ability. Far more data are needed on job performance predictions.

Overall, the test has reasonably high face validity, and shows evidence of some careful developmental work. The manual does a good job of presenting the available data in a relatively readable manner for the average user. However, at present the test should be considered as experimental, and should be used only with substantial caution. Its potential, however, should not be ignored.

Review of the Graduate and Managerial Assessment by RHONDA L. GUTENBERG, Management Consultant, Personnel Decisions, Inc., St. Paul, MN:

The Graduate and Managerial Assessment (GMA) consists of three tests to be used individually, in pairs, or as a three-test battery. The three abilities measured are Verbal, Numerical, and Abstract Reasoning. Each test is intended to discriminate at the upper 12½ percent of the population; thus, their application is likely to be limited to selection and/or identification of the "cream of the crop" (typically in either an academic or work setting). I would like to begin by addressing each test individually and then discuss issues common across the GMA battery. Only Form A of each test was reviewed, so these comments may not apply to Form B.

The GMA-Verbal (GMA-V) is intended to measure one's ability to assess information presented verbally without the requirement of technical or specialized knowledge. The test draws from a number of topics, and the format of a paragraph (stem) followed by four statements is a good method for assessing comprehension. There is, however, one item (page 9, questions 23 and 24) that does require additional specialized knowledge in the opinion of this reviewer.

The instructions state that one should "assume that what is stated in the passage is true—even if it contradicts what you know or believe to be the case in reality." An additional instruction should be included that says something to the effect that it is permissible to utilize other knowledge (not explicitly stated in the paragraph) or common sense to further deduce the veracity of the statements. There are three questions in particular (questions 36, 47, and 48) that do not draw from information found directly in the stem (which would tend to lead the test taker to answer "Can't Tell"); however, they could be answered either True or False when further deductions are made.

There are two questions (questions 19 and 27) that are ambiguous as they are currently worded. And finally, there are four questions (questions 20, 30, 31, and 54) that in the opinion of this reviewer, and others whom I consulted, are keyed with incorrect answers. In our opinion the first three questions cited above (questions 20, 30, and 31) should be answered "Can't Tell." Perhaps additional knowledge (of a more specialized nature) is to be drawn upon to derive the authors' answers. It should be noted, too, that three of the questions (numbers 20, 24, and 36) have rather poor item statistics associated with them. More specifically, all three have means less than .19, item-scale correlations less than .15 (with one equal to -.02), and item-partial correlations less than .08 (with one equal to -.08). This suggests that these items should be examined more carefully if they are to continue to be a part of the GMA-V.

With the above exceptions, the format and level of difficulty of the GMA-V items seem very suitable for its intended purpose.

The GMA-Abstract (GMA-A) is designed to measure one's capacity to think flexibly and to use analytic skills. For each problem there are two squares, each containing four patterns. Below the two squares are five separate patterns, and the required task is to identify to which one of the two squares each pattern belongs. The GMA-A requires the test taker to identify the common element amongst the four patterns in square one that is different from the four patterns in square two and then to test this hypothesis. In my opinion, this is a very challenging and enjoyable test and appears to measure what it is intended to measure. I applaud the test authors for including in the Manual and User's Guide the caveat that one should not assume this test is culture-free (something many might be prone to do because it is a nonverbal test). They go on to explain that "abstract diagrammatic material may be unfamiliar to certain cultural groups." The manual also explains that the GMA-A was developed to identify "potential high fliers." Evidence provided in the manual suggests the test has promise in this area.

The item statistics associated with GMA-A questions 16, 17, 18, and 19 (which all apply to the same problem on page 9) raise some concern. The item means are all less than .09, item-scale correlations are less than .25, and item-partial correlations fall below .18. Perhaps this problem should be eliminated from the test.

Finally, the GMA-Numerical (GMA-N) is intended to measure problem-solving and reasoning as opposed to mechanical arithmetic skills. It appears to be a very appropriate instrument for doing so. The test authors point out that with the availability of calculators, problem-solving skills are far more important than skills in mere calculation. The format is quite good—a short verbal stem, graph, or chart of information is followed by three questions. Sixteen response alternatives are provided for each group of three questions. This format helps eliminate guessing but still provides the ease of scoring a multiple-choice response. Finally, each of the three questions per stem requires a different level of mental-processing complexity. Thus, one can identify the complexity of the items answered incorrectly by the test taker.

The GMA-N (as well as the other two tests) was developed and published in Great Britain. Subtest information is presented in terms of the monetary unit of pounds. Although this is a cultural difference, I do not see it as even a slight obstacle for use in the United States or elsewhere. This is a good test for discriminating quantitative problem-solving skills at the upper level of the population.

Regarding the GMA battery as a whole, there are four areas I would like to address: test administration instructions, the Administrator's Test Record, answer sheets, and the Manual and User's Guide.

In the instructions given to test takers, no reference is made as to whether or not there will be penalties for incorrect answers. The only related comment is to "Work quickly, but not so quickly that you start making unnecessary mistakes." A small point regarding the instructions is that when the test takers are asked to open their booklets and follow instructions, they should be told to which page to turn.

The Administrator's Test Record is a thorough form providing for very detailed information and accurate tracking of tests. There are spaces for two pieces of information, however, that are not clear to me ("Candidates' details" and "Recommendations"), and I think a more thorough explanation of what is meant by these terms is necessary. The answer sheets are a clever, convenient, and efficient mechanism for scoring the various GMA tests.

Finally, the GMA Manual and User's Guide receives praise for its thoroughness and clarity. The intended use and application for each test are described, as are the overall content and development, including the pilot and standardized research. Norms are provided in the manual; however, the authors wisely encourage users to develop local norms and suggest using the published norms until local norms are established. There is a complete discussion of reliability and validity, with accompanying data. Several comments are made to promote user contribution of data to the authors. Data are presented on item analyses and construct validity, and descriptions of concurrent- and predictive-validity studies in progress are provided. The authors are very good at noting any limitations in data and/or interpretation of results.

In Great Britain it may not be of concern; however, in the United States we are interested not only in validity differences due to sex but also in those due to membership in ethnic groups. This area of research has been neglected. One other data omission, in the reviewer's judgment, is significance level or *p*-values in the construct validity data.

Overall, I would recommend use of these tests for discrimination of bright people in the work and academic settings. The GMA-V may need some items revised or the user may want to eliminate the items I have cited earlier. On the whole, though, the GMA-V, GMA-A, and GMA-N are well-written, challenging, well-designed tests. Adequate research has gone into their development, and continuing research is planned and currently under way. The Manual and User's Guide is rather thorough and presents technical information in a very clear manner. Research needs to be conducted on ethnic differences, but otherwise the authors have done a very good job.

[130]

Grammar Test Packet. Purpose: Provides tests over all phases of grammar, punctuation, and capitalization, plus general review. High school students; no date; 15 tests; 1985 price data: $3.95 per complete packet including answer keys; administration time not reported; Kenneth Stratton and George Christian; Stratton-Christian Press, Inc.*

[131]

Gray Oral Reading Tests, Revised. Purpose: To identify students with reading difficulties, to identify strengths and weaknesses of readers, to document progress in regular or special reading programs, and to conduct research. Ages 6-6 to 17-11; 1963–86; GORT-R; 3 scores: Passage, Comprehension, Oral Reading Quotient; individual; 1986 price data: $63 per complete set including examiner's manual ('86, 60 pages), student book, and 25 profile/examiner record forms; $29 per 25 profile/examiner record forms; $16 per student book; $21 per examiner's manual; (15–30) minutes; J. Lee Wiederholt and Brian R. Bryant; PRO-ED, Inc.*

See T3:1007 (32 references) and T2:1681 (11 references); for reviews by Emery P. Bliesmer, Albert J. Harris, and Paul R. Lohnes of an earlier edition, see 6:842.

TEST REFERENCES

1. Little, V. L., & Kendall, P. C. (1978). Note on locus of control and academic achievement in institutionalized juvenile delinquents. *Journal of Abnormal Child Psychology*, 6, 281-283.

2. Cermak, L. S., Goldberg-Warter, J., DeLuca, D., Cermak, S., & Drake, C. (1981). The role of interference in the verbal retention ability of learning disabled children. *Journal of Learning Disabilities*, 14, 291-295.

3. Ryckman, D. B. (1982). Gray Oral Reading Tests: Some reliability and validity data with learning-disabled children. *Psychological Reports*, 50, 673-674.

4. Eskenazi, B., & Diamond, S. P. (1983). Visual exploration of non-verbal material by dyslexic children. *Cortex*, 19, 353-370.

5. Gadow, K. D. (1983). Effects of stimulant drugs on academic performance in hyperactive and learning disabled children. *Journal of Learning Disabled*, 16, 290-299.

6. Gerber, M. J. P., & White, D. R. (1983). Verbal factors in visual recognition memory of poor readers. *Perceptual and Motor Skills*, 57, 851-857.

7. Gittleman, R., & Eskenazi, B. (1983). Lead and hyperactivity revisited: An investigation of nondisadvantaged children. *Archives of General Psychiatry*, 40, 827-833.

8. Lewis, D. O., Shanok, S. S., Grant, M., & Ritvo, E. (1983). Homicidally aggressive young children: Neuropsychiatric and experiential correlates. *The American Journal of Psychiatry*, 140, 148-153.

9. White, M., & Miller, S. R. (1983). Dyslexia: A term in search of a definition. *The Journal of Special Education*, 17, 5-10.

10. Hardman, P. K. (1984). The training of psycho-educational technicians (para-professionals) to administer a screening battery which delineates dyslexia and hyperkinesis. *Journal of Learning Disabilities*, 17, 453-456.

11. Scarborough, H. S. (1984). Continuity between childhood dyslexia and adult reading. *British Journal of Psychology*, 75, 329-348.

12. Sherman, R. G., Berling, B. S., & Oppenheimer, S. (1985). Increasing community independence for adolescents with spina bifida. *Adolescence*, 20, 1-13.

13. Davenport, L., Yingling, C. D., Fein, G., Galin, D., & Johnstone, J. (1986). Narrative speech deficits in dyslexics. *Journal of Clinical and Experimental Neuropsychology*, 8, 347-361.

14. Wolf, M., Bally, H., & Morris, R. (1986). Automaticity, retrieval processes, and reading: A longitudinal study in average and impaired readers. *Child Development*, 57, 988-1000.

15. Werker, J. F., & Tees, R. C. (1987). Speech perception in severely disabled and average reading children. *Canadian Journal of Psychology*, 41 (1), 48-61.

Review of the Gray Oral Reading Tests, Revised by JULIA A. HICKMAN, Assistant Professor of School Psychology, University of Texas at Austin, Austin, TX:

The Gray Oral Reading Tests, Revised (GORT-R) is appropriately billed by its authors as a major revision of the original Gray Reading Test (GORT) (Gray, 1963). The original GORT was a revision of the Standardized Oral Reading Paragraphs developed by William Gray in 1915. The GORT-R, like its predecessors, is an individually administered oral test of reading skills designed to assist diagnosis of reading difficulties in individuals ages 6 years 6 months to 17 years 11 months. The test consists of two alternate forms (A and B) instead of the four forms available on the GORT. Each form includes 13 reading passages of increasing difficulty.

On the GORT-R, the student reads each passage aloud to the examiner who, in turn, records the errors made by the student. Errors made when reading orally are labelled "deviations from print." The examiner must simultaneously record the time it takes the student to read the passage. The number of deviations from print and reading rate are used to derive a Passage Score for each paragraph read by the individual. Passage Scores on each paragraph are then summed to yield an overall Passage Score.

After completing each passage the student is asked five multiple-choice comprehension questions, instead of the open-ended questions used on the original GORT. An overall comprehension standard score is derived by summing the comprehension raw scores on each passage and converting the sum of raw scores to a standard score and percentile score for comprehension. This allows the examiner to make norm-referenced comparisons for an individual student. On the GORT only raw scores in Comprehension were provided, a practice making norm-reference interpretations tedious and prone to error.

The GORT-R manual is well written and relatively complete. The test takes approximately 15 to 30 minutes to administer. Materials required for administration include a student booklet, a stopwatch, and the examiner's manual. These materials are packaged nicely and directions for administration and scoring are easy to understand.

The GORT-R differs from the 1967 GORT in several substantive ways. These changes correct many of the deficiencies of the original GORT noted in previous reviews (e.g., Bliesmer, Harris, Lohnes, 1965). It is somewhat confusing why the authors of the GORT-R repeatedly refer to the 1967 GORT while the same test is elsewhere designated as having been published in 1963 (6:842). The first revision involved renorming the test on a more representative sample of children ages 7 through 17. In addition, several studies investigating the reliability and validity of the new GORT-R were conducted and reported in the manual. The GORT-R was standardized on a sample of 1,401 students between the ages of 7 and 17, from 15 states representing four major geographic regions of the United States. The sample was further representative based on sex, residence, race, and ethnicity. The methods by which the normative sample was chosen are detailed in the test manual.

The manual presents little information regarding examiner qualifications and training necessary to administer the GORT-R. Given the test's content and format, this is an unfortunate oversight. Although on the surface, the GORT-R seems simple and straightforward to administer and score, closer inspection leaves little doubt that the examiner should be well trained in individual testing, test interpretation, as well as the GORT-R.

The importance of prior training is particulary apparent when one considers how reading scores on the GORT-R are calculated and used in remedial programming. The examiner must time the student's rate of reading a specific passage and simultaneously note any errors made when reading orally. The passage scores and the overall Passage Score are dependent on the rate as well as the number of errors made when reading. It is therefore imperative the examiner be very precise in timing reading rate as well as recording reading errors. Accurate decisions can only be made from accurate data.

The manual also presents a detailed error analysis system to use with the GORT-R that is quite easy to execute in terms of marking and recording but rather complicated in terms of classifying and interpreting test data obtained. The examiner would need extensive knowledge of reading processes and terminology to accurately execute this reading analysis system. The authors of the GORT-R are remiss in their failure to state necessary examiner qualifications.

On the other hand, the authors are to be commended for excluding grade-equivalent scores for the GORT-R when it is more popular and at times more financially profitable to make them available. Although the misinterpretation and misuse of grade-equivalent scores have been noted for many years (e.g., Reynolds, 1981), as yet few test authors or publishers have refrained from providing them in test manuals. The use of grade-equivalent scores most often occurs because consumers continue to demand these scores and publishers are hesitant to disappoint consumers. The authors of the GORT-R have chosen to educate the naive consumer regarding the deficiencies of grade-equivalent scores and have followed up on their conclusions by not providing these scores.

The standardization and technical properties of the GORT-R far surpass those of the GORT. Several studies relevant to the reliability and the validity of the GORT-R are presented. Three approaches were used to examine the reliability of the GORT-R. First, Coefficient Alpha formulas were used to calculate the internal consistency reliability of the GORT-R. Alpha is presented for the Comprehension, the Passage, and the Oral Reading Scores of the GORT-R. The resultant values are quite acceptable for both forms across the age range. The values range from an average of .87 on the Passage Scores on Form A to .96 for the Comprehension Score on both forms.

Alternate-forms reliability coefficients also appear adequate, although not excellent, with values of .80 on the Passage Score, .81 on the Comprehension Score, and .83 on the Oral Reading Quotient Score reported. The authors do not report the interval between the administrations of each form which is of primary importance when determining the alternate-form reliability of an instrument (Anastasi, 1982), because the alternate-forms reliability is a measure of the consistency of the trait being measured across forms and not the consistency over time as in test-retest approaches to reliability.

The standard errors of measurement (*SEM*) for the GORT-R are calculated appropriately using internal consistency reliability coefficients and are reported in the manual across the five age ranges for each of the three major scores. The average *SEM* for the standard scores across the age range and forms of the test range from .60 on the Comprehension Score to 3.6 on Form A for the Oral Reading Quotient. Although the *SEM* is presented on the raw scores on the GORT-R, the authors do not elaborate on when the *SEM* may be used to interpret raw scores. The *SEM*s overall are small enough to provide the test user assurance that the obtained score is close to the child's true score.

There is a glaring omission of evidence of scorer reliability on the GORT-R. On a test where the calculation of scores depends so heavily on an examiner's recording of reading errors, it seems important to determine the degree to which different examiners score the same reading passages. This information could be presented in terms of interscorer reliability data.

The authors begin the section on validity with a complete definition of validity taken from Gronlund (1985). The authors are to be commended for attending to such professional detail, although in reality the evidence for validity presented in the manual is not without limitations. For example, the first validation approach involves a discussion of establishing the content validity of the GORT-R. Unfortunately, the authors, while defining content validity correctly, albeit with an incorrect reference to Anastasi (page 32 of manual), suggest the reader reread a previous section of the manual in order to determine evidence for content validity of the GORT-R for themselves. In an otherwise quite detailed manual, this seems like an inexcusable presentation on the authors' part.

Only the concurrent validity of the GORT-R is examined as evidence for the test's criterion-related validity. Several empirical analyses were conducted examining the relationship of GORT-R scores with various measures of reading. In each study, standard scores were appropriately used and each validity coefficient appropriately attenuated to account for the imperfect reliability of the criterion measure.

One of the concurrent-related validity analyses conducted failed to present adequate information regarding the number of children used. This is considered unacceptable evidence of validity. Also, the fourth study reported only teacher ratings of a student's reading ability and the student's score on the GORT-R as evidence of validity. However, the ratings were only of 37 students from two grades. The data reported from this study are the least useful in establishing the concurrent validity of the GORT-R. It is probable the teachers had considerable quantitative and qualitative information regarding the students' reading ability before the GORT-R was administered. Thus, experimenter bias was not controlled and its effects on the obtained data cannot be established. Reliability of the teacher ratings was also not established.

In regard to the construct validity of the GORT-R, the authors compare scores on the GORT-R with age of the students, their language abilities, total school achievement, and intelligence. Although age discrimination and group differentiation provide partial evidence for the GORT-R's construct validity, the finding that GORT-R scores correlate well with measures of language, total achievement, and intelligence fails to provide the necessary remaining evidence of construct validity of the GORT-R. That is, the test is billed as a measure of general oral reading ability and, as such, the construct validity should at least be established by first defining the theoretical construct of oral reading ability then providing evidence that it in fact measures that construct. This could be done by correlating the GORT-R scores with scores on other well-known, accepted oral reading measures thus establishing the convergent validity of the test. This data would be compared to the correlation of scores obtained on the GORT-R with scores on tests unrelated to reading (e.g., math calculation) or with measures of language, intelligence, etc., thus establishing its divergent validity.

Although the authors suggest and encourage the use of other tests to supplement data on the GORT-R in diagnosing reading difficulties, their motives are questionable in that they only suggest the use of tests published by their personal publishing company rather than mentioning solid reading assessment instruments published by other companies.

Despite several minor limitations, the GORT-R should remain a valuable addition in the never ending search for appropriate instruments for the diagnosis and remediation of reading problems. The new normative data and other substantive additions made by the current authors have increased flexibility in use of the test and flexibility in interpretation of its derived scores.

REVIEWER'S REFERENCES

Bliesmer, E. P. (1965). [Review of Gray Oral Reading Test]. In O. K. Buros (Ed.), *The sixth mental measurements yearbook* (pp. 1129-1130). Highland Park, NJ: The Gryphon Press.

Harris, A. J. (1965). [Review of Gray Oral Reading Test]. In O. K. Buros (Ed.), *The sixth mental measurements yearbook* (pp. 1130-1131). Highland Park, NJ: The Gryphon Press.

Lohnes, Paul R. (1965). [Review of Gray Oral Reading Test]. In O. K. Buros (Ed.), *The sixth mental measurements yearbook* (pp. 1131-1132). Highland Park, NJ: The Gryphon Press.

Reynolds, C. R. (1981). The fallacy of "two years below grade level for age" as a diagnostic criterion for reading disorders. *Journal of School Psychology*, 19, 350-358.

Anastasi, A. (1982). *Psychological testing* (5th ed.). New York: Macmillan.

Gronlund, N. E. (1985). *Measurement and evaluation in teaching* (5th ed.). New York: Macmillan.

Review of the Gray Oral Reading Tests, Revised by ROBERT J. TIERNEY, Professor of Educational Theory and Practice, The Ohio State University, Columbus, OH:

The Gray Oral Reading Tests, Revised represents a rather restricted attempt to update the Gray Oral Reading Test, originally published in 1923 and again in 1967. The authors of the revised edition claim they have taken notice of the latest research findings to improve the original battery. Unfortunately, their highly selective and interpretive translation does little to alter a test that is out of step with our current knowledge of reading; indeed, many of the changes implemented in the current edition have created new problems.

For instance, the test emphasizes reading rate, error-free oral reading, and reading comprehension of texts of limited length. Little context and no purpose for reading are provided; and no probes beyond multiple-choice questions are included. In contrast, our knowledge of reading comprehension suggests that readers: (*a*) vary their rate according to the type of texts they read and the purposes they have for reading them; (*b*) perform differently depending upon whether they read short or longer texts and whether they read orally or silently; and (*c*) are apt to offer responses to multiple-choice items that may or may not represent their understandings.

There are also problems with the assumptions underlying the development of this test. To justify the aggregation of scores, the test developers applied item-test discrimination indices as a basis for ensuring homogeneity in student performance across items included in the battery. Homogeneity, however, runs counter to research findings suggesting that any single student's performance is likely to vary relatively unpredictably from one text to another.

Another major problem with the revision of the test is the use of ceilings as a means of expediting the administration of the test. The current authors impose the use of 60% as the criterion students must exceed if they are to continue. Because accuracy with which students will respond oftentimes fluctuates from one passage to the next (regardless of the difficulty level of the passage), the imposition of ceilings is apt to result in the premature termination of testing for some students. In a diagnostic situation it seems arguable whether the cost of artificial deflation resulting in the misrepresentation of a student's performance is worth the price of efficiency.

Finally, a careful study of the psychometric features of the test provided by the current developers suggests some additional problems with validity and reliability. The criterion validity data offered by the authors indicate the test shares only 25 to 30% of its variance with other tests of reading. The reliability of the test, as measured across alternative forms, is of the magnitude of .80. Such a coefficient might support relatively accurate comparisons for groups, but seems somewhat unreliable if individual comparisons are sought.

With these limitations in mind, could a well-meaning, knowledgeable educator accrue some useful information about a student from the Gray Oral Reading Tests, Revised? Given the limitations with the test, educators would need to go beyond the test's scores and beyond what the test developers provide as interpretive guidelines. The authors include some examples of how to interpret test results. Unfortunately, their examples are not well conceptualized. Elsewhere in the manual there are allusions to the fact that the test has been developed with objective rather than subjective interpretation as a goal. This goal remains elusive for the Gray Oral Reading Tests, Revised.

[132]

Group Environment Scale, Second Edition. Purpose: To "measure the social-environmental characteristics of task-oriented, social, and psychotherapy and mutual support groups." Group members and leaders; 1974–86; GES; a part of the Social Climate Scales (T3:222); 10 scores: Cohesion, Leader Support, Expressiveness, Independence, Task Orientation, Self-Discovery, Anger and Aggression, Order and Organization, Leader Control, Innovation; 3 forms: Real Form (Form R), Ideal Form (Form I), and Expectations Form (Form E); 1987 price data: $6 per 25 reusable tests; $1.50 per score key; $4.50 per 50 answer sheets; $3.50 per 50 profiles; $6.50 per manual ('86, 30 pages); $12.50 per specimen set; administration time not reported; Rudolf H. Moos; Consulting Psychologists Press, Inc.*

For reviews by Michael J. Curtis and Robert J. Illback, see 9:453 (4 references); for reviews by David P. Campbell and Robyn M. Dawes, see 8:573; see also T3:1015 (1 reference); for a review of the Social Climate Scales, see 8:681.

TEST REFERENCES

1. Burlingame, G., Fuhriman, A., & Drescher, S. (1984). Scientific inquiry into small group process: A multidimensional approach. *Small Group Behavior*, 15, 441-470.

2. Prestby, J. E., & Wandersman, A. (1985). An empirical exploration of a framework of organizational viability: Maintaining block organizations. *The Journal of Applied Behavioral Science*, 21, 287-305.

3. Evans, N. J., & Jarvis, P. A. (1986). The Group Attitude Scale: A measure of attraction to group. *Small Group Behavior*, 17, 203-216.

4. Hartsough, C. S., & Davis, J. M. (1986). Dimensions of the Group Environment Scale. *American Journal of Community Psychology*, 14, 371-376.

5. Meredith, G. M., & Schmitz, E. D. (1986). Structure of the Group Environment Scale in a seminar-format educational setting. *Perceptual and Motor Skills*, 63, 831-834.

6. Meredith, G. M. (1987). Attributes of group atmosphere as predictors of students' satisfaction in seminar-format classes. *Psychological Reports*, 61, 79-82.

Review of the Group Environment Scale, Second Edition by ARTHUR M. NEZU, Chief, Division of Psychology, Beth Israel Medical Center, New York, NY:

The second edition of the Group Environment Scale (GES) was developed to replace earlier versions (1974, 1981). The new manual provides additional information about the scale's psychometric properties and related research. The GES is one of nine Social Climate Scales developed by Moos and his associates at the Social Ecology Laboratory at Stanford. Social climates are defined as the personality of a setting or environment. Because social climates have been shown to have a strong influence on people in a given setting, assessment of the social climate is suggested as providing important information concerning individuals' behaviors and emotions.

The GES was designed specifically to assess the social climate of various types of groups (task-oriented, social-recreational, and psychotherapy and mutual support groups). It contains 90 items that describe the various characteristics of groups, such as "this is a planning group"; "members often gripe"; and "the rules of the group are clearly understood by members." Respondents are directed to indicate whether they believe each statement to be true or false.

There are 10 GES subscales assessing three underlying dimensions. Within the Relationship domain, there are three subscales (Cohesion, Leader Support, Expressiveness); four subscales comprise the Personal Growth dimension (Independence, Task Orientation, Self-Discovery, and Anger and Aggression); and three subscales are contained within the System

Maintenance and System Change dimensions (Order and Organization, Leader Control, Innovation).

The GES also has three different forms: the Real Form (Form R), which assesses individuals' perceptions regarding actual group settings; the Ideal Form (Form I), which measures people's conceptions of ideal group settings; and the Expectation Form (Form E), which measures the types of expectations that people have concerning new group environments. Forms I and E are not currently available in a published version. The actual test items and instructions are, however, available upon request.

Instructions for test administration and scoring are fairly straightforward and relatively easy. The items themselves are generally readable and are likely to be understood easily by most adult test-takers. Subscale scores for both individuals and for group averages can be converted to standard scores.

Data are provided concerning the subscales' internal consistency (Cronbach's alphas), corrected average item-subscale correlations, test-retest reliability (1 month), and profile stability (4, 8, 12, and 24 months). Overall, this information suggests the GES is a fairly reliable instrument. For example, test-retest correlations range between .65 and .87. Overall GES profiles also appear quite stable over a 2-year period. Whereas there appears to be a moderate degree of subscale intercorrelations (e.g., Expressiveness subscale correlates .51 with Innovation subscale), the authors claim these relations account for an average of less than 10% of the subscale variance.

One major problem that continues to exist, as pointed out by previous *Mental Measurements Yearbook* reviewers, involves the normative data described in the manual. Norms are given by subscale collapsed across a wide variety of groups for both members ($N = 148$ groups) and leaders ($N = 112$ groups), as well as across all members for three different types of groups (i.e., task-oriented, social-recreational, and psychotherapy/mutual support groups). No justification is provided, however, for the manner in which different types of groups are lumped together in any of the three categories. For example, means are obtained for the third category, which includes both inpatient groups and sensitivity groups comprised of psychology students. It is not apparent to the test user how these groups may be inherently similar in nature. No data are presented that refer to any discrete category of group (e.g., outpatient vs. inpatient psychotherapy groups). As such, test users may have difficulty interpreting information gathered about their own group under study in relation to the supposed "norms." Very little information is provided about the groups included in the normative samples concerning actual sampling procedures, number of members per group, age, sex, and socioeconomic status. Therefore, any comparison between obtained GES scores with the available norms may be misleading.

A second major problem concerns the validity of the GES. Although the subscales and items appear to have been developed within a sound conceptual and scientific framework, little is provided in the manual to support the integrity of each of the three dimensions, as well as the 10 subscales. Several studies listed in a reference section purport to impact on the inventory's content and construct validity. However, no systematic attempts are evident to provide for an overall evaluation of the validity of the GES. No factor analytic studies addressing the inherent structure of the GES are mentioned, nor are studies cited relating GES scores to various criterion measures of behaviors of both group members and leaders (e.g., behavioral observation procedures). Because of this overall lack of relevant and concrete validity data, test users are warned to be cautious in interpreting their own obtained results.

In summary, although on face value the GES appears to be firmly grounded in theory and research, the potential identified with its first publication has not yet been fulfilled. Previous reviewers in the *Mental Measurements Yearbooks* have pointed out serious limitations of the GES. Apparently, little has been done to overcome these problems. As such, its utility is limited concerning interpretation and generalization of scores. Any interpretations and inferences about a test user's own group(s) should be made with great care. The GES still holds much promise as a measure of the "personality" of a group. Future revisions of the manual should, however, not continue to make similar mistakes evident in both past and current GES manuals.

[133]

GROW—The Marriage Enrichment Program. Purpose: "An integrated program of assessment, learning activities, and personal development designed to support the efforts of professionals who are working to improve the quality of marital relationships." Married couples; 1982–84; GROW; incorporates a short version of the Adult Personality Inventory as an assessment tool to personalize the marriage enrichment program; 16 scores: Caring, Warm, Sensitive, Trusting, Sociable, Optimistic, Adventurous, Participating, Assertive, Controlling, Confident, Self-reliant, Flexible, Creative, Innovative, Calm; 1986 price data: $50 per complete program including 4 folders with lessons, 2 test booklets, and scoring for one couple; $45 per Introductory Kit including 4 folders with lessons, 2 test booklets, scoring for one couple, and administrator's manual ('84, 18 pages); $3.50 per set of 4 GROW folders; $55 per GROW License (prerequisite to ordering Do-It-Yourself Program); $20 per Do-It-Yourself Program (including 2 test booklets and scoring for one couple); administration time not reported; Thomas J. Henry, Virginia M. Henry, and Samuel E. Krug; MetriTech, Inc.*

Review of GROW—The Marriage Enrichment Program by JAMES R. CLOPTON, Associate Professor of Psychology, Texas Tech University, Lubbock, TX:

GROW is a six-session marriage enrichment program to be used with an individual couple or with a group of couples. The GROW program is designed to help improve a couple's relationship in four areas: (*a*) increasing caring behavior, (*b*) improving communication, (*c*) strengthening negotiating and decision-making skills, and (*d*) clarifying expectations and promoting greater flexibility in role assignments.

During the first session, participants are introduced to the GROW program and complete a 189-item questionnaire. Individualized feedback to each participant, based on the responses to the questionnaire, is incorporated in lessons that are directed at the four goals of the program. In each of the next four sessions, a lesson is given to the couple, there is time for presentation of supplemental material, and for discussion of issues related to the lessons. The couple works on each GROW lesson, both individually and together, during a 2-week period between sessions.

Each lesson begins with a section—"Looking in the Mirror"—that provides personality feedback relevant to that lesson's goal. For example, the goal of the first lesson is to increase caring behavior, and the personality feedback is about the extent to which the person is caring, warm, sensitive, and trusting. In the final GROW session, participants evaluate the program and each couple makes a decision about future work to improve their marriage.

The questionnaire used in the GROW program is a shortened version of the Adult Personality Inventory (API) developed by Samuel E. Krug from the 16 PF item pool (see 9:54 for a review of API). The API has 30 items measuring intelligence, 24 items for evaluating the subject's style of responding to items, and 270 items for scales assessing interpersonal styles (e.g., Sociable, Rebellious), career and life style values (e.g., Practical, Aesthetic), and normal personality traits (e.g., Extraverted, Disciplined). The API items require a fourth-grade reading level, and the subject responds to each item with *Generally True* (T), *Uncertain* (?), or *Generally False* (F). The API has excellent norms, but some API scales are so highly correlated they are nearly identical.

The GROW questionnaire has eliminated the API items that assess response style, but has retained the 30 items that measure intelligence—10 items each that assess vocabulary, arithmetic, and verbal reasoning skills. No rationale is offered for having participants respond to the intelligence items, and no feedback is given about the participant's intelligence. Responses to the other 159 items of the GROW questionnaire contribute to scores for 16 scales, most of which have been given new titles in the GROW program (e.g., Innovative instead of Radicalism), or have been given new titles and have also had the direction of scoring reversed (e.g., Flexible instead of Disciplined). The GROW manual reports that internal consistency reliabilities for the 16 GROW scales ranged from .61 to .85 in one study and from .52 to .86 in another study, with the median reliability coefficient for the scales being about .70. No information is given in the GROW manual about the test-retest reliability or the validity of the 16 scales of the GROW questionnaire.

The goal of marriage enrichment programs, such as the GROW program, is typically described as strengthening good marriages. However, couples attending marriage enrichment programs often have significant personal and interpersonal problems and troubled marriages. Krug and Ahadi (1986) found that GROW participants were less adjusted, less caring, and more hostile than nonparticipant control subjects. Characteristics of program participants could influence the effectiveness of marriage enrichment programs, especially the GROW program, because the participants are mostly on their own as they read their personality feedback and follow structured exercises. Many of these activities ask couples to specify changes they will make to improve their marriage. Marriage enrichment participants may not be open to personality feedback, and may not be able to commit themselves to making changes, unless they have much more direct support and encouragement from a group leader than the GROW program provides.

In summary, the GROW program is a six-session marriage enrichment program that begins with participants completing a questionnaire that is a shortened version of the API. The authors of the GROW program believe a special strength of their program is the inclusion of feedback from the GROW questionnaire in the four lessons given to couples. However, the characteristics commonly found among GROW participants suggest they may not be open to personality feedback, especially when they are on their own as they review that feedback. Users of the GROW questionnaire would have greater confidence in its value if the manual presented evidence of test-retest reliability and validity. Lastly, questionnaire items that assess intelligence should be eliminated because they appear unrelated to the goals of the GROW program.

REVIEWER'S REFERENCE

Krug, S. E., & Ahadi, S. A. (1986). Personality characteristics of wives and husbands participating in marriage enrichment. *Multivariate Experimental Clinical Research*, 8, 149-159.

Review of GROW—The Marriage Enrichment Program by JOSEPH P. STOKES, Associate Professor of Psychology, University of Illinois at Chicago, Chicago, IL:

GROW is an integrated program containing feedback about personal characteristics and structured activities. Conducted with the guidance of a professional facilitator, GROW is designed for couples who are looking for personal growth, as well as for growth in their relationship. Although there is some flexibility in how the program could be administered, typically participants would meet with the professional every other week for about 12 weeks (6 sessions). The program can be implemented with one couple or with several couples meeting as a group.

GROW is implemented in four phases. The first meeting (Phase 1) includes an introduction to the program and the completion of a 189-item questionnaire, which is the basis for individualized feedback given throughout the GROW program. In Phase 2 the individualized GROW lessons are produced by the publisher. The facilitator sends the answer sheets from the questionnaire to a data processing center, which scores the questionnaire and prepares four lessons that include feedback and suggestions based on each individual's responses to the questionnaire. These four lessons, distributed at 2-week intervals, are the basis for Phase 3, the heart of the program. Phase 4 is a session during which participants evaluate the program and decide whether they wish to continue with further professional counseling. GROW "diplomas" are included in the program and may be given during this session to provide a concrete reminder of the GROW experience and to give closure to the GROW program.

Each of the four lessons deals with a particular topic: (*a*) bonding, which targets care and love; (*b*) communications, which builds skills in talking and listening; (*c*) decision making, which teaches problem solving techniques; and (*d*) clarification of roles, which aims to make people more flexible about the role activities in their relationship. Each lesson comprises four activities. The first is feedback based on the individual's responses to the initial questionnaire. For each lesson percentile scores for four characteristics related to the topic under consideration are presented to each participant. For example, in Lesson One, bonding, scores for caring, warmth, sensitivity, and trust are given. Each score is accompanied by a short (2–5 sentence) narrative explaining the score. As a part of the first activity for each lesson, participants complete a 10-item survey designed to increase their awareness of behaviors and attitudes related to the focus of the lesson.

Each lesson contains three other activities relevant to the focus of the lesson. These activities sometimes require the couple to work individually, sometimes together. Often individual work or reflection is followed by joint scoring or planning. For example, in Lesson One participants individually list strengths they see in their partners and think of ways to compliment, affirm, and praise their partners for some of the listed strengths. They then take time to let their partner know what strengths they have listed.

The activities themselves are well chosen and varied. They involve reflection, discussion, and some kind of plan for action or change. The sequence of activities is logical, but there is nothing to prevent a facilitator from omitting an activity or from adding one he or she thinks would be helpful to the couple(s) in the program.

The questionnaire used in the GROW program is a shortened adaptation of the Adult Personality Inventory (Krug, 1984). The GROW manual makes no effort to document the validity of the scales derived from the questionnaire, nor is the manual from the Adult Personality Inventory itself very convincing on this score. Internal consistencies for the GROW scales are reported and range from about .52 to .86, with a median of about .70. The psychometric properties of the scales are not a central issue, however, as the questionnaire is used to provide feedback and to facilitate discussion and self-exploration. This discussion and self-exploration is valuable, even if the feedback itself is off target. Participants should be encouraged to question the feedback and its applicability to them. A responsible GROW facilitator would emphasize this point and make sure the participants were aware of the possible limitations of the measurement device.

In summary, the GROW program provides a useful structured approach for working with couples who are willing to spend time working on their relationship. The program begins with a questionnaire that is sent to the developers for scoring. Responses to the questionnaire provide the basis for feedback that is the initial activity in each of the four GROW lessons. Each lesson also contains other activities the couple completes on their own between sessions with the facilitator. The sessions with the facilitator provide an opportunity for questions and for discussion of problems, but the bulk of the work takes place between sessions. For this reason GROW is appropriate for couples who are able and willing to spend time on their own working with the activities; severely distressed relationships would probably not find the GROW experience helpful. Couples able to work together, with the help of a facilitator, will probably benefit from GROW. Professionals working with couples will appreciate the structure GROW provides and will usually find the GROW progam elicits important issues that, in many cases, can be dealt with in less structured counseling or therapy after the GROW lessons have been completed.

REVIEWER'S REFERENCE

Krug, S. E. (1984). *The Adult Personality Inventory Manual.* Champaign, IL: Institute for Personality and Ability Testing, Inc.

[134]

The Hand Test, Revised 1983. Purpose: "A diagnostic technique that uses pictures of hands as [a] projective medium . . . . the examinee 'projects' by telling what the hand is doing." Ages 6 and over; 1959–83; 41 scores: 24 quantitative scores: Interpersonal (Affection, Dependence, Communication, Exhibition, Direction, Aggression, Total), Environmental (Acquisition, Active, Passive, Total), Maladjustive (Tension, Crippled, Fear, Total), Withdrawal (Description, Bizarre, Failure, Total), Experience Ratio, Acting Out Ratio, Pathological, Average Initial Response Time, High Minus Low Score, plus 17 qualitative scores: Ambivalent, Automatic Phrase, Cylindrical, Denial, Emotion, Gross, Hiding, Immature, Impotent, Inanimate, Movement, Oral, Perplexity, Sensual, Sexual, Original, Repetition; individual; 1987 price data: $7.90 per 25 scoring booklets; $16.20 per set of picture cards; $15.95 per manual ('83, 90 pages plus scoring booklet); (10) minutes; Edwin E. Wagner; Western Psychological Services.*

See 9:464 (16 references), T3:1053 (21 references), 8:575 (29 references), T2:1470 (15 references), and P:438 (12 references); for a review by Goldine C. Gleser and an excerpted review by Irving R. Stone of an earlier edition, see 6:216 (6 references).

TEST REFERENCES

1. Spellacy, F. J., & Brown, W. G. (1984). Prediction of recidivism in young offenders after brief institutionalization. *Journal of Clinical Psychology*, 40, 1070-1074.

2. Graybill, D., MacKie, D. J., & House, A. E. (1985). Aggression in college students who were abused as children. *Journal of College Student Personnel*, 26, 492-495.

3. Panek, P. E., & Rush, M. C. (1985). Response pattern analysis of The Hand Test: Age differences. *Journal of Personality Assessment*, 49, 37-42.

4. Stoner, S. (1985). Test-retest reliability of The Hand Test with institutionalized mentally retarded adults. *Psychological Reports*, 56, 272-274.

5. Wagner, E. E., Alexander, R. A., Roos, G., & Prospero, M. K. (1985). Maximizing split-half reliability estimates for projective techniques. *Journal of Personality Assessment*, 49, 579-581.

Review of The Hand Test by MARCIA B. SHAFFER, School Psychologist, Stueben/Allegany BOCES, Bath, NY:

The Hand Test consists of a series of 10 durable white cards, 3 3/8 by 4 3/8 inches, a size which makes them easy to handle. On nine of the cards is a black outline of a human hand, each in a different position. The tenth card is blank. The subject is asked to tell what each hand is doing.

The test is easily given, particularly by those who are familiar with other projective techniques. A single record form contains the subject's responses and, later, the examiner's scoring. Administration takes from 10–15 minutes, an advantage if one is dealing with impatient clients such as character-disordered adolescents.

The manual is excellent. Instructions to the examiner are clear and detailed. Ways of scoring, both quantitative and qualitative, are described, as are such categories of interpretation as interpersonal, environmental, and maladaptive. A number of different methods of approaching the exegesis of a subject's responses are included. The expected "card pull" for each card is defined. A chapter is devoted to "Indices for Various Diagnostic Groups," indicating both supportive research and illustrative case histories. Studies of the responses of persons afflicted with a variety of psychopathological conditions lend credence to the examiner's diagnostic decisions. Reference is made to the theory of personality called "Structural Analysis," espoused by the originator of the Hand Test, with assurance that neither it nor any other specific theory is necessary for understanding this test. Data on the validity and reliability of the Hand Test are set forth carefully in a section replete with samples of research on which claims for utility are founded. There are discussions of both criterion and construct validity. To generalize, the manual offers the statistical and interpretive data that are essential to the use of this test. The author has done a better than average job of presenting necessary information. And there are, to this reviewer's gratification, numerous cautionary statements with regard to use of the Hand Test, such as "Its use should be restricted to individuals at or beyond the graduate level who are familiar with personality dynamics and projective theory."

In the late 1940s and early 1950s, the field of clinical psychology expanded rapidly, and projective techniques came into prominence. Although the Hand Test appeared later than better known instruments such as the Rorschach and the TAT, its creator, Edwin E. Wagner, identifies with the generation of psychologists whose careers inspired the projective movement. Wagner's manual does, however, indicate one difference between the Hand Test and other projective techniques, most of which purport to tap various levels of emotions. The Hand Test elicits "reactions which are close to the surface and are apt to be expressed in overt behavior." Its revelation of ongoing moods and current events makes the Hand Test a genuine addition to a test battery, producing different rather than corroborative information.

This reviewer's respect for the Hand Test has grown with increasing familiarity. It places less of a burden on the subject than do other projectives. It can be interpreted with the comfortable knowledge that a framework of research surrounds one's insights. It surely would be useful in any setting where clinical psychologists practice. Reports of its results would be of interest to social workers, teachers, judges, and counselors of various persuasions.

[135]

Hanson Silver Management Style Inventory. Purpose: To self report and measure one's own decision-making preferences based on Jung's theory of psychological types. Administrators and leaders; 1981; 4 Management Styles: Sensing Feeling, Sensing Thinking, Intuitive Thinking, Intuitive Feeling; 1988 price data: $3 per inventory; administration time not reported; J. Robert Hanson and Harvey F. Silver; Hanson Silver Strong & Associates, Inc.*

[136]

The Harrington O'Shea Career Decision-Making System. Purpose: "Surveys not only interests, but also values, training plans, and self-ratings of abilities." Grades 7–12 and adults; 1974–85; CDM; 6 scores (Arts, Business, Clerical, Crafts, Scientific, Social) used to identify 3 or more occupational areas, for intensive career exploration, from among 18 clusters (Art Work, Clerical Work, Customer Services, Data Analysis, Education Work, Entertainment, Legal, Literary Work, Management, Manual Work, Math-Science, Medical-Dental, Music Work, Personal Service, Sales Work, Skilled Crafts, Social Services, Technical) and questions in 5 areas (Abilities, Future Plans, Job

Values, Occupational Preferences, School Subject Preferences); 1988 price data: $13 per manual ('82, 102 pages); $9 per audiocassette; $165 per microcomputer edition; $3 per specimen set; (40) minutes; Thomas F. Harrington and Arthur J. O'Shea; American Guidance Service.*

a) SELF-SCORED EDITION. $34 per 25 survey booklets, directions for administration ('82, 6 pages), and interpretive folder ('82, 8 pages); Spanish edition available.

b) MACHINE-SCORED EDITION. 3 scoring reports available: $66 per 25 survey booklets, directions for administration ('82, 2 pages), and profile reports; $70 per 25 survey booklets, directions, and profile reports with group summary report; $8.50 per test with narrative report.

See T3:1059 (3 references); for a review by Carl G. Willis of an earlier edition, see 8:1004.

TEST REFERENCES

1. Galassi, M. D., Jones, L. K., & Britt, M. N. (1985). Nontraditional career options for women: An evaluation of career guidance instruments. *Vocational Guidance Quarterly*, 34, 124-130.

Review of The Harrington O'Shea Career Decision-Making System by CAROLINE MANUELE-ADKINS, Associate Professor Counseling, Department of Educational Foundations, Hunter College of the City University of New York, New York, NY:

The Harrington O'Shea Career Decision-Making System (CDM) is a multidimensional interest inventory measuring several variables hypothesized to contribute to effective career decision making. These variables include: occupational preferences, school subject areas, future plans, job values, abilities, and interests. The authors based their systems on Holland's theory of vocational development. The test has alternative scoring systems for counselor and subject use. The available systems are a self-scoring version, a computerized scoring version, a profile and narrative report, a group-reported scoring report (to provide information to curriculum planners and administrators), and most recently, a microcomputer version (Apple II and IIe and TRS 80 models III). There is also a Spanish version, available only in self-scoring format, and an audiocassette version for poor readers.

In brief, the CDM asks respondents to (*a*) select their first and second occupational preferences from a list of 18 occupational clusters; (*b*) select two school subjects they liked most from a list of 14 subjects; (*c*) identify one future educational or training plan from a list of 9 alternatives; (*d*) select four job values (e.g., security, variety) from 14 values; (*e*) choose 4 abilities from a list of 14; and (*f*) indicate on the interest survey how they feel on a scale of 0, 1, 2 about 120 different activities. As respondents proceed through each section they transfer the information to their summary profile, which produces a career code encompassing dichotomous combinations of crafts, scientific, arts, social, business, and clerical codes. Basically, these codes are renamed Holland codes. Similar to Holland's Vocational Preference Inventory (VPI) and Self-Directed Search (SDS), the codes are matched to different occupational areas.

The CDM survey booklet is easy to read and understand. The directions, for the most part, are clear. However, good reading ability and a sufficient level of motivation to follow through with all the scoring steps are required. The items in the booklet have face validity and there is no item overlap in any of the areas. The self-scoring version is accompanied by an interpretive folder to assist respondents in interpreting each area of their summary profile. This is a well designed and important part of the self-scored CDM. The authors developed it for those clients whose time with a counselor was limited. The interpretive folder fills an important need for a system that may be used without professional assistance. In this respect, the CDM is an advancement over the SDS, which is also self-scored but has until recently not provided interpretive information for the person using it alone. The success of the self-scoring systems depends, of course, on the abilities and motivation of the users.

The manual presents evidence for the validity of the CDM. The items and scale correlations analyses done for the interest section of the CDM indicate that the scales are homogeneous and each item is correlated with its own scale .50 or above. The procedures for developing this part of the CDM are thorough and adequate. The manual also presents evidence for construct validity by illustrating how the CDM interest categories exhibit the same correlational pattern as Holland's hexagonal model (from VPI data). Construct validity is also documented by studies which examine the relationship between CDM codes and Holland codes achieved on the Strong-Campbell Interest Inventory (SCII). For four different samples there is an 88, 89, 95, and 61 percent agreement with the first letter code. Concurrent validity data show the similarity between codes received on the CDM and codes of the occupations of a sample of employed people. In most cases they are very similar. The results were similar for college students' codes and choice of major. The authors state in the manual that they are not concerned with the predictive validity of the CDM. They define its purpose as "self-exploration" and not to "predict the job that an individual will finally enter as a permanent career." Some preliminary predictive validity studies are presented, however, that show the CDM has an average 50% predictive rate for high school students' choice of job or college major (4 years later). Comparison with the SCVIB's predictive validity shows strong similarity. Overall there is good evidence for the validity of the CDM.

Alpha coefficients for the internal consistency of the CDM interest scales range from .91 to .94. Thirty day test-retest reliabilities for the interest scales with high school and college students range from .75 to .94 (average mid .80s). They are slightly less stable for college students over a 5-month period of time. While these reliability estimates are good, they are provided only for the interest scales. Reliability data for the other areas are also necessary. Another concern in terms of this measure is the reliability of the scores obtained among the various scoring systems. The manual reports studies that show .96 and .99 correlations between the student-scored and author-scored interest scales. This is very high interrater reliability but the authors still caution that scores should be checked. These same reliability studies should be done for other areas of the CDM.

Data that are similar, but not as extensive, are presented for the reliability and validity of the Spanish version of the CDM. These compare favorably with the English version. The authors describe their efforts to include language that would be understood by diverse Spanish-speaking cultures and to use more widely understood than literal translations of expressions and phrases in the measure.

Extensive male and female norms are provided for each of the CDM areas for junior high, high school, and college freshmen. Only interest scale norms are provided for the Spanish version (grade 7 through adult), for adults, and for adult CETA participants. Normative data are, therefore, needed for the other CDM areas for these groups. The authors have put a lot of effort into making the CDM gender-fair. It uses neither separate scales by sex nor combined sex scales.

In summary, the CDM appears to be a well-developed measure that is particularly useful if one wants a comprehensive self-scored vocational assessment measure. Because of its similarity to the Holland VPI and SDS measures one has to question the advantages of its use over these other measures. The SDS is simpler to use and the VPI is machine scored rather than self scored. The CDM seems more comprehensive in its coverage and offers more interpretive information than the SDS. Its multiple scoring systems may also be advantageous for meeting the needs of diverse client groups.

[137]

Health and Daily Living. Purpose: "To examine the influence of extratreatment factors on treatment outcome as well as to explore the social resources and coping processes people use to prevent and adapt to stressful life circumstances." Students ages 12–18, adults; 1984–86; HDL; may be administered as an interview or as a questionnaire; 2 levels; 2 forms; form manual ('86, 74 pages) includes all forms and scoring information; price data available from publisher; (30–45) minutes; Rudolf H. Moos, Ruth C. Cronkite, Andrew G. Billings, and John W. Finney; Social Ecology Laboratory, Stanford University Medical Center.*

a) YOUTH FORM. Students ages 12–18; 9 indices: Health-Related (Self-Confidence, Positive Mood, Distressed Mood, Physical Symptoms, Medical Conditions, Health-Risk Behaviors), Social Functioning (Family Activities, Activities with Friends, Social Integration in School).

b) ADULT FORM B. Adults; 47 indices: Health-Related Functioning (Self-Confidence, Physical Symptoms, Medical Conditions, Global Depression, Depressive Mood and Ideation, Endogenous Depression, Depressive Features, Depressed Mood/Past 12 Months, Alcohol Consumption—Quantity, Alcohol Consumption—Quantity/Frequency, Drinking Problems, Smoking Symptoms, Medication Use), Social Functioning and Resources (Social Activities with Friends, Network Contacts, Number of Close Relationships, Quality of Significant Relationship), Family Functioning and Home Environment (Family Social Activities, Family Task Sharing, Tasks Performed by Self, Tasks Performed by Partner, Family Arguments, Negative Home Environment), Children's Health and Functioning (Children's Physical Health Problems, Children's Psychological Health Problems, Children's Total Health Problems, Children's Behavioral Problems, Children's Health-Risk Behaviors), Life Change Events (Negative Life Change Events, Exit Events, Positive Life Change Events), Coping Responses (Active Cognitive Coping, Active Behavioral Coping, Avoidance Coping, Logical Analysis, Information Seeking, Problem Solving, Affective Regulation, Emotional Discharge, Help-Seeking/Mental Health Professional, Help-Seeking/Non-Mental Health Professional), Family Level Composite (Quality of Conjugal Relationship, Family Social Activities, Family Agreement on Task Sharing, Family Agreement on Household Tasks, Family Arguments, Negative Home Environment).

TEST REFERENCES

1. Billings, A. G. (1983). Social-environmental factors among light and heavy cigarette smokers: A controlled comparison with non-smokers. *Addictive Behaviors*, 8, 381-391.

2. Billings, A. G., & Moos, R. H. (1984). Coping, stress, and social resources among adults with unipolar depression. *Journal of Personality and Social Psychology*, 46, 877-891.

3. Cronkite, R. C., & Moos, R. H. (1984). The role of predisposing and moderating factors in the stress-illness relationship. *Journal of Health and Social Behavior*, 25, 372-393.

4. Mitchell, R. E., & Moos, R. H. (1984). Deficiencies in social support among depressed patients: Antecedents or consequences of stress? *Journal of Health and Social Behavior*, 25, 438-452.

5. Billings, A. G., Cronkite, R. C., & Moos, R. H. (1985). Difficulty of follow-up and posttreatment functioning among depressed patients. *Journal of Affective Disorders*, 8, 9-16.

6. Holahan, C. J., & Moos, R. H. (1985). Life stress and health: Personality, coping, and family support in stress resistance. *Journal of Personality and Social Psychology*, 49, 739-747.

7. Billings, A. G., & Moos, R. H. (1986). Children of parents with unipolar depression: A controlled 1-year follow-up. *Journal of Abnormal Child Psychology*, 14, 149-166.

8. Holahan, C. J., & Moos, R. H. (1987). Personal and contextual determinants of coping strategies. *Journal of Personality and Social Psychology*, 52, 946-955.

Review of the Health and Daily Living Form by ARTHUR M. NEZU, Chief, Division of Psychology, Beth Israel Medical Center, New York, NY:

The Health and Daily Living (HDL) Form was designed as a structured procedure to assess various indices of health-related and social functioning, life stressors and strains, and coping responses and social resources. It also includes items covering certain sociodemographic factors. The HDL can be used either in an interview format or as a self-report questionnaire.

In the current HDL manual (1986), the actual forms are included in the appendices—HDL Adult Forms A and B and the Youth Form. Adult Form B is a revision of Form A of the HDL. Form A was originally developed for use in research concerning treatment outcome among alcoholic patients and their families. Form B has been used in longitudinal studies of the outcome of treatment among a depressed patient population and their families. The authors recommend that Form B be used by investigators. The Youth Form is described as suitable for administration to adolescents between the ages of 12 and 18 who are in junior or senior high school.

The HDL appears to have been developed primarily as a research tool to examine the influence of "extratreatment factors on treatment outcome," as well as to evaluate the social resources and coping processes people use in reaction to stressful life circumstances. This work has been conducted within a theoretical framework that specifies the interrelations among the personal and environmental determinants of life stressors and the coping and social resources that moderate the negative effects of such stress on emotional and behavioral adaptation.

The major strength of the HDL lies in its extensive research use by test developers, Moos and his colleagues. In addition to providing norms for the depressed patient population ($N = 424$), means and standard deviations for the HDL indices of a demographically matched community control group ($N = 424$) are also included. Test users can then use the large community sample as potential norms against which to compare their own obtained scores. The depressed patient group can also be used as norms for depression comparisons. Unfortunately, little information beyond the sampling procedure is provided within the manual that describes either sample (e.g., lacking are age, socioeconomic status, religious affiliations, etc.). Whereas references are listed that provide additional information about these samples, specific demographic data should be included in the test manual itself to aid the test user. The authors should remedy this limitation in future revisions of the manual.

With regard to reliability data, internal consistency estimates (alphas) for several of the indices by sample indicate the HDL items have moderate to high levels of internal consistency. However, additional reliability estimates are lacking (e.g., test-retest, item-index correlations). Of major importance is the lack of test-retest coefficients. As such, the stability over time of HDL indices remains unknown. Therefore, if test users wish to use the HDL for either clinical or research purposes, interpretation beyond the particular testing point in time is questionable. It should be pointed out that some of the indices should not be expected to have high levels of test-retest reliability. For example, the amount of experienced negative life events may be quite different between two testing periods over 3 months apart. However, total lack of this information limits the generalizability of test interpretations.

A major limitation of the present manual is the lack of any validity data. Several of the indices have counterparts in the assessment literature that could be compared to assess convergent and discriminant validity. For example, one series of HDL indices involves depressive symptoms. It would be important to know the correlation between these indices and other self-report measures of depression, such as the Beck Depression Inventory (Beck, Ward, Mendelson, Mock, & Erbaugh, 1961). Comparison to the Hamilton Rating Scale for Depression (Hamilton, 1960), a clinical rating scale of patients' depressive symptomatology, could provide information about the criterion validity of these HDL indices.

Several inventories assessing stressful life events also exist (e.g., Life Experiences Survey; Sarason, Johnson, & Siegel, 1978). Again, comparison with these questionnaires could yield important information concerning various HDL psychometric properties. The total lack of validity data severely limits the use of the HDL by the average test user. Further, the use of predetermined weights concerning HDL scoring criterion for the impact of life events is highly questionable (cf. Sarason et al., 1978). Briefly, the variability among individuals experiencing similar life events is rather large. For example, one individual, for a variety of reasons (which may involve variability in coping and social resources), may be less affected by a divorce than another person. To use predetermined weights in scoring ignores this issue.

Normative and psychometric data for the Youth Form are more scanty. Only data for nine indices are included. Test users wishing to use the Youth Form should do so with great caution in interpreting their obtained results.

To summarize, the HDL was developed within the context of a sound conceptual framework concerning the interrelations among stressful life events, coping and social resources, and behavioral and emotional adaptational outcomes. However, limited normative data, and the lack of extensive psychometric data concerning reliability, and especially validity, severely limits its use by the general test consumer. Usage should probably be limited to preliminary types of research investigating various aspects of the authors' conceptual framework. Yet, such investigators may be advised to seek other measurement tools, such as those cited above, that have demonstrated psychometric properties. To use the HDL for the clinical assessment of a particular individual or group is highly risky.

REVIEWER'S REFERENCES

Hamilton, M. (1960). A rating scale for depression. *Journal of Neurology, Neurosurgery, and Psychiatry*, 12, 56-62.

Beck, A. T., Ward, C. H., Mendelson, M., Mock, J., & Erbaugh, J. (1961). An inventory for measuring depression. *Archives of General Psychiatry*, 4, 561-571.

Sarason, I. G., Johnson, J. H., & Siegel, J. M. (1978). Assessing the impact of life changes: Development of the Life Experiences Survey. *Journal of Consulting and Clinical Psychology*, 46, 932-946.

Review of Health and Daily Living by STEVEN P. SCHINKE, Professor, School of Social Work, Columbia University, New York, NY:

STRENGTHS. The Health and Daily Living (HDL) Form is a carefully researched assessment tool. The HDL in its three versions (Adult Form A, Adult Form B, and Youth Form) is suitable for administration as an interview or as a questionnaire. This versatility is a source of considerable strength for the HDL. Besides administration versatility, the HDL has been used to a rich experience of empirical research in the target areas. A great deal of this research, including applications of the HDL, has yielded published papers and other scholarly materials that are retrievable and available in the peer-reviewed literature. As such investigators and clinicians who use the HDL have access to a large body of previous research and normative comparison data.

WEAKNESSES. The HDL is not a short instrument. Form B for Adults, as an illustration, comprises 16 pages of tightly spaced questions. Although the forms contain skip items, most respondents will find themselves faced with a large number of questions about many facets of daily living, mental health, substance use, family members, and personal habits. The HDL form for adults, therefore, gathers its data at a considerable price in administration time, effort, and concentration on the part of the respondent.

The Youth Form of the HDL, however, is surprisingly short. This form occupies only four pages. The form does not include basic demographic questions essential to studying ethnic-racial correlates, family variables, or related factors that adolescent researchers may regard as important. What is more, some questions on the Youth Form do not appear easily interpreted by young persons of less than average intelligence. Illustrative are items concerning asthma, allergies, and weight gain and loss.

Perhaps more serious is the apparent middle-class bias of the Youth Form. Many items on this form assume that youth respondents are actively attending school. Fewer, though no less important items, ask respondents about extracurricular activities associated with middle-class culture. Further, several items require respondents to report on such feelings as their maturity, dependability, confidence, and intelligence. The careful crafting of the adult versions of the HDL, thus, is not paralleled in the youth version.

RELIABILITY, VALIDITY, NORMATIVE DATA. Psychometric parameters for the HDL are evident throughout the manual. Most in abundance are scoring keys and composite indices for the scales. Validity estimates of the HDL, especially for Adult Form B, are based on appropriate comparative samples and appear solid. Most alpha coefficients of internal consistency also seem within acceptable range.

Youth Form psychometrics reflect the authors' research with 70 children of depressed parents and 77 children of "normal" community residents. These parameters on validity and internal consistency appear in the range of acceptable scores, though not grounded on as rich a data base as scores for adult versions.

SUMMARY. Health and Daily Living Forms for Adult A and Adult B versions offer useful clinical and research tools. Albeit somewhat lengthy for administrative purposes, the forms have strong credentials in prior research and in their psychometric properties. Youth forms of the HDL are not as detailed and contain items that appear biased toward verbal, middle-class samples. Despite their minor flaws, all three forms of the HDL should provide valuable data for clinicians and researchers that may not be otherwise available from instruments less well tailored to the HDL's target mental health areas.

[138]

Health Problems Checklist. Purpose: Facilitates "the rapid assessment of the health status and potential health problems of clients typically seen in psychotherapy settings." Adult men, adult women; 1984; no formal scoring procedure; 13 areas: General Health, Cardiovascular/Pulmonary, Endocrine/Hematology, Gastrointestinal, Dermatological, Visual, Auditory/Olfactory, Mouth/Throat/Nose, Orthopedic, Neurological, Genitourinary, Habits, History; no manual; separate forms for men and women; IBM or Apple computer administered version requires 64K (128K-IBM) (80 column card-Apple) and 2 floppy disk drives; 1987 price data: $12.95 per 50 checklists for men or for women or for 25 of each form; $50 per computer version (100 uses); (10–20) minutes; John A. Schinka; Psychological Assessment Resources, Inc.*

Review of the Health Problems Checklist by ROBERT M. KAPLAN, Professor and Acting Chief of Health Care Sciences, and MICHELLE T. TOSHIMA, Ph.D. Candidate, University of California, San Diego, LaJolla, CA:

Psychologists are gaining increasing experience developing measures that are not necessarily psychological in nature. In addition, we are witnessing the increased use of systematic measurement methodologies that are not necessarily tests. The Health Problems Checklist for Men and the Health Problems Checklist for Women are interesting subjects for review in the *Mental Measurements Yearbook* because they are neither tests nor is their focus mental.

The checklists were published in 1984 as part of a series investigating problem areas for adults, adolescents, and children. The checklists include general problem items, as well as health and mental health items. It is important to note that the checklists are not and were never intended by the author to be tests. Thus, there is no manual and no formal scoring procedure.

Each checklist is divided into 11 symptom areas. Although these are identified only by abbreviation in the forms, they represent basic physiological systems, including General Health, Dermatological, Visual, Auditory/Olfactory, Cardiovascular/Pulmonary, Orthopedic, Gastrointestinal, Endocrinological/Hematological, Mouth/Throat/Nose, Neurological, and Genitourinary symptoms. The number of symptoms within these areas varies. For, example there are 26 neurological symptoms, but only 10 orthopedic ones. The women's form has a total of 220 symptoms while the men's form includes 214. The major difference between the two forms is in the genitourinary section. Here some symptoms are sex specific, and six extra items are required for women. In addition to the survey of symptoms, each form includes a section on health habits, current illnesses, medical history, current medication use, and information concerning attending physicians.

The author of the Health Problems Checklist suggests there are four major purposes for the instrument: (*a*) give a client information about his or her own health condition, (*b*) establish rapport while communicating information in conversational terms, (*c*) prepare clients for more formal testing, and (*d*) obtain written documentation about presenting problems.

The checklists were developed through a series of steps. First, a comprehensive list of symptoms was generated through reviews of surveys, text materials, or tests, including those previously developed by the author. The symptoms were then sorted into the basic physiological systems. Those with low base rates were eliminated. The resulting pool of symptoms was then rewritten to meet the criteria of brevity, common language, and inoffensiveness. The pool was next subjected to evaluation by seven physicians, which resulted in further revision, deletion, or addition of items. A second panel of five experts reevaluated the forms and administered them to clients/patients. On the basis of previous revisions and final item revisions from the administration of the checklist to clients/patients, the final instrument of 220 items for women and 214 items for men was completed.

CRITIQUE. The Health Problems Checklist is difficult to evaluate from a psychometric perspective. There is no manual, no peer-reviewed publications describing its use, no formal scoring procedures, and no validity data upon which to anchor inferences. The checklists do, however, provide a formal method for obtaining medical history and information about various systems. The items are very similar to many questions asked by physicians during the history and physical examination. Indeed, the questionnaire is comprehensive.

The value of obtaining comprehensive health information should not be overlooked. This has become apparent in studies of computerized medical decision making. Studies comparing the diagnostic accuracy of humans to computers have usually found the computers to be more accurate. This difference has been attributed to the fact that computers obtain more information prior to making their diagnoses. When human physicians are forced to take a comprehensive history (the Health Problems Checklist would obtain such a detailed history), they have shown diagnostic accuracy comparable to the computers (Schwartz, 1988). Thus, the use of a comprehensive checklist is valuable.

There are some limitations of the checklists as health status measures. For example, several issues pertinent to the assessment of health status are not well addressed (see Kaplan, 1988; Kaplan & Anderson, 1988 for overview of issues). Health status might be conceptualized as having several components. One component involves symptoms; and symptoms are well covered in the checklists. Symptoms are viewed as the subjective component of health status. The second component of health status is dysfunction. There may be several levels of dysfunction for those reporting the same symptoms. For example, the symptom of back pain might cause no limitations in daily activities, or it may cause severe disability. The checklist provides no way of differentiating between these two alternatives. The third component that should be considered is the duration of the problem. A day in pain is not the same as a year in pain. The instructions in the Health Problems Checklist do not ask the respondent to specify when the problem first occurred or how long it lasted. They simply state, "make a check . . . next to each item that applies to you." Those who check joint pain may do so because their legs are temporarily sore after a weekend tennis match or because they have chronic rheumatoid arthritis.

Finally, it is not clear why we need a proprietary list of symptoms in the absence of a meaningful scoring system. As part of their medical training, physicians learn to take a thorough history and run through the major systems during a physical examination. Many health maintenance organizations (HMOs) already use symptom checklists. These lists are available in textbooks and can be reproduced without charge.

In summary, the Health Problems Checklist for Men and the Health Problems Checklist for Women are instruments that were constructed using a systematic methodology. They are comprehensive and may enhance the therapist-client or doctor-patient relationship. Moreover, use of these instruments may help physicians gain more appropriate information prior to making a diagnosis. On the other hand, the checklists cannot serve as measures of health status because they do not consider the impact of the symptoms upon functioning nor do they include duration of the problem. In addition, the checklists do not yield meaningful scores.

REVIEWER'S REFERENCES

Kaplan, R. M. (1988). Health-related quality of life in cardiovascular disease. *Journal of Consulting and Clinical Psychology*, 56, 382-392.

Kaplan, R. M., & Anderson, J. P. (1988). A general health policy model: Update and applications. *Health Services Research*, 23, 203-235.

Schwartz, S. (1988). Computer consultants in the clinic. Keynote address presented at the XXIV International Congress of Psychology. Sydney, Australia, 1988.

[139]

The Henderson-Moriarty ESL/Literacy Placement Test. Purpose: "A placement instrument, a means of identifying literacy learners and assigning them to appropriate classes." Adult learners of English as a second language who have minimal or no oral English skills and minimal or no reading and writing skills in any language using the Roman alphabet; 1982; HELP; "criterion-referenced"; 2 scores: Oral (and reading), and Written (and reading); individual; some test materials must be furnished by the examiner; 1985 price data: $16.95 per examiner's guide ('82, 29 pages) which includes test booklet, test materials, and answer sheets; [15–20] minutes; Cindy Henderson, Pia Moriarty, and Mary Kay Mitchell (illustrations); Alemany Press.*

Review of the Henderson-Moriarty ESL/Literacy Placement Test by CHARLES W. STANSFIELD, Director, Division of Foreign Language Education and Testing, Center for Applied Linguistics, Washington, DC:

INTRODUCTION. The Henderson-Moriarty ESL/Literacy Placement Test (HELP) is a test of oral and written English for low-level learners of English as a second language (ESL). It was designed with the adult Southeast Asian refugee in mind. These examinees often are nonliterate in their native language. For this reason, the HELP assesses certain preliteracy skills as well as some low-level functional literacy skills. The oral language included on the test is also viewed as language that is preliminary to English literacy.

ADMINISTRATION. The HELP should be administered by a bilingual intake worker or teacher. Before the test, the administrator and examinee jointly complete a Background Information form and a First Language Literacy Screening form. These forms require examinees to indicate the language(s) they speak, their trade or occupation, and the number of years of formal schooling and ESL they completed in their native country or in a refugee camp. These questions may be posed in English or in the examinee's native language. In order to determine native language literacy, the administrator asks the examinee to read an introduction to the test that is written in four versions (Lao, Vietnamese, Khmer, and Cantonese) on a single sheet of paper. The administrator notes whether the examinee holds the text right side up and how readily he/she can read aloud. The examiner then administers the 46-item test. Items pertaining to the oral and written scores are not all in separate sections. Instead, they are identified as such on the answer sheet. Items on the oral test are divided into subgroups according to difficulty. If an examinee is unable to respond correctly to the initial items in each subgroup, the examiner may skip the rest of the items in the group. If the examinee does not respond to each question, the examiner may repeat or rephrase the question. Sample restatements of each question are provided in the test booklet. The last 12 written items appear together at the end of the test. Thus, no examiner is needed for this part. At the conclusion of the oral portion, each examinee completes the remainder of the written portion of the test independently, while the examiner continues testing others. Although the test is not timed, complete administration typically takes 20 to 25 minutes.

In order to administer the test, certain stimulus materials (not a part of the kit) must be provided by the examiner. These include an ice cube tray, a telephone, real money (both paper and coins), and a calendar.

TEST CONTENT AND FORMAT. The 46 items on the test consist of 30 oral and 16 written.

There is a healthy variety of item types on the oral portion of the test. Only about half of the oral items require a spoken response. The rest require some action, such as pointing to a person in a picture, to dial a phone number, to pick up the receiver, to circle a picture or a word, to hand a specific amount of money to the examiner, and so on. A number of the oral items involve reading aloud. Examinees must read aloud a date, the time on a clock, digital time (e.g., 12:17), numbers, letters of the alphabet, and isolated words.

On the written portion of the test, examinees must copy a word in upper case, lower case, and cursive writing. They must also arrange letters of the alphabet (given by the examiner) to spell their names. The last 12 items require the examinee to fill out a personal data form that asks for name, address, telephone number, date of birth, sex and marital status (the latter two are in checklist form), signature, and the current date.

SCORING AND SCORE INTERPRETATION. Responses to items on the HELP are scored for *meaningful communication* as opposed to grammatical correctness. Pronunciation is not taken into account unless it impedes communication. On the written portion, spelling is not counted as long as the examiner can recognize the answer. The one exception is that examinees are required to spell their names correctly. The examiner marks on the answer sheet whether each response is correct or incorrect during the oral portion as it is administered. The answer sheet also provides space to record incorrect answers or aspects of test behavior to diagnose later. The total number of oral and written correct answers becomes the score on each portion of the test. These scores are recorded and interpreted separately.

Scores on the HELP can be used to place students into two or three levels of ESL literacy. However, the authors correctly caution the test user to consider examinee background data (i.e., formal schooling, native language literacy, and familiarity with a Roman alphabet) when making a placement. The authors present cutoff scores for two levels of placement at one institution in San Francisco, but recommend appropriately that each program establish its own cutoffs according to local student scores and the number of classes available. While the test reports two scores, the authors note that the "oral and written scores usually fluctuate together" (guide, p.6). Because the test is essentially used for ESL literacy placement, the authors recommend that when the written score is higher than the oral, the written score should determine the placement.

EVALUATION. Judging from its content and format, the HELP appears to be useful for screening newly arrived Southeast Asian refugees for ESL literacy, and perhaps those from other third world countries such as El Salvador. The test is creative because it uses a number of item types involving listening, speaking, reading, and writing, and the artwork is effective. The use of alternative cues in the guide makes it possible to modify the test slightly for pre- and posttesting. The test seems to be culturally fair and appropriate for differentiating among adults who are beginning learners of ESL. However, because the test items and tasks are quite easy, the HELP would not appear useful for placement beyond the beginning or lower levels of ESL.

It is unfortunate that no technical information is presented in the examiner's guide. While the authors state that items are sequenced according to difficulty, no description is given of the test development process. Was the sequencing decided intuitively or was it based on a field testing of the instrument? It is also unfortunate that no information is presented in the guide on the test's reliability or validity. The lack of such information makes it difficult for a school district or institution to justify the use of this test, unless it can gather such information itself. As an alternative, potential test users may want to examine the Basic English Skills Test, which also assesses ESL literacy, though at a somewhat higher level.

[140]

Hogan Personality Inventory. Purpose: "Assesses six dimensions of broad, general importance for personal and social effectiveness" for use in counseling, research, and personnel selection. Age 18–adult; 1985–86; HPI; 13 scores: 6 primary scale scores (Intellectance, Adjustment, Prudence, Ambition, Sociability, Likeability), 6 occupational scale scores (Service Orientation, Reliability, Stress Tolerance, Clerical Potential, Sales Potential, Managerial Potential), and Validity scale score; 1987 price data: $14 or less per 25 reusable test booklets ('86, 4 pages); $7 or less per prepaid answer sheet including the cost of mail-in scoring and reports; $9.25 or less per 25 answer sheets to be used with

Arion II or MICROTEST scoring; $8.50 per manual ('86, 45 pages); scoring services producing interpretive reports available from publisher via prepaid mail-in scoring, Arion II teleprocessing ($7 or less per report) or MICROTEST assessment software ($61 per disk with 10 tests, $292.50 with 50 tests, or $540 with 100 tests, for use with IBM PC or PC/XT); (20–30) minutes; Robert Hogan; National Computer Systems, Inc.*

Review of the Hogan Personality Inventory by JAMES J. HENNESSY, Associate Professor of Psychological and Educational Services, Fordham University, New York, NY:

The Hogan Personality Inventory (HPI) purports to measure six personality dimensions that influence or underlie broad domains of personal and social effectiveness. It is intended for use in counseling, personnel selection, vocational assessment, and research, and may also serve as an early indicator of the need for more in-depth psychological or psychiatric evaluation. It is not, however, a clinical instrument, but is intended for use across a wide spectrum of typical or normal functioning.

The HPI consists of 310 true-false items that yield scores on six primary interpersonal personality dimensions and on six occupational performance scales. Of the 310 items, 212 are keyed on the primary scales, with no item overlap across those scales. Sixteen (16) other items contribute to a Validity scale and the remaining 82 items, together with some items from the primary scales, produce the six occupational performance scales. There is item overlap within the occupational scales, and between them and the primary scales. Users should be cautious, therefore, when interpreting the occupational scales.

The discussion of the socioanalytic personality theory that guided construction of the inventory, and of the factor analytic research literature that influenced the number, characteristics, and names of the six primary scales was superficial and incomplete. As an example, the assertion that *all* modern writers in the field agree that three to six factors adequately describe the trait universe is an overstatement. In addition, the failure to differentiate terms such as *factor*, *dimension*, and *trait* further clouded the presentation.

The six HPI scales, Intellectance, Adjustment, Prudence, Ambition, Sociability, and Likeability, represent the six core traits the author asserts encompass the universe of trait terms members of groups use in evaluating each other. Responses to items indicate how respondents want to be regarded by others, that is, their social identity. These self-imagined reputations are the aspects of personality that influence social and occupational functioning, and are the aspects assessed by the HPI.

Items within the six primary scales are clustered into 43 empirically-validated Homogenous Item Clusters (HIC), which are small groups of content-similar items that in aggregate give meaning to the primary scales. The HICs were constructed to be internally consistent, with items within each more highly correlated with one another than with other items, and with HICs within a scale more highly correlated with each other than with other HICs. A 425-item pool was generated originally and administered over a 5-year period to groups that eventually totalled 1,700 adults. Items that did not meet author-established criteria, primarily related to internal consistency, were deleted, yielding the final 310-item version.

The HPI is self-administered, and is estimated to take approximately one-half hour to complete. Although the items were written at a fourth-grade reading level, it is not likely that adults functioning at that level would be able to *comprehend* the meaning of many items whose conceptual complexity is at a higher level of difficulty. The HPI seems most suitable for individuals who have completed a high school education. Machine- and hand-scoring answer sheets are available, although the manual contains an illustration and directions for the machine version only.

HIC internal consistency was a major factor influencing item selection and, therefore, acceptably high coefficient alpha reliability estimates are reported. The values, based on a sample of 800 adults, range from .39 to .83 for the HICs and from .76 to .89 for the primary scales. The HIC estimates are acceptable, especially in that the lowest estimate is for a HIC that is composed of only three items, and the two others that are below .5 are for HICs having four items. The magnitudes of the estimates for the primary scale are higher than those reported for other widely-used inventories. Test-retest correlations based on a 4-week interval ranged from .74 for the Sociability scale to .99 for the Adjustment scale, values that also are in the acceptable range. The sample size of 90 college students upon which the test-retest estimates are based limits somewhat the confidence a user may place in them.

A major shortcoming of the manual is the omission of any information pertaining to standard errors of measurement and estimate. Guidelines for interpreting scores are based on raw-score cutoffs, above or below which 60% of an undefined, sex-specific population scored. A table of high and low cutoff scores is presented but without any recognition or acknowledgement of measurement error. Differences of only 2 raw-score units separate high and low scorers of both sexes on the Likeability scale, whose internal consistency estimate is .76. Three points separate highs from lows on three of the other 10 comparisons. These 2- and 3-point differences are smaller than an interval bounded by one standard error of measurement around the scores. Almost all of the other differences in cutoff scores between highs and lows overlap in an interval smaller than two standard errors of measurement making interpretation of those differences meaningless. Given the implications for personnel selection and other important decisions attributed by the author to standing in a high or low group, failure to attend to errors of measurement is an egregious oversight.

Internal or factor validity data support the arrangement of HICs on their rationally placed scales. Although the size and composition of the sample on which the factor analysis was derived is not specified, HICs generally are loaded by only one factor, and where they split, their highest loadings are on the desired or expected factor. The intercorrelations between the HPI and California Personality Inventory (CPI) were offered as evidence of concurrent, construct validity. The findings are that similar HPI and CPI scales correlate more highly with each other than with other scales. HPI with Self-Directed Search (SDS) correlations are supportive of HPI primary scale validity. The database from which these findings were derived limits them considerably. The sample was both small ($n = 125$) and composed entirely of U.S. Navy enlisted personnel. Although the findings are encouraging, they provide an insufficient basis on which to rest statements of validity. The MMPI-HPI analysis was based on a small, nonrepresentative sample, thus conclusions based on it must also be cautious ones.

Several studies are cited as evidence of the validity of the HPI in applied settings in which it is used to predict some criterion (e.g., job performance, fitness, proneness to felony). The magnitudes of the many HIC-based multiple correlations often exceeded .50, but their importance and meaning were obscured by poorly-defined or inappropriate criteria, small samples, and infrequent attempts to cross-validate. As just one example of the weakness of the validity studies cited, the HPI primary scales and HICs were correlated with rankings of job performance in a large trucking company. Rankings of 1 were assigned to drivers, of 2 to their immediate supervisors, and 3 to supervisors of supervisors. A canonical correlation analysis was computed and the finding of a very high canonical correlation (.97) between HICs and rankings was cited as evidence of the usefulness of the HPI in predicting successful job performance. No estimate of within-job category performance was obtained leaving one to conclude only that drivers differ from their bosses, who in turn differ from their bosses in some statistically significant, but uninterpretable way. Why one would want a psychological inventory to predict that which is already known (job type in this instance) is not explained.

Normative data are also not reported in sufficient detail. Absolute cutoffs are provided for determining whether or not a respondent's scores are in the high or lower category. Means and standard deviations for men and women respondents are provided for the six primary scales but not for the HICs and Validity scales. Similar data are presented for Whites and Blacks, who differed significantly on four of the six primary scales (not on the Intellectance and Adjustment scales) but the differences are not interpreted substantively. No indication was given as to the significance of the differences between men and women. Nonnormalized *T*-scores, based on the men's group data, are reported on the profile sheet, although no mention of these scores is made in the manual. Apparently they are not needed for interpretations, which are based solely on the cutoff scores. Users can select key words and phrases from the interpretation guide to give meaning to a particular score profile. A user probably would be inclined to place some qualifying adverbs (such as *very*) before key words in instances where raw scores are markedly above or below the cutoffs. It is unfortunate that an inventory that can assess individual differences reliably across a wide range of functioning reduces that information to so few categories. The richness of individuality is lost in favor of categorical typing.

The author indicated that scores ought not be interpreted in isolation and he offered examples wherein specific combinations of high and low scores are suggestive of specific potentials or tendencies. Unfortunately, no evidential basis was provided to support these interpretations, nor were other salient combinations discussed. The primary basis for validating profile interpretation rests on the author's analysis of HPI results for individuals known to him. They were chosen because each represented a distinct Holland personality type, determined by the type of work each performed. HPI descriptors were compared to Holland-type descriptors and the high concordance (qualitatively determined) was cited as evidence of valid test interpretation. This method seems circular in that one starts with a known and structures an analysis to conform to it.

The evidence supporting the reliability and validity of the Occupational Performance Scales is even more scant than that underlying the primary scales. The samples were derived largely from those used above, although the criteria and item configurations differed. Many of the assertions made about the characteristics individuals should possess to succeed at work seem to be based on limited or stereotypic views of the world of work, and the assertions about the qualities employers seek also might not withstand critical analysis. These scales are in the very earliest phase of development and should not be reported to decision makers, or interpreted to respondents. At best they should remain in the domain of experimental test development.

At this point in time a user of the HPI would be able to construct a very general description of an individual's standing on six broad traits. Beyond that broad, and therefore vague, description little can be learned. One cannot decide where an individual's performance places her/him in comparison to some meaningful reference group; a user would be hard-pressed to make and defend personnel decisions in most employment settings; and a counselor would glean little information not already available in the more well-validated SDS and CPI.

Review of the Hogan Personality Inventory by ROLF A. PETERSON, Department of Psychology, The George Washington University, Washington, DC:

The Hogan Personality Inventory was developed to measure major personality dimensions and several occupational performance areas. The inventory represents an attempt to improve upon comprehensive measures of personality.

The strength of the inventory lies in the fact the structure is based on six widely accepted dimensions of personality. The primary areas are made up of several subsets of factors, called HICs (homogeneous item composites) representing the various aspects of the primary area. HICs, across scales, were then selected to measure characteristics relevant to occupational success based on initial development/validity studies.

A case is presented for how self-report is really a self-representation reflecting the personality as "one's reputation" as judged by observers. The fact remains the scale is self-report and subject to the bias of self-report measures. A validity scale is included but serves to assess careless or random responding. Measures of lying, defensiveness, or social desirability are not included.

As seems to be true of all comprehensive personality attributes measures, the attempt to measure global, pervasive traits or, in this case, interpersonal styles, is both a strength and weakness. The attempt to measure multiple global aspects of behavior (personality) serves the goal of supporting personality theory, but results in a relatively complex, weak measuring instrument.

In terms of psychometric and validity data, the Hogan has a number of weak points. Some of the HICs, which should be very related items, have internal alphas of below .50 and some also have quite low 4-week test-retest correlations. Internal reliability is not reported for most of the occupational scales. The six primary scales are better psychometrically than are the HICs.

The validity of the primary personality scales and occupational scales varies with the scales, but in all cases very little data is presented, and, in most cases, the results are marginal in terms of outcome. Two examples can be used to demonstrate the validity data provided in the manual. For "Intellectance, which measures the degree to which a person is perceived as bright, creative and interested in cultural and educational matters" (p. 5 of manual), correlations with the CPI, Holland's Self-Directed Search, and the Armed Forces Vocational Aptitude Battery for a sample of U.S. Navy Enlisted Personnel are provided. Moderate correlations (40s and 50s) are reported for scales with a similar definition. Based on a .26 correlation with Arithmetic Reasoning, a .20 correlation with a pass-fail criterion in technical school, and .18 correlation with grade point in technical school, Hogan concludes that persons scoring high on Intellectance tend to perform well in academic settings. With such low correlations, the predictive value of the scale is questionable.

The Adjustment scale, which appears to be one of the best scales, relates moderately well to a number of other adjustment-based scales and correlates highly (-.76) with the MMPI A scale. The scale does appear to be a good measure of generalized neuroticism.

All validity data are presented in terms of correlations and even when criterion groups are available (felons versus nonfelons) neither ability to classify nor means for groups are provided. For clinical interpretation of the primary scales, a high score has been defined as above the 60th percentile and a low score below the 40th percentile. Data on the validity of these cutoffs are not available.

For the occupational scales, the validity is based on correlations with scales within the inventory and in some cases other scales. Concurrent validity tends to be based on correlations with selected criteria for two or three samples. Again, the correlations are often low and the number of validity studies reported for each scale is marginal at best. The most relevant use of the occupational scales involves the interpretation of the profile pattern of scale scores, but these interpretations are subjective and lack any solid validity evidence.

The conclusions provided for scale meanings and interpretation of scale profiles must be viewed as hypotheses at this time. The scale offers a wealth of opportunity for research to determine the validity, especially predictive validity and criterion validity, of the interpretations of the scales and profile configurations. There is too little established evidence of validity to use the scale as a valid decision-making tool, but the inventory can provide information for general counseling and discussion purposes for vocational guidance activities.

[141]

Home Environment Questionnaire: HEQ-2R and HEQ-1R. Purpose: Measures "dimensions of the child's psychosocial environment that exert specific types of pressure on the child." Grades 4–6; 1983; HEQ; ratings by child's mother; 10 scores: P(ress) Achievement, P Aggression-External, P Aggression-Home, P Aggression-Total, P Supervision, P Change, P Affiliation, P Separation, P Sociability, P Socioeconomic Status; 2 forms: HEQ-2R for use with two-parent families and HEQ-1R for use with single-parent families; 1986 price data: $5 per 25 booklets (specify HEQ-1R or HEQ-2R); $7 per 9 scoring keys (specify HEQ-1R or HEQ-2R); $7 per manual ('83, 22 pages); $30 per specimen set including 25 each HEQ-2R and HEQ-1R, scoring keys, manual and norms; administration time not reported; Jacob O. Sines; Psychological Assessment and Services, Inc.*

TEST REFERENCES

1. Nihira, K., Mink, I. T., & Meyers, C. E. (1984). Salient dimensions of home environment relevant to child development. *International Review of Research in Mental Retardation*, 12, 149-175.

Review of the Home Environment Questionnaire by STEVEN I. PFEIFFER, Director, Institute of Clinical Training and Research, The Devereux Foundation, Devon, PA, and JULIA PETTIETTE-DOOLIN, Department of Psychology, Tulane University, New Orleans, LA:

The Home Environment Questionnaire (HEQ) is an instrument that purports to identify psychosocial factors that exert specific types of environmental press upon a target child. Two HEQ forms are available. Form 2-R consists of 123 true-false items and is designed to assess the environment of a family headed by two parents, whereas Form 1-R, a modification of 2-R, consists of 91 true-false statements applicable for a family headed by one parent. The HEQ (regardless of the form used) is to be completed by the target child's mother or primary caretaker.

The underlying rationale of the questionnaire is Henry Murray's concept of environmental press. Items on the questionnaire are meant to assess those tangible, quantifiable pressures across 10 dimensions: P(ress) Achievement, P Aggression-External, P Aggression-Home, P Aggression-Total, P Supervision, P Change, P Affiliation, P Separation, P Sociability, and P Socioeconomic Status.

The items comprising the 10 scales were included based on an item-scale correlation that equaled or exceeded .30, in conjunction with a general rational-statistical method for scale inclusion. Unfortunately, factor analysis was not employed, and a number of the specific items lack face validity. For example, items of the P Aggression-Home scale vary from "I am often depressed" to "Dirt upsets me a great deal," whereas the item "My husband often loses his temper" is included within the P Affiliation scale. Without factor-analytic-study support, the inclusion of these items may adversely affect respondent cooperation while not contributing to the construct being investigated. In addition, the items that assess each scale differ appreciably in number (ranging from 4 for the Sociability scale to 25 for the Affiliation and Socioeconomic Status scales).

Responses are scored with the assistance of nine transparent scoring templates (provided with the questionnaire packet). Raw scores are calculated for each of the 10 dimensions or scales and then converted to *T*-scores. However, the sample from which the *T*-scores were derived is, unfortunately, quite biased. The sample for the HEQ-2R consisted of 544 mothers of fourth, fifth, and sixth graders, and the sample for the HEQ-1R was composed of 76 mothers of fourth, fifth, and sixth graders. All of the mothers were from a single midwestern city with a population of 24,000, and approximately 95% of the respondents were white. Therefore, the questionnaire is applicable for use only with children in the fourth through sixth grades and should not be used with minority children.

The manual does not provide adequate information concerning application of the *T*-score value. The author states that "clinical experience with the HEQ-2R suggests that a T score above 60 or below 40 on any scale should be considered significant and to warrant further exploration with the parents and the child." This piece of advice, based apparently on the author's personal experience, is sorely lacking in empirical support, and reinforces the use of the scale as an experimental/research instrument.

The manual also describes a method of applying the raw scores from the HEQ scales in a predictive manner. According to the author, the HEQ-2R may "be useful in estimating how much of a child's several specific behaviors can be expected from an 'average child' exposed to the particular environmental press indicated by the HEQ-2R." In order to achieve this predictive objective, the author derived "environmental specification equations" by identifying (through stepwise multiple correlations) the HEQ-2R scales that accounted for a significant portion of the variance in a particular behavioral dimension of the Parent Form of the Missouri Children's Behavioral Checklist (MCBC-P). Therefore, the predictive validity (and essentially the only support for the construct validity of the scale) is assessed by correlating the HEQ results with the results of a second parent questionnaire—a questionnaire that, incidentally, was also designed by the author of the HEQ.

Perhaps the most telling weakness of this scale, in addition to the lack of representative normative data and the dearth of reliability information, is its questionable validity. A number of the items are subject to social desirability factors (e.g., "Other people say that I'm too lenient with ______"), and the manual does not encourage independent observational techniques to support the information obtained from the questionnaire. The mother is the sole informant, and thus a determination of internal reliability is unavailable.

It is safe to caution the present use of the HEQ to experimental and research endeavors. The instrument is to be commended for its conceptual foundation based on a well-articulated theoretical model and for its promise of predicting children's behavior from a more careful understanding of environmental stressors. But large-scale investigations with more representative populations are needed before the HEQ can be considered appropriate for clinical decision making.

[142]

Howell Prekindergarten Screening Test. Purpose: Provides for early identification of children "who may need special assistance to ensure their successful entry into formal education; . . . whose skills seem appropriate for typical kindergarten work; . . . [or those] students with unusually well developed skills which can be most fully enhanced by specially designed educational experiences." Prekindergarten students; 1984; 23 scores: Shapes, Listening Comprehension, Auditory Memory, Colors, Color Words, Vocabulary, Classification, Letter Identification, Rhyming, Letter Writing, Directionality & Spatial Relationships, Consonant Sounds, Visual Motor, Visual Discrimination, Name, Math (Number Identification, Number Writing, Counting Sets, Math Concepts, Addition & Subtraction, Total), Copying, Total; 1986 price data: $17.95 per 10 student test booklets; $12.95 per user's guide and technical manual ('84, 49 pages); $14.95 per specimen set; (60) minutes; Howell Township Public Schools, Joseph P. Ryan (manual) and Ronald J. Mead (manual); Book-Lab.*

Review of the Howell Prekindergarten Screening Test by CARL J. DUNST, Director, Family, Infant and Preschool Program, Western Carolina Center, Morganton, NC:

The Howell Prekindergarten Screening Test is designed to help teachers identify children entering kindergarten who may need supplemental and supportive instructional assistance. The instrument includes 71 items that assess a child's performance in 21 learning areas, including Listening Comprehension, Auditory Memory, Classification, Letter Identification and Writing, Number Identification and Writing, and Addition and Subtraction. The items were selected to tap skills early childhood specialists generally recognize as necessary and important for successful participation in kindergarten classrooms.

The Howell is a group test administered in a paper-and-pencil format. It takes approximately 2 hours to administer. It is recommended that the test be administered in four sittings over a 2-day period. The examiner's manual includes explicit instructions for teachers to follow when administering the test. A filmstrip has been developed in order to facilitate correct administration, scoring, and interpretation of the scale. According to the test developers, the results from the test "can be utilized to develop a diagnostic supplementary educational plan." It must be noted that results are not used for identifying instructional targets for either supplemental or remedial purposes. Rather, the results are used for deciding the next steps to be taken for children whose scores fall below a certain cutoff point, and who, thus, presumably have learning difficulties.

Each of the 71 scale items is scored dichotomously (pass vs. fail). The Howell yields a total scale score, which is simply the sum of the passes on the individual items. (A math subscale score can also be determined.) The total scores are used to classify a child as falling into one of three "score categories": Critical Region (0–30), Regular Performance (31–51), and Very High Performance (52–73). Children in the critical group are thought to need remedial instruction, children in the regular performance category are thought to be prepared for a typical school experience, and children in the very high group are thought to need more challenging educational experiences. The test developers do not provide any rationale, whatsoever, for the parameters of the cutoff points for the score categories, and in no instance is there any discussion of the validity of this categorization scheme.

The method for assigning children to "risk," "nonrisk," and "advanced" categories is especially open to criticism. The selection of cutoff points for assignment of children to the categories appears to have been done either intuitively or based on an approximate tripartite split, and does not appear to have been established empirically. Because no explanation or rationale is provided for the scores demarcating the boundaries of each category, the use of the scale for screening purposes is questionable, especially for children whose scores are close to the cutoff points.

The above criticism is compounded by the fact that no normative or standardization data are presented in the test manual, and no specific information is provided about the subjects (age, sex, parent education, SES, etc.). The Howell was developed in a school district composed of predominantly middle-income families. Consequently, the scale scores may have different meanings depending upon the population being tested. This is not a trivial matter, and caution is warranted in using the Howell even as a screening tool except in cases where scores are either extremely low or high.

The examiner's manual does include numerous bits of data regarding the reliability and validity of the test. The five internal consistency coefficients were all high (Range = .86 to .88) for samples ranging from N s = 186 to

328. Neither short- or long-term test-retest reliability data are reported. Despite the test developers' dismissal of the need for these types of stability indices, such coefficients are needed in order to establish whether the scores allow accurate classification of children administered the scale. This seems especially true because the scale is used primarily with 5-year-olds whose behavior is likely to be affected by taking this type of a paper-and-pencil test. For many children of this age, this test may be their first experience with a paper-and-pencil evaluation.

A number of studies have been conducted with respect to the validity of the Howell. In one study of 229 children, teachers were first asked to classify their students into one of four categories: eligible for compensatory education, possibly needing assistance, prepared for regular program, and eligible for gifted and talented program. Mean Howell scores were then computed for the children assigned to each category. The scores for the four groups were, respectively, 26.0 (*SD* = 7.2), 35.5 (*SD* = 7.8), 43.9 (*SD* = 10.3), and 53.6 (*SD* = 6.9), with all adjacent pair-wise comparisons statistically significant. In a second study, Howell scores were used to group 328 students into low-, middle-, and high-score groups. Eight months later, teachers were asked to assign their students to one of three ability levels (low, middle, high). Cross tabulations of the two sets of data showed identical cell assignments for 64% of the cases. Assignment of only 1.2% of the cases differed by two categories. The "hit" rate for assignment to the high and low groups based on Howell scores is generally impressive. However, examination of the data for the middle ability group, which presumably overlaps considerably with the Regular Performance Category (although no scores are given), suggests difficulties in using the test. Of all the students in the study, teachers assigned 117 to the middle ability group. Only 56 students, or 48%, were properly classified by the Howell scores. Thus, for children bordering around the cutoff points, there is about a 50-50 chance of being assigned to the correct category.

The predictive validity of the Howell was examined in two studies in which Howell scores were used to predict California Achievement Test grade levels and percentile rankings with the measurements taken 1 and 2 years apart. The validity coefficients were .71 and .68, respectively, between the total scale scores and the CAT Reading and Mathematics scores for the 1-year measures, and .64 and .72 for the same comparisons for the 2-year measures. These are quite impressive validity coefficients, and indicate that generally (on the average) children who score low on the Howell at entry into kindergarten are the same youngsters who are likely to score low on the California Achievement Test in the first and second grades, whereas the opposite is true for children who initially score high on the Howell.

SUMMARY. The Howell is a screening instrument designed to identify kindergarten children who may potentially require supplemental or remedial instruction. The results are used to classify a child as being "at-risk," "at-no-risk," or "advanced" in performance. Although the reliability and validity data on the Howell are generally acceptable and in some instances even impressive, none of the data are based precisely on the trichotomized categorization scheme for deciding at-risk status. The major task that remains is to ascertain the degree to which the scoring scheme is reliable and valid. Some type of discriminant analysis is clearly warranted. Until this type of validity study is conducted, users should be cautious in using the Howell for screening purposes.

Review of the Howell Prekindergarten Screening Test by CANDICE FEIRING, Associate Professor of Pediatrics, Robert Wood Johnson Medical School, University of Medicine and Dentistry of New Jersey, New Brunswick, NJ:

The Howell Prekindergarten Screening Test is basically a tool that provides a measure for classifying students entering kindergarten into three groups—high, medium, and low—based on skills believed necessary for beginning kindergarten. The low-performance group may need special assistance to facilitate kindergarten entrance; the medium group has sufficient skills; and the high group is considered advanced and in need of special programming. It must be kept in mind that these three groups are based on norms obtained from a series of samples (*N* = 186–229) from a middle-income community, so that skill levels are based on performance levels necessary to succeed in this type of population. The test is comprised of 73 items easily administered to groups. As a screening tool, the Howell takes a very long time to administer, requiring 2 hours of testing with a recommendation of four sittings over a 2-day period. The items cover 21 skills (see description of test content provided above) believed important by experienced teachers and early childhood experts for kindergarten success. However, these 21 skills cannot be assessed separately as the Howell is a screening tool for general classification of students and is not appropriate for determining children's specific learning profiles.

The psychometric properties of the Howell have been well addressed and the test developers were given technical assistance by the staff at Educational Testing Service. Reliability information on the Howell consists only of information on internal consistency. Split-half reliability, calculated using an odd-even division of items with the Spearman-Brown Prophecy formula to adjust for test length, yielded acceptable levels of internal consistency from .86 to .88 for three independent samples. Test-retest reliability of the Howell was not obtained, the rationales given being the young age of the respondents and the test length. However, it still would have been advisable to obtain an index of the extent to which the Howell reliably classifies children into the same category on two test occasions. An odd-even item split could have been used to create two comparable forms in order to obtain short term test-retest reliability.

Concurrent validity of the Howell was determined by comparing children's test scores to teacher classification of the children into four groups: (1) gifted, (2) regular class, (3) possible assistance, and (4) compensatory program. The teachers who estimated children's skill levels were well experienced with the children's performance and were unaware of the children's test scores. The mean scores on the Howell were shown to be rank ordered as expected (group $1 > 2 > 3 > 4$) given the teacher's estimates, and the observed differences were significant overall for the contrasts of adjacent groups (group $1 > 2$, $2 > 3$, $3 > 4$). While these results are quite acceptable, it would also be useful to have information on the comparison of Howell scores to another instrument (e.g., CIRCUS).

Predictive validity of the Howell was determined in two ways using teachers' rankings and California Achievement Test scores (CAT) as outcome criteria. The teachers' rankings of 328 students into Low, Middle, and High groups were obtained 8 months after a 100-item pilot version of the Howell was administered. The Howell scores were used to classify children into High, Medium, and Low groups and these groups were related to the teachers' subsequent ratings. The agreement between test ranks and teacher rank was moderately good for the High (69%) and Low (78%) groups. For the Middle group, agreement was lower (48%) with children who scored in the Middle group on the Howell often ranked in the High (28%) or Low (20%) group by teachers. Test scores on the Howell for two large samples (N = 138 and 194) were correlated with CAT scores in reading and math. All correlations were significant and ranged from .62 to .72, which is very acceptable predictive validity.

In general, the Howell has acceptable internal consistency and good predictive validity. However, as a screening tool the Howell takes an extremely long time to administer in order to obtain three skill-level classifications for children entering kindergarten. The test developers wisely caution against use of the Howell to measure individual skill areas. The guidelines for test administration and interpretation of scores and psychometric information are clear and well presented in the examiner's manual. In using the Howell, caution should be used in regard to misclassification of children in the middle scoring groups, and it must be kept in mind that this test has been normed on a restricted sample of children from middle-income families. Despite these drawbacks, the Howell has been thoughtfully constructed and initial psychometric findings on a large sample are generally good.

[143]

Human Figures Drawing Test. Purpose: Measures the nonverbal conceptual ability or cognitive maturation of children. Ages 5–0 to 10–11; 1986; HFDT; consists of scoring by examiner for 38 items on child's human figure drawings; 1986 price data: $39 per complete kit including 100 scoring/profile forms and manual ('86, 46 pages); $24 per 100 scoring/profile forms; $17 per manual; (10–15) minutes; Eloy Gonzales; PRO-ED, Inc.*

TEST REFERENCES

1. McCready, K. F., Berry, F. M., & Kenkel, M. B. (1985). Supervised relaxation training: A model for greater accessibility of behavioral interventions. *Professional Psychology: Research and Practice*, 16, 595-604.

Review of the Human Figures Drawing Test by ALLEN K. HESS, Professor of Psychology and Department Head, Auburn University at Montgomery, Montgomery, AL:

The Human Figures Drawing Test (HFDT) purports to measure *cognitive maturation* of children from 5 to 10 years of age. The test materials consist of a 42-page manual and a scoring pad. The score sheet has space for identifying information, the HFDT score (raw, standard, and percentile), other test scores, comments about the test conditions, a comments/recommendation space, and a 38-item scoring section. The manual, in four short chapters, presents an overview of the human figure drawing tests, administration and scoring procedures, interpretation procedures, and construction and statistical characteristics of the HFDT. Two appendices present norms and scoring criteria.

I suppose we can review the highlights and sidelights of human figure drawings in general and this one in particular, review its roots back to the drawings in the caves of Lescaux, review its use to bypass cultural bias in an attempt to assay a "culture free" intelligence, review the ways figure drawings reveal the vicissitudes of emotionality, and split hairs about the difference between figure drawings as measures of intelligence versus measures of cognitive maturation. But simply put, it would be a better use of our space to consider the questions: Why was the HFDT constructed, and does it do anything more for us than other prior tests?

The HFDT yields a single score that is supposed to be diagnostic of a child's placement and programming. The score is putatively indicative of cognitive maturation. Specifically, the test dismisses any and all personality assessment functions of human figure drawings. The manual is careful to indicate that the test portrays the developmental nature of cognitive function. The author's goals were to eliminate contamination of figure drawing test scoring by artistic talent, eliminate subjectivity of scoring, correlate the test with academic achievement, provide age norms, and "update individual items . . . to reflect what today's children are drawing."

Administration and scoring procedures, Chapter 2, are clear, and for the most part, standard. However, children who draw figures smaller than 2 inches in height or begin with a large head that may preclude a complete full figure, are asked to begin anew. Also, the instructions ask for a figure of the child, then one of the opposite sex. Appendix 2 provides examples of scoring criteria to increase scorer reliability. The scoring yields a raw score for the number of correctly drawn items on either drawing; the raw score is converted to a standard score or quotient ($X = 100, S = 15$), and reported along with the percentile equivalent. Aside from a caution against overinterpreting the meaning of low scores, no interpretive guidelines are provided in Chapter 3, entitled Interpretation of the HFDT Results.

Chapter 4 reports the test was developed on 200 children in the 5-, 6-, 7-, 8-, 9-, and 10-year age groups. Data indicate each age group to score 2 or 3 raw score items above the next younger group; the author contends that reaffirms the developmental nature of the HFDT. The 2,400 children in the norming group attended public schools in some 20 states ranging across the country. Gender, race, and urban-rural characteristics parallel the United States general population but test data are not broken down on these variables in the manual. Cronbach alpha coefficients, measuring internal consistency, range from .73 to .85 with corresponding standard errors of measurement ranging from 6 to 8. The manual did not specify whether the normative group, some subsample, or a new sample was used for the reliability estimates, although the text reads as though the normative sample was used. To assess test-retest reliability "50 elementary schools' children grades K, 3, and 5 . . . were tested twice, with a two-week interval between each testing." It is unclear whether the total sample was 50, or 50 in each group for a total of 150. The resulting reliability coefficients were .87 (K), .91 (grade 3), and .89 (grade 5). Three graduate students trained in two 1-hour sessions attained an average scorer reliability of .97 on 30 protocols (10 each from 5-, 8-, and 10-year-old children.)

Construct validation evidence is strongest in the data showing HFDT quotients of 30 students in a gifted program to be 128, while 30 children termed retarded scored 66. No distributions, discriminative functions, or range statistics are provided. Correlations of the HFDT with the Woodcock-Johnson Psychoeducational Battery are .20 (Reading), .52 (Math), and .42 (Written Language) for 50 students of unspecified age and achievement levels. Thirty HFDT protocols were rescored with the Harris system and a .66 resulted. No explanation was offered for these results. Kaufman Assessment Battery for Children correlations with the HFDT were .42 (Sequential composite), .57 (Simultaneous composite), and .52 (Total), while Wechsler Intelligence Scale for Children—Revised correlations were .53 (Verbal), .31 (Performance), and .50 (Full Scale). These provide modest criteria validation supporting the idea that a cognitive function is being tapped by the HFDT.

CONCLUSIONS. If one is interested in a single score putatively tapping cognitive maturation via a nonverbal method, the HFDT is an option. It may be useful for a standardized testing program or a research project because the form is available and convenient. However, one can construct a form for less than 24 cents a sheet, and adapt existing procedures from Harris or other figure drawing tests for less than the $17 42-page manual.

Moreover, the HFDT is not anchored in any theory, nor linked to remedial schema or differential diagnostic taxonomies. Assessment that ends with a single score is fruitless, and even harmful. Testing should serve a positive purpose such as diagnosing particular deficiencies or indicating remediation programs. In fact, the manual views such potentially diagnostic information as a child drawing unusually large or small figures as a contamination, rather than noting such data. The HFDT does yield a score indicative of intelligence but, to repeat a refrain from a Patti Page ballad popular in the 1960s—"Is that all there is?"

Review of the Human Figures Drawing Test by FRANCIS E. LENTZ, JR., Associate Professor of School Psychology and Counseling, University of Cincinnati, Cincinnati, OH:

The Human Figures Drawing Test (HFDT) appears similar in purpose and design to the Goodenough-Harris Draw-a-Person Test (see 7:352 for reviews). Intended to measure "cognitive maturation" (or "nonverbal measure of cognitive ability") in children from 5 to 10 years of age, it produces an "HFDT quotient" with a mean of 100 and *SD* of 15. (This score is not a quotient, however, it is a standard score.) Examinees are asked to draw two figures, one of themselves, and one of the opposite sex. Thirty-eight characteristics of the drawings are scored to produce a raw score that may then be converted to the standard score from six age-based conversion scales (one for each year covered).

VALIDITY. There are a number of problems in attempting to evaluate the purposes for which the HFDT might be valid. First, the construct to be measured by this test is never defined explicitly. A brief discussion of developmental maturation (one term used to describe what the HFDT measures) is provided without theoretical or functional definitions or support related to the test purposes. Further, a network of relationships with other constructs or measures is not delineated. This criticism is unfortunately common for most tests of "cognitive ability" or "intelligence," and is not unique to the HFDT.

Although the manual briefly describes construct, content, and criterion-related evidence for validity, both the logic and the evidence are minimal. In relation to other cognitive measures, correlation coefficients with the Goodenough-Harris (.66, $N = 30$, data for grades 1, 3, and 5), Kaufman Assessment Battery for Children (.52 for total, $N = 60$, no data on sample composition), and Wechsler Intelligence Scale for Children—Revised (WISC-R) (.50 for total IQ, $N = 30$, no data on sample) are reported. These coefficients are not strong, and there are basically no data on the validity studies themselves. In terms of relationship to school achievement, correlations are also reported for the Woodcock-Johnson Psychoeducational Assessment Battery (.20 for reading, .52 for math, and .42 for written language; $N = 50$). Again, no information on the subjects or study methodology is reported. Aside from the very limited sample sizes and sparse information on methodology, these relationships are difficult to interpret in the absence of a theoretical or practical framework, especially because the HFDT appears equally related to cognitive ability measures and to measures of achievement. Certainly, this test cannot be judged as a substitute for either.

Final evidence for validity concerns the test's ability to differentiate across different ages and between identified groups. The former differentiation is critical if the test is to relate to developmental maturity. An examination of distributions of raw scores across ages indicates (and the author reports) significant differences in mean levels across year groups. However, especially from 9.0–10.11, there is a large overlap of derived standard scores. Another study is reported that investigates group differentiation, although once again, information on methods is minimal. These data indicate the mean scores of a group of children ($N = 30$) classified as mentally handicapped and a group of gifted children ($N = 30$) are widely different. This comparison seems senseless; almost any type of measure would differentiate between such widely different groups.

In the introduction to the manual the author suggests that the HFDT is beneficial "to a diagnostician seeking functioning levels for supportive information in placement and programming," and that it "is readily integrated into any battery of tests designed for screening, determining current level of functioning, or identifying deficits." However, what functions and/or deficits are not specified, and the presented data are not sufficiently enlightening. There appears to be an intent that the HFDT produces some measure of cognitive ability; the one example of test interpretation in the manual supports this assumption. However, from the limited data available, an examiner would be ill-advised to use this test to make any decisions inferring limited cognitive development or abilities. Even as a potential screening device for identifying need for more comprehensive student evaluation (for special education placement, for example), the data reported are not sufficiently supportive. In essence, it is not clear on what basis decisions based on this test could be made. As a final caution, the data reported on the norming procedures and resulting norming distribution are extremely sketchy; certainly insufficient for a thoughtful evaluation of their adequacy (the demographics of the norming sample are reasonably well described, although selection procedures are not). Likewise, the author warns against biasing effects of previous drawing experiences and motor problems; no discussion of students with such characteristics in the norming sample is made. In summary, the size of the validity coefficients, the lack of information on methods, the failure to define the measured construct, and ambiguity or lack of information supporting suggested uses are extremely problematic. A positive assessment for any type validity is not currently possible.

RELIABILITY. Three estimates of test reliability are provided: internal consistency, test-retest, and interscorer. For all of these, virtually no information on data collection or analysis is provided, making evaluation difficult. Coefficients of internal consistency measures range from .73 (age 5) to .85 (ages 6 and 10). This is the only estimate of reliability that provides the appropriate *by age* coefficients. Test-retest (2-week interval) estimates are .87 (kindergarten), .91 (grade 3), and .89 (grade 5). The sample size is unclear (either 50 or 150), and (strangely) reliability is reported by grades, not ages. Finally, interscorer reliability, using three trained graduate students and 30 randomly selected protocols from the norming sample (5-, 8-, and 10-year-olds), is reported. The data here are not clear; the author reports analyzing by repeated measures ANOVA, but gives an average correlation coefficient (.97). Likewise, it is unclear if any of the graduate students agree with the original scoring, or if one of them was the original scorer. For this type of estimate, comparison of agreement should be reported in terms of covariation and level.

MANUAL. Instructions for administration seem clear. There are no data on whether administrators who read these directions and are not specifically trained in administration will be accurate scorers (although this seems the likely scenario for field administrators). Parts of the manual contain simplistic and misleading instructions for comparing scores across different tests. The suggestions provided are useful only if both tests assume standard normal distributions and may be misused by naive examiners.

SUMMARY. This test appears easy to administer and scoring criteria seem clear (although data on interscorer reliability were judged inadequate). However, the evidence that the test has valid uses or is reliable is not sufficient in this reviewer's opinion. In fairness to the HFDT, it is also the reviewer's opinion that in terms of determining appropriate interventions for school children who are experiencing academic difficulties, no measure of intelligence, cognitive skills, or maturation, etc., has yet proven useful. However, in making legal decisions about classification and special education placements, examiners should follow regulatory guidelines; I know of none that would find this test acceptable for those purposes.

[144]

Human Information Processing Survey. Purpose: "Assesses processing preference—left, right, integrated, or mixed [brain functioning]." Adults; 1984; HIP Survey; 3 scores: Right, Left, Integrated; 2 forms: Research Edition, Professional Edition; 1985 price data: $46 per 20 surveys, profiles, response forms, and 1 administrator's manual (44 pages) (Research Edition); $46 per 20 surveys, 20 strategy and tactics profiles, and 1 administrator's manual (Professional Edition); $12 per administrator's manual; $10 per specimen set; administration time not reported; E. Paul Torrance, William Taggart (manual), and Barbara Taggart; Scholastic Testing Service, Inc.*

TEST REFERENCES

1. Kienholz, A., & Hritzuk, J. (1986). Comparing students in architecture and medicine: Findings from two new measures of cognitive style. *Psychological Reports*, 58, 823-830.

Review of the Human Information Processing Survey by J. P. DAS, Director, Developmental Disabilities Centre, University of Alberta, Edmonton, Canada:

What can a reviewer say in regard to a test for which there is no empirical or theoretical basis, especially when the test seeks to attribute such multidimensional human behavior as managerial thinking to brain lateralization? The test exposes itself to examination from two established disciplines, neurosciences and cognitive psychology. Split-brain research provides the backdrop against which the test authors spin their highly speculative division of thinking types into scale scores of Right hemisphere and Left hemisphere. Sperry's pioneering work to which only one reference is made in the manual is, significantly, entitled "lateral specialization in the surgically separated hemispheres." Surgically separated is the key term to be remembered by any lay speculator on brain lateralization of cognitive functions. Even in these surgical cases, the two hemispheres have certain ways of communicating with each other. As Gazzaniga (1970) observed, if the right hemisphere makes a wrong decision, the left winces in concern, and then the right realizes its mistake. Put simply, it is a myth to attribute separate and distinct styles of thinking to the left and the right hemispheres of the brain. "The interhemispheric pathways transfer highly specified neural codes that serve to maintain an informational balance across the cerebral midline, and doing so provide mental unity" (Gazzaniga & LeDoux, 1978).

The best that can be said of this test is to give it the status of a "noninvasive measure" and to give it a place beside such other measures as Hiscock and Kinsbourne's left/right hand finger-tapping, and Conjugate Lateral Eye Movements (CLEMs). The Human Information Processing Survey (HIP) is shown to have a marginal r of .36 with CLEMs (35 college students), one of the rare independent studies of concurrent validity (Alberts & McCallum, 1982) that has been carried out on this test. Unfortunately, the noninvasive measure CLEM has doubtful reliability and validity as a test for discriminating between left-right brain functions (see Segalowitz in Obrzut & Hynd, 1986, pp. 200-204). The only other validation study with a recognized noninvasive measure, Dichotic Listening, resulted in a nonsignificant correlation, as reported in the HIP manual.

What the HIP elicits is a self-reported style of thinking that is as much influenced by formal and experiential learning as by task-demands. The latter is determined by knowledge-base and in the case of managerial skills, on the nature of the job and the agency in which the manager works. Tacit knowledge (Wagner & Sternberg, 1986) and some objective measure of planning behavior (Das, 1980) would be able to define the nature of managerial thinking; these will not have the disadvantage of leaning on surgically separated brain processes.

HIP and its predecessor Style of Learning and Thinking (SOLAT) are not valid; but are they reliable? A significant paper on the SOLAT written by authors outside the Torrance group, needs to be discussed in closing this review (Fitzgerald & Hattie, 1983). After noting that creativity should not be linked to left-right hemispheric functions, they comment about the test that "the theoretical bases are weak, there are anomalous and faulty items, misleading scoring, low reliabilities, and a lack of concurrent validity." Even if a few of these comments are found to be justified by a reviewer of this test, it will be difficult to recommend it to the user. This reviewer regards the test to have such an unjustified theoretical base that its validity as a measure of thinking style of left-brained and right-brained people is questionable, hence its unreliability will be of only academic interest to the users. We do not know what the test measures if the theoretical rationale is removed. Unless the user can replace it with a satisfactory rationale, it will be impossible to interpret the test results.

REVIEWER'S REFERENCES

Gazzaniga, M. S. (1970). *The bisected brain*. New York: Appleton-Century-Crofts.

Gazzaniga, M. S., & LeDoux, J. E. (1978). *The integrated mind*. New York: Plenum.

Das, J. P. (1980). Planning: Theoretical considerations and empirical evidence. *Psychological Research*, 41, 141-151.

Alberts, F. L., Jr., & McCallum, R. S. (1982). The relationship among three measures of cognitive style. *Clinical Neuropsychology*, 4, 70-71.

Fitzgerald, D., & Hattie, J. A. (1983). An evaluation of the 'Your Style of Learning and Thinking' Inventory. *British Journal of Educational Psychology*, 53, 336-346.

Segalowitz, S. J. (1986). Validity and reliability of noninvasive lateralization measures. In J. E. Obrzut & G. W. Hynd (Eds.), *Child neuropsychology*, Vol. 1, (pp. 191-208). Orlando: Academic Press.

Wagner, R. K., & Sternberg, R. J. (1986). Tacit knowledge and intelligence in the everyday world. In R. J. Sternberg & R. K. Wagner (Eds.), *Practical Intelligence* (pp. 51-83). Cambridge: Cambridge University Press.

[145]

The Identi-Form System for Gifted Programs. Purpose: "An aid to both the identification of gifted students, and the individualization of programming for these students following selection." Grades K–12; 1982; "incorporates test, performance and anecdotal data in a total assessment of the child"; ratings in 4 areas: Intellectual Abilities, Creative Abilities, Personal Characteristics, Artistic Performing Abilities; 1985 price data: $19.95 each, including 25 rating forms and manual ('82, 216 pages); $2.95 per 25 rating forms; Patricia Weber and Catherine Battaglia; D.O.K. Publishers, Inc.*

Review of The Identi-Form System for Gifted Programs by JAMES O. RUST, Professor of Psychology, Middle Tennessee State University, Murfreesboro, TN:

Identi-Form is really two things at once. It is a book about gifted education as well as a form to be used for identification and programming. The authors go to great lengths to explain their views about educating gifted and talented children. Many of the 200 pages in the book are devoted to describing ideas and philosophy about programs for the gifted. One example is the authors' treatment of the myth of the "overbearing, ego-tripping parent of the gifted child."

Identi-Form may assist program directors by bringing together diverse bits of information. The form offers 28 blank squares for every grade from kindergarten to Grade 12. Squares are provided for IQ, creative flexibility, self-concept, science, work-study performance, and more. A 3-point coding system is used to identify areas of particular strength and to make widely variable information more comparable. Thus, by reducing creative flexibility scores and self-concept scores to the same 3-point scale, the measures apparently become comparable. Following the 3-point transformations, personal strengths may be compared to relative weaknesses in all of the 28 areas.

Identi-Form includes several original checklists and questionnaires for students, parents, and teachers. Although the checklists and questionnaires may be potentially useful, the authors fail to provide basic information about how the questionnaires were constructed. Reliability and validity data are not included. Instead the reader is presented with a number of case studies. The authors have used the Identi-Form for over 4 years, but they do not include empirical support for it or for its scales. Instead Identi-Form is described as a qualitative system and placement decisions are to be based on professional judgment.

Normative data are not included in Identi-Form. Users are expected to create local norms. Cutoff scores are not part of the system either. Rather a range of acceptable scores is to be used flexibly.

The authors make a strong argument that gifted and creative programs should be designed before identification plans are formulated. Assessment systems can be custom designed, therefore, with program characteristics in mind. If educators follow such a sequence, Identi-Form may help organize the identifying material.

Identi-Form may be most useful in providing a framework to evaluate a gifted or creative program. The 28 blank squares per year for an entire K–12 school career could be used to effectively organize a student's performance on evaluative instruments. On the other hand, the 3-point Identi-Form coding procedure may be too crude to be sensitive to gains or losses made by children. The strength of Identi-Form is that it helps bring together a broad array of measures. Program directors may wish to use recording sheets to identify and monitor the students. If so, the Identi-Form may help.

One of Identi-Form's weaknesses is that it leaves too much to be done by individual users. The user has to decide on the appropriate instruments to evaluate the children. While some new questionnaires are included, their reliability and validity remain untested. A second weakness is the colloquial and informal writing style. In addition, references are sometimes incomplete and confusing.

The Baldwin Identification Matrix (Baldwin, 1984) is a system that is similar to the Identi-Form method. Baldwin provides a weighting of diverse data to allow assessment personnel to obtain a single score reflecting the student's overall capacity and talents. The single score can then be used to assist in eligibility decisions and for program evaluation. The Identi-Form is explicitly opposed to weighting systems. The authors prefer to leave final program placement decisions up to the qualitative judgment of a "trained professional." The educator is to weigh students' strengths and weaknesses on a case-by-case basis.

Program directors who consider using the Identi-Form will have to judge whether the convenience of the 28-column response sheet is worth reading and buying a 200-page manual complete with anecdotes and case studies. Another approach would be to make an original template for identifying student candidates and for charting student progress.

REVIEWER'S REFERENCE

Baldwin, A. Y. (1984). *Baldwin Identification Matrix 2* (2nd ed.). New York: Trillium Press.

[146]

Illness Behaviour Questionnaire, Second Edition. Purpose: "To record aspects of illness behaviour, particularly those attitudes that suggest inappropriate or maladaptive modes of responding to one's state of health." Pain clinic, psychiatric, and general practice patients; 1983; IBQ; self-report instrument; 8 scores: 7 factors (General Hypochondriasis, Disease Conviction, Psychological vs. Somatic Perception of Illness, Affective Inhibition, Affective Disturbance, Denial, Irritability) and Whitely Index of Hypochondriasis; price data available from publisher for questionnaire and manual ('83, 60 pages); administration time not reported; I. Pilowsky and N. D. Spence; I. Pilowsky [South Australia].*

TEST REFERENCES

1. Wilson-Barnett, J., & Trimble, M. R. (1985). An investigation of hysteria using the Illness Behaviour Questionnaire. *British Journal of Psychiatry*, 146, 601-608.

2. Clayer, J. R., Bookless-Pratz, C. L., & Ross, M. W. (1986). The evaluation of illness behaviour and exaggeration of disability. *British Journal of Psychiatry*, 148, 296-299.

3. Kellner, R., Wiggins, R. G., & Pathak, D. (1986). Hypochondrial fears and beliefs in medical and law students. *Archives of General Psychiatry*, 43, 487-489.

Review of the Illness Behaviour Questionnaire, Second Edition by MICHELLE T. TOSHIMA, Ph.D. candidate, and ROBERT M. KAPLAN, Professor of Community and Family Medicine, Acting Chief, Division of Health Care Services, University of California, San Diego, La Jolla, CA:

The 62-item Illness Behaviour Questionnaire (IBQ) is designed to assess inappropriate or maladaptive health attitudes. The yes/no items represent seven aspects of illness behavior: General Hypochondriasis, Disease Conviction, Psychological vs. Somatic Concern, Affective Inhibition, Affective Disturbance or Dysphoria, Denial, and Irritability.

The Illness Behaviour Questionnaire was used initially to detect abnormal illness behavior patterns in pain clinic patients. A sample of 100 pain patients referred from a large metropolitan hospital was used for the initial item analysis. More recently, the instrument has been used in assessing a variety of patient populations. Factor analyses using a principal components method with orthogonal rotation are reported in the manual for several patient groups, including myocardial infarction, coronary artery by-pass surgery, and general practice patients. According to the manual, the derived factors were similar across the groups.

Test-retest reliabilities over a 12-week period for the seven scales ranged from .67 to .87. The validity of the IBQ has been assessed through spouse-patient correlations, discriminative studies, and concurrent validity studies. The correlations between the patient's responses and the spouse's perception of the patient's responses ranged from .50 to .78. Discriminant validity studies indicated that pain patients respond differently in comparison to either general practice or psychiatric patients. Concurrent validity was examined only for the Affective Disturbance Scale. Comparisons between the IBQ and the Zung scale ($r = .54$, $p < .001$), the Levine-Pilowsky Depression scale ($r = .56$, $p < .001$), and the Spielberger State Anxiety (r

$= .59, p < .001$), and Trait Anxiety ($r = .76$, $p < .001$) Scales were statistically significant.

The manual presents normative data for a variety of patient populations broken down by sex. Also included for each scale are score frequencies for the patient groups, making it possible for users of the questionnaire to adjust the cutoff points, depending on the specific population being considered. The scoring system, based on the item loadings from the factor analysis can be easily computed by hand or with a computer program. In its final form, scores for the IBQ are summarized graphically in a profile.

CRITIQUE. Using the Science Citation Index, we identified a sample of studies that cited the IBQ. Evaluations of the IBQ were mixed in these studies. McFarlane and Brooks (1988) administered the IBQ and a measure of disease severity to 40 patients diagnosed with rheumatoid arthritis. Two of the IBQ scales (Scale 6—Personal problems caused by disease, and Scale 2—Disease Conviction) were significant correlates of poor health outcomes. In addition, two other scales had lesser associations with poor health outcomes. In a related study, McFarlane and colleagues (1987) administered the IBQ to 30 rheumatoid arthritis patients at entry to a clinic and 3 years later. In contrast to McFarlane and Brooks' (1988) study of arthritis patients, the IBQ did not forecast better or poorer outcomes. Other psychological measures included in the study, however, did differentiate the outcome groups.

Clayers, Bookless, and Ross (1984) administered the IBQ to 164 employees of a public utility and 82 patients who had reported to a hospital in pain, but were diagnosed as neurotic. The public utility employees were divided into two groups: those instructed to exaggerate their symptoms, and those given no such instructions. Although the IBQ differentiated these groups on four scales, it is unclear what a study of such disparate groups actually means.

Several studies have failed to find significant differences between groups responding to the IBQ. For example, Cooper, Wise, and Mann (1985) found that vegetarians and family practice patients did not differ on IBQ scales. Horgan, Davies, Hunt, Westlake, and Mullerworth (1984) were unable to demonstrate pre- and post-operative changes in coronary artery bypass patients using the IBQ. Bassett and Pilowsky (1985) found no differences between groups of pain patients who received either psychodynamic or supportive psychotherapy treatment. Failure to find treatment or group differences is not necessarily grounds for criticizing measures. Some treatments do not work and some groups do not differ. Yet, the meaning of differences, when they are observed, is important to evaluate.

Consider, for example, a study by Pilowsky, Crettenben, and Townley (1985). This investigation demonstrated that poor sleepers were higher on General Hypochondriasis and Disease Conviction than were good sleepers. How does one get a high score on a scale of Disease Conviction? A careful examination of the manual reveals that the Disease Conviction scale is comprised of six items. One of these items is, "Are you sleeping well?" Another item is, "Does your illness interfere with your life a great deal?" If an illness interferes with sleep, we would expect the person to answer in the affirmative. The summary of Disease Conviction, as portrayed in the manual, suggests that individuals scoring high on this scale have symptom preoccupation and tend to reject the doctor's reassurance. The implication is that those scoring high on the scale are neurotic and unappreciative of their medical care providers. Take, for example, patients troubled by severe arthritis. They may not be sleeping well because they are in pain. Further, they will most likely report that the illness interferes with their life a great deal. Lastly, they would probably report yes to another item on the scale, "Do you find that you are bothered by many symptoms?" Thus, the arthritic patient may endorse at least three of the six items on the Disease Conviction scale; but, does this imply any sort of inappropriate or maladaptive attitude?

One of the interesting items on the Disease Conviction scale concerns obedience to the doctor. Item 7 states, "If the doctor told you that he could find nothing wrong with you, would you believe him?" A "No" answer contributes to the scale score. Consider again the patient troubled with arthritis. If a suffering arthritic patient was told by a doctor that nothing was wrong; yet, the patient was indeed experiencing calcification of the joints, would that imply some sort of neurotic response? Surely not! In fact, it would be time to find a new doctor.

What we are suggesting is that the interpretations of the scale scores cannot be undertaken without examining the original items. What information does the IBQ convey? The system does provide a series of scales that are relevant to people with physical illnesses. Some of them consider general hypochondriasis and other aspects of anxiety and worry. However, some of these scales are actually quite brief. For example, five of the seven scales are comprised of only five items. Thus, attributes such as "Affective disturbance" or "Denial" are evaluated based upon a small number of items. We wonder about the reliability of these five-item scales.

Lastly, the manual suggests that three discriminant function analyses revealed "separate though similar discriminant functions," separating pain patients from general practice patients. A closer inspection of the functions raises some questions about their similarity. The three studies were performed on three separate pairs of pain and general/family practice groups. The first and third studies were conducted in Adelaide, South Australia, while the second was completed in Seattle, Washington. In the first study, Factor 2 had the highest positive discriminant function coefficient, while in the other two studies Factor 2 had a modest negative coefficient. Factor 4 had the second highest weight in the third study, but did not significantly contribute to discrimination in the other two analyses. Factor 1 had a strong coefficient in the first study, but did not significantly contribute to the functions in the other two studies and so on. Discriminant function analysis capitalizes on change relationships and the high rates of classification are often attenuated in cross-validation studies. The inconsistencies in the functions may indicate that the accuracy in classification may be somewhat less than reported in the manual. Separating patients who are known to be quite different (i.e., pain vs. general practice) may be less difficult than correctly differentiating patients in similar diagnostic categories. Speculand, Goss, Spence, and Pilowsky (1981) did report that at least two IBQ scales separate intractable from odonogenic pain patients. However, Gordon and Hitchcock (1983) had difficulty finding IBQ differences between trigeminal and non-neuralgic facial pain patients.

In summary, the Illness Behaviour Questionnaire covers rather comprehensively the maladaptive/inappropriate attitudes towards health status. In general, the items are well constructed. The authors have done a great deal of work to develop a useful instrument to assist in measuring health attitudes of patient populations. The test manual is quite comprehensive, explaining in sufficient detail the development of the questionnaire; however, it lacks information needed to interpret the results. Perhaps this information will be offered when a larger number of validity studies have been conducted. Because of limited validity data, statements about IBQ scores may be premature at this time. As mentioned by the authors and supported by the reviewers, the Illness Behaviour Questionnaire is not a replacement for the clinical interview/evaluation, but rather an adjunctive instrument to aid in the diagnostic and evaluative process.

REVIEWER'S REFERENCES

Speculand, B., Goss, A. N., Spence, N. D., & Pilowsky, I. (1981). Intractable facial pain and illness behaviour. *Pain*, 11, 213-219.

Gordon, A., & Hitchcock, E. R. (1983). Illness behaviour and personality in intractable facial pain syndromes. *Pain*, 17, 267-276.

Clayer, J. R., Bookless, C., & Ross, M. W. (1984). Neurosis and conscious symptom exaggeration: Its differentiation by the Illness Behavior Questionnaire. *Journal of Psychosomatic Research*, 28, 237-241.

Horgan, D., Davies, B., Hunt, D., Westlake, G. W., & Mullerworth, M. (1984). Psychiatric aspects of coronary artery surgery: A prospective study. *The Medical Journal of Australia*, 141, 587-590.

Bassett, D. L., & Pilowsky, I. (1985). A study of brief psychotherapy for chronic pain. *Journal of Psychosomatic Research*, 29, 259-264.

Cooper, C. K., Wise, T. N., & Mann, L. S. (1985). Psychological and cognitive characteristics of vegetarians. *Psychosomatics*, 26, 521-527.

Pilowsky, I., Crettenden, I., & Townley, M. (1985). Sleep disturbance in pain clinic patients. *Pain*, 23, 27-33.

McFarlane, A. C., Kalucy, R. S., & Brooks, P. M. (1987). Psychological predictors of disease course in rheumatoid arthritis. *Psychosomatic Research*, 31, 757-764.

McFarlane, A. C., & Brooks, P. M. (1988). Determinants of disability in rheumatoid arthritis. *British Journal of Rheumatology*, 27, 7-14.

[147]

Independent Mastery Testing System for Math Skills. Purpose: "To monitor the student's mastery of basic mathematics skills, to diagnose specific student weaknesses, to recommend a program of further study, and to provide the teacher with a comprehensive record of student progress." Adult students; 1984; IMTS; computer-administered instructional management system; 13 tests: Adding and Subtracting Whole Numbers, Multiplying and Dividing Whole Numbers, Adding and

Subtracting Fractions, Multiplying and Dividing Fractions, Adding and Subtracting Decimals, Multiplying and Dividing Decimals, Percents Skills, Charts and Graphs Skills, Measurement Skills, The Language of Algebra, The Uses of Algebra, Geometry—Angles, Geometry—Plane and Solid Figures; individual, 3 parallel forms of each test; Apple II, Apple II+, Apple IIe, or Apple IIc computer necessary for administration; 1987 price data: $96 per software package including 3 program disks with a backup for each; $35 per individual disk (specify Mastery Disk, Question Disk, or Teacher's Disk); $20 per replacement disk; $7.50 per Math Implementation Manual (63 pages); administration time not reported; Cambridge, The Adult Education Company in association with Moravian College, Bethlehem, PA; Cambridge, The Adult Education Company.*

Review of the Independent Mastery Testing System for Math Skills by RICHARD M. JAEGER, Professor and Director, Center for Educational Research and Evaluation, University of North Carolina at Greensboro, Greensboro, NC:

If the Independent Mastery Testing System for Math Skills (IMTS-M) consists of 13 tests, each of which has three forms, and each form has 20 test items, how many test items compose the entire IMTS-M? [A. 13 B. 39 C. 60 D. 260 E. 780]

Many "word problems" similar to this one appear on each form of the thirteen 20-item tests that compose the IMTS-M. Other items include exclusively numerical stems in standard vertical or horizontal formats. Each item is in five-option, multiple-choice format.

Each test has a varied set of items designed to assess examinees' "mastery" of basic mathematics skills, such as "Adding whole numbers (no carrying)," "Finding averages," "Dividing mixed numbers by fractions and whole numbers," "Understanding algebraic notation through substitution of given values," and "Finding the volume of a solid figure." In total, the 13 tests cover more than 100 hierarchically-arranged mathematics skills. The publisher describes the IMTS-M as "an instructional management system created specifically for the adult learner."

TEST FORMAT. Perhaps the most unusual feature of the IMTS-M is its reliance on an Apple II microcomputer for presentation of test items, recording of examinees' responses, and generation of score reports for examinees and instructors. Examinees need only be taught to select one of three well-labeled diskettes, insert the diskette in the appropriate Apple II disk drive, turn on the microcomputer, and thereafter read and respond to simple menu-presented commands, to complete subtests of the IMTS-M.

The IMTS-M consists of a 60-page Implementation Manual and three diskettes. A "Mastery" diskette prompts examinees for their name and the name of the test they want to take. After supplying responses to these questions, examinees are told to replace the "Mastery" diskette with one labeled "Questions." Twenty test items are presented, one screen at a time. Once the examinee selects a response to an item, a new screen with the next item appears. When all 20 items have been presented, the examinee is prompted to replace the "Questions" diskette with the "Mastery" diskette to learn his/her score on the test. Examinees are given an evaluative statement (e.g., "This unit needs more work" or "Very good!") based on arbitrary "mastery" criteria not stated in the Manual, followed by "You got ______ item(s) correct out of 20, for a percentage score of ______." On request, examinees are shown a listing, by item number, with the letter (A through E) of their selected answer, the letter (A through E) of the correct answer, and the "subskill codes" assessed by the item. However, unless they have been given a printout of items by their instructor, examinees have no opportunity to review the test items at the time they receive this listing.

The third diskette, labeled "Records" is designed for the exclusive use of instructors. It contains programs that (*a*) provide a listing of all items on any test form, either on a computer screen or on a printer; (*b*) provide an alphabetized (by first name) listing of all examinees, together with the test and form numbers they have completed and their raw score and percent correct on each completed form; (*c*) provide a listing for each examinee and each test form completed by the examinee, of the letter (A through E) of the examinee's selected answer to each test item, the letter (A through E) of the correct answer, and the "subskill codes" assessed by the item; and (*d*) provide a listing, for a selected test form, of the number of times each test item has been administered, the number of times examinees answered the test item correctly, and the percentage of times examinees answered the item correctly. Data for these programs are contained in a file that will record results for a maximum of 200 test administrations.

Unfortunately, the computer programs that compose the IMTS-M are primitive, and do not make use of the storage capabilities or analytic potential of the Apple II microcomputer. As a result, there is little obvious advantage to computerized administration of the tests, either for examinees or for instructors. Examinees must reinitiate the Apple II computer every time they want to take a new test, cannot review or modify their answers to items following their initial response selections, and are given no corrective feedback on their performances until they have completed an entire test. Apart from a table of item difficulty values noted earlier, the IMTS-M does not produce any summary information for instructors. To determine the subskill codes of test items that are answered correctly or incorrectly by a large percentage of examinees, instructors must aggregate listings for individuals by hand.

The visual presentation of some items on the Apple II screen impedes, rather than facilitates, correct responses. For example, the elements of items that require addition of compound fractions in vertical format are spaced so closely that they require substantial visual discrimination skills as well as knowledge of addition. What should be solid lines in problems involving fractions are actually dashed lines, with numbers "right adjusted" around the rightmost dash. Since this format differs from the standard one found in arithmetic texts, examinees might be confused by the items.

Items on tests titled Charts and Graphs Skills, The Uses of Algebra, Geometry—Angles, and Geometry—Plane and Solid Figures refer to tables and figures that are printed in the Manual and must be reproduced by the instructor. This use of print-format materials diminishes the administrative convenience of computer-administered testing.

TEST AND MANUAL CONTENT. The Implementation Manual for the IMTS-M contains a "Subskill Code Correlation Table" that lists 141 basic mathematics skills together with page numbers in the Cambridge Book Company's general educational development (GED), pre-GED, and adult basic education (ABE) textbooks that contain instructional materials for each skill. The introduction to the table includes the statement: "There are several subskills included in the chart which have no corresponding test items." The number of skills that fall into this category is not indicated. Although computer-generated listings for examinees and teachers indicate the skills assessed by each item on a test form, the Manual does not contain such a listing for all items on all test forms. Therefore, linking test items to associated preparatory material is a two-step procedure requiring the use of an Apple II computer.

The Manual contains neither a test blueprint nor example test items, so it is difficult to determine the coverage of each test or the relative emphasis given to various mathematics skills. One sentence in the Manual implies that each listed subskill is assessed by three test items, but this is not consistent with the statement, noted earlier, that some subskills are not assessed at all. It is also inconsistent with the fixed number of items, and widely varying number of subskills, attributed to various tests. The only way to determine the content of the IMTS-M is to review each test and carefully analyze each item. This is a tedious task that would be unnecessary if the Manual contained appropriate and sufficient documentation of test content. In its singular attempt to provide psychometric guidance, the Manual contains incorrect statements concerning criterion-referenced testing and a narrative description and corresponding formula for computing item difficulty that are incorrect as well. The Manual recommends that items be judged effective only if their difficulty values (percent correct) are in the range 40 to 60 percent. Although this recommendation would have some rational basis if the IMTS-M were designed to discriminate among examinees of normatively differing abilities, it has no logical foundation when applied to diagnostic, domain-referenced tests. The Manual further states that "The measure of difficulty used in the program is a ratio of the number of times a question was asked to the number of times it was answered correctly." A formula on the same page defines item difficulty as " = (Times Asked/Times Correct) X 100." In both the statement and the equation, the fraction is incorrectly inverted.

TECHNICAL CHARACTERISTICS. The technical characteristics of the IMTS-M are not described in the Manual. The tests are not normed. No reliability evidence is provided. The Manual contains no validity information, save a superficial and incomplete description of the content of the tests. Although computer-generated reports to examinees contain prescriptive suggestions, no evidence on the consistency or validity of these suggestions is provided. The Manual provides no information on the parallelism or comparability of the alternate forms of the IMTS-M tests.

SUMMARY. If the Cambridge Publishing Company's mathematics textbooks for adult basic education have been adopted, the IMTS-M might provide some useful information for guiding examinees' study of those texts. However, in the absence of evidence on the psychometric qualities of the tests, use of the IMTS-M for purposes other than exploratory research by investigators who have completed their own detailed analyses of its items cannot be recommended.

[148]

Infant Screening. Purpose: To identify children as possibly "at risk" of educational, social, and emotional difficulties. Ages 5–6; 1981; screening tests, checklists, and diagnostic tests in the areas of Visual Reception, Auditory Reception, Association Skill, Sequential Skill, Expression (Encoding), and Reading Difficulties; 1988 price data: £3.25 per 10 test booklets; £2.75 per 20 checklists; £4.25 per 25 pupil profiles; £9.50 per teacher's book (73 pages) and 8 diagnostic test cards; administration time not reported; Humberside Education Authority; Macmillan Education Ltd. [England].*

Review of Infant Screening by CATHY F. TELZROW, Psychologist and Director, Educational Assessment Project, Cuyahoga Special Education Service Center, Maple Heights, OH:

The Infant Screening System is described as a three-stage procedure for identifying young children who may be at risk for educational failure. The first stage is a brief teacher-completed checklist, of which there are two forms depending upon the age of the child (Checklist 1 for 5-year-old children and Checklist 2 for children aged 5-10 to 6-3). For the older children, Checklist 2 is supplemented by an Initial Screening Test that can be administered in groups of up to approximately 15 children. The third stage of the Infant Screening System is a lengthy diagnostic test to be administered to children who are identified as "at-risk" by the earlier screening procedures. The system was developed in England; hence the use of the term "infant" refers to children of early school age (approximately 5 to 6$^1/_2$ years).

The theoretical model forming the basis of the Infant Screening System is the psycholinguistic model, which represents receptive, expressive, and association types of processing across auditory and visual channels and representational and automatic levels of organization. The Infant Screening procedure incorporates a method of transactional assessment and hypothesis testing, whereby teachers engage in ongoing formal and informal appraisal of pupils' strengths and weaknesses.

Some portions of the Infant Screening System are heuristically interesting. The initial screening checklists, in particular, appear to include broad behaviors of educational relevance that teachers can respond to rather easily. However, the manual (*Infant Screening: A Handbook for Teachers*) does not indicate how the items included on Checklists 1 and 2 were selected, nor whether or not the items listed have demonstrated validity in predicting school failure or "at risk" status. The Handbook includes an extensive chapter entitled "Remediation," where specific intervention strategies matched to various processes in the system's psycholinguistic model (e.g., visual discrimination, auditory figure-ground perception) are described in detail. Although this section may be of interest to teachers, there is no explanation for how the remedial strategies were designed nor whether or not they have demonstrated validity for improving identified weaknesses. A separate chapter ("Management of Maladaptive Behavior") provides a brief introduction to behavioral principles. Although this chapter might serve as background material for more intensive staff development on the topic of behavior management, it is too incomplete for exclusive use by teachers.

With the exception of a few interesting features, the Infant Screening System must be judged inadequate as an assessment tool. The directions for administering, scoring, and interpreting the components of the Infant Screening System are incomplete and frequently confusing. No data are presented on the procedure used for item selection on the Initial Screening Test. Although the Handbook states "there were three pilot runs," the procedure by which items were deleted or modified during pilot testing is not explained. Technical data are not reported separately for the two-teacher checklists (Checklist 1 and Checklist 2), the Initial Screening Test, and the Diagnostic Test. Instead, the manual states that a group of 594 children, for whom sampling procedures were not specified, "were given the five screening tests and the Carver Word Recognition Test," as well as having their teachers complete "the Bristol Social Adjustment Guide (Children in School) and the checklist for the screening procedure." What is meant by the "five screening tests" is not clear, since the Initial Screening Test has six subtests. From all these tests and screening procedures, a list of 14 variables was generated, and these variables were used in subsequent statistical analyses. Therefore, it is not possible to evaluate the technical qualities of the individual components of the Infant Screening System, nor of the entire system, because all technical data were computed from variables incorporating measures other than those included in the Infant Screening System.

In summary, the Infant Screening System is not recommended as a measure of potential school failure in kindergarten- and first-grade-age children. The absence of any discussion of item selection and validity for certain components of the system (i.e., Checklists 1 and 2 and diagnostic tests) reduces these portions of the system to interesting exercises. Although greater detail is included for the Initial Screening Test, it is not possible to evaluate the technical merits of this component, because all statistical analyses incorporated other measures. Although its restricted sampling complicates its use in some settings, validity data for the Florida Kindergarten Screening Battery (Satz & Fletcher, 1982) suggest this scale is far preferable to the Infant Screening System in identifying children at-risk for school failure.

REVIEWER'S REFERENCE

Satz, P., & Fletcher, J. (1982). *Manual for the Florida Kindergarten Screening Battery*. Odessa, FL: Psychological Assessment Resources.

Review of Infant Screening by STANLEY F. VASA, Professor of Special Education and Communication Disorders, University of Nebraska-Lincoln, Lincoln, NE:

The Infant Screening program is designed to detect children, ages 5 through 6 years of age, who are at risk of having school-related difficulties. The procedures include both teacher observations and judgments and specific screening measures. The program is based on the psycholinguistic model employed in the Illinois Test of Psycholinguistic Abilities (ITPA; Kirk, McCarthy, & Kirk, 1968). Screening tests are provided that measure Visual Reception, Auditory Reception, Association Skill, Sequential Skill, Expression, and Reading Difficulties.

The handbook provides a description of the assessment model, description of the screening tests and materials, remediation guidelines, and guides for dealing with maladaptive behavior. The chapters on remediation and management of maladaptive behavior contribute to the handbook being more of a curriculum guide than a screening test. The remediation section analyzes each of the subtests and provides guides for teacher observations in educational settings. This section overstates the test's power to accurately depict the strengths and weaknesses of a child. In addition, the recommendations provided for the user go beyond the information provided by the tests. The procedures employed are not unique and have a high degree of resemblance to the ITPA subtests.

There is a lack of information about the development of the scale and how items were selected for inclusion. The technical information lacks specificity, and there is not enough information to evaluate the usefulness of the tests in settings other than the ones in which they were developed. No specific information on reliability and validity is provided. The scale is identified as criterion-referenced. The authors report cutoff scores and tables for normal scores, at-risk scores, and moderate to severe difficulties. Unfortunately, no specific description of the standardization population is given beyond the ages of subjects, making the interpretation tables unusable.

The strength of the scale may be in the assessment process utilized. Schools that wish to develop local norms may find the procedures useful. In order to use the screening procedures, it would be necessary to carefully analyze the curriculum of individual programs for agreement with the model utilized by the screening program.

Users should be cautious in making decisions based on the scale. Overall, the content of the scale is a broad-based sampling of abilities and skills of young children. It is fairly ecological in approach and looks at more than basic academic skills.

SUMMARY. The manual accompanying the test appears to be more of a teacher's guide for intervention with young children than a description of the development and psychometric characteristics of this test. The accompanying scale is not well constructed. Concerns regarding this test center on the development of the test items, the standardization sample, and the lack of indicators of concurrent and content validity for the scale. Overall, the Infant Screening program may provide the user with some information, but the lack of standardization data makes interpretations based on the scale suspect.

REVIEWER'S REFERENCE

Kirk, S. A., McCarthy, J. J., & Kirk, W. D. (1968). Illinois Test of Psycholinguistic Abilities. Champaign, IL: University of Illinois Press.

[149]

The Instructional Environment Scale. Purpose: "To systematically describe the extent to which a student's academic or behavior problems are a function of factors in the instructional environment and to identify starting points in designing appropriate instructional interviews for individual students." Elementary students; 1987; TIES; instructional environment evaluations made by assessment professionals for individual students; 12 components: Instructional Presentation, Classroom Environment, Teacher Expectations, Cognitive Emphasis, Motivational Strategies, Relevant Practice, Academic Engaged Time, Informed Feedback, Adaptive Instruction, Progress Evaluation, Instructional Planning, Student Understanding; individual; 1987 price data: $47 per complete kit; $11 per 25 instructional rating forms; $11 per 25 data record forms; $8 per 25 summary/profile sheets; $21 per examiner's manual (66 pages); administration time not reported; James E. Ysseldyke and Sandra L. Christenson; PRO-ED, Inc.*

Review of The Instructional Environment Scale by KENNETH W. HOWELL, Associate Professor of Curriculum and Instruction, College of Education, Western Washington University, Bellingham, WA:

The Instructional Environment Scale (TIES) reflects a much needed reconceptualization of the nature of learning and behavior problems. Specifically the procedure attempts to put into operation the long recognized, but seldom embraced, idea that classroom academic and social behaviors are determined in part by the instructional environment. The authors state that the scale is designed to systematically describe the extent to which problem behaviors are a function of factors in the environment, and to identify starting points for intervention. In order to accomplish these purposes the administrator must engage in a series of interviews and observations that are controlled by a predetermined set of questions and indicators. These efforts are then summarized in the form of ratings on a 4-point ordinal scale and in written notes.

The scale is useful and probably the best instrument of its kind available. However, although the TIES represents a good faith, and generally positive, effort by the authors it does have some flaws. Perhaps the most basic of these are the omission of clear statements about the students and settings for which the TIES is applicable (pilot studies in suburban elementary schools are mentioned—but no descriptions of the students, teachers, or settings are supplied), and the fact that no evidence is supplied to show that anyone has ever benefited from the use of the scale. Evidence of validity is supplied in the form of an excellent literature review, a procedure which seems appropriate for this kind of instrument, but which fails to answer the ultimate question of utility. The review process examined what is popularly referred to as the "teacher effectiveness" literature and led to descriptors that, without a doubt, define the nature of an effective classroom environment. However, given that some of the authors included in this review have cautioned against the application of their own results (Brophy & Good, 1986), evidence of successful utilization is still needed.

Additionally, there are problems of ambiguity inherent in observation and interview procedures which are in evidence in the TIES. To pick two examples, the authors say that a problem exists if a student is not performing at the level the teacher expects, and that the evaluator should continue to observe until s/he feels "comfortable" about rating. However, they supply no guidelines that would allow an evaluator to determine if the teacher's expectation is appropriate, or if their own comfort is justified.

A final criticism deals with the nature of environmental evaluation itself. It is generally recognized that individuals with different learning histories view the same situation differently, and may behave differently as a result (Shuell, 1987). The authors have quite logically chosen to approach the classroom environment from an educator's perspective. In doing so they have developed procedures that filter all information, including a student interview, through the evaluator. As a result the environment that is summarized is the evaluator's environment, not necessarily the student's. The inclusion of more direct summaries of student and peer perceptions (Weinstein, 1985; Moos & Trickett, 1974) would have strengthened the TIES.

REVIEWER'S REFERENCES

Moos, R., & Trickett, E. J. (1974). *Classroom Environment Scale manual*. Palo Alto, CA: Consulting Psychologists Press.

Weinstein, R. S. (1985). Student mediation of classroom expectancy effects. In J. Dusek (Ed.), *Teacher expectancies*. Hillsdale, NJ: Lawrence Erlbaum Associates, Publishers.

Brophy, J., & Good, T. L. (1986). Teacher behavior and student achievement. In M. C. Wittrock (Ed.), *Handbook of research on teaching* (3rd ed.). Macmillan: New York.

Shuell, T. J. (1986). Cognitive conceptions of learning. *Review of Educational Research*, 56, 411-436.

Review of The Instructional Environment Scale by WILLIAM T. MCKEE, Research Associate, and JOSEPH C. WITT, Associate Professor, Louisiana State University, Baton Rouge, LA:

The past several years have witnessed the growing call for both prereferral interventions for children experiencing problems in the regular classroom, as well as increased use of consultation services with classroom teachers. With this change in service delivery focus has come the need to develop instrumentation that provides information enabling teachers to plan adaptions in the classroom learning environment to suit the needs of children who are experiencing difficulties. Recent texts in assessment methods support the view that assessing the learner's instructional environment is an important component of a comprehensive assessment (e.g., Sattler, 1988). In recommending an assessment model for school-based referrals Sattler reiterates the assessment model proposed by the National Academy of Science's Panel on the Selection and Placement of Students in Programs for the Mentally Retarded (Heller, Holtzman, & Messick, 1982). For *any child* who is experiencing academic difficulties two phases of assessment should be followed. In the first phase systematic evaluation of the learning environment should be conducted prior to the use in the second phase of any comprehensive child-based assessment battery. This first phase, environmental assessment, is important both to rule out as causes for child difficulty any deficiencies in the learning environment, as well as for documentation that the child has failed to learn under reasonable alternative instructional approaches. That Sattler heartily endorses such an approach to assessment is gratifying; however, it is only with the development of The Instructional Environment Scale (TIES) that an instrument has become available to aid in the systematic gathering of such data.

The translation of research into practice is not always a smooth one. That is, variables researchers identify as important are not always applied in schools and other settings. However, in the area of environmental assessment the translation of research into practice has been made easier by Ysseldyke and Christenson through their development of TIES. TIES is not so much a test or an instrument as it is a *process* to follow in systematically examining a classroom environment. The noteworthy feature of TIES is that its content mirrors the recent literature so closely. Each component of the instructional environment was selected for inclusion in TIES primarily on the basis of direct evidence from the research literature indicating the component was related to student achievement.

GOALS AND STRUCTURE OF THE INSTRUMENT. The authors state two major purposes for use of this instrument: the description of the extent to which a student's academic or behavior problems are a function of factors in the instructional environment, and the identification of target areas for instructional adaption or intervention in the student's learning environment. Two important assumptions underlie the design and effective use of this type of assessment instrument: (*a*) the instructional environment has a pervasive influence on the amount students learn and how they behave in the classroom and (*b*) the major goal of assessment is to identify elements of the instructional environment that might be changed to better meet the learning needs of the target student. The first assumption is well supported in the literature to which the authors make reference throughout the manual. The second assumption, however, is more contentious. Suggesting a change process is often translated inappropriately as an issue of whether the teacher, the student, last year's teacher, or the parents ought to accept the blame for this child's present poor performance. Without attaching blame, TIES allows a systematic assessment focused on those elements of the classroom environment that are the most important potential targets for classroom-based interventions.

Within the TIES system Ysseldyke and Christenson have conceptualized the classroom environment to be composed of 12 components. Each of these components has a strong research base documenting its relationship to effective teaching. However, as noted by Ysseldyke and Christenson, the individual effects of each variable are not as important as their collective effect:

> The 12 components describe the characteristics of a student's instructional environment. They do not directly evaluate the quality of instruction for a student. It is hypothesized that how the components are combined or delivered during teaching— *due to the synergistic effect* — describes the quality of instruction for an individual student (emphasis added).

In order for users of TIES to obtain data, they must be thoroughly familiar with each of the 12 components. TIES provides detailed descriptions of each of the components and cites research literature supporting the inclusion of each variable. Data on each of the 12 components are obtained by use of three assessment methods: (*a*) teacher interview, (*b*) student interview, and (*c*) classroom observation.

TEACHER INTERVIEW. TIES provides a structured teacher interview that assesses teacher planning, expectations, monitoring, and evaluation procedures. In addition to these questions of primary importance, a more extensive list of teacher interview questions is included in an appendix for special situations in which additional data may be required.

STUDENT INTERVIEW. The structured student interview consists of questions in six areas such as teacher monitoring behaviors and positive and negative consequences for behavior. The primary purpose of the student interview "is to check the student's success rate and understanding of assigned tasks and directions." The authors emphasize it is important to remain aware of the validity of student interview data and to weigh this type of data against other data obtained within TIES. Because data within the TIES system are obtained from multiple people using multiple methods, it is possible to check for convergence of the information obtained.

CLASSROOM OBSERVATION. TIES provides several helpful suggestions about *how*, *when*, and *how often* to conduct a classroom observation. Deciding *what* to observe is a matter of becoming thoroughly familiar with the 12 components of TIES. The record forms provided in TIES allot space in which an observer writes narrative responses for 10 of the 12 components. Cues are provided for some of the components to focus observer attention on particular aspects of that component of the environment. For example, the Classroom Environment component provides cues to observe "management," "time-use," and "climate."

SUMMARY RATINGS. After all the relevant data have been collected, users combine information from several sources relevant to each of the 12 components and make a judgment about the quality of each component of the instructional environment. A global rating on the component "Classroom Environment" would be made by first considering all data from the interviews and observations that provided information about the classroom environment. After careful consideration of such data, the user would rate the environment on a 4-point Likert-type scale ranging from "Not at All Like the Student's Instruction" to "Very Much Like the Student's Instruction." This rating is qualitative in nature and, as the authors suggest, very similar to the rating of movies or restaurants. Thus, if you were asked to rate the quality of a restaurant, you would sample the range of its menu, perhaps on a number of occasions, and observe other important characteristics of your dining experience. There may be particular features that were very positive and others that were very negative. In the end, you would have to assign ratings to reflect the quality of the restaurant in terms, for example, of overall food quality, atmosphere, or value for dollar. A similar process and "mind set" is used for completing the global ratings within TIES. Use of TIES is intended to be flexible. Raters do not have to provide ratings on all components but rather may focus on particular areas of importance for a specific child. Users should allow approximately 20–30 minutes for each of the interviews and at least 30 minutes for classroom observations. However, the total amount of time required for use of the instrument will vary based on the nature of the assessment questions, the variety of instructional settings in which observations are to be made, and the degree of collaboration between the individuals involved in the assessment. Because TIES is intended to lead to interventions, its ideal use is as a starting point for a high degree of teacher involvement and collaboration in interpretation of data and translation into goals for classroom-based interventions.

TECHNICAL ADEQUACY OF THE INSTRUMENT. TIES is not a test in the traditional sense. Rather, it is an instrument to aid the qualitative evaluation of the instructional environment of an individual student. As such, it is difficult to apply the traditional criteria by which such instruments are usually evaluated. Item and scale development procedures are described by the authors as evolving from an extensive review of literature on variables related to positive learning outcomes for students. Factors were selected for inclusion in the scale if they were observable, empirically related to positive academic progress, and repeatedly mentioned in the research literature. Items were then generated that referred to the application of each identified factor for an individual student. The authors report that an original pool of 200 descriptive statements was reduced to 40 representative items on the basis of pilot study results. Use of these items in subsequent studies led to the development of ratings over 12 essential *components* of instruction, with specific factors and original items taken into account.

Although the manual, which is an essential feature of the scale, describes the general nature of the test development procedures and makes reference to pilot studies, no data are reported. For example, the authors do not indicate whether the procedures used to allocate items to components were empirical or more rational and intuitive. Similarly no data are presented with respect to the psychometric characteristics of the instrument during the developmental stages. Reliability data for the final version of the scale are presented in the form of Interclass Correlation Coefficients for 28 observers who rated two teachers from videotaped observations and prepared interview protocols. Reliabilities for these observers ranged from a low of .83 to a high of .96. Although these reliabilities are more than adequate for a scale of this type, the authors do not indicate the stability of ratings (i.e., test-retest) nor do they indicate the level of reliability achieved in conditions of field use. Such data will be an important consideration in future study of this instrument.

With respect to the validity of TIES the authors state that "Validity refers to the extent to which a device measures what its authors say it measures," and acknowledge the importance of establishing evidence for the use of the scale for its intended purposes. The authors present sufficient evidence to support the relation between elements of each component and important student outcomes. This, the authors contend, is evidence for content validity. We believe, in fact, that the authors have done an admirable job of including the most important dimensions of classroom instructional environments demonstrated to be related to student learning outcomes. Such content-related validity is especially important during the development of any instrument of this type. However, current test development standards interpret the demand for validity more broadly to include evidence of the "appropriateness, meaningfulness, and usefulness of the specific inferences made from the test scores" (American Educational Research Association, American Psychological Association, & National Council on Measurement in Education, 1985). Users of TIES will need information that supports the use of ratings of the 12 components for making inferences about required changes in classroom instruction. Important too, will be data to support the appropriateness of application of these ratings to individual students. Several points should be considered here. First, the authors have not presented evidence that classrooms do differ in terms of ratings on TIES, and further, that rating differences are related to differential outcomes for individual students or classes of students. Although it is true that other research has shown differential student outcomes are a function of various instructional variables, it will be necessary to demonstrate these variables as measured by this instrument result in differential outcomes. Second, the literature cited in support of the importance of each of the 12 component constructs is based almost exclusively on evidence of the effectiveness of procedures for *groups* of children rather than individuals. In practice TIES is intended to describe and inform decisions about instructional interventions for individual students. The most glaring omission of validity data is that of criterion-related evidence. How accurately can criterion-related performance be predicted by scale ratings on TIES? Perhaps more important though, is the need for evidence of the treatment utility of TIES assessment of the learning environment. Treatment utility refers to the extent to which treatment outcome is influenced positively by the use of the assessment approach (Hayes, Nelson, & Jarrett, 1987). For example, we would want to demonstrate there is some advantage in using this assessment method over other methods currently available.

A potential problem is that use of this instrument may be seen as teacher evaluation. Users are cautioned that TIES is not a teacher evaluation scale and is not designed to provide comparisons between teachers, schools, or districts. However, the focus of the instructional rating profile on the quality of the individual student's instructional environment leads to valuative interpretations. This might be considered a problem of assessment acceptability. Despite the *potential* usefulness of the rating and the identified intervention decisions, such an approach may easily be perceived as threatening for teachers and other school personnel. This, of course, presents a significant barrier to its effective use. The acceptability of this methodology is an empirical question. Certainly though, effective use will require the user to develop not only skill in use of the instrument but also expert consultative skills that will allow the implementation of the procedure.

TIES is the most systematically developed and comprehensive instrument for assessment of the classroom environment. Earlier efforts in this area (e.g., Englert, 1984; Smith, Neisworth, & Greer, 1978) presented a series of questions and rating scales for teachers to use in self-evaluation of their classroom environment. Other instruments (e.g., Flanders, 1966; Saudargas & Creed, 1980; Whaler, House, & Stambaugh, 1976) have demonstrated good psychometric characteristics and some treatment utility but have a more restricted focus than does TIES.

SUMMARY. Overall, this instrument has the potential to provide extremely useful information for the design of instructional interventions. It is based in sound theory and provides a comprehensive and systematic means for assessing several potentially important areas of the classroom instructional environment. At the present time two major questions related to its use are: Does its use provide accurate data that lead to the development of effective instructional interventions? Can TIES be used with classroom teachers in a way that is acceptable to them? The potential for misuse and misinterpretation of ratings is a particular concern. It is important that TIES be used in a context of "What can be done to improve this child's performance?" rather than the more traditional search for pathology within the child or the search for blame within the child's environment.

The purpose of school-based assessment activities is to solve (and prevent) problems. Traditionally, school psychology and other pupil service specialties have considered relatively few variables as potential contributors to the problems exhibited by a particular child. The variables most often considered are those that can be assessed via the Wechsler Intelligence Scale for Children—Revised (WISC-R), the Wide Range Achievement Test—Revised (WRAT-R), and the Bender-Gestalt administered by a psychologist sitting with the child far away from the classroom. Very often these child-based variables offer little information beyond that required to make a classification decision. Perhaps the greatest value of TIES is as a compendium of a vast range of variables that do markedly affect the learning of school children. The variables described, when properly understood and assessed, offer school-based professionals a road map of potential routes toward classroom-based intervention on behalf of the identified student.

REVIEWER'S REFERENCES

Flanders, N. (1966). *Interaction analysis in the classroom: A manual for observers* (rev. ed.). Ann Arbor, MI: University of Michigan.

Wahler, R., House, A., & Stambaugh, E. (1976). *Ecological assessment of child problem behavior: A clinical package for home, school and institutional setting*. New York: Pergamon Press.

Smith, R. M., Neisworth, J. T., & Greer, J. G. (1978). *Evaluating educational environments*. Columbus, OH: Charles E. Merrill.

Saudargas, R. A., & Creed, V. (1980). *State-event classroom observation system*. Unpublished manuscript, University of Tennessee, Knoxville, TN.

Heller, K. A., Holtzman, W. H., & Messick, S. (Eds.). (1982). *Placing children in special education: A strategy for equity*. Washington, DC: National Academy Press.

American Educational Research Association, American Psychological Asociation, & National Council on Measurement in Education. (1985). *Standards for educational and psychological testing*. Washington, DC: American Psychological Association, Inc.

Hayes, S. C., Nelson, R. O., & Jarrett, R. B. (1987). The treatment utility of assessment: A functional approach to evaluating assessment quality. *American Psychologist*, 42 (11), 963-974.

Sattler, J. M. (1988). *Assessment of children* (3rd ed.). San Diego: Author.

[150]

Instrument Timbre Preference Test. Purpose: "To act as an objective aid to the teacher and the parent in helping a student choose an appropriate woodwind or brass instrument to learn to play in beginning instrumental music and band." Grades 4–12; 1984–85; ITPT; 7 scores: Flute, Clarinet, Saxophone and French Horn, Oboe/English Horn/Bassoon, Trumpet and Cornet, Trombone/Baritone/French Horn, Tuba and Sousaphone; 1986 price data: $39 per complete kit including 100 test sheets, scoring masks, cassette tape, and manual ('84, 53 pages); $13.50 per 100 test sheets; scoring service, $.50 per test available ($10 minimum); (30) minutes; Edwin E. Gordon; G.I.A. Publications, Inc.*

Review of the Instrument Timbre Preference Test by RICHARD COLWELL, Professor of Music and Secondary Education, University of Illinois at Urbana-Champaign, Urbana, IL:

Gordon is the first researcher to suggest that preference for real or an "artificial" timbre is a predictor of success in the study of instrumental music. The claim is that when results of the Instrument Timbre Preference Test are combined with data from his own Musical Aptitude Test and together used to match students with the appropriate musical instrument, this will reduce dropouts and increase achievement in instrumental music. The test is a seven-item forced-choice (which of two timbres do you prefer?) test; seven different timbres are created by the Moog synthesizer, each representing the sound of a specific instrument or a group of related instruments (i.e., Timbre 1 = flute; Timbre 4 = oboe-English horn-bassoon). Gordon pairs each timbre with every other timbre (twice) and asks for a preference between them. The highest possible score for a timbre is 12; for example, if one chose the flute in all of its pairings the flute score would equal 12.

Gordon's sole concern for criterion-related validity was whether experts could match the Moog sound with an actual instrumental timbre. A more appropriate concern for criterion-related validity would be whether the test aids in predicting success on the accepted objectives of school instrumental music. Material in the test manual consists of a mixture of pedagogical suggestions, accurate technical data, unproven hypotheses, and some folklore. This material raises interesting and unanswered questions about what the test actually does measure.

Gordon's data for his control group are based on the responses of 165 nonparticipants in beginning instrumental music; a sample of 159 comparable subjects constitutes the source of data used by this reviewer. Gordon's experimental group consists of 34 nonvolunteers who studied an instrument selected for them on the basis of test scores. Twenty-two of these students completed a year of study.

Gordon obtains the highest mean score (greatest preference) for Timbre 4 (oboe-English horn-bassoon). This preference by students was confirmed by the reviewer's data. Preference for the pseudo-woodwind timbre over the brass timbre by most students was also confirmed. The reviewer, however, also found ethnic differences in preference for various timbres. In a sample of half blacks and half whites, no blacks scored 12 on clarinet timbre and no blacks gave a score of 11 or 12 to trumpets or trombone-baritone. Sixty-eight percent of the black students disliked the tuba (scores of 0–2) as compared to 35 percent of white students. The standard deviation for tuba timbre (7) was 2.73 with a median score of 1.44 for black students. Sex differences need to be investigated before accepting the independence of timbre differences.

The high mean score for double reeds is meaningless and not an indicator that most students should begin instrumental music by studying these instruments. All mean scores are generally irrelevant; the important data are the timbre preference scores of 0–2 and 10–12. These cutoff scores, apparently arbitrarily established by Gordon, are used in recommending or not recommending a particular instrument to a student. Unfortunately, no indication of the size of the student groups falling into these two groups is given in the manual. Our data indicate that Gordon would recommend between 23–34 percent of the students should begin on a double reed instrument; only 1–3 percent should be discouraged. For clarinet 5–10 percent should be encouraged; 1–7 percent discouraged. The similarity of Gordon's mean scores and our mean scores hints that Gordon's data are comparable.

Gordon's argument that a student will be more successful if he or she studies an instrument that has a personally pleasing timbre makes logical sense. Gordon fails to provide data, however, that present students find the timbre of their own instruments unpleasant and whether those who do are unsuccessful or drop out.

Timbre is a factor in preference, but preference is usually more subtle than that measured by Gordon. The difference between a pleasing and an unpleasant sound on an instrument is a finer discrimination than the comparison between a true French horn sound and that putatively attributed to preference for French horn on the test tape. Gordon also hints at this in suggesting that vibrato or special styles added to a timbre would be an invalidating factor. At that point in the manual, however, the author is making an argument for the synthesized sounds rather than for the genuine sounds.

His loose argument on the reasons for success would be disputed by experienced teachers, (e.g., "as much as 3 percent of the reason or reasons for students' success in instrumental music is associated with their physical and psychological well-being and their home and cultural environments"). Home and cultural environment are thought by most teachers to contribute more than 3 percent.

Gordon uses the test manual as much to promote his other publications as to provide data on this test. "*Jump Right In: The Instrumental Series* will prove to be the most appropriate." Gordon also urges use of the Musical Aptitude Profile or one of his two developmental aptitude tests throughout the manual.

Scoring the test requires the use of seven different templates to obtain the seven scores, a cumbersome and time-consuming procedure. Once the scores are recorded, the teacher is to use a colored marker to highlight high and low scores. Scores greater than 2 but less than 10 are presumably not used. As a preference test has no right or wrong answers, there are no norms; reliability is computed by test-retest and validity should be criterion related.

Gordon's pedagogical statements indicate his concern for unidentified talent and for not discouraging any student from instrumental music study. He states that more than 40 percent of the fourth and fifth grade students who score above the 80th percentile on his music aptitude tests do not volunteer to study a musical instrument. A 60 percent success rate in an elective course in any discipline, however, is commendable, even if 100 percent would be better. These extensive pedagogical arguments contribute little to understanding the value of the timbre preference test.

Gordon's test-retest reliability coefficient after one week is about .70. He reports reliability by grade, school, and test, providing 77 reliability figures that range from .46 to .93. Our reliability figures were only slightly lower and as varied. If the score on a single timbre preference is to be used in making a major decision, a user should expect more consistency than a reliability range such as that for timbre 3 (from .55 to .93). Preference is apparently affected by age. For example, Gordon provides data for students in grades 3–8 in one school. At third grade, students generally do not like the clarinet sound, giving it a mean score of 5.2. The preference score increased to 5.8 at fourth grade, 6.6 in fifth, 7.1 in sixth, and then begins to drop off: 6.7 for seventh grade students and 6.3 for eighth graders. The preference ranking is of greater importance. At third grade the clarinet sound is ranked 7 out of 7 but by fifth grade is ranked second, exceeded only by the saxophone-French horn timbre. Preference for clarinet stays second for 3 years only to fall precipitously among eighth graders. In this school, double-reed preference changed from 5.7 (tied for preference 5 or 6) to 8.2 in grade 6. The highest mean score for any timbre at any grade level in any school is 8.2.

Gordon argues the fact that timbre preference is not related to music aptitude contributes to the construct validity of both his aptitude test and this preference test. The argument is weak and negatively constructed. A manual dexterity test would reveal the same low correlation without providing credence for construct validity of either test. The argument for construct validity, along with the test's recommended use, implies that Gordon believes that instrumental timbre preference is an additional component of musical aptitude. Like the extensive reporting of mean scores that are not pertinent to test interpretation, the reporting of low correlations between timbre scores and IQ scores does not advance the argument for predicting success in instrumental music.

When students did not volunteer to study an instrument but were selected based upon their timbre preference as revealed by this test, they did not join the band. Only 20 percent of these students enrolled as opposed to 92 percent and 83 percent of the students from groups where students had selected their own instrument. Selected students, however, were more successful as judged by performance of three études. A preference test that has little relationship to wanting to play the instrument and produce these pleasing timbres yourself is only one of the questions raised by Gordon's research.

Through the publishing of an instrumental-timbre-preference test, GIA and Edwin Gordon have again raised the issue of the components of success in instrumental music. Gordon's conclusion that aptitude plus timbre preference is a more powerful combination than consideration of motivation, home background, and diligence is not convincingly supported by his data. Had the instrumental timbre data been paired with results from an aptitude test other than the author's, a more convincing argument would have been made. The large dropout rate in the experimental school system, the relatively poor quality of the test tape, and the lack of a rigorous test development schema, despite the innovative aspects of providing free use of an instrument for 2 years for nonvolunteers, add up to the need for considerable additional research before Gordon's Instrumental Timbre Preference Test can attain the credibility of his research in musical aptitude.

Review of the Instrument Timbre Preference Test by PAUL R. LEHMAN, Professor and Associate Dean, School of Music, The University of Michigan, Ann Arbor, MI:

Instrumental teachers have long realized that motivation is enormously important in determining success in instrumental study. They also know that one of the most important aspects of motivation is the love that some children seem to have for their instruments, and certainly a part of that magical attraction stems directly from the sound of the instrument.

Gordon has sought to document these bits of conventional wisdom and at the same time to provide a test to help identify students' preferences concerning timbre. His test is based on seven synthesized timbres, each of which is "intended to represent the timbre of one or more woodwind or brass instruments." By using carefully controlled synthesized sounds he eliminates the extraneous factors of dynamics, intonation, tempo, phrasing, and expression (although it sounds as though some of the examples are played more legato than others).

The test is simple and straightforward. Each timbre is paired twice with each other timbre. Thus, there are 12 comparisons for each of the seven timbres. In effect, there are seven separate tests.

The student is asked to indicate whether the melody "sounds better" the first time or the second. According to Gordon, a student who chooses a given timbre 10 or more times reveals a distinct preference for that tone quality and should be encouraged to study an instrument represented by that timbre. His assumption is that, other factors being equal, students will do better if they like the sounds of their instruments.

Some students may show more than one preference. Some may show no preference. Because the test is based on preferences, there is no composite score and no norms are provided.

Based on previous studies, Gordon claims that music aptitudes account for approximately 56% of students' success in beginning instrumental music. Another 4% is related to intelligence, he suggests, while 12% represents error of measurement, and 3% has to do with the students' physical and psychological well being and their home and cultural environments. Of the remaining 25%, according to Gordon, at least 10% is associated with timbre preference.

Because of the nature of the test, the only practical way to determine reliability is by the test-retest method. The reported test-retest reliabilities for the seven timbres, based on 11 groups totaling 642 students in grades 3 through 8 in three schools in the Philadelphia area, are more or less evenly dispersed from .46 to .93, with a median of .72. There is a remarkable lack of central tendency in the reliability coefficients from one group to another within each of the timbres, but one should remember that there are only 12 test items for each timbre.

The ultimate question, of course, is what do the test results mean? The answer must be based in part on how closely the timbres "represent" real instruments. To a musician they do not sound much like the instruments at all. They sound like organ stops. One reason is that they lack the distinctive attack and decay characteristics of real wind instruments. Their harmonic content is not stated.

It is not surprising the trombone and baritone are grouped together and represented by one timbre. It is not especially surprising the French horn is grouped with them. But it is surprising the horn appears a second time sharing a timbre with the saxophone. Can one timbre be sufficiently similar to both the French horn and the saxophone that the test results are valid? How can the test identify a student who might prefer the sound of the horn to all other instruments when the horn is represented by two different timbres?

It would have been possible, of course, to reproduce the sounds of the instruments much more closely. Gordon chose not to do so in order to "represent" more instruments. Some teachers might prefer that he had used timbres more like those of the real instruments even if that meant representing fewer instruments. Several of the instruments included are instruments that most teachers do not start beginners on anyway. The less similar the timbres are to those of actual instruments the less useful the test results are.

As evidence of "criterion-related validity" (but actually representing content validity), a study is reported in which 50 music professors and teachers and 136 members of a university band were asked to name the instrument or instruments "represented by" each timbre. Most members of both groups associated each timbre with more than one instrument, but "at least one actual instrument that the test author had previously associated with each of the timbres . . . was associated with the same timbre by a majority of persons in both groups." Given there were two hearings, and that a written list of instruments was provided to work from, these results scarcely constitute a ringing confirmation that the associations are close.

One way out of this uncertainty is to seek evidence of predictive validity. A longitudinal study is described in which 33 students playing instruments for which they displayed a timbre preference on the Instrument Timbre Preference Test achieved higher scores on three performance measures after 1 academic year of study than did 47 students playing instruments for which they had not displayed a timbre preference. The three measures included an étude prepared in class, an étude prepared independently by the student, and an étude that was sightread. The difference for the combined scores was significant at the .05 level. Still, this is a very small number of cases upon which to base evidence of predictive validity. Additional evidence based on larger samples should be gathered in the future.

This test is the only one of its kind. It is technically excellent. The manual is well written. It bristles with good suggestions and timely caveats. The test is inexpensive and easy to administer in groups. The premise on which it is based is sound. The extent to which instrumental teachers may find it useful will depend entirely on how much confidence they have in the information it yields.

[151]

Interpersonal Style Inventory. Purpose: "Measures an individual's characteristic ways of relating to other people . . . also evaluates style of impulse control and characteristic modes of dealing with work and play." Ages 14 and over; 1977–86; ISI; 15 scores in 5 areas: Interpersonal Involvement (Sociable, Help Seeking, Nurturant, Sensitive), Socialization (Conscientious, Trusting, Tolerant), Autonomy (Directive, Independent, Rule Free), Self-Control (Deliberate, Orderly, Persistent), Stability (Stable, Approval Seeking); 1986 price data: $45 per complete kit including 5 reusable administration booklets ('85, 6 pages); 5 computer-scored answer sheets and manual ('86, 69 pages); $16.50 per 10 administration booklets; $7.50 per computer-scored answer sheet (price includes scoring and computer-generated interpretive report by publisher); $18.50 per manual; (40–45) minutes; Maurice Lorr, Richard P. Youniss, and G. J. Huba (computerized interpretation program and related chapters in manual); Western Psychological Services.*

For reviews by John Duckitt and Stuart A. Karabenick of an earlier edition, see 9:521; see also T3:1173 (1 reference).

TEST REFERENCES

1. Lorr, M., & DeLong, J. A. (1984). Second-order factors defined by the ISI. *Journal of Clinical Psychology*, 40, 1378-1382.

2. Lorr, M., Youniss, R. P., & Stefic, E. C. (1984). Factors common to motives and personality traits. *Psychological Reports*, 55, 119-122.

3. Lorr, M., Nerviano, V. J., & Myhill, J. (1985). Factors common to the ISI and the 16PF Inventories. *Journal of Clinical Psychology*, 41, 773-777.

4. Lorr, M., & DeJong, J. (1986). A short form of the Interpersonal Style Inventory (ISI). *Journal of Clinical Psychology*, 42, 466-469.

Review of the Interpersonal Style Inventory by RANDY W. KAMPHAUS, Assistant Professor of Educational Psychology, University of Georgia, Athens, GA:

The Interpersonal Style Inventory (ISI) is a self-report inventory that, according to the manual, "primarily measures an individual's characteristic ways of relating to other people. It also evaluates style of impulse control and characteristic modes of dealing with work and play. A broad measure of emotional stability versus anxiety has also been included." The scale is designed for use with individuals aged 14 years and older. It consists of 300 true-false items.

Administration of the ISI is straightforward and scoring and interpretation are computer-based. There are no hand-scoring options should an examiner prefer that. The item booklet and machine-readable answer sheet are comprehensible with one exception. It seems that there is a good chance a client could get out of sequence reading the item booklet and placing a response on the scoring sheet. Some procedure, such as putting the items next to the scoring options on the answer sheet would likely facilitate more accurate scoring. The authors also do not present data on the reading level of the items. Some indication of the readability of the items would be helpful to consumers trying to decide whether or not the ISI is appropriate for a particular population.

The standardization procedures for the ISI are highly questionable. The norming sample was comprised of less than 1,000 college students and less than 700 high school students. All of the high school students were from the Baltimore, Maryland area. Sample statistics are not given by socioeconomic status, ethnicity, or other important standardization stratification variables. Furthermore, differences in mean scores were found between high school and college age students on some of the scales. This finding makes it even more unlikely that the norm-referenced scores can be used with confidence for individuals past the typical college age range where *no normative data were collected.*

The test-retest reliability coefficients reported for a sample of college age females are good. No similar data are reported for college age males. Long range stability coefficients for periods ranging from 1 to 3 years were also good, especially when one considers the fact that personality constructs are being measured.

The most impressive aspect of the ISI is the wealth of information on the validity of the scales. Several concurrent validity studies are reported in the manual. Correlations with diverse measures such as the 16PF, and the Edwards Personal Preference Schedule show promise. In addition, a number of differential validity studies have shown that ISI scores can adequately differentiate some clinical samples. The findings regarding these studies, however, are only sketchily described in the manual.

The machine scoring and interpretive procedures are described to some extent in the manual. The various validity checks carried out as part of the scoring service are described in enough detail to give the user confidence that less than valid protocols are likely to be identified. The algorithms for computerized interpretation of the ISI, however, are not described in adequate detail. In lieu of this the reader is referred to a manual for another test that is published by the same publisher. It would be helpful to the ISI user to have this interpretive information reprinted in the ISI manual. The ISI manual does provide helpful interpretive guidelines and procedures, and some interesting sample cases.

In summary, the ISI is a measure of interpersonal style that is easily administered and machine scored and interpreted. It also shows adequate evidence of reliability and validity. The test does have several shortcomings. The standardization sample is limited to adolescents and young adults rendering derived scores as potentially useless for older samples. The manual varies a great deal in quality. It includes generous information on validity and yet does not describe the standardization sample in adequate detail. For clinical purposes the ISI does not possess a research base that is competitive with tests such as the Millon Clinical Multiaxial Inventory-II or the MMPI. On the other hand, the ISI assesses some interesting and unique constructs not assessed by other instruments.

Review of the Interpersonal Style Inventory by GERALD L. STONE, Professor of Counseling

Psychology and Director, University Counseling Service, The University of Iowa, Iowa City, IA:

The Interpersonal Style Inventory (ISI) represents about 20 years of research and development by Lorr and his associates. The ISI has been through several revisions, culminating in Form E, the current version of the Inventory. According to the author, the ISI "primarily measures an individual's characteristic ways of relating to other people." In addition to the interpersonal emphasis, the ISI includes scales concerned with "impulse control" and "characteristic modes of dealing with work and play." The focus is on normal traits, although a broad measure of "emotional stability" has been included.

The ISI is a rationally and empirically constructed instrument using interpersonal constructs based originally on Murray's (1938) work on needs, and expanded through the research and theoretical models concerned with the interpersonal circle (Leary, 1957; Lorr & McNair, 1965).

The inventory contains 300 true-false statements and is intended for use with individuals 14 years of age and older. The self-report inventory is computer scored and evaluates characteristics within five broad areas of personality derived from 14 bipolar dimensions and a Social Approval scale. Each of the 15 component scales is composed of 20 items and balanced for acquiescence. The five higher-order dimensions with their component scales include: Interpersonal Involvement (Sociable, Help Seeking, Nurturant, and Sensitive) Socialization (Conscientious, Trusting, and Tolerant), Autonomy (Directive, Independent, and Rule Free), Self-Control (Deliberate, Orderly, and Persistent), and Stability (Stable and Approval Seeking).

The current form (E) takes about 45 minutes to complete. The true/false format using a computer-scannable answer sheet makes it easy to administer.

The manual describes the general purpose and development, potential uses, administration, and psychometric properties of the instrument. It also contains a chapter on computerized scoring and interpretation by Huba and Lorr. The chapter provides extensive coverage and includes a sample test report with explanations and 10 case studies to facilitate profile interpretation. The test report provides a printout of approximately 15 pages, including (*a*) background information, (*b*) limitations and definitions, (*c*) protocol validity evaluation, (*d*) interpretive summary, (*e*) score profile, (*f*) score level ranking, (*g*) prototype analyses (analysis of probability that the respondent can be considered to be like people in various criterion groups), (*h*) score difference profile, and (*i*) tests for unusual pairs of scores. An appendix describing the profile analysis used in the computerized test report is included. As stated earlier, the information about the test report is extensive; however, there is no disclosure about the decision rules that guide the interpretive statements.

The manual describes the usefulness of the Inventory in providing objective information about how individuals see themselves relating to other people across a variety of social situations, supplemental information for diagnosis and treatment planning, interpersonal information potentially relevant to counseling personnel who are interested in being so counseled, and the breadth and scale construction properties (homogeneous content and relative independence of scales) that make the ISI a preferred instrument for personality research.

Another significant portion of the manual is devoted to examining psychometric properties. The strategy used in developing the ISI appears to be similar to a sequential approach to personality style development (see Jackson, 1970). First, certain bipolar dimensions were selected as a set of rational constructs to represent the specified domains, although, like many other personality tests, there is a lack of an explicit theoretical rationale based on psychological theory to indicate the appropriateness or adequacy of the selected dimensions. After careful construct formulations, efforts were made to suppress response-style variance (e.g., items generated to reflect an intermediate endorsement level, scales defined by balanced keyed statements and social desirability, and the creation of a Social Desirability scale). A number of studies and revisions focused on scale homogeneity. Factor analyses accompanying each of the five revisions are reported to be similar (e.g., stability of primary factors). Scale intercorrelations confirm the relative independence of the scales. Recent factor analytical studies using Form E have confirmed the five higher-order dimensions.

In conducting these various studies, many of which are in published form, norms (*T*-score system) for college and high school male and female students were derived since the norm samples show differences in scale means (e.g., "females are more interpersonally involved"). Unfortunately, no norm tables are provided, but scale correlations for each norm sample are presented.

Reliability data appear to be quite good. Internal consistency reliability (coefficient alpha) is reported to be from .68 to .89 for males and females, with only one coefficient below .70 (Approval Seeking for females). The test-retest stabilities for a sample of females over a 2-week period ranged from .80 to .95. Data are also reported for high school males and females and student nurses on Form D for longer periods of time (medians in .60s for 1 year and slightly lower for 2- and 3-year periods).

A final step in a sequential approach to test evaluation has to do with validity. The ISI manual provides items central to each scale in order to provide an opportunity to assess content validity. These items appear to conform adequately to scale definitions. The manual also provides cross-inventory correlations derived from concurrent validity studies. The evidence suggests that the ISI does in fact measure similarly named constructs found in other inventories such as the Jackson Personality Research Form, the Bentler Personality Inventory, and the Edwards Personality Preference Schedule. The manual also reports the results of studies using a contrasted groups methodology in order to demonstrate criterion-related validity through expected group differences. These studies are difficult to evaluate since the information presented is inadequate and it is unknown what differences were expected before conducting each of the studies.

Finally, the importance of convergent and divergent validity is not overlooked. The factor analyses and scale intercorrelations mentioned earlier satisfactorily address the issue of discriminant validity. In terms of convergent validity, peer and self-ratings were investigated and seem reasonable. The median correlations between ratings and the ISI were .57 for self-ratings and .45 for peer ratings. Some brief information is also reported about construct validity (Lorr & Wunderlich, 1985), but there is little information about the inventory's applied usefulness.

To summarize, the ISI has many strengths, but contained within each strength are unanswered challenges. For instance, the ISI compares quite favorably in terms of basic psychometric properties with highly sophisticated inventories (e.g., Personality Research Form) designed along the lines of Jackson's recommendations (1970). On the other hand, such comparability raises a question of how to determine a preference among these personality inventories. The answer undoubtedly lies in the area of criterion-related validity. On this dimension, the ISI along with comparable inventories are long on psychometric sophistication and potential uses, but short on documented clinical relevance. Another strength/challenge combination is in the continuity and development of the ISI. Lorr and colleagues continue to revise and add new information and procedures. The many years of development are certainly a strength. At the same time, the user has difficulty following the revisions, accounting for the changes, and relating the psychometric evidence to the various revisions. And now the user is asked to cope with computer scoring, prototypical matching, and so on, without adequate information about decision rules and norm tables. A final strength/challenge combination focuses on psychological theory. Although the reference to Murray's needs, and especially the research on the interpersonal circle, is informative and perhaps even unique given the latter's influence on the interpersonal scales, there is a lack of an explicit psychological theory that guides the spectrum of scales used or how the various scales relate to each other. Nevertheless, the strengths outlined above suggest the ISI has promise within a research context, but the challenges also suggest that the relevance of the ISI to the school, clinic, and workplace remains questionable.

REVIEWER'S REFERENCES

Murray, H. A. (1938). *Explorations in personality*. New York: Oxford University Press.

Leary, T. F. (1957). *Interpersonal diagnosis of personality*. New York: Ronald Press.

Lorr, M., & McNair, D. M. (1965). Expansion of the interpersonal behavior circle. *Journal of Personality and Social Psychology*, 2, 823-830.

Jackson, D. N. (1970). A sequential system for personality scale development. In C. D. Spielberger (Ed.), *Current topics in clinical and community psychology Vol. 2* (pp. 61-96). New York: Academic Press.

[152]

Inventory for Client and Agency Planning. Purpose: A "structured instrument to assess the status, adaptive functioning, and service needs of clients." Infant to adult; 1986; ICAP; statistically related to the Scales of Independent Behavior and the Woodcock-Johnson Psycho-Educational Battery; to be completed by "a respondent who has known a client for at least 3 months and who sees him or her on a day-to-day basis"; yields descriptive information in the areas of Client Status, Functional Limitations, Social and Leisure Activities, Service Use; 10 scores: Adaptive Behavior Domains (Motor Skills, Social and Communication Skills, Personal Living Skills, Community Living Skills), Broad Independence, Maladaptive Behavior Indexes (Internalized, Asocial, Externalized, General), Service Level Index; individual; 1988 price data: $30 per 25 record forms ('86, 16 pages); $60 per complete test including 25 record forms and manual ('86, 155 pages); 20(30) minutes; Robert H. Bruininks, Bradley K. Hill, Richard F. Weatherman, and Richard W. Woodcock; DLM Teaching Resources.*

Review of the Inventory for Client and Agency Planning by RONN JOHNSON, Assistant Professor of Educational Psychology, University of Nebraska-Lincoln, Lincoln, NE:

The Inventory for Client and Agency Planning (ICAP) is a structured instrument developed to assess the status, adaptive functioning, and service needs of clients. The ICAP yields descriptive information; identifies diagnostic status, adaptive functional limitations, adaptive behavior skills, problem behaviors; and suggests residential placement, habilitation, and support services. It also purports to help screen, monitor, plan, and evaluate services for handicapped, disabled, and elderly people. The general age range is from less than 1 year to 40 years.

The ICAP also provides information on demographics, diagnostics status, functional limitations, and needed assistance. In addition, it yields data on the following adaptive behavior domains: motor skills, social and communicative skills, personal living skills, community living skills, and broad independence. Problem behaviors, social level, residential placement, daytime program, support services, and social and leisure activities are also reported. A general information and recommendation section is also included as well.

The instrument is presented using a 16-page, self-administered response booklet. It takes about 20 minutes to complete. The booklet allows a respondent, who has known the client for at least 3 months, to record the basic information needed to score the ICAP. The test booklet also contains convenient places for scoring and graphing the results. The authors have provided space for respondent comments. Other useful information in the manual is the distribution of the ICAP norming sample with respect to sex and race in relation to the U.S. population in three age groupings. Sufficient information about test reliability (i.e., internal consistency, test-retest, and interrater reliability) confirmed adequate reliability for ICAP scores. There is also a well-documented section on construct validity, criterion-related validity, and validity of the ICAP service level. The rigorous item selection process supports adequate content validity. The authors also offer sound suggestions for further validity studies.

There are several positive aspects to using the ICAP. The manual is well written, comprehensive, clear, and readable in presentation. The authors offer some rationale for important decisions that were made in the instrument's developmental process and they offer information about their actual developmental procedures. In addition, ICAP scoring procedures, reference tables, and score recording procedures are located in the response (test) booklet. This minimizes the need for checking the manual for tables or charts. Thus, few scoring errors should be made if the procedures are followed by the examiners because of the overall quality of the manual and the response booklet. However, use of the ICAP for decision-making purposes requires either special competencies or specialized training. This training could include an extensive overview of behavioral needs of the clients served. There are other caveats associated with the use of the ICAP.

The adaptive behavior section reports that samples of skill develop across a wide range from infancy to adulthood. Yet the normative data for some age groups, (i.e., 43 and up, 7 to 5) appear underrepresented. Another concern is the limited amount of information available for interpreting the ICAP results. The planning needed for the client and at the program level would be enchanced if the authors offered a more detailed explanation of how the information generated by the ICAP can be applied.

Overall, the ICAP should not be used as a final decision-making measure. Instead, it should be used in two ways. First, it should be used as a preliminary screening device. Second, it may have some merit as a research criterion measure for investigations examining the more global effects of short- and/or long-term training programs.

Review of the Inventory for Client and Agency Planning by RICHARD L. WIKOFF, Professor of Psychology, University of Nebraska at Omaha, Omaha, NE:

PRACTICAL EVALUATION. The response booklet for the Inventory for Client and Agency Planning (ICAP) is attractive, well designed, and efficiently organized. It is easy to read and mark and is laid out in such a way that it would be easy to enter the data into a file for computer analysis.

The booklet may be scored by the user and contains all the necessary profiles for determining the various indexes that are available. Some of the scores are complex in that there are a number of steps required to derive them, but the manual clearly presents the directions. The rationale behind the steps, however, is not always apparent. This is probably more of an advantage than a disadvantage because there is sufficient information given that a person trained in psychometrics can understand the rationale, but others can perform the calculations without having to understand such concepts as standard scores, standard error of measurement, and so forth.

The ICAP provides both categorical and metric information. Categorical information includes the usual demographic data plus information about diagnosed conditions and functional limitations. There are four scales of Adaptive Behavior: Motor Skills, Social and Communication Skills, Personal Living Skills, and Community Living Skills. Each of these scales is marked from *Never or Rarely* (0) to *Does Very Well* (3). Each raw score is the sum of the weighted responses.

Eight Problem Behaviors (Hurtful to Self, Hurtful to Others, Destructive to Property, Disruptive Behavior, Unusual or Repetitive Habits, Socially Offensive Behavior, Withdrawal or Inattentive Behavior, and Uncooperative Behavior) are to be rated for frequency and severity. These ratings are combined to determine four Maladaptive Indexes (Internalized, Asocial, Externalized, and General). Additional information asked for pertains to planning (Residential Placement, Daytime Program, Support Services, and Social and Leisure Activities). There is also room for General Information and Recommendations.

A variety of scores may be determined using different scales. Domain scores are equivalent to the *w*-scores of the Rasch model (Wright & Stone, 1979). They may be transformed through a series of steps into percentile ranks, standard scores with a mean of 100 and a standard deviation of 15, and Normal Curve Equivalents. The latter is a standard score with a mean of 50 and a standard deviation of 21.06 that produces an equal interval scale ranging from 1 to 99 with the end scores being open ended. Relative Performance Indexes may also be determined. These are presented as "predictive statement[s]." They are designed to indicate percentage of independence on a set of tasks that a reference group performed with 90% independence. Other scores include Age Equivalent scores, Maladaptive Behavior Indexes, and an ICAP Service Level. Illustrations and examples of case studies are presented to show how the various scores are calculated and interpreted.

STANDARDIZATION. The adaptive behavior and problem behavior sections of the ICAP were normed on a national sample as part of the standardization for the Scales of Independent Behavior (SIB: Bruininks, Woodcock, Hill, & Weatherman, 1985). Seventy-seven items were chosen for the four ICAP domains from the 226 standardized for the SIB.

Sampling was very carefully done to try to select a sample that was representative of the distribution of the United States population. Stratification and quotas were used for the variables of sex, race, Spanish origin, occupational status, occupational level, geographic region, and type of community. First the communities were sampled and then, for school age subjects, schools were sampled. Finally, subjects were randomly sampled from within the schools. A total of 1,764 subjects were included in the sample. Sample sizes by age ranged from 74 8-year-olds to 177 adults in the 21–42 category. Statistical checks were made to test the influence of population characterisitcs and some weighting was done to correct for over- or underrepresentation. Finally, the norm scores were equated to SIB scores using regression procedures. Additionally, the norming data were statistically anchored to the Woodcock-Johnson norming sample of 4,732 subjects.

RELIABILITY. Reliability is thoroughly discussed in the manual and considerable data are presented concerning several types of reliability. Split-half reliabilities range from .32 to .94 depending on the age group and subtest. Median reliabilities range from .58 for the Motor Skills subscale to .86 for Broad Independence (a composite score). Split-half reliabilities are given for handicapped groups, also. The sample sizes were much smaller, but the reliabilities tended to be significantly larger. Test-retest reliabilities were assessed for all subtests using 29 6–8-year-old subjects and 38 10–11-year-old children. These coefficients ranged from .10 for Socially Offensive Behavior Severity Scale to .97 for Hurtful to Self Frequency Scale. Interrater reliabilities ranged from .87 to .92 after being corrected for effects due to age. Agreement between raters for demographic, diagnostic, and service variables ranged from 66% to 100%, with the most disagreement being for services and social activities items.

VALIDITY. Validity data are extensive and impressive. A large number of studies are presented under the heading of construct validity to demonstrate the developmental aspects of the scales and the differences between various handicapped groups. As predicted, handicapped students scored lower than normals. The differences were quite large for retarded children and were related to degree of severity. The differences were not significant for most subscales for learning-disabled children and children with behavior disorders. Criterion-related studies showed high correlations with the SIB at all age levels and were moderate to high for the Adaptive Behavior Scale—School Edition. Correlations with the Woodcock-Johnson varied from low to high depending on age. Correlations were lowest with handicapped groups. Several multiple discriminant analyses were performed using four adaptive behavior scales and three maladaptive behavior scales as predictors. Criteria included Level of Ability, Levels of Classroom Placement, Levels of Residential Placement, and Levels of Day Placements, and Vocational Programs. All analyses were significant with canonical correlations ranging from .60 to .78. Analyses of covariance indicated there were significant differences in ICAP Service Level Scores for residential placement and levels of daytime services. Finally, content validity is discussed and suggestions are made for further studies.

SUMMARY. The ICAP was developed by "state-of-the-art" psychometric techniques. The inventory is based upon sound psychological concepts and extreme care was taken at every step in its development. The authors used suitable sampling procedures and followed The Rasch model in developing and analyzing items. Norms were carefully prepared and a variety of scores are available. Many studies were presented to indicate the reliability of the various scales and several approaches were discussed to demonstrate validity.

Nevertheless, a few criticisms should be made. First, the authors state the inventory should be administered by individuals who have known the subject for a period of at least 3 months and sees him/her on a day-to-day basis. This was not true of the interviewers who collected the data for the norm sample. It is difficult to predict what effect this might have had. Had this criterion been rigidly followed the technical data might have been even more impressive.

As it was, the reliabilities are quite low in many instances. Although the validity data are very impressive, they vary for different groups. The user needs to be aware of the technical aspects of the specific scales being used.

Another criticism has to do with sample size. While the overall number seems impressive (1,764), because of the many levels of stratification, the actual number of cases at any one level must be quite small, although this information is not given. With age alone considered, one age level had only 74 subjects. This is a rather small number to represent all of the 8-year-olds in the United States.

Finally, no mention is ever made of the effect of language differences on the reliability and validity of the inventory, and yet questions about Primary Language Understood and Hispanic Origin are asked in the descriptive information section and Spanish Origin was used as a stratification variable.

The stated purpose of the test is "to aid in screening, monitoring, managing, planning, and evaluating services for the handicapped, disabled, and elderly people." This reviewer recommends the use of this instrument for these purposes, but with a word of caution. The user should be aware of the differences in reliability and validity for different groups. For this reason it is recommended that local reliability and validity studies be conducted. The use of the inventory as an "aid" should be emphasized. As with any measurement instrument, other sources of information should be used, also.

REVIEWER'S REFERENCES

Wright, B. D., & Stone, M. H. (1979). *Best test design.* Chicago: MESA Press.

Bruininks, R. H., Woodcock, R. W., Hill, B. K., & Weatherman, R. F. (1985). *Development and standardization of the Scales of Independent Behavior.* Allen, TX: DLM Teaching Resources.

[153]

Inventory of Language Abilities, Level II. Purpose: "For use by the classroom teacher in identifying children with possible language learning disabilities." Grades 3–5 and older language disabled students; 1981; a component of the MWM Program for Developing Language Abilities, and an upward extension of the Inventory of Language Abilities (9:526); ratings by each teacher involved with child; behavior checklists in 11 areas: Auditory Reception, Visual Reception, Auditory Association, Visual Association, Verbal Expression, Manual Expression, Auditory Memory, Visual Memory, Grammatic Closure, Visual Closure, Auditory Closure and Sound Blending; individual; 1986 price data: $15 per 25 inventory booklets; administration time not reported; Esther H. Minskoff, Douglas E. Wiseman, and J. Gerald Minskoff; Educational Performance Associates.*

For a review by Rita Sloan Berndt of the Inventory of Language Abilities, see 9:526.

Review of the Inventory of Language Abilities, Level II by LYNN S. BLISS, Associate Professor of Speech, Wayne State University, Detroit, MI:

The Inventory of Language Abilities (ILA) Level II was designed as a screening instrument for a classroom teacher to identify children with "possible language learning disabilities." This instrument is applicable for third, fourth, and fifth grade children, handicapped children, and even junior and senior high school students. It consists of checklists in the areas of: Auditory and Visual Reception, Auditory and Visual Association, Verbal and Manual Expression, Auditory and Visual Memory, Grammatic and Visual Closure, and Auditory Closure and Sound Blending.

Each checklist contains 12 behaviors that are evaluated. The teacher checks those behaviors applicable to each child. A score for each checklist is derived by adding the checks in each area. A profile chart can be filled out delineating a child's strengths and weaknesses in the 11 areas of evaluation. The authors claim that an area having more than 50% of the items checked should receive "special attention."

This inventory is associated with a remediation program, the MWM Program for Developing Language Abilities. Items on the checklist are cross referenced to the educational program. Thus a teacher could identify a child's area of weakness and then refer to the remediation program for specific educational guidelines.

The ILA-Level II reports no reliability, validity, or standardization data. Presumably there are none. High interrater reliability would be doubtful because many of the items are subjective and vague. The directions lack specificity thus increasing the potential for variability among scorers.

Absence of any validity information sheds doubt on the usefulness of this instrument. While many of the individual behaviors on the checklist are appropriate for educational achievement, it is not known whether they are all useful in identifying language learning disabilities (e.g., how does "rarely uses gestures" apply?). Comparison of the results of the inventory with more standardized testing or screening instruments is necessary to assess validity. In addition, there is no theoretical rationale for the selection of the items.

Absence of normative data prohibits any meaningful comparison of a child with his/her peers and fails to determine the ages when each of the behaviors are expected to be mastered. The authors are apparently relying on their intuitions in the construction of this inventory.

In conclusion, the ILA-Level II does not appear to be a useful screening instrument. Without reliability, validity, and normative data, the checklists cannot be used with any degree of confidence. The items are vague and may result in a misleading evaluation of a child. There are adequate screening and evaluation instruments available that would be of more use to a classroom teacher. Furthermore, a skilled classroom teacher would be expected to identify a child with language learning disabilities on his/her own without this inventory.

[154]

Iowa Social Competency Scales. Purpose: Provides "easily administered and objectively scored individual rating instrument for parents relative to the social behavior (competencies) of normal children." Ages 3–12; 1976–82; ISCS; ratings by parents to "measure typical behavior of average (normal) children as they function within the family environment"; 2 levels; 1987 price data: $.10 or less per scale; $10 per manual ('82, 46 pages); administration time not reported; Damaris Pease, Samuel G. Clark, and Sedahlia Jasper Crase; Iowa State University Research Foundation, Inc.*

a) PRESCHOOL. Ages 3–6; 3 forms.

1) *Mother*. 5 scores: Social Activator, Hypersensitivity, Reassurance, Uncooperativeness, Cooperativeness.

2) *Father*. 5 scores: Social Activator, Hypersensitivity, Reassurance, Social Ineptness, Attentiveness.

3) *Combined*. 3 scores: Social Activator, Hypersensitivity, Reassurance.

b) SCHOOL-AGE. Ages 6–12; adaptation of Devereux Elementary School Behavior Rating Scale; 2 forms.

1) *Mother*. 6 scores: Task Oriented, Disruptive, Leader, Physically Active, Affectionate Toward Parent, Apprehensive.

2) *Father*. 5 scores: Capable, Defiant, Leader, Active with Peers, Affectionate Toward Parent.

See 9:532 (2 references).

Review of the Iowa Social Competency Scales by GLORIA E. MILLER, Assistant Professor of Psychology, University of South Carolina, Columbia, SC:

The Iowa Social Competency Scales were designed for research use as a parent-rating instrument for measuring social behavior (competencies) of children ages 3–12. There are five independent scales; mother and father forms for both preschool (ages 3–6) and school-age (6–12) children, and a combined parent form for preschoolers. According to the authors, the major purpose of the scales is "to measure typical behavior of average (normal) children as they function within the family environment."

SCALE CONSTRUCTION. Construction procedures differed across the five scales. The mother and father School-Age Scales have the most extensive developmental history (i.e., dating back to 1973), followed by the mother and father Preschool Scales, and finally, the Combined Preschool Scale. The original school-age version included 35 items representing eight factors of the Devereux Elementary School Behavior Rating Scale developed by Spivack and Swift (1967). The items were modified to fit home or family situations and then evaluated by judges who classified items into the eight categories. Similarly, a panel of developmental experts agreed on the 71 items of the original Preschool Scale that were based on broad areas of social abilities outlined by White and Watts (1973).

In the early stages of development, there was only one scale for use by either parent. However, after the original set of items was subjected to factor analysis in both the school-age and preschool versions, different factor structures emerged for mothers and fathers. The present mother and father forms of the School-Age Scale consist of six factors (26 items) and five factors (33 items), respectively, while the corresponding mother and father forms of the Preschool Scale consist of five factors (34 items) and five factors (29 items), respectively. The results of the final factor intercorrelations for the separate mother and father forms of the School-Age and Preschool Scales are reported in the manual. All forms have demonstrated relatively low factor scale intercorrelations indicating the essential independence of the factors.

The Combined Preschool Scale consists of 19 items involving three factors from the separate mother and father Preschool Scale forms. Fourteen of these items are held in common across the mother and father forms and the remaining five nonoverlapping items have been selected because of their respectable factor loadings (i.e., above .40). The factor analysis on this newly created form has not been reported. However, construct validity was examined in one study using a Campbell and Fiske (1959) model with 92 preschool children. Clear evidence for convergent and discriminant validity was obtained on only one of the three factors (Social Activator).

RELIABILITY. The reported Spearman-Brown reliability scores are satisfactory for the mother ($N = 213$) and father ($N = 262$) School-Age Scales (i.e., range from .47 to .94; median = .90). However, less respectable reliability estimates are reported for the mother ($N = 250$) and father ($N = 186$) Preschool Scales (i.e., range from .47 to .88; median =

.69). No reliability estimates are provided for the Combined Preschool Scale.

VALIDITY. The original item pools for each scale were based on sound theoretical ground, with questions drafted by developmental specialists. In terms of face validity, there is little doubt that these items represented important competencies expected in young children. However, the face validity of the final scale versions may have been compromised because (*a*) there were several stages of unsystematic additions of new items during test construction, and (*b*) the factors that emerge in the final versions are not representative of the dimensions of social behavior posited by the original scales.

NORMS. The normative data are the most disappointing feature of the scales. The sample size on which most of the factor analyses were based are satisfactory; however, it is unclear to what extent the samples were truly representative. Although rural and urban mothers and fathers in eight midwestern states were sampled during scale development, neither the data from the standardization samples nor the mean factor scores presented in the manual are broken down by race, social status, or age. Ideally, we should like to know exactly how the samples were constituted and how the mean factor scores were distributed across different demographic characteristics. At a minimum, norms for different age groups and for different social classes would appear desirable. Without normative data, practical use of the Scales is severely limited.

Another important point about this aspect of the scale construction is that over half of the parents in the standardization samples were participants in an ongoing longitudinal study. To what extent this participation affected the results is, of course, not clear, but subjects in longitudinal research may possess certain personality and motivational characteristics that differ from the population at large.

ADMINISTRATION. Administrative procedures are consistent across the five scales. Parents are asked to rate a series of assertions regarding their child and to base their ratings on "outward behavior you actually observe" in relation to what might be expected in "most children." Each item is rated on a scale of 1 (i.e., almost never) to 5 (i.e., almost always). A rating of 3 indicates that the parent does not know or believes the child behaves "about like the average child." It is unclear whether the test items are to be read to the subject. The wording of some of the items might pose difficulty to adults with less than optimal literacy levels.

Separate factor scores are obtained by summing the ratings for the items associated with each factor of a scale. On the Preschool Scale, where several of the factors contain both positive and negative items, item scores are transformed before summing occurs. Users are cautioned against adding the total raw scores across factors, since there is no evidence that scale factors are additive. Additionally, because each scale differs in the number of factors and item content, the user must treat each of the five scales independently. At the present time, only the Combined form of the Preschool Scale allows for the simultaneous comparison of mother and father ratings.

CONCLUSION. The Iowa Social Competency Scales, like all rating scales, are marked by strong and weak points. In this case, the former outweigh the latter, provided the scales are used for continued research into the development of social competencies in young children. The scales seem to be especially useful with respect to identification of areas of social competencies that characterize school-age children, and these scales probably handle this area as well as any other current rating scale. In particular, these scales are to be commended for attention to social behavior that occurs within family and neighborhood environments. Though there is considerable reason to believe that the scales may eventually be clinically useful for identifying expected levels of social behavior in children, their value in this respect has not as yet been clearly demonstrated.

One of the greatest weaknesses of both the School-Age and Preschool Scales is that, as it stands now, comparisons between the parents of the same child are unwarranted because of the observed factor differences in mothers and fathers. Although theoretically important, the authors never discuss the significance of the observed parental differences. One possibility is that during the standardization process, independent mother and father samples were employed. It is unclear whether similar factor structures would be obtained from a sample population of two-parent families who rated the same child. Although the ability to contrast parents' ratings of children's social competencies has been addressed in the construction of the Combined Preschool Scale, the user is cautioned against its use at this time because of the limited information and research available on this scale.

REVIEWER'S REFERENCES

Campbell, D. T., & Fiske, D. W. (1959). Convergent and discriminant validation by the multitrait-mutimethod matrix. *Psychological Bulletin*, 56, 81-105.

Spivack, G., & Swift, M. (1967). *Devereux Elementary School Behavior Rating Scale Manual.* Devon, PA: The Devereux Foundation.

White, B. L., & Watts, J. C. (1973). *Experience and environment: Major influences on development of the young child* (Vol. 1). Englewood Cliffs, NJ: Prentice-Hall.

[155]

Iowa Tests of Basic Skills, Forms G and H. Purpose: To "provide for comprehensive and continuous measurement of growth in the fundamental skills: vocabulary, reading, the mechanics of writing, methods of study, and mathematics." Grades K.1–1.5, K.8–1.9, 1.7–2.6, 2.5–3.5, 3, 4, 5, 6, 7, 8–9; 1955–86; ITBS; previous edition still available; a component of the Riverside Basic Skills Assessment Program; 1986 price data: $6.15 per 35 pupil profile charts; $6.15 per 35 profile charts for averages; $3 per fall norms booklet; $5.25 per large city norms, Catholic norms, high socioeconomic norms, low socioeconomic norms, 1978–1985 norms conversion tables, standard score norms, or normal curve equivalent norms; $6 per ITBS, TAP and CogAT Preliminary Technical Summary ('86, 91 pages); $13.05 per Manual for School Administrators, Forms G and H ('86, 208 pages); $9 per combined ITBS/TAP Technical Handbook, Form G; $8.40 per Research that Built the Riverside Assessment Program; $3.90 per ITBS Detailed Skills Objectives (Levels 5–14, Form G or Levels 7–14, Form H); $15 per examination kit for Levels 5–14; scoring service available from publisher; A. N. Hieronymus, H. D. Hoover, E. F. Lindquist, K. R. Oberley, N. K. Cantor, D. D. Burbick, J. C. Lewis, E. L. Hyde, A. L. Qualls-Payne, and others listed below; The Riverside Publishing Co.*

a) PRIMARY BATTERY, FORMS G AND H. Grades K.1–1.5, K.8–1.9, 1.7–2.6, 2.5–3.5; 1978–86; 4 levels; $6.42 per 35 reports to parents; $6.84 per 35 class record folders, Levels 5–8.

1) *Early Primary Battery*. Grades K.1–1.5, K.8–1.9; available in Form G (Basic Battery) only; Levels 5 and 6; $5.79 per 35 practice tests for Levels 5 and 6, Form G (including directions for administration); $.99 per directions for administration for practice tests, Levels 5 and 6, Form G; $2.70 per NCS directions for administration (specify Level 5 or 6) ('86, 13 pages/15 pages); $6.69 per Teacher's Guide for Levels 5 and 6, Form G ('86, 72 pages); authors listed above and B. S. Smith, B. S. Loyd, and C. M. Hallenbach.

(*a*) Level 5. Grades K.1–1.5; 5 scores: Listening, Word Analysis, Vocabulary, Language, Mathematics; $36 per 35 MRC machine-scorable test booklets, Level 5, Form G (including Teacher's Guide and materials needed for machine scoring); $27 per 35 hand-scorable test booklets, Basic Battery, Form G, Level 5 (including one class record sheet); $42 per 35 NCS test booklets, Form G, Level 5, Basic Battery (including one directions for administration); $11.25 per one set of MRC scoring masks for Level 5, Form G; 150(195) minutes.

(*b*) Level 6. Grades K.8–1.9; 6 scores: Listening, Word Analysis, Vocabulary, Language, Mathematics, Reading; $42 per 35 MRC machine-scorable test booklets, Level 6, Form G (including Teacher's Guide and materials needed for machine scoring); $28.35 per 35 hand-scorable test booklets, Level 6, Form G (including one class record sheet); $47.10 per 35 NCS test booklets, Form G, Level 6 (including one directions for administration); $13.50 per set of MRC scoring masks for Level 6, Form G; 205(250) minutes.

2) *Primary Battery*. Grades 1.7–2.6, 2.5–3.5; available in Forms G and H; 3 batteries; 2 levels; $7.59 per 35 practice tests for Levels 7 and 8, both forms (including directions for administration); $6.15 per Teacher's Guide, Levels 7 and 8, Forms G and H ('86, 79 pages); $3.30 per directions for administering Form H, Levels 7 and 8 MRC test booklets; $2.70 per NCS directions for administration (specify Level 7, Form G or Level 8, Form G) ('86, 21 pages per booklet); $1.50 per directions for administration for practice tests, Levels 7 and 8, both forms; authors listed above and S. S. Eberly, B. S. Smith, B. S. Loyd, M. A. Whitney, C. M. Hallenbach, K. L. Humphrey, T. B. Lewis, H. V. Monroe, J. J. Peterson, and F. H. Strayer.

(*a*) Level 7. Grades 1.7–2.6; 3 batteries.

(1) Basic Battery. 7 scores: Word Analysis, Vocabulary, Reading Comprehension, Spelling, Mathematics Concepts, Mathematics Problems, Mathematics Computation; $42 per 35 MRC machine-scorable test booklets for Level 7, Form G (including Teacher's Guide and materials needed for machine scoring); $30 per 35 hand-scorable test booklets, Basic Battery, Form G, Level 7; $18 per set of MRC scoring masks for hand scoring MRC Basic Battery

machine-scorable or hand-scorable test booklets; (134) minutes.

(2) Complete Battery. 13 scores: Listening, Word Analysis, Vocabulary, Reading Comprehension, Spelling, Capitalization, Punctuation, Usage and Expression, Visual Materials, Reference Materials, Mathematics Concepts, Mathematics Problems, Mathematics Computation; $45 per 35 MRC machine-scorable test booklets Level 7, Form G (including Teacher's Guide and materials needed for machine scoring); $45 per 35 MRC machine-scorable test booklets Level 7, Form H (including directions for administration and materials needed for machine scoring); $50.52 per 35 NCS test booklets, Form G, Level 7, Complete Battery (including directions for administration); (227) minutes.

(3) Complete Battery Plus Social Studies and Science. 15 scores: Listening, Word Analysis, Vocabulary, Reading Comprehension, Spelling, Capitalization, Punctuation, Usage and Expression, Visual Materials, Reference Materials, Mathematics Concepts, Mathematics Problems, Mathematics Computation, Social Studies, Science; $65.19 per 35 MRC machine-scorable test booklets, Level 7, Form G (including Teacher's Guide and materials needed for machine scoring); (267) minutes.

(*b*) Level 8. Grades 2.5–3.5; details same as for Level 7.

b) MULTILEVEL AND SEPARATE LEVEL EDITIONS, FORMS G AND H. Grades 3, 4, 5, 6, 7, 8–9; 1978–86; 6 levels (Levels 9–14); 3 batteries; $28.50 per 35 Social Studies/Science booklets for Levels 9–14, Form G (including Teacher's Guide); $54.90 per 35 MRC machine-scorable booklets for Level 9, Form G (including directions for administration and materials needed for machine scoring); $33 per 100 practice tests for Levels 9–14 (including 3 directions for administration); $1.95 per answer key booklet (specify Form G, Levels 5–14 or Form H, Levels 7–14); $15 per 35 MRC answer sheets for Forms G and H (including Teacher's Guide, 35 pupil report folders, class record folder and materials needed for machine scoring) (specify Level 9–14); $24 per 100 MRC answer sheets for Forms G and H including materials needed for machine scoring (specify Level 9–14); $114.99 per 500 MRC answer sheets for Forms G and H including materials needed for machine scoring (specify Level 9–14); $33 per 100 combined answer folders for Forms G and H, Iowa Tests of Basic Skills/Cognitive Abilities Test, Form 4, including materials needed for machine scoring (specify Level 9A, 10B, 11C, 12D, 13E, or 14F); $96 per 250 NCS 7010 answer folders for Forms G and H (specify Level 9–14); $12.84 per 100 practice test answer sheets for Levels 9–14; $15.45 per 35 MRC Listening answer folders, Form G, Levels 9–14 (including Teacher's Guide and materials needed for machine scoring); $17.76 per Writing Classroom Test Package (including 35 test booklets, 35 answer folders, Teacher's Guide, and materials needed for local or central scoring), Form G (specify Levels 9–11 or 12–14); $6.42 per 35 "How Are Your Basic Skills?", Levels 9–14 parent teacher report folders for Forms G and H; $6.84 per 35 class record folders, Levels 9–14; $4.50 per Listening Teacher's Guide Levels 9–14, Form G; $1.50 per directions for administration of practice tests for Levels 9–14 ('86, 9 pages); $2.25 per Social Studies/Science Teacher's Guide, Form G; $2.70 per MRC directions for administration for Level 9, Form G; $6.15 per Teacher's Guide for Levels 9–14, Forms G and H ('86, 75 pages); authors listed above and S. S. Eberly, G. B. Bray, L. J. Schuckert, S. D. Rattenborg, D. J. Martin, and D. L. Green.

1) *Basic Battery*. 6 tests: Vocabulary, Reading Comprehension, Spelling, Mathematics Concepts, Mathematics Problem Solving, Mathematics Computation; $3 per Basic Multilevel Battery Test Booklet, Levels 9–14, Form G; (135) minutes.

2) *Complete Battery*. 11 tests: same as in Basic Battery plus Capitalization, Punctuation, Usage and Expression, Visual Materials, Reference Materials; 2 editions; Supplemental Social Studies/Science test also available; $9 per set of MRC scoring masks, Complete Battery (specify Form G, Level 9–14 through Form H, Level 9–14); (256) minutes.

(*a*) Multilevel Edition. $3.87 per Complete Multilevel Battery test booklet, Levels 9–14 (specify Form G or Form H); contains all 11 tests for all 6 levels.

(*b*) Separate Level Edition. $43.50 per 35 Separate Level test booklets, Form G, Complete Battery (including all tests plus Science and Social Studies and directions for administration (specify Level 9–14); $42.15 per 35 Separate Level test booklets, Form H, Complete Battery (including all tests and directions for administration but no Science and Social Studies) (specify Level 9–14); $2.70 per directions for administration for Separate Level Booklets, Levels 9–14 ('86, 21 pages).

For reviews by Peter W. Airasian and Anthony J. Nitko of Forms 7 and 8, see 9:533 (29 references); see also T3:1192 (97 references); for reviews by Larry A. Harris and Fred Pyrczak of Forms 5–6, see 8:19 (58 references); see T2:19 (87 references) and 6:13 (17 references); for reviews by Virgil E. Herrick, G. A. V. Morgan, and H. H. Remmers, and an excerpted review by Laurence Siegel of Forms 1–2, see 5:16. For reviews of the modern mathematics supplement, see 7:481 (2 reviews).

TEST REFERENCES

1. Conrad, K. J., & Eash, M. J. (1983). Measuring implementation and multiple outcomes in a Child Parent Center Compensatory Education Program. *American Educational Research Journal*, 20, 221-236.

2. White, M., & Miller, S. R. (1983). Dyslexia: A term in search of a definition. *The Journal of Special Education*, 17, 5-10.

3. Austin, A. M. B., & Draper, D. C. (1984). The relationship among peer acceptance, social impact, and academic achievement in middle childhood. *American Educational Research Journal*, 21, 597-604.

4. Bloland, R. M., & Michael, W. B. (1984). A comparison of the relative validity of a measure of Piagetian cognitive development and a set of conventional prognostic measures in the prediction of the future success of ninth- and tenth-grade students in algebra. *Educational and Psychological Measurement*, 44, 925-943.

5. Day, K. C., & Day, H. D. (1984). Kindergarten knowledge of print conventions and later school achievement: A five-year follow-up. *Psychology in the Schools*, 21, 393-396.

6. Grabe, M., & Mann, S. (1984). A technique for the assessment and training of comprehension monitoring skills. *Journal of Reading Behavior*, 16, 131-144.

7. Griswold, P. A. (1984). Elementary students' attitudes during 2 years of computer-assisted instruction. *American Educational Research Journal*, 21, 737-754.

8. Harty, H., & Beall, D. (1984). Attitudes toward science of gifted and nongifted fifth graders. *Journal of Research Teaching*, 21, 483-488.

9. Hess, R. D., & McDevitt, T. M. (1984). Some cognitive consequences of maternal intervention techniques: A longitudinal study. *Child Development*, 55, 2017-2030.

10. Hess, R. D., Holloway, S. D., Dickson, W. P., & Price, G. G. (1984). Maternal variables as predictors of children's school readiness and later achievement in vocabulary and mathematics in sixth grade. *Child Development*, 55, 1902-1912.

11. Kashiwagi, K., Azuma, H., Miyake, K., Nagano, S., Hess, R. D., & Holloway, S. D. (1984). Japan-US comparative study on early maternal influences upon cognitive development: A follow-up study. *Japanese Psychological Research*, 26, 82-92.

12. Sanders, J. M. (1984). Faculty desegregation and student achievement. *American Educational Research Journal*, 21, 605-616.

13. Schell, L. M. (1984). Reading Yardsticks. *The Reading Teacher*, 38, 318-321.

14. Wilson, L. R., & Cone, T. (1984). The regression equation method of determining academic discrepancy. *Journal of School Psychology*, 22, 95-110.

15. Zenke, L., & Alexander, L. (1984). Teaching thinking in Tulsa. *Educational Leadership*, 42, 81-84.

16. Abadzi, H. (1985). Ability grouping effects on academic achievement and self-esteem: Who performs in the long run as expected. *The Journal of Educational Research*, 79, 36-40.

17. Blair, J. C., Peterson, M. E., & Viehweg, S. H. (1985). The effects of mild sensorineural hearing loss on academic performance of young school-aged children. *Volta Review*, 87, 87-93.

18. Cummings, O. W., & Hoover, H. D. (1985). Content and score performance comparisons between a survey achievement test and a diagnostic mathematics test. *Measurement and Evaluation in Counseling and Development*, 17, 188-195.

19. Forell, E. R. (1985). The case for conservative reader placement. *The Reading Teacher*, 38, 857-862.

20. Hahn, A. L. (1985). Teaching remedial students to be strategic readers and better comprehenders. *The Reading Teacher*, 39, 72-77.

21. Harty, H., Beall, D., & Scharmann, L. (1985). Relationships between elementary school students' science achievement and their attitudes toward science, interest in science, reactive curiosity, and scholastic aptitude. *School Science and Mathematics*, 85, 472-479.

22. Harty, H., Hamrick, L., & Samuel, K. V. (1985). Relationships between middle school students' science concept structure interrelatedness competence and selected cognitive and affective tendencies. *Journal of Research in Science Teaching*, 22, 179-191.

23. Holmes, B. C., & Allison, R. W. (1985). The effect of four modes of reading on children's comprehension. *Reading Research and Instruction*, 25, 9-20.

24. Kennelly, K. J., & Mount, S. A. (1985). Perceived contingency of reinforcements, helplessness, locus of control, and academic performance. *Psychology in the Schools*, 22, 465-469.

25. Martin, D. J., & Dunbar, S. B. (1985). Hierarchical factoring in a standardized achievement battery. *Educational and Psychological Measurement*, 45, 343-351.

26. McMorris, R. F., Urbach, S. L., & Connor, M. C. (1985). Effects of incorporating humor in test items. *Journal of Educational Measurement*, 22, 147-155.

27. Rothlisberg, B. A., & Dean, R. S. (1985). Reading comprehension and lateral preference in normal readers. *Psychology in the Schools*, 22, 337-342.

28. Smith, E. R. (1985). Community college reading tests: A statewide survey. *Journal of Reading*, 28, 52-55.

29. Taylor, B. M. (1985). Improving middle-grade students' reading and writing of expository text. *The Journal of Educational Research*, 79, 119-125.

30. Tolfa, D., Scruggs, T. E., & Bennion, K. (1985). Format changes in reading achievement tests: Implications for learning disabled students. *Psychology in the Schools*, 22, 387-391.

31. Wise, S. L., Duncan, A. L., & Plake, B. S. (1985). The effect of introducing third graders to the use of separate answer sheets on the ITBS. *Journal of Educational Research*, 78, 306-309.

32. Baglin, R. F. (1986). A problem in calculating group scores on norm-referenced tests. *Journal of Educational Measurement*, 23, 57-68.

33. Dirgi, D. R. (1986). Does the Rasch model really work for multiple choice items? Not if you look closely. *Journal of Educational Measurement*, 23, 283-298.

34. Estes, R. E., Baum, D. L., & Bray, N. M. (1986). Standard and modified administrations of the Iowa Tests of Basic Skills with learning disabled students. *Perceptual and Motor Skills*, 62, 619-625.

35. Griswold, P. A. (1986). Family outing activities and achievement among fourth graders in compensatory educational funded schools. *The Journal of Educational Research*, 79, 261-266.

36. Guida, F. V., Ludlow, L. H., & Wilson, M. (1986). The mediating effect of time-on-task on the academic anxiety/achievement interaction: A structural model. *Journal of Learning Disabilities*, 19, 21-26.

37. Holloway, S. D. (1986). The relationship of mother's beliefs to children's mathematics achievement: Some effects of sex differences. *Merrill-Palmer Quarterly*, 32, 231-250.

38. Juel, C., Griffith, P. L., & Gough, P. B. (1986). Acquisition of literacy: A longitudinal study of children in first and second grade. *Journal of Educational Psychology*, 78, 243-255.

39. Knoff, H. M., Cotter, V., & Coyle, W. (1986). Differential effectiveness of receptive language and visual-motor assessments in identifying academically gifted elementary school students. *Perceptual and Motor Skills*, 63, 719-725.

40. Ladd, G. W., & Price, J. M. (1986). Promoting children's cognitive and social competence: The relation between parents' perceptions of task difficulty and children's perceived and actual competence. *Child Development*, 57, 446-460.

41. Powers, S., Escamilla, K., & Haussler, M. M. (1986). The California Achievement Test as a predictor of reading ability across race and sex. *Educational and Psychological Measurement*, 46, 1067-1070.

42. Uphoff, J. K., & Gilmore, J. (1986). Pupil age at school entrance—How many are ready for success? *Young Children*, 41 (2), 11-16.

43. Hildebrand, M., & Hoover, H. D. (1987). A comparative study of the reliability and validity of the Degrees of Reading Power and the Iowa Tests of Basic Skills. *Educational and Psychological Measurement*, 47 (4), 1091-1098.

44. Kurtz, B. E., & Borkowski, J. G. (1987). Development of strategic skills in impulsive and reflective children: A longitudinal study of metacognition. *Journal of Experimental Child Psychology*, 43, 129-148.

45. Wilson, M., Suriyawongse, S., & Moore, A. (1988). The effects of ceiling rules on the internal consistency reliability of a mathematics achievement test. *Educational and Psychological Measurement*, 48 (1), 213-217.

Review of the Iowa Tests of Basic Skills, Forms G and H by ROBERT L. LINN, Professor of Education, University of Colorado at Boulder, Boulder, CO:

Forms G and H of the Iowa Tests of Basic Skills (ITBS) continue a tradition that began more than half a century ago with the development of the first edition, then called the Iowa Every Pupil Test of Basic Skills, in 1935. As is nicely documented in a Riverside promotional brochure entitled "Research that Built the Iowa Tests of Basic Skills," there has been a steady stream of University of Iowa doctoral dissertations and faculty research related to the ITBS throughout the history of the tests.

One cannot help but be impressed by the scope and depth of this accumulated body of research. It provides the rationale for such specifics as the use of multiple-choice spelling items as valid substitutes for list-dictation tests (see page 81 of the Manual for School Administrators, hereafter referred to as the Manual), the averaging of grade-equivalent (GE) scores (Manual, p. 162), and the rejection of the Rasch model for purposes of vertical equating different levels of an achievement test ("Research that Built the ITBS," p. 10). The research also documents the efforts that have gone into issues of bias (Manual, pp. 156–159) and, as was recently demonstrated by the reliance on the ITBS data base in the Congressional Budget Office (1986; 1987) studies of trends in educational achievement (also see Manual, pp. 148–155), the associated data files provide a valuable resource for addressing a wide range of questions about educational achievement.

TEST CONTENT AND TRADITIONAL EVIDENCE OF VALIDITY. Of course, the research is, perhaps, more compelling for this reviewer than for most teachers and school administrators where the ITBS is used or who must decide upon an achievement test battery for their use. More importantly, as the Manual sensibly advises, the research and statistical results and, for that matter, reviews such as this, can be expected only to assist judgments of potential users and not provide the primary basis for the evaluation. Instead, the potential user is advised that "your final evaluation must rest primarily upon your own critical item-by-item inspection of the test itself and your own analysis of its content in relation to the appropriateness of objectives for your pupils, teachers, school and community" (Manual, p. 73). This is good advice.

Based on a comparison of the item content in relationship to the instructional objectives I would like schools to have, my own evaluation is positive. Given my own biases, I would prefer less emphasis on some skills (e.g., fractions, which for Level 14 are used in 14% of the Concepts items, 41% of the Problem Solving items, and 33% of the Computation items) and more on others. Given the constraints of a standardized survey test battery, however, the content coverage seems excellent. Certainly, the tests attempt to do more than measure factual recall or literal comprehension. However, as the Manual indicates, my evaluation is no substitute for that of educators who are using or considering the ITBS.

The ITBS has gone through all the traditional hoops in providing content-related validity evidence. As is true of other major test batteries, the content specifications are based, in part, on analyses of textbooks and other instructional materials, judgments by curriculum experts, frequency of occurrence of vocabulary, and reviews by "professionals from diverse cultural groups for fairness and appropriateness of content for pupils of different backgrounds: geographic, urban/rural, sex, race, etc." (Manual, p. 74). The specifications are also influenced by feedback from users and by value judgments regarding the importance of the material. Test items are shaped by studies of student errors, item analyses, and studies of differential item performance by gender and racial-ethnic group.

WHAT'S NEW? Forms G and H have much in common with their predecessors, Forms 7 and 8, or, for that matter, Forms 1 thru 6. Changes have been made in the format, in the degree of grade-to-grade overlap, and the number of items per test. Revisions also have been made to bring the test content up to date. With the exception of one of the Language tests, Usage and Expression, however, the Forms G and H tests are designed to measure the same skills as their counterparts in Forms 7 and 8 and the tests have quite similar content specifications.

The addition of "Expression" to the Language Usage test reflects an attempt to go beyond the measurement of a student's ability to recognize correct usage. In the second part of the test students are asked to judge the appropriateness and effectiveness of expression. Although the part 2 items appear to demand different skills than the part 1 items, a comparison of the Form 7 Usage test with the Form G Usage and Expression test in terms of their internal consistencies and correlations with other measures suggests that the constructs being measured are quite similar. In comparison to the earlier Usage test, there is a slight tendency for the Usage and Expression test to have lower correlations with Spelling and Vocabulary while having higher correlations with Reading, Total Work-Study, and Total Mathematics. But the differences in correlations are small.

The change of greatest interest to this reviewer is not in the Basic Battery, but the addition of two new supplements, Listening and Writing, to the Multilevel Battery. Tests obviously send signals as to what is considered important. Regardless of how well essay scores can be predicted from multiple-choice tests, the messages that essay and multiple-choice tests send about the importance of writing are quite different. The addition of essays prompts, even in a supplement, raises the importance of student writing.

SUPPORTING DOCUMENTS AND TECHNICAL BACKUP. The Manual and Teacher's Guides deserve very high marks. They are clearly written and provide solid information and advice. Test administration instructions are easy to follow and consistent with good practice. Good descriptions of the norms and the various types of scores are provided. The Manual is on the required reading list for my introductory educational measurement course, not only as an illustration of a high quality manual, but because of its utility in teaching fundamental measurement principles.

The technical characteristics of the tests and of the standardization studies live up to the standards of the better achievement test batteries. Internal consistency and equivalent-form reliability coefficients are in the expected range (mostly, mid .80s to low .90s). In a number of places the Manual goes beyond the minimum essentials and reports useful information that is often missing from other test manuals. The description of the 1984 standardization sample, for example, gives an indication of school participation rates by including a classification of the schools as to the number that were the first, second, third, or fourth choice or greater according to the random selections within strata. Standard errors of measurement are reported for up to as many as nine GE score intervals, which enables users to identify the GE score ranges where each level of the test provides the most reliable measurement.

SCORE REPORTS. As is true of other major achievement test batteries, the user is presented with a bewildering array of possible score reports (e.g., class lists, student press-on labels, criterion-referenced skills analysis, individual item analyses, class diagnostic reports, building and system averages, narrative reports). Although each report is clearly described in the Manual, it seems unlikely the typical user would get a clear sense of the relative advantages and disadvantages of the various alternatives. On the other hand, typical users are apt to find all they are looking for, and then some, from one of the four standard score reporting plans that are suggested.

LIVING UP TO STATED PURPOSES. Overall, the ITBS comes out with flying colors when the criteria that are traditionally used to evaluate an achievement test battery are applied. The test reliabilities are high. Interpretations are aided by good norms and excellent supporting materials in the Manual and Teacher's Guides. Reasonable evidence of content validity is presented, but users are encouraged to rely on their own careful, item-by-item analyses. However, validity depends on use and interpretation of test scores, which, in turn, depend on purposes of measurement. Thus, to evaluate the tests, it is important to consider the purposes they are intended to serve.

The first two sentences on page 1 of the Manual state the philosophy of educational measurement that has guided the testing program since its inception in simple, albeit demanding, language. "The purpose of measurement is to provide information which can be used in improving instruction. Measurement has value to the extent that it results in better decisions which directly affect pupils." These general statements lead to high expectations, not only for the information the tests provide, but for the uses that are made of the information and the evidence that is provided to support a judgment about the instructional value the tests have when used in particular ways. Together with the nine more specific purposes of the ITBS that are listed (e.g., "determine the developmental level of the pupil in order to better adapt materials and instructional procedures to individual needs and abilities," "diagnose specific qualitative strengths and weaknesses," Manual, p. 1), these statements also provide a framework for evaluating the battery.

Are teachers better able to "adapt materials and instructional procedures to individual needs and abilities" based on the test results? Do they? Is student learning improved when "qualitative strengths and weaknesses" are identified with the ITBS? Is learning better when the tests are used to "indicate the extent to which individual pupils have the specific readiness skills and abilities needed to begin instruction or to proceed to the next step in a planned instructional sequence"? For all the emphasis that we specialists in educational measurement place on hard evidence of validity and quantification, we must rely mostly on logic, anecdotes, and opinions when it comes to answering such questions.

Test manuals do not, and by tradition are not really expected to, provide evidence, either qualitative or quantitative, that the answers to such questions are in the affirmative. Thus, for me to criticize the ITBS for this lack is more a criticism of our accepted professional practice than it is of the ITBS, per se. As is articulated by Messick (in press), however, a broad view of the validation process requires that greater attention be given to the consequences of test use and interpretation. The need for better evidence about the degree to which, and under what conditions, the laudable general and specific purposes of the ITBS are achieved suggests an important research agenda for future University of Iowa doctoral students, and, I might add, the larger educational measurement research community.

REVIEWER'S REFERENCES

Congressional Budget Office. (1986). *Trends in educational achievement.* Washington, DC: Author.

Congressional Budget Office. (1987). *Educational achievement: Explanations and implications of recent trends.* Washington, DC: Author.

Messick, S. (in press). Validity. In R. L. Linn (Ed.), *Educational measurement* (3rd ed.). New York: Macmillan.

Review of the Iowa Tests of Basic Skills, Forms G and H by VICTOR L. WILLSON, Professor of Educational Psychology, Texas A&M University, College Station, TX:

The Iowa Tests of Basic Skills (ITBS) represent the state of the art in multilevel comprehensive test batteries. The name indicates that basic skills are being tested, but that is an unfortunate historical accident, because the tests cover the grade school curricula between kindergarten and grade 9 far more comprehensively than what has come to be associated with basic skills testing in the United States.

The authors present nine purposes for the test. While this is arguably too many, even for a comprehensive test battery, the authors can be given the benefit of the doubt on most of them, even though they do not specifically address validity concerns for most of them. Paraphrased, these purposes are to: 1. Determine the developmental level of the pupil for instruction; 2. Diagnose students' specific strengths and weaknesses; 3. Indicate students' specific readiness skills for instruction; 4. Provide information for instructional grouping; 5. Diagnose group strengths and weaknesses for curriculum change; 6. Compare alternative instructional procedures; 7. Serve as a dependent variable in experimentation; 8. Provide a behavioral model with feedback; and 9. Report performance on basic skills.

Of these nine purposes the test authors have provided the fullest support for the last one, the traditional content purpose for such tests. The reporting provided by the publisher's scoring service is sufficiently rich to allow fulfillment of the third purpose, to diagnose strengths and weaknesses, and the fourth purpose, instructional grouping. Few will quibble with using the tests for comparing institutional units, instructional approaches or for experimentation. The remaining purposes are problematical because of vague definitions and little specific information or validity support. Developmental level is discussed only as an internally derived standard score, and the authors' definition is not consistent with any of the major concepts of development as a psychological, social, and physical construct of the maturation of children in which markers are observed and theoretical progressions are supported. Similarly, the term readiness is used in the third purpose but is discussed only for the Early Primary Battery for ages 5 and 6. Finally, the authors discuss a behavioral model intended to demonstrate expected behaviors and provide feedback. This model simply does not exist, or if it exists is not apparent in the materials provided to teachers. This is not to say such a model could not be developed out of the extensive reports available to the teacher, of which more will be said later. In summary, however, the authors' purposes are not all necessarily well-supported from the normative information provided.

The physical aspects of the tests are excellent. Line drawings are professionally done. Administration instructions to teachers are clear and straightforward to follow. Practice tests are available at all levels for children to improve their test-taking skills prior to regular testing. While practice tests are recommended for children with language handicaps or who have not had testing experience, one might well argue for their use as a normal part of the testing program. Unfortunately, no research reporting use or disuse of practice tests was presented.

Test responses can be obtained in several ways, including responses made directly on the tests (consumable) at the early primary levels and answer sheets that are hand or machine scorable. The tests can be scored locally or scored by the Riverside Scoring Service (RSS) using MRC type answer sheets only. The difference between local scoring and remote electronic scoring is in the wealth of scoring information available from the scoring service. One must balance that against the time lost in sending and receiving information. This has long been a problem in scoring, and the authors give no information regarding the time required for electronic scoring, nor are there any guarantees for turnaround. The instructional usefulness of tests such as the ITBS rests on immediate feedback to the teacher. For this reason hand or local machine scoring is often preferred for beginning-of-school testing. Larger districts will have the resources to develop sophisticated subtest and item analyses comparable to those provided by the scoring service, but smaller districts will rarely be able to do so. It behooves the test developers to expand this area. There are many inexpensive scoring machines now available, and most districts have microcomputers. It is time to let this technology work for small districts.

Norm tables are oriented toward grade equivalents, a well-known proclivity of the Iowa measurement researchers. While the merits of grade equivalents have been long debated, and will not be resurrected here, it was disappointing not to find among the many tables a simple raw-score-to-percentile conversion table. I find this omission unfortunate in an otherwise well-designed set of norm tables. One can convert raw scores to grade equivalents and then apply the grade equivalent-to-percentile conversion table, but it is awkward and hides the distribution of raw scores, which is immediately apparent in direct conversion tables. The authors' use of a Developmental Scale Score (DSS) is questionable. Few school district personnel are trained to understand or correctly interpret such scores. They are confusing at best, potentially harmful through misinterpretation at worst. To their credit the authors have refrained from reliance on latent trait theory in deriving or reporting scaled scores. The potential for confusion in interpreting latent trait parameter estimates outweighs any advantages for school use.

The samples from which the norms were constructed appear to have been carefully developed. Both public and private schools were sampled. Obtaining national samples is a difficult task at best and the ITBS researchers have done as good a job as can be done given the fact that there is no means to compel sampled schools to participate.

Internal consistency reliabilities are provided within level at two testing times (three for kindergarten). As is usual the tests at the lowest levels yielded the lowest values, mostly in the .70s. Reliabilities increase for a given test across level, as is consistent with increasing variance in achievement. A few reliabilities are troublesome, especially those for the computation test M-3, in which for the upper levels the percentage of students completing the test is less than two-thirds. This may be a reliable outcome, but a mathematics teacher would prefer to have information on the items rather than incompletion. If the tests are to be used diagnostically, here is a place where the time limits might be ignored (which obviates the use of norms other than those locally developed). Test M-3 is the only one with this anomaly. Beyond the first several levels the internal consistencies are in the .80s with some in the .90s, quite good for separate tests in such batteries.

Stability reliabilities are provided for intervals of 1 to 5 years. These are difficult to interpret because of their confounding of instructional effects, developmental variance, and ability. Magnitudes of 1-year interval are almost all in the .7 to .9 range, while 2-year interval magnitudes are generally in the mid .7 range. Correlations for 3-year intervals are only slightly lower, with most correlations above .7, none below .60. Users should interpret these statistics with caution.

As was discussed earlier, validities must be interpreted in the context of the purpose for the test. Thus, numerous validity topics must be addressed. The traditional validity of this and most comprehensive test batteries is the content validity of the various tests. Here the authors have done an excellent job, and a very complete book of topic areas gives the item associated with each topic for each level and the difficulty at each test time. An appendix gives objectives and references items to each objective. The area that is missing is reference to any sort of hierarchical or learning taxonomy for items. Not all the items are memory demand items, and some attempt to classify the processes being called upon should be considered. This is not to insist upon Bloom's taxonomy or upon any other, but an indication of the kind of skill or process being called on is surely part of the development requirements for items and could be included for the benefit of teachers and school districts.

The ITBS authors present extensive item information for those who intend to use the test for criterion-referenced test purposes. A feature available in the RSS scoring service is item level information for each child indicating topic areas, items sampling the topic, and correct or incorrect response for each item. This is a step in the right direction, that is, toward true diagnostic use for tests such as the ITBS. The authors are encouraged to continue this emphasis and move toward diagnostic-instructional assistance by providing option level analyses and associated instructional information. While this may sound overly ambitious, such analyses have already been performed in great detail in arithmetic by Brown and Burton (1978). Item level information will be useful to teachers when it is available quickly, points toward specific problems in learning, and suggests instructional stategies of demonstrated potency for remediation. It is expecting too much for the test manuals to contain this information, but either explicit references to such information or companion works should be the goal if the tests are really to be used for the individual diagnostic and instructional purposes claimed for them.

Factor analyses were performed on the test intercorrelations at each level. The authors indicate that analyses consistently yielded three factors, a verbal or reading factor, a mathematics or numerical factor, and a mechanics of language factor. The procedures reported appear appropriate, and while factor analysis results are not provided, it is possible to examine them by using the published intercorrelation matrices in a factor analysis program. The results appear reasonable and support construct validation for the tests.

Criterion-related validity is supported by reports of correlations between ITBS tests and the Cognitive Abilities Test, (CogAT), published with the ITBS. As has been pointed out in previous reviews, the correlations are all moderately high but show little differentiation among the verbal, quantitative, and nonverbal components of the CogAT. This is commonly interpreted as the domination of school achievement by the *g*-factor or crystallized intelligence factor. It is probably an indication of the limitation of achievement tests to measure the more difficult outcomes of schooling related to reasoning, problem solving, and creativity.

Freedom from overt racial and gender bias has been demonstrated by the authors using careful and elaborate procedures. These procedures included content evaluation, differential item function (item bias) analyses, and other research studies. The studies appear to have been carefully conducted in good faith and the authors are commended for their care in addressing these issues so well. Study results consistently showed an absence of overt or statistical bias and should reassure potential purchasers regarding the tests' freedom from gender or racial bias.

The ITBS is not a perfect battery, but it represents the best that modern educational measurement can produce. More is being demanded of all kinds of tests in modern culture, and more will be demanded of the ITBS, particularly in the instruction-testing interface. For users who want an excellent cross-level achievement battery and whose instructional objectives are reasonably reflected in the ITBS's content, these tests can be recommended.

REVIEWER'S REFERENCE

Brown, J. S., & Burton, R. R. (1978). Diagnostic models for procedural bugs in basic mathematical skills. *Cognitive Science*, 2, 155-192.

[156]

Iowa Tests of Educational Development™ [Eighth Edition]. Purpose: "To assess intellectual skills that are important in adult life and provide the basis for continued learning." Grades 9–10, 11–12; 1942–88; ITED™ ; 9 scores: Correctness and Appropriateness of Expression (Test E), Ability to Do Quantitative Thinking (Test Q), Analysis of Social Studies Materials (Test SS), Analysis of Natural Science Materials (Test NS), Ability to Interpret Literary Materials (Test L), Vocabulary (Test V), Use of Sources of Information (Test SI), Composite, Reading Total; 2 forms: X-8, Y-8; 2 levels (Grades 9–10, Level I; Grades 11–12, Level II) in each form; 1988 price data: $44.40 per 25 test booklets with one Directions for Administration (specify Form X-8 or Form Y-8 and test level); $14.55 per 50 MRC answer sheets to be scored by publisher (includes materials needed for machine scoring; specify Level I or Level II); $7.80 per 50 parent communications brochures entitled "ITED Scores and What They Mean"; $1.23 per Directions for Administration ('88, 13 pages); $4.50 per Teacher, Administrator, and Counselor Manual ('88, 87 pages); $5.46 per Norms Booklet ('88, 111 pages); 250(280) minutes; prepared under the direction of Leonard S. Feldt, Robert A. Forsyth, and Stephanie D. Alnot with the assistance of Timothy N. Ansley and Gayle B. Bray; The Riverside Publishing Co.*

For reviews by Edward Kifer and James L. Wardrop of an earlier form, see 9:534 (5 references); see also T3:1193 (14 references); for reviews by C. Mauritz Lindvall and John E. Milholland of an earlier form, see 8:20 (15 references); see T2:20 (85 references); for reviews by Ellis Batton Page and Alexander G. Wesman of earlier forms, see 6:14 (23 references); for reviews by J. Murray Lee and Stephen Wiseman, see 5:17 (9 references); for a review by Eric Gardner, see 4:17 (3 references); for reviews by Henry Chauncey, Gustav J. Froelich, and Lavone A. Hanna, see 3:12.

TEST REFERENCES

1. Albanese, M. A., & Forsyth, R. A. (1984). The one-, two-, and modified two-parameter latent trait models: An empirical study of relative fit. *Educational and Psychological Measurement*, 44, 229-246.

2. Feldt, L. S., Steffen, M., & Gupta, N. C. (1985). A comparison of five methods for estimating the standard error of measurement at specific score levels. *Applied Psychological Measurement*, 9, 351-361.

3. Stockard, J., Lang, D., & Wood, J. W. (1985). Academic merit, status variables, and students' grades. *Journal of Research and Development in Education*, 18 (2), 12-20.

4. Allen, N. J., Ansley, T. N., & Forsyth, R. A. (1987). The effect of deleting content-related items on IRT ability estimates. *Educational and Psychological Measurement*, 47 (4), 1141-1152.

Review of the Iowa Tests of Educational Development [Eighth Edition] by S. E. PHILLIPS, Associate Professor of Measurement, Michigan State University, East Lansing, MI:

Developing an achievement test for high school is more difficult than for lower grade levels. The difficulty is that there is no common or standard curriculum across students or schools. Thus, the earliest high school achievement tests were specific end-of-course examinations. But as the authors of the Iowa Tests of Educational Development (ITED) indicate, "Standardized tests serve their most valuable function . . . when they focus on the extent to which students are achieving the long-range educational goals toward which the various methods and materials converge."

The ITED is designed to measure the important skills of adult daily life. But these are not the skills most educators associate with minimum competency testing. Rather, the test is designed to measure fundamental goals of education, that is, important generalized skills independent of specific coursework or type of curriculum. These generalized skills represent cumulative learning that develops over time as the result of exposure to many kinds of materials and instruction both in and out of school.

The types of items found in the ITED resemble what some educators have recently called "higher order thinking skills." They include multiple-step problems and the integration and synthesis of knowledge; they do *not* include short-term isolated bits of information teachable in short cram sessions. In a recent speech to the Michigan School Testing Conference, Dr. Al Hieronymous, former director of the Iowa Tests of Basic Skills (ITBS), indicated the choice was between measuring what certain groups of kids can do now versus what one thinks they ought to be able to do. ITED has chosen the latter approach and is to be applauded for sticking to the belief in long range outcomes of education at a time of great pressure to test narrow and specifically coachable outcomes.

Perhaps the most frequent criticisms leveled against standardized achievement test batteries today are not technical, but social. Critics charge that such tests are unfair or inappropriate because some groups of students do not do very well. To the extent that malnutrition, crime, lack of sustained effort, failure to complete assignments, poor attendance, and so on interfere with attainment of long range education objectives, those problems must be addressed. But schools should not be forced to give up useful evaluation tools such as standardized tests just because a few educators do not use them wisely. The authors of the ITED carefully describe appropriate uses of the ITED and encourage educators to use a variety of sources of information in making educational decisions. But they also note that, "Unlike grades, [standardized achievement batteries] don't require that differences in teachers' grading standards or differences in courses be taken into account."

The ITED uses a unique overlapping item format like that found in the multilevel ITBS battery. This results in a block of common items included in both Levels I and II. This design strengthens the technical quality of the test by providing a built-in empirical link for placing both test levels on the same developmental scale. The overlapping design allows for more accurate equating than would be possible with two tests of completely different items, content, and difficulty. But it also allows for enough easier unique items in Level I and harder unique items in Level II to provide an adequate floor and ceiling for the battery. Data in the manual suggest that much less than one percent of students receive maximum scores and that only about five percent score below the chance level.

Extensive scaling and equating procedures were completed on the ITED to provide users with useful comparative and normative information. Studies were carefully planned and designed to use the most recent technological developments advantageously. Both traditional and item response theory techniques were utilized. The test manuals provide a concise and understandable summary of the specific steps required to place Forms X-8 and Y-8, for Levels I and II on the common standard score scale of the original edition. The similarity in raw score to standard score conversions for the two forms of the Eighth Edition suggest that the authors were successful in building parallel forms of the test.

The authors made a conscious choice to keep standard scores comparable across editions to facilitate longitudinal growth comparisons. For example, no matter which form, level, or edition a student has taken, a standard score of 15 represents the same level of excellence. The tradeoff is a sacrifice of the comparability of standard scores across subtests as achievement over the years has changed more in some subjects than others. The importance of meaningful growth measures supports the retention of the original scale.

The ITED provides normative information for grades 9, 10, 11, and 12 for three times of year: fall, winter, and spring. This information was obtained by equating the ITED to the Tests of Academic Proficiency (TAP) which had been standardized on a large representative national sample of high school students in 1984. As with all achievement batteries, getting randomly selected districts to participate in standardization studies is difficult. One often must settle for second, third, fourth, or other backup choices and it is probable that users agree to participate more often than nonusers do. But by piggybacking on the ITBS/TAP standardization, ITED was able to benefit from the extensive efforts made to obtain the best possible sample, an effort that probably would have been too costly to replicate.

In addition, because nearly all Iowa schools participate in the Iowa Testing Program, the authors were able to carefully select the sample for the equating study. Sets of anchor items that had been calibrated in the 1984 national standardization sample using a three-parameter conditional logistic model were selected to match the content of the corresponding ITED subtests. The quality of the normative information was also enhanced because the authors combined professional judgement with the appropriate mathematical techniques at all stages of the process. Although some professionals might argue for direct estimation of norms via a separate national sample, the cost of getting school districts already overburdened with too much state and local testing to participate might have resulted in estimation on a much smaller and perhaps less representative national sample.

The ITED emphasizes norms that are simple and easy for the user to understand. The user is given sufficient normative data for appropriate uses of the test but not overwhelmed with numerical data. Two basic kinds of scores are provided: developmental standard scores and percentile ranks. The former address growth; the latter address status within the norm group. Perhaps the greatest advantage of achievement batteries such as the ITED is the provision of developmental scores that make tracking of longitudinal growth possible. Grade equivalents, which tend to lack extrinsic meaning at the high school level, are *not* provided. For the interested user, the manual describes how percentile ranks can be converted to stanines and normal curve equivalents and a conversion table is provided. No separate socioeconomic, urban, parochial, or sex norms are provided. However, the utility of such norms is debatable. Schools may get a false sense of security from good performance in a specialized norm group while not being competitive nationally for their students who wish to go on to college. Given the judgmental reviews conducted to identify any potential sources of bias, the national norms should be adequate for most students. In addition, the authors provide and encourage the use of separately derived norms for school averages.

Validity and reliability data are reasonably complete and well-documented in the manual. Validity is described under the three common headings of content, criterion, and construct. The authors appropriately emphasize content validity. The manual indicates that approximately five times as many items as needed were tried out for the Eighth Edition. This is impressive because it indicates the authors were able to retain only the very best items (using multiple criteria) for the final forms.

In addition to studying the content specifications, the authors suggest that educators who really want to know what the test measures should actually take the test as a student would. The educators should then ask themselves if the items test skills they think their students should be learning. I would add that in cases where the ITED tests skills that a school is not teaching, the educator should ask why not. If the educator is unable to discover a defensible rationale for the choice, the educator might consider the possibility of curriculum revision.

Although, as indicated, judgmental item bias reviews were conducted, no statistical differential item performance data were reported. Because the various statistical techniques seem not to agree with each other or with judgmental reviews, such data might not be particularly helpful to users. But users might be interested in summary data for different sex and ethnic groups if sample sizes are sufficiently large to provide accurate estimates.

Under criterion validity, the manual provides correlations with other measures. These data are as expected. Correlations with grades were in the 60s and 70s for high school and 40s for college. Correlations with ITBS were in the 70s and 80s (.92 with ITBS composite). Correlations with college entrance exams were in the 80s to low 90s (composite) for the ACT and high 80s Verbal (V), low 80s Quantitative (Q) for the SAT. ACT prediction equations are also given by grade and time of year with an emphasis on confidence interval interpretations. Noticeably absent from this section are correlations with other achievement test batteries, including the TAP to which it was equated to obtain national norms.

For construct validity, the manual provides ITED subtest intercorrelations. As expected for subtests that all measure intellectual skills, depend on reading ability, and do not measure statistically independent traits, the battery intercorrelations are reasonably high. They range from the high 60s for Q,E (Q: Ability to Do Quantitative Thinking; E: Correctness and Appropriateness of Expression), and Q,V (V: Vocabulary) to the low 80s for SS,NS (SS: Analysis of Social Studies Materials; NS: Analysis of Natural Science Materials) and SS,L (L: Ability to Interpret Library Materials). No correlations with general ability (IQ) tests or other tests that might demonstrate the convergent/divergent validity of the ITED are given.

The ITED is a highly reliable test. All subtest KR_{20} reliabilities exceed the .85 recommended for individual student decisions, ranging from the high 80s to the mid 90s. Corresponding standard errors of measurement are also provided. One-year interval stability/parallel forms reliabilities ranged from the high 70s to low 90s. The authors indicated the test was too long to obtain traditional parallel forms data.

The authors are to be commended for providing difference score reliability data for all pairs of subtests. These reliabilities were generally in the 40s, 50s, and 60s, which clearly indicated that profile data is not reliable enough for decisions but is suggestive of relative strengths and weaknesses.

The authors also acknowledge that reading ability is a major requirement in all the subtests and that poor readers are unlikely to do well. Like other individual student factors that might affect accurate measurement, lack of adequate reading ability should be considered when interpreting individual student scores.

The authors also provide an interesting treatment of the issue of readability. In addition to calculating the traditional Dale-Chall index which provides an approximate grade level indicator, a normative approach was also presented. An index was calculated which could be compared to that of other written materials such as textbooks, newspapers, and magazines. For example, using this index, the authors note that "the readability of the Test NS passages appears to be somewhat more difficult than the average science textbooks and slightly less difficult than general interest magazine articles on scientific topics." In comparison, the Dale-Chall formula indicated 7th to 11th grade level passages in the same test. The normative technique appeared to alleviate some anomalous results of the traditional indices on the literary passages.

The ITED appears to be relatively unspeeded. Reported completion rates were in the 90s and nearly all items were answered by 95% of the students. In addition, the test authors and publisher have paid close attention to details that make test administration easier for the user. For example, to avoid confusion, separate answer sheets in different colors with correct beginning and ending item numbers for each subtest have been designed for Levels I and II.

In summary, the ITED is an excellent achievement battery. It is a good choice for those interested in assessing the full range of general academic skills at the high school level.

[157]

Irenometer. Purpose: Measures attitudes toward peace. Adults; 1984; no manual; available without charge from author; [12] minutes; Panos D. Bardis; the Author.*

[158]

Jackson Vocational Interest Survey. Purpose: "To assist high school and college students and adults with educational and career planning." High school and over; 1976–85; JVIS; 34 basic interest scale scores: Creative Arts, Performing Arts, Mathematics, Physical Science, Engineering, Life Science, Social Science, Adventure, Nature-Agriculture, Skilled Trades, Personal Service, Family Activity, Medical Service, Dominant Leadership, Job Security, Stamina, Accountability, Teaching, Social Service, Elementary Education, Finance, Business, Office Work, Sales, Supervision, Human Relations Management, Law, Professional Advising, Author Journalism, Academic Achievement, Technical Writing, Independence, Planfulness, Interpersonal Confidence; 1987 price data: $19 per 25 reusable test booklets ('85, 14 pages); $4.75 per 25 hand-scorable answer sheets; $4.75 per 25 profiles; $10.50 per manual ('77, 107 pages); $17.50 per examination kit; $3.25 per basic report (4-page computer report) and $7 per extended report (14-page computer report), available from publisher (cost of each includes machine-scorable answer sheets, printed reports, interpretive guide, and mailing narrative reports); French edition available (test booklets and extended reports only); Spanish edition available (test booklets only); (45–60) minutes; Douglas N. Jackson; Research Psychologists Press, Inc.*

For reviews by Charles Davidshofer and Ruth G. Thomas, see 9:542; see also T3:1204 (1 reference).

TEST REFERENCES

1. Jackson, D. N., Holden, R. R., Locklin, R. H., & Marks, E. (1984). Taxonomy of vocational interests of academic major areas. *Journal of Educational Measurement*, 21, 261-275.

Review of the Jackson Vocational Interest Survey by DOUGLAS T. BROWN, Professor of Psychology and Coordinator of School Psychology, James Madison University, Harrisonburg, VA:

The Jackson Vocational Interest Survey (JVIS) is a multivariate vocational interest device designed for use with adolescents and adults at the high school level and older. The test consists of 289 item pairs that factor into 34 scales composed of 17 items each. It can be hand scored (judged a convenience) or interpreted by computer. The computer-scored version of the instrument is clearly preferable because it yields substantially more information and represents more fairly the basis upon which the test was designed. The vocabulary for individual test items is stated to be at the seventh grade level, but appears to be conceptually much higher than that for certain items.

Jackson has chosen to use a rational/empirical approach for development of this instrument. Thus, a number of vocational interest dimensions were identified in an a priori manner and items developed to measure these dimensions. This contrasts with the technique employed in the Strong Campbell Interest Inventory and other instruments in which items are developed to discriminate among professional or occupational groups. The 34 scales are divided into those dealing with work roles and those with work styles. The work styles dimensions appear to be a combination of expressed needs and personality styles.

The JVIS can be administered individually or in groups. The manual contains adequate instructions for administration and hand scoring. The test takes from 45 minutes to 1 hour to complete, which is reasonable if the computerized scoring technique is employed. This amount of time is excessive for the hand-scored version compared with other comparable instruments.

Norms for the JVIS are based on a variety of samples from colleges, universities, and high school students. Separate norms were developed for males and females. The norm tables presented in the manual appear to be subsets of subjects derived from larger samples collected from colleges and high schools. These subsamples were balanced for sex and other demographic characteristics.

The care with which the JVIS was standardized is exemplary. The items, which are set up in ipsative format, were rationally selected to form the underlying subscales. Extensive confirmatory factor analysis was performed assuming othogonality among factors. Redundant items, or those that produced oblique relationships, were removed. Individual item loadings in the form of biserial correlations range from a mean of .46 to .99. Typical loadings are in the high .60s and low .70s. This level of factor integrity is excellent for a test of this type. Reliability data are also presented for internal consistency and test retest reliability. These coefficients range from .73 to .91 suggesting reasonable stability and internal consistency.

When the JVIS is scored by computer, an individual index of reliability is provided for the person taking the test. This reliability index is essentially a variation of the Spearman Brown Split Half Reliability formula applied to an individual subject. This statistic appears to be interpretable either as a measure of spurious responding or as evidence that a subject has not yet developed consistent job attitudes and interests.

As part of the standardization for the JVIS, occupational profiles were developed by comparing JVIS scaled scores with those obtained on the Strong Vocational Interest Blank (SVIB). Thus, the cluster of scores on the SVIB was used as a predictor to clusters on the JVIS. Through this procedure it was determined that specific patterns of JVIS scaled scores were related to occupational clusters as measured by the SVIB. These include 189 male occupational groups and 89 female occupational groups. The manual presents the mean scale score patterns using the 34 JVIS scales for 278 occupational groups. These groups were then further refined through cluster analysis and yielded 32 occupational clusters.

A number of studies on the validity of the JVIS are presented in the manual. This information appears to have been gathered from a series of rather disjointed studies involving (*a*) prediction of occupational classification, (*b*) concurrent validity analysis with other instruments such as the Strong Vocational Interest Blank, (*c*) prediction of academic college choice, and (*d*) the relationship between the JVIS scaled scores and professional judgment regarding interests of individual subjects. While these validity studies tend to support the integrity of the JVIS, much more extensive research on its validity will be required if it is to reach the status of the more highly developed instruments in this area.

The most useful aspect of the JVIS is its computerized scoring system. The output for this system provides standard score information on each of the 34 primary scales (work roles and work styles). Standard scores are also provided on 10 scales described as general occupational themes (e.g., socialized, helping, conventional, enterprising, communicative) that are theoretically similar to Holland's occupational codes. Standardized score information is provided on 17 academic clusters (e.g., engineering, food science, business). The subject's profile is compared to the 32 occupational classifications and similarities and differences are noted. Based on a subject's top three occupational classifications, a more detailed listing of potential occupations is provided based on the *Directory of Occupational Titles* (*DOT*) code system. Finally, specific references are provided for additional research into the occupational titles drawn from the *DOT*.

The JVIS is a highly sophisticated vocational interest instrument. Its theoretical rationale appears to be well conceptualized and documented. The standardization techniques employed to develop this instrument are in many ways exemplary, especially with regard to the statistical operations employed. Fundamentals of test design such as sample size, reliability, and factor structure have all been attended to with considerable rigor. More information could be presented in the manual with regard to the specific multivariate techniques employed for cluster and pattern analysis. It is impossible to determine, on the basis of the information presented, how these analyses were accomplished. The manual, while attempting to be comprehensive, is often unclearly written and poorly organized. Persons using this test who do not have significant statistical sophistication will find it difficult to understand the structure of the JVIS. In this regard the manual could be rewritten so that less statistically sophisticated users could better conceptualize the structure of this instrument. While this criticism is valid for the JVIS, it is also valid for all instruments using modern multivariate techniques. This underscores the considerable sophistication with which modern instruments are developed compared to their counterparts developed in the 1950s and 1960s.

The JVIS computer output, while exemplary in many ways, could be improved especially through more careful analysis of the general occupational themes. These appear to be added as an afterthought in order to allow the instrument to be more favorably compared with The Self Directed Search.

The JVIS is a comprehensive instrument that can be seriously considered as an alternative to traditional vocational interest instruments. This instrument has considerable theoretical integrity because of its emphasis on work roles and work styles rather than specific occupations. Computer output from the instrument is highly useful and more comprehensive than that derived from other comparable instruments. The JVIS is a relatively young instrument compared to its counterparts and its ability to compete favorably with these instruments will depend heavily on further validation studies.

Review of the Jackson Vocational Interest Survey by JOHN W. SHEPARD, Associate Professor, University of Toledo, Toledo, OH:

PURPOSE AND SCOPE. The Jackson Vocational Interest Survey (JVIS) is comprehensive and thorough in its approach to assessing occupational and educational interests. Test users receive information regarding their interests in distinct career clusters, academic majors as well as their personal work style. Neutral, middle-of-the-road responses, are discouraged through a "forced-choice" format. The JVIS appropriately plays down the listing of specific preferred occupations and encourages user investigation of broad interest groupings and activities. A single form is utilized for the high school, college, and adult populations it services. Unfortunately, test vocabulary is too sophisticated for many high school students and insufficient norms are provided for adult comparisons. Separate forms for each population are recommended. The JVIS appears most appropriate for users interested in pursuing a traditional college curriculum or professional occupations.

USABILITY. The survey's manual is well organized and generally complete. Readers can gain quick access to key data or closely study the text's pages of statistical charts. Test purposes, and administrative and interpretive procedures are clearly described. Practical examples and case studies are provided in a helpful manner. Test costs for the prepaid, computer-scored, 10-page narrative client report are competitive with similar measures (i.e., Kuder, Strong). The JVIS has the added advantage of being hand scorable. (Hand scoring is not time efficient and should be avoided when individualized counselor attention is restricted.) The 10-page interpretive report provides far more information than either the self-scoring procedure or the four-page report. It is well worth its additional cost. With both narrative reports, less-sophisticated test users may be put off by too much data being "packed" into each page. Data are clearly presented through well-labeled charts using standard scores and percentiles. The longer profile presents data on broad career and educational clusters, work style, specific occupational preferences, and career resource materials. The JVIS's suggested 45–60 minute administration time compares favorably with other measures of occupational preference.

TECHNICAL ELEMENTS. A major problem with the JVIS is its inadequate, geographically narrow normative data. The test norms and contents are at least 10 years old. Normative data "borrowed" from Strong were originally obtained in 1971. The test is normed on three groups of approximately 8,000 high school and college students. One set of 1,900 students were selected from the state of Pennsylvania. A group of 4,400 high school students were drawn from the Province of Ontario. A smaller third group was composed of college students randomly selected from 14 American and 2 Canadian universities. As mentioned, normative data for adult comparison were "borrowed" from a 1971 Strong sample. Clearly a fresh, nationally stratified sample of high school, college, and employed adult populations will be necessary if the JVIS is to be considered a viable instrument.

Test reliability is adequate. Medium test-retest coefficients fall in the mid .80s. The coefficients are based on short retest periods of only 1 to 2 weeks. The manual includes insufficient data on concurrent and predictive validity. Future revisions will need to include additional comparisons with established interest surveys and study the JVIS's predictive validity.

SUMMARY. The JVIS has the potential to be one of the best measures of educational/occupational interest. It is time and cost efficient. It is well constructed and is based on sound theoretical constructs. It provides users with a comprehensive, readable manual and interpretive reports. JVIS interpretative results encourage initial exploration of broad career clusters and provide information regarding the use of relevant occupational resource materials. The test must, however, be renormed to be considered ahead of better standardized interest inventories such as the Kuder and the Strong. Separate test forms and norms for high school, college, and adult populations are recommended. Additional data regarding split-half, test-retest reliability, and concurrent and predictive validity should be included in subsequent manuals.

[159]

Job Training Assessment Program. Purpose: Providing a program that assesses a training applicant's likelihood of success in locally available training programs using a machine-scorable paper and pencil test. Job applicants; 1984–85; JOBTAP II; provides a 3-phase process of placement: assessment, planning, and implementation; 8 scores: Basic Work Skills (Speed, Useful Productivity), Inspection/Visualization, Understanding Training and Work Manuals, Applying Training and Work Manual Information, Performing Simple Calculations, Solving Numerical Problems, Following Complex Procedures; 1988 price data: $750 per basic package including test booklets and answer sheets, test administrator's manual ('84, 13 pages), technical manual ('84, 62 pages), score interpretation guide, software to score all answer sheets on an IBM PC-XT or compatible to produce reports; price data available from publisher for practice workbook for participants, resume booklet, portfolio, implementation plan, and technical report; (180) minutes; Raymond G. Wasdyke, Norman E. Freeberg, and Donald A. Rock (technical report); Educational Testing Service.*

Review of the Job Training Assessment Program by JAMES B. ROUNDS, Associate Professor of Educational Psychology, University of Illinois at Urbana-Champaign, Champaign, IL:

Published in 1984, the Job Training Assessment Program (JOBTAP) is an integrated system of vocational assessment and guidance materials and services. In many ways JOBTAP is similar to other vocational appraisal systems: It is comprehensive, furnishing information on the participant's vocational interests, work experiences, job knowledge, job-seeking skills, and cognitive abilities and skills; it relies on an occupational classification, in this case the U.S. Department of Labor (1979) *Guide for Occupational Exploration* (*GOE*), to organize the reporting of scores and to link scores on the interest, work experience, and cognitive ability scales to occupations; and it can be used in occupational decisions, including both individual counseling decisions and institutional decisions. Unlike its major competitor, the USES Aptitude and Interest Testing Program, JOBTAP is not meant to be all things to all users: It is specifically tailored to the needs of employment programs that have locally available job training programs. As such, JOBTAP is designed to be used for workers with at least a sixth-grade reading level who are unemployed or will be shortly and who need to make job training decisions about entry level semiskilled and skilled occupations.

DESCRIPTION. The JOBTAP kit comes with numerous documents including various manuals (Test Administrator's Manual, Management Guide, Technical Manual), test and answer books (Job Finder Checklist, Job Finder Tests-Book 1, Job Finder-Book 2, Job Finder Answer Book), guidance materials (How to Prepare a Resume Booklet, Implementation Plan Worksheet, Portfolio, Job Finder Workbook), and sample reports (Profile of Interest and Work Experience, Profile of Career Skills, Career Development Plan, Counselor's Report, Administrator's Report). Although a brochure is provided with an overview of the materials, it is hard to find pertinent information. I recommend the user begin with the Management Guide. This Guide orders the materials into a three-step program of assessment, planning, and implementation.

The JOBTAP tests are traditional in form and content. The test materials have been carefully edited and the test booklets have clear illustrations and are easy to follow. The Test Administrator's Manual has explicit instructions for administration. An excellent orientation booklet to the cognitive ability tests, The Job Finder Workbook, introduces each type of test item, furnishes an explanation of what the test measures and how the test relates to job performance, and provides a practice examination with key. A variety of score reports are available. Percentile ranks are reported for the cognitive ability and training skill test scales and raw scores for the interest and work experience scales. Missing from the JOBTAP kit are materials describing the score reports and explaining how to interpret and use these scores. It is only with diligent attention to the Technical manual that the user will discover the scores reported for the 28 Training Skill Categories are predicted scores and that the Training Readiness Index scores were prepared by matching interest and skills with GOE career areas rather than with "locally available training programs" as reported on the Career Development Plan.

The Technical Manual is limited to a discussion of the properties of the cognitive ability measures and the Training Skill Category Tests. Missing is information on the development, validity, and reliability of the Interest and Work Experience Checklist. These tests are described as "adapted from the Department of Labor Interest Checklist." Users are also referred to Freeberg and Vitella (1979) for information on how the Job Knowledge and Job Seeking Skills tests were constructed.

TEST CONSTRUCTION. The JOBTAP system began with a review of the various training and employment programs being offered under the Job Training Partnership Act and a survey to identify projected high-demand occupations. The Educational Testing Service's (ETS, 1982) work on the prerequisite skills for training in Military Occupation Specialties was used to specify the skills required for job training in approximately 60 high-demand civilian occupations. From this analysis, 28 skill objectives for training were identified, and 10-item Training Skill Category Tests—again informed by ETS's Department of Defense research—were developed to measure these objectives. These 28 Training Skill Category Tests were then assigned to one or more of the GOE eight career areas, "because they were judged by vocational guidance specialists to be predominant across a number of jobs or work groups in that occupational area." Eight cognitive ability tests were then constructed and the Training Skill Category Tests were each regressed onto these cognitive ability tests. The resulting 28 regression equations are used to estimate a participant's scores on the Training Skill Categories. A small sample of 100 job training participants (in each classification) was used to develop the regression equations, raising serious questions about the generalizability of the weights composing the Training Skill Categories. With interests and training skills linked to the GOE classification, a composite score, the Training Readiness Index (TRI), was constructed by adding the predicted percentile scores for the Training Skill Categories in a career area to the interest percentile score for the same career area.

The Technical Manual describes the rationale and development of JOBTAP in a belabored fashion without providing sufficient detail to evaluate the test development procedures. The following information is not given: the job analysis used to determine the prerequisite skills for training in the Military Occupation Specialties (MOSs), the criteria used to identify 60 MOSs assumed to be applicable to civilian high-demand occupations, the names of these occupations, and the procedures or criteria used to identify and then to classify the 28 skill objectives in GOE interest areas. The latter decision to use the GOE interest areas for grouping the skill requirements seems questionable because there is no evidence that these interest areas or other interest systems classify occupations according to similar task or skill requirements. On the other hand, the manual provides clear descriptions of the cognitive test battery and the contents of the Training Skill Category tests.

STANDARDIZATION. The normative data used for the ability and skill tests come from 1,310 participants at job training sites. The normative sample includes more black participants (48%) than white participants (40%), more females (55%) than males, and a bimodal distribution of years of full-time employment with 31% of the participants reporting less than 1 year and 34% reporting more than 6 years employment. It is impossible to judge the representativeness of the standardization sample because the authors fail to report a sampling design or national statistics on job training participants.

VALIDITY. Appropriately, considerable attention is given to differential validity of the cognitive ability tests and the GOE grouping of the Training Skill Category Tests. Given the general problem of differential validity, the cognitive ability tests are relatively independent when compared to other multiple aptitude batteries. Correlations between tests representing the verbal, numerical, spatial, and basic work skills areas are relatively low, ranging in the middle .30s. As expected, correlations among tests within these domains are high, suggesting considerable redundancy and therefore limitations on their differential predictability. Differential validity data presented for GOE grouping of the Training Skill Category Tests appear reasonable, but the evidence consists of multiple regression results from the development sample rather than from cross-validation samples. Missing from the Technical Manual is information demonstrating that occupations in the GOE interest groupings have similar training skill requirements.

Surprisingly, the 60-page technical manual does not present direct evidence for the recommended uses of the JOBTAP scores. Criterion-related evidence is reported for the cognitive ability tests scores rather than for the Training Skill Category Tests predicted scores or for the Training Readiness Index (TRI) scores. Criteria include number of weeks spent in training and number of training tasks completed during enrollment rather than job training or posttraining performance measures. Evidence is especially needed for the Training Readiness Index because most job training selection or placement decisions will be based on this measure alone. The authors assert that in future JOBTAP development, "the validity of the TRI will be assessed as a predictor of training and job success both as a single index and in terms of appropriate weights to be assigned to each of the two components that form the composite index." Until then, users are cautioned that because the composite includes gender-linked interest preferences, TRI's "effect in assigning individuals to job training areas would tend for half of these job families to have a greater bias toward placing the participant in gender-stereotyped training programs."

RELIABILITY. Internal consistency reliability is provided for the cognitive ability tests and is minimally satisfactory for this type of test. Coefficients range from .97 to .69 with an average of .79. Research is needed to provide reliability estimates for the interest and work experience measures and the Training Readiness Index. Standard errors of measurement are not reported and percentile bands for score interpretation are needed especially for the Training Readiness Index.

SUMMARY. Notwithstanding the 500 dollars for a starter kit, the JOBTAP system will be popular with employment program managers because the assessment program is a self-contained, integrated package of services, with score reports that rank a participant's likelihood of success in various locally available training programs. Nevertheless, the support for the intended uses of JOBTAP scores is not particularly compelling. Until evidence is presented that the JOBTAP scores are related to job training performance, I suggest users rely on the USES Aptitude and Interest Testing Program.

REVIEWER'S REFERENCES

Freeberg, N., & Vitella, P. (1979). *Program for assessing youth employment skills*. Princeton, NJ: Educational Testing Service.

U.S. Department of Labor. (1979). *Guide for occupational exploration*. Washington, DC: U.S. Government Printing Office.

Educational Testing Service. (1982). *U.S. Army M.O.S. Skills Tests, developed for the Training and Doctrine Command (TRADOC)*. Princeton, NJ: Educational Testing Service.

Review of the Job Training Assessment Program by PAUL W. THAYER, Professor and Head of Psychology, North Carolina State University, Raleigh, NC:

JOBTAP is the trademark for "an integrated system of materials and services . . . that leads directly to placement of people in job training programs." It is primarily designed to fulfill the goals of the Job Training Partnership Act, but could be used by other employment or vocational training programs. It is an unusual program in at least two ways: it has a strong research base, and it concentrates on displaced, unskilled, unemployed, or entry-level workers. The goal of JOBTAP is to give guidance information to unemployed workers faced with job and training decisions, as well as to program administrators and counselors.

The individual completes the Job Finder Checklist, made up of a brief series of questions about the individual's background, education, and work experience, a 210-item interest inventory covering activities that might be involved in potential jobs, and a 50-item test of job-seeking skills and job knowledge. This part of the battery is untimed. When examinees finish, they receive a Job Finder Workbook, which they may complete at the testing center or at home. This booklet provides practice exercises before the Job Finder Tests are administered. The individual has an opportunity to practice taking similar items, to score them, and to practice more if the scores are low.

The Job Finder Test—Book 1 includes a Basic Work Skill Test and an Inspection/Visualization Test. The former measures the ability to perform repetitive operations rapidly and accurately. The latter measures the ability to picture a finished object from a pattern. Book 2 contains a Training and Work Manuals Test, a Work Rules and Procedures Test, a Follow-the-Rule Basic Arithmetic Test, and a Find-the-Rule Arithmetic Test. Answer sheets are sent to the Educational Testing Service (ETS), and computer-generated reports are sent to the testing center in about 5 days. Three reports are provided the individual and counselor: a Profile of Interest and Work Experience, based primarily on the background and interest questions in the Job Finder Checklists; a Profile of Career Skills, based upon the rest of the battery; a Career Development Plan, based upon all results, plus information given to ETS by the center as to the availability of local training programs. This last report gives the individual her/his five highest Training Readiness Indices (TRI) indicating the likelihood of success in locally available training programs. The TRI is a combination of the ability measures and interest scores. The individual also gets instruction in how to prepare a resume, and information from the counselor concerning entry into training programs. Thus, the program provides a complete system. It also provides quarterly reports to the center summarizing all data for all individuals for the current quarter and year-to-date.

The test materials are attractively presented and clearly written. The Test Administration Manual is clear and comprehensive, with all the detailed instructions necessary to give the battery under standard conditions. The Technical Manual contains a wealth of information as to the rationale and research done. Some sophistication in statistics, research design, and measurement is needed for full comprehension, but one can follow most of the arguments with basic measurement knowledge. It would be impossible to give a complete picture of all the information in the Technical Manual in the space allowed, so a summary will be given.

The content of the tests is based upon extensive reviews of available training programs and projected high-demand employment opportunities from the Bureau of Labor Statistics. Training and employment opportunities appeared to be greatest in entry level semiskilled and skilled occupations. Training and task analyses revealed that four major cognitive ability domains were involved: figural, symbolic, numerical, and verbal. Capitalizing on the work they had done for the Department of Defense in assessing prerequisite skills for Military Occupational Specialties, they looked for relevant civilian counterparts. Continued analyses determined that 28 basic skills objectives were relevant for the high-demand civilian occupations. (These later served as the basis for developing 28 tests to be used as criteria for the cognitive battery described above.)

The JOBTAP tests were developed so that they would sample across the domains given above, as well as within higher and lower ability levels. Testing began in 1983, with a total of 2,250 unemployed individuals involved. The fact that most examinees answered slightly more than half of the questions correctly is evidence that the tests are set at the appropriate level of difficulty. Further, over 90 percent of participants completed all items. Internal consistency indices are acceptable.

A number of validation studies were conducted. Ideally, all participants would have taken the eight JOBTAP tests and the 28 specific job-skill criterion tests. As time did not permit the ideal, subsets of tests were systematically assigned to random samples of the norming group. Each such sample took the JOBTAP tests and four of the criterion tests, resulting in 63 separate test packets, with nine replications. This procedure "provided the maximum number of data cases for estimating correlations between predictors and criteria, while still providing a sufficient number of estimated correlations among criteria (i.e., across blocks)." Additional studies with a subsample of participants enrolled in training progams used training performance measures as criteria.

Factor analysis is offered as construct validity evidence. Four orthogonal factors account for 85 percent of the variance: verbal, math, spatial, and basic work skills. These are at slight variance with the model upon which the tests were constructed (see above), but the data clearly demonstrate that a single unitary trait is not being measured.

A variety of evidence is offered for concurrent validity. First, the 28 specific job-skills tests were assigned to 8 of the 12 Vocational Interest Areas taken from the Guide for Occupational Exploration (1979): Scientific, Protective, Mechanical, Industrial, Business Detail, Accomodating, Humanitarian, and Leading/Influencing. Evidence is then offered to show different patterns of prediction from the JOBTAP battery to the criteria across these groups. The Mechanical job family, for example, is predicted primarily by Basic Work Skills, Math, and Spatial factors, while Protection is predicted primarily by Basic Work Skills. Similar data using training performance measures support the power of the battery to make differential predictions for various job families.

The national norming sample is made up of 1,310 people, 44 percent male, 52 percent under 25, 81 percent with no more than high school education, 48 percent black, 40 percent white, and 7 percent Hispanic. Mean differences between males and females occur on three JOBTAP tests, with females exceeding males on Speed and Useful Productivity, and males exceeding females on Inspection/Visualization. Ethnic differences are similar to other findings, with whites scoring significantly higher on cognitive skills than blacks or Hispanics. However, the mean differences tend to be consistently smaller than usually found. Results show mean differences of one-third to one-half a standard deviation, rather than the three-quarters to a whole standard deviation usually found. The TRI scores that combine interest and ability scores show fewer significant ethnic and gender differences.

Overall, this new battery has the potential for aiding a group frequently ignored in vocational guidance, the unemployed who are seeking entry-level occupations. ETS has set up a scoring system that permits continuous collection of data so that norms can be improved, and so that better validity data for the TRI scores can be developed. This reviewer hopes that many agencies will utilize this battery. It is a complete system, appears to be easy to use, and should contribute to better utilization of human resources.

REVIEWER'S REFERENCE

U.S. Department of Labor, Employment, and Training Administration. (1979). *Guide for occupational exploration.* Washington, DC: U.S. Government Printing Office.

[160]

JOB-O, 1985–1995. Purpose: "To facilitate self-awareness, career-awareness, and career exploration." Junior high school through adult; 1981–88; JOB-O; also known as Judgement of Occupational Behavior—Orientation; 9 scores: Education, Interest, Inclusion, Control, Affection, Physical Activity, Hands/Tools/Machinery, Problem-Solving, Creativity-Ideas; 1988 price data: $1.45 per test booklet; $.25 per answer insert folder; $2 per administration (Professional) manual ('87, 20 pages); $1.75 per (Supplemental) JOB-O Dictionary ('88, 21 pages); $5 per specimen set including test booklet, insert folder, JOB-O Dictionary, and administration manual; $89 per computer version; Spanish test booklets and answer sheets available; printed version: (60–65) minutes; computer version: (10) minutes; Arthur Cutler, Francis Ferry, Robert Kauk, and Robert Robinett; CFKR Career Materials, Inc.*

For a review by Bruce J. Eberhardt of an earlier edition, see 9:560.

Review of the JOB-O, 1985–1995, by JAMES W. PINKNEY, Associate Professor of Counseling, East Carolina University, Greenville, NC:

The Judgement of Occupational Behavior—Orientation (JOB-O) is presented by the authors as a reusable career assessment inventory that asks the respondent to make reasonable judgments about nine variables relevant to career exploration. The nine variables are self-estimates made by the respondent who then compares those estimates with the requirements of 120 job titles. The job titles are selected by the authors on the basis of being in demand for the coming decade. Other criteria considered in the selection of the job titles are to include job titles for all levels of education and to include job titles for each of the eight interest groups covered by the JOB-O (see descriptive entry above).

The authors suggest that the JOB-O can be used with "all educational levels" and the manual offers activities for grades 8 through 12. They further comment that the JOB-O has been successfully used with sixth graders on up to college and adult populations. The instructions on how to administer the JOB-O include a note that administrative assistance is mandatory "with special education and slower groups."

The respondent first estimates how long he or she wants to go to school (work right out of high school, community college or special school, or 4 or more years of college). The second variable asks the respondent to select one or two interest groups. The next three variables deal with relationship to others and are based on the FIRO-B: inclusion, control, and affection. Variable six deals with the physical aspect of working and is derived from the *Dictionary of Occupational Titles* physical demands scale. The last three variables estimate preferred involvement with hands/tools/machinery, problem-solving, and creativity/ideas. The last seven variables are estimated on a 3-point scale of "usually or often, sometimes or occasionally, and seldom or rarely."

Once the self-estimates have been made the respondent goes through a mechanical procedure of counting "matches" between the self-estimates and the level of each variable needed by each of the 120 job titles. Those job titles with five or more matches are considered to have a score worth exploring and the respondent is then asked to choose three job titles that are most attractive and do some rudimentary research on those three job titles. The respondent is also reminded to look at the related job titles included on the consumable answer sheet. The inventory concludes with suggestions for gathering additional information such as talking with a counselor, visiting people on the job, and career information references. A *JOB-O Dictionary* is available from the publisher and has career information on all job titles mentioned in the JOB-O.

The JOB-O would appear to have some attractive features for many situations. It is straightforward and for most students would be self-administrating and self-scoring. The idea of biennial updating is appealing, and a Spanish version is available. It obviously would be conducive to group administration and in-class career exploration. Many students (and parents) would approve of selecting job titles based on future availability. However, there are several issues the authors do not consider in the manual and the potential user needs to be aware of those issues. In addition, there are severe shortcomings with the manual, and potential users, especially researchers, are likely to be disappointed with how little information is available.

The manual has 18 pages, includes attempts to sell other career-oriented instruments developed by the authors, and the entire section on validity and reliability contains one reported correlation. A 1973 test-retest study found a "90% correlation of obtained job titles (N = 76)." In fact, the only information reported is unpublished research (two studies) and the authors' rationale for not using quantitative relationships. The authors report that 4,800,000 JOB-Os have been administered, which makes the absence of scientific research on the JOB-O's measurement properties alarming. There is insufficient information reported to compare the JOB-O with similar instruments. It is obvious that the authors have not responded to an earlier review of the JOB-O (Eberhardt,

1985). Inspection of the manual's reference list confirms this conclusion: Only one reference cited is dated after 1980 and that is an update of a 1975 article. Based solely on the authors' failure to provide reliability and validity information, the potential user should exercise extreme caution in considering the JOB-O.

Philosophically, one can question the use of a title-oriented, decision-encouraging instrument for junior high and senior high school students. The last page of the answer insert still says "It's Decision Making Time!" Students would need careful explanation about how to use title-specific career information as well as extensive discussion of how accurate and stable such information will be. The idea of using a career inventory with "special education and slower groups" when roughly a third of the job titles require a college degree and/or graduate school is highly unusual.

The idea of including job titles because "those jobs which will be in demand in the next decade" is also questionable at the philosophical level. We have a poor record of predicting occupational trends and societal change is accelerating. Furthermore, selecting a job title based on projected demand discounts personal interest, much of the world of work, and process of career and self-exploration. It may even encourage an unwarranted sense of security in a career choice made too early.

On second thought and closer inspection, some of the attractive aspects of the JOB-O are weakened. The most recent biennial "update" had the following changes: (*a*) assembler became assembler, precision; (*b*) commercial/graphics artist became graphic artist; (*c*) drafter became drafter/CAD; and (*d*) health regulatory inspector became health/regulatory inspector. The JOB-O is simple to complete and conducive to group administrations. The actual task of completing the JOB-O is tedious, and one wonders how attentive and careful students would be. This is not considered in the suggested administration instructions. The issue of realistic, honest self-appraisal is not adequately dealt with, even though it is critical for the JOB-O. Many students might find self-appraisal difficult, uncomfortable, or threatening. Finally, educational persistence is not an easy question for anyone, let alone students in junior or senior high school. The phrasing of the first variable, "How long do you want to go to school?" seems an unfortunate choice. The situation for such students might be more accurately assessed by a simple change in wording such as "How long are you willing to go to school?" or "How long are you planning on going to school?"

CONCLUSION. The JOB-O has an easy reading level and is a straightforward task that uses student self-estimates to identify job titles that match up with those self-estimates. There have been no additions to the manual's lack of reliability and validity data, and extreme caution should be used when considering the JOB-O for use with clients or students. The use of the JOB-O for research purposes is strongly discouraged.

REVIEWER'S REFERENCE

Eberhardt, B. J. (1985). [Review of Judgement of Occupational Behavior—Orientation]. In J. V. Mitchell, Jr. (Ed.), *The ninth mental meansurements yearbook* (pp. 767-769). Lincoln, NE: Buros Institute of Mental Measurements.

[161]

Kaufman Test of Educational Achievement. Purpose: Comprehensive Form: "Provides an analysis of a child's educational strengths and weaknesses in reading, mathematics, and spelling, to identify possible skill areas (e.g., reading comprehension, mathematics computation) needing remediation or enrichment." Brief Form: "Screening of students on global achievement skills to determine the need for follow-up testing and evaluation." Grades 1–12; 1985; K-TEA; 2 forms; individual; 1988 price data: $139 per special edition complete kit including test plates of easily cleaned plastic, manuals, 25 record booklets, sample reports to parents, and in shelf storage boxes for each form; $120 per regular edition complete kit; Alan S. Kaufman and Nadeen L. Kaufman; American Guidance Service.*

a) BRIEF FORM. 4 scores: Reading, Mathematics, Spelling, Battery Composite; $59 per special edition brief form kit including 74 test plates in easel, manual (306 pages), 25 record booklets, sample report to parents, and in shelf storage box; $49 per regular edition brief form kit; $11 per 25 record booklets; $11 per 25 report to parents; $16.25 per manual; (30) minutes.

b) COMPREHENSIVE FORM. 8 scores: Reading Decoding, Reading Comprehension, Reading Composite, Mathematics Applications, Mathematics Computation, Mathematics Composite, Spelling, Battery Composite; $95 per special edition comprehensive form kit including 140 test plates in easel, manual (652 pages), 25 record booklets (including error analyses), sample report to parents, and in shelf storage box; $85 per regular edition comprehensive form kit; $16.75 per 25 record booklets; $12 per 25 report to parents; $27.50 per manual; (60–75) minutes.

Review of the Kaufman Test of Educational Achievement by ELIZABETH J. DOLL, Practicum Coordinator of School Psychology, University of Wisconsin-Madison, Madison, WI:

The Kaufman Test of Educational Achievement (K-TEA) is an educational achievement battery intended to provide both normative and diagnostic information about children's educational abilities. Essential features include the provision of two parallel forms of an educational achievement battery, the provision of a brief achievement battery, and a design that facilitates diagnostic interpretation in addition to standard score data. The K-TEA is sensitive to the need for ease of clinical application and the demands of assessment of young children. Like the other Kaufman test, the Kaufman Assessment Battery for Children (KABC; Kaufman & Kaufman, 1983), the K-TEA employs item units to specify ceiling and basal rules and uses simple, dichotomous scoring rules. The K-TEA manuals meet the highest standards for completeness and comprehensibility.

The two forms of the Kaufman Test of Educational Achievement are independent measures; the Brief Form shares no items in common with the Comprehensive Form. Because the forms are independent, both can be given to the same student, as might be necessary if a student screened for academic deficits was subsequently found to require further evaluation. All students given the Brief Form during standardization were also given the Comprehensive Form, and data are provided showing moderately high correlations between the two forms. Because the forms are correlated, the measures may serve as pre- and post-test measures. As no information is available on possible practice effects between the two forms, it will be important that the forms be administered in counterbalanced order. Users should be aware that there is substantial item overlap between the K-TEA Reading Subtest and the Achievement Subscale of the KABC (Kaufman & Kaufman, 1983). Some degree of overlap also exists between other K-TEA subtests and the KABC, and the manual cautions that these two measures should not be given to the same child.

The normative properties of the Comprehensive Form of the K-TEA are complex. The Comprehensive Form was standardized in both the spring and fall on a well-selected, nationally representative population. The Brief Form was standardized on a smaller but equivalent sample during the fall only, with spring scores extrapolated from data collected on the Comprehensive Form. Transformed scores from all age/grade levels were aggregated into a single distribution, a smoothed curve fit to this distribution, and subtest standard scores were interpolated from this smoothed curve. The process is carefully described and convincingly defended in the manual, but may prove to be the subject of continuing debate among sophisticated statisticians. Unlike many other achievement batteries, students enrolled in special education programs were included in the normative sample for the K-TEA; the inclusion of such students is recommended if the battery is to be truly representative of the school-age population. Users of the K-TEA may compare a student's performance to either fall or spring normative samples using either age or grade norms. Age norms may imply more accuracy than they merit; these are given for 2-month intervals, while an average of only eight students per interval were included in the standardized sample.

The K-TEA is unique among broad range achievement batteries in reporting individual subtest reliabilities equivalent to those of many composite achievement scores. The reliability of individual subtests of the Comprehensive Form are all reported to be at or above .90, while reliabilities of the Brief Form are all reported to be at or above .85. The reliabilities of composite scores are even higher. Because these scores meet the highest standards for score reliabilities, they can be reported with confidence and are well suited for diagnosing strengths or deficits between individual subtests. In the Kaufman tradition, empirical guidelines are established to support comparisons between subtests.

While comparisons between Brief Form subtests are supported, the Brief Form does not lend itself to comparing abilities within skill areas. Brief Form subtests sample all skills within a subject area, but key skills are not sampled at all competency levels. For example, the Reading Subtest includes decoding items in the easier portion of the subtest, but more difficult decoding items are not included. Thus the Brief Form does not provide a complete evaluation of educational achievement skills, and should not be used when comprehensive results are required.

In addition to normative score data, all subtests included in the Comprehensive Form yield an error analysis. For the reading and spelling subtest, the examiner assigns errors to categories differentially based on the nature of the erroneous response. Mathematics errors are preclassified. For example, a child that misses the item "24–15" will receive a "regrouping subtraction" error, whether the error was made in regrouping or in math facts. As a result the mathematical error analysis may be less accurate than those provided for reading and spelling. To facilitate error analyses, the K-TEA provides an interesting procedure for the normative evaluation of error patterns using data on the average number of errors per category made by children showing similar skill development.

Neither the Brief nor the Comprehensive Form of the K-TEA should be used with first graders showing delayed academic skills. Neither form appears to have a sufficient number of items at the level of emerging academic abilities to discriminate between deficient and low normal achievement. For first graders, all subtests of both forms award standard scores higher than two standard deviations below the mean (i.e., within the normal range) to raw scores of 0. This problem does not exist for children in the later grades.

Preliminary validity data have been released with the publication of the K-TEA. Content validity is established with a meticulous description of item development, during which attention was paid to analyses of academic skill development, current textbook content, and the diversity of potential errors. Issues of bias have been addressed by eliminating items demonstrated to be more difficult for one group than the comparison group. A small number of concurrent validity studies are described reporting moderate correlations (between .75 and .85) between the K-TEA and other achievement batteries. These are, as yet, insufficient in number and scope to determine the degree to which the K-TEA and other prominent achievement batteries assess the same skills. Adequate assessment of the validity of the K-TEA must await further study by independent investigators.

In summary, the K-TEA appears to be a well-standardized, reliable measure with some innovative features that may make it the measure of choice for analyzing academic strengths and weaknesses. These include the procedures for error analysis, empirical guidelines for between-subtest comparisons, and the excellent reliabilities reported for individual subtests. Clinically, the measure is simple to administer and may yield a wealth of diagnostically relevant information. The K-TEA should *not* be used in combination with the Achievement Subscale of the KABC, and is not recommended for use with academically delayed first-grade students. The Brief Form is not recommended as a substitute for a comprehensive evaluation of academic skills. Procedures used in the K-TEA development may prove controversial, including the procedures used for score development. While the preliminary validity data included in the manual appear adequate, final evaluation of the validity of the measure must await more complete study by independent investigators.

REVIEWER'S REFERENCE

Kaufman, A. S., & Kaufman, N. L. (1983). Kaufman Assessment Battery for Children. Circle Pines, MN: American Guidance Service.

Review of the Kaufman Test of Educational Achievement by JEROME M. SATTLER, Professor of Psychology, San Diego State University, San Diego, CA:

The Kaufman Test of Educational Achievement (K-TEA) is an untimed, individually administered measure of school achievement for children ages 6 through 18 years. The K-TEA Comprehensive Form contains five subtests: Reading Decoding, Reading Comprehension, Mathematics Applications, Mathematics Computation, and Spelling. Testing time is approximately 1 hour for older children and somewhat less for younger children.

K-TEA SUBTESTS. A brief description of the subtests follows.

The Reading Decoding subtest (60 items) measures the child's ability to identify letters and pronounce phonetic and nonphonetic words. The Reading Comprehension subtest (50 items) measures inferential and literal comprehension of paragraphs of varying lengths. One or two questions about the passage are shown to the examinee, who must respond either by gesture or orally. Items 1 through 8 require a gestural response, whereas items 9 through 50 require an oral response.

The Spelling subtest (50 items) measures spelling ability, using a list of words of increasing difficulty. Each word is both read aloud and used in a sentence. Although examinees generally write the words, those who cannot write can spell the words orally.

The Mathematics Applications subtest (60 items) assesses several arithmetic concepts, particularly as they relate to real-life situations. Questions are presented orally while at the same time the examinee is shown pictures or the questions themselves. The Mathematics Computation subtest (60 items) assesses skills in solving arithmetic word problems spanning the four basic arithmetical operations and complex computational abilities.

The K-TEA provides a systematic approach for evaluating errors on the five subtests. Items on the two mathematical subtests and the Reading Comprehension subtest are classified by the processes or skills they assess. Reading Decoding and Spelling are classified according to the orthographic characteristics (phonemic, morphemic, and syllabic components) of the words.

SCORES. All items are scored 1 (correct) or 0 (incorrect). Raw scores are converted into standard scores ($M = 100$, $SD = 15$) for each subtest as well as for the Composite Score. Age-equivalent and grade-equivalent scores are provided for raw scores. Norms are given for both age and grade.

STANDARDIZATION. The K-TEA was standardized on 1,409 children in the spring normative group and 1,067 children in the fall normative group. The sample was stratified on the basis of grade, sex, geographic region, socioeconomic status, and ethnicity to match U.S. Census data for 1983 in four geographic regions.

RELIABILITY. Split-half reliability coefficients for the Battery Composite are high ($M\ r_{xx} = .98$). The individual subtests show equally impressive split-half reliability coefficients ($M\ r_{xx}$s range from .92 to .95). Test-retest reliability with a sample of 172 students (retest interval from 1 to 35 days) ranged from .83 (Mathematics Computation) to .96 (Spelling and Reading Decoding). An r_{xx} of .97 was reported for the Battery composite. Interrater reliability for the Reading Decoding and Spelling error analysis ranged from .65 to .85.

VALIDITY. Concurrent validity was assessed by correlating the K-TEA with various achievement and ability tests, including the Wide Range Achievement Test, Peabody Individual Achievement Test, K-ABC, Peabody Picture Vocabulary Test—Revised, Stanford Achievement Test, Metropolitan Achievement Test, and Comprehensive Test of Basic Skills. Median coefficients are in the .60s to .80s with appropriate subtest comparisons. Increases in raw scores with grade level constitute evidence of construct validity.

BRIEF FORM. The K-TEA is also available in a brief form that has completely different items. It is intended as a nonoverlapping form that can be administered in approximately 30 minutes. The Brief Form contains three subtests: Reading, Mathematics, and Spelling. Standard scores ($M = 100$, $SD = 15$) are provided for the subtests and the composite. Alternate form reliabilities for the Brief Form (correlations with the Comprehensive Form) range from .80 to .92.

COMMENT ON THE KAUFMAN TEST OF EDUCATIONAL ACHIEVEMENT. The Kaufman Test of Educational Achievement is a well-normed standardized individual test of educational achievement. It provides reliable and valid scores for the basic achievement areas covered in school and offers a procedure for evaluating examinee errors. This latter feature may cause difficulty for the average examiner, and the reliability and validity of the error analysis procedure are questionable. A breakdown of scores for the ethnic groups included in the standardization sample would be helpful. Overall, the K-TEA appears to be a useful instrument for the assessment of academic skills of children from 5 through 18 years of age.

[162]

Keegan Type Indicator. Purpose: Measures perception, judgement, and attitude (extroversion/introversion) based on C. G. Jung's theory of psychological types. Adults; 1980–82; KTI; 3 scores: Extroversion vs. Introversion, Sensation vs. Intuition, Thinking vs. Feeling; user's manual ('80, 13 pages); instructor's manual ('80, 21 pages); price data available from publisher; [20] minutes; Warren J. Keegan; Warren Keegan Associates Press.*

Review of the Keegan Type Indicator by ARLENE C. ROSENTHAL, Educational Psychologist, Lexington, KY:

The Keegan Type Indicator (KTI) is based on Jung's (1921) type theory. His theory ascribes four functions: thinking, feeling, intuition, and sensation to each individual and qualifies them as "superior" and "inferior" with thought and feeling, intuition and sensation as paired opposites. The concept of opposites and complementarity are two of several major concepts associated with Jung (Samuels, 1985). The overall purpose of the indicator seems to be that of self exploration and self discovery. The indicator purportedly reveals an individual's innate tendency towards extroversion or intraversion (i.e., attitudes), sensation versus intuition (i.e., perceiving reality), and thinking versus feeling (i.e., making judgements and decision making).

The user's manual is brief (12 pages); the first half is devoted to describing type theory, which is done pictorially and verbally. The second half is devoted to the implications of type theory, particularly in job settings/situations. That is, typological preferences have "profound implications for the way in which we adapt to life and work" and influence what we do best. The intent of the indicator is to provide an individual with insight into his/her character, strengths, and weaknesses. The indicator reveals an individual's functional superiority in an attempt to provide a framework for understanding how one perceives reality and makes judgements. While describing a typical individual's functional superiority on the above three dimensions, Keegan also recognizes that "The ideal situation would be to fully utilize each function and apply them as circumstances indicate." Frequently, individuals who differ in their superior function each see things not visible to the other. If they share these perspectives this is equivalent to perspective taking in social cognitive terms, the ability to see a situation from another's perspective. In large part the indicator is discussed with regard to organizational settings, for example, "Recognizing the value and validity of different ways of perceiving and decision-making in complementary types is an invaluable managerial insight" and "The history of organizational life is a testimony to two truths; one is the folly of overemphasis of one function; the other is the value of complementarity in organizational life."

Parts of the manual reveal inconsistencies and inaccuracies. The manual states "The value of type theory is not to label ourselves or others, but rather to provide a framework for understanding how we perceive reality and make judgements." Despite these frequent admonitions the manual too frequently does what it purports not to do. Frequent reference is made to "the intuitive," "the feeler," "the thinker," and "the sensation type." For example, the intuitive is best at dealing with the big picture and holistic perception of possibilities while the sensation type, being bound to the present, immediate reality, is often blind to the possibilities and potential developments in a situation.

Although the indicator is recommended as a tool for expanding self knowledge, the test author's concluding statement is that, "No instrument can substitute for self reflection and self knowledge." The manual advises that where one's scores are inconsistent the final analysis must be made by the individual, relying on experience, self reflection, and self evaluation. These statements, in the reviewer's opinion, seem to negate the value of the indicator. Generally, psychological tests are developed to provide individuals with objective and interpretable data. In contrast, the indicator manual recommends that the examinee's subjective evaluation of his standing on the three dimensions be used when scoring is questionable. Form B of the indicator includes a prescoring self evaluation (i.e., pretest) whereby the examinee subjectively reports his/her functional superiority on the three scorable dimensions. The reviewer completed the pretest and was in complete agreement with the final results on the indicator. Obviously a sample of one does not permit generalization to be made. However, it does point up the need to demonstrate empirically that the indicator contributes to self knowledge above and beyond the individual's subjective analyses. Scoring is straightforward; exclusive of administration it takes about 20 minutes or less.

Some statements made in the manual are blatantly incorrect. It is stated that "Today, the theory that the brain is hard wired from birth by genetic forces is widely accepted." Traditionally it has been contended that humans are endowed at birth with a given number of brain cells that gradually die off and are never replaced. More recent evidence contrasts with the "hard-wired" position (Kiester, 1985). First, a phenomenon known as collateral sprouting has been detected when an area of the brain is damaged. This consists of nearby neurons that sprout fibers that grow into the damaged area and assume some of the functions of the old ones. Second, evidence that the brain is capable of lifetime growth has been shown in birds and rats. For example, where rats live in stimulus-rich environments nerve cells enlarge, branch, and make new connections. These findings come from recent research in the area of developmental neurobiology.

The indicator manual is remarkable in its complete absence of psychometric or empirical data on which its constructs are based. The user's manual for the KTI and an Instructions Manual for Trainers, Teachers and Group Facilitators contain not a single statement regarding its technical properties. The former manual is primarily theoretical. The latter manual provides a suggested day plan for a One Day Session Psychological Types Workshop. The workshop itself is comprised of 21 steps and is geared to organizational/managerial settings. Examples of famous individuals are given for each psychological type: thinking, feeling, sensation, and intuitive. Included in the 1-day workshop are the following topics: the ideal organization, strengths and limitations of each of the functions, and group exercises to reveal the applied aspects of type theory. The utility of the KTI seems most relevant to an "encounter group" rather than as a serious psychological test based on demonstrated findings.

In both the users' and instructors' manuals there is a lack of comprehensive, detailed descriptions of empirical testing of Jungian hypotheses. Empirical analyses must demonstrate that the KTI contributes information not available by other means. KTI scores should predict accurately to the variety of constructs it purports to measure.

In conclusion, the KTI should not be used as a psychological test because it lacks the properties of a psychological test (e.g., validity, reliability, etc.). It would seem most useful for (*a*) self exploration and discovery of characteristics that may not be recognized in everyday life, (*b*) providing the individual with alternate perspectives of a situation, and (*c*) highlighting interpersonal and/or group dynamics.

REVIEWER'S REFERENCES

Jung, C. G. (1976). *Psychological types, the collected works of C. G. Jung*, (Vol. 6, Bollingen Series XX). Princeton, NJ: Princeton University Press. (Originally published in German as *Psychologische Typen*, Rascher Verlag, Zurich, 1921)

Samuels, A. (1985). *Jung and the post-Jungians*. London: Routledge.

Kiester, E. (1986). Spare parts for damaged brains. *Science*, pp. 32-38.

[163]

The Kent Infant Development Scale, Second Edition. Purpose: Assesses "the developmental status of infants and young handicapped children." Infants and young handicapped children chronologically or developmentally under 1 year; 1978–85; KID; ratings by parent or caregiver; 6 scores: Cognitive, Motor, Language, Self-Help, Social, Full Scale; individual; Apple II microcomputer required for interactive testing administration via diskette; 1986 price data: $1 per test booklet ('85, 16 pages); $6 per 25 answer sheets; $25 per plastic templates and 10 profile sheets; $15 per manual ('85, 39 pages); $150 per 50 use microcomputer diskette which includes administration and scoring as well as a narrative report; $5 per introductory sample set including test booklet and a prepaid answer sheet for one introductory computer scoring; scoring service available from publisher at $6 per answer sheet processed; German, Dutch, Hispanic, and Castilian versions available; (35–40) minutes; Jeanette Reuter, Lewis Katoff (test booklet), Laura Bickett (manual), and Virginia Dunn (manual for earlier edition); Kent Developmental Metrics.*

For a review by Candice Feiring of an earlier edition, see 9:567; see also T3:1246 (1 reference).

TEST REFERENCES

1. Stancin, T., Reuter, J., Dunn, V., & Bickett, L. (1984). Validity of caregiver information on the developmental status of severely brain-damaged young children. *American Journal of Mental Deficiency*, 88, 388-395.

2. Flexer, C., & Gans, D. P. (1986). Distributions of auditory response behaviors in normal infants and profoundly multihandicapped children. *Journal of Speech and Hearing Research*, 29, 425-429.

Review of The Kent Infant Development Scale, Second Edition by CANDICE FEIRING, Associate Professor of Pediatrics, Robert Wood Johnson Medical School, University of Medicine and Dentistry of New Jersey, New Brunswick, NJ:

The Kent Infant Development Scale (KID) is an instrument to assess the developmental status of normal, at risk, and handicapped children. Overall, considering the empirical work on reliability and validity of the KID, psychometrically sound estimations of developmental ages for research or clinical purposes can be achieved through use of this scale. The manual for the Second Edition is very thorough on the psychometric and administrative aspects of the scale. The internal consistency of the items in each of the five domains is quite high; alpha coefficients are: Cognitive .97, Motor .99, Social .97, Language .95, Self Help .96, and Full Scale .99 (Katoff, 1978). In addition to high internal consistency, the five domains and Full Scale score are highly related. This indicates that each domain, rather than being a separate dimension of developmental age, is a redundant measure of the child's developmental status. This suggests the Full Scale KID score should be used as a total estimate of development (the items contributed by each scale making the instrument more reliable) rather than using domain scores separately as measures of particular skills.

Test-retest reliability studies with normal and severely handicapped children indicate consistency in measurement over short-time intervals (Reuter, Dunn, Stancin, & Moe, 1984). Although the sample size in such studies was small for normal (20–40) as compared to handicapped (100–121) groups, reliabilities were always very high. Test-retest reliability for normal infants ranged between .91 and .94 while test-retest reliability for a severely handicapped sample ranged between .95 and .99. In addition, for the severely handicapped group, item-by-item test-retest reliability is excellent. For example, interjudge reliability between 20 mothers and fathers of normal infants ranged between .85 (Language) and .95 (Full Scale score). On another interjudge reliability study (Reinhardt, 1985) of 50 normal infants rated by their mothers and fathers, the reliabilities ranged from .71 (Language) to .93 (Motor). For a sample of 121 severely handicapped children, interjudge correlations between caregivers familiar with the child (parents, professionals, paraprofessionals) ranged between .92 and .99.

The concurrent validity studies on the KID show encouraging results. In a sample of 38 normal children (Katoff, 1978), developmental ages estimated from the total KID Scale and Bayley Scales of Infant Development were similar and 60% of the correlations between the two instruments were higher than .70. Some concurrent validity work has also been done with a sample of 32 infants at risk due to very low birth weight (Cunningham, 1984). The KID Full Scale score was correlated .59 and .72 with the Bayley Mental and Motor scales. In regard to classification of these infants it was found that 94% of the time the KID Full Scale score and the Bayley Mental score were in agreement. It was also interesting to note some evidence of convergent validity: neurological measures of status and the KID Full Scale score were in good agreement (74–84%). On a sample of 106 severely handicapped children the Full Scale score of the KID yielded a validity coefficient of .86 and .85 with the Bayley Scales of Motor and Mental Infant Development (Stancin, Reuter, Dunn, & Bickett, 1984). This concurrent validity is especially good considering the Bayley is a set of behavior performance items administered by an unfamiliar tester while the KID is a caregiver report measure.

Predictive validity on a sample of 30 normal children indicated that the KID measure administered at 1 year was correlated .32 with the Minnesota Child Development Inventory administered at 4 years. While this relationship is not high and accounts for only 10% of the variance, it is within an adequate range considering the large time interval between testing and the apparent lack of predictive power of other measures from infancy to childhood (Lewis & Starr, 1979). More information on the predictive validity of the KID with severely handicapped children is needed. One study did show a very high short term predictive validity (Hoag, 1983). The Full Scale KID score correlated .97 with itself over a 6-month period. While the stability of the KID measure suggested by this study is certainly desirable it is not informative concerning long term outcomes.

For the clinician, one useful aspect of the KID Scale is that items have been rank ordered within domains according to the percentage of severely handicapped infants passing them. The easiest items are presented first followed by the more difficult ones. Consequently, the clinician can examine the individual infant's performance item by item to determine level from easy to more difficult skill acquisition. By noting the point in item sequencing when an infant consistently fails, the clinician can gain information about what skills need to be targeted for intervention.

Overall, and especially in regard to tracking the growth of severely handicapped children within the first year of mental development, the KID appears to be a good, reliable, and valid instrument. The Full Scale KID score can serve as a good general index of developmental level. The KID yields reliable information provided by parents or paraprofessionals that make it attractive in terms of time, cost, and information benefits. The individual cognitive, motor, social, language, and self-help scales have face validity but have not been shown to have sufficient psychometric differentiation from each other to be used as separate indices of particular skills. However, clinicians can use item grading within domain to describe an infant's level of behavior acquisition from easy to difficult skills.

REVIEWER'S REFERENCES

Katoff, L. (1978). The development and evaluation of the KID Scale (Doctoral dissertation, Kent State University, 1978). *Dissertation Abstracts International*, 39 B2, 98. (University Microfilms No. DDK 78-128780, 122)

Lewis, M., & Starr, M. (1979). Developmental continuity. In J. Osofsky (Ed.), *Handbook of Infant Development*. New York: John Wiley & Sons, Inc.

Hoag, N. (1983). *Short-term developmental progress of severely and profoundly mentally retarded children*. Unpublished master's thesis, Kent State University, Kent, OH.

Reuter, J., Dunn, V., Stancin, T., & Moe, J. (1984). *Caregiver reports on the developmental status of handicapped young children: The Kent Infant Development Scale and the Minnesota Child Development Inventory*. Denver, CO: Symposium presented at the Ninth Annual TASH Conference. (ERIC Document Reproduction Service No. ED 235-608, EC 160 444)

Stancin, T., Reuter, J., Dunn, V., & Bickett, L. (1984). Validity of caregiver information on the developmental status of severely brain-damaged young children. *American Journal of Mental Deficiency*, 88, 388-395.

Reinhardt, C. (in press). Maternal and paternal perceptions of infant development: Their effect on scores of the Kent Infant Developmental Scale (Doctoral dissertation, Kent State University, 1985). *Dissertation Abstracts International*.

Review of The Kent Infant Development Scale, Second Edition by EDWARD S. SHAPIRO, Associate Professor and Director, School Psychology Program, Lehigh University, Bethlehem, PA:

The Kent Infant Development Scale (KID) was designed to provide a measure of infant development from birth through 14 months. Completed as an informant report by a primary caretaker, each item contains a brief sentence describing a specific behavior. The inventory has 252 items each scored as either *Yes*, *Used to do it but outgrew it*, *Is no longer able to do it*, or *No, cannot do it yet*. The authors describe the scale as based on "behavioral theory" but examination of the items and the scale development suggests the scale is more accurately considered a developmental index.

The inventory was constructed by examining existing measures, removing duplicates, and field testing the items on a pilot sample of 100 mothers at well-baby clinics. Normative data were obtained on two samples—one in 1978 ($N = 357$) and one in 1982 ($N = 123$). All normative data apparently came from mothers of presumedly healthy infants in northeastern Ohio. Norms for 1978 represented return rates of about 33% of the contacted mothers.

The scale provides a developmental age (DA) score. In the original edition of the scale, this score was not based on the normative data. In the present edition, however, the DA scores are based on the distribution of mean raw scores and standard deviations from the norm samples.

The scale manual presents a significant amount of data on the psychometric properties of the instrument. Much of the data is from a doctoral dissertation (Katoff, 1978), although other studies using the KID are reported. Reliability data reported from the Katoff (1978) sample were indeed impressive, with internal consistency (alpha coefficients) ranging between .95–.99. Test-retest reliabilities were equally substantial, with correlations ranging from .91 to .94 (mean intertest interval of 69.2 days). Interjudge reliability also was excellent, ranging between .85 and .95.

A potential problem with the reliability, however, may be related to cross-validation studies. Whereas the original sample came from northeastern Ohio, a parallel study conducted in the Rochester, New York and Kingston, Ontario areas found interjudge agreement levels ranging from .71 to .93 across the subscales.

Substantial validity data are presented in the manual. Results of studies suggest the KID correlates well with the Bayley Scales of Infant Development (BSID), the correlations ranging from .82 to .91. Potential problems may be present with this data again, however, given the lower correlations found in the subsequent Reinhardt (1985) study (correlations ranging from .62 to .91 for mothers, and .46 to .88 for fathers).

The authors have examined the use of the KID with infants at risk. Correlations with the BSID with this population ranged from .44 to .84 in one study and between .44 and .72 in another. Overall, the KID does appear to be a potentially effective measure for discriminating infants at risk.

The KID has been investigated as a measure to use with severely handicapped children who are outside the normed age range of the scale. Several studies have employed the scale for children ranging in age from 18 months to 9 years from across the United States. Both interjudge and test-retest correlations with caregivers working with these populations were excellent. Correlations with the BSID ranged from .60 to .91.

The KID scale can be either hand scored or computer scored. Computer printouts offer extensive information and analysis, and can be very helpful. They are not necessary, however, to use the scale.

Interpreting the scale provides data in five basic areas of infant development (Cognitive, Motor, Social, Language, Self-Help). Although useful to compare infant development against same-age peers, the scale obviously has more value when used with high-risk and handicapped infants. Appropriate cautions about the wide range of healthy infant development are offered by the authors. The extensive normative scaling of the measure provides clear indications as to the degree of deviation of the at-risk infants' scores from healthy development.

One of the scale's weak points concerns its mechanism for scoring items. Although use of informant reports can be valuable, they are subject to biases in perception and other variables related to rating scales. The measure may have been vastly improved by using a direct observation format for completing the scale. Serious consideration should be given in future editions to collecting data using direct observation.

One final issue with the KID relates to the prescriptive use of the scale. Although the authors briefly discuss how the measure may be used as a prescriptive tool, it is difficult to see how the scale would be used this way with healthy infants. Among more impaired populations, however, the scale may provide an effective behavioral sequence for establishing a specific infant stimulation program.

Overall, the KID appears to be an excellent infant development measure. Few measures exist that provide as extensive data on the development of healthy infants from birth through 14 months. Although the scale does not seem to have a high degree of potential use with healthy infants, the KID may be very valuable when working with parents of high-risk and handicapped children.

REVIEWER'S REFERENCES

Katoff, L. (1978). The development and evaluation of the KID scale. *Dissertation Abstracts International*, 39/02, 984-B. (University Microfilms No. DDK 78-128780.122)

Reinhardt, C. (1985). Maternal and paternal perceptions of infant development: Their effect on scores of the Kent Infant Development Scale. (Doctoral Dissertation, Kent State University). *Dissertation Abstracts International*, 47/01, 388B.

[164]

Khan-Lewis Phonological Analysis. Purpose: For the "diagnosis and description of articulation or phonological disorders in children of preschool age." Ages 2-0 to 5-11; 1986; KLPA; supplements the Goldman-Fristoe Test of Articulation; 16 scores: Developmental Phonological Processes (Deletion of Final Consonants, Initial Voicing, Syllable Reduction, Palatal Fronting, Deaffrication, Velar Fronting, Consonant Harmony, Stridency Deletion, Stopping of Fricatives and Affricates, Cluster Simplification, Final Devoicing, Liquid Simplification), Nondevelopmental Phonological Processes (Deletion of Initial Consonants, Glottal Replacement, Backing to Velars), Composite; individual; 1988 price data: $42.50 per complete kit including 25 analysis forms, folder, and manual ('86, 112 pages); $28.75 per 25 analysis forms; $10 per folder; $7.50 per manual; (15–40) minutes; Linda M. L. Khan and Nancy Lewis; American Guidance Service.*

Review of the Khan-Lewis Phonological Analysis by DONALD E. MOWRER, Professor of Speech and Hearing Science, Arizona State University, Tempe, AZ:

The Khan-Lewis Phonological Analysis (KLPA) is designed primarily to assist the speech-language pathologist in identifying and categorizing 12 developmental and 3 deviant phonological processes used by children aged 2-0 through 5-11 years (and older) who have moderate to severe articulation problems. A secondary goal is to provide information useful in planning and executing a remedial program. The 35 stimulus pictures (not included) from the Goldman-Fristoe Test of Articulation (GFTA) Sounds-in-Words Subtest (Goldman & Fristoe, 1986) are used to evoke 44 responses from the child. A total of 398 possible errors can be recorded representing the 15 phonological processes. Other errors representing 18 other less common phonological processes can be noted but they are not scored or normed on this test.

A rather high degree of sophistication is required to recognize, interpret, and score the phonological processes presented. The speech-language pathologist should expect to spend from 10 to 15 hours in study of the 103-page KLPA manual. Once understood, scoring and interpreting the process analysis is facilitated using one of the 25 analysis forms provided. The derived composite score representing converted scores of the 12 individual developmental processes can be transformed to a percentile rank and a speech simplification rating of from 0 to 4 allowing for interpretation of the use of the processes from insignificant to excessive. Test scoring should require from 15 to 40 minutes while test administration should require less than 20 minutes. An adequate description of 33 phonological processes is presented.

The KLPA was normed using 852 children ages 2-0 through 5-11 years (about 200 in each of the four age groups) at 41 sites in seven cities in the U.S. The sample was balanced to reflect the U.S. population according to sex, geography, and ethnic background. Children with obvious physical abnormalities were eliminated but no mention was made of screening for hearing acuity. All tests were administered individually by the two authors and responses were entered into a computer program by either one of the two authors or by a graduate assistant.

The authors took great pains to insure the reliability and validity of this test. Three types of reliability are reported. First, 149 children were tested by the same author on two occasions separated by 1 to 2 weeks. A .96 reliability coefficient was obtained for the composite score and .90 for the speech simplification rating. Reliability coefficients were considered adequate for the majority of developmental processes but were quite low for the processes of initial voicing, syllable reduction, and final devoicing (.68, .68, .75). As the authors point out, the discrepancy may have been due to a practice effect. Only 51 children were used in the study of long-term test-retest reliability. The lack of high correlations is explained by the fact that process decline occurs at different rates among different children; nevertheless, there is a tendency for the use of processes to decline with increasing age. Reliability coefficients are lower for individual phonological processes partly because some processes such as deaffrication and palatal fronting have fewer opportunities to occur. Also, one would expect the child's usage of processes to decline substantially after passage of a year. Finally, interrater reliability coefficients were based on a study of 30 children. The audio tape for each of the 30 children was evaluated by two raters. The raters were seven certified speech-language pathologists and three graduate students. With respect to overall use of phonological processes (composite score and speech simplification rating), *r*s of .97 for each score were obtained showing a very high consistency of agreement between evaluators. Some correlations for individual processes were lower as illustrated by an *r* of .58 for final devoicing, yet the correlation for five processes remained above .90.

Information concerning both construct and content validity measures is provided. Construct validity is supported in five areas outlined by the authors. It is unfortunate that when the authors correlated KLPA scores with other tests, they chose not to compare their test with other tests of phonological processes. Instead, they compared the composite score and speech simplification rating with the GFTA Sounds-in-Words Subtest. They found high correlations, ranging from .68 to .87.

With respect to content validity, the 44 test words provide between 6 and 44 opportunities to apply each of 15 phonological processes. For example, cluster simplification is tested in 22 cluster combinations (9 initial, 8 medial, 5 final). Some would argue, as the authors point out, that a few medial clusters (/nd/ in window) should not be classified as true clusters but are really abutting consonants because one consonant arrests the first syllable and the second consonant releases the following syllable. Thus, abutting consonants are not produced in the same way as when both consonants release or arrest a syllable (McDonald, 1964).

Individual sounds are sampled numerous times but not always equally as in the case of the r sound, which is sampled nine times in the post-vocalic position, in four clusters, and only twice in the initial position (consonantal /r/). /s/ is sampled six times in three word positions (2 initial, 3 medial, 1 final) and in only two clusters. No mention is made of the number of times sounds are sampled or the positions in which they occur. One wonders if the GFTA Sounds-in-Words Subtest is the most effective list of sounds sampled to best represent phonological processes. No discussion is presented concerning the rationale for selecting the GFTA as the vehicle for determining use of phonological processes.

Some of the processes are assessed many times (64 times in the case of the consonant harmony process), which might be considered an "overkill," whereas only nine samples of the palatal fronting process are evaluated. The authors cite one reference that states more than four samples are sufficient to analyse a phonological process. Certainly, about 12 examples of each process should comprise an adequate sample.

The single-word versus conversational-speech-sample criticism is addressed by the authors. They cite several references supporting the notion there is little difference between the overall phonological profile of the two response types, but they note single-word responses may not adequately represent the process use of some children.

Finally, the authors found that even though females score slightly higher than males on composite scores and simplification ratings, the overall sex differences are negligible. Differences were found among racial groups studied (whites perform better than blacks) but due to the small number of subjects in some racial groups, the authors recommend caution in attempting to interpret test results of different racial groups.

Scoring the KLPA involves a rather complex process of counting subtotals, obtaining raw scores, converting scores to ratings, determining percentile rank, speech simplification ratings, age equivalent scores, and confidence intervals. The instructions, the 10 sample case studies, plus the arrangement of the scoring sheets are well designed to assist the test giver in determining and placing correct scores in the appropriate places. Age norms and age equivalents are provided for using the composite score (overall use of phonological processes) but ratings of individual processes are not normed because they lack statistical properties of conventional norms. Caution is advised in interpreting differences between two percentile ranks because the ranks are not an equal-interval scale. Also, caution should be observed when making comparisons between two similar percentile ranks because equal ranking would not mean equal process use. It is important the test evaluator bear these facts in mind. Finally, it is advised that standard error of measurement tables be used to establish confidence limits one must use when referring to a child's score.

After completion of the scoring procedure, the last page or Goal Section Worksheet is completed. It is designed to assist the clinician in setting therapy goals according to the order in which the processes should be treated. A phonetic inventory of sounds the child can or cannot produce according to position, as well as problems with clusters, constitutes the final evaluation. Once goals are determined, the authors devote one chapter of their manual to suggestions for remediation. The references used throughout this section suggest the authors are well informed with regard to leading, current therapeutic approaches using the phonological process approach. Although the intent of the authors in providing this section is to be commended, the lack of empirical data regarding field-testing of their remedial approach makes the reader wonder if this section should have been included. There can be no doubt that results of the KLPA can be very useful in assisting one in planning and executing therapy. Diagnosing and planning are the principal purposes in giving the test in the first place. It would seem more suitable if the authors would consider writing a separate text to cover goal setting and remedial topics rather than to include these subjects in a test administration manual. This is not a criticism of the test itself, but rather a suggestion the authors expand upon the final chapters of their manual in a separate publication.

Upon comparing the KLPA with two other current tests designed to assess phonological processes, it would appear the KLPA holds some distinct advantages over other tests. For example, the 174-page manual of a test developed in Britain, Phonological Assessment of Child Speech (Grunwell, 1985), is far more difficult to understand and score than is the KLPA. In fact, to completely understand Grunwell's analysis, it is recommended that two books be read on the subject! The assessment procedure is far more complex than that of the KLPA as is the scoring and interpretation of test results. Shriberg and Kwiatkowski's (1980) Natural Process Analysis also requires careful study of their 175-page manual in order to learn proper administration and scoring techniques. Further, their method of analysis is rather difficult to follow. Neither of these two tests provides data on a large number of subjects nor are reliability or validity checks as extensive as those reported by the authors of the KLPA. Finally, more extensive normative data are presented in the KLPA than are presented in the other two tests. In these respects, I would rate the KLPA in a more favorable light than the two tests just described.

In summary, despite the few limitations both this reviewer and the authors point out, the KLPA should provide the speech-language clinician with a rather quick and thorough evaluation of phonological processes as they are found to occur in the speech of young children. The test would be difficult to administer unless the test giver is familiar with classification and identification of phonological processes.

REVIEWER'S REFERENCES

McDonald, E. T. (1964). *Articulation testing and treatment.* Pittsburgh: Stanwix House.

Shriberg, L. D., & Kwiatkowski, J. (1980). *Natural process analysis.* New York: John Wiley and Sons.

Grunwell, P. (1985). Phonological assessment of child speech. San Diego: College-Hill Press.

Goldman, R., & Fristoe, M. (1986). Goldman-Fristoe Test of Articulation. Circle Pines, MN: American Guidance Service, Inc.

[165]

Kindergarten Screening Inventory. Purpose: To help teachers identify educationally relevant differences among entering kindergarten children. Entering kindergarten children; 1980; KSI; 16 subtests: Naming and Matching (Familiar Objects, Money, Basic Colors, Shapes, Sets, Numerals, Letters), Spatial Relationship Words, Sequence Words and Ordinal Numbers, Sequencing, Counting, Child Writes Own Name, Tracing Basic Strokes, Copying Basic Strokes, Tracing Letters and Numerals, Copying Letters and Numerals; individual; 1985 price data: $9.95 per 32 pupil record forms, set of 6 test cards, and administration manual (8 pages); $3.95 per 32 pupil record forms; administration time not reported; Michael N. Milone, Jr. and Virginia H. Lucas; Zaner-Bloser Co.*

Review of the Kindergarten Screening Inventory by DENNIS C. HARPER, Professor of Pediatrics, The University of Iowa, Iowa City, IA:

The Zaner-Bloser Kindergarten Screening Inventory (KSI) is not a typical early childhood screening instrument. As noted by the authors, the KSI is primarily a placement test for kindergarten programming to be used in conjunction with its instructional companion, the Zaner-Bloser Kindergarten Program-Foundations for Formal Learning. The KSI is a criterion-referenced tool to assist in using the associated prepared kindergarten curriculum. In this respect, the KSI is neither a general screening instrument nor a readiness test for kindergarten entry. The authors emphasize that normative age data were not reported, primarily to encourage the use of local standards in test outcome and interpretation.

The KSI is also described as (*a*) a pre-academic assessment tool; (*b*) a learning experience for the child; (*c*) a broad-based skill assessment tool; (*d*) a pre-post assessment tool to measure pupil growth; and (*e*) an instrument to define instructional groupings for specific educational needs (Sequencing, Matching). This individually-administered tool is more aptly described as a pre-instructional kindergarten survey. The test covers 16 common pre-academic skill areas graded as Introductory Instruction, Skill Refinement Needed, or Mastery Level. Test outcomes are subsequently translated into instructional directives in the Foundations for Formal Learning. The KSI test content was determined by an expert panel who selected items for success in kindergarten. Item inclusion was determined by a 50% pass criterion by a normative sample of kindergarten children. The authors emphasize that no specific data are offered to substantiate the validity or reliability of the KSI and that the test is not intended to stand alone as a general screening tool.

The test kit consists of an eight-page administration manual, a pupil record form, nine test cards of assorted pictures, symbols, and letters, and a list of examiner-supplied common objects. Directions are very clear and the child is prompted with the correct answer if failure occurs. The emphasis is on a positive learning experience regardless of the child's response level.

Examination of the 16 pre-academic skill areas reveals a comprehensive listing satisfactory to most kindergarten teachers. Administration appears easily accomplished by a classroom teacher and the structure of the KSI allows for subject observations as well. The record form and materials are readable by a young child.

The KSI is not a screening test but does represent a reasonably comprehensive pre-academic instructional survey for kindergarten children. The lack of specific psychometric data verifying the validity or reliability remains a shortcoming despite the authors' clarification. The criterion-referenced survey appears to be useful as an individually administered instrument of beginning learning skills when used with its companion instructional program.

Review of the Kindergarten Screening Inventory by SUE WHITE, Assistant Professor of Psychology, Department of Psychiatry, Case Western Reserve University, School of Medicine, Cleveland, OH:

The Kindergarten Screening Inventory (KSI) is designed as an instrument to screen the basic skill areas of the beginning kindergarten student. There are 23 skill areas assessed, each rated on a 7-point scale, which the teacher can use to plan the child's individual educational program using the authors' *Foundations for Formal Learning*. In the reviewer's judgment, the individual skill areas assessed are important ones for a kindergarten child, but the method of evaluating these areas is inadequate. A significant sampling problem occurs in that each of the skill areas only includes six items. Because this test may be administered by a stranger prior to a child's entry into kindergarten, one must recognize that the child's performance has the potential of significant variability. This restricted range of behavioral sampling in a possibly stressful situation may provide the teacher some information about the child, but it hardly seems adequate for program planning. In addition, the tasks of Copying Basic Strokes, Tracing Letters and Numbers, and Copying Letters and Numerals are not presented in optimal fashion: the young child must copy these items from small examples. The scoring standards are extremely simplistic for the fine-motor-drawing items, (e.g., "All copied strokes are similar to models").

Of a more serious concern, however, is that the authors do not present any statistical data to substantiate the skill category labels assigned to score values. The authors suggest that the results can be used to group children with "specific educational needs." Since a small amount of error can result in a child being assigned to a lower category, this practice is not a recommended use of the results of the KSI.

If used at all, the administration of the KSI should be restricted to actual classroom screening and not program planning and grouping of children.

[166]

Kinetic Drawing System for Family and School: A Handbook. Purpose: "Assessing the pervasiveness of a child's difficulties across both the home and school settings; identifying home/family issues which explain school attitudes or behaviors, or school/classroom issues that affect home behaviors (or both); and isolating setting-specific relationships or interactions which contribute to the child's difficulties or may be available as therapeutic resources." Ages 5–20; 1985; KDS; a combination of the Kinetic Family Drawing and Kinetic School Drawing; 5 diagnostic categories: Actions Of and Between Figures, Figure Characteristics, Position/Distance/Barriers, Style, Symbols; individual; 1986 price data: $21.50 per 25 scoring booklets and handbook ('85, 82 pages including scoring booklet); $7.90 per 25 scoring booklets; $15 per handbook; (20–40) minutes; Howard M. Knoff and H. Thompson Prout (handbook); Western Psychological Services.*

TEST REFERENCES

1. Champion, L., Doughtie, E. B., Johnson, P. J., & McCreary, J. H. (1984). Preliminary investigation into the Rorschach response patterns of children with documented learning disabilities. *Journal of Clinical Psychology*, 40, 329-333.
2. Prout, H. T., & Celmer, D. S. (1984). A validity study of the Kinetic School Drawing technique. *Psychology in the Schools*, 21, 176-180.
3. Knoff, H. M., & Prout, H. T. (1985). The Kinetic Drawing System: A review and integration of the Kinetic Family and School drawing techniques. *Psychology in the Schools*, 22, 50-59.
4. Wood, B. (1985). Proximity and hierarchy: Orthogonal dimensions of family interconnectedness. *Family Process*, 24, 487-507.

Review of the Kinetic Drawing System for Family and School: A Handbook by BERT P. CUNDICK, Professor of Psychology, Brigham Young University, Provo, UT:

The Kinetic Drawing System for Family and School: A Handbook is *not* a technical manual that describes the systematic formulation of a test. There is no guiding rationale for the creation of a task. There are no focused scores with accompanying data concerning reliability. There are no norm groups showing the distribution of scores in various kinds of groups and there is no real evidence of systematic attempts to determine validity. In short, this Handbook is not a report of a test; it is rather a compendium of sources regarding a technique that has been used by many people in many different ways.

The technique described in this Handbook consists of two different administration formats with slightly modified sets of instructions. Instruction 1 is, "Draw a picture of everyone in your family, including you, DOING something. Try to draw whole people, not cartoons or stick people. Remember, make everyone DOING something—some kind of action." Instruction 2 is, "I'd like you to draw a school picture. Put yourself, your teacher, and a friend or two in the picture. Make everyone doing something. Try to draw whole people and make the best drawing you can. Remember, draw yourself, your teacher, and a friend or two, and make everyone doing something." After the tasks are finished separate inquiries are made regarding each drawing. A rather lengthy series of questions are suggested that might be presented to the child completing the tasks regarding each person represented in the drawings.

After the drawings and inquiries are completed, it is suggested that the examiner utilize a "scoring booklet" provided for an analysis of the drawings. The scoring booklet consists of various components of five characteristics of the drawings: Actions of and Between Figures; Figure Characteristics; Position, Distance, and Barriers; Style; and Symbols. Subcomponents for each characteristic are also given and the examiner is to indicate whether the component is present or absent.

The subcomponent present or absent element is never used additively to arrive at a global score that has a fixed meaning, rather each element present is given a suggested clinical hypothesis that stems from some published source dealing with the technique.

Nine case studies with background and referral information, observations during assessment, drawings, inquiries, and the characteristics and hypotheses are presented. The background information is sketchy, and the inquiry information very brief. The reviewer expected the presentation of an inquiry protocol with questions and responses. Instead only a limited number of responses were presented. In addition, the inquiry is not scored and, apparently, is not a source of hypotheses, except for those responses which might have veracity and, hence, face validity.

There is a section in the Handbook that presents information regarding norms, reliability, and validity. The major difficulty with this section is that it is a potpourri of information on various scores and interpretative schemes that are not systematically related to the protocol developed by the authors. Hence, they may be of interest to those using figure drawings, but they have limited utility at best when attempting to use the present-absent and hypothesis model partially developed in the Handbook.

In fairness to the authors, they do not purport to have a test; rather they indicate that their approach "primarily involves a hypothesis-generating and hypothesis-testing model, rather than a procedure focused on differential diagnosis . . . the clinician chooses hypotheses to entertain and test further based on his or her knowledge and experience with the child."

The Handbook provides a useful summary of literature related to the use of family drawings. In addition, the protocol developed by the authors could indeed lead one to generate hypotheses. These cookbook formulations might be substantiated by cross validation with independent sources; however, there are no traditional group test data to support such a hope. At present the system developed by the authors is in its infancy; in fact it appears only conceived, yet to be developed.

Review of the Kinetic Drawing System for Family and School: A Handbook by RICHARD A. WEINBERG, Professor, Educational Psychology and Co-Director, Center for Early Education and Development, University of Minnesota, Minneapolis, MN:

This Handbook is an attempt to synthesize current research on and interpretation of the Kinetic Family Drawing (KFD) technique and the Kinetic School Drawing (KSD), both of which were developed in the early 1970s. Knoff and Prout contend that drawings such as these can be used in multiple ways for personality assessment—as a sample of behavior in a semistructured situation, as an "ice-breaker," and especially "as a projective technique which assesses a child's perceptions of relationships among the child, peers, family, school, and significant others."

The Kinetic Drawing System argues the advantage of using both the KFD and KSD, "comparing the two differentially." The authors provide a good summary of the history of projective drawings, highlighting the contributions of Goodenough, Harris, Buck, Machover, and Koppitz. The introduction of action into the KFD family drawings by Burns and Kaufman (1970) ("draw your family *doing* something") is seen as having increased the qualitative and quantitative diagnostic information available in drawings. Developed by Prout and Phillips, the KSD directs attention to interactions in school environments.

Accompanying the Handbook is a sample scoring booklet that includes a list of questions to be asked as part of the inquiry phase, after the child has completed the KFD and the KSD. The inquiry process "attempts to clarify the child's drawing and investigate the overt and covert processes which affected its production." The scoring booklet lists five diagnostic categories used for interpretation: Actions of and Between Figures; Figure Characteristics; Position, Distance, and Barriers; Style; and Symbols. A major portion of the Handbook is a summary of interpretive hypotheses for each characteristic, providing "empirical" data when available as well as indications of clinical evidence. For example, crossing out and redrawing an entire figure may indicate the individual's true or idealized feelings toward the person (Burns & Kaufman, 1970); drawings of a school principal could reflect "significant concerns or conflicts over issues of power, authority, structure, rules" or "may imply the need for a male identification figure" (Sarbaugh, 1982). Thirteen pages of such hypotheses are presented, drawn from a literature dominated by Burns and Kaufman. This material is followed by nine detailed case studies, representing children between the ages of 5 and 16. The latter will be especially intimidating to "non-believers" of projective methods.

In the final and perhaps most important chapter of the Handbook, Knoff and Prout present the psychometric case for the Kinetic Drawing System and its component drawing techniques. In a nutshell, the case continues to be weak (Gersten, 1978; Harris, 1978). There are a few reported normative studies, primarily done in the early 1970s. No new normative data are provided in this Handbook for either the KFD or the KSD. Two major conclusions about the reliability of the KFD are:

1. High interrater reliability can be achieved when scoring criteria are clearly defined and judges are trained adequately. (Four different "objective" scoring systems are presented with limited data on their objectivity.)

2. Poor test-retest stability is reported, but this is interpreted as "suggesting that certain KFD variables are sensitive to children's transitory personality states."

Although limited data on the KFD's validity are presented, one study evaluated the technique's ability to discriminate among children who were clinically labeled. McGregor (1979) concluded that the KFD is not a valid instrument for discriminating "normal" and "clinical" children. Knoff and Prout counter that "the KFD and other projective techniques may still serve a useful function by identifying state-oriented personality/behavioral issues that may be significant to a child." Unfortunately, even less psychometric data are provided for the KSD technique.

In his foreword to the Handbook, Robert C. Burns articulates well the historical tension between the science of psychometrics and the clinical artistry of projective techniques. Burns argues for clinical validity "as a beginning to ask more sophisticated and wise questions." Unfortunately, patience wears thin, waiting for other kinds of validity data. To date, as reflected in this Handbook, the accumulated psychometric underpinnings for projective drawings, in general, and the Kinetic Drawing System for Family and School, in particular, are lean.

Depending upon one's theoretical biases and penchants, cautious use of projectives as a basis for generating clinical hypotheses may have a place in the professional practice of psychology. But the age of accountability, especially in schools, demands that greater psychometric credibility be demonstrated for kinetic drawings. There are multiple steps in approximating the construct validity of our assessment tools (Anastasi, 1986); more vigorous attempts must be made to take these steps in validating drawing techniques.

In summary, the Kinetic Drawing System for Family and School: A Handbook is an excellent synthesis of up-to-date research on and interpretation of kinetic drawing techniques. Unfortunately, however, clinical validity is the primary support offered for their use. While one could confidently recommend the use of kinetic drawings as an "ice-breaker" and "rapport-builder" in the assessment process, one cannot defend the projective interpretive system presented in this Handbook.

REVIEWER'S REFERENCES

Burns, R. C., & Kaufman, S. H. (1970). *Kinetic Family Drawings (K-F-D): An introduction to understanding children through kinetic drawings.* New York: Brunner/Mazel, Inc.

Gersten, J. C. (1978). [Review of Kinetic Family Drawings.] In O. K. Buros (Ed.), *The eighth mental measurements yearbook* (pp. 882-884). Highland Park, NJ: Gryphon Press.

Harris, D. B. (1978). [Review of Kinetic Family Drawings]. In O. K. Buros (Ed.), *The eighth mental measurements yearbook* (pp. 884-886). Highland Park, NJ: Gryphon Press.

McGregor, J. P. (1979). Kinetic Family Drawing Test: A validity study. *Dissertation Abstracts International*, 40, 927B-928B.

Sarbaugh, M. E. A. (1982). Kinetic Drawing-School (KD-S) Technique. *Illinois School Psychologists' Association Monograph Series*, 1, 1-70.

Anastasi, A. (1986). Evolving concepts of test validation. *Annual Review of Psychology*, 37, 1-15.

[167]

Kuder Occupational Interest Survey, Revised (Form DD). Purpose: Measures individual interests in order to "suggest promising occupations and college majors in rank order, based on examinee's interest pattern." Grade 10 through adult; 1956–85; KOIS; includes Vocational Interest Estimates scales identical in content to those of the Kuder Preference Record, Form C and the Kuder General Interest Survey, Form E; 4 types of scores: Dependability, Vocational Interest Estimates (10 areas), Occupational Scales (approximately 100), College Major Scales (approximately 40); 1986 price data: $70 or less per set of materials and scoring for 20 students, including manual ('79, 70 pages) and manual supplement ('85, 14 pages) upon request; $15.95 per Kuder Interpretive Audiocassette; $6.50 per specimen set including survey booklet, interpretive leaflet, general manual, and scoring for one individual; (30–45) minutes; Frederic Kuder, Esther E. Diamond (general manual), and Donald G. Zytowski (manual supplement); Science Research Associates, Inc.*

See T3:1270 (12 references), 8:1010 (41 references), T2:2194 (13 references); for reviews by Robert H. Dolliver and W. Bruce Walsh, and excerpted reviews by Frederick G. Brown and Robert F. Stahmann, see 7:1025 (19 references).

TEST REFERENCES

1. Lange, S., & Coffman, J. S. (1981). Integrative test interpretation: A career counselor tool. *The Vocational Guidance Quarterly*, 30, 73-77.

2. Galassi, M. D., Jones, L. K., & Britt, M. N. (1985). Nontraditional career options for women: An evaluation of career guidance instruments. *Vocational Guidance Quarterly*, 34, 124-130.

3. Jepsen, D. P. (1985). [Test review of the Kuder Occupational Interest Survey, Form DD]. *Measurement and Evaluation in Counseling and Development*, 17, 217-220.

Review of the Kuder Occupational Interest Survey, Revised (Form DD) by EDWIN L. HERR, Professor and Head, Division of Counseling and Educational Psychology and Career Studies, The Pennsylvania State University, University Park, PA:

The 1985 revision of the Kuder Occupational Interest Survey (KOIS, Form DD) uses a format and individual items similar to previous forms of the Occupational Interest Survey, which were revised in 1968, 1975, 1976, and 1979. The KOIS, Revised Form DD, is comprised of a set of 100 triads. For each of these a subject marks a most preferred and a least preferred activity. These subject responses are then compared to patterns of responses of persons in 119 occupational groups (79 with male and 40 with female norm groups) who have met certain criteria for inclusion in the reference group, for example, have been employed in their occupations for a minimum of 3 years and have met standards of job satisfaction. A similar process is implemented to compare inventory-taker's scores to those representing college majors (29 male and 19 female norm groups). Twenty occupations and 12 college majors have both male and female norm groups and are called twin scales. The items in the Revised Form DD of the KOIS are the same as those used in Form D of the Kuder Preference Record and were, in turn, derived from the earlier Kuder Preference Record—Vocational (Form C) and Personal (Form A).

The core of the Kuder Occupational Interest Survey, the V (verification) scale and the occupational and college majors scales, is essentially unchanged from the 1979 version of Form DD. What is changed in the 1985 revision is the report form and the accompanying explanatory material about the KOIS. The new report form consists of information on four different types of scales: (*a*) Dependability; (*b*) Vocational Interest Estimates; (*c*) Occupations; and (*d*) College Majors.

The Dependability Scale includes information many readers will remember as the V-score on earlier forms. In addition, the Dependability Scale score summarizes the number of omitted, spoiled, or unreadable responses as well as the score level below which scores obtained cannot be differentiated from random responding. The 1985 manual supplement clearly addresses the decision rules on which various cautionary statements may be included with the inventory-taker's Dependability Scale score. The Vocational Interest Estimates (VIE) provide the inventory-taker's relative rank of preferences for 10 different kinds of activities. The individual's preferences are compared to men's and women's reference groups in compliance with the Title IX regulation on providing separate sex norms to reduce sex bias in appraisal and counseling materials. The VIEs are reported in rank order by percentiles divided into high (above 75%), average, and low (below 25%). The 1985 Manual supplement also provides a process by which to convert KOIS scale scores into Holland Codes. The Occupations and College Major Scales are essentially unchanged in content since the 1979 version of Form DD. However, a few scales were deleted because of obsolescence or failure to add to the overall list of scale information, and some specialities were merged into single titles to improve interpretability of the scales. These changes are identified in Appendix C of the 1985 Manual Supplement. In both the Occupations and the College Majors Scales, scales are reported in Lambda scores, indices of how similar the inventory-taker's responses are to those of each occupation or college major reference group. This rank order of scores begins with those scales in the top .06 Lambda score range for the individual inventory-taker; these are recommended for primary consideration. Based upon Lambda score ranges of .06, the second group is identified on the Survey Report Form as "These are next most similar" and the third category includes those scales that are more than .12 lambdas from the highest in the list.

There is both an inventory-taker's copy and a counselor's copy of the Survey Report Form. The Report Form for the inventory-taker does not include percentiles, Lambda scores, or V-score but these are provided to the counselor to help the inventory-taker clarify the meaning of the categorical scores (e.g., high, average, low, the next most similar, etc.) on his or her Survey Report Form.

A major intent of the 1985 revision of the KOIS is to make it more usable by the inventory-taker with less intervention required by the counselor. In addition to the major modifications of the Survey Report Form, including extended explanatory material on the back of the form, there is an audio tape available for use with individuals or groups entitled, "Understanding Your KOIS Report Form." The tape uses a narrator interacting with male and female inventory-takers to explain the interpretation of the inventory. The information provided is clear and cast in a format likely to be attractive to adolescents although probably less so to college students and adults. Also available is a booklet and worksheet, entitled *Expanding Your Future*, designed to assist the inventory-taker to identify additional occupational possibilities from their high-ranking KOIS scales. This booklet has not been revised since the 1979 version of Form DD so there are some changes in scale titles and the elimination of others that are not reflected in this material. A revision of the booklet and workbook to make it congruent with the 1985 revision would make this information more useful to the inventory-taker and reduce the need for counselor assistance in working with it.

There is no General Manual for the 1985 Revised Form DD of the Kuder Occupational Interest Survey. Instead, the General Manual available describes the 1979 version of KOIS. There is a Manual Supplement prepared for the 1985 revision. The latter is clearly written and devoted primarily to the 1985 Report Form. It also includes appendices providing scale descriptions of the Vocational Interest Estimates, the top ranking VIEs in Occupational and College Major Scales and changes in occupational and college major scales. The 1979 General Manual includes the technical information pertinent to the development and characteristics of the scales. Since the scales and the items that comprise them have not changed from the 1979 to the 1985 version of the KOIS, the technical information contained in the 1979 General manual continues to be useful to the researcher and to the inventory user.

Earlier reviews of the KOIS, Form DD, in the *Seventh Mental Measurements Yearbook* expressed concerns about the lack of predictive validity reported (Dolliver, 1972; Walsh, 1972). The 1979 General Manual partially rectifies this situation. The results of two predictive validity studies conducted by Zytowski (1976a) and Zytowski and Laing (1978) are reported. In the first of these studies, 882 subjects with usable data were contacted 12 to 19 years after initially taking the Kuder Preference Record—Occupational, containing the same items as the KOIS, in high school or college. At the time of the follow-up, 51 percent of the subjects were employed in an occupation that would have been suggested to them by their scores on the KOIS scales. In the second predictive validity study by Zytowski and Laing, investigators followed up 206 persons who had taken the Kuder Preference Record—Occupational from 12 to 19 years earlier and who were in occupations predictable by one of the 28 KOIS twin scales. The predictive validity of the two sets of own- and other-gender-normed scales, as well as the rank-order correlations between male- and female-normed scales were investigated. According to the manual, "the predictive validity of the two sets of norms was about equivalent, regardless of the gender of the person taking the inventory. Slightly over 43 percent of the sample were in occupations corresponding to their five highest-ranked scales on own-gender norms and . . . more than 50 percent were in occupations corresponding to their five highest-ranked scales on other-gender norms." Such predictive validity studies are useful and positive. More such studies need to be done to enable effective comparisons to be made between the KOIS and the much larger body of predictive data available about the Strong Vocational Interest Blank/Strong-Campbell Interest Inventory (SVIB/SCII).

Another criticism found in the reviews of the KOIS, Form DD in the *Seventh Mental Measurements Yearbook* has to do with the description of reliability and the time lapse intervals reported in the Manual. The 1979 General Manual reports no new reliability studies. Of the four studies reported the time interval of only one is identified as 2 weeks. The time intervals of the other three are not identified. Given the quality of other research on the KOIS reported in the General Manual, a user should expect the reporting of the time intervals for reliability studies would be complete and that more recent studies would be conducted over longer time intervals and with larger *n*s than those now available. A study not reported in the Manual but of relevance to reliability is that of Zytowski (1976b) who computed rank order correlations between the sets of scales on two KOIS profiles of 729 persons obtained 12 or 19 years apart. First administrations occurred at five different ages from 13 to 20. Median Rhos varied from just over .40 for the youngest to .80 for the oldest age at administration. These long term reliabilities are similar to those reported for the SVIB.

In summary, the 1985 revision of Form DD has provided a much improved Survey Report Form. The presentation of scale scores is now clear, comprehensive, and well-explained. Supplementary materials are also helpful in extending the use of the KOIS in relation to Holland Codes, the *Dictionary of Occupational Titles*, and the *Occupational Outlook Handbook*. The KOIS is a well-constructed instrument. Additional predictive validity studies and improved reporting of reliability information are required. On balance, however, the evidence supporting the use of the KOIS continues to be supportive and, indeed, impressive.

REVIEWER'S REFERENCES

Dolliver, R. H. (1972). [Review of Kuder Occupational Interest Survey—Form DD.] In O. K. Buros (Ed.), *The seventh mental measurements yearbook* (Vol. II, pp. 1427-1429). Highland Park, NJ: Gryphon Press.

Walsh, W. B. (1972). [Review of Kuder Occupational Interest Survey—Form DD.] In O. K. Buros (Ed.), *The seventh mental measurements yearbook* (Vol. II, pp. 1429-1431). Highland Park, NJ: Gryphon Press.

Zytowski, D. G. (1976a). Predictive validity of the Kuder Occupational Interest Survey: A 12 to 19 year follow-up. *Journal of Counseling Psychology*, 3, 221-233.

Zytowski, D. G. (1976b). Long-term profile stability of the Kuder Occupational Interest Survey. *Educational and Psychological Measurement*, 36, 689-692.

Zytowski, D. G., & Laing, J. (1978). Validity of other-gender-normed scales on the Kuder Occupational Interest Survey. *Journal of Counseling Psychology*, 3, 205-209.

Review of the Kuder Occupational Interest Survey, Revised (Form DD) by MARY L. TENOPYR, Selection and Testing Director, AT&T, Morristown, NJ:

The Kuder Occupational Interest Survey, although it involves the same items as the previous Kuder Preference Record—Occupational, invokes a revised scoring system and concomitant interpretive guide. The instrument itself consists of 100 triadic items in which the examinee is instructed to mark which one of the three activities he or she likes most and which one he or she likes least. Because each item can have any of six possible combinations of responses, there are 600 potential item response patterns.

The instrument has 119 occupational scales, 48 college major scales, the 10 traditional Kuder generic interest scales, and 8 experimental scales. Women subjects have been the basis for development of 40 of the occupational scales and 19 of the college major scales.

The person taking the inventory should have little difficulty responding accurately. Kuder and Diamond have stated that items are at the sixth-grade reading level, and the excellent printing format should prevent mechanical inaccuracy in response. The items appear to be remarkably resistant to societal change. Terms like "community chest" may be dated and items on television might be substituted for those dealing with radio, but on the whole, it appears that the examinee should have little difficulty understanding the items.

Counselors using the inventory should welcome the new (1985) report form. This appears to be a vast improvement over the previous and somewhat difficult to interpret score report form. The computer-generated report is in four sections. The first of these deals with the dependability of the scores. A plain English printout flags for the counselor scores that may be problematic to interpret. The main basis for the printout is the V-score, a verification score developed to distinguish between those who faked "good" and those who gave sincere responses. The present V-scale is a revision and extension of earlier verification scales developed by Kuder.

The second section of the report form contains vocational interest estimates in terms of the 10 traditional Kuder generic patterns of interest (e.g., mechanical, scientific, and clerical). Scores are reported in terms of percentile ranks for men and women separately. Scores above the 75th percentile are categorized as "high," those below the 25th percentile are designated as "low."

The third section of the report form is concerned with occupations. The scores are reported in terms of lambda (Clemans, 1958), an index of the extent to which an individual's responses are like those of people in selected occupations. A counselor may have some difficulty in working with these scores, and possibly confuse them with the percentile ranks used in the second section of the report.

The fourth section of the report is like the third; the difference is that the examinee's scores are interpreted in terms of persons in college majors instead of persons in occupations. In addition, the results of several experimental scales are provided on the counselor's printout.

The 1985 Kuder DD Manual Supplement provides readable material a counselor might need to interpret the new report form. However, the counselor would be well advised to read thoroughly the full manual for the inventory before he or she proceeds to interpret scores.

The manual itself is a 64-page document that captures the essence of the years of research that have gone into the development of the inventory. The manual provides selected references to assist the reader who wants detailed information on the development of the inventory and the validation of its scales.

The general section of the manual contains material on interest measurement in general, administering the inventory, and interpreting results according to an older reporting system. Although of historic interest, this latter information might be slightly confusing to counselors whose experience is only with the newer 1985 report form. Furthermore, excellent advice on using the inventory in counseling is given in the general section. A useful listing of sources of vocational information is also provided.

The technical section of the manual provides a rationale for the forced-choice format. Its ostensible purpose is to minimize response bias; however, the reader would probably benefit from additional discussion of the drawbacks of the forced-choice format. For example, there should be some indication that the format almost certainly ensures that coefficients of correlation between pairs of scales will be low, when the constructs underlying the scales may not be nearly so independent. Also the fact that the format tends to prevent a person from getting all high or low scores on the generic scales should be strongly pointed out to counselors.

The second section provides the rationale Kuder has used in developing the occupational and college major scales. He contrasts his method, which is based upon differentiation among occupations, with the method used to develop the Strong Vocational Interest Blank (SVIB), which was based on differentiation between occupational groups and people in general.

An informative discussion of the development of the verification (V) scale and subsequent research in section 3 of the manual suggests the use of the V-score as a worthwhile adjunct to score interpretation.

The fourth section reports data suggesting that scoring schemata developed with males can be useful in counseling females. The counselor should read this section carefully lest differences in the absolute level of male and female scores on scales developed on males and those developed on females are misinterpreted.

Validity evidence reported in the manual for the inventory rests heavily on the study of 30 occupations and college majors. Evidence on percentage of misclassification and the extent to which peoples' scores on scales relating to their own occupations or college majors were among their highest scores on the inventory. One would hope this work would be extended beyond the group of 30 scales. The predictive validity data that are presented refer only to previous forms of Kuder inventories. Certainly, reporting of predictive studies for the present form is in order. The 1985 manual supplement similarly does not provide predictive validity data.

Reliability data based on results from some relatively small studies indicate satisfactory stability of scores. However, reliability estimates on both more subjects and more scales are in order.

Factor analytic studies reported in the manual can lead to some confusion. Because of the forced-choice nature of the inventory, appropriate factor analysis is difficult. Also, because Kuder has recently chosen to report again his traditional generic scales, the reader deserves an explanation of the discrepancies between the "factors" emerging from the various analyses and the "factors" on the score report.

A series of useful appendices is included in the manual, but some of them raise questions. For example, it is obvious that data for the occupational groups and college major groups were collected by mail. As a consequence of this methodology, there are some real questions about the effects of percentage return and selective return on the development of scales. This might be a question raised, however, of any undertaking of this sort.

In summary, the Kuder Occupational Interest Survey represents a massive research effort and a welcome addition to the field of interest measurement. In reading test manuals, which of necessity must be brief, there are always unanswered questions. However, with respect to this inventory, the lack of predictive validity data, the failure to provide concurrent validity data beyond that for 30 scales, and the lack of information on the effect of the forced-choice format on interpretation of scores and other data leave much to be desired. This reviewer suggests that rather than issue only a 1985 manual supplement dealing mainly with the interpretation of score reports, Kuder should have updated the whole manual.

Nevertheless, it is commendable that so much research went into the revision of the scoring procedures to make the Kuder Occupational Interest Survey far more useful in vocational guidance than were the older Kuder instruments. The inventory represents a great step forward.

REVIEWER'S REFERENCE

Clemans, W. V. (1958). An index of item-criterion relationship. *Educational and Psychological Measurement*, 18, 167-172.

[168]

La Monica Empathy Profile. Purpose: "To measure and improve a person's ability to care, manage, and provide the empathy needed for optimum performance in fields where personal interaction is intense and frequent." Managers/helpers/teachers in industry, education, and health care; 1980–86; self-administered, self-scored; 5 scores: Nonverbal Behavior, Perceiving Feelings and Listening, Responding Verbally, Respect of Self and Others, Openness/Honesty and Flexibility; 1987 price data: $5.25 or less per instrument (1986, 21 pages include profile, instructions, and scoring information); [15] minutes; Elaine L. La Monica; XICOM, Inc.*

Review of the La Monica Empathy Profile by SUSAN MCCAMMON, Assistant Professor of Psychology, East Carolina University, Greenville, NC:

The La Monica Empathy Profile (LEP) is designed to measure a respondent's use of five subscales (called modes) of empathy. Each of the 30 items (6 from each subscale) contains a pair of behaviors. Respondents choose the alternative that is most typical of their interpersonal behavior when in the role of helper, coach, manager, or teacher. Possible scores range from 0 to 12 on each of the five subscales. The test booklet contains the item pairs, scoring instructions, data collection sheets for background information and a copy of the scores, a graph sheet with percentiles indicated, and a section on score interpretation. The interpretation section describes the uses of each of the five subscales and offers questions for self-examination of low and high subscale scores. Separate documents provided by the publisher and the author (La Monica, 1981, 1988) describe the development of the measure, reliability, validity, and the source of normative data.

La Monica (1988) reported that content validity was pursued through the use of experts, from the helping professions and industry, who separated the items into the five modes and judged social desirability. Test-retest (1-week interval) reliability coefficients were computed based on responses of 32 graduate students in helping professions; values for each subscale ranged from moderate (responding verbally, $r = .39$, $p < .05$) to high (perceiving feelings and listening, $r = .80$, $p < .001$).

Normative data were collected on 371 subjects selected in a quota sample of industrial managers, health care helpers, and teachers in educational systems in the northeast. How subjects were identified and recruited was not stated. When the various demographic and occupational groups were compared, 31 out of 35 tests for differences were nonsignificant, and the few observed differences were described as small in magnitude. Therefore, La Monica concluded the LEP is valid for use in health care, as well as industrial and educational systems—in any interpersonal situation "where the goal of one person is to help another to grow in a more effective direction" (La Monica, 1988, p. 12).

The LEP was based on the Empathy Construct Rating Scale (ECRS), a Likert-type scale which produced only an overall empathy score. La Monica (1981) presented data demonstrating discriminant and content validity, as well as high internal consistency of the ECRS. However, convergent validity was not evident as measured by instruments that focused on peer, self, and client ratings of empathy. Factor analysis of the ECRS items resulted in two factors: well-developed empathy and lack of empathy. Other subscales identified by La Monica were not upheld by the factor analysis. She concluded that "empathy cannot be divided into subscales; it exists as a whole and all elements of it must be present in helpers for it to exist."

La Monica developed the LEP to meet the need for a refined instrument to ascertain the role of empathy in the outcomes of helping interventions. An additional goal was to specify how empathy is best taught and maintained. Although these are important needs, the supporting documents for the LEP do not establish this instrument as the appropriate tool. Several questions remain. The first question concerns the validity of the five modes of empathy. It is clear all five subscales load on the empathy factor and their content is empathy-related. There is no validation, however, of the five as distinct contributors to the overall factor. The conceptual basis for the LEP was drawn primarily from the works of Rogers and Carkhuff, with their emphasis on empathy as the heart of the helping process. The theoretical origin and empirical bases of the five empathy modes are unclear.

The test manual defines empathy as a three-step process in which the helper accurately perceives another's world, the helper communicates that understanding, and the other (i.e., client) perceives the helper's understanding. The five empathy modes emphasize the second step, and do not address the third step at all. In her 1988 document, La Monica mentioned that the LEP can also be used as a rating scale by another person. However, no data were presented regarding its use by another. Perhaps studies relating helper and helpee perceptions are underway. These seem critical to a measure to support this three-step empathy process. Negative results from previous studies reviewed by Kurtz and Grummon (1972) are not encouraging. Significant discrepancies exist between therapists' empathy ratings and those of clients and independent judges.

The reports concerning the LEP and its predecessor ECRS offer no comparison with other measures of therapist-reported empathy. It would be helpful to know how LEP profiles relate to other empathy measures such as Kagan's Affect Sensitivity Scale, the Barrett-Lennard Relationship Inventory, Truax's Relationship Inventory, and Accurate Empathy Scale, or other measures described by Kurtz and Grummon (1972) and Gladstein (1977).

Finally, because the LEP is designed to give information that can enhance interpersonal behavior, data are needed that link measured empathy with helping outcomes. In their review of therapy outcome research, Kurtz and Grummon (1972) reported that of six empathy measures, only client-perceived empathy was predictive of outcome. Data linking performance on the LEP to effective helping are absent from the test booklet. Respondents may compare their scores to norms provided, but no information is provided concerning the success or quality of performance of the members of the normative group. Further, although most members of the various demographic groups did not differ significantly in their LEP profiles, this reviewer still has questions regarding the appropriateness of grouping all the respondents together. Gladstein (1977) differentiated the importance of empathy in psychotherapy versus counseling and asserted there is no clear evidence that empathy plays a prominent role outside of psychotherapy. Clearly more study is needed on the role of empathy in the various helping professions, and the patterns of effective helpers in their use of the five empathy modes. The conceptual and empirical sources of the booklet's self-examination questions for high and low scorers are not reported.

In summary, La Monica (1981) pointed out the problems of inconsistent definitions of empathy and a lack of validity data for empathy measurement instruments. However, more support is needed from studies of the discriminant validity of the five empathy modes and of the convergent validity of the LEP before its usefulness is confirmed. Further, studies linking the empathy modes with helping outcome are also needed.

REVIEWER'S REFERENCES

Kurtz, R. R., & Grummon, D. L. (1972). Different approaches to the measurement of therapist empathy and their relationship to therapy outcomes. *Journal of Consulting and Clinical Psychology*, 39 (1), 106-115.

Gladstein, G. A. (1977). Empathy and counseling outcome: An empirical and conceptual review. *The Counseling Psychologist*, 6 (4), 70-79.

La Monica, E. L. (1981). Construct validity of an empathy instrument. *Research in Nursing and Health*, 4, 389-400.

La Monica, E. L. (1988). A forced-choice measure of empathy: Further reliability and validity. Unpublished manuscript.

Review of the La Monica Empathy Profile by LEADELLE PHELPS, Associate Professor of Educational and Counseling Psychology, University of Missouri-Columbia, Columbia, MO:

The La Monica Empathy Profile (LEP) was designed to measure an individual's level of empathy along five modes: (*a*) Nonverbal Behavior (use of body contact and body language to react and convey messages); (*b*) Perceiving Feelings and Listening (ability and willingness to enter another's world of feelings); (*c*) Responding Verbally (giving messages of encouragement, support, and understanding); (*d*) Respect of Self and Others (belief that one always has rationale for feelings and behaviors); and (*e*) Openness, Honesty, and Flexibility (willingness to share feelings and respond in accordance with one's ethical beliefs). The inventory consists of 30 pairs of statements in which an item whose content purports to fit one of the five modes is compared to an item from one of the other four modes. Within each pair, the examinee is instructed to select which statement is more characteristic of herself/himself. For example, one pair states: A. I allow people to cry and I offer my support; B. I actually seem to feel some of the emotions that another person is experiencing.

The LEP is a refinement of a more lengthy inventory, the Empathy Construct Rating Scale (ECRS) (La Monica, 1980). All items on the LEP were taken from this parent instrument, which consisted of 84 single statements rated by the examinee on a 6-point Likert-type rating scale. As there is no technical manual for either the LEP or the ECRS, all information concerning item development, reliability, and validity had to be specifically requested from the publisher. What one receives upon such a request is a set of photocopied, unpublished manuscripts. The manuscripts (La Monica, 1986, 1987) state that the 84 ECRS items were edited and revised by a pool of experts. Determination of which of the five modes each of the revised 84 items fit into was given to 100 practicing helpers/managers. Based on the "percentage of subjects endorsing each response option, items were placed in their designated subscales" (La Monica, 1986). The percentage criteria for "placement" required that an item have a percent differential of more than 10% between the highest and second highest placement (La Monica, 1987). After deleting 26 items that did not receive at least a 10% higher endorsement in one subscale, the remaining 58 items were paired up based on their similarity of perceived social desirability. Perceived social desirability of each item was judged on a 5-point Likert-type scale by 28 managers/helpers.

After further reduction to eliminate redundancy, the present form of the LEP resulted with 30 paired statements consisting of six items from each of the five modes. Each item was used twice and "were paired equally with items in the 4 remaining subscales" (La Monica, 1986).

The booklet in which the current LEP is sold contains a graph for transferring raw scores from each of the five modes into a percentile rank. The percentiles are based on a sample of 239 practicing managers/helpers/teachers in industry, education, and health care. While the booklet contains no further description of this sample, one of the manuscripts (La Monica, 1987) obtained from the publisher contains a similar graph with an enlarged sample size of 371, of whom 90% are female. (The raw score—percentile equivalencies vary little between the two graphs.)

Having a raw score range of only 12 points, the percentile graph is misleading. For example, there is a spread of over 20% between having a raw score of 5 (35%) as compared to a raw score of 6 (58%) on the Responding Verbally subscale. Further, ipsative scores such as these (i.e., the strength of each subscale or mode is not expressed in absolute terms but in relation to the strength of the individual's other modes) have questionable conversion to normative percentiles. Because the individual responds by expressing a preference of one item over another, two individuals with identical raw scores on the LEP may differ markedly in the absolute strengths of their empathic mode preference. The combination of normative and ipsative frames of reference makes interpretation confusing and rather meaningless.

There are other numerous faults with this instrument. First, the item development is poorly presented, the resulting item pool for each mode of empathy is so small as to be questionable in terms of domain, and the subscales or modes are without theoretical foundation. Second, what little validity and reliability data are available on this instrument were done primarily on the original scale. The terms reliability and validity are never mentioned in the published LEP booklet. It appears the only technical data obtained directly from the newer LEP was a 1-week interval test-retest study that used the "mean subscale scores from 32 subjects . . . enrolled in a graduate degree program" and was reported in one of the unpublished manuscripts (La Monica, 1987). The use of *mean* subscale scores is inappropriate and a 1-week interval is likely too short, thus, resulting in inflated correlations. Finally, validity data are and will be difficult to interpret due to the use of ipsative scores. The author appears to have not taken into account that, with ipsative scores, the mean intercorrelations of the individual modes or subscales should tend to be negative, and the mean correlations of all the scales with any outside variable will approach zero (Hicks, 1970). Due to these artificial constraints, ipsative scores cannot be properly analyzed by the usual correlational procedures.

In summary, this instrument cannot be recommended for general use at this time. Further research needs to be completed regarding its reliability and validity. That technical information available should be clearly presented in a users' manual. This manual should be furnished with purchase of the test. Requiring a user to plough through unpublished and difficult-to-interpret material in order to judge the psychometric qualities of a test is unacceptable.

REVIEWER'S REFERENCES

Hicks, L. E. (1970). Some properties of ipsative, normative, and forced-choiced normative measures. *Psychological Bulletin*, 74, 167-184.

La Monica, E. (1980). Empathy Construct Rating Scale (Copyright transferred to XICOM, Inc., April 3, 1986). Tuxedo, NY: XICOM, Inc.

La Monica, E. (1981). Construct validity of an empathy instrument. *Research in Nursing and Health*, 4, 389-400.

La Monica, E. (1986). *The La Monica Empathy Profile: A forced-choice measure of empathy*. Unpublished manuscript.

La Monica, E. (1987). *A forced-choice measure of empathy: Further reliability and validity*. Unpublished manuscript.

[169]

Language Processing Test. Purpose: "Identifies students' language processing strengths and weaknesses in a hierarchical framework." Ages 5-0 to 11-11; 1985; LPT; 8 Scores: Labeling, Stating Functions, Associations, Categorization, Similarities, Differences, Multiple Meanings, Attributes; individual; yields Standard Scores, Percentile Ranks, and Age Equivalencies; 1985 price data: $42.90 per complete test kit including 20 test forms and examiner's manual ('85, 91 pages); $12.95 per 20 test forms; $29.95 per examiner's manual; (30) minutes; Gail Richard and Mary Anne Hanner; LinguiSystems, Inc.*

Review of the Language Processing Test by THOMAS W. GUYETTE, Assistant Professor of Communication Disorders and Sciences, Rush-Presbyterian-St. Luke's Medical Center, Chicago, IL:

The Language Processing Test (LPT) was developed because the authors felt there was "a void in assessment and remediation materials for students who were experiencing difficulty in assigning meaning to auditory input and subsequently organizing and retrieving the information to formulate an output." The theoretical foundation for the LPT is based on a neuropsychological model of brain organization (e.g., Luria, 1970; 1982). The authors, however, do not describe specifically how the organization of their test (for example, choice and organization of subtests) reflects neurolinguistic concepts of brain organization.

The LPT is composed of two pretests and six subtests. The two pretests evaluate Labeling and Stating Functions. The six subtests of the LPT include Associations, Categorization, Similarities, Differences, Multiple Meanings, and Attributes. The target population for this test is children 5 years of age and older who are suspected of having a language-processing disorder. The LPT manual lists abnormal language behaviors (word retrieval difficulties, inappropriate word usage, nonspecific word usage, etc.) that can be used to identify children needing language-processing evaluation.

The administration and scoring sections of the LPT examiner's manual are, for the most part, comprehensive. Directions for administering the two pretests and six subtests are clear and complete. Guidelines for scoring responses are relatively detailed; however, even with these guidelines it is not always clear how a response is to be scored. Scoring problems result because the examiner must judge the semantic appropriateness of the verbal response. For example, in one subtest (Associations) the student is instructed, "Now tell me what goes with a shoe." For this item "foot" and "another shoe" are acceptable but "boot" is not. What is an examiner to do with answers such as "shoe polish" or "rubbers"? It is not clear if these would be acceptable or unacceptable answers. More examples of correct and incorrect responses would reduce this ambiguity. In addition, it would be helpful to the test user to know the interexaminer consistency for scoring responses of this type.

Justification for selection of test items is supported by research on a preliminary version of the test. In that research, an expanded version of the test was administered to 582 pupils across the appropriate age range. The preliminary version included 20 (rather than 10) items in each subtest. After the initial testing was completed, the data were used to justify selection of 10 items for each subtest. Item selection was based on item difficulty and discrimination indexes.

A second study was conducted on the final version of the LPT in order to establish norms. In this study the test was administered to 970 "normal" subjects. Language- and cognitively-impaired students were eliminated from the sample. The manual gives a good description of the gender and ethnic characteristics of the subjects. Normative data are presented using commonly accepted and easily interpreted statistics such as means, standard deviations, percentiles, and standard scores. Norms are provided for children between the ages of 5 and 11 years.

Unfortunately, the manual does not provide explicit criteria to guide the test user to an appropriate interpretation of the test scores. The authors do suggest that children with language-processing disorders will do better on early subtests than on late subtests, but no cutoff criteria are presented describing when a score on the LPT is indicative of a language-processing deficit and when it is not. Also, since persons with language disorders were not included in the sample, it is not documented how they would perform on these subtests in relation to "normal" peers.

The issue of test validity is not addressed adequately in the LPT manual. Criterion-related validities (predictive and concurrent) are not presented. This deficit may relate to the absence of explicit cutoff criteria used to interpret the test scores. Construct validity evidence is also absent. The authors do argue for the content validity of the LPT, stating that it "was developed following extensive review of available tests and models of language processing, and was constructed to fit the principles espoused by A. R. Luria." The empirical data offered in support of test validity are presented using the "method of internal consistency" to demonstrate the discrimination ability of the test items.

The LPT offers stronger support for test reliability. Tables are presented that clearly display test-retest reliability, split-half reliability, item homogeneity, and standard error of measurement. Overall, these data suggest adequate measurement reliability given the nature of the variable being measured.

In summary, the LPT is a test of language-processing ability in school-age children. The test has several strengths including the care taken in empirically justifying the test items, the clearly presented test norms, and the reliability data. Test weaknesses include ambiguity in the scoring process, the absence of explicit criteria for interpreting test scores, and weak support for test validity. In conclusion, the LPT will probably be most useful to the qualified professional in testing situations where there is no need to have established criteria for test interpretation nor strong support for test validity.

REVIEWER'S REFERENCES

Luria, A. R. (1970). The functional organization of the brain. *Scientific American*, 222 (3), 66-78.

Luria, A. R. (1982). *Language and cognition*. New York: John Wiley & Sons.

Review of the Language Processing Test by LYN HABER, Associate Professor of Psychology, University of Illinois at Chicago, Chicago, IL:

The purpose of the Language Processing Test (LPT) is twofold: to suggest remediation directions and to provide diagnostic information. I would not recommend it for either function.

The LPT is supposedly based on A. R. Luria's model of brain organization. The appeal to neuropsychology sounds impressive but has no foundation here. The specific hierarchy of tasks the authors identify as occurring in the "secondary zone of the temporal lobe" cannot be derived from Luria. The authors even fail to invoke Luria's model properly. Because all responses to the LPT stimuli require verbalization, the tertiary zone of the frontal lobe would appear to be involved in LPT responses as well as the secondary zone of the temporal lobe.

There are five serious problems with the LPT. First, the authors claim a theoretical model of language-processing functions such that the two pretests (Labeling and Stating Functions) and six subtests (Associations, Categorization, Similarities, Differences, Multiple Meanings, and Attributes) are arranged in hierarchical order, gradually increasing in complexity. Given the asserted hierarchy of language-processing tasks, are we to assume that the student who cannot perform at age level on the Similarities subtask has a language-processing difficulty with Similarities as well as the remaining subtests? It would be difficult to justify these particular tasks in this order on a purely theoretical basis and the authors fail to provide statistical evidence such as intercorrelations among individual performances on the subtests, factor analyses, or ordered scaling necessary to support the hierarchical claim. In the absence of these data, a child's performance on any subtest of the LPT reveals, at best, how well performance on these items, scored in this way, compares to that of normal peers of similar age. Beyond using LPT responses as a guide to failed items, there is no justification for believing the more general claims of diagnostic or remedial efficacy.

A second and equally serious problem, which also makes the LPT ineffective for diagnostic or remedial purposes, arises from failure to differentiate among language processes involving input and output. The authors "felt a void in assessment and remediation materials for students who were experiencing difficulty in assigning meaning to auditory input and subsequently organizing and retrieving the information to formulate an output." They assert these "children . . . could not retrieve information previously learned." However, the LPT does not permit the clinician to differentiate among these difficulties. Is the child unable to recognize or organize the information initially (examples of problems of input, in which the information is not "learned" in the first place); is he/she unable to retrieve it (as in some kinds of aphasia); or is the problem one of formulating or organizing the output? The authors fail to include even an object recognition task (usually assumed to be the simplest language-processing task as opposed to labeling, as is claimed here) in order to rule out problems with auditory input.

The authors also blur the critical distinctions between input and output problems in the Discussions of Performance section of the manual. For example, to perform the Differences subtest successfully, the student must focus on critical distinctions rather than secondary ones (possibly an organizational problem). The authors fail to differentiate this type of behavior from the ability to discriminate differences, which is an input problem.

The third problem with the LPT concerns its validity. The LPT was standardized using normal subjects. Excluded from the sample were children previously identified as having mental disabilities, learning/language disabilities, or a known hearing loss. However, these excluded children are the target population of the LPT. The only validity data provided are joint biserial correlations between item and subtest scores. The only information available from the LPT regarding language skills is how close the child is to normal age norms. No evidence is offered that below-age scores are correlated with other indicators of language disabilities or even other existing tests of such disabilities. It is very easy to find test items that correlate with subtest scores; evidence is needed that those items differentiate among children as a function of their language skills.

The fourth problem concerns the reliability of the scoring. No inter- or intraexaminer reliability measures are reported. This is a serious oversight, given the amount of ambiguity present in the scoring of responses. For example, the examiner's manual provides a "reference" of acceptable and unacceptable responses for each subtest. Based on this "reference," the examiner is to judge responses not included in the manual. Because scoring of the subtests is often arbitrary or inexplicable and no rationale is provided for whether responses are acceptable, it is easy to imagine responses the examiner would have no idea how to score. Thus, the validity and reliability of the test are undermined. Some examples of these problems are provided below.

Associations—Item 2: "What goes with *milk*?" *Cow* is listed as incorrect. Item 10: "What goes with *horse*?" *Hay* and *barn* are incorrect. Item 3: "What goes with *hot dog*?" The response *hamburger* is not evaluated.

Categorization—Item 1: "Name three transportation items." The permitted prompt is, "Name three things to travel in." *Trailer* and *camper* are both unacceptable; so are *lamp*, *television*, and *piano* as items of furniture.

Numerous problems exist on other subtests including the final subtest, Attributes, which has a more general flaw than those noted above. The child's response is scored on the basis of eight categories of attributes: function, components, color, accessories/necessities, size/shape, category, composition, and location/origin. A perfect response must touch on all eight categories, but the examiner cannot provide any directed prompts, and the child is never told he must cover all eight categories. What purpose is served by this cumbersome eight-category scoring procedure? Furthermore, unreliable scoring seems likely to arise for this subtest due to the fact that one word may suffice for several categories.

Finally, a fifth problem with the LPT concerns length. The authors claim, on the basis of the normal children sampled, that the entire LPT can be administered in about 30 minutes. Experience suggests several of the individual subtests, especially Similarities and Differences, and Multiple Meanings, would each require close to 30 minutes for learning/language-impaired children. This means the LPT is too lengthy for one session.

For all of these reasons, I do not recommend the LPT. If the clinician wishes to identify the specific language skills included in the LPT (outside a theory of language processing), the WORD Test (Jorgensen, Barrett, Huisingh, & Zachman, 1981) is quite similar and avoids many of the scoring problems of the LPT. (In addition to similarities among the subtests, statistical procedures and their description are virtually identical for the two tests.) If the clinician wishes to assess language behavior within a theoretical description of language, the Test of Language Development—Primary (TOLD-P) (Newcomer & Hammill, 1982), despite many flaws, provides much better insight into the child's general areas of strengths and weaknesses for both diagnostic and remedial purposes. Specifically, the TOLD-P differentiates input and output at several levels of language-processing.

REVIEWER'S REFERENCES

Jorgensen, C., Barrett, M., Huisingh, R., & Zachman, L. (1981). The WORD Test. Moline, IL: LinguiSystems, Inc.

Newcomer, P. L., & Hammill, D. D. (1982). Test of Language Development—Primary. Austin, TX: PRO-ED, Inc.

[170]

Law Enforcement Assessment and Development Report. Purpose: Helps to identify individuals who can become successful law enforcement officers. Applicants for law enforcement positions; 1981–87; LEADR; computer-based analysis from 2 of Cattell's personality questionnaires, Form A of the 16 Personality Factor Questionnaire (9:1136) and Part II of the Clinical Analysis Questionnaire (9:232); questionnaires must be scored by publisher; 4 profile Dimensions (Emotional Adjustment, Integrity/Control, Intellectual Efficiency, Interpersonal Relations), and Performance Indicators; 1987 price data: $21 per 25 reusable test booklets; $7.50 per 25 answer sheets; $12.50 per manual ('87, 51 pages); $27.75 per introductory kit; $28 or less per report; (90) minutes; IPAT Staff; Institute for Personality and Ability Testing, Inc.*

For a review by Lawrence Allen of the earlier edition, see 9:593.

Review of the Law Enforcement Assessment and Development Report by DAVID S. HARGROVE, *Associate Professor and Director of Clinical Training, Department of Psychology, University of Nebraska-Lincoln, Lincoln, NE:*

Law enforcement literature documents the need for instruments that will provide psychological information to assist in the accurate screening and/or selection of police officers. Several personality inventories have been helpful as parts of batteries of tests and other data-gathering procedures. But no single instrument has emerged as clearly superior in identifying and predicting characteristics of psychologically competent officers. There are several reasons for this. First is the criterion problem of defining a psychologically competent officer. This involves the construct validity of a test or instrument and underlies its usefulness in law enforcement screening. The second reason is the issue of determining what the instrument is designed to predict: psychological competence or psychological incompetence. This in part pertains to the specific use to which the instrument is put: whether to separate persons who may have undesirable characteristics or whether to include only those who do possess certain desirable characteristics.

The Law Enforcement Assessment and Development Report (LEADR) is an effort by the Institute of Personality and Ability Testing, Inc. (IPAT), to provide psychological information to assist in the screening and selection of police officers. The Report consists of an interpretive narrative of four dimensions the authors believe are important for law enforcement officers: Emotional Adjustment, Integrity/Control, Intellectual Efficiency, and Interpersonal Relations. These dimensions are taken from Form A of the Sixteen Personality Factor Questionnaire (16 PF; 9:1136) and Part II of the Clinical Analysis Questionnaire (CAQ; 9:232). The 187 items of the 16 PF and the 144 items of the CAQ are bound in a booklet for use with a general purpose computer-based answer sheet. Completed sheets are sent to IPAT for scoring, interpretation, and a report.

The Report is generated by a comparison of a given profile to the 16 PF and CAQ data bank on the critical dimensions. The 16 PF provides normative data for the four critical dimensions. The CAQ provides information for clinical signs and syndromes, which relate to 17 clinical factors. No data are provided on the relationship between the personality factor profile and the clinical signs and syndromes profile. Research is said to be underway to evaluate these relationships.

LEADR is, then, a particular interpretation of one form of the 16 PF (Form A) and the CAQ in a computer-generated report. The Manual points out that it should be interpreted by qualified professionals and that it should also be utilized as one component among several sources of information for selection purposes. Further the Manual warns that local normative data should be collected to facilitate the development of decision rules in specific settings.

Reliability of the LEADR dimensions are based on the use of the 16 PF on 12 samples, none of which are police officers or law enforcement related persons. Reliability data are drawn from the 1986 Administrator's Manual for the 16 PF and do not represent specific administration of the LEADR with law enforcement populations. Reported average short term reliability of the 16 PF is .83, average long term reliability is .64.

Validity data are somewhat more convincing, though certainly not overwhelming. The Manual contains data from 11 validation studies of the LEADR, nine of which were done with law enforcement samples. While both the methods and quality of these studies vary, there is some basis for construct validity of the LEADR dimensions as they are related to the original 16 PF and CAQ scales. Within the limited samples, a growing data bank appears to suggest some relationship between the critical dimensions and those characteristics thought to be associated with positive performance. The weakness of the available validity data is insufficient samples of law enforcement officers' performance to which to relate the

LEADR dimensions. The data certainly are not strong at this point.

The Manual suggests the results of the LEADR be utilized in relationship to other information, such as background checks and medical data. Certainly this is the case, but it is not entirely clear how the LEADR dimensions would relate to other data. The report description and the sample report in the Manual do not give sufficient information to suggest how it may be combined with other information to assist in appropriate decision making.

Generally, review of the LEADR indicates it does not fully produce the results promised in the Manual. At least there do not appear to be sufficient empirical data supporting the use of LEADR for screening and selection purposes in law enforcement settings. More research relating the LEADR dimensions to law enforcement job analyses as well as performance levels will be quite useful in the continued evaluation of the instrument for selection and screening purposes.

[171]

The Lawrence Psychological Forensic Examination. Purpose: "A guide for comprehensive psychological assessments and report writing with clients in the criminal, juvenile and civil justice systems." Juvenile, criminal, and civil justice clients; 1978–83; LAW-PSI; ratings by mental health professional; handbook contains descriptive legal information for report writing, and 3 tests; individual; 1987 price data: $29.50 per handbook ('83, 110 pages); $19.50 per LAW-PSI Reports ('82, 169 pages); Stephen B. Lawrence; Lawrence Psychological Center.*

a) LAWRENCE PSYCHOLOGICAL FORENSIC EXAMINATION. Guided forensic interview to determine precise mental states of mind, life history, or prediction of future client behavior.

b) LAWRENCE MENTAL COMPETENCY TEST. LAW-COMP; to aid clinicians in making judgments needed to determine a client's present legal mental competency to stand trial.

c) LAWRENCE PSYCHOLOGICAL FORENSIC EXAMINATION REPORT EVALUATION. LAW-PSI/EVAL; a rating instrument for evaluating written forensic reports.

Review of The Lawrence Psychological Forensic Examination by SAMUEL ROLL, Professor of Psychology and Psychiatry, University of New Mexico, Albuquerque, NM:

The Lawrence Psychological Forensic Examination is, in reality, not a test or even an examination in the sense of a psychological examination. It is, rather, a compilation of a broad variety of suggestions, information, checklists, guides to administering other tests and compiling information from other test data, legal definitions, excerpts from California jury instructions, and guidelines for probation. It even contains a model of a predeposition agreement for the psychologist to use in working with an attorney, estimated potential blood alcohol concentration depending on type and number of drinks and body weight, sections of DSM-III, a description of the author's own version of personality traits and a sample professional resume. It might more correctly be labeled "Thoughts, checklists, and sundry materials which may be useful in a forensic practice." Its worst general feature is that it is almost unedited and varies in quality from material that is ready for publication to rather poorly xeroxed and unintegrated material from unidentified sources.

One part of the vast amount of information presented is Lawrence's own version of a mental status exam which, like most mental status exams, contains guidelines for the evaluation of general appearance, speech, mood, sensorium, symptoms, etc. It also contains an outline for a life history, a developmental history, a family history, an educational history, a military history, an occupational history, criminal-legal history, medical history, etc. It is more lengthy than most guidelines for a mental status exam and, as expected, more geared to data of value in a forensic setting. As is the case with most mental status exams, it is a guideline for collecting data rather than a psychological test. As such, there are no norms, no reliability data, no validity data, and certainly no indications of conceptual validity or theoretical orientation.

Another component of the Lawrence is the Lawrence Present Mental Competence Test. As is the case with the mental status exam in the Lawrence, it also is not a test in the sense that there are no norms or other psychometric information available describing it to potential users. It does, unlike the mental status exam, have a conceptual orientation because it tries to capture in a structured interview format the legal criteria for mental competency offered by the California penal code. The California criteria match those of most states. Based on those criteria (e.g., that the person can understand the proceedings and can cooperate in the defense) the structured interview aims at collecting two different kinds of information. The first is referred to as "Factual Criterion" and taps the patient's capacity to understand his or her current legal situation, the charges, legal rights, legal issues and procedures, the role of defense counsel, of prosecuting attorney, judge, etc., and the range and nature of possible pleas. The second kind of information, referred to as "Inferential Criterion," includes: capacity to cooperate with counsel, understand the need to provide counsel with information, need to maintain a consistent legal strategy, comprehend counsel's instruction and advice, follow court testimony for contradictions, testify relevantly and protect himself or herself by using available legal safeguards, identify defense witnesses, and avoid mental deterioration throughout the legal proceedings. Based on the information from the interview the psychologist ranks each area as to whether the patient had good or adequate knowledge, no knowledge, or inadequate knowledge. A numerical scale is provided but only as a rough outline or summary of the data. The Competence Test is not designed to be used in conjunction with supporting norms or other psychometric aids.

The companion Lawrence Psychological Forensic Examination Reports is a collection of sample forensic evaluation reports written by Lawrence using the outlines, checklists, interviews, and suggestions that are contained in the Lawrence Psychological Forensic Examination.

In sum, the Lawrence is a kind of outline for an applied textbook in the area of forensic psychology. It certainly would be useful to almost all beginners and to a great many experienced professionals in the area of forensic psychology. None of the material approaches being a "test" with acceptable psychometric properties. Researchers and practitioners looking for a more standardly defined and supported test of competency should check the Competency Screening Test (Lipsitt, Lelos, & McGarry, 1971) with the caution the instrument is appropriate only for subjects who are literate.

REVIEWER'S REFERENCE

Lipsitt, P. D., Lelos, D., & McGarry, A. L. (1971). Competency for trial: A screening instrument. *American Journal of Psychiatry*, 128, 105-109.

[172]

Leadership Skills Inventory. Purpose: "Assess strengths and weaknesses in the area of leadership." Grades 4–12; 1985; LSI; self-administered and self-scored; 9 categories: Fundamentals of Leadership, Written Communication Skills, Speech Communication Skills, Values Clarification, Decision Making Skills, Group Dynamics Skills, Problem Solving Skills, Personal Development Skills, Planning Skills; 1985 price data: $29 per complete kit; $14.95 per 25 inventory booklets; $10.50 per activities manual (52 pages); $14.35 per administration manual (19 pages); $14.95 per computer version; (45) minutes; Frances A. Karnes and Jane C. Chauvin; D.O.K. Publishers.*

Review of the Leadership Skills Inventory by BARBARA A. KERR, Assistant Professor of Counselor Education, The University of Iowa, Iowa City, IA:

The Leadership Skills Inventory (LSI) holds promise as an instrument for self-assessment of leadership skills; more research is needed, however, before it can be used confidently for this purpose. The major difficulty with the inventory lies in the inadequate establishment of its validity.

The LSI comprises nine domains presumed to be related to leadership skills: Fundamentals of Leadership, Written Communication Skills, Speech Communication Skills, Values Clarification, Problem-solving Skills, Personal Skills, and Planning Skills. It is not clear, however, that the construct of "leadership skills" is adequately represented by the instrument. A thorough review of the literature was performed, according to the authors, and the reference list appearing at the end of the manual is a listing of major sources. However, the absence of elements of leadership considered important in much of the social psychology and industrial organizational psychology literature—such as interpersonal influence skills and leadership development skills—is puzzling. A group of adult professionals and a group of youth participants in youth organizations served as panels to review the items developed by the authors, and to make suggestions. The literature review and the use of the panel for item review constituted the only validity research. The use of instruments such as 4-H's Life Skills for Leadership (Miller, 1984) or the Need Dominance Scale of the Edwards Personal Preference Inventory (Edwards, 1953) could have helped to establish concurrent validity. A study comparing the performance of proven young leaders (e.g., successful organization officers) with nonleaders would have lent credibility to claims of construct validity for the LSI. More work is clearly needed before the inventory can be considered to measure what it intends to measure.

The reliability data presented by the authors show the inventory to be internally consistent, with split-half and Kuder-Richardson reliability coefficients mostly in the .80s for the seven regional samples. (A total of 452 students participated in the development of the instrument.) Test-retest reliability was found to be quite low in the one sample featuring this procedure, with six of the subscales having coefficients of .49 and under. Therefore some scales, particularly Fundamentals of Leadership, Personal Skills, and Planning Skills, may lack stability.

The instrument itself is simple, clear, and easily read by most children over 10 years of age. For each category of leadership skills, the respondent is given a set of competency statements followed by Likert 4-point scales anchored by *Almost Always* and *Almost Never*, (e.g., "I know how to get and use written information.") It seems likely that children might learn about the skills of leadership while responding to the inventory.

The authors assume truthful responding to the inventory. In fact, they say that individuals "can obtain a realistic assessment of their current leadership skills. Due to the self-reporting and self-scoring format, individuals can obtain a more objective view of themselves, rather than being rated by others who may be less knowledgeable about the person's individual strengths and weaknesses." This is a novel usage for the word "objective"! Clearly, this instrument is not at all objective, but entirely subjective. Because it is a self-report measure which does not control for socially desirable responding, it would not serve well as a measure of leadership skills for purposes such as identification of potential leaders or selection for leadership positions.

However, the LSI is probably a good self-exploration and learning experience. The authors include a helpful manual of learning activities that form a basis for an experiential learning course in leadership skills. This inventory and activities manual deserve further study.

REVIEWER'S REFERENCES

Edwards, A. L. (1953). *The Edwards Personal Preference Schedule*. New York: The Psychological Corporation.

Miller, R. (1984). *Leader/agents guide/leadership life skills*. Stillwater, OK: Southern Region 4-H Materials.

Review of the Leadership Skills Inventory by STEVEN W. LEE, Assistant Professor of Educational Psychology and Research, University of Kansas, Lawrence, KS:

The Leadership Skills Inventory (LSI) was developed to assess leadership skills of a wide range of individuals (age 9 to adults) in school and youth organizations as well as in business and industry. The LSI kit includes an administration and an activities manual. The activities manual provides many diverse activities designed to help a group leader foster leadership skills among students. The LSI is an untimed test that can be administered in a group or individually. No special training is required of the examiner, and the LSI may be administered orally. The LSI administration manual states that the LSI is a "self-administered, self-scored inventory," although no scoring directions are provided to the examinee on the test form. The scoring for each of the leadership domains is fairly straightforward: The total raw score for each domain is plotted on a profile sheet that provides *T*-score conversions for each domain raw score. The obtained *T* score(s) can then be compared to the normative group. The instructions for administration properly point out that the LSI is an inventory and not a "test." The instructions are sufficiently clear for an understanding of what is to be done, but no examples or sample questions are provided.

Although the manual states that a "thorough review of the literature pertaining to leadership" was done, no clear method of item development is provided in the manual. Two panels of individuals evaluated the generated items and the "suggestions were incorporated." These panels included one group of professional persons from youth organizations and education, while the other group consisted of youths from the same organizations.

The norms are published in the manual; however, the administrative conditions under which the normative data were obtained are not clearly specified, except to say that the teachers were "forwarded the needed number of inventories and the preliminary manual which stated the purpose of the instrument and guidelines for administration." The normative group is comprised of 452 school children with a mean age of 14.6 years. Of this group, 207 were male and 215 were female, and they ranged in age from 9 to 18. The normative sample was obtained from choosing the sample is not provided. No apparent stratification plan for representativeness of the normative sample was employed. As a result, the representativeness of the normative sample of the LSI can be called into question, particularly for important variables such as age, geographic region, rural vs. urban, income levels, or race.

Although normative data were obtained from various states across the U.S., it was not possible to ascertain the rationale for the geographic sampling procedure, because it is not provided in the manual. The manual states that the LSI is designed to assess leadership skills "at the upper elementary, secondary and post-secondary levels," and norms are provided for children ages 9 to 18. However, only a portion of the Louisiana sample (*N* = 107, mean age of 14.4 years) included students below age 12. Therefore, the age group 9 to 11 is inadequately represented within the normative sample. Since the norms are not reported by age, the LSI consumer cannot ascertain whether age differences were found or have been reported in the leadership literature. Scores by age for each leadership domain should be provided. The norms are reported in raw scores. The mean and standard deviation for each leadership domain is provided; however, no other measures of central tendency or variability are reported. Local norms are provided for the states previously mentioned; however, the samples for these norms are small and they vary in age range and male-female demographics. No other stratification characteristics are reported for the local norms in the manual.

The LSI manual reports estimates of internal consistency (Kuder-Richardson) of .78 or above for each leadership domain for the total sample. Somewhat lower estimates of internal consistency were found for the local norms, but none below .65. The domain entitled Fundamentals of Leadership tended to show the lowest estimate of internal consistency, while Group Dynamics displayed the highest. The temporal stability of the LSI was assessed only for the Louisiana sample (*N* = 45). Test-retest reliability estimates ranged from poor to fair in this sample, with the Fundamentals of Leadership domain exhibiting the lowest test-retest reliability (.30 over 4 weeks), and the domain of Speech Communication exhibiting the highest (.67).

No scorer reliability estimates are provided in the manual. In addition, no estimates of the Standard Error of Measurement (*SEM*) are reported. The *SEM* information would help to determine if the scores are sufficiently dependable for the intended use of the LSI.

A paucity of information regarding the validity of the LSI is presented in the manual. Item content validity is purported to exist due to the expertise and creditability of the members of the panels who made suggestions on item content. However, the panels did not include personnel development specialists in business and industry for which the LSI is purportedly useful. No estimates of concurrent or construct validity are reported in the manual. As a result, we do not know whether the leadership domains of the LSI can empirically be shown to exist, nor do we have any idea of their relationship with other measures of leadership characteristics. Further, no plan for gathering these essential validity data is presented. Given these severe psychometric deficits, cautions should be elucidated by the authors as to the limits of generalizability of the results at the LSI; unfortunately, none are provided.

In summary, the LSI is a test which is purported to measure leadership skills. However, due to a lack of concurrent and construct validity estimates, no empirical confirmation is provided for the trait of leadership the LSI purports to measure. Therefore, it is not possible to ascertain whether the construct of leadership exists separate from other personality characteristics, let alone if separate domains exist within the construct of leadership. The internal consistency reliability of the LSI is high, but the data on temporal stability is weak at best. Fundamental information regarding how the items were developed and the rationale for obtaining the normative sample is not provided. The LSI normative group did not appear to be stratified, and has a very small and unrepresentative sample for certain age groups. The best use of the LSI may be as an informal tool to assess an individual's strengths and weaknesses in leadership-type skills and the use of the ideas in the activities manual for intervention strategies.

[173]

Learning-Style Inventory. Purpose: "Designed to help individuals assess their ability to learn from experience." College and adults; 1976–85; LSI; self-administered; 6 scores: Concrete Experience, Reflective Observation, Abstract Conceptualization, Active Experimentation, Abstract/Concrete, Active/Reflective; 1985 price data: $55 per 10 self-scoring test and interpretation booklets; $10 per technical manual ('85, 10 pages); (10) minutes; David A. Kolb; McBer and Company.*

See 9:607 (7 references).

TEST REFERENCES

1. Parker, C. L. (1982). Facilitating career development in a small business. *The Vocational Guidance Quarterly*, 31, 86-89.

2. Ferrell, B. G. (1983). A factor analytic comparison of four learning-styles instruments. *Journal of Educational Psychology*, 75, 33-39.

3. Beutell, N. J., & Kressel, S. S. (1984). An investigation of Kolb's Learning Styles Inventory: Social desirability and normative scoring. *Psychological Reports*, 55, 89-90.

4. Cahill, R., & Madigan, M. J. (1984). The influence of curriculum format on learning preference and learning style. *The American Journal of Occupational Therapy*, 38, 683-686.

5. Marshall, E. A. (1984). Relationship between client-learning style and preference for counselor approach. *Counselor Education and Supervision*, 24, 353-359.

6. Merritt, S. L., & Marshall, J. C. (1984). Reliability and construct validity of ipsative and normative forms of the Learning Style Inventory. *Educational and Psychological Measurement*, 44, 463-472.

7. Ricca, J. (1984). Learning styles and preferred instructional strategies of gifted students. *Gifted Child Quarterly*, 28, 121-126.

8. Hayden, R. R., & Brown, M. S. (1985). Learning styles and correlates. *Psychological Reports*, 56, 243-246.

9. Marshall, E. A. (1985). Relationship between client-learning style and preference for counselor approach. *Counselor Education and Supervision*, 24, 353-359.

10. Marshall, J. C., & Merritt, S. L. (1985). Reliability and construct validity of alternate forms of the Learning Style Inventory. *Educational and Psychological Measurement*, 45, 931-937.

11. Gordon, V. N., Coscarelli, W. C., & Sears, S. J. (1986). Comparative assessments of individual differences in learning and career decision making. *Journal of College Student Personnel*, 27, 233-242.

12. Katz, N. (1986). Construct validity of Kolb's Learning Style Inventory, using factor analysis and Guttman's smallest space analysis. *Perceptual and Motor Skills*, 63, 1323-1326.

13. Pettigrew, F. E., & Buell, C. M. (1986). Relation of two perceptual styles to learning a novel motor skill. *Perceptual and Motor Skills*, 63, 1097-1098.

14. Sims, R. R., Veres, J. G., III, Watson, P., & Buckner, K. E. (1986). The reliability and classification stability of the Learning Style Inventory. *Educational and Psychological Measurement*, 46, 753-760.

15. Sinatra, R., Primavera, L., & Waked, W. J. (1986). Learning style and intelligence of reading disabled students. *Perceptual and Motor Skills*, 63, 1243-1250.

16. Highhouse, S., & Doverspike, D. (1987). The validity of the Learning Style Inventory 1985 as a predictor of cognitive style and occupational preference. *Educational and Psychological Measurement*, 47 (3), 749-754.

17. Veres, J. G., III, Sims, R. R., & Shake, L. G. (1987). The reliability and classification stability of the Learning Style Inventory in corporate settings. *Educational and Psychological Measurement*, 47 (4), 1127-1133.

Review of the Learning-Style Inventory by NOEL GREGG, Director, Learning Disabilities Adult Clinic, College of Education, The University of Georgia, Athens, GA:

The Learning-Style Inventory (LSI) revised in 1985 was developed by David A. Kolb to identify differences among individual learning styles and corresponding learning environments. It is a self-report inventory that purports to measure four dimensions of learning style, namely, Concrete Experience (feeling), Reflective Observation (watching), Abstract Conceptualization (thinking), and Active Experimentation (doing).

The theoretical foundation of the inventory is based upon the Jungian concept of styles or types. The theory predicts fulfillment in adult development is accomplished by higher level integration and expression of nondominant modes of dealing with the world. The LSI model of learning is described as a four-stage cycle that initiates with concrete experiences forming the basis for observation and reflection. The observations are then assimilated into concepts that serve as guides in creating new experiences.

The inventory is made up of 12 simple sentence-completion items written at a clear, accessible reading level. The written directions then require the respondent to rank order four sentence endings that correspond to the four learning modes: Concrete Experience (CE); Reflective Observation (RO); Abstract Conceptualization (AC); and Active Experimentation (AE). The number of most choices relevant to a dimension yields a raw score varying from 12 to 48. The author purports these scores can be used to classify an individual into one of four learning-style types (i.e., converger, diverger, assimilator, and accommodator). No evidence is provided, however, to show that the typology is meaningful; therefore, this format yields ipsative scores. Two combination scores are also obtained that indicate the extent to which the individual emphasizes abstractness over concreteness (AC-CE) and the extent to which he or she emphasizes action over reflection (AE-RO). These raw scores vary from +36 to -36. The entire Learning Style Inventory comes in a self-scoring booklet containing the inventory, the

Learning-Style profile, and the Learning-Style type grid.

Technical specifications for the LSI are provided in a separate 10-page document. The reliability of the LSI for the four basic scales and two combination scores all show good internal reliability as measured by Cronbach's Standardized Scale Alpha ($n = 268$). The combination scores indicate almost perfect additivity (1.0) as measured by Tukey's Additivity test. The author also provides a comparison of LSI 1985 with items from the original LSI as revised. Simplified split-half reliability (Spearman-Brown) figures are described. The standardized percentile scores are based on a sample of 1,446 adults between the ages of 18 and 60. The sample of 638 men and 801 women is described as to age and educational level. While the authors state the norming population is "ethnically diverse," no figures are provided to support this claim. Average raw scale scores for each subtest and combination scores for this sample are provided along with their standard deviations. Finally, the authors provide the intercorrelations among the LSI scales.

Section 9 of the technical document provides a graphic description of the validity relationship between the LSI and career fields of study. This is the only discussion of validity in the manual. No systematic information on convergent-discriminant validity is presented. An overall evaluation of the validity data would be the scales measure what they purport to measure but a more complete and accurate description of criteria needs to be provided. Further documentation on the validity of the LSI is supposedly discussed in *Experimental Learning: Experience as the Source of Learning and Development* (1984) by David Kolb, published by Prentice-Hall.

A review of the research on the LSI indicated that no research has been conducted using the LSI since the middle 1970s. No research could be located that has used the revised LSI. Two additional resources can be bought separately to accompany the LSI. One, a *User Guide for the Learning-Style Inventory* by Donna Smith and David Kolb, is a manual for teachers and trainers. The second resource is the *Personal Learning Guide* by Richard Baker, Nancy Dixon, and David Kolb. This is a guide to increasing one's learning from a training program or course of study. Both books are published by McBer and Company.

In conclusion, the LSI is a promising measurement. It is a quick and reliable self-report instrument measuring learning style. However, further development of the technical manual is needed, as well as research investigating the usefulness of the inventory. Questions of validity will need to await further research.

[174]

LOCO (Learning Opportunities Coordination) A Scale for the Assessment of Coordinated Learning Opportunities in Living Units for People with a Handicap. Purpose: "For indicating to what extent a Living Unit for people with handicaps is able to contribute significantly to their social and personal development and to maintain a level of reasonable independence." Residents of any type of living units where people with a handicap live with the assistance of care givers; 1987; LOCO; can be used in conjunction with P-A-C (Progress Assessment Chart)(9:1003); 4 scores: Basic Training Conditions, Essential Items, Additional Items, Total; 1987 price data: $12 (U.S.) per complete test; administration time not reported; H. C. Gunzburg and A. L. Gunzburg; SEFA (Publications) Ltd. [England].*

[175]

Long Performance Efficiency Test. Purpose: "Measures . . . a subject's potential for satisfactory work performance in any type of job situation." Grade 7 and over; 1983; P.E.T.; individual; 1985 price data: $7.25 per complete test including manual ('83, 11 pages) and set of 3 cards (A, B, C); $5.50 per set of 3 cards; $2.25 per manual; (5–6) minutes; Thomas Rex Long; Stoelting Co.*

Review of the Long Performance Efficiency Test by ROBERT B. SLANEY, Associate Professor of Counseling Psychology, The Pennsylvania State University, University Park, PA:

The Long Performance Efficiency Test consists of three 8 1/2 x 11 cards and involves four colors: red, yellow, green, and blue. Card A prints the four color-words in black ink. Card B prints 1/4-inch squares of the four colors. Card C prints the color-words in red, yellow, green, or blue ink and the color of the ink differs from the meaning of the color-word. For example, the word yellow is printed in red ink. Each color-word or color appears 25 times in random order on each card. On the reverse side of each card, 10 examples of the words or colors are presented to ensure the subject understands the tasks. These cards are presented in order (A, B, C) with the examples preceding the actual tasks. For card A the task is to read the color-words. For card B the color squares are to be named. For card C the task is to name the color of the ink in which the color-word is printed. For example, if the color-word is red but it is printed in green ink then the correct response is green, not red. Responses are timed and uncorrected errors are recorded. The administration takes an estimated 5–6 minutes.

The cards are nicely produced and clearly printed. However, for an instrument that focuses on color, it does not seem unreasonable to wish the yellow were more lemony and less jaundiced looking. The Test Manual is printed in readable type and the writing is generally clear. The Manual consists of nine pages divided into eight sections: Introduction, Test Materials, Administration, Scoring, Correction for Errors, Interpretation, Statistics, and Bibliography. The cards are described succinctly and clear instructions are provided for the administration and recording of the results. Test-retest results over a 1-week period support the reliability of the measure. There does seem to be some confusion about whether the measure may cause anxiety but this is a relatively minor concern. Other minor concerns are apparent when one seeks to determine and interpret the score for the respondent. For each error the average time for the correct responses is added to the total time. No rationale for this correction is presented. It also becomes evident that only card C is considered for errors and total time. The relevance of cards A and B is not addressed. Given the time required for administration, this may not be important but it is an obvious question. More importantly, in order to make sense of the results, once a score is determined, one must enter one of two tables. To do this one needs an IQ score. (Those who have not brought an IQ score, take one step backward.) These tables use norms based on a correlation of -.577 between card C time and IQ or a formula apparently based on a regression equation. No explanations are given for the derivation of these values nor is any additional information provided in their support. The absence of this information raises very basic questions about these values.

Even more basic issues are raised by the statement that describes what the test purportedly measures and the validity data that are provided in support of that statement. The author states that:

> On the basis of extensive research, the test measures with good reliability and empirical validity a subject's potential for satisfactory work performance in any type of job situation. No matter what type of activities or responsibilities is required, skilled, unskilled, or professional, the P.E.T. will identify those least likely to perform and compete successfully (p. 4).

Certainly these statements, notable for their clarity, breadth, and lack of qualification, command attention. After reading these sweeping statements, perhaps even the most optimistic reviewer can be forgiven for turning to inspect the validity data with a certain degree of skepticism. Unfortunately, the data that are provided are neither extensive nor reassuring. In fact, it is difficult not to notice the bibliography contains only two citations and that only one (the author's dissertation, dated 1964) appears relevant to the development of data on the instrument. This may suggest that when the author notes the measure has "been under investigation on and off for almost twenty-four years" that the investigation has perhaps been off considerably more often than it has been on. Although the development of this instrument may have involved gathering data in addition to that gathered in the original dissertation, this is not stated in the Manual.

Apparently, three studies form the basis for the validity of the instrument. The first looked at differences between "producer subjects," that is, subjects "who are successfully employed on the job in the general population" and "nonproducer subjects," (i.e., "unsuccessful, unemployed, and poorly motivated subjects"). Matched on age and IQ, a statistically significant *t*-test indicated the latter group took longer to respond to cards A, B, and C. In commenting on these results the author noted that: "No theoretical considerations are offered at this time regarding the etiology of these differences other than the general diagnostic classifications of neurosis and organic brain syndrome." Although this sentence seems to defy understanding, there is apparently some connection between its intended meaning and the next study which compared "controls, neurotics, and organics." The latter are described elsewhere as "organic brain syndrome cases." It appears the subjects were matched on age and IQ. How that was accomplished is not reported but does raise one's curiosity. The results suggest that "neurotics" take longer than controls but not as long as "organics" to respond to cards A, B, and C although no analyses are reported on these differences. Finally, a comparison between three different age groups (17–24; 25–44; and 45–64) found that older subjects took longer in responding to card C. Again no analyses are reported. The above studies constitute the sum of the validity data provided for the measure.

The descriptions of the validity studies are exceedingly vague. This is particularly true when it comes to describing the subjects and the basis for their selection and classification. For example, the sex of the subjects is not mentioned. Nor is it noted where the subjects came from, who categorized them as "controls, neurotics, or organics," or how this was accomplished. These considerations, as basic as they are, seem secondary to the striking disparity between the stated purpose of the instrument and the studies that were carried out to support its validity. Whether one is struck more by the grandiosity of the stated purpose of the measure, the inadequacy and irrelevance of the validity studies, or the apparent fact that the author appears to believe that support for his measure has been provided, may not be of central importance. However, the total impact of these related concerns is of central importance and suggests this instrument cannot be recommended for any purpose related to measurement.

[176]

Louisville Behavior Checklist. Purpose: "Designed to help parents conceptualize and communicate concerns about their children." Ages 4–6, 7–12, 13–17; 1977–84; LBC; 13 to 20 scales; 3 levels; 1987 price data: $65 per complete kit of any 1 level including 10 reusable questionnaires, 25 answer-profile sheets, scoring keys, 1 WPS test report sheet, and manual ('84, 124 pages); $11.85 per 25 reusable questionnaires; $12.10 per 100 answer-profile sheets; $22.50 per scoring keys; $22.50 per manual; $149.50 per microcomputer edition for IBM or Apple; scoring service, $6.95 or less per questionnaire; administration time not reported; Lovick C. Miller; Western Psychological Services.*

a) FORM E1. Ages 4–6; 20 scales: Infantile Aggression, Hyperactivity, Antisocial Behavior, Aggression, Social Withdrawal, Sensitivity, Fear, Inhibition, Intellectual Deficit, Immaturity, Cognitive Disability, Normal Irritability, Prosocial Deficit, Rare Deviance, Neurotic Behavior, Psychotic Behavior, Somatic Behavior, Sexual Behavior, School Disturbance Predictor, Severity Level.

b) FORM E2. Ages 7–12; 19 scales: same as for Form E1 except Academic Disability replaces Intellectual Deficit, Learning Disability replaces Cognitive Disability, and School Disturbance Predictor is omitted.

c) FORM E3. Ages 13–17; 13 scales: Egocentric-Exploitive, Destructive-Assaultive, Social Delinquency, Adolescent Turmoil, Apathetic Isolation, Neuroticism, Dependent-Inhibited, Academic Disability, Neurological or Psychotic Abnormality, General Pathology, Longitudinal, Severity Level, Total Pathology.

For a review by Betty N. Gordon, see 9:635 (5 references); see also T3:1343 (1 reference).

TEST REFERENCES

1. Fisher, S. G. (1984). Time-limited brief therapy with families: A one-year follow-up study. *Family Process*, 23, 101-106.

2. Gomes-Schwartz, B., Horowitz, J. M., & Sauzier, M. (1985). Severity of emotional distress among sexually abused preschool, school-age, and adolescent children. *Hospital and Community Psychiatry*, 36, 503-508.

3. Krantz, S. E., Clark, J., Pruyn, J. P., & Usher, M. (1985). Cognition and adjustment among children of separated or divorced parents. *Cognitive Therapy and Research*, 9, 61-77.

4. Shafii, M., Carrigan, S., Whittinghill, J. R., & Derrick, A. (1985). Psychological autopsy of completed suicide in children and adolescents. *American Journal of Psychiatry*, 142, 1061-1064.

5. Clingempeel, W. G., & Segal, S. (1986). Stepparent-stepchild relationships and the psychological adjustment of children in stepmother and stepfather families. *Child Development*, 57, 474-484.

6. Funk, J. B., Ruppert, E. S., & Jurs, S. G. (1986). A preliminary investigation of associations between disorders of behavior and language in children with chronic otitis media. *Child Study Journal*, 16, 255-264.

Review of the Louisville Behavior Checklist by FRANCIS E. LENTZ, JR., Associate Professor of School Psychology and Counseling, University of Cincinnati, Cincinnati, OH:

The Louisville Behavior Checklist (LBC) is intended to allow parents to "conceptualize and communicate concerns about their children" and was previously evaluated in *The Ninth Mental Measurements Yearbook* (9:635). Although such instruments are also often used by teachers for the same purposes, there are no normative data for teacher informants. The author suggests that the LBC be interpreted by professional mental health workers as part of a general clinical evaluation.

Since the previous review of the LBC, the manual has been revised; however, the extent of the revisions is unclear, and no new data other than a few additional validity studies published since 1981 (previous revision) are included. The checklist itself and basic accompanying psychometric data remain the same. The evaluation in the previous review (9:635) remains generally adequate in this reviewer's opinion. This review will provide: a brief evaluation of the impact of the new information; some additional comments on reliability and validity; comments on the discussion of case studies within the current manual (it is not certain if these were included in the previous edition; they were not commented upon); and an evaluative summary based on any new conclusions or addenda to the original review.

RELIABILITY. No new data are provided on reliability; the previous data are insufficient for this type of instrument. For retrospective checklists of this sort several types of data on reliability need to be provided for all scores intended to be used (by age, each scale, broad band conglomerates, total scores): internal consistency of discrete scales; across informant (within setting, for example, between parents, or between two educational personnel in a school setting); and test-retest with the same informant and for different informants. Additionally, if individual items are to be used (and uses for individual items are proposed by the author), then similar analyses should be performed per item (across scorer, test-retest, etc.) for both correlation and level differences. Only brief data for internal consistency (all three scales) and test-retest (forms E1 and E2) are reported. These coefficients are generally acceptable. It should be noted that much of the supporting data for form E2 comes from a pilot form (D), and yet response formats and sequences of items were changed in form E2.

VALIDITY. Validity information has been slightly enhanced in the revised manual. One study on form E2 confirms differentiation of group means (on three scales) between "general population and clinical subjects." In addition, studies are reported using the LBC to compare children with cystic fibrosis and their siblings. Unfortunately, the results are reported in a conflicting manner, with both no significant results reported, and then in the next sentence significant differences reported. A second study (details not reported) compared custodial and noncustodial parents of children with separated parents. The degree of cooperative parenting was related to similarity of ratings (no data are reported).

These data do not really alter the conclusions in the previous review. Construct validity (through factor analysis) has not been thoroughly explored; and many scales were not developed through factor analysis, rather a combination of factor analysis and "clinical judgment." There are minimal data on the relationship of the LBC to other similar checklists, or more importantly to direct measures of children's behavior. Norms are very out of date; however, the author reports (briefly) a large 1982 study of the LBC (forms E1–2) in Nevada. This study concludes that samples in the original LBC studies and from Nevada do not show different response patterns. The lack of a national sample, the reported return rates for the original norming study, the use of a different form to derive many norms for form E2, and the lack of extensive validity studies on form E3 remain very serious problems.

There are a series of case profiles reported in the manual. These case interpretations must be considered highly speculative. There are no data on the reliability of profiles, on whether the profiles provided are consistent for various types of children, or on the utility of LBC assessment data for the reported cases. In summary, these case interpretations should not be used except as examples of the author's interpretations. Certainly there is no reason to assume generality across clinicians or cases.

MANUAL. The revised manual remains confusing (a comment on the previous review), to some extent because much of the data reported as describing the current forms were in fact derived from the last pilot form (D).

SUMMARY. There is nothing in the current revision to alter the conclusions of the previous reviewer: support for the LBC, (reliability, validity, and normative information) is not adequate. Readers are referred to the scales developed by Achenbach (Child Behavior Checklist; 9:213) for use by teachers, parents, observers, and children themselves. Although by no means perfect, accompanying documentation is superior to that of the LBC. The LBC may yet prove more useful if additional research is conducted.

[177]

MAC Checklist for Evaluating, Preparing and/or Improving Standardized Tests for Limited English Speaking Students. Purpose: Aids in the review, critique, or preparation of

ESL assessment instruments. ESL test developers, reviewers, and users; 1981; 5 criterion categories: Evidence of Validity, Evidence of Examinee Appropriateness, Evidence of Proper Item Construction, Evidence of Technical Merit, Evidence of Administrative Excellence; 1985 price data: $3.95 per checklist ('81, 71 pages); Jean D'Arcy Maculaitis; the Author.*

Review of the MAC Checklist for Evaluating, Preparing and/or Improving Standardized Tests for Limited English Speaking Students by EUGENE E. GARCIA, Professor/Director, Center for Bilingual/Bicultural Education, Arizona State University, Tempe, AZ:

With the continuing increase of students in U.S. schools whose native language is not English, a variety of educational professionals are called upon to make linguistic, intellectual, and academic assessments of these students. As part of these assessments, standardized instruments are likely to be utilized. In recent years the number of instruments available for the assessment of nonnative English speakers and the demand for the use of these instruments has increased. Moreover, the specific demand on educational personnel to judge the adequacy of these instruments provides evidence of the need for a guide to assist in the evaluation, preparation, and improvement of standardized tests for limited-English-speaking students.

The MAC Checklist provides an examination of the issues that should guide test users in determining the adequacy of a standardized test for use with limited-English student populations. It does so by providing: (*a*) 103 criteria regarding the psychometric and general characteristics of a standardized measure; (*b*) "rights" and tips for test takers; (*c*) selected sources of bilingual tests and testing information; and (*d*) a partial list of selected commercially available English-language measures. The MAC Checklist extracts from the larger testing literature those general aspects of testing that serve to determine a theoretically and methodologically sound measure. In addition, this checklist incorporates specific issues (cultural aspects of items, linguistic diversity, tester bias, etc.) of relevance in the assessment of language minority students. The MAC Checklist professes to be of assistance in test development and modification. Inasmuch as it details the attributes of a "good" test, the MAC Checklist addresses these two issues indirectly. Otherwise, the checklist does not directly deal with test development and modification.

The strength of the MAC Checklist is its direct and satisfactory treatment of standardized test-evaluation criteria. It does provide a useful summary of general test validity, reliability, and administrative criteria. The listing of English-language measures that have become available to educators is useful to professionals unaware of such measures.

Unfortunately for the language-minority professional, the MAC Checklist does not address specific issues of relevance to non-English standardized measures. For determination of educational status and treatment, language-minority students are subjected to assessment of (*a*) the native language, (*b*) English, and (*c*) native language and/or English academic achievement. The MAC Checklist primarily confines itself to issues of relevance to English language measures. In doing so, it is of limited usefulness to the practitioner. Moreover, even in its treatment of English measures, the MAC Checklist does not provide any discussion that will allow a user to determine a yes/no response to a criteria question (e.g., a tester is asked to make a judgement about the test's cultural relevance based on recent research findings; however, a novice test user may have no background to make that judgement).

Most significantly, the MAC Checklist was designed to be of direct assistance to teachers and school administrators. Unfortunately, the vocabulary and terminology used are highly technical and likely to be outside the expertise of a teacher or school administrator. The MAC Checklist is best utilized by the school psychologist or program evaluator. These professionals should already be well versed on test evaluation; however, this summary can be a handy and helpful reference.

As indicated earlier, the MAC Checklist provides one of the few listings of standardized instruments commonly used in language minority education efforts. However, no analysis is provided (i.e., how do these instruments fare when they are evaluated on the criteria identified by the checklist?). Such an analysis would be extremely helpful to the professionals for whom the checklist was developed.

In conclusion, the MAC Checklist can be of assistance in determining the appropriateness of English language measures developed for use with limited-English-proficient students. However, it is not likely to be of significant assistance to individuals who are not already aware of issues related to test theory and application. Moreover, this checklist is restricted to English language measures only.

Review of the MAC Checklist for Evaluating, Preparing and/or Improving Standardized Tests for Limited English Speaking Students by CHARLES W. STANSFIELD, Director, Division of Foreign Language Education and Testing, Center for Applied Linguistics, Washington, DC:

The MAC Checklist is a collection of guidelines for evaluating, selecting, and using standardized tests. The name "MAC" is associated with the author, Jean D'Arcy Maculaitis, who has also written a multilevel English-language-proficiency measure known as the MAC Test. The Checklist presents 103 questions about test materials, organized into groups called criterion categories. The user of the Checklist is to mark "yes" or "no" in a space to the left of each question. The Checklist is intended for test developers, reviewers, and users. It is divided into three parts.

Part I is a four-page introduction that describes the author's purpose and approach to developing the Checklist and gives an overview of the text. This information is interspersed with advice about the analysis of standardized tests.

Part II, Criterion Categories, is the main part of the text. The criterion categories are the question groups for evaluating tests. Category A, validity, contains 22 questions dealing with basic issues, including evidence of content validity, criterion-related validity, the availability of norms, subgroup information, and so on. One guideline asks whether the manual contains correlations between each item and the total score as evidence of validity. This question tends to confuse validity with discrimination. An item can be valid without being discriminating. Also, item discrimination values are not ordinarily reported in a test manual.

The second category of questions deals with examinee appropriateness. These 17 questions are intended to allow the reviewer of a test to assess the degree to which the test is suitable for examinees of specific age or grade levels and cultural or ethnic backgrounds. The questions relate to the relevance of items and pictures to the examinees, the adequacy of test directions, whether a sample test is made available to examinees, the quality of the printing and layout of test materials, and whether the time alloted is adequate and the pacing is appropriate.

The third criterion category, proper item construction, deals with the quality of the test items. These guidelines are the most valuable because most books on measurement slight the art of item writing. Maculaitis brings her test development experience to this section of the Checklist. The guidelines ask the test evaluator to assess whether items are written in concise and clear language, whether clues to the correct answer are found in earlier or subsequent items, whether more than one correct answer is possible for any item, whether all distractors are plausible, and whether assignment of keyed items to position (A, B, C, or D) is random. The author also suggests that items be examined in terms of whether content experts, or native English speakers in the case of an English-as-a-second-language test, could answer them correctly. One perplexing guideline is "Are the number of distractors related to the examinees' age/grade level?" This reviewer is not aware of any research suggesting a different number of distractors as optimum for students of different grade levels.

The fourth category, technical merit, pertains to test reliability. The 17 questions ask about the existence of parallel forms, the discrimination power of the test, the appropriateness of the reliability coefficients reported, and the general quality and usability of the technical manual. Again, a couple of guidelines are questionable. For instance, the author states, "Six months is the recommended maximum time interval between administrations of the same or an equivalent form of the test." The basis for this recommendation is unclear. For example, there is no reason why different forms of a test cannot be administered at the beginning and end of a school year to measure progress on a standardized test.

The final category deals with the quality of the instructions for administering the test. There are 20 questions concerning matters such as the qualifications of test administrators, proctors, and test score interpreters, number of proctors required, and so on. A number of questions pertain to the presentation of score interpretation data, such as the existence of norms for subgroups, and the explanation of standard scores. One unusual guideline asks whether the manual gives different norms for the different types of answer sheets that may be used with the test. Although this guideline may pose a legitimate research question, this reviewer is not aware of such a practice nor that it is even recommended by testing professionals.

Part II of the Checklist presents four appendices. These include lists of 50 basic rights of examinees and 50 hints for examinees in preparing for tests. Although these are useful, it is not apparent why they appear in a document that appears to be aimed at test developers, evaluators, and score users rather than examinees. A third appendix presents sources of information on testing and tests, particularly tests for the nonnative English speaker. The reader is urged to join specific professional organizations, including the National Association for Bilingual Education and Teachers of English to Speakers of Other Languages, to write for specific newsletters, and even to contact specific individuals at the New York State Department of Education. These appendices apparently are reprints of handouts that were used by Maculaitis in the testing workshops she offers in New York and New Jersey. The fourth appendix lists some commercially available tests that appear to satisfy her criteria. Few of these are tests designed for limited-English-proficient students.

Following a references section is a glossary of testing terminology used in the text. The glossary is the weakest section of the text. Many of the terms are explained inadequately. For instance, the author defines the Pearson Product-Moment Reliability Coefficient as "one of several methods used to compute reliability coefficients. (It is the preferred method because it more accurately reflects the differences between and among scores.)" The fact that such coefficients are measures of test-retest or parallel-form reliability is not mentioned. The sentence in parentheses contributes little to the definition, particularly since reliability involves only a single group of examinees.

The MAC Checklist seems to be a collection of handouts from a testing workshop. As such, it contains a number of useful questions that practicing teachers could ask when evaluating standardized tests. Its usefulness is limited to that of supplemental material, however. It should not be relied on or used in lieu of a comprehensive text in educational measurement or the *Standards for Educational and Psychological Testing* (APA, AERA, NCME, 1985). Several of the texts on second language testing listed in the references section of the Checklist would also be more useful than the Checklist. Given its practical format, however, the Checklist may be of some value to a teacher who is in the process of evaluating the suitability of a test for a given purpose and population.

REVIEWER'S REFERENCE

American Psychological Association, American Educational Research Association, & National Council on Measurement in Education. (1985). *Standards for educational and psychological testing*. Washington, DC: American Psychological Association, Inc.

[178]

Macmillan Graded Word Reading Test. Purpose: "To provide a general set of guidelines for the teacher not only on the standard of reading reached by pupils but on what else may need to be required in the reading process." Ages 6–13; 1985; GWRT; individual; 1988 price data: £14.95 per 25 record sheets, teacher's manual (24 pages), and word card; (5–10) minutes; Macmillan Test Unit and Bridie Raban; Macmillan Education Ltd. [England].*

Review of the Macmillan Graded Word Reading Test by BRUCE A. BRACKEN, Associate Professor, Department of Psychology, Memphis State University, Memphis, TN:

The Macmillan Graded Word Reading Test (GWRT) is a sight-word vocabulary scale designed to assess a client's ability to read presented words. The GWRT is packaged in a plastic packet and provides a two-sided stimulus reading chart (two forms), Teacher's Guide, and a tablet of record forms. The test is appropriate for individuals between the ages of 6 years 0 months and 13 years 3 months.

The critique of the GWRT will be divided into three sections: (*a*) manual, (*b*) materials, and (*c*) psychometric adequacy.

MANUAL. The manual (Teacher's Guide) for the GWRT is markedly deficient for a test published in 1985. The user of the GWRT is provided with very little information on such important topics as item construction, item tryouts, item analyses, standardization sample characteristics, interpretation of the test, etc.

In addition to these glaring omissions, the manual is poorly written, with many examples of unclear referents (e.g., they, them), and unsupportable or unusable statements (e.g., "Recording these details is a valuable aid to constructing a suitable teaching programme." In this example, there is no elaboration as to how "these details" will facilitate program development, and in all honesty the solution is less than intuitively obvious.

Rather than providing a sound rationale for the use of sight-word reading tests, the test author provides a defense against common criticisms made toward such tests. It is the opinion of this reviewer that tests should stem from sound theory and rationale rather than in response to one's critics. If the test is theoretically and psychometrically sound, the critics will be hushed.

MATERIALS. The stimulus materials (Word Cards 1 and 2) are eye pleasing in color and layout. Words are nicely spaced and separated. With 50 words per card, the page presents an uncluttered view. Two criticisms of the Word Cards have to do with the size and characteristics of the stimulus words.

First, it is well known that young children read upper case (capital) letters more easily than lower case letters. The easiest words presented on the Word Cards (e.g., the, you, from) should have been printed in an upper case mode to facilitate recognition. These earlier words are larger than the most difficult words by approximately 100 percent in an effort to increase readability. However, this varied letter size leaves one with the feeling they are reading a familiar Snellen Eye Chart, rather than a sight-word list.

Second, more up-to-date reading lists have begun to provide a mix of nonphonetic sight words with those that can be deciphered easily through word-attack strategies (e.g., ache, sword, gnat). Words of this sort truly assess the child's current sight-word reading vocabulary, rather than phonetic deciphering skills.

PSYCHOMETRIC ADEQUACY. The GWRT fails miserably in terms of its demonstration of technical adequacy. The lack of available information on item construction leaves one asking, "Why these words? What kind of item gradient exists? What about content validity?" and so forth. There are no answers to these questions in the Teacher's Guide.

While the Guide provides information on administration and scoring, a minimal number of examples are provided to aid the examiner in those odd cases that eventually surface. The standard scores, converted from obtained raw scores, are also explained minimally. The mean and standard deviation of the standard-score system are not provided, nor are percentile ranks. Thus, the meaning of the converted standard scores is of no greater value than the raw score; neither are easily interpreted in a norm-referenced fashion.

The manual deals with reliability by explaining the test/retest reliability of .85 is an alternate analysis of the KR-21 coefficient of .92. These are not alternate analyses, but both are equally important, depending on which aspect of reliability one is concerned with—stability or internal consistency. This is not explained to the reader and either assumes more psychometric sophistication on the behalf of teachers or the lack of sophistication of the test developer. The samples upon which these coefficients were determined are not described, and the length of the test-retest interval is not identified.

The manual reports nonsignificant sex- or region-related differences. Again, no description of the sample is provided for these studies and the actual obtained scores are not presented in the manual for the reader to inspect.

The standardization sample is not described in detail, and thus its representativeness is unknown. Subject selection according to race, gender, age, socioeconomic, and geographic variables are not described in the Teacher's Guide. However, the manual does reveal that the test was normed in England. Hence, no American norms are available.

The validity of the GWRT rests on a single comparison with the Macmillan Group Reading Test. Not only is this one comparison inadequate in number and description; the comparison of the individual test with its "big brother" group test will surely result in spuriously high correlations.

CONCLUSIONS. This reviewer acknowledges that sight-word reading tests have considerable utility. I have no a priori opposition to them as such. I do believe, however, that tests developed during this current decade should reflect the psychometric advances made during the past century. The publishers of the GWRT seem to have taken a Rip Van Winkle nap and missed out on at least 2 decades of advances in test development. It is recommended that the GWRT not be used, especially in the United States, until it is sufficiently developed to warrant such use. More elaborate development and reporting is needed before this test reaches a minimal standard suitable for public use.

Review of the Macmillan Graded Word Reading Test by DEBORAH B. ERICKSON, Assistant Professor of Psychology, Rochester Institute of Technology and Monroe Community College, Rochester, NY:

The Macmillan Graded Word Reading Test is a 50-word, 5-to-10-minute reading-recognition test developed and standardized in Great Britain. The test is designed to assess reading ability for ages 6 to 14 years. The authors of the test indicate that it is useful, in a qualitative sense, for older students who are below grade level in reading.

The test purports to yield information on grade-level ability and sight vocabulary versus trial and error vocabulary. The test provides for the analysis of errors in word beginnings, word endings, middle of the words, vowels, long vowels, consonant clusters, words inside words, mispronunciations, and reversals. Results are shown through standard scores and reading-age scores.

The test was designed despite recent criticisms toward word-recognition tests. Most reading experts believe reading words in isolation, rather than in context, is of limited use in the interpretation of the total reading process. Also, word-sample sizes are so small in this type of test that any interpretaion about reading ability must be made with extreme caution. However, the authors report that 60% of current teachers use word-recognition tests on a regular basis and will probably continue to use such tests due to their simplicity and speed.

The authors believe a thorough explanation of the limitations of word-recognition tests will reduce the abuse of this type of screening instrument. While the authors emphasize the need for a full battery of diagnostic assessment instruments for a diagnostic/prescriptive analysis of reading, the introduction section of the manual describes the test as allowing teachers to monitor standards, investigate the range of reading attainment in a school or class, and examine individual progress in reading if used at appropriate intervals. The authors indicate this test facilitates analysis of errors yielding diagnostic information that teachers can use to plan educational strategies in the teaching of reading.

The section of the manual describing the directions to be given to students is clear and concise. However, basal levels are not specified. A chart of reasonable starting places is given with directions to credit unread words and to return to an "earlier point" of the test if a mistake is made. While the basal is vague, the ceiling is specific. Failure on five consecutive words ends the test. Directions for scoring are clear and easy to follow. The record sheet is divided into words with columns to allow for the investigation of diagnostic information. The section in the manual discussing the interpretation of the use of this diagnostic information is clear. However, the design to make the word-recognition test more useful by allowing elaborate analysis of errors actually makes the test results more susceptible to abuse. While the use of a word-recognition test may be minimally useful as a screening device, inferring diagnostic information from a sample of 20 to 30 isolated words is not appropriate.

The technical data section of this test does not follow basic test design standards recommended by the joint committee of the American Psychological Association, the American Educational Research Association, and the National Council on Measurement in Education (1985). The sections on item selection, standardization, validity, and reliability are vague and ambiguous.

The item-selection process and the item analysis are not described thoroughly. Standardization of the test was done exclusively in Great Britain. The words and the sequence of difficulty may not be appropriate for use in the United States. While the norming procedure is described in general demographic characteristics, the sample sizes in each area (e.g., sex, residence, geographic area) are not specified. The manual did indicate that updated norms would be made available later due to the small numbers involved in the initial standardization process.

The section on reliability states that "two halves" of the test were correlated, yielding a reliability coefficient of .85. The paragraph then indicates that an alternative method of analysis based on the Kuder-Richardson Formula 21 yielded a reliability of .92. Due to this limited and vague information, the reliability of the test is questionable.

There are other psychometric flaws. Concurrent validity is determined through correlation of the Word Recognition Test with the Macmillan Group Reading Test and with teacher estimates. The validation process is not reported in detail and the one chart demonstrating correlation coefficients is unclear with regard to what comparisons were made. Objective criteria for teacher estimates are also not specified. The lack of information regarding content validity is significant. A systematic examination of item selection and analysis is essential to determine whether the test actually is a representative sample of the behavior domain to be assessed. In addition, reference to construct validity would have been appropriate in light of the controversy over use of word-recognition tests.

SUMMARY. This 50-word, 5-to-10-minute test is designed to yield a reading grade level and a diagnostic evaluation of reading errors. While the directions and interpretation sections of the test manual are generally clear and concise, there are serious concerns with the technical adequacy of the test design. The test manual does not meet the standards recommended by the joint committee of the American Psychological Association, the American Educational Research Association, and the National Council on Measurement in Education (1985). In addition, the exclusive development and standardization in Great Britain limits the use of this test in the United States.

There is a curious paradox in the design of this word-recognition test. The test is a screening instrument with cautions against interpreting a student's total reading ability from 20 to 30 words in isolation. The development of a pattern analysis of these words, however, contradicts the authors' caution against abusing the test in this way.

The test is not recommended for use in the United States. Furthermore, administration and interpretation of any word-recognition test must be done with an awareness of its limitations.

REVIEWER'S REFERENCE

American Educational Research Association, American Psychological Association, & National Council on Measurement in Education. (1985). *Standards for educational and psychological testing*. Washington, DC: American Psychological Association, Inc.

[179]

Macmillan Group Reading Test. Purpose: "A means of monitoring standards of reading and investigating the range of reading attainment in a school or a class." Ages 6–3 to 13–3; 1985; 2 forms; 1988 price data: £4.50 per 25 tests; £4.50 per teacher's manual (23 pages); (30) minutes; The Macmillan Test Unit; Macmillan Education Ltd. [England].*

Review of the MacMillan Group Reading Test by KORESSA KUTSICK, Assistant Professor of Psychology, James Madison University, Harrisonburg, VA:

The MacMillan Group Reading Test is a teacher-administered, multiple-choice test of reading skills. The test was designed for use with children of reading ages 6-3 to 13-3. Two primary reading tasks are included in this test: The first involves picture recognition (students select one of five words that identifies a picture printed in the response booklet); and the second involves sentence completion (one of five words is selected that best fills a blank space in a presented sentence). Two forms of this test (A and B), which are purported to be equivalent forms, are provided. Average administration time is 30 minutes; however, the test has no specific time limit. The MacMillan Group Reading Test provides for transformation of raw scores into standard scores and reading ages.

The overall format of the MacMillan is quite simple. Students complete 48 items that are divided into the two types of tasks discussed above. Due to the limited number of reading tasks presented, the test should be primarily considered a screening tool as opposed to a comprehensive reading test. Publishers of the MacMillan list the utility of this test as: (*a*) a means of obtaining and recording standard reading scores for students; (*b*) a method of comparing student reading skills within a class and within a school; (*c*) an instrument for documenting student progress in reading-skill acquisition; and (*d*) a screening device for identifying students who are poor readers for placement into various kinds of instructional reading groups. Cutoff scores for poor performance are described; however, no diagnostic information regarding specific reading deficiencies can be generated from performances on the MacMillan Group Reading Test.

A Teachers' Guide for the MacMillan is available and discusses administration and scoring procedures in a concise manner. The test is easy to administer and takes little technical skill to score. Clear directions and examples are given regarding the conversion of raw scores to standard scores and reading-age levels.

Psychometric data presented in the Teachers' Guide include information on test construction, reliability, and validity. The MacMillan Group Reading Test was normed on 7,500 students who attended five of the largest school districts in England. This sample was reported to be representative of various geographical areas of the country; however, no information was given as to socioeconomic stratification. The test publishers noted that items and test scores were analyzed to demonstrate that the instrument did not discriminate on the basis of sex or geographical region; however, no specific data were provided to support this statement.

Reliability of the MacMillan Group Reading Test was reported as correlations between the alternate forms of this scale. Positive correlations (ranging from .85 to .94) between these forms across different age levels were reported. No other reliability data were presented.

The validity of the MacMillan Group Reading Test was demonstrated through a number of procedures. Test items were reviewed by teachers for appropriateness of vocabulary and item difficulty. More formal item analyses were not reported. Additional validity measures were obtained by comparing obtained test scores to teachers' estimates of students' reading skills as well as to test scores obtained on other reading instruments. Moderate to high positive correlations were obtained between the MacMillan Group Reading Test and teachers' estimates of reading skills and student performances on the Schonell Graded Word Reading Test, the Holborn Reading Test, the Young Group Reading Test, the Primary Reading Test, the Kent Reading Test, and the MacMillan Graded Word Reading Test. These instruments are commonly used in English infant, junior, and secondary schools.

The MacMillan Group Reading Test appears to be an adequate reading screening tool. Its use in the United States would be limited, however, by the fact that the test was normed in England. For use in England, the test would provide little additional information than that generated by such instruments as the Primary Reading Test or the Kent Reading Test.

In summary, the MacMillan Group Reading Test is a fairly well constructed, easily administered reading-skills screening tool. Its primary advantage appears to be in its brevity. Adequate reliability and validity information is available; however, additional work in this area would enhance this test. The MacMillan Group Reading Test would be most appropriate for use in English schools.

Review of the Macmillan Group Reading Test by GAIL E. TOMPKINS, Associate Professor of Language Arts Education, University of Oklahoma, Norman OK:

The Macmillan Group Reading Test (MGRT) is a multiple-choice word-reading test consisting of 48 items. In the first five items, students select a one-word label for a picture, and in the following 43 fill-in-the-blank items, students select a word to complete a sentence. Two color-coded equivalent forms of the test are available.

The MGRT is published in England, and a few Briticisms and British English spellings are used in the test, restricting its usefulness for American students. One form has three items and the other form has five items with British English spellings (e.g., flavour for flavor) or words with British meanings (e.g., chemist for pharmacist).

The authors cite four purposes for the MGRT: (*a*) to monitor standards of reading, (*b*) to investigate the range of reading attainment in a school or class, (*c*) to assess individual progress with reading, and (*d*) to evaluate the effectiveness of various approaches to reading instruction. The authors acknowledge that the MGRT is less useful in assessing reading fluency and comprehension, and they suggest that criterion-referenced tests and informal testing procedures should also be used in evaluating individual students' reading levels and in determining appropriate placement for reading instruction.

A crucial consideration in choosing this test or any word-reading test is whether emphasis at this level can produce an accurate measure of reading ability. The Teacher's Guide does not address this question except to say that this test should be one test in a battery of reading tests at a teacher's disposal. No information is provided about how the words were selected for inclusion in the test, only that a group of teachers evaluated the appropriateness of the words.

The MGRT can be administered to a class of students with reading ages from 6.3 to 13.3 under normal classroom conditions and within a 30-minute period. The test is not timed, but according to the Teacher's Guide, 30 minutes is adequate time for most students to complete the 48-item test. Clear directions for administering the test are provided. The teacher introduces students to the test using two practice items (one picture item and one fill-in-the-blank sentence item) and then students complete the test independently, by circling the correct word for each test item. At the teacher's discretion, older students may skip the five picture items and begin with the fill-in-the-blank sentence items. Students receive credit for the omitted items when the tests are scored.

The MGRT is hand scored using scoring keys for each form that are included in the Teacher's Guide. Standardized scores and reading-age scores may be calculated from raw scores, and some information is provided in the Teacher's Guide about using the test results and interpreting the standard scores and reading-age scores.

Approximately 7,500 students in five of the largest school districts in England were tested to generate normative data. Validity was estimated in two ways. First, validity estimates were calculated by correlating student scores on MGRT with teacher estimates of these students' reading abilities. Correlations, by grade level, ranged from .76 to .89. Second, validity was established by correlating scores on MGRT with scores on other reading tests. For example, student scores on the MGRT were correlated with their scores on the Macmillan Graded Word Reading Test, and correlations ranged from .70 to .86 according to grade level test. Correlations were also reported for five other reading tests at particular grade levels.

Reliability was estimated through the alternate forms procedure, correlating student scores on Forms A and B. Reliability coefficients by grade level ranged from .85 to .94, indicating a high level of agreement between the two forms. No information is provided on the internal consistency of test items.

In summary, the MGRT appears to be a useful instrument in a teacher's battery of reading tests. It can be quickly administered to a class of students and easily scored to produce standardized scores. A high correlation exists among the MGRT, teachers' evaluations of students' reading achievement, and other word-reading tests. However, the philosphical question of whether the MGRT, a word-reading test, can adequately measure reading achievement remains.

The suitability of the MGRT for American students must be carefully considered. The test was standardized using English students and other reading tests published in Great Britain. Also, Briticisms and British English spellings that American students will find unfamiliar were used in several test items.

[180]

Maculaitis Assessment Program, Commercial Edition. Purpose: "Designed for the purposes of: 1) selection, 2) placement, 3) diagnosis, 4) proficiency and 5) achievement" of non-native speakers of English in grades K–12. ESL students in grades K–3, K–1, 2–3, 4–5, 6–8, 9–12; 1982; MAC: K–12; 6 levels; individual; 1985 price data: $195 per MAC: K–12 sampler set including technical manual (296 pages), examiner's manual (142 pages), and 1 each of all other test materials; $19.10–$31.80 per sampler set for any one level; $32.50 per technical manual; $18.45 per examiner's manual; Jean D'Arcy Maculaitis; The Alemany Press.*

a) BASIC CONCEPTS TEST. ESL students in grades K–3; 8 scores: Color Identification, Shape Identification, 2 Number Identification scores (Counting, Spoken), 2 Letter Identification scores (Alphabet, Spoken), Relationship Identification, Total; (15–20) minutes.

b) MAC K–1. ESL Students in grades K–1. 7 scores: 2 Oral Expression scores (Asking Questions, Connected Discourse), 3 Listening Comprehension scores (Commands, Situations, Minimal Pairs), Vocabulary Recognition, Total; (25–30) minutes.

c) MAC 2–3. ESL students in grades 2–3; 16 scores: 2 Oral Expression scores (Answering Questions, Connected Discourse), 2 Vocabulary Knowledge scores (Identification, Noun Definition), 4 Listening Comprehension scores (Identifying Words, Counting Words, Answering Questions, Comprehending Statements), 6 Word Recognition Skills (Alphabetizing, Recognizing Vowels and Consonants, Recognizing Long and Short Vowels, Using Word Families, Determining Singular and Plural Forms, Recognizing Silent Letters), Reading Comprehension, Total; (79–89) minutes.

d) MAC 4–5. ESL students in grades 4–5. 15 scores: 2 Oral Expression scores (Asking Questions, Connected Discourse), Vocabulary Knowledge, 4 Listening Comprehension scores (Positional Auditory Discrimination, Answering Questions, Comprehending Statements, Comprehending Dialogues), 4 Reading Comprehension scores (Recognizing Homonyms, Recognizing Antonyms, Recognizing Abbreviations, Reading Outcomes), 3 Writing Ability scores (Grammatical Structures, Pictoral, School Information), Total; (119–134) minutes.

e) MAC 6–8. ESL students in grades 6–8; 11 scores: 3 Oral Expression scores (Answering Questions, Asking Questions, Connected Discourse), 3 Listening Comprehension scores (Answering Questions, Comprehending Statements, Comprehending Dialogues), 2 Reading Comprehension scores (Vocabulary, Reading Outcomes), 2 Writing Ability scores (Grammatical Structure, Application Forms), Total; (108–123) minutes.

f) MAC 9–12. ESL students in grades 9–12; 11 scores: same as MAC 6–8; (108–123) minutes.

Review of the Maculaitis Assessment Program by J. MANUEL CASAS, Associate Professor of Counseling Psychology, and DAVID STRAND, PhD Candidate in Counseling Psychology, Department of Education, University of California, Santa Barbara, CA:

Recent increases in the number of immigrants coming into the United States has resulted in a significant increase in the number of students in grades K–12 who are nonnative speakers of English. This increase coupled with consequent legislative action in various states has created a pressing need for instruments that can be used by schools to assess the English proficiency of such students and in turn place them in the most appropriate instructional program. The Maculaitis Assessment Program (MAC) was developed in response to this need.

The test batteries that comprise the MAC were designed to assess the English language competencies of limited-English-proficient (LEP) students in the four basic language skills: listening, speaking, reading, and writing. Relative to each of these skills, the MAC focuses on the functional meaning of language and emphasizes the vocabulary and structures needed by the language learner to respond appropriately in specific situations. Furthermore, the subtests, especially the reading subtest, focus on very important but often overlooked aspects in assessing English proficiency. For instance, "the selection of the correct answer in the reading comprehension subtest must involve interpretation of each passage, not merely matching the words in the choices with the identical words in the passage, thus requiring a careful reading of each passage."

The MAC has both norm-referenced and criterion-referenced applications. Consequently, according to the author, the information it provides can be used by school personnel for a variety of purposes including selection, placement, diagnosis, proficiency, and achievement. Although providing minimal supportive evidence, the test also purports to provide teachers with the opportunity to spot vision problems and gain insight into the affective aspects of the student.

With respect to the content of the test materials, steps were taken to make the test both age and culture appropriate. A unique aspect of the MAC is the inclusion of sample test materials for levels 2–3 and above. The provision of such materials is extremely important for LEP students, who often lack test sophistication and experience. Separate sets of color-coded materials (i.e., booklets, answer sheets, scoring sheets, etc.) are provided for each of the six levels that comprise the test. Although in the long run this may turn out to be a positive attribute of the test, in the short run it gives the MAC a rather voluminous and complex appearance that could potentially discourage testers from using it. To prevent this from happening, the publishers might consider providing workshops to any school district seriously considering using the MAC. Furthermore, future revisions of the MAC should consider the consolidation of all materials into a shorter and more manageable package.

The MAC contains both examiner and technical manuals. The technical manual provides extensive information on validation and standardization procedures, scoring, reporting, understanding, and using test results. The manual states that experts—including professors of tests and measurements, foreign language, and ESL/BE education, and certified ESL/BE classroom teachers—were used to establish content validity. Very methodical piloting procedures were followed to establish the validity of each subtest and of the testing program as a whole. Great care and detail were given to identifying the discriminatory power of the test items. In general, all the validity and reliability data reported throughout the piloting process are very acceptable. Extensive data are provided to demonstrate test fairness and to insure that the MAC is not ethnically or sexually biased for those for whom it was designed. While the MAC provides data showing the relationship between specific subtests and school grades, it would be helpful if future revisions of the test provided information on its concurrent validity vis-a-vis instruments currently used to assess English proficiency.

At present, national norms for the MAC are lacking. Consequently the MAC norms apply only to those urban public school districts and urban private and parochial schools whose enrollment includes non-English proficient and/or limited-English-proficient kindergarten through 12th-grade students from low- and middle-income families. The author does contend, however, that the lack of national norms neither diminishes the appropriateness nor the usefulness of the MAC for any school district. Additional data from varied school districts across the United States are needed to affirm this contention.

The examiner's manual goes into great detail describing the MAC materials and provides information relative to the administration and scoring of the test. Careful reading and use of the examiner's manual will facilitate standardized administration of the MAC.

There is no doubt that much of the information contained in both manuals is a positive attribute of the MAC. Unfortunately, although the author contends the manuals provide information in a quick and concise manner, the fact of the matter is that both manuals are quite formidable in length. The information they provide is exceedingly detailed and, oftentimes, redundant relative to testing in general and the MAC assessment process in particular. For instance, 67 pages of tables are presented to demonstrate that the MAC is not ethnically or sexually biased for those for whom the testing program was designed. In future revisions of the MAC, a careful editing of the manuals should occur in order to ensure that all needed information is provided quickly and concisely.

In summary, the Maculaitis Assessment Program was developed to assess the English language competencies of LEP students. The information it provides can be used for a variety of purposes including selection, placement, diagnosis, proficiency, and achievement. Extensive efforts were taken to demonstrate both its validity and reliability. National norms are lacking; consequently the generalizability of the instrument is somewhat limited. To insure standardization in its administration, detailed procedural information is contained in the examiner's manual. Although the MAC has many positive aspects, the numerous materials provided to assess kindergarten through 12th-grade students give this instrument a voluminous and complex appearance that could potentially discourage testers from using it.

Review of the Maculaitis Assessment Program, Commercial Edition by EUGENE E. GARCIA, Professor/Director, Center for Bilingual/ Bicultural Education, Arizona State University, Tempe, AZ:

The continued growth in the number of language minority students requiring linguistic and educational assessment has challenged present-day test developers. These students come from a variety of native language and cultural backgrounds, necessitating extreme precautions in the administration and interpretation of standardized measures. However, such measures are required by state statutes with the intent of assisting local schools in meeting the needs of these diverse limited-English-proficient students. Few highly reliable, valid comprehensive English language and literacy measures are available for grades K–12. The Maculaitis Assessment Program (MAC) is among these few.

The MAC consists of six assessment packages designed to assist in the selection, placement, and diagnosis of language minority students through the comprehensive evaluation of English language proficiency and English literacy. The theoretical framework of this assessment package considers as important the vocabulary and structural forms needed by a language learner to respond to "real-life" contexts and the diverse communicative needs and functions of the student. At early grade levels the assessment focuses on receptive and expressive proficiency of English vocabulary, phoneme differentiation, interrogatives, connected discourse, letter identification, and other morphological and syntactic abilities. At later grades (grades 2–12), reading and writing assessments are added. Overall, each grade level assessment provides a comprehensive evaluation of a student's English language proficiency by taking into consideration various structural aspects and communicative functions.

Both a highly descriptive examiner's manual and a thorough technical manual serve to inform the potential test administrator. The examiner's manual provides brief but necessary descriptions of the skills tested, theoretical rationale, and the contents of the MAC. A complete description of examiner qualifications and proper testing conditions/preparations is also made available. These descriptions combined with those provided in the actual test booklets assist in assuring appropriate use of this measure. The technical manual provides comprehensive data useful in judging the psychometric adequacy of the instrument including validity, reliability, and score interpretation information. Standardization procedures, populations, and data are available for review. Significantly, data regarding gender and home language background for the norm-referenced populations are available for use in interpreting scores. The authors are to be congratulated for the comprehensiveness and usability of these manuals.

Unfortunately for the language minority professional, the MAC does not address specific issues of relevance to non-English standardized measures. For determination of educational status and treatment, language minority students are subjected to assessment of (*a*) the native language, (*b*) English, and (*c*) native language and/or English academic achievement. The MAC confines itself to measures of relevance to English language and literacy. In doing so, it limits its usefulness to the language minority practitioner.

In summary, the MAC is a comprehensive measure of English language proficiency and English reading and writing. It can be of specific use in the identification of limited English proficiency as well as selected aspects of communicative functions. It is recommended for serious consideration by language minority educational professionals.

[181]

The Major-Minor-Finder, 1986–1996 Edition. Purpose: Provides "the content to help a student to choose a college major of interest and to learn about related career opportunities." Grade 11 through adult; 1978–87; MMF; an exploratory instrument to facilitate college major decision-making; self-scoring; 1986 price data: $1.45 per reusable test booklet (containing one answer insert folder); $.25 per answer insert folder; $2 per administration (Professional) manual ('86, 20 pages); $4 per (Supplemental) College Major Handbook ('87, 72 pages); $6.75 per specimen set including test booklet, insert folder, College Major Handbook, and administration manual; $89 per computer administered version; printed version: (40) minutes, computer version: (10) minutes; Arthur Cutler, Francis Ferry, Robert Kauk, and Robert Robinett; CFKR Career Materials, Inc.*

For reviews by Rodney L. Lowman and Daryl Sander of an earlier edition, see 9:643.

Review of the Major-Minor-Finder, 1986–1996 *Edition, by JAMES W. PINKNEY, Associate Professor, Counseling Center, East Carolina University, Greenville, NC:*

The Major-Minor-Finder (MMF) is intended for use with college-bound high school students, college students, and adults who want to explore college majors. The present version has been "quite drastically revised" in order to be applicable to both 4-year and 2-year college student career planning. The authors suggest that it is most productive in group administrations that stimulate interaction among respondents.

The MMF closely parallels the JOB-O (160) career planning inventory by asking the respondent to make self-estimates on 11 variables and then counting "matches" between the self-estimates and the levels required in college majors. On the back of the answer insert the respondent is asked to research up to five majors with six or more matches. A total of 120 majors are included in the following areas: engineering/environmental design, business, computer/physical science, social sciences/public affairs, agriculture/natural resources, biological sciences, communication and the arts, education, and health professions.

Each major has related jobs on the answer insert with the job most closely related to the major in capital letters. From two to six jobs are listed for both 4-year and 2-year programs. Also available from the authors is a related handbook that offers description of majors, typical courses, job outlook, and where to write for additional information. It parallels the *Occupational Outlook Handbook* and covers all of the MMF majors plus 18 additional majors. The handbook has two appendixes that offer a list of government jobs by major and a summary of federal student financial aid.

The MMF's 11 variables consist of interest areas, educational development, preferred work environments, and desire for working with data, people, and things. A respondent is given the option of choosing one to three of the interest areas noted above. Self-estimates are then made for what level of educational development is sought in terms of reasoning, mathematics, verbal skills, and spatial aptitude/form perception. Next the respondent reads brief descriptions of Holland's six environments and selects three. Self-estimates are then made for desired involvement with data, people, and things. These 11 estimates are then compared with the suggested level needed by each major.

There is an intuitive appeal to the MMF. As a task it would have students take an exhaustive look at most available majors. The fact that it offers job titles related to each major would give students a better feel for where a major might lead. Interacting with friends and counselors about majors in and of itself would be advantageous to many students and the MMF encourages such interaction. Potential users might choose to view the MMF as a structured group activity generating information about possible majors for college-bound high school students or for college students who are undecided about a major. The authors seem to feel that their description of the MMF as a "decision-making, career-oriented instrument" and as an "exploratory instrument to facilitate decision-making" absolves them of presenting any information about the psychometric properties of the MMF.

The manual for the MMF is poorly done and of little use to the potential user interested in helping students explore possible college majors. The directions given for administering the MMF border on the trivial, and completely omit important cautions that are stated in a subsequent section on validity and reliability. The authors "strongly" recommend that students read through all the descriptions of fields of study and related supplementary material before making choices. This information is not included in either the directions for administration or the MMF booklet that students would actually take. The authors also caution the user about the effects of age and experience but, again, this information is not included in either the directions or the MMF booklet. The manual does consistently refer to the MMF as an "exploratory instrument."

Validity and reliability of the MMF are addressed in a philosophical manner and there are little data of any kind. The information presented is suspect because it predates the "drastically revised" version of the current MMF. The authors seem to have confused student response with face validity when they report that over 90% of students were satisfied with the MMF. This statement is not referenced and there is no way to tell if it refers to the current version, earlier versions, or how many students were involved. The evidence for the validity and reliability of the MMF is further weakened by nonreferenced and tangential citations. Predictive validity and construct validity are ignored.

The evidence presented for reliability of the MMF is a single, nonreferenced correlation of 92% for test-retest with $N = 120$. This correlation was obtained on a 1983 version of the MMF, and how it relates to a "drastically revised" version is obscure and not explained by the authors. The authors imply that a nonreferenced statement about the stability of vocational interests further supports the reliability of the MMF. The comment that "reliability is being further tested" (and results can be requested) is irritating at best, and insulting at worst.

CONCLUSION. The task of completing the MMF may have some heuristic value for students making decisions about college majors, but it should be used only with close and extensive supervision. Potential users need to be aware that the manual offers scant information about either validity or reliability even after 13 years of development.

[182]

Management Appraisal Survey. Purpose: "An assessment of managerial practices and attitudes as viewed through the eyes of employees." Employees; 1967–80; companion piece for the Styles of Management Inventory; 5 scores: Overall Leadership Style, Philosophy, Planning, Implementation, Evaluation; user's guide ('80, 4 pages); 1984 price data: $4 or less per survey; administration time not reported; Jay Hall, Jerry B. Harvey, and Martha S. Williams; Teleometrics Int'l.*

See T3:2351 (1 reference); for a review by Abraham K. Korman, see 8:1185 (8 references).

Review of the Management Appraisal Survey by H. JOHN BERNARDIN, Director of Research, College of Business and Public Administration, Florida Atlantic University, Boca Raton, FL:

The Management Appraisal Survey (MAS) is based on the popular "grid theory" of management from Blake and Mouton (1964). There is no rationale or empirical support provided to justify the 12 management situations included in the survey. Both the "grid theory" and the situations appear to be out of step with current research in management and leadership. Despite its popularity and longevity, the "grid theory" has been subjected to few empirical tests and theoreticians have made no attempt to incorporate the thinking or research of contemporary management or leadership studies (e.g., Howell, Dorfman, & Kerr, 1986).

There is (apparently) no manual to accompany the MAS, only a four-page document entitled "A Word About the Management Appraisal Survey and Rating One's Manager." Two of the four pages are norm tables with only provision of the sample size and no other detail on norm development. This is ironic given the contingency theory espoused by the authors. Apparently users are to assume that scores are completely unaffected by occupation, respondent demographics, superior-subordinate structural relationships, method of data collection, and the host of other variables that have been shown to affect perceptions of leader/managerial behavior by subordinates. Research with the Leader Behavior Description Questionnaire (Stogdill, 1963), for example, indicates many factors can affect scores of the leader dimensions. Such factors should be studied in the context of norm refinement and data interpretation with the MAS.

PSYCHOMETRIC ISSUES. No reliability data are reported for the MAS, other than a statement that the instrument has "reliability comparable to the Styles of Management Inventory" (SMI) (Hall & Donnell, 1979). (In a document entitled "Bibliography of Research Studies Utilizing the Instrument," coefficients of stability for the Styles of Management Inventory are reported to range from .69 to .74.) No other reliability data are reported for the MAS.

No validity data are reported for the MAS, except for a correlational study indicating a strong relationship between high task and high relationship orientation (as rated by subordinates) and high managerial achievement. This finding provides additional support for managerial grid theory.

The items on the MAS are identical to those on the Styles of Management Inventory except for the pronouns used in questions. In the "Bibliography of Research Studies Using the [SMI] Instrument" the authors report that "construct validity is high as revealed by canonical analysis of the instrument with the MMPI which yielded two functions significant at the .038 and .09 levels of confidence." It is impossible to interpret this statement without further information and to determine whether these data are at all applicable to the MAS.

There are no formal directions for administrators of the MAS. Issues such as confidentiality, group size required for data aggregation, treatment/weighting of outliers, and specificity of feedback to managers are not discussed despite the fact that such issues have a direct effect on obtained responses. Particularly with regard to subordinate appraisals of managers, the conditions of data collection can have a direct impact on results (Bernardin, 1986). Although the questions on the MAS are not as transparent as those on some instruments, social desirability or response set error could be troublesome. There can be little doubt that subordinates can be affected by the method of data collection and the subsequent use of the data. Without greater information on norm development and the standardization of data collection procedures pursuant to those norms, it is impossible to judge the validity of norms.

Another disturbing feature of the MAS is the use of the sexist language throughout the questionnaire. The authors maintain that pronoun changes could invalidate the norm interpretations. However, there is no evidence that pronoun changes can affect normative data and, of course, very simple procedures exist for ascertaining precise calibrations of response changes for any group of items. The publishers could easily incorporate experimental items into the administration for purposes of determining psychometric equivalence.

CONCLUSION. Given the lengthy and impressive research trail of the Ohio State Leadership Scales, researchers and practitioners interested in comparisons of leader style from the perspective of self and subordinates are on a stronger empirical footing with the Leader Opinion Questionnaire and the Leader Behavior Descriptive Questionnaire (Form XII). As a management development tool, the instruments of assessment from McBer and Company (e.g., the Managerial Style Questionnaire, Subordinate Version) are far superior in terms of theoretical base, directions for administration, feedback to respondents, and face validity. The MAS is in dire need of a manual describing norm development, reliability, validity, administration considerations, and feedback procedures.

REVIEWER'S REFERENCES

Stogdill, R. M. (1963). *Manual for the Leader Behavior Description Questionnaire—Form XII*. Columbus, OH: Bureau of Business Research, Ohio State University.

Blake, R. R., & Mouton, J. S. (1964). *The managerial grid*. Houston: Gulf Publishing Company.

Hall, J., & Donnell, S. (1979). Managerial achievement: The personal side of behavioral theory. *Human Relations*, 32, 77-101.

Bernardin, H. J. (1986). Subordinate appraisal: A valuable source of information about managers. *Human Resource Management*, 25, 421-439.

Howell, J. P., Dorfman, P. W., & Kerr, S. (1986). Moderator variables in leadership research. *Academy of Management Review*, 11, 88-102.

Review of the Management Appraisal Survey by GEORGE C. THORNTON, III, Professor of Psychology, Colorado State University, Fort Collins, CO:

This review begins where Korman (1978) left off in his review in the *Eighth Mental Measurements Yearbook* when he stated, "I do not know how many years it will take to get these types of measures off the market, but the process should begin" (p. 1763). Unfortunately, the Management Appraisal Survey (MAS) and its three companion instruments are still around with no more psychometric justification than was available in 1978.

In light of the recommended use of the MAS as a tool to solicit feedback from subordinates to manager, I am concerned about the complexity of format, the high reading level in the questions, and the complicated nature of the scoring procedure. There is no manual to help the administrator use the questionnaire in practical settings.

The MAS evaluates four basic components of management: Philosophy of Management, Planning and Goal Setting, Implementation, and Performance Evaluation. For each component, the survey asks the subordinate to answer a question regarding three managerial situations. Five alternative answers, representing areas of Blake and Mouton's (1964) grid, are provided for each question. The informant is asked to plot the alternatives on a line graph ranging from *completely uncharacteristic* to *completely characteristic*, relative to how characteristic they are of the manager's behavior.

By this response format, the informant has given each answer a weight ranging from 1 to 10. The informant then places these numerical values under the corresponding lettered alternative on a scoring sheet. Columns are totalled to determine the extent to which the manager incorporates each management style into his or her philosophy, planning, implementation, and evaluation. An overall score also is determined. The leadership styles measured are described as: high concern for people and production; high concern for people, low concern for production; moderate concern for production and people; high concern for production, low concern for people; and low concern for both production and people. The first style is cited as being ideal.

No manual is provided by the publisher and a four-page description addressed to the respondent who has completed the MAS gives only a description of Blake and Mouton's managerial grid theory, a description of the four scales, and norms for 11,311 persons rating their superiors. There are no breakdowns by level, experience, functional area, or industry.

The sum total of psychometric data is provided in a typed attachment to a reference list provided by the authors. According to this information, the median coefficient of stability for the MAS is said to be similar to that of the Styles of Management Inventory (SMI). SMI coefficients range from .69 to .74, and the instrument is said to discriminate between high, average, and low achieving managers and some 13 organizational types. Construct validity is good as revealed through canonical analysis of the SMI with the MMPI, which yielded two functions significant at the .038 and .09 levels of confidence.

No student in my undergraduate class on tests and measurements, and certainly no graduate student in my class on psychometric theory and test construction, would pass the course if he or she turned in such a deficient report of test construction efforts and data to support the instrument. The deductive and rational approach to test construction is a good place to begin, but empirical data should be brought to bear to confirm a test's reliability and validity.

In none of the references supplied by the authors is there any description of the process used to construct the questionnaire, item analysis carried out to refine the questions, internal consistency estimates, correlations among scales, or convergent and discriminant validity. The MAS has been used by its authors in studies of management behavior. For example, it has been found that people who espouse different preferences for styles of management endorse different beliefs in Theory X-Y and different needs in subordinates, and are described by their subordinates as using different degrees and types of employee involvement in decision making (Hall & Donnell, 1985). The instrument has also been used by the authors and others to assess changes in managerial style as a result of management development programs.

It is also worthy of note that Hall's Leadership Appraisal Survey (LAS), virtually identical to the MAS with only "leader" substituted for "manager," was reviewed along with 23 other feedback instruments by a team at the Center for Creative Leadership. Criteria used in the evaluation process included number and type of scales, underlying empirical theory, domains covered, psychometric and face validity, and helpfulness in suggesting corrective actions. The three instruments judged better were the Leadership Behavior Description Questionnaire—Form XII, the MultiLevel Management Survey, and the Management Styles Profile. The theoretical base, the face validity, and the use of the LAS in training is judged adequate, if the organization believes in the Grid approach. On the other hand, the reading level is judged complex and confusing, the psychometric data inadequate, and the interpretation guide "is a semantic thicket . . . compounded by the use of jargon that most managers will not understand." (Morrison, McCall, & DeVries, 1978, p. 220)

I can think of only one situation where I would endorse the use of the MAS. If you have a group of managers and subordinates who were at a well-developed stage of working and training together and you were using the Grid approach, it might be helpful to use the MAS as a conversation starter to illustrate Grid principles and initiate feedback about managerial behavior.

In any other situation, the complexity of wording in the questions, the lack of psychometric justification of the question scales, and the lack of informative norms renders the scores uninterpretable. I would certainly not use the instrument for any decision making, such as promotion, training needs analysis, evaluation of a training program, or for a research study. There are far better instruments available on the market.

REVIEWER'S REFERENCES

Blake, R. R., & Mouton, J. S. (1964). The managerial grid. Houston: Gulf Publishing Co.

Korman, A. K. (1978). [Review of Styles of Leadership and Management]. In O. K. Buros (Ed.), *The eighth mental measurements yearbook* (pp. 1763). Highland Park, NJ: The Gryphon Press.

Morrison, A. M., McCall, M. W., Jr., & DeVries, D. L. (1978). *Feedback to managers: A comprehensive review of twenty-four instruments.* Greensboro, NC: Center for Creative Leadership. (Technical Report No. 8)

Hall, J., & Donnell, S. (1985). The quiet crisis in government. *The Bureaucrat*, 14 (2), 39-44.

[183]

Management Inventory on Modern Management. Purpose: "Developed to cover eight different topics of importance to managers." Managers; 1984; MIMM; self-scored training tool; 8 areas: Leadership Styles, Selecting and Training, Communicating, Motivating, Managing Change, Delegating, Decision Making, and Managing Time, the sum of the 8 areas yielding a Total score; 1987 price data: $27 per 20 tests and answer booklets; $1.50 per manual (12 pages); $3 per specimen set; (20) minutes; Donald L. Kirkpatrick; the Author.*

Review of the Management Inventory on Modern Management by LENORE W. HARMON, Professor of Educational Psychology, University of Illinois, Champaign, IL:

The Management Inventory on Modern Management (MIMM) might be referred to as an achievement test for managers. MIMM items assess knowledge of management principles in eight areas. The author suggests that the MIMM is useful in assessing the need for training, in promoting discussion, in evaluating the effectiveness of training, in providing information for on-the-job "coaching" of managers, and in assisting in the selection of managers. Unfortunately, the effectiveness of the MIMM for any of these purposes is unsubstantiated. The inventory does appear to test for knowledge that would be useful to managers, but no evidence is presented that knowing the things contained in the MIMM contributes to better management. Until such evidence is available, the use of the MIMM for assessing the need for training, evaluating the effectiveness of training, and "coaching" individuals on the job is not indicated. At the least, individuals who wish to use the MIMM for these purposes should review the items and the scoring key to make sure that their preferred management style is reflected in them. The use of the inventory as a vehicle for discussion is nicely complemented by a separate Answer Booklet that contains the reasons for the scoring as well as references that document the reasons. This booklet may be given to the respondent after the inventory is completed.

The manual cautions the reader that the MIMM has not been validated for selection and explains how validation should be done, but this is just one of a long list of things that should have been done but were not. Other omissions include failure to give reasons for the topics selected for coverage by the items, justify the use of an agree-disagree answer format, show that the items for the eight areas are internally cohesive and represent separate factors, provide evidence regarding the stability of the scores (especially important because the use of difference scores is advocated for evaluating training), and present norms for manager aspirants and managers of various levels.

Although the items are based on current research and thinking about management, in its present state the MIMM is no better than inventories published in the typical Sunday newspaper supplement. It is clear that the author understands how to improve the technical basis of his inventory. For instance, he asks users to supply him with information that can be used to compile norms, giving appropriate instructions for collecting group information without compromising confidentiality. It is unfortunate that such steps were not taken prior to publication.

[184]

Management Styles Questionnaire. Purpose: To understand the concept of situational management, recognize the advantages and disadvantages of various styles of management, recognize which style(s) of management are appropriate for a particular work situation, identify one's on-the-job management style, and develop a plan for modifying one's management style. Managers and employees; 1974–83; 4 forms: Generic, Sales, Health Care, Professional; 1987 price data: $6 per set including 1 participant form, 2 companion forms, and scoring and interpretation booklet ('83, 15 pages); $15 per leader's guide (no date, 12 pages); 145(175) minutes; Don Michalak; Michalak Training Associates, Inc.*

Review of the Management Styles Questionnaire by SEYMOUR ADLER, Associate Professor of Applied Psychology, Department of Management, Stevens Institute of Technology, Hoboken, NJ:

The Management Styles Questionnaire (MSQ) was designed for use in a workshop on Situational Management developed by Michalak. The instrument yields scores on the two most commonly studied dimensions of managerial style: task-orientation and people-orientation. The instrument consists of 31 items; 23 of the items are used to measure task-orientation, 15 are used to measure person-orientation.

There are two parallel forms of the questionnaire. One is a self-report instrument completed by the workshop participant him/herself, the other a Companion Form consisting of the same items, suitably rephrased, that is completed by an "employee/co-worker" of the participant. It is recommended the Companion Form be completed by two employees/co-workers of the participants in advance of the workshop. During the course of the workshop, participants learn about Situational Management (building on the work of Blake and Mouton, Reddin, and Hershey and Blanchard), score their own MSQ and those completed by their employees/co-workers, and plot their managerial style scores using the Blake and Mouton 9 x 9 grid. The instrument has been used as part of the Situational Management workshop for over a decade in many organizations.

Although the instrument was originally developed in 1974, there is absolutely no empirical data anywhere to support its validity as a measure of management style. No technical manual exists to provide the potential user with basic descriptive information on the instrument. Furthermore, a search of the literature through 1986 did not yield a single published study that empirically examined the questionnaire or its correlates. Given the existence of far more widely researched measures of the same two constructs—such as the Initiation of Structure and Consideration subscales of the Leader Behavior Description Questionnaire, Form

12—there is little reason for researchers and practitioners to choose the MSQ.

In fairness, the author claims the instrument is intended to be used only within the context of the Situational Management workshop and only for feedback purposes. Leaving aside the generally weak support for the leadership models on which the workshop is based (Yukl, 1981 presents a competent summary of the available evidence), the instrument still may not be well suited to its role in the workshop context. For one, as noted above, there is no evidence the scales actually measure management style. Also, although the Situational Management Model views the two dimensions of style as theoretically independent, there are no data showing that the two scales of the MSQ actually measure these dimensions independently. In fact, some of the individual items on the MSQ are positively weighted in measuring one dimension and negatively weighted in measuring the other dimension, suggesting that the scales may actually be negatively correlated. During the workshop, participants are encouraged to compare their scores on the MSQ with those of their employees and to consider the meaning of any differences that emerge. No guidance is provided as to what sized difference is meaningful. Of even greater concern, participants are instructed to make these comparisons on an item-by-item basis, making it likely that trivial and unreliable item-level differences will be over-interpreted. Finally, it seems doubtful that data from the Companion Forms provide truly meaningful feedback. Participants are simply instructed to give the questionnaire to two "employees/co-workers." It would appear that more meaningful feedback would be provided by employees (not co-workers), by as large a group as possible (not just two), and specifically by those with the best opportunity to observe the participant's behavior as a manager.

At this stage, then, the MSQ can at best be considered an experimental measure of two key dimensions of managerial style. Until clearer definitions of the constructs being measured are articulated, a body of data supporting the construct validity of the instrument assembled, and useful descriptive information (norms, scale intercorrelations, etc.) provided, the instrument would appear to have very limited applicability to practice or research in this area.

REVIEWER'S REFERENCE

Yukl, G. (1981). *Leadership in organizations.* Englewood Cliffs, NJ: Prentice-Hall, Inc.

Review of the Management Styles Questionnaire by WILLIAM I. SAUSER, JR., Associate Vice President and Professor, Office of the Vice President for Extension, Auburn University, Auburn, AL:

Leadership theory—and consequently the measurement of leader behavior—has been progressing steadily over the past several decades (Cook, Hepworth, Wall, & Warr, 1981). Research conducted during the 1940s and 1950s at Ohio State University by Hemphill, Fleishman, Stogdill, and others led to the development of two of the most frequently used leadership assessment instruments, the Leader Behavior Description Questionnaire, and the Leader Opinion Questionnaire. These instruments view leader behavior as multidimensional, and they established wide recognition for two major leadership dimensions: Initiating Structure (organizing to get a task accomplished) and Consideration (looking out for the welfare of group members).

Blake and Mouton (1964) constructed a "managerial grid" based on similar dimensions—"concern for people" and "concern for task"—and argued the most effective leaders were those who demonstrated a high degree of both. Meanwhile, Fiedler's work with the Least Preferred Coworker Scale led him to conclude that the effectiveness of a leader's style was dependent upon the situation in which the leader was functioning. Reddin (1970) and Hersey and Blanchard (1969) supported the concept of situational influences on leadership style effectiveness, and modified Blake and Mouton's grid to reflect these influences.

The Management Styles Questionnaire is also based on the concept of situational effectiveness of leadership styles, and represents a further extension of the work of Reddin and Hersey and Blanchard. The Management Styles Questionnaire is designed as a major component of a training module intended to help workshop participants understand the concepts of situational leadership and, within the context of the workshop, to explore their own styles and develop themselves further as managers. The instrument is clearly intended as a development tool, and seems suitable for that purpose. It also appears well-suited as a research instrument, although its developer does not tout it for that purpose.

The complete kit provides everything an individual reasonably familiar with leadership theory would need to present an informative workshop. The Leader's Guide sets forth objectives for the presentation, lists all materials needed, and outlines activities to be completed prior to, during, and after the workshop presentation. The presentation outline is very detailed, and is designed to be completed in approximately $2^1/_2$ hours.

The Management Styles Questionnaire itself is well presented. The instructions are clear and the items and responses are easy to understand. The instrument contains instructions for self-scoring, and the form is very well designed to facilitate this process. The questionnaire is accompanied by Companion Forms designed to be completed by the workshop participant's subordinates. These forms are also easily scored and provide other viewpoints with which to compare the self-assessments produced using the Participant Form.

The Scoring and Interpretation booklet is designed to further facilitate the learning process. It contains a concise summary of situational leadership theory and helps the participants interpret their own scores in light of this theory. The booklet also contains several exercises and suggestions for developing an increased understanding of the theory and its application. The booklet contains a very thoughtful suggestion for giving feedback to subordinates who provided information on the Companion Forms. The entire package seems well designed to create positive change in the workshop participant's organization.

While the Management Styles Questionnaire appears useful as an educational tool, it does have a glaring weakness which must be overcome before it can be taken seriously as a leadership behavior assessment device. That weakness is the absence of a technical manual! No information is provided regarding norms, reliability, or validity. No research reports are provided to establish the test's utility. While the instrument is face valid and well grounded in theory, there is no empirical evidence presented to support the statements found in the Scoring and Interpretation booklet. Clearly, more research with this instrument is called for. The test developer should carry out or encourage such research and present empirical evidence of the utility of the Management Styles Questionnaire in future revisions of the Leader's Guide and the Scoring and Interpretation booklet.

Given the absence of normative data, the lack of evidence of reliability and validity, and the apparent ease with which the Management Styles Questionnaire can be faked, it is not suitable for use as a personnel selection device. The test developer apparently does not intend it to be used for this purpose, thus he should explicitly label the device "For research and educational use only."

In summary, the Management Styles Questionnaire is a well-designed training device, especially when presented in the context of the workshop outlined in the Leader's Guide. It is well grounded in theory and seems to be an interesting research instrument. The absence of any existing empirical evidence of its reliability and validity, plus the lack of normative data, are serious weaknesses that must be addressed by the test developer if the instrument is to gain widespread professional acceptance. It is not intended, nor is it suitable, for use as an employee selection device.

REVIEWER'S REFERENCES

Blake, R., & Mouton, J. S. (1964). *The managerial grid.* Houston: Gulf Publishing Co.

Hersey, P., & Blanchard, K. H. (1969). *Management of organizational behavior: Utilizing human resources.* Englewood Cliffs, NJ: Prentice Hall, Inc.

Reddin, W. J. (1970). *Managerial effectiveness.* New York: McGraw-Hill.

Cook, J. D., Hepworth, S. J., Wall, T. D., & Warr, P. B. (1981). *The experience of work: A compendium and review of 249 measures and their use.* London: Academic Press.

[185]

Managerial Style Questionnaire. Purpose: "Measures how managers use or do not use power to influence their subordinates' motivation." Persons in managerial situations; 1974-80; MSQ; self-ratings or ratings by subordinates; 6 scores: Coercive, Authoritative, Affiliative, Democratic, Pacesetting, Coaching; 2 forms: manager, subordinate; 1985 price data: $55 per 10 questionnaires and profiles; $20 per 10 subordinate version questionnaires; $10 per trainer's guide ('80, 34 pages); (10–20) minutes; McBer and Company.*

Review of the Managerial Style Questionnaire by H. JOHN BERNARDIN, Director of Research, College of Business and Public Administration, Florida Atlantic University, Boca Raton, FL, and JOAN E. PYNES, Department of Public

Administration and Policy Analysis, Southern Illinois University, Edwardsville, IL:

The Managerial Style Questionnaire (MSQ) consists of 36 forced-choice items that can be completed and self-scored in 15 to 20 minutes. According to the MSQ Trainer's Guide, the MSQ is applicable to all levels of managers, from supervisors to upper-level executives, and can also be used with human services workers who "supervise" or influence clients. The instrument is designed for diagnosis and self-assessment and is not discussed as an instrument for personnel decisions.

The theoretical and empirical justification for the MSQ is work conducted at the Harvard Business School (e.g., McClelland & Winter, 1971) that sought to identify managerial styles that aroused or suppressed the human motives of achievement motivation, affiliation motivation, and power motivation.

The purpose of the MSQ is to measure the extent to which managers use power to influence their subordinates. It is supposed to measure how one sees oneself performing the classic functions of management, (i.e., planning, organizing, motivating, controlling, and coordinating). Six managerial styles are presented (viz., Coercive, Authoritative, Affiliative, Democratic, Pacesetting, and Coaching). The authors do not provide references to previous work or present any empirical data to justify the selection of these six styles.

The MSQ is written in clear, easy-to-understand language. Although the instrument explicates situations when each style is most effective or ineffective, it is nonjudgmental in character—stating that no single managerial style is effective in all situations with all people. This contingency approach is, of course, the generally accepted theory for managerial effectiveness. The language is also carefully guarded so as to provide useful feedback without spawning defensiveness in respondents.

PSYCHOMETRIC ISSUES. The normative data are sparse, with no indication that managerial level has any effect on the percentile norms or has even been studied. This is surprising given the discussion of style x situation interactions on earlier pages of the manual and considerable research which supports the general finding of a style x situation interaction. A total sample of "400 managers from industry, government, military, and educational organizations" is inadequate both in number and description. Also surprising is the failure to find sex effects for any of the subscales, another finding contrary to the literature and perhaps best explained by problems in statistical power.

The relatively small coefficients of stability for managerial style (four of six are below .7) are not surprising given the forced-choice format and the number of items per subscore. Even the reliability of the mean value, the interpretation of which is ambiguous, is below .7. The manual carefully concludes that "compared to other forced-choice instruments consisting of 36 items, MSQ items are reasonably stable." This reviewer cannot disagree, but can hardly understand the rationale for not increasing the number of items beyond 36, given the well-known problems with the forced-choice format.

The reliabilities of the subscale scores are low relative to other managerial style instruments (e.g., Stogdill, 1963), and particularly troublesome given the scoring format for the MSQ and the manual discussion of "dominant" styles. In fact, with the ipsative format, a few changes in responses could result in radical changes in the relative dominance of the various styles. Of course, the reliability of test-retest data based on a sample of only 19 MBA students is highly questionable. Forced-choice instruments typically have reliability problems relative to other rating formats (Bernardin & Beatty, 1984). As it is presently portrayed, the MSQ is designed for self-assessment and diagnosis rather than administrative decisions (e.g., selection, promotion). Research indicates forced-choice formats are only essential in an administrative context (i.e., to control deliberate response distortion). A change in format for the MSQ might enhance the reliability of subscales considerably, with no damage to other psychometric characteristics (Bernardin & Beatty, 1984).

More psychometric data should be provided to support the use of the instrument (e.g., internal consistency, confirmatory factor analysis). Given the scoring format, a profile similarity index on stability (with situation held constant or changed) would also be useful information, given the theoretical proposition underlying the MSQ (i.e., style scores as data points correlated over time and aggregated across individuals).

When addressing the question of MSQ criterion-related validity, the Trainer's Guide states that the MSQ predicts "'hard outcomes' as measured by others or by objective indices such as sales and profits," and goes on to claim that "Democratic and Coaching styles predicted statistically significant ($P < .05$) performance in sales and R & D organizations." The original data on which these claims are made is from McClelland and Burnham (1976), which reports that "In the illustrative company 63 percent of the better managers (those whose subordinates had high morale) scored higher on the democratic or coaching styles of management as compared with only 22 percent of the poor managers, a statistically significant difference." Apparently this is data from only one company and thus does not support the claims of generalized, criterion-related validity across sales and R & D settings. There is no empirical justification for claims made regarding "authoritative" styles.

Further claims for validity are made based on research with the "Organizational Climate Survey Questionnaire." Managerial styles were assessed by measuring the organizational climate as indicated by the subordinates of managers high and low on each managerial style. The Trainer's Guide maintains that subordinates' scores predict such outcome measures as "growth in sales and earnings, return on sales, combat preparedness inspection scores, and personnel turnover rates." A review of the two citations which are given to justify this validity claim again reveals a discrepancy in the conclusions drawn in the Trainer's Guide and the data/discussion in the citations. In fact, there is no empirical justification presented in this research for the claim made regarding style and outcome measures.

The Trainer's Guide indicates that new data are being analyzed to improve the psychometric support for the instrument. Clearly, either appropriate data/citations should be provided or amendments should be made to the strong claims made in the manual for the criterion-related validity of the MSQ.

FEEDBACK GUIDELINES. The section on feedback is clear and helpful. An outline of trainer remarks is provided, with suggestions for handouts and transparencies. A detailed explanation as to how the feedback should be provided is also very useful. The appropriate cautionary note is made regarding the interpretation of the data. Given the reliability problems cited above, emphasis should be placed on this guideline. An outline for a management training module using the MSQ is also provided. In terms of feedback guidelines for this type of instrument, the MSQ Trainer's Guide is well above average.

CONCLUSION. The MSQ is a relatively new instrument with fairly typical psychometric inadequacies related to the forced-choice methodology. Further norm development and improved reliability and validity research would improve this instrument. Relative to other managerial style questionnaires, the MSQ is a useful diagnostic instrument with a strong theoretical base generally supported by other managerial theories and research. In evaluating the entire package (i.e., MSQ Training Manual, Profile and Interpretative Notes, Work Environment Questionnaire), the general conclusion is that valid and helpful information can be gained using the instrument as a diagnostic tool.

REVIEWER'S REFERENCES

Stogdill, R. M. (1963). *Manual for the Leader Behavior Description Questionnaire—Form XII*. Columbus, OH: Bureau of Business Research, Ohio State University.

McClelland, D. C., & Winter, D. G. (1971). *Motivating economic achievement*. New York: The Free Press.

McClelland, D. C., & Burnham, D. H. (1976). Power is the great motivator. *Harvard Business Review*, 54, 100-110.

Bernardin, H. J., & Beatty, R. W. (1984). *Performance appraisal: Assessing human behavior at work*. Boston: Kent-Wadsworth.

[186]

Manager/Supervisor Staff Selector. Purpose: "Measures important intellectual and personality characteristics needed for the successful manager/supervisor." Candidates for managers and supervisors; 1976–84; 7 tests: Problem Solving Ability, Numerical Skills, Fluency, Business, Judgment, Supervisory Practices, CPF (interest in working with people), NPF (emotional stability); 1987 price data: $175–500 (depending on version) per set of tests including manual (no date, 5 pages) and scoring guide; information on scoring service available from distributor; French edition available; (5–15) minutes per test; tests from various publishers compiled, distributed and scored (optional) by Wolfe Personnel Testing & Training Systems, Inc.*

Review of the Manager/Supervisor Staff Selector by ERIC F. GARDNER, Professor of Psychology and Education Emeritus, Syracuse University, Syracuse, NY:

The Manager/Supervisor Staff Selector is a collection of seven tests that have been copyrighted at various times by the following publishers: (*a*) Problem Solving Ability Test, copyright 1984, by Harvard Professional Services (1982), Inc.; (*b*) Numerical Skills Test, copyright 1984, by Harvard Professional Services (1982), Inc.; (*c*) Fluency Test, copyright 1981, by Industrial Psychology, Inc., (prior copyrights 1956, 1947); (*d*) Business Judgment Test, copyright 1977, by Martin M. Bruce, Ph.D., published by Martin M. Bruce, Ph.D., Publishers; (*e*) Supervisory Practices Test, copyright 1976, by Martin M. Bruce, Ph.D., published by Martin M. Bruce, Ph.D., Publishers; (*f*) CPF (Contact Personality Factor) Test, copyright 1982, by R. B. Cattell, J. E. King, and A. K. Schuettler, prior copyright 1954, published by Industrial Psychology, Inc.; (*g*) NPF (Neurotic Personality Factor) Test, copyright 1954, by R. B. Cattell, J. E. King, and A. K. Schuettler, published by Industrial Psychology, Inc.

The three skills tests, which are labeled Problem Solving, Numerical Skills, and Verbal Fluency respectively, consist of three 5-minute tests. The first consists of 30 series items involving both numerical and alphabetical sequences. Although series completion involves one kind of problem solving, the absence of a rationale and validity data makes the claim that the test measures "Job Criteria" defined as "Logic, Problem Solving Ability, Planning and Conceptualizing" sound rather grandiose. The second test consists of 60 questions requiring the ability to use the four fundamental processes with integers and knowledge of the appropriate order when applying these processes. This test, which is offered to measure "Job Criteria" defined as "Numerical Skills and Reason," seems appropriate for measuring numerical skills limited to whole numbers but seems very limited as a measure of Reason. The third skills test labeled "Fluency" consists of three subtests. For Test 1 the subject is to list as many words as he/she can recall that end with the given syllable, for Test 2 as many words as can be recalled with the given prefix, and for Test 3 words with both a given prefix and suffix. This test is taken from the IPI Aptitude Series and has been reviewed in *The Fifth Mental Measurements Yearbook*. The review by Harold Bechtoldt (1959), which covers the entire set of Aptitude-Intelligence Tests published by Industrial Psychology, Inc., concludes "the tests themselves are well designed. . . . an industrial concern might well use these tests in their own long term *research* program, but this reviewer cannot recommend the tests for the selection or classification of job applicants."

Of the four untimed tests, two have been taken from Martin M. Bruce, Ph.D., Publisher (copyrighted 1977 and 1976), and two from IPI (Industrial Psychology, Inc.), copyrighted originally in 1954. The two by Bruce are the Business Judgment Test and the Supervisory Practices Test. The first test consists of 25 items concerning business situations in which a person might find him/herself and must respond accordingly. The second presents 50 questions dealing with common supervisory problems and requires the respondent to assume that he/she is a supervisor and to select the answer he/she believes to be the best. These two tests have been reviewed in *The Fifth* and *The Seventh Mental Measurements Yearbooks*.

Jerome E. Doppelt (1972), in *The Seventh Mental Measurements Yearbook*, makes the following comment about the Business Judgment Test, Revised: "The author suggests two areas of potential uses for the test: selection and training. This reviewer doubts that the instrument will be of much value as a selection device. In training it might have some usefulness as a springboard for discussion." In the same volume Kenneth D. Orton (1972) says: "The test shows promise of being useful in personnel selection, but additional information is needed for that promise to be realized."

The Supervisory Practices Test was reviewed in *The Fifth Mental Measurements Yearbook*. Clifford E. Jurgensen (1959) concluded in his review, "Because of the unreliability of scores for individual predictions, differing 'best' answers in various companies, and absence of information necessary to determine the best answer in some items, this reviewer recommends the test not be used in situations where total scores are obtained."

The last two tests, the 40-item CPF (Contact Personality Factor) and the 40-item NPF (Neurotic Personality Factor), were developed by Raymond B. Cattell in the middle 1950s as part of his extensive factor-analytic studies of personality. Detailed reviews of both of these tests occur in *The Fifth Mental Measurements Yearbook*.

In one of these reviews C. D. Johnson (1959) stressed that "the optimal score on CPF for performance on each job is recommended without sufficient indication as to the kind of evidence leading to the recommendation," and indicated the need for research data on validity. The NPF, which is a companion test to the CPF, was criticized for the same shortcomings by S. B. Sells (1959), who concluded:

> The confidential bulletins which make up the manual for this test present even less information than those for the CPF; item factor loadings have been omitted and no reliability correlations are reported. All of the critical comments incorporated for the CPF apply equally to this test. It is brief; but whether this streamlined test is an adequate measure of the neurotic versus stability factor and whether either the factor or this measure of it has any relevance to job success is still a research problem which should have been investigated by the authors before the test was offered for sale to industrial users. (p. 145)

This current reviewer concurs with the criticisms of the many prior careful and detailed reviews of the five tests in the Manager/Supervisor Staff Selector Battery that has been taken from other published tests. The general overall quality of the items is a positive feature, while the lack of data, especially with respect to validity and job relevance, has been and continues to be a serious deficiency. The first two tests are short, 5-minute tests that contain a reasonable number of familiar type items. There are no data presented about the psychometric characteristics of the items, the reliability of the tests, the source of the data for the tables given to interpret the scores, or validity information relevant to the use of the tests.

In evaluating the Manager/Supervisor Staff Selector, both the individual tests and the total battery are of concern. Unfortunately, the test manual, where one would hope to find the information about the test items, test reliability, normative samples, and test and battery validity, does not even mention these important topics. The one minor exception is a statement referring to a "Major validation study in progress."

The four-page manual contains a general description of the battery, sample questions, and a very ambitious claim for the use of the test as an aid in the selection of all supervisory and management positions—from a very junior level to the most senior. It also specifies the job criteria measured and the type of reports available. The sample report presented contains scores on a percentage scale for six variables and a paragraph describing the strengths and weaknesses of the person under consideration. A hiring recommendation is to be made based on a table indicating six categories with scales from 0 to 100% and ranging from "Do not hire," "Hire only if below average performance is acceptable," "Hire if no better candidate is available," "Hire with qualification," "Hire (Very Good)," to "Hire (Excellent)." However, no information of any kind is given as to how these categories were defined or what population was sampled or to what extent the battery is successful in classifying individuals reliably.

The lack of validity data is especially important in view of the various court decisions stressing the need for job relevance and validity data when making decisions about hiring. In contrast, an instrument that has been validated for various supervisory jobs and that has been shown to have job relatedness is the Supervisory Profile Record (SPR) developed and published by Richardson, Bellows, and Henry. Until validation data are obtained for the Wolfe Manager/Supervisor Staff Selector a company should use this instrument for research purposes only.

From the past lack of information about the effectiveness of most of these tests plus no information about the effectiveness of their inclusion in the Manager/Supervisor Staff Selector, this reviewer can only stress that this battery should not be used for selection, as recommended, until numerous data supporting the statements in the manual are provided.

REVIEWER'S REFERENCES

Bechtoldt, H. (1959). [Review of Aptitude-Intelligence Tests.] In O. K. Buros (Ed.), *The fifth mental measurements yearbook* (pp. 667-669). Highland Park, NJ: Gryphon Press.

Johnson, C. D. (1959). [Review of the IPAT Contact Personality Factor Test.] In O. K. Buros (Ed.), *The fifth mental measurements yearbook* (pp. 140-142). Highland Park, NJ: Gryphon Press.

Jurgensen, C. E. (1959). [Review of the Supervisory Practices Test.] In O. K. Buros (Ed.), *The fifth mental measurements yearbook* (pp. 946-947). Highland Park, NJ: Gryphon Press.

Sells, S. B. (1959). [Review of the IPAT Neurotic Personality Factor Test.] In O. K. Buros (Ed.), *The fifth mental measurements yearbook* (p. 145). Highland Park, NJ: Gryphon Press.

Doppelt, J. E. (1972). [Review of the Business Judgment Test, Revised.] In O. K. Buros (Ed.), *The seventh mental measurements yearbook* (pp. 1488-1489). Highland Park, NJ: Gryphon Press.

Orton, K. D. (1972). [Review of the Business Judgment Test, Revised.] In O. K. Buros (Ed.), *The seventh mental measurements yearbook* (pp. 1489-1490). Highland Park, NJ: Gryphon Press.

[187]

Marital Evaluation Checklist. Purpose: "Provides a brief yet comprehensive survey of the most common characteristics and problem areas in a marital relationship." Married couples in counseling; 1984; MEC; self-administered checklist; 3 areas: Reasons for Marrying, Problems of the Current Relationship, Motivation for Counseling; 1987 price data: $12.95 per 50 checklists including fact sheet (no date, 1 page); (30–40) minutes; Leslie Navran; Psychological Assessment Resources, Inc.*

Review of the Marital Evaluation Checklist by RICHARD B. STUART, Clinical Professor of Psychiatry and Behavioral Sciences, University of Washington, Seattle, WA:

In lieu of a manual, the Marital Evaluation Checklist is furnished with a two-paragraph instruction sheet lacking any mention of reliability or validity data. The first paragraph makes the claim that the instrument furnishes a "comprehensive review of potential problems in three primary areas." However, the prestructured nature of the items precludes the possibility that they can reflect the broad sweep of couples' concerns, which are typically highly individual. The second paragraph advises therapists to summarize problem areas from the separate protocols of both spouses "as a basis for designing priorities in marriage counseling." However, no instruction is offered as to how to weight responses in a fashion that would prioritize them.

The first section of this instrument asks respondents to select any of 77 prestructured alternative reasons for marrying, with a 78th open-ended option. The reasons are divided into interpersonal/emotional, material/economic, social, and personal categories. Several problems are immediately apparent. First, the list is far from exhaustive. Second, many of the alternatives are extremely negative. Indeed, some are so negative as to be highly unlikely choices for someone wishing to make a positive first impression on a marriage therapist (e.g., "for publicity," or "to satisfy a need to dominate someone"). And most importantly, few are correctable by, and therefore relevant to, marriage therapy.

The second section of the instrument concerns current problems in the marriage. It includes 57 prestructured items, and one open-choice alternative in each of four areas; Money and Work, Sex, Personal Characteristics, and Marital Relationship. Respondents are asked to indicate whether they feel the problem is primarily theirs, their spouse's, or shared by both. Here, too, the alternatives are not exhaustive. Presentation of the array of problems may be overwhelming for couples entering therapy because there is no way to indicate which problems are minor in comparison to the others. And asking the partners to assign responsibility for the problem has the potential of forcing them to take positions that may create resistance in a treatment program based on their assuming collective responsibility. Finally, collecting data about problems without at the same time making note of areas of positive functioning will generally lead to dismal therapeutic expectations by counselors and clients.

The third section of the instrument addresses motivation for counseling. Respondents are offered a choice of seven reasons for having sought counseling, seven expectations from therapy, five descriptions of the partner's relative motivation for therapy, and four alternatives of therapeutic goals. Here, too, the alternatives provided are far from exhaustive, as well as being quite heavily negative in tone.

A final, open-ended section solicits respondents' description of other problems or comments.

In summary, lacking the expected establishment of reliability and validity, this instrument has no current research application. Its use by clinicians is likewise ill advised. Fully one-third of it is past-oriented and irrelevant to current therapeutic concerns. It is too narrow to permit couples' expression of the ideographic nature of the concerns. It is so negative as to dampen the chance that either therapists or spouses will salvage any optimism about the chance that the ensuing therapy will have a positive outcome.

[188]

Martinez Assessment of the Basic Skills: Criterion-Referenced Diagnostic Testing of Basic Skills. Purpose: Designed to assist in assessing basic skills in six areas. Learning disabled and mildly to moderately mentally retarded children; 1983; 6 tests: Primary Language Concepts, Counting and Numerals, Time Telling, Spelling, Arithmetic, Reading; individual in part; 1987 price data: $59.95 per complete kit including 5 student profile charts, 5 student response and record booklets for each test, and administration manual ('83, 64 pages); $4.35–$9.05 per 5 student response and record booklets; $2.50 per 5 student profiles; $21.95 per manual; (10–45) minutes per test; David Martinez; ASIEP Education Co.*

Review of the Martinez Assessment of the Basic Skills: Criterion-Referenced Diagnostic Testing of Basic Skills by ROBERT G. HARRINGTON, Associate Professor of Educational Psychology and Research, University of Kansas, Lawrence, KS:

The basic skills curricular approach emphasizes the teaching of key or fundamental skills and knowledge (Staats, 1968). The skill areas selected are said to be basic for later development and learning (Paget & Bracken, 1983). Oftentimes, breadth of objectives may be replaced with a concentration on depth of presumed foundation skills (Lichtenstein & Ireton, 1984). Assessment from this curricular perspective is designed to assess each child's skill level development within each basic skill area so that appropriate curricular objectives for instruction can be selected for individual children and groups of children (Bagnato & Neisworth, 1981).

The Martinez Assessment of the Basic Skills is intended to be a criterion-referenced test developed to assist special and regular education teachers in diagnosing children in kindergarten through ninth grade in six separate subtest areas including Primary Language Concepts, Counting and Numerals, Time Telling, Spelling, Arithmetic, and Reading. No rationale is given as to why these particular skill areas were included out of the multitude of basic skills; nor is there any explanation regarding why these particular grade ranges are covered. Because the source from which the test items were derived was not described it is impossible to judge whether the test content is representative of the most important basic skills in kindergarten through seventh grade.

The Martinez test consists of a very brief test development and examiner's manual, six separate student response and record booklets for each of the six subtests, and a student profile record booklet depicting the specific items passed on each subtest and the percent of items within each subtest mastered by the examinee at the grade levels in which these skills are "commonly taught." Items are scored as either passed or failed. No standard scores or grade equivalents are provided on the Martinez Test and without normative reference points the test is severely limited for making placement decisions, for predicting future school achievement, or for comparing the readiness of students to perform at a particular academic level. Furthermore, it is suggested in the examiner's manual that teachers should use item responses to identify skills yet to be mastered and requiring further instruction. The behavioral objectives matching each item are intended to be used to teach and develop individual education programs for children with skill deficits. According to Martinez the Primary Language Concepts, Time Telling, and Counting and Numerals Tests contain content that may be directly taught because they represent unique skills unto themselves. Of course, it would represent poor test practice to take Martinez's recommendation literally to teach to the test and then presume that increases in test performance upon posttest represent true increases in skill mastery.

In addition to these conceptual problems with the test, the spine of the spiral-bound examiner's manual breaks easily and there are many major typographical errors not only in the examiner's manual but also in the examinee record booklets as well. One such printing error occurs on Subtest J of the Counting and Numerals criterion test covering skills at about the beginning of the second grade level. The unelaborated examiner's instructions simply require the examiner to point to the first four or five lines of numbers on the page and say, "Some numbers are missing." The student's apparent task is to fill in the missing numbers from the sequence. The problem is that there are two "3s" and two "5s" shown within what would otherwise be the standard counting sequence. The brief, understated instructions only add to the confusion on this subtest. The typographical problems and incomplete directions found on this subtest are common throughout the entire test.

The contents of the six basic skills subtests are as follows. The purpose of the 24-item Primary Language Concepts Test is to assess basic receptive language skills such as "over," "under," "inside," and "outside" as well as skills that relate to performance in independent (workbook) classroom activities such as "circle," "underline," "cross-out," and "mark-out." All items range in difficulty from grades K through 1 and each is intended to measure a different concept with the assumption that each of these language concepts will be taught separately.

The 14-item Counting and Numerals Test, with a reported difficulty level in the kindergarten to second grade range, is meant to evaluate beginning mathematical skills such as oral counting, symbol, (numeral) identification, and counting objects.

The 14-item Time Telling Test with items suitable for grades 1–6 is intended to assess time-telling skills as well as five optional items assessing time-telling on a digital clock.

The Spelling Test is divided into three progressively more difficult levels with 12, 4, and 8 items respectively and ranging in difficulty from grades 1–6. The test is primarily a measure of a student's ability to convert symbols to sounds with optional sections on sentence dictation at each level.

The Arithmetic Test has a varying number of items in seven skill areas. These are administered in a hierarchical order of difficulty ranging from grades 1 through 7. The items assess skills in addition, subtraction, multiplication, division, fractions, decimals, and percents.

The Reading Test has four components: a readiness component probing prereading skills; Level 1 probing sound-symbol correspondences; Level II probing irregular sound patterns as well as silent letters; and Level III probing more advanced decoding skills and related word study skills, such as contractions and syllabification.

The six subtests may be administered in any combination; however, depending upon the age of the child, not all of the subtests will be administered. Subtests are administered in either oral or written form. The administration time may vary depending upon the number of subtests administered. Each subtest takes between 10 and 45 minutes for students to complete. Three of the subtests may be administered in a group format as well as individually.

No acceptable evidence of the reliability or validity of this test is offered. Instead, the author says the content validity of the test was evaluated by comparing the test items with instructional programs used in grades K–6 (i.e., elementary school mathematics) and commercially available skill inventories such as the Boehm Test of Basic Concepts (Boehm, 1971), Pre-school Math Inventory (Kraner, 1976), Inventory of Early Development (Brigance, 1978), and the Inventory of Basic Skills (Brigance, 1977). In lieu of psychometric data the Martinez tests are reported to be substantially compatibile with these comparison instruments.

Each item on each subtest is said to have a corresponding behavioral objective to demonstrate the correspondence between the objective and the item. This correspondence is to ensure an easy transition between testing, IEP development, and teaching. Unfortunately several of the subtests include very few items for adequate coverage on a criterion-referenced test and especially for one covering such a wide grade range. For example, the diagnostic reading test, which is supposed to cover from kindergarten to ninth grade, has less than 40 items. The number of items varies across the six subtests and while there may be more than one item per behavioral objective on some of the subtests there is only one item presented per behavioral objective on the Primary Language Concepts Test. Furthermore, some of the basic skills questions use confusing language and even seem redundant. For example, one item on the Primary Language Concepts Test asks the child to, "Mark out the car." This vague instruction is intended to get the child to place a line through a picture of a car. Another question on the same subtest requires the child to "Cross out the car." The exact same response as the previous item is required and appears both redundant and confusing.

The author is correct in stating that many criterion-referenced tests "frequently do not address the reliability question." However, he is incorrect in implying that he is being magnanimous in supplying reliability data for the Martinez Test. Such data are required for criterion-referenced tests according to the *Standards for Educational and Psychological Testing* (AERA, APA, & NCME, 1985). Only one reliability study is reported. The study sample was 25 children (20 nonhandicapped, grades K–8 and 5 mentally retarded and learning disabled, ages 7–13). In this study, the reliabilities of the Primary Language Concepts Test and the Time Telling Test were evaluated using a test-retest analysis with immediate retest. Results showed 99.5% and 90.1% levels of test-retest reliability respectively. Another analysis was applied to render percentages of agreement across items within each of the seven computational areas of the Arithmetic Test. These reported reliabilities ranged between 85.8% and 100%. Finally, an odd-even analysis of the items was conducted to measure the percentage of agreement for the Counting and Numerals Test as well as the Reading and Spelling Tests. These reliabilities were reported to be 93% for the Counting and Numerals Test, between 87% and 100% for the Reading Test, and between 81% and 87% for the Spelling Test. Because the split-half reliabilities for the Spelling and Reading Tests were reported for each level only and not according to the subskills measured in each level of these subtests it is literally impossible to interpret these reported reliabilities. Furthermore, the extremely small sample size, the averaging of the data across grade levels and handicapping conditions, and the lack of replication render these data useless for judging the reliability of the Martinez Test.

In summary, at this time the Martinez Assessment of the Basic Skills should be considered an informal measure of basic skills. In order for the test to be of value as a criterion-referenced instrument it will need to undergo standardization as well as an evaluation of its reliability and validity. The test should not be used to make diagnostic decisions, nor for educational placement decisions. In fact, practitioners considering using the Martinez Test as an informal measure of basic skills should be careful to review the test items to ensure these represent the kinds of curriculum content they wish to evaluate. Furthermore, test users should be prepared to develop their own independent local norms for the test. Fortunately, there are other tests of basic skills readily available that are much better standardized and validated than the Martinez Test. These tests include the Bracken Basic Concept Scale (1984), the Boehm Test of Basic Concepts—Revised (1986), and the Brigance Inventory of Basic Skills (Brigance, 1978).

REVIEWER'S REFERENCES

Staats, A. W. (1968). *Learning, language and cognition.* New York: Holt, Rinehart and Winston.

Boehm, A. (1971). Boehm Test of Basic Concepts. San Antonio, TX: The Psychological Corporation.

Brigance, A. (1978). Brigance Diagnostic Inventory of Basic Skills. N. Billerica, MA: Curriculum Associates, Inc.

Brigance, A. (1978). Brigance Diagnostic Inventory of Early Development. N. Billerica, MA: Curriculum Associates, Inc.

Bagnato, S. J., & Neisworth, J. T. (1981). *Linking developmental assessment and curricula: Prescription for early intervention.* Rockville, MD: An Aspen Systems Corp.

Paget, K. D., & Bracken, B. A. (1983). *The psychoeducational assessment of preschool children.* New York: Grune & Stratton.

Bracken, B. A. (1984). Bracken Basic Concept Scale. San Antonio, TX: The Psychological Corporation.

Lichtenstein, R., & Ireton, H. (1984). *Preschool screening: Identifying young children with developmental and educational problems.* New York: Grune & Stratton.

American Educational Research Association, American Psychological Association, & National Council on Measurement in Education. (1985). *Standards for educational and psychological testing.* Washington, DC: American Psychological Association, Inc.

Boehm, A. (1986). Boehm Test of Basic Concepts—Revised. San Antonio, TX: The Psychological Corporation.

Review of the Martinez Assessment of the Basic Skills: Criterion-Referenced Diagnostic Testing of Basic Skills by DAN WRIGHT, School Psychologist, Ralston Public Schools, Ralston, NE:

The Martinez inventory was developed primarily to assist in monitoring academic skill acquisition by mildly handicapped youngsters in grades K–6. It can be administered by resource or regular classroom teachers, and requires only a modicum of skill at individual assessment. Directions and procedures are reasonably clear, and the consumable test booklets appear well produced and easy to use, if somewhat bland. Test sections require from 10 to 45 minutes each to administer, scoring is straightforward, and results are graphically portrayed on a chart that indicates grade levels at which skills are commonly taught.

It is not evident that a great deal of effort went into the preparation of this inventory. There is no discussion of procedures for item selection or construction, only brief mention that comparison with instructional programs and commercially available skill inventories indicates them to be substantially compatible. Indeed, the Martinez inventory is not actually criterion referenced but objectives referenced; items are keyed to instructional objectives, but there is no indicated plan by which items were selected as representative of clearly defined content domains. This may seem a small point, but it limits sharply the amount of generalization one can make from the results; one cannot legitimately make inferences about examinee ability beyond the items presented. Disregarding this point entirely, there is no evidence that test items are adequate for assessment even of the objectives offered. The only field testing referenced is a single study in which a woefully inadequate sample (5 handicapped and 20 nonhandicapped students in kindergarten through eighth grade) was employed to generate inadequate reliability estimates.

The author acknowledges that inventory users will need to determine whether there is adequate correspondence between the objectives presented and the instructional programs in which students are placed. This reviewer is not a curriculum specialist, but his examination of the materials provided little evidence that the objectives presented were sufficiently comprehensive, that the items assessed objectives adequately or that, above all, the inventory is in any way uniquely appropriate for the mildly handicapped population with whom its use is recommended. It is this last point that is most disquieting. Inventories of this type lend themselves conveniently for use in IEP development and monitoring, with the danger that they may come to *be* the IEP. The questionable adequacy of this particular inventory, its encouraged use as pre- and post-test with programs of supplementary instruction, and an ambiguous discussion on the advisability of teaching directly toward the tests, must cause one to question whether students would demonstrate real or artificial gains. The author comments (favorably, one infers) that if the inventory were used to monitor such an instructional program "criterion test performance should be substantially improved, as such test [*sic*] are sensitive to short term periods of instruction." There appears to be a proclivity to substitute the test for that which it purports to measure, and to thereby encourage its misuse.

In summary, the Martinez inventory is a battery of objectives-referenced tests for which technical adequacy and validity for intended purpose have not been demonstrated. Depending on a user's needs, it may offer some utility; however, to adopt it uncritically for the purposes recommended would be unwise. There is no reason to recommend it over other currently available skills inventories, such as those of the Brigance series.

[189]

Maslach Burnout Inventory, Second Edition. Purpose: Assesses "the different aspects of experienced burnout." Members of the helping professions, including educators; 1981–86; MBI; test titles are Human Services Survey and Educators Survey; 3 subscales: Emotional Exhaustion, Personal Accomplishment, Depersonalization; self-administered; 2 forms: Educators, Human Services; 1987 price data: $5 per 25 Human Services Surveys; $5.50 per 25 Educators Surveys; $4.50 per 25 Educators or Human Services Demographic Data Sheets; $1.25 per score key; $9 per manual (1986, 38 pages); $10 per specimen set; (10–15) minutes; Christina Maslach and Susan E. Jackson; Consulting Psychologists Press.*

For reviews by Jack L. Bodden and E. Thomas Dowd of the original edition, see 9:659 (8 references).

TEST REFERENCES

1. Belcastro, P. A., Gold, R. S., & Grant, J. (1982). Stress and burnout: Physiologic effects on correctional teachers. *Criminal Justice and Behavior*, 9, 387-395.

2. Anderson, M. B. G., & Iwanicki, E. F. (1984). Teacher motivation and its relationship to burnout. *Educational Administration Quarterly*, 20 (2), 109-132.

3. Belcastro, P. A., & Hays, L. C. (1984). Ergophilia . . . ergophobia . . . ergo . . . burnout? *Professional Psychology: Research and Practice*, 15 (2), 260-270.

4. Caccese, T. M., & Mayerberg, C. K. (1984). Gender differences in perceived burnout of college coaches. *Journal of Sport Psychology*, 6, 279-288.

5. Champion, D. F., & Westbrook, B. W. (1984). [Review of the Maslach Burnout Inventory]. *Measurement and Evaluation in Counseling and Development*, 17, 100-102.

6. Eisenstat, R. A., & Felner, R. D. (1984). Toward a differentiated view of burnout: Personal and organizational mediators of job satisfaction and stress. *American Journal of Community Psychology*, 12, 411-430.

7. Fimian, M. J. (1984). Organizational variables related to stress and burnout in community-based programs. *Education and Training of the Mentally Retarded*, 19, 201-209.

8. Gold, Y. (1984). The factorial validity of the Maslach Burnout Inventory in a sample of California elementary and junior high school classroom teachers. *Educational and Psychological Measurement*, 44, 1009-1016.

9. Johnson, A. B., Gold, V., & Knepper, D. (1984). Frequency and intensity of professional burnout among teachers of the mildly handicapped. *College Student Journal*, 18, 261-266.

10. McIntyre, T. C. (1984). The relationship between locus of control and teacher burnout. *British Journal of Educational Psychology*, 54, 235-238.

11. Meier, S. T. (1984). The construct validity of burnout. *Journal of Occupational Psychology*, 57, 211-219.

12. Zabel, M. K., Dettmer, P. A., & Zabel, R. H. (1984). Factors of emotional exhaustion, depersonalization, and sense of accomplishment among teachers of the gifted. *Gifted Child Quarterly*, 28, 65-69.

13. Davis-Sacks, M. L., Jayaratne, S., & Chess, W. A. (1985). A comparison of the effects of social support on the incidence of burnout. *Social Work*, 30, 240-244.

14. Firth, H., McIntee, J., & McKeown, P. (1985). Maslach Burnout Inventory: Factor structure and norms for British nursing staff. *Psychological Reports*, 57, 147-150.

15. Gold, Y. (1985). The relationship of six personal and life history variables to standing on three dimensions of the Maslach Burnout Inventory in a sample of elementary and junior high

school teachers. *Educational and Psychological Measurement*, 45, 377-387.

16. Gold, Y., & Michael, W. B. (1985). Academic self-concept correlates of potential burnout in a sample of first-semester elementary-school practice teachers: A concurrent validity study. *Educational and Psychological Measurement*, 45, 909-914.

17. Kottkamp, R. B., & Mansfield, J. R. (1985). Role conflict, role ambiguity, powerlessness and burnout among high school supervisors. *Journal of Research and Development in Education*, 18 (4), 29-38.

18. Meier, S. T., & Schmeck, R. R. (1985). The burned-out college student: A descriptive profile. *Journal of College Student Personnel*, 26, 63-69.

19. Nagy, S. (1985). Burnout and selected variables as components of occupational stress. *Psychological Reports*, 56, 195-200.

20. Nagy, S., & Davis, L. G. (1985). Burnout: A comparative analysis of personality and environmental variables. *Psychological Reports*, 57, 1319-1326.

21. Nowack, K. M., Gibbons, J. M., & Hanson, A. L. (1985). Factors affecting burnout and job performance of resident assistants. *Journal of College Student Personnel*, 26, 137-142.

22. Pierson-Hubeny, D., & Archambault, F. X. (1985). Role stress and perceived intensity of burnout among reading specialists. *Reading World*, 24 (4), 41-52.

23. Whitehead, J. T. (1985). Job burnout in probation and parole: Its extent and intervention implications. *Criminal Justice and Behavior*, 12, 91-110.

24. Dignam, J. T., Barrera, M., Jr., & West, S. G. (1986). Occupational stress, social support, and burnout among correctional officers. *American Journal of Community Psychology*, 14, 177-193.

25. Jackson, S. E., Schwab, R. L., & Schuler, R. S. (1986). Toward an understanding of the burnout phenomenon. *Journal of Applied Psychology*, 71, 630-640.

26. Jayaratne, S., Chess, W. A., & Kunkel, D. A. (1986). Burnout: Its impact on child welfare workers and their spouses. *Social Work*, 31, 53-59.

27. Kottkamp, R. B., & Travlos, A. L. (1986). Selected job stressors, emotional exhaustion, job satsifaction, and thrust behavior of the high school principal. *The Alberta Journal of Educational Research*, 32, 234-248.

28. Powers, S., & Gose, K. F. (1986). Reliability and construct validity of the Maslach Burnout Inventory in a sample of university students. *Educational and Psychological Measurement*, 46, 251-255.

29. Rafferty, J. P., Lemkau, J. P., Purdy, R. R., & Rudisill, J. R. (1986). Validity of the Maslach Burnout Inventory for family practice physicians. *Journal of Clinical Psychology*, 42, 488-492.

30. Spicuzza, F. J., Baskind, F. R., & Woodside, M. R. (1984). A continuing dialogue on burnout. *Journal of College Placement*, 45 (1), 29-33.

31. Ursprung, A. W. (1986). Incidence and correlates of burnout in residential service settings. *Rehabilitation Counseling Bulletin*, 29, 225-239.

32. Quiqley, T. A., Slack, T., & Smith, G. J. (1987). Burnout in secondary school teacher coaches. *The Alberta Journal of Educational Research*, 33, 260-274.

33. Sarros, J. C., & Friesen, D. (1987). The etiology of Administrator Burnout. *The Alberta Journal of Educational Research*, 33, 163-179.

34. Barone, D. F., Caddy, G. R., Katell, A. D., Roselione, F. B., & Hamilton, R. A. (1988). The Work Stress Inventory: Organizational stress and job risk. *Educational and Psychological Measurement*, 48 (1), 141-154.

Review of the Maslach Burnout Inventory, Second Edition, by DAVID S. HARGROVE, Associate Professor of Psychology, University of Nebraska-Lincoln, Lincoln, NE:

In recent years, human service workers and administrators have become increasingly familiar with the idea of "burnout" among employees, particularly those with considerable direct contact with clientele. This concept has been popularized among the work force and no doubt is used and abused for a variety of purposes related to job performance evaluation. Being "burned out" serves as a common explanation for a wide range of work-related experiences and feelings.

Amidst the popularization of the concept, Maslach and Jackson have presented a serious exception to the usual trite accounts of experiences of "burnout" by workers or advice on how to avoid it by experts. The Maslach Burnout Inventory, Second Edition (MBI) is the result of approximately 8 years of systematic research to understand and measure the concept of "burnout." Directed toward human service professionals with a new form for teachers (Form ED), the MBI was developed to measure components of the "burnout" phenomenon as the authors have conceptualized it. The second edition of the MBI features at least one substantive improvement over the first edition.

Maslach and Jackson believe that "burnout" consists of three components: Emotional Exhaustion, Depersonalization, and reduced Personal Accomplishment. These experiences are thought to be characteristic of human service workers who have intense involvements with other persons. The consequences of "burnout" are thought to be potentially harmful to staff persons, clientele, and the institutions that house them.

The purpose of the MBI is to measure the three identified components of "burnout." Subscale scores are produced for each component. These raw scores are used for interpretation; no summed or weighted total score for the entire inventory has been developed. Thus, to interpret the test, the subscale scores may be compared to normative data and a profile of scores may be plotted to show interrelationships. Various relationships of subscale scores may be interpreted as indicating one of three levels of "burnout."

The test format is a 22-item scale, consisting of statements to be rated on a 0–6 frequency continuum. Each item is a statement about the individual's feelings or attitudes related to his or her work. The statement is rated according to the frequency of occurrence of the feeling or attitude from 0 (never) to 6 (every day). A scoring key is provided that identifies and sums the subscale scores. The emphasis of the scale is on the frequency of occurrence of the individual's feelings or attitudes in relation to certain aspects of the person's work.

The manual is a clearly-written document that traces the development of the MBI, explains its appropriate use, gives necessary instructions, provides reliability and validity data, and offers suggestions for further research. The manual for the second edition of the MBI features a supplement for the use of Form ED, a recently-devised form for teachers.

The MBI was developed from a pool of items collected from previous research interviews and questionnaires and from a review of established scales. The inventory is not theory-driven, but appears to grow from the authors' hypotheses regarding the constructs associated with "burnout." The preliminary form of the MBI contained 47 items that reflected endorsements of both frequency and intensity of the feelings and attitudes. Factor analysis and the establishment of a clear item-selection criterion reduced the total to 22 items.

Reliability of the test is adequately demonstrated in the manual. Subscale coefficients range from .71 to .90 (N = 1,316). Subscale standard errors of measurement ranged from 3.16 to 3.80. Reported test-retest reliability coefficients ranged from .60 to .82 after 2 to 4 weeks (N = 53) and .54 to .60 (N = 248) after 2 years. Reliability coefficients were based on samples not used in item selection.

Reliability data from MBI Form ED are reported to be consistent with those of MBI. Cronbach alpha estimates ranging from .76 to .90 (N = 469) and .72 to .88 (N = 462) are reported from two studies.

Data supporting convergent and discriminant validity are reported in the manual. Convergent validity tables and a useful explanation point out the three subscales are meaningfully related to reported observation by others, such as co-workers or spouses. Additional data are reported relating the subscales to specific dimensions of job performance and personal outcomes. The reported correlation coefficients are modest but statistically significant.

Data suggesting a relationship between MBI and the Job Satisfaction Inventory is presented to show that "burnout" is sufficiently related to job satisfaction (negatively) but also sufficiently distinct to be a different construct. Further, data are presented that demonstrate the MBI is not influenced by social desirability and is not likely to be measuring clinical depression.

The MBI is a systematically developed instrument to measure some constructs that seem to be in the process of becoming defined. Supporting reliability and validity data are adequate for the instrument and its new derivative form (Form ED).

Adequate rationales are presented in the manual for the elimination of the intensity dimension, although that dimension still seems to be pertinent. Whether intensity and frequency of feelings are sufficiently similar is a pertinent issue. However, the relatively strong relationship between the two and the awkwardness of measurement of intensity likely provides the basis for the authors' good judgment to drop it from the inventory.

A problem with the MBI and its manual is the lack of a precise definition of "burnout." The construct seems to be adequately operationalized in the scale, but there is little information regarding the source of the initial items or the hypotheses that may have generated them. Because it is not a theory-driven instrument, it is important to have as much knowledge about the source of the specific items as possible. This information is not presented in the manual. Thus, more data to support the construct validity of the instrument are needed.

Given the lack of a precise definition, it is difficult to know whether "burnout" might be mistaken for other types of job or personal difficulties that manifest themselves in the worklife. Could "burnout," in light of its popularization in the last 10 years, be a convenient label for other issues? Is there a way to discriminate when this occurs? This criticism simply points out there may be a tendency by a given individual to mistakenly attribute issues to "burnout."

Another concern with the MBI is what it does not measure. It is somewhat surprising the ability, or the perception of the ability, to do the job is not considered an important aspect of both satisfaction and "burnout." Does "burnout" presume previous competence in the job?

Third, while there is a warning in the manual not to use the instrument for clinical purposes, it seems likely that some users will employ the test in this manner. It would be helpful to explain the dangers of this type of use and the potential impact of the resulting errors.

Finally, the normative data are not presented in as refined a manner as is desirable. Although the authors do provide a means of collecting demographic data from various samples, the normative data presented in the manual are not broken down into occupational groupings as well as into the variables of sex, race, age, marital status, and education. Certainly one reason for this omission is the insufficient number of cases for each occupational grouping. One would hope that as sufficient data are collected the data will be categorized in that manner. For example, mental health staff should be a single category with comparative data on the sex, race, age, marital status, and education variables presented for that single category.

The Maslach Burnout Inventory, Second Edition is a solidly constructed instrument that continues to be strengthened as additional research is completed. It appears to be particularly useful in a wide range of human service agencies and is related to some important work-related constructs.

Review of the Maslach Burnout Inventory, Second Edition by JONATHAN SANDOVAL, Professor of Education, University of California, Davis, Davis, CA:

The second edition of the Maslach Burnout Inventory (MBI) is evidence of the inventory authors' commitment to furthering the research literature on the phenomenon of burnout in the human services professions. The authors are among the leading researchers in this area and have continued to develop their measurement device.

The second edition differs from the first in that the 22 items are now rated for frequency of occurrence rather than both frequency and intensity of occurrence. The elimination of one of the response dimensions was justified on the basis of the high correlation between frequency and intensity. In addition, the rating of frequency is more concrete than the rating of intensity. As a result of moving to one response dimension, the current edition takes only half the time (as compared to the first edition) for the respondent to complete.

The second edition includes a larger number of norm groups than the first. The new norms are a result of a number of studies that have been done over the last several years. Although the manual does not detail the norm samples, there are references to sources where this information may be found. In addition to a general human services form for use with all mental health and service professionals, there is an additional form available especially for educators. The only difference between the educators' and the human services questionnaire is the substitution of "students" for "recipients" in one third of the items.

The authors recommend two primary uses for the MBI: (*a*) as a research instrument to further our knowledge of the burnout phenomenon and (*b*) as an organizational assessment device to determine if there are substantial numbers of employees who are experiencing burnout in a particular setting. The authors are careful to warn there is not yet sufficient research to justify using scores obtained from individuals for diagnostic purposes or to select individuals for particular interventions. The most appropriate use for the survey is to examine groups of human services workers.

The MBI manual presents data suggesting the inventory has reasonable reliability, especially for research uses. The Emotional Exhaustion scale tends to have a higher reliability coefficient than the other two scales. For the Emotional Exhaustion scale, the alpha coefficient was .90, and a stability coefficient over a 2-to-4-week period was .82. For the Depersonalization scale, the alpha coefficient was .79 and stability coefficient was .60; for the Personal Accomplishment scale, the alpha coefficient was .71 and stability coefficient was .80.

The manual presents an impressive array of data on the validity of the inventory scores. In convergent validity studies, the MBI scores have been correlated with behavior ratings made by knowledgeable informants, with job characteristics that are expected to contribute to burnout, and with other measures of outcome related to burnout. Evidence of discriminant validity is offered suggesting the measures obtained from the MBI are different than job dissatisfaction. Previous Buros reviewers questioned whether or not the construct of Burnout was a useful one, distinct from job satisfaction. This concern has been lessened with increased study of the phenomenon and the scale. However, one study did relate the MBI scores to clinical depression and the similarity of the two constructs should be explored further. In other research, the authors have presented evidence the scale is not unduly influenced by a social desirability response set.

One third of the manual for the second edition is devoted to suggestions for future research on the instrument and a discussion of burnout in education. The authors' devotion of such a high proportion of the manual to these topics emphasizes that this is a research instrument that may have potential for clinical use, but is not presently suitable for such a purpose. The authors acknowledge that more work needs to be done on subscale patterns, group norms, and occupational generalizability. Although it is difficult to argue with the need to do research along the lines suggested, it will continue to be necessary to do independent studies of the reliability and validity of this instrument. The manual is not totally clear on which validity evidence was gathered on the first edition and which was gathered on the second. The convergent validity correlations reported in Table C of the Appendix support the validity, but indicate that reliability and validity may differ within the human services occupations.

In summary the Maslach Burnout Inventory appears to be a well-researched measure of an important construct. The MBI is certainly the instrument of choice to use in research and evaluation endeavors studying the phenomenon of burnout.

[190]

Mastery Test in Consumer Economics. Purpose: Measures knowledge in consumer economics. Grades 8–12; 1984; performance objectives in 15 areas (Consumer in the Marketplace, Consumer in the Economy, Personal Money Management, Consumer Credit Fundamentals, Wise Use of Credit, Food Buying, Housing, Transportation, Furniture/Appliances/Clothing, Personal and Health Services, Banking Services, Saving and Investments, Insurance, Taxes and Government, Consumer in Society), and total score; 1985 price data: $26.50 per test kit including manual (23 pages), 20 test booklets, and 20 answer sheets; $12 per 20 test booklets; $12.50 per 50 answer sheets; $5.50 per manual; $9 per specimen set; STS scoring service, $1.10 per student ($20 minimum); 30(35) minutes; Les Dlabay; Scholastic Testing Service, Inc.*

TEST REFERENCES

1. Thor, A., & Berry, R. E. (1987). A Canadian assessment of consumer education knowledge of prospective teachers. *The Alberta Journal of Educational Research*, 33, 283-291.

Review of the Mastery Test in Consumer Economics by IRVIN J. LEHMANN, Professor of Measurement, Michigan State University, East Lansing, MI:

When I discuss the distinctions between criterion and norm-referenced tests (hereafter referred to as CRTs and NRTs respectively) in my testing courses, I do so in terms of the following differences between the two: (*a*) CRTs are designed to *describe* the strengths and weaknesses of an individual whereas NRTs are designed to *discriminate* among individuals; and (*b*) CRTs have a limited number of instructional objectives with many test items per objective whereas NRTs have a large number of objectives with just one or two items per objective. Both, however, share certain characteristics. For example, the principles generally espoused in measurement textbooks regarding the construction of test items, regardless of what type of test one is developing, are the same: The language should be unambiguous, there should be only one correct answer, there should be no clues in the item to reward the testwise student, etc. In addition, it is necessary for any achievement test, (but especially for CRTs) to demonstrate at least content validity and to offer some type of reliability evidence. Keeping in mind the purposes, psychometric properties, and item-writing practices of any CRT, let us look at the Mastery Test in Consumer Economics (MTCE) in greater detail.

The MTCE is a criterion-referenced test designed for high school students. The test has 45 items grouped into 15 major sections with each section representing a major consumer economic topic. Examples of these topics are The Consumer in the Marketplace, Housing, The Consumer in Society, and Taxes and Government. For each major topic "an overall objective . . . has been developed," and for each of these overall objectives three specific instructional objectives have been written, and one item has been written for each of these three specific objectives.

For example, the major overall objective for MTCE Saving and Investments is "The student will recognize factors related to savings and investments." The three specific instructional objectives are as follows: The student will be able to "(1) recognize the differences among various investments regarding rate of return, (2) identify factors considered by consumers when selecting an investment, and (3) recognize factors which affect stock [market] prices." The major topical sections and the specific instructional objectives within each section are reasonable for a CRT because they meet the requirements of knowledgeable people that a CRT should have a limited number of instructional objectives. However, a CRT, especially a mastery test, should have many test items per instructional objective. In this respect this reviewer feels the MTCE falls short. How confident can a teacher be that Johnny, for instance, has the knowledge needed "to recognize factors which affect food costs among various items" when only one item is used to measure this instructional objective? If I were the teacher, I would be very hesitant to draw any conclusion regarding my students' knowledge of consumer economics based on such a shallow sampling of the domain.

The test author claims content validity on the basis of the following statement: "Selection of test items was based on desired objectives, competencies, and knowledge as set forth in various state education agency and professional organization curriculum guides." This is fine, but what about test authors also consulting textbooks, curriculum specialists, and teachers? Surely sources such as these should have been used in developing the overall test blueprint, but regretfully they were not. This reviewer agrees that for any type of achievement test, be it CRT or NRT, content validity is the sine qua non. Unfortunately, although the test author may also have felt this way, limited information was presented to substantiate the claim for content validity.

There is dispute among some test developers and psychometricians regarding the application of traditional approaches of computing reliability estimates to criterion-referenced tests. Even among those who disagree with the manner in which a CRT's reliability is estimated, however, there is nearly universal agreement that CRTs should present evidence attesting to their reliability. The author of the MTCE apparently disagrees with most measurement persons. He presents no reliability data. Possibly even more disconcerting, at least to this reviewer, is the fact that this psychometric property was not even alluded to in the test manual.

Two other psychometric properties—item difficulty and item discrimination—are a "must" for cognitive tests in general and achievement tests in particular. The author did present data on the former but not on the latter. The average *p*s for the 15 major sections ranged from .33 to .80, with all but two of the average *p*s being over .50. Seven of the sections were somewhat easier, with average *p*s of .70 and higher. This reviewer would have expected a CRT test like the MTCE to be easier. It goes without saying that the MTCE is *not* a mastery test despite the inclusion of mastery in the test name. It should also be noted that the item-validity data must be interpreted with the utmost caution because only 334 students in four Illinois high schools were used to compute the item-analysis statistics. This reviewer would be satisfied with a simple test standardization design; however, the sample description, consisting only of limited information such as the number of subjects, their locale, and their class standing, is inadequate. It is reported that 292 students were upper classmen. But how many were in grades 9, 10, 11, and 12? How many males and females? Surely the author could and *should* have provided the user with more information than "About one-half ($N = 173$) had completed a course in consumer education."

The author is to be commended for the quality of the multiple-choice test items. They are clear, the problem is in the stem, no clues to the correct answer are given the examinee, the options are listed logically, etc. However, this reviewer feels that in a few instances the distractors are not always plausible. And in a few instances one might disagree with the answer keyed as correct. For example, the author states that "The most reliable source of consumer information about a product may be obtained from the label." One of the foils provided is "other consumers." Why is that not correct? Is it not true that the only reliable information provided by the label pertains to the chemical composition of the product, its weight or volume, etc.? This reviewer believes that "the label" is correct only if one interprets consumer information in a very restricted sense. Other than these few instances, however, the quality of the items is very good.

The instructions for test administration are simple and clearly presented. Although it appears the test can be scored only by the publisher, there is no reason why the teacher cannot score the answer sheets. The scoring agency furnishes a score report that presents pupils' performance by objective, the percentage of the group answering each item correctly, the percentage of the group mastering each objective, and how each student performed (mastered/nonmastery/partial mastery) on each item/objective. Although we are told that an examinee must answer all three items to show "mastery" for a particular performance objective, no rationale is provided for this cutoff score.

Although the author supplies the user with a supplementary list of resource materials, little if any information is provided to either help the user teach economics or to help teachers diagnose pupil strengths and weaknesses. And if a CRT serves any useful purpose, it is to assist teachers in gaining a better understanding of their students' strengths and weaknesses. No test that has only three items per major objective can hope to do this validly.

In the final analysis, the test makes a good attempt to demonstrate content validity (albeit not too successfully) but is deficient in demonstrating reliability. The quality of the items is good except for a few instances where some improvement could be made. Regretfully, well written items do not a valid test make. The author is to be commended for using simple, yet realistic situations. If I were a consumer economics teacher I would be very careful to examine the test in relation to its validity and lack of reliability data. I would also be cautious in interpreting the item-analysis data, since the analyses were conducted on a very small, unrepresentative sample.

Review of the Mastery Test in Consumer Economics by LINDA JENSEN SHEFFIELD, Professor of Education and Mathematics, Northern Kentucky University, Highland Heights, KY:

The Administrator's Manual for the Mastery Test in Consumer Economics contains no information on validity or reliability. There is no evidence that either the 15 sections or the 45 individual items were ever analyzed for evidence of validity or reliability. Item difficulty data were obtained from 334 Illinois high school students. Students were from four different high schools—one urban, one rural, one suburban, and one university high school. Of these students, 292 were juniors or seniors, 173 had completed a course in consumer economics, and 161 had not completed such a course. The Administrator's Manual does not describe the students (e.g., gender, ethnicity, SES) in the report of difficulty data. The 334 scores were combined and the percentage of correct responses reported for each of the 45 items and 15 sections.

An overall objective is given for each of the 15 sections and it is then broken down into three more specific objectives for the individual test questions. These were based upon an analysis of goals objectives, competencies, and knowledge as defined by a variety of state education agencies and professional organizations. A list of these resources is included in the Administrator's Manual. A chart cross-referencing sections of the test to chapters in commonly used textbooks is also included, as are lists of supplementary instructional sources, periodicals, and newsletters. It is likely these would be useful to consumer economics teachers.

The tests may be hand scored by the teacher, and an annotated answer key with explanations for correct answers is part of the Administrator's Manual. A scoring service is also available that analyzes each item in terms of whether the item was correct, omitted, or which incorrect response was given. Mastery of each of the 15 sections is reported if the student answered all three questions correctly; nonmastery is reported for 0–1 correct responses, and partial mastery for 2 correct answers. Group scores are provided for both the percent correct and for the percent of mastery. Each student is compared to local norms. No national norms are available.

In summary, the author seems to have based his objectives upon a solid foundation of recommendations from professional organizations and state education agencies. The Administrator's Manual contains much useful information for teachers. Validity and reliability information is sorely needed. The authors may feel that content validity has been addressed through their careful item selection; however, they must do additional work to relate performance on the Mastery Test to performance on other measures. In addition, the small number of questions in each section raises concerns about reliability and adequate coverage of knowledge domains.

[191]

Matrix Analogies Test. Purpose: A nonverbal measure of reasoning designed to be administered as a screening test. Ages 5–17; 1985; 2 forms; 25(30) minutes; Jack A. Naglieri; The Psychological Corporation.*

a) SHORT FORM. MAT-SF; for use when rapid screening of students is desired and when group administration is possible; 1988 price data: $33 per 15 test booklets (19 pages); $17 per 25 self-scoring answer sheets; $17 per specimen set including test booklet, self-scoring answer sheet, and examiner's manual (45 pages).

b) EXPANDED FORM. MAT-EF; for use when "more in depth investigation of nonverbal ability is desired"; individual; $59 per complete kit including stimulus manual, 50 answer sheets, and examiner's manual (82 pages); $30 per stimulus manual; $15 per 50 answer sheets; $15 per examiner's manual.

TEST REFERENCES

1. Naglieri, J. A. (1986). Test-retest reliability of the Matrix Analogies Test—Short Form. *Perceptual and Motor Skills*, 63, 136-138.

Review of the Matrix Analogies Test: Expanded Form by ROBERT F. MCMORRIS, Professor of Educational Psychology and Statistics, DAVID L. RULE, Doctoral Student of Educational Psychology and Statistics, State University of New York at Albany, Albany, NY, and WENDY J. STEINBERG, Associate Personnel Examiner, New York State Department of Civil Service, Albany, NY:

DESCRIPTION. The Matrix Analogies Test (MAT) is an individually administered nonverbal measure of intellectual ability for ages 5 to 17. Raven's-like in format, the items present a visual stimulus with a missing element or sequence. The testee selects the option best completing the stimulus. Variables include size, shape, color, and direction.

Sixty-four items are divided into four 16-item groups. In Group 1, Pattern Completion, a testee "accurately completes the pattern." For Group 2, Reasoning by Analogy, testees "determine how changes in two or more variables converge to result in a new figure." In Group 3, Serial Reasoning, testees "discover the order in which items appear throughout the matrix." With Group 4, Spatial Visualization, testees "imagine how a figure would look when two or more components are combined." The item groups were apparently not derived empirically but by "logical organization."

NORMS. Norms are based on individual testing (under actual test-like conditions) and group testing (a compromise for increasing sample size). The sample seems fairly representative on age, sex, ethnicity, SES, and geographic location. Raw scores for both Item Groups and Total Test may be converted to standard scores, which may then be converted to percentile ranks, NCEs, or stanines.

The author reports a lack of sex or race differences—a welcome and uncommon occurrence among tests of intellectual ability. He also states that a limitation of the Raven's Progressive Matrices (RPM), and thus a major rationale for constructing the MAT, is Raven's lack of U.S. norms. However, U.S. norms for the RPM are now available from The Psychological Corporation. We have not yet obtained these new norms and so leave the user to determine which instrument's norms are more appropriate for the intended interpretation.

RELIABILITY. Median alphas across age groups are .93 for the Total Test and .835 for Item Groups. Test-retest reliability is lower (median = .75), using smaller, less representative samples. Means are given for the "pretest" and "posttest," although the "treatment" was (a presumably standard) 4 weeks of schooling with the 5-point gain likely attributable to practice effects. Standard errors of measurement, given for each age, are based on the alphas.

VALIDITY. The author supports the validity of the MAT in several ways. First, score progression corresponds to age. Second, median correlations of the MAT, based on both normal and special samples, are .52 with the Multilevel Academic Survey Test, .32 with the Stanford Achievement Test, .43 with the Wechsler Intelligence Scale for Children—Revised (WISC-R), and .68 with RPM. Third, gender and racial differences are minimal for groups matched on testing site, age, and father's SES. Fourth, items cluster as a unified measure of nonverbal ability: 83% of the loadings on the first unrotated factor exceed .40. (Caution—the correlations and, therefore, the loadings in the factor analyses are probably inflated because data were combined over four grades.)

Factor analyses did not fully substantiate the four Item Groups. Even using oblique (correlated factors) rotation there were only three distinguishable factors. Only half to two-thirds of a Group's designated items loaded on the expected factor; cross-factor loading was common. Reasoning by Analogy and Serial Reasoning were especially confounded, the former tending to embed within the latter. Nevertheless, the author retained the Reasoning by Analogy items because of their high loadings on the first unrotated factor; whatever these items measure, he considers them a useful measure of the test's overall nonverbal intellectual ability construct. (Oh, *g*! Spearman should be pleased!)

COMMENTARY. Advantages of the MAT over RPM include elimination of color perception deficiency effects (reds and greens are not used) and had included the U.S. norming. This advantage is now lost given the new RPM's norms. However, the MAT continues or introduces several limitations.

The test does not distinguish well in the upper age ranges among testees of superior ability or in the lower age ranges among testees of below average ability. For example, the mean score for 17-year-olds is 52 (out of 64); a 17-year-old only one standard deviation (10.8) above the mean has nearly ceilinged. Although the test is designed for ages 5 to 17, it is unable to differentiate children who are two standard deviations above the mean after age 11. The opposite skewness holds for younger children: For example, the mean for 5-year-olds is 4 or 6% of the items correct/ A greater range of item difficulties could allow differentiation at the extremes but cost in reliability elsewhere. Alternatively, multiple test forms could be developed for smaller age ranges.

No information is given concerning distractor development. We do not know how the distractors were facetted, if they represent particular types of reasoning errors, what those types of errors might be, or whether testees' error choices relate to their ability levels. Investigators have provided such analyses for the RPM. Similarly, we question "matrix dependence." On many items we were able to determine the correct response even without the matrix "stem" being visible, which suggests the distractors need refining.

Referring to the item groupings, the author rightly reminds us that "an item factor analysis seldom, if ever, produces a pattern in which every item in a given subtest loads 'cleanly' on one factor and no other factors." However, something more than the usual unclean loadings may underlie the Reasoning by Analogy items, yet he continues to label these items as a unique factor. For example, when two of the reviewers took the test, they used the same strategy for answering most of the items in Reasoning by Analogy and in Serial Reasoning. A third strategy may supercede what the author thought were two separate strategies. Understanding strategies is important: "A person should never choose the right figure for wrong reasons" (Raven, 1965, p. 20).

Although the author states the Item Groups "should not be overemphasized" and "should not even be considered subtests," his labels tend to encourage such interpretations, as does providing norms for Item Groups. Moreover, an elaborate procedure is used to examine for chance when comparing item-group performance with the total even though the item groups are only partially supported by factor analysis and not studied using other methods. The author seems caught in a dilemma and wishes to resolve it both ways; he would like a one-factor test measuring a single construct plus a differentiated profile of four scores.

In sum, the Matrix Analogies Test appears to be a generally satisfactory test of nonverbal intellectual ability. However, it needs further refinement for assessing extreme abilities at the outer grade levels and refinement of distractors partially to increase matrix dependence and to gain diagnostic information. The dilemma of one versus multiple dimensions/constructs/factors is unsettling; based on processes we used to answer items and on factor analyses, the item groups are only moderately supported. On the positive side, the MAT offers U.S. norms, nonexistent or minimal signs of bias for women and blacks, reduced color-blindness effects, high internal consistency reliability and moderate test-retest reliability, and some validity information. Given the banning of many aptitude measures for special-class placement resulting from the Larry P. case, alternate nonverbal ability tests such as this one deserve consideration.

REVIEWER'S REFERENCE

Raven, J. C. (1965). *Advanced Progressive Matrices, Sets I and*

II: Plan and use of the scale with a report of experimental work. London: H. K. Lewis and Co., Ltd.

[192]

McDermott Multidimensional Assessment of Children. Purpose: Assesses the psychological and educational functioning of children in order to analyze and interpret information, produce objective classifications of childhood normality and exceptionality, and design individualized educational programs. Ages 2–18; 1985; M-MAC; computer-based interpretive system supporting application of selected psychological and educational instruments (Adaptive Behavior Inventory for Children, AAMD Adaptive Behavior Scale—School Edition, Basic Achievement Skills Individual Screener, Bristol Social Adjustment Guides, Conners Teacher Rating Scale, Guide to the Child's Learning Style, Keymath Diagnostic Arithmetic Test, Kohn Problem Checklist, Kohn Problem Checklist and Social Competence Scale, Louisville Behavior Checklist, McCarthy Scales of Children's Abilities, Peabody Individual Achievement Test, Peabody Picture Vocabulary Test—Revised, Revised Behavior Problem Checklist, Stanford-Binet Intelligence Scale, Study of Children's Learning Styles, Stanford Diagnostic Mathematics Test—Red Level, Stanford Diagnostic Mathematics Test—Green Level, Stanford Diagnostic Mathematics Test—Brown Level, Vineland Adaptive Behavior Scales—Survey Form, Vineland Social Maturity Scale—Revised; Wechsler Adult Intelligence Scale—Revised, Wechsler Intelligence Scale for Children—Revised, Wechsler Preschool and Primary Scale of Intelligence, Woodcock-Johnson Tests of Achievement, Wide Range Achievement Tests—Revised, and Woodcock Reading Mastery Tests); 4 levels (corresponding to stages of the assessment process): Identification, Exceptionality, Classification, and Program Design; Classification Level provides 3 operations modes (Standard, Special, and Research) available to yield multidimensional classifications based on 4 dimensions: Intellectual Functioning Dimension, Academic Achievement Dimension, Adaptive Behavior Dimension, and Social-Emotional Adjustment Dimension; Program Design based on one or combination of 4 dimensions: Reading Skills Dimension, Mathematics Skills Dimension, Learning Skills Dimension, and Adaptive Skills Dimension, comprising 54 subskill areas; can be used with an Apple II, IIe, or IIc microcomputer with at least 48K of RAM, 1 or 2 floppy disk drives, and a printer with 80-column capacity; 1985 price data: $1,000 per complete package containing 7 Master and 2 Backup Diskettes enabling user to process 100 Classifications and 100 Individualized Education Programs, and manual ('85, 344 pages); $200 per complete starter set containing 7 Master Diskettes providing for 10 Classifications and 10 IEPs; $150 per starter set (Classification only) containing 5 Master Diskettes providing for 10 Classifications; $125 per starter set (IEP only) containing 2 Master Diskettes providing for 10 IEPs; administration time not reported; Paul A. McDermott and Marley W. Watkins; The Psychological Corporation.*

TEST REFERENCES

1. Glutting, J. J. (1986). The McDermott Multidimensional Assessment of Children: Applications to the classification of childhood exceptionality. *Journal of Learning Disabilities*, 19, 331-335.

Review of the McDermott Multidimensional Assessment of Children by BRUCE A. BRACKEN, Associate Professor of Psychology, Memphis State University, Memphis, TN:

The McDermott Multidimensional Assessment of Children (M-MAC), according to its Systems Manual, is "a comprehensive computer system for use by specialists in assessing the psychological and educational functioning of children ages 2 through 18." The manual goes on to cite three main purposes of the system:

> 1) Empirical analysis and interpretation of test, observation, and interview information. 2) Systematic integration of child demography, empirical information, and professional judgment to render objective classifications of childhood normality and exceptionality. 3) Design of individualized educational programs based on actual performance in fundamental skills areas.

The M-MAC is designed to perform several different functions, some of which are quite useful and some are of limited value. The two major uses of the system are included under the headings of Classification and Program Design. Classification is the part of the M-MAC system that principally does analyses of test results (and other nonstandardized assessment data) entered by the user, and it conducts these analyses using either nonmodifiable "standard" criteria and rules for interpretation or a modifiable "research" mode.

The Classification part of the system is comprehensive, although, at times, somewhat restricting. The Program Design part of the system was a pleasant surprise; Program Design allows the M-MAC user to write individual educational plans (IEPs) and select among behavioral objectives linked to content areas that correspond with academic subjects assessed by the various achievement tests included in M-MAC.

With this preliminary description of the intended use and purpose of the M-MAC, this review will consider conceptual as well as practical aspects of the M-MAC system. This reviewer also wants the reader to be aware that he did not test every aspect of the program, but the major components of M-MAC were tried using a variety of tests and several different subjects.

M-MAC CLASSIFICATION SECTION. Conceptually, the M-MAC Classification section appears to have been developed carefully, with considerable attention paid to the appropriate reporting and interpretation of test data. The M-MAC does not perform analyses that the authors believe are not sufficiently defensible, and this cautious approach may be seen as either an asset or a limitation depending on one's orientation. For example, the analyses conducted on Wechsler Intelligence Scale for Children—Revised (WISC-R) data are limited to the computation of Verbal, Performance, and Full Scale confidence intervals, factor deviation quotients, and the determination of whether significant differences exist between the two subscales. The familiar subtest analysis and interpretation procedure made popular by Kaufman (1979) is not permitted, nor is any confidence level other than the .05 level allowed, unless accessed through the research mode.

While there is not uniformity in opinion among professionals on the usefulness of the Kaufman WISC-R interpretation procedure, it is a system covered in virtually all professional programs that teach interpretation of the WISC-R and is coveted by many psychologists. Regardless of one's orientation, users of the M-MAC are left with the McDermott-Watkins interpretation approach (no WISC-R subtest interpretations and only one level of confidence from which to choose in the standard classification mode). Those professionals who wish to use M-MAC and still conduct standard subtest analyses must do those additional analyses on their own, and there still is no way to integrate that information into the programmed M-MAC printout. The M-MAC does do analyses among scales within an instrument (e.g., among the five subscales within the McCarthy Scales of Children's Abilities) and between instruments (e.g., determining significant discrepancies between intelligence and achievement test scores), but it does not typically make comparisons among subtests.

The M-MAC weaves into the final printout information that is not always appropriate (but can be overridden in some instances). For example, in cases in which there is a significant difference between the WISC-R Verbal and Performance Scales, the printout informs the reader, "Because the Verbal-Performance IQ discrepancy is significant statistically, the Verbal Scale IQ is used as the principal indicator of the child's current level of intellectual functioning." This decision is based in part on a study (Reschly & Reschly, 1979) that concluded that "the Verbal IQ *tends* to be the best predictor of criterion performance." There are obviously situations (e.g., language impairment, cultural disadvantage, auditory impairment) in which the Verbal IQ is not the best descriptor of the child's *overall* intellectual abilities (regardless of criteria), and an insufficient number of studies have been conducted with differing populations to warrant making such a generalization. While the "criterion performance" (presumably school achievement) alluded to by McDermott and Watkins is not spelled out, one should still consider whether this presumed criterion should dictate that examiners treat the Verbal IQ as the "principal indicator of the child's current level of intellectual functioning." To extend this logic further, one could argue for administering only the Verbal Scale, an equally unsound recommendation.

Most individuals who speak of the M-MAC system and who have not actually used the program, believe that its principal value is the elimination of the clerical tasks and error associated with having to look up standard scores, various scale scores, percentile ranks, age equivalents, etc. These individuals expect to enter raw scores into the program and receive a printout outlining the basic psychometric information needed to "classify" the examinee. The M-MAC *does not* provide this clerical service. The system requires that the user perform most of the traditional clerical activities *and then* provide the computer with the results.

Additionally, the system has no procedure for catching clerical errors. This reviewer intentionally entered bogus and inconsistent information into the program (WISC-R subtests that did not correspond with the Verbal, Performance, and Full Scale IQs entered). The system not only did not identify obvious errors, but it conducted the remaining analyses on the erroneous data and provided "clean" looking results. Although such error detection was not intended by M-MAC, it should be recognized that the transposition of data into the system constitutes one more source of error and may reduce the value of the M-MAC program.

Along these lines, this reviewer found himself tiring of the confirmation requests made by the program. The confirmation requests come in response to data entry to ensure that the user did not make a clerical error. As such, the confirmation requests are useful. However, after just four cases I found myself pushing the "Y" key (for yes) to the confirmation request as soon as it appeared on the screen, without consideration of the correctness of the data entered. Hence, the confirmation request did not serve as a stimulus to recheck my entries, but rather was one more nuisance with which to deal. In addition to the standard confirmation requests, the system has an "I don't believe you" confirmation request. After asking the user if everything has been entered correctly and the user responds affirmatively, the program then asks the asinine question, "Are you sure?" This user wanted to respond, "No, I was just kidding!"

Another source of irritation in the M-MAC system stems from the decision to not allow the user to view pertinent classification results from the computer monitor; all classification results are printed only. Users without printers or those who may not have a printer available at the moment, cannot use M-MAC for classification. This is no minor limitation when one considers that not everyone has the luxury of having both a computer and printer readily available. A similarly irritating inconvenience is the monopolistic use of Apple II computers for the M-MAC program. Being employed at an institution where Macintoshes and Zeniths flourish, this reviewer found himself canvassing the entire campus looking for an Apple II. Once having found an appropriate computer, I was evicted midway through my first case due to the limited time that this particular lab was available for general use. The point here is that not everyone owns or cares to own an Apple, and yet not having an Apple available means that the M-MAC is also unavailable.

Also somewhat monopolistic, over half of the tests served by the M-MAC system are published by the Psychological Corporation (the publisher of M-MAC), with the remaining tests representing several different publishers. Some of the tests included in M-MAC and published by the Psychological Corporation should have been excluded due to poor norming (e.g., the Adaptive Behavior Inventory for Children), while other publisher's tests should have been included (e.g., the Kaufman Assessment Battery for Children). The rationale for leaving the K-ABC out of the program is not clear, since the Vineland Adaptive Behavior Scale (conormed with the K-ABC) was included.

M-MAC PROGRAM DESIGN SECTION. Once the user of the M-MAC Classification program determines the child's level of cognitive, achievement, and adaptive functioning, the M-MAC Program Design component then facilitates the determination of appropriate follow-up instruction. Behavioral objectives can be developed in four basic areas: Reading, Mathematics, Adaptive, and Learning subskills. The M-MAC user can select from a large number of objectives in each of the content areas mentioned previously. For example, there are seven Reading Subskill Areas (Letter Identification, Word Recognition, Phonics: Consonant Sounds, Phonics: Vowel Sounds, Word Comprehension: Main Hierarchy, Word Comprehension: Alternate Hierarchy, and Passage Comprehension) and within these seven subskill areas the number of objectives range from two (Word Comprehension: Alternate Hierarchy) to 81 (Passage Comprehension). Likewise, the Mathematics area includes 11 subskill areas dealing with numeration skills and the four basic mathematical functions. Across these subskill areas the range of objectives is from 18 to 111. It should be noted that even though the number of subskills and their objectives are representative of their respective content domains, they are not complete. The major subskills identified could be further reduced to provide finer objectives. However, because of the already comprehensive nature of the Program Design Component, this comment is not intended as a substantive criticism, but rather as a statement of fact.

M-MAC SYSTEMS MANUAL AND MATERIALS. The M-MAC system was designed to be "user friendly" even for the computer novice, and it does in actuality operate very smoothly. However, there is no readily accessible section in the manual that deals with "trouble shooting." Although the program was designed to be used simplistically, the system would have been enhanced greatly by the inclusion of an easily accessed section on "what to do if . . ."; simple programs become very complex when they are not operating as the user had expected, whether due to a program error, computer failure, or the user's lack of experience with computer programs. An index would have done much to help in this trouble-shooting area, but unfortunately the Systems Manual is not indexed.

Although the system does do what the manual indicates, the system does bring out a bit of "octopus" in the user. With two disk drives, nine disks, a key board, printer, and psychoeducational test protocols, a few extra arms (or tentacles) would be very useful for the user of the M-MAC program.

This reviewer also has found that the old saying, "a watched pot never boils" can be changed to "a watched computer never computes." Such is the case with M-MAC. When running through the Classification program the computer screen consistently keeps the user informed of what it is doing. The program also requires the user's active participation as it directs one to insert disk 1 into drive 1, then disk 2 into drive 1, then disk 3 into drive 2, etc. With each insertion the user gets a string of friendly messages such as, "Saving Data, Loading Programs, Clearing Tables, Assessing, Saving Data (again), Loading (again)," etc. Associated with each of these friendly messages is a not so friendly wait, ranging from about 15 seconds to approximately 2 1/2 minutes for the Assessing component. In sum, each case requires 3 to 5 minutes of waiting time; time that cannot effectively be put to use doing something else because the wait at any one program step is too short to "shift gears" into another activity.

Also deemed a waste is the abundance of computer paper required to print the results of each case. The Systems Manual advises that the user ensure that at least 20 pages of paper are available before printing a case. The printout is not particularly well designed, with several sections of the printout requiring only a fraction of a page. At each of these section breaks the printer is then directed to begin a new page. The result is a lot of wasted page space and paper.

Throughout the system the user comes across unorthodox abbreviations and word divisions at the end of lines. For example, while the word *alphabet* is not abbreviated, *alphabetical* is abbreviated as *alphab*. It should be mentioned that all abbreviations are cited in the text of the Systems Manual, but these are not conveniently located in an appendix for easy access. In the context of a sentence it is possible to discriminate the intended meaning, but the selective and inconsistent use of abbreviations is distracting. Also distracting is the unsystematic division of words at the ends of lines. The following are instances of where the M-MAC program has divided words and carried over the remainder of the word to the next line (the slash represents where the division occurs): A/ssociating, i/ndicate, fr/om, wi/th. Many such divisions occur throughout the program, and the result is a product that lacks polish. For the computer "hack" such criticisms may seem minor, even picky. But to those who have come to expect more from computer products, such telegraphic communications add up to major annoyances.

Chapter 8 of the system provides users with technical information from each of the major instruments included in the M-MAC system. Like many assessment related texts (e.g., Salvia & Ysseldyke, 1981) that merely catalog psychoeducational instruments and provide little critique of the instruments' technical characteristics, the technical information provided in the M-MAC system is in some cases sparse and incomplete. While presentation of validity coefficients is made for most instruments, the information is not complete. There is virtually no critical information provided on, or cautions for, such problematic technical psychometric areas of tests as: limited ceilings or floors, steep item gradients, depth of content sampling, standardization or norming data, etc.

In the authors' defense, what they do provide is an impressive battery of statistical procedures designed to "legitimize" and provide the appropriate parameters for careful test interpretation. The analyses McDermott and Watkins performed and/or the considerations they made of tests' technical quality include, but are not limited to: factorial integrity, corrections for simultaneous statistical tests, discrepancies among subscales, regression analyses, estimated true difference analyses, estimated prevalence levels, cutting score criteria, setting confidence levels for scores, and applying nonstandard parameters.

SUMMARY. The M-MAC system provides many notable services for those individuals who conduct psychoeducational evaluations. The somewhat critical tone of this review does not do total justice to McDermott and Watkins, who together have addressed many of the thorny problems associated with effectively combining measurement concerns with assessment realities. The negative aspects of the program outlined in the above review will need to be weighed against the contributions the program may make toward intelligent assessment practices.

Unfortunately, the M-MAC program may stimulate in many a feeling of technological pseudosophistication that exceeds the already lofty point upon which psychometrics have rested for decades. While I personally want to commend the authors of M-MAC for their attention to details and careful program development, I also question whether our current assessment procedures and devices are sufficiently developed to warrant this much attention. Granted, if a system such as M-MAC will improve our classification and placement accuracy and lead to improved instruction and remediation, then the program truly will be a blessing. However, throughout the evaluation of the many components of this program I continually found myself asking, "Are McDermott and Watkins making a silk purse from a sow's ear?"

REVIEWER'S REFERENCES

Reschly, D. J., & Reschly, J. E. (1979). Brief reports on the WISC-R: I. Validity of the WISC-R factor scores in predicting achievement and attention for four sociocultural groups. *Journal of School Psychology*, 17, 355-361.

Salvia, J., & Ysseldyke, J. E. (1981). *Assessment in special and remedial education* (2nd ed.). Boston: Houghton Mifflin Co.

Review of the McDermott Multidimensional Assessment of Children by ALAN S. KAUFMAN, Research Professor of School Psychology, The University of Alabama, Tuscaloosa, AL:

The McDermott Multidimensional Assessment of Children (M-MAC) is not a test; it is a system designed for use with the Apple II series of microcomputers to allow examiners ("competent child specialist(s)") to interpret and integrate data obtained on children ages 2–18 years. The system, which was developed by the first author (McDermott, 1976, 1980), has four levels: (*a*) Identification (background information about the child); (*b*) Exceptionality (factors that may threaten the validity of test scores, e.g., sensory or motor handicaps, cultural or linguistic background); (*c*) Classification (diagnostic hypotheses based on intellectual functioning, academic achievement, adaptive behavior, and social-emotional adjustment); and (*d*) Program Design (the production of specific, objective Individual Educational Programs or IEPs in the areas of Reading, Mathematics, Learning, and Adaptive skills). The two main functions served by the M-MAC are "the empirical *classification* of childhood normality and exceptionality and the *design* of individualized educational programs" (Glutting, 1986).

The M-MAC system, comprised "of over 100 individual programs integrated for use with children" (Glutting, 1986), is equipped to handle input data from a specified set of instruments within the four domains that are applied at the Classification level to determine a child's diagnosis, if any. Over half of these various tests and inventories are published by The Psychological Corporation, the M-MAC's publisher, and the rationale for including or omitting certain instruments is unclear, at best (Bracken, 1986). In view of the authors' goals of classifying children and making meaningful educational recommendations, it is incomprehensible why two instruments that provide intelligence and achievement scores normed on the same population, and that were developed with educational intervention clearly in focus, are excluded from the M-MAC: the Kaufman Assessment Battery for Children (K-ABC) and the Woodcock-Johnson Psycho-Educational Battery. Although the Achievement portion of the Woodcock-Johnson is included in the M-MAC, the nonsensical omission of the Cognitive battery prevents users from taking advantage of the co-norming procedure or the built-in comparisons of ability and achievement that are useful for learning-disabilities diagnosis. Likewise, the exclusion of the commonly used K-ABC prevents examiners from having the choice of the sequential-simultaneous-achievement model for formulating diagnostic hypotheses or generating educational recommendations. Bracken (1986) also feels that the K-ABC and other instruments should have been included, and states: "The rationale for leaving the K-ABC out of the program is not clear, since the Vineland Adaptive Behavior Scale (co-normed with the K-ABC) was included."

Not only is the choice of tests for inclusion or exclusion curious, but the amount of technical information provided for each test or inventory is erratic, varying unpredictably from instrument to instrument. In general, there are insufficient data provided on the standardization samples of most tests, and the reliability and validity data are usually presented too briefly (the McCarthy Scales is a notable exception). Also, the authors do not evaluate the quality of the various tests, or point out limitations that would enhance interpretation.

The M-MAC authors claim that the system is "user-friendly"; after using it several times for practice prior to writing this review, I am inclined to agree. The directions for computer use are straightforward and easy to follow. However, the application of the program to actual cases can become quite tedious, requiring attentive interaction with perhaps 100 screens over a period of 30–45 minutes; demanding the perpetual insertion of various disks into different disk drives; and forcing the user to be patient during the sometimes interminable waits while the computer is performing myriad activities. Turco and Elliott (1986) make the valid point that there are too many "one-way streets" that do not allow a user to correct an error by aborting a subroutine "without having to turn the computer off and losing the data entered to that point." I also concur that users of the M-MAC would benefit by being an "octopus" (Bracken, 1986) or skilled "card dealer" (Turco, 1986).

I wish the manual had been written to be user friendly, but that was not the case; it lacks an index, for example, which is problematic. The introductory chapter is vague and general, and it is unclear where it is leading. I was left with the feeling that a valid system was impossible to develop because of the many seemingly insurmountable pitfalls in the process, although I knew from the M-MAC's advertising campaign that the authors and publisher believe their system to be "comprehensive, . . . objective and flexible, and . . . reliable and empirically valid" (Glutting, 1986). Even the specific microcomputers for which the program was designed are elusive, not being mentioned in the Preface (which dwells on computer use) or in Chapter 1. I found the word "Apple" for the first time on page 10 in Chapter 2, but did not discover that the system was developed for Apple II microcomputers until page 20 in Chapter 3.

The "unfriendliest" aspect of the manual concerns a giant clerical error made by the authors and publisher in the "Standard Mode Case" of Louis J. Rodriguez, the case that serves the vital function of illustrating the standard use of the system. This child is shown as having a Wechsler Intelligence Scale for Children—Revised (WISC-R) Verbal IQ of 94, a Performance IQ of 118, and a Full Scale IQ of 105. However, by examining the scaled scores earned by Louis, it was apparent to me that his Verbal IQ was incorrect. Following up my hunch, I found that a beginning graduate student error was made: adding in Digit Span to compute Verbal IQ. The real Verbal and Full Scale IQs should be 79 and 96, respectively. This 15-point error in Verbal IQ means that the V-P discrepancy is a huge 39 points, not 24 points. The errors in computation affect a good portion of the illustrative case, particularly since the erroneous Verbal IQ is used as the principal indicator of intellectual functioning (79 is Borderline, 94 is Average); hence, the subsequent classifications of "average intellectual functioning," "specific learning disability in reading (provisional)," and "commensurate arithmetic achievement" do not follow from the accurate Verbal IQ of 79. The authors should have caught the error by observing on page 51 that the Verbal Comprehension standard score of 76 was not in the same ballpark as the supposed Verbal IQ of 94. Ironically, throughout the manual the authors preach extreme care in recording data, and emphasize that the output from the program is only as good as the quality of the input. Furthermore, when using the program, the computer repeatedly requests confirmation of the entered data to ensure against examiner error. Whereas the manual error serves to underscore the essential need for clerical accuracy and that no one is above reproach, it still stands in counterpoint to the main message delivered by the authors. It also points to a glaring lack in the system: There is no built-in method for identifying silly or impossible data; if the program simply checked that the sums of Wechsler scaled scores are correct, and that the conversions to IQs are done appropriately, then the authors would have caught the error immediately. Bracken (1986) also urges a checking procedure, noting that when he entered bogus, inconsistent data, the machine accepted them as right and proceeded with the subsequent analyses.

In the Case Study of Louis, as indicated, the authors advocate using the Verbal IQ as the best estimate of his intellectual functioning. They base this decision largely on the fact that verbal intelligence is known to be the best predictor of academic achievement. Yet, they also state that the finding of low Verbal IQ "is consistent with the observation that the child may have limited facility in applying the English language" and that this limited facility "may reduce appreciably the reported results [on a test of achievement] by directly interfering with the child's performance on the BASIS test." If the low Verbal IQ is consistent with a language problem, and that problem may have affected performance on the BASIS, composed of tasks similar to the WISC-R Verbal Scale, then how can the Verbal IQ possibly be the best estimate of that child's mental ability? To me, it is unconscionable to ignore a Hispanic child's Performance IQ of 118 when assessing his or her intellectual ability or potential diagnosis of a specific learning disability.

In short, I disagree with many aspects of the interpretive system applied by McDermott and Watkins to the psychological test data. They use their own system, and do not give users the option to use systems that may be more in keeping with the users' personal philosophies or practices. They discuss several approaches to interpreting the Freedom from Distractibility factor, for example, but make no reference to the procedure I advocate in *Intelligent Testing with the WISC-R* (Kaufman, 1979); they also virtually ignore subtest profile interpretation or analysis of subtest scatter. The authors do not even cite the above mentioned WISC-R book, and although they do cite Sattler's (1982) popular text, they do not systematically incorporate his interpretive procedures in their program. Bracken (1986) points out: "The familiar subtest analysis and interpretation procedure made popular by Kaufman (1979) is not permitted . . . While there is not uniformity in opinion among professionals on the usefulness of the Kaufman WISC-R interpretation procedure, it is a system covered in virtually all professional programs that teach interpretation of the WISC-R and is coveted by many psychologists."

Nonetheless, there is much that is positive about the M-MAC besides its user-friendly nature. The system is indeed comprehensive as it incorporates numerous aspects of test scores and behavior to reach important clinical decisions. The authors' focus on IEPs is laudable and thorough, and is based on a carefully researched foundation. The technical sophistication is outstanding throughout the manual. Psychometric procedures such as the application of the Bonferroni technique, the consideration of the concept of abnormality in the assessment of Verbal-Performance IQ discrepancies, and the definition of specific learning disabilities represent consistently high-level, state-of-the-art thinking and understanding. Yet, despite the empirical focus, the authors do not lose sight of the need to incorporate professional judgment into the decision-making process, to evaluate the validity of all types of data entered into the system, and to carefully consider the impact on test performance of mitigating factors like sensory-motor or linguistic handicaps. Additionally, the M-MAC's comprehensive approach is novel and represents an important conceptual innovation regarding the application of microcomputers to clinical inference; ultimately, that is the most positive feature of the interpretive system.

SUMMARY. The M-MAC is a comprehensive, computer-based assessment system for use with the Apple II series of microcomputers. Its main goals are the empirical classification of childhood exceptionality and the design of individualized educational programs. The major advantages of the M-MAC are the fact that it is "user friendly," it is innovative, its comprehensiveness extends to a well-researched component on educational intervention, it is technically and psychometrically sophisticated, and it gives much weight to professional judgment and to the incorporation of variables such as cultural background that might compromise test scores. However, the M-MAC has a number of disadvantages that limit its usefulness. It overrepresents tests from its publisher, The Psychological Corporation, at the expense of worthy tests like the K-ABC and Woodcock-Johnson. Its manual is confusing and includes a major clerical error in a key Case

Study that is intended to clarify use of the system. The program is geared to a single interpretive approach, one developed by McDermott and Watkins, ignoring alternative approaches that are more popularly used, particularly for WISC-R profiles. Finally, although the program is user friendly, it is still complex to handle all of the materials smoothly, and it can be tedious and frustrating to use. Overall, the M-MAC makes a contribution by virtue of advancing a new concept and helping to bridge the gap between microcomputers and clinical inference. Its primary value lies in providing a starting point for the authors or perhaps someone else to improve on the concept by offering a more heterogeneous choice of instruments and a more eclectic approach to interpretation. In view of its considerable cost and its limitations, I would only recommend the program for examiners who are wedded to the McDermott-Watkins actuarial approach to interpretation or who are primarily interested in deriving benefit from the educational recommendations section of the system.

REVIEWER'S REFERENCES

McDermott, P. A. (1976, September). Actuarial school psychology: A model for efficiency and effect. In G. Snelbecker (Chair), *Actuarial/ecological school psychology: An alternative to the clinical model.* Symposium conducted at the 83rd Annual Convention of the American Psychological Association, Washington, DC.

Kaufman, A. S. (1979). *Intelligent testing with the WISC-R.* New York: John Wiley & Sons, Inc.

McDermott, P. A. (1980). A systems-actuarial method for the differential diagnosis of handicapped children. *Journal of Special Education,* 14, 7-22.

Sattler, J. M. (1982). *Assessment of children's intelligence and special abilities* (2nd ed.). Boston: Allyn & Bacon, Inc.

Bracken, B. A. (1986). Software reviews: McDermott Multidimensional Assessment of Children. *Computers in Human Behavior,* 2, 309-313.

Glutting, J. J. (1986). The McDermott Multidimensional Assessment of Children: Applications to the classification of childhood exceptionality. *Journal of Learning Disabilities,* 19, 331-335.

Turco, T. L. & Elliott, S. N. (1986). Software reviews: McDermott Multidimensional Assessment of Children. *Computers in Human Behavior,* 2, 313-316.

Review of the McDermott Multidimensional Assessment of Children by TIMOTHY L. TURCO, Assistant Professor of Psychology, Lehigh University, Bethlehem, PA, and STEPHEN N. ELLIOTT, Associate Professor of Psychology, University of Wisconsin, Madison, WI:

The McDermott Multidimensional Assessment of Children (M-MAC) is a menu-driven program written for three main purposes: (*a*) to analyze and interpret test, observation, and interview data; (*b*) to objectively classify children ages 2 through 18 years of age by systematically integrating empirical, demographic, and judgmental data; and (*c*) to design individualized educational programs based upon actual performances in skill areas (McDermott, 1985).

PROGRAM DESCRIPTION. The M-MAC has four system levels. The first level is entitled Identification and is basically for gathering demographic data. At this level, a child's name, sex, educational level, age, and evaluation date are collected.

The second level, the Exceptionality level, is an optional level where additional data needed for classification purposes are gathered. At this level, the program user is asked to report the presence and severity (on a 4-point Likert scale) of: (*a*) uncorrected physical handicaps, (*b*) special linguistic features, (*c*) cultural functioning, (*d*) environmental stress, (*e*) educational background, (*f*) general health problems, and (*g*) areas of exceptional abilities.

The third program level is Classification. As described in the manual, the M-MAC classifies children using an empirical mixed categorical multidimensional system that uses a basic skills orientation, objectivity, and behavioristic performance-based criteria.

The M-MAC classifies students using a four-dimensional model. Classification is based on the integration of objective test scores representing: (*a*) intellectual abilities as measured by the Wechsler Intelligence Scale for Children—Revised, Wechsler Preschool and Primary Scale of Intelligence, Wechsler Adult Intelligence Scale—Revised, Stanford-Binet Intelligence Scale, McCarthy Scales of Children's Abilities, or Peabody Picture Vocabulary Test—Revised; (*b*) academic achievement as measured by the Basic Achievement Skills Individual Screener, Peabody Individual Achievement Test, Woodcock Reading Mastery Tests, KeyMath Diagnostic Arithmetic Test, or Wide Range Achievement Tests—Revised; (*c*) adaptive behaviors as measured by the Adaptive Behavior Inventory for Children, AAMD Adaptive Behavior Scale—School Edition, Vineland Adaptive Behavior Scales—Survey Form, Vineland Social Maturity Scale—Revised, or professional judgments and other measures using the AAMD guidelines; and (*d*) social-emotional adjustment as measured by the Bristol Social

Adjustment Guides, Conners Teacher Rating Scale, Kohn Problem Checklist, Kohn Problem Checklist and Social Competence Scale, Louisville Behavior Checklist, Revised Behavior Problem Checklist, or professional judgments and other measures using DSM-III criteria.

The integration of the test scores is based upon nomothetic and ideographic statistical analyses. The M-MAC uses the standard error of measurement of the differences between two obtained scores (Davis, 1964) or estimated prevalence levels (Payne & Jones, 1957; Salvia & Good, 1982; Silverstein, 1981) to assess the Verbal and Performance quotient discrepancies on the Wechsler scales. To aid in the determination of specific learning disabilities, the M-MAC uses regression analysis or estimated true difference analysis. In addition, the M-MAC uses an optional multivariate syndromatic profile analysis to analyze the results of the Bristol Social Adjustment Guide (BSAG).

When performing the classification processes, the M-MAC will use one of three user-selected operation modes. In the standard mode, the M-MAC uses preset cutting scores for determining intellectual giftedness, retardation, achievement problems, and maladjustment. For example, the various levels of mental retardation are based upon AAMD criteria (Grossman, 1977). In the special mode, the examiner can modify the cutting scores and several other program options. The program was designed for applied research and the special mode allows an examiner to modify a number of the M-MAC functions, such as the use of nonstandard parameters for adaptive behaviors and social and emotional adjustment.

In the Program Design level, M-MAC formulates specific Individual Educational Programs (IEPs) with goals stated in behavioral terms. To create an IEP, the program requires the evaluator to enter test scores from one to four user-selected academic areas including (*a*) reading as measured by the Basic Achievement Skills Individual Screener—Reading, Woodcock Reading Mastery Tests, or Stanford Diagnostic Reading Test; (*b*) math as measured by the Basic Achievement Skills Individual Screener—Math, KeyMath Diagnostic Arithmetic Test, or Stanford Diagnostic Mathematics; (*c*) learning as measured by the Study of Children's Learning Styles or Guide to the Child's Learning Style; and (*d*) adaptive behavior skills as measured by the AAMD Parent Interview/Observation of Child. M-MAC contains 1,111 IEP objectives that are ordered hierarchically within each of the subskill academic areas. Based upon each student's performances, M-MAC selects a user-specified number of IEP objectives. The IEP objectives can be sent directly to a printer or can be sent to the computer's screen for review and possible modifications prior to being printed.

The M-MAC user also has the option of having the program provide reference codes for computer-assisted and computer-managed instructional aids with each IEP objective. These codes reference portions of five different programs available from The Psychological Corporation or SouthWest EdPsych Services.

CRITIQUE OF PROGRAM. The M-MAC's 320-page manual and 9 diskettes come neatly housed in a 3 inch x 9 inch x 10.5 inch three-ring binder. Each chapter of the manual is marked clearly with a tab and the manual contains an adequate table of contents. Unfortunately, the manual does not contain an index, so it is occasionally necessary to browse through the table of contents to find a particular topic.

Each of the nine diskettes is marked clearly and color-coded. Thus, finding the proper diskette is not a problem. However, loading, unloading, filing, and unfiling the diskettes was time consuming and cumbersome. This problem was particularly noticeable when the program was used on a computer with only one disk drive.

Despite the need for the M-MAC user to have some skills as a "card dealer," the program is generally easy to use. Both experienced and inexperienced computer-operators should have little difficulty using the program, with only a minimal amount of time studying the M-MAC manual. However, there are a few programming quirks that need to be rectified to make the program more "user friendly." First, with as many diskettes as the M-MAC requires for execution, it would be helpful if some sort of labeling change was made. Ideally, it should be immediately obvious which diskette goes in the machine first.

Once the M-MAC user identifies the correct starting diskette and loads it into drive 1, the program boots itself when the power is turned on. The program's title page appears on the screen. At this point, the program pauses, indefinitely, waiting for input from the user. Unfortunately, the program does not prompt the user to press the "return" key for the program to continue. Oddly, the program accepts only upper-case characters. The program "beeps" when a lower-case character is entered; however, a written prompt on the screen would also be helpful.

In most instances, the program will trap incorrect data entries, such as entering months greater than 12 and trying to enter alphabetic characters where numeric characters belong and vice versa. The program, however, does not trap attempts to enter more than 30 days in September.

One other modification of the program would facilitate ease of use. During the first few times the M-MAC was used, after spending several minutes completing the data required in the Classification level screens, the operator selected to enter the Program Design level. However, after entering the Program Design level, it was realized that the standardized measures needed for this level had not been administered to the student. The operator thus tried to return to the Classification level. Unfortunately, in this area of the program and in several other areas, a user cannot abort a subroutine without having to turn the computer off and losing the data entered to that point. The present version of M-MAC contains many "one-way streets," without a provision to recover. Program users are going to make mistakes, regardless of their level of expertise or level of understanding of the manual. Thus, the existence of unrecoverable areas of the program is a fairly significant programming error. Refined versions of M-MAC should focus on correcting this problem of "one-way streets."

Another feature that is needed in a refined version of the M-MAC concerns the program-planning level. For example, as the program is now written users can print out IEP objectives directly, or they can preview the objectives on the screen, modify them, and print them out later. Although a generic list of hierarchical objectives will be helpful to IEP planners, a person planning the IEPs may routinely want to modify the M-MAC generated objectives. Therefore, if the program was modified to allow the user to save IEP modifications for use with other students, many routine changes in the objectives could be eliminated.

The Apple II version of the M-MAC was used for this review. The program requires an Apple II, Apple II plus, Apple IIc, or an Apple IIe with 48K RAM. The program will support a one- or two-drive system with a 40-column monitor and an 80-column printer.

SUMMARY. The M-MAC provides two worthwhile functions. First, it performs a number of statistical procedures on standardized test data that are too time consuming to be practically and routinely done by hand. The results of these statistical analyses can aid a psychologist in synthesizing evaluation data. Second, the M-MAC also is a useful tool for planning IEPs based upon the results of standardized assessment data. It provides hierarchically ordered IEP behavioral objectives in specific areas and also allows the user to modify program-generated objectives before printing them. In conclusion, M-MAC positively illustrates the application of microcomputing to the assessment of school children, but does not significantly advance the practice of assessment.

REVIEWER'S REFERENCES

Payne, R. W., & Jones, H. G. (1957). Statistics for the investigation of individual cases. *Journal of Clinical Psychology*, 13, 115-121.

Davis, F. B. (1964). *Educational measurements and their interpretation*. Belmont, CA: Wadsworth Publishing.

Grossman, H. J. (1977). *Manual on terminology and classification in mental retardation* (rev. ed.). Washington, DC: American Association on Mental Deficiency.

Silverstein, A. B. (1981). Reliability and abnormality of test score differences. *Journal of Clinical Psychology*, 37, 392-394.

Salvia, J., & Good, R. (1982). Significant discrepancies in the classification of pupils: Differentiating the concept. In J. T. Neisworth (Ed.), *Assessment in special education*. Rockville, MD: Aspen Systems.

McDermott. P. A. (1985). The observation and classification of exceptional child behavior. In R. T. Brown & C. R. Reynolds (Eds.), *Psychological perspectives on childhood exceptionality*. New York: Wiley-Interscience.

[193]

MD5 Mental Ability Test. Purpose: To assess mental ability quickly, easily, and over a wide range of educational and ability levels, in staff selection, placement and counselling. Supervisors to managers; no date on test materials; 1987 price data: £.45 per test booklet; £2.80 per scoring key; £5.50 per manual (17 pages); £7.85 per specimen set; (15) minutes; The Test Agency [England].*

Review of the MD5 Mental Ability Test by M. HARRY DANIELS, Associate Professor of Educational Psychology, Southern Illinois University at Carbondale, Carbondale, IL:

The MD5 Mental Ability Test was developed to provide a quick and easy-to-use test of intelligence for the purpose of selecting managerial and supervisory staff for large commercial organizations. It consists of 57 items selected from a larger item pool and administered in a standardized format. Test items assess both verbal/vocabulary and mathematical skills, including comprehension (1 item), vocabulary/semantic relationships (15 items), symbol relationships—answers as words or parts of words (16 items), alphabetical sequence relationships (6 items), symbol relationships—answers as letters (4 items), relationships between numbers and letters of words (5 items), symbol relationships—answers as numbers (1 item), mathematical relationships (9 items), and mathematical procedures (1 item). Items are arranged in order of increasing difficulty. There is a 15-minute time limit for completion. Thus, the test measures speed as well as power. The MD5 may be administered to individuals or groups as required.

Test materials include a test booklet, a scoring key, and a test manual. Directions for completing the MD5 require that responses to all test items must be made on the test booklet. Answers may be made in either pen or pencil, but erasures are not permitted (mistakes are to be crossed out). Answers require only the use of numbers, letters, or short words. The scoring key consists of a strip of posterboard on which the correct responses for each page of the test booklet are written. Answers are written in vertical columns so that they align with the appropriate answer columns in the test booklet. Clear and concise directions for administering the MD5 are included in the manual.

Scores on the MD5 are determined by totaling the number of items answered correctly; there is no correction for either guessing or error. Raw scores are converted to percentile scores by using the MD5 percentile norms. These norms are based on the results of approximately 3,200 tests completed by middle and lower level managers, supervisors, and applicants for supervisory and managerial positions. Average scores among these groups appear to vary on the basis of education and work experience (the mean score for middle level managers was 39.0; 30.3 for lower level managers; and 26.9 for supervisors).

The manual contains very little information about the psychometric properties of the MD5. Thus, it is not possible to comment about either the internal consistency or the temporal stability of scores. Similarly, there is no empirical evidence concerning the predictive validity of the test, although the publisher asserts that it is "a useful test of mental ability for staff selection and placement at managerial and supervisory levels." On the other hand, evidence is provided demonstrating that MD5 scores correlate highly with the Watson-Glaser ($r = .52$) and the Guilford-Zimmerman II ($r = .62$).

EVALUATION. The MD5 is an example of a mental abilities test designed to serve a particular purpose: to select managerial and supervisory staff. When used with the specific population for which it was developed, it may be a very useful instrument. Due to the paucity of information about the psychometric characteristics of the test, and the lack of any independent evaluations of its content, construction, scoring procedures, and norms, it is difficult to comment on the overall quality of the instrument, or about its usefulness for other populations. The lack of evidence concerning its predictive validity represents an even greater limitation. Instruments like the MD5 are developed for the purpose of making reliable and accurate predictions concerning personnel and training. Considering the vast sums of money spent on such ventures, and the potential impact they may have on human lives, such predictors need to be as reliable and as accurate as possible. Because the MD5 does not provide adequate documentation of its predictive validity, caution should be a guide in its use.

Review of the MD5 Mental Ability Test by DAVID J. MEALOR, Associate Professor of School Psychology, University of Central Florida, Orlando, FL:

The MD5 was developed by Mackenzie Davey and Company "as a quick and easy-to-use test of intelligence," and was first used in 1972 to assist in the selection of supervisory staff for a large commercial organization in the North of England. The instrument was found to make a substantial contribution to the selection of supervisory staff and was extended to more senior levels including graduate management trainees. The author notes the primary focus of the MD5 is on the ability "to deduce relationships and to apply the rules governing them, which are generally considered to be fundamental components of intelligence." How these skills relate to supervisory functions and the weight given them in the selection of supervisory staff is not explained.

The MD5 consists of 57 items arranged in order of increasing difficulty. There is a 15-minute time limit and it is reported that the test is a measure of both speed and power. Examinees are instructed to work as "quickly and accurately as you can." The test can be administered either individually or in a group format. No specialized training on the part of the examiner is required, and the test may be administered by clerical level staff. The item content can be categorized into several areas: comprehension, vocabulary/semantic relationships, symbol relationships (answers as words or parts of words, letters, numbers), alphabetical sequence relationships, relationships between numbers and letters or words, arithmetical relationships, and arithmetical procedures. The manual provides a thorough description of administration and scoring considerations. All items require the examinee to figure out what letter(s) or figure(s) are missing, and to write them in the test booklet. The number of missing elements is determined by the number of asterisks [i.e., (black-white/short-tall/up-****), (2 4 8 16 **)]. Scoring is a simple procedure of placing a scoring key next to the answers written in the test booklet. A raw score is determined by the number of items answered correctly.

A description of the standardization sample is somewhat incomplete. While the author urges the need to construct "local norms" and make comparisons with specifically defined groups, the manual includes "some sets of norms whose data were obtained whilst the test was being developed." Unfortunately, additional demographic data regarding those in the standardization are not provided. This severely limits the use and generalizability of the MD5.

A review of the MD5 raises some serious questions. The technical documentation in the manual is woefully inadequate, and there appear to be a number of weaknesses in the development of the instrument. There is no discussion of how the items were selected or what relationship the item content has with the selection of personnel. Does a high score predict job related success? The test appears to measure a limited domain of cognitive behavior. Reliability and validity information is inadequate at best. It is noted that the instrument can be used with a wide range of educational ability levels, yet no information is presented to support this claim. The author claims there is no significant difference in performance based on sex of examinee. However, male and female performance is compared only with lower level managerial staff. It is unclear if this same pattern would hold true with other groups. A review of the raw score distributions (Appendix 1) is very disturbing. Supervisors appear to do much better than lower level managers, yet when mean scores for the groups are reported (Appendix 2), supervisors' mean scores are lower. No information is presented to determine if the MD5 does what the author intended. Comparative studies with other instruments would be most helpful.

In summary, the MD5 provides insufficient information to determine if it is a valid and reliable instrument. The item type and content limit its use with certain groups. The decision-making process warrants that instruments used be somewhat comprehensive in nature. At this time the MD5 does not appear to be that type of instrument. Significantly more work is needed with the norm groups and to establish the reliability and validity of this test.

[194]

Meadow-Kendall Social-Emotional Assessment Inventory for Deaf and Hearing Impaired Students. Purpose: "Can be used to flag students who need extra attention in particular areas . . . . useful in communicating with parents who are reluctant to admit that their child needs special attention . . . . helpful in implementing an individualized program so that social and emotional areas are emphasized in the curriculum for the child who needs them." Ages 3–6, 7–21; 1983; SEAI; behavior checklist to be completed by adult informant; 2 levels; 1987 price data: $5 per 10 forms; $15 per manual (37 pages); administration time not reported; Kathryn P. Meadow and others listed below; OUTREACH.*

a) PRE-SCHOOL. Ages 3–6; 5 scores: Sociable/Communicative Behaviors, Impulsive Dominating Behaviors, Developmental Lags, Anxious/Compulsive Behaviors, Special Items; Kathryn P. Meadow, Pamela Getson, Chi K. Lee, Linda Stamper, and the Center for Studies in Education and Human Development.

b) SCHOOL-AGE. Ages 7–21. 3 scores: Social Adjustment, Self Image, Emotional Adjustment;

Kathryn P. Meadow, Michael A. Karchmer, Linda M. Petersen, and Lawrence Rudner.

TEST REFERENCES

1. Bolton, B., Turnbow, K., & Marr, J. N. (1984). Convergence of deaf children's sociometric scores and teachers' behavioral ratings. *Psychology in the Schools*, 21, 45-48.

Review of the Meadow-Kendall Social-Emotional Assessment Inventory for Deaf and Hearing Impaired Students by MARILYN E. DEMOREST, Associate Professor of Psychology, University of Maryland-Baltimore County, Catonsville, MD:

Development of the Meadow-Kendall Social-Emotional Assessment Inventory (SEAI) for Deaf and Hearing Impaired Students was motivated by the provision of Public Law 94-142, which requires a comprehensive assessment and individual educational plan for every handicapped child. The SEAI is designed for use by classroom teachers and includes observable behaviors that, at a theoretical level, are expected to reflect the social and emotional development of deaf and hearing-impaired children. One premise underlying the inventory is that development may be influenced by factors such as relative language deprivation and acceptance by significant others.

Test development procedures have ensured the content relevance of the items and the statistical integrity of the resulting scales. Content of the SEAI School-Age form was adapted from the School Behavior Check List (Miller, 1972) in consultation with more than 100 professionals knowledgeable about deaf children. Items use a 4-point response scale ranging from *Very True* to *Very False* and describe both positive and negative behaviors in four categories: (*a*) sociability and interpersonal relationships, (*b*) individual or personal characteristics, (*c*) self-esteem or identity, and (*d*) maturity, responsibility, and independence. A 69-item Research Edition was administered to 2,365 children in 10 residential and day programs from the northeastern, north central, southern, and southwestern regions of the country. Other demographic characteristics of the sample are not reported. Ten items were eliminated for statistical reasons (low response rate, discrimination, or factor loadings) and the resulting 59-item School-Age form yields scores on three scales derived from factor analysis. Because of significant mean differences among some groups, normative data are given by gender and age group for the Social Adjustment and Self Image scales, and by age group for the Emotional Adjustment scale.

The Preschool form was developed with the same rationale and methodology as the School-Age form, which served as a starting point for item construction. A Research Edition containing 70 items was developed in consultation with teachers at the Kendall Demonstration Elementary School and 34 other professionals. Final revision and norming were based on a sample of 857 children from 54 programs in at least 10 states. Characteristics of the sample are more completely described than for the School-Age form. In addition to age and gender, information is provided on geographic distribution of programs by state, type of program, ethnic background of the child, age at onset of deafness, hearing level, and deaf relatives. Item selection procedures resulted in 46 items distributed among four scales. Three additional items related to deafness were retained as "special items" and scored separately, despite the fact that they failed to satisfy inclusion criteria. No rationale for this is given. For Scales 1, 2, and 3, norms are provided by age level and gender to reflect significant differences in mean scores among groups; for Scale 4 subgroup norms were not necessary.

Unpublished data on the reliability and validity of both forms of the SEAI are presented in the test manual but the studies are not described in detail and are quite limited in scope. For the School-Age form interrater reliability, test-retest reliability, and correlations of the scales with an index of sociometric status are reported, but the research is based on a sample of only six children from a single classroom. Some of the coefficients are quite high, but their sampling error is so large that little useful information can be derived. Further evidence of interobserver reliability and convergent validity are provided by two local studies, one conducted in Seattle as part of the evaluation of a social skills curriculum ($N = 61$) and one performed at Gallaudet College in which advisors, dormitory counselors, and parents completed the SEAI for deaf adolescents ($N = 81$) entering the Model Secondary School for the Deaf. Many of the obtained correlation coefficients are significant, and some are moderately high, but very little information is given about the samples and the conditions under which the data were collected. Consequently, the research methods and generalizability of the findings are difficult to assess. The only data reported for the School-Age form that do seem to rest on an adequate data base are the relationships between SEAI scores and the presence of other handicapping conditions in the norm sample. Given that additional handicaps were, predictably, associated with significantly lower scores on all three scales, there is some evidence of construct validity for the SEAI School-Age form.

Preliminary data are also given for the more recently developed Preschool SEAI. Test-retest reliability over a 4-week period was assessed in four preschool programs with a combined sample size of 159 children. Correlations between the SEAI ratings of teachers and teachers' aides are given for one of these programs ($N = 21$) and correlations of the SEAI scales with a global assessment of adjustment (provided by teachers in the norm sample) are also reported. As with the School-Age form, the studies are not reported in detail and are therefore difficult to evaluate.

Given that the SEAI is to be used in formulating an individual educational plan, it is essential that both interobserver and retest reliability be rigorously evaluated. Moreover, internal consistency reliability (coefficient alpha) should be reported for the norm samples since the data are already available. Because the inventories were developed to fill a particular assessment need, other comparable measures are not available for testing concurrent validity. Nevertheless, scores on the SEAI should correlate positively with other measures of social and emotional development as well as with behavioral criteria associated with that construct. Until such validity data become available, content-referenced interpretation of the scores is recommended.

In conclusion, the School-Age and Preschool forms of the SEAI fill an important assessment need for the hearing-impaired population. A judicious combination of theoretical premises, expert judgment, and data analysis has resulted in a set of scales whose potential construct validity appears great. However, there is a critical need for systematic, large-sample studies of the reliability and validity of the scales. Preliminary evidence reported in the manual is promising, but further investigation is needed if the full potential of the scales is to be realized.

REVIEWER'S REFERENCE

Miller, L. C. (1972). School Behavior Check List: An inventory of deviant behavior for elementary school children. *Journal of Consulting and Clinical Psychology*, 38, 134-144.

Review of the Meadow-Kendall Social-Emotional Assessment Inventory for Deaf and Hearing Impaired Students by KENNETH L. SHELDON, School Psychologist, Edgecombe County Schools, Tarboro, NC:

The Meadow-Kendall Social-Emotional Assessment Inventory for Deaf and Hearing Impaired Students (SEAI) was developed in response to the regulations of the Education for All Handicapped Children Act of 1975 (PL 94-142) and the need for an instrument to assess the social and emotional status of hearing-impaired students. Based on developmental theories and research pertaining to mental health problems of hearing-impaired individuals, the SEAI was designed for use with a wide range of hearing losses and to be used in a variety of special education settings. Two inventories were developed, one a revision of the 1980 SEAI for school age children and the other a downward extension of the SEAI for preschool and kindergarten age children. The goals that guided the development of each of these inventories included the sampling of positive and negative classroom behaviors, the creation of reliable subscales, and the generation of a final product that could be easily completed by an adult who has had contact with the student for at least 8 weeks.

SCHOOL-AGE FORM. The standardization sample was representative of both residential and day programs in states representing all but the northwestern United States. Participating sites were voluntary and not randomly selected. Through item analyses, feedback from site participants, and factor analysis, items were deleted and grouped into three subscales.

Interitem reliability (Cronbach's alpha) is in the .90s, indicating adequate item reliability. Based on ratings of six children, interrater reliability between a teacher and counselor varied for each subscale, ranging from .58 to .93. Using the same six students, test-retest reliability ranged from .79 to .86. Some evidence for concurrent validity is provided in a study ($N = 61$) in which the SEAI was correlated with the Health Resources Inventory and the Walker Problem Behavior Identification Checklist. The correlations ranged from .53 to .78. The authors believe that there is "variable but positive support for the meaningfulness of the inventory." The instrument does compare favorably with other behavior rating scales, such as the Burks Behavior Rating Scale, and seems valid. Additional data collection with larger samples is needed.

The SEAI package includes a manual and inventory booklet. The easily read manual includes a helpful scoring and interpretation sample. The inventory booklet is self-contained and includes everything needed to complete and score the inventory. The price of the inventory booklet may be prohibitive for some.

Instructions for completing the 59-item inventory require the informant to compare the child to both hearing and hearing-impaired individuals of similar age. Most items appear to be easily observed, except for item 2, "Kind and considerate," which is not as behaviorally stated as the others. A 4-point scale is used for scoring. Scoring involves some simple calculations which require attention to detail in order to avoid errors. Norms are reported as mean scores, and for two of the subscales the norms for boys and girls are separate. Also, the examiner will need to determine the chronological age since separate norms are reported for ages 7–15 and 16–21. Final scores are reported in deciles.

PRE-SCHOOL AGE FORM. This form is similar in most respects to the School-Age form in administration, scoring, and interpretation. Differences noted are in the developmental sequence of the behaviors sampled and in the norms. Standardization procedures appear to be similar. Once again, the standardization sample was voluntary and not randomly selected. The geographical representation does appear to be more inclusive of all regions. Reliability is similar to the School-Age form and is adequate. There is, however, greater variability in scale reliability, with Scale 4 (anxious, compulsive behaviors) being the least reliable.

The test developers note the lack of validity studies and suggest instruments that can be used to conduct such studies. They do report one study that provides some evidence of validity. Results yielded low to medium correlations between teacher perceptions of the children and teacher ratings of the children using the SEAI. Like most preschool assessment instruments, reliability and validity are difficult to insure due to the changing behaviors of the developing child.

SUMMARY. This reviewer has found the SEAI to be useful in developing individualized treatment programs for hearing-impaired children. Compared to other behavior rating scales normed on hearing individuals, the SEAI is specific to the hearing-impaired population yet appears to measure the most important behaviors necessary for successful integration of any child into the educational setting. The reviewer concurs with the authors' cautions explicitly stated in the manual for using and interpreting the results. The results are only useful if completed after careful observation and should be used to identify students who need extra attention in areas of social and emotional development. Overall, the SEAI is a needed and useful addition to the small but growing list of assessment instruments for the evaluation of hearing-impaired children.

[195]

Measurement of Counselor Competencies: A Self-Assessment. Purpose: "Assesses counselor competencies necessary for the adequate performance of roles and functions." School counselors; 1973–74; ratings by self in 4 areas: Competency Level, Interest Level, Frequency, Demands; no manual (instructions and profile included on test); 1985 price data: $4.75 per manual; administration time not reported; Robert R. Percival, John W. Dahm, and Joseph D. Dameron; Dallas Educational Services.*

Review of the Measurement of Counselor Competencies: A Self-Assessment by RICHARD A. WANTZ, Associate Professor of Educational Psychology and Director of the Counseling Psychology Clinic, College of Education, University of Oklahoma, Norman, OK:

This self-assessment was designed for use by school counselors. The 18-page booklet containing this inventory provides no introduction, rationale (theoretical or otherwise), or references. The amount of time required to administer, score, and profile this inventory is not specified in the test booklet. The items appear to be chosen from some unidentified model regarding school counselors' roles and functions. Some items are broad in scope and difficult to rate. A manual is not provided; in general, the information provided in the inventory book is insufficient.

No evidence is provided regarding the psychometric properties of the instrument including external validity and reliability, nor is any normative data provided. The instrument has not been revised since the early 1970s. For example, a reference is made to the American Personnel and Guidance Association, which is known currently as the American Association for Counseling and Development. Also, since the early seventies the generic term "counselor" is less frequently used without qualifying the type of counselor: school counselor, rehabilitation counselor, marriage and family counselor, employment counselor, public offender counselor, etc. (Wantz, Scherman, & Hollis, 1982; Hollis & Wantz, 1983).

The four broad dimensions assessed—Counseling, Coordination, Consultation, and Organization and Evaluation—are logical but limited as areas to be assessed for a school counselor. No rationale is provided for choosing these or for not including other areas. Not addressed were such areas as career and life style planning, resource and information management, appraisal of students, and computer assisted career guidance systems and other utilizations of computers within an effective school counseling program.

The user would need to carefully match the counseling functions of his or her school against those assessed in this instrument. For example, users are asked to assess their ability to utilize only two specific counseling interaction skills (i.e., the Hill Interaction Matrix and the Carkhuff Communication Scale). No provision is made for substitutions of other methods and techniques. Furthermore, no references are provided for these two approaches. It is unfortunate that a procedure is not provided to allow for adaptation of this instrument to meet local needs. Also it would appear appropriate to incorporate a "not applicable" response within the 1 (low) through 5 (high) response choices.

Profiling and assessment report worksheets are provided, but no assistance is provided in the form of suggested remedial interventions or references.

This instrument might be revised by a school counselor to incorporate specific job responsibilities in a local school setting. Without further research, development, and documentation it offers limited assistance for assessing school counselor competencies. This inventory is not recommended for use in its current state of development.

REVIEWER'S REFERENCES

Wantz, R. A., Scherman, A., & Hollis, J. W. (1982). Trends in counselor preparation: Courses, program emphases, philosophical orientation and experiential components. *Counselor Education and Supervision*, 21, 258-268.

Hollis, J. W., & Wantz, R. A. (1983). *Counselor preparation 1983–1985. Programs, personnel, trends* (5th ed.). Muncie, IN: Accelerated Development Inc.

[196]

Measures of Musical Abilities. Purpose: "Measures, positively, a child's ability to make the kind of basic, elemental judgements that are essential in music making." Ages 7–14; 1966–85; self-administered by tape cassette; 4 tests: Pitch Discrimination, Tonal Memory, Chord Analysis, Rhythmic Memory; 1985 price data: £12.75 per complete set including 25 answer sheets, cassette, and notes for teachers ('85, 8 pages); £2.95 per 25 answer sheets; £5.95 per cassette; £3.95 per notes for teachers; 21(30) minutes; Arnold Bentley; NFER-Nelson Publishing Co., Ltd. [England].*

See T3:1446 (1 reference) and T2:206 (3 references); for reviews by Richard Colwell and John McLeish, and excerpted reviews by Richard R. Bentley and Paul R. Farnsworth, see 7:247 (13 references).

Review of the Measures of Musical Abilities by RICHARD COLWELL, Professor of Secondary Education and Music, University of Illinois at Urbana-Champaign, Urbana, IL:

Only the teacher's manual has been revised since this test was reviewed in the *Seventh Mental Measurements Yearbook* (Buros, 1972, p. 523). Some additional research has been completed, none of which appears to invalidate any of the comments made in the earlier review.

Other than indicating that the terms used in the test are unlikely to confuse young students and suggesting that it is no longer necessary for the testees to sit facing the loud speaker, the revisions in the test manual consist of adding a few paragraphs on the stability of the abilities measured by the test. The test has now been translated into French, German, Japanese, and Spanish and data have been gathered in Israel and some South American countries. The test author, Arnold Bentley, now has data on 11,278 individuals.

The test is a popular measure of music aptitude in many parts of the world, although it continues to be underused in the United States.

The author claims that the test does not measure musical aptitude "in toto," but provides an accurate measure of individual abilities, abilities necessary to make the basic, elemental judgments essential in music making. Recommended uses of the test include selecting students for special music activities and assessing readiness for musical operations that require a level of maturity for success. Most reassuring are Bentley's frequent warnings throughout the manual about the fallibility of his and other tests in predicting the future course of events. If a student were not feeling well or were distracted for some reason when taking the test, the test should be readministered.

Music-education researchers continue to be obsessed with the task of pitch discrimination and the quality of the tools employed in measuring it, concerns that no doubt stem from the importance of playing or singing in tune. Recent research by Janet Mills (1984) challenged the validity of the pitch discrimination subtest of the Measures of Musical Abilities. Mills found that scores were higher on this subtest when the quality of the recording was improved. Mills' argument is that there is enough fluctuation in the pitch of the tones presented to confuse some (the better?) students. Mills is correct on the recording problems, which are undoubtedly made worse by school-quality phonographs and speakers. As Mills reported no discrepancies on the other three subtests, one might assume that she has more confidence in their validity in the measurement of musical aptitude.

Bentley does not provide item-discrimination indices. To him, discrimination is the same as difficulty. Mills (1984) also does not provide data on discrimination, only reporting difficulty data. On the basis of logic alone one can support Mills' claim that the criterion-related validity of the test is improved by her more accurate recording.

Young's research conducted in 1972 revealed a correlation coefficient of .58 when comparing scores on the Bentley with the much longer (2 hours) Musical Aptitude Profile of Edwin Gordon. Young concluded that the validity of the Bentley was "moderately high and a useful test for many assessments in music."

This reviewer administered the test to 142 subjects in 1986 and the results confirmed the stability of the test. K-R 20 reliability was .86 and standard error estimates of 3.39 were obtained with fourth-grade students. Reliability figures reported in research studies using this test have reported consistently a range of .84 to .86, supporting Bentley's original estimate of .85. The mean score has also not changed in 20 years; our American data matched exactly Bentley's British data. Data provided in the new material added to the manual indicate that 90 percent of 30 students who retook the test 6 months after the original administration obtained the same or the next higher or lower grade. Other stability data, 1, 2, 3, and 4 years after original testing, reveal that 87 percent of the students obtain the same or similar scores. Distribution curves compared between 1963 and 1973 by Bentley were the same. He reports an increase of about 4 percent per year (maturation) with a wide range at any single age of about 65 percent.

Our data would indicate that higher scores are now attained by the better students. Norms are provided by grade level. A comparison of Bentley's norms for 9-year-old students with the reviewer's norms for the 1986 study for the same age group revealed the following (the first score in parenthesis representing Bentley norms and the second representing reviewer data): top 10 percent (above 39; above 44); top 70–90 percent (31–38; 38–43); top 30–70 percent (21–30; 27–37); 10–30 percent (15–20; 20–26); and bottom 10 percent (14 and below; 19 and below). The reviewer's 1986 data are similar to that reported by Mills, perhaps lessening the magnitude of the effect that she attributes to the improved recording.

The pitch test, especially with the Mills improved recording, is subject to a ceiling effect that is most noticeable among older students and trained musicians, a comment made in the *Seventh Mental Measurements Yearbook* review (Buros, 1972, p. 523). This ceiling effect is also present with the tonal and rhythmic memory test, the mean score of students who are of junior high school age being 8+ out of a possible 10. Recent work of Vispoel (1986) on the tonal memory component of musical aptitude (comparable to Bentley's tunes subtest) indicates the advantages of adaptive testing in aptitude tests that attempt to provide norms for a wide age span.

Unfortunately, systematic research on music aptitude is sparse. Test authors and sometimes their students investigate selected aspects of their own tests, but impartial and objective research is lacking. Given the British dialect on the recording of the Measures (which young American students initially find distracting), and the quality of the recording, the test accomplishes its purpose amazingly well.

Whatever this test is measuring, especially with the weight given to the chord test where the task is to identify the number of voices being heard (between 1 and 4), it continues to provide a reasonably good indication of probable success in many music activities. The ease of administration and short test length make the Bentley Measures preferable to the aptitude tests of Seashore and Gordon on many occasions.

REVIEWER'S REFERENCES

Buros, O. K. (Ed.) (1972). *The seventh mental measurements yearbook*. Highland Park, NJ: The Gryphon Press.

Mills, J. (1984). The "Pitch" subtest of Bentley's Measures of Musical Abilities: A test from the 1960s reconsidered in the 1980s. *Psychology of Music*, 12 (2), 94-105.

Vispoel, W. (1986). *A computer-administered adaptive test of tonal memory: An application of item response theory to the measurement of musical ability*. Unpublished doctoral dissertation, University of Illinois, Urbana, IL.

[197]

Medical Ethics Inventory. Purpose: Provides "profiles of the value preferences of medical students regarding medical ethical dilemmas." First year medical students; 1982; MEI; 6 scores: Social, Economic, Theoretical, Political, Religious, Aesthetic; 1984 price data: $20 per complete set; [30–40] minutes; Cynthia J. Stolman and Rodney Doran; Cynthia Stolman.*

Review of the Medical Ethics Inventory by JOSEPH D. MATARAZZO, Professor and Chairman, Department of Medical Psychology, School of Medicine, Oregon Health Sciences University, Portland, OR:

The Medical Ethics Inventory (MEI) is a 72-item paper and pencil test designed for use with medical students. Its purpose is to sample the personal values that would guide a future physician faced with ethical dilemmas. The test is composed of 12 clinical cases, each of which presents the physician with an ethical dilemma. The authors began developing the test in 1978 and state in the short, 1982 test manual accompanying the test that the Medical Ethics Inventory "is still in the formative stages of development." Although the 1982 test manual is available only in typed form from the authors, the material in it is readily accessible inasmuch as it is almost identical to the content in the one article on the MEI published to date (Stolman & Doran, 1982).

To produce the MEI the authors used the theoretical framework of values advanced by E. Spranger. This framework was incorporated in the six scales included in the 1930 and 1951 versions of the Study of Values (SOV: 9:1205), published in its third edition (1970) by Allport, Vernon, and Lindzey. Although the six value scales included in the MEI were given the same names as their counterpart SOV scales (Aesthetic, Economic, Political, Religious, Social, and Theoretical), Stolman and Doran used a different format and wrote entirely new items for each scale to better reflect the specific medical context for which their test was constructed. Specifically, from actual clinical cases published in medical journals and textbooks, they constructed 12 separate clinical case histories, each of which involved a not-uncommon ethical dilemma that physicians face (e.g., whether or not to or how to intervene when a profoundly malformed and certainly mentally retarded 3-week-old infant stops breathing). The test taker is then offered six possible considerations or interventions, each of which represents one of the six Spranger values, and is asked to rate on a 5-point scale (from *not at all important* to *extremely important*) each of these six choices that would influence the decision he or she would make. Inasmuch as each of the six values is represented in each of the 12 case histories, and each value must be assigned a rating (later recorded as scores of 1–5), the range of scores for each of the six values any respondent can earn is from 12 (very low on that value) to 60 (very high).

Development of the MEI consisted of the authors culling the literature for the 12 case histories, writing up a potential physician response relating to each of the six values for each case, asking expert "judges" (e.g., a rabbi for the responses based on a religious orientation) to study (and rewrite as necessary) each of the 12 value statements in his or her area of expertise, and then administering the 72-item test to four groups of students. These latter included a group of 151 medical students; a group of 274 students (included among which were 45 social work students, 56 law students, 41 art students, 39 seminary students, 33 chemical engineering students, and 60 commerce students); another group (who also served as the test-retest reliability sample) consisting of 90 psychology students, and a fourth group that included 80 undergraduate students in a medical ethics class.

The results with the 90 psychology students showed the 3-week test-retest reliability of the six scales was moderately high, ranging from .65 for the Theoretical value to .82 for the Religious value scales. However, the internal consistency (studied in the sample of 151 medical students) was only modest; yielding a coefficient alpha for the six scales which ranged from only .46 (Aesthetic) to .67 (Economic).

One of the authors' studies of the validity of the MEI included using the group of 151 medical students and comparing each student's score on the MEI with that earned by the same student on the SOV for each of the six scales. The results revealed that, although there was 28 percent common variance on one bipolar function, overall the "small percentages of shared common variance indicated that the instruments differed in some ways (and that this) difference may be attributed to the differing contextual situations inherent in the medical ethics cases" relevant to the situations tapped by the SOV items.

Other approaches to study of the validity of the MEI involved (*a*) the authors' studying the intercorrelations of each of the six scales (the MEI subscale to subscale *r*s were all positive); and (*b*) examination of the six MEI scales for each of the six subgroups of 274 students with differing majors. Unfortunately, the latter study revealed the subgroups had very similar profiles on the six scales, with the social value response in each case history situation being given the highest rating by each of these five seemingly disparate groups of students.

The authors of the MEI conclude their single published report with the statement that "further research is needed to represent the components of the social dimension of medical ethical decision-making and to proceed with the development of instruments in the area of medical ethics." Although the MEI is a test requiring further development and research, given the increasing frequency with which today's physicians are having to face ethical dilemmas with no easy solution, and the representativeness of the dilemmas portrayed in the 12 case histories included in the MEI, this reviewer believes it is a test worthy of further use as a research instrument.

REVIEWER'S REFERENCE

Stolman, C. J., & Doran, R. L. (1982). Development and validation of a test instrument for assessing value preferences in medical ethics. *Journal of Medical Education*, 57, 170-179.

Review of the Medical Ethics Inventory by GARY B. MELTON, Carl A. Happold Professor of Psychology and Law, University of Nebraska-Lincoln, Lincoln, NE:

The Medical Ethics Inventory (MEI) is intended as an outcome measure in evaluations of medical ethics curricula, "as an aid for values clarification, [and] as a tool for counselors in career planning" (Stolman & Doran, 1982). It is derived from the six-pronged typology of values proposed by Spranger (1928) and incorporated into Allport, Vernon, and Lindzey's Study of Values Test (SOV; 9:1205). The test itself requires Likert-style reponses to six alternatives to each of 12 brief vignettes about dilemmas in medical ethics.

The dilemmas are interesting and reflect a reasonably representative sample of current problems in medical ethics. However, the theoretical underpinnings of the MEI itself are dubious. The typology of values (e.g., aesthetic, political) seems far removed from perspectives on medical ethics. An instrument to tap such perspectives (e.g., deontological; rule-utilitarian; act-utilitarian) would appear to be a more profitable line of inquiry.

In fact, the limited validity data available raise questions about the usefulness of the approach that Stolman and Dolan took. In a study of an apparently selected sample of medical students (75 first-year students at McMaster University, 16 first-year students at SUNY-Buffalo, and 60 upper-class students at Rockford School of Medicine), the relationships between the MEI and the SOV were weak indeed, with only three correlations even reaching statistical significance (Economic, .21; Religious, .45; Social, .19). When small, apparently nonrandom samples of professional students chosen to correspond to the SOV/MEI dimensions took the MEI, few group differences emerged in the weight accorded the various dimensions. Religion students did score higher than the other groups on the religious subscale, and social work students were significantly more likely than the other groups to espouse social values. However, expected relationships on the other dimensions (e.g., aesthetic: art students) were not observed, and the rank ordering of the dimensions was virtually identical across the six groups.

Alphas derived from the medical-student sample showed modest internal consistency (range of .46 to .67). Test-retest correlations in a sample of introductory psychology students across a 3-week interval also were modest (range of .65 to .82). No norms are available.

Research on the MEI is at an early point. However, the studies thus far give no basis for use of the instrument either to measure individual differences (in a values clarification exercise or career counseling) or to assess group differences in evaluation studies. Moreover, no convincing rationale has been presented to validate the choice of scales used to assess ethical preferences in medical decision making.

REVIEWER'S REFERENCES

Spranger, E. (1928). *Types of men; The psychology and ethics of personality*. New York: Hefner.

Stolman, C. J., & Doran, R. L. (1982). Development and validation of a test instrument for assessing value preferences in medical ethics. *Journal of Medical Education*, 57, 170-179.

[198]

Meeker Behavioral Correlates. Purpose: Assesses "major dimensions of intellectual abilities and personality characteristics" for management matching of teams. Industry; 1981; ratings by self in 6 areas: Comprehension, Memory, Leadership, Convergent Production Skills, Creativity, Team Contributions; no manual; 1985 price data: $20 per 10 surveys; [20] minutes; Mary Meeker; SOI Systems.*

Review of the Meeker Behavioral Correlates by WILLIAM I. SAUSER, JR., Associate Vice President and Professor, Office of the Vice President for Extension, Auburn University, Auburn, AL:

Meeker Behavioral Correlates is an unprofessionally developed instrument that is unsuitable for its stated purpose. While it may have some utility for self-assessment or to stimulate discussion of desired characteristics for effective teamwork, it should be afforded no more respect than the "score yourself" questionnaires found in many popular magazines. It certainly should not be seriously considered by organizations seeking an instrument to serve as a basis for selection decisions regarding prospective or current employees.

Meeker Behavioral Correlates consists of 72 words or phrases (e.g., curious, good auditory memory, analytical, able to make changes) arranged under the six headings listed in the test description above. The respondent is directed to "Read each word on the left. Check the boxes which describes (sic) you." Four responses are available for each item: "Most of the time, Some of the time, Once in a while, Others think I am." The directions are unclear as to whether multiple responses to each item are allowed. No scoring instructions are provided.

The list of words and phrases is followed on the instrument with a section titled "How to interpret the bahavioral (sic) correlates." These five paragraphs, purporting to analyze the strengths and weaknesses of the respondent, contain a series of very authoritative statements, such as "Jobs which require rapid and accurate understanding are best carried off by high cognizers." While there may be some evidence in the scientific literature that supports the statements made in this section, no such evidence is presented on the instrument or in any supporting materials. The instrument does, however, contain references to other instruments and training materials that can be purchased from the test developer.

The concluding section of the instrument, "How to interpret team contributions," contains a three-sentence paragraph claiming primarily that the instrument may provide information that "will be helpful for selecting future teams as well as improving existing teams." No specific suggestions beyond asking team members to rate themselves and identify "complimentary (sic) similarities and differences" are provided. The instrument is sold in packets of 10 presumably to facilitate this procedure.

The fact that there is no manual accompanying Meeker Behavioral Correlates is extremely problematic from a professional viewpoint. No normative data are provided, nor is any evidence of reliability or validity presented. The test developer does, however, warn the potential user to be judicious when interpreting various items. For example, one interpretive passage states, "Leadership qualities are varied. Each description has application for different kinds of duties. Select those aspects which seem most likely to make for successes on a given job and for the team."

Although the title of the instrument suggests that test scores might somehow be related to actual job behaviors, no evidence to support this presumption is provided by the test developer. The developer does, however, inform the prospective user that ratings on some of the abilities "can be statistically validated against" scores on other instruments available from the same test developer. No guidance is provided to the user for actually carrying out the essential test validation process.

Clearly this crude, transparently fakable self-report device is unacceptable as a measure of intellectual abilities and personality characteristics. Individuals desiring scientifically defensible measures of comprehension, memory, leadership, and creativity should consult the index for tests reviewed elsewhere in this reference work; numerous alternatives are available.

The concept of using an assessment device to identify individuals who might work effectively together in teams has intrigued researchers for years. While Meeker Behavioral Correlates does not appear suited for this purpose, those interested in this problem may wish to consider using the FIRO-B (9:416), the Learning Style Inventory (9:607), the Myers-Briggs Type Indicator (206), or the Personal Profile System (280). Research with these instruments, while far from conclusive, suggests they may be useful for assembling compatible, productive groups.

The fact that Meeker Behavioral Correlates calls for the respondent to state "Job applying for" at the top of the first page is very disturbing in its implications. An instrument for which there is no shred of evidence of reliability or validity should certainly not be marketed as a possible employment selection device. Any organization considering Meeker Behavioral Correlates for that purpose should immediately abandon the idea.

In summary, Meeker Behavioral Correlates is an unacceptable test. It is poorly conceived and presented, it is not supported with any evidence of reliability or validity, no normative data exist, the directions are unclear, and there are no scoring instructions. The grammatical and spelling errors littering the instrument attest to the sloppiness of its development. Potential users should steer clear of this test, and its developer should withdraw it from the market and either overhaul it to meet at least minimal professional standards or abandon it altogether.

[199]

Meeting Street School P.S.R. Test: Psychological S-R Evaluation for Severely Multiply Handicapped Children. Purpose: "Assesses the abilities of the severely multiply handicapped child," and provides alternate modes of response. Severely multiply handicapped children ages 1–5 and retarded severely multiply handicapped children ages 6–10; 1977; PSR; 2 scales: Auditory Language, Visual-Motor, plus a Tactile Differentiation section; individual; 1985 price data: $35 per complete set including 10 protocols, picture vocabulary cards and response cards, and manual (100 pages); $15 per 10 protocols; administration time not reported; Eileen M. Mullen; Meeting Street School.*

Review of the Meeting Street School P.S.R. Test: Psychological S-R Evaluation for Severely Multiply Handicapped Children by PATRICIA L. MIRENDA, Assistant Professor of Special Education and Communication Disorders, University of Nebraska-Lincoln, Lincoln, NE:

This instrument is designed to help fill the current void that exists in the area of assessment of children with severe multiple handicaps. It is composed of Auditory Language, Visual-Motor, and Tactile Differentiation subscales and is intended to provide a functional age (F.A.) score instead of a mental age (M.A.) score or intelligence quotient (IQ). The items in each subscale are arranged in chronological order from 0–1 month to 60 months for the Auditory and Visual-Motor scales, and from 0–6 months to 6 years for the Tactile Differentiation section. At least one, and up to six, references are provided as evidence for the developmental placement of each of the test items. The references are drawn primarily from assessment instruments that have been standardized for the nonhandicapped population, such as the Bayley Scales, (Bayley, 1969), Užgiris-Hunt Scales (Užgiris & Hunt, 1975), and the Stanford-Binet Intelligence Scale (Terman & Merrill, 1973).

The authors have changed the usual psychological assessment protocol in several ways to accommodate the needs of severely multiply handicapped children. The test (*a*) is not timed, (*b*) is to be administered by examiners who are familiar with severely handicapped children (not necessarily psychologists), and (*c*) provides suggestions for alternate (i.e., nonverbal) responses for most of the test items. The test manual includes information designed to help the examiner identify the stimulus modality (visual, auditory, or both) to which the child is responding. Finally, the examiner is encouraged to focus on the subscales that best suit the child's abilities, and to begin assessment at a level approximately 6 months below the child's anticipated F.A., thus allowing even more individualization and flexibility. The directions for administration of each of the test items are clearly spelled out and include reference to the materials needed, procedure to be used, and alternate responses considered acceptable.

There are also several significant problems with both the construction of the test and the protocol provided for it. First, the term "severely handicapped" is never defined, leaving the potential user in doubt as to whether the test is to be used with children who experience cognitive as well as other handicaps, or with children whose disabilities are primarily motoric and/or sensory in nature. This problem is exacerbated by the rather ambiguous statement in the test manual that "informal test data gathered over the past 2 years" indicates that the test "is particularly effective when testing very young severely multiply handicapped children, ages 1 to 5, and older, *retarded* [italics added] severely multiply handicapped children, ages 6 to 10." The implication here is that the term "severely multiply handicapped" does *not* necessarily refer to a combination of motor/sensory problems plus retardation.

Second, aside from the normative references related to each test item, there are no reliability or validity data provided. In addition, it is unclear whether the authors primarily "borrowed" test items from the references listed, or whether the test items were created specifically for this test, using the normative information contained in the references as a guide. If the former is the case, it is unfortunate that no rationale is provided for how and why particular test items were selected from one test over others. It is also unfortunate that many of the references listed are inaccurate or incomplete, and that no bibliography is supplied for the sources cited. A related problem is that, while the authors note that the end product of the assessment is a functional age (F.A.) score as opposed to either a mental age or IQ score, the differences, if any, between F.A. and M.A. are not clear. The combined result of these ambiguities is that the potential user is left unclear as to how the test was constructed and what the results will indicate.

Third, the test provides no guidelines concerning implications of the assessment results for individual educational planning (I.E.P.) or curriculum development. This failure to discuss educational implications is problematic in that it implicitly encourages the unfortunate practice of basing I.E.P. goals on test items "failed," regardless of whether or not the skills tested by these items are relevant to the student's ability to engage in the meaningful, functional tasks necessary for maximum independence (Brown, Nietupski, & Hamre-Nietupski, 1976). Further, since the test is intended to measure only cognitive development and conceptual understanding, there are no subtest items related to skills in the areas of self-care, recreation/leisure skills, or other adaptive skills. This militates even further against the potential of using the assessment information to identify programming needs in functional curriculum areas.

Given the overall problems related to inadequate definitions of target population, absence of reliability and validity data, ambiguity about how the normative references relate to test development, and lack of direction regarding the implications of test results for educational programming, this evaluation tool appears to fall short of its intended goals. The primary advantages of the Meeting Street P.S.R. Test over already existing assessment tools seem to be the format of the test items and the provision for allowing alternate responses to be counted as "correct." However, the deficits would seem to outweigh the strengths in situations where a straightforward developmental assessment might be indicated.

REVIEWER'S REFERENCES

Bayley, N. (1969). Bayley Scales of Infant Development. New York: The Psychological Corporation.

Terman, L. M., & Merrill, M. A. (1973). Stanford-Binet Intelligence Scale, (3rd rev.). Boston: Houghton-Mifflin Co.

Užgiris, I. C., & Hunt, J. McV. (1975). *Assessment in infancy: Ordinal scales of psychological development*. Urbana, IL: University of Illinois Press.

Brown, L., Nietupski, J., & Hamre-Nietupski, S. (1976). Criterion of ultimate functioning. In M. A. Thomas (Ed.), *Hey don't forget about me!* (pp. 2-15). Reston, VA: Council for Exceptional Children.

Review of the Meeting Street School P.S.R. Test: Psychological S-R Evaluation for Severely

Multiply Handicapped Children by DAVID P. WACKER, Associate Professor, Pediatrics and Special Education, University of Iowa, Iowa City, IA:

The Psychological S-R Evaluation (PSR) utilizes "stimulus and response item content [that] is designed to minimize the physical aspects of the tasks while tapping behavior which demonstrates acquisition of concepts traditionally associated with levels of intellectual development." The PSR consists of two scales: (*a*) Auditory-Language, and (*b*) Visual Motor. Both scales were "designed as a cognitive tool to assess verbal and visual-motor intelligence." Each of the scales consists of a four-step sequence beginning with basic attending behavior and ending with higher level concept formation. For children who have sensory deficits, either scale can be used for assessment. The PSR also contains a Tactile Differentiation Section which is intended to assess "tactile-kinesthetic awareness and discrimination abilities, as well as vestibular integration." The authors suggest that the PSR be used with severely handicapped children who cannot be assessed with traditional measures of intelligence.

The authors report that the PSR has been found to be especially useful in identifying learning styles in young multihandicapped children 1 to 5 years of age. The PSR provides what the authors call a "functional age" score, which is roughly equivalent to mental age scores achieved with other tests. The range in functional ages is from birth through 60 months, with increments ranging from 1 to 6 months. Directions/guidelines are provided for each item and detail the stimulus materials needed (some are included with the test), the testing procedure to be used, and the responses required.

A major strength of the PSR is the manual, which provides good information on who should administer the test, positioning of students, and the purposes of the test. In addition, relatively clear descriptions of all test items are provided.

Unfortunately, no information is provided on test construction, reliability, or validity. Given that the manual was written in 1977, perhaps reliability and validity data are available. If so, these data should be included in the manual. At present, the PSR should be considered an experimental tool of unknown reliability and validity. Additional data are needed before the PSR can be considered for use in applied settings.

[200]

Metropolitan Achievement Test, Sixth Edition. Purpose: "Designed to measure the achievement of students in the major skill and content areas of the school curriculum." Grades K.0–K.9, K.5–1.9, 1.5–2.9, 2.5–3.9, 3.5–4.9, 5.0–6.9, 7.0–9.9, 10.0–12.9; 1931–87; MAT6; 2 batteries and writing test; information regarding numerous customized and package scoring and reporting services available from the publisher; George A. Prescott, Irving H. Balow, Thomas P. Hogan, and Roger C. Farr; The Psychological Corporation.*

a) SURVEY BATTERY. Grades K.0–K.9, K.5–1.9, 1.5–2.9, 2.5–3.9, 3.5–4.9, 5.0–6.9, 7.0–9.9, 10.0-12.9; 1977–86; subtests in Reading and Mathematics available as separates (Grades K.5–12.9); basic batteries without Science and Social Studies available (Grades K.0–12.9); practice tests available; 8 overlapping levels; 1988 price data: $17 per administrator's guide ('87); $17 per test coordinator's handbook ('87, 157 pages); $30 per technical manual ('88, 128 pages); $7.50 per Index of Instructional Objectives for each level; $7.50 per each of several basal textbook resource guides for Reading or Mathematics to link textbooks with appropriate Instructional Reading Level or Instructional Mathematics Level; $20 per National or NonPublic multilevel norms booklet; $15 per National or NonPublic norms booklet for each level; $17 per teacher's manual for each level; $11 per 35 pretest or posttest parent folders for each of first 5 levels or for combined Intermediate/Advanced level; $2.50 per class record form for any one level; $19.50 per 35 cumulative record folders; $2.50 per practice test directions for each of first 5 levels or for combined Intermediate/Advanced level; $195 per Pretest or Posttest Workshop Kits; $15 per examination kit of any one level.

1) *Preprimer*. Grades K.0–K.9; 4 scores: Reading, Mathematics, Language, Total; 2 editions; $20 per 100 practice tests and directions; $27 per set of keys for hand-scorable test booklets or to hand score NCS machine-scorable test booklets; $4.50 per teacher's directions for administering Complete/Basic Battery, Form L ('85, 36 pages); 98(168) minutes in 7 sittings. (a) Hand-Scorable Edition. $49 per 35 Basic Battery test booklets, Form L ('85, 19 pages), including teacher's directions, class record, and 35 practice tests with directions.

(*b*) NCS Machine-Scorable Edition. $73 per 35 Basic Battery test booklets, Form L ('85,

20 pages), including teacher's directions and 35 practice tests with directions.

2) *Primer*. Grades K.5–1.9; 7 scores: Reading (Vocabulary, Word Recognition Skills, Reading Comprehension, Total), Mathematics, Language, Total; 2 editions; $20 per 100 practice tests and directions; $37 per set of keys for Complete/Basic Battery hand-scorable test booklets or to hand score NCS machine-scorable test booklets, $27 per keys for Reading test, $16 per keys for Mathematics test; $4.50 per teacher's directions for administering Survey Battery, Form L ('85, 46 pages); $4.50 per teacher's directions for administering Mathematics Survey test, Form L ('85, 24 pages); $4.50 per teacher's directions for administering Reading Survey tests ('85, 34 pages); 134(204) minutes in 7 sittings.

(*a*) Hand-Scorable Edition. $49 per 35 Basic Battery test booklets, Form L ('85, 31 pages), including teacher's directions and class record; $32 per 35 Reading test booklets('85, 19 pages) or Mathematics test booklets ('85, 11 pages) Form L, including teacher's directions and class record.

(*b*) NCS Machine-Scorable Edition. $73 per 35 Basic Battery test booklets, Form L ('85, 32 pages), including teacher's directions; $49 per 35 Reading test booklets ('85, 20 pages) or Mathematics test booklets ('85, 12 pages), Form L, including teacher's directions.

3) *Primary* 1. Grades 1.5–2.9; 15 scores: Reading (Vocabulary, Word Recognition Skills, Reading Comprehension, Total), Mathematics (Mathematics Concepts, Mathematics Problem Solving, Mathematics Computation, Total), Language (Spelling, Language, Total), Science, Social Studies, Total Basic Battery, Total Complete Battery; 2 editions; 2 forms; $20 per 100 practice tests and directions; $59 per set of keys for Complete/Basic Battery hand-scorable test booklets or to hand score NCS machine-scorable test booklets; $33 per keys for Reading test; $22 per keys for Mathematics test (specify Form L or Form M for each); $4.50 per Complete/Basic Battery directions for administering, Form L ('85, 54 pages); $4.50 per Complete/Basic Battery directions for administering, Form M ('86, 54 pages); $4.50 per directions for administering Reading test, Form L ('85, 30 pages); $4.50 per directions for administering Reading test, Form M ('86, 26 pages); $4.50 per directions for administering Mathematics test, Form L ('85, 26 pages); $4.50 per directions for administering Mathematics test, Form M ('86, 28 pages); 215(315) minutes in 10 sittings.

(*a*) Hand-Scorable Edition. $49 per 35 Basic Battery test booklets, Form L ('85, 40 pages) or Form M ('86, 40 pages); $50 per 35 Complete Battery test booklets, Form L ('85, 48 pages) or Form M ('86, 48 pages); $32 per 35 Reading test booklets, Form L ('85, 22 pages) or Form M ('86, 22 pages); $32 per 35 Mathematics test booklets, Form L ('85, 15 pages) or Form M ('86, 15 pages), all including teacher directions and class record.

(*b*) NCS Machine-Scorable Edition. $73 per 35 Basic Battery test booklets, Form L ('85, 40 pages) or Form M ('86, 40 pages); $80 per 35 Complete Battery test booklets, Form L ('85, 48 pages) or Form M ('86, 48 pages); $49 per 35 Reading test booklets, Form L ('85, 22 pages); $49 per 35 Mathematics test booklets, Form L ('85, 15 pages), all including teacher directions.

4) *Primary* 2. Grades 2.5–3.9; 15 scores: same as 3 above; 2 editions; 2 forms; $20 per 100 practice tests and directions; $69 per set of keys for Complete/Basic Battery hand-scorable test booklets or to hand score NCS machine-scorable test booklets, $37 per keys for Reading test, $22 per keys for Mathematics test (specify Form L or Form M for each); $4.50 per Complete/Basic Battery directions for administering, Form L ('85, 52 pages) or Form M ('86, 52 pages); $4.50 per directions for administering Reading test, Form L ('85, 26 pages) or Form M ('86, 30 pages); $4.50 per directions for administering Mathematics test, Form L ('85, 24 pages) or Form M ('86, 24 pages); 225(315) minutes in 8 sittings.

(*a*) Hand-Scorable Edition. $57 per 35 Basic Battery test booklets, Form L ('85, 44 pages) or Form M ('86, 44 pages); $60 per 35 Complete Battery test booklets, Form L ('85, 52 pages) or Form M ('86, 52 pages); $32 per 35 Reading test booklets, Form L ('85, 26 pages) or Form M ('86, 26 pages); $32 per 35 Mathematics test booklets, Form L ('85, 13 pages) or Form M ('86, 13 pages), all including teacher's directions and class record.

(*b*) NCS Machine-Scorable Edition. $77 per 35 Basic Battery test booklets, Form L ('85, 44 pages) or Form M ('86, 44 pages); $84 per 35 Complete Battery test booklets, Form L ('85, 52 pages) or Form M ('86, 52 pages); $49 per 35 Reading test booklets, Form L ('85, 28 pages); $49 per 35 Mathematics test booklets, Form L ('85, 16 pages); all including teacher's directions.

5) *Elementary*. Grades 3.5–4.9; 16 scores: same as 3 above plus Research Skills; 2 editions; 2

forms; $25 per 100 practice tests and directions; $69 per set of keys for Complete/Basic Battery hand-scorable test booklets or to hand score NCS machine-scorable test booklets, $33 per keys for Reading test, $22 per keys for Mathematics test (specify Form L or Form M for each); $14 per Complete/Basic Battery keys for hand-scorable answer folders (specify Form L or Form M); $8 per Reading test or Mathematics test keys for hand-scorable answer folder (specify Form L or Form M for each); $15 per Complete/Basic Battery keys for hand scoring NCS machine-scorable answer folders (specify Form L or Form M); $8 per Reading test or Mathematics test keys for hand scoring NCS machine-scorable answer folders (specify Form L or Form M for each); $36 per 100 Complete/Basic Battery Form L/M hand-scorable answer folders including 3 class records; $27 per 100 Reading test, Form L/M or Mathematics test, Form L/M hand-scorable answer folders including 3 class records; $36 per 100 Complete/Basic Battery, Form L/M NCS answer folders; $27 per 100 Reading test or Mathematics test, Form L/M NCS answer folders; $730 per 1,500 continuous form NCS answer folders, Form L/M; $4.50 per Complete/Basic Battery ('85, 47 pages), Reading test ('85, 30 pages), or Mathematics test ('85, 28 pages), Form L/M directions for administering; 254(344) minutes in 8 sittings.

(*a*) Hand-Scorable Edition. $57 per 35 Basic Battery reusable test booklets, Form L ('85, 42 pages) or Form M ('86, 42 pages); $60 per 35 Complete Battery reusable test booklets, Form L ('85, 56 pages) or Form M ('86, 56 pages); $32 per 35 Reading test reusable test booklets, Form L ('85, 22 pages) or Form M ('86, 22 pages); $32 per 35 Mathematics test reusable test booklets, Form L ('85, 14 pages) or Form M ('86, 14 pages), all including teacher's directions and class record.

(*b*) NCS Machine-Scorable Edition. $77 per 35 Basic Battery test booklets, Form L ('85, 42 pages) or Form M ('86, 42 pages); $84 per 35 Complete Battery test booklets, Form L ('85, 56 pages) or Form M ('86, 56 pages); $49 per 35 Reading test booklets, Form L ('85, 22 pages); $49 per 35 Mathematics test booklets, Form L ('85, 14 pages), all including teacher's directions.

6) *Intermediate*. Grades 5.0–6.9; 15 scores: Reading (Vocabulary, Reading Comprehension, Total), Mathematics (Mathematics Concepts, Mathematics Problem Solving, Mathematics Computation, Total), Language (Spelling, Language, Total), Science, Social Studies, Research Skills, Total Basic Battery, Total Complete Battery; 2 forms; $25 per 100 Intermediate/Advanced practice tests and directions; $57 per 35 Basic Battery reusable test booklets, Form L ('85, 38 pages) or Form M ('86, 38 pages) and teacher's directions; $60 per 35 Complete Battery reusable test booklets, Form L ('85, 53 pages) or Form M ('86, 53 pages) and teacher's directions; $32 per 35 Reading test reusable test booklets, Form L ('85, 16 pages) or Form M ('86, 16 pages) and teacher's directions; $32 per 35 Mathematics test reusable test booklets, Form L ('85, 14 pages) or Form M ('86, 14 pages) and teacher's directions; $36 per 100 Complete/Basic Battery, Form L/M hand-scorable answer folders including 3 class records; $27 per 100 Reading test, Form L/M hand-scorable answer folders including 3 class records; $27 per 100 Mathematics test, Form L/M hand-scorable answer folders including 3 class records; $36 per 100 Complete/Basic Battery, Form L/M NCS answer folders; $27 per 100 Reading test, Form L/M NCS answer folders; $27 per 100 Mathematics test, Form L/M NCS answer folders; $730 per 1,500 Form L/M continuous form NCS answer folders; $14 per set of keys for Complete/Basic Battery hand-scorable answer folders (specify Form L or Form M); $8 per set of keys for Reading test or Mathematics test hand-scorable answer folders (specify Form L or Form M); $15 per set of keys for hand scoring NCS machine-scorable Complete/Basic Battery answer folders (specify Form L or Form M); $8 per set of keys for hand scoring NCS machine-scorable Reading test or Mathematics test answer folders (specify Form L or Form M for each); $4.50 per Complete/Basic Battery, Forms L & M, directions for administering ('85, 36 pages); $4.50 per Mathematics test, Forms L & M, directions for administering ('85, 24 pages); $4.50 per Reading test, Forms L & M, directions for administering ('85, 21 pages); 244(334) minutes in 9 sittings.

7) *Advanced* 1. Grades 7.0–9.9; 15 scores: same as 6 above; 2 forms; $37 per 35 Basic Battery reusable test booklets, Form L ('85, 34 pages) or Form M ('86, 34 pages) and teacher's directions; $50 per 35 Complete Battery reusable test booklets, Form L ('85, 46 pages) or Form M ('86, 46 pages) and teacher's directions; $32 per 35 Reading test reusable test booklets, Form L ('85, 15 pages) or Form M ('86, 15 pages) and teacher's directions; $32 per 35 Mathematics test reusable test booklets, Form L ('85, 12 pages) or Form M ('86, 12 pages) and teacher's directions; $36 per 100 Complete/Basic Battery, Form L/M hand-scor-

able answer folders including 3 class records; $27 per 100 Reading test, Form L/M hand-scorable answer folders including 3 class records; $27 per 100 Mathematics test, Form L/M hand-scorable answer folders including 3 class records; $36 per 100 Complete/Basic Battery, Form L/M NCS answer folders; $27 per 100 Reading test or Mathematics test, Form L/M NCS answer folders; $730 per 1,500 continuous form NCS answer folders, Form L/M; $14 per Complete/Basic Battery keys for hand-scorable answer folders (specify Form L or Form M); $8 per Reading test or Mathematics test keys for hand-scorable answer folders (specify Form L or Form M); $15 per Complete/Basic Battery NCS machine-scorable answer folders (specify Form L or Form M); $8 per Reading test or Mathematics test keys for hand scoring NCS machine-scorable answer folders (specify Form L or Form M); $4.50 per Complete/Basic Battery, Forms L & M, directions for administering ('85, 35 pages); $4.50 per Reading test, Forms L & M, directions for administering ('85, 22 pages); $4.50 per Mathematics test, Forms L & M, directions for administering ('85, 24 pages); 229(309) minutes in 8 sittings.

8) *Advanced* 2. Grades 10.0–12.9; 12 scores: Reading (Vocabulary, Reading Comprehension, Total), Mathematics, Language (Spelling, Language, Total), Science, Social Studies, Research Skills, Total Basic Battery, Total Complete Battery; 2 forms; $49 per 35 Basic Battery reusable test booklets, Form L ('85, 26 pages) or Form M ('86, 26 pages) and teacher's directions; $50 per 35 Complete Battery reusable test booklets, Form L ('85, 39 pages) or Form M ('86, 39 pages) and teacher's directions; $32 per 35 Reading test reusable test booklets, Form L ('85, 12 pages) or Form M ('86, 12 pages) and teacher's directions; $32 per 35 Mathematics test reusable test booklets, Form L ('85, 8 pages) or Form M ('86, 8 pages) and teacher's directions; $36 per 100 Complete/Basic Battery, Form L/M hand-scorable answer folders including 3 class records; $27 per 100 Reading test or Mathematics test, Form L/M hand-scorable answer folders including 3 class records; $36 per 100 Complete/Basic Battery, Form L/M NCS answer folders; $27 per 100 Reading test or Mathematics test, Form L/M NCS answer folders; $730 per 1,500 continuous form NCS answer folders, Form L/M; $14 per Complete/Basic Battery keys for hand-scorable answer folders (specify Form L or Form M); $8 per Reading test or Mathematics test keys for hand-scorable answer folders (specify Form L or Form M for each); $15 per Complete/Basic Battery keys for hand scoring NCS machine-scorable answer folders (specify Form L or Form M); $8 per Reading test or Mathematics test keys for hand scoring NCS machine-scorable answer folders (specify Form L or Form M for each); $4.50 per Complete/Basic Battery, Forms L & M, directions for administering ('85, 31 pages); $4.50 per Reading test, Forms L & M, directions for administering ('85, 22 pages); $4.50 per Mathematics test, Forms L & M, directions for administering ('85, 20 pages); 175(235) minutes in 6 sittings.

b) DIAGNOSTIC BATTERIES. 1986; 3 tests; designed as instructional planning tools which are statistically equated to scores in the same domain obtained from the Survey battery; all hand-scorable test packages include directions for administering and class record; all NCS machine-scorable test packages include directions for administering, NCS accessory documents, and order for scoring service; all hand-scorable answer document packages include 3 class records; all NCS machine-scorable answer document packages include NCS accessory documents and order for scoring service.

1) *Reading Diagnostic Tests*. Grades K.5–1.9, 1.5–2.9, 2.5–3.9, 3.5–4.9, 5.0–6.9, 7.0–9.9; 6 overlapping levels; 2 forms for all but Primer level; $25 per technical manual ('87).

(*a*) Primer. Grades K.5–1.9; 8 scores: Visual Discrimination, Letter Recognition, Auditory Discrimination, Sight Vocabulary, Phoneme/Grapheme: Consonants, Vocabulary in Context, Reading Comprehension, Total; $21 per 100 practice tests and teacher's directions; $44 per 35 hand-scorable test booklets, Form L ('86, 32 pages); $60 per 35 NCS machine-scorable test booklets, Form L ('86, 32 pages); $37 per set of keys for hand scoring test booklets; $2.50 per class record; $4 per directions for administering ('86, 40 pages); $15 per manual for interpreting ('87, 144 pages); $10 per norms booklet ('86, 35 pages); $7 per examination kit containing test booklet and directions for administering; 133(203) minutes in 7 sittings.

(*b*) Primary 1. Grades 1.5–2.9; 8 scores: Auditory Discrimination, Sight Vocabulary, Phoneme/Grapheme: Consonants, Phoneme/Grapheme: Vowels, Vocabulary in Context, Word Part Clues, Reading Comprehension, Total; $21 per 100 practice tests with teacher's directions; $44 per 35 hand-scorable test booklets, Form L or Form M ('86, 36 pages); $66 per 35 NCS machine-scorable test booklets, Form L or Form M ('86, 36 pages); $42 per set of keys for hand scoring test booklets (specify Form L or

Form M); $2.50 per class record; $4.50 per directions for administering, Form L or Form M ('86, 40 pages); $15 per manual for interpreting ('87, 156 pages); $15 per norms booklet ('86, 46 pages); $7 per examination kit containing test booklet and directions for administering; 52(212) minutes in 6 sittings.

(*c*) Primary 2. Grades 2.5–3.9; 7 scores: Sight Vocabulary, Phoneme/Grapheme: Consonants, Phoneme/Grapheme: Vowels, Vocabulary in Context, Word Part Clues, Reading Comprehension, Total; $21 per 100 practice tests with teacher's directions; $44 per 35 hand-scorable test booklets, Form L or Form M ('86, 36 pages); $66 per 35 NCS machine-scorable test booklets, Form L or Form M ('86, 36 pages); $42 per set of keys for hand scoring test booklets (specify Form L or Form M); $2.50 per class record; $4.50 per directions for administering, Form L or Form M ('86, 32 pages); $15 per manual for interpreting ('87, 144 pages); $15 per norms booklet ('86, 46 pages); $7 per examination kit containing test booklet and directions for administering; 122(172) minutes in 5 sittings.

(*d*) Elementary. Grades 3.5–4.9; 7 scores: Phoneme/Grapheme: Consonants, Phoneme/Grapheme: Vowels, Vocabulary in Context, Word Part Clues, Rate of Comprehension, Reading Comprehension, Total; $28 per 100 practice tests with teacher's directions; $44 per 35 hand-scorable test booklets, Form L or Form M ('86, 28 pages); $66 per 35 NCS machine-scorable test booklets, Form L or Form M ('86, 28 pages); $32 per set of keys for hand scoring test booklets (specify Form L or Form M); $9 per set of keys for scoring hand-scorable answer documents (specify Form L or Form M); $12 per set of keys for hand scoring NCS machine-scorable answer documents (specify Form L or Form M); $47 per 100 hand-scorable answer documents (specify Form L or Form M); $55 per 100 NCS machine-scorable answer documents (specify Form L or Form M); $2.50 per class record; $4.50 per directions for administering, Forms L/M ('86, 36 pages); $15 per manual for interpreting ('87, 151 pages); $15 per norms booklet ('87, 47 pages); $7 per examination kit containing test booklet and directions for administering; 124(174) minutes in 5 sittings.

(*e*) Intermediate. Grades 5.0–6.9; 8 scores: Phoneme/Grapheme: Consonants, Phoneme/Grapheme: Vowels, Vocabulary in Context, Word Part Clues, Rate of Comprehension, Skimming and Scanning, Reading Comprehension, Total; $28 per 100 Intermediate/Advanced practice tests with teacher's directions; $44 per 35 test booklets, Form L or Form M ('86, 16 pages); $9 per set of keys for scoring hand-scorable answer documents (specify Form L or Form M); $12 per set of keys for hand scoring NCS machine-scorable answer documents (specify Form L or Form M); $55 per 100 NCS machine-scorable answer documents (specify Form L or Form M); $47 per 100 hand-scorable answer documents (specify Form L or Form M); $2.50 per class record; $4.50 per directions for administering, Forms L/M ('86, 32 pages); $15 per manual for interpreting ('87, 160 pages); $15 per norms booklet ('87, 56 pages); $7 per examination kit containing test booklet, directions for administering, and hand-scorable answer documents; 134(184) minutes in 5 sittings.

(*f*) Advanced 1. Grades 7.0–9.9; 5 scores: Vocabulary in Context, Rate of Comprehension, Skimming and Scanning, Reading Comprehension, Total; $44 per 35 test booklets, Form L or Form M ('86, 16 pages); $9 per set of keys for scoring hand-scorable answer documents (specify Form L or Form M); $12 per set of keys for hand scoring NCS machine-scorable answer documents (specify Form L or Form M); $47 per 100 hand-scorable answer documents (specify Form L or Form M); $55 per 100 NCS machine-scorable answer documents (specify Form L or Form M); $2.50 per class record; $4.50 per directions for administering, Forms L/M ('86, 24 pages); $15 per manual for interpreting ('87, 144 pages); $15 per norms booklet ('86, 52 pages); $7 per examination kit containing test booklet, directions for administering, and hand-scorable answer documents; 79(109) minutes in 3 sittings.

2) *Mathematics Diagnostic Test*. Grades 1.0–2.9, 2.5–3.9, 3.5–4.9, 5.0–6.9, 7.0–9.9; 5 overlapping levels; 1 form (Form L); $15 per technical manual ('88, 107 pages).

(*a*) Primary 1. Grades 1.0–2.9; 5 scores: Numeration, Geometry and Measurement, Problem Solving, Computation: Whole Numbers, Total; $21 per 100 practice tests with teacher's directions, $44 per 35 hand-scorable test booklets ('86, 25 pages); $66 per 35 NCS machine-scorable test booklets ('86, 26 pages); $34 per set of keys for hand scoring test booklets; $2.50 per class record; $4.50 per directions for administering ('86, 32 pages); $15 per manual for interpreting ('87, 120 pages); $15 per norms booklet

('86, 31 pages); $7 per examination kit containing test booklet and directions for administering; 130(190) minutes in 6 sittings.

(*b*) Primary 2. Grades 2.5–3.9; 5 scores: same as *a* above; $21 per 100 practice tests and teacher's directions; $44 per 35 hand-scorable test booklets ('86, 22 pages); $66 per 35 NCS machine-scorable test booklets ('86, 22 pages); $34 per set of keys for hand scoring test booklets; $4.50 per directions for administering ('86, 29 pages); $15 per manual for interpreting ('87, 120 pages); $15 per norms booklet ('86, 29 pages); $7 per examination kit containing test booklet and directions for administering; 117(159) minutes in 4 sittings.

(*c*) Elementary. Grades 3.5–4.9; 5 scores: same as *a* above; $28 per 100 practice tests and teacher's directions; $44 per 35 hand-scorable test booklets ('86, 24 pages); $66 per 35 NCS machine-scorable test booklets ('86, 24 pages); $34 per set of keys for hand scoring test booklets; $9 per set of keys for scoring hand-scorable answer documents; $12 per set of keys for hand scoring NCS machine-scorable answer documents; $45 per 100 hand-scorable answer documents; $45 per 100 NCS machine-scorable answer documents; $2.50 per class record; $4.50 per directions for administering ('86, 30 pages); $15 per manual for interpreting ('87, 120 pages); $15 per norms booklet ('86, 30 pages); $7 per examination kit containing test booklet and directions for administering; 127(167) minutes in 4 sittings.

(*d*) Intermediate. Grades 5.0–6.9; 7 scores: Numeration, Geometry and Measurement, Problem Solving, Computation: Whole Numbers, Computation: Decimals and Fractions, Graphs and Statistics, Total; $28 per 100 Intermediate/Advanced 1 practice tests and teacher's directions; $45 per 35 test booklets ('86, 27 pages); $9 per set of keys for scoring hand-scorable answer documents; $12 per set of keys for hand scoring NCS machine-scorable answer documents; $45 per 100 hand-scorable answer documents; $45 per 100 NCS machine-scorable answer documents; $2.50 per class record; $4.50 per directions for administering ('86, 31 pages); $15 per manual for interpreting ('87, 140 pages); $15 per norms booklet ('86, 30 pages); $7 per examination kit containing test booklet, directions for administration, and hand-scorable answer documents; 175(235) minutes in 6 sittings.

(*e*) Advanced 1. Grades 7.0–9.9; 7 scores: same as *d* above; $44 per 35 test booklets ('86, 23 pages); $9 per set of keys for scoring hand-scorable answer documents; $12 per set of keys for hand scoring NCS machine-scorable answer documents; $45 per 100 hand-scorable answer documents; $45 per 100 NCS machine-scorable answer documents; $2.50 per class record; $4.50 per directions for administering ('86, 30 pages); $15 per manual for interpreting ('87, 140 pages); $15 per norms booklet ('86, 36 pages); $7 per examination kit containing test booklet, directions for administration, and hand-scorable answer documents; 137(187) minutes in 5 sittings.

3) *Language Diagnostic Tests*. Grades 1.0–2.9, 2.5–3.9, 3.5–4.9, 5.0–6.9, 7.0–9.9; 5 overlapping levels; 1 form (Form L); $15 per technical manual ('87).

(*a*) Primary 1. Grades 1.0–2.9; 7 scores: Listening Comprehension, Punctuation and Capitalization, Usage, Written Expression, Spelling, Study Skills, Total; $20 per 100 practice tests and teacher's directions; $55 per 35 hand-scorable test booklets ('86, 20 pages); $77 per 35 NCS machine-scorable test booklets ('86, 19 pages); $36 per set of keys for hand scoring test booklets; $2.50 per class record; $4.50 per directions for administering ('86, 40 pages); $15 per manual for interpreting ('87, 112 pages); $15 per norms booklets ('86, 31 pages); $7 per examination kit containing test booklet and directions for administering; 115(155) minutes in 4 sittings.

(*b*) Primary 2. Grades 2.5–3.9; 7 scores; same as *a* above; $20 per 100 practice tests and teacher's directions; $55 per 35 hand-scorable test booklets ('86, 26 pages); $77 per 35 NCS machine-scorable test booklets ('86, 26 pages); $36 per set of keys for hand scoring test booklets; $2.50 per class record; $4.50 per directions for administering ('86, 39 pages); $15 per manual for interpreting ('87, 120 pages); $15 per norms booklet ('86, 29 pages); $7 per examination kit containing test booklet and directions for administering; 130(190) minutes in 6 sittings.

(*c*) Elementary. Grades 3.5–4.9; 7 scores: same as *a* above; $28 per 100 practice tests and teacher's directions; $55 per 35 hand-scorable test booklets ('86, 30 pages); $77 per 35 NCS machine-scorable test booklets ('86, 31 pages); $42 per set of keys for hand scoring test booklets; $12 per set of keys for scoring hand-scorable answer documents; $15 per set of keys for hand scoring NCS machine-scorable answer documents; $49 per 100 hand-scorable answer documents; $55 per 100 NCS machine-scorable answer documents; $2.50 per class record; $4.50 per directions for administering ('86, 36 pages); $15 per manual for interpreting ('87, 111 pages); $15 per norms booklet ('86, 31 pages); $7 per examination kit containing test booklet and directions for administering; 150(210) minutes in 6 sittings.

(*d*) Intermediate. Grades 5.0–6.9; 6 scores: Punctuation and Capitalization, Usage, Written Expression, Spelling, Study Skills, Total; $28 per 100 Intermediate/Advanced 1 practice tests with teacher's directions; $55 per 35 test booklets ('86, 28 pages); $12 per set of keys for scoring hand-scorable answer documents; $15 per set of keys for hand scoring NCS machine-scorable answer documents; $49 per 100 hand-scorable answer documents; $55 per 100 NCS machine-scorable answer documents; $2.50 per class record; $4.50 per directions for administering ('86, 29 pages); $15 per manual for interpreting ('87, 112 pages); $15 per norms booklet ('86, 31 pages); $7 per examination kit containing test booklet, directions for administering, and hand-scorable answer documents; 120(160) minutes in 5 sittings.

(*e*) Advanced 1. Grades 7.0–9.9; 6 scores: same as *d* above; $55 per 35 test booklets ('86, 23 pages); $12 per set of keys for scoring hand-scorable answer documents; $15 per set of keys for hand scoring NCS machine-scorable answer documents; $49 per 100 hand-scorable answer documents; $55 per 100 NCS machine-scorable answer documents; $2.50 per class records; $4.50 per directions for administering ('86, 27 pages); $15 per manual for interpreting ('87, 112 pages); $15 per norms booklet ('86, 36 pages); $7 per examination kit containing test booklet, directions for administering, and hand-scorable answer documents; 105(155) minutes in 5 sittings.

c) WRITING TEST. Purpose: A free-response, work-sample test that provides norm-referenced information about students' writing achievement. Grades 2.5–4.9, 5.0–8.9, 9.0–12.9; 1986; 3 levels; 2 forms; test may be sent to publisher where it will be holistically and/or analytically scored; $15 per manual for interpreting ('87, 54 pages); $20 per norms and technical information booklet ('87, 51 pages); 20(30) minutes.

1) *Elementary*. Grades 2.5–4.9; $15 per 35 test folders, Form L or Form M ('86, 4 pages).

2) *Middle-School/Junior High*. Grades 5.0–8.9; $15 per 35 test folders, Form L or Form M ('86, 4 pages).

3) *High School*. Grades 9.0–12.9; $15 per 35 test folders, Form L or Form M ('86, 4 pages).

For reviews by Edward H. Haertel and Robert L. Linn see 9:699 (30 references); see also T3:1473 (89 references); for reviews by Norman E. Gronlund and Richard M. Wolf and an excerpted review by Joseph A. Wingard and Peter M. Bentler of an earlier edition, see 8:22 (41 references); see also T2:22 (20 references) and 7:14 (25 references); for reviews by Henry S. Dyer and Warren G. Findley of an earlier edition, see 6:16 (16 refernces); for a review by Warren G. Findley, see 4:18 (10 references); see also 3:13 (7 references); for reviews by E. V. Pullias and Hugh B. Wood, see 2:1189 (3 references); for reviews by Jack W. Dunlap, Charles W. Odell, and Richard Ledgerwood, see 1:874. For reviews of subtests, see 8:283 (1 review), 8:732 (2 reviews), 6:627 (2 reviews), 6:797 (1 review), 6:877 (2 reviews), 6:970 (2 reviews), 4:416 (1 review), 4:543 (2 reviews), 2:1458.1 (2 reviews), 2:1551 (1 review), 1:892 (2 reviews), and 1:1105 (2 reviews).

TEST REFERENCES

1. Sherer, M. (1983). The incarceration period and educational achievements of juvenile delinquents. *Criminal Justice and Behavior*, 10, 109-120.

2. White, M., & Miller, S. R. (1983). Dyslexia: A term in search of a definition. *The Journal of Special Education*, 17, 5-10. Edition (1978)):

3. Chandler, H. N. (1984). The American public school: Yes, we have no standards. *Journal of Learning Disabilities*, 17, 186-187.

4. Farr, R., & Beck, M. (1984). Validating the "instructional reading level" score of the Metropolitan Achievement Tests. *Journal of Research and Development in Education*, 17 (2), 55-64.

5. Farr, R., Courtland, M. C., & Beck, M. D. (1984). Scholastic aptitude test performance and reading ability. *Journal of Reading*, 28, 208-214.

6. Flexer, B. K. (1984). Predicting eighth-grade algebra achievement. *Journal for Research in Mathematics Education*, 15, 352-360.

7. Fredrick, D., Mishler, C., & Hogan, T. P. (1984). College freshman mathematics abilities: Adults versus younger students. *School Science and Mathematics*, 84, 327-336.

8. Ham, R., Fucci, D., Cantrell, J., & Harris, D. (1984). Residual effect of delayed auditory feedback on normal speaking rate and fluency. *Perceptual and Motor Skills*, 59, 61-62.

9. Hanna, G. (1984). The use of a factor-analytic model for assessing the validity of group comparisons. *Journal of Educational Measurement*, 21, 191-199.

10. Horn, W. F., & O'Donnell, J. P. (1984). Early identification of learning disabilities: A comparison of two methods. *Journal of Educational Psychology*, 76, 1106-1118.

11. Katz, I., & Singer, H. (1984). The substrata-factor of reading: Subsystem patterns underlying achievement in beginning reading. *National Reading Conference Yearbook*, 33, 298-307.

12. Lindeman, D. P., & Goodstein, H. A. (1984). An evaluation of the Yellow Brick Road Test through a full prediction-performance comparison matrix. *Journal of School Psychology*, 22, 111-117.

13. Lloyd, J., & Barenblatt, L. (1984). Intrinsic intellectuality: Its relations to social class, intelligence, and achievement. *Journal of Personality and Social Psychology*, 46, 646-654.

14. Olejnik, S. F., & Algina, J. (1984). Parametric ANCOVA and the rank transform ANCOVA when the data are conditionally non-normal and heteroscedastic. *Journal of Educational Statistics*, 9, 129-149.

15. Roberge, J. J., & Flexer, B. K. (1984). Cognitive style, operativity, and reading achievement. *American Educational Research Journal*, 21, 227-236.

16. Sadoski, M., & Page, W. D. (1984). Miscue combinations scores and reading comprehension: Analysis and comparison. *Reading World*, 24 (1), 43-53.

17. Steele, K. J., Battista, M. T., & Krockover, G. H. (1984). Using microcomputer-assisted mathematics instruction to develop computer literacy. *School Science and Mathematics*, 84, 119-124.

18. Swanson, B. B., & Mason, G. E. (1984). Measuring early reading progress: Some non-traditional measures. *Journal of Educational Research*, 78, 90-96.

19. Swanson, H. L. (1984). Effect of cognitive effort on learning disabled and nondisabled readers' recall. *Journal of Learning Disabilities*, 17, 67-74.

20. Swanson, H. L. (1984). Effects of cognitive effort and word distinctiveness on learning disabled and nondisabled readers' recall. *Journal of Educational Psychology*, 76, 894-908.

21. Weithorn, C. J., Kagen, E., & Marcus, M. (1984). The relationship of activity level ratings and cognitive inpulsivity to task performance and academic achievement. *The Journal of Child Psychology and Psychiatry and Allied Disciplines*, 25, 587-606.

22. Wilkinson, L. C. (1984). Research currents: Peer group talk in elementary school. *Language Arts*, 61, 164-169.

23. Evans, E. D. (1985). Longitudinal follow-up assessment of differential preschool experience for low income minority group children. *Journal of Educational Research*, 78, 197-202.

24. Lemons, R., & Malatesha, R. N. (1985). Improving reading through training to listen. *Perceptual and Motor Skills*, 60, 788-790.

25. Limbrick, E., McNaughton, S., & Glynn, T. (1985). Reading gains for underachieving tutors and tutees in a cross-age tutoring programme. *The Journal of Child Psychology and Psychiatry and Allied Disciplines*, 26, 939-953.

26. Medina, M., Jr., Saldate, M., IV, & Mishra, S. P. (1985). The sustaining effects of bilingual instruction: A follow-up study. *Journal of Instructional Psychology*, 12, 132-139.

27. Mitman, A. L. (1985). Teachers' differential behavior toward higher and lower achieving students and its relation to selected teacher characteristics. *Journal of Educational Psychology*, 77, 149-161.

28. Saldate, M., IV, Mishra, S. P., & Medina, M., Jr. (1985). Bilingual instruction and academic achievement: A longitudinal study. *Journal of Instructional Psychology*, 12, 24-30.

29. Schmidt, S., & Perino, J. (1985). Kindergarten screening results as predictors of academic achievement, potential, and placement in second grade. *Psychology in the Schools*, 22, 146-151.

30. Siders, J. A., Siders, J. Z., & Wilson, R. M. (1985). A screening procedure to identify children having difficulties in arithmetic. *Journal for Research in Mathematics Education*, 16, 356-363.

31. Sizemore, B. A. (1985). Pitfalls and promises of effective schools research. *Journal of Negro Education*, 54, 269-288.

32. Swanson, B. B. (1985). Teacher judgments of first-graders' reading enthusiasm. *Reading Research and Instruction*, 25, 41-46.

33. Tolfa, D., Scruggs, T. E., & Bennion, K. (1985). Format changes in reading achievement tests: Implications for learning disabled students. *Psychology in the Schools*, 22, 387-391.

34. Weithorn, C. J., & Marcus, M. (1985). High-active children and achievement tests: A two-year follow-up. *Psychology in the Schools*, 22, 449-458.

35. Baglin, R. F. (1986). A problem in calculating group scores on norm-referenced tests. *Journal of Educational Measurement*, 23, 57-68.

36. Dirgi, D. R. (1986). Does the Rasch model really work for multiple choice items? Not if you look closely. *Journal of Educational Measurement*, 23, 283-298.

37. Helfeldt, J. P., Henk, W. A., & Fotos, A. (1986). A test of alternative cloze test formats at the sixth-grade level. *The Journal of Educational Research*, 79, 216-221.

38. Hilgers, T. L. (1986). How children change as critical evaluators of writing: Four three-year case studies. *Research in the Teaching of English*, 20, 36-55.

39. Ritter, S., & Idol-Maestas, L. (1986). Teaching middle school students to use a test-taking strategy. *The Journal of Educational Research*, 79, 350-357.

40. Sadoski, M., & Lee, S. (1986). Reading comprehension and miscue combination scores: Further analysis and comparison. *Reading Research and Instruction*, 25, 160-167.

41. Stanovich, K. E., Nathan, R. G., & Vala-Rossi, M. (1986). Developmental changes in the cognitive correlates of reading ability and the developmental lag hypothesis. *Reading Research Quarterly*, 21, 267-283.

42. Wintre, M. G. (1986). Challenging the assumption of generalized academic losses over summer. *The Journal of Educational Research*, 79, 308-312.

43. Zimmerman, B. J., & Pons, M. M. (1986). Development of a structured interview for assessing student use of self-regulated learning strategies. *American Educational Research Journal*, 23, 614-628.

44. Noble, E. J. (1987). Redressing the negative influence of socioeconomic status gender in a treatment facility school. *The Alberta Journal of Educational Research*, 33, 137-143.

Review of the Metropolitan Achievement Test, Sixth Edition by ANTHONY J. NITKO, Professor of Education, University of Pittsburgh, Pittsburgh, PA:

The Sixth Edition of the Metropolitan Achievement Test (MAT6) measures pupils' command of basic skills in the curricular areas of vocabulary, reading, mathematics, spelling, language, science, social studies, and writing. Selected items from several curricular area subtests are also used to form separate research and higher-order thinking skills scores. Most standardized test batteries claim to serve two purposes: (*a*) improving within classroom decisions, such as helping to diagnose each student's strengths and weaknesses in an area, and (*b*) improving educational decision making that occurs outside the classroom, such as evaluating programs, curricula, and schools. The MAT6 is no exception in this regard. Unlike many other batteries, however, the MAT6 reflects exceptional effort towards attainment of these purposes.

As readers of the *Mental Measurements Yearbooks* may notice, the claim that a single multilevel survey battery can serve both goals cited above has never been substantiated by classroom-level empirical research. Most standardized multilevel survey tests serve the second purpose better than the first, because they contain too few items that correspond to the broad array of within classroom instructional objectives that a student must attain in a curricular area. The MAT6, as did its predecessor MAT5, uses a two-stage assessment strategy. The first stage is the Survey Test Battery and the second is a Diagnostic Battery focusing on language, mathematics, and reading skills. The Survey Battery measures educational development in a general way and is intended to be used for making general statements about a student's achievements and for facilitating school, curriculum, and program evaluation decisions. The more detailed and highly specific information about a student's performance in the curricular areas of language usage, mathematics, and reading—information that is necessary for classroom planning and individualized instruction—is obtained from the Diagnostic Test Battery.

The advantage of the MAT6 system is that the Survey and the Diagnostic tests are connected statistically and substantively so they work together in a two-stage testing program. For example, the common area tests were developed together; the Survey tests were built by sampling items from the Diagnostic tests; the common area tests were normed simultaneously, the interpretive materials were integrated into a unified scheme; and the two-stages are based on a common philosophy, format, and reporting procedure.

A disadvantage of this two-stage testing procedure is the large amount of time needed to complete both stages and the possibly long turnaround time between giving the tests and receiving the computerized analyses. Because the two components may be administered separately, a school district may find it feasible to administer the Survey subtests only on a sampling basis and to use the Diagnostic Battery for within classroom instructional improvement.

MULTILEVEL NATURE OF THE TESTS. The survey battery spans kindergarten through 12th grade with eight levels. Not all curricular areas are measured at every level (see the test entry). Reading, Mathematics, and Language begin at the Preprimer level with dictated tests. Vocabulary is added at the Primer level. Spelling, Science, Social Studies, and Higher Order Thinking Skills are added at the Primary 1 level. Research Skills are added at the Elementary level. The Writing Test, which is a supplement to the MAT6, spans grades 2 through 12.

A presumed advantage of using a multilevel battery is its potential for out-of-level testing (i.e., administering a test at a level that is closer to a student's functional level of educational development than is the student's actual grade placement). It would be difficult to recommend out-of-level testing with the MAT6 because of practical considerations stemming from the tests' design. First, there are no validated locator tests available, thus leaving the burden of selecting the appropriate test level for a student entirely on the shoulders of the test coordinator and/or the teacher. Second, the discrete nature of many of the objectives for a level make it difficult to test comparable material with easier items. Third, if out-of-level testing were to be done on a wide scale, students would need to be removed from their normal classroom locations and regrouped by level for purposes of administering the tests. With few exceptions, within a curricular area, each level has a different length, testing time, directions, sample items, amount of dictation, and thematic appeal to students. The excellent Test Coordinator's Handbook notes these difficulties, but is less than emphatic in discouraging out-of-level testing.

VALIDITY. The MAT6 materials present evidence of the validity of some of the score interpretations recommended by the authors, but not all of the important ones. The authors' rationale for including each MAT6 subtest and the contents of the instructional domain measured by each subtest are exceptionally well explained in the series of Teacher's Manual for Interpreting that accompany both the Survey and Diagnostic Batteries. These are so well done that it would be foolhardy to attempt to use any component of the MAT6 without having read the appropriate Teacher's Manual. The manual thoroughly explains the authors' rationale for including content and skills, their view of the stages of educational development within each curricular area, the degree to which their view matches with current textbook series and classroom practices, the specific objectives that are tested in each curricular area, how they derived special scores for an area (e.g., independent, instructional, and frustration levels), why each type of test item format is used, and how the test results may be used to teach the skills within the area. Separate publications contain complete lists of MAT6 objectives and detail the chapter and verse in several popular reading and mathematics textbooks that correspond to each objective. The thoroughness with which the domain descriptions and curricular analyses are reported and interpreted is to be commended. The MAT6 probably sets an industry standard in this aspect of achievement test reporting. It is easy to see from these reports that the test items are representative samples from their respective domains.

Only the local school personnel can answer the important question of whether the test items adequately represent local curriculum objectives. Most schools would probably conclude that at a general level the important *basic skills* espoused for elementary schools in reading, mathematics, language usage, science, and social studies have at least a few items on the test. Each school has the burden of providing evidence that its emphases and priorities are well matched to the MAT6 before it is purchased. Because the authors' points of view and domain specifications are so clearly articulated, a school district should have very little difficulty in determining this match. The Test Coordinator's Handbook provides suggestions for reviewing and selecting tests.

Whether most local high schools would subscribe to the content, scope, and sequence of the MAT6 is less certain. Although the test content seems appropriately easy (or difficult, depending on your viewpoint) for high school students, it also seems to be much less matched to learning goals that are often espoused for this educational level. Focusing assessment on basic skills seems much less desirable at the high school level than at the elementary level.

Of special concern when considering using MAT6 with high school students, is the measurement of higher order thinking skills. Schools have made serious efforts to explicitly teach higher order thinking skills in all subject areas, especially in high schools. The authors of the MAT6, no doubt correctly, rationalize this category of skills as requiring the application of knowledge in several curricular areas rather than viewing this as a distinct area. The authors develop a higher order thinking skill score using selected items which are part of the Reading Comprehension, Mathematics Problem Solving, Science, and Social Studies tests. It is difficult for the test user to "see" all of these items because they are scattered throughout several tests. Studying the list of objectives identified as measuring these skills is not an appropriate alternative to studying the items themselves. The items do appear to test whether a student is able to think about the material presented, at least certain aspects of the material. Recent educational trends have emphasized developing generalized problem-solving abilities, teaching students to analyze critically events that occur daily, encouraging the development of appropriate knowledge structures and schema, and requiring students to understand the bases of complex social and technological developments. From this perspective, MAT6 items appear to require less (perhaps different) higher order thinking, application of intellectual skills to solve "real world" problems, and critical analysis than, for example, the Iowa Tests of Educational Development (ITED). If higher order thinking and application of skills and knowledge are important reasons for using a standardized test at the high school level, one should carefully compare the MAT6 test items with those on other tests, such as the ITED, before making a decision.

Although the rationales for domains, items, and various scores are clearly and logically articulated, the authors present little or no empirical evidence to support many of the interpretations that they recommend. This is not to say their recommendations are inappropriate, but it is to say that much more evidence than content delineation is needed. For instance, the item formats for reading comprehension break new ground in using "purpose questions" (claimed to be advanced organizers) immediately before each passage. A passage discussing the etymology of the term "OK," for example, is preceded by the bold-faced and boxed questions, "Where did we get the term OK?" These "purpose questions" are supposed to help students focus their "attention on important text elements" and to "help them bring to mind background knowledge needed for comprehending the passage." If this in fact happens, then these items represent a different definition of reading comprehension assessment than has typically been measured on reading tests in survey batteries. Further, although some readers approach daily reading tasks using implicit "purpose questions," such questions are seldom presented for the daily reader of print materials. The MAT6 may, in fact, have a superior method for assessing reading comprehension. Proper validation evidence is needed, however, to support this approach and to demonstrate its superiority over other assessment procedures.

Several types of scores accompany MAT6 recommendations for test use. Among these are instructional levels (for Mathematics and Reading), research skills scores, higher order thinking skills scores, skills priorities, cluster scores, and achievement-ability comparison ranges. The MAT6 materials defend each of the scores and their associated interpretations on logical grounds. Behind each interpretation lies one or more "constructs" and implied usages that need to be more completely validated. For example, if students are placed at their instructional level in mathematics, will they learn mathematics skills more rapidly and, consequently, narrow the gap between themselves and their peers who are not so placed? This is an empirical question that could be answered, at least partially, by data from school-based studies. The preliminary technical manual sloughs off such interpretive questions because "Construct validity is more complex and difficult to interpret." The fundamental interpretive framework of each test, although logically built, needs to have a solid, MAT6-specific, research footing. This concern echoes the *Standards for Educational and Psychological Testing* (AERA, APA, & NCME, 1985) that state, "If validity for some common interpretation has not been investigated, that fact should be made clear, and potential users should be cautioned about making such interpretations" (p. 13).

The preliminary technical manual states that the MAT6 is expected to correlate significantly with other achievement measures, but offers no MAT6-specific data to support this claim. Such correlational data and the authors' interpretation would be particularly helpful to persons wishing to switch to a MAT6 adoption. These data would be helpful also in trying to understand the extent to which the authors' MAT6 interpretations are valid.

The MAT6 Writing test does provide correlational data to support the interpretations of its score. This test consists of a drawing depicting a scene involving people, usually school-aged children and adults. Examinees are instructed to write what is happening in the scene and what will happen next. The basic thematic content of the picture changes with the test level to accomodate students' interests, but the instructions remain the same. The students are given 20 minutes to complete their writing. The data indicate that two trained readers will typically rank the same writing samples in a similar, but not identical, order. Correlations are in the .80–.89 range. Second, the Writing Sample score correlates moderately with scores from the various subtests of the Survey Battery, typically being in the .50–.59 range. This level of correlation is consistent with the interpretation that the Writing test taps a skill that is different from the Survey Battery. Correlations with the Survey Language subtest and the subtests of the Language Diagnostic Test are somewhat higher, supporting the relationship of language skill to assessed writing skill. The Otis-Lennon School Ability Test (OLSAT) correlates between .38 and .63 with the Writing score at various levels of schooling, with the correlations in the high school student sample being at the higher end of this range. This finding indicates that a student's general school ability is reflected in the student's writing, but that there is not complete overlap of these measures. Claims are made that the scores are not influenced by the themes of the pictures, the length of writing time, penmanship (except for completely illegible papers which are not scored), and so on. Data to support such claims would be useful.

The preliminary technical manual provides several uninterpreted tables of intercorrelations among the MAT6 subtests and with the OLSAT. These are generally high with the expected exceptions: The mathematics and spelling subtests correlate least with the other subtests. Interestingly, the OLSAT correlations tend to be among the lowest in these tables, and are rather low for data collected on children placed below grade 6. This pattern of intercorrelations would indicate that the school should be very cautious in interpreting the achievement/ability comparison scores that are found on the individual student reports. Teachers should use more information than the OLSAT scores in order to judge a student's school learning potential, at least to the extent that this learning is measured by the MAT6.

RELIABILITY. KR20 reliabilities are reported for the subtest scores and total scores of the Survey and Diagnostic Batteries. Raw score standard errors of measurement based on these KR20s are around 2.5 points for the subtests, 3.0 points for the composites (Reading, Mathematics, Language total scores), and about 7.0 for the complete Survey Battery. No reliability coefficients are reported for the higher order thinking score. Although the authors have "not deemed [it] necessary," test-retest reliability coefficients would add to the interpretability of the scores. The stability of the scores over various lengths of time is not only of interest to the construct interpretation of the scores, but is also of use in making decisions about how long to wait before administering another achievement test to students. Alternate forms test-retest coefficients are reported for the group of students who participate in the equating study. This short time interval between testings precludes the use of these coefficients to help interpret retestings planned over longer time periods, such as Fall to Spring school testing programs.

Some important reliability information is not provided. The authors encourage cluster analyses interpretations, but provide little help about the extent to which teachers are likely to be misled because of measurement error when they use cluster scores as indicators of skill mastery. Indices of decision consistency have long been recommended as aids for criterion-referenced interpretations, but these indices have not been calculated. Because the extent to which teachers are likely to be misled by using cluster analyses and objectives-based profiles to interpret MAT6 scores is unknown, users are cautioned not to interpret these scores without routinely using concomitant evidence that is not part of the MAT6 battery.

SCALES AND NORMS. The MAT6 provides the usual variety of score scales including percentile ranks, grade equivalents, and expanded standard scores. Standardization took place during the 1984–1985 school year. Fall (October) and Spring (April) empirical norms are available. There is no indication that there are plans for annual renorming, so these norms will be several years old when readers have access to this review. The norm group is a representative national sample, at least as far as is practical. Schools invited to participate sometimes decline to do so and must be replaced, so true representation is usually an ideal rather than a reality. The characteristics of the students comprising the norm group should be noted. First, all were required to participate in MAT6 practice tests. Second, the school agreed to include all handicapped children who were able to be tested in a standardized situation except for the trainable, severely, and profoundly mentally handicapped students. The proportion of the norm group that is handicapped has not been reported in the preliminary technical manual. Users of the MAT6 (and other survey batteries) should be aware of the "Lake Wobegon effect" (see Haney, 1988) when interpreting norms that are several years old and which may not be comprised of the same mix of students as are in local schools. Separate nonpublic school norms are provided. Norms for building and school averages are not reported but should be because the MAT6 claims to be useful in curriculum and program evaluations and these types of norms are helpful for these purposes.

SUMMARY. The MAT6's two-component system is a feasible solution to the duel between classroom and district-wide testing needs which schools must satisfy. Because the two components are closely related, schools may consider providing all teachers with the MAT6's diagnostic tools, but using the Survey Battery on a sampling basis only to satisfy district-wide needs. The strengths of the MAT6 seem to be in providing quality measurement at the elementary school level (K–8) where it does a good job of sampling basic skills. The tests appear to be less useful for high schools concerned with measuring students' general educational development, abilities that extend beyond the basic skills, and application of knowledge in settings beyond the classroom. Because the MAT6 has excellent interpretative materials for teachers to use and has extensive lists of objectives that are keyed to reading and mathematics textbook series, it should be relatively easy to match the content of the MAT6 to local instructional objectives. Such specificity does not come without some dangers, however. Teachers who believe that a standardized test will be used to judge their teaching abilities may feel pressured to narrow the scope of their instructional efforts to only those objectives found on the test. The specificity provided by the MAT6 makes this undesirable practice more easily implemented. The fundamental shortcoming of the MAT6 is the same one pointed out in a review of MAT5 (Linn, 1984): There is only a limited amount of evidence to support the appropriateness of the interpretations and uses the test authors suggest.

REVIEWER'S REFERENCES

American Educational Research Association, American Psychological Association, & National Council on Measurement in Education. (1985). *Standards for educational and psychological testing*. Washington, DC: American Psychological Association, Inc.

Linn, R. L. (1985). [Review of Metropolitan Achievement Tests, 5th Edition (1978)]. In J. V. Mitchell, Jr. (Ed.), *The ninth mental measurements yearbook* (pp. 965-968). Lincoln, NE: Buros Institute of Mental Measurements.

Haney, W. M. (Ed.). (1988). Special issue of *Educational-Measurement: Issues and Practice*, 7 (2).

Review of the Metropolitan Achievement Test, Sixth Edition by BRUCE G. ROGERS, Professor of Educational Psychology and Foundations, University of Northern Iowa, Cedar Falls, IA:

The Metropolitan Achievement Test (MAT) has been a strong competitor in the field of achievement tests for over half a century. Originally developed to measure student achievement in the New York City Public Schools, it was first published for general use in 1931 and successive editions have been frequently hailed as among the better tests available. Previous reviewers have had some strong criticisms of certain editions, but the authors and editors have shown a willingness to attempt to correct many of the perceived weaknesses.

The sixth edition of this test (MAT6) continues the innovations introduced in the fifth edition (MAT5), thus, many of the observations made in reviews of the MAT5 in *The Ninth Mental Measurements Yearbook* (9:699) are still appropriate. The present review will not duplicate those observations.

A significant change that was introduced in MAT5, and continued in the sixth edition, is the division of the test into a "two component system." The Survey component is intended to provide global, overall information, while the Diagnostic component is designed to provide more specific information. For each of the two components, both normative interpretations and objective-referenced interpretations are given. Each component has separate batteries in the basic skills areas of Reading, Mathematics, and Language, and the Survey component also contains subtests in Science, Social Studies, and Research Skills. According to the Teacher's Manual, a description of how these two testing components are to be integrated into a single program is presented in an Administrator's Guide. However, this Guide was yet to be published at the time this review was written.

A Practice Test is available for each level. These preparatory materials are useful for students who have not had previous experience in taking multiple-choice tests of this nature. Since these practice tests are nonsecure, they can be discussed with students and parents.

For the large majority of students, it will be appropriate to administer the level of the test corresponding to the grade level of the student. For some mainstreamed students, it may be difficult for the teacher to determine the most suitable level. Unfortunately, that determination was not addressed in the Teacher's Manual or the Directions for Administration. Discussions of this matter, and suggested procedures, are provided with batteries such as the California Achievement Tests (41).

The format of the booklets makes the items easy to read. The items are arranged on each page with sufficient white space and printed with a print size appropriate for each grade level. An attempt was made to keep the difficulty of the passages in the Reading test comparable to the reading difficulty of basal readers. Toward this end, a vocabulary control formula and a readability formula were employed, but no descriptions of procedures or results are to be found in the available manuals.

At the Primary level and Elementary level, both hand-scorable and machine-scorable booklets are available. The hand-scorable booklets are printed with black ink on white paper, and the machine-scorable booklets are printed in dark purple ink on light purple paper. Many studies of print and paper color have been done, usually indicating the desirability of the traditional black on white. It is not indicated in the manuals why color was introduced into the machine-scorable forms. Evidence concerning the implied assumption of equivalence of the two different print modes with respect to pupil performance should be reported.

MAT6 is divided into six levels, each of which contains more than one grade. A district could administer this test battery every year by using alternate forms for the multiple grades in the same level.

In the development of this test, the test blueprints and items were submitted to various panels of experts for review of content, grammar, item quality, and cultural and sexual bias. Users might find it helpful to have some evidence that these panels of outside experts agreed that the materials were in harmony with professional standards. Likewise, it would be appropriate to have evidence concerning potential cultural and sexual bias from studies that compared pupil performance by race and by sex.

VALIDITY. The validity of an achievement test is primarily judged with respect to its content. After examining school textbooks in each area to be tested, the authors developed a list of instructional objectives to represent the content of a national core curriculum. Some information is provided concerning the materials used in the reading area, but a more complete list of textbooks consulted in all areas would be informative. For each of the areas of Reading, Mathematics, and Language, the detailed objectives and test levels are reported in a two-dimensional table, with item numbers shown in the cells of the table. More abbreviated tables are shown for the other three test areas in the Survey battery. In addition, for the Science and Social Studies tests, items were assigned to the Behavioral Classifications of Knowledge, Comprehension, Inquiry Skills, and Critical Analysis. Curriculum experts were asked to review the items and blueprints for the tests; no data are shown as to the extent to which the experts agreed upon the appropriateness of the materials. The Teacher's Manual repeats the oft-used phrase that test users can best evaluate the test by a careful examination of the contents, but, since that is a time-consuming process, data on consensus of experts would be useful to support the content validity of the tests.

The discussion of criterion-related validity refers only to the Otis-Lennon School Ability Test. It is not made clear why an intelligence test should be the criterion for an achievement test. The correlations with intelligence tests would be more meaningful if presented under evidence for construct validity. Construct validity evidence is briefly mentioned, with an allusion to available data. Although details may not be necessary, a summary of those data would strengthen that commentary. There are no criterion scores that are exactly suitable for use with achievement tests, however, teacher grades in appropriate courses would certainly be relevant.

STANDARDIZATION AND NORMS. The standardization procedure began with the selection of a national probability sample, stratified in terms of socio-economic index, school district enrollment, geographic region, and public versus nonpublic (both Catholic and non-Catholic). On each of these stratification variables, and also with respect to ethnic group, comparisons of data from the sample schools with United States Census data show reasonably good agreement, although lower socio-economic groups tend to be somewhat over-represented. The success of any standardization effort depends upon the willingness of invited school districts to participate in the program. Of those school districts that were first invited to participate, only about one-fourth accepted; this necessitated two additional rounds of invitation. There is some evidence (Baglin, 1981) that the more affluent districts may be less likely to accept such an invitation, and thus, in subsequent regular administrations, grade equivalent scores (GEs) may be spuriously high. Norm data were collected both fall and spring, but no acceptance rates were shown for the spring. The authors are to be commended in reporting the percentage of first acceptances; such details should also be reported for the subsequent rounds.

The socio-economic index used as a stratification variable was defined as follows: "The SES Index for each school district was computed by summing median family income (in thousands of dollars) and the percentage of adults over twenty-five years of age who have completed high school" (Teacher's Manual, Survey Battery, Elementary, p. 153). "Median family income and percent of high school graduates were weighted so that the education variable contributed approximately twice the variance as did the income variable. . . . The socio-economic data reported for each school district included median family income and median years of schooling of adults in the community" (Preliminary Technical Manual, pp. 16, 17). Interpretation of this SES index presents certain difficulties. First, although the educational variable and the income variable are easily understood individually, their sum is not as readily conceptualized. A rationale needs to be given. Second, clarification is lacking on what educational statistics were to be combined, median years of schooling or percentages of high school graduates, and exactly how they were weighted to form the combination. Finally, it is not clear whether the original variables were a representation of the school district or the entire community. In some instances those regions may be congruent, but in others they are not. Each of these points needs further clarification in the technical manuals.

Several types of derived scores are available to users, including percentile ranks, stanines, scaled scores, normal curve equivalents, grade equivalents (GEs), achievement/ability comparisons, and performance indicators. For each of these, both uses and limitations are discussed, but more discussion is needed in recommending which scores are most meaningful for reporting results to parents and students. The sections on the proper uses and limitations of grade equivalents are particularly well written, and will likely find acceptance by both "advocates" and "detractors" of those scores. However, the definition of GE may cause some confusion. As an example, a grade equivalent of 4.2 is said to refer to the second month of the fourth grade. Most readers will associate that with the month of October; however, an accompanying table identifies it with November. Perhaps it would be simpler to define the grade equivalent in terms of achievement at the end of a named month, which, for this example, would be the end of October in the fourth grade. It is to the credit of the authors that they caution against the overinterpretation of discrepant GEs, by explaining that GEs differing by more than 2 years from the actual grade placement of the student have very little meaning other than signifying scores in the extremes of the distribution for that grade. Misinterpretations of grade equivalents in the chance range of the distribution are of particular concern at the upper grade levels. For example, consider the Reading Comprehension Test at the Advanced 2 level (designed for grades 10 through 12), which contains 50 four-option items. If a student tossed a coin to answer each item, the mathematically expected score would be 12.5, corresponding to a GE of 3.3. A typical third grader taking this high school level test would be likely to get a score near this value, since he or she would probably have to guess randomly on each item, but the score would not represent a valid measure of reading comprehension ability. Although this problem is not unique to the MAT6, such misinterpretations could be reduced by excluding from the table those GE values corresponding to raw scores in the chance range.

MAT6 was normed along with the Otis-Lennon School Ability Test (OLSAT), permitting comparisons between the achievement score predicted for a child from the OLSAT and the actual MAT6 achievement score. In the norm data, discrepancy scores were converted to stanines, and then separated into three categories, three stanine values per category. Because the lower and upper categories are essentially the lower and upper quarters of the distribution, it would probably have been simpler had the distribution of discrepancy scores been divided by quartiles originally. Students represented in these upper and lower groups are commonly called overachievers and underachievers. The concepts of overachievement and underachievement can be useful when properly employed, but the Teacher's Manual does not provide explicit directions or examples of proper interpretation and application. The manual would be strengthened with further clarification and discussion of these concepts.

A stated major emphasis in MAT6 is the intent to permit both norm-referenced and objective-referenced interpretations for each of the components, Survey and Diagnostic. However, the objective-referenced scores have a norm-referenced characteristic. As an example, for each of the content clusters in the Survey component, the raw score and number possible score are reported, along with a Performance Indicator labeled low, average, or high. This Performance Indicator shows the student's performance on the cluster as compared to the national standardization group. Thus, this interpretation is in part norm-referenced. Instructional Reading Level (IRL) scores are said to be "criterion-referenced scores" because they are based upon the percent of questions answered correctly. These scores are then reported in terms of the level at which the student should be instructed. This is essentially a norm-based interpretation, since it compares the student with pupils of a given grade level. The authors have gone to great lengths to produce Basic Resource Textbook Guides for each of the major reading series to help properly place the pupil in a basal reader, using the IRL score. This yields valuable information for the teacher, but to label the IRL score a "criterion referenced score" is likely to be confusing.

In the Diagnostic Tests, performance is reported more specifically. On each skill test (e.g., Vocabulary In Context), raw scores, number possible score, national percentiles, and stanines are reported, along with a teaching suggestion of Reteach, Practice, or Apply. Each skill test report is further subdivided into performance by objectives, showing raw score, number possible, and whether or not the pupil's score reached the criterion for that objective. Although the criterion score is reported for each objective, the manual does not explicate how that criterion score was established. Explanation of these matters in subsequent revisions of the manuals may remove the ambiguity and permit more meaningful objective-referenced and criterion-referenced interpretations.

RELIABILITY. Both the Survey and Diagnostic tests were normed in the fall and spring of 1984–1985. The Preliminary Technical Manual reports reliability data for only the Survey component. Interpretations of the Diagnostic scores are also dependent upon the availability of reliability data, particularly because the subtests are relatively short. Additional reliability data are needed for these scores.

For the Survey component, two measures of reliability are reported for each subtest. KR20 reliability coefficients are reported for every grade, while alternate form coefficients are reported for one selected grade within each level. Most of the subtest values are between .80 and .89, departures being more often in the higher direction. No reliability data are presented for the content clusters, so the user has no way of assessing stability of those scores, except by estimating them with the Spearman-Brown formula. Perhaps when the complete Technical Manual appears, it will contain data on this point. Until then, the user of these scores lacks sufficient supporting data.

Each subtest percentile score is reported on the Individual Report as both a point value and graphically as a band based on the standard error of measurement. These displays will be easily interpreted by teachers, parents, and students, which is clearly a strength of MAT6.

MANUALS AND SUPPORTING LITERATURE. Six types of manuals were originally planned to help users of MAT6.

(1) The Teacher's Manuals give enough information for teachers to interpret all the test reports they are likely to receive. For each test, there is a section on the development of skills across levels, factors to consider in interpreting scores, and several "tips for teaching." The "tips" appear to be pedagogically sound, but it would be useful if information or data to indicate effectiveness were provided. For both the Survey and Diagnostic components, the manuals at the various levels are quite complete, each containing over 150 pages. Because these publications may be too lengthy to be read by the typical busy teacher, Pre-test and Post-test Workshop Kits were planned to help administrators explain the content of the tests to their staff. The Pre-test Workshop is a well organized introduction to the MAT6, consisting of a script, overhead transparencies, and handouts. Although the script is detailed and easy to read, it will require a reasonable amount of preparation time by a person who is very familiar with the test to properly adapt the workshop to the particular testing situation. The printed script covers the purpose of the test, the major parts of the test (illustrated with sample items on transparencies), and the use of answer documents. The transparencies are easy to read, except for a few which have so much fine print that they might better be presented on handouts. For teachers who have not had experience with the MAT6, this workshop can be an efficient 1-hour overview that will help them explain the purpose and function of the test to both pupils and parents. The Post-Workshop covers much of the interpretation of tests as presented in the Teacher's Manual, and provides overhead transparencies and handouts for duplication. It is designed for a workshop of 60–90 minutes, and contains materials that are definitely attractive and informative. An administrator may find this kit to be a useful tool for stimulating group discussion on the proper interpretation of tests.

(2) A Basal Textbook Resource Guide is provided for several of the major textbook series in Reading and Mathematics. Each guide contains a match between the MAT6 objectives and page numbers in the particular text. These guides will be particularly useful to a teacher in

interpreting the class summary reports. For content clusters in which achievement is lower than expected, the teacher can locate specific pages in textbooks and workbooks as aids in instructional planning.

(3) The Norms booklets, which contain tables for converting raw scores to scaled scores, percentile ranks, and grade equivalents, will be particularly useful in instances in which the hand scoring of a test is necessitated. (Of course, when the tests are machine scored, these derived scores are automatically printed.)

(4) The Test Coordinator's Handbook is an informative guide for planning and coordinating the entire testing program. The program is divided into 25 steps, each described in detail, with suggested times and samples of checklists, worksheets, etc., for making the process efficient with a large group. This volume will be most valuable for test coordinators of moderately large districts to help them keep track of important details. (The 78 detailed pages may prove formidable to the superintendent of a small district who needs very compact instructions; perhaps a guide sheet could be prepared for this purpose.)

(5) Not yet available is an Administrator's Guide, which is described as discussing the actual administration and interpretation procedures in detail.

(6) A Preliminary Technical Manual has been produced, but the complete manual was unavailable as of this writing. It is unfortunate that it was decided to release MAT6 before some of the supporting manuals were complete. This practice has also been followed by other publishers, and it certainly complicates test evaluation and score interpretation.

SUMMARY. The MAT series has a long history as a well-developed achievement test. MAT6 is consistent with this background, and is suitable for schools that wish to emphasize skills that are widely accepted as basic and fundamental. Items are well-written, booklets are attractive, score reports are easily read, and the manuals now available contain helpful suggestions for teachers. For scores on the subtests, there is good empirical evidence to support normative interpretations, but for scores on the content clusters there is somewhat weaker evidence. The criterion-referenced scores are useful, but would benefit from more empirical support. Overall, the test is well constructed, and educators who find the test objectives compatible with local curricula should give careful consideration to adopting MAT6 as a part of their school testing programs.

REVIEWER'S REFERENCE

Baglin, R. F. (1981). Does "nationally" normed really mean nationally? *Journal of Educational Measurement*, 18, 97-107.

[201]

Miller Motivation Scale. Purpose: "To measure behavior related to motivation." College students and adults; 1986; MMS; 8 scores: Creative, Innovative, Productive, Cooperative, Attention, Power, Revenge, Give-Up; 1987 price data: $6.25 per 25 test booklets (7 pages); $12 per manual (53 pages); $3.50 per test for scoring service available from publisher; (30–60) minutes; Harold J. Miller; META Development [Canada].*

Review of the Miller Motivation Scale by DANIEL J. MUELLER, Professor of Educational Psychology, Indiana University, Bloomington, IN:

The Miller Motivation Scale (MMS) is a self-report personality inventory designed to promote "self-understanding" for clients in counseling settings. Each of the eight scales has 20 items. Six response categories, ranging from "Very much like me" to "This does not apply to me" are used. Items are standard-type personality items, asking about beliefs, preferences, and behaviors. The use of the word "motivation" in the title seems entirely arbitrary. Instructions for administration are clear. The general appearance of the instrument is neat and professional.

The psychometric quality of the instrument is very poor. Test-retest reliabilities are mixed. Three of the eight scales have reliabilities in the .80s. But four scales have reliabilities below .65; these should not be used for individual decision-making or counseling purposes. Internal consistency data for individual scales are lacking—a serious omission for scales of this nature. An alpha of .87 is reported for four of the scales combined, and an alpha of .77 for the other four. This seems to argue for using two composite scores in interpretation of results rather than the eight separate scale scores, but the author does not suggest this.

Evidence of enormous construct overlap across scales comes from correlational and factor analytic data found in the manual. Of the 28 scale intercorrelations, 12 are .50 and above;

two are in the .70s. Principal components factor analysis of the scale intercorrelations resulted in two very large factors. Factor loadings are not reported, but according to the manual the first factor is dominated by four of the scales, and the second factor includes substantial variance from *all* of the scales. The factor structure clearly does not support the existence of eight separate constructs.

Under the label "Concurrent Validity" the manual presents correlations of the eight MMS scales with two other personality inventories and several Structure of Intellect scales. (Probably this should be called construct validity.) No validity hypotheses are proferred. Nonetheless, after each table the author concludes that whatever significant correlations have been found constitute evidence of validity. In fact, with the exception of the Creative and Innovative scales (which seem to be measuring almost the same thing) there is no empirical evidence that the scales are measuring what it is claimed they are measuring.

In addition to overly optimistic conclusions about the validity of the scales, the Manual has several shortcomings. The language is often awkward and stilted, and there are many tense and person inconsistencies. In addition there are a number of typos and misspellings. In one instance a table row (Table 5) contains an incorrect scale name. Explanations of technical psychometric procedures are sometimes uninterpretable.

Further, there are several examples of serious psychometric and statistical misunderstandings. The square root of each reliability coefficient is presented in a table correctly labeled "Upper Limits of Validity." Then, below the table, the author implies that these are actually indices of validity. For one scale with a maximum possible validity of .94 the author says, "The maximum validity indicates there is . . . a 6% variance between what the test proports [sic] to measure . . . and what it actually measures" (p. 18). Regarding factor analysis the author maintains that, "the principal component solution requires as many components [factors] as there are variables" (p. 14). And item analysis is said to contribute to the validity of a scale (p. 8).

But the worst aspect of the manual is the suggested interpretations. Here the author makes completely unsubstantiated claims. There are even inconsistencies. For example: "If either of these scores [revenge or give-up scales] is beyond the 35th percentile, they will start to have a negative impact on the individual's life" (p. 23). "Scores from the 26th to the 75th percentile indicate a normal level of revenge motivation" (p. 29). "Scores from the 26th . . . to the 75th percentile indicate a normal level of give-up motivation" (p. 29).

"Individuals [above the 76th percentile on the creative scale] spend much of their waking time either thinking about or doing creative things. Sometimes [their] imagination is so vivid that it causes slight fear . . . " (p. 25).

"If the individual has scores above the 50th percentile on revenge [,] and power scores above the 50th percentile, you can expect the individual to act out their [sic] revenge motivation . . . " (p. 24).

"If you find scores above the 75th percentile [on the cooperative scale] you are likely to find . . . people who seem to be unable to function independently" (p. 24).

"You may find scores approximately equal on all subscales . . . The result is a house divided against itself" (p. 24).

Raw scores are converted to percentiles, and reported to respondents in a bar graph. Norms are based on 500 college students from several majors—apparently a convenience sample. Respondents' scores on each scale are explained by an interpretive summary, which is simply a compilation of phrases from the items they endorsed on that scale. While this may be a safe interpretive strategy, it is not very insightful.

In summary, the Miller Motivation Scale is a very weak psychological instrument. It should not be used for individual decision-making or counseling purposes. For most scales there is simply no empirical reason to believe the scales are measuring what the author claims they are. For purposes of diagnosing motivations for behavior, a counselor would be on much safer ground to use an established value inventory, such as the Surveys of Personal, or Interpersonal Values by Leonard Gordon (SRA) or the Career Orientation Placement and Evaluation Survey (COPES) by Knapp and Knapp (EdITS), or a needs assessment instrument such as the Edwards Personal Preference Schedule (EPPS) by Allen Edwards (The Psychological Corporation). Personal adjustment, which seems to be an interest of the MMS author, could better be measured with the Personal Orientation Inventory by Everett Shostrom (EdITS).

Review of the Miller Motivation Scale by DENISE M. ROUSSEAU, Associate Professor of Organization Behavior, Kellogg School of Management, Northwestern University, Evanston, IL:

Designed to measure behavior related to the eight dimensions of Creativity, Innovation, Productivity, Cooperation, Attention, Power, Revenge, and Giving Up, the Miller Motivation Scale (MMS) is a 160-item computer-scored self-report questionnaire. As part of the computer scoring, written individualized subscale interpretations are made available to users. Accompanying this feedback is a counseling plan. It is intended to be used as a problem-solving guide by people with little counseling training as well as by experienced professionals.

The inventory's items include measures of behavioral intent (e.g. "I try to be perfect in everything I do"), preferences (e.g., "I like to solve practical problems"), self-reported behavior (e.g., "I set goals and meet my goals"), and others' perceptions of the focal person (e.g., "People have told me that I have a negative attitude"). The test developer infers that all of these dimensions reflect motivation and that "there is a cause-effect relationship between motivation and behavior." Use of the inventory requires the assumption that (*a*) the subscales measure different types of motives and (*b*) the collection of intentions, preferences, and self-described behaviors and perceptions can be equated. The manual provides no evidence for the validity of these assumptions and no discussion of the theoretical underpinnings of these particular eight subdimensions. (Why this particular set?) Similar inventories have sought to focus on only one type of item (e.g., preferences, Super & Nevill, 1985; self described behavior, Lafferty, 1974). The manual concludes:

> There appears to be a reasonable relationship between motivation, thoughts and behaviors. Even though it is not possible to say to what degree motives cause certain thought patterns or thought pattern cause behavior, it reasonable [sic] to say that there is some degree of cause effect [sic] relationship between the three variables. (p. 7)

Five subscales are intended to measure general functional aspects of motivation (Creative, Innovative, Productive, Cooperative, and Power) and three subscales are intended to tap dysfunctionals (Attention Getting, Revenge, Give-Up). The MMS includes, therefore, five subscales to tap positive or functional motives and three subscales assessing negative or dysfunctional ones. However, two of the functional or fulfillment-oriented dimensions reflect motives or thinking styles that other researchers and inventories have treated as negative. Cooperative includes the security a person gets from being part of a group and Power includes elements of taking charge and control, both of which have been treated as distinct from and perhaps counter to motives of encouragement and self-fulfillment (Lafferty, 1973; Maslow, 1954; McClelland, Atkinson, Clark, & Lowell, 1953). Thus, there is some concern the MMS underrepresents presumably dysfunctional styles and is not consistent with content theories of motivation in the specification and labelling of its dimensions.

Items comprising each subscale were assigned to subscales a priori and the appropriateness of this assignment gauged by item to item-total correlations. No item-level factor analysis was reported, suggesting that further evidence of the subscales' construct validity is needed. The high intercorrelations among the subscales, especially those involving the subscale Creative, suggest that acquiescence bias might exist in the subjects' responses, inflating individuals' overall scores (Nunnally, 1967). Concern over the conceptualization of various scales is exacerbated by such findings as the high positive intercorrelations of Power with Revenge and Give-up, subscales which should be negatively related with Power were its classification as a fulfillment style correct. The principle components analysis described in the manual yielded two factors (no rotation is reported) but unfortunately the loadings of each scale on these factors are not presented. The unrotated components analysis is difficult to interpret and adds little to our understanding of the empirical dimensionality of the subscales. No evidence for the criterion-related validity of the instrument (e.g., correlations with actual behavior) is reported.

Test-retest reliabilities (over an approximately 10-week period) ranged from .58 to .89. I am dubious of the manual's claim that these reliabilities indicate that what the test purports to measure and what it actually measures overlap considerably (e.g., 23%). These test-retest reliabilities or stability coefficients indicate that whatever the subscales measure, it is relatively stable over 10 weeks, but they say nothing about how well it taps "what the test purports to measure."

A minor concern regarding scoring of the test by respondents is the instruction to skip a number on the answer sheet when respondents wish to indicate "0" as their response. A "not applicable" or "I never do this category" would be preferable to prevent respondents from mistakenly answering the subsequent questions(s) in the blank intended to signify "0."

This inventory appears to be in a developmental or exploratory phase, with the author continuing to conduct research on its psychometric properties. At present, it is perhaps best to withhold judgment on its construct validity until more data are in. I could not recommend it for use at present as a counseling tool or a measure of motivation without further explication of its conceptual underpinnings and evidence of construct validity.

REVIEWER'S REFERENCES

McClelland, D. C., Atkinson, J. W., Clark, R. A., & Lowell, E. L. (1953). *The achievement motive*. New York: Appleton-Century-Crofts, Inc.

Maslow, A. H. (1954). *Motivation and personality*. New York: Harper.

Nunnally, J. C. (1967). *Psychometric theory*. New York: McGraw-Hill.

Lafferty, J. C. (1973). Level 1: Lifestyles Inventory Self-Description. Plymouth, MI: Human Synergistics.

Nevill, D. D., & Super, D. E. (1986). The Values Scale: Research Edition. Palo Alto, CA: Consulting Psychologists Press.

[202]

Multidimensional Aptitude Battery. "Designed to provide a convenient objectively-scorable measure of general aptitude or intelligence in the form of a profile containing five verbal and five performance subtest scores." High school and adults; 1982–84; MAB; 13 scores: 6 Verbal (Information, Comprehension, Arithmetic, Similarities, Vocabulary, Total), 6 Performance (Digit Symbol, Picture Completion, Spatial, Picture Arrangement, Object Assembly, Total), Total; 1987 price data: $22 per machine-scorable examination kit including manual ('84, 94 pages), verbal battery booklet and answer sheet, performance battery booklet and answer sheet, and 1 coupon for computerized scoring; $33 per hand-scorable examination kit including same material as machine-scorable kit but with scoring templates and record form rather than coupon; $57.50 per 35 test booklets for verbal or performance battery; $16.50 per 35 answer sheets for verbal or performance battery; $6.50 per 35 record forms; $13.75 per scoring templates; $22 per cassette tape; $10.50 per manual; $3.50 per 6-page computer report; 35(50) minutes per battery; Douglas N. Jackson; Research Psychologists Press, Inc.*

TEST REFERENCES

1. Krieshok, T. S., & Harrington, R. G. (1985). A review of the Multidimensional Aptitude Battery. *Journal of Counseling and Development*, 64, 87-89.

2. Vernon, P. A., Nador, S., & Kantor, L. (1985). Reaction times and speed-of-processing: Their relationship to timed and untimed measures of intelligence. *Intelligence*, 9, 357-374.

3. Sternberg, R. J. (1986). Haste makes waste versus a stitch in time? A reply to Vernon, Nador, and Kantor. *Intelligence*, 10, 265-270.

4. Vernon, P. A. (1986). He who doesn't believe in speed should beware of hasty judgments: A reply to Sternberg. *Intelligence*, 10, 271-275.

5. Vernon, P. A., & Kantor, L. (1986). Reaction time correlations with intelligence test scores obtained under either timed or untimed conditions. *Intelligence*, 10, 315-330.

Review of the Multidimensional Aptitude Battery by SHARON B. REYNOLDS, Assistant Professor of Education, Texas Christian University, Fort Worth, TX:

The Multidimensional Aptitude Battery (MAB) attempts to translate the basic ideas of the Wechsler intelligence measures into a format suitable for group administration. There are verbal and performance sections, each with its own test booklet, answer sheet, and scoring template. The answer sheets are standardized to correspond to the format of the test booklets. The test materials are color coded for each scale. The test booklet and answer sheet have a clear, readable format. Instructions and practice items are included in the test booklet.

MANUAL. An extensive manual is provided, including chapters describing the purpose, administration, scoring and standardization, construction, and psychometric properties of the MAB. The 12-page introduction to the manual includes a general description of the MAB, and a summary of constructs and theories of intelligence. The presentation is thorough and provides an adequate basis for understanding the place of the MAB in the context of the general notion of intelligence testing.

The description of the item selection and scale construction is preceded by a general discussion of test construction. The procedure for selecting items was clearly and thoroughly described. The items retained were selected after a series of item analyses. These analyses are described in detail in the manual. Empirical data are presented in support of the 7-minute time limit that was adopted as standard for the MAB.

Scale intercorrelations and factor analyses yielded support for the subscales being divided into Verbal and Performance scales. These data are fully described in the manual.

ADMINISTRATION AND SCORING. All necessary information for administration of the instrument is provided in an easily understandable form. Verbatim instructions are included in the manual. A cassette tape of instructions is also available. The test may be scored manually or by computer. Templates are provided for manual scoring. The templates are easy to use and are color coded to match the appropriate answer sheet to further reduce the probability of error. The MAB record form provides a simple way to record the scores and convert the raw scores to scaled scores. The layout of the record form and step-by-step directions make the recording and presentation of the scores simple and clear. The standard scores are converted to a Verbal IQ, a Performance IQ, and a Full Scale IQ by consulting an age-appropriate table provided in the manual. There are instructions for estimating a full scale score from administration of fewer than the standard five Performance scales.

STANDARDIZATION. The instrument was standardized by equating (calibrating) the MAB with the Wechsler Adult Intelligence Scale—Revised (WAIS-R). A thorough description of the method of equating was given, including the theoretical justification in terms of the application of sampling theory to test standardization. Adequate empirical evidence is presented to support the decision to use linear equating. The standardization group is adequately described as to both number and type of subject in the sample. The sample was heterogeneous with respect to age, gender, and source. The equating procedure was comprehensive and well described.

RELIABILITY AND VALIDITY. Reliabilities were computed for each age group from 15 to 20. The sample was adequate in size and was composed of males and females. These Kuder-Richardson Formula 20 reliabilities range from .94 to .97 for the Verbal Scale, .95 to .98 for the Performance Scale, and .96 to .98 for the Full Scale. Reliability data based on weighted composites, verbal/performance composite, and separately timed halves are also reported. Test-retest subtest reliabilities ranged from .83 to .97 (Verbal Scale) and from .87 to .94 (Performance Scale). Verbal Scale reliability was .95, Performance Scale was .96, and Full Scale was .97. All subscale reliabilities are reported, as are the standard errors of measurement.

Validity was assessed primarily by correlations with the WAIS-R. These correlations compare favorably with WAIS/WAIS-R correlations, which are also reported. Factor analyses of the MAB and the WAIS-R demonstrated marked congruence between the respective Verbal and Performance factors, with congruence coefficients of .97 for the Verbal factor and .96 for the Performance factor.

SUMMARY. The MAB appears to be a very good alternative to the WAIS-R in settings where group administration is appropriate. It has the advantages of standardized group administration without sacrificing reliability and validity. The empirical support for the test is impressive. The materials are easy to understand and use. The information provided in support of the instrument is thorough and provides an adequate basis for interpreting scores and evaluating the appropriateness of the test for the user's setting.

Review of the Multidimensional Aptitude Battery by ARTHUR B. SILVERSTEIN, Professor of Psychiatry, University of California, Los Angeles, CA:

For years, the instruments David Wechsler devised for the measurement and appraisal of adult intelligence have been among the most successful of all psychological tests, both scientifically and commercially. Douglas N. Jackson's intent in designing the Multidimensional Aptitude Battery (MAB) was to evaluate the degree to which it is possible to incorporate some of the positive features of Wechsler's scales into a test that does not require individual administration and scoring by a specially trained psychologist or psychometrist.

Like Wechsler's scales, the MAB consists of two groups of subtests: Five Verbal subtests are contained in one booklet, and five Performance subtests in another. Separate answer sheets that may be either hand or machine scored are provided for each booklet. Nine of the subtests have the same names as in Wechsler's scales (Digit Span is omitted and Spatial replaces Block Design), but the specific items are original and a multiple-choice format is employed throughout. Examiner's instructions are standardized so the test can be administered by cassette, available from the publisher. Seven minutes are allowed for each subtest, and each half of the battery is said to require about 50 minutes for complete administration. For comparison, the Wechsler Adult Intelligence Scale—Revised (WAIS-R) is said to require from 60 to 90 minutes (of professional time) to administer.

Raw scores on the 10 subtests are first transformed into scaled scores with a mean of 50 and a standard deviation of 10 (on Wechsler's scales the scaled scores have a mean of 10 and a standard deviation of 3). The scaled scores for the two halves of the battery are summed separately to yield Verbal and Performance scores, and these two sums are added to yield a Full Scale score. Finally, the Verbal, Performance, and Full Scale scores are converted into IQs with a mean of 100 and a standard deviation of 15 (just as with Wechsler's scales), or alternatively, to standard scores with a mean of 500 and a standard deviation of 100 (as with the Scholastic Aptitude Test). A table is also provided so that an individual's subtest scores can be compared with those of people in the same age group, as for pattern analysis.

The procedure used to standardize the MAB is remarkable, for it was equated directly to the WAIS-R, using a rather small ($N = 160$) and extremely heterogeneous sample that took both tests: university and senior high school students, hospitalized psychiatric patients, and probationers from court-imposed prison sentences, of both sexes and ranging in age from 16 to 35 years. (Yet norms are provided for age groups up to 70–74.) In a partial check on the validity of the equating procedure, a large ($N > 5{,}000$) sample of Canadian high school students obtained an average Full Scale IQ of 103 on the MAB, which is very close to the expected value. Data are also given on the correlations between the MAB and the WAIS-R for a subset of the subjects in the equating sample. These range from .44 to .89 for the subtests and from .79 to .94 for the three scales, roughly comparable to the correlations between the WAIS-R and its predecessor, the 1955 WAIS. Nevertheless, much more research is required before scores on the MAB can be considered equivalent to those on the WAIS-R.

Additional information on the psychometric properties of the MAB includes internal consistency and test-retest reliability coefficients (generally $>.95$ for the three scales), data on the effects of speededness (they do not appear excessive), and the results of several factor analyses (yielding the same Verbal Comprehension and Perceptual Organization factors that are commonly found in Wechsler's scales).

Practitioners who stress the distinction between the psychological assessment of intelligence and the psychometric testing of intelligence (e.g., Matarazzo, 1972) will doubtless regard the MAB with skepticism (some, perhaps, with horror). Its author acknowledges that clinical observation of a subject's test-taking behavior is sometimes helpful, and that mentally retarded and some psychotic patients require individual administration, but he maintains that for most people individual administration is not only costly but unnecessary. Those who share this view are likely to find the MAB an attractive alternative.

REVIEWER'S REFERENCE

Matarazzo, J. D. (1972). *Wechsler's measurement and appraisal of adult intelligence.* Baltimore: Williams & Wilkins.

[203]

Multilevel Academic Survey Test. Purpose: "Intended for use by school personnel who make decisions about student performance in reading and mathematics." Grades K–8 and high school students with reading or mathematics skill deficits; 1985; MAST; 1988 price data: $30 per examination kit including Grade Level test booklet, self-scoring answer sheet, Curriculum Level record form, examiner's manual (189 pages with Curriculum Level test cards); Kenneth W. Howell, Stanley H. Zucker, and Mada Kay Morehead; The Psychological Corporation.*

a) GRADE LEVEL TEST. Grades K–8 and high school students with reading or mathematics skill deficits; may be administered independently or in combination with Curriculum Level Test; 3 forms; $18 per 25 test booklets (12 pages); $11 per 25 self-scoring answer sheets.

1) *Primary Form.* Grades K–2; individual; (10–15) minutes.

2) *Short Form.* Grades 3–12; 22(27) minutes.

3) *Extended Form.* Grades 3–12; administered to students who have taken the Short Form when larger sample of performance is required; 30(35) minutes.

b) CURRICULUM LEVEL TEST. Grades K–8; "criterion-referenced"; 14 scores: Reading (Graded Oral Reading, Graded Comprehension, Timed Rereading, Diagnostic Oral Reading, Comprehension Problem Checklist), Mathematics (Basic

Facts Screening Test, Addition Test, Subtraction Test, Multiplication Test, Division Test, Fractions Test, Decimals/Ratios/Percents Test, Problem Solving Test, Applications Content Test); $18 per 25 record forms; (1–5) minutes per test.

Review of the Multilevel Academic Survey Test by ELLEN H. BACON, Assistant Professor, Western Carolina University, Cullowhee, NC:

The Multilevel Academic Survey Test (MAST) is designed for use by educational professionals who work with students having academic difficulty in math or in reading. The manual states the test is useful for both differentiating students on normative comparisons and measuring performance of students on specific content objectives. The MAST combines norm-referenced and criterion-referenced measures into one instrument.

The Multilevel Academic Survey Test consists of a Grade Level Test and a Curriculum Level Test. The Grade Level Test is a norm-referenced instrument including a Primary Form, a Short Form (22 minutes), and an Extended Form (additional 30 minutes). The Curriculum Level Test is a criterion-referenced test for reading and math skills and also contains informal diagnostic measures for analyzing error patterns in both reading and math. The tests can be used independently or in combination.

The combination of these measures offers the special educator or remedial teacher the tools to compare a student's performance with his age and grade peers, to determine specific skills needed by the student, and to analyze the student's errors in reading and math. The MAST fills a need that remedial teachers have for identifying instructional levels for students with delays in reading and math. The tests are easy to administer and score and are economical in cost. Because the tests are devised so the teacher can use only as many tests as needed to provide information on a student, the MAST is economical in terms of administration time.

GRADE LEVEL TEST. The manual claims the Grade Level Test can be used to determine placement in a special program. Although this test could be useful to a teacher who needs a quick screening instrument or an estimate of a child's performance to begin criterion-referenced testing, the test should not be used to place students in special education classes. The test lacks the reliability needed for such use. Reliability of the test was determined by two methods, test-retest correlations to indicate stability over time and by internal consistency to indicate stability over items in the test. Test-retest reliability should be .90 or above for tests used for placement decisions (Salvia & Ysseldyke, 1985). Less rigorous standards require, at least, .80 for educational decision making (Berdine & Meyer, 1987). Of the 24 test-retest correlations on the Grade Level Test, calculated on four forms at six grade levels (3–8), only four were above or equal to the .80 level and none reached the .90 level. The median coefficient across grades was .68 for Short Form Reading; .72 for Extended Form Reading; .71 for Short Form Mathematics; and .75 for Extended Form Mathematics.

To measure internal consistency, the statistical procedure KR20 was used. Interpretation of this reliability information is limited as the KR20 procedure should not be used with timed tests or tests that are not completed by all those being tested (Gronlund, 1981).

On other technical considerations the MAST is adequate to very good. The case for content validity is strong, based on the texts and programs from which items were developed. Criterion-related validity is moderately high, based on correlations with the Iowa Test of Basic Skills ranging from .59 to .81 for the reading Short Form and Extended Form tests and from .54 to .85 for the mathematics Short Form and Extended Form tests.

The norm sample is adequate with over 200 subjects at each grade level. The sample is well described and is representative of the U.S. population by age, grade, sex, and geographical region. Administration and scoring procedures are clearly presented and the norm tables are easy to use. The authors should be commended for providing the standard error of measurement (*SEM*) at each grade level, instructions on how to use the *SEM*, and a place for recording confidence intervals on the record sheet.

Although age and grade norms are provided, the authors caution against interpretation of scores by age and grade levels. The manual also cautions users that the test measures only skills from K–8 even though it provides norms up through grade 12. Users should heed these cautions to avoid misinterpretation of test norms.

CURRICULUM LEVEL TEST. The Curriculum Level Test is designed to complement the normative data from the Grade Level Test by providing a criterion-referenced test assessing a series of specific skills required for reading and math in grades K–8. There are a total of 23 tests including two sets of graded reading passages and seven mathematics tests. Each test is designed to assess clearly stated academic objectives and appropriate criteria for mastery are listed for each objective. The tests include Graded Oral Reading Tests, Graded Comprehension Tests (including a maze completion subtest), Timed Rereading Tests, and Diagnostic Oral Reading Tests. The diagnostic reading test includes instructions on collecting and analyzing error samples. The mathematics tests include Basic Facts Screening Tests, Arithmetic Operations Tests, Problem Solving Tests, and Applications Content Tests.

Content validity should be evaluated by how well the test reflects and measures the content being taught in a particular curriculum. Individual users will have to make their own assessment of how well the test matches their curriculum, but the Curriculum Level Test is based on an extensive analysis of major reading and math texts for grades 1–8. The manual also presents data on how criteria for mastery were determined for the maze completion items.

Reliability coefficients for a few of the tests are reported. Alternate-form reliability for maze completion is .90 with split-half reliability ranging from .71 to .98. Test-retest reliability is reported for the timed oral reading task (.64–.88) and written computation (.81–.86). The time interval was, however, only one day. These correlation coefficients should be interpreted very cautiously with such a brief retest interval. The authors can be commended for reporting reliability data for a criterion-referenced test, but much of the evidence presented is difficult to interpret due to the nonstandard collection and analysis of data.

SUMMARY. The MAST is a fine addition to the assessment tools available to educators and should fill a need for many remedial and special education teachers. The first section of the test provides a quick placement test, the Grade Level Test, for determining a student's approximate academic level. However, this test should not be used for placing a student into special education or remedial services, until stronger evidence of reliability of the scores is provided. The second section of the test is a criterion-referenced test, the Curriculum Level Test. This test provides teachers with measures to determine which skills a student is lacking in reading and math, and methods to analyze the students' errors. While the MAST does not meet its goal of providing a norm-referenced test useful in placement decisions, the test does fill a need for informal and diagnostic measures helpful to teachers in planning academic programs.

REVIEWER'S REFERENCES

Gronlund, N. E. (1981). *Measurement and evaluation in teaching*. New York: Macmillan Publishing Co., Inc.

Salvia, J., & Ysseldyke, J. E. (1985). *Assessment in special and remedial education* (2nd ed.). Boston: Houghton Mifflin Co.

Berdine, W. H., & Meyer, S. A. (1987). *Assessment in special education*. Boston: Little Brown & Co.

Review of the Multilevel Academic Survey Test by THOMAS G. HARING, Assistant Professor of Special Education, University of California, Santa Barbara, CA:

The Multilevel Academic Survey Test (MAST) was designed for educators who assess or instruct students with academic difficulties and who desire a rapid method of assessing levels of achievement in reading and computational skills. The authors state the MAST can be used both as a screening device to assist in the identification of students with special education needs and as a tool for determining instructional needs. The test assesses reading and mathematic skills typically included in curricula from kindergarten through eighth grade by the use of several interrelated tests: (*a*) The Grade Level Test is a norm-referenced achievement test and comes in three forms—Primary (kindergarten through second grade), Extended Form (grades 3 through 12), and Short Form (a shorter version of the Extended Form); and (*b*) the Curriculum Level Test, which is a series of criterion-referenced tests used to determine instructional needs. Parts of the MAST are individually administered (The Primary Form and the Curriculum Level Test), while other subtests allow for group administration (the Grade Level Tests).

DESCRIPTION OF THE GRADE LEVEL TEST. The Primary Form of the Grade Level Test contains 71 items and takes 10–15 minutes to administer. The reading portion assesses a student's ability to imitate sounds, produce sounds when shown letters, identify letters within words that correspond to given sounds, read single words, and read sentences. The mathematics section assesses skills, such as counting, number recognition, addition, and subtraction. The administration and scoring of the test is generally straightforward. The directions for administering the test would be improved by changing the ordering of information. Instructions concerning required testing materials seem inconveniently out of place five pages before the rest of the directions.

The Short Form of the Grade Level Test is a timed test taking 22 minutes to complete. The test is comprised of two reading passages. Reading ability is assessed with a modified cloze procedure (with multiple choice rather than free response). Every fifth word is omitted and the student must select one of three options. Younger students with learning disabilities may have some difficulty in mastering the answer form because they must simultaneously remember the question number, and the number (1, 2, or 3) of their answer, and then find their place again within the passage. The mathematics section consists of 24 computational problems ranging from simple addition to converting a fraction into a percentage. Scoring the test is made very simple by having an answer key underneath the student's answer form that is automatically keyed by the student through a dry transfer.

The Extended Form of the Grade Level Test is given in conjunction with the Short Form. It takes approximately one hour to give both forms. The Extended Form expands upon the Short Form by including three additional reading passages for which traditional multiple-choice questions assess reading comprehension (with 14 additional items). The mathematic section contains 18 items and assesses students' abilities to solve word problems. This section of the test is particularly noteworthy in that the students respond to the problems by selecting the correct operation within a multiple-choice format. Thus, the ability to apply the correct strategy is separated from computational ability.

DESCRIPTION OF THE CURRICULUM LEVEL TEST. The Curriculum Level Test is designed to assist in making recommendations about a student's instructional needs in reading and arithmetic. The Curriculum Level Reading Test contains five criterion-referenced tests to assess possible causes of a student's reading problems and specifies seven profiles of performance difficulties. The authors state that subtests should be individually selected for each student based on the results of the Grade Level Test and that, in general, one to three subtests should be administered to each student. The subtests of the Curriculum Level test are:

1. The Graded Oral Reading Test consists of eight short reading passages written at the difficulty levels associated with first through eighth grades. The test administrator calculates the student's rate (correct words per minute) of oral reading, number of errors per 100 words, and accuracy (number of correctly read words per 100 words). Guidelines are provided to assess the student's current grade level, the level at which the student can read independently, and the level at which the student can read with assistance and feedback. The test is easy to administer and should provide a quick assessment of the grade level at which a student functions.

2. The Graded Comprehension Test consists of four comprehension questions following each passage in the Graded Oral Reading Test and a passage with every fifth word removed in a modified cloze format with three multiple-choice options. The test assesses the student's comprehension of grade level passages.

3. The Timed Rereading Test consists of readministering the highest level passage in the Graded Oral Reading Test on which a student was 90% accurate. The purpose of the test is to determine if a student's oral reading rate improves with practice. If a student's rate increases by a set criteria, the authors recommend that rate be emphasized within the student's instructional program.

4. The Diagnostic Oral Reading Test is employed to collect a sample of reading errors. As a student orally reads a graded passage, the tester records each error verbatim. Based on the coding of six types of errors (e.g., hesitations), the test administrator is instructed to analyze these errors and categorize them into three types of errors (e.g., Type 1: The error does not make semantic or syntactic sense in the context of the passage's meaning). The scoring of the test requires the use of a sophisticated coding scheme for which a more detailed scoring protocol is needed with operational definitions of the scoring categories. As presented, this subtest would require considerable practice to

reliably score as a student orally reads. Although reliability data are provided for a sample of 25 teachers who categorized error types *after* the authors recorded the errors made by one student, there are no data provided to assess whether or not teachers can reliably score passages as students orally read with this system.

5. The Comprehension Problem Profile is a checklist comprised of seven prerequisite skills (e.g., "The student knows what the words in the passage mean") assessed by 33 questions (e.g., "Can discuss unstated ideas accurately"). After the questions are answered for each prerequisite, an overall judgment is made following three options: Adequate, Instruction Needed, Additional Testing Needed. The authors state the information needed to complete the profile can be gathered from testing, interviewing former teachers, or other available sources of information. No data are provided to evaluate the reliability of the results obtained by the profile. It would appear the reliability and validity of this information is based on the quality of information available to the examiner and the skill of the examiner in observing reading difficulties.

After several subtests are administered, the authors provide guidelines to identify a learning (and error pattern) profile characterizing the student's performance. The greatest strength of the Curriculum Level Test is the close linkage between the results of the reading subtests and the specific recommendations for instructional content and method. The authors base their recommendations on sound pedagogic grounds that are well referenced to state-of-the-art research into reading problems and instructional techniques. Test users who have a relatively sophisticated background in reading instruction should find these guidelines and recommendations helpful in planning instruction. Less sophisticated users may have difficulty in detecting the error patterns identified by the authors and may have difficulty in translating the suggestions into actual instructional episodes. A flow chart showing key decision points and their consequences for planning instruction would be a helpful future addition to the test.

The MAST also provides Curriculum Level Mathematics Tests. The test assesses accuracy of basic arithmetic facts, automaticity (rate) of basic arithmetic facts, patterns of errors in basic operations on whole numbers and rational numbers, errors in solving word problems, and difficulties with measurement concepts by use of five subtests. A guide sheet is provided to aid detection of specific computational errors. Recommendations are given after each subtest as to what type of instruction is needed or if further testing is indicated. As with the reading subtests, the skills needed for competent arithmetic performance are only sampled, the tests are by no means an exhaustive survey of all the skills that underlie reading or arithmetic performance, for which more comprehensive criterion-referenced tests should be employed.

TECHNICAL EVALUATION. The content validity of the test appears to be high for elementary-aged students in that a large sample of basal texts were reviewed, curriculum strands from several school districts were consulted, and the authors have previously conducted an extensive review of curricula for the construction of earlier criterion-referenced tests. The authors employed a one parameter model (based on item difficulty) for selecting items. Other statistical criteria for item selection, particularly an item discrimination index, would be an improvement.

The test is predominately composed of items selected from kindergarten through sixth grade. By high school grades, the sampling of items is so sparse that an increase of one item in the raw score can, in some cases, increase the grade equivalent more than two to three grades. The test should not be used to assess secondary-aged pupils because of the limitation in the number of items and because the items are not written with age-appropriate themes or content.

The test was standardized with a sample of 3,500 students from kindergarten through twelfth grade. Although this sample size is not large by achievement test standards, information in the manual compares the demographic characteristics of the sample to U.S. census data allowing readers the opportunity to directly assess the comparability of the sample. Students from 13 school districts sampling every region of the country comprised the norming group. Although the sampling was broad, the northeast was underrepresented in the sample (8.7% in the sample vs. 22.1% in the U.S. population) and the west was overrepresented (34.8% in the sample vs. 18.9% in the U.S. population). More importantly, the sampled districts were predominately in small towns or rural areas, no major urban centers were surveyed. The standardization sample was, however, generally representative of the U.S. population in terms of race, income of parents, and other social status indicators with the exception of students from Hispanic backgrounds, who are underrepresented.

The authors should be commended for the thoroughness of the reporting of the technical characteristics of the test. In total, 23 different tables of reliability and validity data are provided and sufficient detail is given in the tables for users to evaluate the test. A critical characteristic to be judged by users is the efficiency of the Grade Level Test as an achievement test as compared to other more comprehensive achievement tests. The authors compare the Short Form of the MAST and the Long Form to the comparable subtests of the Iowa Test of Basic Skills (which takes 90 minutes to administer the related subtests). The correlations between the two forms of the MAST and the Iowa Test of Basic Skills are moderately high, but not overly impressive. For the Short Form, the range in correlations across grades was .54 to .77 with a mean of .68. The Long Form ranged from .56 to .85 with a mean of .71. Thus, as an achievement test, test users must weigh the time savings afforded by the MAST against the lowering of accuracy of measurement inherent in a less comprehensive test. Certainly, the more than doubling of the time needed for administration of the longer version of the MAST must be justified with data relative to predictive validity.

The usefulness of the test in screening groups to identify learning disabled students was also assessed. A sample of 39 students identified as learning disabled was matched to a sample of nonidentified students on the basis of age, sex, race, and Hispanic origin. A discriminate analysis (which was not fully described) was conducted to identify a criteria for categorization as learning disabled. When used as a screening test with this criteria, 74% of the group already categorized as LD was identified by the MAST as LD. Using the same criteria, 28% of the nonlearning-disabled sample was identified as LD. Thus, if this criteria were employed (which is not possible because it is not specified) a relatively high percentage of the typical school population would require extensive follow-up testing to more accurately determine if special services are needed. Thus, further cost/efficiency data are required to assess whether the savings realized by using a less comprehensive achievement test such as the MAST are balanced by the costs of extra testing necessitated by this rate of false positives.

The thoroughness in the development of the MAST is evidenced by the measures of construct validity provided. Construct validity is assessed by examining the intercorrelations among subtests (these were positive and moderately high), a discriminate analysis of the performance of LD and nonLD students on portions of the test, a factor analysis of the reading scores (which indicates two interpretable factors that seem to be determined by item format), and correlations with a test of reasoning ability. The test of reasoning ability was the Matrix Analogies Test—Short Form given to 2,800 students. The mean correlations across grade levels for the reading subtests was .47 (Short Form) and .55 (Long Form) and for the math subtests it was .48 (Short Form) and .58 (Long Form). These are moderate correlations, but not unusual when compared to other reported correlations between achievement and reasoning ability, which average .8 when corrected for attenuation (Jensen, 1973).

Data on reliability indicate the Multilevel Academic Survey Test produces moderately consistent results. Test-retest reliabilities for the Reading subtest (Short Form) ranged from .59 to .72 with a mean of .68, and for the Long Form, ranged from .67 to .81 with a mean of .74. The section on standard error of measurement is clearly presented and would be a good resource for explaining this statistic to practitioners.

Two forms of validity are reported for the Curriculum Level Test. Split half reliability ranged from .71 to .98 with a mean of .83. Data were also collected and reported for the validity of the mastery criteria indicating that students at specific grade levels can be expected to show mastery of the items as written.

SUMMARY. The MAST is not a single test with a single purpose. It attempts to provide an initial screening instrument, an achievement test, and a criterion-referenced assessment system. For any of these purposes, more comprehensive achievement tests or criterion-referenced tests would give more reliable and more detailed information and would be preferable. However, that said, the tests have several strengths including the care taken in their development and the quality of the instructional recommendations given. Given that all special education programs require periodic assessments on each child, a more rapid, time-efficient test such as the MAST is needed. Although the curriculum recommendations are a major strength, the amount of clinical skill needed in the interpretation of the subtests necessitates these recommendations be viewed as hypotheses requiring an empirical test by the classroom teacher and rejected if progress is not made.

REVIEWER'S REFERENCE

Jensen, A. R. (1973). *Educability and group differences.* New York: Harper & Row, Publishers.

[204]

Multilevel Informal Language Inventory. Purpose: "Designed to measure a child's level of functioning in the production of critical semantic relations and syntactic constructions." Ages 4–12; 1982; MILI; no scores, semantic and syntactic developmental profiles in 8 areas: Verbs, Nominals, Modification, Interrogatives, Negation, Combining Propositions, Adverbs/Prepositions, Associative Language; individual; 1988 price data: $69 per complete set including examiner's manual (111 pages), picture manual, and 12 record forms; $15 per 12 record forms; $45 per picture manual; $25 per examiner's manual; (40–60) minutes; Candace Goldsworthy and Wayne Secord (picture manual); The Psychological Corporation.*

Review of the Multilevel Informal Language Inventory by ELIZABETH M. PRATHER, Professor of Speech and Hearing Science, Arizona State University, Tempe, AZ:

The Multilevel Informal Language Inventory (MILI) was designed to provide an efficient means of sampling 44 specific syntactic and semantic targets. Developmental profiles based on normal syntactic acquisition patterns are included. Ordering of constructions within syntactic categories is based upon a composite of findings from earlier research of Bloom and Lahey (1978), deVilliers and deVilliers (1972), Miller (1981), and others. A check-sheet of semantic relations is provided, but sequenced order is not specified.

The MILI is designed solely for intrachild comparisons. The author uses multiple levels of tasks and probes to increase the child's opportunities to perform, to help the clinician select targets for an intervention program, and to monitor progress during the training program. No norms are provided and comparisons between children or among age-level counterparts are inappropriate.

The examiner's manual is clearly written and includes considerable detail on ways to analyze language samples. The picture manual is appropriate; it includes colored drawings with sufficient detail to provide clarity. Pictured and verbal stimuli are used to sample language at various task levels: (*a*) general survey level similar to traditional language sampling, as in "Tell me everything you can about this picture"; (*b*) specific survey stories based on story-retell from sequenced pictures; and (*c*) direct probes. None of the direct probes uses immediate imitation; rather three different elicitation levels are used for each potential target behavior (evoked spontaneous, elicited, and receptive understanding). For the user who wants a prepared set of stimuli to elicit language samples and a record form which provides a simple check-off system, the MILI may be very useful.

The MILI has major weaknesses. Field testing was completed with 45 children aged 4 to 12 years, but only to determine whether test stimuli produced desired responses (to allow for the revision or elimination of confusing or inappropriate stimuli). No intrasubject (test-retest) or interexaminer reliability is provided, and neither are age-level norms. Further, this test is much more effective in analyses of syntactic structures than in analyses of semantic relations, a fact recognized by the author.

The MILI is not recommended when normative comparisons are important, such as in documenting a need for speech-language services. It could, however, provide an efficient procedure for obtaining and profiling syntactic productions and identifying the child's use of various semantic relations. In recommending the MILI, I am assuming that intrasubject reliability data will be provided in a future revision.

REVIEWER'S REFERENCES

deVilliers, P. A., & deVilliers, J. G. (1972). Early judgments of semantic and syntactic acceptability by children. *Journal of Psycholinguistic Research*, 1, 299-310.

Bloom, L., & Lahey, M. (1978). *Language development and language disorders.* New York: Wiley.

Miller, J. F. (1981). *Assessing language development in children: Experimental procedures.* Baltimore: University Park Press.

Review of the Multilevel Informal Language Inventory by ROBERT RUEDA, Visiting Associate Professor of Curriculum, Teaching, and Learning, University of Southern California, Los Angeles, CA:

DESCRIPTION OF TEST. This inventory was designed to provide a developmental profile of language functioning, specifically in the areas of semantic relations and syntactic constructions. The manual suggests that this measure would be appropriately used for screening, diagnostic assessment, and ongoing assessment. Although the Multilevel Informal Language Inventory (MILI) is individually administered, it was not designed as a norm-referenced measure, but as a tool for intra-individual comparison.

The content of the MILI was based upon a review of research "on the acquisition of oral language production in children up to the approximate age at which they enter school (5 to 6 years)." The primary references used for this purpose are provided in the manual. As the introductory description points out, the items covered by this inventory are semantic relations and syntactic constructions.

The authors of the MILI have attempted to incorporate a multilevel approach to assessment, and there are three distinct ways in which this multilevel approach is embedded either in the administration procedures or the test content. First, an attempt was made to follow an approximate developmental ordering of test items within each category assessed. For example, the probe for the present progressive verb form precedes the past irregular form since this is the assumed order of developmental acquisition. Second, the inventory proceeds from less structured to more structured levels of observation. For example, the contexts for observations move from free description of a page-size cartoon-like drawing, to a somewhat more structured retelling of a story based on a series of cartoon drawings, and finally to direct probes of specific syntactic and semantic items. The third multilevel feature of the MILI is found in the administration procedures of the direct probes for specific language features. Probes may be presented to children either at the evoked spontaneous level, the elicited level, or the receptive level, thus providing an indication of the conditions under which the child was able to produce the linguistic structure being assessed.

Although the manual indicates that the MILI underwent field testing, little detailed information is provided. Forty-five children, including 15 "normal" children and 30 children "who had previously been diagnosed as language delayed and/or disordered" were administered a draft of the inventory. However, there was no information on where the field testing took place nor was any specific description of the subjects provided. The only type of validity discussed with respect to the MILI was content validity. Given the presentation in the manual on the derivation of the content of the test, the content validity of the test appears adequate.

ADMINISTRATION AND SCORING. The test authors appropriately caution that this measure should be used in conjunction with natural observation and standardized test procedures. In fact, the manual states "Use of MILI assumes that the child has already been administered one or more formal assessments of language, i.e., standardized tests or batteries, and that some estimate of his overall degree of delay/disorder has been made."

The MILI does not yield numerical scores, but rather provides separate developmental profiles for semantic relations and for syntactic features, which are taken as a summary of a child's level of language functioning. A positive feature of the syntactic profile is that it indicates the conditions under which the child produced specific target items (evoked spontaneously, specifically elicited, or responded to at the receptive level only). The MILI allows a great deal of clinical leeway in terms of specific administration procedures, order of presentation, selection of the entry level of assessment, etc. This is both a strength and a weakness. On the one hand, clinical sensitivity can be used to facilitate maximum performance levels of students without violating the structure or assumptions of the MILI. On the other hand, the clinician needs to have considerable experience, a firm grasp of language development, and well-developed clinical skills in order to effectively deal with the lack of rigid administration guidelines.

The administration time should be 15–20 minutes per session (if more than one session is needed), and results of the first session should be used to determine specific targets and levels to assess for the second administration. This procedure is meant to avoid making awkward and time-consuming test-time decisions. Overall, the manual provides adequate, clear administration instructions, and the scoring sheet appears to be well thought out. The cartoon-like drawings which are used as stimulus materials in the MILI appear to be attractive and interesting, at least to children at the lowest ages for which the inventory was designed. The stimulus drawings maintained the interest and elicited a substantial amount of language from 4-year-olds to whom it was shown by the reviewer.

The introduction in the manual provides a straightforward discussion of language assessment, which is balanced and sensitive to various aspects of testing language proficiency. In addition, the authors clearly state the assumptions guiding development of the test.

SUMMARY AND CONCLUSION. Overall, this inventory appears to fulfill what the authors promise. However, there are some factors that need consideration by clinicians using this inventory. For example, the manual states that "An underlying assumption of such measures [informal assessment instruments] is that the task will closely approximate the child's typical performance and thereby provide a representative sample of that child's current language behavior." Nevertheless, the MILI does incorporate many elements of standardized test situations, such as tape recording (where appropriate), marking of scoring forms by the clinician while recording responses, and having children interact individually with a strange adult in a test-like context around school-like tasks. It should be kept in mind that there is mounting evidence from many disciplines that both linguistic and cognitive behaviors are tremendously sensitive to contextual variations, especially in the case of young children and minority children. Given this information, the clinician needs to be aware that some of the "test-like" features of the MILI may serve to counteract the intent of the MILI to "elicit the most natural language behavior from the child." As a simple example, some children might respond very differently in a group or peer communicative context. In all fairness, the authors caution that "a child's failure to produce the intended target should first be viewed as a failure of the stimuli to elicit the target rather than as clear-cut evidence that the child is unable to produce the target under any conditions." In addition, the authors stress that the MILI should not be used as the sole indicator of language functioning. Nevertheless, clinicians will need to exercise clinical judgement in the use and interpretation of the MILI with minority and non-English-speaking students.

There are some specific features of the MILI that merit caution when used with very young children. At younger ages, for example, it is possible that the survey stories may confound short term memory capacity with language skills, especially if a child interprets the task as a strict retelling (not rephrasing) of the story provided by the clinician. Also, the survey scenes used as a stimulus for the general language sample may confound discrimination skills with linguistic features. Finally, several items appear to tap labeling (vocabulary) skills, for example, where the child's task is to "tell me about this picture."

At the more advanced levels, some of the items appear to tap cognitive rather than strictly linguistic features. For example, level AL-1 (creating words) seems, at least in part, to tap divergent thinking skills. In addition, some of the items such as AL-4 (word meanings in context) seem more like items from an intelligence test, (e.g., "How many centimeters are there in a parking meter?").

A final consideration in the use of the MILI is that the focus on specific features of syntax and semantic relations encourages a somewhat decontextualized approach to language intervention. Although the MILI has a somewhat narrow focus, it is true that the test does not promise more than it delivers, and it certainly was not meant to be used in isolation. However, the relatively recent emphasis on context as a key factor in language and development by sociolinguists, educational anthropologists, and others, should encourage consideration of the role of contextual factors and the process of natural language acquisition in a comprehensive language assessment and intervention program.

[205]

The Multiple Affect Adjective Check List, Revised. Purpose: Measures positive and negative affects as traits or states. Ages 20–79; 1960–85; MAACL-R; previous edition still available; 5 basic scores: Anxiety, Depression, Hostility, Positive Affect, Sensation Seeking, and 2 summary scores: Dysphoria, and Positive Affect and Sensation Seeking; 2 forms: State and Trait; 1987 price data: $6.50 per 25 hand-scoring or machine-scoring State or Trait forms; $10 per set of handscoring keys; $2.50 per manual ('85, 29 pages); $3.50 per bibliography ('85, 33 pages); $5.50 per specimen set including one copy of each form and manual); $1 per answer form for scoring service available from publisher; 5(10) minutes; Marvin Zuckerman and Bernard Lubin; EdITS/Educational and Industrial Testing Service.*

See 9:734 (47 references), T3:1547 (108 references), 8:628 (102 references), and T2:1293 (56 references); for reviews by E. Lowell Kelly and Edwin I. Megargee of an earlier edition, see 7:112 (60 references); see also P:176 (28 references).

TEST REFERENCES

1. Rohsenow, D. J. (1982). Control over interpersonal evaluation and alcohol consumption in male social drinkers. *Addictive Behaviors*, 7, 113-121.

2. Suedfeld, P., Ramirez, C., Deaton, J., & Baker-Brown, G. (1982). Reactions and attributes of prisoners in solitary confinement. *Criminal Justice and Behavior*, 9, 303-340.

3. Ellickson, J. L. (1983). Representational systems and eye movements in an interview. *Journal of Counseling Psychology*, 30, 339-345.

4. Fordyce, M. W. (1983). A program to increase happiness: Further studies. *Journal of Counseling Psychology*, 30, 483-498.

5. Alter, R. C. (1984). Abortion outcome as a function of sex-role identification. *Psychology of Women Quarterly*, 8, 211-233.

6. Barbaree, H. E., & Davis, R. B. (1984). Assertive behavior, self-expectations, and self-evaluations in mildly depressed university women. *Cognitive Therapy and Research*, 8, 153-172.

7. Chaplin, W. F., & Goldberg, L. R. (1984). A failure to replicate the Bem and Allen study of individual differences in cross-situational consistency. *Journal of Personality and Social Psychology*, 47, 1074-1090.

8. Cragan, M. K., & Deffenbacher, J. L. (1984). Anxiety Management Training and Relaxation as Self-Control in the treatment of generalized anxiety in medical outpatients. *Journal of Counseling Psychology*, 31, 123-131.

9. Crandall, J. E. (1984). Social interest as a moderator of life stress. *Journal of Personality and Social Psychology*, 47, 164-174.

10. Farley, R. C. (1984). Training in rational-behavior problem solving and employability enhancement of rehabilitation clients. *Rehabilitation Counseling Bulletin*, 28, 117-124.

11. Gotlib, I. H. (1984). Depression and general psychopathology in university students. *Journal of Abnormal Psychology*, 93, 19-30.

12. Greenstein, S. M. (1984). Pleasant and unpleasant slides: Their effects on pain tolerance. *Cognitive Therapy and Research*, 8, 201-210.

13. Haskett, R. F., Steiner, M., & Carroll, B. J. (1984). A psychoendocrine study of Premenstrual Tension Syndrome: A model for endogenous depression. *Journal of Affective Disorders*, 6, 191-199.

14. Hertsgaard, D., & Light, H. (1984). Anxiety, depression, and hostility in rural women. *Psychological Reports*, 55, 673-674.

15. Ingram, R. E. (1984). Information processing and feedback: Effects of mood and information favorability on the cognitive processing of personally relevant information. *Cognitive Therapy and Research*, 8, 371-386.

16. Johnson-Sabine, E. C., Wood, K. H., & Wakeling, A. (1984). Mood changes in bulimia nervosa. *British Journal of Psychiatry*, 145, 512-516.

17. King, D. A., & Heller, K. (1984). Depression and the response of others: A re-evaluation. *Journal of Abnormal Psychology*, 93, 477-480.

18. Lang, A. R., Verret, L. D., & Watt, C. (1984). Drinking and creativity: Objective and subjective effects. *Addictive Behaviors*, 9, 395-399.

19. Light, H. K. (1984). Differences in employed women's anxiety, depression, and hostility levels according to their career and family role commitment. *Psychological Reports*, 55, 290.

20. Martin, D. J., Abramson, L. Y., & Alloy, L. B. (1984). Illusion of control for self and others in depressed and nondepressed college students. *Journal of Personality and Social Psychology*, 46, 125-136.

21. Miller, L. S., & Funabiki, D. (1984). Predictive validity of the Social Performance Survey Schedule for component interpersonal behaviors. *Behavioral Assessment*, 6, 33-44.

22. Mitchell, J. E., & Madigan, R. J. (1984). The effects of induced elation and depression on interpersonal problem solving. *Cognitive Therapy and Research*, 8, 277-285.

23. Peck, D. F., Morgan, A. D., MacPherson, E. L. R., & Bramwell, L. (1984). The Multiple Affect Adjective Check List: Subscale intercorrelations from two independent studies. *Journal of Clinical Psychology*, 40, 123-125.

24. Plante, T. G., & Denney, D. R. (1984). Stress responsivity among dysmenorrheic women at different phases of their menstrual cycle: More ado about nothing. *Behaviour Research and Therapy*, 22, 249-258.

25. Powell, M., & Hemsley, D. R. (1984). Depression: A breakdown of perceptual defence. *British Journal of Psychiatry*, 145, 358-362.

26. Pretty, G. H., & Seligman, C. (1984). Affect and the overjustification effect. *Journal of Personality and Social Psychology*, 46, 1241-1253.

27. Schare, M. L., & Lisman, S. A. (1984). Self-statement induction of mood: Some variations and cautions of the Velten procedure. *Journal of Clinical Psychology*, 40, 97-99.

28. Schare, M. L., Lisman, S. A., & Spear, N. E. (1984). The effects of mood variation on state-dependent retention. *Cognitive Therapy and Research*, 8, 387-408.

29. Veleber, D. M., & Templer, D. I. (1984). Effects of caffeine on anxiety and depression. *Journal of Abnormal Psychology*, 93, 120-122.

30. Abrahamson, D. J., Barlow, D. H., Sakheim, D. K., Beck, J. G., & Athanasiou, R. (1985). Effects of distraction on sexual responding in functional and dysfunctional men. *Behavior Therapy*, 16, 503-515.

31. Brown, N. W. (1985). Assessment measures that discriminate between levels of DUI clients. *Psychological Reports*, 56, 739-742.

32. Carey, M. P., & Burish, T. G. (1985). Anxiety as a predictor of behavioral therapy outcome for cancer chemotherapy patients. *Journal of Consulting and Clinical Psychology*, 53, 860-865.

33. Dobson, K. S. (1985). Defining an interactional approach to anxiety and depression. *The Psychological Record*, 35, 471-489.

34. Dobson, K. S. (1985). An analysis of anxiety and depression scales. *Journal of Personality Assessment*, 49, 522-527.

35. Farber, S. S., Felner, R. D., & Primavera, J. (1985). Parental separation/divorce and adolescents: An examination of factors mediating adaptation. *American Journal of Community Psychology*, 13, 171-185.

36. Friedrich, W. N., Tyler, J. D., & Clark, J. A. (1985). Personality and psychophysiological variables in abusive, neglectful, and low-income control mothers. *The Journal of Nervous and Mental Disease*, 173, 449-460.

37. Gackenbach, J. I., & Auerbach, S. M. (1985). Sex-role attitudes and perceptual learning. *The Journal of Social Psychology*, 125, 233-243.

38. Gotlib, I. H., & Beatty, M. E. (1985). Negative responses to depression: The role of attributional style. *Cognitive Therapy and Research*, 9, 91-103.

39. Hasher, L., Rose, K. C., Zacks, R. T., Sanft, H., & Doren, B. (1985). Mood, recall, and selectivity effects in normal college

students. *Journal of Experimental Psychology: General*, 114, 104-118.

40. Kirschenbaum, D. S., Tomarken, A. J., & Humphrey, L. L. (1985). Affect and adult self-regulation. *Journal of Personality and Social Psychology*, 48, 509-523.

41. Klein, H. A., & Rennie, S. E. (1985). Temperament as a factor in initial adjustment to college residence. *Journal of College Student Personnel*, 26, 58-62.

42. Koverola, C., Manion, I., & Wolfe, D. (1985). A microanalysis of factors associated with child-abusive families: Identifying individual treatment priorities. *Behaviour Research and Therapy*, 23, 499-506.

43. Mehlman, R. C., & Snyder, C. R. (1985). Excuse theory: A test of the self-protective role of attributions. *Journal of Personality and Social Psychology*, 49, 994-1001.

44. Ruderman, A. J. (1985). Dysphoric mood and overeating: A test of Restraint theory's disinhibition hypothesis. *Journal of Abnormal Psychology*, 94, 78-85.

45. Shaw, J. B., & Weekley, J. A. (1985). The effects of objective work-load variations of psychological strain and post-work-load performance. *Journal of Management*, 11, 87-98.

46. Tuffin, K., Hesketh, B., & Podd, J. (1985). Experimentally induced learned helplessness: How far does it generalize? *Social Behavior and Personality*, 13, 55-62.

47. Young, L., & Humphrey, M. (1985). Cognitive methods of preparing women for hysterectomy: Does a booklet help? *British Journal of Clinical Psychology*, 24, 303-304.

48. Adam, K., Tomeny, M., & Oswald, I. (1986). Physiological and psychological differences between good and poor sleepers. *Journal of Psychiatric Research*, 20, 301-316.

49. Anderson, C. A., & Ford, C. M. (1986). Affect of the game player: Short term effects of highly and mildly aggressive video games. *Personality and Social Psychology Bulletin*, 12, 390-402.

50. Asso, D. (1986). The relationship between menstrual cycle changes in nervous system activity and psychological, behavioural and physical variables. *Biological Psychology*, 23, 53-64.

51. Brand, A. G., & Powell, J. L. (1986). Emotions and the writing process: A description of apprentice writers. *The Journal of Educational Research*, 79, 280-285.

52. Cash, T. F., Rimm, D. C., & MacKinnon, R. (1986). Rational-irrational beliefs and the effects of the Velten Mood Induction Procedure. *Cognitive Therapy and Research*, 10, 461-467.

53. Clark, D. A. (1986). Cognitive-affective interaction: A test of the "specificity" and "generality" hypotheses. *Cognitive Therapy and Research*, 10, 607-623.

54. Daiss, S. R., Bertelson, A. D., & Benjamin, L. T., Jr. (1986). Napping versus resting: Effects on performance and mood. *Psychophysiology*, 23, 82-88.

55. Dougherty, K., Templer, D. I., & Brown, R. (1986). Psychological states in terminal cancer patients as measured over time. *Journal of Counseling Psychology*, 33, 357-359.

56. Gard, P. R., Handley, S. L., Parsons, A. D., & Waldron, G. (1986). A multivariate investigation of postpartum mood disturbance. *British Journal of Psychiatry*, 148, 567-575.

57. Glynn, S. M., & Ruderman, A. J. (1986). The development and validation of an eating self-efficacy scale. *Cognitive Therapy and Research*, 10, 403-420.

58. Gotlib, I. H., & Meyer, J. P. (1986). Factor analysis of the Multiple Affect Adjective Check List: A separation of positive and negative affect. *Journal of Personality and Social Psychology*, 50, 1161-1165.

59. Haley, W. E., & Strickland, B. R. (1986). Interpersonal betrayal and cooperation: Effects on self-evaluation in depression. *Journal of Personality and Social Psychology*, 50, 386-391.

60. Harris, R. N., Snyder, C. R., Higgins, R. L., & Schrag, J. L. (1986). Enhancing the prediction of self-handicapping. *Journal of Personality and Social Psychology*, 51, 1191-1199.

61. Herbert, J., Moore, G. F., de la Riva, C., & Watts, F. N. (1986). Endocrine responses and examination anxiety. *Biological Psychology*, 22, 215-226.

62. Higgins, E. T., Bond, R. N., Klein, R., & Strauman, T. (1986). Self-discrepancies and emotional vulnerability: How magnitude, accessibility, and type of discrepancy influence affect. *Journal of Personality and Social Psychology*, 51, 5-15.

63. Kraemer, D. L., & Hastrup, J. L. (1986). Crying in natural settings: Global estimates, self-monitored frequencies, depression and sex differences in an undergraduate population. *Behaviour Research and Therapy*, 24, 371-373.

64. Liu, T. J., & Steele, C. M. (1986). Attributional analysis of self-affirmation. *Journal of Personality and Social Psychology*, 51, 531-540.

65. Madigan, R. J., & Bollenbach, A. K. (1986). The effects of induced mood on irrational thoughts and views of the world. *Cognitive Therapy and Research*, 10, 547-562.

66. Mullins, L. L., Peterson, L., Wonderlich, S. A., & Reaven, N. M. (1986). The influence of depressive symptomatology in children on the social responses and perceptions of adults. *Journal of Clinical Child Psychology*, 15, 233-240.

67. Nickel, E. J., Lubin, B., & Rinck, C. M. (1986). The new MAACL scales with adolescents: Preliminary reliability and validity determinations. *Adolescence*, 21, 81-86.

68. Overholser, J. C., & Beck, S. (1986). Multimethod assessment of rapists, child molesters, and three control groups on behavioral and psychological measures. *Journal of Consulting and Clinical Psychology*, 54, 682-687.

69. Peterson, C., Zaccaro, S. J., & Daly, D. C. (1986). Learned helplessness and the generality of social loafing. *Cognitive Therapy and Research*, 10, 563-570.

70. Saranson, I. G., Saranson, B. R., & Shearin, E. N. (1986). Social support as an individual difference variable: Its stability, origins, and relational aspects. *Journal of Personality and Social Psychology*, 50, 845-855.

71. Schwartz, D. P., Burish, T. G., O'Rourke, D. F., & Holmes, D. S. (1986). Influence of personal and universal failure on the subsequent performance of persons with Type A and Type B behavior patterns. *Journal of Personality and Social Psychology*, 51, 459-462.

72. Snyder, C. R., Lassegard, M., & Ford, C. E. (1986). Distancing after group success and failure: Basking in reflected glory and cutting off reflected failure. *Journal of Personality and Social Psychology*, 51, 382-388.

73. Suominen-Troyer, S., Davis, K. J., Ismail, A. H., & Salvendy, G. (1986). Impact of physical fitness on strategy development in decision-making tasks. *Perceptual and Motor Skills*, 62, 71-77.

74. Davis, M. H., Hull, J. G., Young, R. D., & Warren, G. G. (1987). Emotional reactions to dramatic film stimuli: The influence of cognitive and emotional empathy. *Journal of Personality and Social Psychology*, 52, 126-133.

75. Essau, C. A. (1987). Type A personality and discrepancies between self-report and heart-rate responses to stress. *Perceptual and Motor Skills*, 64, 544-546.

76. Follette, V. M., & Jacobson, N. S. (1987). Importance of attributions as a predictor of how people cope with failure. *Journal of Personality and Social Psychology*, 52, 1205-1211.

77. Klein, H. (1987). The relationship of temperament scores to the way young adults adapt to change. *The Journal of Psychology*, 121, 119-135.

78. Metalsky, G. I., Halberstadt, L. J., & Abramson, L. Y. (1987). Vulnerability to depressive mood reactions: Toward a more powerful test of the diathesis-stress and causal mediation components of the reformulated theory of depression. *Journal of Personality and Social Psychology*, 52, 386-393.

79. Miller, S. M. (1987). Monitoring and blunting: Validation of a questionnaire to assess styles of information seeking under threat. *Journal of Personality and Social Psychology*, 52, 345-353.

80. Pyszczynski, T., Holt, K., & Greenberg, J. (1987). Depression, self-focused attention, and expectancies for positive and negative future life events for self and others. *Journal of Personality and Social Psychology*, 52, 994-1001.

81. Smith, M. A., & Houston, B. K. (1987). Hostility, anger, expression, cardiovascular responsibility, and social support. *Biological Psychology*, 24, 39-48.

82. Stephens, R. S., Hokanson, J. E., & Welker, R. (1987). Responses to depressed interpersonal behavior: Mixed reactions in a helping role. *Journal of Personality and Social Psychology*, 52, 1274-1282.

83. Swann, Jr., W. B., Griffin, Jr., J. J., Predmore, S. C., & Gaines, B. (1987). The cognitive-affective crossfire: When self-consistency confronts self-enhancement. *Journal of Personality and Social Psychology*, 52, 881-889.

84. Vitkus, J., & Horowitz, L. M. (1987). Poor social performance of lonely people: Lacking a skill or adopting a role? *Journal of Personality and Social Psychology*, 52, 1266-1273.

Review of The Multiple Affect Adjective Check List, Revised by JOHN A. ZARSKE, Director, Northern Arizona Psychological Services, P.C., Flagstaff, AZ:

The Multiple Affect Adjective Check List, Revised (MAACL-R) represents a revision of an earlier version first published by Zuckerman and Lubin in 1965. The previous version of the MAACL required revision due to problems affecting the test's discriminant validity. Prior to its revision, the MAACL generated considerable research activity. Included with the MAACL manual is a bibliography of over 700 of these studies, indexed according to various research and clinical topic areas. With the improved norms and psychometric properties of the MAACL-R, it is anticipated that a host of similar, new studies and clinical uses shall emerge for this popular test.

The authors have done a commendable job of addressing the several problems of the MAACL (i.e., high correlations between the subscales, acquiescence response set, and the independence of positive and negative affect scores). Additionally, the manual includes a thorough and scientific treatment of strengths and weaknesses of the revised edition. Included in the manual are several new validity and reliability studies, a comprehensive discussion of the factor analytic investigations that led to the development of the new scales, and details regarding administration, scoring, normative data, and demographic factors affecting the MAACL-R. In all, it appears the authors have made substantial improvements for a test that has already enjoyed a vast amount of research attention and use in clinical practice.

SCORING AND ADMINISTRATION. Scoring is a simple and straightforward procedure as described in the manual. Basically, all checked adjectives for the various scales are counted to compute a raw score for each of the scales or scale groupings (i.e., broader factor scales) and transformed into *T* scores using appendices in the back of the manual. The test publisher provides an optical scanning service for machine scoring but this reviewer was unable to establish under what conditions the user may score the test without relying upon the scoring service. The manual indicates that "local" scoring may be done "under arrangement with the test publisher." However, a one-page mailer that accompanied the manual suggests that hand-scoring keys are available (none were included in the specimen set).

Administration is simple and the test is completed in under 5 minutes in most circumstances. For the Trait form, the respondent is asked to check those adjectives which "generally apply"; for the State version, those which apply "at the present time."

VALIDITY. As mentioned above, the main problem with the MAACL was that the three subscales (Anxiety, Depression, and Hostility) were correlated with each other between .7 and .9. Research studies demonstrated that when a respondent was exposed to a stressor, concurrent changes would occur in all three scales. Correlational studies comparing the MAACL scales with other assessment tools (observer ratings and questionnaires), typically revealed that the Anxiety and Depression scales had adequate convergent validity but not discriminant validity. To address this problem, the authors conducted a series of factor-analytic studies that resulted in a five-factor solution: Anxiety (A), Depression (D), Hostility (H), Positive Affect (PA), and Sensation Seeking (SS). The A, D, and H scales (i.e., the Negative Affect scales) now show correlations in the range of .4 to .6, revealing an improvement in the discriminant validity of these scales. However, there is still a significant intercorrelation among these scales, leading the authors to postulate a broader Dysphoria Factor, composed of these three subfactors. The PA and SS scales are significantly correlated as well, hypothetically combining to form a Positive Affect factor. Correlational studies between these two broader Positive and Negative Affect factors show evidence for convergent and discriminant validities, suggesting a new and more useful structure for the MAACL-R.

Several other validity studies are reported in the manual for various populations using peer ratings and single clinical observer ratings correlated with MAACL-R scaled scores. Peer ratings showed the highest correlation but even the observer correlations were adequate. The authors also correlated the MAACL with the Lorr Poms and the MMPI. Correlations between the Poms and MAACL were greatest for college students. The MMPI-MAACL study suggests the PA scale shows merit in predicting depression in several psychiatric diagnostic groups. Sufficient validity studies are lacking for the Sensation Seeking scale in both the Trait and State forms, indicating a need for further studies regarding this scale's construct validity.

RELIABILITY. All scales show adequate internal reliability with the exception of the Sensation Seeking scale. Of course, the Trait scales would be expected to show higher reliability coefficients and this is supported by the data. All scales, except the Positive Affect scale, show satisfactory reliabilities for periods up to 8 weeks.

NORMS. As part of the MAACL-R revision process, norms were developed for the Trait form. Analysis of information presented in the manual suggests that the Trait-form norms are based on a representative nationwide sample with proportional representation for sex, racial, regional, educational, and financial distributions in the United States. The new norms will probably result in greater research and clinical use of the MAACL-R Trait form. The norms for the State form are restricted and based only on a sample of 538 midwestern students examined in groups. As such, norms for the State version are not representative. This suggests a need for restandardization with a larger, more representative sample. The authors address this particular weakness directly in the manual and suggest that despite the lack of standardization, test-retest comparisons may still be conducted using existing State *T* scores as such comparisons are within subjects.

In summary, the MAACL-R is a psychometrically improved version of the popular MAACL. The Trait form is now standardized and new validity studies cited in the manual suggest direct clinical applications in assessment of affect and affective characteristics. The MAACL-R also shows promise for pre- and post-treatment measures of therapeutic effectiveness on a broad range of variables, including emotional aspects of health, stress, and stress management, as well as differential diagnosis. With its improved psychometric foundation, it is anticipated that the MAACL-R will continue to find considerable utility in psychological research and evaluation of treatment effectiveness.

[206]

Myers-Briggs Type Indicator. Purpose: "To identify, from self-report of easily recognized reactions, the basic preferences of people in regard to perception and judgment, so that the effects of each preference, singly and in combination, can be established by research and put to practical use." Grades 9–16 and adults; 1943–85; MBTI; based on personality theory of C. G. Jung; 4 scores: Extraversion vs. Introversion, Sensing vs. Intuition, Thinking vs. Feeling, Judgment vs. Perception; 3 forms available: F, G, abbreviated version; 1987 price data: $9.50 per 25 Form F or G question booklets; $12 per 25 abbreviated version question booklets; $6.50 per 50 answer sheets; $10 per handscoring keys; $5.50 per 50 individual report forms; $20 per manual ('85, 319 pages); $3 per specimen set; $200 per complete MBTI software program (IBM PC or IBM-compatible personal computer); CAPT scoring service, $6 or less per test; (30–40) minutes; Katharine C. Briggs, Isabel Briggs Myers, and Mary H. McCaulley (revised manual); Consulting Psychologists Press, Inc.*

For a review by Anthony J. DeVito, see 9:739 (19 references); see also T3:1555 (42 references); for a review by Richard W. Coan, see 8:630 (115 references); see also T2:1294 (120 references) and P:177 (56 references); for reviews by Gerald A. Mendelsohn and Norman D. Sundberg and an excerpted review by Laurence Siegel, see 6:147 (10 references).

TEST REFERENCES

1. Kerr, B. A. (1983). Raising the career aspirations of gifted girls. *The Vocational Guidance Quarterly*, 32, 37-43.

2. Pinkney, J. W. (1983). The Myers-Briggs Type Indicator as an alternative in career counseling. *The Personnel and Guidance Journal*, 62, 173-177.

3. Buchanan, D. R., & Bandy, C. (1984). Jungian typology of prospective psychodramatists: Myers-Briggs type indicator analysis of applicants for psychodrama training. *Psychological Reports*, 55, 599-606.

4. Carlson, R., & Williams, J. (1984). Studies of Jungian typology: III Personality and marriage. *Journal of Personality Assessment*, 48, 87-94.

5. Geer, C., Ridley, S. E., & Roberts, A. (1984). Jungian personality types as a predicator of attendance at the Black College Day march. *Psychological Reports*, 54, 887-890.

6. Grasha, A. F. (1984). Learning styles: The journey from Greenwich Observatory (1796) to the college classroom (1984). *Improving College & University Teaching*, 32, 46-53.

7. Guthrie, T. C., Jr., & Gehman, W. S. (1984). Effects of positive suggestions on mood states. *Educational and Psychological Measurement*, 44, 315-329.

8. Hicks, L. E. (1984). Conceptual and empirical analysis of some assumptions of an explicitly typological theory. *Journal of Personality and Social Psychology*, 46, 1118-1131.

9. Mill, J. (1984). High and low self-monitoring individuals: Their decoding skills and empathic expression. *Journal of Personality*, 52, 372-388.
10. Rovezzi-Carroll, S., & Fitz, P. A. (1984). Predicting allied health major fields of study with selected personality characteristics. *College Student Journal*, 18, 43-51.
11. Thomas, C. R. (1984). Regression of Myers-Briggs Type scales. *Psychological Reports*, 55, 568.
12. Tzeng, O. C. S., Outcalt, D., Boyer, S. L., Ware, R., & Landis, D. (1984). Item validity of the Myers-Briggs Type Indicator. *Journal of Personality Assessment*, 48, 255-256.
13. Westman, A. S., & Canter, F. M. (1984). Diurnal changes on the Myers-Briggs Type Indicator: A pilot study. *Psychological Reports*, 54, 431-434.
14. Baker, D. R. (1985). Predictive value of attitude, cognitive ability, and personality to science achievement in the middle school. *Journal of Research in Science Teaching*, 27, 103-113.
15. Borrello, G. M., & Thompson, B. (1985). Correlates of selected test-wiseness skills. *Journal of Experimental Education*, 53, 124-128.
16. Carlson, J. G. (1985). Recent assessments of the Myers-Briggs Type Indicator. *Journal of Personality Assessment*, 49, 356-365.
17. Eison, J., & Pollio, H. R. (1985). A multidimensional approach to the definition of college students' learning styles. *Journal of College Student Personnel*, 26, 434-443.
18. Feeney, S., & Chun, R. (1985). Effective teachers of young children. *Young Children*, 41 (1), 47-52.
19. Goldsmith, R. E. (1985). Sensation seeking and the sensing-intuition scale of the Myers-Briggs Type Indicator. *Psychological Reports*, 56, 581-582.
20. Hicks, L. E. (1985). Is there a disposition to avoid the fundamental attribution error? *Journal of Research in Personality*, 19, 436-456.
21. Hopkins-Best, M., Wiinamaki, M., & Yurcisin, A. (1985). Career education for college women with disabilities. *Journal of College Personnel*, 26, 220-223.
22. Kelly, E. J. (1985). The personality of chessplayers. *Journal of Personality Assessment*, 49, 282-284.
23. Kreienkamp, R. A., & Luessenheide, H. D. (1985). Similarity of personalities of flight instructors and student-pilots: Effect on flight training time. *Psychological Reports*, 57, 465-466.
24. Mills, J., Robey, D., & Smith, L. (1985). Conflict-handling and personality dimensions of project-management personnel. *Psychological Reports*, 57, 1135-1143.
25. Sipps, G. J., Alexander, R. A., & Friedt, L. (1985). Item analysis of the Myers-Briggs Type Indicator. *Educational and Psychological Measurement*, 45, 789-796.
26. Ward, R. A., & Loftus, E. F. (1985). Eyewitness performance in different psychological types. *Journal of General Psychology*, 112, 191-200.
27. Ware, R., Yokomoto, C., & Morris, B. B. (1985). A preliminary study to assess validity of the Personal Style Inventory. *Psychological Reports*, 56, 903-910.
28. Barrett, L., & Connot, R. (1986). Knowing student personality can help school, classroom, activity participation. *NASSP Bulletin*, 70 (487), 39-45.
29. Buchanan, D. R., & Taylor, J. A. (1986). Jungian typology of professional psychodramatists: Myers-Briggs Type Indicator analysis of certified psychodramatists. *Psychological Reports*, 58, 391-400.
30. Burton, L. (1986). Relationship between musical accompaniment and learning style in problem solving. *Perceptual and Motor Skills*, 62, 48-50.
31. Cann, D. R., & Donderi, D. C. (1986). Jungian personality typology and the recall of everyday and archetypal dreams. *Journal of Personality and Social Psychology*, 50, 1021-1030.
32. Carey, J. C., Hamilton, D. L., & Shanklin, G. (1986). Does personality similarity affect male roommates' satisfaction? *Journal of College Student Personnel*, 27, 65-69.
33. Gordon, V. N., Coscarelli, W. C., & Sears, S. J. (1986). Comparative assessments of individual differences in learning and career decision making. *Journal of College Student Personnel*, 27, 233-242.
34. Hai, D. M., Ziemelis, A., & Rossi, J. (1986). Personality types: Comparison of job applications and applicants. *Psychological Reports*, 59, 1119-1125.
35. Kerr, B. A. (1986). Career counseling for the gifted: Assessments and interventions. *Journal of Counseling and Development*, 64, 602-604.
36. Leiden, L. I., Veach, T. L., & Herring, M. W. (1986). Comparison of the abbreviated and original versions of the Myers-Briggs Type Indicator personality inventory. *Journal of Medical Education*, 61, 319-321.
37. Schurr, K. T., Houlette, F., & Ellen, A. (1986). The effects of instructors and student Myers-Briggs Type Indicator characteristics on the accuracy of grades predicted for an introductory English composition course. *Educational and Psychological Measurement*, 46, 989-1000.
38. Stoltenberg, C. D., Pace, T., & Maddux, J. E. (1986). Cognitive style and counselor credibility: Effects of client endorsement of Rational Emotive Therapy. *Cognitive Therapy and Research*, 10, 237-243.
39. Thompson, B., & Borrello, G. M. (1986). Construct validity of the Myers-Briggs Type Indicator. *Educational and Psychological Measurement*, 46, 745-752.
40. Sipps, G. J., & Alexander, R. A. (1987). The multifactorial nature of extraversion-introversion in the Myers-Briggs Type Indicator and Eysenck Personality Inventory. *Educational and Psychological Measurement*, 47 (3), 543-552.
41. Corman, L. S., & Platt, R. G. (1988). Correlations among the Group Embedded Figures Test, the Myers-Briggs Type Indicator and demographic characteristics: A business school study. *Perceptual and Motor Skills*, 66 (2), 507-511.
42. Schurr, K. T., Ruble, V. E., & Henriksen, L. W. (1988). Relationship of Myers-Briggs Type Indicator personality characteristics and self-reported academic problems and skill ratings with Scholastic Aptitude Test scores. *Educational and Psychological Measurement*, 48 (1), 187-196.

Review of the Myers-Briggs Type Indicator by JERRY S. WIGGINS, Professor of Psychology, The University of British Columbia, Vancouver, Canada:

During the last decade, the role of personality theory in guiding the construction and evaluation of personality tests has received increasing emphasis. Historically, this emphasis may be traced to the introduction of the notion of construct validity first proposed by Cronbach and Meehl (1955) and subsequently elaborated by such writers as Loevinger (1957) and Jackson (1971). Although the construct point of view has gained wider acceptance as a set of principles, there have been few attempts to implement these principles in practice. The Myers-Briggs Type Indicator (MBTI) is a notable exception to this trend and the fact that it has been largely ignored by proponents of the construct point of view illustrates a feature of construct validity that is seldom discussed: "Unless substantially the same nomological net is accepted by the several users of the construct public validation is impossible . . . . A consumer of the test who rejects the author's theory cannot accept the author's validation" (Cronbach & Meehl, 1955, p. 291).

The MBTI is an excellent example of a construct-oriented test that is inextricably linked to Jung's (1923) theory of psychological types. A slightly modified version of Jung's theory determined the substantive, structural, and external considerations involved in all stages of the construction and evaluation of this instrument. Hence, it is not surprising that the MBTI is held in high regard by many who subscribe to this aspect of Jungian theory. It is also not surprising that those who do not accept the tenets of the theory reject, or more typically ignore, the considerable body of evidence regarding the validity of the MBTI that now exists. Even though the familiar construct of "extraversion" is central to dimensional theories of personality such as those of Eysenck and Cattell, the Jungian construct of an "extraverted attitude" as a dynamic component within a psychological *type* is embedded in a very different nomological net. The validity of the MBTI can be evaluated independently of the total corpus of Jung's writings but it cannot be fairly appraised outside the more delimited context of Jung's theory of psychological types. As with any construct-oriented test, both the validity of the test and the validity of the theory are at issue.

The principal stumbling block to more widespread acceptance of the MBTI lies in the structural model of bipolar discontinuous types to which the test authors are firmly committed. The attitudes of extraversion versus introversion (EI), the perceptual styles of sensing versus intuition (SN), the judgmental styles of thinking versus feeling (TF), and the orientations to the outer world of judgment versus perception (JP) are all assumed to be genuine dichotomies with true zero points. On the basis of responses to forced-choice items (e.g., one keyed E and the other I), the difference between points on two scales determines the respondent's preference (ties are not permitted). Preferences are indicated by a letter designation (e.g., E) and a number indicating strength of the preference (e.g., 25); the former was considered by Myers to be more important than the latter. The four preferences are assumed to interact in complex nonlinear ways to produce one of 16 psychological *types* (e.g., ESTJ), and this is reflected in the manner in which dominant, auxiliary, and inferior functions are identified for extraverts and introverts.

Evidence bearing on the structural-dynamic model underlying the MBTI is of a different form than evidence bearing on the more traditional continuous multivariate model in which variables are assumed to combine in an additive fashion. This would include, among other things: (*a*) direct evidence of bimodal distributions of preference scores; (*b*) indirect evidence of discontinuities between bipolar preferences when the two halves of the bipolar preference scales are plotted against a third variable; (*c*) evidence of the temporal stability of type classification over time; and (*d*) frequency distributions of types within and between criterion groups that are in accord with theoretical expectations. From the studies described in the MBTI manual, it would appear that evidence of the first kind is nonexistent; evidence of the second kind is only occasionally suggestive (e.g., the slopes of the distributions of E and I scales appear to differ when plotted against ratings of gregariousness); evidence of the third kind is somewhat disappointing (e.g., over periods of time ranging from 5 weeks to 6 years, the proportion of four-variable profile types that remain the same seldom exceeds 50%); and evidence of the fourth kind is often promising (e.g., the type distributions of creative architects, mathematicians, research scientists, and writers strongly support the notion of intuitive types).

For those who would prefer to interpret the MBTI as a set of four, normally-distributed, bipolar continuous scales, there is a wealth of external validity information presented in the extensive manual (actually a handbook) that provides a reasonably consistent picture of what the individual scales do and do not measure. Those whose commitment to the dimensional perspective is less tenacious are urged to peruse this manual in its entirety for a full description of the most notable attempt, to date, to develop measures of Jung's psychological types.

REVIEWER'S REFERENCES

Jung, C. G. (1923). *Psychological types.* Translated by H. Godwyn Baynes. London: K. Paul, French, Trubner & Co., Ltd.; New York: Harcourt, Brace & Co., Inc.

Cronbach, L. J., & Meehl, P. E. (1955). Construct validity in psychological tests. *Psychological Bulletin*, 52, 281-302.

Loevinger, J. (1957). Objective tests as instruments of psychological theory. *Psychological Reports*, 3, 635-694.

Jackson, D. N. (1971). The dynamics of structured personality tests: 1971. *Psychological Review*, 78, 229-248.

[207]

National Assessment of Educational Progress Released Exercises: Citizenship and Social Studies. Purpose: "A continuing, congressionally mandated national survey of knowledge, skills, understanding, and attitudes of young Americans" in the fields of citizenship and social studies. Ages 9 and 13 and 17; 1969–82; NAEP; released-exercise set, which is approximately 1/4 of complete assessment package administered to national sample of the specified age groups in 1981–82 (Third Assessment); manual entitled *Citizenship and Social Studies Objectives,* 1981–82 *Assessment,* 5 objectives: Demonstrates Skills Necessary to Acquire Information, Demonstrates Skills Necessary to Use Information, Demonstrates an Understanding of Individual Development and the Skills Necessary to Communicate With Others, Demonstrates an Understanding of and Interest in the Ways Human Beings Organize/Adapt to/Change Their Environments, Demonstrates an Understanding of and Interest in the Development of the United States; price data available from publisher; released exercises are in the public domain and may be copied without restriction; manual ('80, 39 pages); National Assessment of Educational Progress; Educational Testing Service.*

Review of the National Assessment of Educational Progress Released Exercises: Citizenship and Social Studies by GARY J. ROBERTSON, Director, Test Division, American Guidance Service, Inc., Circle Pines, MN:

Upon completion of the third national assessment of citizenship/social studies in 1981–1982, 64 of the exercises were released so that state and local school districts might make use of these in their own assessment programs. The exercises are best viewed as an item bank, with each item keyed to a particular objective developed by the National Assessment of Educational Progress (NAEP). Released exercises are in the public domain and may be reproduced without restriction. A state or local education authority would find the NAEP item bank useful if there was agreement between the NAEP and local curriculum objectives.

According to the explanatory materials provided with the exercises, the NAEP citizenship/social studies objectives and subobjectives were developed over a period of 1 year by content experts and subsequently reviewed by several hundred educators and lay persons. The list of reviewers is impressive in its scope. Exercises written to measure the NAEP objectives are of three types: objective (multiple-choice or true-false), open ended, or a combination of objective and open ended. Exercises vary from a single multiple-choice or completion item to items with multiple parts using mixed formats.

Of primary concern for an item bank such as this is the quality of objectives and the items that measure these objectives. The process used to develop the objectives seems to have resulted in a comprehensive, useful content structure. There are some excellent items measuring the higher order cognitive processes of application and synthesis of knowledge. A number of the two-option items, however, are not impressive and one wonders if multiple-choice items might not have provided better measurement of those objectives. Exercise 402006, for example, uses a two-option format for each of eight separate items. Seven of these items are keyed to option one, with only one keyed to option two. An acquiescence response set for position would provide faulty data in this case and illustrates a well-known problem with any two-option item type.

Interpretation of the exercise results can be accomplished by use of the *p*-values obtained from a national probability sample of 9-, 13-, and 17-year-olds tested in the NAEP survey. *P*-values of modal grade groups (grades 4, 8, and 11) are also provided. For a given exercise, the *p*-values are available for 1–3 of the age or grade groups, depending upon the number of ages (or grades) at which the exercise was administered in the national survey. Formulas for computing the standard error of the *p*-values are given but there is practically no discussion or illustration of how these are to be used.

This reviewer feels NAEP should provide more information to assist consumers in the use and interpretation of results obtained from the local administration of these exercises. As with any test, there is the possibility of misuse of these exercises if they are used as the basis for making incorrect inferences about the success of local educational effort and curricular effectiveness. NAEP has not addressed these issues in the scanty material disseminated with the exercise set.

In conclusion, the 64 NAEP exercises released from the 1981–82 citizenship/social studies assessment of 9-, 13-, and 17-year-olds may be helpful to state and local education agencies whose curricular objectives match those of NAEP and who have the resources to guide proper use and interpretation of the results.

[208]

National Assessment of Educational Progress Released Exercises: Mathematics. Purpose: "A continuing, congressionally mandated national survey of knowledge, skills, understanding, and attitudes of young Americans" in the field of mathematics. Ages 9 and 13 and 17; 1969–82; NAEP; released-exercise set, which is approximately 1/4 of complete assessment package administered to national sample of the specified age groups in 1981–82 (Third Assessment); manual entitled *Mathematics Objectives,* 1981–82 *Assessment*; 11 scores: process levels (Mathematical Knowledge, Mathematical Skill, Mathematical Understanding, Mathematical Application, Attitudes Toward Mathematics), content areas (Numbers and Numeration, Variables and Relationships, Shape/Size/Position, Measurement, Statistics/Probability, Technology); price data available from publisher; released exercises are in the public domain and may be copied without restriction; manual ('81, 44 pages); National Assessment of Educational Progress; Educational Testing Service.*

[209]

National Business Competency Tests: Accounting Procedures Test—Trial Edition. Purpose: Measures marketable productivity in the area of accounting procedures. High school and college and adults; 1984; no manual; 5 tasks: General Accounting Procedures, Payroll Records, Bank Reconciliation, Worksheet for a Merchandising Business, Journalizing and Posting; 1985 price data: $.75 per test; $.75 per scoring key; (100) minutes; National Business Education Association.*

[210]

National Business Competency Tests: Office Procedures Test. Purpose: "To help teachers and employers determine whether prospective employees (students) are ready for entry-level office jobs, excluding typewriting tasks." High school and college and adults; 1981; 21 jobs: Filling Out a Job Application Form, Office Services (Comparing Words and Numbers, Proofreading, Editing, Mail Activities, Telephoning), Indexing and Filing (Alphabetizing, File Labels, Sequencing Numbers, Subject Captions, Geographic Filing, File Drawers), Payroll (Time Report, Computing the Payroll Journal), Accounting Services (Deposit Slip, Checkbook, Purchase Order, Purchase Invoice), Computation (Computing Cost of Dresses, Computing the Loss on Sales at Below Standard Prices, Computing Revenue Earned on Slacks Sold at Varying Prices); 1985 price data: $.75 per test; $.75 per manual (4 pages); (100) minutes; National Business Education Association.*

Review of the National Business Competency Test: Office Procedures Test by BRUCE J. EBERHARDT, Associate Professor of Management, University of North Dakota, Grand Forks, ND:

The National Business Competency Test: Office Procedures Test (NBC-OPT) was developed to assess the readiness of high school and college students for entry-level office jobs, excluding typewriting tasks. Examination of the content of the test indicates that it possesses face validity. Many of the tasks normally assigned to an entry-level office worker are included in the test.

The test is comprised of two separate parts. The first part consists of 12 jobs covering a variety of office services in addition to the completion of a job application. The jobs are typical of those engaged in by first-level office workers. The second part of the test includes nine jobs involving simple computations and accounting services.

The test can be administered to groups and the publisher suggests that the two separate parts can be given on two different days. The test is timed in that each part should be completed within a 50-minute time limit. The 2-day, 50-minute administration lends itself nicely for testing in high school and college courses in office procedures or secretarial practice. In the four-page manual, users are provided with a general explanation of the test. The publisher offers the suggestion that students' motivational level could be increased by incorporating NBC-OPT results into students' final grades.

The instructions for administration recommend that students be required to use ball point pens in completing the test. In addition, calculators and extra paper may be made available for the computations. However, if each student has access to a calculator, the recommended time for completion of the second part is 25 to 38 minutes. No explanation is given for the range of time allowed when a calculator is used. For those concerned with standardization of testing conditions, this is a decided weakness.

Although the NBC-OPT appears to possess adequate content and face validity, there are several glaring weaknesses associated with its very sparse four-page manual. The first such weakness involves the scoring of the test. Thirty-four of the 238 possible points on Part 1 of the test are allocated to the completion of a job application form. The instructions for scoring the application form suggest that "Every item should be neatly and correctly filled in for 34 points." Given that it may be very difficult for test users to assess the correctness of certain responses and that estimations of neatness are susceptible to variations in individual perceptions, the scoring of the job application form is open to a great deal of subjectivity. Another problem with the recommended scoring of the test concerns the granting of bonus points. Test scorers are provided with easily interpreted scoring keys for the remaining 20 jobs; however, the scoring instructions once again permit subjectivity on the part of the scorer. The manual states that up to five bonus points can be given for completion of Part 1 before the time allowed and that an extra bonus point can be given for each completed job that is accurate and neat. This allows for a substantial amount of discretion on the part of the test scorers, and standardization of scoring procedures suffers as a result.

The major weakness of the test manual is the total lack of data on the reliability and validity of the test. Additionally, normative data are missing. Cutoff scores are provided for each part to judge "superior" and "good" performance. However, no mention is made of how these standards were developed or the nature of the sample on which they were developed. The manual states that "The NBEA [National Business Education Association] Test Committee recommends that research individuals and groups gather data to report performance norms and indexes of validity and reliability to NBEA. In such cases, a scoring and evaluation guide should be prepared for the participating teachers to assure uniformity of test administration and scoring." It should be noted that the National Business Education Association has been criticized (in *Mental Measurements Yearbook* reviews over the years) for failing to supply test validation data, and has not yet attempted to rectify this major deficiency.

In summary, the NBC-OPT appears to possess both face and content validity. It should prove to be a useful assessment device for teachers of high school and college courses in office procedures or secretarial practice. Users should, however, take care to ensure standardization of administration conditions and scoring. On the other hand, the test cannot be recommended to employers as a selection tool in the hiring of entry-level office workers. Before such a use can be supported, evidence of the reliability and validity of the test and normative performance data must be documented in the manual.

Review of the National Business Competency Tests: Office Procedures Test by WILBUR L. LAYTON, Professor of Psychology, Iowa State University, Ames, IA:

This test was constructed by a committee of the National Business Education Association. The test user is advised to tell "students that they are participating in a national project to help teachers and employers determine whether prospective employees (students) are ready for entry-level office jobs, excluding typewriting tasks." From this statement I infer that the test was constructed as part of a national assessment project. There is no further indication of how the tests might be used.

The test consists of two parts, each given in 50 minutes. Part 1, Office Services, includes 12 jobs. The jobs include things such as completion of a job application, checking, proofreading, telephoning, and mail services. Part 2 consists of nine jobs involving computation and accounting services such as payroll, accounting forms, and computation. According to the manual the jobs "are typically found in the office." No further evidence of content validity is given.

The two parts are intended for administration to students in office procedures, secretarial practice, or cooperative office education. The test "may be used with high school and college populations" according to the manual.

Under the heading "Standards" the manual states point expectations for "superior" and "good" students. No normative data are presented. Jobs are expected to be completed, neat, and accurate. No objective definitions are given for these criteria.

Scoring key models are presented in the manual. Test users are advised to follow their "usual practices and standards for evaluating basic skills and job performance."

The manual contains the following statement: "The NBEA Test Committee recommends that research individuals and groups gather data to report performance norms and indexes of validity and reliability to NBEA." This recommendation is commendable; however, the tests meet few if any of the published test standards. Until evidence of content and other forms of validity and reliability are available, the tests should be used with great caution and only as classroom exercises by a knowledgeable teacher.

[211]

National Business Competency Tests: Secretarial Procedures Test. Purpose: "To help teachers and employers determine whether prospective secretarial employees (students) are ready for entry-level jobs." Secondary and postsecondary students completing a secretarial program; 1983; 6 tasks: Filling Out a Job Application Form, Secretarial Procedures Information, Editing, Priority Assignments, Calendar Notations, Letter and Envelope; 1985 price data: $.75 per test; $.75 per manual (4 pages); (100) minutes; National Business Education Association.*

Review of the National Business Competency Tests: Secretarial Procedures Test by MICHAEL RYAN, Clinical Psychologist, West Side Family Mental Health Clinic, P. C., Kalamazoo, MI:

The National Business Competency Tests: Secretarial Procedures Test purports to measure the secretarial skills of secondary and post-secondary students completing a secretarial program. It consists of two parts which should be administered on consecutive days. A ball-point pen is required for the first day and a typewriter for the second day. The tests take a total of 100 minutes to administer. On the first part, students are asked to fill out a job application, answer a multiple choice test on secretarial procedures, and perform a proofing and editing task. On the second part, students prioritize six tasks and then complete them. These tasks include typing minutes, a letter, an agenda, a purchase order, and a memo. In addition, each student is asked to update an employer's calendar. The directions for Part 1 are straightforward and understandable. However, the directions for Part 2 are more complex and somewhat confusing. The strength of these tests lies in the broad range of secretarial skills they measure. In addition to the clerical tasks, such as proofing, these tests ask the student to perform more cognitive tasks such as prioritizing time. A variety of typing skills are measured on Part 2. The author should be commended for the breadth of secretary abilities measured in this instrument.

However, these tests are wholly lacking in the psychometric information that is needed to make them useful to the educator, employer, or researcher. The brief (four-page) test manual includes little of the information deemed essential in the *Standards For Educational and Psychological Testing*, which was prepared by a joint committee of the American Educational Research Association, the American Psychological Association, and the National Council on Measurement in Education (AERA et al, 1985). Strict scoring procedures, normative data, reliability data, and validity data are absent. Although scoring procedures for Part 1 are straightforward, scoring on Part 2 is somewhat confusing, and the manual ends by stating "follow your usual practices and standards for evaluating basic secretarial skills and job performance." Because such procedures and standards may vary greatly, this section is of questionable reliability and scores become meaningless.

The manual provides a cutoff score of 170 (85 points for each section) to indicate a good student at the secondary or post-secondary levels. However, no information was given as to how this cutoff was determined and no other normative data were provided. Furthermore, no information was provided to suggest differences in performance in regard to age, sex, or minority group membership. Although comprehensive norms would be preferable, at minimum separate means and standard deviations for secondary and post-secondary students are required to make these tests meaningful. In addition, normative data on intercorrelations on each subtest are also essential to understand the interrelationships among tests.

The authors have provided no reliability data. Therefore, it cannot be determined whether these tests will yield consistent scores over time. Furthermore, without consistent and clear scoring procedures, low reliability would be expected.

Finally, although the test purports to "help teachers and employers determine whether prospective secretarial employees (students) are ready for entry level jobs," the manual offers no validity studies whatsoever. At most, the manual states that reviewers of the tests, (unspecified) as well as the committee that developed the tests, judged these items to be significant measures of secretarial competency. This hardly suffices to prove this instrument's validity.

At first glance, the National Business Competency Test appears to possess content validity. It provides a reasonable sample of the skills needed by a typical secretary. However, the lack of consistent scoring procedures and normative data bring into question the validity of this instrument. In addition to a more rigorous psychometric foundation for this test, studies of predictive and concurrent validity are necessary. Correlations with job performed and other established tests would help substantiate the author's claims that this instrument measures secretarial skills.

Finally, the manual offers no discussion of what results mean or how to use results to remediate deficits. It is reasonable to assume that deficits on some tests are more significant than others. For example, a deficit in the knowledge of office procedures seems more detrimental than an inability to type an office memo. If this test is for use by educators, recommendations for remediating specified deficits would be extremely helpful.

In summary, the National Business Competency Tests: Secretarial Procedures Test, has some potential because of the diversity of the abilities that are measured; yet it cannot be recommended for use by educators, employers, or researchers because of a lack of consistent scoring procedures, reliability data, normative data, and validity data. Furthermore, the manual needs to include a more comprehensive discussion of the test's uses and appropriate populations. The test developers would do well to develop a clear and more consistent system of scoring, perform reliability and normative studies, and evaluate the validity of these measures against other secretarial tests and the actual success of students in secretarial positions. A similar test that provides more psychometric information, but still is somewhat flawed, is the Office Skills Test published by Science Research Associates.

REVIEWER'S REFERENCE

American Educational Research Association, American Psychological Association, & National Council on Measurement in Education. (1985). *Standards for educational and psychological testing*. Washington, DC: American Psychological Association, Inc.

Review of the National Business Competency Tests: Secretarial Procedures Test by PAUL W. THAYER, Professor and Head of Psychology, North Carolina State University, Raleigh, NC:

The Secretarial Procedures Test presents some interesting problems for the reviewer. It has been prepared by a committee of business-procedures educators for the purpose of measuring secretarial skills. The contents look very interesting to this reviewer. I would, for example, want my secretary to know many of the things required: calling an 800 number instead of a billable number, choosing the appropriate mail service, delivering an urgent message to me during an important meeting with minimal disruption, editing rough copy, setting work priorities, etc. The test certainly has high face validity.

Unfortunately, it suffers from a host of deficiencies. I requested information concerning a number of these, but answers were not forthcoming within the time allowed for this review. The manual does not contain answers to the questions that many test users would have.

Despite my impression of face validity, there is no information as to how the contents of the test were determined. There is no indication of a series of job or curriculum analyses. Because one doesn't know the universe of possible test items, it is hard to say how representative the item sample is.

There are also some peculiarities with regard to administration instructions. The option to give the test in one or two sittings is possible, and extra points for completing part of the test early can be given. The impact of these procedures on the scoring system is not explained, nor is the rationale for them given. Further, we are informed that good students should receive 85 or more points (out of 100) on each part of the test. No other normative information is given. There are also some unusual instructions for scoring which might inadvertently penalize a student twice for an error. Students are penalized for incorrect priority assignments, and for failure to complete assignments. As different assignments get different weights, incorrect priority assignment may result in extra penalties for failing to complete a given task.

There is also a serious error in the "calendar notation" section. The student is to take two telephone memos and correct the boss's calendar. The calendar in the test booklet is already corrected and is identical to that in the scoring key booklet.

Most serious is the failure to provide any normative, reliability, or validity data. The NBEA Test Committee recommends that researchers collect such data and submit them to NBEA. The reviewer hopes that will be done. Given the mistakes and inadequate information on psychometric properties, one cannot recommend this instrument.

[212]

National Business Competency Tests: Typewriting Test. Purpose: To determine a prospective typist's skill level. High school and college and adults; 1979; 7 parts: Straight Copy, Statistical Copy, Filling in Lines on a Form, Business Letter, Table, Report Manuscript, Business Form; 1985 price data: $.75 per test; $.75 per manual (4 pages); (100) minutes; National Business Education Association.*

Review of the National Business Competency Tests: Typewriting Test by WILBUR L. LAYTON, Professor of Psychology, Iowa State University, Ames, IA:

This test was constructed by a committee of the National Business Education Association. According to the manual, the test is to be administered to students in advanced typing courses and may be used with both high school and college student populations. There are two parts to the test. Part one was designed to measure basic keystroking skills: speed and accuracy on straight copy and on statistical copy (5 minutes). Part two was designed to measure in 50 minutes, the ability to do practical typing jobs which are evaluated on (*a*) form and arrangement of typed matter, (*b*) accuracy of copy produced, (*c*) time used to complete the work, and (*d*) ability to follow directions.

Part one tasks are said to be of average difficulty. The manual contains no information about how average difficulty was determined. Part two consists of five typing jobs. Presumably these are "typical jobs performed by office typists." No information is presented on how the jobs were selected.

There are no norms presented in the manual. Under the heading "Standards" the test user is advised to "use your own departmental standards" for part one. For part two the "Standards" lists expectations for "better students who have finished advanced typewriting." The standards section also says, "the test construction committee judges that the test meets the usual requirements of validity and reliability." No evidence is presented.

This typewriting test may be useful to typing teachers. It may meet their need for a classroom exercise. It appears to be no better than what an experienced teacher could generate. The manual is totally inadequate. Details of the construction of the tests are not given. There is no information about norms, reliability, and validity. Given the increasing use of microcomputers and word processors one wonders if this test is obsolete. In any event this "test" is recommended for use only as a classroom exercise in typing courses.

[213]

The National Tests of Basic Skills. Purpose: Designed to help schools improve instruction, communicate with parents, and summarize district data on student learning. Preschool–K.5, K.0–K.9, K.6–1.5, 1.0–1.9, 1.6–2.9, 2.6–3.9, 3.6–4.9, 4.6–5.9, 5.6–6.9, 6.6–7.9, 7.6–8.9, 8.6–10.9, 10.6–12.9, 11.6–college; 1985; 14 levels; 1987 price data: $13.55–$15.40 per 10 test booklets and examiner's manual for each level; $10.60 per 35 answer sheets; $12.75 per 35 answer folders; $10.60 per answer key for all levels; $8.50 per teacher's guide for Level P–D, E–J, or K–M; $47.70 per specimen set of all levels; $15.90 per specimen set of Levels P–D or K–M; $21.20 per specimen set of Levels E–J; American Testronics.*

a) LEVEL P. Preschool–K.5; 11 scores: Visual Matching, Combining Information, Silly Pictures, Visual Oddities, Generalization, Auditory Attention, Auditory Picture Closure, Auditory Picture Rhymes, Auditory Comprehension, Developmental Mathematics, Total; examiner paced.

b) LEVEL A. K.0–K.9; 7 scores: Listening Comprehension, Alphabet Knowledge, Letter Recognition, Sound Recognition, Word Matching, Mathematics, Total; (109) minutes.

c) LEVEL B. K.6–1.5; 7 scores: Word Attack, Listening Comprehension, Vocabulary, Reading Comprehension, Language Expression, Mathematics, Total; (123) minutes.

d) LEVEL C. Grades 1.0–1.9; 9 scores: Word Attack, Vocabulary, Reading Comprehension, Language Expression, Mathematics Computation, Mathematics Concepts and Applications, Social Studies, Science, Total; (163) minutes.

e) LEVEL D. Grades 1.6–2.9; 11 scores: same as *d* plus Spelling, Language Mechanics; (193) minutes.
f) LEVEL E. Grades 2.6–3.9; 12 scores: Vocabulary, Reading Comprehension, Spelling, Language Mechanics, Language Expression, References, Mathematics Computation, Mathematics Concepts, Mathematics Applications, Social Studies, Science, Total; (228) minutes.
g) LEVEL F. Grades 3.6–4.9; scores same as *f*; (261) minutes.
h) LEVEL G. Grades 4.6–5.9; scores and time same as *g*.
i) LEVEL H. Grades 5.6–6.9; scores and time same as *g*.
j) LEVEL I. Grades 6.6–7.9; scores and time same as *g*.
k) LEVEL J. Grades 7.6–8.9; scores and time same as *g*.
l) LEVEL K. Grades 8.6–10.9; 11 scores: Vocabulary, Reading Comprehension, Spelling, Language Mechanics, Language Expression, Written Expression, Mathematics Computation, Mathematics Concepts and Applications, Social Studies, Science, Total; (177) minutes.
m) LEVEL L. Grades 10.6–12.9, scores and time same as *l*.
n) LEVEL M. Grades 11.6–college; scores and time same as *l*.

Review of The National Tests of Basic Skills by CLINTON I. CHASE, Director, Bureau of Evaluative Studies and Testing, and Professor of Educational Psychology, Indiana University, Bloomington, IN:

The National Tests of Basic Skills is a new (1985 copyright) achievement battery designed to assess basic skills from prekindergarten to college level. There are 14 overlapping test levels: tests P, A, and B covering the preschool level; B through G covering grades 1 to 6; and H through M covering the junior and senior high schools and college. The skills to be tested are placed at the grade level where they presumably receive greatest emphasis. For example, test level D (grades 1.6–2.9) contains a subtest in word attack skills; this subtest does not appear in later tests. A subtest in use of references is found in test levels E through J (grades 2.6–8.9), but not elsewhere. The basic skills that cross all levels are vocabulary, reading comprehension, spelling, language mechanics, language expression, written expression, mathematics computation, mathematics concepts and applications, social studies, and science.

Only one form of the test is currently available. This somewhat limits the use of the National Tests in a continuing testing program. The tests are good enough that one would hope that a second (and third) form of the tests will be forthcoming.

A variety of scores are available to users: raw scores, grade equivalents, equal interval scores, normal curve equivalents, percentile ranks, and stanines. Many teachers and most parents may find this array of data confusing, but the manuals and the printouts contain well done explanatory notes that help even statistically unsophisticated users get the most out of the data.

Test reliabilities are not listed in the manual, but the standard errors for total skill scores are. They range from .3 to .4 of a grade equivalent. Standard errors are not available for other scoring systems. The standard errors are often more useful in interpreting scores than are the coefficients that underlie them. Nevertheless, the typical test user also prefers to see the coefficients when judging the quality of the tests.

The tests are based on content validity derived from an examination of basal textbook series, state and school system curriculum guides, recommendations of national curriculum organizations, and advice of curriculum specialists. All items were reviewed by a panel to identify sex, ethnic, or racial bias. The names of the panel are listed in the manual, and they do, indeed, list persons with reputations in the area of test bias. The manuals contain tables of specifications indicating the contents of each skill test at each level. Schools can use these tables to match tests to their particular instructional programs. Also, in the development of the test items, the readability level was assessed as at or below the grade level at which the test is aimed. This feature of the test allows children to deal with the content area concepts without being limited by difficulties in reading. Scores on the science test, for example, are consequently more likely to be tied to science knowledge, not science knowledge confounded by reading problems. Unfortunately the method for assessing readability is not mentioned.

Included in the teachers' manual is a description of the steps followed in pretesting the items. These steps follow accepted psychometric procedures very closely. The fundamentals of test construction appear to have been carefully applied. One feature is missing, however. The geographic location of the students in the item pretests and in the standardization samples is not provided, nor is the number of students in the norming groups at each grade level. This information would be very useful in estimating the representativeness of the samples in terms of either a national population or in terms of the clientele of a given local school that may wish to employ the test. Also, the mean IQ of the standardization sample would be helpful in describing the students tested.

Three teachers' manuals are provided, each covering a set of tests at adjacent levels. The manuals are well done. They are concise and to the point, do not involve technical language, but do include many helpful guides to interpretation of the tests. The manuals will not only improve a teacher's ability to use and interpret the tests, but will also teach a great deal about test construction and about the statistics that go into test results.

Manuals are also provided for test administration. These, too, are concise and focused on the essentials of the task at hand. The instructions to be read to the class are boxed in and on a screened grey background, nicely set off from the rest of the print, making the instructions easy to locate and present to the class. The test booklets are easy to work with and have sketches to increase the informality of the test atmosphere.

In sum, the authors of the National Tests of Basic Skills have carefully followed the procedures of content validity in developing their tests to assess the basic skills presumably taught in schools at all levels. They have written a very useful manual in a concise and direct manner, and printed the tests in a functional format. The tests are limited in that there is only one form at this time. Nonetheless, school systems should give the National Tests careful consideration when choosing an achievement test.

[214]

The NEO Personality Inventory. Purpose: "A concise measure of the five major dimensions or domains of normal adult personality." Adults; 1978–85; NEO-PI; 2 forms: Form S (self-reports), Form R (observer ratings); 23 scores: Neuroticism (Anxiety, Hostility, Depression, Self-Consciousness, Impulsiveness, Vulnerability, Total), Extraversion (Warmth, Gregariousness, Assertiveness, Activity, Excitement-Seeking, Positive Emotions, Total), Openness (Fantasy, Aesthetics, Feelings, Actions, Ideas, Values, Total), Agreeableness, Conscientiousness; IBM or Apple computer-administered version requires 64K 80-column card, 2 floppy disk drives-Apple; 128K and 1 floppy disk drive-IBM; 1987 price data: $42 per complete kit including 10 reusable test booklets, 25 Form S profile forms, 25 Form S answer sheets, scoring keys, and manual ('85, 48 pages); $9.50 per 10 reusable test booklets; $7.50 per 25 answer sheets; $6 per 25 profile forms; $12 per set of scoring keys; $10 per manual; $24 per introductory kit including manual, scoring keys, 1 of each test booklet, scoring key, and answer sheet; $95 per computer version; (30) minutes; Paul T. Costa, Jr. and Robert R. McCrae; Psychological Assessment Resources, Inc.*

TEST REFERENCES

1. Costa, P. T., Jr., McCrae, R. R., & Holland, J. L. (1984). Personality and vocational interests in an adult sample. *Journal of Applied Psychology*, 69, 390-400.

2. McCrae, R. R. (1986). Well-being scales do not measure social desirability. *Journal of Gerontology*, 41, 390-392.

3. McCrae, R. R., & Costa, P. T., Jr. (1986). Personality, coping, and coping effectiveness in an adult sample. *Journal of Personality*, 54, 385-405.

4. McCrae, R. R., Costa, P. T., Jr., & Busch, C. M. (1986). Evaluating comprehensiveness in personality systems: The California Q-Set and the five-factor model. *Journal of Personality*, 54, 430-446.

5. McCrae, R. R. (1987). Creativity, divergent thinking, and openness to experience. *Journal of Personality and Social Psychology*, 52, 1258-1265.

6. McCrae, R. R., & Costa, P. T., Jr. (1987). Validation of the five-factor model of personality across instruments and observers. *Journal of Personality and Social Psychology*, 52, 81-90.

Review of The NEO Personality Inventory by ROBERT HOGAN, McFarlin Professor of Psychology, University of Tulsa, Tulsa, OK:

The test authors' goal for the NEO Personality Inventory (NEO-PI) is to provide users with a concise measure of "the five major dimensions or domains of adult personality traits." The scales on many personality inventories have a certain arbitrary quality to them—they are either based on selected elements of traditional theories of personality or on the author's intuitive notions about the structure of personality. In contrast, the NEO-PI is grounded in the mainstream of research over the past 25 years and this is so, in part, because the test authors have been themselves major contributors to that research tradition. They start from the position that there is a growing consensus among personality researchers that the language of ordinary person description—the trait vocabulary—can be parsimoniously organized in terms of five broad dimensions. The NEO-PI is one of the first inventories explicitly designed to assess the five dimensions identified by 50 years of factor analytic research.

The primary scales are Neuroticism, Extraversion, Openness, Agreeableness, and Conscientiousness. The first three of these are composed of six more specific scales that measure facets of the primary or global dimensions. Scores are provided for both the facets and the primary scales. The NEO-PI was carefully developed and this is reflected in its excellent psychometric properties: Internal consistency reliabilities for the facets vary between .60 and .86; for the scales these values are .85 and .93. Test-retest reliabilities range between .66 and .92 for the facets and .86 to .91 for the scales. A facet-level factor analysis suggests that the structure of the first three scales is clear and unambiguous.

The test authors are commendably concerned with the problem of validity. Correlations presented in the manual with the Eysenck Personality Inventory, the Guilford-Zimmerman Temperament Survey, the Loevinger sentence completion test, Holland's Self-Directed Search, and various measures of well-being, suggest good discriminant and convergent validity. Even more persuasive, however, are the correlations reported with spouse and peer ratings—these are significant and substantial, often in the .50 to .70 range.

Four aspects of the NEO-PI warrant special mention. First, the test was developed and validated on a sample of adult men and women rather than college students or mental patients, and this enhances our confidence regarding its general applicability and utility. Second, the test is consistent with what we have learned over the past 50 years about the structure of the trait lexicon. Third, in a refreshing break with the past, the authors offer data and logical analyses to support the view that social desirability does *not* make test scores ambiguous. Finally, although the test authors are psychometric craftsmen, their test development activities were primarily guided by a search for psychological meaning—it is delightful to see substance take precedence over form.

The test has some shortcomings, although these appear to be issues that could be resolved through additional research. The first problem is that only three of the five scales are fully developed; clearly the test authors were in a hurry to get into print. In addition, there are only 363 men in the normative sample, and that group is older and *much* better educated than the population in general. Third, it is not entirely clear what the Openness scale measures. The scale parallels the well-known culture dimension of the five-factor model, but Costa and McCrae give it a political dimension not present in the original scheme; thus, high scorers on Openness favor civil disobedience as well as being interested in the life of the mind.

On balance, however, the NEO-PI is one of the most interesting and well-developed measures of normal personality to appear in 20 years. The test authors have used the NEO-PI very effectively in their research in health psychology, and one suspects the test would work well in other applied settings as well. Although not nearly as well validated as, for example, the California Psychological Inventory, the NEO-PI may ultimately prove to be quite useful in practical applications.

[215]

New England Pantomime Tests. Purpose: "Designed to investigate the nonverbal sending and receiving abilities of aphasic and other communicatively disordered adults." Communicatively disordered adolescents and adults; 1984; 4 tests: Pantomime Recognition Test (Forms A, B), Pantomime Expression Test, Pantomime Referential Abilities Test; individual; 1988 price data: $69 per complete set including manual (36 pages); administration time not reported; Robert J. Duffy and Joseph R. Duffy; PRO-ED, Inc.*

Review of the New England Pantomime Tests by RUSSELL L. ADAMS, Director, Psychology Internship Program, University of Oklahoma Health Sciences Center, Oklahoma City, OK:

The purpose of the New England Pantomime Tests is to measure quantitatively and presumably qualitatively the nonverbal sending and receiving abilities of aphasic patients and other communicationally impaired adults. All the norms are based on adult populations; however, the manual states the test can be used for children. There are actually four different tests included. These tests are the Pantomime Recognition Test, (Forms A and B), the Pantomime Expression Test, and the Pantomime Referential Abilities Test.

The manual states that nonverbal communication behaviors are important to the clinician, especially the speech therapist, because patients use nonverbal pantomimes as compensatory or augmenting mechanisms for communication. The test can be given prior to and following speech therapy in an effort to quantify improvement in sending or receiving ability of nonverbal communication. Because the test is standardized, the therapist can compare the efficacy of different therapeutic approaches.

The test, in this reviewer's opinion, is probably not appropriate for routine inclusion in most psychological or neuropsychological batteries because the amount of information gained by the test normally does not justify the time involved in gathering the data. If a specific question arises concerning the patient's ability to send or receive nonverbal communication signals, then the test could be helpful. The test may well be helpful to speech therapists or speech pathologists. The following is a brief description of each of the four tests.

PANTOMIME RECOGNITION TEST. The Pantomime Recognition Test is a nonverbal task that measures the subject's ability to recognize pantomime acts as being associated with common objects. For example, using this test, the examiner demonstrates the use of a cup for drinking, using pantomime actions. The patient's task is to point to the cup from an array of four pictures presented visually. The specific approach the examiner is to use in pantomiming drinking from a cup is clearly delineated in the manual. To pantomime drinking from a cup, the examiner is instructed to use one hand, beginning with tips of thumb and index finger almost touching and parallel to table. The side of the palm should be touching the table. The examiner is told to bring the hand close to the mouth, rounding lips slightly, and rotating the hand until the index finger is superior to the thumb. The examiner is then instructed to move the hand away from the mouth.

The written description of the pantomimes can be used in conjunction with a videotape demonstration of the pantomimes, which is available presumably from the publisher. However, specific information on how to order the videotape or the cost of the tape is not available in the manual.

Form A of the Pantomime Recognition Test contains 46 items and Form B contains 40. Specific data concerning the length of time for administration of the test are not presented in the manual. Form A differs from Form B in that Form B was developed to make the responses more difficult for aphasic patients by including distractors that are semantically related to the target object. Norms for Form B are not currently available, so this makes interpretation of the performance of a given patient on the test problematic. Norms for Form A, however, are available for three groups of patients: left hemisphere damaged, right hemisphere damaged, and normal controls. The manual provides no statistical tests to show whether the performance of aphasics is significantly different from the performance of the right hemisphere group or the control group. The mean for the aphasic patients on this test was 39.6 while the mean for the right hemisphere damaged group was 43.8. Thus the aphasia patients performed just 5 points lower on this test than did the right hemisphere group.

No test-retest reliability information on the instrument was given for the Pantomime Recognition Test. Given the fluctuation in attention seen in many brain-damaged patients, such data would be helpful in future updates of the test.

PANTOMIME EXPRESSION TEST. In this test the patient is asked to demonstrate the function of an object through pantomime. The patient's performance is videotaped and later scored according to a 16-point scoring system. The Pantomime Expression Test can be considered a measure of expressive deficit while the Pantomime Recognition Test could be considered a measure of pantomime reception deficit.

The interrater reliability of scores for the expression test was computed for only 10 aphasic patients. The correlation was .98. The intrascorer reliability for one score after a 1-year interval was .94 for 13 aphasic patients. This individual scorer looked again at the videotapes that had been made a year earlier.

The norms for 46 aphasic, 25 right hemisphere damaged, and 10 controls were presented. Again, no statistical tests were presented to determine if these groups differ significantly, although inspection of the table would certainly suggest that they do. No data are presented on important factors such as age, education, sex, length of time since onset of aphasia, etiology of aphasia, etc., of the subject population.

An important finding is that no subject in the control group or in the right-hemisphere-damaged group scored as low as the average patient (as measured by either the mean or the median) in the aphasic group. This strikingly low performance of the aphasic group was not found on the Pantomime Recognition Test.

PANTOMIME REFERENTIAL ABILITIES TEST. This test measures the ability of the patient to demonstrate the function of an object to a receiver (not the examiner) to the point that the receiver has obtained sufficient information to identify the object from an array of four pictures. This test differs from the Pantomime Expression Test in that the latter requires the patient's performance to be compared with that described on a 16-point scale. The Pantomime Referential Test uses the same 23 items as the Pantomime Expression Test; however, the distractors are different. At least one of the distractors requires the same location in space or body topography as the target. For example, for the target item "apple," a distractor of a cigarette is given. Both are associated with the mouth area. The more difficult distractor makes the test a more complicated one. No reliability or validity data are presented in the manual on this test. Because the patient demonstrates the function of an object to a receiver (not the examiner), the ability of reviewers is an important consideration. Receivers may differ greatly in the amount of information they need to recognize the pantomime. No data are presented in the manual concerning "receiver" reliability.

SUMMARY. The advantages of the Pantomime Abilities Tests are that they look at nonverbal pantomime communications skills of aphasia from both the receptive and expressive viewpoint. One recent study by the authors not described in the manual demonstrates that Wernicke's (fluent) aphasics were also relatively fluent on the Pantomime Fluency Test, while Broca's (nonfluent aphasics) were relatively nonfluent on the Pantomime Expression Test. Thus the study demonstrated distinct differences in the pantomime fluency in these two aphasic groups which are similar to differences in their speech fluency. In another study involving the test, the test authors concluded that aphasic patients' pantomime expressive deficits are not caused by general intellectual deficits or limb apraxia; instead, these deficits are associated with a central symbolic disorder or a verbal mediation deficit.

The manual does not present concrete descriptions and case examples on how to use this test with a clinical population. The clinician is given no guidance as to why he/she should utilize this test or how it would be utilized. Perhaps the test could best be described as a research instrument in a state of development.

In summary, the tests are interesting ones, particularly because of their theoretical import (i.e., do aphasics also have an underlying impairment to communicate nonverbally through pantomime?). Some of the New England Pantomime Tests must be considered as still under construction because of the lack of adequate norms and validity and reliability studies. The tests would probably not be appropriate for regular inclusion in most neuropsychological batteries or psychological batteries because it is not clear how the results would be used clinically.

Review of the New England Pantomime Tests by JOHN A. COURTRIGHT, Professor and Chair of Communication, University of Delaware, Newark, DE:

The authors of the New England Pantomime Tests (NEPT) have used earlier versions and individual sections of these tests in their published research on aphasia (e.g., Duffy, Duffy, & Pearson, 1975; Duffy & Duffy, 1981; Duffy, Duffy, & Mercaitis, 1984). This has been excellent, trend-setting work, where the primary goal has been to investigate the causal antecedents of aphasic deficits. Unfortunately, the transition from research instrument to published test has resulted in several serious omissions. Users of the NEPT willing to take the time and energy to explore the authors' research may find these omissions less critical. Without this exposure, however, information essential to the understanding and evaluation of the NEPT is simply not available in the test manual.

The most obvious and certainly most perplexing of these omissions is the lack of a definitive statement of purpose. What performance domain is being measured? To what evaluative or diagnostic purpose would scores from the several sections of the NEPT be put? The test manual fails to address these questions in any meaningful way. The authors suggest that nonverbal behaviors should be of interest to clinicians because of their "potential uses as compensatory or augmentative procedures for dealing with deficits in verbal/linguistic skills." This represents the beginnings of a rationale for constructing such a test, but it does not address the use or purpose of the tests per se.

There is only one statement in the manual that speaks directly to the NEPT's purpose: "The New England Pantomime Tests can serve as a standardized measure of pre- and posttraining abilities in studies of the efficacy of clinical procedures designed to enhance communicative functioning through nonverbal modes." What abilities? What procedures? What nonverbal modes? Do the authors intend, as the previous quotation implies, for the NEPT to be solely a research instrument for "studies" of therapeutic effectiveness? Certainly, the manual provides only the vaguest conception of what diagnostic or therapeutic ends the NEPT was designed to serve. As a result, the content validity of these tests is virtually impossible to evaluate.

This absence of a specific purpose also surfaces in the administration and scoring of one of the four tests: the Pantomime Referential Abilities Test (PRAT). In discussing the scoring of this test, the authors state, "Various scores may be obtained." After briefly outlining the measures obtained by Duffy et al. (1984), the authors conclude, "Other measures of accuracy, efficiency, or effectiveness of the subject's performance may also be devised."

Are users of this test really expected to devise other measures? Devise them for what purpose? With what degree of content and criterion-related validity could this be done? The authors seemingly place the burden for test construction and validation on the user, instead of accepting this essential responsibility for themselves. In the research arena, investigators frequently use instruments for a variety of unintended purposes, and thus must assume the responsibility for providing evidence of the reliability and validity of these "devised" measures.

In the clinical setting, however, clinicians have neither the time nor, in many cases, the methodological skills to explore the reliability and validity of their diagnostic instruments. Moreover, they should not be expected to investigate these issues, particularly for published instruments they have purchased! This is the responsibility of the NEPT's authors—a responsibility they have not fulfilled in these test materials.

These several concerns notwithstanding, the most salient omissions from the test manual are the complete absence of any discussion of validity, accompanied by an incomplete treatment of reliability. I will address the issue of reliability first. Although reliability is treated a bit differently for each of the four NEPT tests, it is always approached from the standpoint of scorer or rater reliability. Thus, for example, the authors claim no need to address the reliability of the two Pantomime Recognition Tests, because "there is little room for error in the examiner's recording of the response." Similarly, when presenting the reliability of the Pantomime Expression Test (PET), only interscorer reliability is considered, but the statistic used to calculate this value is not disclosed.

While it is important and necessary to know that independent scorers are highly consistent on these tests, it is, perhaps, more important to be apprised of the *internal* consistency of the tests themselves. Are the 46 items comprising the Pantomime Recognition Test measuring the same phenomenon? What about the 23 items for the PET and the Pantomime Referential Abilities Test (PRAT)? Several different indices of reliability could have provided this essential information, and the omission of internal consistency information must be considered a serious shortcoming.

Equally serious, of course, is the absence of any discussion of the validity of the four tests that comprise the NEPT. Much of this information—particularly information relevant to concurrent validity—is presented in detail in the authors' several research monographs. Moreover, those presentations make a convincing case that the four subtests of the NEPT are each related to established indices of communicative deficits in aphasics, the most notable being the Porch Index of Communicative Ability (PICA).

Despite availability elsewhere, some synthesis or summary of these findings should have been offered in the test manual. Test users have an important practical need to know what other major indices are related to the test they are using. This is especially true in the case of the NEPT, because competent clinicians dealing with aphasic clients will routinely administer the PICA. Given (*a*) the consistently high correlation (across several studies) of these two instruments, and (*b*) the authors' failure to articulate a definitive evaluative/diagnostic purpose (i.e., a performance domain) for the NEPT, one must question what nonredundant information would be obtained by administering the NEPT. The authors almost certainly have an answer to this question, but it is not made apparent in the test materials.

In conclusion, the NEPT is a set of four individual tests for which the transition from research instrument to published test has been less than successful. Information essential for a user to critically evaluate the NEPT is simply not provided. Because no domain of behavioral performance or skill is articulated, it is impossible to evaluate the content validity of the NEPT. In addition, evidence for concurrent validity, which exists in published research reports, is not presented in the test materials. Finally, reliability is incompletely treated as only the agreement among raters, rather than as additionally the internal consistency of the instruments. As a consequence, the user of the NEPT cannot be certain exactly what behavioral phenomenon is being measured, nor how accurately that measurement is being performed. Given these shortcomings and omissions, I cannot recommend the NEPT for general use by speech and language clinicians. The PICA remains a much better and more widely accepted diagnostic instrument.

REVIEWER'S REFERENCES

Duffy, R. J., Duffy, J. R., & Pearson, K. L. (1975). Pantomime recognition in aphasics. *Journal of Speech and Hearing Research*, 18, 115-132.

Duffy, R. J., & Duffy, J. R. (1981). Three studies of deficits in pantomimic expression and pantomimic recognition in aphasia. *Journal of Speech and Hearing Research*, 24, 70-84.

Duffy, R. J., Duffy, J. R., & Mercaitis, P. A. (1984). Comparison of the performances of a fluent and nonfluent aphasic on a pantomimic referential task. *Brain and Language*, 21, 260-273.

[216]

New Macmillan Reading Analysis. Purpose: For "diagnosis and assessment in remedial or clinical settings [and] assessing reading progress in the early Junior years." Ages 6–11; 1985; NMRA; 2 scores: Accuracy, Comprehension; individual; 3 approximately equivalent forms (Form A, Form B, Form C); 1988 price data: £7.50 per Test Reader ('85, 41 pages); £4.50 per 25 Analysis Sheets (A, B, or C); £6.50 per Teacher's Guide ('85, 80 pages); administration time not reported; Denis Vincent, Michael de la Mare, and Helen Arnold (consultant); Macmillan Education Ltd. [England].*

Review of the New Macmillan Reading Analysis by ROGER BRUNING, Professor of Educational Psychology, University of Nebraska-Lincoln, Lincoln, NE, and CAROLYN COLVIN MURPHY, Assistant Professor of Teacher Education, San Diego State University, San Diego, CA:

The New Macmillan Reading Analysis (NMRA) is an individually-administered oral reading inventory designed for elementary-age children. Children are asked to read passages aloud, then to answer oral comprehension questions over them. Both oral reading and comprehension performance are recorded; separate scores can be derived from each. According to its designers, the NMRA is "a flexible test for which a variety of uses are possible."

The present reviewers are, however, less positive than the test developers about the NMRA. Several factors limit its utility in its current form. Some limitations are inherent in the nature of an informal reading inventory. Others, however, might have been avoided by better test development practices.

First, construction of the test does not appear to have been guided by a clear conceptualization of reading processes or their assessment. For instance, no serious theoretical rationale is presented for coupling oral reading with comprehension assessment, for selection of the reading passages, for construction of the comprehension questions, nor for selecting the "target words" for the Words in Context scale. The Accuracy score for oral reading is based on aggregating a variety of errors—inaccuracies, inserting words not in the text, omitting words, reversing two or more separate words, and refusing to read a word—that may or may not have an underlying process in common. When readers are tested orally for comprehension, they may look back at the passage, but "extended re-reading, or word-by-word search" is to be prevented. The illustrations, available for each passage, play an unspecified role in both oral reading and comprehension assessment.

Second, the normative information presently provided for the NMRA cannot be considered as sufficient. The standardization sample was approximately 600 students in 71 Primary schools in two London boroughs. These students had obtained "average" scores for their age group on another reading test. The authors state the restrictions imposed by individual testing precluded a national sampling; nonetheless, little confidence can be placed in the representativeness of the present norms. For a larger U.K. audience and, obviously, for possible overseas users of the NMRA, the available norms have the potential to be misleading. Also, at this point there is no empirical evidence of concurrent validity by which to judge the NMRA.

Because it was developed in England, the NMRA contains a number of instances of English language usage that would be unfamiliar to American students. If the test is marketed in the U.S., these would be problematic. For instance, the first (easiest) passage of Form C contains the sentence, "She came off her bike on the way," an expression unfamiliar to American youngsters. Other passages contain occasional phrases such as "The . . . eighteen-storey block of flats fell down" and "was director of a sweet factory." U.S. test administrators also would encounter potentially unfamiliar terminology in the manual (e.g., Junior school, backward readers) that could contribute to difficulty in judging the measure.

In sum, the NMRA appears to have been published somewhat prematurely and its use in its present form is not recommended. The test developers must provide a clearer perspective on their conception of reading and reflect this perspective in the choices they make in passage selection, use of illustrations, and assessment of accuracy and comprehension. The norms must be better developed and the test validated against other standardized reading tests if it is intended that the test be used throughout the U.K. and distributed in other English-speaking countries.

Review of the New Macmillan Reading Analysis by ROBERT C. CALFEE, Professor of Education, School of Education, Stanford University, Stanford, CA:

The New Macmillan Reading Analysis (NMRA) is best described as a "formalized" informal reading inventory. According to the manual, this individually administered test requires 10 to 15 minutes to administer. The skillful practitioner who takes full advantage of the clinical potential of the instrument is likely to spend much longer on administration and a substantial amount of additional time to interpret the findings.

NMRA is actually three different instruments. Administered and scored in one fashion, the instrument yields *age equivalent* ranges in oral reading accuracy and text comprehension; these measures are similar to grade equivalents, but with upper and lower limits rather than a point-estimate. Administered and scored in another manner leads to Rasch scale scores. Finally, the manual gives instructions for qualitative assessment of student strengths and weaknesses through behavioral observations and miscue analysis.

The manual provides a clear account of the concepts underlying the instrument, instructions for administration, scoring, and interpretation of the findings, and a description of the norming process. Though complex, the ideas are well organized and quite readable.

The strengths of this instrument are its clinical orientation and its value as a model for professional assessment of literacy. The test unfortunately has several limitations, some endemic to the field of reading, some specific to this particular device:

PASSAGES. The core of NMRA is a set of 18 passages divided into three "forms" of six passages each. The passages, which serve to assess both decoding and comprehension, are graded from easy (first grade-ish) to hard (11-year-olds had to make mistakes). More difficult passages are longer, have tougher vocabulary, and are about less familiar topics. The style varies widely (story snippets, advertisements, recipes, and so on). As the manual notes, strange alterations were made to the most difficult levels in order to generate mistakes. The result is a hodgepodge, exacerbated by idiosyncratic illustrations. I think the designers would have done better to pick a single genre across forms and levels.

QUESTIONS. The assessment of comprehension is a problem today; contemporary theories of text structure provide a foundation for generating questions, but these ideas have yet to influence practice. It is not surprising the comprehension questions in NMRA are a motley. Most of the questions focus on details of the text. Some ask about vocabulary (e.g., What word in the story means ______?). Others ask for inference or opinion. The manual gives normative answers, but these leave something to be desired; in many instances "any suitable response" leaves it to the tester to decide. None of the questions are at a "meta-"level; you will not find questions like "Who were the characters?" "What was the plot?" "What was the major topic?"

DECODING AND COMPREHENSION. The texts are not chosen on the basis of orthographic patterns, and so unintended barriers easily crop up. *Strange*, *danced*, and *stared* may seem of little consequence to the literate adult. The pronunciations of G and C in the first two words are quite rare, however, and "vowel-plus-R" patterns are notoriously problematic. The assessment of decoding accuracy in this instrument is scattershot at best. A second limitation is that comprehension level is limited by decoding skill. That is, if the student cannot translate a text, he or she has no opportunity to demonstrate comprehension skill. Not surprisingly, decoding and comprehension are highly correlated in the norming data.

Perhaps the most interesting feature of this test is the frank discussion of reliability and the norming process. Reliability is assessed by both alternate-form and internal-consistency indices. The coefficients range from a low of .58 to a high of .94, with a median in the mid-80s. The manual is apologetic about the low values, but is also quite informative about the reasons—in a nutshell, interrater reliability is critical. The fieldworkers varied in administration, recording, and even scoring. "Why not improve standardization of the raters?" you might ask. In fact, the discussion carries a more significant message. If instruments like NMRA are to see widespread use, then we need to improve the training of those practitioners who employ the instruments. This manual, more than any other with which I am familiar, lays this issue on the line.

While NMRA has a number of interesting features, I cannot recommend it for general use. Practitioners would do better to select texts, questions, and other tasks suitable to their local situations. The NMRA norming population is quite limited, and Rasching weak data does not lead to meaningful scores. Finally, the passages contain a number of idiosyncracies unique to Great Britain, and are unlikely to make sense in other places.

[217]

New Zealand Item Bank: Mathematics. Purpose: To provide teachers with a test in "new" mathematics and also to provide teachers with practical help in developing their own classroom tests. Year 3, 4, 5, 6, 7 in Australian school systems and Std. 2, 3, 4, Form I, II in New Zealand school systems; 1980; 6 levels each containing ten or more broad topics in mathematics; no manual, information pamphlet (8 pages) included in Level 2 booklet; 1987 price data: A$25 per complete set; administration time not reported; New Zealand Department of Education; distributed by Australian Council for Educational Research [Australia].*

Review of the New Zealand Item Bank: Mathematics by VICTOR L. WILLSON, Professor of Educational Psychology, Texas A&M University, College Station, TX:

This item bank of mathematics items for elementary grades does what it is intended to do, gives teachers an extensive set of items referenced to objectives. A brief pamphlet is provided listing four purposes for the item bank: (*a*) "To provide test material which is related to the objectives of the mathematics syllabus and uses the conventions of the commonly used textbooks and guide notes"; (*b*) "To provide a bank of test items [written by teachers] that have been tried out on appropriate age groups of children and are free from ambiguities, inconsistencies and other faults"; (*c*) "To provide information about the likely difficulty level of items"; (*d*) "To provide behavioural objectives that indicate the areas of the syllabus and the kinds of abilities that the items are intended to assess." Three purposes are well met. It is difficult to assess anything about the second purpose, however, because no information on standardization groups is provided.

The items may be reproduced by the purchaser but are copyrighted and cannot be indiscriminately distributed. The items are organized by levels 2 to 6 corresponding roughly to our grades 3 to 7. An evaluation of the objectives indicates that some are taught at later grades in the U.S. than in New Zealand or Australia. For each unit a specification table is given that sets out a topic by ability process (recall, computation, understanding, and application); items measuring these elements are listed for the cells of the table. On following pages objectives are listed side by side with the items, typically one item per objective. The printing quality is adequate. With each item is a code consisting of none to four asterisks, indicating easy (no asterisk, .8 difficulty) to hard (four asterisks,

<.3 difficulty) items. It is not known if the items were field tested before or after instruction. There is absolutely no description of any samples used to try out or select the items, so the difficulty levels provided by the authors must be viewed cautiously. No discrimination information is provided, although the developers assure the potential buyer that only items that "discriminate between the mathematically more able and less able pupils" were selected. No validity data are provided and users must decide for themselves upon content validity of the items.

All items are in multiple-choice format. Most of them could easily be converted into supply type items. Definition items are probably best left as they are. The developers note that many items were constructed so as to incorporate common mistakes as incorrect options. The developers could have done a great service by providing item analysis information such as choice frequency, teachers' notes regarding remediation strategies for specific errors, and persistence of errors and misconceptions. Clearly, the diagnostic-prescriptive area in mathematics education has been productive in the last decade. It is time test developers acknowledge and incorporate such information into their tests. Mathematics education has been a leader in this movement, and developers of mathematics tests, in particular, should be sensitive to the unambiguous research findings supporting the importance of diagnosis and prescription (e.g., Brown & Burton, 1978).

A teacher with a photocopier can cut and paste together tests from this item bank with little difficulty. A computer-based version of the item banks would be helpful. There are, however, many line drawings that would not be printed easily with current technology. Some differences in word usage, drawings, and convention will need to be changed for a U.S. school usage, but the revisions would not be extensive.

Many teachers in the elementary grades could improve their testing by having this set available. The financial outlay is quite modest because for a school district it is a one-time cost. Even with the limited item analysis information the item bank is recommended as a useful addition to teachers' files.

REVIEWER'S REFERENCE

Brown, J. S., & Burton, R. R. (1978). Diagnostic models for procedural bugs in basic mathematical skills. *Cognitive Science*, 2, 155-192.

[218]

NIIP Engineering Arithmetic Test EA4. Purpose: Used as a selection instrument for courses, apprenticeships, and occupations. Age 15–adult; 1936–80; one of five subtests of the NIIP Engineering Selection Test Battery (T3:1582); 1987 price data: £4.75 per 10 test booklets; £2.25 per marking key; £1.50 per instruction card; £9.35 per manual for entire battery ('80, 52 pages); 20(25) minutes; National Institute of Industrial Psychology; NFER-Nelson Publishing Co., Ltd. [England].*

[219]

NOCTI Student Occupational Competency Achievement Test: Commercial Foods. Purpose: To measure the individual's occupational competency in commercial foods. Students in vocational and technical programs; 1987; test available to individual teachers and schools for local administration; 9 scores for Written part (Total and 8 subscores); 6 scores for Performance part (Total and 5 subscores); 2 parts: Written, Performance; Written test booklet (18 pages); Performance test booklet (8 pages); examiner's guide (12 pages); for more complete information, see 9:773; price data available from publisher; 180(195) minutes for Written part, 180(195) minutes for Performance part; National Occupational Competency Testing Institute.*

[220]

NOCTI Student Occupational Competency Achievement Test: Computer Programming. Purpose: To measure the individual's occupational competency in computer programming. Students in vocational and technical programs; 1985; test available to individual teachers and schools for local administration; 10 scores for Written part (Total and 9 subscores); 4 scores for Performance part (Total and 3 subscores); 2 parts: Written, Performance; Written test booklet (15 pages), 2 parts; Performance test booklet (3 pages); examiner's guide (7 pages); for more complete information, see 9:773; price data available from publisher; 180(195) minutes for Written part, 240(260) minutes for Performance part; National Occupational Competency Testing Institute.*

[221]

NOCTI Student Occupational Competency Achievement Test: Construction Masonry. Purpose: To measure the individual's occupational competency in construction masonry. Students in vocational and technical programs; 1985; test available to individual teachers and schools for local administration; 10 scores for Written part (Total and 9 subscores); 2 scores for Performance part (Total and 1 subscore); 2 parts: Written, Performance; Written test booklet (26 pages); Performance test booklet (7 pages); examiner's guide (9 pages); for more complete information, see 9:773; price data available from publisher; 180(195) minutes for Written part, 195(210) minutes for Performance part; National Occupational Competency Testing Institute.*

[222]

NOCTI Student Occupational Competency Achievement Test: Electronics. Purpose: To measure the individual's occupational competency in electronics. Students in vocational and technical programs; 1988; test available to individual teachers and schools for local administration; 6 scores for Written part (Total and 5 subscores), 6 scores for Performance part (Total and 5 subscores); 2 parts: Written, Performance; Written test booklet (20 pages); Performance test booklet (8 pages); examiner's guide (14 pages); for complete information see 9:773; price data available from publisher; 180(195) minutes for Written part, 180(195) minutes for Performance part; National Occupational Competency Testing Institute.*

[223]

NOCTI Student Occupational Competency Achievement Test: Graphic Arts. Purpose: To measure the individual's occupational competency in graphic arts. Students in vocational and technical programs; 1986–87; test available to individual teachers and schools for local administration; an individual may take any 1, 2, or all 3 choices for Performance part; 8 scores for Written part (Total and 7 subscores); 18 scores for Performance part (Choice 1 [Subparts 1–5 and Total], Choice 2 [Subparts 6–10 and Total], Choice 3 [Subparts 11–15 and Total]); 2 parts: Written, Performance; Written test booklet ('86, 18 pages); Performance test booklet ('87, 16 pages); examiner's guide ('87, 30 pages); for complete information, see 9:773; price data available from publisher; 180(195) minutes for Written part, 150–450(480) minutes for Performance part; National Occupational Competency Testing Institute.*

[224]

NOCTI Student Occupational Competency Achievement Test: Truck and Bus Mechanics. Purpose: To measure the individual's occupational competency in truck and bus mechanics. Students in vocational and technical programs; 1987; test available to individual teachers and schools for local administration; 10 scores for Written part (Total and 9 subscores), 6 scores for Performance part (Total and 5 subscores); 2 parts: Written, Performance; Written test booklet (14 pages); Performance test booklet (5 pages); examiner's guide (9 pages); for complete information, see 9:773; price data available from publisher; 180(195) minutes for Written part, 200(220) minutes for Performance part; National Occupational Competency Testing Institute.*

[225]

NOCTI Teacher Occupational Competency Test: Air Conditioning, Heating and Refrigeration. Purpose: To measure the individual's occupational competency in air conditioning, heating, and refrigeration. Teachers and prospective teachers; 1986; test administered at least twice a year at centers approved by the publisher; 9 scores for Written part (Total and 8 subscores), 3 scores for Performance part (Process, Product, Total); 2 parts: Written, Performance; Written test booklet ('86, 26 pages); Performance test booklet ('86, 20 pages); examiner's copy of Performance test ('86, 26 pages); manual for administering NOCTI TOCT Performance tests ('86, 17 pages); manual for administering NOCTI TOCT Written tests ('86, 20 pages); price data available from publisher; 180(195) minutes for Written part, 360(380) minutes for Performance part; National Occupational Competency Testing Institute.*

For a review of the NOCTI program, see 8:1153 (6 references).

[226]

NOCTI Teacher Occupational Competency Test: Airframe and Powerplant Mechanic. Purpose: To measure the individual's occupational competency in airframe and powerplant mechanics. Teachers and prospective teachers; 1973–86; test administered at least twice a year at centers approved by the publisher; 9 scores for Written part (Total and 7 subscores), 3 scores for Performance part (Process, Product, Total); 2 parts: Written, Performance; Written test booklet ('86, 39 pages); Performance test booklet ('86, 7 pages); examiner's copy of Performance test ('86, 13 pages); manual for administering NOCTI TOCT Performance tests ('86, 17 pages); manual for administering NOCTI TOCT Written tests ('86, 20 pages); price data available from publisher; 180(195) minutes for Written part, 360(395) minutes for Performance part; National Occupational Competency Testing Program.*

For a review of the NOCTI program, see 8:1153 (6 references).

[227]

NOCTI Teacher Occupational Competency Test: Appliance Repair. Purpose: To measure the individual's occupational competency in appliance repair. Teachers and prospective teachers; 1986; test administered at least twice a year at centers approved by the publisher; 8 scores for Written part (Total and 7 subscores), 3 scores for Performance part (Process, Product, Total); 2 parts: Written, Performance; Written test booklet ('86, 25 pages); Performance test booklet ('86, 23 pages); examiner's copy of Performance test ('86, 35 pages); manual for administering NOCTI TOCT Performance tests ('86, 17 pages); manual for administering NOCTI TOCT Written tests ('86, 20 pages); price data available from publisher; 180(195) minutes for Written part, 360(380) minutes for Performance part; National Occupational Competency Testing Institute.*

For a review of the NOCTI program, see 8:1153 (6 references).

Review of the NOCTI Teacher Occupational Competency Test: Appliance Repair by RICHARD C. ERICKSON, Professor and Chair, Department of Practical Arts and Vocational-Technical Education, University of Missouri-Columbia, Columbia, MO:

The NOCTI Appliance Repair test is one of a growing number of NOCTI Teacher Occupational Competency Tests. Each is designed to assess the technical knowledge and manipulative skills of those who need to present objective evidence of their trade competence in order to be certified as vocational teachers or to obtain academic credit from an institution that recognizes NOCTI examination as a basis for granting credit for work experience. This test, like all the other NOCTI tests, has a two-part format—a written test and a performance test.

The written test contains 200 multiple-choice items distributed as follows: electrical fundamentals, 44 items; power tools and small appliances, 12 items; major heating devices, 24 items; kitchen equipment, 31 items; laundry equipment, 24 items; refrigeration, 45 items; and electronics, 20 items. Generally, the items are very well written. This reviewer found only a few that were unclear or did not conform to accepted guidelines for preparing multiple-choice items. However, nearly all the items concentrate on assessing mastery of factual knowledge. Too few items are devoted to assessing higher order cognitive processes, particularly the application of problem-solving skills. These skills are of prime importance to tradespersons.

The scope of the competencies to be demonstrated and assessed in the performance test appears to be adequate. A total of 18 job-related tasks are included in the performance booklet. Examinees are required to complete nine mandatory tasks and four others of their choosing from among the remaining nine. This, of course, means that different examinees are exposed to differing test requirements. This suggests their obtained scores would not be comparable. The performance evaluation form provided with the test is to be used by the performance examiners in rating both process- and product-related aspects of the tasks. The form includes a recommended listing of criteria or expectations for each area of concern to be rated. Ratings for each process and product area of concern are made on 5-point scales and are to indicate whether the examinee's performance or product is typical of a/an extremely skilled, above average, average, below average, or inept worker. The performance evaluation worksheet appears to achieve its purpose. However, this reviewer feels that variation in performance examiners' expectations could be controlled to an even greater degree if the directions to the examiners included detailed definitions of the descriptor for each position on the 5-point scale, "extremely skilled . . . inept worker."

The Appliance Repair test is a revision of the NOCTI Major Appliance Repair test. A committee was used to "validate" the modifications made in the earlier test. No attempt was made to field test the revised test. Therefore, statistical information important for judging the reliability, level of difficulty, and ability to discriminate between qualified and unqualified examinees is not available for the Appliance Repair test. Users are referred to normative data and reliability estimates developed for the Major Appliance Repair test. At their very best, descriptive statistics for the earlier test must be considered poor substitutes for validity, reliability, and normative information and data for this revision. The only viable option for users at this time is to develop estimates of reliability and validity, local norms, and perhaps expectancy tables based upon local experience with the Appliance Repair test.

A test manual of the type that should accompany standardized achievement tests needs to be developed for this test. Much of the content needed for such a manual has been developed. However, relevant validity and reliability information and data, adequate norms, and guidelines and aids for interpreting and using the results of this test must be developed and included in the manual.

In summary, it is this reviewer's opinion that the Appliance Repair test is a major step forward in developing a standardized means of assessing the trade competency of appliance repairpersons who desire to become instructors of their trade. The test appears to be a good test. It is the only one of its kind that is readily available. The National Occupational Competency Testing Institute simply must build upon this effort and develop an accompanying test manual that includes adequate validity and reliability data and norms, as well as expectancy tables, suggested cutoff scores, and/or other aids for interpreting locally obtained scores. To do so would contribute much to the purpose and intent of the NOCTI testing program.

[228]

NOCTI Teacher Occupational Competency Test: Auto Body Repair, Forms A and D. Purpose: To measure the individual's occupational competency in auto body repair. Teachers and prospective teachers; 1973–87; test administered at least twice a year at centers approved by the publisher; 11 scores for Written part (Total and 10 subscores), 3 scores for Performance part (Process, Product, Total); 2 parts: Written, Performance; 2 equivalent forms: A, D; Written test booklet ('85, 23 pages); Performance test booklet ('85, 5 pages); examiner's copy of Performance test ('85, 8 pages), manual for administering NOCTI TOCT Performance tests ('86, 17 pages); manual for administering NOCTI TOCT Written tests ('86, 20 pages); price data available from publisher; 180(195) minutes for Written part, 340(360) minutes for Performance part (Form A), 285(305) minutes for Performance part (Form D); National Occupational Competency Testing Institute.*

See 9:777 (1 reference); for a review of the NOCTI program, see 8:1153.

[229]

NOCTI Teacher Occupational Competency Test: Brick Masonry. Purpose: To measure the individual's occupational competency in brick masonry. Teachers and prospective teachers; 1986; test administered at least twice a year at centers approved by the publisher; 10 scores for Written part (Total and 9 subscores), 3 scores for Performance part (Process, Product, Total); 2 parts: Written, Performance; Written test booklet ('86, 24 pages); Performance test booklet ('86, 19 pages); examiner's copy of Performance test ('86, 26 pages); manual for administering NOCTI TOCT Performance tests ('86, 17 pages); manual for administering NOCTI TOCT Written tests ('86, 20 pages); price data available from publisher; 180(195) minutes for Written part, 340(360) minutes for Performance part; National Occupational Competency Testing Institute.*

For a review of the NOCTI program, see 8:1153.

Review of the NOCTI Teacher Occupational Competency Test: Brick Masonry by THOMAS S. BALDWIN, Practicing Psychologist, Chapel Hill, NC:

This test contains two major parts, a written and a performance test. The test was developed through a committee of professionals in brick masonry who followed a number of techniques of job analysis to develop the content of the test. A high degree of content validity is thereby insured in both the written and performance parts of the test. The 200-item written test covers nine areas organized around content, in considerable detail. In addition, the performance portion of the subtest contains six "jobs," such as "Construct A Brick Chimney" that the candidate must complete. Both written and performance subtests are administered in regional test centers approved by NOCTI. Test security is given extremely high priority. Locally approved examiners evaluate performance subtests for both "process" and "product," based on a 5-point scale ranging from "Extremely Skilled Worker" to "Inept Worker."

The concept of measuring the actual performance aspects of a trade represents a real advancement in standardized achievement testing, which traditionally is limited to paper-and-pencil tests. The logistics of performance assessment are enormous and NOCTI is to be commended for implementing its concept of regional test centers and trained examiners.

Unfortunately, the care and precision that NOCTI has followed in developing the Brick Masonry Test does not extend to reporting psychometric data on the test. An annual set of norms for the test is published, but they contain no instructions and are confusing and virtually impossible to interpret. Mean, standard deviation, and standard error of measurement are reported in percentages with no explanation to permit the uninitiated to interpret them. Individual score reports are not accompanied by adequate explanations of the data and border on being uninterpretable. Attempts to obtain more specific information directly from NOCTI were not successful.

An even more serious problem with the NOCTI Brick Masonry Test is the lack of data on reliability, intercorrelation of written subtests, intercorrelations of performance subtests, and correlations between written and performance tests. Information obtained from NOCTI indicated that they do annual analyses of test performance that include determination of reliability, but this reviewer was advised that no such information had been published since the discontinuance of the NOCTI Technical Supplement in 1982. The 1982 data are not applicable to the current test.

In its present form the NOCTI Brick Masonry Test can reasonably be considered to have a high degree of content validity. Reliabilities, correlations between performance and subtests, standard errors of measurement, etc., are not available and thereby significantly restrict the usefulness of this test. The potential user must, therefore, accept the adequacy of such important psychometric characteristics on faith or rely on other means of testing competency in teachers and potential teachers.

SUMMARY. NOCTI's excellent conceptualization of the cognitive and performance aspects of brick masonry and careful test development are to be commended. NOCTI has fallen severely short, however, in its responsibility to provide potential users and researchers with sufficient psychometric data to permit informed decision making regarding the potential utility of the test.

[230]

NOCTI Teacher Occupational Competency Test: Building and Home Maintenance Services. Purpose: To measure the individual's occupational competency in building and home maintenance services. Teachers and prospective teachers; 1986; test administered at least twice a year at centers approved by the publisher; 10 scores for Written part (Total and 9 subscores), 3 scores for Performance part (Process, Product, Total); 2 parts: Written, Performance; Written test booklet ('86, 20 pages); Performance test booklet ('86, 11 pages); examiner's copy of Performance test ('86, 20 pages); manual for administering NOCTI TOCT Performance tests ('86, 17 pages); manual for administering NOCTI TOCT Written tests ('86, 20 pages); price data available from publisher; 180(195) minutes for Written part, 300(330) minutes for Performance part; National Occupational Competency Testing Program.*

For a review of the NOCTI program, see 8:1153 (6 references).

Review of the NOCTI Teacher Occupational Competency Test: Building and Home Maintenance Services by GARY E. LINTEREUR, Associate Professor of Technology, Northern Illinois University, DeKalb, IL:

These written and performance tests were developed to enable candidates to verify their experience and demonstrate their competence as a tradesperson in the building and home maintenance services. These tests were developed and reviewed with the expertise of tradespersons in the occupation.

The written test has an explicit manual for administering the 3-hour test which includes a list of materials needed, directions for the examiner, instructions for the candidates, and helpful hints for administering the test. The 19-page test consists of 162 multiple-choice questions with four responses to choose from. The topics tested are: floor stripping, refinishing and buffing (27 questions); carpet care (9 questions); general electricity and repair (24 questions); plumbing (40 questions); general cleaning (24 questions); building security/fire prevention/records (6 questions); employee supervision/relations (11 questions); painting (10 questions); and heating (11 questions). The questions are well written and provide a range from easy but necessary safety items to more technical problem-solving situations. The questions reflect a "job-entry level" depth of knowledge and the topics covered are appropriate for the occupation. A qualified candidate should easily finish the written test in the time allotted.

The performance test has an explicit manual for administering the test which includes: a preliminary checklist, materials needed, preparing the shop, information for the examiner, instructions for the candidates, and other information to help administer the test. The candidate is evaluated on a 5-point Likert scale from an "extremely skilled worker" to an "inept worker." The tasks evaluated are: general cleaning of an office or classroom and a restroom or shower/locker room (45 minutes), floor stripping/refinishing/buffing (1 hour), carpet care—extraction: dry foam/spin clean methods (45 minutes), welding—arc and/or gas or soldering copper (30 minutes), electrical repair—duplex outlets/switches/ballasts (45 minutes), small hand/power tools (30 minutes), and interior/exterior painting (45 minutes). Each task is well written telling the candidate specifically what to do to observe safety considerations and follow clean-up procedures. If all tasks are assigned, the test would take about 5 hours to complete. The tasks are appropriate for the occupation.

In summary, the written and performance tests will give the examiner a very good idea of the candidate's competence as a beginning tradesperson. The performance test has a well-developed evaluation form and identifies criteria and safety considerations the candidate should follow. Reliability, validity, and normative data were not supplied with the test manuals as well as recommended cutoff scores for success in the trade. However, the data obtained will give the examiner valuable information regarding a candidate. Future development of the test should include attention to psychometric concerns.

[231]

NOCTI Teacher Occupational Competency Test: Commercial Art. Purpose: To measure the individual's occupational competency in commercial art. Teachers and prospective teachers; 1985–86; test administered at least twice a year at centers approved by the publisher; 6 scores for Written part (Total and 5 subscores), 3 scores for Performance part (Process, Product, Total); 2 parts: Written, Performance; Written test booklet ('85, 13 pages); Performance test booklet ('85, 6 pages); examiner's copy of Performance test ('85, 9 pages); manual for administering NOCTI TOCT Performance tests ('86, 17 pages); manual for administering NOCTI TOCT Written tests ('86, 20 pages); price data available from publisher; 180(195) minutes for Written part, 300(330) minutes for Performance part; National Occupational Competency Testing Institute.*

For a review of the NOCTI program, see 8:1153 (6 references).

Review of the NOCTI Teacher Occupational Competency Test: Commercial Art by GARY E. LINTEREUR, Associate Professor of Technology, Northern Illinois University, DeKalb, IL:

These written and performance tests were developed to enable candidates to verify their experience and demonstrate their competence as a tradesperson in the commercial art field. These tests were developed and reviewed with the expertise of tradespersons in the occupation.

The written test has an explicit manual for administering the 3-hour test, which includes a list of materials needed, directions for the examiner, instructions for the candidates, and helpful hints for administering the test. The 12-page test consists of 125 multiple-choice questions with four responses to choose from. The topics tested are: design and typography (21 questions), drawing and rendering (44 questions), production (21 questions), printing (23 questions), and general (16 questions). The questions are well written at the "job-entry level"; depth of knowledge and the topics are appropriate for the occupation. A qualified candidate should easily finish the written test in the time allotted.

The performance test has an explicit manual for administering the test which includes: a preliminary checklist, materials needed, preparing the shop, information for the examiner, instructions for the candidates, and other information to help administer the test. The candidate is evaluated on a 5-point Likert scale from an "extremely skilled worker" to an "inept worker." The tasks evaluated are: rough layout for a sport magazine ad (1 1/2 hours), black and white tonal layout rendering for a newspaper ad (2 hours), and keyline/mechanical production art (1 1/2 hours). Each task is well-organized and requires material and equipment to be provided by the candidate. The tasks also require the examiner to provide examples or references. The examiner should be careful not to lead or guide the candidate by providing examples that are easily copied.

In summary, the written and performance tests will give the examiner a very good idea of the candidate's competence as a beginning tradesperson. The written test is comprehensive in nature and the performance test has a well-developed evaluation form. Reliability, validity, and normative data were not supplied with the test manuals, nor were recommended cutoff scores for success in the occupation. However, the data obtained will give the examiner valuable information useful in decision making regarding a candidate.

[232]

NOCTI Teacher Occupational Competency Test: Computer Science Examination for Secondary Teachers. Purpose: To measure the individual's occupational competency in computer science. Teachers and prospective teachers; 1986; test administered at least twice a year at centers approved by the publisher; 6 scores for Written part (Total and 5 subscores), 3 scores for Performance part (Process, Product, Total); 2 parts: Written, Performance; Written test booklet (20 pages); Performance Test booklet ('86, 14 pages); examiner's copy of Performance test (23 pages); manual for administering NOCTI TOCT Performance tests (17 pages); manual for administering NOCTI TOCT Written Tests (20 pages); price data available from publisher; 180(195) minutes for Written part, 360(375) minutes for Performance part; National Occupational Competency Testing Program.*

For a review of the NOCTI program, see 8:1153.

[233]

NOCTI Teacher Occupational Competency Test: Diesel Mechanic. Purpose: To measure the individual's occupational competency in diesel mechanics. Teachers and prospective teachers; 1986; test administered at least twice a year at centers approved by the publisher; 8 scores for Written part (Total and 7 subscores), 3 scores for Performance part (Process, Product, Total); 2 parts: Written, Performance; Written test booklet ('86, 24 pages); Performance test booklet ('86, 7 pages); examiner's copy of Performance test ('86, 20 pages); manual for administering NOCTI TOCT Performance tests ('86, 17 pages); manual for administering NOCTI TOCT Written tests ('86, 20 pages); price data available from publisher; 180(195) minutes for Written part, 240(260) minutes for Performance part; National Occupational Competency Testing Program.*

For a review of the NOCTI program, see 8:1153 (6 references).

[234]

NOCTI Teacher Occupational Competency Test: Electrical Construction and Maintenance. Purpose: To measure the individual's occupational competency in electrical construction and maintenance. Teachers and prospective teachers; 1986–87; test administered at least twice a year at centers approved by the publisher; 7 scores for Written part (Total and 6 subscores), 3 scores for Performance part (Process, Product, Total); 2 parts: Written, Performance; Written test booklet ('87, 25 pages); Peformance test booklet ('87, 11 pages); examiner's copy of Performance test ('87, 38 pages); manual for administering NOCTI TOCT Performance tests ('86, 17 pages); manual for administering NOCTI TOCT Written tests ('86, 20 pages); price data available from publisher; 180(195) minutes for Written part, 275(295) minutes for Performance part; National Occupational Competency Testing Program.*

For a review of the NOCTI program, see 8:1153.

[235]

NOCTI Teacher Occupational Competency Test: Electrical Installation. Purpose: To measure the individual's occupational competency in electrical installation. Teachers and prospective teachers; 1973–86; test administered at least twice a year at centers approved by the publisher; 8 scores for Written part (Total and 7 subscores), 3 scores for Performance part (Process, Product, Total); 2 parts: Written, Performance; Written test booklet ('86, 26 pages); Performance test booklet ('86, 10 pages); examiner's copy of Performance test ('86, 20 pages); manual for administering NOCTI TOCT Performance tests ('86, 17 pages); manual for administering NOCTI TOCT Written tests ('86, 20 pages); price data available from publisher; 180(195) minutes for Written part, 300(320) minutes for Performance part; National Occupational Competency Testing Institute.*

See 9:788 (1 reference); see also T3:1601 (1 reference); for a review by Alan R. Suess, see 8:1139 (1 reference). For a review of the NOCTI program, see 8:1153.

[236]

NOCTI Teacher Occupational Competency Test: Electronics Communications. Purpose: To measure the individual's occupational competency in electronics communications. Teachers and prospective teachers; 1986–87; test administered at least twice a year at centers approved by the publisher; 11 scores for Written part (Total and 10 subscores), 3 scores for Performance part (Process, Product, Total); 2 parts: Written, Performance; Written test booklet ('87, 28 pages); Performance test booklet ('87, 12 pages); examiner's copy of Performance test ('87, 28 pages); manual for administering NOCTI TOCT Performance tests ('86, 17 pages); manual for administering NOCTI TOCT Written tests ('86, 20 pages); price data available from publisher; 180(195) minutes for Written part, 180(195) minutes for Performance part; National Occupational Competency Testing Program.*

See 9:789 (1 reference); for a review by Emil H. Hoch, see 8:1140. For a review of the NOCTI program, see 8:1153.

[237]

NOCTI Teacher Occupational Competency Test: Heavy Equipment Mechanic. Purpose: To measure the individual's occupational competency in heavy equipment mechanics. Teachers and prospective teachers; 1986; test administered at least twice a year at centers approved by the publisher; 11

scores for Written part (Total and 10 subscores), 3 scores for Performance part (Process, Product, Total); 2 parts: Written, Performance; Written test booklet ('86, 23 pages); Performance test booklet ('86, 8 pages); examiner's copy of Performance test ('86, 17 pages); manual for administering NOCTI TOCT Performance tests ('86, 17 pages); manual for administering NOCTI TOCT Written tests ('86, 20 pages); price data available from publisher; 180(195) minutes for Written part, 345(400) minutes for Performance part; National Occupational Competency Testing Program.*

For a review of the NOCTI program, see 8:1153 (6 references).

[238]

NOCTI Teacher Occupational Competency Test: Industrial Electronics. Purpose: To measure the individual's occupational competency in industrial electronics. Teachers and prospective teachers; 1974–86; test administered at least twice a year at centers approved by the publisher; 10 scores for Written part (Total and 9 subscores), 3 scores for Performance part (Process, Product, Total); 2 parts: Written, Performance; Written test booklet ('86, 26 pages); Performance test booklet ('86, 31 pages); examiner's copy of Performance test ('86, 64 pages); manual for administering NOCTI TOCT Performance tests ('86, 17 pages); manual for administering NOCTI TOCT Written tests ('86, 20 pages); price data available from publisher; 180(195) minutes for Written part, 240(260) minutes for Performance part; National Occupational Competency Testing Institute.*

See 9:793 (1 reference); for a review by Emil H. Hoch, see 8:1142. For a review of the NOCTI program, see 8:1153.

[239]

NOCTI Teacher Occupational Competency Test: Machine Trades. Purpose: To measure the individual's occupational competency in machine trades. Teachers and prospective teachers; 1973–86; test administered at least twice a year at centers approved by the publisher; 11 scores for Written part (Total and 10 subscores), 3 scores for Performance part (Process, Product, Total); 2 parts: Written, Performance; Written test booklet ('86, 21 pages); Performance test booklet ('86, 11 pages); examiner's copy of Performance test ('86, 23 pages); manual for administering NOCTI TOCT Performance tests ('86, 17 pages); manual for administering NOCTI TOCT Written tests ('86, 20 pages); price data available from publisher; 180(195) minutes for Written part, 330(350) minutes for Performance part; National Occupational Competency Testing Institute.*

See 9:795 (1 reference); see also 8:1144 (1 reference). For a review of the NOCTI program, see 8:1153.

Review of the NOCTI Teacher Occupational Competency Test: Machine Trades by THOMAS S. BALDWIN, Practicing Psychologist, Chapel Hill, NC:

The NOCTI Machine Trades Test is administered periodically in approved testing centers around the country. It is an ambitious undertaking in that it measures both cognitive skills through a written test as well as performance skill on a representative sampling of jobs that would be routinely performed by someone in the machine trades.

Content validity of the written test is assured through the use of a test development team. The initial responsibility of this team was to develop an "occupational data base" using a variety of sources of information about the occupation. The team then converted this data base into a series of 160 items that make up the 10 parts of the written test. Since the team is responsible not only for item writing but for periodic revisions of test content, one can have reasonable confidence that a high degree of content validity is built into the test.

The performance part of this test consists of four "jobs," such as "Grind Threading Tool," that the candidate is required to perform. Performance of this part of the test is scored for both "Process" and "Product." The process score consists of a rating of a variety of items, such as "Correct Measuring Practices," each of which is rated on a scale of A to E, with A representing "Extremely Skilled Worker" and E representing "Inept Worker." Each "item" in the process evaluation is, of necessity, somewhat subjective. However, a degree of specificity is built into the examiners manual that should insure clarity and, therefore, reliability. The "Product" score for each of the jobs in the performance part of the test is far more objective, frequently involving measurements of physical dimensions. The same evaluation key is used in deriving the product score. The total score is the unweighted sum of the Process and Product scores.

Unfortunately, the psychometric characteristics of this test are largely unknown. NOCTI publishes an annual set of norms for the test but these are quite confusing. The norms include data on each of the 10 subparts of the written test as well as Process, Product, and Total performance tests. Means, standard deviations, and standard errors are presented in percentile form and defy interpretation. For example, the mean on a four-item subtest is reported as being 62.6% while the mean on a 37-item subtest is reported to be 62.1%. The annually published norms provide no information on interpretation of the data and, therefore, remain somewhat of a mystery.

Part of the material made available to this reviewer included The Teacher Occupational Competency Test Packet, which includes the statement that new tests are pilot tested and "the results are analyzed using item analysis and standard reliability techniques KR-20 and Cronbach's alpha." No such information was provided for this review nor was the reviewer able to get such information by contacting NOCTI. This reviewer was advised that a technical supplement was published in the past and contained reliability data on this test. This technical supplement, however, was discontinued in 1982 and current information is not available.

SUMMARY. Conceptually, the NOCTI Machine Trades Test is sound and meets an important need in vocational education. Operationally, NOCTI has insured content validity through the use of a committee of professionals who are proficient in machine trades. This is true for both the written and performance parts of the test. NOCTI does not, however, provide potential users of this test with adequate psychometric data by which its merits can be judged. A decision regarding the utility of this test must, therefore, be made on faith. Unfortunately, alternative standardized tests do not exist. Given its 15-year history, this reviewer does not feel that NOCTI has lived up to its responsibilities for providing adequate evidence that the machine trades test meets minimal psychometric standards necessary for using it for its intended purposes.

[240]

NOCTI Teacher Occupational Competency Test: Tool and Die Making. Purpose: To measure the individual's occupational competency in tool and die making. Teachers and prospective teachers; 1986–87; test administered at least twice a year at centers approved by the publisher; 11 scores for Written part (Total and 10 subscores), 3 scores for Performance part (Process, Product, Total); 2 parts: Written, Performance; Written test booklet ('87, 23 pages); Performance test booklet ('87, 9 pages); examiner's copy of Performance test ('87, 17 pages); manual for administering NOCTI TOCT Performance tests ('86, 17 pages); manual for administering NOCTI TOCT Written tests ('86, 20 pages); price data available from publisher; 180(195) minutes for Written part, 330 (350) minutes for Performance part; National Occupational Competency Testing Program.*

For a review of the NOCTI program, see 8:1153.

[241]

Nutrition Achievement Tests. Purpose: Measures achievement of nutrition knowledge. Grades K–12 and adults; 1979–85; 4 tests; National Dairy Council and Iowa State University (Tests 1, 2, and 3), National Dairy Council and University of Illinois at Chicago (Test 4); National Dairy Council.*

a) TEST 1. Grades K–2; 1979–80; publisher suggests that questions 1 through 20 be used for kindergarten pupils, 1 through 30 for first grade, and all 40 questions for second grade pupils; price data for manual ('80, 41 pages) including Tests 1, 2, and 3 which may be reproduced for local use available from local Dairy Council; (20–45) minutes.

b) TEST 2. Grades 3–4; 1979–80; publisher suggests that questions 1 through 30 be used for third grade pupils and all 40 questions be used for fourth grade pupils; (20–60) minutes.

c) TEST 3. Grades 5–6; 1979–80; (20–60) minutes.

d) TEST 4. Grades 7–12 and adults; 1985; price data for manual ('85, 16 pages) including Test 4 and hand-scorable answer sheet which may be reproduced for local use, and answer key available from local Dairy Council; (40) minutes.

[Note: The publisher advised in April 1989 that this test will be discontinued.]

[242]

Oaster Stressors Scales. Purpose: To index an individual's level of stressors by using derived trait scales. Adults; 1983; 4 profiles: Classic/Overload Stressor Pattern of Type A Behavior, Overload Stressor Pattern, Underload Stressor Pattern/ Goal-Blocked Type A, Type B Behavior Pattern; price data available from publisher; administration time not reported; Thomas R. Oaster; the Author.*

[243]

Occupational Aptitude Survey & Interest Schedule: Aptitude Survey. Purpose: Measures the career development of students. Grades 8–12; 1983; OASIS-AS; intended to be used with Occupational Interest Schedule; 6 scores: Vocabulary, Computation, Total (General Ability), Spatial Relations, Word Comparison, Making Marks; 1985 price data: $46 per complete test kit including manual (42 pages), 10 tests, 50 student profile and answer sheets, and scoring stencil; $14 per 10 tests; $18 per 50 student profile and answer sheets; $18 per manual; 35(45) minutes; Randall M. Parker; PRO-ED, Inc.

Review of the Occupational Aptitude Survey and Interest Schedule: Aptitude Survey by RODNEY L. LOWMAN, Director, Corporate Mental Health Programs, Occupational Health Service, and Faculty, Divisions of Medical Psychology and Occupational Medicine, Duke University Medical Center, Durham, NC:

The Occupational Aptitude Survey and Interest Schedule: Aptitude Survey (OASIS-AS) is intended to be like foreign automakers' answer to Detroit: a sleeker, more efficient, and in many ways, better version of the old gas-guzzling models. Analysis suggests that this instrument is an evolutionary, not revolutionary, product. By traditional standards of test validation much work remains to be done. If one word were to be used in evaluating this test it would be "promising." However, if the test is to become more than an isolated oasis in the midst of a dry and lately rather infertile desert, much more research will be required. This research should be directed especially to some troubling aspects of the validity evidence currently available.

There is little question that the five aptitudes which the OASIS-AS attempts to measure are well established as related to vocational success. Individually, these factors can be predictive of success in certain employment situations and, as a group, are generally of value in counseling high school students, the primary target population for this battery. The authors correctly note the limitations of the two major existing multiaptitude test batteries, the Differential Aptitude Test (DAT) and the General Aptitude Test Battery (GATB). Both tests were excellent measures in their day, but they have problems, including the length of time needed to complete the instruments and, in the case of the GATB, its unavailability until recently to those outside certain government employment services. The need for an updated, reliable, valid, but shortened instrument to measure these particular aptitudes is clear.

By this standard, the OASIS has laid a good foundation on which to build. The reliability evidence for the test, though based in certain instances (especially the split-half and test-retest data) on rather small samples, is generally within professionally acceptable standards. The OASIS-AS normative data includes a national sample of about 1,400 individuals. This sample is racially imbalanced (blacks are inadequately represented and no breakdown is provided for those of Hispanic or Oriental origin). The sample is also geographically imbalanced (too many rural testees). The manner of selecting schools for inclusion in the sample is not adequately specified. Measures of central tendency for the item difficulty levels are not provided.

Except for two subtests (Making Marks and Word Comparison), the OASIS-AS is described as being primarily a power test. However, the question of the extent to which the remaining subtests are also speed tests is inadequately addressed in the manual. By its design, the OASIS-AS is a *shortened* version of longer multiaptitude batteries. The apparent hope is that the same precision of aptitude measurement can be accomplished in less time. Indeed, the longest OASIS-AS subtest is 12 minutes; the shortest, 1 minute. While shortening does not necessarily occur at the expense of validity, the extent to which the OASIS-AS has become a speeded measure needs more research attention. This question is especially important in the case of those examinees who have the desired aptitude but who do not respond well in timed situations.

Test format and instructions are clear, except that examinees are not told that the test extracts no penalty for guessing. The booklet and test items are printed in an attractive format. However, the apparent intent to condense the Vocabulary and Computation subtests to a single page results in some very small print, especially for Computation. Students with uncorrected visual deficits may be needlessly penalized by this format.

The test falls short in the validation area. The OASIS-AS was patterned after the five factors on the GATB. However, the test manual reports only the results of a second order factor analysis (suggesting two factors), not the prior factor analyses which were said to have been conducted. It is important to know whether five factors emerged from the primary factor analyses. If not, what are the subtests really measuring, apart from the labels the author assigned to them? Moreover, the OASIS-AS does not provide evidence of adequate validation using external criteria. Although a few studies (again with small *N* s) are cited that present correlations between OASIS-AS and other measures of aptitude or ability (generally suggesting that the OASIS-AS measures something akin to the GATB), it must be emphasized that the OASIS-AS is a new test and as such needs to be validated against external criteria, not just other tests.

Does the OASIS-AS meet minimally acceptable standards for commercial publication? Probably, but barely so. As an instrument for further exploration and research, it is a promising start. As a test to guide career choices and possibly for employment selection, the user should proceed with caution (especially with minorities) pending additional studies.

The authors correctly note that "the OASIS-AS should not be used as the sole predictor of job performance in a specific occupation." However, the counseling uses suggested for the OASIS-AS go beyond the validity evidence. Especially problematic is the inclusion of suggested "minimal aptitudes" needed for a variety of occupations. Although it is difficult to determine from the inadequate description in the test manual, these cutoff norms appear to be based on the GATB rather than the OASIS-AS. An example of the dangers of using this "minimal aptitudes" construct is illustrated by the case of Gloria, who is described as having "the requisite aptitudes for any of the 120 occupations listed." Any measure which suggests that the same examinee has equally sufficient aptitude for computer-applications engineer, dairy farm manager, and arc welder would appear not to be measuring aptitudes at a sufficient level of specificity to be valid or useful.

Finally, insofar as the OASIS-AS is to be used as a general aptitude battery for counseling, there are areas of omission which are mildly troublesome. Here, the OASIS-AS is no oasis. It uses the same "tried (or is it 'tired'?) and true" measures of, essentially, academic aptitude. What about the student with artistic talents? The budding executive or manager? The psychotherapist? The garage mechanic? Will these individuals, who may present rather lackluster profiles on the OASIS-AS, be discouraged from pursuing their "natural talents"? Evidence has begun to emerge that artistic, social, and mechanical aptitudes are rather independent of some of the aptitudes tapped by the OASIS. (See for example, Gardner, 1983; Lowman, Williams, & Leeman, 1985.) One would like to see this battery (or some other) expand the old repertoire to include other types of "intelligence." If counseling is the goal, it is time to move beyond those aptitudes which are primarily academic and provide a measure for general counseling purposes which will tap into more of the diversity of human abilities than is captured by measures like the OASIS-AS.

SUMMARY. This could be an important new measure of basic aptitudes, primarily academic. It is a bit early in its development to advocate its use on a widespread basis, but assuming the authors and their colleagues get on with the research needed, there is great hope for this shortened multi-aptitude test battery. Although it may be criticized for omitting some important measures of aptitude (e.g., social, mechanical, artistic) the OASIS-AS hopefully will be shown to measure in only minutes what many aptitude batteries have taken many hours to do. Those with the time to administer the longer GATB or DAT will probably get more predictably reliable and valid results, but for a general screen and as a test for further validation efforts, the OASIS-AS offers much promise.

REVIEWER'S REFERENCES

Gardner, H. (1983). *Frames of mind: The theory of multiple intelligences.* New York: Basic Books.

Lowman, R. L., Williams, R. E., & Leeman, G. E. (1985). The structure and relationship of college women's primary abilities and vocational interests. *Journal of Vocational Behavior,* 27, 298-315.

Review of the Occupational Aptitude Survey and Interest Schedule: Aptitude Survey by KEVIN W. MOSSHOLDER, Associate Professor of Management, Auburn University, Auburn, AL:

The Occupational Aptitude Survey and Interest Schedule (OASIS) is a vocational exploration and career development tool for use with junior high and high school students. Only one part of OASIS, the Aptitude Survey (AS), is discussed here. The OASIS-AS is a multiple aptitude test that includes the following subtests: Vocabulary (verbal), Computation (numerical), Spatial Relations (spatial), Word Comparison (perceptual), and Making Marks (manual dexterity). The Vocabulary and Computation scores may be combined to yield a general ability score.

Published in 1983, the OASIS-AS was constructed with the idea of providing a commercially available test of multiple aptitudes encompassing the dominant factors measured by the General Aptitude Test Battery (GATB). Exploratory and Procrustes factor analyses of GATB correlation matrices were performed and interpreted as indicating that five factors underlie the GATB subtests. These factors became the constructs on which the OASIS-AS was based. Traditional item-analysis techniques were employed to construct the Vocabulary, Computation, and Spatial Relations subtests. Item-total correlations for items comprising these subtests were in the .2 to .6 range. Because Word Comparison and Making Marks were speeded subtests, standard item analysis was not used with these subtests.

Norms for the OASIS-AS were developed from a sample of 1,398 8th- through 12th-grade students residing in 11 states. The sample was predominantly white and urban, though balanced for sex. Norm tables are available in terms of percentiles, stanines, and 5-point scores. The latter are useful for comparing student scores with purported minimal aptitude requirements of various occupations.

Appropriate forms of reliability (alpha, split-half, alternate-forms, test-retest) were used to check the reliability of the five subtests. The subtests were equally reliable for males and females. Overall, the median reliability for all subtests was approximately .85, with Spatial Relations being at the low end of the range and Making Marks at the high end of the range. It should be noted that some reported reliabilities were corrected for range restriction, while others were not. Where corrected reliabilities were reported, corresponding uncorrected reliabilities should have been, but were not listed.

The validity of the OASIS-AS is reported largely in terms of concurrent criterion-related validities for subtests. Subtests of the OASIS-AS were matched and correlated with counterpart subtests from the Iowa Tests of Educational Development (ITED), SRA Achievement Series, and the GATB. Convergent validities, correlations between subtests measuring similar aptitudes, were best for OASIS-AS/GATB matches, ranging from .53 to .87. This is not surprising given that the OASIS-AS was developed with the GATB in mind. Convergent validities with ITED and SRA subtests were really only meaningful for the Vocabulary and Computation subtests of the OASIS-AS. Average correlations were approximately .70 for the Vocabulary subtest and .50 for the Computation subtest. The Spatial Relations, Work Comparison, and Making Marks subtests exhibited low to moderate correlations with verbally or numerically-loaded subtests of the ITED and SRA series.

The OASIS-AS manual is understandable, containing basic psychometric information like that described above, as well as standardized instructions for giving and scoring the subtests. The manual explains test features, and by using examples, discusses ways that the OASIS-AS might be used for counseling. Male and female norms for both grade 8–10 and grade 11–12 aggregates are reported. A table listing minimum aptitudes for 120 occupations keyed to OASIS-AS subtests is also included.

The major strength of the OASIS-AS ultimately may be its ties with the GATB, since much occupational information is keyed to the GATB. This linkage could prove beneficial when counseling students about occupational choices; however, whether the OASIS-AS can meet this objective is uncertain. There are several points concerning the OASIS-AS that may limit its utility. First, the supposition that there are five factors underlying the GATB, the five measured by the OASIS-AS, is based on an intercorrelation matrix for GATB subtests from 100 high school seniors. In order to show that these five factors could be found in data from other samples, Procrustes procedures were utilized. Such methods are notorious for yielding hypothesized factors, even in the face of many other equally plausible factor structures. Better confirmatory procedures are available and should have been used. One cannot be sure how well OASIS-AS covers the GATB construct domain until more research is completed.

Perhaps because the test was developed recently, validational evidence is not as complete as would be desired. Correlating the OASIS-AS with tests (ITED and SRA series) not designed as multiple aptitude tests does not permit completely meaningful subtest comparisons. As previously noted, convergent validities were best for OASIS-AS/GATB comparisons. However, these comparisons were based on the responses of only 72 students. Also, convergent validity may be the easiest standard for new tests to meet.

Discriminant validity, differentiation among subtests regarding what they measure, is harder to demonstrate. Data presented as supporting OASIS-AS discriminant validity was not rigorously assessed (as per a multitrait, multimethod paradigm), and is only adequate at best. It is also suggested in the manual that examining OASIS-AS subtest intercorrelations and/or factor-analyzing them is a partial means of assessing construct validity. Though not incorrect, the utility of such actions vis-a-vis construct validity is very marginal. Information about the predictive validity of the OASIS-AS with respect to any criteria of occupational success is completely omitted. Though the recency of the OASIS-AS may partly explain this shortcoming, such information is vital and must be sought.

There are other minor negative points that should be noted. The OASIS-AS has no apparent means for machine scoring. This deficiency could present extra work for counselors. Another undesirable feature is the inclusion of IQ and GATB equivalents in a conversion table, although users are cautioned about converting OASIS-AS scores in this manner. However, even printing such information creates the potential for abuse. Finally, the sampling procedures used to develop the normative sample may not have been ideal. That is, no statistically systematized sampling plan is mentioned. In fairness, demographics of the sample are fully described.

Given its current state of development, any summary judgment about the OASIS-AS must be mixed. Evidence for its reliability appears sufficient. However, more and better validational data must be gathered before one should consider this test as an alternative to some other multiple aptitude tests (e.g., Differential Aptitude Battery). The goal of providing a commercially available parallel to the GATB is laudable. Whether or not it can be attained is, at present, unknown. Use of the OASIS-AS for research and comparative purposes is encouraged. Those who wish to use it for actual counseling are advised to proceed with caution and restraint.

[244]

Occupational Aptitude Survey & Interest Schedule: Interest Schedule. Purpose: "Developed to assist students in grades 8–12 in formulating educational and vocational goals and generally in career planning." Grades 8–12; 1983; OASIS-IS; intended to be used with Occupational Aptitude Survey; 12 scores: Artistic, Scientific, Nature, Protective, Mechanical, Industrial, Business Detail, Selling, Accommodating, Humanitarian, Leading-Influencing, Physical Performing; 1985 price data: $47 per complete test kit including manual (42 pages), 25 tests, 50 profiles, and 50 answer sheets; $9 per 25 tests; $12 per 50 profiles; $12 per 50 answer sheets; $18 per manual; $49 per scoring and interpretation software package; (35) minutes; Randall M. Parker; PRO-ED, Inc.*

TEST REFERENCES

1. Parker, R. M., & Green, D. (1987). Construct validity of the OASIS Inventory Schedule. *Educational and Psychological Measurement*, 47 (3), 755-757.

Review of the Occupational Aptitude Survey and Interest Schedule: Interest Schedule by CHRISTOPHER BORMAN, Professor, Department of Educational Psychology, Texas A&M University, College Station, TX:

The Occupational Aptitude Survey and Interest Schedule (OASIS) was developed "to assist junior high and high school students in vocational exploration and career development." The OASIS consists of two separate instruments—the Aptitude Survey (AS) and the Interest Schedule (IS). This review pertains only to the Interest Schedule. The IS has 240 items that are scored on a 3-point scale using the terms *like*, *neutral*, and *dislike*. This interest instrument has 12 scales with 20 items per scale. Of the 20 items for each scale, half of the items are occupational titles and the other half are job activities.

The OASIS-IS is built upon interest research conducted by the U.S. Employment Service and the early work of Cottle (1950). This research led to the identification of 12 interest factors, and the 240 items in the IS were selected to represent these 12 interest factors. Each of the 12 scales is briefly described in the test manual.

The test was standardized and normed on a sample of 1,398 students in grades 8–12 living in 11 states across the United States that seem to be representative of the country. About equal numbers of males and females were used in the sample, and the manual compares the sample to 1980 census data based on region of the country, gender, enthnicity, and urban or rural residence. Separate male and female norms are presented along with combined norms. Scores are presented in percentiles and stanines.

Alpha and test-retest reliabilities were employed in the development of the OASIS-IS. Two tables present alpha reliabilities for 260 students in grades 8, 10, and 12, and for 177 males and females, respectively. The coefficients for the 12 scales range from .85 to .95 indicating very respectable internal consistency for the OASIS-IS. Test-retest reliability was computed from data on 54 junior high and high school students over a 2-week interval, with the reliability coefficients ranging from .66 to .91 for the 12 OASIS-IS subscales. One of the most useful types of reliability evidence for an interest inventory is consistency over time, and the test-retest reliability data indicate that the IS scales are relatively stable over time.

The validation techniques used for the OASIS-IS included content and construct validity. Content validity was demonstrated by showing that the occupational titles and occupational activities listed in the OASIS-IS are representative of all the occupations listed in the *Guide for Occupational Exploration* (U.S. Department of Labor, 1979). Based on the information given in the manual, this instrument appears to have items representative of all the occupations listed in this Department of Labor publication. Factor analysis was used to provide evidence for the construct validity of the IS, and the analyses indicated that the 12 factors or components extracted could be identified as corresponding to one of the IS scales with one possible exception. This evidence seems to support the construct validity of the instrument. In this reviewer's opinion, the most serious shortcoming of the OASIS-IS is a lack of evidence of predictive validity. This absence of predictive validity data is a condition common among interest inventories, but it is a serious weakness because interest inventories are based on the assumption that predictions can be made from the scores. Although the purpose of this test may be to encourage exploration and not predict specific behaviors, information on the predictive validity of the instrument would still be helpful.

The OASIS-IS is untimed, but most examinees should be able to complete the instrument within 30 minutes. Directions for administration of the OASIS-IS are clear and easy to follow. Scoring is facilitated by a published scoring form. Unless the computer version of the instrument is used, the test must be hand scored, and this could be quite time consuming if more than just a few answer sheets have to be scored at one time. A machine-scoring service for the OASIS-IS would be helpful. Getting the scores for the 12 scales from the back of the scoring form to the front of the form and then recording the corresponding percentiles and stanines is somewhat awkward and could lead to mistakes in recording the results.

The OASIS-IS manual gives general guidelines for interpreting an interest inventory, and then specific guidelines for interpreting the OASIS-IS results are given. These guidelines are clear and present excellent suggestions for interpreting the test results. Also, the manual refers test administrators to several very useful resource books that have particular relevance to the OASIS-IS.

A microcomputer version of the OASIS-IS is now available for use on the Apple II+, IIe, and IIc personal computers. This program administers, scores, profiles, and provides interpretative information regarding an examinee's scores on the OASIS-IS. A separate small manual describes the background of the test, gives instructions for using the computer program, and offers several guidelines or suggestions for interpreting the results. The instructions for using this software package are clear and easy to follow. If a printer is available with the microcomputer being used, the computer program will print a profile of an examinee's scores; otherwise, the scores (percentiles and stanines) can be copied on the scoring form and profile sheet used with the paper-and-pencil version. Although this computer program presents a profile of an individual's scores and some general interpretative information, the program does not analyze the test results or provide an opportunity for the examinee to interact with the computer. One real advantage of the computer program is that the computer scores the test rather quickly.

The OASIS-IS was published in 1983 and remains a relatively new entrant to the interest-inventory market. The OASIS-IS does offer the potential for being a useful and respected instrument. Reliability data indicate respectable internal consistency and stability over time. Evidence is presented supporting the content and construct validity of the OASIS-IS, but there is no data on the predictive validity of the instrument. Therefore, the OASIS-IS should be used with caution until evidence supporting the predictive validity of the instrument is available. The test manual presents convincing evidence that the OASIS-IS was normed on a sample of students in grades 8–12 that is quite representative of students in the United States in this age group. The microcomputer version of the OASIS-IS offers another means of administering and scoring the instrument, but the full potential of a computer program is not realized because the program does not interpret individual test results or interact with the individual taking the test.

REVIEWER'S REFERENCES

Cottle, W. C. (1950). A factorial study of the Multiphasic, Strong, Kuder, and Bell inventories using a population of adult males. *Psychometrika*, 15, 25-47.

U.S. Department of Labor. (1979). *Guide for occupational exploration*. Washington, DC: U. S. Government Printing Office.

Review of the Occupational Aptitude Survey and Interest Schedule: Interest Schedule by RUTH G. THOMAS, Associate Professor, College of Education, University of Minnesota, St. Paul, MN:

The basis for development of the OASIS Interest Schedule (OASIS-IS) is worker trait research. Twelve empirically-derived, occupational interest factors were identified from the factor analysis of 307 activity items covering all worker trait groups. This research, conducted by the U.S. Employment Service, defined the domains which served as the basis for the writing of the OASIS-IS items.

Recent concerns about sex bias in occupational interest inventories and their interpretation are addressed in the OASIS-IS by: (*a*) using as its basis factors that are reportedly invariant by sex, (*b*) screening scale items for sex bias, and (*c*) providing both separate and combined norms for females and males.

Items are of two types: job titles and work activities. The *Guide for Occupational Exploration* (U.S. Department of Labor, 1979) was the source document for item development. The approach to development of the OASIS-IS beyond the identification of the original 12 interest factors is content oriented. Both items and occupations were keyed to the 12 domains on a logical basis. No evidence of empirical validation of items to occupations is provided. Item-total score correlations provided the basis for item inclusion in each scale.

While no systematically derived reading level information is provided, the OASIS-IS uses straightforward nontechnical language which should be understandable to most students in the age groups for which it is intended.

The OASIS-IS provides a profile of peer-normed percentile and stanine scores on 12 occupational interest scales that correspond to the original 12 interest factors. A computerized version of the interest schedule is available. This computer program offers immediate feedback to the student but provides less total information than does the paper-and-pencil version, omitting the stanine scores included on the original scoring sheet. However, even the paper-form version of the OASIS-IS does not provide as much information to the student as other established interest inventories. Many other inventories provide scores on other types of scales in addition to occupational interest scales.

The OASIS-IS was normed on a national sample of approximately equal numbers of male and female students in grades 8–12. Descriptive information about the norm group is provided and the manual is explicit about the norm group biases toward white, urban populations. The method by which the normative sample was drawn is not described, nor are the dates of norm data collection provided. The development of local norms is encouraged.

The manual deals with complex psychometric concepts and properties of the OASIS-IS in language aimed at a general population of users. It explains basic measurement concepts in a very readable and understandable fashion. The language used in the discussion of raw scores is of some concern since it refers to "correct" responses and to "performance," which inappropriately implies ability interpretations rather than interest interpretations.

Test-retest reliability coefficients for the 12 interest scales are slightly lower than those for the interest scales on the Strong-Campbell SVIB SC-II. While alpha internal consistency reliability coefficients are reported for three grade levels, only one standard error of measurement is reported for each subscale. The procedures and criteria used for drawing the reliability subsamples from the norm group are not explained. Means and standard deviations on each of the 12 subscales are provided for a larger norm group but not for the reliability subsamples.

Content and construct validity are identified in the OASIS-IS manual as the two types of validity most relevant to the purposes of the inventory. The purposes of the inventory are described in various sections as vocational exploration and career development, vocational goal setting, and measuring interests in a variety of occupations. It is clearly stated that the OASIS-IS is not intended for selection or prediction uses. The absence of a prediction element, particularly in relation to goal setting, is limiting in that it does not allow interpretations of scores in terms of predicted occupational satisfaction, success, entry, or tenure.

The use of judges or other types of verification of content validity is not reported, and therefore the validity of assignment of items and occupations to the 12 scales appears to be based solely on logical analysis.

Construct validity is based on data collected as part of the interest schedule development process. No research using the OASIS-IS is reported. Construct validity data is based on factor analysis and is totally internal to the inventory. It would be strengthened by empirical anchoring of scale items to occupational groups.

A means of checking for response bias with respect to social desirability and scale position is provided by two validity scales, which are designated as research scales because of their need for further empirical validation. Appropriate precautions regarding their use are given.

The length of time required to complete the interest schedule (identified as 30 minutes) is within the attention span and energy levels of the intended audience. No particular qualifications of users are indicated. Suggestions for user orientation are given. Administration and scoring instructions are detailed and could be followed by most education and counseling professionals. A hand-scoring procedure and form is provided and is reasonably simple to use. The lack of a machine-scoring option for the paper form may be a disadvantage when dealing with large numbers of students. Detailed instructions for providing interpretive feedback to students are given.

Users of the OASIS-IS should have at their disposal two publications recommended by the Interest Schedule author for use in interpreting OASIS-IS results and linking them to specific occupations: *Guide for Occupational Exploration* and *Worker Trait Group Guide*. Although the manual provides a limited summary of this type of information, it would be most helpful to have the more complete information provided in these two publications. The table in the manual appendix that is intended to link occupational titles, OASIS-IS item numbers, *Dictionary of Occupational Titles* (*DOT*) codes, and occupational interest areas to the 12 occupational interest scales is not adequately labeled for ease of interpretation. The 12 broad interest areas are not explicitly identified in the table. One can eventually infer what is missing in the table and supply it, but this is a needless task for users.

The strengths of the OASIS-IS include attention to sex bias concerns regarding occupational interest inventories, control of the scoring process by the user, and the availability of immediate computerized student feedback and scoring. Less sophisticated users might find the OASIS-IS less overwhelming and more understandable than more complex inventories with multiple dimensions. Weaknesses include the limited information the OASIS-IS provides to students and the lack of empirical, occupationally-anchored validation of scale items.

It would be difficult to recommend this interest schedule over a well established inventory like the Strong-Campbell SVIB SC-II if the goal is to provide maximum information to the student. The practical logistical advantages the OASIS-IS offers may outweigh information considerations in some instances.

[245]

Oetting's Computer Anxiety Scale. Purpose: "To provide a general measure of computer anxiety." College students; 1983; COMPAS; for research only; 8 subscale scores: Hand Calculator, Trust, General Attitude, Data Entry, Word Processing, Business Operations, Computer Science, Overall; Overall scale only for short form (10 questions from long form) and parallel forms (first or last halves of long form); norms for entering freshmen only; 1985 price data: $50 per 100 long form; $12 per manual ('83, 36 pages) including tests, scoring keys, scoring forms, and profile summary; [15] minutes; E. R. Oetting; Rocky Mountain Behavioral Science Institute, Inc.*

Review of Oetting's Computer Anxiety Scale by BENJAMIN KLEINMUNTZ, Professor of Psy-

chology, University of Illinois at Chicago, Chicago, IL:

At the risk of questioning the purpose and rationale of 90 percent or more of the psychological tests published over the years and reviewed in these pages, I seriously challenge the importance of predicting computer anxiety. But even if one were to argue that it is meaningful to do so—an argument that would probably revolve around the issue of the computer's increasingly important role in our society and the possibility that it frightens some people some of the time—the test manual does not help us out in this regard. Nowhere does Oetting indicate the redeeming societal (i.e., clinical, industrial, practical) value of identifying, discovering, or predicting such anxiety. For example, is it a disabling disorder that warrants remediation? Does it interfere with one's performance in school, at work, or in the home? Or is it simply an inconvenience that deprives some people of their God-given privilege of participating in our high-tech society?

On the other hand, if one were to assume that it is important to measure or predict computer anxiety, then Oetting's Computer Anxiety Scale (COMPAS) is certainly the test to select. Its manual is admirably prepared in the best psychometric tradition, and the two forms of the test—Long Form (48 items) and Short Form (10 items)—are certainly to the point, and seem to have high face validity. These are advantages that should not be underestimated, given the general slovenliness and/or commercialism that one often finds in test manuals.

Oetting's manual for the COMPAS appropriately begins with a caveat that the test should be used "*only* for research purposes" and "should not be used for selection if there could be negative consequences from that selection." It then formulates a general theory of computer anxiety by reviewing some of the highlights of trait and state anxiety, and concludes that computer anxiety is concept-specific, a term intended to provide "the theoretical underpinning of the COMPAS." Content-specific anxiety, Oetting believes, "may be the most useful construct for clinical practice or for many different kinds of research" and he defines it as "anxiety associated with a specified, clearly defined, and limited situation." The definition strikes me as being closer to the classical notion of phobia than to anxiety, given that the source of the emotional response is known.

Definitional considerations aside, Oetting's manual provides clear descriptions of the COMPAS and its scoring and interpretation. The internal consistency reliability data are admirably expressed in the form of Cronbach's alpha, which ranges from .88 for the Short Form to .96 for the Long Form based on 435 entering freshmen to Colorado State University. The parallel forms reliability of the test ranges from .94 to .96, and the internal consistency reliability of the subscales ranges from .71 (Business Operations) to .87 (General Attitude). The validity coefficients range from a low of .19 when the test is correlated with the criterion of Theme or Term Paper Anxiety measure, .40 with Suinn's Math Text Anxiety, .48 with the Science Test Anxiety, and a resounding .70 with a measure of computer *test* anxiety, which is a measure of "taking examinations where you would have to use a computer." No cross-validation data are presented.

Intercorrelations of COMPAS' seven subscales (Hand Calculator, Trust, General Attitude, Data Entry, Word Processing, Business Operations, and Computer Science) range from .07 to .71. These correlations, based on the normative sample of 435 entering freshman and 279 sophomores, tend to average around .50. They are all positive, and are correctly interpreted as showing that most of the subscales are related to an underlying common theme. They also help identify clusters of items that tap different dimensions of computer anxiety.

To summarize, the COMPAS is psychometrically sound, but its rationale for being is not immediately apparent. It would seem, moreover, that any subject who is afraid of computers would be as likely to say Yes or No to the following direct question as he/she would to the COMPAS' 48 or 10 item forms: "Are you afraid of, or made nervous by the idea of operating a computer?"

Review of Oetting's Computer Anxiety Scale by STEVEN L. WISE, Assistant Professor of Educational Psychology, University of Nebraska-Lincoln, Lincoln, NE:

Computers are playing an increasingly pervasive role in our society. Encounters with computers now commonly occur at home, in the workplace, and in many other aspects of our daily lives. This recent proliferation of computer use has produced an interest in the anxieties that may occur when people interact with computers. The Computer Anxiety Scale (COMPAS) was developed to measure these types of anxieties. The COMPAS is a 48-item attitude scale designed to provide a general measure of computer anxiety as well as measures of anxiety in particular situations involving computers.

The user is cautioned that the COMPAS should be used only for research purposes. The rationale behind this admonishment is unclear. Although it is true that the construct of computer anxiety is relatively new and has not been extensively studied, commercially-distributed anxiety scales are commonly used in clinical settings. A clinical interpretation of scores obtained using the COMPAS would not appear to represent a misuse of this instrument.

The items of the COMPAS were developed to measure a wide range of computer-related anxieties. I found some of the subscales to be more relevant to computer use than others. The Hand Calculator subscale, for example, appears to be, at best, marginally related to computer anxiety.

Each COMPAS item consists of a statement describing a situation involving a computer, followed by a 5-point rating scale using bipolar adjectives as scale endpoints. For a number of the items, the adjectives were not consistently used. For instance, across three of the items the adjective "anxious" is paired with "confident," "relaxed," and "comfortable," respectively. The double-barreled nature of some of the adjective pairings is particularly evident in combinations such as "anxious-confident."

The psychometric evidence for the COMPAS is fully described in the user's manual. The internal consistency reliability estimates for overall computer anxiety, across the various forms of the scale, are quite high. The reliabilities of the individual subscales are markedly lower, ranging from .71 to .87, although this is not surprising since each subscale is based on only four items. Also, while many items are reverse-keyed, the items within each subscale are all keyed in the same direction. This allows for the possibility of response sets distorting the subscale scores. Evidence for both content and construct validity of the COMPAS is well presented. It is clear that the test author paid close attention to validity issues when developing the COMPAS.

The manual contains detailed scoring information for the COMPAS. The scoring instructions, while unambiguous, are often very awkward to follow. For instance, the scoring of the subscales involves simultaneous manipulation and alignment of test form, transparent scoring key, and subscale scoring form. I generally found the scoring instructions to be unnecessarily difficult to use.

The user's manual also contains a scale profile sheet on which to plot the relative subscale and overall computer anxiety levels for a respondent. On this profile sheet there are interpretive statements beside several of the scale values. However, no evidence is provided to support the matching of the scale values with these interpretive statements. The manual implies that these statements follow from a direct interpretation of the rating scale used in the items. For example, the author claims that a score falling in the middle of the score range is indicative of a moderate level of anxiety. Without empirical evidence that people who are moderately anxious do, in fact, score in the middle of the score range, it is difficult to assess the validity of the author's claim. I recommend that the interpretive statements on the COMPAS profile sheet be used cautiously.

In summary, I feel that the overall computer anxiety scale of the COMPAS will be quite useful in measuring the levels of anxiety that people feel when interacting with computers. I am less confident in the utility of the COMPAS subscales, due primarily to modest reliabilities and susceptibility to response sets.

[246]

Ohio Apparel and Accessories Achievement Test. Purpose: "For evaluation and diagnosis of vocational achievement for the improvement of instruction." Grades 11–12; 1982–88; available only as a part of the Ohio Vocational Education Achievement Test Program; 11 scores: Cashiering, Merchandise Display, Sales, Stockkeeping and Inventory Control, First Line Management, Product Knowledge, Receiving and Marking Merchandise, Support Functions, Customer Services, Obtain Employment, Total; Part 1 ('84, 18 pages), Part 2 ('84, 18 pages); program manual ('88, 41 pages); program instructions to test administrators ('88, 32 pages); 1988 price data: materials are not for sale, all must be returned; use and scoring fee: $2.50 per student (non-Ohio schools in March), $3.50 per student at all other times, $1.25 per student (Ohio schools in March only); 240(250) minutes in 2 sessions; Instructional Materials Laboratory, Ohio State University.*

Review of the Ohio Apparel and Accessories Achievement Test by RICHARD C. ERICKSON, Professor and Chair, Department of Practical Arts and Vocational-Technical Education, University of Missouri-Columbia, Columbia, MO:

The Ohio Apparel and Accessories Achievement Test is one of a battery of 39 achievement tests designed to measure skills and understanding in specific vocational areas. The basis for this test is the duties, tasks, and activities that would be performed by entry-level employees in the retail clothing industry. These tasks and their related duties and activities were derived from a comprehensive analysis of those tasks performed by retail personnel in both large and small establishments. The test contains a total of 342 items. Each item included in the test is directed toward assessing student achievement with respect to one of the 337 activities identified in the analysis. Moreover, the items do not focus on assessing recall of specific facts alone. As dictated by the activities identified in the analysis, items also are focused on assessing skills in problem solving, data analysis, application of principles, abstract thinking, and the like. With an occasional exception here and there, all items are clearly written and conform to accepted guidelines for preparing multiple-choice items. The exceptions are a few items where the item stem does not set the task. In these few instances, students are required to read the stem and all of the alternatives before they can be sure of what task is being posed by the item.

K-R20 and K-R21 reliability estimates for 70 high school juniors are reported to be .977 and .973, respectively and .969 and .964, respectively for 35 high school seniors. While the magnitude of these estimates is certainly adequate, the number of students upon which they are based ranges from marginal ($N = 70$) to inadequate ($N = 35$). Also, because users are given and are encouraged to use 11 subtest scores, reliability estimates should be provided for each of the subtests. They are not provided.

Of more importance, however, is the absence of data with regard to the validity of this test. Crosswalking individual test items with their associated activities in the task analysis that formed the basis for this test has assured this reviewer that the test has considerable content validity. But, no data are presented in the test materials to assist users in determining whether or not this test would, for example, be useful in predicting students' success on the job after high school graduation. The test materials do indicate that "a validation study of the new tests is done during the first year of administration." This includes an evaluation of test results for high school juniors and seniors and for job incumbents with less than 2 years of employment in this occupation. The precise nature of this evaluation activity is not described except to say that, in the end, "test items not contributing favorable (sic) to the test are revised or eliminated." This reviewer tends to view this "validation study" to be a study to improve the internal consistency (reliability) of the test and not one to demonstrate test validity.

The program manual and instructions to test administrators are well written and contain information, instructions, and aids that are very useful to the test user. However, they only partially fulfill the need for the comprehensive test manual that has not been developed for this test.

In summary, this reviewer finds the Ohio Apparel and Accessories Achievement Test to be a significant contribution to testing in vocational education. It is the first and currently the only test of its kind. An exceptionally fine task analysis was conducted to form the basis of its development. It contains a large number of items and, collectively, they cover an adequate sampling of the work activities identified in the task analysis. Finally, this reviewer would recommend that a test manual be developed for this test and that it include the data and information normally included in such a manual, particularly the descriptive statistics and other results of efforts to study this test's validity and reliability.

[247]

Ohio Auto Mechanics Achievement Test. Purpose: "For evaluation and diagnosis of vocational achievement for the improvement of instruction." Grades 11–12; 1959–88; available only as a part of the Ohio Vocational Education Achievement Test Program; 14 scores: Lubrication and Prevention Maintenance, Service and Repair Engine, Service and Repair Cooling Systems, Service and Repair

Fuel and Exhaust Systems, Service and Repair Ignition Systems, Personal Development, Service and Repair Cranking and Charging Systems, Service and Repair Accessory Systems, Service and Repair Transmissions and Drive Line, Service and Repair Emission Systems, Service and Repair Brake Systems, Service and Repair Steering and Suspension Systems, Service and Repair Heating/Ventilation and Air Conditioning, Total; Part 1 ('88, 19 pages), Part 2 ('88, 16 pages); program manual ('88, 41 pages); program instructions to test administrators ('88, 32 pages); 1988 price data: materials are not for sale, all must be returned; use and scoring fee: $2.50 per student (non-Ohio schools in March), $3.50 per student at all other times, $1.25 per student (Ohio schools in March only); 240(250) minutes in 2 sessions; Instructional Materials Laboratory, Ohio State University.*

Review of the Ohio Auto Mechanics Achievement Test by HANK CAMPBELL, Associate Professor of Industrial Technology, Illinois State University, Normal, IL:

This test is specifically designed to measure the cognitive skill of an individual enrolled in a vocational program. Test results may be helpful to teachers, supervisors, administrators, potential employers, or persons interested in pursuing a career in auto mechanics. Parts I and II of the test require a minimum of 5 hours of administration. Test results are an indicator of degree of cognitive achievement and in some small part, the problem-solving capabilities of the test taker.

The two-part test includes test section I, consisting of 183 multiple-choice questions, including Lubrication; Preventative Maintenance and Shop Management; Mechanical Engine Repair; Cooling Systems, Fuel and Exhaust Systems; Ignition Systems; Personal Development; Cranking and Starting Systems; Accessory Systems; Transmissions and Drive Links; Emission Systems; Braking Systems; and Steering and Suspension and Heating and Air Conditioning Systems. Basic math skills are required for the Shop Management and Personal Development sections, but no use of calculators is permitted during the test. Part II has 181 items.

The test results are based on 1985 data. Analysis of test results suggests a K-20 reliability of .959 for juniors (N = 1,666) with a standard error of 8.871 and .979 for seniors (N = 1,717) with a standard error of 8.731. The K-21 results were .955 with standard error of 9.294 for juniors and .977 with standard error 9.137 for seniors.

Each section of multiple-choice questions was clearly written with an OPSCAN answer sheet provided to facilitate scoring.

The recent exam did contain printing errors and word usage errors. Also the content reflected traditional engine and automotive system design. Tremendous component changes have been made on present automobiles requiring knowledge of different nomenclature, understanding of electronics, hook-up for volt-ohm meters, computer logic for fuel injections and emission controls, and sophisticated accessory components. Many of these topics and necessary concept areas were not present within the test. Although the test should be a benchmark indicator assessing fundamental mechanic knowledge, it should not be assumed that good test performance assures a student to be capably educated to transfer that knowledge toward contemporary mechanical/electrical automotive systems.

[248]

[Ohio] Building Maintenance Achievement Test. Purpose: "For evaluation and diagnosis of vocational achievement for the improvement of instruction." Grades 11–12; 1986–88; available only as a part of the Ohio Vocational Education Achievement Test Program; 12 scores: Carpentry, Masonry, Electrical, Heating/Air Conditioning, Painting/Decorating, Plumbing, Welding, Flooring, Custodial, Grounds and Landscape, Personal Development, Total; Part 1 ('86, 16 pages), Part 2 ('86, 17 pages); program manual ('88, 41 pages); program instructions to test administrators ('88, 32 pages); 1988 price data: materials are not for sale, all must be returned; use and scoring fee: $2.50 per student (non-Ohio schools in March), $3.50 per student at all other times, $1.25 per student (Ohio schools in March only); 240(250) minutes in 2 sessions; Instructional Materials Laboratory, Ohio State University.*

Review of the Ohio Building Maintenance Achievement Test by GARY E. LINTEREUR, Associate Professor of Technology, Northern Illinois University, DeKalb, IL:

Ohio vocational teachers and specific building trades workers developed a *Task/Activity Analysis for Building Maintenance* curriculum guide from which the achievement test was designed. Test results will be useful to the extent the task analysis is appropriate for the user's purpose. No content or concurrent validity statements are made, but the description of the test development is at least face valid. The primary purpose of the test is improvement of instruction. It is strongly recommended that teachers do not see or administer the achievement test in their area as this might encourage teaching toward a test rather than geographical vocational needs. The data obtained should be helpful to supervisors and area leaders in assessing programs and instruction.

The paper-and-pencil test is administered over 3 days with the California Short Form Test of Academic Aptitude first (1 hour), followed by 2 days of administering Part 1 and Part 2 of the achievement test (2–2 1/2 hours each). The administration manual is very well written and easy to follow. Helpful suggestions for testing handicapped or disadvantaged students are provided.

The multiple-choice four-response achievement test questions are not simply recall in nature. Students are asked to solve problems, analyze data, use knowledge of principles, react to generalizations, use abstract thinking, and synthesize information. The publisher reports for juniors ($N = 207$), a K-20 of .969, K-21 of .966 with a standard error of measurement 8.684 and 9.094 respectively. The standard deviation was 49.32. Seniors ($N = 118$) show a K-20 of .960, K-21 of .956 with a standard error of measurement of 8.838 and 9.269 respectively. The standard deviation for this group was 44.19.

The user may not purchase the materials and all test materials are to be returned to the publisher. The school will receive a computer print-out of student scores by grade level and in rank order. Student subtest, subtotal, and total scores are reported as well as school median and means. A percentile norm sheet is also provided to allow for comparisons between school/state, student/class, and student/state.

In summary, the achievement test is very well developed, written, and should be very useful in evaluating 11th and 12th grade vocational building maintenance programs. The user should keep in mind this is not a building construction test, but rather directed toward building maintenance. The instructional goals were based on the needs of building maintenance workers in the state of Ohio and test generalizability should be considered for a specific location. Although program improvement is the paramount goal, teachers will find the results helpful for personal and course evaluation, and students will have useful information regarding career selection.

[249]

Ohio Child Care Achievement Test. Purpose: "For evaluation and diagnosis of vocational achievement for the improvement of instruction." Grades 11–12; 1986–88; available only as a part of the Ohio Vocational Education Achievement Test Program; 10 scores: Assist in Managing the Center, Assist in Maintaining Facilities and Supplies, Aid in Program Planning, Conduct Routine Activities, Assist Infant/Toddler Instruction, Assist Pre-School Instruction, Assist Elementary School Instruction, Assist Exceptional Children Instruction, Personal Development, Total; Part 1 ('86, 18 pages), Part 2 ('86, 20 pages); program manual ('88, 41 pages); program instructions to test administrators ('88, 32 pages); 1988 price data: materials are not for sale, all must be returned; use and scoring fee: $2.50 per student (non-Ohio schools in March), $3.50 per student at all other times, $1.25 per student (Ohio schools in March only); 240(250) minutes in 2 sessions; Instructional Materials Laboratory, Ohio State University.*

[250]

Ohio Clerk Typist Achievement Test. Purpose: "For evaluation and diagnosis of vocational achievement for the improvement of instruction." Grades 11–12; 1982–88; available only as a part of the Ohio Vocational Education Achievement Test Program; 11 scores: Letters/Memos and Envelopes, Filing, Proofreading and Editing, Mail Procedures, Employment Procedures/Human Relations, Reports/Manuscripts and Forms, Accounting/Calculating, Telephone and Receptionist Duties, Machine Transcription/Word Processing, Reprographics, Total; Part 1 ('84, 17 pages), Part 2 ('84, 18 pages); program manual ('88, 41 pages); program instructions to test administrators ('88, 32 pages); 1986 price data: materials are not for sale, all must be returned; use and scoring fee: $2.50 per student (non-Ohio schools in March), $3.50 per student at all other times, $1.25 per student (Ohio schools in March only); 240(250) minutes in 2 sessions; Instructional Materials Laboratory, Ohio State University.*

Review of the Ohio Clerk Typist Achievement Test by VIRGINIA E. CORGAN, Associate Professor of Vocational and Adult Education, University of Nebraska-Lincoln, Lincoln, NE:

This test consists of 333 multiple-choice questions divided into two parts. Part I has 167 items and Part II has 166 items. Although this multiple-choice format has some strengths (e.g., ease of checking, objective), the skills/knowledge tested by such items are not the same as performance measures in typing or other clerical tasks. Those using the Ohio Clerk Typist Achievement Test must assume the examinees are already competent in typing and in proofreading or be prepared to administer other tests.

Twenty-five questions concern the typing of letters, memos, and envelopes. The questions cover much of the basic knowledge a typist needs; they are similar to questions that all typing instructors use for pencil-and-paper tests. The typist, however, may not have the typing skill to be a competent typist. Accuracy of keystroking and speed of typing are the primary ingredients for success in typing. These things cannot be assessed by multiple-choice items.

The fundamental rules related to filing and handling mail are appropriately tested by the available items. The Proofreading and Editing Section is made up of 28 multiple-choice items. Here again, the most logical type of testing would be a performance task testing the examinee's use of proofreading marks and/or ability to read them and perform accordingly.

The test contains an employment procedures/human relations section with 50 multiple-choice questions. This section reflects an Ohio requirement that all vocational programs contain a section on "Personal Development." This reviewer noted that some items require test takers to respond with answers specific to certain curricular material. The section may be inappropriate for many schools.

In Part II of the Clerk Typist Test multiple-choice items cover typing knowledge regarding reports, manuscripts, and forms. Test items are well written and cover the essential rules for documents of varying types. If incorporated with the typing of a document it would give teachers useful feedback.

The Accounting/Calculation section of the test has a large number of items that require a limited understanding of accounting principles. Most items would be categorized as business arithmetic. An item referring to punched cards, now a historical process, was obviously overlooked in any test revision.

Knowledge of telephone and receptionist duties is applicable to the clerk typist occupation. Items in this area necessitate students' use of reasoning skills.

The section on machine transcription/word processing is concerned primarily with the process of transcribing documents using typewriter, electronic, or word-processing equipment. The items are marred by the use of historical terms. It is apparent the test requires a revision. Terms such as "automated typewriters," "indicator slip," and "correspondence secretary" (a term coined in the 70s which did not catch on) are used throughout. The obsolete terms threaten the items' validity. Even excellent items would be insufficient in this area, however, because production of a transcript is the most important learning outcome to be tested.

Reprographics, the last section of this test, is clearly outdated. The processes discussed are those that were prevalent in the mid 70s. The 1980s clerk typist does not operate an offset machine, and the inefficient methods and poor quality of the fluid process and the mimeograph process are long gone. This section will hold little meaning to current students.

The items were based on task analyses. These analyses have not kept pace with changing business technology and procedures. The test lacks up-to-date reliability estimates and provides no validity information. The content is based on antiquated equipment and procedures.

Although the test has some good sections, the pragmatic teacher will choose a test that first evaluates the productivity of the clerk typist with equipment in the 1980s office. Multiple-choice items are appropriate to evaluate format and principles. These must be revised frequently, however, to reflect changing conditions.

[251]

Ohio Community and Home Services Achievement Test. Purpose: "For evaluation and diagnosis of vocational achievement for the improvement of instruction." Grades 11–12; 1982–88; available only as a part of the Ohio Vocational Education Achievement Test Program; 12 scores: Communicating Information, Giving Personal Care, Taking Vital Signs, Lifting/Moving/Transporting Patients, Assisting with Special Care Procedures, Assisting with Nutritional Needs, Caring for Infants and Children, Assisting with Recreational Activities, Bed Making and Laundry Care, Providing Housekeeping Services, Personal Development, Total; Part 1 ('88, 18 pages), Part 2 ('88, 18 pages); program manual ('88, 41 pages); program instructions to test administrators ('88, 32 pages); 1988 price data: materials are not for sale, all must be returned; use and scoring fee: $2.50 per student (non-Ohio schools in March), $3.50 per student at all other times, $1.25 per student (Ohio schools in March only); 240(250) minutes in 2 sessions; Instructional Materials Laboratory, Ohio State University.*

[252]

Ohio Construction Electricity Achievement Test. Purpose: "For evaluation and diagnosis of vocational achievement for the improvement of instruction." Grades 11–12; 1973–88; available only as a part of the Ohio Vocational Education Achievement Test Program; 12 scores: Basic Electricity, National Electric Code, Planning and Layout, Rough-in Wiring, Finish Wiring, Safety, Service Entrance, Motors and Controls, Low-Voltage Systems, Electrician's Mathematics, Personal Development, Total; Part 1 ('84, 20 pages), Part 2 ('84, 19 pages); program manual ('88, 41 pages); program instructions to test administrators ('88, 32 pages); 1988 price data: materials are not for sale, all must be returned; use and scoring fee: $2.50 per student (non-Ohio schools in March), $3.50 per student at all other times, $1.25 per student (Ohio schools in March only); 240(250) minutes in 2 sessions; Instructional Materials Laboratory, Ohio State University.*

Review of the Ohio Construction Electricity Achievement Test by ALAN R. SUESS, Professor of Industrial Technology and Education, Purdue University, West Lafayette, IN:

The Ohio Construction Electricity Achievement Test is one of a series of tests designed by the Instructional Materials Laboratory (IML) at The Ohio State University. It has several stated goals, including evaluation of both instruction and student learning. The item budget for this and all other "Ohio" tests is based on the task/activity analysis produced by the IML. As a result, the test can only be as good as the occupational analysis upon which it is based and the extent to which the test questions, in fact, reflect the analysis.

If the evaluation of both teaching and learning are goals of this particular test, then serious concern is immediately evident. First, questions 1 to 26 relate to basic theory or Ohm's law—content not a part of the task/activity analysis. Second, the directions specifically prohibit the use of slide rules and calculators. Nine of these early questions require participants to extract a square root, compute least common denominators, manipulate reciprocals, or use other calculations common to AC/DC circuits. Later, the test booklet contains a 20-question section titled "Electrician's Math" and several relatively sophisticated personal finance questions. This artificial rigor appears out of place in an era of solar-powered "credit card" calculators. Craftpersons who need to make on-the-job calculations have available a durable, inexpensive, and reliable calculator as near as their shirt pocket or tool box tray.

Another concern is the section devoted to the National Electric Code (NEC). Historically, the NEC has had very few changes year-to-year. The recent past has been characterized by widespread revisions in the code. This examination has a 1984 copyright which predates many significant NEC changes. As time passes, there will be increased problems of currency of code items.

The test has several problems caused by format or context. For example, five questions are asked about a kitchen electrical plan reduced in scale to a size so small that one must assume that the symbol next to three-way switches is a three. Three adjacent questions about a duplex outlet use identical alternatives, effectively creating a three-item, four-response matching question. A question about thermal insulation is included in a section devoted to electrical insulation codes and standards. The stems of several questions are so general that they will likely reward the average student and cause great consternation to the most able. If the participant knows that relays are an important factor in low-voltage wiring, three virtually identical questions are "gifts."

There is only one serious omission in the test. Although several questions are asked about electrical conduit and electrical metallic tubing fittings, no questions are devoted to the calculations necessary for bending allowances or appropriate installation and use of fittings for either system. Because there are both code requirements and applied mathematics applications of this important commercial and industrial wiring practice, its omission is questionable.

Despite the preceding comments, there is much to recommend this test for its intended use—vocational electricity students. Many of the questions are based on the ability of students to read actual tables common to the trade. The section on personal development includes a number of items on personal banking, installment credit, job application procedures, grievance procedures, and similar occupationally relevant topics. These questions are well conceived and posed in realistic situations that probe the participant's understanding of the topics. There is a reasonable balance between the several task areas such as single-phase, three-phase, and low-voltage wiring, service entrance installation, rough-in, and finish wiring. Motors and controls are also well handled for a test at this level.

[253]

Ohio Data Processing Achievement Test.

Purpose: "For evaluation and diagnosis of vocational achievement for the improvement of instruction." Grades 11–12; 1981–88; available only as a part of the Ohio Vocational Education Achievement Test Program; 9 scores: Performing Data Entry, Providing Clerical Support, Using Software, Performing Business Applications, Operating Computer Systems, Performing Accounting Functions, Analyzing and Designing Business Systems, Progressing in the Work Environment, Total; Part 1 ('88, 19 pages), Part 2 ('88, 22 pages); program manual ('88, 41 pages); program instructions to test administrators ('88, 32 pages); 1988 price data: materials are not for sale, all must be returned; use and scoring fee: $2.50 per student (non-Ohio schools in March), $3.50 per student at all other times, $1.25 per student (Ohio schools in March only); 240(250) minutes in 2 sessions; Instructional Materials Laboratory, Ohio State University.*

TEST REFERENCES

1. Altschuld, J. W., Hines, C. V., & Rinderer, R. E. (1983). Further evidence in support of the construct validity of Ohio's Vocational Achievement Test program. *Journal of Industrial Teacher Education*, 21 (1), 3-13.

Review of the Ohio Data Processing Achievement Test by VIRGINIA E. CORGAN, Associate Professor of Vocational and Adult Education, University of Nebraska-Lincoln, Lincoln, NE:

The Ohio Data Processing Achievement Test is hopelessly outdated in content. This problem is so pervasive this reviewer cannot imagine a valid use for the test.

This test is described as useful in curriculum improvement activities and not meant to be a screening device or provide predictive information concerning examinees' performance as data processors. The reported validation study involved first-year instruction students (11th grade), second-year instruction students (12th grade), and persons who had been in the occupation no more than 2 years. No results of this study are provided. The authors merely state the test has been validated.

Content validity is discussed in terms of a Task/Activity Analysis. This analysis is purportedly reviewed to be kept current with actual occupational practices.

As with other tests in the Ohio series, this one records impressive internal reliabilities. Samples of junior ($N = 932$) and senior ($N = 989$) test takers provided K-20 reliabilities of .967 and .974, respectively.

A careful review of this test failed to reveal for whom the test is meant. Its content does not match any current job roles or functions known to this reviewer. Is the test for people who are simply working in the machine room of a large computing system? These people learn their jobs from "on-the-job-training" not from a curriculum. Certainly the test is not directed toward programmers. Programmers are working primarily with systems; seldom would they be found laboring over the writing of programs in several of the languages cited in the tests. Obviously, the test is not written for analysts, either.

The operations defined by the test are equally outdated. Operation of keypunch/verifier equipment, key-disk equipment, the burster, decollator, automatic data-processing equipment, and card sorter are of only historical interest. Modern business processing equipment is long past the equipment cited above.

This reviewer must assume the test lacks current and comprehensive validity and reliability information. The test as now written will not be helpful to instructors who are preparing students to be effective in today's business organizations.

[254]

Ohio Dental Assisting Achievement Test.

Purpose: "For evaluation and diagnosis of vocational achievement for the improvement of instruction." Grades 11–12; 1970–88; available only as a part of the Ohio Vocational Education Achievement Test Program; 11 scores: Dental Anatomy, Dental Emergencies, Preventive Dentistry, Infection Control, Chairside Assisting, Dental Specialties, Dental Laboratory, Radiology, Dental Office Management, Personal Development, Total; Part 1 ('82, 16 pages), Part 2 ('88, 22 pages); program manual ('88, 41 pages); program instructions to test administrators ('88, 32 pages); 1988 price data: materials are not for sale, all must be returned; use and scoring fee: $2.50 per student (non-Ohio schools in March), $3.50 per student at all other times, $1.25 per student (Ohio schools in March only); 240(250) minutes in 2 sessions; Instructional Materials Laboratory, Ohio State University.*

TEST REFERENCES

1. Altschuld, J. W., Hines, C. V., & Rinderer, R. E. (1983). Further evidence in support of the construct validity of Ohio's Vocational Achievement Test program. *Journal of Industrial Teacher Education*, 21 (1), 3-13.

[255]

Ohio Diversified Health Occupations Achievement Test. Purpose: "For evaluation and diagnosis of vocational achievement for the improvement of instruction." Grades 11–12; 1975–88; available only as a part of the Ohio Vocational Education Achievement Test Program; 12 scores: Anatomy and Physiology, Asepsis and Sterilization, Vital Signs, Acute Care Nursing, Ward Clerk, Emergency First Aid, Long Term Care Nursing, Home Health Aide, Medical Assisting and Laboratory, Dental Assisting, Personal Development/Employment Skills and Ethics, Total; Part 1 ('85, 14 pages), Part 2 ('85, 16 pages); program manual ('88, 41 pages); program instructions to test administrators ('88, 32 pages); 1988 price data: materials are not for sale, all must be returned; use and scoring fee: $2.50 per student (non-Ohio schools in March), $3.50 per student at all other times, $1.25 per student (Ohio schools in March only); 240(250) minutes in 2 sessions; Instructional Materials Laboratory, Ohio State University.*

[256]

Ohio Drafting Achievement Test. Purpose: "For evaluation and diagnosis of vocational achievement for the improvement of instruction." Grades 11–12; 1962–88; available only as a part of the Ohio Vocational Education Achievement Test Program; 15 scores: Geometric Shapes and Construction, Orthographic and Auxiliary Projection, Pictorial Drawing, Sectional Views, Production/Working Drawings, Fastening Methods, Industrial Materials and Processes, Dimensions and Tolerancing, Intersections and Developments, Mechanics, Architectural Drawings, Structural and Civil Drawings, Electrical and Electronic Drawings, Personal Development, Total; Part 1 ('86, 23 pages), Part 2 ('86, 23 pages); program manual ('88, 41 pages); program instructions to test administrators ('88, 32 pages); 1988 price data: materials are not for sale, all must be returned; use and scoring fee: $2.50 per student (non-Ohio schools in March), $3.50 per student at all other times, $1.25 per student (Ohio schools in March only); 240(250) minutes in 2 sessions; Instructional Materials Laboratory, Ohio State University.*

For a review by Richard A. Swanson of an earlier edition, see 8:1160; see also T2:2428 (1 reference).

Review of the Ohio Drafting Achievement Test by GARY E. LINTEREUR, Associate Professor of Technology, Northern Illinois University, DeKalb, IL:

Ohio vocational teachers and drafters developed a *Task-Activity Analysis for Drafting Occupations* curriculum guide from which this achievement test was designed. Test results will be useful to the extent the task analysis is appropriate for the user's purpose. No content or concurrent validity information is given, but the description of the test development does seem appropriate. The primary purpose of the test is improvement of instruction and it is strongly recommended that teachers do not see or administer the achievement test in their area as this might encourage teaching toward a test rather than geographical vocational needs. The data obtained should be helpful to supervisors and area leaders in assessing programs and instruction.

The paper-and-pencil test is administered over 3 days with the California Short Form Test of Academic Aptitude first (1 hour), followed by 2 days of administering Part 1 and Part 2 of the achievement test (2–2½ hours each). The administration manual is very well written and easy to follow. Helpful suggestions for testing handicapped or disadvantaged students are provided.

The multiple-choice four-response achievement test questions are not simply recall in nature. Students are asked to solve problems, analyze data, use knowledge of principles, react to generalizations, use abstract thinking, and synthesize information. The publisher reports for juniors ($N = 602$) a K-20 of .959, K-21 of .954 with a standard error of measurement of 8.780 and 9.300 respectively. The standard deviation was 43.36. Seniors ($N = 478$) show a K-20 of .964, K-21 of .959 with a standard error of measurement of 8.827 and 9.420 respectively. The standard deviation for this group was 46.52.

The user may not purchase the materials and all test materials are to be returned to the publisher. The school will receive a computer print-out of student scores by grade level and in rank order. Student subtest, subtotal, and total scores are reported as well as school medians and means. A percentile norm sheet is also provided to allow for comparisons between school/state, student/class, and student/state.

In summary, the achievement test is well developed, written, and should be very useful in evaluating 11th and 12th grade vocational drafting programs. The instructional goals measured by the test were based on the needs of drafters in the state of Ohio. Thus, test generalizability should be considered for a specific location. Although program improvement is the paramount goal, teachers and other personnel will find the results helpful for personal and course evaluation, and students may gain useful information regarding career selection.

[257]

Ohio Electronics Achievement Test. Purpose: "For evaluation and diagnosis of vocational achievement for the improvement of instruction." Grades 11–12; 1973–88; available only as a part of the Ohio Vocational Education Achievement Test Program; 10 scores: DC Circuits, AC Circuits, Solid State Circuits, Analog Circuits, Digital Circuits, Control/Processor Operations, Test Equipment, Electrical/Electronic Systems and Subassemblies, Personal Development, Total; Part 1 ('88, 24 pages), Part 2 ('88, 24 pages); program manual ('88, 41 pages); program instructions to test administrators ('88, 32 pages); 1988 price data: materials are not for sale, all must be returned; use and scoring fee: $2.50 per student (non-Ohio schools in March), $3.50 per student at all other times, $1.25 per student (Ohio schools in March only); 240(250) minutes in 2 sessions; Instructional Materials Laboratory, Ohio State University.*

[258]

Ohio Farm Management Achievement Test. Purpose: "For evaluation and diagnosis of vocational achievement for the improvement of instruction." Grades 11–12; 1982–88; available only as a part of the Ohio Vocational Education Achievement Test Program; 12 scores: Plan and Supervise Work, Analyze Farm Records, Buildings and Structures, Finance Farm Operations, Maintain Inventory of Supplies, Plan Crop Enterprise, Market Farm Products, Plan Livestock Enterprise, Equipment and Machinery, General Management Duties, Employment Procedures, Total; Part 1 ('83, 15 pages), Part 2 ('88, 17 pages); program manual ('88, 41 pages); program instructions to test administrators ('88, 32 pages); 1988 price data: materials are not for sale, all must be returned; use and scoring fee: $2.50 per student (non-Ohio schools in March), $3.50 per student at all other times, $1.25 per student (Ohio schools in March only); 240(250) minutes in 2 sessions; Instructional Materials Laboratory, Ohio State University.*

TEST REFERENCES

1. Altschuld, J. W., Hines, C. V., & Rinderer, R. E. (1983). Further evidence in support of the construct validity of Ohio's Vocational Achievement Test program. *Journal of Industrial Teacher Education*, 21 (1), 3-13.

Review of the Ohio Farm Management Achievement Test by GEORGE WARDLOW, Assistant Professor of Agricultural Education, University of Minnesota, St. Paul, MN:

This test is available from among several in the Ohio Vocational Achievement Tests. These occupational tests were developed to measure skills and understanding in each of several vocational areas. According to the program manual, they are designed to measure student abilities to: solve problems, analyze data, recall specific facts, use knowledge of principles, react to generalizations, use abstract thinking in specific situations, and put together parts to form a complete structure. It is in consideration of these objectives the following review is prepared.

The Farm Management Test, copyrighted in 1982, is one of several in Agricultural Education designed to measure student abilities in various agriculture areas. It consists of two parts and includes the sections: Plan and Supervise Work, Analyze Farm Records, Buildings and Structures, Finance Farm Operations, Maintain Inventory of Supplies, Plan Crop Enterprise, Market Farm Products, Plan Livestock Enterprise, Equipment and Machinery, General Management Duties, and Employment Procedures.

The approximately 300 items are representative of the overall content of farm management education at the high school level. The questions are well written and free of bias. Appropriate distractors are included in the solution choices for each item. When compared with other tests from the Agricultural Education area of the Ohio battery, some overlap of content was found. For example, several of the questions are also included on the Production Agriculture Test. However, because farm management is seldom taught or learned in isolation from production agriculture, some overlap is appropriate. One concern might be any geographic regionality implied in the proportion of items related to specific agricultural practices. Because the test is an Ohio product, other regions in the country might have different emphases in the proportion of agricultural items in specific content areas.

The test is successful at addressing the objectives of measuring student ability to recall specific factual information and knowledge of general principles. However, because of the constraints of a timed objective test covering a wide range of content, and because measurement of student abstract thinking abilities is a complex problem, it falls short of its objectives of measuring student abilities to use abstract thinking and to put parts together to form a complete structure.

The instruction booklet for test administrators is very well done with complete step-by-step instructions for administering the test. The program manual includes a discussion of the development of the tests and reliability and validity tests. Upon completion of the test, a comprehensive set of analyses are returned to the school. This information includes individual and group data in both raw score and percentile rank form. Ohio norms have been established and are provided for reference.

The test was developed by professional educators in agriculture based on a comprehensive occupational task analysis, tested and revised to insure validity of the instrument. Reliability estimates based upon the Kuder-Richardson 20 and 21 procedures as applied to a test sample of 155 Ohio high school juniors and seniors in agriculture are included in the program manual. The listed reliability estimates are in the .95 to .97 range with a standard error of measurement in the 7.9 to 8.4 range.

In summary, the Ohio Farm Management Test addresses well its objectives of measuring student abilities relative to factual information and principles related to farm management education. It is a well-prepared and well-tested instrument. It should be noted that other measures do exist commercially to assess student abilities in this area. A current one is under production by a major national testing service at the time of this writing.

[259]

Ohio Heating, Air Conditioning, and Refrigeration Achievement Test. Purpose: "For evaluation and diagnosis of vocational achievement for the improvement of instruction." Grades 11–12; 1976–88; available only as a part of the Ohio Vocational Education Achievement Test Program; 9 scores: Install Heating Systems, Install Refrigeration and Air Conditioning Equipment, Troubleshoot Refrigeration and Air Conditioning Equipment, Service and Repair Refrigeration and Air Conditioning Equipment—Electrical, Service and Repair Refrigeration and Air Conditioning Equipment—Mechanical, Troubleshoot/Service and Repair Oil Heating Systems, Troubleshoot/Service and Repair Alternate Heating Systems, Personal Development, Total; Part 1 ('86, 21 pages), Part 2 ('86, 20 pages); program manual ('88, 41 pages); program instructions to test administrators ('88, 32 pages); 1988 price data: materials are not for sale, all must be returned; use and scoring fee: $2.50 per student (non-Ohio schools in March), $3.50 per student at all other times, $1.25 per student (Ohio schools in March only); 240(250) minutes in 2 sessions; Instructional Materials Laboratory, Ohio State University.*

[260]

Ohio Horticulture Achievement Test. Purpose: "For evaluation and diagnosis of vocational achievement for the improvement of instruction." Grades 11–12; 1979–88; available only as a part of the Ohio Vocational Education Achievement Test Program; 12 scores: Soil and Plant Science, Greenhouse Operations, Interior Plantscape Service, Landscape Services, Turf Services, Retail Floriculture, Nursery, Garden Center, Fruit and Vegetable Production, Equipment and Mechanics, Personal Development, Total; Part 1 ('86, 19 pages), Part 2 ('86, 20 pages); program manual ('88, 41 pages); program instructions to test administrators ('88, 32 pages); 1988 price data: materials are not for sale, all must be returned; use and scoring fee: $2.50 per student (non-Ohio schools in March), $3.50 per student at all other times, $1.25 per student (Ohio schools in March only); 240(250) minutes in 2 sessions; Instructional Materials Laboratory, Ohio State University.*

Review of the Ohio Horticulture Achievement Test by JERRY L. PETERS, Associate Professor of Education, Purdue University, West Lafayette, IN:

The 1986 Ohio Horticulture Achievement Test is designed to measure occupational skills and knowledge of the vocational area of horticulture. The two-part test contains a total of 363 multiple-choice questions covering 11 major occupational task areas of horticulture. Each of the two parts of the test is to be administered on a separate day. Time requirements recommended of 2 to 2½ hours each day seem adequate.

The description of the care with which the test items were developed from an occupational analysis of the skills and the knowledge necessary to perform the tasks of a person working in horticulture is impressive. The authors indicate that Occupational Tasks/Activity Analyses are reviewed each year to ensure applicability to current occupational practices and requirements.

The test itself is printed for easy readability and each major occupational task area is identified. Graphic illustrations used are clearly presented.

An instructional manual (1986) for test administrators, designed to accompany the various Ohio Vocational Education Achievement Tests including the test under review, offers very explicit, easy-to-follow instructions. The authors have done an excellent job of developing a generic instructional manual for their achievement tests without weakening the directions for the test administrator and the student taking the test. Directions to the student, found on the front page of the test booklets, are in bold print and are easy to follow.

Test reliability scores, computed by Kuder-Richardson Formula 20 and 21 coefficients, are based on a sampling of 434 juniors and 383 seniors. Reliability coefficients range from .96 to .97 respectively. Data for job incumbents who have been employed in the occupation for less than 2 years are not given.

The authors have put together a very thorough technical manual that presents information on the development and suggested use of all Ohio Vocational Education Achievement Tests. The 1986 manual offers data regarding the reliability and validity of the tests; provides examples of test items covered on each test and the occupational task area covered under each test; makes suggestions concerning the use of the tests for instructor and student appraisal; and describes the type of information and data returned to the schools and the norming procedures used. Page 2 of the manual makes reference to an annual percentile norm sheet, which is to be found on page 27. However, examples of the percentile norm sheet are found in the Appendices on pages 35 and 37.

It is strongly recommended by this reviewer that before a school or instructor decides to administer this achievement test, careful review be made of the Horticulture Task/Activity Analysis document that identifies several of the tasks involved in the horticulture occupation. This document was used in the development of the achievement test and it is this reviewer's concern that a school/instructor not using this document to assist in the development of the horticulture curriculum may find the interpretation of the test results misleading.

In summary, this reviewer is quite impressed with the amount of time and effort put forth to develop an occupational achievement test for horticulture in the state of Ohio. This is a test which could be administered in other states. Horticulture teachers should be using this test to help improve instruction in their vocational programs throughout the United States.

[261]

Ohio Lithographic Printing Achievement Test. Purpose: "For evaluation and diagnosis of vocational achievement for the improvement of instruction." Grades 11–12; 1976–88; available only as a part of the Ohio Vocational Education Achievement Test Program; 11 scores: Layout and Design, Composing, Proofing, Paste-up, Camera and Film Processing, Personal Development, Stripping, Platemaking and Proofs, Offset Presses, Finishing Operations, Total; Part 1 ('85, 16 pages), Part 2 ('85, 14 pages); program manual ('88, 41 pages); program instructions to test administrators ('88, 32 pages); 1988 price data: materials are not for sale, all must be returned; use and scoring fee: $2.50 per student (non-Ohio schools in March), $3.50 per student at all other times, $1.25 per student (Ohio schools in March only); 240(250) minutes in 2 sessions; Instructional Materials Laboratory, Ohio State University.*

[262]

Ohio Machine Trades Achievement Test. Purpose: "For evaluation and diagnosis of vocational achievement for the improvement of instruction." Grades 11–12; 1958–88; available only as a part of the Ohio Vocational Education Achievement Test Program; 12 scores: Benchwork, Inspection and Measuring Instruments, Drilling Machines, Turning Machines, Sawings and Special Operations, Layout and Blueprint, Milling, Abrasive Machining, Heat Treating and Applied Science, N.C./C.N.C., Personal Development, Total; Part 1 ('85, 18 pages), Part 2 ('85, 19 pages); program manual ('88, 41 pages); program instructions to test administrators ('88, 32 pages); 1988 price data: materials are not for sale, all must be returned; use and scoring fee: $2.50 per student (non-Ohio schools in March), $3.50 per student at all other times, \$1.25 per student (Ohio schools in March only); 240(250) minutes in 2 sessions; Instructional Materials Laboratory, Ohio State University.*

See T2:2427 (2 references).

Review of the Ohio Machine Trades Achievement Test by THOMAS S. BALDWIN, Practicing Psychologist, Chapel Hill, NC:

Development of the Ohio Machine Trades Achievement Test follows standards often discussed but seldom achieved in the development of such instruments. Content validity was insured by the establishment of a test development committee consisting of subject matter experts and a representative of the Instructional Materials Laboratory (IML). The committee's initial task was to develop a comprehensive task/activity analysis for machine trades (165 pages). Based on this detailed analysis the committee then developed test items, which were field tested and analyzed following standard item analysis procedures.

An approach to establishing construct validity was to administer the test to first year students (11th grade), second year students (12th grade), and job incumbents with no more than 2 years of experience. After further revision, the test was made available to schools that have approved vocational programs. Test security is given extremely high priority. Even instructors in the machine trades area are not permitted to see the test to prevent the tendency to teach specifically for good performance on the test.

The administration manual, although generic for the entire IML series, is highly detailed and insures standardized conditions in test administration. The test administrator is even provided guidance in dealing with "Special Needs" students such as the handicapped, disadvantaged, etc.

The administration of this test requires 3 days, the first of which is devoted to administration of the California Short Form Test of Academic Aptitude (SFTAA). The inclusion of such a test as a frame of reference provides many interesting possibilities for use with the achievement test, although this is not dealt with very adequately in the test materials. For example, while KR-20 reliabilities .88, .90, and .93, are reported for the nonlanguage, language, and total sections of the SFTAA based on a sample of 16,000 11th grade students, no correlations of this test are given with the Ohio Machine Trades Achievement Test. Instructors are, therefore, left to their own resources to know how this test relates to the achievement test that is the primary purpose of the program.

The Ohio Machine Trades Achievement Test itself consists of two parts, both of which are organized around subject matter content areas and appear to follow very closely the task/activity analysis. Part 1 of the test (162 items) and Part 2 (183 items) cover 11 subject matter areas including "Personal Development." The last section is not specific to machine trades and deals with more general questions such as computing overtime wages, how much to tip a waiter, etc. Parts 2 and 3 of the test require 2 hours of actual testing time each.

Unfortunately, the care and detail with which this test has been developed and administered does not carry over into the reports of its psychometric merits. Basic data, including the median, mean, standard deviation, KR-20 and KR-21 reliabilities, and standard errors of measurement for KR-20 and KR-21 are reported for total score for both Juniors ($N = 916$) and Seniors ($N = 878$). Reliabilities are exceptionally high (.96 and .97). Unfortunately, means and reliabilities are not reported for the various subtests nor are intercorrelations among the various subtests. Furthermore, as noted above, correlations with the SFTAA are not reported, leaving the user to decide for him or herself the utility of this reference test.

It should be noted the excellent data on reliability of tests calls into question the overall efficiency of the test. At present the test requires 3 days to administer and a total of 5 to 6 hours of administration time. By reducing to one half its present length, the achievement test reliabilities would suffer only a modest decrease. Furthermore, the inclusion of the SFTAA requires an additional day of testing as well as scoring and reporting the results. This is particularly important in view of the rather poorly defined uses that the SFTAA has for the consumer. It might be advisable for IML to examine the alternative of a 1-day program and weigh the modest decrease in reliability and questionable loss of utility by eliminating the SFTAA, against the reduced time and cost involved in the current 3-day program.

As noted above the goal of this test is program evaluation which will lead to improvement of instruction. Materials supplied for review list a number of potential student benefits. Among the latter are providing "information to teachers and counselors for job placement"; "The teacher and student will have evaluative information concerning the students (sic) ranking in local and state settings"; and "Students should obtain a better understanding of themselves and their potential." These legitimate individualized uses seem to be inconsistent with the statement that "These tests are not designed to be used as a counseling instrument." It is not entirely clear why this disclaimer is included in the manual because the use of the instrument for such individualized purposes appears to be legitimate for such a well developed and carefully administered test.

Finally, it should be mentioned that the Ohio Machine Trades Achievement Test is a paper-and-pencil test. It appears to measure very thoroughly and with a high degree of reliability those aspects of performance that can be measured through the use of paper-and-pencil testing procedures. The test does not measure the ability of a student to apply such knowledge to actual performance on various tasks required in machine trades. Of course, the test does not purport to measure such performance. However, in fairness to the potential test user this shortcoming of the test should at least be acknowledged.

SUMMARY. The Ohio Machine Trades Achievement Test was conceived to meet a very significant need in vocational education. The care with which the test was conceptualized, developed, and administered appears to meet the most rigorous standards of test development. Unfortunately, the reported data regarding the psychometric merit of the test do not meet such standards. Although the test has exceptionally high measures of internal consistency, length of subtests, subtest reliabilities, subtest intercorrelations, and the relationship of the achievement test to the reference test (SFTAA) are not reported. Additionally, the test currently requires 3 days for administration and the IML should be encouraged to consider the marginal gains they are achieving over a program that could be administered in 1 day. Nevertheless, the test remains a sophisticated instrument that measures what it purports to measure with a high degree of accuracy. It is strongly recommended to potential users.

[263]

Ohio Masonry Achievement Test. Purpose: "For evaluation and diagnosis of vocational achievement for the improvement of instruction." Grades 11–12; 1982–88; available only as a part of the Ohio Vocational Education Achievement Test Program; 11 scores: Prepare Materials and Establish the Work Area, Lay Brick and Block to a Line, Lay Brick and Block with a Plumb Rule, Construct Fireplaces and Chimneys, Construct Arches, Miscellaneous Masonry Construction, Concrete Masonry, Surveying, Welding and Cutting, Personal Development, Total; Part 1 ('88, 20 pages), Part 2 ('88, 21 pages); program manual ('88, 41 pages); program instructions to test administrators ('88, 32 pages); 1988 price data: materials are not for sale, all must be returned; use and scoring fee: $2.50 per student (non-Ohio schools in March), $3.50 per student at all other times, $1.25 per student (Ohio schools in March only); 240(250) minutes in 2 sessions; Instructional Materials Laboratory, Ohio State University.*

TEST REFERENCES

1. Altschuld, J. W., Hines, C. V., & Rinderer, R. E. (1983). Further evidence in support of the construct validity of Ohio's Vocational Achievement Test program. *Journal of Industrial Teacher Education*, 21 (1), 3-13.

Review of the Ohio Masonry Achievement Test by THOMAS S. BALDWIN, Practicing Psychologist, Chapel Hill, NC:

This test is a well-conceived and carefully developed test covering the field of brick and block masonry in considerable detail. The test development began with a thorough task/activity analysis, which is some 87 pages in length. Each activity is analyzed in terms of tools and materials, safety hazards, science, etc., necessary to complete the activity. This task/activity analysis forms the basis for item construction which was done by a committee of subject matter experts and a representative of the Instructional Materials Laboratory (IML). The steps involved in test development are carefully set forth and represent a thorough approach to achievement test construction.

The test is used by virtually all Ohio secondary schools offering approved programs in brick and block masonry and by a number of schools located in other states. The test requires 3 days to administer, the first day being devoted to the administration of The California Short Form Test of Academic Aptitude (SFTAA; 1970), which contains a language and nonlanguage section. This test is intended to provide a frame of reference by which instructors and others can evaluate the achievement of individual students on various subtests in the actual achievement test. The second and third days are devoted to the administration of Part 1 (154 items) and Part 2 (145 items) of the achievement test.

The test is organized around 10 sections or subtests, nine of which deal directly with brick and block masonry while the tenth, Personal Development, deals with items such as what to do with an R.S.V.P. invitation, basic information contained in Robert's Rules of Order, and basic questions about filling out an employment application.

The Instructions to Test Administrators manual, while generic to the entire IML Series, is very detailed and has been revised each year from 1979 through 1986. Test security is given high priority and even instructors are not permitted to see the test to counteract the tendency to teach toward the test.

The Achievement Test Program manual states that the test is designed for "evaluation and diagnosis of vocational achievement for the improvement of instruction." It further states specifically that it is *not* designed to be used as a counseling instrument. Nevertheless, in a different section of the manual the test is suggested as a means of providing "information to teachers and counselors for job placement," as a means by which "teacher and student will have evaluative information concerning the student's ranking and in local and state standings," and to provide the student with "a better understanding of themselves and their potential." The manual seems somewhat inconsistent in this respect and may be doing a disservice to potential users by not placing more emphasis on the legitimate individualized uses of the test.

Unfortunately, the psychometric data accompanying this test are not as detailed and comprehensive as the procedures followed in developing the test. Total test (not including the SFTAA) median, mean, standard deviation, KR-20 and KR-21 reliabilities, and KR-20 and KR-21 standard errors of measurement are reported. Reliability coefficients are quite high for the total test. For Juniors, based on an N of 162, the manual reports KR-20 reliability of .97 and a KR-21 reliability of .97. For Seniors, based on an N of 149, KR-20 reliability is .97 and KR-21 reliability is .96. Unfortunately, no information is provided on subtest reliabilities, for which scores are reported. Nor are means, intercorrelations, or even the number of items in each of the 10 subtests given.

The utility of the SFTAA is mostly left up to the potential test user to determine. The manual does report means, standard deviations, KR-20 reliabilities, and standard error of measurement based on a sample of 16,000 11th grade students. How the SFTAA relates to the other sections of the test is not dealt with in the manual. For example, the simple matter of correlation between the SFTAA scores and subtest and total test scores of the achievement test are not reported. Therefore, it is not clear how one should interpret the achievement test results as they relate to the SFTAA.

Content validity appears to have been assured through the use of well-qualified item-writing committees, a careful task/activity analysis, and item analysis. In addition, empirical data are available that support the concept of construct validity, specifically the difference in means between Juniors and Seniors. However, individuals who have been engaged in the occupation were also administered the test, although no data are reported for this group.

One has to question the marginal benefits of taking 3 days to administer the Ohio Masonry Achievement Test. By a rearrangement of items within Part 1 and Part 2, parallel forms of the test could be developed with minimum sacrifice in reliability. Furthermore, the use of the SFTAA in conjunction with the achievement test is not clearly set forth. Because three separate days and 5 to 6 hours of testing time are currently required, IML should look at the benefits currently achieved versus the benefits of a 1-day, 2½-hour session that could be accomplished by eliminating the SFTAA and by reducing the achievement test length by half.

Finally, it should be noted that this test is a measure of cognitive knowledge and ability associated with brick and block masonry. The test does not address the performance or psychomotor aspect of the work of a mason. IML does not state that this is a purpose of the test, but they also do not mention that this very significant component of job performance is not measured by this particular test.

SUMMARY. The Ohio Masonry Achievement Test is a carefully developed instrument and consumers can have considerable confidence regarding its content validity. There is some evidence of construct validity, although this could easily be expanded. As a whole the test appears reliable and to have many potential uses in vocational education. The stated purpose of the test, improving instructional programs, is an important objective. Perhaps IML should consider other uses of the test such as individual counseling. The test is an excellent, if somewhat time consuming, test of those aspects of masonry that can be measured with paper and pencil.

[264]

Ohio Medical Assisting Achievement Test. Purpose: "For evaluation and diagnosis of vocational achievement for the improvement of instruction." Grades 11–12; 1974–88; available only as a part of the Ohio Vocational Education Achievement Test Program; 14 scores: Personal Development, Body Systems, Clinical Skills, Medications, Medical Office Skills, Sterilization, Laboratory Skills, E.K.G., X-Ray, Diet and Nutrition, First Aid, Medical Terminology, Medical Office Computations, Total; Part 1 ('84, 18 pages), Part 2 ('84, 18 pages); program manual ('88, 41 pages); program instructions to test administrators ('88, 32 pages); 1988 price data: materials are not for sale, all must be returned; use and scoring fee: $2.50 per student (non-Ohio schools in March), $3.50 per student at all other times, $1.25 per student (Ohio schools in March only); 240(250) minutes in 2 sessions; Instructional Materials Laboratory, Ohio State University.*

[265]

Ohio Production Agriculture Achievement Test. Purpose: "For evaluation and diagnosis of vocational achievement for the improvement of instruction." Grades 11–12; 1982–88; available only as a part of the Ohio Vocational Education Achievement Test Program; 13 scores: Beef Production, Small Grain Production, Sheep Production, Soybean Production, Crop Chemical Application, Agricultural Construction, Operator Equipment Maintenance, Dairy Production, Corn Production, Swine Production, Forage Production, Employment Procedures, Total; Part 1 ('84, 16 pages), Part 2 ('83, 16 pages); program manual ('88, 41 pages); program instructions to test administrators ('88, 32 pages); 1988 price data: materials are not for sale, all must be returned; use and scoring fee: $2.50 per student (non-Ohio schools in March), $3.50 per student at all other times, $1.25 per student (Ohio schools in March only); 240(250) minutes in 2 sessions; Instructional Materials Laboratory, Ohio State University.*

Review of the Ohio Production Agriculture Achievement Test by JERRY L. PETERS, Associate Professor of Education, Purdue University, West Lafayette, IN:

The 1986 Ohio Production Agriculture Achievement Test is designed to measure occupational skills and knowledge of production agriculture. The two-part test contains a total of 349 multiple-choice questions covering 12 major occupational task areas of production agriculture. Each of the two parts of the test is to be administered on a separate day. Time requirements recommended of 2 to 2 1/2 hours each day seem adequate.

The description of the care with which the test items were developed from an occupational analysis of the skills and the knowledge necessary to perform the tasks of a person working in production agriculture is impressive. The authors indicate that Occupational Tasks/Activity Analyses are reviewed each year to ensure applicability to current occupational practices and requirements.

The test itself is printed for easy readability and each major occupational task area is identified. Graphic illustrations used are clearly presented.

An instructional manual (1986) for test administrators, designed to accompany the various Ohio Vocational Education Achievement Tests including the test under review, offers very explicit, easy-to-follow instructions. The authors have done an excellent job of developing a generic instructional manual for their achievement tests without weakening the directions for the test administrator and the student taking the test. Directions to the student, found on the front page of the test booklets, are in bold print and are easy to follow.

Test reliability scores, computed by Kuder-Richardson Formula 20 and 21 coefficients, are based on a sampling of 157 juniors and 112 seniors. Reliability coefficients range from .96 to .97 respectively. Data for job incumbents who have been employed in the occupation for less than 2 years are not given.

The authors have put together a very thorough technical manual that presents information on the development and suggested use of all Ohio Vocational Education Achievement Tests. The 1986 manual offers data regarding the reliability and validity of the tests; provides examples of test items covered on each test and the occupational task area covered under each test; makes suggestions concerning the use of the tests for instructor and student appraisal; and describes the type of information and data returned to the schools and the norming procedures used. Page 2 of the manual makes reference to an annual percentile norm sheet, which is to be found on page 27. However, examples of the percentile norm sheet are found in the Appendices on pages 35 and 37.

It is strongly recommended by this reviewer that before a school or instructor decides to administer this achievement test, careful review be made of the Production Agriculture Task/Activity Analysis document that identifies several of the tasks involved in the production agriculture occupation. This document was used in the development of the achievement test and it is this reviewer's concern that a school/instructor not using this document to assist in the development of the production agriculture curriculum may find the interpretation of the test results misleading. It is also important to note that several of the test questions refer specifically to Ohio and therefore would be inappropriate for someone taking this test from another state.

In summary, this reviewer is quite impressed with the amount of time and effort put forth to develop an occupational achievement test for production agriculture in the state of Ohio. Test administration outside of Ohio must be done cautiously. Test questions specific to Ohio should be changed. Production agriculture teachers in Ohio should be using this test to help improve instruction in their vocational programs.

Review of the Ohio Production Agriculture Achievement Test by GEORGE WARDLOW, Assistant Professor of Agricultural Education, University of Minnesota, St. Paul, MN:

The Ohio Production Agriculture Achievement Test is available from among several in the Ohio Vocational Achievement Tests battery. These occupational tests were developed to measure skills and understanding in a number of vocational areas. According to the program manual, they are designed to measure student abilities to: solve problems, analyze data, recall specific facts, use knowledge of principles, react to generalizations, use abstract thinking in specific situations, and put together parts to form a complete structure. It is in consideration of these objectives the following review is prepared.

The Production Agriculture Achievement Test, copyrighted in 1983, is one of several in Agricultural Education designed to measure student abilities in various agriculture areas. It consists of two parts and includes the sections: Beef Production, Small Grain Production, Sheep Production, Soybean Production, Crop Chemical Application, Agricultural Construction, Operator Equipment Maintenance, Dairy Production, Corn Production, Swine Production, Forage Production, and Employment Procedures.

The approximately 350 items are representative of the overall content of production agriculture education at the high school level. The questions are well written and free of bias. Appropriate distractors are included in the solution choices for each item. When compared with other tests in the Agricultural Education area of the Ohio battery, some overlap of content was found. For example, several of the questions are also included on the farm management test. An additional concern might be any geographic regionality implied in the proportion of items related to specific agricultural practices. Because the test is an Ohio product, other regions in the country might have different emphases in the proportion of agricultural items in specific content areas.

The test is successful at addressing the objectives of measuring student ability to recall specific factual information and knowledge of general principles. However, because of the constraints of a timed objective test centering on a wide range of content, and the difficulty in measuring student abstract thinking abilities, it falls short of its objectives of measuring student abilities to use abstract thinking and to put parts together to form a complete structure.

The instruction booklet for test administrators is very well done with complete step-by-step instructions for administering the test. The program manual includes a discussion of the development of the tests and of tests for reliability and validity. Upon completion of the test, a complete set of analyses are returned to the school. This information includes individual and group data in both raw score and percentile rank form. Ohio norms have been established and are provided for reference.

The test was developed by professional educators in agriculture based on a comprehensive occupational task analysis, tested and revised to insure validity of the instrument. Reliability estimates based upon the Kuder-Richardson 20 and 21 procedures as applied to a test sample of 269 Ohio high school juniors and seniors in agriculture are included in the program manual. The listed reliability estimates are in the .97 range with a standard error of measurement in the 8.5 to 8.9 range.

In summary, the Ohio Production Agriculture Achievement Test succeeds in measuring student abilities relative to factual information and principles related to production agriculture education. It is a well-prepared and well-tested instrument. It should be noted that other measures do exist commercially to assess student abilities in this area. A current one is under production by a major national testing service at the time of this writing.

[266]

Ohio Small Engine Repair Achievement Test. Purpose: "For evaluation and diagnosis of vocational achievement for the improvement of instruction." Grades 11–12; 1984–88; available only as a part of the Ohio Vocational Education Achievement Test Program; 16 scores: Tools and Fasteners, Fuel and Exhaust Systems, Cooling and Lubrication Systems, Short Block and Governor Systems, Charging and Electrical Systems, Starting Systems, Mechanics Mathematics, Ignition Systems, Valve Train Systems, Troubleshooting, Lawn and Garden Equipment, Motorcycle Equipment, Marine Equipment, Snowmobile Equipment, Business and Shop Operations, Total; Part 1 ('84, 15 pages), Part 2 ('84, 15 pages); program manual ('88, 41 pages); program instructions to test administrators ('88, 32 pages); 1986 price data: materials are not for sale, all must be returned; use and scoring fee: $2.50 per student (non-Ohio schools in March), $3.50 per student at all other times, $1.25 per student (Ohio schools in March only); 240(250) minutes in 2 sessions; Instructional Materials Laboratory, Ohio State University.*

Review of the Ohio Small Engine Repair Achievement Test by HANK CAMPBELL, Associate Professor of Industrial Technology, Illinois State University, Normal, IL:

This test seeks to determine the degree to which an individual comprehends the fundamental concepts associated with servicing small internal combustion engines. The two-part test requires 4 hours to administer with 2 hours for each of the two parts. The test could be used by high school instructors, private and public technical school instructors, or potential employers wanting to determine examinees' factual knowledge about small engine systems. The test seems to test for a high proficiency in component memorization rather than for skills in solving challenging problems.

Part I includes questions related to specific nomenclature and practices when servicing small one- and two-cycle gasoline engines. Seven sections of the 174-item test feature questions on Tools and Fasteners, Fuel and Exhaust Systems, Cooling and Lubrication Systems, Short Block and Governor Systems, Charging and Electrical Systems, Starting Systems, and Mechanics Mathematics. An attempt was made to distribute equally questions related to each topic section; however, combined, the sections on Fuel and Exhaust, Cooling and Lubrication Systems, and Mechanics Mathematics comprise about 15% of Part I.

Part II tests student knowledge of Ignition Systems, Valve Train Systems, Troubleshooting, Lawn and Garden Equipment, Motorcycle Equipment, Marine Equipment, Snowmobile Equipment, and Business and Shop Operations. The 164 questions challenge the learner to respond to many factual items with only a limited number of problem-solving questions. The section on Business and Shop Operations is a curious mix of questions ranging from parliamentary procedures to determining correct specifications for a piece of equipment to be taken from a common specification sheet of a manufacturer's service manual. Only about three questions require any math computation skill.

Test reliability coefficients were computed for juniors and seniors who participated in the achievement test program in 1984 or 1985. (The manual is unclear about the date.) For juniors ($N = 152$) the KR-20 was .970. The standard error of measurement was 8.236. The KR-21 yielded .966 with a standard error of measurement of 8.768. Seniors ($N = 130$) fared slightly better with the KR-20 of .984 and a standard error of measurement of 8.097, and with the KR-21 of .982 and a standard error of measurement of 8.588.

These 1984 tests are in need of revision. Although the basic concepts are not dated, substantial changes in ignition systems, fuel systems, and emission requirements for small engines have occurred. The test lacks emphasis on concepts of electronics and computerized test equipment needed to service some small engines. There have been substantial changes in tax laws and how they apply to small businesses. Greater test emphasis should be applied toward testing for problem-solving and mathematical skill.

This test should yield a measure of acquired knowledge about small engine mechanics but not necessarily yield information as to how one might perform as a mechanic or technician. The results of this test along with some type of performance test could be viewed as good indicators of entry level skill for this technical area.

[267]

Ohio Word Processing Achievement Test. Purpose: "For evaluation and diagnosis of vocational achievement for the improvement of instruction." Grades 11–12; 1982–88; available only as a part of the Ohio Vocational Education Achievement Test Program; 11 scores: Typing and Transcription, Reprographics, Word Processing Concepts and Procedures, Business Transactions, Proofreading and Editing, Automated Word Processing Equipment, Receptionist Duties, Composition and Dictation, Records Management, Employment Procedures, Total; Part 1 ('84, 17 pages), Part 2 ('84, 19 pages); program manual ('88, 41 pages); program instructions to test administrators ('88, 32 pages); 1988 price data: materials are not for sale, all must be returned; use and scoring fee: $2.50 per student (non-Ohio schools in March), $3.50 per student at all other times, $1.25 per student (Ohio schools in March only); 240(250) minutes in 2 sessions; Instructional Materials Laboratory, Ohio State University.*

Review of the Ohio Word Processing Achievement Test by VIRGINIA E. CORGAN, Associate Professor of Vocational and Adult Education, University of Nebraska-Lincoln, Lincoln, NE:

The Task/Activity Analysis upon which the Ohio Word Processing Achievement test is based is excellent. The tasks required, the materials and equipment used, and the procedures are spelled out very well. The group of word-processing instructors from Ohio vocational schools who assembled this analysis provided an excellent document.

The first section of this two-part test has 54 multiple-choice questions regarding the format of documents and transcription techniques. The rules for formatting are very like those of the clerk typist examination, and the transcription rules are primarily the simple ones published by a major dictation/transcription equipment manufacturer in the 70s. These rules have been used for many years and there is little likelihood that they will change. This reviewer found it interesting that where centering titles was queried, the test taker was required to know placement in terms of a typewriter scale; operators using word-processing programs use electronic centering procedures. Few offices can afford the inefficiency of the typewriter for word processing.

The Reprographics section includes 18 multiple-choice questions; 13 of these items include references to the spirit duplicator, mimeograph, and offset processes. This reviewer found the task analysis (basis of the test) to have little reference to such historical processes. The task analysis, too, had a relatively brief section on reprographics as would be expected for a word-processor occupation. Consequently, entries about reprographic equipment of a historical type seem to be particularly inappropriate for an up-to-date occupational program.

Word Processing Concepts and Procedures is a section of 33 items; a few of these may also be open to question on grounds that they are out of date today.

The section on business transactions primarily involves simple computations. There are 20 entries to relate to the three activities associated with business transactions in the task analysis. The items are basic, and though a word processor would seldom be responsible for these computations, the rationale for their inclusion may be that all occupational curricula should include such items. This reviewer would not disagree with such a principle.

Proofreading and Editing, a responsibility of the word processor occupation, has 40 entries in Part I of the test. The task analysis gives little space to the function of proofreading though it is implicit in the processing of documents. Multiple-choice entries include a good selection of problems, from spelling and word division to identification of correct grammar and proofreaders' marks.

Requiring a test taker to insert the correct proofreading marks in a selection or requiring a test taker to process a selection that is marked could be of greater value than the multiple-choice questions for testing proofreading.

Part II of the test checks the processor's knowledge of word-processing equipment. These 56 questions are more indicative of present-day word processing. Up-to-date terminology is used and the questions are written in a manner that assumes the student is using electronic equipment. Where equipment brands are cited, this reviewer would prefer entries to be rewritten.

There are 38 items regarding receptionists' duties. Telephone skills are tested, and entries regarding receptionist duties, procedures for public relations, for making travel arrangements, and planning company tours are all in agreement with the task analysis.

The student's understanding of letter composition and dictation rules is tested in Composition and Dictation, and tests for understanding of simple filing and of file processes (microfilm, fiche, etc.) are tested in Records Management. Both of these sections were correctly derived from the task analysis and are well done.

Employment Procedures, as in all Ohio tests, has items concerning procedures in applying for the specific occupation. The entries are practical and in line with the philosophy of the vocational curricula to include information about seeking a position.

The Word Processing Achievement Test is a good test. This reviewer believes that such a test used in conjunction with an assessment method that actually tests the transcription of documents would be a valid test of skill and knowledge for an occupational curriculum. Without the skill testing it is conceivable that a student could not perform well enough to be prepared for such positions. Although authors of the tests state: "The occupational tests were developed to measure skills and understanding in specific vocational areas" (Ohio, 1986) current test items cannot measure skills.

The test authors note the tests are validated for use only in educational programs at the 11th and 12th grade levels and are not to be used for evaluating individuals for pre-employment screening (Rinderer, 1986). The authors mention the tests were validated in the first year of administration (1982) against job incumbents employed no more than 2 years in the occupation. Like others of the Ohio tests, specific validity procedures or coefficients are not cited.

Instructions for giving the tests are clear. The testing service is a total package program from the Ohio Vocational Instructional Materials Laboratory. All scoring is done there. KR-20 reliabilities of .964 for Juniors and .977 for Seniors (591 Juniors and 506 Seniors) are reported for this test.

Scores are returned to schools with percentile norm sheets provided so that a teacher can determine how a student or class ranks in comparison to other test takers. Test norms appear to be valid as one analyzes the test scores and their increases from the junior level to senior level.

With validity information provided, a skill test administered, and questionable items removed, this test would be a useful tool. The authors should pay special attention to frequent revisions of the items because equipment improves rapidly in the office occupations.

REVIEWER'S REFERENCES

Instructional Materials Laboratory. (1986). The Ohio Vocational Education Achievement Test Program. Columbus, OH: Author.

Rinderer, R. E. (1986). Ohio Vocational Achievement Tests (Memo, February 14, 1986). Columbus, OH: Instructional Materials Laboratory, Ohio State University.

[268]

Oral Motor Assessment and Treatment: Improving Syllable Production. Purpose: "Designed for use with children who have subtle difficulties with rapid, accurate syllable production." Ages 4–11; 1985; 3 parts: reliability training to assess oral motor performance, Oral Motor Assessment Scale, treating oral motor discoordination; 4 scores: Accuracy, Smooth Flow, Rate, Total; individual; 1988 price data: $54 per manual (62 pages) and 2 treatment and assessment cassette tapes; administration time not reported; Glyndon D. Riley and Jeanna Riley; PRO-ED, Inc.*

Review of Oral Motor Assessment and Treatment: Improving Syllable Production by ROBERT RUEDA, Visiting Associate Professor of Curriculum, Teaching, and Learning, University of Southern California, Los Angeles, CA:

The Oral Motor Assessment and Treatment Program is a three-part system designed for "children who have subtle difficulties with rapid, accurate, syllable production," and is meant to improve "the phonological system and fluent production of syllables." The manual appropriately cautions that this program may or may not be helpful for children with overt physical disorders involving difficulty in breathing, swallowing, and other nonverbal motor systems (e.g., cerebral palsy). Additionally, the manual suggests that this program should be used only as a part of an overall management plan, since some cases may involve factors beyond the scope of this program. The test is individually administered and the equipment needed includes a high quality tape recorder with an external microphone and a stopwatch that can be read to one-tenth of a second.

The three parts of the program include: (*a*) Reliability Training needed for administration of the scale, (*b*) the Oral Motor Assessment Scale, and (*c*) the Oral Motor Discoordination Training Program. Each of these will be discussed in turn.

RELIABILITY TRAINING. The reliability training is provided on a single audiotape, and a separate worksheet is provided to allow the listener to follow each part of the training. The tape provides samples of types of errors, which are then scored by the listener and compared to a standard provided by the authors. In addition, this tape provides a section on timing the rate of production of various samples of grouped syllable sets. Normative rates based upon two empirical studies are provided for children between the ages of 3–13, with extrapolated norms for some syllable sets at the 3–5 year age level. The last part of the first tape contains samples of syllable production errors, which are then scored and compared to a standard provided by the authors.

The training appears to be well thought out and clearly presented. The training does take some time to work through, but is essential for later use of the assessment scale. The most difficult aspects were correctly scoring the grouped syllable sequences once an error was made on the tape, and timing the rate of production. The syllable sets are timed to the tenth of a second, and it takes some effort to obtain the level of precision suggested in the manual. This is not a trivial consideration, since the norms at the lower age levels contain gradations as small as one-tenth of a second separating different age groups. In fact, analysis of variance of rate measures between the various age groups, as indicated in the normative data, did not reach significance.

ADMINISTRATION OF THE OMAS. The OMAS is based on previous versions of oral motor performance measures developed by the same authors. The specific areas of syllable production assessed in this program include accuracy (including distortion errors and voicing errors), flow (including coarticulation errors, even flow, and sequencing errors), and rate. Three syllable sets are used as the basis for scoring these categories, based upon their use in previous research in which norms were calculated. The syllable sets that the child is asked to produce are first modeled by the clinician, at age-appropriate rates, and the child's response is taped for later scoring. Scores are assigned in each of the categories, and are based on the number of errors (as indicated on the scoring sheet provided). The score for rate is based upon standard deviation units from the age-appropriate norms. Overall scores are provided for accuracy, smooth flow, and rate, and these are summed for an overall total score ranging from 0–42.

The part-to-whole correlations, based upon 103 "normal children" reported in the manual for the separate areas of the scale (not including total scores), ranged from .30 for distortions to .67 for rate. Although all correlations were significant, it seems that the scale measures distinct aspects of syllable production. Factor analysis of the scale might help clarify the relationships between the various subscales. In addition to these data, three studies of interobserver reliability conducted by the authors produced reliability coefficients ranging from .83 to .99. However, the reliability of the scale with wider use by clinicians trained only with the audiotape remains to be seen. Validity data for the OMAS was somewhat less complete. For example, it is reported that 69% of 54 children who stuttered were 1.5 standard deviations away from normal expectations on oral motor discoordination, and a comparable figure was reported for a smaller sample of 17 students. However, this means that approximately 30% of these students scored within normal limits. Since the test is designed for children who have "subtle difficulties," it might be expected that these percentages would be higher. An additional study involving the comparison of scoring judgments of syllable sets with spectographic analysis was inconclusive.

Age-graded normative data are provided in the manuals for 206 children from ages 4 through 11. The manual does not indicate where or when the data were collected.

THE OMAS TRAINING PROGRAM. The training program is designed to impact the accuracy, smooth flow, and rate of syllable set production. Guidelines, based on OMAS scores, are provided for the selection of appropriate cases for treatment. The basic procedure is based upon the clinician's modeling the target syllable set and the child's imitation of the modeled performance. Syllable sets of increasing complexity are used as a basis for the training, and the manual as well as the audiotape provides suggestions, examples of appropriate reinforcement procedures, etc.

SUMMARY. The most positive aspect of this test is the attempt to link reliability training, assessment, and treatment into a single package. The manual is clear, well-written, and simple to follow, with an appropriate amount of detail. In spite of these positive features, however, there is a need for a wider data base on reliability and validity using practitioners in actual clinical settings. In addition, one potential problem with the scale is that the repeated production of nonsense syllables required of children may confound oral motor coordination with factors related to attention. Finally, it is not at all clear how the production of nonsense syllables generalizes to everyday language use. Given the increasing attention to function as well as form in the study of language development and assessment, this type of decontextualized approach may need to be evaluated carefully with respect to an overall language development program.

Review of Oral Motor Assessment and Treatment: Improving Syllable Production by SHELDON L. STICK, Professor, Department of Special Education and Communication Disorders, The University of Nebraska-Lincoln, Lincoln, NE:

The Oral Motor Assessment and Treatment Program was designed for use with children between 4 and 11 years of age who present subtle difficulties with rapid and accurate syllable production. The authors' stated purpose is to describe selected aspects of motor activity that commonly are associated with speech sound production. The intent is to provide a self-training package to enable a user to reliably assess selected motor aspects of speech production. A 14-level treatment program, based on the authors' model, accompanies the assessment training. Included in the purchase price are two audio cassettes that repeat information contained in the manual and also present examples of selected oral motor activity. The manual has three major sections: (1) Reliability Training To Assess Oral Motor Performance, (2) Oral Motor Assessment Scale (OMAS), and (3) Treating Oral Motor Discoordination.

CRITIQUE. As indicated earlier, this three-part Oral Motor Assessment and Treatment Program is aimed at improving syllable production. Empirically it would seem that any program that sets out to systematically increase the rate of production and length of units involved in the production would stand a reasonable chance of being successful, and that practitioners probably would welcome the addition of such an instrument. As a vehicle for improving syllable production, the Oral Motor Assessment and Treatment Program might be a reasonable approach. However, the data provided in the manual do not support its use as anything more than a procedure for assessing nonsense-syllable production and as an outline for training children to produce nonsense syllables at a more rapid rate.

The first major section of the manual addresses reliability training for an individual who would be using the program. It is in this section that the authors present their definitions of the three major categories of syllable production: Accuracy, Smooth Flow, and Rate. These three factors were identified as selected oral motor behaviors commonly observed among individuals who stuttered and/or who presented articulation disorders. It was noteworthy that the authors did not use the same terminology consistently throughout the rest of the manual. That was particularly distracting for the category of Smooth Flow. It is the authors' prerogative to define terms as they elect; however, it would have been helpful had they explained why they elected to deviate from more commonly accepted definitions. For example, the category of accuracy included distortions (lack of precision) and voicing errors (substitution of a voiced cognate for the target consonant). It is possible for a child to substitute a voiceless sound for the target sound, and other types of speech sound substitutions might appear as well as cognate substitutions. Perhaps the authors view these other forms of speech sound substitutions as within the purview of phonological processes. If so, it would have been helpful for such a clarification to be made at the outset of the manual instead of at the very end where they discuss which groups of children might benefit from the Oral Motor Assessment and Treatment Program.

Under the category of Smooth Flow the authors discussed three subareas: coarticulation, even spacing, and correct sequencing. Even spacing might be interpreted as an aspect of Rate, and it is not clear why the authors elected to put this subarea under Smooth Flow. Furthermore, the definition of correct sequencing would seem to have some elements of coarticulation, and it is not apparent why the two areas were not combined. The category of Rate is addressed mainly from the point of view of being slower than a so-called normal standard. There is some reference throughout the manual to a more rapid rate, but the norms presented address only slower than normal rates of speech production.

Training tape 1.1 is transcribed in the manual, so the individual seeking the training from this program has both auditory as well as visual input. There are some problems with this tape, as with the three other tapes, in that it contains an uncommon amount of noise, variation in apparent quality of production, unusual amounts of breathiness on the part of a speaker, apparently unusual cadence (rate), and, possibly, misarticulated speech sounds. The impression is that the tapes lack the professional quality one would expect when purchasing such a program. However, despite the apparent shortcomings of the tapes a listener can develop an understanding of the authors' intentions for Accuracy and Smooth Flow. It would be helpful if the manual contained a number of detachable copies of the various forms referenced for use during the training process instead of having to constantly flip pages or make photocopies of all forms. The manual contains what is referred to as a transcript of the tape, but it is not an exact transcription, which can become disturbing. Also, the writing style in the manual is not precise, and during the first part of the manual the authors' intention is not always apparent. Listening to the tape clarifies the ambiguity.

The second side of the first cassette tape is divided into two sections. The first section provides examples of varying rates that are referenced to an accompanying table in the manual (Table 1). In Table 1 data are presented as time in seconds required to perform selected syllable sets 10 times. Under the 50th percentile is a column heading entitled "Standard Deviation Mean." It is not clear whether that is intended to be the standard error of measurement or whether, in fact, a number of samples were averaged and that figure represents the average of all the standard deviations. Regardless, it would be helpful if information were provided on how that mean score was obtained. The samples presented on training tape 1.3 were acknowledged to be of less than good quality. However, the amount of noise present made judging the samples difficult; in some instances, it might prove detrimental for individuals attempting to become proficient in the use of the instrument.

The second major section of the manual addresses the development of the instrument and presents information on administration and scoring of the various subscales. Some reorganization of this part of the manual probably would be in order because scoring criteria are addressed before the reliability and validity information, but the last part of the section explains the administration and scoring. Perhaps the administration and scoring instruction should precede the scoring criteria and item selection sections. Training tape 2.1 accompanied this part of the manual and, as with both sides of the first training tape, there were numerous problems with this tape. For example, there was variability in terms of the carrier phrase presented to the presentation of the stimulus model in both intensity and in the actual length of time. Furthermore, the samples varied in overall intensity as a consequence of the speaker apparently attempting to get all of the syllables produced in a single breath. With the clinician holding the external microphone approximately 2 inches from a child's mouth (as recommended in the manual), this would seem to be a difficult task to accomplish without creating some distraction and/or unnaturalness in the gathering of the data. Directions for obtaining the sample state that the model presented should be at a rate that is challenging or at a faster rate than would be expected for a child at a given age. However, earlier in the manual the authors commented on the fact that presentation of a model at an uncomfortably rapid rate might cause the child's speech syllable production to deteriorate. That was substantiated by an example on the tape. Yet, during the administration and scoring section the authors recommend doing just that procedure. It is not clear why they suggest presenting a model in a manner that is likely to obtain less than an optimum performance from a subject. Several paragraphs later, the authors address this very issue of rate for presentation of the model and stress the importance of presenting age-appropriate rates.

The scoring criteria vary according to the major category and the subareas within the categories. It is not an easy process to follow, but with practice can be implemented. It was noted that the scoring criteria varied without an apparent explanation. For example, under the major category of Accuracy the distortion errors are scored as follows: No errors would be assigned a score of 0; 1–2 errors assigned a score of 1; and 3 or more errors would be assigned a score of 2. The second subarea in the major category of Accuracy, voicing, is scored as follows: No errors equaled 0; 1–2 errors apparently equaled 1; 3 or more errors equaled 3. It should be noted that there was an apparent typographical error in the scoring criteria because the manual stated that 1–2 errors equaled a point value of 3, whereas in the sample score profile form it listed 1–2 errors as receiving a value of 1. There were also other apparent typographical errors in the manual.

Two types of reliability were reported. Part-whole reliability was determined by using 103 normal children, ages 4 through 8, and correlating their scores for each of the major categories and subareas within the categories with the total Oral Motor Assessment Scale (OMAS). All of the correlation coefficients were reported as being statistically significant beyond the .001 level. The total Accuracy category had a correlation of .46, with the two subareas of distortion and voicing having correlations of .30 and .33 respectively. These were by far the lowest correlations with the total OMAS. The total Smooth Flow correlation with the OMAS was .83, with no subunit having a correlation lower than .52. Rate correlated .67 with the OMAS. It would seem that the Accuracy category probably reflects phonological aspects of speech production and, as such, is not truly an index of oral motor ability. Furthermore, since Rate had just one item considered in the correlation coefficient, and it had the single highest correlation with the total OMAS, that could be viewed as a means for obtaining an estimate on oral motor ability without doing the other subunit analyses. There were no data provided on similar correlation coefficients with children presenting articulation or stuttering problems.

The two aspects of validity reported were content and construct validity. For content validity the authors stated that since this was the third generation of an assessment instrument, by implication it was more valid than its predecessors. Furthermore, using the second generation instrument the authors reported that 69% of 54 children who stuttered were 1.5 standard deviations below the mean score expected on oral motor abilities. Using the OMAS the authors reported that 12 of 17 children who stuttered scored 1.5 standard deviations above the mean ("above meaning poorer performance"). This would support what was reported with the second generation instrument.

Construct validity evidence included a statement by the authors that the OMAS had a "close" relationship with the second generation of the instrument and that this relationship implied construct as well as content validity. Also, the authors stated that the OMAS total score had a correlation of .67 with a procedure suggested by Fletcher (1972); however, Fletcher's reference was not included in the reference list. The remainder of the discussion on construct validity was fragmented and confusing and ended with the authors' statement that construct validity seemed adequate, but that further study was necessary. It is questionable whether the authors provided reasonable information in terms of content or construct validity. It seems that the data provided do little beyond indicating that the instrument has face validity.

Normative data apparently were based on 206 children between 4 and 11 years of age. There was no indication of how the children were selected nor any background information on the children in terms of demographics and/or speech sound production skills. Means and standard deviations were reported for four age groupings: age 4, age 5, ages 6–7, and ages 8–11. There were variable numbers of subjects in each group. Means and standard deviations were reported by age group for the three major categories and then for the total OMAS. When the total scores are examined they show higher means and standard deviations for each of the younger groups, and the authors comment on that difference. However, they do not indicate whether there is any statistically significant difference among any of the groups. Furthermore, the central tendency data are then arranged into levels of oral motor discoordination for each of the age groups without any explanation as to why certain levels are associated with a given number of points. In general, the information provided on the norm group was not adequate for a reader to judge whether the sample selected was representative of a normal population. Additionally, it was unclear why the authors elected to apparently extrapolate, without any explanation, cutoff levels for the oldest age group (8–11) to children of 12 and 13 years of age.

The third major section of the manual addressed a treatment program for oral motor discoordination. It focused on a systematically more complex sequence of syllables throughout a 14-level hierarchy, but there was no clear explanation as to why the various stimuli were selected as opposed to using other stimuli. It was unclear why at least a full page of the treatment section of the manual repeated, verbatim, what was on the first two pages of the manual.

A problem apparent in the training section of the manual, which occurred throughout the entire manual, was that the style of writing was not clear, and individual readers have to infer the intent of the authors. Distracting noise on training tapes was also a problem. Training tape 2.2, which presented examples of oral motor treatment, probably had the least amount of distracting noise. However, the speaker, as on the other training tapes, had apparent misarticulations. It is not known whether the misarticulations were due to the recording mechanism or the individual's manner of speaking. However, these misarticulations were apparent and distracting.

The authors' apparent intent in preparing the Oral Motor Assessment and Treatment Program was to prepare a procedure by which individuals could become reliable in terms of identifying three aspects of what were termed oral motor behaviors observable during syllable production, assessing those oral motor behaviors in a manner that would be reliable, and then providing a systematic treatment program, if necessary. In terms of assisting individuals in the identification of various aspects of speech syllable production, the OMAS does provide some direction, but practicing clinicians will need to decide whether they want to focus on the three major categories identified as reflecting oral motor behaviors (Accuracy, Smooth Flow, and Rate). The present edition of the OMAS does not provide sufficient information to determine whether the data were gathered in a reliable manner, nor is there sufficient information to indicate that the assessment protocol is valid. Furthermore, the poor quality of the accompanying audio tapes and the oftentimes confusing style of writing in the manual raise questions about the instrument's usefulness. Ultimately, each professional will need to decide whether the OMAS has sufficient merit to warrant its purchase.

[269]

Our Class and Its Work. Purpose: "To measure those teaching behaviors believed to contribute to student achievement in the classroom." Grades 3–12; 1983; OCIW; self-report instrument; 8 scales: Didactic Instruction, Enthusiasm, Feedback, Instructional Time, Opportunity to Learn, Pacing, Structuring Comments, Task Orientation, plus Total; user manual (13 pages); technical manual (47 pages); price data available from publisher; administration time not reported; Maurice J. Eash and Hersholt C. Waxman; Maurice J. Eash.*

TEST REFERENCES

1. Anderson, R. N., Greene, M. L., & Loewen, P. S. (1988). Relationship among teacher's and student's thinking skills, sense of efficacy, and student achievement. *The Alberta Journal of Educational Research*, 34, 148-165.

Review of Our Class and Its Work by JAMES R. BARCLAY, Professor of Educational and Counseling Psychology, University of Kentucky, Lexington, KY:

The Our Class and Its Work inventory is an instrument of 40 items designed to be administered in grades 3–12 to measure teaching behaviors believed to contribute to student achievement. Test materials include a brief user's manual and a technical report. Both appear to be available from the authors at the

College of Education, University of Illinois at Chicago.

The inventory is described in the technical manual as the end product of a chain of research. This research included item analysis, scale formation and deletion, and the final form of the inventory that includes eight scales: Didactic Instruction, Enthusiasm, Feedback, Instructional Time, Opportunity to Learn, Pacing, Structuring Comments, and Task Orientation. The reliability studies appear to support the integrity of these scales. Validity studies include ratings of teachers by one principal and correlations with achievement tests.

The overall impression in reviewing this instrument is that it is very premature to make any judgment about it. Its use has been limited, and it appears to have been applied in various research-related studies only in the Chicago area. Item response alternatives define a 4-point system from *strongly agree* (4) to *strongly disagree* (1). Norms are not provided for interpretation but ranges of scores are divided into four statements. For example, if the total score is from 120–160, the judgment recorded is: "the teacher probably obtains increased achievement from most students." If the total score is below 80 the judgment is: "the teacher probably does *not* obtain increased achievement from most students." Scoring includes a number of items that must be scored negatively.

On the positive side, the scales appear to be related to dimensions that researchers have identified as important in teaching effectiveness. The research underlying the development of items is clear and documents the empirical reasoning used by the authors. On the negative side it is clear that this is a research effort, not a commercial one. Details of scoring may be confusing to some users. Norms are not available, and the interpretation of results is highly tentative.

In summary, much more work should be done with this inventory, relating it to the emotional and affective dimensions of teachers and students. In addition, the use of the inventory for assessment and possible remediation should be documented against other instruments and longitudinal outcomes. At present, it is a research instrument that might be used by researchers, but it does not seem ready in any way to be used for evaluating classroom-climate variables.

Review of Our Class and Its Work by F. CHARLES MACE, Associate Professor, Graduate School of Applied and Professional Psychology, Rutgers University, Piscataway, NJ:

Our Class and Its Work (OCIW) is a self-report questionnaire designed to solicit student appraisals of their teachers' instructional skills in grades 3–12. The instrument consists of 40 items selected to measure the following constructs or scales believed to be predictive of effective instruction: (*a*) Didactic Instruction, (*b*) Enthusiasm, (*c*) Feedback, (*d*) Instructional Time, (*e*) Opportunity to Learn, (*f*) Pacing, (*g*) Structuring Comments, and (*h*) Task Orientation. Each item describes an observable teacher or student activity. Students are asked to judge the extent to which each statement accurately describes their class using a *strongly agree*, *agree*, *disagree*, or *strongly disagree* format. Depending on the value of the summed raw scores, the authors suggest the following predictions: The teacher (*a*) probably (raw score = 120–160), (*b*) somewhat inconsistently (80–120), or (*c*) probably does not (below 80) obtain increased achievement from most students. The validity of these predictions and the utility of the instrument are perhaps best understood by examining the questionnaire's psychometric properties.

SAMPLES USED IN DEVELOPING THE OCIW. The OCIW is not a standardized instrument in the usual sense (i.e., norms have not been established for different grade levels against which raw scores are compared). However, during the course of the OCIW's development, various versions of the instrument were administered to approximately 1,500 students in over 100 classrooms in grades 2 through 12. The characteristics of these samples included students from public and parochial schools, urban and suburban districts, and black, Hispanic, and white racial groups. Thus, the OCIW has been extensively field tested with a wide variety of students and, as the authors note, this experience was useful in eliminating items that were vague, unreliable, or poor discriminators. In future versions of the OCIW, the authors may wish to consider establishing norms by grade and perhaps general subject matter. Student responses to many of the items could be expected to vary across grades and subject matter, thus substantially altering the interpretability of the total score. For instance, responses to item 25 ("Students are allowed to select activities on their own") are likely to be very different from a third-grade class than from tenth-grade algebra students.

RELIABILITY. Internal consistency and test-retest reliability have been established for the instrument. Intercorrelations among items were high, with total test reliability estimated at .85 and individual scale reliabilities ranging from .84 to .92. This level of internal consistency suggests a tendency for students to rate individual teachers consistently across the 40-item questionnaire. That is, teacher instructional skills generally appear to be rated by students as either "good" or "bad" (given the limited range of rating options). However, this pattern of ratings seems at odds with probable reality. It seems unlikely that teachers/classrooms are consistently favorable or unfavorable along the eight dimensions assessed by the OCIW, but rather that teachers are skilled in some areas and less so in others. Such a hypothesis is testable by assessing the correspondence between student ratings and direct observations of classroom events (see following discussion of validity).

Test-retest reliabilities assessed at a 5-month interval were rather low, ranging from .38 to .82 (6 of 8 scales were .58 or lower). As the authors note, it is not unusual to find test-retest reliabilities in this range after a long retest interval, and this may actually be expected as students and teachers adjust to one another during the course of the school year.

A measure of reliability that is perhaps more relevant to the assessment of teacher instructional skills is the extent to which students in a given class provide comparable ratings of their teacher (i.e., interrater reliability). If ratings among students in the same class are disparate, we have less confidence in the correspondence between ratings and actual classroom events. Future versions of the OCIW could be strengthened by assessing interrater reliability which, in this reviewer's opinion, is more meaningful than measures of internal consistency and stability for the assessment of instructional skills.

VALIDITY. The authors report the results of several analyses that assessed the predictive validity of the OCIW. Findings generally showed that, when combined with previous measures of student achievement, some OCIW scales added significantly to the prediction of post achievement gains over and above the predictions based on previous achievement scores alone. It is important to note, however, that the contribution of OCIW scores to the total error variance accounted for was small and substantially less than the contribution of prior achievement despite its statistical significance. Thus, compared to other available measures (e.g., classroom achievement, standardized achievement scores, IQ), the meaningful predictive power of the OCIW appears minimal.

The stated purpose of the OCIW is to "measure those teaching behaviors believed to contribute to student achievement in the classroom." Given this objective it is important to demonstrate that the instrument is capable of providing accurate measures of teachers' instructional skills. Although the authors discuss some of the shortcomings of direct observation, repeated observational measures generally provide the most accurate representation of the subject matter available. Demonstrating the concurrence between student ratings on the OCIW and direct classroom observations is a necessary step in establishing the validity of the instrument; this should be undertaken in future versions of the OCIW.

An important limitation of the OCIW that is common to many rating scales is the instrument's insensitivity to various dimensions of behavior and the conditions under which it occurs. For instance, the *strongly agree* to *strongly disagree* format provides little or no information about the frequency, duration, celeration, latency, and interresponse time of the behaviors in question. Further, the scale does not indicate the prevailing context in which various classroom events occur. It is doubtful, for example, that a classroom is noisy or fraught with interruptions across all situations. To the extent that an assessment device can provide specific information about the dimensions of behavior and conditions under which it is likely to occur, it can be useful in planning and evaluating the effectiveness of interventions.

APPLICATIONS. Beyond its contribution to predicting future achievement, few applications of the OCIW are discussed in the manual. Although the instrument should be used with caution to assess instructional skills until it has been validated, the OCIW has potential applications in the following areas. First, the device could be very useful to assess student opinions or perspectives of their teachers' own perspectives and may set the occasion for reconciling these differences. Second, OCIW ratings may be useful in teacher-training programs to provide student teachers with feedback on how their teaching tactics are perceived by students prior to entering the profession. Third, OCIW scores may be one of several measures used by principals to evaluate teacher performance. Fourth, the OCIW may be useful in instructional research as a measure of social validity or to supplement classroom observational measures.

To summarize, the OCIW has a number of positive features that recommend its use. It has benefited from several revisions, each of which was prompted by research findings on the instrument's psychometric properties. Also contributing to the device's improvement has been its extensive field testing with heterogeneous groups of students. The history of the OCIW and its current characteristics are described in a well-written and scholarly manual. On the negative side, the instrument has not been adequately validated for assessing instructional skills, it has limited predictive validity, and it is generally insensitive to various dimensions of behavior. If the revision process continues to address these issues, the OCIW is likely to become an important instrument in the assessment of teaching skills.

[270]

Parent/Family Involvement Index. Purpose: "Measure of the extent to which parents are involved in their child's special education program." Parents with children in special education programs; 1984–85; P/FII; ratings by teachers; 13 scores: Contact With Teacher, Participation in the Special Education Process, Transportation, Observations at School, Educational Activities at Home, Attending Parent Education/Consultation Meetings, Classroom Volunteering, Involvement With Administration, Involvement in Fund Raising Activities, Involvement in Advocacy Groups, Disseminating Information, Involvement Total, Total; 1985 price data: $2.50 per index and mimeographed paper ('85, 21 pages); (12–15) minutes; John D. Cone, David D. DeLawyer, and Vicky V. Wolfe; John D. Cone.*

Review of the Parent/Family Involvement Index by MARILYN FRIEND, Assistant Professor of Learning, Development, and Special Education, Northern Illinois University, DeKalb, IL:

The Parent/Family Involvement Index (P/FII), developed by the West Virginia University Affiliated Center for Developmental Disabilities and the West Virginia Department of Health, is designed to be an easily administered and scored measure of parents' participation in the education of their handicapped children. The index consists of 63 specific statements describing parent activities in 12 education-related areas. Teachers, aides, or others familiar with the parents indicate one of four responses for each item: yes, no, don't know (DK), or not applicable (NA). A 13th area, overall involvement, is scored on a 6-point scale (1 =*not at all involved*, 6 = *extremely involved*). Separate responses for a mother and a father can be recorded on a single index. Three types of scores can be tabulated for the P/FII: (*a*) a score for each of the 12 areas; (*b*) a total score calculated by summing scores across areas; and (*c*) an overall rating, simply the score obtained for the 13th area. The first two types of scores are percentages of "yes" responses in relation to "yes" and "no" responses. DK and NA responses are excluded from all analyses.

A variation of a paper published in *Exceptional Children* (Cone, DeLawyer, & Wolfe, 1985) serves as the technical manual for the P/FII, and the manual is an appropriate starting point for a discussion of the many problems with the index. In terms of appearance, the manual is poorly arranged and badly reproduced, its single-spacing and fuzzy mimeographed print making it extremely difficult to read. In addition, three tables discussed in the text were missing from the paper.

The manual describes the instrument's development in excruciating detail. Index items were generated based on a literature search for which no parameters were included, and items were grouped on the basis of authors' judgment. Initial field testing resulted in a revision in format, the addition of 13 items, and the rewording of others. No rationale is presented for any of the changes.

The validity of the final version of the instrument is not adequately addressed. While some items clearly have face validity (e.g., "Parent has attended an IEP conference in the school setting"), others seem to have little to do with parents' participation in their handicapped children's education (e.g., "Parent has baby-sat for another handicapped child and/or has been part of a baby-sitting or respite service for parents of handicapped children"). The authors did not employ the relatively simple strategy of submitting items to an expert panel for review. The validity of the index is also suspect because of the exclusion of all DK and NA responses from scoring. A teacher answering only a few items, but positively, could rate parents as more involved than a teacher completing most items but with several negative responses. Nowhere in the manual is this anomaly addressed.

The authors determined the reliability of the P/FII using two methods. First, the instrument's internal consistency was assessed. This strategy is not particularly convincing since relatively high KR-21 values are not necessarily desirable when an instrument purports to measure distinct components of a single phenomenon. Second, interrater reliability was calculated. This was accomplished by having the aides of an unknown number of the 65 special education teachers included in the field test complete an additional P/FII for 24% ($N = 55$) of the 229 families involved in the study. Although such interrater reliability is desirable, the authors did not convincingly establish the independence of these ratings. Finally, test-retest reliability, defined here as a rater's judgments for the same cases across a short period of time (an important consideration), was simply not assessed.

Misleading norms are reported for the index. Although the information in the index booklet states the field test families came from three states and encourages users to compare parents with the included "profiles of normal scores" for mothers and fathers, the manual explains that all families were from middle Atlantic states and primarily from rural areas. Further, 79% of handicapped students in the families were in preschool or elementary school, 61% of them were either trainable mentally retarded or learning disabled, and 65% were enrolled in self-contained classes. The limitations of the reported norms are not mentioned.

From a lengthy list of additional weaknesses with the P/FII, the following three should be noted: (*a*) Several sets of items are hierarchical and thus not independent, and the effect of this factor on scores is not considered by the authors; (*b*) no type of factor analysis or cluster analysis was used to establish the 12 scales; and (*c*) numerous correlations between demographic variables and index scores are reported in a discussion of predicting parent involvement through the use of this index. In order to appropriately address this last issue, a regression analysis should have been completed.

In summary, the P/FII is too technically flawed to systematically assess parent involvement in handicapped students' education. However, because the items are for the most part objective and apparently representative of a wide range of parent involvement levels, it could be appropriately used as a reminder for educators on how to actively involve parents, or as a checklist for inviting parents to select school activities in which they would like to assist educators. Thus, it has a purpose, although not the one intended by its developers.

REVIEWER'S REFERENCE

Cone, J. D., DeLawyer, D. D., & Wolfe, V. V. (1985). Assessing parent participation: The Parent/Family Involvement Index. *Exceptional Children*, 51, 417-424.

Review of the Parent/Family Involvement Index by KORESSA KUTSICK, Assistant Professor of Psychology, James Madison University, Harrisonburg, VA:

The Parent/Family Involvement Index (P/FII) was designed to assess the level of parent participation in their handicapped child's education. The Index is completed by a classroom teacher or educational aide who is familiar with the handicapped child's family. The scale consists of 63 items reflecting parental activities which are broken into 12 categories of involvement: Contact with Teacher, Participation in Special Education Process, Transportation, Observations at School, Educational Activities at Home, Attending Parent/Education Consultation Meetings, Classroom Volunteering, Parent-Parent Contact and Support, Involvement with Administration, Involvement in Fund Raising Activities, Involvement in Advocacy Groups, and Disseminating Information. A 13th area summarizes a rater's overall impression of the level of parent involvement with the child's educational program.

Instructions for completing the P/FII are straightforward and clear-cut. Raters are asked to check Yes, No, NA (not applicable), or DK (don't know) for each item as it describes a child's parent. Separate inventories may be completed for the mother and father. The composite list of items appears very complete and covers a wide range of parental activities.

Three types of scores may be generated from the P/FII. These include: (*a*) area scores summarizing each of the 12 different categories of parent involvement; (*b*) a total score which quantifies parental involvement across all 12 areas; and (*c*) an overall rating which is the rater's response to the 6-point Likert-scale items comprising area 13 of the index. Calculating the area and total scores of the P/FII are slightly confusing tasks. Raters must follow verbal descriptions of mathematical formulas in order to generate the 12 area scores and the total score. It seems that the inclusion of a printed formula where raters could plug in data and perform the necessary mathematical operations would have simplified the scoring process. Guidelines for interpreting the three scores are also vague. Procedures include transferring area, total, and overall rating scores to a rather crowded profile. A description of a "perfectly" average score is provided, but no specific information is given as to how far scores can vary from average and still be considered "normal." There are also no clear indicators of how to interpret high and low scores.

Psychometric properties of the P/FII are perhaps the weakest characteristics of this instrument. No reliability or validity data are presented in the Index materials. A supplemental paper (Cone, DeLawyer, & Wolfe, 1985) provided by the authors explains test construction procedures and the norming sample, as well as reliability and validity data. Normative data were developed from the scores of 226 mothers and 168 fathers who had handicapped children in special education programs. The majority of these parents were from rural or semi-rural areas. The sample did not reflect stratified U.S. population statistics. A truly randomized selection of families was not achieved. Reliability data presented in the supplemental paper consisted of reported high interrater and moderate internal consistency values. No clear validity data have been established for this instrument, although it would appear to meet criteria for adequate face and content validity.

The major strengths of this test lie in its purpose and heuristic value. The authors stated that the scale could be utilized in identifying possible needs of parents in terms of their involvement with the education of their special-needs child. Results could lead to recommendations for family interventions. The tool could also be used as a program evaluation measure where documenting changes in parent involvement in a particular education process is necessary. The index should still be considered an experimental scale, however, until additional reliability and validity studies can be conducted. The authors should also be encouraged to develop a parent-completed version of this index. Such a measure would provide direct assessment of parents' perceptions of involvement in their child's educational experiences. It also seems as if it would be necessary to interpret the various scores generated by the P/FII in light of parental sociological conditions. For example, it would seem possible that a single mother who works full time to support three children would have different involvement scores than a married mother of one child who did not work outside the home. It may not be reasonable to expect the same involvement activities from both of these parents. Currently, the P/FII does not incorporate information such as marital or employment status into the interpretation of the index scores.

In summary, the Parent/Family Involvement Index holds promise of being a useful evaluation device. Due to the lack of psychometric data and need for revising the instrument, however, its current applied use should be limited. Further development of this instrument is encouraged.

REVIEWER'S REFERENCE

Cone, J. D., DeLawyer, D. D., & Wolfe, V. V. (1985). Assessing parent participation: The Parent/Family Involvement Index. *Exceptional Children*, 51, 417-424.

[271]

Parenting Stress Index. Purpose: "Identifies parent-child systems under stress." Parents of children below 10 years of age; 1983–86; PSI; 16 scores: 7 Child Domain scores (Adaptability, Acceptability, Demandingness, Mood, Distractibility/Hyperactive, Reinforces Parent, Total), 8 Parent Domain scores (Depression, Attachment, Restrictions of Role, Sense of Competence, Sense of Isolation, Relationship With Spouse, Parental Health, Total), Total Stress, plus optional Life Stress scale score; 1987 price data: $3.50 per reuseable test booklet; $.75 or less per self-scoring answer sheet; $.10 per profile sheet; $14.50 per manual ('86, 74 pages); $27.50 per specimen set; $109 per 25-use computer scoring and interpretive report program (specify IBM-PC or Apple II); administration time not reported; Richard R. Abidin and Brenda Loyd (manual); Pediatric Psychology Press.*

TEST REFERENCES

1. Kazak, A. E., & Marvin, R. S. (1984). Differences, difficulties and adaptation: Stress and social networks in families with a handicapped child. *Family Relations*, 33, 67-77.

2. Adamakos, H., Ryan, K., Ullman, D. G., Pascoe, J., Diaz, R., & Chessare, J. (1986). Maternal social support as a predictor of mother-child stress and stimulation. *Child Abuse and Neglect*, 10, 463-470.

3. Bendell, R. D., Culbertson, J. L., Shelton, T. L., & Carter, B. D. (1986). Interrupted infantile apnea: Impact on early development, temperament, and maternal stress. *Journal of Clinical Child Psychology*, 15, 304-310.

Review of the Parenting Stress Index by FRANK M. GRESHAM, Professor of Psychology, Louisiana State University, Baton Rouge, LA:

The Parenting Stress Index (PSI) is a parent rating instrument designed to measure "parenting stress." The PSI supposedly measures stressful aspects of the parent-child system including child characteristics, parent (mother) characteristics, and life stress events. Although the PSI would appear to be a measure of stress (as indicated in the title), this is never directly stated in the manual. Stress is never defined in the manual and only passing references are made to the stress literature (e.g., Lazarus, 1966; Rahe, 1974; Selye, 1952, 1974). It appears from reading the manual that the author equates temperamental characteristics of children with stress. For example, the author draws heavily upon the New York Longitudinal Study (Thomas, Chess, & Birch, 1968) to describe his conception of "stress."

The manual provides a totally inadequate theoretical development of the stress construct. In fact, using the author's description of "stress," it appears that virtually everything in this and seven other solar systems are subsets of the superordinate construct of stress. For example, child characteristics on the PSI include Hyperactivity, Demandingness, Mood, and so forth. Parent characteristics include Depression, Social Isolation, Health, Restrictions of Role, and the like. The manual never provides an explanation of how these variables supposedly interact. Are child characteristics independent variables producing changes in parent characteristics (i.e., dependent variables)? Are parent characteristics independent variables producing changes in child characteristics? The author provides no conceptual guidance whatsoever in assisting readers in viewing stress within a theoretical framework. This is most likely because the author has no theoretical understanding of the stress concept, at least as evidenced by the absence of a theoretical discussion of stress in the manual.

It appears that the impetus for developing the PSI was based more upon the author's personal experiences as a parent and as a psychologist in a medical facility than upon sound empirical or theoretical knowledge of the stress literature. The manual's description of the fundamental basis of the PSI, what it is designed to measure, and how it attempts to measure it, is disjointed, poorly organized, and not particularly well written.

ITEM FORMAT AND SCALES. The PSI contains 101 items, most of which are rated by a parent (mother) on a 1 to 5 Likert-type scale (*Strongly Agree, Agree, Not Sure, Disagree,* or *Strongly Disagree*). The Child Domain contains 47 items spread across six subscales: (*a*) Adaptability (11 items), (*b*) Acceptability (7 items), (*c*) Demandingness (9 items), (*d*) Mood (5 items), (*e*) Distractibility/Hyperactivity (9 items), and (*f*) Reinforces Parent (6 items). The Parent Domain contains 54 items spread across seven subscales: (*a*) Depression (9 items), (*b*) Attachment (7 items), (*c*) Restrictions of Role (7 items), (*d*) Sense of Competence (13 items), (*e*) Social Isolation (6 items), (*f*) Relationship With Spouse (7 items), and (*g*) Parent Health (5 items). There is an optional scale called the Life Stress Scale containing 19 items. Scores are reported in raw scores and percentile ranks for the Total Score, Child Domain, Parent Domain, and all subscales.

NORMATIVE DATA. The PSI was standardized on 534 parents who visited small group pediatric clinics in central Virginia. The normative sample was 92% white and 6% black consisting of mothers whose ages ranged from 18 to 61 years (mean age = 29.8 years). The socioeconomic status level based upon family income was unrepresentative of the U.S. population with 25% of the sample earning less than $10,000 per year and 25% of the sample earning over $20,000 per year. The normative sample was also unrepresentative of the U.S. population in terms of educational level of parents, with over 33% of the sample having graduated from college, graduate school, or professional school. The manual contains a supplemental set of norms for fathers based upon 100 males; however, it is unclear whether these fathers were spouses of some of the mothers in the normative sample. Demographic characteristics of the fathers are not reported in the manual.

In summary, the standardization sample of the PSI is unrepresentative of the U.S. population in terms of geographic region, family income, educational level of parents, racial distribution, and marital status of the mother. The author of the PSI elected to use a sample of convenience rather than a sample of substance in standardizing the PSI. As such, any interpretation of scores obtained on individuals from other geographic regions, income levels, educational backgrounds, and so forth is risky, at best.

RELIABILITY. The PSI is not reliable enough to make individual interpretations of scores obtained from the subscales as recommended by the author in the Clinical Interpretations section of the manual. Internal consistency estimates (coefficient alphas) of the Child Domain subscales range from .62 to .70 (median = .64). Coefficient alphas for the Parent Domain subscales range from .55 to .80 (median = .73). These alphas do not meet minimally acceptable standards of reliability for research purposes, much less for individual clinical interpretations. The manual presents a number of profiles based upon scatter in the subscales. A good example of this is what the manual calls the "Crisis Profile" in which the interpretation is that there is a high potential for child abuse given a profile of this sort. This represents a totally inappropriate use and interpretation of the PSI given the extremely low reliability estimates of virtually all subscales. It would appear that the author does not realize the constraints on the validity of subscales resulting from errors of measurement (i.e., unreliability). Legal uses of the so-called "Crisis Profile" in abuse and/or custody cases should be easily dissolved through expert testimony regarding the unreliability of the PSI subscales. The only reliability estimates meeting minimally acceptable standards for clinical interpretation are the Child Domain score (.89), the Parent Domain score (.93), and the Total Stress score (.95).

Stability estimates for the PSI were established in a series of four studies reported in the manual. Sample sizes for these studies ranged from 15 subjects to 54 subjects. The stability of the PSI over a 1–3-month period appears to be approximately .70 for the Child Domain, .80 for the Parent Domain, and .92 for the Total Stress score. No stability estimates are reported for the 13 individual subscales. Based upon the data reported in the manual, the PSI does not meet minimally acceptable standards of stability.

VALIDITY. The manual reports a series of abstracts supporting the validity of the PSI. Five types of validity are presented in the manual: (*a*) Concurrent Validity, (*b*) Construct Validity, (*c*) Predictive Validity, (*d*) Discriminant Validity, and (*e*) Factorial Validity. Many of the abstracts reported used a contrasted groups design (group differentiation) to support the construct validity of the PSI. Most of the investigations reported only show differences between groups on a few of the PSI subscales. Given the poor reliability of the subscales, the differences between groups reported in the manual are most likely Type I errors due to errors of measurement.

One study reported in the manual showed a correlation between the PSI and trait anxiety of .84. This, in fact, argues against the construct validity of the PSI as a measure of stress because it would appear that the PSI is redundant with the construct of trait anxiety (i.e., the measures are congruent).

The manual offers little convincing evidence that the PSI is actually a measure of stress. Instead, the PSI appears to be measuring a duke's mixture of parental and childhood behavior problems/psychopathology, primarily with error. Part of the difficulty with the PSI is that the author never provides a theoretical nor an empirical definition of stress. As such, the research done with the instrument has no roadmap or direction. Validity studies reported in the manual appear to be a shotgun approach to test validation lacking focus and integration.

SUMMARY. The PSI is a poorly standardized, unreliable, and invalid measure of stress. Users of the PSI should be aware that whatever it is that is being measured with the PSI is being measured with a great deal of error. Moreover, profile interpretations of the PSI as suggested in the manual represent the worst form of "subtest scatter" analysis and yield data that are virtually meaningless given the unreliability of the subscales. The use of the PSI in clinical settings to make important decisions for families cannot be recommended.

REVIEWER'S REFERENCES

Selye, H. (1952). *The story of adaptation syndrome, told in the form of informal illustrated lectures.* Montreal: Acta, Inc.

Thomas, A., Chess, S., & Birch, H. G. (1968). *Temperament and behavior disorders in children.* New York: New York University Press.

Lazarus, R. S. (1974). *Psychological stress and the coping process.* New York: McGraw-Hill.

Rahe, R. H. (1974). The pathway between subjects' recent life changes and their near-future illness reports: Representative results and methodological issues. In B. S. Dohrenwend & B. P. Dohrenwend (Eds.), *Stressful life events: Their nature and effects* (pp. 73-86). New York: Wiley.

Selye, H. (1974). *Stress without distress.* Philadelphia: Lippincott.

Review of the Parenting Stress Index by RICHARD A. WANTZ, Associate Professor of Educational Psychology and Director of Counseling Psychology Clinic, College of Education, University of Oklahoma, Norman, OK:

The Parenting Stress Index (PSI) is a product of approximately three decades of research, study, and development and has evolved through six refinements. The development of this index has been conducted in a highly professional manner consistent with sound procedures for developing assessment devices. In the PSI manual, Richard Abidin, states: "The Parenting Stress Index was designed to be an instrument whose primary value would be to identify parent-child systems which were under stress and at risk for the development of dysfunctional parenting behaviors or behavior problems in the child involved." The PSI is recommended for this use as a screening, diagnostic, and research instrument for Caucasian parents of children below 10 years of age.

Thorough documentation of the evolution and theoretical rationale is provided in the 74-page manual. Evidence indicating content, concurrent, construct, discriminant, and factorial validity is provided. Evidence of construct validity is demonstrated through significant correlations between the PSI Child Domain Score and the Child Behavior Problems Checklist and between the PSI Parent Domain Score and the State-Trait Anxiety Scale. The Total Score on the PSI was found to be significantly correlated with both Trait and State Anxiety.

PSI scores have been found to be related to involvement in parent education, marital satisfaction, parental role satisfaction, behavioral observations, Bayley Scales of Infant Development scores, and Achenbach Child Behavior Checklist scores.

Reported discriminant validity evidence includes examining PSI scores of mothers of "normal" children and mothers of special-needs children (e.g., mothers of children with nonambulatory cerebral palsy, mental retardation). The PSI was also used successfully to discriminate between physically abusive and nonabusive mothers, amount of husband support, and single and married mothers. Three factor analyses of the PSI are reported. These analyses tend to be supportive of the PSI organization. Inspection of this data indicates that the Child and Parent Domains are distinct scales but that these subscales are also moderately correlated.

Adequate internal consistency and stability coefficients are reported. Alpha reliability coefficients of .95 are reported for the Total Stress Score. Test-retest reliability coefficients ranging from .55 to .82 for the Child Domain, .69 to .91 for the Mother Domain, .70 to .71 for the Parent Domain, and .69 to .96 for the Total Stress Score are reported.

The normative group consisted of 534 predominantly white parents. A description of the norm group is provided. The normative sample could be improved by the addition of data for nonwhite populations, male parents, age variations of parents, and differentiation of parents with total family income above $20,000.

The clinical interpretation and case discussion sections of the manual are clearly written and thorough. In addition to an explanation of Domain Scores, a profile and discussion are presented for a family representing each of the following conditions: normal, in crisis, separation anxiety, and permissive parent. Also, typical profiles are presented for families of cerebral palsied, abused, hyperactive, developmentally delayed, autistic, and normal nursery school children and children with attention deficit disorder and from unwanted unmarried pregnancies, but without discussion of the profiles.

The merits of the PSI far outweigh negative aspects; however, the user will find the discussion of the inventory administration procedures lacking. The amount of time required for administering, scoring, and profiling is not indicated. Computer-assisted scoring and interpretive reports are available for on-site use. Neither optimum conditions for administration of the PSI nor the reading level of items is specified.

The PSI is recommended as a screening, diagnostic, and research instrument for use with parents of children below 10 years of age. The results should be both useful and reliable.

[272]

Pediatric Early Elementary Examination. Purpose: Provides standardized observation procedures "to help clinicians characterize children's functional health and its relationship to neurodevelopmental and physical status." Ages 7–9; 1983; PEEX; publisher suggests should be used only as one contribution toward a multifaceted evaluation; 5 major sections: Developmental Attainment, Neuromaturation, Task Analysis, Associated (behavioral) Observations, General Health Assessment; individual; 1986 price data: $49 per complete set including 12 record forms, 12 response booklets ('83, 16 pages), PEEX kit, stimulus booklet ('83, 48 pages), and manual ('83, 48 pages); $22 per 12 record forms and 12 response booklets; $8 per stimulus book; $15 per PEEX Kit (includes ball, paper clip, wooden block, key, rubber band, and Eye-Hand Board); $5.50 per examiner's manual; $6 per specimen set containing record form and examiner's manual; (40–50) minutes; Melvin D. Levine and Leonard Rappaport (examiner's manual); Educators Publishing Service, Inc.*

Review of the Pediatric Early Elementary Examination by J. JEFFREY GRILL, Professor of Special Education, The College of Saint Rose, Albany, NY:

The Pediatric Early Elementary Examination (PEEX) is intended for use with children 7 to 9 years of age by "health care and other [unspecified] professionals to derive empirical descriptions of a school child's development and functional neurological status." Intended for use in a multidisciplinary evaluation, and designed to be more comprehensive than a developmental screening test, the PEEX is difficult to categorize. According to the authors, "The PEEX does not produce a specific score or diagnosis. Instead, it generates a functional profile—a description of strengths, weaknesses, and stylistic preferences . . . [which] can have significant implications for educational planning, counseling, the use of medication, and general programming for success in childhood."

While the PEEX is neither a screening nor a diagnostic instrument, it further defies classification because it is neither norm- nor criterion-referenced. In essence, it allows the user to administer a standardized set of tasks to elicit performances and behaviors. These are then rated with varying degrees of subjectivity. Ratings are largely dependent on the user's familiarity with the normal developmental progression of children's performance on the tasks used in the PEEX.

Although the PEEX focuses on a narrow developmental range, it was not developed in isolation. For children between 4 and 6 years of age, the senior author developed the Pediatric Examination of Educational Readiness (9:928) and for those from 9 to 15 years, the Pediatric Examination of Educational Readiness at Middle Childhood (273) is available.

The PEEX consists of 32 tasks distributed among seven assessment categories: (1) fine motor function (e.g., imitative finger movement); (2) visual-fine motor function (e.g., copying geometric forms); (3) visual processing (e.g., direct matching); (4) temporal-sequential organization (e.g., counting aloud); (5) linguistic function (e.g., following verbal instructions); (6) gross motor function (e.g., hopping in place); and (7) recall (e.g., recalling words and objects used earlier in the assessment). The record form is arranged so that examiners may record not only specific pass/fail performances for each item, but also note specific observations about developmental attainment, neuromaturation, cognitive tempo, and task analysis. It is these sections of the PEEX that seem to be of greatest import to the authors and of potential value to users. Additional sections of the carefully and cleverly contrived (although complex) record form allow for the recording of general health assessment information and of associated observations about selective attention, modality-specificity, adaptation to examination, and affective observations.

The various tasks of the PEEX are not new or innovative; they consist of the types of items widely used in standard, neurological, gross-motor, perceptual-motor, linguistic, and memory evaluations. What is of value here is the emphasis placed on the observation of *how* a child performs the tasks, and the delineation of several possible "hows" (i.e., with or without associated movements and other neurological signs), at what level (relative to age-appropriate expectancies) of performance, at what tempo or pace. Not surprisingly, this strength of the instrument is its weakness, for without any normative data whatsoever, these observations must remain highly subjective and utterly dependent on the knowledge and experience of the examiner. One suspects that the authors have extensive experience in this sort of evaluation and that they have made a valiant effort to codify what they know so that this experience will be of use to others. Clearly, the PEEX represents an extraordinary effort to make that knowledge available; yet the authors miss the mark, primarily because of a few, significant problems.

First, no descriptive data on norms are offered, although the reader can infer from the acknowledgements in the manual that youngsters from Brookline, Boston, and Melrose, Massachusetts participated in the development of the PEEX. Such an inference hardly substitutes for actual data. No information is presented about the numbers of children, the numbers of "normal" and dysfunctional children, or the ratio of girls to boys who participated. This lack of norms is particularly troublesome, even in light of the authors' strong recommendation that local norms be established, because with no norms available, even an experienced examiner will have little basis for the interpretation of an individual child's performance. Furthermore, the development of local norms, although appropriate, may result in biased norms because the PEEX is likely to be used only with children who evidence some degree of dysfunction, rather than with adequately functioning children.

The second problem is the total absence of reliability and validity data. For an instrument that purports to yield information that can have "significant implications," such data are essential. The total absence of this critical information in the manual renders the PEEX useless except to record observations. The reference to one published article reporting some validation and reliability research does not suffice for what should be in the manual.

The third problem is the absence of clearly described implications of various kinds of performance on the PEEX. To be sure, the authors frequently note relationships between specific kinds of performance and their actual or presumed causes. For example, for the verbal instructions task the authors state, "the first three directions are identical to the last three. This may entrap youngsters who have a tendency to deteriorate over time." Aside from the semantic error (i.e., a youngster's performance, not the youngster, may deteriorate over time), this statement is typical of the authors' frequent and careful explanations of the subtleties of performance to be observed during administration of the PEEX. For this the authors are to be commended. Nonetheless, such explanations are not, in themselves, implications of anything.

The manual's Appendix includes an example of a completed PEEX record form for an 8 year 4 month old boy referred because of poor reading skills and problems of concentration. This example is most useful, but the two-paragraph narrative preceding the completed form offers only minimal, summary information, and simply alludes to implications for school programming. A better, more complete approach would have included a detailed narrative with specific implications, followed by a second example using a different child who evidenced different problems so that differences in performance on the PEEX could be more easily understood in relation to differences in reported (school) problems.

In summary, the PEEX provides an opportunity to observe subtle signs of neurological dysfunction through a standardized array of tasks assumed or demonstrated to be related to success in school. However, the lack of any data on norms, reliability, and validity, renders this instrument much less useful to clinicians than it could be. The inclusion of such data along with more and more-detailed examples (including specific implications) would make the PEEX highly valuable.

Review of the Pediatric Early Elementary Examination by NEIL H. SCHWARTZ, Associate Professor of Psychology, California State University, Chico, Chico, CA:

The Pediatric Early Elementary Examination (PEEX), according to its authors, is a "'middle level' evaluation tool that enables health care and other professionals to derive empirical descriptions of a school child's development and functional neurological status." The authors are careful to point out that the instrument "does not produce a specific score or diagnosis." Rather it yields "a functional profile—a description of strengths, weaknesses, and stylistic preferences."

Following close inspection, I found this description accurate and fair, neither an overstatement of utility nor a deception of value. In essence, the instrument is intended to be used as a comprehensive screening tool to: (*a*) infer an examinee's level of neurodevelopmental maturation and (*b*) assist in determining whether further assessment may be needed to explain some various behavioral difficulties for which the examinee was probably referred.

I believe that the instrument succeeds in both endeavors. Furthermore, it is well appointed in appearance, layout, and design. Instructions for administration and scoring are clear and easy to follow. Finally, although there are some disappointing aspects inherent in the instrument that I will discuss later, for the most part it is a valuable instrument, with two of its features meriting special notation.

First, the descriptions provided for both the six test sections and the six principal developmental areas are informative, well presented, and well explained for the space alloted—particularly the sections on Neuromaturation, Associated Observations, Temporal-Sequential Organization, and Linguistic Function. For example, the authors point out effectively the importance of "soft neurological signs" and caution the test user in the insignificance of a few behavioral elicitations of them. In addition, the inclusion of the Task Analysis section is refreshing since it differentiates between input and output modalities of information processing. Finally, the treatment given to attention deficits is especially well presented. The differentiation between pervasive primary and secondary attention problems is important, and it is good to see the difference delineated.

Second, the instructions for each task are very clear and easy to follow, with clear rationales for eliciting and scoring an examinee's performance. The materials are durable and the record form is especially well designed—particularly in light of the number and complexity of the task requirements. Moreover, the inclusion of two checkpoints for making observations of associated test-taking behaviors is a clever idea, one that helps to ensure that the behaviors will be assessed systematically and not be overlooked. Indeed, the behavioral observations identified to be assessed are a representative, meaningful sample of important aspects of selective attention, adaptation to an examination, and affect.

However, there are several glaring elements of the instrument that are extremely disappointing. Perhaps the most conspicuous is the absence of norms. The authors state that there have been a series of preliminary studies on normal volunteer children in several middle-class communities, along with some pilot testing of a clinic for youngsters with learning disorders, both of which have been used to establish norms for each item on the PEEX. However, the authors identify only one pertinent investigation in their reference list, and no norms are contained in the manual or accompany the test.

I found this condition to be both disappointing and rather deceiving, the latter because the test user is advised, in bold face, to determine and establish local norms because a number of "community-based" variables will influence performance on the PEEX. Of course, sophisticated test users will recognize that this cautious advisement is really a moot point and is absolutely no substitute for the provision of norms. It is puzzling why the authors go ahead and list approximate developmental attainments in four levels to judge the adequacy of performance. It is also impossible to discern how these levels were obtained.

A related psychometric component of the instrument also requires attention because it is presented confusingly in the manual. That is, the authors state that test users should adhere to the guidelines set forth in the manual because "much of the standardization has been based upon the precise manner of administration." Of course, this advice is essential for a standardized instrument that will yield meaningful data for interpretation. However, why "much" rather than *all* of the instrument was standardized is an enigma. It is also not essential for an instrument to be standardized when there are no norms to which an examinee's performance will be compared. In fact, most would define the term standardization as the administration of a carefully constructed test to a large, representative sample of people under standard conditions for *the purpose of determining norms*.

Finally, no data are offered for reliability or validity. This may not be a really serious omission since there are no norms and the instrument is actually a tool for making systematic observations of behavior to be used in making recommendations for further assessments. However, since test users will probably have to administer the instrument many times before they approach a reliable level of administration and scoring, some data would be very helpful on interexaminer reliability and the practice-time characteristics of the examiners when high reliability indices were reached.

There are other detractions I found with the instrument, but their inclusion is not space-justified because they are relatively minor. On the other hand, although there are some serious omissions of psychometric test-properties that have been discussed above, I believe the instrument is still of value for use under prescribed conditions. Specifically, if its use is restricted to screening where descriptive statements are solicited to shed explicative light on the neurodevelopmental maturation of a 7- to 9-year-old child, the instrument will have high utility. It is, perhaps, one of the most comprehensive *screening* devices I have seen to be restricted in use for making recommendations of further assessments.

[273]

Pediatric Examination of Educational Readiness at Middle Childhood. Purpose: "To generate part of a functional profile or empirical description of a child's development and current neurological status." Ages 9–15; 1984–85; PEERAMID; publisher suggests should only be used as a part of a multifaceted evaluation; 6 major sections: Minor Neurological Indicators, Fine Motor Function, Language, Gross Motor Function, Temporal-Sequential Organization, Visual Processing; individual; 1986 price data: $56.50 per complete set including 12 record forms, 12 response booklets, stimulus booklet ('84, 20 pages), PEERAMID kit (not necessary for examiners having PEEX kit, see 272), examiner's manual ('85, 80 pages); $28 per 12 response booklets and 12 record forms; $8 per stimulus booklet; $14 per PEERAMID kit (containing eye-hand board, cup, and ball); $6.50 per examiner's manual; $7 per specimen set including record form and examiner's manual; administration time not reported; Melvin D. Levine; Educators Publishing Service, Inc.*

Review of the Pediatric Examination of Educational Readiness at Middle Childhood by CATHY W. HALL, Director, School Psychology, Fort Hays State University, Hays, KS:

The Pediatric Examination of Educational Readiness at Middle Childhood (PEERAMID) for ages 9–15 is an upward extension of the Pediatric Early Elementary Examination (PEEX) (Levine, 1983) for ages 7–9 years and the Pediatric Examination of Educational Readiness (PEER) (Levine, 1982) for ages 4–6 years. The PEERAMID is said to focus on a young adolescent's neurological status and development. All three tests have features in common, but are also specific to developmental issues relevant to each age grouping. The PEERAMID does not provide an overall score. The authors are also quite specific in stating the PEERAMID should never be used in isolation, but should be part of a multifaceted evaluation.

There are six major sections of the PEERAMID: Minor Neurological Indicators, Fine Motor Function, Language, Gross Motor Function, Temporal-Sequential Organization, and Visual Processing. A seventh area involving Selective Attention is also assessed at four checkpoints. In addition to these, at the end of the record form, are a behavioral observations sheet, a general health assessment that should be completed by a physician or nurse, a task analysis form, and an overall summary grid. The organization of the PEERAMID is such that higher ratings indicate better performance.

The PEERAMID is divided into three age ranges: 9–10 years old, 11–12 years old, and 13–14 years old. Criteria for the analysis of performance are based on these age ranges and are denoted throughout the record form by Group I, Group II, and Group III (9–10 years, 11–12 years, and 13–14 years, respectively). While no specific information regarding time for administration was noted in the manual, it would appear the wide range of tasks and number of tasks covered would result in a minimum administration time of 3 to 4 hours.

The rationale behind the PEERAMID is: "to survey neurodevelopmental areas that may be associated with academic difficulties in this age group." The results of the PEERAMID lead to a description of the child's functioning rather than specific scores or one overall global score.

It is the opinion of this reviewer that the key word in the rationale is "may." While the PEERAMID points to several indicators of dysfunction, there are also numerous studies that have found these same indicators to occur in children who do not display any type of dysfunction. The authors of the test point this out, but no information is given regarding the frequency with which these indicators are seen in children displaying difficulties as opposed to those children with the same indicators who do not exhibit problems. This lack of information leaves the examiner with questions regarding the frequency of indicators occurring in children having problems as opposed to the frequency of occurrence in children without problems, and the correlation of the indicators with various dysfunctions. Studies are referenced in the manual regarding this issue, but no specific data are given.

No standardization, validity, or reliability data are included in the manual. This is a major weakness of the instrument and must limit its use. The manual does state that local norms should be obtained and modifications made whenever possible. Current normative data are available by writing the authors. However, the available normative data are extremely limited and are based on a sample of adolescents from three public schools in New England. Clearly, the standardization work on the instrument is incomplete. This reviewer has additional concerns with the concept of "modifying" the normative data. Cultural, socioeconomic, and regional differences may certainly exist, but an appropriately developed assessment instrument reflects these variations in well-developed normative data and item analyses. Properly prepared instruments do not leave "modifications" to the discretion of each individual administrator.

The manual states the PEERAMID is "a neurodevelopmental assessment procedure for use by health care and other professionals." It is the opinion of this reviewer that few professionals without extensive training in neuropsychology would be qualified to use the current instrument and/or to interpret test results in an appropriate fashion. The PEERAMID appears to be based on an approach very similar to that of Luria's neuropsychological assessments, and focuses on an individual, case-by-case evaluation. While there is nothing wrong with this approach, it does require a great deal of skill. The authors discuss that each test section is not a "pure" measure of certain abilities, but that there is a great deal of overlap in brain functions. Someone who does not have the proper background in neuropsychology would not be competent to determine the various neural functions required by each task. Without such expertise, making a differential diagnosis would be impossible. It is the reviewer's opinion the authors do not stress the necessary expertise of the examiner sufficiently, nor are cautions as explicitly noted in the PEERAMID manual as they are in the PEER manual. A test does not produce an "instant expert," rather valid utilization of an evaluation instrument requires expertise on the part of the examiner.

An additional concern is that the PEERAMID manual does not stress the need for supervised training in the administration and scoring of the assessment instrument. The manual does state: "To minimize the effects of subjective judgment, a person who is to administer the PEERAMID should undergo some reliability testing whenever possible." This is quite different from the PEER manual, which is explicit in underscoring the need for training: "A person administering the PEER should have received supervised training from professionals who have had experience with it . . . . Although every effort has been made to make this manual as comprehensive as possible, it is unlikely that one can become proficient at the PEER merely by reading the instructions." (Levine, 1982, p. 5)

SUMMARY. The PEERAMID has tremendous potential as a research instrument in the area of childhood neurodevelopment. Knowledge of neurodevelopment in children is incomplete. Many questions are yet to be answered. However, any neurodevelopmental battery must be used with caution, and administered and scored by someone with knowledge in neurophysiology. Neurodevelopmental assessments are not, and realistically cannot be, constructed to be so inclusive that all areas of functioning can be assessed discretely. Due to the complexity of higher level processing of information, it is difficult to make precise distinctions between the different functions. They work in close, interdependent concert.

Although the PEERAMID has potential as a research instrument, its use as a standardized assessment battery raises serious concerns. Standardization research must be conducted with the PEERAMID. More explicit cautions regarding examiner qualifications and how to interpret the instrument should be provided. The instrument is not yet ready to be part of a decision-making process about children and adolescents.

REVIEWER'S REFERENCES

Levine, M. D., & Schneider, E. A. (1982). Pediatric Examination of Educational Readiness. Cambridge, MA: Educators Publishing Service, Inc.

Levine, M. D., & Rappaport, L. (1983). Pediatric Early Elementary Examination. Cambridge, MA: Educators Publishing Service, Inc.

Review of the Pediatric Examination of Educational Readiness at Middle Childhood by JAN N. HUGHES, Associate Professor of Educational Psychology, Texas A&M University, College Station, TX:

The stated purposes of the Pediatric Examination of Educational Readiness at Middle Childhood (PEERAMID) are (*a*) to generate a functional profile of a child's development and current neurological status; (*b*) to assist in the diagnosis of specific learning disabilities; and (*c*) to suggest therapeutic interventions. Unfortunately, none of these goals are achieved by the PEERAMID. The theoretical and empirical rationale for the test is poorly conceptualized and articulated, and the most basic psychometric standards are not met.

The PEERAMID manual does not provide even minimal information required by potential test users to evaluate the test or to use it in clinical practice. Data on reliability or validity of scores are virtually absent, and only scant information on test development and standardization is provided.

The normative data are based on "studies of children from three public school systems in New England blue- and white-collar communities." Not provided are the number of children in the normative sample, data on relevant demographic variables (e.g., sex, race, size of communities), data on other relevant variables (e.g., school achievement, intelligence), or information on the method of sampling. For each of 31 test items or groups of test items, normative keys are provided. These keys state the "normal" score range on the specific item or group of items for children in each of three age groups: 9- and 10-year-olds, 11- and 12-year-olds, and 13- and 14-year-olds. Children who score below the normal range fail the item or group of items. The percentage of children scoring within the normal range is not given, nor are measures of central tendency or variability provided. Therefore, the test user cannot meaningfully interpret a child's normative score, using these keys. The lack of meaningful normative data is especially appalling in a test billed as a developmental test.

No data on reliability of any type are provided. Because scores are based on single items or on a few items, the reliability of these scores is highly questionable. Because the scoring of many of the items is subjective, the lack of data on interrater agreement is a critical shortcoming.

Although the test's title and its statement of purpose emphasize the educational benefit of the test, no data on the relationship of test scores to educational criteria are provided, nor is the lack of such data mentioned as a shortcoming. Throughout the manual, vague and unsubstantiated claims are made that poor performance on certain tasks is associated with other learning problems. For example, it is stated that children who have fine-motor dyspraxia do poorly on the paper graph subtest. Also, "youngsters who have problems with Category Naming may have generalized problems with word finding (i.e., dysphasia)." Typically, no empirical evidence is offered in support of the assertions.

The PEERAMID is based on the reasoning that learning problems are a result of neuromaturational delays. Yet, no critical summary of the relevant extant literature is provided. Levine appears to accept noncritically the well-publicized myths of the learning disabled child. For example, Levine cites Orton's (1937) discredited work on the relationship between mixed hand preference and learning problems. Levine states that minor neurological indicators suggest "central nervous system inefficiency" and a lack of "fine tuning" of central nervous system function. From that assumption, he concludes these children need help with study skills. Thus, the theoretical and empirical underpinnings of the PEERAMID are inadequate.

A task analysis grid is provided to assist the test user in determining a child's strengths and weaknesses. Due to the lack of adequate normative data, the scores on which this grid is based are of questionable meaningfulness. Furthermore, there is no empirical evidence to support these groupings. Thus, the test user's interpretation depends solely on the user's clincial acumen and fund of basic neuropsychological information.

The recommended qualifications of test examiners and of persons interpreting test results are not stated. Some medical background is required to interpret instructions for test administration. Given the lack of adequate normative scores and evidence of reliability and validity, test results are likely to be misinterpreted and overgeneralized by test users who lack a strong knowledge base in neuropsychology and learning disabilities.

Instructions for test administration are adequate, but several scoring criteria require subjective judgements. For example, on the Category Naming Test, ease of production is scored 0, 1, or 2, according to the following criteria: 0 = considerable hesitancy, prolonged effort; 1 = some hesitancy; 2 = ease of production (quick response), no hesitancy. The average time necessary for administering the test is not stated; however, it is too lengthy a test to serve as a useful screening device. Levine does not describe the PEERAMID as a screening measure, but suggests it should be a part of a comprehensive assessment that includes a family and social history, medical evaluation, intellectual assessment, and achievement testing. The unique contribution of the PEERAMID to such a comprehensive assessment is not clearly stated, nor is empirical evidence of its clinical utility offered.

Because the test is at times described in the manual as a test of educational readiness, a test of development, and a test of neurological status, it is difficult to know what alternative tests to suggest in its place. An examination of the test items and recommended interpretations suggest the test is intended to be a test of neuropsychological aspects of learning problems. The Halstead Neuropsychological Test Battery for Children (HNTB-C; 9:463) is a far superior test for this purpose. The HNTB-C is a well-researched test that provides a comprehensive view of a child's neuropsychological functioning. Administration of the HNTB-C requires a highly trained and experienced clinical neuropsychologist. Given the complexity of neuropsychological assessment, interpretations will always require considerable training and experience in neuropsychology. The PEERAMID can be faulted for not specifying the level of training and experience required to make meaningful interpretations based on PEERAMID scores and for failing to meet basic psychometric standards for standardization, reliability, and validity.

[274]

People Performance Profile. Purpose: Designed to determine how employees perceive their organization, their work team, and themselves. Organization members; 1985; 3 areas: Personal Performance, Work Team Performance, Organization Performance; 1985 price data: $295 per complete set including work-team guide (30 pages), leader's guide (31 pages), and scoring and reporting for 1–15 participants; administration time not reported; Bob Crosby, John Scherer (profile), and Gil Crosby (guide); University Associates, Inc.*

Review of the People Performance Profile by SEYMOUR ADLER, Associate Professor of Applied Psychology, Department of Management, Stevens Institute of Technology, Hoboken, NJ:

The People Performance Profile (PPP) is an organizational survey instrument designed to diagnose organizational effectiveness across 20 dimensions that are presumed to have impact on productivity and employee satisfaction. The authors have designed the instrument to be used as the basis of an organizational development process. A Leader's Guide and a Work-Team Guide are provided to structure the intervention process meant to accompany administration, analysis, and feedback of the PPP.

The instrument itself contains 190 items, divided into three sections, and takes from 30–45 minutes to complete. Completed forms are submitted to the test publisher for analysis. Results are presented on both an organizational level and on a subgroup level. To protect the anonymity of respondents, subgroups must contain at least four members in order to be separately analyzed.

Section I of the questionnaire addresses the organization-level factors of planning, management procedures, motivational climate, and physical environment. In addition, an organizational stress score is calculated from some unspecified subset of items in this section. Section II addresses the work-team factors of supervision, role clarity, communications, conflict management, problem-solving, meeting effectiveness, job satisfaction, and group productivity. Section III, which organizations may or may not want to include in the survey, addresses personal fitness and includes subsections on health habits, exercise, nutrition, alcohol and drug use (the only dimension excluded from the survey feedback provided to participants), interpersonal support, time management, and personal stress management. In addition, respondents indicate those dimensions they would be interested in seeing improve. Finally, many of the 20 subsections described above are in fact comprised of even more detailed multi-item subscales from which separate scores are calculated.

In sum, then, the PPP appears to be comprehensive in scope while measuring organizational attitudes and perceptions at a detailed level. As such, researchers and practitioners might find the PPP useful in exploratory research.

Unfortunately, technical documentation for the PPP is inadequate to address basic questions concerning the reliability and construct validity of the 20 dimension scores derived from the PPP, let alone the more detailed subscores provided as output. Consequently, at this point the PPP cannot be recommended as an instrument of demonstrated value. In the one study cited, 40 employees in four work groups—two effective and two ineffective—completed the PPP on two occasions, 1 month apart. The correlation between the two administrations of the survey is reported as $r = .95$. Presumably, "total PPP score" was correlated over two administrations, although no mention is made anywhere in the support materials, or in the computer analysis of the PPP, of an overall score, nor is it clear what such a score would mean. No reliability analysis of any sort—internal consistency or stability—is provided for any of the PPP dimension or subscale scores.

Users might also like to know the extent to which the scales on the PPP are intercorrelated, especially because some of the items included as work-team level items appear to address organization-level factors. For example, among the items presumably relating to communication within the immediate work group are those that address organization-wide communication from top management. Unfortunately, an overall correlation matrix is not provided. The only validity data reported are from a concurrent study which showed, for a sample of 40 employees in four work groups, that—on an overall profile basis—group effectiveness related significantly to PPP responses. On the whole, then, the publishers provide wholly inadequate data to support their claim that the instrument "has the highest reliability and validity achievable" (PPP Research and Validity Summary, undated).

Some potential users might find the very title of this instrument objectionable, because it implies that the attitudinal and perceptual dimensions measured help determine performance in organizations. This implication is strengthened by the opening sentence of the introduction to the survey, which refers to employee productivity. Unfortunately, this approach perpetuates the myth held by many managers that the organizational climate and attitudinal dimensions measured on the PPP have a demonstrated impact on productivity. More suitable is the description provided in the accompanying Guides that describes the PPP as a survey of the work environment.

Finally, those considering the PPP for exploratory research might want to revise the response scale utilized in the instrument. Virtually all 190 items are rated on a 5-point frequency scale (from "never" to "always") although the vast majority of items are more suitably rated on an agreement Likert-type scale.

Review of the People Performance Profile by LARRY COCHRAN, Associate Professor of Counselling Psychology, The University of British Columbia, Vancouver, British Columbia, Canada:

Apparently, the People Performance Profile is designed to be used as a part of a pre-set organizational effectiveness program for working teams within organizational settings. Members of a working team first complete an 11-page survey. The answer sheets are then computer scored. When the scores for the group are returned to the organization, two meetings are held for the working team, conducted by a guide in accordance with a 30-page guidance manual. Using the tabulated responses the working team is oriented toward improving the work situation rather that blaming personalities, and becomes acquainted with the interpretive scale by identifying group strengths and weaknesses. Items with low scores suggest problem areas. The team is then led to exemplify problems, brainstorm solutions, and make recommendations to their supervisor. Essentially, it is a test-referenced program for increasing the productivity and quality of life of a working team.

The survey is composed of 190 items such as "my supervisor coordinates the work of my team well." Each item is rated on a 5-point scale ranging from *always*, *frequently*, *occasionally*, *seldom*, to *never*. The survey has three major sections with subsections under each. Organizational performance indicators include subsections on planning, management procedures, motivational climate, physical environment, and organizational stress. Work-team performance indicators include supervision, role clarity, communications, conflict management, problem solving, meeting effectiveness, job satisfaction, and group productivity. Personal fitness indicators include health habits, exercise, nutrition, alcohol and drug use, interpersonal support, time management, and personal stress management. The items are transparent with an obvious positive or negative answer. Indeed, subsection instructions are educational, indicating what, for instance, good supervision is. For truthful answers, the authors rely upon the test rationale, which is that the test provides a way "to determine what needs to be done to make your organization a healthier, happier, better place." Individual profiles are not returned. Rather, team scores are returned for each item, subsection, and section, along with frequencies of response for scale points. The scoring scale ranges from 0 to 6 with labels of critical, marginal, functional, good, excellent, and superior.

The test items are clear, seem well-constructed, and appear to have content validity. The survey of issues is broad and reasonably conceived, although it would be desirable if a manual presented a theory that suggested the items or described free responses of workers to determine if coverage is as broad as it appears.

Unfortunately, there is no test manual. There is no indication of how scores were derived, why responses require computer scoring, or what the scores mean with reference to a norm group. There is no indication of how the test was constructed, nor any evidence for reliability and validity. The survey has the appearance of a test, but no substance whatever in the sense that no standards for tests are satisfied.

Without reliability, validity, and norming group evidence, the survey is more of a checklist than a test. It might be argued that this is enough for the use envisioned. That is, it organizes team member responses so the team can concentrate upon problematic issues for correction. However, there are two difficulties with this position. First, if the survey is posed as a test, it should meet acceptable standards or at least provide evidence of an attempt to meet them. Second, the responses are returned as scores and there is no evidence that these scores accurately represent what they are purported to mean. For example, how would one know if a team characterized as functional by this test actually was functional, whatever functional might mean in this context? Would an improvement of scores reflect an improvement in work productivity, worker satisfaction, or what? Are some sections more important than others? Do the sections really measure different things? There are no answers to these and other questions, and no research context to know how to interpret the scores or gauge their significance.

The survey has such strong face validity and fits so well as a basis for the work-team meetings that one can almost be lulled into thinking that the lack of evidence does not matter. That is, the test items provide a focus for problem-solving discussions. What could be clearer? However, it does matter. For example, suppose that with further evidence, one found that a functional score for, say, role clarity was actually very low with reference to norms for productive and satisfied work teams. The work team would no doubt miss it, concentrating instead upon presumably very low scores from other sections. In short, they could be distracted away from areas that might really make a difference in their setting. Norms, along with other statistics, provide a way to highlight areas upon which to focus with some degree of confidence and a way to interpret the meaning of the aggregated scores. The People Performance Profile is woefully lacking in this very basic and essential information.

[275]

Performance Levels of a School Program Survey. Purpose: "For diagnosing and assessing current offerings of a school program with reported levels of performance." School teachers and administrators; 1979; PLSPS; 9 ability scores: General Intellectual Abilities, Specific Academic Abilities, Leadership Abilities, Creative Productive Thinking Abilities, Psychomotor Abilities, Visual-Performing Arts Abilities, Affective Abilities, Vocational-Career Abilities, Total, and 11 survey scores: Measurement, Enrichment, Acceleration, Individualization, Recognition, Special Activities, Special Personnel, Staff Development, Student Mentors, Out of School/Class Activities, Total; 1985 price data: $14.95 per complete kit including survey materials for 30 participants and manual ('79, 16 pages); (60) minutes; Frank Williams; D.O.K. Publishers, Inc.*

Review of the Performance Levels of a School Program Survey by TIMOTHY Z. KEITH, Associate Professor of School Psychology, Virginia Tech University, Blacksburg, VA:

The Performance Levels of a School Program Survey (PLSPS) is designed to assess whether a school measures and develops eight abilities believed to be important for all school programs. The extent to which schools foster those abilities is measured through a survey administered to teachers and administrators.

The PLSPS attempts to assess a school program's development of General Intellectual Abilities, Specific Academic Abilities, Leadership Abilities, Creative Productive Thinking Abilities, Psychomotor Abilities, Visual-Performing Arts Abilities, Affective Abilities, and Vocational-Career Abilities. Within each of these eight areas, the PLSPS includes one question designed to assess each of the following 10 dimensions: Measurement ("Are there means provided for measuring leadership abilities of students in your class or school?"), Enrichment ("Do you select students who perform well on creative thinking tasks for future experiences requiring such skills in your class or school?"), Acceleration ("Are students identified as intellectually bright accelerated in grade or subject level?"), Individualization ("Are talented students assigned to work with music and art teachers from your staff on artistic activities over and beyond that offered all students?"), Recognition and Reward ("Are academic achievers provided opportunities to pursue advanced work or interest areas as a reward for academic excellence?"), Special Activities ("Do you provide specific lessons and class activities for students which would purposely integrate their emotional along with their academic development?"), Special Personnel ("Are there provisions in your class or school for parent and community involvement in physical education and health programs for students?"), Staff Development ("Is staff development provided for training teachers what vocational-career opportunities are available for students in the local community?"), Student Mentors ("Are intellectually bright students used in and around the school to help others?"), and Out-Of-School/Class Activities ("Are identified leaders excused from classes to participate in further leadership activities in or out of school?"). For each question, respondents are directed to give their impressions of the extent to which their school program develops the activities highlighted in each question; possible ratings are: *not being done* (scored 0), *rarely being done* (1), *usually being done but need more* (2), and *adequately being done, leave as is* (3). The questionnaire is easy to use, although many of the items are difficult to rate.

The manual for the PLSPS is short, and although simple to follow, few details are provided concerning anything other than scoring. The introduction, for example, states the survey was derived from "extensive research dealing with how gifted and creative children learn." Yet none of that research is cited anywhere in the manual, and there is no evidence presented to support the notion that the areas and dimensions the survey is designed to measure are, in fact, important components of an effective school program. Furthermore, there is little attempt to justify the extension of findings from gifted students to the education of students in general. Rather, the author simply states that "by looking at what determines good education for gifted and talented students, one can then relate these findings into better education for most other students." Finally, there is no rationale provided in the manual for the suggested use of the PLSPS at all grade levels in a district, even though it seems likely the abilities and dimensions assessed should be of varying importance at different age levels.

The administration and scoring of the PLSPS is straightforward. Ideally, it is administered to an entire school or district staff, both teachers and administrators, in a group setting. Each item is weighted by its rating (0 to 3) with the ratings summed across ability areas and across dimensions. The eight ability areas and the 10 dimensions are then separately rank ordered from highest score to lowest score. The author suggests the primary interpretation be based on those ranks; areas and dimensions ranked highly should be interpreted as strengths in the school or district program and those areas ranked the lowest should be considered as weaknesses. Obviously, using this approach, even very effective schools will have weaknesses according to the survey, and even ineffective schools will have strengths according to the survey. The raw scores on the eight ability levels may also be summed to provide a total score (averaged across respondents) for the survey. The interpretation of this total score is unclear. The manual simply reports the mean score and range of scores for a sample of 450 teachers and administrators.

The manual reports this is the third version of the PLSPS; two earlier versions of the scale were field-tested and revisions made based on the results of those field tests. Yet details concerning the groups surveyed, the results of those surveys, or the modifications made to the survey are not provided. The only normative information provided in the manual is the range and mean of total scores for a sample of approximately 450 teachers and administrators. Even this group is not described. In fact, it is impossible to determine whether the total mean score reported is based on the final version of the scale or one of the earlier versions of the scale. It is similarly unclear how or where this sample was collected and how the total score should be interpreted.

Reliability and validity information are similarly scant and vague. The author reports a test-retest correlation of .61 for a sample of 51 teachers and administrators over a 6-month period. The score on which the reliability is based is not specified. Presumably the reliability coefficient is based on the total raw score, but it is unclear whether this reliability estimate is based on the current version of the scale or one of the earlier field-tested versions. Finally, no information, even grade level, is reported concerning the sample of teachers and administrators used to calculate reliability. Validity information presented in the manual is restricted to content validity; again the information is vague. The manual reports that "six specialists in evaluation and measurement of gifted and talented educational programs" evaluated the scale and that "all reported the scale was a valid and useful instrument for assessing a broad spectrum of total human development."

SUMMARY. The PLSPS is an interesting effort to assess a school or district's efforts toward development of various skills and abilities in children. And although the intent of the scale is intriguing, in its present form the PLSPS cannot be recommended for purposes other than research. To fulfill its intended purpose, the PLSPS first needs a much stronger grounding in research, not just research about gifted children, but research concerning school attributes that produce high quality education for all children. The scale should be adequately standardized and interpretable norms presented. The reliability and validity of all recommended scores should be demonstrated, with particular attention devoted to establishing the criterion-related validity of the scale. Specifically, the author should provide evidence that the areas assessed by the scale are, in fact, important for an effective school program.

Review of the Performance Levels of a School Program Survey by LESLIE T. RASKIND, School Psychologist, Gwinnett County Public Schools, Lawrenceville, GA:

The Performance Levels of a School Program Survey (PLSPS) is a questionnaire and rating scale designed to survey teachers' and/or administrators' perceptions of how well their school district develops the total human potential of all students. Eight abilities are included for rating, such as General Intellectual Skill, Leadership, Affective Development, etc. (listed in the test descriptive entry above as ability scores). Additionally, ratings can be grouped according to 10 methods of developing students' abilities, such as Providing Enrichment, Special Activities, Use of Student Mentors, etc. (listed above as survey scores).

The PLSPS is designed to assess the school program's effectiveness in developing the eight abilities for most students. However, the specific questions are posed in terms of how well accelerated or talented students are served. The author's rationale is that gifted and regular students vary only in terms of degree of ability, not in kind or type of skills possessed. Because extensive research is available documenting effective ways of educating accelerated students, a survey of gifted education could serve as a blueprint for improving regular education.

The PLSPS consists of an eight-page questionnaire in which 80 items are rated on a 4-point scale ranging from *not being done* to *adequately being done*. Most items request additional qualitative, short-form responses such as who provides a service, how often it is provided, and how many students are served. The author estimates that less than an hour is needed to complete the survey, with scoring taking about 30 minutes. Scoring directions take three pages in the manual, but seem fairly simple; each check is weighted and summed, and total weighted scores are rank ordered. Scores might also be averaged across raters, but the author advises separate comparisons of teacher's perceptions with those of administrators. The only normative data given are a range of total weighted scores and a mean score from surveys completed by approximately 450 teachers and administrators. No other description of the normative group is given. The norms are based on a mixed sample, in spite of the author's admonition to compare teachers and administrators separately. Separate norms should have been provided.

The author states that interpretation of scores is best done by studying the lowest ranked abilities and then meeting with "competent professionals trained in program design to consider modifications." The author indicates that high ranks are rarely found, so that interpretation is best focused on the lowest ranks obtained. The PLSPS purports to be only an initial screening device, and so does not offer suggestions or references for further assessment and remediation of deficiencies.

The PLSPS is designed to provide an efficient and economical survey instrument. Certainly, ease of administration and scoring are strong points of this survey. The instrument is extremely economical in terms of cost. The author has attempted to meet recommended standards by providing information on test construction, reliability, and validity in the manual.

Regarding construction, there were two field tests and three revisions of the PLSPS in six western states. Only the first sample is described, consisting of 435 teachers and principals of schools serving kindergarten through twelfth grade. Only one reliability study was reported consisting of a test-retest study over 6 months. A finding of moderate reliability resulted. The sample was a small mixed group of teachers and administrators ($N = 51$). The small size and lack of descriptive information are limitations of this single study.

Content validity data were gathered by soliciting judgments from six specialists in evaluation of gifted programs. This seems to be one type of validity check for the PLSPS, but specialists in regular education evaluation should have been included because the PLSPS purports to apply to most students, gifted and regular.

This reviewer's most serious concern regarding the PLSPS is the assumption that it can be used validly to survey the offerings of a total school program. If information is desired on all students, why not directly ask teachers to assess the 8 ability areas and 10 survey areas for all students? Although research on gifted education can surely be useful in studying mainstream practices, it seems the indirect method of asking about gifted education and applying results to regular education creates an unnecessary extrapolation. Self-reports are fraught with measurement problems, and a more direct method of asking about regular education (when generalizations are to be made to regular education) would seem to improve the PLSPS. Alternatively, the author could present his instrument as a way of assessing gifted programs.

Less serious concerns include the fact that no directions are printed on the rating form. The form is somewhat self-explanatory, but questions could arise as to whether all questions must be answered and whether the rater is to score the total number of checks on each page, or leave that portion blank. Additionally, some directions should have been given for the use of the short-answer qualitative data. Otherwise, asking for such specific information seems to strain the good graces of the rater. Lastly, this reviewer felt that the test is too short (80 items) to derive the 18 scores. The grid-system used to develop the 18 scores contributed to items that seemed very repetitive. The author may be trying to investigate too many areas with too few items.

The PLSPS was found to be an economical survey in which the author attempted to adhere to accepted standards in reporting reliability, validity, and test construction information directly in the manual. However, this reviewer feels the PLSPS is better suited to be used as a survey of a gifted and talented program rather than to survey an entire curriculum. The PLSPS could be said to be an initial screening device, but to say the PLSPS diagnoses and assesses current offerings of a total school program overstates its usefulness.

[276]

Personal Opinion Matrix. Purpose: Surveys the impressions and reactions of those who are managed. Employees; 2 scores: Managerial Review, Climate; no manual (instructions for administration and scoring included on test); 1984 price data: $4.50 per test; administration time not reported; Jay Hall; Teleometrics Int'l.*

Review of the Personal Opinion Matrix by GREGORY H. DOBBINS, Assistant Professor of Psychology, Louisiana State University, Baton Rouge, LA:

The Personal Opinion Matrix is designed to measure the task and relationship orientation of managers and organizations. It is divided into two major sections. The first section, the Managerial Strategy Matrix, assesses the extent to which a manager is task oriented (i.e., motivated to accomplish goals and objectives; concerned with the more universal compensations like salary, working conditions, and fringe benefits) and relationship oriented (i.e., concerned about the well-being and needs of subordinates, interacts openly and sensitively with subordinates, and responds to individuals based upon altruistic values). The second part of the scale, the Organizational Culture Matrix, assesses the extent to which an organization's structure and reward policies are task and relationship oriented. The instrument may be completed by both managers and subordinates.

The basic concept behind the Personal Opinion Matrix is that effective managers and organizations are *both* task and relationship oriented. This conclusion is based upon a series of studies conducted by the authors (Hall, 1976; Hall & Donnell, 1979). Using a concurrent design, they found that high task and high relationship oriented managers made rapid career progress. The authors interpreted these findings as supporting the notion that "a collaborative, participative High Task-High Relationship managerial style typifies High Achievers who integrate maximum concern for task and relationship demands" (Hall & Donnell, 1979, pp. 97–98).

An alternative explanation for the above findings should also be considered. It seems plausible, if not likely, that high achievement managers were assigned more demanding jobs than were low achievement managers, and these more difficult assignments may have prompted a high task and high relationship orientation. Since the authors used a concurrent design, it is impossible to determine whether high task and high relationship managerial behavior *resulted* in high achievement or was a *consequence* of high achievement.

Even if one accepts the premise that high task and high relationship orientation produces high achievement, there are still several reasons to question the use of the Personal Opinion Matrix. First, the authors have not demonstrated that the instrument is valid. In fact, past research cited as support for the scale (e.g., Hall & Donnell, 1979) used two other instruments to assess task and relationship orientation: the Styles of Management Inventory (Hall, Harvey, & Williams, 1963) and the Managerial Appraisal Survey (Hall, Harvey, & Williams, 1970). Second, the reliability of the Personal Opinion Matrix is also unknown. Third, the authors do not present means, standard deviations, norms for the instrument, or correlations between subscales. Fourth, the interpretative guide is woefully inadequate and does not describe the manner in which the instrument was developed or present the scale's psychometric characteristics. In short, the Personal Opinion Matrix fails to meet most criteria of the *Standards for Educational and Psychological Testing* (APA, AERA, NCME, 1985).

The actual format of the Personal Opinion Matrix is also problematic. Respondents are presented with a matrix of 18 descriptions and are asked to select the eight that are most characteristic of their management style and the eight that are most characteristic of their organization. An extremely complex scoring procedure is applied to these selections to calculate the task and relationship orientation of the manager and the task and relationship orientation of the organization. The rationale behind the scoring algorithm and scale format is not clear. Simpler scoring procedures and rating formats would be less confusing and perhaps, more effective.

The authors emphasize that the Personal Opinion Matrix was developed to provide managers with feedback concerning their managerial style which should, in turn, serve as a catalyst for positive change. Unfortunately, until the psychometric properties and theoretical orientation of the instrument are supported, organizations may be wasting their time and resources with it. Even more disconcerting is the possibility that the instrument may provide managers with inaccurate feedback that could, in turn, result in decreased performance (Ilgen, Fisher, & Taylor, 1979).

Future research should determine the psychometric properties of the Personal Opinion Matrix. At a minimum, it should: (*a*) determine the reliability of each subscale; (*b*) determine the correlation between scores on each subscale and managerial effectiveness; (*c*) provide means, standard deviations, and norms for each subscale; and (*d*) develop a scoring procedure that is less cumbersome.

In summary, since the psychometric properties of the Personal Opinion Matrix are unknown, I would not recommend its use in organizations. Better instruments are available, such as the Initiating Structure and Consideration Subscales of Form XII of the Leader Behavior Description Questionnaire (Stogdill, 1963). Although the Personal Opinion Matrix may have a positive effect on group functioning, it could also decrease effectiveness if it is not reliable and valid. Client organizations should demand that management consulting firms use only those assessment instruments that have demonstrated acceptable psychometric characteristics and are accompanied by comprehensive technical manuals.

REVIEWER'S REFERENCES

Hall, J., Harvey, J. B., & Williams, M. S. (1963). *Styles of management inventory*. Conroe, TX: Telemetrics International.

Stogdill, R. M. (1963). *Manual for the Leader Behavior Description Questionnaire—Form XII*. Columbus, OH: Bureau of Business Research, Ohio State University.

Hall, J., Harvey, J. B., & Williams, M. S. (1970). *Management appraisal survey*. Conroe, TX: Telemetrics International.

Hall, J. (1976). To achieve or not: The manager's choice. *California Management Review*, 18 (4), 5-18.

Hall, J., & Donnell, S. M. (1979). Managerial achievement: The personal side of behavioral theory. *Human Relations*, 32, 77-101.

Ilgen, D. R., Fisher, C. D., & Taylor, M. S. (1979). Consequences of individual feedback on behavior in organizations. *Journal of Applied Psychology*, 64, 349-371.

American Educational Research Association, American Psychological Association, & National Council on Measurement in Education. (1985). *Standards for educational and psychological testing*. Washington, DC: American Psychological Association, Inc.

[277]

Personal Outlook Inventory. Purpose: "Predicts the probability of employee theft before a person is hired." Prospective employees; 1983; POI; 5 scores: Personal Demographics, General Activity Level, Social and Moral Values, Satisfaction With Personal Circumstances, Risk-Taking Behavior; technical report (14 pages); 1985 price data: $18 or less per inventory; administration time not reported; Selection Research Publishing; Wolfe Personnel Testing and Training Systems, Inc.*

[The publisher advised in September, 1987 that this test has been discontinued.]

Review of the Personal Outlook Inventory by ROBERT M. GUION, University Professor Emeritus of Psychology, Bowling Green State University, Bowling Green, OH:

Interest seems to be growing in using tests to tackle the problem of employee theft. This inventory is said to differ from other so-called honesty tests in that it has been developed and validated against actual theft reports.

It is not theory-based. The Technical Report, the only manual available, says that the five component parts (the subscores, for which no interpretations are offered) are related to a presumably generalized trait, "propensity to steal." This contention is based on an extensive literature review." There is no discussion of the general propensity or of the relationship of the component traits to it, so a user can have only a vague idea of what, if anything, is being measured by this 37-item inventory. The report ignores many debatable issues. For example, on what basis is it assumed that "propensity to steal" is a general or stable trait? Are components such as high activity level and great willingness to take risks causally associated with theft, or is the relationship in the opposite direction? In many jobs, these would be considered desirable traits. How does the logic of the inventory distinguish between desirable and undesirable activity and risk taking?

The answer is not available, largely because there is no articulated logic. This inventory was developed in a strictly empirical tradition. A 378-item pool was developed and divided into two sets, set A with 178 items and set B with 200. Each set was given to recently hired employees in several stores of a retail chain (a different chain for each set). Subsequent records of those fired for theft were kept for 9 months. These cases made up one category of a dichotomous criterion with those still employed after 9 months making up the other. Voluntary terminations were excluded. For each data set, two-thirds of the data were used for item analysis, and the other third was held back for cross validation. In the primary samples, items with significantly different response rates in the two criterion categories were identified. In the holdout groups, total scores (not subscores) based on these items gave validity coefficients of .43 and .23. No reliability data are reported.

Nor are other important technical data reported. No norms (other than means and standard deviations) are provided. No item statistics are reported, even for the 37 items retained, nor were they determined within the holdout group. The level of significance required for item retention is not mentioned. The probability level required for significance is not reported. The problem of multiple significance tests, particularly severe with 378 nonindependent tests, is not mentioned. In each item set, approximately 10% of the items were keyed as significant, an unimpressive proportion when one considers that (*a*) the number of cases was apparently quite large, although not given, so very small differences are significant at any level; (*b*) the inclusion of each item in the final inventory rests on a single unreplicated significance test; and (*c*) the number of items in the pool was very large, making the usual problem of multiple significance tests extremely severe.

A further analysis of 549 cases "drawn from" data set B included 177 people terminated for theft and 372 others. However, only 270 of the 549 were in the holdout group. These selected cases give a higher point-biserial correlation (.39) than reported for the full data set from which they were drawn (.23). The basis for selecting cases is not clear; indeed, it is not clear why this analysis was done. One interest expressed in the Technical Report is compliance with the Uniform Guidelines, and this particular analysis does attempt to provide data for ethnic subgroups. Oddly enough, it offers ethnic group correlations not only for cases drawn from the cross-validation sample but also for those from the original item-analysis group and for the whole set of 549 cases including cases from both groups. We cannot say why these latter two sets of data were reported, but the impression of technical naivete is strong. The impression is enhanced when cross-validation subgroup analyses are reported for 22 blacks and 10 Spanish—samples clearly too small for sensible conclusions.

Other data on the use of the inventory sustain that impression. One study reports a kind of program evaluation, presented as evidence of "operational validity" of the 37-item test. Four stores using the test in preemployment screening had a 68% decrease in terminations for theft; four others without the test had a 29% increase. These data seem impressive at first, but alternative interpretations are plausible and uninvestigated. To what extent is the dramatic decrease due to the predictive validity of the test, and to what extent can it be attributed to the test as a sign that the theft problem is getting serious management attention, thereby increasing risk of getting caught? Some decrease due to the use of a valid predictor could be expected, but its storewide effect would be diluted by the presence of employees not so screened. Yet the effect reported here seems anything but diluted.

Other operational validity data show mean scores for those fired for theft, in each of 2 years, 2 points below the means for all people hired (including those later fired for theft). This very small difference raises ethical and utility problems not considered in the Technical Report. These problems are not limited to this particular inventory; they are common to efforts to screen out potential thieves. But how ethical would it be for a company to decide to reject people for having a general "propensity to steal," and tagging them so in company records, on the basis of inventory scores? The question suggests that users should be very sure they know what they are doing by having very strong validity data. For this inventory, the available validity data are sparse; although suggestive, they are far from convincing. The utility questions require attention to the relative costs of false positives and false negatives; these issues are not examined in the Technical Report.

In short, unanswered questions about logic, item analyses, predictive or follow-up validity, and utilities at different score levels are serious enough to cast doubt on the use of the inventory for anything beyond exploratory research.

Review of the Personal Outlook Inventory by KEVIN R. MURPHY, *Professor of Psychology, Colorado State University, Fort Collins, CO:*

Employee theft is thought to account for over a billion dollars in annual losses in the retail industry alone. A variety of techniques, including polygraph examination, honesty testing, and voice analysis have been suggested as methods of reducing theft. The Personal Outlook Inventory (POI) represents a relatively new instrument designed to meet this same goal. In particular, the POI is promoted as a scientifically sound instrument that predicts the likelihood that a prospective employee will steal. The test is specifically recommended for use in personnel selection; the POI manual claims that the inventory complies with all legal regulations and that it has been shown to be highly effective in reducing theft.

The POI is an empirically keyed inventory, similar to the Minnesota Multiphasic Personality Inventory or the Strong-Campbell Interest Inventory. That is, POI items were selected on the basis of their success in discriminating employees who are caught stealing from those who are not. As with other empirically keyed inventories, the acid test of the POI rests on its ability to predict theft in some sample other than the samples used in developing the test. Little evidence exists that the POI meets this criterion.

The technical manual for the POI presents two classes of evidence that at first appear to support the validity of the POI: (*a*) cross-validation studies and (*b*) studies of operational validity. Close examination of this evidence suggests that the case for the validity of the POI is quite weak. First, the cross-validation studies employ a design that essentially guarantees a high cross-validated correlation (*r*) even when significant overfitting exists; this design is especially inappropriate for empirically keyed tests (Murphy, 1983, 1984). In each of three cross-validation studies described in the technical manual, a sample of employees was randomly divided into derivation and cross-validation subsamples, and that test was used to predict theft in the cross-validation subsamples. The test manual cites the high levels of cross validity as evidence of the validity of the inventory. In fact, the large cross validities are no indication of the usefulness of the test, but rather reflect the fact that the derivation and validation subsamples are (and by design must be) very similar, and that an empirically keyed test that works well in the derivation subsample *must* also work well in the cross-validation subsample (see Murphy, 1983 for an extended critique of this cross-validation design). Thus, these studies present no credible evidence that the test generalizes to samples other than those used in test development. Since empirically keyed tests can take substantial advantage of chance, this sort of evidence is crucial.

Second, the operational validity studies that describe the effects of using the POI in the field are both poorly designed and poorly reported, making their interpretation difficult. For example, the manual reports that four stores that used the test experienced a 68% decrease in negative references (persons previously terminated for theft), while four other stores that did not use the test reported a 29% increase. We do not know whether the test itself, the very fact that some stores used a test and others did not, or some other irrelevant characteristic (e.g., store location) is responsible for this difference. Later, test scores in an undetermined number of stores are reported for 1980 and 1981. These scores indicate that individuals fired for theft had lower scores than the total group hired, but it is not clear whether these differences are statistically significant, or whether differences in range restriction have been taken into account. Finally, the manual notes that in another setting (*N* is once again unspecified), the number of employees discharged with scores in the "reject," "questionable," and "acceptable" ranges were 6%, 2%, and .6%, respectively. The manual does not indicate whether these differences are significant.

In addition to the unimpressive validity evidence cited above, the test shows little evidence of reliability. A reliability coefficient of .58 is reported. Although the manual is unclear about the method used in estimating reliability, it appears that this coefficient describes the internal consistency of the POI. An internal consistency measure is hardly appropriate for an empirically derived test such as the POI, but even if it was appropriate, a coefficient of .58 would not indicate an acceptable level of reliability.

The technical manual is deficient in several respects. First, normative data are not reported in sufficient detail. For example, the mean and standard deviation in the theft group (M = 28.1, $S.D.$ = 6.6) and the nontheft group (M = 35.0, $S.D.$ = 6.6) of the test development sample are presented, but these statistics do not provide a sufficient basis for setting cutting scores or for interpreting individual scores. Second, the manual is filled with minor inconsistencies. For example, the POI is described as a 35-item test in the manual, but in fact is comprised of 37 items. Third, redundant statistics are often presented as if they conveyed new information. For example, we are told that the differences between the means of the theft and nontheft groups are significant, and that the point-biserial correlation between test scores and group membership is also significant. The significance test for the point-biserial *r* is in fact exactly the same as the test of the difference between group means.

The most important difficulty with the manual is the ambiguity in describing test-development procedures. We are told that two experimental forms, A and B, were used, and that 16 of 178 items (Form A) and 26 of 200 items (Form B) discriminated theft from nontheft groups. It is not clear whether the operational validity studies described earlier employed Form A, Form B, or some combination of both. The POI is described as being made up of 35 selected items, but it is not clear how these items relate to the items on Forms A and B. The manual implies that these items were somehow selected from the 42 discriminators from Forms A and B, but gives no detail. In addition, a potentially serious confounding exists, since at least some of the data involved in the development of Form B were also used in developing weights for the POI. In addition, the manual fails to discuss the relationships between the weights derived for Forms A and B and the POI weights. Assuming that items from Forms A and B were used in the POI, it is reasonable to ask whether the same weights were derived in the different item analyses. That is, it would be useful to know whether items that discriminated theft from nontheft groups in the original analyses of Forms A and B also discriminated between groups in the item analysis conducted for the POI.

The manual does not state whether the POI has adverse impact. However, the scores of Black and Hispanic members of the test-development sample were somewhat lower than the scores of whites. In the light of these data, the claim put forth in the promotional materials that the POI complies with all legal regulations must be examined in terms of the evidence provided. Evidence concerning reliability and validity reviewed above suggests that this claim is overstated. Some features of test scoring suggest additional problems. The inventory yields scores on five separate scales; practically no detail regarding these scales is given in the manual. These five scores are sent to the publisher, who returns a single score that is described as indicating the probability of theft. Apparently, scores are reported on a 4-point scale, anchored as *low risk*, *moderate risk*, *substantial risk*, and *extreme risk*. There is no indication of the actual risk levels asociated with these labels or of the scoring procedures used to transform scale scores to a single risk measure.

In summary, the POI is advertised as a valid tool for reducing employee theft. The available evidence does not support this interpretation. Unfortunately, it is difficult to identify a superior test that can be used for this same purpose; there is little evidence that paper-and-pencil tests or physiological measures such as the polygraph provide valid predictors of theft (Lykken, 1970; Sackett & Harris, 1984). The POI claims to be superior to its competitors; those claims are yet to be validated.

REVIEWER'S REFERENCES

Lykken, D. (1979). The detection of deception. *Psychological Bulletin*, 86, 47-53.

Murphy, K. (1983). Fooling yourself with cross-validation: Single sample designs. *Personnel Psychology*, 36, 111-118.

Murphy, K. (1984). Cost-benefit considerations in choosing among cross-validation methods. *Personnel Psychology*, 37, 15-22.

Sackett, P., & Harris, M. (1984). Honesty testing for personnel selection: A review and critique. *Personnel Psychology*, 37, 221-245.

[278]

Personal Problems Checklist. Purpose: "To facilitate the rapid assessment of an individual's problems as seen from that person's point of view." Adults; 1984; 13 areas: Social, Appearance, Vocational, Family and Home, School, Finances, Religion, Emotions, Sex, Legal, Health and Habits, Attitude, Crises; no manual; 1987 price data: $12.95 per 50 checklists; $50 per computer version (100 uses); IBM or Apple computer-administered version requires 128K-IBM (64K and 80-column card-Apple) and 2 floppy disk drives; (10) minutes; John A. Schinka; Psychological Assessment Resources, Inc.*

Review of the Personal Problems Checklist by HAROLD R. KELLER, Associate Professor of Psychology and Education, Syracuse University, Syracuse, NY:

The Personal Problems Checklist (PPC) for Adults is one of a series of similar checklists, including the PPC-Adolescent, Children's Problems Checklist (completed by the child's parent or guardian), Marital Evaluation Checklist, and Health Problems Checklist. The PPC-Adult is designed to facilitate rapid assessment of an individual's problems from the client's own perspective. It represents a survey instrument of 208 common problems in 13 areas. The instrument is self-explanatory, and no manual is provided.

The author (Schinka, personal communication, February 1986) indicated that items were selected from existing surveys, tests, and texts. Items were sorted logically into domains. The author apparently eliminated items with low baserates. Baserates for problem endorsements by adults can be empirically determined and would be a helpful addition to the literature. Items were then evaluated by a panel of expert judges (7–10 doctoral level clinicians). This unspecified evaluation served as the basis of item revision, deletion, and addition. The revised items were evaluated by a second panel of expert judges in an unspecified manner with unspecified criteria. It is stated that some of the expert judges administered the PPC to clients. The final item revision was made on the basis of this second evaluation. This kind of content validation procedure is not unusual for a survey instrument of this sort, but it would be helpful to the user to know more about the nature of the evaluation and the evaluation criteria.

In addition to the primary purpose of the checklist (i.e., surveying the client's common problems), the Psychological Assessment Resources catalog and the author suggest that the PPC serves other useful purposes, including helping to establish rapport, preparing clients for more formal testing procedures, and providing written documentation of presenting problems. Social validity is a concept that refers to the consumer's (or client's) satisfaction with the process and outcome of treatment. The claim that the PPC helps establish rapport can be tested empirically within the context of social validity research and other measures of rapport. The author reported one study in progress concerned with clinician satisfaction, comparing the PPC-Adult and Mooney Problem Checklist. With regard to preparing the clients for more formal testing procedures, I assume the followup intake discussion with the client contributes to this preparation as well as the PPC.

Providing written documentation of presenting problems is perhaps the most important and clearly demonstrable outcome of the use of the PPC. Clinical interviews, which are indirect measures of client problems, are the most frequently used assessment strategies, regardless of theoretical approach to treatment. Numerous reliability problems exist with the clinical interview as a primary measure for problem identification. Direct recording of problems is the most reliable method of identifying client problems (Hay, Hay, Angle, & Nelson, 1979). However, because the author does not report baserates for the problems eliminated or included on the PPC, we do not know how exhaustive the item list is. Users should carefully record problems not on the PPC that clients identify in followup interviews. Audio recording with an interview schedule and/or problem checklist (allowing for problems not specified on the schedule or checklist) provides the most reliable information for problem identification (Hay et al, 1979).

In summary, the PPC-Adult is an efficient, easy-to-administer survey of problems as seen from the client's perspective. It provides written documentation of presenting problems, an important component to problem identification. Only content validation exists for the checklist, but the validation procedures are unspecified for the user. Problem endorsement baserates are needed with this and other similar instruments. Claims regarding the PPC-Adult and its role in establishing rapport and in preparing clients for more formal assessment are unsubstantiated.

REVIEWER'S REFERENCE

Hay, W. M., Hay, L. R., Angle, H. V., & Nelson, R. O. (1979). The reliability of problem identification in the behavioral interview. *Behavioral Assessment*, 1, 107-118.

[279]

Personal Problems Checklist for Adolescents. Purpose: "To identify relevant problems, establish rapport, and provide written documentation of presenting problems consistent with community standards of care." Adolescents; 1985; 13 areas: Social and Friends, Appearance, Job, Parents, Family and Home, School, Money, Religion, Emotions, Dating and Sex, Health and Habits, Attitudes and Opinion, Crises; no manual; IBM or Apple computer-administered version requires 128K-IBM (64K and 80-column card-Apple) and 2 floppy disk drives; 1987 price data: $12.95 per 50 checklists; $50 per computer version; (10–20) minutes; John A. Schinka; Psychological Assessment Resources, Inc.*

Review of the Personal Problems Checklist for Adolescents by BRIAN K. MARTENS, Assistant Professor of Psychology and Education, Syracuse University, Syracuse, NY:

The adolescent version of the Personal Problems Checklist (PPC) is a self-report rating scale composed of 240 brief descriptive phrases purported to survey 13 problem areas common to adolescents. Respondents are instructed to place a check by each problem with which they are now troubled and to place a check next to as well as circle each problem with which they are now troubled and perceive as causing "the most trouble at this time."

The three-paragraph descriptive material that accompanies the scale (no manual has been developed) states that the PPC can be completed by most adolescents in 10 to 20 minutes and can be used with "any adolescent who is literate and has at least low average intelligence." Scoring of the scale is described as being accomplished by "summarizing the problem areas and important item endorsements." The enclosed descriptive material reports further that the PPC is intended as a survey measure for identification of relevant problems, establishing rapport, and providing written documentation of presenting problems for adolescents in the 13-to-17-year age range.

In its favor, the list of 240 items included in the PPC appears comprehensive and the scale reportedly can be completed in a short amount of time. In contrast, several aspects of the scale itself, as well as information contained in the accompanying material are at best incomplete and in some cases misleading to potential users. The 3-point response format (no mark, check, check with a circle around the item) seems tedious and one questions why a more conventional Likert-type format with descriptive anchors was not used. In addition, many items are ambiguously worded (e.g., "not understanding the attitudes of others"), and other items may be potentially threatening to the respondent (e.g., "friend or family member committing suicide"). Finally, the statement about scoring of the scale is misleading since the PPC is not scored nor are summary data provided concerning the items (telephone communication with author, June 5, 1986). These aspects of the scale should be stated plainly in the accompanying descriptive material.

INTENDED USE. In the absence of data concerning client reactivity to the PPC or the relationship of scale completion to ratings of treatment acceptability/therapist desirability, claims that the scale establishes rapport cannot be made. Moreover, since data are lacking that compare responses on the PPC (a self-report measure) to more extensive therapist-directed interview procedures, the extent to which the PPC documents actual presenting problems identified and addressed in subsequent client contacts is problematic.

Statements that the scale is intended for use with any adolescent in the "13 to 17 year age range" who is "literate and has at least low average intelligence" are appropriate if there are data in support of such claims. However, there is no information available that indicates how the restriction on age was determined, what level of literacy (e.g., vocabulary, knowledge of grammar) is required for scale completion, or how the required intellectual level was determined (e.g., comparative pilot study or mere clinical judgement). Again, statements made in the descriptive material are not valid without supporting data or more detailed explanations of derivation.

SCALE DEVELOPMENT. Although not reported in the checklist materials, the author indicated (telephone communication, June 5, 1986) that the PPC was developed in the following manner. First, item lists were generated based upon review of existing surveys, tests, and texts pertaining to intake interviewing. Items were then sorted logically into content domains with duplicate and low baserate items eliminated. Finally, the resulting item pool was evaluated independently by two panels of expert judges, the first being composed of doctoral level clinicians. The composition of the second panel was not specified.

Although the parallel-panels method is an appropriate procedure for enhancing content validity of a scale (Ghiselli, Campbell, & Zedeck, 1981), the subjective procedure of sorting items "logically" into domains is questionable given the availability of empirically derived methods. Since logical sorting was the method selected, criteria employed for item pooling should be identified in the accompanying materials. However, since the items are neither summarized nor scored, their grouping into domains serves no purpose beyond convenience for the clinician, rendering the grouping method a non-issue. Finally, since no mention is made of attempts to control for item vocabulary level, the ability of adolescents in the 13-to-17-year age range to comprehend the scale is unknown.

PSYCHOMETRIC CHARACTERISTICS. No information concerning the psychometric properties of the PPC beyond use of the parallel-panels method of construction is available. Thus, although the user may have some confidence that the majority of potential problems with which the adolescent population is faced appear on the PPC, the internal consistency of the scale, its test-retest reliability, its relation to more extensive interview procedures (concurrent validity), and its role in treatment development (treatment validity) are unknown. Although the author reported one study in process employing the adolescent version of the PPC, it is unclear when the resulting information will be made available to the consumer.

SUMMARY. The adolescent version of the PPC is a self-report, structured survey checklist for use during the intake interview. The PPC covers a large number of problem areas and reportedly can be completed in a short amount of time. Responses to the items are neither summarized nor scored, some items may be threatening to the respondent, vocabulary level of the scale may or may not be appropriate for its intended population, and there is no available information concerning scale reliability or validity.

REVIEWER'S REFERENCE

Ghiselli, E. E., Campbell, J. P., & Zedeck, S. (1981). *Measurement theory for the behavioral sciences*. New York: W. H. Freeman.

Review of the Personal Problems Checklist for Adolescents by TONI E. SANTMIRE, Associate Professor of Educational Psychology, University of Nebraska-Lincoln, Lincoln, NE:

The Personal Problems Checklist for Adolescents is a 240-item self report instrument designed to be used with adolescents in the 13–17 age range. Items are statements descriptive of feelings or characteristics. These are grouped into 13 problem areas ranging in length from 12 to 24 items. Respondents are asked to check those statements reflecting problems they are currently having and to circle those they feel are worst or causing them the most trouble.

There is no manual provided for the checklist. A one-page descriptive sheet suggests the purpose of the list is to assess and evaluate adolescents. Although the purposes for which such assessment might be carried out are not specified, the implication seems to be the results are intended to be used as a preliminary assessment of presenting problems of adolescents referred for clinical evaluation.

The limited documentation provided for the checklist provides no information regarding the source of the items, the basis for grouping the items into categories, or any data about the rates with which various populations of adolescents normally endorse different items. There is no way of assessing how exhaustive the list of problems is.

The lack of such information means this instrument is one that should be used with considerable care and with the exercise of well-informed professional judgment. It certainly is appropriate to ask individuals what they perceive their problems to be. A combination of such self-report measures and structured interviews in conjunction with other measures provides a reliable means of identifying problems for further exploration in adults. However, there are some cautionary notes that need to be made in using such an instrument with an adolescent population. In the first place, an ability to accurately describe problems areas might be expected to be less well developed in younger populations. In the second place, willingness to disclose problems is an important issue, particularly in clinical populations of adolescents. A third difficulty is that adolescence is a period of life in which there are a number of normative stresses typical of the period. Careful attention needs to be given to differentiating those perceived problems typical of adolescents in general and those that typify adolescents whose problems are either more severe or of an unusual nature. Documentation for this checklist does not permit the user to make adequate judgments about any of these issues.

A careful reading of the checklist on the part of this reviewer led to concerns about some variability in the items in terms of how adolescents, particularly adolescents of different ages and circumstances, might respond to them.

Some items are ones that might be more problematic to adults than to adolescents (e.g., "having a bad attitude toward school"). Others are likely to be endorsed only rarely (again, particularly a younger adolescent) (e.g., behaving in strange ways). Some of the problem statements in the checklist appear to be representative of the normal range of adolescent concerns (e.g., not fitting in with peers and feeling lonely) and would be readily endorsed by almost anyone in that age range. Still others appear to be concerns indicative of clinical populations (e.g., behaving in strange ways). These are examples of ambiguities in the items and how good they are as a means for establishing what adolescents perceive their problems to be. Such ambiguities would be answered easily with the appropriate data, data that would be relatively easy to gather.

Based on the absence of reliability and validity information for the checklist as a whole or the problem areas individually, use of this instrument for research into the nature and extent of adolescent problems or for assessment of presence of particular adolescent problems in populations of adolescents should be avoided.

In summary, if used strictly as an indication of those problems adolescents are willing to report, this instrument may be a source of specific problems to explore in further assessment procedures. Users should be careful not to make any interpretations of the test beyond responses to individual items (e.g., that because a particular respondent checks several problems in the "social" area, that individual is characterized by generalized problems with social relationships or as having more than usual problems in the area). There should be no assumption that an exhaustive survey of problems has been made. In addition, the relation of individual problems to normal adolescent problems needs to be ascertained independently of the results of this checklist. An instrument such as the Porteus Problem Checklist (286), normed on appropriate populations, and providing data regarding the frequency and nature of problems reported by a wide variety of adolescents, might be more efficient and useful for the stated purposes than is this checklist.

[280]

Personal Profile System. Purpose: "Helps people identify their behavioral style and pinpoints what they might do to become more effective and successful people." Employees; 1977–83; self-report instrument; 1985 price data: $7.50 per profile booklet; $10 per manual ('83, 70 pages); (60–360) minutes depending upon preferred program format; published by Performax Systems International, Inc.; distributed by Development Publications.*

Review of the Personal Profile System by ELLEN MCGINNIS, Assistant Professor of Special Education, University of Wisconsin-Eau Claire, Eau Claire, WI:

The goal of the Personal Profile System, originally published in 1979 and revised in 1983, is to help "people identify their behavioral style and pinpoints what they might do to become more effective and successful people." The Personal Profile is based on William M. Marston's theory that behavior can be viewed according to four clusters: Dominance, Inducement of Others, Steadiness, and Compliance. These behavioral clusters, according to Marston, could be described along two axes: Process Oriented and Product Oriented.

The Personal Profile is comprised of 24 descriptors, modified from Marston's 1928 work by Geier (1967). In completing this self-report scale, the user is instructed to rate each descriptor as *most* descriptive and *least* descriptive of himself/herself. These choices are then placed on three graphs yielding profiles of the person's behavior in reaction to others' expectations, in reaction to stress or pressure, and according to the interaction of the environment and the individual's response style.

The measure is designed to be self-scored and self-interpreted and is suggested for a workshop in the training/development of adults and high-school-age youth. The manual contains sections on theory, reliability and validity, administration, applications, and suggested use.

The theoretical base of the Personal Profile System and its focus on increasing individuals' understanding of their own behavioral patterns in relationship to environmental factors have value in increasing personal effectiveness. A serious concern with this instrument is its lack of reported research. While the authors state the instrument shows good reliability and validity, they provide the user with virtually no data to support these claims.

The manual refers to a study of 300 Minnesota dentists using the system, but neglects to provide the reader with statistical specifics. The manual also refers to studies involving "hundreds of thousands of people" but does not provide specific results or references, stating that these studies "are not widely available" or "cannot be included in this packet because of their confidential nature." The authors do briefly describe one study of 100 subjects who were given the Personal Profile System, the Tennessee Self-Concept Scale (TSC), and the Personal Orientation Inventory (POI). According to the authors, items on the Personal Profile System highly correlated with items on the other two measures. However, the authors fail to report complete information and conclude: "The dimensions of the Personal Profile are sufficiently represented within the POI and the TSC to assume that some of the underlying attributes of the POI and TSC are also being measured by the scales of the Personal Profile. Not having the scores on the subscales for each of the POI and TSC, it is not possible to get a direct relationship between the Personal Profile and reported scores on the POI and TSC." Clearly, such vague and incomplete information regarding the construct or convergent validities of the Personal Profile is unacceptable.

While the theory behind this instrument holds promise in increasing individuals' awareness of their behavioral styles in interactions with environmental conditions, the clear lack of data to support this instrument should preclude its use.

REVIEWER'S REFERENCES

Marston, W. M. (1928). *Emotions of normal people.* New York: Harcourt, Brace.

Geier, J. G. (1967). A trait approach to the study of personalities and their roles in task situations. *The Journal of Communication,* 17, 316-323.

[281]

Personality Inventory for Children, Revised Format. Purpose: "Provides comprehensive and clinically relevant descriptions of child behavior, affect, and cognitive status, as well as family characteristics, for children and adolescents ages 3 through 16 years." Ages 3–16; 1977–84; PIC; manual entitled *Multidimensional Description of Child Personality: A Manual for the Personality Inventory for Children, Revised 1984*; 33 scale scores: 16 profile scales: Lie, Frequency, Defensiveness, Adjustment, Academic Achievement, Intellectual Screening, Development, Somatic Concern, Depression, Family Relations, Delinquency, Withdrawal, Anxiety, Psychosis, Hyperactivity, Social Skills, plus 17 experimental scales: Adolescent Maladjustment, Aggression, Asocial Behavior, Cerebral Dysfunction, Delinquency Prediction, Ego Strength, Excitement, Externalization, Infrequency, Internalization, Introversion-Extraversion, K (identifies denial of symptoms), Learning Disability Prediction, Reality Distortion, Sex Role, Social Desirability, Somatization; child's guardian completes the test, author recommends administering the test to the child's biological mother; 1986 price data: $125 per complete kit including 10 test booklets, 25 profiles for ages 3–5, 25 profiles for ages 6–16, 100 answer sheets, 1 set of scoring templates, manual ('84, 164 pages), revised format manual supplement ('82, 111 pages), and 2 computerized scoring reports; $12.50 per 10 test booklets; $12.10 per 100 profile forms for parts I and II or parts III and IV; $12.10 per 100 answer sheets; $29.50 per scoring keys for parts I, II, and III; $24.50 per manual; $16.50 per revised format manual supplement; $149.50 per microcomputer edition; WPS scoring service, $7.40 or more per test; administration time not reported; Robert D. Wirt (manual and test), David Lachar (manual and manual supplement), James K. Klinedinst (manual), Philip D. Seat (manual and test), and William E. Broen (test); Western Psychological Services.*

For reviews by Cecil R. Reynolds and June M. Tuma of an earlier edition, see 9:949 (5 references); see also T3:1796 (5 references).

TEST REFERENCES

1. Achenbach, T. M., & Edelbrock, C. S. (1984). Psychopathology of childhood. *Annual Review of Psychology,* 35, 227-256.

2. Barad, S. J., & Hughes, H. M. (1984). Readability of the Personality Inventory for Children. *Journal of Consulting and Clinical Psychology,* 52, 906-907.

3. Berg, R. A., Bolter, J. F., Ch'ien, L. T., & Cummins, J. (1984). A standardized assessment of emotionality in children suffering from epilepsy. *Clinical Neuropsychology,* 6, 247-248.

4. Breen, M. J., & Barkley, R. A. (1984). Psychological adjustment in learning disabled, hyperactive, and hyperactive/learning disabled children as measured by the Personality Inventory for Children. *Journal of Clinical Child Psychology,* 13, 232-236.

5. Forbes, G. B. (1984). Clinical utility of the McVaugh and Grow rules for the detection of faking on the Personality Inventory for Children. *Journal of Clinical Psychology,* 40, 1205-1209.

6. McAuliffe, T. M., & Handal, P. J. (1984). PIC delinquency scale: Validity in relation to self-reported delinquent acts. *Criminal Justice and Behavior,* 11, 35-46.

7. Witt, P. H., & Handal, P. J. (1984). Person-environment fit: Is satisfaction predicted by congruency, environment, or personality? *Journal of College Student Personnel,* 25, 503-508.

8. Cornell, D. G. (1985). External validation of the Personality Inventory for Children—Comment on Lachar, Gdowski and Snyder. *Journal of Consulting and Clinical Psychology,* 53, 273-274.

9. Daldin, H. (1985). Faking good and faking bad on the Personality Inventory for Children—Revised, shortened format. *Journal of Counseling and Clinical Psychology,* 53, 561-563.

10. Fowler, R. D. (1985). Landmarks in computer-assisted psychological assessment. *Journal of Consulting and Clinical Psychology,* 53, 748-759.

11. Gdowski, C. L., Lachar, D., & Kline, R. B. (1985). A PIC profile typology of children and adolescents: 1. Empirically derived alternative to traditional diagnosis. *Journal of Abnormal Psychology,* 94, 346-361.

12. Harrington, R. G., & Marks, D. (1985). The Adjustment Scale of the PIC as a screening measure for behaviorally disordered children. *The Psychological Record*, 35, 465-470.
13. Lachar, D., Gdowski, C. L., & Snyder, D. K. (1985). Consistency of maternal report and the Personality Inventory for Children: Always useful and sometimes sufficient—reply to Cornell. *Journal of Consulting and Clinical Psychology*, 53, 275-276.
14. Reynolds, W. M., Anderson, G., & Bartell, N. (1985). Measuring depression in children: A multimethod assessment investigation. *Journal of Abnormal Child Psychology*, 13, 513-526.
15. Byrne, J. M., Backman, J. E., Gates, R. D., & Clark-Touesnard, M. (1986). Interpretation of the Personality Inventory for Children—Revised (PIC-R): Influence of cognitive impairment. *Journal of Abnormal Child Psychology*, 14, 287-296.
16. Hulbert, T. A., Gdowski, C. L., & Lachar, D. (1986). Interparent agreement on the Personality Inventory for Children: Are substantial correlations sufficient? *Journal of Abnormal Child Psychology*, 14, 115-122.
17. Nicassio, P. M., LaBarbera, J. D., Coburn, P., & Finley, R. (1986). The psychosocial adjustment of the Amerasian refugees: Findings from the Personality Inventory for Children. *The Journal of Nervous and Mental Disease*, 174, 541-544.
18. Nussbaum, N. L., & Bigler, E. D. (1986). Neuropsychological and behavioral profiles of empirically derived subgroups of learning disabled children. *Clinical Neuropsychology*, 8, 82-89.
19. Nussbaum, N. L., Bigler, E. D., & Koch, W. (1986). Neuropsychologically derived subgroups of learning disabled children: Personality/behavioral dimensions. *Journal of Learning Disabilities*, 19, 57-67.
20. Monastra, V. J., Kovaleski, M., & Kurkjian, J. (1987). Neuropsychological deficit and learning disability in children with psychiatric disorders: A preliminary report. *Psychological Reports*, 61, 110.

Review of the Personality Inventory for Children, Revised Format by HOWARD M. KNOFF, Associate Professor of School Psychology, University of South Florida, Tampa, FL:

The Personality Inventory for Children, Revised Format (PIC) is an objective personality assessment tool that was developed for use with children and adolescents, ages 3 through 16, to provide "comprehensive and clinically relevant descriptions of child behavior, affect, and cognitive status, as well as family characteristics" (Wirt, Lachar, Klinedinst, & Seat, 1984). Historically, the PIC administration booklet was first published by Wirt and Broen in 1958 followed by norms collected between 1958 and 1962 based on a sample of public school children (N = 2,390) primarily from the Minneapolis public schools. In 1977, the first PIC manual was published (*a*) summarizing the many subsequent studies and dissertations addressing the construction of the PIC scales, their respective reliabilities and validities, and their actuarial interpretations; and (*b*) providing other much-needed technical and statistical information about the test. In 1979, Lachar and Gdowski published the *Actuarial Assessment of Child and Adolescent Personality: An Interpretive Guide for the Personality Inventory for Children Profile*, which provided actuarial interpretations of the various PIC scales based on a sample of 431 children and adolescents evaluated at the Lafayette Clinic (Detroit, MI) between December 1975 and April 1977. Finally, in 1984, two updated manuals were published: *Multidimensional Description of Child Personality: A Manual for the Personality Inventory for Children* by Wirt, Lachar, Klinedinst, and Seat; and *Personality Inventory for Children: Revised Format Manual Supplement* by Lachar, describing a reorganized PIC and the test's most recent data and information.

In its current version, the PIC consists of 600 true/false items that are completed by an adult who has lived continuously with the child being assessed or referred and/or who is thoroughly familiar with the child. Research with the PIC has indicated the child's mother or maternal surrogate is the best respondent to the PIC and, indeed, this is advised given the test's normative data, which are based on maternal responses. Compared with the 1977 version of the PIC, only the order of the 600 items has been changed; that is, the revised PIC consists of the same items, scale development procedures, standardizations and norms, and basic interpretations as its predecessor. Thus, the PIC still consists of the same 3 validity, 1 general screening, 12 clinical, and 17 supplemental or experimental scales. Scoring, meanwhile, can be completed by hand, through scannable answer sheets scored by the test publisher, or by using a microcomputer diskette that can both administer the test and score its individual responses.

Despite the maintenance of its 600 items, the PIC's reorganization has some inherent logic and benefit. For example, those items specific to the 17 supplemental scales now comprise the last 179 PIC items (items 421 to 600); practitioners not interested in them can simply advise respondents to delete them from consideration. Further, the first 420 items are organized such that three cumulative (or hierarchical) levels of clinical specificity can be chosen: Part I (items 1 to 131), which includes the Lie Scale and the test's four broad-band factor scales (Undisciplined/Poor Self-Control, Social Incompetence, Internalization/Somatic Symptoms, Cognitive Development); Part II (items 1 to 280), which includes the above scales *and* the shortened versions of the 2 other validity scales, the general screening scale, and the 12 clinical scales; and Part III (items 1 to 420), which includes the four broad-band factor scales and the full versions of all the validity, screening, and clinical scales. This item reorganization is a significant improvement in that (*a*) respondents no longer need to complete all 600 PIC items—often an exhaustive and cost-inefficient task; (*b*) hand scoring is less cumbersome—the first 280 items have been placed on one side of the answer sheet, thus eliminating the need to turn the sheet and reposition the scoring grid for each scale of Parts I and II; and (*c*) the clinician can choose the level of clinical specificity desired based on the client's needs and the assessment goals.

Because the PIC items, scale development procedures, and standardizations and norms have not changed, many previous concerns about the test (Reynolds, 1985; Tuma, 1985) also have not changed. These concerns will be reviewed briefly through discussions of the PIC's scale construction, testing procedures, standardization and norms, and reliability and validity. A final section will review the organization and contents of the new manuals with a view toward future needs and directions.

SCALE CONSTRUCTION. The PIC validity, screening, and clinical scales were constructed either through empirical methods (specifically, the Defensiveness, Adjustment, Achievement, Intellectual Screening, Delinquency, Psychosis, and Hyperactivity scales) or through "rational" strategies (all remaining scales), where expert judges nominated specific items that were then empirically tested with specific, clinically-relevant samples. Most of the empirically derived scales utilized a scale construction technique developed by Darlington (Darlington & Bishop, 1966), which maximizes test item usage, item validity, scale validity, and item usefulness. This technique and its application to create the various scales were well described in the PIC manual. The construction of the rationally derived scales, however, was not well detailed in the manual and requires greater description before they can be fully evaluated. For example, while it is assumed that different sets of judges were used to nominate specific items for each scale, this is only an assumption. The manual needs to identify each scale's judges and the judging process and criteria more explicitly. For example, in the development of the Lie Scale, "five clinicians familiar with the PIC" nominated items that now comprise that scale. We have no idea who these clinicians were (what sex, what level of professional experience, what racial or socioeconomic background), what their true familiarity with the PIC was, or what instructions or judgment processes were specified or available to them (e.g., did they make decisions individually or in groups, after discussion or blindly?). To comprehensively analyze the PIC, such information needs to be stated in the manual—not just in citations, which often refer to difficult-to-obtain dissertation work.

The dependence on external citations, in the absence of description and detail, occurs frequently in the PIC manual, both in discussing the rational development of the nine scales constructed with that approach and in demonstrating the soundness and utility of each scale's usefulness and ability to discriminate among discrete clinical groups. While the studies behind the citations do accomplish their goal, greater description of these studies in the manual would facilitate a broader understanding of the PIC. Such description should include, minimally, a complete description of the subjects in each study so that the integrity of the clinical sample and the generalizability of each study's results to other samples or geographic areas can be assessed. Despite these shortcomings, the manual does a nice job of revealing the factor groupings of specific items within each scale, the items shared across more than one PIC scale, and the correlations between each scale and the other PIC scales. This information is invaluable, allowing a more detailed interpretation of the PIC. Yet again, a more complete description of the sample used to generate these data would provide a better clinical context and a sounder process of profile interpretation.

TESTING PROCEDURES. Echoing an earlier review by Reynolds (1985), there are some significant difficulties related to the testing procedures recommended for the PIC. First, the norms are based on the responses of mothers whose children were being assessed and/or referred; thus profiles of PICs completed by anyone other than a child's mother may have some undetermined degree of variability or error. Second, the length of the scale and its completion in more than one sitting or setting may cause response contamination, especially when the respondent converses with a significant other about the test items or is influenced by a negative interaction with the referred child in the midst of the scale's completion. Finally, the scale's length and scoring and interpretation complexity may discourage the clinician from using multiple respondents such that a more rounded, multiperspective picture of the child is available. This creates a dependence on the expertise and knowledge of one respondent, and, pragmatically, the clinician often does not have a choice as to who that respondent will be. While the latter two concerns are more in the control of the clinician, the initial concern suggests the need for separate norm tables for, minimally, maternal and paternal respondents. This need is further supported by research, cited in the manual itself, which demonstrates that PIC profiles from mother-father pairs often differ substantially.

Other concerns related to the PIC's testing procedures include: (*a*) the lack of a specific time frame to guide a parent's responses, (*b*) the presence of some items that require respondent supposition or conjecture, and (*c*) the PIC's scaling method. The lack of a specified time frame for parental responses (e.g., "please respond to the PIC given your child's behavior *over the past month*") not only introduces additional respondent error to the profiling and interpretation process (because we cannot be sure that an individual respondent's time frame matches the "average" time frame of the standardization sample, whatever that time frame might be), but it also makes idiographic interpretation difficult because a parent's responses may reflect *different* time frames from question to question. Clearly, this variable needs to be controlled in any new standardization of this test; at the present time, studies demonstrating optimal time frames for both clinical and pragmatic diagnosis and interpretation are needed. Similarly, the presence of items where respondents must "guess" at an answer because they have not actually observed the behavior in an appropriate setting (e.g., "my child is usually a leader in groups") decreases the clinical accuracy of the PIC. In addition, the response format chosen for the PIC (i.e., a "yes" or "no" answer instead of choosing one alternative from a 5- or 7-point Likert scale) may oversimplify the actual situation, thus requiring additional follow-up and clinician interviewing. While these concerns may be addressed in the context of a comprehensive personality assessment, these limitations to interpretation should be identified and discussed in the PIC manual.

To its credit, the PIC directions, as presented in the administration booklet, are straightforward and understandable, and its individual items require a sixth- to seventh-grade reading level, an admirable achievement in contrast with other personality assessment tools. The revised answer sheet also appears easy to use, and the true-false format does facilitate the response pace needed to complete the test in a reasonable time frame. In short, while the test's administration procedures with respect to the respondents have been well-designed, some concerns are evident when considering who actually responds to the PIC and in what time and behavioral context they are responding.

STANDARDIZATION AND NORMS. The PIC was normed between 1958 and 1962 on an extremely large sample of 2,390 children from the greater Minneapolis area (81.5% from the Minneapolis Public Schools and the majority of the rest from a local medical center), with approximately 100 boys and 100 girls at each of 11 age levels between the ages of 5 1/2 and 16 1/2 years. The norms for the preschool scales are based on a doctoral dissertation published in 1979 that consisted of protocols from 102 boys and 90 girls ages 3 to 5. While the original norms were a monumental achievement for their time, they are now unacceptable for clinical use. They are dated, geographically localized, their stratification was weak and now is passé, and the social and societal perceptions of normality and abnormality on which they are based certainly differ from the early 1960s. Further, given the development of new scales and new scale items during the 1970s as described in the manual, one is unsure as to whether the norms can still be applied. The preschool norms, meanwhile, cannot be evaluated given only the dissertation reference provided in the manual. Indeed, the preschool sample, its stratification, geographic origin, and generalizability are not discussed. The manual states that "(t)he relatively small size of the preschool normative sample and the limited experiences in which the PIC has been applied to this age group clearly suggest that additional effort is necessary to document the validity that has been demonstrated for latency-aged children and adolescents," yet the PIC profile for these ages was still published for clinical and diagnostic use. Clearly, these norms should be considered untested and experimental, and should not have been published for general use.

Other concerns with the PIC's standardization and norms relate to the separation of the norms into two age levels (ages 3 to 5 and 6 to 16), which are profiled for analysis and interpretation. The manual notes that, of the 32 PIC scales, the norms for 18 of these scales statistically differ across sex while 23 scales significantly differ across age. The manual goes on to minimize these significant age differences, without revealing the actual ANOVA results in any tabular form, stating that they lack any practical clinical importance except for the narrow-band Intellectual Screening and broad-band Cognitive Development scales. As noted by Tuma (1985), these differences are not so easily dismissed and the criterion studies in Lachar and Gdowski's 1979 monograph suggest that age is an important variable across many of the PIC scales—certainly important enough to warrant individual Sex X Age tables. Nonetheless, with the separation of the norms into only two broad 3 to 5- and 6 to 16-year-old age groups, a significant, potential loss of clinical accuracy, discriminability, and interpretability now exists. Can we assume that the constructs of depression or delinquency, for example, are similar at both the 6- and 16-year-old levels? Developmentally, the research would not support this assertion, yet empirically this is the interpretation that similar PIC *T*-scores on these respective scales would suggest.

These standardization and normative concerns can be most comprehensively addressed only through a national, stratified, census-driven restandardization of the PIC, which additionally provides separate Sex X Age (and perhaps racial) norm tables. With the PIC's rich clinical history, sound scale development methods and procedures, and good psychometric qualities to draw on, it appears that now is a most logical time for this to occur. Further, a restandardization of the scale will clearly solidify its place in any personality assessment battery and retire one of its major criticisms. Without a restandardization, the PIC's clinical utility will continue to be questioned, and the field will lose a tool of great importance.

Aside from the need for new PIC norms, one final norm-specific concern, related to the scaling of the Intellectual Screening scale and the Cognitive Development factors, can be corrected now. While the manual defines the age groups into which these two areas are separated as, for example, age 6 = 5-7 through 6-6 years, age 7 = 6-7 through 7-6 years, etc., this is not specifically stated as such on the PIC profile protocol. The protocol, in fact, only identifies separate profile scales for age 6, 7, 8, etc. If one missed the short paragraph on page 34 of the manual, assumed that age 7 on the protocol meant children aged 7-0 to 7-11 years, and profiled a 7-9 year old male's raw score of 17 on the Intellectual Screening scale on the 7- (instead of 8) year-old profile line, a 7-point *T*-score error would be made. This error would result in less concern by the clinician (the raw score results in a *T*-score of 64) than would be warranted, because the true *T*-score falls in the clinically significant range at 71T. This potential error can be easily avoided by having the inclusive age ranges, as defined in the manual, clearly identified on the PIC protocol.

RELIABILITY AND VALIDITY. The same three test-retest reliability studies cited in the 1977 manual appear in the revised manual. Excluding the PIC's 17 experimental scales, these reliabilities ranged from .46 (Defensiveness) to .94 with a mean reliability coefficient of .86 for a psychiatric, outpatient sample ($N = 34$); from .50 (Defensiveness) to .89 with a mean of .71 for a sample of normal children ($N = 46$); and from .68 (Somatic Concerns) to .97 with a mean of .89 for a different sample of normal children. Across the three studies, the length of time between two testings ranged from an average of 15 days to 51 days.

One internal consistency reliability study was described in the revised manual based on a heterogeneous clinic sample ($N = 1,226$); no other descriptive information about the sample was provided. The internal consistency estimates ranged from .57 (Intellectual Screening) to .86 with a mean alpha of .74. The manual noted these estimates are comparable to similar personality assessment measures, and that the PIC scales were constructed to favor heterogeneous item groupings within scales as opposed to across scales.

Finally, a number of studies reporting mother-father interrater reliabilities were discussed.

Reliabilities here for the PIC profile scales ranged from .34 (Frequency) to .68 with a mean of .57 for a sample of normal children ($N = 146$); from .21 (Defensiveness) to .79 with a mean of .64 for a clinical sample ($N = 84$); and averaged .66 for the 13 clinical scales for a sample of children seen for a psychiatric evaluation ($N = 360$). Evaluations of the latter study and an additional study cited with autistic children are difficult given the lack of complete background data and the absence of tables with the individual scale correlations.

Given the separate constructions of many of the PIC scales, the reliability fluctuations noted are not surprising. However, their presence does call for caution and consideration of each PIC scale when scale by scale interpretation is necessary. The mother-father interrater reliabilities, as noted above and in the manual, were lower than those for individual mothers' test-retest reliabilities. Thus again, given the presence of maternal report data within the norms and throughout most of the reliability and validity studies, caution is necessary when interpreting profiles generated through father reports. Finally, it should be noted that the Manual Supplement contains reliability (and validity) studies and data for the four broad-band factors, some using the same samples that generated the individual scale data cited above.

With respect to validity, the PIC manual documents a vast array of studies, most specific to its separate scales and related to their construction, and most addressing concurrent, convergent, or discriminant validity. One factor analytic study is also reported from a clinic sample ($N = 764$) of various presenting problems whereby five more homogeneous factors accounting for 98.4% of the variance were derived from the separate profile scales. The four final broad-band factors were generated through a factor analysis of data from a sample of 1,226 children evaluated at the Lafayette Clinic; these data, however, are reported in the Manual Supplement. Regardless, both sets of derived factors are fairly consistent, and overlap significantly with those factors typically reported by other objective, empirically-based personality assessment tools. Rather than review the impressive number of individual validity studies, it will only be noted in summary that they create an excellent foundation for the PIC. This foundation, however, requires additional work, optimally after a national restandardization, to fully validate the PIC as a sound clinical, diagnostic tool that can be used with diverse populations across the United States.

CRITIQUING THE PIC AND ITS REVISED MANUAL. In general, the PIC is a significant contribution to the field of personality assessment. It is fairly easy to administer and score, its manuals are written in understandable language, and the authors appear to have an appropriate understanding of its complexity and limitations. With its reorganization, its administration can be more individualized to a clinician's assessment needs, and concerns about its length are less relevant. Its interpretation, however, is quite complex, and the clinician will need to consult the revised manual, the manual supplement, *and* the actuarial monograph to begin to get a diagnostic "feel" for the instrument. Indeed, as noted by Tuma (1985), further research will be necessary before each scale assumes its own unique clinical "gestalt," moving beyond a simple interpretation of its individual items.

Within the manual itself, a number of strengths can be noted: the authors (*a*) emphasized the need to thoroughly review all of the PIC manuals and guides before using the instrument; (*b*) clearly described the qualifications for a PIC user; (*c*) provided a six-step interpretive process for using the PIC and noted its place within a multimethod assessment battery; (*d*) furnished a number of case studies to exemplify unusual patterns of PIC responding or typical patterns from various clinical populations; and (*e*) continually noted areas that require additional research and/or documentation before final procedural or interpretive conclusions can be made.

A chief concern with the manual is that it is not all-inclusive. Data discussing the construction and interpretation of the broad-band factors and the shortened clinical scales (the "S"-scales) are found exclusively in the manual supplement. Actuarial interpretations for the scales are found only in this supplement or in the 1979 actuarial monograph. The PIC authors emphasize that *T* scores over 70T do not necessarily indicate clinical significance and that each scale has unique levels of *T* score significance and interpretation, yet this interpretive information is not provided in the test's "primary" manual. The PIC manual *cannot* stand alone, yet some clinicians will likely consult only this manual to the detriment of many children and their families. There is only one solution: a rewriting and integration of all three current PIC manuals into a *single*, all-inclusive manual dealing with all of the test's development, psychometric, and interpretive characteristics.

SUMMARY. The PIC has enormous potential as an objective personality assessment measure for the evaluation of children and adolescents. It has a well-documented history, a variety of clinically important and well-constructed scales, an actuarial base that should facilitate sound interpretation and diagnostic decision-making, and a research foundation supporting its good psychometric potential. The revised PIC's item reorganization was both logical and beneficial; the addition of the shortened scales increases the scales' flexible use, and the placement of the experimental scale items at the end of the test allows clinicians to more easily exclude them when they are not required. Despite this potential and its utility in personality assessment and other research, the PIC's clinical/diagnostic use is questionable at the present time. The instrument's chief need is an appropriately stratified, national restandardization. Its documentation and supportive materials sorely need integration into a single, all-inclusive manual that fully describes important studies rather than simply citing them. Both of these concerns now preclude the psychometric and interpretive confidence that a tool of its magnitude should command. The 1970s and early 1980s have seen a great deal of research with the PIC. It is now time to use this research and experiential base and bring the PIC to where it can be used as it was intended—to assist in the comprehensive assessment of child and adolescent personality, the generation of reliable and valid interpretations and diagnostic decisions, and the development of sound intervention directions addressing psychological and mental health needs. Most assuredly, the mental health community will wait for the PIC to realize its great potential.

REVIEWER'S REFERENCES

Lachar, D., & Gdowski, C. L. (1979). *Actuarial assessment of child and adolescent personality: An interpretive guide for the Personality Inventory for Children Profile.* Los Angeles: Western Psychological Services.

Lachar, D. (1982). *Personality Inventory for Children (PIC): Revised format manual supplement.* Los Angeles: Western Psychological Services.

Wirt, R. D., Lachar, D., Klinedinst, J. K., & Seat, P. D. (1984). *Multidimensional description of child personality: A manual for the Personality Inventory for Children* (Revised 1984 by D. Lachar). Los Angeles: Western Psychological Services.

Reynolds, C. R. (1985). [Review of the Personality Inventory for Children]. In J. V. Mitchell (Ed.), *The ninth mental measurements yearbook* (pp. 1154-1157). Lincoln, NE: Buros Institute of Mental Measurements.

Tuma, J. M. (1985). [Review of the Personality Inventory for Children]. In J. V. Mitchell (Ed.), *The ninth mental measurements yearbook* (pp. 1157-1159). Lincoln, NE: Buros Institute of Mental Measurements.

[282]

Personality Research Form, 3rd Edition. Purpose: Yields "a set of scores for personality traits broadly relevant to the functioning of individuals in a wide variety of situations." Grade 6–college, adults; 1965–87; PRF; previous edition (9:950) still available; 6 forms; 1987 price data: $19 per 25 reusable test booklets (specify form); $5 per scoring template (specify Form E, A/B, or AA/BB); $4.75 per 25 answer sheets; $4.75 per 25 profiles (specify Form E, A/B, or AA/BB); $8 per manual ('84, 72 pages); $27.50 per examination kit including 10 reusable booklets, manual, scoring template, 25 answer sheets, and 25 profiles (specify form); Douglas N. Jackson; Research Psychologists Press, Inc.*

a) FORM A. Age 16–Adult; 1965–85; 15 scores: Achievement, Affiliation, Aggression, Autonomy, Dominance, Endurance, Exhibition, Harmavoidance, Impulsivity, Nurturance, Order, Play, Social Recognition, Understanding, Infrequency; (30–45) minutes.

b) FORM B. Parallel form to Form A.

c) FORM AA. College students; 1965–85; 22 scores: same as for Form A and Form B plus Abasement, Change, Cognitive Structure, Defendence, Sentience, Succorance, Desirability; (40–70) minutes.

d) FORM BB. Parallel form to Form AA.

e) FORM E. Grade 6–Adult; 1974–87; 22 scores: same as Form AA; slightly modified version may be administered by cassette tape for individuals with limited verbal skills; $.15 per machine-readable answer sheet; $17 per cassette tape; $7 per manual entitled *Manual for Audio Presentation of the Personality Research Form-E* ('81, 59 pages) for use with PRF tape; $4 per basic report (2-page computer report); $7 per extended report (11-page computer report); also available in French (booklets only); Spanish edition (booklets only): (30–45) minutes.

f) FORM G. Business and industry; 1984; 20 scores: same as Form E except Infrequency and Desirability items are omitted; exclusively computer scored form yielding both basic and extended computerized reports; (30–45) minutes.

See 9:950 (42 references); see also T3:1798 (116 references); for a review by Robert Hogan of an earlier edition, see 8:643 (132 references); see also T3:1322 (23 references); for reviews by Anne Anastasi, E. Lowell Kelly, and Jerry Wiggins, and excerpted reviews by John O. Crites, Lonnie D. Valentine, Jr., and Ruth Wessler with Jane Loevinger of an earlier edition, see 7:123 (27 references); see also P:201 (13 references).

TEST REFERENCES

1. Williams, R. L., Gutsch, K. U., Kazelskis, R., Verstegen, J. P., & Scanlon, J. (1980). An investigation of relationships between level of alcohol use impairment and personality characteristics. *Addictive Behavior*, 5, 107-112.

2. Gaddy, C. D., Glass, C. R., & Arnkoff, D. B. (1983). Career involvement of women in dual-career families: The influence of sex role identity. *Journal of Counseling Psychology*, 30, 388-394.

3. Banks, S., Mooney, W. T., Mucowski, R. J., & Williams, R. (1984). Progress in the evaluation and prediction of successful candidates for religious careers. *Counseling and Values*, 28, 82-91.

4. Bates, J. E., & Bayles, K. (1984). Objective and subjective components in mothers' perceptions of their children from age 6 months to 3 years. *Merrill-Palmer Quarterly*, 30, 111-130.

5. Bond, C. R., & McMahon, R. J. (1984). Relationships between marital distress and child behavior problems, maternal personal adjustment, maternal personality, and maternal parenting behavior. *Journal of Abnormal Psychology*, 93, 348-351.

6. Borders, L. D., & Fong, M. L. (1984). Sex-role orientation research: Review and implications for counselor education. *Counselor Education and Supervision*, 24, 58-69.

7. Davidson, W. B. (1984). Personality correlates of the Matching Familiar Figures Test in adults. *Journal of Personality Assessment*, 48, 478-482.

8. Diener, E., Larsen, R. J., & Emmons, R. A. (1984). Person x situation interactions: Choice of situations and congruence response models. *Journal of Personality and Social Psychology*, 47, 580-592.

9. Duniluk, J. C., & Herman, A. (1984). Parenthood decision-making. *Family Relations*, 33, 607-612.

10. Egeland, B., & Farber, E. A. (1984). Infant-mother attachment: Factors related to its development and changes over time. *Child Development*, 55, 753-771.

11. Hedlund, B. L., & Lindquist, C. U. (1984). The development of an inventory for distinguishing among passive, aggressive, and assertive behavior. *Behavioral Assessment*, 6, 379-390.

12. Lalonde, R. N., & Gardner, R. C. (1984). Investigating a causal model of second language acquisition: Where does personality fit? *Canadian Journal of Behavioural Science*, 16, 224-237.

13. Lanyon, R. I. (1984). Personality assessment. *Annual Review of Psychology*, 35, 667-701.

14. Lefcourt, H. M., Martin, R. A., & Saleh, W. E. (1984). Locus of control and social support: Interactive moderators of stress. *Journal of Personality and Social Psychology*, 47, 378-389.

15. Littlefield, C., & Fleming, S. (1984). Measuring fear of death: A multidimensional approach. *Omega*, 15, 131-138.

16. Meier, S. T. (1984). The construct validity of burnout. *Journal of Occupational Psychology*, 57, 211-219.

17. Morey, L. C., Skinner, H. A., & Blashfield, R. K. (1984). A typology of alcohol abusers: Correlates and implications. *Journal of Abnormal Psychology*, 93, 408-417.

18. Moser, R. S. (1984). The measurement of role taking in young adults. *Journal of Personality Assessment*, 48, 380-387.

19. Paunonen, S. V. (1984). Optimizing the validity of personality assessments: The importance of aggregation and item content. *Journal of Research in Personality*, 18, 411-431.

20. Peacock, A. C., & O'Shea, B. (1984). Occupational therapists: Personality and job performance. *The American Journal of Occupational Therapy*, 38, 517-521.

21. Peterson, C. A. (1984). "Hedonism" is no fun. Notes on Burgess's "Hedonism" construct. *British Journal of Criminology*, 24, 296-300.

22. Preston, J. M. (1984). Referential communication: Some factors influencing communication efficiency. *Canadian Journal of Behavioral Science*, 16, 196-207.

23. Scarpello, V., & Whitten, B. J. (1984). Multitrait-multimethod validation of personality traits possessed by industrial personnel in research and development. *Educational and Psychological Measurement*, 44, 395-404.

24. Tunnell, G. (1984). The discrepancy between private and public selves: Public self-consciousness and its correlates. *Journal of Personality Assessment*, 48, 549-555.

25. Assor, A., & Assor, T. (1985). Emotional involvement in marriage during the last trimester of the first pregnancy: A comparison of husbands and wives. *The Journal of Psychology*, 119, 243-252.

26. Brook, J. S., Gordon, A. S., & Whiteman, M. (1985). Stability of personality during adolescence and its relationship to stage of drug use. *Genetic, Social, and General Psychology Monographs*, 111, 319-330.

27. Burisch, M. (1985). I wish it were true: Confessions of a secret deductivist. *Journal of Research in Personality*, 19, 343-347.

28. Coye, R. W. (1985). Characteristics of participants and nonparticipants in experimental research. *Psychological Reports*, 56, 19-25.

29. Dobson, K. S. (1985). Defining an interactional approach to anxiety and depression. *The Psychological Record*, 35, 471-489.

30. Erdle, S., Murray, H. G., & Rushton, J. P. (1985). Personality, classroom behavior, and student ratings of college teaching effectiveness: A path analysis. *Journal of Educational Psychology*, 77, 394-407.

31. Fowler, P. C. (1985). Factor structure of the Personality Research Form-E: A maximum likelihood analysis. *Journal of Clinical Psychology*, 41, 377-381.

32. Gifford, R., & Gallagher, T. M. B. (1985). Sociability: Personality, social context, and physical setting. *Journal of Personality and Social Psychology*, 48, 1015-1023.

33. Greenglass, E. R., & Borovilos, R. (1985). Psychological correlates of fertility plans in unmarried women. *Canadian Journal of Behavioural Science*, 17, 130-139.

34. Harackiewicz, J. M., Sansone, C., & Manderlink, G. (1985). Competence, achievement orientation, and intrinsic motivation: A process analysis. *Journal of Personality and Social Psychology*, 48, 493-508.

35. Harris, J. G., Jr. (1985). Congruence of temporal stability of multimethod profiles: A new pair of personality variables. *Journal of Personality*, 53, 586-602.

36. Holden, R. R., Fekken, G. C., & Jackson, D. N. (1985). Structured personality test item characteristics and validity. *Journal of Research in Personality*, 19, 386-394.

37. Holden, R. R., Mendonca, J. D., & Mazmanian, D. (1985). Relation of response set to observed suicide intent. *Canadian Journal of Behavioural Science*, 17, 359-368.

38. Hundleby, J. D., & Loucks, A. D. (1985). Personality characteristics of young adult migraineurs. *Journal of Personality Assessment*, 49, 497-500.

39. Josiassen, R. C., Shagass, C., Roemer, R. A., & Straumanis, J. J. (1985). Attention-related effects on somatosensory evoked potentials in college students at high risk for psychopathology. *Journal of Abnormal Psychology*, 94, 507-518.

40. Leak, G. K., Millard, R. J., Perry, N. W., & Williams, D. E. (1985). An investigation of the nomological network of social interest. *Journal of Research in Personality*, 19, 197-207.

41. Mitchell, C. M., Davidson, W. S., II, Redner, R., Blakely, C., & Emshoff, J. G. (1985). Nonprofessional counselors: Revisiting selection and impact. *American Journal of Community Psychology*, 13, 203-220.

42. Newcomb, M. D. (1985). The role of perceived relative parent personality in the development of heterosexuals, homosexuals, and transvestites. *Archives of Sexual Behavior*, 14, 147-164.

43. Norcross, J. C., Prochaska, J. O., & Hambrecht, M. (1985). Levels of Attribution and Change (LAC) Scale: Development and measurement. *Cognitive Therapy and Research*, 9, 631-649.

44. Paunonen, S. V., & Jackson, D. N. (1985). On ad hoc personality scales: A reply to Burisch. *Journal of Research in Personality*, 19, 348-353.

45. Paunonen, S. V., & Jackson, D. N. (1985). The validity of formal and informal personality assessments. *Journal of Research in Personality*, 19, 331-342.

46. Ramanaiah, N. V., Heerboth, J. R., & Jinkerson, D. L. (1985). Personality and self-actualizing profiles of assertive people. *Journal of Personality Assessment*, 49, 440-443.

47. Saunders, D. M., Fisher, W. A., Hewitt, E. C., & Clayton, J. P. (1985). A method for empirically assessing volunteer selection effects: Recruitment procedures and responses to erotica. *Journal of Personality and Social Psychology*, 49, 1703-1712.

48. Swimmer, G. I., & Ramanaiah, N. V. (1985). Convergent and discriminate validity of selected assertiveness measures. *Journal of Personality and Social Psychology*, 49, 243-249.

49. Whittemore, P. B., Burstein, A. G., Loucks, S., & Schoenfeld, L. S. (1985). A longitudinal study of personality changes in medical students. *Journal of Medical Education*, 60, 404-405.

50. Blustein, D. L., Judd, T. P., Krom, J., Viniar, B., Padilla, E., Wedemeyer, R., & Williams, D. (1986). Identifying predictors of academic performance of community college students. *Journal of College Student Personnel*, 27, 242-249.

51. Brucker, N. M., Barrow, V. L., & Blick, K. A. (1986). Traits of endurance and affiliation as self-schemata in memory. *Perceptual and Motor Skills*, 63, 962.

52. Emmons, R. A., & Diener, E. (1986). An interactional approach to the study of personality and emotion. *Journal of Personality*, 54, 371-384.

53. Emmons, R. A., & Diener, E. (1986). Situation selection as a moderator of response consistency and stability. *Journal of Personality and Social Psychology*, 51, 1013-1019.

54. Emmons, R. A., Diener, E., & Larsen, R. J. (1986). Choice and avoidance of everyday situations and affect congruence: Two models of reciprocal interactionism. *Journal of Personality and Social Psychology*, 51, 815-826.

55. Fowler, P. C. (1986). Confirmatory maximum likelihood factor analyses of the Personality Research Form-E. *Journal of Clinical Psychology*, 42, 302-306.

56. Harris, M. J., & Rosenthal, R. (1986). Counselor and client personality as determinants of counselor expectancy effects. *Journal of Personality and Social Psychology*, 50, 362-369.

57. Jandorf, L., Deblinger, E., Neale, J. M., & Stone, A. A. (1986). Daily versus major life events as predictors of symptom frequency: A replication study. *The Journal of General Psychology*, 113, 205-218.

58. Labouvie, E. W., & McGee, C. R. (1986). Relation of personality to alcohol and drug use in adolescence. *Journal of Consulting and Clinical Psychology*, 54, 289-293.

59. Larsen, R. J., & Seidman, E. (1986). Gender schema theory and sex role inventories: Some conceptual and psychometric considerations. *Journal of Personality and Social Psychology*, 50, 205-211.

60. Retzlaff, P., Gibertini, M., Scolattin, M., Laughna, S., & Sommers, J. (1986). The Personality Adjective Inventory: Construction, reliability, and validity. *Educational and Psychological Measurement*, 46, 963-971.

61. Richardson, A. M., & Piper, W. E. (1986). Leader style, leader consistency, and participant personality effects on learning in small groups. *Human Relations*, 9, 817-836.

62. Riggio, R. E., & Friedman, H. S. (1986). Impression formation: The role of expressive behavior. *Journal of Personality and Social Psychology*, 50, 421-427.

63. Vaux, A., Phillips, J., Holly, L., Thomson, B., Williams, D., & Stewart, D. (1986). The Social Support Appraisals (SS-A) Scale: Studies of reliability and validity. *American Journal of Community Psychology*, 14, 195-219.

64. Werner, P. D., & Pervin, L. A. (1986). The content of personality inventory items. *Journal of Personality and Social Psychology*, 51, 622-628.

65. Winston, R. B., Jr., & Polkosnik, M. C. (1986). Student Developmental Task Inventory (2nd Edition): Summary of selected findings. *Journal of College Student Personnel*, 27, 548-559.

66. Basinger, K. S., & Gibbs, J. C. (1987). Validation of the Sociomoral Reflection Objective Measure—Short Form. *Psychological Reports*, 61, 139-146.

67. Lee, D. J., King, D. W., & King, L. A. (1987). Measurement of the Type A behavior pattern by self-report questionnaires: Several perspectives on validity. *Educational and Psychological Measurement*, 47 (2), 409-423.

68. Tetlock, P. E., & Kim, J. I. (1987). Accountability and judgment processes in a personality prediction task. *Journal of Personality and Social Psychology*, 52, 700-709.

Review of the Personality Research Form, 3rd Edition by ROBERT HOGAN, McFarlin Professor of Psychology, University of Tulsa, Tulsa, OK:

Tests can be evaluated in terms of four general questions. The first concerns what the test measures and why; this asks about the conceptual foundations of the test. The Personality Research Form (PRF) is designed to assess, depending on the form, 15 to 22 dimensions of normal personality originally defined by Henry Murray (1938) in his *Explorations in Personality*. These dimensions appear on other standardized inventories as well as the PRF, so the choice is well precedented. Nonetheless, these variables were chosen primarily, one senses, because they were there, and because they have name recognition value in the personality research community. The test author regards these as traits, whereas Murray thought they were needs. This discrepancy further suggests the dimensions were chosen for expeditious rather than conceptual reasons.

The second question concerns how the scales on the test were constructed. For the PRF the answer is, "elaborately." The scale construction procedures for the PRF were the most detailed of any standard personality inventory. The result is a set of scales with high internal consistency, minimal overlap, good test-retest reliability, and minimal item ambiguity. It is also apparent from the manual that the test author has taken great pains to develop scales that are relatively free of acquiescence and social desirability response bias. Because the test author spent his early career arguing these response biases render most standard inventories uninterpretable, one suspects a major incentive for the construction of the PRF was to avoid the problem alleged to plague earlier tests. Not everyone shares the test author's deep concern about the effects of acquiescence and social desirability, however.

The third question concerns the psychometric properties of the test. The technical qualities of the PRF are, in a word, excellent. There are 12 tables of normative data, and four tables of scale intercorrelation matrices. KR20 reliabilities for the standard scales vary between .78 and .94; parallel form reliabilities vary between .60 and .85; odd-even reliabilities vary between .50 and .91; in all cases the median reliability coefficients are in the high .80 range. The manual contains a wealth of information regarding the psychometric characteristics of the PRF scales; from the perspective of formal test theory, the scales are well constructed indeed.

The final question concerns how useful a test is in terms of: (*a*) illuminating the psychological meanings of the constructs that have been scaled; and (*b*) providing a credible characterization of individuals. Here we are concerned with "validity in use." This is not, however, a topic that interests the test author, who notes on page 43 of the test manual that "a thorough discussion of validity must await publication in normal research outlets." Nonetheless, the Third Edition of the manual contains substantially more validational data than the earlier versions. Correlations between scale scores and peer ratings are substantial, and there is an abundance of tables containing correlations between the PRF and other well-established inventories. Careful study of these tables suggests the PRF scales may be performing as they should—nonetheless, the reader must make this determination because the test author is primarily concerned with other, technical issues.

What, then, are we to conclude about this test that first appeared in 1967? On the one hand, it is technically excellent and is well suited for what the author sees as the primary use of the test—as a tool for "general research in personality." On the other hand, the test (like any test) has some shortcomings. It has a slightly dated feel to it—it is based on a 50-year-old conceptual model and it is untouched by recent developments in personality research (e.g., the "Big Five" theory). Moreover, the author has little interest in practical applications—the scales on the profile sheet, for example, are organized alphabetically rather than in terms of their psychological or empirical coherence. Despite the technical excellence of the PRF, users interested in uncovering psychological meanings may find tests like the California Psychological Inventory or the Myers-Briggs Type Indicator more useful. This is a test designed primarily for psychometricians and personality researchers and only secondarily for test users.

Review of the Personality Research Form, 3rd Edition by JERRY S. WIGGINS, Professor of Psychology, The University of British Columbia, Vancouver, Canada:

The Personality Research Form (PRF) has been available as a commercial test for almost 20 years, and although the final verdict is not in, there would appear to be a consensus among earlier reviewers on several points. From its inception the PRF has been viewed as an exceptionally promising and welcome addition to the realm of normal personality testing primarily because of its psychometric soundness, the elegance of its scale construction procedures, and the restraint and modesty of the test author with respect to claims regarding applications. Opinions on the shortcomings of the PRF have been more varied and include: a lack of clarity concerning which samples were employed in the various stages of scale construction and evaluation, a lack of complete reliability data for all forms of the test, and a lack of reported correlations with certain other widely used inventories (e.g., Edwards Personal Preference Schedule, EPPS). But perhaps the most frequently expressed disappointment, with respect to the first two editions of the PRF manual, was the lack of validity studies and of noncollege normative data that would permit the application of the PRF to applied settings.

The third edition of the PRF manual does not differ substantially from the second edition. New normative data on Form E are presented for male and female adult samples, for a stratified random sample of college students, and for a group of juvenile offenders. Additional odd-even reliability data are reported for PRF-E in psychiatric and college samples. Both test-retest and parallel form reliabilities are reported for Forms AA and BB. The 42 tables in the manual have been rearranged to improve readability, but the sheer amount of data presented still occasionally detracts from the narrative.

Form G of the PRF is now available for those who wish to avail themselves of computerized scoring and interpretive services. In terms of item content, PRF-G is PRF-E minus the 16 items of the Infrequency scale. The absence of this scale is not considered serious because irregularities in responding can be detected by computer and because the obvious lack of face validity of the Infrequency items may present problems in some applied settings. Although there is, no doubt, an increasing demand for computerized scoring of the PRF, Jackson is to be commended for continuing to make available PRF-E with appropriate scoring keys and normative data. Despite the convenience of computerized scoring and interpretation, there is still much to be said for having direct knowledge of the item content of scales and of the evidential basis of interpretations.

The most notable changes in the recent PRF manual are an expanded section on empirical evaluation of the PRF and a new bibliography that has increased from less than two pages in the previous manual to nine full pages in the present one. Not all the references are to PRF validity studies, but it is clear from examination of the titles that a considerable amount of research has been conducted on the PRF. Test authors are sometimes damned whether they do or they do not collect their own validity data. Those who rely on the efforts of other workers may be regarded as shirking their responsibilities, while those who report only data collected by themselves and their students may be viewed with suspicion. The validity studies cited in the most recent PRF manual strike a favorable balance between these two extremes. Jackson, together with his students and colleagues, continues to amass evidence regarding PRF correlates. At the same time, the PRF and its individual scales are being investigated by an increasing number of other workers in a variety of settings and contexts.

Jackson observes that: "Thorough discussion of validity must await publication in normal research outlets" and provides mainly citations categorized under a dozen or more broad areas of application. One hopes, however, that such a thorough discussion, in the form of an integrated survey of PRF literature, will eventually be forthcoming. Only then will it be clear how widely, and in what contexts, the PRF should be applied.

The goals of the PRF as originally stated were: "first, to develop sets of personality scales and an item pool which might be useful in personality research, and secondly, to provide an instrument for measuring broadly relevant personality traits in settings such as schools and colleges, clinics and guidance centers, and in business and industry." That the author has succeeded so admirably in realizing the first goal is of no small consequence to the field of personality research. One of many possible examples of this is the basic structure content scaling procedures developed by Jackson and Helmes (1979):

> One of the side benefits of the care with which the PRF was constructed is that it has provided an item pool whose psychometric properties are sound enough to permit applications of the fine-grained scaling procedures of Jackson and Helmes. This opens up the possibility of a very productive cycle of basic and applied research. Analyses of the process of item responding should have implications for the construction of better items, which in turn could provide more clear-cut stimuli for further studies of the item response process, etc. (Wiggins, 1986, p. 229).

The second goal has not yet been fully realized, although the steady accumulation of research on the PRF evident from the present manual suggests there is movement in this direction. In the interim, I would recommend PRF-E over any other inventory of Murray's needs (e.g., EPPS) on substantive, structural, and external grounds.

REVIEWER'S REFERENCES

Jackson, D. N., & Helmes, E. (1979). Basic structure content scaling. *Applied Psychological Measurement*, 3, 313-325.

Wiggins, J. S. (1986). Epilog. In A. Angleitner and J. S. Wiggins (Eds.), *Personality assessment via questionnaires: Current issues in theory and measurement* (pp. 225-234). New York: Springer-Verlag.

[283]

Phase II Profile Integrity Status Inventory and ADdendum. Purpose: "Measures a person's status regarding honesty in the work place," the ADdendum elicits information about an examinee's use and abuse of alcohol and drugs. Job applicants and employees in staff positions; 1978–82; 8 scores: Ability to Rationalize Dishonesty, How Often a Person Thinks or Plans About Doing Something Dishonest, Basic Honest Attitudes, Basic Dishonest Attitudes, Major Admissions of Dishonesty, Minor Admissions of Dishonesty, Lie, Total; 2 forms:

Prospective Employees, Current Employees; 1985 price data: $15 or less per self-score or PACE (Profile Assessment by Computer Evaluation) answer sheet for prospective employees (includes ADdendum alcohol and drug disclosure form) or for PACE answer sheet for current employees (included with each 10 answer sheets is reusable question booklet, set of scoring templates, and test administration guide ['82, 16 pages]); $3 per additional question book; $3 per additional set of templates and test administration guide; Profile Assessment by Computer Evaluation (PACE) allows for immediate assessment via toll-free number with printout of computer evaluation following by mail, included with cost of PACE answer sheets for prospective employees, additional $5 per answer sheet assessment charge for current employees; price information for IBM compatible self-scoring computer-administered version available from publisher; available in Spanish for PACE version for prospective employees only; (25–30) minutes; Gregory M. Lousig-Nont; G. M. Lousig-Nont & Associates, distributed by R. B. Ishmael & Associates.*

Review of the Phase II Profile Integrity Status Inventory and ADdendum by BENJAMIN KLEINMUNTZ, Professor of Psychology, University of Illinois at Chicago, Chicago, IL:

The assignment to review the Phase II Profile Integrity Status Inventory and its ADdendum, Alcohol Drug Abuse Disclosure Form brings to mind a story told by Lykken (1980) in his superb book on the uses and abuses of lie detectors. Lykken describes the case of a nun who was denied employment with B. Dalton Bookstores after having "failed" an honesty test. Sister Terressa, according to the story, had been rejected for a part-time job with the Minneapolis branch of the store because (or so she was told) she had obtained the lowest score that they had ever seen. Her subsequent testimony before The Minnesota Legislature in 1976 was responsible, in part, for the Minnesota statute that forbids the use in employment applications of polygraphs, voice stress analyzers, or any device that purports to test the honesty of current or prospective employees.

It was not the intent of this legislation to mandate that one has a statutory right to any job for which one applies and is qualified. But this law does imply that people do have a right to be "fairly considered" for employment, which means not to be rejected on the basis of irrelevant information about them. This right is reaffirmed for minority groups by the Equal Employment Opportunity Commission's (EEOC) guidelines that stipulate that psychological tests are irrelevant as preemployment screening devices if validity cannot be demonstrated.

Honesty, of course, is relevant to most jobs, especially those that place the prospective employee in a situation of trust. Therefore, a test that claims to measure and predict honesty is potentially relevant and fair. But it will only qualify as relevant and fair if honesty is indeed measured. Hence the question of fairness in the case of Sister Terressa revolves around whether or not she was fairly denied a job on the basis of a valid test that measures honesty.

The claims for the Phase II Profile's ability to detect dishonesty are no different than those made by the honesty testing industry at large. One accompanying flyer, for example, states that "It's a great feeling when you know you've hired an honest, dependable employee . . . you can have that great feeling every time with the Phase II Profile." Other claims in the brochure are that it is "developed by a professional . . . (M.A., M.S.D.D., A.C.P., C.P.P. Noted Criminologist and Polygraph Expert) . . . is psychologically validated . . . does not violate EEOC hiring standards . . . (has the approval of) . . . a Staff Psychologist with a Ph.D. from Brigham Young University . . . gives you valuable insight . . . (and a 'guarantee' of) . . . complete satisfaction." The skeptical prospective user can also find comfort in the testimonials from satisfied customers at TeleCheck ("the employees we have hired since [using Phase II] are fantastic"); Radio Shack ("I anticipate acquiring a minimum total of 10,000 each over a 12 month period"); Brown's Sporting Goods of Peoria, Illinois ("the Profile Tests . . . have proven to be invaluable in determining the calibre of personnel"); and from the President of Restaurant Operations, also of Peoria, Illinois, in a letter which claims that since beginning to use the test "on or about November 6, 1981 . . . we were $10.00 over in our cash control . . . after having lost over $180 in cash in thirty days . . . and had improved our food cost by one full percentage point."

In the event that the prospective user is not convinced by these testimonials, he or she is offered further reassurance by the author of the Phase II. "Dishonesty is a matter of opportunity, need and attitude . . . all three must be present. Our test effectively ferrets out those whose attitude will predispose them to steal whenever the need and opportunity arise." Claims are based on two solid case histories, one of which is partially presented here. "She passed our interviewing process with flying colors. Her references were of the best. There wasn't a single hint of dishonesty in her work history of bookkeeping for our biggest competitor. That's why we were shocked when we discovered that she was pocketing checks from our customers." Guess what finally solved her "desolate" employer's problem? Of course, The Phase II Profile. The second case history is equally fatuous.

For a glimpse at the rationale and evidence for these claims, the prospective user can turn to four sources: A Test Administration guide, a Report on Statistical Validation Studies, a Report on Adverse Impact Studies, and a letter from the Law Offices of Jenner and Block, a prestigious Chicago law firm that "analyzed" one of its client's tests (Phase II) in the context of the EEOC Uniform Guidelines on Employer Selection Procedures.

The Test Administration Guide is a clearly written booklet that takes great care in instructing the user how to "count all of the marks which fall inside each of the 7 different symbols (Diamonds, Hexagons, Triangles, Squares, Tombstones [sic], Arrows, and Circles) . . . before you call the toll free number." It also instructs the user to be prepared to give the PACE OPERATOR your PACE AUTHORIZATION NUMBER, and so on. The guide also provides interpretations of specific score values within each of these categories. Thus, for example, we learn that the 10 diamonds represent the "Lie Scale" and a score of 10 represents 100% truthful responses, 9 is a 90% truthful attempt by the subject, and so on. We also learn that "The 'lie scale' is used to make sure people are not trying to phoney the test and make themselves look perfect."

The 10 hexagons "indicate how much a person thinks or plans about doing something dishonest." The 14 triangles "show a person's ability to rationalize dishonesty." The 31 squares "represent attitudes we have found statistically associated with individuals having dishonest attitudes." The 7 tombstones "represent minor admissions of dishonesty, or acts of dishonesty that happened quite some time ago." The 25 arrows "indicate actual admissions of dishonesty, or that the person would do something dishonest if given the chance." We also learn that "98 to 100% of the people who mark arrows have been involved in serious activity involving dishonesty." Finally, there are 48 circles that "represent attitudes we have found statistically are associated with basically honest individuals (71%)." Of course, no evidence supporting these interpretive claims, or how interpretations were determined, nor the score values accompanying such claims appear in the published research literature. But more importantly, nowhere do they provide evidence in the accompanying manual, "Statistical Validation Report." This is a clear violation of the EEOC Guidelines that indicate that the meaning of test scores as well as their cutting scores and how they were derived must be stipulated.

In the "Test Administration Guide," the publishers also include an example of an optional Confidential Phase II Profile Pace Computer Report addressed to the Personnel Director of the client (i.e., company). There the Personnel Director (not necessarily a psychologist nor anyone with even an elementary or a high school education) learns that the applicant took "too long" to complete the test, has a "poor attitude regarding honesty," resembles a "confirmed thief," "rationalizes (his) dishonesty," and has stolen "$5 from jobs in the last two years" as well as $25 in "merchandise from all jobs." Again, no supporting evidence is provided that these are valid or accurate statements. But no matter, because we are urged to "be sure to use both tests" to provide confirmation of the applicants' unfitness for employment. However, the authors do admit that the ADdendum, Alcohol Drug Abuse Disclosure Form "is not perfect." It is a good deal less than perfect. It is useless, as I indicate below.

The brochure called "Statistical Validation Studies" describes three studies conducted by D. L. Ennis, a Ph.D. Psychologist, who designed these statistical studies to provide evidence that the Phase II Profile Integrity Status Inventory was valid. The first study reports a .97 reliability (where "1.0 would indicate a perfect relationship") with a level of significance at greater than .001 for 60 unspecified subjects. Absolutely no validity information is provided, which possibly goes unnoticed by most prospective users (e.g., lawyers, personnel managers) because reliability and validity are commonly confused with one another. The second study used 660 unspecified subjects, half of whom "passed their preemployment polygraph" and half "failed it and admitted various activities of theft." Aside from using the highly fallible criterion of polygraph tests (see Kleinmuntz and Szucko, 1982, 1984; OTA, 1983; Szucko & Kleinmuntz, 1981), the publishers provide no validity coefficients, but do state that the "statistics indicate a very definite correlation between Phase II Profile Scores and subsequent pre-employment polygraph test results," whatever that means. The third study used research tactics similar to the previous one, except with fewer subjects (240), again unspecified, and divided these into halves consisting of those who passed and failed the polygraph exam. This time a Pearson Product Moment correlation coefficient of -.64 is reported, which would suggest a highly valid relationship—unless, of course, one examines the wording used to define the thieves and the amounts they presumably stole: They "failed" the polygraph and "admitted they had in fact lied" and also (admitted) to activities of "theft." As indicated earlier, to have "failed" a polygraph may be a badge of honesty, given that the false positive rate (innocents classified as guilty) runs as high as 55 percent in some studies (Horvath, 1977) and according to a whole host of studies (OTA, 1983), is at least a 50-50 proposition for most honest persons. But more to the point, admitting to thefts is not necessarily a confession of untruthfulness; rather, it might very well be a sign of honesty in that one is admitting to have taken something during the course of a lifetime. In addition, admitting to taking some vague amount of money is a meaningless criterion of theft. For example, Study III indicates that "only subjects whose admissions were $100 or less were used in this study." Whom does this include? It could include people who truthfully admitted to taking $1.00, $2.00, or any amount up to $99.99. How does this disqualify them for employment?

Not a shred of evidence is presented regarding the standardization, reliability, or validity of their highly touted ADdendum, Alcohol Drug Abuse Disclosure Form. But this does not deter the distributors from interpreting the meaning of various scores and of warning employers to "exercise caution in considering this person for employment" when certain scores are achieved because "you must realize that people have a tendency to minimize their admissions." Did it occur to this test's developers that some people may actually maximize or exaggerate their transgressions, especially when socialization has been of the "straight-arrow" variety?

This issue of minimizing or maximizing admissions takes us full circle to Sister Terressa's probable admission of theft on the B. Dalton's honesty examination and her "failing" score. I want to reemphasize that such an admission—no matter what the merchandise or dollar amount—is an act of honesty, not dishonesty. Clearly, it is more likely that honest rather than dishonest people admit to having been dishonest at one time in their lives, and therefore are the ones most likely to "fail" these tests. Moreover, the logic of this and most other honesty tests seems to be that if one has thoughts about thefts; or has knowledge of people stealing from employers; or has information or a perception about the extent of theft in our society; or, worst of all, if one has a lenient attitude toward theft (drugs, alcohol, or violence), then one is dishonest. But the fallacy in this form of reasoning should be apparent. "It is not likely that most people who recommend leniency are thieves. It is not true that all those who see this as a sinful place are great sinners themselves" (Lykken, 1980, p. 201).

Having argued that the rationale, standardization, and psychometric evidence for the Phase II all leave something to be desired, I now turn to a brief review of the distributors' Adverse Impact Studies brochure and their attorneys' testimonial that "we see nothing in the Uniform Guidelines which precludes use of the Phase II Profile as a measure of employee honesty." The Adverse Impact brochure consists of thumbnail descriptions of three studies. One of these studies used 33 unspecified white and 33 equally unspecified black applicants whose mean scores were "insignificant at the .05 level indicating that the Phase II Profile is racially nondiscriminatory." The second study consisted of 40 male and 40 female job applicants—again, not described in terms of age, race, education, socioeconomic group, and so on. The "difference in the . . . scores was found to be insignificant at the .05 level," this time demonstrating that the test "is nondiscriminatory as to sex." And the third study was conducted with "30 job applicants under age

35" (15?, 18?, 21?, 25?, 29?) and "30 job applicants over age 40" (41?, 51?, 61?, 69?) and "the significance was in favor of the protected group (40 and over)." The conclusion? The Phase II Profile does not have adverse impact on racially, sexually, and age-protected classes. Of course, this is nonsense because it is impossible to infer these conclusions from test scores alone, especially because they were obtained from nonspecified subjects who could have been successful applicants and because—and I quote from the Jenner and Block Law Offices letter—"an employer's overall employment practices" need to be assessed as well as "the employer's general position concerning equal employment opportunity, including its affirmative action plan and results achieved under the plan." Consequently, the Law firm's concluding reassurance to its client that, "we see nothing . . . which precludes use of the Phase II Profile," is wrong by its own understanding of the meaning of adverse impact as contained in the Guidelines. What is worse, this reassurance is seriously misleading as well to prospective users because the test scores and the arbitrary test score cutting points for honesty versus dishonesty were not properly validated—at least not according to any of the existing *Standards for Educational and Psychological Testing* (AERA, APA, & NCME, 1985).

There is also a Spanish version of The Phase II Profile Integrity Status Inventory. Absolutely no data are provided to indicate that any standardization, reliability, or validity studies were conducted for this version. It is safe to assume, therefore, that this inventory is at least as flawed psychometrically as its English counterpart. This is unfortunate because persons taking this test are protected class individuals, and thus more susceptible to being victimized by test scores that signify nothing about them.

Given the information reviewed, I conclude that the use of so-called honesty tests to make hiring or promotion decisions are on the same shaky ground as are the polygraphs against which they were validated, and are the equivalent of a random procedure. Individuals may just as well use a lottery because both methods randomly and unfairly deny persons access to certain jobs on the basis of irrelevant and flawed information. In that sense they are themselves dishonest devices. They are dishonest toward employers because they reject many potentially productive workers, hence causing greater costs than savings. And they are dishonest toward prospective employees because they constitute an unfair method of screening. Therefore, no corporate user should waste money and time denying employment on the basis of this questionable tool and no person should be denied the opportunity for a job on the basis of scores from this instrument. It is my contention that it is illegal and unethical to do so in the case of minority or protected class applicants, and it is unethical and unconscionable to do so in all other instances.

REVIEWER'S REFERENCES

Horvath, F. (1977). The effect of selected variables on interpretation of polygraph records. *Journal of Applied Psychology*, 62, 127-136.

Lykken, D. T. (1980). *A tremor in the blood: Uses and abuses of the lie detector*. New York: McGraw-Hill.

Szucko, J. J., & Kleinmuntz, B. (1981). Statistical versus clinical lie detection. *American Psychologist*, 36, 488-496.

Kleinmuntz, B., & Szucko, J. J. (1982). On the fallibility of lie detection. *Law and Society Review*, 17, 85-104.

Office of Technology Assessment (OTA). (1983). *Scientific validity of polygraph testing: A research review and evaluation*. Congress of the United States, Washington, DC. (OTA-TM-H-15).

Kleinmuntz, B., & Szucko, J. J. (1984). A field study of the fallibility of polygraphic lie detection. *Nature*, 308, 449-450.

Sackett, P. R., & Harris, M. M. (1984). Honesty testing for personnel selection: A review and critique. *Personnel Psychology*, 37, 221-245.

American Educational Research Association, American Psychological Association, & National Council on Measurement in Education. (1985). *Standards for educational and psychological testing*. Washington, DC: American Psychological Association, Inc.

Review of the Phase II Profile Integrity Status Inventory and ADdendum by KEVIN L. MORELAND, Consultant, NCS Professional Assessment Services, Minneapolis, MN:

The Phase II Profile includes three components, two of which will be reviewed here. The Integrity Status Inventory (ISI) is "a psychological paper and pencil test that . . . measures a person's status regarding honesty in the work place" (Lousig-Nont, 1985). The ADdendum is "a uniquely designed disclosure form to elicit information regarding alcohol and drug abuse" (Lousig-Nont, 1985). (The In House Security Survey, a counterpart of the ISI designed to assess the "integrity status" of current employees, will not be reviewed here.)

ITEMS AND INSTRUCTIONS. The ISI comprises 116 items in the seven content categories listed in the test description preceding this review. There are true-false, yes-no, and multiple-choice questions. The following true-false question gets at Ability to Rationalize Dishonesty: "Sometimes a person may have a good reason to steal from a place where they work." The ADdendum is composed of 21 multiple-choice questions. Seven questions ask how many times the respondent has purchased, used, used at work, or sold various drugs; several similar questions ask the last time one engaged in these activities. The final seven questions ask about alcohol use. An example of the latter is: "How many times have you missed work because of intoxication? Refuse [to answer], Daily, I lost count, . . . , 1 or 2 times, I never have." Both of these portions of the Phase II Profile are available in Spanish as well as English.

Because the items on both portions of the Profile are "clear purpose" (cf. Sackett & Harris, 1985), the author has employed "[p]sychologically structured directions . . . worded in such a way as to lower the threshold of reluctance to admit [deviance]" (Lousig-Nont, 1985). For example, the ADdendum exhorts the respondent:

> Our computer studies have shown that over 98% of the people that say they have used Marijuana 16 to 50 times, have also purchased Marijuana. So, if you mark you have used Marijuana 16 to 50 times, and try to lie about the fact that you may also have purchased Marijuana, the questionnaire knows that there is a high probability that you are not telling the TRUTH. (Lousig-Nont, 1981)

SCORING, NORMS, AND INTERPRETATION. Complete raw scoring information for the ISI was not available to this reviewer. It is clear that the items in six of the seven content categories (the publisher reported that the Minor Admissions of Dishonesty do not correlate with polygraph results) are weighted and combined to form the Total Score, which is used in decision making. The ADdendum is scored by computing a weighted raw score for each of the items. Different weighting schemes are used for each of the three types of ADdendum items.

No norms are offered for the ISI or the ADdendum. Cutting scores of undescribed origin are offered for the ISI Total Score and each of the ADdendum items.

Interpretation of the ISI is straightforward: Total Scores less than 140 are characteristic of those who admit theft, scores greater than 147 are characteristic of those who do not admit theft, and those scoring between 140 and 147 are about equally split between the two groups. Interpretation of the ADdendum is more complex. There are several rules for combining the results of the "how much" questions with the "how recent" questions in a configural manner.

RELIABILITY. One reliability study of 60 subjects yielded a 10-day test-retest reliability coefficient of .97 for the ISI Total Score (Lousig-Nont, 1982a). No reliability studies were reported for the ADdendum.

VALIDITY. Two validity studies of the ISI used theft admissions during polygraph examinations as criteria (Lousig-Nont, 1982a). In one, the standard cutting scores accurately identified 89% of two equal-sized groups ($N =$ 330) of admitted thieves and those not admitting to theft. A second study of 240 subjects yielded a correlation of -.636 between ISI Total Scores and self-reported dollar amount stolen. A validity study of questionable relevance given the purpose of the ISI, involved separating 28 welders laid off in a reduction of force from 25 peers chosen for retention (McCarty & McCarty, undated). The ISI outperformed 14 measures of aptitude, health, and personality in this study. No validity data were available for the ADdendum.

ADVERSE IMPACT. Three studies employing samples of 30–40 subjects per group yielded no mean ISI Total Score differences between blacks and whites or men and women; those over the age of 40 had higher mean scores than those under 35 (Lousig-Nont, 1982b). An undated photocopied sheet, partly typed and partly handwritten, provided by the publisher reported the 80/20 test of compliance with federal guidelines comparing a sample of 45–58 black and Hispanic men and women with 623 white subjects. These data indicated compliance with federal guidelines for all the protected groups except Hispanic men. A handwritten note indicated that new data had boosted the pass rate for Hispanic males to 79% that of the white males, but no further details were offered. No adverse impact data were available for the ADdendum.

SUMMARY AND EVALUATION. Unlike the publishers of many of the "clear purpose" honesty tests based on polygraph examinations, the publishers of the Phase II Profile have clearly recognized the need to establish the credibility of their instruments within the community of psychometric scientists. Unfortunately, at this time, they have made only the barest of starts. Obviously, few reliability and validity data are available for the ISI and none for the ADdendum. The available data are reported in very cursory fashion. I have provided almost as much detail in this brief review as is available in the published studies. Finally, there is controversy over the use of polygraph results as validity criteria (cf. Sackett & Harris, 1985). In my view, these instruments should not be used to make practical hiring decisions absent local validation.

REVIEWER'S REFERENCES

Lousig-Nont, G. M. (1981). Phase II Profile ADdendum. Las Vegas, NV: Lousig-Nont & Associates.

Lousig-Nont, G. M. (1982a). *Phase II Profile statistical validation studies*. Las Vegas, NV: Lousig-Nont & Associates.

Lousig-Nont. G. M. (1982b). *Phase II Profile adverse impact studies*. Las Vegas, NV: Lousig-Nont & Associates.

Lousig-Nont, G. M. (1985). *It's a great feeling when you know you've hired an honest, dependable employee*. Las Vegas, NV: Lousig-Nont & Associates.

Sackett, P. R., & Harris, M. M. (1985). Honesty testing for personnel selection: Review and critique. In H. J. Bernardin & D. A. Bownas (Eds.), *Personality assessment in organizations* (pp. 236-276). New York: Praeger.

McCarty, T., & McCarty, J. J. (undated). *Employee theft: One solution to this increasing problem*. Joliet, IL: R. B. Ishmael & Associates.

[284]

Phonological Assessment of Child Speech. Purpose: A guide for the phonological analysis and assessment of children's pronunciation patterns. Children referred for speech therapy; 1985; PACS; 8 scores: The Phonetic Inventory, The System(s) of Contrasts, Polysystemic Description, Phonotactic Possibilities, Assessment of Communicative Adequacy, Assessment of Developmental Status, Identification of Diagnostic Categories, Identification of Treatment Aims; individual; 1986 price data: £17.50 per set of photocopy masters of all worksheets and manual ('85, 180 pages); administration time not reported; Pamela Grunwell; NFER-Nelson Publishing Co., Ltd. [England].*

Review of the Phonological Assessment of Child Speech by KATHRYN W. KENNEY, Clinical Supervisor in Speech-Language Pathology, Department of Speech & Hearing Science, Arizona State University, Tempe, AZ:

TEST CONSTRUCTION. The Phonological Assessment of Child Speech (PACS) is a workbook of procedures designed to identify pronunciation patterns and indicate which require modification for more effective communication. The PACS can be used with normally developing, developmentally delayed, and developmentally disordered children. The author recommends use of the PACS with children who exhibit severe phonetic and phonological problems. The clinician may use any or all of the procedures with a particular child.

The first procedure is a Phonetic Inventory of the child's consonant productions by place and manner of production, and a distribution of consonant singletons and clusters by syllable structure. Single words of varying length and complexity are analyzed. There is a separate section for analyzing words in context; the author, however, cautions readers that connected speech may influence consonant production and advises against the analysis of utterances affected by context.

The next four procedures comprise the contrastive analyses. The System of Contrasts describes the child's use of singleton and cluster phones to signal contrasts in meaning. Polysystemic Description is an analysis of contrastive phones for three word structures: syllable initial word initial, syllable initial within word, and syllable final word final. Phonotactic Possibilities categorizes productions by syllable structure: monosyllables, disyllables with stress on the first syllable, disyllables with stress on the second syllable, and polysyllabic words. Within each of these procedures the child's productions are compared with the adult target system to provide the Assessment of Communicative Adequacy.

In the Phonological Process Analysis, Grunwell describes simplification processes two ways: structural, which include modification of syllable and word structure; and systemic, which describe simplifications of systematic contrasts. Both normal and idiosyncratic processes are analyzed. The child's phonological processes are compared with normal performance on the Developmental Profile Chart in the Assessment of Developmental Status. Five patterns of deviant phonological processes are proposed in the Identification of Diagnostic Categories: persisting normal processes, chronological mismatch, unusual/idiosyncratic processes, variable use of processes, and systematic sound preference. The last section, Identification of Treatment Aims, contains guidelines for planning therapy.

VALIDITY. The author does not presume that phonological processes have psychological reality as patterns of cognitive operations. As a result the PACS incorporates components from several phonological theories including those of Shriberg and Kwaitkowski (1980), Sommerstein (1977), Menn (1976), Ingram (1976), and Stampe (1985).

Most phonologists concur that a satisfactory phonological analysis should consist of procedures that are exhaustive, replicable, and predictive. Grunwell adds seven "clinical" requirements for a good phonological analysis:

1. Describe the pronunciation patterns in a child's speech.
2. Discriminate between normal and deviant patterns in a child's speech.
3. Indicate the effect of the child's patterns on communication.
4. Compare the child's patterns with developmental norms.
5. Identify different patterns of pronunciation disorders.
6. Define treatment priorities.
7. Identify changes in pronunciation patterns over time.

The author does not demonstrate empirically how the PACS meets these criteria for validity. On the surface the PACS appears capable of meeting the three phonological criteria. With multiple procedures to choose from, the PACS is almost certainly the most exhaustive phonological analysis published. The manual, with Grunwell's two other texts (Grunwell, 1981; Grunwell, 1982), provides a clear description of the procedures that should allow replicable and predictable data analysis. Without empirical evidence, however, it is impossible to determine if the PACS meets the two clinical objectives.

RELIABILITY. The author provides no data on interexaminer or intraexaminer reliability. She indicates, instead, that good descriptions of the procedures result in reliable instruments. She has spent considerable effort to make the procedures clear. The author strongly recommends that the user read the manual, her two texts, and Ingram (1976) prior to using the PACS. These texts are referred to extensively in the PACS manual and are prerequisite to the comprehension of many procedures. Most of the PACS manual is devoted to test administration and scoring, including the appendices containing examples of two completed protocols.

NORMATIVE DATA. Although no attempt was made to provide normative data with the PACS, a developmental profile is provided. The chart shows "stages" of phonological processes development based upon linguistic development (Crystal, Fletcher, & Garman, 1976; Crystal, 1982). Grunwell indicates these "stages" are somewhat arbitrarily forced into age ranges and must be interpreted with flexibility. She suggests a future undertaking would be empirical research using the PACS to define the phonetic and phonological characteristics of specific organic and developmental speech and language disorders.

USE OF THE TEST. The PACS is time consuming to learn, administer, and score. Prior to administration one must read the 170-page manual and a good portion of three other texts. Because the author intended for PACS users to analyze spontaneous speech, time must be spent obtaining a representative sample of the child's conversation. To reduce administration time, responses from an articulation test could be used for analysis because specific methods for obtaining the sample are not proscribed. The amount of time needed to score the PACS would vary considerably depending upon how many of the seven analyses are completed. In her preface the author acknowledges the PACS "needs a proving period of clinical trials." In its current form the PACS could be considered an experimental version of a phonological analysis. Its early distribution will allow users to collect data concerning its efficacy. Considering the limited validity and reliability information, it is difficult to recommend the use of this time-consuming procedure to clinicians.

SUMMARY. As an instrument to assess phonological development of a child's speech the PACS lacks empirical evidence of validity, reliability, and normative data. It could be used experimentally with another instrument with proven validity and reliability.

REVIEWER'S REFERENCES

Crystal, D., Fletcher, P., & Garman, M. (1976). *The grammatical analysis of language disability: A procedure for assessment and remediation.* London: Edward Arnold.

Ingram, D. (1976). *Phonological disability in children.* London: Edward Arnold.

Menn, L. (1976). Evidence for an interactionist-discovery theory of child phonology. *Papers and Reports on Child Language Development*, 12, 169-177. Stanford: Stanford University.

Sommerstein, A. H. (1977). *Modern phonology*, Baltimore: University Park Press.

Shriberg, L. D., & Kwaitkowski, J. (1980). *Natural process analysis (NPA).* New York: Macmillan Publishing Co., Inc.

Grunwell, P. (1981). *The nature of phonological disability in children*. London: Academic Press.
Crystal, D. (1982). *Profiling linguistic disability*. London: Edward Arnold.
Grunwell, P. (1982). *Clinical phonology*. London: Croom Helm.
Stampe, D. (1985). *A dissertation on natural phonology*. New York: Garland Publishing, Inc.

[285]

The Poppleton Allen Sales Aptitude Test. Purpose: "Designed to measure those attributes which are of importance for effective selling." Adults; 1984; PASAT; 15 factors: Administrative Effectiveness, Social Sophistication, Emotional Resilience, Dynamism, Economic Motivation, Empathy, Competitiveness, Organisational Ability, Work Commitment, Emotional Stability, Self-sufficiency, Verbal Fluency, Determination, Self-confidence, Entertaining; 1987 price data: £3.75 per test; £2.50 per answer sheet; £34 per manual (131 pages); £40 per specimen set; (20–30) minutes; S. Poppleton, E. Allen, and D. Garland; The Test Agency [England].*

Review of The Poppleton Allen Sales Aptitude Test by LARRY COCHRAN, Associate Professor of Counselling Psychology, The University of British Columbia, Vancouver, British Columbia, Canada:

The Poppleton Allen Sales Aptitude Test (PASAT) is an untimed test of personality designed specifically to measure traits presumed important for selling occupations. It is composed of 126 items, 99 of which are rated on a 5-point scale ranging from *very rarely* to *almost always*, and 27 of which are rated on a 4-point scale ranging from *very rarely* to *frequently*. The raw scores are converted to percentile ranks based upon norm groups of 138 salesmen and 58 saleswomen. The test yields a sales personality profile on 15 factors such as administrative effectiveness and dynamism.

Test items were initially generated by job analysis and a critical incidents interview study of salespersons. Most items concern a particular behavior in a type of situation, rather than beliefs or attitudes. The items do not concern sales behaviors, but analogous behaviors of everyday life. A person is asked to estimate the frequency of each behavior in one's life. Items were chosen in a series of studies involving criteria of significant correlation with sales volume and interrelationship with other items. The 15 factors emerged from a principal components analysis involving 136 people and 74 items (which involved item combinations).

Generally, the factors show moderate to good internal consistency and stability although there are some exceptions. In studies of salesmen, all but two factors correlated significantly with objective sales criteria and eight correlated significantly with supervisory ratings. For saleswomen, the evidence is much weaker. Although the primary use of the test is to screen applicants, there is no predictive validity available. Construct validity was assessed by factor correlations with the 16 Personality Factor Questionnaire and with supervisory ratings of questionnaire items relevant to each factor.

The validational evidence is mixed. Validity problems arise because of the low number of subjects in the norming group, because effectiveness criteria are open to extraneous influences, and because different job tasks are relevant for different selling jobs. However, part of the difficulty might involve the test itself. Concurrent validity is strongest. A factor that correlates significantly with performance one year tends to correlate significantly the second year. However, a number of factors that did not correlate significantly the first year were also found to be significant the second year.

Construct validity for the test is weaker. For one sample, most of the hypothesized relations between the 15 PASAT factors and the 16PF factors were confirmed, but for another sample, eight were not confirmed and five were partially confirmed. In another study, seven PASAT factors correlated significantly with targeted performance ratings for men while only three correlations for women were significant. Correlations among the factors tend to be strong, suggesting that the test might benefit from a regrouping of items into fewer but perhaps stronger factors. Some of the factors contain only four items at present, and whatever contribution they make to external validity might be due to overlap with other factors.

Validational evidence for saleswomen is weak in comparison to salesmen, and there is the possibility that some factors do not have the same meaning for women as they do for men. For example, self confidence for women correlated negatively with overall performance ratings in one study. Two of its five items concern talking with strangers, which could mean something very different to a woman than to a man. This factor, for instance, correlates negatively with the L scale of the 16PF, meaning that women with presumably more self confidence are more trusting and accepting rather than suspicious.

The data reported in the technical manual suggest there might be different profiles that are predictive of good salespersons. For example, in a study correlating factors with 16 aspects of job performance, 14 of the 15 factors yielded significant correlations, but nine of those factors involved significant negative correlations. Thus, salespersons who are higher on administrative effectiveness might be better at planning work in advance ($r = .27$), but worse on expressing oneself easily ($r = -.29$). If so, correlations with a single effectiveness index might mask varying strengths influencing effectiveness. One salesperson might owe his or her success to different strengths than another. Although this generates considerable complexity, it also holds open the possibility that sales managers might facilitate salespersons in quite different ways.

In general, the strength of PASAT is the task-relevant and criterion-referenced construction of test items. Its weaknesses are that the internal structure of the test requires sharpening into stronger and more differentiated factors, and that the validity for saleswomen is weaker and more uncertain than for salesmen. The test norms are more nominal than substantive; the test could not be used in an organization without developing its own norms and factor validities. It is best to view the PASAT as promising, experimental, and still in the process of development. As the authors recommend, the test's use as a screening instrument ought to be preceded by a careful study of each particular organization. Local norms, reliabilities, and validities must be established in each new setting.

Review of The Poppleton Allen Sales Aptitude Test by DAVID O. HERMAN, President, Measurement Research Services, Inc., Jackson Heights, NY:

Applied psychologists have long sought measures of personality or temperament to forecast performance on sales jobs. Tests of general ability have often proved only moderately successful as measures of sales aptitude, and it is natural to look to noncognitive domains for improved prediction. The Poppleton Allen Sales Aptitude Test (PASAT) is the outcome of an intensive research effort in Great Britain to develop just such a measure.

Most of the developmental research on the PASAT is based on samples of individuals employed in commercial sales; the commodities involved are life insurance, chemicals, brewery products, and advertising space. A few studies of reliability and of the correlation of the PASAT and other measures are based on groups of students in business and management. Thus the instrument has been developed on samples relevant to its purpose.

The PASAT had its beginnings in a study of personality factors related to sales performance. The initial item pool was based on critical-incident material gathered from interviews in two life insurance organizations. Inspection of the critical incidents suggested 12 general types of job behavior, and items were drafted to fit each category. Particular effort was made to focus the items on behavior in specific situations that would be familiar to all job applicants.

The items went through a series of three systematic, well-considered pilot studies designed to maximize the internal consistency of the initial 12 subscales, to minimize correlation with unintended subscales, and to correlate with external criteria of sales effectiveness. The final 15 PASAT factors are derived, however, from a factor analysis of the items surviving the three tryouts. Possibly the wide range in the number of items making up the 15 factors can be traced to this shift in test-construction strategy at the end of the development process.

The 126 items of the published edition of the test are clear in meaning with very few exceptions. Two items refer to consulting one's "diary." This term is likely to be misunderstood in the United States.

The questionnaire is divided into two sections. The 99 items of Section 1 are statements describing personal behavior, many referring to work situations. Examinees are to rate on a 5-point scale how closely each statement has applied to them in the past. The 27 items of Section 2 describe how other people have perceived the subject. These are to be rated on a 4-point scale according to how frequently each statement has been true of the examinee. Two kinds of answer documents are available—optically readable, and hand scorable. The directions for administration are clear and complete.

Raw scores on the PASAT factors are basically the sum of ratings given to the items of each scale. Ten of the 15 subscales include items that are negatively worded and thus reflect the negative pole of the intended construct. For each of these subscales ratings on the negative items are subtracted from the sum of ratings for the positive items; constants are then added to the resulting scores, presumably to eliminate any negative raw scores. Unhappily the hand-scoring answer sheet is so designed as to require considerable mental arithmetic, and users should recheck all scoring routinely.

To help interpret scores, the PASAT manual offers norms from a sample of 76 life insurance salesmen, from a pooled group of 138 salesmen from the advertising, brewery, and chemical industries, and from a relatively small sample of 58 women in advertising sales. The manual also includes a discussion of "Motivational distortion," or what others often call "faking good." Although no explicit quantitative measure of faking is provided, the manual suggests that high scores on several factors are a sign of such faking. Limited research suggests that six of the factors are particularly subject to this kind of response distortion.

Alpha coefficients are presented for a group of 120 life insurance salesmen, and ranged from .55 to .90 with a median of .69. Such a picture of internal consistency gives little support to the use of the PASAT for individual predictions. It is evident the number of items contributing to the 15 factors partly accounts for some of the low coefficients; the median alpha is .67 for the eight factors with between 4 and 6 items, and .81 for the seven factors with between 7 and 23 items.

The low reliabilities add to other problems in interpreting scores on some of the very short scales. Factor 6 (Empathy), for example, is one of those measured by only four items. The table of norms for 138 salesmen shows that raw scores of 13, 14, 15, and 16 on this factor correspond to percentiles of 27, 46, 62, and 81. Thus single points of raw score can have a large effect on percentile rank. Furthermore the alpha coefficient for this factor was .67. Clearly, some PASAT factors are not pulling their weight.

The validity of the PASAT in terms of its relationship to job criteria obtained concurrently with test scores was studied for varied employee samples. A number of statistically significant relationships between PASAT factors and job-performance measures were found, where the criteria were new business obtained (life insurance), commissions earned and ratings of overall performance (advertising), and ratings of sales effectiveness (chemicals). The PASAT's relationship to criterion ratings for brewery salesmen was less clear.

The construct validity of the PASAT was explored through studies of its relationship with scores on Cattell's 16 Personality Factor Questionnaire, and through factor analytic evidence. Correlations with the Cattell questionnaire were studied for a group of students in business and management, and for men and women (separately) in advertising sales. The results were generally in line with the authors' hypotheses and indicated significant areas of overlap between the two instruments. The 15 PASAT scores were factor analyzed for the same three groups. Although the three factor structures bore clear similarities, there were also differences among them that the Technical Manual seeks to explain in more detail than is probably warranted. For one thing, the male and female advertising samples contain only 43 and 31 cases, which suggest strongly the factor loadings of the 15 scores may be unstable.

EVALUATION AND RECOMMENDATION. In view of its stated purpose, the PASAT's firm grounding in sales-related job behaviors is perhaps its strongest feature. Other positive features are its extensive tryout and refinement on relevant employee groups, and some suggestive validation efforts. On the other hand, the impression of scale reliability must be called mixed, and hand-scoring procedures appear to invite error.

Employers wishing to use questionnaire data to supplement other selection techniques for identifying sales potential may consider the PASAT a candidate for their selection research, but cautions must be taken. Individual intepretations of the PASAT may not be highly reliable.

[286]

Porteous Problem Checklist. Purpose: Identifies adolescent problems. Ages 12–18; 1985; 9 areas: Parents, Peers, Employment, Authority, Self-Centred Concerns, Boy-Girl, Oppression, Delinquency, Image; manual ('85, 48 pages); 1987 price data: £5.50 per 10 self-scoring questionnaires; £9.50

per specimen set (must be purchased to obtain manual); (20–30) minutes; Murray A. Porteous; NFER-Nelson Publishing Co., Ltd. [England].*

Review of the Porteous Problem Checklist by GLORIA A. GALVIN, Assistant Professor of Psychology and Director, School Psychology Training Program, Ohio University, Athens, OH:

The Porteous Problem Checklist (PPC) was developed to better understand the nature of English and Irish adolescents' problems. It is recommended for use in screening and for diagnosis of a range of social, emotional, and personal problems faced by adolescents. The PPC is a 68-item self-report inventory for boys and girls ages 12 to 16 on which the respondents indicate, "yes, sometimes, or no" to a series of statements such as, "I worry that I might be going mad." The PPC is divided into two 34-item sections labeled Part 1 and Part 2. The author recommends using the 68-item inventory for in-depth assessment of adolescents' concerns and using the individual parts for screening purposes or for use as pre- and post-measures to assess, for example, if treatment has been successful.

The PPC items have been grouped into nine types of adolescent problems or worries called Problem Sets which are labeled Parents, Peers, Authority, etc. Raw scores on the PPC are translated into percentile ranks for each of the Problem Sets, thus indicating the percentage of the norm group that was exceeded by the respondent in amount of problems claimed. Normative comparisons are possible for each of two age groups (12–14.5, 14.5–16), in each sex, and each cultural group (English and Irish).

The PPC was developed out of the author's expressed clinical need for an efficient inventory. Unfortunately, clinical and intuitive decisions rather than sound measurement practices have dominated the development of the PPC.

The norm groups, although large (1,496 English and 1,401 Irish), are inadequately described. Participants were selected from schools in urban, rural, and inner city areas, comprised both sexes, and were ages 12 to 16. However, no percentages by sex, locale, or social class are presented. Nor is a comparison with current census data made. Yet the author claims a "representative cross-section" for the norm groups. It appears that norm-group size has been used as the measure of adequacy instead of documented representativeness.

The scale development has been a mixture of opinion and factor analysis. After preliminary testing of items, the resultant pool was submitted to a factor analysis separately for the English and Irish groups with only the former reported in the manual. The evidence presented indicates one strong factor and a total of seven factors with eigenvalues greater than 1.0. Yet, nine factors (i.e., Problem Sets) were retained in order to "retain flexibility" and to give the PPC "a broader coverage in terms of meaningful content areas." An examination of the nine Problem Sets reveals that 26 of the 68 items are present on more than one Problem Set; therefore, the nine Problem Sets cannot be interpreted as separate distinct types.

Internal consistency reliabilities for the Problem Sets range from .72 to .87 indicating moderate to good internal consistency. Stability coefficients presented for a 2-week period were only .50 to .65, casting doubt on the usefulness of the PPC as a pre- and post-test of change. The manual also presents a table of internal consistency of the Problem Sets in relation to the halves (Part 1 and Part 2) of the PPC from which they are derived. These correlations range from .86 to .95 suggesting that the PPC is measuring one general factor, and this might be a more appropriate use of the PPC rather than attempting to interpret separate factors. Unfortunately, the manual does not provide a table for interpreting the total score.

Although no evidence in the manual is labeled validity, the author does present several instances of the relationship of the PPC to other variables. For example, the PPC was shown to have modest correlations with external locus of control (.42), teenage ethnocentricism (.53), and teen agreement with traditional values (-.30). These data do suggest that teens who score high on the PPC tend to be those who would indicate problems on other measures; however, the usefulness of the PPC for indicating the specific types of problems and the extent of problems remains to be established.

Finally, a few comments are in order about the test materials. The PPC is cumbersome to hand score, and transferring the point values to the appropriate Problem Set scales is likely to result in clerical errors. In addition, the tables in the manual list the Problem Set scales in an order different from the order on the test booklet, which creates confusion when retrieving values from the tables in the manual.

In summary, the PPC items are based on reasonable clinical judgment and the scores from it show modest, positive relationship to other problem indices. The claim for the PPC as a diagnostic instrument does not seem warranted because the scales are not independent. Use as a pre- and post-measure does not appear appropriate because the test-retest reliabilities are fairly low. Furthermore, the norm groups are inadequately described. The PPC does have potential as the basis for discussion with teens who have responded to it, and this modest use which the author suggests is, perhaps, the best use for this inventory.

Review of the Porteus Problem Checklist by TONI E. SANTMIRE, *Associate Professor, Department of Educational Psychology, University of Nebraska-Lincoln, Lincoln, NE:*

The Porteus Problem Checklist is a 68-item, self-report inventory of adolescent problems that may be divided into two 34-item equivalent forms. An extensive procedure was used to develop items descriptive of typical adolescent problems and to which adolescents would respond readily. This resulted in a 94-item list that was administered to representative samples of 1,401 Irish and 1,496 English adolescents. The final form of the checklist grew out of subjecting these data to analyses for item placement in problem sets and for item ability to discriminate adolescents who reported problems at greater frequency than their peers.

The checklist is quite readable and easy to complete and score. Raw scores on the nine problem areas are derived by a system that provides more weight to problem statements indicated as being frequently characteristic of the adolescent than those scored as sometimes characteristic of the adolescent. Raw scores are converted to percentiles through the use of tables derived from the Irish and English data. The author recommends that a percentile of 75, indicating that 75% of the standardization population reported fewer problems in the area, be used as a preliminary indication of problem areas needing further exploration.

When the full scale is used tables are provided for age ranges from 12–14.5 and 14.5–16 and for boys and girls for each nationality. When the shorter forms are used the table for converting to percentiles retains the nationality distinctions but loses the sex and age range distinctions. This is appropriate, given reported differences in patterns of problem areas in the two cultural groups and the lower reliability of the shorter forms. It does, however, lead to some potential problems in interpreting the results from the short forms. It is possible for an individual to receive higher percentile ranks on both short forms than on the long form, probably because of sex and age differences. It could result in some problems with interpretation using the short forms when a problem area score ranks above the 75th percentile on each of the two short forms and below the 75th percentile on the long form. It is possible for the user to deduce where this will occur from the data presented in various tables, but it takes careful analysis to do it. The user should be alerted to this potential problem.

A quick assessment of overall problem status is provided by counting the number of items reported as being a problem on the first short form and comparing that with a percentile table. Again, a percentile value over 75 is suggested as an index of a frequency of problems that might indicate a need for further exploration of problem status.

In addition to the tables from which percentile ranks are determined, there are tables for each problem area indicating the frequency of responses to each item in the standardization population and the correlation of the item with the overall problem set score. This should be of excellent assistance to both the clinician or counselor in exploration of problem areas and to the researcher interested in particular aspects of adolescence. One needs to exercise care in using and interpreting percentiles, as the author notes, but the tables are clear and easy to use.

Another index provided is a "Clinical Indicator Ratio" (CIR). This was derived by sending the 94-item version of the checklist to 20 psychologists, psychiatrists, and social workers working with clinical populations of adolescents. They were requested to identify those items that they thought were descriptive of adolescents who were experiencing serious disturbance as opposed to those that described the normal range of adolescent problems. Items nominated by 50% or more of the clinicians were included in the final form.

The CIR is calculated by dividing the weighted score on the clinician-identified items by the absolute number of problems reported over the 64 items. Data are provided on the percent of the standardization sample whose CIR was below various levels in order to give the clinician an index of where a given adolescent stands relative to average adolescents on these items. Again, the author recommends this be used as a basis for further study, not an absolute indicator of clinical problems. The validity of the CIR has only been established through the nomination procedure. This is a very useful and important characteristic of this instrument and future research into the construct validity of the CIR is important.

The correlations of the short forms with each other and with the long form, and the reliabilities of the forms are acceptable, with Alpha coefficients ranging from .72 to .87 for the long form. A test-retest reliability study was undertaken yielding correlations on the problems area scores ranging from .50 to .65. The author correctly states that test-retest reliability is low on this type of instrument because normal adolescent problems fluctuate rapidly and often decline with time. These low reliabilities should not dissuade the potential user from considering this instrument although they do mean that dated problem checklist results should not be used as a basis for clinical work or for research designed to correlate scores with other, contemporaneous data.

The author suggests that uses of the inventory include initial screening of large adolescent populations for the occurrence of problems that might need to be dealt with, as an aid to speeding up problem definition in counseling sessions, as a means of promoting self reflection in adolescents, as an indicator of potential clinical problems, and for research on adolescence. The manual has been clearly designed to support such uses and presents the necessary data from the standardization study clearly.

The author recognizes the validity of problem checklists of this nature depends upon the cooperation of the individuals completing them and observes there is a small percentage of perfectly normal adolescents who prefer not to disclose their problems. Given the manner in which items were selected, it may also be that there are some problem areas not tapped by the test, providing no assurance that this is an exhaustive list of adolescent problems. It is clear from the normative data that there are cultural differences in the frequency of reporting of problems in various areas.

One of the most useful features of this checklist is its attempt to distinguish between those adolescents who are clinically disturbed as opposed to those who are simply having greater than average frequency of fairly typical adolescent problems. Adolescence is a time of considerable subjectively felt worries, most of which go along with the developmental nature of the period. For many research and school purposes it is useful and important to be able to identify normative problems and distinguish them from those of a more serious nature. The checklist is well designed for this purpose.

Overall, this is a well-conceived, professionally developed checklist. Its documentation does not make indefensible claims for the instrument and provides all of the information that a person needs to use the checklist for its stated purposes. It seems well suited for use in England and Ireland. The data presented on national differences in scores on the problem areas and some wordings peculiar to those populations suggest that it should be revised and normed for American or other cultural groups before it is used outside of England and Ireland.

[287]

Portland Problem Behavior Checklist—Revised. Purpose: "Developed to aid school and mental health personnel to identify problem behaviors, make classification or diagnostic decisions, and evaluate counseling and behavioral consultation procedures." Grades K–12; 1984; PPBC; 4 to 6 scores (depending on age and sex): Conduct Problems, Academic Problems, Anxiety Problems, Peer Problems, Personal Problems, Total; individual; 1987 price data: $10.95 per 25 male or female checklists; $21.95 per manual (28 pages); administration time not reported; Steven A. Waksman; ASIEP Education Co.*

TEST REFERENCES

1. Waksman, S. A. (1984). Assertion training with adolescents. *Adolescence*, 19, 123-130.

Review of the Portland Problem Behavior Checklist—Revised by TERRY A. STINNETT, Professor of School Psychology, University of Wisconsin-Whitewater, WI:

DESCRIPTION AND PURPOSE. The Portland Problem Behavior Checklist—Revised (PPBC-

R) is a 29-item, Likert-type, behavior-rating scale designed for use with students enrolled in grades kindergarten through 12. Each test item is a description of inappropriate behavior and is to be rated from 1 (no problem) to 5 (severe) by a classroom teacher or teachers who have daily contact with the target student, based upon observation or first-hand knowledge. Separate protocols are provided for male and female students. All items fall into one of 5 factor analytically determined scales: Conduct Problems, Peer Problems, Personal Problems, Academic Problems, and Anxiety Problems. Three additional spaces are provided for teachers to specify and rate behaviors that are not contained in the checklist. These items are not included in the scoring. Factor scores are calculated by adding the individual item raw scores that comprise each factor and are transferred to a profile on the protocol. Percentile ranks are listed on the right and left of the profiled raw scores.

The purpose of the PPBC-R is for data collection as a screening device or as a supplemental instrument in a more comprehensive assessment process. Data collected with the PPBC-R might then be used to identify problem behaviors, to design and evaluate counseling and behavioral interventions, to make classification or diagnostic decisions, for research and program evaluation, and to identify behaviors to be included on an exceptional student's Individual Education Plan (IEP).

ITEM DEVELOPMENT. During the 1976–77 school year, teachers referring students to a school mental health program in Portland, Oregon were asked to state the three problems of greatest concern about each referred student. Two hundred seventy-five specific problems were submitted. Instead of factor analyzing these problem statements, 29 of the most frequently stated problems were selected and included in the checklist. The items were reported to represent the concerns of teachers working with Headstart, elementary, middle, and high school students and thus face validity was obtained. The author suggests this procedure also insured content validity. However, it does not seem likely that a 29-item checklist adequately samples and represents in appropriate proportions the child-behavior problems that might result in teacher referral.

STANDARDIZATION. The Portland Problem Behavior Checklist (PPBC) was originally normed in 1977–78 on 217 randomly selected students from three elementary schools and one middle school in Portland, Oregon. The instrument was renormed during the 1982–83 school year. A random sample of 306 kindergarten through 12th grade students was selected from 10 schools in the greater metropolitan area of Portland, Oregon. Separate norms are used for males, grades kindergarten–6; females, grades kindergarten–6; males, grades 7–12; and females, grades 7–12 (males, K–6, $n = 81$; females, K–6, $n = 81$; males 7–12, $n = 79$; females, 7–12, $n = 65$). The normative data significantly limit the usefulness of the PPBC-R. Sample size was small and regionalized, therefore, the norms are likely to be unrepresentative of the U.S. population. Second, the manual does not provide an adequate description of the demographic characteristics of the normative sample such as race, socioeconomic status, or other sampling variables. As a result, potential users of the PPBC-R should proceed with caution as the appropriateness of normative comparisons cannot be adequately evaluated.

Another major problem with the PPBC-R involves the type of scores that can be derived from the collected data. Tables are provided to convert raw scores only to percentile rank scores. The test protocol has dashed lines on the profile diagrams at the 90th, 95th, and 98th percentiles. However, the significance of the dashed lines is not further explained and might easily confuse a naive test user. The author does indicate in the manual that percentile scores indicate the percentage of students in the standardization sample who received that score or a lower score. Since percentile rank scores are considered to be ordinal level measurement, the usefulness of the data collected with the PPBC-R for making comparisons is limited. Although the author suggests that interventions can be evaluated with pretest and posttest teacher ratings on the PPBC-R, such comparisons would not be appropriate with percentile rank scores. Also comparisons between the PPBC-R and other instruments becomes problematic.

PSYCHOMETRIC PROPERTIES. The PPBC-R was factor analyzed and item loadings of .40 were used as the cutoff criterion for inclusion in a factor. Factor analyses of other scales designed to identify child-behavior problems have been consistent in defining four large groups of problems: conduct, personality, inadequacy-immaturity, and socialized delinquency (Evans & Nelson, 1977). The PPBC-R factors do not completely correspond with those general problem-behavior areas but do represent other factors that have been identified as problem-behavior areas (e.g., Edelbrock & Achenbach, 1984; Walker, 1970).

One concern regarding the PPBC-R factor scores is the small number of items that comprise certain PPBC-R factors. The factor of Peer Problems (females, Grades K–6) is composed of raw scores from only two items and the factors of Anxiety Problems and Personal Problems (females, Grades 7–12) are each calculated using the raw scores from only three items. In addition, the Personal Problems factor (Males, Grades 7–12) is comprised of only two items and the Anxiety Problems and Peer Problems factors (males, Grades 7–12) are each calculated using the raw scores from only three items each. Users would have more confidence in these factors if the factors were made up of a larger number of items. The original 275 referral problems could have been submitted to an item factor analysis and more items could have been included in the scale based upon those results.

Split-half and test-retest reliabilities are quite adequate. Split-half reliability of the PPBC-R was estimated using coefficient alpha and was .94 (n = 306) for the entire sample. Split-half reliability coefficients are also reported by gender. Test-retest reliability was estimated after a 1-month interval using a random sample of 239 students from grades kindergarten through high school and was estimated to be .81. Test-retest correlation coefficients are also reported by gender and by grade. Specific item reliabilities and interrater reliabilities are also reported but are not as adequate. The mean item reliability coefficient was .71 and individual item reliabilities ranged from .34 to 1.00. Interrater reliability for the total score was estimated to be .54. Because the interrater and item reliability coefficients are somewhat low, PPBC-R users should make only cautious inferences about the target student based on the teacher's rating. A safeguard procedure could be to obtain multiple ratings on the target child and to obtain data with alternate methods (e.g., systematic behavioral observation).

Construct validity of the PPBC-R was assessed by correlating the PPBC-R with the AML Checklist and the Walker Problem Behavior Identification Checklist. Correlation coefficients of .57 and .66 were obtained. These correlations are somewhat low, but the PPBC-R author does not address these low correlation coefficients. The PPBC-R was also correlated with the Piers-Harris Children's Self Concept Scale and the Waksman Social Skills Rating Scale. Correlation coefficients of .49 and .65 were obtained. The author also reports a study where PPBC-R ratings of students who received at least 1 month of psychological treatment showed more improvement than did a control group. Finally, a comparison of total scores of 24 emotionally disturbed in residential placement and a random sample drawn from the norm group of middle school students was completed. The groups were noted to be significantly different (t = 4.97, p <.001). The relationship between the PPBC-R and direct observations of behavior needs to be established.

SUMMARY AND LIMITATIONS. The PPBC-R has limited usefulness as a behavior rating scale. The author fails to address any of the scale's limitations in the test manual and overstates the potential uses and advantages of the PPBC-R. Small sample size and regionalized norms are likely to be unrepresentative of the population. The lack of information on race and socioeconomic variables limits the ability of PPBC-R users to evaluate the appropriateness of normative comparisons. Comparisons between the PPBC-R and other instruments and assessment of intervention effects are problematic because the instrument yields only percentile rank scores. Interrater and specific item reliabilities are not adequate for behavior rating scales. In conclusion, the PPBC-R might be recommended for use only as a screening instrument, however, the Walker Problem Behavior Identification Checklist or the Child Behavior Checklist would likely be better selections.

REVIEWER'S REFERENCES

Walker, H. M. (1970). Walker Problem Behavior Identification Checklist test and manual. Los Angeles: Western Psychological Services.

Evans, I. M., & Nelson, R. O. (1977). Assessment of child behavior problems. In A. R. Ciminero, K. S. Calhoun, & H. E. Adams (Eds.), *Handbook of Behavioral Assessment*. New York: John Wiley & Sons.

Edelbrock, C., & Achenbach, T. M. (1984). The teacher version of the Child Behavior Profile: I. Boys aged 6-11. *Journal of Consulting and Clinical Psychology*, 52, 207-217.

Review of the Portland Problem Behavior Checklist—Revised by JOHN G. SVINICKI, Powell Associates, Inc., Austin, TX:

The Portland Problem Behavior Checklist is a 29-item screening test for identifying problem behaviors. The three to five factors (depending on age and sex) are interpreted by plotting them on a profile form that yields a percentile rank for each factor. There are some minor problems such as a poorly written manual, references to tables that are not in the manual, and directions for using the checklist forms that do not match the forms themselves. These minor problems will not be detailed here because they are, in a sense, irrelevant due to the severity of the three major problems to be discussed.

The first major problem with the Portland Problem Behavior Checklist has to do with the factors derived from the checklist. The standardization data were factor analyzed *separately* for the following groups: male, kindergarten through sixth grade (n = 81); male, seventh through twelfth grade (n = 79); female, kindergarten through sixth grade (n = 81); and female, seventh through twelfth grade (n = 65). The resulting factors were different for each group. This, in and of itself, is not a problem. More important is the question of the stability of factors derived from such small samples. Beyond that issue, however, are other issues as well. Whatever one thinks about factor analyzing 29 items with data from 65 to 81 students (depending on the group), the factors that resulted in this case pose some interesting problems. For example, several of the factors have only 2 or 3 items in them. A factor with so few items could very easily turn out to be unreliable and, hence, of little meaning. Those items that did not have a factor loading of .4 or greater on any factor were put in a category called "other." The real problem is that the "other" category contains important problem behaviors, yet this category does not show up on the interpretive profile. Given the general rationale for conducting a factor analysis, it is appropriate that "other" is *not* on the profile because it is not, technically, a factor, but this means that several problem behaviors are not included in the analysis of a given student's problem behavior. For example, examining the factors for females, kindergarten through sixth grade, one finds three factors plus the "other problems" category: Conduct Problems has 8 items, Peer Problems has 2 items, Personal Problems has 8 items, and the "Other Problems" category has 11 items. Included in the "Other Problems" category are important behaviors such as drug abuse, stealing, lack of independence, and low academic achievement; but no measure of the severity of these problems can be obtained for students in this group. A list of 29 problem behaviors seems small enough as it is but then to be left with only 18 to evaluate seems to eliminate any usefulness the checklist might have had in the first place.

A related problem is that it appears some of the factor names are not accurate descriptions of the factor content. Because the factor name will be used as shorthand for the item content, that name should describe the content as accurately and completely as possible. Some teachers might wonder why being inattentive is a "personal" problem for a sixth grade female but an "academic" problem for a seventh grade female. Although the manual contains some statements describing why the factors are configured as they are, the difficulty of interpreting the results of this checklist is of sufficient magnitude to make one question its value as well as the conceptual framework from which it was developed. If nothing else, answering questions from teachers and parents about the meaning of the results could be especially problematic.

The second major problem with the Portland Problem Behavior Checklist is that reliability and validity data are presented only for the total score. Unfortunately, the total score does not appear on the interpretive profile. As a result, the Portland Problem Behavior Checklist lacks any evidence of reliability and validity for factor scores even though these scores provide the only basis for interpreting Portland Problem Behavior Checklist results. Considering the small number of items in some of the factors, the absence of factor reliability data is particularly troublesome. In addition to being irrelevant to interpreting Portland Problem Behavior Checklist results, the reliability and validity data presented for the total score are mixed. The samples of teachers and students from which the data were obtained are not adequately described. The data presented for concurrent validity of the total score are, at best, moderate and the rationale for selecting some of the concurrent measures is not clear.

The third major difficulty with the Portland Problem Behavior Checklist is that the percentile ranks were derived from a total sample of 306 students (162 students in grades K–6 and 144 students in grades 7–12). A breakdown of the sample by grade is not presented. The entire sample was selected from schools in Portland, Oregon. In addition to the small sample (given the large grade range), the geographical limitation of the sample makes use of the "normative" data questionable, at best, for test users in other parts of the country.

In short, the Portland Problem Behavior Checklist is not an appropriate instrument to use for assessing problem behavior. There are several conceptual and practical problems with the factors that make interpretation of the results of the Portland Problem Behavior Checklist difficult or impossible. The normative data are based on a small sample of students in Portland, Oregon and there is no evidence presented to establish that the factor scores are reliable and valid measures. The potential for misuse of Portland Problem Behavior Checklist scores is very great. Given the severe deficiencies of the Portland Problem Behavior Checklist with regard to current test construction standards, users should select another instrument for assessing problem behaviors in students. The Behavior Evaluation Scale (McCarney, Leigh, & Cornbleet, 1983) is an instrument that can be reliably and validly used to assess problem behavior in students. The Behavior Rating Profile (Brown & Hammill, 1983) is another instrument that possesses good reliability and validity. These instruments were standardized with national samples and meet most of the current standards for test development.

REVIEWER'S REFERENCES

Brown, L. L., & Hammill, D. D. (1983). Behavior Rating Profile. Austin, TX: PRO-ED, Inc.

McCarney, S. B., Leigh, J. E., & Cornbleet, J. A. (1983). The Behavior Evaluation Scale. Columbia, MO: Educational Services.

[288]

Power Base Inventory. Purpose: "Designed to measure the kinds of power which a manager (or supervisor) chooses to use with subordinates." Managers and supervisors; 1985; self-administered; 6 scores: Information, Expertise, Goodwill, Authority, Reward, Discipline; manual (20 pages including inventory); 1987 price data: $5.25 per each 1–99 inventories (minimum order $20); (10) minutes; Kenneth W. Thomas; XICOM, Inc.*

Review of the Power Base Inventory by RABINDRA N. KANUNGO, Professor of Psychology and Management, McGill University, Montreal, Quebec, Canada:

The main purpose of the Power Base Inventory is to assess the reasons for subordinates' compliance with supervisors' wishes when these wishes are expressed in different ways (e.g., suggestions, directions, requests, orders, etc.). The theoretical basis of the inventory is the typology of social power and influence processes developed by French and Raven (1959). Ordinarily, operationalization of the French and Raven typology of social power deals with five bases of power: reward, coercive, legislate, expert, and referent. The Power Base Inventory is designed to measure these five power bases plus a sixth, referred to as information power. The possibility of informational influence was suggested by French and Raven (1959) but was not considered to be a primary source of power. By accepting the informational influence as a separate primary source of supervisory power and measuring it independently, the Power Base Inventory appears more inclusive in scope compared to other measures (e.g., Kanungo, 1980; Student, 1968).

In addition to the inclusiveness criterion, the Inventory is different from other measures of French and Raven social power framework in yet another way. The Inventory is designed to assess the six bases of supervisory power through supervisor's perception of subordinate's reasons for compliance. The common practice, however, following French and Raven's theoretical rationale, is to use subordinates' own perceptions of their reasons for compliance (Podsakoff & Schriesheim, 1985). Since the Inventory is meant to reveal supervisor's rather than subordinates' response, the scores cannot be interpreted as true indications of subordinates' reasons for compliance. Rather the scores indicate supervisor's perceptions of subordinates' reasons, and being one step farther removed from subordinates' reasons, such perceptions may be influenced by unknown attributional errors.

The Inventory uses a paired comparison format with 30 paired items designed to measure six power bases. The range of scores for each power base is 0 to 10. The use of multiple items forced-choice technique is a considerable improvement over other single item questionnaire formats (e.g., Kanungo, 1980) for drawing a comparative profile of six power bases. In spite of such improvements, there are serious problems with content validity. For instance, one finds no information on item construction and no justification for item content.

A careful examination of the items reveals that several items in the Inventory appear too general and vague. Such items are open to different interpretations. For example, Item 27A, "They have to agree with the facts that I use for support," can be interpreted two ways. Subordinates may agree because of the merits of the facts (informational influence) or because the facts are used by a superior (legitimate power base).

Furthermore, inclusion of several direct attributional statements such as Item 17A, "They enjoy doing what they can for me," creates problems. Inclusion of such items enhances the possibility of attributional and social desirability errors. It would be more appropriate to use only behavioral items such as Item 12B, "I show them how to properly interpret and deal with the situation, so that we agree."

A different type of problem affecting content validity stems from changing the referents across items. The Inventory uses some items that reflect the supervisor's direct perception of resources under his/her control and other items that reflect the supervisor's perception of similar resources through the eyes of subordinates. Item 25B, "I am able to get them to see why I am right" is an example of the former type, and Item 26B, "They think I could be tough with them if I had to" is an example of the latter type.

It is not clear whether an adequate sampling of the content domain was achieved. A cursory look at the five to seven items reflecting each power base reveals the item content to be very narrow. In addition, the dimensionality of a given domain remains unknown, as does the internal consistency of items measuring a given power base. Failure to provide such information makes assessment of construct validity difficult.

There is no information on how the six power bases are related to each other. Without such data, it is hard to justify informational influence as a primary power base separate from the influence exerted through supervisor's expertise.

The Inventory provides descriptions of how to score and interpret profiles of individual respondents. Percentile data based on the profiles of 317 managers from a variety of organizations are provided to serve as norms. Although the norms are useful, this information is hardly adequate considering the lack of data on reliability, dimensionality, stability, and validity of the Inventory.

A qualitative description of six bases of "managerial power," the conditions under which each power base is effective, and the interpretation of high and low scores are useful appendages from a practitioner's point of view. However, no information is available demonstrating the effectiveness of a given power under specific conditions (i.e., criterion-related validity). Furthermore, there is no information on conditions under which two or more power bases in combination may be more effective than such power bases operating in isolation.

In summary, the Power Base Inventory does not represent a reliable and valid standardized instrument for measuring bases of managerial power. Hence it cannot be useful as a diagnostic tool to identify the nature of a manager's influence over subordinates. However, it can be used during training sessions as a structured exercise or a training tool that can sensitize managers to the nature of the social influence processes within organizations.

REVIEWER'S REFERENCES

French, J. R. P., & Raven, B. (1959). The bases of social power. In D. Cartwright (Ed.), *Studies in social power*, (pp. 150-167). Ann Arbor, MI: Institute for Social Research.

Student, K. R. (1968). Supervisory influence and work group performance. *Journal of Applied Psychology*, 52, 188-194.

Kanungo, R. N. (1980). *Biculturalism and Management*. Toronto: Butterworths.

Padsakoff, P. M., & Schriesheim, C. A. (1985). Field studies of French and Raven's bases of power: Critique, reanalysis, and suggestions for future research. *Psychological Bulletin*, 97, 387-411.

Review of the Power Base Inventory by CHARLES K. PARSONS, Professor of Management, Georgia Institute of Technology, Atlanta, GA:

The Power Base Inventory provides a measure of a manager's perception of his/her bases of power over his/her subordinates. The instrument is based primarily on the work of French and Raven (1959). The instrument yields scores on six scales representing six bases of managerial power. These scales are (*a*) Information, (*b*) Expertise, (*c*) Goodwill, (*d*) Authority, (*e*) Reward, and (*f*) Discipline. The test booklet contains one page of introduction, three pages of forced choice items (a total of 30 item pairs), one page for self scoring the instrument, one page for graphing a power base profile, and nine pages of score interpretation. There is also a page where the respondent is asked to provide background data to be sent along with the data sheet back to the authors of the instrument.

The instructions for the forced choice items are clear. The respondent is forewarned that some item pairs may appear equally descriptive, but is instructed to choose one item from each of the 30 item pairs. The items appear to be approximately matched on social desirability, though no data concerning social desirability were provided. This might cause some uneasiness among respondents because there are likely to be times when they feel both statements are equally descriptive (or nondescriptive) of their beliefs.

For each of the 30 item pairs, the respondent simply circles the item (A or B) that is more characteristic of his/her subordinates' reasons for compliance. Some of the items are used more than once in a different pair. The basis for item construction was not included in the materials that this reviewer saw. The power base tapped by each item is apparent to one who knows the French and Raven typology.

The respondent can score the instrument by circling the letter of the item chosen for each pair on a special scoring sheet. The number of items are totaled for each of six scales. Scores can range from 0 to 10 for each scale. Because of the ipsative nature of the scales, the respondent cannot get the maximum (or minimum) number of points on all scales.

Scores on each scale can be converted to percentiles using a chart provided by the authors. The norming group is described as "317 managers in a variety of organizations." It should be noted that the authors encourage the respondent to send a copy of his/her data sheet and background information to the authors. This action leads this reviewer to believe that more specific norming data will be provided in the future.

The interpretation of scores includes a description of each of the six power bases. The descriptions are brief but clear. There are also descriptions of situations when use of each power base is desired and what is required to use this power base effectively.

Finally, there are warning signals for respondents who scored high or low on a particular scale. The signals are meant to be diagnostic and help the manager determine why he/she tends to hold certain beliefs. These warning signals are provided for high and low scorers on all six scales.

No validity or reliability data were provided to this reviewer. The construct of managerial power bases deserves further research. It is hoped that the authors will provide data in the future concerning the relationships between scores on the six scales and other managerial behaviors. Because the interpretations of the scales are situational and normative (certain power bases are more appropriately used in certain situations), research needs to be conducted to substantiate the suggestions offered as part of this instrument.

REVIEWER'S REFERENCE

French, J. R. P., & Raven, B. (1959). The bases of social power. In D. Cartwright (Ed.), *Studies in social power* (pp. 150-167). Ann Arbor, MI: Institute for Social Research, University of Michigan.

[289]

Preschool and Kindergarten Interest Descriptor. Purpose: "Identify children with attitudes and interests usually associated with preschool and kindergarten creativity." Ages 3–6; 1983; PRIDE; downward extension of the Group Inventory for Finding Creative Talent; scale for rating by parents; 4 dimension scores: Originality, Imagination-Playfulness, Independence-Perseverance, Many Interests; 1984 price data: $55 per complete set including manual (10 pages), and 30 scales; $10 per specimen set; scoring service included in the cost of the test; (20–35) minutes; Sylvia B. Rimm; Educational Assessment Service, Inc.*

Review of the Preschool and Kindergarten Interest Descriptor by GLORIA A. GALVIN, Assistant Professor and Director, School Psychology Training Program, Ohio University, Athens, OH:

The Preschool and Kindergarten Interest Descriptor (PRIDE) was developed as a screening measure for young children who may qualify for programs for the creatively gifted. The inventory contains 50 questions to which parents respond regarding their own or their child's interests and behaviors. The responses are made on a Likert-type scale. Given the question, "My child likes to do hard puzzles," parents may check " *no*," " *to a small extent*," "*average*," "*more than average*," or "*definitely*." Group administration of the inventory to parents while visiting school is recommended.

In order to score the inventory, it must be sent to a scoring service that promises to return results within 1 month of receipt. The results are reported in percentile ranks and Normal Curve Equivalent scores for the total PRIDE inventory and in stanines for the four dimensions of the PRIDE, reportedly based on factor analysis of the inventory. Perhaps it is an understandable business decision not to allow users to score the inventory themselves; however, this requirement does introduce a significant delay in receiving the results for use in decision making. This is a problem in a screening device that should be followed by more focused assessment of creativity on those who have been screened "in." The length of time needed to receive screening results adds significantly to the amount of time in the overall assessment process.

The PRIDE inventory has several attractive features. It is brief and easy to administer; parents will not find the questions at all threatening and should, in fact, find them easy to answer. The use of parents as respondents allows for assessment of young children who would not be good candidates for self-report methods. Finally, PRIDE offers a substitute for teacher-nomination methods of identifying creative children that have been found unsatisfactory.

Unfortunately, there are also significant problems with the PRIDE inventory in regard to purpose and development. Its purpose is described in the manual as, "to screen children 'into' a program and not 'out' of a program." No cutoff scores are provided nor recommended to be developed from local norms. Although the purpose of screening should be to be overly inclusive (and to follow screening with additional assessment of those screened "in"), failure to screen anybody "out" seems to leave the PRIDE inventory without a clear purpose. Given the stated purpose, the author does not feel constrained to provide any information regarding the decision-making efficiency of PRIDE. The issue of false positives and false negatives has been avoided. Rather, users are told that students not selected by high PRIDE scores may be selected by other means such as teacher nomination, even though it is the criticisms of teacher nomination (Rimm, 1984) that has spurred the development of PRIDE.

The psychometric data gathered during the development of the PRIDE inventory appears promising. However, the data are only minimally reported. Internal consistency reliability is reported for the total inventory as .92; however, no further information is provided on the subjects upon whom this was based nor on the details of that study. More importantly, no assessment of test stability or interrater (e.g., mother, father) reliability is presented, and these would both be useful in judging the value of this instrument.

Three studies of criterion-related validity are reported. Subjects numbered 62, 18, and 14 children, respectively. Two significant correlations (.50, .38) are reported for two of the subject groups between PRIDE and a composite criterion score based on a drawing of a picture, a "brief dictated story," and a teacher rating. This evidence is promising; however, two of the sample sizes are very small and details about the subjects and the study are not given, making judgment of the quality of the evidence impossible.

Construct validity for the PRIDE is asserted based on the evidence that test items were taken from preschool characteristics of creative children reported in papers by scholars in the area of creativity. Furthermore, the PRIDE is reported to contain four dimensions determined by factor analysis. Unfortunately, the factor analysis is not reported in the manual other than to indicate that it was performed and to name the factors (dimensions) obtained from the analysis. No report is made of how many items make up each dimension, the number of subjects on which the analysis was based, or how reliable the factors are. The norm group for the PRIDE is reported as 114 children representing urban, rural, and suburban areas. No further description as to age, sex, or any other relevant characteristics is provided. If the purported factor analysis was based on the norm group, the sample is too small to yield reliable results from a factor analysis of a 50-item inventory.

In summary, the PRIDE is a good first step towards development of a creativity screening measure for preschoolers that may eventually prove to be more useful than teacher nomination. The items have face validity and have been derived from several research sources. What is needed is an effort to administer the PRIDE to a large representative sample that could be the basis for a carefully described normative population. Then factor analytic, reliability (consistency, stability, and interrater), and validity studies need to be carried out and reported to the potential user in the manual. As currently presented, the PRIDE costs approximately $1.33 per administration and requires the examiner to wait a month for results of questionable value.

REVIEWER'S REFERENCE

Rimm, S. (1984). The characteristics approach: Identification and beyond. *Gifted Child Quarterly*, 28, 181-187.

Review of the Preschool and Kindergarten Interest Descriptor by SUE WHITE, Assistant Professor of Psychology, Case Western Reserve University, School of Medicine, Cleveland, OH:

According to the author, this assessment instrument was designed "in order to provide an easy to administer, reliable and valid instrument for use in screening preschool and kindergarten children for programs for the creatively gifted." This questionnaire consists of 50 items to which a parent responds on a 5-point scale. Scoring is to be done only by the test publisher and is included in the original cost of the test. The author indicates that this test is to be used to include a child in a creativity program, but admits that a low score should not be allowed to restrict a child's admission if the teacher feels such would be appropriate. This reviewer believes, however, that all children at this age (3–5 years) should be included in any such creativity programs.

Psychometrically this test does not meet adequate standards as its norms are based on "114 children representing urban, suburban and rural populations." The extremely small sample coupled with the lack of other demographic information makes this test unacceptable for applicability to a larger population, especially for providing for the tracking of children at a very young age. The test manual provides very scanty data relative to reliability and validity. It is felt that this test should be avoided and is inappropriate for the purpose for which it was designed.

[290]

Preschool Behavior Rating Scale. Purpose: Measures the level of children's preschool behavioral skills in the psychomotor, cognitive, and social areas. Day care, Head Start, or nursery school children ages 3–6; 1980; PBRS; ratings by teachers; 9 scores: Coordination, Expressive Language, Receptive Language, Environmental Adaptation, Social Relations, Total, Language Skills, Socialization Skills, Psychomotor Skills; individual; 1986 price data: $7 per basic packet including blank scale and manual ('80, 23 pages); $2 per blank scale; $6.50 per manual; $3.50 per technical monograph; William F. Barker and Annick M. Doeff; Child Welfare League of America, Inc.*

Review of the Preschool Behavior Rating Scale by MARY LOU KELLEY, Assistant Professor of Psychology, Louisiana State University, Baton Rouge, LA:

The Preschool Behavior Rating Scale (PBRS) is a 20-item instrument for assessing preschoolers' psychomotor, cognitive, and social skills. The scale is completed by teachers on children aged 3–6 who are enrolled in a daycare or preschool program. As described in the scoring manual, the PBRS can be used to: (*a*) screen for developmental delays; (*b*) identify children in need of further evaluation; (*c*) objectively monitor children's skill acquisition over time; (*d*) guide teachers' selection of appropriate curriculum; and (*e*) evaluate program effectiveness.

The items are grouped into five domains: Coordination, Expressive Language, Receptive Language, Environmental Adaptation, and Social Relations. All items are written using a Guttman scaling format with 4–5 response choices. Item choices range from lower to higher skill levels. Raters are required to select the response choice closest to the actual behavior of the child.

In part, each item is intended to assess a child's skill level within a very broad area. In doing so, the measure can be completed in a short period of time and yields information about a variety of skills relevant to preschoolers' adaptive functioning.

The manual emphasizes evaluating children based on observed behavior rather than the child's potential. Although objectivity is emphasized, many of the items appear to lack adequate specificity for obtaining objective ratings. For example, the item used to assess fine motor skills contains response choices ranging from "1. Generally unable to use or manipulate preschool materials requiring fine motor skills, eye-hand coordination (e.g., crayons, scissors, buttoning, or unbuttoning)," to "3. Occasional awkwardness in using these materials," to "5. Easily and deftly uses preschool materials." As the above example indicates, the language of many of the items may be too complex and the discriminations too fine for some preschool teachers to accomplish easily.

The behaviors assessed by the test reportedly were chosen because they occur in a preschool setting, are observable, and are relevant to development. Although the skills covered by each item reportedly were evaluated by mental health workers and educators, they were not derived through empirical methods. In addition, given the brevity of the test it is not clear whether the items adequately represent the skill area or whether the skill areas covered by the test accurately reflect those important to preschoolers' adaptive functioning.

The PBRS has been normed on a heterogeneous sample of children (N = 1,367). Norms are available at 6-month intervals for both male and female children aged 3–6 years. However, the number of subjects per group is, in some cases, relatively small. Based on these normative data, children are categorized as typical, questionable, and atypical for each of the five skill areas. The authors stress that this categorization is not to be used for diagnostic purposes. However, the manual does not specify clearly how the test results are to be used to accomplish the stated purposes of the test.

The manual accompanying the test is generally well written. Like the text itself, however, the instructions for completing the test may be difficult for some preschool teachers to interpret. Furthermore, adequate information regarding the misuses of test data is not provided.

A significant amount of research has been conducted on the reliability and validity of the PBRS. Correlation coefficients were computed to assess interobserver agreement, internal consistency, and alternate-item-format reliability. The interobserver reliability coefficient for the total score was .89. However, the manual did not specify how these data were obtained (e.g., amount of training the teachers received prior to completing the instrument). Split-half and alternate-item-format reliability coefficients were acceptable. However, the authors did not adequately assess exact agreement between raters. They also did not adequately validate whether item choices were "true" Guttman scales as neither the coefficient of reproducibility nor scalability was obtained. In some instances the scale items appeared to be difficult to distinguish from one another or did not appear to represent a "true" sequence of skills.

Factor analytic studies supported the validity of the PBRS. The results of the factor analysis yielded three relatively nonoverlapping factors (Language, Social, and Psychomotor).

The predictive validity of the PBRS was evaluated by assessing the degree to which the test differentiated between children with and without a "problem." The authors did not specify criteria for subject selection. The results indicated that total test scores did not differentiate the two groups. However, when scores for all items were entered into the discriminant analyses, only 15% of the atypical children and 7% of the typical children were misclassified.

The PBRS has a number of positive features. The test is brief, relatively easy to complete and score, and apparently reliable. In spite of the positive features of the test, the test items lack specificity and in my opinion are fairly ambiguous and susceptible to rater bias. In addition, the authors failed to specify how the respondents are to use the information to accomplish the purported purposes of the test. Reliability and validity studies relevant to the stated purposes of the test have not been conducted to an adequate degree. In attempting to efficiently assess a wide variety of skills, the authors may have failed to develop a test that can be consistently administered. Unfortunately, the manual does not provide sufficient training in the interpretation and uses of test data and thus information obtained from the test could be easily misused by individuals unfamiliar with test administration and interpretation. Thus, I do not recommend use of this test for the purposes cited in the manual.

Review of the Preschool Behavior Rating Scale by F. CHARLES MACE, Associate Professor, Graduate School of Applied and Professional Psychology, Rutgers University, Piscataway, NJ:

DESCRIPTION AND PURPOSE. The Preschool Behavior Rating Scale (PBRS) is designed to assess psychomotor, cognitive, and social skills of children ages 3–6 who are enrolled in day care settings or Head Start programs. The main purposes of the PBRS are (*a*) to facilitate screening of preschoolers to identify those who show signs of developmental problems (without diagnosing or categorizing children), and (*b*) to permit monitoring of progress in preschool behavioral skill development over time.

After a minimum of 4 weeks observation, teachers are asked to rate individual children on 20 items, each of which consists of four or five Guttman-scaled options. These options describe observable skills ordered from lower to higher skill levels according to a developmental perspective. For purposes of interpretation, PBRS items are grouped in the following ways: (*a*) Total Score (all 20 items); (*b*) 3 Factor Scores (Language, Socialization, and Psychomotor Skills); and (*c*) 5 Subscores (Coordination, Expressive and Receptive Language, Environmental Adaptation, and Social Relations). Within each of these groupings, summed ratings are compared to norms by sex and age group (6-month intervals) and are classified as either Typical, Questionable, or Atypical.

STANDARDIZATION. Norms for the PBRS were established on a sample of 1,367 children. Sampling procedures were not reported. The sample included male and female children of low and high socioeconomic status (SES), black and white racial groups, and ages ranging from 36 to 71 months. Statistical analyses showed that, of the four groupings (sex, SES, race, and age), PBRS scores differed significantly only by age and sex. On the basis of these findings, separate norms were developed for males and females at six different, 6-month interval age groupings. The norms for future versions of the PBRS could be strengthened by (*a*) describing the sampling procedures, (*b*) obtaining multiregional samples, and (*c*) including Hispanic children.

RELIABILITY. Pearson product-moment correlations were computed for interrater, split-half, and alternate forms reliability. The most important of these for an instrument measuring behavior—interrater reliability—showed that independent ratings of children by pairs of teachers correlated highly (generally $>.80$) for the PBRS total, three factor groupings, and five subscore groupings. One exception was the Coordination subscore, for which the median correlation was .65. This high level of correspondence between independent ratings of child behavior increases our confidence that the instrument provides reasonably accurate measures of the behaviors surveyed.

Split-half and alternate forms reliability for the PBRS total were .94 and .98, respectively. These values suggest a high degree of internal consistency among rating-scale items.

VALIDITY. Three types of validity have been assessed for the PBRS: face, factorial, and concurrent validity. With respect to face validity, PBRS items were constructed, in part, on the basis of interviews with nonprofessional and professional mental health workers and educators after they examined the scale. In general, the resulting items correspond to observable child behaviors that require few inferences regarding hypothetical conditions or motives. Although generally reflecting observable behaviors, some items are ambiguous, leading to difficulties with scoring and interpretation. For example, many item options include multiple parts (e.g., item VIII: 1 "Generally avoids joining groups, disrupts or does not participate appropriately"). In such cases it is not clear how to score and interpret the item if the child exhibits some but not all of the behaviors. Guidelines for dealing with this problem are discussed in the manual, but they are complicated and seem unlikely to be followed.

Another factor contributing to the ambiguity of some items is option differentiation based on terms such as "generally," "markedly," and "occasional" (e.g., item II). Without specific criteria which differentiate such options on the basis of amount of behavior exhibited, the validity of these items is questionable.

A final concern regarding the development of the PBRS items is the lack of empirical evidence for the developmental ordering of item options. Although most item options seem to follow a logical developmental sequence, some do not. For example, it seems questionable that children normally progress from "almost never initiates any activity" to "can usually find a variety of acceptable activities" (item XV). Empirical validation of these developmental sequences would greatly strengthen the PBRS.

Factor analysis of PBRS items resulted in a solution with a clearly determined factor structure. Thus, there is empirical evidence for the existence of three factors (Language, Social, and Psychomotor Skills).

One of the most important characteristics of a screening device is its ability to discriminate those in need of additional evaluation or services. Discriminant function analyses on low SES children revealed that the PBRS, in combination with age and sex information, could differentiate between typical children and children previously diagnosed as having a problem. Only fifteen percent of atypical children and seven percent of typical children were misclassified. It is important to note that this level of differentiation was found only when all item scores were used.

Two shortcomings of the PBRS concern the scale's insensitivity to important dimensions of behavior (e.g., frequency, duration, latency, etc.) and the absence of research showing a correspondence between PBRS scores and actual child behavior. Insensitivity to dimensions of behavior places limits on the use of the scale beyond screening purposes. The authors suggest in the manual that the PBRS may be used for program development and evaluation. In this reviewer's opinion, the PBRS is not well suited for these purposes. Program development requires detailed information regarding specific skill strengths and deficits as well as the conditions that promote and inhibit their display. Such information is best obtained through curriculum-based assessment and direct observation. Similarly, program evaluation is best achieved via repeated measures of behaviors that have been targeted for improvement.

The problem of unestablished score-behavior relationships is common to behavior rating scales. In the case of the PBRS, concern is diminished somewhat by high levels of interrater reliability, which are suggestive of accurate measurement. However, the PBRS could be at the forefront of behavior rating scales if future versions addressed the problems of insensitivity to dimensions of behavior and score-behavior relationships.

In summary, the Preschool Behavior Rating Scale appears to be among the best screening devices for teachers to identify children who may have problems in the development of language, social, or psychomotor skills. Its principal strengths are the ability to facilitate agreement between independent raters and to identify those children in need of further evaluation or services. Future versions of the PBRS would be strengthened by expanding its norm groups, increasing sensitivity to various dimensions of behavior, and establishing the correspondence between PBRS scores and actual child behavior. Until these objectives are achieved, the scale should be used principally for screening purposes.

[291]

Preschool Development Inventory. Purpose: "A screening inventory designed to help identify children with developmental and other problems which may interfere with the child's ability to learn." Ages 3–0 to 5–5; 1984; parent's report of child's current functioning; 1985 price data: $6 per 25 question/answer sheets and mimeographed manual (7 pages); administration time not reported; Harold Ireton; Behavior Science Systems, Inc.*

Review of the Preschool Development Inventory by R. A. BORNSTEIN, Assistant Professor of Psychiatry, Departments of Psychiatry and Psychology, Ohio State University, Columbus, OH:

The Preschool Development Inventory (PDI) appears to be a condensation of the Minnesota Child Development Inventory (MCDI) and the Minnesota Preschool Inventory (MPI), both by the same author. Not surprisingly, the Preschool Development Inventory has the same goal, that is, the identification of children with developmental problems that could contribute to learning problems. It is unclear whether the author conceptualizes the PDI as a substitute for the previous tests, or as a "screening device" to be followed in some instances by the other inventories. Given the apparently extensive overlap of items, it may be that the PDI represents a cost- and time-effective substitute for the other measures.

The normative data base is that reported for the MCDI. That sample was sufficiently large, but (as emphasized in a previous review of the MCDI) permits generalization primarily to white, middle-class families. The PDI then suffers similar constraints. The PDI is divided into five sections. Two sections request parents to respond to questions regarding general development or specific problems. The other three sections elicit narrative descriptions aimed at obtaining parent's concerns and perceptions about the child.

The first section contains 60 items from the MCDI, and covers seven developmental areas. The items included in the PDI are described as "among the most age-discriminating items of the MCDI," although the basis for this item selection is not explicitly presented. Furthermore, the balance of item selection in the various areas is very uneven, with 33 of the items related to Language Comprehension (19) or Expressive Language (14). This very likely contributes to the differential sensitivity of the test. A child's score is compared with the mean of children who are 25% younger, and those below this cutoff are described as delayed. This operational definition has some appeal, but is not without problems. No information is provided about the variability of performance in the normal sample, which is likely to be considerable. It would be helpful to know the accuracy of the test using other types of cutoffs, such as two standard deviations from the mean of normals. No formal classification studies have been included in the manual.

The authors suggest using a cutoff score based on the combination of males and females from the normal sample. While the author is aware of the different base rates of children with delays, he suggests that a case can be made for identifying more males than females as delayed. There is some merit to this view, but there is an insufficient discussion of the issues, and no data are presented to justify the use of combined scores. If in fact males do develop more slowly than females, the intent of the test should be to identify "abnormal" delay, and thus sex-specific cutoffs should be employed. Fortunately, the author provides such sex-specific cutoff scores. The remainder of the PDI essentially serves as a broad outline for a structured interview of the parent.

In essence the PDI is an amalgamation of two previous tests. The two primary components of the test are a general developmental scale that is poorly balanced in depth of inquiry in various areas, and an outline for a structured interview. The PDI appears to be shorter and more efficient than the previous tests, and its value may be in terms of its cost and time savings. It is more likely to be useful in screening settings where potential obstacles to learning may not be readily apparent. This is consistent with the author's goals for the test, and he carefully acknowledges that the test is not intended as a substitute for more formal testing. As a screening device, the test may be a time- and cost-efficient adjunct to the early identification of children with possible developmental delays.

[292]

The Preverbal Assessment-Intervention Profile. Purpose: "Developed as an individualized assessment for severely and multihandicapped preintentional learners." Low functioning handicapped infants and children; 1984; PAIP; 7 scores for Stage One (developmental ages 0–1 month): Motor, Communication, Visual Awareness of Objects, Auditory Awareness of Sounds, Earliest Interaction Patterns, Reflex/Motor, Tactile Acceptance/Defensiveness; 6 scores for Stage Two (developmental ages 1–4 months): Motor, Communication, Visual Attending, Auditory Attending, Social Bond Attending, Reflex/Motor; 5 scores for Stage Three (developmental ages 4–8 months): Motor, Communication, Orienting to Objects, Orienting to Persons, Reflex/Motor; individual; 1987 price data: $14.95 per 5 assessment record booklets; $29.95 per assessment manual (46 pages); administration time not reported; Patricia Connard; ASIEP Education Co.*

Review of The Preverbal Assessment-Intervention Profile by PATRICIA MIRENDA, Assistant Professor of Special Education and Communication Disorders, University of Nebraska-Lincoln, Lincoln, NE:

The Preverbal Assessment-Intervention Profile (PAIP) was designed to evaluate sensorimotor and prelinguistic behaviors in individuals labelled severely/profoundly retarded and/or multihandicapped. The assessment manual provides protocols for determining the level at which to begin detailed assessments, as well as protocols for the in-depth assessments themselves. In addition, the manual includes a section related to developing goals and personalized objectives based on the assessment results.

The PAIP assessment is designed more as an observational protocol than as a test per se. That is, unlike many assessments used with individuals who are handicapped, there is not a series of predetermined items or skills that are either "passed" or "failed" by the person being tested. Rather, the assessment involves a series of detailed observations and analyses of learner behavior in a number of sensorimotor areas during both naturalistic and contrived interactions. The result is a profile of learner responses and initiations to caregivers under a number of conditions. This unusual mode of assessment is intuitively appealing in that it allows a great deal of flexibility to the examiner; provides for many alternative response modes by the learner; and, perhaps most importantly, potentially results in an increased appreciation by the examiner of the subtle responses (called communiques in the PAIP) of the severely handicapped individual to a variety of environmental events. Unlike most assessments that might be used with severely multihandicapped learners, this instrument provides a structure for *learning about* the person being assessed rather than simply assigning a developmental age score based on some arbitrary set of tasks.

There are several problems, however, that militate against the usefulness of the instrument. The major problem is that the protocols are extremely complex and time-consuming and would seem to be virtually impossible to utilize in a classroom situation by examiners (e.g., teachers) who have not received fairly extensive training in the assessment format. The protocols require that the examiner possess finely-tuned behavioral observation and recording skills as well as an appreciation of the subtleties of learner-caregiver interactions. Further, the directions for conducting many of the observations are so detailed that they are quite confusing and would require several careful readings by an examiner in order to understand exactly how each protocol is to be administered. In several instances, the manual contains terms that require specialized knowledge; however, these terms are left undefined. For example, the Assessment Record for Reflex/Motor Skills (Stage 3, Form C, page 32 of the manual) contains items such as "A.T.N.R. Inhibited" and "S.T.N.R. Inhibited," which require considerable knowledge of primitive reflex patterns in order to be relevant. ("A.T.N.R. Inhibited" means that the asymetric tonic neck reflex, a primitive reflex pattern normally seen in infants and elicited by turning the head to the side, does not occur. "S.T.N.R. Inhibited" means that the symetric tonic neck reflex, elicited in normal infants by extending or flexing the neck, does not occur.) In attempting to go beyond the traditional "pass-fail" assessment format (a commendable goal in itself), the author(s) seem to have gotten so entrenched in detail that the result is an extremely complex and very confusing instrument.

In addition to this major drawback, there are some rather serious flaws with the test reliability and validity studies as reported in the manual. First, the interobserver reliability measures reported (average percent agreement = 92%) are misleading in that the calculations were completed after the observers received a *total of 12 hours* of lecture, recitation, and simulation training in the assessment protocols. Thus, the calculations would seem to indicate that the *training* was effective in teaching the observers to use the instrument reliably, but not that the instrument as it stands alone (i.e., without training) produces reliable results. In addition, the test-retest reliability report states that "all [15 individuals involved] received the same communication and reflex/motor stage placement during both testing situations." However, since there are only three stages possible for placement, this level of agreement could be easily achieved even if the specific results of the detailed profiles varied widely between the two testing sessions. Finally, the validity measure correlates the scores reported in five areas on the PAIP with analogous scores on the Early Learning Accomplishment Profile (ELAP). The latter test is not well known and is apparently quite new, as it does not appear in the most recent *Mental Measurements Yearbook* (Mitchell, 1985). Thus, it is difficult to assess the strength of the validity correlations provided for the PAIP since these depend, in turn, on the degree of validity of the ELAP for which no information is available.

Finally, the PAIP is not clear concerning the question of how the assessment results are translated in educational programs once the assessment has been completed. The test format provides a procedure to translate the observational data into a series of scores; however, these scores seem to have no bearing on the intervention goals that might be produced and serve no other discernible purpose aside from summarization of the test results. Thus, the suggestions provided for developing goals and objectives flow directly from the observational records themselves; this has the advantage of allowing maximum utilization of the results for each learner on an individualized basis. However, the suggested goals and objectives provided in the manual are problematic in that they tend to emphasize teaching tasks that are largely nonfunctional (and, for learners over the age of 5, chronological-age-inappropriate) in nature. That is, the goals and objectives are unlikely to result in the learner's ability to participate in meaningful domestic, recreation/leisure, vocational, and/or general community activities in integrated settings (Brown, Branston, Hamre-Nietupski, Pumpian, Certo, & Gruenewald, 1979; Brown, Falvey, Vincent, Kaye, Johnson, Ferrara-Parrish, & Gruenewald, 1980). The result may be that, after expending considerable energy in learning to conduct and in administering the assessment, the examiner is left with a large amount of very detailed information that is difficult to translate into meaningful goals, activities, and/or programs. As a tool that has the potential for teaching adults to observe and appreciate the unique and subtle behaviors exhibited by learners labelled severely/profoundly and/or multiply handicapped, the PAIP has much to offer. However, as an assessment instrument to aid in the development of functional, meaningful programs for this population, the instrument falls far short of its intended purpose.

REVIEWER'S REFERENCES

Brown, L., Branston, M. B., Hamre-Nietupski, S., Pumpian, I., Certo, N., & Gruenewald, L. (1979). A strategy for developing chronological-age-appropriate and functional curricular content for severely handicapped adolescents and young adults. *Journal of Special Education*, 13, 81-90.

Brown, L., Falvey, M., Vincent, L., Kaye, N., Johnson, F., Ferrara-Parrish, P., & Gruenewald, L. (1980). Strategies for generating comprehensive, longitudinal, and chronological-age-appropriate individualized education programs for adolescent and young-adult severely handicapped students. *Journal of Special Education*, 14, 199-215.

Mitchell, J. V., Jr. (Ed.). (1985). *The ninth mental measurements yearbook*. Lincoln, NE: The Buros Institute of Mental Measurements.

Review of The Preverbal Assessment-Intervention Profile by DAVID P. WACKER, Associate Professor of Pediatrics and Special Education, The University of Iowa, Iowa City, IA:

The Preverbal Assessment-Intervention Profile (PAIP) was "developed to assist specialists in answering the question, 'What can we do to help this child learn to communicate needs and wants?'" According to Connard, the administrative procedures of the PAIP "provide for an indepth probe that allows the examiner to obtain representative samples of an individual's abilities within the natural setting. Discrete behaviors indicative of the individual's information processing abilities (interactions with things), communication abilities (interactions with people), and motor abilities are observed and recorded." The PAIP uses a "Piagetian sensorimotor framework" to evaluate the responding of severely handicapped persons who function within the first three sensorimotor stages of development (birth to 8 months). To assist these individuals in obtaining intentional communication behavior, Connard argues that an assessment must be first conducted to "ascertain information relative to the child's ability to communicate awareness, attending, and orienting." Once these behaviors have been identified, intervention programs can then be developed which build on the child's current skills and hopefully promote greater communication ability. The PAIP, therefore, is solidly based within the developmental orientation, and was developed specifically for use with the lowest functioning individuals within the severe/profound range of functioning.

The PAIP is comprised of four sections: (*a*) a preliminary evaluation of communication and motor abilities for deciding further assessment needs; (*b*) a diagnostic profile of variations in age-stage levels of functioning across several areas; (*c*) a narrative section arranged by developmental and functional areas providing descriptions of the child's current level of functioning, deficits, and instructional needs; and (*d*) a listing of developmentally based learning goals and objectives "to assist in appropriate program planning" (based on the results of assessment). The assessment manual provides a description of how each of these sections should be administered, how the data should be recorded in the record booklet, and also provides an example to assist the examiner in understanding how to administer the test.

To use the PAIP, the examiner begins by completing the Preliminary Placement Evaluation Profile. This can be completed either through interview, direct observation in natural situations, or through elicited responding. The preliminary placement evaluation is used as a screening procedure to determine at which stage of development the child is functioning, and consists of very few items (6 communication and 4 motor items at Stage 1). Scoring of each item (e.g., "Is the learner aroused by human voices?") is conducted by indicating "Yes," "No," or "Not applicable." The child's performance on these items is then used to determine if assessment should be conducted at a higher level (Stage 2) or if a diagnostic assessment within that stage appears appropriate. The diagnostic evaluation is then conducted to assess individual patterns of performance within a given stage of development. These patterns of performance provide the information needed to "design and implement effective intervention programs" using the goals and objectives sheets provided in the record booklet.

Connard reports that the PAIP was developed by reviewing 26 instruments used in facilities serving severely handicapped persons. An initial item pool of 785 behaviors was field-tested with 20 teachers of severely handicapped infants, children, and adults. The results of the field test led to the inclusion of the current items using the present format. No further information is provided on the construction of the test or how individual items were specifically selected.

Two reliability studies are reported in the manual. The first study evaluated interrater agreement across 25 pairs of observers each of whom assessed two severely handicapped individuals, while the second reported test/retest reliability over an average of 26 days with 15 severely handicapped persons. Interrater agreement was collapsed across all items within a stage, and ranged from 88% to 96% agreement. No data are provided for the test-retest reliability, except that the students "received the same communication and reflex/motor stage placement during both testing situations."

One validity study is also reported in the manual, where the communication and reflex/motor placement scores of the PAIP were correlated with skill areas from the Early Learning Accomplishment Profile for 35 severely handicapped persons. Five Spearman rank correlation coefficients were computed resulting in correlation coefficients ranging between .84 and .94.

In interpreting these findings, Connard states that the results of these studies "strongly suggest that the PAIP can be used reliably and validly with severely, profoundly, and multihandicapped individuals." Although these preliminary data are positive, it is premature to conclude that the test is either reliable or valid. For example, no data are provided on the intercorrelations across items or stages, and no data are provided on how successful children are in programs based on the results of assessment.

Of potential concern is the administration of the PAIP with untrained examiners. A great deal of flexibility is present in the administration procedures, which may limit the overall generalizability of the findings. For example, the directions for the Stage One Preliminary Placement Evaluation indicate that the learner should be observed "in a variety of situations." No guidelines are given regarding how many environments should be sampled, what activities should be available, how long the observation periods should be, etc. With respect to the items (e.g., "Is the learner visually aroused by humans?"), no specific criteria are provided to evaluate this behavior, especially if inconsistent behavior occurs. For the interrater agreement investigation, Connard reported that observers received at least 4 hours of training. Given the flexibility available in the administration of the test, it would seem that at least this amount of training would be needed for examiners to achieve acceptable levels of interrater agreement.

In summary, the data presented in the manual regarding the reliability and validity of the PAIP are positive, but should be considered as preliminary data. Given the great amount of flexibility in the administration of the test, it will probably be necessary for examiners to receive at least some training (and possibly extensive training) prior to the use of the test in applied settings. Although the use of the PAIP may prove useful for programs that already emphasize a strong developmental orientation to training, it should be used with some caution given the lack of reliability and validity data reported in the manual. Especially important to note is the fact that no data are provided that establish a link between the assessment and intervention components of the PAIP.

[293]

Printing Performance School Readiness Test. Purpose: Identifies preschool children exhibiting an excessive number of form errors in printing as an early warning sign of later school failure. Ages 4–6; 1985; PPSRT; individual; 1986 price data: $60 per portfolio including spiral binder containing presentation material, 500 response sheets, 100 scoring sheets, and manual ('85, 54 pages); $20 per 500 response sheets and 100 scoring sheets; (10–15) minutes; Marvin L. Simner; Guidance Centre [Canada].*

Review of the Printing Performance School Readiness Test by CAROL MARDELL-CZUDNOWSKI, Professor of Educational Psychology and Special Education, Northern Illinois University, DeKalb, IL:

This is an easy test to administer and score and appears to have high test-retest and interrater reliability. Children are tested individually in a nontimed, nonthreatening situation. Testers may be classroom teachers or nurses; the primary requirement is that they are familiar with the standardized procedures in the manual and the scoring criteria. Administration and scoring takes approximately 10 to 15 minutes per child. Prekindergarten children are requested to copy the 41 letters or numbers, one at a time, while kindergarten children are requested to draw what they have seen from memory following a 2–3 second exposure.

The scoring criteria are presented clearly with ample completed response sheets that allow for practice and familiarity with the criteria. One idiosyncracy needs to be noted. If a child traces over a letter but the overall form of the final reproduction closely resembles the letter in the spiral binder this is not scored as a form error; however, if the child realizes a mistake has been made midway through printing or even after the construction and then self-corrects, only the child's first attempt is scored.

The author assumes that as children get older, they will make fewer form errors. However, it is reported in the manual that the mean error score of children at mean age of 4-10 is 14.8 while the mean error score of children at mean age of 5-3 is 16.3. Although the authors recommend three cutoff scores depending on a child's age, it appears that it is not possible to have different "form error" score cutoff points for the two age groups cited above, when in actuality the older group made more errors (according to the results from the normative sample). On the other hand, separate cutoff scores at the end of kindergarten appear appropriate. Thus the use of two, rather than three, different cutoff points is recommended (one before kindergarten instruction; one after kindergarten instruction).

As a norm-referenced test, the size of the sample is adequate, but the sample appears to be based upon one readily available population. Means and standard deviations are given for the three age groups, but internal consistency and standard errors of measurement are not presented.

Concurrent validity was established on the basis of two sets of criterion measures: standardized test performance and academic performance in school. Both appear to be satisfactory. Predictive validity was calculated separately for the three different testing times. Using teachers' evaluations and eliminating children who were not clearly "good" or "poor" because they would be ambiguous, the cutoff points correctly identified 70–80% of all the at-risk children while achieving an overall classification hit rate in the vicinity of 80%. This hit rate may be considered quite good for a brief screening test.

The author takes care to point out that this test should be used for preliminary screening only because it is not possible to determine whether a child has not been successful due to perceptual, motor, perceptual/motor integration, and/or attention problems. He also discusses the fact that certain in-class behaviors will aid in identifying those children who did not do well on the Printing Performance School Readiness Test (PPSRT) (false positives) but really do not need early assistance. However, he does not discuss the children who will be missed by this test (false negatives), who may remember the letter or number and draw it adequately but still may have language or conceptual problems that will interfere with school success.

On the basis of this screening, further testing is recommended for those children for whom the at-risk odds are 1:1 or higher. The author even names a few specialized instruments that may be used before making any recommendations regarding early intervention. It would be much easier for the test user if the author used something more common (e.g., *z*-score, percentile, standard score) than at-risk odds. On the other hand, the author should be commended for encouraging school districts to develop locally adjusted norms which take into consideration different age and promotion criteria.

[294]

Problem Management Survey. Purpose: "Measures the perceptions you and your coworkers hold of how you manage the problems and opportunities that arise in your job." Employees; 1982; self-scoring; 8 scores: Valuing, Priority Setting, Information Gathering, Definition of Cause, Idea Getting, Decision Making, Involvement, Planning; 2 versions: participant, other; 1985 price data: $55 per 10 participant surveys and profile and interpretive notes (11 pages); $20 per 10 other surveys; (20) minutes; McBer and Co.*

[The publisher advised in November, 1987 that this test has been discontinued.]

Review of the Problem Management Survey by GREGORY H. DOBBINS, *Assistant Professor of Psychology, Louisiana State University, Baton Rouge, LA:*

The Problem Management Survey is based upon the experiential learning model and focuses on the problem-solving activities of managers. It asks managers to indicate the frequency with which they engage in 48 problem-solving behaviors. The items are designed to measure managerial approaches to the four stages of problem solving: (*a*) Situation Analysis, (*b*) Problem Analysis, (*c*) Solution Analysis, and (*d*) Implementation Analysis. In addition, the instrument assesses whether the respondent approaches each of the four stages from either operations management (i.e., based upon analytic processes) or innovation management (i.e., based upon intuition/participation). Thus, the Problem Management Survey assesses eight functional areas of management: (*a*) Priority Setting (analyzing the situation with operations management); (*b*) Valuing (analyzing the situation with innovation management); (*c*) Definition of Cause (analyzing the problem with operations management); (*d*) Information Gathering (analyzing the problem with innovation management); (*e*) Decision Making (solving the problem with operations management); (*f*) Idea Getting (solving the problem with innovation management); (*g*) Planning (implementing the solution with operations management); and (*h*) Involvement (implementing the solution with innovation management). Each of the eight subscales contains six items.

The Problem Management Survey has two major assets. First, it is based upon the experiential learning model and focuses on problem-solving behaviors. This theoretical orientation is a welcomed change from the typical leadership/management instrument that attempts to categorize managers as either "person-oriented" or "task-oriented" (e.g., *Situational Leadership*, Hersey & Keilty, 1980). Second, the instrument is easily scored by managers, thus providing quick feedback concerning their strengths and weaknesses. Remedial training programs can be developed based upon the results of the instrument.

Although the rationale behind the Problem Management Survey is intuitively appealing, the validity of the experiential learning model has not been demonstrated. In fact, the only data cited in direct support of the approach are several quotes by either practicing managers or management trainers. Until the theoretical orientation of the instrument is validated, organizations may be wasting their time and resources with it. Even more disconcerting is the possibility that the instrument may provide managers with inaccurate feedback which could, in turn, result in decreased performance (Ilgen, Fisher, & Taylor, 1979).

Even if the authors could present empirical support for their theoretical orientation, I could not recommend the use of the Problem Management Survey in its present form. The instrument violates almost all of the guidelines of the *Standards for Educational and Psychological Testing* (AERA, APA, NCME, 1985). The technical manual does not present any information about reliability, validity, standard error of measurement, means, or variance of the instrument. Furthermore, the independence of the eight subscales is questionable, and since normative data are not presented, the user is unable to determine what represents a high or low score on each dimension.

Numerous other problems exist with the Problem Management Survey. Since all items are positively worded, response bias could contaminate scores. In addition, the instrument is extremely transparent, and supervisors could fake responses to receive any score they desired. Furthermore, some of the items do not appear to be measuring the appropriate construct. Finally, the technical guide is inadequate and does not describe scale development, appropriate uses for the scale, or report any psychometric information.

Although there are glaring problems with the instrument, the Problem Management Survey may have great potential for organizations. Its focus on problem solving is intuitively appealing and in sharp contrast to most leadership/management questionnaires. It is unfortunate that the authors either did not adequately develop the instrument or failed to describe such development. At a minimum, the authors should (*a*) Determine coefficient-alpha and test-retest reliability for each subscale; (*b*) analyze the 48 items to see if they load on the eight a priori determined factors; (*c*) determine the correlation between scores on the instrument and managerial effectiveness; and (*d*) provide means, standard deviations, and norms for each subscale.

In summary, although the Problem Management Survey may have great potential, I would not recommend its use until its psychometric properties are evaluated. Given the potential utility of the instrument, I strongly urge the authors to conduct such work at once. Although management training instruments like the Problem Management Survey may have a positive effect on the productivity of an organization, they could also have negative effects if they are not reliable and valid. Thus, all test publishers and client organizations should demand reliable and valid managerial assessment instruments with comprehensive technical manuals. Hopefully, the authors of the Problem Management Survey will respond to this call.

REVIEWER'S REFERENCES

Ilgen, D. R., Fisher, C. D., & Taylor, M. S. (1979). Consequences of individual feedback on behavior in organizations. *Journal of Applied Psychology*, 64, 349-371.

Hersey, P., & Keilty, J. W. (1980). *Situational leadership: Leadership scale.* San Diego, CA: Learning Resources Corporation.

American Educational Research Association, American Psychological Association, & National Council on Measurement in Education. (1985). *Standards for Educational and Psychological Testing.* Washington, DC: American Psychological Association, Inc.

[295]

Problem-Solving Decision-Making Style Inventory. Purpose: Provides feedback on one's perception of problem-solving and decision-making styles of self or others. High school and college and adults in organizational settings; 1982; self-administered questionnaire; ratings by self or other on 4 problem-solving and decision-making styles: Delegative, Facilitative, Consultative, Authoritative; no manual (administrative and scoring instructions included in instrument); 1984 price data: $2.95 per test booklet; administration time not reported; Paul Hersey and Walter E. Natemeyer; University Associates, Inc.*

Review of the Problem-Solving Decision-Making Style Inventory by DAVID N. DIXON, Professor and Department Chair of Counseling and Psychology Services, Ball State University, Muncie, IN:

The Problem-Solving Decision-Making Style Inventory consists of two forms, one completed by the person being rated and one completed by another person, that attempt to describe the typical style a person uses to solve problems and make decisions. The two forms consist of 12 items each that are administered in a weighted, forced-choice format. Thus, for each of four dimensions (Authoritative, Consultative, Facilitative, and Delegative) two items for each dimension are paired with the two items for each of the other three dimensions.

The inventory is more appropriately a measure of administrative style as it pertains to solving problems and making decisions. It does not consider dimensions such as impulsivity or means-ends analysis, major dimensions of problem-solving from a more internal, information-processing perspective.

There is no manual for the inventory; thus no reliability, validity, or normative data are available. For an inventory that costs $2.95 for each two-page test booklet, the user receives very little that describes the development of the inventory or information about how the inventory can validly be used.

The inventory seems to be loosely related to a Situational Leadership Model of management. This is never made explicit and whether the inventory does, in fact, measure the supportive/directive dimensions as suggested is purely speculative.

This inventory, until further developed and reported upon, is indicative of the lack of consideration of psychometrics in the management field. Until such time as this inventory and other similar administrative style inventories demonstrate they are reliable, valid instruments, consumers are strongly admonished to avoid use. Buyer beware!

Review of the Problem-Solving Decision-Making Style Inventory by PAUL MCREYNOLDS, Professor of Psychology, University of Nevada-Reno, Reno, NV:

The Problem-Solving Decision-Making Style Inventory (PDSI) is a short self-administered and self-scored form intended for use in conjunction with the theory of situational leadership developed by Paul Hersey and Kenneth Blanchard (1982). In order to describe and evaluate the PDSI it will be helpful first to briefly summarize this underlying theory.

The theory deals primarily with leadership in management situations, but is held also to be applicable in educational and family settings. Two dimensions of leadership—one concerning directive (task-oriented) behaviors and the other concerning supportive (relationship) behaviors—are posited. By considering these two dimensions together four leadership styles are defined. Thus, Style A involves high directive behavior and low supportive behavior (Authoritative style). Style B emphasizes high directive and also high supportive behavior (Consultative style); in Style C directive behavior is low, but supportive behavior is high (Facilitative style); and in style D both directive and supportive behaviors are low (Delegative style).

The PDSI attempts to apply this model to two aspects of leadership—problem-solving and decision-making. One form of the inventory is devised to assay these two aspects in terms of the way the subject perceives his or her own behaviors, and an alternate form is designed to reveal how the subject perceives the problem-solving and decision-making behaviors of a specific other individual. The PDSI is a four-page form. Page 2 is the actual inventory. The other pages consist of instructions for self-administration, self-scoring, and interpretation. The inventory includes 12 items, each item consisting of two statements concerning how a person might behave in a problem-solving or decision-making situation, with each statement representing one of the four leadership styles (e.g., "Share ideas and attempt to reach consensus on a decision" reflects the Facilitative style). The subject is requested to answer each item by distributing a total of 3 points between the two statements. These values are then summed in such a way as to represent the relative dominance in the subject's responses of given problem-solving and decision-making styles.

The situational leadership theory of Hersey and Blanchard is plausible and worthy of respect. Further, the PDSI appears, in principle, to reflect the basic postulates of the theory. The PDSI cannot, however, be recommended as an adequate instrument for assessing individuals with respect to the different styles subsumed by the theory. The inventory is too brief (each style is represented by only two statements, which when paired with each of the other three styles yield the 12 items), and lacks the necessary psychometric bases to function as a diagnostic instrument. Moreover, it is this reviewer's understanding (personal conversation with Paul Hersey) that the PDSI authors do not conceive of the inventory as a test in the usual sense of accurately measuring individuals, but rather think of it as primarily an instructional exercise to use in classes, management workshops, lectures, and the like. Certainly, the format and clarity of the form should make it an excellent device for illustrating certain aspects of the theory of situational leadership, provided it is made clear to participants that the form cannot adequately serve to provide valid information on individuals.

Because of the possibility, however, that some workers might be tempted to employ the PDSI as a formal assessment instrument, it should be noted that internal consistency, reliability, and validity data on the instrument have not been reported, nor have the intercorrelations among the different style scores. There is no manual, and the only information on interpretation of the form is that on the form itself. No doubt an adequate test to assess situational leadership variables could be constructed, but the PDSI, at least as presently developed, does not constitute such an instrument.

In sum, the PDSI appears to be useful as an instructional aid in delineating the situational leadership theory, but it is not appropriate for use as a psychological test.

REVIEWER'S REFERENCE

Hersey, P., & Blanchard, K. H. (1982). *Management of organizational behavior: Utilizing human resources* (4th ed.). Englewood Cliffs, NJ: Prentice-Hall.

[296]

Process Technician Test. Purpose: "To evaluate the knowledge of industrial process workers in specific subject areas." Applicants or incumbents for jobs where process knowledge is a necessary part of training or job activities; 1985; PTT; 9 scores: Lubrication, Welding and Mechanical, Electrical, Chemical, Inspection, Metal Testing, Computers, Statistical Process Control, Total; 1986 price data: $10 per reusable test booklet; $40 per 500 answer sheets; manual ('85, 16 pages) and hand scoring keys also available from publisher; 120(130) minutes; Roland T. Ramsay; Ramsay Corporation.*

Review of the Process Technician Test by RICHARD C. ERICKSON, Professor and Chair, Department of Practical Arts and Vocation-

al-Technical Education, University of Missouri-Columbia, Columbia, MO:*

The Process Technician Test was developed for use with applicants or incumbents for jobs where process knowledge is a necessary part of training or job activities. More specifically, the developer intended for scores on this test to be predictive of job performance measures in jobs requiring processing knowledge and skills.

The test contains a total of 195 multiple-choice items distributed as follows: Lubrication, 12 items; Welding and Mechanical, 40 items; Electrical, 25 items; Chemical, 31 items; Inspection, 31 items; Metal Testing, 30 items; Computers, 15 items; and Statistical Process Control, 11 items. Nearly all items are clearly written and conform to accepted guidelines for preparing multiple-choice items. They provide what appears to be a good sample of the lower levels of the cognitive aspects of a process technician's work; knowledge of terminology and specific facts that are important to this occupation. Items that are designed to assess higher level cognitive skills are not included in this instrument.

Of particular concern is the omission of items designed to assess examinees' ability to make applications, an area of major importance to this occupation. The basis for the subject areas and terms included in this test was the judgment of three experts—a general manager, an operations manager, and a process engineer. A formal on-the-job task analysis (involving incumbent process technicians and focusing on the tasks performed and the tools and equipment and work aids used by these workers) would have been a more appropriate basis for the development of this test.

Norms and other descriptive statistics provided by the publisher are based upon a sample of 84 (75 male and 9 female) former metal processing workers. This reviewer sees as concerns here (*a*) small sample size and (*b*) the use of former workers from a technologically advancing occupational field. The K-R20 reliability estimate (.90) and the standard error of measurement (8.1) reported for this test suggest that the test might be adequate when used in making decisions regarding groups of persons. Item analysis data (difficulty index and point-biserial r for each item) indicate that 10 percent of the items are negatively correlated with total test score. Others show little or no correlation. Reliability of this test could and should be increased. A modified Angoff technique was used to derive a cutoff score with a preceding range of marginal scores for use in making individual selection decisions. Caution should be exercised when using this test and these derived scores to compare or to make decisions about individuals.

The most serious shortcoming of this test is that the publishers provide no empirical data upon which to judge its validity. The test may be considered to have a degree of content validity because it was developed with the assistance of experts who were knowledgeable of the job duties of electrogalvanizing process technicians. However, neither construct validity (as might be demonstrated by finding successively higher mean scores for higher levels of observed performance on the job) nor predictive validity (as might be shown by finding a high correlation between test scores and supervisors' ratings sometime after initial employment) have been demonstrated. At present one is at a loss to interpret what a given obtained score means based on the data for this test as reported.

In summary, the Process Technician Test is a very specialized test and probably the only one of its kind. It is composed of items that appear to be well written. It has an excellent set of administration instructions. Its format and printing are of a professional quality. However, while the test does have potential for evaluating the knowledge of both incumbent and potential process technicians, further attention should be given to (*a*) upgrading items where needed to increase test reliability and (*b*) conducting the research needed to demonstrate the relationship between specific levels of performance on this test and various levels of acceptable and unacceptable performance on the job. Otherwise, users of this test will have to do this type of research and generate the local norms, expectancy tables, and the like that are needed in order to interpret scores and make decisions based on these scores.

[297]

Productivity Assessment Questionnaire. Purpose: Assesses an employee's opinions about productivity in the organization in which they work. Employees; 1984; self-administered and self-scored; 11 areas: Policy, Leadership, Objectives, Inputs, Performance, Technology, Work Procedures, HRD,

Work Quality, Managerial Skills, Quality of Work Life; no manual; price data available from publisher; administration time not reported; Robert C. Preziosi; Source Publications, Inc.*

Review of the Productivity Assessment Questionnaire by ROBERT M. GUION, University Professor Emeritus, Bowling Green State University, Bowling Green, OH:

This inventory has 44 items, each with a 4-point response scale, providing 11 scores, each presumably measuring an "area of productivity." Some item content is like a job satisfaction survey, some like an organizational climate questionnaire, some like a leadership questionnaire—all raising a question about the validity of the items as measures of productivity, however defined. The use of only four items per scale raises a reliability question. With no manual of any kind, the usual reliability and validity questions, questions about norms or, indeed, the suitability of the items for different work settings, have no answers either for practitioners or for researchers. A letter to the publisher requesting technical data was not answered.

Standards (or technical recommendations) detailing information that should be included in a manual for tests or related instruments have been published in 1954, 1966, 1974, and 1985. What justification can a test developer have for selling a psychometric instrument without providing evidence of meeting at least some of the standards? Without at least some technical information, no firm evaluation is possible, but this reviewer doubts whether these scales merit the attention of potential users.

[298]

Program Self-Assessment Service. Purpose: "To assist colleges and universities that are carrying out departmental or program reviews at the undergraduate level." Faculty members, students majoring in the department, and recent graduates; 1986; PSAS; results are summarized and reported for groups only; 16 scores: Environment for Learning, Scholarly Excellence, Quality of Teaching, Faculty Concern for Students, Curriculum, Departmental Procedures, Available Resources, Student Satisfaction With Program, Internship/Fieldwork/Clinical Experiences, Resource Accessibility, Employment Assistance, Faculty Work Environment, Faculty Program Involvement, Faculty Research Activities, Faculty Professional Activities, Student Accomplishments; 3 forms: Faculty, Students, Alumni; 1986 price data: $.50 per questionnaire (specify Faculty, Student or Alumni); no charge for transmittal forms; $.10 per confidential envelope (includes cost of opening envelopes at ETS); processing by publisher at $1.50 per questionnaire plus $50 per Summary Data Report; $20 per optional subgroup report; (30–45) minutes; Educational Testing Service.*

Review of the Program Self-Assessment Service by DARRELL L. SABERS, Professor of Educational Psychology, University of Arizona, Tucson, AZ:

The Program Self-Assessment Service (PSAS) includes a set of three questionnaires, each for a different intended respondent group, namely, undergraduates, alumni, and faculty members. Some items are common to all three questionnaires, while others are unique to each form. Additional items may be provided by the institution using the service. There are adequate procedures to allow respondents to remain anonymous. The PSAS plan is the type most likely to be followed by an institution desiring information from its respondents, and is supported by a scoring and reporting service.

Because no interpretation is suggested for the results, it is appropriate that there are no data supporting reliability and validity and that there are no norms or standardization sample. However, there are "Preliminary Comparative Data" available at this writing and more complete data are promised. This review will focus on the appropriateness of the preliminary data anticipating the comments will be useful in assessing the data available later.

The PSAS is purported to "reflect the particular concerns of undergraduate departments and programs" and therefore its validity should be judged by the degree to which the concerns included in the questionnaire reflect the concerns of the institution. However, because there is provision for including as many as 20 questions developed by the institution, the critique should focus on items included rather than items omitted. There is no need for "content" validity as usually defined because there is no curriculum with which to compare the table of specifications for the questionnaire.

The items are clearly written and should be understood easily by the intended users. Part 1 of the questionnaire uses a format that is criticized by Converse and Presser (1986) because each item asks for both agreement and intensity of feeling. Although this item type is clearly suspect with respect to including two constructs in each item, the popularity of Likert scales demonstrates that the problem is common. However, the reader of a report will have to decide whether "agree strongly" to a statement like "The program is academically demanding for most students" means the respondent agrees strongly that the program is demanding (to some unknown degree) or agrees that it is very demanding. No one interpretation is clear, though many are chosen by various readers of such reports.

A few items appear to be of questionable quality or to be categorized incorrectly, but most items are acceptable. A questionable placement, for example, is one item regarding service on an editorial board of a journal placed in the category of research. This item may belong more correctly in the category of professional activities.

The sample report and the booklet presenting comparative data are easy to read and present useful information. However, they suggest a potential problem with interpreting results. Responses from faculty, students, and alumni are presented for easy comparison with no regard for the precision of the data. In one display the results are presented as a bar extending from unity to the mean for each group, rather than as a confidence interval around each mean. With this display, group responses resulting from small samples may be judged to be more important than is justified due to sampling error. Using the bar to represent the mean plus and minus two standard errors (or plus and minus one standard deviation) would be much more useful to the reader. All comparisons, across groups within years and across years, should be presented as confidence intervals. In the comparison data, using the bar to show the standard deviation across programs would aid interpretation. Summaries that now present number of respondents, means, and standard deviations of responses could present the standard error of the mean as well.

There are serious problems with the preliminary comparative data based on responses from 13 colleges. Although 85% of the students surveyed attended part time, 88% of the alumni for those same institutions reported that they had attended full time. How meaningful are such data for providing a basis for interpreting results of other institutions when they are misleading for the colleges assessed?

There are a number of meaningless composites of items reported as summary scores. Item scores are summed across item types; that is, items rated from agree to disagree are combined with items rated from poor to excellent, presumably because all have four response categories. Another problem is a composite that represents a combination of items measuring different variables or factors. In the summary of the alumni questionnaire, four items about the college's help in obtaining employment are combined with the item "how helpful were letters sent directly to employers without knowing of openings." Why should the adequacy of a college's placement service be judged by the helpfulness of letters sent without the assistance of the placement service?

Regional differences in alumni's approximate annual income are ignored in the report of comparative data. One would expect more complete and useful reporting of comparative data when the data are available. Given the necessity for publisher scoring of the surveys, a more adequate data base should be available in a short time.

None of the potential misuses of the PSAS is suggested by the publisher. It may be impossible to identify a suggested misuse of a program that doesn't purport to do anything but contribute to "the improvement of undergraduate programs," since how this contribution is to be made is not stated, and no specific interpretations of any data are suggested. However, no cautions against misuse are mentioned in the material for the PSAS.

In summary, the PSAS can be recommended for an institution desiring information on items included in the PSAS in order to save developmental time and costs while obtaining much of the same data as a completely customized questionnaire. However, great care should be taken to avoid misinterpretation of the summary data report and the comparative data provided by the publisher.

REVIEWER'S REFERENCE

Converse, J. M., & Presser, S. (1986). *Survey questions: Handcrafting the standardized questionnaire*. (Quantitative Applications in the Social Sciences Series No. 07-063). Beverly Hills: Sage.

[299]

Psychosocial Adjustment to Illness Scale. Purpose: "Designed to assess the quality of a patient's psychosocial adjustment to a current medical illness or its residual effects." Medical patients or their immediate relatives; 1983; PAIS; 8 scores: Health Care Orientation, Vocational Environment, Domestic Environment, Sexual Relationship, Extended Family, Social Environment, Psychological Distress, Total; individual; 2 versions: interview, self-report; 1987 price data: $3 per reuseable interview booklet; $.70 per reuseable self-report booklet; $17.50 per manual (56 pages); (20–30) minutes; Leonard R. Derogatis and Maria C. Lopez (manual); Clinical Psychometric Research.*

Review of the Psychosocial Adjustment to Illness Scale by CABRINI S. SWASSING, Psychologist, Central Ohio Psychiatric Hospital, Columbus, OH:

This scale consists of two forms, a semistructured interview and a self-report inventory. Each form is comprised of 46 questions covering a total of seven psychosocial domains. The items are intended to assess the patients themselves or, with slight changes in format, their spouses, parents, or other relatives. The Psychosocial Adjustment to Illness Scale (PAIS and PAIS-R) is meant to provide three levels of information: overall adjustment, areas of relative assets and liabilities, and unique aspects of the individual's adjustment to illness.

It is not clear from the instructions in the manual who is to conduct the personal interview. However, the questions would seem to indicate a need for the interviewer to be medically knowledgeable about the patient's illness. The self-report scale (PAIS-SR) is in the form of a consumable booklet and has instructions for completion printed in the booklet. It is recommended that if the self-report form is to be administered by mail, there should be an additional page of instructions. However, none is included.

Although the authors state the two forms are equivalent, there appear to be considerable and unnecessary differences in the wording and meaning of the two forms. The time frame for both forms is the past 30 days or, if the patient is in the hospital, the 30 days preceding hospitalization.

Scoring is relatively simple, requiring only addition and subtraction. However, instructions are difficult to understand. Half of the scores on the PAIS-SR must be "reflected" (i.e., subtracted from three) to eliminate possible response set. After adding the sum of each domain, these scores are then converted to standardized *T*-scores using the tables provided. A *T*-score of 62 or higher indicates clinical levels of psychological distress. There are score/profile forms available for each of the four normed groups as well as a non-normed scoring form.

Information regarding reliability and validity of the scales is limited. There are only two norming groups for each form of the scales, and these groups are small, biased, and limited in type of illness. The PAIS, or structured interview, groups consist of one group of 120 lung cancer patients (all male) and 272 renal dialysis patients (57% male). The PAIS-SR norming groups consist of 170 cardiac patients (92% male) and 114 mixed cancer patients (36% male). There are no norms for relatives of patients.

Internal consistency reliability is provided for 269 renal dialysis, 89 lung cancer, and 69 cardiac patients. With two exceptions, reliability coefficients range from .62 to .93. No information is provided for the mixed cancer patients regarding internal consistency reliability. While the authors state the scales are stable over time, no data are provided to support this claim. Interrater reliabilities for the PAIS are provided for 17 breast cancer and 37 Hodgkins disease patients. Reliability coefficients range from .56 to .86 for these small samples.

Factor analysis was used to determine construct validation for 120 lung cancer patients. In the analysis, seven substantive dimensions were identified accounting for 63% of the variance. Interrelationships among the separate domains and the total scores appear to be appropriate in that the domains show little correlation with each other and a greater correlation with the total scores. Predictive validity, or the usefulness of an instrument to predict or discriminate among specific outcomes, was statistically significant with the PAIS on five of the seven domains and the total score when administered to these 120 lung cancer patients.

In summary, the PAIS and the PAIS-SR are at this time in the early stages of usefulness. Parts of the manual are unclear, and the two forms of the scale do not appear to be equivalent. In general, instructions for administration and scoring are ambiguous and difficult to understand. The scales would be easier to use if the two forms were more similar in wording and format.

Reliability and validity information is based on small, biased, and strictly defined samples. There is a need for more norms based on larger groups and representing a variety of illnesses. At this time the scales have not been used extensively enough to provide these norms. As more data become available, these scales could be helpful in identifying patients having difficulty in adjusting to various illnesses. With this knowledge, more support and information might be provided for them. Until more data are available, however, the utility of these scales is limited.

[300]

The Pyramid Scales. Purpose: "Assesses adaptive behavior in handicapped persons of all ages." Handicapped persons ages birth–adult; 1984; "criterion-referenced"; behavior checklist for measuring adaptive behavior by directly observing client or by interviewing adult informant; 20 specific-objective scales: Sensory (Tactile Responsiveness, Auditory Responsiveness, Visual Responsiveness), Primary (Gross Motor, Eating, Fine Motor, Toileting, Dressing, Social Interaction, Washing/Grooming, Receptive Language, Expressive Language), Secondary (Recreation/Leisure, Writing, Domestic Behavior, Reading, Vocational, Time, Numbers, Money); individual; 1984 price data: $28 per complete set including 50 answer/profile sheets; $12 per 50 answer/profile sheets; $18 per manual (76 pages including test); (30–45) minutes; John D. Cone; PRO-ED, Inc.*

Review of The Pyramid Scales by JOHN G. SVINICKI, Evaluation Specialist, Powell Associates, Inc., Austin, TX:

The adequacy of an assessment instrument can best be judged within the context of the purposes for which it was developed and will be used. Clearly it is possible for an instrument to be acceptable for some uses but not for other uses. This is the case for The Pyramid Scales, which is a comprehensive set of scales of adaptive behavior and designed to be criterion and curriculum referenced. According to the test manual, these scales are intended to be used (*a*) to generally describe the level of adaptive behavior of an individual, (*b*) to plan educational programs, and (*c*) for evaluation purposes. The Pyramid Scales is acceptable for the first of these (general descriptive purposes) but not for the other two purposes. The reasons why The Pyramid Scales is inadequate for planning educational progams and evaluation fall into two categories: (*a*) its relationship to the curriculum in use and (*b*) its reliability and validity.

The first of these problems revolves around how closely The Pyramid Scales matches the curriculum on which the individual educational plan (IEP) is being developed. Once The Pyramid Scales has been administered and general training needs established, the user must conduct another, more detailed, assessment based on the curriculum system being used. The author indicates that this can be accomplished readily using The West Virginia System Curriculum or any other curriculum system. This additional assessment is undoubtedly easy if one is using The West Virginia System Curriculum because it appears that The Pyramid Scales is tied very closely to it. In fact, one gets the strong impression that The Pyramid Scales, formerly known as The West Virginia Assessment and Tracking System, is actually a screening test for The West Virginia System Curriculum. The degree of the match between The Pyramid Scales and other curriculum systems is not as clear as the test manual implies. Therefore, users will have to determine to what degree the curriculum they are using matches The West Virginia System Curriculum or The Pyramid Scales. This could be a very time consuming task. If there is not a screening test for the curriculum being used, this might be worth doing. However, there are several instances in which the behavior being assessed by The Pyramid Scales is not clear. This lack of clarity will lead to difficulty when it comes to specifying instructional objectives for persons failing an item or determining whether the curriculum in use matches The Pyramid Scales.

Another problem arises when interpreting Pyramid Scale scores. The test manual indicates that, because The Pyramid Scales is criterion referenced, the score on each scale represents the "percentage of adequate or competent performance in an area." Actually, this is not always, or perhaps even usually, true. As an example, the area score (in the Primary and Secondary Zones) is a ratio of the number of subitems passed to the maximum number of subitems. However, the maximum number of subitems does *not* include any subitem that was scored "N" (no opportunity to observe) or "P" (physiologically incapable). As a result, a severely orthopedically impaired person could have a very high percentage score in a motor area and be incapable of performing virtually any of the skills involved. Such an outcome would yield an extremely misleading profile of that person's skills. There are some actions users could take to remedy this situation. Some suggestions for dealing with too many "N" responses are made, although the issue of too many "P" responses is not directly addressed. One alternative not mentioned is that users could adopt a multiple-score system. For example, one could calculate a second score for each area based on the total set of skills (i.e., including Ns and Ps). The user would then be in a position to make descriptive statements such as, "In the fine motor area, Johnny scored 75% on those items observed (or of which he is physiologically capable) and 25% on the total set of skills." Such a statement would more accurately reflect the person's level of adaptive behavior. This could be of crucial importance when the information will impact program placement. This adaptation would also be important in using the "minimum required competency" profiles mentioned later.

The second reason for the inadequacy of The Pyramid Scales is the lack of evidence for its reliability and validity. With regard to the data presented to establish the reliability, validity, and usefulness of The Pyramid Scales, the author states "Indeed, much of the technical data reported in this manual were collected with earlier versions of the measure." Given the extensive revisions The Pyramid Scales went through to reach its current form, this means that virtually no data are presented to establish the technical properties of The Pyramid Scales in its current form. However, this is less of a problem if the use of The Pyramid Scales is restricted to providing general descriptions than if it is used for evaluation or program planning of any kind. When the purpose of The Pyramid Scales is to provide a general description of the level of adaptive behavior, the data probably are sufficient to establish test-retest reliability and internal consistency.

Should reliability and validity data be collected for the current form of the test, the following issues should be considered. Even if the data had been collected with the current version of The Pyramid Scales, the evidence presented to establish the reliability and validity would still be weak. Because the primary source of information for The Pyramid Scales is an interview, the test manual addresses the issue of the accuracy of information obtained from an informant. Two dependent measures were used to compare information obtained from an informant to that obtained through direct observation. The first measure was a correlation between the area (scale) scores obtained with each method. The second measure is one the author terms the "mean percent agreement" score. This agreement score was calculated for each student by determining the area score obtained with each method and dividing the smaller score by the larger one. The agreement scores for the students were then summed and divided by the sample size to obtain the mean percent agreement score. The author argues that the agreement score is the best measure to use in this and other circumstances, saying that it "is a more stringent test of accuracy . . . because it requires exact agreement on individual scores rather than merely their same relative placement within the group." While this may be true, neither of these measures is as good as a measure that compares item (or subitem) scores instead of area scores. It is not very difficult to construct an example in which there are no instances of item agreement and yet there is 100 percent agreement on the area score, which is the sum of the item scores. This may not be a problem in a norm-referenced instrument but it can be a major problem in a criterion-referenced one, particularly if one of the purposes is to develop specific instructional objectives from the item results. This is one of the stated purposes for The Pyramid Scales and the data presented do not establish the reliability of The Pyramid Scales for this purpose. The content (face) validity of The Pyramid Scales is good, which is characteristic of most adaptive behavior scales that have a curriculum base. The data presented to establish other types of validity are weak.

One of the most interesting possible uses for The Pyramid Scales and other adaptive behavior measures is detailed in the discussion on developing "minimum required competency" profiles for programs. Properly validated, these profiles could be extremely useful in identifying when an individual has the appropriate skills and skill levels to enter special programs.

From a test construction perspective it is clear The Pyramid Scales fails to meet the standards for reliability and validity necessary for it to be useful for many aspects of IEP development, program planning, and evaluation. In fact, The Pyramid Scales itself is not well suited for those functions (unless, perhaps, one has adopted The West Virginia System Curriculum). The primary role of The Pyramid Scales is to provide a *general* description of the level of adaptive behavior of an individual. In this capacity, the issues of reliability and validity become less crucial, though they can never be ignored. An in-depth assessment based on the curriculum in use is required to fulfill the IEP, program-planning, and evaluation functions discussed. It is the reliability of that assessment instrument and the validity of the curriculum upon which it is based that are essential. It would be beneficial, of course, if reliability and validity data were collected with the current version of The Pyramid Scales, these data were analyzed on an item or subitem basis, and some of the confusing aspects of the test and manual were clarified. However, in its current form, The Pyramid Scales is adequate for general descriptive purposes. In this sense, The Pyramid Scales can be viewed as a screening test for a program-specific curriculum-based assessment.

[301]

A Questionnaire Measure of Individual Differences in Achieving Tendency. Purpose: Measures an individual's achievement motivation. Adult; 1969–78; 1986 price data: $28 per test kit including scales, scoring directions, norms, and test manual; (15) minutes; Albert Mehrabian; the Author.*

For review by Jayne E. Stake of an earlier edition, see 9:682; see also T3:1442 (1 reference).

Review of A Questionnaire Measure of Individual Differences in Achieving Tendency by TIMOTHY S. HARTSHORNE, Assistant Professor of Counseling and School Psychology, Wichita State University, Wichita, KS:

A Questionnaire Measure of Individual Differences in Achieving Tendency (QAT) is a 38-item research instrument designed to measure, with more objectivity than TAT type instruments (McClelland, Atkinson, Clark, & Lowell, 1953), need for achievement. The QAT is designed particularly to reflect the theory of Atkinson (1964) regarding risk-taking and aspiration among low and high achievers. While research instruments need not meet the same standards as clinical tests, the flaws in test construction, reliability and validity, and scoring procedures seriously detract from the QAT even for research purposes.

The QAT is a revision of earlier scales developed by the author. Its development, description, and technical data are described in an article by Mehrabian and Bank (1978). The item pool was developed to reflect aspects of achieving tendency found in the literature. No other criteria are described (e.g., research studies with quality designs). Steps were taken throughout test development to insure a lack of correlation with social desirability (as measured by Crowne & Marlowe, 1960). While this may be appropriate, no theoretical justification was given for a lack of relationship between achieving tendency and the tendency to give socially desirable answers.

As an early step in test development, the authors factor analyzed a pool of 184 items administered to 261 subjects. Results were used to group items and eliminate redundancy. Because factor analysis is so sensitive to sampling error, researchers are cautioned to have as large a difference between items and subjects as possible. Nunnally (1967), for example, recommends 10 times as many subjects as items (or variables).

Another problem in this test's development is that all subjects have been undergraduate students. Their ages are not reported, but one can assume only that they are typical college students. Thus there is no evidence to support the use of the QAT with 18- to 21-year-olds who are not in college, or with older adults. Is it not likely, however, that achieving tendency might be quite different, or at least expressed differently by these groups? Thus the utility of the QAT, even as a research instrument, is quite restricted.

Reliability data were collected from 76 male and 66 female undergraduates, a rather small sample of that restricted group. A reliability coefficient of .91 was found using the Kuder-Richardson formula 20 (KR-20). While that is certainly high enough for a research instrument, KR-20 requires that items be scored 0 or 1 (right or wrong). Each item on the QAT is scored on a 9-point scale. The appropriate statistic would have been Cronbach's alpha, which may in fact be what was used.

Validity data are much weaker, and still based on the 142 undergraduates. The authors point first to a correlation of .02 with social desirability, but because the test was constructed by selecting items that did not correlate with Crowne and Marlowe's instrument, this finding is not surprising, and certainly not evidence of validity, particularly with no theoretical discussion of how the achieving tendency and social desirability constructs interact. As further evidence of validity the authors point to a lack of response bias because scoring direction for the items is balanced. That is hardly evidence. Concurrent validity is presented with correlations of .74 with "Jackson's (1967) achievement scale" (presumably the Jackson Personality Inventory; T3:1203) and .59 with the first author's previous scale for males and .68 with his scale for females. While these correlations are all statistically significant, they are not very high, and the low correlations with the latter two scales are particularly curious. If they are all measures of achieving tendency, should they not show a higher relationship?

Very little information for scoring, and no information for interpreting, other than norms, are provided. Because the scoring direction of the items is balanced, scores for the positive and negative statements are summed separately, and then the latter are subtracted from the former. While this may seem straightforward, the 9-point scale for scoring each item ranges from +4 to -4. This means that for a person with a relatively high achieving tendency, their sum on the negatively worded statements will be a negative number. When that negative number is subtracted from the positive score on the positively worded items, the effect is to add. This, while reasonable, is confusing, and should have been addressed on the brief instruction sheet that accompanies the scale.

Norms, in the form of means and standard deviations are provided for males, females, and total. However, these are based on only 142 undergraduates (from somewhere).

In summary, the QAT cannot be recommended on the evidence available to support it. It should be used only by researchers with a desire to further establish its merits.

REVIEWER'S REFERENCES

McClelland, D. C., Atkinson, J. W., Clark, R. A., & Lowell, E. L. (1953). *The achievement motive*. New York: Appleton-Century-Crofts.

Crowne, D. P., & Marlowe, D. (1960). A new scale of social desirability independent of psychopathology. *Journal of Consulting Psychology*, 24, 349-354.

Atkinson, J. W. (1964). *An introduction to motivation*. Princeton, NJ: Van Nostrand.

Nunnally, J. C. (1967). *Psychometric theory*. New York: McGraw-Hill.

[302]

Quick-Score Achievement Test. Purpose: "Designed as a quick, reliable, and valid measure of school achievement." "To identify students who need help in school work and to indicate their specific areas of difficulty." Ages 7-0 to 17-11; 1987; Q-SAT; 5 scores: Writing, Arithmetic, Reading, Facts, Composite; individual; 2 equivalent forms: A, B; 1987 price data: $57 per complete kit; $11 per 25 student record form A or B; $15 per 50 summary/profile sheets; $24 per examiner's manual (62 pages); (30–60) minutes; Donald D. Hammill, Jerome J. Ammer, Mary E. Cronin, Linda H. Mandlebaum, and Sally S. Quinby; PRO-ED, Inc.*

Review of the Quick-Score Achievement Test by CLEBORNE D. MADDUX, Department Chairman, Curriculum and Instruction, University of Nevada-Reno, Reno, NV

The Quick-Score Achievement Test (QSAT) appears to be designed as a competitor to the popular Wide-Range Achievement Test—Revised (WRAT-R) (Jastak, Jastak, & Wilkinson, 1984). The manual is clearly written, administration is simple and straightforward, and excellent examples are provided to aid the novice in understanding how basals and ceilings are obtained. The manual is clearly superior to that of the WRAT-R, and test administration and scoring is simpler and less likely to produce errors. Unfortunately, the QSAT suffers from many of the same shortcomings as the WRAT-R, particularly the problem of limited sampling of behaviors.

The QSAT consists of four untimed subtests including Writing, Arithmetic, Reading, and Facts. Each subtest yields raw scores, percentiles, and standard scores (m = 10, s = 3). A global score, called the General Achievement Quotient (m = 100, s = 15) can be derived.

WRITING. The Writing subtest consists of 22 graded sentences to be written from dictation. Each of the sentences has a punctuation or capitalization form and a spelling word taught at the same grade level. Each item is scored "1" or "0," and all three elements in an item must be correct to receive credit. The manual states that the primary writing skill measured is "mechanics."

The problem of conceptualizing writing ability as skill in spelling, punctuation, and capitalization is obvious. The manual unsuccessfully attempts to justify this decision by citing a study that reported "highest" correlations between writing mechanics and other writing skills including vocabulary, theme, and penmanship. The authors fail to establish that writing is synonymous with mechanical skills; that vocabulary, theme, and penmanship are the most important elements of writing; or that one subtest should treat three mechanical skills.

ARITHMETIC. The Arithmetic subtest consists of 40 items purporting to measure skill in calculation. The items consist almost entirely of mechanical algorithms, as does the same subtest of the WRAT-R. Construction of yet another test that relies totally on measurement of calculation skills to assess Arithmetic achievement can only serve to exacerbate the problem of instructional overemphasis on these skills and underemphasis on other, more important mathematical skills. This problem of emphasis has been of widespread concern in recent years to experts in math education.

READING. The Reading subtest consists of a list of 40 graded words to be read orally by the subject. Items are scored correct or incorrect based solely on pronunciation. The subtest could more accurately be titled "Reading Recognition," because comprehension is not assessed. The manual incorrectly states that comprehension is incorporated in the subtest.

FACTS. The Facts subtest consists of 20 orally administered questions. The manual states that the test is designed to measure basic school-taught facts in four or five subject areas. Science, social studies, health, and language arts are always mentioned, humanities is sometimes added to the list. An obvious problem is the extremely small portion of the curriculum sampled by this subtest. Twenty questions are purported to measure knowledge of basic facts in science, social studies, health, language arts, and humanities for children ages 7-0 to 17-11.

NORMATIVE DATA. The QSAT was normed between March and June of 1986 with a sample of 1,495 students from 15 states. The sample appears to be roughly representative of the national population with respect to sex, place of residence, race, geographic distribution, ethnicity, and age. No information is provided on grade level, socioeconomic standing, or numbers/types of handicapped students in the normative sample.

RELIABILITY. Internal consistency was investigated for 550 subjects. Reliability figures (coefficient alpha) are reported for five age groups on both forms of all subtests and for global scores. The subtest coefficients range from .76 to .95. All of the lower coefficients involve the Facts subtest. Ninety percent of the reported subtest alphas are at least .80, with 53% reaching .90. Internal reliabilities for global scores range from .94 to .96.

Equivalent forms reliability for subtests was computed for 1,380 subjects who took both forms in a single testing session. Correlation coefficients were computed (with effects of age partialed out) for the four subtests and range from .85 to .96 (only the Facts subtest was below .90). Composite reliability using Guilford's (1954) formula was .95.

Test-retest reliability with equivalent forms was computed for 115 students in six states who took both forms at least 1 day apart. No demographic data are supplied for this group. Age was partialed out and resulting coefficients were as follows: Writing, .83; Arithmetic, .96; Reading, .86; Facts, .77. Reliability coefficient for global score (Guilford's formula) was .94.

VALIDITY. The manual states that two kinds of evidence are presented for content validity (*a*) rationale for test content and format, and (*b*) item analysis data. Problems with the rationale presented for each subtest have been dealt with above. The item analysis deals primarily with internal consistency and item difficulty, rather than the actual content validity.

Data on criterion-related validity consists of attenuated correlations between QSAT subtest and global scores, and various scores from the SRA Achievement Series (SRA), the California Achievement Tests (CAT), and the Iowa Tests of Basic Skills (ITBS). These correlations are not broken down by age or grade and have been computed for extremely small subsamples (SRA, $n = 73$; CAT, $n = 81$; ITBS, $n = 111$). Furthermore, these subsamples appear to be samples of convenience consisting of those subjects whose records happened to contain scores on these achievement tests. Correlations with WRAT-R scores are notably absent.

Data on construct validity consist of studies of age differentiation, interrelationships among QSAT subtests, group differentiation, and grade differentiation. Correlations with age for the entire standardization sample ranged from .62 to .82. Intercorrelations between subtests ranged from .20 to .68 and were all significant. Group differentiation was studied by examining scores of only 47 students. No factor analytic work is reported.

SUMMARY. The QSAT is an individually administered, norm-referenced test, apparently intended to compete with the WRAT-R. The QSAT compares favorably with regard to quality of the manual and ease of administration and scoring. However, the test suffers from many of the same weaknesses as the WRAT-R.

Reliability appears to be adequate for all subtests except Facts. Information on validity is scanty and has yet to be established. The primary problem with the test is its narrow coverage of the curriculum areas included. Given these problems, it can only be concluded that the QSAT adds little, if anything, to the state of the art of individual achievement testing.

REVIEWER'S REFERENCES

Guilford, J. P. (1954). *Psychometric methods* (2nd ed.). New York: McGraw-Hill.

Jastak, J. F., Jastak, S., & Wilkinson, G. S. (1984). Wide Range Achievement Test—Revised. Wilmington, DE: Jastak Associates, Inc.

[303]

Rahim Organizational Conflict Inventories. Purpose: "Designed to measure three independent dimensions of organizational conflict: Intrapersonal, Intragroup, and Intergroup" (ROCI-I) and "designed to measure five independent dimensions that represent styles of handling interpersonal conflict: Integrating, Obliging, Dominating, Avoiding, and Compromising" (ROCI-II). Managers; 1983; ROCI; 2 tests; 1987 price data: $20.50 per 50 answer sheets; $10 per professional manual (27 pages); $12 per specimen set; M. Afzalur Rahim; Consulting Psychologists Press, Inc.*

a) RAHIM ORGANIZATIONAL CONFLICT INVENTORY—I. ROCI-I; organizational conflict; 3 scales: Intrapersonal, Interpersonal, Intergroup; separate answer sheets must be used; $8.50 per 25 tests; (6) minutes.

b) RAHIM ORGANIZATIONAL CONFLICT INVENTORY—II. ROCI-II; styles of handling interpersonal conflict; 5 scales: Integrating, Obliging, Dominating, Avoiding, Compromising; separate answer sheets must be used; $11.50 per 25 test booklets; (8) minutes.

TEST REFERENCES

1. Rahim, M. A. (1983). Measurement of organizational conflict. *Journal of General Psychology*, 109, 189-199.

2. Rahim, M. A., & Psenicka, C. (1984). Comparison of reliability and validity of unweighted and factor scales. *Psychological Reports*, 55, 439-445.

3. Rahim, M. A. (1985). A strategy for managing conflict in complex organizations. *Human Relations*, 38, 81-89.

Review of the Rahim Organizational Conflict Inventories by GEORGE C. THORNTON, III, Professor of Psychology, Colorado State University, Fort Collins, CO:

Both of these inventories are based on sound theory and rationale, have been developed through careful and extensive empirical methods, have shown superior psychometric properties, and have demonstrated their usefulness in research and practice. The manual is a model of thorough and clear reporting of the types of information one needs to understand the background, quality, and appropriateness of the tests for potential users.

Theoretical development of the concepts measured by the two questionnaires is well documented. Work started with Rahim's dissertation in 1976, spans a series of published papers evaluating the instruments and their concepts, and continues up to the current (1986) development of a conflict management study group and plans for the first international congress on managing conflict in 1987.

The questionnaires, answer sheets, and scoring forms are clear, efficient, and easy to use as self-administered materials. The Rahim Organizational Conflict Inventory—I (ROCI-I) consists of 21 questions and takes 6 minutes to complete, yet gives reliable measures of intrapersonal, intragroup, and intergroup conflict. There are a total of 28 items in the Rahim Organizational Conflict Inventory—II (ROCI-II) measuring five styles of handling interpersonal conflict; the informant responds to slightly modified versions of these statements in describing how he or she interacts with the boss, subordinates, and peers.

The development of both questionnaires involved the analysis of prior instruments, careful item preparation based on theoretical formulations, tryouts of initial item pools, item analyses, subjective discussions with users to ensure clarity, and revisions to prepare the final forms. The test development efforts included measurement of the social desirability of items, initial factor analyses to confirm item loadings on hypothesized factors, and subsequent factor analyses on separate groups to test stability of the constructs, item-scale correlations, and correlations among scales.

The psychometric properties of the resulting scales are impressive. The ROCI-I scales show internal consistency in the high .70s and .80s; test-retest correlations range from .74 to .85 over a 1-week period. The correlations among the three scales are .27, .37, and .32. The scales do not correlate significantly with age, experience, or two measures of response bias (social desirability and a "lie" scale). Validity evidence is equally supportive. In addition to the factor analytic results, the scales correlate negatively (as would be expected) with measures of organization climate, job satisfaction, and perceptions of organization effectiveness.

Similarly impressive data exist for the ROCI-II. Internal consistency reliabilities are somewhat lower (alphas range from .72 to .77), but test-retest correlations range from .60 to .83 (mean = .76). These indices are considerably higher than reliabilities reported for similar instruments. Intercorrelations among the scales are very low (absolute values are .08 to .31 with a median of .12), indicating that separate behavioral styles are being measured. The use of an obliging style is correlated negatively (-.20 to -.13) with age and experience, but the other styles are not correlated with these demographics. Only the integrating scale was correlated, to a small degree, with response-style measures. Thus, it appears the ROCI-II is not contaminated by these demographic variables and response biases.

Only marginal correlations were found between the ROCI-II and measures of personality and perceived organizational effectiveness. This is an area where more research needs to be done, including evidence that self-reports correlate with behavior measures of approaches to conflict situations.

Detailed norms are presented in the manual. For the ROCI-I there are general norms for managerial and collegiate groups. Within the managerial groups, separate means and standard deviations are presented for respondents at different organizational levels, functional areas, and educational levels. Differences revealed by analysis of variance among these groups for certain scales are reported; none are very large. Within the collegiate sample, means and standards are reported for subgroups of sex and educational level. Similar breakdowns for norms on the ROCI-II are reported. Again, few meaningful differences are present across the demographic variables.

The most interesting bit of normative data on the ROCI-II, which really addresses the validity of the instrument, is the consistent difference in the use of these styles when interacting with different referent people. Managers report that they tend to use obliging, dominating, and avoiding styles with bosses, the integrating style with subordinates, and the compromising style with peers.

In summary, these inventories have much to recommend them. They are devised from well developed theoretical positions, they were constructed with great care, and they have proven psychometric soundness. In addition, the manual is thorough and well presented, and there continues to be active research and collaboration in the area. I recommend their use for organizational diagnosis of and research on conflict and conflict management.

[304]

Randt Memory Test. Purpose: Functions "as a global survey and evaluation of patients' complaints concerning their memory." Ages 20–90; 1983–86; RMT; 10 scores: Acquisition Recall (Five Items Acquisition, Paired Words Acquisition, Short Story Verbatim, Digit Span, Incidental Learning), Delayed Recall (Five Items Recall, Paired Words Recall, Picture Recall, General Information), and Memory Index; individual; 5 alternative forms included for repeated measurement, Program for Computer-Aided Administration and Scoring also available (Apple II+, IIc, or IIe); 1986 price data: $75 per complete test including 10 administration booklets, 5 sets of picture cards, and manual ('86, 36 pages); $18 per 50 administration booklets; $40 per computer scoring program including diskette and manual of instructions; (20–25) minutes; C. T. Randt and E. R. Brown; Life Science Associates.*

TEST REFERENCES

1. Drew, R. H., Templer, D. I., Schuyler, B. A., Newell, T. G., & Cannon, W. G. (1986). Neuropsychological deficits in active licensed professional boxers. *Journal of Clinical Psychology*, 42, 520-525.

Review of the Randt Memory Test by JOSEPH D. MATARAZZO, Professor and Chairman, Department of Medical Psychology, School of

Medicine, Oregon Health Sciences University, Portland, OR:

The Randt Memory Test (RMT) was developed by a physician-psychologist team (C. T. Randt, M.D. and E. R. Brown, Ph.D.) from the Department of Neurology, New York University, School of Medicine. Designed to help assess both short term and long term memory functions, the RMT consists of seven different subtests: General Information, Five Items, Repeating Numbers, Paired Words, Short Story (recall), Picture Recognition, and Incidental Learning. The test yields seven individual subtest scores, from which three summary scores (Acquisition, Recall, and Memory Index) are derived. The sum for the Acquisition (or new learning) score is obtained from a subject's scores on five (all but General Information and Picture Recognition) of the seven subtests. The sum for the Recall (retention) score is derived from five (all except Repeating Numbers and Incidental Learning) of these same seven subtests. The test administration format permits an examination of immediate memory (e.g., via the Reading Numbers subtest), short-delay memory (evaluated following an interpolated activity), and 24-hour recall (for which the examinee is queried by telephone on a few of the items administered the day before). A unique feature of the RMT is that the *raw* score for each subject in an age group (i.e., 20–29, 30–40, . . . 80–89) is converted to a *scaled* score utilizing tables of norms and a procedure not unlike that used in each of Wechsler's intelligence scales.

To permit repeat examination of short and long term memory functions the RMT has five alternate forms for which research reveals good test-retest reliability. Data on the latter were derived from reexamination after 10–14 days of 20 normal adult *S*s using alternate forms A and B of the test, plus 26 adult VA hospital inpatients using alternate forms C and D (Brown, Randt, & Osborne, 1983), as well as from Cronbach Alpha values obtained from alternate forms administration (Fioravanti, Thorel, Ramelli, & Napoleoni, 1985).

Franzen, Tishelman, Smith, Sharp, and Friedman (1989) reported test-retest coefficients (using form A) and on the equivalency of forms A and B. These researchers found fairly low test-retest reliability over 1- and 2-week intervals (.38 for Acquisition, .51 for Recall, and .52 for the Memory Quotient). The reliabilities associated with the parallel forms were somewhat higher (.72 for Acquisition, .69 for Recall, and .76 for the Memory Quotient). Overall, none of these coefficients are robust enough to support confidence in the clinical use of the test.

Administration time for the seven subtests during a complete examination (by use of any of the five alternate forms) averages 30 minutes; whereas an average of 5 to 10 minutes is required for administering the 24-hour delayed-recall examination. An Italian version of the items has been developed by Fioravanti, Thorel, Ramelli, and Napoleoni (1985).

Except for the studies cited above, published research on the RMT is scarce. Specifically, in the single journal publication to date by Randt, Brown, and Osborne (1980), and in the 30-page Administration Manual (Randt & Brown, 1983), the test authors provide (with almost no discussion) only the tables by which to convert raw scores into scaled scores. The conversion scores in these tables were based on a study of 349 normal individuals, ages 20–89. The data in these tables do not include 74 clinical patients with a mean age of 63, who also were studied by the authors.

No mention of research on the validity of the RMT is included in the 1983 Manual. However, some preliminary validity results are available in one article and two book chapters. Specifically, the tables published by Randt, Brown, and Osborne (1980) showing the mean score obtained by 200 *S*s in each of six age groups (20–29, 30–39 . . . 70–79) reveal that (*a*) the expected drop in the average memory score for *S*s across this cross-sectional, 60-year age span, and (*b*) very poor mean memory scores for the clinical group of 24 patients (mean age 63) relative to those of the 48 *S*s in the 60–69-year-old subgroup of normal individuals. The two subsequently published book chapters (Brown, Randt, & Osborne, 1983; Osborne, Brown, & Randt, 1982) contain little additional information and briefly describe what essentially were similar findings following the authors' increase in the size of their sample of normal *S*s from 200 to 300, and an increase in the clinical sample from 48 to 61 *S*s.

The second author of the RMT shared with this reviewer that the test should be considered a research and not yet a clinical instrument. He indicated that, given the costs involved, and because federal funds for its continued development were not available, further development and more adequate standardization of the RMT has had to be postponed.

The RMT has features both different from and similar to the outdated, but still very popular, Wechsler Memory Scale (Wechsler & Stone, 1945). A common feature is that four of the seven subtests of the RMT (General Information, Repeating Numbers [Digit Span], Short Story recall, and Paired Words) have counterparts in the Wechsler Memory Scale (WMS) and thus any individual's relative performance should be comparable on the two tests. In fact, the *r* between scores on the WMS and the RMT is .73 (Brown, Randt, & Osborne, 1983). Unique features of the RMT are *(a)* the above cited conversion of raw scores into aged-normed scale scores, *(b)* the differences between the two tests in their three remaining subtests, *(c)* the RMT's assessment of recall following a standardized interpolated activity, and *(d)* the RMT delayed recall score. These last two are features not found in the Wechsler Memory Scale but which are found in a number of today's popular clinical neuropsychological assessment batteries.

The RMT is considered by its developers to be in its earliest stages of development. Until standardization is completed on the requisite larger samples of normal and clinical samples of different age and diagnostic groups and until more evidence is gathered on reliability and validity, interested clinicians who need an age-normed omnibus test of memory may wish to use the Wechsler Memory Scale (Wechsler & Stone, 1945), a scale which the Psychological Corporation currently is restandardizing and which should be available during 1988. However, if the RMT were to be more adequately developed, its novel features could make it a useful, clinical neuropsychological assessment instrument.

REVIEWER'S REFERENCES

Wechsler, D., & Stone, C. P. (1945). Wechsler Memory Scale. New York: The Psychological Corporation.

Randt, C. T., Brown, E. R., & Osborne, D. P., Jr. (1980). A memory test for longitudinal measurement of mild to moderate deficits. *Clinical Neuropsychology*, 2, 184-194.

Osborne, D. P., Jr., Brown, E. R., & Randt, C. T. (1982). Qualitative changes in memory function: Aging and dementia. In S. Corkin, J. H. Groudon, K. L. Davis, E. Usdin, & R. J. Wurtman (Eds.), *Alzheimer's disease: A report of progress*. (Vol. 19, pp. 165-169). New York: Raven Press.

Brown, E. R., Randt, C. T., & Osborne, D. P., Jr. (1983). Assessment of memory disturbances in aging. In A. Agnoli, G. Crepaldi, P. F. Spano, & M. Trabucchi (Eds.), *Aging brain and ergot alkaloids*. New York: Raven Press.

Randt, C. T., & Brown, E. R. (1983). *Randt Memory Test, administration manual*. Bayport, NY: Life Sciences Associates.

Fioravanti, M., Thorel, M., Ramelli, L., & Napoleoni, A. (1985). Reliability between the five forms of the Randt Memory Test and their equivalence. *Archives of Gerontology and Geriatrics*, 4, 357-364.

Franzen, M. D., Tishelman, A., Smith, S., Sharp, B., & Friedman, A. (1989). Preliminary data concerning the test-retest and parallel-forms reliability of the Randt Memory Test. *The Clinical Neuropsychologist*, 3, 25-28.

[305]

Reading Appraisal Guide. Purpose: "Suggests ways to gain a clear picture of an inefficient reader's total problem, including attitude to reading as well as an evaluation of the students reading ability." Children with reading problems; 1979; individual; 1987 price data: A$8.25 per complete set including guide text (79 pages) and tally sheet for miscue analysis; administration time not reported; Barbara Johnson; Australian Council for Educational Research [Australia].*

[306]

Reading Comprehension Test DE. Purpose: "A test of reading which measures understanding of whole and sometimes quite complex passages, rather than single sentences." Ages 10-0 to 12-10; 1963–76; a component of the Reading Tests Series; 1986 price data: £4.25 per 10 tests ('70, 10 pages); £1.95 per manual ('76, 9 pages); (50) minutes; E. L. Barnard, The National Foundation for Educational Research in England and Wales; NFER-Nelson Publishing Co., Ltd. [England].*

Review of the Reading Comprehension Test DE by DOUGLAS K. SMITH, Professor of Psychology and Director School Psychology Program, University of Wisconsin-River Falls, River Falls, WI:

The Reading Comprehension Test DE presents eight passages (seven prose and one verse) and a total of 50 questions about them. The majority of questions are multiple choice in nature. Selected questions require a written response that is usually a direct quotation from the passage. The test is untimed and students are to complete as much of the test as they can.

The passages are drawn primarily from English literature. The author of the test indicates that "considerable numbers of passages and questions were tried out, and statistical analysis performed to establish items which were of a satisfactory level of difficulty throughout the age-range, and which were also discriminating satisfactorily between children in this age-group." Additional details, however, are not provided. Thus, it is not possible to determine the adequacy of this phase of test development.

Standardization occurred between 1971 and 1973 using 13,949 children, (7,076 male, 6,873 female), ages 10 years, 2 months to 12 years, 8 months from local authority areas and a city area in the northwest of England. Data regarding socioeconomic status of the students are lacking. Information was not provided on selection procedures for the school districts used in standardization.

Instructions for this measure of reading comprehension are clear. Students read each passage silently and then answer the four to eight questions on each passage. Administration time is usually less than 50 minutes and the test can be administered in a group setting. Standardized scores (mean of 100 and standard deviation of 15) are provided with scores extrapolated at ages 10 years, 0 months to 10 years, 1 month and 12 years, 9 months to 12 years, 10 months. In addition, the questions for each passage (script) have been categorized by the author into (*a*) global understanding, (*b*) detail, (*c*) inference, and (*d*) understanding the use of individual words or phrases. Thus, students' scores can be used to determine their place in relation to other students and to determine the types of questions answered incorrectly. The author notes the categories do overlap to some extent and other categorization systems may exist.

Reliability was calculated by the Kuder-Richardson (Formula 20) procedure for a random sample of 317 scripts from one of the areas in the standardization sample and yielded a reliability coefficient of .96. Test-retest reliability data are not presented. Validity information is not provided in the Manual of Instructions.

Although the test has "face" validity and uses reading passages from such works as *Doctor Doolittle*, *The Ancient Mariner*, and *History of England*, validity studies with other tests or measures of reading comprehension are not reported. Limited data on standardization and reliability are presented. Although the test appears to measure reading comprehension, as measured by the understanding of reading passages rather than sentences, concerns are present in the areas of standardization, reliability, and validity. The age range appropriate for the test (ages 10-0 to 12-10) is also a limitation in terms of the general usefulness of the test.

[307]

Reading Diagnosis. Purpose: "Help to show you a students' strength and weaknesses in general reading ability (oral reading), silent reading comprehension, phonics, sight word vocabulary, meaning vocabulary and other areas." Grades 1–6; 1981; battery of informal tests and interest inventories in 10 areas: Oral Reading Comprehension, Silent Reading Comprehension, Phonics, Sight Vocabulary, Meaning Vocabulary, Letters and Numerals, Spelling, Handwriting, Vision and Hearing, Student Interests; individual; no manual, instructions on administering, scoring, and interpreting each test contained in test battery booklet; 1985 price data: $20 per test battery booklet; administration time not reported; Edward B. Fry; Jamestown Publishers.*

[The publisher advised in September, 1987 that this test is out-of-print.]

Review of Reading Diagnosis by IRA E. AARON, Professor Emeritus of Reading Education, and SYLVIA M. HUTCHINSON, Professor of Reading Education, University of Georgia, Athens, GA:

Reading Diagnosis: Informal Reading Inventories is intended to give a teacher or clinician a system for collecting student information in order to assist in selecting appropriate materials for instruction. In the hands of a person knowledgeable about reading instruction, the instrument could provide useful diagnostic reading information and also serve as a very rough estimate of reading levels.

The publication is packaged well, with thick pages and spiral binding, and with clear divisions between sections. Permission is also granted for duplication of pages needed for record keeping; record sheets for most subsections also are available from the publisher in packages of 30 or 40 copies.

Most traditional published inventories establish instructional and other levels on the basis of students' oral and/or silent reading of selections and responses to comprehension questions over the selections. In contrast, in this inventory Independent, Instruction, and Frustration levels are established merely from the oral reading of short paragraphs, that is, 14 words at easy first-grade level, 64 words at hard third-grade level, and 56 words at seventh-grade level. The 10 paragraphs range in difficulty from "easy first grade" to "seventh grade." According to the author, the paragraph labeled "seventh grade" is "indicative of popular adult and nonacademic or nontechnical secondary reading levels." Criterion requirements vary from level to level: Independent level ranges from 86 percent accuracy up to 98 percent, Instruction level from 71 percent to 97 percent, and Frustration level from 64 percent to 95 percent. As the author points out, the short selections sacrifice reliable and valid estimates for brevity of testing time. Using this pronunciation criterion alone for estimating levels appears less valid than the usual procedure, because comprehension is much more than merely pronouncing words.

The three multiple-choice comprehension subtests consist of a 12-item test for use with the first- and second-grade level readers, a 10-item test for third-grade level readers, and another 10-item test for seventh-grade level readers. According to test descriptions, questions for the two 10-item tests are taken from the National Assessment of Educational Progress (NAEP) materials. No information was offered about how these items were selected or from which NAEP administration they were taken. The items actually were taken from the approximately 100 items released following the 1970–71 NAEP assessment. Five items of each test are classified as Literal and five as Inferential questions, in keeping with the NAEP classification. As the author indicates, the brevity of the tests limits their preciseness. The percent passing each of the NAEP items refers to the 9-year-old and 13-year-old subjects who took the test in 1970–71. That information is of limited usefulness in diagnosis.

The phonics section consists of an 18-item Brief Phonics Survey and a 99-item Phonics Criterion Test, both based upon subjects' pronunciations of "nonsense words." The teacher may use either or both forms with a child, depending upon need and time available. Instructions for the Brief Phonics Survey fail to tell the Examiner whether correctness is based upon vowel and consonant pronunciation or just upon the one indicated (as Easy Consonants) on the Record Sheet. The instructions are adequate for the Phonics Criterion Test. The longer test is comprehensive and should match most skills teachers may be teaching. However, two minor errors were noted on the Record Sheet: a long, final *E* (as in *use*) is labeled as a long, open syllable rule, and *gh* in *weigh* is labeled as a "silent blend."

Both Sight Vocabulary tests, the 300-word Instant Words Criterion Test and the 30-word Extended Instant Words Test, are based upon the book 3,000 *Instant Words*, by the same publisher. More information about the selection of the 3,000 words should have been included in the instructions.

The Letter and Numeral Recognition Test, assessing children's ability to identify upper and lower case letters, 26 numerals, and 5 symbols, can be used to test limited aspects of reading readiness and primer/first grade reading of numerals and symbols. The Spelling Tests give a basis for estimating roughly how many words the student knows of 300 and 3,000 instant words from which test words were taken. For those teachers wanting to evaluate students' handwriting, the Handwriting Test, based on the Ayres Handwriting Scale, may be used, though this test may have little relationship to reading ability in some children. The Vision and Hearing Tests are too crude and imprecise to be of much value, though the observation checklists of vision and hearing are useful reminders for teachers.

The Student Interest inventories and the Parent/Guardian Information form should be adequate for their purposes. The School Records form is limited mainly to data on age, grade, and standardized test results. Information on current basal reader instructional level of the student would also be useful, as well as reading strengths and weaknesses from the previous year, which some schools record at the end of each school term. The first five pages of the eight-page Reading Diagnosis Summary form are of limited use for assessing specific strengths and weaknesses, because the entries are of total scores only, which are of more use in screening than diagnosis.

Reading Diagnosis: Informal Reading Inventories is a collection of information-gathering materials that, despite some shortcomings, could be used by a knowledgeable teacher in assessing strengths and weaknesses in reading. The instrument would likely be less useful in determining reading levels than the typical published reading inventory. A college teacher or staff development director might use parts of the publication in helping teachers and potential teachers to learn more about diagnosing reading difficulties. However, most currently available published reading inventories would be at least as useful—and probably more useful—to teachers in most classroom settings. Even better would be inventories based upon the materials that the students are reading and using in instruction, thus making the testing and teaching materials comparable.

[308]

Reading Evaluation and Diagnostic Screen. Purpose: An evaluative and diagnostic tool to determine sensory deficiencies relating to reading and spelling. Ages 4–15; 1983; READS; experimental form; 4 scores: Letter Memory, Say Words, Distal Quadrant, Total; individual; 1987 price data: $58.88 per complete set of materials including copies of supporting articles, recording sheets, outline figure chart, pointer, fat and thin pencils, manual (88 pages); (20) minutes; Alvin H. Shapiro; LISCOR [Canada].*

Review of the Reading Evaluation and Diagnostic Screen by EDITH S. HEIL, Administrative Assistant for Special Programs, Crowley Independent School District, Crowley, TX:

The Reading Evaluation and Diagnostic Screen (READS) was developed by the author to identify the reasons for students' inabilities to sound through words, sequence letters in spelling, or print words without reversals. There are five subtests in the READS: printing the lower case alphabet, printing sounded-out letters, letter-sequence memory, speech articulation, and the body-image. The directions for administration are easy to follow but the format as one moves from one section to another requires the examiner to be very familiar with the directions and just mark responses on the answer sheet. In the printing of symbol-sound subtest, one repetition for testing of each letter is permitted, but in letter memory no repetition is permitted. After seven consecutive errors, the examiner should cease administering the letter memory section, but continue the whole test subsection for other portions.

Printing the lower case alphabet is rather straightforward; the student either knows the sequence or not. Letters missed by the student may provide clues concerning poor visual memory. Printing sounded-out letters, however, appears to skip a progression in the analysis of possible reading errors. The student is asked to print the sound that he/she hears. Reversals and inversions are counted as errors. Counting errors for reversals and inversions does not test whether the sound is heard accurately, but whether the information can be transferred to paper in letter form. Speech pathologists often use the Lindamood Auditory Conceptualization Test to ascertain whether a child can recognize that two different sounds are being spoken. The child demonstrates recognition with different colored tiles. This test is a quicker (8-minute average) evaluation of auditory processing than is the READS subtest.

The READS norm population is from the London, Ontario area. Students were between the ages of 4 and 16. Teachers selected 11 boys and 11 girls in each grade level. Test users will want to investigate the appropriateness of this standardization group as compared to their target populations before using READS.

The READS defines reading as "recognition reading" or word calling. The Wide Range Achievement Test (WRAT) was used to measure the norm population in recognition reading. Many reading scholars might question the premise that comprehension skills are not prerequisite to reading. If test consumers were interested in only recognition reading skills, the READS may be an adequate screening device.

Screening on the READS gave examiners information to pursue for additional diagnosis of physical causes of reading failure. Students were neither dyslexic nor learning disabled. Many of the case studies reported in the manual involved remediations that were medical in nature (i.e., hearing losses, physical brain injury).

READS seems to be a more reliable measure for children under age 10, as indicated in Table 4 of the manual. The numbers in each group are rather small, however, and more standardization work should be done.

The author suggests remediation for certain READS profiles through the use of a high frequency auditory trainer called the "Whisper." A review of the test and information in the manual should perhaps cover this phonological weakness in more detail.

The READS, although still in its experimental stage, does look promising for the identification of potential auditory and visual deficits characteristic of many normal IQ students who are exhibiting reading difficulties. The reviewer would encourage the author to refine and norm the test more adequately. There are few tests addressing specifically the identification of dyslexia that are not closely related to one specific remediation technique. The READS could fill a need in this area.

Review of the Reading Evaluation and Diagnostic Screen by DIANE J. SAWYER, Associate Professor of Education, Syracuse University, Syracuse, NY:

The Reading Evaluation and Diagnostic Screen (READS) is still in a developmental stage and is a revised form of an earlier work called the Shapiro Dyslexia Test (SDT) (Shapiro, 1983). READS differs from the SDT in that one subtest (Rapid Visual Perception) has been dropped and a second, Blending Ability, has been renamed Say Words. READS is available from the author, who reports it will be further modified as more information is gathered from users. Specifically, test-retest reliability and national (Canadian) norms are yet to be established, and validity information is being gathered. Information regarding reliability and validity is not presented in the test materials.

READS is rooted in the perspective that reading difficulties (serious delays in acquiring mastery over decoding) occur as a consequence of sensory and/or motor deficits/defects. The various subtests purport to tap sequential memory (Write Alphabet and Letter Memory), visual/verbal association (Write Sounds), the ability to coordinate the articulation of multisyllable words (Say Words), and the projection of body awareness (Distal Quadrant).

READS, as the manual is presently written, is confusing to both administer and interpret. For example, the "Instructions and Scoring" section of the manual indicates the first subtest requires the subject to write the lower case letters of the alphabet on an unlined sheet of paper. A preceding description of the contents of READS notes that a fat and a thin pencil are included. However, at no place in the instructions is the examiner directed to offer a subject choice of either of these pencils. One finds this information in one of the eight supporting articles accompanying the test.

Directions for scoring the Write Alphabet subtest indicate that "score consists of all abc's correct after error subtraction." Errors are said to include omitted letters, letters made to face the wrong way (reversed), or upside down/downside up (inverted). Because READS is intended for ages 4–15, a negative score could be obtained using this scoring procedure. No discussion of this issue appears. Further, when one considers the differences in exposure to instruction in the alphabet between 4-year-olds and 10- or 14-year-olds it would seem the right minus wrong approach to scoring this subtest would serve to misrepresent the competencies of young children. No discussion of this issue is provided. However, a table of grade equivalents for READS scores shows a score of 5 on this subtest as equivalent to P.K. .8 (the eighth month of pre-kindergarten). This simply is not reasonable unless the right minus wrong and omitted scoring procedure was suspended for 4- and 5-year-olds. No discussion of the derivation of this table appears in the manual.

Scoring procedures for the second subtest, Write Sounds, raise similar questions not addressed by the author. The subject is asked to write the letter that stands for a sound the examiner will say (e.g., "y" as in yet). The examiner gives 10 sounds. The score is the number correct, but reversed and inverted letters, as well as incorrect letters are considered errors. Among the letters to be written are "p" and "n." Four- and 5-year-olds frequently confuse the orientation of these letters producing "q" and "backwards n" (child is not requested to use lower case letters only). Although the child, in this instance, would have achieved the correct letter/sound correspondence, credit could not be given.

The author introduces further confusion in the fourth subtest, Say Words. In the manual this subtest is subtitled "Articulation." The examiner is directed to listen for errors including "1) sound distortions, 2) sound substitutions, and 3) sound omissions" as the subject repeats multisyllable words given by the examiner. In the articles accompanying the test, however, Say Words is described (Shapiro, 1983) as a syllabication task intended to tap blending ability and, by inference, it is related to issues involved in achieving adequate articulation (Shapiro, 1985). What is/are the underlying capacities/processes this subtest is intended to assess? How should performance be interpreted?

Scores present another source of confusion. Raw scores, total score, scaled scores, and standard score are all recorded on the record sheet. Raw scores for each subtest are first converted to scaled scores developed for different ages. Total score is defined as the combined raw score totals of only three subtests (Letter Memory, Say Words, and Distal Quadrant). A standard score conversion (for different age groups) is available only for the total raw score. The rationale for omitting the first two subtests from consideration of the total score is not given. The standard score is said to be "predictive," but this label is not discussed. Presumably, the standard score may be considered predictive of decoding status because the author states, "the standard scores should reliably agree with standard scores from reading (decoding) tests." The rationale for this type of prediction is not discussed. If the standard score obtained for the performance of a 4- or 5-year-old predicts the child is likely a nonreader (extremely poor decoder), the information seems to hold little significance. It would be important only if the standard score predicted very poor decoding at the end of first or second grade. The author makes no such claim.

READS is clearly a test that is still in the process of becoming. While it may be of some use to researchers, it should not be considered for general use in schools. READS does not provide a *R*eading *E*valuation as is suggested in the title; not one task demands that a subject engage in a decoding act. The author's claim that "READS measures word-decoding" is not supportable. READS might be a diagnostic screen for abilities that might impede acquisition of decoding skills. The author's research is beginning to establish the basis for such use (Shapiro, 1986; Shapiro & Mistal, 1986). More work is needed.

Those interested in a test of decoding skills with potential for identifying and assisting in educational planning for dyslexics are advised to consider the Decoding Skills Test (78) by E. Richardson and B. DiBenedetto. For an additional review of this test consult the June, 1987 issue of *Topics in Language Disorders*.

REVIEWER'S REFERENCES

Shapiro, A. H. (1983). A new brief dyslexia test. *Reading Improvement*, 20, 45-49.

Shapiro, A. H. (1985). Children's language disorders. *Ontario ACLD Communique*, 14 (2), 3.

Shapiro, A. H. (1986). Projection of body image and printing the alphabet. *Journal of Learning Disabilities*, 19, 107-112.

Shapiro, A. H., & Mistal, G. (1986, February). ITE-aid auditory training for reading and spelling-disabled children: A longitudinal study of matched groups. *The Hearing Journal*, pp. 14-16.

[309]

Reading Skills Checklists. Purpose: "Designed to provide teachers with a practical tool for assessing an individual's progress toward mastery of reading skills in any reading program." Grades K–3, 4–6, junior high; 1978; checklist should be maintained by teacher and passed on as the student moves from grade to grade; 3 levels: Primary, Intermediate, Junior High; individual; no manual; general directions (no date, 2 pages); 1988 price data: $12.39 per 30 Primary checklists; $13.14 per 30 Intermediate checklists; $14.61 per 30 Junior High checklists; administration time not reported; Therese Horan, M. Plunkett, Marcella Kucia, Nancy Kirby, and Angela Waldron; Modern Curriculum Press.*

Review of the Reading Skills Checklists by RICHARD L. ALLINGTON, Professor of Education and Chair, Department of Reading, State University of New York at Albany, Albany, NY:

The Reading Skills Checklists are presented straightforwardly as record-keeping materials, without pretense of any theoretical or empirical foundation. No discussion of the source of the various skill items is offered and, likewise, no evidence of any sort of verification of psychological, psychometric, or pedagogical reality of the skills is included. Of course, given the paucity of available evidence concerning the reliable identification of isolable reading set skills, one could hardly have expected a strong rationale to be offered. Given these significant limitations, one must question the utility of the Checklists.

On a purely practical level, setting aside questions of reliability and validity, the Checklists present a confusing array of items with little direction on how the teacher might assess mastery, although it is stated that an *X* should be placed in the appropriate box when mastery is determined. For instance, on the Primary Individual Reading Skills Checklist, Readiness—Kindergarten Level, one item asks the teacher to indicate when mastery of "Answers specific questions" is achieved. This item is grouped under the Auditory Discrimination heading. Under the Visual Discrimination heading, another single item asks the teacher to indicate mastery for "Connects dots, walks a balance beam, cuts, pastes, buttons, zips, snaps, laces, hooks, and ties." Another item asks an indication of mastery of "Forms correct usage patterns" under the Oral Expression Skills heading.

In the other primary-level checklists there is a pattern of redundancy in many areas. For grade 2, under the Word Recognition heading, the teacher is to indicate mastery of "Recognizes all 220 Dolch basic sight words," while on the grade 3 checklist, "Recognizes with ease 220 Dolch basic sight words," is a nearly identical item. How one differentiates between "Recognizes" and "Recognizes with ease" is left to the user. Also at grade 3 one encounters items under the Comprehension Skills heading that ask the teacher to indicate mastery of "Sees relationships" and "Applies phonics rules independently."

These patterns continue throughout the remaining checklists. Other problems are evident also, with one grade 4 item asking for an indication of mastery of the suffix "ance (state of being), e.g., balance" and another the prefix "com (with), e.g., combine." Both of these are obviously inaccurate examples of the affix structure. On the junior high school level, the Checklists ask teachers to indicate, under Oral Reading Skills, when mastery of "Reads to a group without distracting mannerisms" is achieved and when "Folk haiku" can be identified as a literary form.

In short, this reviewer can find nothing to recommend the use of the Reading Skills Checklists. The advertised "practicality" and "comprehensiveness" of the Checklists is not borne out under analysis, and the omission of information on how the items were selected or compiled undermines any potential use in classrooms.

[310]

Reading Test AD. Purpose: Tests reading comprehension. Ages 8-0 to 10-7; 1970–78; a component of the Reading Tests Series (see T3:2003); 1986 price data: £2.75 per 10 tests ('70, 4 pages); £1.50 per manual ('78, 8 pages); 15(20) minutes; A. F. Watts, The National Foundation for Educational Research in England and Wales; NFER-Nelson Publishing Co., Ltd. [England].*

Review of the Reading Test AD by PETER W. AIRASIAN, Professor of Education, Boston College, Chestnut Hill, MA:

The Reading Test AD is a test of reading comprehension that is part of the larger Reading Test Series used in England and Wales. The present edition is a restandardization of an earlier version.

TEST DEVELOPMENT. The test contains 35 items of the incomplete sentence variety in which the test taker is required to underline in the test booklet the one of five presented words that best completes the sentence. The sentences are graded from relatively simple to quite complex. The language (chemist, tobacconist, sack) and spelling (programmes) of some of the items make them inappropriate for use in the United States.

The Manual of Instructions contains very little information about the development of the test. The nature of the construct measured is not specified other than to say the test is a reading test. There is much more to reading than the skill called for in these test items. The items are obviously graded, but the manner of grading is not stated. The inferences it is appropriate to make on the basis of test scores are not indicated. Although there may be other materials that provide the information indicated above, the Manual of Instructions does promise information about the test and does provide relatively detailed information on reliability, choice of an appropriate scoring formula, and comparisons of performance on Reading Test AD to performance on Reading Test BD. It does not seem too much to ask that some information about test development, the construct measured, and the validity of the test also be provided in the Manual of Instructions.

NORMS AND SCORES. The current version of the test is a restandardization based on 9,363 children selected using a "stratified random technique designed to make it representative of the population in England and Wales." The technique is not described. Scores are reported separately for second year junior (ages 8+ to 9+ years old) and third year junior (9+ to 10+ years old) students. Raw scores are converted to standard scores (mean = 100, standard deviation = 15) by entering the proper grade level norms and finding the intersection of a pupil's raw score and age in years and months. Each pupil is compared to pupils of his/her same age, rather than to pupils at the same grade level. This score format seems restrictive as regards instructional decisions, and would have little use for testing in the United States. Percentile rank by grade would be easily obtained and useful information.

VALIDITY AND RELIABILITY. There is no validity information provided in the Manual of Instructions and the reader is given no guidance regarding the construct measured by the test or the inferences that are appropriate to make from the scores. The scores do have high internal consistency reliability (.92) for each of the grade levels for which the test is designed. Information about the standard error is also provided, along with a very concise and well done description of how to use the standard error of measurement in interpreting test scores.

SUMMARY. The documentation, standardization, norms, and technical support for the Reading Test AD are less than required by the Test Standards. This test is not applicable to educational institutions in the United States, for many technical and language/culture reasons.

Review of the Reading Test AD by ANTHONY J. NITKO, Professor of Education, University of Pittsburgh, Pittsburgh, PA:

The Reading Test AD appears to be identical to a 1950s test, the Sentence Reading test. The current version consists of 35 items. Each item is a sentence with a word missing at the end. Students must select from among five choices the one word that correctly completes the sentence. There is a 15-minute time limit to complete the test. The test is intended for use with 8-to-10-year-olds in the United Kingdom.

The test manual is poorly done. In no way does it meet the professional criteria for test manuals articulated by the Standards for Educational and Psychological Testing (AERA, APA, & NCME, 1985). The test's technical quality and development procedures are summarized in two and one-half pages. Basic information which a user of the test needs to interpret the scores obtained from it is missing. For instance, anyone intending to use this test with students should know (*a*) the purpose for which it was constructed, (*b*) the developer's rationale for limiting a reading test to one narrow item format, (*c*) the instructional uses to which the scores are intended to be put, (*d*) the specific suggestions which teachers might be given for using the tests in their classrooms, and (*e*) the body of evidence that is used to validate the developer's interpretations of the test scores. All of this information is lacking. Purchasing this test without having this information in hand cannot be recommended.

The 35 sentences comprising this test are ordered in difficulty. No information is provided, however, concerning just how difficult they are for children currently attending school. Even item data from the most recent standardization (1977) are missing. Information about currently enrolled students' performance on individual items is essential for a narrow test of this type whose content has not changed over the last 35 years. The vocabulary and thematic content of the sentences, and the background and experience of the children who read them, are critical factors to consider when interpreting the results of any reading test. Unfortunately, this test is especially loaded in its assumptions about the background and cultural experiences of today's children. Because of its lack of empirical research on the test's validity, this test cannot be recommended as a suitable measure of any child's reading ability.

Most of the items are oriented to a white, male-dominated, privileged community. Only two items refer explicitly to females (one refers to a telephone receptionist, the other to a tired old lady). Seven items refer explicitly to males, usually as active and intelligent persons (e.g., a clever uncle, an ambitious musician). Such blatant gender stereotyping has long disappeared in modern reading tests.

The test was standardized on a sample of second and third year juniors (8–10-year-olds) in 1977. Although the manual claims that the sample is representative of England and Wales, the data presented are too sparse to support this claim. No information is provided, for example, on how the sample was selected or on how those included in the sample compare to the population of 8- to 10-year-olds attending school. No information is provided about the enrollment sizes of the schools included, their geographic locations within England and Wales, the socioeconomic status of the students, the educational tracks tested, or the extent to which handicapped children were excluded from testing. Raw scores are referenced to standard scores within age groups of 1-month intervals (e.g., 8 years, 1 month; 8 years, 2 months). This seems completely unnecessary for a reading test. The standard score scale has a mean of 100 and a standard deviation of 15. This is an unfortunate choice of metric because such scores may be confused easily with deviation IQ scores on students' records. Percentile ranks would be much more meaningful but are not provided.

Kuder-Richardson reliabilities of .92 are reported. This is not surprising given the narrow content and format of the test. If the test is to be used for educational purposes, information on the stability of children's scores over time is important to obtain. Test-retest data for the Reading Test AD are not reported. A study with 8- and 9-year-olds using Reading Test AD and (one month later) Reading Test BD is reported. This study is a poorly designed attempt to establish the equivalence of the AD and BD versions. To overcome procedural flaws in the data collection design, an attempt is made to statistically adjust the results to eliminate effects of sequential testing (which are confounded with practice effects) and effects that are "maturational." The data do not support the equivalence of the two forms. The test cannot be recommended if there is no evidence that the scores students obtain are stable over time or over different samples of sentences.

The raw scores are "corrected" by an unusual procedure. A student is awarded 1 point credit for each item answered correctly up to the place on the test "at which a gap of FIVE consecutive wrong answers occurs." No credit is given for correct answers beyond this point. Further, if the first five items are answered incorrectly or omitted, the student is given a score of zero.

The rationale offered for this scoring procedure is that a five-item "gap" indicates that a student has stopped using reading comprehension ability and that any items answered correctly after the gap are answered on the basis of guessing and/or "associated word recognition." The converse of this rationale, that word recognition plays no role in reading comprehension and that students do not use guessing strategies and word recognition skills in comprehending the "pre-gap" sentences, is not discussed. There was an attempt in 1955 to study the relationship between the number-right-after-the-gap-score (called the "tail-end score") and the number-right-before-the-gap-score (called the "corrected score"). The developer concludes, "The relationship between 'tail-end' and corrected scores may mean nothing more than that the less a child's corrected score the more opportunity he has for making a "tail-end" score, and it is unprofitable to speculate on the precise function involved." If a score adjustment cannot be demonstrated to improve the validity of the test, why use it?

SUMMARY. The Reading Test AD is a narrow measure of reading achievement. Because (*a*) its content is dated, limited in scope, and oriented toward privileged white males; and (*b*) the developer has provided no evidence to validate the claim that the test measures reading comprehension as this term is generally defined, the Reading Test AD cannot be recommended for use as either an instructional tool for teachers or a curriculum evaluation tool for evaluators. Given the large number of modern and professionally developed standardized reading tests in the marketplace, there is no reason for purchasing this test.

REVIEWER'S REFERENCE

American Educational Research Association, American Psychological Association, & National Council on Measurement in Education. (1985). *Standards for educational and psychological testing*. Washington, DC: American Psychological Association, Inc.

[311]

Reading Test SR-A and SR-B. Purpose: "Provide a means of estimating the reading attainment of primary school children." Ages 7-6 to 11-11; 1970-82; 2 similar tests: SR-A and SR-B; 1986 price data: £2.25 per 10 tests for either SR-A or SR-B, £1.75 per combined manual ('79, 17 pages); 20(25) minutes per test; Brian Pritchard, The National Foundation for Educational Research in England and Wales; NFER-Nelson Publishing Co., Ltd. [England].*

Review of the Reading Test SR-A and SR-B by ROBERT C. CALFEE, Professor of Education, School of Education, Stanford University, Stanford, CA:

The Reading Test SR-A/B is a 48-item group-administered sentence completion test designed to assess the reading achievement of primary school children. Each item is of the form: My dog can (talk, sing, fly, bark, draw). The student's task is to underline the word that is semantically appropriate to the context. The most difficult items deal with unfamiliar vocabulary and contexts; assuming that the student can decode the words, the primary demand is vocabulary knowledge.

The test demands are relatively slight, administration is fast and easy, and scoring would be straightforward if the test were converted to a multiple choice response format. As a screening device the instrument might have some advantages—it is fast and cheap. The reliability indices (intra-year internal consistencies) fall in the mid-.80s, somewhat low given the homogeneity of the task and the items.

I cannot recommend the instrument to most readers, however, because of several limitations. First, it will not be clear in most instances what is being assessed. Decoding skill, vocabulary knowledge, and background information are all intertwined in the task. The procedure provides no information about comprehension ability. The instrument is a thin reed whether used for student placement, diagnostic assessment, or program evaluation. The manual is quite skimpy—less than three pages of prose, and most of that on the technical aspects of norming and scoring. The instrument was developed in Great Britain, and details of the language as well as the norming population limit the utility outside of the country. Better alternatives exist.

Review of the Reading Test SR-A and SR-B by MARIAM JEAN DREHER, Associate Professor of Education, Department of Curriculum and Instruction, University of Maryland, College Park, MD:

The Reading Test SR-A and its alternate form SR-B require a child to read incomplete sentences and choose a correct last word from among either four or five choices. These sentence completion tests are intended to estimate "the reading attainment of primary school children." A prospective user of SR-A and SR-B should consider whether exclusive use of sentence completion adequately taps the reading skills being stressed in the user's reading program. For instance, because only single sentences are used, students' comprehension of connected discourse is not assessed. Thus, the tests would not match the curricular emphasis of a reading program that stresses the comprehension of passages and stories.

The author of SR-A and SR-B acknowledges the limitations of sentence completion and attempts to eliminate them by stating, "The tests do not claim to measure all aspects of reading skill but sentence completion tasks do correlate highly with other measures of reading." Unfortunately that statement is not elaborated. No information is provided on other reading measures which correlate with SR-A and SR-B or with any other sentence completion tests. Indeed, no information at all is offered regarding the validity of the tests.

SR-A and SR-B are intended for use in the first through fourth years of elementary school. Reliability coefficients ranging from .85 to .88 are reported for each school year and each test form. No correlations between the two test forms are given.

The author calculated the reliability coefficients using an index of interitem consistency (Kuder-Richardson Formula 21). But he justifies his choice of this form of reliability estimate by arguing that the procedure is acceptable because it is associated with test-retest correlation. If test-retest correlation is what the author considered ideal, it is unclear why another procedure was used. It is also unclear why the test-retest correlation would be ideal for this type of test since such a reliability procedure is aimed at establishing stability or consistency of performance over time. Yet the purpose of SR-A and SR-B is apparently to make inferences about students' ability to read at a given time; ongoing instruction should make this level of knowledge change over time. Consequently, a measure of interitem consistency such as was actually used appears to be appropriate and the justification of it in terms of an association with test-retest correlation is confusing.

The SR-A was standardized on 13,886 first through fourth year elementary school students ranging in age from 7 years 9 months to 11 years 8 months. A stratified random sampling procedure was used to make the sample representative of students in England and Wales. This sample was used to construct norm tables in which raw scores are converted to standard scores on the basis of year in school and a pupil's age. Norms for SR-B were constructed by calibrating the performance of 3,099 additional students against the original norms.

Standard scores are easily obtained from the norm tables. However, negligible information is provided to assist test users in interpreting the test scores once they are obtained. Test users are simply told that the standard scores have a mean of 100 and a standard deviation of 15. In addition, a very brief discussion of standard error of measurement is included that would be of questionable value to anyone not already very familiar with the concept.

The SR-A and SR-B can be administered quickly and easily. Students are given 20 minutes to work on the 48 items. However, a redesign of the first page of the test booklet should be considered because the first six items are in full view as children fill in identifying information and complete the practice items. Rather than allowing faster students to get a head start on this speeded test by reading ahead, the author should begin the test on the second page.

Each test form covers a wide range of difficulty because the test is to be used across first through fourth year elementary school levels; norms extend from ages 7 years 6 months to 11 years 11 months. Although such a range of difficulty may avoid the problem of ceiling and floor effects that exist when a test of more limited range is given at a particular grade level, there is a trade-off with such a wide-ranged approach. With only 48 items on each form, the difficulty of the items accelerates rapidly. Therefore, beginners may quickly find the test too difficult and perhaps become discouraged.

One must assume the author intends SR-A and SR-B to be used to track progress over the four grade levels for which the test is targeted. If so, then a discussion is needed of appropriate intervals for administering the test and appropriate use of the alternate forms. The manual for SR-A and SR-B offers no information on how the two forms are to be used. For instance, does the author recommend giving one form at the beginning of each school year and the other at the end? Or perhaps the test is to be given yearly with the two forms given in alternate years so that students encounter the same test only twice. Possible problems that may be encountered in administering the same test more than once to the same students should also be discussed in the manual.

In summary, although the Reading Tests SR-A and SR-B are easy to administer and score, the manual presents no information on the validity of the tests and next to nothing to help users interpret students' scores. In addition, the one sentence description of the purpose does not explicate such questions as why two forms are provided or how these two forms should be used in tracking students' progress over the first through fourth years in elementary school. If the SR-A and SR-B are to be useful tests, the manual needs to include a good deal more information and to clarify much of what is included. In addition, test users outside of England and Wales should develop local norms before using the tests for any important educational decision making.

[312]

Receptive One-Word Picture Vocabulary Test. Purpose: Assesses a child's ability to verbally identify pictures of objects. Ages 2-0 to 11-11; 1985; ROWPVT; individual; 1988 price data: $46 per manual (47 pages), test plates, and 25 record forms; Spanish forms available; (10–15) minutes; Morrison F. Gardner; Academic Therapy Publications.*

Review of the Receptive One-Word Picture Vocabulary Test by JANICE A. DOLE, Assistant Professor of Educational Studies, University of Utah, Salt Lake City, UT:

The Receptive One-Word Picture Vocabulary Test (ROWPVT) is a norm-referenced, individually administered test designed to assess "a child's receptive single-word vocabulary." The test consists of a set of 100 plates, ordered in difficulty. Each plate has four pictures on it. The child is asked to identify the picture that matches the word presented orally by the examiner. For example, the child is shown a plate with black and white line drawings of objects such as a ball, a shoe, a doll, and a bicycle, and is asked to point to the shoe. The test can be administered to children from ages 2 through 11 years 11 months in 10 to 15 minutes.

ADMINISTRATION AND SCORING. The ROWPVT is a straightforward, easy-to-administer test. Directions for establishing basals and ceilings and for scoring the test are adequate. Appropriate cautions are provided for the examiner, and the manual points out potential difficulties in testing. However, it would be useful if the directions were scripted in boldface. Scripted directions help ensure the standardization of testing, and directions in boldface are especially helpful for examiners.

Directions for administering the test to Spanish-speaking children are included in the Administration and Scoring section of the manual. These directions are wholly inadequate for the administration and interpretation of the test to Spanish-speaking children.

No standardization of the Spanish version was undertaken. Nor was the test administered to any Spanish-speaking children as part of the actual standardization process. Finally, the manual states that the test can be administered to Spanish-speaking children to assess English vocabulary, and then "a program of English development can be initiated." However, this instrument is inadequate for setting up a remedial English program because the test measures only a small portion of language acquisition.

NORMATIVE INFORMATION. Standardization was accomplished by administering the ROWPVT to 1,128 children in the San Francisco Bay area. Raw scores were converted to standard scores based on the norms from the Expressive One-Word Picture Vocabulary Test (EOWPVT), a test developed by the same author. The ROWPVT was designed and normed as a companion to the EOWPVT.

The standardization procedures described for the ROWPVT must be regarded as inadequate. The test appears to have been standardized on a relatively homogeneous sample of subjects in San Francisco, California. Socio-economic and ability levels of the subjects in the sample were not adequately reported. It is indicated that "Parents brought the very young children to the Child Development Center [at Children's Hospital in San Francisco] to be tested." It is not clear whether parents were asked to bring their children in, or whether they brought their children in for other reasons. The latter case would result in a nonrepresentative sample of subjects.

Norms for this test include standard scores comparable to those on the EOWPVT, stanines, language ages, and percentile ranks. The manual is particularly good in discussing the use and interpretation of these derived scores. Examiners with a rudimentary knowledge of descriptive statistics should be able to understand the manual's description of each of these scores, what the scores mean, and how they can be used in evaluating performance.

RELIABILITY AND VALIDITY. Reliability is determined by Cronbach's alpha. These correlation coefficients, as well as standard errors of measurement (*SEM*) for raw scores and standard scores, are reported in 6-month intervals for ages 2 through 5 and 1-year intervals for ages 6 through 12. Coefficients ranged from .81 to .93, with a median of .90. *SEM* for raw scores ranged from 2.37 to 3.79 with a median of 3.33. These figures are regarded as adequate, although test-retest reliability should be reported as well.

Content and criterion-related validity are discussed for the ROWPVT. The manual reports that "pictures and verbal descriptions that represented words and pictures that children are typically exposed to" were selected for possible inclusion in the test. These words were then reviewed and evaluated by teachers and speech and language pathologists. How representative are these words of the domain of "receptive vocabulary?" The answer to this question is important for establishing the content validity of this test. A dilemma arises if more abstract words or words that can't be easily translated into pictures are part of what we agree to be "receptive vocabulary." No data are provided to answer this concern.

However, even if we can demonstrate that the words on this test do not reflect the full scope of receptive vocabulary, it is still possible for the author to support the validity of the test by demonstrating its convergent and discriminant validity. Unfortunately, data are not provided to adequately address these issues. The manual reports an average correlation coefficient of .42 between the ROWPVT and the Vocabulary subtests of the WPPSI and the WISC-R. But this correlation is not adequate for establishing the convergent validity of the ROWPVT, or, for that matter, the manual's assertion of criterion-related validity.

Unfortunately, there are no additional criterion-related measures which would help establish the ROWPVT's validity or would explain why the ROWPVT does differ so much from the Weschler tests. Since the ROWPVT and the EOWPVT correlate so highly ($r = .89$), it is likely that these two tests measure largely the same constructs. But what are they, and how do they relate to language? This information is not provided.

These questions point out a larger problem related to the test and the manual. There is no theoretical rationale presented for the ROWPVT. The manual states that the test is designed to provide norms comparable to the EOWPVT. An examiner can use information from both tests to compare a child's performance on receptive versus expressive vocabulary. But the manual does not provide a rationale for these measures. How do expressive and receptive vocabulary relate to overall language ability? And what would be the advantage of giving one or both of these tests over other, more global measures of language?

A final problem is reflected in the stated purpose for the test. It is stated in the manual that information can be gleaned about differences in language skills caused by language impairment, language delay, bilingualism, and a host of other factors. Then the examiner is told that poor performance on the test could be due to another variety of factors, including problems in hearing, auditory discrimination, auditory memory, visual memory, etc. In fact, so many factors are included that it is difficult to evaluate what an examiner would know based on the results of this test, and what an examiner would do with what s/he finds out.

SUMMARY. The ROWPVT is an individually administered test designed to be a companion test to the EOWPVT and to measure receptive knowledge of single words. The test is easy to administer, score, and interpret. The standardization procedures reported for the test are inadequate. No theoretical rationale is given for the test. For example, the manual does not provide sufficient information for the examiner to understand how this test fits into a framework for measuring language abilities. Inadequate information is provided to the examiner for understanding the test's usefulness in assessing potential language problems. Finally, reported reliabilities for this test are adequate, but insufficient evidence is provided in the manual to establish the validity of the test. In light of the revisions and new standardization of the Peabody Picture Vocabulary Test—Revised (PPVT-R), I would recommend PPVT-R over this competitor as a measure of receptive vocabulary. Further study and additional data are needed to warrant confidence in the ROWPVT as a superior alternative to the PPVT-R.

Review of the Receptive One-Word Picture Vocabulary Test by JANICE SANTOGROSSI, Instructor of Special Education and Communication Disorders, University of Nebraska-Lincoln, Lincoln, NE:

The Receptive One-Word Picture Vocabulary Test (ROWPVT) is an untimed, individually administered measure of single-word receptive vocabulary which was designed to accompany the Expressive One-Word Picture Vocabulary Test (EOWPVT). The ROWPVT and the EOWPVT yield similar scores ($r = .89$), which makes possible direct comparisons between the two measures.

The ROWPVT contains 100 items arranged in order of increasing difficulty. The use of a basal (highest eight consecutive correct responses) and ceiling (lowest six incorrect responses out of eight consecutive items) makes administration of all the items unnecessary. The author employed evaluations by classroom teachers and speech-language pathologists and item analysis of the frequency of correct responses to each item to determine item selection and sequence.

The author states that the ROWPVT requires 10 to 15 minutes to administer and 5 minutes or less to score. Trial administration and scoring by this reviewer supported the author's claim. For the purpose of achieving consistent presentation, the author includes a pronunciation guide for stimulus words in the test manual.

The illustrations for the ROWPVT are arranged horizontally, four pictures to a 5 1/2 by 11 inch page in a spiral bound book. The author states that he arranged the pictures in a single, horizontal row based on a survey of 1,000 psychologists who presumably reported that left-to-right scanning is easier for young children.

The illustrations for the ROWPVT are rather crude line drawings. The poor quality of the illustrations is also a long-recognized drawback of the ROWPVT's predecessor, the EOWPVT. In addition, many of the drawings in the ROWPVT have inappropriate size relationships to each other (e.g., page 4, on which the drawings of the flower, fan, and leaf are approximately the same size as the drawing of the tree).

The examiner subtracts the number of errors from the number of the ceiling item to obtain the raw score. The raw score can be converted to a language age, standard score, and stanine score. The use of these types of scores is an improvement over the IQ score and mental age scores used for the EOWPVT. This reviewer suggests, however, that the author would have been better advised to use another term such as "receptive vocabulary age" or "age equivalent" instead of "language age," because receptive vocabulary is only one component of language.

To aid in interpretation the author provides the standard error of measurement (*SEM*) for raw scores and standard scores at each age level.

Direct comparisons may be made between the child's performance on the ROWPVT and the EOWPVT using the standard scores. The author provides the standard error of difference for the two tests and suggests that a standard score difference of 9 or more points reflects a true difference in receptive versus expressive vocabulary while a difference of less than 9 points is indicative of error of measurement.

The author employed Cronbach's alpha, to determine the internal consistency of the ROWPVT. The reliability of coefficients for each age level range from .81 to .93 with a median of .90. The *SEM*s for raw scores range from 2.37 to 3.79 with a median of 3.33. For standard scores, the *SEM*s range from 3.97 to 6.53 with a median of 4.50. The reliability coefficients are below .90 for the 2-0 to 2-5, 2-6 to 2-11, 3-6 to 3-11, 9-0 to 9-11, and 11-0 to 11-11 age levels. The reliability data indicate adequate support for the consistency of the ROWPVT in measuring receptive vocabulary, except at those age levels indicated (i.e., where reliability coefficients are below .90). No test-retest reliability data are presented.

The author reports information about three kinds of validity: content, item, and criterion-related. The author established content validity by having classroom teachers and speech-language pathologists evaluate the pictures and verbal descriptions to determine the pictures and words to which children are typically exposed at home or at school. Pictures and verbal descriptions with possible ethnic, regional, or gender bias and words that could not be translated into Spanish were excluded from the final form of the ROWPVT. In addition, the author had classroom teachers and speech-language pathologists assign items to age levels. Item validity was established, according to the author, "by the retention of only those items that yielded a greater percent passing as chronological age increases." These are subjective methods of establishing content and item validity. In addition, the author provides no information concerning the experience or qualifications of the professionals he consulted, the criteria used to make judgements, or the extent of agreement among the professionals.

The author examined the criterion-related validity of the ROWPVT by correlating raw scores from the ROWPVT with raw scores from the vocabulary subtests of the Wechsler Preschool and Primary Scale of Intelligence (WPPSI) and the Wechsler Intelligence Scale for Children—Revised (WISC-R) for 935 children in the standardization sample. These correlation coefficients range from .23 to .70 with a median of .42. The author adds that additional criterion-related validity can be inferred from the high correlation (r = .89) between raw scores for the ROWPVT and the EOWPVT. The reported correlations are inadequate for establishing the criterion-related validity of the ROWPVT. This reviewer wonders why the author chose to compare the ROWPVT to the vocabulary subtests of the WPPSI and the WISC-R, since the latter, in contrast to the ROWPVT, require the child to verbally express the meanings of words. A more appropriate comparison would be to the Peabody Picture Vocabulary Test—Revised (PPVT-R), which is more like the ROWPVT. The author includes no information concerning attempts to establish the construct validity of the ROWPVT.

The similarity of the ROWPVT to the PPVT-R in purpose and design makes comparison of the two measures inevitable. In most respects, the PPVT-R is clearly superior to the ROWPVT. Most notable of the PPVT-R's advantages when compared to the ROWPVT is the size and composition of the standardization sample. The ROWPVT was normed on 1,128 children from the San Francisco Bay area, the PPVT-R on 4,200 children nationwide selected to approximate the 1970 census data. In addition, the quality and amount of reliability and validity data, the existence of two forms, and the applicability to a wider age range make the PPVT-R the clear choice for a measure of receptive vocabulary.

SUMMARY. The ROWPVT is a quick, easy method for estimating a child's single-word receptive vocabulary. Its best feature is that its norms are equivalent to those of the EOWPVT, which makes it possible to compare a child's receptive and expressive vocabulary scores. The superiority of the PPVT-R to the ROWPVT, however, is unquestionable. Further research to establish the test-retest reliability and validity of the ROWPVT, more extensive normative studies, and improvement of the illustrations are needed before this reviewer would recommend use of the ROWPVT over the PPVT-R as the better measure of receptive vocabulary.

[313]

Recognition Memory Test. Purpose: "Geared to detect minor degrees of memory deficit across a wide age range of the adult population." Adult patients referred for neuropsychological assessment; 1984; RMT; 2 scores: Words, Faces; individual; 1986 price data: £34.25 per complete kit; £25 per set of test booklets; £3.50 per 25 record forms; £5.95 per manual (16 pages); administration time not reported; Elizabeth K. Warrington; NFER-Nelson Publishing Co., Ltd. [England].*

TEST REFERENCES

1. Kapur, N. (1987). Some comments on the technical acceptability of Warrington's Recognition Memory Test. *British Journal of Clinical Psychology*, 26, 144-146.

Review of the Recognition Memory Test by RUSSELL L. ADAMS, Director, Psychology Internship Program, University of Oklahoma Health Sciences Center, Oklahoma City, OK:

This test, which is a measure of recognition memory of both words and faces, was designed to detect *minor* degrees of memory deficits in patients with known or suspected memory disorders.

The test consists of two separate instruments—Recognition Memory for Words (RMW) and Recognition Memory for Faces (RMF). In the Recognition Memory for Words Test, the patient is presented with 50 words of 4 to 6 letters in length. The words are frequently occurring words in the English vocabulary. The words are presented at the rate of one word every 3 seconds. The patient is then presented with a card containing 50 word pairs. Each pair contains a word previously presented and a distractor. The subject's task is to select the word previously presented.

The Recognition Memory for Faces is an analogous task except the test stimuli consist of 50 photographs of unfamiliar faces. After presentation of 50 faces, the patient is asked to select the previously presented face from a pair of two faces. Fifty such pairs are presented.

The test has some very strong assets. The test manual presents data on 310 volunteer subjects, ranging in age from 18 to 70. Separate norms are presented for three age groups: <40, ages 40–54, ages >55. Age norms are important because there is a clear decrement in the memory scores of normative subjects in the older age groups. More importantly, however, the manual also presents the results of 134 patients with right-hemisphere lesions and 145 patients with left-hemisphere lesions. These lateralized-brain-injured patients were further divided into frontal-, parietal-, temporal-, or occipital-lesion groups. The fact that this test has such a large sample of patients with lateralized damage sets it aside from most other memory measures. Getting documented cases of lateralized disorders is very difficult.

Although the manual states the pathology in these lateralized groups includes 65% neoplastic lesions and 31% vascular lesions, the reader does not know the exact type of lesions, the chronicity of the lesions, or whether testing was done prior to or after surgery. These factors can greatly affect memory disorders and, in this reviewer's opinion, should have been reported in the manual. The manual also presents performance data on a group of 112 patients with documented cerebral atrophy as measured by the CT scan. The degree of atrophy was separately assessed by both (*a*) width of sulci and (*b*) width of ventricles on a 5-point scale. Patients with obvious marked dementing processes were not included. Apparently the decision to exclude these patients was made on clinical grounds when it was felt that patients were not up to the demands of this rather complicated memory task. This procedure effectively eliminated patients with severe dementia. Unfortunately, the implication of this approach is that it would be difficult to do repeat testing of patients with progressive memory disorders who at the time of retest may be in the severe range, because no norms are available on the more significantly demented patients. The manual, however, clearly points out that this test is for patients with mild memory disorder. Of course, one test cannot be expected to do everything.

The fact that the test has both a verbal-memory measure and a nonverbal-memory measure is another real asset, because the dominant hemisphere is thought to play a major role in the verbal memory and the nondominant hemisphere in the nonverbal memory. The manual presents the very important finding that there was a highly significant impairment in the right-hemisphere-lesion groups on the RMF, while there was no corresponding impairment on the RMW. Similarly, the patients with lesions in the left hemisphere were impaired on both the RMW and the RMF compared with the normal subjects. However, as expected, the left-hemisphere group was significantly worse than the right-hemisphere group on the RMW measure. In addition, the right-hemisphere group performed significantly poorer on the RMF than the left-hemisphere group. This finding would make the test useful in separating right-hemisphere-damaged from left-hemisphere-damaged patients. However, one must be careful to note this is only one of many measures that must be used in order to differentiate these two groups. The actual percent of patients with deficit scores (poorer than the performance of 95% of the normal patients) was seldom over 40%. That would mean that 60% of the brain-injury group would be misclassified as would 5% false positives in the normative sample.

No data are presented concerning an overall measure of recognition memory that would be obtained by adding together the performance scores on the RMF and RMW. Such data may be important, especially in diffuse brain-injured patients. Psychometric theory would suggest that the more items the memory measure has, the higher the reliability of the measure would be. Why this information was not included in the manual is unknown.

Also, it was noted that there was no parallel form of the test available. Again, no test can be perfect, but such parallel forms are helpful for repeat testing of a progressive disorder such as memory impairment.

Unfortunately, the reliability coefficients of these measures were not presented. Granted, test-retest reliability would be inappropriate in a memory measure because once the test is given, the patient would likely remember much of this material on the next presentation. However, some type of internal consistency reliability estimate would be in order. If parallel forms of the test were available, the reliability between these two parallel measures would also be helpful.

The manual presents data in a very scientific and appropriate manner. The test user is likely to benefit from the scholarly approach of the author. It would be helpful, however, to have a section in the manual demonstrating how performance on this test could be helpful in clinical planning. Perhaps case examples would be helpful. Also I think a section dealing with possible problems in using the instrument would be useful.

The various tables presented in the manual did not present summary information concerning false positives, false negatives, hits, and misses when the test was used with various subgroups. Such information is clearly of great importance and should be included in future revisions of the test.

In summary, the Recognition Memory Test is an excellent measurement tool. The manual presents detailed information, not only on normal test performance, but also on lateralized lesions and patients with diffuse atrophy. Moreover, the performance of patients who have lesions in particular lobes of each hemisphere is described. I would anticipate frequent use of this test in the future.

Additional studies need to be conducted and cross-validation studies undertaken. However, given the fact that this test was copyrighted only in 1984, such data may well be forthcoming in future revisions. The test has some advantages over the Wechsler Memory Scale because the Wechsler Memory Scale, as described in its manual, dilutes the various memory components of the test by averaging scores. After reviewing the test manual, this reviewer (who, parenthetically, had not used the test previously) will start to include it periodically in his test battery. This reviewer would suggest that future revisions of this test include some measure of free recall of the words rather than just recognition memory. Free recall of words could simply be obtained prior to the recognition-memory portion of the test. Similarly, perhaps the test could further be expanded by having a delayed-component recognition memory obtained 30 minutes after the initial recall. Delayed recognition may well result in additional clinical data.

[314]

Revised Children's Manifest Anxiety Scale. Purpose: "Designed to assess the level and nature of anxiety in children and adolescents from 6 to 19 years old." Ages 6–19; 1985; RCMAS; revision and published version of the Children's Manifest Anxiety Scale (CMAS); 5 scores: Physiological Anxiety, Worry/Oversensitivity, Social Concerns/Concentration, Total Anxiety, Lie; 1986 price data: $33 per complete kit including 100 test sheets, scoring key, and manual (106 pages); $16.50 per 100 test sheets; $7.50 per scoring key; $12.75 per manual; (10–15) minutes; Cecil R. Reynolds and Bert O. Richmond; Western Psychological Services.*

TEST REFERENCES

1. Reynolds, C. R. (1983). Test bias: In God we trust; all others must have data. *The Journal of Special Education*, 17, 241-260.

2. Argulewicz, E. N., & Miller, D. C. (1984). Self-report measures of anxiety: A cross-cultural investigation of bias. *Hispanic Journal of Behavioral Sciences*, 6, 397-406.

3. Paget, K. D., & Reynolds, C. R. (1984). Dimensions, levels and reliabilities on the Revised Children's Manifest Anxiety Scale with learning disabled children. *Journal of Learning Disabilities*, 17, 137-141.

4. Strauss, C. C., Forehand, R., Frame, C., & Smith, K. (1984). Characteristics of children with extreme scores on the Children's Depression Inventory. *Journal of Clinical Child Psychology*, 13, 227-231.

5. Reynolds, C. R. (1985). Multitrait validation of the Revised Children's Manifest Anxiety Scale for Children of high intelligence. *Psychological Reports*, 56, 402.

6. Strauss, C. C., Forehand, R., Smith, K., & Frame, C. L. (1986). The association between social withdrawal and internalizing problems of children. *Journal of Abnormal Child Psychology*, 14, 525-535.

7. Hooper, S. R. (1987). Concurrent validity of the common belief inventory for students. *Perceptual and Motor Skills*, 64 (1), 331-334.

Review of the Revised Children's Manifest Anxiety Scale by FRANK M. GRESHAM, Professor of Psychology, Louisiana State University, Baton Rouge, LA:

The Revised Children's Manifest Anxiety Scale (RCMAS) is a 37-item self-report instrument designed to measure the level and degree of anxiety in children and adolescents. The RCMAS is designed for children and youth between the ages of 6 and 19 years and, according to the manual, has a third-grade reading level. The authors claim the RCMAS can be administered in a group testing situation for children 9½ years and older. The manual recommends the instrument be individually read to children in grades K–3 and to nonreaders. Children respond to each of the 37 items by marking a Yes or No response.

The authors provide a succinct yet informative review of the anxiety literature and relate the RCMAS to a theoretical conceptualization of anxiety. The manual is well-written and extremely well-organized. Potential users of the scale can easily locate major aspects of the test such as development, administration, scoring, standardization, and psychometric characteristics. Unlike many scales of this nature, the RCMAS manual contains the essential components of test development and could serve as a model for how to organize a test manual. The authors are obviously very knowledgeable of test development standards and exemplify this knowledge in the manual.

SCALE DESCRIPTION AND COMPONENTS. The RCMAS consists of five scores: (*a*) Total Anxiety, (*b*) Physiological Anxiety, (*c*) Worry/Oversensitivity, (*d*) Social Concerns/Concentration, and (*e*) Lie Scale. The Total Anxiety score is based upon 28 items with 9 items comprising the Lie Scale. The authors correctly advise that the three anxiety subscales should be interpreted cautiously because of limited reliability levels and should be used only as an aid in hypothesis generation.

The Total Anxiety Score is expressed as a T score ($M = 50$, s $= 10$) and the subscales are expressed as scale scores ($M = 10$, s $= 3$). Percentile ranks are provided for each of the RCMAS scores. Norms are provided at 1-year intervals and for each ethnic/sex combination for blacks and whites. The authors recommend the use of norms separated by age, ethnicity, and sex. The manual points out the literature is inconclusive regarding demographic differences in anxiety. The Lie Scale is a positive feature of the instrument and is designed to detect acquiescence, social desirability, or faking of responses.

STANDARDIZATION. The RCMAS was standardized on 4,972 children between the ages of 6 and 19 years. The standardization sample contained 2,208 white males (44%), 2,176 white females (44%), 289 black males (5.8%), and 299 black females (6%). The sample was obtained from children in 13 states and more than 80 school districts from all major geographic regions of the U.S. The sample was not stratified according to SES although the authors believe that "an excellent cross-section of school children was obtained." The manual, however, provides no data to support this statement. Rural and urban areas were equally represented in the standardization sample. Approximately 600 children in the sample were classified as handicapped (i.e., educably mentally retarded, learning disabled, or gifted).

In summary, the standardization sample appears to be representative of the U.S. population, but the authors do not provide contrasts with census data to document how closely the standardization sample tracks the U.S. population. Users of the instrument can, however, be reasonably confident the RCMAS has a well-standardized and representative sample.

RELIABILITY. The manual reports internal consistency estimates (coefficient alphas) for white and black males and females for each of the 12 age levels for the Total Anxiety score. Standard errors of measurement for the Total Anxiety score are also provided to assist users in interpretation of individual scores. Reliability estimates ranged from .42 (Age 6, black females) to .87 (Age 12, black males and Age 15, black males). Reliability estimates collapsed across the 12 age levels ranged from .79 to .85 (median = .82). Of the 48 coefficient alphas reported across age, race, and sex, 17 alphas fall below .80. As such, users should be cautious in using the RCMAS for these groups given the low internal consistency estimates.

Coefficient alphas are also reported for each of the three anxiety subscales and the Lie Scale. Most of these alphas fall below .80, some far below (.15) indicating poor domain sampling. Individual anxiety subscales are too unreliable to merit interpretation for most persons in the standardization sample.

The manual reports less data concerning the stability of the instrument. One study reported in the manual found a stability coefficient of .68 for the Total Anxiety score and .58 for the Lie Scale score for 534 children tested 9 months apart. Stability estimates increase dramatically when the interval between testings is shorter. For example, the manual reports a .98 stability estimate for the Total Anxiety score over a 3-week interval. The relatively low stability coefficients for the Total Anxiety score over a 9-month interval and the relatively high stability coefficients over a 3-week interval seems to argue against the RCMAS as a measure of trait anxiety as the test authors claim. If in fact the RCMAS is a measure of trait anxiety, then one would not expect such dramatic differences in the stability of the trait at various time intervals. All stability estimates reported in the manual are for children below grade 7. No stability data are reported for junior and senior high school students.

In summary, the Total Anxiety score is reliable enough across most ages to permit reliable interpretations. The anxiety subscales, however, should not be interpreted because of large errors of measurement contained in the scores. Stability estimates for the Total Anxiety score are sketchy, but encouraging. The RCMAS needs further research investigating the stability of the instrument at upper age levels (i.e., ages 13–19 years).

VALIDITY. The RCMAS manual focuses upon the development of construct validity for the instrument. The RCMAS is considered by the authors to be a measure of trait anxiety: that is, a lasting predisposition to experience anxiety in a variety of settings. As previously mentioned, the 9-month stability coefficient for the RCMAS was only .68 arguing against the RCMAS as a measure of trait anxiety. The manual does, however, report higher correlations between the RCMAS Total Anxiety score and a measure of trait anxiety (r = .67) than between Total Anxiety and a measure of state anxiety (r = .10).

The factor analysis of the RCMAS standardization sample used a common-factor model inserting communalities in the diagonal and rotating to an orthogonal solution. The authors state that Varimax rotation maximizes the variance accounted for by each factor and is of maximum utility when one is interested in clinical or applied use.

A Varimax (orthogonal) solution indicates that at a theoretical level the factors are assumed to be uncorrelated. This makes neither theoretical nor empirical sense. Theoretically, one would not expect the various facets of anxiety to be uncorrelated, particularly for a measure that purports to be a measure of trait anxiety. If there is a large general anxiety factor in the RCMAS as the authors suggest and if the RCMAS is a measure of trait anxiety, then one would expect the various minor factors to be correlated. Empirically, the correlation between the RCMAS factors range from .49 to .85 (median = .67), suggesting correlated factors and an oblique solution.

A major error in the RCMAS is the presentation of a five-factor solution showing the factor structure of the scale. The factor loadings for each of the three anxiety factors are not particularly large (.26 to .61) and the solution did not show a particularly good simple structure. There are a number of items that load on more than one factor thereby clouding the interpretability of the factor structure.

An even more serious error in the five-factor solution as reported by the authors is that the factor matrix accounts for 200% of the variance. Obviously, this is mathematically impossible. The authors have also incorrectly calculated the percent of variance accounted for by each factor. For example, the authors claim Factor I (Physiological Anxiety) accounts for 34% of the variance (Eigenvalue = 2.24). Actually, Factor I accounts for only 6% of the variance (2.24/37 = .06). Similar errors occur for each factor. The authors are using an unknown algorithm for calculation of percent variance accounted for by each factor. Test users should be aware the factor analysis presented in the manual contains inadequate information to correctly interpret the factor analysis.

The manual also inappropriately refers to a validity study as a multitrait-multimethod (MTMM) investigation. A MTMM refers to the measurement of two or more traits using two or more methods in which both traits and methods are crossed. The study reported in the manual is simply a concurrent validity study and cannot address convergent or discriminant validity.

In summary, validity data for the RCMAS are sparse and the test authors appear to have botched the factor analysis of the instrument. The standardization data should be refactored before test users can have faith in the dimensions underlying the RCMAS. This, however, may be a moot issue given the unreliability of the RCMAS subscales.

SUMMARY. The RCMAS appears to be a well-standardized self-report measure of anxiety. The standardization sample is based upon a large and what appears to be a representative sample of children and adolescents. Internal consistency reliability of the Total Anxiety score is adequate for individual interpretation but the reliabilities of the anxiety subscales are too low for separate subscale interpretation. The manual reports a paucity of data on stability of the RCMAS. Validity data for the instrument are sparse and the authors have apparently completed an inappropriate factor analysis of the scale. Future work with the scale, particularly the factor analysis, should be undertaken. The RCMAS may develop into one of the better measures of anxiety in children and adolescents.

Review of the Revised Children's Manifest Anxiety Scale by KRISTA J. STEWART, Associate Professor of Psychology, Tulane University, New Orleans, LA:

The Revised Children's Manifest Anxiety Scale (RCMAS) was developed in 1978 in order to address criticisms of the original Children's Manifest Anxiety Scale (CMAS; Castenada, McCandless, & Palermo, 1956). Goals for revision of the scale were to: (*a*) create an objective measure of children's anxiety suitable for group administration; (*b*) keep administration time to the minimum required for accurate, valid assessment; (*c*) make the reading level of items suitable for elementary school students but yet make the instrument one that could be used throughout the school years; (*d*) cover areas of anxiety not measured by the CMAS and determine whether anxiety would best be treated as unidimensional or multidimensional; (*e*) develop large-scale norms and information on the anxiety scores of diverse groups of children; and (*f*) make sure that all items meet the criteria for a good test item. The test developers have carefully attempted to meet each of these goals.

The RCMAS, entitled on the test sheet "What I Think and Feel," contains 37 self-report, yes-no items, 28 of which comprise the three anxiety subscales and 9 of which comprise the Lie subscale. Test items are written in statement form on approximately a third grade level. The test can be administered individually or in a group, although the authors suggest group administration only to children 9 1/2 years old or older. Items should be read by the examiner to first and second graders.

The Total Anxiety score and the Anxiety subscale scores are determined by the number of "yes" responses to the anxiety items. The Lie Score is determined by "yes" responses to the Lie subscale items and is used to determine if the child was making a valid attempt to respond to the Anxiety Scale or rather was simply marking "yes" to every item or trying to please the examiner. Thus, all questions are keyed in the "no" direction, a somewhat undesirable feature of the test. Three of the lie items contain negatives and are, as the authors acknowledge, potentially confusing.

The manual for this test, copyrighted in 1985, is excellent and might serve as a model for individuals developing tests. The authors discuss in a clear and cogent manner their rationale and the procedures followed for every stage of development of the test from its conception to the final product. Explanations of less familiar procedures are provided, and strengths and limitations of the test are explicitly stated.

The manual begins with a discussion of the construct of "anxiety" and how it has been measured in the past, a description of the RCMAS, and a notation of limitations of the RCMAS in the measurement of anxiety. Information is presented on administration, scoring, and interpretation of the test. Norms are provided for the total normative sample and also for each ethnic/sex combination for blacks and whites at 1-year intervals (except for years 17–19, which are collapsed into one interval). Included are interpretive explanations of each subscale and six case studies in which the RCMAS has been used as part of a complete psychoeducational battery. The authors provide details on the development and standardization of the test and include information on the tryout instrument as well as on the national norming of the RCMAS. Finally, the authors report on the psychometric properties of the test.

The authors have taken great care in the development of the RCMAS. From the 73 items of the tryout test instrument (42 Anxiety items and 11 Lie items adapted from the CMAS and 20 new items), the authors retained for the RCMAS the 28 Anxiety items and 9 Lie items that met the stated quantitative criteria for good test items. The national norming was then undertaken with children representing 13 states from all major geographic regions of the United States. The standardization sample for the test was 4,972 black and white, male and female children between the ages of 6 and 19 and included 600 special education children. The authors describe the procedures followed in deriving the standard scores for the test and include tables in the manual appendix for converting raw scores to scaled scores and percentiles.

Internal consistency reliability estimates are reported for the Total Anxiety Score for the test development sample and its comparison sample, the standardization sample, and several special populations. Most reliability estimates are above .80 with the exception of those for black females; at ages 6, 8, 10, and 11, reliability coefficients are significantly lower for black females than for white females at the same ages. The authors urge that special care be taken when using the RCMAS with black females under 12 years of age. Also, coefficient alpha reliability estimates are presented for each of the four subscales and, considering the brevity of the subscales, are good (mostly in the .60s), particularly for the Lie subscale (consistently in the .70s and .80s after age 8). Test-retest reliabilities are reported for two samples. Results suggest excellent reliability over a short interval (in the .90s for a 3-week interval between testings) and reasonable stability over a longer interval (.68 for a test interval of 9 months), thus supporting the usefulness of the RCMAS in assessing chronic anxiety in children. Based on coefficient alpha reliability estimates, the authors present standard errors of measurement by age, sex, and race thus enabling the test user to easily calculate a confidence interval for any child tested.

In order to establish the validity of the RCMAS, the authors report factor analyses of the responses of the test development sample, the standardization sample, and other special samples. For the full standardization sample, as well as for males only, females only, blacks only, and whites only, three anxiety and two lie factors emerged consistently. The three anxiety factors constituted the Anxiety subscales. The two lie factors resulted from a split of those Lie subscale questions containing and not containing negatives. To further support the construct validity of the RCMAS, the authors report convergent and divergent validity of the scale under conditions of concurrent administration of the State-Trait Anxiety Inventory for Children (STAIC; Spielberger, 1973). The RCMAS showed a large, significant correlation with the Trait scale of the STAIC (.85) but a low correlation with the State scale (.24). The authors note that the magnitude of the correlation between the STAIC Trait scale and the RCMAS suggests that the two scales may be used as alternate forms. Also, a study using multitrait-multimethod procedures is reported and provides support for the construct validity of the RCMAS.

Finally, information is presented on evaluation of item bias for ethnicity and sex. The authors report that the presence of biased test items was statistically confirmed but that the significant Item x Ethnicity x Sex interaction term accounted for less than 1% of the total variation in test performance and thus appears to have minimal impact on test score variation.

In summary, the RCMAS is a carefully constructed revision of the original CMAS with psychometric properties that support its usefulness as a measure of the trait of anxiety with children of school age. Some caution needs to be taken, however, when the scale is used with black females under age 12, for whom reliability estimates have been found to be low.

REVIEWER'S REFERENCES

Castaneda, A., McCandless, B., & Palermo, D. (1956). The children's form of the Manifest Anxiety Scale. *Child Development*, 27, 317-326.

Spielberger, C. D. (1973). *Preliminary manual for the State-Trait Anxiety Inventory for Children ("How I Feel" Questionnaire)*. Palo Alto, CA: Consulting Psychologists Press.

[315]

Rhode Island Test of Language Structure.

Purpose: "Provides a measure of English language development—a profile of the child's understanding of language structure—and assessment data." Hearing-impaired children ages 3–20, hearing children ages 3–6; 1983; RITLS; primarily designed for use with hearing-impaired children, "both a criterion-referenced and norm referenced instrument"; measures syntax response errors for 20 sentence types, both simple and complex, including relative and adverbial clauses, subject and other complements, reversible and nonreversible passives, datives, deletions, negations, conjunctives, and embedded imperatives; individual, can be administered orally or in signed English; 1986 price data: $56 per complete kit including booklet with illustrations, 10 analysis sheets, 10 response sheets, and manual ('83, 112 pages); $49 per test booklet; $9 per 10 response forms and 10 analysis sheets; (30) minutes; Elizabeth Engen and Trygg Engen; PRO-ED, Inc.*

Review of the Rhode Island Test of Language Structure by LYNN S. BLISS, Associate Professor of Speech, Wayne State University, Detroit, MI:

The Rhode Island Test of Language Structure (RITLS) was designed for two purposes: to provide information about a child's level of language development and to give educators information for planning a child's educational program. It focuses on the comprehension of syntactic structures using a picture-verification task. The RITLS has been standardized on a hearing-impaired as well as a normal-hearing sample.

The emphasis of the RITLS is on syntax. The authors made it clear the aim is to have the child respond to syntactic structure in the absence of contextual and other extralinguistic cues. The RITLS consists of 100 stimulus items divided into 50 simple and 50 complex constructions. The stimuli consist of a wide range of syntactic constructions. Morpheme structures were deleted because they are not perceptually salient and are difficult for hearing-impaired individuals to notice.

The RITLS was developed for use as both a criterion- and a norm-referenced instrument. As the first option, the RITLS can be used to describe a child's performance with respect to specific syntactic structures. Normative data were obtained in order to expand the usefulness of the RITLS as a norm-referenced test.

The RITLS consists of a test manual, a picture booklet with instructions, a scoring sheet that provides a place to record the number of the picture to which the child pointed so that an error analysis can be made, and an analysis sheet enabling the examiner to determine specific strengths and weaknesses in syntactic comprehension. The stimuli can be presented in one of two manners: oral or oral in combination with signing. Percentiles and *T* scores (standard scores with a mean of 50 and a standard deviation of 10) are presented along with guidelines for interpretation and educational planning. An examination time of 30 minutes is suggested.

Reliability, validity, and standardization data were reported within two contexts: a pilot study and a standardization study to develop normative data. The pilot study was designed to evaluate the test by comparing hearing and hearing-impaired children. Ninety-one kindergarten hearing children and 69 hearing-impaired children, ranging in age from 5 to 16 years, made up the sample. The hearing-impaired children exhibited a wide range of etiologies and hearing losses and were enrolled in the Rhode Island School for the Deaf. The pilot study used either signing and oral or oral-only for the hearing-impaired children, depending on with which communication style the child was most familiar. The results were used primarily as a basis for modifying the test stimuli.

Normative data were collected in a second study consisting of 364 hearing-impaired and

283 hearing children. The hearing-impaired children were divided into the following age groups: 5–7 years (65 children); 8–10 years (107 children); 11–13 years (92 children); 14–16 years (73 children); and 17+ years (27 children). The hearing children were divided into the following age groups: 3½ years (31 children); 4 years (75 children); 5 years (71 children); and 6 years (106 children). In this study all hearing-impaired children received the stimuli in a combined oral and signing approach. Most of the hearing-impaired children had profound sensorineural losses.

Kuder-Richardson Formula 20 correlations in the pilot study were .72 for the hearing children and .88 for the hearing-impaired children. From the larger standardization study, Kuder-Richardson Formula 20 results were .89 for the hearing-impaired group and .89 for the hearing children. Factor analyses of intercorrelations among the scores for each of the 20 sentence types (.28) and among the 100 items (.08) suggested, according to the authors, little redundancy in the test. The authors assert the factor analysis data supplement the reliability information. A split-half reliability coefficient obtained from the pilot test data was .91. When a subset of the children was retested later, the test-retest reliability coefficient was .62. No similar data are presented for the second study.

Information concerning validity is provided in terms of a general discussion concerning content-oriented and construct validity. The content-oriented validity was addressed by improving the content of the RITLS instead of correlating its scores with those of outside measurements. Items were improved by modifying the stimuli on the basis of the data obtained in the pilot study. The authors claim content validity is demonstrated because clearly defined linguistic structures are used in the RITLS. Construct validity was in terms of a description of items difficult for hearing-impaired and hearing children.

The RITLS has advantages and disadvantages. The advantages are: The inclusion of hearing-impaired individuals as part of the standardization group—this is useful for educators working with such children; the RITLS is easy to administer, score, and interpret; and there is a variety of syntactic structures and exemplars for investigation. The disadvantages are: The reliability and validity information is inadequate and needs to be expanded; over-reliance on syntax without consideration of the pragmatic aspects of comprehension; the omission of morphemes may fail to pick up mildly impaired children; lack of a complete test subject description; limited number of minority individuals will prevent generalization of the results; and absence of a method of error analysis misses valuable data interpretation.

In summary, the RITLS focuses on the comprehension of syntactic structures. Its standardization populations are hearing children from 3½ to 6 years and hearing-impaired individuals from 5 to over 17 years. A picture-verification task is used to assess children's ability to comprehend a variety of simple and complex sentences. It is very thorough and relatively quick to administer and score. Absence of adequate reliability and validity information warrant the user be cautious when using this test as a norm-referenced measure.

Review of the Rhode Island Test of Language Structure by JOAN I. LYNCH, Associate Professor of Language Science, University of Texas Health Science Center at Houston, Houston, TX:

The stated goal of the Rhode Island Test of Language Structure (RITLS) is to provide a measure of language development and to assist in educational planning. The domain of this test is language comprehension, particularly comprehension of syntax. The test contains 100 sentences representing, according to the authors, the syntactic range of the English language. The sentences are divided into 20 different Sentence Types with 10 types of Simple Sentences and 10 types of Complex Sentences. Each of the Sentence Types occurs five times thus allowing the test to be used as both a criterion-referenced instrument and a norm-referenced test. The RITLS has no base or ceiling and all 100 items must be given. Administration time is about 25 to 35 minutes for normal hearing children and about twice as long for the hearing impaired.

Comprehension is operationalized as the child's ability to point to the one of three pictures that best illustrates the sentence the examiner has said and/or signed using signed English. The manual contains general guidelines for administering the test. The test may be given by teachers, speech therapists, or anyone familiar with testing. Normative data by age group are provided for the normal hearing and the hearing impaired. The raw score is obtained by counting the number of errors. A percentile score and a *T* score can then be established from the tables provided. The Sentence Types are also ordered according to their level of difficulty. The authors recommend the test results be used with the hearing impaired to identify the type(s) of sentences difficult for the child in order to make placement decisions and to plan class work. They recommend the test might be used with normal hearing children in the following ways: (*a*) to screen preschool children; (*b*) to ascertain school readiness; (*c*) to provide entry/exit criteria for bilingual programs; and (*d*) to determine the type of program appropriate for the child.

In their consideration of validity, the authors indicate they focused on content and construct validity. They support construct validity by comparing their order of mastery of different sentence types with research studies of language acquisition and with studies of the language of the deaf. However, certain problems with test construction may adversely affect the validity of this test. The stated purpose of the test is to measure the child's knowledge of syntactic structures; however, in many instances the test may actually be measuring semantic knowledge. This is due to problems with the pictorial foils. For example in item 14, "The ball was thrown by the boy," the first picture shows a boy throwing a ball, the second a girl throwing a ball, and the third a boy throwing a stick. The contrasts are between boy/girl and ball/stick. A child who understood only the simple words BOY and BALL could score correctly in the absence of any knowledge of the Passive Nonreversible, which is the sentence type being tested. A number of other Simple Sentences of various types could be correctly identified if the child distinguished between man/woman or boy/girl. In item 4, which tests the Dative sentence type, a child who understood the verb GIVING could score correctly because this verb occurs only in the correct choice. Because it is possible to use strategies other than syntactic knowledge to decode an utterance, other likely strategies (e.g., gender distinction) must be controlled in the foils. It is unfortunate the authors chose not to correlate the results of this test with other tests of comprehension without these same weaknesses.

The choice of test sentence types may adversely influence the examiner's ability to predict whether a particular child might be expected to have problems comprehending language in real life situations. The authors have included several rarely used sentence types like Non-Initial Subject. Thus sentences such as (71) "It is the boy who the dog is following," and (79) "The one who is calling the boy is the girl," are given equal weight in the scoring system with more common sentence types like Relative Clauses or Adverbial Clauses. The authors have excluded such common sentence types as Questions. They justify the omission of questions by pointing out the difficulties of testing forms like the imperative and questions using a pictorial format. However, they chose to include imperatives and exclude questions.

Based upon information in the manual, evidence of test reliability is weak. Of primary concern is that although the authors recommend the use of RITLS with a variety of normal hearing children (e.g., bilingual, those with suspected language problems, and as a screening instrument), no data are included on the actual use of the test with these populations. The reported test-retest reliability of .62 does not appear acceptable despite the authors' suggestion this was due to language development. No mention is made of interexaminer reliability despite the fact the test was administered by different professionals at the various schools.

Test standardization procedures are also problematic. The pilot version was standardized on 91 kindergarten children with no known language/learning problem and on 69 hearing-impaired children between 5 and 16 years of age. The norming sample consisted of 283 normal-hearing children from English-speaking homes attending seven different rural, urban, and suburban schools in Rhode Island. Approximately equal numbers of boys and girls represented all ethnic and socioeconomic groups in the state. The 364 hearing-impaired subjects were enrolled in schools for the deaf in Rhode Island (25%), Massachusetts (15%), New Jersey (13%), and North Carolina (47%). The number of boys and girls was approximately equal and they ranged in age from 5 to over 17 years. No information was provided regarding their ethnic or socioeconomic status nor was there any reference to their scholastic aptitude or achievement levels. Only two of the subgroups, the 6-year-old normal hearing and the 8–10-year-old hearing impaired, met the APA criteria of 100 subjects per subgroup. Thus, the number of subjects in most groups is inadequate. The geographic distribution was limited to New England or the Eastern coast and may underrepresent some ethnic groups and socioeconomic levels. Because a strength of this test is its emphasis on the hearing-impaired population, the lack of specificity regarding this group is a loss. Comparisons of the scores based upon severity of hearing loss, type of training (oral versus total), and presence of other problems would be of importance. The choice of hearing-impaired subjects entirely from schools for the deaf is also a problem. The performance of children with equally severe hearing losses who were being mainstreamed into regular classes would be important when considering the norms for the hearing impaired.

While the focus of this test on the hearing-impaired population appears to fill a void among the current tests of language comprehension, the problems with validity, reliability, and the standardization group would need to be resolved before the RITLS could be recommended over other existing tests of language structure. Its strong resemblance to, at least, one other well-standardized and widely-used test of language comprehension (Test of Auditory Comprehension of Language, 1985 Revision) makes the use of that test preferable for most of the populations for which the authors recommend the RITLS. However, the RITLS appears to make a contribution to the assessment of the hearing impaired especially as a criterion-referenced measure to assist in class placement and program planning.

[316]

Rogers Criminal Responsibility Assessment Scales. Purpose: "To quantify essential psychological and situational variables at the time of the crime and to implement criterion-based decision models for criminal responsibility." Criminals; 1984; R-CRAS; criterion-referenced; completed immediately following a review of clinical records, police-investigative reports, and the final clinical interview with the patient-defendant; 5 scales: Patient Reliability, Organicity, Psychopathology, Cognitive Control, Behavioral Control; individual; 1987 price data: $22 per test kit including manual (62 pages) and 15 examination booklets; $14.50 per 15 examination booklets; $40 per 50 examination booklets; $8.50 per manual; administration time not reported; Richard Rogers; Psychological Assessment Resources, Inc.*

Review of the Rogers Criminal Responsibility Assessment Scales by ROBERT J. HOWELL, Professor of Psychology and Director of Clinical Psychology, Brigham Young University, and R. LYNN RICHARDS, Doctoral Student, Brigham Young University, Provo, UT:

The Rogers Criminal Responsibility Assessment Scales (R-CRAS) are designed to provide a systematic approach to evaluations of criminal responsibility. The scales are divided into two parts. Part I consists of 30 questions designed to establish the degree of impairment on psychological variables significant to the determination of insanity. Part II consists of a decision model for determination of criminal responsibility based upon the American Law Institute (ALI) Standard of Insanity. Part II also contains decision models for Guilty-But-Mentally-Ill (GBMI) and M'Naghten (latest agreed upon spelling is McNaughten) Standards. However, these last two decision models have not been empirically validated, therefore their use is restricted to research only.

The 30 items in Part I result in a composite rating ranging from 0–6, which is made from the integration of multiple sources of information. Questions 1–25 are used in determining insanity based upon the criteria of the American Law Institute (ALI) Standard of Insanity. The questions are divided into five scales designed to assess Patient Reliability, Organicity, Psychopathology, Cognitive Control, and Behavioral Control at the time of the alleged crime. Questions 26–30 are designed to assess criteria for the GBMI and M'Naghten standards of insanity.

Qualifications of forensic examiners using the R-CRAS include a Ph.D. in clinical or counseling psychology, or being a board certified or board eligible psychiatrist. Examiners must have substantial experience in forensic evaluations prior to employing the R-CRAS or obtain supervision from a professional who is so qualified. The R-CRAS is not a substitute for solid clinical training and specialized forensic experience.

The internal consistency of the R-CRAS as measured by Cronbach's alpha coefficient was .28 for Patient Reliability (two items), .52 for Organicity (five items), .80 for Psychopathology, .64 for Cognitive Control (four items), and .77 for Behavioral Control (seven items). A rigorous test of interrater reliability completed at an average interval of 2.7 weeks resulted in kappa reliability coefficients for the R-CRAS decision variables of .48 for Malingering, 1.00 for Organicity, .79 for Psychiatric Disorder, .75 for Loss of Cognitive Control, .80 for Loss of Behavioral Control, .89 for Loss of Control Due to Disorder, and .94 for Meeting the ALI Standard.

Construct validity was chosen as the most appropriate type of test validity because of the absence of meaningful criteria to establish criterion-related validity. Construct validity was divided into three components: substantive, structural, and external. Substantive validity is supported in light of the fact that the individual items on the R-CRAS were derived from the ALI Standard of Insanity. The structural validity of the R-CRAS was examined from two approaches. First, evidence is presented from three different studies indicating that distinct patterns of score evaluations do distinguish the sane from the insane, thus supporting the ALI construct of insanity. The second approach to structural validity is based upon the results of two-stage discriminant analysis in which the utilization of the R-CRAS summary scales correctly classified a high (83.3%) to exceptionally high (98.7%) percentage of clinically evaluated sane and insane subjects. Canonical loadings from the discriminant analysis are highly consistent with the ALI construct of insanity with each scale making a contribution to the final clinical opinion. The canonical loadings reported are: (*a*) Patient Reliability .41, (*b*) Organicity .63, (*c*) Psychopathology .69, (*d*) Cognitive Control .50, and (*e*) Behavioral Control .78. The third component of R-CRAS construct validity is its external validity, which was established by comparing the legal disposition of 93 legal cases with R-CRAS data. Although legal outcome is confounded by many variables outside of the psychological state of the person at the time of the crime, there was 95.2% agreement in the determination of sanity, and 73.3% agreement in the determination of insanity.

The R-CRAS is limited in examining the area of organic impairment because the range of organic impairment data is restricted. Therefore, examiners are cautioned to request thorough intellectual, neurological, and neuropsychological assessments in order to avoid the omission of organic impairment in the decision-making process. The second limitation involves the use of the GBMI and M'Naghten standards. As the R-CRAS now stands these standards are included only for research purposes and data from them should not be made available to the courts until such a time when their reliability and validity have been empirically established.

[317]

Safe Driver Attitude Test. Purpose: Measures "the attitudes of drivers, including handicapped and learning disabled adolescents, toward certain driving situations." Driver education students; 1981; 2 sets of scores: Profile of Responses, Numerical Score of Responses; test administered by cassette tape and filmstrips; 2 parts: General Driving Situations, Highway and Country Driving; 1986 price data: $59 per complete kit including ditto for student answers and profiles, 2 filmstrips, cassette, and teacher's guide ('81, 4 pages); (10–11) minutes per part; Russell L. Carey, Dawn Bashara, and Harry Schmadeke; Educational Activities, Inc.*

Review of the Safe Driver Attitude Test by BRUCE G. ROGERS, Associate Professor, Department of Educational Psychology and Foundations, University of Northern Iowa, Cedar Falls, IA:

The Safe Driver Attitude Test (SDAT) was designed, as its name implies, to measure those attitudes of automobile drivers likely to affect performance in actual driving situations. According to the stated purpose, the test was designed to be appropriate for a wide variety of drivers. It is intended to be used at the beginning of a driver education program to aid in identifying specific needs of that particular group and thus assist in adapting subsequent instruction to student needs. It is also recommended for use again at the end of the course to assess possible attitude changes. The test materials include two film strips and an audiotape.

Development of this instrument began with the specification of an affective model for defensive driving that included the attitudes (or intervening variables) of Egoism, Emotionalism, Cautiousness, Cooperation, Confidence, and Communication. After these terms were defined with explanations and illustrative behaviors, items related to them were formulated to elicit "the student's initial affective reaction" to simulations of actual driving dilemmas. In each item the student is asked to choose among three alternatives based upon the intervening variables. Unfortunately, the Teacher's Guide does not detail the development of the test, nor does it provide a method for interpreting the scores in terms of the intervening variables. Perhaps such a scheme originally existed; the principal author provided this reviewer with a copy of a draft of the model, but a request to the publisher for further technical information produced only the Teacher's Guide. The user is thus left with a great void in interpreting the responses.

Directions and procedures for administration are clear and simple. The directions ask the student to mark what the student actually *would* do if the driver, rather than what the student thinks *should* be done. Each item is then described by the narrator and presented on five frames. The first frame shows the situation, such as a stalled car. The narrator describes this situation and asks, "What would you do?" Three alternatives are described and shown on separate frames. Finally, the printed alternatives are shown and the student is asked to circle the appropriate letter on the answer sheet. The total test consists of 19 situations. The scoring key ranks the alternatives in each item from least desirable to most desirable and assigns numbers on a scale of 1 to 3. A sheet is provided to display the results as a profile of the individual items and as total scores. No rationale is given for the rankings of the alternatives; in some cases, students and instructors may challenge this ordering. Empirical data showing the degree of consensus among experts who ranked the choices would be appropriate evidence to substantiate the validity of the interpretations of the profiles and the total test scores.

The two filmstrips and the audio cassette tape convey a professional approach. The filmstrips show scenes that are well planned, colorful, and clearly photographed. The narrator's voice on the cassette tape distinctly articulates the script. The language of both the narrator's script and the test items appears appropriate for a very wide range of students at the high school level.

The Teacher's Guide consists of one and one-half pages of descriptive information followed by the script of the text. Unfortunately, the brief exposition neglects technical characteristics. The topics of reliability, validity, and norms are not even mentioned. Inasmuch as the test was purportedly developed and tried out in a number of schools, it is surprising that indices of internal consistency are not shown, or that correlations with cognitive measures of driving skills are not displayed. The lack of any distributions of scores is also surprising. The Teacher's Guide urges the teacher to "follow up" with "standard teaching approaches" to improve student attitudes, but no suggestions are given as to how to interpret the scores to accomplish that task. A technical manual with appropriate data and substantive suggestions for teachers would considerably enhance usability of this instrument.

There appears to be a semantic contradiction between the directions to the students and the descriptive information in the Teacher's Guide. As the filmstrip presentation begins, students are told "this is not a test, and your answers will not be graded." But the word "test" is contained in the title of this instrument and is used at least five times in the descriptive information. Furthermore, the teacher is told how to "score" the test, according to the desirability of the responses, so the test is "graded." Perhaps it would be better for the teacher to tell the students their responses will not affect their grades in the driver training program.

This test is different from others purporting to measure driving attitude, in that it is an audio-visual presentation of incidents rather than a collection of declarative statements with which the students indicate their degree of agreement. The realism of the situations would appear to make the SDAT an instrument worthy of psychometric study.

SUMMARY. The Safe Driver Attitude Test appears to be a carefully developed instrument for assessing the attitudes of drivers toward dilemmas in actual driving situations. Inasmuch as the audio-filmstrip presentation is relatively short, the physical quality of the materials is good, and the text of the script is clearly written, students are likely to remain interested and attentive throughout the session. But, unfortunately, the supporting information provided by the publisher fails to meet the technical standards expected of educational measures. The manual provides neither an adequate rationale for the test development nor an explanation of item selection and item analysis. Directions for administration are clear, but no instructions for interpreting the scores are given, either in terms of the purported intervening variables or in terms of normative data. Evidence for reliability and validity is totally absent in the published materials. The lack of information and data on these topics will make it very difficult for teachers in driver education classes to make the type of informed and defensible interpretations that will be of value to them in designing instruction to fit the needs of the students.

[318]

Salamon-Conte Life Satisfaction in the Elderly Scale. Purpose: "Designed to reliably measure life satisfaction among the aged in a variety of settings." Older adults; 1984; LSES; 9 scores: Daily Activities, Meaning, Goals, Mood, Self-Concept, Health, Finances, Social Contacts, Total; 1987 price data: $21.95 per complete kit including 50 test booklets, 50 scoring sheets, and manual (27 pages); (15–25) minutes; Michael J. Salamon and Vincent A. Conte; Psychological Assessment Resources, Inc.*

Review of the Salamon-Conte Life Satisfaction in the Elderly Scale by DAVID N. DIXON, Professor and Department Chair of Counseling and Psychology Services, Ball State University, Muncie, IN:

The Life Satisfaction in the Elderly Scale (LSES) is one of many scales in this area. The authors establish a place for this new scale primarily on the basis of inadequate psychometric information for previous scales and expanded coverage of important domains of life satisfaction.

The LSES provides a total satisfaction score and eight subscale scores. The chosen subscales are consistent with those definitions of satisfaction found in the literature. Five of the domains of satisfaction (Daily Activities, Meaning, Goals, Mood, and Self-Concept) are also assessed by Life Satisfaction Index scales developed by Neugarten, Havighurst, and Tobin (1961). The three additional subscales are Health, Finances, and Social Contacts.

Reliability data support the internal consistency and stability of the total scale. Coefficient alpha reliabilities of .93 and .92 and test-retest reliability coefficients of .67 (6 month) and .90 (1 month) are reported. Subscale reliabilities are adequate for most subscales; however, the Goals and Self-Concept subscales are questionable (coefficient alpha reliabilities of .60, .50 and .61, .47 respectively for two different samples).

Validity data, derived by factor analysis and cluster analysis procedures, generally support the subscale structure of the LSES. These data also raise questions about the Goals and Self-Concept subscales.

No criterion-related validity is presented in the manual. Minimally, it would be useful to know how the LSES correlates with other measures of life satisfaction.

The authors report normative data from 600 individuals with total scores broken down by age groups. They encourage the development of local norms in order to consider unique characteristics of the population of interest. They state that older adults suffering from impaired physical functioning would have lower subscale scores on Health and Mood and that a clinically depressed population would be expected to score lower on Mood, Meaning, and Self-Concept. However, no norms are presented to support these assertions. For the total scale and subscales to be most useful, data for these clinical populations need to be gathered.

Instructions for administration and scoring are clear. Instructions for interpretation, unfortunately, go well beyond the current stage of development of the LSES. Four case studies are presented in the manual to illustrate how scores on the LSES are interpreted. Interpretation of scores for individuals fails to consider measurement principles such as standard error of measurement. Whether changes in subscale scores of 2 or 3 points have any clinical significance lacks validation, and the user of the LSES should be very cautious about interpreting individual scores until further research is completed.

Overall, the LSES appears to be an acceptable measure of life satisfaction. The content, as reflected by the subscales, is comprehensive. The total scale and some of the subscales are reliable. Further validity studies of the subscales are needed to provide a basis for individual interpretation.

REVIEWER'S REFERENCE

Neugarten, B. L., Havighurst, R. J., & Tobin, S. S. (1961). The measurement of life satisfaction. *Journal of Gerontology*, 16, 134-143.

Review of the Salamon-Conte Life Satisfaction in the Elderly Scale by NANCY A. BUSCH-ROSSNAGEL, Associate Professor of Psychology and Research Associate, Hispanic Research Center, Fordham University, Bronx, NY:

The authors of this scale criticize the scales frequently used to assess the well-being of the elderly population (i.e., Life-Satisfaction Indices, [LSI] devised by Neugarten, Havighurst, & Tobin, 1961) because of "the lack of information regarding the psychometric properties" and because "the domain of life satisfaction encompasses a larger number of issues than the five" constructs used by Neugarten et al. The Salamon-Conte Life Satisfaction in the Elderly Scale (LSES) has been designed to overcome these limitations. Thus, the LSES includes the five life-satisfaction constructs of the LSI—taking pleasure in daily activities, regarding life as meaningful, goodness of fit between desired and achieved goals, positive mood, and positive self-concept—and adds three more—perceived health, financial security, and social contacts.

The LSES contains 40 items, five for each subscale, on a 5-point Likert scale. Most of the items are written in the first person. To score the subscales, the far left anchor is always given a score of 1, the next anchor is given a score of 2 and so on, so that the far right anchor is given a score of 5. This scoring procedure means that the "best" response, reflecting high satisfaction, would be a column of "Xs" down the far right anchor. No information is given about the possibility of response bias generated by this scoring procedure. The scores are written on a scoring sheet patterned to allow for easy summation to obtain the subscale score by adding down the columns; the total score is computed by summing the subscale scores.

Three different samples were used to examine reliability. The first consisted of 408 subjects, ages 55 to 90, who lived in the community. The second sample contained 241 subjects affiliated with health care providers, including in-patient and ambulatory care services and visiting nurse services provided in the subjects' own homes. The third sample consisted of 50 subjects, ages 65 to 89, residing in a housing complex for older adults. Information about both internal consistency and test-retest reliability is provided. The coefficient alphas for the total score were .93 and .92 for the first two samples respectively. The reliabilities for the subscales ranged from .60 to .79 and .47 to .78 for the first two samples respectively. The lower reliabilities were found for the subscales of Goals and Self-Concept. Six-month test-retest for 120 subjects of the first sample was .67 for the total score. One-month test-retest reliability for the third sample was .90 for the total scale and above .88 for all subscales.

Information about construct and concurrent validity is provided. The authors state the items were reviewed by a panel of four experts to establish their face validity, but no information about this process is given. More specific information about construct validity is provided by means of factor analysis and cluster analysis. A principal components analysis with the data from Sample 1 indicated that eight factors adequately summarized the data. Factor rotation, using an eight-factor solution, indicated that the subscales of Health and Finance are well determined by each of two factors. However, the loadings for the other six factors did not identify the other subscales as coherently. Using the data from Sample 2, a cluster analysis indicated that four of the five items from five of the subscales cluster together. The subscales of Self-Concept, Goals, and Daily Activities did not show such clear patterns.

A study of concurrent validity used a sample of 75 subjects who were applying to a preventative health care program. The data obtained on these subjects included the LSES, information about health background, psychosocial information, and physical assessments. Unfortunately, the authors provide no specific information about how the data other than the LSES were scored or coded, so it is impossible to interpret their table of chi-squares and correlations.

Additional concurrent validity information was obtained using the second sample. These subjects were recruited from six different types of settings. ANOVAs were used to examine group differences in the total and subscale scores. The total scores and the subscales of Daily Activities, Meaning, and Health significantly differentiated among the groups. The authors state the other subscales are "related to personal characteristics not expected to correlate with participation in health services." However, it is not clear that this was an a priori hypothesis.

The available norms are based on scores from elderly persons living primarily in the Northeastern United States, and the authors state the norms should be considered preliminary. While the sample appears to be heterogeneous in regard to age, sex, socioeconomic status, and so on, the sample is not compared to the population at large. The authors suggest establishing local norms, but do not follow their own advice of cross-tabulating norms against demographic data such as sex, service unit, or income level. The norms are separated by age group: 55–60, 61–65, etc.; the last age group is "over 80." The norms are presented as quantiles for the total scores and average quantiles for the subscales scores. The authors also suggest that the LSES may be useful for individualized assessment and present four case studies as illustrations. The preliminary nature of the norms requires that other diagnostic tools be used when developing individual treatment plans and monitoring progress.

The LSES is an adequate measure of life satisfaction among the elderly. The manual provides more psychometric information about the LSES than is easily obtainable for the widely-used LSI (Neugarten et al, 1961). While the reliability of the total score of the LSES is high, the validity evidence is mixed. The information about concurrent validity is not presented in enough detail to allow for evaluation. Construct validity information suggests that more work is needed on item development, and studies of groups that should differ on the subscales related to personal characteristics are needed to further establish validity in this area. As the authors note, further work on the norms is needed.

REVIEWER'S REFERENCE

Neugarten, B. L., Havighurst, R. J., & Tobin, S. S. (1961). The measurement of life satisfaction. *Journal of Gerontology*, 16, 134-143.

[319]

Sales Staff Selector. "Evaluates the suitability of candidates of all levels of experience for the position of Sales Representative." Candidates for sales representatives; 1954–84; 7 tests: Numerical Skills, Problem Solving Ability, Fluency, Sales Comprehension, Sales Motivation, C.P.F. (interest in working with people), N.P.F. (emotional stability); 1987 price data: $125–400 per person per set of tests including grading and a personalized report on each person, manual (no date, 6 pages), and scoring guide; information on scoring service available from distributor; French edition available; (5–15) minutes per test; tests from various publishers compiled, distributed, and scored (optional) by Wolfe Personnel Testing & Training Systems, Inc.*

Review of the Sales Staff Selector by PHILIP G. BENSON, Assistant Professor of Management, New Mexico State University, Las Cruces, NM:

The Sales Staff Selector (SSS) consists of a battery of seven tests, all of which are proposed as predictors of success in sales positions. The manual suggests the test is useful in selection of personnel for all levels and types of sales and marketing positions, and for individuals with all levels of previous experience.

At the outset, it is notable that the test should be viewed as an experimental instrument in its present form. The manual is five pages in length, presents no data on validity, has no real norms (although a rough indicator of cut scores is provided), and generally lacks the kind of data needed to make a clear interpretation of the potential usefulness of the test in practice. The publisher points out that a validation study is underway, and is willing to assist in local validation efforts (if a minimum of 30 applicants are provided) at no cost beyond that of the tests themselves. Potential users would be well advised to participate in such a study, as far too little is known to use the test without local data on validity.

One point of interest about the Sales Staff Selector is that the subtests are themselves published tests, many of which have been reviewed in previous editions of the *Mental Measurements Yearbook* (*MMY*). Potential users of the SSS should, in particular, refer to the *Ninth MMY* entries for the "Fluency" scale (9:552—no review), the "Sales Motivation Inventory" scale (9:1067), the "CPF" scale (9:552—no review), and the "NPF" scale (9:552—no review). Note that entry 9:552, while it does not contain a new review of the scales indicated, does refer the reader to all earlier *MMY* reviews of these scales.

The first scale deals with Numerical Skills, and consists of a series of math problems. These problems vary in difficulty, but clearly the 5-minute time limit is too short for most people to complete all 60 items. While a speeded test of mathematical calculation may be appropriate for certain sales positions (e.g., retail clerks), it is not clear the speeded component is appropriate for higher level marketing positions. In addition, each problem is set up on a single line and is to be solved from left to right. While computational space is provided, if basic math is the construct to be measured, there is no clear reason to structure the problems in this way other than to save paper. If such a structure represents a confound, it would be best avoided.

The second scale, Problem Solving Ability, is parallel in construction to the Numerical Skills scale. It differs, however, in that the problems require logical and analytical skills; each item gives a list of four alphanumeric characters or groupings and requires that the test taker supply the fifth to complete a logical series. Again, the difficulty of individual items varies considerably, and the reason such a test is universally applicable to sales and marketing occupations is not provided. It seems obvious, however, the scale would share significant amounts of variance with tests of general intelligence.

The Fluency scale requires the test taker to generate lists of words that have a specified beginning or ending, measuring a form of verbally-based divergent production. Again, the precise reason the test should predict success in all sales and marketing positions is not clear. According to the manual, it taps into the construct of "communication skills," but this reviewer would expect other forms of verbal/communication skills to be more relevant to the interpersonal aspects of sales work.

The Sales Comprehension scale is certainly face valid, and has promise. Questions deal with basic sales principles, and tend to be appropriate for someone with college-level marketing courses. The content of items varies, including door-to-door sales, insurance, service industries, and others. While retailing questions are included, they represent a small portion of the total. The test overall seems most appropriate for door-to-door sales and corporate sales.

The Sales Motivation Inventory was reviewed at length in the *Ninth MMY* (9:1067). Previous reviewers suggest this test has potential, but agree that greater detail is required on validity of the test in predictive situations. It is unfortunate the manual for the Sales Staff Selector fails to review the data from earlier research on this and other subscales. In addition, it is still not clear the extent to which scale transparency makes fakability of this scale, which is an interest test, a problem in selection applications.

The next two scales, C.P.F. and N.P.F., are part of the Employee Attitude Series published by Industrial Psychology, Inc., and are also available through the Institute for Personality and Ability Testing (IPAT). The scales measure "Contact Personality" and "Neurotic Personality" Factors, and are included here as measures of desire for "people contact" (i.e., general introversion/extroversion) and emotional stability. While the constructs seem valuable in selecting sales representatives, it would, again, be useful to have better data in the test manual.

In assembling the SSS, the publisher neglected to format the various subscales for use as a battery. The result is that the test seems "piecemeal," as various portions use different paper, different styles of production, etc. In addition, much redundant information is collected; thus, the test taker's name is collected on five of the subscales (and also on the general information sheet), company and date are asked repeatedly, etc. The likely impression to be made on the test taker is negative.

In the general instructions, it is pointed out that there are two sections of tests. The first includes timed tests, while the second set of tests are untimed. Unfortunately, the instructions, which point out that one's score is based on the number of correct answers and that speed and accuracy are both important, are included with the description of the untimed tests (which have no right or wrong answers, as pointed out within the instructions for individual tests).

Thus, a serious reservation can be raised with the SSS. If a potential user is reading this review, he or she likely is sophisticated enough to consider the various options available to test users. Given that reliability and validity data are not presented for the SSS, given that the battery gives the impression of having been constructed from a variety of other sources (which it was), and given the variety of positions that are included within the sales and marketing area, there is no clear reason why potential users should not just assemble their own tests as appropriate to their specific needs.

All of this is not to imply that the SSS is without merit. The tests included have in some cases been well developed, and for the most part the tests have very high face validity for many sales positions. The SSS is very likely to show predictive validity in a number of settings. However, without documentation of such validity, it is just as easy for potential users to find their own collections of tests as to use the battery presented here.

Review of the Sales Staff Selector by RICHARD W. JOHNSON, Adjunct Professor of Counseling Psychology and Counselor Education, and Associate Director of University Counseling Service, University of Wisconsin-Madison, Madison, WI:

The Sales Staff Selector consists of seven subtests drawn from a variety of sources for the purpose of evaluating sales applicants. As noted below, five of the seven subtests have been reviewed in previous editions of the *Mental Measurements Yearbooks* (*MMY*). Numerical Skills and Problem Solving Ability are published by Wolfe Personnel Testing & Training Systems, Inc., the distributor of the Sales Staff Selector. Fluency, CPF (Contact Personality Factor), and NPF (Neurotic Personality Factor) are published by Industrial Psychology, Inc., as part of the Job-Tests Program (6:774). The Sales Comprehension Test (5:947) and Sales Motivation Inventory, Revised (9:1067) are both products of Martin M. Bruce Publishers.

The first three subtests measure cognitive abilities. Numerical Skills, a 5-minute timed test, evaluates ability to perform simple arithmetic. Problem Solving Ability, another 5-minute timed test, asks respondents to determine the last item in a progressive series of numbers or letters. Fluency, which is called "Communication Skills" in the test report, comprises three 2-minute timed tests in which respondents write all the words they can think of that begin or end with a particular syllable. For each of these subtests, the item content appears to be more limited in its scope than the name of the test would imply.

The fourth subtest, Sales Comprehension, taps job knowledge. This 30-item, multiple-choice test effectively differentiates between salespeople and nonsalespeople and to a lesser extent, between successful and unsuccessful salespeople. According to previous reports (5:947), the test scores are not correlated with general intelligence, that is, they provide important information separate from that obtained from tests of cognitive ability.

The next two subtests, Sales Motivation and CPF, assess the applicant's desire to interact with and influence people. The Sales Motivation subtest consists of 75 items selected by empirical means to distinguish between salespeople and nonsalespeople while the CPF subtest contains 40 items derived by factor analysis to measure the introversion-extroversion dimension of personality. Although the two tests were developed by different techniques, much of the item content for the two tests is similar. Scores on the two tests are probably highly intercorrelated; however, no information concerning this matter is reported. Both of these subtests are highly fakable.

Finally, the NPF scale is a 40-item measure of personal stability based on factor analysis. Its items assess emotional balance in a variety of circumstances. Intuitively, this factor would seem to be important in identifying rational, well adjusted salespeople who pursue their work conscientiously and effectively; however, the research evidence available to support this belief is weak.

The distributor has provided no information regarding the psychometric qualities of the test battery. The short test manual provides only sample questions, limited information on test administration and scoring, and a sample report. No normative data, reliability coefficients, or validity measures are presented. The author of the manual notes a "major validation study in progress," but no further information is offered despite the fact that it has been over 10 years since the test battery was introduced.

I was unable to obtain specific information in regard to the scoring of the subtests or the manner in which the subtest scores are combined. A scoring guide is advertised, but the publisher did not provide one for review. According to the manual, the total test scores range from 0 to 100. These scores are divided into six categories for the purpose of making recommendations. The relationship between the specific hiring recommendations and actual job success is unknown.

The manual claims the Sales Staff Selector may be used to aid in the selection of a wide range of sales applicants at all levels of experience (e.g., inside sales/order desk, sales applicants without prior experience, sales professionals with experience, sales service applicants at all levels of experience, and marketing candidates). No data are presented to support this claim. The manual also states that Wolfe Personnel Testing Systems "will undertake, at no cost but for the tests, a validation study on the Wolfe Sales Staff Selector." This practice is commendable; however, there is no evidence available to indicate that any such studies have actually been completed.

In summary, I cannot recommend the Sales Staff Selector because of lack of information concerning most of the subtests (except for Sales Motivation and Sales Comprehension) and the manner in which they are combined to arrive at a hiring recommendation. As a possible alternative, I would suggest the ETSA Tests, a comparable test battery about which more is known. Under any circumstances, the test battery should be validated by means of local research and supplemented by additional information (e.g., biographical data and supervisor ratings) to ensure its most effective use in sales personnel selection (Churchill, Ford, Hartley, & Walker, 1985).

REVIEWER'S REFERENCE

Churchill, G. A., Jr., Ford, N. M., Hartley, S. W., & Walker, O. C., Jr. (1985). The determinants of salesperson performance: A meta-analysis. *Journal of Marketing Research*, 22, 103-118.

[320]

Santa Clara Inventory of Developmental Tasks. Purpose: Enables "the classroom teacher to assess her students' readiness skills and to structure an individual developmental program for each child." Preschool through age 7; 1980; IDT; a component (available separately) of the Santa Clara Plus; 9 skill areas: Social/Emotional, Motor Coordination, Visual Motor Performance, Visual Perception, Visual Memory, Auditory Perception, Auditory Memory, Language Development, Conceptual Development; individual; 4 difficulty levels: Preschool age, 5–5.5 years, 6–6.5 years, 7 years; some test materials (e.g., beads, construction paper, pencils, coins) must be supplied by examiner; 1987 price data: $59.95 per complete Inventory (246 pages) with teacher's manual and supportive resources; $39.95 per Spanish Edition (to be used with English Edition); administration time not reported; William L. Gainer, Richard L. Zweig, Phyllis W. Dole, Sandra A. Watt, Florence Bergman, Mary Covello, Ruth Holland, Richard Knowles, L. J. McClenahan, Barbara Semenoff, and Allan Wiley; Zaner-Bloser Co.*

TEST REFERENCES

1. Spillman, C. V., & Lutz, J. P. (1985). Focus on research: Criteria for successful experiences in kindergarten. *Contemporary Education*, 56, 109-113.

Review of the Santa Clara Inventory of Developmental Tasks by KENNETH A. KAVALE, Professor, Division of Special Education, The University of Iowa, Iowa City, IA:

The Santa Clara Inventory of Developmental Tasks (IDT) is designed to assess students' readiness skills as represented by milestones in their development. The IDT consists of 72 tasks appropriate for children from preschool (no basal age given) to 7 years of age. The IDT serves primarily as a screening device and provides developmental information for nine skill areas: Social/Emotional (12 tasks), Motor Coordination (11 tasks), Visual Motor Performance (10 tasks), Visual Perception (9 tasks), Visual Memory (8 tasks), Auditory Perception (7 tasks), Auditory Memory (6 tasks), Language Development (5 tasks), and Conceptual Development (4 tasks). The tasks are arranged into four levels of difficulty: preschool, 5–5$^1/_2$ years of age, 6–6$^1/_2$ years of age, and 7 years of age. The individual tasks within each skill area are sequenced so they become progressively more difficult and increasingly more abstract.

The IDT need not be administered at one time. Scoring is based on a 3-point scale with zero (0) indicating the task is beyond the child's developmental level, one (1) indicating that the child has partially mastered the task but not to complete mastery, and two (2) indicating that the child has demonstrated the prescribed criterion level. The 72 items are scored on a Developmental Profile that presents a hierarchical and sequential rendering of developmental patterns.

The IDT is packaged in a loose-leaf binder that includes an Observation Guide describing how to measure each task. For each of the 72 tasks, a description is provided as well as the procedures and materials used for assessing the task, and the criteria for evaluating performance. The binder also includes 21 spirit masters used as worksheets for particular tasks, task cards used for eight tasks, a description of required teacher-assembled materials for 11 tasks, and a resource guide listing educational activities and materials for enhancing performance on 60 tasks.

The IDT lacks, however, the technical information necessary to make judgments about its value as a developmental assessment. For example, no information is provided about the theoretical foundation for the IDT. How were the individual tasks chosen? Are they sequenced in a way that accurately parallels development? A sound conceptual base is a necessary prerequisite for developmental measures in order to judge the rationale and logic of the chosen task sequence. Visual motor performance on the IDT, for example, includes 10 tasks beginning with Follow Moving Target with Eyes and ending with Copy a Diamond. Do the 10 tasks form a natural progression? Are the tasks appropriate for the targeted age levels? There is no information about the way the test evolved. It, therefore, remains problematic whether or not the IDT is suitable for assessing development.

Psychometric information is also missing from the IDT. No reliability data are reported for either individual tasks or any of the nine skill areas. The lack of reliability data makes it difficult to judge the consistency and stability of teachers' scoring. At a minimum the percent of interrater agreement should be reported in order to assess the inherent variability of tasks on the IDT. Similarly, no validity data are reported. To be useful, some form of construct and predictive validity should be reported in order to assess whether or not the IDT is, in fact, providing appropriate information about developmental patterns. Finally, no information is presented about scoring criteria. Although there is an assumed normative basis for a 0, 1, or 2 score, no information is provided as to how criterion levels were established. In summary, no technical information about the IDT is reported. The lack of even any citations about where such information might be obtained leaves the user with no basis for making judgments about the IDT.

It is thus difficult to properly evaluate the IDT in its present form. The only property it possesses presently is face validity but this is hardly a sufficient criterion. More technical data are needed before the IDT can be used with confidence. The IDT may or may not be a suitable developmental measure. That judgement cannot be made with the data currently provided. It is incumbent upon the authors and publisher to provide the data necessary for evaluating the IDT. Until that time, the IDT cannot be recommended.

Review of the Santa Clara Inventory of Developmental Tasks by ESTHER SINCLAIR, Associate Professor of Psychiatry and Biobehavioral Sciences, UCLA School of Medicine, University of California, Los Angeles, Los Angeles, CA:

The Santa Clara Inventory of Developmental Tasks (IDT) is a battery of 72 individual tasks sequenced by chronological age into nine skill areas appropriate for children from preschool (aged 2-9 approximately) through age 7. The IDT was developed primarily as a screening device to enable the classroom teacher to determine what specific skills students had already mastered in the areas of Social/Emotional Development, Motor Coordination, Visual Motor Performance, Visual Perception, Visual Memory, Auditory Perception, Auditory Memory, Language Development, and Conceptual Development. These scores presumably relate to the children's readiness levels for reading and mathematics instruction and help the teacher determine appropriate classroom instructional levels. The IDT yields a developmental profile in each of the nine skill areas sequenced into four levels of difficulty.

The manual provides clear, succinct explanations of each of the 72 tasks and indicates what additional materials or teacher preparation may be necessary for the administration of each of the tasks. The procedures are very specific and easy to follow. Spirit masters for the student response portion and the developmental profile are included.

The scoring criterion for each of the 72 tasks is based on a 3-point scale and specific to the task. For example, in the skill area of Social/Emotional Development, the task measuring ability to cope with frustration (A-3) is scored according to the child's ability to deal with a frustrating situation in a socially acceptable way by reacting within the limits of acceptable classroom behavior. A score of 0 indicates unacceptable behavior. A score of 1 indicates that the child sometimes reacts acceptably. Finally, a score of 2 indicates that the child reacts to frustration within limits of acceptable classroom behavior.

The authors state that it is not necessary to administer the entire test to each student. Indeed, all of the skill areas, with the exception of Social/Emotional Development, may be administered on an individual basis by teachers, consultants, or other examiners in or out of the classroom setting. The observations necessary to score the Social/Emotional component must be made in a classroom setting by someone with some degree of sophistication regarding children's behavior and emotional functioning.

Normative data are decidedly lacking. Numerous attempts were made to contact the senior editor listed in the IDT manual but his phone number was not listed and a complete address was not given. The sequence of developmental tasks seems valid in terms of face validity in all skill areas except Social/Emotional Development. For example, Communication Skills (A-1) seems to be a more difficult skill to master than Proud of Accomplishments (A-4). No explanation of how these skills were chosen or ordered was provided in the manual. Perhaps this information is included in the Santa Clara Plus of which the IDT is a component. However, the Santa Clara Plus was not available to the reviewer. In addition, no reliability or validity data were mentioned in the manual.

The four difficulty levels of the IDT are divided into Pre-school age, 5–5.5 years, 6–6.5 years, and 7 years. The Language Development skill area does not include any tasks at the Preschool difficulty level. Furthermore, auditory skills, perception, and memory skills are extremely limited in this age group as well. This severely limits the usefulness of this instrument with a prekindergarten population. The IDT might be useful for a developmentally disabled population as the tasks for the skill area of Motor Coordination include creeping and walking. These are developmental skills most preschool children have already mastered.

In summary, the IDT is an easy-to-use screening instrument that appears to have more limited usefulness and generalizability than the preschool to 7-year age range suggests. The remediation activities for each of the 72 skill areas appear both skill and age appropriate. However, the authors should have reported on their standardization procedures, if any, and on methods of item analysis. The rationale for inclusion of the various tasks in the manual should have also been provided.

[321]

Scales of Independent Behavior. Purpose: "Designed to assess behaviors needed to function independently in home, social, and community settings." Infants through adults; 1984–85; SIB; Part Four of the Woodcock-Johnson Psycho-Educational Battery; a short form scale, an early development scale, and a measure of problem behaviors are also available in the test materials; 14 subscales: Gross-Motor Skills, Fine-Motor Skills, Social Interaction, Language Comprehension, Language Expression, Eating and Meal Preparation, Toileting, Dressing, Personal Self-Care, Domestic Skills, Time and Punctuality, Money and Value, Work Skills, Home/Community Orientation; individual; 1988 price data: $110 per complete program including easel-style test book, examiner's manual (196 pages), and 25 response booklets; $20 per 25 response booklets; $18 per technical manual entitled *Development and Standardization of the Scales of Independent Behavior* ('85, 157 pages); $109 per microcomputer scoring program; (60) minutes; Robert H. Bruininks, Richard W. Woodcock, Richard F. Weatherman, and Bradley K. Hill; DLM Teaching Resources.*

Review of the Scales of Independent Behavior by BONNIE W. CAMP, Professor of Pediatrics and Psychiatry, University of Colorado School of Medicine, Denver, CO:

The Scales of Independent Behavior (SIB) assess both Adaptive Behavior and Problem Behavior over the age range of infancy to adulthood. In the Adaptive Behavior domain there are 14 subscales containing 226 items, an Early Developmental Scale, and a Short Form Scale with 32 items each. In the Behavior Problem domain there are 4 subscales with 8 items. The items are descriptions of concrete behaviors. For the Adaptive Scales, the respondent is asked to rate the subject on a 4-point Likert scale depending on whether the subject can (or could) do the task completely without help or supervision *never or rarely even if asked* (0) to *does very well, always or almost always, without being asked* (3). For the Behavior Problem items (Hurtful to Self, Hurtful to Others, Destructive of Property, Disruptive Behavior, Unusual or Repetitive Habits, Socially Offensive Behavior, Withdrawal or Inattentive Behavior, and Uncooperative Behavior) the respondent is asked to rate the subject on a 5-point Likert scale for frequency and severity.

This scale is administered individually but does not require an extensive background in test administration; the necessary procedures can be learned by a variety of personnel. It is presented in an easel form with three or four items on each page along with four response boxes repeated on each page. Items are arranged in order of increasing difficulty. The 11 types of scores available for each scale include scores for normative comparisons (age scores, percentile ranks, standard scores, stanines, and normal curve equivalents), instructional functioning scores (instructional ranges, relative performance indexes, functioning levels), and adjusted adaptive behavior functioning scores (expected age scores, expected cluster scores, percentile ranks based on age and cognitive ability). The adjusted score is particularly interesting because it takes both age and cognitive ability into account. Problem Behavior scores are age adjusted.

Data on standardization, research, and development are included in a separate publication *Development and Standardization of the Scales of Independent Behavior* (Bruininks, Woodcock, Weatherman, & Hill, 1985). The items developed for the SIB were written with the goal of presenting precise behavioral statements, representing a broad range of independent and adaptive behaviors and minimizing needs for verbal comprehension and memory. A Rasch analysis procedure was used in item analysis and scaling of items in each subscale. The "norming sample" consisted of a stratified random sample of 1,764 normal subjects from 40 communities ranging from infancy to 40 years and balanced in terms of the national distribution of sex, race, occupation, geographic location, and type of community. Extensive analysis of the effect of population characteristics (including sex) on SIB scores revealed only low and inconsistent contributions. Reliability studies included analysis of internal consistency, interexaminer reliability, test-retest reliability, and reliability in handicapped samples. With very few exceptions, reliability coefficients were above .70 and most were in the high 80s and 90s.

A number of studies are presented to support the validity of the SIB as a measure of both adaptive and maladaptive behavior. These include studies demonstrating the ability of the SIB to distinguish between handicapped and nonhandicapped groups, different ages, and different settings. Significant correlations with other instruments assessing both adaptive and maladaptive behavior are also presented along with results of studies demonstrating significant differences in pattern of scores for different groups of handicapped children and children requiring different levels of special education service.

The authors appear to have been successful in their goal of developing an instrument that is easily learned, employs precise behavioral statements, and provides useful information about the adaptive functioning of normal and handicapped persons. The inclusion of problem behaviors as well as traditional adaptive behaviors is an extremely useful addition to this type of scale. The background data are impressive in describing the quality of work that went into preparing the content of the scale, collecting the normative data, and studying reliability and validity. The manual describing the test construction is written so clearly and comprehensively it could be used as a model for students of test construction. Nevertheless, one may deplore the practice of publishing a test manual without presenting even minimal technical information on reliability and validity.

A major drawback of the SIB is the form of presentation. The use of a cumbersome easel requiring the examiner to flip the pages after each group of three or four items detracts from ease of administration and the weight makes it unlikely that examiners will always keep it on hand. Surely the publishers will provide a form where all questions are in a test booklet. At present, the Vineland Adaptive Behavior Scales (Sparrow, Balla, & Cicchetti, 1984) which cover most of the same material on adaptive behavior, require less equipment and seem easier to administer. Even so, the SIB is a welcome addition to the armamentarium for assessing adaptive behavior and promises to become a leading instrument for this purpose.

REVIEWER'S REFERENCES

Sparrow, S. S., Balla, D. A., & Cicchetti, D. V. (1984). Vineland Adaptive Behavior Scales. Circle Pines, MN: American Guidance Service.

Bruininks, R. H., Woodcock, R. W., Weatherman, R. F., & Hill, B. K. (1985). *Development and standardization of the Scales of Independent Behavior*. Allen, TX: DLM Teaching Resources.

Review of the Scales of Independent Behavior by LOUIS J. HEIFETZ, Professor of Special Education, School of Education, Syracuse University, Syracuse, NY:

According to the Scales of Independent Behavior's (SIB) technical manual

(*Development and Standardization of the Scales of Independent Behavior*, Bruininks, Woodcock, Weatherman, & Hill, 1985, pp. 3–4), the SIB was designed for several purposes: (*a*) "to identify individuals who lack adaptive functional independence in particular settings"; (*b*) to help set goals for Individualized Education or Individualized Program Plans; (*c*) to aid in the selection and placement of individuals for specialized programs of education and training; and (*d*) to assess pre/post effects of intervention, as part of individual case management, program evaluation, or formal research. Like other measures of adaptive behavior, the SIB does not involve direct observation of the person being evaluated. Instead, the SIB scales are completed during a semistructured interview with a respondent (e.g., teacher, parent, case-worker) who is thoroughly familiar with the behavior of the person under scrutiny.

The SIB contains 226 items of adaptive behavior, arranged into the 14 subscales (domains) listed above (14–18 items per subscale). These subscales can be grouped into four nonoverlapping clusters: Motor Skills (consisting of the Gross-Motor and Fine-Motor subscales); Social Interaction and Communication Skills (consisting of the Social Interaction, Language Comprehension, and Language Expression subscales); Personal Living Skills (consisting of the Eating and Meal Preparation, Toileting, Dressing, Personal Self-Care, and Domestic Skills subscales); and Community Living Skills (consisting of the Time and Punctuality, Money and Value, Work Skills, and Home/Community Orientation subscales). The SIB also yields an overall index of Broad Independence (Full Scale), encompassing all 14 subscales. The Broad Independence Short Form (an alternative to the Full Scale version) contains 32 of the 226 total items, representing all 14 subscales. Another measure of Broad Independence—the Early Development Scale—is used with individuals below the developmental age of 2.5 years. It contains 32 lower-level items drawn from 12 of the 14 SIB subscales.

In addition to these indices of adaptive functioning, the SIB includes various measures "for identifying problem behavior that often limits personal adaptation and community adjustment" (p. 9 of technical manual). Analogous to the 14 adaptive behavior subscales are eight problem behavior areas (domains), each containing 6–12 specific examples of problem behavior. These areas can be grouped into three nonoverlapping clusters: Internalized Maladaptive Behavior (consisting of the Hurtful to Self, Unusual or Repetitive Habits, and Withdrawal or Inattentive Behavior areas); Externalized Maladaptive Behavior (consisting of the Hurtful to Others, Destructive to Property, and Disruptive Behavior areas); and Asocial Maladaptive Behavior (consisting of the Socially Offensive Behavior and Uncooperative Behavior areas). An overall index of General Maladaptive Behavior encompasses the information from all eight areas of problem behavior. There is no short-form measure of problem behavior to parallel the Broad Independence Short Form.

SCORING THE SIB. Scoring methods are substantially different for adaptive behavior items and problem behavior items. Each item on the Behavior Problem Scale receives two separate ratings: one for frequency of occurrence (a 6-point scale ranging from "never" to "one or more times an hour"); another for severity (a 5-point scale ranging from "not serious/not a problem" to "extremely serious/a critical problem"). After various mathematical transformations, each of the eight problem areas can be plotted on a two-dimensional grid whose axes represent separate stanine scores for frequency and severity. Three levels of seriousness of behavior problems are shown by differently shaded sections of the grid.

Adaptive behavior items are scored in a very different manner, using a single 4-point scale for each item. However, each point on the scale has multiple meanings, reflecting *frequency* (how often the person does the task completely, without help or supervision), *quality* (how well the task is done), and *initiative* (whether the person needs to be asked to perform the task). This scoring system, which forces three separate aspects of adaptive functioning into a single continuum, raises conceptual and practical questions that are potentially serious. It is generally agreed that the assessment of adaptive functioning should reflect what a person regularly does, not just what a person is capable of doing. In other words, the measurement of adaptive behavior must address both capacity (skills, abilities) and motivation (one's willingness to apply these skills in fulfillment of societal expectations for responsible behavior).

This perspective reflects the fact that capacity and motivation are independent, such that one's level of capacity is not tightly linked to one's motivation to apply that capacity. For example, a person of limited capacity might regularly and appropriately make use of that capacity, while another person with much greater capacity might not be motivated to use that capacity adaptively.

Unfortunately, the adaptive behavior items on the SIB do not provide for separate scoring of a person's ability to perform and motivation to perform. For example, an item-score of 3 indicates the following about a person's task performance: "does the task very well [quality] . . . always or almost always [frequency] . . . without being asked [initiative]." A score of 1 indicates: "does the task, but not well, or about one-fourth of the time (may need to be asked)" (p. 7 of technical manual). How, then, would we score a person who does the task very well, but only rarely does it, even when asked? A score of 2 might seem reasonable, except that the SIB scoring system assigns to a score of 2 a meaning that in no way fits this person's performance: "does the task fairly well, or about three-fourths of the time (may need to be asked)." In short, an implicit assumption of the SIB's item-scoring system is that higher levels of skill, greater regularity of performance, and less need to be asked to perform the task all go hand in hand. This fundamental assumption is not stated explicitly by the authors, is not verified by them, and is not, in fact, tenable. A better scoring system would involve separate ratings of ability and willingness to perform each of the task items (similar to the separate ratings of frequency and severity for the behavior problem items), along with a clear procedure for combining those separate scores into a composite rating of adaptiveness. The current scoring system—with its force fitting of quality, frequency, and initiative—confronts interviewers with a large number of "judgment calls" to make. Furthermore, the questionable method of item-level scoring raises concerns about the higher-level indices derived from the item-scores (i.e., subscale scores, cluster scores, and Broad Independence measures).

CALIBRATION AND NORMING PROCEDURES. Successive stages of item analysis and modification were conducted under the Rasch model of scale development. An advantage of Rasch-calibrated tests is that comparable changes in ability level (e.g., from a 50% success level to a 75% success level on a given set of items) are reflected in comparable changes in test scores (e.g., a 10-point increase on the W-scale transformed scores), in *any* skill area and at *any* skill level. This characteristic of Rasch scaling techniques simplifies the interpretation of SIB scores.

SIB norms were derived from interviews with 1,764 respondents, reporting on the behavior of subjects ranging from 3 months to 44 years. A painstaking procedure of sampling and weighting was used to approximate the 1980 U.S. Census data in terms of sex, race, occupational status and level, geographic region, and type of community. As part of the norming procedure, Full Scale Broad Independence scores were analyzed for possible biases related to demographic variables other than age. These analyses revealed only negligible influences. In part, this reflects scrupulous efforts to minimize sex bias in the construction and selection of test items. Because of the success of these efforts, there was no need to provide separate SIB norms by sex; norms are organized simply by age. One other noteworthy feature of the SIB norms is their direct comparability to the Broad Cognitive Ability measure of the Woodcock-Johnson Psycho-Educational Battery. In order to create this useful comparability, the authors conducted a series of equating studies at 15 different age levels.

RELIABILITY OF SIB SCORES. In describing the internal consistency of scores of adaptive behavior (the 14 subscales, 4 clusters, and overall index of Broad Independence), the authors report split-half (odd vs. even items) correlations with Spearman-Brown corrections. For each subscale, reliabilities are reported separately for 13 different age groups (youngest, 3-to-11 months; oldest, 29-to-44 years). The 182 correlations range from .00 to .95. Only 93 of these correlations (51%) are at least .80, and only 15 of them (8%) are at least .90. The authors contend that low reliabilities reflect "floor effects" in younger groups (where nearly all individuals have zero scores on some subscales) or "ceiling effects" in older groups (where nearly all individuals have perfect scores on some subscales). Yet, even when overall reliabilities are computed for the combined age levels, only 5 of the 14 subscales

(36%) achieve a correlation of .80, and none of them reaches .90. Thus, at the level of subscale scores of adaptive behavior, the SIB's internal consistency is only sporadically adequate. When the 14 subscales are collapsed into the four cluster scores, internal consistencies improve substantially. For the 13 separate age groups, the 52 correlations range from .64 to .95. Of these, 48 (92%) reach or exceed .80, while 29 (56%) reach or exceed .90. When the separate age groups are combined, internal consistencies of cluster scores rise even higher: Motor Skills = .83; Social and Communication Skills = .89; Personal Living Skills = .93; and Community Living Skills = .92. For the overall index of Broad Independence, internal consistencies are uniformly high for the 13 age groups, ranging from .95 to .97. The Short Form scale, however, has much lower internal consistencies, ranging from .67 to .88 and reaching .80 in only 2 of the 13 age groups (15%). In summary, internal consistency is excellent for Broad Independence, good for cluster scores, highly variable for subscale scores, and generally inadequate for the Short Form. No data are provided for the internal consistency of the maladaptive behavior indices.

In describing test-retest reliability, the authors do not provide adequate evidence of the stability of SIB scores. Test-retest samples are small and narrow, and their reliabilities are often low. Data were collected on two samples of nonhandicapped, elementary-school students—29 6-to-8-year-olds and 38 10-to-11-year-olds. These two small samples, which do not even span the elementary-school age range, cannot be used to generalize about the stability of SIB scores across the broad spectrum of age and ability levels covered by the SIB. Among the 6-to-8-year-olds, subscale reliabilities range from .67 to .94, with only four of 14 subscales (29%) reaching at least .90. Reliabilities are even lower among the 10-to-11-year-olds, ranging from .51 to .88, with only six subscales reaching at least .80 and none reaching .90. When the 14 subscales are collapsed into the four cluster scores, reliabilities improve, ranging from .86 to .96 for the 6-to-8-year-olds and ranging from .71 to .88 for the 10-to-11-year-olds. The overall index of Broad Independence has a test-retest reliability of .96 for the 6-to-8-year-olds and .87 for the 10-to-11-year-olds. In short, there are very limited data on the stability of SIB scores, showing adequate-to-excellent reliability for Broad Independence and the four cluster scores (except for Motor Skills among the 10-to-11-year-olds). Subscale reliabilities are generally lower and much more variable—several of them are inadequate—with 10-to-11-year-olds tending to have less reliable scores than 6-to-8-year-olds.

The technical manual also provides some limited data on interrater reliability (the consistency of scores reported by different interviewers of the same respondent). In one study, interviews with 31 respondents were tape recorded and then scored independently by two other raters. (No information is provided about the characteristics of the individuals whose adaptive behavior was being described. Thus, the generalizability of the findings is unknown.) Correlations were computed between the two tape-raters and between each tape-rater and the original interviewer. All correlations for adaptive and maladaptive cluster scores and full-scale scores were in the high .90s. However, these correlations are artificially inflated by the fact that all three raters dealt with a single interview protocol from each respondent, instead of protocols that were both independently generated and independently scored. In another, more realistic test of interrater agreement, the SIB was independently completed by the teachers and teacher aides of 39 retarded adolescents. For adaptive cluster scores, correlations ranged from .74 to .86; for maladaptive cluster scores, correlations ranged from .69 to .81. The data from these two samples—one artificial, the other limited to retarded adolescents—fail to demonstrate adequate interrater reliability for the wide range of populations to which the SIB is meant to be applied.

VALIDITY OF SIB SCORES. Information on the validity of the SIB comes from several sources. Data from the norming sample show that the adaptive behavior scores improve systematically from lower to higher age levels (the pattern for maladaptive scores is less pronounced and less consistent). Scores on Broad Independence and the adaptive behavior clusters were correlated with factor scores from the AAMD Adaptive Behavior Scale (School Edition) in two samples. With 10-to-17-year-olds (72 nonhandicapped and 10 mildly/moderately retarded students), the correlations ranged from .45 to .87. With 10-to-12-

year-olds (47 nonhandicapped and 5 mildly/moderately retarded students in regular classes), correlations ranged from .59 to .91. SIB maladaptive cluster scores were correlated with scores on the six scales from the Quay-Peterson Revised Behavior Problem Checklist, in a sample of 185 6-to-19-year-olds who had been classified as "behavior disordered" by their school districts. Most correlations were either of modest size or statistically insignificant. For five of the six Quay-Peterson scales, no correlations with SIB scores exceeded .40.

In addition to these correlations between SIB scores and scores from other instruments, the authors present several comparisons of nonhandicapped and variously handicapped/labeled samples. In each comparison, the nonhandicapped group was drawn from the national norming sample and matched with the handicapped individuals on sex and age. Most, but not all, comparisons showed significantly higher adaptive behavior scores or significantly lower maladaptive behavior scores in the nonhandicapped groups. In general, greater discrepancies were evident with the more severely handicapped comparison groups. Finally, a series of discriminant analysis studies was used to explore how accurately SIB cluster scores (adaptive, maladaptive, or both together) could discriminate among levels of retardation (nonretarded vs. mildly retarded vs. moderately retarded persons), among degrees of school "mainstreaming" (full-time regular classroom vs. part-time special education classroom vs. full-time special classroom vs. segregated school placement), or between nonhandicapped and behavior-disordered groups. In the four reported analyses, various combinations of SIB cluster scores predicted group membership accurately in 76%, 78%, 68%, and 86% of cases, respectively. These were superior to predictions made on the basis of chance (and proportional assignment to groups of different sizes), which would have been accurate in 48%, 38%, 31%, and 50% of cases, respectively.

The evidence for validity is more difficult to interpret than the evidence for reliability. With reliability, the higher the correlation between two scores, the better. For example, two respondents reporting on the same individuals would, ideally, show perfect agreement (interrater reliability). Similarly, separate reports on the same individuals within a short span of time should also, ideally, agree perfectly (test-retest reliability). With validity, however, the interpretation of correlations can be quite ambiguous. For example, for the early-childhood subjects in the norming sample (549 children), the authors report a (second-degree) curvilinear correlation of .96 between chronological age and Broad Independence scores. In other words, 92% of the variance in Broad Independence scores is associated with differences in children's *chronological* ages. Yet, we know clinically and empirically that there is substantial variance in adaptive behavior among children of the same chronological age, which suggests that the reported correlation of .96 is excessive. Indeed, a lower correlation might actually speak more strongly to the validity of SIB scores. For another example of the ambiguity of validity data, consider the discriminant analyses summarized earlier. One of these dealt with students who had been classified as "nonretarded," "mildly retarded," or "moderately retarded" *on the basis of their school placements*. Scores on the SIB adaptive clusters accurately predicted the type of placement for 76% of the students. However, because school placements are not always made properly, we can derive very different meanings from this analysis. For concrete illustration, assume that only 80% of the students had been placed appropriately by their districts. If SIB scores exactly reproduced the districts' placements, then the SIB decisions would have 100% agreement with school district decisions, even though the SIB decisions were only 80% appropriate. Conversely, if the SIB scores produced placement decisions that were 100% appropriate (i.e., perfectly valid), the SIB decisions would show only 80% agreement with district decisions. Because we have no independent knowledge of which students were placed appropriately and inappropriately by their districts, we also do not know if the 76% agreement with these placement decisions is a true reflection of the SIB's validity, too high, or too low.

This sort of ambiguity arises whenever SIB scores are being correlated with other variables that are, themselves, only indirect measures of adaptive behavior (e.g., diagnostic label, type of school placement, intelligence test scores, or scores on other interview or survey instruments dealing with an absent person's adaptive/maladaptive behavior). Much of this ambiguity could be eliminated by correlating SIB scores with data from direct observations of subjects' behavior by trained, objective observers. This would directly address the core question of validity—how well an instrument actually measures what it was designed to measure. Unfortunately, none of the analyses reported in the SIB technical manual take this direct tack, leaving a critical gap in the evidence for the SIB's validity. Other gaps relate to the SIB's sensitivity to actual changes in an individual's adaptive behavior. The technical manual provides cross-sectional data from the norming sample, showing successive increases in adaptive behavior scores across separate groups of progressively higher ages. There are not, however, any longitudinal data on changes in SIB scores as individuals age. Ideally, for example, the increase in SIB scores displayed by normative 3-year-olds from one year to the next should be very similar to the original differences between the normative 3-year-olds and the normative 4-year-olds. If the longitudinal differences were either notably smaller or notably larger than the cross-sectional differences, this finding would raise serious questions about the SIB's reactivity (i.e., ways in which a person's current SIB scores might be distorted by previous administrations of the SIB). Of particular concern, such reactivity would undermine the validity of the SIB as a pre/post measure in evaluating the effects of interventions designed to improve adaptive behavior. The technical manual does not present any data on this use of the SIB, even though the authors explicitly suggest using the SIB in pre/post evaluations.

SUMMARY. The SIB currently presents somewhat of a "jagged profile." Certain aspects of its development and norming are quite strong—thoughtful selection of scale content; use of Rasch scaling techniques; precise matching of the norming sample to 1980 census data. Also, some of the reliability data are robust, and aspects of the validity data are compelling. On the other hand, various aspects of reliability and validity have been ignored altogether or addressed with samples too limited for broad generalization. Some of the data reported in the technical manual show areas where validity or reliability are not necessarily adequate.

Individuals needing to assess functional skills could include, whenever possible, data based on *direct observation* of the person being assessed. Such data are readily gathered on many aspects of adaptive functioning covered in the SIB and other indirect-report instruments. The direct observational data are not only informative in their own right, but also permit inferences about the wider accuracy/inaccuracy of the indirect data from the interviewed informant. Another recommendation is to gather interview data independently from two or more informants on the same areas of adaptive functioning. Both recommendations involve attempts at "triangulation" in order to make the data more credible. This, of course, could apply to *any* of the indirect-report instruments.

In comparative terms, the SIB is psychometrically one of the better indirect-report measures of adaptive behavior—considerably stronger, for example, than the AAMD Adaptive Behavior Scale (9:3) (institutional instrument [Nihira, Foster, Shellhaas, & Leland, 1975] or school version [Lambert & Windmiller, 1981]), the Adaptive Behavior Inventory 9; Brown & Leigh, 1986), or the original Vineland (T3:2557; Doll, 1965), but not quite as strong as the 1984 revision of the Vineland (381; Sparrow, Balla, & Cicchetti, 1984).

REVIEWER'S REFERENCES

Doll, E. A. (1965). Vineland Social Maturity Scale. Circle Pines, MN: American Guidance Service. (Originally published in 1953.)

Nihira, K., Foster, R., Shellhaas, M., & Leland, H. (1975). AAMD Adaptive Behavior Scale for Children and Adults, 1974 Revision. Washington, DC: American Association on Mental Deficiency.

Lambert, N., & Windmiller, M. (1981). *Diagnostic and technical manual, revised, AAMD Adaptive Behavior Scale—School Edition.* Monterey, CA: CTB/McGraw-Hill.

Sparrow, S., Balla, D., & Cicchetti, D. (1984). *Interview edition, expanded form manual, Vineland Adaptive Behavior Scales.* Circle Pines, MN: American Guidance Service.

Brown, L., & Leigh, J. (1986). Adaptive Behavior Inventory. Austin, TX: PRO-ED, Inc.

[322]

Schaie-Thurstone Adult Mental Abilities Test. Purpose: "Measuring the mental abilities of adults." Ages 22–84; 1985; STAMAT; consists of many items from the Thurstone Primary Mental Abilities Test Form 11–17; 7 scales: Recognition Vocabulary, Figure Rotation, Letter Series, Number Addition, Word Fluency, Object Rotation, Word Series; manual (86 pages); price data available from publisher; (50–60) minutes; K. Warner Schaie; Consulting Psychologists Press, Inc.*

Review of the Schaie-Thurstone Adult Mental Abilities Test by ERIC F. GARDNER, Professor of Psychology and Education Emeritus, Syracuse University, Syracuse, NY:

The Schaie-Thurstone Adult Mental Abilities Test (STAMAT) is presented as a research and assessment tool for measuring the mental abilities of adults. It consists of two forms. Form A, for adults, is "essentially the Thurstone Primary Mental Abilities Test Form 11-17 (PMA) with new adult norms." Form OA, for the "Older Adult," contains the same tests as Form A augmented by two tests paralleling two of the original tests but using stimuli less abstract and more familiar to adults.

This reviewer believes that there are very few tests that have been so thoroughly and critically reviewed in previous editions of *The Mental Measurements Yearbooks* as the Thurstone Primary Mental Ability Tests. Previous reviews, beginning with *The Second Mental Measurements Yearbook* (Buros, 1940), and continuing in each subsequent edition up to and including *The Seventh Mental Measurements Yearbook* (Buros, 1972), have pointed out the large number of deficiencies of past editions as well as what are described as partial improvements. The most recent reviews in *The Seventh Mental Measurements Yearbook* by Richard Schutz (Schutz, 1972) and M. Y. Quereshi (Quereshi, 1972) stress that many of the needed improvements have not been made and that the tests have outlived their usefulness.

Quereshi says, "The PMA tests served an important purpose as research tools in the advancement of the multiple factor notion of ability but have not fulfilled the practical promise of differential educational or vocational measurement" (Quereshi, 1972, p. 1066). Schutz is even more critical: "Neither a modern researcher nor a practitioner is likely to find it an attractive new buy, considering the other models available to him" (Schutz, 1972, p. 1067).

In view of these rather devastating criticisms, one could legitimately ask why Schaie selected the PMA tests for his extensive research. Schaie addresses this issue directly and makes a special point that the reason he selected the Thurstone tests for his work, in contrast with other possibilities, was because of their theoretical basis. Although this is a desirable objective, it should be pointed out that attempts to devise tests for intellectual abilities have been based on theories associated with three alternative hypotheses: (*a*) that the measurement of "general" intelligence is of major importance (e.g., Stanford-Binet and Otis-Lennon tests); (*b*) that different kinds of intelligence are of major importance and, therefore, each should be measured (e.g., Thurstone tests); and (*c*) that both the "general factor" of intelligence and specialized "group factors" should be measured.

The PMA, although representing only one of the various models of mental abilities stressing hypothesis *b*, has seen steady growth and has been the basis for a number of competing tests. A plausible additional explanation for its choice is that Schaie began his extensive research program in gerontology, which requires long-range longitudinal studies, years ago with data from the PMA and such studies require a constant stimulus. Of great importance is the fact that previous reviewers have indicated that the PMA tests are sound and well constructed, that the test items are well written, and the directions clear. This reviewer concurs. In any event, the use and improvement of the Primary Mental Abilities Test for the adult level is a defensible choice.

The major deficiencies have been addressed by Schaie through his gerontological research the past 20 years, and he has taken steps to rectify them. Specifically, he has: (*a*) focused on a specific portion of the age range; (*b*) defined the purpose of the Schaie-Thurstone Adult Mental Abilities Test as a research instrument; (*c*) presented data, both cross sectional and longitudinal, over an extensive period of time; (*d*) used a methodology relating both kinds of data (cross-sectional and longitudinal); (*e*) shown the interrelationships among the variables for different age groups; (*f*) shown stability over time (3 years, 7 years, 14 years, and 21 years); (*g*) presented norms separately for each sex as well as the combined group for age groups extending from 22–28-year-olds to 78–84-year-olds; (*h*) adapted a more suitable format for Form OA (Older Adult); (*i*) presented two additional tests in Form OA with stimuli more suitable for older adults; and (*j*) addressed the issue of validity directly and presented substantial amounts of data.

The manual is well written and contains the supporting data for the statements made about the tests. Data for both validity and reliability are presented and discussed in a relevant fashion. The stability indices for the 21 years of longitudinal data are amazingly high and consistent. The correlation coefficients for the three separate cohorts with a 7-year test-retest span for Form A ranged from a low of .72 to a high of .86 for the individual tests. The stability over a 21-year span for 120 of the subjects for the same tests ranged from .77 to .82. The consistency on Form OA for 256 persons, ages 55 to 85, who were followed for 3 years ranged from .80 to .86. Several of the tests are sufficiently short so as to give relatively large standard errors of measurement in spite of their respectable reliability coefficients. This matter would be serious if differential diagnosis of individuals is attempted.

An extensive discussion with considerable supporting data of content, concurrent, predictive, and construct validity is presented in the manual. Schaie makes the important point that "intelligence tests have typically been constructed to predict performance in educational or vocational entry," whereas the purposes for adult intelligence tests may stress other needs. In particular, they should be validated in terms of situations involving specific competencies, especially those related to independent living. Very little work has been done in this area and Schaie expresses hope that the STAMAT will be used for research in this field.

Voluminous tables of norms for each subtest in Form A as well as for a weighted total score are given for each sex and the total group. The individual test scores are converted to standard *T*-scores by sex for each age of nine age groups extending from 22–29 to 78–84. Composite intellectual ability norms expressed as deviation IQ equivalents with a mean of 100 and standard deviation of 15 are given for each sex over the nine age groups. Also, composite educational aptitude indices expressed as standard scores with a mean of 50 and standard deviation of 10 are tabled. Similar tables of norms are included for Form OA, but there are no composite intellectual ability scores or composite educational aptitude scores for this Older Adult form.

In conclusion, the Schaie-Thurstone Adult Mental Abilities Test is based upon the previous work of the Thurstones; the long range research program by Schaie has made available two instruments, measuring important cognitive variables and with excellent psychometric characteristics, for research on the mental abilities of adults.

REVIEWER'S REFERENCES

Buros, O. K. (Ed.). (1940). *The second mental measurements yearbook*. Highland Park, NJ: Gryphon Press.
Buros, O. K. (Ed.). (1972). *The seventh mental measurements yearbook*. Highland Park, NJ: Gryphon Press.
Quereshi, M. Y. (1972). [Review of SRA Primary Mental Abilities, 1962 Edition]. In O. K. Buros (Ed.). *The seventh mental measurements yearbook* (pp. 1064-1066). Highland Park, NJ: Gryphon Press.
Schutz, R. E. (1972). [Review of SRA Primary Mental Abilities, 1962 Edition]. In O. K. Buros (Ed.). *The seventh mental measurements yearbook* (pp. 1066-1068). Highland Park, NJ: Gryphon Press.

[323]

The Schedule of Recent Experience. Purpose: "To find out whether—and how often—stress-producing events have occurred in [a client's] life during the recent past." Patients/clients of all ages; 1981–86; SRE; questionnaires for children under age 13 should be completed by their mothers; 2 forms: one-year test scale, three-year test scale; 1987 price data: $20 per 50 1-year forms; $30 per 50 3-year forms; $35 per folder including 50 1-year forms, template, and manual ('86, 19 pages); $50 per folder including 50 3-year forms, template, and manual; administration time not reported; Marion E. Amundson, Cheryl A. Hart, and Thomas J. Holmes; University of Washington Press.*

TEST REFERENCES

1. Woody, J. D., Colley, P. E., Schlegelmilch, J., Maginn, P., & Balsanek, J. (1984). Child adjustment to parental stress following divorce. *Social Casework: The Journal of Contemporary Social Work*, 65, 405-412.
2. Barnett, B., & Parker, G. (1986). Possible determinants, correlates and consequences of high levels of anxiety in primiparous mothers. *Psychological Medicine*, 16, 177-185.
3. Rabins, P. V., Brooks, B. R., O'Donnell, P., Pearlson, G. D., Moberg, P., Jubelt, B., Coyle, P., Dalos, N., & Folstein, M. F. (1986). Structural brain correlates of emotional disorder in multiple sclerosis. *Brain*, 109, 585-597.

Review of The Schedule of Recent Experience by GERALD L. STONE, Professor of Counseling Psychology and Director, University Counseling Service, The University of Iowa, Iowa City, IA:

The Schedule of Recent Experience (SRE), according to the authors, "is a paper-and-pencil questionnaire which elicits information about the occurrence of particular events in an individual's recent life experience." Historically, the SRE is linked to the life chart approach of Meyer. The life chart displayed patient-generated information about their life situations and emotional responses chronologically, by year and age, and in a separate column were listed related diseases. Beginning in 1949, one of the authors (Holmes) and colleagues adopted the life chart method and used it in a large systematic study of some 5,000 cases, resulting in the selection of the life events for the SRE because of their occurrence prior to the onset of illness or clinical symptoms.

The SRE format has changed considerably, culminating in a self-report questionnaire requiring identifying data and information about recent experience with 42 life events. These life events generally represent the ordinary, but also sometimes encompass extraordinary transactions and major areas of significance in the social world: family, marriage, occupation, residence, peer relations, education, health, religion, and so on.

Respondents are to record the number of times each of the 42 items occurred in particular time periods. The time intervals requested can be modified such as 10 years, 3 years, 1 year, daily reports, or a specified time period before and after an event.

Frequency data (i.e., number of life events experienced) were used in earlier applications of the SRE in assessing the relationship of social change to many diseases. In order to enhance precision, Holmes and Rahe (1967) developed the Social Readjustment Rating Scale (SRRS). Psychophysics methodology for measuring sensation magnitude and intensity was influential in the approach for assigning weights to each of the SRE items. A sample of 394 subjects completed the SRE items plus Christmas. They provided magnitude estimations for the amount of change associated with each item, relative to marriage, which was given the arbitrary value of 500. The mean score, divided by 10, for each item for the entire sample was calculated, arranged in rank order, and these resulting values are used to weight the relative impact of the SRE life events.

The SRE items endorsed by respondents can be tallied either as frequency data for each time period or a life change score can be derived using the values of the SRRS in a weighted item frequency calculation (Life Change Score equals the sum of Item Frequency times Scale Value), although these two methods are highly correlated.

The manual describes the general purpose and development, scoring and administration procedures, psychometric properties, statistical considerations, and modifications for special populations. Appendices provide copies of the SRE, SRRS, scoring and coding guidelines, and an illness history form.

Before addressing the psychometric properties, it should be noted that the manual addresses some special modifications of the SRE including an interview format and discussion of item modifications customized for special populations including children, athletes, college students, and military personnel. Moreover, research-based criteria have been established to evaluate life change scores (e.g., over 300 Life Change Score = 80% chance of illness in the near future, and so on).

The SRE and SRRS appear to be empirically constructed instruments with little theoretical consideration given to the selection of the items. Some effort was given to the question of response style variance by wording each SRE item to reflect change rather than psychological meaning or social desirability, yet the effect of social desirability on SRE responding is still a possible influence (see Lei & Skinner, 1980).

Recent interest in stress research has focused on the psychometric soundness of life-event checklists. Reliability coefficients for the SRE range from .78 to .83 for short test-retest intervals (range from 2 weeks to 5 months). As expected, considerably lower coefficients (e.g., r = .34) are presented for longer administration intervals (2 years). It should be noted that the authors are sensitive to reliability considerations as indicated by a list of several issues in the manual including administration time interval; the age, education, and intelligence of the subjects; the time interval the subjects are requested to recall life events; the wording and format of the items; and the relative salience of the SRE events. In a more general sense, the test-retest strategy is limited by the dynamic nature of life events, pretest sensitization effects within short-interval retesting, and the apparent inconsistent recall of specific items (although the number of items may be similar).

Some validity data are presented through retrospective and prospective studies focusing on the predictability of health change occurring after life change. In one study, young resident physicians who experienced a mild life crisis (150–190 life change score) in one year showed a 37% chance of health change. Those who experienced a moderate life crisis (200–299) showed a 51% chance of health change the following year, while those who experienced a major life crisis (300 and above score) showed a 79% chance of health change during the next year. In another study involving medical students, 86% with high life change scores, 48% with moderate life change scores, and 33% with low life change scores experienced major health changes. Most research employing a correlational strategy to detect an association between psychological stress measured by the SRE and health status tend to be in the .20 to .30 range. Of course, one must view those validity data within a problematic context of restricted range and variability. In addition to questionable reliability data, the manual describes summary data about the frequency of occurrence of 40 SRE items for various groups—prisoners, pregnant women, college students, and others. It seems that many of the SRE items occur infrequently.

In summary, like many empirically based instruments, the SRE has some substantive weaknesses resulting from a lack of theoretical explication and strategic attention to possible response and/or personality style bias. Although the SRE has benefitted from the long empirical tradition associated with relating psychosocial stress and health, it also has been the focus of numerous criticisms. It has been argued that the reliability and validity of the SRE are unknown since most of the SRE reliability studies have employed an inappropriate strategy and the problems of restricted range and variability may indicate an underestimation of validity estimates. Furthermore, questions have arisen about the importance of using weighted or unweighted items or whether the number of events endorsed is a reflection of stimulus-defined stress or more an assessment of the respondents' subjective world of how they feel at the time of test administration. Given the controversy surrounding the general issue of assessment in the area of stress and health and the emergence of competitors such as the Hassles Scale and the Life Experience Survey, the old adage of "more research is needed" is appropriate here—research characterized by more psychometric sophistication.

REVIEWER'S REFERENCES

Holmes, T. H., & Rahe, R. H. (1967). The Social Readjustment Rating Scale. *Journal of Psychosomatic Research*, 11, 213-218.

Lei, L., & Skinner, H. A. (1980). A psychometric study of life events and social readjustment. *Journal of Psychosomatic Research*, 24, 57-65.

Review of The Schedule of Recent Experience by JOHN A. ZARSKE, Director, Northern Arizona Psychological Services, P.C., Flagstaff, AZ:

The Schedule of Recent Experience (SRE) represents one of the best-known methods for determining the frequency of occurrence of various stress-producing events in an individual's recent past. Having its roots in Meyer's (1951) "Life Chart" procedure for medical diagnosis, the SRE emerges as a major contribution to medical and behavioral researchers and clinicians entrusted with the important task of examining the social context of illness and health.

The SRE is a paper-and-pencil questionnaire containing 42 common human events (i.e., gaining a new family member, major personal injury or illness, death of a close family member, major change in financial state) allowing computation of scores referred to as "Life Change Units" (LCU). Numerous research studies described in the manual demonstrate the utility of the LCU in predicting the likelihood of illness. Each patient is asked to indicate the number of times each of the 42 events listed on the SRE has occurred during specific time periods. There are two forms of the SRE, one of the time frame 0–12 months and the other divided into four time periods (0–6 months; 6–12 months; 1–2 years; 2–3 years). The manual also provides appendices that allow the examiner to modify the time periods recorded in the SRE to include daily occurrences, monthly occurrences, and even time periods ranging to 10 years. As such, the instrument appears flexible and can be adapted to a wide range of research and clinical needs. The authors also provide an illness history chart that, together with the core SRE items, can be used for the purpose of conducting structured interviews.

Only one paragraph in the manual is devoted to validity. The authors point out that items were empirically selected for their observed occurrence prior to the onset of illness in two samples of medical school students and young resident physicians. In this regard, the SRE is indeed unique among the various life events scales. However, the authors could improve the SRE manual substantially by expanding their treatment of validity to address many of the complicated issues that surround the concept of stress and its measurement. For example, the

SRE is based on Selye's (1956) concept of stress as the physical and psychosocial change brought about by particular events, irrespective of the level of desirability of the events. The SRE assumes that stress is quantifiable in terms of the number of events experienced. Such a conceptualization of stress assumes a linear relationship between stress and illness and fails to deal with the "stress" that can arise when certain life events fail to occur in people's lives. Similarly, recent studies demonstrate significant differences in estimating the weights associated with different life events for samples with dissimilar demographic backgrounds (Chiriboga, 1977; Hough, Fairbanks, & Garcia, 1976; Miller, Bentz, Aponte, & Brogan, 1974). These studies suggest individual differences and situational factors also may influence a person's perception of stress and challenge the view of stress as a nonspecific consequence of isolated life events. These studies also present a challenge to the practice of assigning standard weights to various life events and suggest standard weights might be most useful when derived from specific populations. Indeed, modifications of the SRE for different populations are numerous and the authors point out this fact in the manual. However, they could go a step further by providing a more thorough discussion of the rationales for a population-specific approach.

Another issue not addressed in the manual relates to the content validity of the SRE and the method used for item selection. Presumably, items were selected as they were endorsed by the two samples as having occurred prior to the onset of illness. Such an approach has benefits in that the item pool is small and therefore administration time is brief (under 20 minutes). However, using a brief list of life events can result in a skewed distribution of scores for patients who earn low event totals, thus attenuating possible stress-criterion relationships that may exist (Hurst, 1979; Perkins, 1982). An alternative is to use what Perkins (1982) calls the "comprehensive approach," which uses a broader sample of relevant events that may yield a more accurate appraisal of life stress. The user of the SRE can accommodate a more comprehensive approach by asking the respondent to include life events that are not among the 42 items. To do so would require an extended interview but may provide more relevant and useful data for the clinician, especially when working with referrals who earn low LCU scores.

The manual describes several reliability studies and these studies generally suggest the SRE has adequate reliability. The authors appropriately address some of the factors that negatively influence the instrument's reliability and the discussion is straightforward and cogent. The authors point out that significantly less material is recalled for the more distant time periods and that more salient life events are likely to be remembered when compared with less salient events. The authors also address the effects of IQ, education, and age on the SRE's reliability.

Besides this instrument's obvious relevance to medical and behavioral research, the SRE has much to offer in the clinical arena, especially for psychiatrists and psychologists interested in preventative behavioral health. The SRE can be used to assist the clinician in identifying patients whose lifestyles and life changes place them at risk for the development of physical illness, and it has considerable heuristic value for treatment planning. In its current form, the instrument appears most valid when used with individuals in the 25–55 year age range. The manual provides a list of suggestions that are directly relevant to prevention and can assist the clinician in linking the LCU to meaningful interventions for the patient. The SRE may also be useful in the area of psychiatric and psychological diagnosis. Many behavioral scientists use the Diagnostic and Statistical Manual III (DSM III; Spitzer, 1980) multiaxial system for diagnostic and treatment planning purposes. Indeed, use of the DSM III is required for insurance reimbursement in many states. The SRE may ultimately represent a method for improving the interrater reliability of clinical judgments related to DSM III Axis IV (Severity of Psychosocial Stressors) and Axis V (Highest Level of Adaptive Functioning, Past Year).

Despite the apparent difficulties posed by a stimulus-oriented approach to stress, the SRE appears to have considerable utility as a predictive measure of illness. Additionally, the SRE is truly a methodological breakthrough because of its ability to provide a single quantitative index for the largely qualitative concept of "stress." The authors have made a major contribution with the development of the SRE.

REVIEWER'S REFERENCES

Meyer, A. (1951). The life chart and the obligation of specifying positive data in psychopathological diagnosis. In E. E. Winters (Ed.), *The collected papers of Meyer. Vol. 3: Medical teaching*. Baltimore: Johns Hopkins Press.

Selye, H. (1956). *The Stress of Life*. New York: McGraw-Hill.

Holmes, T. H., & Rahe, R. H. (1967). The Social Readjustment Rating Scale. *Journal of Psychosomatic Research*, 11, 213-218.

Miller, F. T., Bentz, W. K., Aponte, J. F., & Brogan, D. R. (1974). Perception of life crisis events: A comparative study of rural and urban samples. In B. S. Dohrenwend & B. P. Dohrenwend (Eds.), *Stressful life events: Their nature and effects*. New York: John Wiley.

Hough, R. L., Fairbanks, D. T., & Garcia, A. M. (1976). Problems in the ratio measurement of life stress. *Journal of Health and Social Behavior*, 17, 70-82.

Chiriboga, D. A. (1978). Life event weighting systems: A comparative analysis. *Journal of Psychosomatic Research*, 22, 47-55.

Hurst, M. W. (1979). Life changes and psychiatric symptom development: Issues of content, scoring, and clustering. In J. E. Barrett, R. M. Rose, & G. L. Klermon (Eds.), *Stress and mental disorder*, (pp. 17-36). New York: Raven.

American Psychiatric Association. (1980). *Diagnostic and Statistical Manual of Mental Disorders, Third Edition*. Washington, DC: American Psychiatric Association.

Perkins, D. V. (1982). The assessment of stress using life events scales. In L. Goldberger & S. Breznitz (Eds.), *The handbook of stress*, (pp. 320-331). New York: The Free Press.

[324]

School Environment Preference Survey. Purpose: "Designed to measure the student's commitment to the set of attitudes, values and behaviors that have been characteristically fostered and rewarded in traditional school environments." Grades 4–12; 1978; SEPS; 5 scores: Self-Subordination, Traditionalism, Rule Conformity, Uncriticalness, Structured Role Orientation; 1987 price data: $6.50 per 25 survey forms; $10 per hand-scoring keys; $2.50 per manual (17 pages); $5 per specimen set; (10–15) minutes; Leonard V. Gordon; EdITS.*

Review of the School Environment Preference Survey by JOAN SILVERSTEIN, Assistant Professor of Psychology and Director, School Psychology Program, Montclair State College, Upper Montclair, NJ:

The School Environment Preference Survey (SEPS) was designed to assess attitudes, values, and behaviors fostered and reinforced in traditional school settings, including acceptance of authority, identification with the institutional subculture, close adherence to rules of conduct, and disinclination to question what is taught. The survey, a downward extension of the Work Environment Preference Schedule (WEPS), designed for adults in the work environment (Gordon, 1973), is based on the assumption that a syndrome of personality characteristics, which may be identified in the earlier years, predisposes students to accept values and behaviors that are fostered in traditional school environments.

The SEPS provides an overall measure of structured role orientation (*So*), defined as the external process of indoctrination and/or reinforcement of particular norms and values as it occurs in the school setting, and the internalization by the individual of these norms and values. *So* consists of four components: Self-subordination (S)—(a desire to comply with the wishes of and to please one's teacher); Traditionalism (T)—("a need to identify with one's school and to conform to the general student norm"), Rule Conformity (R)—("a desire for the security that following rules and regulations affords"); and Uncriticalness (U)—("an uncritical acceptance of the opinions of teachers").

The survey, consisting of 24 items organized in a Likert-response format, is designed for use as a self-administered scale with students from 4th through 12th grades. The questions have been read to third graders. The survey can be completed in approximately 15 minutes. Hand scoring is straightforward with a template; machine scoring is also available. Scores are generated for each of the subscales and for *So*.

Construct validity was determined, for *So* only, by determining the degree of correspondence between the construct at the student and adult levels. Internal analyses and factor analyses were employed to check item-subscale allocation. Items were then arranged in the repeating order by subscale: S, T, R, U; S, T, R, U; etc. Coefficient alpha reliabilities for the *So* score range between .86 to .88 for grades 6, 8, and 10. Reliability coefficients for the subscales are lower, generally in the .64 to .76 range, but in the .49 to .59 range for U.

Separate percentile norms are presented for combined grade levels 5–6, 7–9, and 10–12. The author urges the development of local norms. All major regions of the country were reported to be represented, and students of varying socioeconomic status and racial composition were selected; however, no data regarding the distribution of these variables are presented in the manual. When interpreting scores, it is important to remember that a high percentile value is not necessarily favorable. A negative correlation between high percentile ranking on the SEPS and aptitude scales was cited in one study. As the author cautions, the scores are merely descriptive and must be interpreted in the context of other data including intelligence level, age, and actual behavior.

The suggested uses of the test are: individual counseling, vocational education, classroom planning, placement, value clarification, and evaluation. However, several serious concerns about the underlying constructs and design of the survey lead to a recommendation that the survey not be used in its current form for such activities as evaluation, placement, or counseling.

The design issues involve the length of the scale, the composition of the Traditionalism subscale, and the potential for development of an acquiescence response set. The survey is too short for what it claims to accomplish. At least 40 items, rather than 24, are necessary for a Likert-response format with four subscales. Based on visual inspection, the Traditionalism scale appears to tap two different, often conflicting, components: the belief that students should always speak well of their school and the belief that students should conform to the school's peer group subculture.

Because all statements are phrased so that agreement corresponds to the acceptance of the traditional school norm, an acquiescence response set may develop. No attempt was made to control for response set because it was considered to be a characteristic of the structured role orientation construct. However, acquiescence response set becomes a confounding factor in the interpretation of findings. Similarly, random placement of items would have been desirable rather than maintaining the consistent item order S, T, R, U throughout the survey.

More important than these technical problems are those concerning underlying constructs and the potential uses of the test. The survey deals with a specific set of values that, on inspection, appear to correspond closely to an authoritarian orientation. Despite warnings to the contrary, there is a danger that test users will interpret high percentiles as desirable and low percentiles as negative, particularly because many traditional schools do subscribe to authoritarian values. Therefore, the test could result in yet another means for classifying students, with little obvious benefit, and the potential for harm.

Because the test items are all phrased to reflect traditional values, the survey provides no useful information about students who do not fit this pattern, except to tell us what they do not believe. In fact, low percentile students could hold a wide variety of beliefs and exhibit a wide range of behaviors. For example, creative students and alienated students could both, conceivably, receive low scores. Therefore, the test, in its current form, appears to provide no information for any important educational decisions. Similarly, the usefulness of the survey for evaluation of attitude sets seems to be limited by the narrowness of the attitudes, values, and beliefs that are tapped. Even when used as a vehicle to stimulate class discussion, the set of values described in the SEPS seems limited to specific types of occupations. Attitudes and values tapped by the SEPS seem more appropriate to low level bureaucratic workers than to executives in decision-making positions.

In summary, any potential usefulness of the SEPS in its current form appears to be outweighed by the narrowness of its scope and the potential for harm through the development of a new method of classifying students based on a narrow set of values and attitudes. The survey might be of greater descriptive utility if it were modified to represent a broader range of attitudes, values, and beliefs.

[325]

School Subjects Attitude Scales. Purpose: Measures group (classroom) attitudes toward school subjects. Grades 5–12; 1982–83; for measurement of classroom groups rather than individual students; 3 scores: Evaluative, Usefulness, Difficulty; norms for Alberta, Canada classrooms only; 1987 price data: $1.50 per 10 answer sheets; $1 per manual for administrators ('83, 159 pages); scoring service for users outside Alberta available from Psican Consulting Ltd.; (20) minutes; V. R. Nyberg and S. C. T. Clarke; Learning Resources Distribution Centre [Canada].*

Review of the School Subjects Attitude Scales by BARBARA PERRY-SHELDON, Associate Professor of Education, North Carolina Wesleyan College, Rocky Mount, NC:

The development of the School Subjects Attitude Scales (SSAS) during 1978–79 was initiated and funded by the Alberta, Canada Department of Education. As in many school systems, Alberta included positive attitudes as part of its goals at all grade levels and perceived a need for assessing attitudes especially when changes in curricula were planned.

The SSAS is intended to assess group and not individual attitudes toward a school subject. The SSAS is a one-page form to be completed by each student in a class. It has directions on the back and questions for demographic data and a rating scale of 24 semantic pairs (e.g., nice/awful, lively/listless [inactive, lazy], complicated/simple) on the front. Each of the three subscales, Evaluative, Usefulness, or Difficulty, contains eight semantic pairs. The student fills in a circle for *very much*, *a bit*, *neither*, *a bit*, or *very much*, between each pair. The administrator's manual includes norms for Alberta, general information, and an article in the appendix describing the development of the SSAS.

Teachers may administer the form if anonymity is stressed, but the authors encourage a neutral administrator and a minimum of monitoring to reduce faking. Instructions on the form are supplemented by more detailed ones in the manual. Administration time may be 20 minutes for first time users, but usually takes 5 minutes.

The items may be hand or machine scored. The score range for each eight-pair subscale is 8 to 40. (The manual mistakenly says there are five pairs.) Scores over 24 indicate a positive attitude for each subscale. Hand scoring is simple, but averaging and then using one of the 98 norm tables to identify the percentile rank could require considerable time. A formula for adjusting scores for sex differences for single-sex classes is included with the norms.

After deciding to use the bipolar word format, the authors identified 100 word pairs. After review and use with a few students the number was reduced to 46. These were then split into two instruments and administered to over 700 fifth and eighth graders. A factor analysis indicated that three factors accounted for 57% of the variance; these became the subscales. The 24 strongest pairs were then cross-validated on a new sample. Each factor analysis yielded similar results.

An academic magnet school, two schools with diverse cultural backgrounds, and other easily accessible schools were chosen nonrandomly for testing reliabilities. Reliabilities based on individual student responses ranged from .96 on the Evaluative scale to .91 for Usefulness, and .82 for the Difficulty scale at grade 5. Those for the eighth grade were almost identical. Test-retest reliabilities after 1 month were much lower, from .37 to .68. The instrument was then modified by the addition of some definitions for the words and testing at grade 11 was added. Test-retest results 1 week apart yielded reliabilities of .61 to .86 with the highest being for the eleventh grade. The short retesting time could acocunt for the higher values. Reliability estimates for class means from fifth and tenth grade samples during the norming phase were at or above .92 for Evaluative and Usefulness and ranged from .73 to .93 for Difficulty. The reliabilities seem strong for an attitude scale.

Validity was assessed by comparing ratings of courses at grades 5 and 8 to the teachers' identification of students with the most or least positive attitudes. There was significant agreement. When ratings were compared to students' stated preferences for a subject, there was significant agreement. Analyses of ratings by various subgroups—sex, type of school, and cultural group—tended to yield expected differences and offered support for the validity of the instrument.

Norms for early, middle, and end of year were developed because the authors hypothesized that attitudes vary over time. Stratified samples of schools by urbanization and grade served as the norming group, but private schools and self-contained special education classes were excluded. The norms represent adjusted values for a given test time. The reason for adjusting was not clearly explained and may be unnecessary. The usefulness of the norms outside of Alberta is limited.

In conclusion, the SSAS can be viewed as a promising instrument for assessing attitudes. There are few such standardized measures. Its coverage of all academic subjects and easily-administered format are enhanced by optional machine scoring. It must be remembered that it is intended for reporting class means and not individual student attitudes. Because the validity studies indicated the SSAS results agreed with teachers' projections of students' attitudes and there was a significant relationship between the students' expressed preferences and the results of the instrument, one might conclude that it would be simpler to ask opinions rather than using the SSAS. Also, the scale may indicate a preference for a course, but the results do not say whether the curriculum, the teacher, the instructional climate or other things shaped the attitudes. The authors have provided a simple, reliable instrument that could be useful for researching attitudes, but one requiring further testing development.

[326]

The Schutz Measures: Elements of Awareness (Clinical and Research Edition). Purpose: "Measures various aspects of human functioning and human relationships." Junior high and over; 1982–83; for research and experimental use; 4 tests; 1987 price data: $7 per manual ('83, 19 pages); $9 per specimen set; (20) minutes per test; Will Schutz; Consulting Psychologists Press, Inc.*

a) ELEMENT B (BEHAVIOR). Measures interpersonal contact, control over others, and openness; 12 scales: Expressed, Received, Perceived, and Wanted scales for each of 3 areas (Inclusion, Control, Openness); $7.75 per 25 tests; $15 per 50 response sheets and interpretive guides.

b) ELEMENT F (FEELINGS). Measures feelings related to significance, competence, and likeability; 12 scales: Expressed, Received, Perceived, and Wanted scales for each of 3 areas (Significance, Competence, Likeability); prices same as *a* above.

c) ELEMENT S (SELF-CONCEPT). Measures "behavior and feelings directed toward the self"; 12 scales: Perceived and Wanted scales in 3 behavior areas: Inclusion, Control, Awareness; Perceived and Wanted scales in 3 feeling areas: Significance, Competence, Likeability; prices same as *a* above.

d) ELEMENT R (RELATIONSHIPS). Measures dyadic interpersonal characteristics; 24 scales: Expressed, Received, Perceived, and Wanted scales for each of 6 areas: Inclusion, Control, Openness, Significance, Competence, Likeability; $16 per 50 tests; $15 per 50 response sheets and interpretive guides.

Review of The Schutz Measures: Elements of Awareness (Research Edition) by WILLIAM P. ERCHUL, Assistant Professor of Psychology, North Carolina State University, Raleigh, NC:

OVERVIEW. The Schutz Measures consist of four 54-item questionnaires, each designed to assess different facets of interpersonal (Elements B, F, and R) and intrapersonal (Element S) functioning. The instrument is based on one of the few formally stated and well-developed theories of interpersonal behavior—FIRO, or Fundamental Interpersonal Relations Orientation (Schutz, 1958). The Schutz Measures reflect the author's current thinking regarding FIRO and, as such, three of four Elements can be considered revisions and/or extensions of previously released FIRO scales. Thus, Element B is similar to FIRO-B; Element F, FIRO-F; and Element R, MATE (Marital ATtitude Enquiry) (Schutz, 1966). Element S, Self-Concept, presents a dimension new to FIRO.

Like their predecessors, the Elements are comprised of a series of nine-item Guttman-type scales. Elements B, F, and S have 12 scales each and Element R has 24 scales. Respondents are instructed to rate items (e.g., "I join social groups") on a 6-point continuum ranging from *definitely not true* (1) to *especially true* (6). A subject's score on a given scale is not the sum of the item ratings, but rather a number from 0 to 9 indicating the degree to which the scale name (e.g., "I include people") is endorsed.

The Schutz Measures appear to improve upon the FIRO scales in several ways. First, examinees are instructed to respond to all Element items twice, initially rating items indicating their present condition (e.g., "I feel competent") and then rating items indicating a future, desired condition (e.g., "I want to feel competent"). Score discrepancies resulting from this procedure may facilitate the determination of personal growth goals. Second, a simplified scoring method presents the opportunity for respondents to score their own protocols. In a group setting, exercising this option may result in a significant savings of examiner time and effort.

Before reviewing the test's psychometric properties, it should be noted that the front cover and title page of the booklet supplied with the specimen set are erroneously labelled Professional Manual, despite the fact the text refers to the booklet as the Preliminary Manual. This oversight seriously misrepresents the developmental state of the instrument. However, it is emphasized that The Schutz Measures are in a very early developmental stage; potential users are reminded that presently the test is a "research edition" and therefore unsuitable for psychodiagnostic and treatment purposes.

STANDARDIZATION AND NORMS. Data from 200 to 312 subjects were used to generate descriptive statistics for the 60 total scales contained in the four Elements. Means tabulated by age (five groups ranging from "under

20" to "over 49") and sex for all scales are presented, but standard deviations are not given and the composition of the sample is not clearly specified. Most subjects were college students but no information regarding their socioeconomic status, ethnic origin, or psychological characteristics is offered. It seems doubtful that the sample employed was a representative one. Also, scores from specific groups (e.g., Middle-Eastern students) on particular scales are mentioned in passing, but it is not clear whether or not these scores contributed to the overall scale means. Perhaps due to the relatively small sample size, no percentiles, standard scores, or standard errors are given.

RELIABILITY. Guttman coefficients of reproducibility are at or above the generally accepted criterion of .90 (Shaw & Wright, 1967) for 49 of the 60 scales. The other scales offer coefficients ranging from .85 to .89, which overall suggests the scales are unidimensional and reliable. If the test is to be used with a variety of populations as its author recommends, then additional scalogram analyses are advised because scalability of items may be population-specific (Shaw & Wright, 1967). No test-retest reliability is reported, which is very surprising in light of the fact Schutz advocates that the test be utilized in pre-post comparisons. These data need to be compiled.

VALIDITY. It is remarkable that the word "validity" never appears in the 15-page manual. Users are informed only that the Elements' "similarity to . . . the thoroughly studied FIRO scales may create a presumption that many of their statistical properties will be similar." Assuming this presumption is correct, caution still is warranted because the FIRO scales in general appear to have questionable criterion-related validity and weak construct validity (Lifton, 1985). Although the FIRO-B tends to fare better psychometrically than the other FIRO scales, overall the argument of test comparability by analogy is unconvincing. Extensive efforts to document the content, criterion-related, and construct validity of The Schutz Measures should be undertaken. A reliable but unvalidated test is of limited use.

SUMMARY. The Elements of Awareness is an updated version of the FIRO scales, which are based on Schutz's theory of interpersonal relations. The test presently is in a very early developmental stage and perhaps is viewed most fairly as incomplete rather than psychometrically inadequate. Major concerns noted in this review include a vaguely defined norming sample, scant reliability data, and indirect validity support. If these areas of concern are addressed satisfactorily, there is reason to believe the Elements of Awareness will have even greater utility than the well-known FIRO scales. Currently, however, use of the test should be limited to research and experimental applications.

REVIEWER'S REFERENCES

Schutz, W. C. (1958). *FIRO: A three-dimensional theory of interpersonal behavior.* New York: Rinehart & Company, Inc.

Schutz, W. C. (1966). *The interpersonal underworld.* Palo Alto, CA: Science and Behavior Books.

Shaw, M. E., & Wright, J. M. (1967). *Scales for the measurement of attitudes.* New York: McGraw-Hill Book Company.

Lifton, P. D. (1985). [Review of The FIRO Awareness Scales]. In J. V. Mitchell, Jr. (Ed.), *The ninth mental measurements yearbook* (pp. 578-579). Lincoln, NE: Buros Institute of Mental Measurements.

[327]

Screening Assessment for Gifted Elementary Students. Purpose: "To obtain information that is helpful in identifying children for gifted classes that emphasize aptitude, achievement, and/or creativity." Ages 7-0 to 12-11; 1987; SAGES; 4 scores: Reasoning, School-Acquired Information, Divergent Production, SAGES Quotient; individual in part; 1987 price data: $64 per complete kit; $15 per 50 profile and response sheets; $29 per picture book; $23 per examiner's manual (61 pages); (30–90) minutes; Susan K. Johnsen and Anne L. Corn; PRO-ED, Inc.*

Review of the Screening Assessment for Gifted Elementary Students by E. SCOTT HUEBNER, Department of Psychology, Western Illinois University, Macomb, IL:

The Screening Assessment for Gifted Elementary Students (SAGES) is a screening test designed "to obtain information that is helpful in identifying children for gifted classes." It consists of three subtests: Reasoning (RSG), School-Acquired Information (SAI), and Divergent Production (DP). In addition to identifying gifted students, the authors suggest the test may be used (*a*) to assess a child's strengths and weaknesses in aptitude, achievement, and creativity and (*b*) as a research instrument to study giftedness.

The Reasoning subtest, which was designed to assess aptitude, consists entirely of two kinds of items—analogies and classification. The SAI subtest samples academic achievement through requiring students to read items involving math, social studies, and science using a multiple-choice format. A single composite score indexes performance on this subtest. The final subtest, Divergent Production, measures one facet of creativity, that is, fluency. For this subtest, the examinee views a matrix of pictures or figures and generates a list of as many item groups (i.e., items that can be grouped together on some logical basis) as s/he can in 3 minutes. In my opinion, the limited number of item types suggests unduly narrow definitions of reasoning, academic achievement, and creativity.

The test manual is well-written. Administration and scoring standards are detailed clearly and applied easily. The test materials are attractive and interesting to students. In general, the SAGES is user friendly.

Raw scores can be converted to percentiles and standard scores (*M*ean = 10; *SD* = 3). To the authors' credit, age and grade equivalent scores are not provided, avoiding the ambiguity associated with these scores (Reynolds, 1981).

Item analysis data are reported thoroughly in the manual. Inspection of the data for each age level reveals some interesting observations. First, there is a general trend for a decrease in difficulty levels as age increases, except for the SAI with normal students. Most importantly, the SAI is likely too easy for 11- and 12-year-old gifted students as the median difficulty levels are .88 and .84 respectively for these ages. Otherwise, the other subtests do seem to discriminate effectively at the upper ages and levels of ability. Users should note, however, the test does not necessarily discriminate well at the lower levels of ability. For example, a score of 1 on the SAI earns a standard score of 6 for children from ages 7-0 to 9-5.

The manual includes comprehensive standardization information. Norms are provided for two groups—a normal sample and a gifted sample. To obtain the normal sample, SAGES was administered to 1,567 children from 16 states. Normal children were defined "as those currently enrolled in regular classrooms." For the gifted sample, SAGES was administered to 1,595 gifted children from 21 states. Gifted children were identified as "those currently enrolled in gifted classrooms."

The characteristics of the two groups in terms of sex, age, race, ethnicity, domicile, geographic location, and parental education are reported in the manual. However, according to the manual, "Since demographic characteristics of a national gifted standardization are unavailable, it was not possible to compare percentages with those of the United States population." With regard to the normal sample, the demographics compare favorably with the following exceptions. First, the North Central region is underrepresented (8% vs. 25%) while the South (51% vs. 34%) and the West (29% vs. 20%) were overrepresented. Second, the percentage of college-educated parents is overrepresented (61% vs. 34%). Given the well-documented relationships between socio-economic status (SES) and intelligence and achievement, the raw score points needed to achieve a given score are probably greater than the points needed in a more representative sample. Thus, the user must exercise some caution in the use of the norms, particularly if considering using the test as an intellectual screening device with regular students.

Reliability information is limited to internal consistency estimates for the RSG and SAI subtests and interscorer reliability for the DP subtest. Correlations are reported for the normal and gifted samples across each age level. Coefficients range from .86 to .89 (median = .87) for normal students on the RSG subtest. For the gifted sample, coefficients range from .82 to .91 (median = .87) on the RSG subtest. On the SAI subtest, correlations range from .85 to .95 (median = .93) for normal students and from .88 to .92 (median = .90) for gifted students. RSG coefficients are acceptable for screening purposes but do not quite meet the standard of .90 or above suggested for *individual* decisions (e.g., Nunnally, 1978; Salvia & Ysseldyke, 1981). Interscorer reliability for the DP subtest is good (94% for pictures and 100% for figures). Test-retest data are not reported for any of the subtests.

Validity data are promising, but sparse. Content validity is not addressed adequately in the manual. Support for criterion-related validity is limited to concurrent validity studies. Correlations with the Wechsler Intelligence Scale for Children—Revised (WISC-R), Ross Test of Higher Cognitive Processes, Short Form Test of Academic Aptitude, Iowa Tests of Basic Skills, and California Achievement Tests are reported and are generally adequate. However, the correlations between the RSG and other aptitude measures are quite modest. For example, the highest correlation between the RSG and the aptitude measures is with the WISC-R ($r = .51$) and is surprisingly lower than the WISC-R and SAI correlation ($r = .73$). In addition to the relationships reported, I would like to see studies assessing correlations between SAGES subtests and teacher ratings and between the DP subtest and more well-accepted tests of creativity (e.g., Torrance Tests of Creative Thinking). Predictive validity studies are also essential, particularly for the RSG subtest. In summary, much research remains to be completed, particularly to provide adequate support for the RSG as a measure of aptitude.

According to the manual, support for construct validity is provided through the positive correlations between SAGES and age and by mean score differences between normals and gifted at each age level, favoring the latter. While such information is useful, factor analytic studies of the structure of SAGES are an essential prerequisite to evaluating the construct validity of the test. Interestingly, even data regarding intercorrelations among the three subtests are omitted.

The use of this test with minority students may be particularly problematic. Although minority students were carefully represented in the standardization samples, information concerning item and/or test bias is not presented in the manual. Given the current controversy surrounding the assessment of aptitude in minority children, I would like to see research related to differential content (i.e., item), construct, and criterion-related validity. Without such information, the user must be especially cautious in using the test with minority students.

In summary, SAGES shows promise, but must be studied further. Additional validation work needs to be accomplished, including studies involving minority students. Factor analytic studies are especially needed to provide information pertaining to the structure of the test before it can be used to assess strengths and weaknesses across the various domains. At this time, the test is perhaps best used cautiously as one source of information in screening middle and upper SES, white students for gifted classes.

REVIEWER'S REFERENCES

Nunnally, J. S. (1978). *Psychometric theory*. New York: McGraw-Hill.

Salvia, J., & Ysseldyke, J. E. (1981). *Assessment in special and remedial education*. Boston: Houghton Mifflin.

Reynolds, C. R. (1981). The fallacy of "two years below grade level for age" as a diagnostic criterion for reading disorders. *Journal of School Psychology*, 19, 350-358.

[328]

A Screening Deep Test of Articulation. Purpose: "Provide the speech clinician with a tool which permits quick observation of a child's articulation of several commonly misarticulated consonants in a variety of phonetic contexts." Grades K–3; 1968–76; SDTA; individual; 1987 price data: $35 per test book/manual ('76, 69 pages), 250 individual record sheets, and 100 teacher's report forms; $4.95 per 50 individual record sheets or 50 teacher's report forms; administration time not reported; Eugene T. McDonald; Communication Skill Builders, Inc.*

See T3:2103 (9 references) and T2:2090 (1 reference); for reviews by Edgar R. Garrett and Harold A. Peterson, see 7:968 (2 references).

Review of A Screening Deep Test of Articulation by WILLIAM O. HAYNES, Associate Professor, Department of Communication Disorders, Auburn University, Auburn, AL:

According to the test manual, A Screening Deep Test of Articulation (SDTA) is designed to "provide the speech clinician with a tool which permits quick observation of a child's articulation of several commonly misarticulated consonants in a variety of phonetic contexts." Further, McDonald suggests that the longitudinal data included in the test "may assist the clinician in identifying, at an early age, children who are 'at risk' for failure to develop mature articulation without speech training." The SDTA is one of the few tests that provide such data in a screening measure for articulation. The author recommends the development of regional/local norms for use by practicing clinicians because the longitudinal data included in the test were developed on children in Pennsylvania.

The SDTA is based on the assumption that the syllable is the basic physiological unit of speech and that consonants can either initiate or terminate a syllable. It is also assumed that it is important to observe consonants not as singletons, but as members of abutting pairs. Thus, like the McDonald Deep Test of Articulation (MDTA, McDonald, 1964), the SDTA does not assess consonants in isolation or single words but typically in CVCCVC canonical shapes with the target phoneme either initiating the second syllable or terminating the first syllable. The test also was not designed to consider the occurrence of phonological processes in children's speech, so like the MDTA it is limited in its scope of viewing articulation as primarily sensorimotor behavior. The SDTA uses pairs of color pictures to elicit bisyllabic productions from children (e.g., bat-man, sheep-dog, match-rake, etc.). The pictures are attractive and the SDTA is compact and efficiently arranged. The test elicits ten productions each of the phonemes /s/, /l/, /r/, /ch/, /sh/, /th/, /k/, /f/, and /t/. McDonald indicates that these phonemes were selected because they are most frequently misarticulated in young children. The voiced cognates are not included because it is assumed they are articulated similarly.

A critical variable in the administration of the SDTA is the elicitation of responses from the child. The manual states "It is essential that the individual being tested link the two monosyllables into a bisyllable. Any interruption between the pair of monosyllables would interfere with the coarticulations which influence how a sound is made." In this reviewer's experience, some children may have difficulty performing this task exactly according to the above specifications; however, McDonald did succeed with a relatively large pilot sample. There are also six practice pictures prior to the actual test items to help accustom the child to the task. During the test administration, the examiner must evaluate several sounds simultaneously in the bisyllables. Specifically, of the 31 test pictures the examiner must listen for two phonemes in 11 of the trials, three phonemes in 12 of the trials, and four phonemes in 8 of the trials. The record forms are logically arranged for the clinician to score correct or incorrect responses on phonetically pretranscribed versions of each bisyllable. These correct/incorrect judgments are ultimately transferred to a "phonetic profile" that indicates how many correct responses occurred in the 10 contexts for each of the nine phonemes tested in the 31 trials. In this way, the clinician can see in graphic form the phonemes with the fewest contexts correct. A similar phonetic profile form is included for distribution to classroom teachers.

The SDTA was piloted on 521 children from Pennsylvania who completed all phases of a longitudinal study. Children were administered the SDTA at the beginning and end of kindergarten, beginning and end of first grade, the beginning of second and the beginning of third grades. According to the manual, the subjects had no hearing impairments, physical problems, or academic difficulties severe enough to make the child repeat a grade. The children represented a broad range of socioeconomic classes; however, there was no breakdown as to sex of the subjects. Fifty testers administered the SDTA during the longitudinal study. The only reliability data reported were interjudge and intrajudge figures of at least 80% agreement for incorrect/correct judgments. These reliability figures may have been higher if fewer sounds were scored simultaneously per word by the examiners. No data were available on test-retest reliability since McDonald feels that this type of measure is "inappropriate for determining the reliability of an articulation test with young children whose articulation is variable." According to the author, a strength of the SDTA is its capacity to assess such variability of production.

The longitudinal data are reported as proportions of children at each testing time from K–3 who correctly articulated each consonant in from 1 to 10 contexts. Specific guidelines are provided in the manual regarding implications for case selection based on production of each of the nine sounds tested. McDonald says that clinicians should not solely use the SDTA to decide on case selection. He recommends that a Deep Test of Articulation and a spontaneous sample are warranted before final scheduling takes place. An especially potent predictor, according to McDonald, is a pattern where children exhibit two testing periods with zero contexts correct on any sound. He recommends further screening of children who had fewer than three contexts correct on any consonant at the beginning of kindergarten or first grade. Regarding the validity of the SDTA, no data are provided other than for /s/ and /r/ but McDonald states that "In general we find that children who produce a sound correctly in all SDTA contexts are usually not judged to misarticulate the sound in spontaneous speech."

The administration time is not specifically stated in the manual, but certainly should be under 5 minutes. The age range from K–3 is useful for prediction purposes; however, there are no data for use with younger or older children. Recent research comparing the SDTA with other available screening measures (Templin-Darley Screening Test and Predictive Screening Test of Articulation) has shown that children given all three tests failed them for different reasons and only 3 of 91 children failed all three tests (Ritterman, Zook-Herman, Carlson, & Kinde, 1982). This suggests that the criteria for case selection should include more than SDTA performance.

REVIEWER'S REFERENCES

McDonald, E. T. (1964). A Deep Test of Articulation. Pittsburgh: Stanwix House, Inc.

McDonald, E. (1968). *Articulation testing and treatment.* Pittsburg: Stanwix House, Inc.

Ritterman, S., Zook-Herman, S. L., Carlson, R. L., & Kinde, S. W. (1982). The pass/fail disparity among three commonly employed articulatory screening tests. *Journal of Speech and Hearing Disorders*, 47, 429-433.

Review of A Screening Deep Test of Articulation by JOAN I. LYNCH, Associate Professor of Language Science, University of Texas Health Science at Houston, Houston, TX:

When A Screening Deep Test of Articulation (SDTA) was published in 1968 it represented an advance in articulation testing. The SDTA is based upon the author's sensory-motor approach to speech sound production as a ballistic movement. In contrast to the traditional tests available at that time, this test was the first to stress the effects of coarticulation and to emphasize the syllable as the basic unit of speech. Using a controlled context of two-syllable utterances, each of nine consonant sounds was sampled in 10 different phonemic contexts. This process allowed for analysis of the range of correct productions depending upon the phonemic context and acknowledged that inconsistency had diagnostic and prognostic implications. The 1976 revision reflects the same philosophy and retains the same format and stimulus items as the original test.

The test was designed to be used with children between kindergarten and third grade for the purpose of identifying those children who are "at risk" for continuing misarticulation and in need of speech therapy. The test consists of a single spiral notebook containing the manual and the stimulus pictures. There are test plates with two pictures per page. The child is instructed to "put the two little words together to make one big word." Six practice plates are also included to train the child to name the two pictures as one word (i.e., CUP + CAKE or MATCH + TOOTH).

Among the 90 tested positions are 16 syllable initial or arresting positions, 15 syllable final or releasing positions, 28 instances when the consonants function together (compound) or when the releasing consonant abuts an arresting consonant, and 2 instances when the consonant is between two vowels. Administration time ranges from approximately 3 minutes to over 17 minutes with a mean of approximately 6 minutes (Prather & Kenney, 1986). As the child produces each "big word" the examiner must record the production of between two and four consonants. The production of each consonant may be noted as correct or incorrect or the examiner may record the exact phoneme produced by the child. However, in analyzing the results only correct productions are counted.

The author indicates that his purpose was to design a test that would measure a child's ability to produce consonant sounds and to assist in determining if a kindergarten or first grade child needed articulation therapy. The purpose was not to judge intelligibility. Given this purpose, the interpretation of the score made by each child is critical. A major change in the 1976 revision is the addition of a revised method of interpretation. Instead of the single table and profile provided in 1968, there are now separate tables for each consonant so that the number of correct contexts can be compared with the norming population at each of six different ages: Beginning Kindergarten, Ending Kindergarten, Beginning First, Ending First, Beginning Second, and Beginning Third Grade. The revised manual also provides a discussion section regarding the implications of these scores for case selection for therapy.

The validity of a test is largely a product of its construction. Although the author explains the rationale for several decisions regarding test construction, these have not been tested experimentally. The author indicates that he chose the nine consonants for the test because they are the ones "most frequently misarticulated." In addition, he indicates that only voiceless consonants are included because there is a close relationship in the production of cognates. This test is unique because of controlled sampling of phonetic context; however, the manual provides no rationale for the choice of context. For example, why is /-sf-/ measured twice while /sp/ and /sn/ are not sampled at all? Another problem concerns the assumption that children will pronounce the two stimulus words as a single long word even though many of these big words are semantically meaningless (e.g., MATCH TOOTH; BRUSH FIVE). There may be a tendency for children to insert a pause between these two words thus decreasing the likelihood that the child is actually producing the type of utterance the test is intended to measure.

The author indicated that he was not going to attempt to determine concurrent validity. However, the manual does contain the scores of 73 children whose production of /s/ and /r/ were compared with ratings of spontaneous speech. The children who had no errors on the SDTA were not judged to have errors in spontaneous speech. Finally, test-retest reliability studies were not done because the author felt that the 10 presentations of each sound made that step "inappropriate."

The normative data for this test differ from standardization data for most other tests in that this was a longitudinal rather than a cross-sectional study. The original population consisted of 818 kindergarten children in Blair County, Pennsylvania who were tested at the beginning of kindergarten. The same children were subsequently retested at the end of kindergarten, the beginning of and end of first grade, the beginning of second grade, and the beginning of third grade. Of the original children, 521 were available throughout the study. None of these children had hearing loss, observable physical problems, or repeated any grades. The author did not specifically control for socioeconomic status but instead reported the 1970 census data for Blair County. Fifty trained examiners administered all tests and inter- and intratester agreement was at least 80%.

In summary, the 1976 revision of the SDTA still lacks the usual measures of validity and reliability and its longitudinal norms were not compared to any other criterion group. The author has chosen not to provide any discussion regarding the place of coarticulation testing as compared to traditional articulation testing or to tests utilizing distinctive feature theory or phonological process theory. The latter two theories have had considerable influence on testing since the SDTA was first published. Despite these drawbacks, the SDTA is founded upon a theoretical base that has not been challenged and remains relevant. The test can be recommended as a supplement to other articulation tests. Its brief administration and scoring time make this supplemental use practical. The only caution suggested is that examiners must be able to accurately score multiple phonemes as the child says each of the "big words." Because of the nature of the norming procedure for the SDTA, clinicians who can use only a single screening test may need to rely upon screening tests that have better established norms.

REVIEWER'S REFERENCE

Prather, E. M., & Kenney, K. W. (1986). Coarticulation testing of kindergarten children. *Language, Speech & Hearing Services in Schools*, 17, 285-291.

[329]

Secretarial Staff Selector. Purpose: "Evaluates the suitability of candidates of all levels of experience for the position of secretary." Candidates for secretaries and office administrators and executive assistants; 1966–84; 9 tests: Numerical Skills, Problem Solving Ability, Attention to Details, Manual Dexterity, Alphabetizing and Filing, Clerical Skills Series Grammar and Punctuation, Clerical Skills Series Spelling-Vocabulary, C.P.F. (interest in working with people), N.P.F. (emotional stability-optional); 1987 price data: $45–225 per person per set of tests including manual (no date, 6 pages) and scoring guide; information on scoring service available from distributor; French edition available; (5–15) minutes per test; tests from various publishers compiled, distributed, and scored (optional) by Wolfe Personnel Testing & Training Systems, Inc.*

Review of the Secretarial Staff Selector by MICHAEL RYAN, Clinical Psychologist, West Side Family Mental Health Clinic, Kalamazoo, MI:

The Secretarial Staff Selector was designed to assess the abilities of candidates for several types of office positions such as: senior clerk, secretary, administrative assistant, or word processing operator. It consists of nine subtests that were compiled from three different test publishers (Harvard Professional Services, Martin M. Bruce, and Industrial Psychological Corporation). The first seven tests are timed and take a total of 45 minutes to administer. The last two tests, measuring aspects of personality functioning, are optional and are untimed. In general, the directions for the first seven tests are clear with adequate examples for each task. However, the format for the last two tests is somewhat confusing and awkward, in that the subject has to read the directions and then turn the test booklet over to complete each test. Scoring can be done by the client or by Wolfe Personnel Testing & Training Systems, Inc. with the protocol being sent or read over the telephone. If scored by the publisher, test results are summarized in a one- or three-page report representing the subject's performance on each of the subtests. The report offers a short narrative summarizing the subject's abilities and hiring recommendations. The decision to hire or not appears to be based on an overall score.

The strengths of these tests lie in the broad range of abilities they measure. In addition to basic clerical and filing skills, the tests also look at manual dexterity and analytical skills. Given the variety of responsibilities that can occur in an office setting, this diverse information could be extremely helpful. The authors should be commended for the breadth of secretarial abilities measured in this instrument. Furthermore, administration of the instrument is very easy and could be done in a group setting.

However, the test manual is completely lacking the psychometric information deemed essential in the *Standards for Educational and Psychological Testing*. The standards were prepared by a joint committee of the American Psychological Association, The American Educational Research Association, and the National Council on Measurement in Education (1985). Information on normative data, reliability data, and validity data are absent. Even upon inquiry, Wolfe Personnel Testing & Training Systems, Inc. was unable to provide this information. Although scoring procedures appear to be straightforward, these procedures are not reported in the manual and are available only upon request.

Although the manual provides cutoff scores for hiring, no information is given as to how these scores were obtained. No normative data are provided. Furthermore, no information was available to suggest differences in performance with regard to age, sex, or minority group membership. These data are essential to determine when use of the Secretarial Staff Selector is appropriate. In addition to normative data, intercorrelations among subtests are also necessary to understand the interrelationship among tests. Furthermore, the authors have provided no reliability data. Therefore, it cannot be determined whether these tests will yield consistent scores over time. When making critical hiring decisions, the reliability of an instrument is essential.

Although the Secretarial Staff Selector purports to evaluate the abilities of candidates for secretaries, office administrators, and executive assistants, the manual offers no validity studies, whatsoever. The manual alludes to a major validity study in progress. However, upon inquiry, the authors were unable to provide any information concerning this or any other study. It could be argued that because of the wide range of abilities the Secretarial Staff Selector attempts to measure and the obvious relationship of these skills to office procedures, this instrument possesses content validity. However, the lack of information concerning normative data, reliability, and validity casts doubt on the test's usefulness. In addition to more complete psychometric information concerning the foundation of these tests, studies of predictive and concurrent validity are also necessary. Correlations with job performance and other established tests would help substantiate the authors' claims that this instrument measures applicants' abilities.

Finally, the manual offers no discussion of the significance of differing results or how scores relate to the wide range of jobs within an office setting. It is reasonable to assume that a secretarial job demands different skills than an executive assistant. Therefore, performance on some subtests may be more highly correlated to success in certain kinds of jobs. An understanding of how the subtests relate to each other and the performance of different jobs is necessary for the future employer.

In short, the Secretarial Staff Selector has potential because of the diversity of abilities that it measures. However, it cannot be recommended for use by potential employers, vocational counselors, or researchers because of a lack of information concerning scoring, normative data, reliability, and validity. Furthermore, the manual needs to include a more comprehensive discussion of the test uses and appropriate populations. The test publishers would do well to include in their manual more information concerning scoring, how norms were obtained, and the test's reliability. Finally, it is critical they evaluate the validity of these measures against other secretarial tests and the actual success of individuals in different secretarial staff positions. A similar test that provides more psychometric information, although still somewhat flawed, is the Office Skills Test (1977).

REVIEWER'S REFERENCES

Science Research Associates, Inc. (1977). Office Skills Test. Chicago: Science Research Associates, Inc.

American Psychological Association, American Educational Research Association, & National Council on Measurement in Education. (1985). *Standards for educational and psychological testing*. Washington, DC: American Psychological Association, Inc.

[330]

The Self-Directed Search: A Guide to Educational and Vocational Planning—1985 Revision. Purpose: "Developed to create a scientifically sound and practical simulation of the vocational counseling experience by using a self-administered, self-scored, and self-interpreted vocational assessment booklet and compatible file of occupational possibilities." High school and college and adults; 1970–87; SDS; 6 scores (Realistic, Investigative, Artistic, Social, Enterprising, Conventional) for each of 3 scales (Activities, Competencies, Occupations) and for Self-Ratings of Abilities, Summary; 2 forms: standard, Form E ("simplified for a 4th grade reading level"), 1987 price data: $75 per 10 mail-in prepaid test booklets/answer sheets; $30 per 25 standard booklets and 25 occupations finders; $30 per 25 Form E booklets and 25 jobs finders; $19.50 per 25 alphabetized occupations finders; $27 per 20 college majors finders; $150 per computer version (50 uses); IBM or Apple computer-administered version requires 64K, 80-column card, 2 floppy disk drives (Apple); 256K and 2 disk drives (IBM); $12 per professional manual ('85, 102 pages); $9 per manual supplement ('87, 51 pages); (40–60) minutes; John L. Holland; Psychological Assessment Resources, Inc.*

Canadian Edition: 1985; edited by Lewis Miller; also available in French; Guidance Centre [Canada].

For a review by Robert H. Dolliver of an earlier edition, see 9:1098 (12 references); see also T3:2134 (55 references); for a review by John O. Crites and excerpted reviews by Fred Brown, Richard Seligman, Catherine C. Cutts, Robert H. Dolliver, and Robert N. Hansen, see 8:1022 (88 references); see also T2:2211 (1 reference).

TEST REFERENCES

1. Kerr, B. A. (1983). Raising the career aspirations of gifted girls. *The Vocational Guidance Quarterly*, 32, 37-43.

2. Winer, J. L., Wilson, D. D., & Pierce, R. A. (1983). Using the Self-Directed Search—Form E with high school remedial reading students. *The Vocational Guidance Quarterly*, 32, 130-135.

3. Costa, P. T., Jr., McCrae, R. R., & Holland, J. L. (1984). Personality and vocational interests in an adult sample. *Journal of Applied Psychology*, 69, 390-400.

4. Dawis, R. V., & Sung, Y. H. (1984). The relationship of participation in school activities to abilities and interests in a high school student sample. *Journal of Vocational Behavior*, 24, 159-168.

5. Furnham, A., & Schaeffer, R. (1984). Person-environment fit, job satisfaction and mental health. *Journal of Occupational Psychology*, 57, 295-307.

6. Healy, C. C., & Mourton, D. L. (1984). The effects of an abbreviated Self-Directed Search on the career decision competencies of community college students. *Vocational Guidance Quarterly*, 33, 55-62.

7. Healy, C. C., Mourton, D. L., Anderson, E. C., & Robinson, E. (1984). Career maturity and the achievement of community college students and disadvantaged university students. *Journal of College Student Personnel*, 25, 347-352.

8. Hollinger, C. L. (1984). The impact of gender schematic processing on the Self Directed Search responses of gifted and talented female adolescents. *Journal of Vocational Behavior*, 24, 15-27.

9. Iachan, R. (1984). Measures of agreement for incompletely ranked data. *Educational and Psychological Measurement*, 44, 823-830.

10. Pichl, H. A., & Clark, A. K. (1984). Congruency, achievement, and the Self Directed Search. *Canadian Counsellor*, 18, 79-86.

11. Aronowitz, A., Bridge, R. G., & Jones, P. (1985). Sex bias in the Self-Directed Search Investigative subscale. *Journal of Vocational Behavior*, 26, 146-154.

12. Elliott, T. R., & Byrd, E. K. (1985). Scoring accuracy of the Self-Directed Search with ninth-grade students. *Vocational Guidance Quarterly*, 34, 85-90.

13. Galassi, M. D., Jones, L. K., & Britt, M. N. (1985). Nontraditional career options for women: An evaluation of career guidance instruments. *Vocational Guidance Quarterly*, 34, 124-130.

14. Healy, C. C., & Mourton, D. L. (1985). Congruence and vocational identity: Outcomes of career counseling with persuasive power. *Journal of Counseling Psychology*, 32, 441-444.

15. Lowman, R. L., Williams, R. E., & Leeman, G. E. (1985). The structure and relationship of college women's primary abilities and vocational interests. *Journal of Vocational Behavior*, 27, 298-315.

16. Neimeyer, G. J., & Ebben, R. (1985). The effects of vocational interventions on the complexity and positivity of occupational judgments. *Journal of Vocational Behavior*, 27, 87-97.

17. Kerr, B. A. (1986). Career counseling for the gifted: Assessments and interventions. *Journal of Counseling and Development*, 64, 602-604.

18. Schwartz, R. H., Andiappan, P., & Nelson, M. (1986). Reconsidering the support for Holland's congruence-achievement hypothesis. *Journal of Counseling Psychology*, 33, 425-428.

19. McCrae, R. R. (1987). Creativity, divergent thinking, and openness to experience. *Journal of Personality and Social Psychology*, 52, 1258-1265.

Review of The Self-Directed Search: A Guide to Educational and Vocational Planning—1985 Revision by M. HARRY DANIELS, Associate Professor of Educational Psychology, Southern Illinois University at Carbondale, Carbondale, IL:

Since its initial publication in 1971, John Holland proposed that the Self-Directed Search (SDS) would provide vocational counselors with a "self-administered, self-scored, and self-interpreted vocational counseling tool" that could be used to serve a large portion of the adolescent and adult population. Additionally, he intended that the SDS would provide a framework for users to organize occupational and personal information and would be a means for researchers to investigate both the theoretical and practical utility of its underlying typology. Holland has achieved his purposes.

The SDS is based on Holland's theory of vocational choice, which postulates the existence of six types of work environments: Realistic (R), Investigative (I), Artistic (A), Social (S), Enterprising (E), and Conventional (C). The theory also states that most people can be categorized into one of six matching personality types, and that individuals will seek out environments in which they will have the greatest opportunity to act out those values, interests, and competencies consistent with their personality. The SDS represents a popular means for conducting a search for the proper person-environment match. It is widely used as the vocational instrument of choice with adolescent, young adult, and adult populations throughout the United States and in several other countries. Related research has stimulated a reexamination of the vocational counseling process as well as improvements in the instrument itself.

Its apparent usefulness notwithstanding, the SDS and its underlying typology have been the focus of frequent evaluation and criticism. Issues related to the presence of cultural, gender, or age biases represent the most persistent and frequent criticisms. Other concerns have focused on the simplicity of Holland's personality typology, the problems associated with self-scoring and self-interpretation, the unavailability of appropriate and adequate statistical procedures to utilize essential psychological constructs (e.g., differentiation and consistency) when interpreting or comparing results, and the lack of adequate support materials to guide users' career information-seeking behavior.

Although it appears to be virtually unchanged from the 1977 version, the 1985 version of the SDS both addresses and answers most of the criticisms previously leveled against it. The goals in developing the 1985 revision were (*a*) to make the new SDS more practical and easier to use, (*b*) to increase the benefits of the SDS, (*c*) to make assessment more scientific, (*d*) to consider the evaluations of test reviewers and users, and (*e*) to weigh the implications of Title IX, the *Standards for Educational and Psychological Testing*, and the NIE guidelines. It is my judgment that Holland achieved the majority of his goals.

As with previous versions, the SDS consists of an assessment booklet and an Occupations Finder (OF). The assessment booklet consists of six scales: Occupational Daydreams (up to eight self-identified occupations can be listed), Activities (11 items for each of the six personality types), Competencies (11 items for each of the six personality types), Occupations (14 items for each of the six personality types), and two Self-Estimates (two 7-point scales for each of the six personality types). Except for Occupational Daydreams, all of the scales are used to calculate the total score for each of the six personality types (each total score equals the sum of the five raw scores). The ordinal relationship of the magnitude of the three highest total scores determines the three-letter Holland occupational code. (It is recommended that the Occupational Daydreams section be used as a cross-validation of the obtained occupational code.) Once obtained, the summary code represents a simple way of organizing information about occupations. Users are directed to search the OF for every possible ordering of their three-letter code. Form E (Easy) of the SDS, which contains the same sections but with fewer items per section and different labels for each section, is available for use with individuals with limited reading skills. There is also a separate OF for Form E.

Revising approximately one-fourth of the items (59 of 228) with the intent of increasing the validity of the scales and of eliminating gender and age biases represents one of the major changes in the new SDS. This change should not be interpreted to mean that Holland has set aside his position that gender does influence career choices. According to Holland, gender bias is a complex social-emotional issue that involves more than reducing mean differences between sexes. It is his contention that "anyone can write items that make men and women look alike. It is another matter to write items that will withstand the variety of standard psychometric and content validity tests (Holland, 1985, p. 375)." There is a growing body of literature supporting the validity of Holland's view that gender does influence career. Assuming that such a conclusion is indeed valid, it would not be unreasonable to argue that the accurate assessment of those influences by instruments like the SDS would promote rather than prohibit satisfactory career choices.

Other important differences between the old and the new SDS includes enlarging the OF to include "all of the most common occupations in the United States," rewriting the directions to improve clarity of understanding, and providing a more useful list of resources in the assessment booklet. This revision of the OF represents a marked improvement over previous ones. The actual number of occupations increased from 500 to 1,156, which accounts for "approximately 99% of all workers." As before, individual occupations included in the OF are arranged according to personality types and subtypes. Occupational subtypes are also arranged according to the general educational development (GED) that an occupation requires according to the *Dictionary of Occupational Titles*, (DOT). Most occupations are also designated by their current DOT number. The availability of the revised OF greatly enhances the potential of the SDS to stimulate career information-seeking behavior.

The 1985 SDS Professional Manual is as impressive as its predecessor. It contains a total of 69 tables (37 in the text and 32 in the appendices), four figures, and 35 SDS profiles. (The chapter on the interpretation and use of the SDS is most informative. Questions concerning score consistency and score differentiation as well as other problems related to scoring and interpreting the SDS are addressed through the interpretation of 35 profiles.) The lack of tables of contents for these information sources greatly reduces their utilization. One entire appendix is devoted to normative data (i.e., percentile ranks, mean scores, frequency of code combinations, and distribution of people and jobs). Another appendix contains an eight-page alphabetical listing of occupational classifications and codes. Two appendices emphasize scoring accuracy, and one contains technical information for the 1985 revision. The reference section has been updated, but otherwise is almost identical to the one in the 1977 Revision.

Estimates of the internal consistency of the 1985 SDS are slightly higher overall than those reported for the 1977 version. For the Summary Scales, 69% had higher alphas, 17% showed no change, and 14% had lower alphas. The range of summary-scale alphas varied by age and gender. For ages 14–18, estimates for females ranged from .81 (Realistic) to .91 (Investigative), while males ranged from .81 (Social) to .92 (Realistic). For ages 19–25, alphas ranged from .87 (Social) to .92 (Artistic and Enterprising) for females, and from .83 (Social) to .92 (Artistic) for males. Estimates for females in the 26–74 age range varied between .85 (Artistic and Social) to .91 (Realistic, Enterprising, and Conventional), and between .87 (Artistic) to .93 (Investigative and Realistic) for males. No estimates of the temporal stability of the 1985 SDS were reported in the Professional Manual. The concurrent validity of the 1985 SDS, which is determined by assessing the "percentage of hits" (i.e., the percentage of a sample whose high-point code and occupational code agree), is comparable to that reported for the 1977 version.

Although many of the limitations of previous versions of the SDS have been satisfactorily addressed, others persist. Two problems are of special concern. The first is the use of raw score data to determine total scores and, subsequently, the summary codes. Holland has provided a detailed rationale for his use of raw scores, and many of his arguments are good ones. However, his arguments fail to provide a satisfactory explanation of the practice, especially in light of the construction of the instrument. Holland describes the SDS as having four sections (totaling 228 items) that are used to determine the summary codes. Because the scales do not contain the identical number of items, they contribute unequally to the total scores. Activities and Competencies have 11 items for each of six scales, while Occupations has 14 items per scale. Self-Estimates contains 12 items (two sets of six ratings, each rating corresponding to a type). Because raw scores rather than standard scores are used to calculate the total score for each type, Occupations contributes more to the total than either Self-Estimates, Activities, or Competencies, and Self-Estimates contributes more than either Activities or Competencies. Such a scoring protocol places undue emphasis on fantasy as opposed to experience, which may result in unrealistic and unsatisfactory career choices. (This explanation becomes more plausible if occupations are considered as an "objectively determined" set of occupational daydreams.)

The second concern is Holland's inconsistent use of his typology in the different sections. In three of the sections (Activities, Competencies, and Occupations), the typology serves as a framework for listing items (each item of each scale in each section has an assigned value of 1). In the Self-Estimates section, however, the types become items, and the items may have an assigned value ranging from 1–7. Such a practice maximizes the weighted value of the very thing (occupational type) that is being determined. (It is conceivable, for example, that the sum of the Self-Estimates could total 14, which is more than 25% of even the largest possible score, and which may represent up to 100% of an obtained score). It also raises questions about the necessity of including all the items from each of the other sections. Finally, it may represent a potential source of the reported confusion about the scoring procedures.

In sum, the 1985 version of the SDS reflects Holland's continuing commitment to provide vocational clients, counselors, and researchers with an accurate, inexpensive, and simple means for addressing questions that are related to occupational choice. Its popularity among practitioners and researchers alike is testimony to its perceived utility and effectiveness. The expanded OF will enhance its use as a stimulus for vocational exploration. Despite its many positive features, however, it is important to remember that it may not be the instrument of choice for all clients, and that some clients will need to see a counselor even after completing the SDS. (According to the manual the SDS will only satisfy the vocational assistance needs of approximately 50% of the people.) Similarly, users need to remember that the SDS, like other vocational choice instruments, has limited predictive validity. This limitation notwithstanding, the SDS remains an excellent vocational counseling tool that can be used with most adolescents and adults.

REVIEWER'S REFERENCE

Holland, J. L. (1985). Author biases, errors, and omissions in an evaluation of the SDS Investigative Scale: A response to Aronowitz, Bridge and Jones (1985). *Journal of Vocational Behavior*, 27 (3), 374-376.

Review of The Self-Directed Search: A Guide to Educational and Vocational Planning—1985 Revision by CAROLINE MANUELE-ADKINS, Associate Professor, Counseling, Department of Educational Foundations, Hunter College of the City University of New York, New York, NY:

The Self-Directed Search (SDS) is a self-administered, self-scored, and self-interpreted inventory of a person's occupationally related characteristics. The purpose of the SDS is to provide people with "a vocational counseling experience by simulating what a person and counselor might do together in several interviews." The SDS was developed from Holland's Vocational Preference Inventory and is based on his theory of vocational choice.

The Holland theory proposes that "most people can be categorized as one of six personality types labeled realistic, investigative, artistic, social, enterprising, or conventional." The theory also predicts that work environments can be classified in the same way because specific work environments are dominated by people who share the same "interests, competencies, and outlook on the world," (e.g., a social work environment is dominated by many social personality types). Good vocational choices then consist of helping people find a work environment congruent with their personality orientation. The SDS operationalizes this theory by providing people with information about their personality types and by helping them identify occupations congruent with their types.

The 1985 version of the SDS consists of an assessment booklet divided into six sections. These include Occupational Daydreams, Activities (liked and disliked), Competencies (activities performed well or poorly), Occupations (interesting or uninteresting), and Self-Estimates (high to low ratings of various abilities). The last section is a scoring section in which a three-letter summary code is obtained for the person's personality types. Accompanying the booklet is the Occupations Finder in which occupations are classified according to personality type and subtypes, and a *Dictionary of Occupational Titles* (*DOT*) with required educational level. The 1985 version of the SDS is similar to the 1977 version except that 59 of the 228 items were revised and the Occupations Finder has been increased from 500 to 1,156 occupations. According to the manual, the scoring directions were also changed to "stimulate completing of the SDS and to increase understanding of the results." These appear, however, to be minor changes. Form E of the SDS is for people with limited reading skills. It is similar to the standard form except that it is shorter (203 items) and a two-letter rather than three-letter code is obtained. No mention is made in the manual as to whether this form was revised for the 1985 edition.

The SDS is easy to read and understand. Each scale includes items that are clearly worded and obviously related to the area being assessed. In this revision efforts were made to make the items more contemporary and in some instances more occupationally related (e.g., social activities such as going to a party or dance have been replaced by items such as teaching in a college or taking a human relations course). A possible item-related problem appears in the content of the Conventional Competencies subscale. Items in that scale are so consistently directed at secretarial and office competencies that many females who have these competencies may receive an inflated Conventional score. Including more diverse Conventional Competency items may alleviate this problem.

Directions for taking and scoring the SDS appear to be clear but questions have been raised about the accuracy of client self-scoring of the SDS. Studies on the 1977 version of the SDS indicate that about 40% of a sample of high school students made errors in scoring. Some of these were minor and did not affect the accuracy of the 3-point code. The manual does caution that "the scoring of the SDS should be supervised and checked." One area of scoring and interpretation that may need more attention is the Occupational Daydreams section. The instructions for this section include obtaining a three-letter code (in the Occupations Finder) for each of the career choices or aspirations listed, and then later comparing these codes to the person's summary code. The problem is that scoring directions for this part tend to minimize the importance and significance of the information obtained. First, the scoring is not part of the primary scoring directions but is buried under "some next steps" which may be easily ignored or skimmed over by some test takers. Second, the directions do not fully explain to the self-scorer what similarities or disagreements may mean. They are advised only that the codes should have some resemblance to each other and that if there is no relation they should talk to a counselor or friend. Because the manual points out that these comparisons provide extremely important information about the nature of a person's choices and agreement between codes is valuable for predicting actual career choices, more specific instructions seem warranted. Disagreements imply the person is making noncongruent choices. Evidence of self-concept clarity and confusion can also be obtained by looking at these comparisons. Thus it would seem important to include this area in the primary scoring directions and to point out to the self-scorer more extensively what agreements and disagreements might mean.

Extensive information is presented in the manual regarding the validity, reliability, and norming of the SDS. These areas of the manual could be improved in their clarity of presentation. The item content and format demonstrate good content validity. One of the purposes of this revision was to increase validity by reducing item overlap across scales, by writing better items, by omitting items with extreme endorsement rates for males and females, and by making items more applicable to a broader age range. This revision's summary scale intercorrelations indicate they are similar to the correlational hexagon pattern obtained on studies done with the earlier versions. Predictive validity studies done over time are not presented for this version but studies on the earlier versions indicate that the SDS has moderate validity for predicting actual occupational choice. The Occupations Finder is an integral part of the SDS. Many studies described in the manual seem to indirectly address the question of the accuracy of the codes assigned to various occupations. More direct studies, (e.g., testing many different occupational groups to determine their actual Holland code), would provide more evidence for the validity of the occupational codes.

Extensive normative data are also supplied in the manual. Different age groups (including high school, college, and adult) are consistently described with respect to their percentile ranks, mean scores, and frequency of code occurrences for both scale scores and summary code scores. What is missing are normative data regarding the performance of different samples on Form E. Populations with literacy problems for whom norms would be useful include people who are high school dropouts, disadvantaged, learning disabled, and people for whom English is a second language. As in previous editions, women receive different Holland codes than men. For the 1985 revision female average scores, ranked from highest to lowest, were Social (33.56), Enterprising (26.14), Artistic (23.50), Conventional (21.27), Investigative (20.47), and Realistic (14.36). Male average scores, ranked from highest to lowest, were Enterprising (27.57), Social (26.68), Realistic (24.39), Investigative (23.43), Artistic (20.45), and Conventional (19.35). These findings indicate that results on the SDS are still gender-related and reflect the cultural differences of males and females in this society.

The SDS is promoted as an inventory requiring little assistance from a counselor. In fact, the manual indicates the SDS alone is sufficient for about 50% of the test takers. For a measure that is supposed to "stand on its own" it is paradoxical to find such extensive information available in the manual to assist the counselor with SDS interpretation and almost no information available to the test taker who is attempting to understand it without guidance. This problem is somewhat alleviated with the 1985 edition because this revision includes a new booklet by Holland entitled "You and Your Career." The booklet provides users with some basic theoretical concepts, (e.g., descriptions of the different personality types). The usefulness of the booklet should be highlighted for users. All test takers should have access to it as a means of helping them understand their SDS results more completely.

The SDS has been well received and extensively used. Its strengths are that it meets the objectives the author set out for it—to produce a simple self-report, self-scoring measure that could be used by a wide variety of people. It is well grounded in theory and has an extensive cadre of research studies providing evidence for its validity and reliability. The SDS is, however, a measure requiring more assistance from a counselor than is acknowledged in the manual. The SDS compares quite favorably to other self-administered and handscored measures (e.g., the Career Decision Making System).

REVIEWER'S REFERENCE

Harrington, T. F., & O'Shea, A. J. (1982). The Harrington-O'Shea Career Decision-Making System. Circle Pines, MN: American Guidance Service.

[331]

Sequenced Inventory of Communication Development, Revised Edition. Purpose: Functions as a diagnostic assessment to evaluate the communication abilities of normal and retarded children. Ages 4 months through 4 years; 1975–84; SICD; individual; 2 scales; some test accessories (e.g., paper, coins, and picture book) must be assembled locally; 1986 price data: $250 per complete kit (includes 50 each of Receptive Scales, Receptive Behavioral profiles, Receptive Processing profiles, Expressive Scales, Expressive Behavioral profiles, and Expressive Processing profiles; 100 items used in the administration of the test; instruction manual ['84, 79 pages], and test manual ['84, 117 pages]; all in a plastic carrying case); $25 per 50 sets of Receptive Scales and 2 profiles or Expressive Scales and 2 profiles; $30 per instruction manual and test manual; $20 per test manual only; $20 per instruction manual only; $35 per 25 Spanish-language forms with pictures; Spanish translation included in test manual and separate Spanish-language forms with pictures are available; (30–75) minutes; Dona Lea Hedrick, Elizabeth M. Prather, and Annette R. Tobin, with contributions by Doris V. Allen, Lynn S. Bliss, and Lillian R. Rosenberg; University of Washington Press.*

a) RECEPTIVE SCALE. 3 scores: Awareness, Discrimination, Understanding.

b) EXPRESSIVE SCALE. 4 scores: Imitating, Initiating, Responding, Verbal Output.

For reviews by Barbara W. Hodson and Joan I. Lynch of the earlier edition, see 9:1109 (4 references); see also T3:2159 (4 references).

TEST REFERENCES

1. Tsai, L. Y., & Beisler, J. M. (1983). The development of sex differences in infantile autism. *British Journal of Psychiatry*, 142, 373-378.

2. Allen, D. V., & Robinson, D. O. (1984). Middle ear status and language development in preschool children. *American Speech and Hearing Association*, 26 (6), 33-37.

3. Conti-Ramsden, G, & Friel-Patti, S. (1984). Mother-child dialogues: A comparison of normal and language impaired children. *Journal of Communication Disorders*, 17, 19-35.

4. Jago, J. L., Jago, A. G., & Hart, M. (1984). An evaluation of the total communication approach for teaching language skills to developmentally delayed preschool children. *Education and Training of the Mentally Retarded*, 19, 175-182.

5. Klecan-Aker, J. S., & Lopez, B. (1984). A clinical taxonomy for the categorization of pragmatic language functions in normal preschool children. *Journal of Communication Disorders*, 17, 121-131.

6. Funk, J. B., Ruppert, E. S., & Jurs, S. G. (1986). A preliminary investigation of associations between disorders of behavior and language in children with chronic otitis media. *Child Study Journal*, 16, 255-264.

Review of the Sequenced Inventory of Communication Development, Revised Edition by CAROL MARDELL-CZUDNOWSKI, Professor of Educational Psychology, Counseling, and Special

Education, Northern Illinois University, DeKalb, IL:

STANDARDIZATION OF THE NORMATIVE SAMPLE. In this revision of the Sequenced Inventory of Communication Development, Revised Edition (SICD-R), the small, original normative sample of 252 children was supplemented with additional samples of young children. The largest supplemental sample of 609 children included 276 Black children, but the age range was 31–48 months whereas the test begins at 4 months. Thus, the norms of the revised version for children between 4 and 30 months are based on only white children. This weakness is particularly striking because separate norms are advocated for use with Black children.

A strength of the revised manual is that several cited studies indicate use of the SICD-R with special populations (e.g., autistic, "difficult-to-test," hearing impaired, Eskimo). Even a Spanish translation has been included in the revised manual and Spanish scoresheets are available. Unfortunately, the SICD-R has not been normed with normally developing, monolingual Spanish-speaking children. This oversight may limit the test's usefulness unless local norms are developed. In addition, the size of the sample in the lower age range is not adequate. It does not approach 100 or more subjects for each age level.

ITEM ANALYSIS, CENTRAL TENDENCY, AND VARIABILITY. The manual provides an adequate report of the quantitative methods used to study and control for item difficulty and evidence concerning item validity. A useful addition in the manual is a comparison of the original normative data with the more recent data on the 609 children mentioned above. Means, standard deviations, and four percentage levels (the latter available only on the original sample) are given by age level (and race for the more recent data). Standard errors of measurement are missing and are critical in understanding if scores reported by 4-month age increments are meaningful discriminations.

VALIDITY. Construct validity is enhanced by the test's reliance on both behavioral and language processing models. Communication behaviors and receptive and expressive language skills are assessed independently. A problem, however, is the limited number of items at some age levels or in some of the interpretative categories. For example, there are only two items for syntactic receptive processing and two items for initiating motor responses in the expressive behavioral category. On the other hand, there are 37 items measuring verbal responding in the expressive behavior category.

Careful selection of test items from many well-established sources and the authors' own extensive experience are cited as evidence of content validity. However, no data related to either concurrent validity or predictive validity are provided in the manual. Correlations between the scores derived from the SICD-R (RCA = receptive communication age and ECA = expressive communication age) and the Peabody Picture Vocabulary Test (PPVT) score are provided but these cannot be interpreted because the number of subjects making up the sample is not provided.

RELIABILITY. Both test-retest reliability and interexaminer reliability are within acceptable levels, but must be viewed with caution. Small numbers of subjects were used in the empirical reliability research.

ADMINISTRATION PROCEDURES. The instruction manual is clearly written to enable examiners to duplicate the administration and scoring procedures used during test standardization. All test items are administered either directly to the child or through parent report. Total testing time depends on the age of the child but ranges from 30 to 75 minutes. The transfer of scores to the behavioral or processing profiles is both cumbersome and time-consuming, despite the usefulness of the process.

The stated purpose of the SICD-R is to assist clinicians "in remedial programming for the deviant child" (p. 47). Again, on page 52 of the manual it is stated that "the SICD-R was designed to aid the *diagnostician* in determining the child's level of functioning in the areas defined by the Behavioral and Processing Models of Communication. The description of the child's behaviors according to normative information assists in the evaluative aspect of *diagnosis*." (Emphasis added.) The point is that the SICD-R is really a diagnostic test, not a screening test. It leads to programs and intervention strategies and appears to do so in a meaningful way. Missing data concerning concurrent and predictive validity becomes an even more significant deficit of the test under these circumstances.

TESTER QUALIFICATIONS. Although the general administration instructions indicate that the examiner should practice test administration with at least six children at different age levels before using the test clinically, there is no mention of qualifications regarding field of training or level of expertise required of examiners. It is obvious, however, that examiners would need to know normal language development as well as individualized testing practices to make appropriate interpretations. The manual does provide a number of helpful case examples.

MATERIALS. The sturdy, tackle-type box is easy to carry and works well in keeping test items separated and easy to view. Both receptive and expressive language cards include a picture of a pipe. This picture may be a bit dated. Some of the materials are not very durable but, overall, they appear appealing to most children in this age range.

In summary, the revised edition of the SICD is an improvement over the original test but still leaves problems for the practitioner who wants to utilize a technically adequate test. The practitioner would have to weigh the pros (racial norms for children between 31–48 months; Spanish translation and scoresheet; independent assessment of receptive and expressive language skills; evidence of content validity; acceptable reliability levels; clearly written administration manual; appealing materials) against the cons (only white norms for children between 4–30 months; no Spanish norms; no standard errors of measurement; uneven emphasis of some language aspects for interpretive purposes; no evidence of concurrent or predictive validity; time-comsuming profiling). The use of local norms would solve a few of the problems but the authors should be encouraged to resolve the other issues in the near future.

Review of the Sequenced Inventory of Communication Development, Revised Edition by MARY ELLEN PEARSON, Professor of Special Education, Mankato State University, Mankato, MN:

INTRODUCTION. The Sequenced Inventory of Communication Development (SICD) was originally published in 1975; it was revised in 1984 and named the Sequenced Inventory of Communication Development, Revised Edition (SICD-R). The inventory includes both parental report and observation of communication behaviors for children from 4 to 48 months. The inventory also includes a 50-item language sample; an additional articulation test is recommended but not included.

PURPOSE. The authors of the SICD-R identify the following three purposes for the inventory: (*a*) determine broad long-range communication goals for remedial programming, (*b*) establish broad areas of communication development that may need further in-depth assessment, and (*c*) assign developmental ages to receptive and expressive communication.

CONTENTS. The SICD-R kit includes the 100 material items used in the administration of the inventory. Eighty-two of these items are three dimensional and generally of high interest to children. Eighteen of the items are acceptable line drawings, and six additional items are easily provided by the examiner.

The kit also contains an improved Instruction Manual with clear general directions for administration, scoring, and computation of basals, ceilings, developmental ages, and Mean Length Response (MLR).

The SICD-R includes Receptive and Expressive Scale forms for recording a child's answers. These answers can be transferred to a Behavioral Profile form or to a Processing Profile form or to both. The Behavioral Profile facilitates an analysis of Awareness, Discrimination, Understanding, Imitation, Initiation, Response, Motor, Vocal, and Verbal. The Process Profile facilitates analysis of Semantics, Syntax, Pragmatics, Perceptual, and Phonological.

The kit also includes a Test Manual that provides the information addressed in the sections that follow.

TECHNICAL WORK. The reliability, validity, and norm information is the same as that provided in the 1975 inventory with the addition of a field study completed in Detroit. The original data were collected on 252 children, 21 children at each of the twelve 4-month age groups. The children were chosen to reflect the social makeup of Seattle, Washington, with equal representation from low, middle, and high income levels. The children were Caucasian, from monolingual homes, and were believed to have normal hearing, language, physical, and mental development. A second set of norm information is included reflecting the Detroit area.

NORM INFORMATION. Mean scores and standard deviations are provided for each of the 12 age groups; however, the developmental ages assigned must be considered tentative because the sample sizes are small, some developmental ages and chronological ages do not match, and no percentiles are provided (see also McCauley & Swisher, 1984).

RELIABILITY. *Test-retest* reliability data were collected for 10 children, and the authors report 92.8% agreement on items for tests administered by the same examiner 1 week apart. *Interrater* reliability data were collected for 16 children, and the authors report 96% agreement on items watched simultaneously by two raters; no interrater reliability data are reported for separate examinations. Finally, two of the authors independently assigned receptive and expressive communication ages for 21 children and report 90.48% agreement. Reliability data are acceptably high; however, too few subjects are included.

CONTENT VALIDITY. The content of the SICD-R was developed from "well-established sources" and from the clinical experience of the authors; the face and content validity of the inventory are well accepted. There should be more items at each grade level, however, to insure high levels of content validity.

CONSTRUCT VALIDITY. The SICD-R fits most current constructs of language, including a broad communication system, pragmatics, and the traditional components of language.

An important aspect of language development is changes over the age range. The authors do provide mean scores reflecting differences but they do not match the chronological ages closely enough. The additional data from the Detroit field study do not satisfy the questions raised concerning construct validity.

PREDICTIVE VALIDITY. The authors do not report data to support the ability of the SICD-R to identify children with delays because "such a result seemed so obvious." They do indicate the inventory has been given to children with delays and that such children scored below the means. Some of these studies appear in the Special Populations section of the Test Manual. These data need clarification in the Validity section of the Manual because they can support the validity of the test. Predictive validity is especially important when developmental ages are assigned.

Allen, Bliss, and Timmons (1981) reported that clinicians' judgments of delay and SICD identification of delay were significantly correlated; but 61.5% of the children who were identified as delayed by clinicians scored normal on the SICD, and 50.0% of the children identified as delayed by the SICD were identified as normal by the clinicians.

CONCURRENT VALIDITY. The authors present data for the 126 three- and four-year-olds who took the Peabody Picture Vocabulary Test (PPVT) and the SICD. The PPVT is a measure of receptive vocabulary and correlates significantly with both the receptive (.8097) and the expressive (.7553) portions of the SICD. The SICD expressive portion also correlates significantly with MLR (.7613). These data do provide concurrent validity for the SICD. Moderate correlations are expected because the inventory is a broader measure of communication. Future revisions of the inventory could include further discussion and support for concurrent validity.

SPECIAL POPULATIONS. The authors provide some information for testing children with autism, hearing impairments, Yup'ik Eskimo heritage, and children who are difficult to test. Clinicians would welcome standardized adapted procedures and norms for these and other groups in the future. A Spanish version of the inventory is included in the Test Manual although norms are not available.

SUMMARY.

Advantages. The SICD-R kit is complete, and the inventory is given in a standard manner with clear directions for administration and scoring.

The test is well suited for testing very young children and includes interesting materials, assessment of a wide range of communication behaviors (Owens, Haney, Giesow, Dooley, & Kelly, 1983), and parental reports.

Two different profiles are available for analysis which reflect accepted, as well as current, approaches to assessment and remediation. In addition, case studies are provided to aid in analysis. The inventory satisfactorily meets the purpose of determining goals for program planning, and the language sample and MLR provide additional information for programming.

Disadvantages. The major disadvantages concern the following two purposes for giving the inventory: screening and assigning communication ages. The test may be used to help determine areas in need of further assessment, but it should not be the sole screening instrument because clear cutoff scores and its appropriateness (validity) as a screening instrument have not been provided. In addition, the assignment of communication ages is problematical. If they are used to help determine programming after a child is identified as delayed, they may be acceptable. However, the authors and other clinicians do use the test to identify delays. Reliability data are provided on too few children, and validity data are not complete enough to warrant its use for determining delays. In addition, some ages have too few items, means were developed on too few children, and percentiles and standard scores are not provided. The additional data provided from the Detroit study do not answer the questions concerning norms, reliability, and validity.

CONCLUSION. The SICD-R has been well received and has many strengths, but the communication ages must be viewed as tentative and should not be the only data for deciding on the presence of a delay.

REVIEWER'S REFERENCES

Allen, D. V., Bliss, L.S., & Timmons, J. (1981). Language evaluation: Science or art? *Journal of Speech and Hearing Disorders*, 46, 66-68.

Owens, R. E., Jr., Haney, M. J., Giesow, V. E., Dooley, L. F., & Kelly, R. J. (1983). Language test content: A comparative study. *Language Speech and Hearing Services in Schools*, 14, 7-21.

McCauley, R. J., & Swisher, L. (1984). Psychometric review of language and articulation tests for preschool children. *Journal of Speech and Hearing Disorders*, 49, 34-42.

[332]

Signals Listening Tests. Purpose: "Assist in identifying students who are not meeting minimum standards in listening." Grades 3, 5; 1982; 3 objectives: Listening for the Main Idea, Following Geographical Directions, Following Instructions; test administered by cassette tape; 1 form for each of 2 levels: grade 3, 5; 1985 price data: $75 per 2-level sets including 30 tests for each level, directions for administering (19 pages) for each level, and technical manual (27-32 pages) for each level; $40 per 1-level set; $.95 per test; $8 per technical manual; $10 per specimen set; (35) minutes; Project Signals; Project SPOKE.*

Review of the Signals Listening Test by MARTIN FUJIKI, Associate Scientist, Parsons Research Center, Bureau of Child Research, University of Kansas, Parsons, KS:

The Signals Listening Test is designed to provide the test user with an effective means of quickly screening a classroom of third or fifth grade children for listening problems. To do this, performance is evaluated in three tasks: Listening for the Main Idea, Following Geographical Directions, and Following Instructions.

Because the test is designed to be administered to an entire classroom, it may be a highly efficient means of screening large numbers of children. Additionally, the tape-recorded instructions insure consistency from administration to administration. However, just as these procedures have certain advantages, they also bring certain disadvantages to the testing situation. For example, any test simultaneously administered to large numbers of individuals is subject to certain problems. Some children may perform poorly because they did not understand the directions. Other children may do well because they are helped, although inadvertently, by other students. The fact that the test directions are tape recorded, and that the examiner is instructed not to stop the tape, may add to these difficulties. Test users should consider their specific needs in relation to these advantages and disadvantages in using this test.

A discussion of content validity is presented in the statistical manual; however, criterion validity and construct validity are not addressed. Some discussion of construct validity would have been especially helpful in that the term "listening" is a particularly nebulous one. It is difficult to determine if the test is designed to identify children with specific clinical deficits, or children who are generally within normal developmental limits but whose listening skills are not as refined as those of their peer group.

On a related note, it is likely that a variety of disorders might cause a child to fail the test. For example, children with attending problems, language comprehension disorders, memory difficulties, and auditory acuity problems might be expected to have difficulty. Although this is not necessarily a weakness in a screening measure (depending upon what behaviors one considers to fall within the domain of listening), it is a consideration that the potential test user should keep in mind.

The administration instructions are generally well written, and the test itself is easy to administer. The testing materials are acceptable. The cassette-tape recordings used in testing are professionally done, both with respect to recording quality and content.

There is one point of possible confusion between the statistical manual and the test administration manual having to do with the cutoff point between passing and failing the test. The administration manuals for both forms of the test state, "Most students will score between 13 and 15 correct out of 15 items." This statement can be interpreted to indicate that a score of 12 or lower is failing. However, in the statistical manual for both forms, it is stated that, "A school system which wishes to maintain a criteria [sic] of seventy-five percent correct will consider a raw score of 12 or above as passing the Listening Basic Skills test and a raw score of 11 or below as indicating non-competency." The first statement could be misinterpreted by test users.

It is clearly stated in the administration directions and the statistical manual for both grade levels that the test is a screening instrument. As such, it can be used to identify only those children who are candidates for further evaluation, and cannot differentiate levels of acceptable performance (e.g., fair, good, excellent). This caution might be logically extended by also stating that the test cannot be used to identify treatment goals. Although the child is presented with three specific tasks, performance on any one of these tasks is not sampled in great enough detail to allow in-depth interpretation of performance.

The test manuals for both levels emphasize the need for further evaluation once a child fails the test. This is of particular importance in that, as noted previously, failure may stem from a variety of sources. Further assessment will be critical in providing such children with proper services. Discussion of this point is not intended as criticism, but is provided to emphasize the importance of close adherence to guidelines presented by the test designers.

In summary, the Signals Listening Test, Grades 3 and 5, can be a useful assessment tool if used within the guidelines specified in the test manual. Test users should be aware of the behaviors that constitute listening as identified and probed by this test measure. Unfortunately, determining what specific behaviors are actually measured by the Signals Listening Test is a task largely left to the test user. Although the test lacks sensitivity to specific types of problems, it may provide the clinician or teacher with an efficient screening tool if the user's concept of listening is similar to that represented by the test.

[333]

Silver Drawing Test of Cognitive and Creative Skills. Purpose: Designed to assess levels of ability in three areas of cognition: sequential concepts, spatial concepts, and association and formation of concepts. Ages 6 and over; 1983; SDT; 4 scores: Predictive Drawing, Drawing From Observation, Drawing From Imagination, Total; 1984 price data: $35 per complete kit including manual (95 pages), 10 test booklets, and 1 individual/classroom record sheet; $18 per specimen set; (30) minutes; Rawley A. Silver; Ablin Press.*

Review of the Silver Drawing Test of Cognitive and Creative Skills by CLINTON I. CHASE, Director, Bureau of Evaluative Studies and Testing, Indiana University, Bloomington, IN:

The Silver Drawing Test of Cognitive and Creative Skills (SDT) is based on the idea that cognitive skills are evident in visual as well as in verbal conventions, and that drawing can be an avenue of cognitive expression paralleling verbal expression. From this perspective, drawing takes the place of language as the primary channel of receiving and expressing ideas.

The test is divided into three parts. In the Predictive Drawing section, which purports to assess sequencing of concepts, outline drawings are provided and the test taker draws a line or lines to elaborate the outline. For example, an outline of a full soda glass is provided and the client is told to show how the picture would look if a few sips were taken from the glass. Spatial concepts are assessed in the Drawing From Observation section. Here an arrangement of objects (a can, a rock, a cylinder) is given to the client and the task is to draw a picture of the arrangement. In the Drawing From Imagination section, the ability to associate form and concept is tested. In this part of the test, the examinee is given two pages with six pictures on each page. The instructions are to take one picture from each page and combine them into a single picture. Scoring is based not only on selection and combination, but also on originality.

Tests of psychological constructs must rely on the adequacy of their nomological net for validity. Although some research is cited by Silver in the manual (the tests involve Piagetian concepts and, in part, rest on research in the deficiencies found among reading disabled youngsters), there is no theory of cognition or cognitive development spelled out as a base for the construct validity of the tests. This is a serious deficiency in that no guide is provided to determine which classes of behaviors are tied to the construct and which are not. Silver has assumed that increasing age should be correlated with increasing test scores, and that the test should correlate with other intelligence and achievement tests. The empirical data related to the convergent validity of the Silver test are, however, a bit bewildering. For example, the three Silver test scores are correlated .32, .03, and .31 with the Metropolitan Achievement Test Reading score and .36, -.15, and .37 with the SRA Achievement Series Mathematics score. No rationale is provided on why these tests were chosen to establish "validity" or how these tests should relate to the Silver test. If the Silver test is a measure of general cognitive ability, the correlations should have been much more substantial. Indeed, these figures would be better evidence for discriminant validity, but the presentation of the data suggests they are intended to be evidence of convergent validity.

The Silver tests were also correlated with the Wechsler Intelligence Scale for Children Performance IQ (why not the Verbal, too?) and with IQs from the Otis Lennon School Ability Test. Here correlations at best were .39 (Imagination with the Otis Lennon) and at worst .05 (Observation with the Otis Lennon). Normally one would expect that correlations between tests intended to measure cognitive functioning would be higher than this. The lack of a clearly defined construct for the Silver test means there is little or no basis for deciding how the test should relate to anything.

Reliability is assessed by two methods: correlation among scorers and the test-retest method. The evidence for acceptable interrater reliability is tenuous because of the small number of cases involved. For example, in one study seven judges scored tests of six children; in another, 10 judges' data were correlated with the scores of the instructor who was teaching the judges to score; in a third case, an art therapist's scores for nine mentally retarded children were correlated with the scores for these children reported by the test author. The correlations are typically moderate to high, but one must wonder about their usefulness because of the small group sizes. Data on the means and standard deviations generated in these studies are not given and would be useful for prospective test users.

The test-retest data do not fare much better. The time lapse between the two testings is not provided, but the coefficients ranged from .56 for Imagination to .84 for Observation. Unfortunately, the data were based on only 12 learning-disabled children, where the range of scores is likely to be constricted. Although the correlations are cited as significantly larger than zero, they are unimpressive as reliability coefficients given that the time between the testings is not provided and that the coefficients are based on only one small sample.

Silver reviews some studies in which the Silver tests have been used. These studies suffer from the same problem as those used to establish reliability data—the number of cases is typically very small (less than 20). For this reason the conclusions must be regarded as, at best, tentative.

The manual provides only a page and a half of instructions for administration and 5 pages of scoring instructions, with several pages of sample drawings and their scores. Judgment plays such a large role in scoring that these few pages devoted to test administration and scoring seem inadequate. In actually trying out the tests, however, I found that I could at least find my way through the procedures based on these parsimonious leads. The greatest difficulties come in the scoring, especially in deciding what was "creative." Much more detail (and theory) would have been an aid to the scorer.

In sum, the Silver tests represent a novel idea, but are lacking in a solid theoretical foundation. No information is provided to relate Silver's conceptualization of cognitive and creative skills to other behaviors or test scores thought to represent cognitive and creative abilities. The data on reliability and on application of the test are based on too few cases to allow a reasonable conclusion about the utility of the tests. Until the psychometric qualities of the Silver tests are more clearly established, these tests should be used only as experimental tools. Their design and departure from typical paper-and-pencil cognitive measures are intriguing but not convincing.

Review of the Silver Drawing Test of Cognitive and Creative Skills by DAVID J. MEALOR, Associate Professor of School Psychology, University of Central Florida, Orlando, FL:

The Silver Drawing Test of Cognitive and Creative Skills (SDT) is a carefully thought out instrument that allows drawing to take "the place of language as the primary channel for receiving and expressing ideas." The premise of the SDT is that art and art activities can be a language of cognition paralleling language skills and may yield more meaningful information for some groups of children and adults than traditional measures of intelligence and achievement. The objective of the test is to assess the effectiveness of educational and therapeutic programs as well as monitor individual progress with pretest and posttest measures. The SDT is appropriate for age ranges from 6 years to adult and can be administered either individually or in a group format by teachers, therapists, or psychologists. The SDT is comprised of three subtests: Predictive Drawing (responses are scored for sequencing, horizontality, and verticality), Drawing from Observation (responses scored for left-right, above-below, and front-back), and Drawing from Imagination (responses scored for selecting, combining, and representing). Each subtest reportedly measures specific areas of cognition. Predictive Drawing assesses sequential concepts, Drawing from Observation assesses spatial concepts, and Drawing from Imagination assesses the ability to associate and form concepts. Although there is no time limit, administration should take less than 20–30 minutes. Examinees are given a test booklet in which to complete their drawings. Scoring principles are based on the works of Piaget and Inhelder as well as Bruner and his associates. Performance in each area is rated from 0–5 points for a maximum subtest score of 15. The maximum total score is 45. Raw scores can be converted to percentile ranks and *T*-scores.

While it is apparent that a great deal of effort has gone into the development of the SDT, several perplexing issues surface. The most noticeable involves the technical documentation found in the test manual. It is insufficient at best. As the author notes, "to compare the scores of particular children with typical scores," the standardization group was comprised of 513 children, ages 7 to 16, in heterogeneous classes from nine schools. Sample sizes for grades ranged from 16 (tenth) to 106 (fourth). Five of the classes were located in New York, one each in New Jersey, Pennsylvania, California, and Canada. Twenty subjects comprised the adult group. Unfortunately, no demographic data are presented regarding the individuals selected. How "typical" this group is remains unclear.

The reliability and validity information is inadequate in scope. Reliability investigations are reported by interscorer and test-retest methods. All are comprised of limited sample sizes and did not appear to include those in the standardization group. Of particular concern to this reviewer is the manner in which the reliability information is presented. While the correlation coefficients are high, in two of the studies raters participated "in a series of training sessions." The third and fourth studies "were undertaken to determine the adequacy of the scoring guidelines for scorers who did not participate in training sessions." The two raters selected for "non-training" were a university director of art therapy and a registered art therapist. The generalizability of their performance to regular classroom teachers and psychologists without special training is suspect. Yet, no mention of the need for training in scoring techniques appears in the administration section of the manual. The manual does contain a number of drawings with examples of scoring. It would be beneficial for potential users if explanations for assigned scores were included with the examples.

As the author notes, the purpose of the statistical development was to determine if test items in the SDT "were related primarily to age and cognitive maturity, with scores increasing as children grow older" and "to test the hypothesis that scores on the test can be used to assess intellectual functioning." Statements made are intended to lead the reader to believe that skills measured by the SDT "are closely related to the skills measured by commonly used tests of intellectual excellence." Based on information presented in the manual, it is most difficult to find any empirical support for these claims. More care is needed in the construction of the statistical tables.

In summary, the author provides theoretical support for the SDT. However, it is uncertain that this instrument does what it purports to do.

If scores increase with age, is a high score indicative of creativity? In its present form reliability of scoring is questionable. The author has put a great deal of effort into the development of an instrument that is surely needed. An instrument such as the SDT can assist in the measurement of nonverbal concept formation, visual-motor coordination, spatial relations, and visual perception. However, substantially more work is needed in the development of norms and support for the reliability and validity of this instrument.

[334]

The Singer-Loomis Inventory of Personality (Experimental Edition). Purpose: "Assessing personality factors that may help an individual in self-understanding and in utilizing skills, talents, and abilities to better deal with interactions between the self and the environment." High school and college and adults; 1984; SLIP; self-report measure of cognitive style based on Jung's typology; profile of 8 scores: Introverted, Extroverted, for each of 4 functions (Thinking, Feeling, Sensing, Intuition); 1987 price data: $12 per 25 tests; $28 per 50 answer sheets and scoring forms; $5 per manual (23 pages); $6 per interpretive guide (46 pages); (30–40) minutes; June Singer and Mary Loomis; Consulting Psychologists Press, Inc.*

TEST REFERENCES

1. Hurley, J. R., & Cosgro, M. A. (1986). An interpersonal-Jungian interface: Links of divergent personality measures. *Journal of Clinical Psychology*, 42, 469-474.

Review of The Singer-Loomis Inventory of Personality by RICHARD B. STUART, Clinical Professor of Psychiatry and Behavioral Sciences, University of Washington, Seattle, WA:

The Singer-Loomis Inventory of Personality (SLIP) is a self-report measure intended to help individuals develop better self-understanding and improve the utilization of their skills, talents, and abilities in interpersonal and environmental interactions. The authors are careful to stress that their test does not measure intelligence, emotional stability, or aptitude. But they do suggest a wide range of potential applications from career planning to sampling consumer preferences, and from matching potential patients with therapists and/or therapeutic methods to identifying similarities and differences between spouses. The manual states the potential applications of the SLIP are "limited only by the imagination of those who seek a better understanding of self and others." However, no guidelines, illustrations, or validation for any application of the test data are presented. Indeed, the Interpretive Guide accompanying the SLIP identifies 28 somewhat overlapping "cognitive mode interactions" containing predictions that seem to greatly outdistance the scope of the items comprising the instrument. Application of test results along the suggested lines in clinical settings is unwarranted until such use is experimentally validated.

The SLIP contains 120 items asking respondents to indicate on a 5-point scale (*never . . . always*) how often they consider themselves likely to make each of 8 different responses in 15 different situations. Both the responses (e.g., "be shocked and express my sadness to the person who called") and the situations (e.g., "I have just been told on the telephone that someone very close to me has died suddenly. I would . . .") are clearly worded and understandable to the high school and older population for which the SLIP was designed. Administration of the instrument took approximately 20 minutes in a pretest conducted by the reviewer.

The SLIP, now in its third "experimental" form, is designed to identify respondents' tendencies toward introversion and extroversion in Jungian terms. Because the authors reject Jung's assumptions concerning the bipolarity of thinking and feeling, and of perception and intuition, their instrument generates eight personality types reflecting an interaction of these orientations, modes, and functions.

The SLIP purportedly treats personality types in state and trait terms, although no data are presented to establish the stability of responses over time or across situations. To control for response bias, SLIP scores are computed as percentages of response totals, yielding a measure of the relative strength of scales within but not between individuals. Reasonable alpha reliability scores were obtained from an almost all white sample. The authors suggest, without basis, the values would be close to those "calculated from a more balanced population."

Content validity was tested via peer review of item content. Construct validity was tested via factor analysis, which generated four factors explaining only 26.27 percent of the total variance. While not noted in this context, the authors do report that 72 percent of the subjects tested revealed a different superior function on the SLIP as opposed to the Gray-Wheelwright Jungian Type Survey, and 46 percent had different superior functions on the SLIP as opposed to the Myers-Briggs Type Indicator. The authors ascribe this to the fact that their measure rejects the bipolarity assumption accepted by authors of the more widely used tests. It is also possible that these differences may indicate validity problems inherent in the SLIP. Finally, criterion validity was addressed through studies employing an earlier version of the SLIP to differentiate the personality types of artists and psychotherapists, and of artists adopting different expressive styles.

In summary, the SLIP should prove to be of interest to Jungian therapists who regard personality constructs as continuous rather than as bipolar. The instrument is easy to understand, administer, and score. Its stability over time has not yet been well established, nor has its validity been well tested. Because of the nature of the test, it is doubtful that norms can be established, much less confidently interpreted. Therefore, the instrument is better adapted to applications of therapy than to personality research.

[335]

Situation Diagnosis Questionnaire. Purpose: To understand the concept of situational management, recognize situations in which various management styles are most appropriate, identify the management style(s) most appropriate for the individual's situation, and develop a plan to use a more appropriate management style on the job. Managers and employees; 1974–83; 1987 price data: $6 per set including 1 participant form, 2 companion forms, and scoring and interpretation booklet ('83, 10 pages); $15 per leader's guide ('83, 15 pages); 115(135) minutes; Don Michalak; Michalak Training Associates, Inc.*

Review of the Situation Diagnosis Questionnaire by RABINDRA N. KANUNGO, Professor of Management and Psychology, Faculty of Management, McGill University, Montreal, Quebec, Canada:

The Situation Diagnosis Questionnaire (SDQ) is designed primarily for use in training sessions for managers. With the help of SDQ, the training program is supposed to achieve the following four objectives for the participant managers: (*a*) The managers would be able to understand the concept of "situational management"; (*b*) they would develop an appreciation of the appropriateness of different "management styles" for different situations; (*c*) they would identify the management style(s) appropriate for their own job situations; and finally, (*d*) they would be able to articulate the specific manner in which they can use the appropriate management style in their job.

In order to achieve these objectives, the trainer is provided with a Leader's Guide that spells out the specific step-by-step details of the training session including the time needed for each step. Overall, the design of the training session and the packaging of the SDQ materials (e.g., questionnaire forms, scoring and interpretation booklet, and the Leader's Guide) are done quite well, with trainers' needs in mind.

The four objectives listed above and specified in the Leader's Guide appear quite sound and attractive from the practitioner's point of view. However, the "situation management" and "management styles" constructs that form the basis of SDQ are conceptually ambiguous and hence provoke serious questions about the content validity of SDQ as a measuring or diagnostic instrument of work situation characteristics requiring specific management styles.

The theoretical rationale for SDQ is derived from the earlier works on the managerial grid (Blake & Mouton, 1964) and contingency or situational theory of leadership (Hersey & Blanchard, 1977). Several management styles are identified on the basis of two dimensions of "concern for task" and "concern for people". For instance, managers showing low levels of both people and task concerns are characterized as showing an "administrator" style of management, whereas managers showing high levels of both task and people concerns are labelled as showing a "team" approach to management. Such labelling of management styles on the basis of two very broad and vaguely defined dimensions of managerial behavior is simplistic and confusing. Broadly defined categorization of managers' behavior overlooks many important distinctions between different aspects of each category of behavior. The simplistic dichotomy between people and task concerns expresses the behavioral dimensions of looking after the "needs-of-the-task" versus the "needs-of-the-subordinates." This dimension, however, is confused with "direction and control" versus "participation" of subordinates. Such confusion is reflected in the SDQ scoring and interpretation booklet by equating "autocratic control" of managers as "task" concern, and "permissiveness" of managers as "people" concern. In actual practice, a manager can use either autocratic or participative styles of management while trying to meet the needs of either task or people under his/her supervision. For such reasons, current theories of organizational leadership (Yukl, 1981) have argued in favour of making a clear distinction between participation behavior (decision-centralization dimension) and behavior showing "task" or "people" concern.

The type of conceptual ambiguity mentioned above is reflected in the item contents of SDQ. Hence, the content validity of SDQ is suspect. The SDQ items represent various work situation characteristics but are scored in terms of the styles of management most appropriate for such situational characteristics. However, the criterion-related validity of the items is difficult to judge in the absence of any empirical data. One simply does not know how the items were chosen and whether in fact a given situational characteristic requires a specific management style. Furthermore, some items are scored to represent a fit for both "task" and "people" concern and some others represent a fit for "administrative concern" (defined as being low on both task and people concern) along with task or people concern. Items representing such combinations, particularly of the latter type, are not very meaningful without proper content validity checks.

The use of SDQ in a training session requires a participant manager to previously obtain two subordinates' perception of the work situation using the "Companion" forms. The subordinates' characterization of the work situation is compared with the participant's own perception in order to arrive at a more realistic recognition of the work situation. The participant is then encouraged to think of specific behaviors (management style) most appropriate to his/her situation. Such procedure achieves the objectives of getting feedback from subordinates and developing an awareness of how to behave in the future for managerial effectiveness. Although the procedure is commendable, the questionable content validity of the questionnaire casts a shadow of doubt on the effectiveness of such training to achieve stated objectives.

In summary, the SDQ provides a convenient training package with explicit instructions to the trainers. It can be used as a training tool in both organizational and academic settings. However, considerable caution needs to be exercised in interpreting the item contents and the management styles profiles based on SDQ, primarily because of the weak conceptual basis of the "task-people concern" dichotomy of managerial behavior and the lack of data on the criterion-related validity of the measure.

REVIEWER'S REFERENCES

Blake, R., & Mouton, J. S. (1964). *The managerial grid.* Houston: Gulf Publishing Co.

Hersey, P., & Blanchard, K. H. (1977). *Management of organizational behavior: Utilizing human resources* (3rd ed.). Englewood Cliffs, NJ: Prentice-Hall.

Yukl, G. A. (1981). *Leadership in organizations.* Englewood Cliffs, NJ: Prentice-Hall.

Review of the Situation Diagnosis Questionnaire by CHARLES K. PARSONS, Professor of Management, Georgia Institute of Technology, Atlanta, GA:

The Situation Diagnosis Questionnaire provides a measure of a manager's work situation. This information is then used to suggest an appropriate style of management to fit the situation. The instrument and suggestions are based on the work of Blake and Mouton (1964), Reddin (1967), and Hersey and Blanchard (1969). The explicit purpose of the authors of the Situation Diagnosis Questionnaire is to assess the manager's situation at work rather than the manager's current style. The instrument yields scores on three situational scales: (*a*) the required task-orientation, (*b*) the required people-orientation, and (*c*) the required pure administrative orientation. There is a test booklet for the participating manager, test booklets for two employees or coworkers, and a scoring and interpretation booklet.

The Participant form is designed to be self-administered and completed before attending a workshop on situational management. The instructions on this form are minimal. The workshop leader is supposed to prepare a cover letter to accompany the form and hopefully give further explanation as to the purpose of the instrument. There are 21 items that purportedly assess important aspects of the work situation such as presence of quantifiable output, intellectual versus physical task demands, existence of clear procedures for work performance, and so forth. The items are answered on a 5-point verbally anchored scale (from 0 to 4). The verbal anchors are 4 = *almost always*, 3 = *regularly*, 2 = *often*, 1 = *sometimes*, 0 = *almost never*. This reviewer was a bit confused by the implied frequency scale and how the scale points were determined. Do most respondents believe "regularly" is more frequent than "often"? The participants are instructed (in the cover letter) to bring the completed instrument to the workshop.

Companion forms are sent to two coworkers or employees of the participant. The Companion forms are to be completed and returned to the personnel department (or whoever is coordinating the program). The instructions on this form are also minimal. The cover letter can provide some more information. The same 21 items from the Participant form are included on the Companion form. The response scale is the same. The two completed Companion forms are taken to the workshop on situational management.

The author of the instrument gives a step-by-step Leader's Guide for sending out instruments. There are also sample cover letters that would accompany the Participant Form and Companion Form. The sample cover letters are clearly written. I would suggest to potential users that some further explanation be given to the participants and coworkers concerning the nature of the information to be disclosed. Suggestions for respondents would be to be honest, to realize that the instruments are not for evaluating anyone's job performance, to understand that the results will not affect jobs or assignments, and so forth. One final point of interest is the fact that the author shows no preferences concerning the use of coworkers or employees as "companions," though he later notes that the responses could be quite different depending on the perspective.

Scoring of both the Participant Form and Companion Form occurs at the workshop. The Scoring and Interpretation Booklet gives directions on deriving and interpreting scores on three scales: the required task orientation (T-scores), the required people orientation (P-scores), and the required administrative orientation (A-scores). The T-scores and P-scores are plotted on a grid similar to that used by Blake and Mouton. In addition, the A-score is interpreted as meaning the degree to which the manager should act as a pure administrator.

The Scoring and Interpretation Booklet describes the meaning of various combinations of T-scores and P-scores, but is deficient in explaining what is meant by the Administrative style of management. This is additionally troublesome because users who are familiar with Blake and Mouton's Managerial Grid will have little trouble understanding the T-score/P-score combinations and labels, but will probably struggle (as did this reviewer) to understand the meaning and rationale for the A-scores.

The Leader's Guide gives suggestions on helping participants interpret differences between their responses and those on the Companion form. The meaning of these differences (or similarities) could potentially be quite beneficial to the manager, especially if the Companion forms were those of employees rather than coworkers.

In the materials seen by this reviewer, there was no evidence of normative, reliability, or validity data. Many of the 21 items included in the instrument are used in two of the three scales. Without any evidence of scale homogeneity or discriminant or convergent validity, this approach to scoring is questionnable. Some psychometric evidence should be made available so that users can better judge the merits of the scales.

One strength of the instruments is that they are part of a package of workshop exercises and discussion. The user can benefit from the author's experience in using the scales. Discussion questions and exercises are included as part of the Leader's Guide.

Another strength of the package is that independent observations of the work situation are obtained from employees or coworkers. Therefore, differences between perceptions of different people must be confronted and become part of the training exercise. This reduces the likelihood of purely socially desirable responding.

Finally, because the diagnosis of work situations leads to a discussion of "appropriate management styles," this reviewer would recommend further research on the effectiveness of the situational management approach.

An alternative training package that is based on situational management is that of Fiedler (1967). In Fiedler's contingency theory of leadership, people have a more or less stable disposition to be People-oriented or Task-oriented. Upon assessing their work situation, Fiedler suggests that leaders try to change the situation to be compatible with their style. The advantage of the Fiedler approach is that a great deal of research has been done on the leadership model, the measure of leader disposition (the Least Preferred Coworker Scale), and a specific training program called Leader Match. The user has a much better idea of the characteristics of the instrumentation and effectiveness of the training program in various settings.

REVIEWER'S REFERENCES

Blake, R. R., & Mouton, J. S. (1964). *The managerial grid.* Houston: Gulf Publishing Co.

Fiedler, F. E. (1967). *A theory of leadership effectiveness.* New York: McGraw-Hill.

Reddin, W. J. (1967). The 3-D management style theory. *Training and Development Journal*, 21, 8-17.

Hersey, P., & Blanchard, K. H. (1969). Life cycle theory of leadership. *Training and Development Journal*, 23, 26-34.

[336]

Sklar Aphasia Scale, Revised 1983. Purpose: "Developed as a clinical procedure to provide systematic information about the severity and nature of language disorders following brain damage in adults." Brain damaged adults; 1966–83; SAS; 5 scores: Auditory Decoding, Visual Decoding, Oral Encoding, Graphic Encoding, Total Impairment; individual; 1986 price data: $45 per complete kit including 25 test booklets, stimulus cards, and manual ('83, 25 pages); $11.85 per 25 test booklets; $22.50 per set of stimulus cards; $12.50 per manual; administration time not reported; Maurice Sklar; Western Psychological Services.*

See T3:2213 (1 reference); for a review by Manfred J. Meier, see 8:976 (1 reference); for reviews by Arthur L. Benton and Daniel R. Boone of the original edition, see 7:970; see also P:247 (2 references).

TEST REFERENCES

1. Thompson, C. K., & McReynolds, L. V. (1986). Wh interrogative production in agrammatic aphasia: An experimental analysis of auditory-visual stimulation and direct-production treatment. *Journal of Speech and Hearing Research*, 29, 193-206.

Review of the Sklar Aphasia Scale, Revised 1983, *by LINDA CROCKER, Professor of Foundations of Education, University of Florida, Gainesville, FL:*

The 1983 edition of the Sklar Aphasia Scale (SAS) is the second revision since the original publication of the SAS in 1966. The current edition features pictorial stimuli (rather than actual objects used in earlier editions) and some updated normative data. The test author suggests that this scale is intended for use by examiners with a general background knowledge of common speech and language disorders, but the manual does provide fairly clear functional definitions for a variety of clinical terms often used in classification and discussion of speech disorders.

The SAS is administered in two parts. The first part is an informal but structured interview requiring approximately 15 minutes for completion. The interview is designed to allow the examiner to form an initial impression of the client's functional level, estimating the overall degree of impairment on a 3-point scale. The primary usefulness of this interview would appear to be establishing rapport with the client and/or screening clients who may be too severely disabled to participate in the formal testing procedure that follows the interview. Because one of the tasks in the formal interview requires reading a passage, the examiner should check to insure that the client has minimal literacy skills and normal intelligence before administration of this test.

The second part of the SAS is composed of five 25-item subtests in which each item is rated by the examiner on a 0–4-point scale (with high scores indicating greater degree of impairment). Some subjective judgement on the part of the examiner is required for scoring the items, but the scoring criteria are straightforward and the instructions for numeric scoring are easy to follow. A particularly helpful feature of the manual is the inclusion of an illustrative case study to demonstrate subtest and total score interpretation.

The normative data for interpretation of the subtest and total scores are based on a relatively small sample ($N = 69$). Subscale and total score ranges are divided into three broad categories ranging from minimal-mild to severe. Placement of the cutting scores that discriminate between these diagnostic categories was determined empirically from the frequency distribution data of the norming sample. This process raises serious questions about use of these diagnostic categories in score interpretation, particularly for clients who score near the cutting scores.

Another question that might be raised about the new edition of the SAS is whether substitution of pictorial stimuli for actual objects in the naming tasks has an effect on examinee performance. Results of a study comparing examinee performance on 10 items using pictured stimuli and the same items using objects are reported. Although significant differences occurred for performance on only 3 of the 10 items, this investigation was based on an extremely small sample (11 subjects), which greatly reduced the chance of observing statistically significant differences. Thus evidence of similar performance on the two types of items is not convincing.

A decided shortcoming of the SAS is apparent in the psychometric data reported. Reliability evidence consists of only one investigation, and the data reported are for interrater reliability for a German translation of the scale. No internal consistency estimates for the subscales or total test are reported although these could have been readily determined from the responses of the standardization sample. Even more serious is the lack of any evidence of test-retest reliability.

Validity evidence is presented in the form of a variety of studies dating back to 1963. Results of factor analytic studies give some general support to organization of the scale into subscales, and correlational studies of the SAS and other measures of aphasia and verbal aptitude offer some evidence of construct validity. Users must be willing to assume that these results have applicability for the present edition since no validation studies with the current edition of the scale are reported.

In summary, the strengths of the SAS include its breadth of coverage, subscales of reasonable length, factor analytic evidence to support the subscale structure, clear instructions for scoring, and an illustrative case study to aid users in interpretation of test results. The author's suggestions for future research needed with this scale deserve attention. The weaknesses of this test include the small standardization sample, diagnostic categories of questionable stability, lack of essential reliability data, and lack of recent research on the scale's validity. Considering the lengthy history of this instrument, it is disappointing that these weaknesses were not addressed in the recent revision.

Review of the Sklar Aphasia Scale, Revised 1983, by LAWRENCE J. TURTON, Professor of Speech-Language Pathology, Indiana University of Pennsylvania, Indiana, PA:

The 1983 version of the Sklar Aphasia Scale (SAS) is the third version of this instrument. No significant changes were made in test design. The SAS continues to assess four areas: Auditory Decoding, Visual Decoding, Oral Encoding, and Graphic Encoding. The only change in the test stimuli was a substitution of pictures for objects in the Auditory Decoding subtest. New norms were obtained on 69 aphasic patients and cutoff points were identified from these data to create three impairment categories: mild, moderate, and severe. The last change, integration of the Preliminary Interview into the protocol booklet, was not central to the test and will not be addressed in this review.

The significance of the revision of the SAS is what was omitted rather than what was changed. This is the third review of this test in the *Mental Measurements Yearbooks* (Benton & Boone, 1972; Meier, 1978). In the first set of reviews, Benton expressed serious reservations about the SAS due to the poor quality of test design and standardization procedures. Meier's review stressed the same problems and this reviewer is in complete concurrence with their concerns. Unfortunately, these concerns were ignored by the author and publisher in the current revision of the SAS.

The only reliability indices reported for the SAS were taken from a study done in Germany in 1977 and consist of percentage of agreement measures for interrater reliability. There are no reliability indices to indicate that scores and severity ratings are stable. Given the fact that this test was designed to be administered in the hospital setting shortly after onset of problems, this failure is a most serious deficiency. Yet the author has failed to address the problem after 20 years of marketing and numerous complaints by reviewers.

The scoring for the SAS consists of a 5-point scale (0 = correct, 4 = incorrect or no response). Although broad descriptions for each category are included in the manual, there are no indices for reliability of the ratings as they are used by certified clinicians or by subtests. The author fails to point out that for many of the items the 5-point scale may not be applicable. For example, virtually the entire Auditory Decoding subtest requires yes/no responses (either oral or manual). Without specific scoring protocols, clinicians must decide on their own whether a response is delayed (1), assisted (2), or distorted (3). A clinician can create his/her own standards and score a response differently than a colleague, resulting in a different final score and severity rating. If a yes/no standard is used, only options 0 and 4 are possible for an item.

There is very little to be said about the validity measures in the manual. They were derived from mini-studies using the first version of the SAS, which did not use the 5-point scale. Furthermore, the tests used for comparison no longer constitute state-of-the-art aphasia diagnosis. The change in the scoring system was a major change; indeed, it resulted in a new test with new standards. However, users are expected to rely upon reliability and validity measures computed from a totally different set of scoring standards. This is one more critical testing concept ignored in the preparation of this revision.

The author reports new standardization data on 69 patients selected on the basis of availability from five states and an unspecified number of treatment sites. The data from these patients constitute the new norms in the form of profiles for the severity categories. These norms, however, are only as good as the reliability of the data collection procedures. Once again, the author fails to provide the user with this important information. The fact that these norms were collected from geographically disparate sites with small samples at each site suggests that different examiners may have done the testing. If this is true, the lack of reliability indices takes on greater prominence. Very simply, the norms cannot be accepted as having any degree of validity as presented in the manual.

Despite the negative reviews, this test has managed to survive over 20 years and the publisher was willing to invest in a new edition. From a clinical perspective, this test is a good *screening* device. It provides a clinician with a fast method of obtaining global information to use to advise family and medical staff on appropriate steps to follow in establishing a rehabilitation program. However, it should not be used for a true diagnostic evaluation from which a comprehensive program will be designed. The problems of reliability and validity raise the possibility of serious errors in classification and identification of the total pattern of aphasia.

[337]

The SOON Test. Purpose: Assesses "the ways a subject organizes and relates needs to each other in a temporal sequence." Adults; no date on test materials; also called the Sequential Organization of Needs Test; 22 base needs: Abasement, Achievement, Affiliation, Aggression, Autonomy, Blame Avoidance, Counteraction, Defendance, Deference, Dominance, Exhibition, Gratitude, Harm Avoidance, Inference Avoidance, Nurturance, Order, Play, Rejection, Sentience, Sex, Succorance, Understanding; no manual; 1984 price data: $3 per test including scoring; administration time not reported; Jay L. Chambers; the Author.*

Review of the SOON Test by DOUGLAS T. BROWN, Professor of Psychology and Coordinator of School Psychology, James Madison University, Harrisonburg, VA:

The SOON Test (Sequential Organization of Needs Test) is an instrument that appears to be based on Henry A. Murray's theory of constructive needs systems. This theory posits that personality style is reflected in the basic need structure expressed by an individual. The test is composed of 22 items posed in the form of situations corresponding to Murray's original 20 needs, plus those of Gratitude and Blame Avoidance. The subject is asked to read each needs statement and to choose, from the other 21 needs statements, the situations that would immediately precede and follow the situation described. Each of the 22 statements is, therefore, referenced against all other statements (needs). The array of needs statements chosen by subjects represents their motivational schema, known as their diachronic motivation system.

Administration of the test is confusing and fraught with possible sources of error. The directions to the subject are also confusing and difficult to interpret. In taking the test, the subject must constantly scan all 22 items in order to choose responses. The possibility of primacy or recency affecting choices is great. Subjects will probably find this test frustrating to take, thus increasing the probability of random responding. The probability of error due to reading miscue is also substantial.

The SOON Test is scored by computer. An analysis is performed of the frequency of the 22 needs chosen as before and after statements in the test. In addition, an elaborate interactive analysis is performed on all 22 needs statements in terms of interactive choices made by the subject. Thus, needs systems which tend to be cyclical (e.g., Achievement to Affiliation to Aggression to Achievement) are identified. The summary data produced by the computer scoring of this test includes cyclical patterns of motivation, the frequency with which each need is chosen, and a count of whether each need is chosen as a before or after statement. The computer output lacks clarity and is difficult to interpret.

A three-page description of administration, scoring, and interpretation is provided with the SOON Test. The test does not have a manual per se. The author cautions the test is experimental and that normative data are not yet available to allow interpretation of the various scores provided. Very little information is provided on the theoretical rationale for this instrument. No information is provided on reliability or validity. Virtually no psychometric properties of the test are described in the literature provided. The major function of the manual seems to be that of providing information on the analysis of data from the test. Even this information is presented in a puzzling and atheoretical manner. Generally, the information provided is inadequate to allow a determination regarding the efficacy of this instrument.

One can only speculate about the reasons the SOON Test is being sold in its present format. Even as an experimental instrument, it is theoretically uninterpretable and could lead to misuse by those not aware of its limitations. While the frequency with which subjects choose individual needs may be of some interest (if normative data are collected), the procedure described for analyzing the diachronic motivation system is purely fanciful. The only legitimate uses of this test would be in the development of norms and standardization procedures in order to establish its psychometric properties. The absence of this information in a published instrument is disquieting. In addition, a much stronger theoretical base is required if the SOON Test is to achieve some semblance of integrity. In the meantime, under no circumstances should the instrument be used for applied assessment of any type. Even the use of the instrument in research should be limited to establishing its psychometric properties at this time.

[338]

The Southern California Ordinal Scales of Development. Purpose: Provide a clear guide to what is profitable to teach a given child at a given time. Multihandicapped, developmentally delayed, and learning disabled children, and normal children; 1977-85; SCOSD; a Piagetian-based assessment system; 6 scales: Cognition, Communication, Social-Affective Behavior, Practical Abilities, Fine Motor Abilities, Gross Motor Abilities; individual; 1988 price data: $18–$25 per scale including manual ('85, 61–182 pages) and 10 record booklets; $7–$10 per 25 record booklets; (60–120) minutes per scale; Donald I. Ashurst, Elaine Bamberg, Julika Barrett, Ann Bisno, Artice Burke, David C. Chambers, Jean Fentiman, Ronald Kadish, Mary Lou Mitchell, Lambert Neeley, Todd Thorne, and Doris Wents; Foreworks.*

Review of The Southern California Ordinal Scales of Development by CAMERON J. CAMP, Associate Professor of Psychology, University of New Orleans, New Orleans, LA:

The 1985 edition of The Southern California Ordinal Scales of Development (SCOSD) consists of six scales—Cognition, Communication, Social-Affective Behavior, Practical Abilities, Fine Motor Abilities, Gross Motor Abilities—that were "designed to be used especially with developmentally and learning disabled children," though "they are equally effective with all other children." The SCOSD is said to differ from most other intelligence and ability tests in three ways: "(1) It is criterion-referenced rather than norm-referenced; (2) assessment procedures are flexible rather than fixed; (3) the scoring system takes into account the quality as well as the quantity of responses."

Criterion-referencing is achieved by basing the scales on Piagetian theory and methodology. "Each scale is divided according to the levels and stages that Piaget describes in his writings on human development." Therefore, test items are arranged according to the four major periods or stages of Piaget's theory: Sensorimotor (appearing at approximately 0–24 months of age), Preoperational (2–7 years), Concrete Operational (7–11 years), and Formal Operations (11+ years). Sensorimotor is further divided into six (sub)stages, while Preoperational is subdivided into two (sub)stages. Within stages, items are grouped according to specific concepts or abilities. For example, in the Cognition scale at the Sensorimotor stage, (sub)stage 4, the ability to know that an object exists even though it cannot be directly perceived is tested using the set of items grouped under the heading "Awareness of Object Constancy." Items here include Finds Hidden Object Under a Cloth, Retrieves Object Hidden Under a Cup or Box, Recognizes Reversal of Objects, and Looks for Contents of Box.

The administration of these scales is flexible in that the materials used are chosen by individual test administrators. "You are encouraged to vary materials to suit your needs, the children's handicaps, or a particular child's observed interests or cultural background." For example, in the Social-Affective Behavior scale at Preoperational stage, (sub)stage 2, one of the items under the heading "Self-Awareness" is Shows Interest in Projects. Materials can be clay, blocks, drawing materials, or any others the examiner wishes to use. Through observation, the examiner determines if the child "shows interest in planning small projects with definite goals in mind, carries her plans to completion, and shows regard for meeting some standard." Uses Language To Express Feeling, another item under the "Self-Awareness" heading, can be measured through spoken language, gesture, signing, or (with nonverbal children) through body gestures and/or facial expression. Examiners are encouraged to "observe the subject in his/her natural environment, using materials that are readily available and familiar." If a child doesn't perform a task that the examiner believes to be within his or her ability, a parent or teacher may administer the item in the presence of the examiner. Limits testing and repeated presentations of some of the same items are also encouraged.

Scoring reflects quality of responses. Test items are "passed" when the child exhibits a minimum level of performance. If passed, an item is scored according to the following criteria: Sometimes Observed (SO)—ability or concept only seen in highly structured environments; Frequently Observed (FO)—ability or concept seen with moderate structuring, but is in transition and is not automatic; or Regularly Observed (RO)—ability or concept is typical mode of functioning and is generalizable. Scores on items are used to create a developmental profile for each scale. Three levels of development are derived for each child. These are: Functional level—highest stage of development (Sensorimotor, Preoperational, etc.) in which the child obtains RO scores for at least 66 percent of items; Basal Level—highest stage in which the child obtains RO scores on all items; and Ceiling Level—highest stage at which a child passes one or more items with a score of SO or above. Items which a child cannot "pass" because a sensory or physical deficit prevents the demonstration of a concept or ability are labelled "Not Applicable" and are omitted in computing Functional, Basal, and Ceiling levels.

All six scales have separate manuals, though general instructions, references, and validation data are identical in all manuals. Responses are made in answer booklets that accompany each scale. Scales vary in length and in the number of items used at each stage. For example, the Cognition scale has many more items at the Formal Operations stage than the Gross Motor Skills scale, as would be expected.

Test items were selected from existing tests and research literature "on the basis of empirical evidence of validity." The field study sample used to "standardize" the scales was composed of 508 children, 505 of whom were classified as having some type of disability based on "diagnostic impression." Data were gathered from 1977 to 1980. Males comprised approximately 65 percent of the sample. Anglos comprised 68 percent of the sample, Hispanics 20 percent, and Blacks 6 percent. The geographic region from which the sample was selected is not mentioned (presumably it is Southern California). Disability categories included severely emotionally disturbed (20 percent), TMR (13 percent), aphasia (13 percent), deafness (13 percent), multihandicapped (23 percent), among others. Mean chronological ages for each disability category ranged from 102 months for aphasics to 131 months for TMRs. The manual contains the statement that "Criterion-group validity is easily established by a visual comparison of scores between groups," but this point is never elaborated nor are the figures being referenced totally clear as to how this validation is established.

Mean scores for each disability group for each scale are shown in the manuals in a series of tables and figures. However, these mean scores are given in terms of "months." It is unclear how these scores were derived. Presumably, a child with a Basal level of Concrete Operations (7–11 years) was given a score of 11 years (132 months), though this is unspecified in the manuals. This "mental age," however it was computed, was then somehow compared to IQ. Thus, the manual contains the statement that ceiling levels are "roughly equivalent to expected IQ measures for various categories of handicaps," but no correlational data are cited to support this statement. The manual also contains the claim that for disability groups where program admission required an IQ within 1 standard deviation of national norms, "the Ceiling scores very closely approximate the chronological ages." Basal and Functional levels were consistently below Ceiling levels. The manual therefore includes the claim that "these findings indicate that instruction based upon age and measured IQ is not appropriate for children in these categories. Rather, the levels at which they are routinely proficient (Basal and Functional) provide a more realistic foundation for instructional planning." No other attempts to relate Scale scores to other measures of intelligence are to be found.

No data on test-retest reliability are reported, nor are there data on reliability between different examiners. Internal consistency of the six scales was studied using Cronbach's alpha after assigning unweighted numeric values to the criterion-referenced designations used in the scales. "Almost all items show correlations above .75."

The strength of the SCOSD is its solid connection with Piaget's work. The test uses many of his tasks in an ordering that is consistent with his theory, and is a truly "developmental" scale. Central concepts such as object permanence are tested with multiple items, materials, and operations. Other strengths include the flexibility/adaptability of procedures and the attempt to give qualitative scores to responses. The item instructions are stated clearly, and the manuals are well designed for ease of use while testing. The focus of the SCOSD is to allow the development of educational programs based on abilities and concepts that a child has mastered, which is a worthwhile goal.

The weaknesses of the SCOSD, paradoxically, derive from the same sources as its strengths. A "thorough grounding in Piagetian developmental theory" is required if valid assessments are to be made using such flexible procedures and qualitative scoring. Thus, reliability is probably at risk with this instrument. Given that Piaget's ideas about intelligence are far removed from the individual differences approach of standardized intelligence testing, concurrent validity is difficult to achieve. No real effort to assess concurrent validity is found in these materials. The use of Functional, Basal, and Ceiling levels also seems inappropriate. Labelling a child as a "Concrete Operational" child is simply of little use. Piaget's concepts of decalage (both horizontal and vertical) would seem to militate against the use of such labels. It would seem to be best to look at profiles across tasks rather than to assign a child to a stage. Even adults will not always generalize formal operational thought to all tasks, as Piaget himself noted.

Finally, by adhering so closely to Piaget's theory, the SCOSD also is open to the general criticisms of Piaget's theory. Though space does not allow an elaboration of these criticisms, it should be sufficient to note that educators and psychologists who are not enamored with Piaget's work will not wish to develop the expertise necessary to administer these scales, nor will they likely accept the validity of the SCOSD as a means of assessing the abilities and concepts it purportedly measures.

SUMMARY. The Southern California Ordinal Scales of Development represent an attempt to use Piagetian theory to create a standardized assessment battery for use with disabled children. Its chief strength is that it is based on a widely-known and respected theory which describes cognitive development in a cohesive, developmental framework from birth to adolescence. It is also flexible and adaptable for use with a wide variety of populations, and allows qualitative measurement of performance. Its weaknesses are the high level of familiarity with Piagetian theory needed to administer the Scales, the lack of data on reliability and concurrent validity, and the attempt to attach stage labels to children based on performance with these tasks. The Scales may best be used as a means of creating a developmental profile of abilities which seem to be automatic, partially obtained, or lacking. These data might be useful in constructing educational or training programs, if there is sufficient understanding of how such abilities relate to specific academic behaviors. The SCOSD is not a "standardized" test in the classic use of the term, and should not be viewed as a substitute for more traditional intelligence tests.

Review of The Southern California Ordinal Scales of Development by ARLENE C. ROSENTHAL, Educational Psychologist, Lexington, KY:

The Southern California Ordinal Scales of Development are comprised of six developmental scales. The scales are comprised of approximately 500 items. The instrument was developed to provide a guide for what is profitable to teach a given child at a given time. Although the scales were developed for use with developmentally and learning disabled children the authors report that "they are equally effective with all other children." The scales draw on the developmental theories of Jean Piaget. They are (*a*) criterion as opposed to norm referenced, (*b*) comprised of flexible as opposed to fixed administration procedures, (*c*) scored qualitatively as well as quantitatively, and (*d*) used to obtain a Basal, Functional, and Ceiling Level.

There is no single comprehensive manual; each scale has its own manual and scoring form. Each manual is divided into 14 sections: General Instructions, Scale Instructions, Sensorimotor Stages 1–6, Preoperational Stages 1–2, Concrete Operations, Formal Operations, Technical, and Appendix.

The authors emphasize that these scales are criterion-referenced measures rather than norm-referenced measures. The issue of norm- versus criterion-referenced tests in the overall pupil evaluation and instructional process is controversial. In most assessment processes both types are generally used and each has its advantages and disadvantages. Perhaps most important is that the selected test match the purpose of the assessment. Each item on this test is criterion referenced and is scored as pass or fail. Each passed item is then scored qualitatively (i.e., how often it is observed). Generally, all items of a scale need not be administered to obtain a Basal, Functional, or Ceiling Level.

Performance on the scales is used to provide information about a child's overall range of functioning (e.g., areas of strength). Analysis of a child's profile can be used to "produce comprehensive individualized education plans." Essentially, the scales serve a diagnostic prescriptive function and are, purportedly, particularly suitable in teaching the handicapped. Careful analysis of performance on many traditional, standardized tests will also reveal areas of deficits and strengths. The ordinal scales are not remarkable in this sense.

The general instructions section of each manual describes procedures to ensure reliable administration, scoring, and interpretation. Each of the manuals contains additional administration and scoring directions unique to the abilities assessed. In the general instructions section, directions for administering each scale cover: procedure, method of communication, item repetition, time, materials, structure of the environment, and alternative methods of administration. In the technical section the authors indicate that instruction based on the Basal and Functional Levels "provide a more realistic foundation for instructional planning," whereas the Ceiling Level is the "least stable foundation for planning instruction."

A brief description of each scale will be provided below. The scale of Fine Motor Abilities assesses dexterity, perceptual motor, and graphomotor abilities at each of Piaget's developmental levels. The Cognition Scale assesses the development of: (*a*) methods of problem solving, (*b*) classification processes, and (*c*) linguistic and intellectual processes that require reasoning, logical thought, and the understanding of causality. The scale of Gross Motor Abilities assesses strength, balance, mobility, and coordination which, when combined, form the basis of many large muscle motor tasks. Items on this scale assess abilities ranging from simple reflexes to complicated motor actions. The scale of Practical Abilities assesses personal independence and the capacity to care for basic needs. The Communication Scale assesses oral and gestural expression, which together comprise total communication. Receptive and expressive behavior are assessed independently in each of four areas: (*a*) Awareness of Self and Environment, (*b*) Imitation, (*c*) Communicative Mediation, and (*d*) Symbolization. The scale of Social-Affective Behavior assesses: (*a*) self awareness, that is, emotional responses, self-initiated activities, and self image; and (*b*) relationships with others: awareness of others, responses to others, initiation of interaction with others, acquisition of social norms, development of sensitivity to others, and acquisition of social values.

The flexibility of the scales permits the examiner to adapt the assessment procedures to the needs of the child. In exchange for this flexibility, the examiner must be well grounded in Piagetian theory, assessment techniques, and clinical acumen. This is stated explicitly by the authors although a paragraph later they state "given some understanding of Piagetian epistemology, anyone can administer them." The examiner must react quickly to the examinee's performance and must not waiver deciding in which direction to proceed. The scales offer tips on how to conduct such interviews in order to solicit the most useful information and ancillary behaviors to observe (e.g., delayed responses).

Prior to utilizing the scales it is highly recommended that the examiner be familiar with each item in the six scales in order to establish Functional, Basal, and Ceiling Levels in a timely manner. Inadequate preparation for this task on the part of the examiner would seem to militate against the valid use of the results.

Technical data are provided in each scale manual and the data reported are identical in all six manuals. Why the general instructions, technical data, and bibliography are repeated verbatim in each of the six manuals is unclear, although presumably for convenience. The scales were administered to several hundred children collected over a 3-year period. Samples from this population were selected to provide data for item analysis and reliability studies. Each technical data section contains three tables reporting, respectively: (*a*) demographic characteristics, (*b*) type and frequency of various handicaps, and (*c*) mean Functional, Basal, and Ceiling Level scores in all scales for each handicap, and (*d*) analysis of variance across all handicaps all of which were statistically significant at the .001 level. Of 508 children, the socioeconomic status of approximately 35% are professional with the remainder including the unemployed, semi-skilled, and skilled craftsmen. The majority are of White or Hispanic background with 12.2% of Black, Asian Indian, or other ethnicity. Children ranged in age from, approximately, 8 years to 11 years. Of 508 children only .6% were in the regular classroom, 20.1% were severely emotionally disturbed/autistic, 30.8% were mentally retarded, and 23.5% multiply handicapped.

Approximately half a page each is given to the issues of validity and reliability. The validity of the scales is asserted by having selected items from existing developmental scales based on *normally developing* children at each level of development. This seems questionable given that items were empirically selected based on normal children but are to be used with handicapped youngsters. The authors suggest that criterion group validity is easily established by statistically significant differences between diagnostic groups on Basal, Functional, and Ceiling Levels. A single F-test across the standardization samples is given such that while an overall statistically significant result is achieved, the reader does not know what groups are responsible for this overall result. That is, there are no post-hoc analyses. With respect to reliability, a 250-page printout of reliability tables for each scale is available upon special request. The manual reports that almost all items show correlations above .75 "indicating excellent internal consistency."

It is distressing and erroneous that the authors claim the test assesses intelligence as well as ability. Intelligence is a controversial construct and current research suggests there may be a number of "intelligences" (e.g., social, artistic, etc.). There is not one piece of evidence given that relates performance on the scales to the more widely used measures of intelligence. Users of the scales should be aware of this, and this test in no way should be used to assess intellectual capacity. It is further stated that "The Ceiling levels are roughly equivalent to expected IQ measures for the various categories of handicap." There are several problems with this. First, expected IQ is not defined. Second, the manner in which the authors make the conceptual leap from Ceiling Level to IQ is unclear and therefore not interpretable. What this statement suggests is that an examiner can determine a child's Ceiling Level and extrapolate an IQ score based on the figures in the manual for the appropriate group. Third, Ceiling Levels are provided for each of the six scales. The unstated suggestion is that an "expected IQ" score can be obtained for each scale giving a "communication IQ," "gross motor IQ," etc. Clearly this paradigm is questionable given the oft debated construct of "intelligence."

In summary, the scales seem to be useful if used in a clinical versus an "absolute" (i.e., numerical) sense. The scales were developed to identify, developmentally, a child's placement in a variety of areas. The scales seem to do this and are appropriate for this purpose. While the scales are criterion referenced for the purpose of providing a total picture of a child's abilities, the manuals do not suggest a single intervention nor how to interpret/summarize the plethora of results. Given that intervention is the purported aim of this test, the lack of suggestions is a shortcoming. It would be useful to provide some continuity from the test results to the practical world (i.e., classroom). Psychometrically the test is touted as criterion versus norm referenced. That's fine. But more complete validity and reliability data are required before a practitioner can use the instrument with confidence.

Currently, numerous texts and periodicals address assessment of special or exceptional children in the same areas as do these scales. I would recommend that currently available commercial tests be used instead of, or in addition to, these scales. Tests in each area can be found in many special education assessment texts, in various test catalogues, and in the *Mental Measurements Yearbooks*. It is also of note that of approximately 30 references, only 2 are more recent than 1975 and approximately 16 appeared prior to 1970. The area of special education, in general, has undergone great change since 1975. The references given by the authors are outdated and do not integrate recent research.

The behaviors assessed in the early stages of this instrument have limited application to exceptional child assessment. Additionally, given that the scales are for prescriptive programming for the school-aged child, recommendations for interface with the school are absent. Generally, to receive special education in the school system the student must go through several stages in the assessment program. How the results of the scales fit into this process is not explained.

The scales attempt to do too much and cover too many areas, so that their utility in any one area is diminished. Again, the user should be cautious in making the conceptual leap from performance on the scales to intellectual capacity. The quantitative measurement of intellectual capacity has a long and rich heritage. Evidence that the scales measure intellectual capacity is lacking and should not supplant/uproot the more traditional measures. The scales represent a first step towards building an assessment model of intelligence.

[339]

Sports Emotion Test. Purpose: "Designed to show how an athlete responds affectively to a competition." High school through adult athletes; 1980–83; SET; 24 scores: 4 scores (Intensity, Concentration, Anxiety, Physical Readiness) for 6 different points in time (24 Hours Before, At Breakfast, Just Before, After Start, At Peak, Something Wrong); 1982 price data: $50 per 100 scales and profiles; $15 per manual ('83, 75 pages); (10–20) minutes; E. R. Oetting and C. W. Cole (profile); Rocky Mountain Behavioral Science Institute, Inc.*

Review of the Sports Emotion Test by ROBERT D. BROWN, Professor of Educational Psychology, University of Nebraska-Lincoln, Lincoln, NE:

The Sports Emotion Test (SET) is a self-report scale asking athletes to indicate how they feel when they are performing in athletic competition. The SET is made up of four scales: Anxiety, Intensity, Concentration, and Physical Readiness. The Anxiety Scale is intended to capture feelings of anxiety, the Intensity Scale indicates whether or not the athlete is "psyched up," the Concentration Scale suggests how well the athlete is able to focus on the event, and Physical Readiness indicates the athlete's perceptions of how well his or her body is working. The author stresses that these are measures of the athlete's perceptions of his or her emotional state and these may or may not reflect physiological anxiety or readiness.

Each scale is a semantic differential consisting of six bipolar adjectives with specific concepts as the stimulus for each item within the differential. The concepts are: "How I feel" for the Anxiety and Intensity scales, "What my thoughts are like" for the Concentration scale, and "What my body is like" for the Physical Readiness scale. Each scale is administered six times at different periods prior to and during competition. There is no testing period for after the competition per se, but rather athletes are asked to indicate how they feel after "something goes wrong."

A scoring template is provided and normative data are available based on slightly over 100 athletes. Most of these were male and female college athletes from Colorado State University, but the group included a few high school and professional athletes as well. The author emphasizes the norms may not be as helpful as noting how the individual athlete responds to different periods of time surrounding the competition and how the responses may vary by scale. A validity-check process (to determine whether or not the respondent answered honestly) is described and several individual SET profiles are presented with helpful case illustrations of a particular athletes' performances and unique problems.

The manual provides an interesting discussion of anxiety and other emotions believed to be related to athletic performance. Rather fine, but important, distinctions are made between perceptions and physiological effects and between anxiety and intensity.

The manual includes a more than adequate discussion of overall validity and the validity of each scale. Three psychologists served as judges of the content validity. All items in the current version of the SET were correctly sorted into the scale categories. Cluster analysis was used to assess discrimant validity. A separate cluster analysis was done for each scale using 118 athletes.

The author is to be commended for the excellent presentation of the cluster-analysis results. A spherical graph of the results provides a clear portrayal of the summary of the analyses suggesting that the items do cluster within the scale categories and that the scales are relatively independent of each other.

Evidence for construct validity is also presented for each scale. The empirical evidence (e.g., patterns of concentration before and during a race) are consistent with expectations, though based on limited sample sizes. Internal consistency measures of reliability resulted in Cronbach alphas ranging from .83 to .94 across time periods and scales. Test-retest reliability was .85 for Anxiety, .79 for Intensity, .75 for Concentration, and .70 for Physical Readiness. These latter indices of reliability were based on a sample of 18 athletes.

The work that this manual traces and the manual itself could easily serve as a model for independent test developers. The author considers and confronts most of the major steps and concerns in test and scale construction. Theory development is briefly but adequately explored, reliability and validity issues are addressed, and case illustrations make it possible for potential users to see how the instrument might be used.

Not everyone is likely to agree with the theoretical premises of the SET. Psychologists are still debating the causes and effects of stress and even coaches disagree on when athletes should be "psyched up" or how important it is for them to be "fired up." Further research with this instrument may help our understanding.

Users need to remember that this is a self-report instrument and in most instances depends on recall. It undoubtedly suffers from limitations as do all self-report instruments. Further research with athletes completing appropriate scales at the moments related to competition rather than depending upon recall may be fruitful, though the reactive effects of being tested need to be considered.

The evidence is too limited at this point to use the SET for predictive purposes. As the author cautions, the SET is primarily a research tool. It has the potential, however, for being useful for individual counseling with athletes without paying attention to normative information. Group or individual conversations with a trained psychologist around issues raised by the SET could not only improve the athletes' performances but could also result in a clearer and enhanced self-concept. This in itself could be a major accomplishment within a society in which adolescent and post-adolescent athletes often find themselves under severe stress.

Review of the Sports Emotion Test by ROBERT P. MARKLEY, *Professor of Psychology, Fort Hays State University, Hays, KS:*

The Sports Emotion Test is a set of scales attempting to measure a performer's emotional responses to a situation involving athletic competition. The scales ask the performer to provide self ratings of their feelings and reactions to the stress of competition on four theoretically derived dimensions (Anxiety, Intensity, Concentration, and Physical Readiness). The athlete is asked to retrospect about emotional feelings experienced at six times: 24 hours before competition, breakfast on the day of a meet, just before competition, just after the start of competition, at the peak of a competition, and "just after something goes wrong." Twenty-two check-mark responses are required at each time period. When the competitor completes the entire test, there are 24 scores that can be profiled in a variety of ways. Available from the publisher are a test booklet, a profile sheet, and a technical handbook.

This test attempts to capture some good ideas: that emotional responses (Anxiety) are situationally specific, are different at various times within a situation, are multidimensional, and that one's evaluative construction of stress and arousal is perhaps as important as the actual presence of physiological stress and arousal responses. The test's Anxiety dimension assesses the athlete's perception of the amount of emotional or physiological arousal that is interpreted by the athlete as anxiety. The authors postulate a phenomenal distinction between Anxiety feelings and the emotional Intensity the performer experiences. They suggest that the profile (over time) of Intensity is different than the profile for Anxiety. For example, in successful athletes anxiety often drops after the start of a meet while intensity stays constant or increases.

The Concentration dimension asks whether the athlete can stay attentionally focussed upon the performance or is distracted and experiences anxiety-related thought interference. The authors report some construct validity data for this scale from prior test-anxiety research. The Physical Readiness scale measures perceptions of bodily strength and coordination, for example, how weak (or powerful) the legs feel at a particular time before or during a meet.

Cronbach alpha reliabilities are reported ranging from .83 to .94 for a sample of $N = 118$ university, high school, and professional athletes. Test-retest reliability is a problematic concept when dealing with these sorts of idiographic measures of affective responses. These measures are specific to a particular point in the time course of a specific event; however, the authors report small sample estimates that range from .85 (Anxiety scale) to .70 (Physical Readiness scale).

Content, discriminant, and some construct validity data are provided in the test manual. Three qualified judges agreed about the scale placement of each item. A cluster analysis of data from the 118 athletes located items from each scale in separate clusters. The Anxiety scale is essentially identical to a previous scale published by the same authors in the 1960s. Validity data for the previous scale are reported in the manual. The other three dimensions represent new scales for which very limited validity data are presented.

The manual contains some discussion of scale profiles. These may be useful to a clinician working with a client on a sports-related performance-anxiety problem. Such a clinician will have to acquire some experience using the test with several clients and, because there is no single simple score, the user must also be one who enjoys the intellectual challenge of interpreting the spaghetti strands of multiple profiles.

The idea embodied in this instrument, of assessment at various times prior to and during an athletic event, is a good one. It is not clear, however, that this set of scales, with a wealth of measures, would be more useful than something simpler, for example, Martens' (1977) shortened form of the State Anxiety Inventory, as a situational measure of competition anxiety. Also, I am unconvinced that the Intensity or Concentration subscales are valid assessments of physiological arousal. In particular, the issue of the personal meaning one gives to various physical states—"I am excited and therefore am going to perform well (or poorly,)"—is not clearly addressed. The opportunity for more experimental research is clear. For example, it may be possible to construct modifications of the scales to deal with other performance-anxiety situations (e.g., music, theater, speech, and so on).

This test may be a useful tool to examine the dynamics of performance and anxiety in the sports setting. What is missing is evidence of refereed published research using this instrument. It is my opinion that an author's responsibility extends beyond simply publishing the test and manual. Test users will benefit from carefully researched demonstrations of the substantive usefulness of the test.

REVIEWER'S REFERENCE

Martens, R. (1977). Sport Competition Anxiety Test. Champaign, IL: Human Kinetics Publishers.

[340]

Standardized Reading Inventory. Purpose: For evaluating students' reading abilities. Children with reading ability not exceeding eighth grade level; 1986; SRI; "criterion-referenced"; 2 scores: Word Recognition, Comprehension; individual; 2 forms: A and B; 1987 price data: $47 per complete kit including student booklet, 50 summary/record sheets, and examiner's manual ('86, 139 pages); $16 per student booklet, $13 per 50 summary/record sheets; $21 per examiner's manual; (15–60) minutes; Phyllis L. Newcomer; PRO-ED, Inc.*

Review of the Standardized Reading Inventory by KENNETH W. HOWELL, Associate Professor of Curriculum and Instruction, College of Education, Western Washington University, Bellingham, WA:

The Standardized Reading Inventory (SRI) is a traditionally formatted instrument for making decisions about the decoding and comprehension skills of students. These decisions are based on students' reading of passages and words in isolation. The reading passages were developed by merging word lists generated by grade level from five reading series. Passage difficulty was controlled by assuring the inclusion of "Key Words" recognized because of their use at the same level in two or more series. Information on the number of sentences, average words per sentence, total words, and number of key words is supplied for each passage. Passage difficulty, as indicated by some sort of readability formula is not supplied. Factual, inferential, and lexical comprehension questions follow the reading of each passage.

Reading inventories provide an evaluator the opportunity to observe a reader's skill in a short period of time. The SRI offers the evaluator about the same information offered by any number of other inventories in that students read passages and answer questions. The actual purpose of the Inventory is not clearly stated although the introductory chapter makes reference to the determination of reading competence, confirmation of placement in reading, and recognition of instructional level (as opposed to frustration level and/or independent level). This final purpose is described in spite of the author's own caution that the Independent/Instruction/Frustration construct lacks validation.

The manual does a fair job of reviewing the difficulties encountered in generating passages that can be used to place students into specific levels of reading programs. What it does not do is provide any support for the activity itself. Instead, the author seems to assume that text selection is a worthwhile undertaking and that difficulty levels in reading are best defined by the words occurring in a passage (as opposed to a set of phonetic and/or language skills). The passages themselves are shown to be appropriately ordered by difficulty, but their actual utility is never documented. Additionally, while the procedure for recognizing the score boundaries between levels (Instructional/Independent/Frustration) is explained, no evidence is provided to demonstrate that students at the frustration level are frustrated or that those at the instructional level learn anything.

Some studies are provided in an attempt to document the SRI's validity; however, these are not well described and appear to be quite limited. The claim for concurrent validity of the entire inventory, for example, is made on the basis of correlations between scores obtained from 30 fifth grade students. The claim for test-retest reliability is based on the performance of 30 third grade students, rereading only three of the test's 20 passages after a 1-week interval. Little if any support for the validity or reliability of the comprehension items is provided. Of particular concern is the author's failure to identify the instructional programs used on the students selected for the reliability and validity studies. Given that different series teach different things, and that different tests sample different things, it is likely that an instrument valid for one series will not be valid for another (Jenkins & Pany, 1978; Shapiro & Derr, 1987).

The author states that the SRI is a criterion-referenced device. However, the test is not standardized as a criterion-referenced test should be and, in fact, few criteria are even supplied. For example, the Summary/Record sheet prompts the evaluator to rank various work attack and comprehension skills as good, adequate, or poor without supplying any definition of these levels. Similarly, the student's reading rate, which in this case is referred to as a "Reader Characteristic" rather than a skill, is to be scored as problematic or acceptable in the absence of any rate criteria.

In summary, the SRI does not seem to have any attributes that would cause one to select it over other similar instruments. In fact, there is every indication an evaluator would get as good or better information by having students read out of their own books.

REVIEWER'S REFERENCES

Jenkins, J. R., & Pany, D. (1978). Standardized achievement tests: How useful for special education? *Exceptional Children*, 44, 448-453.

Shapiro, E. S., & Derr, T. F. (1987). An examination of overlap between reading curricula and standardized achievement tests. *Journal of Special Education*, 21, 59-67.

Review of the Standardized Reading Inventory by CLEBORNE D. MADDUX, Department Chairman, Curriculum and Instruction, University of Nevada-Reno, Reno, NV:

The Standardized Reading Inventory (SRI) is similar in format and administration to common informal reading inventories. There are two forms, each consisting of 10 graded word recognition lists (20 words per list) and 10 sets of graded comprehension passages (Preprimer, Primer, and grades 1–8 inclusive). Subjects read words orally from the lists and each item is scored 1 or 0. Comprehension paragraphs are read first. During this reading, word recognition errors are recorded including omissions, insertions, substitutions, and requests for help. Unlike many informal reading inventories, hesitations, mispronunciations, repetitions, and self-corrections are not counted as errors. Subjects are then directed to silently reread the passage, and the examiner asks a series of comprehension questions. Scoring identifies independent, instructional, and frustration reading levels.

The SRI manual is clearly and simply written. Test procedures and scoring criteria are adequately explained and illustrated, with the exception of procedures for deriving listening comprehension level, which is defined in the manual and listed on the Summary/Record Sheet but not included in the procedures or instructions.

TECHNICAL CONSIDERATIONS. The SRI is not a norm-referenced instrument. However, the manual provides standardization information and data related to reliability and validity. Although these data are insufficient, the information represents an improvement over other informal reading inventories. Most other tests are the result of much less rigorous methods of word selection and passage development, and treat reliability and validity even more superficially than does the SRI.

Unlike many informal reading inventories, readability formulae were not employed to create the reading passages of the SRI. Instead, graded word lists were created by compiling words introduced at each level in five common basal reading series (*Scott, Foresman Basics in Reading*, *Houghton Mifflin Reading Series*, *HBJ Bookmark Reading Program*, *Macmillan Reading Series*, and *Ginn Reading Series*). Passages were then written for each level using words introduced at that level by at least two reading series. Factual, inferential, and lexical questions were generated for each passage and administered to a group of 288 average readers.

VALIDITY. Content validity is addressed through an analysis of the performance of 288 average readers in grades 1 through 4 drawn from three elementary schools and a middle school in a suburban school district near Philadelphia. No demographic data such as socioeconomic status or gender are presented for these students. Reading level was determined by (*a*) scores on tests found at the end of their basal readers (*Scott, Foresman Basics in Reading*), or (*b*) scores on the Stanford Achievement Test. No information is provided on reliability or validity of the basal reader test, time of administration, competence of examiner, etc. All subjects were administered both forms of the SRI and means and standard deviations were computed for each level for number of word recognition errors. For each passage, the instructional level was set at plus or minus one standard deviation from the mean; independent level requires scores exceeding one standard deviation above the mean; and frustration level begins with scores that exceed one standard deviation below the mean.

Ten to 15 comprehension questions were asked of all students in this sample. Results were used to set criteria for elimination of inappropriate questions and to determine error ranges for independent, instructional, and frustration levels.

These empirical approaches to defining passage difficulty are a definite improvement over exclusive reliance on readability formulae or acceptance of levels as stated by textbook publishers. If the subjects had comprised a large, representative sample, these procedures would have been excellent. Given the small sample, however, application of various readability formulae would have provided useful comparisons with the more empirical process. One additional problem is the manual does not state how the 20 words for each graded word recognition word list were chosen from the master word list.

No evidence is presented for predictive validity. An inadequate study of concurrent validity is reported in which the total number of SRI words recognized correctly and number of comprehension questions answered correctly were correlated with scores on the Word Reading and Reading Comprehension subtests of the Stanford Achievement Test. Attenuated correlation coefficients of .74 and .69 were computed for recognition and comprehension, respectively. The sample consisted of only 30 fifth graders in a single school.

Construct validity is investigated by seeking to establish that scores on the SRI are related to chronological age and to intelligence, that SRI scores will differentiate between good and poor readers, and that Word Recognition and Comprehension scores are interrelated. The methods used to establish these facts are inadequate due to lack of evidence for the representative nature of the samples, small sample sizes, and failure to make use of subjects from all grade levels. For example, the study of differentiation between good and poor readers used only 20 "poor readers" and 20 "capable readers" from the eighth grade. No demographics are presented and the manual does not give the cutoff score used to classify the students.

RELIABILITY. The subsample used to investigate test-retest reliability is unacceptably small ($n = 30$), restricted to one grade level (third), and presented without demographic data. Coefficients range from .83 to .92. Alternate-form reliability data were computed for the original 288 students and range from .71 to .97. Five of the seven coefficients below .80 appear below the third grade level. Unacceptably low coefficients are reported for Word Recognition at the preprimer (PP) and primer levels (.79, .72) and for Comprehension at PP, and grades 1, 2, 6, and 8 (.78, .74, .71, .78, .78). Interscorer reliability was also investigated and appears to be adequate.

SUMMARY. The SRI is a standardized, non norm-referenced reading inventory with a format similar to typical informal reading inventories (IRI). It differs from IRIs in the empirical base underlying word list and passage construction, and in procedures devoted to establishing reliability and validity. Unfortunately, however, the samples used in these procedures are frequently unacceptably small and not demonstrably representative. Reliability and validity are not established. Technically, the test could be severely criticized in comparison with other well-standardized, norm-referenced tests. In comparison with other informal reading inventories, however, the SRI compares favorably, and should be regarded as a positive, although not sufficient step in the right direction.

[341]

Standardized Test of Computer Literacy and Computer Anxiety Index (Version AZ), Revised. Purpose: Measures general computer literacy and identifies students who have computer related anxieties. Students in introductory computer literacy courses; 1984; STCL and CAIN; 2 tests; 1984 price data: $2.10 per test booklet including achievement and anxiety tests with answer sheets (publisher scoring costs included); $5 per manual ('84, 37 pages); multiple group scoring results available from publisher for additional fee of $.50 per student; Michael Simonson, Mary Montag (manual and achievement test), and Matt Maurer (manual and anxiety survey); Iowa State University Research Foundation, Inc.*

a) STANDARDIZED TEST OF COMPUTER LITERACY (VERSION AZ), REVISED. Measures achievement in computer literacy; 3 scores: Computer Systems, Computer Applications, Computer Programming; may be administered in one session or in separate sessions for each of 3 sections; $1.75 per "Achievement Test" only with answer sheets (publisher scoring costs included); 90(105) minutes.

b) COMPUTER ANXIETY INDEX. Test booklet title is Computer Opinion Survey; $.50 per "Computer Opinion Survey" only with answer sheets (publisher scoring costs included); administration time not reported.

Review of the Standardized Test of Computer Literacy and Computer Anxiety Index (Version AZ), Revised, by RON EDWARDS, Professor of Psychology and Director of School Psychology Training, University of Southern Mississippi, Hattiesburg, MS:

The Standardized Test of Computer Literacy (STCL) and the Computer Anxiety Index (CAIN) are two independent but simultaneously developed tests packaged together and described in a single manual. The STCL is described in the manual as a "competency based test of general computer literacy . . . most appropriately used to determine the progress made by students in an introductory computer literacy course." The STCL can be used to "evaluate individual and class progress" and the "test item analysis information can be used to identify group strengths and weaknesses." The STCL's 80 multiple-choice items are purported to assess 70 competencies organized into three sections: Computer Systems, Computer Applications, and Computer Programming. The manual lists each competency and the item (or items) assessing each competency. Each section requires 30 minutes to administer. All three sections can be administered in one testing session (not recommended) or each section can be administered separately.

The CAIN was "designed to identify students who have computer related anxieties." The CAIN purportedly can be used at the beginning of a computer literacy course to identify anxious students or at the end of a course to assess changes in computer anxiety. The CAIN consists of 26 items purported to assess nine competencies. It is untimed and said to take about 10 minutes to complete. Unlike the STCL, no information regarding item/competency relationships is provided.

Completed answer sheets for both the STCL and the CAIN must be returned to the publisher for scoring. Both individual and group scores, including item analyses, are available but the exact nature of the scores provided is not specified.

DEVELOPMENT OF THE STCL. Most of the information pertaining to the development of the STCL and the CAIN was obtained from a draft manuscript supplied to this reviewer and, presumably, available from the publisher or authors. The manual itself provides only minimal information and users are referred to two unpublished master's theses for details. Considerable attention was devoted to development of a definition of computer literacy and to the identification of relevant competencies. Some of the competencies are relatively specific behavioral objectives while others are very similar to the domains associated with criterion-referenced measures. Items were then developed to assess each competency. However, the majority of competencies are assessed by only one item and one competency has no associated item. Thus, any attempt to infer mastery of specific competencies is inappropriate.

A group of 152 students who had just completed a college-level computer literacy course served as the normative group for the STCL. No other descriptive information about the normative group is provided. The manual includes *M*s, *SD*s, ranges, reliability estimates, frequency distributions, and a raw score to percentile table. The performance level of the norm group seems somewhat low but is difficult to evaluate without more information regarding the students and the course they had completed. The manuscript reports data for an additional sample of 296 undergraduate and 45 graduate students from six states (no other information is provided) but these data are not included in the manual.

The manual provides *M*s, *SD*s, ranges, frequency distributions, and a raw score to percentile table for the CAIN based on the performance of a group of 614 subjects that included college students, junior high students, teachers, business professionals, computer users, and others. Curiously, the manuscript describes a norm group of 1,943 subjects. All of the data for certain subgroups were apparently incorporated into the manual norms but for others only a portion was included. For example, the manuscript reports data for 1,088 junior high students but only 247 are included in the manual table. Why some data were not used or how certain subjects were selected for inclusion is not discussed.

RELIABILITY AND VALIDITY. The test manual provides only minimal information regarding the reliability (primarily test-retest) of the STCL and the CAIN. No validity information for either the STCL or the CAIN is provided in the manual. The manuscript reports the results of one unimpressive validity study for the CAIN.

As described in the manual, the uses for the STCL are very limited and some of the suggested uses are questionable. It was designed to assess the computer literacy of students who have completed a college level course. As such, the test might be of value in assessing the post-course achievement level of students. However, it is doubtful that instructors would want to use the test results in determining course grades. Although the authors suggest the STCL can be used to assess ongoing progress, the normative data were collected only for students who had completed a full course. It is not clear how the results could be used to assess ongoing progress. In addition, the manual's suggestion that group strengths and weaknesses can be identified is questionable because the majority of competencies are assessed by only one item.

Uses for the CAIN are somewhat more apparent. However, far more data supporting the validity of the CAIN are needed before it could be used with any confidence.

The term "competency based" used by the authors may be somewhat misleading to users. It may suggest the STCL and the CAIN are criterion-referenced tests. They are not. A more appropriate designation would be "objective-referenced." Actually, it is difficult to characterize the STCL and CAIN: Their development incorporated many of the steps recommended for criterion-referenced tests, the test items are objective-referenced, and the statistical treatment and scores provided are more characteristic of norm-referenced tests. The development process was characterized by exceptional attention to some factors and insufficient or no attention to others.

SUMMARY. The STCL and the CAIN are best viewed as norm-referenced tests of computer literacy and computer attitudes. Given the sparsity of data provided for the normative groups, the extent to which the norms can be generalized is unknown. Interpretation of scores in anything other than a norm-referenced manner is probably inappropriate. The manual is woefully inadequate in its current form and needs substantial revision. In the absence of further validity data, the tests should be used only as research instruments or as supplementary information for assessing student progress.

Review of the Standardized Test of Computer Literacy and Computer Anxiety Index (Version AZ), Revised by KEVIN L. MORELAND, Consultant, NCS Professional Assessment Services, Minneapolis, MN:

The Standardized Test of Computer Literacy (STCL) was developed to measure aspects of computer literacy that were identified in a review of the literature. The test consists of two main components that are actually packaged as separate instruments, an achievement battery, and the Computer Anxiety Index (CAIN). The achievement battery comprises 80 multiple-choice questions spread across three subscales designed to assess knowledge of Computer Applications, Computer Systems, and Computer Programming. The following question comes from the Computer Programming section: "Computer language used often for scientific and engineering applications. PILOT, LOGO, BASIC, COBOL, FORTRAN." The CAIN is composed of 26 questions like "I enjoy using computers," with which the respondent expresses his or her degree of agreement on a 6-point scale.

The STCL items appear to have been developed with unusual care. The authors first developed an operational definition of computer literacy. They then developed operational definitions of the four components of computer literacy that formed the basis for the three achievement subscales and the CAIN. These definitions were used to cull the literature for computer competencies and in soliciting competencies from 90 computer education specialists. A list of 79 computer competencies was thus developed.

Fifteen computer literacy specialists were asked to draft items tapping the 70 achievement competencies. Detailed guidelines were provided to those drafting the items. An initial pool of 186 items was pilot tested on samples of approximately 20 college students who had completed a computer literacy course and 20 who had not. Specific guidelines were established by which to reject items on the basis of poor psychometric properties. In addition, nine "computer specialists" were asked to judge the congruence between a test item and the competency it was written to assess. Eighty questions survived the pilot test. Those 80 questions were administered to a new group of 152 computer-literate college students. This final pilot test gave rise to "minor revisions" resulting in the achievement battery currently under review.

The CAIN items were developed to assess "the fear or apprehension felt by an individual when using computers, or when considering the possibility of computer utilization" (Administrator's Manual). Development of the CAIN items is not described in detail, but an unpublished manuscript provided to this reviewer indicated that they "were pilot tested in a manner similar to the one described for the verification of the achievement items." The items were not carefully edited: "If I use a computer, I could (sic) get a better picture of the facts and figures." In addition, it appears to this reviewer that the CAIN is more appropriately characterized as a general measure of attitudes about computers and their use. For example, it seems eminently possible to disagree with the statement "A computer could make learning fun" without feeling anxious or fearful about computers.

RELIABILITY. The total achievement score has demonstrated good internal consistency (KR20): .86 in the initial pilot test and .87 in a sample of 341 college students collected for normative purposes. Estimates of internal consistency of the subscales are available only for the 152 students in the final pilot study. The latter are less satisfactory, ranging from .64 to .75. The test-retest reliability of the achievement battery has not been reported. Both the internal consistency (coefficient alpha = .94) and the test-retest reliability (.90 over a 3-week interval) of the CAIN are high. Unfortunately, except for the fact the test-retest sample comprised teacher education students, important characteristics of the samples used to make these estimates have not been reported (e.g., sample sizes, demographic characteristics, means, standard deviations).

NORMS. Normative data for the achievement battery are based on 341 college students from six states. Forty-five of these students were graduate students in teacher education. Neither the other students nor the institutions they were attending have been described. A wider array of individuals compose the 1,943-member CAIN normative group: junior high school students, college students, teachers, adults with formal computer training, adults who routinely use computers, and a small catchall "other" group. No further description of these samples has been published.

VALIDITY. To date one study of the STCL's content validity has been completed. Thirty-four computer education specialists (from among the 90 who helped define the content of the STCL) were asked to evaluate the (*a*) definitions used in the tests' development; (*b*) list of competencies used in the tests' development; (*c*) test items; and (*d*) instruments as a whole. These experts were mildly positive about the STCL. Their evaluations were consistently around 3.5 on a 5-point scale where 3 = unsure and 5 = positive.

SUMMARY AND EVALUATION. Presently, the strength of the STCL lies in the careful definition of its content coverage and the careful development of items to tap the chosen content domains. This makes the results of the content validity investigation described above disquieting. One suspects the problem lies with the evaluative instrument used in the study rather than with the STCL. In any case, further study will be required in order to reach any definitive conclusions about the usefulness of the STCL.

[342]

Stanford-Binet Intelligence Scale, Fourth Edition. Purpose: "An instrument for measuring cognitive abilities that provides an analysis of the pattern as well as the overall level of an individual's cognitive development." Ages 2–adult; 1916–86; S-B; Third Revision is still available; 20 scores: Verbal Reasoning (Vocabulary, Comprehension, Absurdities, Verbal Relations, Total), Abstract/Visual Reasoning (Pattern Analysis, Copying, Matrices, Paper Folding and Cutting, Total), Quantitative Reasoning (Quantitive, Number Series, Equation Building, Total), Short-Term Memory (Bead Memory, Memory for Sentences, Memory for Digits, Memory for Objects, Total), Total; individual; 1987 price data: $297 per complete examiner's kit; $24.30 per 35 record booklets ('86, 40 pages); $24 per Guide for Administering and Scoring the Fourth Edition ('86, 196 pages); $15 per Examiner's Handbook ('87, 171 pages); $8.55 per Technical Manual ('86, 142 pages); administration time not reported; Robert L. Thorndike, Elizabeth P. Hagen, Jerome M. Sattler, Elizabeth A. Delaney (Examiner's Handbook), and Thomas F. Hopkins (Examiner's Handbook); The Riverside Publishing Co.*

See 9:1176 (41 references), T3:2289 (203 references), 8:229 (176 references), and T2:525 (428 references); for a review by David Freides, see 7:425 (258 references); for a review by Elizabeth D. Fraser and excerpted reviews by Benjamin Balinski, L. B. Birch, James Maxwell, Marie D. Neale, and Julian C. Stanley, see 6:536 (110 references); for reviews by Mary R. Haworth and Norman D. Sundberg of the second revision, see 5:413 (121 references); for a review by Boyd R. McCandless, see 4:358 (142 references); see also 3:292 (217 references); for excerpted reviews by Cyril Burt, Grace H. Kent, and M. Krugman, see 2:1420 (132 references); for reviews by Francis N. Maxfield, J. W. M. Rothney, and F. L. Wells, see 1:1062.

TEST REFERENCES

1. Bouchard, T. J., Jr. (1983). Do environmental similarities explain the similarity in intelligence of identical twins reared apart? *Intelligence*, 7, 175-184.

2. Hartsough, C. S., Elias, P., & Wheeler, P. (1983). Evaluation of a nonintellectual assessment procedure for the early screening of exceptionality. *Journal of School Psychology*, 21, 133-142.

3. Morrison, G. M., & Borthwick, S. (1983). Patterns of behavior, cognitive competence, and social status for educable mentally retarded children. *The Journal of Special Education*, 17, 441-452.

4. Teglasi, H., & Freeman, R. W. (1983). Rapport pitfalls of beginning testers. *Journal of School Psychology*, 21, 229-240.

5. Tsai, L. Y., & Beisler, J. M. (1983). The development of sex differences in infantile autism. *British Journal of Psychiatry*, 142, 373-378.

6. Wilson, R. S., & Matheny, A. P., Jr. (1983). Mental development: Family enviroment and genetic influences. *Intelligence*, 7, 195-215.

7. Adams, J. L., Campbell, F. A., & Ramey, C. T. (1984). Infants' home environments: A study of screening efficiency. *American Journal of Mental Deficiency*, 89, 133-139.

8. Bickett, L., Reuter, J., & Stancin, T. (1984). The use of the McCarthy Scales of Children's Abilities to assess moderately mentally retarded children. *Psychology in the Schools*, 21, 305-312.

9. Bradley, R. H., & Caldwell, B. M. (1984). The relation of infants' home environments to achievement test performance in first grade: A follow-up study. *Child Development*, 55, 803-809.

10. Deckner, C. W., Soraci, S. A., Jr., Blanton, R. L., & Deckner, P. O. (1984). The relationships among two experimental and four psychometric assessments of abnormal children. *Journal of Clinical and Child Psychology*, 13, 157-164.

11. Flynn, J. R. (1984). The mean IQ of Americans: Massive gains 1932 to 1978. *Psychological Bulletin*, 95, 29-51.

12. Furrow, D. (1984). Social and private speech at two years. *Child Development*, 55, 355-362.

13. Guidubaldi, J., & Perry, J. D. (1984). Concurrent and predictive validity of the Battelle Development Inventory at the first grade level. *Educational and Psychological Measurement*, 44, 977-985.

14. Hoffman-Plotkin, D., & Twentyman, C. T. (1984). A multimodal assessment of behavioral and cognitive deficits in abused and neglected preschoolers. *Child Development*, 55, 794-802.

15. Honig, A. S. (1984). Risk factors in infants and young children. *Young Children*, 39 (4), 60-73.

16. Kaufman, A. S. (1984). K-ABC and controversy. *The Journal of Special Education*, 18, 409-444.

17. Kohlberg, L., Ricks, D., & Snarey, J. (1984). Childhood development as a predictor of adaptation in adulthood. *Genetic Psychology Monographs*, 110, 91-172.

18. Maheady, L., Maitland, G., & Sainato, D. (1984). The interpretation of social interactions by mildly handicapped and nondisabled children. *The Journal of Special Education*, 18, 151-159.

19. Martin, N. D. T., Snodgrass, G. J. A. I., & Cohen, R. D. (1984). Idiopathic infantile hypercalcaemia—A continuing enigma. *Archives of Disease in Childhood*, 59, 605-613.

20. McCall, R. B. (1984). Developmental changes in mental performance: The effect of the birth of a sibling. *Child Development*, 55, 1317-1321.

21. McGowan, R. J., & Johnson, D. J. (1984). The mother-child relationship and other antecedents of academic performance: A causal analysis. *Hispanic Journal of Behavioral Sciences*, 6, 205-224.

22. Mehrens, W. A. (1984). A critical analysis of the psychometric properties of the K-ABC. *The Journal of Special Education*, 18, 297-310.

23. Miller, L. B., & Bizzell, R. P. (1984). Long-term effects of four preschool programs: Ninth- and tenth-grade results. *Child Development*, 55, 1570-1587.

24. Obrzut, A., Nelson, R. B., & Obrzut, J. E. (1984). Early school entrance for intellectually superior children: An analysis. *Psychology in the Schools*, 21, 71-77.

25. Odom, S. L., Deklyen, M., & Jenkins, J. R. (1984). Integrating handicapped and nonhandicapped preschoolers: Developmental impact on nonhandicapped children. *Exceptional Children*, 51, 41-48.

26. Ramey, C. T., & Campbell, F. A. (1984). Preventive education for high-risk children: Cognitive consequences of the Carolina Abecedarian Project. *American Journal of Mental Deficiency*, 88, 515-523.

27. Ramey, C. T., Yeates, K. O., & Short, E. J. (1984). The plasticity of intellectual development: Insights from preventive intervention. *Child Development*, 55, 1913-1925.

28. Ritvo, E. R., Freeman, B. J., Yuwiler, A., Geller, E., Yokota, A., Schroth, P., & Novak, P. (1984). Study of fenfluramine in outpatients with the syndrome of autism. *The Journal of Pediatrics*, 105, 823-828.

29. Runco, M. A. (1984). Teachers' judgements of creativity and social validation of divergent thinking tests. *Perceptual and Motor Skills*, 59, 711-717.

30. Sternberg, R. J. (1984). The Kaufman Assessment Battery for Children: An information-processing analysis and critique. *The Journal of Special Education*, 18, 269-279.

31. Tobey, E. A., & Cullen, J. K., Jr. (1984). Temporal integration of tone glides by children with auditory-memory and reading problems. *Journal of Speech and Hearing Research*, 27, 527-533.

32. Zins, J. E., & Barnett, D. W. (1984). A validity study of the K-ABC, the WISC-R, and the Stanford-Binet with nonreferred children. *Journal of School Psychology*, 22, 369-371.

33. Berbaum, M. L., & Moreland, R. L. (1985). Intellectual development within transracial adoptive families: Retesting the confluence model. *Child Development*, 56, 207-216.

34. Blackwell, S. C., Dial, J. G., Chan, F., & McCollum, P. S. (1985). Discriminating functional levels of independent living: A neuropsychological evaluation of mentally retarded adults. *Rehabilitation Counseling Bulletin*, 29, 42-52.

35. Cardoso-Martins, C., Mervis, C. B., & Mervis, C. A. (1985). Early vocabulary acquisition by children with Down syndrome. *American Journal of Mental Deficiency*, 90, 177-184.

36. Coleman, M., Sobel, S., Bhagavan, H. N., Coursin, D., Marquardt, A., Guay, M., & Hunt, C. (1985). A double blind study of vitamin B6 in Down's syndrome infants. Part 1-Clinical and biochemical results. *Journal of Mental Deficiency Research*, 29, 233-240.

37. Covin, T. M., & Sattler, J. M. (1985). A longitudinal study of the Stanford-Binet and WISC-R with special education students. *Psychology in the Schools*, 22, 274-276.

38. Cunningham, C. C., Glenn, S. M., Wilkinson, P., & Sloper, P. (1985). Mental ability, symbolic play and receptive and expressive language of young children with Down's syndrome. *The Journal of Child Psychology and Psychiatry and Allied Disciplines*, 26, 255-265.

39. Durham, T. W. (1985). Extrapolated Stanford-Binet IQs for severely and profoundly retarded adults. *Psychological Reports*, 56, 189-190.

40. Gunn, P., & Berry, P. (1985). The temperament of Down's syndrome toddlers and their siblings. *The Journal of Child Psychology and Psychiatry and Allied Disciplines*, 26, 973-979.

41. Hewitt, K. E., Carter, G., & Jancar, J. (1985). Ageing in Down's syndrome. *British Journal of Psychiatry*, 147, 58-62.

42. Kashani, J. H., Carlson, G. A., Horwitz, E., & Reid, J. C. (1985). Dysphoric mood in young children referred to a child development unit. *Child Psychiatry and Human Development*, 15, 234-242.

43. Kavale, K. A., & Nye, C. (1985). Parameters of learning disabilities in achievement, linguistic, neuropsychological, and social/behavioral domains. *Journal of Special Education*, 19, 443-458.

44. Kistner, J., White, K., Haskett, M., & Robbins, F. (1985). Development of learning-disabled and normally achieving children's causal attributions. *Journal of Abnormal Child Psychology*, 13, 639-647.

45. Klanderman, J., Devine, J., & Mollner, C. (1985). The K-ABC: A construct validity study with the WISC-R and Stanford-Binet. *Journal of Clinical Psychology*, 41, 273-281.

46. Latorre, R. A. (1985). Kindergarten screening: A cross-validation of the Florida Kindergarten Screening Battery. *The Alberta Journal of Educational Research*, 31, 174-190.

47. Marcell, M. M., & Jett, D. A. (1985). Identification of vocally expressed emotions by mentally retarded and nonretarded individuals. *American Journal of Mental Deficiency*, 89, 537-545.

48. Plomin, R., & DeFries, J. C. (1985). A parent-offspring adoption study of cognitive abilities in early childhood. *Intelligence*, 9, 341-356.

49. Richardson, S. A., Koller, H., & Katz, M. (1985). Appearance and mental retardation: Some first steps in the development and application of a measure. *American Journal of Mental Deficiency*, 89, 475-484.

50. Rose, S. A., & Wallace, I. F. (1985). Cross-modal and intramodal transfer as predictors of mental development in full-term and preterm infants. *Developmental Psychology*, 21, 949-962.

]P521 Rose, S. A., & Wallace, I. F. (1985). Visual recognition memory: A predictor of later cognitive functioning in preterms. *Child Development*, 56, 843-852.

52. Sinclair, E., Forness, S. R., & Alexson, J. (1985). Psychiatric diagnosis: A study of its relationship to school needs. *Journal of Special Education*, 19, 333-344.

53. Templer, D. I., Schmitz, S. P., & Corgiat, M. D. (1985). Comparison of the Stanford-Binet with the Wechsler Adult Intelligence Scale—Revised: Preliminary report. *Psychological Reports*, 57, 335-336.

54. Wasserman, G. A., Allen, R., & Solomon, C. R. (1985). At-risk toddlers and their mothers: The special case of the physical handicap. *Child Development*, 56, 73-83.

55. Wilson, R. S. (1985). Risk and resilience in early mental development. *Developmental Psychology*, 21, 795-805.

56. Breitmayer, B. J., & Ramey, C. T. (1986). Biological nonoptimality and quality of postnatal environment as codeterminants of intellectual development. *Child Development*, 57, 1151-1165.

57. Carvajal, H., & Weyand, K. (1986). Relationships between scores on Stanford-Binet IV and Wechsler Intelligence Scale for Children—Revised. *Psychological Reports*, 59, 963-966.

58. Chomsky, C. (1986). Analytic study of the tacloma method: Language abilities of three deaf-blind subjects. *Journal of Speech and Hearing Research*, 29, 332-347.

59. Goldstein, D. J., Smith, K. B., & Waldrep, E. E. (1986). Factor analytic study of the Kaufman Assessment Battery for Children. *Journal of Clinical Psychology*, 42, 890-894.

60. Harris, K. R. (1986). The effects of cognitive behavior modification on private speech and task performance during problem solving among learning-disabled and normally achieving children. *Journal of Abnormal Child Psychology*, 14, 63-76.

61. Hewitt, K. E., Fenner, M. E., & Torpy, D. (1986). Cognitive and behavioural profiles of the elderly mentally handicapped. *Journal of Mental Deficiency Research*, 30, 217-225.

62. Karnes, F. A., Whorton, J. E., Currie, B. B., & Cantrall, S. W. (1986). Correlations of scores on the WISC-R, Stanford-Binet, the Slosson Intelligence Test, and the Developing Cognitive Abilities Test for intellectually gifted youth. *Psychological Reports*, 58, 887-889.

63. Kashani, J. H., Horwitz, E., Ray, J. S., & Reid, J. C. (1986). DSM-III diagnostic classification of 100 preschoolers in a child development unit. *Child Psychiatry and Human Development*, 16, 137-147.

64. Lewis, M., Jaskir, J., & Enright, M. K. (1986). The development of mental abilities in infancy. *Intelligence*, 10, 331-354.

65. Lidz, C. S., & Ballester, L. E. (1986). Diagnostic implications of McCarthy Scale General Cognitive Index/Binet IQ discrepancies for low-socioeconomic-status preschool children. *Journal of School Psychology*, 24, 381-385.

66. Maisto, A. A., & German, M. L. (1986). Reliability, predictive validity, and interrelationships of early assessment indices used with developmentally delayed infants and children. *Journal of Clinical Child Psychology*, 15, 327-332.

67. Mannarino, A. P., & Cohen, J. A. (1986). A clinical-demographic study of sexually abused children. *Child Abuse and Neglect*, 10, 17-23.

68. Mattison, R. E., Humphrey, F. J., II, Kales, S. N., & Wallace, D. J. (1986). An objective evaluation of special class placement of elementary schoolboys with behavior problems. *Journal of Abnormal Child Psychology*, 14, 251-262.

69. Mundy, P., Sigman, M., Ungerer, J., & Sherman, T. (1986). Defining the social deficits of autism: The contribution of non-verbal communication measures. *Journal of Child Psychology and Psychiatry and Allied Disciplines*, 27, 657-669.

70. Palisin, H. (1986). Preschool temperament and performance on achievement tests. *Developmental Psychology*, 22, 766-770.

71. Rantakallio, P., & von Wendt, L. (1986). Mental retardation and subnormality in a birth cohort of 12,000 children in Northern Finland. *American Journal of Mental Deficiency*, 90, 380-387.

72. Rice, T., Corley, R., Fulker, D. W., & Plomin, R. (1986). The development and validation of a test battery measuring specific cognitive abilities in four-year-old children. *Educational and Psychological Measurement*, 46, 699-708.

73. Roth, F. P., & Spekman, N. J. (1986). Narrative discourse: Spontaneously generated stories of learning-disabled and normally achieving students. *Journal of Speech and Hearing Disorders*, 51, 8-23.

74. Silva, P. A. (1986). A comparison of the predictive validity of the Reynell Developmental Language Scales, the Peabody Picture Vocabulary Test and the Stanford-Binet Intelligence Scale. *British Journal of Educational Psychology*, 56, 201-204.

75. Silva, P. A., Chalmers, D., & Stewart, I. (1986). Some audiological, psychological, educational and behavioral characteristics of children with bilateral otitis media with effusion: A longitudinal study. *Journal of Learning Disabilities*, 19, 165-169.

76. Simmons, C. H., & Zumpf, C. (1986). The gifted child: Perceived competence, prosocial moral reasoning, and charitable donations. *The Journal of Genetic Psychology*, 147, 97-105.

77. Singer, L. (1986). Long-term hospitalization of failure-to-thrive infants: Developmental outcome at three years. *Child Abuse and Neglect*, 10, 479-486.

78. Spitz, H. H. (1986). Disparities in mentally retarded persons' IQs derived from different intelligence tests. *American Journal of Mental Deficiency*, 90, 588-591.

79. Taylor, A. E., Saint-Cyr, J. A., & Lang, A. E. (1986). Frontal lobe dysfunction in Parkinson's disease: The cortical focus of neostriatal outflow. *Brain*, 109, 845-883.

80. Wasserman, G. A., Shilansky, M., & Hahn, H. (1986). A matter of degree: Maternal interaction with infants of varying levels of retardation. *Child Study Journal*, 16, 241-253.

81. Carvajal, H., & Gerber, J. (1987). 1986 Stanford-Binet Abbreviated Forms. *Psychological Reports*, 61, 285-286.

82. Carvajal, H., Gerber, J., Hewes, P., & Weaver, K. A. (1987). Correlations between scores on Stanford-Binet IV and Wechsler Adult Intelligence Scale—Revised. *Psychological Reports*, 61, 83-86.

83. Ernhart, C. B., Marler, M. R., & Morrow-Tlucak, M. (1987). Size and cognitive development in the early preschool years. *Psychological Reports*, 61, 103-106.

84. Gollob, H. F., & Reichardt, C. S. (1987). Taking account of time lags in causal models. *Child Development*, 58, 80-92.

85. Karnes, F. A., & D'Ilio, V. R. (1987). Correlations of scores on verbal and non-verbal measures of intelligence for intellectually gifted students. *Perceptual and Motor Skills*, 64 (1), 101-102.

86. Loveland, K. A. (1987). Behavior of young children with Down syndrome before the mirror: Exploration. *Child Development*, 58, 768-778.

87. Lukose, S. (1987). Knowledge and behavior relationships in the memory ability of retarded and nonretarded students. *Journal of Experimental Child Psychology*, 43, 13-24.

88. Whorton, J. E., & Karnes, F. A. (1987). Correlation of Stanford-Binet Intelligence Scale with various other measures

used to screen and identify intellectually gifted students. *Perceptual and Motor Skills*, 64, 461-462.

89. Zarnegar, Z., Hocevar, D., & Michael, W. B. (1988). Components of original thinking in gifted children. *Educational and Psychological Measurement*, 48 (1), 5-16.

Review of the Stanford-Binet Intelligence Scale, Fourth Edition by ANNE ANASTASI, Professor Emeritus of Psychology, Fordham University, Bronx, NY:

This revision of the Stanford-Binet is the most extensive ever undertaken, including basic changes in content coverage, administration, scoring, and interpretation, as well as a complete restandardization on a representative national sample. Continuity with the earlier editions was maintained in part by retaining many of the item types from the earlier forms. Even more important is the retention of the adaptive testing procedure, whereby each individual takes only those items whose difficulty is appropriate for his or her performance level.

ADMINISTRATION AND SCORING. In this edition, adaptive testing is achieved by a two-stage process. In the first stage, the examiner gives the Vocabulary Test, which serves as a routing test to select the *entry level* for all remaining tests. Where to begin on the Vocabulary test depends solely on chronological age. For all other tests, the entry level is found from a chart reproduced on the record booklet, which combines Vocabulary score and chronological age. In the second stage, the examiner follows specified rules to establish a *basal level* and a *ceiling level* for each test on the basis of the individual's actual performance.

Unlike the age grouping followed in earlier editions, items of each type are now placed in separate tests in increasing order of difficulty. Item difficulty is incorporated in the scoring by recording the item number of the highest item administered, from which is subtracted the total number of attempted items that were failed. There are 15 tests, chosen to represent four major cognitive areas: Verbal Reasoning, Quantitative Reasoning, Abstract/Visual Reasoning, and Short-Term Memory. No one individual, however, takes all 15 tests, because some are suitable only within limited age ranges. In general, the complete battery may include from 8 to 13 tests, depending on the test taker's age and performance on the routing test. For some testing purposes, moreover, special abbreviated batteries of 4 to 8 tests are suggested in the Guide.

Testing procedures are facilitated in several ways. Four item books, conveniently designed for flip-over presentation, display stimulus material on the test taker's side and condensed directions on the examiner's side. For most tests, each item has only one correct answer, available to the examiner on the record booklet and in the item books. All items are passed or failed according to specified standards. Five tests call for free responses, thus requiring the use of expanded scoring guidelines included in the Guide.

STANDARDIZATION AND NORMS. The standardization sample comprised slightly over 5,000 cases between the ages of 2 and 23 years, tested in 47 states (including Alaska and Hawaii) and the District of Columbia. The sample was stratified to match the proportions in the 1980 U.S. Census in geographic region, community size, ethnicity, and sex. Socioeconomic status, assessed by parental educational and occupational levels, revealed some overrepresentation at the upper and underrepresentation at the lower levels. This imbalance was adjusted through differential weighting of frequencies in the computation of normative values.

Raw scores on each of the 15 tests are converted to Standard Age Scores (SAS); these are normalized standard scores with mean of 50 and standard deviation of 8, within each of 30 age levels (ranging from 4-month intervals for ages 2 to 5 to a single interval for ages 17-11 to 23-11). The record booklet provides a chart for plotting a profile of the SASs on each test administered. It would have been desirable to give the test user some further guidance in the interpretation of this profile, beyond the simple statement in the Guide that the profile "shows at a glance the strengths and weaknesses of the examinee's cognitive abilities." At the very least, there should have been a reference to the table of minimum significant differences in the Appendix of the Technical Manual. Not all users will read the Technical Manual, much less its Appendices. It might also have been helpful to give the user some overall guidelines to follow, such as plotting score bands (± *SEM*) and observing overlap, as is done in some published group tests. To be sure, the present procedure is a marked improvement over the traditional clinical practice of comparing performance on subjectively grouped items of unknown reliability. Nevertheless, the technical improvements introduced in this regard could have been carried a bit farther through integration of available data in the Guide.

The normative tables also provide SASs for the four cognitive areas and for a composite score on the entire scale. These SASs have a mean of 100 and a standard deviation of 16, thus using the same units as the deviation IQs of the earlier editions. In addition, the normative tables permit the examiner to find SASs for any desired combination of two or more area scores ("partial composites"). For example, a combination of verbal and quantitative reasoning corresponds closely to scholastic aptitude and may be of particular interest in academic settings. In the introductory discussions in both Guide and Technical Manual, this composite is designated a measure of "crystallized abilities," in contrast to the "fluid-analytic abilities" identified with the single area score in abstract/visual reasoning. This distinction is of questionable value and is not well supported by the Stanford-Binet data themselves. The "fluid-analytic score" seems to be more a measure of spatial ability than of abstract-visual reasoning. Of the four tests in this area, only Pattern Analysis has a substantial loading on the abstract-visual factor; the other three tests have their major nongeneral loading in specificity factors (Technical Manual). Although introduced in discussing the theoretical rationale for the Fourth Edition, the crystallized-fluid distinction does not play a significant part in the actual processing of scores. The available procedures permit considerable flexibility in combining and interpreting area scores. For the well-qualified and sophisticated user, this is an advantage.

RELIABILITY AND VALIDITY. K-R 20 reliabilities were found for each 1-year age group in the standardization sample for ages 2 to 17, and for the 18–23-year group. Reliabilities of the composite score ranged from .95 to .99. Reliabilities were also high for the four cognitive area scores; although varying with the number of tests included, they ranged from .80 to .97. For the separate tests, most reliabilities fell in the .80s and low .90s, except for Memory for Objects, a short, 15-item test whose reliabilities ranged from .66 to .78. In general, all reliabilities tended to be slightly higher at the upper age levels. *SEM*s are also reported for each test, each area score, total composite, and all partial composites. Some retest reliabilities (2–8 month intervals) showed coefficients in the .90s for composite score, but the other results are difficult to interpret because of small samples, restricted ranges on some tests, and an appreciable practice effect.

Beginning with a hierarchical model of cognitive abilities, the test construction process (spanning some 8 years) pursued the dual goal of retaining as many item types as possible from the earlier editions while incorporating current ability constructs. Of the final tests, nine evolved from earlier item types, six used new types. Field trials on different age groups provided data for both quantitative and qualitative item analyses, including item-fairness reviews, as well as intercorrelations and factor analyses of preliminary tests. For the final scale, intercorrelations of all scores within the 17 age groups of the standardization sample were used in confirmatory factor analyses. By far the largest loadings were on a general factor. There was also some support for the area scores, although the identification of the abstract/visual factor appears questionable, and the evidence for a memory factor is weak, especially in the Bead Memory test. Special studies were conducted on "non-exceptional samples" and on exceptional samples (gifted, mentally retarded, and learning disabled) to find (*a*) correlations with Stanford-Binet (Form L-M), Wechsler scales, and the Kaufman Assessment Battery for Children (K-ABC), and (*b*) performance level on composite and area scores. In general, all the results conformed to expectations.

OVERVIEW. This basic restructuring of a well-established clinical instrument shows a high level of technical quality in its test construction procedures. At this stage, its principal limitation centers on communications with test users, especially in clinical settings. This limitation has been met in part by the publication of the optional Examiner's Handbook (Delaney & Hopkins, 1987). This volume includes cautions regarding possible misuse of scores, together with examples of clinical interpretations and some illustrative case reports. Moreover, it provides thorough and sophisticated procedures for profile analysis of subtest scores, which are lacking in the Guide and the Technical Manual.

REVIEWER'S REFERENCE

Delaney, E., & Hopkins, T. (1987). *Stanford-Binet Intelligence Scale examiner's handbook: An expanded guide for fourth edition users.* Chicago: The Riverside Publishing Company.

Review of the Stanford-Binet Intelligence Scale, Fourth Edition by LEE J. CRONBACH, Fellow, Center for the Study of Families, Children, and Youth, Stanford University, Stanford, CA:

This essentially new instrument (hereafter, SB4) is not much like the Stanford-Binet of former years. Traces of the thinking of Terman and Merrill survive in SB4 and its manuals—notably, some wise counsel on how to conduct individual tests. Many of the 15 subtests are ingenious modifications and extensions of tasks devised by Binet or Terman; others are adapted from the Cognitive Abilities Test (CogAT), the group test of Thorndike and Hagen; one, Matrices, descends from Spearman. The structure resembles that of CogAT, setting out to measure four correlated dimensions: Short-Term Memory, plus Verbal, Quantitative, and Abstract/Visual Reasoning. These combine into a Composite SAS ("standard age score"). I shall refer to the scores as M, V, Q, A, and CSAS. For possible supplementary use, the tester also records subtest scores.

Six subtests have a low floor and a high ceiling: Vocabulary, Comprehension, Quantitative, Pattern Analysis, Bead Memory, and Memory for Sentences. Two further subtests top out in early adolescence; three more have floors near the 12-year level, and four serve from age 7 upward. Above age 7, the older Stanford-Binet was predominantly a verbal test, whereas SB4 has a balance of the four dimensions at age 7 and above. Although Q and M are measured by few subtests at earlier ages, the sections are weighted equally in obtaining the CSAS.

Easy and hard items within a subtest often differ in character. In Pattern Analysis, for example, easy items use a three-piece formboard; intermediate items require matching a model made of cubes by arranging one to four cubes that have patterned faces; and in advanced items intricate printed designs are to be reproduced with many cubes. (This is the only subtest with strict time limits.) The brief verbal directions for A subtests are supplemented by sufficient pantomime to reduce the influence of listening comprehension.

My impression is that SB4 is less game-like than some other individual tests and will be less attractive to children. Some items call for choice response. Less can be inferred from styles and strategies when interaction with materials and with the examiner is reduced; and perhaps SB4 will elicit fewer idiosyncratic, clinically suggestive responses than the Wechsler Intelligence Scale for Children (WISC) or the traditional SB. A countervailing virtue is that the austerity of SB4 encourages conservative interpretation.

ADMINISTRATION AND SCORING. SB4 is efficient to administer. Items within a subtest are ordered by difficulty, which ascends rapidly; each pair of items is labeled with a letter. Vocabulary is given first as a "routing" test. Subsequently, M, V, Q, and A subtests are interspersed. Entering a chart with the subject's age and the performance on Vocabulary pinpoints a letter that identifies the level at which every further subtest is to begin. When the examinee has trouble on a subtest at this entry level, the tester backs down to where the person consistently passes. Otherwise, the examiner works upward until items are consistently failed. The examinee finds few items very easy or very hard, and encounters together all items of the same kind (an improvement over Binet's format). The examiner must judge rapidly whether to credit a response, deny credit, or probe further; scoring guides are succinct and handy.

Test development sought to enhance objectivity, subtest homogeneity, and comparability over ages. The publisher reports only a fraction of the findings made during test development. Thus, when a clinician tells me that items in a certain subtest are ordered incorrectly, according to her trials with children, I cannot review the authors' evidence for their ordering.

Some judgments can be questioned. I regret that the authors catered to tradition with an archaic 100 ± 16 scale for CSAS and for section SAS scores, then introduced for subtests an unprecedented 50 ± 8 scale. I favor the 50 ± 10 scale for all standard scores, to facilitate communication. If a child scores zero on a subtest (not rare at ages 2 and 3), the subtest is treated as spoiled and not counted. This would bias upward the section score, and could be critical in evaluating the severity of mental handicaps. Many Vocabulary and Comprehension items have more than one defensible answer, and usually any of them is credited. For "Why do people read newspapers?" answers listed in the scoring guide include "To find out what the news is," "Because it's fun," "To see what's on TV," and "Because the TV is broken." Full credit is given to any of the first three, none to the fourth. I doubt that there is empirical evidence to justify such scoring; from my armchair, I prefer Wechsler's principle of giving greater credit for a more basic answer.

The norming plan specified selection of communities, schools, and classrooms. Children were tested after their parents mailed to the publisher an agreement to participate. Parents from high occupational and educational strata responded more often and are overrepresented. Weighting adjusted the score distributions, but undersampling of lower strata reduces the accuracy of the norms. A side effect: the manual's statistical tables vary between unweighted and weighted calculations. This makes it hard to pursue some technical questions.

For a subtest too easy or too hard to be given to all members of an age sample, the reliabilities and correlations with other subtests are hard to interpret; some calculations are restricted to abler examinees, others to less able ones. Toward the end of the age range for such a subtest, norms were created by extrapolation. The procedures seem appropriate, but the extrapolation makes it more important than usual not to take seriously the numerical value of a low score.

RELIABILITY OF SCORES AND CONTRASTS. Users are given poor information on accuracy. The manual relies almost wholly on KR20 coefficients for subtests, compositing them into reliability coefficients for sections and CSAS. Because of the termination rule, items within subtests are not independent and all coefficients are inflated. The presentation, especially in Appendix F on differences between scores required for "significance," is misleading.

Far too little was invested in retest studies; retests, with a time lapse of 4 months or so, were made on fewer than 60 cases at age 5 and at age 8. The retest coefficients imply a standard error for CSAS nearly twice as great as those based on KR20. It seems likely that CSAS retest reliability is around .90. In small samples, the correlations of CSAS with IQ from Wechsler Preschool and Primary Scale of Intelligence (WPPSI) and Wechsler Intelligence Scale for Children—Revised (WISC-R) were .80 and .83, respectively. Retests with a change of examiners should be made on 100 cases at each early age and at spaced later ages; reliabilities for all contrasts in the profile should be reported; and, to minimize memory effects, the coefficients for subtests and broader scores should be derived from the stepped-up correlation of odd items on the first trial with even items on the second (and vice versa).

Until near-term stability is verified, it is especially important to be wary of measurement error at the lowest ages and in a section score based on one or two subtests. The full SB4 requires somewhat more testing time than its competitors, and shortened scales must be considered dubious until their reliability is established.

How useful is the profile? As the test is planned primarily to measure four categories of ability, subtest-specific factors constitute noise rather than signal. Therefore, I treat subtests as random representatives of their domains in evaluating how well each section score measures its postulated latent trait. For age 9, my coefficients are: CSAS, .91; V, .84; M, .73; A, .71; Q, .64. Coefficients tend to be larger in adolescence, lower in early childhood. These "domain validity" coefficients count subtest-specific variance as error, but not instability from session to session. (See Tryon, 1957; for a similar analysis of WPPSI, see Cronbach, Gleser, Rajaratnam, & Nanda, 1972, pp. 234-256, under "Universe 3.") Surprisingly, domain true scores for Q and A correlate perfectly at age 9.

Are differences between CSAS and a section SAS meaningful? It would be exceedingly liberal to take seriously a part-whole contrast having a domain validity of .40; V and M generally satisfy this standard at ages 8 and above, whereas Q and A almost never do. This conclusion appears consistent with the authors' factor analyses.

To speak in practical terms, assume that someone wants to identify persons whose true scores on a dimension are 1/2 standard deviation above or below their true Composite scores, and not persons with smaller differences. At the ages where V is most reliable an examiner with 100 cases, flagging V-minus-CSAS differences "significant at the .05 level," would have about

5 hits (worthwhile true difference, flagged), 5 misses, and 10 false positives. These proportions would not become more encouraging with other cut scores or a section other than V. So SB4 profile shape provides nothing beyond suggestions to be checked with additional evidence.

The SB4 selection of content is plausible especially for school-related testing, and the general factor is strong. At age 9, 88 per cent of the within-occasion variance comes from the child's *attention and adaptation to intellectual demands from an authority figure*. It appears entirely safe to impute importance to CSAS, on the basis of the vast body of research on ability to reason and to learn. Although CSAS appears to measure most English-speaking persons well, it of course does not indicate how well a person with limited command of English can function in his or her own community.

COMPARISON WITH OTHER TESTS. Further research on stability, especially at ages 2 through 6, may show SB4 to be as accurate as its competitors; I shall compare tests on the assumption that this uncertainty is resolved favorably. SB4 is shaped much less by clinical aims and experience than the competing batteries (or Binet's own scale). It concentrates on quantifying the attribute that a century of psychometrics has proved central to educational and vocational success. The unique feature of SB4 is continuity of subtests over a wide age range. This enables one to compare scores over a span of 20 years; but not many testers need to do that.

Testers familiar with a Wechsler scale can take advantage of years of personal experience and published suggestions for interpretation. They may find Wechsler performance subtests more informative for diagnosing educational difficulties and for cases with language handicaps than subtests of SB4. SB4 provides more information on memory than Wechsler scales do, and its well-engineered subtests may take on subtle interpretations as experience accumulates. Those who take norms most seriously may be uneasy with WISC-R and WPPSI norms compiled in the early 1970s, but when these tests and SB4 were given to the same children the Wechsler means ran only 3–5 IQ points higher. (I understand that new norms for WPPSI will soon be available, with a renormed WISC-R in a few years.)

The Kaufman Assessment Battery for Children (K-ABC) evidently assembled a better standardization sample than SB4. I surmise that it outdoes SB4 with respect to children's responsiveness to the tasks, and the richness of clinical clues in the performance. The sections of K-ABC are more distinct than those of SB4, and clinicians who like its structure of scores and norms are unlikely to find SB4 appealing. (SB4 V correlates .87 with K-ABC "Achievement," so the two instruments give similar weight to verbal abilities.) SB4 does not present separate norms for the disadvantaged; some users of K-ABC or the Wechsler-related System of Multicultural Pluralistic Assessment (SOMPA) will regret this, but I do not.

The McCarthy scales, despite out-of-date norms, appear to be the instrument of choice at early ages. For individualized educational planning in the primary grades, the British Ability Scales and Feuerstein's LPAD (Learning Potential Assessment Device) have special virtues. If SB4 has advantages over WISC-R and K-ABC for measurement at later ages, the case has not been made.

REVIEWER'S REFERENCES

Tryon, R. C. (1957). Reliability and behavior domain validity: Reformulation and historical critique. *Psychological Bulletin*, 54, 229-249.

Cronbach, L. J., Gleser, G. C., Nanda, H., & Rajaratnam, N. (1972). *The dependability of behavioral measurements: Theory of generalizability for scores and profiles*. New York: John Wiley & Sons, Inc.

[343]

Statements About Schools Inventory. Purpose: "Measures the extent to which high schools meet the needs of their students for a safe, stable environment . . . for interpersonal relationships . . . for success and achievement . . . and for personal growth." Students and teachers; 1981–85; SAS; 4 scales: Security, Social, Esteem, Self-Actualization; preliminary manual ('81, 14 pages); 1987 price data: $.20 per inventory (self-administered and self-scored); $100 plus $.20 per inventory for self-administration and publisher scoring and interpretation (partial service); $300 plus expenses for publisher to administer, score, and interpret 100–150 students and all volunteer teachers (complete service); [20–30] minutes; Gerald R. Smith, Thomas B. Gregory, and Richard B. Pugh; the Authors.*

[344]

Stenographic Skill-Dictation Test. Purpose: "Measures speed and accuracy in taking shorthand notes from dictated material." Applicants for stenographic positions; 1950–83; formerly called Test for Stenographic Skill; 3 scores: Difficulty Level, Dictation Speed, and Read-Back Ability; test may be administered orally or by cassette recording; 1987 price data: $96 per complete test kit including album with 5 cassette tapes and instruction manual ('83, 21 pages); $24 per cassette tape; $23 per instruction manual; administration time not reported; E. F. Wonderlic; E. F. Wonderlic Personnel Test, Inc.*

For additional information and reviews by Reign H. Bittner and Clifford E. Jurgensen of an earlier version, see 4:459.

Review of the Stenographic Skill-Dictation Test by VIRGINIA E. CORGAN, Associate Professor of Vocational and Adult Education, University of Nebraska-Lincoln, Lincoln, NE:

The Stenographic Skill-Dictation Test consists of five cassettes on which are recorded short business letters. The first cassette is a warm-up to be given prior to dictation of any test cassettes. The business letters on the cassettes are dictated at varying speeds, from 40 words per minute to 120 words per minute. The warm-up cassettes are letters at 40 and 60 words per minute, progressing to 120 words a minute.

If the test examiner prefers to dictate the tests, prints of the letters are available in test materials. These printed letters are accompanied by charts to aid the dictator in pacing the material at the speed desired.

The recorded letters are not done in office-style dictation. The dictator's voice is very clear, the enunciation perfect, and the dictation given in a well-modulated, male voice. Punctuation marks are not dictated and dictation of the salutation is not included within the timing. All letters are exactly 100 words.

In addition to the speed of dictation, a second factor considered is Difficulty Level. The difficulty level refers to Syllable Density. There are three levels incorporated into these materials: 140s, 160s, and 180s. Business teachers know these measures as syllabic intensity (s.i.). The measure is a count of the number of syllables per 100 words. The number 140 means that 100 words have 140 syllables, or in business-teacher terms: syllabic intensity is 1.4. In other words, averaged, every word has 1.4 syllables. The syllable density count allows for variations, such as 141, 142, etc.

Another measure provided by the Stenographic Skill-Dictation Test is the length of sentence. The easier letters in the series (s.i. 140, 160) usually have six sentences each and these are most often simple sentences. The higher-speed letters contain five to seven sentences, and these sentences generally will be compound and complex sentences. It is possible to control only the length and type of sentences in the test by choosing letters of 1.4 and 1.6 syllabic intensity or of 1.8 syllabic intensity.

The directions accompanying the test cassettes and letter copies are clear and the test easy to administer. The literature accompanying the test discusses this test as a pre-occupational test designed for placement of a stenographer within a business. The assumption is that the applicant who performs well at top difficulty and speed levels will be suited to certain positions. A qualifier to this assumption is the examiner must have comparative scores between the applicant and those persons who have been previously hired on the basis of like tests.

The test materials laud its "instant results." A statement from the test manual describes this test as being quicker than comparable measures, because the applicant merely reads the letter back from shorthand notes instead of transcribing it on a typewriter. The justification given for reading instead of typing is that typing speed is usually measured by a separate test and that with familiarity in a given job, a stenographer's dictation and typing rates will increase.

In giving the test, it is up to the examiner to find the highest speed and the highest difficulty level at which the applicant can take shorthand. Grades are assigned to the test as follows:

> A letter read back easily with no errors is "A" quality; a letter read accurately with two or less errors is "B"; a satisfactory letter with three or more errors or changes (which make sense) receives "C."

> Three scoring symbols are used: I, II, or III gives the difficulty level of 140-, 160-, or 180-syllable density; 60, 80, 100, etc. represent the dictation speed; and A, B, C, D is assigned to the "read-back" ability.

An added statement to scoring directions is that to judge the neatness of typing, the test taker may be asked to transcribe a letter that was *successfully* read back. Again it is noted that typing skill should be measured separately.

The test measures the variables we knew to be important for competent office performance in an earlier decade. New variables may deserve attention. This reviewer was troubled by the word content of the letters. There is not a technical word within any of the 13 letters in the set. Current business letters are replete with highly technical words and phrases. The mundane words making up the test selections should be adjusted to more realistically reflect modern business realities.

The numbers used in the test materials are easily remembered, relatively short examples. Clippinger and Hammer (1987) in their recent machine transcription research found that "the concentration of number expressions and syllabic intensity of words have greater effects . . . on performance accuracy." They further concluded that concentration of number expressions "affected both speed and accuracy of machine transcription performance."

The average syllabic intensity (s.i.) of business correspondence years ago was determined to be 1.6 (Perry, 1968). Therefore, to provide a warmup below 1.6 may be helpful to put test applicants at ease, but to test at any rate below 1.6 seems out of order.

Each letter, as was pointed out, is precisely 100 words long. A person who has taken shorthand knows many secretaries can retain enough of the sentences to play "catch-up" at the end of a 100-word letter. A person could, thus, conceivably take a single 100-word letter at 140 words a minute, but if given a 300-word letter could not function at that speed.

The difficulty level of the copy used in the tests is considered only in syllable density (syllabic intensity) and in length of sentences. In typewriting when the three factors of high frequency words, stroke intensity, and syllable intensity were examined, the best single index of difficulty appeared to be high frequency words in typewriting (Bell, 1950). This reviewer would advocate that test letters should have a variety of sentence structures with letters containing unlike numbers of sentences for an office-style test.

The fact the stenographer is not required to type the dictated letters makes this just a shorthand skill test. A single 100-word letter may not even be indicative of true shorthand skill. A more valid test would be dictation of several letters to be transcribed on typewriter or word processor, rather than to read back each letter immediately after recording it as required in current directions.

This reviewer does not agree with the test authors that typing should be tested separately. Even if such a test were to be given, a typing test is not indicative of a transcription test in which spelling, punctuation, number sense, and the "sense" of a letter must be taken into consideration. It is these components of the stenographic tasks that are really important. If an individual can take shorthand at 140 words a minute but cannot transcribe it into a mailable letter, the stenographic skill is of little import. Although the read-back method provides a rapid analysis of skills, this simplicity may be error-prone.

No indication of the reliability or validity of the test was given by test authors. Instead, as cited earlier, the test examiner is left to rate the candidate's test against other tests taken by stenographers engaged in the company, or against other applicants. Thus, test results may be rated differently company by company.

The test has good potential. Most employers who require testing are giving similar types of tests. Overall, the following changes should be considered. Some of these changes could be accomplished by the test administrator. (*a*) Include letters with syllable density of not less than 160, and increase density to 200. (*b*) Incorporate words in the current economic news and update the language. Occasionally use some large numbers. (*c*) Use letters of varying size, 100 to 200 words per letter and use some feminine voices. (*d*) Dictate a series of two to three letters and require these to be transcribed into mailable copy.

REVIEWER'S REFERENCES

Bell, M. L. (1950). *Some factors of difficulty in typewriting copy.* Unpublished doctoral dissertation, University of Oklahoma, Norman, OK.

Perry, D. (1968). *An analytical comparison of the relative word-combination frequencies of business correspondence with phrase frequencies of selected shorthand textbooks.* University of North Dakota, Grand Forks, ND.

Clippinger, D. A., & Hammer, J. N. (1987). *A study of factors contributing to the difficulty of voice-recorded text.* (Report to Delta Pi Epsilon Research Foundation). St. Peter, MN: Delta Pi Epsilon National Office.

Review of the Stenographic Skill-Dictation Test by MICHAEL J. STAHL, Professor and Head, Department of Management, School of Business, Clemson University, Clemson, SC:

The Stenographic Skill-Dictation Test is easy to understand and administer. Stenographic skills are evaluated across a variety of controlled speed levels (words per minute) and complexity levels (syllables per line).

The test can be administered either via prerecorded tapes or an administrator reading the material. Herein lies the only apparent shortcoming. To quote from the Foreword: "The dictation of the Test letters to the applicant may be accomplished by using the professionally recorded Stenographic Skill Dictation Cassette Tapes, or you may read the Test letters directly to the applicant yourself. The Cassette Tapes provide an easy to use, accurate method of administering the test. Of course by dictating the Test letters yourself, you may gain additional information about the ease and confidence of the applicant." Using the tapes with some applicants and reading to others creates uneven testing conditions. The differential testing conditions could dramatically influence the results. The user is encouraged to determine exactly which behaviors are to be evaluated (i.e., stenographic skills and/or ease and confidence of the applicants) and then consistently evaluate all applicants on that basis using either the prerecorded tapes or reading the transcript.

[345]

The Stetson Reading-Spelling Vocabulary Test. Purpose: To determine achievement levels in reading and spelling and to determine whether or not a student should receive instruction in the Reading-Spelling Vocabulary Program, and if so, to predict at which lesson instruction should begin. Grades 1–14; 1983–86; RSVT; "norm-referenced and criterion-referenced"; equivalent forms A and B for each of 4 subtests at 4 levels can be administered as Reading test or Spelling test; 1988 price data: $59 per complete program; $16 per replacement chart (form A or B) and 50 record forms; $17 per manual ('84, 72 pages); Elton G. Stetson; PRO-ED, Inc.*

a) READING TEST. Grades 1–12; individual; [5] minutes.

b) SPELLING TEST. Grades 2–14; uses same word lists as Reading test; $14 per pad of 50 spelling record forms; [30] minutes.

[Note: The publisher advised in April 1989 that this test is now out of print.]

Review of The Stetson Reading-Spelling Vocabulary Test by THOMAS J. KEHLE, Professor of Educational Psychology, University of Connecticut, Storrs, CT:

The underlying rationale of the Stetson Reading-Spelling Vocabulary Test (RSVT) is that less than .3 of one percent of the total words available in the English language are employed in 90 percent of everyday communication—including writing, speaking, and reading. Consequently, the author assumed that mastery over the core vocabulary of the 1,000 frequently used words (out of an available pool of 350,000) would enhance literacy and improve reading skills and written expression. Identification of the frequently employed words has resulted in the development of a 900-word vocabulary list, termed the Reading-Spelling Vocabulary Program (RSVP). This list is divided into 60 lessons, each comprised of 15 vocabulary words, arranged in an increasing order of difficulty from the primary grades through high school.

The RSVT was designed as a short placement test to determine the level of the student's ability and a starting point for instruction. The RSVT has two equivalent forms that, according to the author, can be employed as both a criterion placement and a norm-referenced test. The purpose of the RSVT is to determine reading and spelling achievement, and whether or not the student should receive instruction, and at what level, in the 900-word RSVP. Further, the author has developed the Stetson Reading-Spelling Approach (SRSA), a five-step system to teach students with identified deficits to read and spell vocabulary words.

The Stetson Reading-Spelling Vocabulary Test (RSVT) contains 120 words. These 120 words were obtained, through a random selection procedure, from the 900-word RSVP. The 120-word RSVT is divided into four 30-word sections arranged in an increasing order of difficulty. However, the 30 words in each section are not arranged in order of increasing difficulty. It is assumed by the author that RSVT's word list is one of the most reliable methods of predicting reading achievement, and that the production-type spelling test, requiring the subject to write the words from dictation, is one of the most reliable methods of determining spelling achievement. When employed to evaluate reading achievement, the RSVT is designed for students in grade levels 1 through 9, or for students in grades 10 or above who are suspected of possessing reading skills below the ninth-grade level. When employed as a production-type spelling test, the RSVT is considered by the author to be valid for students in grade levels 2 through 14.

The instructions for administration and scoring are clearly presented in the manual. With respect to the reading test, raw scores are easily converted to grade-equivalent scores; in addition, the purported norm-referenced scores can be used as a criterion placement to aid instructional intervention, and in the development of individual education plans. The reading test's alternate form was designed to aid in the assessment of instructional gains. With respect to the spelling test, the administration can be designed for either groups or individual students. As in the case of the reading test, raw scores are easily converted to grade-equivalent scores; in addition, they can be employed to determine instructional placement, and in the design of individual education plans. The spelling test also has an alternate form.

Support for the reliability of the RSVT reading test is based on a single investigation of children from one middle-class school district. This study involved 266 nonrandomly selected subjects enrolled in grades 1 through 9 who were reading on grade-level. The equivalent-form reliability coefficient reported was exceptionally high—.995. It is unclear how the .99 reliability coefficient was obtained. Data are not presented for each of the nine grade levels tested; presumably the .995 is based on all 266 students in the entire grade range 1 through 9. This wide range of achievement undoubtedly contributes to the inflation of the reliability coefficient. A serious omission is the lack of a table of means and standard deviations as a function of grade level and sex.

The validity data presented for the RSVT reading test included the same 266 subjects used to determine the reliability. The validity study involved comparison of RSVT scores with Wide Range Achievement Test (WRAT) total scores. The correlation between RSVT Form A and the WRAT was .86; the correlation between RSVT Form B and the WRAT was .85. No means and standard deviations were presented as a function of grade level or sex.

In another study, using 65 remedial readers from grades 2 through 11, the relationship between the RSVT reading test and the Woodcock Reading Mastery Test (WRMT) Word Identification subtest was .93. The relationship between the RSVT and the WRMT Comprehension subtest was .86. Omitted are the correlations between the RSVT and the other subtests of the WRMT, and means and standard deviations as a function of grade level and sex.

Support for the reliability of the RSVT spelling test is also based on a single investigation. This study involved 1,371 students enrolled in grades 2 through 14. Equivalent-form reliability coefficients were derived for each grade level. The coefficients ranged from .81 to .97 with an average of .89. The internal-consistency coefficients ranged from .89 to .96 with a mean of .93.

Support for the validity of the RSVT spelling test is based on the same investigation of 1,371 students used to determine the test's reliability. Raw scores from the RSVT spelling test were compared with raw scores obtained from the spelling subtest of the WRAT. The coefficients ranged from .77 to .91 with a mean of .84.

The standardization of the RSVT reading test is insufficient and seriously limits the use of the instrument. The standardization sample was not randomly selected and was based on a single investigation involving one middle-class school district. No information is presented on race, ethnicity, social class, or other demographic characteristics. Means and standard deviations as a function of grade level and sex were also omitted. Similarly, the standardization of the RSVT spelling test, although more detailed than the reading test, is still deficient.

In summary, the RSVT is a system purporting to provide normative and criterion-referenced information about students' reading and spelling achievement. Test results are then employed to select instructional interventions or design individual education plans. The attempt to relate assessment to intervention is laudable. However, what support is presented in the manual for the reliability and validity of both the reading and spelling tests is restrictive. Adequate normative data are missing. Given the dearth of investigations employing the RSVT and the fact that the standardization sample is insufficient and not representative, the use of the instrument should be limited to attempts at further development and refinement. Development of adequate standardization for the instrument and further investigations employing the RSVT may demonstrate it as an economical means of reading-achievement assessment. Further, the RSVT may be beneficial in that it does appear to provide well-designed interventions based on the diagnostic information obtained. However, the basic assumption of the RSVT system (i.e., increased mastery over the core vocabulary would enhance the student's literacy in reading and writing) remains untested. Given the extent of current development of the RSVT, employing the RSVT for placement, or in the design of interventions, would not be warranted.

Review of The Stetson Reading-Spelling Vocabulary Test by TIMOTHY Z. KEITH, Associate Professor of Education and Psychology, Virginia Polytechnic Institute and State University, Blacksburg, VA:

The Stetson Reading-Spelling Vocabulary Test (Stetson) is a list of 120 common words used to estimate student achievement in reading and spelling. The same word list is used for both the spelling and the reading tests; students read the words aloud for the reading test and write the words for the spelling test. Two 120-word lists (Forms A and B) are available.

The Stetson word lists are subsets of the 900-word list of the Stetson Reading-Spelling Vocabulary Program (Program), which is intended as a list of the most commonly used words in speaking, reading, and writing. The Program was developed by comparing and combining the word lists from 14 high-frequency-word studies of children and adults (e.g., the Dolch list of 220 basic sight words). The criteria used to choose words appear sound. Following selection, the words were ranked by teachers in order of their presumed difficulty and grouped into four levels. Each of the four levels was further subdivided into 15 "lessons," for a total of 60 lessons.

To create the Stetson from the Program, four words were chosen at random from each lesson, with two words assigned to Form A and two to Form B. The Levels from the Program were retained in the test; each form contains four subtests corresponding to the Levels in the Program. The ranking of words by difficulty was not retained within subtests, however. Instead, word order was scrambled within subtests to minimize frustration that might result when students reach their ceiling.

Separate test forms are used for the reading and the spelling tests; these, along with a training manual and reading chart, comprise the Stetson kit. The materials are clear and the manual is straightforward. The sections on administration are very good, and a section on teaching reading and spelling vocabulary may be helpful. The sections on reliability and validity are misleading.

The reading tests are administered individually by having examinees read the entire 120-item word list. The spelling test may be administered individually or in groups; the entire list is also used. Although a "cut-time" method of administration is also described (involving the administration of selected subtests), it is not the preferred method. This need to administer the entire test seems a weakness of the Stetson. First, it makes the test unnecessarily long (the 5-minute estimate for completion of the reading test probably applies to the cut-time method). Second, the procedure may be frustrating for many examinees and examiners. If the author is truly concerned about avoiding frustration, it would make more sense to arrange the words in order (based on standardization data rather than teacher opinion) and establish basal and ceiling rules for the test.

The Stetson is intended for two primary purposes: to provide an estimate of students' reading and spelling achievement, and to act as a criterion-referenced placement test into the Program. Consequently, raw scores may be converted into grade equivalents and can be used in an "instructional placement" chart. Both scoring methods have problems. Grade equivalents are the only type of normative score provided. The meaning of the scores is stated incorrectly in the manual. The instructional planning/placement scoring is intended to allow placement of students into appropriate lessons in the Program based on their performance on the four subtests of the Stetson. But the logic behind the placement conversions is suspect; it assumes that students will miss words in the same order as in the Program word list. This is an especially questionable assumption because the order of that list was based on teacher opinion rather than actual student data.

No information is presented in the Stetson manual concerning the norming of the scale. Information concerning reliability and validity is presented, but much of that information is inaccurate or misleading. For example, there are errors in the discussion of the meaning of reliability (the effect on reliability of homogeneity and heterogeneity is reversed), and the manual labels the concurrent validity estimates presented as predictive validity.

Reliability and validity information concerning the Stetson as a reading test appear impressive but are undoubtedly inflated. The manual reports an alternate-forms reliability estimate of .995 for the reading test. This coefficient was calculated, however, using raw scores from an extremely extended range of students in grades 1 through 9. Concurrent validity was estimated by correlating the Stetson with the Wide Range Achievement Test (WRAT) and the Woodcock Reading Mastery Test, but again it appears the raw scores on the Stetson were correlated with developmental scores on the two criterion measures (raw or grade scores on the WRAT and mastery scores on the Woodcock) across a very wide age and grade range. Thus, reliability and validity estimates of the reading scale are inflated by the extended age ranges used, and should be ignored. Users should also ignore the author's implication that the high correlation found between the Stetson and the Woodcock Reading Comprehension test (.86) demonstrates the validity of word recognition tests as measures of reading. Given the extended age range used, the Stetson would likely correlate almost as highly with a math test.

More adequate information is presented concerning the reliability and validity of the Stetson as a spelling test; all correlations were computed separately for each grade level. The median alternate-forms reliability estimate was .89 (range .81 to .97) for a sample of 1,371 students in grades 2 through 14; median split-half reliability was .93 for both forms (range .89 to .96). To establish concurrent validity, raw spelling scores from the Stetson and the WRAT were correlated separately for each grade level in the sample; validity estimates ranged from .77 (grades 6 and 13) to .91 (grade 4; median coefficient = .84).

SUMMARY. The Stetson could provide a valuable assessment of children's, adolescents', and adults' ability to read and spell common vocabulary; it does not do so in its present form. There are problems with the structure of the scale, the norms are not described, and there is little information concerning the reliability and validity of the scale, especially when used as a reading test. To fulfill its intended purpose, the Stetson words should be placed in an empirically derived order (both in the test and in the larger Program), basals and ceilings should be established, a careful standardization program should be undertaken and accurately described in the manual, and the reliability and validity of the scale should be established. Other types of derived scores should be available, and the validity of the scale as a placement device into the Program should be established. Until these weaknesses are remedied, the use of the Stetson should be limited to a screening test for use in placement into the Stetson Program and as a research instrument. At present, the WRAT, despite its limitations (cf. Matuszek, 1985; Saigh, 1985), probably provides a better estimate of reading and spelling vocabulary.

REVIEWER'S REFERENCES

Matuszek, P. (1985). [Review of Wide Range Achievement Test.] In J. V. Mitchell, Jr. (Ed.), *The ninth mental measurements yearbook* (pp. 1734-1736). Lincoln, NE: Buros Institute of Mental Measurements.

Saigh, P. A. (1985). [Review of Wide Range Achievement Test.] In J. V. Mitchell, Jr. (Ed.), *The ninth mental measurements yearbook* (p. 1736). Lincoln, NE: Buros Institute of Mental Measurements.

[346]

Stress Analysis System. Purpose: Helps to identify possible sources of negative stress in ones life and recognize the symptoms of stress and provides techniques for modifying ones reactions to stress. Adults; 1983–85; self-administered, self-scored; 6 scores: Type A, Anger In, Situational, Health, Accountability, Interpersonal; 1985 price data: $6.50 per booklet ('85, 13 pages) including test and profile; administration time not reported; P. B. Nelson, K. M. Schmidt, and Noel Nelson; Interdatum, Inc.*

Review of the Stress Analysis System by MARY LOU KELLEY, Assistant Professor of Psychology, Louisiana State University, Baton Rouge, LA:

The Stress Analysis System is a 114-item instrument designed to evaluate the amount of stress experienced by an individual across six different domains. The test is apparently completed, scored, and interpreted by the test taker. The stated purpose of the test is to help the respondent identify sources of negative stress and recognize symptoms of stress. Test materials include a number of techniques for modifying reactions to stress. The test is packaged in a professional and appealing manner. The test booklet is divided into several sections including directions for completing and interpreting the results of the test, discussion of the nature and types of stress, and a description of various interventions for alleviating specific types of stress.

The instructions for completing and scoring the test are simple and straightforward. The respondent determines whether each statement is true or false. Next, the test taker sums the items endorsed in each of six areas. Scores obtained in each area are plotted on a profile that indicates the degree to which a given score reflects low or high stress levels.

The six areas of stress purportedly measured by the test are described as:

1. The Type "A" Controller Personality. This personality type is characteristic of individuals who are high achieving, driven to succeed, never happy with their performance, and have a strong desire to control themselves and their environment.

2. The Anger-In Personality. This type is characteristic of individuals who are unassertive and/or find it difficult to express feelings.

3. Situational Stress and Life Readjustments. These items reflect stress due to life changes such as a divorce.

4. Corollary Health Habits. Health habits are measured by items on substance abuse, diet, and exercise.

5. Low Accountability/Victim Syndrome. This pattern is characteristic of individuals who do not assume responsibility for their circumstances, believe they have little influence over their environment, or blame others for their shortcomings or problems.

6. Interpersonal Stress. These stressors are related to a lack of adequate social support.

The items making up each of the six areas appear to correspond with the author's descriptions of types of stress, thus demonstrating face validity, at least. The items themselves are brief and clear. The stress domains targeted on the test correspond to commonly held notions about stress and are, in fact, constructs with some research support in terms of their relationship to stress reactions. However, the authors did not provide any data on or description of test construction. Apparently, the items were intuitively selected and grouped rather than empirically derived.

With regard to other aspects of reliability and validity, absolutely no data were provided on the psychometric characteristics of the test. Thus, it is not known whether the test measures what it is intended to measure or in any way is a useful instrument. Although the profile sheet indicates whether a score represents a low or high amount of stress in a specific domain, the authors did not substantiate empirically the validity of their stress "barometers." The references cited as support for the stress domains and treatment suggestions incorporated in the test are, primarily, self-help books. No mention was made of any data available in support of the instrument.

A serious concern related to the use of the Stress Analysis System is that the test manual offers an array of interventions for reducing stress yet fails to mention the importance of professional help in assisting individuals in stress management. Discussions on alleviating stress present fairly sound advice, yet do not mention the difficulty that may be experienced by many individuals who attempt to carry out the suggestions. Nor did the authors mention any of the negative consequences that may be encountered when a suggestion is used incompetently, ineffectively, or just used at all. For example, the authors discuss the importance of communicating assertively yet fail to mention that changes in one's assertiveness may not always be well received by important people in the subject's life.

In summary, the Stress Analysis System is a slickly-packaged instrument designed to assist individuals in evaluating the degree to which they experience stress. Test materials provide information on methods of alleviating stress. The instrument is apparently completed, scored, and interpreted by the test taker. As the authors did not report any data on the reliability, validity, or standardization of the test, the utility of the test is unknown. Therefore, I recommend that the test not be used for any purpose other than research aimed at establishing its psychometric characteristics. Results from the test have unknown validity and reliability and, in my opinion, could be easily misinterpreted by individuals unfamiliar with psychological evaluation.

Review of the Stress Analysis System by JAYNE E. STAKE, Professor of Psychology, University of Missouri-St. Louis, St. Louis, MO:

P. B. Nelson developed the first version of the Stress Analysis System (SAS) in 1978. The

SAS was originally designed for use in training physicians to be better aware of psychological factors in stress-related disease. The items were rationally derived, based upon stress theory. The current form of the SAS was first published in 1981.

The SAS comprises six scales purported to measure six factors that can lead to stress: Type A tendencies, involving preoccupation with time and results; Anger In tendencies, the inability to express anger appropriately; Situational, the number of major adjustments and changes experienced within the past 12 months; Health, hazardous health habits, including poor eating patterns, smoking, and excessive alcoholic consumption; Accountability, the tendency to see oneself as a victim, rather than in control of one's life situation; and Interpersonal, problems in interpersonal relationships.

Also included in the SAS booklet are directions for obtaining a score for each scale, a Stress Profile for charting the six scores, information for interpreting the meaning of each scale, and suggestions for possible changes in behavior and attitudes for participants scoring high on the scales.

There are virtually no data available regarding the psychometric properties of the SAS. Information regarding the reliability and validity of the scales has not been obtained. Of prime importance is the lack of evidence demonstrating that scores on any of the scales are associated with stress-related disease. This is a key assumption made by the authors, and it has not been tested.

A related psychometric problem is that no information is available to justify the scaling of items on any of the six measures. Participants are instructed that if they have scored above a certain level on each scale they have a high potential for stress symptoms. There is no evidence provided to substantiate a relationship between the stated cutoff scores and stress symptoms.

An additional limitation of the SAS is that the internal consistency of the scales has not been established. The authors have assumed that each scale measures one factor in stress-related disease, but the scales may not be factorially pure. This possibility is most evident in the Accountability scale, which includes a number of items that may not be closely related to one another. That is, items on the scale may measure more than one factor or dimension, leading to a summary score of unknown properties. A factor-analysis study is clearly needed.

On the positive side, the SAS provides a clear and helpful explanation to the layperson about the relationship between stress factors and health problems. Participants who are high scorers are given a rationale for changes in their attitudes and life styles, and specific suggestions for changes are provided for each of the six scales. The suggestions could provide a beginning for those seeking better ways of coping with and avoiding stress.

In summary, the SAS has some potential as a self-help tool for diagnosing potential sources of stress and for finding new strategies for reducing stress. Scores should be interpreted with caution, however, as the validity of the scales has not been established.

[347]

Stress Audit. Purpose: "Samples the magnitude and types of stress [and stress symptoms] experienced by the respondent and assesses relative vulnerability to stress." Adults; 1983–87; self-administered; 16 scores: Situational (Family, Individual Roles, Social Being, Environment, Financial, Work/School), Symptom (Muscular System, Parasympathetic Nervous System, Sympathetic Nervous System, Emotional, Cognitive System, Endocrine, Immune System), Vulnerability, Total Situational Stress, Total Symptoms; 1987 price data: $20 per specimen set including Stress Audit booklet, profile sheet, and manual ('87, 44 pages); [20–30] minutes; Lyle H. Miller, Alma Dell Smith, and Bruce L. Mehler (manual only); Biobehavioral Associates.*

Review of the Stress Audit by ROLF A. PETERSON, Professor of Psychology, The George Washington University, Washington, DC:

The Stress Audit is a comprehensive measure of the factors associated with stress problems in that it assesses both perception of past and future problems and a full range of physical and emotional stress reactions. Additionally, a Vulnerability scale involving health habits and social support is provided. The Vulnerability scale was developed to measure variables that moderate or buffer the effect of stressors. The measurement of stressors, stress reaction, and a moderator variable in one scale is unique within the stress area, except for the Parenting Stress Index (Abidin, 1983) which has more limited dimensions and relates to a special population. A reasonable amount of normative data is available for stress clinic clients and college students. Some data are available for an adult workforce. The scale has good internal consistency reliability and test-retest reliability for 1 week, 2 weeks, and 6 weeks. As expected, the lowest test-retest reliabilities are for a 6-week period (.54 to .72) and are consistent with an environment in which stressors and reactions can change rapidly. The .63 6-week test-retest reliability coefficient for the vulnerability scale is somewhat low because it measures support and habits that would be expected to be quite stable over a 6-week period of time.

The major concerns with the scale are the validity of the individual scales and the validity of the measure as a whole. Interscale correlations suggest an appropriate factor structure and semi-independence of the subscales. On the other hand, criterion group and quasi-experimental studies raise serious questions about the validity of the scale or, at least, suggest data are needed for groups more clearly expected to show differences on stressor and stress reaction measures. The mean scores for the college sample and the stress clinic samples appear very similar and no statistical comparison between the two groups is offered. Presumably, large differences should be present if the stress clinic clients were experiencing moderate to severe stress problems. Data on treatment effects were not presented in the manual. The primary validity study presented is the comparison of scores for students just prior to final exams and 6 weeks later. All scales show significant *t*-test differences in the expected direction, but the changes are small and it is unclear if the changes are clinically meaningful. This also raises a question as to interpretation because an increase in recognition of stressors and an arousal reaction may be appropriate reactions to coping with demands as long as the reactions are within reasonable limits. Another analysis that compares students who work to nonworking students finds that working students report significantly fewer stressors and stress reactions. Although the results are interpreted to support the Stress Audit as a valid measure, the reasons working students might have fewer stressors and fewer stress reactions than nonworking students are not clear.

Another major issue existing in terms of the validity of the diagnostic information regarding need to change or seek help (for example, in one test format the measure is presented as a self-evaluation tool) is that a *T* score above 50 is defined as having a problem with stress. This arbitrary definition is based on the general assumption that we live in a stressful environment and frequently must deal with multiple stressors. No experimental evidence is offered that *T* scores in the 50 to 70 range have deleterious effects, nor is it suggested that high scores should exist over some period of time before change is definitely needed. The prescriptions for change and treatment suggested in the manual are consistent with published treatment data but the issue of the validity of scores remains.

The scale was well constructed in terms of general stress models and the empirical evidence on stressors, stress reactions, and moderate variables. The comprehensive format of the Stress Audit and the reliability of the scales forms the basis for a potentially highly valuable measurement instrument in the area of stress research and services. Prior to adoption of this scale for formal use, validity of the scales and profiles must be demonstrated. For the time being, the scale would appear to be of great value as a structured interview procedure for use in a clinical setting to obtain information on stressors and reactions along with other interview information. REVIEWER'S REFERENCE

Abidin, R. R. (1983). Parenting Stress Index. Brandon, VT: CPPC.

[348]

Stress Management Questionnaire. Purpose: Identifies how one responds to life stressors and copes with stress. Adults and adolescents; 1983–87; SMQ; manual title is *Stress Management Training System*; 11 scores: Stress Coping Skills (Hostility, Perfectionism, Time-Orientation, Disappointment, Negative Mood, Under Achievement, Tension), Stress Effects (General Stress, Life/Work Satisfaction), Stressors (Life Events, Hassles/Concerns); 2 forms: participant, companion; completed by self and by a close companion; 1987 price data: $7.95 per system (including Stress Management Questionnaire—Participant Form, Stress Management Questionnaire—Companion Form, Stress Management Scoring Form, and Stress Management Guide); $17.95 per manual ('86, 64 pages); (20–25) minutes; James C. Petersen; The Assessment Centre.*

Review of the Stress Management Questionnaire by JAYNE E. STAKE, Professor of Psychology, University of Missouri-St. Louis, St. Louis, MO:

The Stress Management Questionnaire (SMQ) is designed as a broad-based system of measures to diagnose problems in stress management behaviors and current life stressors. The assumptions underlying the SMQ are cognitive-behavioral in nature and are explicitly stated in the test manual. They include the basic tenet that stress-related health problems can be ameliorated through better coping strategies and altered thinking patterns.

James Peterson began work on the scale in 1976. He assembled a set of questionnaiure items designed to test "Type A" behavior and several other factors associated with health. He indicates the questionnaire underwent a number of revisions during the period, 1976–1982, but provides no information about the early forms of the SMQ.

The current form of the SMQ includes seven "Stress Coping Skills" subscales: Hostility, Perfectionism, Time-Orientation, Disappointment, Negative Mood, Under Achievement, and Relaxation; two "Effects of Stress" subscales: General Stress (physical symptoms of stress) and Life/Work Satisfaction; and two "Stressors" subscales: Life Events and Concerns. A pamphlet, the "Stress Management Questionnaire Report" provides instructions so that participants can calculate their subscale scores and chart their "Personal Stress Profile." The "Stress Management Guide" provides descriptions of each subscale and suggestions for participants who score high on each subscale. In addition, a "Companion Form" of the SMQ is available for the purpose of obtaining others' perceptions of a participant's behavior and life situation.

An earlier form of the questionnaire was evaluated in 1982 by Peterson and Lawrence. An unpublished paper describing the results of this study (Peterson & Lawrence, 1982) provides the only psychometric data available on the SMQ. In this study, 285 employees from six companies, including line staff, management, and supervisors, were tested. The subjects' responses to the SMQ were factor analyzed as a means of testing the structure of the subscales. Based on factor loadings of individual items, some reorganization of the subscales was undertaken, resulting in the current form of the test. This refinement of the subscales on the basis of empirical data is a strength of the SMQ. Unfortunately, such test development is rarely done for multiscaled tests of this type.

eterson and Lawrence have failed, however, to cross validate their revised scale with a second sample of subjects. The need to cross validate is especially important in this instance because of the size and nature of the 1982 sample. It was a relatively small sample and may not be representative of the average employee in the work setting. Although the sample was described as being stratified and randomly selected, it included a disproportionate number of women (64%) and a disproportionate number indicating no alcohol consumption (54%).

A related problem is that the scaling of the items in each subtest is based on the scores from the sample of 285. This is a small sample to rely upon for scaling the items. Clearly, there are some problems with the scaling of some of the subtests. First, the Life Events scale does not appear to have been appropriately scaled. According to the SMQ profile, the average person experiences between 9 and 10 events from the Life Events list within a 12-month period. Given the relatively rare occurrence of any one of the events (e.g., divorce, death, major financial loss), this number is certainly inaccurate.

A second problem with the scaling is a basic assumption underlying the scaling process. The authors designated low, medium, and high scores for each subscale on the basis of the 1982 sample. Furthermore, they state that individuals scoring in those ranges are at low, moderate, and high risk for stress-related health problems. The authors did not have sufficient information to make this judgment, and it may well be that the average subject in the sample was not at moderate risk. Hence, the manual's statement that scores in the medium range should be identified as a cause for concern may be false and misleading.

An additional scaling problem is evident in the General Stress and Life Events scales. In the case of General Stress, symptoms (e.g., headaches, racing pulse) are added to form a summary score. Given the scaling for this subtest, an individual could indicate "very frequent" headaches, and might, in fact, suffer from debilitating stress-related migraines, yet score low on this scale of the physical effects of stress. The same problem is evident for the Life Events scale; subjects could indicate a small number of very disruptive life events (e.g., loss of job, jail term) and yet appear to be low on life stressors. Individual life events should have been weighted to reflect the severity of the disruption likely to be caused by each event.

There are no reliability data on the SMQ. Internal consistency and test-retest measures should be, but are not available. There are some validity data from the 1982 study, providing a mixed picture of positive and negative findings. Some stress coping scales were related to health problems, life/job satisfaction, number of hours worked, and level of work responsibility. However, other tested relationships failed to confirm the authors' expectations. Negative Mood and Relaxation did not correlate with stress effects nor with the Life Events scale. Also, subjects' smoking, alcohol consumption, and exercise did not relate to the stress coping scales. Hence, there is only modest support for the validity of the scales.

SUMMARY AND RECOMMENDATIONS. The SMQ represents an effort to provide a set of factorially pure subscales to measure stress coping skills and attributions, stress symptoms, and life stressors. It is designed so that it can be self-administered, self-scored, and self-interpreted. It was developed primarily for use in stress management training programs in business and mental health settings.

Although some work has been done to test the underlying factor structure and validity of the scales, critical psychometric data are not available, including reliability coefficients and cross validation data. Also, some scales have failed to correlate in expected directions. Furthermore, the scaling of the subscales was based on too limited a sample and on untested assumptions.

Peterson and Lawrence (1982) made several statements regarding future directions in the development of the SMQ. These include a rescaling of the stress symptoms and the life stressor scales and an expansion of the normative sample. These efforts, in addition to gathering reliability and validity data, are needed before the SMQ can be strongly recommended. In the meantime, subscale scores should be interpreted with caution, as they may provide misleading information. With that caution, the SMQ may prove useful in stress management programs to provide a beginning for the exploration of self-defeating behaviors and attitudes and for identification of life stressors and stress symptoms.

REVIEWER'S REFERENCE

Petersen, J. C., & Lawrence, H. (1982). *Validation study of the Stress Management Questionnaire.* Unpublished manuscript.

[349]

Structure of Intellect Learning Abilities Test. Purpose: "Designed to assess a wide variety of cognitive abilities or factors of intelligence in children and adults." Preschool–adult; 1975–85; SOI-LA; 7 forms; 1986 price data: $37.50 per set of stimulus cards required to administer all Forms except Form P and Form RR; $24.50 per manual ('85, 165 pages); $12.50 per technical data manual ('81, 134 pages); $7.40 per teachers guide ('85, 33 pages); Mary Meeker, Robert Meeker, and Gale H. Roid (manual); Western Psychological Services.*

a) FORM A. Grade 2–adult; 1975–85; 26 subtests in 5 test areas: Cognition (Cognition of Figural Units, Cognition of Figural Classes, Cognition of Figural Systems, Cognition of Figural Transformations, Cognition of Symbolic Relations, Cognition of Symbolic Systems, Cognition of Semantic Units, Cognition of Semantic Relations, Cognition of Semantic Systems), Memory (Memory of Figural Units, Memory of Symbolic Units—Visual, Memory of Symbolic Systems—Visual, Memory of Symbolic Units—Auditory, Memory of Symbolic Systems—Auditory, Memory of Symbolic Implications), Evaluation (Evaluation of Figural Units, Evaluation of Figural Classes, Evaluation of Symbolic Classes, Evaluation of Symbolic Systems), Convergent Production (Convergent Production of Figural Units, Convergent Production of Symbolic Systems, Convergent Production of Symbolic Transformations, Convergent Production of Symbolic Implications), and Divergent Production (Divergent Production of Figural Units, Divergent Production of Semantic Units, and Divergent Production of Symbolic Relations) yielding 14 general ability scores: Cognition, Memory, Evaluation, Convergent Production, Divergent Production, Figural, Symbolic, Semantic, Units, Classes, Relations, Systems, Transformations, and Implications; $95 per complete kit containing 5 each of Forms A and B, manual, scoring keys, stimulus cards, and 100 worksheets and profiles; $10.75 per package of 5 test booklets; $25 per set of scoring keys (for all forms except Form P and Form RR); $12.10 per pad of 100 worksheets and profiles; $37.50 per

set of stimulus cards (for all forms except Form P and Form RR); (150–180) minutes.
b) FORM B. Alternative to Form A.
c) GIFTED SCREENING FORM (FORM G). Grade 2–adult; 1975–85; 12 subtests from Form A which best predict gifted status; $9.60 per package of 5 test booklets; (60–90) minutes.
d) ARITHMETIC-MATH FORM (FORM M). Upper elementary or intermediate students having difficulties with math concepts; 1975–85; 12 subtests from Form A relating to arithmetic, mathematics, and science; $9.90 per package of 5 test booklets; (60–90) minutes.
e) READING FORM (FORM R). Grade 2–adult; 1975–85; 12 subtests from Form A relating to reading, language arts, and social science; $9.90 per package of 5 test booklets; (60–90) minutes.
f) PRIMARY FORM (FORM P). Grades K–3; 1975–85; formerly called Process and Diagnostic Screening Test; 11 subtests similar to Form A, 5 measuring figural abilities, 3 measuring symbolic abilities and 3 measuring semantic abilities; $13.50 per package of 5 test booklets; $22.50 per set of scoring keys; (60–90) minutes.
g) READING READINESS FORM (FORM RR). Young children and new readers; 1985; 10 subtests similar to Form A measuring skills basic to reading; $10.75 per package of 5 test booklets; (60–90) minutes.

For reviews by William E. Coffman and Donald A. Leton of an earlier form, see 9:1197 (2 references); see also T3:2320 (2 references).

TEST REFERENCES

1. O'Tuel, F. S., Ward, M., & Rawl, R. K. (1983). The SOI as an identification tool for the gifted: Windfall or washout? *Gifted Child Quarterly*, 27, 126-134.
2. Roid, G. H. (1984). Construct validity of the figural, symbolic, and semantic dimensions of the Structure-of-Intellect Learning Abilities Test. *Educational and Psychological Measurement*, 44, 697-702.
3. Ebmeier, H., Dyche, B., Taylor, P., & Hall, M. (1985). An empirical comparison of two program models for elementary gifted education. *Gifted Child Quarterly*, 29, 15-19.
4. Roid, G. (1985). Limitations of the test reviewing process: A response to Clarizio and Mehrens. *Gifted Child Quarterly*, 29, 121-123.
5. Vida, R. M., & Vargas, Q., III. (1985). A study of cognitive development and verbal fluency. *Journal of Research and Development in Education*, 18 (4), 11-18.

Review of the Structure of Intellect Learning Abilities Test by JACK A. CUMMINGS, Associate Professor and Director of School Psychology Program, Department of Counseling and Educational Psychology, Indiana University, Bloomington, IN:

Meeker, Meeker, and Roid (1985) describe the Structure of Intellect Learning Abilities Test (SOI-LA; Meeker & Meeker, 1985) as a "series of test forms designed to assess a wide variety of cognitive abilities or factors of intelligence in children and adults." Guilford's major categories of "operations," "contents," and "products" are sampled by the SOI-LA. Operations refer to intellectual processes, or what an individual does with raw information. Operations include: cognition, memory, evaluation, convergent production, and divergent production. Contents are defined as different types of information, for example, figural contents are represented by images, shapes, and concrete objects, while symbolic contents (letters, numbers, and musical notes) provide the foundation for semantic content. The abstract representativeness of the semantic content is what qualitatively differentiates it from symbolic content. Guilford also listed a behavioral dimension as part of contents, but as noted by Roid (1985) it is not part of the SOI-LA. Products are the outcomes of cognitive activity. They include: units, classes, relations, systems, tranformations, and implications.

According to Meeker et al. (1985) the major purpose of the SOI-LA is to provide a profile of an individual's cognitive strengths and weaknesses. Because the SOI-LA measures up to 26 separate cognitive abilities, it is suggested that the results provide a sound basis for educational placement and individualized instruction. Under the heading of major uses, Meeker et al. list gifted screening/prescription of enrichment materials, diagnosis of learning disabilities, and diagnosis of possible reasons for underachievement, as well as other comparable functions for which the SOI-LA has been widely used.

STANDARDIZATION. In 1980, pupils were sampled in grades 2–6. Between 349 and 474 pupils were included in the sample at each of the five grade levels. Boys and girls were represented in roughly equivalent numbers at each level. All pupils were drawn from six school districts. Half of the districts were located in California, with one district located in southern Indiana, one in Oklahoma, and one on the Texas-Mexico border. No data are reported on the socioeconomic status of the children or the ethnic/racial composition of the sample. Nor are data reported on the percentage of children coming from each of the four states represented in the sample.

It is impossible to judge the adequacy of the norms for Forms A and B of the Intermediate and Adult levels. Meeker et al. (1985) "accumulated" data for the normative sample from "computerized score files of students in grades 7 to 12." They report that the students came from gifted, special education, and regular education programs. The adult norms (ages 18–55) were assembled "from CETA programs, career-counseling centers, the SOI Testing Center in El Segundo, California, and in-service training programs in industrial firms." The time period in which these subjects were sampled was not specified, nor was a breakdown of subjects by age level. The Primary Form was normed in 1982 and included subjects from six states. The Primary Form was normed on pupils in grades K–3. Again important data are not reported for those who were included in this sample.

ADMINISTRATION AND SCORING. The SOI-LA was designed to be administered individually or in a group format. Individual administration is recommended when the examinee is a nonreader or nonwriter. The SOI-LA may be given by either a teacher or paraprofessional. In the SOI-LA manual the importance of standard testing procedures is stressed. However, the authors suggest that minor variations in test procedure are permissible when "common sense" implies that the standardized procedures are inappropriate. No examples of permissible minor variations are given in the manual, nor are examples of deviations from standardized procedure which would invalidate the use of norms. This is a significant omission given that relatively unsophisticated (in measurement terms) users may administer the SOI-LA. More specificity is needed in this section of the manual.

Forms A and B require approximately 3 hours to administer. Most of the subtests are 3 to 5 minutes in length, with four requiring 10 minutes and one taking 15 minutes to administer. Rather than attempt administration of the entire test in a single sitting, it is recommended that two separate sessions be used with more sessions being appropriate with handicapped children.

The oral directions reflect careful consideration of wording. In general, the wording flows naturally and is comprehensible for the intended audience. In situations where students are likely to misunderstand directions, as in the Memory of Symbolic Systems—Auditory Subtest, the teacher is warned to monitor carefully the students' responses to ensure they understand that the digits are to be written in backward order. Additionally, the teacher is warned to observe for students writing the numbers from right to left. The directions clearly spell out what the teacher should do when the various situations arise.

RELIABILITY. For the vast majority of subtests, interjudge reliability is a nonissue due to the convergent nature of the acceptable responses. However, for two subtests, Divergent Production of Figural Units and Divergent Production of Semantic Units, it is necessary to scrutinize carefully the consistency of independent scorers. In the former subtest the examinee's creativity is tapped by having the child make each of 16 squares into something different. For the latter subtest the examinee is asked to write a story about a drawing from the previous subtest. In the manual (Meeker et al., 1985) it is noted that studies of interrater reliability are regularly completed at the SOI Institute. They report that the interjudge reliability coefficients range from .75 to .85 for Divergent Production of Figural Units and .92 to 1.0 for Divergent Production of Semantic Units. An investigation by Thompson and Anderson (1983) also revealed adequate interjudge reliability on these two subtests. The interjudge reliability is particularly noteworthy because scoring of open-ended responses is often fraught with excessive subjectivity and tends to be notoriously unreliable. However, the reliability coefficients reported for the SOI-LA indicate that independent judges are able to score consistently the open-ended responses.

Test-retest stability is also reported in the manual. For the 26 separate ability measures, the stability coefficients (Form A) ranged from .35 to .88, with a median coefficient of .57. It should be noted that the test-retest interval was 2 to 4 weeks. Only 4 of the 26 coefficients were equal to or exceeded .75. This indicates that caution must be exercised when interpreting subtest scores other than the four stable subtests: Cognition of Figural Units, Cognition of Semantic Units, Convergent Production of Symbolic Transformation, and Convergent Production of Symbolic Implications as well as Convergent Production of Symbolic Systems for Form B. The stability coefficients for the five Operations ranged from .65–.90. Both Divergent Production and Memory fell below

.75, with coefficients of .65 and .69 respectively. The three Content stability coefficients all exceeded .80, whereas the coefficients for Products ranged from .72 to .87 with the median being .80. Stability was also problematic for Form P (grades K–3). For the separate ability subtests at the kindergarten level the median coefficient was .54. The median coefficients were .54, .53, and .56 for the first, second, and third grade levels, respectively.

Stability data are not reported for intermediate or adult levels, nor for Forms G or M. Measures of internal consistency are also not reported in the manual.

Because equivalent forms are available (Forms A and B), the alternate form reliability is important to consider. The basic question is whether an individual's score on Form A would be comparable to the same individual's score if Form B had been used. Only 3 of 26 ability tests achieve adequate alternate form reliability. These three were Cognition of Semantic Units, Convergent Production of Symbolic Systems, and Convergent Production of Symbolic Implications. Interestingly, all of these were mentioned above as being among the most stable. Two of the five operations had alternate form coefficients below .75: Divergent Production, .63, and Memory, .69. All Content alternate form coefficients were above .75. Four of the six Products alternate form coefficients fell below .75: Classes, .65; Relations, .70; Transformations, .74; and Implications, .74.

The alternate form data as a whole indicate that it is not appropriate to conclude that performance on 26 separate ability measures would be equivalent across Forms A and B (with the exceptions noted above). However, much greater confidence can be placed in the parallel nature of the scores across Forms A and B for Contents, Operations, and Products.

Clarizio and Mehrens (1985) point out that another significant omission in the technical manual is the failure of the authors to take into account the reliability of difference scores. Given the large number of scores and the emphasis on profile interpretation, one would expect to find a discussion of the standard error of difference as well as profile analysis. This same point was echoed by Coffman (1985) in a previous Buros review, that is, the test authors fail to recognize the importance of the standard error of measurements (*SEMs*) associated with the 26 ability scores. The 26 relatively unreliable ability measures contribute to large *SEMs*, which in turn result in large differences needed to conclude that there is a reliable difference between two subtests. As such even though differences may appear large, the reliability of the difference score may indicate that such differences are not statistically stable.

VALIDITY. To paraphrase Clarizio and Mehrens (1985), it may be that SOI-LA represents an attempt to slice the intellectual pie too thinly. From Guilford's SOI model of 120 abilities, Meeker and Meeker (1975) reduced the number to 26. The manual as well as related research does not provide empirical support for the notion that there are 26 unique intellectual abilities. In fact, many have questioned the theoretical adequacy of the SOI model (Eysenck, 1973; Horn, 1985; Jensen, 1980; Maker, 1982; McNemar, 1964; and Vernon, 1979). Most critics question whether each of the separate factors have a sufficient amount of variance for which other factors cannot account. Roid (1985) asserts that major theorists and prominent researchers have not been critical of the SOI-LA, but rather Guilford's (1967) model of 120 abilities. However, even with the Meeker and Meeker's (1975) reduction to 26 abilities, the criticisms are still valid.

CONCLUSIONS. The SOI-LA (Meeker & Meeker, 1975) has been harshly criticized by previous Buros reviewers (Coffman, 1985; Leton, 1985). Likewise, the recent revision of the SOI-LA (Meeker & Meeker, 1985) was criticized on almost every psychometric dimension by Clarizio and Mehrens (1985). The present reviewer is in general accord with Clarizio and Mehrens (1985), Coffman (1985), and Leton (1985). One of the authors of the test manual (Roid, 1985) responded to Clarizio and Mehrens' (1985) critique.

Roid (1985) concluded that the Clarizio and Mehrens (1985) analysis was overly negative and failed to take into account the "practicalities" of test development associated with a highly complex scale. He questioned whether the SOI-LA should be discarded on the basis of the "strict standards of Clarizio and Mehrens" (Roid, 1985). However, the standards to which Roid refers are not those of Clarizio and Mehrens, rather the standards are the collective judgement of a series of committees that received input from researchers, test publishers, test developers, and practitioners. The culmination of the input resulted in the *Standards for Educational and Psychological Testing* (AERA, APA, & NCME, 1985). This being the case, the present reviewer does not view the limitations of the SOI-LA as trivial, but rather as essential prerequisites to the informed use of the measure. The present reviewer's summary of serious limitations associated with the SOI-LA includes:

1. The standardization sample (Form A and B) lacks genuine geographic representativeness, data on socioeconomic status, and information on the ethnicity/race of the subjects.

2. The stability of the vast majority of the 26 separate ability measures is not adequate.

3. The reliability coefficients between the alternate forms (A and B) were low. This indicates that these two forms are not parallel.

4. Due to the large number of subtest scores, a more sophisticated approach should be considered for interpretation. The approach must take into account the reliabilities (standard error of measurement) associated with each subtest.

Despite the limitations, the SOI-LA is not without its assets:

1. Compared with existing cognitive and academic achievement measures, the SOI-LA assesses divergent production, an operation omitted from the forementioned measures.

2. A teacher's guide (Meeker, 1985) is available for teaching students whose skills are deemed deficient. This instructional focus is noticeably absent in the manuals of other measures of cognitive ability. Unfortunately, Meeker (1985) takes a deficit approach to training (i.e., when a specific skill is low, remediation is provided with the goal being to increase the functioning level of that specific skill to some criterion level). An alternative perspective would employ strengths to circumvent a child's weaknesses (Reynolds, 1981).

3. The teacher's oral directions are well written and situations that arise in typical administrations are anticipated in the section on instructions.

In advertising brochures, the publisher claims an additional asset of the SOI-LA (i.e., it provides an alternative to traditional intelligence tests). In the wake of the Larry P. decision, the SOI-LA is alleged to provide a means to "measure cognitive abilities without using an IQ test." The present reviewer views the SOI-LA as a cognitive abilities test with more shared variance with traditional intelligence/achievement tests than unique variance (with the exception of the measures of divergent production). After consideration of the norms, reliability, validity, and interpretative problems, this reviewer believes the Wechsler scales, Kaufman Battery, and recently revised Stanford-Binet are superior alternatives if one needs a measure of cognitive functioning. If one needs measures of achievement the Woodcock-Johnson Psycho-Educational Battery (Part II), and the Kaufman Test of Educational Achievement are superior alternatives when the administration format is individual. If group administration is indicated, options include the California, Metropolitan, and Stanford achievement tests. All offer alternatives with adequate norms, reliability, and validity.

REVIEWER'S REFERENCES

McNemar, Q. (1964). Lost: Our intelligence? Why? *American Psychologist*, 19, 871-882.

Guilford, J. P. (1967). *The nature of human intelligence*. New York: McGraw-Hill Book Company.

Eysenck, H. J. (1973). *The inequality of man*. London: Temple Smith.

Meeker, M., & Meeker, R. J. (1975). Structure of Intellect Learning Abilities Tests. El Segundo, CA: SOI Institute.

Vernon, P. E. (1979). *Intelligence: Heredity and environment*. San Francisco: W. H. Freeman.

Jensen, A. R. (1980). *Bias in mental testing*. New York: Free Press.

Reynolds, C. R. (1981). Neuropsychological assessment and the habilitation of learning: Considerations in the search for the aptitude X treatment interaction. *School Psychology Review*, 10, 343-349.

Maker, C. J. (1982). *Teaching models in education of the gifted*. Rockville, MD: Aspen Systems Corporation.

Thompson, B., & Andersson, B. V. (1983). Construct validity of the divergent production subtests from the Structure-of-Intellect Learning Abilities Test. *Educational and Psychological Measurement*, 43, 651-655.

American Educational Research Association, American Psychological Association, & National Council on Measurement in Education. (1985). *Standards for educational and psychological testing*. Washington, DC: American Psychological Association, Inc.

Clarizio, H. F., & Mehrens, W. A. (1985). Psychometric limitations of Guilford's Structure-of-Intellect model for identification and programming of the gifted. *Gifted Child Quarterly*, 29, 113-120.

Coffman, W. E. (1985). [Review of Structure of Intellect Learning Abilities Test.] In J. V. Mitchell, Jr. (Ed.), *The ninth mental measurements yearbook* (pp. 1486-1488). Lincoln, NE: Buros Institute of Mental Measurements.

Horn, J. L. (1985). Remodeling old models of Intelligence. In B. B. Wolman (Ed.), *Handbook of intelligence: Theories, measurements, and applications*. New York: John Wiley and Sons.

Leton, D. A. (1985). [Review of Structure of Intellect Learning Abilities Test.] In J. V. Mitchell, Jr. (Ed.), *The ninth mental measurements yearbook* (pp. 1488-1489). Lincoln, NE: Buros Institute of Mental Measurements.

Meeker, M. (1985). *A teacher's guide for the Structure of Intellect Learning Abilities Test.* Los Angeles: Western Psychological Services.

Meeker, M., & Meeker, R. J. (1985). Structure of Intellect Learning Abilities Test. Los Angeles: Western Psychological Services.

Meeker, M., Meeker, R. J., & Roid, G. H. (1985). *Structure of Intellect Learning Abilities Test (SOI-LA) manual.* Los Angeles: Western Psychological Services.

Roid, G. (1985). Limitations of the test reviewing process: A response to Clarizio and Mehrens. *Gifted Child Quarterly*, 29, 121-123.

Review of the Structure of Intellect Learning Abilities Test by DIANNA L. NEWMAN, Assistant Professor of Education, University at Albany/SUNY, Albany, NY:

The Structure of Intellect Learning Abilities Test (SOI-LA) is a series of tests designed to measure a variety of cognitive skills for second graders through adults. The tests are based on Meeker and Meeker's adaptation of Guilford's model of the intellect and provide a profile of a student's learning ability by presenting as many as 26 separate subscores. Each subscore is derived from a subtest assessing one of the factors of Guilford's model of intellect and represents a three-dimensional concept of ability (operations, contents, products).

There are seven basic forms of the SOI-LA. Forms A and B are equivalent comprehensive forms that include all 26 subscores. These two forms are appropriate for grade 2 through adults. The Gifted Screening Form (Form G) is a selected series of subtests from Form A that have been shown to best predict gifted status. This form provides information similar to that of the Stanford-Binet plus information on Divergent Production Abilities that include creative responses. The Arithmetic-Math Form (Form M) and the Reading Form (Form R) are both subsets of Form A that can be used to assess strengths and weaknesses of students in the respective areas. Both tests assess the prerequisites to the cognitive skills necessary to successful progress and may be used with students who are having difficulty in these areas. The Primary Form (Form P) and the Reading Readiness Form (Form RR) were designed for younger children and use larger type and figures to identify items. The Primary Form, for students in grades K–3, assesses students' reading and cognitive skills including figural, symbolic, and semantic abilities. The Reading Readiness Form measures skills associated with basic reading.

USES OF SOI-LA. The basic philosophy of SOI-LA is that all children have intelligence; thus, the instrument may fulfill a variety of uses. The first and primary use is the assessment of "what kind" of intelligence the test-taker has; thus, the test is appropriate for planning curriculum and instruction for remedial, general, and gifted students. Documentation in the manual provides evidence supporting the use of the test with gifted, learning disabled, educationally handicapped, and underachieving students. The student profiles may also be used to analyze programmatic strengths and weaknesses in the specific areas of math and reading, leading to prescriptions of specific teaching materials for individuals as well as curriculum design and evaluation.

ADMINISTRATION AND SCORING. The SOI-LA can be easily administered and scored by a classroom teacher or a paraprofessional. Administration can take place in either a group setting or individually. Individual administration is required for nonreading or nonwriting students. Forms A and B, which yield the largest number of subscores, require approximately 2 1/2 to 3 hours to administer. The specialized tests (Forms G, M, R, P, and RR) use only selected subtests and hence require only approximately 1 to 1 1/2 hours of test time. The authors suggest that the examiner determine the number of sessions for testing based on student age and ability; however, a minimum of two sessions is suggested for administration of Forms A and B. Although the tests are to be timed if norms are to be used for interpretation, administrators may provide students with additional time for uncompleted items by marking the last item completed within the time period. This allows the computation of two scores, one based on norms to be used for comparative purposes, the second based on ability only to be used for diagnostic and prescriptive purposes.

Directions for administering Form A and Form B are easy to read and follow. The standard format for each subtest is a brief description of the test or tasks (for examiner use only), specific instructions for the examiner and the examinee, and clear guidelines for time limits. Most of the subtests can be given in any order. Those requiring a certain sequence are clearly identified.

Clear instructions are also provided for the Gifted, Math, Primary, Reading, and Reading

Readiness Forms. The manual does not suggest additional training for examiners using these forms. It should be noted, however, that these forms might better be administered by an examiner with more training in test administration than the typical classroom teacher has had. On these forms, the instructions to both examiner and examinee are complex and may result in confusion for both administrator and respondent.

Directions for scoring the subtests are complete and detailed. The manual not only provides the scoring keys but also provides acceptable options for responses such as lists of synonyms and the use of colloquial equivalents. Sample responses for figural and semantic units with associated scoring are also provided. Directions for the establishment of a student profile and interpretation of scores are comprehensive and clear.

THEORETICAL AND TECHNICAL REPRESENTATION. There can be little question about the quantity of theoretical and technical support for the SOI-LA. Based on the theory proposed by Guilford and adapted to education by Meeker and Meeker, there is an abundance of theoretical and empirical evidence to support the inventory. The manual provides three sections presenting this material to the reader. The overall description of the inventory presents a concise description of Meeker and Meeker's adaptation of Guilford's model and its contribution to test theory. A later chapter presents an indepth examination of the procedure used to standardize the test and to determine reliability and validity. Additional studies supporting and expanding upon these characteristics are also provided along with a complete list of references. This particular chapter is especially beneficial to thosc who are training examiners because it provides an excellent example of the procedures necessary to establish an inventory.

The last chapter in the manual, "Research and Evaluation Studies," presents a summary of studies indicating the successful use of the inventory in training students and increasing mastery of subject material. This chapter emphasizes the use of the instrument in supporting the underlying theory of the Structure of Intellect Model. Studies specific to certain populations (e.g., special education, gifted, and general education students) are presented and summarized in terms of the effects of training on specific abilities. The chapter may be of special use to those in academic or research settings as it concludes with suggestions for future research on the model and on the instrument.

SUMMARY AND CONCLUSIONS. The Structure of Intellect Learning Abilities Test is a series of tests that assess a variety of cognitive skills based on Meeker and Meeker's adaptation of Guilford's theory of intellect. The test provides a series of subscores reflecting a complex array of skills categorized by operations, contents, and products. The instrument can be used in its total form (Form A or B) to assess general ability, or various subscales can be used to assess specific areas such as math or reading. Although originally developed for assessment of elementary-aged children in general education, parts of the test have now been expanded and validated to include assessment of gifted, special education, handicapped, and remedial students ranging from kindergarten through adults.

The basic forms of the test are easily administered and scored by teachers or paraprofessionals. Group settings are appropriate for most of the inventory, however, some tests do require individualized administration.

There is an abundance of materials in the public domain, including the manual, accompanying literature, and published works, that support the use of the instrument as a means of assessing intelligence in educational settings. Of key importance, however, is that inventory users and interpreters accept and are prepared to use the developers' philosophy that the test measures not "how much" intelligence but "what kind." This premise allows for the variety of uses the developers advocate, and supports the emphasis on subscores. One of the most positive aspects of this already well-documented material is that the authors encourage additional validation and research using both their model and their instrument. Both researchers and test users considering this inventory would be well advised to examine current data bases for continued information on the status of the instrument. The potential of the instrument and its concomitant research is expanding at a rapid pace and will continue to do so.

[350]

Structured Pediatric Psychosocial Interview. Purpose: "Assists school-aged children and adolescents in expressing their affective distress and life concerns." Ages 5–19; 1979–85; SPPI; 9 subscale scores: Fretfulness, Impetuosity, Adherence, Emulation, Doubtfulness, Obdurateness, Composure, Unhappiness, Resentfulness, and 3 composite scores: Feeling, Relating, Thinking; individual; 1987 price data: $14 per 25 interview booklets; $15 per manual ('85, 102 pages); $29 per computer scoring program; (20) minutes; Thomas E. Webb and Chris A. Van Devere; Fourier Inc.*

TEST REFERENCES

1. Webb, T. E., VanDevere, C. A., & Ott, J. S. (1984). A comparative study of affective distress in elementary school children and adolescents. *Elementary School Guidance & Counseling*, 18, 188-193.

2. Webb, T. E., Singleton, C. R., Laplace, A. C., & Vandevere, C. A. (1986). Genetic influence in the expression of affectivity: Twin study of children and adolescents. *The Journal of Genetic Psychology*, 147, 279-281.

Review of the Structured Pediatric Psychosocial Interview by WAYNE C. PIERSEL, Associate Professor of Educational Psychology, University of Nebraska-Lincoln, Lincoln, NE:

The Structured Pediatric Psychosocial Interview (SPPI) is designed to elicit children's and adolescents' expressions of their life's concerns and affective distress. The SPPI is a structured interview that is organized into 50 broad questions containing a total of 169 followup inquiries, open ended questions or sentence completion type items, and an optional section to explore motivations regarding drug usage. A total of 198 scoreable responses can be generated if the entire interview is administered. The manual indicates the interview can be administered and scored in approximately 30 minutes.

The SPPI questions are apportioned across four scales of Feeling, Relating, Thinking, and Impetuosity. There are nine subscales labeled Fretfulness, Impetuosity, Adherence, Emulation, Doubtfulness, Obdurateness, Composure, Unhappiness, and Resentfulness. The authors specifically note the SPPI is not intended to function as a diagnostic tool and should not be employed to arrive at specific psychiatric diagnoses. The authors intend for this interview to facilitate clinicians arriving at a subjective estimate of the child's or youth's latent psychological processes or traits that are thought to underlie the individual's current emotional state. More specifically, the structured interview is intended to help children and youth verbally express their psychosocial concerns and to assist the interviewer in determining the presence of abnormal levels of stress. The present version of the SPPI is a revision of an interview schedule developed initially by the authors in the 1970s.

The normative sample is comprised of 492 children aged 5 to 12 and 523 adolescents aged 13 to 19. All of the participants attended public schools in northeastern Ohio. The authors provide sufficient information on the standardization sample to enable the reader to conclude that this sample approximates the population of the United States. Tables for converting raw scores from the four scales and the nine subscales into scaled scores are provided for males and females for five age groups. In a unique aspect, the manual also provides norms based on the gender of the interviewer. To the extent the sex of the interviewer interacts with the sex of the child or youth being interviewed, these score conversion tables are a welcome addition.

The test manual is reasonably well constructed and the chapter on psychometric properties is fairly complete. Data are provided on the four major scales including internal consistency coefficients, temporal stability, and interviewer agreement or reliability. The data in the manual indicate a wide range of reliability coefficients across the different scales and ages. For example, internal consistency coefficients range from a low of .43 for Impetuosity for the 8–12-year-old group to a high of .93 for Feeling for the 5–7-year-old group. The interrater reliability coefficients are based on a sample of 12 cases and range .42 for Thinking to .97 for Impetuosity. Test-retest stability correlations vary from .37 for a 12–24-month interval on the Relating scale to .60 for a 1–4-month interval for the Relating scale. Depending on the use of the interview and the derived scores, the various estimates of reliability suggest only minimal adequacy.

The authors devote several pages in an effort to establish the validity of the SPPI through the use of various factor analytic techniques. The factor analysis does provide a high degree of support for the grouping of the nine subscales onto the four major scales. However, no description or empirical data are provided regarding how the authors located or placed individual items or questions on each of the subscales. In terms of concurrent validity the authors provide correlational data to illustrate comparisons with intelligence and achievement measures with the scales. These data indicate minimal relation to these measures. The correlations establish some degree of discriminant validity. No data concerning convergent validity are available.

To establish criterion validity, the manual describes one study conducted by the authors where the mean scores of a group of hospitalized youth were compared with a sample of 100 youth drawn from the standardization sample. On three of the four scales (Feeling, Relating, and Impetuosity) the means were significantly different with the maladjusted group attaining higher scores. It must be noted, however, that the absolute differences were relatively small detracting from the clinical or practical utility of the SPPI to differentiate those youth who are experiencing problems from those youth who are viewed as normal. $A major limitation of this interview instrument and the manual is that the extensive clinical interpretation provided contains no references to empirical literature to support the many inferences made. The practice of profile analysis (e.g., the comparison of the relative scores on the various scales and subscales) is highly questionable given the lack of empirical support. The authors' discussion is presented in such a way as to suggest that the resulting interpretations are well established and verified conclusions. In fact, the authors appear to be resorting to clinical mystique in discussing the many kinds of "rich clinical" information this instrument is purported to uncover from the subject's unconscious. There is no empirical support regarding the treatment utility of such approaches and the authors present no data regarding the treatment value of their interview scale.

Aside from the limited psychometric adequacy of a test and lack of empirical support for many of the suggested clinical interpretations, the practical utility of the SPPI is probably the most important question that a potential user has to answer. Unfortunately, this reviewer feels the SPPI has little or no practical application. Achenbach and McConaughy (1987) note that interview data are typically limited to one context and one interaction partner and are most useful when systematically paired with other data. The SPPI authors' deliberate efforts to avoid assessing traditional traits and symptoms viewed as comprising major diagnostic categories (viz., *DSM III-R*) render the instrument of no practical value. The information obtained in the interview cannot be systematically compared to other sources of data. The instrument does not qualify as a research tool, it is not useful for psychiatric diagnoses, and is not useful for planning or evaluating treatment. Merely assessing a child's or youth's level of discomfort or stress is relatively meaningless in isolation from some intended outcome such as reducing the stress or identifying the source of the stressors. There are many other instruments and processes that are better suited to identifying specific child problems and child stressors. This reviewer is hard pressed to conceive of any situation where this interview schedule would be the preferred technique.

If the authors can provide at some point, criterion validity, then this interview scale may have utility. Until that time, professionals would more productively use their time and energy in identifying specific client problems and identifying contributors to those problems through direct client interviews following formats as suggested by Gross (1984) and Ollendick and Cerny (1981). Direct observation and the use of well-developed behavior checklists such as the Child Behavior Checklists by Achenbach and Edelbrock (1983), which include parallel scales for parents, teacher, and youth to complete, are preferred assessment processes. The goal of developing structured interviews to generate data that can be quantified is certainly commendable. Such efforts would be better served: (*a*) by relating the standardized quantifiable interview to other existing instruments, (*b*) by directly linking the structured interview to an accepted diagnostic system with clearly defined behaviors, or (*c*) by linking the interview to a clearly articulated theoretical framework. In its present form, the Structured Pediatric Psychosocial Interview has little to offer.

REVIEWER'S REFERENCES

Ollendick, T. H., & Cerny, J. A. (1981). *Clinical behavior therapy with children*. New York: Plenum Press.

Achenbach, T. M., & Edelbrock, C. (1983). Child Behavior Checklist. Burlington, VT: University of Vermont, Department of Psychiatry.

Gross, A. M. (1984). Behavioral interviewing. In T. H. Ollendick & M. Hersen (Eds.), *Child behavior assessment: Principles and procedures* (pp. 61-79). Elmsford, NY: Pergamon Press.

Achenbach, T. M., & McConaughy, S. H. (1987). *Empirically based assessment of child and adolescent psychopathology: Practical applications.* Newbury Park, CA: Sage Publications.

American Psychiatric Association. (1987). *Diagnostic and statistical manual of mental disorders* (3rd ed., revised). Washington, DC: Author.

Review of the Structured Pediatric Psychosocial Interview by RICHARD A. WEINBERG, Professor of Child Psychology and Educational Psychology, and Director, Center for Early Education and Development, University of Minnesota, Minneapolis, MN:

The Structured Pediatric Psychosocial Interview (SPPI) is a serious attempt to develop a systematic, standardized, norm-referenced interview technique that samples a child's expression of "psychosocial concerns" and "aids the listener's detection of abnormal distress." A child's or adolescent's interview protocol is compared with response characteristics of a sample of over 1,000 public school pupils from northeastern Ohio, between the ages of 5 to 19 years. Although geographic diversity is not provided, many demographic characteristics of the sample are proportional to those of the national population. Normative groups associated with responder's age and sex as well as the sex of the interviewer provide the bases for generating standardized scaled scores from raw subscale scores.

Developed in a pediatric medical center, the basic interview consists of approximately 50 question scenarios printed in a booklet format. For children over 8 years old, some sentence completion items are included, and finally, a brief, optional section deals with chemical abuse and delinquency issues.

The scoring booklet is clearly organized, allowing the interviewer to quickly compute raw scores, converted scaled scores for the nine subscales, and composite scores for the major scaling dimensions, and to draw a profile of scores. A software program for automating scores is also available.

Regular and technical scoring options are well articulated in the manual and are easily accessible to the interviewer. Not all reactions to an inquiry are scored, "only those which have demonstrated empirical relevance to the SPPI's scaling parameters." The interviewer is also cautioned that scores are estimates of the presence of traits, not of trait intensity. A chapter on technical coding helps the interviewer deal with coding dilemmas when scoring item responses. Two "illustrative protocols" are used to model scale interpretation and score meaning as well as to offer suggestions for summarizing the "subjective" nature of the interview.

The manual provides good support for the reliability of the scaling, citing evidence for internal consistency, interrater agreement, and temporal stability. The validity of the SPPI is grounded in a sophisticated "Structural Factor" model. Several large protocol samples were subjected to exploratory factor analyses, resulting in the four hypothetical dimensions along which children describe their affective experience and life concerns. To verify empirically their postulated model, Webb and Van Devere applied the LISREL technique to the simultaneous factor analysis of weighted subscale data from large child and adolescent inpatient samples ($N = 862$). The resulting "goodness of fit" index of .96 suggests that the obtained factor structure does approximate the SPPI model well. Cross-validation of the model with a sample of developmentally delayed/handicapped children corroborated the "goodness of fit."

Proof of the adequacy of the SPPI in discriminating groups of maladjusted and normal children is documented, with the exception that the Relating scale appears not to be sensitive to longstanding disturbance. The authors recommend putting the Relating scale into perspective by comparing it with the overall profile of other scales.

Unfortunately the comprehensive and well-written manual is blemished by poor proofreading and careless footnoting, which can be quite frustrating to the reader and should be remedied in reprintings of the manual. Also, a more comprehensive discussion of the studies conducted on the SPPI and other modes of assessment would have been helpful.

Traditionally, clinicians have extolled the value of interview data in the assessment process. The SPPI, a standardized, norm-referenced technique, brings increased psychometric credibility to the interview. Although limited to an interviewee's perception of affective distress and life concerns, the SPPI could be a valuable tool for experienced health care and educational professionals who develop the necessary administration, scoring, and interpretive skills.

[351]

Student Rights Scales. Purpose: Determines student and teacher perceptions of student rights in junior and senior high school. Grades 7–12; 1982; SRS; for research use only; 5 subscales: General Rights, Due Process, Academic Self Determination, Freedom of Expression, Personal Conduct; price data available from publisher for manual ('82, 9 pages including test); administration time not reported; T. R. F. Oaster; the Author.*

Review of the Student Rights Scales by STEVEN W. LEE, Assistant Professor of Educational Psychology and Research, University of Kansas, Lawrence, KS:

The Student Rights Scales—Revised (SRSR) was designed to measure and "compare student and teacher perceptions" of rights that students have in junior high and high school. The manual states that the SRSR was designed for use with students and teachers, but parents are also listed as possible respondents. The SRSR materials include a manual and a copy of the Student Rights Scale. According to the manual, the "best use of the current form of the SRSR is as a research tool." The manual presents little research on the topic of student rights. Some of the relevant literature on student rights provided in the accompanying studies should be incorporated in the manual.

The SRSR is an untimed test that apparently can be administered individually or in groups. However, little information about the appropriate administrative conditions is reported in the manual. The directions for self administration are reported on the first page of the test form with two examples. The directions for administration are clear, but the method of scoring the protocol is not discernable due to discrepancies in the procedure for item weighting. No information on interpretation of the scale is provided either in the manual or on the test form. The SRSR purports to measure five categories of students' rights, identified by the following subscales: General Rights, Due Process, Personal Conduct, Academic Self Determination, and Freedom of Self-Expression.

Apparently the items on the SRSR were generated in a study by Oaster (1983), who reports that "several school teachers were involved in the generation of original item stems." The items in the current form of the SRSR were divided into five "rights categories" on the basis of item intercorrelations and a literature review by Price, Babcock, and Oaster (1982). However, these item intercorrelations could not be found in the above mentioned study. Not only is the development of items for the SRSR not clear in the manual; the development of the "subscales" is equally mysterious.

The norms for the SRSR are provided for 113 students, grades 7 through 12 in two rural school districts. These students volunteered to complete the instrument in their social studies classes. No stratification of the sample was attempted. While the scale is not recommended for clinical or educational uses, the fact that the SRSR has not been sufficiently normed or standardized deserves more emphasis in the manual.

While norms may not be important when the SRSR is used as a research tool, the reliability and validity of the scales are essential. A coefficient alpha of .74 was reported for Form 1. Identical forms with Likert-scale choice points ranging from 3 to 9 yielded coefficient alpha reliabilities ranging from .65 (Form 3) to .78 (Form 7). No estimates of temporal stability or interrater reliabilities were reported in the manual.

Some evidence of content validity exists simply by virtue of a rational examination of the test items. However, no empirical evidence is reported in the manual for the validity of the SRSR as a measure of students' or teachers' perceptions of rights in school. No factor analytic or concurrent validity studies are reported that may help to confirm the SRSR as a measure of students' rights. Furthermore, other than the item intercorrelations, which the manual states are reported in a manuscript by Oaster (1983), no empirical evidence exists for the identified subscales of the SRSR. The item intercorrelations reported to be in Oaster (1983) were not found. These concerns suggest the SRSR cannot demonstrate empirically that it measures what it purports to measure. With these fundamental problems of reliability and validity in mind, the SRSR manual should provide cautions regarding the use of the scale and the limits of generalizability. Unfortunately, the manual does not provide the necessary cautions.

In summary, the SRSR was designed as a research instrument to measure students' and teachers' perceptions of students' rights in school. The procedure used to develop items for the SRSR was not clearly stated in the manual and appears to lack scientific rigor. Because little information was provided in the manual regarding research in the area of students' rights and the development of the SRSR, definite conclusions regarding the theory and development of the SRSR are difficult to draw. A research scale should demonstrate adequate reliability and validity even though completely developed norms are not essential. The norms for the SRSR are quite insufficient. While this is not a major problem in a research scale, more cautions against the use of the SRSR clinically or educationally should be provided in the manual. The internal consistency of the SRSR appeared adequate (coefficient alpha = .74) but no estimates of temporal stability or interrater reliabilities are provided. With the exception of content validity, the SRSR manual offers no empirical support for the scale as a measure of students' rights nor of its subscales. More fundamental research in the area of temporal stability, interrater reliability, and concurrent and construct validity are needed before the SRSR can be considered a viable tool measuring perceptions of students' rights.

REVIEWER'S REFERENCES

Price, L. B., Babcock, S. K., & Oaster, T. R. (1982, February). *Teacher and student perceptions of student rights.* Paper presented at the meeting of the American Association of Colleges for Teacher Education. Houston, TX.

Oaster, T. R. F. (1983). *Reservation and off-reservation parent, teacher and student perceptions of student rights.* Kansas City: University of Missouri-Kansas City. (ERIC Document Reproduction Service No. ED 220 740)

Review of the Student Rights Scales by DAVID MOSHMAN, Associate Professor of Educational Psychology, University of Nebraska-Lincoln, Lincoln, NE:

Public school controversies have made student rights a matter of national attention. Do students have a right to encounter a variety of books, ideas, and points of view? To express their own views? To make curriculum decisions? To wear what they please? To pray in school? Do they have a right to freedom from religious indoctrination? From searches of their desks, lockers, clothes, and bodies? From corporal punishment? Do they have a right to due process if accused of wrongdoing? To equal protection and opportunity regardless of race? Regardless of sex?

Although all of the above questions are raised frequently and have been the subject of substantial legal controversy, relatively little is known about the attitudes of parents, teachers, administrators, and students themselves on these issues. The purpose of the Student Rights Scales is to assess attitudes toward a wide range of student rights. It is a worthy aim.

Unfortunately, the psychometric properties of the scale are, at present, not well established. The items themselves cover a range of rights that are divided into five subscales: General Rights, Due Process, Personal Conduct, Academic Self-Determination, and Freedom of Self-Expression. The subscales do cover a variety of important rights and the distinctions among them are reasonable. On the other hand, there is little attempt to show that these scales adequately encompass the relevant domain or that the differentiation of the student rights domain into these five categories is legally, theoretically, or empirically justified. Why not, for example, a category labeled something like Equal Protection and Opportunity?

In several studies using the scale, the coefficient alpha estimate of reliability has ranged from .52 to .79. The meaning of these figures is unclear in that the populations tested were quite diverse, the samples were usually small, the test itself varied from study to study as items were added or dropped, and even *within* several of the studies items judged inappropriate were dropped prior to calculating reliability. Given these limitations, it cannot be said that the test has been convincingly normed for any definable population.

In its present state of development, the Student Rights Scales cannot be considered a definitive assessment device. Nevertheless, its existence does focus attention on an area worthy of serious research. Do students, teachers, administrators, and parents differ in their overall level of support for student rights? Does this support vary as a function of category of rights (e.g., free speech vs. due process)? Does it vary as a function of individual personality, social class, or school climate? How does *attitude* toward student rights (which is what these scales assess) relate to *knowledge* about relevant legal, moral, or educational considerations? In the absence of other measures, the Student Rights Scales may be useful as a beginning strategy to address questions of this sort. In the course of such research, however, the scale itself must be scrutinized and improved.

[352]

Stuttering: Parental Diagnostic Questionnaire, Revised Edition. Purpose: Assists "the speech pathologist in the evaluation, prevention and treatment of stuttering in children." Ages 3–6; 1978–87; PDQ; ratings by parent, teacher, or guardian; 3 scores: Speech Behaviors, Parental Attitudes, Parental Responses; 1988 price data: $29 per 25 each questionnaires, profiles, normative data and worksheets, and instructions ('87, 1 page); (15) minutes; Dennis C. Tanner; PRO-ED, Inc.*

[353]

Styles of Training Index. Purpose: Designed to help identify training styles, or orientations, in terms of how much of two concerns a person shows: a concern for what is being taught, a concern for who is being taught. Instructors; 1974–83; 1987 price data: $4 per index and scoring and interpretation booklet ('83, 11 pages); [60] minutes; Don Michalak; Michalak Training Associates, Inc.*

Review of the Styles of Training Index by SUSAN J. SCHENCK, Associate Professor of Special Education, College of Charleston, Charleston, SC:

The Styles of Training Index consists of two booklets—a self-analysis questionnaire and a scoring/interpretation booklet. There was no accompanying manual with information concerning construction or validation of the instrument.

The self-analysis questionnaire consists of 41 statements concerning training styles. Respondents are to indicate on a scale of 3 (*Very Much Like Me*) to 0 (*Hardly Like Me*) how each statement reflects their own training style. Scores are recorded in two columns, one reflecting concern for what is taught and the other concern for who is taught. Total scores from each column are then placed on a graph and perpendicular lines are drawn. The intersection of these lines, according to the authors, indicates ones training style. Scoring can be somewhat confusing and care must be taken when transferring scores from the Participant Booklet to the Scoring/Interpretation Booklet.

The four Training Styles identified are: Integrated, Student-Centered, Administrative, and Traditional. There is no discussion concerning how these training styles were identified. The interpretation section of the Scoring/Interpretation Booklet merely gives a general description of each training style and then describes the differences among the four areas given five specific areas: Assumptions About the Students, Motivation, Use of Tests, Methods Used in Class, and Interpersonal Communications in Class. The discussion of the differences consists merely of a two-to-three-sentence paragraph explaining how each training style reacts to the specific area. The Interpretation section concludes with a brief statement about identifying those areas, or styles, one might wish to change. There is no discussion as to the method(s) one might employ to make any desired changes.

Of critical importance is the complete lack of validity data concerning the questionnaire. Validation is required to determine if the questionnaire does indeed measure what it purports to measure, in this case training style. Without information provided concerning the development and subsequent validation of the Styles of Training Index, as well as information concerning the identification of the various training styles, one is left with the question as to the accuracy of the results.

The Styles of Training Index may provide users with some insight into their characteristics related to training/teaching. However, due to the lack of information concerning test construction and development, care needs to be taken when interpreting the results. As with many self-analysis questionnaires, the Styles of Training Index should be used only for very superficial self-exploration. Without evidence of predictive validity, even this use may be of no importance.

Review of the Styles of Training Index by BRUCE SHERTZER, Professor of Education, Purdue University, West Lafayette, IN:

The Styles of Training Index and its accompanying scoring and interpretation booklet do not provide any direct statement about its purpose or the conditions for which it is designed to be used. Nor does a Leader's Guide speak to these matters. The Index is a self-administered, -scored, and -profiled inventory from which the individual identifies his or her training style and then decides upon behaviors to be changed. This reviewer infers from what is depicted on the front cover of the scoring and interpretation booklet that the rationale upon which the Index is based is that feedback about training behaviors leads to awareness and that leads to change. This review, presumably, could serve as a test of that rationale.

A concern for What Is Taught and a concern for Who Is Being Taught are the two factors from which a training style is derived. Michalak states that these two concerns are independent variables but does not provide any evidence to justify the assertion. And it is true that traditionally content and student have been viewed as independent variables in teaching. This position is illustrated by the old saw: First teacher, "I teach arithmetic"; second teacher, "I teach children." But equally long ago, a third teacher said "I teach children arithmetic."

Inspection of the 22 items that comprise the What-Is-Taught component reveals three of them probe testing practices and six other items question what the instructor would do in certain situations such as students falling asleep, disagreeing with the instructor, or engaging in an activity other than what the class is doing. This reviewer concluded that 13 of the 22 items addressed *how* content is taught or evaluated, rather than *what* is taught. Examination of the 19 items comprising the Who-Is-Being-Taught component reveals much the same story in that 8 of the 19 items were classified by this reviewer as being more concerned with *how* content is taught rather than *who* is being taught. The content validity of these subscales is questionable.

Directions for scoring, ordering, and graphing What and Who scores are presented clearly, simply, and without using sexist terminology. The intersection of the How and Who scores on the X and Y axes yields one of four possible training styles, that is, administrative, integrated, student centered, or traditional. No explanation is given as to how the author determined cutoff points or positioned the four styles.

Michalak describes the four training styles, using quantifications (high or low) of concerns for what and who is being taught. Low concerns for the two variables place an instructor in an administrative style, and high concerns for both in an integrated style. High concern for what is being taught and low concern for who is being taught represent a traditional style and the reverse loadings are characteristic of a student-centered style. If this reviewer were an administrator, questions would be asked about the aptness of the label, administrative, to characterize instructors with little interest in content or involvement with students. And is traditional really the opposite of student centered? Why not use the designation, content centered?

Michalak identifies how each training style diverges in assumptions made about students, beliefs about motivation, use of tests, instructional methods, and interpersonal communications in class. There is no evidence given to support the statements about each style's assumptions and characteristics. A saving grace is that modifiers (e.g., might be, tends to, seems to, are perhaps) are used to dilute the force of the statements. Although the author asserts that no style or orientation is right or wrong, the integrated style is in the highest position on the graph. Statements about the behaviors of that training style in the matter of tests, methods, etc., further serve to highlight it as the most desirable training style.

Michalak stated (November, 1987 telephone conversation) that about 40 percent of trainees were classified as having an integrated style. But for those classified otherwise who want to change their classification, an exercise for doing so is provided in the Scoring and Interpretation Booklet. These individuals inspect the items for which they scored the lowest (least like them or strongly disagree) associated with the lowest scored who or what concern. The author noted that making "minor adjustments," by doing more of the behaviors associated with a few items will produce change. And it is true that elevating responses to two or three items would place many trainees beyond the cutoff points established for an integrated style. One need not feel bad or uncomfortable with oneself when just a little minor adjustment is necessary for being an integrated trainer!

At first inspection this reviewer thought the Styles of Training Index might well tap elements involved in a contingency model for both the design and delivery of training set forth by Morton and Kurtz (1982). Their model takes into account three interacting instructional variables: task, relationship, and situation. The task dimension includes trainer activities such as formulation of objectives, sequencing instructional activities, behaviors used to guide the instructional process, and presentation of learning activities. The relationship dimension consists of establishing a climate for learning, building trainer-trainee trust, and responding to trainee needs throughout the course of training.

The situational dimension includes factors such as the sponsoring institution's commitment to the training, quality of physical facilities, and the cultural background, involvement, knowledge, and skill level brought by trainees to training. But until more information about the Index is provided, judgments about what constructs it taps are not feasible.

The Index and its acompanying scoring and interpretation booklet and Leader's Guide are viewed by the author (as stated in the November telephone call) as "broad-brush experimental training materials." To justify even that use, however, the author-publisher owes consumers more information about the purpose, construction, reliability, and validity of the Index. Until that is done, this reviewer doubts the Index can be used to induce any enduring change in trainer behaviors.

REVIEWER'S REFERENCE

Morton, T. D., & Kurtz, P. D. (1982). Conditions affecting skills learning. In E. K. Marshall and P. D. Kurtz (Eds.), *Interpersonal helping skills* (pp. 394-422). San Francisco: Jossey-Bass, Inc., Publishers.

[354]

Survey of Personal Values. Purpose: "Measure certain critical values that help determine the manner in which individuals cope with the problems of everyday living." High school and college and adults; 1964–84; SPV; self-administered; test identical to 1965 edition, some additional material provided in manual; 6 scores: Practical Mindedness, Achievement, Variety, Decisiveness, Orderliness, Goal Orientation; 1987 price data: $33 per 25 tests; $5.50 per scoring stencil; $10 per examiner's manual ('84, 49 pages); (15) minutes; Leonard V. Gordon; Science Research Associates, Inc.*

See T3:2370 (5 references) and T2:1409 (5 references); for a review by Gene V Glass, see 7:148 (6 references); see also P:263 (3 references).

Review of the Survey of Personal Values by WILLIAM P. ERCHUL, Assistant Professor of Psychology, North Carolina State University, Raleigh, NC:

The Survey of Personal Values (SPV) is a brief, self-administered instrument that reportedly measures temperaments and values that influence a person's behavior. Such information may be useful for the purposes of personnel selection, vocational guidance, and individual counseling. Before proceeding further, two observations regarding the SPV are warranted. First, the word "personal" in its title refers to the author's claim that the SPV assesses the individual's values in coping with life's problems; Gordon's Survey of Interpersonal Values (a companion test) purports to measure a different set of values concerned with one's interpersonal relationships. Second, the SPV's use of the word "values" is somewhat misleading; as has been noted previously, the test more accurately measures "broad areas of interest" rather than "values" (Glass, 1972). Thus, potential users should be aware that the SPV is not concerned with "values" in the sense of standards by which good/evil and moral/immoral behavior is evaluated.

The SPV employs a forced-choice format and consists of 30 sets of three statements. Within each triad, the respondent is instructed to choose the statement considered "most important" and the statement judged "least important." Each triad presents statements matched for social desirability drawn from three different value dimensions. In all, six dimensions (i.e., scales) are represented: Practical Mindedness (being materialistically-oriented); Achievement (accepting and successfully completing challenging tasks); Variety (engaging in diverse and novel activities); Decisiveness (stating and defending one's opinions); Orderliness (approaching matters in an organized, systematic way); and Goal Orientation (having task-oriented, problem-solving tendencies). Decisiveness and Goal Orientation derive from Guilford's Convergent Thinking and Dislike of Ambiguity factors, respectively; the remaining four scales were developed from "a review of the relevant literature."

Interestingly, scale intercorrelations are such that an ordering of the scales resembling a circumplex model (e.g., Leary, 1957; Olson, Sprenkle, & Russell, 1979) is possible. Two major axes, Organization-Fluidity and Challenge-Security define this model, and individual scales cluster around each of the four poles. Gordon appropriately acknowledges the model's preliminary nature and its oversimplification of human behavior. It is, however, conceptually intriguing and merits further attention.

NORMS. Percentile ranks based on raw scores for each of the six scales are presented for eight nonoccupational and two occupational groups: vocational ninth grade male (N = 1,096), vocational ninth grade female (N = 1,571), high school male (N = 1,644), high school female (N = 1,392), vocational junior college male (N = 2,311), vocational junior college female (N = 587), college male (N = 984), college female (N = 1,080), "workers in routinized jobs" (N = 1,461), and managerial (N = 1,089). These numbers appear adequate and can be expected to grow through further test development. The composition of the entire sample seems to be representative of the U.S. in general, although minority group representation data are unavailable for the college and occupational groups. Finally, no standard errors or standard scores are offered, but percentile ranges based on equal standard score intervals are given to aid in interpretation.

RELIABILITY. Using coefficient alpha, internal consistency for the six scales ranges from .77 (Achievement) to .87 (Variety). The test-retest reliability over a 7–10 day period extends from .74 (Decisiveness) to .92 (Variety) as calculated on scores of 97 college students. Reliability coefficients for a 1-year interval collapsed across four educational levels range from .38 (vocational ninth graders' scores on Practical Mindedness) to .74 (eleventh graders' scores on Orderliness), with a mean 1-year test-retest reliability of .58 (N = 207). Taken together, these figures indicate the SPV to be a reliable instrument.

VALIDITY. The manual cites over 20 studies concerned with establishing the validity of the test. In terms of concurrent validity, the SPV scales (with the exception of Variety) correlate significantly with logically related scales of Cattell's Sixteen Personality Factor Questionnaire, and five of six SPV scales correlate significantly with either the Economic or Aesthetic scale of the Allport-Vernon-Lindzey Study of Values. In addition, SPV scores appear to be unrelated to cognitive ability and Caucasian/Black racial class membership (when socioeconomic status is held constant). Other correlational findings raise questions such as: Why are measures of authoritarianism, dogmatism, and self-esteem all significantly related to most SPV scales? And why are the disparate constructs of Acquiescence (Couch & Keniston, 1960) and Authoritarianism (Adorno, Frenkel-Brunswik, Levinson, & Sanford, 1950) both positively related to Practical Mindedness? One begins to wonder what the SPV scales actually measure.

The author relies largely on the contrasting-group approach to establish construct validity; however, in most cases, there are no generally agreed-upon, a priori hypotheses regarding group performance that data can support or fail to support. For example, are faculty members expected to have lower scores on Goal Orientation and Orderliness than their students? Gordon apparently believes so, and presents these results to support the test's construct validity. The strongest argument for using a contrasting-group approach can be made for the Achievement scale, for which meaningful comparisons between groups (e.g., enrolled students and drop-outs) can be and are made. As a final note, Gordon's inclusion of cross-cultural research is inherently interesting, but does little to convince one of the SPV's validity.

SUMMARY. Numerous refinements of the SPV have occurred since the time of Glass' (1972) review. Specifically, the test presents better norms developed on more diverse populations and acceptable long-term reliability data. However, basic questions surrounding the test's validity still remain (e.g., What do the individual scales actually measure?). In the final analysis, the SPV appears to have risen above the status of a research instrument but continues to walk in the shadow of the more well-established Study of Values.

REVIEWER'S REFERENCES

Adorno, T. W., Frenkel-Brunswik, E., Levinson, D. J., & Stanford, R. N. (1950). *The authoritarian personality*. New York: Harper & Row.

Leary, T. (1957). *Interpersonal diagnosis of personality*. New York: Ronald Press Co.

Couch, A., & Keniston, K. (1960). Yeasayers and naysayers: Agreeing response set as a personality variable. *Journal of Abnormal and Social Psychology*, 60, 151-174.

Glass, G. V. (1972). Review of Survey of Personal Values. In O. K. Buros (Ed.), *The seventh mental measurements yearbook* (Vol. 1, pp. 359-360). Highland Park, NJ: The Gryphon Press.

Olson, D. H., Sprenkle, D. H., & Russell, C. S. (1979). Circumplex model of marital and family systems: I. Cohesion and adaptability dimensions, family types, and clinical applications. *Family Process*, 18, 3-28.

Review of the Survey of Personal Values by RODNEY L. LOWMAN, Director, Corporate Division, Personal Assistance Service, Occupational Health Service, and Faculty, Divisions of Medical Psychology and Occupational Medicine, Duke University Medical Center, Durham, NC:

In reviewing the Survey of Personal Values (SPV), one is reminded of Peter Drucker's old differentiation between organizational efficiency and effectiveness. Efficiency, said Drucker, is doing the job right, while effectiveness is doing the right job. The SPV is more problematic concerning *what* it measures than for *how* it goes about the process of measuring it. It is the test's conceptualization of values that raises the most concern.

What are values? How do they relate to decisions and behaviors that are of interest to psychologists who would use such a test, presumably, to advise and counsel persons about real-life choices and decisions? Does this test really measure values or some related construct such as vocational interests? These are important, and largely unanswered, questions raised by this measure. The answers matter a great deal because they help to determine whether this test is of use outside of a very narrow research context and they guide the question of whether this is the most efficient test of its genre.

Conceptually, this measure is rather confused. It comes narrowly close to being a set of items (or scales) in search of constructs to measure. The closest definition of "values" provided is "the relative importance individuals ascribe to various activities." The "various activities" measured here include six scales of what are presumed to be stable (typological) characteristics of persons: Practical Mindedness, Achievement, Variety, Decisiveness, Orderliness, and Goal Orientation. In post-hoc analyses, these scales are said to reduce to two underlying dimensions: Organization-Fluidity and Challenge-Security. Yet, the loadings on each scale do not add up to a conceptually satisfactory (much less elegant) solution. The Challenge-Security dimension seems especially muddled.

Although the SPV's test manual has been revised and updated, the instrument was last revised over 20 years ago (1965). The format requires the respondent to select the items in each of 30 triads that are most and least liked. No formal validity or fakability scales are incorporated. Although norms are provided for high school students, the measure remains one requiring a fairly high degree of reading comprehension and test sophistication. It is difficult to imagine the test being used with students or others of below average intelligence and reading level.

Normative data are included for several groups. Unfortunately, the data are not adequately elaborated as to geographic, racial, and socioeconomic distributions. Although minorities were included in the normative samples, no breakdown for each race is provided. (Buried in the manual's validity section are normative data for Japanese college students and Indian high school students.) Norms are provided for two industrial samples (managers and "workers in routinized jobs"), but only combined sample data are presented (without age, sex, or experience level breakdowns). Given the profound societal changes of the last 20 years, a need for new normative data and more sophisticated elaboration of norms is suggested.

An abundance of types of validity evidence is presented on behalf of the SPV: factorial, correlations with other tests, and descriptive data for groups of known characteristics. The test is differentiated from abilities, but in considering its relationship with other personality-like variables, the author follows an unfortunate practice of correlating the SPV with other tests produced by him, (viz., the Survey of Interpersonal Values, the Gordon Personal Profile, the Gordon Personal Inventory, and the Work Environment Preference Schedule). Both with his own instrumentation and when comparing the SPV with other measures, the samples are small and the results rather mixed. For example, in correlating scores of 58 Peace Corps volunteers on the SPV and the more widely known Allport-Vernon-Lindzey Study of Values, four of the latter's values (Theoretical, Social, Political, and Religious) have no statistically significant correlations with any of the SPV scales. Although some of the correlations with the Economic and Aesthetic values are in an interpretable direction, there is a statistically significant negative correlation of "Economic Man" with scores on the SPV's achievement scale, and its modest correlation with Goal Orientation is not statistically significant. Whatever the SPV is measuring, it would appear to be something rather different from what is measured by the Study of Values. Similarly, some of the correlations between the SPV and scores on the 16PF for a sample of 172 men make good sense (e.g., Goal Orientation with the 16PF's self-discipline measure), but many do not (e.g., Variety with scales described as "tense, suspicious, and apprehensive"; no correlation between "Practical-Imaginative" scale on the 16PF and the Practical Mindedness scale on the SPV, etc.).

Validity concerns are also raised by the data provided for various occupational groups. This is particularly troubling since the SPV is suggested by its author to be appropriate for use in personnel selection as well as student-counseling contexts. At first, one is impressed with the finding, in three samples of managers from diverse cultural settings, that Achievement and Goal Orientation are the first and second highest scoring patterns for each group. However, in reviewing the normative data provided for 44 occupational samples cited in the Appendix to the test manual, it is noted that in 29 of these diverse occupations, Goal Orientation was the highest endorsed scale (in two additional cases, it ties for first place). In all but three of the remaining cases, Achievement Orientation was the highest score. If there is a theory to explain why record clerks, high school teachers, chemical sales representatives, and retail chain managers all share the same pattern of highest-held values, it is certainly not elaborated. The test author also includes, without discussion, data indicating that a sample of prisoners scored higher on the SPV's achievement scale than did a sample of college students, community college students, and a variety of high school students.

The careful reader is left with the conclusion that there is considerable confusion about exactly what is being measured by this test and a need for clarification before it can usefully be applied in clinical practice. Differential validity for the various scales is insufficiently demonstrated. Whether the test indeed measures "values" as the author contends is open to question. Moreover, variables such as "variety" and "goal orientation" may be more appropriate for describing characteristics of jobs or of the *interaction* between individuals and jobs rather than regarded as typological characteristics of persons. Longitudinal research to assess changes in persons over time as they interact with jobs or other life circumstances of known dimensions is recommended in order to better understand this issue.

Finally, the author's suggestions concerning possible uses for personnel selection are troublesome, especially the author's contention of the need for situational validation. In the context of the manual's 1984 copyright date, this recommendation suggests a curious unfamiliarity with the personnel selection literature of the last decade moving the field toward validity generalization and away from the situational specificity approach advocated by the author.

SUMMARY. The SPV itself was last revised in 1965 and there are only two references in the current (1984) manual as recent as the 1980s. This measure has had many reliability and validity studies, but remains problematic for contemporary use. Although it appears to measure its constructs reliably, there is a much more ambiguous pattern to the validity data presented. There is evidence that the test is measuring something different from abilities. There is less evidence that it is measuring something different from vocational interests.

When this test (and the more widely utilized Survey of Values) were first promulgated, there was a scarcity of tests on the commercial market and the absence of conceptual clarity was perhaps more understandable. Today, there are thousands of tests readily available for a wide variety of personality and vocational constructs and conceptual specificity is appropriately demanded. Considerable updating of this instrument and its research literature are called for if the SPV is to be of more than passing historical interest.

[355]

Survey of Student Opinion of Instruction.

Purpose: For "obtaining student opinion of instruction for use in instructional development and faculty evaluation." High school systems; 1985; separate questionnaires to be completed by students and instructor; provides Class Summary, Instructor Summary, Unit Summary Report, and Comprehensive Summary; 9-track magnetic tape or 8-inch diskette containing all local data may be provided as part of standard report package; 6 factors: Instructor Commitment to Student Learning, Instructor's Communication Skills, Testing and Evaluation, Learning and Understanding, Classroom Supervision and Organization, Instructor Preparation and Enthusiasm; price data including processing for reports available from publisher; (20) minutes; Summa Information Systems, Inc.*

Review of the Survey of Student Opinion of Instruction by KATHRYN CLARK GERKEN, Associate Professor, College of Education, The University of Iowa, Iowa City, IA:

As part of the evaluation process, most instructors in institutions of higher education ask for students' opinions of their instruction. Often, instructors develop their own evaluation forms or use forms created at their institution or forms available commercially. The Summa Survey of Student Opinion of Instruction is a new instrument to evaluate high school instruction.

The Student Opinion of Instruction User's Guide is a 10-page brochure that describes the purpose and procedures for using the Summa Survey System. Sample instructions for a coordinator, proctor, and instructor are also given. The brochure is clearly written and illustrates the contents of each questionnaire and summary report. This reviewer has two copies of the User's Guide, both with a 1985 copyright, but with some differences in content. One User's Guide states that the six factors identified by factor analysis of the first 21 questionnaire items are: Instructor Commitment to Student Learning, Instructors Communication Skills, Testing and Evaluation, Learning and Understanding, Classroom Supervision and Organization, and Instructor Preparation and Enthusiasm. Whereas the other User's Guide states that the six factors are: Instructor Commitment to Student Learning, Instructor Preparation and Organization, Instructor-Student Interaction, Testing, Course Objectives, and Course Assignments. The only other difference noted in these Guides is the fourth level of the summary is labeled "Institution Summary" in one Guide and "Comprehensive Summary" in the other guide. Neither Guide indicates the population of students for whom the survey is intended (secondary or post-secondary or both). However, personal communication with Summa Information Systems (September 18, 1987) confirmed the survey was intended for students in grades 9–12.

The User's Guide or brochure states the Summa Survey System is made up of nationally validated instruments, with normative and comprehensive summaries, that it is more economical than local development, provides reports in 30 days, and has guaranteed accuracy.

The brochure also provides guidelines for the appropriate use of student ratings. These guidelines are well thought out and adhere to the professional standards for test use that are discussed in the *Standards for Educational and Psychological Testing* (AERA, APA, & NCME, 1985).

It is clear from the brochure the survey is comprehensive in scope. Student opinions of instruction for 21 "core" items that might be common to all classes, an overall rating of teaching effectiveness, up to 17 optional items provided by Summa, and up to 11 specific local items comprise the test.

A scale from 5 to 1 where 5 means "strongly agree" and 1 means "strongly disagree" is used for each item on the questionnaires. Means are calculated by using numerical values for the responses and are based on the total number of responses for each summary level. The instructor questionnaire allows an instructor to respond to items dealing with class conditions, such as size, physical environment, quality of textbooks, etc., and add five optional items.

Four levels of summary reports are provided: Class, Instructor, Unit, Institution or Comprehensive. The following information is reported in the class and instructor summary: percent distributions of student responses to each questionnaire item, item means, and comparison means for the unit and comprehensive levels. The class summary also contains responses from the Instructor Questionnaire, whereas the Instructor Summary contains a Factor Mean Report, gives the means and standard deviations for each of the six factors for the instructors, the instructors unit, and for the institution. The Unit Summary Report combines all the student responses within a unit (this could be a subject area or a school within a district or both), gives percent distribution, unit means, and comprehensive comparison or institution means. The frequencies for instructors' responses from all of the Instructor questionnaires for that unit are also given. The Comprehensive or Institution Summary combines the student responses for all classes and gives the percent distribution and comprehensive mean for each item, as well as frequencies for instructors' responses on the Instructor Questionnaire.

Summa also provides a 10-page brochure that gives a description of the uses, benefits, contents, and configuration of the Summa Instructional Survey for Microcomputer (SIS).

The uses and contents are the same as for the Survey of Student Opinion of Instruction, but school personnel can set up their own times to survey classes and analyze the data. The developers believe use of SIS will make instructional development and teacher evaluation easier, more precise, and more efficient. Thus,

Summa has created instructional surveys that can be used by schools with microcomputers (IBM PCs or compatible) or by schools that send all materials to Summa for scoring and summary reports. What is not clear is which system would be most economical. The price of the microcomputer system was provided in materials this reviewer requested from Summa ($895.00 for SIS program and User's Guide package) but the price for questionnaires, scoring, and processing of reports for the initial survey was not provided.

The User's Guide or brochures are what is ordinarily provided to a potential consumer. The brochures do not, however, contain all of the information needed to be an informed consumer. None of the brochures report how the survey was developed, how reliability and validity were determined, or the appropriate age range for the test. The additional information was requested from Summa and the two-page paper they sent entitled "Design and Validity" does provide some of the needed information. The paper indicates that in 1979, Summa reviewed the use of existing surveys to determine what might be needed in a new system. Summa attempted to avoid the weaknesses in other systems by providing a way for faculty members to comment on conditions beyond their control, conducting reliability and validity studies, and providing normative or comprehensive summaries in their reports.

However, Summa does not provide information regarding the initial development of items for the surveys in the additional paper. Were instructors surveyed? Were items borrowed from other surveys? Was there field testing of the items? What is known is that a factor analysis of 90,000 student responses to the first 21 items on the survey identified six factors. However, as already stated, these factors have different names in different publications by Summa.

The brief paper reports that a national sample of 96,000 surveys was divided into various subgroups (grade level, geographic region, etc.) and factor loadings for all the subgroups were invariant. The Design and Validity report also states that internal consistency was established by high correlations between the responses of random pairs of students within classes, among all pairs of students by class, and between the mean responses on each item for equal partitions within classes. Reliabilities are reported as above .90 for classes of 17 or more. It is also reported that stability coefficients for a sample of 20 classes (chosen to represent class level, discipline, class size, and type of institution) were obtained from pre/post comparisons of student responses 2 weeks before the end of the course with responses at the end of the final examination. The stability coefficients ranged from .80 to .95 with an average of .87. No additional information is provided regarding the validity and reliability of the surveys.

In summary, the Student Opinion of Instruction and the Summa Instructional Survey are up-to-date surveys of instruction designed to aid in instructional development and faculty evaluations in high school settings. The surveys are identical in content and differ only in the procedures for administering, scoring, and reporting the results. A unique feature of the surveys is the instructor survey, which allows for instructors' input regarding conditions beyond their control.

The brochures describing the surveys are brief and clearly written and provide appropriate cautions about the use of the surveys. However, neither the brochures nor the additional information provided to this reviewer by Summa contain essential information needed to evaluate the technical and practical usefulness of the instrument.

It is important to know how these surveys were developed and if they are appropriate for a diverse group of secondary schools. Two widely used surveys of instruction that Summa believes measure similar factors to the Summa surveys are the Student Instructional Report (SIR) (ETS, 1973) and Instructional Development Effectiveness Assessment (IDEA) (Hoyt & Owens, 1975). These instruments provide the information needed to evaluate their practical and technical usefulness for college level instruction.

At a minimum this same information is needed for the Summa surveys. Summa needs to rewrite their brochures in order to make sure all information is identical and to include specific information regarding the development of the surveys and how reliability and validity were established. It appears that construct validity and perhaps content validity has been addressed but not criterion-related validity.

If these surveys are to be used in instructional development and faculty evaluation, studies demonstrating the validity of these uses must be conducted. Cohen (1981) suggests student ratings of instruction should show a strong relationship to student achievement, and his meta-analysis of multisection validity studies supports this. Such investigations are needed with the Summa surveys. In addition, instructional development studies, measuring changes in instruction and student opinions are important future research priorities.

REVIEWER'S REFERENCES

Educational Testing Service. (1973). Student Instructional Report. Princeton, NJ: Author.

Hoyt, D. P., & Owens, R. E. (1975). *Instructional Development Effectiveness Assessment*. Manhattan, KS: Center for Faculty Evaluation and Development.

Cohen, P. A. (1981). Student ratings of instruction and student achievement: A meta-analysis of multisection validity studies. *Review of Educational Research*, 51 (3), 281-309.

American Educational Research Association, American Psychological Association, & National Council on Measurement in Education. (1985). *Standards for educational and psychological testing*. Washington, DC: American Psychological Association, Inc.

Summa Information Systems, Inc. (1987). *Summa Information Systems Student Opinion of Instruction Survey: Design and Validity*. Unpublished manuscript.

Review of the Survey of Student Opinion of Instruction by RICHARD A. SAUDARGAS, Associate Professor of Psychology, University of Tennessee, Knoxville, TN:

The Survey of Student Opinion of Instruction is designed for use with any type of curriculum and instructional mode. The accompanying User's Guide is brief and nontechnical. The student questionnaire has three parts. The first part contains 22 statements each rated on a 5-point scale from *strongly agree* to *strongly disagree*. Each question is typically found on surveys of this kind. There are questions about classroom organization, examinations, use of class time, preparation of instructor, etc. The second part contains 17 optional statements from which the instructor may select those considered most appropriate for the students to answer. A few of these statements relate to specific attributes of the instructor, others relate to specialty courses such as laboratory courses, and others ask about the student (e.g., grade level, grade-point average). The third part contains answer blanks for up to 10 questions which can be provided by the instructor.

The instructor's questionnaire consists of 10 statements about the course. Again the questions are typical, asking about the text, the students, etc. There are five response blanks for optional questions.

After the questionnaires are completed, the answer sheets are sent to the publisher for scoring. According to the User's Guide, four levels of reports are returned. These consist of a class summary, an instructor summary, a unit or department summary, and a comprehensive summary. The class summary provides data for each class completing the questionnaire. The instructor summary provides data for all the classes for each instructor. The unit or department summary provides data for each department (e.g., English). The comprehensive summary gives data for all classes. Summary data supplied include number of respondents, percent distributions for each question, item mean, and standard deviations. In addition to the usual data, the instructor summary report contains data on six factor analytically derived dimensions. The instructor, unit, and institution (i.e., school) means and standard deviations are reported next to each factor.

In the Interpreting Your Results section of the User's Guide, the Factor Means Report is called the "single most important part of the Instructor Summary." The six factors contain different numbers of items ranging from 2 to 5. The User's Guide provides no information about how these factors were obtained, characteristics of the sample, *N* size, factor loadings, type of factor analysis, or whether individuals or classes were used for the unit of analysis. Nor does the User's Guide provide a reference to obtain this information. The rest of this section discusses and gives examples of interpreting the Factor Means Report. Basically, if an instructor's mean is different from a comparison mean (i.e., unit mean) by one-half a standard deviation, the difference is considered significant. Examples are given to help clarify this idea. While one may quibble with whether one-half a standard deviation is significant, at least the variability of the student responses is being considered. Because so much other summary information is provided, it would have been helpful if the significant differences had been flagged rather than requiring the users to calculate the differences by hand.

In an Appropriate Use of Student Ratings Section of the User's Guide, several guidelines and cautions are given. Apparently the publishers were concerned enough about the misuses of this instrument they put the guidelines in boldface and in a different type. These guidelines include being certain enough (i.e., appropriate number of) students answer the survey, taking into account the course and instructor characteristics, and using multiple sources of information when making teaching performance decisions. These guidelines are applicable to all instruments of this type, and it was appropriate for the publisher to include them in the User's Guide.

One issue common to all surveys of this kind is they never ask the students or instructor to indicate how important the item being rated is. It is up to the consumer to decide relative importance. For example, students in a class may agree the instructor does not do something very well. At the same time, if asked, the students may also agree that a particular behavior is not very important. Such additional information certainly would temper the interpretaton of that particular item.

In summary, the Survey of Student Opinion is a fairly good instrument of its type. There are no surprises in the kinds of questions it asks or the information provided to the consumer. If a school system were committed to regular course evaluations and did not want to develop its own, this Survey would be worth considering. Indeed the primary advantage of this instrument is that scoring and summary reports are provided. A nice feature is that the instructor, institution, or school district can write items specific to their situation. No norms are provided and are not necessary for an instrument of this type. Over time, a local school district, school, or teacher could accumulate enough data to establish local norms or baseline data.

[356]

Systems Programming Aptitude Test. Purpose: "To evaluate the aptitude and potential of systems programming candidates of all experience levels, for work in all types of systems programming tasks." Systems programmers; 1979–83; SPAT; 1987 price data: $200 per complete set including manual (no date, 6 pages) and scoring service; (180–240) minutes; Jack M. Wolfe; Wolfe Personnel Testing & Training Systems, Inc.*

Review of the Systems Programming Aptitude Test by SAMUEL JUNI, Associate Professor of Counselor Education, New York University, New York, NY:

The SPAT consists of five programming problems requiring respondents to respond in writing to a variety of computer-language style instructions. Contrary to the author's introductory statement, "lower level" applicants would find the test very difficult and would be lost very quickly. The symbols and algorithms in the problem are not defined for the novice, and presume a working familiarity with computer languages. "P" and "Q," for example, are used freely, with no explanation that these symbols are intended to represent any number, algebra style. "Replace" is used freely, presumably meaning to "cross out," but never defined explicitly.

Problems are worded in a cumbersome and particularly difficult style. Commas are shunned. It took this reviewer three passes to punctuate correctly the first problem sentence. The following quote illustrates typical circumlocutions pervading the test: "Change the number appearing in the instruction on Line 11 by increasing it by the number appearing on the line referred to in that instruction." Although the test is reportedly untimed, such encumbrances are unnecessary.

Other than the address of a scoring service, no information is given on test scoring procedures or criteria. Subjects are instructed to hand in all computations and work materials; presumably these, too, are used in evaluating the subject and arriving at a score.

The interim validation study (May, 1981) lists eight different job traits measured by the test: (1) superior logical ability, (2) accuracy, (3) ability to reason with symbols, according to stated definitions, (4) understanding and observing highly complex relationships, (5) deducing generalizations from a series of specific cases, (6) ability to precisely interpret intricate specifications and definitions, (7) analyzing a problem not solvable by trial and error alone, and (8) high attention to detail. No data are presented on the source of these factors, nor are data presented on how items were constructed, by whom they were constructed, or their relationship to these factors.

Subjects are instructed to explain their reasoning in solving problems if it is not "readily apparent" from calculations. It is implied that such explanations enter into scoring, yet a subject's skills at knowing and explaining what is not "readily apparent" are clearly beyond the bounds of the test.

In the absence of other information, it appears that scoring for the test is subjective, categorizing protocols with a wide range of possible responses of various lengths and complexity, where incorrect solutions still can merit partial credit and correct solutions may still merit reductions in credit. The distillation of such test data into a single score is most likely unreliable and psychometrically suspect.

Validity data are presented for 37 systems programming candidates (28 men and 9 women) who were hired by clients of the testing company which designed the test. Scores ranged from 41% to 100% with a mean of 86.6 and a standard deviation of 13.16. Supervisors rated these candidates 6 months later on a 5-point scale ranging from "marginal" to "excellent" (mean = 3.76, standard deviation = .97). The reported correlation between test scores and supervisors' rating was .33 ($p < .05$).

This interim validation report is deficient on several counts: (*a*) What were the criteria for the supervisor's ratings? (*b*) How many supervisors were used and what were the interrater reliabilities? (*c*) What were the qualifications of the supervisors? (*d*) Were supervisors blind to the SPAT scores of employees? (*e*) By using only candidates who were hired, the validity of the test with respect to "poor" candidates is severely limited. (*f*) Were SPAT scores used to determine hiring? If so, this presents another confounding source of error.

The predictive validity, represented by $r =$ .33, accounts for 10% of the variance in supervisor ratings. Such a level does not support the use of the SPAT in personnel selection. The author also presents data showing females scoring higher than males. The relationship is untestable for statistical significance because of the low number of females in the group.

Based on the data presented, the SPAT is not recommended as an evaluative tool.

Review of the Systems Programming Aptitude Test by DAVID MARSHALL, Associate Professor of Computer Science, The Texas Woman's University, Denton, TX:

The Systems Programming Aptitude Test (SPAT) claims to measure the following "essential traits of a systems programming position": logical ability, accuracy, symbolic reasoning, understanding of highly complex relationships, deduction of generalizations from specific cases, ability to interpret intricate definitions and specifications, ability to analyze problems which cannot be solved solely by trial and error, strong attention to detail, and ability to clearly document. Further, the authors claim the test predicts job performance as a systems programmer.

The SPAT consists of five untimed problems presented in increasing order of difficulty. These items usually require 3 to 4 hours for completion in one uninterrupted, unassisted sitting. Primarily the problems involve following complex sets of instructions and documenting one's work.

The first problem is a set of five interrelated number series completion items. These types of items also appear in other computer aptitude tests because they are presumed to measure ability to detect internal, structured order. Though untimed, the examinee is urged to move along in the test after 35 minutes work, and then return to the problem after completing the others.

The second, third, and fourth problems each amount to an exercise in methodically following a complicated set of instructions and writing down one's maneuvers and the results thereof at each step. The instructions are written in English and symbols similar to computer programming language statements. These problems have content validity for assessing basic skills that trained computer programmers must possess in order to read flowcharts and poorly documented computer programs in an effort to decipher the algorithms.

The fifth problem involves locating certain elements in a data display, given very complicated verbal definitions regarding the structure of the display, and computing their sum. This item has content validity for assessing the same skills as problems two, three, and four, as well as some programming knowledge and cognitive skills possessed by expert database and operating systems programmers.

While each problem has a correct solution, the kinds of strategies attempted, quality of documentation, and types of errors made can earn points for the examinee; thus all work must be shown on the test booklet. The test is scored at the testing firm "by categorizing different types of errors and deducting different point values for errors, varying with the severity." A total score and its percentile equivalent are reported, with a narrative description of examinee's strengths, weaknesses, and potential in systems programming. The manual does not specify the error categories, how the narrative is composed in view of the test score and errors made, or even whether the scoring process is completely objective.

CRITICISMS. The test manual provides no information about the development of the test, no formal definition of systems programming aptitude beyond the stated "essential traits," and no information about the role of each test problem in measuring the job traits. One job trait is improperly stated, that of deducing generalizations from particulars. Arriving at a generalization given specific cases is *induction* rather than deduction.

While the test may adequately assess ability to accurately follow complicated instructions, the test does not appear to directly assess the major job trait of ability to create algorithms, to write computer programs, and to invent sets of instructions, in a job-relevant way. This weakness may not prove crucial because the test is designed for trained programming candidates who presumedly are able to, given a problem statement, create a program or system of programs for solving the problem. However, ability to follow instructions does not necessarily imply either the ability for or interest in computer programming, and the test manual provides no rationale or data to support such an implication.

The manual cites no empirical evidence whatsoever in support of the SPAT as a measure of the stated job traits or systems programming aptitude, or as a valid predictor of job success. There is no information regarding test reliability and validity. Though sparse, the information on test scoring suggests that conventional methods of estimating internal consistency reliability may not be applicable. Interrater and test-retest reliabilities are not reported.

One validation study is reported in a separate document, but is of questionable value. Thirty-seven job candidates at 18 different sites took the SPAT, and 6 months after hiring they were rated by their supervisors on a 5-point scale of Marginal (1), Acceptable (2), Good (3), Very Good (4), and Excellent (5). A correlation between the SPAT and ratings was reported as .33, $p < .05$, but the type of correlation procedure used was not specified. The reviewer recomputed the correlation on the raw data listed in the report, with the following results: Pearson $r = .347$, $p < .02$; Spearman rho $= .261$, $p > .05$; Kendall Tau-b $= .204$, $p > .05$. Given that the supervisor rating criterion cannot be considered an interval level measure and that some might argue ordinal properties for percentile scores, the latter two nonparametric correlations may be more appropriate to use in assessing the SPAT-ratings relationship. Both values are undesirably low and not statistically significant. Of greater concern is the lack of evidence that the ratings were either reliable or valid correlates of job success. The manual does not give information about procedures used to assess interrater reliability or rating validity. The results of this small sample study do not constitute adequate evidence of predictive validity.

The SPAT should be correlated with measures of intelligence and other aptitudes and abilities, both related and unrelated to computer programming, and with valid, reliable job performance criteria. Such work will enable the establishment of construct and predictive test validities. At this time such evidence does not exist.

The test manual includes a percentile norm table, but no information is given regarding its development. The norm sample appears to have been 662 "experienced candidates" mentioned only in a separate table of descriptive sample statistics. Over a third of the percentile entries are marked with an asterisk which referred to a footnote that read: "Differences due to time factor." The reviewer found it impossible to interpret the footnote, and no explanation was given in the manual.

In summary, the SPAT has content validity for measuring some of the stated job criteria, but does not appear to directly measure computer programming ability or interest for trained candidates. The test mainly requires examinees to follow complex instruction sets. The manual makes many claims as to what the SPAT measures and how it can be used in selection and promotion activities, but such claims are not supported empirically. The lack of evidence regarding validity, reliability, actual usefulness in personnel selection, and sex or race biases in the test weigh heavily against using the SPAT as a selection device until such evidence is presented. Research on the reliability and validity of the test should be conducted and the test manual should be rewritten to contemporary standards of completeness regarding test development and scoring, normative information, and reliability and validity.

[357]

Taylor-Johnson Temperament Analysis. Purpose: Provides "an evaluation in visual form showing the respondent's feelings about himself or herself at the time when he or she answered the questions," and also provides "a measure of interpersonal perception." Secondary school students, college students and adults; 1941–85; T-JTA; revision of the Johnson Temperament Analysis; self or criss-cross testing; 9 trait scores: Nervous vs. Composed, Depressive vs. Lighthearted, Active-Social vs. Quiet, Expressive-Responsive vs. Inhibited, Sympathetic vs. Indifferent, Subjective vs. Objective, Dominant vs. Submissive, Hostile vs. Tolerant, Self-disciplined vs. Impulsive, (plus Test-Taking Attitude Scale); 8 computer report scales: 1 validity scale (Consistency), 4 supplemental scales (Adequacy of Self-Image [Self-Esteem], Emotional Pressure [Stress], Alienating, Persuasive/Influential), and 3 supplemental predictive scales (Leadership [Preference/ Potential], Interpersonal Relationships [Potential for Success in Marriage], Family Relationship Skills [Parenting Effectiveness Potential]) yielded only by interpretive program in addition to 9 basic trait scores; 3 forms; 1988 price data: $85 per basic package, option A including 5 question booklets (choice of Regular, Non-Criss-Cross, Secondary Form-S), 50 handscoring answer sheets, 50 profiles (shaded or sten), handscoring stencils, pens, ruler, manual ('84, 74 pages); $98 per expanded basic package, option B including 10 question booklets (Regular or Secondary Form-S), 100 handscoring answer sheets, handscoring stencils, 100 profiles, pens, ruler, and test manual; $108 per comprehensive: basic + secondary package, option C including 5 Regular question booklets, 5 Secondary Form-S question booklets, 100 handscoring answer sheets, handscoring stencils, 50 student sten profiles, 50 shaded profiles, pens, ruler, student sten norms ('80, 4 pages); $60 per computer scoring package, option D including 10 question booklets (choice of Regular, Non-Criss-Cross, Secondary Form-S), 50 computer scoring answer sheets and manual; $15 per military scoring training packet; $8 per 10 reusable question booklets (Regular, Non-Criss-Cross, or Secondary Form-S); $12.50 per 100 handscoring or PPI computer scoring service answer sheets; $27.50 per set of handscoring stencils; $35 per set of military handscoring stencils; $12.50 per 100 profiles (choice of regular shaded, shaded without zone designations, regular sten, student sten); $2 per locator-and-profiling ruler; $50 per manual; $19.50 per handbook ('85, 175 pages); $12.50 per student sten norms; $10 per practice scoring training packet; $6.50 per copy of "The AWOL Syndrome" ('71, 20 pages); $5 per reference list; $10 per norms for Spanish-speaking Americans; computer scoring, profiling, and interpretive reports available from publisher, $5 per answer sheet for scoring and profiling, $20 per complete Criss-Cross testing (4 answer sheets, 5 profiles) scoring and profiling; $20 per self test scoring, profiling, interpretive report; $50 per complete Criss-Cross scoring, profiling, 4 interpretive reports; German, French, and Portuguese editions available; (30–45) minutes; original edition by Roswell H. Johnson, revision by Robert M. Taylor, Lucile P. Morrison (manual), W. Lee Morrison (handbook and Secondary Edition question booklet), James C. Berbiglia ("The AWOL Syndrome"); Psychological Publications, Inc.*

a) REGULAR EDITION. Adults and college students (reading level grade 8 and over); 1941–85.

1) *[Criss-Cross Form]*. May be used to evaluate self or significant other.

2) *Non-Criss-Cross Form*. Used only for self testing.

b) SECONDARY EDITION, FORM-S. Secondary school students and adult poor readers (minimum grade 5 reading level); 1972–85; used only for self testing.

See T3:2396 (1 reference); for additional information and a review by Robert F. Stahmann, see 8:692 (18 references); see also T2:840 (3 references); for a review by Donald L. Mosher of an earlier edition of *a*, see 7:572 (1 reference); see also P:264 (3 references) and 6:130 (10 references); for a review by Albert Ellis of the original edition, see 4:62 (6 references); for a review by H. Meltzer of the original edition, see 3:57.

Review of the Taylor-Johnson Temperament Analysis by CATHY W. HALL, Assistant Professor of Psychology, East Carolina University, Greenville, NC:

The previous edition of the Taylor-Johnson Temperament Analysis (T-JTA) has been reviewed in both the Seventh and Eighth Editions of the *Mental Measurements Yearbook* (Mosher, 1972, [7:572]; Stahmann, 1978, [8:692]). The 1984 revision updated the norms for the General Population and College Student (1966–67) and norms for adolescents (1973 & 1974).

There are three T-JTA question booklet editions: Regular Edition, Regular Non-Criss-Cross Edition, and Secondary Edition. The Regular Edition and Regular Non-Criss-Cross

Edition are appropriate for the general population of adults and college students with a minimum reading level of eighth grade. The Secondary Edition Question Booklet requires a minimum reading level of fifth grade and is recommended for the age range of 13–18 years as well as poor adult readers. There is no time limit for the administration of the T-JTA, but it usually requires 30–45 minutes. The questions consist of 180 items equally divided among nine bipolar traits: Nervous (vs. Composed), Depressive (vs. Lighthearted), Active-Social (vs. Quiet), Expressive-Responsive (vs. Inhibited), Sympathetic (vs. Indifferent), Subjective (vs. Objective), Dominant (vs. Submissive), Hostile (vs. Tolerant), and Self-Disciplined (vs. Impulsive). In addition to these nine bipolar traits, trait score combinations can be assessed. These score combinations include: Anxiety Pattern, Withdrawal Pattern, Dominant-Hostile Pattern, Dependent-Hostile Pattern, Emotionally Inhibited-Blocked Pattern, and Emotionally Repressed Pattern. If the examiner chooses to utilize the computerized scoring and interpretation service from Psychological Publications, supplemental scales are also available. Some examples of the computer-generated scales are: Adequacy of Self-Image, Emotional Pressure, Leadership Potential, Potential for Successful Marital Adjustment, and Potential for Successful Parenting. These scales are not available through hand-scoring procedures.

The T-JTA scales are not useful with people who exhibit extreme maladjustments. The scales are designed to aid in the early identification of problem areas prior to the development of acute problems.

The examinee can respond to the 180 items on the T-JTA Regular Edition as they apply to himself/herself (Self test) or as they apply to a significant other (Criss-Cross test). The Criss-Cross test is beneficial in marital counseling. The format may help subjects gain self-understanding as well as insights into the significant other. Each examinee fills out the record form twice: once as it applies to himself/herself, and once as it applies to the significant other. The present reviewer concurs with Stahmann (8:692) that this is a "unique and valuable feature of the test."

Reliability and validity data are presented in the T-JTA manual. Reliability studies include test-retest correlation coefficients, split-half correlations, and Hoyt's analysis of variance approach. Correlations for 1- to 3-week intervals on the nine scales ranged from .62 to .90. Split-half reliability studies and reliability estimates by the analysis of variance procedure also proved to be adequate for the T-JTA.

Efforts to establish test validity include empirical validity studies comparing professional clinical ratings to the T-JTA scores. In addition, "self-rated" test results were compared with "other-rated" (Criss-Cross) test results. Validity studies, referenced in the manual, report the relationships of T-JTA scales to the Sixteen Personality Factor Questionnaire (16PF) and the Minnesota Multiphasic Personality Inventory (MMPI). The relationships among the measures support the construct validity of the T-JTA.

Standardization data are provided in the T-JTA manual. The General Population *N* was 3,942 (2,316 males and 1,626 females). The College Student *N* was 3,926 (1,644 males and 2,282 females). The Secondary Population (ages 13–18) *N* was 10,071 (5,045 males and 5,026 females). The 1984 norms for use in scoring the Criss-Cross test for each population group are also included in the T-JTA manual. The 1984 Secondary norms are a combination of the 1973 High School norms with the 1977 Secondary norms.

The norms are representative of age and sex, but are limited in geographical and socioeconomic representation (i.e., 49.01% of the General Population sample is from California with the remaining normative data coming from 32 other states).

The manual is well constructed and provides appropriate cautions concerning interpretation and use of the T-JTA. It also provides step-by-step instructions for scoring, conversion of raw scores, and plotting of results. The manual provides a practice packet with profile forms for plotting results of two Self tests and two Criss-Cross tests.

In addition to the three portions of the T-JTA already described, there is also a supplement for use in the early identification of potential absent-without-leave (AWOL) military personnel. The research conducted with the AWOL scale has methodological flaws especially in terms of controlling for extraneous variables. The results support the provision of preventive counseling, but should not be seen as prediction data. The term AWOL is also somewhat misleading. The T-JTA was used to identify extreme personality traits, not to predict specific misconduct.

The T-JTA instrument is very well constructed. The norm group is not representative, but in general the T-JTA follows sound test construction procedures. The authors appear to be aware of the need to keep the T-JTA updated and current.

The Criss-Cross scoring available from this test has been previously viewed as a unique and highly useful feature. The present reviewer concurs with this viewpoint and feels this aspect of the T-JTA has a great deal to offer the practicing family therapist in evaluating interpersonal relations.

REVIEWER'S REFERENCES

Mosher, D. L. (1972). [Review of Taylor-Johnson Temperament Analysis]. In O. K. Buros (Ed.), *Seventh mental measurements yearbook* (Vol. II, pp. 959-960). Highland Park, NJ: Gryphon Press.

Stahmann, R. F. (1978). [Review of Taylor-Johnson Temperament Analysis]. In O. K. Buros (Ed.), *Eighth mental measurements yearbook* (Vol. I, pp. 1111-1112). Highland Park, NJ: Gryphon Press.

Review of the Taylor-Johnson Temperament Analysis by PAUL MCREYNOLDS, Professor of Psychology, University of Nevada-Reno, Reno, NV:

The origin of the Taylor-Johnson Temperament Analysis (T-JTA) goes back to 1941, when Roswell Johnson published the Johnson Temperament Analysis (JTA). In the 1960s the JTA was extensively revised by Robert Taylor and Lucile Morrison and published as the Taylor-Johnson Temperament Analysis (T-JTA). Since that time extensive normative data, updated to 1984, have been collected.

The T-JTA consists of 180 questions, to each of which the subject is requested to answer "decidedly yes" or "mostly so"; "undecided"; or "decidedly no" or "mostly not so." The 180 items are comprised of 20 items for each of nine personality variables (e.g., Nervous vs. Composed; see listing in test entry above), with no item overlap. Eighteen of the items were empirically selected, on the basis of correlations with the Minnesota Multiphasic Personality Inventory (MMPI) K Scale, to constitute an Attitude Scale for use in assessing test-taking bias. In addition to the 10 scales just noted, interpretation involves the inspection of certain trait patterns (e.g., Anxiety pattern, made up of values on Nervous, Depressive, and Subjective scales). A number of supplemental computer-scored scales (see test entry above), presumably more experimental, are also available. The middle or "undecided" response category (termed "Mids") is also accorded interpretative significance. The T-JTA is available in three different test formats, two for adults and one for adolescents. The items in the latter form, though designed to include the same content as in the adult forms, are in some instances worded in simpler English. Of the two adult formats the items in one are worded with respect to the subject (e.g., "Are you by nature a forgiving person?"), and in the other with respect to a specific other person (e.g., "Is ______ by nature a forgiving person?").

Independent norms, stated in terms of percentiles and stens, and updated to 1984, are provided for the general population, college students, and adolescents, each separately for males and females. In terms of numbers (*N*s = 3,942 for general population, 3,926 for college students, and 10,071 for adolescents), representations of each gender, geographic distribution, and socio-economic levels, the norms, with respect to contemporary America, appear quite solid, better than for most inventories. Ethnic minorities appear to be adequately represented in the secondary school samples, but this question cannot be evaluated with certainty for the other groups from data in the manual. Reliability (test-retest and odd-even) for the nine basic scales, as reported in the manual for samples of presumably typical subjects, are satisfactory to good, but are somewhat lower, though still acceptable, for a sample of military offenders (Fraas & Fox, 1973). Reliability data for computer scales are not reported.

The manual for the T-JTA and the accompanying handbook are, within the limitations noted below, quite good. The nature, background, and purposes of the test are explained clearly, and the clinical applications of the instrument, particularly in couples counseling, are adequately developed. A special feature of one form of the T-JTA Profile sheet (on which the subject's results are plotted) is that it includes shaded portions to suggest which trait scores are within a desirable range, and which are outside that range. While such a method can, in principle, facilitate test interpretation, the particular areas shaded and the gradations in shading utilized on the special T-JTA form are not adequately explained or justified in the manual, and until (and unless) sufficient supporting data are provided this form should be employed in only an extremely tentative way.

Though not a crucial fact to T-JTA users, it may be observed that despite its name the instrument is not, in the accepted meaning of the term, a measure of temperaments, analogous to the Temperament Inventory or to Buss and Plomin's (1975) Temperament Survey. Rather, the T-JTA is a personality inventory of the same genre as the California Psychological Inventory and the Personality Research Form. In this context it has a number of attractive qualities. It is reasonably brief, and its nine basic scales assess conventional and important traits. The various alternative formats provide the user with a number of options. Perhaps the test's most noteworthy feature is the arrangement, noted above and referred to as criss-cross testing, by which an assessor can compare a subject's profile with a profile on the same person completed by someone else. Though this procedure is possible with any inventory, it is facilitated by the T-JTA format and is especially useful in marital counseling, an area in which the T-JTA has been widely utilized. Further, the T-JTA format, as well as its trait labels, enhances the feasibility of sharing test results openly with a client.

This reviewer's major reservation concerning the T-JTA is the question of its validity. Although the scales appear to have considerable face validity, the main objective evidence for validity presented in the manual consists of correlations of T-JTA trait scores with MMPI and 16PF (Sixteen Personality Factor) variables. While the resulting coefficients are informative, the lack of symmetry between the MMPI and 16PF dimensions and the T-JTA scales makes the comparisons strained, and certainly not sufficient to demonstrate test validity. The manual states that research employing clinical ratings and the results of criss-cross testing provide support for validity, but no specific data and no references are given. What is needed is a series of studies specifically designed to objectively evaluate the validity of the different T-JTA scales. Ideally, this should involve correlations of each of the scales separately with relevant criteria, including non-self-report criteria. For example, the correlations between the Depression Scale and clinical ratings of depression, as well as with the Beck Depression Inventory, could be determined. The manual does include a study by Romoser indicating a reasonable degree of independence of the scales, but this does not attest to their validity. It also includes a study by Berbiglia (1971) indicating a particular T-JTA pattern among military AWOL offenders, but this conclusion was not supported by Fraas and Fox (1973).

To sum up, my overall evaluation of this T-JTA is positive, but guarded. Although the test has many attractive features, there is a danger that it will be adopted into routine clinical use before the validity of its scales has been adequately established. Hopefully, research will be forthcoming to further assay T-JTA's validity and to elaborate its range of applicability.

REVIEWER'S REFERENCES

Berbiglia, J. C. (1971). *The AWOL syndrome.* Los Angeles: Psychological Publications.

Fraas, L. A., & Fox, L. J. (1973). Counseling from the Taylor-Johnson Temperament Analysis AWOL syndrome. *Measurement and Evaluation in Guidance*, 6, 111-116.

Buss, A. H., & Plomin, R. (1975). *A temperament theory of personality development.* New York: Wiley.

[358]

Teacher Assessment of Grammatical Structures. Purpose: "Developed to evaluate a child's understanding and use of the grammatical structures of English and to suggest a sequence for teaching these structures." Ages 2–4, 5–9, 9 and over; 1983; TAGS; 3 ratings per level on Imitated, Prompted, or Spontaneous Production; ratings are based on informal administration in classroom or therapy setting; individual; 3 levels; 1985 price data: $6 per 25 rating forms per level; $15 per manual (203 pages); administration time not reported; Jean S. Moog and Victoria J. Kozak; Central Institute for the Deaf.*

a) TAGS-P, PRE-SENTENCE LEVEL. Ages up to 6 years for hearing impaired, ages 2–4 for language impaired children; receptive and expressive skills.

b) TAGS-S, SIMPLE SENTENCE LEVEL. Ages 5–9 years for hearing impaired, ages 3 and over for language impaired children; expressive skills.

c) TAGS-C, COMPLEX SENTENCE LEVEL. Ages 8 and over for hearing impaired, 3.5 and over for language impaired.

Review of the Teacher Assessment of Grammatical Structures by ELIZABETH M. PRATHER,

Professor of Speech and Hearing Science, Arizona State University, Tempe, AZ:

Teacher Assessment of Grammatical Structures (TAGS) is a series of rating forms designed primarily for use by teachers of hearing-impaired children. It is reportedly also appropriate for rating normal-hearing children with serious delays in English syntax. The authors suggest that the forms are useful for (*a*) specifying the child's use of syntactic structures, (*b*) planning language instruction, (*c*) measuring and recording progress, and (*d*) reporting to parents.

No normative data have been provided to interpret a child's level of performance; the grammatical structures on each of the three forms, however, are listed in an "expected order of development." The sequenced orders were determined by the authors from experiences in teaching the hearing impaired, experiences with standardized language tests, knowledge of normal language development, and understanding how teaching the hearing-impaired parallels normal language development.

The TAGS closely resembles in content and format the Grammatical Analysis of Elicited Language (GAEL) (Moog, Kozak, & Geers, 1983). There are, however, important differences. The GAEL was standardized on hearing-impaired (aged 3 to 12 years) and normal-hearing children (aged 2 1/2 to 5 1/2 years) for use in a formal test setting. The TAGS provides no standardization data and no reliability or validity data. Teachers are asked to rate each structure as *Acquired* or *Emerging* from observations made during classroom activities. The teacher notes whether the child comprehends, imitates, shows prompted production, or shows spontaneous production by checking the appropriate box. The acquired-emerging distinction is made on the basis of ease of facility with which the child comprehends or uses the structure. Criteria for ratings are specified and teachers are encouraged to observe the child in enough situations to make accurate judgments.

The TAGS was developed to chart a child's understanding and use of structures in everyday environments. This information could be used to plan instructional targets and to assign children to appropriate instructional groups. Because the structures are ordered developmentally, the forms might serve as a guide to the selection of the next targets.

It would be inappropriate to categorize the TAGS as a test. It is a series of check sheets designed to help teachers observe a child's comprehension, imitation, and production of various grammatic forms. With our current emphasis on functional communication and pragmatics, these forms limited to grammar seem almost outdated.

It is unfortunate that no evidence of validity is provided. One wonders whether teachers' ratings would closely resemble those completed by trained observers within the classroom. It would also be of interest to know how a child's GAEL performance (in a structured testing session) compares to the TAGS ratings completed by the teacher. These data are not provided.

The usefulness of the TAGS would depend upon (*a*) the degree of emphasis a given teaching program places on grammatic development, and (*b*) the ability of the classroom teacher to observe and record accurately the various aspects of grammatical language.

REVIEWER'S REFERENCE

Moog, J. S., Kozak, V. J., & Geers, A. E. (1983). *Grammatical analysis of elicited language*. St. Louis, MO: Central Institute for the Deaf.

Review of the Teacher Assessment of Grammatical Structures by KENNETH G. SHIPLEY, *Professor and Chairman, Department of Communicative Disorders, Laboratory School-MS* 80, *California State University-Fresno, Fresno, CA:*

The Teacher Assessment of Grammatical Structures (TAGS) consists of an instructional manual and different rating forms for evaluating aspects of hearing-impaired children's abilities with a variety of syntactic constructions. The three scales generally correspond to children's language development and language age.

TAGS-P focuses on six types of language constructions. These include single words, two-word combinations, three-word combinations, pronouns, wh-questions, and tense markers. TAGS-S attempts to evaluate children's use of six more advanced constructions which range from noun modifiers (e.g., adjectives to demonstratives) to questions (e.g., *where* to modals like *can* and *may*). Each of these more advanced constructions is subdivided into four to six levels of specific language substructures.

The third form, TAGS-C, views six even more complex sentence-level constructions. Categories range from certain types of nouns to various question types. Again, each of these six categories contains four to six levels of substructures available for evaluation. Thus, the three rating forms include more than 220 language features and structures available for evaluation.

Each of the three TAGS rating forms is administered by teacher observation. Essentially, the teacher is looking for the presence or absence of the specific words or structures under study in various classroom situations. Productions are rated as follows: imitated productions, prompted productions, and spontaneous productions. Based on multiple observations, each structure is subsequently rated as being acquired, emerging, or a possible teaching objective.

There are several very positive aspects of the TAGS. Among the most positive are the range and large number of language features that can be evaluated. Other positive features include the readability of the manual and some of the teaching examples and appropriate cautions that are outlined in the manual. For example, the authors caution that:

> Since not all possible structures are included on the TAGS rating forms, the teacher should not let the forms limit what is taught, but . . . as a guide to organize instruction. Rather than dictating what to teach, the TAGS rating forms should serve as a reminder of the wide variety of structures possible and should stimulate the teacher to think of others.

Although there are several strengths of TAGS, there are also several major weaknesses that must be noted. The most noticeable problems are the failure to address issues of validity or reliability. Validity seems to be assumed, but neither data nor an ample review of appropriate literature are presented to the reader. This is particularly apparent in the 203-page instructional manual, which contains only two fully cited references and four nonreferenced bibliographic works by TAGS' senior author.

There are vague references to validity issues as when the authors state the belief that teachers know the child best and indicate that teacher ratings are based on multiple observations. However, this does not speak to the instrument's basic validity. This surfaces as a problem because the authors recommend using a developmental teaching sequence and present vertical teaching levels for "the sequence for teaching [language] structures within each grammatical category." Unfortunately, a number of these sequences fail to correspond to the current literature on children's language development. The authors offer little evidence to substantiate the developmental sequences, and no direct data are offered to the reader.

There is also a very sparse discussion of reliability issues. Reliability is affected by a variety of factors: observer's backgrounds, their training and experience, the time they have to study a child, and their knowledge of language and its development. In the absence of more precise information on how these factors affect the administration and scoring of the TAGS, users must remain cautious about the test's reliability.

In summary, TAGS presents a novel and structured method for viewing language and its development with hearing-impaired youngsters. It has been used in a number of settings and has an appearance of relatively good face validity. However, educators and clinicians need to read the manual very carefully, understand the appropriate applications of such a model, and be judicious in their consideration of the validity and reliability issues posed within this review.

[359]

A Teacher Attitude Inventory: Identifying Teacher Positions in Relation to Educational Issues and Decisions. Purpose: "Indicator of teacher attitudes regarding philosophical issues and contrasting educational practices." Teachers; 1986; TAI; for evaluation and research purposes; 5 scores: Controlling, Rigidity, Individualism, Professionalism, Total; 1986 price date: $19.95 per complete kit including 25 Inventories, 25 scoring sheets, and manual ('86, 16 pages); $6 per 25 Inventories; $6 per 25 scoring sheets; $10 per manual; (10–15) minutes; Joanne Rand Whitmore; United Educational Services, Inc.*

Review of A Teacher Attitude Inventory: Identifying Teacher Positions in Relation to Educational Issues and Decisions by MARY HENNING-STOUT, Assistant Professor of Counseling Psychology, Lewis and Clark College, Portland, OR:

The Teacher Attitude Inventory (TAI) is a descriptive instrument designed to measure teacher attitudes relative to two divergent philosophical positions regarding education. This scale was originally developed to serve as a measure of the effectiveness of an inservice program designed to "encourage teachers to break away from traditional methods and to experiment with new alternatives; to attend more to individual students and their emotional needs; and to individualize instruction more often in order to increase pupil success and opportunities for self-correction." Thus, the original intent of the scale was to gauge movement toward more flexible, child-centered attitudes toward teaching.

In the 16-page manual accompanying the scale, the author suggests that application of the TAI in other educational settings could occur for purposes of evaluation and research. A number of potential uses for the inventory are presented in the manual and discussed below. Among these uses is the evaluation of prevailing attitudes to illustrate intraorganizational matches, for example, among teachers and between teachers and administrators or teachers and students.

ADMINISTRATION. The TAI takes the form of a questionnaire with 24 items. These items are presented in a 5-point Likert-type format with two contrasting educational positions at the opposite poles (e.g., "Schools are too structured these days" vs. "A major problem in today's schools is a lack of well defined structure"). Teachers indicate their position relative to these statements by marking an "X" in one of the five blanks between them. The TAI is reported to require 10–15 minutes for completion.

The author suggests that the inventory be administered in an atmosphere that encourages "unreserved self-disclosure" of educational philosophy by establishing "an open, trusting, nonjudgmental climate for 'testing.'" Although this suggestion would seem to lead to the most candid responses to the TAI, contriving such an environment would seem to be an organizational intervention that could contaminate the data gathered. This would especially be the case if the TAI were being administered in any sort of descriptive manner (i.e., for describing current attitudes in a particular educational setting). The author does briefly suggest that, for use in more rigid organizations, the TAI should be administered in such a way that the responses are anonymous. Her other suggestions for informing the respondents of the nature and use of the inventory include ethical considerations that are impressively complete.

Along with the 25 questionnaire copies included in the standard inventory packet, there are 25 scoring sheets for tabulating individual responses. This useful sheet allows for tabulation of a total score and four subscale scores. The subscales identified are intuitive and, according to the author, have not been verified with factor analysis. These subscales include items reflecting the following dimensions: "Controlling vs. Releasing, Rigidity vs. Flexibility, Individualism vs. Group-Orientation, and Interest vs. Disinterest in Professionalism." The author suggests that these subscale scores should be used with caution and that the total score seems of greater value.

PSYCHOMETRIC PROPERTIES. One distracting feature of the TAI is the significant number of typographical errors in both the manual and questionnaire. This weakness is mentioned in this section of the review because additional evidence of careless construction of the manual detracts significantly from the claims regarding the inventory's psychometric properties. The report of the project for which this scale was developed is referred to quite frequently as a source for additional statistical information. There is also frequent reference in the manual to a section of that text that would explain and present such data. No such section exists. Therefore, in spite of the author's convincing prose regarding the inventory's content validity (factor analysis reportedly supported the dichotomous nature of the polar stems) and predictive validity (evidence that attitudes indicated match with behavioral practices), the lack of supporting data presentation requires the consumer to take a great deal "on faith."

The description of the scale's construction also leaves several questions. The author reports that the items making up the scale were selected by "the research staff" as fitting with one of the dichotomous styles. There is no indication of the criteria used to select these questions. Again, the author reports successful item analysis, test-retest results, and within- and between-scale correlations but provides no data to support her statements.

A review of the project report to which the author frequently refers (Whitmore, 1974) did provide the statistical results of efforts to establish the psychometric viability of this instrument. Reliability was described as moderate and seemed low for one of the two school districts tested in the original application of this instrument. Construct validity was established with factor analysis, which verified the dichotomy represented by the items but failed to support the existence of the postulated subscales. Predictive validity was weakly supported by the data in the project report.

Whitmore (1974) called for additional research to establish the psychometric strength of the instrument. The original project employing the TAI was completed in the early 1970s. Apparently no research in response to the report author's call has occurred. The 1985 manual cites no other research beyond the 1974 project report.

PRACTICAL AND RESEARCH UTILITY. The author of the TAI presents an impressive number of practical uses for this scale. The TAI could be used by school building administrators to determine the most effective match between teachers and children with specific learning needs (e.g., more "rigid" teachers with children requiring more structure). Findings could also be used to group teachers in teams according to their educational views or to match an administrator's characteristics with those of the teachers with whom s/he will work. Measurement of faculty attitudes regarding education could guide program planners in deciding which approaches would be most effective in a given school or classroom. TAI results could also provide information useful for determining faculty development needs.

This inventory also seems to have a variety of potential uses for research. Results could be used to determine the correlation between faculty positions on the scale and the relative success of specific programs. The original use of the TAI was to measure attitude change in a pre-post test design. This use is potentially generalizable. Finally, the TAI could be used as a covariate in studies considering the success of district- or state-wide programs. The utility of this inventory is restricted only by its incomplete development as described in the preceding section.

In summary, the TAI has significant potential as a practical and research tool for individuals involved in the planning and evaluation of educational programs and organizations. The incompleteness of the inventory in its current presentation restricts its utility. Without verification of the psychometric strength of the TAI, the consumer would be remiss in choosing this inventory for any but descriptive uses, and then without reliance on the reportedly dichotomous items as accurately representative of disparate behavioral tendencies.

REVIEWER'S REFERENCE

Whitmore, J. R. (1974). *A Teacher Attitude Inventory: Identifying Teacher Positions in Relation to Educational Issues and Decisions.* (Research and Development Memorandum No. 118). Stanford, CA: Stanford University, Stanford Center for Research and Development in Teaching.

Review of A Teacher Attitude Inventory: Identifying Teacher Positions in Relation to Educational Issues and Decisions by SYLVIA ROSENFIELD, Professor of School Psychology, Temple University, Philadelphia, PA:

A Teacher Attitude Inventory (TAI), a self-report questionnaire for elementary school teachers, was developed as an indicator of teacher attitudes about philosophical issues related to contrasting educational practices. Specifically, the instrument attempted to divide teachers along a continuum between two contrasting styles: (*a*) Style One was assigned to "traditional, teacher-centered" methodology; (*b*) Style Two represented progressive, pupil-centered approaches and experimentation. Characteristics of the contrasting basic styles are described in the manual. In addition, the scale itself was divided by the author into four theoretical subscales: Rigidity, Controlling, Professionalism, and Individualism.

The instrument contains 24 items, divided into the four theoretical subscales (Rigidity, Controlling, Professionalism, and Individualism), each consisting of six items. Items were constructed by preparing statements to reflect basic attitudes along these dimensions; each statement was paired with its opposite to formulate an item. Teachers place a mark on a 5-point Likert scale between the paired dichotomous statements, expressing their tendency to agree or disagree with one of the statements in each pair.

Administration time is considered by the authors to be 10 to 15 minutes. Suggestions are given to facilitate teacher responding, including sensitivity to issues of confidentiality and explanation of the purpose of the questionnaire. Two sample items are included in the manual. Scoring is done by hand using an individual scoring sheet that enables the scorer to group the items on the subscales and indicates which 13 items are reverse scored.

The TAI was developed for a field-based project of the Stanford Center for Research and Development in Teaching (SCRDT). This project was designed as an intervention in an elementary school with a predominantly black, low SES population. The objective of the inservice program, which formed the basis of the project, was to enable the teachers to "break away from traditional methods and to experiment with new alternatives." The inventory was developed to measure the change in teacher attitudes as a result of the inservice training.

The manual indicates that SCRDT Research and Development Memorandum No. 118 (Whitmore, 1974) contains the bulk of the technical data on the TAI. No data on reliability and validity are presented in the manual itself, although there are some general statements about the research presented in the Memorandum. The Memorandum, which can be obtained for cost of xeroxing and mailing from the Center for Educational Research, cautions with the following statement: "At this stage, there is not enough evidence of the reliability and validity of the instrument for its use to be extended beyond that of qualified researchers desiring to obtain more data." No additional data are provided in the TAI Manual since the publication of the 1974 Memorandum, however.

The data presented in the Memorandum are essential to the potential user of the TAI. It is important, for example, to know that there is little evidence in the Memorandum to support the use of subscores, although the test scoring sheet continues to divide the items into the four hypothesized subscales. Factor analysis of the TAI did not support either a 2-factor or a 4-factor construct, but rather suggested a general factor. In addition, the samples used in the initial construction and validation of the questionnaire are limited to two California school districts. One was the predominantly low-SES black community with a tradition of emphasizing the 3-Rs and with firm discipline and control of pupils as the principal concern of the teachers (the district in which the inservice was provided). The contrasting district was a predominantly white, middle class community, with teachers who were frequently engaged in some form of innovative experiment in grouping or instruction. The descriptions of the schools were based on the direct experience of the test author.

Statistical analysis of the original questionnaire, which consisted of 40 items, is not reported in the Memorandum. On the revised 24-item TAI, interitem correlations were low to moderate, with low correlations between similar items. Whitmore (1974) suggested that errors may have occurred in the original pairing of statements assumed to be dichotomous and/or in assigning items to subscales. Coefficients of internal consistency for the total test varied between .76 and .84 for the samples at different times, indicating some degree of internal consistency. Test-retest reliability is hard to evaluate on the data provided, given the long period of time between testings (October and May). In the middle class school, without an intervention project, the questionnaire was moderately stable over the year (.66 for total score on an N of 29). Primary teachers appeared to be more stable than intermediate teachers, but the sample was small.

Validation studies included a factor analysis, with both a 4-factor and a 2-factor rotation examined. The findings, as noted above, indicated that one general attitude factor is the best fit for the inventory. Low reliabilities on individual items suggest caution in the use of the factor analysis results, however.

Criterion-related validity was also attempted, to predict whether teachers observed as exhibiting behavior described as Style One (traditional "3-R" teacher behavior) would receive significantly lower scores on the TAI than teachers behaving as described by Style Two (innovative, experimental teaching behavior). There were, however, large within-group variances and lack of consistent differences between groups, although Whitmore notes that differences between group means were usually in the predicted direction. There were significant differences between teachers in the two districts (which Whitmore had described as reflecting the two different styles) on TAI Total, Rigidity, and Controlling scale means; these findings were due to differences between the intermediate teachers in the two districts. Based on the informal descriptions of the two districts by Whitmore, the instrument did seem to validate her perception of the attitudes displayed. Although Whitmore provides cutoff scores for differentiating teachers as Style One or Style

Two in the manual, there does not seem to be a sound empirical foundation for their use, and she concludes the Memorandum with a call for norms to be obtained on large heterogeneous samples.

Whitmore concludes the test manual with a caution: "Until there is more extensive testing of the reliability and validity of the instrument . . . , users should be cautious and tentative in using test scores in practical decision making." The instrument as developed thus far has, in fact, very limited reliability and validity data, with no compelling case for the subscales. No additional research on the TAI is reported by Whitmore between the 1974 Memorandum and the publication of the manual in 1985. However, given the increasing interest in adaptive instruction and the continuing interest in evaluating the effectiveness of inservice training, the inventory may be useful to researchers in education who are interested in teacher style and its underlying philosophical base.

REVIEWER'S REFERENCE

Whitmore, J. R. (1974). *A Teacher Attitude Inventory: Identifying Teacher Positions in Relation to Educational Issues and Decisions.* (Research and Development Memorandum No. 118). Stanford, CA: Stanford University, Stanford Center for Research and Development in Teaching.

[360]

Teacher Role Survey (Revised). Purpose: "To measure teachers' expectancies for internal or external control of important aspects of the work of teaching." Elementary, secondary, or technical school teachers; 1986; TRS; 3 factors: Recognition, Teaching/Learning Process, Attitudes of Parents and Society; price data available from publisher; administration time not reported; Darrell E. Anderson and Wayne R. Maes; Wayne R. Maes.*

Review of the Teacher Role Survey (Revised) by SUSAN J. SCHENCK, Associate Professor of Special Education, College of Charleston, Charleston, SC:

The Teacher Role Survey (Revised) consists of 24 pairs of contrasting statements "one indicating a belief in personal influence over important dimensions of the teacher's role and the other expressing a belief in the potency of external factors" (Anderson & Maes, 1988). Respondents are requested to read each statement pair, pick the statement that best reflects their belief, and mark on an answer sheet (which was not included) a value of '1' or '0' for each statement. Scoring is accomplished by totaling the number of '1' values received. No information was presented to indicate the meaning of the scores.

The only information about validity, reliability, and normative data was contained in a research paper that discussed the construction of the original Teacher Role Survey and *not* the Revised Survey. Without information specific to the revised instrument, the survey is of questionable value. However, the initial development of the survey appears adequate based on the limited information provided.

There was no test manual, and in light of the previous comments concerning reliability, validity, and normative data, this is not surprising. The original Teacher Role Survey was normed on a group of 321 teachers either currently teaching and/or enrolled full or part time in graduate education programs. All participants came from a limited geographical area. The representativeness of the normative sample is highly questionable.

As to the interpretation of the results of the Teacher Role Survey (Revised), one is left hanging. There is no discussion related to interpretation of scores. Also lacking are instructions to the examiner concerning administration time, testing conditions, scoring guidelines, and so on.

In its present form, the Teacher Role Survey (Revised) does not meet acceptable standards. The only use for the Survey would seem to rest in the area of research concerned with teacher locus of control. However, additional data are required prior to being able to determine if the Teacher Role Survey (Revised) is an accurate measure of locus of control. More detailed information is required in the following areas: reliability and validity data on the Revised edition; expanded and more representative normative data; instructions concerning administration; and finally, a discussion concerning the interpretation of results.

REVIEWER'S REFERENCE

Anderson, D. E., & Maes, W. (1988). The relationship between teacher locus of control and selected indices of stress. Manuscript submitted for publication.

[361]

Team Effectiveness and Meeting Strategy. Purpose: "Designed to evaluate the effectiveness of group process." Groups or teams; 1977; T.E.A.M.S.; ratings by individuals and group of team effectiveness; 18 scores: Skill Factors (Situation Analysis, Purpose and Objectives, Identifying Problems, Generating Alternatives, Evaluating Alternatives and Selection of Solutions, Making Decisions), Quality Factors (Role and Task Definition, Emphasizing Facts, Standards, Judgment, Verification, Total), Acceptance Factors (Group Involvement and Participation, Your Effort Counts, Support Climate, Trust Level, Commitment Level, Total); 1987 price data: $18 per kit including 8 response forms, group skills profile, worksheet for improvement, 4 reprints from *Creative Management*, and Leader's Guide (10 pages); [30–60] minutes; Norman R. F. Maier, J. Clayton Lafferty, Glenn J. Morris, and Janice E. Brown; Human Synergistics.*

Review of the Team Effectiveness and Meeting Strategy by LYLE F. SCHOENFELDT, Professor of Management, Texas A&M University, College Station, TX:

As the Leader's Guide accompanying the Team Effectiveness and Meeting Strategy (TEAMS) suggests:

> All of us spend a lot of time in meetings. We look at these sessions as a necessary evil. We need meetings to identify and solve problems . . . to help assure reaching the level of quality and acceptance required to make decisions work.

Whether we look at meetings as a necessary evil or in a more positive light, TEAMS is designed to assist meeting participants to understand the dynamics of their sessions, to pinpoint specific strengths and weaknesses, and to help in making group interactions more productive.

The heart of the procedure is a TEAMS evaluation system, a questionnaire completed by each member of an ongoing group. The questionnaire calls for 60 ratings along with yes-no responses to 20 summary questions, 30 ratings and 10 questions each with respect to elements of meeting *quality* and meeting *acceptance*. Each rating anchors the intersection of a grid resulting from the crossing of the six Skill Factors of: (*a*) Situation Analysis, (*b*) Purpose and Objective, (*c*) Identifying Problems, (*d*) Generating Alternatives, (*e*) Evaluation and Selection, and (*f*) Making Decisions, with the five Quality Dimensions of (*a*) Role and Task Definition, (*b*) Emphasizing Facts, (*c*) Standards, (*d*) Judgments, and (*e*) Verification, and the five Acceptance Dimensions of: (*a*) Group Involvement and Participation, (*b*) Your Effort Counts, (*c*) Support Climate, (*d*) Trust Level, and (*e*) Commitment Level. The ratings are in the form of "We can improve our meetings by . . ." followed by a statement. For example, the item "honestly seeking more information from varied sources" is designed to measure the Skill Factor Situation Analysis and the Quality Dimension of Role and Task Definition. As another example, the item "making sure each person recognizes purpose of objectives and is willing to work to achieve them" measures the Skill Factor of Purpose and Objective and the Acceptance Dimension of Commitment Level.

Each rating is along the 4-point scale from *No change desired* to *Serious change desired*. An example of a Quality Dimension summary (yes-no) question is the statement, "Too little time was allocated for discussing important topics." An Acceptance Dimension summary question is "Very few members really contributed to the decision."

Scoring is by adding responses within rows (Quality or Acceptance Dimensions) and columns (Skill Factors). The five Quality Dimension scores and five Acceptance Dimension scores are then added to produce respective Quality and Acceptance process totals. The number of yes answers to the 10 Quality and 10 Acceptance summary questions are then added to the respective process scores to give Quality and Acceptance totals, which can each range between 0 and 100.

The individual scores are plotted on an Acceptance-Quality grid. The 18 separate scores, six Skill scores, the five each Quality and Acceptance scores, and two respective Quality and Acceptance totals, are transferred to a worksheet and are averaged for all group participants. Also, included with the materials is a group skills profile on which the 18 averages are plotted. The resulting graph is designed to give a clear picture of how the group perceives the effectiveness of the meetings.

A 10-page Leader's Guide provides hints for using TEAMS. Users are told the instrument is more valuable when used in a scheduled work session so that it will be "more than an academic exercise." In keeping with the process orientation of the instrument, the user is cautioned to announce its use beforehand. "Use with an unprepared committee may cause anxiety or hostility."

Four session plan options are described. Each outline covers purposes, time required (1 1/2 to 4 hours in one session depending on the option selected or 1 1/4 hours spread over two sessions), physical setting, materials and resources, and procedure. Three of the options presume an ongoing group, while the fourth involves a group exercise followed by TEAMS. As an aside, four booklets, chapters from an early 1960s book by Norman R. F. Maier, are included. The Leader's Guide suggests reading these as sources of insights into what makes effective sessions. The materials are somewhat dated and do not track directly with the skill factors or dimensions described.

Meetings occur for different purposes. Can TEAMS be expected to improve the effectiveness of different types of meetings? What score areas indicate need for improvement versus satisfactory skill, quality, or acceptance? Should a level of agreement among members of an ongoing group be expected? What does it indicate if members agree versus disagree on dimensions? Do groups using TEAMS feel it improved the effectiveness of their meetings? These questions bear on the reliability, validity, and norms of TEAMS, and all are open issues. Although TEAMS is not a test in the usual sense, some of the standards for tests bear on the effectiveness of TEAMS. No information is provided on any areas of reliability or validity that would allow the consumer to evaluate the potential effectiveness. No information is provided on scores of various types of groups that would permit users to know to what degree scores should be considered indications of problems. These problems exist despite the availability of TEAMS for over a decade.

In summary, the TEAMS survey system may improve the effectiveness of groups when used in one of the options suggested, but absolutely no evidence is offered to support this assertion. The user information that is provided is clear but very brief. Group participants may have trouble responding to the 60 items or 20 summary questions because some will not apply to their group. Use of TEAMS could easily "cost" one-half a person-work-week, depending on the option selected. If the group members do not feel the benefit is equal the cost, the hostility against which the Leader's Guide cautions may be unavoidable.

[362]

Test Behavior Checklist. Purpose: "To provide a systematic and quantifiable means of recording the relevant behaviors observed over the course of psychological testing." Ages 4 through adolescence; 1986; TBC; behavior checklist for use during psychological testing; 3 areas: General Information, Test-Taking Approach and Behavioral Characteristics, Personality and Social Characteristics; individual; 1987 price data: $10 per 25 test booklets; $9 per manual (24 pages); $17 per specimen set including 25 test booklets and manual; (5–10) minutes; Glen P. Aylward and Robert W. MacGruder; Clinical Psychology Publishing Co., Inc.*

Review of the Test Behavior Checklist by LEADELLE PHELPS, Associate Professor of Educational and Counseling Psychology, University of Missouri-Columbia, Columbia, MO:

The Test Behavior Checklist (TBC) was developed as an instrument to assist professionals in recording the observed behaviors of children and adolescents as they are being tested. The recording instrument is a four-page document consisting of descriptive rating scales. The first section, General Information, requires the examiner to fill in demographic data, followed by checking the appropriate descriptions of motor skill development, articulation/language, activity level, and test-taking anxiety. The remainder of the TBC consists of two areas: Test-Taking Approach and Behavioral Characteristics (consisting of 10 behavioral indices) and Personality and Social Characteristics (with 3 behavioral indices). Each of the behavioral indices contains five Likert-type rating options, ranging from one descriptive extreme to the other. For example, one of the indices under the area of Test-Taking and Behavioral Characteristics is "Fear of Failure" with the five rating options ranging from "showed no signs of worry concerning failure; appeared almost lackadaisical" to "excessive fear of failure present; may have attempted to see examiner's scoring or at least asked repeatedly about correctness of answers." Another example is "Cooperativeness," part of the Personality and Social Characteristics area, with the five choices ranging from resistive to examiner and uncooperative to excessively eager to please.

As an aid in psychological evaluation and reporting, the TBC is a psychometrically simple tool. There is no total score or any points assigned, no standardization or norm groupings for comparisons, no reliability coefficients reported, and no indications of a validity assessment. Although it is obvious the authors were not seeking to market a sophisticated scale, the lack of even an interrater reliability statistic or an analysis of content validity is inappropriate.

Checklists are subject to many sources of error variance due to the observational method of data collection. Halo effects, leniency errors, proximity errors, social desirability effects, and situational factors all affect the reliability of a given score. These sources of error variance can be checked quite easily by evaluating scorer variance. Interrater reliability coefficients should always be reported on measures such as the TBC. The authors seem to understand this need. Yet they report data on a sample of only 30 children by stating that "Our interrater agreement for a specific test session has ranged from 88% to 96% during field testing, where two raters viewed the same examination session. Agreement was considered to exist only if both raters endorsed the identical response descriptor" (test manual). Why the authors did not calculate a coefficient of reliability is unclear.

Further, the validity of any checklist is highly dependent upon the behavioral descriptors incorporated therein. The language, depth, and scope of the behavioral indices is an important component. The manual contained no discussion regarding the construction or content analysis of the instrument's descriptors. Users are left a small space at the end of the TBC for additional comments if other noteworthy behavior(s) occurred. However, as examiners we often look only for those behaviors specified. Therefore, an analysis of at least the content validity of this instrument would be considered an essential component. Yet an overview of the manual found not a single instance of the word "validity." Further, an extensive literature review located no other reliability, validity, or technical data on the TBC.

The manual included three examples of TBC results and subsequent paragraphs that had been developed for inclusion in the behavioral observation section of each youngster's psychological report. These examples are helpful in illustrating the ease and practical application of the instrument.

In the absence of more data regarding reliability (e.g., interrater and internal consistency coefficients would be well advised) and validity (e.g., content analysis and concurrent validity coefficients measured against other available checklists such as Sattler's 1982 28-item Behavior and Attitude Checklist), the TBC cannot be recommended as a psychometrically sound assessment tool at this time.

REVIEWER'S REFERENCE

Sattler, J. M. (1982). Behavioral and Attitude Checklist. In J. M. Sattler (Ed.), *Assessment of children's intelligence and special abilities* (2nd ed.) (p. 497). Boston: Allyn and Bacon.

[363]

Test for Auditory Comprehension of Language, Revised Edition. Purpose: Provides a means of assessing a child's auditory-comprehension, helps to identify individuals having receptive language disorders, helps to guide the clinician toward specific areas that need additional testing, and provides a means of measuring change in auditory comprehension. Ages 3–10; 1973–85; TACL-R; guidelines for use with adults are provided; 4 scores: Word Classes and Relations, Grammatical Morphemes, Elaborated Sentences, Total; individual; 1988 price data: $105 per examiner's manual ('85, 195 pages), test book, and 25 individual record forms; $20 per 25 individual record forms; $23 per examiner's manual; $109 per microcomputer scoring program; (10–20) minutes; Elizabeth Carrow-Woolfolk; DLM Teaching Resources.*

See T3:2472 (25 references); for reviews by John T. Hatten and Huberto Molina, see 8:454 (6 references); see also T2:997A (2 references).

TEST REFERENCES

1. Fey, M. E., & Leonard, L. B. (1984). Partner age as a variable in the conversational performance of specifically language-impaired and normal-language children. *Journal of Speech and Hearing Research*, 27, 413-423.

2. Terrell, B. Y., Schwartz, R. G., Prelock, P. A., & Messick, C. K. (1984). Symbolic play in normal and language-impaired children. *Journal of Speech and Hearing Research*, 27, 424-429.

3. Tallal, P., Stark, R. E., & Mellits, D. (1985). The relationship between auditory temporal analysis and receptive language development: Evidence from studies of developmental language disorder. *Neuropsychologia*, 23, 527-534.

4. Beitchman, J. H., Nair, R., Clegg, M., & Patel, P. G. (1986). Prevalence of speech and language disorders in 5-year-old kindergarten children in the Ottawa-Carleton region. *Journal of Speech and Hearing Disorders*, 51, 98-110.

5. Brinton, B., Fujiki, M., Winkler, E., & Loeb, D. F. (1986). Responses to requests for clarification in linguistically normal and language-impaired children. *Journal of Speech and Hearing Disorders*, 51, 370-378.

6. Dollaghan, C., & Kaston, N. (1986). A comprehension monitoring program for language impaired children. *Journal of Speech and Hearing Disorders*, 51, 264-271.

Review of the Test for Auditory Comprehension of Language—Revised by NICHOLAS W. BANKSON, Professor and Chair, Department of Communication Disorders, Boston University, Boston, MA:

The Test for Auditory Comprehension of Language—Revised (TACL-R) is an improved version of the original TACL. The need for a revision was based on studies and critiques of the original test. While the test organization, format, and construction of the TACL-R are similar to the original, there is substantial increase in the depth of performance assessed with the revised version.

The TACL-R is an individually administered test for measuring auditory comprehension of language. Specifically, test items are organized into three, 40-item sections, with each section assessing several linguistic categories. Section I assesses word classes and relations, and is comprised of 33 single word stimuli (e.g., girl, box, round, giving), and seven items that involve "word relations" (e.g., a bird and a cat; riding a little bicycle). Included among the single word stimuli are several items from each of the following categories: nouns, verbs, modifiers/qualifiers, quantity, and direction.

Section II is called Grammatical Morphemes, and is comprised of short sentence verbal stimuli (e.g., The circle is around the car) that are designed to reflect semantic modulations of other structures, such as specificity, number, aspect, tense, and mood. Items reflecting each of the following categories are included in this section: prepositions, pronouns (the manual provides the rationale for placement of pronouns in this section, rather than Section I), noun number, noun case, verb tense, verb number, noun-verb agreement, and derivational suffixes. Section III, Elaborated Sentences, assesses comprehension of more complex sentences of various types including interrogatives, negatives, active and passive voice, direct and indirect object, embedded and partially and completely conjoined sentences.

Each stimulus item is comprised of a word or sentence presented by the examiner, and a corresponding pictorial plate that has three black and white line drawings. One of the three pictures for each item illustrates the meaning of the word, morpheme, or syntactic structure being tested. The other two pictures illustrate either two semantic or grammatical contrasts of the stimulus, or one contrast and one decoy. The subject is required to point to the picture that he or she believes best represents the meaning of that which is spoken by the examiner. Test items within each section are ordered according to difficulty. Basal and ceiling rules for scoring are provided. Although the test manual indicates that the average testing time is 10 minutes, children with language difficulties are likely to require more time.

The TACL-R Examiner's Manual is a more thorough manual than is often available for speech and language tests. Items such as the theoretical base of the test, the revision process, item selection, test standardization, reliability and validity, and interpretation and use of the test, represent individual chapters in this manual. The test user can obtain a great deal of information about assessment of language comprehension, test construction, and the nature of TACL-R with this manual.

Several measures of test reliability are reported. Standard errors of measurement are reported for each section by age groupings, and are relatively low. Internal consistency is demonstrated with a split-half reliability of .96 for the total score. Test-retest reliabilities range from .89 to .91 across the various age levels. Because test scoring is a straightforward, objective procedure, intertester reliability was not reported.

Three types of validity assessments are reported for the TACL-R. Content validity is supported by descriptions of the rationale and procedures involved in item selection, including examination of the instrument by numerous reviewers and test users. One emergent issue is the relationship between language comprehension and sentence length. In other words, an examiner may wonder whether a child's failure on an item is a function of item complexity or the length of the stimulus itself. This question was addressed by correlating the percentage of subjects in the norming and in the clinical samples that passed each item in Section III, Elaborated Sentences, with the number of syllables in each item. On the basis of these figures the author reported "this amount of variance represents such a negligible effect when compared to the remaining variance (92.2% to 98.8%), that one can confidently conclude that item length has little effect on a subject's performance on the TACL-R."

Construct validity is demonstrated through data indicating that subject performance is better on simpler as opposed to complex items, that performance improves with age, and that subjects identified as having language disorders performed more poorly than normals. Concurrent validity is reflected in high correlation between scores on the TACL-R and each of the following: the original TACL; Auditory Association, Auditory Reception, and Grammatic Closure subtests of the Illinois Test of Psycholinguistic Abilities; the Peabódy Picture Vocabulary Test; the Sequences Inventory of Communication Development; and the Stanford-Binet Intelligence Scale.

Normative data on the TACL-R are provided for children ages 36–119 months and for grades kindergarten through four. Raw scores can be transformed to percentile ranks, *z*-scores, and *T* scores. Non-normalized standard scores are also provided for use with extremely low or high scores. The norming sample represented four geographical regions of the United States, and included 1,003 children, including a total of 161 from ethnic/minority groups. In addition, three levels of family occupation groups were included in the sample.

Although the current trend in language assessment is away from the administration of formal tests that focus on one aspect of language behavior (in this instance auditory comprehension), the test can be highly useful if norm referenced data on a language skill is needed. This would be the case if one needs to know where a particular child stands with regard to his or her peer group, or one wishes to measure changes in behavior over time. The careful work undertaken on this instrument will allow one to use the instrument with confidence for such purposes.

Assuming the clinicians who use the TACL-R may be as interested in guidelines for remediation as in normative data, we must also consider the instrument from this perspective. Although knowing the section level(s) (I, II, III) in which a client has difficulties has clinical utility, of more interest may be the specific categories within each section that may have posed problems. While the score form for the original TACL provided for this type of analysis, the revised scoring form does not. Rather, the clinician must consult page 92 of the Examiner's Manual and do his/her own item analysis. Since this process is cumbersome, the test would be improved, in my opinion, by more readily accommodating this type of analysis through the scoring form. I would see this type of analysis being primarily of benefit to clinicians in the early years of their career, since it provides a way of structuring observations that often come more readily to experienced diagnosticians.

In summary, this test is as thorough a formal measure of auditory comprehension of language as is on the market. The revised form represents careful and systematic efforts by the author to develop a standardized test that measures particular facets of auditory comprehension in a controlled situation. It can be particularly useful as part of a comprehensive language evaluation of children referred for language disorders.

Review of the Test for Auditory Comprehension of Language—Revised by *WILLIAM O. HAYNES, Associate Professor, Department of Communication Disorders, Auburn University, Auburn, AL:*

The Test for Auditory Comprehension of Language—Revised (TACL-R) has been changed significantly from the previous editions of the TACL. Carrow-Woolfolk and her associates have done a competent job of researching, piloting, and presenting the TACL-R. All aspects of the revision are explained in detail in a 185-page examiner's manual. The documentation is extensive and a significant improvement over the 30 pages of explanation and data that preceded the 1973 version of the test. The plan for the revision of the TACL was well thought out and systematically completed. The revisions began with a thorough literature review including surveys of working clinicians, published reviews of the TACL, and studies published between 1971–85. The literature review also included new information on language development and the processes involved in comprehension. Pilot administrations of the TACL-R were used to evaluate needed changes in test items and scoring conventions. The revision plan resulted in alterations in the general format of the test, standardization methods, and the documentation provided in the manual.

THEORETICAL FRAMEWORK AND PURPOSE. A criticism of the TACL had been that it was not broad enough to really assess comprehension and that it focused on literal meanings of linguistic forms (Rees and Shulman, 1978). In short, the TACL did not measure comprehension as it occurs in the natural environment with discourse situations, idiomatic usage, metaphoric language, and inferencing. The TACL-

R is quite clear in its stated purpose: It was not designed to test all aspects of comprehension, just literal meanings in a very specific examination context. Thus, the TACL-R does not purport to be an all-inclusive comprehension measure, which would be all but impossible to design. Many authorities have recommended nonstandardized assessment of comprehension, but still there remains a need for standardized instruments to help determine if behavior falls within the range of normal variation. The TACL-R certainly does not claim to do anything it does not accomplish. The examiners' manual has many disclaimers and cautions regarding test theory, interpretation, and use. These are appropriate and useful for both novice and experienced test users. An informative review of comprehension theory, ways to measure comprehension, test content, standardized versus nonstandardized approaches, comprehension in language disordered populations, and comparisons of the content and format of various comprehension tests is included.

GENERAL FORMAT. Several changes have been made in the organization of the test. First, the Spanish version of the instrument has been eliminated. Second, the TACL-R is divided into three sections which analyze the comprehension of word classes and relations, grammatical morphemes, and elaborated sentences (coordination, negatives, imperatives, passives, subordination, and embedding). The section on elaborated sentences has been greatly expanded in the TACL-R. A third change is the expansion of the age range, from a ceiling age of 6-11 to 9-11. Fourth, the picture stimuli have been redrawn and include more minorities. Fifth, the sections are organized in developmental order according to Brown (1973). A final format change is that basal and ceiling scores have been established so that the time of test administration can be more efficiently related to both lower and higher achieving children.

STANDARDIZATION. The norms for the TACL-R were based on 1,003 normal language children between 3-0 and 9-11 years. In addition, 60 normal adults, 234 speech/language disordered children, 16 hearing impaired children, 11 mentally retarded children, and 7 adult aphasic patients were tested. The normal subjects were selected using stratified random sampling. There were a variety of geographical, occupational, and minority populations represented. Several reliability coefficients were calculated on the TACL-R. Standard errors of measurement are available for each grade and age level on all three sections and appear acceptable. Both split-half and test-retest reliabilities were well within acceptable limits. The manual includes a discussion of content validity, construct validity, and criterion-related validity. The normal age groups differed significantly from one another and the norm sample also differed significantly from a sample of language impaired children in a series of comparisons. The TACL-R was correlated with the Illinois Test of Psycholinguistic Abilities (ITPA), Peabody Picture Vocabulary Test (PPVT), Sequenced Inventory of Communicative Development (SICD), and the Stanford-Binet Intelligence Scale; the majority of correlations were significant. Finally, the normative sample showed no significant performance difference among groups based on sex, socioeconomic status, or ethnic origin. Thus, the author suggests that only a single set of norms is necessary for scoring.

The inclusion of normalized standard scores in addition to percentile ranks is an improvement over earlier editions. The TACL-R provides *z*-scores, *T* scores, deviation quotients, and normal curve equivalents in addition to percentile ranks for age and grade level. A table of age equivalent scores is also included. The inclusion of standard scores allows more precise interpretation and comparison of TACL-R scores with other tests.

ADMINISTRATION AND SCORING. The TACL-R takes between 5–20 minutes to administer depending on the child. Strict guidelines are provided regarding instruction, establishing basal and ceiling levels, marking responses, and use of the tables to convert raw scores to any of the measures mentioned in the previous section. It is recommended that the scores be graphically displayed on the record form as standard scores with the confidence intervals calculated using the *SEM* data provided in tabular form. The final two chapters in the manual are devoted to test interpretation and case examples.

In sum, this reviewer feels that the TACL-R is a well-designed and psychometrically sound instrument for evaluating limited aspects of comprehension. Carrow-Woolfolk realistically views the TACL-R as a general guide that may suggest problem areas in need of further exploration with specific informal measures.

[364]

Test for Examining Expressive Morphology. Purpose: "Developed to help clinicians evaluate expressive morpheme development with children whose language skills range from three to eight years of age." Ages 3-0 to 8-12; 1983; TEEM; individual; 1987 price data: $24.95 per complete set including 25 scoring forms, test, and manual (43 pages); $10 per 25 scoring forms; (5–7) minutes; Kenneth G. Shipley, Terry A. Stone, and Marlene B. Sue; Communication Skill Builders.*

Review of the Test for Examining Expressive Morphology by DORIS V. ALLEN, Professor of Audiology, Wayne State University, Detroit, MI:

The Test for Examining Expressive Morphology (TEEM) is a well-constructed instrument that provides information about a child's development of bound morphemes. The test contains 54 items distributed as follows: present progressive (4), plurals (14), possessives (7), third person singular (7), past tense (12), and derived adjectives (10). A picture-presentation format is used, accompanied by sentence-completion statements by the examiner, such as "Here is a boat. Here are two ______." The pictures are standard black-and-white line drawings similar to those used in many other instruments for young children. The test booklet is approximately 5 x 8 inches and spiral bound—a convenient size and format for presentation. Average test time is 6.5 minutes.

The instrument was thoroughly researched in its preliminary as well as its final stages. Prestandardization testing was conducted with 40 normally developing children ranging in age from 3 years through 6 years 12 months. Construct validity and concurrent validity were estimated for this sample; estimates of validity were above .8 and the choice of criterion for each was logical. High inter- and intratester reliability were also obtained (.95 and .94).

Standardization on 500 children, ages 3 through 7 years 12 months, followed. Descriptions of various characteristics of the sample and where/how the children were obtained are reported, important information for users. The results of data analyses for age and sex differences are described. At the youngest age levels (3-year-olds), significant differences at 6-month age intervals were reported, while differences at 12-month intervals were significant at 4 years and older. Sex differences were not found at any age level. The data for the standardization sample and the prestandardization sample were comparable even though the samples differed in terms of size, location, and researcher. Thus, the test deserves to be characterized as well researched and well documented.

The instructions for administration and scoring are clear and detailed. Directions for interpretation of scores are given with suggestions for intervention/therapy programs. The authors point out the limitations of their instrument and make suggestions for alternate procedures (e.g., language samples or presentation of additional items testing the target concept) to confirm morphemes for which the child may need clinical intervention.

Overall, this is a well-designed instrument that should be useful to speech-language pathologists who wish to evaluate expressive morpheme development in children. It is a test designed for clinical use—examiners should be knowledgeable about child language development and experienced in phonetics, both for recording responses and for hearing subtle differences between endings. The authors are to be especially commended for the manual—it is a model of clarity and completeness while remaining brief and direct.

Review of the Test for Examining Expressive Morphology by JANICE A. DOLE, Assistant Professor of Educational Studies, University of Utah, Salt Lake City, UT:

The Test for Examining Expressive Morphology (TEEM) was developed "to help clinicians evaluate expressive morpheme development" in young children. The individually administered test consists of 54 items designed to measure children's correct use of six major morphemes (present progressive, plurals, possessives, third person singulars, past tense, and derived adjectives). Children are presented with a stimulus picture and asked to complete a target sentence, (e.g., "Here is a boat. Here are two ______."). The test is designed to be used with children ranging from 3 to 8 years of age.

ADMINISTRATION AND SCORING. The test is simple and straightforward to administer. Directions in the manual are clear. Examiners are presented with helpful information about what to do if children do not respond appropriately to the practice items. The information also details how much prompting can be given legitimately.

Explicit information about scoring the responses also is found in the manual. Care is taken to caution the examiner not to count subtle speech idiosyncracies as errors. In addition, sample test protocols are provided to demonstrate the entire scoring procedure. The scoring procedures are easy to follow, and should present no problems for examiners.

NORMATIVE INFORMATION. The TEEM was standardized by comparing the results of tests administered to a group of 40 subjects in Reno, Nevada (prestandardization) to a group of 500 subjects in Fresno, California (standardization). Preschools and schools used during standardization were selected to represent "middle class" populations and achievement test scores near the "national median." Students in both samples were said to exhibit "normal speech, language, and hearing abilities."

Statistical results from the prestandardization and standardization samples are quite similar. Reliability coefficients and age differences were comparable, and no significant differences in scores emerged between the two groups. Despite these similarities, the standardization of the TEEM must be regarded as inadequate. Larger sample sizes and a more heterogeneous population are needed to justify placing confidence in this test.

RELIABILITY. Test-retest reliability was determined by having a clinician administer the test to 12 randomly selected children on two occasions. An r of .94 was reported, a correlation sufficiently high to establish more than adequate reliability. But, considerably larger numbers of students are needed to have any confidence in the reported reliability. Intertester reliability was determined by having different clinicians administer the test to 12 different, randomly selected children. The obtained scores were then used to calculate an intertester reliability of .95. Again, this correlation is high and would, with larger samples of students, buttress confidence in the reliability of the test.

VALIDITY. The manual reports data on three types of validity: content, construct, and concurrent. The reporting of content validity is confusing. I had to reread different parts of the manual to see how content validity was established. The allomorph variations used in the test were determined through research on children's language development at different ages. The stimulus word items, the morphemes, were selected from lists of words children first learn and lists of words for primary readers. These words were then tested for familiarity with normal preschoolers. These procedures appear to be adequate for establishing content validity.

Construct and concurrent validity present more serious problems for interpretation. First, the manual states that research indicates that morpheme development is "related to children's overall language development and, to a lesser degree, their age." Construct validity therefore was determined by correlating the TEEM scores with children's ages. A Pearson r of .87 was reported. This correlation, in and of itself, is not adequate to establish the construct validity of the TEEM. After all, we know that many cognitive as well as linguistic abilities improve with age—children's abilities to infer, to recall, and to remember, etc. A better indicator of the test's validity would be to correlate the test with an established test of children's overall early language development. The Test of Early Language Development (TELD) is one such measure, and this reviewer would have far more confidence if the TEEM correlated highly with a language measure such as the TELD. Or, better still, the TEEM should be correlated with a battery of language measures which clearly reflect the language abilities of children. Thus the manual is inadequate in providing sufficient evidence for the construct validity of the TEEM.

The manual does report the correlation between the TEEM and the Peabody Picture Vocabulary Test (PPVT), and this correlation of .8 is used as evidence for the concurrent validity of the TEEM. But the TEEM manual states that the PPVT is a language measure, when, in fact, it is not. The PPVT is a vocabulary test, and therefore inadequate for demonstrating either the construct or concurrent validity of the TEEM. The correlation of .84 between the PPVT and the TEEM is problematic, because it suggests that the TEEM measures something very similar to what the PPVT measures—perhaps natural language development, intelligence, or both.

There are additional problems with the validity of the TEEM. The manual states that the test could be administered by a "clinician or an educator," but why would either want to give this test? Research clearly demonstrates, and this test corroborates the fact that morphologic development advances with age and is part of natural language development. Why, then, would someone give this test as opposed to a test that measures more globally expressive and/or receptive language? One answer might be to screen children who are having language problems in this particular area. This use of the test is hinted at in the manual, which indicates that "the TEEM may be useful for. . . . language-delayed or language-disordered children," but absolutely no information or guidance is provided for clinicians or educators about how to use the test for this purpose. Furthermore, the test was not administered to any language-delayed or disordered children as part of the standardization process. Is there any relationship between children who are language-delayed and low scores on this test? The answer to this question is important for determining the usefulness of the TEEM with this particular population.

Another reason to give the TEEM might be to diagnose certain morphological problems exhibited by second language learners or dialect differences exhibited by nonstandard speakers of English. These purposes are also suggested in the manual, but no assistance is provided as to what differences might be found, or what those differences might suggest for remediation. The manual does caution the clinician about interpreting and reporting results obtained from nonstandard speakers of English, but this caution is inadequate.

SUMMARY. The TEEM is an individually administered measure of young children's morphological development. It is a quick, easy-to-administer test, but its usefulness to clinicians and educators is questionable. First, the standardization sample must be regarded as inadequate. Second, reliability coefficients, though high, were established with very small samples. Third, the test has not been adequately correlated with more global language measures.

Perhaps the biggest problem with this test is that clinicians and educators who might want to use the test are not provided with enough information in the manual to guide them beyond the administration and scoring of the test. How should clinicians interpret the test results? What do they mean? And what should clinicians do with the information? Should they teach morphemes and allomorphs directly? What are the consequences of direct teaching for different language abilities of children? And how does morphological development relate to overall language development? Until some of these practical, philosophical, and research questions are answered, consumers might be well advised to seek more global measures of language development.

[365]

Test of Adolescent Language—2. Purpose: "To identify students whose scores are significantly below those of their peers and who might profit from interventions designed to improve language proficiency, to determine areas of relative strength and weakness in language abilities, to document progress in language development as a consequence of special intervention programs, and to serve as a measurement device for research efforts designed to investigate language behaviors of adolescents." Ages 12-0 through 18-5; 1980–87; TOAL-2; 19 scores: 8 subtest scores (Listening/Vocabulary, Listening/Grammar, Speaking/Vocabulary, Speaking/Grammar, Reading/Vocabulary, Reading/Grammar, Writing/Vocabulary, Writing/Grammar), 11 composite scores (Adolescent Language Quotient, Listening, Speaking, Reading, Writing, Spoken Language, Written Language, Vocabulary, Grammar, Receptive Language, Expressive Language); individual in part; 1987 price data: $82 per complete kit including 10 student books (12 pages), 50 student answer sheets, 50 summary/profile sheets, and manual ('87, 79 pages); $16 per 10 student books; $32 per 50 student answer sheets; $15 per 50 summary/profile sheets; $23 per examiner's manual; $59 per software scoring system designed for use with an Apple II+, IIc, or IIe system and 80-column printer; (60–180) minutes; Donald D. Hammill, Virginia L. Brown, Stephen C. Larsen, and J. Lee Wiederholt; PRO-ED, Inc.*

For a review by Robert T. Williams of an earlier edition, see 9:1243.

Review of the Test of Adolescent Language—2 by ALLEN JACK EDWARDS, Professor of Psychology, Southwest Missouri State University, Springfield, MO:

The Test of Adolescent Language (TOAL) was published in 1980 as a measure of oral, written, receptive, and expressive language abilities of adolescents. In 1987, the revision, now called TOAL-2, became available. One might assume that, because of research, feedback on use, and applications with adolescents, the authors and publisher made significant and helpful changes in the manual and/or the test. By and large, such an assumption is questionable. With only a few additions the review of the TOAL by Williams (9:1243) could be repeated for TOAL-2.

As would be expected, the strengths of TOAL remain in TOAL-2. The test is professionally designed and printed, with clean drawings, competent instructions, clear suggestions, and helpful examples. Designed principally for both normative comparisons and diagnostic analyses, the authors continue to maintain, as they did with TOAL, that the test results may be used with equal success for accountability of intervention programs and as a research device. The former is not documented in the manual, and the latter is more conspicuous for absence of evidence than presence in the 7 years between editions.

STANDARDIZATION. TOAL-2 used a sample of 2,628 students in grades 6 through 12 from 21 states and 3 Canadian provinces. The sample is slightly smaller than for TOAL, but with four additional states. Demographics are fully described, and are improved over what they were with TOAL.

Statistical analysis not only follows procedures used with TOAL, but often cites TOAL data. That is, support for TOAL-2 is the procedural-factual evidence from the first form. The authors justify this step by pointing out the 1987 version differs from the 1980 form only in the fact that several items were added to all but one subtest to develop a lower testing "floor." Users had informed the authors that language-deficient students were often unable to establish a basal. To assess differences that resulted from the addition of the items, 100 protocols were drawn from the norming sample of TOAL-2 and scored with and without the new items. The resulting coefficients were in the .90s for both subtests and composites. Although anything less would have been astounding, the authors maintain this result warrants using TOAL data as equivalent to results that might have been found with TOAL-2. Although the assumption may be valid, the opportunity to offer current, useful data and to sample in a way to assure greater acceptance of the test's quality was lost. In addition, correction of several questionable or flawed procedures pointed out by Williams (9:1243) is lacking.

Where TOAL-2 used new samples, test characteristics show improvement. For example, item analysis data are more convincing, and there is greater reliability as measured by coefficient alpha. Criterion validity remains suspect, despite evidence from two additional studies done with TOAL. In each relevant study, correlation coefficients are moderate even though statistically significant.

In judging construct validity, the authors use four criteria. First, they say subtests should show mean increases by age with strong relationships between age and performance. The results obtained for the TOAL-2 standardization group are not impressive. Small gains in means from ages 12 thru 18 are found. Coefficients between age and performance are low, all in the .20s and .30s. The authors explain that such results for adolescents and their language abilities have been found for other tests. One can say, then, that the criterion is inadequate for judging construct validity, or that TOAL-2 lacks validity on this dimension.

A second criterion is the interrelation among subtests. For TOAL-2, the coefficients range from .31 to .61. Such values, though statistically significant, lack practical import. The third and fourth criteria, cognitive processes involved and language differentiation, report only data from TOAL.

The authors conclude that TOAL-2 is both reliable and valid as a measure of language abilities in adolescents. This reviewer feels that such a statement may be too strong. The assumptions underlying data reported are debatable in some instances. The call for research results is to be applauded, and should help substantiate the strengths of the test, while providing bases for improvement.

SUMMARY. TOAL-2 is a modestly-refined version of a test designed to measure the language abilities of adolescents. Norm-referenced in its assessment, the instrument reflects a three-dimensional model: semantic and syntactic language both in spoken and written form, and employing receptive and expressive systems. The rationale underlying the test and its components remains a major strength.

Minor changes in content (reflected in adding items to provide more floor for language-impaired students) and scoring on subjectively-evaluated subtests to reduce inconsistencies are the only modifications done. Thus, the user of TOAL-2 is using TOAL, and most of the statistical data are based on TOAL.

Although the instrument is appealing in its approach and professional in its production, this reviewer believes more convincing evidence is needed before users can be confident in TOAL-2 scores, interpretations, and applications.

Review of the Test of Adolescent Language—2 by DAVID A. SHAPIRO, Assistant Professor of Communication Disorders, School of Education and Psychology, Western Carolina University, Cullowhee, NC:

The Test of Adolescent Language—2 (TOAL-2, 1987) is very similar in scope and format to the Test of Adolescent Language (TOAL, 1980). The authors contend that "The two versions of the test are essentially the same. The only difference is that the 1987 version added a few items at the lower levels of all subtests except Listening/Vocabulary." This was done in response to examiners of the earlier version who reported difficulty in establishing a basal for young adolescents with language disorders.

The specific purposes for using the TOAL-2 are clearly stated, and are identified in the descriptive information preceding this review. The authors caution that the results of the TOAL-2 are most meaningful in the context of and when compared to data from other related sources. The design of the eight subtests is based upon a three-dimensional test model including forms (spoken and written language), features (semantics/vocabulary and syntax/grammar), and systems (receptive and expressive operations) of language. Therefore, the subtests assess adolescents' oral and written, receptive and expressive language abilities in terms of both vocabulary and grammar.

The instructions provided in the test manual for test administration and scoring are clearly stated. Particular strengths include the discussions of eligibility criteria, examiner competence, and basals and ceilings. Six of the eight subtests can be administered to groups of students; the remaining two (Speaking/Vocabulary, Speaking/Grammar) must be given individually. The average time required to give the entire test is reportedly 1 hour and 45 minutes. This reviewer found the reported time to be an underestimation. However, testing time varies with many factors. Although no time limits are imposed on the individual subtests, any student who takes longer than his peers in a group administration is "encouraged to finish as rapidly as possible." This procedure could pressure an individual and thereby challenge the validity of his/her scores.

All printed stimuli are contained in the Student Booklet. Except for the Speaking/Vocabulary and Speaking/Grammar subtests, the student indicates all responses in the Student Answer Booklet by crossing out the letters corresponding to stimuli presented or by writing responses. Responses are scored either as correct (receiving 1 point) or incorrect (receiving 0 points). Subtests include the following: (*a*) Listening/Vocabulary—This 35-item subtest is intended to assess knowledge of vocabulary and multiple meanings. The examiner directs the student to select two of four pictures that relate best to the stimulus words presented orally. (*b*) Listening/Grammar—Tapping the ability to recognize similar ideas in different spoken grammatical forms, the examiner reads three sentences to the student who then selects the two with nearly equivalent meanings (35 items). (*c*) Speaking/Vocabulary—In order to assess the student's ability to use vocabulary in spoken sentences, the examiner directs the student to construct a sentence using each of 25 stimulus words presented orally. The examiner either records each sentence verbatim or only the score for each sentence. (*d*) Speaking/Grammar—Assessing the student's ability to use different grammatical forms in spoken language, this subtest utilizes a sentence-imitation task. The 30 stimuli are of increasing length and complexity. (*e*) Reading/Vocabulary—Emphasizing relational rather than referential meaning, this subtest directs the student to read three stimulus words that are related to a common concept, and to select two words from four possible responses that are most closely associated with the stimulus words (30 items). (*f*) Reading/Grammar—This 25-item subtest measures the student's ability to recognize similar meanings in sentences that have different grammatical forms. When given five sentences to read, the student selects the two that have the closest meaning. (*g*) Writing/Vocabulary—Assessing the appropriateness of word use and meaning in written form, the examiner directs the student to compose a sentence using each of the words listed (30 words). (*h*) Writing/Grammar—To determine how well students use syntax in writing, series of sentences of increasing length and complexity are presented with directions to formulate a single sentence incorporating the meaningful elements (30 items).

These eight subtests provide a comprehensive system for assessing selected aspects of adolescent language. In the listening and reading subtests, selection of two responses, rather than one, reduces the chance of successful guessing. The guidelines and examples of correct and incorrect responses provided in the manual for the speaking and writing subtests are particularly helpful for scoring. The space provided in the speaking and writing subtests for verbatim recording provides a useful opportunity for more in-depth language analysis.

Several other aspects of the test administration warrant careful attention. (*a*) The methods used for recording responses may yield occasional student confusion. For example, crossing out the letter corresponding to the selection of correct responses appears counterintuitive. Having the students transfer responses from the Student Booklet to the Student Answer Booklet, especially in the listening and reading subtests, adds complexity to already challenging tasks. (*b*) The format of both the Student Booklet and Student Answer Booklet is complex. For example, the Listening/Vocabulary subtest presents eight different items, each containing four possible responses, the corresponding letter selections, and the item numbers (i.e., 72 bits of information) on a single page in the Student Booklet. This task, therefore, requires certain visual, attentional, and fine motor prerequisites for students. (*c*) Several procedures used to sample and score representative language behaviors are questionable. In the Listening/Grammar subtest, for example, the student is required to remember the three sentences read by the examiner, their order, and their relative association to A, B, and C, before processing to discover the two that are most alike. The component task requirements might confound the intended task. The authors state that mispronunciations and use of nonstandard English should not be counted as errors in the Speaking/Vocabulary subtest, but should be in the Speaking/Grammar subtest. Likewise, there is greater tolerance for errors in the Writing/Vocabulary subtest than in the Writing/Grammar subtest. Both the rationale for these instructions and the procedures for distinguishing among error types could be strengthened. Analysis of these error patterns could provide valuable information, only if the examiner elects to write out the response verbatim (i.e., the authors provide the examiner that choice). The procedures utilized in the Speaking/Grammar subtest (i.e., sentence-imitation) are questionable from an ecological perspective. In other words, although the authors justified the procedures used, inferences regarding a student's ability to use different grammatical forms in spoken language must be considered as tentative based upon the method of elicitation. Lastly, while scoring responses as correct/incorrect might facilitate quantification, this method tends to obscure individual differences and overlook the linguistic significance of creative "errors."

The authors present a very clear and useful section for analyzing and interpreting results. The sample case study presented on the Summary and Profile Sheet, sample Observation Report Sheet, and sample Written Report Form are all very helpful. All tables are clear and easy to read. Perhaps one of the most valuable sections is "Reasonable Cautions in Interpreting Scores." Examiners should read this closely. The resources for further assessment and programming, annotated bibliography, and reference list are useful. A software scoring system is available.

The technical aspects of the test are presented clearly. These include discussions of item analysis, standardization and normative information, reliability, and validity.

The authors address item analysis in terms of item difficulty and item discriminating power. Mean difficulty level of approximately 50% and a range between 15% and 85% serve as criteria. Three hundred protocols (50 students at each age level between 12 and 18-5) were systematically drawn for analysis. All of the median coefficients (not means) of discrimination are statistically significant. Thirty-six of the 48 median percentages of difficulty are within the acceptable range. The remaining 12 medians that are not within range are justified in terms of the addition of "easy" items to seven of the eight subtests, aforementioned.

The TOAL-2 was standardized on a sample of 2,628 students in all age intervals in 21 states and three Canadian provinces. No students identified as handicapped are included. The demographic data reported (sex, residence, race, ethnicity, and geographic region) are within 5 percentage points of national averages. The sample is representative of nonhandicapped students enrolled in school.

The normative information addresses the standardized scores associated with the subtests, quotients associated with the composites, and why neither age nor grade equivalents are computed.

Standard scores have a mean of 10 and a standard deviation of 3 to remain comparable with other related tests. The rationale and procedures for preparing the normative tables are logical and presented clearly.

Quotients for the composite variables are derived by pooling the standard scores of the subtests that comprise the individual composites. Fifty students at each age between 12-0 and 18-5 were drawn randomly from the standardization sample. The resulting quotients have a mean of 100 and a standard deviation of 15 and thus are comparable with other tests of intelligence and school achievement.

Grade equivalents are not provided because the authors contend that traits being measured on the TOAL-2 are not clearly grade related. Age equivalents are not reported because the authors feel they have little meaning when applied to older children and adults.

The authors address the test's reliability based upon error variance related to content sampling, time sampling, and interscorer differences. To be considered reliable, a coefficient of .80 is a minimum. The research reported to support the reliability and validity of the TOAL-2 used either the 1980 or 1987 version. Based upon a correlational study demonstrating the equivalency of the TOAL and TOAL-2, the authors contend that the research results pertaining to the earlier version can be applied to the most recent edition. In this study, 100 test protocols were randomly drawn from the normative sample and scored with and without the new items. The resulting coefficients for the subtests ranged from .91 to .97, and for the composites from .94 to .99.

Internal consistency reliability was investigated using coefficient alpha computed on 300 students used in the item analysis. Relating to the subjects' internal consistency, all of the reported coefficients reach or exceed .80, the minimum level for indicating educational usefulness. Pertaining to the composite scores, all but one of the coefficients reach or exceed .90. Standard errors of measurement range from 2 to 5. These data indicate the TOAL-2 has sufficient internal consistency reliability.

The time sampling reliability (for the TOAL only) is reported from a 2-week test-retest of 52 subjects ranging in age from 11 to 14. The test-retest coefficients for the subtest range from .74 to .90. Three subtests fell below the .80 criterion: Listening/Vocabulary (.78), Listening/Grammar (.74), and Spoken/Grammar (.79). The test-retest coefficients associated with the composite scores ranged from .82 to .98. Because of the small number of subjects used, the three test-retest coefficients for subtests not meeting criterion, and the absence of time sampling data for TOAL-2, this reviewer remains cautious regarding the authors' interpretation that "the TOAL-2 scores are stable over time."

Interscorer reliability was investigated (presumably for the TOAL only) by having six people score the answer booklets of 15 ninth-grade students. The range of mean coefficients was from .87 to .98, and of percentage of agreement from 82 to 100. Although the scorer reliability looks good, several inconsistencies are reported. The authors repeatedly refer to the scorer reliability of the TOAL in the text, yet in the summary (Table 9) refer to the Scorer Reliability Coefficients for the TOAL-2 subtests. Also, the reference to Table 8 on page 49 should be a second reference to Table 9.

Evidence for content validity, criterion-related validity, and construct validity is provided. The content validity is supported adequately by discussion of the rationale and format of the test and item selection. However, this reviewer remains cautious regarding choice of format.

Evidence for criterion-related validity is reported in three investigations correlating the TOAL (only) with seven criterion tests. The significant correlations demonstrate at least a "high" relationship.

Construct validity is established adequately through various studies supporting age differentiation, subtest interrelationships, relationship of the TOAL to tests of intelligence and other tests of cognitive ability, and group differentiation of the TOAL among nonhandicapped, mentally retarded, and learning disabled students. The construct is supported further by a coherent model and clearly stated assumptions, questions, and hypotheses.

In summary, the TOAL-2 is very similar to the TOAL, and is a carefully developed and comprehensive system for assessing selected aspects of adolescent language. Mindful of the authors' Specific Purposes for Using the TOAL-2 and Reasonable Cautions in Interpreting Scores, potential users will find this test useful as one aspect of an assessment and intervention program.

[366]

Test of Articulation Performance—Diagnostic. Purpose: "Designed to provide information that is useful in planning and implementing remedial programs." Ages 3–8; 1983; TAP-D; 6 areas: Isolated Words, Distinctive Features, Selective Deep Test, Continuous Speech, Stimulability, Verbal Communication Scales; Verbal Communication Scales available as separate; individual; 1985 price data: $68 per test kit including manual (53 pages), diagnostic picture cards, 25 test forms, and complete verbal communication scales; $12 per 25 test forms; $25 per diagnostic picture cards; $18 per verbal communication scales; $17 per manual; no time limit; Brian R. Bryant and Deborah L. Bryant; PRO-ED, Inc.*

Review of the Test of Articulation Performance—Diagnostic by NICHOLAS W. BANKSON, Professor and Chair, Department of Communication Disorders, Boston University, Boston, MA:

Bryant and Bryant have made a commendable attempt to develop in a single articulation assessment instrument the breadth of phonological sampling that is called for in a diagnostic battery. Although there are some notable shortcomings, there are also some very positive attributes to this multi-step assessment tool.

First, by assessing two consonants in each of 81 stimulus words, an acceptable sample is obtained of consonant productions in single words. The scoring sheet is designed to reflect the fact that most phonemes are sampled more than three times and is organized so that the examiner can record the percentage of time a sound is produced correctly in the isolated words sample. The scoring sheet also facilitates a place, manner, and voicing pattern analysis (erroneously referred to in the test as a "distinctive feature" analysis).

The Test of Articulation Performance—Diagnostic (TAP-D) calls for stimulability testing of error productions at syllable, word, and sentence levels. Continuous speech is also assessed using the same words sampled in the isolated words portion of the instrument. Continuous speech can be assessed either through sentences that are imitated, or a list of sentences that are read. A truly unique aspect of the instrument consists of guidelines for the clinician to use stimulus words to assess "adjacent phonemes," or in other words to perform a "deep test" on selected error productions.

Test reliability is well documented as far as internal consistency and test-retest performance are concerned. Although interjudge reliability for scoring the instrument is reported as 95% among eight judges, the exact procedure for determining reliability is not reported. Whether this figure reflects point-to-point agreement or some overall averaging of correct/incorrect judgements is not clear. Intrajudge reliability on the instrument is not reported. Concurrent and construct validity of the test are acceptable.

A major shortcoming of an instrument such as this, which seeks to be broad based enough to be considered "diagnostic" and also includes phonological pattern analysis among its aims, is the manner in which patterns among errors are analyzed. The place-manner-voicing analysis mentioned earlier is fine, but is a very basic type of pattern analysis. Current emphasis on phonological process occurrence and analysis suggests that some type of process analysis could strengthen the instrument. By transcribing all segments in the 81 stimulus words and then looking for processes among these transcriptions, response data could be more efficaciously analyzed. Clinically, phonological process analysis has been shown to be more relevant than distinctive feature-type pattern analysis; however, as indicated earlier, this instrument does not really facilitate the distinctive feature-type pattern analysis that clinicians look for when they see this term.

Although the instrument provides for a deep test analysis of error productions, the procedures for doing this are cumbersome. The examiner must determine the contexts he/she wishes to test by reviewing the contextual possibilities among the stimulus words and then employ selected stimulus pictures. It would save considerable examiner time if the manual prescribed the items that could be used for contextual testing of each target sound.

Clinicians should be aware that the instrument does not assess all consonant sounds, but only those "that occurred most frequently" on two measures of sound productions. In addition, vowel sounds are not formally assessed. Consonant blends are tested. The instrument does not include a sample of "spontaneous" continuous speech (not imitated, not read), which is something that should be a part of any articulation assessment that is considered "diagnostic" in nature.

An interesting procedure that is related to the phonological assessment, and yet is a separate instrument, is the Verbal Communication Scale. There are three separate scales: student, teacher, and parent scales. These scales, which include separate sets of 20–25 questions each, are designed to assess attitudes toward the clients' speech and language. This information may ultimately be of value in case selection and/or treatment. Limited reliability and validity data are presented. However, the ultimate value of the instrument will be determined by the extent to which a clinician may make practical use of the information. The student scale appears to have value for older children, and the other scales may have value with particular parents and teachers.

The test manual is clear and concise in its presentation; however, the background information regarding phonology/articulation is often superficial and dated. For example, the term "articulation" is used throughout, even though the term "phonology" is increasingly being used in the literature. The inappropriate use of the term "distinctive features" has already been cited. Although the manual indicates that articulation and intelligence are related, this statement is true only for those with below normal intelligence. Information contained in the manual could easily be corrected and made more substantial and does not constitute a flaw of the instrument itself.

In summary, this test pulls together procedures that traditionally have been a part of separate tests that have been used together as a phonological/articulation test battery. Physical properties of this test (black and white pictures, small print for scoring sheet) may make it hard to compete with some of the existing, more attractively produced instruments. In addition, the lack of normative data may decrease its viability compared to other instruments. In spite of these limitations, however, the TAP-D can provide clinicians with a reasonably comprehensive sample of a client's phonological/articulatory productions.

Review of the Test of Articulation Performance—Diagnostic by LAWRENCE J. TURTON, Professor of Speech-Language Pathology, Indiana University of Pennsylvania, Indiana, PA:

The Test of Articulation Performance—Diagnostic (TAP-D) is an ambitious attempt to provide a comprehensive test for articulation disorders. Bryant and Bryant have taken the major step of trying to include multiple testing modes and analytical procedures in one testing battery. The TAP-D consists of single word stimuli, deep-testing, and sentence testing through imitation or reading. Not all tests are administered to each child; the tests administered depend upon the age level of the child. The manual provides for analysis by percent correct, coarticulation effects, error pattern, distinctive features, phonetic inventory, continuous speech, and stimulability. Only phonological analyses are omitted as a possible source of interpretive data for a clinician.

The core stimulus for virtually all of these analyses is a set of 81 words depicted with line drawings to test 23 consonants in the word-initial or word-final positions, 12 blends, and 13 vowels. The words were selected from standard word lists to control for familiarity and age. All of the analyses except continuous speech and stimulability are computed on the responses to words. The deep-testing is performed on those phonemes judged by the clinician to be misarticulated and is accomplished by combining pictures from the single word stimuli. Clinicians will find this very awkward because the picture cards are relatively large and are not bound, making attempts to combine them into spondaic word patterns most difficult.

Only the responses to single words testing word-initial or word-final are incorporated into the distinctive feature analysis. For some reason, the authors decided to disregard responses for blends or sentence stimuli from this analysis. Indeed, clinicians need to be aware of the fact that the "distinctive feature" analysis is actually a phonetic feature analysis and not truly a distinctive feature analysis. This decision is most remarkable in light of the fact that the authors indicate in the manual that they reviewed all the primary sources on distinctive features but still elected to adopt an analysis that stresses phonetic features.

The decision to use a phonetic feature model preempts the need to do the phonetic inventory described separately from the "distinctive feature" analysis, if the clinician includes all instances of the production of a sound disregarding correctness (Turton, 1973). Furthermore, inclusion of the data from the sentences would strengthen this analysis because the words are embedded in the sentences in such a way that all responses are utterance-medial and will yield more information on coarticulation effects.

Clinicians will also get a more accurate percentage of correctness in the single word test if they ignore the vowel productions and divide the total correct for consonants by 146 rather than 164 (74 for initial position; 72 for final). There are so few instances of vowels in the test that there is a high probability that the children will produce them correctly and the percentage derived from the computation will be inflated.

Bryant and Bryant are to be congratulated for actually attempting to obtain data on the reliability and validity of their instrument. It was most refreshing to open a manual on an articulation test and find a comprehensive section on these critical measures. Unfortunately, except for two measures, they apparently used only normal children in the standardization studies. Their data base would have been strengthened considerably if they had repeated the reliability and validity studies with samples of children who misarticulate. Reliability can be demonstrated easily with normal children who make few errors, yielding virtually exact patterns of variance on all measures. Clinicians need to know how stable scores are with children who have problems.

Validity studies provide some evidence of the appropriateness of this test with handicapped children. One construct-validity study involved a comparison between normal and misarticulating children. The differences between the groups were statistically significant at the .001 level, suggesting that the test could distinguish between two different populations. The most striking observation based upon the validity studies is that the TAP-D correlates so highly with other instruments that one has to question why it should be chosen over older tests. Bryant and Bryant fail to point out that using their test would be more efficient because a clinician has all the various testing modes available in one packet. This fact would preclude the need for a school clinician to carry multiple tests as she/he travels from school to school, a strong argument in its favor.

Included in the test packet is a set of attitudinal scales called the Verbal Communication Scales. These scales are designed to be administered to the child using a yes/no response or to parents or teachers using a Likert-type scale. Standardization data and percentiles are included in a separate manual. However, the authors do not provide an analytical system to allow a clinician to use the data in the decision-making process. The scales are an interesting attempt to highlight the social impact of an articulation disorder but they are not central to the decision to place a child in therapy. More importantly, the authors do not provide specific treatment procedures to help the clinician and child cope with the social impact other than articulation treatment.

The TAP-D fails at the same clinical step as most of its predecessors. Decision making is left totally to the discretion of the individual clinician. There are no norms or standards available to suggest who is placed in treatment or the course of treatment. Indeed, a clinician can ignore the elaborate analyses described in the manual and make the diagnostic decisions on the basis of any standard she/he selects. Once again, the profession has an elaborate set of stimuli to purchase but no standards for determining whether a child is normal or handicapped. Consequently, clinicians would be wise to save money and create their own set of testing stimuli and make decisions from the responses to those stimuli.

REVIEWER'S REFERENCE

Turton, L. J. (1973). Diagnostic implications of articulation testing. In W. D. Wolfe & D. J. Goulding (Eds.), *Articulation and learning* (pp. 195-218). Springfield, IL: Charles C. Thomas.

[367]

Test of Articulation Performance—Screen. Purpose: "To detect those children who have significant articulation problems and who probably need further diagnostic articulation assessment and therapy." Ages 3–8; 1983; TAP-S; individual; 1985 price data: $38 per test kit including manual (38 pages), screen picture book, and 50 record forms; $11 per 50 record forms; $15 per manual; (10) minutes; Brian R. Bryant and Deborah L. Bryant; PRO-ED, Inc.*

Review of the Test of Articulation Performance—Screen by BARBARA LAPP GUTKIN, Speech-Language Clinician, Lincoln Public Schools, Lincoln, NE:

The Test of Articulation Performance—Screen (TAP-S) is an articulation screening test designed to detect those children between the ages of 3 and 9 who have significant articulation problems and who may need further diagnostic articulation assessment and therapy. The test consists of 31 items. Each of these items contains an isolated word with key English phonemes included. Each word is elicited spontaneously using the stimulus pictures and sentences as prompts. For children who experience difficulty with this format, a repetition of the examiner's pronunciation is scored. Results are compared to national norms for both the spontaneous and imitative formats. Raw scores can be converted into quotients, percentiles, or age equivalents. Administration time is less than 5 minutes.

In contrast to many other articulation tests, the whole-word scoring procedure is used rather than just targeting particular phonemes in words. In the whole-word scoring procedure, an item can be scored as correct only if every sound in the word is articulated correctly. The authors claim they chose this method because, in comparative testing, the two scoring methods were statistically equivalent and the whole-word method was easier to use.

Items containing certain phonemes were chosen based on each phoneme's frequency of occurrence in the speech of children. The authors indicated that research shows misarticulation of frequently used phonemes reduces intelligibility more than the misarticulation of seldomly used phonemes.

The TAP-S normative sample contained 1,014 children residing in 18 states. The sample was a reasonable approximation of 1980 census data in terms of the demographic variables of sex, residence, occupation of parents, and geographic area. Among the more notable discrepancies between the national and normative sample was a 6% underrepresentation of black children. The manual fails to indicate: (*a*) whether children with speech or other relevant handicaps were included in the normative sample, and (*b*) the number of subjects in each age group. These are potentially serious omissions in judging the adequacy of the norming group.

The authors report a variety of data regarding the reliability of the TAP-S. Internal consistency reliability, as measured by coefficients alpha and Kuder-Richardson 20, range from a low of .88 to a high of .97. A 4-day and a 1-week test-retest analysis yielded reliability coefficients of .94 and .93 respectively. Using the isolated words component of the Test of Articulation Performance—Diagnostic (Bryant & Bryant, 1983), which includes the 31 items of the TAP-S, the authors found a .95 and .98 alternate form reliability for preschool and kindergarten groups, respectively. Interrater reliability among speech language clinicians was reported as 90%.

While the reliability data reported in the manual are quite supportive of the TAP-S, it is important to note that many of these data are based on limited samples of subjects. For example, virtually all of the reliability data were gathered exclusively in Texas. The reported test-retest reliability statistics were based on a total sample of less than 60 children. Likewise, the interrater reliability data reflected the level of agreement among only eight clinicians in reference to five children. Beyond this, these eight raters were graduate students and, thus, may not be representative of field-based practitioners.

Information pertaining to content, criterion-related, and construct validity are each reported in the manual. The content validity of the TAP-S rests upon the normative work of Wepman and Hass (1969) and the Child Study Committee of the International Kindergarten Union (1928) investigating the frequency of phoneme occurrence in children's speech. It is difficult to know whether these dated norms are still valid in the late 1980s. The criterion-related validity of the TAP-S is based on studies correlating test scores with the Arizona Articulation Proficiency Scale (Fudala, 1970), the Word Articulation subtest of the Test of Language Development—Primary (Hammill & Newcomer, 1982), and the professional judgment of examiners who collected the standardization data for the TAP-S. While the correlations between the Arizona and the Word Articulation subtest were quite substantial

(.70 and .90 respectively), these studies were conducted on a limited sample of children (52 children between the ages of 3 and 6 in Austin, Texas). The correlation between TAP-S scores and examiners' professional judgments of children's articulation proficiency was only moderate (i.e., $r =$ .58).

Construct validity for the TAP-S was based on a number of indices. For example, the authors report a correlation of .43 between TAP-S scores and subjects' ages. This finding is consistent with the fact that articulation improves with age. The relationship between TAP-S scores and intelligence was assessed using the Slosson Intelligence Test (Slosson, 1982). As one would expect, the results indicated a moderate positive correlation ($r = .64$). Finally, TAP-S scores of children exhibiting speech problems were compared to matched sets of children with no apparent articulation difficulties. Speech-impaired children earned significantly poorer TAP-S scores. Unfortunately, although the authors indicate the degree of statistical significance between the score obtained by these groups of children, they fail to report the magnitude of score differences.

In summary, the TAP-S appears to be a useful screening measure of articulation for children between the ages of 3 and 9. It provides users with articulation quotients, norms for both spontaneous and imitative responses, and age equivalents. The normative, reliability, and validity data appear to provide adequate support for the TAP-S. The information in the manual and the studies upon which these conclusions are based is, however, often quite scanty.

REVIEWER'S REFERENCES

Child Study Committee of the International Kindergarten Union. (1928). *The vocabulary of children before entering the first grade.* Baltimore.

Wepman, J. M., & Hass, W. (1969). *A spoken word count (children—ages 5, 6 and 7).* Chicago: Language Research Associates.

Fudala, J. B. (1970). Arizona Articulation Proficiency Scale: Revised. Los Angeles: Western Psychological Services.

Hammill, D. D., & Newcomer, P. L. (1982). Test of Language Development: Intermediate. Austin, TX: PRO-ED, Inc.

Slosson, R. L. (1982). Slosson Intelligence Test. East Aurora, NY: Slosson Educational Publications, Inc.

Bryant, B. R., & Bryant, D. L. (1983). Test of Articulation Performance—Diagnostic. Austin, TX: PRO-ED, Inc.

Review of the Test of Articulation Performance—Screen by E. CHARLES HEALEY, *Associate Professor of Speech-Language Pathology, University of Nebraska-Lincoln, Lincoln, NE:*

TEST OVERVIEW. The two necessary attributes of any screening test of articulation are the small expenditure of time needed to perform the test and the limited yet representative sampling of speech-sound production. The Test of Articulation Performance—Screen (TAP-S) satisfies both needs. This assessment instrument has been adequately tested and standardized. Complete reliability and validity data are presented along with explanations of how the data were obtained.

STRENGTHS. This test is one of the easiest formal articulation screening tests to use and administer. The test manual is well organized and easy to comprehend. The form used to record each child's response and other relevant evaluation information is small and compact, making it suitable for most types of permanent record files. Administration of the test is brief (less than 5 minutes) and the results can be compared to normative data. The population, age groups, and individuals for which this test is designed are clearly specified.

The authors provide a cogent and concise explanation of how TAP-S was developed and the data-based rationale for the selected test items. An outstanding feature of the test is the extensive presentation of information on the standardization procedures. Professionals requiring a data-based test will find the TAP-S highly useful. This test was nationally normed according to sex, residence of the children (urban/rural), race, geographic area, and occupation of the parents (white-collar/blue-collar workers). Reliability data include internal consistency, test-retest, interrater, alternate form, and standard error of measurement. The authors provide reliability data for five different age groups. The brief but informative definition and explanation of each type of reliability measure obtained is a strength that will make the test attractive to practicing professionals as well as students in training. Similar positive comments can be made about the section on test validity. Definitions of content, criterion-related, and construct validity are provided. Results are reported for thc validity studies and are conducted under each of these rubrics. These studies typically involved small numbers of subjects.

Finally, the authors assist professionals in the interpretation of the results of the TAP-S. Helpful suggestions are given relative to the reporting of scores and how to cope with regional dialects and the establishment of local norms. The authors encourage clinicians and researchers to submit suggestions for improving the test.

WEAKNESSES. The weaknesses of this screening device are few and relatively minor given the nature and purpose of the test, which is to detect, not diagnose, articulation problems. One major weakness is the single-word response required by the child. Many misarticulating children can produce accurate productions in isolated words. Thus, naming pictures is a simple, efficient method of assessing articulation but it does not provide a representative sample of articulation during connected speech. Articulatory screening tests such as the Stephens Oral Language Screening Test (SOLST) require a connected utterance from the child. Tests like the SOLST would probably give a more realistic analysis of a child's articulatory ability than would the TAP-S.

Although the black and white line drawings of the pictures used in the test are adequately illustrated, they could be problematic in holding the attention of children 3 and 4 years of age. Colored drawings or photographs of real objects of each item would be an improvement in the instrument.

Finally, although no age norms are available, the authors suggest that the TAP-S can be given to children above the age of 8 years 11 months. This suggestion should be disregarded because use with nonnormed ages encourages misuse of the TAP-S. Clearly, children older than the age norms established for this test would require more extensive testing than this test could provide.

SUMMARY. The TAP-S provides speech-language pathologists and researchers with an efficient, simple-to-use, standardized articulatory screening device for children 3 to 9 years of age. Single-word responses are required through pictures, a sentence prompt, or by imitation from the examiner. Although this form of testing is efficient, it does not allow for an evaluation of speech in a connected context. However, the major strengths of this test are the extensive documented studies and research that went into the development and construction of the test. National normative data are provided according to age, race, geographical location, and parent occupation. Test reliability and validity data are well documented, explained, and delineated.

REVIEWER'S REFERENCE

Stephens, M. I. (1977). Stephens Oral Language Screening Test. Peninsula, OH: Interim Publishers.

[368]

Test of Computational Processes. Purpose: Provides "an assessment tool that identifies which basic computational skills a student possesses or does not possess and a data base for comparing a student's skills with those of other students." Grades 1–8; 1985; TCP; "criterion-referenced" and norm referenced; 8 scores: Adding Whole Numbers, Subtracting Whole Numbers, Multiplying Whole Numbers, Dividing Whole Numbers, Fraction Computation, Decimal Computation, Measurement Knowledge, Total; 4 overlapping levels (grades 1, 2, 3, 4–8) in a single booklet; 1986 price data: $50 per set including 25 test booklets and examiner's manual ('85, 96 pages); $20 per 25 test booklets; (20–80) minutes; Neldon D. Kingston; DLM Teaching Resources.*

Review of the Test of Computational Processes by PATTI L. HARRISON, Assistant Professor, Area of Behavioral Studies, College of Education, The University of Alabama, Tuscaloosa, AL:

The Test of Computational Processes (TCP) is an untimed test of basic computational skills designed to measure a student's ability to add, subtract, multiply, and divide using whole numbers, decimals, and fractions. The author states the test can be used with students in grades 1 through 8, although it has particular value for students in grades 3 through 8. Testing time ranges from 20 minutes for grade 1 students to 80 minutes for grade 8 students. The TCP can be group or individually administered.

The TCP comprises seven subtests that require students to manually solve answers to arithmetic problems, as well as write answers to questions about basic arithmetic facts. The problems in each of the subtests appear to support their face validity. The author indicates the test is both a norm-referenced and criterion-referenced instrument. Norms are available for the Total score. Criterion-referenced data include a content (e.g., column addition, multiplying two-digit whole numbers, dividing decimals) and error (e.g., confusing operations, regrouping problems, alignment difficulties) analysis. Other suggested uses of the TCP include determining specific strengths and weaknesses, placing students in appropriate learning environments, planning instruction, and monitoring progress.

The record form for the TCP is well-designed, uses bold printing for the problems, and has adequate space for students' computations. The score summary and content and error analysis are on the back page of the form; thus, scoring may be cumbersome. The author suggests the back page be torn off when reviewing the computations for the analysis, but it probably would have been better to include the score summary and content and error analysis on a separate form.

The manual is well written and has most of the characteristics of a "good" test manual. The author includes detailed descriptions of development, administration, and scoring of the TCP and thoughtfully provides an extensive set of appendices containing, for example, general and expanded answer keys, a case illustration, and frequently asked questions about the TCP.

TECHNICAL INFORMATION. The development of the TCP items is described as a 12-year process that included review of textbooks, practice exercises, students' computations, and articles and publications. A detailed discussion of this process is provided. The author does not include instructional objectives or a test blueprint, but the descriptions of each item contained in an appendix and the content and error analysis on the record form allow test users to determine if the TCP assesses what is taught in their particular school curricula. It should be noted that some content areas contain only one or two items, perhaps resulting in a limited behavior sample. The manual also reports each item's difficulty for grades 1 to 8 in the standardization sample.

The standardization sample for the TCP is extremely limited. Six school districts in Idaho and Wyoming participated in the standardization. Although the author indicates there are approximately equal numbers of males and females and 7 percent minority students, he does not report the size of the communities or other needed information. Testing was conducted with 3,475 subjects in the Fall and 3,240 subjects in the Spring.

The Total score, Critical score (based on the computation problems only), and Process score (based on computational algorithms only) can be converted to percentile ranks, standard scores, and grade equivalents. Tables for Fall and Spring testing are available for each score and the author gives appropriate cautions about using the norms when test dates deviate from the Fall and Spring dates. The tables for percentile ranks support the inadvisability of using these norms with grades 1 and 2 and perhaps even grades 3 and 4. Small differences in raw score points yield extremely large differences in percentile ranks. Grade equivalents were developed through linear interpolation and no curve fitting was done. Thus, the grade equivalents do not reflect the normal, *nonlinear* developmental progression of math skills and probably should not be used. In addition, Fall and Spring grade equivalents were developed. The author should have used data from both the Fall and Spring testings to develop one set of grade equivalents. Such a process would have resulted in interpolation over a 6-month span instead of a 12-month span.

Internal consistency (split-half) reliability coefficients are reported and are high, ranging from .87 to .99. For some reason, the entire standardization sample was not used to compute split-half coefficients and the reliability sample sizes are too small, ranging from 25 to 54. The samples are not described and the manual does not indicate if the coefficients are based on Fall or Spring testings. Standard errors of measurement for raw scores in Fall and Spring testings are reported. Interscorer agreement was investigated. Although it appears that interscorer agreement is high, the procedures used to compute agreement levels were nontraditional and are described in such a vague manner that it is difficult to determine what was actually done.

Content validity is the only evidence of validity discussed in the manual and is supported by the 12-year process used to develop items. Criterion-related and construct validity studies that investigate each of the suggested uses of the TCP are needed.

ADMINISTRATION AND SCORING. The test administration procedures are explained clearly in the manual. The author states that administration does not require specialized training. The author suggests that only certain parts of the test be administered to each grade. Because the author's suggestions are based on the performance of the limited standardization sample, test users should determine that each part is appropriate for their students.

Directions for scoring are also explained clearly. Scoring requires specialized training and thorough knowledge of mathematics because of the extremely comprehensive procedures. The manual includes many excellent aids for scoring, including step-by-step procedures, diagrams, charts, and samples. An extensive content and error analysis can be conducted. The author provides directions for comparing individual item scores to item difficulties obtained from standardization. This procedure should be conducted with great caution because of the limited nature of the standardization sample and the low reliability of item scores.

CONCLUSIONS. This reviewer concludes with a somewhat mixed appraisal of the TCP. The comprehensive development of the items is impressive. The manual is extremely well-written and will be a valuable aid for those professionals who administer and score the TCP. However, the standardization sample is limited to two states and the reliability data are questionable. Validity is supported by content evidence only. A norm-referenced approach to using the TCP is not recommended, unless test users wish to establish local norms.

An informal, diagnostic approach to using the TCP will be valuable for many teachers. The thorough content and error analyses provide suggestions of deficiencies in computational skills. Teachers should be aware that some of the content areas provided limited samples of behavior and that they must determine the content validity for their own curricula before using the TCP. However, the TCP can serve as a basis for teachers to develop more extensive items or their own diagnostic tests.

Review of the Test of Computational Processes by KEVIN S. MCGREW, School Psychologist, St. Cloud Community Schools, St. Cloud, MN:

The Test of Computational Processes (TCP) is a criterion- and norm-referenced test of basic mathematical skills. Items are organized into the seven domains of Adding, Subtracting, Multiplying, and Dividing Whole Numbers, Fraction and Decimal Computation, and Measurement Knowledge. Both individual and group administration are possible by a wide range of school personnel. The individual and group administration directions are clearly written and easy to master.

SCORING AND INTERPRETATION. Scoring involves three different scoring procedures. The General Scoring Standards operationalize right/wrong item scoring through a list of 13 scoring rules, a number of which have four to six subrules. Raw scores can be converted into three summary scores. The Total score summarizes performance across all 122 items. The Critical score summarizes performance on 107 purely arithmetic items (i.e., nonmeasurement items). The Process score is the number of correct algorithms used in 92 selected items. All three summary scores can be expressed as raw scores, percentile ranks, standard scores, or grade equivalents. The 8-point Process Scoring Standards are used to determine whether appropriate computational algorithms are used when solving the problems. Finally, the Diagnostic Scoring Procedures consists of Content Analysis and Specific Error Pattern Analysis checklists. Content Analysis identifies the types of items passed/failed by content area. Specific Error Pattern Analysis is the classification of errors according to an 11-category classification scheme. All three scoring standards are operationally defined, but the sheer number of scoring rules requires significant time to master. Although most scoring rules make logical sense, the validity of the scoring procedures rests on the test author's background and experiences. The scoring standards were not subjected to an expert review process. All scoring information is summarized on a convenient summary page.

TEST CONSTRUCTION. The 122 TCP items were selected from a criterion-referenced perspective to represent the essential computational skills needed in life-skills application. Because content or domain specification is probably the most important aspect of criterion-referenced test development, the TCP's failure to adequately describe this step is a significant problem. The domain specification presented in the manual fails to provide the information needed to judge the relationship between the items and the intended math domains. Instead of providing a rigorous behavioral domain definition, the manual indicates only that the selected items were based on a review of the literature and approximately 12 years of testing, research, and observation by the test's author. The failure to describe a rigorous domain specification process is a major weakness of this criterion-referenced measure.

Items within content domains are ordered by item difficulty (percent of norming subjects correctly solving each item by grade level). Because traditional item analysis indices (e.g., item difficulty and discrimination) are not as germane to criterion-referenced tests, this form of item difficulty information would suffice for a criterion-referenced test. However, the TCP is also a norm-referenced test. The manual fails to present the item analysis information necessary to evaluate the items from a norm-referenced perspective.

TECHNICAL QUALITIES. The TCP was standardized on approximately 6,000 subjects in six school districts in Idaho and Wyoming. Half of the sample was tested during either the Spring or Fall of 1982. Sample sizes at each grade level (range of 344–457 for Spring; range of 375 to 510 for Fall) are quite adequate for norm development. Although the size of the standardization group is impressive, the use of six school districts in only two states raises questions about the representativeness of the sample. This concern is compounded by the failure to adequately describe the norming sample. Although the sample is characterized by a nearly even distribution of males and females, the only other descriptive information presented in the manual is the statement that approximately 7% of the sample consisted of minority students. No sample characteristic data (e.g., SES variables, specific minority representation, etc.) are presented to allow an evaluation of the sample's representativeness as compared to the U.S. Census data.

As would be appropriate for a criterion-referenced test, the manual places major emphasis on the TCP's content validity. The previous comments on the poorly described domain specification process makes it difficult to clearly evaluate the TCP's content validity. No other basic validity data (i.e., criterion-related and/or construct validity) are presented to support the TCP's use as a norm-referenced measure of basic math computational processes. Split-half (odd/even) internal consistency estimates for the three summary scores range from .87 to .99, with most in the mid .90s. These values indicate the total scores have adequate reliability. In addition, users can estimate the precision of the total scores from standard errors of measurement presented in the manual. Test-retest reliability is not reported. Considering the judgement required in the complex scoring procedures, interscorer agreement is a significant concern with the TCP. A study using 20 different scorers suggests good interscorer agreement. Given the importance of interscorer reliability for the TCP, this reviewer views the failure to provide other analyses (e.g., variance component analysis based on generalizability theory) as a weakness in the test's development.

The normative scores available (e.g., percentile ranks, standard scores, grade equivalents) must be interpreted with caution. Separate Fall (.2 of the school year) and Spring (.8 of the school year) scoring tables are provided. Different percentile-rank tables, based on separate Fall and Spring cumulative frequency distributions, are presented in the manual. The use of separate Fall and Spring norms introduces the problem of accurately representing the performance of students tested at times discrepant from the .2 or .8 portions of the school year.

Separate Fall and Spring grade equivalent tables are presented in the manual. The grade equivalent tables were obtained by calculating the median scores for each grade level, and then estimating the intervening grade equivalents by interpolation. The manual states that although most norm-referenced tests use curve fitting procedures to develop grade equivalents, the interpolation procedure was employed because the TCP is primarily a criterion-referenced test. A plot of both the Fall and Spring total score medians by time of year tested (as presented in the manual) reveals a systematic, curvilinear relationship. This reviewer easily fit a curve to these points and found that a single grade equivalent table could have been generated. Instead of providing a single grade equivalent table across grades 1–8 (the result of this curve fitting procedure), the user is left with separate Fall and Spring tables. Furthermore, the grade equivalents generated by this reviewer's curve fitting varied from the test manual grade equivalents for the same raw scores. These findings raise concerns about the accuracy of the separate Fall and Spring grade equivalent tables.

SUMMARY. The TCP is described as both a criterion- and norm-referenced measure of basic math skills. Test administration and interpretation are straightforward and adequately described in the manual. The TCP's strength lies in the clinical information generated by the three scoring systems. Two of the scoring systems have the potential to provide valuable insights into the "why" of a student's mathematical performance. Users intent on using the TCP as a criterion-referenced measure are urged to review the individual items to determine if they adequately represent the math skill domain they intend to assess. Although the total TCP scores appear to have adequate internal consistency reliability, all other technical characteristics of the test are questionable. The standardization sample is geographically restricted and poorly described. No empirical validity data are presented. The use of Fall and Spring norms, as well as the failure to generate a single table of grade equivalents through curve fitting procedures, instills little confidence in the accuracy and meaningfulness of the TCP norm-referenced scores. The TCP is not recommended for use as a norm-referenced test. For users with mathematical backgrounds and time to master the scoring systems, the TCP may provide useful clinical insights into a student's math performance.

[369]

Test of Early Socioemotional Development. Purpose: Measures the social and emotional competence of young children. Ages 3–7; 1984; TOESD; downward extension of Behavior Rating Profile; ratings by students, teachers, and parents; 4 ratings: Student, Teacher, Parent, Sociogram; 1984 price data: $44 per complete test including 50 copies of each rating form and manual (62 pages); $11 per 50 rating forms; $15 per manual; (10–30) minutes for student rating scale; administration time not reported for other scales; Wayne P. Hresko and Linda Brown; PRO-ED, Inc.*

Review of the Test of Early Socioemotional Development by ELIZABETH J. DOLL, *Practicum Coordinator for School Psychology, University of Wisconsin-Madison, Madison, WI:*

Authors of the Test of Early Socioemotional Development (TOESD) were cognizant of the need to assess the socioemotional competence of young children with ratings from multiple informants and settings. For this purpose, they standardized a set of three behavior-rating scales and a sociometric procedure on the same population of young children. This model of multiple measures developed on a common population deserves careful attention.

Authors of the TOESD were also sensitive to needs for ease of administration of the measure. Items on the Student Rating Scale were carefully composed so as to be clear when read to young children. The TOESD Teacher Rating Scale and Parent Rating Scale can be easily completed during a conference or left with the adults for completion at their convenience. The TOESD also includes a Sociogram.

The manual suggests that TOESD scores are indicative of the severity of socioemotional deficiencies. However, severity of deficits should not be confused with the range or variety of deficits. Lower scores on the TOESD would result when students evidence many problematical behaviors whether or not these deficits are equivalent in importance. It would be inappropriate to use such scores as indices of the severity of deficit behaviors.

While the authors declare the TOESD to be a measure of socioemotional competence, the TOESD rating scales appear to be more appropriate for assessing deficiency. A measure of competence should include some items describing appropriate socioemotional behaviors, while all items on both the Teacher Rating Scale and Parent Rating Scale are descriptions of negative behaviors. Only the Student Rating Scale includes both positive and negative items. Parent and Teacher raters may find the omission of positive behaviors offensive. A measure of socioemotional competence should identify children who are precocious in their socioemotional skills as well as those who are deficient. However, a review of the raw score conversion tables for the TOESD indicates that while all scales convert easily to scores up to three standard deviations below the mean, they do not differentiate between students with average and above average socioemotional skills. Users who require a measure of socioemotional competence may be better served by the Vineland Adaptive Behavior Scales (Sparrow, Balla, & Cicchetti, 1984).

The TOESD does provide a convenient set of rating scales that can be compared with one another because they are normed on the same sample of children. However, comparisons among the different measures are informal, achieved by "eyeballing" a graphic profile of all available ratings. While the manual suggests that some patterns of ratings might be indicative of disturbance, there is no predictive validity evidence presented in support of such interpretations. Users would be cautioned to draw no firm conclusions from the profile of scores in the absence of empirical support for these.

A descriptive table in the manual is presented as evidence that the normative sample used for the TOESD approximates the 1983 census data for most important socioeconomic categories. However, the manual does not describe how this sample was selected. Given that Teacher Rating Scales were included for all children in the normative group, it must be assumed even preschool children were enrolled in some form of educational or daycare program. As attendance at such a program is very likely to affect socioemotional development, the TOESD may be inappropriate for use with any child who does not have a history of preschool attendance.

Reliability data included in the manual show adequate internal consistency and test-retest reliability for the Parent and Teacher Rating Scales. The reliability of the Student Rating Scale is more problematic, but would be appropriate for a screening measure. There are no reliability data provided for the Sociogram, and the authors note the reliability of sociometric measures with very young children is not good. Because of this omission, use of the Sociogram is not recommended.

Validity data presented in the manual are insufficient to establish the TOESD as an acceptable measure of socioemotional development. Assessing the validity of a preschool socioemotional scale is problematic because of the difficulty in identifying an appropriate criterion measure of socioemotional skill at the preschool level, and because of the lack of consensus on whether or not socioemotional competence differs from similar constructs such as adaptive behavior or social skills. The authors assessed validity by correlating the Test of Early Socioemotional Development with three other measures of socioemotional competence. Two of these, the Basic School Skills Inventory—Diagnostic (Hammill & Leigh, 1983) and the Behavior Evaluation Scale (McCarney, Leigh, & Cornbleet, 1983), are less than 3 years old and consequently have not yet undergone independent evaluations to establish reputations as appropriate measures of socioemotional competence. The third measure, the Behavior Rating Profile (Brown & Hammill, 1983), is a poor choice because all of its items were included in the original item pool to develop the TOESD. Because these two measures share many items, the correlation between them is spuriously high. Finally, the authors note that because of the very high correlations between the Behavior Rating Profile (BRP) and the TOESD, the validity data for the BRP can be transferred to interpretations of the TOESD. In fact, the two measures were developed on different age groups. Even if the measures were found to be equivalent at the overlapping age levels, it cannot be assumed that correlational relationships found to exist in older children will automatically generalize to younger children.

In summary, the three rating scales of the Test of Early Socioemotional Development appear to measure socioemotional deficits. These have been standardized on an acceptable normative population and their reliability appears adequate. However, neither the validity of the Rating Scale Scores nor of the interscale comparisons has been demonstrated to be satisfactory. Because of this the TOESD Rating Scales would not be appropriate for use except for research purposes. The use of the sociometric scale is not recommended under any circumstances in the absence of data supporting its reliability.

REVIEWER'S REFERENCES

Brown, L., & Hammill, D. D. (1983). Behavior Rating Profile. Austin, TX: PRO-ED.

Hammill, D. D., & Leigh, J. E. (1983). Basic School Skills Inventory—Diagnosis. Austin, TX: PRO-ED.

McCarney, S. B., Leigh, J. E., & Cornbleet, J. A. (1983). Behavior Evaluation Scale. Austin, TX: PRO-ED.

Sparrow, S. S., Balla, D. A., & Cicchetti, D. V. (1984). Vineland Adaptive Behavior Scales. Circle Pines, MN: American Guidance Service.

[370]

Test of Gross Motor Development. Purpose: To identify, plan instructional programs, assess individual student progress, evaluate programs, and serve as a measurement instrument in research involving gross motor development. Ages 3–10; 1985; TGMD; 3 scores: Locomotor Skills, Object Control Skills, Gross Motor Development Quotient; individual; additional materials must be supplied by examiner; 1985 price data: $19 per 50 student record books; $19 per manual (43 pages); (15) minutes; Dale A. Ulrich; PRO-ED, Inc.*

Review of the Test of Gross Motor Development by LINDA K. BUNKER, Professor, Curry School of Education, University of Virginia, Charlottesville, VA:

The Test of Gross Motor Development (TGMD) was developed by Dale Ulrich to assess locomotion and object control skills in children aged 3–10. The primary purpose of the TGMD is to identify children who are significantly behind their peers in gross motor skill development to verify their eligibility for special physical education services. Among the items tested in the locomotion subtest are the run, gallop, hop, leap, horizontal jump, skip, and slide. Object control skills that are assessed include the two-hand strike, stationary ball bounce, catch, kick, and overhand throw.

TGMD was developed in such a way as to make it easy to administer, even by persons with little physical education training. For example, the author hoped that regular classroom teachers might use the instrument in order to detect children who needed special assistance, or to evaluate their own curricula related to motor development.

Ulrich also specified the test was designed to fill a void in the available instruments related to developmental aspects of gross motor skills. As Ulrich points out, most previous instruments have been norm-referenced tests, focusing on the end product of movements (time, speed, accuracy), rather than on the process of movement or the motor pattern itself. Because of the limitations of other measures, evaluators had little choice but to label children in terms of norms, and were provided no information concerning how to intervene to facilitate motor pattern development once a child was evaluated.

TESTING MANUAL AND MATERIALS. The testing materials provide not only adequate information about TGMD itself, but also some very useful philosophical background. The manual makes clear how the author selected the items, and why he feels they will be important in the assessment of a child's motor skills.

There are clear instructions to the examiner, and an important note regarding the skill or competency required to be an effective examiner (e.g., ability to toss a ball underhand over 15 feet). Each item specifies the equipment needed and the instructions to be provided by the examiner. It is the examiner's responsibility to supply the needed materials (no materials are included with the manual), therefore, keeping the cost of the kit to a minimum.

The manual is extremely clear and understandable. Each item is illusrated (with multisex and multicultural children), and carefully described in terms certainly understandable by most teachers. Examiners are instructed to have each child attempt the skill three times. If the child demonstrates the criterion of interest 2 of 3 times, it is scored a pass (= 1 point).

Students are scored on a pass/fail basis for three to four criteria on each skill. This is a very workable number of criteria, and can be managed easily by examiners of various levels of training in motor development. However, it could be argued that having only three or four criteria does not allow for fine discriminations to be made between various stages of performance. For example, the overhand throw specifies as its second criterion: "rotation of hip and shoulder to a point where the nondominant side faces an imaginary target." Actually, the mature pattern would be characterized by sequential timing with the hips rotating after the shoulders start back, and reversed on the forward motion, with hips starting first, followed by de-rotation of the shoulders.

Test materials come with a "student record book" that includes an opportunity to record descriptive data as well as the results of the test. Examiners are asked to record the sex, age, and grade level of each child. Criterion scores are then translated into standard scores and eventually into percentiles. An examiner can also note other observations made during the testing session (e.g., distractibility, problems with cross-lateral integration). The entire testing time requires approximately 15 minutes per child.

TGMD also provides specific information about translating the results of this test into recommendations for Individual Educational Plans for children needing special services. This is an important contribution of these materials that will assist a teacher in complying with various public laws.

References are provided to inform the reader about test development and the test's philosophical underpinnings. Only a small amount of published research is currently available employing the TGMD, because of its recent publication. An extensive review of the instrument was done by Langendorfer (1986).

PSYCHOMETRIC PROPERTIES. The test manual provides information about the development of the test items. Specific criteria used in developing the items are provided, accompanied by data on the discriminating power of each item at each age. Such data are critical in evaluating the relevance of a test and its appropriateness for various students.

Sampling procedures seemed to be quite appropriate and were carefully described in the manual. Test reliability is reported in terms of stability (.49–.53), interscorer (.53–.81), and internal-consistency (.67–.93) measures. In terms of validity, Ulrich reports measures based on both the norm- and criterion-referenced elements. Initial content validity was determined by use of an "expert jury," accompanied by a principal components method of factor analysis with varimax rotation. In addition, external validity was checked based on the hypothesis that mentally retarded children would score significantly lower than "normal" children. All measures of reliability and validity fell within acceptable ranges.

The test criteria were based on descriptions of mature motor patterns. The use of such criteria represents a philosophical choice limiting the observability of natural transitions in the maturing of a motor skill. For example, in the overhand throw there are no differences mentioned about the timing of observable rotation versus the transfer of weight, even though we know that one occurs developmentally before the other. Thus it might be argued the criteria do not really describe the development of the motor skill, but rather describe the characteristics of the mature pattern. This absence of developmental or intermediate characteristics between the initial and mature pattern is a weakness.

There are two difficulties with the available norms. First, the age ranges are split into whole year increments, even though there is a great deal of motor difference between a 3-year-old who is 36 months and one who is 47 months old. Secondly, norms are not provided for boys versus girls. Although it is true that most differences in early-childhood gross motor skills are a result of experience, and not gender, there are still obvious differences between the performance of motor patterns in boys and girls. The absence of separate male and female norms is a significant weakness if the test is used as a normative measure, but is not a major problem as a criterion-referenced instrument.

COMPARABLE TESTS. There at three other tests that are comparable to the TGMD in terms of appropriate gross motor measures: the Bruininks-Oseretsky Test of Motor Proficiency (Bruininks, 1978), the Fundamental Motor Pattern Assessment (FMPA) Instrument (McClenaghan & Gallahue, 1978), and the I CAN assessment procedures (Wessel, 1976).

The Bruininks-Oseretsky test includes many elements that may be of interest to the practitioner (e.g., 46 items or 14 items on the short form). However, it is essentially a norm-referenced test, and therefore does not contain the criteria essential for educational planning. The FMPA is a criterion-referenced test assessing fundamental patterns of walking, running, jumping, throwing, catching, and kicking. Reassessment is done in terms of three global criteria: initial stage, elementary stage with improved coordination and integration, and the mature state of coordinated, adultlike performance. The I CAN materials are the most sophisticated of the measures, and include more criteria for each skill. This sophistication has the definite advantage of providing more specific information. It also requires, however, more sophistication to use and a longer administration time.

SUMMARY. Data generated by the TGMD represent the ability of a child (ages 3–10) to perform various elements of 12 motor skills. The results can be interpreted in both a norm- and criterion-referenced manner. Overall, this test is an exceptionally good initial screening device to identify children requiring specific placements or support services. I would recommend its use by classroom teachers or agencies. The most comprehensive understanding of a child's gross motor skills may be gained by combining the use of the TGMD with an expert assessment using an instrument such as the I CAN.

REVIEWER'S REFERENCES

Wessel, J. A. (1976). I can curriculum. Northbrook, IL: Hubbard Scientific Co.

Bruininks, R. H. (1978). Bruininks-Oseretsky Test of Motor Proficiency. Circle Pines, MN: American Guidance Service.

McClenaghan, B. A., & Gallahue, D. L. (1978). *Fundamental movement: A developmental and remedial approach*. Philadelphia: Saunders.

Langendorfer, S. (1986). Books and media review: Test of Gross Motor Development. *Adapted Physical Activity Quarterly*, 3, 186-190.

Review of the Test of Gross Motor Development by RON EDWARDS, Professor of Psychology and Director of School Psychology Training, University of Southern Mississippi, Hattiesburg, MS:

The Test of Gross Motor Development (TGMD) was developed to assess motor skills frequently taught to children from 3 to 10 years of age. The TGMD was designed to be used by a wide variety of professionals with minimal training; to allow for both norm- and criterion-referenced interpretations; and to assess the sequence of motor skills rather than their products. The TGMD measures 12 gross motor skills grouped into two subtests (Locomotor Skills and Object Control Skills) in children 3 to 10 years of age. The manual suggests the TGMD can be used to: (*a*) identify children who are significantly behind their peers in gross motor skill development and should be eligible for special education services in physical education, (*b*) plan an instructional program in gross motor skill development, (*c*) assess individual student progress in gross motor skill development, (*d*) evaluate gross motor skills instructional programs, and (*e*) serve as a measurement instrument in research involving gross motor development.

The TGMD can be administered by a wide range of individuals and requires approximately 15 minutes to complete. Examiners are encouraged to practice administration of certain items and observation of performance prior to administration. The manual provides an excellent discussion of general testing considerations for unsophisticated examiners. The test materials include only a Student Record Book and an Examiner's manual. A variety of other necessary materials (primarily balls of various types) must be supplied by the examiner. Although having to supply these materials is an inconvenience, the materials are easily obtained and inexpensive. Administration and scoring of the TGMD is presented very clearly in the manual. Scoring is facilitated by descriptions of three or four performance criteria for each item including illustrations of correct performance for each criterion. Raw scores for each subtest can be converted to standard scores and percentiles. Tables for converting subtest raw scores at each age level to standard scores ($M = 10$, $SD = 3$) and/or percentiles are provided along with a table for converting the sum of the subtest standard scores to a Gross Motor Development Quotient ($M = 100$, $SD = 15$). A handy table showing the relationship among percentile ranks, standard scores, normal curve equivalents, *T*-scores, *z*-scores, and stanines is also included. The manual includes a very good discussion of the interpretation of TGMD results. This section provides guidelines for the interpretation of raw scores, subtest percentiles, subtest standard scores, and gross motor development quotients. For instructional programming purposes, tables are provided showing (*a*) the age at which 60% of the standardization sample achieved all of the performance criteria for each of the 12 skills assessed, and (*b*) the age at which 60% and 80% achieved each of the performance criteria. Especially welcome is a section discussing cautions in interpreting test results including a discussion of the *SEm*. The *SEm* for subtest raw scores and standard scores by age level is provided as well as the *SEm* for subtest and gross motor development composite standard scores.

DEVELOPMENT OF THE TGMD. Although there is little discussion of how the specific skills to be assessed were selected, there is a good discussion of the procedures used in item selection and the development of performance criteria. The normative sample ($N = 909$) included 101 to 153 children at each of the eight age levels. The sample was drawn from eight states and stratified to resemble census data on gender, race, community size, and geographic region variables. Overall the sampling was adequate with minor underrepresentation of rural children and children from the south and overrepresentation of urban children and children from the north central and west regions. Of greater significance is the minimal number of minority children included in the sample. Although the overall percentage of minority children matches the census data, an average of less than 20 minority children per age group were included.

RELIABILITY AND VALIDITY. The test manual provides extensive reliability and validity information relative to both norm-referenced and criterion-referenced uses of the TGMD. Test-retest reliability (unspecified interval) was based on a sample of only 10 children representing the age range of the TGMD with 20 students in an undergraduate adaptive physical education course serving as raters. Whether less knowledgeable raters would achieve equivalent results is an important question. Internal consistency was assessed with 25 children at each age level using Spearman-Brown corrected split-half procedures. An important addition for use of the TGMD as a criterion-referenced instrument is a study evaluating the reliability of mastery decisions for both normal and handicapped children using 70% and 85% mastery standards. Several validity studies are reported including content validity assessed by expert judges; and construct validity assessed by factor analysis, increased scores across ages, performance differences between normal and mentally retarded children, assessment of performance standards by judges, and a study showing that the effects of motor skill instruction are reflected by changes in test performance.

SUMMARY. The TGMD is a well-constructed test of gross motor skills for young children. The standardization sample is generally adequate although caution should be exercised when interpreting the results for minority children. Additional reliability information for larger samples of children and with different types of examiners would be useful. On the other hand, the manual is unusually comprehensive and reports several types of information not often included in test manuals. The manual is exceptionally well-written and should be easily understood by both inexperienced and sophisticated examiners. Sufficient information is provided to facilitate appropriate use of the TGMD as either a norm-referenced or criterion-referenced instrument. Individuals needing a specific measure of gross motor skills for norm-referenced comparisons or for criterion-referenced instructional planning should consider the TGMD.

[371]

Test of Pragmatic Skills, Revised Edition. Purpose: Designed to provide information on children's use of language to signify conversational intent. Ages 3-0 to 8-11; 1985–86; optional language sampling supplement is provided in test materials; 5 scores: Playing With Puppets, Playing With Pencil and Sheet of Paper, Playing With Telephones, Playing With Blocks, Total; individual; 1987 price data: $59 per manipulatives, manual (23 pages), and 25 scoring forms; $24.95 per 25 scoring forms; administration time not reported; Brian B. Shulman; Communication Skill Builders.*

Review of the Test of Pragmatic Skills, Revised Edition by MARTIN FUJIKI, Associate Scientist, Parsons Research Center, Bureau of Child Research, University of Kansas, Parsons, KS

In recent years pragmatics has attracted increased attention from individuals interested in language disorders in children. With this increased interest has come the need for clinical tools to assess this area. The Test of Pragmatic Skills is an attempt to address this need.

The Test of Pragmatic Skills is designed to assess "children's use of language to signify conversational intent." As such, the test examines the child's ability to produce 10 different "conversational intentions." This is done in four assessment tasks (playing with puppets, playing with pencil and sheets of paper, playing with telephones, and playing with blocks). In each of these tasks, the examiner provides the child with various probes (questions and statements) designed to elicit various speech acts. The child receives a score representing his/her performance on each of the four tasks, as well as a mean composite score. These scores are used to compare the child's performance to that of the normative population.

The value of calculating scores for each of the individual assessment tasks is questionable. Although the normative data suggest that certain tasks are more difficult than others for various age groups, there does not appear to be any diagnostic significance in these differences. If there is specific information to be gained from these scores, it is not indicated in the manual. The test user should be aware that scores for specific intentions (e.g., requesting) are not provided.

High interexaminer and test-retest reliability figures are reported in the test manual; however, internal consistency is not addressed. Test validity is only briefly discussed. For example, the entire discussion of the test's construct and content validity is as follows: "To ensure that the Test of Pragmatic Skills sampled pragmatic behavior, a variety of speech acts and assessment contexts was included in the test construction. The test elicits conversational intentions from the child in a variety of guided play contexts. The test's theoretical bases substantiate and describe its construct and content validity." Although more extensive, the discussion of criterion-related validity is also limited. Such a brief treatment of validity is unacceptable in a standardized measure. Without further data, the validity of this measure is questionable. Further, the situations in which the conversational intentions are elicited are relatively limited compared to the number of situations a child deals with each day.

The manual implies that information from the test may be used to identify treatment targets (see discussion on page 10 of the manual). In this regard, the author states that specific deficit areas may be identified by examining the summary sheet and score sheet, and that specific attention should be focused on items receiving a score of 1 or 0 (the two lowest scores possible on a 0 through 5 scale). It is the opinion of this reviewer that specific treatment decisions cannot be made on the basis of these test results alone. Any attempt to do so would be at best problematic for the following reasons. First, the test evaluates specific conversational intentions on a limited number of trials in a limited conversational setting. As such it does not test a broad spectrum of behaviors. Further, the test items are not analyzed in enough detail to make a sound clinical decision possible. Before it would be possible to confidently make treatment decisions regarding the child's ability to produce a specific conversational intention, the behavior would have to be observed in a variety of situations on numerous occasions.

Secondly, there are a number of other linguistic deficits outside the realm of pragmatics that might be the basis for a low score on this instrument. For example, a child with severe verbal apraxia might produce limited responses, and thus earn a poor score, even though the child might not demonstrate specific pragmatic difficulties. To the author's credit, it is noted in the test manual that this instrument should be used in conjunction with other language assessment tools.

The Language Sampling Supplement is an optional section of the test evaluating four aspects of discourse: verbal turntaking, speaker dominance, topic maintenance, and topic change. A major weakness of this supplement is the simplified manner in which these parameters are examined. For example, consider topic maintenance and topic change. As viewed by the Language Sampling Supplement, topic maintenance and change are examined only in terms of how long the child talks on topic. However, such a procedure fails to deal with a number of significant variables. For example, topic maintenance may be heavily influenced by the speaker's interest and knowledge of the topic, the speaker's social relationship with the listener, and the conversational situation.

No normative data are provided for the Language Sampling Supplement. To be fair, this measure is an informal procedure, and as such might not be expected to provide norms. However, the question of separating normal from disordered behavior is one of central importance, and the test user is left to his/her own devices to make this decision. Because current research has not definitively specified normative information on these conversational parameters, this is an extremely difficult task. Further, the casual manner in which these behaviors are approached in the manual may suggest to some test users that these judgments can be made confidently on the basis of linguistic intuition. This is a questionable assumption. Those users who are searching for clinical guidelines will be disappointed.

In summary, although the Test of Pragmatic Skills provides the clinician with a certain amount of structure with which to view pragmatic behavior, it also has a number of limitations. When the advantages of using the test are considered in conjunction with these limitations, the Test of Pragmatic Skills, Revised Edition has little to offer the clinician that could not be obtained in a traditional language sample.

Review of the Test of Pragmatic Skills, Revised Edition by BARBARA LAPP GUTKIN, Speech-Language Clinician, Lincoln Public Schools, Lincoln, NE:

The Test of Pragmatic Skills by Brian B. Schulman is a unique language test designed to measure the ability of children ages 3 years to 8 years 11 months to use language appropriately in different natural contexts. Given the growing body of literature on the importance of pragmatic language abilities, a standardized measure designed to evaluate these abilities in young children is essential. The Test of Pragmatic Skills purports to address this need. Responses are quantified through a norm-referenced standardized test that is more conversational and naturalistic than most standardized language measures currently available. Children's abilities to express specific conversational intentions through speech acts are measured. A list of 10 conversational intentions probed by the test (e.g., requesting information, rejection, responding, informing) is provided by the author along with a description of behaviors the child could exhibit to demonstrate these intentions. To understand the intention or purpose of the child's speech acts, the discourse must be viewed in the context of the conversation, observing both the verbal and nonverbal cues used by the speaker to express meaning to the listener.

The author operationalizes his purpose through the use of four tasks likely to be of high interest to young children: puppet play, a pencil and paper task, toy telephones, and wooden blocks. A clinician, while taking on the role of a child's playmate, is able to systematically observe a child's performance in using language for varying speech acts in the listener and speaker roles. During administration, video taping or audio taperecording with written notes on nonverbal behaviors is crucial for the accurate recording and scoring of results. Responses are rated for their appropriateness in the conversational context and for response length on a 5-point scale.

When scoring responses, this test provides greater flexibility than found in the majority of commercially available language tests because responses can receive full credit even if the response does not contain the specific words shown on the sample response form. Because specific words are not required, children who may feel uncooperative during the test administration or who do not know certain information can receive credit for context-appropriate expressions of negative intentions such as statements like "I don't know" or "I don't want to tell you."

For children who approximate or exceed the mean performance value on the Test of Pragmatic Skills or for whom the clinician thinks the problem lies in discourse rather than specific conversational intention, the author provides the Language Sampling Supplement. The use of this supplement is optional. Specific discourse behaviors that can be evaluated in the Language Sampling Supplement include verbal turntaking, speaker dominance, topic maintenance, and topic change. The author describes various formulas for analyzing the discourse behaviors but supplies no theoretical or statistical basis for his analysis.

Unfortunately, the Test of Pragmatic Skills is quite weak from a psychometric perspective. For example, the manual does not provide enough information regarding the reliability of the test. While impressive interexaminer and test-retest (3-week interval) reliability coefficients are reported (.92 and .96, respectively), these data are the result of only two studies. Above and beyond this, the manual devotes a total of only five sentences to these topics, leaving the reader with no clear understanding of the quality of these studies. There is no examination of internal consistency reliability, a crucial oversight in light of the fact that task scores are combined to yield a total score. Most importantly, even though clinicians are encouraged to determine deficit areas based on subjects' performance on small groups of items (e.g., items pertaining to informing), there is absolutely no information regarding the reliability of these item clusters.

The validity section of the manual is also inadequate. Content and construct validity are dismissed by noting that "a variety of speech acts and assessment contexts was included in the test construction" and that "the test elicits conversational intentions from the child in a variety of guided play contexts." No data or meaningful theoretical discussions are provided. Criterion-related validity is based entirely on the analysis of two subjects from the standardization sample by two clinicians, and a very brief analysis of how predictive validity could be investigated in the future.

The Test of Pragmatic Skills suffers from a number of other technical shortcomings. First, the standardization sample includes only middle-class Anglo children and thus, as acknowledged in the manual, may not be appropriate for children from diverse racial and socioeconomic backgrounds. While the authors state that the standardization sample geographically reflects the 1980 U.S. Census, no data are presented to support this claim. Second, the norm tables provided in the manual transform raw scores into percentiles rather than standard score units; this makes the interpretation of test scores unnecessarily cumbersome. Finally, the manual fails to present the intercorrelations among children's scores on the four tasks. As a result, it is not possible to assess the adequacy of the prescribed method of combining these four scores into a Mean Composite Score.

In summary, the Test of Pragmatic Skills is an exploratory attempt to provide clinicians and researchers with a standardized instrument for assessing children's language in a natural context. As such, it is one of the few tests that provide information that is appropriate for use within the increasingly important pragmatic perspective of language development and language disorders. The Test of Pragmatic Skills is thus an important addition to our body of existing tools for assessing language. Unfortunately, the test is seriously flawed from a technical perspective. Substantial additional research is needed to assess its reliability and validity. Clinicians would be well advised to exercise considerable caution when using this test in their daily practice.

[372]

Test of Reading Comprehension: A Method for Assessing the Understanding of Written Language, Revised Edition. Purpose: "Designed to help the practitioner make better educational decisions in situations where reading comprehension abilities are involved." Ages 7-0 to 17-11; 1978–86; TORC; 9 scores: General Vocabulary, Syntactic Similarities, Paragraph Reading, Sentence Sequencing, Reading Comprehension Quotient, Mathematics Vocabulary, Social Studies Vocabulary, Science Vocabulary, Reading Directions; individual; 1986 price data: $68 per complete kit including examiner's manual ('86, 78 pages), 10 student booklets, 50 copies of subtest 7, 50 answer sheets, and 50 profile sheets; $13 per 10 student booklets; $13 per 50 answer sheets; $13 per 50 profile sheets; $13 per 50 copies of subtest 7; $21 per examiner's manual; administration time not reported; Virginia L. Brown, Donald D. Hammill, and J. Lee Wiederholt; PRO-ED, Inc.*

For reviews by Brendan John Bartlett and Joyce Hood of an earlier edition, see 9:1270; see also T3:2456 (1 reference).

TEST REFERENCES

1. Moyer, J. C., Sowder, L., Threadgill-Sowder, J., & Moyer, M. B. (1984). Story problem formats: Drawn versus verbal versus telegraphic. *Journal for Research in Mathematics Education*, 15, 342-351.

2. Paris, S. G., Cross, D. R., & Lipson, M. Y. (1984). Informed strategies for learning: A program to improve children's reading awareness and comprehension. *Journal of Educational Psychology*, 76, 1239-1252.

3. Threadgill-Sowder, J., Sowder, L., Moyer, M. B., & Moyer, J. C. (1984). A case against telegraphing math story problems for poor readers. *The Reading Teacher*, 37, 746-748.

4. Neville, D. D., & Searls, E. F. (1985). The effect of sentence-combining and kernel-identification training on the syntactic componet of reading comprehension. *Research in the Teaching of English*, 19, 37-61.

Review of the Test of Reading Comprehension: A Method for Assessing the Understanding of Written Language, Revised Edition by JAMES A. POTEET, Professor of Special Education, Ball State University, Muncie, IN:

The Test of Reading Comprehension: A Method for Assessing the Understanding of Written Language, Revised Edition (TORC) is a standardized, norm-referenced, untimed silent reading test of reading comprehension that can be administered to individuals and to groups. The test is for students of ages 7 years 0 months through 17 years 11 months. The age range of the earlier edition of the test was 6-6 to 14-6 years. The approximate time requirements for individual student administration as stated in the manual range from 1 1/2 to 3 hours.

The test is comprised of eight subtests: (1) General Vocabulary, (2) Syntactic Similarities, (3) Paragraph Reading, (4) Mathematics Vocabulary, (5) Social Studies Vocabulary, (6) Science Vocabulary, (7) Reading the Directions of School Work, and (8) Sentence Sequencing. Subtests 1, 2, 3, and 8 comprise the General Reading Comprehension Core; the remaining subtests are termed "Diagnostic Supplements." Seven of the subtests are in multiple-choice format; one subtest (Subtest 7—Reading the Directions of Schoolwork) requires a variety of written responses as might be found in a typical student workbook (i.e., circling numbers, completing sentences, writing words in alphabetical order, etc.). For the multiple-choice subtests, the examiner has the option of asking the student to put the responses on a separate answer sheet or, if this procedure is confusing to the student, to write the answer directly in the Student Booklet containing the test items and the response choices. For Subtest 7, each student must use a separate sheet.

ADMINISTRATION AND SCORING. The verbal directions for each subtest given by the examiner seem "wordy" and could be confusing to the student. For example, for the sample items in subtests 1, 4, 5, and 6 the instructions ask the student to find the words "in the box" when the words, while separated from the choices, are not actually in a "box." Also, the student is asked to "put an X over" the letter beside the selected response; a more clear approach would be to ask the student to "put an X ON" the letter beside the selected response. However, because permission is given to vary the specific instructions to insure the student understands the task requirements, pointing to the stimulus words in the sample items and explaining the marking procedures should not be a problem when using the test with individual students.

The manual does not state if it is permissible to tell the student any unknown word if the student asks. One is left to presume that such help is not permitted because the directions specify for the student to "do the rest of the items by yourself."

Instructions are given for group administration. This procedure allows students to work items beyond the actual ceiling used in scoring. The change is necessary due to the somewhat complicated procedures for determining ceilings on some subtests. For example, the subtests are terminated for five subtests when the student misses three of five consecutive items; other subtests are terminated when the student misses two or more of the five questions in Paragraph Reading, or attains any two consecutive items with scores of 3 or lower on Sentence Sequencing. The example given in the manual for computing ceilings should be helpful to the test user. There is a typographical error on the example on page 23 in the number of points for scoring subtest 8. All students begin with the first item, so no basal is established.

The scoring procedures are somewhat complex because varying points can be given for the different items in the Sentence Sequencing subtest. The correct responses are given in a TORC Answer Key, which should help simplify scoring for the remaining subtests. In general, the scoring procedures are no more complicated than some other tests currently used in special education.

USE OF RESULTS. A profile is used to plot the scores. A place for the student's grade placement is not on the profile sheet even though the manual says it is. The profile has space for recording identifying data and characteristics of the student, test results, to whom the information was released, administrative, environmental, and student conditions, and interpretations and recommendations as well as a brief summary of the characteristics of the test itself. The section in the manual telling the examiner how to compute the chronological age has several numerical errors. There is no explanation of how to deal with the number of "days" in a student's calculated chronological age when using the tables that are given in years and months. Raw score points should be transferred to Section II of the profile sheet, not Section I as stated in the manual. Directions for determining the standard scores from the tables are initially confusing because the standard scores are not "written next to the raw score" as stated in the manual. An example of a complete profile is given and may be helpful to the test user, but the table is found in Figure 5, not Figure 4 as stated in the manual.

Although the manual states that "much diagnostic value" is found in comparing the Reading Comprehension Quotient with scores from a general measure of conceptual ability having a mean of 100 and a standard deviation of 15, the procedures and cautions in doing so are not specified. Several examples of cognitive tests are given including the Slosson Intelligence Scale for Children and Adults (1983). The Slosson, however, has a standard deviation of 16, not 15. The shading on the profile sheet is obviously drawn to show the "average" area including plus and minus one standard deviation for the standard scores for the subtests, but the shading does not precisely delineate these limits and could be somewhat confusing. No provisions are made on the profile sheet to account for the standard error of measurement of the subtests, the Reading Comprehension Quotient, or for a comparison test of aptitude or IQ, which may be written in on the profile sheet. Therefore, meaningful differences among the plotted scores are open to confusion and misinterpretation by test users who do not consider the confidence intervals of the separate scores. Differences between scores that are both practically and statistically significant are not detailed on the profile sheet.

The authors wisely suggest the use of "reasonable caution" in using the TORC results because the test is viewed as an *ability* test measuring only certain aspects of reading comprehension. They emphasize the need for additional child study for more specific information about the student's skills. Also, they do not advocate the remediation of skills represented by the specific subtests (except Reading Directions). They further point out that the scores "do not provide a suitable or sufficient basis for planning instructional programs. . . they should not serve as the basis for an individual education plan." They also note the examiner should be aware of environmental conditions that might lead to sources of error in the test results. In addition, they appropriately suggest that deviations from standardized procedures be used to probe the student's responses if necessary. Results from such a "modified assessment technique" (Hargrove & Poteet, 1984) must not be used in calculating the student's score, however.

ITEM SELECTION. Item selection was based on responses from 120 students in Austin, Texas in grades 2 through 6 who attended a private parochial school. Characteristics of the students were not included. Procedures to control for the effects of possible ethnic or socioeconomic bias in the items were not mentioned.

The index of item difficulty (percent of students passing each item) should be close to .50 to allow for maximum discrimination between potentially easy and difficult items although higher indices are favored for tests with a multiple-choice format such as the TORC. The purpose of item analysis using the index of item difficulty (i.e., $p = .50$) is to select items closest to this index to use in the final edition of a test. Such an analysis is not reported in the manual. Instead, the median indices of item difficulty are reported on items that were actually used in the final form of the test. These indices were based on 550 protocols, 50 at each age level of 7 through 17, drawn randomly from the standardization population. The median p was reported for each age for seven subtests (except for ages 15–17 for the Reading Directions test because it is not administered to this age group). Of the 74 median p values given, ranging from .0 through .96, 28 (38%) fall below .50. The lower p values are found for ages 7 and 8 suggesting that lower percentages of students passed items at these age levels and that the items are very difficult at these age levels. Conversely, the higher p values are found for the older age levels suggesting the items for the adolescent students are relatively easy. Of the ps reported, 16 (22%) lie from .40 through .60 (i.e., .50 ± .10).

The point biserial correlation method was used to determine item discrimination. The choice of this particular method instead of others, such as the index of discrimination (D) is not clear. In any case, the reported values suggest the items are highly correlated with total scores of the subtests reflecting good internal consistency.

STANDARDIZATION. Standardization procedures for the 1986 edition of the TORC included "most of the students who made up the 1978 normative group." It is unclear if the students were readministered the new test; the manual states that "the sample was augmented in the spring of 1985." Current TORC users were contacted to obtain students "more or less representative" of their area. In addition, teams of examiners were sent to the four census regions to obtain samples. Although not randomly selected and, therefore, not truly representative, the sample of 2,492 students in 13 states is, according to the manual, similar to the percentages of sex, residence (urban, rural), and geographic area of the population reported in the Statistical Abstract of the United States (1985). Additional information about IQ, ethnicity, socioeconomic status, handicapping conditions, etc., describing the sample is missing, making the norming information incomplete.

SCORES. Deviation standard scores, with a mean of 10 and standard deviation of 3, and percentiles are given for each subtest. Scores from the four subtests that comprise the General Comprehension Core are summed to obtain a Reading Comprehension Quotient, actually a "Sped" score (standard score with mean of 100 and a standard deviation of 15). The remaining four subtests comprise the Diagnostic Supplements and are reported only by the deviation standard scores separately for each subtest.

The authors of the TORC are to be commended for not including grade equivalents in their package of score options. Their rationale is clearly expressed in the manual. Other test authors should follow their example.

RELIABILITY. Evidence of acceptable internal consistency reliability is clearly presented in tables giving the reliability coefficients and standard errors of measurement. Of the 96 coefficients reported, 76 (79%) are .90 or above, 19 (20%) are between .80 and .89, and one is .73.

Using 59 low socioeconomic students ages 8 to 11 years in Kansas City, Missouri, test-retest reliability coefficients for the subtests ranged from .64 to .86; the coefficient for the Reading Comprehension Quotient was .91. Clearly additional research is needed to establish the test's stability for different populations of interest.

VALIDITY. The authors have done a good job of developing the theoretical rationale of reading comprehension guiding their test development. They view reading comprehension as an active, constructive language process in which interaction between the text structure and the knowledge the student brings to the test must occur for comprehension to be realized. The authors point out the TORC subtests reflect behaviors believed to be "representative, but not inclusive, of that construct."

The tests constructed by the authors "require the student to 'construct' meaning through the development of increasingly difficult relationships." Skills in constructing meaning are measured in a number of ways on subtests making up the General Comprehension Core subtests. For example, on General Vocabulary, the student must conceptualize the relationship of three stimulus words (yellow, red, blue) and select *two* of the four responses (black, grass, green, eyes); on Syntactic Similarities the student must select *two* of the five stimulus sentences that are most identical in meaning; on Paragraph Reading the student must select the best title, recall details, and select a possible and an unlikely inference; and on Sentence Sequencing the student must reorder the five randomly ordered sentences to make a sensible paragraph. The authors give a rationale for each subtest.

To establish the construct validity of the TORC these subtests should be shown to relate highly with other indicators of the theoretical constructs on which the test is based. Likewise, weak relationships to other measures of different theoretical constructs would assist in distinguishing the cognitive/psycholinguistic theories of reading comprehension on which the TORC was constructed. In the manual, the authors' view of construct validity is reflected by their evidence to show that (*a*) "the means get larger as the ages of the subjects increase," (*b*) the subtests are moderately positively correlated, (*c*) the differences between the means of poor and good readers were statistically significant beyond the 1% level of confidence, and (*d*) the median correlations of the subtests were moderately correlated with tests of intelligence, math, and language arts. These tests were the Short-Form Test of Academic Aptitude, the Wechsler Intelligence Test for Children—Revised (WISC-R), the California Achievement Test (CAT), the Comprehensive Test of Basic Skills (CTBS), the Peabody Individual Achievement Test (PIAT), and the Science Research Associates (SRA) Achievement Series. It seems to this reviewer that these tests are unlikely to reflect the theoretical constructs of reading comprehension on which the TORC was based. Additional work is needed, therefore, to establish construct validity.

Content-related validity is evidenced by the degree to which the items represent the domain of the test's content—in this case, cognitive/psycholinguistic theories of reading comprehension. The authors' explanation of the construction of the items for some of the subtests may contribute to this type of validity. However, the Paragraph Reading subtest seems to reflect the traditional approach to the assessment of reading comprehension.

Criterion-related validity is evidenced by scores on a test being systematically related to outcome criteria that are of primary interest as determined by school personnel. The value of criterion-related validity studies depends on the relevance of the criterion measure used (AERA, APA, & NCME, 1985). The outcome criteria logical for use with the TORC would seem to be teacher grades or eligibility for programs offering remedial programming for low achieving students. Predictive and concurrent designs could be appropriate to determine evidence of criterion-related validity. The TORC manual reports three investigations using five different and varied samples of students (*N*s = 54, 50, 94, 55, 28; Grades 2 & 3, 4 & 5, and unspecified for the three remaining samples; Types = probably regular class, regular class, students attending public school, disabled readers, and residential treatment center adolescent girls). Significant correlations were obtained between the subtests and reading tests on the CAT, CTBS, SRA, and PIAT. The logical value of these criteria measures would be questioned by some test users.

MANUAL. There are several mistakes in the manual, possibly simple typographical errors, but they do contribute to some confusion for the test user. Some examples follow. A 1969 reference is given as an example of a "most recent" cognitive study. In the material following a major heading of "Eligibility Criteria" it is unclear what the discussion is dealing with in terms of eligibility for *what*. The authors point out the "standardization sample included populations of typical children from various geographical areas, ethnic and linguistic backgrounds, and socioeconomic classes." Only the geographic areas of the sample are actually specified. The authors state the test of silent reading comprehension is appropriate for students who speak with a dialect, with articulation problems, and who are deaf (and can be administered the test by signing). Norms are not provided for these types of students, and scores made by these special populations can be compared to only the "general" norm group on which the test was standardized as the manual suggests.

The authors wisely point out the examiner qualifications as being formal training in assessment practices, usually through college courses or special workshops. The manual also contains a section offering responses to diagnostic questions and many useful references that would be appropriate for the interested test user to read for instructional strategies. Guidelines for reporting test results and aids to interpretation are also given in the manual.

Before a potential test user should decide to use the TORC, he or she should carefully review the theoretical rationale on which this test is based to determine if this test matches the construct of reading comprehension that is used in a given locale. In addition, the evidence of validity and the item difficulty for the age levels at which the test would be used should be carefully scrutinized, as well as the procedures for administration and scoring, the time limits required, and the specific tasks required of the students. Any current or new user of this test should acquire a corrected Table P available from the publisher.

REVIEWER'S REFERENCES

Hargrove, L. J., & Poteet, J. A. (1984). *Assessment in special education: The education evaluation*. Englewood Cliffs, NJ: Prentice-Hall.

American Educational Research Association, American Psychological Association, & National Council on Measurement in Education. (1985). *Standards for educational and psychological testing*. Washington, DC: American Psychological Association, Inc.

Review of the Test of Reading Comprehension: A Method for Assessing the Understanding of Written Language, Revised Edition by ROBERT J. TIERNEY, Department of Educational Theory and Practice, The Ohio State University, Columbus, OH:

The 1986 revision of the Test of Reading Comprehension is an update of the first edition, which appeared in 1978. The revision does not differ substantially from the first edition. Norms have been updated, additional technical analyses have been conducted, and justification for the test has been extended. The main subtests, which constitute the general core of reading comprehension, now subsume the Sentence Sequencing, as well as the General Vocabulary, the Syntactic Similarities, and the Paragraph Reading subtests. The optional subtests (content area vocabulary tests and directions of school work) remain.

The authors appear to be responding to past critics of the test in their discussion of the test's rationale:

> The 1978 edition of the Test of Reading Comprehension: A Method for Assessing the Understanding of Written Language (TORC) represented a significant departure from traditional ways of viewing and measuring reading comprehension. The years since its initial publication have been characterized by intense professional interest in the subject. An examination of recent literature . . . shows that the original ideas embodied in the TORC not only remain compatible with today's view of reading comprehension but continue to represent an appropriate norm-referenced approach to its measurement.

Unfortunately, the authors' claims exceed what the test actually offers. The subtests that constitute the core reflect a rather limited view of reading comprehension. The Paragraph Reading test incorporates the use of passages that are limited in length and variety. The longest text is approximately 130 words. The authors pride themselves on the "content-free" nature of the paragraphs by avoiding topics from the content areas. At a time when reading programs tend to be including a larger percentage of content area reading materials, the exclusion of such passages is actually a limitation rather than a virtue. The probes of paragraph understanding are hampered by the failure to provide even the most minimal context clues (e.g., the paragraphs are devoid of titles or statement of source) and the use of multiple-choice test items that assumes a single correct answer when, in fact, more than one answer is oftentimes plausible.

The General Vocabulary test invites students to engage in a conceptual sorting task with 25 words presented in isolation from even a sentence context. As an instructional technique to enhance conceptual understanding, the task may be reasonable; as a test intended to reflect how readers enlist vocabulary knowledge during reading it seems problematic. The Sentence Sequencing test requires students to reorder a random list of related events in accordance with a predetermined arrangement. Unfortunately, the authors do not consider the possibility of plausible variations in sequence that are likely to arise. The test of Syntactic Similarity requires readers to engage in detailed syntactic analyses: The reader is presented with five syntactically similar sequences and clauses (what is the difference between a sequence and a clause?) involving similar ideas from which he or she must choose two that match. Again, the testmakers have developed tasks that go beyond the demands of reading.

In addition to these concerns, aspects of the development and interpretation of the test are based on problematic assumptions. For example, the authors base the development of subtests on the notion that items within subtests should be homogeneous. This assumption runs counter to findings from numerous studies of individual differences in reading comprehension suggesting that students' responses vary across passages and tasks in ways for which correlational coefficients cannot adjust. The authors also seem to be willing to accept reliability coefficients (test-retest, homogeneity of variance) around the .80 level. A more conservative estimate of .90 would seem more reasonable for discriminating across individual performance on subtests.

It should not be assumed the testmakers themselves do not recognize the limitations of their test. In their manual, they provide the following caveats: "We would suggest reasonable caution in the use of the TORC results . . . . The scores only serve as a reference point at a particular time. By providing suggestions for individual diagnostic follow-up, we have tried to call attention to the point that test results do not deal with causation . . . . Test scores . . . do not provide . . . a sufficient basis for planning instructional programs . . . . We would reemphasize the point that the TORC was developed to measure only certain aspects of reading abilities and performance." Furthermore, the test authors offer suggestions for adaptive assessment to probe students' understanding of the tasks. For example, they suggest that teachers might have students explain their choice of answers.

How should prospective users regard TORC? The most distressing aspect of the test is the tenuous relationship between what TORC measures and what reading comprehension is. Indeed, the extent to which the TORC correlates with other measures of reading comprehension suggests the TORC is as good as the tests it purports to replace. The developers of the TORC do reconcile themselves with some of these limitations. In accordance with the aforementioned discussion of caveats, the authors discourage either direct translations to instruction or any type of conclusions based solely on these tests.

[373]

Test of Word Finding. Purpose: Assists "professionals in the assessment of children's word finding skills" and "provides a structure for describing a child's naming behavior . . . with respect to accuracy, speed, substitution types, and the presence of gestures and extra verbalizations." Ages 6-6 to 12-11; 1986; TWF; 5 sections: Picture Naming: Nouns, Sentence Completion Naming, Description Naming, Picture Naming: Verbs, Picture Naming: Categories; yielding 4 scores: Comprehension, Accuracy, Item Response Time, Word Finding Profile; individual; 2 levels: Primary, Intermediate (on 1 overlapping form); tape recorder and stopwatch required to tape-record section 1 for calculation of item response time; 1988 price data: $110 per complete set including easel-binder test book ('86, 363 pages), 25 response booklets ('86, 8 pages), administration, scoring and interpretation manual ('86, 159 pages), and technical manual ('86, 127 pages); $20 per 25 response booklets; (20–30) minutes; Diane J. German; DLM Teaching Resources.*

Review of the Test of Word Finding by MAVIS DONAHUE, Associate Professor, College of Education, University of Illinois at Chicago, Chicago, IL:

The Test of Word Finding (TWF) is a new instrument designed to fill an important gap in oral language assessment, that is, a reliable and valid means of assessing the accuracy and speed of naming single words by elementary school students. Although word-finding problems in children have been a well-known clinical phenomenon for a number of years, formal assessment has been problematic. Language therapists attempting to identify and describe these deficits have had to rely on informal observation of free speech samples or standardized tests with questionable conceptual frameworks and less than optimal standardization and norming samples (Fried-Oken, 1987; Hall & Jordan, 1987). However, recent research suggests that language impairments in early childhood often resurface as word-finding problems in the elementary and secondary school years. Further, word-finding skills have been found to be significantly related to academic achievement, suggesting that a test like the TWF may be useful for identifying children at risk for reading and math problems.

The TWF consists of 5 naming subtests: Picture Naming: Nouns, Picture Naming: Verbs, Picture Naming: Categories, Sentence Completion Naming, and Description Naming. The Picture Naming: Nouns, Picture Naming: Verbs, and Picture Naming: Categories subtests use a "confrontation naming" format where pictures are presented and the child is asked to rapidly provide a single-word name. The Sentence Completion Naming and Description Naming subtests require the child to listen and "fill in the blank" (e.g., "you part your hair with a ______[comb]") or answer a question (e.g., "What is a chart that shows the days, weeks and months of the year and is used to make appointments [calendar]?").

Accuracy and response time measures are equally important in describing word-finding ability, enabling the examiner to categorize children into one of four naming profiles: Fast and Inaccurate, Slow and Inaccurate, Fast and Accurate, and Slow and Accurate (surprisingly, the least frequent profile among both language-impaired and normal subjects). Case studies illustrate these profiles. A valuable feature of the TWF is a detailed description of error-analysis procedures (i.e., qualitative analyses of typical strategies a child might use to attempt to retrieve a word). Error analysis is an essential prerequisite to designing individual intervention techniques.

The TWF is unique in that it is grounded in an extensive research base, representing the culmination of the author's series of studies on learning-disabled children's word-finding abilities. The technical manual is a wealth of information. It includes not only a careful research review, but also a discussion of important factors influencing word-finding performance that underlie the design of the test (e.g., nature of the target word, stimulus context). The extensive test development procedures and standardization efforts are described in detail, and represent an excellent model for other test developers to follow.

The TWF was standardized on 1,200 children in six grades and 18 states, a sample matching 1980 U.S. Census data on all stratification variables. Children with documented word-finding problems made up 3% of this sample. There is evidence of good internal consistency (for both normal children and subjects with word-finding problems) and test-retest reliability (normal subjects only). Concurrent validity with commonly used word-finding measures was established for normal and language-impaired children. Construct validity was demonstrated through factor analysis, intercorrelations between accuracy and response time measures, and by data indicating that the TWF discriminates groups of children by age and expressive language ability.

The administration, scoring, and interpretation manual is clearly and carefully written, and the test is generally easy to administer. However, in light of the importance of response time as well as accuracy, the task of recording student responses and monitoring a stop watch while smoothly and quickly turning pages requires a great deal of practice, certainly more than the five trial administrations recommended in the manual.

One major conceptual difficulty in the assessment of word-finding skills is that the inability to rapidly name a picture or concept may be a symptom of at least three kinds of language deficits: a lack of knowledge of or exposure to the word; an incomplete or partial acquisition, resulting in storage of the word in less elaborate form in semantic memory; and/or difficulty in accessing a word that is adequately represented in semantic memory (Kail & Leonard, 1986).

The TWF is the only word-finding measure that provides a means for ruling out the first hypothesis. This is done by including an informal receptive vocabulary measure for every target word in the naming subtests. For each item incorrectly named, the child is asked to identify the word by selecting it from an array of four pictures. (Inexplicably, two items per page are usually presented, resulting in two rows of four pictures each in a block of eight pictures. This not only increases the visual-perceptual demands of the task superfluously, but is also very confusing.) To increase the likelihood that most children could easily comprehend these items, only words recognized by 95% of the normative sample on this comprehension task were included.

However, implicit in the TWF model is the assumption that adequate performance on the comprehension subtest in conjunction with inaccurate and/or slow naming can be interpreted as difficulty in the retrieval phase of word naming. Certainly, a child's ability to differentiate the correct picture from three rather dissimilar distractors (e.g., "calf" is accompanied by pictures of a rabbit, a pig, and a horse) gives some evidence the child has heard the word before and has acquired some aspects of its meaning. However, it does not allow the clinician to conclude the child has stored the word in the fully elaborated form needed to rapidly gain access to it. Recent research on the word-finding skills of language-impaired children (Kail & Leonard, 1986) found primary support for deficits in lexical storage rather than retrieval strategies.

In sum, for a new instrument, there is considerable evidence that the TWF has excellent psychometric properties, and shows great promise for both research and clinical purposes. However, test users should keep in mind that the difficulty in differentiating naming problems due to incomplete semantic storage versus genuine retrieval deficits is unresolved. Because the two diagnoses have very different implications for intervention approaches, this is an essential issue that deserves further research.

REVIEWER'S REFERENCES

Kail, R., & Leonard, L. B. (1986). Word-finding abilities in language-impaired children. *ASHA Monographs*, 25, 1-39.

Fried-Oken, M. (1987). Qualitative examination of children's naming skills through test adaptations. *Language, Speech, and Hearing Services in Schools*, 18, 206-216.

Hall, P. K., & Jordan, L. S. (1987). An assessment of a controlled association task to identify word-finding problems in children. *Language, Speech, and Hearing Services in Schools*, 18, 99-111.

Review of the Test of Word Finding by PRISCILLA A. DRUM, Associate Professor of Education, Graduate School of Education, University of California at Santa Barbara, Santa Barbara, CA:

The Test of Word Finding, published 1986, is a clinical assessment instrument for a special population of children in elementary school who are suspected of having a mild form of aphasia that interferes with learning. The basic thrust of the test is to identify children who know the target words, such as chin, beard, pipe, but are unable to produce them in speech as quickly and accurately as a normative sample of children without word-finding disorders.

TEST DESCRIPTION. The primary form, grades 1 and 2, and the intermediate form, grades 3 through 6, differ only in that the older group has more items in most of the five subsections: (*a*) Picture Naming: Nouns (22 and 28 items for the two forms), (*b*) Sentence Completion Naming where children must produce the last word of a sentence read to them (10 and 12 items), (*c*) Description Naming where a sentence is read aloud to the child describing a common object that the child then names (12 and 13 items), (*d*) Picture Naming: Verbs (20 and 21 items), and (*e*) Picture Naming: Categories (16 items for both, but the intermediate start at item 3). The last section, comprehension assessment, goes over each of the incorrectly answered items of the preceding tests. The administrator names the word and the child points to the appropriate picture. The instructions, the sample items, and the pictures for this test are well done. If the examiner does administer the comprehension section and the child knows the words, then the previous item responses can be considered as reliable measures of the child's speed and accuracy in naming words.

Completion time for all items in the three naming subtests and accuracy on each test are the major performance measures with a correction procedure based on the comprehension assessment. Also, the average response time for each item in the Picture Naming: Nouns subtest is calculated. This measure is time consuming for the tester and is done only when completion time is excessive. Because no specific rationale is provided for this calculation, and the procedures—sum all responses and divide by the number of responses—are markedly similar to completion time, it probably should be ignored. The secondary measure, gestures and nontask verbalizations, is good descriptive information that all clinicians should note for any test.

The scoring procedures are clear with sufficient examples of both acceptable synonyms and error responses. The four profiles could be useful for subsequent research. The two profiles that designate word-finding problems, Fast and Inaccurate Namers and Slow and Inaccurate Namers, could eventually be tied to different types of problems. The Slow but Accurate Namers might also provide information on learning.

VALIDITY. The theoretical perspective of this test is based on an examination of the word-finding ability in an extensive review of studies of adults with neurological disorders, fewer studies of children who exhibit neurological problems, and correlational studies with learning-disabled students, dyslexic readers, and children with oral language problems. Slower naming responses and more errors are prevalent in the studies cited. As in all correlational studies, however, the possibility exists that word-finding problems are simply a manifestation of some general problem that would interfere with tactile, labelling, classifying, or any other performance task.

No study is cited that indicates improving children's word-finding skills will also improve their general academic performance or specific subskills such as decoding abilities. The test does not differentiate among different types of reading disabilities nor among different groups of learning-disabled children. Perhaps, subsequent research studies will document specific uses for the test. But until this information is available, the Word Finding Test is simply one of many tests that can predict a child is likely to have learning problems.

RELIABILITY. Numerous reliability measures are presented in the manual, along with clear explanations of how the results were obtained. The test-retest, internal consistency, and goodness-of-fit results are acceptable, particularly for the younger children in the standardization sample and the 59 children who have word-finding problems.

STANDARDIZATION. The stratified random sampling for the standardization of the test includes 1,200 children without word-finding problems or 200 at each grade from 18 different states. The stratification design also includes children from different racial or ethnic backgrounds, different community sizes, three levels of parental educational level, as well as approximately equal numbers of boys and girls. The proportionate representation in the stratification cells is based on the 1980 U.S. Census. The 40 children with word-finding difficulties are also described by the stratification variables. Results on the test are supplied for both groups, so a test user can compare a child's response with either the normative group or with the responses of children with linguistic handicaps.

RECOMMENDATION. In summary, the Test of Word Finding is a reliable instrument for either a clinician or a researcher who wants a measure of a child's accuracy and rate in naming known words. However, the purposes for using the test are ambiguous. It is unclear how test results will contribute to classification decisions or to instructional methods.

[374]

Test of Written Spelling [Revised Edition].

Purpose: "Assesses the student's ability to spell words whose spellings are (*a*) readily predictable in sound-letter patterns, (*b*) words whose spellings are less predictable (i.e., the demons), and (*c*) both types of words considered together." Grades 1–12; 1976–86; TWS-2; 3 scores: Predictable Words, Unpredictable Words, Total; 1986 price data: $32 per complete kit including manual ('86, 42 pages), and 50 answer sheets; $13 per 50 answer sheets; $21 per manual; (15–25) minutes; Stephen C. Larsen and Donald D. Hammill; PRO-ED, Inc.*

For reviews by John M. Bradley and Deborah B. Erickson of an earlier edition, see 9:1279 (1 reference).

Review of the Test of Written Spelling [Revised Edition] by DEBORAH B. ERICKSON, Assistant Professor of Psychology, Rochester Institute of Technology, and Monroe Community College, Rochester, NY:

The Test of Written Spelling [Revised Edition] (TWS-2) is designed to assess written spelling from ages 5 to 18. Larsen and Hammill describe an unmet need for adequate spelling assessment and instruction. They define spelling skills as the ability to properly arrange letters in words. They cite research supporting the contention that analysis of the student's knowledge of English orthographic rules and memorization of specific nonconforming exceptions provides an adequate basis for the assessment of spelling ability. Their suggested testing approach thus divides spelling of

English words into two categories: those that follow orthographic rules ("predictable words") and those that do not ("unpredictable words"). The authors suggest that this division will assist teachers in planning an appropriate instructional program. In adherence to the new emphasis on creating tests to directly assist in the educational process, these authors sought to develop a test of written spelling that could be linked to an educational program of spelling. However, caution should be exercised before planning a total educational program in spelling from a test of 100 words covering 12 grades.

The manual developed for the TWS-2 is clear and concise. It follows the guidelines of reporting test construction data recommended by the joint committee of the American Educational Research Association, the American Psychological Association, and the National Council on Measurement in Education (1974). The thoroughness with which the authors have described the purpose of the test, the directions to administer and interpret the test, and the technical development of the test are commendable.

Specifically, the administration and scoring section of the manual details the basal, ceiling, and scoring procedures. The interpretation section gives examples of how to use the profile of scores. Scores are reported in percentiles and standard scores. Grade equivalents are not given due to the recent controversy and dissatisfaction over the abuse of grade equivalent scores. In the development section of the TWS-2, differences from the TWS are outlined. Item selection was redone to allow for the extension into upper grades. Five basal series and an upper level vocabulary series were used in the selection of the words. Item analyses consisted of item difficulty data and item discrimination indices (point biserial correlations). Normative data include a thorough description of demographic characteristics of the sample population.

Test-retest reliability and internal-consistency data are reported in the TWS-2 manual. The test-retest reliability coefficients for the total scores on the test range from .91 to .99 with a median of .96. Coefficient alpha reliabilities range from .92 to .98 with a median of .98. Reliability estimates indicate that the test can be accepted as a consistent measure of written spelling ability. However, sample sizes of the studies were limited to 20 students per grade in each of grades 1–8 for the interval from 6 to 18 years for the coefficient alpha data. Future revisions should consider larger sample sizes representative of all age and grade levels.

Content validity is inferred through a thorough discussion of the item-selection process. Concurrent validity for the TWS-2 is based upon studies of its predecessor, the TWS. Concurrent validity of the TWS was established through correlations with other measures of spelling in studies of 63 students in 3 different fourth grade classrooms in Austin, Texas. Demonstrating equivalence of the TWS and the TWS-2 was attempted by comparing 300 cases of similar items from the TWS and the TWS-2. From this comparison the authors concluded that the studies reported in the 1976 manual support the validity of the present TWS-2. While all other aspects of the test manual used rigorous methods of test development, it is disappointing that concurrent test validity was approached in this manner. Again, future revisions should expand upon this study. Construct validity is inferred through a focus upon the developmental nature of spelling ability. The authors compared the spelling ability of younger and older children and of normal and learning-disabled students. Studies comparing different populations indicated that the TWS-2 does discriminate between groups of students with different spelling abilities. This evidence for the discriminatory power of the test is a significant factor in establishing validity of the TWS-2.

SUMMARY. The revisions of the test manual and the additional information regarding the discriminatory power of the TWS-2 make this test an excellent screening instrument for assessing written spelling ability. Spelling is a complex function and the TWS-2 does not assess all aspects of the spelling process. However, it is useful in analyzing a student's strengths and weaknesses in spelling predictable and unpredictable words. This analysis can assist a teacher to develop appropriate teaching strategies for spelling. Further diagnostic assessment is recommended before developing a total educational program in the area of spelling.

REVIEWER'S REFERENCE

American Psychological Association, American Educational Research Association, & National Council on Measurement in Education. (1974). *Standards for educational and psychological tests.* Washington, DC: American Psychological Association.

Review of the Test of Written Spelling [Revised Edition] by RUTH M. NOYCE, Professor of Curriculum and Instruction, The University of Kansas, Lawrence, KS:

Using a dictated word format, the Test of Written Spelling (TWS-2) measures the ability of students in grades 1 through 12 to spell both "predictable" and "unpredictable" words. It is composed of two subtests, one comprised of words conforming to the rules of English orthography and the other made up of irregular words. The test has two unique features that separate it from other commercial spelling tests. One is the capacity to provide diagnostic information relative to specific teaching strategies; the other is the requirement that the examinee actually write the word. Both features contribute to the appeal of the instrument when it is compared to existing tests. Most commercial spelling tests report general progress without discriminating between rule-governed words and "spelling demons"; therefore, they are not useful for the purpose of identifying the specific problems of individuals. In addition, the majority of current tests require the examinee to select a correctly-spelled word from among four or five choices, a practice which has been criticized by some authorities for possibly reinforcing incorrect spellings. While most current formats measure editing ability, they do not determine the student's capability to correctly spell words in written form without a visual stimulus.

The theoretical base for TWS-2 is derived from the research of Hanna, Hanna, Hodges, and Rudorf (1966), who reported that knowledge of the linguistic nature of English orthography is useful to spellers due to the fact that a considerable number of spellings are rule-governed. The authors of TWS-2 have taken this into account, maintaining that teachers need a valid tool for identifying specific error patterns in order to accurately diagnose a pupil's spelling difficulties.

An excellent test manual provides a clear explanation of procedures for administering the TWS-2. Examiners are instructed to allow 15 to 25 minutes for administration and advised that young or immature pupils may require two or more sessions to complete the test, because they are required to write dictated words. The use of entry levels, basals, and ceilings is thoroughly explained in the manual. Five consecutive items must be answered correctly in the establishment of a basal. Otherwise, the examiner returns to the entry point (determined by grade level) and tests downward until five consecutive items are answered correctly. The examiner says the word in isolation, reads a sentence from the manual containing the word, and then repeats the word, while the examinee writes the word on a response form. The words written by the subject are scored "correct," earning one point, or "incorrect," receiving no credit, and the raw score is the sum of the correct answers. Each subtest yields raw scores, percentiles, and standard scores that are recorded on a summary form on the reverse side of the word-list page written by the student. This information is recorded graphically in the form of a profile on the Summary/Response Form.

Illustrative features of the test manual that are particularly helpful to the examiner are a completed sample Summary/Response Form and a chart showing the relationship of TWS-2 words to the word lists of five current (1982–84) spelling programs. A glossary of pronunciation symbols is also included. Adequate information for interpreting the three types of scores is provided. However, no grade equivalents are given, due to dissatisfaction expressed over their use since the 1976 edition of the test. The authors acknowledge a recommendation from the International Reading Association requesting test publishers not to provide this information. The problem becomes obvious when the reader of the test manual observes the inconsistency with which words are placed at grade levels in the five spelling series. Grade level placement is not a stated purpose of the developers of this instrument, who purport to have created a valid device for measuring individual progress in spelling and for determining the kinds of instruction needed to remedy spelling problems.

The validation data reported are satisfactory. Content validity was addressed through controlled item-selection and item-analysis procedures. Words for grades 9 through 12 were selected from the EDL Reading Core Vocabulary; words for the elementary grades were derived from the EDL list and current spelling programs for grades 1 through 8. The criteria for word selection were that the word could be easily categorized as rule-governed or irregular and that the word appear in the five current basal spelling program word lists compared by the authors. Concurrent validity data indicate substantial correlation with the spelling subtests of four well-established tests: California Achievement Tests (CAT), Durrell Analysis of Reading Difficulty (DARD), SRA Achievement Series (SRA), and Wide Range Achievement Test (WRAT).

Adequate normative data were collected from a nationally representative sample of 3,805 children and reported as standard scores and percentile ranks. The developers report acceptable results from both test-retest and internal consistency reliability estimates. In this revised version of the test, the reliability at younger age levels has been strengthened.

The TWS-2 appears to measure what it was designed to measure efficiently and consistently. It is a well-constructed, easily-administered test to be used in diagnosing and prescribing for spelling instruction. Its unique purpose is to distinguish between the ability to spell rule-governed words and the ability to spell irregular words. However, the extent of its utility is difficult to predict. An underlying assumption is that children who don't "spell by the rules" can be taught to do so by learning certain rules that have "broad application." Spelling authorities are not in agreement about this issue. The value of the TWS-2 as a diagnostic tool for educators will be directly proportionate to the willingness of teachers to follow up the testing by modifying instructional practices.

REVIEWER'S REFERENCE

Hanna, P. R., Hanna, J. S., Hodges, R. G., & Rudorf, E. H. (1966). *Phoneme-grapheme correspondences to spelling improvement.* Washington, DC: Office of Education, United States Department of Health, Education, and Welfare.

[375]

Tests of Achievement and Proficiency, Forms G and H. Purpose: To "provide efficient and comprehensive appraisal of student progress toward widely accepted academic goals in the basic skill areas." Grades 9–12; 1978–86; TAP; second component of the Riverside Basic Skills Assessment Program; 2 forms; 4 overlapping levels (levels 15–18); 1986 price data: $43.50 per 35 separate level test booklets (specify Level 15–18) and 1 Directions for Administration ('86, 17 pages); $1.26 per Form G answer key booklet ('86, 5 pages); $9 per MRC scoring masks (specify level); $96 per 250 NCS 7010 answer sheets (specify level); $15 per 35 MRC answer sheets (specify level) and Teacher's Guide ('86, 51 pages), 35 pupil report folders, 1 class record folder, and materials needed for machine scoring; $24 per 100 MRC answer sheets (specify level) including materials needed for machine scoring; $114.99 per 500 MRC answer sheets (specify level) including materials needed for machine scoring; $33 per 100 combined MRC answer folders (specify level) for Tests of Achievement and Proficiency, Forms G and H and Cognitive Abilities Tests, Form 4 (includes materials needed for machine scoring); $6.15 per 35 pupil profile charts; $6.15 per 35 profile charts for averages; $6.42 per 35 pupil report folders; $6.84 per 35 class record folders; $6.15 per Teacher's Guide for Levels 15–18 for Forms G & H; $2.70 per Directions for Administration for Separate Level Booklets, Form G; $3 per Fall Norms booklet, Form G; extensive scoring services available from publisher; Dale P. Scannell in cooperation with Oscar M. Haugh, Alvin H. Schild, and Gilbert Ulmer; The Riverside Publishing Co.*

a) BASIC BATTERY. Grades 9–12; 8 scores: Reading Comprehension, Mathematics, Written Expression, Using Sources of Information, Total, plus an Applied Proficiency Skills score and Minimum Competency Scores for Reading and Mathematics; $3 per Basic Battery multilevel test booklet for Levels 15–18; 160(200) minutes.

b) COMPLETE BATTERY. Grades 9–12; 10 scores: Reading Comprehension, Mathematics, Written Expression, Using Sources of Information, Social Studies, Science, Total, plus an Applied Proficiency Skills score and Minimum Competency Scores for Reading and Mathematics; $3.87 per Complete Battery multilevel test booklet for Levels 15–18; 240(280) minutes.

c) SUPPLEMENTS. Grades 9–12 (Levels 15–18); Listening, Form G; $13.89 per 35 MRC answer folders (specify level), including Teacher's Guide and materials needed for machine scoring; Writing, Form G; $9.36 per 35 answer folders with test prompts (specify level), including Teacher's Guide and materials needed for local or central scoring.

For reviews by John M. Keene, Jr. and James L. Wardrop of an earlier edition, see 9:1282.

TEST REFERENCES

1. Morgenstern, C. F., & Renner, J. W. (1984). Measuring thinking with standardized science tests. *Journal of Research in Science Teaching*, 21, 639-648.

2. Schell, L. M. (1984). Reading Yardsticks. *The Reading Teacher*, 38, 318-321.

Review of the Tests of Achievement and Proficiency, Forms G and H by ELAINE CLARK, Assistant Professor of Educational Psychology, University of Utah, Salt Lake City, UT:

The Tests of Achievement and Proficiency (TAP), Form G, replace the earlier version, Form T. The revision was intended to reflect modifications in the curriculum for grades 9 through 12, and to update the test content and objectives. The TAP are a part of the Riverside Basic Skills Assessment Program; other tests include the Iowa Tests of Basic Skills (ITBS) and the Cognitive Abilities Test (CogAT). ITBS tests are designed to measure skills in reading, language, work-study, and mathematics in grades kindergarten through 9; social studies and science in grades 1 through 8; and writing and listening skills in grades 3 through 8. The CogAT is designed to measure verbal, quantitative, and nonverbal reasoning abilities in grades kindergarten through 12.

Major additions to the TAP include a Writing Test, a Listening Test, and a 15-item questionnaire. Although several new items have been added, the existing subtests are essentially unchanged from the earlier edition. The Reading Comprehension subtest maintains an emphasis on secondary school reading assignments; however, readings that pertain to out-of-school topics have also been added. The Mathematics subtest continues to focus on understanding fundamental math concepts and applying those to everyday problem solving. The Written Expression subtest still emphasizes composition, use of language, and problems with writing. The Using Sources of Information, which was designed to assess a student's independent ability to solve problems by locating information, now includes an exercise on flow chart interpretation. The Social Studies subtest places greater emphasis on historical topics; and finally, the Science subtest focuses on the content and processes of earth and space sciences.

For the most part, Form G has retained the basic goal of its predecessor, that is, an emphasis on the application of knowledge and skills rather than specific content (e.g., geography, literature). In fact, the Applied Proficiency Skills score is still computed to reflect student competence in applying math and communication skills to solving problems in daily living. Test users who elect to use this score should keep in mind that it is a derived, or nonscale score based on 63 "selected" items from the Reading Comprehension, Mathematics, Written Expression, and Using Sources of Information tests. Items having particular relevance to interpreting tabular and graphic material, use of reference materials, communication of ideas in writing, and the mathematical solution to problems are included. The only rationale given for selecting some items from the four tests, and not others, is that some items have more direct and common application than others. On the basis of a raw score count of these "selected" items, students are classified as having high, medium, or low proficiency. Surprisingly, there are no empirical data to support the validity of this score. A similar situation can be found with the Minimum Competency Score, a standard score that is intended to assess whether a student has minimum competency in reading and mathematics. Minimum competency is judged relative to the median score of eighth grade students; however, no reason is given for selecting this level as the criterion. Furthermore, there is an absence of empirical data to support the use of this score.

Adequate attention was paid to the content validity of the TAP; consequently, the items measure basic skills of secondary students. The procedures used, and specifications for determining item selection, placement, and distribution of emphases are described satisfactorily. Furthermore, the items were assessed for ethnic and gender bias using both qualitative (panel of judges comprised of males and females of various ethnic backgrounds) and quantitative (traditional and item response theory techniques) means. Individual test items were categorized in terms of both the skill and content measured. Whereas the basis for categorization varies somewhat from test to test, the selection criteria for individual categories is consistent, that is, "useful and practical"; however, submitting the test items to factor analysis would have yielded more statistically sound information, and could have provided some support for the construct validity of the TAP. While construct validity is based on relatively weak data (e.g., intercorrelations among subtests), concurrent validity is neglected.

The reliability coefficients of the tests are at least .82. In fact, the majority are greater than .90. These coefficients compare favorably with that of similar tests, of similar length. Unfortunately, all reliabilities are KR-20 estimates. There is a section in the Preliminary Technical Manual titled, "Long-term stability of Iowa Tests of Basic Skills and Tests of Achievement and Proficiency scores," but no discussion follows pertaining to the TAP.

The standardization of Form G took place in 1984 and 1985. Fifty-two thousand students from 155 schools were tested. Schools were stratified according to size of enrollment (range from below 600 to above 100,000); geographic region (New England/Mideast, Southeast, Great Lakes/Plains, West/Far West); and socioeconomic status (based on years of education and income). The standardization procedures are adequately described and the sample appears nationally representative.

The test materials are user friendly. Four test levels, 15, 16, 17, and 18 have been developed to reflect the general achievement and curriculum of students in grades 9, 10, 11, and 12, respectively. The author should be commended on the use of levels to test students who might be measured more accurately with a lower or higher level test than their grade would suggest. The test materials are available in separate test booklets and a multilevel booklet. The multilevel booklets may be purchased for the Basic Battery (excludes the Social Studies and Science tests) and the Complete Battery. The instructions for administration and scoring are generally clear. With the exception of the two new supplementary tests, Writing and Listening, a multiple-choice format is used. The multiple-choice items can be computer scored by the Riverside Scoring Service, or hand scored using MRC (Measurement Research Center) templates.

The Writing and Listening tests are not included with the other test booklets. Instead, these tests are published separately, along with a Teacher's Guide. There is little information in the Preliminary Teacher's Guide other than a brief mention of "holistic" scoring (e.g., analyzing for style of expression, mechanics, remembering main ideas), test item number, and working time (each test requires 40 minutes, the same amount of time as the other six achievement tests). The Writing and Listening test materials were not available for review; however, the format seems to be an improvement over a multiple-choice method of assessing these particular skills.

Information about the tranformation of raw scores to standard scores, grade equivalents, percentile ranks for pupils and schools, and stanines may be found easily in the manuals. The standard score scale for Form G is reported to "differ slightly" from that of the earlier forms. The author states that it is linked to the developmental standard score for the ITBS. Because the earlier form was similarly "linked," the difference must be the inclusion of kindergarten in the ITBS norms.

In summary, the TAP shares many of the strengths and weaknesses of its predecessor. The procedures for test development and standardization are sound, and the test materials are well written and sensibly organized; however, further data are needed to support the validity and stability (e.g., test-retest reliabilities) of the TAP. Furthermore, without validity data, test users should be cautious interpreting the Minimum Competency score and the Applied Proficiency Skills score. Nonetheless, the TAP compares favorably with other group achievement batteries, and is suitable for continued use as a measure of "basic skills."

[376]

Thinking About My School. Purpose: Measures "student perceptions of the school environment and feelings about their school." Grades 4–6; 1985; TAMS; 6 scores: Power, Social, Work, Teachers, Liking for School, Total; 1986 price data: $19.95 per complete kit including 50 student questionnaires, 50 scoring sheets, and manual ('85, 16 pages); $6 per 50 scoring sheets; $10 per manual; (30–60) minutes; Joanne Rand Whitmore; United Educational Services, Inc.*

Review of Thinking About My School by S. E. PHILLIPS, Associate Professor of Measurement, Michigan State University, East Lansing, MI:

Thinking About My School (TAMS) is a 47-item survey designed to measure students' attitudes and opinions about their school environment. The survey was designed originally to evaluate intervention in a troubled elementary school with low achieving, minority children. For each short positive or negative statement, TAMS uses a 4-point Likert scale of frequency of occurrence from *not at all* to *always*. TAMS was written for use in grades 4, 5, and 6. The author indicates, however, it could also be used with modifications in grades 2–12, but provides the user with no guidance as to what those modifications should be.

The most serious drawback for the user of TAMS is that much of the data that could aid the user in understanding what TAMS measures are not included in the manual. At several points, the user is referred to research bulletins not included with the test materials. This makes it very difficult to evaluate the technical quality of the survey. It would be very helpful if some of these data could be included in the manual.

Another major concern is the appropriate level of interpretation for the survey. The author lists both individual and group interpretations but states that "TAMS results are most valuable to stimulate dialogue with an individual student." Conversely, the manual also suggests that confidentiality is an important factor in obtaining meaningful results. Students would probably provide more honest responses if their answers remain anonymous. In addition, reliabilities reported for the subscales (generally in the .60s) are too low for making individual student decisions. Although the total score reliability is .92, it is not clear how this score alone could provide meaningful interpretation for an individual student. Thus, I would encourage users to limit their interpretations to group aggregated data.

It is also not clear from the manual what sample was used to calculate the reliabilities. It might have been more informative to present reliabilities separately for each grade. It would also be useful to have a stability coefficient, perhaps for a 2-week interval, to determine the short-term consistency of responses that the user might expect with this survey.

The author indicated the research group had difficulty responding to the Likert format and recommended that users provide practice before administering the survey. It would be easier for the user to follow this suggestion if the samples in the directions were included in a box at the beginning of the survey instrument. The directions were generally well written but were a bit contradictory in telling students to think carefully about each question but to respond fairly quickly.

Interpretation of the results is problematic. One must accept, for example, that student power in the school is a positive attribute. The author appears to rely heavily on judgment and "face validity" to substantiate the validity of TAMS. A process aimed at content validity is described but there appears to have been no formal tryout process. Although at some point in the scale-development process, item-scale correlations and factor analyses were apparently obtained and used for decisions on final inclusion, none of these data are included in the manual. There are 10 miscellaneous items that are not included in any of the five subscales; perhaps they should be eliminated. About one fourth of the statements are negative; the rest are positive. A more even balance might be important to control response biases.

In judging the items and subscales, it would also have been helpful to know whether the items/scales tended to discriminate between schools identified as having positive versus negative climates. There is no indication whether ethnicity or gender affected responses to the instrument. In short, there are no comparisons for any meaningful groups. The author indicates that survey scores and profiles were related to teacher identification of students with behavioral problems but presents no data to support this assertion.

As the author indicates, the administration of a survey instrument to a low achieving population presents serious concerns about the validity of the results. The author stresses proper motivation, reading the items aloud to the students, and practice with the answer format to encourage valid responses. But no data are presented to indicate the success of such procedures. One has only the author's statement that "Such an instrument was expected to provide the most accurate method of attitude assessment attainable."

Perhaps the most useful feature of the TAMS is that it "forces us to look at more objective evidence of the nature of our school climate and allows us to analyze it more systematically." To the degree this is true, TAMS may make an important contribution to school evaluation. The author also indicates, however, that, "All interpretations must be regarded as tentative or speculative until verified through other communication with the student(s) and behavioral observations." Thus, it is not clear what information the user derives from TAMS that is additional or different from that already available through informal communication with students and student observations.

Review of Thinking About My School by SYLVIA ROSENFIELD, Professor, School Psychology Program, Temple University, Philadelphia, PA:

Thinking About My School (TAMS) is a self-report questionnaire designed for students in grades 4, 5, and 6. Its purpose is to measure student perceptions of the school environment and feelings about school, particularly related to five elements that are, according to the manual, considered to influence student feelings about school: "(*a*) peer relations and the general social atmosphere of the peer culture; (*b*) teachers and administrators; (*c*) assigned class work; (*d*) power to influence events or opportunities to share in decision making; and (*e*) general feelings about attending their school."

The instrument itself consists of 47 items, divided into four scales of 8 items each: Power, Social (peer relations), Work, and Teachers; one scale of 5 items: Liking for School; and a miscellaneous set of 10 items regarded as valuable but not clearly belonging to any of the scales (e.g., item 25: "I would like to see many things change in my school"). The items are phrased in simple language. The response format is a 4-point scale, labeled in words (not at all, once in a while, often, all the time) that respondents check to describe how they feel about their school with respect to each item. Respondents mark their answers directly on the two-page scale (although the manual says four pages). This response method is meant to reduce any errors children might make in transferring responses to an answer sheet. Statements are read to the children to avoid contamination with poor reading ability. Sample items are included in the instructions. The author indicates the scale can be administered comfortably in 30 minutes, with an additional 15 to 30 minutes allowed for practice, questions, and possible rest breaks. A scoring sheet, which facilitates subscale score calculation, is provided. Thirteen items are reverse scored to counteract a potential acquiescent response set.

TAMS was originally developed in the early 1970s for use in a Stanford field-based research project. The project was designed to help teachers develop more constructive student behavior and more positive attitude in a "distressed" school with a predominantly black, low SES population. The scale was created because no appropriate instrument was available to measure attitude towards school of subjects similar in age and background to those in the project.

The technical adequacy of the TAMS manual is limited. The only data reported in the manual are the alpha coefficients for internal consistency in the initial research use of the TAMS with pupils in grades 4 through 6. The alpha for the total score was .92. Subscales varied from .60 to .76. No validity data are reported. The manual suggests face validity; indicates that TAMS scale scores and total scores were accurate in discriminating groups of students identified by teachers and research staff as differing in their attitudes towards schools; and concludes that test results are most valuable in stimulating dialogue with individual or groups of students. The potential test user is referred to Research and Development Memorandum No. 125: *Thinking About My School (TAMS): The Development of an Inventory to Measure Pupil Perception of the Elementary School Environment* (Whitmore, 1974), for further details.

The data presented in Memorandum No. 125, however, confirm that TAMS has a limited technical base. All the data reported are obtained from subjects in the school involved in the research project briefly described above, severely restricting the generalizability of the results. Factor analyses failed either to confirm the theoretical subscales or to generate more unambiguous and valid scales. It is unclear, therefore, why the author continues to include instructions to score the subscales. The author reports poor reliability, even between items intended to have the same meaning. A number of recommendations are made to reword items (all items involving the word "power") and drop items (19, 24, 38), none of which are done in the published version of the test. Further she suggests the accuracy of responses to negative items should be evaluated further. While concluding the scale may be as reliable as measures of attitude, the author indicates there was evidence of undesirably large response error. This was, perhaps, attributable to the specific characteristics of the population from which the sample was drawn.

Given the poor reliability, it is not surprising that limited validity evidence was found. The author suggests some evidence of concurrent validity for the subscales based on correlations of specific TAMS scales with other instruments administered to the sample. Examination of these data, however, does not reveal unique relationships of subscales with related external criteria. There is little evidence of predictive validity and many inconsistencies in results. The author concludes that it is "wise to delay conclusions about the reliability and validity of

TAMS until data can be collected and analyzed from other samples in varying conditions."

As a result of the above conclusion, it is hard to understand why the author published the scale in 1985 without collecting further data to demonstrate its technical adequacy. Further, providing scoring instructions for the theoretical subscales, which were not supported by factor analyses, and failure to follow the specific recommendations regarding item modification in Memorandum No. 125 (Whitmore, 1974), are puzzling. As it stands, the instrument consists of a list of potentially useful items, with some preliminary data and suggestions for modification.

Whitmore (1974) acknowledges the lack of research on measuring student attitudes, the dearth of instruments for assessing them, and the measurement problems involved in developing scales. To her credit, she has attempted to develop such an instrument for an age range and population that has received little attention in this literature. TAMS may be useful to researchers in this area who would be interested in further refinement of the scale. However, without further data collection, the scale as now presented has a severely limited technical base. Further research on the reliability of the scale, use with other populations (as well as replication with similar populations), and modification of the items and the scales should be undertaken, along with the development of validity information. This information is vital so that test users can judge the appropriateness of TAMS for their specific needs.

REVIEWER'S REFERENCES

Whitmore, J. R. (1974). *Thinking About My School (TAMS): The development of an inventory to measure pupil perception of the elementary school environment* (Research and Development Memorandum No. 125). Stanford, CA: Stanford University, Stanford Center for Research and Development in Teaching. (The Memorandum is currently available from the Center for Educational Research, Stanford University, Stanford, CA 94305).

[377]

Thomas-Kilmann Conflict Mode Instrument. Purpose: Assesses "an individual's behavior in conflict situations." Managers; 1974; self-administered, self-scored; 5 scores: Competing, Collaborating, Compromising, Avoiding, Accommodating; 1987 price data: $4.50 per instrument ('74, 16 pages including test and general information); [15] minutes; Kenneth W. Thomas and Ralph H. Kilmann; XICOM, Inc.*

TEST REFERENCES

1. Dickson, G. L. (1984). Conflict management style: A staff development program. *Journal of College Student Personnel*, 25, 167-168.

2. Yarnold, P. R. (1984). Note on the multidisciplinary scope of psychological androgyny theory. *Psychological Reports*, 54, 936-938.

3. Duane, M. J., Azevedo, R. E., & Anderson, U. (1985). Behavior as an indication of an opponent's intentions in collective negotiations. *Psychological Reports*, 57, 507-513.

4. Mills, J., Robey, D., & Smith, L. (1985). Conflict-handling and personality dimensions of project-management personnel. *Psychological Reports*, 57, 1135-1143.

Review of the Thomas-Kilmann Conflict Mode Instrument by RICHARD E. HARDING, Vice President, Research, Selection Research, Inc., Lincoln, NE:

The Thomas-Kilmann Conflict Mode Instrument was designed to "assess an individual's behavior in conflict situations." Conflict situations were defined as situations where the concerns of two people appear to be incompatible. According to the authors, two basic dimensions of behavior were used to define the five modes with regard to dealing with conflict. The two dimensions were assertiveness and cooperativeness. To measure these two dimensions, five modes were identified which were labeled Competing, Collaborating, Compromising, Avoiding, and Accommodating.

The instrument is composed of a series of 30 pairs of statements. Each statement of each pair is associated with one of the five conflict-handling modes. Thus, there are 12 statements associated with competing, 12 with collaborating, etc. Respondents are asked to choose one of the statements for each of the 30 pairs, the statement that best describes their own typical behavior. Respondents are also directed to select one statement from each pair even if neither statement is consistent with their own individual behavioral patterns.

Scoring the instrument is completed by identifying how many statements are circled for the Competing, Collaborating, Compromising, Avoiding, and Accommodating modes. Each mode score could range from 0 to 12. A percentile ranking is used to place each score for the five modes into a high, middle, or low area. The high area was defined to be a percentile rank of 75 or above, and the low area was defined to be at the percentile rank of 25 percent or below. A middle area between 25 and 75 was also defined.

After scoring, respondents are informed that there are no right answers. Additionally, all five modes are listed as being useful in some situations, "each represents a set of useful social skills." The authors then state, "To help you judge how appropriate your utilization of the five modes is for your situation, we have listed a number of uses for each mode—based upon lists generated by company presidents." There are, additionally, from one to five questions listed for each of the modes if one scored either high or low on a particular mode. The reason for these questions is to help respondents focus on "warning signals for the overuse or underuse of each mode." Thus, the authors claim the instrument is designed to help individuals define their personal conflict position and how they relate to the requirements of each conflict situation.

The warning signals associated with each mode were developed from lists generated by company presidents. There was no indication of the number of company presidents involved or any specific information about how these lists were developed.

There are additional areas that help to pinpoint modes on which the individual scored high or low. One of the statements in the test manual is, "Each possible score is graphed in relation to the scores of managers who have already taken the Thomas-Kilmann Conflict Mode Instrument." One wonders how many managers there were but, upon further examination, finds on the next page under the percentile table that there were 339 practicing managers at middle and upper levels of business and government organizations used in developing the percentile tables. No description of these managers is provided, leaving serious concerns about why and how they were selected. There are no indications of the methodology or the analytic techniques used.

The test itself is accompanied by a section entitled "Scoring and Interpreting the Thomas-Kilmann Conflict Mode Instrument." As a test manual, it is lacking in detail. There are no sections in the test manual regarding test development, standardization, reliability, or validity. The manual serves only as a source of direction for administering the test and/or scoring the test.

A three-page document entitled "Question and Answer Reference For The Leader; Questions Most Often Asked About The Thomas-Kilmann Conflict Mode Instrument," is sent with each order for the instrument. Questions answered in this three-page document are: (1) How thoroughly has the Thomas-Kilmann Conflict Mode Instrument been tested? (2) What's the difference between collaborating and compromising? (3) Wouldn't my scores vary if I thought of different specific situations when I filled out the instrument? (4) Doesn't the word "collaborating" have negative overtones? (5) What if my scores don't seem to fit me?

Claims are made in this document that extensive testing has not been completed on the instrument because it may take 10 years or more to thoroughly validate an instrument. Other claims are that the scores on the modes are "assessing behaviors—i.e., the interpersonal 'processes' that an individual uses in conflict situations, not necessarily the decisions they reach." In terms of the reliability of scores, the statement is made, "However, tests of the Instrument indicate that scores are fairly consistent when people take the test on separate occasions." This statement is made with no data provided in this document as evidence.

Another issue of concern was found in Question 5, which stated, "What if scores don't seem to fit me?" A statement made in relation to this question is:

> In the past, this question has usually meant that the instructions were misunderstood, the test scored incorrectly, or the meaning of the scores misinterpreted. Otherwise, the scores are usually close enough to the person's own perceptions of his/her behavior that the question doesn't come up.

The question and answer reference ends with a statement that:

> However, it is useful to remember that any measuring device is, at best, only accurate in most instances. This person may be the exception. For this reason, it's always dangerous to proclaim (or to accept) instrument results as gospel truth. The results of any psychological instrument should be viewed as more data about the individual—to be compared with other data which he has about himself. It is a starting place to begin asking questions about oneself—to help put one's behavior into perspective.

One thought that came to mind while reading this statement was—what if this page is lost and not with the instrument? What are the possible implications regarding the misinterpretation of the results for the individual completing the instrument?

In summary, the test manual and the question-and-answer reference pages raised more questions about using the instrument than either document answered. Many basic questions are left unanswered, such as, the methodology used in developing the instrument, reliability issues, validity issues, and strong documentation for appropriate use of the instrument.

After contacting the publisher (XICOM, Inc.), a reprinted journal article from *Educational and Psychological Measurement* was received by this reviewer. The title of this article was "Developing A Forced-Choice Measure of Conflict-Handling Behavior: The 'Mode' Instrument" by Ralph H. Kilmann and Kenneth W. Thomas. This article was informative regarding the development of the Thomas-Kilmann Conflict Mode Instrument. Addressed in this 10-year-old article were validity and reliability issues, but no specific item statistics were presented. However, another call to XICOM, Inc. revealed that this article is not included when the Conflict Mode Instrument is sent to purchasers.

This instrument may be of value for research purposes, but any use beyond that should be exercised with extreme caution. In addition, the test manual or accompanying materials must be improved to meet existing standards so that users can be fully informed as to the instrument's psychometric qualities.

Review of the Thomas-Kilmann Conflict Mode Instrument by RONN JOHNSON, Assistant Professor of Educational Psychology, University of Nebraska-Lincoln, Lincoln, NE:

The Thomas-Kilmann Conflict Mode [*M*anagement *O*f *D*ifferences *E*xercise] Instrument (MODE) is a measure of interpersonal conflict-handling modes. The five interpersonal conflict-handling modes the instrument was designed to measure are: (*a*) Competing, (*b*) Collaborating, (*c*) Compromising, (*d*) Avoiding, and (*e*) Accommodation. The test materials are presented in an 18-page booklet that presents 30 pairs of statements. Example: A. I like to solve problems by myself; B. I usually consult with others while solving a problem. Respondents are asked to endorse the one statement from each pair that is most characteristic of their own behavior. A number of the items are repeated.

The directions for administering the conflict-mode instrument are clear. It is easy to self-administer, score, and graph. The entire scoring and graphing process takes about 15 minutes. The highest possible score for each skill is 12, occurring if the respondent chooses the statement for a given mode as being more personally characteristic than the other mode it was paired with. The lowest possible score for each skill is 0, given when the respondent fails to choose the statement representing a particular mode in the 30 comparisons presented.

The above mentioned test booklet also contains self-scoring procedures and a graph for the results that depict the respondent scores. Interpretation information is also available for the five modes of handling conflict as well as high or low scores. In addition to this, the authors have included diagnostic questions that may serve as guidelines for the overuse and underuse of each mode.

The authors report reliability and concurrent test validity. The internal consistency coefficients are as follows: .43 Accommodating, .62 Avoiding, .58 Compromising, .65 Collaborating, .71 Competing. The average alpha coefficient for the mode is .60, while the average for the Lawrence-Lorsch and Hall instruments were .45 and .55, respectively. The average test-retest reliability for the MODE instrument is .64, while the average for the Lawrence-Lorsch instrument is .50, the Blake-Mouton .39, and the Hall instrument is .55. Concurrent test validities using the other three conflict-handling instruments on each of the five conflict modes provide evidence of convergence. In addition, some support was reported for substantive validity. However, external validity is a major area of concern for the MODE.

This concern for external validity is directly expressed in the need to control for factors of social desirability. The authors report a study using the items of the MODE instrument where an aggregate of self-ratings yielded 4 percent of the variance that was attributed to the social desirability value of the items. This 4 percent variance was contrasted with an average of 80 percent variance for three other similar instruments (i.e., Blake-Mouton, Lawrence-

Lorsch, & Hall). Further, when social desirability over all modes was examined, 17 percent of the variance among aggregate scores on the five modes in the MODE instrument can be accounted for by social desirability. The variance of 17 percent was in contrast to an average variance of 90 percent for the other previously mentioned instruments. In spite of these findings, it cannot be stated with certainty that the MODE instrument controls for distortions in self-descriptions any better than other instruments. Individuals who describe themselves positively on either social desirability scale also rate themselves as more collaborating on all four instruments.

The MODE test does not tell you how effective a person is at using a particular mode. Yet, the authors indicate the conflict-mode instrument helps "you judge how appropriate your utilization of the five modes is for your situation." This implies a need for knowledge of the person's ability to use that particular mode. That is, a person could have a high score on Comprising and may know the situations where this mode should or should not be used but may not have the personal or intellectual abilities needed to implement that mode. In other words, the interaction between the level of social confidence and complex situations will determine the effective use of a particular mode.

A related concern is the author's report that no one person can be characterized as having a single, rigid style of dealing with conflict. They further indicate the instrument is designed to assess the mix (e.g., Avoidance and Compromising) of the conflict-handling modes. However, they do not provide extensive interpretive data on the various combinations (e.g., high Competing and low Compromising). Furthermore, no attention is given to conflicts involving three or more people, or cross-cultural, or cross-gender conflicts. For example, how, if at all, the conflict modes change if a black female top manager, who is high on Competing, interacts with a white male subordinate who may also be high on the same mode? The slow advent of racial minorities and women into the executive work force makes the information about their conflict-mode dynamics of critical importance.

Overall, I have found the MODE instrument to be a useful tool in stimulating discussions about conflict modes. It is easy and quick to self-administer, score, and graph. However, we have become more concerned for standards of educational and psychological tests, and have become more sophisticated in our awareness of these standards. This reviewer believes the conflict-MODE instrument is of limited value in understanding the comprehensive picture of conflict MODES. This criticism is based partially on the conceptualization of conflict modes measured and partially on the limited information reported in the manual on the interpretation of the test. The manual should be updated and improved by including better normative and interpretive information as well as a more complete review of the research conducted using the Conflict Mode Instrument. Nevertheless, the conflict MODE has value as a research tool and a supplemental instrument, especially if the user reads the booklet carefully and understands the conceptualization of the constructs being measured.

[378]

Trainee Performance Sample. Purpose: "To be utilized to assist in making vocational skill learning placements of severely retarded individuals." Severely mentally retarded adolescents and adults; 1982; TPS; 5 scores: Verbal, Model, Prompt, Learning, Total; individual; 1987 price data: $750 per complete set including administration manual (101 pages), and technical manual (26 pages); (20–30) minutes; Larry K. Irvin and Russell M. Gersten; Ideal Developmental Labs.*

Review of the Trainee Performance Sample by JOHN M. TAYLOR, Executive Director, Developmental Disabilities Center, Boulder, CO:

The Trainee Performance Sample (TPS) was created to assist in making vocational placement decisions for severely and profoundly retarded adults and adolescents. The test incorporates a "process" assessment approach, or the measurement of the examinee's ability to benefit from instruction during the testing process. As a standardized vocational skills assessment instrument suited for use with severely retarded adults and adolescents, the test is most satisfactory.

The TPS was standardized originally in 1976 on a sample of over 300 severely retarded adults in a large state institution. The test was revised in 1979 to improve content validity of the items, expand the range of subjects to include persons classified in the low range of moderate retardation, and to better examine the reliability and validity of the test.

The final standardization sample of the 1979 revision of the TPS included 149 adults classified as "severely or low-moderately retarded." The subjects were from 10 facilities (community and state institutions), and all were over the age of 16. Test-retest reliability, obtained from a random sample of 26 subjects, was .93. Internal consistency reliabilities ranged from .64 to .86 for the various subtests, and was .93 for the TPS total scores. Reliabilities were lowest for the severely and profoundly retarded adolescent population in the sample, and for the "guidance" or "prompt" subscale.

Criterion validity scores between the TPS total scores and subsequent performance on an assembly and sorting task are reasonably high (ranged from -.57 to -.66) and demonstrate the TPS total score can predict with some accuracy the future vocational performance of an individual on sorting and assembly tasks: the higher the TPS score, the fewer trials, errors, and time to meet criterion. Construct validity was assessed by comparing the mean total scores for community-based versus institutionalized residents (contrasted groups). The results revealed sufficient sensitivity of the TPS as indicated by significant differences in the mean percent correct for each group.

The basic test consists of various sorting/assembly items (cards, brackets, nuts and bolts, wire, blocks) neatly packaged in a sturdy briefcase. The test itself examines three dimensions (type of instruction, nature of the task, and number of objects involved in the task) for each item presented. Types of instruction include verbal directions, model/match-to-sample, and physical guidance. The task attributes that were varied for each item included: difficult discriminations, coordinated two-hand movements, and sequencing of steps. In addition, the number of objects within the TPS items were varied. Final item selection resulted in 25 items being included in the TPS.

The TPS is designed to be administered by a "skilled" examiner (with, the authors recommend, at least several months experience teaching severely handicapped persons) in a single 30-minute session. The administration manual is well written, and the instructions for both the administration and scoring of each item are reasonably straightforward and clear. Anyone with psychometric experience should have no difficulty with the TPS. The TPS yields five major types of scores: Verbal, Imitation or Modeling, Physical Guidance or Prompt, Learning (familiarity with material/tasks, and new learning), and Total score. Also provided with the test is a "TPS Interpretation Form," which enables one to identify and record the major results of the test, and transfer the findings to a written report.

If there is a major fault with the TPS, it is that current vocational training and employment for the severely handicapped is now active in vocational areas different from those upon which the TPS was built. The TPS was designed to permit habilitation professionals to determine the level and type of training needed for an individual to learn bench-type sorting and assembly skills. In the past few years, vocational placements for even the most severely handicapped have forced us to raise dramatically our expectations. Sheltered workshop settings that required bench-type sorting and assembly skills are no longer the sole workplace for the severely handicapped. There are now more options available to all, and the push for "prevocational," "supported," and "competitive" employment work sites for the severely handicapped limits the extent of the applicability of the TPS.

In summary, the TPS appears to be a relatively quick and useful assessment device for making training decisions at job sites requiring sorting and assembly skills. Although the validity of certain subtests (e.g., Verbal) is less than acceptable, it is very possible this problem reflects difficulty with complex verbal communication with severely retarded individuals, and not an insurmountable problem with the TPS.

Review of the Trainee Performance Sample by LELAND C. ZLOMKE, Clinical Director of the Intensive Training Service, and BRENDA R. BUSH, Psychologist, Beatrice State Developmental Center, Beatrice, NE:

DESCRIPTION. The Trainee Performance Sample (TPS) is a revision of the original TPS developed by Bellamy and Snyder in 1976. The instrument attempts to measure the vocational competency of mentally retarded subjects by examining both the subjects' skills to complete small task components and their competency in learning vocational skills. The TPS also seeks to bridge a perceived gap between task-specific assessments and traditional norm-referenced measures of performance and learning abilities.

Included in the TPS package is an administration manual (101 pages), technical manual (26 pages), scoring forms (100), interpretation forms (100), and a case of materials (approximately 93 pieces). The materials range from paper clips to acrylic blocks with nuts and bolts. The administration manual provides well-detailed administration directions with examiner prompts and standardization requirements. Also provided is an excellent discussion of factors complicating the vocational assessment of both product and process skills in severely handicapped subjects. The instrument is expected to be completed in a single 20–30 minute session. The session is composed of the presentation of 25 individual items. Each item has a two-trial format. The second trial allows for examination of response consistency or ability to benefit from prompting and training.

SCORING. Scores provided include raw scores to be transformed into percentages (correct responses/total items) per domain. The resultant percentages are then classified into three general categories for comparison to behaviorally anchored narratives. Interpretation of final results provide information to make vocational placement and training decisions for adolescents and adults displaying low-moderate through profound mental retardation. The information includes predictions of the level and type of resources needed to adequately teach the individuals sedentary sorting and assembly skills. Five major scores and two clinical information scores are provided through a TPS administration. The major scores for each subject include: Verbal Receptivity, Imitative Skills, Prompting and Physical Guidance, Overall Learning Skills, and Total Test Score. The two clinical scores include Resistance to Prompts, and No Responses. Each of the domain scores has a behaviorally anchored narrative description of predicted resource requirements for adequate training.

The TPS has indeed standardized the assessment procedure, but also claims to provide information on the amount and type of training resources that a severely retarded person may be expected to require relative to other similar clients in specific types of tasks. However, only percentages, describing trial successes divided by opportunities, are interpreted through comparisons with several seemingly arbitrary behaviorally anchored narratives. There is no reference to the norm group's performance on such tasks. More useful information would have included at least a percentile table or some mention of central tendency or dispersion.

ITEM GENERATION. It is unclear how the TPS items were derived. The information in the manual indicates that items were selected that "representatively sampled the domain of tasks and instructional methods commonly used in vocational training for severely retarded individuals." Also mentioned was a test blueprint based on a recognized model training program. This blueprint was used to revise items. Items were further selected for: (*a*) difficult discriminations, (*b*) coordinated two-hand movements, (*c*) sequencing of steps, and (*d*) conjunctive stimulus control. It is difficult to discern from this limited explanation the process used to determine the criterion for item retention and it appears that no empirical evidence (e.g., item discrimination, reliability, or validity measures) was used in the selection process.

SAMPLE. A "community-based definition" of severe and low-moderate retardation, rather than a traditional IQ measure, was used for initial selection of subjects. One hundred seventy-one adults and 56 adolescents all with no major physical or visual impairments comprised the initial sample. An additional 26 community-based adults were selected, from a sample of 227, for the retest data. No explanation was given for how these 26 were chosen.

RELIABILITY. Internal consistency estimates were calculated for all TPS scores. Coefficient alphas ranged from .91–.93 on the total TPS score. However, the subgroups of items (verbal, model, prompt) had internal consistency ratings from .64–.86. These analyses were conducted on only seven or nine items per subgroup. Test-retest reliability appeared adequate ($r_{tt} = .93$) after a 2-week interval.

VALIDITY. Concurrent validity was determined through correlations with the Supervisor Checklist. This newly created measure was analyzed by the TPS authors and achieved a reliability estimate of .95. More research should be conducted before the Supervisor Checklist is deemed an acceptable indicator of concurrent validity. Additionally, the TPS was correlated with the Peabody Picture Vocabulary Test (PPVT) in order to achieve a rough estimate of correlation with a standardized intelligence test. However, the PPVT is most accurately described as a rapid measure of vocabulary (Anastasi, 1982) and is not acceptable clinically as a standardized measure of intelligence. A correlation with an intelligence measure is of questionable use in any case.

The Technical Manual also includes information on criterion and construct validity. A criterion-validation study showed significant negative correlation between TPS scores and subsequent required training trials, errors, and prompts needed for subjects to reach production criterion. The TPS does apparently correlate with performance on assembly and sorting tasks. However, no empirical evidence is presented to recommend vocational training resource levels nor to demonstrate a relationship between TPS scores and the level and type of resources required to train such individuals. Construct validity was assessed in a study comparing community versus institutionalized subjects. The results showed higher scores by the community-based subjects. However, none of several confounding factors, such as uncontrolled subject selection by group, curriculum differences, and previous learning experiences, were discussed.

SUMMARY. The developers of the TPS have made an effort to present an instrument capable of assessing the vocational skills, primarily sedentary bench work, of severely handicapped individuals. The assessment is conducted under well-specified standardized conditions and contains well-structured behavioral samples explained in an organized and understandable fashion. The test materials are well designed and useful, however, the $750 cost seems very expensive.

A substantial amount of psychometric research has been conducted with the TPS. The standardization procedures, reliability, and initial validity studies are commendable. However, the item selection and predictive validity remain considerably lacking in empirical support. The developers have a norm sample but fail to use it as a comparative measure, choosing instead to interpret results against a set of arbitrary narrative descriptions and percentage criterion. The provision of percentiles, measures of central tendency, and dispersion would, at least, lend more credence to interpretations of individual subject scores. This information, together with a study examining the predictive validity of TPS scores with an actual set of needed vocational resources for clients, would greatly enhance the confidence that clinicians could have in using the results of the TPS to make placement and training decisions.

REVIEWER'S REFERENCE

Anastasi, A. (1982). *Psychological testing* (5th ed.). New York: Macmillan Publishing Co., Inc.

[379]

The Values Scale, Research Edition. Purpose: "To measure intrinsic and extrinsic life-career values." High school through adults; 1985–86; VS; developed as part of the international Work Importance Study; 21 scores: Ability Utilization, Achievement, Advancement, Aesthetics, Altruism, Authority, Autonomy, Creativity, Economic Rewards, Life Style, Personal Development, Physical Activity, Prestige, Risk, Social Interaction, Social Relations, Variety, Working Conditions, Cultural Identity, Physical Prowess, Economic Security; 1987 price data: $13.50 per 25 reusable test booklets; $14.50 per 50 answer sheets; price data for profiles available from publisher; $10 per manual ('86, 46 pages); $11 per specimen set; scoring services available from publisher; (30–45) minutes; Donald E. Super and Dorothy D. Nevill; Consulting Psychologists Press, Inc.*

Review of The Values Scale, Research Edition by DENISE M. ROUSSEAU, Associate Professor of Organization Behavior, Kellogg School of Management, Northwestern University, Evanston, IL:

The Values Scale (VS) was developed as a vocational and career choice diagnostic, as a counseling tool, and needs survey. It assesses the values that individuals seek to find in various life roles and the relative importance of the work role as a means of value realization. It contains 106 items assessing 21 intrinsic and extrinsic values, requiring 30 to 45 minutes to administer. Hand scoring of the VS is possible when the number of respondents is small. The VS can also be mailed to the publisher for scoring when accompanied by payment. The VS was designed to be used with upper elementary or middle school students as well as with employed adults in semi-skilled, skilled, clerical, sales, professional, and managerial occupations.

The values measured are: Ability Utilization, Achievement, Advancement, Aesthetics, Altruism, Authority, Autonomy, Creativity, Economic Rewards, Life Style, Personal Development, Physical Activity, Prestige, Risk, Social Interaction, Social Relations, Variety, Working Conditions, Cultural Identity, Physical Prowess, and Economic Security (the latter three applicable only to some countries).

No conceptual model underlying the 21 scales is found in the VS manual. The scales reflect a wide range of motives and activities, intrinsic and extrinsic. The absence of a framework underlying the scales makes it difficult to gauge its thoroughness and theoretical representativeness. Nonetheless, its scales are linked to many commonly used concepts in the vocational literature (e.g., achievement, economic reward).

This assessment system was developed by an international consortium of vocational psychologists. The VS is intended to be employed as part of a Development Assessment Model outlining the psychological and situational factors that affect vocational choice and adjustment. This model allows counselor and counselee to assess career readiness and assist in making vocational career decisions. The VS provides critical data on the motives and orientations of young adults, which can be juxtaposed along with occupation-characteristic data to forecast fit. The manual indicates that different VS forms exist for use in different countries. These different forms are not described.

NORMS. At present no norms are available for the VS based upon representative samples (the manual does include means and standard deviations from 3,000 American youths and adults, based upon a convenience sampling). Thus, career counseling using the VS should be conducted using an ipsative (intraindividual) interpretation.

PSYCHOMETRIC PROPERTIES. Alpha (internal consistency) reliabilities are above .70 for all scales based upon samples from 686 high school and 1,042 college students (though varying somewhat in other samples). Test-retest reliabilities appear to be above .50 for all scales (based on college student samples). The time interval involved, however, is not reported. Given the fluctuations in internal consistency and stability across samples, factor scores are currently being developed to provide more reliable indices.

Construct validity is an issue with the VS because the factor structure reported from a sample of 1,728 high school and college students indicates simultaneous loadings by several scales on more than one factor. Substantial intercorrelations exist among many scales (i.e., $>.65$). Factor structure appears to vary across samples, especially when age groups differ. The authors postulate these differences reflect age changes suggestive of a progression in value structure. Currently, research is being conducted on the factor structure and construct validity of the VS. Predictive validity analyses linking the VS to behavior or adjustment are not yet available. At present it is not possible to confirm the construct or criterion-related validity of the VS. Further research is needed.

CONCLUSIONS. Although validation studies are not yet complete, a systematic effort is underway to examine and enhance the validity of The Values Scale. The evidence currently available suggests it will be a useful and psychometrically sturdy inventory assessing values pertaining to vocational and career choice. It is also a potentially useful device for researchers investigating cross-cultural differences in values and needs in the labor force. Use of the instrument should be restricted to research or exploratory applications until further psychometric data are available.

Review of The Values Scale, Research Edition by ROBERT B. SLANEY, Associate Professor of Counseling Psychology, The Pennsylvania State University, University Park, PA:

The Values Scale (VS) was developed to measure 21 intrinsic and extrinsic values related to values or satisfactions that "most people seek in life." There are 106 items, five per scale, with a final item included only when the scale is administered in cross-national studies. The scale is neatly printed with a cover page, two pages of items, and a final page that provides a grid for determining the respondent's occupational group. The front page of the answer sheet collects demographic data and the reverse side provides directions for responding, an example of a question, and the responses that are to be used. These range from 1 which means "Of little or no importance" to 4 which means "Very important." The answer sheets can be machine or hand scored. The items are conveniently arranged on the answer sheet to facilitate hand scoring. Scores equal the sum of the endorsed responses for the scale items. The accompanying Manual, labelled as a "Research Edition" consists of 41 pages including 26 tables, and is nicely produced and printed.

A unique and appealing aspect of the development of this scale is that it was designed to be used in national and cross-national research. It is related to Super's work as coordinator of the Work Importance Study (WIS), an "informal consortium of autonomous research teams in a dozen countries in Europe, North American, and Australia, with corresponding members in Asia and Africa." In developing the scale each national team reviewed its national literature and shared the review with the consortium. Based on these reviews the WIS group decided to "develop an instrument to measure work and general values." Working groups from different countries wrote definitions of each value. These definitions were discussed, revised, reviewed, and revised again. Then sample items were written following the approach used to create the definitions. These items were reviewed and revised and assigned to at least two diverse national teams for refinement. These items were then circulated prior to the next meeting where they were reviewed yet again and possibly revised.

The national teams also translated the items into their own languages, reviewed the translation, and pilot tested the items. A 1980 version of the Values Scale contained 10 items for each of the 23 original scales. In the U.S. these scales were administered to two samples of high school and college students. Item-scale correlations and item-factor analyses were derived. Each national team identified the scales it considered worth keeping and selected the five best items, considering the best mix of general and work-specific items. In a 1981 meeting the teams decided which scales to drop and which to retain based on the data gathered. Finally, each scale was reduced to five items, two measuring general values, two measuring work-specific values, and a final item, measuring either, that was selected empirically. At this point, data have been gathered on Portuguese, Yugoslavian, Australian, and Canadian (in English and French) samples. The U.S. samples have been mainly samples of convenience and the authors note that a more adequate norm group is being gathered. Regardless, the Manual focuses on the U.S. results and the comments below will concentrate on these findings.

Alpha coefficients on high school, college, and adult samples were generally above .70 although they were clearly lower than those found for high school and college samples using the previous 10 item scales. Test-retest data on two college samples were rather disappointing. For the first sample, six scales had correlations below .70 and for the second sample nine of the scales were below .70. Overall, the reliability of the scales raises some questions about the confidence one can place in the individual scale scores. The reliabilities also raise questions about the authors' contention that ipsative interpretations of the scale are acceptable.

A curious feature of the Manual is that the validity of the scale is addressed in two chapters, first under "Use and Interpretation" and again under "Development, Reliability, and Validity." Face validity does appear to be adequate, as the authors suggest, although items on several scales seem quite similar if not repetitious. Still, when the authors note that "face validity . . . was assured by the writing of items according to the agreed upon definitions of the values" the word "assured" seems excessive. It is also quite noticeable that the Manual does not present the definitions of the values that were agreed upon. However, even more basic concerns are evident in inspecting the data on construct validity. Here the authors note that: "The most important types of validity data are those that show that the instrument actually measures what theory has said it should measure." Although it is not clear what is being referred to as theory in this instance, a very basic concern for the instrument is whether the individual scales measure what they suggest they measure. No studies were reported that directly addressed this issue.

The studies that are reported are difficult to evaluate because they are often unpublished or were reported at meetings and not easily available. A study by Yates that was available is reported in the Manual as follows:

> In a nationwide sample of 383 military personnel, Yates (1985) found that Realistic individuals significantly valued Physical Prowess more than did Enterprising types and, less expectedly, that Social types valued Economic Security more than did Realistic.

In fact, the most striking aspect of this study is the lack of differences that were found considering the study used five of the Holland types and 21 values. In the same study Yates looked for differences by grouping subjects according to age. No specific hypotheses were presented but the results were interpreted as supportive of the construct validity of the scale. Without clear predictions based on theory or, at least, carefully reasoned rationales, the possibility of interpreting the findings as confirming what was expected seems problematic. The results of Yates' study may be interesting but they seem difficult to justify as clear support for the construct validity of the instrument.

When comparisons of high school, college, and adult males and females yielded no statistically significant sex differences, the authors, though sophisticated researchers, inspected trends. The same occurred for age and educational levels where differences were apparently expected but not found. Data on concurrent validity for an Australian sample appeared somewhat tangential but generally supportive of several of the scales. Studies from other countries also yielded data that appeared to be consistent with the scale meanings. Factor analytic results also were supportive but not unequivocal. Overall, although preliminary data are generally supportive, there is a clear need for additional studies that address the construct validity of the scales of this instrument in a direct and unequivocal manner. An analysis of these issues requires a more adequate norm group.

Based on the validity data for the scales of this instrument it was appropriate and encouraging for the authors to label the Manual as a "Research Edition." Other statements in the Manual are less encouraging. For example, the authors state that "the VS can be used with upper elementary or middle school pupils." It is unclear how the authors reached that conclusion. They also state that the "VS is now ready . . . . for exploratory use in career and vocational counseling." Although the use of the word exploratory seems well advised there is a danger that readers will not emphasize the exploratory use of the scale. This danger seems especially likely because the authors suggest the scales can be used in an ipsative manner and they provide a sample case that demonstrates such use in counseling. No rationale or data are provided in support of the ipsative use of the scale in career counseling. Until additional data are provided on a more adequate norm group, including reliability and especially construct validity data, any suggested use seems premature.

[380]

The Vane Kindergarten Test (1984 Revision). Purpose: "Evaluate the intellectual and academic potential and behavior adjustment of young children." Ages 4–6; 1968–84; VKT; 4 scores: Perceptual Motor, Vocabulary, Drawing a Man, Total; 1987 price data: $8 per 50 record sheets; $7.50 per manual ('84, 61 pages); (30) minutes; Julia R. Vane; Clinical Psychology Publishing Co., Inc.*

See T3:2548 (4 references) and T2:528 (7 references); for reviews by Dorothy H. Eichorn and Marcel L. Goldschmid, see 7:428 (3 references).

TEST REFERENCES

1. Kaplan, H. B. (1985). A comparison of the Vane Kindergarten Test with the WPPSI and a measure of self-control. *Psychology in the Schools*, 22, 277-282.

2. Schmidt, S., & Perino, J. (1985). Kindergarten screening results as predictors of academic achievement, potential, and placement in second grade. *Psychology in the Schools*, 22, 146-151.

*Review of The Vane Kindergarten Test (*1984 *Revision) by DAVID W. BARNETT, Associate Professor, School Psychology, University of Cincinnati, Cincinnati, OH:*

The Vane Kindergarten Test (VKT) is a screening measure developed to assist with the identification of cognitive and social behaviors related to early school success or failure. However, the reader is also given the unwarranted impression that the VKT yields an adequate estimate of intelligence and enables the *determination* (emphasis added) of the effects of motivation, attention, perceptual skills, and behavior on performance. The scale is intended for use by school psychologists.

The VKT is comprised of three subtests: Perceptual Motor, Vocabulary, and Intelligence ("a Man subtest"). In addition, a number of unstructured observations are suggested.

PERCEPTUAL MOTOR SUBTEST. This subtest is similar to many other drawing tasks such as the Bender-Gestalt and the Geometric Design subtest of the Wechsler Preschool and Primary Scale of Intelligence (WPPSI). The author states that performance on this subtest is related to early reading and writing skills, and difficulties are possibly indicative of a "developmental lag." If the performance is extremely "poor," central nervous system dysfunction (or brain injury) is implicated. Only three forms are included in the scale: a square, a cross formed by double lines, and a hexagon. Each is drawn three times.

VOCABULARY. Verbal expressive skills are required. The child is asked to define 11 words similar to the words on the WPPSI Vocabulary subtest and other language tests. General information is an important determinant of success on this subtest.

MAN SUBTEST. The child is asked to draw a person, a technique similar to that used in other tests (e.g., Harris, 1963; Koppitz, 1968). Details and features of the drawing contribute to the developmental scoring, yielding a "man IQ." In addition, various psychopathological signs found in the literature on children's drawings are used to evaluate adjustment (e.g., absence of mouth, grotesque drawing).

ADDITIONAL OBSERVATIONS. Although the author refers to a section describing additional measures, no objective guidelines are offered for the subsequent observations. One "measure" is the child's skill in writing his or her name. The author states that a child's skill in this task "contains a number of clues that are helpful in reaching an evaluation regarding the child's motivation, learning ability, and perceptual motor development." A second category includes test observations of such factors as hand dominance, attention, following directions, self-control, cooperation and turn taking, interference, motivation, spontaneity, and related behaviors.

RESTANDARDIZATION. The original VKT was published in 1968. The present norms are based on the performance of 800 children, ages 4 to 6-5, from three states (New Jersey, New York, and Vermont). Equal numbers of boys and girls were included at each age level and the 1980 census was used as a guide for selection based on occupation, rural versus urban residence, and racial group (described as white and nonwhite). Non-English-speaking children were not represented. Sample selection procedures are not adequately described.

VALIDITY. Each subtest is substantially correlated with the full score (Perceptual Motor = .78; Vocabulary = .74; Man = .82; N = 800). The intercorrelations between the subtests are at a high, but reasonable level (e.g., the highest, between Man and Perceptual Motor, is .58).

Four studies reported correlations between the VKT and the Stanford-Binet. The median correlation was .73. Two studies reported correlations between the VKT and the WPPSI (.70, $N = 33$; .75, $N = 18$).

Various achievement measures also have been used to study the validity of the VKT. The range of correlations was from .52 ($N = 213$), based on a comparison between the VKT given in kindergarten and the Stanford Achievement test given one year later, to .60 ($N = 304$), the correlation between the VKT administered in kindergarten and the Stanford Achievement test given in third grade.

Other studies reported the use of the VKT with test batteries and other types of tests. In general, the VKT was substantially correlated with other academic, language, and perceptual motor measures.

RELIABILITY. Test-retest reliability information was examined in six different samples with various intervals between tests. The results ranged from a high of .97 ($N = 14$, 1-week interval) to .70 ($N = 29$, 5-to-6-week interval).

ADMINISTRATION AND SCORING. The Perceptual Motor and Man subtests can be group administered to 10–12 children. The Vocabulary subtest is individually administered. Scoring instructions for the Man and Vocabulary subtests are clearly presented with sufficient examples of successful and unsuccessful performances.

An IQ is derived for each subtest. Tables enable the determination of IQ relative to the child's age and performance. One month increments are used. The three subtests are simply averaged to obtain a "Full IQ."

Mental age equivalents of subtest scores are available from ages 3-9 to 7-6 for the Perceptual Motor subtest, ages 4-0 to 8-0 on the Vocabulary subtest, and 3-0 to 10-3 for the Man subtests. However, it should be noted that many of these ages were *not* included in the standardization and information is not presented on the derivation of the mental ages.

CONCLUSIONS. The evidence for both validity, and, to a lesser extent, reliability of the VKT seems to be comparable to individually administered IQ tests for preschool children. However, numerous preschool measures correlate in a similar manner and the concerns identified below preclude the recommendation of the VKT as a screening measure.

The psychometric development of the scale does not use contemporary techniques or suggested guidelines for scale development. Information is not included concerning the construction of the IQ tables. Standard scores are not used.

Concerns can be raised with respect to the labeling of subscales (e.g., *Man* IQ), misleading floor and inadequate ceiling (e.g., a child of 6-11 with a perfect score receives an IQ of 105), derivation of composite scores, derivation of mental ages for children not included in standardization, the standardization itself, and other factors. The standard deviations of subtests range from 15.1 (Perceptual Motor) to 20.3 (Vocabulary) at various ages. Reliabilities of subtests and standard errors for all scales are not included in the manual. No guidelines are suggested for interpretations of subtests or for screening decisions. The case studies included serve as testimonials and are potentially misleading.

The most important criticism of the VKT is conceptual in nature. Many contemporary reviews of preschool screening suggest that this process should be curricular based, ongoing, include adult or caregiver behaviors in addition to child behaviors as targets of assessment, and be systematic. Assessment tasks should have direct links to interventions. The use of the VKT as a screening instrument is inconsistent with these guidelines.

REVIEWER'S REFERENCES

Harris, D. B. (1963). *Children's drawings as measures of intellectual maturity*. New York: Harcourt, Brace & World.

Koppitz, E. M. (1968). *Psychological evaluation of children's human figure drawings*. New York: Grune & Stratton.

Review of The Vane Kindergarten Test (1984 Revision) by WILLIAM B. MICHAEL, Professor of Education and Psychology, University of Southern California, Los Angeles, CA:

The 1984 edition of The Vane Kindergarten Test (VKT) represents a revision of the earlier 1968 form, which has been designed to evaluate not only the intellectual and academic potential of young children, but also their behavioral adjustment. The first two of the three parts of the VKT, which can be administered to groups of 10 to 12 children at one sitting, include the following: (*a*) the Perceptual Motor Subtest, in which the examinee is directed to make copies of three boxes, three crosses, and three hexagons, and (*b*) the Man Subtest, in which the child draws a picture of an entire man. The third part of the VKT, which is individually administered, is named Vocabulary Subtest. It requires the examinee to tell the examiner what each of 11 different words means. The instructions for administration and scoring of the three parts of the VKT are clear, detailed, and quite specific. Examiners would be expected to be qualified school psychologists. Specific criteria (signs) have been given to the examiner so that he or she can use them during the process of test taking as indicators of behavioral characteristics associated with difficulties or problems in perceptual-motor development and emotional-social adjustment. In addition, the examiner is also urged to observe test behaviors that might suggest possible deficiencies in motivation or cognitive functioning.

In the restandardization of the VKT, substantial effort has been expended to obtain a representative population of children under 6-6 years of age relative to socio-economic level, urban or rural background, ethnicity, and sex. Selected from an initial population of more than 2,000 children, the final standardization sample of 800 consisted of (*a*) subgroups of 100 boys and 100 girls within each of three age levels of 4-6 to 4-11 years, 5-0 to 5-5 years, and 5-6 to 5-11 years, and (*b*) subgroups of 50 boys and 50 girls at ages 4-0 to 4-5 years and 6-0 to 6-5 years. Although efforts were made to allocate percentages of children in the various strata according to the population distribution throughout the United States, all those tested came only from the states of New York, New Jersey, and Vermont. In this restandardization, one of the main objectives was to correct for inflation in test scores that had occurred subsequent to 1968. A second goal was to simplify the scoring system for the Man Subtest. To minimize scoring errors, certain test items requiring difficult judgmental decisions concerning the appropriateness of responses were eliminated. A comparatively simple scoring system of 31 points was devised. The test author has recommended that this new system should be used only with young children, as it may underestimate the intellectual level of very bright children of 6-6 to 7-0 years. She also has suggested that for older children the well-known Goodenough scoring method be applied to the Man Subtest.

The restandardization effort has led to the generation of a considerable amount of new normative, reliability, and validity data. In the case of normative data, three kinds of evidence are represented by (*a*) mean IQs and standard deviations of the normative population relative to each of the three subtests and the full scale for each age subgroup as well as for the total population, (*b*) mean IQs and standard deviations on the same measures according to sex of child and occupation of parent, and (*c*) IQs converted from raw scores on each of the subtests by each month of chronological age over an age span from 3-6 to 6-11 years.

Virtually all reliability data were cited in the form of test-retest coefficients involving the use of comparatively small samples. Seven reported coefficients varied between .70 to .97 with an approximate median value of .81. Evidence that might be considered indicative of the internal consistency of the VKT was apparent in coefficients among the subtests for the total sample of 800 children. Coefficients of .43, .58, and .45 were found between the Perceptual Motor and Vocabulary, Perceptual Motor and Man, and Vocabulary and Man subtests, respectively.

Concurrent validity data have been presented in terms of the corrrelation of the VKT with other widely used standardized measures of intelligence. The range of correlation coefficients found in five different samples fell between .62 and .76 with a median value of approximately .74. Predictive validity information has been reported in the form of coefficients between the VKT and three different, widely employed standardized tests of achievement. The five validity coefficients varied between .52 and .60 with a median entry of .59. Additional evidence for validity was cited in the form of correlations between the VKT and other types of tests indicative of perceptual-motor and cognitive development. The resulting validity coefficients were comparable to those already mentioned.

Additional noteworthy features occur in the manual. Studies pertaining to the performance of minority populations on the VKT have been cited, although the information presented is not sufficient to permit any reliable degree of generalization. Of potential assistance in the interpretation of subtest and full-scale IQ scores is Chapter 5 of the manual. This chapter includes six case studies that are anchored to detailed information presented in the form of reproductions of drawings representing the two nonverbal parts of the test. These case studies also provide information on vocabulary responses, age of child, school attended, handedness, and IQs earned on the three subtests as well as on the full scale.

In summary, the VKT is a relatively easy test to administer and to score in the hands of a well-trained school psychologist. The 1984 revision furnishes what may be considered quite adequate normative and interpretive score information on each subtest as well as on the full scale. Although additional data on reliability and validity would be welcome, the initial evidence has been quite promising. In comparison with other widely used measures of early childhood perceptual-motor and cognitive development, the VKT would appear to be comparable, if not possibly superior, in its psychometric adequacy and clinical usefulness.

[381]

Vineland Adaptive Behavior Scales. Purpose: "Assess personal and social sufficiency of individuals from birth to adulthood." Birth through 18–11 and low functioning adults, ages 3 through 12–11; 1935–85; revision of the Vineland Social Maturity Scale; semi-structured interview for Survey and Expanded Forms; 3 editions; 13 scores: 3 Communication scores (Receptive, Expressive, Written), 3 Daily Living scores (Personal, Domestic, Community), 3 Socialization scores (Interpersonal Relationships, Play and Leisure Time, Coping Skills), 2 Motor Skills scores (Gross, Fine), Adaptive Behavior Composite, Maladaptive Behavior (optional for Survey and Expanded Forms only); individual; Spanish edition available; American Guidance Service.*

a) INTERVIEW EDITION, SURVEY FORM. Birth through 18–11 and low functioning adults; 1935–84; general assessment of adaptive strengths and weaknesses; 1988 price data: $16.50 per 25 record booklets; $8.75 per 25 reports to parents; $19 per manual ('84, 313 pages); $27 per starter set (includes 10 record booklets, manual, and 1 report to parents); (20–60) minutes; Sara S. Sparrow, David A. Balla, and Domenic V. Cicchetti.

b) INTERVIEW EDITION, EXPANDED FORM. Birth through 18–11 and low functioning adults; 1935–84; comprehensive assessment of adaptive behavior for program planning; $39.50 per 25 item booklets and 25 score summary and profile reports; $10 per 25 reports to parents; $14 per 25 program planning reports; $25 per manual ('84, 334 pages); $50 per starter set (includes 10 item booklets, 10 score summary and profile reports, 1 program planning report, 1 report to parents, and manual); (60–90) minutes; Sara S. Sparrow, David A. Balla, and Domenic V. Cicchetti.

c) CLASSROOM EDITION. Ages 3 through 12–11; 1985; an assessment of adaptive behavior in the classroom; $16.50 per 25 questionnaire booklets; $9.50 per 25 reports to parents; $14.50 per manual ('85, 186 pages); $21 per starter set (includes 10 questionnaire booklets, manual, and 1 report to parents); (20) minutes; Sara S. Sparrow (test, report), David A. Balla (test, report), Domenic V. Cicchetti (test, report), and Patti L. Harrison (manual).

For a review of the Survey Form and Expanded Form by Iris Amos Campbell, see 9:1327 (8 references); see T3:2557 (38 references), 8:703 (23 references), T2:1428 (50 references), P:281 (21 references), 6:194 (20 references), and 5:120 (15 references); for reviews of an earlier edition by William M. Cruickshank and Florence M. Teagarden, see 4:94 (21 references); for reviews by C. M. Louttit and John W. M. Rothney and an excerpted review, see 3:107 (58 references); for reviews by Paul H. Furfey, Elain F. Kinder, and Anna S. Starr, see 1:1143.

TEST REFERENCES

1. Goldstein, D. J. (1985). Accuracy of parental report of infants' motor development. *Perceptual and Motor Skills*, 61, 378.

2. Guidubaldi, J., & Cleminshaw, H. (1985). Divorce, family health, and child adjustment. *Family Relations*, 34, 35-41.

3. Janos, P. M., Fung, H. C., & Robinson, N. M. (1985). Self-concept, self-esteem, and peer relations among gifted children who feel "different". *Gifted Child Quarterly*, 29, 78-82.

4. Oakland, T., & Houchins, S. (1985). A review of the Vineland Adaptive Behavior Scales, Survey Form. *Journal of Counseling and Development*, 63, 585-586.

5. Altepeter, T., Moscato, E. M., & Cummings, J. A. (1986). Comparison of scores of hearing-impaired children on the Vineland Adaptive Behavior Scales and the Vineland Social Maturity Scale. *Psychological Reports*, 59, 635-639.

6. Goldstein, D. J., Smith, K. B., & Waldrep, E. E. (1986). Factor analytic study of the Kaufman Assessment Battery for Children. *Journal of Clinical Psychology*, 42, 890-894.

7. Guidubaldi, J., Cleminshaw, H. K., Perry, J. D., Nastasi, B. K., & Lightel, J. (1986). The role of selected family environment factors in children's post-divorce adjustment. *Family Relations*, 35, 141-151.

8. McCallum, R. S., Helm, H. W., Jr., & Sanderson, C. E. (1986). Local norming and validation of an adaptive behavior screening unit. *Educational and Psychological Measurement*, 46, 709-718.

9. O'Connor, L., & Schery, T. K. (1986). A comparison of microcomputer-aided and traditional language therapy for developing communication skills in nonoral toddlers. *Journal of Speech and Hearing Disorders*, 51, 356-361.

Review of the Vineland Adaptive Behavior Scales by JEROME M. SATTLER, Professor of Psychology, San Diego State University, San Diego, CA:

The Vineland Adaptive Behavior Scales (VABS) is a revision of the Vineland Social Maturity Scale published by Doll in 1935. The VABS assesses the social competence of handicapped and nonhandicapped individuals from birth through age 19. The VABS requires that a respondent familiar with the behavior of the individual in question answer behavior-oriented questions posed by a trained examiner (interviewer) or complete a questionnaire. There are three versions of the VABS: Survey Form, Expanded Form, and Classroom Edition.

Adaptive behavior—the principal focus of measurement—is defined as the ability to perform daily activities required for personal and social sufficiency. In each version of the scale adaptive behavior is measured in four domains: Communication, Daily Living Skills, Socialization, and Motor Skills. The combination of these four domains forms the Adaptive Behavior Composite. The Survey and Expanded Forms also include a Maladaptive Behavior domain.

Each domain is designed to evaluate various adaptive skills. The Communication domain samples receptive, expressive, and written communication skills. The Daily Living Skills domain evaluates personal living habits, domestic task performance, and behavior in the community. The Socialization domain focuses on interactions with others, including play, use of free time, and responsibility and sensitivity to others. The Motor Skills domain evaluates gross and fine motor coordination. Finally, the Maladaptive Behavior domain deals with undesirable behaviors that may interfere with adaptive behavior.

The Survey Form contains 297 items administered over a 20- to 60-minute period. The Expanded Form, which takes approximately 60 to 90 minutes to administer, contains 577 items, including the 297 items on the Survey Form. It was constructed to provide a comprehensive measure of adaptive behavior and to aid in designing educational, habilitative, and treatment programs. The Classroom Edition contains 244 items, designed for children from 3 years, 0 months to 12 years, 11 months of age. It provides an assessment of adaptive behavior in the classroom. This form is designed to be completed by the child's teacher in approximately 20 minutes.

SCORES. All three versions of the Vineland have $M = 100$ and $SD = 15$ for the four domain scores and for the Adaptive Behavior Composite. "Unfortunately, the means and SDs vary considerably from age group to age group" (Silverstein, 1986). These fluctuations mean that (*a*) both the standard errors of measurement and the bands of error reported in the manual are only rough approximations, (*b*) critical differences needed to evaluate significant differences among domain scores also may be only rough approximations, and (*c*) it is difficult to compare individuals across ages or perform longitudinal comparisons for the same individual. Silverstein advises caution in using the VABS standard scores for any of these purposes.

STANDARDIZATION. The standardization sample for the Survey and Expanded Forms closely matched the population as described by 1980 U.S. census data. The ages of the 3,000 individuals in the sample ranged from newborn to 18 years, 11 months. Stratification variables included sex, race or ethnic group, geographical region, community size, and parents' educational level. Norms are provided from birth to 18 years, 11 months. From birth through 1 year, norms are broken into 1-month increments, from 2 through 5 years, into 2-month increments; from 6 through 8 years, into 3-month increments; and from 9 through 18 years, into 4-month increments. Separate norms also are provided for mentally retarded, emotionally disturbed, and physically handicapped children and adults.

The Classroom Edition had a representative sample of 2,984 students, ages 3 years, 0 months to 12 years, 11 months, again selected to conform to 1980 U.S. census data, and used the same stratification variables as the other forms.

RELIABILITY. Three measures of reliability were reported in the manual—split-half, test-retest, and interrater reliability. Split-half reliability coefficients for the Survey Form are as follows: For the Communication domain, split-half reliabilities range from .73 to .93 ($Mdn\ r_{xx} = .89$); for the Daily Living Skills domain, they range from .83 to .92 ($Mdn\ r_{xx} = .90$); for the Socialization domain, they range from .78 to .94 ($Mdn\ r_{xx} = .86$); and for the Motor Skills domain, they range from .70 to .95 ($Mdn\ r_{xx} = .83$). The Adaptive Behavior Composite split-half reliability coefficients range from .84 to .98 ($Mdn\ r_{xx} = .94$), and the Maladaptive Behavior domain coefficients range from .77 to .88 (IMdn $r_{xx} = .86$).

Split-half reliability coefficients for the Expanded Form were estimated based on the Survey Form and adjusted by the Spearman-Brown formula. For Communication, estimates of split-half reliabilities range from .84 to .97 ($Mdn\ r_{xx} = .94$); for Daily Living Skills, they range from .92 to .96 ($Mdn\ r_{xx} = .95$); for Socialization, they range from .88 to .97 ($Mdn\ r_{xx} = .92$); and for Motor Skills, they range from .83 to .97 ($Mdn\ r_{xx} = .91$). The Adaptive Behavior Composite reliability estimates range from .94 to .99 ($Mdn\ r_{xx} = .97$); estimated split-half reliability coefficients for the Maladaptive Behavior domain are identical to those for the Survey Form.

Test-retest reliability for the Survey Form (2- to 4-week retest interval) are in the .80s and .90s. No test-retest reliabilities were computed for the Expanded Form.

Interrater reliability coefficients for the Survey and Expanded Forms range from .62 to .75.

In the Survey Form, standard errors of measurement range from 3.4 to 8.2 over the four domains, and from 2.2 to 4.9 ($M\ SE_m = 3.6$) for the Adaptive Behavior Composite. In the Expanded Form, standard errors of measurement range from 2.4 to 6.2 over the four domains and from 1.5 to 3.6 ($M\ SE_m = 2.6$) for the Adaptive Behavior Composite.

VALIDITY. Concurrent validity was established by correlating the Vineland Adaptive Behavior Scales with various tests. An $r = .55$ was reported with the original Vineland. With normal samples, correlations between the Vineland Adaptive Behavior Composite and several intelligence and ability tests were as follows: r s $= .32$ and .37 with the Kaufman Assessment Battery for Children (K-ABC) Mental Processing and Achievement scales, respectively, and $r = .28$ with the Peabody Picture Vocabulary Test—Revised (PPVT-R). Correlations with the Wechsler Intelligence Scale for Children (WISC) or Wechsler Intelligence Scale for Children—Revised (WISC-R) were .52 for emotionally disturbed children, .70 for visually handicapped children, and .47 for hearing-impaired children, correlations with the Hayes-Binet and Perkins-Binet were .82 and .71, respectively, for visually handicapped children.

The manual reports relationships between the VABS Adaptive Behavior Composite and various demographic variables. Whereas females obtained scores that were .5 to 5.3 points higher than those of males, there was less than a 4.6 point difference, on the average, among racial or ethnic groups. Level of parents' education was an important factor, however. Those children whose parents had attended 4 or more years of college scored on the average 8.3 points higher than did children whose parents had less than a high school education. Regional differences were minor (less than 4.0 points), and community size had virtually no effect.

The manual also provides tables for equating the Adaptive Behavior Composite on the Survey and Expanded Forms with Social Quotients and Deviation Social Quotients from the Vineland Social Maturity Scale and with standard scores on the K-ABC Mental Processing Composite, Achievement Scale, and Nonverbal Scale.

COMMENT ON THE VINELAND ADAPTIVE BEHAVIOR SCALES. The Vineland Adaptive Behavior Scales is a potentially useful tool for the assessment of adaptive behavior. Difficulties still exist with the scales, however, despite the care and effort that have gone into the revision. Silverstein's (1986) analysis seriously questions the norming procedures. The fluctuations in the means and *SD*s of the standard scores from age group to age group are a problem, particularly with mentally retarded individuals. Of less serious concern are difficulties in framing questions, eliciting appropriate responses, and scoring responses (Oakland & Houchins, 1985). (Some items require knowledge that informants may not possess. For example, in the Communication domain, informants must tell whether the child says at least 100 recognizable words, uses irregular plurals, and prints or writes at least 10 words from memory.) Further research will be needed to evaluate how adequately the VABS assesses adaptive behavior.

REVIEWER'S REFERENCES

Oakland, T. D., & Houchins, S. (1985). Testing the test: A review of the Vineland Adaptive Behavior Scales, Survey Form. *Journal of Counseling and Development*, 63, 585-586.

Silverstein, A. B. (1986). Nonstandard standard scores on the Vineland Adaptive Behavior Scales: A cautionary note. *American Journal of Mental Deficiency*, 91, 1-4.

[382]

Vocational Preference Inventory, 1985 Revision. Purpose: "To assess personality . . . also useful for assessing vocational interests." High school and college and adults; 1953–85; VPI; "a personality-interest inventory composed entirely of occupational titles"; 11 scales: Realistic, Investigative, Social, Conventional, Enterprising, Artistic, Self-Control, Masculinity-Femininity, Status, Infrequency, Acquiescence; Apple or IBM computer administered version requires 64K, 80-column card-Apple (128K-IBM) and 2 floppy disk drives; 1987 price data: $6 per 25 reusable test booklets; $11 per 50 sets of answer sheets and profiles; $1.50 per score key; $9 per manual ('85, 36 pages); $125 per computer version (50 uses); (15–30) minutes; John L. Holland; Psychological Assessment Resources, Inc.*

For reviews by James B. Rounds and Nicholas A. Vacc and James Pickering of an earlier edition, see 9:1342 (19 references); see T3:2581 (45 references); for an excerpted review by W. Bruce Walsh of an earlier edition, see 8:1028 (175 references); see also T2:1430 (48 references); for reviews by Joseph A. Johnston and Paul R. Lohnes, see 7:157 (39 references); see also P:283 (31 references); for reviews by Robert L. French and H. Bradley Sagen of an earlier edition, see 6:115 (13 references).

TEST REFERENCES

1. Pelhan, J. P., & Fretz, B. R. (1982). Racial differences and attributes of career choice unrealism. *The Vocational Guidance Quarterly*, 31, 36-42.

2. Varvil-Weld, D. C., & Fretz, B. R. (1983). Expectancies and the outcome of a career development intervention. *Journal of Counseling Psychology*, 30, 290-293.

3. Wiggins, J. D., & Moody, A. (1983). Identifying effective counselors through client-supervisor ratings and personality-environmental variables. *The Vocational Guidance Quarterly*, 31, 259-269.

4. Knapp-Lee, L., Michael, W. B., & Grutter, J. (1984). Relationship of the COPSystem, Form P Interest Inventory (COPS-P) scales to Vocational Preference Inventory scales (VPI): Construct validity of scales based on professed occupational interest in a college sample. *Educational and Psychological Measurement*, 44, 455-461.

5. Miller, M. J., Greco, E. A., Parette, H. P., & Kemp, E. L. (1984). On using the Vocational Preference Inventory with incarcerated men. *Psychological Reports*, 54, 832-834.

6. Slaney, R. B. (1984). Relation of career indecision to changes in expressed vocational interests. *Journal of Counseling Psychology*, 31, 349-355.

7. Wiggins, J. D. (1984). Personality-environmental factors related to job satisfaction of school counselors. *Vocational Guidance Quarterly*, 33, 169-177.

8. Winchell, A. E. (1984). Conceptual systems and Holland's theory of vocational choice. *Journal of Personality and Social Psychology*, 46, 376-383.

9. Iacono, C. U., & Darden, J. (1985). VPI-SAS: Using SAS as an aid for evaluating Holland's Vocational Preference Inventory. *Educational and Psychological Measurement*, 45, 193-194.

10. Johnson, R. G. (1985). Microcomputer assisted career exploration. *Vocational Guidance Quarterly*, 34, 296-304.

11. Monahan, C. J., & Muchinsky, P. M. (1985). Intrasubject predictions of vocational preference: Convergent validation via

the decision theoretic paradigm. *Journal of Vocational Behavior*, 27, 1-18.

12. Royalty, G. M., & Magoon, T. M. (1985). Correlates of scholarly productivity among counseling psychologists. *Journal of Counseling Psychology*, 32, 458-461.

13. Schell, B. H., & Zinger, J. T. (1985). An investigation of self-actualization, job satisfaction, and job commitment for Ontario funeral directors. *Psychological Reports*, 57, 455-464.

14. Sedge, S. K. (1985). A comparison of engineers pursuing alternate career paths. *Journal of Vocational Behavior*, 27, 56-70.

15. Taylor, N. B., & Pryor, R. G. L. (1985). Exploring the process of compromise in career decision making. *Journal of Vocational Behavior*, 27, 171-190.

16. Hodgkinson, G. P. (1986). A note concerning the comparability of the standard and automated versions of the Vocational Preference Inventory. *Journal of Occupational Psychology*, 59, 337-339.

17. Pryor, R. G. L., & Taylor, N. B. (1986). On combining scores from interest and value measures for counseling. *Vocational Guidance Quarterly*, 34, 178-187.

Review of the Vocational Preference Inventory, 1985 Revision by JOHN W. SHEPARD, Associate Professor of Education, Counselor and Human Services Education, University of Toledo, Toledo, OH:

The Vocational Preference Inventory (VPI), 1985 Revision, is substantially the same as its 1977 predecessor. With few exceptions, the test's theoretical basis, purpose, format, item content, and technical properties remain constant. New or old, it accomplishes its stated purposes as a brief personality test and interest inventory.

While not a comprehensive test of personality, the VPI does provide useful information regarding work style, work typology, and interest in specific occupations. It does not, however, inform users of the broad occupational clusters they may need to explore initially before pursuing a given vocation.

The test is based on Holland's six work typologies: Realistic, Investigative, Artistic, Social, Enterprising, and Conventional (RIASEC). It appears appropriate for adolescents and adults of normal intellect. Reported typology codes and code weightings are ordered in a manner compatible with Holland's *Occupational Finder* and *Dictionary of Holland Occupational Codes*. Appropriately, the Revision has substituted the scale title Investigative for Intellectual. Test items have been structured so that the instrument is more appropriate for use by females.

The VPI is easily administered, scored, and interpreted. It is one of the more time- amd cost-efficient interest inventories. It is based on sound theoretical constructs.

While the manual is well organized and understandable, it does not contain up-to-date data regarding normative, reliability, and validity studies. Cited research, indicating past versions of the VPI have possessed adequate reliability and validity, are 10 to 25 years old. It is recommended the manual be amended to fully describe contemporary studies of the 1977 and 1985 VPI. It is also recommended the Masculinity-Femininity scale be deleted or renamed using nongender language. The author's claim that this scale can be used as a check against "faking" suggests a possible title change to "Validity Scale."

In summary, the VPI effectively provides information regarding a user's work personality/style and interests. It is improved over the 1977 version for it allows users to easily translate occupational codes (RIASEC) to specific occupational titles. It would be most effectively utilized in concert with other measures of interest and personality. The test's technical properties need to be comprehensively studied and described in the manual.

Review of the Vocational Preference Inventory, 1985 Revision by NICHOLAS A. VACC, Professor and Coordinator of Counselor Education, University of North Carolina, Greensboro, NC:

The Vocational Preference Inventory (VPI) is comprised of a listing of 160 occupational titles divided among 11 scales (i.e., Realistic, Investigative, Artistic, Social, Enterprising, Conventional, Self-Control, Masculinity-Femininity, Status, Infrequency, and Acquiescence). To complete the inventory, individuals indicate whether they like or dislike the occupations listed.

Although originally developed to assess personality, the VPI is used primarily for assessing vocational interests. As reported by the author, the instrument has been used as (*a*) a brief personality inventory for employed adults and high school and college students, (*b*) a helpful addition to a battery of personality inventories, (*c*) an interest inventory, and (*d*) an assessment technique for the investigation of career theory and behavior. Most vocational counselors would agree that the merit of the VPI is in assessing occupational interest using the Realistic (R), Investigative (I), Artistic (A), Social (S), Enterprising (E), and Conventional (C) scales as formulated in Holland's theory of careers.

As indicated in the manual, persons completing the VPI should have at least normal intelligence and be over 14 years of age. It is also recommended that the inventory be used and interpreted "only in combination with other psychosocial information such as age, sex, educational level, field of training, and current occupational status."

The 1985 Edition of the VPI is the eighth revision, containing four new or revised occupational titles. Item 51 was changed from Power Shovel Operator to Hunting or Fishing Guide, item 91 was changed from Filling Station Worker to Electronic Technician, and item 111 was shortened from Long Distance Bus Driver to Bus Driver. Item 88, Department Store Manager, was interchanged with item 135, Sports Promoter. These changes were made to reduce the weighting of items toward males.

Three short Research Forms (i.e., A, B, and C), developed for use in investigations or surveys for which a brief assessment of vocational interests is desirable, have been added with the 1985 Revision. These forms are not for use with individuals. Items from six scales of the 1977 Revision (i.e., Realistic, Intellectual, Artistic, Social, Enterprising, and Conventional) were organized into Forms A and B, each of which consists of 42 items. Form A is comprised of *unbalanced* items and Form B contains *balanced* items. (*Unbalanced* items are those with endorsement rate differences for females and males ranging from 11% to 35%; *balanced* items are those with female-male endorsement rate differences from 1% to 11%.) Form C, which is a shortened version of Form B, consists of 30 items. Further comment on the Research Forms is impossible because of insufficient information in the manual.

The 1985 Edition is, for all practical purposes, identical to the seventh edition. Changes have been made in four items as mentioned above; the form of the answer sheet, profile sheet, and scoring template has been redesigned; the manual has been updated to include changes made in the instrument during the seventh revision; and approximately 12 additional references have been included in the manual. The profile form and manual now use a single letter abbreviation for each of the six scales. Revisions in the manual include the elimination of sexist language, additional examples of scale interpretations, additional case illustrations for females, and improved organization and "flow" of content.

The 1985 Edition contains a limited amount of new validity or reliability data. This information is helpful, but is not particularly substantive and does not appreciably affect previous psychometric evaluations of the instrument. In general, the changes and updating undertaken in the 1985 Edition could have been addressed during the seventh revision and thus saved consumers from having to purchase new test materials within a short period of time.

In summary, the 1985 revision of the VPI is an improved edition because of the updating of the manual and profile sheets, and the instrument is recommended as being helpful for career exploration. The major advantages of using the VPI, in addition to its theory-base relationship with Holland's Self-Directed Search Instrument, are its low cost and the short amount of time needed for administering and scoring.

For an instrument that is often used by vocational counseling professionals, additional data need to be systematically collected for the purpose of addressing unresolved psychometric issues. Concerns about the validity and reliability of the instrument, as cited by reviewers in previous editions of *The Mental Measurements Yearbook*, have yet to be addressed.

[383]

Waksman Social Skills Rating Scale. Purpose: "Developed to assist psychologists, educators, and other clinicians to identify specific and clinically important social skill deficits in children and adolescents." Grades K–12; 1983–84; WSSRS; 3 scores: Aggressive, Passive, Total; individual; separate forms for males and females; 1987 price data: $5.45 per 25 male or female rating forms; $21.95 per manual ('84, 15 pages); administration time not reported; Steven A. Waksman; ASIEP Education Co.*

Review of the Waksman Social Skills Rating Scale by HAROLD R. KELLER, Associate Professor of Psychology and Education, Syracuse University, Syracuse, NY:

The Waksman Social Skills Rating Scale (WSSRS) was designed to aid in the assessment of social competence or specific social skills. After carefully defining social competence as those abilities required to perform competently at a social task, the author indicates that the WSSRS was developed "to identify specific and clinically important social skill deficits in children and adolescents." It is apparent from examination of the items and the two factors on the scale (Aggressive and Passive domains) that the focus of the scale is upon problematic behaviors. The behavior descriptors for the items were selected as representative of behaviors taught by a number of social skills training programs. While the programs cited train specific social competencies, the WSSRS items address problematic behaviors.

The 21 items on the scale were selected on the basis of ratings of 29 original items by 50 mental health professionals and/or educators and 50 graduate students in counseling psychology. The raters were asked to judge whether the behaviors were "important for a child's development" on a scale of 0–5 (with 5 indicating extreme importance). To be retained in the final pool, an item had to have a mean rating over 2.5 and at least 50% of the ratings for that item had to be 3, 4, and 5.

Administration and scoring of the WSSRS is very simple, with each behavior rated on a scale of 0 (never) to 3 (usually). Domain subtotal and total scores are easily obtained, as are corresponding percentile scores from the profile table on the front of the respective rating forms for males and females. The rating forms and manual indicate the WSSRS should be completed by classroom teachers, counselors, or childcare workers who have "daily contact with the child or adolescent." There is no indication of a minimum period of familiarity or daily contact with the child before ratings are done. Classroom teachers who had had the students enrolled in their classes for a minimum of 2 months did the ratings for the normative sample. In order to make valid normative comparisons, the manual should state explicitly that ratings be made only after a minimum of 2 months contact with the student. Further, it should be noted that behavior ratings by teachers do not correlate consistently highly with those of mental health professionals (Achenbach & Edelbrock, 1978), so the source of the ratings must be considered.

The normative sample consists of 331 students in kindergarten through high school, randomly selected from 10 schools in the metropolitan area of Portland, Oregon. Given the limited nature of the sample, much more descriptive information is needed in order for users to judge the comparability of their settings and children with those of the normative sample. What was the basis for selecting the 10 schools? Are the schools public or private? The sample must be described more specifically in terms of numbers of children by grade, gender, race, socioeconomic status, or census tract data. The explicit basis for the grade grouping in the norm tables is not provided, though the groupings fit elementary school, middle school, and high school breakdowns.

The factor analysis appears to be appropriate. Consistent with the apparent focus of the WSSRS on problematic behaviors rather than on social skills and competence, the factors identified appear to match closely the primary factors that emerge from factor analyses of most behavior problem rating scales. That is, the Aggressive and Passive domains appear to be versions of externalizing (undercontrolled) and internalizing (overcontrolled) factors obtained in previous research (Achenbach & Edelbrock, 1978). Research is needed on the WSSRS within the context of multitrait (or multibehavior), multimethod designs to determine whether this scale and its factors are any different from already existing, high-quality, general behavior problem rating scales (e.g., the Child Behavior Checklist, Achenbach & Edelbrock, 1983). The author did correlate the WSSRS with the Portland Problem Behavior Checklist (Waksman, 1980; Waksman & Loveland, 1980) and found a substantial relationship between the measures. This result raises the question of whether the WSSRS is a measure of social skills, or an alternative behavior problem checklist.

The internal consistency reported was very high (.92). Test-retest reliabilities were moderately high (.63 to .74). Interrater reliabilities showed mixed results, being particularly low for the Passive domain with a randomly selected sample of high school students and a small sample of emotionally disturbed children. Such interrater reliabilities are, of course, subject to rater differences, setting differences, and/or setting specificity of behaviors.

The author attempted to demonstrate validity by a comparison group approach. Rating scale scores differentiated significantly among the normative sample and two small samples of emotionally disturbed children in the public schools and a residential setting, with the residential children having the highest scores. The samples were very small (7 and 32, respectively) and genders and ages are not specified. A comparison group approach involving emotionally disturbed children appears to be based upon the assumption that emotionally disturbed children are children with social skills deficits. A more appropriate comparison would be to identify groups with and without social skills, as determined by independent assessment of social skills. Then, in addition to mean score differences, information on hit/miss ratios would be very helpful. However, more importantly, a critical validity test would involve determining the relationship among WSSRS ratings and independent measures of social skills. As indicated earlier, a multitrait (or multibehavior), multimethod design is needed to determine the relationship of the WSSRS with other social skills measures and its independence from general behavior problem rating scales.

The author suggests a number of uses for the WSSRS, including identification of students and behaviors for social skills training programs, behavioral interventions, and for individual education programs. In addition, the author suggests the scale can be used to evaluate social skills training programs or other counseling programs. However, no studies of treatment validity are presented, and there is no indication of the measure's sensitivity to interventions.

In summary, the WSSRS is an easily administered and scored rating scale, though a minimum time frame for the rater to gain familiarity with the child or adolescent is not specified. The normative sample is quite limited and largely unspecified, a limitation making it difficult for users to determine comparability to their own children and settings. Reliabilities are mixed, particularly for the Passive domain. Validity data are extremely limited, particularly as they relate to suggested uses for the scale. Perhaps most importantly, the author has failed to present data to demonstrate the scale is assessing the stated skills (i.e., social skills), independent of behavior problems.

REVIEWER'S REFERENCES

Achenbach, T. M., & Edelbrock, C. S. (1978). The classification of child psychopathology: A review and analysis of empirical efforts. *Psychological Bulletin*, 85, 1275-1301.

Waksman, S. A. (1980). *The Portland Problem Behavior Checklist test and manual*. Portland, OR: Enrichment Press.

Waksman, S. A., & Loveland, R. J. (1980). The Portland Problem Behavior Checklist. *Psychology in the Schools*, 17, 25-29.

Achenbach, T. M., & Edelbrock, C. S. (1983). *Manual for the Child Behavior Checklist and the Revised Child Behavior Profile*. Burlington, VT: Author.

Review of the Waksman Social Skills Rating Scale by ELLEN McGINNIS, Assistant Professor of Special Education, University of Wisconsin-Eau Claire, Eau Claire, WI:

The Waksman Social Skills Rating Scale (WSSRS) is a brief normative checklist (21 items) designed to screen children and adolescents with social skill deficits. Possible uses suggested by the author include identifying students with social skills deficits and evaluating success of special counseling or social skills training programs.

The scale consists of 9 behavioral descriptors which factor into the "Aggressive domain" and 12 factoring into the "Passive domain." The rating scale is designed for use by classroom teachers, counselors, or child care workers who rate the descriptors on a 4-point scale of 0 (never) exhibited by this child to 3 (usually) exhibited.

The author, recognizing the limitations of using only rating scales to assess social skills, suggests this scale be used as only one piece of information to identify social skills deficits in children and also encourages completion of the scale by more than one educator due to the variability of student behavior.

Research suggests that many handicapped children are deficient in social skills. With the current interest in and development of social skills training programs, methods to assess these deficits are in high demand. The WSSRS, while having a strength in its prescriptive nature, falls short in many critical areas.

First, the brevity of the scale, while allowing for quick administration, measures a very narrow range of behaviors. Additionally, the majority of the behavioral descriptors are related to teacher acceptability. This scale does not attend adequately to behaviors related to positive relationships with peers.

Other serious drawbacks relate to psychometric issues. The descriptors comprising each of the subscales are grouped together under the headings "Passive" or "Aggressive," which may create a serious biasing effect. If the author believed that this grouping of the rating scale descriptors was desirable, statistical procedures should have been done to rule out possible biasing effects of this format.

The sample size of 331 was randomly selected from one metropolitan area, resulting in a small normative sample size when broken down into subsamples (male, female, grades K–5, grades 6–8, and grades 9–12) for units of comparison. For example, the norms for females in grades 6–8 were based on a sample of only 43 pupils. In addition, by grouping several grade levels together for normative purposes, the author has failed to attend to critical age differences found with other rating scale measures (i.e., Matson, Rotatari, & Helsel, 1985).

While the author has suggested that the WSSRS does discriminate between a normal group ($N = 32$) and a group of emotionally disturbed students ($N = 32$), the latter group was comprised of youngsters in residential treatment facilities. The user should be cautioned that this scale may discriminate only between normal and severely emotionally disturbed groups of youngsters, as adequate information was not provided on a sample of less severely handicapped youth.

Although the author stated that WSSRS scores were highly correlated with scores on the Portland Problem Behavior Checklist, this was not the case across all subgroups. Additionally, test-retest correlations were not high, especially for scores in the Passive domain. Test-retest item correlation coefficients were also below .55 on one-third of the items of this rating scale.

With the increase in awareness of the need to assess children's social behaviors for identification and documentation of the effectiveness of interventions, social skills rating scales will be in demand. While the Waksman Social Skills Rating Scale allows for quick administration, is prescriptive in nature, and does provide the user with a normative base, it seeks to measure only a narrow range of social behaviors, and the scale itself and the norms provided are of highly questionable utility. Those interested in using a social skills rating scale would be wise to look for alternatives, such as the Matson Evaluation of Social Skills with Youngsters (Matson, Rotatori, & Helsel, 1985). The Matson scale, while still in need of additional research, has more items and is more realistically evaluated by its authors.

REVIEWER'S REFERENCE

Matson, J. L., Rotatori, A. F., & Helsel, W. J. (1985). Development of a rating scale to measure social skills in children: The Matson Evaluation of Social Skills with Youngsters (MESSY). *Psychopharmacology Bulletin*, 21 (4), 855-868.

[384]

Watson-Barker Listening Test. Purpose: Measures adult interpersonal listening abilities. Adults in business, professions, and college; 1984; may be self-scored for awareness training; 6 scores: Evaluating Message Content, Understanding Meaning in Conversations, Understanding and Remembering Information in Lectures, Evaluating Emotional Meanings in Messages, Following Instructions and Directions, Total; test administered by audio cassette; 3 forms: Form A (for pre-testing), Form B (for post-testing), and Short Form (for demonstration and listening awareness); The Short Form is available with or without background distractions; 1985 price data: $79.95 per test package (Form A or Form B) including 20 test booklets, 20 self-scoring answer sheets, audio cassette, narrative script, and facilitator's guide ('84, 32 pages); $119.95 per test package for both Form A and Form B including all above listed materials for each form; $49.95 per Short Form test package including 10 test booklets, answer key, 10 self-scoring answer sheets, audio cassette, and set of instructions; $25 per 10 test booklets (Specify Form A, Form B, Half A/Half B, Short Form); $25 per 100 self-scoring answer sheets; 30(40) minutes; Kittie W. Watson and Larry L. Barker; SPECTRA Communication Associates.*

Review of the Watson-Barker Listening Test by JAMES R. CLOPTON, Associate Professor of Psychology, Texas Tech University, Lubbock, TX:

The Watson-Barker Listening Test assesses listening comprehension in adults. It is administered (to an individual or group) by playing the tape-recorded instructions and test material. There are two forms of the test (Forms A and B). Each form has 50 items divided into five parts and takes 30 minutes to complete. The test requires the subject to evaluate the content and implications of messages (Part I) and conversations (Part II), to remember details from descriptions (Part III) and instructions (Part V), and to understand the emotional significance of messages (Part IV). A 20-item short form of the test is available, as are versions of the test that include distractions—background noises such as business machinery and conversation.

Instructions, listening material, and test questions for Form A and Form B are all on one audio cassette tape. The tape-recorded instructions are clear and easy to follow, and the high quality of the tape recording should insure that the test can be administered even with an inexpensive tape player. However, detailed information is included with the test material about the use of high-quality sound equipment to eliminate tape noise.

The Watson-Barker Listening Test is designed for use with college students and adults in business and professional jobs, and normative data are available for both groups. Specifically, the means and standard deviations are reported for the five parts and for the total score. The authors report that test scores differ significantly depending on whether the test is administered individually or in a group setting, but separate norms are not available for those two types of administration.

The most significant problems with the Watson-Barker Listening Test are inadequate reliability and a lack of convincing evidence of validity. The correlation between Form A and Form B (r = .42), which is far below an acceptable level of reliability (.80 or higher), indicates that most variability in test scores is error variance. The authors did not report whether Form A and Form B were administered at the same time or with an interval between administrations. Consequently, the low reliability may be only a result of inconsistent responding to the two different item samples, or may also reflect the test's lack of temporal stability. In addition, a separate study, cited by the authors, reported a lack of internal consistency for the test.

The authors report that experts on listening have praised the test. Such praise cannot be construed as content validity, however, because no description of expert involvement in test development is provided. Unspecified correlations between the Watson-Barker Listening Test and other measures of listening are mentioned. Investigating the validity of the Watson-Barker Listening Test will be difficult until the authors give a clear definition of listening comprehension. For example, the authors consider listening skills to be more than mere attention. They are critical of other measures of listening skills as being mostly measures of general intelligence, but do not specify the expected relationships between listening comprehension and other intellectual abilities. If listening skills contribute to general intelligence and are dependent on attention and concentration, then the Watson-Barker Listening Test should have moderate correlations with intelligence tests and with other measures of attention, concentration, and short-term memory.

The authors provide no evidence that each part of their test assesses a separate listening skill. The content of the test suggests that different abilities are being assessed, but not necessarily five different abilities corresponding to the five parts of the test. For example, Part III and Part V would seem to assess the same skill—the ability to remember details. In contrast, the items in Part IV apparently measure a different skill—the ability to understand the emotional significance of short messages. The authors do not report the correlations among the five parts of the test, however, nor the results of factor analyses of test items.

In conclusion, the Watson-Barker Listening Test has clear, easy-to-follow directions and normative information for college students and for adults in business and professional jobs. Before the test can be used with confidence, however, improved reliability and evidence of validity are needed.

Review of the Watson-Barker Listening Test by JOSEPH P. STOKES, Associate Professor of Psychology, University of Illinois at Chicago, Chicago, IL:

The Watson-Barker Listening Test uses audiotaped materials to test five aspects of listening ability: (*a*) interpreting the meaning of messages, (*b*) understanding meaning from dialogue/conversation, (*c*) understanding and remembering information from short lectures, (*d*) hearing emotional meaning from *how* something is said rather than *what* is said, and (*e*) understanding and remembering instructions/directions. These five types of listening are intuitively appealing, although the authors present no information about how these types of listening were chosen or about how they are correlated with one another. The authors mention factor analytic studies, but these are not described.

The Watson-Barker Listening Test is available in alternate forms (A and B), as well as in a short form suitable for demonstration or listening-awareness purposes. Forms A and B each contain 50 multiple-choice items divided equally into the five sections representing aspects of listening ability. Stimulus materials are presented on a 30-minute audiotape. The test is interesting to take and contains items with a variety of content, much of it relevant to business settings. Norms are provided from two samples: over 4,000 undergraduates at 4-year universities and over 500 business and professional people enrolled in communications training seminars. The audiotape and accompanying materials are carefully prepared, although for one item the correct answer is not one of the choices.

In a paper presented at the Speech Communication Association Convention, Watson and Barker (1985) presented evidence for the reliability and validity of this test. The evidence is neither very convincing nor very encouraging. The alternate forms of the test are not highly correlated (r = .42), and research during the developmental stages of the test (Roach & Fitch-Hauser, 1984) showed "little inter-item consistency." Surprisingly, coefficient alpha or another measure of internal consistency is not reported for either the total score or for any of the five subtest scores of the Watson-Barker Listening Test. Claims of validity are supported by significant correlations between the total score of the Watson-Barker and both the Kentucky Comprehensive Listening Test and the Receiver Apprehension Test. The magnitude of these correlations is not reported, although the authors admit the shared variance between the Watson-Barker and the Kentucky Test was "surprisingly low."

In summary, because of the limited and discouraging evidence for the reliability and validity of the Watson-Barker Listening Test, it is not suitable as an instrument for evaluation or selection in business settings. Problems with discriminant validity seem inherent in a listening test. How is it possible to differentiate listening skills from general intelligence and memory? Reading ability is another potentially confounding factor, at least when response options must be read as in the Watson-Barker. Respondents with limited reading skills would not have time to read the multiple choices and respond before the next stimulus item was presented on the audiotape. The Watson-Barker Listening Test will, however, be useful as a device for increasing awareness about listening or as a tool for use in training programs focusing on listening and communication.

REVIEWER'S REFERENCES

Roach, D. A., & Fitch-Hauser, M. (1984, March). *A comparison of three modes of administering listening tests.* Paper presented at the International Listening Association Convention, Scottsdale, AZ.

Watson, K. W., & Barker, L. L. (1985, November). *Listening assessment: The Watson-Barker Listening Test.* Paper presented at the Speech Communication Association Convention, Denver, CO.

[385]

[Re Wechsler Intelligence Scale for Children—Revised.] The Explorer. Purpose: A microcomputer system designed to "provide a simple and efficient method of analyzing WISC-R scores." 1983; various reports available: subtest reports, reports with descriptions of all subtests, hypotheses as to why the child scored high or low, scatterplot of all the scaled subtest scores, scatterplot of the factor scores, and various combinations of reports; system requirements: TRS-80 Model III or IV (TRS-80 version) or an Apple II+ or IIe, 2 disk drives, an 80-column printer, and at least 48K of random access memory; 1988 price data: $65 per TRS-80 or Apple diskette and manual (19 pages); Booney Vance, Charles Paparella, and Charles Piazza; Academic Therapy Publications.*

Review of [Re Wechsler Intelligence Scale for Children—Revised], The Explorer by J. P. DAS, Professor of Educational Psychology, University of Alberta, Edmonton, Canada:

This software and the accompanying manual are intended to analyze Wechsler Intelligence Scale for Children—Revised (WISC-R) results. The materials are especially helpful, the authors say, for school psychologists who administer the WISC-R 100 or more times a year. Although The Explorer is not purported to be a program useful in diagnosing and treating exceptionality, it is billed as an aid to understanding the children who are being evaluated. This distinction between diagnosis and understanding is a difficult one for the reviewer to discern.

The major problems with The Explorer are in the interpretations provided for subtest scores and the insensitivity of these interpretations to differences between widely different cases. Some examples of these interpretive problems are given later in this review. The WISC-R subtests are not meant to be used by themselves as their individual reliabilities vary widely; this is well known in the literature. The authors try to allay concerns about subtest interpretations by categorizing the subtest scores into "factor scores." The accepted meaning of a factor score involves the determination of the subtest factor loadings, through factor analysis, that are then used to calculate the factor scores of the individuals tested. This is obviously not the connotation of the term "factor score" as used in The Explorer. What is worse, it is claimed that the "factor score" computations are justified by "sound research"/ No reference could be found for this claim nor for the special sense in which the term is used.

Some more specific comments on The Explorer are given below. Two frequent users of the WISC-R tried out the program and reported their observations for use in this review. The Explorer program examines each subtest in isolation. Evidently, The Explorer scores the subtests as very low, low, average, high, or very high. There is a matrix of these five levels x 12 subscales of the WISC-R, each of which has a discrete hypothesis. The Explorer output includes the appropriate hypothesis from this matrix for each subscale. The usefulness of these hypotheses is questionable. For example, when subtest scaled scores of 15 were input for all subtests, except a score of 5 for Arithmetic, the hypothesis was exactly the same as that for scores that would be obtained by a child who is mentally deficient. "Poor scores may indicate that the student has poor concentration, and possible high anxiety. It may show that the student has poor achievement possibly due to rebellion against authority or from a cultural disadvantage."

Provided below are further examples of how The Explorer performs in two cases referred for clinical work. The two cases (Jason and Shayla) were entered into the program for analysis. Jason was 1 to 2 years behind in school subjects and he was referred for testing to determine if he was learning disabled. Jason scored in the average range on the WISC-R. During the testing he displayed distractible behavior. This distractibility was evident in the WISC-R results (FD Factor). His lowest scores of the computer program's factor analysis were Distractibility and Sequencing (both 6). But he did not have a serious sequencing problem. The Explorer could not offer an independent interpretation of distractibility.

The second case concerns Shayla who was performing close to grade level in school subjects but whose mother felt that Shayla was a gifted under-achiever. Shayla scored in the superior range on the WISC-R with her lowest scores on Digit Span and Coding subtests. The clinician suspected that Shayla had trouble with short-term memory tasks. This suspicion was confirmed by further testing. On The Explorer's factor analysis, her lowest factors were Distractibility and Sequencing, which received the same interpretation given to Jason.

Many of the hypotheses in the interpretations contain strong language such as "rebellion against authority," "compulsive tendencies," "student's familial and/or cultural background may be disadvantaged." This kind of statement should be made with utmost care and certainly only by someone who has applied a high degree of clinical skill in developing such conclusions.

Overall, I suspect that clinicians interested in careful diagnosis and comprehensive understandings of children's intellectual functioning will not find many reasons to use The Explorer. The so-called factor scores have little theoretical basis for making valid interpretations; in any case, the interpretations may be misleading because of their total reliance on one or two subtests. The Explorer's advantages are easy storage and retrieval of records. The two strengths do not compensate for concerns about the content of the test interpretations generated by the program.

Review of [Re Wechsler Intelligence Scale for Children—Revised], The Explorer by FRED M. GROSSMAN, *Associate Professor of Special Education and Communication Disorders, University of Nebraska-Lincoln, Lincoln, NE, and* MARTIN J. WIESE, *School Psychologist, Wilkes County Schools, Wilkesboro, NC:*

The Explorer computer program is designed to provide assistance in interpreting the Wechsler Intelligence Scale for Children—Revised (WISC-R). It is intended to be used after the WISC-R has been administered and the subtests have been scored. The program recognizes patterns of strengths and weaknesses, and prints out clinical and educational hypotheses based on an individual's WISC-R subtest scaled scores and IQs. In addition to assisting the clinician interpret scores, the program also has a data storage and retrieval capability. Assessment data from the WISC-R can be stored in files that can include the names and results of up to

50 individuals. There is no limit to the number of files that can be used with the program, but only one file can be accessed at a time.

The Explorer is designed to run on a TRS-80 Model III/IV or an Apple II series computer. It requires two disk drives, an 80-column printer, and at least 48K of random-access memory. The program is provided on a single diskette that contains the Explorer program itself and a text file containing hypotheses used by the main program. The diskette and a manual are conveniently packaged in a vinyl folder. The manual is well written and provides adequate instructions for operating the program. It takes the user step-by-step through the data entry, editing, and reporting procedures. Also included in the manual is a list of factors and their component subtests (e.g., Freedom from Distractability: Arithmetic, Digit Span, and Coding) and a bibliography of materials related to WISC-R interpretation.

The Explorer provides a printed report that includes a statement describing each of the 12 subtests, subtest scores, and a brief verbal description of the child's level of performance. Strengths and weaknesses are identified and hypotheses are generated for scores outside the normal range (subtest scaled scores from 8 to 12 are considered within the normal range). The report identifies discrepancies between Verbal and Performance IQ scores and provides hypotheses about such discrepancies. The program also categorizes the child's subtest scaled scores into 22 research and clinically derived subtest groupings. These recategorized scores are determined by averaging the scaled scores for the group of subtests associated with a particular grouping. The program can optionally provide a scatterplot of the subtest scaled scores, factor scores, subtest grouping scores, and a printout of a normal curve for the child's IQ scores.

CRITIQUE. After the user starts up the program the main menu appears and provides the options of creating a new file or accessing data from an existing file. If there is no existing file the user must exit the program and format a new disk for information storage. As mentioned above, the program requires a dual-drive system and the program requires that the blank, unformatted diskette be placed into the second drive to be formatted. Although dual-drive systems are becoming less expensive and more common, the program could have a larger user base if it would allow use with single-drive systems. Even though the requirement of two disk drives seems an unnecessary requirement, it is wise to keep the main program and data on separate disks, as this program demands. Once the program is running and a data disk has been formatted, it is possible to begin entering data.

When the input mode is selected from the second menu, the user is presented with the data entry screen that requests the child's name, demographic data, and WISC-R scores. The data entry screen requires the user to progressively fill out a series of blanks. Error checking by the program is minimal. The program readily accepts values for the child's age, subtest scores, and IQ scores far outside valid ranges. Invalid entries are detected when a report is printed out rather than during data entry. If an error is made during data entry, it can be corrected after all the values for that record are entered. The edit option allows corrections to be made to specific values, but again, error checking is not evident. As an example, when the child's last name is entered initially the program limits entry to 15 letters. However, in the edit mode it is possible to enter a surname well beyond the 15-letter limit even though doing so will cause the program to stop functioning whenever the record is accessed.

Data entry allows one to build up a file of up to 50 records. As a data storage and retrieval system, the program allows the user to review records and search for specific records by the child's last name. In the event of two or more children in the file having identical surnames, the program presents each record, alphabetized by the child's first name, and queries whether the desired record has been selected or if searching should continue. This procedure is effective in selecting records for output; however, it does not function if one wishes to delete a specific record from the active file. In an instance of duplicate surnames, the "Kill a Record" choice does not provide a "search further" option, but merely selects one record with the desired surname. If this is not the record to be deleted, the program stops searching and returns to an alternate menu. One way to circumvent this problem is to use the edit mode to change the information in the record to be deleted. By changing the child's first name to "AAAA" it would be selected before other records containing the identical surname and can then be deleted. It would be best not to have identical surnames in the same file, but this limits the usefulness of the program's record retrieval capability.

The Explorer allows a variety of report formats. The user can select the following options: (*a*) Subtest Report Only: Provides report of the student's scores and indicates whether they are high, normal, or low; (*b*) Report With Descriptions: Gives subtest scores with a description of each subtest; (*c*) Subtest Report, Descriptions, and Hypotheses: Provides subtest scores, subtest descriptions, and hypotheses which attempt to explain high or low subtest scaled scores; (*d*) Subtest Report, Descriptions, Hypotheses, and Scatterplot: Includes all of the above and a scatterplot of the subtest scaled scores, subtest grouping scores, and a printout of a normal curve; (*e*) Scatterplot Only: Printout of scatterplot and normal curve representation.

Subtest scaled scores 7 and below have been selected to indicate a weakness and scores 13 and above have been selected to indicate a strength. This approach compares the child's subtest scores to the normative group data only and does not make comparisons with the child's own average performance on each scale, as recommended by Kaufman (1979) and Sattler (1982). By failing to make intraindividual comparisons of subtest scores, the program may erroneously identify strengths and weaknesses where none exist. In addition to identifying strengths and weaknesses of an individual's performance based upon comparisons with the normative sample, it would be appropriate to use ipsative comparisons as well.

As an option, the program provides hypotheses that attempt to explain high or low subtest scaled scores. These hypotheses are subtest specific and, thus, assume each subtest to be a measure of a unique ability. Although Kaufman (1975) found ample specificity for most of the subtests, inadequate specificity was found for Similarities (ages 9½ to 16½) and Object Assembly (for all ages). Even with these two exceptions, Kaufman (1979) warns that examiners should not make specific inferences about individual subtests, but emphasizes the importance of evaluating performance on groups of subtests in terms of shared abilities. The Explorer disregards these recommendations and provides hypotheses based upon single subtest scores.

In addition to the hypotheses generated, the program will categorize the child's subtest scaled scores into factor scores and subtest grouping scores. These scores are determined by calculating the average scaled score for the group of subtests which comprise a given factor or grouping. These scores are calculated and presented as part of the scatterplot option. As with the subtest scaled scores, factor scores and subtest grouping scores are categorized as below average, average, or above average based upon normative comparisons. The scores are presented in a scatterplot to provide a visual aid to the interpretation of subtest performance; however, this type of profile analysis is inadequate for making comparisons between factor scores and determining significant differences in selected abilities.

As part of the scatterplot printout, the program includes a representation of a normal curve for the child's IQ scores. The result is a crude representation of a normal curve with the child's IQ scores printed beneath it. This feature appeared to be rather useless, other than to provide a rough estimate of percentile ranks for each of the IQ scores.

Several programming flaws became evident as the reviewers used The Explorer. As a record storage and retrieval system, the program operated erratically. Although the manual does not state so, the program should be used with the Caps Lock key on. The program distinguishes uppercase from lowercase letters and if a record is stored under the name "JONES," it cannot be retrieved if the user requests the record under the name "Jones." A second problem occurs when one attempts to exit the "Report Output" option. After selecting "Report Output" from the menu and the type of report desired, the user is presented with a request to enter the last name of the child. At this point the user has the option of entering the name or exiting the report function; however, the reviewers could not exit by following the instructions on the screen. Instead of leaving the report option, the program began printing a report with all of the values set to zero or left blank. It was also noticed that the program does not advance the printer paper to the top of a new page when appropriate, but prints continuously.

Interpretation of WISC-R subtest scaled scores is a controversial matter and several methods exist. The Explorer provides one method of interpreting the WISC-R and generates predictive statements about a child's general cognitive functioning and subtest specific strengths and weaknesses. Regardless of the reviewers' disagreement with the method used for analysis of the WISC-R, The Explorer lacks the sophistication and polish of a professionally written program. The Explorer would be more useful to the practitioner if it contained adequate error checking procedures and support of lowercase letters, and corrected the program bugs mentioned above.

REVIEWER'S REFERENCES

Kaufman, A. S. (1975). Factor analysis of the WISC-R at eleven age levels between 6½ to 16½ years. *Journal of Consulting and Clinical Psychology*, 43, 135-147.

Kaufman, A. S. (1979). *Intelligent testing with the WISC-R.* New York: John Wiley and Sons, Inc.

Sattler, J. M. (1982). *Assessment of children's intelligence and special abilities*. Boston: Allyn and Bacon, Inc.

[386]

[Re Wechsler Intelligence Scale for Children—Revised]. WISC-Riter 'Complete'. Purpose: Provides a computer-assisted "psychological report based on a student's performance on the WISC-R." Ages 6–16; 1986; educator enters child's WISC-R subtest scores as well as grade equivalent and standard scores from any achievement test into computer program; requires IBM PC or Apple IIc or IIe (2 drives) computer and printer; 1986 price data: $495 per complete program including 2 program disks, manual (38 pages), and resource book of educational recommendations; $99 per additional disk after purchase of a program; Charles L. Nicholson; Southern MicroSystems.*

Review of the WISC-Riter 'Complete' for the Wechsler Intelligence Scale for Children—Revised by SYLVIA SIBLEY, School Psychologist, Highland Park I.S.D., Dallas, TX:

The WISC-Riter 'Complete' provides an individualized psychoeducational report based on data from students' Wechsler Intelligence Scale for Children—Revised (WISC-R) profiles and achievement test standard scores. Users of this program enter WISC-R subtest scores and Verbal, Performance, and Full Scale IQ scores. To obtain an in-depth report, the author recommends that all 12 subtests be administered (i.e., including Digit Span and Mazes). Reading, Spelling, and Arithmetic grade equivalent scores, percentiles, and standard scores from the standardized achievement test of the examiner's choice are also entered. A convenient Data Input Form is provided to facilitate entry of appropriate data. The subsequent report provides: subtest evaluations, standard score interpretations, Verbal and Performance Scales achievement, 95% confidence ranges, strengths and weaknesses in overall ability, severe discrepancy levels for Verbal, Performance, and Full Scale IQ's, ranges of learning disability achievement levels for Verbal and Performance IQ scores, factor analytic interpretations, possible reasons for elevated or depressed subtest scaled scores, and educational recommendations for remediation of deficit areas.

MATERIALS. The WISC-Riter 'Complete' program is available for use on an Apple IIc or IIe (80-column card, two drives, and 128K memory) or an IBM Personal Computer and Compatibles. The manual and disk are conveniently packaged in a vinyl folder. The program also includes a resource book of educational recommendations; however, it was not available for review. The main menu allows data to be recorded and reviewed, printed, and/or stored. It is also possible to read data from a disk file or save it to a disk file. Files may also be catalogued on a disk. The completed report is about seven pages in length.

CRITIQUE. This program earns an "A+" for providing easy-to-follow directions both in the manual and on the screen. Ease of input combined with the convenience of the Data Input Form could easily make data entry a clerical function. As well as directions, the manual includes development and technical data and a page-by-page explanation of the report. Appendices contain the Data Input Form, definitions of factors, explanation of abbreviations, and bibliography.

The program bases its analysis and report on IQ scores, scaled scores, and achievement test data. Internal scatter within a subtest, quality of responses, and examiner/student interaction are not taken into account. However, the report can be edited to allow interjection of examiner observations and impressions into the final report. The manual provides an explanation of the rationale for each component of the report.

The report addresses the possibility of a learning disability by comparing achievement test standard scores with Verbal IQ scores and Performance IQ scores. If an achievement test standard score is 11 to 16 points below WISC-R IQ, the report states that "achievement is below the expected level," while a 17-point (or greater) discrepancy yields this statement: "Achievement is significantly below the expected level." Because many school districts use the one standard deviation discrepancy method to determine eligibility for special education services on the basis of a learning disability, the above program statements may require additional explanation. For instance, in the case of an 11-point discrepancy, parents or teachers may need information on why the student does not qualify as learning disabled, despite the report assertion that "achievement is below the expected level." Obviously, the key words are "significantly below."

The manual notes the program user may alter these discrepancy values if "the school system utilizes a different value to determine significant over or under achievement." The examiner can also edit the report to make the eligibility issue clearer.

The report is very nicely presented although it is lengthy (seven pages). Demographic data appear at the beginning of the report. WISC-R subtest scaled scores and percentiles are presented in tabular form as are achievement test data and factor analytic interpretations. This aids in a quick visual review of the test data.

In field testing, the hypotheses presented to account for performance on the intellectual and achievement tests were of some concern. The manual contains the following caution: "There have been many attempts to diagnose emotional problems with the WISC, WISC-R or WAIS. Most of these have not been successful and the results have not been encouraging." The author continues: "The WISC-R is not to be the definitive method of diagnosing emotional problems, but may provide clues of possible problems . . . . Only *tentative* emotional and/or adjustment statements can be derived from it. *Caution is urged in this area*."

Despite this warning, which is reiterated in the report, personality factors and emotional indicators that could possibly be influencing the student's scores are stated. For instance, "possible paranoid personality" was listed (among other hypotheses) for a relatively high Comprehension score. For a low Coding score, "possible anxiety" and "possible depression" were proposed. Although caution is strongly urged, field testers expressed doubt about any benefit or usefulness of these hypotheses appearing in a psychoeducational report. The possibility of overinterpretation by school personnel or alarm by parents may outweigh the benefit that could be served by including these personality statements.

Recommendations for remediation are practical and instructionally oriented. The report also refers the examiner to the Teacher's Guide (Nicholson & Alcorn, 1983) for additional suggestions. Although basically helpful, field testers noted some simplistic generalizations and relatively superficial remarks in this section (for instance, "In order to obtain good grades, Joe needs an adequate memory . . . . Provide memory training if memory is poor.").

TECHNICAL ASPECTS. No major problems were noted in operating the program or in printing the report. A few minor typographical errors were found (for instance, "sub:ests" for "subtests," "verbatum" for "verbatim," and "scale scores" for "scaled scores"). Additionally, the demographic data does not require input of the student's sex. Therefore, in the prose of the Recommendations section, "(s)he" is used as the pronoun to refer to the student. This seems rather awkward and impersonal, and could easily be corrected. Further, with so many "unisex" names (for instance, Taylor, Shannon, Morgan), it was suggested that "sex" be added to the demographic data at the beginning of the report.

CONCLUSION. The general response to this program and the completed report is positive. The WISC-Riter 'Complete' will be a useful addition to educational software libraries. This program provides a comprehensive interpretation of the WISC-R and achievement test data including information that will assist educators in understanding a student's specific strengths and weaknesses. Hypotheses are proposed to account for performance and helpful recommendations are offered for remediation of deficits.

REVIEWER'S REFERENCE

Nicholson, C. L., & Alcorn, C. L. (1983). *Educational applications of the WISC-R: A handbook of interpretive strategies & remedial recommendations*. Los Angeles: Western Psychological Services.

[387]

Weller-Strawser Scales of Adaptive Behavior for the Learning Disabled. Purpose: "To assess the adaptive behavior of the learning disabled student." Learning disabled students ages 6–12, 13–18; 1981; WSSAB; ratings by teachers; 5 scores: Social Coping, Relationships, Pragmatic Language, Production, Total; individual; 2 levels: Elementary and Secondary; 1987 price data: $33 per complete kit including 25 elementary or secondary forms and manual ('81, 112 pages) in vinyl folder; $15 per 50 elementary or secondary forms; $15 per manual; $15 per specimen set including sample forms and manual; administration time not reported; Carol Weller and Sherri Strawser; Academic Therapy Publications.*

See 9:1359 (1 reference).

TEST REFERENCES

1. Strawser, S., & Weller, C. (1985). Use of adaptive behavior and discrepancy criteria to determine learning disabilities severity subtypes. *Journal of Learning Disabilities*, 18, 205-211.

Review of the Weller-Strawser Scales of Adaptive Behavior for the Learning Disabled by THOMAS G. HARING, *Assistant Professor of Special Education, University of California, Santa Barbara, CA:*

The purpose of the Weller-Strawser Scales of Adaptive Behavior for the Learning Disabled (WSSAB) is to discriminate students with learning disabilities who have mild to moderate impairments in adaptive behavior from those with severe problems in adaptive behavior. The scales are intended to provide a profile of adaptive behavior across four areas: Social Coping, Relationships, Pragmatic Language, and Production. The publication of these scales is noteworthy because the area of adaptive behavior has been largely neglected within the field of learning disabilities and an increased focus on adaptive behavior, especially in secondary programs, might ensure that the graduates of special education programs are maximally employable and independent in adult life.

There are two scales provided, one for elementary-aged students and one for secondary-aged students. There are 35 items across the four subscales for each of the scales. Two descriptors are provided for each item and the test user indicates which descriptor is more accurate. The Social Coping subscale consists of eight items and includes measures of a student's ability to appropriately anticipate upcoming events, handle criticism, and manage time. The Relationships subscale consists of eight items that include assessment of the age-appropriateness of a student's friendships and social skills. The Pragmatic Language subtest, which consists of nine items, includes measures of the student's ability to interpret gestures, facial expressions, and feelings of others. The 10-item Production subscale measures a student's ability to transfer a skill to new tasks, follow through with tasks, ask for help if needed, and properly organize work space.

Items that sample the skills necessary for conducting oneself independently in school, community, and home settings are considered central to the construct of adaptive behavior. The universe sampled by the WSSAB is not referenced to the complex skills needed to live independently and productively. The Weller-Strawser Scales defines the construct of adaptive behavior solely in terms of social skills and task-related skills that, while important, is a narrow sample of the skills that are critical to a comprehensive assessment of adaptive behavior.

The major difference between the WSSAB and other tests of adaptive behavior (e.g., the AAMD Adaptive Behavior Scales and the Vineland Adaptive Behavior Scales) is that the WSSAB was developed with specific reference to the field of learning disabilities. That is, the items were generated by interviewing teachers of students with learning disabilities to identify behaviors they felt were related to adaptive behavior; the scale was normed on learning disabled students; and the authors specifically exclude the use of the WSSAB on any student who is not learning disabled.

Scoring and interpreting the WSSAB is straightforward and can be done in a time-efficient manner. The norms are developed such that students are placed into one of two broad categories: mild to moderate adaptive behavior problems or moderate to severe adaptive behavior problems. Although this procedure simplifies scoring, the philosophic underpinnings of a test developed for an exceptional population that does not allow for the *possibility* of rating a student as nonimpaired is difficult to defend. The manual provides a lengthy chapter of remedial activities that may prove helpful to practitioners.

TECHNICAL EVALUATION. An initial version of the WSSAB was developed on the basis of interviews with teachers. Next, the items were tested with 236 students from six states. Many details are missing in the description of this initial testing including the number of teachers who participated, the states and cities where the testing occurred, and the makeup of the sample in terms of ethnic diversity and Hispanic background. The WSSAB should not be used with students from ethnically and linguistically underrepresented groups.

Although the WSSAB is norm referenced, it does not provide age or grade norms. Instead it is normed at two levels: elementary (which lumps all elementary-aged students together) and secondary (which lumps all secondary-aged students together). Thus, at best, the WSSAB provides a broad picture of how well a student is functioning with reference to a heterogeneous group of either 154 elementary-aged students or 82 secondary-aged students.

Problems with the norming procedures are further compounded because the authors first piloted a longer version of the test with this same sample, then subjected the items from this longer version to an item selection analysis. During the item selection process, in addition to changing the content of the test from this initial tryout, the authors also changed the scoring format of the test. The problem arises because rather than readministering the revised test to a new sample to determine the norms, the original tests were recalculated based on the revisions to determine the norms. This is problematic because the alteration of the content and scoring format of the test may have caused an alteration of the way teachers responded to the items. Thus, the norms, as calculated, may have been different had the teachers employed the final version of the test. Given this problem, the small sample sizes employed, and lack of detail concerning the sampling procedures used, the adequacy of the norms must be questioned.

The authors provide two estimates of reliability: internal consistency and interrater reliability. The split-half reliability ranged from .94 to .96 across the four subscales. The split-half reliability for the entire scale was .99. Intercorrelations between the subtests ranged from .88 to .91 with a median of .90. These high internal consistency estimates and high intercorrelations between subtests indicate the designation of the four subtests is not substantiated and the subtests of the WSSAB measure essentially the same trait. In my review of the content of the WSSAB, I believe the main construct sampled by the WSSAB could be summarized as social maturity. With such high intercorrelations attempting to conduct a profile analysis across the four subscales, as the authors suggest, would be essentially meaningless.

With any checklist-type measure of adaptive behavior the most important types of reliability are interobserver reliability and test-retest reliability. Interobserver reliability was assessed with two teachers who shared teaching responsibility for 63 elementary-aged students and two teachers who shared responsibility for 19 secondary-aged students. The correlation between the two teachers was .88 (elementary) and .89 (secondary). This degree of interobserver agreement is impressive for a scale of this type; however, more extensive data are needed with a larger sample of raters. A major weakness is that no data are provided to assess test-retest reliability.

In addition to the analysis of intercorrelations, construct validity was further assessed by computing point biserial correlations between the WSSAB scores of the norm sample and the teachers' judgement of the severity of each individual's adaptive ability (severely impaired or moderately/mildly impaired). The correlation between the WSSAB and the teachers' subjective evaluation was .99. Thus, the scale can be expected to be an accurate reflection of teachers' judgements of social maturity. Unfortunately, no data are provided to assess the relationship between the WSSAB and other numerical criteria such as other adaptive behavior scales, ratings of vocational preparation, community awareness, or popularity with peers.

SUMMARY. The WSSAB is unique. However, potential users of this test should be aware of its technical shortcomings and problems with content validity. In particular, the development of the norms was problematic due to small sample sizes, changes in the test from the initial version to the final version without new norm data, and the categorization of students into only two categories (moderate to severe vs. mild to moderate) without finer grade or age norms. In addition, there are no data to evaluate test-retest reliability. Given the small sample size of secondary students, I would not recommend the use of this test beyond grade school. Even for elementary-aged students, users should be aware that the test represents a restricted portion of the adaptive behavior domain.

Existing adaptive behavior scales, of which the Vineland ABS can be considered an exemplar of the state-of-the-art, although developed for mentally retarded students, could be used for students with learning disabilities because age norms are provided that are referenced to the performance of nonhandicapped people. Although several of the subscales are relevant only for much lower functioning students, many of the subscales can be used. A scale developed specifically for students with learning disabilities that sampled complex adaptive behavior skills such as public transportation skills, filling out government forms and job applications, comparative shopping skills, following written instructions for assembling household items, as well as social maturity would be an important addition to the literature.

[388]

Wichita Auditory Processing Test. Purpose: "To determine whether the rate at which speech is heard will affect a listener's comprehension of speech." School-age children; 1984; WAPT; a vocabulary pre-test is given to determine whether the basic noun and verb vocabulary used in the WAPT is known by the listener; test administered by cassette tape; 10 sentences scored at each of four rates of speaking; individual; 1985 price data: $68 per complete kit including response plates, cassette tape, 55 score sheets, and user's manual (42 pages); administration time not reported; Robert L. McCroskey; PRO-ED, Inc.*

[The publisher advised in January 1988 that this test is no longer available.]

Review of the Wichita Auditory Processing Test by MALCOLM R. MCNEIL, Professor, Department of Communicative Disorders, University of Wisconsin, Madison, WI:

The general goal of the Wichita Auditory Processing Test (WAPT) is to detect individuals having difficulty with rate of auditory language processing. Specific goals appear to be the differential identification of clinical subgroups [i.e., children with (*a*) articulation disorders, (*b*) learning disabilities, (*c*) mental retardation, (*d*) dialectical differences, and (*e*) normal elderly persons]. This differential diagnosis is to occur from differential performance across speech rate conditions on the WAPT. The test was designed for use by audiologists and speech-language pathologists but can be used by school psychologists/psychometrists and special educators. Qualification for use is "Any individual who is sensitive to requirements for administering a standardized test."

The test manual is inconsistent within itself, but lists three prerequisites for valid test use. Patients must have (*a*) visual acuity within normal limits or corrected to normal; (*b*) eye-hand coordination sufficient to locate and touch or mark the picture selected as a match with the sentence that was heard, and (*c*) basic vocabulary as determined by a pretest or parent/teacher report.

The test attempts to assess the accuracy of auditory comprehension of various syntactic forms through a four-choice picture-pointing paradigm. Four sets of 10 sentences are presented at different speech rates (175 words per minute [wpm], 87 wpm, 250 wpm, and 135 wpm). The construction of the tapes for the two rates that are slower (expanded) than normal (87 wpm and 135 wpm) and the fast (compressed rate, 250 wpm) were achieved with the Varispeech I electronic speech compressor/expander and possess the characteristic sound distortion associated with that rate manipulator.

The test has a vocabulary pretest designed to assess the vocabulary used in the actual test. It is recommended that 100 percent identification be achieved before proceeding with the rate-altered subtests of the WAPT. The syntactic structure tested is the same for each of the rate conditions; however, the lexical item used to test that structure differs among conditions. This is important because equivalent linguistic forms of the task have not been established, making differences among rate conditions difficult to interpret. This caution is warranted in spite of the pretest that assesses lexical knowledge because lexical access can be greatly affected by the load given to the syntactic operation required. The order of administration for each rate condition is constant for each subject. There are no data presented to demonstrate the lack of an order effect for any of the subject populations for which the test is intended.

The WAPT test manual presents sufficient literature supporting the potential importance of speech rate as a factor in the differential performance of the various pathological groups from normal (nonpathological) subjects. However, no data are presented using the published version of the WAPT supporting this literature review. The test does not appear to be based upon a specific model of auditory-linguistic processing, and construct validity is not explicitly addressed in the manual. However, the manual does offer sufficient evidence from its literature review for the interaction of stimulus rate and auditory processing to justify the need for a valid and standardized instrument such as the WAPT.

The test manual claims concurrent validity for the WAPT by successful identification and classification of the various pathological groups and by its correlation with other diagnostic tests; however, no data supporting these two forms of concurrent validity are presented. The manual does not explicitly address content or predictive validity. No tester (intra- or inter-judge) or subject (test-retest) reliability data are presented.

The WAPT appears to be adequately standardized in the sense that an explicit set of administration procedures, test stimuli, and scoring procedures have been established. The test has not, however, been standardized in the sense of establishing a database for comparison purposes and offers no reference data on the subjects for whom it was designed (normal or pathological).

Without the provision of additional validity data (concurrent, content, and predictive), reliability data, and adequate comparative or reference data, the Wichita Auditory Processing Test cannot be recommended for any of the purposes for which it was designed.

[389]

Wide Range Achievement Test—Revised. Purpose: "To measure the codes which are needed to learn the basic skills of reading, spelling, and arithmetic." Ages 5-0 to 11-11, 12-0 to 75; 1940–84; WRAT-R; 3 scores: Reading, Spelling, Arithmetic; individual in part; 2 forms; 2 levels; reading and spelling lists available on cassette tape for examiner training or group administration of spelling test; 1987 price data: $10 per 25 test forms (level 1 or level 2); $15 per 10 large print edition test forms (level 1 or level 2); $10 per set of 2 plastic word list cards; $25 per tape cassette; $20 per manual ('84, 82 pages); $45 per starter set including test forms for both Level 1 and Level 2, set of plastic cards, and manual; large print edition available; (15–30) minutes; Sarah Jastak, Gary S. Wilkinson, and Joseph Jastak (earlier editions); Jastak Associates, Inc.*

For reviews by Paula Matuszek and Philip A. Saigh of an earlier edition, see 9:1364 (103 references); see also T3:2621 (249 references), 8:37 (117 references), and T2:50 (35 references); for reviews by Jack C. Merwin and Robert L. Thorndike of an earlier edition, see 7:36 (49 references); see also 6:27 (15 references); for reviews by Paul Douglas Courtney, Verner M. Sims, and Louis P. Thorpe of the 1946 edition, see 3:21.

TEST REFERENCES

1. Epperson, D. L., Hannum, T. E., & Datwyler, M. L. (1982). Women incarcerated in 1960, 1970, and 1980: Implications of demographic, educational, and personality characteristics for earlier research. *Criminal Justice and Behavior*, 9, 352-363.

2. August, G. J., Stewart, M. A., & Holmes, C. S. (1983). A four-year follow-up of hyperactive boys with and without conduct disorder. *British Journal of Psychiatry*, 143, 192-198.

3. Berg, R. A., Ch'ien, L. T., Bownan, W. P., Ochs, J., Lancaster, W., Goff, J. R., & Anderson, H. R., Jr. (1983). The neuropsychological effects of acute lymphocytic leukemia and its treatment—a three year report: Intellectual functioning and academic achievement. *Clinical Neuropsychology*, 5, 9-13.

4. Elliott, S. N., Piersel, W. C., & Galvin, G. A. (1983). Psychological re-evaluations: A survey of practices and perceptions of school psychologists. *Journal of School Psychology*, 21, 99-105.

5. Epstein, M. H., & Cullinan, D. (1983). Academic performance of behaviorally disordered and learning-disabled pupils. *The Journal of Special Education*, 17, 303-307.

6. Feitel, B., & Sano, M. (1983). Intellectual assessment of young adult chronic patients. *Hospital and Community Psychiatry*, 34, 1153-1155.

7. Fogel, L. S., & Nelson, R. O. (1983). The effects of special education labels on teachers' behavioral observations, checklist scores, and grading of academic work. *Journal of School Psychology*, 21, 241-251.

8. Gettinger, M., & Lyon, M. A. (1983). Predictors of the discrepancy between time needed and time spent in learning among boys exhibiting behavior problems. *Journal of Educational Psychology*, 75, 491-499.

9. Lomax, R. G. (1983). Applying structural modeling to some component processes of reading comprehension development. *The Journal of Experimental Education*, 52, 33-40.

10. McDermott, P. A., & Watkins, M. W. (1983). Computerized vs. conventional remedial instruction for learning-disabled pupils. *The Journal of Special Education*, 17, 81-88.

11. Morrison, G. M., Forness, S. R., & MacMillan, D. L. (1983). Influences on the sociometric ratings of mildly handicapped children: A path analysis. *Journal of Educational Psychology*, 75, 63-74.

12. Silverstein, A. B., Brownlee, L., Legutki, G., & MacMillan, D. L. (1983). Convergent and discriminant validation of two methods of assessing three academic traits. *The Journal of Special Education*, 17, 63-68.

13. Thurber, S., & Walker, C. E. (1983). Medication and hyperactivity: A meta-analysis. *Journal of General Psychology*, 108, 79-86.

14. White, M., & Miller, S. R. (1983). Dyslexia: A term in search of a definition. *The Journal of Special Education*, 17, 5-10.

15. Ysseldyke, J., Algozzine, B., & Epps, S. (1983). A logical and empirical analysis of current practice in classifying students as handicapped. *Exceptional Children*, 50, 160-166.

16. Aram, D. M., Ekelman, B. L., & Nation, J. E. (1984). Preschoolers with language disorders: 10 years later. *Journal of Speech and Hearing Research*, 27, 232-244.

17. Barth, J. T., Macciocchi, S. N., Ranseen, J., Boyd, T., & Mills, G. (1984). The effects of prefontal leucotomy: Neuropsychological findings in long term chronic psychiatric patients. *Clinical Neuropsychology*, 6, 120-123.

18. Bissell, J. C., & Clark, F. (1984). Dichotic listening performance in normal children and adults. *The American Journal of Occupational Therapy*, 38, 176-183.

19. Blachman, B. A. (1984). Relationship of rapid naming ability and language analysis skills to kindergarten and first-grade reading achievement. *Journal of Educational Psychology*, 76, 610-622.

20. Black, J. L., Collins, D. W. K., Deroach, J. N., & Zubrick, S. (1984). A detailed study of sequential saccadic eye movements for normal- and poor-reading children. *Perceptual and Motor Skills*, 59, 423-434.

21. Black, J. L., Collins, D. W. K., DeRoach, J. N., & Zubrick, S. R. (1984). Smooth pursuit eye movements in normal and dyslexic children. *Perceptual and Motor Skills*, 59, 91-100.

22. Bookman, M. O. (1984). Spelling as a cognitive-developmental linguistic process. *Academic Therapy*, 20, 21-32.

23. Cermak, S. A., & Ayres, A. J. (1984). Crossing the body midline in learning-disabled and normal children. *The American Journal of Occupational Therapy*, 38, 35-39.

24. Champion, L., Doughtie, E. B., Johnson, P. J., & McCreary, J. H. (1984). Preliminary investigation into the Rorschach response patterns of children with documented learning disabilities. *Journal of Clinical Psychology*, 40, 329-333.

25. Chandler, H. N. (1984). The American public school: Yes, we have no standards. *Journal of Learning Disabilities*, 17, 186-187.

26. Christie, D., DeWitt, R. A., Kaltenbach, P., & Reed, D. (1984). Hyperactivity in children: Evidence for differences between parents' and teachers' perceptions of predominant features. *Psychological Reports*, 54, 771-774.

27. Cohen, R. L., Netley, C., & Clarke, M. A. (1984). On the generality of the short-term memory/reading ability relationship. *Journal of Learning Disabilities*, 17, 218-221.

28. Colligan, R. C., & Bajuniemi, L. E. (1984). Multiple definitions of reading disability: Implications for preschool screening. *Perceptual and Motor Skills*, 59, 467-475.

29. Copeland, A. P., & Reiner, E. M. (1984). The selective attention of learning-disabled children: Three studies. *Journal of Abnormal Child Psychology*, 12, 455-470.

30. DeWolfe, A. S., & Ryan, J. J. (1984). Wechsler Performance IQ > Verbal IQ index in a forensic sample: A reconsideration. *Journal of Clinical Psychology*, 40, 291-294.

31. Dishion, T. J., Loeber, R., Stouthamer-Loeber, M., & Patterson, G. R. (1984). Skill deficits and male adolescent delinquency. *Journal of Abnormal Child Psychology*, 12, 37-54.

32. Dorman, C., Hurley, A. D., & Laatsch, L. (1984). Prediction of spelling and reading performance in cerebral palsied adolescents using neuropsychological tests. *Clinical Neuropsychology*, 6, 142-144.

33. Doyle, B. A., & Higginson, D. C. (1984). Relationships among self-concept and school achievement, maternal self-esteem and sensory integration abilities for learning disabled children, ages 7 to 12 years. *Perceptual and Motor Skills*, 58, 177-178.

34. Elbert, J. C. (1984). Short-term memory encoding and memory search in the word recognition of learning-disabled children. *Journal of Learning Disabilities*, 17, 342-345.

35. Eno, L., & Woehlke, P. (1984). Relationship between grammatical errors on Rotter's Scale and performance on educational tests for students suspected of having learning problems. *Perceptual and Motor Skills*, 58, 75-78.

36. Frane, R. E., Clarizio, H. F., & Porter, A. (1984). Diagnostic and prescriptive bias in school psychologists' reports of a learning disabled child. *Journal of Learning Disabilities*, 17, 12-15.

37. Friedrich, D., Fuller, G. B., & Davis, D. (1984). Learning disability: Fact and fiction. *Journal of Learning Disabilities*, 17, 205-209.

38. Garrison, W., Earls, F., & Kindlor, D. (1984). Temperament characteristics in the third year of life and behavioral adjustment at school entry. *Journal of Clinical Child Psychology*, 13, 298-303.

39. Grossman, F. M., & Clark, J. H. (1984). Concurrent validity of WISC-R factor scores for educable mentally handicapped children. *Perceptual and Motor Skills*, 58, 227-230.

40. Guidubaldi, J., & Perry, J. D. (1984). Concurrent and predictive validity of the Battelle Development Inventory at the first grade level. *Educational and Psychological Measurement*, 44, 977-985.

41. Hale, R. L., & McDermott, P. A. (1984). Pattern analysis of an actuarial strategy for computerized diagnosis of childhood exceptionality. *Journal of Learning Disabilities*, 17, 30-37.

42. Hall, R. J., Reeve, R. E., & Zakreski, J. R. (1984). Validity of the Woodcock-Johnson Tests of Achievement for Learning-Disabled Students. *Journal of School Psychology*, 22, 193-200.

43. Halperin, J. M., Gittelman, R., Klein, D. F., & Rudel, R. B. (1984). Reading disabled hyperactive children: A distinct subgroup of Attention Deficit Disorder with hyperactivity? *Journal of Abnormal Child Psychology*, 12, 1-14.

44. Harvey, S., & Seeley, K. R. (1984). An investigation of the relationships among intellectual and creative abilities, extracurricular activities, achievement, and giftedness in a delinquent population. *Gifted Child Quarterly*, 28, 73-79.

45. Huesmann, L. R., Eron, L. D., Lefkowitz, M. M., & Walder, L. O. (1984). Stability of aggression over time and generations. *Developmental Psychology*, 20, 1120-1134.

46. Karnes, F. A., Whorton, J. E., & Currie, B. B. (1984). Correlations between the Wide Range Achievement Test and the California Achievement Test with intellectually gifted students. *Psychological Reports*, 54, 189-190.

47. Karnes, F. A., Whorton, J. E., & Currie, B. B. (1984). Correlations between WISC-R IQs and Wide Range Achievement Test grade equivalents for intellectually gifted students. *Psychological Reports*, 54, 69-70.

48. Kaufman, A. S. (1984). K-ABC and controversy. *The Journal of Special Education*, 18, 409-444.

49. Lindgren, S. D., & Richman, L. C. (1984). Immediate memory functions of verbally deficient reading-disabled children. *Journal of Learning Disabilities*, 17, 222-225.

50. Lindsey, J. D., & Armstrong, S. W. (1984). Performance of EMR and learning-disabled students on the Brigance, Peabody, and Wide Range Achievement Tests. *American Journal of Mental Deficiency*, 89, 197-201.

51. Lomax, R. G. (1984). A component processes model of reading comprehension development: A comparison of normal and learning disabled children. *National Reading Conference Yearbook*, 33, 308-316.

52. Mattes, J. A., Boswell, L., & Oliver, H. (1984). Methylphenidate effects on symptoms of attention deficit disorder in adults. *Archives of General Psychiatry*, 41, 1059-1063.

53. Meltzer, L. J., Levine, M. D., Karniski, W., Palfrey, J. S., & Clarke, S. (1984). An analysis of the learning styles of adolescent delinquents. *Journal of Learning Disabilities*, 17, 600-608.

54. Newman, R. S. (1984). Children's achievement and self-evaluations in mathematics: A longitudinal study. *Journal of Educational Psychology*, 76, 857-873.

55. Niklason, L. B. (1984). Nonpromotion: A pseudoscientific solution. *Psychology in the Schools*, 21, 485-499.

56. Nolen, P., & McCartin, R. (1984). Spelling strategies on the Wide Range Achievement Test. *The Reading Teacher*, 38, 148-158.

57. Obrzut, A., Nelson, R. B., & Obrzut, J. E. (1984). Early school entrance for intellectually superior children: An analysis. *Psychology in the Schools*, 21, 71-77.

58. Olson, J., & Midgett, J. (1984). Alternative placements: Does a difference exist in the LD populations? *Journal of Learning Disabilities*, 17, 101-103.

59. Perlmutter, B. F., & Bryan, J. H. (1984). First impressions, ingratiation, and the learning disabled child. *Journal of Learning Disabilities*, 17, 157-161.

60. Phelps, L., Rosso, M., & Falasco, S. L. (1984). Correlations between the Woodcock-Johnson and the WISC-R

for a behavior disordered population. *Psychology in the Schools*, 21, 442-446.

61. Punnett, A. F., & Steinhauer, G. D. (1984). Relationship between reinforcement and eye movements during ocular motor training with learning disabled children. *Journal of Learning Disabilities*, 17, 16-19.

62. Ryan, M. C., Miller, C. D., & Witt, J. C. (1984). A comparison of the use of orthographic structure in word discrimination by learning disabled and normal children. *Journal of Learning Disabilities*, 17, 38-40.

63. Scarborough, H. S. (1984). Continuity between childhood dyslexia and adult reading. *British Journal of Psychology*, 75, 329-348.

64. Schiller, J. J. (1984). Neuropsychological foundations of spelling and reading difficulty. *Clinical Neuropsychology*, 6, 255-261.

65. Schneider, B. H., & Byrne, B. M. (1984). Predictors of successful transition from self-contained special education to regular class settings. *Psychology in the Schools*, 21, 375-380.

66. Schulte, A., & Borich, G. D. (1984). Considerations in the use of difference scores to identify learning-disabled children. *Journal of School Psychology*, 22, 381-390.

67. Siegel, L. S., & Linder, B. A. (1984). Short-term memory processes in children with reading and arithmetic learning disabilities. *Developmental Psychology*, 20, 200-207.

68. Sinatra, R. C., Stahl-Gemake, J., & Berg, D. N. (1984). Improving reading comprehension of disabled readers through semantic mapping. *The Reading Teacher*, 38, 22-29.

69. Spellacy, F. J., & Brown, W. G. (1984). Prediction of recidivism in young offenders after brief institutionalization. *Journal of Clinical Psychology*, 40, 1070-1074. Edition):

70. Wilson, L. R., & Cone, T. (1984). The regression equation method of determining academic discrepancy. *Journal of School Psychology*, 22, 95-110.

71. Wolff, D. E., Desberg, P., & Marsh, G. (1985). Analogy strategies for improving word recognition in competent and learning disabled readers. *The Reading Teacher*, 38, 412-416.

72. Worland, J., Weeks, D. G., Janes, C. L., & Strock, B. D. (1984). Intelligence, classroom behavior, and academic achievement in children at high and low risk for psychopathology: A structural equation analysis. *Journal of Abnormal Child Psychology*, 12, 437-454.

73. Wright, L. (1984). Modifying the Bond and Tinker formula for use with low IQ adolescents. *Journal of Reading*, 28, 224-227.

74. Altepeter, T., & Handal, P. J. (1985). A factor analytic investigation of the use of the PPVT-R as a measure of general achievement. *Journal of Clinical Psychology*, 41, 540-543.

75. Baker, E. L., White, R. F., & Murawski, B. J. (1985). Clinical evaluation of neurobehavioral effects of occupational exposure to organic solvents and lead. *International Journal of Mental Health*, 14 (3), 135-158.

76. Brown, R. T., & Alford, N. (1984). Ameliorating attentional deficits and concommitant academic deficiencies in learning disabled children through cognitive training. *Journal of Learning Disabilities*, 17, 20-26.

77. Brown, R. T., Wynne, M. E., & Medenis, R. (1985). Methylphenidate and cognitive therapy: A comparison of treatment approaches with hyperactive boys. *Journal of Abnormal Child Psychology*, 13, 69-87.

78. Carnine, D., Gersten, R., Darch, C., & Eaves, R. (1985). Attention and cognitive deficits in learning-disabled students. *Journal of Special Education*, 19, 319-331.

79. Cohen, N. J., Gotlieb, H., Kershner, J., & Wehrspann, W. (1985). Concurrent validity of the internalizing and externalizing profile patterns of the Achenbach Child Behavior Checklist. *Journal of Consulting and Clinical Psychology*, 53, 724-728.

80. Connelly, J. B. (1985). Published tests—which ones do special education teachers perceive as useful? *Journal of Special Education*, 19, 149-155.

81. Dalby, J. T. (1985). Taxonomic separation of attention deficit disorders and developmental reading disorders. *Contemporary Educational Psychology*, 10, 228-234.

82. Derr, A. M. (1985). Conservation and mathematics achievement in the learning disabled child. *Journal of Learning Disabilities*, 18, 333-336.

83. Estes, R. E., Hallock, J. E., & Bray, N. M. (1985). Comparison of arithmetic measures with learning disabled students. *Perceptual and Motor Skills*, 61, 711-716.

84. Feldman, M. J. (1985). Evaluating pre-primer basal readers using story grammar. *American Educational Research Journal*, 22, 527-547.

85. Fischer, F. W., Shankweiler, D., & Liberman, I. Y. (1985). Spelling proficiency and sensitivity to word structure. *Journal of Memory and Language*, 24, 423-441.

86. Fletcher, J. M. (1985). Memory for verbal and nonverbal stimuli in learning disability subgroups: Analysis by selective reminding. *Journal of Experimental Child Psychology*, 40, 244-259.

87. Guy, E., Platt, J. J., Zwerling, I., & Bullock, S. (1985). Mental health status of prisoners in an urban jail. *Criminal Justice and Behavior*, 12, 29-53.

88. Heilbrun, A. B., Jr., & Heilbrun, M. R. (1985). Psychopathy and dangerousness: Comparison, integration and extension of two psychopathic typologies. *British Journal of Clinical Psychology*, 24, 181-195.

89. Hilgert, L. D., & Treloar, J. H. (1985). The relationship of the Hooper Visual Organization Test to sex, age, and intelligence of elementary school children. *Measurement and Evaluation in Counseling and Development*, 17, 203-206.

90. Humphreys, L. G., Rich, S. A., & Davey, T. C. (1985). A Piagetian test of general intelligence. *Developmental Psychology*, 21, 872-877.

91. Kraft, R. H. (1985). Laterality and school achievement: Interactions between familial handedness and assessed laterality. *Perceptual and Motor Skills*, 61, 1147-1156.

92. Kupke, T., & Lewis, R. (1985). WAIS and neuropsychological tests: Common and unique variance within an epileptic population. *Journal of Clinical and Experimental Neuropsychology*, 7, 353-366.

93. Lowman, R. L., Williams, R. E., & Leeman, G. E. (1985). The structure and relationship of college women's primary abilities and vocational interests. *Journal of Vocational Behavior*, 27, 298-315.

94. Lueger, R. J., Albott, W. L., Hilgendorf, W. A., & Gill, K. J. (1985). Neuropsychological and academic achievement correlates of abnormal WISC-R Verbal-Performance discrepancies. *Journal of Clinical Psychology*, 41, 801-805.

95. Margolis, R. B., Greenlief, C. L., & Taylor, J. M. (1985). Relationship between the WAIS-R and the WRAT in a geriatric sample with suspected dementia. *Psychological Reports*, 56, 287-292.

96. Mayberry, W., & Gilligan, M. B. (1985). Ocular pursuit in mentally retarded, cerebral-palsied, and learning-disabled children. *The American Journal of Occupational Therapy*, 39, 589-595.

97. Moon, C., Marlowe, M., Stellern, J., & Errera, J. (1985). Main and interaction effects of metallic pollutants on cognitive functioning. *Journal of Learning Disabilities*, 18, 217-221.

98. Newville, L., & Hamm, N. H. (1985). Content validity of the WRAT and grade level achievement of primary grade students. *Journal of School Psychology*, 23, 91-93.

99. Ormrod, J. E. (1985). Proofreading *The Cat in the Hat*: Evidence for different reading styles of good and poor spellers. *Psychological Reports*, 57, 863-867.

100. Ormrod, J. E. (1985). Visual memory in a spelling matching task: Comparison of good and poor spellers. *Perceptual and Motor Skills*, 61, 183-188.

101. Reilly, T. P., Drudge, O. W., Rosen, J. C., Loew, D. E., & Fischer, M. (1985). Concurrent and predictive validity of the WISC-R, McCarthy Scales, Woodcock-Johnson, and academic achievement. *Psychology in the Schools*, 22, 380-382.

102. Reitsma-Street, M., Offord, D. R., & Finch, T. (1985). Pairs of same-sexed siblings discordant for antisocial behaviour. *British Journal of Psychiatry*, 146, 415-423.

103. Saldate, M., IV, Mishra, S. P., & Medina, M., Jr. (1985). Bilingual instruction and academic achievement: A longitudinal study. *Journal of Instructional Psychology*, 12, 24-30.

104. Shelton, T. L., Anastopoulos, A. D., & Linden, J. D. (1985). An attribution training program with learning disabled children. *Journal of Learning Disabilities*, 18, 261-265.

105. Sherman, R. G., Berling, B. S., & Oppenheimer, S. (1985). Increasing community independence for adolescents with spina bifida. *Adolescence*, 20, 1-13.

106. Sinclair, E., Forness, S. R., & Alexson, J. (1985). Psychiatric diagnosis: A study of its relationship to school needs. *Journal of Special Education*, 19, 333-344.

107. Smith, E. R. (1985). Community college reading tests: A statewide survey. *Journal of Reading*, 28, 52-55.

108. Treiman, R. (1985). Phonemic awareness and spelling: Children's judgments do not always agree with adults'. *Journal of Experimental Child Psychology*, 39, 182-201.

109. Vance, B., Kitson, D., & Singer, M. G. (1985). Relationship between the standard scores of Peabody Picture Vocabulary Test—Revised and Wide Range Achievement Test. *Journal of Clinical Psychology*, 41, 691-697.

110. Wagner, S. R. (1985). Handedness and higher mental functions. *Claremont Reading Conference Yearbook*, 49, 258-266.

111. Webster, R. E. (1985). The criterion-related validity of psychoeducational tests for actual reading ability of learning disabled students. *Psychology in the Schools*, 22, 152-159.

112. Wright, P. G., & Friesen, W. J. (1985). The Carlson Psychological Survey with adolescents: Norms and scales reliabilities. *Canadian Journal of Behavioural Science*, 17, 389-399.

113. Wurtz, R. G., Sewell, T., & Manni, J. L. (1985). The relationship of estimated learning potential to performance on a learning task and achievement. *Psychology in the Schools*, 22, 293-302.

114. Ackerman, P. T., Anhalt, J. M., & Dykman, R. A. (1986). Arithmetic automatization failure in children with attention and reading disorders: Associations and sequela. *Journal of Learning Disabilities*, 19, 222-232.

115. Bellemare, F. G., Inglis, J., & Lawson, J. S. (1986). Learning disability indices derived from a principal components analysis of the WISC-R: A study of learning disabled and normal boys. *Canadian Journal of Behavioural Science*, 18, 86-91.

116. Berninger, V. W. (1986). Normal variation in reading acquisition. *Perceptual and Motor Skills*, 62, 691-716.

117. Brown, R. T., Borden, K. A., Wynne, M. E., Schleser, R., & Clingerman, S. R. (1986). Methylphenidate and cognitive therapy with ADD children: A methodological reconsideration. *Journal of Abnormal Child Psychology*, 14, 481-497.

118. Burton, L., & Elliott, R. N., Jr. (1986). Evaluation of a mathematics peer-tutoring program. *Journal of College Student Personnel*, 27, 80-81.

119. Catts, H. W. (1986). Speech production/phonological deficits in reading-disordered children. *Journal of Learning Disabilities*, 19, 504-508.

120. Corning, W. C., Steffy, R. A., Anderson, F., & Bowers, P. (1986). EEG "maturational lag" profiles: Follow-up analyses. *Journal of Abnormal Child Psychology*, 14, 235-249.

121. Dalby, J. T., & Williams, R. (1986). Preserved reading and spelling ability in psychotic disorders. *Psychological Medicine*, 16, 171-175.

122. Davenport, L., Yingling, C. D., Fein, G., Galin, D., & Johnstone, J. (1986). Narrative speech deficits in dyslexics. *Journal of Clinical and Experimental Neuropsychology*, 8, 347-361.

123. Fowler, P. C. (1986). Cognitive differentiation of learning-disabled children on the WISC-R: A canonical model of achievement correlates. *Child Study Journal*, 16, 25-38.

124. Gersten, R., Carnine, D., Zoref, L., & Cronin, D. (1986). A multifaceted study of change in seven inner-city schools. *Elementary School Journal*, 86, 257-276.

125. Goldstein, H. S. (1986). Conduct problems, parental supervision, and cognitive development of 12- to 17-year-olds. *Psychological Reports*, 59, 651-658.

126. Guidubaldi, J., Cleminshaw, H. K., Perry, J. D., Nastasi, B. K., & Lightel, J. (1986). The role of selected family environment factors in children's post-divorce adjustment. *Family Relations*, 35, 141-151.

127. Hinshaw, S. P., Carte, E. T., & Morrison, D. C. (1986). Concurrent prediction of academic achievement in reading disabled children: The role of neuropsychological and intellectual measures at different ages. *Clinical Neuropsychology*, 8, 3-8.

128. Holmes, C. S. (1986). Neuropsychological profiles in men with insulin-dependent diabetes. *Journal of Consulting and Clinical Psychology*, 54, 386-389.

129. Jason, L. A., Pillen, B., & Olson, T. (1986). Comp-tutor: A computer-based prevention program. *The School Counselor*, 34, 116-122.

130. Juel, C., Griffith, P. L., & Gough, P. B. (1986). Acquisition of literacy: A longitudinal study of children in first and second grade. *Journal of Educational Psychology*, 78, 243-255.

131. Livesay, J. R. (1986). Clinical utility of Wechsler's deterioration index in screening for behavioral impairment. *Perceptual and Motor Skills*, 63, 619-626.

132. McCue, P. M., Shelly, C., & Goldstein, G. (1986). Intellectual, academic and neuropsychological performance levels in learning disabled adults. *Journal of Learning Disabilities*, 19, 233-236.

133. Miezejeski, C. M., Jenkins, E. C., Hill, A. L., Wisniewski, K., French, J. H., & Brown, W. T. (1986). A profile of cognitive deficit in females from fragile X families. *Neuropsychologia*, 24, 405-409.

134. Newsome, G. L., III. (1986). The effects of reader perspective and cognitive style on remembering important information from texts. *Journal of Reading Behavior*, 18, 117-133.

135. Nici, J., & Reitan, R. M. (1986). Patterns of neuropsychological ability in brain-disordered versus normal children. *Journal of Consulting and Clinical Psychology*, 54, 542-545.

136. Nussbaum, N. L., & Bigler, E. D. (1986). Neuropsychological and behavioral profiles of empirically derived subgroups of learning disabled children. *Clinical Neuropsychology*, 8, 82-89.

137. Nussbaum, N. L., Bigler, E. D., & Koch, W. (1986). Neuropsychologically derived subgroups of learning disabled children: Personality/behavioral dimensions. *Journal of Learning Disabilities*, 19, 57-67.

138. Pennington, B. F., McCabe, L. L., Smith, S. D., Lefly, D. L., Bookman, M. O., Kimberling, W. J., & Lubs, H. A. (1986). Spelling errors in adults with a form of familial dyslexia. *Child Development*, 57, 1001-1013.

139. Perlick, D., Stastny, P., Katz, I., Mayer, M., & Mattis, S. (1986). Memory deficits and anticholinergic levels in chronic schizophrenia. *American Journal of Psychiatry*, 143, 230-232.

140. Reid, N. (1986). Wide Range Achievement Test: 1984 revised edition. *Journal of Counseling and Development*, 64, 538-539.

141. Reynolds, C. R. (1986). Wide Range Achievement Test (WRAT-R), 1984 edition. *Journal of Counseling and Development*, 64, 540-541.

142. Sarazin, F-A., & Spreen, O. (1986). Fifteen year stability of some neuropsychological tests in learning disabled subjects with and without neurological impairment. *Journal of Clinical and Experimental Neuropsychology*, 8, 190-200.

143. Sears, N. C., & Johnson, D. M. (1986). The effects of visual imagery on spelling performance and retention among elementary students. *The Journal of Educational Research*, 79, 230-233.

144. Sears, N. C., & Johnson, D. M. (1986). The effects of visual imagery on spelling performance and retention among elementary students. *Journal of Educational Research*, 79, 230-233.

145. Shapiro, A. H. (1986). Projection of body image and printing the alphabet. *Journal of Learning Disabilities*, 19, 107-111.

146. Sinclair, E., & Alexson, J. (1986). Factor analysis and discriminant analysis of psychoeducational report contents. *Journal of School Psychology*, 24, 363-371.

147. Spruill, J., & Beck, B. (1986). Relationship between the WAIS-R and Wide Range Achievement Test—Revised. *Educational and Psychological Measurement*, 46, 1037-1040.

148. Stevenson, H. W., & Newman, R. S. (1986). Long-term prediction of achievement and attitudes in mathematics and reading. *Child Development*, 57, 646-659.

149. Stiffman, A. R., Jung, K. G., & Feldman, R. A. (1986). A multivariate risk model for childhood behavior problems. *American Journal of Orthopsychiatry*, 56, 204-211.

150. Vance, B., Fuller, G. B., & Lester, M. L. (1986). A comparison of the Minnesota Perceptual Diagnostic Test Revised and the Bender Gestalt. *Journal of Learning Disabilities*, 19, 211-214.

151. Vance, H. R., Hankins, N., & Brown, W. (1986). Predictive validity of the McCarthy Screening Test based on Wide Range Achievement Test. *Psychological Reports*, 59, 1060-1062.

152. Voeller, K. K. S. (1986). Right-hemisphere deficit syndrome in children. *American Journal of Psychiatry*, 143, 1004-1009.

153. Wharry, R. E., & Kirkpatrick, S. W. (1986). Vision and academic performance of learning disabled children. *Perceptual and Motor Skills*, 62, 323-336.

154. Beden, I., Rohr, L., & Ellsworth, R. (1987). A public school validation study of the achievement sections of the Woodcock-Johnson Psycho-educational Battery with learning disabled students. *Educational and Psychological Measurement*, 47 (3), 711-717.

155. Dorman, C. (1987). Verbal, perceptual, and intellectual factors associated with reading achievement in adolescents with cerebral palsy. *Perceptual and Motor Skills*, 64, 671-678.

156. Elkind, M. A., Cohen, J. C., Glenwick, D. S., & Roth, J. L. (1987). Relation of scores on the Open Middle Test to self control and academic achievement of inner-city fourth grade children. *Perceptual and Motor Skills*, 64 (1), 87-93.

157. Famularo, R., & Fenton, T. (1987). The effect of methylphenidate on school grades in children with attention deficit disorder without hyperactivity: A preliminary report. *The Journal of Clinical Psychiatry*, 48, 112-116.

158. Huesmann, L. R., Eron, L. D., & Yarmel, P. W. (1987). Intellectual functioning and aggression. *Journal of Personality and Social Psychology*, 52, 232-240.

159. Lovett, M. W. (1987). A developmental approach to reading disability: Accuracy and speed criteria of normal and deficient reading skill. *Child Development*, 58, 234-260.

160. Werker, J. F., & Tees, R. C. (1987). Speech perception in severely disabled and average reading children. *Canadian Journal of Psychology*, 41 (1), 48-61.

161. Whorton, J. E., & Karnes, F. A. (1987). Correlation of Stanford-Binet Intelligence Scale with various other measures used to screen and identify intellectually gifted students. *Perceptual and Motor Skills*, 64, 461-462.

Review of the Wide Range Achievement Test—Revised by ELAINE CLARK, Assistant Professor of Educational Psychology, University of Utah, Salt Lake City, UT:

The Wide Range Achievement Test—Revised (WRAT-R) is the most recent of five revisions of the original 1936 test. As with most revised editions, this test was intended as a refinement and restandardization of the earlier version. Although the test looks different than its predecessors (e.g., spiral-bound test manual and separate and different colored test forms for the two levels), the content and format are virtually unchanged. The items are identical to the 1965 test edition except for the addition of two counting problems and one subtraction problem to Level 1 of the Arithmetic subtest, and the addition of 10 simple arithmetic items to Level 2. The correlation coefficients between the two editions range from .91 to .99. Nonetheless, the authors report that substantive, though not necessarily perceptible, changes have been made that contribute to the psychometric soundness of the measure.

The Rasch model for item analysis and scaling was used. It is unclear, however, in what way the results of these analyses were used. For example, although the rank order of item difficulty was different for White and non-White samples on the two versions of the Arithmetic subtest, the WRAT-R items and order of presentation are virtually the same as on the WRAT.

Standard scores and grade equivalents were revised based on the newly developed and extended norms. The normative data have been extended to include individuals between the ages of 65 and 75. Norms are now available for individuals ranging in age from 5 years, 0 months, to 74 years, 11 months. Like the earlier version, the WRAT-R has two levels: Level 1 for children ages 5 years, 0 months, to 11 years, 11 months; and Level 2 for persons over 12 years of age.

STANDARDIZATION. The standardization sample of 5,600 was stratified by age (28 age groups, each with 200 persons), sex, race (White/non-White), geographic region, and community residence (metropolitan/non-metropolitan). Unfortunately, with the exception of age, no demographic characteristics of the sample are described in the manual. The rationale underlying the decision to collapse all non-White individuals into one group is absent. For example, there is no information about the individuals who comprise the non-White group. Without such information, it is impossible to evaluate the representativeness of the sample; however, the limited information presented suggests that it was not representative. For instance, Illinois was the only state to represent the entire north central region, a region which is comprised of 26% of the U.S. population (according to the 1982 Rand McNally *Commercial Atlas and Marketing Guide*, which is used as the source of the population figures cited in the WRAT-R manual). Sampling from 1 of 12 north central states, of course, is no more disturbing than sampling 5 of 13 states in the west region, a region where 19% of the U.S.

population reside. Without a breakdown of subjects according to states, and other variables on which the sample was stratified, there is no way of evaluating the representativeness of the sample.

The description of procedures used during the standardization are similarly inadequate. The authors do not describe specifically how the subjects were recruited or selected; in fact, randomization procedures were reportedly abandoned with the "difficult-to-find" adult subjects.

RELIABILITY. Consequent to selecting test items using the Rasch model, indices of person and item separation were used, in part, to assess reliability. With the exception of a coefficient of .82 for Level 1 Arithmetic, all median coefficients across subtests for person separation (test reliability) and item separation (sample reliability) are above .91. Test users who are unfamiliar with the Rasch scaling techniques may find it difficult to understand what these coefficients mean. Test-retest reliabilities were calculated for 81 individuals in Level 1 and 67 individuals in Level 2. Given the relatively small sample size, it would have been beneficial to have demographic information about this group. Without a sample description and information regarding the testing procedure (e.g., length of time between the two administrations), all the test user knows is that the coefficients for Level 1 subtests range from .94 to .97, and for Level 2 the range is .79 to .90. Further elaboration and clarification would have been helpful.

VALIDITY. The authors state that "the content validity of the WRAT-R is apparent." What is apparent to this reviewer is that the test has "face validity." Considering the fact that the parameters of the WRAT-R domains (e.g., Reading, Spelling, and Arithmetic) are not adequately defined, content validity cannot be judged. Furthermore, given the stated purpose of the test, "to measure the codes which are needed to learn the basic skills of reading, spelling, and arithmetic," it is not at all clear what the test is measuring. Nonetheless, the authors use the Rasch analysis of item difficulty as a source of evidence. The inclusion of both easy and difficult items does not constitute content validity. The evidence provided by the author for construct validity comes from two sources, item separation coefficients and increasing raw scores with age. However, it is unclear how item separation coefficients pertain to construct validity. Similarly, there is little support for concurrent validity. Not only is minimal information provided, but the studies referred to in the manual pertain to the 1978 version of the WRAT instead of the WRAT-R. Despite the similarity in content of the WRAT and WRAT-R, studies using the new version would be more meaningful.

ADMINISTRATION AND SCORING. The instructions for administering and scoring the individual subtests are clearly presented, as are the procedures for converting raw scores to standard scores and grade equivalents. What is not clear is the procedure used to "smooth" the raw data, nor the reason behind the procedure. In any case, the resultant standard scores have a mean of 100 and standard deviation of 15. The presentation of the grade equivalents has been changed, and now reflects more accurately the ordinal nature of the data. For example, instead of reporting an equivalent of 4.8 (eighth month of the fourth grade), a 4E (end of fourth grade) is reported. Since it is unclear whether the assignment of grade equivalents is arbitrary or based on objective indices, standard scores should be used for score comparisons.

Interpretation of test scores seems further confounded by the fact that test users may administer the test individually or in a group (the training cassette tape can be used for group administrations). Furthermore, the examiner may administer the subtests in a "convenient" order, a provision that was also made for examiners during standardization. Not only are there no data to suggest that the scores derived under the various conditions are comparable, there are no separate norms.

SUMMARY. Perhaps the worst thing that can be said about the WRAT-R is that the more it changes, the more it stays the same. At the present time there is no evidence to suggest that the WRAT-R is an improvement over previous editions. Although the publishing company has indicated to the reviewer that it no longer plans to publish the Diagnostic and Technical Manual as once intended, they will be publishing six monographs pertaining to (*a*) studies of the WRAT/WRAT-R and other instruments; (*b*) comparisons between the WRAT and WRAT-R; (*c*) reliability; (*d*) case studies; (*e*) test development; and (*f*) validity. These monographs should fill in some of the information missing in the Administration Manual. This test seems to have potential as a research and clinical tool; however, until documentation is available, test users should be cautious when using the test to assist in the diagnosis of learning disabilities, help determine personality structure, or check school achievement for vocational assessment, job placement, and training. The fact that this test can be administered and scored quickly will continue to contribute to its popularity. And like its predecessors, the WRAT-R will undoubtedly continue to be one of the most widely used instruments to estimate academic achievement.

Review of the Wide Range Achievement Test—Revised by PATTI L. HARRISON, Assistant Professor of Behavioral Studies, College of Education, The University of Alabama, Tuscaloosa, AL:

The Wide Range Achievement Test—Revised (WRAT-R) is the sixth edition of the popular test that was first published in 1936. Like the earlier versions, the WRAT-R contains three subtests: Reading (recognizing and naming letters and words), Spelling (writing symbols, name, and words), and Arithmetic (solving oral problems and written computations). The authors of the WRAT-R stress that the test is designed to measure basic school codes rather than comprehension, reasoning, and judgement processes. General uses for the test described in the manual include comparing achievement of one person to another, determining learning ability or learning disability, comparing codes with comprehension in order to prescribe remedial programs, and informally assessing error patterns to plan instructional programs.

The items of the WRAT-R are virtually unchanged from earlier versions. The Reading and Spelling subtests contain no changes, while the Arithmetic subtest contains a few additional problems. The administration and scoring procedures also remain unchanged, with a few exceptions that are mostly cosmetic in nature.

The major change intended by the authors of the WRAT-R, and their primary goal in restandardization, was improvement of the psychometric qualities of the test. Critics of previous editions pointed out inadequate standardization and questionable reliability and validity as major problems. The authors of the WRAT-R undoubtedly attempted to answer the criticisms. This review addresses the extent to which they were successful.

DEVELOPMENT AND STANDARDIZATION. One of the new features incorporated into the WRAT-R is the use of the Rasch item-response-theory model. The manual contains a description of the basic premises of the Rasch model, but gives little information about how the model was actually applied to test development. The manual and a later publication (Jastak Associates, in press) describe the use of Rasch item difficulty estimates to determine that the items ranged from easy to hard. However, the estimates were not used to determine the order of item administration, a logical use of the item statistics because the cutoff rule of 10 consecutive errors on the Reading and Spelling subtests assumes the items are administered in order of difficulty. The manual also indicates that the Rasch model was used to investigate item bias, but this approach to item bias is recognized as inappropriate (Shepard, Camilli, & Williams, 1984). More details about the use of the Rasch model have been promised in forthcoming publications; however, no information was available at the time of this review (three years after the WRAT-R was published).

In contrast to earlier editions, a stratified national sampling plan was used for the standardization of the WRAT-R. A total of 5,600 subjects, or 200 subjects in each of 28 age groups from 5 to 74 years, composed the sample. Stratification variables included age, sex, race, geographical region, and metropolitan versus nonmetropolitan residence. The efforts to obtain a representative national sample are laudable, but concerns about the standardization procedures result in questions about the adequacy of the sample.

Socioeconomic status was not used as a stratification variable, although research clearly shows that socioeconomic status has a stronger relationship with achievement than does race or many other variables. In addition, race was designated as white versus nonwhite, a questionable practice. Perhaps the greatest concern is the failure to describe the actual composition of the sample. Population percentages for each stratification variable, taken from a Rand McNally guide instead of U.S. census reports, are reported in the manual, but there is no indication that the WRAT-R sample matched these percentages. One piece of evidence to support that the percentages were not matched is the states included in the norming program. For example, a total of 17 states were used during standardization, but only one state was located in the north central region of the country.

The characteristics of the adult sample are so vague and confusing that the use of the WRAT-R with individuals above age 18 is probably not advisable. The authors state, "Because of the difficulty in selecting an adult sample, randomization was not as carefully followed." A need to carefully consider amount of higher education is described, but there is no indication of the number of college graduates in the sample. College students (but not college graduates) were excluded from the sample for some reason, resulting in a biased sample. The authors indicate that correction of the norms was necessary to make the results more sensible, but test users should wonder what the WRAT-R norms indicate for adult subjects.

The manual contains adequate guidelines for interpreting the standard scores, percentile ranks, and grade equivalents obtained from the WRAT-R. The authors recommend wisely that only standard scores be used for making subtest comparisons, but do not provide standard errors of difference. The norm tables were constructed to provide standard scores for half-year age intervals at younger ages and wider intervals at older ages. Quarter-year age intervals at younger ages would be more appropriate, given the rapid development of achievement skills at younger ages.

RELIABILITY AND VALIDITY. The Rasch analysis provided person-separation and item-separation values and these are given as evidence of internal consistency. Traditional internal-consistency data, such as split-half or alpha coefficients, are not provided and are needed. Test-retest reliability coefficients range from .79 (Level 2 Arithmetic) to .97 (Level 1 Spelling), but are virtually useless. No indication of the time interval between test and retest is given and the coefficients are based on small samples for only a few age groups in the school-age range. The authors recommend the practice of using standard errors of measurement when interpreting scores, but the values are questionable since they are based on the test-retest reliability coefficients.

One of the major sources of criticism about previous editions was lack of evidence for content validity. Although the current manual provides little information about content validity, a report by Jastak Associates (in press) addresses the issue in greater detail. The following evidence is given for content validity: The first edition sampled dictionaries to obtain reading and spelling items, Rasch statistics support the wide range of item coverage, the test exhibits evidence of internal consistency, there is a developmental progression of raw scores, WRAT-R subtests have moderately high correlations with Woodcock-Johnson achievement subtests, and the format of administration is similar to classroom activities. None of this evidence supports content validity and test users cannot be assured that the WRAT-R systematically and adequately samples the content taught in today's schools.

The manual supplies two sources of evidence for construct validity: person and item-separation values and increasing raw scores with age. As indicated by Anastasi (1982), internal consistency and developmental progression of scores are necessary but insufficient conditions for construct validity. The raw score means obtained by the standardization sample also do not indicate a clear developmental progression. Some adjacent age groups have small differences in raw score means. The means for 18-to-19-year-olds are always lower than the means for 16-to-17-year-olds, presumably because of the exclusion of college students.

The evidence for concurrent validity consists primarily of a summary of studies comparing the WRAT with other achievement tests. The manual reports very high correlations (i.e., .91 to .99) between the WRAT and WRAT-R, but the correlations were calculated using the WRAT-R norm sample and an "arbitrary" sample of previously administered WRATs. It appears that the correlations are not based on a sample of subjects who took both tests. A few recent studies not presented in the manual investigated concurrent validity. Spruill and Beck (1986a) found WRAT/WRAT-R correlations of .98, .97, and .71 for the Reading, Spelling, and Arithmetic subtests, respectively. Merrill (1985) reports correlations of .70 to .85 for the WRAT-R and Woodcock-Johnson achievement tests. Jastak Associates (1985) found correlations ranging from .37 to .72 for the WRAT-R subtests and WISC-R Verbal, Performance, and Full scales. Smith and Smith (1986) report correlations ranging from .21 to .64 for the WRAT-R subtests and WISC-R Verbal and Performance scales. Spruill and Beck (1986b) found correlations of .47 to .71 for the WRAT-R subtests and WAIS-R Verbal, Performance, and Full scales.

CONCLUSIONS. Does the WRAT-R meet psychometric standards for an achievement test? This reviewer must answer "No" given available information. Although there seem to be some improvements over earlier editions, the development of the WRAT-R either did not include many recommended practices or the authors did not report them. There are many questions about the applications of the Rasch model, and the standardization sample is not described in enough detail to determine adequacy. Traditional internal consistency coefficients are not available and test-retest reliability coefficients are questionable. Content validity is not supported and information about construct and concurrent validity is limited.

The general uses of the WRAT-R given in the manual are not supported by the test's psychometric qualities. There is no supporting evidence that the WRAT-R can be used for placement of children into special education and remedial programs or for prescribing instruction. Some practitioners justify their use of the WRAT-R by saying, "I use it for screening purposes only." There is no support for this use, either. Using the WRAT-R for screening may result in a great disservice to students. The WRAT-R yields a limited sample of behavior. Although the WRAT-R measures codes, an important aspect of achievement, it does not measure comprehension. A child with comprehension problems could obtain high scores and, thus, not be identified as a child with special academic needs.

REVIEWER'S REFERENCES

Anastasi, A. (1982). *Psychological testing* (5th ed.). New York: MacMillan.

Shepard, L., Camilli, G., & Williams, D. M. (1984). Accounting for statistical artifacts in item bias research. *Journal of Educational Statistics*, 9, 93-128.

Jastak Associates. (1985). *WRAT-R/WISC-R correlations.* Wilmington, DE: Author.

Merrill, K. H. (1985). *Analysis: The new WRAT-R compared with Woodcock-Johnson achievement and WISC-R.* Unpublished manuscript, Mesa Public Schools, Mesa, AZ.

Smith, T. C., & Smith, B. L. (1986). The relationship between the WISC-R and WRAT-R for a sample of rural referred children. *Psychology in the Schools*, 23, 252-254.

Spruill, J., & Beck, B. (1986a). Relationship between the WRAT and WRAT-R. *Psychology in the Schools*, 23, 357-360.

Spruill, J., & Beck, B. (1986b). Relationship between the WAIS-R and Wide Range Achievement Test—Revised. *Educational and Psychological Measurement*, 46, 1037-1040.

Jastak Associates. (in press). *WRAT-R monograph #1: Content validity*. Wilmington, DE: Author.

[390]

Wide-Span Reading Test. Purpose: Assesses a "child's skills in decoding printed symbols into meaningful sounds of language, in fitting meanings to groups of sounds, and in construing the structural relationship of meanings in their total semantic and syntactical context." Ages 7-10 to 14-11; 1972–84; 2 parallel forms, Form A and Form B; 1986 price data: £20.95 per introductory set containing 25 reusable pupils' booklets Forms A and B, 50 answer sheets, and teachers' manual ('83, 36 pages); £6.35 per 25 pupils' booklets, Form A or B; £2.35 per 25 answer sheets; £3.80 per teachers' manual; £4.25 per specimen set containing one each pupils' booklets Forms A and B, answer sheet, and teachers' manual; 30(40) minutes; Alan Brimer; NFER-Nelson Publishing Co., Ltd. [England].*

See T3:2625 (1 reference); for additional information and reviews by David J. Carroll and William Yule, see 8:747.

Review of the Wide-Span Reading Test by MARIAM JEAN DREHER, Associate Professor of Education, Department of Curriculum and Instruction, University of Maryland, College Park, MD:

The Wide-Span Reading Test is intended to assess the reading comprehension level of students aged 7 through 14 years who are in the first through fourth years of junior school and the first through fourth years of secondary school. Students' raw scores on this test are converted to standard scores based on year in school and chronological age in years and months. In addition to standard scores, a nominal scale score can be derived, which is said to represent a student's highest level of functioning. This level is determined by locating the last place in the test where a student has three out of four consecutive items correct; the nominal score is then the item number of the middle of the three correct answers. Although these nominal scores are said to be meaningful on their own, their value is not completely clear; however, there is a table to convert them to reading ages.

The test was standardized on a sample of 7,503 students who are said to represent the different types of schools and locations in

England and Wales. However, no information is given to indicate how the sample was selected. There is also no indication of when the test was standardized. Although the test manual was revised in 1984, the test itself was copyrighted in 1972. If the standardization was conducted for the 1972 test, then the sample may be 15 or more years old and therefore may no longer be an appropriate reference group.

The Wide-Span Reading Test presents students with unrelated pairs of sentences. One sentence in each pair has a missing word that must be filled in by selecting an appropriate word from the other sentence. For example, students are asked to fill the blank in "Turn ______ the light" with one of the words from the sentence, "One of them went out the door and into the street."

By having students engage in a series of such tasks, the author of the test claims that "level of reading comprehension" will be measured. However, the author acknowledges that the test does not assess "the sustaining of comprehension throughout continuous passages." This limitation seems a critical one because a major goal of reading-comprehension instruction, and therefore of comprehension assessment, is most certainly to produce students capable of comprehending continuous passages.

Because the task requirement of the test is limited to the comprehension of single sentences, with some degree of reference to a second sentence, it appears that the type of comprehension measured is rather narrow. In fact, the test seems to have more in common with vocabulary rather than comprehension measures. Moreover, the task requirement does not appear to reflect typical modes of responding during common reading activities. Nevertheless, it is possible that performance on these paired sentence completion exercises might be correlated with aspects of reading comprehension that are important for teachers to know. However, no data are presented to support such a claim. Indeed, no information on the validity of the test is offered.

Reliability data are provided by reporting the intercorrelation of the two forms of the Wide-Span Reading Test, Forms A and B. Since the correlation between the two forms at each grade level ranges from .89 to .95, the two forms appear to be measuring much the same thing.

The instructions for administering the test are straightforward. However, since the manual stresses the need to time the 30-minute work period accurately to the second, it is odd that the first four items are in view on the first page while instructions and examples are being discussed. Since accuracy in timing is so important, the test items should begin on the next page to avoid having students read ahead.

The scoring procedures are clear except for an instruction to enter the total number correct in a cell marked "I" at the bottom of the answer sheet. Since there are several cells at the bottom of the page, but none marked "I," users may be confused. Apparently the intended cell is the one marked l on the answer sheet.

Besides measuring level of reading comprehension, another purpose of the Wide-Span Reading Test is "to indicate the areas of reading skill within which low-scoring children may have difficulty." To achieve this purpose, teachers are directed to have students take the test in the usual manner (i.e., students are given 30 minutes to work on the test beginning at the designated starting point for their grade level). Then, immediately afterward, students are instructed to go back to a specific earlier point and work those problems as well. Because first and second year junior school students begin the test at item 1, they of course do not have to go back; but all other students do.

There are some problems with the instructions for using the test for diagnosis. First, the section opens with a sentence that seems to say that the diagnostic use is only for third year juniors and up: "The method of working the test for the purposes of diagnosis (third year juniors and above only) is . . ." Actually, the sentence is misleading because the test is claimed to be useful diagnostically even for the younger grades. Second, teachers are given contradictory instructions regarding how long students should be allowed to work once they are sent back to earlier test sections. Teachers are told to "Allow as much time as is necessary for each child to reach the point at which he first began." But then the very next sentence says "Allow no more than thirty minutes."

After scoring the students' responses, teachers are to identify which students have at least 10 errors within a specified set of items for their grade level. The author notes that only those students' papers can be marked diagnostically.

The teacher is then to examine each incorrect item within the designated set and classify the error as a decoding, linguistic (syntax), or vocabulary error. The error is to be marked "decoding" if the student has inverted letter order, or omitted, substituted, or added letters "which detract from the phonetic representation of the word." The question arises as to whether an error in writing can be equated with ability to decode, but the point is not discussed.

A key is provided to guide teachers in categorizing linguistic and vocabulary errors. For instance, for the sentence "When logs ______, smoke rises," students are to select the missing word from "Brush up the leaves and burn them." The correct answer is "burn." The diagnostic answer key indicates that if the incorrect response is "brush," it is a vocabulary error. However, it is not always clear why a given response is classified in a certain way. Why, for instance, could not "brush" be a decoding error? Errors can also be coded as being from two "error" categories. But the marking key gives no examples to assist teachers in making such a judgement.

If half or more of the total errors occur in any of the three areas, then the claim is made that a "positive diagnostic indication is given" that indicates "prima facie evidence of the general nature of the handicap that contributes to the child's reading comprehension difficulty." However, because no evidence is offered regarding the validity or reliability of the results, it does not seem worthwhile to expend the effort required to obtain this diagnostic information. Indeed, even if teachers make the effort, they are told that the lack of "diagnostic indication" does not rule out a reading difficulty. Moreover, even when a "diagnostic indication" is found, more specific diagnosis is recommended. Consequently, it would seem more productive simply to omit the diagnostic use of this test. Instead, teachers could give an in-depth diagnostic measure to students who do not do well in reading.

In summary, although the Wide-Span Reading Test is reliable and easy to administer, there is no information on its validity for the stated purpose of assessing students' reading comprehension level. Moreover, neither reliability nor validity data are provided for the diagnostic use of the test. The manual's acknowledgement that the test does not measure the comprehension of continuous passages, along with the lack of data on how the test correlates with different aspects of typical reading, should signal prospective users to consider carefully whether this test meets their needs.

Review of the Wide-Span Reading Test by PRISCILLA A. DRUM, Associate Professor of Education, Graduate School of Education, University of California at Santa Barbara, Santa Barbara, CA:

The purpose of the Wide-Span Reading Test is to measure the level of reading comprehension "within the range defined by the beginning of competent silent reading and the full development of reading comprehension effectiveness." The test was developed and normed in Great Britain in 1972. The 1984 revision is limited to changes in the test manual, for both the actual tests and the standardization sample appear to be those obtained in 1972.

DESCRIPTION. This is a group test with exactly 30 minutes allotted for answering the questions after the preliminary instructions are provided. There are two forms of the test, Form A and Form B, so pre- and post-tests can be given to measure increases in level of comprehension. The intercorrelations between the two forms are quite high, ranging from .89 to .95 for the eight grades tested, with relatively small estimates of the standard error of measurement. However, parallel-forms reliability is the only type of reliability information provided; no test-retest, internal consistency, or item data are given.

The standardization sample appears adequate, though again, only the number and sex at each grade are noted. The manual attests to the representativeness of the sample for types of schools and geographical regions throughout England and Wales. No breakdown is provided.

FORMAT. This test differs from the typical question-stem and multiple-choice-recognition formats of most reading achievement tests. The format of the test is a modified Cloze, with each item consisting of two sentences placed side by side on the page. The stem sentence on the right side has one word deleted. The deleted item can occur at any position within the sentence from the first to the last word. The task is to select the most appropriate word from the sentence on the left side to complete the meaning of the stem sentence on the right side. The number of choices depends on the length of the left sentence, from 6 to 22 words. The guessing factor of selecting one out of four or five choices is avoided. Also, the answer cannot be selected without examining both sentences.

STUDENT LEVEL. The age range given for the test is 7-0 to 14-11 years, or the four junior years and the first four secondary years in English schools (equivalent to second grade through ninth grade in the United States). The item suggested for beginning the test increases from item 1 for the first and second junior years up to item 57 for the fourth secondary year. However, the average performance of 7-year-olds is 1 to 6 items correct and for 8-year-olds 3 to 12 items correct. Since the intent is to measure competent silent reading comprehension, this test should probably not be used until the third year of school. Also, the number of items available for the fourth secondary year, 24 items, is too few to establish adequate discrimination between students of differing abilities. Based on data from the "second occasion" (or second testing) tables, a raw score of one item correct is equivalent to a -1.33 standard deviation for a 14-year-old on the fourth year test, while the same score for a 14-year-old on the 35-item third year test is equivalent to a -2.40 standard deviation. The age for testing and the raw scores have not changed, only the entry level and the number of items available have. Thus, the effective range for this test is somewhat more limited than that recommended by the author.

The sentence items do increase in difficulty, but not just in the manner described in the manual (i.e., "complexity of the incomplete sentence, the embeddedness of the missing word in the second sentence, and the counter-suggestions of inappropriate alternatives"). Both the target and the cue sentences do increase in length, resulting in more elaborated phrases and dependent clauses. However, the target sentence for item 1, Form B, ends with a subordinate clause. Passive constructions and the use of verbals are more prevalent in the later items. But the two major sources of difficulty are the decreasing frequency of the vocabulary used and the changing content of the sentences from familiar, concrete events to abstractions and/or more technical information. The lack of any systematic description for the content of this test beyond the phrases quoted above is the major weakness of this test.

VALIDITY. The test looks like a reading comprehension test; it has face validity. But there is no reference in the manual to any theory of reading comprehension; no model is provided for levels of comprehension. In fact, there is no attempt to provide any type of validity information. How the test was developed and evaluated cannot be determined. The conversion tables for reading age, percentile rankings, and standard scores indicate that older students have more correct answers, but do these scores correlate with school performance measures or with subsequent educational attainments? These questions are not answered. More than this, if a class or a school performs poorly as compared with similar grades in the normative sample, what instruction should be provided? Without attention to construct and content validity, a score on this test can only provide comparative standings. Items are not categorized into types, nor is any item data provided except for a few brief notes on the recommended diagnostic procedures.

The diagnostic portion of the test would be difficult to implement and the results not particularly informative if done. The test administrator would have to decide in advance to proceed with the diagnostic phase because it follows immediately after the regular 30-minute test. The students in the third year and beyond now begin at a designated item prior to the item where they initially began. Each student is given an additional 30 minutes to answer the earlier items and to "look over the work you have already done." The error responses are then individually scored as indicating decoding problems (any type of misspelling), linguistic problems (selection of any word from the cue sentence other than the correct choice or an incorrect choice that is identified as a vocabulary error), and vocabulary problems (selection of a designated vocabulary word error from the cue sentence). Ten or more errors in any of the three error categories indicate the general nature of the child's reading difficulties. It is noted that an error can indicate conjoint problems, for instance, both linguistic and vocabulary. Again, no rationale is provided for the diagnostic procedures, nor any substantiation that 10 or more errors do identify a general problem area. There appears to be little point, even if feasible, to follow the diagnostic steps.

RECOMMENDATION. In summary, the Wide-Span Reading Test is an imaginative test of reading comprehension that could be useful in numerous research studies in both timed and untimed sessions to see if those students who do not have knowledge of the vocabulary used could figure out the answers by using the information in both the cue and the target sentence. As described, this test provides a measure of a student's ability to evaluate vocabulary in context. Also, major test publishers in the United States should examine this test as a basis for constructing reading comprehension tests. The format offers many ideas for better testing procedures.

However, this test cannot be recommended for classroom testing; too much of the information required by the American Psychological Association's *Standards for Educational and Psychological Testing* (AERA, APA, NCME, 1985) is simply not provided, particularly answers concerning the validity of the test.

REVIEWER'S REFERENCE

American Educational Research Association, American Psychological Association, & National Council on Measurement in Education. (1985). *Standards for educational and psychological testing*. Washington, DC: American Psychological Association, Inc.

[391]

Woodcock Reading Mastery Tests—Revised. Purpose: Measures "several important aspects of reading ability." Kindergarten through adult; 1973–87; WRMT-R; 6 test scores: 4 Reading Achievement tests (Word Identification, Word Attack, Word Comprehension, Passage Comprehension); 2 Readiness tests (Letter Identification, Visual-Auditory Learning), and a Supplementary Letter Checklist; 5 derived scores for clusters (Readiness, Basic Skills, Reading Comprehension, Total Reading—Full Scale, Total Reading—Short Scale; individual; 2 forms: G, H (includes Reading Achievement tests only); 1988 price data: $149 per Form G and Form H combined kit including Form G and Form H test plates in easel, 25 test records for each form, sample Form G+H test record, pronunciation guide cassette, sample report to parents, and examiner's manual ('87, 182 pages); $89.50 per Form G complete kit including Form G test plates in easel, 25 Form G test records, and additional materials as in combined kit; $84.50 per Form H complete kit including Form H test plates in easel, 25 Form H test records, and additional materials as in combined kit; $16 per 25 Form G or Form H test records; $12 per 25 Form G+H test records; $10 per 25 report to parents forms; $8 per pronunciation guide cassette; $20 per examiner's manual; (40–45) minutes entire battery, (15) minutes Short Scale; Richard W. Woodcock; American Guidance Service.*

See T3:2641 (17 references); for reviews by Carol Anne Dwyer and J. Jaap Tuinman, and excerpted reviews by Alex Bannatyne, Richard L. Allington, Cherry Houck (with Larry A. Harris), and Barton B. Proger of the 1973 edition, see 8:779 (7 references).

TEST REFERENCES

1. Cahill, J. (1981). Towards model refinement in compensatory education: Comparison of intervention programs and paraprofessional screening measures. *American Journal of Community Psychology*, 9, 731-749.

2. McHugh, L. M., & Buss, R. R. (1981). Diagnostic and prescriptive decisions made by specialists and classroom teachers: Quadratic assignment as a reliability measure. *National Reading Conference Yearbook*, 30, 137-143.

3. Appelbaum, A. S., & Tuma, J. M. (1982). The relationship of the WISC-R to academic achievement in a clinical population. *Journal of Clinical Psychology*, 38, 401-405.

4. Deno, S. L., Mirkin, P. K., & Chiang, B. (1982). Identifying valid measures of reading. *Exceptional Children*, 49, 36-45.

5. Gold, P. C., & Horn, P. L. (1982). Achievement in reading, verbal language, listening comprehension and locus of control of adult illiterates in a volunteer tutorial project. *Perceptual Motor Skills*, 54, 1243-1250.

6. Alexander, P. A., White, C. S., & Mangano, N. (1983). Examining the effects of direct instruction in analogical reasoning on reading comprehension. *National Reading Conference Yearbook*, 32, 36-42.

7. Duffy, G. G., Book, C., & Roehler, L. R. (1983). A study of direct teacher explanation during reading instruction. *National Reading Conference Yearbook*, 32, 295-303.

8. Prasse, D. P., Siewert, J. C., & Breen, M. J. (1983). An analysis of performance on Reading Subtests from the 1978 Wide Range Achievement Test and Woodcock Reading Mastery Test with WISC-R for learning disabled and regular education students. *Journal of Learning Disabilities*, 16, 458-461.

9. Simpson, R. G., & Eaves, R. C. (1983). The concurrent validity of the Woodcock Reading Mastery Tests relative to the Peabody Individual Achievement Test among retarded adolescents. *Educational and Psychological Measurement*, 43, 275-281.

10. Bos, C. S., & Filip, D. (1984). Comprehensive monitoring in learning disabled and average students. *Journal of Learning Disabilities*, 17, 229-233.

11. Breen, M. J., Lehman, J., & Carlson, M. (1984). Achievement correlates of the Woodcock-Johnson Reading and Mathematics subtests, Key Math, and Woodcock Reading in an elementary aged learning disabled population. *Journal of Learning Disabilities*, 17, 258-261.

12. Calhoun, M. L., & Allegretti, C. L. (1984). Processing of short vowels, long vowels, and vowel digraphs by disabled and non-disabled readers. *Perceptual and Motor Skills*, 59, 951-956.

13. Chandler, H. N. (1984). The American public school: Yes, we have no standards. *Journal of Learning Disabilities*, 17, 186-187.

14. Mann, V. A., & Liberman, I. Y. (1984). Phonological awareness and verbal short-term memory. *Journal of Learning Disabilities*, 17, 592-599.

15. Sandoval, J. (1984). Repeating the first grade: How the decision is made. *Psychology in the Schools*, 21, 457-462.

16. Simpson, R. G., Haynes, M. D., & Haynes, W. O. (1984). The relationship between performance on the Wepman Auditory Discrimination Test and reading achievement among adolescents. *Educational and Psychological Measurement*, 44, 353-358.

17. Thomas, B. (1984). Early toy preferences of four-year-old readers and nonreaders. *Child Development*, 55, 424-430.
18. Wilson, L. R., & Cone, T. (1984). The regression equation method of determining academic discrepancy. *Journal of School Psychology*, 22, 95-110.
19. Connelly, J. B. (1985). Published tests—which ones do special education teachers perceive as useful? *Journal of Special Education*, 19, 149-155.
20. Franklin, M. R., Jr., Fullilove, R. M., & Sabers, D. L. (1985). Woodcock analogies: Effect of additional practice and instruction for learning-disabled students. *Journal of Learning Disabilities*, 18, 521-523.
21. Hahn, A. L. (1985). Teaching remedial students to be strategic readers and better comprehenders. *The Reading Teacher*, 39, 72-77.
22. Horn, C. C., & Manis, F. R. (1985). Normal and disabled readers' use of orthographic structure in processing print. *Journal of Reading Behavior*, 17, 143-161.
23. Katz, R. B., & Shankweiler, D. (1985). Repetitive naming and the detection of word retrieval deficits in the beginning reader. *Cortex*, 21, 617-625. Tests—Revised):
24. Kistner, J. A. (1985). Attentional deficits of learning-disabled children: Effects of rewards and practice. *Journal of Abnormal Child Psychology*, 13, 19-31.
25. Reynolds, C. R., Willson, V. L., & Chatman, S. P. (1985). Regression analyses of bias on the Kaufman Assessment Battery for Children. *Journal of School Psychology*, 23, 195-204.
26. Scruggs, T. E., Bennion, K., & Lifson, S. (1985). An analysis of children's strategy use on reading achievement tests. *Elementary School Journal*, 85, 479-484.
27. Sherman, R. G., Berling, B. S., & Oppenheimer, S. (1985). Increasing community independence for adolescents with spina bifida. *Adolescence*, 20, 1-13.
28. Stanovich, K. E. (1985). Cognitive determinants of reading in mentally retarded individuals. *International Review of Research in Mental Retardation*, 13, 181-214.
29. Caskey, W. E., Jr. (1986). The use of the Peabody Individual Achievement Test and the Woodcock Reading Memory Tests in the diagnosis of a learning disability in reading: A caveat. *Journal of Learning Disabilities*, 19, 336-337.
30. Catts, H. W. (1986). Speech production/phonological deficits in reading-disordered children. *Journal of Learning Disabilities*, 19, 504-508.
31. Fuchs, L. S., Fuchs, D., & Tindal, G. (1986). Effects of mastery learning procedures on student achievement. *The Journal of Educational Research*, 79, 286-291.
32. Howell, M. J., & Manis, F. R. (1986). Developmental and reader ability differences in semantic processing efficiency. *Journal of Educational Psychology*, 78, 124-129.
33. Kamhi, A. G., & Catts, H. W. (1986). Toward an understanding of developmental language and reading disorders. *Journal of Speech and Hearing Disorders*, 51, 337-347.
34. Manis, F. R., Szeszulski, P. A., Howell, M. J., & Horn, C. C. (1986). A comparison of analogy- and rule-based decoding strategies in normal and dyslexic children. *Journal of Reading Behavior*, 18, 203-218.
35. Voeller, K. K. S. (1986). Right-hemisphere deficit syndrome in children. *American Journal of Psychiatry*, 143, 1004-1009.
36. Henderson, J. G., Jr. (1987). Effects of depression upon reading: A case study for distinguishing effortful from automatic processes. *Perceptual and Motor Skills*, 64 (1), 191-200.
37. Manis, F. R., Savage, P. L., Morrison, F. J., Horn, C. C., Howell, M. J., Szeszulski, P. A., & Holt, L. K. (1987). Paired associate learning in reading-disabled children: Evidence for a rule-learning deficiency. *Journal of Experimental Child Psychology*, 43, 25-43.
38. Simpson, R. G., & Halpin, G. (1987). The effects of altering the ceiling criterion on the passage comprehension test of the Woodcock Reading Mastery Test. *Educational and Psychological Measurement*, 47 (1), 215-221.

Review of the Woodcock Reading Mastery Tests—Revised, by ROBERT B. COOTER, JR., Associate Professor of Elementary Education, Brigham Young University, Provo, UT:

INTRODUCTION. The Woodcock Reading Mastery Tests (WRMT) were first published in 1973 by American Guidance Service offering reading professionals a unique blend of norm- and criterion-referenced measures. However, the WRMT was almost instantly plunged into controversy. For proponents, the tests offered a rather comprehensive diagnostic review of important reading skill areas along with impressive and robust normative data. On the other hand, critics of the WRMT considered the splintering of the reading act into five subskill areas an intolerable perversion yielding questionable diagnoses.

American Guidance Service recently (1987) released the Woodcock Reading Mastery Tests—Revised. This review will briefly describe the WRMT-R, compare the revised tests to their earlier version, and examine how the authors have attempted to retain elements praised by proponents while adding new components to satisfy the critics.

DESCRIPTION. The Woodcock Reading Mastery Tests—Revised (WRMT-R) are a battery of individually administered reading tests surveying several aspects of the reading act primarily for student levels ranging from kindergarten through college senior. While the manual is reportedly written to assist the inexperienced examiner, its level of sophistication is such that formal training would be desirable, such as through graduate courses in reading diagnosis.

The WRMT-R is comprised of six tests (Visual-Auditory Learning, Letter Identification, Word Identification, Word Attack, Word Comprehension, and Passage Comprehension), and a two-part supplementary letter checklist, all contained in an easel kit. Two forms of the WRMT-R are available (Forms G and H) to assist teachers and researchers needing pre- and posttest measurements. The first test, Visual-Auditory Learning, is a seven-item exercise borrowed from the Woodcock-Johnson Psycho-Educational Battery (Woodcock & Johnson, 1977). Its purpose is to measure the subject's ability to learn to read unfamiliar graphic symbols that represent familiar words, then translate sequences of these symbols which have been connected to form sentences. A vocabulary totaling 26 words and two word endings (-ing, -s) is presented.

Letter Identification is the second test consisting of 51 items that require subjects to recognize alphabet characters in a variety of type forms. A new Supplementary Letter subtest has been added that presents letters only in the sans serif type style commonly used in basal reading materials. This addition is apparently in response to critics who complained that the 1973 Letter Identification test required subjects to read type styles uncommon to most published materials.

The Word Identification and Word Attack tests remain essentially unchanged. As with the 1973 version, the Word Identification test requires subjects to identify words in isolation. There are 106 items on each form arranged in order of difficulty. The Word Attack test consists of 45 nonsense words, beginning with simple one-syllable patterns (e.g., ip, din) and progressing to more complex combinations (e.g., ceisminadolt, gnouthe). While the use of nonsense words on reading assessment measures has been attacked by critics, the authors defend the practice stating "the task faced by a subject encountering a nonsense word closely simulates the real-life task of a person encountering an unknown-though real-word." An audio cassette is provided to help examiners learn the desired pronunciations.

Word Comprehension is the most changed test in the battery. It is comprised of three subtests—Antonyms, Synonyms, and Analogies. The Analogies subtest has been retained from the 1973 edition wherein students are required to supply the final word in a four-word sequence (e.g., on-off: in-_______). Critics of the 1973 WRMT stated that analogies comprise only one type of comprehension, and note that it is a rather sophisticated comprehension task at that. The WRMT-R authors have responded by adding an Antonyms or word opposites subtest (e.g., up-down, south-*north*), and a Synonyms subtest (e.g., mug-cup, dad-*father*). An added feature of the Word Comprehension test allows examiners to evaluate students across four reading vocabularies—General Reading, Science-Mathematics, Social Studies, and Humanities.

Passage Comprehension is the final test which utilizes a modified cloze format. This 68-item exercise requires students to identify key words missing from each passage selected from various reading materials (e.g., textbooks, newspapers, and "typical" household and business documents).

The primary differences between the WRMT-R and the 1973 version seem to be the addition of the Visual-Auditory Learning test, the inclusion of two new subtests in the Word Comprehension test, the expansion of norms tables to include adults, new procedures for computing the Summary of Scores, and the inclusion of diagnostic profiles for comparing supplementary test scores (WRMT-R Manual, 1987).

ADMINISTRATION AND SCORING. The administration guidelines in the WRMT-R manual are precise and exceptionally well-written. Included is a Checklist for Examiner Training Activities to assist both experienced and inexperienced examiners in completing training activities with the new form. Each of the reading tests has a title page in the Easel Kit directing the examiner to the appropriate starting points. The basal and ceiling criteria for each of the tests are six or more consecutive items either passed or failed. However, it is suggested that entire pages be completed even if the ceiling level is reached at midpage.

A variety of information can be derived from the raw scores. Stating that interpretation "of a subject's test performance should only be done to produce information that will actually be utilized," the authors suggest that three "degrees" or levels of evaluation may be derived from the WRMT-R. In the first degree, the examiner obtains grade equivalent scores, instructional ranges, and strengths and weaknesses among the skills measured. Interpretations to the second degree provide more normative information; and third degree interpretations provide such data as age and grade equivalents, a variety of standard scores, standard error of measurement confidence bands for percentile ranks, standard scores, and the Relative Performance Index or RPI (known as the Relative Mastery Score on the 1973 edition). Although the manual states that only 15 to 30 minutes would be required to complete all three levels of interpretation, 45 to 60 minutes may actually be needed in many cases.

In order to ease the burden of scoring the WRMT-R and to help assure accuracy, the publishers have developed a microcomputer software package called ASSIST. As with the 1973 ASSIST package for the WRMT, this is a user friendly, menu-driven program compatible to most IBM PC and Apple II series microcomputers. After demographic information and raw scores are entered into the microcomputer, conversion of raw scores to age and grade equivalents, percentile rankings, standard scores, and other interpretations mentioned above occurs within seconds. The ASSIST package is well worth the investment and will quickly repay examiners in time saved.

TECHNICAL DATA. The WRMT-R was normed on a sample of 6,089 subjects in what has been described as 60 geographically diverse communities. Communities were selected with respect to socioeconomic characteristics matching the 1980 U.S. Census. Of this number, 4,201 subjects were in grades K–12, 1,023 subjects were considered college/university students, and the remaining 865 subjects were categorized as age 20 to over 80 and not enrolled in college. Subjects were randomly selected using a stratified sampling design which controlled for specific community and subject variables. Data were analyzed using the Rasch (1960) model.

Reliabilities were calculated using the split-half procedure and were corrected for length with the Spearman-Brown formula. Split-half reliability coefficients for each of the tests ranged from a low of .34 (grade 5 of the Letter Identification test) to a high of .98 (grade 1 of the Word Identification test). Median split-half reliability coefficients ranged from .84 to .98 for Forms G or H.

Two sources of evidence are discussed regarding validity of the WRMT-R. Content validity refers to the match between test items and the curriculum that has been taught (Farr & Carey, 1986). Under this heading evidence should be presented indicating that the test items are representative of not only the curriculum, but also the psychological processes involved in the reading act for each grade/age level surveyed. However, no direct evidence is presented to substantiate content validity. The authors state that the WRMT-R items were developed with the assistance of "outside experts" and experienced teachers, but sources of the items are not revealed.

Concurrent validity indicates how effective a test is as compared to other similar tests in measuring a student's behavior. Again, it is difficult to find support for this aspect of validity in what has been presented by the authors. The first table (Table 5.4) presents correlation statistics between the WRMT-R with the Woodcock-Johnson Reading Tests. Because both tests were authored by the same individual, it seems implausible that this exercise constitutes a comparison between "independent criterion measures." The second table presents correlation statistics between the 1973 version of the WRMT and selected reading measures, but not data pertaining to the 1987 revised forms. Thus, satisfactory evidence regarding any validity aspect of the WRMT-R is lacking, leaving users to decide for themselves the appropriateness of these tests.

COMMENTS AND EVALUATION. Much has been written in recent months regarding the state of reading assessment. Some have stated categorically that instruments like the WRMT-R are useless and represent a bygone age that viewed the reading act in a fractured or splintered way. Others have indicated that standardized reading measures still have a place in the future when used intelligently, as part of an overall evaluation (Calfee, 1987). It is the latter philosophy which tempers these brief closing comments.

The WRMT-R authors have seemingly made a good faith effort to address some of the criticisms of the 1973 version. New subtests have been added to the Comprehension test to better represent current theory, explanations have been offered for the Word Attack test format, and an optional Supplementary Letter Checklist is provided which uses standard letter forms only.

Other improvements include expanded norms for adult students, provisions for examiner training, an extremely useful and informative examiner's manual, and the ASSIST microcomputer package for scoring. Reliability estimates are generally quite high, but appropriate tables should be consulted to determine the appropriateness of a given test for specific students.

Some criticisms of the 1973 WRMT remain valid for the revised edition. First and perhaps foremost is that reading is assessed in fragments rather than holistically. While this feature allows for more reliable testing, validity suffers proportionately. Second, by attempting to serve subjects from kindergarten to old age, it is doubtful that any will be served well.

Finally, the WRMT-R has some problems with administration and scoring. The tests can be very long and tedious for students. Scoring errors occur frequently for beginning examiners as they work through the numerous tables. Obviously, the ASSIST microcomputer software program could help examiners avoid these problems in scoring, but that presumes an additional outlay of funds for software, not to mention a microcomputer.

In summary, the Woodcock Reading Mastery Tests—Revised is a reliable instrument useful in measuring some aspects of the reading process. Used in conjunction with the more valid process-oriented measures, the WRMT-R can potentially contribute to a thorough review of a subject's reading growth.

REVIEWER'S REFERENCES

Woodcock, R. W., & Johnson, M. B. (1977). Woodcock-Johnson Psycho-Educational Battery. Allen, TX: DLM Teaching Resources.

Laffey, J. L., & Kelley, D. (1979). Test review: Woodcock Reading Mastery Tests. *The Reading Teacher*, 33 (3), 335-339.

Farr, R., & Carey, R. F. (1986). *Reading: What can be measured?* (2nd ed.). Newark, DE: International Reading Association.

Calfee, R. C. (1987). The school as a context for assessment of literacy. *The Reading Teacher*, 40 (8), 738-743.

Review of the Woodcock Reading Mastery Tests—Revised, by RICHARD M. JAEGER, Professor and Director, Center for Educational Research and Evaluation, University of North Carolina at Greensboro, Greensboro, NC:

This battery of individually administered tests is claimed to assess important aspects of reading readiness and reading ability for examinees of widely differing age and education. Norms are provided for pupils and students from the beginning of kindergarten through the senior year in college, and for out-of-school adults beyond age 75.

As was true of the 1973 edition of the Woodcock Reading Mastery Tests (WRMT), two forms of the battery are provided. Form G alone contains a 134-item Visual-Auditory Learning Test and a 51-item Letter Identification Test, in addition to Supplementary Letter Checklists composed of 27 capital letters and 36 lowercase letters. The two test scores are combined to form a "Reading Readiness Cluster" score. Both Form G and Form H of the WRMT-R contain Word Identification tests (106 items per form), Word Attack tests (45 items per form), Word Comprehension tests (146 items per form), and Passage Comprehension tests (68 items per form). An examinee's performances on Word Identification and Word Attack are averaged to compute a Basic Skills Cluster score; performances on Word Comprehension and Passage Comprehension are averaged to compute a Reading Comprehension Cluster score. Applications that require two assessments of examinees' reading performances, such as pretreatment/posttreatment evaluations of instructional programs, are made feasible by the existence of two forms of the WRMT-R.

REVISIONS SINCE 1973. The 1973 edition of the WRMT has been expanded in a number of ways. A Visual-Auditory Learning test has been added. Together with the Letter Identification test, which was present in the 1973 battery, this test yields a Readiness Cluster score. The Word Comprehension test of the 1973 edition has been generalized through the addition of subtests that require generation of antonyms and synonyms of stimulus words. The verbal analogies items in the 1973 edition have been retained in this test. Stimulus words have been purposefully selected from content areas labeled "General Reading," "Science-Mathematics," "Social Studies," and "Humanities." The Examiners Manual includes instructions for computing separate vocabulary scores in the four content areas, in addition to a total Word Comprehension score. Derived scores on two of the tests, Word Identification and Passage Comprehension, can be averaged to produce a "Short Scale Total Reading Score," should an examiner wish to avoid administration of the entire battery.

A norm-referenced score that is peculiar to the WRMT-R, termed the "Relative Performance Index (RPI)" is represented as a ratio, in contrast to a logically similar score termed the "Relative Mastery Score" in the 1973 battery. Information on the derivation of this score scale is not provided in the Examiners Manual. The age range of the norms tables has been expanded considerably, and a number of nomographs have been developed for recording scores in ways that yield approximate 68-percent prediction intervals for common derived-score scales, such as grade equivalent units, deviation-IQ-like standard scores, and percentile ranks.

TEST CONTENT. Although the admonition "don't judge a book by its cover" should always be applied when selecting a test, it is particularly applicable to the WRMT-R. The tasks contained in this test battery are unique, and often differ substantially from those of other batteries with similar test and subtest titles. Thus the measurement claims of the Examiners Manual should be considered thoughtfully as the items in each subtest are carefully examined. The Visual-Auditory Learning test was originally published as a part of the Woodcock-Johnson Psycho-Educational Battery in 1977. It is claimed to be a "miniature 'learning-to-read' task," in that it requires the association of common, mostly single-syllable words with figural patterns. Many of the contrived figures support obvious semantic links with the words they represent, although some do not. For example, a stylized stick figure wearing an appropriate hat is associated with a stimulus word for a person with an occupational title that is common in children's stories. Although reading Japanese Kanji characters obviously requires the formation of visual-auditory linkages of the sort measured by the WRMT-R Visual-Auditory Learning test, it is not obvious that the skill measured by this test generalizes to the auditory-visual linkages required by printed or written English. As a case in point, the figures in the test have neither phonemic correlates nor compositional regularity across words.

One would expect a test titled Letter Identification to require oral naming of the letters of the alphabet in response to common printed forms, including the typefaces often found in children's books, newspapers, and other widely read sources. However, the WRMT-R Letter Identification test presents the letter of the alphabet in a wide variety of forms, including upper and lower case, roman, italic, bold type, serif and sans serif type faces, cursive, and several relatively obscure fonts that are seen only in documents produced by those who are fascinated with the capabilities of Macintosh microcomputers, such as London and Calligraphy. According to the Examiners Manual, these items "may measure associational skills or form constancy." Their value in assessing commonly accepted conceptions of readiness to read is not obvious, nor is it likely they assess the same construct as the items that present letters in more typical forms and formats. This latter observation is especially pertinent because each of the WRMT-R tests is scaled through the use of a Rasch item response theory model that assumes all items measure a single ability dimension.

The Word Identification test contains few surprises. An examiner presents lists of three to nine printed stimulus words, and asks the examinee to pronounce each one. The words contained in the test range from those found in early elementary school readers to polysyllabic tongue-twisters likely to be familiar only to persons whose leisure hours are spent perusing the *Oxford English Dictionary*. The Manual advises examiners to attend to the strategies examinees use when faced with unfamiliar words, presumably as a device for assessing their reliance on phonics or purely visual cues. Oral identification of individually presented words has been faulted as a useful measure of sight vocabulary, because examinees cannot make use of semantic context cues.

The Word Attack test contains nonsense words composed of two to three letters (in the lowest-numbered items) to 13 letters and four syllables (in some of the highest-numbered items). The test is claimed to assess examinees' phonic and structural analysis abilities when faced with unfamiliar real words. Detailed analyses of errors on specific phonemes are recommended, unfortunately without accompanying cautions on the possibly low reliability of such interpretations.

The Word Comprehension test requires antonyms or synonyms in response to stimulus words that vary widely in length and obscurity, as well as single-word completion of analogies of the form '*a* is to *b* as *c* is to ______.' Although the Examiners Manual claims this subtest measures knowledge of word meanings, verbal reasoning ability would also appear to be strongly tapped. The diagnostic and prescriptive value of a low score on this subtest are not obvious, nor is its usefulness for instructional planning.

The Passage Comprehension test presents tasks that differ markedly from those contained in other widely used reading comprehension tests. Each test item presents from one to three sentences. A single word has been omitted from each stimulus passage, and the examinee must supply the missing word orally when shown the stimulus passage in printed form. Twenty-two of 68 stimulus passages have an accompanying drawing, but examinees whose reading level is judged by the examiner to be at least at Grade 6 would begin the test with more-difficult items that do not have such drawings. Many of the drawings portray stereotypically gender-linked activities (men in business suits having a conference, and women in domestic roles or with responsibility for child care; boys engaged in contact sports and girls in comparatively passive or pastoral scenes), and all of the persons portrayed are obviously majority whites in clothing that suggests economic security. The use of such gender stereotypic and ethnically restricted stimulus materials is inconsistent with Standard 3.5 of the 1985 *Standards for Educational and Psychological Testing* which states:

> When selecting the type and content of items for tests and inventories, the test developers should consider the content and type in relation to cultural backgrounds and prior experiences of the variety of ethnic, cultural, age, and gender groups represented in the intended population of test takers. (Conditional).

It is also inconsistent with the widespread efforts of major test and textbook publishers to eliminate instructional and examination materials that perpetuate racial, ethnic, and gender stereotypes and to eliminate materials that might advantage some groups of examinees or students in ways that are irrelevant to the objectives of assessment or instruction.

FORMAT AND INSTRUCTIONS. The physical format of the WRMT-R is attractive and sturdy. The test materials are clearly printed on heavy, nonreflective stock that is ring bound in a test booklet that folds out to form a triangular easel. When arranged as suggested in the Examiners Manual, the directions for administration will thus be visible to the examiner, and the stimulus materials will be readily visible to both the examinee and the examiner. The Examiners Manual contains very detailed training materials and instructions for administration, scoring, and interpretation of the WRMT-R, including checklists for assessing the knowledge and preparation of examiners. In this respect, the WRMT-R is a model of sound measurement practice.

TECHNICAL CHARACTERISTICS. The norming samples for the WRMT-R were carefully developed, with appropriate attention to representation of the 1980 U.S. population on a large number of demographic variables. Individual test responses were weighted in an attempt to match the marginal distributions of these variables to the distributions reported for the 1980 U.S. Census of Population. The publisher's success in achieving representativeness for particular norm groups (e.g., first graders) is unknown, as is the degree of success in matching multivariate distributions of demographic characteristics (e.g., central-city white males). The sizes of norming samples reported for selected grade levels and for the overall college and adult populations ranged between 242 and 1,023. These sample sizes afford estimates of percentile ranks that are, at worst, within plus or minus 5 points of true values, with 95 percent confidence.

Norming data for the school-age samples were collected continuously over a 2-year time period. The Examiners Manual claims that this procedure affords accurate percentile rank norms for an examinee's exact age (to the nearest month), and accurate grade-equivalent and age-equivalent values to the nearest tenth of a school year or the nearest month of age, for grades kindergarten through college senior and ages 5 years to 18 years 11 months respectively. In fact, the empirical base for specific age or grade-level percentile rank norms was limited (e.g., an average of 50 subjects at any month of the first grade completed the Word Identification test), and the accuracy and precision of the resulting norms depends on the quality and appropriateness of an undescribed interpolation procedure.

The WRMT-R was "equated" to selected tests from the G-F-W Sound-Symbol Tests and the Woodcock-Johnson Psycho-Educational Battery. The Examiners Manual states that these tests were placed on a common scale. No information on the methodology or the quality of the equating is provided; the equating was based on only 600 cases (which is often insufficient to reduce equating errors to tolerable levels); and the equating of nonparallel tests is inherently suspect. Scoring sheets for the WRMT-R contain "Diagnostic Profiles" that purport to provide comparative information on examinees' performances on these tests on common grade equivalent and Rasch-model-based scales. Although the recommended procedures for using these Profiles are appropriately attentive to the influence of random measurement errors, they ignore bias errors that might result from faulty test equating. Profiles of examinees' scores that include tests outside the WRMT-R should therefore be interpreted cautiously.

Reliabilities reported for the WRMT-R are limited to split-half estimates that were inflated using the Spearman-Brown formula. It is unfortunate that stability coefficients are not reported for the four tests that are common to Forms G and H. Of 34 split-half reliability estimates reported for within-grade or within-age-group samples and test scores on a single form of the WRMT-R, 68 percent were at least .90, 26 percent were between .80 and .89, and 6 percent were less than .80. (The smallest coefficient, .34 for the Letter Identification test administered to fifth graders, demonstrates the ineffectiveness of this test beyond the early elementary school years.) Thus at least two-thirds of the tests were sufficiently reliable for individual diagnoses when used with the standardization samples. However, the Examiners Manual contains numerous claims that the WRMT-R is useful for detailed diagnoses of examinees' reading problems, and the scoring sheets provide spaces for recording several dozen categories of word attack errors in addition to scores on subtests of the Word Comprehension test. On page 36 of the Examiners Manual we find: "Analysis of individual errors can be used as a rich resource with direct implications for planning instruction." No reliability information is provided for such error scores or for subtest scores, but random measurement error would certainly contribute substantially to decisions based on individual test items or small groups of items.

Limited validity data are provided for the WRMT-R. Brief rationales for the content of tests that contribute to the Diagnostic Profiles are given under the heading "Content Validity." Correlations between four of the WRMT-R tests, the full-scale and short-scale Total Reading scores of the WRMT-R, and the Woodcock-Johnson Reading Tests are given for small samples of first-, third-, fifth-, and eighth-graders. These correlations fluctuate substantially across grades, are often modest in size, and with disturbing frequency, are lower for noncorresponding tests than for corresponding tests. For example, in the sample of fifth-graders, the correlation between the Woodcock-Johnson Letter-Word Identification test and the WRMT-R Passage Comprehension test is larger than the correlation between the Woodcock-Johnson Passage Comprehension test and the WRMT-R Passage Comprehension test.

The only other concurrent validity data provided are for the Total Reading score of the 1973 edition of the WRMT and total reading scores of five other widely used batteries. These correlations range between .78 and .92 for samples of 40 to 86 examinees. Although these correlations support the contention that the original WRMT and other reading assessment tests share substantial common variance, they provide no support for the diagnostic interpretations of WRMT-R scores recommended in the Examiners Manual.

Matrices of correlations among the WRMT-R tests and composite scores are provided for five grade-level samples of examinees in addition to college students and adults. Through Grade 11, the skills assessed by the WRMT-R become increasingly differentiated for higher-level grades, and at every grade and age, indicate that the components of the WRMT-R measure distinguishable skills.

CONCLUSIONS. The Woodcock Reading Mastery Tests—Revised provide a unique approach to the measurement of skills associated with reading, as well as normative information for examinees who differ greatly in educational level and age. However, the diagnostic value and instructional planning value of the WRMT-R are debatable, and the evidence offered in support of the reliability and validity of the WRMT-R for the purposes suggested in the Examiners Manual must be judged inadequate. It would be well to regard the results of administering the WRMT-R as tentative hypotheses, to be confirmed through the use of more extensive assessment procedures or intensive observation of examinees performances on "real" reading tasks.

[392]

Word Processing Test. Purpose: "Designed to measure two of the most important operating abilities: inputting and editing material." Applicants and employees; 1985; WPT; 4 scores: Text Input, Table Input, Text Edit, Table Edit; 2 forms: A, B; individual; 1988 price data: $295 per complete kit including 5 test booklets, manual (19 pages), 10 personal scoring records, scoring keys, and edit disk; $195 per 10 input/edit test booklets; $49.50 per 25 personal scoring records; $90 per input/edit scoring keys; $95 per edit disk; $30 per manual; $49 per examination kit (includes test booklet, manual, and personal scoring record); (35) minutes; The Psychological Corporation.*

Review of the Word Processing Test by ROBERT FITZPATRICK, Lecturer, University of Pittsburgh, Pittsburgh, PA:

Typists and secretaries are often selected, and occasionally evaluated on the job, on the basis of a test of typing speed and accuracy. The typist-secretary job family is evolving to become the word-processing-operator job family. The Word Processing Test (WPT) is an extension of the typing test to measure skill in certain aspects of the word processing functions of input and edit, for both text and tabular materials.

The initial version of the WPT is designed for use only with WANG word processing equipment. An IBM version is planned.

The Text Input subtest calls for the examinee to input (type) a business letter exactly as shown, from typed copy. The Table Input subtest is the same, except that the content consists almost entirely of five columns of four-digit numbers. The manual provides no rationale for the choice of material, but implies that it is typical of word processing tasks in business. The text material is said to be "of moderate difficulty."

In the Text Edit and Table Edit subtests, the examinee is to modify material already in the computer, following hand-printed directions on a printed copy of the material. The text and table are similar to those in the Input subtests. Presumably, the examinee is to use various special function keys to insert, delete, move, underline, and otherwise modify parts of the text and table. Typically, there is more than one way to make a given modification, so there is no assurance that the examinee will have used a variety of the function keys.

Detailed and complex scoring directions are given for each subtest. The directions are clear and generally sensible. However, training or conscientious study of the directions appears necessary if scorers are to be accurate and consistent.

In each subtest, the score is a function of both speed and accuracy, with a fairly high weight given to accuracy. Users may wish to consider using separate speed and accuracy scores or a different weighting of errors. However, the normative, reliability, and intercorrelation data are based on the publisher's scoring method.

Percentile norms are provided for 90 employed word processing operators, 57 operators registered with temporary service agencies, and 85 business school students. Large organizations should develop their own norms, and the publisher should expand the available norms for the benefit of small users.

Alternate form reliability coefficients and standard errors of measurement are based on a sample of only 52. The coefficients are highly satisfactory, ranging from .85 to .92, but a larger sample is needed to insure their stability.

No criterion-related validity evidence is reported in the manual. Construct-related evidence is limited to intercorrelations of the subtests, suggesting appropriate degrees of overlap.

The manual asserts: "The validity of the Word Processing Test is inherent in its content." It is true that the content of the WPT bears a superficial resemblance to much word processing work. One may question, however, whether this resemblance is sufficient to produce an adequate degree of validity for typical applications.

Organizations considering using the WPT should compare the test content with the results of their own job analyses. Many users may find differences of some importance. For example, the WPT requires only that the examinee copy material exactly and follow precise directions in modifying it. But typists—and, one presumes, word processing operators—in many organizations must decide about spacing and placement of material on the page. In these organizations, ability to follow straight copy and directions may account for only a little or no part of the job.

The word-processing-operator job family will no doubt continue to evolve. If the evolution is in the direction of more regimentation and less use of judgment by the operator, the WPT may be especially useful. If job tasks and responsibilities evolve in other directions, it seems likely that the WPT will be less applicable.

The WPT is a carefully developed test, with excellent administrative and scoring directions. It is currently limited to use with WANG word processing equipment. For organizations that can confirm its claim to content validity, the WPT should be of value.

[393]

Word Processor Assessment Battery. Purpose: "Measure specific skills and abilities necessary for success in word processing." Word processing students and operators; 1984; WPAB; 3 parts; 1987 price data: $60 per 10 test booklets; $25 per audio dictation cassette for Part III; $25 per examiner's manual (39 pages); Steven J. Stanard; Science Research Associates, Inc.*

a) PART I—MACHINE APTITUDE. 3 scores: Section One, Section Two, Total; 15 minutes per section.

b) PART II—TYPING SPEED AND ACCURACY. 3 scores: Typing Speed, Errors, Net Speed; 5 minutes.

c) PART III—MACHINE TRANSCRIPTION. 4 scores: Punctuation, Spelling, Format, Total; 20 minutes.

Review of the Word Processor Assessment Battery by ROBERT FITZPATRICK, Lecturer, University of Pittsburgh, Pittsburgh, PA:

The Word Processor Assessment Battery (WPAB) is based on an analysis of the word processing operator job. Although the job analysis is described only briefly in the Examiner's Manual, it is apparent that the WPAB was designed to parallel major aspects of the word processor's work.

PART I: MACHINE APTITUDE. The instructions say that Part I "is designed to measure your ability to think logically using word processing concepts." Given a list of codes and their meanings, the examinee is to determine the codes appropriate to each of 30 simulated word processing situations or tasks. In 12 of the items, simple arithmetic calculations are also required.

Some parts of the instructions and some of the code explanations seem unclear (e.g., "Start your answer from where the project is in the problem"). The examinee should "not rely on any word processing knowledge or experience you may have!" Nevertheless, some experienced people may use prior knowledge; it is not obvious whether this would be a net advantage or disadvantage to the examinee.

Examinees write their responses in the Test Battery Booklet, which is not reusable. The process of hand scoring has been made convenient, but will be laborious with large numbers of examinees.

The manual presents three types of reliability information: internal consistency correlations (by KR-20), standard errors of measurement, and parallel forms correlations (with Form B, not for sale at the time of this writing). These data suggest an adequate degree of reliability.

Percentile norms, based on 308 word processing students and 559 experienced word processing operators, are presented in the manual. Score distributions for 53 black students and 25 experienced black operators are also shown.

The manual describes criterion-related validity evidence for two groups of students and two groups of experienced word processing operators. The combined samples number about 350. Validity coefficients for the total score range from .21 to .56 with a weighted mean of .36.

The manual does not argue for the content-related validity of Part I. On the contrary, it says the test "does not necessarily need to resemble job duties since it is a criterion-valid test." But there is evidence of content-related validity, because test content parallels job content in several respects (if the job in the user's organization is similar to those jobs represented in the job analysis).

Construct-related validity evidence is weak; it is not at all clear just what Part I is measuring. Curiously, the manual claims a degree of construct-related validity in asserting "the test appears to also measure the mental abilities needed to understand the quasi-computer functions of word processing equipment."

As is often the case with a new test, the validity data are skimpy. In view of the way in which Part I was developed, its similarities to tests that have been valid for clerical jobs over many years, and the initial criterion-related validity coefficients, it may be argued that it should be reasonably valid for appropriate jobs. On the other hand we have little basis for predictions about the ways in which word processing will be done in the future; a degree of caution in asserting validity for this category of jobs for any test is appropriate.

PART II: TYPING SPEED AND ACCURACY. In Part II, the examinee is to type a letter, from copy consisting of a typed letter with several long-hand insertions, on a page provided in the Test Battery Booklet. The passage was intended to be of "average reading difficulty." The instructions tell the examinee not to stop to correct typing errors; some could argue this is unrealistic if the aim is to simulate the job, but it is a reasonable compromise from a measurement point of view.

The manual recommends that word processing equipment be used for the test only by examinees "who have experience on the brand used by your company. All others should be tested on a typewriter." The manual does not question the possibility the test might measure different skills when used with different types of equipment.

Three scores are suggested: typing speed in five-stroke words per minute, number of errors (as defined with reasonable clarity in the manual), and net typing speed (typing speed minus errors). The formula for net typing speed is, of course, arbitrary; some users may wish to weight errors differently or to dispense entirely with a score purporting to represent both quantity and quality of production.

Percentile norms with typewriter are reported for 600 experienced operators and almost 400 students, and with word processing equipment for 100 experienced operators.

The manual reports test-retest reliability coefficients of .84, .89, and .87 for the three scores with a sample of 57 word processing students. More reliability data are needed.

No criterion-related or construct-related validity evidence is presented. The manual contains evidence for a reasonable degree of content-related validity, because the task and passage seem representative of much word processing work.

PART III: MACHINE TRANSCRIPTION. The examinee's task in Part III is to listen to a taped voice dictating a letter and to type that letter on a page provided in the Test Battery Booklet. The speed of dictation is not reported.

Examinees who do not complete the letter in the 20-minute time limit or whose letters are obviously not "mailable" are counted as having failed Part III. The passing letters are scored for only a sampling of the possible errors and imperfections. A score is derived from punctuation (10 items), spelling (19 items), and format (5 items) subscores. The manual provides no information about subscore means and variances; it seems likely that format contributes little to the total score variance. The scoring system probably makes for good scoring accuracy but may produce some anomalous results. More information about the scoring and the scores is needed.

The manual presents a table of means and standard deviations for 340 experienced operators and 170 students. (In the 1984 version of the manual, there are two errors in this table: The total mean for experienced operators should be 30.57 and the mean for white students should be 30.11.) Test-retest reliability is estimated from a sample of 57 to be .80; more data are needed.

The content-related validity evidence for Part III is similar to that for Part II. No criterion-related or construct-related validity evidence is presented.

OVERALL EVALUATION. The WPAB represents a praiseworthy effort to provide a systematic and comprehensive set of selection procedures for word processing operator jobs. The packaging, in one nonreusable booklet, is convenient if all three parts are used, but wasteful if only one is used.

If the word processing job family remains similar to that of typist and secretary, the WPAB will probably be valid, although one wishes for more evidence more completely presented. If the job family evolves in other directions, the WPAB may or may not be appropriate. The alternatives to the WPAB seem no more attractive. Many using organizations likely will find the WPAB to be congruent with their definitions of word processing operator jobs; for these organizations, it is recommended.

[394]

Work Aptitude: Profile and Practice Set.

Purpose: "Designed specifically to sample the more common abilities needed for the range of jobs to which educational leavers with minimal qualifications can apply." Ages 15–17; 1985; 6 tests: Using Words, Using Your Eyes, Working With Numbers, How Things Work, Being Accurate, Thinking Logically; 1988 price data: £18.95 per 5 test booklets; £3.75 per 30 answer sheets; £6.95 per scoring keys; £9.50 per teacher's manual (32 pages); £10 per specimen set; (5) minutes per test; Saville & Holdsworth Ltd.; Macmillan Education Ltd. [England].*

Review of the Work Aptitude: Profile and Practice Set by KEVIN R. MURPHY, Professor of Psychology, Colorado State University, Fort Collins, CO:

The Work Aptitude: Profile and Practice Set is a vocational counseling tool designed to help "educational leavers with minimum qualifications" in three ways: (*a*) by providing practice with standardized testing techniques, (*b*) by diagnosing strengths and weaknesses in work-related aptitudes, and (*c*) by suggesting methods of developing areas of current weakness. The assumption behind this test is that individuals will be required to take aptitude tests when applying for jobs, and that reductions in test anxiety, increases in test-taking skills, accurate diagnoses of strengths and weaknesses, and efforts to develop work-related aptitudes will all lead to increased employment opportunities.

In evaluating this test, it is useful to consider separately its use as a practice test and its use as an instrument for diagnosis and development. As a practice test, the Work Aptitude: Profile and Practice Set has several exemplary features. First, the subtests are generally representative of tasks that are included on many employment tests. The Using Words and Working With Numbers subtests are similar to standard tests of reading comprehension and basic arithmetic. The Using Your Eyes and Being Accurate tests resemble several embedded figure tests and tests of clerical speed and accuracy. The How Things Work test is very similar to the Bennett Mechanical Comprehension Test (T3:282). Only the Thinking Logically subtest is unique. Second, the test provides very clear directions and detailed descriptions of the test administration procedures. The test provides practice with a wide variety of item types and response formats, and does so in a nonthreatening situation. Although the test is relatively short (total testing time is one hour), the examinee has ample opportunity to practice many of the types of items that are most likely to appear on employment tests. On the whole, this test provides a good opportunity to develop and practice the most basic test-taking skills, and may reduce anxiety at future testings.

Evaluation of the test as an instrument for diagnosis and development is a more complex matter involving both the technical characteristics of the test and the feasibility of substantial development of the abilities tapped by this test. Evidence for the technical adequacy of the test is quite mixed. Evidence for reliability and construct validity is based on a very small sample ($N = 42$), and is somewhat inconclusive. Coefficient alphas for the six subtests are reasonably high, ranging from .50 to .92, with a mean of about .75. Scale intercorrelations are presented, but minimal interpretation is given. In this sample, scale intercorrelations ranged from .39 to .70, with a mean of .53. It is not clear whether the correlations are evidence in favor of construct validity or evidence against construct validity. If the aptitudes measured by this test are assumed to be orthogonal, these correlations would indicate a low level of validity. If it is assumed that the true correlations, corrected for attenuation, are all reasonably high, and invariant from test to test, these data would suggest a high level of construct validity.

Test norms are based on a sample ($N = 589$) that appears to be reasonably representative, and should allow for a clear interpretation to test scores. Unfortunately, the norm table uses a five-division grade system, in which the top 10% of the normative sample form one group (Grade A), the next 20% form the next group (Grade B), and so on. It is not clear that use of such broad categories presents any clear advantage; as the manual notes, a difference of one point could change the norm grade from A to B. No explicit guidelines are presented for determining whether scores on one subtest are significantly higher than scores on another. Given the high correlation among subtests, a relatively substantial difference in test scores would be needed to provide convincing evidence that significant differences exist in work-related aptitudes.

The evidence presented in the test manual does not support the use of this test in diagnosing strengths and weaknesses. First, no evidence is presented to show that the test measures what it is designed to measure. Given the similarity of the subtests to well-established measures of related abilities, it is likely that the tests do possess some level of construct validity, but the question is not even addressed in the test manual. Second, the value of diagnostic feedback based on this test is not well established. Here, the test manual presents an extremely mixed bag. On the one hand, the manual presents very detailed advice regarding feedback, together with examples of job activities that involve each of the aptitudes measured by the test. On the other hand, little evidence is presented linking specific strengths and weaknesses to chances for occupational success. Assume, for example, that an individual was at the 50th percentile in How Things Work, and the 30th percentile in Being Accurate, and at the 70th percentile in Thinking Logically. It is not clear what level of test performance is too low (or too high) for which occupations.

The manual presents suggestions for developing areas in which examinees receive low scores. For example, the manual suggests that scores on tests involving reading comprehension might be improved by reading newspapers or doing crossword puzzles. The use of catalogues, timetables, and reference books is suggested as a method of improving clerical accuracy. The manual does not present any evidence regarding: (*a*) the likelihood that these activities will, in fact, affect the abilities measured by these tests, and (*b*) the amount of change that can reasonably be expected if these activities are pursued. Several of the abilities measured by this test appear to be stable individual differences that might be quite difficult to change. The developmental feedback suggested in the manual may be both unfair and unrealistic; it may be difficult in a short period of time, to produce a meaningful change in any of the attributes measured by this test.

In summary, the Work Aptitude: Profile and Practice Set is probably more useful as a practice test than as an instrument for diagnosis and development. It is clear that individuals who are entering the work world must be prepared to take standardized tests, and the practice and familiarization provided by this test will probably be useful. The use of this test in diagnosis is less well documented; tests such as the USES General Aptitude Test Battery (9:1304) might be preferable for this purpose. The use of this test in developing areas of weakness is even more tenuous. Evidence has not been presented to show this test validly identifies areas of strengths and weaknesses, or that activities provided in the test manual will have a substantial impact on the aptitudes measured by the test.

[395]

World Government Scale. Purpose: Measures attitudes toward world government. Students; 1985; no manual; available without charge from author; [12] minutes; Panos D. Bardis; the Author.*

[396]

The Written Expression Test. Purpose: To "measure written expression objectively." Grades 1–6; 1979–82; WET; 5 scores: Productivity, Mechanics, Handwriting, Maturity, Composite; 1986 price data: $34.95 per test including picture stimulus, scoring forms, and manual ('82, 58 pages); (30) minutes; Clark Johnson and Sharon Hubly; Rocky Mountain Education Systems.*

Review of The Written Expression Test by NOEL GREGG, Director, Learning Disabilities Adult Clinic, College of Education, The University of Georgia, Athens, GA:

The Written Expression Test (WET) was developed in 1978 as a tool that would "measure written expression objectively." A major objective of the instrument was to be easy and quick for classroom teachers to administer to students either individually or in groups. Because it requires showing the students a picture to write about and then takes 5–7 minutes to score, this goal was accomplished. Unfortunately, this particular instrument fails to meet the typical standards of psychometric quality that clinicians have grown to expect from measurement tools used for either clinical or research purposes.

The major weakness of the WET is that it was not based upon any theoretical foundation of written language. While the authors purport to be interested in writing as a "coherent task," the majority of the skills measured are mechanical in nature (i.e., grammar, spelling, handwriting). In the past, written language was investigated only by identifying grammatical types and numbers of sentences produced rather than with the text as a whole. Currently, theorists have attempted to integrate linguistic, psychological, and cultural research to heighten the understanding of the processes involved in the production of written language, particularly the development of form. Much of form is developed in written language by cohesion and coherence, aspects the authors of WET have given little or no attention. Also, the lack of any measure of sense of audience is interesting because this is a key element that contributes to a student's use of form and mechanics. In the authors' attempt to provide measures of interest to "teachers rather than linguists" they have developed a very superficial evaluation tool that ignores the process of writing abilities and looks only at the end product.

The inventory itself consists of an administration manual and an 8 x 10 picture stimulus. The color photograph is of a scene of three elementary students engaged in an activity. While the authors state the picture was "picked because it elicited good compositions from elementary students at all grade levels" they never provide data to document this statement. The manual is a xerox copy of the original typed edition providing a somewhat unprofessional document. The style in which the manual is written is awkward and there are a number of internal contradictions.

A written language composite score is obtained by adding the raw scores of four subtests that include: Productivity, Mechanics, Handwriting, and Maturity. Scaled scores can also be obtained for each of the individual subtests. In the first description of the subtests the authors state that "productivity is simply the number of words in a composition." However, in the scoring section they include both number of words and number of clauses as indexes that comprise the Productivity subtest. No rationale is provided the reader for the counting of clauses. The number of words is used to calculate the ratio norms. These are norms based on the errors per 100 words in a composition. The Mechanics subtest is comprised of spelling, punctuation, and grammar scores. A Handwriting score is obtained by comparing a student's writing sample to a set of criteria that rates it from 1 to 5. Maturity of written language is arrived at by adding a phrase length score (dividing number of clauses in the story by the total number of words), vocabulary development score (number of different words that contain three or more syllables), and a paragraph development and abstractness of theme score (compared to a 7-point scale). All scoring is done as the word or phrase is intended to be written not as it is actually written by the student. A misspelled "word is counted as only one error no matter how many times it is actually misspelled or how many different ways it is misspelled."

The only measure of reliability reported was interrater reliability. However, this was based on only 30 protocols from the first, second, and third grade norming samples. These protocols were randomly chosen and independently scored by each of the authors. The scores were then correlated. The interrater reliabilities ranged from .71 to .99. The authors report that two other reliability studies were conducted but the data had not been analyzed. This reliability information was not available for inspection although the authors promised a technical manual would be published at the end of 1982.

The only reported validity study compared the WET to the Comprehensive Test of Basic Skills (CTBS) reading vocabulary and reading comprehension. It would have been more appropriate to correlate the WET with the Test of Written Language (Hammill & Larsen, 1978). The authors promise further validity studies in the technical manual, which is unavailable.

Scaled scores found in the WET were based on the protocols of more than 660 students. The norms were based on populations from Colorado, Florida, and Wisconsin. However, 80% of the sample came from a predominantly middle-class suburban population. Data on socioeconomic levels and ethnic groups were provided in the administration manual. Scaled scores were provided on individual charts for grades 1 through 6. Means and standard deviations of all subtests were included, as well as a chart describing the scaled scores, percentile equivalents, standard scores, and significance.

Despite the growing interest in the evaluation of written composition, the WET does not appear to be adequate for use either as a research or a clinical instrument. The WET appears to be very similar in format to the Test of Written Language (Hammill & Larsen, 1978) without the excellent reliability and validity data this instrument provides clinicians. Also, the theoretical foundation of the WET is not explained, the development of the instrument unreported, and considerations of psychometric quality unobserved. Therefore, the WET cannot be recommended as an instrument for measuring written language.

REVIEWER'S REFERENCE

Hammill, D. D., & Larsen, S. C. (1978). The Test of Written Language. Austin: PRO-ED, Inc.

Review of The Written Expression Test by LYN HABER, Associate Professor of Psychology, University of Illinois at Chicago, Chicago, IL:

The Written Expression Test (WET) is intended to enable the classroom teacher to measure a student's expressive writing skills objectively. Two interesting and unusual aspects of the WET are that it evaluates written language as a coherent task, instead of as isolated subtests; and it attempts to measure expressive ability as well as mechanics of writing.

The WET has other important practical features: It can be administered either individually or to an entire class; it can be scored in about 5 minutes; and it can be scored by the classroom teacher without additional training.

The picture stimulus provided is an interesting color photograph. The instructions the teacher gives the child(ren) are excellent. In contrast, the accompanying administration and scoring manual is hastily and poorly written, with numerous typographical errors. Scoring instructions are accompanied by examples of scored protocols. The examples are very valuable (more are needed), but the demonstrated scoring is inconsistent with and sometimes contradictory to the instructions provided. The section on Interpretation of Scores is extremely inadequate.

Appropriate validity and reliability measures do not appear in the WET manual (the authors state these data are being collected and analyzed, and will be published at the end of 1982).

The purpose of the WET is to measure written language skills (as opposed to other abilities, such as oral language and reading ability). These abilities are generally highly correlated. In order for the WET to measure written language rather than some general intelligence or language factor, the best validity measure would be to ask teachers to identify two groups of children: those with good writing skills who are poor oral storytellers, and those with poor writing skills who are good oral storytellers. If the WET can discriminate between these two groups, the authors would have evidence the WET measures written expression rather than general scholastic ability or intelligence. (The manual describes a related validity measure, in which an unspecified number of teachers each selected the six best and six poorest writers—grades unspecified. This does not discriminate between written and other kinds of expressive abilities.)

A second and equally critical validity measure is also required: a factor analysis of the raw scores of the tests. The authors group together, for example, under Mechanics three subtests: Spelling, Punctuation, and Grammar. Are these three skills really related? Productivity includes the subtests Number of Words and Number of Clauses, but Clause Length is grouped under Maturity. Should not Clause Length be grouped under Productivity? A factor analysis, based on a sufficient number of children at each grade level, would provide an objective basis for grouping the subtests. Further, the authors weight the subtests equally in obtaining a total score. A regression analysis of the correlations among the subtests would provide a rationale for how to weight the different subtests, weightings that well might change as a function of grade.

The authors mention a test-retest reliability study, using alternative picture stimuli. The results are not provided (but are promised for 1982). The only reliability measure actually presented is interrater reliability between the two authors. A proper interrater study should use teachers, who are the intended scorers of the test and who are presumably less trained than the two authors. The correlations between the two authors would be expected to be the highest possible. In fact, between the two authors' scorings, correlations were very high for the measures requiring only straightforward counting procedures, and barely above significance levels for those involving judgment (i.e., Handwriting and Maturity). These findings reveal the main difficulty with the WET: Several of the present scoring procedures are not objective enough, and therefore not reliable.

Difficulties with scoring range from trivial to profound. As an example of a trivial difficulty, consider the following instruction for scoring the subtest Number of Words: "Tokens such as numbers, addresses, and phrases such as 'OK' are counted as a single word." Now score the sentence: "Tom said, 'Hi. My address is 130 Elm Street.'" Did you count the address as one word? The manual scores this sentence as having nine words.

As an example of more problematic scoring instructions, a number of the examples of errors under Grammar are Black English: "He go fast," "When he be old."

The most judgmental, nonobjective categories to be scored are Abstraction, Handwriting Quality, and Letter Formation.

Abstraction (a subtest of Maturity) is an interesting and important attempt to measure the sophistication of the child's story. Scoring ranges from 1–7 and rigorous descriptions are needed, along with better evidence of interrater agreement. Maturity would be an important measure to expand. As an example of an additional measure of Maturity, does the student represent all three children shown in the stimulus photograph?

The two handwriting measures are simply judgment calls. The manual includes examples of handwriting rated 1 through 5 at each grade level, but even the authors differed in scoring protocols (their interrater agreement was only .71).

Norming procedures for the WET involve between 100 and 120 children per grade. For each grade separately, the raw scores on each subtest are translated into scaled scores based on percentile ranks, so that it is possible to determine where a particular subtest score stands in relation to the normative grade group. The present sample size is barely adequate.

The scaled scores are valuable for revealing a child's status on each subtest relative to his grade-mates. However, this procedure does not permit the teacher to judge across grades. The teacher cannot discover that a child is two grades behind in his or her mechanics, for example. This point should be explained in the manual.

The Interpretation of the Scores section of the manual is extremely poor. A low Productivity score, for example, "may indicate the student wasn't in the mood to write, or was not inspired by the picture." How is the teacher to tell? The authors state their "findings indicate that this happens less than 5%" of the time. What findings are those? Which "this"—wrong mood or wrong picture? We are then told the most common reason for a low Productivity score is poor writing skills. "The association of how well a child can write and how many words he or she writes . . . is fairly high." This assertion is at the heart of the validity claim: It depends on a correlation that is not presented.

In conclusion, the WET needs additional work in order to establish its validity and reliability. Only then can it be said to measure written expression, and to do so objectively. However, it is a teacher-usable, interesting attempt to measure written language in context.

CONTRIBUTING TEST REVIEWERS

IRA E. AARON, Professor Emeritus of Reading Education, University of Georgia, Athens, GA

RUSSELL L. ADAMS, Director, Psychology Internship Program, University of Oklahoma Health Sciences Center, Oklahoma, OK

SEYMOUR ADLER, Associate Professor of Applied Psychology, Department of Management, Stevens Institute of Technology, Hoboken, NJ

PETER W. AIRASIAN, Professor of Education, Boston College, Chestnut Hill, MA

DORIS V. ALLEN, Profesor of Audiology, Wayne State University, Detroit, MI

RICHARD L. ALLINGTON, Professor of Education and Chair, Department of Reading, State University of New York at Albany, Albany, NY

ANNE ANASTASI, Professor Emeritus of Psychology, Fordham University, Bronx, NY

ELLEN H. BACON, Assistant Professor of Special Education, Western Carolina University, Cullowhee, NC

THOMAS S. BALDWIN, Practicing Psychologist, Chapel Hill, NC

NICHOLAS W. BANKSON, Professor and Chair, Department of Communication Disorders, Boston University, Boston, MA

JAMES R. BARCLAY, Professor of Educational and Counseling Psychology, University of Kentucky, Lexington, KY

DAVID W. BARNETT, Associate Professor, School Psychology, University of Cincinnati, Cincinnati, OH

PHILIP G. BENSON, Assistant Professor of Management, New Mexico State University, Las Cruces, NM

H. JOHN BERNARDIN, Director of Research, College of Business and Public Administration, Florida Atlantic University, Boca Raton, FL

RITA SLOAN BERNDT, Associate Professor of Neurology, University of Maryland School of Medicine, Baltimore, MD

LYNN S. BLISS, Associate Professor of Speech, Wayne State University, Detroit, MI

CHRISTOPHER BORMAN, Professor of Educational Psychology, Texas A&M University, College Station, TX

R. A. BORNSTEIN, Assistant Professor of Psychiatry and Psychology, Ohio State University, Columbus, OH

BRUCE A. BRACKEN, Associate Professor of Psychology, Memphis State University, Memphis, TN

LINDA E. BRODY, Assistant Director, Study of Mathematically Precocious Youth (SMPY), The Johns Hopkins University, Baltimore, MD

DIANE BROWDER, Associate Professor of Special Education, Lehigh University, Bethlehem, PA

DOUGLAS T. BROWN, Professor of Psychology and Coordinator of School Psychology, James Madison University, Harrisonburg, VA

ROBERT D. BROWN, Professor of Educational Psychology, University of Nebraska-Lincoln, Lincoln, NE

ROGER S. BRUNING, Professor of Educational Psychology, University of Nebraska-Lincoln, Lincoln, NE

LINDA K. BUNKER, Professor, Curry School of Education, University of Virginia, Charlottesville, VA

NANCY A. BUSCH-ROSSNAGEL, Associate Professor of Psychology and Research Associate, Hispanic Research Center, Fordham University, Bronx, NY

BRENDA R. BUSH, Psychologist, Beatrice State Developmental Center, Beatrice, NE

KATHARINE G. BUTLER, Professor of Communication Sciences and Disorders, and Director of Center for Research, Syracuse University, Syracuse, NY

ROBERT C. CALFEE, Professor of Education, School of Education, Stanford University, Stanford, CA

BONNIE W. CAMP, Professor of Pediatrics and Psychiatry, University of Colorado School of Medicine, Denver, CO

CAMERON J. CAMP, Associate Professor of Psychology, University of New Orleans, New Orleans, LA

HANK CAMPBELL, Associate Professor of Industrial Technology, Illinois State University, Normal, IL

C. DALE CARPENTER, Associate Professor of Special Education, Western Carolina University, Cullowhee, NC

J. MANUEL CASAS, Associate Professor of Counseling Psychology, University of California, Santa Barbara, CA

CLINTON I. CHASE, Director, Bureau of Evaluative Studies and Testing, and Professor of Educational Psychology, Indiana University, Bloomington, IN

ELAINE CLARK, Assistant Professor of Educational Psychology, University of Utah, Salt Lake City, UT

JAMES R. CLOPTON, Associate Professor of Psychology, Texas Tech University, Lubbock, TX

LARRY COCHRAN, Associate Professor of Counselling Psychology, The University of British Columbia, Vancouver, British Columbia, Canada

NICHOLAS COLANGELO, Professor and Chair of Counselor Education, University of Iowa, Iowa City, IA

RICHARD COLWELL, Professor of Music and Secondary Education, University of Illinois at Urbana-Champaign, Urbana, IL

ROBERT B. COOTER, JR., Associate Professor of Elementary Education, Brigham Young University, Provo, UT

VIRGINIA E. CORGAN, Associate Professor of Vocational and Adult Education, University of Nebraska-Lincoln, Lincoln, NE

GIUSEPPE COSTANTINO, Clinical Director, Sunset Park Mental Health Center of Lutheran Medical Center, Brooklyn, NY, and Research Associate, Hispanic Research Center, Fordham University, Bronx, NY

JOHN A. COURTRIGHT, Professor and Chair of Communication, University of Delaware, Newark, DE

LINDA CROCKER, Professor of Foundations of Education, University of Florida, Gainesville, FL

LEE J. CRONBACH, Fellow, Center for the Study of Families, Children, and Youth, Stanford University, Stanford, CA

JACK A. CUMMINGS, Associate Professor and Director of School Psychology Program, Department of Counseling and Educational Psychology, Indiana University, Bloomington, IN

BERT P. CUNDICK, Professor of Psychology, Brigham Young University, Provo, UT

M. HARRY DANIELS, Associate Professor of Educational Psychology, Southern Illinois University at Carbondale, Carbondale, IL

J. P. DAS, Director, Developmental Disabilities Centre, University of Alberta, Edmonton, Alberta, Canada

DAVID A. DECOSTER, Vice President for Student Affairs, Indiana University of Pennsylvania, Indiana, PA

MARILYN E. DEMOREST, Associate Professor of Psychology, University of Maryland-Baltimore County, Catonsville, MD

ROBERT E. DEYSACH, Associate Professor of Psychology, University of South Carolina, Columbia, SC

DAVID N. DIXON, Professor and Department Chair of Counseling and Psychology Services, Ball State University, Muncie, IN

GREGORY H. DOBBINS, Assistant Professor of Psychology, Louisiana State University, Baton Rouge, LA

JANICE A. DOLE, Assistant Professor of Educational Studies, University of Utah, Salt Lake City, UT

ELIZABETH J. DOLL, Practicum Coordinator of School Psychology, University of Wisconsin-Madison, Madison, WI

GEORGE DOMINO, Professor of Psychology, University of Arizona, Tucson, AZ

MAVIS DONAHUE, Associate Professor, College of Education, University of Illinois at Chicago, Chicago, IL

MARIAM JEAN DREHER, Associate Professor of Education, Department of Curriculum and

Instruction, University of Maryland, College Park, MD

PRISCILLA A. DRUM, Associate Professor of Education, Graduate School of Education, University of California at Santa Barbara, Santa Barbara, CA

CARL J. DUNST, Director, Family, Infant and Preschool Program, Western Carolina Center, Morganton, NC

BRUCE J. EBERHARDT, Associate Professor of Management, University of North Dakota, Grand Forks, ND

ALLEN JACK EDWARDS, Professor of Psychology, Southwest Missouri State University, Springfield, MO

RON EDWARDS, Professor of Psychology and Director of School Psychology Training, University of Southern Mississippi, Hattiesburg, MS

STEWART EHLY, Associate Professor of School Psychology, The University of Iowa, Iowa City, IA

STEPHEN N. ELLIOTT, Associate Professor of Educational Psychology, University of Wisconsin-Madison, Madison, WI

WILLIAM P. ERCHUL, Assistant Professor of Psychology, North Carolina State University, Raleigh, NC

DEBORAH B. ERICKSON, Assistant Professor of Psychology, Rochester Institute of Technology and Monroe Community College, Rochester, NY

RICHARD C. ERICKSON, Professor and Chair, Department of Practical Arts and Vocational-Technical Education, University of Missouri-Columbia, Columbia, MO

CANDICE FEIRING, Associate Professor of Pediatrics, Robert Wood Johnson Medical School, University of Medicine and Dentistry of New Jersey, New Brunswick, NJ

AMY FINCH-WILLIAMS, Associate Professor of Speech/Language Pathology, University of Wyoming, Laramie, WY

COLLEEN FITZMAURICE, Graduate Associate, Louisiana State University, Baton Rouge, LA

ROBERT FITZPATRICK, Lecturer, University of Pittsburgh, Pittsburgh, PA

HAZEL M. FOX, Professor of Human Nutrition, Emeritus, University of Nebraska-Lincoln, Lincoln, NE

MARILYN FRIEND, Assistant Professor of Learning, Development, and Special Education, Northern Illinois University, DeKalb, IL

DOUGLAS FUCHS, Associate Professor of Special Education, George Peabody College, Vanderbilt University, Nashville, TN

LYNN S. FUCHS, Assistant Professor of Special Education, George Peabody College, Vanderbilt University, Nashville, TN

MARTIN FUJIKI, Associate Scientist, Parsons Research Center, Bureau of Child Research, University of Kansas, Parsons, KS

GLORIA A. GALVIN, Assistant Professor of Psychology and Director, School Psychology Training Program, Ohio University, Athens, OH

EUGENE E. GARCIA, Professor/Director, Center for Bilingual/Bicultural Education, Arizona State University, Tempe, AZ

ERIC F. GARDNER, Professor of Psychology and Education Emeritus, Syracuse University, Syracuse, NY

KATHRYN CLARK GERKEN, Associate Professor of Education, The University of Iowa, Iowa City, IA

MARIBETH GETTINGER, Associate Professor of Educational Psychology, University of Wisconsin-Madison, Madison, WI

NOEL GREGG, Director, Learning Disabilities Adult Clinic, College of Education, The University of Georgia, Athens, GA

FRANK M. GRESHAM, Professor of Psychology, Louisiana State University, Baton Rouge, LA

J. JEFFREY GRILL, Professor of Special Education, The College of Saint Rose, Albany, NY

FRED M. GROSSMAN, Associate Professor of Special Education and Communication Disorders, University of Nebraska-Lincoln, Lincoln, NE

ROBERT M. GUION, University Professor Emeritus of Psychology, Bowling Green State University, Bowling Green, OH

RHONDA L. GUTENBERG, Management Consultant, Personnel Decisions, Inc., St. Paul, MN

BARBARA LAPP GUTKIN, Speech-Language Clinician, Lincoln Public Schools, Lincoln, NE

THOMAS W. GUYETTE, Assistant Professor of Communication Disorders and Sciences, Rush-Presbyterian-St. Luke's Medical Center, Chicago, IL

LYN HABER, Associate Professor of Psychology, University of Illinois at Chicago, Chicago, IL

CATHY W. HALL, Assistant Professor of Psychology, East Carolina University, Greenville, NC

RICHARD E. HARDING, Vice President, Research, Selection Research, Inc., Lincoln, NE

DAVID S. HARGROVE, Associate Professor and Director of Clinical Training, Department of Psychology, University of Nebraska-Lincoln, Lincoln, NE

THOMAS G. HARING, Assistant Professor of Special Education, University of California, Santa Barbara, CA

LENORE W. HARMON, Professor of Educational Psychology, University of Illinois, Champaign, IL

DENNIS C. HARPER, Professor of Pediatrics, The University of Iowa, Iowa City, IA

ROBERT G. HARRINGTON, Associate Professor of Educational Psychology and Research, University of Kansas, Lawrence, KS

PATTI L. HARRISON, Assistant Professor of Behavioral Studies, College of Education, The University of Alabama, Tuscaloosa, AL

STUART N. HART, Associate Professor of Educational Psychology, Indiana University-Purdue University at Indianapolis, Indianapolis, IN

BRUCE W. HARTMAN, Professor of Education, Seton Hall University, South Orange, NJ

TIMOTHY S. HARTSHORNE, Assistant Professor of Counseling and School Psychology, Wichita State University, Wichita, KS

WILLIAM O. HAYNES, Associate Professor of Communication Disorders, Auburn University, Auburn, AL

E. CHARLES HEALEY, Associate Professor of Speech-Language Pathology, University of Nebraska-Lincoln, Lincoln, NE

LOUIS J. HEIFETZ, Professor of Special Education, School of Education, Syracuse University, Syracuse, NY

EDITH S. HEIL, Administrative Assistant for Special Programs, Crowley Independent School District, Crowley, TX

ALFRED B. HEILBRUN, JR., Professor of Psychology, Emory University, Atlanta, GA

JAMES J. HENNESSY, Associate Professor of Psychological and Educational Services, Fordham University, New York, NY

MARY HENNING-STOUT, Assistant Professor of Counseling Psychology, Lewis and Clark College, Portland, OR

STEPHAN A. HENRY, Director of Research and Evaluation, Topeka Public Schools, Topeka, KS

DAVID O. HERMAN, President, Measurement Research Services, Inc., Jackson Heights, NY

EDWIN L. HERR, Professor and Head, Division of Counseling and Educational Psychology and Career Studies, The Pennsylvania State University, University Park, PA

ALLEN K. HESS, Professor of Psychology and Department Head, Auburn University at Montgomery, Montgomery, AL

JULIA A. HICKMAN, Assistant Professor of School Psychology, The University of Texas at Austin, Austin, TX

A. DIRK HIGHTOWER, Associate Director, Center for Community Study, Psychology Department, University of Rochester, Rochester, NY

ROBERT HOGAN, McFarlin Professor of Psychology, University of Tulsa, Tulsa, OK

STEPHEN R. HOOPER, Assistant Professor of Psychiatry, Psychology Section Head, The Clinical Center for the Study of Development and Learning, University of North Carolina School of Medicine, Chapel Hill, NC

KENNETH W. HOWELL, Associate Professor of Curriculum and Instruction, College of Education, Western Washington University, Bellingham, WA

ROBERT J. HOWELL, Professor of Psychology and Director of Clinical Psychology, Brigham Young University, Provo, UT

E. SCOTT HUEBNER, Associate Professor, Department of Psychology, Western Illinois University, Macomb, IL

JAN N. HUGHES, Associate Professor of Educational Psychology, Texas A&M University, College Station, TX

SYLVIA M. HUTCHINSON, Professor of Reading Education, University of Georgia, Athens, GA

RICHARD M. JAEGER, Professor and Director, Center for Educational Research and Evaluation, University of North Carolina at Greensboro, Greensboro, NC

RICHARD W. JOHNSON, Adjunct Professor of Counseling Psychology and Counselor Education, and Associate Director of University Counseling Service, University of Wisconsin-Madison, Madison, WI

RONN JOHNSON, Assistant Professor of Educational Psychology, University of Nebraska-Lincoln, Lincoln, NE

BARRY W. JONES, Associate Professor of Communicative Disorders, San Diego State University, San Diego, CA

SAMUEL JUNI, Associate Professor of Counselor Education, New York University, New York, NY

RANDY W. KAMPHAUS, Assistant Professor of Educational Psychology, University of Georgia, Athens, GA

RABINDRA N. KANUNGO, Professor of Psychology and Management, McGill University, Montreal, Quebec, Canada

ROBERT M. KAPLAN, Professor of Community and Family Medicine, and Acting Chief of Health Care Sciences, University of California, La Jolla, CA

ALAN S. KAUFMAN, Research Professor of School Psychology, The University of Alabama, Tuscaloosa, AL

KENNETH A. KAVALE, Professor and Chair, Division of Special Education, The University of Iowa, Iowa City, IA

THOMAS J. KEHLE, Professor of Educational Psychology, University of Connecticut, Storrs, CT

TIMOTHY Z. KEITH, Associate Professor of School Psychology, Virginia Tech University, Blacksburg, VA

HAROLD R. KELLER, Associate Professor of Psychology and Education, Syracuse University, Syracuse, NY

MARY LOU KELLEY, Assistant Professor of Psychology, Louisiana State University, Baton Rouge, LA

KATHRYN W. KENNEY, Clinical Supervisor in Speech-Language Pathology, Department of Speech & Hearing Science, Arizona State University, Tempe, AZ

BARBARA A. KERR, Assistant Professor of Counselor Education, The University of Iowa, Iowa City, IA

BENJAMIN KLEINMUNTZ, Professor of Psychology, University of Illinois at Chicago, Chicago, IL

HOWARD M. KNOFF, Associate Professor of School Psychology, Department of Psychological Foundations, University of South Florida, Tampa, FL

DEBORAH KING KUNDERT, Assistant Professor, Educational Psychology and Statistics, SUNY-Albany, Albany, NY

KORESSA KUTSICK, Assistant Professor of Psychology, James Madison University, Harrisonburg, VA

WILBUR L. LAYTON, Professor of Psychology, Iowa State University, Ames, IA

STEVEN W. LEE, Assistant Professor of Educational Psychology and Research, University of Kansas, Lawrence, KS

PAUL R. LEHMAN, Professor and Associate Dean, School of Music, The University of Michigan, Ann Arbor, MI

IRVIN J. LEHMANN, Professor of Measurement, Michigan State University, East Lansing, MI

FRANCIS E. LENTZ, JR., Associate Professor of School Psychology and Counseling, University of Cincinnati, Cincinnati, OH

ROBERT L. LINN, Professor of Education, University of Colorado at Boulder, Boulder, CO

GARY E. LINTEREUR, Associate Professor of Technology, Northern Illinois University, DeKalb, IL

RODNEY L. LOWMAN, Director, Corporate Mental Health Programs, Occupational Health Service, and Faculty, Divisions of Medical Psychology and Occupational Medicine, Duke University Medical Center, Durham, NC

JOAN I. LYNCH, Associate Professor of Language Science, University of Texas Health Science at Houston, Houston, TX

F. CHARLES MACE, Associate Professor, Graduate School of Applied and Professional Psychology, Rutgers University, Piscataway, NJ

CLEBORNE D. MADDUX, Department Chairman, Curriculum and Instruction, University of Nevada-Reno, Reno, NV

CAROLINE MANUEL-ADKINS, Associate Professor Counseling, Department of Educational Foundations, Hunter College of the City University of New York, New York, NY

CAROL MARDELL-CZUDNOWSKI, Professor of Educational Psychology, Counseling, and Special Education, Northern Illinois University, DeKalb, IL

ROBERT P. MARKLEY, Professor of Psychology, Fort Hays State University, Hays, KS

DAVID MARSHALL, Associate Professor of Computer Science, The Texas Woman's University, Denton, TX

BRIAN K. MARTENS, Assistant Professor of Psychology and Education, Syracuse University, Syracuse, NY

JOSEPH D. MATARAZZO, Professor and Chairman, Department of Medical Psychology,

School of Medicine, Oregon Health Sciences University, Portland, OR

JAMES J. MAZZA, University of Wisconsin-Madison, Madison, WI

SUSAN MCCAMMON, Assistant Professor of Psychology, East Carolina University, Greenville, NC

ELLEN MCGINNIS, Assistant Professor of Special Education, University of Wisconsin-Eau Claire, Eau Clair, WI

KEVIN S. MCGREW, School Psychologist, St. Cloud Community Schools, St. Cloud, MN

WILLIAM T. MCKEE, Research Associate, Louisiana State University, Baton Rouge, LA

ROBERT F. MCMORRIS, Professor of Educational Psychology and Statistics, State University of New York at Albany, Albany, NY

MALCOLM R. MCNEIL, Professor, Department of Communicative Disorders, University of Wisconsin, Madison, WI

PAUL MCREYNOLDS, Professor of Psychology, University of Nevada-Reno, Reno, NV

DAVID J. MEALOR, Associate Professor of School Psychology, University of Central Florida, Orlando, FL

GARY B. MELTON, Carl A. Happold Professor of Psychology and Law, University of Nebraska-Lincoln, Lincoln, NE

WILLIAM B. MICHAEL, Professor of Education and Psychology, University of Southern California, Los Angeles, CA

GLORIA E. MILLER, Associate Professor of Psychology, University of South Carolina, Columbia, SC

PATRICIA L. MIRENDA, Assistant Professor of Special Education and Communication Disorders, University of Nebraska-Lincoln, Lincoln, NE

KEVIN L. MORELAND, Consultant, NCS Professional Assessment Services, Minneapolis, MN

DAVID MOSHMAN, Associate Professor of Educational Psychology, University of Nebraska-Lincoln, Lincoln, NE

KEVIN W. MOSSHOLDER, Associate Professor of Management, Auburn University, Auburn, AL

DONALD E. MOWRER, Professor of Speech and Hearing Science, Arizona State University, Tempe, AZ

ROBERT R. MOWRER, Assistant Professor of Psychology and Sociology, Angelo State University, San Angelo, TX

DANIEL J. MUELLER, Professor of Educational Psychology, Indiana University, Bloomington, IN

CAROLYN COLVIN MURPHY, Assistant Professor of Teacher Education, San Diego State University, San Diego, CA

KEVIN R. MURPHY, Associate Professor of Psychology, Colorado State University, Fort Collins, CO

GWENDOLYN NEWKIRK, Professor and Chairman, Department of Consumer Science and Education, University of Nebraska-Lincoln, Lincoln, NE

DIANNA L. NEWMAN, Assistant Professor of Education, University at Albany/SUNY, Albany, NY

ARTHUR M. NEZU, Chief, Division of Psychology, Beth Israel Medical Center, New York, NY

ANTHONY J. NITKO, Professor of Education, University of Pittsburgh, Pittsburgh, PA

JANET A. NORRIS, Assistant Professor of Communication Disorders, Louisiana State University, Baton Rouge, LA

RUTH M. NOYCE, Professor of Curriculum and Instruction, The University of Kansas, Lawrence, KS

KEVIN E. O'GRADY, Assistant Professor of Psychology, University of Maryland, College Park, MD

JUDY OEHLER-STINNETT, Assistant Professor, University of Wisconsin-Whitewater, Whitewater, WI

ROBERT E. OWENS, JR., Associate Professor of Speech Pathology, State University of New York, Geneseo, NY

KATHLEEN D. PAGET, Associate Professor, Department of Psychology, University of South Carolina, Columbia, SC

CHARLES K. PARSONS, Professor of Management, Georgia Institute of Technology, Atlanta, GA

MARY ELLEN PEARSON, Professor of Special Education, Mankato State University, Mankato, MN

BARBARA PERRY-SHELDON, Associate Professor of Education, North Carolina Wesleyan College, Rocky Mount, NC

JERRY L. PETERS, Associate Professor of Education, Purdue University, West Lafayette, IN

CHARLES A. PETERSON, Staff Clinical Psychologist, VA Minneapolis Medical Center, and

Clinical Assistant Professor, Department of Psychology, University of Minnesota, Minneapolis, MN

HAROLD A. PETERSON, Director, Clinical Services and Professor of Audiology and Speech Pathology, University of Tennessee-Knoxville, Knoxville, TN

ROLF A. PETERSON, Professor of Psychology, The George Washington University, Washington, DC

STEVEN I. PFEIFFER, Director, Institute of Clinical Training and Research, The Devereux Foundation, Devon, PA

JULIA PETTIETTE-DOOLIN, Department of Psychology, Tulane University, New Orleans, LA

LEADELLE PHELPS, Associate Professor of Educational and Counseling Psychology, University of Missouri-Columbia, Columbia, MO

S. E. PHILLIPS, Associate Professor of Measurement, Michigan State University, East Lansing, MI

NICK J. PIAZZA, Assistant Professor, Department of Counselor Education, The University of Toledo, Toledo, OH

WAYNE C. PIERSEL, Associate Professor of Educational Psychology, University of Nebraska-Lincoln, Lincoln, NE

JAMES W. PINKNEY, Associate Professor of Counseling, East Carolina University, Greenville, NC

EDWARD A. POLLOWAY, Professor of Education, Lynchburg College, Lynchburg, VA

C. DALE POSEY, Licensed Psychologist, C. M. E. Psychology Consultants, Boca Raton, FL

G. MICHAEL POTEAT, Assistant Professor of Psychology, East Carolina University, Greenville, NC

JAMES A. POTEET, Professor of Special Education, Ball State University, Muncie, IN

ELIZABETH M. PRATHER, Professor of Speech and Hearing Science, Arizona State University, Tempe, AZ

JOAN E. PYNES, Department of Public Administration and Policy Analysis, Southern Illinois University, Edwardsville, IL

LESLIE T. RASKIND, School Psychologist, Gwinnett County Schools, Lawrenceville, GA

SHARON B. REYNOLDS, Assistant Professor of Education, Texas Christian University, Fort Worth, TX

R. LYNN RICHARDS, Doctoral Student, Brigham Young University, Provo, UT

GARY J. ROBERTSON, Director, Test Division, American Guidance Service, Inc., Circle Pines, MN

BRUCE G. ROGERS, Professor of Educational Psychology and Foundations, University of Northern Iowa, Cedar Falls, IA

SAMUEL ROLL, Professor of Psychology and Psychiatry, University of New Mexico, Albuquerque, NM

SYLVIA ROSENFIELD, Professor of School Psychology, Temple University, Philadelphia, PA

ARLENE C. ROSENTHAL, Educational Psychologist, Lexington, KY

MICHAEL J. ROSZKOWSKI, Research Psychologist, The American College, Bryn Mawr, PA

JAMES B. ROUNDS, Associate Professor of Educational Psychology, University of Illinois at Urbana-Champaign, Champaign, IL

DENISE M. ROUSSEAU, Associate Professor of Organization Behavior, Kellogg School of Management, Northwestern University, Evanston, IL

ROBERT RUEDA, Visiting Associate Professor of Curriculum, Teaching, and Learning, University of Southern California, Los Angeles, CA

DAVID L. RULE, Doctoral Student of Educational Psychology and Statistics, State University of New York at Albany, Albany, NY

JAMES O. RUST, Professor of Psychology, Middle Tennessee State University, Murfreesboro, TN

MICHAEL RYAN, Clinical Psychologist, West Side Family Mental Health Clinic, Kalamazoo, MI

JANE A. RYSBERG, Associate Professor of Psychology, California State University, Chico, CA

DARRELL L. SABERS, Professor of Educational Psychology, University of Arizona, Tucson, AZ

JONATHAN SANDOVAL, Professor of Education, University of California, Davis, Davis, CA

TONI E. SANTMIRE, Associate Professor of Educational Psychology, University of Nebraska-Lincoln, Lincoln, NE

JANICE SANTOGROSSI, Instructor of Special Education and Communication Disorders, University of Nebraska-Lincoln, Lincoln, NE

JEROME M. SATTLER, Professor of Psychology, San Diego State University, San Diego, CA

RICHARD A. SAUDARGAS, Associate Professor of Psychology, University of Tennessee, Knoxville, TN

WILLIAM I. SAUSER, JR., Associate Vice President and Professor, Office of the Vice President for Extension, Auburn University, Auburn, AL

DIANE J. SAWYER, Associate Professor of Education, Syracuse University, Syracuse, NY

SUSAN J. SCHENCK, Associate Professor of Special Education, College of Charleston, Charleston, SC

STEVEN P. SCHINKE, Professor, School of Social Work, Columbia University, New York, NY

RICHARD J. SCHISSEL, Associate Professor and Chair, Department of Speech Pathology and Audiology, Ithaca College, Ithaca, NY

LYLE F. SCHOENFELDT, Professor of Management, Texas A&M University, College Station, TX

FREDRICK A. SCHRANK, Associate Academic Dean, Griffin College, Tacoma, WA

NEIL H. SCHWARTZ, Associate Professor of Psychology, California State University, Chico, Chico, CA

MARCIA B. SHAFFER, School Psychologist, Steuben/Allegany BOCES, Bath, NY

DAVID A. SHAPIRO, Assistant Professor of Communication Disorders, School of Education and Psychology, Western Carolina University, Cullowhee, NC

EDWARD S. SHAPIRO, Associate Professor and Director, School Psychology Program, Lehigh University, Bethlehem, PA

LINDA JENSEN SHEFFIELD, Professor of Education and Mathematics, Northern Kentucky University, Highland Heights, KY

KENNETH L. SHELDON, School Psychologist, Edgecombe County Schools, Tarboro, NC

JOHN W. SHEPARD, Associate Professor of Education, Counselor and Human Services Education, University of Toledo, Toledo, OH

BRUCE SHERTZER, Professor of Education, Purdue University, West Lafayette, IN

KENNETH G. SHIPLEY, Professor and Chairman, Department of Communicative Disorders, Laboratory School-MS80, California State University-Fresno, Fresno, CA

SYLVIA SIBLEY, School Psychologist, Highland Park I.S.D., Dallas, TX

ARTHUR B. SILVERSTEIN, Professor of Psychiatry, University of California, Los Angeles, CA

JOAN SILVERSTEIN, Assistant Professor of Psychology and Director, School Psychology Program, Montclair State College, Upper Montclair, NJ

ESTHER SINCLAIR, Associate Professor of Psychiatry and Biobehavioral Sciences, UCLA School of Medicine, Los Angeles, CA

ROBERT B. SLANEY, Associate Professor of Counseling Psychology, The Pennsylvania State University, University Park, PA

CORINNE ROTH SMITH, Associate Professor of Special Education and Rehabilitation, Syracuse University, Syracuse, NY

DOUGLAS K. SMITH, Professor of Psychology and Director School Psychology Program, University of Wisconsin-River Falls, River Falls, WI

JEFFREY K. SMITH, Associate Professor of Educational Psychology, Rutgers, The State University, New Brunswick, NJ

MICHAEL J. STAHL, Professor and Head, Department of Management, School of Business, Clemson University, Clemson, SC

JAYNE E. STAKE, Professor of Psychology, University of Missouri-St. Louis, St. Louis, MO

CHARLES W. STANSFIELD, Director, Division of Foreign Language Education and Testing, Center for Applied Linguistics, Washington, DC

WENDY J. STEINBERG, Associate Personnel Examiner, New York State Department of Civil Service, Albany, NY

KRISTA J. STEWART, Associate Professor of Psychology and Director of the School Psychology Training Program, Tulane University, New Orleans, LA

SHELDON L. STICK, Professor, Department of Special Education and Communication Disorders, The University of Nebraska-Lincoln, Lincoln, NE

TERRY A. STINNETT, Professor of School Psychology, University of Wisconsin-Whitewater, Whitewater, WI

JOSEPH P. STOKES, Associate Professor of Psychology, University of Illinois at Chicago, Chicago, IL

GERALD L. STONE, Professor of Counseling Psychology and Director, University Counseling Service, The University of Iowa, Iowa City, IA

DAVID STRAND, Counseling Psychologist, University of Colorado, Boulder, CO

RICHARD B. STUART, Clinical Professor of Psychiatry and Behavioral Sciences, University of Washington, Seattle, WA

ALAN R. SUESS, Professor of Industrial Technology and Education, Purdue University, West Lafayette, IN

JOHN G. SVINICKI, Evaluation Specialist, Powell Associates, Inc., Austin, TX

CABRINI S. SWASSING, Psychologist, Central Ohio Psychiatric Hospital, Columbus, OH

JOHN M. TAYLOR, Executive Director, Developmental Disabilities Center, Boulder, CO

CATHY F. TELZROW, Psychologist and Director, Educational Assessment Project, Cuyahoga Special Education Service Center, Maple Heights, OH

MARY L. TENOPYR, Selection and Testing Director, AT&T, Morristown, NJ

PAUL W. THAYER, Professor and Head of Psychology, North Carolina State University, Raleigh, NC

RUTH G. THOMAS, Associate Professor of Education, University of Minnesota, St. Paul, MN

GEORGE E. THORNTON, III, Professor of Psychology, Colorado State University, Fort Collins, CO

ROBERT J. TIERNEY, Professor of Educational Theory and Practice, The Ohio State University, Columbus, OH

C. ALAN TITCHENAL, Nutrition Education Consultant, Office of School Food and Nutrition Services, Long Island City, NY

GAIL E. TOMPKINS, Associate Professor of Language Arts Education, University of Oklahoma, Norman, OK

MICHELLE T. TOSHIMA, Ph.D. Candidate, University of California, San Diego, La Jolla, CA

TIMOTHY L. TURCO, Assistant Professor of School Psychology, Lehigh University, Bethlehem, PA

LAWRENCE J. TURTON, Professor of Speech-Language Pathology, Indiana University of Pennsylvania, Indiana, PA

NICHOLAS A. VACC, Professor and Coordinator of Counselor Education, University of North Carolina, Greensboro, NC

STANLEY F. VASA, Professor of Special Education and Communication Disorders, University of Nebraska-Lincoln, Lincoln, NE

DAVID P. WACKER, Associate Professor of Pediatrics and Special Education, The University of Iowa, Iowa City, IA

RICHARD A. WANTZ, Associate Professor of Educational Psychology and Director of Counseling Psychology Clinic, College of Education, University of Oklahoma, Norman, OK

GEORGE WARDLOW, Assistant Professor of Agricultural Education, University of Minnesota, St. Paul, MN

JAMES L. WARDROP, Associate Professor of Educational Psychology, University of Illinois at Urbana-Champaign, Champaign, IL

RICHARD A. WEINBERG, Professor of Child Psychology and Educational Psychology, and Director, Center for Early Education and Development, University of Minnesota, Minneapolis, MN

SUE WHITE, Assistant Professor of Psychology, Case Western Reserve University, School of Medicine, Cleveland, OH

MARTIN J. WIESE, School Psychologist, Wilkes County Schools, Wilkesboro, NC

JERRY S. WIGGINS, Professor of Psychology, The University of British Columbia, Vancouver, Canada

RICHARD L. WIKOFF, Professor of Psychology, University of Nebraska at Omaha, Omaha, NE

WILLIAM K. WILKINSON, Research Associate, Northern Arizona University, Flagstaff, AZ

ROBERT T. WILLIAMS, Associate Professor of Occupational and Educational Studies, Colorado State University, Fort Collins, CO

VICTOR L. WILLSON, Professor of Educational Psychology, Texas A&M University, College Station, TX

STEVEN L. WISE, Assistant Professor of Educational Psychology, University of Nebraska-Lincoln, Lincoln, NE

JOSEPH C. WITT, Associate Professor of Psychology, Louisiana State University, Baton Rouge, LA

DAN WRIGHT, School Psychologist, Ralston Public Schools, Ralston, NE

JAMES E. YSSELDYKE, Professor of Educational Psychology, University of Minnesota, Minneapolis, MN

JOHN A. ZARSKE, Director, Northern Arizona Psychological Services, P.C., Flagstaff, AZ

PAUL F. ZELHART, Associate Academic Vice President and Professor of Psychology, East Texas State University, Commerce, TX

LELAND C. ZLOMKE, Clinical Director of the Intensive Training Service, Beatrice State Developmental Center, Beatrice, NE

INDEX OF TITLES

This title index lists all the tests included in The Tenth Mental Measurements Yearbook. *Citations are to test entry numbers, not to pages—e.g.,* 54 *refers to test* 54 *and not page* 54. *(Test numbers along with test titles are indicated in the running heads at the top of each page, while page numbers, used only in the Table of Contents but not in the indexes, appear at the bottom of each page.) Superseded titles are listed with cross references to current titles, and alternative titles are also cross referenced.*

An (N) *appearing immediately after a test number indicates that the test is a new, recently published test, and/or that it has not appeared before in a Buros Institute publication. An* (R) *indicates that the test has been revised or supplemented since last reviewed in a* Mental Measurements Yearbook.

INDEX OF ACRONYMS

This Index of Acronyms refers the reader to the appropriate test in The Tenth Mental Measurements Yearbook. *In some cases tests are better known by their acronyms than by their full titles, and this index can be of substantial help to the person who knows the former but not the latter. Acronyms are only listed if the author or publisher has made substantial use of the acronym in referring to the test, or if the test is widely known by the acronym. A few acronyms are also registered trademarks (e.g., SAT); where this is known to us, only the test with the registered trademark is referenced. There is some danger in the overuse of acronyms, but this index, like all other indexes in this work, is provided to make the task of identifying a test as easy as possible. All numbers refer to test numbers, not page numbers.*

AAD: Ability-Achievement Discrepancy, 2
AAI: Academic Advising Inventory, 3
ABI: Adaptive Behavior Inventory, 9
ACDM: Assessment of Career Decision Making, 16
ACLC: Assessment of Children's Language Comprehension, 1983 Revision, 17
ACT: The Activity Completion Technique, 8
ADS: Alcohol Dependence Scale, 12
AIDS: Assessment of Intelligibility of Dysarthric Speech, 19
AIM: Achievement Identification Measure, 5
ALST: Adolescent Language Screening Test, 10
ASA: Articulation Screening Assessment, 14
ASCVIS: Armed Services-Civilian Vocational Interest Survey, 13
A.S.S.E.T.S: A.S.S.E.T.S.—A Survey of Students' Educational Skills, 20

BAB: Behaviour Assessment Battery, Second Edition, 29
BBCS: Bracken Basic Concept Scale, 33
BDAE: Boston Diagnostic Aphasia Examination, 15
BDI: Battelle Developmental Inventory, 25
BDP: Brief Drinker Profile, 70
BIAB: Brief Index of Adaptive Behavior, 34
BIC: Bury Infant Check, 38
BLCT: Basic Language Concepts Test, 23
Boehm-R: Boehm Test of Basic Concepts—Revised, 32
BPI: Bipolar Psychological Inventory, 31
BPS: BRIGANCE® Preschool Screen, 36
BRP: Behavior Rating Profile, 27
BRS: Behaviordyne Retirement Service, 28
BSI: The Brief Symptom Inventory, 35
BSID: Bayley Scales of Infant Development, 26

CABS: Childrens Adaptive Behavior Scale, Revised, 55
CADL: Communicative Abilities in Daily Living, 69
CAI: Career Assessment Inventory—The Enhanced Version, 43
CAIMI: Children's Academic Intrinsic Motivation Inventory, 54
CAIN: Computer Anxiety Index, 341
CALIP: Computer Aptitude, Literacy, and Interest Profile, 72
CAML: Coarticulation Assessment in Meaningful Language, 64
CAP Inventory: The Child Abuse Potential Inventory, 50
CAP: Clinical Articulation Profile, 63
CAS: Children's Abilities Scales, 53
CAS: Cognitive Abilities Scale, 65
CAST: The Children of Alcoholics Screening Test, 52
CAT/E&F: California Achievement Tests, Forms E and F, 41
CCAT: Canadian Cognitive Abilities Test, Form 3, 42
CCT: Computer Competence Tests, 73
CDI: Career Directions Inventory, 44
CDM: The Harrington O'Shea Career Decision-Making System, 136
CDP: Comprehensive Drinker Profile, 70

WSSAB: Weller-Strawser Scales of Adaptive Behavior for the Learning Disabled, 387
WAPT: Wichita Auditory Processing Test, 388
WRAT-R: Wide Range Achievement Test—Revised, 389
WRMT-R: Woodcock Reading Mastery Tests—Revised, 391
WPT: Word Processing Test, 392
WPAB: Word Processor Assessment Battery, 393
WET: The Written Expression Test, 396

CLASSIFIED SUBJECT INDEX

The Classified Subject Index classifies all tests included in The Tenth Mental Measurements Yearbook *into 16 major categories: Achievement, Developmental, Education, English, Fine Arts, Foreign Languages, Intelligence and Scholastic Aptitude, Mathematics, Miscellaneous, Neuropsychological, Personality, Reading, Sensory-Motor, Social Studies, Speech and Hearing, and Vocations. Each category appears in alphabetical order and tests are ordered alphabetically within each category. Each test entry includes test title (first letters capitalized), population for which the test is intended (lower case), and the test entry number in* The Tenth Mental Measurements Yearbook. *All numbers refer to test entry numbers, not to page numbers. Brief suggestions for the use of this index are presented in the introduction.*

ACHIEVEMENT

California Achievement Tests, Forms E and F, grades K.0–K.9, K.6–2.2, 1.6–3.2, 2.6–4.2, 3.6–5.2, 4.6–6.2, 5.6–7.2, 6.6–8.2, 7.6–9.2, 8.6–11.2, 10.6–12.9, see 41

Diagnostic Achievement Test for Adolescents, grades 7–12, see 92

Iowa Tests of Basic Skills, Forms G and H, grades K.1–1.5, K.8–1.9, 1.7- -2.6, 2.5–3.5, 3, 4, 5, 6, 7, 8–9, see 155

Iowa Tests of Educational Development™[Eighth Edition], grades 9–10; 11–12, see 156

Kaufman Test of Educational Achievement, grades 1–12, see 161

Maculaitis Assessment Program, Commercial Edition, ESL students in grades K–12, see 180

Metropolitan Achievement Tests, Sixth Edition, grades K.0–K.9, K.5–1.9, 1.5–2.9, 2.5–3.9, 3.5–4.9, 5.0–6.9, 7.0–9.9, 10.0–12.9, see 200

Multilevel Academic Survey Test, grades K–8 and high school students with reading or mathematics skill deficits, see 203

The National Tests of Basic Skills, preschool–college, see 213

Quick-Score Achievement Test, ages 7-0 to 17-11, see 302

Tests of Achievement and Proficiency, Forms G and H, grades 9–12, see 375

Wide Range Achievement Test—Revised, ages 5-0 to 11-11, 12-0 to 75, see 389

DEVELOPMENTAL

The ABC Inventory to Determine Kindergarten and School Readiness, ages 3.5–6.5, see 1

A.S.S.E.T.S.—A Survey of Students' Educational Talents and Skills, kindergarten–grade 3, grades 4–6, see 20

Battelle Developmental Inventory, birth to 8 years, see 25

Bayley Scales of Infant Development, ages 2–30 months, see 26

Behaviour Assessment Battery, Second Edition, severely mentally handicapped children and adults, see 29

Bracken Basic Concept Scale, ages 2-6 to 7-11, ages 5-0 to 7-0, see 33

BRIGANCE® Preschool Screen, ages 3–4, see 36

Bury Infant Check, children in second term of infant school, see 38

EDUCATION

ENGLISH

FINE ARTS

FOREIGN LANGUAGES

INTELLIGENCE AND SCHOLASTIC APTITUDE

MATHEMATICS

MISCELLANEOUS

Test Behavior Checklist, ages 4 through adolescence, see 362
Vineland Adaptive Behavior Scales, birth through 18-11 and low functioning adults, see 381
Watson-Barker Listening Test, adults in business, professions, and college, see 384
Weller-Strawser Scales of Adaptive Behavior for the Learning Disabled, learning disabled students ages 6–12, 13–18, see 287

NEUROPSYCHOLOGICAL

Human Information Processing Survey, adults, see 144
Sklar Aphasia Scale, Revised 1983, brain damaged adults, see 336

PERSONALITY

The Activity Completion Technique, high school and over, see 8
Alcohol Dependence Scale, problem drinkers, see 12
Autistic Behavior Composite Checklist and Profile, autistic or emotionally handicapped students, see 21
Basic Living Skills Scale, grades 3–8, see 24
Behavior Rating Profile, ages 6-6 through 18-6 and/or grades 1–12, see 27
Bipolar Psychological Inventory, college and adults, see 31
The Brief Symptom Inventory, psychiatric patients and non-patients, see 35
The Child Abuse Potential Inventory, Form VI, male and female parents or primary caregivers who are suspected of physical child abuse, see 50
The Children of Alcoholics Screening Test, school-age children of possible alcoholics, see 52
Children's Academic Intrinsic Motivation Inventory, grades 4–8, see 54
Children's Problems Checklist, ages 5–12, see 56
Comprehensive Drinker Profile, problem drinkers and alcoholics, see 70
Coping Inventory, ages 3 through adults, see 74
Decision Making Inventory, high school and college students, see 77
Defense Mechanisms Inventory, adolescents, adults, and elderly, see 79
Diagnostic Interview for Borderline Patients, patients, see 95
Eating Disorder Inventory, ages 12 and over, see 100
The Edinburgh Questionnaires (1982 Edition), adults, see 102
Family Relationship Inventory, young children, adolescents, and adults, see 112
The Golombok Rust Inventory of Sexual Satisfaction, sex therapy clients, see 127
Gordon Personal Profile—Inventory, grades 9–16 and adults, see 128
The Hand Test, Revised 1983, ages 6 and over, see 134
Hanson Silver Management Style Inventory, administrators and leaders, see 135
Hogan Personality Inventory, age 18–adult, see 140
Illness Behaviour Questionnaire, Second Edition, pain clinic, psychiatric, and general practice patients, see 146
Interpersonal Style Inventory, ages 14 and over, see 151
Iowa Social Competency Scales, ages 3–12, see 154
Keegan Type Indicator, adults, see 162
Kinetic Drawing System for Family and School: A Handbook, ages 5–20, see 166
La Monica Empathy Profile, managers/helpers/teachers in industry, education, and health care, see 168
Leadership Skills Inventory, grades 4–12, see 172
Learning-Style Inventory, college and adults, see 173
Louisville Behavior Checklist, ages 4–17, see 176
Maslach Burnout Inventory, Second Edition, members of the helping professions, including educators, see 189
Meadow-Kendall Social-Emotional Assessment Inventory for Deaf and Hearing Impaired Students, ages 3–21, see 194
Meeker Behavioral Correlates, industry, see 198
Miller Motivation Scale, college students and adults, see 201
The Multiple Affect Adjective Check List, Revised, ages 20–79, see 205
Myers-Briggs Type Indicator, grades 9–16 and adults, see 206
The NEO Personality Inventory, adults, see 214
Oaster Stressors Scales, adults, see 242
Oetting's Computer Anxiety Scale, college students, see 245
Parenting Stress Index, parents of children below 10 years of age, see 271
Personal Outlook Inventory, prospective employees, see 277
Personal Problems Checklist, adults, see 278
Personal Problems Checklist for Adolescents, adolescents, see 279
Personal Profile System, employees, see 280
Personality Inventory for Children, Revised Format, ages 3–16, see 281
Personality Research Form, 3rd Edition, grade 6–college, adults, see 282
Phase II Profile Integrity Status Inventory and ADdendum, job applicants and employees in staff positions, see 283
Porteous Problem Checklist, ages 12–18, see 286
Portland Problem Behavior Checklist—Revised, grades K–12, see 287
Problem-Solving Decision-Making Style Inventory, high

READING

SENSORY-MOTOR

SOCIAL STUDIES

SPEECH AND HEARING

Articulation Screening Assessment, preschool and elementary, see 14
The Assessment of Aphasia and Related Disorders, Second Edition, aphasia patients; ages 5.5–59, see 15
Assessment of Fluency in School-Age Children, ages 5–18, see 18
Assessment of Intelligibility of Dysarthric Speech, adult and adolescent dysarthric speakers, see 19
CLASS—The Cognitive, Linguistic and Social-Communicative Scales, ages birth through 72 months, see 59
Clinical Articulation Profile, young children, see 63
Coarticulation Assessment in Meaningful Language, ages 2.5–5.5, see 64
Communicative Abilities in Daily Living, aphasic adults, see 69
Comprehensive Screening Tool for Determining Optimal Communication Mode, low functioning non-speaking clients, see 71
Developmental Articulation Profile, ages 3.0–7.3, see 88
Evaluating Acquired Skills in Communication, language age 3 months to 8 years: mentally impaired, developmentally delayed, preschool language delayed, emotionally handicapped, autistic impaired, see 109
Goldman Fristoe Test of Articulation, ages 2 and over, see 126
Khan-Lewis Phonological Analysis, ages 2-0 to 5-11, see 164
Oral Motor Assessment and Treatment: Improving Syllable Production, ages 4–1, see 268
Phonological Assessment of Child Speech, children referred for speech therapy, see 284
A Screening Deep Test of Articulation, grades K–3, see 328
Stuttering: Parental Diagnostic Questionnaire, Revised Edition, ages 3–6, see 352
Test for Auditory Comprehension of Language, Revised Edition, ages 3– 10, see 363
Test for Examining Expressive Morphology, ages 3-0 to 7-12, see 364
Test of Articulation Performance—Diagnostic, ages 3–8, see 366
Test of Articulation Performance—Screen, ages 3–8, see 367
Wichita Auditory Processing Test, school-age children, see 388

VOCATIONS

Armed Services-Civilian Vocational Interest Survey, high school through adult, see 13
Assessment of Career Decision Making, adolescents and adults, see 16
Business Analyst Skills Evaluation, candidates for non-computer Business Analyst positions, see 39
Career Assessment Inventory—The Enhanced Version, junior high school and above, see 43
Career Directions Inventory, high school and college and adults, see 44
Career Profile System, insurance sales representatives and candidates for insurance sales representative positions, see 45
Career Survey, grade 7 through adults, see 46
Certified Picture Framer Examination, individuals actively involved in the business of picture framing for one year, see 48
Clerical Staff Selector, candidates for clerks, see 62
Communications Profile Questionnaire, managers and employees, see 68
Computer Aptitude, Literacy, and Interest Profile, high school and adults, see 72
Correctional Officers' Interest Blank, applicants for jobs in penal institutions and correctional agencies, see 75
Data Entry Operator Aptitude Test, candidates for data entry operators, see 76
Dental Assistant Test, dental assistant applicants, see 81
Dental Receptionist Test, dental receptionist applicants, see 82
Electronic and Instrumentation Technician Test, applicants or incumbents for jobs where electronics and instrumentation knowledge is a necessary part of training or job activities, see 106
Food Protection Certification Test, food industry personnel, see 119
The Harrington O'Shea Career Decision-Making System, grades 7–12 and adults, see 136
Jackson Vocational Interest Survey, high school and over, see 158
Job Training Assessment Program, job applicants, see 159
JOB-O, 1985–1995, junior high school through adult, see 160
Kuder Occupational Interest Survey, Revised (Form DD), grade 10 through adult, see 167
Law Enforcement Assessment and Development Report, applicants for law enforcement positions, see 170
Long Performance Efficiency Test, grade 7 and over, see 175
The Major-Minor-Finder, 1986–1996 Edition, grade 11 through adult, see 181
Management Appraisal Survey, employees, see 182
Management Inventory on Modern Management, managers, see 183
Management Styles Questionnaire, managers and employees, see 184
Managerial Style Questionnaire, persons in managerial situations, see 185

PUBLISHERS DIRECTORY AND INDEX

This directory and index gives the addresses and test entry numbers of all publishers represented in The Tenth Mental Measurements Yearbook. *Please note that all numbers in this index refer to test entry numbers, not page numbers. Publishers are an important source of information about catalogs, specimen sets, price changes, test revisions, and many other matters.*

Ablin Press, P.O. Box 184, Mamaroneck, NY 10543: 333

Academic Therapy Publications, 20 Commercial Blvd., Novato, CA 94947-6191: 83, 312, 385, 387

Addiction Research Foundation, 33 Russell Street, Toronto, Ontario, M5S 2S1, Canada: 12

Alemany Press (The), 2501 Industrial Parkway West, Hayward, CA 94545: 139, 180

American College Testing Program, 2201 North Dodge Street, P.O. Box 168, Iowa City, IA 52243: 6, 7

American Guidance Service, Publishers' Building, P.O. Box 99, Circle Pines, MN 55014-1796: 126, 136, 161, 164, 381, 391

American Printing House for the Blind, Inc., 1839 Frankfort Avenue, P.O. Box 6085, Louisville, KY 40206-0085: 32

American Testronics, P.O. Box 2270, Iowa City, IA 52244: 46, 213

ASIEP Education Co., P.O. Box 12147, 3216 NE 27th Ave., Portland, OR 97212: 188, 287, 292, 383

The Assessment Centre, P.O. Box 64867, Tucson, AZ 85740-1867: 348

Australian Council for Educational Research, P.O. Box 210, Hawthorn, 3122 Victoria, Australia: 4, 217, 305

Panos D. Bardis, University of Toledo Sociology Department, Toledo, OH 43606: 157, 395

Barnell Loft, Ltd., 958 Church St., Baldwin, NY 11510: 93

Behavior Science Systems, Inc., P.O. Box 1108, Minneapolis, MN 55440: 291

Behaviordyne, Inc., 994 San Antonio Road, P.O. Box 10994, Palo Alto, CA 94303-0997: 28

The Ber-Sil Co., 3412 Seaglen Drive, Rancho Palos Verdes, CA 90274: 30

Biobehavioral Associates, 1101 Beacon Street, Brookline, MA 02146: 347

Book-Lab, 500 74th Street, North Bergen, NJ 07047: 142

Wm. C. Brown Co., Publishers, 2460 Kerper Blvd., Dubuque, IA 52001: 61

CAMBRIDGE, The Adult Education Co., 888 Seventh Avenue, New York, NY 10106: 147

Camelot Unlimited, 5 North Wabash Avenue, Suite 1409, Chicago, IL 60602: 52

Center for the Study of Evaluation, University of California, Los Angeles, 145 Moore Hall, Los Angeles, CA 90024-1521: 67

Central Institute for the Deaf, 818 South Euclid, St. Louis, MO 63110: 358

CFKR Career Materials, Inc., P.O. Box 437, Meadow Vista, CA 95722-0437: 13, 160, 181

Jay L. Chambers, Center for Psychological Services, College of William and Mary, Williamsburg, VA 23185: 337

Child Welfare League of America, Inc., Publications Department, 440 First Street, N.W.-Suite 310, Washington, DC 20001: 290

Childcraft Education Corp., 20 Kilmer Road, P.O. Box 3081, Edison, NJ 08818-3081: 89

Clinical Psychology Publishing Co., Inc., (CPPC), 4 Conant Square, Brandon, VT 05733: 362, 380

Clinical Psychometric Research, Inc., Campbell Building, Suite 302, 100 W. Pennsylvania Avenue, Towson, MD 21204: 35, 299

Communication Skill Builders, 3830 East Bellevue, Box 42050, Tucson, AZ 85733: 21, 64, 109, 110, 328, 364, 371

John D. Cone, School of Human Behavior, United States

International University, 10455 Pomerado Road, San Diego, CA 92131: 270
Consulting Psychologists Press, Inc., 577 College Ave., Palo Alto, CA 94306: 17, 60, 75, 122, 132, 189, 206, 303, 322, 326, 334, 379
CTB/McGraw-Hill, Del Monte Research Park, 2500 Garden Road, Monterey, CA 93940-5380: 41
Curriculum Associates, Inc., 5 Esquire Road, North Billerica, MA 01862- 2589: 36, 108

Dallas Educational Services, P.O. Box 831254, Richardson, TX 75083-1254: 24, 125, 195
Development Publications, 5605 Lamar Road, Bethesda, MD 20816-1398: 280
Diagnostic Specialists Inc., 1170 North 660 West, Orem, UT 84057: 31
DLM Teaching Resources, One DLM Park, Allen, TX 75002: 25, 152, 321, 363, 368, 373
DMI Associates, 615 Clark Avenue, Owosso, MI 48867: 79
D.O.K. Publishers, Inc., P.O. Box 605, East Aurora, NY 14052: 111, 145, 172, 275

Dr. Maurice J. Eash, Director, Institute of Learning and Teaching, University of Massachusetts at Boston, Boston, MA 02125: 269
EdITS/Educational and Industrial Testing Service, P.O. Box 7234, San Diego, CA 92107: 205, 324
Educational Activities, Inc., P.O. Box 391, Freeport, NY 11520: 317
Educational Assessment Service, Inc. W6050 Apple Road, Watertown, WI 53094: 5, 289
Educational Performance Associates, Inc., 600 Broad Avenue, Ridgefield, NJ 07657: 153
Educational Research Centre, Test Department, St. Patrick's College, 66 Richmond Road, Dublin 3, Ireland: 96, 97
Educational Studies & Development, 1357 Forest Park Road, Muskegon, MI 49441: 1
Educational Testing Service, Publication Order Services, P.O. Box 6736, Princeton, NJ 08541-6736: 119, 159, 207, 208, 298
Educators Publishing Service, Inc., 75 Moulton Street, Cambridge, MA 02238-9101: 272, 273

Charles G. Fast, Publisher, Route 1, Novinger, MO 63559: 113
Fearon Education, 500 Harbor Boulevard, Belmont, CA 94002: 98
Foreworks, Box 9747, North Hollywood, CA 91609: 338
Fourier, Inc., P.O. Box 125, Akron, OH 44308: 350
Functional Resources Enterprises, 2734 Trail of the Madrones, Austin, TX 78746: 123

G.I.A. Publications, Inc., 7404 South Mason Avenue, Chicago, IL 60638: 150
Guidance Centre, Faculty of Education, University of Toronto, 10 Alcorn Avenue, Toronto, Ontario M4V 2Z8, Canada: 293

Hanson Silver Strong & Associates, Inc., Box 402, Moorestown, NJ 08057: 135
Hayes Publishing, Ltd., 3312 Mainway, Burlington, Ontario L7M 1A7, Canada: 91
Heinemann Publishing Australia Pty Ltd., 85 Abinger Street, P.O. Box 133, Richmond, Victoria 3121, Australia: 124
Houghton Mifflin, One Beacon Street, Boston, MA 02108: 37
Human Synergistics, Inc., 39819 Plymouth Road, Plymouth, MI 48170: 103, 361
Humanics Limited, P.O. Box 7447, Atlanta, GA 30309: 55

Ideal Developmental Labs, P.O. Box 27142, West Allis, WI 53227: 378
Institute for Personality and Ability Testing Inc., P.O. Box 188, Champaign, IL 61820-0188: 170
Instructional Materials Laboratory, The Ohio State University, 842 Goodale Blvd., Columbus, OH 43212: 246, 247, 248, 249, 250, 251, 252, 253, 254, 255, 256, 257, 258, 259, 260, 261, 262, 263, 264, 265, 266, 267
Interdatum, Inc., 600 Montgomery Street, 37th Floor, San Francisco, CA 94111: 346
The Interstate Printers & Publishers, Inc., 19 North Jackson Street, P.O. Box 50, Danville, IL 61834-0050: 18
Iowa State University Research Foundation, Inc., Child Development Department, 101 Child Development Building, Research Laboratories, Ames, IA 50011: 154
Iowa State University Research Foundation, Inc., Instructional Resources Center, Quadrangle Building, Iowa State University, Ames, IA 50011: 341
R.B. Ishmael & Associates, Phase II Profile Division, 2705 South Black Road, Suite 5, Joliet, IL 60435: 283

Jamestown Publishers, P.O. Box 9168, Providence, RI 02940: 307
Jastak Associates, Inc., P.O. Box 4460, Wilmington, DE 19807: 114, 389

Warren Keegan Associates Press, 210 Stuyvesant Avenue, Rye, NY 10580: 162
Kent Developmental Metrics, 1325 S. Water Street, P.O. Box 845, Kent, OH 44240: 163
Donald L. Kirkpatrick, 1920 Hawthorne Drive, Elm Grove, WI 53122: 183

Lawrence Psychological Center, 407 East Gilbert St., Suite 6, San Bernardino, CA 92404: 171
Lea & Febiger, 600 Washington Square, Philadelphia, PA 19106-4198: 15
Learning Publications, Inc., Box 1326, 5351 Gulf Dr., Holmes Beach, FL 33509: 20
Learning Resources Distribution Centre, 12360–142nd Street, Edmonton, Alberta T5L 4X9, Canada: 325
Life Science Associates, One Fenimore Road, Bayport, NY 11705: 304
Life Insurance Marketing and Research Association, Inc., P.O. Box 208, Hartford, CT 06141: 45
LinguiSystems, Inc., 716 17th Street, Moline, IL 61265: 169
LISCOR, 809 Dundas Street East, London, Ontario N5W 2Z8, Canada: 308
Pamela S. Ludolph, Counseling Center, The University of Michigan, 1007 Huron St., Ann Arbor, MI 48104-1690: 95

Macmillan Education Ltd., Registered Office, 4 Little

Essex Street, London, WC2R 3LF, England: 148, 178, 179, 216, 394
Macmillan Publishing Co., 866 Third Avenue, New York, NY 10022: 22
Jean D'Arcy Maculaitis, Ph.D., P.O. Box 56, Sea Bright, NJ 07760: 177
Dr. Wayne R. Maes, University of New Mexico, Dept. of Counselor Education, Mesa Vista Hall 4021, College of Education, Albuquerque, NM 87131: 360
Marathon Consulting & Press, P.O. Box 09189, Columbus, OH 43209-0189: 77
McBer and Company, 137 Newbury Street, Boston, MA 02116: 173, 185, 294
Meeting Street School, 667 Waterman Avenue, East Providence, RI 02914: 199
Albert Mehrabian, University of California, Department of Psychology, 405 Hilgard Avenue, Los Angeles, CA 90024: 51, 301
META Development, 23 Marquis Crescent, Regina, Saskatchewan, S4S 6J8, Canada: 201
MetriTech, Inc., 111 N. Market Street, Champaign, IL 61820: 133
Michalak Training Associates, Inc., 875 Pinto Place, South, Tucson, AZ 85748-7921: 68, 184, 335, 353
Midwest Publications, Inc., P.O. Box 448, Pacific Grove, CA 93950: 107
Modern Curriculum Press, Customer Service Dept., 13900 Prospect Road, Cleveland, OH 44136: 94, 309

National Business Education Association, 1914 Association Drive, Reston, VA 22091: 209, 210, 211, 212
National Computer Systems, Inc., P.O. Box 1416, Minneapolis, MN 55440: 43, 140
National Dairy Council, 6300 North River Road, Rosemont, IL 60018-4233: 40, 117, 118, 241
National Occupational Competency Testing Institute, 318 Johnson Hall, Ferris State College, Big Rapids, MI 49307: 219, 220, 221, 222, 223, 224, 225, 226, 227, 228, 229, 230, 231, 232, 233, 234, 235, 236, 237, 238, 239, 240
Nelson Canada, 1120 Birchmount Road, Scarborough, Ontario, M1K 5G4, Canada: 42
NFER-Nelson Publishing Co., Ltd., Darville House, 2 Oxford Road East, Windsor, Berkshire SL4 1DF, England: 11, 29, 38, 49, 53, 102, 127, 129, 196, 218, 284, 286, 306, 310, 311, 313, 390

Thomas R. Oaster, School of Education, University of Missouri-Kansas City, 5100 Rockhill Road, Kansas City, MO 64110-2499: 242, 351
The Ontario Institute for Studies in Education, 252 Bloor Street West, Toronto, Ontario M5S 1V6, Canada: 121
OUTREACH, Pre-College Programs, KDES PAS6, Gallaudet University, Washington, DC 20002: 194

Pediatric Psychology Press, 320 Terrell Road, West, Charlottesville, VA 22901: 271
Pfizer, 235 East 42nd Street, New York, NY 10017: 95
I. Pilowsky, University of Adelaide, Department of Psychiatry, Royal Adelaide Hospital, Adelaide, South Australia 5001: 146
Precision People, Inc., 3452 North Ride Circle, S., Jacksonville, FL 32217: 86
PRO-ED, Inc., 8700 Shoal Creek Blvd., Austin, TX 78758-6897: 9, 10, 14, 19, 27, 58, 59, 63, 65, 69, 72, 84, 85, 87, 88, 92, 99, 120, 131, 143, 149, 215, 244, 268, 300, 302, 315, 327, 340, 345, 352, 365, 366, 367, 369, 370, 372, 374, 388
Professional Picture Framers Association, 4305 Sarellen Road, Richmond, VA 23231: 48
Project SPOKE, Vincent IGO Administration Center, South Street, Foxboro, MA 02035: 332
Psychological Assessment and Services, Inc., P.O. Box 1031, Iowa City, IA 52244: 141
Psychological Assessment Resources, Inc., P.O. Box 998, Odessa, FL 33556-0998: 8, 54, 56, 70, 100, 104, 138, 187, 214, 278, 279, 316, 318, 330, 382
The Psychological Corporation, 555 Academic Court, San Antonio, TX 78204-0952: 26, 32, 33, 73, 128, 191, 192, 200, 203, 204, 392
Psychological Publications, Inc., 5300 Hollywood Blvd., Los Angeles, CA 90027: 112, 357
Psytec Inc., P.O. Box 300, Webster, NC 28788: 50

Ramsay Corporation, Boyce Station Offices, 1050 Boyce Road, Pittsburgh, PA 15241: 106, 296
Research Psychologists Press, Inc., P.O. Box 984, 1110 Military St., Port Huron, MI 48061-0984: 44, 158, 202, 282
The Riverside Publishing Co., 8420 Bryn Mawr Avenue, Chicago, IL 60631: 66, 155, 156, 342, 375
Rocky Mountain Behavioral Science Institute, Inc., P.O. Box 1066, Fort Collins, CO 80522: 245, 339
Rocky Mountain Education Systems, 9400 W. 10th Avenue, Lakewood, CO 80215: 396

Scholastic Testing Service, Inc., 480 Meyer Road, P.O. Box 1056, Bensenville, IL 60106-8056: 34, 74, 144, 190
Science Research Associates, Inc., 155 North Wacker Drive, Chicago, IL 60606-1780: 23, 167, 354, 393
SEFA (Publications) Ltd., The Globe, 4 Great William Street, Stratford- upon-Avon, CV37 6RY, England: 174
Slosson Educational Publications, Inc., P.O. Box 280, East Aurora, NY 14052: 57, 101
Gerald R. Smith, Chair, Department of Curriculum and Instruction, Education 337, Indiana University, Bloomington, IN 47405: 343
Social Ecology Laboratory, VA Medical Center, 3801 Miranda Avenue, Palo Alto, CA 94304: 137
SOI Systems, P.O. Box D, Vida, OR 97488: 81, 82, 198
Source Publications, Inc., P.O. Box 8089, Atlanta, GA 30306: 297
Southern Micro Systems, P.O. Box 2097, Burlington, NC 27216: 2, 386
SPECTRA Communication Associates, P.O. Box 5031, Contract Station 20, New Orleans, LA 70118: 384
Stoelting Company, 620 Wheat Lane, Wood Dale, IL 60191: 115, 175
Cynthia J. Stolman, 19 Fenton Dr., Short Hills, NJ 07078: 197
Stratton-Christian Press, Inc., Box 1055, University Place Station, Des Moines, IA 50311-0055: 130
Student Development Associates, Inc., 110 Crestwood Drive, Athens, GA 30605: 3
Summa Information Systems, Box 2172, Greenville, NC 27834: 355

INDEX OF NAMES

This analytical index indicates whether a citation refers to authorship of a test, a test review, or a reference for a specific test. Numbers refer to test entries, not to pages. The abbreviations and numbers following the names may be interpreted as follows: "test, 73" indicates authorship of test 73; "rev, 186" indicates authorship of a review of test 186; "ref, 50r" indicates a reference (unnumbered) in one of the "Reviewer's References" sections for test 50. Names mentioned in cross references are also indexed.

SCORE INDEX

This Score Index lists all the scores, in alphabetical order, for all the tests included in The Tenth Mental Measurements Yearbook. *Because test scores can be regarded as operational definitions of the variables measured, sometimes the scores provide better leads to what a test actually measures than the test title or whatever else is available. The Score Index is very detailed, and the reader should keep in mind that a given variable (or concept) of interest may be defined in several different ways. Thus the reader should look up these several possible alternative definitions before drawing final conclusions about whether tests measuring a particular variable of interest can be located in the* 10th MMY. *If the kind of score sought is located in a particular test or tests, the reader should then read the test descriptive information carefully to determine whether the test(s) in which the score is found is (are) consistent with reader purpose. Used wisely, the Score Index can be another useful resource in locating the right score in the right test. As usual, all numbers in the index are test numbers, not page numbers.*

CODE OF FAIR TESTING PRACTICES IN EDUCATION

Prepared by the Joint Committee on Testing Practices

The Code of Fair Testing Practices in Education states the major obligations to test takers of professionals who develop or use educational tests. The Code is meant to apply broadly to the use of tests in education (admissions, educational assessment, educational diagnosis, and student placement). The Code is not designed to cover employment testing, licensure or certification testing, or other types of testing. Although the Code has relevance to many types of educational tests, it is directed primarily at professionally developed tests such as those sold by commercial test publishers or used in formally administered testing programs. The Code is not intended to cover tests made by individual teachers for use in their own classrooms.

The Code addresses the roles of test developers and test users separately. Test users are people who select tests, commission test development services, or make decisions on the basis of test scores. Test developers are people who actually construct tests as well as those who set policies for particular testing programs. The roles may, of course, overlap as when a state education agency commissions test development services, sets policies that control the test development process, and makes decisions on the basis of the test scores.

The Code has been developed by the Joint Committee on Testing Practices, a cooperative effort of several professional organizations, that has as its aim the advancement, in the public interest, of the quality of testing practices. The Joint Committee was initiated by the American Educational Research Association, the American Psychological Association, and the National Council on Measurement in Education. In addition to these three groups, the American Association for Counseling and Development/Association for Measurement and Evaluation in Counseling and Development, and the American Speech-Language-Hearing Association are now also sponsors of the Joint Committee.

Code of Fair Testing Practices in Education. (1988) Washington, D.C.: Joint Committee on Testing Practices. (Mailing Address: Joint Committee on Testing Practices, American Psychological Association, 1200 17th Street, NW, Washington, D.C. 20036.)

The Code presents standards for educational test developers and users in four areas:

A. Developing/Selecting Tests
B. Interpreting Scores
C. Striving for Fairness
D. Informing Test Takers

Organizations, institutions, and individual professionals who endorse the Code commit themselves to safeguarding the rights of test takers by following the principles listed. The Code is intended to be consistent with the relevant parts of the *Standards for Educational and Psychological Testing* (AERA, APA, NCME, 1985). However, the Code differs from the Standards in both audience and purpose. The Code is meant to be understood by the general public; it is limited to educational tests; and the primary focus is on those issues that affect the proper use of tests. The Code is not meant to add new principles over and above those in the Standards or to change the meaning of the Standards. The goal is rather to represent the spirit of a selected portion of the Standards in a way that is meaningful to test takers and/or their parents or guardians. It is the hope of the Joint Committee that the Code will also be judged to be consistent with existing codes of conduct and standards of other professional groups who use educational tests.

A. Developing/Selecting Appropriate Tests*

Test developers should provide the information that test users need to select tests.

Test users should select tests that meet the purpose for which they are to be used and that are appropriate for the intended test-taking populations.

Test Developers Should:

1. Define what each test measures and what the test should be used for. Describe the population(s) for which the test is appropriate.
2. Accurately represent the characteristics, usefulness, and limitations of tests for their intended purposes.
3. Explain relevant measurement concepts as necessary for clarity at the level of detail that is appropriate for the intended audience(s).
4. Describe the process of test development. Explain how the content and skills to be tested were selected.
5. Provide evidence that the test meets its intended purpose(s).
6. Provide either representative samples or complete copies of test questions, directions, answer sheets, manuals, and score reports to qualified users.
7. Indicate the nature of the evidence obtained concerning the appropriateness of each test for groups of different racial, ethnic, or linguistic backgrounds who are likely to be tested.
8. Identify and publish any specialized skills needed to administer each test and to interpret scores correctly.

Test Users Should:

1. First define the purpose for testing and the population to be tested. Then, select a test for that purpose and that population based on a thorough review of the available information.
2. Investigate potentially useful sources of information, in addition to test scores, to corroborate the information provided by tests.
3. Read the materials provided by test developers and avoid using tests for which unclear or incomplete information is provided.
4. Become familiar with how and when the test was developed and tried out.
5. Read independent evaluations of a test and of possible alternative measures. Look for evidence required to support the claims of test developers.
6. Examine specimen sets, disclosed tests or samples of questions, directions, answer sheets, manuals, and score reports before selecting a test.
7. Ascertain whether the test content and norm group(s) or comparison group(s) are appropriate for the intended test takers.
8. Select and use only those tests for which the skills needed to administer the test and interpret scores correctly are available.

B. Interpreting Scores

Test developers should help users interpret scores correctly.

Test users should interpret scores correctly.

Test Developers Should:

9. Provide timely and easily understood score reports that describe test performance clearly and accurately. Also explain the meaning and limitations of reported scores.
10. Describe the population(s) represented by any norms or comparison group(s), the dates the data were gathered, and the process used to select the samples of test takers.

Test Users Should:

9. Obtain information about the scale used for reporting scores, the characteristics of any norms or comparison group(s), and the limitations of the scores.
10. Interpret scores taking into account any major differences between the norms or comparison groups and the actual test takers. Also take into account any differences in test administration practices or familiarity with the specific questions in the test.

*Many of the statements in the Code refer to the selection of existing tests. However, in customized testing programs test developers are engaged to construct new tests. In those situations, the test development process should be designed to help ensure that the completed tests will be in compliance with the Code.

11. Warn users to avoid specific, reasonably anticipated misuses of test scores.

11. Avoid using tests for purposes not specifically recommended by the test developer unless evidence is obtained to support the intended use.

12. Provide information that will help users follow reasonable procedures for setting passing scores when it is appropriate to use such scores with the test.

12. Explain how any passing scores were set and gather evidence to support the appropriateness of the scores.

13. Provide information that will help users gather evidence to show that the test is meeting its intended purpose(s).

13. Obtain evidence to help show that the test is meeting its intended purpose(s).

C. Striving for Fairness

Test developers should strive to make tests that are as fair as possible for test takers of different races, gender, ethnic backgrounds, or handicapping conditions.

Test Developers Should:

14. Review and revise test questions and related materials to avoid potentially insensitive content or language.

15. Investigate the performance of test takers of different races, gender, and ethnic backgrounds when samples of sufficient size are available. Enact procedures that help to ensure that differences in performance are related primarily to the skills under assessment rather than to irrelevant factors.

16. When feasible, make appropriately modified appropriately forms of tests or administration procedures available for test takers with handicapping conditions. Warn test users of potential problems in using standard norms with modified tests or administration procedures that result in non-comparable scores.

Test users should select tests that have been developed in ways that attempt to make them as fair as possible for test takers of different races, gender, ethnic backgrounds, or handicapping conditions.

Test Users Should:

14. Evaluate the procedures used by test developers to avoid potentially insensitive content or language.

15. Review the performance of test takers of different races, gender, and ethnic backgrounds when samples of sufficient size are available. Evaluate the extent to which performance differences may have been caused by inappropriate characteristics of the test.

16. When necessary and feasible, use appropriately modified forms of tests or administration procedures for test takers with handicapping conditions. Interpret standard norms with care in the light of the modifications that were made.

D. Informing Test Takers

Under some circumstances, test developers have direct communication with test takers. Under other circumstances, test users communicate directly with test takers. Whichever group communicates directly with test takers should provide the information described below.

Test Developers or Test Users Should:

17. When a test is optional, provide test takers or their parents/guardians with information to help them judge whether the test should be taken, or if an available alternative to the test should be used.

18. Provide test takers the information they need to be familiar with the coverage of the test, the types of question formats, the directions, and appropriate test-taking strategies. Strive to make such information equally available to all test takers.

Under some circumstances, test developers have direct control of tests and test scores. Under other circumstances, test users have such control. Whichever group has direct control of tests and test scores should take the steps described below.

Test Developers or Test Users Should:

19. Provide test takers or their parents/guardians with information about rights test takers may have to obtain copies of tests and completed answer sheets, retake tests, have tests rescored, or cancel scores.

20. Tell test takers or their parents/guardians how long scores will be kept on file and indicate to whom and under what circumstances test scores will or will not be released.

21. Describe the procedures that test takers or their parents/guardians may use to register complaints and have problems resolved.

Note: The membership of the Working Group that developed the Code of Fair Testing Practices in Education and of the Joint Committee on Testing Practices that guided the Working Group was as follows:

Theodore P. Bartell
John R. Bergan
Esther E. Diamond
Richard P. Duran
Lorraine D. Eyde
Raymond D. Fowler
John J. Fremer (Co-chair, JCTP and Chair, Code Working Group)
Edmund W. Gordon
Jo-Ida C. Hansen
James B. Lingwall
George F. Madaus (Co-chair, JCTP)
Kevin L. Moreland
Jo-Ellen V. Perez
Robert J. Solomon
John T. Stewart
Carol Kehr Tittle (Co-chair, JCTP)
Nicholas A. Vacc
Michael J. Zieky
Debra Boltas and Wayne Camara of the American Psychological Association served as staff liaisons

Additional copies of the Code may be obtained from the National Council on Measurement in Education, 1230 Seventeenth Street, NW, Washington, D.C. 20036. Single copies are free.